CH00708994

1999/2000	2000/01	2001/02	2002/03	2003/04	2004/05		Para No.
10%	10%	10%	10%	10%	**10%**	Starting rate	3
£1,500	£1,520	£1,880	£1,920	£1,960	**£2,020**	Starting rate limit	3
20%	20%	20%	20%	20%	**20%**	Lower rate	3, 5
—	—	—	—	—	**—**	Lower rate limit (taxable income)	3, 5
23%	22%	22%	22%	22%	**22%**	Basic rate	3, 5
£26,500	£26,880	£27,520	£27,980	£28,540	**£29,380**	Basic rate band (taxable income)	3, 5
£28,000	£28,400	£29,400	£29,900	£30,500	**£31,400**	Basic rate limit (taxable income)	3, 5
40%	40%	40%	40%	40%	**40%**	Higher rate	3, 5
10%	10%	10%	10%	10%	**10%**	Schedule F ordinary rate	9
32.5%	32.5%	32.5%	32.5%	32.5%	**32.5%**	Schedule F upper rate	9
—	—	£5,200	£5,290	—	—	Children's tax credit (10%)	18
—	—	£5,200	£10,490	—	—	—year of birth	
						PERSONAL ALLOWANCES	
£4,335	£4,385	£4,535	£4,615	£4,615	**£4,745**	Personal	14
£1,970	—	—	—	—	—	Married couple's	15
							14, 15
£5,720	£5,790	£5,990	£6,100	£6,610	**£6,830**	Age — Personal (65 or over)	
£5,980	£6,050	£6,260	£6,370	£6,720	**£6,950**	— Personal (75 or over)	
£5,125	£5,185	£5,365	£5,465	£5,565	**£5,725**	— Married couple's (65 or over or, for 2000/01 onwards, born before 6.4.1935)	
£5,195	£5,255	£5,435	£5,535	£5,635	**£5,795**	— Married couple's (75 or over)	
£16,800	£17,000	£17,600	£17,900	£18,300	**£18,900**	— Income limit	
£1,970	£2,000	£2,070	£2,110	£2,150	**£2,210**	— Minimum where income limit exceeded	
£1,970	£2,000	—	—	—	—	Widow's bereavement (death before 6.4.00)	16
£1,970	—	—	—	—	—	Addition re child if claimant single or claimant's spouse ill	17
£1,380	£1,400	£1,450	£1,480	£1,510	**£1,560**	Blind Persons	19
						CLASS 4 NIC	
6%	7%	7%	7%	8%	**8%**	— Rate	
£7,530– £26,000	£4,385– £27,820	£4,535– £29,900	£4,615– £30,420	£4,615– £30,940 plus 1% on excess	**£4,745– £31,720** plus 1% on excess	— Band	
						DISCRETIONARY TRUST INCOME	
34%	34%	34%	34%	34%	**40%**	Flat rate	
25%	25%	25%	25%	25%	**32.5%**	Schedule F trust rate	

Tolley's
Income Tax
2004–05

89th Edition

by
David Smailes FCA
Andrew Flint MA CTA

Members of the LexisNexis Group worldwide

United Kingdom	LexisNexis UK, a Division of Reed Elsevier (UK) Ltd, Halsbury House, 35 Chancery Lane, LONDON, WC2A 1EL, and 4 Hill Street, EDINBURGH EH2 3JZ
Argentina	LexisNexis Argentina, BUENOS AIRES
Australia	LexisNexis Butterworths, CHATSWOOD, New South Wales
Austria	LexisNexis Verlag ARD Orac GmbH & Co KG, VIENNA
Canada	LexisNexis Butterworths, MARKHAM, Ontario
Chile	LexisNexis Chile Ltda, SANTIAGO DE CHILE
Czech Republic	Nakladatelství Orac sro, PRAGUE
France	Editions du Juris-Classeur SA, PARIS
Germany	LexisNexis Deutschland GmbH, FRANKFURT and MUNSTER
Hong Kong	LexisNexis Butterworths, HONG KONG
Hungary	HVG-Orac, BUDAPEST
India	LexisNexis Butterworths, NEW DELHI
Ireland	LexisNexis, DUBLIN
Italy	Giuffrè Editore, MILAN
Malaysia	Malayan Law Journal Sdn Bhd, KUALA LUMPUR
New Zealand	LexisNexis Butterworths, WELLINGTON
Poland	Wydawnictwo Prawnicze LexisNexis, WARSAW
Singapore	LexisNexis Butterworths, SINGAPORE
South Africa	LexisNexis Butterworths, DURBAN
Switzerland	Stämpfli Verlag AG, BERNE
USA	LexisNexis, DAYTON, Ohio

© Reed Elsevier (UK) Ltd 2004

Published by LexisNexis UK

A CIP Catalogue record for this book is available from the British Library.

ISBN 0 7545 2544 9

Typeset by Interactive Sciences Ltd, Gloucester

Printed and bound in Great Britain by CPI Bath

Visit LexisNexis UK at www.lexisnexis.co.uk

About This Book

This is the 89th edition of Tolley's Income Tax, a detailed and comprehensive commentary on the current law and practice relating to UK income tax. It includes coverage of all the relevant provisions of **Finance Act 2004**, plus all other relevant material to **1 July 2004**, e.g. statutes, statutory instruments, court cases, Special Commissioners' decisions, internet statements, press releases, concessions, Statements of Practice, Revenue Tax Bulletins, Revenue Manuals and other publications. The law and practice for at least six years prior to 2004/05 are also covered. Chapter 95 summarises the relevant provisions of the current Finance Act.

The chapters are arranged alphabetically for ease of reference. An index and tables of statutes and leading cases also provide quick reference to the subject matter and to the law. Numerous worked examples are given throughout the book. There is a 12-year summary of rates and allowances inside the front cover. The inside back cover contains the main tax rates for the current year and a table of the main taxable social security benefits.

Income tax legislation is consolidated from time to time and is also currently being rewritten in its entirety, albeit over a number of years. The approach adopted to citation of references is summarised overleaf.

This book is derived from a text originally written by Eric L Harvey FCA and updated over many years by Glyn Saunders MA. The publishers and current authors are grateful to Eric and Glyn for their invaluable contributions.

Comments and suggestions for improvement are always welcome.

TOLLEY

Consolidation and Rewriting of Tax Enactments

With effect generally for 1988/89 and subsequent years of assessment (and for companies' accounting periods ending after 5 April 1988), the *Taxes Acts* provisions relating to income tax and corporation tax are consolidated in the *Income and Corporation Taxes Act 1988* (*ICTA 1988*). The consolidation does not affect the application of the provisions concerned, but references to provisions which ceased to have effect before 6 April 1988 are omitted, as is the commencement date of the consolidated provisions (unless still relevant to application of the current provisions).

This section continues, as in previous years, to set out the position for the six years before 2004/05, i.e. for 1998/99 to 2003/04, but occasional references are still required to earlier years. In strictness, the legislation applicable to years before 1988/89 is that in force prior to the consolidation referred to above, and the Revenue (while acknowledging that 'on previous consolidation, inspectors, Commissioners and taxpayers alike got used to the new references in dealing with previous periods'), have indicated that claims etc. for those years should refer to the statute then applicable.

Accordingly, the approach which has been adopted to statutory references in this issue is as follows:

(i) Remaining references to the previous consolidation Act are in the form '*ICTA 1970, s XXX*' or '*ICTA 1970, Sch XX*'. Where there has been no change in the legislation in the last six years, no statutory reference other than that for *ICTA 1988* is quoted.

(ii) Where the legislation has changed during the last six years, the earlier provisions continue to be described in the text, and the appropriate earlier statutory reference is quoted. Legislation current during that six years but now repealed is similarly dealt with. Where any part of the current legislation was introduced during that six years, the commencement date is quoted, but the statutory reference for that date is generally omitted.

(iii) In any case where a claim or election for a year before 1988/89 may be involved, the appropriate earlier statutory reference is quoted. The earlier reference is also given in certain cases where the reference may have achieved a particular familiarity, e.g. in the case of *sections 154(2), 189* or *460 of ICTA 1970*.

(iv) Where a full pre-consolidation statutory reference is required, this may be obtained from Tolley's Income Tax 1987/88 or an appropriate earlier edition.

(v) The Table of Statutes in this edition includes all references to earlier legislation appearing in the text (as above).

A similar approach has been adopted on the consolidation of the enactments relating to capital allowances in the *Capital Allowances Act 1990*, which took effect generally for chargeable periods ending after 5 April 1990, and to those relating to corporation tax on capital gains in the *Taxation of Chargeable Gains Act 1992*, which took effect generally for chargeable periods beginning after 5 April 1992.

Following the re-enactment of the capital allowances legislation in the *Capital Allowances Act 2001* as part of the 'simplification' programme, both the old and the new references are quoted in the text, as the revised wording and layout of the legislation may be relevant, particularly in cases where minor changes have been incorporated. See 10.1 CAPITAL ALLOWANCES as regards the election for deferment of the commencement of any such changes. A similar approach has been adopted in relation to the *Income Tax (Earnings and Pensions) Act 2003*, and see 75.1 SCHEDULE E—EMPLOYMENT INCOME as regards commencement.

Contents

The following subjects are in the same alphabetical order in this section. A detailed index and tables of cases and statutes are at the end of the section.

Contents

Contents

Abbreviations and References

ABBREVIATIONS

ACT	=	Advance Corporation Tax.
CAA	=	Capital Allowances Act.
CA	=	Court of Appeal.
CCA	=	Court of Criminal Appeal.
CCAB	=	Consultative Committee of Accountancy Bodies.
CES	=	Court of Exchequer (Scotland).
Cf.	=	compare.
CGT	=	Capital Gains Tax.
CGTA 1979	=	Capital Gains Tax Act 1979.
CIR	=	Commissioners of Inland Revenue ('the Board').
Ch D	=	Chancery Division.
CJEC	=	Court of Justice of the European Communities.
CS	=	Scottish Court of Session.
DSS	=	Department of Social Security.
EC	=	European Communities.
ECHR	=	European Court of Human Rights.
EEC	=	European Economic Community.
EU	=	European Union.
Ex D	=	Exchequer Division (now absorbed into Chancery Division).
FA	=	Finance Act.
FII	=	Franked Investment Income.
FRS	=	Financial Reporting Standard
HC	=	High Court.
HC(I)	=	High Court of Ireland.
HL	=	House of Lords.
ICAEW	=	Institute of Chartered Accountants in England and Wales.
ICTA	=	Income and Corporation Taxes Act.
IHT	=	Inheritance Tax.
IHTA 1984	=	Inheritance Tax Act 1984.
IR	=	Inland Revenue.
ITEPA 2003	=	Income Tax (Earnings and Pensions) Act 2003.
KB	=	King's Bench Division.
LIFFE	=	London International Financial Futures Exchange.
NI	=	Northern Ireland.
PC	=	Privy Council.
PDA	=	Probate, Divorce and Admiralty Division. (Now Family Division).
QB	=	Queen's Bench Division.
RI	=	Republic of Ireland (Eire).
s	=	Section.
SC(I)	=	Irish Supreme Court.
Sch	=	Schedule.
SI	=	Statutory Instrument.
SP	=	Inland Revenue Statement of Practice.
Sp C	=	Special Commissioners.
SR&O	=	Statutory Rules and Orders.
SSAP	=	Statement of Standard Accounting Practice.
TCGA 1992	=	Taxation of Chargeable Gains Act 1992.

TMA 1970	=	Taxes Management Act 1970.
VAT	=	Value Added Tax.
VATA 1994	=	Value Added Tax Act 1994.

REFERENCES

AER	=	All England Law Reports (Butterworths, Halsbury House, 35 Chancery Lane, London WC2A 1EL).
ATC	=	Annotated Tax Cases (Gee & Co. (Publishers) Ltd., South Quay Plaza, 183 Marsh Wall, London E14 9FS).
ITC	=	Irish Tax Cases (Government Publications, 1 and 3 G.P.O. Arcade, Dublin 1).
LTR	=	Law Times Reports.
SC	=	Special Commissioners.
SLR	=	Scottish Law Reporter.
SLT	=	Scots Law Times.
SSCD	=	Simon's Tax Cases Special Commissioners' Decisions (Butterworths, as above).
STC	=	Simon's Tax Cases (Butterworths, as above).
STI	=	Simon's Tax Intelligence (Butterworths, as above).
TC	=	Official Tax Cases (H.M. Stationery Office, P.O. Box 276, SW8 5DT).
TLR	=	Times Law Reports.
TR	=	Taxation Reports (Gee & Co., as above).

The first number in the citation refers to the volume, and the second to the page, so that [1995] 1 AER 15 means that the report is to be found on page fifteen of the first volume of the All England Law Reports for 1995. Where no volume number is given, only one volume was produced in that year.

Some series have continuous volume numbers.

Where legal decisions are very recent and in the lower courts, it must be remembered that they may be reversed on appeal. But references to the official Tax Cases ('*TC*') may generally be taken as final.

In English cases, Scottish and N. Irish decisions (unless there is a difference of law between the countries) are generally followed but are not binding, and Republic of Ireland decisions are considered (and vice-versa).

Acts of Parliament, Cmnd. Papers, 'Hansard' Parliamentary Reports and Statutory Instruments (SI) formerly Statutory Rules and Orders (SR & O)) are obtainable from The Stationery Office (bookshops at 49, High Holborn, WC1V 6HB and elsewhere; orders to P.O. Box 276, London SW8 5DT). Telephone orders should be made to 020-7873 9090. **Hansard** references are to daily issues and do not always correspond to the columns in the bound editions. **N.B.** Statements in the House, while useful as indicating the intention of enactments, have no legal authority if the Courts subsequently interpret the wording of the Act differently, but see 4.22 APPEALS for circumstances in which evidence of parliamentary intent may be considered by the Courts.

Abbreviations and References

BOOKS

Inland Revenue explanatory publications may be obtained from local tax offices (except where otherwise stated — see list in Chapter 37) and are mostly free. Most are also on the internet.

Inland Revenue Press Releases and Statements of Practice are obtainable individually from Inland Revenue Information Centre, SW Wing, Bush House, Strand, London WC2B 4RD (tel. 020–7438 6420/5), and are published on the Revenue's website (http:/www.inlandrevenue.gov.uk/ news/press.htm).

Tolley's Corporation Tax 2004/05 is the companion publication to Tolley's Income Tax and sets out the application of the taxing statutes to the income and capital gains of companies up to 1 July 2004 and including the 2004 Finance Act.

Tolley's Capital Gains Tax 2004/05 is a detailed guide to the statutes and case law up to 1 July 2004 and including the 2004 Finance Act. Also includes the charge to corporation tax on chargeable gains. In the same alphabetical format as Tolley's Income Tax and Tolley's Corporation Tax.

Tolley's Inheritance Tax 2004/05 is a detailed guide to the statutes and case law up to 1 July 2004 and including the 2004 Finance Act.

Tolley's Value Added Tax 2004/05 is a comprehensive guide to value added tax, covering legislation, Customs & Excise notices and leaflets and all other relevant information. It is published in two editions, up to 31 January 2004 and up to 1 July 2004 and including the 2004 Finance Act.

Tolley's Tax Computations 2004/05 contains copious worked examples covering income tax, corporation tax, capital gains tax, inheritance tax and value added tax.

Tolley's Income Tax, Corporation Tax and **Capital Gains Tax Workbooks 2004/05** contain comprehensive, clearly presented and up-to-date examples covering income tax, corporation tax and capital gains tax respectively.

Tolley's Yellow Tax Handbook 2004/05 contains the text of the current primary and secondary legislation relating to the main direct taxes, plus non-statutory material. Includes Finance Act 2004.

Tolley's Tax Cases 2004 contains over 2,500 summaries of cases up to 1 January 2004 relevant to current legislation.

Tolley's National Insurance Contributions 2004/05 is the definitive guide to the law and practice relating to this increasingly important 'tax'.

Tolley's Capital Allowances 2004/05 is a detailed and comprehensive guide to all aspects of capital allowances. Includes coverage of Finance Act 2004.

Tolley's Tax Losses is the leading publication covering relief for income and capital losses incurred by individuals and companies. Includes copious worked examples.

Tolley's Practical Tax is a fortnightly newsletter containing news, articles and items of practical use to all involved with UK tax. By subscription only.

1   Allowances and Tax Rates—Applicable to individuals

1.1   This chapter provides a general introduction to UK income tax. All rates and allowances for at least the last six years are included. Changes are shown for and from the year in which they commenced with current rates etc. in **bold type**. A separate **twelve-year summary** of rates and allowances appears inside the front cover.

Headings in this chapter are:

1.2   The **Fiscal Year** (or 'year of assessment' or 'tax year') runs from **6 April to 5 April** (e.g. the fiscal year 2004/05 is from 6 April 2004 to 5 April 2005 inclusive). **Total Income** (see 1.6 below) less **Personal Allowances** (see 1.14–1.19 below) equals **Taxable Income**.

1.3   **RATES OF TAX — 2004/05** [*ICTA 1988, s 1(2); FA 2004, s 23; SI 2004 No 772*]

	Rate	On Taxable Income	Cumulative tax
Starting Rate	10%	0–£2,020	£202
Basic Rate	22%	£2,021–£31,400	£6,665.60
Higher Rate	40%	Over £31,400	

The figure of £2,020 is known as the starting rate limit and the figure of £31,400 as the basic rate limit. [*ICTA 1988, s 1(2A)(3); FA 1999, s 22(2)(3)*].

Where income tax at the basic rate has been deducted from income, and that income is chargeable (in whole or part) at the starting rate (before 1999/2000, at the lower rate), repayment of the excess tax deducted may be claimed. [*ICTA 1988, s 1(6A); FA 1992, s 9(8); FA 1999, s 22(6)*].

A lower rate of **20%** is applied to savings income to the extent that such income does not exceed the basic rate limit (treating it as the highest part of an individual's income). For 1999/2000 onwards, the starting rate applies to such income instead of the lower rate to the extent that it falls within the starting rate band. For 2004/05 onwards, the lower rate is extended to chargeable event gains on life policies. See 1.9 below. Before 1999/2000 the lower rate also applied to income chargeable under Schedule F (i.e. UK company dividends etc. together with related tax credits), or income of the same nature received from non-UK resident companies, but see 1.9 below as regards the special rates applicable to such income from 6 April 1999. [*ICTA 1988, ss 1A, 207A; FA 1993, s 77; FA 1996, s 73, Sch 41 Pt V(1); FA 1999, s 22(7); FA 2000, s 32*].

See 81.5 SETTLEMENTS as regards rate applicable to certain trust income. See 1.13 below as to indexation of tax bands.

Scottish variable rate. With effect for 2000/01 and subsequent years of assessment, the Scottish Parliament has the power to increase or reduce the basic rate of income tax in any year of assessment by up to three percentage points (in half-point steps). The rate so varied will apply to the income of Scottish taxpayers other than income from savings or distributions to which the lower or Schedule F rate applies (see 1.9 below). An individual is treated as a Scottish taxpayer in relation to any year of assessment if he is treated as UK resident for income tax purposes (see 65 RESIDENCE, ORDINARY RESIDENCE AND DOMICILE) and either:

(*a*)   he spends at least as much time during the year in Scotland as elsewhere in the UK;

(*b*)   he is a member of Parliament for a Scottish constituency, a member of the European Parliament for Scotland or a member of the Scottish Parliament; or

(*c*)   his principal UK residence is located in Scotland for at least as much of the tax year as it is not located in Scotland and he spends at least part of the tax year in that Scottish residence.

[*Scotland Act 1998, Pt IV*].

See also Revenue Press Release 23 February 1998 for a Government technical paper commenting on the tax varying power of the Scottish Parliament, and setting out the Government's policy intentions where that power interacts with other parts of the tax system.

1.4   **EARLIER HISTORY**

For 1973/74 onwards, a unified income tax system replaced the previous dual structure of income tax and surtax on the incomes of individuals. A single graduated tax, comprising a basic rate and higher rates, became applicable to all income, whether earned or unearned, and an investment income surcharge commenced as an additional flat rate charge on investment incomes exceeding certain limits. [*FA 1971, ss 32–39, Schs 6, 7; FA 1972, ss 65, 66*]. Earned income relief as such was abolished. [*FA 1971, s 32(2)*]. For 1978/79 and 1979/80 a lower rate applied to the first slice of taxable income. [*FA 1978, s 14; FA 1980, s 18(2)*]. The investment income surcharge was abolished for 1984/85 onwards. [*FA 1984, Sch 7 para 1*].

For rates of tax for 2003/04 to 1998/99, see 1.5 below.

1.5   **RATES OF TAX—2003/04 TO 1998/99**

Starting, basic and higher rate for 2003/04 [*ICTA 1988, s 1(2); FA 2003, s 131; SI 2003 No 840*]

	Rate	On Taxable Income	Cumulative tax
Starting Rate	10%	0–£1,960	£196
Basic Rate	22%	£1,961–£30,500	£6,474.80
Higher Rate	40%	Over £30,500	

Starting, basic and higher rate for 2002/03 [*ICTA 1988, s 1(2); FA 2002, s 26; SI 2002 No 707*]

	Rate	On Taxable Income	Cumulative tax
Starting Rate	10%	0–£1,920	£192
Basic Rate	22%	£1,921–£29,900	£6,347.60
Higher Rate	40%	Over £29,900	

Starting, basic and higher rate for 2001/02 [*ICTA 1988, s 1(2); FA 2001, ss 50, 51; SI 2001 No 638*]

	Rate	On Taxable Income	Cumulative tax
Starting Rate	10%	0–£1,880	£188
Basic Rate	22%	£1,881–£29,400	£6,242.40
Higher Rate	40%	Over £29,400	

Starting, basic and higher rate for 2000/01 [*ICTA 1988, s 1(2); SI 2000 No 806; FA 2000, s 31*]

	Rate	On Taxable Income	Cumulative tax
Starting Rate	10%	0–£1,520	£152
Basic Rate	22%	£1,521–£28,400	£6,065.60
Higher Rate	40%	Over £28,400	

Starting, basic and higher rate for 1999/2000 [*ICTA 1988, s 1(2); SI 1999 No 597; FA 1999, ss 22(1), 23*]

	Rate	On Taxable Income	Cumulative tax
Starting Rate	10%	0–£1,500	£150
Basic Rate	23%	£1,501–£28,000	£6,245
Higher Rate	40%	Over £28,000	

Lower, basic and higher rate for 1998/99 [*ICTA 1988, s 1(2); SI 1998 No 755; FA 1998, s 25*]

	Rate	On Taxable Income	Cumulative tax
Lower Rate	20%	0–£4,300	£860
Basic Rate	23%	£4,301–£27,100	£6,104
Higher Rate	40%	Over £27,100	

1.6 **TOTAL INCOME**

of an individual is the sum of income from all sources, calculated in accordance with tax legislation, after all allowable deductions from each source of income have been made, less certain charges etc. (see 1.10 below). [*ICTA 1988, s 835*]. See also 27 EXCESS LIABILITY.

See Revenue Relief Manual Re 50 *et seq.*

Exemptions. See list under 28 EXEMPT INCOME.

Simon's Direct Tax Service. See E1.401 *et seq.*

1.7 **EARNED INCOME**

'Earned income' is any income arising to an individual:

   (i) which is charged to tax under *ITEPA 2003* (employment (including share-related) income, pension income and social security income), other than jobseeker's allowance (see 83.3 SOCIAL SECURITY) and certain returns of surplus pension contributions (see 58.2(*n*) PENSION INCOME) (and see (iv) below as regards annuities). Before 6 April 2003, the various categories of income falling within this definition were specified. [*ICTA 1988, s 833(4)(a), (5)(a)–(d); ITEPA 2003, Sch 6 para 108(3)(4)*];

   (ii) from any property attached to or forming part of the general earnings from any office or employment (and see *Recknell Ch D 1952, 33 TC 201*). [*ICTA 1988, s 833(4)(b); ITEPA 2003, Sch 6 para 108(3)*];

(iii) from the *personal* carrying on of a trade, profession or vocation (including certain POST-CESSATION RECEIPTS (62) chargeable under *ICTA 1988, s 103* or *s 104* [*ICTA 1988, s 107*] and Lloyd's underwriting profits [*FA 1993, s 180*], see 89.3 UNDER-WRITERS AT LLOYD'S). [*ICTA 1988, s 833(4)(c)*]. This does not include: a sleeping partnership; trustees carrying on business for minors etc. (*Shiels' Trustees CS 1914, 6 TC 583*) (except, in practice, where a trustee carrying on such a business is himself a beneficiary — see also *Dale HL 1953, 34 TC 468*, and *White v Franklin CA 1965, 42 TC 283*); interest received by solicitor on bank deposits made out of clients' funds in his hands (*Brown v CIR HL 1964, 42 TC 42; Northend v White Ch D 1975, 50 TC 121*);

(iv) (notwithstanding (i) above) from annuities under PERSONAL PENSION SCHEMES (60) or RETIREMENT ANNUITIES (66), so far as attributable to contributions on which relief has been given, and partnership retirement annuities as specified in *ICTA 1988, s 628* (see 53.15 PARTNERSHIPS). [*ICTA 1988, ss 619(1), 628(1), 643(3)*];

(v) being inventor's income from patents [*ICTA 1988, s 529*] (see under 54 PATENTS);

(vi) from the distribution of assets of body corporate carrying on mutual business to certain recipients [*ICTA 1988, s 491(5)*], see Tolley's Corporation Tax under Mutual Companies;

(vii) from the sale of earnings for capital sum [*ICTA 1988, s 775(2)*], see 3.9 ANTI-AVOIDANCE;

(viii) from the sale of know-how by non-trading vendor who devised it [*ICTA 1988, s 531(6)*], see 71.57 SCHEDULE D, CASES I AND II; and

(ix) from furnished holiday lettings [*ICTA 1988, s 503*], see 69.8 SCHEDULE A.

1.8   **INVESTMENT (OR UNEARNED) INCOME**

is the income *other than earned income* included in the total income. It includes the following.

(i) **Annual payments** either made otherwise than by an individual, or made in pursuance of an 'existing obligation' (but see below). This includes **annuities** (except that the capital portion of a purchased life annuity or annuity certain is exempt from tax, and certain retirement annuities are treated as earned income, see 1.7(iv) above) and, to the extent outlined below, **maintenance payments** (alimony) under a Court Order or enforceable agreement. Such income may be received after deduction of income tax at the basic rate (but most maintenance payments made after 5 April 1989 (see 47.8 MARRIED PERSONS) are made without deduction of tax as are certain annual payments made under tax avoidance schemes (see 3.18 ANTI-AVOIDANCE)). The gross amount of annual payments is assessable on the recipient but a credit is given for tax deducted (which means that if tax at the basic rate is deducted *and* the recipient is only liable to basic rate tax, there is no further liability).

An annual payment made by an individual, or by a Scottish partnership in which at least one partner is an individual, and (for 1999/2000 and earlier years) not made in pursuance of an 'existing obligation', does not form part of the taxable income of the person to whom it is made or of any other person, but excluded are payments of interest, payments due before 6 April 2000 under charitable covenants, payments made for *bona fide* commercial reasons in connection with the payer's trade, profession or vocation and payments within 3.18 ANTI-AVOIDANCE. This rule also applies to payments treated as income of the payer under *ICTA 1988, ss 660A, 660B* (see 81.13–81.18 SETTLEMENTS) *even if* made under an 'existing obligation', which means, for example, that a payment under a pre-15 March 1988 non-charitable deed of covenant will not count as the income of the recipient for tax purposes.

An '*existing obligation*' means a binding obligation under

(*a*)   a Court Order made, whether or not in the UK, before 15 March 1988, or applied for before 16 March 1988 and made before the end of June 1988, or

(*b*)   a deed executed, or written agreement made, before 15 March 1988 and received by an inspector of taxes before the end of June 1988, or

(*c*)   an oral agreement made before 15 March 1988, written particulars of which were received by an inspector before the end of June 1988, or

(*d*)   a Court Order or written agreement made after 14 March 1988 or a maintenance assessment or maintenance calculation under the Child Support Act 1991 (or NI equivalent) which replaces, varies or supplements an order or agreement within these provisions, but only if

(i)   the obligation is for a person to make periodical payments of maintenance (excluding instalments of a lump sum) to or for the benefit of his or her divorced or separated spouse, or to any person under 21 for his own benefit, maintenance or education, or to any person for the benefit etc. of a person under 21, and

(ii)   the previous order etc. was for the benefit etc. of the same person.

A payment to or for the benefit of a person who attained the age of 21 before the due date of the payment but after 5 April 1994 which is made in pursuance of an obligation within (*a*), (*b*) or (*c*) above is deemed *not* to have been made in pursuance of an existing obligation (and payments within (*b*) and (*c*) above to those aged 18 and over are disregarded — see 47.8 MARRIED PERSONS). This treatment is extended to payments made after 5 April 1996, in pursuance of an obligation within (*a*) above, to or for the benefit of a child who attained the age of 21 before 6 April 1994.

Payments due between a husband and wife at a time when they are living together are, notwithstanding (*a*)–(*d*) above, effectively regarded as being other than in pursuance of an existing obligation.

[*ICTA 1988, s 347A; FA 1988, s 36, Sch 3 para 32; F(No 2)A 1992, s 62(2); FA 1994, s 79(2); FA 1995, Sch 17 para 4(1); FA 1996, s 149; FA 1999, Sch 20 Pt III(6); FA 2000, s 41(2)(9); Child Support, Pensions and Social Security Act 2000, ss 26, 86, Sch 3 para 9; SI 1992 No 2642*].

Maintenance payments received under existing obligations and falling due before 6 April 2000 are taxable only to the extent of the aggregate amount of such payments received from the same person which formed part of the recipient's taxable income (before the above-mentioned deduction) for 1988/89; such payments will usually be receivable without deduction of tax at source (but see 47.8 MARRIED PERSONS for exceptions). In addition, where the payments are received from a divorced or separated spouse, the recipient may claim a maximum deduction equal to the married couple's allowance (see 1.15 below). No deduction may be made in respect of payments due at a time when the beneficiary has remarried. Payments received from a divorced or separated spouse include payments received by a third party for the benefit of the person concerned and payments received by that person for the maintenance of a child of the family, being a person under 21 who is a child of both parties to the marriage or has been treated by them both as a child of their family, but excluding a child who has been boarded out with them by a public authority or voluntary organisation.

Maintenance payments falling due **after 5 April 2000**, whether or not under an existing obligation, do not form part of the recipient's income for tax purposes.

1.9 Allowances and Tax Rates—Applicable to individuals

[*FA 1988, ss 37, 38, 40, Sch 3 para 33; FA 1994, Sch 26 Pt V(1); FA 1999, s 36(7)(8), Sch 20 Pt III(6); FA 2004, Sch 17 para 10(3)*].

See also 47.8 MARRIED PERSONS.

Simon's Direct Tax Service. See B5.3.

(ii) **Dividends etc. and other savings income.** See 1.9 below for the special provisions applicable to such income.

(iii) **Property income** assessed under SCHEDULE A (69) other than from furnished holiday lettings (see 69.8).

1.9 DIVIDENDS AND OTHER SAVINGS INCOME

Dividends etc. In addition to receiving the cash amount of a UK dividend or other qualifying distribution, a UK resident receives a 'tax credit' of a proportion of the dividend etc. received. For payments made before 6 April 1999, this is found by the formula

$$\frac{I}{100 - I}$$

where I is the lower rate of income tax, expressed as a percentage, for the year of assessment. Thus the tax credit is one-quarter of the dividend etc. No tax credit is available in respect of 'foreign income dividends' within *ICTA 1988, Pt VI, Ch VA* (see Tolley's Corporation Tax under Foreign Income Dividends) or certain other payments treated as if they were foreign income dividends (see 3.20 ANTI-AVOIDANCE). Foreign income dividends are, in any event, abolished after 5 April 1999.

From 6 April 1999, the tax credit is a fixed proportion (the 'tax credit fraction') of the dividend etc. This is initially set at one-ninth.

The income assessable on the UK resident is the sum of the dividend etc. and the attached tax credit, with the tax credit being available against the liability.

For 1998/99 and earlier years, income from UK dividends etc. which would otherwise be chargeable at the basic rate is instead chargeable at the lower rate, so that the liability thereon is fully satisfied by the tax credit. The tax credit may generally be repaid if the allowances are not exhausted by other income, and if dividend etc. income exceeds the basic rate limit, it is taxed at the higher rate (with a tax credit at the lower rate). For this purpose, the dividend etc. income is (together, for 1996/97 onwards, with other savings income) treated as the top slice of income (see below).

For 1999/2000 onwards, following the change referred to above in the rate of tax credit, special rates of tax apply to income from dividends etc. (but not to other types of savings income, see below). Where the income falls within the basic rate limit (treating dividend etc. income as the top slice of income), the rate is the 'Schedule F ordinary rate', initially set at 10%, so that the liability is met by the tax credit. To the extent that the income exceeds the basic rate limit, the rate is the 'Schedule F upper rate', initially set at 32.5% (equivalent to a further liability of 25% of the amount of the dividend etc., which is the same as that applicable before 6 April 1999). Also from 6 April 1999, the provisions for payment of the tax credit (e.g. where there are unused personal allowances) are abolished, and tax credits may only be set against liability in respect of qualifying distributions brought into charge (see 2.3(ii) ALLOWANCES AND TAX RATES—EXAMPLES). See, however, 28.13, 28.24 EXEMPT INCOME for a five-year extension of tax credit payments in certain cases.

The Schedule F ordinary rate or, before 6 April 1999, the lower rate applies equally to non-qualifying UK company distributions and (unless taxable on the remittance basis under *ICTA 1988, s 65(5)(b)*, see 73.5 SCHEDULE D, CASES IV AND V) income consisting of foreign dividends etc. chargeable under Schedule D, Case V, which do not, however, carry a tax credit.

[*ICTA 1988, ss 1A, 1B, 14(3), 207A, 231, 231A; FA 1993, ss 77, 78(1)(3); FA 1996, s 73, Sch 41 Pt V(1); F(No 2)A 1997, ss 30, 31*].

The definition of 'excess liability' throughout the *Taxes Acts* is amended to take account of the above provisions. See also 81.5 SETTLEMENTS as regards income of discretionary trusts and 71.72 SCHEDULE D, CASES I AND II as regards dealers in securities.

No tax credit. A UK resident (other than a company) who is not entitled to a tax credit on a distribution is treated as having paid Schedule F ordinary rate tax (before 6 April 1999, lower rate tax) on the distribution. Any Schedule F upper rate tax (before 6 April 1999, higher rate tax) is reduced by the tax so treated as paid. The income is not available to cover tax on charges (see 1.10 below) and the notional tax deducted is not repayable. Where non-entitlement to a tax credit in respect of a qualifying distribution arises from the recipient being non-UK resident (and not a company) or, before 6 April 1999, from the distribution being a 'foreign income dividend' (see above), the distribution is for these purposes grossed up at the Schedule F ordinary rate of tax (before 6 April 1999, the lower rate of tax). [*ICTA 1988, ss 233(1)(1A), 246C, 246D; F(No 2)A 1992, s 19(4); FA 1993, Sch 6 para 2; FA 1994, Sch 16 para 1; FA 1996, s 122(3)–(5), Sch 6 paras 5, 28, Sch 27 para 2, Sch 41 Pt V(1); F(No 2)A 1997, s 31, Sch 4 para 6, Sch 6 para 3; FA 2004, Sch 24 para 1(3)–(6)*]. See also 81.5 SETTLEMENTS as regards income of discretionary trusts.

Certain payments (and other items normally treated as distributions) made by a company for the redemption, repayment or purchase of its own shares are not treated as distributions [*ICTA 1988, s 219*] and consequently have no tax credit and are not treated as income (but see 71.72 SCHEDULE D CASES I AND II as regards dealers in securities). See Tolley's Corporation Tax regarding purchase by a company of its own shares.

A non-resident individual who claims personal allowances (see 51.10 NON-RESIDENTS AND OTHER OVERSEAS MATTERS) is entitled to a tax credit in respect of any qualifying distribution as if he were resident in the UK. [*ICTA 1988, s 232*].

Tax credits set off or repaid which ought not to have been set off or repaid may be assessed, the tax due on such an assessment being payable (subject to the normal appeal procedures) within 14 days after the issue of the notice of assessment. [*ICTA 1988, s 252*].

See Simon's Direct Tax Service D1.401, D1.402.

Savings income (including interest). 'Savings income' is chargeable to income tax at the lower rate (provided in the case of an individual that it is not chargeable at the starting rate or the higher rate — see below). This applies to 'savings income' received by any person other than a discretionary trust (see 81.5 SETTLEMENTS) or unauthorised unit trust (see 90.2 UNIT TRUSTS). The starting rate of income tax applies to savings income for 1999/2000 onwards to the extent that it falls within the starting rate band (treating savings income as the second top slice of income below dividends etc. — see below). Where tax is deductible at source (see below) from 'savings income', then (regardless of the recipient's status) the deduction is at the lower rate. See Revenue Press Release 9 November 1999 as regards tax repayments due for 1999/2000 where liability is at the starting rate and the taxpayer is not within self-assessment. Where, exceptionally, basic rate tax has been deducted at source, repayment of the excess tax deducted can be claimed. For these purposes, *'savings income'* comprises:

(*a*) any income chargeable under SCHEDULE D, CASE III (72), *except for* annuities and other annual payments that are not interest (see 1.8(i) above and 22.10 DEDUCTION OF TAX AT SOURCE) and rents etc. under *ICTA 1988, s 119* (see 22.14 DEDUCTION OF TAX AT SOURCE); *however*, purchased life annuities (see 22.11(*c*) DEDUCTION OF TAX AT

SOURCE, and including those excluded under 22.11(*c*)(i)) are *not* excluded and the lower rate thus applies;

(*b*)   foreign income chargeable under SCHEDULE D, CASES IV AND V (73) and equivalent to income within (*a*) above but arising from securities or other possessions outside the UK, *except for* income so chargeable on the remittance basis (see 73.5 SCHEDULE D, CASES IV AND V) and payments made out of a foreign estate of a deceased person and chargeable under Case IV (see 21.3 DECEASED ESTATES);

(*c*)   (for 1998/99 and subsequent years) amounts chargeable under the accrued income scheme, other than certain charges on trustees (see 74.5 *et seq.* SCHEDULE D, CASE VI); and

(*d*)   (for 2004/05 and subsequent years) chargeable event gains on life policies etc. (though in this case the tax treated as paid at source is notional and not refundable) (see 45.13 LIFE ASSURANCE POLICIES).

Until 5 April 1999, it additionally includes UK company distributions and '*equivalent foreign income*' (i.e. foreign company distributions chargeable under SCHEDULE D, CASES IV AND V (73) which would be chargeable under SCHEDULE F (76) if the paying company were UK-resident (subject to the same exceptions as apply under (*b*) above)). See above as regards dividends and other such distributions after 5 April 1999 and generally.

Savings income is chargeable at the higher rate to the extent that it falls within an individual's higher rate band. If the income has suffered lower rate tax at source, excess liability is payable at the difference between the higher and lower rates. For the purpose of determining this extent, savings income is, until 5 April 1999, treated as the top slice of income, but before taking into account income chargeable under *ITEPA 2003, ss 401–416* (payments and benefits on termination of office or employment — see 18.5 COMPENSATION FOR LOSS OF EMPLOYMENT). From 6 April 1999, dividends and other distributions (and equivalent foreign income) are treated as the top slice and savings income as the next slice. For all years, chargeable event gains on life policies etc. (see 45.13 LIFE ASSURANCE POLICIES) have priority over both dividends etc. and other savings income for all purposes, including the computation of top-slicing relief on such gains. For 2004/05 onwards, *except for the purposes of top-slicing relief,* life assurance gains that do *not* carry a notional tax credit have the same priority as any other savings income; examples are certain friendly society policies (see 31.4 FRIENDLY SOCIETIES) and offshore policies (see 45.19 LIFE ASSURANCE POLICIES).

[*ICTA 1988, ss 1A, 4(1A), 833(3); FA 1996, s 73; FA 1997, Sch 18 Pt VI(2); F(No2)A 1997, s 31; FA 1998, s 100; FA 1999, s 22(7); FA 2000, s 32; ITEPA 2003, Sch 6 para 108(2); FA 2003, s 173, Sch 35 paras 1, 5*].

For whether solicitors' client account interest is savings income, see 44.2 INTEREST RECEIVABLE.

Interest is receivable under deduction of tax at source where it is annual interest paid *by* a company (including a partnership of which a company is a member), *by* a local authority, or *to* a person whose usual place of abode is outside the UK [*ICTA 1988, s 349(2)(3)*], including interest on company debentures and other securities. Bank and building society interest is excluded, but deduction of tax is imposed under separate provisions. See 7.2 BANKS and 8.3 BUILDING SOCIETIES for further details and for exceptions. Otherwise, interest is generally receivable gross. See 28.16 EXEMPT INCOME for interest on 'TESSAs' and other tax-exempt interest, and see also 33 GOVERNMENT STOCKS.

1.10   DEDUCTIONS IN COMPUTING TOTAL INCOME

The following are deductible to the extent indicated in arriving at total income (see 1.6 above).

(i)   **Charges on income**, i.e. sums paid under legal obligation and which may or must be paid under deduction of tax (see 22.2, 22.3 DEDUCTION OF TAX AT SOURCE). These consist of annuities and patent royalties and (subject to the wide exclusions referred to below) annual payments. *[ICTA 1988, s 348(1)(2)(a), s 349(1)]*.

Annual payments. There is a general exclusion from relief against total income, subject to the exceptions referred to below. See 1.8(i) above for details of annual payments and 22 DEDUCTION OF TAX AT SOURCE (and 47.8 MARRIED PERSONS as regards maintenance payments) for the circumstances in which income tax at the basic or lower rate should be deducted. The payer, having deducted tax at source, will be assessed to that tax to the extent, if any, that it exceeds the tax he has borne on his income. *[ICTA 1988, s 350(1)(1A); FA 1996, Sch 6 paras 8, 28]. If he fails to deduct tax*, he obtains no relief for the payment. *[ICTA 1988, s 276; FA 1994, Sch 8 para 11]*. No deduction is made from total income for excess liability purposes for certain annual payments made under tax avoidance schemes (see 3.18 ANTI-AVOIDANCE).

An annual payment made by an individual, or by a Scottish partnership in which at least one partner is an individual, and falling due after 14 March 1988 is excluded from relief as a charge on the income of the person making it. Exceptions are

(*a*)   payments under 'existing obligations' (see 1.8(i) above, and also below as regards maintenance payments),

(*b*)   payments of interest (but see (ii) below),

(*c*)   payments due before 6 April 2000 under charitable covenants,

(*d*)   payments made for *bona fide* commercial reasons in connection with the payer's trade, profession or vocation, and

(*e*)   payments within *ICTA 1988, s 125* (see 3.18 ANTI-AVOIDANCE).

As regards (*a*) above, a payment treated as income of the payer under *ICTA 1988, ss 660A, 660B* (see 81.13–81.18 SETTLEMENTS) is not a charge on the income of the payer even if made under an 'existing obligation', which would apply for example to a payment due and made after 5 April 1995 under a pre-15 March 1988 non-charitable deed of covenant.

[ICTA 1988, s 347A(1)(2); FA 1988, s 36(1)(3); FA 1995, Sch 17 para 4(1); FA 1999, Sch 20 Pt III(6); FA 2000, s 41(2)(9)].

See 47.8 MARRIED PERSONS for special rules regarding maintenance payments, in particular the reduced relief for payments within (*a*) above up to 1999/2000 and the general abolition of such relief for 2000/01 onwards (from which time such payments attract a limited relief and then only if they are qualifying maintenance payments).

(ii)   **Interest payable** by the taxpayer insofar as it is allowable for tax purposes and has not been allowed as a deduction in computing profits. Higher rate relief is denied in certain cases. For 1999/2000 and earlier years, most mortgage interest is relieved either by deduction at source under MIRAS or by way of a reduction in tax payable; such interest is *not* deductible in arriving at total income. Mortgage interest relief is abolished after 5 April 2000. See 43.3 INTEREST PAYABLE.

(iii)   **Qualifying donations** to charities before 6 April 2000 (see 14.16 CHARITIES). (See 14.12 CHARITIES as regards relief for qualifying donations made after 5 April 2000.) *[FA 1990, s 25(6) as originally enacted]*.

(iv)   **Losses** relieved under *ICTA 1988, ss 380, 381* (see 46.3, 46.10 LOSSES). *[ICTA 1988, ss 380(1), 381(2)]*.

(v) (Before 6 April 1999) costs of a **qualifying course of vocational training** (see 92 VOCATIONAL TRAINING RELIEF). [*FA 1991, s 32(2); FA 1999, s 59*].

(vi) **Post-cessation expenditure** (see 62.4 POST-CESSATION RECEIPTS AND EXPENDITURE). [*ICTA 1988, s 109A(1); FA 1995, s 90*].

(vii) **Post-employment deductions** (see 75.26 SCHEDULE E—EMPLOYMENT INCOME). [*ITEPA 2003, s 555(2); FA 1995, s 92(1)*].

Deductions as above are, subject to any express provisions to the contrary, treated as reducing income of different descriptions in the order which will result in the greatest reduction in tax liability. [*ICTA 1988, s 835(4)*].

See Revenue Relief Manual Re 73, 100 *et seq.*

Simon's Direct Tax Service. See E1.501 *et seq.*

See also 27 EXCESS LIABILITY.

1.11 CLAIMS

Allowances unclaimed or not deducted from assessments (and relief for unused tax credits on dividends or tax suffered by deduction at source) may be claimed within five years after 31 January following the tax year for which the claim is made. [*TMA 1970, s 43; FA 1994, ss 196, 199(2)(a), Sch 19 para 14*]. See 16 CLAIMS. But relief is given only in respect of tax actually borne by the claimant, i.e., no relief on income the tax on which he is entitled to charge at the basic rate against, or deduct from any payment to, any other person. [*ICTA 1988, ss 256(3)(c)(ii), 276; FA 1994, s 77(1), Sch 8 para 11*]. Allowances depend upon 'the facts as they exist at the time' and cannot afterwards be withdrawn (or fresh assessments made) by reason of facts 'which arose after the year of assessment' (*Dodworth v Dale KB 1936, 20 TC 285*).

See 6 BANKRUPTCY for claims by bankrupts.

1.12 NON-RESIDENTS

pay income tax at the full rates on chargeable income, with none of the following reliefs except those available to Commonwealth subjects etc. (see 51.10 NON-RESIDENTS AND OTHER OVERSEAS MATTERS) and under certain DOUBLE TAX RELIEF (24) agreements. See, however, 65.5 RESIDENCE, ORDINARY RESIDENCE AND DOMICILE as regards year permanent residence begins or ends.

1.13 INDEXATION OF PERSONAL RELIEFS AND TAX THRESHOLDS

Unless Parliament otherwise determines, the starting rate band, the basic rate band, the higher rate bands (where applicable), the children's tax credit and certain personal reliefs are increased by the same percentage as the percentage increase (if any) in the retail price index (or any substitute index) for the September preceding the year of assessment over that for the previous September. The resultant figure in the case of tax rate bands (other than the starting rate band) and income limits is rounded up to the nearest £100 and in the case of the starting rate band and the personal reliefs to the nearest £10. The personal reliefs affected are the personal allowance, the married couple's allowance, the blind person's allowance and, for 2002/03 only, the children's tax credit at 1.18 below.

The new figures are specified in a statutory instrument by HM Treasury before the year of assessment, but (for 1999/2000 and subsequent years) no change is required in PAY AS YOU EARN (55) deductions or repayments before 18 May in the year of assessment (15 June for 2003/04 for changes to rate bands only). [*ICTA 1988, ss 1(4)(5A)(6), 257C; FA 1988, s 33,*

Sch 3 para 5; FA 1993, s 107; FA 1997, s 56(2)(3); FA 1998, s 27(2); FA 1999, ss 22(4), 25, 30(3); FA 2001, s 53(4)(7); FA 2002, s 27; Tax Credits Act 2002, Sch 6; ITEPA 2003, Sch 6 para 35; FA 2003, s 132; SI 2003 No 962].

1.14   **PERSONAL ALLOWANCE** [*ICTA 1988, s 257; FA 1988, s 33; SI 1995 No 3031; FA 1996, ss 74, 134, Sch 20 para 13; SI 1996 No 2952; FA 1997, s 55; SI 1998 Nos 755, 2704; FA 1999, s 24; SI 1999 Nos 597, 3038; SI 2000 No 806; SI 2000 No 2996; SI 2001 No 3773; FA 2002, ss 28, 29; SI 2002 No 2930; SI 2003 No 3215; FA 2004, s 24*]

The personal allowance is available to all claimants (subject to the rules relating to non-UK residents, see 51.10 NON-RESIDENTS AND OTHER OVERSEAS MATTERS).

For	1998/99	£4,195
For	1999/2000	£4,335
For	2000/01	£4,385
For	2002/02	£4,535
For	2002/03	£4,615
For	2003/04	£4,615
For	**2004/05**	**£4,745**

Where the claimant is at any time in the year of assessment aged 65 (or aged 75) or over, or would have been but for his or her death in that year, a higher allowance is available. Where total income exceeds an income limit, that higher allowance is reduced by one half of the excess until the allowance is the same as the ordinary personal allowance. By concession, contributions to personal pension schemes after 5 April 2001 are deducted from the individual's total income for this purpose (relief otherwise being given only by deduction of tax or, in the case of higher rate relief, by extension of the basic rate band). (Revenue Pamphlet IR 1, A102). The income level at which the higher allowance ceases is shown in the right hand column below.

		Personal allowance		Income	Maximum income	
		65 to 74	75 or over	limit	65 to 74	75 or over
For	1998/99	£5,410	£5,600	£16,200	£18,630	£19,010
For	1999/2000	£5,720	£5,980	£16,800	£19,570	£20,090
For	2000/01	£5,790	£6,050	£17,000	£19,810	£20,330
For	2001/02	£5,990	£6,260	£17,600	£20,510	£21,050
For	2002/03	£6,100	£6,370	£17,900	£20,870	£21,410
For	2003/04	£6,610	£6,720	£18,300	£22,290	£22,510
For	**2004/05**	**£6,830**	**£6,950**	**£18,900**	**£23,070**	**£23,310**

Subject to any express provisions to the contrary, deductions to be made from a person's total income, including the personal allowance, are to be treated as reducing income of different descriptions in the order which will result in the greatest reduction of his income tax liability. [*ICTA 1988, s 835(4)*]. See 14.12 CHARITIES as regards deductions from income in respect of qualifying charitable donations.

See 1.13 above as to indexation.

See 47.4 MARRIED PERSONS as regards certain transitional reliefs.

1.15   **MARRIED COUPLE'S ALLOWANCE** [*ICTA 1988, ss 256, 257A; FA 1988, s 33; FA 1994, ss 77(1)(2)(6)–(10), 78, Sch 8 para 1; SI 1995 No 3031; FA 1996, s 134, Sch 20 para 14; SI 1996 No 2952; FA 1998, s 27(1); SI 1998 No 755; SI 1999 No 597; FA 1999, ss 31, 32, 35; SI 2000 No 806; SI 2000 No 2996; SI 2001 No 3773; SI 2002 No 2930; SI 2003 No 3215*]

The married couple's allowance is **abolished** for 2000/01 and subsequent years of assessment **except** in the case of couples one of whom was born before 6 April 1935, for which see further below. Subject to this, the allowance is available (subject to the rules relating to non-UK residents, see 51.10 NON-RESIDENTS AND OTHER OVERSEAS MATTERS) to a claimant who is, at any time in the year of assessment, a married man whose wife is living with him (see 47.5 MARRIED PERSONS). For polygamous marriages under Moslem law, see *Nabi v Heaton CA 1983, 57 TC 292*, in which, at the Revenue's request, the taxpayer's appeal from the Ch D decision against him was allowed by consent.

For	1998/99	£1,900
For	1999/2000	£1,970

Tax relief for the married couple's allowance is given at a reduced rate of 15% up to and including 1998/99, and 10% thereafter. The allowance is no longer given as a deduction from total income, but is given instead by means of a reduction in the claimant's income tax liability. The reduction is the smaller of the specified percentage (i.e. 10% for 1999/2000) of the allowance and what would otherwise be the claimant's total income tax liability. For this purpose, 'total income tax liability' is before deducting any double tax relief and excludes any basic rate tax deducted at source from charges on income or other payments (and is before giving credit for tax suffered at source on the claimant's income and tax credits on dividends). Other reductions in income tax liability are made before that for married couple's allowance.

No more than one allowance may be claimed for any year of assessment, and where marriage takes place during the year of assessment (and the husband had not previously in that year been entitled to the married couple's allowance), the allowance is reduced by one-twelfth for each fiscal month (i.e. ending on 5 May, 5 June etc.) of the year ending before the date of the marriage.

A man marrying in a year of assessment and otherwise entitled to the additional personal allowance in respect of children (see 1.17 below) may elect that the marriage be disregarded for the purposes of both that allowance and the married couple's allowance. [*ICTA 1988, s 261; FA 1988, Sch 3 para 6; FA 1999, s 33*].

Where death takes place during the year of assessment, the full allowance is available for that year. The allowance is not reduced if the husband remarries during the year in which his wife dies.

See 1.13 above as to indexation.

See 47.1, 47.4 MARRIED PERSONS as regards transfer of allowances and certain transitional reliefs.

Spouse reaching age 65 before 6 April 2000. As indicated above, following the general abolition of the married couple's allowance for 2000/01 and subsequent years of assessment, it continues to be available at the 10% rate where either spouse was born before 6 April 1935. In such cases (and also for years prior to 2000/01), where the claimant or his wife is at any time in the year of assessment aged 65 (or aged 75) or over, or would have been but for his or her death in that year, a higher allowance is available (but with relief restricted, and calculated, as above). Where the claimant's total income exceeds an income limit (as in 1.14 above), that higher allowance is reduced by one half of the excess (less any reduction made in the claimant's personal allowance age increase, see 1.14 above) until the allowance is the same as the ordinary married couple's allowance. As a consequence of the abolition of the ordinary married couple's allowance for 2000/01 and subsequent years of assessment, the minimum figure is based on the ordinary 1999/2000 figure above, indexed for future years in the normal way (see 1.13 above).

For	2000/01	£2,000
For	2001/02	£2,070
For	2002/03	£2,110
For	2003/04	£2,150
For	**2004/05**	**£2,210**

The maximum income level at which the higher allowance ceases is shown in the right hand columns below.

		Married couple's allowance		Income limit	Maximum income	
		65 to 74	75 or over		65 to 74	75 or over
For	1998/99	£3,305	£3,345	£16,200	£21,440	£21,900
For	1999/2000	£5,125	£5,195	£16,800	£25,880	£26,540
For	2000/01	£5,185	£5,255	£17,000	£26,180	£26,840
For	2001/02	£5,365	£5,435	£17,600	£27,100	£27,780
For	2002/03	£5,465	£5,535	£17,900	£27,580	£28,260
For	2003/04	£5,565	£5,635	£18,300	£29,120	£29,480
For	**2004/05**	**£5,725**	**£5,795**	**£18,900**	**£30,100**	**£30,480**

The figures in the right hand column may vary where entitlement to the higher allowance is by virtue of the wife's age rather than the husband's, or where the wife is 75 or over.

For 2001/02 and 2002/03, a man entitled to claim the married couple's allowance cannot claim the children's tax credit (see 1.18 below). At any time when a woman is married to and living with such a man, she is regarded as having no child resident with her. She can thus only claim the children's tax credit for a year of assessment if there is a time during the year when she is *not* married to and living with him. Any person may, however, elect (by notice to the Revenue) to disclaim the married couple's allowance for any year of assessment, and where such an election is in force the person is treated as not entitled to claim it for that year (so that entitlement to the children's tax credit may arise). Children's tax credit is abolished for 2003/04 onwards.

1.16   **WIDOW'S BEREAVEMENT ALLOWANCE** [*ICTA 1988, ss 256, 262; FA 1988, Sch 3 para 7; F(No 2)A 1992, Sch 5 para 7; FA 1994, s 77(1)(5)(8)(9), Sch 8 para 9; FA 1998, s 27(1); FA 1999, ss 34, 35; SI 2000 No 806*]

These provisions cease to have effect in relation to deaths after 5 April 2000.

Where a married man whose wife is living with him dies, his widow is entitled to an allowance for the year of his death, and for the following year provided she does not remarry before the beginning of that year, of an amount equal to the basic married couple's allowance (see 1.15 above) for the year, in addition to any other available reliefs. The allowance is still due if the couple stopped living together before the husband's death, provided that they separated in the year of death and are still married at the time of his death. (Revenue Independent Taxation Handbook, In 523, 524).

For	1998/99	£1,900
For	1999/2000	£1,970
For	2000/01	£2,000

Tax relief for the allowance is given at a reduced rate of 15% up to and including 1998/99, and 10% for 1999/2000 and 2000/01, and is given by means of a reduction in the widow's income tax liability. The reduction is the smaller of the specified percentage (i.e. 10% for 2000/01) of the allowance and what would otherwise be the widow's total income tax liability. For this purpose, 'total income tax liability' is as defined in 1.15 above, except that it is before any reduction on account of married couple's allowance (see below).

Where a widow is entitled for the year of her husband's death both to the bereavement allowance and (as a result of an election (see 47.1 MARRIED PERSONS)) to the whole or part of the married couple's allowance, the married couple's allowance is given by way of reduction in the late husband's income tax liability of the year of death, to the extent that there is sufficient liability to cover it. The widow is entitled to a reduction by reference to any excess allowance.

Attempts have been made by *widowers* to claim an equivalent allowance on the grounds of sex discrimination in breach of the *European Convention on Human Rights*. These have proved unsuccessful (see *R (oao Wilkinson) v CIR CA, [2003] STC 1113*), even though the Board are known to have settled 'out of court' a claim made to the European Court of Human Rights.

These provisions cease to have effect in relation to deaths after 5 April 2000.

1.17   **ADDITIONAL RELIEF IN RESPECT OF CHILDREN** [*ICTA 1988, ss 256, 259–261A; FA 1988, ss 30, 35, Sch 3 paras 5, 6; F(No 2)A 1992, Sch 5 paras 5, 6; FA 1994, s 77(1)(3)(4)(8)(9), Sch 8 paras 6–8; FA 1996, s 134, Sch 20 paras 17, 18; FA 1998, ss 26, 27(1); FA 1999, s 33*]

This relief is abolished for 2000/01 and subsequent years.

A relief equal in amount to the married couple's allowance (see 1.15 above) is claimable by

(i)   any woman who is not throughout the year of assessment married and living with her husband,

(ii)   a man who is neither married and living with his wife for the whole or part of a year of assessment nor entitled to the transitional personal reliefs available to certain separated couples (see 47.4(*c*) MARRIED PERSONS), and

(iii)   an individual who, for the whole or part of a year of assessment, is married, the spouse being totally incapacitated (physically or mentally) throughout the year (for which see Revenue Independent Taxation Handbook, In 594),

who has a 'qualifying child' resident with him/her for the whole or part of the year.

For	1998/99	£1,900
For	1999/2000	£1,970

Relief under (i) and (ii) above is not available for the year of separation, for which special provisions apply (see below).

The relief is given at a reduced rate of 15% up to and including 1998/99, and 10% for 1999/2000, and is given by means of a reduction in the claimant's income tax liability. The reduction is the smaller of the specified percentage (i.e. 10% for 1999/2000) of the additional relief and what would otherwise be the claimant's total income tax liability. For this purpose, 'total income tax liability' is as defined in 1.15 above, except that it is before any reduction on account of married couple's allowance and/or widow's bereavement allowance.

A claimant is entitled to only one relief for a year of assessment no matter how many 'qualifying children' are resident with him/her during the year. A woman is not entitled to relief under (i) above for a year of assessment during any part of which she is married and living with her husband unless the 'qualifying child' is resident with her during a part of the year when she is not married and living with her husband.

A man marrying in a year of assessment may claim that his marriage be disregarded for the purposes of both this relief and the married couple's allowance (see 1.15 above).

Where an unmarried couple live together as husband and wife at any time in the year of assessment, and they would both otherwise be entitled to claim the additional relief, then neither of them will be entitled to the relief in respect of any child other than the youngest of the children for whom either of them could otherwise claim relief, i.e. relief to the couple is restricted to one allowance.

A '*qualifying child*' must be born in, or under sixteen at the commencement of, the year of assessment or over sixteen and receiving full-time instruction at a university, college, school or other educational establishment or undergoing full-time training by an employer (for not less than two years) for a trade, profession or vocation. A child who enrols on a two year YTS training programme normally satisfies this latter condition. See generally Revenue Independent Taxation Handbook, In 653–655. The child must be resident with the claimant for the whole or part of the year, and must be a 'child of the claimant' or, if not, must be under eighteen and maintained for the whole or part of the year at the claimant's expense. 'Custody' of child is not required.

The Revenue consider that, to be 'resident with' the claimant, a child must have his or her home with the claimant. While it is possible for a child to have more than one home, it is not accepted that any short visit, e.g. for a holiday, makes the place so visited a home. (Revenue Tax Bulletin November 1992 p 44, and see Revenue Independent Taxation Handbook, IN 640).

'*Child of the claimant*' includes a stepchild, an illegitimate child whose parents have married each other after his birth and a child adopted under the age of eighteen.

Age of child. A child is 'over sixteen' or 'over eighteen' at the beginning of a year of assessment if its sixteenth or eighteenth birthday falls either on the first day of that year (i.e. 6 April) or during the previous year.

Apportionment of the relief may be made between two or more persons as may be agreed between them or, failing agreement, in proportion to the length of the periods the child resided with them respectively during the year. Failing agreement, the apportionment is to be made by the appellate General Commissioners for the division in which one of the claimants resides (or Special Commissioners if none of the claimants resides in the United Kingdom). Each claimant is entitled to make oral or written representations.

The Board may direct that a claim to relief which requires apportionment be dealt with by the Commissioners. Where an individual is apportioned amounts in respect of two or more children, his total relief is limited to the lesser of the sum of those amounts and the full relief available for one child. An individual is not entitled to relief in respect of the same child as another person if he alone is entitled to relief in respect of another child.

Year of separation. The additional relief is available in the year of assessment of 'separation' to a spouse with whom a qualifying child resides during the year but after the separation, but not where it is already available to that spouse under (iii) above. The amount of the relief is reduced by any married couple's allowance available to the spouse (see 1.15 above, 47.1 MARRIED PERSONS), unless that allowance has been transferred to that spouse because the other spouse's income was insufficient fully to utilise the allowance (see 47.1 MARRIED PERSONS). Only one relief is available to a spouse, regardless of the number of qualifying children resident with the spouse. The relief is given at a reduced rate, and by means of an income tax reduction, as above.

Where another person is entitled to the additional relief in respect of the same child, whether under this or under the general provision, the total relief (which may not exceed the married couple's allowance) is apportioned between them (subject to the same procedural rules as apply in relation to the general provision above). '*Separation*' for these purposes means separation under a Court order or deed of separation or in circumstances that it is likely to be permanent.

This relief is abolished for 2000/01 and subsequent years.

1.18　Allowances and Tax Rates—Applicable to individuals

1.18　CHILDREN'S TAX CREDIT [*ICTA 1988, s 257AA, Sch 13B; FA 1999, ss 30, 35, Sch 3; FA 2000, ss 34, 39(9); FA 2001, ss 52, 53, Sch 11; Tax Credits Act 2002, Sch 6; SI 2002 No 707; SI 2003 No 962*]

This relief is abolished for 2003/04 and subsequent years.

For **2001/02 and 2002/03**, an income tax reduction (a '*children's tax credit*') is available by reference to the following amount to a claimant with whom a 'qualifying child' (or more than one) is resident during the whole or part of the year.

| For | 2001/02 | £5,200 |
| For | 2002/03 | £5,290 |

For 2002/03 only, if any 'qualifying child' was born during the year of assessment, the amount is increased by £5,200 for that year.

The amount is, however, reduced by £2 for every £3 of the claimant's income in respect of which income tax is chargeable at the higher rate or Schedule F upper rate (see 1.3, 1.9 above) for the year. See also 1.15 above as regards interaction with married couple's allowance for couples at least one of whom was born before 6 April 1935.

The income tax reduction is the smaller of 10% of the available amount and what would otherwise be the claimant's total income tax liability. For this purpose 'total income tax liability' is before deducting any double tax relief and excludes any basic rate tax deducted at source from charges on income or other payments (and is before giving credit for tax suffered at source on the claimant's income and tax credits on dividends). The reduction is made before that for the married couple's allowance (where still applicable, see 1.15 above).

A '*qualifying child*' is a child under 16 who either is a child of the claimant (including an illegitimate child or stepchild) or is maintained by, and at the expense of, the claimant for any part of a year of assessment.

For **2003/04** onwards, children's tax credit is **abolished**, as a consequence of the introduction in April 2003 of the 'child tax credit', a new social security type of benefit payable direct to the main child carer. See 83.7 SOCIAL SECURITY.

Child living with more than one adult: married and unmarried couples. Special provision is made for cases where, at any time in a year of assessment, a child (the '*relevant child*') is a qualifying child in relation to both of a husband and wife living together or a man and a woman living together as husband and wife. These are referred to below as the 'partners', and as the 'higher-earning' or 'lower-earning' partner by reference to total income for the year. If both partners have the same total income, they may elect for one of them to be treated as the lower-earning partner, and if they do not make an election neither of them is entitled to the children's tax credit for the year. The lower-earning partner is not entitled to the children's tax credit in respect of the relevant child, except that if neither partner is liable to higher rate or Schedule F upper rate tax on any part of his or her income, then, if the lower earning partner so claims, the amount by reference to which the credit is given is divided equally between the partners. Alternatively, again where no higher rate etc. liability, the partners may elect, by notice to the Revenue, for the whole of the amount to be allocated to the lower earning partner. Such an election may be for one year or for a number of consecutive years and must be made before the start of the year (or first year) for which it is to have effect on the basis of assumptions about the partners' incomes for that year. It may be made on such assumptions during the year (or first year) for which it is to have effect provided that:

(*a*)　it is made during the first 30 days of that year following written notification having been given to the Revenue before the start of the year of the intention to make the election; or (*b*)   the partners marry in that year; or

(*c*)   the partners start to live together as man and wife during that year; or

(*d*)   a relevant child becomes resident with the partners in that year, no relevant child having previously been resident with them during that year; or

(*e*)   it is assumed that the lower-earning partner in that year will have been the higher-earning partner in the previous year; or

(*f*)   (for 2002/03) a relevant child is born in that year.

The election may be withdrawn by the making of another election superseding the first or by notice to the Revenue by either partner. In the latter case, the withdrawal has effect for the year of assessment in which the notice is given and for subsequent years. An election for one year in any event does not have effect for the next year or for subsequent years where the lower-earning partner in the second year was the higher-earning partner in the first.

Where a partner whose children's tax credit exceeds his or her total income tax liability for a year of assessment gives notice to the Revenue, the other partner will be entitled to the excess amount by reference to which the credit is available, in addition (where relevant) to any existing entitlement. The notice must be given on or before the fifth anniversary of the 31 January next following the end of the year of assessment, in such form as the Board may determine, and is irrevocable.

Child living with more than one adult: other cases. Special provision is also made for cases where a child is a qualifying child in relation to two or more persons (the 'taxpayers') with whom he is resident at the same or different times during a year of assessment and the above provisions for married and unmarried couples do not apply. The amount by reference to which the credit is given is divided amongst all such people who make a claim either as agreed between all the taxpayers concerned or, in default of agreement, as determined by the General Commissioners for a division in which one of the taxpayers resides (as the Revenue directs), or, if all the taxpayers are non-resident, by the Special Commissioners. The case is heard in the same manner as an appeal, with any of the taxpayers being entitled to appear and be heard or to make written representations. A taxpayer may aggregate amounts allotted under this provision in respect of a number of children, but not so as to total more than the full amount available in respect of a single child (and for 2002/03 and subsequent years, if any of the children in respect of whom the taxpayer was or could have been allotted a proportionate credit was born during the year, the maximum is the double amount available in respect of such a child).

Combined cases. Where, in any year of assessment, a child is a relevant child for the purposes of the provisions relating to married and unmarried couples (as above) and either

(i)   it is a relevant child in relation to more than one pair of partners, or

(ii)   the provisions for other cases described above would apply to it for that year but for the fact of its being a relevant child under the married and unmarried couples provisions,

the provisions for other cases described above are first applied, treating each pair of partners under the married and unmarried couples rules as a single person to whom the amount to be allotted is determined, and the married and unmarried couples provisions then apply to each pair of partners by reference to the amount so allotted to them.

Changes of circumstances. Where a 'relevant event' takes place in a year of assessment in relation to a child, and either the child is, immediately before the event, a qualifying child in relation to both parties to the event, or as a result of the event the child becomes, or stops being, a qualifying child in relation to any person, then all the above provisions apply in relation to the child's residence as if each of the following were a separate year of assessment:

(A)   the period ending with the day before the first (or only) such event;

(B)   the period starting with the day of the last (or only) such event; and

(C)   any period starting with the day of one such event and ending with the day before the next,

except that, for 2002/03, this does not apply in determining whether a double allowance is due for the year as a result of a child having been born during that year.

The amount by reference to which the credit is given is apportioned to such periods at the rate of 1/365th for each day in a period. A person's income is, however, taken as his or her income for the whole year and not just for the period concerned. A '*relevant event*' is the marriage of a man and a woman, or their starting to live together as husband and wife, or a husband and wife ceasing to live together, or a man and woman who have been living together as husband and wife (without being married) ceasing to do so.

Revenue guidance. For guidance on the application of these provisions, including numerous examples, see Revenue Independent Taxation Manual IN 1300 *et seq.*

This relief is abolished for 2003/04 and subsequent years.

1.19   **BLIND PERSONS** [*ICTA 1988, s 265; FA 1988, Sch 3 para 8; FA 1994, s 82; FA 1996, ss 75, 134, Sch 20 para 19; FA 1997, s 56; SI 1998 No 755; SI 1999 No 597; SI 2000 No 806; SI 2001 No 638; SI 2002 No 707; SI 2002 No 2930; SI 2003 No 3215*]

For	1998/99	£1,330
For	1999/2000	£1,380
For	2000/01	£1,400
For	2001/02	£1,450
For	2002/03	£1,480
For	2003/04	£1,510
For	**2004/05**	**£1,560**

Allowance as above may be claimed if a person is, throughout the whole or part of the year, registered as blind under *National Assistance Act 1948, s 29* (or Scottish or NI equivalent).

By concession, a person becoming entitled to the blind person's allowance by being registered during the year will (subject to the normal time limit for claims) also be given the allowance for the previous year if, at the end of that year, the evidence on which the registration was based (e.g. the ophthalmologist's certificate) had already been obtained. (Revenue Pamphlet IR 1, A86).

For transfer of allowances between spouses, see 47.1 MARRIED PERSONS.

See 1.14 above re *ICTA 1988, s 835(4)* (order of set-off), which applies equally to blind person's allowance.

1.20   For Life Assurance Relief, see 45.1 *et seq.* LIFE ASSURANCE POLICIES. For relief for medical insurance premiums, see 48 MEDICAL INSURANCE. For Mortgage Interest Relief, see 22.13 DEDUCTION OF TAX AT SOURCE and 43.6 *et seq.* INTEREST PAYABLE. For relief for Pension Contributions, see 60 PERSONAL PENSION SCHEMES (AND STAKEHOLDER PENSIONS), 66 RETIREMENT ANNUITIES and 67 RETIREMENT SCHEMES FOR EMPLOYEES.

2   Allowances and Tax Rates—Examples

The following examples illustrate the method of calculating tax payable **for 2004/05**. References in brackets are to items above (under 1 ALLOWANCES AND TAX RATES).

2.1   A **single person** aged under 65 receives earned income of £15,000, net building society interest of £488 and national savings bank ordinary account interest of £130.

		£	£
(1.7)	Earned income		15,000
(1.9)	Building society interest received	488	
	Tax deducted ($\frac{20}{80}$)	122	
		—	610
	National savings bank ordinary account interest		
	(£130 less £70 exempt)		60
(1.6)	Total income		15,670
(1.14)	*Deduct* Personal allowance		4,745
	Taxable income		£10,925
(1.3)	Tax liability (non-savings income):		
	£2,020 at 10%		202.00
	£8,235 at 22%		1,811.70
(1.9)	(savings income):		
	£670 at 20%		134.00
			2,147.70
	Deduct tax deducted from interest		122.00
	Tax payable		£2,025.70

2.2   **Repayment claim.** A single person aged under 65 years receives earned income of £2,950 (no tax having been deducted under PAYE), plus bank deposit interest of £1,600 (net of £400 tax deducted at source).

		£
(1.7)	Earned income	2,950
(1.9)	Bank deposit interest (£1,600 + £400)	2,000
(1.6)	Total income	4,950
(1.14)	*Deduct* Personal allowance	4,745
	Taxable income	£205
(1.9)	Tax liability: £205 at 10% (starting rate)	20.50
	Deduct Tax deducted at source	400.00
	Income tax repayable	£379.50

2.3   **Dividend taxation.** (i) A married man has income from self-employment assessable in 2004/05 of £29,400. He also receives UK dividends in that year of £8,100 (with tax credit attached £900). Both he and his wife were under 65 at 5 April 2000 (so that no married couple's allowance is due).

		£	£
(1.7)	Earned income	29,400	
(1.9)	Dividends (incl. tax credit)	9,000	
(1.6)	Total income	38,400	
(1.14)	*Deduct* Personal allowance	4,745	
	Taxable income	33,655	
(1.3)	Tax liability on non-dividend income:		
	£2,020 at 10% (starting rate)		202.00
	£22,635 at 22%		4,979.70
(1.9)	Tax liability on dividends: (£31,400 – £24,655 =)		
	£6,745 at 10% (Schedule F ordinary rate)		674.50
	£2,255 at 32.5% (Schedule F upper rate)		732.87
			6,589.07
	Deduct Tax credit on dividends		900.00
	Income tax payable		£5,689.07

(ii) A widow aged 68 has a taxable pension of £4,160 and net dividend income of £30,240.

		£	£	£
(1.7)	Earned income		4,160	
(1.9)	Dividends	30,240		
(1.9)	Tax credit ($\frac{1}{9}$)	3,360		
			33,600	
(1.6)	Total income		37,760	
(1.14)	*Deduct* Personal allowance		4,745	
	Taxable income		£33,015	
(1.3)	No tax liability on non-dividend income (covered by personal allowance)			Nil
(1.9)	Tax liability on dividends:			
	£2,020 at 10% (starting rate)			202.00
	£29,380 at 10% (Schedule F ordinary rate)			2,938.00
	£1,615 at 32.5% (Schedule F upper rate)			524.87
				3,664.87
	Deduct Tax credit on dividends:			
	£33,015 at 10% (note (*a*))			3,301.50
	Income tax payable			£363.37

Notes

(*a*)   Tax credits deductible are restricted to those on the amount of dividends brought into charge to tax (see 1.9 ALLOWANCES AND TAX RATES). In this case, £585 of dividends are covered by excess of personal allowance over non-dividend income.

(*b*)   No age-related personal allowance is available — as total income is too far in excess of £18,900 income limit (see also 2.4 below).

2.4   **Age increase in personal/married couple's allowance.** A married man aged 78 has a total income of £23,500 (which does not include any dividend or savings income).

		£	£
(1.6)	Total income	23,500	23,500
(1.14)	Income limit	18,900	
(1.15)			
	Excess	4,600	
(1.14)	Personal allowance (75 and over)	6,950	
	Less reduction for excess ($\frac{1}{2} \times 4,600$)	2,300	
		4,650	
	Since this is below the basic personal allowance of £4,745, the reduction is limited to £2,205 and the full £4,745 is allowable		4,745
	Taxable income		£18,755
(1.3)	Tax liability: £2,020 at 10%		202.00
	£16,735 at 22%		3,681.70
			3,883.70
(1.15)	*Deduct* Married couple's allowance £5,700 (see below) at 10%		570.00
	Tax payable		£3,313.70
(1.15)	Married couple's allowance (75 and over)		5,795
	Less reduction for excess	2,300	
	less reduction in personal allowance	2,205	95
			£5,700

2.5   **Transfer of married couple's allowance.** A married man aged 68 at 5 April 2000 has a total income for 2004/05 of £8,330. His wife, aged under 65, has a total income of £10,500. She elects to receive one-half of the minimum married couple's allowance. Neither spouse has any savings or dividend income.

Husband		£
(1.6)	Total income	8,330
(1.14)	Personal allowance	6,830
	Taxable income	£1,500

2.5 Allowances and Tax Rates—Examples

(1.3)	Tax liability: £1,500 at 10%	150.00
(1.15)	*Deduct* Married couple's allowance (£5,725 − ½ × £2,210) = £4,620 £4,620 at 10% = £462.00 but restricted to	150.00
	Tax payable	Nil

Wife

(1.6)	Total income	10,500
(1.14)	Personal allowance	4,745
	Taxable income	£5,755

(1.3)	Tax liability: £2,020 at 10%	202.00
	£3,735 at 22%	821.70
		1,023.70
(1.15)	*Deduct* Married couple's allowance (under election) £1,105 (£2,210 × ½) at 10%	110.50
	Tax payable (subject to below)	£913.20

The unused balance of the husband's married couple's allowance is (£462 − £150) × $\frac{100}{10}$ = £3,120. On a claim, this may be transferred to the wife, who will then be entitled to a further income tax reduction of £312 (£3,120 at 10%), reducing tax payable to £601.20.

3 Anti-Avoidance

Cross-references. See CAPITAL ALLOWANCES at 9.8, 9.22 and 9.38(C) for sales between connected persons and 9.35 re certain leasing arrangements; 24 DOUBLE TAX RELIEF for amounts taxed abroad; 43.2(ii) INTEREST PAYABLE for certain interest; 45.5 LIFE ASSURANCE POLICIES for withdrawal of life assurance relief; 46.8 LOSSES for restrictions relating to the use of losses in a trade, profession or vocation; 52 OFFSHORE FUNDS; 53.9–53.11 PARTNERSHIPS for restrictions on loss reliefs and interest reliefs due to non-active partners; 53.13 PARTNERSHIPS in relation to certain company partnership arrangements; 53.17, 53.18 PARTNERSHIPS for restrictions on loss reliefs and interest reliefs due to, respectively, limited partners and members of limited liability partnerships; 69.16 and 69.17 SCHEDULE A for certain transactions in short leases; 74.5 *et seq.* SCHEDULE D, CASE VI for accrued income scheme; 81.13–81.20 SETTLEMENTS for provisions treating income of settlements as income of settlor.

Other sources. See Tolley's Anti-Avoidance Provisions.

3.1   **For the general approach of the Courts** to transactions entered into solely to avoid or reduce tax liability, leading cases are *Duke of Westminster v CIR HL 1935, 19 TC 490; W T Ramsay Ltd v CIR, Eilbeck v Rawling HL 1981, 54 TC 101; CIR v Burmah Oil Co Ltd HL 1981, 54 TC 200* and *Furniss v Dawson (and related appeals) HL 1984, 55 TC 324.* See also *Cairns v MacDiarmid CA 1982, 56 TC 556; Ingram v CIR Ch D, [1985] STC 835; Craven v White and related appeals HL 1988, 62 TC 1; Shepherd v Lyntress Ltd Ch D 1989, 62 TC 495; Moodie v CIR and Sinnett HL 1993, 65 TC 610; Hatton v CIR Ch D, [1992] STC 140; Ensign Tankers (Leasing) Ltd v Stokes HL 1992, 64 TC 617; Countess Fitzwilliam and Others v CIR and related appeals HL, [1993] STC 502; Pigott v Staines Investment Co Ltd Ch D 1995, 68 TC 342; CIR v McGuckian HL 1997, 69 TC 1;* and *MacNiven v Westmoreland Investments Ltd HL 2001, 73 TC 1.*

The classical interpretation of the constraints upon the Courts in deciding cases involving tax avoidance schemes is summed up in Lord Tomlin's statement in the *Duke of Westminster* case that ' . . . every man is entitled if he can to order his affairs so that the tax attaching . . . is less than it otherwise would be.' The case concerned annual payments made under covenant by a taxpayer to his domestic employees, which were in substance, but not in form, remuneration. The judgment was thus concerned with the tax consequences of a single transaction, but in *Ramsay*, and subsequently in *Furniss v Dawson*, the Courts have set bounds to the ambit within which this principle can be applied in relation to modern sophisticated and increasingly artificial arrangements to avoid tax. *Ramsay* concerned a complex 'circular' avoidance scheme at the end of which the financial position of the parties was little changed, but it was claimed that a large CGT loss had been created. It was held that where a preconceived series of transactions is entered into to avoid tax, and with the clear intention to proceed through all stages to completion once set in motion, the *Duke of Westminster* principle does not compel a consideration of the individual transactions and of the fiscal consequences of such transactions taken in isolation.

The HL opinions in *Furniss v Dawson* are of outstanding importance, and establish, inter alia, that the *Ramsay* principle is not confined to 'circular' devices, and that if a series of transactions is 'preordained', a particular transaction within the series, accepted as genuine, may nevertheless be ignored if it was entered into solely for fiscal reasons and without any commercial purpose other than tax avoidance, even if the series of transactions as a whole has a legitimate commercial purpose.

However, in *Craven v White* the House of Lords indicated that for the *Ramsay* principle to apply all the transactions in a series have to be pre-ordained with such a degree of certainty that, at the time of the earlier transactions, there is no practical likelihood that the

3.1 Anti-Avoidance

transactions would not take place. It is not sufficient that the ultimate transaction is simply of a kind that was envisaged at the time of the earlier transactions.

The inheritance tax case *Fitzwilliam v CIR* appears to further restrict the application of the *Ramsay* principle, in that the HL found for the taxpayer in a case in which all their Lordships agreed that, once the scheme was embarked upon, there was no real possibility that the later transactions would not be proceeded with. There is, however, some suggestion that a decisive factor was that the first step in the transactions took place before the rest of the scheme had been formulated. Again, in the case of *MacNiven v Westmoreland Investments Ltd* it was held that the *Ramsay* principle did not apply where a company loaned money to a subsidiary to enable it to pay up outstanding interest and thus crystallise tax losses. The interest had been paid within the meaning of the legislation and the manner in which the payment was funded was irrelevant.

See ICAEW Guidance Note TR 588 'Furniss v Dawson' for guidance on the Revenue approach to the application of the principles outlined above.

Simon's Direct Tax Service. See A1.314–A1.317.

Anti-avoidance legislation is intended to counteract transactions designed to avoid taxation, but *bona fide* transactions may sometimes be caught also. The provisions relating to individuals (some of which may also relate to companies) are detailed below and as further indicated in the cross-references above. For provisions relating only to companies, see Tolley's Corporation Tax — and see Tolley's Capital Gains Tax for CGT provisions.

3.2   Cancellation of tax advantages from certain transactions in securities. [*ICTA 1988, ss 703–709*].

3.3   Sale of right to annuities, dividends or interest. [*ICTA 1988, s 730*].

3.4   Treatment of price differential on sale and repurchase of securities. [*ICTA 1988, ss 730A, 730B*].

3.5   Income received on securities held for one month or less. [*ICTA 1988, ss 731–735*].

3.6   'Manufactured' dividends or interest. [*ICTA 1988, ss 736A–738, Sch 23*].

3.7   Transfer of assets abroad. [*ICTA 1988, ss 739–746*].

3.8   Transfer pricing. [*ICTA 1988, s 770A, Sch 28AA*].

3.9   Capital sums received in lieu of earnings. [*ICTA 1988, ss 775, 777, 778*].

3.10   Transactions in land. [*ICTA 1988, ss 776–778*].

3.11   Land sold and leased back. [*ICTA 1988, s 779*].

3.12   Land sold and leased back. [*ICTA 1988, s 780*].

3.13   Leases of assets other than land. [*ICTA 1988, ss 781, 783, 784*].

3.14   Leases of assets (other than land) previously owned for trade etc., by taxpayer. [*ICTA 1988, s 782*].

3.15   Loan transactions. [*ICTA 1988, s 786*].

3.16   Persons exempt from tax (restrictions regarding pre-acquisition dividends etc., received on 10% holdings). [*ICTA 1988, ss 235, 236*].

3.17   Persons exempt from tax (restriction regarding certain bonus issues). [*ICTA 1988, s 237*].

3.18   Annual payments for non-taxable consideration. [*ICTA 1988, s 125*].

3.19   Dealings in commodity futures. [*ICTA 1988, s 399*].

3.20   Companies buying their own shares and other special dividends. [*FA 1997, s 69, Sch 7*].

3.21   Futures and options. [*ICTA 1988, s 127A, Sch 5AA*].

3.22   Arrangements to pass on value of dividend tax credit. [*F(No 2)A 1997, s 28*].

3.23   Benefits from pre-owned assets. [*FA 2004, s 84, Sch 15*].

Disclosure of tax avoidance schemes. *FA 2004* imposes a disclosure obligation on promoters of certain tax avoidance schemes and in some cases on persons entering into transactions under such schemes. See 3.24 below.

3.2   **CANCELLATION OF TAX ADVANTAGES FROM CERTAIN TRANSACTIONS IN SECURITIES** [*ICTA 1988, ss 703–709*]

Where, in consequence of transaction(s) in securities (including interests in companies not limited by shares, and such transaction(s) coupled with liquidation of a company), *combined with* any of the relevant circumstances mentioned below, a person is able to obtain a tax advantage, the Board of Inland Revenue may make adjustments counteracting that advantage (having first given notice of their intention to do so), unless the person concerned is able to show that the transactions were made (1) for *bona fide* commercial reasons or in the ordinary course of investment management, and (2) without tax advantages being their main object, or one of their main objects. [*ICTA 1988, s 703*]. For 'transactions in securities' see *CIR v Joiner HL 1975, 50 TC 449* (in which a variation of rights prior to a liquidation was held to be such a transaction) and *CIR v Laird Group plc HL, [2003] STC 1349* (in which the payment of a dividend representing previously undistributed profits was held not to be). For '*bona fide* commercial reasons' see *Laird Group* in the *Ch D ([2001] STC 689)* and *CIR v Brebner HL 1967, 43 TC 705, Clark v CIR Ch D 1978, 52 TC 482* and *Marwood Homes Ltd v CIR, Tribunal 1998, [1999] SSCD 44*. In *Lewis (as a trustee of the Redrow Staff Pension Scheme) v CIR (Sp C 218), [1999] SSCD 349*, a distribution by way of purchase of its own shares by a company from the trustees of its pension scheme, pursuant to legislation requiring the trustees to reduce their holding, was held to be a transaction carried out by the trustees both for *bona fide* commercial reasons and in the ordinary course of investment management.

The relevant circumstances are those where a person:

A   in connection with (i) the distribution, transfer or realisation of a company's profits, income, reserves or other assets, or (ii) a sale or purchase of securities followed by the purchase or sale of the same or other securities, *receives an abnormal amount* (see definition below) *by way of dividend* (or other qualifying distribution, see *ICTA 1988, s 14(2)*) which is taken into account for purposes of (*a*) tax exemption or (*b*) setting-off losses against profits or income or (*c*) group relief (see *ICTA 1988, s 402*) or (*d*) (before 6 April 1999) calculating a company's advance corporation tax liability, or (*e*) (before 2 July 1997) the application of a surplus of franked investment income under *ICTA 1988, s 242* or *s 243*, or (*f*) payments within *ICTA 1988, s 348* or *s 349(1)*, or (*g*) setting against income of interest paid, or (*h*) the application of franked investment income in relation to 'shadow ACT' computations (see Tolley's Corporation Tax under Advance Corporation Tax), or

B   in connection with A(i) and (ii) above, *becomes entitled to a deduction from profits because of a decrease in value of securities* held, formerly held, or sold which arises from payment of a dividend thereon or from any other dealing with a company's assets (or where another company obtains the benefit of such a deduction by way of group relief), or

C   in consequence of a transaction whereby (see *CIR v Garvin HL 1981, 55 TC 24* and *Bird v CIR HL 1988, 61 TC 238*, and contrast *Emery v CIR Ch D 1980, 54 TC 607*)

another person has received or subsequently receives an abnormal amount (see definition below) by way of dividend, or has become, or subsequently becomes, entitled to a deduction, as in B above, *receives a consideration not taxable as income* (apart from the present provisions) representing the value of a company's trading stock, future receipts, or assets which are, or would otherwise have been, available for distribution (see *CIR v Brown CA 1971, 47 TC 217*) as dividend, and which, in the case of a company incorporated abroad, do not represent a return of capital to subscribers, or

D   in connection with the distribution of the profits, income, reserves or other assets of a company (including any body corporate) under the control of *five or fewer persons*, or whose shares are not listed and dealt in on the Stock Exchange (but excluding in either case any company under control of one or more companies to which D does not apply), *receives a consideration not taxable as income* as in C above, or

E   in connection with (i) the transfer of the assets of a company to which D above applies, to another such company, or (ii) a transaction in securities in which two or more such companies are concerned, receives, in the form of *share capital or securities* of such a company, any non-taxable consideration representing the value of distributable assets of such a company. (Adjustments under this heading may be made immediately if the consideration consists of securities or redeemable share capital, but in the case of non-redeemable share capital *not unless*, and until, *that capital is repaid* (including repayments in liquidation).)

[*ICTA 1988, s 704; FA 1996, s 175; F(No 2)A 1997, Sch 8 Pt II(4); FA 1998, Sch 3 para 33; SI 1999 No 358, reg 23*].

C, D and E above are in practice unlikely to apply unless the company in question has (or has recently had) distributable reserves. (Revenue Inspector's Manual IM 4516–4518).

See Revenue Tax Bulletin November 1992 p 37 for the Revenue view on the application of these provisions in relation to payments of intra-group dividends outside any group income election.

For **other cases** under C and D above, see *CIR v Cleary HL 1967, 44 TC 399; Anysz v CIR Ch D 1977, 53 TC 601; Williams v CIR HL 1980, 54 TC 257; CIR v Wiggins Ch D 1978, 53 TC 639*. In determining 'under the control' in D, the relevant date is the date of the dividend (*CIR v Garvin above*).

An abnormal amount by way of dividend etc. is one which substantially exceeds either

(*a*)   a normal return on the consideration provided for the shares, with market value at time of acquisition used if less than consideration or if no consideration provided, and, in determining 'normal return', regard will be had to length of time the shares were held and other distributions received in respect of them, or

(*b*)   the proportion of the dividend arising during ownership (where the dividend is at a fixed rate and the recipient sells, disposes of, or acquires an option to sell, the securities within six months of purchase). [*ICTA 1988, s 709(4)–(6)*].

'Dividend' includes interest and any other qualifying distribution. The amount of a qualifying distribution includes the related tax credit for these purposes (*CIR v Universities Superannuation Scheme Ltd Ch D 1996, 70 TC 193*). In the case of a purchase by a company of its own shares treated as a distribution under *ICTA 1988, s 209(2)(b)* (see Tolley's Corporation Tax under Distributions), it was held that the return was not abnormal (*CIR v Sema Group Pension Scheme Trustees CA 2002, 74 TC 593*).

Tax advantage means any relief or repayment (or increases thereof) or avoidance or reduction of a charge or assessment to tax, whether effected by receipts accruing as non-taxable or by deductions from profits or gains. It is made clear that this includes a dividend tax credit, or (before 6 April 1999) the payment of an amount in respect of a dividend tax credit. [*ICTA 1988, s 709(1)(2A); FA 1997, s 73; F(No 2)A 1997, Sch 4 para 19*].

For 'tax advantage' see *CIR v Cleary HL 1967, 44 TC 399* (tax advantage obtained where taxpayers' company purchased shares from them) and contrast *CIR v Kleinwort, Benson Ltd Ch D 1968, 45 TC 369* (no tax advantage where merchant bank purchased debentures with interest in arrear shortly before redemption). The decision in *Sheppard and another (Trustees of the Woodland Trust) v CIR (No 2) Ch D 1993, 65 TC 724* that no tax advantage could arise where relief was obtained by virtue of charitable exemption was doubted in *CIR v Universities Superannuation Scheme Ltd Ch D 1996, 70 TC 193*, in which the opposite conclusion was reached. Prior to the hearing of the latter case, the Revenue had, in any event, indicated that they would continue to proceed under *ICTA 1988, s 703* on the footing that tax-exempt bodies obtain a tax advantage whenever they receive abnormal dividends, since they considered that there would have been good grounds for challenging the earlier decision had it not been for a defect in the assessment under appeal. This continues to be the Revenue approach. (Revenue Tax Bulletin August 1993 p 90, April 1998 p 537, October 1998 pp 590–592). For the quantum of the tax advantage, see *Bird v CIR HL 1988, 61 TC 238*. On the question of whether a tax advantage was a 'main object' of a transaction, see *Marwood Homes Ltd v CIR, Tribunal 1998, [1999] SSCD 44*. See also *Laird Group plc v CIR Ch D, [2001] STC 689*.

Procedure.

(i)   The Board must notify person (or personal representatives if deceased [*ICTA 1988, s 703(11)*]) that they have reason to believe *section 703* may apply to him in respect of transaction(s) specified in notification. [*ICTA 1988, s 703(9)*]. See *Balen v CIR CA 1978, 52 TC 406*. No assessment may be made later than six years after the chargeable period to which the tax advantage relates. [*ICTA 1988, s 703(12)*].

(ii) Person notified may make, within 30 days, statutory declaration that in his opinion *section 703* does not apply and state supporting facts and circumstances. [*ICTA 1988, s 703(9)*]. For acceptance of late statutory declarations, see Revenue Tax Bulletin April 1999 p 656.

(iii) The Board must then either take no further action or send declaration together with certificate that they see reason to take further action (and any counter-statement they wish to submit) to tribunal (appointed by Lord Chancellor) which will decide either (*a*) there is no prima facie case for proceeding further (against this the Crown cannot appeal) or (*b*) there is such a case. [*ICTA 1988, s 703(10)*]. The taxpayer is not entitled to see the Board's counter-statement nor to be heard by the tribunal (*Wiseman v Borneman HL 1969, 45 TC 540*). See also *Howard v Borneman HL 1975, 50 TC 322* and *Balen v CIR CA 1978, 52 TC 406*.

(iv) If tribunal decides there is a case, or *if no statutory declaration is made by taxpayer*, the Board will make adjustments to counteract the specified tax advantages and notify the taxpayer. [*ICTA 1988, s 703(3)*].

(v)   Taxpayer may, within 30 days, appeal to Special Commissioners against adjustments. After appeal has been heard and determined either side may, by notice within 30 days to the Special Commissioners, require the appeal to be re-heard by the tribunal, with usual rights of further appeal by case stated in the High Court. As regards re-hearing applications, see *Marwood Homes Ltd v CIR, [1998] SSCD 53* (for the tribunal decision in which see *[1999] SSCD 44*). [*ICTA 1988, ss 705–705B; SI 1994 No 1813; FA 1998, Sch 3 para 34*].

(vi) The Board have power to require of any person information (within 28 days of written notice) relevant to transaction(s) which it appears to the Board may give rise to a liability on that person under these provisions. [*ICTA 1988, s 708*]. For the way in which the Board should exercise these powers, see *R v CIR (ex p Preston) HL 1985, 59 TC 1.*

(vii) The application of these provisions is outside self-assessment, so that returns should be made without having regard to a possible charge (although taxpayers may wish to draw the inspector's attention to any correspondence with the Business Tax Clearance Team (see below) in connection with any particular transaction). Enquiries into the possible application of these provisions will accordingly be carried out independently of any enquiry into the self-assessment return (see 68.6 RETURNS). (Revenue Tax Bulletin April 2000 pp 742, 743).

Distributions etc. For 1998/99 and earlier years, there are provisions whereby income tax paid by a person under D or E above may be treated by a company as advance corporation tax. Advance corporation tax is abolished after 5 April 1999. [*ICTA 1988, s 703(4)–(6); FA 1993, Sch 6 para 12; FA 1998, Sch 3 para 32(3)(5)*]. With effect for assessments made after 5 April 1999, the income tax payable by a person under D or E above is limited to that which would arise in respect of a qualifying distribution of an amount equal to the consideration referred to in D or E above (as appropriate) received on the same day as that consideration. [*ICTA 1988, s 703(3A); FA 1998, Sch 3 para 32(2)(4)*].

Clearance. Taxpayer may take the initiative by submitting to the Board particulars of any transaction effected or contemplated; the Board may, within 30 days of receipt, call for further information (to be supplied within 30 days). Subject to this, they must notify their decision within 30 days of receipt of the particulars or further information, and if they are satisfied that no liability arises the matter is concluded as regards that transaction by itself, provided that all facts and material particulars have been fully and accurately disclosed. [*ICTA 1988, s 707*]. The Revenue is not obliged to give reasons for refusal of clearance but where the applicant has given full reasons for his transactions the main grounds for refusing clearance will be indicated. A refusal to give clearance indicates that counteraction would be taken if the transaction were completed. (Revenue Pamphlet IR 131, SP 3/80, 26 March 1980).

Applications for clearance should be directed to Business Tax Clearance Team, Fifth Floor, 22 Kingsway, London WC2B 6NR for the attention of Mohini Sawhney (or, if market-sensitive information is included, Margaret Draper). Applications may be faxed to 020-7438 4409 or emailed to reconstructions@gtnet.gov.uk (in both cases after telephoning Margaret Draper (on 020-7438 6585) if market-sensitive information is included). A hard copy need not then be sent. Only a single application need be made as above for clearances under any one or more of: *ICTA 1988, s 707* (as above), *ICTA 1988, s 215* (demergers), *ICTA 1988, s 225* (purchase of own shares), *TCGA 1992, s 138(1)* (share exchanges), *TCGA 1992, s 139(5)* (reconstructions involving the transfer of a business), *TCGA 1992, s 140B* (transfer of a UK trade between EU Member States), *TCGA 1992, s 140D* (transfer of a non-UK trade between EU Member States) and *FA 2002, Sch 29 para 88* (various clearances under the corporation tax intangible assets regime). (Revenue Internet Statement 23 October 2002).

Revenue 'Working Together' Bulletin August 2001 pp 8, 9 contain a checklist of the items of information whose omission from clearance applications most commonly causes delay in the processing of applications.

Simon's Direct Tax Service. See A7.1.

3.3 **SALE OF RIGHT TO ANNUITIES, DIVIDENDS OR INTEREST — INCOME ASSESSABLE ON SELLER** [*ICTA 1988, s 730; FA 1996, Sch 7 para 23; FA 2002, Sch 25 para 51*]

Where the owner of securities sells or transfers the right to the interest, dividends, annuities etc. therefrom *but not to the securities themselves*, such interest etc. is treated for tax purposes as income of that owner (or, where the owner is not the beneficial owner, of the beneficiary entitled to the income) and no other person, for the fiscal year in which the right to receive the interest was sold. If the interest etc. on the securities is paid gross, an assessment under Schedule D, Case VI is made on the owner unless he shows that the proceeds of any sale etc. have been taxed as above. If tax would have been chargeable on the remittance basis on the interest etc. under Schedule D, Cases IV or V, the Case VI assessment is correspondingly limited to the amounts remitted. The Board have power to obtain information.

For company accounting periods beginning after 30 September 2002, *section 730* does not have effect for the purposes of the loan relationships legislation (see Tolley's Corporation Tax under Loan Relationships).

This section applies chiefly to coupons sold through agents abroad not liable to deduct tax (Hansard 27 June 1938 col 1575), but it may have a wider application.

Simon's Direct Tax Service. See A7.4.

3.4 **TREATMENT OF PRICE DIFFERENTIAL ON SALE AND REPURCHASE OF SECURITIES (REPO AGREEMENTS)** [*ICTA 1988, ss 730A, 730B, 730BB; FA 1995, s 80; FA 2003, Sch 38*]

Subject to the exception mentioned below, where a person (the 'original owner') has transferred securities to another person (the 'interim holder') under an agreement to sell them entered into on or after 1 May 1995, and the original owner or a CONNECTED PERSON (19) is required to buy them back under, or in consequence of the exercise of an option (whether a put or a call option) acquired under, the same or a 'related' agreement at a different price, the difference between the sale and repurchase price is treated for income and corporation tax purposes as a payment of interest which:

(*a*) where the repurchase price is greater than the sale price, is made by the repurchaser on a deemed loan from the interim holder of an amount equal to the sale price; and

(*b*) otherwise is made by the interim holder on a deemed loan from the repurchaser of an amount equal to the repurchase price.

In either case, the deemed interest is treated for income and corporation tax purposes as becoming due when the repurchase price becomes due and, accordingly, as paid when that price is paid. For income and corporation tax purposes (other than those of the current provisions and *ICTA 1988, ss 737A, 737C* — see 3.6 below), and for the purposes of *TCGA 1992* (unless *TCGA 1992, s 263A*, see below, applies), the repurchase price is treated as reduced by the amount of the deemed interest where (*a*) above applies or as increased by that amount where (*b*) above applies. For the purposes of *ICTA 1988, s 209(2)(d)* (interest treated as a distribution, see Tolley's Corporation Tax under Distributions) any deemed interest payment under (*a*) above is deemed to be interest in respect of securities issued by the repurchaser and held by the interim holder; for 2003/04 and earlier years, this also applied for the purposes of *ICTA 1988, s 209(2)(da)* (now repealed).

The repurchase price, in a case where *ICTA 1988, s 737A* (see 3.6 below) applies (or would apply were it in force in relation to the securities in question) is that price which is or would be applicable by virtue of *ICTA 1988, s 737C(3)(b), (9)* or *(11)(c)*. For agreements made after 8 April 2003, in cases involving the exercise of an option (whether a put or a call option), the sale price must be adjusted for any consideration given for the option (except where such consideration is brought into account under the derivative contracts provisions for companies (see Tolley's Corporation Tax under Financial Instruments and Derivative Contracts).

For corporation tax purposes, deemed interest under these provisions is treated as payable under a loan relationship, in respect of which the debits and credits to be brought into account are trading or non-trading according to the extent to which the repurchase is in the course of activities forming an integral part of the company's trade. Any foreign exchange gain or loss arising on the original sale price over the period of the sale and repurchase agreement is to be similarly treated under the loan relationship rules; *ICTA 1988, s 730BB*, which applies to agreements made after 8 April 2003, is designed to provide clarity of treatment for such gains and losses. See Tolley's Corporation Tax under Loan Relationships.

For purposes other than corporation tax, the Revenue generally accept that the deemed interest is short interest, except where it is clear that the transaction was entered into as a substitute for long term finance, and in particular where it is clear finance was arranged in this way specifically to avoid deduction of tax at source. (Revenue Tax Bulletin December 1995 p 266).

The exception referred to above disapplies these provisions (unless regulations under *ICTA 1988, s 737E*, see 3.6 below, otherwise provide) if the agreement(s) in question are non-arm's length agreements, or if all the benefits and risks arising from fluctuations in the market value of the securities accrue to, or fall on, the interim holder.

The Treasury has power to make regulations providing for an amount of deemed interest under these provisions to fall within the exemptions for pension business of insurance companies, for exempt approved pension schemes or superannuation funds or certain other such schemes, or for funds held for personal pension schemes or retirement annuity contracts. See *SI 1995 No 3036* (as amended).

See also *SI 1998 No 3177, regs 16, 17* as regards securities which, prior to their repurchase, are converted from currencies of States which have adopted the euro into euros.

[*ICTA 1988, ss 730A, 730BB; FA 1995, s 80(1)(5); FA 1996, Sch 14 para 37; FA 2002, Sch 25 para 52; FA 2003, Sch 38 paras 5, 10–12, 16, 20, 21(2)(3); FA 2004, Sch 42 Pt 2(2)*].

Where the above provisions apply (or would apply were the sale and repurchase price different), the acquisition and disposal by the interim holder, and (except where the repurchaser is or may be different from the original owner) the disposal and acquisition (as repurchaser) by the original owner, are disregarded for capital gains tax purposes. This does not, however, apply:

(A)   where the repurchase price falls to be computed by reference to provisions of *ICTA 1988, s 737C* (see 3.6 below) which are not in force in relation to the securities when the repurchase price becomes due; or

(B)   if the agreement(s) in question are non-arm's length agreements, or if all the benefits or risks arising from fluctuations in the market value of the securities accrue to, or fall on, the interim holder; or

(C)   in relation to any disposal or acquisition of qualifying corporate bonds (see Tolley's Capital Gains Tax under Qualifying Corporate Bonds) where the securities disposed of by the original owner, or those acquired by him or another person as repurchaser, are not such bonds.

See also *SI 1998 No 3177, regs 14–18* as regards conversions of securities from currencies of States which have adopted the euro into euros.

[*TCGA 1992, s 263A; FA 1995, s 80(4)(5)*].

Interpretation. For the above purposes, the following apply.

(i)   Agreements are 'related' if entered into in pursuance of the same arrangement.

(ii)   References to buying back securities include buying back similar securities, and 'repurchase' is construed accordingly. Securities are 'similar' if they give entitlement to the same rights against the same persons as to capital, interest and dividends, and to the same enforcement remedies. Where securities are converted from the currency of a State which has adopted the euro into euros (a *'euroconversion'*), the new securities are treated as 'similar' (see *SI 1998 No 3177, regs 3, 14*).

(iii) 'Securities' has the same meaning as in *ICTA 1988, s 737A* (see 3.6 below).

[*ICTA 1988, s 730B; FA 1995, s 80(1)*].

The Treasury has broad powers to make regulations providing for the above provisions to apply with modifications (including exceptions and omissions) in relation to cases involving any arrangement for the sale and repurchase of securities where the obligation to repurchase is not performed, or the repurchase option not exercised, or where provision is made by or under any agreement:

(*a*)   for different or additional securities to be treated as, or included with, securities which, for the purposes of the repurchase, are to represent securities transferred in pursuance of the original sale; or

(*b*)   for any securities to be treated as not included with securities which, for repurchase purposes, are to represent securities transferred in pursuance of the original sale; or

(*c*)   for the sale or repurchase price to be determined or varied wholly or partly by reference to fluctuations, in the period from the making of the agreement for the original sale, in the value of securities transferred in pursuance of that sale, or in the value of securities treated as representing those securities, or for any person to be required, where there are such fluctuations, to make any payment in the course of that period and before the repurchase price becomes due.

Regulations may also make such modifications in relation to cases where corresponding arrangements are made by an agreement, or by related agreements, in relation to securities which are to be redeemed in the period after their sale, those arrangements being such that the vendor (or a person connected with him), instead of being required to repurchase the securities or acquiring an option to do so, is granted rights in respect of the benefits that will accrue from their redemption. They may also provide for modifications in relation to cases involving any arrangement for the sale and repurchase of securities in relation to which there is an agreement which would not have been entered into by persons dealing at arm's length.

[*ICTA 1988, s 737E; FA 1995, s 83(1); FA 2003, Sch 38 paras 8, 13, 21(2)*].

Although of wider general application, these provisions were introduced as part of a package of measures designed to facilitate an open market in the sale and repurchase of gilt-edged securities ('gilt repos'). See also 3.6 below, 33.3 GOVERNMENT STOCKS, 71.72 SCHEDULE D, CASES I AND II and Tolley's Corporation Tax under Income Tax in Relation to a Company. For a brief overview of the changes made by *FA 2003* to the tax provisions on sale and repurchase agreements, see Revenue Tax Bulletin August 2003 pp 1052, 1053.

Simon's Direct Tax Service. See A7.13.

3.5   **INCOME RECEIVED ON SECURITIES HELD FOR ONE MONTH OR LESS —**
or held for more than one month but not more than six months *and either* purchase or sale was not at current market price *or* agreement regarding sale was made at, or before, purchase (see *ICTA 1988, s 731(3); FA 1996, Sch 20 para 36*). [*ICTA 1988, ss 731–735*].

Effects as regards various classes of recipient are as in (*a*) to (*d*) below.

In calculating period of one or six months, sale under prior option is regarded as a sale at option date [*ICTA 1988, s 731(4)*], and a sale of 'similar securities' is taken into account.

3.5 Anti-Avoidance

[ICTA 1988, s 731(5)(10)]. A purchase or sale effected as a direct result of the exercise of a 'qualifying option' (broadly, a traded or financial option within *TCGA 1992, s 144(8)*) is treated as being at current market price (and so excluded from these provisions) if the first buyer acquired, or became subject to, the option on arm's length terms. *[ICTA 1988, s 731(4A)–(4C); FA 1991, s 55]*. The *'appropriate amount'* is the pre-acquisition portion of the dividend, interest etc. calculated from last 'ex-div' day. *[ICTA 1988, s 735(3); FA 1996, Sch 38 para 9]*. See *ICTA 1988, s 735(4)* (as amended) if no last 'ex-div' day. In the case of (*a*) below, the portion taken is of net interest after deduction of tax and the amounts of actual dividends. In the case of (*b*), (*c*) and (*d*) below, it is the gross amount of interest and the amounts of dividends plus related tax credits. In all cases, special rules apply in relation to foreign income dividends within *ICTA 1988, Pt VI, Ch VA* (prior to their abolition after 5 April 1999). *[ICTA 1988, s 731(9)–(9B), s 735(1)(2); FA 1994, Sch 16 para 17; F(No 2)A 1997, Sch 6 para 14]*.

These provisions do not apply where the purchaser is required by the purchase agreement to make to the vendor, before his re-sale of the securities, a payment representative of the interest, or where the purchaser is treated by *ICTA 1988, s 737A(5)* (see 3.6 below) as being required to make a payment representative of a dividend on them. *[ICTA 1988, s 731(2A); FA 1995, s 81]*.

Where there is a 'repo agreement' in relation to any securities, neither their purchase or repurchase, nor their sale or sale back, is taken into account under these provisions. The securities purchased by the original owner from the person to whom securities were sold under the agreement (the *'interim holder'*) are instead treated under these provisions as the same securities, and as purchased at the same time, as his original holding. This does not, however, apply if the agreement(s) under which the arrangements are made are on non-arm's length terms, or if the interim holder bears any of the benefits or risks of market value fluctuations before the securities are repurchased. There is a *'repo agreement'* if the original owner sells the securities in pursuance of an agreement, and under the same or a related agreement either:

- is required to buy back the securities, either as a result of a straightforward obligation or the interim holder's exercise of an option; or

- acquires an option to buy them back which he subsequently exercises; or

- is entitled to receive from the interim holder an amount equal to any redemption proceeds.

See *ICTA 1988, s 730B* (under 3.4 above) for 'related agreements', 'securities' and the extended meaning of 'buying back' securities.

[ICTA 1988, s 731(2B)–(2F); FA 1997, s 77; FA 2003, Sch 38 paras 6, 21(2)].

(*a*) **Share dealers.** The net 'appropriate amount' of the interest etc. is treated for all tax purposes as a reduction of the purchase price. This treatment does not apply if the interest falls to be taken into account in computing the first buyer's Schedule D, Case I or II profits (see 71.72 SCHEDULE D, CASES I AND II). It also does not apply to overseas securities if *ICTA 1988, s 732(4)* complied with.

[ICTA 1988, s 732; FA 1990, s 53; FA 1991, s 56; FA 1996, Sch 41 Pt V(21); F(No 2)A 1997, s 26].

See *ICTA 1988, s 731(7)(8)* regarding change in ownership, or commencement, of trade.

The Board may make regulations by statutory instrument, effective from a day to be appointed therein, imposing conditions for the exclusion of market makers to apply, and making appropriate provision in regard to recognised investment exchanges other than the Stock Exchange. *[ICTA 1988, s 738(1)]*.

32

(b)   **Person entitled to exemption from tax.** Exemption does not extend to the gross 'appropriate amount' of the interest etc. and any annual payment out of the interest etc. is treated as not paid out of taxed income. [*ICTA 1988, s 733*].

(c)   **Traders other than share dealers** (whether company or not). The gross 'appropriate amount' of the interest etc. and tax thereon is ignored in calculating loss repayment claim under *ICTA 1988, s 380* or *s 381* (see 46.3, 46.10 LOSSES). [*ICTA 1988, s 734(1)*].

(d)   **Companies other than share dealers.** The gross 'appropriate amount' and tax thereon is ignored for tax purposes except that net equivalent is treated as capital distribution in calculation of chargeable gain. [*ICTA 1988, s 734(2)*].

'Securities' are defined to exclude those within the accrued income scheme (see 74.5 *et seq.* SCHEDULE D, CASE VI). [*ICTA 1988, s 731(9)*].

Simon's Direct Tax Service. See A7.3.

3.6   **'MANUFACTURED' DIVIDENDS OR INTEREST**

The provisions of *ICTA 1988, s 736A, Sch 23A* (introduced by *FA 1991, s 58, Sch 13*) have effect in relation to certain cases (see (a)–(c) below) where, under a contract or other arrangement for the transfer of shares or securities, a person is required to pay to the other party an amount representing a dividend or payment of interest thereon.

Where these provisions apply, the intention is that both payer and recipient of the amount in question should be in the same position, for tax purposes, as if the payment had in fact been a dividend or payment of interest. See *Schedule 23A paras 2–6* (as amended) for the detailed mechanism by which this is achieved in each case. See also *FA 1998, s 102* (introducing, *inter alia*, *ICTA 1988, ss 231AA, 231AB*) for the denial of tax credits in certain cases involving stock lending or repurchase agreements, and for provisions to secure the position following the abolition of advance corporation tax from 6 April 1999. Where a person receives a real or manufactured dividend in respect of UK shares acquired under a repo or stock lending arrangement on terms requiring him to manufacture an equivalent payment, amendments made by *FA 2004, Sch 24* seek to ensure that the manufactured payment is deductible only from the dividend receipt (or so much of it as is chargeable to tax) and not from total income as previously; and then only if the dividend is received in the same tax year as that in which the person makes the manufactured payment or in the preceding or following tax year. In addition, no tax is treated as having been paid at source on the dividend received. These amendments have effect from, broadly, 5 November 2003 where the person concerned is an individual and 17 March 2004 where that person is a trust, though certain of the changes are deferred until 22 July 2004.

The circumstances in which these provisions apply are as follows.

(a)   *Manufactured dividends on UK equities.* This applies where one of the parties to a transfer of UK equities is required to pay the other an amount (a '*manufactured dividend*') representative of a dividend thereon. Special provisions apply in relation to foreign income dividends within *ICTA 1988, Pt VI, Ch VA* (until their abolition after 5 April 1999).

(b)   *Manufactured interest on UK securities.* This applies where one of the parties to a transfer of UK securities is required to pay the other an amount ('*manufactured interest*') representative of a periodical payment of interest thereon. (See Tolley's Corporation Tax under Loan Relationships special cases for the corporation tax treatment of manufactured interest.)

(c)   *Manufactured overseas dividends.* This applies where one of the parties to a transfer of overseas securities (including, before 1 April 2001, quoted Eurobonds held in a recognised clearing system, see 22.3 DEDUCTION OF TAX AT SOURCE) is required to pay the other an amount (a '*manufactured overseas dividend*') representative of an overseas dividend thereon.

As regards (*c*) above, the Board was able before 1 November 2003 to arrange for manufactured overseas dividends to be paid without deduction of tax in certain cases where a double taxation agreement is in force with the territory in which the recipient of the dividend (not being UK resident) is resident. See *SI 1993 No 1957* as amended by *SI 1995 No 1551* and *SI 1996 No 2654* and revoked by *SI 2003 No 2581*. From 1 November 2003, the general requirement for the payer to deduct and account for tax in relation to payments of manufactured overseas dividends to non-UK recipients is removed by *SI 2003 No 2582*.

There are provisions to counteract any artificial allocation of a payment between the manufactured dividend or interest and any associated stock lending fee.

With effect after, broadly, 1 July 2004, a company is not entitled to any tax relief for a manufactured payment to the extent that it is made in pursuance of arrangements that have an unallowable purpose, i.e. a purpose that is not among the business or other commercial purposes of the company. See Tolley's Corporation Tax for details.

The Treasury may make 'dividend manufacturing regulations' for the purposes of these provisions which may, *inter alia*, extend the circumstances in which (*a*)–(*c*) above may apply. See *SI 1993 No 2004* (amended by *SI 1995 No 1324, SI 1996 Nos 1229, 2643, SI 1997 Nos 987, 988, 2706, SI 2001 No 403* and *SI 2003 No 2582*) and *SI 1996 No 1826* (amended by *SI 1996 No 2642*).

[*ICTA 1988, s 736A, Sch 23A; FA 1991, s 58, Sch 13 para 1; FA 1993, Sch 6 para 19; FA 1994, s 123(2)–(5)(7), s 124; FA 1995, s 82; FA 1996, s 159(4)–(9), Sch 14 para 52; FA 1997, Sch 10 paras 4, 7(2), 10–13, 16(1); F(No 2)A 1997, s 24(13), Sch 6 para 17; FA 2000, Sch 40 Pt II(17); FA 2004, s 137, Sch 24; SI 1992 No 173; SI 1992 No 1346; SI 1993 No 933; SI 1997 No 991*].

A payment which is representative of a qualifying distribution made before 6 April 1999 consisting of a payment by a company on the redemption, repayment or purchase of its own shares, or on the purchase of rights to acquire its own shares, is treated as if it were representative of a dividend on the shares concerned. [*FA 1997, Sch 7 para 7(3); F(No 2)A 1997, Sch 8 Pt II(12)*].

The Treasury has power to make regulations providing for any manufactured payment within *Schedule 23A* to be treated as falling within the exemptions for pension business of insurance companies, for exempt approved pension schemes or superannuation funds or certain other such schemes, or for funds held for personal pension schemes or retirement annuity contracts. [*ICTA 1988, s 737D; FA 1995, s 83(1)*]. See *SI 1995 No 3036* (as amended) as regards payments after 1 January 1996.

Stock lending arrangements. Special rules apply to stock lending arrangements. Where, under such an arrangement, interest (including dividends) on stock transferred is paid to a person other than the lender, with no provision for the lender to receive a payment representative of that interest, *Schedule 23A* (and regulations thereunder) apply as if the borrower were required to make, and did make, such a payment on the date the interest it represents is paid. For deemed payments made after 2 October 2000, the borrower is not entitled to any deduction in computing profits or gains for income or corporation tax purposes or against total income or (as the case may be) total profits, and (in the case of a company) no amount for which a deduction is so prohibited may be surrendered by way of group relief. [*ICTA 1988, s 736B; FA 1997, Sch 10 paras 3, 7(1); FA 2001, s 84; SI 1997 Nos 987, 991, 992, 993; SI 1999 No 621*].

See generally Revenue Inspector's Manual IM 4345 *et seq*. Guidance notes to help people in the financial markets to comply with the tax rules on manufactured payments are available on the Revenue's website.

Sale and repurchase of securities. *ICTA 1988, Sch 23A* above and the dividend manufacturing regulations thereunder apply where a person (the 'transferor') agrees to sell any 'securities', and under the same agreement (or under another agreement under the same arrangement) he (or a person connected with him (within *ICTA 1988, s 839*)) is required to buy back the same or 'similar' securities (whether as a result of a straightforward obligation or the exercise of a put option), or acquires an option (which he subsequently exercises) to buy them back, and either of the following two sets of conditions is fulfilled. The first set of conditions is that:

(*a*)   as a result of the transaction, a dividend on the securities is receivable by a person other than the transferor;

(*b*)   the agreement(s) do not contain a requirement for an amount representative of the dividend to be paid to the transferor on or before the date the repurchase price becomes due; and

(*c*)   it is reasonable to assume that the repurchase price took into account the fact that the dividend was receivable by a person other than the transferor.

The second set of conditions (relevant only to agreements made after 8 April 2003) is that:

(*a*)   a dividend which becomes payable in respect of the securities is receivable otherwise than by the transferor;

(*b*)   the transferor (or a person connected with him) is required to make a payment representative of the dividend;

(*c*)   there is no requirement for a person to pay to the transferor an amount representative of the dividend on or before the date the repurchase price becomes due; and

(*d*)   it is reasonable to assume that, in arriving at the repurchase price, account was taken of these circumstances.

The provisions apply as if the person from whom the securities are repurchased (or from whom the transferor has the right to repurchase them) were required under the arrangements for transfer of the securities to pay the transferor an amount representative of the dividend mentioned in (*a*) above, and a payment were accordingly made by that person to the transferor on the date the repurchase price of the securities becomes due. For the corporation tax treatment of such deemed payments, see Tolley's Corporation Tax under Loan Relationships (special cases).

'*Securities*' means UK equities and securities and overseas securities (as under *ICTA 1988, Sch 23A para 1(1)*), and securities are '*similar*' if they carry the same entitlement as to capital and interest (or dividends) and the same enforcement remedies. Where securities are converted from the currency of a State which has adopted the euro into euros (a '*euroconversion*'), the new securities are treated as 'similar' (see *SI 1998 No 3177, regs 3, 14*). References in *ICTA 1988, s 737A* to dividends are, in the case of UK securities, to periodical payments of interest, and in the case of overseas securities, to overseas dividends (as under *ICTA 1988, Sch 23A para 1(1)*).

There are special provisions (in *ICTA 1988, s 737C*) for determining the amount of the deemed manufactured dividend or interest for these purposes, and for a corresponding adjustment to be made for tax purposes to the repurchase price of the securities.

See also *SI 1998 No 3177, reg 17* as regards securities which, prior to their repurchase, are converted from currencies of States which have adopted the euro into euros.

3.7 Anti-Avoidance

[*ICTA 1988, ss 737A, 737B, 737C; FA 1994, s 122; FA 1996, s 159(1)(3), Sch 6 paras 19, 28; FA 1997, Sch 10 para 11(2), Sch 18 Pt VI(10); FA 2003, Sch 38 paras 1–3, 7, 17, 21(1)(2); SI 1995 No 1007; SI 1996 No 2645*].

The Treasury has broad powers to make regulations providing for *ICTA 1988, ss 737A–737C* to apply with modifications (including exceptions and omissions) in relation to cases involving any arrangement for the sale and repurchase of securities where the obligation to repurchase is not performed, or the repurchase option not exercised, or where provision is made by or under any agreement:

(*a*) for different or additional securities to be treated as, or included with, securities which, for the purposes of the repurchase, are to represent securities transferred in pursuance of the original sale; or

(*b*) for any securities to be treated as not included with securities which, for repurchase purposes, are to represent securities transferred in pursuance of the original sale; or

(*c*) for the sale or repurchase price to be determined or varied wholly or partly by reference to fluctuations, in the period from the making of the agreement for the original sale, in the value of securities transferred in pursuance of that sale, or in the value of securities treated as representing those securities, or for any person to be required, where there are such fluctuations, to make any payment in the course of that period and before the repurchase price becomes due.

Regulations may also make modifications in relation to cases where corresponding arrangements are made by an agreement, or by related agreements, in relation to securities which are to be redeemed in the period after their sale, those arrangements being such that the vendor (or a person connected with him), instead of being required to repurchase the securities or acquiring an option to do so, is granted rights in respect of the benefits that will accrue from their redemption.

See *SI 1995 No 3220* as regards such modification in cases where securities are redeemed rather than being repurchased, and where other securities are substituted for those originally transferred.

[*ICTA 1988, s 737E; FA 1995, s 83(1); FA 2003, Sch 38 paras 8, 21(2)*].

See also 3.5 above and, as regards application of accrued income scheme to such securities, 74.22 SCHEDULE D, CASE VI.

Simon's Direct Tax Service. See A7.8.

3.7 **TRANSFER OF ASSETS ABROAD** — income **payable to person abroad assessable on UK resident in certain circumstances** [*ICTA 1988, ss 739–746*]

Liability of transferor. Where, as a result of a transfer of assets, either alone or in conjunction with any associated operations (see below), income becomes payable to non-residents, or to persons not domiciled in the UK, then the following provisions apply.

(*a*) If, by virtue of the transfer, either alone or in conjunction with associated operations (see *Vestey v CIR HL 1979, 54 TC 503* overruling *Congreve v CIR HL 1948, 30 TC 163*; and also *CIR v Pratt and Others Ch D 1982, 57 TC 1*), the transferor, being an individual ordinarily resident in the UK, has power to enjoy, forthwith or in the future, any income of a non-resident or non-domiciled person which would be taxable if it were the income of the resident individual received in the UK, that income is deemed, for all tax purposes, to be the income of that individual.

(*b*) If such a resident individual receives, or is entitled to, any capital sum by way of loan etc. (see *Lee KB 1941, 24 TC 207*), or other non-income payment not for full consideration, which is in any way connected with the transfer etc., the income which, by virtue of the transfer etc., has become payable to the non-resident or non-domiciled person is deemed for all tax purposes to be income of the resident. A sum which a third person receives, or is entitled to receive, at the individual's direction or by assignment of the right to receive it, is treated as such a capital sum. There is no deemed income for a year of assessment in respect of a loan to the individual which has been wholly repaid before the beginning of that year.

These provisions do not apply if the Board are satisfied (subject to review by the Special Commissioners) that avoidance of tax was not a main purpose of the transfer or associated operations, or that they were *bona fide* commercial transactions not designed for the avoidance of tax. [*ICTA 1988, ss 739, 741*]. For successful appeals against Revenue refusals of relief, see *Beneficiary v CIR (Sp C 190), [1999] SSCD 134* (in which the grounds were that a transfer involved tax mitigation rather than tax avoidance) and *Carvill v CIR (Sp C 233), [2000] SSCD 143* (in which the Special Commissioner accepted that the transfer had been for *bona fide* commercial purposes).

In the case of *CIR v Willoughby HL 1997, 70 TC 57*, the Revenue's refusal of exemption under *section 741* in relation to 'personal portfolio bonds' (the holder of which has a degree of control of the management of the underlying investments but no proprietary interest therein) was overturned on appeal. For the treatment of then open cases, and past cases, affected by this decision, see Revenue Press Release 18 December 1997.

For income arising after 25 November 1996 (regardless of when the transfer of assets took place), it is made clear by *FA 1997, s 81* that these provisions apply:

(I)   regardless of whether or not the individual with power to enjoy the income was ordinarily resident in the UK when the transfer of assets took place. This reverses the decision in *CIR v Willoughby HL 1997, 70 TC 57* on this point and is stated by the Revenue to confirm their long-standing practice;

(II) where the purpose of the transfer is the avoidance of any form of direct taxation, and not just income tax (again apparently confirming long-standing Revenue practice).

Where a non-UK resident or domiciled person realises a profit from the discount on a relevant discounted security (see 72.5 SCHEDULE D, CASE III), it is treated for these purposes as income of that person. [*FA 1996, Sch 13 para 12*].

For the above purposes an individual is deemed to have power to enjoy income of a non-resident or non-domiciled person if

(i)   the income is so dealt with by *any* person so as to benefit the individual at some point of time, whether as income or not, or

(ii) the income increases the value to the individual of assets held by him or for his benefit, or

(iii) the individual receives, or is entitled to receive, at any time any benefit provided out of the income, or out of money available by the effect of associated operations on that income or assets representing it, directly or indirectly, or

(iv) the individual may obtain beneficial enjoyment of the income in the event of the exercise of one or more powers, by whomsoever exercisable and whether with or without the consent of any other person, or

(v)   the individual is able to control application of the income,

regard being had to the substantial effect of the transfer and associated operations and bringing into account all resultant benefits to the individual whether or not he has rights in law or equity to those benefits. [*ICTA 1988, s 742(2)(3)*].

3.7 Anti-Avoidance

Companies incorporated abroad, or regarded under double taxation arrangements as resident outside the UK, are, for this purpose, always to be treated as resident abroad, even if technically resident in UK. [*ICTA 1988, s 742(8); FA 1990, s 66*].

Reference to an individual includes the individual's wife or husband. [*ICTA 1988, s 742(9)(a)*].

For *premiums on leases etc.* in the case of persons resident in the Republic of Ireland but not in UK, see *ICTA 1988, s 746*.

Income falling under the above headings is not chargeable at the basic (or lower) rate to the extent that it has borne such tax by deduction. From 6 April 1999, this applies equally to Schedule F ordinary rate tax. The charge is under SCHEDULE D, CASE VI (74), except that, from 6 April 1999, dividends and certain similar classes of income are brought within the normal provisions relating to income chargeable under SCHEDULE F (76). A non-domiciled individual is only chargeable on any income *deemed* to be his if he would have been chargeable if it had in fact been his income. All deductions and reliefs to be given to the individual assessed as if he had actually received the income. If it is received subsequently, not again assessed. [*ICTA 1988, s 743; FA 1996, Sch 6 paras 20, 28; F(No 2)A 1997, Sch 4 para 20*]. Appeals are to Special Commissioners. [*TMA 1970, s 46B(4)(c)*].

The Board have power to demand from any person, under penalty, particulars of transactions where he acted for others (even if he considers no liability arises), and of what part he took in them. [*ICTA 1988, s 745; FA 1989, Sch 12 para 17; FA 1995, Sch 17 para 18; FA 1996, Sch 37 para 2*]. These powers limited in the case of *solicitors* (but not accountants or others), and *bankers* are not obliged to furnish particulars of any *ordinary* banking transactions carried out in the *ordinary* course of a banking business. 'Bank' for this purpose is defined by *ICTA 1988, s 840A* (see 7.1 BANKS). See *Royal Bank of Canada Ch D 1971, 47 TC 565*, where held particulars required were not ordinary banking transactions and *Clinch v CIR QB 1973, 49 TC 52* for powers of Revenue.

See *Philippi v CIR CA 1971, 47 TC 75* for burden on taxpayer to prove that avoidance was not a purpose.

'*Associated operation*'. See *ICTA 1988, s 742(1)* and *Corbett's Exors CA 1943, 25 TC 305; Bambridge HL 1955, 36 TC 313* and *Fynn CD 1957, 37 TC 629*.

For general principles see the above cases and *Cottingham's Exors CA 1938, 22 TC 344; Beatty cases KB 1940, 23 TC 574; Lord Howard de Walden CA 1941, 25 TC 121; Aykroyd KB 1942, 24 TC 515; Latilla HL 1943, 25 TC 107; Sassoon CA 1943, 25 TC 154; Vestey's Exors HL 1949, 31 TC 1; Ramsden Ch D 1957, 37 TC 619; Chetwode v CIR HL 1977, 51 TC 647; Vestey (Nos 1 & 2) HL 1979, 54 TC 503; CIR v Schroder Ch D 1983, 57 TC 94; CIR v Brackett Ch D 1986, 60 TC 134, 639; CIR v Botnar CA, [1999] STC 711*.

Liability of non-transferor. Where, as a result of a transfer of assets, either alone or in conjunction with associated operations (see above), income becomes payable to a non-resident, or to a person not domiciled in the UK, *and* an individual ordinarily resident in the UK who is not liable as the transferor under *ICTA 1988, s 739* (see above) receives a benefit provided out of those assets, then the following provisions apply to benefits received and relevant income arising after 9 March 1981 irrespective of when the transfer or associated operations took place. They do not, however, apply if the Board are satisfied (subject to review by the Special Commissioners) that avoidance of tax was not a main purpose of the transfer or associated operations, or that they were *bona fide* commercial transactions not designed for the avoidance of tax (and see above). [*ICTA 1988, ss 740(1), 741*].

Where a non-UK resident or domiciled person realises a profit from the discount on a relevant discounted security (see 72.5 SCHEDULE D, CASE III), it is treated for these purposes as income of that person. [*FA 1996, Sch 13 para 12*].

The value of the benefit, up to the amount of relevant income of years of assessment up to and including the year in which received, is treated as income of the resident individual for all tax purposes for that year and charged under Schedule D, Case VI. Any excess of benefit is carried forward against relevant income of subsequent years and taxed accordingly. [*ICTA 1988, s 740(2)(4)*].

'*Relevant income*' of a year of assessment is any income arising in that year to a non-resident or non-domiciled person and which by virtue of the transfer or associated operations mentioned above can directly or indirectly be used for providing a benefit for the resident individual or enabling a benefit to be provided for him. [*ICTA 1988, s 740(3)*].

An individual domiciled outside the UK is not taxable on a benefit not received in the UK in respect of any 'relevant income' on which, if he had received it, he would not, because of his domicile, have been taxable. *ICTA 1988, s 65(6)–(9)* (income applied outside UK treated in certain cases as received in UK, see 64.4 REMITTANCE BASIS) applies as if the benefit were income arising from possessions outside the UK. [*ICTA 1988, s 740(5)*].

Where a benefit otherwise giving rise to a charge under these provisions is in whole or part a capital payment subject to certain capital gains tax charges, it is to that extent treated as having already been treated as income under these provisions. [*ICTA 1988, s 740(6); TCGA 1992, Sch 10 para 14; FA 2000, Sch 26 para 6*].

The provisions of *ICTA 1988, ss 742(8)–(10), 745* apply, see above.

Exclusion of double charge. No income can be charged more than once under the above provisions and where there is a choice as to persons to be assessed the Board may allocate income as appears just and reasonable. The Board's decision is appealable to the Special Commissioners. Income is treated as having been charged to tax

(A)   in full, where charged under *ICTA 1988, s 739* as income;

(B)   to the extent of the value of any benefit charged under (iii) above, and

(C)   to the amount of relevant income taken into account in charging any benefit under *ICTA 1988, s 740*. [*ICTA 1988, s 744*].

Trustees and personal representatives. In relation to benefits received on or after 15 June 1989, relevant income for *section 740* purposes (see above) includes income arising to trustees or personal representatives before 6 April 1989, notwithstanding that one or more of the trustees or personal representatives was not resident outside the UK, unless they have been charged to tax in respect of that income. [*FA 1989, s 111(8)*].

Accrued income on certain securities. See 74.30 SCHEDULE D, CASE VI as regards deemed income arising on transfer of certain securities.

Controlled foreign companies. See also Tolley's Corporation Tax under Controlled Foreign Companies as regards *ICTA 1988, ss 739, 740* relief in certain cases where a charge is made in respect of profits of such companies.

Revenue interpretation. For an article giving the Revenue interpretation of a number of aspects of these provisions, see Revenue Tax Bulletin April 1999 pp 651, 652.

Simon's Direct Tax Service. See E1.721 *et seq*.

3.8   **TRANSFER PRICING**

For 1998/99 and earlier years of assessment (see below for the later position), where either the buyer or the seller (being a 'body of persons' or a partnership) is controlled by the other party to the contract, or both are such bodies controlled by the same person(s), any sale (including letting and hiring of property, grant or transfer of rights or licences, or giving of business facilities (for which see *Waterloo plc v CIR (Sp C 301), [2002] SSCD*

95)) at a price other than market price at the time of completion or, if earlier, of giving possession may (if the Board of Inland Revenue so direct) be adjusted by the Revenue as follows.

(i)   If the price is **below** market price, the latter is substituted in computing the *seller's* profits unless the buyer, being a UK resident trader, is entitled to deduct the price paid in computing his own profits.

(ii) If the price is **above** market price, the latter is substituted in computing the *buyer's* profits unless the seller, being a UK resident trader, would have to bring in, as a trade receipt, the price received. [*ICTA 1988, s 770*].

The extension of these provisions to the 'giving of business facilities' is capable of bringing the making of interest-free loans within their scope (*Ametalco UK v CIR; Ametalco Ltd v CIR (Sp C 94), [1996] SSCD 399*).

'*Control*', for this purpose, means power of a person (including nominees and certain connected persons, and their nominees), by shareholding or voting power (whether direct or through another company) or under articles of association, to secure that the company's affairs are conducted according to that person's wishes. It includes, for partnerships, the right to a share of more than one-half of the firm's assets or profits. For whether control at company meeting is necessary, see *Irving v Tesco Stores Holdings Ltd Ch D 1982, 58 TC 1*. As to trustee holdings, see *CIR v Lithgows CS 1960, 39 TC 270*. [*ICTA 1988, ss 773(2)(3), 840*].

The Board may serve notices specifying the information required (with penalties for non-compliance) on a *company* if it or an associated company was party to a relevant transaction. If one party to a transaction which may be within *ICTA 1988, s 770* is a non-resident 51% subsidiary of a UK parent, notice may be served on the parent for access to the books etc. of the subsidiary (subject to appeal to Special Commissioners). An inspector may in certain circumstances and with the Board's authority enter premises to examine books etc.

Where a direction is given, all necessary adjustments are made, by assessment, repayment or otherwise, to give effect to it. [*ICTA 1988, s 770(3)*]. This applies equally to adjustment of open assessments (*Glaxo Group Ltd and Others v CIR CA 1996, 68 TC 166*). Appeals involving questions arising from directions are to that extent to be referred to and determined by the Special Commissioners. [*ICTA 1988, s 772(8)*].

Nothing in *section 770* is to affect the operation of any provisions of *CAA 1990*. [*ICTA 1988, s 773(1)*].

For an article on the application of the transfer pricing rules to employee share scheme costs, in particular in relation to the decision in *Waterloo plc v CIR (Sp C 301), [2002] SSCD 95* referred to above, see Revenue Tax Bulletin February 2003 pp 1002–1007.

In 1995 and 1996, the OECD published its report 'Transfer Pricing Guidelines for Multinational Enterprises and Tax Administrations' and supplementary material, containing guidelines on the general principles to be applied in determining transfer prices for tax purposes. These can be purchased from HMSO outlets. An article in the Revenue Tax Bulletin October 1996 pp 345–349 sets out the Revenue's position on those guidelines and also provides some practical guidance on the operation of the Mutual Agreement Procedure contained in UK double taxation conventions.

An Inland Revenue leaflet 'The Transfer Pricing of Multinational Enterprises' is also available from the Board, drawing attention to the UK provisions and to the Board's powers.

See Simon's Direct Tax Service B3.1827.

For 1999/2000 and subsequent years of assessment, and subject to transitional arrangements (see below), *sections 770–773* are replaced by a new *ICTA 1988, s 770A, Sch*

28AA. [*FA 1998, s 108(1)(2)(5), Sch 16*]. *Schedule 28AA* is to be construed so as best to secure consistency between the effect given to the basic rules of the *Schedule* (under *paragraph 1*, see below) and the principles of the OECD model tax convention and transfer pricing guidelines. [*ICTA 1988, Sch 28AA para 2*]. The guidelines are currently published by the OECD as 'Transfer Pricing Guidelines for Multinational Enterprises and Tax Administrations', and can be purchased from HMSO outlets. An article in the Revenue Tax Bulletin October 1996 pp 345–349 sets out the Revenue's views on those guidelines and provides practical guidance on the operation of the mutual agreement procedure contained in UK double taxation conventions. See also the Revenue leaflet 'The Transfer Pricing of Multinational Enterprises'.

The scope of these transfer pricing rules is extended by *FA 2004* **for 2004/05 onwards** to transactions both parties to which are in the UK, but there are exemptions for small and medium-sized businesses; this is incorporated within the coverage below and see also under Transitional provisions. See http://www.inlandrevenue.gov.uk/international/transfer-pricing.htm for further guidance.

See Tolley's Corporation Tax under Transfer Pricing for matters relevant only to companies, in particular the rules on so-called 'thin capitalisation'.

Schedule 28AA applies where provision (the '*actual provision*') has been made or imposed as between two persons (the '*affected persons*') by means of a transaction or series of transactions, and at the time the provision was made or imposed either

(I)   one of the affected persons was directly or indirectly participating in the management, control or capital of the other, or

(II)   there was a person or persons who was or were directly or indirectly participating in the management, control or capital of each of the affected persons.

Except as below, if the actual provision differs from the provision which would have been made at arm's length as between independent enterprises (or if no provision would have been so made) and confers a 'potential advantage' in relation to UK taxation on one of the affected persons or (whether or not the same advantage) on each of them, the profits and losses (and certain items treated as losses) of the potentially advantaged person, or of each of them, are computed for tax purposes as if the arm's length provision had been made or imposed (or, as the case may be, no provision made) instead of the actual provision. The resulting increase in profits etc. is often referred to as the transfer pricing adjustment.

A 'transaction' for these purposes includes schemes or arrangements of any kind, understandings and mutual practices (whether or not legally enforceable), and a 'series' of transactions includes a number of transactions entered into in pursuance of, or in relation to, the same scheme or arrangement. A series of transactions is not prevented from being regarded as the means by which provision has been made or imposed between two persons by reason only that there is no transaction in the series to which both those persons are parties, or one or more transactions to which neither of them is a party, or that the parties to any scheme or arrangement in pursuance of which the transactions are entered into do not include one or both of them.

A person is for these purposes treated as directly participating in the management, control or capital of another person at a particular time if and only if, at that time, the other person is a body corporate or partnership which that person controls (within *ICTA 1988, s 840*, see 19.8 CONNECTED PERSONS). Similarly indirect participation requires that the person (the '*potential participant*') either would be taken to be participating directly if certain rights and powers (see *ICTA 1988, Sch 28AA para 4(3)–(6)(10)–(12)*), including future rights and powers, were attributed to him, or is one of a number of 'major participants' in the other person's enterprise. A person is a '*major participant*' in another person's enterprise when the other person is a body corporate or partnership, and he is one of two persons who

3.8 Anti-Avoidance

control (as above) the other person, each of whom has at least 40% of the holdings etc. giving that control (again after attribution of certain rights and powers as above).

The actual provision confers a *'potential advantage'* on a person in relation to UK taxation where its effect, compared to that of the corresponding arm's length provision, would be a reduction in chargeable profits or increase in losses (or conversion of profits into losses) of that person for any chargeable period. Where, however, for 2003/04 and earlier years, the following conditions are satisfied in relation to each of the persons as between whom an actual provision was made, no such potential advantage is conferred on either of them:

(*aa*) they are within the charge to income or corporation tax in respect of profits arising from the activities in relation to which the actual provision was made or imposed (and not exempt in respect of all or any part of the income or profits from those activities), and where it is an income tax charge which applies, they are UK-resident for all chargeable periods for which it so applies;

(*bb*) they neither have an entitlement to a foreign tax credit in any chargeable period in relation to profits from such activities, nor would have any such entitlement if there were any such profits or if they exceeded a certain amount; and

(*cc*) the amounts taken into account in computing profits or losses from such activities for any chargeable period in relation to which (*aa*) above is satisfied do not include any income from which a deduction is made for foreign tax (where no credit is allowable).

For 2004/05 onwards, any income of a non-resident that is 'excluded income' (within 51.1 NON-RESIDENTS AND OTHER OVERSEAS MATTERS or corporation tax equivalent) is left out of account in determining whether there is any reduction in chargeable profits etc.

[*ICTA 1988, Sch 28AA paras 1–5, 14; FA 2004, s 30(2), s 31(2), s 37(1)(2)*].

Exemptions. For 2004/05 onwards, with the exceptions below, the above transfer pricing adjustment does not apply in computing profits/losses of a potentially advantaged person for a tax year for which that person is a 'small enterprise' or a 'medium-sized enterprise'. For this purpose, a *'small enterprise'* is one defined as such in the Annex to *Commission Recommendation 2003/361/EC* published by the EC on 6 May 2003 (as modified by *ICTA 1988, Sch 28AA para 5D(3)–(6)*) and a *'medium-sized enterprise'* is one which falls within the category of micro, small and medium-sized enterprises as defined in that Annex (as modified) but is not a 'small enterprise'. Broadly, the entity must meet the following criteria (see Revenue guidance at www.inlandrevenue.gov.uk/international/small-medium-ent.pdf).

	Maximum number of staff	And less than *one* of these limits	
		Annual turnover	*Balance sheet total*
Small enterprise	50	10 million euros	10 million euros
Medium-sized enterprise	250	50 million euros	43 million euros

'Balance sheet total' means, broadly, total assets (without netting off liabilities). Associated entities etc. must be taken into account in determining whether the criteria are met. The modifications made to the Annex ensure, in particular, that qualification as small or medium-sized depends on the entity's data for the tax year under review and without reference to past history.

A small or medium-sized enterprise may make an irrevocable election to disapply the exemption for a particular tax year. The Revenue may itself over-ride the exemption for *medium-sized* enterprises for any tax year (in relation to one or more particular provisions made or imposed) by issuing a *'transfer pricing notice'* to the potentially advantaged person. A transfer pricing notice can be given only after an enquiry has been opened into the person's tax return (and an enquiry can be opened for this purpose). That person can appeal against the notice (within 30 days) but only on the grounds that he is not a medium-sized (as opposed to a small) enterprise. A person in receipt of a transfer pricing notice has 90 days in which to make the necessary amendments to his tax return, beginning on the date of issue of the notice or, where relevant, the date the appeal against the notice is finally determined or abandoned. Failure to do so results in the return becoming an incorrect return (so that penalties potentially apply — see, for example, 57.3 PENALTIES). The enquiry into the tax return cannot be closed until either the amendment is made or the 90-day period expires. (See 68.6 *et seq.* RETURNS for enquiries into returns generally.)

The exemption does not apply to either a small or a medium-sized enterprise in relation to an actual provision made or imposed if, at the time the provision is made or imposed, the other affected person or a 'party to a relevant transaction' is a 'resident' of a 'non-qualifying territory' (regardless of whether he is also a resident of a 'qualifying territory'). A person is a *'party to a relevant transaction'* if the actual provision was imposed by means of a series of transactions and he was a party to one of more of them. For these purposes, a person is a *'resident'* of a territory if he is liable to tax there by reason of his domicile, residence or place of management, unless he is so liable only in respect of income from sources in that territory or capital situated there. *'Qualifying territory'* means the UK or any territory with which the UK has a double tax agreement (see 24.2 DOUBLE TAX RELIEF) containing a standard non-discrimination provision (see Revenue guidance at www.inlandrevenue.gov.uk/international/small-medium-ent.pdf for a list of countries with which the UK had an appropriate agreement at 1 April 2004). *'Non-qualifying territory'* is construed accordingly. However, territories may also be designated as 'qualifying' or 'non-qualifying' by Treasury regulations made for the purposes of these provisions.

[*ICTA 1988, Sch 28AA paras 5B–5E; TMA 1970, s 9A(4); FA 2004, s 30(9), s 31(4), s 37(1)(2), Sch 5 para 1*].

An exemption also applies with effect from, broadly, 1 April 2004 where the potentially advantaged person is a pre-existing dormant company (see Tolley's Corporation Tax under Transfer Pricing for details).

Elimination of double counting. Where a potential advantage is conferred (as above) on only one of the affected persons (the *'advantaged person'*), and the other person (the *'disadvantaged person'*)

- (for 2004/05 onwards) is within the charge to income tax or corporation tax in respect of profits arising from the activities in relation to which the actual provision was made or imposed, or

- (for 2003/04 and earlier years) is within (*aa*) above (or would be if any exemption from tax were disregarded),

then (except as below) the disadvantaged person may claim application of the arm's length provision rather than the actual provision (over-riding any applicable time limits for the necessary adjustments). Such a claim may only be made if the arm's length provision has similarly been applied in the case of the advantaged person (in his return or following a determination, see below), and the computations in the case of each of them on that basis must be consistent. The claim must be made within two years of the making of the return or the giving of the notice taking account of the determination, as the case may be, and a claim based on a return which is subsequently the subject of such a notice may be amended within two years of the giving of the notice. (These time limits may be extended in certain cases where the Board fails to give proper notice to disadvantaged persons, see below.)

Where such a claim is made, it is assumed, as respects any foreign tax credit which has been or may be given to the disadvantaged person, that that foreign tax does not include tax which would not be or have become payable if the arm's length provision had also been

3.8 Anti-Avoidance

substituted for the purposes of that tax, and that the profits from the activities in relation to which the actual provision was made or imposed and in respect of which the tax credit relief arises are reduced to the same extent as they are treated as reduced by virtue of the claim.

Where the application of the arm's length provision in a computation following such a claim involves a reduction in the amount of any income, and that income also falls to be treated as reduced under *ICTA 1988, s 811(1)* by an amount of foreign tax (where credit relief is not available), the former reduction is treated as made before the latter, and the deductible foreign tax excludes that paid on so much of the income as is represented by the amount of the former reduction.

Any adjustment to double tax reliefs as above may be given effect by set-off against any relief or repayment arising from the claim, and may be made without regard to any time limit on assessments or amendments.

For 2004/05 onwards, where one or more payments ('*balancing payments*') are made to the advantaged person by the disadvantaged person to compensate for the transfer pricing adjustment, they are not taken into account in computing either person's taxable profits or allowable losses to the extent that they do not in aggregate exceed the 'available compensating adjustment'. The '*available compensating adjustment*' is the difference between the profits/losses of the disadvantaged person computed on the basis of the actual provision and those profits/losses computed on the basis that the disadvantaged person makes a claim as above to apply the arm's length provision instead.

Also for 2004/05 onwards, a claim by the disadvantaged person to apply the arm's length provision does not affect the amount he is required to bring into account as closing trading stock or work in progress for any accounting period of his which ends on or after the last day of the accounting period of the advantaged person in which the actual provision was made or imposed. In the absence of such a rule, the benefit to him of applying the arm's length provision would effectively be delayed until the stock were sold or the work in progress realised.

[*ICTA 1988, Sch 28AA paras 6, 6A, 7, 7A; FA 2001, s 88, Sch 29 para 35(3)(4); FA 2004, s 30(3)–(6), s 32(2), s 37(1)(2)*].

The above rules are modified where the advantaged person is a 'controlled foreign company' (see Tolley's Corporation Tax under Transfer Pricing for details).

Capital allowances and capital gains. These provisions do not generally affect the computation of capital allowances or balancing charges under *CAA 2001*, or of capital gains or allowable losses under *TCGA 1992*, and do not require any income or losses to be treated as on capital rather than revenue account. However, for 2004/05 onwards, this does *not* apply for the purposes of the rules above on Elimination of double counting. [*ICTA 1988, Sch 28AA para 13; CAA 2001, Sch 2 para 68; FA 2004, s 32(4), s 37(1)(2)*].

Interest paid. For 2004/05 onwards, where a person pays interest under the actual provision and a transfer pricing adjustment falls to be made, such that some or all of the interest paid is disallowed, the disallowed interest is not chargeable on the recipient under Schedule D, Case III if he makes a claim under the Elimination of double counting provisions above. [*ICTA 1988, s 28AA, para 6E; FA 2004, s 35(4), s 37(1)(2)*].

Determinations requiring the sanction of the Board. A determination of an amount falling to be brought into account under these provisions, other than in certain cases where an agreement has been reached between the Board and the person concerned (see *FA 1998, s 110(5)–(7)*), requires the Board's sanction. Where such a determination is made for the purpose of giving a closure notice, giving a discovery notice amending a partnership return or making a discovery assessment, and the notice of the closure, amendment or discovery assessment is given to any person without the determination, so far as taken into account in the notice or assessment, having been approved by the Board, or without a copy of the Board's approval having been served on that person at or before the time the notice was given, the closure or amendment notice or discovery assessment is deemed to have been given or made (and in the case of an assessment notified) as if the determination had not been taken into account. The approval must apply specifically to the case in question and the amount determined, but may otherwise be given (either before or after the making of the determination) in any such form or manner as the Board may determine. An appeal relating to a determination approved by the Board may not question the Board's approval except to the extent that the grounds for questioning the approval are the same as the grounds for questioning the determination itself. [*FA 1998, s 110; FA 2001, s 88, Sch 29 para 38(2)*]. For the requirement that the Revenue give notice of determinations to persons who it appears to them may be 'disadvantaged persons' (as above) by reference to the subject-matter of the determination, see *FA 1998, s 111* as amended.

Appeals. An appeal against an amendment of a return, the refusal of a claim or a discovery assessment or determination involving the application of *Schedule 28AA* lies to the Special Commissioners. Where the appeal relates to any provision as between two persons each within the charge to income tax or corporation tax in respect of profits arising from the activities in relation to which the actual provision was made or imposed (for 2004/05 onwards — previously each within (*aa*) above), each person is entitled to appear before and be heard by the Special Commissioners, or to make written representations to them, and the Commissioners must determine that aspect of the appeal separately from any other, that separate determination being treated as made in an appeal to which each of those persons was a party. [*ICTA 1988, Sch 28AA para 12; FA 2004, s 30(8), s 37(1)(2)*].

Miscellaneous. Amounts brought into account in respect of exchange gains and losses and financial instruments/derivative contracts adjustments are not subject to application of an arm's length provision as above, but this does not affect the application of *Schedule 28AA* for the purposes of *FA 1993, ss 136, 136A* or (for accounting periods beginning after 30 September 2002) *FA 1996, Sch 9 para 11A* or *FA 2002, Sch 26 para 27* in the case of certain loan interest (see Tolley's Corporation Tax under Exchange Gains and Losses, Financial Instruments and Derivative Contracts and Loan Relationships). [*ICTA 1988, Sch 28AA para 8; FA 2002, Sch 23 para 21, Sch 27 para 15*]. There are also special provisions relating to transactions involving oil and gas [*ICTA 1988, Sch 28AA paras 9, 10*] and to 'ring-fenced' oil and gas exploration activities. [*ICTA 1988, Sch 28AA para 11*].

The provisions apply to unit trust schemes (see 90.1 UNIT TRUSTS) as if they were bodies corporate, with appropriate modification. [*ICTA 1988, Sch 28AA para 14(5)*].

Transitional provisions. *Schedule 28AA* does not apply in the case of any potentially disadvantaged person as respects the consequences, at any time before 17 March 2001, of the difference between an actual and an arm's length provision if:

(1)   the actual provision is made or imposed under contractual arrangements entered into by that person before 17 March 1998;

(2)   the control requirement in (I) or (II) above (as the case may be) is satisfied in the case of the actual provision and that person only by his indirect participation as a major participant in the other person's enterprise (see above);

(3)   that person's rights and obligations under the actual provision have not been varied or continued by a transaction entered into after 17 March 1998 and before that time; and

(4)   that person is not, and has not been, a party to any transaction by virtue of which he could, in the period between 17 March 1998 and that time, have secured the variation or termination of those rights and obligations.

[*FA 1998, s 108(6)*].

3.8 Anti-Avoidance

The amendments made by *FA 2004* (which, in particular, extend the scope of the transfer pricing rules to transactions both parties to which are in the UK and introduce exemptions for small and medium-sized enterprises) apply for the purpose of computing profits/losses for 2004/05 onwards (regardless of when the actual provision is or was made or imposed), but a period of account straddling 5 April 2004 is deemed to be split, for these purposes only, into two periods, the first ending on 5 April 2004 and the second beginning on 6 April 2004, with the amendments applying only in relation to the second period. (For corporation tax purposes, the amendments apply for accounting periods beginning on or after 1 April 2004, with similar provision for splitting accounting periods straddling that date.) [*FA 2004, s 37*].

For 2004/05 and 2005/06 only, certain penalty provisions are relaxed as follows. The penalty imposed by *TMA 1970, s 12B* for failure to keep and preserve records (see 68.5 RETURNS) does not apply in relation to such records as might have been needed to submit a correct and complete return so far as concerns the use of arm's length prices. For the purpose of the penalty imposed by *TMA 1970, s 95* (or, for partnerships, *TMA 1970, s 95A*) for submitting an incorrect return (see 57.3 PENALTIES), a person is not regarded as having negligently done so by reason only of a failure to keep or preserve any such records. A comparable let-out applies in respect of the penalty under *TMA 1970, s 99* on agents for assisting in preparing incorrect returns (see 57.7 PENALTIES). [*FA 2004, s 33*].

See generally Simon's Direct Tax Service B3.18.

For an article on the application of the transfer pricing rules to employee share scheme costs, in particular in relation to the decision in *Waterloo plc v CIR (Sp C 301), [2002] SSCD 95* referred to above in relation to pre-1999/2000 periods, see Revenue Tax Bulletin February 2003 pp 1002–1007.

The Revenue International Division, Room 311, Melbourne House, Aldwych, London WC2B 4LL may be approached for pre-transaction guidance on the likely tax treatment in particular cases when financial arrangements are in the process of being put in place. See Revenue Tax Bulletin October 1998 pp 579–582 for guidance on the record-keeping required for self-assessment under the above provisions and on the application of the provisions to financial transactions and arrangements; December 1998 pp 603–605 for guidance on penalties under those provisions; April 2000 pp 740–742 for the practical implications of the new regime for non-UK resident landlords; and August 2002 pp 943–947 for guidance on the nature of the risk assessment carried out by the Revenue before undertaking a transfer pricing enquiry and a suggested timetabling framework for such enquiries.

Advance pricing agreements. A taxpayer may apply to the Board for an agreement, on a prospective basis, on the resolution of complex transfer pricing issues relating to any one or more of the following matters which fall, or might fall, to be determined.

(*a*)   The attribution of income to a branch or agency, or permanent establishment of a company, through which the taxpayer has been carrying on, or is proposing to carry on, a trade in the UK.

(*b*)   The attribution of income to any permanent establishment of the taxpayer (wherever situated) through which he has been carrying on, or is proposing to carry on, any business.

(*c*)   The extent to which income which has arisen or which may arise to the taxpayer is to be taken for any purpose to be income arising outside the UK.

(*d*)   The treatment for tax purposes of any provision operating between the taxpayer and any 'associate' of his. Persons are '*associates*' for this purpose if (as in (I) and (II) above in relation to *Schedule 28AA*) one directly or indirectly participates, at the time of the making or imposition of the provision, in the management, control or capital of the other, or the same person or persons so participate in the management, control or capital of each of them (with further special provision in relation to sales of oil).

(*e*)   The treatment for tax purposes of any provision operating between a 'ring fence trade' carried on by the taxpayer and any other activities the taxpayer carries on. A *'ring fence trade'* for this purpose is a trade which is treated as a separate trade under *ICTA 1988, s 492(1)* (oil extraction activities, see Tolley's Corporation Tax under Oil Companies), or would be so treated if a different trade were also carried on.

The application must set out the taxpayer's understanding of what would, in his case, be the effect, in the absence of any agreement, of the provisions in relation to which clarification is sought, and in what respects clarification is required. He must also propose how the clarification might be effected in a manner consistent with that understanding.

Where the Board and the taxpayer have entered into such an agreement (an 'advance pricing agreement' or 'APA') in relation to a chargeable period, then (except as below) any questions relating to those matters are, to the extent provided for in the APA, to be determined in accordance with the APA rather than by reference to the legislative provisions which would otherwise have applied. However, where the relevant matter falls within (*d*) or (*e*) above and not within (*a*), (*b*) or (*c*) above, the only legislative provisions which can be displaced are those contained in *Schedule 28AA* (as above). Where an APA relating to a chargeable period beginning or ending before the date of the APA provides for the manner in which consequent adjustments are to be made, those adjustments are to be made in the manner provided for in the APA.

An APA does not, however, have effect in relation to the determination of any question which relates to:

(i)   a time after that from which an officer of the Board has revoked the APA in accordance with its terms; or

(ii)   a time after or in relation to which any provision of the APA has not been complied with, where the APA was conditional upon compliance with that provision; or

(iii)   any matter as respects which any other essential conditions have not been, or are no longer, satisfied.

The APA must contain a declaration that it is made for the purposes of *FA 1999, s 85*. It may be made on or after 27 July 1999 and may apply in relation to any chargeable period ending on or after that date (and this may include periods ending before the date of the APA). It is for the Board to ensure that the APA is modified so as to be consistent with any double taxation arrangements.

Where the APA makes provision for its modification or revocation by the Board, this may take effect from such time (including a time before the modification or revocation) as the Board may determine.

Any party to an APA must provide the Board with all such reports and other information as he may be required to provide under the APA or by virtue of any request made by an officer of the Board in accordance with its terms.

An APA is deemed never to have been made where, before it was made, the taxpayer fraudulently or negligently provided the Board with false or misleading information in relation to the application for the APA or in connection with its preparation, and the Board notifies the taxpayer that the APA is nullified by reason of the misrepresentation. A penalty not exceeding £10,000 may apply for so giving such false or misleading information.

[*FA 1999, ss 85, 86*].

Effect of APA on third parties. Where an APA has effect in relation to any provision between the taxpayer and another person, then in applying the 'double counting' rules (see above) of *Schedule 28AA* to the other person, the arrangements set out in the APA similarly apply in determining any question as to

(A)   whether the taxpayer is a person on whom a potential advantage in relation to UK taxation is conferred by the actual provision, or

(B)   what constitutes the arm's length provision in relation to the actual provision.

This is subject to any APA made between the Board and the other person. The notice requirements of *FA 1998, s 111* are correspondingly amended.

[*FA 1999, s 87*].

For a detailed explanation of how APAs are administered, see Revenue Pamphlet IR 131, SP 3/99, 31 August 1999 (as revised). The contact address for APA applications and other information is Assistant Director (APAs), Revenue Policy, International, Business Tax Group (APAs), Victory House, 30–34 Kingsway, London WC2B 6ES (tel. 020–7438 7758; fax 020–7438 6106) or, where oil taxation is involved, Deputy Director (APAs), Revenue Policy, International, Oil Taxation Office (APAs), Melbourne House, Aldwych, London WC2B 4LL (tel. 020–7438 7579; fax 020–7438 6910). See also Revenue Tax Bulletin October 1999 pp 697, 698 for a note on the scope of agreements, and for procedural guidance relating to bilateral agreements in the light of the Revenue's experiences and observations in concluding agreements with treaty partners under double tax treaty mutual agreement procedures.

See Simon's Direct Tax Service B3.1850 *et seq.*

Arbitration Convention. The Convention (*90/436/EEC*) on the elimination of double taxation in connection with the adjustment of profits of associated enterprises requires Member States to adopt certain procedures and to follow the opinion of an advisory commission in certain cases of dispute relating to transfer pricing adjustments (although it appears that no such commission has ever been appointed). If the appropriate Protocol to the Convention is ratified, the Convention will continue in force until December 2004, with automatic five-year extensions thereafter unless the signatory States decide otherwise (see Revenue Tax Bulletin August 1998 pp 575, 576). *ICTA 1988, s 815B* makes provision for domestic legislation and agreements to be over-ridden where necessary under the Convention, and *ICTA 1988, s 816(2A)* and *FA 1989, s 182A* provide the necessary information powers and confidentiality requirements in relation to disclosures of information to an advisory commission. [*F(No 2)A 1992, s 51*]. See Revenue Tax Bulletin October 1997 pp 465–467 for guidance on Arbitration Convention procedures. Enquiries about the application of the Convention may be made to Andrew Hickman, Inland Revenue, International Division, Victory House, 30–34 Kingsway, London WC2B 6ES (tel. 020–7438 6916, fax. 020–7438 7629) or, in relation to sales of oil etc., to Janice Cross, Oil Taxation Office, Melbourne House, Aldwych, London WC2B 4LL (tel. 020–7438 7579, fax. 020–7438 6910).

See Simon's Direct Tax Service B3.1854, F4.6.

3.9   **CAPITAL SUMS RECEIVED IN LIEU OF EARNINGS** [*ICTA 1988, ss 775, 777, 778*]

Where

(i)   transactions or arrangements are made (having as their *main* object, or one of their main objects, the avoidance or reduction of income tax) which enable some other person to enjoy profits, gains, income, copyrights, licences or rights etc., deriving, directly or indirectly, from occupational activities, past or present, which an individual (whether resident in the UK or not [*ICTA 1988, s 775(9)*]) carries on wholly or partly in the UK, and

(ii)   in connection therewith, or in consequences thereof, that individual obtains, for himself or for some other person, *a capital amount* (i.e. any amount not otherwise includible in any computation of income for tax purposes [*ICTA 1988, s 777(13)*])

any such amount is (subject to certain exceptions, as below) to be treated as *earned income* of that individual, assessable under Schedule D, Case VI, arising when the capital sum is receivable (or, if it consists of property or a right, when it is sold or realised [*ICTA 1988, s 775(7)*]). [*ICTA 1988, s 775(1)–(3), (8)*].

Exemptions. Capital amounts from the disposal of

(*a*)   shares in a company, so far as their value is attributable to the value of the company's business as a going concern, or

(*b*)   assets (including goodwill) of a profession or vocation, or a share in a professional or vocational partnership, so far as their value is attributable to the value of the profession etc., as a going concern.

But the above exemptions do not apply to any part of the capital amount which represents any part of the going-concern value of the business, profession etc., as above, materially deriving from prospective income etc., from the individual's activities in the occupation, whether as partner or employee, for which he has not received full consideration (disregarding all capital amounts). [*ICTA 1988, s 775(4)–(6)*].

Where the person charged to tax is not the one for whom the capital amount was obtained (see (ii) above) he may recover from the latter person any part of that tax which he pays (for which purpose the Revenue will supply, on request, a certificate of income in respect of which tax has been paid). [*ICTA 1988, s 777(8)*].

The various provisions applicable to *ICTA 1988, s 776*, which are listed in 3.10 below under 'General', also apply for purposes of this section.

Simon's Direct Tax Service. See **E1.702** *et seq.*

3.10   **TRANSACTIONS IN LAND** [*ICTA 1988, ss 776–778*]

The following provisions apply to all persons, whether UK residents or not, if all or any part of the land in question is in the UK. [*ICTA 1988, s 776(14)*].

Where

(*a*)   land (or any property deriving its value from land) is acquired with the sole or main object of realising a gain from disposing of it, or

(*b*)   land is held as trading stock, or

(*c*)   land is developed with the sole or main object of realising a gain from disposing of it when developed,

any capital gain from disposal of the land or any part of it (i.e. any amount not otherwise includible in any computation of income for tax purposes [*ICTA 1988, s 777(13)*]) which is realised (for himself or for any other person) by the person acquiring, holding or developing it (or by any connected person, as defined by *ICTA 1988, s 839* (see 19 CONNECTED PERSONS), or a person party to, or concerned in, any arrangement or scheme to realise the gain indirectly or by a series of transactions) is, subject as below, treated for all tax purposes as income of the person realising the gain (or the person who transmitted to him, directly or indirectly, the opportunity of making that gain [*ICTA 1988, s 776(8)*]) assessable, under Schedule D, Case VI, for the chargeable period in which the gain is realised. [*ICTA 1988, s 776(1)–(3)*]. See *Yuill v Wilson HL 1980, 52 TC 674* and its sequel *Yuill v Fletcher CA 1984, 58 TC 145; Winterton v Edwards Ch D 1979, 52 TC 655*; and

3.10 Anti-Avoidance

Sugarwhite v Budd CA 1988, 60 TC 679. Bona fide transactions, not entered into with tax avoidance in view, may be caught by the legislation—see *Page v Lowther and Another CA 1983, 57 TC 199*.

'*Land*' includes buildings, and any estate or interest in land or buildings. [*ICTA 1988, s 776(13)(a)*].

'*Property deriving its value from land*' includes any shareholding in a company, partnership interest, or interest in settled property, deriving its value, directly or indirectly, from land, and any option, consent or embargo affecting the disposition of land. [*ICTA 1988, s 776(13)(b)*]. See, however, 'Exemptions' below.

Land is '*disposed of*' for the above purposes if, by any one or more transactions or by any arrangement or scheme (whether concerning the land or any property deriving its value therefrom), the property in, or control over, the land is effectively disposed of. [*ICTA 1988, s 776(4)*]. Any number of transactions may be treated as a single arrangement or scheme if they have, or there is evidence of, a common purpose. [*ICTA 1988, s 776(5)(b)*]. See also under 'General' below.

For the date of the capital gain where instalments involved, see *Yuill v Fletcher CA 1984, 58 TC 145*.

Exemptions.

(i) An individual's gain made from the *sale etc., of his residence* exempted from capital gains tax under *TCGA 1992, s 222* or which would be so exempt but for *TCGA 1992, s 224(3)* (acquired for purpose of making a gain). [*ICTA 1988, s 776(9)*].

(ii) A gain on the sale of *shares in a company holding land as trading stock* (or a company owning, directly or indirectly, 90% of the ordinary share capital of such a company) *provided that* the company disposes of the land by normal trade and makes all possible profit from it, and the share sale is not part of an arrangement or scheme to realise a land gain indirectly. [*ICTA 1988, s 776(10)* and see *Chilcott v CIR Ch D 1981, 55 TC 446*].

(iii) (If the liability arises solely under (*c*) above.) Any part of the gain fairly attributable to a period *before the intention was made* to develop the land. [*ICTA 1988, s 776(7)*].

Gains are to be computed 'as is just and reasonable in the circumstances', allowance being given only for expenses attributable to the land disposed of, and the following may be taken into account.

(A) If a leasehold interest is disposed of out of a freehold, the Sch D, Case I treatment in such a case of a person dealing in land (see 71.67 SCHEDULE D, CASES I AND II).

(B) Any adjustments under *ICTA 1988, s 99(2)(3)* for tax on lease premiums. [*ICTA 1988, s 776(6)*].

Where the computation of a gain in respect of the development of land (as under (*c*) above) is made on the footing that the land or property was appropriated as trading stock, that land etc., is also to be treated for purposes of capital gains tax (under *TCGA 1992, s 161*) as having been transferred to stock. [*ICTA 1988, s 777(11)*].

Where, under *ICTA 1988, s 775* or *s 776*, tax is assessed on, and paid by, a person other than the one who actually realised the gain, the person paying the tax may recover it from the other party (for which purpose the Revenue will, on request, supply a certificate of income in respect of which tax has been paid). [*ICTA 1988, s 777(8)*].

Clearance. The person who made or would make the gain may (if he considers that (*a*) or (*c*) above may apply), submit to his Inspector of Taxes particulars of any completed or proposed transactions. If he does so the inspector must, within 30 days of receiving those particulars, notify the taxpayer whether or not he is satisfied that liability under this section does not arise. If the inspector is so satisfied no assessment can thereafter be made on that gain, provided that all material facts and considerations have been fully and accurately disclosed. [*ICTA 1988, s 776(11)*].

General. See *ICTA 1988, s 777(2)(3)* for provisions to prevent avoidance by the use of indirect means to transfer any property or right, or enhance or diminish its value, e.g., by sales at less, or more, than full consideration, assigning share capital or rights in a company or partnership or an interest in settled property, disposal on the winding-up of any company, partnership or trust etc. For ascertaining whether, and to what extent, the value of any property or right is derived from any other property or right, value may be traced through any number of companies, partnerships and trusts, at each stage attributing property held by the company, partnership or trust to its shareholders etc., 'in such manner as is appropriate to the circumstances'. [*ICTA 1988, s 777(5)*]. Where the person liable is non-resident, the Board may direct that any part of an amount taxable under these provisions on that person be paid under deduction of tax as if made other than out of taxable income. [*ICTA 1988, s 777(9)*].

For the above purposes the Revenue may require, under penalty, any person to supply them with any particulars thought necessary, including particulars of

(I)   transactions etc., in which he acts, or acted, on behalf of others, and

(II) transactions etc., which in the opinion of the Revenue should be investigated, and

(III) what part, if any, he has taken, or is taking, in specified transactions etc. (Under this heading a *solicitor* who has merely acted as professional adviser is not compelled to do more than state that he acted and give his client's name and address.) [*ICTA 1988, s 778*].

The transactions of which particulars are required need not be identified transactions (*Essex v CIR CA 1980, 53 TC 720*).

Simon's Direct Tax Service. See **B3.636** *et seq.*

3.11   **LAND SOLD AND LEASED BACK — TAX DEDUCTIONS FOR RENT ARE LIMITED TO COMMERCIAL RENT** [*ICTA 1988, s 779; FA 1995, Sch 6 para 27; ITEPA 2003, Sch 6 para 101*]

Where, after 14 April 1964, land (or any interest or estate in land) is transferred from one person to another (by sale, lease, surrender or forfeiture of lease etc.) and

(*a*)   under a lease of the land, or any part of it, granted then or subsequently by the transferee to the transferor, or

(*b*)   as a result of a transaction or transactions affecting the land or interest,

the transferor, or any person associated with him, becomes liable to pay any lease rent (including any premium treated as rent — see 69.17 SCHEDULE A), or rent charge on, or connected with, the land which would be allowable

(i)   as a deduction from trading profits, or

(ii)   in computing profits or losses under Case VI, or

(iii) as a management expense under *ICTA 1988, s 75* or *s 76*, or

(iv)   against employment income, under *ITEPA 2003, s 336*, or

(v)   as a deduction in computing profits from woodlands, or

(vi)   in computing profits under Schedule A,

the allowance for tax purposes in respect of that rent or other payment (apart from any portion which properly relates to services, tenant's rates, or the use of assets other than land) is limited to the commercial rent of the land to which it relates for the period for which the payment is made. In the case of a lease, '*commercial rent*' means the open-market rent, at the time the actual lease was created, under a lease whose duration and repair terms are the same as under the actual lease but stipulating a rent payable at uniform intervals at a uniform rate, or progressively increasing proportionately to any increases provided by the actual lease. For other transactions, it is the open market rent which would be payable under a tenant's repairing lease (as defined by *ICTA 1988, s 779(12)*) for the period over which payments are to be made, or 200 years if they are for a longer period or are perpetual.

Any part of a payment which is disallowed under the above provisions may be carried forward as an addition to the next subsequent payment, and so on. All payments for the same period are amalgamated, including apportioned parts of periods which overlap. A payment for a period falling, wholly or partly, beyond one year from the date of payment is treated as being for the year commencing with the date on which it is paid. [*ICTA 1988, s 779(5)–(7)*].

'Associated persons'.

A.   Husband and wife, their relatives and spouses,

B.   the trustee of a settlement and the settlor or any person associated with him,

C.   a person and any body, or bodies of persons (including partnerships) which he, or any persons associated with him, or he and any persons associated with him, controls (as under *ICTA 1988, s 840*, see 19.8 CONNECTED PERSONS and note that, in the case of a partnership, control means the right to more than a half share in assets or income),

D.   any bodies of persons associated with the same person under C above,

E.   joint owners of the land etc. the subject of disposal, including their associates,

F.   the transferor and any other transferor acting in concert, or reciprocally, with him, and their associates,

G.   any two or more companies participating in the reconstruction, or amalgamation, of a company or companies. [*ICTA 1988, s 779(11), s 783(10); FA 1995, Sch 17 para 19*].

Simon's Direct Tax Service. See **B3.647**.

3.12   **LAND SOLD AND LEASED BACK — PROPORTION OF CAPITAL SUM RECEIVED IS TO BE TAXED AS INCOME IN CERTAIN CIRCUMSTANCES** [*ICTA 1988, s 780; FA 1988, s 75*]

As regards arrangements as in *ICTA 1988, s 779* (see 3.11 above), made after 21 June 1971, where the lease when sold has no more than 50 years still to run and the period for which the premises are leased back is 15 years or less, the increased rent payable, so far as it does not exceed a commercial rent (see 3.11 above), is allowable as a deduction from profits, but of the consideration received by the lessee for giving up the original lease (or undertaking to pay an increased rent) a proportion equivalent to one-fifteenth of that consideration multiplied by the number of years by which the term of the lease-back falls short of 16 years will be treated as assessable income, not capital. Appropriate adjustment to be made where the lease-back is of part only of the property previously leased. For the above purposes the term of the new lease is deemed to end on any date whereafter the rent payable is reduced, or, if the lessor or lessee has power to determine the lease or the lessee has power to vary its terms, on the earliest date on which the lease can be so determined or varied.

Simon's Direct Tax Service. See **B3.648**.

3.13   **LEASES OF ASSETS OTHER THAN LAND — CAPITAL SUM RECEIVED BY PERSON WHO PAYS LEASE RENTALS IS TAXABLE — to the extent of tax allowances on such lease rentals** [*ICTA 1988, ss 781, 783, 784*]

Where any payment under a lease, created after 14 April 1964, of any asset not falling under *ICTA 1988, s 779* (see 3.11 above) or *s 782* (see 3.14 below), is allowable

(i)   as a deduction from trading profits, or

(ii)   in computing profits or losses under Schedule D, Case VI, or in respect of woodlands, or

(iii)   as a management expense under *ICTA 1988, ss 75, 76* or

(iv)   against employment income under *ITEPA 2003, s 336*,

then if at any time the person making the payment has obtained, or obtains, a capital sum (i.e. any money, or money's worth, not chargeable as profits etc., of a trade, profession, or from woodlands nor chargeable under Case VI) in respect of the lessee's interest in the lease (including by surrender to the lessor, assignment, subleasing, or receipt under insurance — and see *ICTA 1988, s 783*), or any person associated with the payer has obtained a capital sum for an interest in the asset, the recipient of that capital sum is assessed, under Case VI, for the year in which the capital sum was obtained, on a figure equal to the amount of the payment under the lease which is allowable for tax purposes as above (or the effectively allowable part of it, where the whole or part of the period in which the payment would normally be allowed is not a basis period for assessment), subject to the overriding limitation that the amount(s) so charged shall not exceed the capital sum received (or, where the lease is a hire-purchase agreement, that sum less the recipient's capital expenditure on the asset — see *ICTA 1988, s 784*).

Apportionments are made in the case of recipients who are partners or persons with a joint interest in the asset. 'Associated persons' are as listed in A to E of 3.11 (relating to *ICTA 1988, s 779*) above. [*ICTA 1988, s 783(10)*]. Assessments to give effect to the above provisions may be made up to five years after 31 January following the tax year in which the allowable payment was made or, for corporation tax purposes, six years after the end of the accounting period in which it was made. [*ICTA 1988, s 781(8); FA 1996, s 135, Sch 21 para 21*].

Simon's Direct Tax Service. See **B3.661** *et seq.*

3.14   **LEASES OF ASSETS (OTHER THAN LAND) PREVIOUSLY OWNED FOR TRADE ETC. BY TAXPAYER — deductions for lease rentals are limited to commercial rent** [*ICTA 1988, s 782*]

Any payment under a lease, created after 14 April 1964, of any asset (other than land or an interest in land) which at any time prior to the lease was used for the purpose of the lessee's trade (or any other trade carried on by him) and was then owned by the person carrying on the trade in which it was used is limited, in computing profits or losses of the lessee's trade, to the commercial rent of the asset for the period covered by the payment, i.e. a rent representing a reasonable return, by uniform instalments at uniform intervals over the remainder of the asset's anticipated normal working life (as under *ICTA 1988, s 782(6)*), on its market value at the time the lease was created. *ICTA 1988, s 782(3)–(5)* contains similar provisions (disallowed payments carried forward etc.) to *ICTA 1988, s 780(4)–(6)* — see 3.11 above.

Simon's Direct Tax Service. See **B3.664**.

3.15 Anti-Avoidance

3.15   **LOAN TRANSACTIONS** [*ICTA 1988, s 786; FA 1996, s 159(1); SI 1996 No 2645*]

Where, with reference to lending money or giving credit (or varying the terms of a loan or credit):

    (i)   a transaction provides for the payment of an *annuity or other annual payment* — that payment is treated as if it were of annual interest. [*ICTA 1988, s 786(3)*];

    (ii)   any person *assigns, surrenders, waives or forgoes* income on property (without a sale or transfer of the property) — that person is assessable under Schedule D, Case VI, on a sum equal to the income assigned, surrendered, waived etc. [*ICTA 1988, s 786(5)*];

    (iii)   if credit is given for the purchase price of property and during the subsistence of the debt, the purchaser's rights to income from the property are suspended or restricted — he is treated for the purpose of (ii) above as if he had made a surrender of that income. [*ICTA 1988, s 786(6)*].

Transactions with CONNECTED PERSONS (19) are included.

Simon's Direct Tax Service. See E1.555.

3.16   **PERSONS EXEMPT FROM TAX — RESTRICTION REGARDING PRE-ACQUISITION DIVIDENDS ETC. RECEIVED ON 10% HOLDINGS** [*ICTA 1988, ss 235, 236; FA 1993, s 78(6), Sch 6 para 3; FA 1997, s 70; F(No 2)A 1997, Sch 4 para 7*]

An exempt person will not be able to recover a tax credit in respect of any part of a distribution made before 6 April 1999 related to profits (as defined — see *ICTA 1988, s 236 as amended*) arising before acquisition of the shares if the shares held (together with any associated holding) are 10% or more of that class. The income will not then be exempt from tax and will become liable to tax, or, as the case may be, additional tax at the difference between the lower rate and the rate applicable to trusts (see 81.5 SETTLEMENTS) in force when the distribution is made and will not be available for purposes of *ICTA 1988, s 348* and *s 349(1)*, nor may interest paid within *ICTA 1988, s 353* be set against it. These provisions do not apply to certain payments treated as qualifying distributions (see 3.17 below). See *CIR v Sheppard and another (Trustees of the Woodland Trust) (No 2) Ch D 1993, 65 TC 724* for attribution of profits to a distribution where waiver resulted in whole distribution being received although only 60% of shares held.

These provisions are **repealed** for distributions made **on or after 6 April 1999**.

Simon's Direct Tax Service. See A7.1202.

3.17   **PERSONS EXEMPT FROM TAX — RESTRICTION REGARDING CERTAIN BONUS ISSUES** [*ICTA 1988, s 237; FA 1993, Sch 6 para 3; FA 1994, Sch 9 para 2; F(No 2)A 1997, Sch 4 para 7*]

Where, before 6 April 1999, 'bonus issues' are treated as a distribution by virtue of *ICTA 1988, s 209(3), s 210*, or *s 211*, a recipient entitled to exemption from tax or the setting-off of losses against income shall have such bonus issue and related tax credit ignored in the repayment or loss calculation and be liable to tax as in 3.16 above on such bonus issue unless it represents a normal return, as defined. Such 'bonus issues' are not available for purposes of *ICTA 1988, s 348* and *s 349(1)*, nor may interest paid and otherwise deductible under *ICTA 1988, s 353* be set against them.

These provisions are **repealed** for distributions made **on or after 6 April 1999**.

Simon's Direct Tax Service. See A7.1203.

3.18   **ANNUAL PAYMENTS FOR NON-TAXABLE CONSIDERATION** [*ICTA 1988, s 125; FA 1989, s 109(2); FA 1995, Sch 17 para 2, Sch 29 Pt VIII(8)*]

Any payment (whenever the liability to make it was incurred, but subject to exceptions as below) of an annuity or other annual payment charged with tax under SCHEDULE D, CASE III (72), not being interest, and made for a consideration which is *not wholly* included in the income for tax purposes of the person making the annual payment, shall be paid without deduction of tax and not allowed as a deduction from, or a charge on, his income for the purposes of income tax and corporation tax. Certain admission rights in return for annual payments to charities are disregarded for this purpose (see 14.17(*b*) CHARITIES).

Exceptions to the above provisions are any payments (i) which fall within 81.17(i) or (ii) SETTLEMENTS, or (ii) to an individual for surrendering, assigning or releasing an interest in settled property to a person having a subsequent interest, or (iii) of any annuity granted in the ordinary course of a business of granting annuities, or (iv) any annuity charged on an interest in settled property and granted before 30 March 1977 by an individual to a company whose business was wholly or mainly in acquiring such interests or which was carrying on life assurance business in the UK. For Scotland, reference to settled property refers to property held in trust. For position prior to these provisions see *CIR v Plummer HL 1979, 54 TC 1*, and *Moodie v CIR and Sinnett HL 1993, 65 TC 610*, in which the decision in *Plummer* on similar facts was reversed on *Ramsay* principles (see 3.1 above).

A payment to which these provisions apply is excluded from the *FA 1988* provisions as to the non-deductibility and exemption from tax of certain annual payments falling due after 14 March 1988 (see 1.8(i) and 1.10(i) ALLOWANCES AND TAX RATES).

Simon's Direct Tax Service. See E1.503.

3.19   **DEALING IN COMMODITY FUTURES — WITHDRAWAL OF LOSS RELIEF** [*ICTA 1988, s 399; FA 1997, s 80(4); FA 2002, Sch 27 para 4*]

If, apart from *ICTA 1988, s 128* and *TCGA 1992, s 143(1)* (see 71.22 SCHEDULE D, CASES I AND II), gains arising in the course of dealing in commodity or financial futures or qualifying options would, for income tax purposes, constitute profits or gains chargeable under Schedule D other than as profits of a trade, any loss arising in the course of that dealing is not allowable against profits or gains chargeable under Schedule D. This does not apply to a loss arising from a transaction to which *ICTA 1988, Sch 5AA* applies (see 3.21 below).

Where there is a trade of dealing in commodity futures carried on in partnership in which one or more partners is a company and arrangements are made or a scheme effected (whether by the partnership agreement or otherwise) after 5 April 1976 so that the sole or main benefit expected from the partnership is tax relief under *ICTA 1988, s 380* (trading losses set-off against general income of an individual) or *ICTA 1988, s 393A(1)* (trading losses set-off against total profits of a company) or *ICTA 1988, s 381* (losses in early years of a trade set-off against general income of an individual in earlier years), such relief will not be given. Where relief has been given, it will be withdrawn by an assessment under Schedule D, Case VI.

Simon's Direct Tax Service. See D2.408.

3.20   **COMPANIES BUYING THEIR OWN SHARES AND OTHER SPECIAL DIVIDENDS** [*FA 1997, s 69, Sch 7; F(No 2)A 1997 ss 24(14), 25, 36(3), Sch 6 para 21, Sch 8 Pt II (8)(9)(11)(12)*]

The special treatment described below applies to qualifying distributions, made after 7 October 1996 and **before 6 April 1999** by UK-resident companies, which fall within either or both of the following.

3.20 Anti-Avoidance

(a)   Payments made on the redemption, repayment or purchase by the company of its own shares, or on the purchase of rights to acquire its own shares (see Tolley's Corporation Tax under Purchase by a Company of its Own Shares).

(b)   Distributions in relation to which there are any kind of arrangements by virtue of which one or more of the 'specified matters' is or was to any extent made in any way referable to, or to the carrying out of, a transaction in securities (within *ICTA 1988, s 703*, see 3.2 above). This does not apply where that transaction was completed before 8 October 1996 unless some or all of the arrangements were made on or after that date. The '*specified matters*' are whether the distribution is made, the time it is made, its form and its amount.

Subject to the exceptions and modifications referred to below, such distributions are treated as foreign income dividends ('FIDs', see 1.9 ALLOWANCES AND TAX RATES and Tolley's Corporation Tax under Foreign Income Dividends) with effect from 8 October 1996, over-riding the election for such treatment under *ICTA 1988, s 246A*. The dividend certificate must state that the distribution is a FID by virtue of these provisions.

Distributions treated as income of trustees. Where a distribution within (a) above is or has been made to trustees (other than trustees of a unit trust scheme within *ICTA 1988, s 469* (see 90.2 UNIT TRUSTS)), or passed on to them through personal representatives, the 'relevant part' (and a corresponding part of the deemed FID) is treated as income within *ICTA 1988, s 686* to which the rate applicable to trusts accordingly applies (see 81.5 SETTLEMENTS). The '*relevant part*' of the distribution is so much (if any) as does not fall to be treated as income of the settlor and is not income either

(i)   within *ICTA 1988, s 686(2)(a)* (i.e. income to be accumulated or which is payable at the trustees' or any other person's discretion), or

(ii)   arising under a trust established for charitable purposes only, or

(iii)   from investments or deposits or other property held for pension purposes (as under *ICTA 1988, s 686(2)(c)*).

There are consequential changes to *section 686* to ensure that income defrayed to meet trust management expenses is taxable only at the basic or lower rate of tax, as appropriate.

See SETTLEMENTS at 81.5 and generally.

Exceptions. The following distributions are excluded from the application of these provisions in the circumstances described.

(1)   *Stock options.* A distribution is not within (b) above solely because it is made in consequence of an election in respect of a stock dividend option (see 85.1 STOCK DIVIDENDS).

(2)   *Fixed rate preference share dividends.* A dividend on a fixed rate preference share (as defined) is not within (b) above by reason only that a specified matter is made referable to the issue terms.

(3)   *Pre-sale distributions.* An 'excepted pre-sale distribution' is not within (b) above if the only transactions in securities to which any of the specified matters are referable are 'relevant transactions'.

A distribution is an '*excepted pre-sale distribution*' if, on or within 14 days of the making of the distribution, there is a '*major change in the ownership*' of the distributing company, i.e. if a single person acquires a holding of, or two or more persons between them acquire holdings together amounting to, 75% or more of its ordinary share capital. A '*relevant transaction*' is any transaction in securities by which any such holding is acquired. In comparing a person's holdings at any two dates, he is to be treated at the later date as having acquired whatever he did not hold at the earlier date, irrespective of intervening acquisitions and disposals. It is beneficial ownership which is considered, and comparisons are made in percentage terms throughout. Acquisitions of shares on death are left out of account, as is any gift which was unsolicited and made without regard to these provisions. Where the existence of extraordinary rights or powers renders ownership of the ordinary share capital an inappropriate test of change of ownership, holdings of all kinds, or of any particular kind, of share capital, voting power or any other special kind of power may be taken into account instead.

(4)   *Manufactured dividends.* Payment of an amount consisting of a manufactured dividend (within *ICTA 1988, Sch 23A*, see 3.6 above) is generally excluded from the operation of these provisions. However, where that amount is representative of a distribution to which these provisions apply, the payment is deemed to be such a distribution, except insofar as *Schedule 23A* makes different provision in relation to the payment. Where the distribution of which that amount is representative is within (*a*) above, the payment is treated for the purposes of *Schedule 23A* as representative of a dividend on the shares concerned in the redemption etc.

(5)   *Dividends within groups of companies.* See Tolley's Corporation Tax under Groups of Companies as regards exclusion from these provisions of certain distributions subject (before 6 April 1999) to a group income election under *ICTA 1988, s 247*.

Authorised unit trusts. For the treatment of distributions within these provisions in the distribution accounts of authorised unit trusts, see 90.1 UNIT TRUSTS.

For the Revenue's views on the scope of these provisions, with a number of illustrative examples, see Revenue Tax Bulletin June 1997 pp 429–434.

These provisions are repealed for distributions made after 5 April 1999.

3.21   **FUTURES AND OPTIONS — TRANSACTIONS WITH GUARANTEED RETURNS** [*ICTA 1988, s 127A, Sch 5AA; FA 1997, s 80, Sch 11; FA 1998, s 99; FA 2002, s 78, Sch 27 paras 14, 25*]

(See the note at the end of this section as regards replacement of these provisions for corporation tax purposes by specific corporation tax provisions.)

The special provisions described below apply to a 'disposal of futures or options' if it is one of two or more 'related' transactions, and it is reasonable to assume that a main purpose of the transactions, taken together, is or was to produce a 'guaranteed return', either from the disposal itself or together with another such disposal or disposals. The likely effect of the transactions, and/or the circumstances in which they, or any of them, is or are entered into, are taken into account for this purpose. For accounting periods ending after 25 July 2001, the provisions also apply to a transaction if it is one of the disposals of futures or options to which *FA 1996, s 93A* (inserted by *FA 2002, s 76*) refers (see Tolley's Corporation Tax under Loan Relationships).

A disposal is a '*disposal of futures or options*' if it consists in a disposal of one or more 'futures' or 'options' or of any combination thereof. A '*future*' is any outstanding rights and obligations under a commodity or financial futures contract, and an '*option*' is one listed on a recognised stock or futures exchange or otherwise relating to currency, shares, stock, securities, an interest rate or rights under a commodity or financial futures contract. The existence or timing of a disposal is determined in accordance with *TCGA 1992, ss 143(5)(6), 144, 144A* (see Tolley's Capital Gains Tax under Disposal) and other relevant provisions of that *Act*, modified as necessary for this purpose, on the assumption that all futures are assets. However, a disposal consisting in the grant of an option, which precedes at least one 'related' transaction (or 'associated' transaction within *FA 1996, s 93A*) which is a disposal other than the grant of an option, is deemed for these purposes to be made at the time of (or of the first) such subsequent disposal (except insofar as the provisions of *TCGA 1992* referred to above require the grant of an option and the transaction entered into to fulfil obligations under the option to be treated as a single transaction, and determine the time at which that single transaction is treated as entered into).

Transactions are '*related*' or '*associated*' for these purposes if they are entered into in pursuance of a scheme or arrangements (including understandings of any kind, whether or not legally enforceable). This may include transactions with different parties, or with parties different from the parties to the scheme or arrangements. It also includes any case in which it would be reasonable to assume, from the likely effect of the transactions and/or the circumstances in which they, or any of them, is or are entered into, that neither or none of them would have been entered into independently of the other(s).

A '*guaranteed return*' is produced wherever risks from fluctuations in the subject matter to which the futures or options (or their value) are referable are so eliminated or reduced as to produce a return equating, in substance, to interest and not significantly attributable (otherwise than incidentally) to any such fluctuations. This includes any case where a main reason for the choice of subject matter is that it appears that there is no (or only an insignificant) risk that it will fluctuate. The return from one or more disposals is for these purposes that represented by the total net profits or gains (or all but an insignificant part of those profits or gains), aggregating where appropriate profits or gains of persons who are 'associated' (as specially defined) in relation to the disposals.

Profits or gains realised from a transaction to which these provisions apply (whether capital or not) are treated as income of the person by whom they are realised, chargeable under SCHEDULE D, CASE VI (74) for the chargeable period in which the disposal takes place. There are exclusions for profits or gains within the financial instruments provisions of *FA 1994, Pt IV, Ch II* (see Tolley's Corporation Tax under Financial Instruments and Derivative Contracts) or arising to an authorised unit trust within *ICTA 1988, s 468* (see 90.1 UNIT TRUSTS), and for so much of any profits or gains as is chargeable under Case I or Case V of Schedule D on the person to whom they arise. A loss sustained after 4 March 1997 is similarly a Case VI loss within *ICTA 1988, s 392* or *s 396* for the chargeable period of the disposal. The profits or gains (or losses) are not otherwise brought into account for tax purposes (other than as receipts for a Case I computation for life insurance companies under *FA 1989, s 83*, see Tolley's Corporation Tax under Life Insurance Companies).

The charge is extended to cases where there are related (or associated) transactions one of which is or would be the creation or acquisition of a future or option, and another of which is or would be the running of the future to delivery or the exercise of the option, and the latter transaction is not treated under the current provisions as a disposal of a future or option. (Transactions are related or associated for this purpose if they would be but for *TCGA 1992, s 144(2)* or *(3)*, which in certain cases treat the grant or exercise of an option and the transaction in fulfilment of the obligations under the option as a single transaction, see Tolley's Capital Gains Tax under Disposal.) The current provisions then apply to the parties to the future or option as if there was a disposal of the future or option under the arrangements for the related or associated transactions immediately before the future runs to delivery or, as the case may be, the option is exercised. The disposal is treated, in the case of a person whose rights and entitlements under the future or option have a market value at that time, as at that value, or in the case of any other person as made for nil consideration with costs equivalent to those required at arm's length to obtain release of his obligations and liabilities under the future or option. There are special provisions preventing double charge or relief under the current provisions and capital gains tax (or corporation tax on chargeable gains), for which see *ICTA 1988, Sch 5AA para 4A(5)–(10)*.

Trusts. Where profits or gains are treated as income arising to trustees under these provisions, *ICTA 1988, s 686* (rate applicable to trusts, see 81.5 SETTLEMENTS) applies to so much of that income as is not treated as income of the settlor. The exclusion of income within *section 686(2)(c)* (income arising under charitable trusts or from property held for certain retirement benefit or personal pension schemes) applies equally for this purpose.

Transfer of assets abroad. Any profit or gain realised by a person resident or domiciled outside the UK from a transaction within these provisions is treated as income becoming payable to that person under *ICTA 1988, ss 739, 740* (see 3.7 above) in determining whether a UK ordinarily resident individual has an income tax liability in respect of the profit or gain.

Insurance companies. For the purposes of *ICTA 1988, s 432A* (see Tolley's Corporation Tax under Life Insurance Companies), income and losses under these provisions are generally treated as gains or losses accruing on the disposal of an asset.

Recovery of assets under Proceeds of Crime Act 2002, Pt 5. Where the transfer of futures or options is a *Pt 5* transfer under *Proceeds of Crime Act 2002* (as in 9.2(xi) CAPITAL ALLOWANCES) and no compensating payment is made to the transferor, it is not treated as a disposal for the purposes of these provisions. [*Proceeds of Crime Act 2002, Sch 10 paras 8, 10*].

Note. These provisions **cease to apply for the purposes of corporation tax for accounting periods beginning after 30 September 2002,** being replaced thereafter by specific corporation tax provisions (to similar effect) in *FA 2002, Sch 26 para 6* and *FA 1996, s 93A* (see Tolley's Corporation Tax under Financial Instruments and Derivative Contracts and under Loan Relationships).

Simon's Direct Tax Service. See **B7.204A**.

3.22 **ARRANGEMENTS TO PASS ON VALUE OF DIVIDEND TAX CREDIT** [*ICTA 1988, s 231B; F(No 2)A 1997, s 28*]

Special provisions apply where:

(*a*)   a person ('A') is entitled to a tax credit in respect of a qualifying distribution;

(*b*)   arrangements (as widely defined) subsist such that another person ('B') obtains, whether directly or indirectly, a payment representing any of the value of the tax credit;

(*c*)   the arrangements (whether or not made directly between A and B) were entered into for an 'unallowable purpose'; and

(*d*)   had B been entitled to and received the distribution when it was made, he would not have been entitled to payment of the tax credit and, if a company, could not have used the income consisting of the distribution to frank a distribution made in the same accounting period (after using any actual franked investment income).

They apply equally where an amount representing any of the value of the tax credit is applied at the direction of, or otherwise in favour of, some other person, as if that other person had obtained a payment representing that value.

Where these provisions apply:

(i)   no claim may be made for payment of the tax credit or for set-off against tax on other income;

(ii)   the income consisting of the distribution is not regarded as franked investment income; and

(iii)   no transitional charity relief payment (see 14.6 CHARITIES) may be claimed.

This does not, however, apply to the extent that the tax advantage otherwise obtained under the arrangements is cancelled or reduced by any other provision. 'Tax advantage' for this purpose is as under *ICTA 1988, s 709* (see 3.2 above), but also includes the obtaining of a payment representing any of the value of a tax credit where, had the person obtaining the payment been entitled to and received the distribution when it was made, he would not have been entitled to payment of the tax credit and, if a company, could not have used the income consisting of the distribution to frank a distribution made in the same accounting period (after using any actual franked investment income).

Arrangements are entered into for an *'unallowable purpose'* if any person is a party to the arrangements for purposes which include a purpose other than a business or commercial purpose (which includes the efficient management of investments). The purpose of obtaining a tax advantage for any person is not a business or commercial purpose unless it is not a main purpose of entering into the arrangements.

3.23   **BENEFITS FROM PRE-OWNED ASSETS** [*FA 2004, s 84, Sch 15*]

Subject to certain exemptions, a *de minimis* limit and a transitional right to elect to disapply these provisions (with inheritance tax (IHT) consequences), an income tax charge applies **for 2005/06 onwards** as described below on the annual benefit of using property previously owned by the user and not disposed of by him at arm's length. The legislation is intended to counter avoidance schemes which bypass the IHT 'gifts with reservation' rules, for which see Tolley's Inheritance Tax, but is not restricted to cases where such schemes have been used.

The main charge applies where an individual (whether alone or together with others) occupies any land or is in possession of, or has the use of, any chattel and *either* of the following two conditions is met.

The *first condition* is that, at some time after 17 March 1986, the individual owned the land or chattel, or owned other property the proceeds of disposal of which were applied, directly or indirectly, by another person towards the acquisition of the land or chattel, and the individual has disposed of all or part of his interest in the land, chattel or other property other than by way of an 'excluded transaction' (see below).

The *second condition* is that, at some time after 17 March 1986, the individual has provided, directly or indirectly but other than by way of an 'excluded transaction', any of the consideration given by another person for the acquisition of the land or chattel or of any other property the proceeds of disposal of which were applied by another person towards the acquisition of the land or chattel.

The above references to land include an interest in land, ownership of a chattel means sole or joint ownership, and references to the acquisition or disposal of any property generally include acquisitions and disposals of an interest in that property.

A disposition which creates a new interest in land or a chattel out of an existing interest is treated as a part disposal of the existing interest.

Where the above applies to an individual at any time in 2005/06 or any subsequent tax year, then subject to the exemptions from charge detailed below, the chargeable amount computed as below is treated as income of his, chargeable to income tax, for the tax year in question.

Excluded transactions. Any of the following disposals of the land, chattel or other property in question is an *'excluded transaction'* for the purposes of the first condition above:

- a disposal of the individual's entire interest in the property (except for any right expressly reserved by him over the property) by a transaction made at arm's length with a person not connected with him or by a transaction such as might be expected to be made at arm's length between persons not connected with each other;

- a transfer of the property to the individual's spouse (or, by court order, to his former spouse);

- a gift (or a transfer for the benefit of a former spouse made in accordance with a court order) by virtue of which the property became settled property in which the individual's spouse or former spouse has an interest in possession which either still subsists or has come to an end on the death of the spouse or former spouse;

- a disposition which is exempt from IHT under *IHTA 1984, s 11* (dispositions for maintenance of family);

- an outright gift to an individual which is covered by the IHT annual exemption or small gifts exemption.

For the purposes of these provisions, *ICTA 1988, s 839* (see 19 CONNECTED PERSONS) applies to determine whether or not persons are connected with each other but as if a relative also included an uncle, aunt, nephew or niece and as if 'settlement', 'settlor' and 'trustee' had the meaning they have for IHT purposes.

For the purposes of the second condition above, the provision by the individual of consideration for another person's acquisition of property is an '*excluded transaction*' if

- the other person is the individual's spouse (or, where the transfer has been ordered by the court, his former spouse); or

- on its acquisition the property became settled property in which the individual's spouse or former spouse has an interest in possession which either still subsists or has come to an end on the death of the spouse or former spouse; or

- the provision of the consideration was an outright gift of money made at least seven years before the individual first occupied the land in question or had possession of, or the use of, the chattel in question; or

- the provision of the consideration is a disposition which is exempt from IHT under *IHTA 1984, s 11* (dispositions for maintenance of family); or

- the provision of the consideration is an outright gift to an individual which is covered by the IHT annual exemption or small gifts exemption.

Exemptions from charge. The charge under these provisions does not apply by reference to any property at a time when that property would fall to be treated for IHT purposes as property which, in relation to the individual concerned, is property subject to a reservation (or would fall to be so treated were it not for specified IHT exemptions). See generally Tolley's Inheritance Tax under Gifts with Reservation. This exemption also applies at any time where property deriving its value from the property in question would fall to be so treated; however, if such other property reflects some of, but substantially less than the whole of, the value of the property in question, the exemption does not apply but the chargeable amount is scaled down accordingly.

The charge does not apply by reference to any property at a time when the individual's estate for IHT purposes includes that property or includes other property whose value is derived from it. If such other property reflects some of, but substantially less than the whole of, the value of the original property, the exemption does not apply but the chargeable amount is scaled down accordingly. This exemption (or partial exemption) is subject to anti-avoidance provision where the value of the estate is reduced by certain associated liabilities.

The provisions do not apply to a person for any tax year during which he is not UK-resident. If in any tax year a person is UK-resident but not UK-domiciled (as defined for IHT, not income tax, purposes — see Tolley's Inheritance Tax under Domicile), the provisions apply to him only if the land or chattel is situated in the UK. In applying the provisions to a person previously domiciled outside the UK, no regard is to be had to any property which is 'excluded property' as defined for IHT purposes (see Tolley's Inheritance Tax under Excluded Property).

The Treasury may confer additional exemptions by regulations. See below for *de minimis* limit.

The chargeable amount. In the case of an individual chargeable under these provisions as a result of his occupation of **land**, the amount chargeable to tax in respect of any tax year is the 'appropriate rental value' less any payments made, under a legal obligation, by the individual to the owner for his occupation of the land. The *'appropriate rental value'* is

$$R \times \frac{DV}{V}$$

where R = the 'rental value' of the land, V = the value of the land, and DV = (depending on the circumstances) (i) the value of the interest in the land that the individual disposed of or (ii) such part of the land's value as can reasonably be attributed to the other property that the individual disposed of, or (iii) (where it is the second condition above that is met) such part of the land's value as can reasonably be attributed to the consideration provided by the individual. So, in the most straightforward case where the individual disposed of the whole of the land he now occupies, the value of DV/V will be one and the tax charge will be on the rental value (subject to any deduction for payments made). Where it is the first condition above that is met and the disposal (whilst not being an excluded transaction as above) was a money sale of the individual's entire interest in the land or other property at less than market value, DV is scaled down proportionately so as to only take account of the gift element.

The *'rental value'* of land is the rent that would have been payable by the individual for the tax year if the land had been let to him at an annual rent equal to that which might reasonably be expected under a standard lease under which the landlord bears the cost of repairs, maintenance and insurance and the tenant pays all taxes, rates and other charges usually paid by a tenant. Regulations may prescribe the continuing use of such rental value for subsequent tax years (subject to any prescribed adjustments).

In the case of an individual chargeable under these provisions as a result of his use or possession of a **chattel**, the amount chargeable to tax in respect of any tax year is the 'appropriate amount' less any payments made, under a legal obligation, by the individual to the owner for his use or possession of the chattel. The *'appropriate amount'* is

$$N \times \frac{DV}{V}$$

where N = a notional amount of interest (at a rate to be prescribed by regulations) on the value of the chattel, and V and DV have similar meanings as in the above formula for land.

Where the individual is within these provisions during part only of a tax year, references above to the tax year, as regards both land and chattels, are to that shorter period within the tax year. The date at which *valuations* are to be made for these purposes is to be prescribed by statutory instrument, which may also prescribe the continuing use of such valuations for subsequent tax years (subject to any prescribed adjustments).

De minimis **limit.** A person is not chargeable under these provisions for a particular tax year if, for that year, the aggregate of any amounts given by the above formulae and (where applicable) the chargeable amount for intangible property in a settlement (see below) is £5,000 or less. Note that in determining whether or not the *de minimis* applies, no deduction is made at this stage for any payments made under legal obligation by the individual for occupation of land or for use or possession of chattels; it is thus possible for a tax charge to arise on an amount equal to or less than the *de minimis*.

Miscellaneous. The **value** of any property for the purposes of these provisions is its open market value, disregarding any potential reduction on the ground that the whole of the property is placed on the market at the same time.

A disposition made in relation to an interest in a deceased person's estate is disregarded for the purposes of these provisions if, by virtue of *IHTA 1984, s 17*, it is not a transfer of value for IHT purposes. This takes into account **instruments of variation, disclaimers etc.** — see Tolley's Inheritance Tax under Deeds Varying Dispositions on Death. So, for example, an individual is not treated as having formerly owned and disposed of any property simply by virtue of a will or intestacy that was subsequently varied.

A person who merely acts as **guarantor** in respect of a loan taken out by another person to acquire a property is not regarded for the purposes of these provisions as having thereby funded the acquisition.

Where for any tax year amounts are chargeable, in respect of a person's occupation of any land or his use or possession of any chattel, both under these provisions and, under *ITEPA 2003*, as **earnings** (including benefits in kind), the charge under *ITEPA 2003* takes priority and the charge under these provisions is limited to the excess (if any) of the amount otherwise chargeable under these provisions over the amount chargeable as earnings.

Transitional election to disapply these provisions. An election may be made, in prescribed form, to disapply the above provisions by reference to any particular property, with the consequence described below. Such election has effect for the first tax year for which a charge under these provisions would otherwise arise by reference to enjoyment of the property in question (or any substituted property) and for all subsequent tax years. It must be made no later than **31 January** following that first tax year (unless reasonable excuse can be shown for a late election) and can be revoked or varied (but only by the chargeable person and not by his personal representatives) at any time on or before the deadline for making it. The consequence of the election is that, for as long as that person continues to enjoy the property (or any substitute property), the property is treated for IHT purposes as property subject to a reservation; it will thus potentially attract an IHT charge if the person dies whilst continuing to enjoy the property or within seven years after ceasing to do so (see Tolley's Inheritance Tax under Gifts with Reservation). Where, in the absence of an election, the charge to income tax would arise by reference to only a proportion of the value of the property, only a proportion of the property is treated as property subject to a reservation. The foregoing references to enjoyment of property are to occupation of the property where it is land and to use or possession of the property where it is a chattel.

Intangible property comprised in a settlement. Also included in these provisions is a charge on certain intangible property comprised in a settlement in which the settlor has an interest. The charge applies where

(*a*)   the terms of a settlement, as they affect any property comprised in it, are such that any income arising from the property would be treated by virtue of *ICTA 1988, s 660A* (see 81.17 SETTLEMENTS) as the settlor's income (but *not* where it would be so treated only because the settlor's spouse could benefit from the settlement); and

(*b*)   that property includes any intangible property (meaning any property other than chattels or interests in land) which is, or which represents, property which the settlor settled, or added to the settlement, after 17 March 1986.

Where the above applies at any time in a tax year, an amount is treated as income of the settlor for that tax year. That amount is N minus T, where N is a notional amount of interest (at a rate to be prescribed by regulations) on the value of the intangible property in (*b*) above and T is the amount of income tax and/or capital gains tax payable (if any) by the settlor under specified enactments including *ICTA 1988, s 660A*, so far as that tax is attributable to that property.

The exemptions etc. described above apply equally in relation to this charge. Where for any tax year a person would be chargeable under the above provisions by reason of his enjoyment of any land or chattel and also by reference to intangible property which derives its value (wholly or partly) from that land or chattel, he is chargeable only under whichever provision produces the greater chargeable amount; and only that amount is taken into account for the purposes of applying the *de minimis* limit above.

With appropriate modifications, the transitional election above is also available, with similar consequences, in relation to the charge on intangible property.

3.24   **DISCLOSURE OF TAX AVOIDANCE SCHEMES**

With effect on and after **1 August 2004**, *FA 2004* imposes obligations, as outlined below, on promoters of certain tax avoidance schemes, and in some cases on persons entering into transactions under such schemes, to disclose those schemes to the Inland Revenue. The primary legislation provides the framework for these disclosure rules, with the detail to be provided by regulations made by statutory instrument. Three sets of draft regulations were published on 17 May 2004 as follows. The draft *Tax Avoidance Schemes (Information) Regulations 2004* sets out the procedural rules for disclosures, dealing with the manner and timing of disclosure and the information to be provided. The draft *Tax Avoidance Schemes (Prescribed Descriptions of Arrangements) Regulations 2004* applies the disclosure rules initially to certain arrangements related to financial products and certain arrangements connected with employment (in both cases with the features described in those regulations) and limits the scope of the rules to income tax, corporation tax and capital gains tax advantages. The draft *Tax Avoidance Schemes (Promoter and Prescribed Circumstances) Regulations 2004* exclude from the definition of 'promoter' a company providing taxation services to another company in the same 51% group. Also on 17 May 2004, the Revenue made available on their website their detailed draft guidance notes on these disclosure rules, entitled 'Tackling Direct Tax Avoidance: Disclosure Requirements', which cover both the primary and draft secondary legislation.

On 22 June 2004, it was announced that certain changes will be made to the draft regulations before they become final. These changes will 'ensure that only those at the heart of a scheme or arrangement, and capable of meeting the obligations, will be treated as promoters' and 'ensure the financial products test is easier to apply in practice'. The regulations will now also set transitional commencement rules, as follows.

- Where the 'relevant date' (see below under Obligations of promoters) falls on or after 1 August 2004, the initial time limit for making disclosure will be 30 September 2004.

- Promoters will not be required to disclose arrangements involving *financial products* marketed from 18 March 2004 or 23 April 2004 (as appropriate — see below) unless the relevant date falls after 21 June 2004. They will be given until 31 October 2004 to disclose financial product arrangements with a relevant date falling after 21 June 2004 and before 1 August 2004.

- Promoters will still be required to disclose arrangements involving *employment products* where the relevant date falls on or after 18 March 2004 or 23 April 2004 (as appropriate) but will be given until 31 October 2004 to disclose employment product arrangements where the relevant date falls before 1 August 2004.

(Revenue Press Release 22 June 2004).

Obligations of promoters. A 'promoter' must provide the Board with specified information on any 'notifiable proposal' within a stipulated period (5 business days according to the draft regulations) after the *'relevant date'*, i.e. the date on which he makes the proposal available for implementation by any person or, if earlier, the date he first becomes aware of any transaction forming part of arrangements implementing the proposal. A person is a *'promoter'* in relation to a 'notifiable proposal' if, in the course of a 'relevant business', he is to any extent responsible for the design of the proposed arrangements or he makes the 'notifiable proposal' available for implementation by others. A *'notifiable proposal'* is a proposal for arrangements which, if entered into, would be *'notifiable arrangements'*, i.e. arrangements falling within any description prescribed by regulations (see above) which enable (or might be expected to enable) any person to obtain a tax advantage (as widely defined) and are such that the main benefit, or one of the main benefits, that might be expected from them is the obtaining of that advantage.

There is a separate requirement for a 'promoter' to provide the Board with specified information relating to notifiable arrangements (as above) and to do so within a stipulated period (again expected to be 5 business days) after the date on which he first becomes aware of any transaction forming part of those arrangements; but this does not apply if the arrangements implement a proposal which has been notified as above. A person is a *'promoter'* in relation to notifiable arrangements if, by virtue of his having made the proposal available for implementation, he is a promoter in relation to a notifiable proposal (as above) which is implemented by those arrangements or if, in the course of a 'relevant business', he is to any extent responsible for the design of the arrangements or the organisation or management of the arrangements.

A *'relevant business'* is any trade, profession or business which involves the provision to other persons of taxation services or is carried on by a bank or a securities house. Where companies form a 51% group, anything done by one group company for the purposes of another company's relevant business is brought within the above disclosure requirements.

Where two or more persons are promoters in relation to the same proposal or arrangements, notification by one promoter discharges the obligations of the others. If a promoter has discharged his obligations in relation to a proposal or arrangements, he is not required to notify proposals or arrangements which are substantially the same as those already notified (whether or not they relate to the same parties).

The above obligations do not apply in the case of any notifiable proposal for which the relevant date (as above) fell before 18 March 2004, any notifiable arrangements which implement such a proposal or any notifiable arrangements which include a transaction entered into before that date.

Obligation of person dealing with non-UK promoter. A person who enters into any transaction forming part of notifiable arrangements in relation to which there is a non-UK resident promoter (and no UK resident promoter) must himself provide the Board with specified information relating to those arrangements. He must do so within a prescribed period (again expected to be 5 business days) after entering into the transaction. This obligation is discharged if a promoter makes disclosure of the notifiable proposal for the arrangements in question. It does not apply in relation to any notifiable arrangements which include a transaction entered into before 23 April 2004.

Obligation of parties to notifiable arrangements not involving a promoter. A person who enters into any transaction forming part of notifiable arrangements in respect of which neither he nor any other person in the UK has an obligation as above must himself provide the Board with specified information relating to those arrangements. This does not apply in relation to any notifiable arrangements which include a transaction entered into before 23 April 2004. According to the draft regulations, he may make such disclosure at any time after the date of the transaction and before he is first required to quote a reference number for the arrangements (see below).

Reference numbers allocated to arrangements. Where a person has made a disclosure as above, the Board may allocate a reference number to the arrangements in question and must notify the number to that person within 30 days after the disclosure. A promoter who is providing services to a client in connection with notifiable arrangements must pass on to the client the reference number for those arrangements or for arrangements which are substantially the same as those arrangements. He must do so within 30 days after the date he first becomes aware of any transaction forming part of the arrangements or, if later, the date on which the reference number is notified to him by the Board.

According to the draft regulations, a party to any notifiable arrangements giving rise to an income tax or capital gains tax advantage must quote the allocated reference number in his personal tax return for the year in which the number is notified to him (or, if earlier, the year in which the tax advantage is expected to arise) and in all subsequent returns until the advantage ceases to apply to him. He must also quote the tax year in which, or the date on which, the advantage is expected to arise. Comparable provisions apply for corporation tax. For arrangements connected with employment, the obligation falls on the employer to quote the reference number etc. in the annual return on form P35 for the appropriate tax year. Persons not required to file a tax return or, as the case may be, a P35 return must instead provide the Revenue with specified information no later than what would have been the filing date for such a return.

Penalties. The maximum penalty for failure to comply with any of the disclosure obligations above is £5,000 (such penalty to be determined by the Special Commissioners). In the case of continuing failure after such a penalty is imposed, there is a daily penalty of up to £600 per day. Penalties of the same level apply if a promoter fails in his duty to notify a reference number to a client.

A party to notifiable arrangements who fails to give the reference number as required (for example, by including it in his tax return) is liable to a penalty of £100 for each scheme (i.e. each set of notifiable arrangements) to which the failure relates. A second such failure within a period of 36 months gives rise to a penalty of £500 per scheme. A third or subsequent failure within 36 months gives rise to a penalty of £1,000 per scheme. The pre-existing penalty regime for incorrect tax returns is, however, disapplied in relation to any such failure.

Legal professional privilege. These provisions do not require the disclosure of privileged information, i.e. information with respect to which a claim to legal professional privilege (or Scottish equivalent) could be maintained in legal proceedings.

[*TMA 1970, s 98C; FA 2004, ss 306–319*].

4 Appeals

Cross-references. See 16.3 CLAIMS for appeals in respect of claims made outside returns; 30.7 FRAUDULENT OR NEGLIGENT CONDUCT for investigatory powers of Revenue; 52.7 OFFSHORE FUNDS; 56.3, 56.4 PAYMENT OF TAX for payment of tax in relation to appeals; 57.11, 57.13, 57.14 PENALTIES for appeals relating to penalties; 65.8 RESIDENCE, ORDINARY RESIDENCE AND DOMICILE.

Simon's Direct Tax Service A3.5, A3.7, E1.838.

The Department for Constitutional Affairs has produced a leaflet: 'Tax Appeals: A Guide to Appealing against Decisions of the Inland Revenue on Tax and Other Matters', which replaces Inland Revenue leaflet IR 37 from July 2004. The leaflet should be available from Revenue offices and enquiry centres.

The headings in this chapter are as follows.

4.1 INTRODUCTION

An appeal may be made against:

(*a*)   any assessment other than a self-assessment (see 5.2 ASSESSMENTS);

(*b*)   any conclusion stated, or amendment made, by a closure notice on completion of an enquiry into a personal, trustees' or partnership return (see 68.9 RETURNS);

(*c*)   any Revenue amendment (of a self-assessment) made, during an enquiry, to prevent potential loss of tax to the Crown (see 68.10 RETURNS);

(*d*)   any amendment of a partnership return where loss of tax is 'discovered' (see 5.3 ASSESSMENTS).

Notice of appeal must be given, in writing to the officer of the Board concerned and specifying grounds of appeal, within 30 days after the date of issue of the assessment in (*a*) above, the closure notice in (*b*) above or the notice of amendment in (*c*) or (*d*) above. An appeal within (*c*) above cannot be heard and determined until the enquiry has been completed. An appeal within (*a*)–(*d*) above cannot question the Revenue's exercise of the 'Crown Option' (see 68.6 RETURNS). The Appeal Commissioners may allow the appellant to put forward grounds omitted from the notice of appeal, if satisfied that the omission was not wilful or unreasonable. [*TMA 1970, ss 31, 31A; FA 2001, s 88, Sch 29 para 11(1)*].

The above provisions apply as from, broadly, 11 May 2001, though comparable provisions applied previously, the changes being in consequence of the revised procedure at 68.9 RETURNS for completion of an enquiry. [*FA 2001, Sch 29 para 11(2)*]. An appeal may be made in similar fashion against Revenue amendments made under the rules in 68.10, 68.13 RETURNS to a self-assessment (or partnership statement) following completion of an enquiry before 11 May 2001, or against a disallowance (or partial disallowance) of a claim or election included in a return (now covered by (*b*) above and no longer a separate matter). [*TMA 1970, s 31(1)(1AA)(1A)(2)(5)(6) as previously enacted; FA 1994, ss 196, 199(2)(a), Sch 19 para 7; FA 1996, Sch 19 para 6*].

An appeal within (*a*) above is to the Special Commissioners if the assessment was made either by the Board or under *ICTA 1988, s 350* (see 22.3 DEDUCTION OF TAX AT SOURCE). Otherwise, appeals are normally to the General Commissioners, subject to specific statutory exceptions and subject also to the appellant's right of election, similar to that outlined in 4.3 below, to bring an appeal before the Special Commissioners. However, where a question was referred to the Special Commissioners (see 68.11 RETURNS) during an enquiry into a return, an appeal within (*b*), (*c*) or (*d*) above relating to that return must also be to the Special Commissioners (unless they otherwise direct), and this applies even if notice of referral was given but subsequently withdrawn. [*TMA 1970, s 31(3)(4)(5A)–(6) as previously enacted, ss 31B–31D; FA 1984, Sch 22 para 3; FA 1996, Sch 22 para 4; FA 2001, s 88, Sch 29 para 11; SI 1984 No 1836*].

A number of enactments give the right of appeal against a decision of the Board or an officer of the Board in specified circumstances or a Revenue notice or determination (see e.g. *SI 2003 No 2682, reg 18* as regards PAYE codings). Such rights are referred to in the appropriate section of this work. Further, certain matters are dealt with as appeals (see e.g. 71.73 SCHEDULE D, CASES I AND II as regards disputes as to the transfer price of trading stock on a discontinuance). There is, however, no right of appeal against a determination of liability made by the Revenue in the event of non-submission of a self-assessment tax return (see 68.12 RETURNS). For appeals in connection with claims and elections made outside the tax return, see 16.3 CLAIMS.

Unless otherwise stated or required by context, the remainder of this chapter applies to all appeals and matters treated as appeals.

An appeal once made cannot be withdrawn unilaterally (*R v Special Commrs (ex p Elmhirst) CA 1935, 20 TC 381; Beach v Willesden General Commrs Ch D 1981, 55 TC 663*) but see 4.5 below for the withdrawal of appeals by agreement and 4.18 *et seq.* below regarding appeals to the High Court.

For postponement of tax pending appeal and payment of tax on determination of the appeal, see respectively 56.3 and 56.4 PAYMENT OF TAX.

Broadly similar provisions to those described in this chapter apply to corporation tax appeals. See Tolley's Corporation Tax under Assessments and Appeals and Self-Assessment.

4.2   TIME LIMIT FOR APPEALS ETC.

The normal time limit for giving notice of appeal is as stated in 4.1 above (but see e.g. 65.8 RESIDENCE, ORDINARY RESIDENCE AND DOMICILE as regards special time limits in certain cases). There is no time limit for appeals against PAYE codings. A **late appeal** may be accepted by the inspector or the Board if satisfied that there was reasonable excuse for the delay. If it is not accepted, the Revenue must refer the application to the Commissioners (normally the General Commissioners) for their decision. [*TMA 1970, s 49*]. If they refuse, their decision is not subject to appeal by way of stated case (*R v Special Commrs (ex p Magill) QB (NI) 1979, 53 TC 135*), but is subject to judicial review (see *R v Hastings and Bexhill General Commrs and CIR (ex p Goodacre) QB 1994, 67 TC 126*, in which a refusal was quashed and the matter remitted to a different body of Commissioners). *TMA 1970, s 49* confers upon the Commissioners a broader discretion than that of the inspector; they should take interests of justice into account; lack of reasonable excuse is potentially relevant but not conclusive (*R (oao Browallia Cal Ltd) v General Commrs QB, [2004] STC 296*).

4.3 ELECTION TO BRING APPEAL BEFORE SPECIAL COMMISSIONERS

Except as referred to at 4.1 above, and subject to 4.4 below, an appeal is normally brought before the General Commissioners. An appellant may, however, elect instead to bring an appeal within 4.1(*a*)–(*d*) above before the Special Commissioners, either when the appeal is made or separately but within the time limit for making the appeal. Such an election is, however, disregarded if the appellant and the inspector (or other officer of the Board) so agree in writing before the appeal is determined, or if before the appeal is determined the inspector (or other officer) refers the election to the General Commissioners (after notifying the appellant) and they so direct. They must give such a direction unless satisfied that the appellant has arguments to present or evidence to adduce on the merits of the appeal. Such a direction may be revoked at any time before determination of the appeal if that condition is subsequently satisfied. The decision to give or revoke a direction is final. [*TMA 1970, s 31(5A)–(5E) as previously enacted, s 31D, s 46(1); FA 1984, Sch 22 para 3; FA 2001, s 88, Sch 29 para 11*]. See also 4.4 below as regards transfers of proceedings between the General and Special Commissioners.

4.4 JURISDICTION OF APPEAL COMMISSIONERS

Certain questions which may be in dispute on appeal (but not necessarily the entire appeal) must be determined by the Special Commissioners. The questions concerned involve the application of provisions on SETTLEMENTS (81), DECEASED ESTATES (21), liability on transfers of assets abroad (see 3.7 ANTI-AVOIDANCE) and in respect of controlled foreign companies (see Tolley's Corporation Tax under Controlled Foreign Companies), and liability in relation to territorial sea and designated areas (see 51.12 NON-RESIDENTS AND OTHER OVERSEAS MATTERS). They also include any question as to the value for the purposes of capital gains tax or corporation tax on chargeable gains of any unquoted shares or securities in a UK resident company (any question for those purposes as to the value of any land or lease of land being determined by the relevant Lands Tribunal). [*TMA 1970, ss 46B, 46D; FA 1996, Sch 22 para 7; FA 1998, Sch 19 paras 24, 26; FA 2001, s 88, Sch 29 paras 27, 29; ITEPA 2003, Sch 6 para 129*].

Where, on an appeal, the question in dispute concerns a claim made (in a tax return) to the Board or made under any one or more specified provisions, the question must be determined by the Special Commissioners. The specified provisions cover double taxation relief, management expenses of the owner of mineral rights, exemptions for certain friendly societies, trade unions and employers' associations, and reliefs in respect of royalties, copyright payments etc. This applies in relation to appeals against conclusions and amendments following an enquiry into a return and appeals against certain Revenue amendments to returns and self-assessments to prevent loss of tax. [*TMA 1970, s 46C; FA 1996, Sch 22 para 7; FA 2001, s 71(4), s 88, Sch 24 para 2, Sch 29 para 28*]. Comparable provisions apply under *TMA 1970, Sch 1A* (see 16.3 CLAIMS) as regards claims not included in returns.

Appeals to the General Commissioners for which election for transfer to the Special Commissioners could be made may, if the parties so apply and the Commissioners consent, be transferred to the Special Commissioners (and *vice versa*) despite the expiry of the time

4.4 Appeals

limit for election as above or the making of such an election. [*TMA 1970, s 44(3)*]. In addition, the General Commissioners may arrange that an appeal brought before them be transferred to the Special Commissioners, with the Special Commissioners' consent, if, after considering any representations made to them by the parties to the appeal, the General Commissioners consider that, because of the complexity of, or likely time required to hear, the appeal, it should be so transferred. [*TMA 1970, s 44(3A); FA 1984, Sch 22 para 5; SI 1984 No 1836*].

The Lord Chancellor has powers, by regulation, to provide for the transfer of appeals between the General and Special Commissioners or between General Commissioners for different divisions, and for varying the number of General or Special Commissioners required or permitted to hear appeals. Different provision may be made for different cases and different circumstances. [*TMA 1970, s 46A; F(No 2)A 1992, Sch 16 para 3*]. See *SI 1994 Nos 1811–1813* and 4.7 *et seq.* below.

The Special Commissioners go on circuit to the chief provincial towns, but appeals to them may generally by arrangement be heard in London, which is usually more convenient if it is intended to engage counsel.

Rules for assigning procedures to General Commissioners. For proceedings relating to income tax or capital gains tax for 1996/97 and subsequent years (except those concerning PAYE or partnerships or where the Board otherwise direct, see below), either the taxpayer or an officer of the Board (whichever commences the proceedings) may elect by notice to the other in writing for the proceedings to be heard in the division in which is situated either the taxpayer's place of residence, his place of business (as defined) or his place of employment (as defined and regardless of whether the proceedings are in connection with the employment). An officer may make the election if the taxpayer fails to exercise his right to do so when giving notice of appeal or otherwise commencing proceedings or at such later time as the Board allow. (In practice, the Revenue will accede to a request by an employee subsequent to the appeal being made but before it is set down for hearing (and notwithstanding an election by the inspector as above) for the hearing to be in the Division in which he resides or in any other Division the employee nominates. See Revenue Tax Bulletin May 1993 p 70 and February 1997 p 387.) The taxpayer's election is irrevocable. The division for PAY AS YOU EARN (55) appeals is governed by the *Income Tax (Pay As You Earn) Regulations 2003 (SI 2003 No 2682)* except to the extent that the appellant elects as above. Proceedings relating to a partnership to which a partner is a party are brought before the division in the place where the partnership business is, or is mainly, carried on. For proceedings relating to corporation tax (or income tax where a UK resident company is a party) under self-assessment, there are rules similar, but suitably modified, to those above for income tax and capital gains tax.

Notwithstanding the above, the Board may direct that specified proceedings be brought before the General Commissioners for a specified division. An officer of the Board must serve on the taxpayer written notice stating the effect of the direction, and the taxpayer may object in writing within 30 days of the notice being served, in which case the direction has no effect. The Board may also give directions for determining the appropriate division, other than in PAYE appeals, where there is no place of residence, business or employment (or corporation tax equivalents) as described above, or where that place would otherwise be outside the UK; procedure is as above except that the taxpayer has no right of objection.

The parties to proceedings may supersede the above rules by coming to an agreement that the proceedings be brought before the General Commissioners for a division specified therein. The rules are also subject to specified provisions in relation to which two or more parties other than the Revenue are involved (which have their own rules), to regulations under *TMA 1970, s 46A* (see above) and to regulations for capital gains tax appeals (see Tolley's Capital Gains Tax under Appeals).

[*TMA 1970, s 44(1)(2), Sch 3; FA 1988, s 133(2); FA 1996, Sch 22 para 10, Sch 41 Pt V(12); ITEPA 2003, Sch 6 para 142*].

Comparable rules under earlier legislation were held to be directory and not mandatory (*CIR v Adams CA 1971, 48 TC 67; Murphy v Elders Ch D 1973, 49 TC 135*). A determination of the General Commissioners cannot be invalidated for want of jurisdiction if there was no objection to jurisdiction before the determination. [*TMA 1970, s 44(4)*]. See also *R v Kingston & Elmbridge Commrs QB 1972, 48 TC 75; R v St Pancras Commrs QB 1973, 50 TC 365; Parikh v Birmingham North Commrs CA, [1976] STC 365*.

Simon's Direct Tax Service. See E1.839.

4.5   **SETTLEMENT OF APPEALS BY AGREEMENT**

Where agreement, written or otherwise, has been reached at any time between the Revenue and the appellant or agent on his behalf on any appeal to General or Special Commissioners, against any assessment or decision under appeal, the assessment or decision as upheld, varied, discharged or cancelled by that agreement, is treated as if it had been determined on appeal, provided that

(*a*)   the taxpayer may withdraw from the agreement by giving written notice within 30 days of making it, and

(*b*)   oral agreements are of no effect unless confirmed in writing by either side (the date of such confirmation then being the effective date of the agreement).

[*TMA 1970, s 54*].

The agreement must specify the figure for assessment or a precise formula for ascertaining it (*Delbourgo v Field CA 1978, 52 TC 225*). The inspector has no power unilaterally to 'vacate' an assessment (*Baylis v Gregory CA, [1987] STC 297*). An agreement only covers the assessments which are the subject of the appeal, and does not bind the Revenue for subsequent years, e.g. where relievable amounts are purported to be carried forward from the year in question (*MacNiven v Westmoreland Investments Ltd HL 2001, 73 TC 1*). See also *Tod v South Essex Motors (Basildon) Ltd Ch D 1987, 60 TC 598*. For the extent to which further assessments or error or mistake relief claims are permissible if an appeal has been determined by agreement, see 5.3 ASSESSMENTS.

The issue of an amended notice of assessment by the inspector does not of itself constitute an agreement under *TMA 1970, s 54*, nor can a lack of response by the taxpayer constitute acceptance of an offer (*Schuldenfrei v Hilton CA 1999, 72 TC 167*). For the general requirements for an agreement, see *Cash & Carry v Inspector (Sp C 148), [1998] SSCD 46*.

An agreement under *TMA 1970, s 54* does not prevent an assessment being revised to correct an error, where the effect of the error was that the common intention of the parties was not recorded by the agreement (*R v HMIT ex p Bass Holdings Ltd QB 1992, 65 TC 495*). An agreement based on a mutual mistake of fact was thereby vitiated, so that the taxpayer could proceed with his appeal (*Fox v Rothwell (Sp C 50), [1995] SSCD 336*).

A taxpayer cannot withdraw an appeal made to Commissioners (see 4.1 above) but if, having appealed, he, or his agent acting in that appeal, gives the inspector oral or written notice of his desire not to proceed, then, unless the inspector gives written notice of objection within 30 days thereof, the appeal is treated as if settled by agreement, as above, at the date of the taxpayer's notification. [*TMA 1970, s 54(4)*].

An appeal that has been settled by the taxpayer's trustee in bankruptcy cannot subsequently be reopened by the taxpayer (*Ahajot (Count Artsrunik) v Waller (Sp C 395), [1994] SSCD 151*).

4.6 Appeals

THE HANDLING OF TAXPAYERS' APPEALS

Appeal meetings must be notified to the appellant and the inspector (or other Revenue party). In practice the inspector normally gives details of appeals ready for hearing to the Clerk to the Commissioners who, after consulting the inspector and, in important appeals, the taxpayer or his agent as appropriate, makes the necessary arrangements, notifies the inspector and issues notices of the hearing to the appellant. In some Divisions he may, by arrangement, also notify the appellant's agent. See also 4.9, 4.16 below.

4.7 **APPEAL COMMISSIONERS — INTRODUCTION**

The Lord Chancellor has wide regulatory powers in relation to the practice and procedure to be followed in connection with appeals, including the power to make different provision for different cases and different circumstances. Regulations may also provide for the transfer of appeals between the General and Special Commissioners or between General Commissioners for different divisions, and for varying the number of General or Special Commissioners required or permitted to hear appeals. [*TMA 1970, ss 46A, 56B–56D; F(No 2)A 1992, Sch 16 paras 3, 4; FA 1994, s 254*]. With effect from 1 September 1994, regulations [*SI 1994 No 1812*] were brought in governing the jurisdiction of the General Commissioners and the procedure for proceedings before them (see 4.8–4.13 below). Similar regulations [*SI 1994 No 1811*] were simultaneously brought into effect in relation to the Special Commissioners (see 4.14–4.17 below), and *SI 1994 No 1813* made consequential and complementary amendments to other enactments.

Simon's Direct Tax Service. See A3.5.

4.8 **GENERAL COMMISSIONERS**

Constitution of tribunal. Two or more, but not more than five, General Commissioners for a division may hear any proceedings. [*SI 1994 No 1812, reg 2*]. They will themselves decide which one of them will preside at the hearing. Where possible at least three will sit, and, with the consent of all the parties, proceedings may be continued by one or more of them. [*SI 1994 No 1812, reg 11*]. For the effect of personal business connection between a Commissioner and a party to proceedings, see *R v Holyhead Commrs (ex p Roberts) QB 1982, 56 TC 127*.

The Clerk to the Commissioners, who is frequently a local solicitor, normally attends the meeting to take minutes and to advise them as required, but a meeting without a Clerk would not be invalid (*Venn v Franks CA 1958, 38 TC 175*).

4.9 **Preparation for hearing.** *Listing and notice of hearing.* Except in relation to proceedings under *TMA 1970, s 100C* (see 57.14 PENALTIES), any party to the proceedings may serve notice on the Clerk to the Commissioners that he wishes a date for the hearing to be fixed, on receipt of which the Clerk must send notice to each party of the place, date and time of the hearing. Unless the parties otherwise agree, or the Commissioners otherwise direct, the date must not be earlier than 28 days after the date of the Clerk's notice. [*SI 1994 No 1812, reg 3*].

Witnesses. A General Commissioner, on the application of any party to the proceedings, may issue a witness summons (in Scotland, a witness citation) requiring any person in the UK either to attend the hearing of those proceedings to give evidence or to produce any relevant document in his possession, custody or power. The party applying for issue of the summons is responsible for its service (for which see *reg 4(3)*), and attendance may not be required within seven days of service unless the witness informs the Clerk that he accepts shorter notice. That party must also agree to meet the witness' reasonable travelling expenses. The witness may apply, by notice served on the Clerk, for the Commissioners to set aside the summons (in whole or part), on which application the party on whose application the summons was issued is entitled to be heard.

Except in Scotland, a witness so summoned to give evidence may only be cross-examined by the party on whose application the summons was issued if the Commissioners decide that the witness is a hostile witness and give leave.

A witness cannot be compelled to give evidence or produce documents which he could not be compelled to give or produce in an action in a court of law. An auditor or tax adviser (within *TMA 1970, s 20B(10)*) cannot be compelled to produce any document which he would not be obliged to deliver or make available by notice under *TMA 1970, s 20(3)* or *(8A)* (having regard to *TMA 1970, s 20B(9)–(13)*), and copies of, or of parts of, documents may similarly be produced in certain cases (see 30.7 FRAUDULENT OR NEGLIGENT CONDUCT).

In the event of failure by a witness to attend in obedience to the summons, or refusal to be sworn or to affirm, or refusal to answer any lawful question or to produce a document he is required to produce by the summons, the Commissioners may summarily determine a penalty not exceeding £1,000, to be treated as tax charged by an assessment and due and payable.

[*SI 1994 No 1812, reg 4*].

Joint hearings. The Commissioners have powers to direct that two or more proceedings, in one or more divisions, with common issues be heard at the same time or consecutively within one division, either of their own motion or on an application by any of the parties to any of those proceedings. All the parties must be notified, and are entitled to be heard before such a direction is given. On the giving of a direction, the Clerk must send notice of its date and terms to all parties. [*SI 1994 No 1812, reg 6*]. The Commissioners have an inherent power to deal with two or more appeals simultaneously where the appellants' affairs are so intermingled as to be incapable of separation, and where they are satisfied that it would result in no injustice to either party (*Johnson v Walden; King v Walden CA 1996, 68 TC 387*).

Postponements and adjournments. The Commissioners may postpone or adjourn the hearing of any proceedings, the Clerk being responsible for notifying all parties of the place, date and time of the postponed or adjourned hearing (unless announced before an adjournment in the presence of all parties). Where a hearing is adjourned for the obtaining of further information or evidence, the Commissioners may direct the parties regarding the disclosure of such information or evidence prior to resumption. [*SI 1994 No 1812, reg 8*]. In *Packe v Johnson Ch D 1991, 63 TC 507*, a determination was quashed because of the Commissioners' refusal to consider all relevant information in deciding to refuse an adjournment at a second hearing.

Other matters in preparation for hearing. There are also regulations dealing with the agreement of documents [*SI 1994 No 1812, reg 5*], the joinder of additional parties to the proceedings [*SI 1994 No 1812, reg 7*] and the admission of expert evidence. [*SI 1994 No 1812, reg 9*].

4.10 **Hearing and determination of proceedings.** Where proceedings are commenced after 30 December 2002, the hearing is in public. The Commissioners may, however, direct (dependent on certain criteria, e.g. national security, interests of justice, protection of private life etc., and subject to all parties having opportunity to make representations) that all or part of a hearing be in private, such direction to be made of their own volition or on the application (by written notice to the Clerk) of any or all of the parties. In such circumstances, they may also direct that *information* about the proceedings should not be made public. Certain persons with official responsibilities may be present at *any* hearing, and may remain present during, but not take part in, the Commissioners' deliberations. With the consent of the parties, the Commissioners may permit any other person to attend an otherwise private hearing. They may exclude a person from all or part of any hearing on grounds of disruptive or potentially disruptive conduct. Before 31 December 2002, hearings were in private, though with similar provision as above as to the presence of others. [*SI 1994 No 1812, reg 13; SI 2002 No 2976, regs 1, 10*].

Power to obtain information. The Commissioners may, at any time before final determination of the proceedings, serve on any party to the proceedings (other than the Revenue) notice requiring that party, within a specified time,

(*a*)   to deliver such particulars as may be required to determine any issue of the proceedings, and

(*b*)   to make available for inspection by the Commissioners or by an officer of the Board such specified or described books, accounts etc. in his possession or power as may, in their opinion, contain information relevant to the proceedings.

For unsuccessful challenges relating to the issue of notices under these and the similar powers previously contained in *TMA 1970, s 51*, see *Johnson v Blackpool General Commrs and CIR CA 1997, 70 TC 1, Eke v Knight CA 1977, 51 TC 121, Khan v Newport General Commrs and CIR Ch D 1994, 70 TC 239* and *Slater Ltd v Beacontree General Commrs Ch D 2001, 74 TC 471*.

The Commissioners may summarily determine a penalty (to be treated as tax charged in an assessment and due and payable) of up to £300 for failure to comply with such a notice, plus up to £60 per day for continuing failure after such a penalty is determined. Any officer of the Board (and the Commissioners in the case of (*b*)) may, at all reasonable times, take copies of, or extracts from, any such particulars, books etc. [*SI 1994 No 1812, reg 10*].

Representation at hearing. A party to the proceedings may be represented by any person, except that the Commissioners may, if satisfied that there are good and sufficient reasons for doing so, refuse to permit a party to be represented by a particular person, not being a legally qualified person or a current member of an incorporated society of accountants. In practice, most bodies of Commissioners permit the taxpayer to be represented by any person who they are satisfied is competent to present the appellant's case. The Revenue may be represented by a barrister, advocate, solicitor or any officer of the Board. [*SI 1994 No 1812, reg 12*]. The Revenue representative is normally an inspector. The secretary or 'other proper officer' represents a company (the liquidator, or (following *Enterprise Act 2002*) the administrator, if one has been appointed). [*TMA 1970, s 108; FA 2003, Sch 41 para 2*].

Failure to attend hearing. Where a party fails to attend or be represented at a hearing of which he has been duly notified, the Commissioners may postpone or adjourn a hearing or (unless satisfied that there is good and sufficient reason for such failure, and after considering any written or other representations) hear and determine the proceedings. [*SI 1994 No 1812, reg 14*]. Determinations in the absence of the taxpayer or his agent have been upheld where notice of the meeting was received by the appellant (*R v Tavistock Commrs (ex p Adams) QB 1969, 46 TC 154; R v Special Commr (ex p Moschi) CA, [1981] STC 465* and see *Fletcher & Fletcher v Harvey CA 1990, 63 TC 539*), but Commissioners were held to have acted unreasonably in refusing to re-open proceedings when taxpayer's agent was temporarily absent when the appeal was called (*R & D McKerron Ltd v CIR CS 1979, 52 TC 28*). Where the taxpayer was absent through illness, a determination was quashed because the Commissioners, in refusing an adjournment, had failed to consider whether injustice would thereby arise to the taxpayer (*R v Sevenoaks Commrs (ex p Thorne) QB 1989, 62 TC 341* and see *Rose v Humbles CA 1971, 48 TC 103*). See also *R v O'Brien (ex p Lissner) QB, 1984 STI 710* where the determination was quashed when the appellant had been informed by the inspector that the hearing was to be adjourned.

Procedure and evidence at hearing. The Commissioners have wide discretion as to the manner in which the proceedings are conducted, and should seek to avoid inappropriate formality. They may require any witness to give evidence on oath or affirmation, and may admit evidence which would be inadmissible in a court of law (and see *Taylor v Cox (Sp C 163), [1998] SSCD 179* for the acceptance of computer-generated documents in evidence). Evidence may be given orally or, if they so direct, by affidavit or statement recorded in a document (and they may, on their own motion or on the application of any party, at any stage require the personal attendance as a witness of the maker of such a statement or affidavit or the person who recorded the statement). They may take account of the nature and source of any evidence, and the manner in which it is given, in assessing its truth and weight. The parties may be heard in any order, but are entitled to give evidence, to call witnesses, to question witnesses (including other parties who give evidence), and to address the Commissioners both on the evidence and on the subject matter of the proceedings. [*SI 1994 No 1812, reg 15*]. A party to the proceedings cannot insist on being examined on oath (*R v Special Commrs (in re Fletcher) CA 1894, 3 TC 289*). False evidence under oath would be perjury under criminal law (*R v Hood Barrs CA [1943] 1 AER 665*). A taxpayer was held to be bound by an affidavit he had made in other proceedings (*Wicker v Fraser Ch D 1982, 55 TC 641*). A remission to Commissioners to hear evidence directed at the credit of a witness was refused in *Potts v CIR Ch D 1982, 56 TC 25*. Rules of the Supreme Court under which evidence can be obtained from a witness abroad cannot be used in proceedings before the Commissioners (*In re Leiserach CA 1963, 42 TC 1*). As to hearsay evidence under *Civil Evidence Act 1968*, see *Forth Investments Ltd Ch D 1976, 50 TC 617* and *Khan v Edwards Ch D 1977, 53 TC 597*.

The inspector is entitled to ask the Commissioners to exercise their powers to increase an assessment, and to adduce evidence in support of his application (*Glaxo Group Ltd and others v CIR CA 1996, 68 TC 166*).

The Commissioners are under no obligation to adjourn an appeal for the production of further evidence (*Hamilton v CIR CS 1930, 16 TC 28; Noble v Wilkinson Ch D 1958, 38 TC 135*), and were held not to have erred in law in determining assessments in the absence abroad of the taxpayer (*Hawkins v Fuller Ch D 1982, 56 TC 49*).

The taxpayer has no general right to conduct his appeal in writing without attending the hearing (*Banin v Mackinlay CA 1984, 58 TC 398*), although written pleadings may, at the Commissioners' discretion, be taken into account (*Caldicott v Varty Ch D 1976, 51 TC 403*).

In reaching their decision, the Commissioners may not take into account matters appropriate for application for judicial review (*Aspin v Estill CA 1987, 60 TC 549*). They do not generally have the power to review on appeal the exercise of a discretion conferred on the Revenue by statute (see *Slater v Richardson & Bottoms Ltd Ch D 1979, 53 TC 155; Kelsall v Investment Chartwork Ltd Ch D 1993, 65 TC 750*), although in certain cases such power of review is itself statutory; see e.g. *SI 1993 No 743, reg 10(4)*, which in effect reversed the decision in *Richardson & Bottoms Ltd* above.

For the extent to which Commissioners may use their local knowledge, see *Forest Side Properties (Chingford) Ltd v Pearce CA 1961, 39 TC 665*.

Onus of proof. The onus is on the appellant to displace an assessment (but see 30.2 FRAUDULENT OR NEGLIGENT CONDUCT for onus on Crown to prove fraud or wilful default (now fraudulent or negligent conduct) to support extended time limit assessments). See *Brady v Group Lotus Car Companies plc CA 1987, 60 TC 359* where the onus of proof remained with the taxpayer where the amount of the normal time limit assessment indicated a contention of fraud. The general principle emerges in appeals against estimated assessments in 'delay cases' which, before the introduction of self-assessment, made up the bulk of appeals heard by the General Commissioners. For examples of cases in which the

4.11 Appeals

Commissioners confirmed estimated assessments in the absence of evidence that they were excessive, see *T Haythornthwaite & Sons Ltd v Kelly CA 1927, 11 TC 657; Stoneleigh Products Ltd v Dodd CA 1948, 30 TC 1; Rosette Franks (King St) Ltd v Dick Ch D 1955, 36 TC 100; Pierson v Belcher Ch D 1959, 38 TC 387*. In a number of cases, the Courts have supported the Commissioners' action in rejecting unsatisfactory accounts (e.g. *Cain v Schofield Ch D 1953, 34 TC 362; Moll v CIR CS 1955, 36 TC 384; Cutmore v Leach Ch D 1981, 55 TC 602; Coy v Kime Ch D 1986, 59 TC 447*) or calling for certified accounts (e.g. *Stephenson v Waller KB 1927, 13 TC 318; Hunt & Co v Joly KB 1928, 14 TC 165; Wall v Cooper CA 1929, 14 TC 552*). In *Anderson v CIR CS 1933, 18 TC 320*, the case was remitted where there was no evidence to support the figure arrived at by the Commissioners (which was between the accounts figure and the estimated figure assessed), but contrast *Bookey v Edwards Ch D 1981, 55 TC 486*. The Commissioners are entitled to look at each year separately, accepting the appellant's figures for some years but not all (*Donnelly v Platten CA (NI) 1980, [1981] STC 504*). Similarly, the onus is on the taxpayer to substantiate his claims to relief (see *Eke v Knight CA 1977, 51 TC 121; Talib v Waterson Ch D, [1980] STC 563*).

For the standard of proof required in evidence, see *Les Croupiers Casino Club v Pattinson CA 1987, 60 TC 196*.

4.11 **The Commissioners' decision.** The Revenue representative must not be present while the Commissioners are deliberating their decision unless the other party or parties (or their representative(s)) are also present (*R v Brixton Commrs KB 1912, 6 TC 195*). The Commissioners' determination was quashed where the Clerk had discussed the case with Revenue representatives between hearing and announcement of determination (*R v Wokingham Commrs (ex p Heron) QB, 1984 STI 710*).

If, on an appeal, it appears to the Commissioners

(*a*)   that the appellant is over- or under-charged by a self-assessment, or

(*b*)   that any amounts in a partnership statement (see 68.13 RETURNS) are excessive or insufficient, or

(*c*)   that the appellant is over- or under-charged by an assessment other than a self-assessment,

they must reduce or increase the assessment or amounts accordingly, but otherwise the assessment or statement stands good. The Commissioners are given the power to vary the extent to which a claim or election included in a tax return is disallowed following an enquiry. (Separate rules apply to claims and elections made outside the tax return, for which see 16.3 CLAIMS.) In a case within (*c*) above, the Commissioners can normally only reduce or increase the amount assessed, and this determines the appeal; they are not obliged to determine the revised tax payable. In a case within (*b*) above, an officer of the Board must amend the partners' own tax returns to give effect to the reductions or increases made. These provisions apply as from, broadly, 11 May 2001, although comparable provisions applied previously (i.e. under self-assessment for 1996/97 onwards and for company accounting periods ending on or after 1 July 1999), the changes being in consequence of the revised procedures for completion of an enquiry (see 68.9 RETURNS). [*TMA 1970, s 50(6)–(9); F(No 2)A 1975, s 67(2); FA 1994, ss 196, 199(2)(3), Sch 19 para 17; FA 1996, Sch 19 para 7; FA 2001, s 88, Sch 29 para 30; SI 1994 No 1813*].

See 42.2 INTEREST AND SURCHARGES ON UNPAID TAX and 57.2 PENALTIES for Commissioners' options in an appeal against a surcharge or late filing penalty, which turn on the question of whether the appellant had a 'reasonable excuse' for non-compliance.

Any decision is by a majority of the Commissioners hearing the proceedings, with the presiding Commissioner having a casting vote where necessary. The final determination may be announced orally at the end of the hearing or may be reserved. In either case, the Clerk to the Commissioners must send to each party a notice (including in most cases details of the procedure for appeals from the General Commissioners) setting out the determination, and unless the determination was given at the hearing, the date of such notice is the date of the determination. [*SI 1994 No 1812, reg 16; SI 1999 No 3293, reg 3*]. Where the Clerk announced the decision wrongly, it was held that the correct decision stood good (*R v Morleston & Litchurch Commrs KB 1951, 32 TC 335*) (and see 4.13 below under heading *Irregularities*).

A determination may not be based on a conclusion reached in contradiction of an agreed fact without notice of the likelihood of reaching such a conclusion having been given before or at the hearing (*Parmar (t/a Ace Knitwear) v Woods Ch D 2002, 74 TC 562*).

Where Commissioners determined appeals in principle and held a further hearing to adjust assessments, their action in refusing to admit further evidence for the taxpayer at the later hearing was upheld (*R v St Marylebone Commrs (ex p Hay) CA 1983, 57 TC 59*). They are entitled, however, to alter their decision in principle at a later hearing (*Larner v Warrington Ch D 1985, 58 TC 557*). See also *Gibson v Stroud Commrs Ch D 1989, 61 TC 645*.

A decision of the Commissioners is not legally binding on them or any other Commissioners in any other proceedings, even on appeal by the same taxpayer against a similar assessment for another year (*CIR v Sneath CA 1932, 17 TC 149* and cf. *Edwards v 'Old Bushmills' Distillery HL 1926, 10 TC 285; Abdul Caffoor Trustees PC 1961, 40 ATC 93*).

Review of the Commissioners' final determination. A decision of the Commissioners is generally final and conclusive [*TMA 1970, s 46(2)*], but the Commissioners may review and set aside or vary their final determination on the application of any party or of their own motion where they are satisfied that either

(*a*)   it was wrongly made as a result of administrative error, or

(*b*)   a party entitled to be heard failed to appear or be represented for good and sufficient reason, or

(*c*)   relevant information had been supplied to the Clerk or to the appropriate inspector or other Revenue officer prior to the hearing but was not received by the Commissioners until after the hearing.

A written application for such a review must be made to the Commissioners not later than 14 days after the date of the notice of the determination (or by such later time as the Commissioners may allow), stating the grounds in full. Where the Commissioners propose of their own motion to review a determination, they must serve notice on the parties not later than 14 days after the date of the notice of the determination.

The parties are entitled to be heard on any such review or proposed review. If practicable, the review is to be determined by the Commissioners who decided the case, and if they set aside the determination, they may substitute a different determination or order a rehearing before the same or different Commissioners. A decision to vary or substitute a final determination is to be notified in the same way as the original determination (see above).

[*SI 1994 No 1812, reg 17*].

See 4.24 below as regards application for judicial review where the Commissioners have acted unfairly or improperly.

4.12   **Special procedure.** *Proceedings relating to tax on chargeable gains.* Where material, the market value of an asset or the apportionment of an amount or value is, if so required by any party, to be recorded in the final determination. They may be proved in any proceedings relating to tax on chargeable gains by a certificate signed by the Clerk to the Commissioners (in certain cases the clerk or registrar of another tribunal), or by the inspector where the appeal was settled by agreement, stating the material particulars. [*SI 1994 No 1812, reg 18; SI 1999 No 3293, reg 4*].

Reference to other tribunals. Certain questions relating to the value of land or of a lease of land must be referred to the appropriate Lands Tribunal, and questions in relation to unquoted shares and to certain specified claims must be referred to the Special Commissioners (see *TMA 1970, ss 46B, 46C, 46D* at 4.4 above). The instant proceedings are to be determined without awaiting the outcome of such referral. [*SI 1994 No 1812, reg 19; SI 1999 No 3293, reg 5*].

4.13   **Miscellaneous.** *Irregularities.* Any irregularity resulting from failure to comply with regulations or with any Commissioners' direction given before a final determination is reached, shall not, of itself, render the proceedings void, and before reaching that determination the Commissioners may, and if they consider that any person has been prejudiced by the irregularity must, give such direction as they think just to cure or waive any irregularity which comes to their attention. Clerical errors in any document recording a direction or decision of the Commissioners may be corrected by any of the Commissioners concerned (or by the Clerk if all the Commissioners have died or ceased to be Commissioners) by certificate under his hand. [*SI 1994 No 1812, reg 24*].

Notices must be in writing unless the Commissioners authorise them to be given orally. [*SI 1994 No 1812, reg 25*].

Service of any notice or document (other than a witness summons, see 4.9 above) may be by post, by (legible) facsimile transmission etc. or by delivery at the proper address. [*SI 1994 No 1812, reg 26(1)*]. The persons and addresses to whom and which a document may be sent or delivered are set out in *SI 1994 No 1812, reg 26(2)(3)*, and the provisions for substituted or waived service in certain cases in *SI 1994 No 1812, reg 27*.

Penalties. Any appeal against summary penalties determined under regulations as at 4.7 above lies to the High Court (in Scotland, the Court of Session). [*TMA 1970, s 53; SI 1994 No 1813*].

Guidance notes on Appeals to the General Commissioners (TAXGUIDE 4/00) were published in June 2000 by the Tax Faculty of the ICAEW. The National Association of Tax Commissioners also publish on their website (www.natax.org.uk) useful notes for appellants on what they may expect of General Commissioners.

Appointment and protection of General Commissioners. See 35.3 INLAND REVENUE: ADMINISTRATION.

4.14   **SPECIAL COMMISSIONERS**

Except as otherwise stated or required by context, the provisions applicable to the General Commissioners (see 4.7–4.13 above) apply equally to the Special Commissioners, with the variations and additions described at 4.15–4.17 below.

An explanatory booklet 'Appeals and Other Proceedings before the Special Commissioners' (October 1994) dealing with procedural and other points is available free of charge from the Clerk to the Special Commissioners, 15/29 Bedford Avenue, London WC1B 3AS (tel. 020–7631 4242) and at www.financeandtaxtribunals.gov.uk There is also a supplement available on 'IR35 Appeals'.

4.15   **Constitution of tribunal.** Any one, two or three of the Special Commissioners may hear any proceedings. If two or three Commissioners are sitting, the Presiding Special

Commissioner, or, if he is not sitting, the Commissioner nominated by him, shall preside at the hearing. With the consent of all parties, proceedings may be continued by any one or two of the Commissioners unless the Presiding Special Commissioner otherwise directs. [*SI 1994 No 1811, regs 2, 13*].

4.16   **Preparation for hearing.** *Listing and notice of hearing.* Before notifying the parties of the place, date and time of a hearing, the Clerk to the Commissioners must satisfy himself that the Special Commissioners have jurisdiction over the proceedings and that he has sufficient particulars for determination. The Presiding Special Commissioner may direct that such notifications are not to be sent. [*SI 1994 No 1811, reg 3*].

General power to give directions. The Commissioner(s) have wide direction-giving powers, on the application of any of the parties to proceedings or of their own motion. Applications by the parties (otherwise than during the hearing) must be in writing to the Clerk, and if not made with the consent of all the parties, must be served by the Clerk on any affected party, who may object. [*SI 1994 No 1811, reg 4*].

Witnesses. The maximum penalty which the Commissioner(s) may summarily determine for failure to attend or refusal to be sworn or affirm, to answer any lawful question or to produce documents as required is £10,000. [*SI 1994 No 1811, regs 5, 24(2)*].

Preliminary hearing. Where it appears to a Special Commissioner that any proceedings would be facilitated by holding a preliminary hearing, he may, on the application of a party or of his own motion, give directions for such a hearing to be held. The Clerk to the Special Commissioners must give to all the parties 14 days' notice (or such shorter time as the parties agree or the Commissioner sees fit to impose) of the time and place of the hearing. On a preliminary hearing, the Commissioner has wide direction-giving powers, and may, if the parties so agree, determine the proceedings without any further hearing. [*SI 1994 No 1811, reg 9*]. See 4.17 below as regards powers of Commissioner to obtain information on preliminary hearing of any proceedings. For a refusal by a Special Commissioner to determine a preliminary point of law, see *Investment Trust v CIR (Sp C 173), [1998] SSCD 287.*

4.17   **Hearing and determination of proceedings.** Hearings before the Special Commissioner(s) are normally in public. Where proceedings are commenced after 30 December 2002, rules equivalent to those for the General Commissioners in 4.10 above apply as regards private hearings in certain cases and the right to attend. Broadly similar rules applied before 31 December 2002, although an explicit direction for a hearing to be in private was required only where the application was made by the Revenue. [*SI 1994 No 1811, reg 15; SI 2002 No 2976, regs 1, 6*]. See *Businessman v Inspector of Taxes (Sp C 374), [2003] SSCD 403* for a direction that the whole hearing be in private for the protection of the taxpayer's private life.

Power to obtain information. The powers of General Commissioners to obtain information apply to both a preliminary hearing before a Special Commissioner and to the hearing of the proceedings, except that the specific penalty provisions for failure to comply with a notice do not apply (although the general penalty for failure to comply with Commissioner's direction, see below, *does* apply). [*SI 1994 No 1811, regs 10, 24(1)*].

The Commissioners' decision. The recording of the Commissioner(s)' decision must contain a statement of the facts found and the reasons for the determination. After reserving the final determination, the Commissioner(s) may give a written decision in principle on one or more of the issues arising, and adjourn the making of the final determination until after that decision has been issued and any further questions arising from it have been agreed by the parties or decided by the Commissioner(s) after hearing the parties. A decision in principle must contain a statement of the facts and the reasons for the decision, and these need not be repeated in the document recording the final determination. [*SI 1994 No 1811, reg 18; SI 1999 No 3292, reg 4*].

Review of the Commissioners' decision in principle may proceed in the same way as a review of a final determination. [*SI 1994 No 1811, reg 19*].

Publication of decisions in principle or final determinations. The Presiding Special Commissioner may arrange for the publication of such reports of decisions in principle and final determinations as he considers appropriate. If the proceedings (or any part) were held in private, he must ensure that the report is in a form which, so far as possible, prevents the identification of any person whose affairs are dealt with. [*SI 1994 No 1811, reg 20*]. An application for non-publication of a decision on the grounds of inadequate anonymity, or for publication of a short summary only, was refused by the Presiding Special Commissioner in *Y Co Ltd v CIR (Sp C 69), [1996] SSCD 147*. The policy on anonymisation was quoted as: 'In cases where anonymisation is required, the Presiding Special Commissioner will seek to achieve this in co-operation with the parties. If a decision or determination cannot be anonymised to the complete satisfaction of the party requiring it, the Presiding Special Commissioner's policy is to report it in as anonymised a form as he, in consultation with the Special Commissioner[s] deciding the case, considers to be appropriate. To this there is one exception, which is that no report will be published where the decision cannot be effectively anonymised and to report it would defeat the ends of justice, e.g. where particulars of a secret process would otherwise have to be disclosed or in cases where minors were involved. The Presiding Special Commissioner will consider cases falling outside this exception on their merits.' A substantial number of cases (averaging some 50 per year from early 1995) is now reported, and these are referred to in the text of this publication where relevant. The Special Commissioners expect to have their attention drawn in appropriate cases to any of their previous published decisions which is relevant, unless superseded by a higher court decision. The Revenue consider that, whilst not creating any binding legal precedent, these decisions may be relevant in other cases, particularly if not appealed against, but that it would be inappropriate to enter into any discussion of a case which is, or may be, the subject of appeal to the High Court. (Revenue Tax Bulletin October 1995 pp 258, 259).

Orders for costs. The Commissioner(s) may make an order awaiting costs (in Scotland expenses) of, or incidental to, the hearing of any proceedings against any party who has, in their opinion, acted wholly unreasonably in connection with the hearing, but not without giving that party the opportunity of making representations against the award. The award may be of all or part of the costs of the other party or parties, such costs to be taxed in the county court (in Scotland the sheriff court) if not agreed. In Northern Ireland, the Commissioners may determine the costs. [*SI 1994 No 1811, reg 21*]. For cases in which costs were awarded, see *Scott and another (trading as Farthings Steak House) v McDonald (Sp C 91), [1996] SSCD 381* and *Robertson v CIR (No 2) (Sp C 313), [2002] SSCD 242* (on taxpayer application) and *Phillips v Burrows (Sp C 229A), [2000] SSCD 112, Morris and another v Roberts (Sp C 407), [2004] SSCD 245* (on Revenue application). For cases in which costs were refused, see *Salt v Young (Sp C 205), [1999] SSCD 249* (on Revenue application) and *Carter v Hunt (Sp C 220), [2000] SSCD 17, Self-assessed v Inspector of Taxes (No 2)(Sp C 224), [2000] SSCD 47, Powell v Jackman (Sp C 338), [2002] SSCD 488* and *Lavery v Macleod (No 2) (Sp C 375), [2003] SSCD 413* (on taxpayer application). Only in 'a very rare case' would the Court interfere with the Commissioners' decision as regards costs (see *Gamble v Rowe Ch D 1998, 71 TC 190*, where a refusal of costs was upheld).

Penalty for failure to comply with Commissioner(s)' direction. The Commissioner(s) may summarily determine a penalty of up to £10,000 for any such failure, to be treated as if it were tax charged in an assessment and due and payable. [*SI 1994 No 1811, reg 24(1)(3)*].

4.18   **APPEALS TO THE HIGH COURT — INTRODUCTION**

Prior to the determination of an appeal by the Commissioners, the Court may be prepared to consider an application seeking a determination as to whether the Revenue may make use of certain 'tax-altering' provisions in relation to the assessments under appeal (*Balen v CIR Ch D 1976, 52 TC 406*; *Beecham Group plc v CIR Ch D 1992, 65 TC 219*). In general, 'there is an absolute exclusion of the High Court's jurisdiction only when the proceedings seek relief which is more or less co-extensive with adjudicating on an existing open assessment . . . the more closely the High Court proceedings approximate to that in their substantial effect, the more ready the High Court will be, as a matter of discretion, to decline jurisdiction.' (*Glaxo Group Ltd and others v CIR Ch D 1995, 68 TC 166*).

Simon's Direct Tax Service. See A3.7.

4.19   **APPEALS FROM THE GENERAL COMMISSIONERS**

Case stated procedure. Within 30 days of the date of final determination of an appeal (or of the variation or substitution of such a determination, see 4.11 above), any party dissatisfied with the determination as being erroneous in point of law (for which see e.g. *Billows v Robinson CA 1991, 64 TC 17*) may serve notice on the Clerk requiring the Commissioners to state and sign a case for the opinion of the High Court (in Scotland the Court of Session, in Northern Ireland the Court of Appeal (NI)), setting forth the facts and final determination of the Commissioners. See *Grainger v Singer KB 1927, 11 TC 704* as regards receipt of the case. The 30 day time limit for requesting a case does not apply to the payment of the fee (*Anson v Hill CA 1968, 47 ATC 143*). The Commissioners may serve notice on the person who required the stated case requiring him, within a specified period of not less than 28 days, to identify the question of law on which he requires the case to be stated. They may refuse to state a case until such notice is complied with, or if they are not satisfied that a question of law is involved, or if the requisite fee (see below) has not been paid. A requirement for a case to be stated becomes invalid if the determination to which it relates is set aside or varied. After 31 December 1999, the case stated procedure does not apply to a final determination by the General Commissioners of an appeal in which a question has been referred to another tribunal (the Lands Tribunal or the Special Commissioners, see *TMA, ss 46B, 46C, 46D* at 4.4 above) and all appeal rights have been exhausted. [*SI 1994 No 1812, regs 20, 23; SI 1999 No 3293, reg 6*].

A fee of £25 is payable to the Clerk by the person requiring the case before he is entitled to have it stated. [*TMA 1970, s 56(3); SI 1994 No 1813*]. A single case may have effect as regards each of a number of appeals heard together (*Getty Oil Co v Steele and related appeals Ch D 1990, 63 TC 376*).

If the taxpayer dies, his personal representatives stand in his shoes (*Smith v Williams KB 1921, 8 TC 321*).

Although the case stated procedure envisages the determination of the proceedings before the Commissioners, where an appeal has been decided in principle but there may be considerable delay in reaching figures for the formal determination, the Court will accept a case stated in principle (see e.g. *Rank Xerox Ltd v Lane HL 1979, 53 TC 185*).

The case stated procedure is not open to a successful party to an appeal (*Sharpey-Schafer v Venn Ch D 1955, 34 ATC 141*), but where another party requires a case, the successful party may invite the Commissioners to include in the case an additional question relating to another ground on which the Commissioners had found against it (*Gordon v CIR CS 1991, 64 TC 173*). In the case of a partnership, the procedure is available to any one of the partners, with or without the consent of the others (*Sutherland & Partners v Barnes & Gustar CA 1994, 66 TC 663*).

4.20 Appeals

4.20   **Consideration of draft case.** Within 56 days of receipt of a notice requiring a stated case (or of the Commissioners being satisfied as to the question of law involved), the Clerk must send a draft of the case to all the parties. Written representations thereon may be made to the Clerk by any party within 56 days after the draft case is sent out, with copies to all the other parties, and within a further 28 days further representations may similarly be made in response. Any party to whom copies of representations are not sent may apply to the Clerk for a copy. The validity of a case after it has been stated and signed (see 4.21 below), and of any subsequent proceedings, is not affected by a failure to meet these time limits or by a failure to send copies of representations to all parties. [*SI 1994 No 1812, reg 21*].

An application for the taxpayer's name to be withheld was refused (*In re H Ch D 1964, 42 TC 14*) as was an application for the deletion of a passage possibly damaging the taxpayer (*Treharne v Guinness Exports Ltd Ch D 1967, 44 TC 161*). An application for judicial review on the ground that the case did not cover all matters in dispute was refused in *R v Special Commrs (ex p Napier) CA 1988, 61 TC 206*. In *Danquah v CIR Ch D 1990, 63 TC 526*, an application for the statement of a further case was refused where the case did not set out all the questions raised by the taxpayer in the originating motion by which he had sought an order directing the Commissioners to state a case. The proper course was for the taxpayer to apply for remission of the case for amendment under *TMA 1970, s 56(7)*. See also *Consolidated Goldfields plc v CIR Ch D 1990, 63 TC 333* (dealt with further at 4.22 below) in which a request to remit a case to the Commissioners for further findings of fact was refused.

4.21   **Preparation and submission of final case.** As soon as may be after the final date for representations (see 4.20 above and see *McKinney v Hagans Caravans (Manufacturing) Ltd CA(NI) 1997, 69 TC 526*), the Commissioners, after taking into account any representations, must state and sign the case. In the event of the death of a Commissioner, or of his ceasing to be a Commissioner, the case is to be signed by the remaining Commissioner(s) or, if there are none, by the Clerk. The case is then sent by the Clerk to the person who required it to be stated, and the other parties notified accordingly.

In England, Wales and Scotland, the party requiring the case must transmit it to the High Court (in Scotland, the Court of Session) within 30 days of receiving it, and at or before the time he does so must notify each of the other parties that the case has been stated on his application and send them a copy of the case. The fact that the same case may have been transmitted timeously by another party, where there are cross-appeals, does not relieve the appellant of the requirement to transmit the case timeously if his appeal is to be heard (*Petch v Gurney CA 1994, 66 TC 743*). The case must be *received* by the High Court (or Court of Session) within the 30 day time limit (*New World Medical Ltd v Cormack Ch D, [2002] STC 1245*). It is mandatory (*Valleybright Ltd (in liquidation) v Richardson Ch D 1984, 58 TC 290; Petch v Gurney CA 1994, 66 TC 743*), and may run from the date the case is received by the taxpayer's authorised agent (*Brassington v Guthrie Ch D 1991, 64 TC 435*) (these latter three cases having been determined under the similar earlier provisions of *TMA 1970, s 56(4)*). The notification (and copy) to the other parties is required only to give 'adequate notice' of the appeal and not to be 'too long delayed' (*Hughes v Viner Ch D 1985, 58 TC 437*). In Northern Ireland, slightly different rules apply (and see *CIR v McGuckian CA (NI) 1994, 69 TC 1*).

[*SI 1994 No 1812, regs 22, 23*].

4.22   **The Hearing.** The High Court (or Court of Session or Court of Appeal (NI)) hears and determines any question(s) of law arising on the case, and may reverse, affirm or amend the determination of the Commissioners, or may remit the matter to the Commissioners with the opinion of the Court thereon, or may make such other order as seems to it fit. In certain circumstances, this may include the power to uphold an assessment as if it had been made under a section other than that under which it was in fact made (*CIR v McGuckian CA (NI) 1994, 69 TC 1*). The Court may also cause the case to be sent back for amendment (see further below). An appeal from the decision of the High Court lies (in England and Wales) to the Court of Appeal and thence (with leave) to the House of Lords. In certain cases, 'leap-frog' appeals direct from the High Court to the House of Lords may be permitted under *Administration of Justice Act 1969, s 12* (see e.g. *Fitzleet Estates Ltd v Cherry HL 1977, 51 TC 708*). In the case of an appeal against a decision on an appeal against an assessment, tax must be paid in accordance with the Commissioners' decision. Following the decision on appeal, any tax overpaid is refunded with such interest as the Court may allow, and any amount undercharged is due and payable 30 days after the inspector issues a notice of the amount due. [*TMA 1970, s 56(6)–(9); SI 1994 No 1813*].

Once set down for hearing, a case cannot be declared a nullity (*Way v Underdown CA 1974, 49 TC 215*) or struck out under *Order 18, rule 19 of the Rules of the Supreme Court* (*Petch v Gurney CA, 66 TC 743*), but the appellant may withdraw (*Hood Barrs v CIR (No 3) CA 1960, 39 TC 209*, but see *Bradshaw v Blunden (No 2) Ch D 1960, 39 TC 73*). Where the appellant was the inspector and the taxpayer did not wish to proceed, the Court refused to make an order on terms agreed between the parties (*Slaney v Kean Ch D 1969, 45 TC 415*).

The Court may, however, return a case for amendment. [*TMA 1970, s 56(7)*]. In *Consolidated Goldfields plc v CIR Ch D 1990, 63 TC 333*, the taxpayer company's request that the High Court remit a case to the Commissioners for further findings of fact was refused. Although the remedy was properly sought, it would only be granted if it could be shown that the desired findings were (*a*) material to some tenable argument, (*b*) reasonably open on the evidence adduced, and (*c*) not inconsistent with the findings already made. See also *Carvill v CIR Ch D 1996, 70 TC 126*. However, in *Fitzpatrick v CIR CS 1990, [1991] STC 34*, a case was remitted where the facts found proved or admitted, and the contentions of the parties, were not clearly set out, despite the taxpayer's request for various amendments and insertions to the case, and in *Whittles v Uniholdings Ltd Ch D 1993, 68 TC 528*, remission was appropriate in view of the widely differing interpretations which the parties sought to place on the Commissioners' decision (and the case was remitted a second time (see *[1993] STC 767*) to resolve misunderstandings as to the nature of a concession made by the Crown at the original hearing and apparent inconsistencies in the Commissioners' findings of fact). See also *Bradley v London Electric plc Ch D, 70 TC 155*. If a case is remitted, the taxpayer has the right to attend any further hearing by the Commissioners (*Lack v Doggett CA 1970, 46 TC 497*) but the Commissioners may not, in the absence of special circumstances, admit further evidence (*Archer-Shee v Baker CA 1928, 15 TC 1; Watson v Samson Bros Ch D 1959, 38 TC 346; Bradshaw v Blunden (No 2) Ch D 1960, 39 TC 73*), but see *Brady v Group Lotus Car Companies plc CA 1987, 60 TC 359* where the Court directed the Commissioners to admit further evidence where new facts had come to light suggesting the taxpayers had deliberately misled the Commissioners. Errors of fact in the case may be amended by agreement of the parties prior to hearing of the case (*Moore v Austin Ch D 1985, 59 TC 110*). See *Jeffries v Stevens Ch D 1982, 56 TC 134* as regards delay between statement of case and motion for remission.

A new question of law may be raised in the Courts on giving due notice to the other parties (*Muir v CIR CA 1966, 43 TC 367*) but the Courts will neither admit evidence not in the stated case (*Watson v Samson Bros Ch D 1959, 38 TC 346; Cannon Industries Ltd v Edwards Ch D 1965, 42 TC 625; Frowd v Whalley Ch D 1965, 42 TC 599*, and see *R v Great Yarmouth Commrs (ex p Amis) QB 1960, 39 TC 143*) nor consider contentions evidence in support of which was not produced before the Commissioners (*Denekamp v Pearce Ch D 1998, 71 TC 213*).

Following the decision in *Pepper v Hart HL 1992, 65 TC 421* (see 75.16 SCHEDULE E—EMPLOYMENT INCOME), the Courts are prepared to consider the parliamentary history of legislation, or the official reports of debates in Hansard, where all of the following conditions are met.

(*a*)   Legislation is ambiguous or obscure, or leads to an absurdity.

(*b*)   The material relied upon consists of one or more statements by a Minister or other promoter of the Bill together if necessary with such other parliamentary material as is necessary to understand such statements and their effect.

(*c*)   The statements relied upon are clear.

For the requirements preliminary to reference to extracts from Hansard in any hearings, see Supreme Court Practice Direction issued 20 December 1994 (*1995 STI 98*).

Many Court decisions turn on whether the Commissioners' decision was one of fact supported by the evidence, and hence final. The Court will not disturb a finding of fact if there was reasonable evidence for it, notwithstanding that the evidence might support a different conclusion of fact. The leading case is *Edwards v Bairstow & Harrison HL 1955, 36 TC 207*, in which the issue was whether there had been an adventure in the nature of trade. The Commissioners' decision was reversed on the ground that the *only* reasonable conclusion from the evidence was that there had been such an adventure. For a discussion of the application of this principle, see *Milnes v J Beam Group Ltd Ch D 1975, 50 TC 675*.

A Court decision is a binding precedent for itself or an inferior Court except that the House of Lords, while treating its former decisions as normally binding, may depart from a previous decision should it appear right to do so. For this see *Fitzleet Estates Ltd v Cherry HL 1977, 51 TC 708*. Scottish decisions are not binding on the High Court but are normally followed. Decisions of the Privy Council and of the Irish Courts turning on comparable legislation are treated with respect. A Court decision does not affect other assessments already final and conclusive (see 5.5 ASSESSMENTS) but may be followed, if relevant, in the determination of any open appeals against assessments and in assessments made subsequently irrespective of the years of assessment or taxpayers concerned (*Re Waring decd Ch D, [1948] 1 AER 257*; *Gwyther v Boslymon Quarries Ltd KB 1950, 29 ATC 1*; *Bolands Ltd v CIR SC(I) 1925, 4 ATC 526*). Further, a Court decision does not estop the Crown from proceeding on a different basis for other years (*Hood Barrs v CIR (No 3) CA 1960, 39 TC 209*). A general change of practice consequent on a Court decision may affect error or mistake relief (see 16.7 CLAIMS) or retrospective employment income assessments under *ITEPA 2003, s 709* (see 75.2(vi) SCHEDULE E—EMPLOYMENT INCOME).

For joinder of CIR in non-tax disputes, see *In re Vandervell's Trusts HL 1970, 46 TC 341*.

4.23   **APPEALS FROM THE SPECIAL COMMISSIONERS**

In the case of an appeal to the Special Commissioners, if the appellant or the Revenue is dissatisfied in point of law with a decision (whether in principle or on final determination) or with a decision varying or substituting such a decision, appeal may (except in certain Lands Tribunal cases) be made to the High Court. Under *Order 55* of the Supreme Court Practice, the appeal must be lodged in the High Court within 28 days from the date on which notice of the decision is given. Further appeal may be made to the Court of Appeal and thence (with leave) to the House of Lords. A 'leap-frog' appeal to the Court of Appeal may be made if all the parties agree, the Commissioners certify that a point of law is involved relating wholly or mainly to the construction of an enactment which was fully argued and considered before them, and the leave of the Court of Appeal has been obtained. In Scotland appeals are to the Court of Session, in Northern Ireland to the Court of Appeal (NI), and thence in either case to the House of Lords. When a decision against which an appeal has been made is set aside or varied (see 4.17 above), the appeal is treated as withdrawn.

In the case of an appeal against a decision on an appeal against an assessment, tax must be paid in accordance with the Commissioners' decision. Following the decision on appeal, any tax overpaid is refunded with such interest as the Court may allow, and any amount undercharged is due and payable 30 days after the inspector issues a notice of the amount due.

[*TMA 1970, ss 56A, 58; SI 1994 No 1813; SI 1999 No 3294*].

For case law applicable equally to appeals from the General and Special Commissioners, see 4.19 *et seq.* above.

4.24   JUDICIAL REVIEW

A taxpayer who is dissatisfied with the exercise of administrative powers may in certain circumstances (e.g. where the Revenue has exceeded or abused its powers or acted contrary to the rules of natural justice, or where the Appeal Commissioners have acted unfairly or improperly) seek a remedy in one of the prerogative orders of mandamus, prohibition or certiorari. This is now done by way of application for judicial review under *Supreme Court Act 1981, s 31* and *Order 53 of the Rules of the Supreme Court.*

The issue on an application for leave to apply for judicial review is whether there is an arguable case (*R v CIR (ex p Howmet Corporation and another) QB, [1994] STC 413*). The procedure is generally used where no other, adequate, remedy, such as a right of appeal, is available. See *R v Special Commrs (ex p Stipplechoice Ltd) (No 1) CA 1985, 59 TC 396, R v HMIT (ex p Kissane and Another) QB, [1986] STC 152, R v Sevenoaks Commrs (ex p Thorne) QB 1989, 62 TC 341, R v Hastings and Bexhill General Commrs and CIR (ex p Goodacre) QB 1994, 67 TC 126* and *R v CIR (ex p Ulster Bank Ltd) CA 1997, 69 TC 211.*

There is a very long line of cases in which the courts have consistently refused applications where a matter should have been pursued through the ordinary channels as described above. See, for example, *R v Special Commrs (ex p Morey) CA 1972, 49 TC 71*; *R v Special Commrs (ex p Emery) QB 1980, 53 TC 555*; *R v Walton General Commrs (ex p Wilson) CA, [1983] STC 464*; *R v Special Commrs (ex p Esslemont) CA, 1984 STI 312*; *R v Brentford Commrs (ex p Chan) QB 1985, 57 TC 651*; *R v CIR (ex p Caglar) QB 1995, 67 TC 335.* See also, however, *R v HMIT and Others (ex p Lansing Bagnall Ltd) CA 1986, 61 TC 112* for a successful application where the inspector issued a notice under a discretionary power on the footing that there was a mandatory obligation to do so, and *R v Ward, R v Special Commr (ex p Stipplechoice Ltd) (No 3) QB 1988, 61 TC 391*, where insufficient notice was given of revision of an accounting period under *ICTA 1988, s 12(8)* prior to appeal hearing.

In *R v CIR (ex p J Rothschild Holdings) CA 1987, 61 TC 178*, the Revenue were required to produce internal documents of a general character relating to their practice in applying a statutory provision, but in *R v CIR (ex p Taylor) CA 1988, 62 TC 562* discovery of internal Revenue correspondence was refused as there was no material indication that it had any bearing on the question of whether the decision taken by the inspector could be challenged. In *R v CIR (ex p Unilever plc) CA 1996, 68 TC 205*, an application for judicial review for a Revenue decision to refuse a late loss relief claim was successful. The Revenue's refusal was 'so unreasonable as to be, in public law terms, irrational' in view of an administrative procedure established with the company over many years of raising assessments on estimates of net taxable profits, adjusted when the final accounts became available without regard to the loss claim time limit. A confirmation by the local inspector that capital allowances were available in relation to an enterprise zone property trust scheme was not binding where the promoters were aware that clearance applications were required to be made to a specialist department, and failed to disclose that the scheme involved 'artificial provisions' (*R v CIR (ex p Matrix-Securities Ltd) HL 1994, 66 TC 587*). As regards informal advice by the Revenue generally, they were not bound by anything less than a clear, unambiguous and unqualified representation (*R v CIR (ex p MFK Underwriting Agencies Ltd) QB 1989, 62 TC 607*), and in *R v CIR (ex p Bishopp and another) QB, [1999] STC 531*, an application for judicial review of informal advice given by the Revenue in relation to a proposed transaction was refused. See generally 35.6 INLAND REVENUE: ADMINISTRATION. See also *R v CIR (ex p Camacq Corporation) CA 1989, 62 TC 651*, where a Revenue decision to revoke its authorisation to pay a dividend gross was upheld, and *R v CIR (ex p S G Warburg & Co Ltd) QB 1994, 68 TC 300*, where a decision not to apply a published practice was upheld. The underlying facts in *Carvill v CIR (No 2); R (oao Carvill) v CIR Ch D, [2002] STC 1167* were that in two separate appeals relating to different tax years, income from an identical source had been held liable to tax for some years (the earlier years) but not others. An application for judicial review of the Revenue's refusal to refund tax, and interest on tax, paid for the earlier years was rejected; the assessments for those years were valid assessments which the Special Commissioner in question had had jurisdiction to determine, and the taxpayer the right to challenge, and those assessments had not been set aside. A further application for judicial review on the grounds that the Revenue's refusal to repay was unfair was similarly dismissed (*R (oao Carvill) v CIR (No 2) QB, [2003] STC 1539*).

See 30.7 FRAUDULENT OR NEGLIGENT CONDUCT as regards challenges to the validity of notices under *TMA 1970, s 20*.

The first step is to obtain leave to apply for judicial review from the High Court. Application for leave is made *ex parte* to a single judge who will usually determine the application without a hearing. The Court will not grant leave unless the applicant has a sufficient interest in the matter to which the application relates. See *CIR v National Federation of Self-employed and Small Businesses Ltd HL 1981, 55 TC 133* for what is meant by 'sufficient interest' and for discussion of availability of judicial review generally, and cf. *R v A-G (ex p ICI plc) CA 1986, 60 TC 1*.

Time limit. Applications must be made **within three months** of the date when the grounds for application arose. The Court has discretion to extend this time limit where there is good reason, but is generally very reluctant to do so. See e.g. *R v HMIT (ex p Brumfield and Others) QB 1988, 61 TC 589 and R v CIR (ex p Allen) QB 1997, 69 TC 442*. Grant of leave to apply for review does not amount to a ruling that application was made in good time (*R v Tavistock Commrs (ex p Worth) QB 1985, 59 TC 116*).

Simon's Direct Tax Service. See A3.9.

4.25   **COSTS**

Costs may be awarded by the Courts in the usual way. In suitable cases, e.g. 'test cases', the Revenue may undertake to pay the taxpayer's costs. There is no general provision for the award of costs of appearing before Commissioners, but see 4.17 above as regards award of costs of Special Commissioners' hearings against parties acting 'wholly unreasonably'. Costs awarded by the Courts may include expenses connected with the drafting of the Stated Case (*Manchester Corporation v Sugden CA 1903, 4 TC 595*). Costs of a discontinued application for judicial review were refused where the Revenue was not informed of the application (*R v CIR ex p Opman International UK QB 1985, 59 TC 352*). Law costs of appeals not allowable for tax purposes (*Allen v Farquharson KB 1932, 17 TC 59; Rushden Heel and Smith's Potato cases HL 1948, 30 TC 298 & 267*, and see *Spofforth KB 1945, 26 TC 310*).

5   Assessments

Cross-references. See 71.3–71.11 SCHEDULE D, CASES I AND II for bases of assessments on business profits. As regards particular assessments see also 27.1 EXCESS LIABILITY; 30 FRAUDULENT OR NEGLIGENT CONDUCT; 53 PARTNERSHIPS; 75 SCHEDULE E—EMPLOYMENT INCOME and 55 PAY AS YOU EARN for assessments on employment income; 81 SETTLEMENTS for assessment on trust income.

Simon's Direct Tax Service A3.2.

SELF-ASSESSMENT (78) **was introduced for income tax and capital gains tax with effect from 1996/97 and, for corporation tax, for accounting periods ending on or after 1 July 1999.** The rules for assessments other than self-assessments were accordingly substantially revised. However, many aspects of the self-assessment provisions are couched in similar terms to those previously applicable, so that the case law relating to pre-self-assessment periods may continue to be of relevance and continues to be covered here.

5.1   ASSESSMENTS — PRE-SELF-ASSESSMENT

(**Note.** The references to *TMA 1970* in this paragraph are to that Act prior to amendment in connection with the commencement of self-assessment.)

Assessments to tax are made by inspectors, or their delegates [*TMA 1970, s 113(1A)(1B)*] and notices of assessment are served, which must also state the date issued and the time limit for making APPEALS (4). [*TMA 1970, s 29(1)(2)(5); F(No 2)A 1975, s 44(5)*]. Assessments may, where income is charged for a year of assessment on the amount arising in that year, be raised during the year, subject to later adjustment. [*TMA 1970, s 29(1)(c); FA 1988, s 119*]. The assessment must include a statement of the tax actually payable (*Hallamshire Industrial Finance Trust Ltd v CIR Ch D 1978, 53 TC 631*). A taxpayer may request the inspector (on form 64–8) to provide a copy of any assessment to an agent. An assessment becomes binding if not appealed against within 30 days of the date of issue. [*TMA 1970, s 31; F(No 2)A 1975, s 67(1)*]. The inspector's power of assessment is not limited to persons or sources of income within the area of his tax office (*R v Tavistock Commrs (ex p Adams) CA 1971, 48 TC 56*). See 4.4 APPEALS for jurisdiction of Commissioners on appeal.

In the absence of a satisfactory return the inspector may make an assessment to the best of his judgment. [*TMA 1970, s 29(1)(b)*]. As to this, see *Van Boeckel v C & E Commrs QB 1980, [1981] STC 290*, relating to the comparable VAT provision of *FA 1972, s 31(1)*, *Blackpool Marton Rotary Club v Martin CA 1989, 62 TC 686* and *Phillimore v Heaton Ch D 1989, 61 TC 584*.

An assessment defective in form or containing errors may be validated by *TMA 1970, s 114(1)* if the person and income assessed are apparent, e.g. where the person assessed was later found to have received the income as trustee (*Martin v CIR CS 1938, 22 TC 330*). See also *Fleming v London Produce Co Ltd Ch D 1968, 44 TC 582, Hart v Briscoe Ch D 1977, 52 TC 53* and *Vickerman v Mason's Personal Representatives Ch D 1984, 58 TC 39*. But where the assessment was under Schedule D, Case VII it was held that *section 114(1)* could not be used to treat the assessment as under Case I (*Bath & West Counties Property Trust Ltd v Thomas Ch D 1977, 52 TC 20*, although for special reasons, including the Crown option between Cases, the Court used its powers under *TMA 1970, s 56(6)* to alter the assessment, for which see also *CIR v McGuckian CA(NI), [1994] STC 888*) or to validate an assessment where wrong year of assessment had been entered through a copying error (*Baylis v Gregory CA, [1987] STC 297*).

Income under Schedules A or D is assessable on the person receiving or entitled to it. [*ICTA 1988, ss 21(1), 59(1)*]. Trustees, guardians etc. are assessable in respect of income of incapacitated persons including minors (see 15.3 CHILDREN) and there are provisions for charging non-residents through agents etc. (see 51.3 NON-RESIDENTS AND OTHER OVERSEAS MATTERS) but these provisions do not preclude the non-resident himself being assessed if he can be reached (*CIR v Huni KB 1923, 8 TC 466; Whitney v CIR HL 1925, 10 TC 88*).

An assessment once made cannot be 'vacated' (*Baylis v Gregory*, above).

In making assessments, the Revenue has an option, where more than one Case of Schedule D is applicable, to elect to tax under the Case which is most advantageous to it (*Liverpool London and Globe Insurance Co v Bennett HL 1913, 6 TC 327*). This case related to unremitted foreign interest, which could not then be assessed under Case IV, but the Revenue successfully contended that it formed part of the taxpayer's '*trading profits*' assessable under Case I (and cf. *Butler v Mortgage Co of Egypt CA 1928, 13 TC 803*).

But there is no such power of selection between the Schedules. 'A subject matter of taxation properly assessed ... under one Schedule, cannot be brought into assessment under another Schedule' (Lord Dunedin and Lord Tomlin in *Salisbury House Estate v Fry HL 1930, 15 TC 266*). And see *Sywell Aerodrome Ltd v Croft KB 1941, 24 TC 126; Mitchell & Edon v Ross HL 1961, 40 TC 11*.

An assessment is made on the date on which the inspector authorised to make it signs a certificate in the appropriate assessments volume that he made certain assessments including the assessment in question (*Honig v Sarsfield CA 1986, 59 TC 337*).

Time limits. An assessment or additional assessment cannot be made later than six years from the end of the tax year to which it relates (or accounting period in the case of a company) [*TMA 1970, s 34*] except in cases of FRAUDULENT OR NEGLIGENT CONDUCT (6) [*TMA 1970, ss 36–41; FA 1989, s 149*] or where there is specific statutory provision for later assessment. But assessments on personal representatives in respect of deceased's income before death must be made within three years after end of tax year in which death occurred. [*TMA 1970, s 40(1)*]. See also 30.4 FRAUDULENT OR NEGLIGENT CONDUCT regarding deceased persons.

5.2   ASSESSMENTS — SELF-ASSESSMENT

All assessments which are not self-assessments must (unless otherwise provided) be made by an officer of the Board, notice of such assessment to be served on the person assessed stating the date of issue and the time limit for making APPEALS (4). The assessment may not then be altered except as expressly provided under the *Taxes Acts*. All income tax falling to be assessed other than by self-assessment may be included in a single assessment, notwithstanding that the liability may have arisen under more than one Schedule. [*TMA 1970, s 30A; FA 1994, ss 196, 199(2)(a), Sch 19 para 5*].

Time limits. The normal time limit for the making of an assessment to income tax or capital gains tax is five years after 31 January following the year of assessment. [*TMA 1970, s 34(1); FA 1994, ss 196, 199(2)(a), Sch 19 para 10*]. The extended time limit in cases of fraudulent or negligent conduct is twenty years after 31 January following the year of assessment (and see 30.3 FRAUDULENT OR NEGLIGENT CONDUCT). [*TMA 1970, s 36(1); FA 1994, ss 196, 199(2)(a), Sch 19 para 11(1)*]. The latest time for assessing the personal representatives of a deceased person is three years after 31 January following the year of assessment in which death occurred. [*TMA 1970, s 40(1)(2); FA 1994, ss 196, 199(2)(a), Sch 19 para 12*].

In relation to employment income, pension income or social security income chargeable to tax for 2004/05 or any subsequent year but received in a tax year later than that for which it is chargeable, an assessment can be made at any time within six years after the tax year in which the income is received. [*TMA 1970, s 35; FA 2004, Sch 17 para 3*].

5.3   **FURTHER ASSESSMENTS ON 'DISCOVERY'**

Pre-self-assessment. If an inspector or the Board 'discover' that income has not been assessed or has been under-assessed or that excessive relief has been given, a further assessment can be made. [*TMA 1970, s 29(3)(4)*]. The existence of an assessment under appeal capable of being increased and determined in the correct amount does not preclude the making of a further assessment and the consequent determination of both the original assessment and the further assessment (*Duchy Maternity Ltd v Hodgson Ch D 1985, 59 TC 85*). Discovery has been given a very wide meaning by the Courts. There is a discovery by the inspector if he comes to the honest conclusion that there has been under-assessment (*R v Kensington Commrs (ex p Aramayo) HL 1915, 6 TC 279, 613; R v St Giles etc. Commrs (ex p Hooper) KB 1915, 7 TC 59*; but see *Scott and another (trading as Farthings Steak House) v McDonald (Sp C 91), [1996] SSCD 381* for a case in which the Special Commissioner found that there had been no honest *bona fide* discovery by the inspector). It has been established in a number of cases that *a change of opinion* or rectification of an error by the Revenue, including an arithmetical error in calculating the tax, without the ascertainment of any new facts amounts to discovery and this is so notwithstanding that the former opinion had been notified to the taxpayer (*Brodie's Trustees v CIR KB 1933, 17 TC 432; Williams v Grundy Trustees KB 1933, 18 TC 271; British Sugar Mfrs Ltd v Harris CA 1937, 21 TC 528; CIR v Mackinlay's Trustees CS 1938, 22 TC 305; Steel Barrel Co Ltd v Osborne (No 2) CA 1948, 30 TC 73; Commercial Structures Ltd v Briggs CA 1948, 30 TC 477; Jones v Mason Investments Ch D 1966, 43 TC 570; Vickerman v Mason's Personal Representatives Ch D 1984, 58 TC 39*). (See 56.8 PAYMENT OF TAX for remission of tax in cases of official error.) A further assessment may be made on incomplete information supplied on behalf of the taxpayer (*McLuskey's Executrix v CIR CS 1955, 36 TC 163*) and successive further assessments are permissible (*Cansick v Hochstrasser Ch D 1961, 40 TC 151*). See also *Beatty v CIR Ch D 1953, 35 TC 30; Multipar Syndicate Ltd v Devitt KB 1945, 26 TC 359*. A Court decision does not estop the Crown from proceeding on a different basis for other years (*Hood Barrs v CIR (No 3) CA 1960, 39 TC 209*).

If in the determination of an appeal *including a determination by agreement under TMA 1970, s 54* (see 4.5 APPEALS) a matter has been adjudicated or agreed, the Revenue cannot re-open the matter by making a further assessment (*Cenlon Finance Co Ltd v Ellwood HL 1962, 40 TC 176*) or by adjusting a further assessment made for an unrelated reason (*Sun Chemical Ltd v Smith (Sp C 340), [2002] SSCD 510*). However, the matter must have been dealt with specifically (*Kidston v Aspinall Ch D 1963, 41 TC 371; Young v Duthie Ch D 1969, 45 TC 624; Skinner v Berry Head Lands Ltd Ch D 1970, 46 TC 377; Parkin v Cattell CA 1971, 48 TC 462*) or clearly have been raised by implication, so that an inspector of average experience must have appreciated it was being made (*Olin Energy Systems Ltd v Scorer HL 1985, 58 TC 592*). A further assessment is not precluded where an appeal was settled by an agreement based on trading profits which were incorrectly stated (*Gray v Matheson Ch D 1993, 65 TC 577*). For a case in which assessments raised under *ICTA 1988, s 770* (transfer pricing, see 3.8 ANTI-AVOIDANCE) were discharged, the relevant licensing agreements having been submitted to the inspector prior to a *section 54* agreement, see *Newidgets Manufacturing Ltd v Jones (Sp C 197), [1999] SSCD 193*.

Similar considerations apply in determining whether an agreement under *TMA 1970, s 54* prevents a taxpayer making an error or mistake relief claim under *TMA 1970, s 33* (see 16.7 CLAIMS) (and see *Grafton Ltd v CIR (Sp C 172), [1998] SSCD 278*).

The Revenue have issued a Statement of Practice setting out their view of the application in practice of the case law outlined above in relation to pre-self assessment periods. The following are listed as specific circumstances in which there are clearly no grounds for *not* making discovery assessments:

(*a*)   profits or income have not earlier been charged to tax because of any form of fraudulent or negligent conduct;

(b) the inspector has been misled or misinformed in any way about the particular matter at issue;

(c) there is an arithmetical error in a computation which had not been spotted at the time agreement was reached, and which can be corrected by the making of an in date discovery assessment;

(d) an error is made in accounts and computations which it cannot reasonably be alleged was correct or intended, e.g. the double deduction from taxable profits of a particular item (say group relief).

The Statement of Practice also makes it clear that, by concession, the principles determining the making of a further assessment following settlement of an appeal by agreement will also be applied where agreement is reached prior to the issue of an assessment. Also by concession, whether or not there has been an appeal, a discovery assessment will not be made where, although the matter in question may not have been the subject of a specific agreement within the case law principles outlined above, the inspector's decision was based on full and accurate disclosure and was a tenable view, so that the taxpayer could reasonably have believed the inspector's decision to be correct. (Revenue Pamphlet IR 131, SP 8/91, 26 July 1991 as revised).

See 16.8 CLAIMS as regards the making of claims etc. relevant to further assessments.

Self-assessment periods. If an officer of the Board or the Board 'discover', as regards any person (the taxpayer) and a chargeable period (i.e. for income tax and capital gains tax purposes, a year of assessment), that

(a) any income or chargeable gains which ought to have been assessed to tax (see 78.2 SELF-ASSESSMENT) have not been assessed, or

(b) an assessment is or has become insufficient, or

(c) any relief given is or has become excessive,

then with the exceptions below, an assessment (a discovery assessment) may be made to make good to the Crown the apparent loss of tax. In limited circumstances, a discovery assessment may be made even though the deadline for opening an enquiry into the return (see 68.6 RETURNS) has not passed (see Revenue Tax Bulletin August 2001 pp 875, 876).

No discovery assessment may be made, in respect of a chargeable period, where a return under *TMA 1970, s 8* or *s 8A* (see 68.2 RETURNS) has been delivered,

(1) if it would be attributable to an error or mistake in the return as to the basis on which the liability ought to have been computed and the return was, in fact, made on the basis, or in accordance with the practice, generally prevailing at the time when it was made; or

(2) unless either

(a) the loss of tax is attributable to fraudulent or negligent conduct by the taxpayer or a person acting on his behalf (for an example of which see *Hancock v CIR (Sp C 213), [1999] SSCD 287*), or

(b) at the time when an officer of the Board either ceased to be entitled to enquire (see 68.6 RETURNS) into the return or informed the taxpayer of the completion of his enquiries, he could not have been reasonably expected, on the basis of the information so far made available to him (see below), to be aware of the loss of tax.

For the purposes of (2)(b) above, information is regarded as having been made available to the officer if it has been included in

(i) the return (or accompanying accounts, statements or documents) for the chargeable period concerned or for either of the two immediately preceding it, or

(ii)   a partnership return (see 68.13 RETURNS), where applicable, in respect of the chargeable period concerned or either of the two immediately preceding it, or

(iii)   any claim for the chargeable period concerned, or

(iv)   documents etc. produced for the purposes of any enquiries into such a return or claim,

or is information the existence and relevance of which could reasonably be expected to be inferred from the above-mentioned information or are notified in writing to the Revenue. See also below.

An objection to a discovery assessment on the grounds that neither (*a*) nor (*b*) in (2) above applies can be made only on an appeal against the assessment. (See 4.1 APPEALS for right of appeal.)

[*TMA 1970, s 29; FA 1994, s 191(1), s 199(2)(a); FA 2001, s 88, Sch 29 para 22*].

See 78.7 SELF-ASSESSMENT as regards due date of payment.

A change of Revenue opinion on information previously made available to them is not grounds for a discovery assessment.

Particularly in large or complex cases, the standard accounts information details and other information included in the tax return (see 68.2 RETURNS) may not provide a means of disclosure adequate to avoid falling within (2)(*b*) above. The submission of further information, including perhaps accounts, may be considered appropriate but will not necessarily provide protection against a discovery assessment beyond that arising from submission of the return alone. The reasonable expectation test (see (2)(*b*) above) must be satisfied. Where voluminous information beyond the accounts and computations is sent with the return, the Revenue recommend that there should be a brief indication of the relevance of the material. The Revenue will accept that for *TMA 1970, s 29* purposes documents submitted within a month of the return 'accompany' it (see (i) above) provided the return indicates that such documents have been or will be submitted. They will consider sympathetically a request that this condition be treated as satisfied where the time lag is longer than a month. (Revenue Press Release 31 May 1996 and Tax Bulletin June 1996 pp 313–315).

The categories in (i)–(iv) above constitute an exhaustive definition of 'information made available to an officer of the Board' for the purpose of (2)(*b*) above; an officer is not precluded from making a discovery assessment simply because some other information (not normally part of the officer's immediate checks) might be available (in the instant case a form P11D) that might place doubt on the sufficiency of the self-assessment (*Langham v Veltema CA, [2004] STC 544*).

See Simon's Direct Tax Service A3.1607, E1.815. See also generally Revenue Assessment Procedures Manual AP 2144–2160.

See 16.8 CLAIMS for extended time limits for claims where a discovery assessment is made in a case where neither fraudulent nor negligent conduct is involved.

Amendment of partnership return on discovery. Provisions broadly similar to those described above apply as regards an understatement of profits or excessive claim for relief or allowance in a partnership statement (see 68.13 RETURNS), although the Revenue's remedy in this case is to amend the partnership return, with consequent amendment of partners' own returns. [*TMA 1970, s 30B; FA 1994, ss 196, 199(2)(a), Sch 19 para 6; FA 1995, s 115(5); FA 1998, Sch 19 para 14; FA 2001, s 88, Sch 29 para 24*]. See 4.1 APPEALS for right of appeal.

5.4   **DOUBLE ASSESSMENT**

The taxing acts 'nowhere authorise the Crown to take Income Tax twice over in respect of the same source for the same period of time' (Lord Sumner in *English Sewing Cotton Co HL*

5.5 Assessments

1923, 8 TC at *513*). An *alternative* income tax assessment may, however, be raised in respect of transactions already the subject of a final CGT assessment (*Bye v Coren CA 1986, 60 TC 116*), and where more than one of a number of alternative assessments become final and conclusive, the Crown may institute collection proceedings in respect of any one (but not more than one) of them (*CIR v Wilkinson CA 1992, 65 TC 28*). For alternative assessments generally, see *Lord Advocate v McKenna CS, [1989] STC 485*.

Where there has been double assessment for the same cause and for the same chargeable period a claim may be made to the Board (with right of appeal to the Commissioners having jurisdiction to hear appeals against the assessment, or the later of the assessments, to which the appeal relates) for the overcharge to be vacated. [*TMA 1970, s 32*]. See 16.7 CLAIMS for error or mistake relief.

5.5 FINALITY OF ASSESSMENTS

An assessment cannot be altered after the notice has been served except in accordance with the express provisions of the *Taxes Acts* (e.g. where the taxpayer appeals — see 4 APPEALS). [*TMA 1970, s 29(6) as originally enacted; TMA 1970, s 30A(4); FA 1994, Sch 19 para 5*]. Where over-assessment results from an *error or mistake* in a return, see 16.7 CLAIMS. An assessment as determined on appeal or not appealed against is final and conclusive (but see 56.12 PAYMENT OF TAX for application of 'equitable liability').

6 Bankruptcy

(See also Revenue Pamphlet IR 4.)

Simon's Direct Tax Service A3.1107.

6.1   Income received by trustee during bankruptcy is not income of bankrupt for purposes of claiming personal allowances, etc. (*Fleming CS 1928, 14 TC 78*). Trustee is assessable on such income including profits of bankrupt's business continued by him notwithstanding requirement to hand over to creditors (*Armitage v Moore QB 1900, 4 TC 199*). And see *Hibbert v Fysh CA 1962, 40 TC 305* (bankrupt assessable on remuneration retainable by him). The trustee continues generally to act following the death (undischarged) of the bankrupt as if he or she were still alive.

For the Revenue approach to dealing with personal insolvency under SELF-ASSESSMENT (78), see Revenue Tax Bulletin April 1998 pp 530, 531.

See 56.7 PAYMENT OF TAX for Crown Priority and 57.18 PENALTIES for penalties awarded against a bankrupt. See also Tolley's Capital Gains Tax under Settlements.

7 Banks

Simon's Direct Tax Service D4.11.

7.1   For the tax treatment of banks themselves, and for certain exemptions, see Tolley's Corporation Tax (under Banks).

Interest payable in UK to a UK bank, and interest paid by a UK bank, are both payable gross (see 22.3(ii) DEDUCTION OF TAX AT SOURCE) except as detailed in 7.2 below, but payments by individuals to banks of certain home mortgage interest are made after deduction of tax, see 22.13 DEDUCTION OF TAX AT SOURCE. For savings bank interest etc., see 28.16 EXEMPT INCOME.

In general, the term 'bank' is defined by reference to the carrying on of a *bona fide* banking business, but for certain purposes it is specially defined as:

(*a*)   the Bank of England;

(*b*)   a person who has permission under *Financial Services and Markets Act 2000, Pt 4* to accept deposits (excluding building and friendly societies, credit unions and insurance companies);

(*c*)   an EEA firm within *Financial Services and Markets Act 2000, Sch 3 para 5(b)* which has permission under *para 15* of that *Schedule* (as a result of qualifying for authorisation under *para 12(1)*) to accept deposits; or

(*d*)   an international organisation of which the UK is a member and which is designated as a bank for the particular purpose by Treasury order (e.g. the European Investment Bank, see *SI 1996 No 1179*).

(Before 1 December 2001, (*b*) and (*c*) above were replaced by the following:

(*b*)   an institution authorised under the *Banking Act 1987*;

(*c*)   a European authorised institution (within the *Banking Co-ordination (Second Council Directive) Regulations 1992*) in relation to the establishment of a branch of which the requirements of *Sch 2 para 1* of those regulations have been complied with.)

See 3.7 ANTI-AVOIDANCE, 14.10 CHARITIES, 22.3(ii) DEDUCTION OF TAX AT SOURCE, 68.15 RETURNS.

[*ICTA 1988, s 840A; FA 1996, Sch 37 para 1(1); SI 2001 No 3629, Article 46; SI 2002 No 1409*].

Returns. Banks must make returns of interest paid to depositors, see 68.15 RETURNS.

7.2   **DEDUCTION OF TAX FROM INTEREST** [*ICTA 1988, ss 480A–482; FA 1990, Sch 5 paras 7–12; SI 1990 No 2232; FA 1991, ss 75, 82; SI 1992 Nos 12–15; F(No 2)A 1992, Sch 8 para 4; SI 1992 No 3234; FA 1993, ss 59, 183(2); SI 1994 No 295; FA 1995, s 86; SI 1995 No 1370; FA 2000, s 111(3)(6); SI 2001 Nos 405, 406; SI 2001 No 3629, Article 39; SI 2002 No 1968*]

Any 'deposit-taker' paying or crediting interest on a 'relevant deposit' must deduct therefrom a sum representing income tax thereon (at the lower rate for the year of assessment in which the payment is made), unless the conditions for gross payment contained in *The Income Tax (Deposit-takers) (Interest Payments) Regulations 1990 (SI 1990 No 2232)* (see below) are met. Income tax chargeable under SCHEDULE D, CASE III (72) on such interest is computed on the full amount of the interest arising in the year. *ICTA 1988, s 349* (see 22.3 DEDUCTION OF TAX AT SOURCE) does not apply to such payments.

The deposit-taker must treat all deposits as relevant deposits unless satisfied to the contrary, but if so satisfied may treat a deposit as not being a relevant deposit until he comes into possession of information reasonably indicative that the deposit is, or may be, a relevant deposit.

For these purposes '*deposit-taker*' means the Bank of England, persons authorised under the *Banking Act 1987* (or municipal bank within that *Act*) or the *Financial Services and Markets Act 2000*, the Post Office (until its dissolution), any local authority and any other deposit-taker prescribed by Treasury order. A 'European deposit-taker' (see *SI 1992 No 3234 as amended*) is included, as is (from 1 October 2002) any authorised person (i.e. under *Financial Services and Markets Act 2000*) whose business consists wholly or mainly of dealing as principal in 'financial instruments' (as defined) (see *SI 2002 No 1968*). A '*relevant deposit*' (subject to the exclusions below) is a deposit where either:

(*a*)   the person beneficially entitled to any interest is an individual (or the persons so entitled are all individuals), or is a Scottish partnership all the partners of which are individuals; or

(*b*)   the person entitled to the interest receives it as the personal representative of a deceased individual (but note particularly the ordinary residence requirement at (xii) below); or

(*c*)   (from 6 April 1996) the interest arises to the trustees of a discretionary or accumulation trust (as under *ICTA 1988, s 686*, see 81.5 SETTLEMENTS). This does not apply to deposits made before 6 April 1995 unless the deposit-taker has, since that date but before the making of the payment, been notified by the Board or the trustees that the interest is income of such a trust (and the Board has wide information powers in relation to such notices). The form of notification by the trustees is laid down by *SI 1995 No 1370*, under which payments may continue to be made gross for up to 30 days after receipt of notice (whether by the trustees or by the Revenue) where deduction within that period has not become reasonably practicable. Notification may be cancelled by the Revenue where appropriate. There were transitional provisions treating the source as ceasing where a payment on a deposit made before 6 April 1996 was brought within the scheme before 6 April 1998.

Excluded are:

(i)   deposits in respect of which a CERTIFICATE OF DEPOSIT (12) has been issued for £50,000 or more (or foreign equivalent at the time the deposit is made) and which are repayable within five years;

(ii)   non-transferable deposits of £50,000 or more (or foreign equivalent at the time the deposit is made) repayable at the end of a specified period of not more than five years;

(iii)   a '*qualifying deposit right*', i.e. a right to receive an amount in pursuance of a deposit of money under an arrangement under which no certificate of deposit has been issued, although the person entitled to the right could call for the issue of such a certificate, which otherwise meets the conditions in (i) above;

(iv)   debentures (as defined in *Companies Act 1985, s 744*);

(v)   loans made *by* a deposit-taker in the ordinary course of his business;

(vi)   debts on securities listed on a recognised stock exchange;

(vii)   deposits in a '*general client account deposit*', i.e. a client account, other than an account for specific clients, if the depositor is required by law to make payments representing interest to any of the clients whose money it contains;

(viii) Lloyd's UNDERWRITERS (89) premiums trust funds;

(ix) (before 1 December 2001) deposits by Stock Exchange money brokers (recognised by the Bank of England) in the course of business as such a broker;

(x) deposits held at non-UK branches of UK resident deposit-takers;

(xi) deposits with non-UK resident deposit-takers held other than in UK branches; and

(xii) deposits in respect of which the 'appropriate person' has declared in writing (or, from 6 April 2001, by electronic means) to the deposit-taker that:

    (1) where (*a*) above applies, the individual (or all of the individuals) concerned is (are), at the time of the declaration, not ordinarily resident in the UK; or

    (2) where (*b*) above applies, the deceased, at the time of his death, was not ordinarily resident in the UK; or

    (3) where (*c*) above applies, at the time of the declaration the trustees are not UK resident and do not have any reasonable grounds for believing that any of the beneficiaries (as defined for this purpose) is a UK ordinarily resident individual or a UK resident company.

The '*appropriate person*' is any person beneficially entitled to the interest, or entitled to receive it in his capacity as a personal representative or trustee, or to whom it is payable. The declaration must be in such form, and contain such information, as is required by the Board, and must include an undertaking to notify the deposit-taker should any individual concerned become ordinarily resident in the UK, or the trustees or any company concerned become resident in the UK, or any UK ordinarily resident individual or UK-resident company become a beneficiary of the trust to which the declaration relates. The Revenue have powers to review all declarations received by a deposit-taker. For declarations made before 6 April 2001, a certificate by the deposit-taker is required in cases where the declaration of non-ordinary residence does not include the depositor's permanent address, but from that date the address must be included in any such declaration. Declarations in similar terms made to a building society which converts to company status (see 8.3, 8.6 BUILDING SOCIETIES) are, by concession, treated as having been made to the successor company. (Revenue Pamphlet IR 1, A69).

The deposit-taker has to treat all deposits as relevant deposits unless satisfied to the contrary, but if so satisfied can treat a deposit as not being a relevant deposit until he comes into possession of information reasonably indicative that the deposit is, or might be, a relevant deposit.

The Treasury and the Board are given wide powers to alter the legislation by statutory instrument, in particular in relation to the declaration required at (xii) above.

In the case of depositors who make the appropriate declaration for their deposit to be excluded from being a relevant deposit (see (xii) above) to a deposit-taker other than a bank, the normal deduction rules under *ICTA 1988, s 349(2)* are disapplied by *section 349(3)(h)* (introduced by *FA 1993, s 59*) as they are disapplied in the case of banks by *section 349(3)(a)* (and see Revenue Press Release 21 January 1993).

The collection procedure of *ICTA 1988, Sch 16* applies, *mutatis mutandis*, to such payments whether or not the deposit-taker is UK-resident.

For repayment claims on behalf of persons incapable of managing their own affairs, see Revenue Tax Bulletin April 1996 p 301.

IR Savings, Pensions, Share Schemes may be contacted for technical advice in relation to the basic rate tax scheme on 0151–472 6156.

Gross payment may be made where the person beneficially entitled to the interest is UK ordinarily resident (see 65.6 RESIDENCE, ORDINARY RESIDENCE AND DOMICILE) and has supplied the appropriate certificate to the deposit-taker to the effect that he is unlikely to be liable to income tax for the year of assessment in which the payment is made or credited (taking into account for this purpose all interest arising in the year of assessment concerned which would, in the absence of such a certificate, be received under deduction of lower or basic rate tax). The certificate must be in prescribed form and must contain the name, permanent address, date of birth and (where applicable) national insurance number of the person beneficially entitled to the interest, and the name (and if necessary branch) of the deposit-taker and account number. It must also contain an undertaking to notify the deposit-taker if the person beneficially entitled to the payment becomes liable to income tax for the year in which the payment is made or credited. Revenue Explanatory Leaflet IR 110 outlines the conditions for certification (which are described in detail below) and contains the appropriate form R85 on which registration may be made (and of which further copies may be obtained from the Revenue website and from banks, building societies and local authorities). It also explains the procedure for reclaiming tax deducted, using form R40, where no registration is in place. Provision is made from 6 April 2001 for use of electronic forms of communication.

Such a certificate may only be given by:

(i)   a depositor aged 16 or over at the beginning of the year of assessment in which the payment is made or credited, or who attains age 16 during that year, who is beneficially entitled to the payment; or

(ii)   the parent or guardian of a person beneficially entitled to the payment who is under 16 at the beginning of that year; or

(iii)   a person authorised by power of attorney to administer the financial affairs of the person beneficially entitled to the payment; or

(iv)   the parent, guardian, spouse, son or daughter of a mentally handicapped person, or any person appointed by a court to manage the affairs of a mentally handicapped person; or

(v)   a person appointed by the Secretary of State to receive benefits on behalf of a person who is for the time being unable to act.

A certificate may not be given where the payment is treated as income of a parent of the person beneficially entitled to the payment, or where the Board has issued a notice in relation to the account concerned requiring deduction of tax (see below).

The certificate must be supplied before the end of the year of assessment in which the payment is made or credited, or, in the case of a certificate given by a person who will attain 16 years of age during a year of assessment, before the end of that year.

A person who gives such a certificate fraudulently or negligently, or fails to comply with any undertaking contained in the certificate, is liable under *TMA 1970, s 99A* (introduced by *FA 1991, s 82*) to a penalty up to £3,000.

Tax deducted from payments in a year prior to receipt of a certificate relating to that year may be refunded, and a like amount recovered by the deposit-taker from the Board, provided that a certificate of deduction of tax (see 22.7 DEDUCTION OF TAX AT SOURCE) has not been furnished to the depositor prior to receipt of the gross payment certificate.

In Revenue Press Release 13 August 1992, the Revenue position as regards incorrect certification for gross payment was explained. In asking those who had registered to reconsider their position (and, if appropriate, to ask for their registration with the bank or building society to be cancelled), the Revenue made clear that where, as a result of their audited sample, cases of incorrect registration were identified, gross payment would cease and tax (and possibly interest and penalties) would be imposed in respect of any interest already received. No interest and penalties would be applied in cases of simple misunderstanding of the position, and a penalty would be considered only where false or fraudulent declarations had knowingly been made on the registration form (or there had been a deliberate failure to cancel the registration).

A certificate ceases to be valid:

(*a*)   where the deposit-taker is notified (as above) that the person beneficially entitled to the payment is liable to income tax for the year in which the payment is made;

(*b*)   where it was given by a parent or guardian, at the end of the year of assessment in which the person beneficially entitled to the payment attains 16 years of age;

(*c*)   where it was given by a person who attained 16 years of age during the year of assessment in which a payment was made or credited, but who was not the holder of the account to which the certificate relates, and that person fails to become the holder before the first payment is made or credited after the end of that year of assessment;

(*d*)   where the deposit-taker is notified that the person by or on whose behalf the certificate was given has died; and

(*e*)   where the Board, having reason to believe that a person beneficially entitled to a payment of interest has become liable to income tax, give notice requiring the deposit-taker to deduct tax from payments of interest made, more than 30 days after the issue of the notice (or from earlier payments, if practicable), to or for the benefit of that person on a specified account held by or on behalf of that person.

A notice under (*e*) above must be copied to the person to whom it refers, and a further certificate in respect of the account referred to in the notice may not be given by or on behalf of that person (unless the notice is subsequently cancelled, see below).

A notice under (*e*) above may be cancelled (and the deposit-taker and person referred to in the notice so informed) if the Board are satisfied that the person referred to in the notice was not at the date of the notice, and has not since become, liable to income tax, or is no longer so liable.

Certificates of non-liability given by a building society which converts to company status are, by concession, treated as having been given to the successor company. (Revenue Pamphlet IR 1, A69).

Joint accounts. The position as regards certification by each of joint holders of an account is considered separately. Payments are apportioned equally to each joint holder, and tax deducted in respect of that part of a payment to which certification does not apply. The deposit-taker may, however, deduct tax from the whole of payments in respect of joint accounts where certification does not apply to all the joint holders, after giving notice to the Board of its intention to do so (which notice the deposit-taker may subsequently cancel).

Information. The Board may by notice require any deposit-taker (within not less than 14 days) to furnish them with such information (including books, records etc.) as they require, in particular

(I)   for verification of payments made without deduction of tax and of the validity of certification for gross payment, and

(II)   for verification of the amount of tax deducted from payments of interest (but this does not include copies of books, records etc. from which the depositor can be ascertained).

Copies of the deposit-taker's books, records etc. must be made available when required by the Board. Certificates for gross payment must be retained for at least two years after they expire.

Subject to *FA 1989, s 182(5)* (see **36.4** INLAND REVENUE: CONFIDENTIALITY OF INFORMA-TION), information obtained under these provisions may not be used other than for the purposes of the provisions or for the ascertainment of the tax liability of the deposit-taker or of the person beneficially entitled to interest paid without deduction of tax to whom the information relates.

The Board may also make regulations providing for the exclusion from its information powers of accounts held by non-UK ordinary residents or non-UK resident trustees.

For Revenue audit powers and further information powers, see *SI 1992 Nos 12, 15* as amended.

The Revenue have published a Code of Practice (No 4) setting out their standards for the carrying out of inspections of tax deduction schemes operated by financial intermediaries.

8 Building Societies

Simon's Direct Tax Service D4.7.

8.1 For years up to and including 1985/86, a Building Society normally entered into special arrangements with the Revenue. For the years 1986/87 to 1990/91 inclusive, this system was replaced by regulations (see *SI 1986 No 482 as amended*) made by statutory instrument by the Board, although the revised system operated on broadly similar lines to the previous arrangements. [*ICTA 1988, s 476*].

For 1991/92 and subsequent years, building societies deduct lower or basic rate tax from interest payments unless a certificate is supplied to the effect that the recipient is unlikely to be liable to income tax for the year. [*ICTA 1988, s 477A; FA 1990, s 30, Sch 5*]. Regulations provide for the detailed implementation of the scheme (see *The Income Tax (Building Societies) (Dividends and Interest) Regulations 1990, SI 1990 No 2231* as amended).

For these purposes, a building society is one within the meaning of the *Building Societies Act 1986*. [*ICTA 1988, s 832(1)*].

8.2 **Returns.** Building societies are required to make returns of dividends and interest paid to investors. [*TMA 1970, s 17; SI 1986 No 482; FA 1990, s 92; SI 1990 No 2231; F(No 2)A 1992, s 29*]. See 68.15 RETURNS.

8.3 **INTEREST AND DIVIDENDS PAID TO INVESTORS** [*ICTA 1988, ss 477A, 482A; TMA 1970, s 99A; FA 1990, Sch 5 paras 4, 10; SI 1990 No 2231; FA 1991, ss 52, 75, 82, Sch 11; SI 1992 Nos 10, 11, 2915; SI 1994 No 296; SI 1995 No 1184; SI 1996 No 223; FA 2000, s 111(4)(6), s 145(10)(11); SI 2001 No 404; SI 2001 No 3629, Article 128*]

Except in the case of certain marketable securities (see below), building societies are required under regulations (*SI 1990 No 2231*) made under *ICTA 1988, s 477A* to deduct a sum representing income tax (at the lower rate for the year of assessment in which the payment is made) thereon from all payments or credits of dividends or interest in respect of shares in, deposits with or loans to the society, unless gross payment is authorised under the conditions described below. The deduction requirements of *ICTA 1988, s 349* (see 22.3 DEDUCTION OF TAX AT SOURCE) do not apply to such payments. Whether or not gross payment applies, such interest etc. is chargeable under SCHEDULE D, CASE III (72) on the current year basis.

For repayment claims on behalf of persons incapable of managing their own affairs, see Revenue Tax Bulletin April 1996 p 301.

IR Savings, Pensions, Share Schemes may be contacted for technical advice in relation to the tax deduction scheme on 0151–472 6156.

Gross payment. Interest and dividends are payable without deduction of tax where, at the time of payment, they fall into one of the following categories.

(*a*)   A payment to an individual not ordinarily resident in the UK who is beneficially entitled to the payment, or jointly so entitled with other such individuals.

(*b*)   A payment to trustees of a trust in the income of which no person has an interest apart from individuals not ordinarily resident in the UK.

(*c*)   A payment to personal representatives in respect of an investment (or another investment representing an investment) forming part of the estate of a deceased person who was not ordinarily resident in the UK at the time of his death.

(d)   A payment to a charity exempt under *ICTA 1988, s 505(1)(c)*.

(e)   A payment to a pension fund approved under *ICTA 1988, s 592(1)* or whose application for approval is under consideration.

(f)   A payment of interest on a bank loan.

(g)   A payment under a CERTIFICATE OF DEPOSIT (12) issued after 5 April 1983 under which the society is obliged within five years of issue to pay £50,000 or more (exclusive of interest); or on a non-transferable sterling deposit of £50,000 or more for a fixed period of less than five years (which, for deposits made after 5 April 1991, must prohibit partial withdrawals or additions). Such certificates of deposit and other non-transferable deposits may be denominated in a foreign currency, the equivalent £50,000 limit being determined at the time of the deposit.

(h)   A payment on a deposit by a subsidiary of a building society with its parent society (where an election for gross payment is in force).

(i)   A payment for the purposes of an approved personal pension scheme (see 60.2 PERSONAL PENSION SCHEMES).

(j)   A payment in respect of a general client deposit account (see 7.2(vii) BANKS).

(k)   A payment to a local authority within *ICTA 1988, s 842A*.

(l)   A payment into a Lloyd's UNDERWRITERS (89) premiums trust fund.

(m)   All payments to companies (defined to include all bodies corporate and unincorporated associations other than partnerships and local authority associations), health service bodies (within *ICTA 1988, s 519A*) and trustees of unit trust schemes (within *Financial Services and Markets Act 2000, s 237(1)*).

(n)   A payment in respect of a 'qualifying deposit right' (as defined below).

(o)   A payment in respect of an investment held at a non-UK branch.

(p)   A deemed interest payment under *ICTA 1988, s 730A(2)* (price differential on sale and repurchase of securities, see 3.4 ANTI-AVOIDANCE).

(q)   A payment to trustees of a discretionary or accumulation trust (within *ICTA 1988, s 686*, see 81.5 SETTLEMENTS) where the trustees are non-UK resident and all beneficiaries (as widely defined) are either non-UK ordinarily resident individuals (or Scottish partnerships comprising such individuals) or non-UK resident companies.

(r)   (From 6 April 2001) a payment of interest in respect of cash received in connection with a sale and repurchase agreement to which *ICTA 1988, s 730A* (see 3.4 ANTI-AVOIDANCE) applies, and which is required as a result of a variation in the value of the securities concerned as security for performance by the parties to the agreement of their obligations thereunder.

Gross payment also applies where the person beneficially entitled to the interest is UK ordinarily resident (see 65.6 RESIDENCE, ORDINARY RESIDENCE AND DOMICILE) and has supplied the appropriate certificate to the society to the effect that he is unlikely to be liable to income tax for the year of assessment in which the payment is made or credited (taking into account for this purpose all interest arising in the year of assessment concerned which would, in the absence of such a certificate, be received under deduction of lower or basic rate tax). The conditions for certification, and related Revenue information powers, are similar to those described at 7.2 BANKS in relation to gross payment to non-ordinary residents.

Scottish partnerships consisting only of individuals not ordinarily resident in the UK are within the requirements at (a) and (b) above. A payment within (a)–(e) or (i) above may not be made gross unless the society has a written (or, from 6 April 2001, electronic) declaration in a prescribed form from the investor certifying that the relevant conditions are met. This requirement also applies to most companies and to unit trust scheme trustees.

Interest payments completely exempt from income tax (e.g. under ISAs, TESSAs or SAYE schemes or personal equity plans (see 28.13, 28.16, 28.24 EXEMPT INCOME)) are also paid gross. See also below as regards interest on 'quoted Eurobonds'.

Where payments are made gross, liability arises on the recipient under Case III of Schedule D.

Marketable securities. Dividends or interest paid in respect of shares or securities (other than 'qualifying certificates of deposit' or a 'qualifying deposit right') listed, or capable of being listed, on a recognised stock exchange when the dividend etc. became payable are not within the regulations under *ICTA 1988, s 477A* referred to above, but are subject to deduction of tax under *ICTA 1988, s 349* unless the securities are within the 'quoted Eurobonds' exclusion (see 22.3(ii) DEDUCTION OF TAX AT SOURCE). 'Permanent interest bearing shares' (see Tolley's Corporation Tax under Building Societies) issued by a society are within these provisions.

A '*qualifying certificate of deposit*' is a CERTIFICATE OF DEPOSIT (12) for £50,000 or more (exclusive of interest) (or foreign equivalent at the time of the deposit) repayable within five years. A '*qualifying deposit right*' is a right to receive an amount in pursuance of a deposit of money under an arrangement under which no certificate of deposit has been issued, although the person entitled to the right could call for the issue of such a certificate, which otherwise meets the same conditions as a qualifying certificate of deposit. [*ICTA 1988, s 349(3A)(3B)(4), s 477A(1A); FA 1991, Sch 11 paras 1, 2; F(No 2)A 1992, Sch 8 paras 2, 3*].

Code of Practice. The Revenue have published a Code of Practice (No 4) setting out their standards for the carrying out of inspections of tax deduction schemes operated by financial intermediaries.

Simon's Direct Tax Service. See **D4.727–D4.730.**

8.4 **INTEREST PAYABLE TO BUILDING SOCIETIES**

Payments to a building society in respect of advances normally comprise capital repayment plus interest. The interest portion will, for interest paid before 6 April 2000, generally be 'relevant loan interest' which will be paid under deduction of tax by most borrowers (see 22.13 DEDUCTION OF TAX AT SOURCE). Otherwise, no tax is deductible from such payments but the payer is given tax relief (subject to certain restrictions, see 43.5 *et seq.* INTEREST PAYABLE) on the interest portion each year (either by adjustments in PAYE coding or by discharge or repayment).

Where building society interest is paid in connection with a trade, profession or vocation and the payer's income is not sufficient for relief to be given in full, any unrelieved balance may be carried forward against subsequent profits as under *ICTA 1988, s 385*, or used in a terminal loss claim under *ICTA 1988, s 388.* [*ICTA 1988, s 390*]. See under 46 LOSSES.

8.5 **TAX LIABILITY OF A BUILDING SOCIETY ITSELF**

See Tolley's Corporation Tax (under Building Societies).

8.6 **TRANSFER OF BUILDING SOCIETY BUSINESS TO COMPANY**

The acquisition by members of shares on such a transfer is granted certain reliefs from capital gains tax and from treatment as a distribution. [*FA 1988, s 145, Sch 12; TCGA 1992, ss 216, 217*]. See Tolley's Corporation Tax under Building Societies.

Declarations made as to the ordinary residence of depositors and certificates of non-liability given to societies (see 8.3 above) are treated as having been made or given to the successor company. (Revenue Pamphlet IR 1, A69).

Simon's Direct Tax Service. See **D4.771–D4.773**.

9 Capital Allowances

Cross-references. See 14.19 CHARITIES for gifts of plant or machinery to charities; 75.46 SCHEDULE E—EMPLOYMENT INCOME as regards allowances for vehicles used in employment.

Simon's Direct Tax Service Part B2.

Other sources. See Tolley's Capital Allowances (published annually).

9.1   The law relating to capital allowances was consolidated in *Capital Allowances Act 2001* (*CAA 2001*) as part of the Tax Law Rewrite programme. *CAA 2001* also made some (relatively minor) changes to pre-existing law and, subject to the election below, has effect as respects capital allowances (and balancing charges) falling to be made for income tax periods of account ending after 5 April 2001 and for corporation tax accounting periods ending after 31 March 2001. [*CAA 2001, s 579*]. Where a change in the law effected by *CAA 2001* alters the tax consequences for a 'relevant chargeable period' of a transaction or event occurring before the 'relevant date', the person affected may elect for that change not to have effect as regards that chargeable period. With the exception noted in 9.2(vi) below (and also applied in 9.2(vii) below), a *'relevant chargeable period'* is a chargeable period (see 9.2(i) below) ending on or straddling the relevant date. The *'relevant date'* is 6 April 2001 for income tax purposes and 1 April 2001 for corporation tax purposes. Where the same transaction or event so affects more than one person, an election by one is of no effect unless all elect. For income tax purposes, an election must be made on or before the first anniversary of 31 January following the tax year in which the relevant chargeable period ends. For corporation tax purposes, it must be made within two years after the end of the relevant chargeable period. [*CAA 2001, s 577(1), Sch 3 para 8*].

Capital allowances (balancing charges) are a deduction from (addition to) the profits etc. of trades and other qualifying activities in arriving at the taxable amount. The amount of depreciation charged in the accounts of a business is not so allowed. For a full list of qualifying activities in relation to which plant and machinery allowances are available, see 9.24 below. Certain other allowances are given only in relation to trades, some only in relation to particular kinds of trade, and some additionally given against particular sources of non-trading income — details are given in the relevant section of the chapter (see list of headings below).

For income tax purposes, capital allowances/balancing charges are treated as trading expenses/receipts of the period of account (see 9.2(i) below) to which they relate. The same applies throughout for corporation tax purposes, but by reference to the corporation tax accounting period. [*CAA 2001, ss 2, 6; CAA 1990, ss 140, 144; FA 1994, s 211*]. See also 9.2(i) and (xi) below.

Capital allowances are granted in respect of certain types of expenditure detailed in 9.3–9.52 below. See the corresponding chapter of Tolley's Corporation Tax for matters with special relevance to companies.

Headings in this chapter are as follows.

9.2	Matters of general application	9.10	**Industrial buildings**
9.3	Agricultural buildings and works	9.11	— qualifying buildings
		9.12	— qualifying expenditure
9.5	Cemeteries and Crematoria	9.13	— initial allowances
9.6	Dredging	9.14	— writing-down allowances
9.8	Dwelling-houses let on assured tenancies	9.15	— balancing allowances and charges
9.9	Flat conversion		

9.2   MATTERS OF GENERAL APPLICATION

(i) **Meaning of 'chargeable period' and 'period of account'.** For capital allowances purposes, as regards income tax, a '*chargeable period*' is a 'period of account'. As regards corporation tax, a chargeable period is a corporation tax accounting period.

For persons carrying on a trade, profession or vocation, a '*period of account*' means a period for which accounts are drawn up, except that where such a period exceeds 18 months, it is deemed to be split into two or more periods of account, beginning on, or on an anniversary of, the date on which the actual period begins. Exceptionally, where there is an interval between two periods of account, it is deemed to form part of the first such period, and where two periods of account overlap, the common period is deemed to form part of the first such period only.

For non-traders, a period of account is a tax year.

[*CAA 2001, s 6; CAA 1990, ss 140, 160, 161(2); FA 1994, ss 211, 212*].

See the examples at 9.33 below.

(ii) **Claims.** Capital allowances are given only if a claim is made. Such a claim can only be made by inclusion in the annual tax return (subject to the very limited exceptions at *CAA 2001, s 3(4)(5)*). [*CAA 2001, s 3, Sch 2 para 103(2); CAA 1990, s 140(3); FA 1994, s 211; FA 1998, Sch 18 para 79*]. See 68.4 RETURNS as regards amendments to income tax returns, and the time allowed for making them. See the corresponding chapter of Tolley's Corporation Tax for the rules on amendments to, and withdrawal of, capital allowances claims made in company tax returns. For corporation tax accounting periods ending after 30 September 1993 and before 1 July 1999, capital allowances claims by companies had to be included in the annual tax return or amended return, but were subject to special time limits, for which see Tolley's Corporation Tax.

(iii) **Capital expenditure.** References in the capital allowances legislation to the incurring of capital expenditure and the paying of capital sums exclude any sums allowed as deductions in computing the payer's profits or earnings and sums payable under deduction of tax. Corresponding rules apply as regards the receipt of such sums. [*CAA 2001, s 4, Sch 3 para 9; CAA 1990, s 159(1)(1A); FA 1997, Sch 15 paras 7, 9; FA 1998, Sch 5 para 60; ITEPA 2003, Sch 6 para 247*].

(iv) **Time expenditure incurred.** Capital expenditure (other than that constituted by an 'additional VAT liability' — see (viii) below) is generally treated, for capital allowances purposes, as incurred as soon as there is an unconditional obligation to pay it, even if all or part of it is not required to be paid until some later date. However, expenditure is treated as incurred on a later date in the following circumstances.

- Where any part of the expenditure is not required to be paid until a date more than four months after the date determined as above, it is treated as incurred on that later date.

- Where an obligation to pay becomes unconditional earlier than in accordance with normal commercial usage, with the sole or main benefit likely to be the bringing forward of the chargeable period in which the expenditure would otherwise be treated as incurred, it is instead treated as incurred on the date on or before which it is required to be paid.

Where, as a result of an event such as the issuing of a certificate, an obligation to pay becomes unconditional within one month after the end of a chargeable period, but at or before the end of that chargeable period the asset concerned has become the property of, or is otherwise attributed under the contract to, the person having the obligation, the expenditure is treated as incurred immediately before the end of that chargeable period.

The above provisions do not override any specific rule under which expenditure is treated as incurred later than the relevant time given above.

[*CAA 2001, s 5; CAA 1990, s 159(2)–(8); FA 1991, Sch 14 para 14; FA 1994, Sch 26 Pt V(24)*].

Simon's Direct Tax Service. See **B2.104**.

(v) **Exclusion of double allowances.** Where an allowance is made to a person under one of the following codes of allowances, he cannot obtain an allowance under another of those codes in respect of that expenditure or the provision of any asset to which that expenditure related:

- agricultural buildings allowances (9.3 below);

- allowances for expenditure on dredging (9.6 below);

- allowances for dwelling-houses let on assured tenancies (9.8 below);

- allowances for expenditure on flat conversion (9.9 below);

- industrial buildings allowances (9.10–9.23 below);

- allowances for mineral extraction (9.39–9.49 below);

- research and development (formerly scientific research) allowances (9.52 below).

Similarly, no allowance under any of the above codes can be made in respect of any expenditure that has been allocated to a plant and machinery pool (see 9.28 below), and on which a plant or machinery allowance (or balancing charge) has consequently been given (or made), or any related asset (as above); and expenditure which has attracted an allowance under any of the above codes (and any related asset) cannot be allocated to a plant and machinery pool.

Additional rules apply under *CAA 2001, s 9* to prevent double allowances in relation to plant or machinery treated as fixtures (as at 9.34 below).

[*CAA 2001, ss 7–10, Sch 3 para 10; CAA 1990, s 147; FA 1993, Sch 13 para 13; FA 1997, Sch 16 para 7*].

Where an item of expenditure qualifies for more than one type of capital allowance, it is the taxpayer's choice as to which to claim, but he cannot alter his choice in later years. (Revenue Capital Allowances Manual CA 16000).

Simon's Direct Tax Service. See B2.114.

(vi) **Expenditure met by another's contributions.** Subject to the exceptions below, a person is not regarded as incurring expenditure for capital allowances purposes (other than for dredging — see below) to the extent that it is met, or will be met, directly or indirectly by another person or by a *'public body'*, i.e. the Crown or any government or public or local authority (whether in the UK or elsewhere). For the scope of 'public authority', see *McKinney v Hagans Caravans (Manufacturing) Ltd CA(NI) 1997, 69 TC 526*. There is an exception where the expenditure is met by a Regional Development Grant or NI equivalent (for which see *SI 1995 No 611, SI 1997 No 660, SI 1999 No 719, SI 2001 No 810* and predecessor orders). (Note that applications for Regional Development Grants were not accepted after 31 March 1988, but NI equivalents do continue.) Expenditure met by insurance or other compensation money due in respect of a destroyed, demolished or defunct asset is not excluded from allowances (though this exception did not apply for the purpose of research and development (formerly scientific research) allowances before *CAA 2001* had effect).

As regards allowances for dredging (see 9.6 below), the above is replaced by a rule to the effect that a person is not regarded as incurring expenditure for the purposes of his trade or future trade to the extent that it is met, or will be met, directly or indirectly by a public body or by capital sums contributed by another person *for purposes other than those of the fore-mentioned trade.*

The main rule above (but not the rule for dredging) is disapplied, and allowances are thus available, if the contributor is not a public body and can obtain neither a capital allowance on his contribution by virtue of (vii) below nor a deduction against profits of a trade, profession or vocation. Where *CAA 2001* has effect (see 9.1 above), and for the purposes of plant and machinery allowances only, this is extended to cover profits of any qualifying activity within 9.24(iii)–(vi) below. In relation to this particular change in law, the *'relevant chargeable period'* for the purposes of the election in 9.1 above (to defer the application of *CAA 2001*) is the earliest chargeable period for which the tax consequences of the transaction or event are altered — this exception to the rule recognises that a contribution might be made before the relevant date in 9.1 above to expenditure incurred in a chargeable period beginning after that date.

[*CAA 2001, ss 532–536, Sch 2 para 19, Sch 3 paras 106–108; CAA 1990, ss 134(8), 153; ICTA 1988, s 91(9), s 532(1)*].

The main rule above is also disapplied in relation to certain contributions by pools promoters towards football ground improvements, despite their being an allowable deduction in the pools promoter's business (see 71.75 SCHEDULE D, CASES I AND II). [*FA 1990, s 126; CAA 2001, Sch 2 para 72*].

9.2 Capital Allowances

Repaid grants. Where a grant which has been deducted from expenditure qualifying for capital allowances (as above) is later repaid (in whole or part), the repayment will, by concession, be treated as expenditure qualifying for capital allowances. Where allowances were restricted in respect of a contribution from a person (other than a public body) who himself obtained either a capital allowance under (vii) below or a trading deduction for his contribution (as above), this treatment is dependent upon the repayment falling to be taxed on the recipient through a balancing charge or as a trading receipt. (Revenue Pamphlet IR 1, B49 as revised).

Simon's Direct Tax Service. See B2.111.

(vii) **Contribution allowances.** Contributors towards another person's capital expenditure on an asset may receive allowances ('*contribution allowances*') where the contribution is for the purposes of a trade or 'relevant activity' carried on (or to be carried on) by the contributor, and where the expenditure would otherwise have entitled the other person (assuming him not to be a public body) to agricultural buildings, industrial buildings, plant and machinery or mineral extraction allowances. Contribution allowances are not available where the contributor and the other person are CONNECTED PERSONS (19). A '*relevant activity*' is a profession or vocation or, where *CAA 2001* has effect and for the purposes of plant and machinery allowances only, an activity within 9.24(iii)–(vi) below; the same comments apply as in (vi) above as regards this particular change in the law.

Contribution allowances are such as would have been made if the contribution had been expended on the provision for the contributor's trade etc. of a similar asset and as if the asset were at all material times used for the purposes of the contributor's trade etc. (so that balancing adjustments do not apply to such contributions). As regards plant and machinery, the contributor's deemed expenditure can only be allocated to a single asset pool (see 9.28 below). On a transfer of the trade etc., or part thereof, the allowances (or part) are subsequently made to the transferee.

In relation to agricultural buildings and industrial buildings allowances, the conditions are satisfied if the contribution is made for the purposes of a trade etc. carried on by a tenant of land in which the contributor has an interest. Entitlement to writing-down allowances passes to any person becoming entitled to the interest held by the contributor at the time of the contribution.

[*CAA 2001, ss 537–542, Sch 3 paras 109, 110; CAA 1990, ss 154, 155; FA 1990, Sch 13 para 5; FA 2001, s 67, Sch 19 Pt II paras 3, 4*].

Capital contributions towards expenditure on dredging are treated as expenditure incurred by the contributor on that dredging. [*CAA 2001, s 543; CAA 1990, s 134(8)*].

Simon's Direct Tax Service. See B2.112.

(viii) **VAT capital goods scheme.** Under the VAT capital goods scheme, the input tax originally claimed on the acquisition of certain capital assets is subject to amendment within a specified period of adjustment in accordance with any increase or decrease in the extent to which the asset is used in making taxable, as opposed to exempt, supplies for VAT purposes. The items covered by the scheme are limited to land and buildings (or parts of buildings) worth at least £250,000 and computers (and items of computer equipment) worth at least £50,000. See Tolley's Value Added Tax under Capital Goods Scheme for a full description.

Special capital allowances provisions apply where a VAT adjustment is made under the capital goods scheme. These affect allowances for industrial buildings, plant and machinery and research and development (formerly scientific research), and the provisions specific to each are described in the appropriate sections of this chapter. General definitions and provisions are described below.

'*Additional VAT liability*' and '*additional VAT rebate*' mean, respectively,

- an amount which a person becomes liable to pay, or

- an amount which he becomes entitled to deduct

by way of adjustment under the VAT capital goods scheme in respect of input tax. Generally (but see below), such a liability or rebate is treated as incurred or made on the last day of the period

- which is one of the periods making up the applicable VAT period of adjustment under the VAT capital goods scheme, and

- in which occurred the increase or decrease in use giving rise to the liability or rebate.

However, for the purpose of determining the chargeable period (see (i) above) in which it accrues, an additional VAT liability or rebate is treated as accruing on whichever is the relevant day below.

- Where the liability or rebate is accounted for in a VAT return, the last day of the period covered by that return.

- If, before the making of a VAT return, Customs and Excise assess the liability or rebate, the day on which the assessment is made.

- If the trade (or other qualifying activity — see 9.24 below) is permanently discontinued before the liability or rebate has been accounted for in a VAT return and before the making of an assessment, the last day of the chargeable period in which the cessation occurs.

Where an allowance or charge falls to be determined by reference to a proportion only of the expenditure incurred or a proportion only of what that allowance or charge would otherwise have been, a related additional VAT liability or rebate is similarly apportioned.

[*CAA 2001, ss 546–551; CAA 1990, s 159A; FA 1991, Sch 14 para 14; FA 1994, Sch 26 Pt V(24)*].

Simon's Direct Tax Service. See B2.103, B2.104.

(ix) **Composite sales** may be apportioned by Appeal Commissioners regardless of any separate prices attributed in the sale agreement. [*CAA 2001, ss 562–564; CAA 1990, ss 150, 151*]. See *Fitton v Gilders & Heaton Ch D 1955, 36 TC 233*, and *Wood v Provan CA 1968, 44 TC 701*.

(x) **Finance leasing.** See 71.58 SCHEDULE D, CASES I AND II as regards restrictions on capital allowances where certain finance leasing arrangements are involved. See also 9.28, 9.38(A)(C) below.

(xi) **Recovery of assets under** *Proceeds of Crime Act 2002, Pt 5. Proceeds of Crime Act 2002, Pt 5 Ch 2* provides for the recovery, in civil proceedings before the High Court (or, in Scotland, the Court of Session), of property which is, or represents, property obtained through 'unlawful conduct' (as defined in the *Act*). If the Court is satisfied that any property is recoverable under the provisions, it will make a '*recovery order*', vesting the property in an appointed trustee for civil recovery. Alternatively, the Court may make an order under *section 276* of the *Act* staying (or, in Scotland, sisting) proceedings on terms agreed by the parties. The vesting of property in a trustee for civil recovery or any other person, either under a recovery order or in pursuance of a *section 276* order, is known as a *Pt 5* transfer. A *'compensating payment'* may in some cases be made to the person who held the property immediately before the transfer. If the order provides for the creation of any interest in favour of that person, he is treated as receiving (in addition to any other compensating payment) a compensating payment equal to the value of the interest. [*Proceeds of Crime Act 2002, ss 240(1), 266(1)(2), 276, 316(1), 448, Sch 10 para 2*].

Where the property in question is plant or machinery, the relevant interest in an industrial building or in a flat (within 9.9 below), or an asset representing qualifying expenditure on research and development (within 9.52 below), there are provisions to ensure that the *Pt 5* transfer has a tax-neutral effect, unless a compensating payment is made to the transferor in which case its amount and/or value must be brought into account as a disposal value or, as the case may be, as proceeds from a balancing event. [*Proceeds of Crime Act 2002, Sch 10 paras 12–29*].

(xii) **Avoidance affecting proceeds of balancing event.** An anti-avoidance rule has been introduced to prevent a balancing allowance being created or increased by means of any tax avoidance scheme that depresses an asset's market value and thus the amount to be brought into account on a balancing event (e.g. a sale) or as a disposal value. The rule denies entitlement to a balancing allowance, though the unrelieved balance of expenditure immediately after the event must be computed as if the allowance had been made. The rule applies to allowances for industrial buildings, agricultural buildings, flat conversion expenditure, dwelling-houses let on assured tenancies and mineral extraction (but not, for example, to plant and machinery allowances). It applies in relation to any event occurring after 26 November 2002 that would otherwise occasion a balancing allowance, except where it occurs in pursuance of a contract entered into on or before that date and is not consequent upon the exercise after that date of any option or right. [*CAA 2001, s 570A; FA 2003, s 164*].

Simon's Direct Tax Service. See **B2.244.**

9.3   **AGRICULTURAL BUILDINGS AND WORKS**

The current code of capital allowances for agricultural buildings and works (as described below) applies to expenditure incurred **on or after 1 April 1986 (1 April 1987** where it was incurred under a contract entered into before 14 March 1984). [*CAA 2001, Sch 3 para 82; CAA 1990, s 123*].

Qualifying buildings etc. Writing-down, and previously (in certain cases) initial, allowances (see below) are given in respect of capital expenditure incurred for the purposes of 'husbandry' on the construction of buildings (such as farmhouses (but see (*b*) below), farm buildings or cottages), fences or other works. [*CAA 2001, s 361(1)(2); CAA 1990, ss 123, 124(1), 124A; FA 1993, Sch 12 paras 2, 3*]. 'Capital expenditure on construction' includes preliminary demolition costs (unless already taken into account for industrial buildings allowance purposes, see 9.15 below), expenditure on reconstruction, alteration or improvement and architect's fees, and 'other works' includes e.g. drainage and sewage works, water and electricity installations, walls, shelter belts of trees, silos, farm roads, land reclamation and hedge demolition. (Revenue Capital Allowances Manual CA 40100, 40200). Cottages occupied by retired farm workers and buildings constructed to provide welfare facilities for employees may qualify for allowances, as may farm shops to the extent that they sell produce of the farm. (Revenue Capital Allowances Manual CA 40100). *'Husbandry'* includes any method of intensive rearing of livestock or fish on a commercial basis for the production of food for human consumption, and also 'short rotation coppice' (see 71.47(*i*) SCHEDULE D, CASES I AND II). [*CAA 2001, s 362; CAA 1990, s 133(1); FA 1995, s 154(1)*].

Market gardening, whether of plants or flowers or for the production of food, is treated in the same way as farming for allowance purposes, and a house which is the centre of such operations is treated as a farmhouse (see (*b*) below). (This commentary is not included in the current Revenue Capital Allowances Manual but was previously at CA 4509 and is presumed still to be of application.)

Qualifying expenditure. Allowances are available where a person who has a 'freehold' or 'leasehold' interest in land in the UK occupied wholly or mainly for the purposes of husbandry incurs capital expenditure on qualifying buildings etc. (as set out above) for the purposes of husbandry on that land. The building etc. on which the expenditure is incurred does not have to be on the land in question, e.g. a farmworker's cottage in a nearby village might qualify (this commentary, although not included in the current Revenue Capital Allowances Manual having previously been at CA 4504 and being presumed still to be of application). A *'freehold'* interest in land is the fee simple estate in the land or an agreement to acquire that interest (or Scottish equivalent), and a *'leasehold'* interest is the interest of a tenant in property subject to a lease (including an agreement for a lease if the lease term has begun and any tenancy, but excluding a mortgage). The expenditure is *'qualifying expenditure'* except that:

(*a*)   expenditure on the acquisition of the land or rights over the land is excluded;

(*b*)   a maximum of one-third of expenditure on the construction of a farmhouse may qualify (reduced as is just and reasonable where the accommodation and amenities are disproportionate to the nature and extent of the farm). For the meaning of 'farmhouse', see *Lindsay v CIR CS 1953, 34 TC 289, CIR v Whiteford & Sons CS 1962, 40 TC 379, Korner v CIR HL 1969, 45 TC 287,* and Revenue Capital Allowances Manual CA 40100 (including the circumstances in which it may be accepted that a farm has two farmhouses); and

(*c*)   only a just and reasonable proportion of expenditure on assets (other than the farmhouse) only partly used for the purposes of husbandry on the land in question may qualify.

[*CAA 2001, ss 361(1)(2), 363, 369, 393, Sch 3 para 81; CAA 1990, ss 123, 124(1)(2), 124A(4), 125(1), 133(1)(6)*].

As regards *buildings etc. bought unused,* similar provisions apply as in the case of industrial buildings (see 9.12 below), modified to take account of the restrictions and exclusions referred to above. [*CAA 2001, ss 370, 374; CAA 1990, ss 127, 127A, 133(7); FA 1993, Sch 12 paras 5, 6*].

Where a person is entitled to different 'relevant interests' (see below) in different parts of the land, the expenditure is apportioned on a just and reasonable basis, and these provisions apply separately to the expenditure apportioned to each part. (This is now provided for by *CAA 2001, s 371,* but the Revenue consider that the requirement for apportionment was implicit in the provisions applying before *CAA 2001* came into effect (see 9.1 above). See Note 49 in Annex 2 to the Explanatory Notes to the 2001 Capital Allowances Bill.)

Initial allowances. An initial allowance was available to a person incurring qualifying expenditure under a contract entered into in the twelve-month period **1 November 1992 to 31 October 1993 inclusive,** or for the purpose of securing compliance with obligations incurred under a contract entered into during that period, but not for expenditure incurred under a contract entered into for the purpose of securing compliance with obligations under a contract entered into before 1 November 1992. The qualifying building must have come to be used for the purposes of husbandry before 1 January 1995, and, if this condition was not satisfied or if the building first came to be used for purposes other than husbandry, any initial allowance given will have been withdrawn. The initial allowance was **20%** of the expenditure incurred, and was given for the chargeable period related to the incurring of the expenditure. For income tax purposes and, as regards company accounting periods ended after 30 September 1993, for corporation tax purposes, either a smaller initial allowance could be claimed or the initial allowance not claimed at all; for earlier accounting periods, a company could disclaim the initial allowance in whole or in part by giving written notice to the inspector within two years after the end of the accounting period concerned. [*CAA 1990, s 124A(1)–(3), (5)–(7); FA 1993, Sch 12 para 3*].

Writing-down allowances are made to the person who for the time being has the '*relevant interest*' in relation to the qualifying expenditure, i.e. (except as follows) the interest in the land in question to which the person incurring the expenditure was entitled when the expenditure was incurred. If there is more than one such interest and one was reversionary on all the others, that one is the relevant interest. The creation of a lease to which the relevant interest is subject is disregarded for these purposes. Where an interest in land has been conveyed or assigned by way of security subject to a right of redemption, it will still be treated as belonging to the person with the right of redemption. [*CAA 2001, ss 361(3), 364–366; CAA 1990, ss 123(1), 125(1)–(4), 126(4), 133(4)*]. When a leasehold relevant interest is surrendered or reverts, the interest into which it merges becomes the relevant interest, unless a new lease takes effect on the extinguishment. Otherwise, on a leasehold relevant interest coming to an end, if a new lease is granted to the former lessee, the lessee is treated as continuing to have the same relevant interest. (Under *CAA 2001* this applies equally where the new lease is of only part of the land subject to the old lease. This makes statutory the approach previously adopted in practice, see Change 42 listed in Annex 1 to the Explanatory Notes to the 2001 Capital Allowances Bill.) If the new lease is granted to a person other than the former lessee, the relevant interest is treated as acquired by the new lessee if he makes a payment to the former lessee for the assets representing the expenditure in question. In any other case, the interest of the landlord under the former lease is treated as becoming the relevant interest. [*CAA 2001, ss 367, 368; CAA 1990, ss 125(4), 126(4)(5)*].

A person is entitled to an allowance for any chargeable period (see 9.2(i) above) at any time during which he is entitled to the relevant interest. Allowances are given at the rate of **4% p.a.** of the qualifying expenditure (or such lesser amount as may be claimed) during a period of 25 years beginning on the first day of the chargeable period (of the person incurring the expenditure) during which the expenditure was incurred, so as to give aggregate allowances (including any initial allowance) up to the amount of that expenditure. If the buildings etc. in fact come to be first used other than for the purposes of husbandry, no writing-down allowance can be made in respect of the related expenditure and any allowance previously given is withdrawn. A writing-down allowance could be given for the same chargeable period as an initial allowance under *CAA 1990, s 124A* (see above) in respect of the same expenditure, but only if the building etc. came to be used for the purposes of husbandry before the end of that chargeable period. [*CAA 2001, ss 372–374; CAA 1990, s 123, s 124(2), s 124B; FA 1993, Sch 12 para 3*]. If the conditions are met when the expenditure is incurred and the first use is for the purposes of husbandry, allowances continue throughout the writing-down period without regard to any change of use of the building in later years. (Revenue Capital Allowances Manual CA 41100).

Transfer of relevant interest. Where a person entitled to allowances in respect of capital expenditure as above ceases to own the relevant interest in the land (or part of the land) giving rise to that entitlement, and another person acquires that interest, the right to the writing-down allowances (or appropriate part) is transferred to the new owner of the interest (proportionate allowances being given where the transfer falls during a chargeable period (see 9.2(i) above) of either the former or the new owner). See below as regards allowances where the transfer is a 'balancing event'. [*CAA 2001, s 375; CAA 1990, s*

126(1)–(3); FA 1993, Sch 12 para 4(1)(2); FA 1994, Sch 26 Pt V(24)]. If, by virtue of a transfer of the relevant interest, the total allowances which were or could have been claimed (disregarding any anti-avoidance etc. restrictions on balancing allowances) during the writing-down period would otherwise be less than the amount of the expenditure, then the difference is made up in the chargeable period in which the writing-down period ends. [*CAA 2001, s 379; CAA 1990, s 126(6)*].

Balancing events. A '*balancing event*' occurs when the relevant interest in land (or part) is acquired by another person (see above) or when the building etc. (or part) on construction of which the expenditure was incurred is demolished, destroyed, or otherwise ceases altogether to be used, *provided that* a written election to that effect is made. (Before the enactment of *CAA 2001* (see 9.1 above), the words 'ceases to exist as such' rather than 'ceases altogether to be used' were employed. See Change 44 listed in Annex 1 to the Explanatory Notes to the 2001 Capital Allowances Bill.) The election must be made (i) for income tax, within twelve months after 31 January following the tax year in which ends the chargeable period in which the balancing event occurs, and (ii) for corporation tax, within two years after the end of such chargeable period. The election must be made jointly in the case of acquisition of the relevant interest, but otherwise by the former owner only. An election may not be made by a person outside the charge to income or corporation tax, nor if the sole or main benefit of an acquisition was the obtaining of an allowance or greater allowance (but ignoring *CAA 2001, ss 568, 573* (previously *CAA 1990, s 157*), see below). [*CAA 2001, ss 381, 382; CAA 1990, s 129; FA 1993, Sch 12 para 8; FA 1994, Sch 26 Pt V(24); FA 1996, s 135, Sch 21 para 33*].

Where a balancing event occurs in a chargeable (or basis) period for which an allowance would otherwise have been available, no such allowance is made, but a balancing adjustment arises for that period on or to the person entitled to the relevant interest immediately before the balancing event. If the residue of expenditure immediately before the balancing event (i.e. after deducting any allowances previously given and adding any balancing charges previously made) exceeds any sale, compensation etc. receipts, a balancing allowance equal to that excess is made (subject to the anti-avoidance rule at 9.2(xii) above). If any sale, compensation etc. receipts exceed that residue, a balancing charge is made equal to the excess (but limited to the allowances previously given to the person on whom the charge arises). Allowances made to a husband before 6 April 1990 in respect of his wife's relevant interest are treated as having been made to the wife for these purposes on a balancing event on or after that date. [*CAA 2001, ss 377, 380, 383–388, Sch 3 para 80; CAA 1990, s 128; FA 1993, Sch 12 para 7; FA 1994, Sch 26 Pt V(24)*].

Where a balancing event occurs on the transfer of the relevant interest, the writing-down allowances available to the new owner consist of the residue of expenditure (see above) immediately before the balancing event, plus any balancing charge or less any balancing allowance consequent on that event, spread over the period from the balancing event to the end of the original 25 year writing-down period. For this purpose, any balancing allowance which (on that or any previous balancing event) has been reduced or denied under *CAA 2001, s 389* or *CAA 1990, s 130* (see below) is treated as having been made in full. [*CAA 2001, ss 376, 378; CAA 1990, ss 129(3), 130(3); FA 1994, Sch 26 Pt V(24)*].

Making of allowances and charges. An initial, writing-down or balancing adjustment for a chargeable period is given or made in taxing a trade. If no trade is carried on in that chargeable period, then allowances and charges are treated as expenses and receipts of a Schedule A business (see 69.3 SCHEDULE A) or, where the taxpayer is not, in fact, carrying on such a business, of a deemed Schedule A business. [*CAA 2001, ss 391, 392; CAA 1990, s 132; FA 1995, Sch 6 para 35; FA 1998, s 38, Sch 5 para 59*]. See also 9.2(i)(ii)(xi) above, and see 69.12 SCHEDULE A as regards Schedule A losses.

9.4 Capital Allowances

There are **connected person** and **anti-avoidance provisions** in respect of certain balancing events, similar to those applicable to industrial buildings allowances (see 9.22(i) below). [*CAA 2001, ss 389, 390, 567, 568, 570(1), 573; CAA 1990, ss 130, 133(8)(9), 157, 158(5)*].

Simon's Direct Tax Service. See B2.5.

9.4   *Example*

Farmer Jones prepares accounts annually to 31 December and has incurred the following expenditure

		£
12.1.99	Extension to farmhouse	12,000
3.6.2000	Construction of cattle court	15,000
26.4.01	Erection of barn	10,000
15.10.04	Replacement barn for that acquired on 26.4.01 which was destroyed by fire in September 2004. The insurance proceeds totalled £5,200	20,000

The agricultural buildings allowances are as follows.

Date of expenditure £	Cost £	Residue brought forward £	Allowances WDA 4% £	Residue carried forward £
1999/2000 (period of account — year to 31.12.99)				
12.1.99	4,000		160	3,840
2000/01 (period of account — year to 31.12.2000)				
12.1.99	4,000	3,840	160	3,680
3.6.2000	15,000		600	14,400
	£19,000	£3,840	£760	£18,080
2001/02 (period of account — year to 31.12.01)				
12.1.99	4,000	3,680	160	3,520
3.6.2000	15,000	14,400	600	13,800
26.4.01	10,000		400	9,600
	£29,000	£18,080	£1,160	£26,920
2002/03 (period of account — year to 31.12.02)				
12.1.99	4,000	3,520	160	3,360
3.6.2000	15,000	13,800	600	13,200
26.4.01	10,000	9,600	400	9,200
	£29,000	£26,920	£1,160	£25,760

Date of expenditure	Cost	Residue brought forward	Allowances WDA 4%	Residue carried forward
	£	£	£	£

2003/04 (period of account — year to 31.12.03)

Date of expenditure	Cost	Residue brought forward	Allowances WDA 4%	Residue carried forward
12.1.99	4,000	3,360	160	3,200
3.6.2000	15,000	13,200	600	12,600
26.4.01	10,000	9,200	400	8,800
	£29,000	£25,760	£1,160	£24,600

2004/05 (period of account — year to 31.12.04)

(i) No election for a balancing adjustment

Date of expenditure	Cost	Residue brought forward	Allowances WDA 4%	Residue carried forward
12.1.99	4,000	3,200	160	3,040
3.6.2000	15,000	12,600	600	12,000
26.4.01	10,000	8,800	400	8,400
15.10.04	20,000		800	19,200
	£49,000	£24,600	£1,960	£42,640

(ii) Election for a balancing adjustment

Date of expenditure	Cost	Residue brought forward	Allowances WDA 4%	Residue carried forward
12.1.99	4,000	3,200	160	3,040
3.6.2000	15,000	12,600	600	12,000
15.10.04	20,000		800	19,200
	£39,000	£15,800	£1,560	£34,240

Balancing allowance

	£
Proceeds	5,200
Written-down value	8,800

Balancing allowance   £3,600

9.5   CEMETERIES AND CREMATORIA [*ICTA 1988, s 91*]

Cemeteries. In computing profits of a trade consisting of or including the carrying on of a cemetery, a deduction as a trading expense of any period is allowed for

(i)   *cost of land* (including cost of levelling, draining or making suitable) *sold for interments,* or in relation to which *interment rights are sold,* in that period, and

(ii)   a *proportion* (based on ratio of number of grave spaces sold in the period to that number plus those still available) of the *residual capital expenditure* at the end of the period. *Capital expenditure* for this purpose is expenditure on any building or structure (excluding dwelling houses) and underlying or surplus land, likely to have little or no value when the cemetery is full. (Certain expenditure before the 1954/55 basis period is excluded.) The *residue* is the balance of such expenditure after

115

deducting amounts previously allowed under this section and any sale or insurance etc. receipts in respect of assets (the subject of such expenditure) sold or destroyed.

Changes of ownership of the trade (whether otherwise treated as a discontinuance or not) are ignored — allowances continue as they would to the original trader. [*ICTA 1988, s 91(5)*].

For the treatment of lump sums for grave maintenance etc., see Revenue Business Income Manual BIM 52505, 52510.

Crematoria attract similar allowances, substituting memorial garden plots for cemetery land, grave-spaces or interments. [*ICTA 1988, s 91(7)*]. See also *Bourne v Norwich Crematorium Ch D 1967, 44 TC 164*.

For the treatment of expenditure and receipts in connection with the provision of niches and memorials, see Revenue Business Income Manual BIM 52520, 52525.

Simon's Direct Tax Service. See **B3.1131, B3.1132**.

Example

GE, who operates a funeral service, owns a cemetery for which accounts to 31 December are prepared. The accounts to 31.12.04 reveal the following

(i)	Cost of land representing 110 grave spaces sold in period	£3,400
(ii)	Number of grave spaces remaining	275
(iii)	Residual capital expenditure on buildings and other land unsuitable for interments	£18,250

The allowances available are £

(*a*)   Item (i) 3,400

(*b*) $\dfrac{110}{110 + 275} \times £18,250$ 5,214

£8,614

Note

(*a*)   £8,614 will be allowed as a deduction in computing GE's Schedule D, Case I profits for the period of account ending on 31 December 2004.

9.6   **DREDGING** [*CAA 2001, ss 484–489; CAA 1990, ss 134, 135*]

Writing-down, balancing and, previously, initial allowances may be claimed for capital expenditure on **dredging** incurred for the purposes of a *qualifying trade* (provided that neither industrial buildings allowances (see 9.10 below) nor plant and machinery allowances (see 9.24 below) are available in respect of the same expenditure).

'*Dredging*' must be done in the interests of navigation, and either

(i)   the qualifying trade must consist of the maintenance or improvement of navigation of a harbour, estuary or waterway, or

(ii)   the dredging must be for the benefit of vessels coming to, leaving or using docks or other premises used in the qualifying trade.

It includes removal, by any means, of any part of, or projections from, any sea or inland water bed (whether then above water or not), and the widening of any inland waterway.

A *'qualifying trade'* is one either within (i) above or within the industrial buildings allowance definitions at 9.11(*a*)–(*c*) below. Expenditure only partly for a qualifying trade is apportioned as may be just and reasonable, and for this purpose, where part only of a trade qualifies, the qualifying and non-qualifying parts are treated as separate trades.

[*CAA 2001, ss 484, 485; CAA 1990, s 134(1)(6), s 135(1)(3)*].

Initial allowances were given for the year of assessment in whose basis period the expenditure was incurred at the following rates.

From 6 April 1956 —   10%
From 15 April 1958 —   15% (5% where certain investment allowances were payable between 8 April 1959 and 16 January 1966).

[*CAA 1968, s 67(1)(a)(8), Sch 1*].

Initial allowances were **abolished** for expenditure incurred **after 31 March 1986**, unless incurred before 1 April 1987 under a contract entered into before 14 March 1984 by the person incurring the expenditure. [*FA 1985, s 61*].

Writing-down allowances are given to the person for the time being carrying on the trade during a writing-down period of 25 years (50 years for expenditure incurred before 6 November 1962) beginning with the first day of the chargeable period in which the expenditure was incurred, subject to an overall restriction on allowances (initial and writing-down) of the amount of the expenditure. No allowance is given for a chargeable period in which a balancing allowance arises (see below). The rates of allowance, fixed by the date expenditure was incurred, are as follows (although a lesser amount may be claimed).

Before 6 November 1962 — 2% p.a.
From 6 November 1962 — 4% p.a.

[*CAA 2001, ss 487, 489, Sch 3 para 103; CAA 1990, s 134(1), s 135(2), s 146; FA 1994, s 211(2), s 213(9), Sch 26 Pt V(24)*].

Expenditure incurred for a trade before it is carried on attracts allowances as if it were incurred on the first day on which the trade was carried on. Similarly, expenditure incurred in connection with a dock etc. with a view to occupying it for the purposes of a qualifying trade other than one within (i) above attracts allowances as if it were incurred when the dock etc. is first so occupied. [*CAA 2001, s 486*]. Slightly different rules applied before *CAA 2001* came into effect (see 9.1 above and Change 57 listed in Annex 1 to the Explanatory Notes to the 2001 Capital Allowances Bill). [*CAA 1990, ss 134(7), 135(2)*].

A **balancing allowance** is given for the chargeable period of *permanent discontinuance* of the trade, equal to expenditure incurred less initial and writing-down allowances given, to the person last carrying on the trade. The allowance includes expenditure incurred before 6 April 1956, but in relation to such expenditure, all possible allowances (other than initial allowances) are deemed to have been given in respect of 1955/56 and earlier years as if the provisions introduced by *FA 1956* had always been in force.

Permanent discontinuance includes sale of the business (unless it is a sale between CONNECTED PERSONS (19), or without change of control, or one the sole or main benefit of which appears to be a capital allowance advantage), but not deemed discontinuance under *ICTA 1988, s 113* (change in person(s) carrying on trade) or certain corporation tax provisions.

[*CAA 2001, s 488, Sch 3 para 104; CAA 1990, s 134(2)–(4)*].

9.7 Capital Allowances

Contributions to expenditure. See 9.2(vi)(vii) above.

Simon's Direct Tax Service. See **B2.8**.

9.7 *Example*

D is the proprietor of an estuary maintenance business preparing accounts to 30 June. Expenditure qualifying for dredging allowances is incurred as follows.

	£
Year ended 30.6.03	4,000
Year ended 30.6.04	5,000

On 2 January 2005, D sells the business to an unconnected third party.

The allowances available are

Date of expenditure	Cost	Residue brought forward	Allowances WDA 4%	Residue carried forward
	£	£	£	£
2003/04 (year ended 30.6.03)				
2003	4,000	—	160	£3,840
2004/05				
Year ended 30.6.04				
2003	4,000	3,840	160	3,680
2004	5,000	—	200	4,800
			£360	£8,480

Six months ending 2.1.05

Balancing allowance	£8,480

Total allowances 2004/05 (360 + 8,480)	£8,840

9.8 **DWELLING-HOUSES LET ON ASSURED TENANCIES** [*CAA 2001, ss 490–531; CAA 1990, ss 84–97*]

Legislation was introduced by *FA 1982* to give capital allowances on capital expenditure incurred by an '*approved body*' (i.e. a body specified by the Secretary of State under *Housing Act 1980, s 56(4)*), on the construction of buildings consisting of, or including, dwelling-houses let on assured and certain other tenancies, after 9 March 1982 and before 1 April 1992. [*CAA 2001, ss 490(1), 491, 492; CAA 1990, ss 84, 96(3)*]. The provisions were substantially modified following repeal of the relevant sections of the *Housing Act 1980* by the *Housing Act 1988*.

A dwelling-house is a '*qualifying dwelling-house*' when it is let on a tenancy being an assured tenancy within *Housing Act 1980, s 56* (or, not being an assured shorthold tenancy, within *Housing Act 1988*) and continues to qualify at any time when

(i) it is subject to a regulated tenancy or a housing association tenancy (as defined in the *Rent Act 1977*), and

(ii) the landlord under the tenancy either is or has been an approved body.

[*CAA 2001, s 490(2)–(5); CAA 1990, s 86(1)(2)(4), s 97(1)*].

A dwelling-house does not qualify

(*a*) unless the landlord is a company (applicable to expenditure contracted and incurred after 4 May 1983, or where a person other than a company becomes entitled to the 'relevant interest' after that date) and either is entitled to the relevant interest in the dwelling-house or is the person who incurred the capital expenditure on the construction of the building containing it; or

(*b*) if the landlord is a housing association approved under *ICTA 1988, s 488* (co-operative housing association) or is a self-build society under the *Housing Associations Act 1985*; or

(*c*) if the landlord and tenant, or a company of which the tenant is a director, are CONNECTED PERSONS (19); or

(*d*) if the landlord is a close company and the tenant is a participator, or associate of a participator, in that company; or

(*e*) if the tenancy is part of a reciprocal arrangement between the landlords or owners of different dwelling-houses designed to counter the restrictions in (*c*) or (*d*) above.

[*CAA 2001, ss 504, 505; CAA 1990, s 86*].

Capital expenditure attributable to a dwelling-house is limited to £60,000 if it is in Greater London and £40,000 elsewhere, and is:

(A) where the building consists of a single qualifying dwelling-house, the whole of the expenditure on its construction;

(B) where the dwelling-house forms part of a building, (i) the proportion of capital expenditure attributable to that dwelling-house, and (ii) such proportion of the capital expenditure on any common parts of the building as is just and reasonable, but not exceeding one-tenth of the amount in (i).

[*CAA 2001, s 511; CAA 1990, s 96(1)(2)*].

The acquisition of, or of rights in or over, any land is not included in expenditure incurred on the cost of construction of a building for these purposes. Any capital expenditure incurred on repairs is treated as if incurred on the construction for the first time of that part of the building. [*CAA 2001, s 493; CAA 1990, ss 93(1), 97(2)*].

Buildings bought unused. The provisions in *CAA 2001, ss 502, 503* or *CAA 1990, s 91* are similar to those in *CAA 2001, ss 295, 296* or *CAA 1990, s 10*, for which see 9.12, 9.13 below.

Expenditure met by another's contributions. See 9.2(vi) above.

Initial allowances were, and **writing-down allowances** are, given in a similar manner, at similar rates and under similar conditions as for industrial buildings, for which see 9.13, 9.14 below. [*FA 1982, Sch 12 para 1; FA 1984, s 58, Sch 12 para 3; CAA 2001, ss 507–510, 519; CAA 1990, ss 85, 87(7)(8); FA 1994, s 213(7), Sch 26 Pt V(24)*].

References to 'temporary disuse' [*CAA 2001, s 506(2); CAA 1990, s 89(2)*], 'residue of expenditure' [*CAA 2001, ss 512, 523–528; CAA 1990, s 90*], and 'relevant interest' [*CAA 2001, ss 495–498, 500; CAA 1990, s 95*] should be taken as they apply for industrial buildings allowances, but it should be noted that the creation of a subsidiary interest (e.g. leasehold out of freehold) does not transfer the relevant interest.

9.9 Capital Allowances

Balancing allowances and charges are made in a similar manner and under similar conditions as for industrial buildings in *CAA 2001, s 314 et seq.* or *CAA 1990, s 4* (see 9.15 below). [*CAA 2001, s 513 et seq.; CAA 1990, ss 87, 88; FA 1994, Sch 26 Pt V(24)*].

Where *cessation of qualifying use occurs* otherwise than by sale or transfer of the relevant interest, that interest is treated as having been sold at the time of cessation at the open market price. [*CAA 2001, s 506(1); CAA 1990, s 89(1)*].

Making of allowances and charges. Allowances and charges are made in a similar way as they apply to lessors and licensors of industrial buildings, for which see 9.17 below. [*CAA 2001, s 529; CAA 1990, ss 92, 140–145; FA 1995, Sch 6 para 34; FA 1998, s 38, Sch 5 para 58*].

Holding over by lessee etc. Where the relevant interest in relation to the capital expenditure incurred on the construction of a building is an interest under a lease, the following provisions apply. The lease will be treated as continuing where (i) with the consent of the lessor, a lessee remains in possession of any building after his lease ends and without a new lease being granted, (ii) where a lease ends and a new lease is granted to the same lessee under an option available in the first lease, and (iii) where a lease ends and another lease is granted to a different lessee who pays a sum to the first lessee (i.e. the transaction is treated as an assignment). However, where a lease ends and the lessor pays any sum to the lessee in respect of the building, the transaction is treated as if the lease had come to an end by reason of its surrender in consideration of the payment. [*CAA 2001, s 499; CAA 1990, s 94*].

Connected persons and other anti-avoidance provisions. The provisions of *CAA 2001, ss 567–570* (and forerunners) apply to certain sales as they apply to sales of industrial buildings (see 9.22 below) but an election is only available if both the seller and the buyer are, at the time of the sale (or were at any earlier time), approved bodies. Any transfer of relevant interest which is not a sale will be treated as a sale other than at market price under these provisions but there is no balancing allowance or charge if the dwelling-house is treated as having been sold for a sum equal to the residue of expenditure before the sale. [*CAA 2001, ss 569(5), 570(4), 573; CAA 1990, ss 87(5), 88(4), 158(3)*]. See also the anti-avoidance rule at 9.2(xii) above.

Simon's Direct Tax Service. See B2.9.

9.9 **FLAT CONVERSION**

For expenditure incurred **on or after 11 May 2001**, subject to the conditions below, 100% capital allowances (known as flat conversion allowances) are available for qualifying expenditure (see below) on converting former residential space above shops and other commercial premises in the UK into flats for letting or on renovating such flats. [*CAA 2001, ss 393A–393W; FA 2001, s 67, Sch 19 Pt I*]. The allowances are available only against rental income under SCHEDULE A (69) (though see 69.12 as regards relief for Schedule A losses).

Flat conversion allowances are available to the person (including a company) who incurred the qualifying expenditure and has the 'relevant interest' in the flat. [*CAA 2001, s 393A(2)*]. The *'relevant interest'* in relation to qualifying expenditure is determined in similar manner, with appropriate modifications, as for industrial buildings allowances (see 9.14 below), except that for the present purposes it cannot be transferred by the grant or surrender of a lease. In its simplest form, the relevant interest is the interest in the flat to which the person incurring the expenditure was entitled when it was incurred. [*CAA 2001, ss 393F, 393G*]. As regards termination of leases, provisions similar to those of *CAA 2001, s 359* apply (see 9.14 below). [*CAA 2001, s 393V*]. *'Lease'* is defined (as are related expressions accordingly), and in particular includes an agreement for a lease whose term has begun and a tenancy. [*CAA 2001, s 393W*].

For these purposes, a '*flat*' is a separate set of premises (covering one or more floors) forming part of a building and divided horizontally from another part. [*CAA 2001, s 393A(3)*]. See below for 'qualifying flat'.

Qualifying expenditure means capital expenditure incurred on, or in connection with,

- the conversion of part of a 'qualifying building' into a 'qualifying flat';

- the renovation of a flat in a 'qualifying building' if the flat is, or will be, a 'qualifying flat'; or

- repairs to a 'qualifying building', to the extent that they are incidental to either of the above (and for this purpose repairs are treated as capital expenditure if disallowable in computing Schedule A profits),

other than expenditure incurred on, or in connection with,

- the acquisition of, or of rights in or over, land,

- the extension of a qualifying building (except to the extent necessary to provide access to a 'qualifying flat'),

- the development of adjoining or adjacent land, or

- furnishings or chattels.

The part of the building being converted, or the flat being renovated, must have been unused, or used only for storage, throughout the 12 months immediately preceding the commencement of the work.

[*CAA 2001, s 393B(1)–(4)*].

For a building to be a '*qualifying building*':

- all or most of its ground floor must be 'authorised for business use';

- its construction must have been completed before 1 January 1980 (disregarding any extension completed on or after that date but before 1 January 2001);

- it must have no more than four storeys above ground floor (disregarding an attic storey, unless used, or previously used, as a dwelling or part of a dwelling); and

- at time of construction, all such storeys must have been primarily for residential use.

[*CAA 2001, s 393C(1)(3)(4)*].

'*Authorised for business use*' is defined by reference to specified uses designated in the relevant ratings rules for England and Wales, Scotland and NI. [*CAA 2001, s 393C(2)*]. Included are retail shops, food and drink outlets, premises offering financial and professional services, other offices, medical and dental practices, and premises used for research and development and industrial processes which can be carried out in residential areas (Revenue Budget Notes REV BN 15, 7 March 2001).

For a flat to be a '*qualifying flat*':

(*a*)   it must be in a qualifying building;

(*b*)   it must be suitable for letting as a dwelling (disregarding any temporary unsuitability where previously suitable);

(*c*)   it must be held for short-term letting, i.e. on leases of five years or less;

(*d*)   it must be accessible by some means other than via the ground floor business area;

(*e*)   it must have no more than four rooms (disregarding kitchens and bathrooms of whatever area, and closets, cloakrooms and hallways of no more than five square metres in each case);

(*f*)   it must not be a 'high value flat';

(*g*)   it must not be (or have been) created or renovated as part of a scheme involving the creation etc. of one or more 'high value flats'; and

(*h*)   it must not be let to a person connected (within *ICTA 1988, s 839* — see 19 CONNECTED PERSONS) with the person who incurred the conversion or renovation expenditure.

[*CAA 2001, s 393D(1)–(4)*].

A flat is a '*high value flat*' if the 'notional rent' exceeds the relevant limit below.

No. of rooms (as in (e) above)	Greater London	Outside Greater London
1 or 2	£350 per week	£150 per week
3	£425 per week	£225 per week
4	£480 per week	£300 per week

The '*notional rent*' is the rent that could reasonably have been expected, at the time expenditure on the conversion etc. work is first incurred, if the work had been completed and the flat was then let furnished, on a shorthold tenancy (not applicable in NI), other than to a CONNECTED PERSON (19), and otherwise than for any additional payment, such as a premium.

[*CAA 2001, s 393E(1)–(5)(7)*].

The above definitions of qualifying expenditure, qualifying building and qualifying flat and the above notional rent limits may be amended by Treasury regulations. [*CAA 2001, s 393B(5), s 393C(5), s 393D(5), s 393E(6)*].

Initial allowances. The initial allowance is **100%** of the qualifying expenditure, may be claimed in whole or in part, and is made for the chargeable period (see 9.2(i) above) in which the expenditure is incurred. The initial allowance is not available if the flat is not a qualifying flat at the time it is first suitable for letting as a dwelling or if the person who incurred the expenditure sells the relevant interest (see above) before that time; any initial allowance already made is withdrawn in such circumstances. [*CAA 2001, ss 393H, 393I*].

Writing-down allowances (WDAs) are available where the expenditure has not been wholly relieved by an initial allowance. The annual WDA is **25%** of the qualifying expenditure, on a straight line basis, proportionately reduced or increased if the chargeable period is less or more than a year, and may be claimed in whole or in part. The WDA cannot exceed the residue, i.e. the unrelieved balance, of the qualifying expenditure. The person who incurred the expenditure is entitled to a WDA for a chargeable period if *at the end of that period*:

- he is entitled to the relevant interest (see above) in the flat;

- he has not granted, out of the relevant interest, a long lease (exceeding 50 years) of the flat for a capital sum; and

- the flat is a qualifying flat.

There is nothing to prevent a WDA being given in the same chargeable period as an initial allowance for the same expenditure.

[*CAA 2001, ss 393J–393L, 393Q, 393R*].

Balancing allowances and charges. If a 'balancing event' occurs, a balancing adjustment, i.e. a balancing allowance or balancing charge, is made to or on the person who incurred the qualifying expenditure and for the chargeable period in which the event occurs. If more than one balancing event occurs, a balancing adjustment is made only on the first of them. **No balancing adjustment** is made in respect of a balancing event occurring **more than seven years** after the time the flat was first suitable for letting as a dwelling. Any of the following is a '*balancing event*':

(i)   the sale of the relevant interest (see above) in the flat;

(ii)   the grant, out of the relevant interest, of a long lease (exceeding 50 years) of the flat for a capital sum;

(iii)   (where the relevant interest is a lease) the coming to an end of the lease otherwise than on the person entitled to it acquiring the reversionary interest;

(iv)   the death of the person who incurred the qualifying expenditure;

(v)   the demolition or destruction of the flat;

(vi)   the flat's otherwise ceasing to be a qualifying flat.

The proceeds of a balancing event depend upon the nature of the event and are as follows.

(1)   On a sale of the relevant interest, the net sale proceeds receivable by the person who incurred the qualifying expenditure.

(2)   On the grant of a long lease, the capital sum involved or, if greater, the premium that would have been paid in an arm's length transaction.

(3)   In an event within (iii) above, where the persons entitled to, respectively, the lease and the superior interest are CONNECTED PERSONS (19), the market value of the relevant interest in the flat at the time of the event.

(4)   On death, the residue (see below) of qualifying expenditure.

(5)   On demolition or destruction, the net amount received for the remains by the person who incurred the qualifying expenditure, plus any insurance or capital compensation received by him.

(6)   On the flat's otherwise ceasing to be a qualifying flat, the market value of the relevant interest in the flat at the time of the event.

If the residue, i.e. the unrelieved balance, of qualifying expenditure immediately before the event exceeds the proceeds of the event (including nil proceeds), a balancing allowance arises, equal to the excess. (This is subject to the anti-avoidance rule at 9.2(xii) above.) If the proceeds exceed the residue (including a nil residue), a balancing charge arises, normally equal to the excess but limited to the total initial and writing-down allowances previously given to the person concerned in respect of the expenditure.

[*CAA 2001, ss 393M–393P*].

Note that, by virtue of *CAA 2001, s 572*, a surrender for valuable consideration of a leasehold interest is treated as a sale (for equivalent proceeds), and thus falls within (1) above (if not caught by (3) above).

Any proceeds of sale of the relevant interest or other proceeds of a balancing event are, if attributable to both, apportioned on a just and reasonable basis between assets representing qualifying expenditure and other assets, and only the first part taken into account as above. [*CAA 2001, s 393U*].

Demolition costs. Where a qualifying flat is demolished, the net cost (after crediting any money received for remains) of demolition borne by the person who incurred the expenditure is added to the residue of qualifying expenditure immediately before the demolition, and is thus taken into account in computing the balancing adjustment; no amount included in gross demolition costs can then attract capital allowances of any kind. [*CAA 2001, s 393S*].

9.10 Capital Allowances

Making of allowances and charges. If the taxpayer's interest in the flat is an asset of a Schedule A business (see 69.3 SCHEDULE A) carried on by him at any time in the chargeable period (see 9.2(i) above) in question, allowances/charges under these provisions are treated as expenses/receipts of that business. If the above is not the case, he is deemed to be carrying on a Schedule A business anyway, and allowances/charges given effect accordingly. [*CAA 2001, s 393T*]. See 69.12 SCHEDULE A as regards relief for Schedule A losses.

Connected persons and other anti-avoidance provisions. The provisions at 9.22(i) below for industrial buildings allowances apply equally to flat conversion allowances, *except* that the election to treat a sale etc. as being at tax written-down value is *not* available in the instant case. [*CAA 2001, ss 567–570, 573, 575(1), 577(4); FA 2001, s 67, Sch 19 Pt II paras 5–7*].

Revenue guidance. See generally Revenue leaflet IR 2007 'Capital Allowances for Flats over Shops' or the notes on the Revenue's website at www.inlandrevenue.gov.uk/specialist/flatsovershops.htm.

Simon's Direct Tax Service. See B2.10.

9.10 INDUSTRIAL BUILDINGS

Allowances are given in respect of certain capital expenditure (see 9.12 below) on industrial buildings (see 9.11 below), and are available to traders and to lessors and licensors of industrial buildings for use by traders. The main elements of the scheme of allowances are dealt with as follows

Simon's Direct Tax Service. See B2.2.

9.11 **Qualifying buildings.** An 'industrial building' is a building or structure, or part of a building or structure, in use either

(*a*)   for the purposes of a trade, or part of a trade (see (A) below), consisting of

    (i)   the manufacture or processing of goods or materials, or

    (ii)   after 9 March 1982, the maintaining or repairing of goods or materials (but not goods etc. employed by the person carrying out the repair or maintenance in any trade or undertaking unless that trade etc. itself qualifies the building as an industrial building), or

    (iii)   the storage of (*a*) raw materials for manufacture, (*b*) goods to be processed, (*c*) goods manufactured or processed but not yet delivered to any purchaser, or (*d*) goods on arrival in the UK from a place outside the UK, or

    (iv)   the working of mines, oil wells etc. or foreign plantations, or

    (v)   agricultural operations on land not occupied by the trader, or

    (vi)   catching fish or shellfish; or

(*b*)   for the purposes of

    (i)   a transport, dock, inland navigation, water, sewerage, electricity, hydraulic power, bridge or tunnel undertaking, or

(ii)   in relation to any chargeable or basis period ending after 5 April 1991, a toll road undertaking or, for expenditure incurred after 5 April 1995, a 'highway undertaking' (see below); or

(c)   for the welfare of workers employed in a trade or undertaking within (a) or (b) above; or

(d)   as a sports pavilion for the welfare of workers employed in any trade; or

(e)   as a qualifying hotel (see 9.18 below).

As regards (a) above, following the decision in *Bestway (Holdings) Ltd v Luff Ch D 1998, 70 TC 512*, the Revenue changed their view in two respects.

(A)   Previously they had considered that, provided it was self-contained, anything done in the course of a trade was part of a trade for this purpose. Their revised view is that, whilst the activities in question do not need to be self-contained, they must be a significant, separate and identifiable part of the trade carried on. (Revenue Capital Allowances Manual CA 32300).

(B)   They previously considered the main test under (a)(iii) above to be whether the further conditions as to use of the goods or materials stored were satisfied. They have now adopted the Court's preliminary test that the determining factor in deciding whether a building is used for storage is the purpose for which the goods or materials are kept or held — it is used for storage only if the purpose of keeping them there is their storage as an end in itself and not some other purpose. (Revenue Capital Allowances Manual CA 32224).

This change of view is most likely to be significant in wholesale trades where it has previously been accepted that there was a qualifying part trade of storage of goods or materials to be used in the manufacture of other goods or materials or subjected to a process. For allowances to continue to be available, the storage must be conducted as a purpose and end in itself, not just as a necessary and transitory incident of the conduct of the wholesale business. Where claims have previously been accepted under the earlier view, the revised view should be applied to claims for chargeable periods ending after 31 December 1999. (Revenue Tax Bulletin December 1999 pp 710, 711).

As regards (b) above, *CAA 2001* omits the previous reference to 'a trade carried on in a mill, factory or other similar premises'. This is because case law indicates that all trades within the earlier provision are subsumed within (a)(i) above (see Note 45 in Annex 2 to the Explanatory Notes to the 2001 Capital Allowances Bill).

A building the whole of which is in use partly for qualifying and partly for non-qualifying purposes may qualify for allowances in full provided that the qualifying use is at least 10% of the total use. (Revenue Capital Allowances Manual CA 32315). See also *Saxone Lilley & Skinner (Holdings) Ltd* below.

Excluded from the definition of 'industrial building' are buildings or structures in use as, or as part of, dwelling-houses, retail shops, showrooms, offices or hotels (but see 9.18 below as regards expenditure on hotels after 11 April 1978), or for purposes ancillary thereto. See Revenue Capital Allowances Manual at CA 32312 for what is an 'office' for these purposes, and at CA 32313 for purposes 'ancillary' to those of a retail shop. In *Girobank plc v Clarke CA 1998, 70 TC 387*, a bank document and data processing centre was held not to be an office. In *Sarsfield v Dixons Group plc CA 1998, 71 TC 121*, a warehouse used by a group distribution company for receiving, storing and delivering goods purchased by the group for sale from its shops was held to be used for purposes ancillary to those of the group's retail shops. Where only part of a building or structure, representing 25% (10% for expenditure incurred before 16 March 1983 or deemed so incurred under *CAA 1990, s 10(1)(2)*, see 9.12 below) or less of the total cost, falls within these exclusions, the whole building or structure continues to qualify. Note that when alterations, extensions etc. or changes in use result in the 25% limit being exceeded, no amendment is made to allowances for chargeable (or basis) periods before that of the change, and allowances continue to be available in respect of that part of the building or structure not excluded. Similarly, where the 25% condition commences to be met, allowances are available for the whole of the building or structure only for the chargeable (or basis) period of the change and subsequent periods.

Buildings or structures constructed for occupation by, or welfare of, employees in mines, oil wells etc. or foreign plantations, and likely to have little or no value on the ending of the working of the mine etc. or of the foreign concession, also qualify.

Buildings or structures *outside the UK* can only qualify if the trade for which they are in use is assessable under Schedule D, Case I. A building or structure used by more than one licensee of the same person only qualifies if each of the licensees uses the building or structure, or his part of it, for the purposes of a trade as above under licences granted after 9 March 1982.

[*CAA 2001, ss 271(1)(2), 274–278, 280, 282, 283, Sch 3 paras 57, 59, 74; CAA 1990, ss 14, 18; FA 1991, s 60(4)(10); FA 1993, s 113(6); FA 1995, ss 99(5), 101*].

A *'highway undertaking'* (see (*b*)(ii) above) means so much of any undertaking relating to the design, building, financing and operation of roads as is carried on for the purposes of, or in connection with, the exploitation of 'highway concessions'. A *'highway concession'*, in relation to a road, means any right, in respect of public use of the road, to receive sums from the State, or, in the case of a toll road, the right to charge tolls. [*CAA 2001, ss 274(1), 341(4)(5); CAA 1990, s 21(5AA); FA 1995, s 99(7); FA 2001, s 69, Sch 21 para 6*].

(*c*) above is regarded by the Revenue as including canteens, day nurseries, garages, hard tennis courts, hostels and indoor sports halls. It does not, however, include buildings or structures excluded as above from being 'industrial buildings' (e.g. a grocery shop with extended hours for the convenience of workers, or holiday accommodation). Also as regards (*c*) above, the workers for whose welfare a building or structure is provided must be workers engaged directly in the productive, manufacturing or processing side of the business, rather than office staff or management, although the whole of a building or structure provided for staff generally may qualify provided use by production workers is not negligible. Similarly, use by outsiders as well as workers does not exclude the building or structure from relief. (Revenue Capital Allowances Manual CA 32320).

For cases in which industrial buildings allowances were **refused** see *Dale v Johnson Bros KB(NI) 1951, 32 TC 487* (warehouse — contrast the non-tax case *Crusabridge Investments Ltd v Casings International Ltd Ch D 1979, 54 TC 246*); *CIR v National Coal Board HL 1957, 37 TC 264* (colliery houses capable of alternative use); *Bourne v Norwich Crematorium Ch D 1967, 44 TC 164* (furnace chamber etc.); *Abbott Laboratories Ltd v Carmody Ch D 1968, 44 TC 569* (separate administrative block); *Buckingham v Securitas Properties Ltd Ch D 1979, 53 TC 292* (building used for wage packeting); *Vibroplant Ltd v Holland CA 1981, 54 TC 658* (depots of plant hire contractor, but now see (*a*)(ii) above); *Copol Clothing Co Ltd v Hindmarch CA 1983, 57 TC 575* (inland storage of goods imported in containers); *Carr v Sayer Ch D 1992, 65 TC 15* (quarantine kennels, claimed under (*a*)(iii)(*d*) above); *Girobank plc v Clarke CA 1998, 70 TC 387* (bank document and data processing centre); *Bestway (Holdings) Ltd v Luff Ch D 1998, 70 TC 512* (cash-and-carry wholesale warehouse); and *Sarsfield v Dixons Group plc CA 1998, 71 TC 121* (warehouse used by retail group distribution company for receiving, storing and delivering goods).

For cases where allowances were **granted**, see *CIR v Lambhill Ironworks Ltd CS 1950, 31 TC 393* (drawing office); *Kilmarnock Equitable Co-operative Society Ltd v CIR CS 1966, 42 TC 675* (coal packing not ancillary to retail shop); *Saxone Lilley & Skinner (Holdings) Ltd v CIR HL 1967, 44 TC 122* (warehouse for shoes both bought and manufactured).

Temporary disuse. A building or structure which falls temporarily out of use after a period in which it qualified as an 'industrial building' is treated as continuing to so qualify during disuse. [*CAA 2001, s 285; CAA 1990, s 15*]. All disuse other than that preceding demolition or dereliction is in practice regarded as temporary.

Simon's Direct Tax Service. See B2.203 *et seq.*

9.12   **Qualifying expenditure** is the cost of construction of the building or structure including the cost of preparing, cutting, tunnelling or levelling land, but excluding expenditure on the land itself or on rights therein. [*CAA 2001, ss 272(1), 294; CAA 1990, ss 1(1), 3(1), 21(1)*]. A just and reasonable apportionment is required to exclude unallowable expenditure (and see *Bostock v Totham Ch D 1997, 69 TC 356* as regards the basis of such apportionment). [*CAA 2001, s 356; CAA 1990, s 21(3)*]. Anything with four walls and a roof is a building for these purposes, provided that it is of a reasonably substantial size. Anything smaller may be a structure. A structure is something which has been artificially erected or constructed, and which is distinct from the surrounding earth, e.g. roads, paved car parks or tennis courts, tunnels, culverts, bridges, walls and fences. (Revenue Capital Allowances Manual CA 31110, 31120). The fees of professionals involved in the design and construction of a building or structure (e.g. architects, quantity surveyors and engineers) are also included. (Revenue Capital Allowances Manual CA 31400). Expenditure on repairs which is, exceptionally, disallowable as capital expenditure in computing profits is treated as the cost of constructing that part of the building or structure [*CAA 2001, s 272(2)(3); CAA 1990, s 12*], and the cost of preparing etc. land as a site for the installation of plant or machinery is, if no relief would otherwise be available under industrial buildings or plant and machinery allowances, treated as attracting allowances as if the plant or machinery were a building or structure. [*CAA 2001, s 273; CAA 1990, s 13*]. Where, for the purpose of erecting a new building or structure on the same site, costs are incurred in demolishing an existing building or structure, and the costs cannot be taken into account in calculating a balancing adjustment (see 9.15 below) on the demolished building or structure (e.g. because more than 25 (or 50) years has elapsed since it was first used), the demolition costs may be treated as expenditure on construction of the new building or structure. (Revenue Capital Allowances Manual CA 31400).

Roads on an industrial trading estate most of the buildings on which are industrial buildings will themselves be treated as industrial buildings. [*CAA 2001, s 284; CAA 1990, s 18(8)*].

See 9.25 below for certain expenditure on existing buildings or structures treated as being on plant or machinery.

The following are considered by the Revenue to be excluded from being qualifying expenditure: expenditure on obtaining planning permission (although if a builder's costs are inclusive of such expenditure, no apportionment will be made); capitalised interest; public enquiry costs; land drainage and reclamation and landscaping; and legal expenses. (Revenue Capital Allowances Manual CA 31400).

Abortive expenditure. Expenditure (including professional fees) incurred on the construction of a building or structure which never becomes an industrial building (e.g. because it is never completed) cannot be qualifying expenditure. (Revenue Capital Allowances Manual CA 31410).

Buildings bought unused. If the 'relevant interest' (see 9.14 below) in a building or structure is sold before it is used, the purchaser (the last purchaser if more than one before the building or structure is used) is treated as having incurred on its construction, at the time the purchase price becomes payable, the lesser of the actual cost of construction and the net purchase price of the interest (excluding any part attributable to the land, see Revenue Capital Allowances Manual CA 31305). Where the original expenditure was incurred by a builder as part of his trade of constructing such buildings or structures with a view to sale, the purchaser's deemed construction cost is the net purchase price paid by him or, if there have been previous sales unused, the lesser of the net purchase price paid by him and the net price paid to the builder on the first sale. (Note that this latter provision does not apply for agricultural buildings allowances purposes, for which the provisions are otherwise similar.) [*CAA 2001, ss 294–296, 299, 300; CAA 1990, s 10(1)–(3)*]. Except where the purchase price is specially defined by virtue of an election under *CAA 2001, s 290* or *CAA 1990, s 11* (see 9.14 below), the net purchase price of the interest includes acquisition costs, i.e. legal fees, surveyors' fees and stamp duty. (Revenue Capital Allowances Manual CA 33520).

The initial allowance under *CAA 1990, s 2A* (see 9.13 below) could be claimed by the purchaser (or last purchaser) of an unused building or structure regardless of the date of sale providing some or all the actual construction expenditure fell within those provisions, i.e. it was incurred in, broadly, the year ending 31 October 1993. It could also be claimed where the actual construction expenditure was incurred by a builder (as above) *at any time* before 1 November 1993, the sale occurred between 1 November 1992 and 31 October 1993 inclusive and the vendor had been entitled to the relevant interest since before 1 November 1992. Such construction expenditure was deemed for these purposes to fall within *section 2A*. In both circumstances, it remained a condition that the building or structure came to be used before 1 January 1995 (see 9.13 below). Where only part of the actual construction expenditure was within *section 2A*, the purchaser's deemed construction cost was computed as above and then divided into a *section 2A* element qualifying for the initial allowance and a residual element qualifying only for writing-down allowances. The *section 2A* element was the proportion of the deemed expenditure that corresponded to the proportion of actual construction expenditure that was within *section 2A*. [*CAA 2001, Sch 3 para 77; CAA 1990, s 10(3A), s 10C(1)–(10); FA 1993, s 113(3)(4)*].

Appropriation from trading stock. A building or structure appropriated by a builder from trading stock to capital account (with a corresponding market value credit to profit and loss) and let as an industrial building, is eligible for writing-down allowances based on the construction cost (rather than on the transfer value). Initial allowances were not available in these circumstances. (This commentary is not included in the current Revenue Capital Allowances Manual but was previously at CA 1212 and is presumed still to be of application.)

Arrangements having an artificial effect on pricing. Where certain 'arrangements' have been entered into relating to, or with respect to, any interest in or right over a building or structure, special rules apply for determining any amount which is to be taken to be:

(*a*)   for the purposes of the provisions relating to buildings bought unused or, after use, from original builder or, in certain cases, within two years after first use (see above and 9.19 below), the sum paid on the sale of the relevant interest, and

(*b*)   for the purposes of allowances and charges generally (see above and 9.13–9.19 below), the amount of any proceeds from a subsequent balancing event where a person is deemed under any of the provisions referred to in (*a*) above to have incurred expenditure on the construction of the building or structure of an amount equal to the price paid on a sale of the relevant interest.

Where these provisions apply, the amount falling to be determined is reduced to the extent that the sale price or the amount of the sale etc. moneys is more than it would have been if the arrangements had not contained the provision in (iii) below.

The '*arrangements*' in question are those

(i)   entered into at or before the 'specified time',

(ii)   having the effect at that time of enhancing the value of the relevant interest in the building or structure, and

(iii)   containing any provision having an artificial effect on pricing,

and as regards (iii) above, arrangements are treated as containing such a provision to the extent that they go beyond what, at the time they were entered into, it was reasonable to regard as required by the prevailing market conditions in similar arm's length transactions. For examples of the sort of arrangements considered by the Revenue to be most likely to be used, see Revenue Capital Allowances Manual CA 39620.

The '*specified time*' is the time of the fixing of the sale price:

(A)   in relation to the determination of an amount within (*a*) above, for the sale in question; and

(B)   in relation to the determination of an amount within (*b*) above, for the sale by reference to which the amount of the deemed expenditure fell to be determined.

These provisions do not apply if the sale price referred to became payable before 29 November 1994 (6 April 1995 where the price was fixed under a contract entered into before 29 November 1994).

[*CAA 2001, ss 357, 564(3), Sch 3 para 78; CAA 1990, s 10D; FA 1995, s 100*].

Simon's Direct Tax Service. See **B2.222** *et seq.*

9.13   **Initial allowances.** In general, initial allowances were **abolished** for expenditure incurred after 31 March 1986, or after 31 March 1987 in the case of expenditure incurred after 13 March 1984 under a contract entered into before 14 March 1984 by the person incurring the expenditure. [*FA 1984, Sch 12 para 1*]. However, they continue at a rate of 100% for certain expenditure in enterprise zones (see 9.19 below), and were temporarily reinstated at a rate of 20% for general expenditure incurred in, broadly, the year ended 31 October 1993 (see below). They also continue to be available at the appropriate rate in respect of any additional VAT liability (see 9.2(viii) above) in respect of such expenditure. [*CAA 2001, ss 305, 306, 346, Sch 3 paras 75–77; CAA 1990, ss 1(1), 2A; FA 1991, Sch 14 para 2*].

Initial allowances were temporarily reintroduced in respect of qualifying expenditure (see 9.12 above) incurred under a contract entered into in the twelve-month period **1 November 1992 to 31 October 1993 inclusive** or for the purpose of securing compliance with obligations incurred under a contract entered into during that period, but not for expenditure incurred under a contract entered into for the purpose of securing compliance with obligations under a contract entered into before 1 November 1992. The qualifying building or structure must have come to be used before 1 January 1995, and if this condition was not satisfied, any initial allowance given will have been withdrawn. The initial allowance was **20%** of the expenditure incurred. These provisions did not apply where initial allowances would otherwise have been available as above. They do apply to qualifying hotels (see 9.18 below), and also in respect of any 'additional VAT liability' (see 9.2(viii) above) incurred in respect of expenditure falling within these provisions. [*CAA 2001, Sch 3 paras 75–77; CAA 1990, s 2A; FA 1993, s 113(1)*].

The general conditions for the grant of initial allowances apply to the temporary allowances as above and (subject to the special provisions described in 9.19 below) to the 100% enterprise zone allowances generally in the same way as they applied to the pre-1984 allowances. The allowances are available to a person incurring qualifying expenditure (see 9.12 above) on a building etc. which is to be in use as an 'industrial building' (see 9.11 above) for a trade carried on by that person or by his lessee or, for licences granted after 9 March 1982, by his licensee. [*CAA 2001, s 305, Sch 3 para 64; CAA 1990, s 1(1)(4)*]. See also 9.12 above as regards buildings or structures bought unused. An initial allowance is given for the chargeable period in which the expenditure is incurred. [*CAA 2001, s 306(3); CAA 1990, s 1(1)*]. Expenditure for the purposes of a trade incurred by a person about to carry it on is treated as if incurred on the day the trade is actually commenced, but this applies only for the purpose of determining the chargeable period for which the allowance may be made (and not, for example, to determine the availability or otherwise of an initial allowance under *CAA 1990, s 2A* — see above). [*CAA 2001, s 306(4); CAA 1990, s 1(10)*]. See also 9.2(iv) above generally as to the time at which expenditure is treated as being incurred.

Expenditure taken into account for the purposes of certain grants or payments specified by the Treasury for the purpose are excluded from initial allowances. [*CAA 2001, s 308, Sch 3 para 65; CAA 1990, s 1(7)–(9)*]. See also 9.2(vi) above.

Initial allowances may be claimed in whole or part. [*CAA 2001, s 306(2); CAA 1990, s 1(5); FA 1990, Sch 17 para 2*]. They are withdrawn if, when the building or structure comes to be used, it is not an 'industrial building', or (in relation to the vendor) if it is sold before being used. [*CAA 2001, s 307; CAA 1990, s 1(6)*].

Earlier rates of initial allowance were as follows.

After 5 April 1944	— 10%	
After 5 April 1952	— Nil	
After 14 April 1953	— 10%	
After 6 April 1954	— Nil	
After 17 February 1956	— 10%	
After 14 April 1958	— 15%	
After 7 April 1959	— 5%	
After 16 January 1966	— 15%	
After 5 April 1970	— 30%	(40% if building or structure in development or intermediate area or N. Ireland)
After 21 March 1972	— 40%	
After 12 November 1974	— 50%	(20% on hotels and 100% in enterprise zones and on certain small workshops, from later dates, see 9.18, 9.19 and 9.21 below)
After 10 March 1981	— 75%	(— as above —)
After 13 March 1984	— 50%	(— as above, omitting reference to workshops from 27 March 1985 —)
After 31 March 1985 to 31 March 1986	— 25%	(— as above —)

Simon's Direct Tax Service. See B2.232 *et seq.*

9.14   **Writing-down allowances** are available where a qualifying building or structure (see 9.11 above) is in use as such (or in temporary disuse following such use, see 9.11 above) at the end of a chargeable period. They are available to the person entitled to an interest which is the 'relevant interest' in the building or structure at the end of that period. A writing-down allowance can be given for the same chargeable period as an initial allowance (see 9.13 above) in respect of the same expenditure.

For expenditure incurred between 6 April 1946 and 5 November 1962 inclusive, the rate of allowance is 2% p.a.

For expenditure incurred **after 5 November 1962**, the rate of allowance is **4% p.a.** (but see 9.19, 9.21 below as regards 25% annual allowances in certain cases) or such smaller amount as may be claimed.

The allowances are calculated on the qualifying expenditure (see 9.12 above) incurred, and continue until the 'residue of expenditure' is nil. The annual writing-down allowance is available in full where the expenditure is incurred during the chargeable period, but is proportionately reduced or increased where the chargeable period is less or more than twelve months. [*CAA 2001, ss 309, 310, 312, Sch 3 para 66; CAA 1990, s 3(1)(2)(4); FA 1994, s 213(2), Sch 26 Pt V(24)*]. For lessors of industrial buildings, however, the chargeable period is the year of assessment itself, so that the full allowance is available regardless of the date of commencement of letting in the year. [*CAA 2001, s 6(2); CAA 1990, s 160(5); FA 1994, s 212(1)*].

Where an 'additional VAT liability' (see 9.2(viii) above) is incurred in respect of any qualifying expenditure, the amount of the liability qualifies for writing-down allowances as if it were additional capital expenditure incurred on the construction in question; the 'residue of expenditure' is increased by that amount at the time the liability accrues. For chargeable periods ending after the time the liability accrues, writing-down allowances are given of the proportion of the residue of expenditure immediately after that time which the length of the chargeable period bears to the length of the period from the date of the incurring of the liability to the 25th anniversary of the first use of the building or structure for any purpose. Similar provisions apply where an 'additional VAT rebate' (see 9.2(viii) above) is made, the residue being reduced by the amount thereof (but see 9.15 below where the rebate exceeds the residue). [*CAA 2001, ss 311, 347, 349–351; CAA 1990, s 3(2A)–(2C), s 8(12A); FA 1991, Sch 14 paras 3, 5(2); FA 1994, Sch 26 Pt V(24)*].

If the 'relevant interest' in a building or structure is sold, and the sale is a balancing event (see 9.15 below), subsequent writing-down allowances are given to the purchaser and are calculated on the 'residue of expenditure' immediately after the sale, spread over the period from the date of sale to the 25th anniversary of the first use of the building or structure for any purpose (50th anniversary for expenditure incurred before 6 November 1962). [*CAA 2001, s 311, Sch 3 para 67; CAA 1990, s 3(3); FA 1994, Sch 26 Pt V(24)*].

For a sale *before 18 December 1980* (or pursuant to a contract made before that date) at a time when the building or structure was not in use as an 'industrial building', so that no balancing adjustment arose (see 9.15 below), writing-down allowances to the purchaser (for subsequent chargeable (or basis) periods at the end of which the building or structure has reverted to use as an 'industrial building') continue at the rate after the most recent sale while in use as an 'industrial building' or, if there has been no such sale, the full 4% (or 2%) rate. [*CAA 1968, s 2; FA 1981, s 74*].

'*Residue of expenditure*' is original capital expenditure

minus all industrial buildings and research and development (or scientific research) allowances (see 9.52 below) granted, including balancing allowances, and

minus 'notional writing-down allowances' for periods, following first use of the building or structure for any purpose, at the end of which the building or structure was not in use as an 'industrial building', and

plus any balancing charges made, and

plus or *minus* any 'additional VAT liability' or 'additional VAT rebate' (see 9.2(viii) above) incurred or made in respect of that expenditure.

Where the Crown is entitled to the relevant interest for a period immediately before a sale etc., allowances and charges which could have been made if the building or structure had been in use by a non-corporate trader entitled to that interest for that period are taken into account for this purpose. For sales etc. after 28 July 1988, this treatment applies also to prior entitlement by any person not within the charge to income or corporation tax.

Where a balancing charge arises on the excess of allowances given over adjusted net cost following a sale after non-qualifying use (see 9.15 below), the residue after the sale is restricted to the net sale proceeds.

9.14 Capital Allowances

[*CAA 2001, ss 313, 332–339, 348, Sch 3 paras 72, 73; CAA 1990, s 3(2A)(b), s 8; FA 1991, Sch 14 paras 3(1), 5; FA 1994, s 213(3), Sch 26 Pt V(24)*].

'*Notional allowances*' are calculated on the original qualifying expenditure or, if the building etc. has subsequently been sold in circumstances giving rise to a balancing adjustment (see 9.15 below), at the appropriate rate following that sale. [*CAA 2001, s 336(3)(4); CAA 1990, s 8(7)*].

'*Relevant interest*' is, in relation to any expenditure incurred on the construction of the building or structure, the interest (freehold or leasehold) in that building or structure to which the person who incurred the expenditure was entitled when he incurred it. If there is more than one such interest, and one was reversionary on all the others, the reversionary interest is the relevant interest. The creation of a subordinate interest (e.g. leasehold out of freehold) does not generally transfer the relevant interest (but see below). An interest arising on or as a result of completion of construction is treated as having been held when the expenditure was incurred. If a leasehold relevant interest is extinguished by surrender, or by the person entitled to it acquiring the interest reversionary on it, the interest into which it merges becomes the relevant interest. A highway concession (see 9.11 above) is not generally an interest in a road, but is treated as the relevant interest where the person who incurred expenditure on construction of the road was not then entitled to an interest in the road but was entitled to the highway concession in respect of it. [*CAA 2001, ss 286–289, 342; CAA 1990, ss 20, 21(2); FA 1991, s 60(5); FA 1995, s 99(6)*].

But where a lease of more than 50 years is granted out of a 'relevant interest' the lessor and the lessee may jointly elect for allowances to apply to the leasehold interest. The grant of the lease is then regarded as a sale to the lessee, the capital sum as the purchase price, and the lessee's interest as replacing all the lessor's relevant interest. The election is not available if lessor and lessee are 'connected persons' (unless the lessor controls the lessee and has statutory functions) or if the sole or main benefit which may be expected to accrue to the lessor is a balancing allowance (see 9.15 below). The election must be in writing to the inspector within two years after the date on which the lease takes effect. [*CAA 2001, ss 290, 291; CAA 1990, s 11*].

Requisitioned land. Allowances may be available for buildings on land requisitioned by the Crown. See *CAA 2001, s 358; CAA 1990, s 16(1)–(3)*.

Termination of leases. (i) Where a lease ends and the lessee, with the lessor's consent, remains in possession without a new lease being granted, the lease is treated as continuing. (ii) A new lease granted on the termination of an old lease on exercise of an option available under the old lease is treated as a continuation of the old lease. (iii) If on termination of a lease the lessor pays any sum to the lessee in respect of a building comprised in the lease, the lease is treated as surrendered in consideration of the payment. (iv) If, on the termination of a lease, a lessee who is granted a new lease makes a payment to the lessee under the old lease, the two leases are treated as the same lease, the old lessee having assigned it to the new lessee for payment. [*CAA 2001, s 359; CAA 1990, s 16(4)–(7)*].

Buildings bought after use. Where a person carrying on a trade, consisting wholly or partly of the construction of buildings or structures with a view to their sale, incurs expenditure on such a construction and after the building or structure has been used, he sells the relevant interest in the course of the trade, the purchaser is entitled to allowances as if the original expenditure had been capital expenditure and all appropriate writing-down allowances and balancing allowances or charges (see 9.15 below) had been made to or on the vendor. Normally, the effect will be that the purchaser obtains allowances on the lesser of the net purchase price and the cost of construction. This provision applies in any case where the purchase price becomes payable after 26 July 1989. [*CAA 2001, s 297, Sch 3 para 60; CAA 1990, s 10(4)(5)*]. Previously, a similar rule operated by extra-statutory concession. (Revenue Pamphlet IR 1, B20).

Simon's Direct Tax Service. See **B2.234** *et seq.*

9.15   **Balancing allowances and charges.** A balancing allowance or charge may arise to or on the person entitled to the 'relevant interest' (see 9.14 above) in a building or structure when it is sold, destroyed or permanently put out of use, or when the relevant interest is lost on termination of a lease or foreign concession, or when a highway concession (see 9.11 above) is brought to or comes to an end (see also below), *provided that* that event occurs within 25 years (50 years for expenditure incurred before 6 November 1962) of the building or structure's first being used. On a sale etc. **after 17 December 1980** (unless pursuant to a contract made on or before that date) of a building or structure which has been an industrial building (or used for research and development (before 6 April 2000, scientific research), see 9.52 below) throughout the 'relevant period', the balancing adjustment is calculated as follows. If the 'residue of expenditure' (see 9.14 above) immediately before the sale etc. exceeds the proceeds of any sale, insurance, salvage or compensation, the difference is allowed as a balancing allowance (subject to the anti-avoidance rule at 9.2(xii) above); if it is less, the difference is the subject of a balancing charge. Where the building or structure has at any time in the 'relevant period' been neither an 'industrial building' nor in use for research and development (or scientific research), a balancing charge will be made to recover all allowances given where the proceeds of sale, insurance, salvage or compensation equal or exceed the 'starting expenditure'. Where those proceeds are nil or less than the 'starting expenditure', a balancing allowance will be given (or a balancing charge made) on the excess of the 'adjusted net cost' of the building or structure over the allowances given (or *vice versa*). For this purpose, the allowances given include all industrial buildings, research and development (or scientific research), and mills, factories or exceptional depreciation allowances, and any balancing charge raised may not exceed the total of such allowances, less any balancing charges previously made. Allowances made to a husband before 6 April 1990 in respect of his wife's relevant interest are treated as having been made to the wife for this purpose on a balancing event on or after that date.

'*Relevant period*' means the period beginning at the time when the building or structure was first used for any purpose and ending with the event giving rise to the balancing adjustment, unless there have been previous sales, when the relevant period begins on the day following the last sale.

'*Starting expenditure*' means the expenditure incurred on the construction of the building or structure (less any balancing charge made in respect of an 'additional VAT rebate' — see below) or, in the case of a second-hand building or structure, the residue of expenditure (see 9.14 above) at the beginning of the relevant period, together (in either case) with the net cost of demolition (see below) if appropriate.

'*Adjusted net cost*' means the amount by which starting expenditure exceeds the proceeds, reduced in the proportion that the period of qualifying use bears to the relevant period.

[*CAA 2001, ss 314(1)–(4), 315, 316, 318–324, 343, 350(5), Sch 3 paras 68–70; CAA 1990, s 4; FA 1991, Sch 14 para 4(4)(5); FA 1994, Sch 26 Pt V(24); FA 1995, s 99(3); FA 2000, Sch 19 para 8*].

Successive sales etc. during non-use as industrial building. Where there are two or more sales etc. in a period during which a building or structure is not an 'industrial building', a balancing adjustment arises only on the first such sale etc. [*CAA 2001, s 314(5); CAA 1990, s 4(2); FA 1991, Sch 14 para 4(2)*].

Additional VAT rebate. Where an 'additional VAT rebate' (see 9.2(viii) above) is made in respect of qualifying expenditure, and this exceeds the residue of expenditure (see 9.14 above), a balancing charge, equal to the excess, will be made. [*CAA 2001, s 350; CAA 1990, s 4(1)(e)(2A); FA 1991, Sch 14 para 4(1)(3)*].

In the case of a *highway concession* (see above), no balancing adjustment arises (and writing-down allowances continue) where, on the coming to an end of the concession, the period for which it was granted is extended, i.e. the person entitled to it is granted a renewal of the concession in respect of the whole or part of a road, or he or a CONNECTED PERSON (19) is granted a new concession in respect of the same road (or part of it or a road of which it is part). Where the extension relates to part only of a road, a 'just and reasonable' apportionment is made to determine the expenditure in respect of which a balancing adjustment arises. [*CAA 2001, s 344; CAA 1990, s 4(2AA)(2AB); FA 1995, s 99(4)*].

Buildings for miners etc. Special provisions apply to certain balancing allowances arising in the chargeable period in which a trade consisting of or including the working of a source of mineral deposits ceases, but which cannot be given effect because of an insufficiency of profits. Where the allowances are in respect of buildings occupied by, or for the welfare of, persons employed at or in connection with the working of the source, and they arise because of the source ceasing to be worked or the coming to an end of a foreign concession, the allowances may (subject to restrictions) be carried back to earlier chargeable periods. [*CAA 2001, s 355; CAA 1990, s 17*].

On a sale etc. **before 18 December 1980** (or pursuant to a contract made before that date), a balancing adjustment arose only when the building or structure was in use as an 'industrial building' at the time of the sale etc. Any balancing adjustment which did arise was calculated as follows. If the 'residue of expenditure' (see 9.14 above) immediately before the sale etc. exceeded the proceeds of any sale, insurance, salvage or compensation, the difference was allowed as a balancing allowance; if it was less, the difference was the subject of a balancing charge, subject to two restrictions:

(*a*)   the charge may not exceed the total of industrial buildings, scientific research, and mills, factories or exceptional depreciation allowances given; and

(*b*)   where during any part of the 'relevant period' (see below) the building or structure has not attracted writing-down or scientific research allowances, the charge is reduced to the proportion which the parts of the 'relevant period' which were included in basis periods for which such allowances were given bears to the whole of the 'relevant period'. For this purpose the '*relevant period*' is the period from first use of the building or structure to date of the sale etc. or, if that date is not the last day of a basis period, the most recent day before the sale etc. which was the last day of a basis period.

A restriction similar to that in (*b*) above could be placed on balancing allowances on election by the vendor. [*CAA 1968, s 3 as originally enacted*].

Demolition. The net cost (after crediting sales of materials and scrap) of demolition borne by the person on whom a balancing adjustment arises is added to 'residue of expenditure' for balancing allowance and balancing charge calculations (and those costs are then not taken into account for capital allowance purposes except in the case of dwelling-houses let on assured tenancies, see 9.8 above). [*CAA 2001, s 340; CAA 1990, s 8(12)*]. Where this is not possible (e.g. because more than 25 (or 50) years has elapsed since the building or structure was first used), and if the holder of the relevant interest demolishes the building or structure for the purpose of erecting a new building or structure on the same site, the demolition costs may be treated as expenditure by the holder on construction of the new building or structure. (Revenue Capital Allowances Manual CA 31400).

See also 9.22(i) below as regards certain transactions between connected persons and other anti-avoidance provisions.

Simon's Direct Tax Service. See **B2.237** *et seq.*

9.16   *Examples*

Writing-down allowances and balancing adjustments
Prior to commencing business on 1 June 1994, P incurred the following expenditure.

	£
10.1.94 Plot of land	50,000
20.2.94 Clearing and levelling site	20,000
20.4.94 Construction of factory	500,000
	£570,000

The factory was brought into use for a qualifying purpose on commencement of trade, and remained in such use until 1 May 2004, when it was sold to Y for £550,000, being £480,000 for the factory and £70,000 for the land. P drew up accounts annually to 31 May. Y draws up accounts to 30 April, having commenced trading on 1 May 2004, and uses the factory for a qualifying purpose.

The allowances available to P are as follows.

Period of account ended			Residue of expenditure £
31 May 1995	Qualifying expenditure		520,000
	Writing-down allowance	4% of £520,000	(20,800)
			499,200
31 May 1996	Writing-down allowance for 8 years	4% of £520,000 × 8	(166,400)
1997			
1998			
1999			
2000			
2001			
2002			
2003			
			332,800
31 May 2004	Sale proceeds		(480,000)
	Balancing charge		£147,200

9.16   Capital Allowances

The allowances available to Y are as follows.

Date of first use	1.6.94
Date of purchase by Y	1.5.04
Number of years remaining	15 years 1 month
Residue of expenditure	£480,000

Y is therefore entitled to writing-down allowances of £31,824 p.a. until total allowances reach £480,000. His first writing-down allowance will be given for the period of account 1.5.04 to 30.4.05.

Note

(*a*)   No allowances are due on the cost of the land (see 9.12 above).

Non-qualifying purposes and balancing adjustments

A, B and C entered into partnership in 1976 and prepare accounts annually to 31 March. The partnership incurred £40,000 of capital expenditure in 1986 (and before 31 March 1986) on the construction of a building which was brought into use as an industrial building on 1 April 1987. After three years of use for a qualifying industrial purpose, it was used for three years, from 1 April 1990 to 31 March 1993, for non-qualifying purposes after which the original qualifying activity was resumed until the building was destroyed by fire.

The fire occurred on 1 October 2004 with an insurance recovery of (i) £50,000 (ii) £35,000. The partnership's industrial buildings allowance position for the period of account 1 April 2004 to 31 March 2005 will be as follows.

Year ended 31 March 2005: Balancing charge

(i) *Proceeds exceed cost*		
Actual allowances given	note (*a*)	£30,800
Balancing charge		£30,800

		£
(ii) *Proceeds less than cost*		
Net cost (£40,000 – £35,000)		5,000
Reduction $\dfrac{3y}{17y\ 6m}$	note (*b*)	(857)
Adjusted net cost		4,143
Allowances given	note (*a*)	30,800
Excess		£26,657
Balancing charge		£26,657

Notes

(*a*)   Allowances given in previous years are

136

	£
Initial allowance £40,000 × 25%	10,000
Writing-down allowances £40,000 × 4% × 13	20,800
	£30,800

Writing-down allowances would not have been given for the three years 1991/92 to 1993/94 as the building was not an industrial building at the end of the basis period for each of those years (see 9.14 above).

(*b*)   In example (ii), the net cost is reduced by the proportion which the period of non-qualifying use bears to the total period from first use to date of balancing event (see 9.15 above).

9.17   **Making of allowances and charges.** For traders, allowances and charges are given effect in calculating profits (see 9.1 above and see also below). This applies equally to professions and vocations (see Change 36 in Annex 1 to the Explanatory Notes to the 2001 Capital Allowances Bill). [*CAA 2001, s 352; CAA 1990, ss 9(2), 140(2); FA 1994, s 211*]. Allowances must be claimed in the annual tax return (see 9.2(ii) above). A highway undertaking (see 9.11 above) is treated as a trade. [*CAA 2001, s 341(1); CAA 1990, ss 21(5A), 140(6)*].

Allowances to, and charges on, traders are treated as trading expenses and receipts [*CAA 2001, s 352(1); CAA 1990, s 140; FA 1994, s 211*] and are calculated by reference to events in periods of account (see 9.2(i) above).

Temporarily unused buildings. Where an allowance or charge falls to be made in a period during which a building or structure is temporarily out of use but deemed still to be an industrial building (see 9.11 above) and, since it was last used as such, the trade in question has ceased (or, where the relevant interest was subject to a lease, or the building or structure used under licence, the lease or licence has come to an end), such allowances and charges are dealt with in the same way as those falling to be made to or on lessors (see below). Where a balancing charge falls to be made on any person following such a period of temporary disuse, and the most recent use was as an industrial building for the purposes of a trade carried on by that person which has since ceased, the same deductions can be made from the charge as can be made under *ICTA 1988, s 105* from a post-cessation receipt (see 62.1 POST-CESSATION ETC. RECEIPTS AND EXPENDITURE) (without prejudice to the deduction of any amounts allowable against the balancing charge under other provisions). [*CAA 2001, s 354; CAA 1990, s 15(2)(2A)(3), s 15ZA, s 15A; FA 1996, Sch 39 para 1(2)(4); FA 1998, s 38, Sch 5 paras 48–50, Sch 27 Pt III(4)*].

Lessors (and licensors) of industrial buildings may claim allowances for a tax year. Allowances and balancing charges are treated as expenses and receipts of a Schedule A business (see 69.3 SCHEDULE A) or, if the lease or licence is an asset of an overseas property business, of that business. Where it is not an asset of any property business, allowances and charges are treated as expenses and receipts of a deemed Schedule A business. See 69.12 SCHEDULE A as regards Schedule A losses. [*CAA 2001, s 353; CAA 1990, ss 9, 141, 161(2A); FA 1994, Sch 26 Pt V(24); FA 1995, Sch 6 para 29; FA 1997, Sch 18 Pt VI (11); FA 1998, s 38, Sch 5 para 47*].

For allowances to companies generally, see Tolley's Corporation Tax.

Simon's Direct Tax Service. See **B2.241** *et seq.*

9.18   Capital Allowances

9.18   **Hotels.** Expenditure incurred after 11 April 1978 and before 1 April 1986, or before 1 April 1987 under a contract entered into before 14 March 1984 by the person incurring the expenditure, on construction or extension of a 'qualifying hotel' attracted an initial allowance of 20% and writing-down allowances of 4% p.a.. The 20% initial allowance under *CAA 1990, s 2A* for expenditure incurred in, broadly, the year ending 31 October 1993 (see 9.13 above) applied equally to 'qualifying hotels'. For subsequent expenditure, 'qualifying hotels' attract writing-down allowances as industrial buildings in the normal way (see 9.14 above). Certain expenditure on fire safety and thermal insulation may be treated as on plant and machinery, see 9.25 below.

A *'qualifying hotel'* must have accommodation in building(s) of a permanent nature and be open for at least four months during April–October, and whilst open during those months: (i) must have at least ten letting bedrooms, i.e. private bedrooms for letting to the public generally and not normally in same occupation for more than a month; (ii) must offer sleeping accommodation consisting wholly or mainly of letting bedrooms; and (iii) its services must normally include providing breakfast and evening meals, making beds and cleaning rooms. The provision of breakfast and dinner must be offered as a normal event in the carrying on of the hotel business and must not be exceptional or available only on request. (Revenue Pamphlet IR 131, SP 9/87, 22 September 1987). Buildings provided (and in use) for the welfare of employees are regarded as part of a qualifying hotel. Accommodation which, when the hotel is open during April–October, is normally used as a dwelling by an individual carrying on (including in partnership) the hotel (or by a member of his family or household) is excluded (unless the proportion of the total cost attributable to excluded accommodation is less than 25% (10% before 16 March 1983), in which case the whole of the expenditure qualifies).

The meeting of the above conditions at any time during a chargeable period is determined by reference to their being met during a twelve month period as follows. If the hotel was in use for the trade throughout the twelve months ending with the last day of the chargeable period, it is that twelve month period. If the hotel was first used for the purposes of the trade after the beginning of such a period (or the ten-bedroom requirement commenced to be met after the beginning of such a period), it is the twelve months from commencement (or from the requirement being first met). The conditions are not met at any time in a chargeable period after the hotel has ceased altogether to be used. An hotel in temporary disuse (see 9.11 above) ceases to qualify two years after the end of the chargeable period in which it fell out of use. An hotel outside the UK may qualify provided that the profits etc. are assessable under Schedule D, Case I.

Balancing adjustments arise on a balancing event falling within *CAA 2001, s 315* or *CAA 1990, s 4* (see 9.15 above) (whether or not the hotel is at the time a 'qualifying hotel') or, if the hotel ceases to qualify and there is no such balancing event within two years of the end of the chargeable period in which it ceases to qualify, at the end of that two years, when the hotel is treated as having been sold at market value. The latter 'two-year' rule does not apply to qualifying hotels in enterprise zones (see 9.19 below).

[*CAA 2001, ss 271(1)(b), 279, 282, 283, 285, 317, Sch 3 para 58; FA 1978, s 38, Sch 6; FA 1985, s 66; CAA 1990, ss 7, 19; FA 1990, Sch 13 para 1; FA 1994, Sch 26 Pt V(24)*].

Simon's Direct Tax Service. See B2.252 *et seq.*

9.19   **Enterprise zones.** An 'enterprise zone' is an area designated as such by the Secretary of State (or by Scottish Ministers, the National Assembly for Wales or, for NI, the Department of the Environment). [*CAA 2001, s 298(3); CAA 1990, s 21(4); FA 2001, s 69, Sch 21 para 5*]. Areas designated are as follows.

Zones whose ten-year life expires after 31 March 2004

Ashfield, see East Midlands (No 7)
Barnsley, see Dearne Valley
Bassetlaw, see East Midlands (No 4)
Dearne Valley (Nos 1 to 6) (from 3 November 1995, *SI 1995 No 2624*)
Derbyshire (NE), see East Midlands (Nos 1 to 3)
Doncaster, see Dearne Valley
Easington, see East Durham
East Durham (Nos 1 to 6) (from 29 November 1995, *SI 1995 No 2812*)
East Midlands (Nos 1 to 3) (from 3 November 1995, *SI 1995 No 2625*)
East Midlands (No 4) (from 16 November 1995, *SI 1995 No 2738*)
East Midlands (No 7) (from 21 November 1995, *SI 1995 No 2758*)
Holmewood, see East Midlands (Nos 1 to 3)
Rotherham, see Dearne Valley
Tyne Riverside (North Tyneside) (No 1) (from 19 February 1996, *SI 1996 No 106*)
Tyne Riverside (North Tyneside) (No 2) (from 26 August 1996, *SI 1996 No 1981*)
Tyne Riverside (North Tyneside and South Tyneside) (from 21 October 1996, *SI 1996 No 2435*)

Zones whose ten-year life expired before 1 April 2004

Allerdale, see Workington (Allerdale)
Arbroath, see Tayside (Arbroath)
Belfast (from 21 October 1981, *SR 1981 No 309*)
Clydebank (from 3 August 1981, *SI 1981 No 975*)
Corby (from 22 June 1981, *SI 1981 No 764*)
Delyn (from 21 July 1983, *SI 1983 No 896*)
Dudley (Round Oak) (from 3 October 1984, *SI 1984 No 1403*)
Dudley (not Round Oak) (from 10 July 1981, *SI 1981 No 852*)
Dundee, see Tayside (Dundee)
Flixborough, see Glanford (Flixborough)
Gateshead (from 25 August 1981, *SI 1981 No 1070*)
Glanford (Flixborough) (from 13 April 1984, *SI 1984 No 347*)
Glasgow (from 18 August 1981, *SI 1981 No 1069*)
Hartlepool (from 23 October 1981, *SI 1981 No 1378*)
Inverclyde (from 3 March 1989, *SI 1989 No 145*)
Invergordon (from 7 October 1983, *SI 1983 No 1359*)
Isle of Dogs (from 26 April 1982, *SI 1982 No 462*)
Kent (NW) (zones 1 to 5 only) (from 31 October 1983, *SI 1983 No 1452*)
Kent (NW) (zones 6 and 7 only) (from 10 October 1986, *SI 1986 No 1557*)
Lanarkshire (Hamilton) (from 1 February 1993, *SI 1993 No 23*)
Lanarkshire (Monklands) (from 1 February 1993, *SI 1993 No 25*)
Lanarkshire (Motherwell) (from 1 February 1993, *SI 1993 No 24*)
Lancashire (NE) (from 7 December 1983, *SI 1983 No 1639*)
Liverpool (Speke) (from 25 August 1981, *SI 1981 No 1072*)
London, see Isle of Dogs
Londonderry (from 13 September 1983, *SR 1983 No 226*)
Lower Swansea Valley (from 11 June 1981, *SI 1981 No 757*)
Lower Swansea Valley (No 2) (from 6 March 1985, *SI 1985 No 137*)
Middlesbrough (Britannia) (from 8 November 1983, *SI 1983 No 1473*)
Milford Haven Waterway (North Shore) (from 24 April 1984, *SI 1984 No 443*)
Milford Haven Waterway (South Shore) (from 24 April 1984, *SI 1984 No 444*)
Newcastle (from 25 August 1981, *SI 1981 No 1071*)
Rotherham (from 16 August 1983, *SI 1983 No 1007*)

9.19 Capital Allowances

Salford Docks (from 12 August 1981, *SI 1981 No 1024*)
Scunthorpe (Normanby Ridge and Queensway) (from 23 September 1983, *SI 1983 No 1304*)
Speke, see Liverpool (Speke)
Sunderland (Castletown and Doxford Park) (from 27 April 1990, *SI 1990 No 794*)
Sunderland (Hylton Riverside and Southwick) (from 27 April 1990, *SI 1990 No 795*)
Swansea, see Lower Swansea Valley and Lower Swansea Valley (No 2)
Tayside (Arbroath) (from 9 January 1984, *SI 1983 No 1816*)
Tayside (Dundee) (from 9 January 1984, *SI 1983 No 1817*)
Telford (from 13 January 1984, *SI 1983 No 1852*)
Trafford Park (from 12 August 1981, *SI 1981 No 1025*)
Wakefield (Dale Lane and Kingsley) (from 23 September 1983, *SI 1983 No 1305*)
Wakefield (Langthwaite Grange) (from 31 July 1981, *SI 1981 No 950*)
Wellingborough (from 26 July 1983, *SI 1983 No 907*)
Workington (Allerdale) (from 4 October 1983, *SI 1983 No 1331*)

Advantageous provisions apply to expenditure on the construction of an industrial building, which for this purpose includes a 'qualifying hotel' or a 'commercial building or structure', which is incurred (or contract entered into) within ten years of the inclusion of the site in an enterprise zone. Expenditure incurred more than 20 years after a site was first included in an enterprise zone does not attract enterprise zone allowances, regardless of when the contract for the expenditure was entered into. [*CAA 2001, ss 271(1)(b), 298; CAA 1990, ss 1(1)(2), 17A; FA 1990, Sch 13 para 1; F(No 2)A 1992, Sch 13 para 10*].

'*Qualifying hotel*' has the same meaning as in 9.18 above. (Note that any hotel not qualifying under this heading will qualify as a commercial building.)

'*Commercial building or structure*' means a building or structure which is used for the purposes of a trade, profession or vocation or as an office for any purpose, but does not include any building in use as, or as part of, a dwelling house. [*CAA 2001, s 281; CAA 1990, s 21(5)*].

The allowances given are as follows.

An initial allowance of 100% is given but the full amount need not be claimed. If any part of the initial allowance is not claimed, then **writing-down allowances at 25% p.a.** of cost on the straight line basis will apply to the unclaimed balance. [*CAA 2001, s 306(1)(2), s 310(1)(a); CAA 1990, ss 1, 6; FA 1990, Sch 17 para 2*].

For the general provisions relating to industrial buildings allowances, see 9.11 *et seq.* above. As regards enterprise zone allowances, the following special rules apply.

(i)　*Date expenditure incurred. CAA 2001, s 306(4)* (or *CAA 1990, s 1(10)*)(pre-trading expenditure treated as incurred on first day of trading, see 9.13 above) do not apply in determining whether expenditure attracts enterprise zone allowances (i.e. whether it is incurred at a time when the building or structure is in an enterprise zone).

As regards buildings or structures bought unused, where the purchase price becomes payable after 15 December 1991, the normal rules under *CAA 2001, ss 294–296* (or *CAA 1990, s 10*) apply (see 9.12 above), except that:

(*a*)　where some or all of the actual construction expenditure is incurred (or incurred under a contract entered into) within ten years of the inclusion of the site in an enterprise zone, a corresponding proportion of the purchaser's deemed expenditure is treated as giving rise to entitlement to enterprise zone allowances, notwithstanding that it may be deemed to have been incurred outside that ten-year period;

(b)   where (a) does not apply, the purchaser's deemed expenditure is treated as not giving rise to entitlement to enterprise zone allowances, notwithstanding that it may be deemed to have been incurred during the ten-year period.

Where some of the actual construction expenditure fell within (a) above and some or all of the balance could qualify for a 20% initial allowance by virtue of the provisions in 9.12 above, the above provisions and those in 9.12 above interacted. The purchaser could thus obtain a 100% enterprise zone initial allowance on part of his deemed expenditure and the 20% initial allowance on another part or, where appropriate, on the balance.

[*CAA 2001, ss 300, 302, Sch 3 para 61; CAA 1990, ss 10A, 10C(11); F(No 2)A 1992, Sch 13 paras 2–7, para 14; FA 1993, s 113(4)*].

(ii)   *Buildings purchased within two years of first use.* Where some or all of the construction expenditure on a building or structure first used after 15 December 1991 is incurred (or incurred under a contract entered into) within ten years of the inclusion of the site in an enterprise zone, and the 'relevant interest' (see 9.14 above) is sold during the two years (but see below) following the first use of the building or structure (whether or not there have been any sales while the building or structure was unused), then on that sale (or the first such sale) the normal balancing allowance or charge rules apply to the vendor (see 9.15 above), but the purchaser is deemed to have incurred expenditure on purchase of a building or structure bought unused (see 9.12 and (i) above). A proportion of the deemed expenditure corresponding to the proportion of the actual construction expenditure which was incurred within ten years of the inclusion of the site in the enterprise zone is treated as giving rise to entitlement to enterprise zone allowances, notwithstanding that it may be deemed to have been incurred outside the ten-year period. The balance of the deemed expenditure does not attract enterprise zone allowances. If the purchase is directly from a person who constructed the building or structure in the course of a trade of constructing such buildings or structures for sale, the part of the purchaser's deemed expenditure which does *not* attract enterprise zone allowances is calculated by reference to the actual expenditure of the vendor if that is less than the price actually paid by the purchaser. [*CAA 2001, ss 301, 303, 304, Sch 3 para 62; CAA 1990, s 10B; F(No 2)A 1992, Sch 13 paras 8, 9, 15*]. The two year period is extended to 31 August 1994 where it would otherwise end within the period beginning 13 January 1994 and ending 31 August 1994, and the relevant interest was sold within that period and outside the two year period. [*CAA 2001, Sch 3 para 63; FA 1994, s 121*].

(iii)   *Plant and machinery* forming an integral part of a building or structure was not subject to the restriction of first-year allowances to lessors under *CAA 1990, s 22(4)* (see 9.35 below) (and see now below). [*CAA 1990, s 22(5)*].

(iv)   *Balancing charge on realisation of capital value.* Where capital expenditure on construction of a building or structure in an enterprise zone has been incurred (or is deemed to have been incurred) under a contract entered into after 12 January 1994 (or which becomes unconditional after 25 February 1994), and 'capital value' is received in respect of the building or structure, a balancing charge (but not a balancing allowance) may arise. This applies generally where the payment is made (or an agreement to make it made) seven years or less after the date of the agreement relating to the expenditure (or the date on which that agreement became unconditional). Where, however, there are certain guaranteed exit arrangements, it applies throughout the normal balancing adjustment period (i.e. 25 years from first use, see 9.15 above).

'*Capital value*' is realised when a sum is paid which is attributable to an interest in land to which the relevant interest in the building or structure in question is or will be subject, e.g. where a lease is granted out of the relevant interest, unless *CAA 2001, s 290* (or *CAA 1990, s 11*)(see 9.14 above) applies to the grant of that interest. There are detailed provisions as to the form and amount of the capital value, and as to its attribution to the grant of the interest. See Revenue Capital Allowances Manual CA 37730 *et seq.*

[*CAA 2001, ss 327–331, Sch 3 para 71; CAA 1990, s 4(1)(dd)(9A), s 4A; FA 1994, s 120*].

(v)   *Partially completed buildings.* For the Revenue interpretation of the allowances available where a partially completed building or structure is acquired in an enterprise zone, see Revenue Tax Bulletin June 1998 p 553.

(vi)   It should be noted that where a building or structure in an enterprise zone is sold and the purchaser is *not* treated as having incurred expenditure on its construction, the residue of expenditure (if any) is allowed over the balance of the period of 25 years from first use of the building etc., and not at the 25% writing-down rate (see Revenue Capital Allowances Manual CA 37375).

An 'additional VAT liability' (see 9.2(viii) above) incurred in respect of qualifying expenditure, within ten years of the inclusion of the site in the enterprise zone, is itself qualifying expenditure for the chargeable period in which the liability accrues. [*CAA 2001, s 346; CAA 1990, s 1(1A); FA 1991, Sch 14 para 1*]. Where a 100% initial allowance was not claimed on the expenditure to which the additional VAT liability relates, a 100% allowance may nevertheless generally be claimed for the additional VAT liability. If less than the full 100% allowance is claimed for the additional VAT liability, writing-down allowances for the whole of the expenditure on the building or structure in question will be recomputed as under 9.14 above, resulting in a substantial reduction in the rate of annual allowance.

For balancing adjustments after non-qualifying use, see 9.15 above. For transfers between connected persons etc., see 9.22(i) below.

For the special treatment for tax purposes of investors in enterprise zone property schemes, see *SI 1988 No 267* and *SI 1992 No 571* (and see Revenue Inspector's Manual IM 4213 *et seq.*).

Plant or machinery. Expenditure on plant or machinery, or on thermal insulation treated as plant or machinery under 9.25(ii) below, which is to be an integral part of an industrial or commercial building in an enterprise zone may be treated as part of the expenditure on construction of the building or structure, and so attract the 100% initial allowance. A claim for expenditure on plant or machinery to be so treated does not prevent a subsequent purchaser of the building or structure from claiming plant and machinery allowances on that expenditure and industrial buildings allowances on the fabric of the building. (This commentary is not included in the current Revenue Capital Allowances Manual, but was previously at CA 1060 and is presumed still to be of application.)

Simon's Direct Tax Service. See B2.262 *et seq.*

9.20   *Examples*

(i)

In 2002, J, a builder, incurred expenditure of £400,000 on the construction of a building in a designated enterprise zone. The whole of the expenditure was incurred (or contracted for) within ten years of the site's first being included in the zone. In January 2003, he sold the building unused to K for £600,000 (excluding land). In February 2003, K let the building to a trader who immediately brought it into use as a supermarket. K claims a reduced initial allowance of £50,000. In March 2005, he sells the building to L for £750,000 (excluding land).

K's allowances are as follows.

		£	Residue of expenditure £
2002/03	Qualifying expenditure		600,000
	Initial allowance (maximum 100%)	50,000	
	Writing-down allowance 25% of £600,000	150,000	
	Total IBA due	200,000	(200,000)
2003/04	Writing-down allowance	150,000	(150,000)
			250,000
2004/05	Writing-down allowance	—	—
	Sale proceeds		(750,000)
			£500,000
	Balancing charge (restricted to allowances given)		£350,000

Notes

(a) K's qualifying expenditure would normally be the lesser of cost of construction and the net price paid by him for the building. However, on purchase from a builder, whose profit on sale is taxable as a trading profit, his qualifying expenditure is equal to the net price paid for the relevant interest (excluding the land). See 9.12, 9.19(i) above.

(b) K's allowances and balancing charges are treated as expenses and receipts of a Schedule A business. See 9.17 above. K could have claimed a 100% initial allowance in 2002/03 if he had so wished.

(c) Providing the building continues to be used for a qualifying purpose, L can claim writing-down allowances over the remainder of the 25-year writing-down period. His qualifying expenditure is restricted to £600,000, i.e. the residue of expenditure (£250,000) plus the balancing charge on K. See 9.14 above.

(d) In this example, the first sale after the building was first used took place just over two years after the date of first use. If the sale had taken place within two years after first use, the balancing charge on K would have been computed in the same manner, but L could have claimed an initial allowance and 25% writing-down allowances as if he had bought the building unused. His qualifying expenditure would again have been restricted to £600,000, being the lesser of the price paid by him for the relevant interest in the building and that paid on the original purchase by K from the builder. See 9.19(ii) above.

(ii)

The facts are as in (i) above, except that, of the £400,000 construction expenditure actually incurred, only £360,000 is incurred (or contracted for) within ten years of the site's first being included in an enterprise zone, and the first sale occurred after the expiry of that ten-year period.

9.21 Capital Allowances

K's qualifying expenditure of £600,000 (arrived at as in (i) above) is divided into an enterprise zone element and a non-enterprise zone element.

The enterprise zone element is

$$£600,000 \times \frac{360,000}{400,000} = £540,000$$

The non-enterprise zone element is $£600,000 - £540,000 = £60,000$

The non-enterprise zone element does not qualify for enterprise zone allowances. See 9.19(i) above. (It could have qualified for normal IBAs if the building had been an industrial building.)

K's allowances are as follows.

		£	Residue of expenditure £
2002/03	Qualifying expenditure (enterprise zone element)		540,000
	Initial allowance (maximum 100%)	50,000	
	Writing-down allowance (25% of £540,000)	135,000	
		185,000	(185,000)
2003/04	Writing-down allowance	135,000	(135,000)
			220,000
2004/05	Writing-down allowance	—	—
	Sale proceeds £750,000 × $\dfrac{540,000}{600,000}$		(675,000)
			£455,000
	Balancing charge (restricted to allowances given)		£320,000

L's qualifying expenditure is £540,000, i.e. the residue of £220,000 plus the balancing charge of £320,000 on K.

Note

(*a*)   The apportionment of sale proceeds in 2004/05 is considered to be 'just and reasonable'.

9.21   **Small and very small workshops.** Expenditure incurred after 26 March 1980 and before 27 March 1985 on the construction of an industrial building (or permanently separated part of a larger building or structure, intended and suitable for separate occupation, but common facilities are excepted) of, before 27 March 1983, 2,500 square feet or less, and, after 26 March 1983 and before 27 March 1985, 1,250 square feet or less of gross internal floor space (including ancillary works) qualified for an initial allowance of 100% with similar rights to reduce or disclaim this and receive writing-down allowances of 25% as described in 9.19 above. Similarly the provisions stated at (i), (iii) in 9.19 above applied also to small workshops. [*FA 1980, s 75, Sch 13 Pt I; FA 1982, s 73*]. (Revenue Pamphlet IR 131, SP 6/80, 9 July 1980). For balancing adjustments after non-qualifying use, see 9.15 above. For transfers between connected persons etc., see 9.22(i) below.

See Revenue Pamphlet IR 131, SP 4/80, 26 March 1980 for the application of these provisions where individual units in a larger development did not exceed 2,500 square feet.

The limit of 1,250 square feet could be exceeded in certain cases where existing buildings were converted into separate units. [*FA 1983, s 31*].

9.22   **GENERAL MATTERS.**

(i)   *Connected persons and other anti-avoidance provisions.* Special provisions apply to sales of industrial buildings where

(*a*)   the sale results in no change of control, or

(*b*)   the sole or main benefit apparently arising is the obtaining of an industrial buildings allowance.

Paragraph (*a*) also covers sales between CONNECTED PERSONS (19), and (*b*) includes cases where the anticipated benefit is a reduction in a charge or the *increase* of an allowance. Normally, where these provisions apply, market value is substituted for purchase price (if different), and this also applies to transfers other than by way of sale. However, provided that (*b*) above does not apply, for sales within (*a*) above and other transfers the parties may elect for the substitution of the residue of expenditure (see 9.14 above) if this is lower than market value, and for any subsequent balancing charge on the buyer to be calculated by reference to allowances etc. of both buyer and seller. Such an election is *not* available if the circumstances are such that an allowance or charge which otherwise would or might fall, in consequence of the sale, to be made to or on *any* of the parties to the sale cannot fall to be made. The election must be made within two years after the sale. The election also covers qualifying hotels and commercial buildings etc. in enterprise zones. [*CAA 2001, ss 567–570, 573, 575(1), 577(4); CAA 1990, ss 21(6)(7), 157, 158; FA 1993, s 117(2)(4)(5); FA 1994, s 119(1)*].

Balancing allowances (see 9.15 above) are restricted on sales after 13 June 1972 where the relevant interest (see 9.14 above) in an industrial building is sold subject to a subordinate interest (e.g. in a sale and lease-back) and either

(1)   the seller, the purchaser of the interest, and the grantee of the subordinate interest (or any two of them) are CONNECTED PERSONS (19), or

(2)   the sole or main benefit appears to be the obtaining of an industrial buildings allowance.

In such cases the net sale proceeds are increased, in determining any balancing allowance, by

(A)   where less than a commercial rent is payable under the subordinate interest, the difference between actual sale proceeds and market value had a commercial rent been payable, and

(B)   the amount of any premium receivable for the grant of the subordinate interest and not chargeable under *ICTA 1988, s 34* (see 69.16 SCHEDULE A),

but not by more than is required to eliminate any balancing allowance. Special provisions apply if the terms of the subordinate interest are varied before the sale.

The residue of expenditure (see 9.14 above) following the sale is, however, calculated as if the balancing allowance had been made without the application of these provisions.

[CAA 2001, ss 325, 326; CAA 1990, s 5].

(ii)   *Double allowances.* See 9.2(v) above.

(iii)   *Partnerships* are entitled to industrial buildings allowances in respect of qualifying expenditure (see 9.12 above) on industrial buildings (see 9.11 above).

On a change of partnership, if the trade etc. is treated as continuing, unexhausted allowances are carried forward, and subsequent balancing adjustments (see 9.15 above) made as if the new partnership had carried on the trade etc. before the change. [*CAA 2001, ss 557, 558; CAA 1990, s 152(3); FA 2001, s 69, Sch 21 para 4(2)*]. See also (iv) below as regards allowances on successions to trades.

(iv)   *Successions.* Where a trade etc. changes hands (other than in certain partnership changes (see (iii) above)), then unless the change is not treated as discontinued (see 53.5 PARTNERSHIPS), any asset transferred, without being sold, to the new owner for continuing use in the trade is treated as sold at market value on the date of change, although no initial allowance is available to the new owner. [*CAA 2001, ss 557, 559; CAA 1990, s 152(1)(2)*].

9.23   'KNOW-HOW'

Expenditure incurred after 31 March 1986. Expenditure on acquiring 'know-how' (so far as not otherwise deductible for income tax or corporation tax purposes) gives rise to writing-down and balancing allowances (and balancing charges) where the person acquiring it either:

(i)   is then carrying on a trade for use in which it is acquired; or

(ii)   subsequently commences such a trade (in which case the expenditure is treated as incurred on commencement); or

(iii)   acquires it with a trade (or part) in which it was used, and either the parties to the acquisition make the appropriate joint election under *ICTA 1988, s 531(3)(a)* (see 71.57 SCHEDULE D, CASES I AND II) or the trade was carried on wholly outside the UK before the acquisition.

The same expenditure may not be taken into account in relation to more than one trade.

Expenditure is, however, *excluded* where the buyer and seller are bodies of persons (which includes partnerships) under common control.

[*CAA 2001, ss 452(1), 454, 455; ICTA 1988, ss 530(1)(7), 531(7)*].

'*Know-how*' means any industrial information and techniques of assistance in (*a*) manufacturing or processing goods or materials, (*b*) working, or searching etc. for, mineral deposits, or (*c*) agricultural, forestry or fishing operations. [*CAA 2001, s 452(2)(3); ICTA 1988, s 533(7)*]. For expenditure on offshore divers' training courses treated as on know-how, see Revenue Capital Allowances Manual CA 74000.

All qualifying expenditure of a trade is pooled, and:

(1)   if the 'available qualifying expenditure' exceeds the 'total disposal value', a writing-down allowance is available of **25%** of the excess, proportionately reduced or increased where the period is less or more than one year, or if the trade has been carried on for part only of a chargeable period (and subject to any lesser amount

being claimed), *except that* if the chargeable period is that of permanent discontinuance of the trade, a balancing allowance of **100%** of the excess is available;

(2)   if the 'total disposal value' exceeds the 'available qualifying expenditure', a balancing charge arises of **100%** of the excess.

'Available qualifying expenditure' in a pool for a chargeable period consists of qualifying expenditure allocated to the pool for that period and any unrelieved qualifying expenditure brought forward in the pool from the previous chargeable period (usually referred to as the written-down value brought forward). In allocating qualifying expenditure to the pool, rules identical to those for patent rights at 9.50(i) and (ii) below must be observed.

The *'total disposal value'* is the aggregate of any disposal values to be brought into account for the period, i.e. the net sale proceeds (being capital sums) from any disposal of know-how on which qualifying expenditure was incurred (but excluding any sale the consideration for which is treated as a payment for goodwill under *ICTA 1988, s 531(2)* (see 71.57 SCHEDULE D, CASES I AND II)). (The restriction to capital sale proceeds is introduced by *CAA 2001* (see 9.1 above) — see Change 55 in Annex 1 to the 2001 Capital Allowances Bill.)

The allowances and charges are given effect as deductions or receipts of the relevant trade.

[*CAA 2001, ss 456–463; ICTA 1988,s 530(2)–(5)(8)*].

For receipts arising from sales of know-how, see also 71.57 SCHEDULE D, CASES I AND II.

Expenditure incurred before 1 April 1986. A *writing-down allowance* of one-sixth per annum of the expenditure incurred was available during the six years beginning with the chargeable period in whose basis period the expenditure was incurred. A *balancing allowance* was given of the expenditure unallowed on the trade ceasing during that six years. [*ICTA 1988, s 530(6)–(8) prior to repeal*]. There were no provisions for a balancing charge.

Simon's Direct Tax Service. See B2.615 *et seq.*

9.24   **PLANT AND MACHINERY**

Qualifying expenditure and activities. Allowances are available in respect of 'qualifying expenditure' incurred by a person carrying on a trade or other 'qualifying activity'. Subject to 9.25, 9.26 below and to other specific exclusions, expenditure is *'qualifying expenditure'* if it is 'capital expenditure' (see 9.2(iii) above) incurred on the provision of plant or machinery wholly or partly for the purposes of the qualifying activity carried on by that person, and as a result of which that person owns the plant or machinery (for which see the paragraph on 'Ownership' in 9.27 below). [*CAA 2001, s 11; CAA 1990, ss 22(1), 24(1)*]. See 9.30(C) below as regards partial use for other purposes. Provided these tests are met (but subject to specific restrictions — see, for example, 9.38(C) below), it is irrelevant whether or not the object of the person incurring the expenditure was, or included, the obtaining of capital allowances (see *Barclays Mercantile Business Finance Ltd v Mawson CA 2002, [2003] STC 66*, a case involving complex 'finance leasing' arrangements). Expenditure incurred for the purposes of, and prior to the commencement of, a qualifying activity is treated as incurred on the first day on which the activity is carried on. [*CAA 2001, s 12; CAA 1990, s 83(2)*].

Any of the following is a *'qualifying activity'*:

(i)   a trade, profession or vocation;

(ii) an employment or office (excluding any duties the earnings for which are taxable on the remittance basis — see 75.6 SCHEDULE E—EMPLOYMENT INCOME);

(iii) a Schedule A business (see 69.3 SCHEDULE A) or overseas property business (see 73.4 SCHEDULE D, CASES IV AND V);

(iv) a furnished holiday lettings business (see 69.8 SCHEDULE A);

(v) any of the concerns listed in *ICTA 1988, s 55(2)* (mines, quarries and sundry other undertakings) (not applicable before *CAA 2001* had effect, see 9.1 above, unless the concern qualified as a trade);

(vi) the management of an investment company;

(vii) special leasing, i.e. the hiring out of plant or machinery otherwise than in the course of another qualifying activity (see 9.37 below);

but, for chargeable periods ending after 20 March 2000 (and other than for the purposes of 9.35 and 9.38(C) below), to the extent only that the profits therefrom are within the charge to UK tax (or would be if there *were* any profits).

[*CAA 2001, ss 15–18, 19(1), 20; CAA 1990, ss 27–29, 61(1), 83(2A), 161(2A); FA 1998, Sch 5 para 61; FA 2000, s 75(1)(6); ITEPA 2003, Sch 6 para 248*].

As regards (iii) and (vii) above, expenditure in providing plant or machinery for use in a dwelling-house (or flat — see Revenue Capital Allowances Manual CA 20020, 20040) is not qualifying expenditure. Expenditure on plant and machinery partly for such use is apportioned as is just and reasonable. [*CAA 2001, s 35; CAA 1990, ss 28A(3)(4), 61(2)*].

As regards (ii) above, the plant or machinery must be *necessarily* provided for use in performing the duties of the employment etc. and, from 6 April 2002, mechanically propelled road vehicles and cycles are excluded. [*CAA 2001, s 36; CAA 1990, s 27(2); FA 2001, s 59*]. See 75.46 SCHEDULE E—EMPLOYMENT INCOME for the special provisions relating to private vehicles and cycles before that date. Plant provided by a vicar so as to give visual sermons was held not to comply with this requirement (*White v Higginbottom Ch D 1982, 57 TC 283*). With minor exceptions, expenditure on plant or machinery for providing business entertainment is excluded [*CAA 2001, s 269, Sch 2 para 51; ICTA 1988, s 577(1)(c)*], as is certain expenditure incurred by members of the House of Commons, the Scottish Parliament or the Wales or Northern Ireland Assemblies in or in connection with the provision or use of residential or overnight accommodation. [*CAA 2001, s 34; CAA 1990, s 74; FA 1999, Sch 5 para 2(3)*].

Whether plant or machinery is acquired new or second-hand is generally irrelevant (but see 9.38(C) below as regards certain sales between connected persons etc.). Allowances in respect of leased assets are available to the lessor and not the lessee, irrespective of the accounting treatment adopted. (Revenue Press Release 27 October 1986). See, however, 9.34 below as regards fixtures which become part of land or buildings. A *share* in plant or machinery can qualify for allowances [*CAA 2001, s 270; CAA 1990, s 83(4)*].

Any still unrelieved expenditure incurred before 27 October 1970, and not brought within the then current rules by *FA 1976, s 39*, is outside the scheme of allowances described in this chapter. [*CAA 2001, Sch 3 para 55; CAA 1990, s 82(1)*]. A different scheme applies, for detailed coverage of which see the 1981/82 and earlier editions.

The main elements of the scheme of allowances are dealt with as follows.

Simon's Direct Tax Service. See B2.3.

9.25   **Eligible expenditure.** The capital expenditure eligible for allowances includes that on alteration of existing buildings incidental to the installation of plant or machinery for the purposes of a trade or other qualifying activity [*CAA 2001, s 25; CAA 1990, s 66*] and on demolition of plant or machinery which it replaces [*CAA 2001, s 26(1)(2); CAA 1990, s 62(1)(a)(2)*]. Costs of moving plant from one site to another and re-erecting it, so far as not deductible in computing profits, qualify for allowances (Revenue Capital Allowances Manual CA 21190). Capital expenditure on animals and other living creatures kept for the purposes of farming or any other trade, or on shares in such animals etc., is excluded. [*CAA 2001, s 38; CAA 1990, s 82(2); FA 2000, s 76*].

Meaning of plant or machinery: leading cases. Plant and *machinery* are not statutorily defined. *Machinery* is accordingly given its ordinary meaning, but *plant* has been considered in many cases. It includes apparatus kept for permanent employment in the trade etc., but a line is drawn between that which performs a function in the business operations (which may be plant) and that which provides the place or setting in which these operations are performed (which is not). See *Cole Bros Ltd v Phillips HL 1982, 55 TC 188* (electric wiring and fittings in department store held not to be plant) and *St. John's School v Ward CA 1974, 49 TC 524* (prefabricated school buildings held not to be plant) and contrast *CIR v Barclay, Curle & Co Ltd HL 1969, 45 TC 221* (dry docks, including cost of excavation, held to be plant) and *CIR v Scottish & Newcastle Breweries Ltd HL 1982, 55 TC 252* (lighting and decor of licensed premises held to be plant). If an item used for carrying on a business does not form part of the premises and is not stock-in-trade, then it is plant (*Wimpy International Ltd v Warland CA 1988, 61 TC 51*).

Permanent employment demands some degree of durability, see *Hinton v Maden & Ireland Ltd HL 1959, 38 TC 391* (shoe manufacturer's knives and lasts, average life three years, held to be plant). In practice, a life of two years or more is sufficient, and this applies equally as regards animals functioning as apparatus with which a trade is carried on (see Revenue Capital Allowances Manual CA 21100, 21220).

Held to rank as plant. Movable office partitions (*Jarrold v John Good & Sons Ltd CA 1962, 40 TC 681*); mezzanine platforms installed in a warehouse (but not ancillary lighting) (*Hunt v Henry Quick Ltd Ch D 1992, 65 TC 108*); swimming pools for use on caravan site (*Cooke v Beach Station Caravans Ltd Ch D 1974, 49 TC 514*); grain silos (*Schofield v R & H Hall Ltd CA(NI) 1974, 49 TC 538*); barrister's books (*Munby v Furlong CA 1977, 50 TC 491*); Building Society window screens (*Leeds Permanent Building Society v Proctor Ch D 1982, 56 TC 293*); light fittings (*Wimpy International Ltd v Warland CA 1988, 61 TC 51*); synthetic grass football pitch (*Anchor International Ltd v CIR (Sp C 354), [2003] SSCD 115*).

9.25 Capital Allowances

In relation to certain 'qualifying films' (broadly, British or European films), a *film production* business producing and retaining a master print of a film with an anticipated life of two years or more may elect to treat the cost as capital expenditure on plant (for details, see 71.48 SCHEDULE D, CASES I AND II). [*F(No 2)A 1992, s 40D; CAA 2001, Sch 2 para 82; CAA 1990, s 68(9)–(9C)*]. See *Ensign Tankers (Leasing) Ltd v Stokes HL 1992, 64 TC 617* for relief to investor in film production partnership. Otherwise, see now 71.48 SCHEDULE D, CASES I AND II for relief for production costs treated as revenue expenditure and for special relief for preliminary expenditure.

Held not to be plant. Stallions (*Earl of Derby v Aylmer KB 1915, 6 TC 665*); wallpaper pattern books (*Rose & Co Ltd v Campbell Ch D 1967, 44 TC 500*); canopy over petrol-filling station (*Dixon v Fitch's Garage Ltd Ch D 1975, 50 TC 509*); ship used as floating restaurant (*Benson v Yard Arm Club Ltd CA 1979, 53 TC 67*); false ceilings (*Hampton v Fortes Autogrill Ltd Ch D 1979, 53 TC 691*); a football stand (*Brown v Burnley Football Co Ltd Ch D 1980, 53 TC 357*); an inflatable tennis court cover (*Thomas v Reynolds Ch D 1987, 59 TC 502*); shop fronts, wall and floor coverings, suspended floors, ceilings and stairs etc. (*Wimpy International Ltd v Warland, Associated Restaurants Ltd v Warland CA 1988, 61 TC 51*); permanent quarantine kennels (allowances having been granted for movable kennels) (*Carr v Sayer Ch D 1992, 65 TC 15*); lighting ancillary to mezzanine platform installation qualifying as plant (*Hunt v Henry Quick Ltd Ch D 1992, 65 TC 108*); a planteria (a form of glasshouse, see also below) (*Gray v Seymours Garden Centre (Horticulture) CA 1995, 67 TC 401*); access site and wash hall containing car wash equipment (*Attwood v Anduff Car Wash Ltd CA 1997, 69 TC 575*); housing for underground electricity sub-station (*Bradley v London Electricity plc Ch D 1996, 70 TC 155*); golf putting greens (*Family Golf Centres Ltd v Thorne (Sp C 150), [1998] SSCD 106*); an all-weather horse racing track (*Shove v Lingfield Park 1991 Ltd CA, [2004] STC 805*).

In *McVeigh v Arthur Sanderson & Sons Ltd Ch D 1968, 45 TC 273*, held that cost of blocks etc. of a wallpaper manufacturer (admitted to be plant) should include something for the designs but the designs, following *Daphne v Shaw KB 1926, 11 TC 256*, were not plant. (*Daphne v Shaw* has since been overruled by *Munby v Furlong* above.)

Interest etc. on money borrowed to finance purchases of plant and charged to capital, held not eligible for capital allowances (*Ben-Odeco Ltd v Powlson HL 1978, 52 TC 459* and cf *Van Arkadie v Sterling Coated Materials Ltd Ch D 1982, 56 TC 479*). It is understood that the Revenue consider this exclusion to apply also to architects' fees and preliminary expenses on plant included in building works (Tolley's Practical Tax 1983 p 28, and see also ICAEW TAXline March 1993, para 40).

Lighting. The extent to which lighting and lighting systems may qualify as plant, i.e. as part of the business apparatus as opposed to the setting, is discussed on the Revenue website at www.inlandrevenue.gov.uk/capital_allowances/eca_guidance.htm#lightingappendix   An office lighting system incorporating anti-glare lighting throughout to enable effective use of personal computers may be plant, for example.

Cable television. The cost of provision and installation of ducting in connection with construction of cable television networks is regarded as expenditure on plant or machinery (Revenue Press Release 15 March 1984).

Glasshouses are likely to be accepted as plant only where, during construction, sophisticated environmental control systems are permanently installed, incorporating e.g. a computer system controlling heating, temperature and humidity control, automatic ventilation systems and automatic thermal or shade screens (Revenue Tax Bulletins November 1992 p 46, June 1998 p 552). See, for example, *Gray v Seymours Garden Centre (Horticulture) CA, 67 TC 401*, where a 'planteria' was held to be premises. See also 9.26 below and, as regards whether glasshouses are 'long-life assets', 9.30(G) below.

See generally Revenue Capital Allowances Manual CA 21000 *et seq.*

Certain expenditure on buildings, as below, is treated for capital allowance purposes as being on plant and machinery (unless tax relief could otherwise be obtained). On any disposal, the disposal value (see 9.29 below) in respect of expenditure within (i)–(iii) below is taken as nil [*CAA 2001, s 63(5); CAA 1990, ss 67(1), 69(1), 70(1)*].

(i) *Fire safety expenditure* incurred in a trade or other qualifying activity in taking steps specified in a notice under *Fire Precautions Act 1971, s 5(4)* (or which might have been so specified but were in fact specified in a document from the fire authority on application for a fire certificate under that *Act*) and similarly for expenditure incurred in order to avoid restriction of use of premises by a prohibition notice under *section 10* of that *Act*. [*CAA 2001, ss 27, 29; CAA 1990, s 69*]. Applies to NI by concession (Revenue Pamphlet IR 1, B16 as revised). Applies by Order to hotels and boarding houses (*SI 1972 No 238*) and to premises of factories, offices, shops and railways with minimum of 10 employees (*SI 1976 No 2009*). *Lessors of such premises* may claim allowances on contributions (see 9.2(vii) above) towards tenants' qualifying expenditure or own similar direct expenditure (Revenue Pamphlet IR 1, B16 as revised).

(ii) Expenditure on *thermal insulation of existing industrial building* by a person occupying the building for the purposes of a trade carried on by him or letting the building in the course of a Schedule A business or overseas property business.

[*CAA 2001, ss 27, 28; ICTA 1988, s 32(1B)(1C); CAA 1990, s 67; FA 1994, Sch 26 Pt V(24); FA 1995, Sch 6 paras 8(3), 32; FA 1997, Sch 15 paras 1, 5, Sch 18 Pt VI(11); FA 1998, s 38, Sch 5 para 56, Sch 27 Pt III(4); FA 2001, s 69, Sch 21 para 1*].

(iii) *Sports ground expenditure* incurred by a person carrying on a trade or other qualifying activity to comply with a safety certificate issued or to be issued under the *Safety of Sports Grounds Act 1975* or certified by local authority as falling within requirements if such certificates had been (or could have been) applied for. Also, expenditure incurred by a trade in respect of a 'regulated stand' (as defined by the *Fire Safety and Safety of Places of Sport Act 1987*) to comply with a safety certificate (as defined by that *Act*) issued for the stand or to take steps specified by the local authority as being necessary under the terms, or proposed terms, of such a safety certificate issued, or to be issued, by it. [*CAA 2001, ss 27, 30–32; CAA 1990, s 70*]. See also 9.2(vi)(vii) above as regards certain contributions to expenditure.

(iv) *Hotels and restaurants.* The Revenue regard as eligible for capital allowances expenditure on *apparatus* to provide electric light or power, hot water, central heating, ventilation or air conditioning, alarm and sprinkler systems. Also on cost of hot water pipes, baths, wash basins etc. Also expenditure on alterations to *existing* buildings which is incidental to the installation of plant and machinery. (CCAB Statement, 9 August 1977.) See now *Cole Bros Ltd v Phillips HL 1982, 55 TC 188* and *CIR v Scottish & Newcastle Breweries Ltd HL 1982, 55 TC 252*.

See 9.26 below for provisions restricting allowances for certain expenditure on buildings and structures.

Where it appears that any sums, not otherwise taxable, are to be payable, directly or indirectly, to the owner of plant or machinery in respect of, or to take account of, the *whole* of the **depreciation** of that plant or machinery, the expenditure incurred in providing that plant or machinery for the purposes of the qualifying activity is not qualifying expenditure. [*CAA 2001, s 37; CAA 1990, s 80(1)*]. As regards subsidies towards *partial* depreciation, see 9.38(J) below.

Expenditure on security assets. Except where tax relief could otherwise be obtained, expenditure by an individual, or partnership of individuals, carrying on a trade or any other qualifying activity within 9.24(i), (iii) or (iv) above, in connection with the provision for or use by the individual, or any of them, of a security asset (being an asset which improves personal security), is treated as if it were capital expenditure on plant or machinery. On any disposal the disposal value (see 9.29 below) is taken as nil. They apply only where certain conditions, very similar to those described in 71.71 SCHEDULE D, CASES I AND II, are satisfied, both as regards the provision or use of the asset and the type of asset that may qualify. An appropriate proportion of the expenditure may qualify in cases where the asset is intended to be used *only partly* to improve personal physical security. [*CAA 2001, ss 27, 33, 63(5); CAA 1990, ss 71, 72*]. See also 75.38 SCHEDULE E—EMPLOYMENT INCOME.

Computer software. Where capital expenditure is incurred after 9 March 1992 on the acquisition of computer software for the purposes of a trade or other qualifying activity, the software, if it would not otherwise be plant, is treated as such for capital allowances purposes. Similarly, where capital expenditure is incurred after that date in acquiring for such purposes a right to use or otherwise deal with computer software, both the right and the software are treated as plant provided for the purposes of the qualifying activity and (so long as entitlement to the right continues) as belonging to the person incurring the expenditure.

Where, after 9 March 1992, a right is granted to another person to use or deal with the whole or part of software or rights which are treated as plant, and the consideration for the grant consists of (or would if it were in money consist of) a capital sum, a disposal value (see 9.29 below) has to be brought into account (unless the software or rights have previously begun to be used wholly or partly for purposes other than those of the qualifying activity, or the activity for which they were used has been permanently discontinued). The amount of the disposal value to be brought into account is the net consideration in money received for the grant, plus any insurance moneys or other capital compensation received in respect of the software by reason of any event affecting that consideration. However, market value is substituted where the consideration for the grant was not, or not wholly, in money, or where

- no consideration, or money consideration less than market value, was given for the grant,

- there is no charge under *ITEPA 2003* (i.e. on employment, pension or social security income), and

- the grantee cannot obtain plant and machinery or research and development (formerly scientific research) allowances for his expenditure or is a dual resident investing company connected with the grantor.

Where a disposal value falls to be calculated in relation to software or rights, then for the purpose of determining whether it is to be limited by reference to the capital expenditure incurred (see 9.29 below), that disposal value is increased by any disposal value previously falling to be brought into account as above in respect of the same person and the same plant.

[*CAA 2001, ss 71–73, Sch 3 para 18; CAA 1990, s 24(6A), s 26(1)(ea)(eb)(ec)(2AA), s 67A; F(No 2)A 1992, s 68; FA 1994, Sch 26 Pt V(24); ITEPA 2003, Sch 6 para 251*].

See also 71.62 SCHEDULE D, CASES I AND II.

Enterprise zones. Expenditure on plant or machinery which is to be an integral part of an industrial or commercial building in an enterprise zone may qualify for 100% industrial buildings allowance. See 9.19 above.

Simon's Direct Tax Service. See B2.305 *et seq.*

9.26   **Restrictions on eligible expenditure.** For expenditure incurred after 29 November 1993 (subject to transitional provisions, see below), legislation was introduced by *FA 1994, s 117* (see now *CAA 2001, ss 21–24*) to exclude certain expenditure from the definition of plant and machinery for capital allowances purposes. Assets which have been held to be plant under specific court decisions continue to qualify for plant and machinery allowances, and assets not covered by the *FA 1994* provisions remain subject to prevailing case law on plant. (Revenue Press Release 17 December 1993).

Transitional provisions. Expenditure was not affected by the above-mentioned provisions where it was incurred before 6 April 1996 in pursuance of a contract entered into either before 30 November 1993 or for the purposes of securing compliance with obligations under a contract entered into before that date. [*FA 1994, s 117(2)*].

General exceptions. Expenditure falling within any of *CAA 2001, ss 28–33, 71* and *F(No 2)A 1992, s 40D* or earlier equivalents (relating to thermal insulation, fire safety, safety of sports grounds, security assets, computer software, and films, tapes and discs — see 9.25 above) is not affected by the provisions described below. [*CAA 2001, s 23(1)(2); CAA 1990, Sch AA1 para 4; FA 1994, s 117(1)*].

Expenditure on buildings which does not qualify for allowances. Expenditure on the construction or acquisition of a building will not qualify for plant and machinery allowances where it is incurred after 29 November 1993 (subject to the above transitional provisions and general exceptions and to the specific exceptions listed at (1)–(33) below). For these purposes the expression 'building' includes:

- any assets incorporated in the building;

- any assets which, although not incorporated in the building (because they are movable or for some other reason), are nevertheless of a kind which are normally incorporated into buildings; and

- any of the following:

  (i)   walls, floors, ceilings, doors, gates, shutters, windows and stairs;

  (ii)   mains services, and systems, of water, electricity and gas;

  (iii) waste disposal systems;

  (iv)   sewerage and drainage systems;

  (v)   shafts or other structures in which lifts, hoists, escalators and moving walkways are installed; and

  (vi)   fire safety systems.

[*CAA 2001, s 21; CAA 1990, Sch AA1 para 1(1)(2)(4), para 5(1); FA 1994, s 117(1)*].

Expenditure on structures which does not qualify for allowances. 'Structure' means a fixed structure of any kind, other than a building. A structure is 'any substantial man-made asset' (see Revenue Press Release 17 December 1993).

Expenditure on the construction or acquisition of a structure or any other asset listed immediately below, or on any works involving the alteration of land, will not qualify for plant and machinery allowances where it is incurred after 29 November 1993 (subject to the above transitional provisions and general exceptions and to the specific exceptions listed at (1)–(33) below).

- A tunnel, bridge, viaduct, aqueduct, embankment or cutting.

- A way, hard standing (such as a pavement), road, railway, tramway, a park for vehicles or containers, or an airstrip or runway.

- An inland navigation, including a canal or basin or a navigable river.

- A dam, reservoir or barrage (including any sluices, gates, generators and other equipment associated with it).

- A dock, harbour, wharf, pier, marina or jetty, or any other structure in or at which vessels may be kept or merchandise or passengers may be shipped or unshipped.
- A dike, sea wall, weir or drainage ditch.
- Any structure not included above, except
    (i) a structure (other than a building) within the definition of an 'industrial building' (see 9.11 above),
    (ii) a structure in use for the purposes of a gas undertaking, or
    (iii) a structure in use for the purposes of a trade consisting in the provision of telecommunications, television or radio services,

    and see *Anchor International Ltd v CIR (Sp C 354), [2003] SSCD 115*, in which a synthetic football pitch was held not to be within this exclusion.

[*CAA 2001, s 22, Sch 3 para 13; CAA 1990, Sch AA1 para 2(1)(2)(4), para 5(1); FA 1994, s 117(1)*].

Specific exceptions. The above exclusions do not affect the question as to whether expenditure on any of the items listed in (1)–(33) below qualifies for plant and machinery allowances. Note that items (1)–(16) below do not include any asset whose principal purpose is to insulate or enclose the interior of a building or to provide an interior wall, floor or ceiling which (in each case) is intended to remain permanently in place.

(1) Any machinery (including devices for providing motive power) not within any other item in this list.

(2) Electrical systems (including lighting systems) and cold water, gas and sewerage systems provided mainly to meet the particular requirements of the qualifying activity, or provided mainly to serve particular plant or machinery used for the purposes thereof.

(3) Space or water heating systems; powered systems of ventilation, air cooling or air purification; and any ceiling or floor comprised in such systems.

(4) Manufacturing or processing equipment; storage equipment, including cold rooms; display equipment; and counters, checkouts and similar equipment.

(5) Cookers, washing machines, dishwashers, refrigerators and similar equipment; washbasins, sinks, baths, showers, sanitary ware and similar equipment; and furniture and furnishings.

(6) Lifts, hoists, escalators and moving walkways.

(7) Sound insulation provided mainly to meet the particular requirements of the qualifying activity.

(8) Computer, telecommunication and surveillance systems (including their wiring or other links).

(9) Refrigeration or cooling equipment.

(10) Fire alarm systems; sprinkler and other equipment for extinguishing or containing fires.

(11) Burglar alarm systems.

(12) Strong rooms in bank or building society premises; safes.

(13) Partition walls, where movable and intended to be moved in the course of the qualifying activity.

(14) Decorative assets provided for the enjoyment of the public in hotel, restaurant or similar trades.

(15)   Advertising hoardings; signs, displays and similar assets.

(16)   Swimming pools (including diving boards, slides and structures on which such boards or slides are mounted).

(17)   Any glasshouse constructed so that the required environment (namely, air, heat, light, irrigation and temperature) for the growing of plants is provided automatically by means of devices forming an integral part of its structure; see also below.

(18)   Cold stores.

(19)   Caravans provided mainly for holiday lettings. (Under *CAA 2001, s 23(5)*, 'caravan' includes, in relation to a holiday caravan site, anything treated as such for the purposes of the *Caravan Sites and Control of Development Act 1960* (or NI equivalent). Before *CAA 2001* had effect (see 9.1 above) the definition in *section 29(1)* of the fore-mentioned 1960 Act was adopted by concession, see Revenue Pamphlet IR 1, B50.)

(20)   Buildings provided for testing aircraft engines run within the building.

(21)   Movable buildings intended to be moved in the course of the qualifying activity.

(22)   The alteration of land for the purpose only of installing plant or machinery.

(23)   The provision of dry docks.

(24)   The provision of any jetty or similar structure provided mainly to carry plant or machinery.

(25)   The provision of pipelines, or underground ducts or tunnels with a primary purpose of carrying utility conduits.

(26)   The provision of towers provided to support floodlights.

(27)   The provision of any reservoir incorporated into a water treatment works or any service reservoir of treated water for supply within any housing estate or other particular locality.

(28)   The provision of silos provided for temporary storage; or storage tanks.

(29)   The provision of slurry pits or silage clamps.

(30)   The provision of fish tanks or fish ponds.

(31)   The provision of rails, sleepers and ballast for a railway or tramway.

(32)   The provision of structures and other assets for providing the setting for any ride at an amusement park or exhibition.

(33)   The provision of fixed zoo cages.

Before *CAA 2001* had effect (see 9.1 above), these rules operated slightly more restrictively in that the exceptions at (18)–(21) above applied only in relation to buildings, and certain of the other exceptions applied only in relation to structures (see the 2000/01 and earlier editions).

As regards expenditure on *glasshouses* (item 17 above), see 9.25 above for the Revenue approach to allowances for such expenditure, and 9.30(G) below as regards whether glasshouses are 'long-life assets'.

[*CAA 2001, s 23(3)–(5); CAA 1990, Sch AA1 para 1(3)(4), para 2(3)(4), para 5(1)(2)); FA 1994, s 117*].

Interests in land. Expenditure on the provision of plant or machinery does not include expenditure incurred after 29 November 1993 (subject to the above transitional provisions) on the acquisition of an interest in land, but this restriction does not apply to any asset which is so installed or otherwise fixed in or to any description of land as to become, in law, part of that land. 'Land' does not include buildings or other structures but is otherwise as defined in *Interpretation Act 1978, Sch 1*. 'Interest in land' for these purposes has the same meaning as in *CAA 2001, s 175* (allowances for fixtures — see 9.34 below). [*CAA 2001, s 24; CAA 1990, Sch AA1 paras 3, 5; FA 1994, s 117(1)*].

Simon's Direct Tax Service. See B2.308.

9.27   **First-year allowances.** A person is entitled to a first-year allowance (FYA) for a chargeable period (see 9.2(i) above) in respect of any 'first-year qualifying expenditure' which he incurs in that period on plant and machinery which he owns (see below under *Ownership*) at some time during that period. He may claim the allowance in respect of the whole or a part of the first-year qualifying expenditure. In determining for these purposes the time at which expenditure is incurred, *CAA 2001, s 12* (pre-commencement expenditure — see 9.24 above) is disregarded. Otherwise, see 9.2(iv) above as regards the date on which expenditure is treated as having been incurred.

Subject to the exclusions below, qualifying expenditure (as in 9.24 above) is *'first-year qualifying expenditure'* if it is incurred

(*a*)   **after 1 July 1997** by a **'small or medium-sized enterprise'**, in which case the maximum FYA is as follows:

    (i)   (except where (ii) below applies) **40%** (of the amount of the expenditure) for expenditure incurred **after 1 July 1998** (but long-life assets are excluded);

    (ii)   (in the case of a **'small enterprise'** only (as distinct from a 'small or medium-sized enterprise')) **50%** for expenditure incurred within the tax year **2004/05** only (or, for corporation tax purposes, within the 12 months beginning 1 April 2004) (but long-life assets remain excluded); and

    (iii)   **50%** for expenditure incurred **before 2 July 1998** (12% in the case of long-life assets — see 9.30(G) below); or

(*b*)   **after 31 March 2000 and before 1 April 2004** by a **'small enterprise'** (as distinct from a 'small or medium-sized enterprise') on **'information and communications technology'**, in which case the maximum FYA is **100%**; or

(*c*)   **after 11 May 1998 and before 12 May 2002** by a **'small or medium-sized enterprise'** on the provision of plant and machinery for use primarily in **Northern Ireland**, in which case the maximum FYA is **100%**; or

(*d*)   **after 31 March 2001** by any person on **'energy-saving plant or machinery'** which is unused and not second-hand, in which case the maximum FYA is **100%** (available for income tax periods of account ending after 5 April 2001 and corporation tax accounting periods ending after 31 March 2001); or

(*e*)   **after 16 April 2002 and before 1 April 2008** by any person on cars first registered after 16 April 2002 which are either **'electrically-propelled'** or have **'low carbon dioxide emissions'**, and which are unused and not second-hand, in which case the maximum FYA is **100%**; or

(*f*)   **after 16 April 2002 and before 1 April 2008** by any person on plant or machinery, unused and not second-hand, installed at a **'gas refuelling station'** for use solely for or in connection with refuelling vehicles with natural gas or hydrogen fuel, in which case the maximum FYA is **100%**; or

(*g*)   **after 16 April 2002** by a company on plant or machinery for use wholly for the purposes of a **'ring fence trade'** within *ICTA 1988, s 501A* (petroleum extraction activities, see Tolley's Corporation Tax under Oil Companies), in which case the maximum FYA is **100%** (reduced to **24%** where the plant etc. is a long-life asset, see 9.30(G) below); (the relief is, however, withdrawn where the plant etc. is used for less than five years in such a trade, see *CAA 2001, s 45G; FA 2002, Sch 21 para 4*); or

(*h*)   **after 31 March 2003** by any person on '**environmentally beneficial plant or machinery**', unused and not second-hand, in which case the maximum FYA is **100%** (but long-life asset expenditure, see 9.30(G) below, does not qualify).

Exclusions. FYAs are not available under *any* of (*a*)–(*h*) above in the circumstances listed below (and note also the exclusion of long-life assets from (*a*)(i) and (*a*)(ii) above and from (*h*) above).

   (i)   The expenditure is incurred in the chargeable period in which the qualifying activity is permanently discontinued.

  (ii)   The expenditure is incurred on the provision of a '*car*', defined for these purposes (by *CAA 2001, s 81*) as a mechanically propelled road vehicle which is neither (1) of a construction primarily suited for the conveyance of goods or burden of any description nor (2) of a type not commonly used as a private vehicle and unsuitable for such use; a 'car' thus includes a motor cycle.

         As regards (2), see employee benefits case of *Gurney v Richards Ch D, [1989] STC 682* (fire brigade car equipped with flashing light held within excluded class), decided on similarly worded legislation (see 75.18 SCHEDULE E—EMPLOYMENT INCOME). See also *Bourne v Auto School of Motoring Ch D 1964, 42 TC 217* (driving school cars) and *Roberts v Granada TV Rental Ltd Ch D 1970, 46 TC 295* (mini-vans etc.).

         This exclusion does *not* apply as regards (*e*) above, in relation to which the above definition of 'car' applies but with the specific inclusion of any mechanically-propelled road vehicle of a type commonly used as a hackney carriage, and the specific exclusion of motorcycles.

 (iii)   The expenditure is on a ship or railway asset of a kind excluded from being a long-life asset (see 9.30(G)(iii)(iv) below).

  (iv)   The plant or machinery would be a long-life asset but for the transitional provisions of *CAA 2001, Sch 3 para 20* (see 9.30(G) below).

   (v)   The expenditure is on plant or machinery for leasing (whether or not in the course of a trade). For this purpose, 'leasing' expressly includes the letting of a ship on charter or of any other asset on hire. This exclusion does *not* apply as regards expenditure incurred after 16 April 2002 within (*d*), (*e*) or (*f*) above or expenditure within (*h*) above.

         Expenditure by a company on plant and machinery to be used by its subsidiary in return for an annual charge fell within the exclusion (*M F Freeman (Plant) Ltd v Jowett (Sp C 376), [2003] SSCD 423*).

         In an article published initially on their website and subsequently in their Tax Bulletin, the Revenue announced a change of view concerning the supply by a business of plant or machinery with an operator. Where the equipment is to be operated solely by the operator thus provided, the Revenue now accept that this is the provision of a service and not merely plant hire. FYAs are not excluded in such a case. Previously, this applied only where overall supervision and control rested with the operator and not, as is usual, with the hirer; the change of view cannot be used to reopen closed periods. They also now accept that the provision of building access services by the scaffolding industry (but not simply the supply of scaffolding poles etc. for use by others) is the provision of a service. (Revenue Internet Statement 2 June 2003; Revenue Tax Bulletin August 2003 p 1054).

(vi) The provision of the plant or machinery is connected with a change in the nature or conduct of a trade or business carried on by a person other than the person incurring the expenditure on its provision, and the obtaining of an FYA was the main benefit, or one of the main benefits, which could reasonably be expected to arise from the making of the change.

(vii) The provision of the plant of machinery is by way of gift (see 9.38(D) below).

(viii) The plant or machinery was previously used by the owner for purposes other than those of the qualifying activity (see 9.38(E) below).

(ix) The plant or machinery is acquired by means of a transaction with a connected person (within *ICTA 1988, s 839* — see 19 CONNECTED PERSONS), or a sale and leaseback (or sale and finance leaseback) transaction, or a transaction the sole or main benefit of which would be the obtaining of a plant and machinery allowance (see *CAA 2001, ss 217, 223, 232; CAA 1990, ss 75, 76(1), 76A(1); F(No 2)A 1997, s 46(2)(3)*).

Also excluded from (*b*) above (expenditure on information and communications technology) is expenditure incurred after 25 March 2003 on software (including software rights) if the person incurring the expenditure does so with a view to granting to another person a right to use or otherwise deal with any of the software in question. This is intended to exclude the *sub-licensing* of software rights; *leasing* activities were already excluded by virtue of (v) above.

Also excluded from (*c*) above (expenditure for NI purposes) is expenditure on long-life assets (see 9.30(G) below), on aircraft or hovercraft or on goods vehicles for use in a trade consisting primarily of the conveyance of goods, and unauthorised expenditure on plant or machinery for use primarily in agriculture, fishing or fish farming or in any transportation, storage, preparation, processing or packaging activities carried out in bringing any agricultural produce, fish or fish product to market. Expenditure is unauthorised for this purpose unless it is authorised by the Department of Agriculture and Rural Development in Northern Ireland, and provision is made for the necessary exchange of information between the Revenue and that Department. Expenditure is also excluded where, when it is incurred, the person incurring it intends the plant or machinery to be used partly outside NI, and there are arrangements (of which the transaction under which the expenditure is incurred forms part) from which the main benefit, or one of the main benefits, which could reasonably be expected to be the obtaining of an FYA (or greater FYA) in respect of so much of the expenditure as is attributable (on a just and reasonable basis) to the intended use outside NI. There are also provisions for the withdrawal of FYAs if, within two years of the expenditure being incurred (five years where the expenditure concerned exceeds £3.5 million), and at a time when the plant or machinery belongs to the person who incurred it (or a connected person), the primary use to which it is put is a use outside NI, or it is held for use otherwise than primarily in NI. Any person whose return is rendered incorrect by such a change of use must (subject to penalty) amend the return within three months of becoming aware that it has become incorrect.

Definitions. '*Small or medium-sized enterprise*' is defined for the purposes of (*a*) and (*c*) above by reference to the *Companies Act 1985, s 247* (or NI equivalent) definition of 'small or medium-sized company'. Broadly, the requirement is that two of the following three conditions are fulfilled: that the turnover not exceed £22.8 million; that the assets not exceed £11.4 million; and that there be not more than 250 employees. (For accounting periods ended before 30 January 2004, the two monetary thresholds were £11.2 million and £5.6 million respectively — there is provision to prevent the benefit of the increased limits being brought forward by a change of accounting date — see Revenue Press Release 30

January 2004 and *SI 2004 No 16*.) If an enterprise which previously qualified fails to satisfy this requirement over two consecutive financial years, it will cease to qualify with effect from the second of those years, and an enterprise which did not previously qualify but which satisfies the requirement over two consecutive financial years will qualify with effect from the second of those years. In the case of a company which is a member of a group of companies, the requirements apply to the group as a whole. For expenditure incurred after 11 May 1998 (but not for the purposes of the allowances available for expenditure incurred before 2 July 1998, or for the purposes of those available for expenditure incurred thereafter where the contract was entered into before 12 May 1998), the group which has to be considered in this context includes any international group of which the company is a member.

'*Small enterprise*' is similarly defined for the purposes of (*a*)(ii) and (*b*) above, but by reference to the *Companies Act 1985* definition of 'small company', i.e. where two of the following three conditions are fulfilled: that the turnover does not exceed £5.6 million; that the assets are not more than £2.8 million; and that there be not more than 50 employees. (For accounting periods ended before 30 January 2004, the two monetary thresholds were £2.8 million and £1.4 million respectively — there is provision to prevent the benefit of the increased limits being brought forward by a change of accounting date — see Revenue Press Release 30 January 2004 and *SI 2004 No 16*.)

'*Information and communications technology*' is divided for the purposes of (*b*) above into three classes: computers and associated equipment (but excluding computerised control or management systems or other systems that are part of a larger system whose principal function is not processing or storing information); other qualifying equipment (i.e. WAP and third generation mobile telephones and data network reception and transmission devices for use with television sets, and similar devices capable of receiving and transmitting information from and to data networks); and software (i.e. the right to use or otherwise deal with software for the purposes of equipment within the first two classes). The class of 'other qualifying equipment' may be further defined or added to by Treasury order.

'*Energy-saving plant or machinery*', for the purposes of (*d*) above, is plant or machinery which, either at the time the expenditure is incurred or at the time the contract for its provision is entered into, is of a description specified by Treasury order *and* meets the energy-saving criteria specified by Treasury order for plant or machinery of that description. Expenditure incurred, or incurred under a contract entered into, after 31 March 2001 but before 16 July 2001 (the date of making of the first Treasury order) qualifies if it would have done so had that order already been made when the expenditure was incurred. A Treasury order may identify qualifying plant or machinery by reference to lists of technology or products issued by the relevant Secretary of State; the first order refers to the Energy Technology Product List (ETPL) initially published on 1 April 2001 (and available at www.eca.gov.uk). An order may also provide that, in specified cases, no FYA is to be given under (*d*) above unless a '*relevant certificate of energy efficiency*' is in force, i.e. a certificate issued by the Secretary of State, the Scottish Ministers, the Welsh Assembly or the relevant NI department, or by persons authorised by them, to the effect that a particular item, or an item constructed to a particular design, meets the relevant energy-saving criteria. The first order so specifies certain combined heat and power equipment. With effect after 4 August 2003, component based fixed systems falling within the technology class 'automatic monitoring and targeting equipment' (see below) were also specified. If a certificate is revoked, it is treated as having never been in issue, with the result that FYAs under (*d*) above will not have been available. Subject to penalty under *TMA 1970, s 98* for non-compliance, a person who has consequently made an incorrect tax return must give notice to the Revenue, specifying the amendment required to the return, within three months of his becoming aware of the problem. Technology classes initially included in the ETPL, subject to the appropriate criteria, certification or product approval, were boilers, combined heat and power, lighting, motors and drives, pipework insulation, refrigeration and thermal screens. The following were added with effect after 4 August 2002: heat pumps for space heating, radiant and warm air heaters, compressed air equipment and solar thermal systems. With effect after 4 August 2003, automatic monitoring and targeting equipment was added. If one or more components of an item of plant and machinery qualify under these provisions, but the whole item does not, normal apportionment rules are disapplied, and instead the first-year qualifying expenditure under (*d*) above is limited to the amount (or aggregate amount) specified in the ETPL for that component (or those components); where relevant, each *instalment* of expenditure falls to be apportioned in the same way as the whole. See generally the detailed Guidance Notes published on the Revenue website on 13 March 2002.

For the purposes of (*e*) above, a car has '*low carbon dioxide emissions*' if it is first registered on the basis of an EC certificate of conformity, or a UK approval certificate, which specifies a carbon dioxide emissions figure of 120g/km or less (a combined figure not exceeding that limit where more than one figure is specified). In the case of a bi-fuel car (whether petrol/road fuel gas or diesel/road fuel gas), the limit applies by reference to the lowest figure specified by the certificate (the lowest combined figure where more than one figure is specified for each fuel). The 120g/km limit is variable by Treasury order. A car is '*electrically-propelled*' if is propelled solely by electrical power derived from an external source or from a storage battery not connected to any source of power when the car is in motion. See also Revenue Capital Allowances Manual CA 23153.

For the purposes of (*f*) above, a '*gas refuelling station*' is any premises (or part) where mechanically-propelled road vehicles are refuelled with natural gas or hydrogen fuel. Plant or machinery installed for use solely for or in connection with such refuelling includes any storage tank for such fuels, any compressor, pump, control or meter used in the refuelling and any equipment for dispensing such fuels to vehicles' fuel tanks.

'*Environmentally beneficial plant or machinery*', for the purposes of (*h*) above, is plant or machinery which, either at the time the expenditure is incurred or at the time the contract for its provision is entered into, is of a description specified by Treasury order *and* meets the environmental criteria specified by Treasury order for plant or machinery of that description. A Treasury order may identify qualifying plant or machinery by reference to technology lists or product lists issued by the relevant Secretary of State. The intention is to promote the use of technologies, or products, designed to remedy or prevent damage to the physical environment or natural resources (Revenue Press Release BN 26, 9 April 2003); the first order refers to the Water Technology Product List (WTPL) initially published in April 2003 (and available at www.eca-water.gov.uk). Expenditure incurred, or incurred under a contract entered into, after 31 March 2003 but before 11 August 2003 (the date of making of the first Treasury order) qualifies if it would have done so had that order already been made when the expenditure was incurred or the contract entered into. An order may provide that, in specified cases, no FYA is to be given under (*h*) above unless a '*relevant certificate of environmental benefit*' is in force, i.e. a certificate issued by the Secretary of State, the Scottish Ministers, the Welsh Assembly or the relevant NI department, or by persons authorised by them, to the effect that a particular item, or an item constructed to a particular design, meets the relevant environmental criteria (though the first order makes no such provision). If a certificate is revoked, it is treated as having never been in issue, with the result that FYAs under (*h*) above will not have been available. Subject to penalty under *TMA 1970, s 98* for non-compliance, a person who has consequently made an incorrect tax return must give notice to the Revenue, specifying the amendment required to the return, within three months of his becoming aware of the problem. Technology classes initially included in the WTPL, subject to the appropriate criteria or product approval, are water meters, flow controllers, leakage detection equipment, low flush toilets and efficient taps. If one or more components of an item of plant and machinery qualify under these provisions, but the whole item does not, normal apportionment rules are disapplied, and instead the first-year qualifying expenditure under (*h*) above is limited to the amount (or aggregate amount) specified in the WTPL for that component (or those components); where relevant, each *instalment* of expenditure falls to be apportioned in the same way as the whole.

[*CAA 2001, ss 39–52, Sch 3 paras 14, 48–50; CAA 1990, s 22(1)(1AA)(3C)–(3H)(6B)–(7)(10), ss 22A, 22AA, 22B, 22C, 50(2); FA 1990, Sch 17 para 3; F(No 2)A 1997, s 42; FA 1998, ss 83–85; FA 1999, s 78; FA 2000, ss 70–72; FA 2001, s 65, Sch 17, Sch 33 Pt II(4); FA 2002, ss 59, 61–63, Sch 19 paras 2–5, Sch 20, Sch 21 Pt 1; FA 2003, ss 165–167, Sch 30; FA 2004, s 142; SI 1999 No 2119; SI 2001 No 2541; SI 2002 No 1818; SI 2003 Nos 1744, 2076*].

In general, where expenditure has qualified for an FYA (including a universal FYA — see below), any 'additional VAT liability' (see 9.2(viii) above), incurred in respect of that expenditure at a time when the plant or machinery in question is provided for the purposes of the qualifying activity, also qualifies — at the same rate and for the chargeable period in which the liability accrues. Where *CAA 2001* has effect (see 9.1 above), it is made clear that an additional VAT liability incurred at a time when the plant or machinery is used for overseas leasing other than protected leasing (see 9.35 below) does not qualify for an FYA, and nor does such a liability qualify if incurred at a time when an FYA given on the original expenditure has fallen to be withdrawn under the NI provisions above. However, there is nothing in *CAA 2001* to prevent an FYA in respect of an additional VAT liability from being available in the chargeable period in which the qualifying activity is permanently discontinued, notwithstanding exclusion (i) above, where the liability (but not the original expenditure) is incurred in that period; on a strict interpretation, this was not previously the case. [*CAA 2001, ss 236, 237, Sch 3 paras 46–50; CAA 1990, s 22(1A)(1B); FA 1991, Sch 14 para 6*].

Partial use for non-trade etc. purposes results in FYAs being scaled down as is just and reasonable. [*CAA 2001, s 205; CAA 1990, s 79; FA 1971, Sch 8 para 5; FA 1985, Sch 14 para 2*]. See 9.30(C) below as regards writing-down allowances in such cases.

See 9.38(J) below for the scaling down of FYAs where it appears that a *partial depreciation subsidy* will be payable.

See 9.38(G) below for the denial of FYAs on plant and machinery treated as changing hands by virtue of certain partnership changes and other *successions*.

Ownership. Before *CAA 2001* had effect (see 9.1 above), the question of whether a person *owns* plant and machinery at some time in the chargeable period in which the expenditure is incurred was expressed in terms of whether it *belonged* to him at some time during the chargeable period related to the incurring of the expenditure. [*CAA 1990, s 22(1)*]. 'Belongs' has its ordinary meaning and normally entails a right of disposition over the thing possessed. See also *Bolton v International Drilling Co Ltd Ch D 1982, 56 TC 449, Ensign Tankers (Leasing) Ltd v Stokes HL 1992, 64 TC 617, Melluish v BMI (No 3) Ltd HL 1995, 68 TC 1* and *BMBF (No 24) Ltd v CIR Ch D, [2002] STC 1450*. Following the decision in *Stokes v Costain Property Investments Ltd CA 1984, 57 TC 688*, specific provisions were introduced to determine entitlement to allowances for plant or machinery which are fixtures (see 9.34 below). See 9.38(A) below as regards plant and machinery acquired on hire-purchase, and 9.38(K) below as regards certain expenditure incurred by a lessee under the terms of a lease. For ownership of certain assets transferred under oil production sharing contracts to the government or representative of the production territory, see *CAA 2001, s 171 (formerly CAA 1990, s 64A introduced by FA 2000, s 81)*. The change in terminology in *CAA 2001* is not intended to be a change in the law.

Universal FYAs (no longer available). FYAs were previously available universally (as opposed to being specifically targeted as above) at the following rates.

After 26 October 1970	— 60%	*After* 13 March 1984	— 75%
After 19 July 1971	— 80%	*After* 31 March 1985	— 50%
After 21 March 1972	— 100%		

Universal FYAs were subject to the same general conditions being satisfied as to ownership of the plant or machinery and the expenditure being qualifying expenditure (see 9.24 above). Claims could be made for all or part of the allowances available. They were generally **abolished** for expenditure **after 31 March 1986**, although they continued at the 100% rate for expenditure incurred before 1 April 1987 in certain cases involving pre-14 March 1984 contracts.

As a temporary measure, universal FYAs were reinstated at a rate of **40%** in respect of expenditure incurred **after 31 October 1992 and before 1 November 1993**, disregarding the effect of *CAA 1990, s 83(2)* (pre-commencement expenditure — see 9.24 above), and in respect of any 'additional VAT liability' (see 9.2(viii) above) incurred (at whatever time) in relation to such expenditure.

Exclusions similar to those for targeted FYAs in (i) and (ix) above applied for universal FYAs. In addition, the following did not qualify for universal FYAs.

(A)   Cars, defined as in (ii) above, except where provided wholly or mainly for a trade of hire to, or carriage of, members of the public (i.e. not where hiring etc. is limited to a certain class of customers, such as business connections or group companies), but see also below.

(B)   Certain assets used for leasing (see 9.35 below).

[*CAA 2001, Sch 3 paras 46, 47(1)–(3); CAA 1990, s 22(1)(3B)(4)(a)(b); FA 1993, s 115*].

The exception in (A) above for hire etc. cars applies only if the vehicle was either not normally on hire etc. to the same person (or a person connected with him, see 19 CONNECTED PERSONS) for a period of 30 or more consecutive days or for 90 or more days in any 12-month period; or was provided to a person who himself satisfied those conditions in using it wholly or mainly for a trade of hire etc. to members of the public (e.g. a taxi driver). These restrictions do not, however, apply to vehicles supplied for the use of persons receiving a social security mobility allowance, disability living allowance or war pensioners' mobility supplement and certain other like payments. [*CAA 1990, ss 22(4)(b), 36; SI 1991 No 2874*].

As regards partial use for non-trade purposes, partial depreciation subsidies, and successions, the same comments apply as for targeted FYAs above.

Ships (postponement of FYAs). Where a ship qualifies for an FYA (and note the exclusion at (iii) above), the person entitled may, by written notice, *postpone* all or part of the allowance. The amount to be postponed must be specified in the notice. Where an FYA is claimed in respect of part only of the qualifying expenditure, the above applies in respect of the FYA claimed. The time limit within which notice must be given is (i) for income tax, twelve months after 31 January following the tax year in which ends the chargeable period for which the allowance is due, and (ii) for corporation tax, two years after the end of the chargeable period. Available qualifying expenditure for writing-down allowances (see 9.28 below) is computed as if the postponed FYA had, in fact, been made. Postponed FYAs may be claimed over one or more subsequent chargeable periods. [*CAA 2001, s 130(1)(3)–(6), s 131(1)(2)(4)(7); CAA 1990, s 30; FA 1990, Sch 17 para 7; FA 1993, Sch 13 para 3; FA 1996, s 135, Sch 21 para 27*]. See 9.30(B) below for postponement of writing-down allowances and deferment of balancing charges.

Simon's Direct Tax Service. See B2.320 *et seq.*

9.28   **Pooling, writing-down allowances and balancing adjustments.** Qualifying expenditure (as in 9.24 above) is *pooled* for the purpose of determining entitlement to writing-down allowances and balancing allowances and liability to balancing charges. In addition to the *main pool* for each qualifying activity, there may be a *single asset pool* and/or a *class pool*, and qualifying expenditure falling to be allocated to either of the latter (see 9.30, 9.35, 9.38(J) below) cannot be allocated to the main pool.

For each pool of qualifying expenditure, a **writing-down allowance (WDA)** is available for each chargeable period (see 9.2(i) above) other than the 'final chargeable period' and is equal to a maximum of **25%** of the amount (if any) by which 'available qualifying expenditure' exceeds the total of any disposal values (see 9.29 below) falling to be brought into account. See 9.30(G) below (long-life assets) and 9.35(*a*)(*b*) below (overseas leasing) for exceptions to the 25% rate. The WDA is proportionately reduced or increased if the chargeable period is less or more than a year, or if the qualifying activity has been carried on for part only of the chargeable period. A claim for a WDA may require it to be reduced to a specified amount. For the 'final chargeable period', a **balancing allowance** is available, equal to the excess (if any) of (1) 'available qualifying expenditure' over (2) total disposal values. If, for *any* chargeable period, (2) exceeds (1), there arises a liability to a **balancing charge**, equal to that excess.

The '*final chargeable period*', as regards the main pool, is the chargeable period in which the trade or other qualifying activity is permanently discontinued. As regards a single asset pool, it is normally the first chargeable period in which a disposal event (see 9.29 below) occurs. As regards class pools, see 9.30(G) (long-life assets) and 9.35(*a*) (overseas leasing) below.

'*Available qualifying expenditure*' in a pool for a chargeable period consists of qualifying expenditure allocated to the pool for that period and any unrelieved qualifying expenditure brought forward in the pool from the previous chargeable period (usually referred to as the written-down value brought forward). There are rules requiring an allocation to a pool in specific circumstances, for example where an item falls to be transferred from one type of pool to another, and prohibiting the allocation of certain excluded expenditure. These are listed in *CAA 2001, s 57(2)(3)* and are covered elsewhere in this chapter where appropriate. See below for special provisions applicable to finance lessors. See 9.38(C) below as regards restrictions under connected persons and other anti-avoidance provisions.

In allocating qualifying expenditure to the appropriate pool, the following rules must be observed (and see below for interaction with first-year allowances).

(*a*)   Qualifying expenditure can be allocated to a pool for a chargeable period only to the extent that it has not been included in available qualifying expenditure for an earlier chargeable period. (Before *CAA 2001* had effect, see 9.1 above, there was some doubt as to whether qualifying expenditure could be allocated to a pool for a chargeable period later than that in which it was incurred, except where a first-year allowance had been given in the immediately preceding period (though this seems to have been accepted in practice). For chargeable periods covered by *CAA 2001*, this doubt is removed and, in addition, there is now nothing to prohibit the allocation of *part only* of a particular amount of qualifying expenditure for a particular chargeable period.)

(*b*)   Qualifying expenditure cannot be allocated to a pool for a chargeable period earlier than that in which it is incurred.

(*c*)   Qualifying expenditure can be allocated to a pool for a chargeable period only if the person concerned *owns* the plant or machinery at some time in that period. (Before *CAA 2001* had effect, see 9.1 above, this was expressed in terms of the item *belonging* to that person, but no change in the law is intended; see 9.27 above and 9.34 below for meaning of 'belongs'. See 9.38(K) below as regards certain expenditure by a lessee.)

Where an 'additional VAT liability' (see 9.2(viii) above) is incurred in respect of qualifying expenditure, at a time when the plant or machinery in question is provided for the purposes of the qualifying activity, it is itself expenditure on that plant or machinery and may be taken into account in determining available qualifying expenditure for the chargeable period in which it accrues.

The net cost of demolition of plant and machinery demolished during a chargeable period, and not replaced, is allocated to the appropriate pool for that chargeable period.

Interaction with first-year allowances. If a first-year allowance (FYA) (see 9.27 above) is made in respect of an amount of first-year qualifying expenditure, none of that amount can be allocated to a pool for the chargeable period in which the expenditure is incurred, and only the balance (after deducting the FYA) can be allocated to a pool for a subsequent chargeable period.

However, expenditure which qualifies for an FYA for a chargeable period is not excluded from being allocated to a pool for that period if either (1) the FYA is not claimed or (2) it is claimed in respect of part only of the expenditure (in which case the remaining part can be so allocated). Before *CAA 2001* had effect (see 9.1 above), an election was required to allocate the expenditure to the pool if (1) applied. The time limit for the election is (i) for income tax, twelve months after 31 January following the tax year in which the chargeable period ends, and (ii) for corporation tax, two years after the end of the chargeable period. For chargeable periods covered by *CAA 2001*, no such election is required.

If an FYA is made in respect of an amount of qualifying expenditure, at least some of the balance (after deducting the FYA) must be allocated to a pool for a chargeable period no later than that in which a disposal event (see 9.29 below) occurs in relation to the item in question. It will usually be beneficial to choose to allocate the whole balance. A nil balance (following a 100% FYA) is deemed to be so allocated. Such allocation is necessary to enable a disposal value to be properly brought into account. Before *CAA 2001* had effect (see 9.1 above), a similar rule applied but only if a disposal value fell to be brought into account for the chargeable period related to the incurring of the expenditure; the change in law is a consequence of the removal of doubt referred to in (*a*) above.

[*CAA 2001, s 26(3)–(5), ss 53–59, 65, 235; CAA 1990, s 24(1)–(5), s 25(1)–(5)(9), s 41(1)(c), s 62(1)(b)(2); FA 1990, s 60, Sch 17 paras 5, 6; FA 1991, Sch 14 para 7; FA 1994, s 118(6), s 213(4), Sch 26 Pt V(24); FA 1996, s 135, Sch 21 para 26; FA 2000, ss 73, 74; FA 2001, Sch 20 para 5(2)*].

See *Example (C)* at 9.31 below.

Finance lessors. For expenditure incurred after 1 July 1997 (or in the following twelve months under a contract entered into on or before that date), only a proportion of capital expenditure during a chargeable period on the provision of plant or machinery for leasing under a 'finance lease' (see 9.38(C) below) may be brought in as available qualifying expenditure for that period. The proportion is the same as the proportion of the chargeable period which falls after the time the expenditure was incurred, so that e.g. only one-quarter is brought in where expenditure is incurred three months before the end of a twelve-month period. This does not apply where a disposal value (see 9.29 below) is brought in in respect of the plant or machinery in the same period. The balance of the expenditure may be brought in in the following chargeable period or periods. [*CAA 2001, s 220, Sch 3 para 44; CAA 1990, s 25(5A)–(5C); F(No 2)A 1997, s 44*]. See Revenue Tax Bulletin June 1998 pp 539–544 for a general article on how these and associated capital allowance restrictions are intended to operate. In particular the following apply in relation to the instant provisions.

- As a transitional measure, up to the end of 2001, lessors may agree with the local inspector to adopt a mean expenditure date for weekly or monthly batches of small items, or some other form of simplified calculation giving broadly the correct result. Thereafter, any basis adopted must ensure that no more than the correct amount is included in qualifying expenditure, e.g. by using the end rather than the mean date for batched items.

- Where the limit on allowances for cars costing over £12,000 applies (see 9.30(A) below), it operates after the restriction under these provisions.

- Where the plant or machinery is a fixture let under an equipment lease and does not belong to the lessor at any time during the chargeable period in which the expenditure is incurred, because the lessee has not commenced trading (see 9.34(b) below), no allowances are due for that period. The restriction thus does not apply, and the expenditure is brought in in full in the period in which the fixture first belongs to the lessor (i.e. in which the lessee starts to trade). If the lessee starts to trade during the period in which the expenditure is incurred, the expenditure is apportioned from the date the expenditure is incurred, and not from the date the lessee starts to trade.

See also 9.38(A)(C) below, 71.58 SCHEDULE D, CASES I AND II as regards finance lease allowance restrictions.

Simon's Direct Tax Service. See B2.332 *et seq.*

9.29 **Disposal events and values.** Where a person has incurred qualifying expenditure (see 9.24 above) on plant or machinery, a **disposal value** must be brought into account for a chargeable period (see 9.2(i) above) in which any one of the following **disposal events** occurs (but normally only in relation to the first such event to occur in respect of that plant or machinery).

(i) The person ceases to own the plant or machinery.

(ii) He loses possession of it, and it is reasonable to assume the loss is permanent.

(iii) It has been in use for 'mineral exploration and access' (see 9.40(a) below) and the person abandons it at the site where it was so in use.

(iv) It ceases to exist as such (by reason of its destruction, dismantling or otherwise).

(v) It begins to be used wholly or partly for purposes other than those of the qualifying activity.

(vi) The qualifying activity is permanently discontinued.

The amount to be brought into account depends upon the nature of the event.

(a) On a sale (other than one within (b) below), it is the net sale proceeds plus any insurance or capital compensation received (by the person concerned) by reason of any event affecting the sale price obtainable.

(b) On a sale at less than market value, it is market value, unless

    (i) the buyer (not being a dual resident investing company connected with the seller) can claim plant or machinery or research and development (formerly scientific research) allowances for his expenditure, or

    (ii) the sale gives rise to a charge to tax under *ITEPA 2003* (i.e. on employment, pension or social security income),

in which case (a) above applies.

(c) On demolition or destruction, it is the net amount received for the remains, plus any insurance or capital compensation received.

(*d*)   On permanent loss (otherwise than within (*c*) above), or, where *CAA 2001* has effect (see 9.1 above), on abandonment as in (iii) above, it is any insurance or capital compensation received.

(*e*)   On permanent discontinuance of the qualifying activity preceding an event in (*a*)–(*d*) above, it is whatever value would otherwise have applied on the occurrence of that event.

(*f*)   On a gift giving rise to a charge to tax on the recipient under *ITEPA 2003* (i.e. on employment, pension or social security income), it is nil. (Before *CAA 2001* had effect, see 9.1 above, a similar result was achieved slightly differently in that no disposal value was required to be brought into account in such circumstances). See also Revenue Capital Allowances Manual CA 23250.

(*g*)   On any other event, it is market value at the time of the event.

However, the disposal value is in all cases limited to the qualifying expenditure incurred on the plant or machinery by the person in question. In addition, where *CAA 2001* has effect (see 9.1 above), there is no requirement to bring a disposal value into account if none of the qualifying expenditure in question has been taken into account in determining the person's available qualifying expenditure (see 9.28 above) for any chargeable period up to and including that in which the disposal occurs. As regards both these rules, see also 9.38(C)(i) below as regards certain transactions between connected persons.

Additional VAT rebates. Where an 'additional VAT rebate' (see 9.2(viii) above) is made in respect of an item of qualifying expenditure, a disposal value of an equivalent amount must be brought into account (on its own or as an addition to any other disposal value brought into account for that item) for the chargeable period in which the rebate accrues. Any disposal value brought into account for a subsequent chargeable period is limited to the original qualifying expenditure less all additional VAT rebates accrued in all chargeable periods up to (but not including) that chargeable period. If the disposal value is itself the result of an additional VAT rebate, it is limited to the original qualifying expenditure less *any* disposal values brought into account as a result of earlier events. (Before *CAA 2001* had effect, see 9.1 above, reference here to earlier events did not include the making of additional VAT rebates.)

[*CAA 2001, ss 60, 61, 62(1), s 63(1), s 64(1)(5), ss 238, 239; CAA 1990, s 24(6)(7)(8), s 26; FA 1991, Sch 14 paras 7(2), 8; FA 1994, Sch 26 Pt V(24); ITEPA 2003, Sch 6 paras 249, 250*].

The rules at (*b*)(ii) and (*f*) above where there is a charge to tax under *ITEPA 2003* (previously under Schedule E) are understood to apply where there would be such a charge but for the exemptions in 18.5, 18.6 COMPENSATION FOR LOSS OF EMPLOYMENT (AND DAMAGES) (Tolley's Practical Tax 1984 p 114).

See 9.38(C)(ii) below for certain anti-avoidance rules.

Simon's Direct Tax Service. See B2.334.

9.30   **Items excluded from the main pool of qualifying expenditure** are as follows.

(A) Cars costing over £12,000 acquired for purposes of a trade or other qualifying activity. For this purpose, 'car' is as defined at 9.27(ii) above, but with the exclusion of hire etc. cars as at 9.27(A) above and cars qualifying for first-year allowances under 9.27(*e*) above. Qualifying expenditure (see 9.24 above) on a car costing over £12,000 can only be allocated to a *single asset pool* (see 9.28 above). Writing-down allowances (WDAs) are limited to a maximum of £3,000 per chargeable period (proportionately reduced or increased for chargeable periods of less or more than a year).

Separate rules apply to reduce the maximum WDA in cases involving contributions towards capital expenditure (as in 9.2(vi)(vii) above) and partial depreciation subsidies (as in 9.38(J) below). If the car begins to be used *partly* for purposes other than those of the qualifying activity, the single asset pool continues and no disposal value is brought into account. For a chargeable period in which such part use exists, the WDA and any balancing allowance or charge is reduced to such amount as is just and reasonable (though the full amount is deducted in arriving at any unrelieved qualifying expenditure carried forward).

For expenditure incurred before 11 March 1992 or under a contract entered into before that date, these provisions apply to cars costing over £8,000 and by reference to a maximum WDA of £2,000.

[*CAA 2001, ss 74–78, 81, 82, Sch 3 para 19; CAA 1990, s 34(1)–(3)(5), s 35(1), s 36; F(No 2)A 1992, s 71; FA 1994, s 213(5)(6); FA 2002, Sch 19 para 6; SI 1991 No 2874*].

See 9.38(C)(ii) below for special rule determining the disposal value of a car within these provisions on a sale etc. to which the anti-avoidance provisions there mentioned apply. See 71.58 SCHEDULE D, CASES I AND II as regards expenditure on *hiring* a car whose retail price when new exceeded £12,000 (previously £8,000).

See Simon's Direct Tax Service B2.342.

Cars costing £12,000 or less. Cars costing £12,000 or less previously had to be included in a class pool (see 9.28 above). This requirement is abolished, for periods of account ending after 5 April 2000 and corporation tax accounting periods ending after 31 March 2000 (subject to election to defer this for one year), and qualifying expenditure on such cars may now be allocated to the main pool (unless excluded for other reasons, e.g. partial use for non-trade etc. purposes — see (C) below). For expenditure incurred before 11 March 1992 or under a contract entered into before that date, these provisions applied to cars costing £8,000 or less. See 9.35(*a*) below.

(B) Ships. Qualifying expenditure (see 9.24 above) on the provision of a ship for the purposes of a trade or other qualifying activity can only be allocated to a *single asset pool* (see 9.28 above), known as a *single ship pool*. This does not apply if

- an election is made to exclude such treatment (see below); or

- the qualifying activity is one of special leasing (see 9.37 below); or

- the ship is otherwise provided for leasing (which expressly includes letting on charter), *unless* it is not used for 'overseas leasing' (other than 'protected leasing') at any time in the 'designated period' *and* it appears that it will be used only for a 'qualifying purpose' in that period (see 9.35 below for meaning of expressions used here).

When a disposal event occurs in relation to a single ship pool, the available qualifying expenditure (see 9.28 above) in that pool for the chargeable period in question is transferred to the '*appropriate non-ship pool*' (i.e. the pool to which the expenditure would originally have been allocated in the absence of the single ship pool rules), and the single ship pool is brought to an end with no balancing allowance or charge. The disposal value is brought into account in the pool now containing the qualifying expenditure. In addition to the circumstances at 9.29 above, a disposal event occurs if a ship is provided for leasing or letting on charter and begins to be used otherwise than for a 'qualifying purpose' at some time in the first four years of the 'designated period' (see 9.35 below as regards expressions used).

If the ship ceases to be used by the person who incurred the qualifying expenditure, without his having brought it into use for the purposes of the qualifying activity, then, in addition to any adjustments required as above, any writing-down allowances (WDAs) previously made (or postponed — see below) are withdrawn, and the amount withdrawn is allocated to the 'appropriate non-ship pool' (see above) for the chargeable period in question.

A person who has incurred qualifying expenditure on a ship may elect, for any chargeable period, to disapply the single ship pool provisions in respect of

- all or part of any qualifying expenditure that would otherwise be allocated to a single ship pool in that period, or

- all or part of the available qualifying expenditure (see 9.28 above) already in a single ship pool,

with the result that the amount in question is allocated to the 'appropriate non-ship pool' (see above). The time limit within which the election must be made is (i) for income tax, twelve months after 31 January following the tax year in which ends the chargeable period in question, and (ii) for corporation tax, two years after the end of the chargeable period.

Postponement of WDAs. A person entitled to a WDA for a chargeable period in respect of a single ship pool may, by written notice, postpone all or part of it to a later period. The amount to be postponed must be specified in the notice. Where a reduced WDA is claimed, all or part of the reduced amount may be postponed. The time limits for giving notice are the same as for the election referred to immediately above. Available qualifying expenditure (see 9.28 below) is computed as if the postponed WDA had, in fact, been made. Postponed WDAs may be claimed over one or more subsequent chargeable periods. See 9.27 above for postponement of first-year allowances.

[*CAA 2001, ss 127–129, s 130(2)(7), s 131(1)(3)–(7), ss 132, 133, 157(1); CAA 1990, ss 31–33, 40(4); FA 1990, Sch 17 para 8; FA 1993, s 116(1)(4); FA 1994, Sch 26 Pt V(24); FA 1996, s 135, Sch 21 paras 28, 29; FA 1998, Sch 5 para 52*].

Deferment of balancing charges on qualifying ships. Balancing charges on ships may be deferred and set against subsequent expenditure on ships for a maximum of six years from the date of disposal. A claim for deferment of the whole or part of a balancing charge may be made by the shipowner where a disposal event within 9.29(i)–(iv) above occurs after 20 April 1994 in relation to a 'qualifying ship' (the old ship). A *'qualifying ship'* is, broadly, a ship of a sea-going kind of 100 gross registered tons or more, excluding offshore installations (as now defined by *ICTA 1988, s 837C* — for earlier definition, see *CAA 2001, s 153 as originally enacted*) and ships of a kind used or chartered primarily for sport or recreation (but passenger ships and cruise liners are not so excluded). The provisions also apply to ships of less than 100 tons in cases where the old ship is totally lost or is damaged beyond worthwhile repair. A ship brought into use in the trade on or after 20 July 1994 must within three months of first use (unless disposed of during those three months) be registered in the UK, the Channel Islands, Isle of Man, a colony (as to which see Revenue Tax Bulletins April 1995 p 208, June 1998 p 553), a European Union State or a European Economic Area State and must continue to be so until at least three years from first use or, if earlier, until disposed of to an unconnected person. It is a further condition that no amount in respect of the old ship has been allocated to an overseas leasing pool (see 9.35 below), a 'partial use' single asset pool (see (C) below), a 'partial depreciation subsidy' single asset pool (see 9.38(J) below) or a pool for a qualifying activity consisting of special leasing (see 9.37 below).

The balancing charge on the old ship is in effect calculated as if allowances had been granted, and the charge arises, in a single ship pool, with appropriate assumptions where that is not, in fact, the case (see *CAA 2001, s 139*, or for earlier chargeable periods *CAA 1990, s 33B*).

Deferment is achieved by allocating the amount deferred to the 'appropriate non-ship pool' (see above) for the chargeable period in question, so that it is effectively set against the disposal value brought into account in that pool (see above) as a result of the disposal event concerned. The *maximum deferment* is the *lowest* of (i) the amount treated as brought into account in respect of the old ship under *CAA 2001, s 139* (see above), (ii) the amount to be expended on new shipping (see below), so far as not already set against an earlier balancing charge, in the six years starting with the date of disposal of the old ship, (iii) the amount which, in the absence of a deferment claim, would have been the total balancing charge for the chargeable period in question in the appropriate non-ship pool, and (iv) the amount needed to reduce the profit of the trade or other qualifying activity to nil (disregarding losses brought forward), no deferment being possible if no such profit has been made. If the amount actually expended within (ii) above turns out to be less than the amount deferred, the amount of the deficiency is reinstated as a balancing charge for the chargeable period to which the claim relates. (Before *CAA 2001* had effect (see 9.1 above), the amount calculated at (iii) above could also include balancing charges in certain other pools and may therefore have been a larger amount.)

Where an amount is expended on new shipping within the six-year period allowed and is attributed by the shipowner, by notice to the Revenue, to any part of an amount deferred, an amount equal to the amount so matched is brought into account as a disposal value, for the chargeable period in which the expenditure is incurred, in the single ship pool to which the expenditure is allocated, thus reducing the amount on which allowances may be claimed on the new ship. No amount of expenditure can be attributed to a deferment if there is earlier expenditure on new shipping within the said six-year period which has not been attributed to that or earlier deferments. An attribution may be varied by the trader by notice to the inspector within a specified time (see *CAA 2001, s 142*, or for earlier chargeable periods *CAA 1990, s 33F(4)* and *FA 1995, s 98(6)(b)*).

For the purposes of these provisions, an amount is expended on new shipping if it is qualifying expenditure, incurred by the claimant wholly and exclusively for the purposes of a qualifying activity, on a ship (the new ship) which will be a qualifying ship (see above) for at least three years from first use or, if earlier, until disposed of to an unconnected person. Expenditure is treated as incurred by the claimant if it is incurred by a successor following a partnership change (see 53.5 PARTNERSHIPS) or company reconstruction (see Tolley's Corporation Tax) in consequence of which the qualifying activity was not treated as discontinued. Expenditure incurred on a ship which has belonged to either the shipowner or a connected person within the previous six years or which is incurred mainly for tax avoidance reasons does not qualify. The expenditure must be allocated to a single ship pool. If an election is made to disapply the single ship pool provisions, the expenditure is deemed never to have been expenditure on new shipping (but must nevertheless be treated as such in matching expenditure with deferments, so that the election prevents further matching of amounts already deferred). Expenditure does not qualify if the overseas leasing provisions at 9.35 below come to apply to the new ship.

For income tax purposes, the claim for deferment must be made within twelve months after 31 January following the tax year in which ends the chargeable period of deferment. Before the current year basis of assessment applied, the claim had to be made within two years after the end of that chargeable period. For corporation tax purposes, the provisions relating to capital allowances claims apply also to claims for deferment. Where a claim for deferment is found to be erroneous as a result of subsequent circumstances, the shipowner must, within three months after the end of the chargeable period in which those circumstances first arise, notify the Revenue accordingly (failure to do so incurring a penalty under *TMA 1970, s 98*); consequential assessments may be made within twelve months after notice is given, notwithstanding normal time limits.

Where the disposal giving rise to the balancing charge occurs on or after 29 April 1996, there is provision for the balancing charge to be set against expenditure on new shipping by another member of the same *group of companies* as the shipowner (within *ICTA 1988, Pt X, Ch IV*, see Tolley's Corporation Tax under Groups of Companies). Such expenditure is, however, excluded where the ship ceases to be owned by the fellow group member without being brought into use for the purposes of a qualifying activity, or where, within three years of being so brought into use, a disposal event occurs in respect of the ship (although these exclusions do not apply in the case of total loss of, or commercially irreparable damage to, the ship). Expenditure is similarly excluded where the group relationship between the two companies ceases after the expenditure is incurred and within three years after the ship is first brought into use (again disregarding events after the total loss etc. of the ship).

[*CAA 2001, ss 134–158, Sch 3 para 24; CAA 1990, ss 33A–33F; FA 1995, ss 94–98; FA 1996, Sch 35; FA 2004, Sch 27 paras 9, 11; SI 1996 No 1323; SI 1997 No 133*].

See Simon's Direct Tax Service B2.350–B2.353.

(C) Plant and machinery partly used for non-trade etc. purposes. Qualifying expenditure (see 9.24 above) incurred partly for the purposes of the trade or other qualifying activity and partly for other purposes can only be allocated to a *single asset pool* (see 9.28 above). (See 9.27 above as regards first-year allowances.) Where in other cases plant or machinery *begins to be used* partly for other purposes, such that a disposal value falls to be brought into account (see 9.29(v) above) in a pool, an amount equal to the disposal value is allocated to a single asset pool for the chargeable period in question (but see (A) above as regards cars costing over £12,000). In respect of a single asset pool under these provisions, writing–down allowances and balancing allowances and charges are reduced to such amount as is just and reasonable (though the full amount is deducted in arriving at any unrelieved qualifying expenditure carried forward).

Where, after 20 March 2000, circumstances change such that the proportion of use for purposes other than those of the qualifying activity increases during a chargeable period, and the market value of the plant or machinery at the end of the period exceeds the available qualifying expenditure (see 9.28 above) in the pool for that period by more than £1 million, then if no disposal value would otherwise fall to be brought into account for the period, a disposal value must be brought into account (equal to market value — see 9.29(*g*) above) and, in the next or a subsequent chargeable period, an equivalent amount may be allocated to a new single asset pool as if it were qualifying expenditure newly incurred.

[*CAA 2001, ss 206–208, Sch 3 para 42; CAA 1990, ss 79, 79A; FA 1990, Sch 17 para 14; FA 1994, Sch 26 Pt V(24); FA 2000, s 75(2)(6)*].

See also *Kempster v McKenzie Ch D 1952, 33 TC 193* and *G H Chambers (Northiam Farms) Ltd v Watmough Ch D 1956, 36 TC 711* and Revenue Capital Allowances Manual CA 23530, 27100 as regards further adjustment for any element of personal choice.

See Simon's Direct Tax Service B2.359.

(D) Plant and machinery in respect of which a **partial depreciation subsidy** is received (see 9.38(J) below).

(E) Plant and machinery used for overseas leasing (see 9.35 below).

(F) Short-life assets. A person who has incurred qualifying expenditure (see 9.24 above) on an item of plant or machinery may elect for it to be treated as a short-life asset, provided it is not an excluded item (see list below). There is no requirement as to the expected useful life of the item, but short-life asset treatment will be of no practical benefit where the item remains in use for five years or more. The time limit for the election, which is irrevocable, is (*a*) for income tax, twelve months after 31 January following the tax year in which ends the chargeable period in which the expenditure (or earliest expenditure) is incurred, and (*b*) for corporation tax, two years after the end of the chargeable period.

In general, inspectors will require sufficient information in support of an election to minimise the possibility of any difference of view at a later date (e.g. on a disposal) about what was and was not covered by the election, and to ensure that it does not incorporate any excluded items (see list below). Where separate identification of short-life assets acquired in a chargeable period is either impossible or impracticable, e.g. similar small or relatively inexpensive items held in very large numbers, perhaps in different locations, then the information required in support of the election may be provided by reference to batches of acquisitions. (Revenue Pamphlet IR 131, SP 1/86).

Each of the following items of plant or machinery is excluded from being a short-life asset.

(i) A car, defined as at 9.27(ii) above with the exception of cars hired out to persons receiving certain disability allowances or mobility supplements. (Before *CAA 2001* had effect, see 9.1 above, it would appear that this exclusion was narrower in that *all* hire etc. cars within 9.27(A) above were excepted from it).

(ii) A ship.

(iii) An item which is the subject of special leasing (see 9.37 below).

(iv) An item acquired partly for the purposes of a trade or other qualifying activity and partly for other purposes.

(v) An item which is the subject of a partial depreciation subsidy (see 9.38(J) below).

(vi) An item received by way of gift or whose previous use by the person concerned did not attract capital allowances (see 9.38(D)(E) below).

(vii) An item the expenditure on which is within the long-life asset provisions (see (G) below).

(viii) An item provided for leasing, unless it will be used within the 'designated period' for a 'qualifying purpose' (see 9.35 below as regards these expressions), and with the exception in any case of cars hired out to persons receiving certain disability allowances or mobility supplements.

(ix) An item leased overseas such that it attracts only a 10% writing-down allowance (see 9.35(*a*) below).

(x) An item leased to two or more persons jointly such that *CAA 2001, s 116* applies (see 9.35(*f*) below).

(xi) An item qualifying for a universal first-year allowance (see 9.27 above) other than the reinstated allowance for expenditure in the twelve months to 31 October 1993. (An item qualifying for one of the targeted first-year allowances at 9.27(*a*)–(*h*) above is *not* automatically excluded from short-life asset treatment.)

Qualifying expenditure in respect of a short-life asset can only be allocated to a *single asset pool* (see 9.28 above), known as a *short-life asset pool*. If no disposal event within 9.29(i)–(vi) above occurs in any of the chargeable periods ending on or before the fourth anniversary (referred to below as the '*four-year cut-off date*') of the end of the chargeable period in which the expenditure is incurred (or the first such period in which any of it was incurred), the short-life asset pool is brought to an end on the four-year cut-off date but with no balancing allowance or charge and no denial of a writing-down allowance for the final period. The item ceases to be a short-life asset and the available qualifying expenditure in the pool is allocated to the main pool for the first chargeable period ending *after* the four-year cut-off date.

The following applies where short-life asset treatment has been claimed on the basis that the item has been provided for leasing, but will be used within the 'designated period' for a 'qualifying purpose' (so is not excluded by (viii) above). (See 9.35 below as regards expressions used here.) If, at any time in a chargeable period ending on or before the four-year cut-off date (as above), the item begins to be used otherwise than for such a purpose, and that time falls within the first four years of the 'designated period', the short-life asset pool is brought to an end at that time but with no balancing allowance or charge and no denial of a writing-down allowance for the final period. The item ceases to be a short-life asset and the available qualifying expenditure in the pool is allocated, for the chargeable period in which that time falls, to the main pool (or, where appropriate and prior to its abolition, to the separate class pool for cars — see (A1) above and 9.35(*a*) below).

If at any time before the four-year cut-off date (as above), a short-life asset is disposed of to a connected person (within *ICTA 1988, s 839* — see 19 CONNECTED PERSONS), short-life asset treatment continues in the connected person's hands (though the original four-year cut-off date remains unchanged). If both parties so elect (within two years after the end of the chargeable period in which the disposal occurs), the disposal is treated as being at a price equal to the available qualifying expenditure (see 9.28 above) then in the short-life asset pool, and certain anti-avoidance provisions on transactions between connected persons are disapplied. If no election is made, the anti-avoidance provisions at 9.38(C) below apply in full, and the exception at 9.29(*b*)(i) above is disapplied (so that market value can be substituted for a lesser sale price even where the buyer is entitled to capital allowances).

If a disposal event occurs in respect of a short-life asset pool such that the pool ends and a balancing *allowance* arises (see 9.28 above), and an 'additional VAT liability' (see 9.2(viii) above) is subsequently incurred in respect of the item concerned, a further balancing allowance of that amount is given for the chargeable period in which the additional VAT liability accrues.

The Revenue accept that it may not be practicable for individual pools to be maintained for every short-life asset, especially where they are held in very large numbers. Statement of Practice SP 1/86 sets out examples of acceptable bases of computation where the inspector is satisfied that the actual life in the business of a distinct class of assets with broadly similar average lives, before being sold or scrapped, is likely to be less than five years.

[*CAA 2001, ss 83–89, 240; CAA 1990, ss 37, 38, 40(4); FA 1991, Sch 14 para 9; F(No 2)A 1992, s 68(7); FA 1993, s 116(1)(4), Sch 13 para 4; FA 1994, Sch 26 Pt V(24); FA 1996, s 135, Sch 21 para 30; FA 1997, Sch 14 para 3; ITEPA 2003, Sch 6 para 252*].

See *Example (A)* at 9.31 below.

See *Simon's Direct Tax Service* B2.343.

(G) Long-life assets. There are special provisions for chargeable periods ending on or after 26 November 1996 relating to certain 'long-life asset expenditure'. These do not apply to expenditure incurred before 26 November 1996, or to expenditure incurred before 1 January 2001 under a contract entered into before 26 November 1996 (except that the later start date does not apply to any increased expenditure resulting from a variation of the contract on or after 26 November 1996). '*Long-life asset expenditure*' is qualifying expenditure (as in 9.24 above) incurred on the provision of a 'long-life asset' for the purposes of a qualifying activity (but see below for exclusions by reference to a monetary limit).

Subject to below, a '*long-life asset*' is plant or machinery which it is reasonable to expect will have a useful economic life of at least 25 years (or where such was a reasonable expectation when the plant or machinery was new, i.e. unused and not second-hand). For these purposes, the useful economic life of plant or machinery is the period from first use (by any person) until it ceases to be, or to be likely to be, used by anyone as a fixed asset of a business. Where part only of capital expenditure on an item of plant or machinery falls within these provisions, that part and the remainder are treated as expenditure on separate items, any necessary apportionments being made on a just and reasonable basis. As an introduction to a detailed discussion of what constitutes a long-life asset (including twelve examples), the Revenue have stated that they 'will generally accept the accounting treatment as determining whether an asset is long-life provided it is not clearly unreasonable'. (Revenue Tax Bulletin August 1997 pp 445–450). For whether glasshouses (for which see generally 9.25 and 9.26(17) above) are long-life assets, see Revenue Tax Bulletin June 1998 p 552. For aircraft, see Revenue Tax Bulletin June 1999 pp 671, 672, April 2000 pp 739, 740 and December 2003 pp 1074, 1075.

The following *cannot* be long-life assets.

(i) Fixtures (see 9.34 below) in, or plant or machinery provided for use in, a building used wholly or mainly as a dwelling-house, showroom, hotel, office or retail shop or similar retail premises, or for purposes ancillary to such use.

(ii) Cars, as defined at 9.27(ii) above.

(iii) (In relation to expenditure incurred before 1 January 2011) ships of a seagoing kind, other than offshore installations (as now defined by *ICTA 1988, s 837C* — for earlier definition, see *CAA 2001, s 94 as originally enacted*), and not of a kind used or chartered primarily for sport or recreation (which expression does not encompass passenger ships or cruise liners).

(iv) (In relation to expenditure incurred before 1 January 2011) 'railway assets' used only for a 'railway business' (as defined).

Long-life asset expenditure which is incurred wholly and exclusively for the purposes of a qualifying activity, and which does not require allocation under other rules to a single asset pool, can only be allocated to a *class pool* (see 9.28 above), known as the *long-life asset pool*. The final chargeable period (see 9.28 above) of a long-life asset pool is that in which the qualifying activity is permanently discontinued.

Writing-down allowances for a chargeable period in respect of long-life asset expenditure (whether in the long-life asset pool or a single asset pool) are restricted to 6% (instead of the normal 25% or, where the overseas leasing rules in 9.35(*a*) below apply, 10%), proportionately reduced or increased if the chargeable period is less or more than a year, or if the qualifying activity has been carried on for part only of the chargeable period. A claim for a writing-down allowance may require it to be reduced to a specified amount. Where plant and machinery allowances have been claimed for long-life asset expenditure, any earlier or later expenditure on the same asset for which allowances are subsequently claimed, unless excluded by (i)–(iv) above, is treated as also being long-life asset expenditure if it would not otherwise be so. This over-rides the exclusion of expenditure within the monetary limit referred to below.

Where a disposal value less than the 'notional written-down value' would otherwise fall to be brought into account in respect of long-life asset expenditure which has attracted restricted allowances as above, an adjustment may be required. Where the event giving rise to the disposal value is part of a scheme or arrangement a main object of which is the obtaining of a tax advantage under these provisions, the 'notional written-down value' is substituted for the disposal value. The *'notional written-down value'* is qualifying expenditure on the item in question less maximum allowances to date, computed on the assumptions that the expenditure was not excluded from being long-life asset expenditure by the operation of the monetary limit below and that all allowances have been made in full.

Monetary limit. Expenditure is not long-life asset expenditure if it is expenditure to which the monetary limit (see below) applies and it is incurred in a chargeable period for which that limit is not exceeded. The limit applies to expenditure incurred by an individual, he devotes substantially the whole of his time in that chargeable period to the carrying on of the qualifying activity for the purposes of which the expenditure was incurred. In the case of a partnership of individuals, at least half the partners must satisfy the requirement as to devotion of time, but a company falls outside that requirement. In any case, the monetary limit does not apply to the following types of expenditure:

● expenditure on a share in plant or machinery; or

● a contribution treated as plant or machinery expenditure under *CAA 2001, s 538* (see 9.2(vii) above); or

● expenditure on plant or machinery for leasing (whether or not in the course of a trade).

The monetary limit is £100,000, proportionately reduced or increased for chargeable periods of less or more than a year and, as regards companies, divided by one plus the number of associated companies (as under *ICTA 1988, s 13* — see Tolley's Corporation Tax under Small Companies Rate). For the purpose of applying the monetary limit, all expenditure under a contract is treated as incurred in the first chargeable period in which any expenditure under the contract is incurred.

Transitional rule for second-hand assets. A second-hand asset is excluded from the long-life asset provisions if

● the previous owner properly claimed plant and machinery allowances for expenditure on its provision,

● his expenditure did not fall to be treated as long-life asset expenditure, and

● his expenditure would have fallen to be so treated if the long-life asset rules (apart from this transitional rule) had always been law.

A provisional claim to 25% writing-down allowances may be made by a purchaser on this basis, before the vendor has made the appropriate return, provided that reasonable steps have been taken to establish that entitlement will arise, and that the appropriate revisions will be made, and assessments accepted, if entitlement does not in the event arise (Revenue Tax Bulletin August 1997 p 450).

[*CAA 2001, ss 56(5), 65(1), 90–104, Sch 3 para 20; CAA 1990, ss 38A–38H, 83(1); FA 1997, Sch 14; FA 2004, Sch 27 paras 8, 11*].

For an article explaining how the Revenue interpret and operate these provisions, see Revenue Tax Bulletin August 1997 pp 445–450. For their application to modern equipment used in the printing industry, see Revenue Tax Bulletin February 2002 pp 916, 917.

See *Example (B)* at 9.31 below.

See Simon's Direct Tax Service B2.344.

9.31   *Examples*

(A) Short-life assets
A runs a small business. He prepares trading accounts to 30 September each year, and buys and sells machines, for use in the trade, as follows.

	Cost	Date of acquisition	Disposal proceeds	Date of disposal
Machine X	£40,000	30.4.99	£13,000	1.12.2000
Machine Y	£25,000	1.9.99	£4,000	1.12.03

A elects under what is now *CAA 2001, s 83* for both machines to be treated as short-life assets. His main pool of qualifying expenditure brought forward at the beginning of period of account 1.10.98–30.9.99 is £80,000.

A's capital allowances are as follows.

	Main Pool £	Short-life asset pools Machine X £	Machine Y £	Total Allowances £
Period of account 1.10.98–30.9.99				
WDV b/f	80,000			
Additions		40,000	25,000	
FYA 40%		(16,000)	(10,000)	26,000
WDA 25%	(20,000)	—	—	20,000
	60,000	24,000	15,000	£46,000
Period of account 1.10.99–30.9.2000				
WDA 25%	(15,000)	(6,000)	(3,750)	£24,750
	45,000	18,000	11,250	
Period of account 1.10.2000–30.9.01				
Disposal		(13,000)		
Balancing allowance		£5,000		5,000
WDA 25%	(11,250)		(2,813)	14,063
				£19,063
	33,750		8,437	
Period of account 1.10.01–30.9.02				
WDA 25%	(8,437)		(2,109)	£10,546
	25,313		6,328	
Period of account 1.10.02–30.9.03				
WDA 25%	(6,328)		(1,582)	£7,910
	18,985		4,746	
Period of account 1.10.03–30.9.04				
Transfer to pool	4,746		(4,746)	
	23,731		—	
Disposal	(4,000)			
	19,731			
WDA 25%	(4,933)			£4,933
WDV c/f	£14,798			

Note

The fourth anniversary of the end of the chargeable period in which the expenditure is incurred is 30.9.03 (the four-year cut-off date). The balance of expenditure on Machine Y is thus transferred to the pool in the period of account 1.10.03–30.9.04, this being the first chargeable period ending after the four-year cut-off date.

(B) Long-life assets

B prepares trading accounts to 31 December. In the year to 31 December 2002, he has built new factory premises for use in his trade, which include a building mainly in use as offices (on which 20% of the cost of the premises is expended). Industrial buildings allowances are available on the construction expenditure. The main plant and machinery pool written-down value at 1 January 2002 is £800,000, and the disposal value to be brought into account in respect of plant and machinery in B's previous premises is £720,000. Machines installed in the new factory cost £920,000. No first-year allowances are available.

He also claims, for the year to 31 December 2002, plant and machinery allowances for expenditure of £520,000 incurred on fixtures integral to the new premises, which are agreed to have an expected life in excess of 25 years. Of this expenditure, it is agreed £120,000 should be apportioned to the offices.

On 1 May 2003 he incurs additional expenditure on upgrading the fixtures of £19,000, none of it relating to office fixtures.

On 1 October 2004 he moves to new premises, disposing of the old premises for a consideration including £425,000 relating to the integral fixtures (of which £95,000 relates to the office fixtures) and £510,000 relating to other plant and machinery.

Plant and machinery in the new premises costs £960,000, none of which relates to integral fixtures (which are included in the industrial buildings allowances claim for the new premises).

The plant and machinery allowances computations for relevant periods are as follows.

	Main Pool £	Long-life asset pool £	Total allowances
Year ending 31.12.02			
WDV b/f	800,000	—	
Additions (see note (*a*))	1,040,000	400,000	
Disposals	(720,000)	—	
	1,120,000	400,000	
WDA	280,000	24,000	£304,000
WDV c/f	840,000	376,000	
Year ending 31.12.03			
Additions (see note (*b*))	—	19,000	
	840,000	395,000	
WDA	210,000	23,700	£233,700
WDV c/f	630,000	371,300	
Year ending 31.12.04			
Additions	960,000	—	
Disposals	(605,000)	(330,000)	
	985,000	41,300	
WDA (see note (*c*))	246,250	2,478	£248,728
WDV c/f	£738,750	£38,822	

Notes

(*a*)   Expenditure on fixtures provided for use in offices is excluded from being long-life asset expenditure (regardless of whether the office building itself attracts industrial

176

buildings allowances because it represents not more than 25% of the overall cost of premises otherwise qualifying).

(b)   Additional expenditure on existing long-life assets is within the provisions even if within the annual monetary limit.

(c)   The long-life asset pool comes to an end only on permanent discontinuance of the trade and not before. Allowances therefore continue to be given at 6% p.a. on the residue of expenditure on long-life assets despite their having been disposed of.

(C) Pooling, writing-down allowances, cars, partial non-business use, acquisitions from connected persons and balancing adjustments

A is in business as a builder and demolition contractor. His business qualifies as a small business for the purposes of first-year allowances. He makes up his accounts to 5 April. The accounts for the year to 5 April 2005 reveal the following additions and disposals.

	£
Additions	
Plant	
Dumper Truck	5,000
Excavator	32,000
Bulldozer	20,000
	£57,000
Fittings	
Office furniture	£2,000
Motor Vehicles	
Land Rover	6,000
Van	5,000
Car 2	12,200
Car 3	2,000
	£25,200

Disposals	Cost	Proceeds
	£	£
Excavator	32,000	30,000
Digger loader	15,000	4,000
Car 1	14,200	4,200
Fittings	3,500	500

The dumper truck was bought second-hand from Q, brother of A, but had not been used in a trade or other qualifying activity. The truck had originally cost Q £6,000, but its market value at sale was only £2,000.

The excavator was sold without having been brought into use.

The bulldozer and Car 3 were both purchased from P, father of A and had originally cost P £25,000 and £3,500 respectively. Both assets had been used for the purposes of a qualifying activity. In both cases, the price paid by A was less than the market value.

Car 1 sold and the new Car 2 are both used for private motoring by A. Private use has always been 30%. Car 3 is occasionally borrowed by A's daughter, and the private use proportion is 20%.

9.31 Capital Allowances

The written-down values at 5 April 2004 of the main plant and machinery pool and Car 1 are £7,500 and £3,900 respectively.

The plant and machinery allowances for the 12-month period of account ending on 5 April 2005 are

	Expenditure qualifying for FYAs 40%	Main Pool 25%	Car 3 partial use pool 25%	Expensive car pools — Car 1	Car 2	Total allowances
	£	£	£	£	£	£
WDV b/f		7,500		3,900		
Additions						
Excavator (note (*a*))	32,000					
Dumper truck (notes (*b*)(*c*))		2,000				
Bulldozer (notes (*b*)(*d*))		20,000				
Furniture	2,000					
Land Rover and van	11,000					
Cars			2,000		12,200	
	45,000					
FYA (50%)	(22,500)					22,500
Transfer to pool (£32,000 less 50% (note (*a*))	(16,000)	16,000				
	6,500					
Disposals						
Excavator		(30,000)				
Digger		(4,000)				
Fittings		(500)				
Audi				(4,200)		
		11,000	2,000	(£300)	12,200	
WDA (25%)		(2,750)	(500)			3,250
WDA (restricted)					(3,000)	3,000
Private use restriction:						
Car 2 — £3,000 @ 30%						(900)
Car 3 — £500 @ 20%						(200)
Transfer to pool	(£6,500)	6,500				
WDV c/f		£14,750	£1,500		£9,200	
Total allowances						£27,650

Balancing charge (Car 1) £300 less 30% private use   (£210)

Notes

(*a*) First-year allowances (9.27 above) and writing-down allowances (9.28 above) are available even though an item of plant or machinery is disposed of without being brought into use, always provided that the expenditure is qualifying expenditure (see 9.24 above). See 9.28 above as regards the requirement, where a first-year allowance has been given, to allocate the expenditure to a pool for a chargeable period no later than that in which a disposal event occurs.

(*b*)   No first-year allowance is available in respect of an item of plant or machinery purchased from a connected person. See 9.27(ix) above.

(*c*)   Qualifying expenditure on the dumper truck is restricted to the lowest of

   (i)   market value;

   (ii)   capital expenditure incurred by the vendor (or, if lower, by a person connected with him);

   (iii)   capital expenditure incurred by the purchaser.

See 9.38(C) below.

(*d*)   Qualifying expenditure on the bulldozer is the lesser of A's actual expenditure and the disposal value brought into account in the vendor's computations (see 9.38(C) below). (The vendor's disposal value would have been market value but for the fact that the purchaser is himself entitled to claim capital allowances on the acquisition (see 9.29(*b*)(i) above).) A's qualifying expenditure is thus equal to his actual expenditure. The same applies to the purchase of Car 3.

(*e*)   Car 2, by virtue of its costing over £12,000, is allocated to a single asset pool (see 9.30(A) above), and the same applied to Car 1. Car 3 is allocated to a single asset pool by virtue only of its being used for non-business purposes (see 9.30(C) above). See note (*d*) above as regards the amount of qualifying expenditure to be brought into account in respect of Car 3.

(*f*)   The writing-down allowance on Car 2 is restricted to £3,000 before adjustment for private use (see 9.30(A) above).

9.32   **Making of allowances and charges.** The following applies for both income tax and for corporation tax. In its relevance for income tax purposes to trades, professions and vocations, it applies where the current year basis of assessment has effect, which, for capital allowances purposes, is 1997/98 onwards (except in the case of trades etc. commenced after 5 April 1994, where it has effect from the outset). See the 2003/04 and earlier editions as regards the preceding year basis previously in operation and for provisions applicable to the Schedule A activities of companies before 1 April 1998.

Where the qualifying activity is within 9.24(i) or (iii)–(v) above, plant and machinery allowances are treated as expenses of, and balancing charges are treated as receipts of, the trade, profession, vocation, Schedule A business, overseas property business, furnished holiday lettings business or *ICTA 1988, s 55(2)* concern. Where the qualifying activity is an employment or office (as in 9.24(ii) above), allowances are given as deductions from taxable earnings and balancing charges are themselves treated as earnings. [*CAA 2001, ss 247–252, 262; CAA 1990, ss 27(1), 28A(1), 29(1), 73(1), 140(2)(4), 144(2), 161(5); FA 1994, s 211; FA 1997, Sch 15 paras 3, 4; FA 1998, Sch 5 para 61; ITEPA 2003, Sch 6 para 253*].

Allowances and charges are computed for income tax purposes by reference to events in periods of account (see 9.2(i) above) and for corporation tax purposes by reference to events in company accounting periods. [*CAA 2001, ss 2(1), 6(1); CAA 1990, ss 140(1), 144(1), 161(2); FA 1994, ss 211, 212(2)*].

See 9.37 below as regards a qualifying activity of special leasing (as in 9.24(vii) above).

9.33   Capital Allowances

See 9.2(ii) above as regards the *claiming* of capital allowances.

Simon's Direct Tax Service. See B2.380 *et seq.*

9.33   *Examples*

Periods of account
James commences business on 1 October 2003 preparing accounts initially to 30 September.
He changes his accounting date in 2005, preparing accounts for the 15 months to 31
December 2005. The following capital expenditure is incurred.

	Plant	Car
	£	£
Year ended 30 September 2004	12,000	4,000 (no private use)
Period ended 31 December 2005	7,500	
Year ended 31 December 2006	4,000	

An item of plant was sold for £500 (original cost £1,000) on 25 September 2005. James'
business is a small business for the purposes of first-year allowances. None of the plant
additions occurred during the period 6 April 2004 to 5 April 2005 (in which case the rate
of first-year allowance would have been 50%).

Profits *before* capital allowances but otherwise as adjusted for tax purposes are as follows.

	£
Year ended 30 September 2004	18,000
Period ended 31 December 2005	25,000
Year ended 31 December 2006	24,000

The capital allowances are

	Qualifying for FYAs	Main pool	Allowances
	£	£	£
Year ended 30.9.04			
Qualifying expenditure	12,000	4,000	
FYA 40%	(4,800)		4,800
WDA 25%		(1,000)	1,000
	7,200		
Transfer to pool	(7,200)	7,200	
WDV at 30.9.04		10,200	
Total allowances			£5,800
15 months ended 31.12.05			
Additions	7,500		
Disposals		(500)	
		9,700	
FYA 40%	(3,000)		3,000
WDA 25% × $\frac{15}{12}$		(3,031)	3,031
	4,500	6,669	
Transfer to pool	(4,500)	4,500	
WDV at 31.12.05 c/fwd		11,169	
Total allowances			£6,031

180

	Qualifying for FYAs £	Main pool £	Allowances £
WDV b/fwd		11,169	
Year ended 31.12.06			
Additions	4,000		
FYA 40%	(1,600)		1,600
WDA 25%		(2,792)	2,792
	2,400	8,377	
Transfer to pool	(2,400)	2,400	
WDV at 31.12.06		10,777	
Total allowances			£4,392

Taxable profits for the accounting periods concerned are

	Before CAs £	CAs £	After CAs £
Year ended 30 September 2004	18,000	5,800	12,200
Period ended 31 December 2005	25,000	6,031	18,969
Year ended 31 December 2006	24,000	4,392	19,608

Taxable profits for the first four years of assessment of the business are

	£	£
2003/04 (1.10.03–5.4.04) (£12,200 × $\frac{6}{12}$)		6,100
2004/05 (y/e 30.9.04)		12,200
2005/06 (1.10.04–31.12.05)	18,969	
Deduct Overlap relief £6,100 × $\frac{3}{6}$	3,050	15,919
2006/07 (y/e 31.12.06)		19,608

Notes

(*a*) Capital allowances are calculated by reference to periods of account and are treated as trading expenses (see 9.1, 9.2(i), 9.32 above).

(*b*) Where a period of account exceeds 12 months, writing-down allowances are proportionately increased (see 9.28 above).

Period of account exceeding 18 months

Bianca commenced business on 1 October 2002 preparing accounts initially to 30 June. She changes her accounting date in 2004/05, preparing accounts for the 21 months to 31 March 2005. The business qualifies as a small business for the purposes of first-year allowances. The following capital expenditure is incurred.

	Plant £	Car £
Period ended 30 June 2003	24,000	16,000 (no private use)
Period ended 31 March 2005	10,000	
Year ended 31 March 2006	2,150	

9.33 Capital Allowances

Of the £10,000 of expenditure incurred in the 21-month accounting period to 31 March 2005, £3,000 was incurred in January 2004 and £7,000 in the nine months to 31 March 2005.

An item of plant is sold for £675 (original cost £1,000) on 3 November 2005.

Profits *before* capital allowances but otherwise as adjusted for tax purposes are as follows.

	£
Period ended 30 June 2003	30,000
Period ended 31 March 2005	75,000
Year ended 31 March 2006	50,000

The capital allowances are

	Qualifying for FYAs £	Main pool £	Car £	Total allowances £
9 months ended 30.6.03				
Qualifying expenditure	24,000		16,000	
FYA 40%	(9,600)			9,600
WDA £3,000 × $\frac{9}{12}$			(2,250)	2,250
	14,400			
	(14,400)	14,400		
WDV at 30.6.03		14,400	13,750	
Total allowances				£11,850
12 months ended 30.6.04				
Additions	3,000			
FYA 40%	(1,200)			1,200
WDA 25%		(3,600)		3,600
WDA £3,000			(3,000)	3,000
	1,800	10,800		
Transfer to pool	(1,800)	1,800		
WDV at 30.6.04		12,600	10,750	
Total allowances				£7,800
9 months ended 31.3.05				
Additions	7,000			
Disposals			(675)	
		11,925		
FYA 50%	(3,500)			3,500
WDA 25% × $\frac{9}{12}$		(2,236)	(2,016)	4,252
	3,500	9,689		
Transfer to pool	(3,500)	3,500		
WDV at 31.3.05 c/fwd		13,189	8,734	
Total allowances				£7,752

	Qualifying for FYAs £	Main pool £	Car £	Total allowances £
WDV b/fwd		13,189	8,734	
Year ended 31.3.06				
Additions	2,150			
FYA 40%	(860)			860
WDA 25%		(3,297)	(2,184)	5,481
	1,290	9,892		
Transfer to pool	(1,290)	1,290		
WDV at 31.3.06		£11,182	£6,550	
Total allowances				£6,341

Taxable profits for the periods of account concerned are

	Before CAs £	CAs £	After CAs £
Period ended 30 June 2003	30,000	11,850	18,150
Period ended 31 March 2005	75,000	(7,800 + 7,752)	59,448
Year ended 31 March 2006	50,000	6,341	43,659

Taxable profits for the first four years of assessment of the business are

	£	£
2002/03 (1.10.02 – 5.4.03) (£18,150 × $\frac{6}{9}$)		12,100
2003/04 (1.10.02 – 30.9.03):		
1.10.02 – 30.6.03	18,150	
1.7.03 – 30.9.03 (£59,448 × $\frac{3}{21}$)	8,493	26,643
2004/05 (1.10.03 – 31.3.05) (£59,448 × $\frac{18}{21}$)	50,955	
Deduct Overlap relief	(12,100)	38,855
2005/06 (y/e 31.3.06)		43,659

Notes

(a)   Where a period of account for capital allowances purposes would otherwise exceed 18 months, it is broken down into shorter periods, the first beginning on the first day of the actual period and each subsequent period beginning on an anniversary of the first day of the actual period. No period can therefore exceed 12 months. See 9.2(i) above.

(b)   The capital allowances computed for the notional periods of account referred to in (a) above are deductible in aggregate in arriving at the adjusted profit for the actual accounting period.

(c)   An accounting period exceeding 18 months cannot normally result in an immediate change of basis period. However, the conditions of *ICTA 1988, s 62A* do not have to be satisfied if the change of accounting period occurs in the second or third year of assessment of a new business, as in this example. See 71.7 SCHEDULE D, CASES I AND II.

9.34   Capital Allowances

Fixtures. For expenditure incurred after 11 July 1984 (but excluding, for chargeable periods ending after 23 July 1996, expenditure under a contract entered into on or before that date, or pursuant to an obligation in a lease, or agreement for a lease, entered into on or before that date), there are special provisions to determine entitlement to allowances on fixtures, i.e. plant or machinery which, by law, becomes part of the building or land on which it is installed or otherwise fixed, including any boiler or water-filled radiator installed as part of a space or water heating system. A dispute may arise as to whether fixtures have, in law, become part of a building or land. Where two or more persons' tax liabilities are affected by the outcome of such a dispute, the question is determined for tax purposes by the Special Commissioners, before whom all those persons are entitled to appear and be heard or to make written representations. [*CAA 2001, s 172(1)(2), s 173, s 204(1)–(3); CAA 1990, s 51(1)–(2A)(7); FA 1997, Sch 16 para 2(5)(6); FA 2000, s 78*].

In *J C Decaux (UK) Ltd v Francis (Sp C 84)*, *[1996] SSCD 281*, automatic public conveniences and other street furniture such as bus shelters were held to be fixtures forming part of the land (and see (*a*) below).

These provisions determine ownership for capital allowances purposes of plant or machinery that is (or becomes) a fixture and determine entitlement to allowances in each of the various circumstances described at (*a*)–(*f*) below. Before *CAA 2001* had effect (see 9.1 above), the provisions also denied allowances to any person other than the person to whom plant or machinery was thereby treated as belonging. The provisions do not affect the entitlement of a contributor towards capital expenditure (see 9.2(vii) above). [*CAA 2001, s 172(1)(2)(5); CAA 1990, s 51(1)(8)*]. See after (*f*) below for provisions determining cessation of ownership (and consequent disposal values), acquisition of ownership in certain cases and restrictions of qualifying expenditure where allowances previously claimed.

Although the rules apply strictly on an asset-by-asset basis, the Revenue accept that in practice they may be applied to groups of assets provided that this does not distort the tax computation (Revenue Tax Bulletin June 1998 p 552).

For the purposes of the fixtures provisions, an '*interest in land*' means

  (i)   the fee simple estate in the land,

  (ii)   in Scotland, in the case of feudal property prior to abolition of feudal tenure, the estate or interest of the proprietor of the *dominium utile*, and in any other case, the interest of the owner,

  (iii) a lease (defined for these provisions in relation to land as any leasehold estate in (or, in Scotland, lease of) the land (whether a head-lease, sub-lease or under-lease) or any agreement to acquire such an estate (or lease)),

  (iv)   an easement or servitude,

  (v)   a licence to occupy land,

and any agreement to acquire an interest as in (i)–(iv) above. Where an interest is conveyed or assigned by way of security subject to a right of redemption, the interest is treated as continuing to belong to the person having the redemption right. [*CAA 2001, ss 174(4), 175, Sch 3 para 29; CAA 1990, s 51(3)(4)*]. As regards (v) above, for the Revenue view of when a licence to occupy land exists for these purposes, see Revenue Tax Bulletin June 2000 p 761.

See generally Revenue Capital Allowances Manual CA 26000 *et seq*.

  (*a*)   *Expenditure incurred by holder of interest in land.* Where a person having an interest in land incurs capital expenditure on plant or machinery which becomes a fixture in relation to that land, for the purposes of a trade or other qualifying activity, then, subject to the election in (*b*) or (*f*) below, the fixture is treated as belonging to that person. If there are two or more such persons, with different interests, the only interest to be taken into account for this purpose is

(i)   an easement or servitude, or any agreement to acquire same;

(ii)   if (i) does not apply to any of those interests, a licence to occupy the land;

(iii)   if neither (i) nor (ii) applies to any of those interests, that interest which is not directly or indirectly in reversion on any other of those interests in the land (in Scotland, that of whichever of those persons has, or last had, the right of use of the land).

[*CAA 2001, s 176; CAA 1990, s 52; FA 2001, s 66, Sch 18 para 3*].

In *J C Decaux (UK) Ltd v Francis (Sp C 84), [1996] SSCD 281*, suppliers to local authorities of automatic public conveniences and other street furniture such as bus shelters, which were held to be fixtures forming part of the land, were held not to have an interest in the land.

(*b*)   *Expenditure incurred by equipment lessor.* An 'equipment lease' exists where

● a person incurs capital expenditure on an item of plant or machinery for leasing,

● an agreement is entered into for the lease, directly or indirectly from that person (the '*equipment lessor*'), of the item to another person (the '*equipment lessee*'),

● the item becomes a fixture, and

● the item is not leased as part of the land in relation to which it is a fixture.

Such an agreement, or a lease entered into under such an agreement, is an '*equipment lease*'. Provided that

(i)   under the equipment lease, the plant or machinery is leased for the purposes of a trade or other qualifying activity carried on (or to be carried on in future) by the equipment lessee,

(ii)   it is not for use in a dwelling-house,

(iii)   the equipment lessee is within the charge to UK tax on profits from the qualifying activity for use in which the equipment is leased (but see below for supersession of this requirement),

(iv)   the equipment lessor and equipment lessee are not CONNECTED PERSONS (19),

(v)   if the expenditure on the fixture had been incurred by the equipment lessee, he would have been entitled to allowances under (*a*) above,

the equipment lessor and equipment lessee may jointly elect for the fixture to be treated, from the time the expenditure is incurred by the equipment lessor (or, if later, from the commencement of the lessee's qualifying activity), as owned by the lessor and not the lessee.

Where the following conditions are met, (i), (iii) and (v) above do not have to be satisfied (and the potentially later start date of the election is not relevant).

(1)   the plant or machinery becomes a fixture by being fixed to land which is neither a building nor part of a building;

(2)   the lessee has an interest in that land when he takes possession of the plant or machinery under the equipment lease;

(3)   under the terms of the equipment lease the lessor is entitled, at the end of the lease period, to sever the plant or machinery from the land to which it is then fixed, whereupon it will be owned by the lessor;

(4)   the nature of the plant or machinery and the way it is fixed to the land are such that its use does not, to any material extent, prevent its being used, after severance, for the same purposes on different premises; and

(5)   the equipment lease is such as falls under generally accepted accounting practice (see 71.30 SCHEDULE D, CASES I AND II) to be treated in the accounts of the equipment lessor as an operating lease.

For 2000/01 and subsequent years and for corporation tax accounting periods ending after 20 March 2000, the requirement at (iii) above is repealed, having been superseded by the general exclusion of non-UK taxable activities in 9.24 above. The general exclusion applies even where (1)–(5) above are met.

In relation to agreements entered into before 19 March 1997, the election is not available where the lessee's trade was not being carried on at the time of the agreement, and the waiver of certain requirements (as above) where conditions (1)–(5) above are satisfied does not apply. For expenditure incurred by the equipment lessor before 24 July 1996, conditions (ii) and (iii) above do not apply, and (v) above is replaced by a requirement that, if the expenditure had been incurred by the equipment lessee, the equipment would, under (a) above, have been treated as belonging to him (for which see *Melluish v BMI (No 3) Ltd HL 1995, 68 TC 1*).

The time limit for the election is (A) for income tax, within twelve months after 31 January following the tax year in which ends the equipment lessor's chargeable period in which the expenditure is incurred, and (B) for corporation tax, within two years after the end of the equipment lessor's chargeable period in which the expenditure was incurred.

Where expenditure is incurred on or after 28 July 2000 and before 1 January 2008 on plant or machinery consisting of a boiler, heat exchanger, radiator or heating control installed in a building as part of a space or water heating system, and the equipment lease is approved under the Affordable Warmth programme by the Secretary of State (or the responsible Scottish, Welsh or NI body), these provisions have effect without (i)–(iii) and (v) above having to be satisfied. If the approval is withdrawn, it is treated as never having had effect. The taxpayer must notify the inspector, within three months of his becoming aware that a return of his has become incorrect by reason of the withdrawal of approval, of the amendments to the return required in consequence of the withdrawal, subject to penalties for failure.

[*CAA 2001, s 174(1)–(3), ss 177–180, 203, Sch 3 paras 30–33; CAA 1990, s 53; FA 1996, s 135, Sch 21 para 31; FA 1997, Sch 16 para 3; FA 2000, s 75(5)(6), s 79; FA 2002, Sch 40 Pt 3(16)*].

See (f) below as regards expenditure incurred by an energy services provider.

(c)   *Expenditure included in consideration for acquisition of existing interest in land.* Where a person acquires a pre-existing interest in land to which a fixture is attached, for a consideration in part treated for capital allowance purposes as being expenditure on provision of the fixture, the fixture is treated as belonging to the person acquiring the interest. This applies equally where the fixture in question was previously let under an 'equipment lease' (see (b) above) and, in connection with the acquisition, the purchaser pays a capital sum to discharge the equipment lessee's obligations under that lease. For income tax periods of account ending after 5 April 2001 and corporation tax accounting periods ending after 31 March 2001, it also applies where the fixture was provided under an energy services agreement (see (f) below) and, in connection with the acquisition, the purchaser pays a capital sum to discharge the client's obligations under that agreement.

Where the purchaser acquired the interest before 24 July 1996, the above applied with the additional condition that either no person had previously been entitled to allowances on the fixture, or any person previously so entitled has been or is required to bring in a disposal value (other than by virtue of an 'additional VAT rebate' — see 9.2(viii) above) in respect of the fixture.

[*CAA 2001, s 181(1)(4), s 182(1), 182A(1), Sch 3 paras 34, 35; CAA 1990, s 54; FA 1991, Sch 14 para 10; FA 1997, Sch 16 paras 2, 4, 5; FA 2001, s 66, Sch 18 paras 5, 6*].

Where the above provisions would otherwise apply, they are treated as not applying (and as never having applied) where the following conditions are met.

(A)   Before *CAA 2001* had effect (see 9.1 above):

    (i)   an interest in any land in which the whole or part of the land to which the fixture is attached is comprised is held by any person immediately after the time of the above acquisition (where that time is after 23 July 1996);

    (ii)   that interest is not the one acquired by the purchaser;

    (iii)   the person in (i) above is treated as the owner of the fixture (other than under *CAA 1990, s 154* (contributions to expenditure — see 9.2(vii) above)) immediately before the time referred to in (i) above, in consequence of his having incurred expenditure on its provision; and

    (iv)   that person is entitled to, and claims, an allowance in respect of that expenditure.

(B)   Where *CAA 2001* has effect (see 9.1 above):

    (i)   a person is treated as the owner of the fixture (other than under *CAA 2001, s 538* (contributions to expenditure — see 9.2(vii) above)) immediately before the time of the above acquisition, in consequence of his having incurred expenditure on its provision; and

    (ii)   that person is entitled to, and claims, an allowance in respect of that expenditure.

Where any person becomes aware that a return of his has become incorrect because of the operation of this provision, the necessary amendments to the return must be notified to the Revenue within three months of his becoming so aware, subject to penalties for failure.

[*CAA 2001, s 181(2)(3), s 182(2)(3), s 182A(2)(3), s 203; CAA 1990, ss 51(6A), 56A; FA 1997, Sch 16 para 2(4)(7), paras 4, 9; FA 2001, ss 66, 69, Sch 18 paras 6, 11, Sch 21 para 2(1)–(3)*].

(*d*)   *Expenditure incurred by incoming lessee: election to transfer lessor's entitlement to allowances.* Where a person with an interest in land to which a fixture is attached grants a lease and he would (or if chargeable to tax would) be entitled, for the chargeable period in which the lease is granted, to capital allowances in respect of the fixture, and the consideration given by the lessee falls, in whole or in part, to be treated for plant and machinery allowances purposes as expenditure on the provision of the fixture, an election is available to the lessor and lessee. They may jointly elect (by notice to the Revenue within two years after the date on which the lease takes effect) that, from the grant of the lease, the fixture is treated as belonging to the lessee and not to the lessor. No such election is available if lessor and lessee are CONNECTED PERSONS (19), or (where the lease was granted before 24 July 1996) if it appears that the sole or main benefit to the lessor from the grant of the lease and the election would be enhanced capital allowances or a reduced balancing charge; see now the anti-avoidance provision at *CAA 2001, s 197* below. The instant provisions apply to the entering into of an agreement for a lease as they apply to a grant of a lease. [*CAA 2001, ss 174(4), 183, Sch 3 para 36; CAA 1990, s 55; FA 1997, Sch 18 Pt VI (12)*].

(e)   *Expenditure incurred by incoming lessee: lessor not entitled to allowances.* Where

- a person with an interest in land to which a fixture is attached grants a lease,

- the provisions at (*d*) above do not apply, because the lessor is not entitled to capital allowances in respect of the fixture,

- before the lease is granted, the fixture has not been used for the purposes of a trade or other qualifying activity by the lessor or a person connected with him (see 19 CONNECTED PERSONS), and

- the consideration given by the lessee includes a capital sum falling, in whole or in part, to be treated for plant and machinery allowances purposes as expenditure on the provision of the fixture,

the fixture is treated as belonging to the lessee from the time the lease is granted.

Where the lease was granted before 24 July 1996, these provisions applied with the additional condition that at the time of grant no person had previously become entitled to an allowance in respect of any capital expenditure incurred on the provision of the fixture. Where the lease is granted on or after that date, rules similar to those of *CAA 2001, s 181(2)(3), s 182(2)(3), s 182A(2)(3), s 203* at (*c*) above apply instead (by reference to the time of grant).

[*CAA 2001, s 184, Sch 3 para 37; CAA 1990, ss 52, 56; FA 1997, Sch 16 paras 3, 4, 6; FA 2001, s 69, Sch 21 para 2(4)*].

(f)   *Expenditure incurred by energy services provider.* An '*energy services agreement*' is an agreement entered into by an 'energy services provider' and his client that provides, with a view to the saving or more efficient use of energy, for

- the design of plant or machinery or of systems incorporating it,

- the obtaining and installation of the plant or machinery, and

- its operation and maintenance,

and under which any payment by the client in respect of the operation of the plant or machinery is wholly or partly linked to the energy savings or increased energy efficiency. An '*energy services provider*' is a person carrying on a qualifying activity consisting wholly or mainly in providing energy management services. [*CAA 2001, s 175A; FA 2001, s 66, Sch 18 para 2*].

For income tax periods of account ending after 5 April 2001 and corporation tax accounting periods ending after 31 March 2001, where

- an energy services agreement is entered into,

- the energy services provider incurs capital expenditure after 31 March 2001 under the agreement on an item of plant or machinery,

- the item becomes a fixture,

- at the time the item becomes a fixture, the client has an interest in the land in relation to which it is a fixture but the provider does not,

- the item is neither leased nor used in a dwelling-house,

- the operation of the item is carried out wholly or substantially by the provider or a person connected with him, and

- provider and client are not CONNECTED PERSONS (19),

the energy services provider and the client may jointly elect for the fixture to be treated, from the time the expenditure is incurred, as owned by the former and not the latter. This opens the way for the energy services provider to claim 100% first-year allowances where his expenditure is within 9.27(*d*) above. The election must be made on or before the first anniversary of 31 January following the tax year in which ends the income tax period of account in which the expenditure is incurred, or within two years after the end of the corporation tax accounting period in which it is incurred. If the client would not have been entitled to allowances under (*a*) above if he had incurred the expenditure himself, the election is available only if the item belongs to the technology class 'Combined Heat and Power' in the Energy Technology Criteria List (see 9.27 above), as specified by Treasury order *SI 2001 No 2541*, or to any other class of plant or machinery specified for this purpose by Treasury order; the intention is that, in such specified cases, allowances to the provider are not to be denied only because the client is a non-taxpayer. [*CAA 2001, s 180A; FA 2001, s 66, Sch 18 para 4*]. See also Revenue Capital Allowances Manual CA 23150.

Cessation of ownership

(A) If a person is treated as owning a fixture under *CAA 2001, s 176* (see (*a*) above) *s 181, 182* or *182A* (see (*c*) above), *s 183* (see (*d*) above) or *s 184* (see (*e*) above), he is treated as ceasing to be the owner if and when he ceases to have the 'qualifying interest'. The '*qualifying interest*' is the interest in the land in question, except that where (*d*) or (*e*) above apply it is the lease there referred to. There are rules (see *CAA 2001, s 189*) for identifying the qualifying interest in special cases.

(B) Where, under (*d*) above, the lessee begins to be treated as owning the fixture, the lessor is treated as ceasing to own it at that time.

(C) Where a fixture is permanently severed from the building or land, such that it is no longer owned by the person treated as owning it, he is treated as ceasing to own it at the time of severance.

(D) Where an equipment lessor is treated as owning a fixture (see (*b*) above) and either he assigns his rights under the equipment lease or the financial obligations of the equipment lessee (or his assignee etc.) are discharged, the equipment lessor is treated as ceasing to own the fixture at that time (or the earliest of those times).

(E) Where an energy services provider is treated as owning a fixture (see (*f*) above) and either he assigns his rights under the energy services agreement or the financial obligations of the client (or his assignee etc.) are discharged, the energy services provider is treated as ceasing to own the fixture at that time (or the earliest of those times).

[*CAA 2001, ss 188–192A; CAA 1990, s 57(2)–(5)(7), s 58(1)(5); FA 2001, s 66, Sch 18 paras 7, 8*].

The *disposal value* to be brought into account in relation to a fixture depends upon the nature of the event.

(1) On cessation of ownership under (A) above due to a sale of the qualifying interest (other than where (2) below applies), and subject to the election below, it is that part

of the sale price that falls (or would, if there were an entitlement, fall) to be treated for plant and machinery allowances purposes as expenditure by the purchaser on the provision of the fixture.

(2) On cessation of ownership under (A) above due to a sale of the qualifying interest at less than market value (unless the buyer (not being a dual resident investing company connected with the seller) can claim plant or machinery or research and development (formerly scientific research) allowances for his expenditure, in which case (1) above applies), it is the amount that, if that interest were sold at market value (determined without regard to the disposal event itself) at that time, would be treated for plant and machinery allowances purposes as expenditure by the purchaser on provision of the fixture.

(3) On cessation of ownership under (A) above where neither (1) or (2) above applies but the qualifying interest continues (or would do so but for being merged with another interest), it is an amount determined as in (2) above.

(4) On cessation of ownership under (A) above due to the expiry of the qualifying interest, it is any capital sum received by reference to the fixture, or otherwise nil.

(5) On cessation of ownership under (B) above, and subject to the election below, it is that part of the capital sum given by the lessee for the lease as qualifies for plant and machinery allowances as the lessee's expenditure on the fixture.

(6) On cessation of ownership under (C) above, it is market value at time of severance.

(7) On cessation of ownership under (D) above, it is the consideration for the assignment or, as the case may be, the capital sum, if any, paid to discharge the equipment lessee's financial obligations.

(8) On cessation of ownership under (E) above, it is the consideration for the assignment or, as the case may be, the capital sum, if any, paid to discharge the client's financial obligations.

(9) On permanent discontinuance of the trade or other qualifying activity followed by the sale of the qualifying interest, it is an amount determined as in (1) above.

(10) On permanent discontinuance of the qualifying activity followed by demolition or destruction of the fixture, it is the net amount received for the remains, plus any insurance or capital compensation received.

(11) On permanent discontinuance of the qualifying activity followed by permanent loss (other than as in (10) above) of the fixture, it is any insurance or capital compensation received.

(12) On the fixture's beginning to be used wholly or partly for purposes other than those of the qualifying activity, it is that part of the sale price that would fall to be treated for plant and machinery allowances purposes as expenditure by the purchaser on the provision of the fixture if the qualifying interest were sold at market value.

If, before 24 July 1996, a person is treated as ceasing to own a fixture by virtue of (A), (B) or (C) above, and another person incurs expenditure on the fixture, allowances are not available on so much (if any) of that expenditure as exceeds the former owner's disposal value.

[*CAA 2001, s 196, Sch 3 para 41; CAA 1990, s 26(1)(f), s 57(1), s 58(2)(4)(5), s 59; FA 1997, Sch 18 Pt VI(12); FA 2001, s 66, Sch 18 para 10*].

Where the event concerned occurs after 23 July 1996, fixtures are treated as disposed of at their 'notional written-down value' (if greater than would otherwise be the case) where the disposal event is part of a scheme or arrangement having tax avoidance (whether by increased allowances or reduced charges) as a main object. The '*notional written-down value*' is qualifying expenditure on the item in question less maximum allowances to date, computed on the assumption that all allowances have been made in full. [*CAA 2001, s 197; CAA 1990, s 59A; FA 1997, Sch 16 para 5*].

A special election is available where the disposal value of fixtures falls to be determined under (1) or (5) above at a time on or after 19 March 1996. Subject as below and to *CAA 2001, ss 186, 187* (see below) and *s 197* (above), the seller and purchaser (or, where (5) above applies, the lessor and lessee under (*d*) above) may jointly elect to fix the amount so determined at a figure not exceeding either the capital expenditure treated as incurred on the fixtures by the seller (or lessor) former owner or the actual sale price (or capital sum). The remainder (if any) of the sale price (or capital sum) is attributed to the other property included in the sale. The notice of election must be given within two years after the interest is acquired (or the lease granted), and is irrevocable. A copy must also accompany the return of the persons making the election. The notice must contain prescribed information and must quantify the amount fixed by the election, although if subsequent circumstances reduce the maximum below that fixed, the election is treated as being for that reduced maximum amount. There are provisions for the determination of questions relating to such elections by Appeal Commissioners. Where any person becomes aware that a return of his has become incorrect because of such an election (or because of subsequent circumstances affecting the election), the necessary amendments to the return must be notified to the Revenue within three months of his becoming so aware, subject to penalties for failure. [*CAA 2001, ss 198–201, 203, 204(4)–(6); CAA 1990, s 51(6A), ss 59B, 59C; FA 1997, Sch 16 para 2(4)(7), paras 6, 9; FA 1999, Sch 11 para 6*]. In practice, the Revenue normally accept an election covering a group of fixtures, or all the fixtures in a single property, but not one covering fixtures in different properties (e.g. where a portfolio of properties is sold) (Revenue Tax Bulletin June 1998 p 552).

Acquisition of ownership in certain cases. If, on the termination of a lease, the outgoing lessee is treated under (A) above as ceasing to own a fixture, the lessor is thereafter treated as the owner. This applies in relation to a licence as it does in relation to a lease. [*CAA 2001, s 193; CAA 1990, s 57(6)*].

The following apply where an election is made under (*b*) above (election to treat fixture as owned by equipment lessor), and either

- the equipment lessor assigns his rights under the equipment lease; or

- the equipment lessee's financial obligations under the lease (or those of his assignee etc.) are discharged (on the payment of a capital sum).

If the former applies, then, from the time of the assignment, the fixture is treated as belonging to the assignee for capital allowance purposes, and the consideration for the assignment treated as consideration given by him on provision of the fixture. If the assignee makes any further assignment, he is treated under this provision as if he were the original lessor.

If the latter applies, the capital sum is treated as consideration for the fixture, and the fixture is treated from the time of the payment as belonging to the equipment lessee (or to any other person in whom his obligations under the lease have become vested).

[*CAA 2000, ss 194, 195; CAA 1990, s 58(2)–(5)*].

The same applies, with appropriate modifications, where the election in question was under (*f*) above (election to treat fixture as owned by energy services provider). [*CAA 2001, ss 195A, 195B; FA 2001, s 66, Sch 18 para 9*].

Restriction of qualifying expenditure where allowance previously claimed. Where

   (i)   a fixture is treated under these provisions as belonging to any person (the current owner) in consequence of his incurring capital expenditure on its provision;

  (ii)   the plant or machinery is treated (other than under *CAA 2001, s 538* — contributions to expenditure, see 9.2(vii) above) as having belonged at a 'relevant earlier time' to a person (who may be the same as the person within (i) above) in consequence of his incurring expenditure other than that within (i) above; and that person, having claimed a plant and machinery allowance for that expenditure, must bring a disposal value into account *by reason of an event occurring after 23 July 1996,*

so much (if any) of the expenditure referred to in (i) above as exceeds the 'maximum allowable amount' is left out of account in determining the current owner's qualifying expenditure or, as the case may be, is taken to be expenditure which should never have been so taken into account.

A '*relevant earlier time*' is any time before the earliest time when the plant or machinery is treated as belonging to the current owner in consequence of the expenditure referred to in (i) above. The relevant earlier time does not, however, include any time before an earlier sale of the plant or machinery other than as a fixture and other than between CONNECTED PERSONS (19).

The '*maximum allowable amount*' is the sum of the disposal value referred to in (ii) above and so much (if any) of the expenditure referred to in (i) above as is deemed under *CAA 2001, s 25* (installation costs, see 9.25 above) to be on provision of the plant or machinery. Where (ii) above is satisfied in relation to more than one disposal event, only the most recent event is taken into account for this purpose.

Where any person becomes aware that a return of his has become incorrect because of the operation of this provision, the necessary amendments to the return must be notified to the Revenue within three months of his becoming so aware, subject to penalties for failure.

[*CAA 2001, ss 185, 203, Sch 3 para 38; CAA 1990, ss 51(6A), 56B; FA 1997, Sch 16 para 2(4)(7), paras 4, 9*].

Where

  (I)   a person has claimed industrial buildings allowances for expenditure partly on the provision of plant or machinery, and transfers the relevant interest in the building concerned; and

 (II)   the transferee, or any other person to whom the plant or machinery is subsequently treated under these provisions as belonging, claims plant and machinery allowances for expenditure incurred thereon *at a time after 23 July 1996* when it is a fixture in the building,

the qualifying expenditure in respect of which the claim in (II) above is made is restricted to the '*relevant amount*', i.e. the proportion of the consideration for the transfer referred to in (I) above attributable to the fixture. It is assumed for this purpose that the transfer was a sale for an amount equal to the residue of expenditure (see 9.14 above) immediately after the transfer.

A similar restriction applies where research and development (formerly scientific research) allowances have previously been claimed.

[*CAA 2001, ss 186, 187, Sch 3 paras 39, 40; CAA 1990, ss 56C, 56D; FA 1997, Sch 16 para 4; FA 2000, Sch 19 para 8*].

Simon's Direct Tax Service. See B2.355 *et seq.*

Finance leasing. See 71.58 SCHEDULE D, CASES I AND II as regards restrictions on capital allowances where certain finance leasing arrangements are involved. See also 9.28 above, 9.38(A)(C) below.

9.35 **Overseas leasing.** *History.* Legislation regarding capital allowances on plant and machinery provided for leasing (not just overseas leasing) was first introduced in 1980 and was mainly concerned with restricting the availability of universal first-year allowances (see 9.27 above). Further legislation introduced in 1982 restricted, and in some cases prohibited, writing-down allowances on plant and machinery leased to non-UK resident lessees in certain circumstances. Following the phasing out of universal first-year allowances, much of the original legislation was no longer appropriate and the leasing provisions were widely amended by the *Finance Act 1986* but so as to broadly retain those relating to overseas leasing. The current provisions are contained in *CAA 2001, ss 105–126.*

Current provisions. For the purposes of these provisions, a 'lease' includes a sub-lease, with 'lessor' and 'lessee' being construed accordingly, and 'leasing' is regarded as including the letting of any asset on hire or of a ship or aircraft on charter (and see *Barclays Mercantile Industrial Finance Ltd v Melluish Ch D 1990, 63 TC 95* at (*d*) below). [*CAA 2001, s 105(1); CAA 1990, s 50(1)(2)*].

For the purposes of the provisions described below, plant or machinery is used for overseas leasing if it is leased to a person who

(1) is not resident in the UK, and

(2) does not use the plant or machinery exclusively for earning profits chargeable to UK tax (which includes profits from exploration or exploitation activities carried on in the UK or its territorial sea).

Where there is a chain of leases, the Revenue now consider that the provisions apply where any lessee in the chain falls within (1) and (2) above. Their view had previously been that only the end lessee need be considered, and they will act in accordance with their earlier view for leasing arrangements entered into before 19 April 1999, or within three months after that date where the principal terms had been agreed in writing before that date (e.g. in an agreed term-sheet or accepted offer letter) and had not materially altered in the intervening period. (Revenue Tax Bulletin April 1999 p 654).

For the purpose of (2) above, profits chargeable to UK tax do not include profits in respect of which the trader etc. is entitled to tax relief under a double taxation agreement. This does not apply in the case of leases entered into before 16 March 1993 for which, in addition, the use of the plant or machinery does not have to be *exclusively* for the purposes stated.

[*CAA 2001, s 105(2)–(4), Sch 3 para 21; CAA 1990, ss 42(1), 50(3A); FA 1993, s 116(2)–(4)*].

The provisions described below apply in relation to 'new expenditure'. *'New expenditure'* means expenditure incurred after 31 March 1986 on plant and machinery other than certain cars costing £12,000 or less (see (*a*) below), provided that it is not 'old expenditure'. *'Old expenditure'* means, broadly, expenditure incurred before 1 April 1986, although certain post-31 March 1986 expenditure was included in the term under transitional provisions, as was post-31 March 1986 expenditure qualifying for a universal (as opposed to targeted) first-year allowance (see 9.27 above) other than the temporarily reinstated 40% allowance for expenditure in the twelve months to 31 October 1993. See the 2000/01 and earlier editions for coverage of 'old expenditure' (and see (*a*) below).

[*CAA 1990, s 50(3); FA 1993, Sch 13 para 11(1); F(No 2)A 1997, s 42(6); FA 1998, s 85(4); FA 2000, s 71(2)*].

The provisions referred to above are as follows.

(*a*) *Separate pooling and restriction of writing-down allowances.* Separate pooling provisions apply to qualifying expenditure (see 9.24 above) if it is incurred on the provision of plant or machinery for leasing and if that plant or machinery is at any time in the 'designated period' (see (*c*) below) used for overseas leasing other than 'protected leasing' (see (e) below). They do not apply to long-life asset expenditure (see 9.30(G) above) or to expenditure which can only be allocated to a single asset pool (see 9.28 above). Qualifying expenditure meeting the above conditions can only be allocated to a *class pool* (see 9.28 above), known as the *overseas leasing pool*. The final chargeable period (see 9.28 above) of the overseas leasing pool is the chargeable period at the end of which circumstances are such that no further disposal values (see 9.29 above) could fall to be brought into account.

Writing-down allowances on qualifying expenditure meeting the above conditions are restricted to **10% p.a.** (instead of the normal 25% p.a.).The restriction applies whether such expenditure falls to be allocated to the overseas leasing pool or to a single asset pool (including, where *CAA 2001* has effect, see 9.1 above, a pool for partial non-business use as in 9.30(C) above). The 10% rate does not, however, displace the 6% rate applicable to long-life asset expenditure (see 9.30(G) above). The 10% allowance is proportionately reduced or increased if the chargeable period is less or more than a year, or if the qualifying activity has been carried on for part only of the chargeable period. A claim for a writing-down allowance may require it to be reduced to a specified amount.

[*CAA 2001, ss 56(5), 65(4), 107, 109; CAA 1990, s 41(1)–(4)(6), s 42(2); FA 1990, Sch 17 para 9; FA 1997, Sch 14 paras 4, 5; FA 2000, s 74(1)*].

When plant or machinery in the overseas leasing pool is disposed of to a CONNECTED PERSON (19) (otherwise than on certain partnership changes/company reconstructions, as listed in (b) below, where the qualifying activity is treated as continuing) the disposal value to be brought into account (see generally 9.29 above) is its market value or, if lower, its original cost, and the person acquiring it may claim allowances on the same value. [*CAA 2001, s 108; CAA 1990, s 41(5)*].

Cars costing £12,000 or less (£8,000 for expenditure incurred before 11 March 1992 or under a contract entered into before that date), and which are not leased so as to be otherwise within these provisions, previously had to be included in a similar class pool, but *not* the same pool as that used for overseas leasing. This car pool also included certain 'old expenditure' (see above) on plant or machinery provided for leasing. The separate pooling requirement is, however, abolished for periods of account ending after 5 April 2000 and corporation tax accounting periods ending after 31 March 2000, except that an election may be made to treat the abolition as deferred by one year in any particular case. Any unrelieved qualifying expenditure brought forward from the immediately preceding chargeable period in the separate pool is included in the main pool of qualifying expenditure for the chargeable period for which abolition has effect. [*CAA 1990, s 41(1)(b)(c)(4); FA 2000, s 74*].

(b) *Prohibition of allowances.* No writing-down or balancing allowances are available in respect of qualifying expenditure meeting the conditions in (a) above if the plant or machinery is used other than for a 'qualifying purpose' (see (d) below) *and*

(i) there is more than one year between consecutive payments due under the lease, or

(ii) any payments other than periodical payments are due under the lease or under any collateral agreement, or

(iii) any payment expressed monthly under the lease or any collateral agreement is not the same as any other such payment, but disregarding variations due to changes in rates of tax, capital allowances, interest which is linked with rates applicable to inter-bank loans or changes in premiums for insurances of any kind by a person not connected with the lessor or lessee, or

(iv)   either the lease is for a period exceeding 13 years or there is any provision for its extension or renewal or for the grant of a new lease such that the leasing period could exceed 13 years, or

(v)   at any time, the lessor or CONNECTED PERSON (19) could be entitled to receive from the lessee or any other person a payment (not insurance money) of an amount determined before expiry of the lease and referable to the value of the plant or machinery at or after that expiry (whether or not the payment relates to a disposal of the plant or machinery).

[*CAA 2001, s 110; CAA 1990, s 42(3)*].

Where allowances (including any first-year allowance) have been made (and not fully withdrawn under the excess relief provisions in (*g*) below) but by reason of any event in the 'designated period' (see (*c*) below) the expenditure is brought within the above provisions, the net allowances are clawed back by means of a balancing charge. For this purpose only, the allowances made are determined as if the item of plant or machinery in question were the only item, i.e. as if it had not been pooled. A disposal value equal to the balance of the expenditure is also brought into account so as to effectively remove the item from the pool. Where the item was acquired from a CONNECTED PERSON (19), or as a part of a series of transactions with connected persons, allowances made to those persons are also taken into account in computing the balancing charge, with any actual consideration on a connected persons transaction being ignored and with the amount of such allowances being adjusted 'in a just and reasonable manner' where balancing allowances/charges have already been made in respect of the item in question. This does not apply in the case of transactions between connected persons on which the qualifying activity was treated as continuing under *ICTA 1988, s 113(2)* or *s 114(1)* (partnership changes treated as a continuation) or *ICTA 1988, s 343(2)* (company reconstruction without change of ownership). [*CAA 2001, ss 114, 115; CAA 1990, s 42(4)–(9); FA 1993, Sch 13 para 6; FA 1998, s 85(4); FA 2000, s 71(2)*].

(*c*)   '*Designated period*'. For the purposes of these provisions, the '*designated period*' is the period of ten years after the item of plant or machinery in question is first brought into use by the person who incurred the expenditure. It is, however, brought to an end at any time within that ten-year period at which that person ceases to own the item, disregarding any disposal to a CONNECTED PERSON (19) or on a partnership change treated as a continuation under *ICTA 1988, s 113(2)* or disregarded under *ICTA 1988, s 114(1)*. For leases entered into before 16 March 1993, the ten-year period was reduced to one of four years if the plant or machinery was used for a 'qualifying purpose' (see (*d*) below); for later leases, this continues to apply only for the purposes of the provisions for separate pooling of ships (see 9.30(B) above) and short-life assets (see 9.30(F) above). [*CAA 2001, 106; CAA 1990, s 40(4)(5); FA 1993, s 116(1)*].

(*d*)   '*Qualifying purpose*'. Plant or machinery on which a person (the buyer) has incurred expenditure is used for a '*qualifying purpose*' at any time if, at that time:

(i)   the lessee uses it for the purposes of a qualifying activity without leasing it; and had the lessee bought the plant or machinery himself at that time, his expenditure would have fallen to be wholly or partly included in his available qualifying expenditure (see 9.28 above) for a chargeable period; or

(ii)   the buyer uses it for 'short-term leasing' (see (*e*) below); or

(iii)   the lessee uses it for 'short-term leasing' and is either UK resident or so uses it in the course of a qualifying activity carried on in the UK; or

(iv)   the buyer uses it for the purposes of a qualifying activity without leasing it.

For the purposes of (ii) and (iv) above, where the plant or machinery is disposed of to a connected person, or on a partnership change treated as a continuation under *ICTA 1988, s 113(2)* or disregarded under *ICTA 1988, s 114(1)*, the new owner is treated as the 'buyer'.

[*CAA 2001, ss 122, 125; CAA 1990, s 39(1)–(5)(10); FA 1993, Sch 13 para 5(1)*].

As regards the reference to 'leasing' in (i) above, the word is to be construed in accordance with the narrow test applicable to leases of land, so that distribution agreements entered into by film lessee companies were not leases for these purposes but arrangements entered into in the ordinary course of their businesses (*Barclays Mercantile Industrial Finance Ltd v Melluish Ch D 1990, 63 TC 95*).

Ships, aircraft and transport containers. Without prejudice to (i)–(iv) above, a ship is also used for a '*qualifying purpose*' at any time when it is let on charter in the course of a trade of operating ships if the lessor is resident, or carries on his trade, in the UK and is responsible as principal (or appoints another person to be responsible in his stead) for navigating and managing the ship and for defraying substantially all its expenses except those directly incidental to a particular voyage or charter period. The same applies with necessary modifications in relation to aircraft. However, neither ship nor aircraft chartering qualifies if the main object, or one of them, of the chartering (or of a series of transactions of which the chartering was one) was the obtaining by any person of an unrestricted writing-down allowance (or a universal first-year allowance for expenditure in the twelve months to 31 October 1993 — see 9.27 above). A transport container is also used for a '*qualifying purpose*' at any time when it is leased in the course of a trade carried on in the UK or by a UK resident if either the trade is one of operating ships or aircraft and the container is at other times used by the trader in connection with such operation, or the container is leased under a succession of leases to different persons who, or most of whom, are not connected with each other. [*CAA 2001, ss 123, 124, Sch 3 para 23; CAA 1990, s 39(6)–(9); FA 1993, Sch 13 para 5(2)*].

(e) '*Protected leasing*' means 'short-term leasing' (see below) or, in the case of a ship, aircraft or transport container, its use for a qualifying purpose (see (*d*) above). [*CAA 2001, s 105(5); CAA 1990, ss 42(1), 50(3)*].

'*Short-term leasing*' means leasing an item of plant or machinery in such a manner

(i) that (A) the number of consecutive days for which it is leased to the same person will normally be less than 30 and (B) the total number of days to the same person in any period of 12 months will normally be less than 90; or

(ii) that (A) the number of consecutive days for which it is leased to the same person will not normally exceed 365 and (B) the aggregate of the periods for which it is leased to lessees not falling within (*d*)(i) above in any period of 4 consecutive years within the 'designated period' (see (*c*) above) will not exceed 2 years.

For the above purposes, persons who are connected with each other (see 19 CONNECTED PERSONS) are to be treated as the same person. Where plant or machinery is leased from a group of items of similar description and not separately identifiable, all the items in the group may be treated as used for short-term leasing if substantially the whole of the items in the group are so used.

[*CAA 2001, s 121; CAA 1990, s 40(1)–(3)*].

(f) *Joint lessees.* The following applies where an item of plant or machinery is leased (otherwise than by 'protected leasing' — see (*e*) above) to two or more persons jointly, and at least one of the joint lessees is a person within (1) and (2) above (definition of overseas leasing). An unrestricted writing-down allowance is due if the lessees use the item for the purposes of a qualifying activity or activities (but not for leasing) but only to the extent that it appears that the profits therefrom throughout the 'designated period' (see (c) above), or the period of the lease if shorter, will be chargeable to UK income tax or corporation tax. The part of the expenditure so qualifying for unrestricted allowances is treated as if it were expenditure on a separate item of plant or machinery (outside the overseas leasing pool) with the remaining part treated as expenditure within the overseas leasing provisions, with such apportionments as are necessary.

Excess relief is recoverable under (g) below if at any time in the designated period while the item is so leased, no lessee uses it for the purposes of a qualifying activity the profits of which are chargeable to UK tax as above (referred to below as 'eligible use') or if, at the end of the designated period, it appears that the actual extent of eligible use was less than anticipated. In the latter case the amount of excess relief recoverable is in proportion to the reduction in eligible use and any disposal value subsequently brought into account is apportioned to the extent of the eligible use as determined at the end of the designated period.

The above provisions (including the clawback of excess relief) apply in respect of the temporarily reinstated 40% universal first-year allowance for expenditure incurred in the twelve months to 31 October 1993 as they apply in respect of writing-down allowances.

[*CAA 2001, ss 116, 117, Sch 3 para 22; CAA 1990, s 43(1)–(3), 44; FA 1993, Sch 13 paras 7, 8; FA 1997, Sch 14 para 6*].

(g)   *Recovery of excess relief.* Where expenditure has qualified for a normal 25% writing-down allowance (or for a first-year allowance) and the plant or machinery is used for overseas leasing (other than 'protected leasing'— see (e) above) at any time in the 'designated period' (see (c) above), any 'excess relief' is recovered. This is achieved by means of a balancing charge of an amount equal to the excess relief, to be made on the person who owns the item when it is first so used, for the chargeable period in which it is first so used. The item is removed from its existing pool by means of a disposal value equal to the item's written-down value for capital allowances purposes at the end of that period. The '*excess relief*' is the excess, if any, of the allowances made, up to and including the chargeable period in question, over the maximum allowances that could have been made if the expenditure had been within (a) or (b) above from the outset. The allowances made are determined for this purpose as if the item in question were the only item, i.e. as if it had not been pooled with any other item of plant or machinery. The sum of the excess relief and the disposal value is then allocated to the appropriate pool (usually the overseas leasing pool) for the following chargeable period.

Where the person on whom the balancing charge falls to be made acquired the item in question from a CONNECTED PERSON (19), or as part of a series of transactions with connected persons, the allowances taken into account in computing the excess relief include the allowances made to such person(s), any consideration passing between them for the item being ignored. The amount of excess relief is adjusted 'in a just and reasonable manner' where balancing allowances/charges have been made on any of the transactions. However, these modifications do not apply in the case of transactions between connected persons in respect of which the qualifying activity was treated as continuing by virtue of *ICTA 1988, s 113(2)* or *s 114(1)* (partnership changes treated as a continuation) or *ICTA 1988, s 343(2)* (company reconstruction without change of ownership). (Before *CAA 2001* had effect, see 9.1 above, this list of provisions also included *CAA 1990, s 77*, see 9.38(G) below, but it is thought this may have been an error, as that provision does not operate in the same way as the others mentioned.)

In the case of a ship, any allowance previously postponed (see 9.27, 9.30(B) above) cannot be made for any chargeable period in or after that in which the ship is first used for overseas leasing (other than protected leasing) within the designated period. The total of any such allowances is instead allocated to the appropriate pool for the following chargeable period as if it were itself qualifying expenditure.

[*CAA 2001, ss 111–113; CAA 1990, s 46; FA 1990, Sch 17 para 10; FA 1993, Sch 13 para 9; FA 1994, Sch 26 Pt V(24); FA 1997, Sch 14 para 7; F(No 2)A 1997, s 42(6); FA 1998, s 85(5); FA 2000, s 71(3)*].

(*h*)   *Information* must be provided to the Revenue, by the then owner, where expenditure on plant or machinery has qualified for a normal 25% writing-down allowance (or for a first-year allowance) and the item is subsequently used for overseas leasing (other than 'protected leasing'— see (*e*) above) at any time in the 'designated period' (see (*c*) above). Information must also be provided to the Revenue, by the lessor, where plant or machinery is leased to joint lessees as described in (*f*) above and, in addition, if circumstances occur such that excess relief is recoverable. In all cases, the time limit for providing the information is three months after the end of the chargeable period in which the item is first so used (or the said circumstances occur), extended to 30 days after the informant came to know that the item was being so used (if he could not reasonably have been expected to know earlier).

Where expenditure has not yet qualified for a normal 25% writing-down allowance or a first-year allowance or for either and the item is used for overseas leasing which is protected leasing, a claim for a first-year allowance or writing-down allowance thereon must be accompanied by a certificate describing the protected leasing.

[*CAA 2001, ss 118–120, 126; CAA 1990, ss 44(2), 48, 50(3); FA 1990, Sch 17 para 12; FA 1993, Sch 13 para 10; FA 1994, Sch 26 Pt V(24); FA 1997, Sch 14 para 8; F(No 2)A 1997, s 42(6); FA 1998, s 85(5); FA 2000, s 71(3)*].

Restriction of first-year allowances. The targeted first-year allowances at 9.27(*a*)–(*h*) above are *not* generally available in respect of expenditure on plant or machinery for leasing (see 9.27(v) above for details and exceptions). Such expenditure is not automatically precluded from qualifying for the temporarily reinstated 40% universal first-year allowance for expenditure incurred in the twelve months to 31 October 1993 (see 9.27 above), but *is* so precluded if

(I)   it appears that the expenditure would fall within (*a*) or (*b*) above such that writing-down allowances would be restricted or prohibited (but see below re joint lessees); or

(II)   the expenditure is incurred after 13 April 1993, the person to whom the plant or machinery is to be, or is, leased (or a person connected with him) used the plant or machinery for any purpose at any time before its provision for leasing, *and* the plant or machinery does not fall into any of the following qualifying categories:

- plant or machinery which it appears will be used only for a 'qualifying purpose' (see (*d*) above) in the 'designated period' (see (*c*) above);

- plant or machinery which is to be an integral part of a building qualifying for enterprise zone allowances (see 9.19 above);

- plant or machinery fixed to a building or land of which the person incurring the expenditure is the lessor, where a transfer of his interest in the building etc. would operate to transfer his interest in the plant or machinery; and

- cars hired out to persons receiving certain disability allowances or mobility supplements.

Preclusion under (I) above does not apply to the extent that it appears that the plant or machinery will be leased to joint lessees as described at (*f*) above, such that (*a*) and (*b*) above are disapplied in respect of all or part of the expenditure. See (*f*) above for the potential clawback of the allowance in specified circumstances.

[*CAA 2001, Sch 3 para 47(4)–(8); CAA 1990, s 22(4)(c)(5)(6)(6A)(11), s 43(4); FA 1993, s 115(3), Sch 13 para 7; SI 1991 No 2874*].

Simon's Direct Tax Service. See **B2.345** *et seq.*

9.36   *Examples*

Separate pooling

L has a leasing business preparing accounts annually to 31 May. In the year to 31 May 2004, his expenditure included the following.

		£
(i)	Machine 1, leased to M Ltd, a UK-resident company for the purposes of its trade	20,000
(ii)	Machine 2, leased to N, a UK-resident individual, for private use	8,000
(iii)	Machine 3, leased to P, a non-UK resident, for his overseas trade	16,000
(iv)	Fixtures and fittings for use in L's business	2,000
(v)	Car used by L entirely for business	6,000

At 1 June 2003, there is a written-down value of £40,000 brought forward in L's main plant and machinery pool.

The leasing in (iii) above is not 'protected leasing' (see 9.35(*e*) above), but neither does it fall within 9.35(*b*) above (prohibition of allowances). None of the expenditure qualifies for first-year allowances.

L's plant and machinery allowances for the year ended 31 May 2004, assuming no capital expenditure other than as listed above, are as follows.

	Main Pool £	Overseas leasing pool £	Total allowances £
WDV b/f	40,000		
Additions	36,000	16,000	
WDA 25%	(19,000)		19,000
WDA 10%		(1,600)	1,600
WDV c/f	£57,000	£14,400	
Total allowances			£20,600

Notes

(*a*)   Machines 1 and 2 go into the main plant and machinery pool, as do the fixtures and fittings and the car. Machine 3 goes into an overseas leasing pool under 9.35(*a*) above.

9.36   Capital Allowances

(b)   The writing-down allowance for Machine 3 is restricted to 10%.

Recovery of excess relief

M, who has a 30 September accounting date, incurred expenditure of £16,000 in March 2002 on a machine leased to Q Ltd, a company trading in the UK. In May 2004, Q Ltd terminated the lease and M then leased the machine, with effect from June 2004, to P Ltd, a company resident in Panama, for the purposes of its trade there. The leasing was not 'protected leasing' (see 9.35(e) above).

A balancing charge arises in the period of account to 30.9.04 as follows.

Actual allowances

	£	Total allowances £
Expenditure (y/e 30.9.02)	16,000	
WDA 25% for y/e 30.9.02	4,000	4,000
	12,000	
WDA 25% for y/e 30.9.03	3,000	3,000
	9,000	
WDA 25% for y/e 30.9.04	2,250	2,250
Balance of expenditure	£6,750	
Total allowances claimed		£9,250

Notional allowances

	£	Total allowances £
Expenditure (y/e 30.9.02)	16,000	
WDA 10% for y/e 30.9.02 note (a)	1,600	1,600
	14,400	
WDA 10% for y/e 30.9.03	1,440	1,440
	12,960	
WDA 10% for y/e 30.9.04	1,296	1,296
	£11,664	
Notional allowances		£4,336

Balancing charge, equal to the excess of actual allowances over notional allowances, for y/e 30.9.04   £4,914

M will then be deemed to have incurred qualifying expenditure of £11,664 (equal to the balance of expenditure plus the balancing charge) for the year ended 30.9.05, i.e. the chargeable period following that in which the change of use arose, and will then be entitled to writing-down allowances of 10% for that and subsequent chargeable periods. The expenditure will constitute, or form part of, an overseas leasing pool under 9.35(a) above.

Notes

(a) Notional writing-down allowances are restricted to 10% notwithstanding the fact that the machine was used for a qualifying purpose up to May 2004. It is used for overseas leasing (other than protected leasing) at some time in the 'designated period' (see 9.35(a) above).

(b) In practice, the machine would originally have been included in the main plant and machinery pool. For the purpose of calculating the balancing charge, it is assumed to have been the only item of plant and machinery qualifying for writing-down allowances. For the year ended 30 September 2004, a disposal value equal to the residue of expenditure (£6,750) must be brought into account in the main pool, so as to effectively remove the item from that pool.

(c) If the expenditure had qualified for a first-year allowance, this also enters into the calculation of excess relief and is thus effectively clawed back.

9.37 **Special leasing** is the hiring out of plant or machinery otherwise than in the course of a trade or other qualifying activity. It is itself a qualifying activity for the purpose of claiming plant and machinery allowances. However, plant or machinery provided for use in a dwelling-house or flat is excluded from being qualifying expenditure. See 9.24 above.

Where a person hires out more than one item of plant and machinery, he has a *separate qualifying activity* in relation to each item. A qualifying activity of special leasing begins when the plant or machinery is first hired out. It is permanently discontinued if the lessor permanently ceases to hire it out. (Before *CAA 2001* had effect, see 9.1 above, the legislation was ambiguous as to whether a balancing allowance, see 9.28 above, could arise in this situation, but it is clear that it can arise under *CAA 2001*.) [*CAA 2001, s 19(2)–(4); CAA 1990, s 61(1)*].

Manner of making allowances and charges for special leasing. For *income tax*, a plant and machinery allowance is given effect by deduction from the person's income for the tax year in question from qualifying activities of special leasing. If, however, the plant or machinery was not used for the whole (or for a part) of the tax year for the purposes of a qualifying activity carried on by the *lessee*, the allowance (or a proportionate part) can only be set against the lessor's income from that particular qualifying activity of special leasing. A claim for an allowance may be made outside a tax return. Any excess of allowances over the income for a tax year against which they may be set is carried forward without time limit against future such income. A balancing charge is taxed as income under Schedule D, Case VI and is included in the income against which an allowance may be set as above.

Broadly similar rules for allowances apply for *corporation tax*, by reference to company accounting periods rather than tax years. A balancing charge is treated as income from special leasing.

[*CAA 2001, s 3(4), ss 258, 259; CAA 1990, ss 73, 83(1), 141, 145(1)(2); FA 1995, Sch 6 para 33; FA 1996, s 135, Sch 21 para 34; FA 1997, Sch 18 Pt VI(11); FA 1998, s 38, Sch 5 para 57, Sch 27 Pt III(4)*].

Simon's Direct Tax Service. See B2.385.

9.38 **PLANT AND MACHINERY — MISCELLANEOUS**

(A) **Hire-purchase and similar contracts.** The following applies where a person incurs capital expenditure, on the provision of plant or machinery for the purposes of a trade or other qualifying activity, under a contract providing that he shall or may become the owner of it on performance of the contract. One example of such a contract is a hire-purchase agreement. That person is treated for the purposes of plant and machinery allowances as the sole owner of the plant or machinery for as long as he is entitled to the benefit of the contract. When the plant or machinery is brought into use for the purposes of the qualifying activity, the full outstanding capital cost (i.e. excluding the hire or interest element) attracts capital allowances immediately. Any such capital payments made before it is brought into use attract allowances as they fall due.

If the contract is not completed, and the person above does not, in fact, become the owner of the plant or machinery, he is treated as ceasing to own it when he ceases to be entitled to the benefit of the contract. The resulting disposal value (see 9.29 above) depends on whether the plant or machinery has been brought into use for the purposes of the qualifying activity. If it has, the disposal value is

(i) the total of any capital sums received by way of consideration, compensation, damages or insurance in respect of the person's rights under the contract or the plant or machinery itself, plus

(ii) the capital element of all instalments treated as paid (see above) but not, in fact, paid.

This is subject to the over-riding rule that the disposal value cannot exceed the qualifying expenditure brought into account (see 9.29 above).

If the plant or machinery has not been so brought into use, then where *CAA 2001* has effect (see 9.1 above), the disposal value is the total in (i) above (but see below as regards assignments). Previously, no specific rule was provided in such a case, so disposal value was equal to market value by virtue of 9.29(*g*) above.

[*CAA 2001, ss 67, 68, Sch 3 para 15; CAA 1990, s 60*]. See 71.58 SCHEDULE D, CASES I AND II as regards hire-purchase agreements relating to cars whose retail price when new exceeded £12,000.

The above rules do not apply to expenditure incurred on 'fixtures' within *CAA 2001, ss 172–204* (see 9.34 above), and if (at a time on or after 28 July 2000) plant or machinery which has been treated under the above rules as owned by a person becomes such a fixture, he is treated as ceasing to own it at that time (unless it is treated as belonging to him under *sections 172–204*). [*CAA 2001, s 69, Sch 3 para 16; CAA 1990, s 60A; FA 2000, s 80*].

With effect for chargeable periods ending on or after 2 July 1997, the above rules similarly do not apply (except in relation to deemed ownership of the asset concerned) to expenditure incurred after 1 July 1997 (unless it is incurred before 1 July 1998 under a contract entered into on or before 1 July 1997) on the provision of plant or machinery for leasing under a 'finance lease' (see (C) below). [*CAA 2001, s 229(3), Sch 3 para 44; CAA 1990, s 60(2A); F(No 2)A 1997, s 45*]. See Revenue Tax Bulletin June 1998 pp 539–544 for a general article on how these and associated capital allowance restrictions are intended to operate. In particular it is noted that the commencement rules for the fore-mentioned restriction apply before the rule above for bringing in capital costs before they are actually incurred, so that where the asset is brought into use by the lessor in a chargeable period ending on or after 2 July 1997, only expenditure actually incurred before that date (or before 2 July 1998 under an existing contract) can be brought into account at that time. See also 9.28 above, (C) below and 71.58 SCHEDULE D, CASES I AND II as regards finance lease allowance restrictions.

If the person entitled to the benefit of a hire-purchase or similar contract assigns that benefit before the plant or machinery is brought into use, and the assignee's allowances fall to be restricted under the anti-avoidance provisions at (C)(ii) below, both the disposal value and the expenditure against which it is set are increased by the capital expenditure he would have incurred if he had wholly performed the contract. The same applies in finance lease cases. This is to protect the assignee against an undue repression of qualifying expenditure by reference to the assignor's disposal value (see (C)(ii) below). [*CAA 2001, s 229*]. Before

CAA 2001 had effect (see 9.1 above), a similar rule as to acceleration of expenditure operated under *CAA 1990, s 25(6)*, though in more limited circumstances.

See Simon's Direct Tax Service B2.340.

(B) Abortive expenditure. The rules at (A) above for hire-purchase and similar contracts can equally be applied to expenditure under other contracts which proves to be abortive. A disposal value falls to be brought into account as in (A) above when the contract fails to be completed. Thus, for example, plant and machinery allowances can be obtained in respect of a non-refundable deposit paid on an item of plant or machinery which is never actually supplied, notwithstanding the fact that the item is never owned by the person incurring the expenditure.

(C) Connected persons and other anti-avoidance measures. See 19 CONNECTED PERSONS for the definition of that term for these purposes.

(i)   For disposals of plant or machinery acquired as a result of transaction(s) between connected persons, the limit on the disposal value (see 9.29 above) is to the greatest amount of qualifying expenditure incurred on it by any of the participants in the transaction(s) (after deducting any 'additional VAT rebates' made — see 9.2(viii) above).

The normal absence of any requirement to bring a disposal value into account if none of the qualifying expenditure in question has been taken into account in determining available qualifying expenditure (see 9.29 above) does not apply if the person concerned acquired the plant or machinery as a result of such transaction(s) as are mentioned above *and* any earlier participant was required to bring a disposal value into account. Instead, the current participant's qualifying expenditure is deemed to be allocated (if this is not actually the case), for the chargeable period in which the current disposal event occurs, to whichever pool is appropriate, thus requiring the bringing into account of a disposal value (which is then subject to the above-mentioned limit).

[*CAA 2001, s 62(2)–(4), s 64(2)–(5), s 239(5)(6); CAA 1990, s 26(3)(4); FA 1991, Sch 14 para 8(3)*].

(ii)   Where plant or machinery is purchased from a connected person, or in a 'sale and leaseback transaction', or in transaction(s) from which the sole or main benefit appears to be the obtaining of a plant and machinery allowance, no first-year allowances (where otherwise relevant) are available (see 9.27(ix) above), and, in determining the buyer's qualifying expenditure, there is disregarded any excess of his expenditure (including any 'additional VAT liability' incurred in respect thereof — see 9.2(viii) above) over the disposal value to be brought into account by the seller. Where no such disposal value is to be brought into account (e.g. where the seller is non-UK resident), the buyer's qualifying expenditure (if otherwise greater) is restricted to the lesser of

(*a*)   market value at time of sale, and

(*b*)   the capital expenditure, if any, incurred by the seller or any person connected with him,

with modifications to allow for 'additional VAT liabilities' and 'rebates' — see 9.2(viii) above.

For these purposes, a sale is a *'sale and leaseback transaction'* if the plant or machinery

(A)   continues to be used for the purposes of a 'qualifying activity' carried on by the seller, or

(B)   is used at some time after the sale for the purposes of a 'qualifying activity' carried on by the seller (or by a connected person other than the buyer) without having been used in the meantime for the purposes of any other 'qualifying activity' except that of leasing the plant or machinery.

For the purposes of these provisions, a '*qualifying activity*' is any activity within 9.24(i)–(vii) above regardless of whether or not profits therefrom are within the charge to UK tax.

These restrictions do not apply to the supply of unused plant or machinery in the ordinary course of the seller's business. Also, for chargeable periods ending before 12 May 1998, where the plant or machinery had not before the sale been used in a qualifying activity carried on by the seller or any person connected with him, first-year allowances (where otherwise relevant) were available, on the lesser of (*a*) and (*b*) above (if less than actual expenditure).

The above provisions apply to contracts for future delivery, hire-purchase etc. contracts, and hire-purchase etc. contract assignments as they apply to direct sales.

[*CAA 2001, s 213(1)(2), ss 214–218, 230–233, 241, 242; CAA 1990, ss 75, 76; FA 1991, Sch 14 para 11; FA 1998, s 85(8)(9)*].

The 'sole or main benefit' restriction referred to above does not generally apply to straightforward finance leasing transactions (*Barclays Mercantile Industrial Finance Ltd v Melluish Ch D 1990, 63 TC 95*). However, with effect for expenditure incurred on or after 2 July 1997 (unless incurred before 2 July 1998 under a pre-2 July 1997 contract), the above rules are extended to further restrict allowances in the case of 'sale and finance leasebacks'. A '*sale and finance leaseback*' is a transaction which either

- meets one of the conditions at (A) and (B) above, or

- in which the plant or machinery is used at some time after the sale etc. for the purposes of a non-qualifying activity carried on by the seller (or by a connected person other than the buyer) without having been used in the meantime for the purposes of a 'qualifying activity' (defined as above) except that of leasing the plant or machinery,

where the availability of the plant or machinery for the use in question is a direct or indirect consequence of its having been leased under a 'finance lease'.

Where an item of plant or machinery is the subject of a sale and finance leaseback, the buyer's qualifying expenditure (*and* in this case the seller's disposal value, if any) is further limited to the item's notional written-down value, computed on the assumption that all available allowances have been made in full. There are also restrictions on the qualifying expenditure of any future owner of the item. Where the finance lessor has substantially divested himself of any risk that the lessee will default, the lessor's expenditure does not qualify for plant and machinery allowances at all (and this applies regardless of any election as below). Modifications to these rules allow for any 'additional VAT liabilities' and 'rebates' — see 9.2(viii) above.

A '*finance lease*' is any arrangements for plant or machinery to be leased or made available such that the arrangements (or arrangements in which they are comprised) would fall, in accordance with generally accepted accounting practice (see 71.30 SCHEDULE D, CASES I AND II), to be treated in the accounts of one or more of those companies (including any consolidated group accounts) as a finance lease or as a loan.

With effect from 28 July 2000, in the case of sale and leaseback (and sale and finance leaseback) transactions within the above provisions, a joint (irrevocable) election may be made by the seller (or assignor) and the lessor (within two years of the sale etc.) provided that

- the seller (or assignor) incurred capital expenditure on acquiring the plant or machinery unused (and not second-hand) and not under a transaction itself within the above provisions,

- the sale etc. takes place not more than four months after the plant or machinery is first brought into use for any purpose, and

- the seller (or assignor) has not claimed capital allowances for the expenditure or included it in a pool of qualifying expenditure.

The effect of the election is that no allowances are made to the seller (or assignor) in respect of the expenditure, and that allowances which are accordingly available to the lessor are given by reference to the lesser of his expenditure and the amount in (*b*) above, i.e. disregarding the current market value at the time of the sale etc. (and, in the case of sale and finance leasebacks, the item's notional written-down value).

[*CAA 2001, ss 219, 221–228, 243–245, Sch 3 paras 45, 51; CAA 1990, ss 76(7), 76A, 76B, 82A; F(No 2)A 1997, ss 46, 47; FA 2000, s 77; FA 2001, s 69, Sch 21 para 3; FA 2002, Sch 40 Pt 3(16)*].

(iii)   Where a disposal value is required to be brought into account in respect of a car costing over £12,000 (previously £8,000) (see 9.30(A) above) on a sale (or on the performance of a contract) within any of the provisions in (ii) above, the disposal value is equal to the lesser of market value at the time of the event and the capital expenditure incurred (or treated as incurred) on it by the person disposing of it. The new owner is treated as having incurred capital expenditure on the car of the same amount. [*CAA 2001, s 79; CAA 1990, s 34(4)*].

(iv)   In a case where an item of plant or machinery is the subject of a sale and finance leaseback (as defined above) and the seller's disposal value falls to be restricted as in (ii) above, further anti-avoidance provisions apply in relation to periods ending after 16 March 2004 (but subject to the transitional provisions below) so as to limit the amount of lease rentals deductible in computing the lessee's income or profits. The amount deductible is limited to the aggregate of the finance charges shown in the accounts and the depreciation that would have been charged if the value of the item at the beginning of the leaseback had been taken for this purpose to be equal to the restricted disposal value.

In the period of account in which the leaseback terminates,

- the above restriction on deductible lease rentals does not apply to any refund of lease rentals;

- the aforementioned aggregate is increased by a proportion of the net book value of the item immediately before the termination, such proportion to be computed in accordance with a formula in *CAA 2001, s 228B(4)*;

- (other than where a pre-17 March 2004 leaseback terminates before that date) the lessee's income/profits from the qualifying activity for the purposes of which the leased item was used immediately before the termination are increased by a proportion of the original consideration on the sale less the restricted disposal value, such proportion to be computed in accordance with a formula in *CAA 2001, s 228C(3)*.

The above rules do not apply to a lessee who became the lessee by means of an assignment of the lease.

For the above purposes and those below, a '*termination*' of a leaseback includes an assignment of the lessee's interest, the making of any other arrangements under which a person other than the lessee becomes liable to make payments under the leaseback and any variation as a result of which the leaseback ceases to be a finance lease.

In any case in which the above restriction on the lessee's deductible lease rentals potentially applies (or would do so if he had not obtained his interest by way of assignment), the following apply in computing the income/profits of the *lessor* for a period of account. Amounts receivable by the lessor under the leaseback are included as income without netting off any amounts due by the lessor to the lessee. However, amounts receivable are not included as income to the extent that they exceed the aggregate of the gross earnings under the leaseback as shown in the lessor's accounts (effectively the finance charge element of the lease rentals) and a proportion of the restricted disposal value, such proportion to be computed in accordance with a formula in *CAA 2001, s 228D(4)*. These rules do not apply if the lessee became the lessee by means of an assignment of the lease made before 17 March 2004.

Where the leaseback terminates and the lessor disposes of the plant or machinery in circumstances such that the resulting disposal value is limited under the general rule in 9.29 above (disposal value of plant or machinery to be limited to qualifying expenditure incurred on its acquisition) or by that rule as modified under (i) above, then, in computing the lessor's income/profits for the period of account in which termination occurs, any amount refunded to the lessee is deductible only to the extent that it does not exceed the limited disposal value. This does not apply in the case of a pre-17 March 2004 leaseback terminating before that date.

Special provision is made for cases in which accounts are not drawn up in accordance with generally accepted accounting practice (GAAP). Additionally, the above rules are adapted, insofar as they relate to the lessee, in a case where the leaseback does not fall under GAAP to be treated in the lessee's accounts as a finance lease but does fall to be so treated in the accounts of a person connected with the lessee. If the leaseback falls to be so treated in the accounts of neither the lessee nor a person connected with him, those rules are disapplied. In that case, however, where the term of the leaseback begins after 17 May 2004, the lessee's income/profits for the period of account during which it begins are increased by the sale consideration less the restricted disposal value.

Where plant or machinery, whilst continuing to be the subject of a sale and finance leaseback, is leased to the original owner, or a person connected with him, under an operating lease (meaning, for this purpose, a lease that does not fall under GAAP to be treated in the lessee's accounts as a finance lease) commencing after 17 May 2004, the following apply. In computing the income/profits of the lessee (i.e. the lessee under the operating lease), the deduction for operating lease rentals is restricted to the 'relevant amount'. In computing the income/profits of the lessor (i.e. the lessor under the operating lease), amounts receivable by him under the operating lease are included as income without netting off any amounts due by the lessor to the lessee. However, amounts receivable are not included as income to the extent that they exceed the 'relevant amount'. In each case, the *'relevant amount'* is the maximum amount of finance lease rentals deductible in computing the finance lessee's income/profits (see above). In applying these rules, such apportionments are to be made as are just and reasonable where only some of the plant or machinery subject to the sale and finance leaseback is also subject to the operating lease.

Lease and finance leasebacks. The above rules also apply, again in relation to periods ending after 16 March 2004 (subject to the transitional provisions below), to a 'lease and finance leaseback' but with appropriate modifications; in particular, depreciation is disregarded in computing the finance lessee's lease rentals and the above limitation on the finance lessor's income/profits applies by reference only to the gross earnings under the leaseback. A '*lease and finance leaseback*' occurs if a person leases plant or machinery to another in circumstances such that, had it been a sale, the transaction would have been a sale and finance leaseback as defined in (ii) above (except that the availability of the plant or machinery for the use in question must in this case be a *direct* consequence of its having been leased under a finance lease). For this purpose, a person is regarded as leasing an item of plant or machinery to another person only if he grants him rights over the item for consideration and is not required to bring all of that consideration into account under the plant and machinery capital allowances code; there is a let-out where the last condition is met only because a joint election under *CAA 2001, s 199* was made by lessor and lessee before 18 May 2004 in relation to a fixture (see 9.34 above under Cessation of ownership).

Transitional provisions. In relation to any leasebacks whose term commenced before 17 March 2004, transitional rules seek to preserve the pre-existing treatment of lease rentals payable before that date or in respect of any period ending before that date and a time proportion of lease rentals payable for periods straddling that date. For the effect on the lease rental deductions due to the lessee, see *FA 2004, Sch 23 paras 2, 3*; for the equivalent rules affecting computation of the lessor's income/profits, see *FA 2004, Sch 23 paras 7, 8*.

The increase in the lessee's income/profits for the period of account in which the leaseback terminates is capped, in accordance with a formula in *FA 2004, Sch 23 para 5*, if a pre-17 March 2004 leaseback terminates early, i.e. other than by expiry of its term.

The increase in the lessee's income/profits for the period of account in which the leaseback terminates is abated if a pre-17 March 2004 leaseback terminates early, the lessee reacquires ownership of the plant or machinery and the lessee's capital expenditure on reacquisition is itself restricted under (ii) above. If the restriction equals or exceeds the increase in profits/income, the increase is cancelled; in other cases, the increase is reduced by the restriction. However, the increase is reinstated in modified form if a disposal event (see 9.29 above) occurs in relation to the whole or part of the plant or machinery within six years after the leaseback terminates. See *FA 2004, Sch 23 para 6*.

Where a pre-17 March 2004 lease and finance leaseback terminates and the finance lessee then disposes of the plant or machinery, there is provision for his chargeable gain to be reduced for capital gains tax purposes. See *FA 2004, Sch 23 para 10*.

See Tolley's Capital Allowances for more detail on these transitional provisions.

[*CAA 2001, ss 228A–228J; FA 2004, s 134, Sch 23*].

See Simon's Direct Tax Service B2.365, B2.366, B2.368, B2.369.

See Revenue Tax Bulletin June 1998 pp 539–544 for a general article on how these and associated capital allowance restrictions are intended to operate. In particular the article considers sale and leaseback by novation or new contract, or on defeased terms, and assets with long build times. See also 9.28 above, (A) above and 71.58 SCHEDULE D, CASES I AND II as regards finance lease allowance restrictions.

See (G) below as regards succession to a trade or other qualifying activity carried on by a 'connected person'.

(D) Where plant or machinery received by way of gift is brought into use for the purposes of a trade or other qualifying activity carried on by the donee, the donee is entitled to writing-down allowances as if he had purchased it from the donor at the time it is brought into use and at its market value at that time. Where the gift was brought into use between 1 November 1992 and 31 October 1993 inclusive, the donee's deemed expenditure qualified for the temporarily reinstated 40% first-year allowance (see 9.27 above), but such deemed expenditure cannot qualify for any of the targeted first-year allowances introduced subsequently. [*CAA 2001, ss 14, 213(3), Sch 3 paras 12, 43; CAA 1990, s 81; FA 1993, Sch 13 para 12(1)*]. See Simon's Direct Tax Service B2.303.

(E) Previous use outside trade etc. Where a person brings into use, for the purposes of a trade or other qualifying activity carried on by him, plant or machinery which he previously owned for purposes not entitling him to plant and machinery allowances in respect of that activity, writing-down allowances are calculated as if the trader etc. had, at the time of bringing it into use, incurred expenditure on its acquisition equal to its market value at that time. Actual cost, if less, is substituted for market value where the plant or machinery is brought into trade etc. use after 20 March 2000. The actual cost for this purpose is reduced to the extent that it would have been reduced under the anti-avoidance provisions of *CAA 2001, s 218* or *s 224* or earlier equivalents (see (C) above) had it been expenditure on plant or machinery for use in the qualifying activity.

Where the plant or machinery was brought into use between 1 November 1992 and 31 October 1993 inclusive, the deemed expenditure qualified for the temporarily reinstated 40% first-year allowance (see 9.27 above); such first-year allowances were not, however, available where plant or machinery was transferred from one qualifying activity to another carried on by the same person and was brought into use in the second activity after 13 April 1993. Expenditure deemed to be incurred under these provisions does not qualify for any of the targeted first-year allowances introduced subsequently.

[*CAA 2001, s 13, Sch 3 para 11; CAA 1990, s 81; FA 1993, Sch 13 para 12; FA 2000, s 75(3)(6)*].

See Simon's Direct Tax Service B2.303.

(F) Partnerships are entitled to allowances in respect of an item of plant or machinery used for the trade or other qualifying activity carried on by the partnership, and owned by one or more partners without being partnership property. Any transfer of the item between partners, whilst it continues to be so used, does not require a disposal value to be brought into account. These provisions do not apply if such an item is *let* by one or more partners to the partnership or otherwise made available to it in consideration of a tax-deductible payment. [*CAA 2001, s 264; CAA 1990, s 65*].

Following a change in the persons carrying on a trade or other qualifying activity in partnership, other than one resulting in the activity being treated under *ICTA 1988, s 113(1)* (see 53.5 PARTNERSHIPS) or *s 337(1)* (see 71.15 SCHEDULE D, CASES I AND II) as permanently discontinued, allowances are subsequently given and balancing charges subsequently made as if the new partnership had carried on the activity before the change. For this purpose, a '*qualifying activity*' does not include an office or employment but otherwise includes any of the activities at 9.24(i)–(vii) above regardless of whether or not the profits therefrom are within the charge to UK tax. [*CAA 2001, s 263; CAA 1990, s 78(3)(4); FA 2001, s 69, Sch 21 para 4(1)*]. See (G) below as regards partnerships treated as discontinued and successions to trades generally.

See Simon's Direct Tax Service B2.390.

(G) Successions. Where a trade or other qualifying activity changes hands (other than in certain partnership changes — see (F) above) unexhausted allowances may not be carried forward to the new owner. Where the 'qualifying activity' is treated under *ICTA 1988, s 113(1)* (see 53.5 PARTNERSHIPS) or *s 337(1)* (see 71.15 SCHEDULE D, CASES I AND II) as permanently discontinued, any plant or machinery transferred, without being sold, to the new owner for continuing use in the qualifying activity is treated as sold at market value on the date of change, although no first-year allowance (where otherwise applicable) is available to the new owner. For this purpose, a '*qualifying activity*' does not include an office or employment but otherwise includes any of the activities at 9.24(i)–(vii) above regardless of whether or not the profits therefrom are within the charge to UK tax. These provisions apply equally to plant or machinery not in use but provided and available for use for the purposes of the qualifying activity. Where *CAA 2001* has effect (see 9.1 above), they apply only to plant and machinery actually owned by the predecessor. [*CAA 2001, s 265; CAA 1990, s 78(1)(5)*].

If a beneficiary succeeds to a 'qualifying activity' (as above) under a deceased proprietor's will or intestacy, he may elect for written-down value to be substituted (if less) for market value. [*CAA 2001, s 268, Sch 3 para 53; CAA 1990, s 78(2)(2A)(5); FA 1990, Sch 13 para 3*].

Where a person succeeds to a trade or other qualifying activity carried on by a person 'connected' with him, each is within the charge to UK tax on the profits, and the successor is not a dual resident investing company, they may jointly elect, within two years after the date of change, for plant or machinery to be treated as transferred at a price giving rise to neither a balancing allowance nor a balancing charge. This applies to plant or machinery which immediately before and after the succession is owned by the person concerned and either in use, or (where *CAA 2001* has effect — see 9.1 above) provided and available for use, for the purposes of the qualifying activity, and regardless of any actual sale by the predecessor to the successor. Allowances and charges are subsequently made as if everything done to or by the predecessor had been done to or by the successor. Where *CAA 2001* has effect, it is expressly provided that the deemed sale takes place when the succession takes place.

For this purpose, persons are '*connected*' if

(*a*)   they are CONNECTED PERSONS (19) within *ICTA 1988, s 839*, or

(*b*)   one of them is a partnership in which the other has the right to a share of assets or income, or both are partnerships in both of which some other person has the right to such a share, or

(*c*)   one of them is a body corporate over which the other has control (within *CAA 2001, s 574*), or both are bodies corporate, or one a body corporate and one a partnership, over both of which some other person has control.

An election in relation to a succession occurring after 26 July 1989 precludes the application of *CAA 2001, s 104* (disposal value of long-life assets in avoidance cases — see 9.30(G) above), *CAA 2001, s 265* (see above) and the similar provisions in *CAA 2001, s 108* (see 9.35(*a*) above), and their forerunners. First-year allowances would appear to be precluded by 9.27(ix) above.

These provisions did not apply in this form to successions occurring before 29 July 1988.

[*CAA 2001, ss 266, 267, Sch 3 para 52; CAA 1990, s 77; FA 1997, Sch 14 para 9*].

See Simon's Direct Tax Service B2.390.

(H) A renewals basis is generally available as an alternative to capital allowances. A deduction is allowed in computing profits of the cost of a replacement item less the proceeds of sale (or scrap value) of the item replaced. Where, however, the replacement item is an improvement on that replaced, the deduction is restricted to the cost of replacing like with like. See *Caledonian Railway Co v Banks CES 1880, 1 TC 487; Eastmans Ltd v Shaw HL 1928, 14 TC 218; Hyam v CIR CS 1929, 14 TC 479*.

Cost of renewals of trade implements, utensils etc. are allowed as a deduction under *ICTA 1988, s 74(1)(d)*, but cf. *Hinton v Maden & Ireland Ltd HL 1959, 38 TC 391* and also see *Peter Merchant Ltd v Stedeford CA 1948, 30 TC 496* (provision for future renewals not allowable). Replacement of parts is allowed under general principles so far as identity of plant or machinery is retained. For further details of 'renewals basis' and change from renewals basis to normal capital allowances and *vice versa*, see Revenue Pamphlet IR 1, B1 as revised and Revenue Business Income Manual BIM 46935, 46950, 46955.

See Simon's Direct Tax Service B2.312.

A **valuation basis** is a variation of renewals basis in which a class of assets, for example spare parts for plant and machinery, are dealt with in a similar way to trading stock, involving opening and closing valuations. For further detail, and for change from capital allowances to valuation basis, see Revenue Business Income Manual BIM 46940, 46960.

(J) Partial depreciation subsidies, i.e. sums, not otherwise taxable on the recipient, are payable to him, directly or indirectly, by any other person in respect of, or to take account of, *part* of the depreciation of plant or machinery resulting from its use in the recipient's trade or other qualifying activity.

Where it appears that a partial depreciation subsidy will be payable, a first-year allowance (where available — see 9.27 above) can nevertheless be given, but must be scaled down as is just and reasonable (though the full amount is deducted in arriving at the balance of expenditure available for writing-down allowances).

Qualifying expenditure (see 9.24 above) which has been the subject of a partial depreciation subsidy can only be allocated to a *single asset pool* (see 9.28 above). Where qualifying expenditure has otherwise been allocated to a pool and a partial depreciation subsidy is received for the first time in respect of it, it must be transferred to a single asset pool. This is achieved by bringing in a disposal value (equal to market value — see 9.29(g) above) in the original pool for the chargeable period in which the subsidy is paid and allocating an equivalent amount to the single asset pool. Writing-down allowances and balancing allowances and charges in respect of the single asset pool are reduced to such amounts as are just and reasonable (though the full amount is deducted in arriving at any unrelieved qualifying expenditure carried forward).

[*CAA 2001, ss 209–212; CAA 1990, s 80(2)–(7); FA 1990, Sch 17 para 15*].

See 9.25 above as regards subsidies towards the whole of such depreciation. See 9.2(vi)(vii) above as regards contributions by others towards *expenditure* qualifying for plant and machinery and other capital allowances.

See Simon's Direct Tax Service B2.360.

(K) A lessee required to provide plant or machinery under the terms of the lease (including any tenancy), and using it for the purposes of a trade or other qualifying activity, is treated as if he owned it (for as long as it is used for those purposes), but is not required to bring in a disposal value (see 9.29 above) on termination of the lease. If

- the plant or machinery continues to be so used until termination of the lease,

- the lessor holds the lease in the course of a qualifying activity, and

- on or after termination, a disposal event occurs at a time when the lessor owns the plant or machinery,

the *lessor* is required to bring in a disposal value, for the chargeable period in which the disposal event occurs, in the pool to which the expenditure would have been allocated if incurred by the lessor. These rules do not, however, apply where the plant or machinery becomes, by law, part of the building in which it is installed or attached (see 9.34 above) under a lease entered into after 11 July 1984 unless pursuant to an agreement made on or before that date. [*CAA 2001, s 70, Sch 3 para 17; CAA 1990, s 61(4)(8)*].

9.39   **MINERAL EXTRACTION**

Mineral extraction allowances are available in respect of qualifying expenditure (see 9.40 below) incurred by a person carrying on a 'mineral extraction trade'. A *'mineral extraction trade'* is a trade consisting of or including the working of a source of *'mineral deposits'*, i.e. such deposits of a wasting nature including any natural deposits or geothermal energy capable of being lifted or extracted from the earth. A *'source of mineral deposits'* includes a mine, an oil well and a source of geothermal energy. [*CAA 2001, s 394; CAA 1990, s 98(1), s 121(1)(2), s 161(2)*]. A *share* in an asset may qualify for mineral extraction allowances. [*CAA 2001, s 435; CAA 1990, s 121(5)*].

The main elements of the code of mineral extraction allowances are dealt with as follows.

9.40	Qualifying expenditure and first-year qualifying expenditure	9.44	Disposal events and values
		9.45	Balancing allowances
9.41	Limitations on qualifying expenditure	9.46	Making of allowances and charges
9.42	Second-hand assets	9.47	Plant and machinery allowances
9.43	First-year and writing-down allowances and balancing adjustments	9.48	— example
		9.49	Transition to current code of allowances

Simon's Direct Tax Service. See **B2.4.**

9.40   **Qualifying expenditure and first-year qualifying expenditure.** *'Qualifying expenditure'* means capital expenditure, incurred for the purposes of a mineral extraction trade, on

(a)   *'mineral exploration and access'* (i.e. searching for or discovering and testing the mineral deposits of any source, or winning access to any such deposits),

(b)   acquisition of a *'mineral asset'* (i.e. any mineral deposits or land comprising mineral deposits, or any interest in or right over such deposits or land) (subject to the limitations in 9.41 below),

(c)   construction of works, in connection with the working of a source of mineral deposits, which are likely to become of little or no value when the source ceases to be worked,

(d)   construction of works which are likely to become valueless when a foreign concession under which a source of mineral deposits is worked comes to an end.

Included in (a) above is abortive expenditure (including appeal costs) on seeking planning permission for the undertaking of mineral exploration and access or the working of mineral deposits. Expenditure on the acquisition of, or of rights over, mineral deposits or the site of a source of mineral deposits falls into (b) rather than (a) above.

However, the following are *not* qualifying expenditure:

•   expenditure on the provision of plant or machinery (except certain pre-trading expenditure — see below), and see 9.47 below;

•   expenditure on acquisition of, or of rights in or over, the *site* of any works in (c) or (d) above;

•   expenditure on works constructed wholly or mainly for processing the raw products, unless the process is designed to prepare the raw products for use as such;

•   (subject to *CAA 2001, s 415* — see below) expenditure on buildings and structures for occupation by, or welfare of, workers;

211

- expenditure on a building constructed *entirely* for use as an office;

- expenditure on the office part of a building or structure constructed *partly* for use as an office, where such expenditure exceeds 10% of the capital expenditure on construction of the whole building.

[*CAA 2001, ss 395–399, 400(1), 403(1)(2), 414; CAA 1990, ss 105, 121(1)*].

Qualifying expenditure also includes capital contributions, for the purposes of a mineral extraction trade carried on outside the UK, to the cost of accommodation buildings, and certain related utility buildings and welfare works, for employees engaged in working a source, provided that the buildings or works are likely to be of little or no value when the source ceases to be worked, that the expenditure does not result in the acquisition of an asset, and that relief is not due under any other tax provision. [*CAA 2001, s 415; CAA 1990, s 108*]. Net expenditure incurred on the restoration of the site of a source of mineral deposits (or land used in connection with working such a source) within three years after the cessation of the trade is also qualifying expenditure, treated as incurred on the last day of trading, unless relieved elsewhere. [*CAA 2001, s 416; CAA 1990, s 109*].

Pre-trading expenditure for the purposes of a mineral extraction trade is treated as incurred on the first day of trading. This applies equally to pre-trading expenditure on mineral exploration and access, but in determining whether such expenditure is qualifying expenditure within (*a*) above, the following limitations apply.

(i)   In the case of pre-trading expenditure on plant or machinery which is used at a source but is sold, demolished, destroyed or abandoned before commencement of the mineral extraction trade, qualifying expenditure is limited to net expenditure after taking account of sale proceeds, insurance money or capital compensation.

(ii)   In the case of pre-trading exploration expenditure other than on plant or machinery, qualifying expenditure is limited to net expenditure after taking into account any reasonably attributable capital sums received before the first day of trading.

In either case, if mineral exploration and access is not continuing at the source on the first day of trading, qualifying expenditure is further limited to net expenditure incurred in the six years ending on that day.

[*CAA 2001, s 400(2)–(5), 401, 402, 434; CAA 1990, ss 105(2), 106, 107, 120*].

Qualifying expenditure (as above) incurred by a company **after 16 April 2002** is '*first-year qualifying expenditure*' if it is incurred wholly for the purposes of a 'ring fence trade' within *ICTA 1988, s 501A* (petroleum extraction activities, see Tolley's Corporation Tax under Oil Companies), subject to the exclusion of expenditure on:

(A)   acquisition of mineral assets (see (*b*) above); and

(B)   acquisition of an asset representing expenditure incurred by a connected company (within *Sec 839*, see 19 CONNECTED PERSONS), including any results obtained from any search, exploration or enquiry on which mineral exploitation and access expenditure was incurred.

For this purpose, *CAA 2001, ss 400(4), 434* (see above), which treat certain expenditure as having been incurred on the first day of trading, do not apply.

[*CAA 2001, ss 416A–416C; FA 2002, Sch 21 para 9*].

Simon's Direct Tax Service. See B2.406 *et seq.*

9.41   **Limitations on qualifying expenditure.** Qualifying expenditure within 9.40(*b*) above (acquisition of mineral asset) is limited in the following circumstances.

If the mineral asset is an interest in land, an amount equal to the 'undeveloped market value' of the interest is excluded. '*Undeveloped market value*' is the market value of the interest at the time of acquisition ignoring the mineral deposits and assuming that development of the land (other than that already lawfully begun or for which planning permission has already been granted) is, and will remain, unlawful. Where the undeveloped market value includes the value of buildings or structures which, at any time after acquisition, permanently cease to be used, their value at acquisition (exclusive of land and after deducting any net capital allowances received in respect of them) is treated as qualifying expenditure incurred at the time of cessation of use. These provisions operate by reference to the actual time of acquisition, regardless of any different time given by the pre-trading expenditure provisions at 9.40 above. They do not apply where an election is made under *CAA 2001, s 569* or its forerunner (election to treat connected persons transactions as made at written-down value). [*CAA 2001, ss 403(3), 404, 405, Sch 3 para 84; CAA 1990, s 110*].

Where a deduction has been allowed under *ICTA 1988, s 87* in respect of a premium under a lease (see 69.17 SCHEDULE A), the qualifying expenditure allowable in respect of the acquisition of the interest in land to which the premium relates is correspondingly reduced. [*CAA 2001, s 406; CAA 1990, s 111*].

Simon's Direct Tax Service. See B2.410.

9.42   **Second-hand assets.** Where

(*a*)   an asset is acquired from another person, and

(*b*)   either that person or any previous owner incurred expenditure on it in connection with a mineral extraction trade,

the buyer's qualifying expenditure is restricted to the seller's qualifying expenditure on the asset less net allowances given to him. If an oil licence (or an interest therein) is acquired, the buyer's qualifying expenditure is limited to the amount of the original licence fee paid (or such part of it as it is just and reasonable to attribute to the interest). However, these restrictions do not affect amounts *treated* under rules below as qualifying expenditure on mineral exploration and access. In relation to a mineral asset situated in the UK, the restrictions do not apply to an acquisition under a pre-16 July 1985 contract, and the reference above to previous owners excludes any person who has not been the owner at any time after 31 March 1986.

Where

(i)   the purchased asset above is a mineral asset, and

(ii)   part of its value is properly attributable to expenditure on mineral exploration and access incurred as in (*b*) above,

so much if any of the buyer's expenditure as it is just and reasonable to attribute to the part of the value in (ii) above (not exceeding the amount of original expenditure to which it is attributable) is treated as qualifying expenditure on mineral exploration and access, with the remainder treated as expenditure on acquisition of a mineral asset. In relation to an asset situated in the UK, this rule does not apply to an acquisition under a pre-16 July 1985 contract, and the reference to previous owners excludes any person who has not been the owner at any time after 31 March 1986. In relation to claims made after 25 November 1996, expenditure deducted by a previous owner in computing taxable profits is excluded for these purposes from the original expenditure.

Where

- capital expenditure is incurred in acquiring assets for a mineral extraction trade from a person (the seller) who did *not* carry on a mineral extraction trade, and

- the assets represent expenditure on mineral exploration and access incurred by the seller,

the buyer's qualifying expenditure is limited to the amount of the seller's expenditure. Assets include any results obtained from any search, exploration or inquiry on which the expenditure was incurred. This restriction does not apply if the asset is an interest in an oil licence acquired by the buyer after 12 September 1995; in this case, so much if any of the buyer's expenditure as it is just and reasonable to attribute to the part of the value of the licence attributable to the seller's expenditure (but limited to the amount of that expenditure) is treated as qualifying expenditure on mineral exploration and access, with the cost of the oil licence being reduced by the buyer's expenditure so attributable (without limitation).

Where a mineral asset is transferred between companies under common control, and no election is made under *CAA 2001, s 569* or its forerunner (election to treat connected persons transactions as made at written-down value), the buyer's expenditure is limited to that of the seller. However, this does not affect amounts *treated* under rules above as qualifying expenditure on mineral exploration and access. Where the asset is an interest in land, the limitations at 9.41 above generally apply as if the buyer acquired the interest when the seller acquired it (or, in the case of a sequence of such transactions, when the first seller acquired it).

[*CAA 2001, ss 407–413, Sch 3 paras 85–87; CAA 1990, ss 113–118; FA 1997, s 66*].

Simon's Direct Tax Service. See B2.411 *et seq.*

9.43   **First-year and writing-down allowances and balancing adjustments.** For each item of first-year qualifying expenditure (see 9.40 above), a **first-year allowance (FYA)** of up to **100%** is available for the chargeable period in which the expenditure is incurred. No FYA is available, however, to the extent that a transaction is attributable to any scheme, agreement or understanding, whether or not legally enforceable, a main purpose of which is the obtaining of a first-year allowance which would not otherwise have been available (or of a greater allowance than would otherwise have been available).

For each item of qualifying expenditure (see 9.40 above), a **writing-down allowance (WDA)** is available for each chargeable period (see 9.2(i) above) and is equal to a set percentage (as below) of the amount (if any) by which 'unrelieved qualifying expenditure' exceeds the total of any disposal values falling to be brought into account as in 9.44 below. The WDA is proportionately reduced or increased if the chargeable period is less or more than a year, or if the mineral extraction trade has been carried on for part only of the chargeable period.

In the circumstances listed at 9.45 below, a **balancing allowance** is available, instead of a WDA, equal to the excess (if any) of (1) 'unrelieved qualifying expenditure' over (2) total disposal values. (This is subject to the anti-avoidance rule at 9.2(xii) above.) If, for any chargeable period, (2) exceeds (1), there arises a liability to a **balancing charge**, normally equal to that excess but limited to net allowances previously given (including, where a balancing charge arises in respect of first-year qualifying expenditure incurred in the period, any FYA given on that expenditure). A claim for a WDA *or* a balancing allowance may require it to be reduced to a specified amount.

Rates of WDA are as follows:

Acquisition of a mineral asset (see 9.40(b) above)	10% p.a.
Other qualifying expenditure	25% p.a.

'*Unrelieved qualifying expenditure*' means qualifying expenditure (other than first-year qualifying expenditure) incurred in the chargeable period and the tax written-down value brought forward (i.e. net of allowances and any disposal values) of qualifying expenditure (including first-year qualifying expenditure) incurred in a previous chargeable period. If a disposal receipt falls to be brought into account in the case of first-year qualifying expenditure for the chargeable period in which it was incurred, any balance of that expenditure after deducting any FYA given in respect of it is treated as unrelieved qualifying expenditure *but only* for the purpose of determining whether there is a balancing allowance or charge for that period and, if so, the amount of such an allowance or charge.

[*CAA 2001, ss 416D–419; CAA 1990, ss 98, 100; FA 1994, s 213(8); FA 2002, Sch 21 paras 11–13].*

The net demolition costs (i.e. the excess, if any, of demolition costs over money received for remains) of an asset representing qualifying expenditure is added to that expenditure in determining the amount of any balancing allowance or charge for the chargeable period of demolition, and is not then treated as expenditure incurred on any replacement asset. [*CAA 2001, s 433; CAA 1990, s 103*].

There is no provision for pooling expenditure (cf. plant and machinery at 9.28 above). In practice, the Revenue do not object to the grouping together of assets for computational convenience, provided individual sources are kept separate and assets attracting different rates of WDA are not grouped with each other. However, where a disposal value falls to be brought into account or a balancing allowance arises, it will sometimes be necessary to reconstruct separate computations for individual items of expenditure previously grouped. (Revenue Capital Allowances Manual CA 50410).

Simon's Direct Tax Service. See **B2.419** *et seq.*

9.44   **Disposal events and values.** A disposal value must be brought into account (by deduction from unrelieved qualifying expenditure — see 9.43 above), for the chargeable period in which the event occurs, on the occurrence of any of the following events.

(i)   An asset representing qualifying expenditure (see 9.40 above) is disposed of or permanently ceases to be used for the purposes of a mineral extraction trade (whether because of cessation of trade or otherwise).

(ii)   A mineral asset begins to be used (by the trader or another person) in a way which constitutes development which is neither 'existing permitted development' nor development for the purposes of a mineral extraction trade. Development is '*existing permitted development*' if, at the time of acquisition, it had already lawfully begun or the appropriate planning permission had already been granted.

(iii)   In a case not within (i) or (ii) above, a capital sum is received which, in whole or in part, it is reasonable to attribute to qualifying expenditure.

The amount to be brought into account depends upon the nature of the event.

(a)   On an event within (i) or (ii) above, it is an amount determined in accordance with the list at 9.29(a)–(g) above (disregarding (f), the reference to abandonment at (d) and the text immediately following the list). However, if the asset is an interest in land, the amount so ascertained is then restricted by excluding the '*undeveloped market value*', determined as in 9.41 above but by reference to the time of disposal.

(*b*)   On an event within (iii) above, it is so much of the capital sum as is reasonably attributable to the qualifying expenditure.

[*CAA 2001, ss 420–425; CAA 1990, ss 99, 112; FA 1994, Sch 26 Pt V(24); ITEPA 2003, Sch 6 para 254*].

In relation to sales at other than market value, the connected person and other anti-avoidance provisions, and election potential, of *CAA 2001, ss 567–570* (and forerunners) apply with appropriate modifications for mineral extraction allowances as they do for industrial buildings allowances (see 9.22(i) above).

Simon's Direct Tax Service. See B2.420.

9.45   **Balancing allowances.** A person is entitled to a balancing allowance (instead of a writing-down allowance) for a chargeable period if

- the chargeable period is that in which the first day of trading falls, and either the qualifying expenditure is pre-trading expenditure on plant or machinery within 9.40(i) above or it is pre-trading exploration expenditure within 9.40(ii) above where mineral exploration and access is not continuing at the source on the first day of trading; or

- the qualifying expenditure was on mineral exploration and access, and in that chargeable period he gives up the exploration, search or inquiry to which the expenditure related, without subsequently carrying on a mineral extraction trade consisting of or including the working of related mineral deposits; or

- in that chargeable period he permanently ceases to work particular mineral deposits, and the qualifying expenditure was on mineral exploration and access relating solely to those deposits or on the acquisition of a mineral asset consisting of those deposits or part of them; but where two or more mineral assets are comprised in, or derive from, a single asset, the above applies only when *all* the relevant mineral deposits cease to be worked; or

- the qualifying expenditure falls within *CAA 2001, s 415* (capital contributions to certain buildings or works for benefit of employees abroad — see 9.40 above), and in that chargeable period, the buildings or works permanently cease to be used for the purposes of or in connection with the mineral extraction trade; or

- the qualifying expenditure was on the provision of any assets, and in that chargeable period any of those assets is disposed of or otherwise permanently ceases to be used for purposes of the trade; or

- the qualifying expenditure is represented by assets, and in that chargeable period those assets are permanently lost or cease to exist (due to destruction, dismantling or otherwise) or begin to be used wholly or partly for purposes other than those of the mineral extraction trade; or

- the mineral extraction trade is permanently discontinued in that chargeable period.

[*CAA 2001, ss 426–431; CAA 1990, s 101; FA 1994, Sch 26 Pt V(24)*].

Simon's Direct Tax Service. See B2.421.

9.46   **Making of allowances and charges.** Mineral extraction allowances (or balancing charges) are given (or made) as trading expenses (or trading receipts) in calculating the profits of the mineral extraction trade. [*CAA 2001, s 432; CAA 1990, ss 104, 140, 144; FA 1994, s 211*].

Simon's Direct Tax Service. See B2.423.

9.47   **Plant and machinery allowances.** Plant and machinery is normally excluded from relief under the current provisions, but certain pre-trading expenditure may qualify (see 9.40 above). The normal plant and machinery rules (see 9.24 *et seq.* above) apply to plant and machinery provided for mineral exploration and access in connection with a mineral extraction trade. [*CAA 2001, ss 159, 160; CAA 1990, s 83(1)(6)*]. Where such expenditure (limited to capital expenditure where *CAA 2001* has effect — see 9.1 above) is incurred prior to the date of commencement of a mineral extraction trade and the plant or machinery is still owned at that date, it is treated as if sold immediately before that date and re-acquired on that date. The capital expenditure on re-acquisition is deemed to be equal to the actual expenditure previously incurred. [*CAA 2001, s 161, Sch 3 para 25; CAA 1990, s 63*].

9.48   *Example*

X has for some years operated a mining business with two mineral sources, G and S. Accounts are prepared to 30 September. On 31 December 2003 the mineral deposits and mineworks at G are sold at market value to Z for £80,000 and £175,000 respectively. A new source, P, is purchased on 30 April 2004 for £170,000 (including land with an undeveloped market value of £70,000) and the following expenditure incurred before the end of the accounting period ended 30 September 2004.

	£
Plant and machinery	40,000
Construction of administration office	25,000
Construction of mining works which are likely	
to have little value when mining ceases	50,000
Staff hostel	35,000
Winning access to the deposits	150,000
	£300,000

During the year to 30 September 2004, X also incurred expenditure of £20,000 in seeking planning permission to mine a further plot of land, Source Q. Permission was refused.

Residue of expenditure brought forward		£
(based on accounts to 30 September 2003)		
Mineral exploration and access	– Source G	170,000
	– Source S	200,000
Mineral assets	– Source G	95,250
	– Source S	72,000

The mineral extraction allowances due for the year ending 30 September 2004 are as follows.

9.48 Capital Allowances

	£	£
Source G		
Mineral exploration and access		
WDV b/f	170,000	
Proceeds	175,000	
Balancing charge	£5,000	(5,000)
Mineral assets		
WDV b/f	95,250	
Proceeds	80,000	
Balancing allowance	£15,250	15,250
Source S		
Mineral exploration and access		
WDV b/f	200,000	
WDA 25%	(50,000)	50,000
WDV c/f	£150,000	
Mineral assets		
WDV b/f	72,000	
WDA 10%	(7,200)	7,200
WDV c/f	£64,800	
Source P		
Mineral exploration and access		
Expenditure	150,000	
WDA 25%	(37,500)	37,500
WDV c/f	£112,500	
Mineral assets		
Expenditure note (*c*)	100,000	
WDA 10%	(10,000)	10,000
WDV c/f	£90,000	
Mining works		
Expenditure	50,000	
WDA 25%	(12,500)	12,500
WDV c/f	£37,500	
Source Q		
Mineral exploration and access		
Expenditure note (*b*)	20,000	
WDA 25%	(5,000)	5,000
WDV c/f	£15,000	
Total allowances (net of charges)		£132,450

Notes

(a)   Allowances are not due on either the office or staff hostel although the hostel may qualify for industrial buildings allowances (see 9.11 above). The plant and machinery qualify for plant and machinery allowances (see 9.24 above) rather than for mineral extraction allowances (see 9.47 above).

(b)   Abortive expenditure on seeking planning permission is qualifying expenditure as if it were expenditure on mineral exploration and access (see 9.40 above).

(c)   The undeveloped market value of land is excluded from qualifying expenditure (see 9.41 above).

9.49   **Transition to current code of allowances.** The current code of allowances, as described at 9.39–9.46 above was introduced for expenditure incurred after 31 March 1986 (though a trader could elect to continue to apply the old code to certain expenditure incurred in the twelve months to 31 March 1987). Any unrelieved balance of expenditure at 1 April 1986 (or 1 April 1987 where applicable) under the old code was treated for the purposes of the current code as expenditure incurred on that day for the purposes for which the original expenditure was actually incurred. If expenditure had been fully relieved under the old code but the assets remained in use, the current code applies as if the expenditure had been incurred on 1 April 1986 and had been fully relieved under the current code (thus enabling balancing charges to accrue subsequently).

Expenditure on mineral exploration and access, or on acquisition of mineral assets, or on construction of certain works, which did not qualify for allowances under the old code because either the trade, or output from the source, had not commenced, or for some other reason, was treated as incurred on 1 April 1986 and relieved as appropriate under the new code.

Special rules apply where the old code expenditure on a mineral asset included the acquisition of an interest in land. The undeveloped market value of that interest was not excluded from the relievable expenditure where some relief had already been given under the old code, but nor is such value excluded under 9.44(a) above from any disposal value to be brought into account.

In making balancing charges where old code expenditure has been brought under the new code, allowances given under the old code will be taken into account together with those given under the new code.

[*CAA 2001, Sch 3 para 88; CAA 1990, s 119*].

Simon's Direct Tax Service. See B2.455.

9.50   **PATENT RIGHTS**

Allowances are available, and balancing charges made, in respect of 'qualifying expenditure' on the purchase of patent rights, i.e. the right to do or authorise the doing of anything which would, but for that right, be a patent infringement. The obtaining of a right to acquire future patent rights and the acquisition of a licence in respect of a patent are each treated for these purposes as a purchase of patent rights. '*Qualifying expenditure*' may be either

- '*qualifying trade expenditure*', i.e. capital expenditure incurred by a person on purchase of patent rights for the purposes of a trade carried on by him and within the charge to UK tax; or

- '*qualifying non-trade expenditure*', i.e. capital expenditure incurred by a person on purchase of patent rights if the above does not apply but any income receivable by him in respect of the rights would be liable to tax.

Expenditure incurred by a person for the purposes of a trade he is about to carry on is treated as if incurred on the first day of trading, unless all the rights in question have been sold before then. The same expenditure cannot be qualifying trade expenditure in relation to more than one trade.

The grant of a licence in respect of a patent is treated as a sale of part of patent rights. The grant by a person entitled to patent rights of an exclusive licence, i.e. a licence to exercise the rights to the exclusion of the grantor and all others for the remainder of their term, is, however, treated as a sale of the whole of those rights.

[*CAA 2001, ss 464–469; ICTA 1988, ss 520(1)–(3), 533(1)–(3)(5)(6)*].

Expenditure incurred after 31 March 1986

Qualifying expenditure is pooled for the purpose of determining entitlement to writing-down allowances and balancing allowances and liability to balancing charges. A separate pool applies for each separate trade and for all qualifying non-trade expenditure.

For each pool of qualifying expenditure, a **writing-down allowance (WDA)** is available for each chargeable period (see 9.2(i) above) other than the 'final chargeable period' and is equal to a maximum of **25%** of the amount (if any) by which 'available qualifying expenditure' exceeds the total of any disposal values falling to be brought into account. The WDA is proportionately reduced or increased if the chargeable period is less or more than a year, or if (where relevant) the trade has been carried on for part only of the chargeable period. A claim for a WDA may require it to be reduced to a specified amount. For the 'final chargeable period', a **balancing allowance** is available, equal to the excess (if any) of (1) 'available qualifying expenditure' over (2) total disposal values. If, for *any* chargeable period, (2) exceeds (1), there arises a liability to a **balancing charge**, equal to that excess.

The '*final chargeable period*', as regards a pool of qualifying trade expenditure, is the chargeable period in which the trade is permanently discontinued. As regards a pool of non-qualifying trade expenditure, it is the chargeable period in which the last of the patent rights in question either comes to an end (without any such rights being revived) or, where *CAA 2001* has effect (see 9.1 above), is wholly disposed of.

'*Available qualifying expenditure*' in a pool for a chargeable period consists of qualifying expenditure allocated to the pool for that period and any unrelieved qualifying expenditure brought forward in the pool from the previous chargeable period (usually referred to as the written-down value brought forward).

In allocating qualifying expenditure to a pool, the following must be observed.

(i) Qualifying expenditure can be allocated to a pool for a chargeable period only to the extent that it has not been included in available qualifying expenditure for an earlier chargeable period. (Before *CAA 2001* had effect, see 9.1 above, there was some doubt as to whether qualifying expenditure could be allocated to a pool for a chargeable period later than that in which it was incurred. For chargeable periods covered by *CAA 2001*, this doubt is removed and, in addition, there is now nothing to prohibit the allocation of *part only* of a particular amount of qualifying expenditure for a particular chargeable period.)

(ii) Qualifying expenditure cannot be allocated to a pool for a chargeable period earlier than that in which it is incurred.

(iii) Qualifying expenditure cannot be allocated to a pool for a chargeable period if in any earlier period the rights in question have come to an end (without any of them being revived) or have been wholly disposed of.

[*CAA 2001, ss 470–475; ICTA 1988, s 520(2)(4)–(6), s 521(1), s 528(1); FA 1994, s 214(4), Sch 26 Pt V(24)*].

A *disposal value* falls to be brought into account for a chargeable period in which a person sells the whole or part of any patent rights on the purchase of which he has incurred qualifying expenditure. The disposal value is equal to the net sale proceeds (limited to *capital* sums where *CAA 2001* has effect — see 9.1 above), except that:

(1) it cannot exceed the qualifying expenditure incurred on purchase of the rights in question; and

(2) where the rights were acquired as a result of a transaction between CONNECTED PERSONS (19) (or a series of such transactions), (1) above shall have effect as if it referred to the greatest capital expenditure incurred on the purchase of those rights by any of those connected persons.

[*CAA 2001, ss 476, 477; ICTA 1988, s 521(2)–(4); FA 1994, Sch 26 Pt V(24)*].

Connected persons and anti-avoidance. Where a person incurs capital expenditure after 26 July 1989 on the purchase of rights either from a connected person (see 19 CONNECTED PERSONS), or so that it appears that the sole or main benefit from the sale and any other transactions would have been the obtaining of an allowance under these provisions, the amount of that expenditure taken into account as qualifying expenditure may not exceed an amount determined as follows:

(*a*) where a disposal value (see above) falls to be brought into account, an amount equal to that value;

(*b*) where no disposal value falls to be brought into account, but the seller receives a capital sum chargeable under Schedule D, Case VI (see 54.5 PATENTS), an amount equal to that sum;

(*c*) in any other case, an amount equal to the smallest of

- market value of the rights;

- the amount of capital expenditure, if any, incurred by the seller on acquiring the rights;

- the amount of capital expenditure, if any, incurred by any person connected with the seller on acquiring the rights.

[*CAA 2001, s 481, Sch 3 para 102; ICTA 1988, s 521(5)–(7); FA 1989, Sch 13 para 27*]. Previously, the restriction was by reference to the disposal value only. See also (2) above.

Making of allowances and charges. An allowance (or balancing charge) in respect of qualifying *trade* expenditure is given effect as a trading expense (or trading receipt). [*CAA 2001, s 478; CAA 1990, ss 140, 144; ICTA 1988, ss 528(1), 532(1); FA 1994, s 211*].

An allowance in respect of qualifying *non-trade* expenditure is set against the person's 'income from patents' for the same tax year/corporation tax accounting period, with any excess being carried forward without time limit against such income for subsequent tax years/accounting periods. A balancing charge is taxed under Schedule D, Case VI for income tax and charged to corporation tax as income from patents. For these purposes, '*income from patents*' embraces royalties and similar sums, balancing charges under these provisions, and receipts from the sale of patent rights taxable under *ICTA 1988, s 524* or *s 525* (see 54.5, 54.6 PATENTS). [*CAA 2001, ss 479, 480, 483; ICTA 1988, s 528(2)–(4), s 533(1)*].

Expenditure incurred before 1 April 1986

Qualifying expenditure incurred before 1 April 1986 is allowable in full, by equal annual writing-down allowances, over a writing-down period of whichever is the shortest of

- seventeen years,

- (where applicable) the period covered by the rights purchased, and

- if the rights purchased begin a year or more after the date from which the patent became effective, and are not for a specified period, seventeen years less the number of complete years from the patent becoming effective to the rights being purchased (subject to a minimum writing-down period of one year),

beginning with the chargeable period in which, or in whose basis period, the expenditure is incurred. Each item of expenditure is dealt with separately, rather than being pooled. The annual writing-down allowance is reduced (or increased) for chargeable periods of less than (or more than) twelve months.

No writing-down allowance is given for a chargeable period in which, or in whose basis period, any of the following events occur.

(A)   The rights come to an end without subsequently being revived.

(B)   The rights (or remaining rights) are sold, the net proceeds of sale being

    (i)   less than the unallowed expenditure, or

    (ii)   greater than the unallowed expenditure.

(C)   Part of the rights is sold, the net proceeds of sale being greater than the unallowed expenditure.

Where (A) or (B)(i) apply, a *balancing allowance* is given on the unallowed expenditure (less net capital sale proceeds, if any) provided that writing-down allowances have been given in respect of the rights (or would have been given but for the sale etc.).

Where (B)(ii) or (C) apply, a *balancing charge* is made on the excess of net capital sale proceeds over unallowed expenditure (but limited to total writing-down allowances given in respect of the rights).

Where part of the rights is sold but (C) does not apply, writing-down allowances for the chargeable period in question and subsequent chargeable periods are recalculated after deducting net capital sale proceeds from the unrelieved expenditure.

Allowances are given, and balancing charges made, in a similar manner as for post-31 March 1986 expenditure above.

[*CAA 2001, Sch 3 paras 92–101; ICTA 1988, ss 522, 523, 528(1), 533(1); FA 1994, Sch 26 Pt V(24)*].

Connected persons and anti-avoidance. There are provisions for the substitution of market value for sale consideration on certain 'sole or main benefit' transactions, sales without change of control and sales between connected persons, subject in the latter cases to an election for unrelieved expenditure to be substituted instead. [*CAA 1990, ss 157, 158; ICTA 1988, s 532*]. However, where the inventor is the seller, no such election was available unless he sold to own controlled company at less than market value, in which case allowances and charges (and, if the purchaser agreed, capital gains tax) could by concession be based on actual price paid (Revenue Pamphlet IR 1, B17).

Trading partnerships and successions are treated in the same way as for industrial buildings allowances (see 9.22(iii)(iv)).

See 54 PATENTS for treatment of patent royalties and capital sums received, and 71.63 SCHEDULE D, CASES I AND II for trading income and expenses re patents.

Simon's Direct Tax Service. See B2.601–B2.609.

9.51   *Example*

P, who prepares accounts to 31 December, acquires three new patent rights for trading purposes.

	Date	Term	Cost
Patent 1	20.2.86	21 years	£6,800
Patent 2	19.4.03	15 years	£4,500
Patent 3	5.10.04	5 years	£8,000

On 1.10.04 P sold his rights under patent 1 for £4,200 and on 1.12.04 he sold part of the rights under patent 2 for £2,000.

The allowances for each patent are

Patent 1	£
Expenditure	6,800
1987/88 (basis period — y/e 31.12.86)	
WDA $\frac{1}{17}$ × £6,800	(400)
	6,400
1988/89 to 1996/97 inclusive	
WDA $\frac{1}{17}$ × £6,800 × 9 years	(3,600)
	2,800
Y/e 31.12.97 to y/e 31.12.03 inclusive	
WDA $\frac{1}{17}$ × £6,800 × 7 years	(2,800)
	Nil
Y/e 31.12.04	
Disposal proceeds	(4,200)
Balancing charge	£4,200

Patents 2 and 3	Pool	WDA
Y/e 31.12.03		
	£	£
Expenditure (patent 2)	4,500	
WDA 25%	(1,125)	£1,125
	3,375	
Y/e 31.12.04		
Expenditure (patent 3)	8,000	
Disposal proceeds (patent 2)	(2,000)	
	9,375	
WDA 25%	(2,344)	£2,344
WDV c/f	£7,031	

9.52   **RESEARCH AND DEVELOPMENT (FORMERLY SCIENTIFIC RESEARCH)**

'Qualifying expenditure' incurred by a trader on (for 2000/01 onwards and for corporation tax accounting periods ending after 31 March 2000) 'research and development' (R & D) or (for earlier tax years and accounting periods) 'scientific research' attracts an allowance equal to 100% of the expenditure. A claim for an allowance may require it to be reduced to a specified amount (but the part of the allowance thus forgone cannot be claimed for a later chargeable period). References below to R & D, except in the definition thereof, also embrace scientific research.

'*Qualifying expenditure*' is capital expenditure incurred by a trader on R & D related to the trade and undertaken directly or on his behalf (i.e. by an agent or other person in a similar contractual relationship, see *Gaspet Ltd v Elliss CA 1987, 60 TC 91*). It includes such expenditure incurred before commencement of the trade (pre-commencement expenditure). Expenditure potentially leading to or facilitating an extension of the trade is related to that trade, as is expenditure of a medical nature specially related to the welfare of workers in the trade. A just and reasonable apportionment may be made of capital expenditure only partly qualifying.

Expenditure on the acquisition of, or of rights in or over, land cannot be qualifying expenditure, except insofar as, on a just and reasonable apportionment, such expenditure is referable to a building or structure already constructed on the land, or to plant or machinery which forms part of such a building or structure, and otherwise qualifies as R & D expenditure.

Expenditure on R & D includes all expenditure incurred for carrying out (or providing facilities for carrying out) R & D. Expenditure on the acquisition of rights in, or arising out of, R & D is, however, excluded. Also excluded is expenditure on provision of a *dwelling*, except where not more than 25% of the expenditure (disregarding any 'additional VAT liability' or 'rebate' — see 9.2(viii) above) on a building consisting partly of a dwelling and otherwise used for R &D is attributable (on a just and reasonable apportionment) to the dwelling, in which case the dwelling can be ignored and the whole of the building treated as used for R & D.

An 'additional VAT liability' (see 9.2(viii) above) incurred in respect of qualifying expenditure is itself qualifying expenditure, provided the same person still owns the asset in question and it has not been demolished or destroyed.

Making of allowances. The allowance is given as a trading expense of the chargeable period (see 9.2(i) above) in which the expenditure is incurred (or, in the case of pre-commencement expenditure, the chargeable period in which the trade commences). An allowance in respect of an additional VAT liability is similarly given, but by reference to the time the *liability* is incurred.

[*CAA 2001, ss 437(1), 438–441, 447, 450, Sch 3 paras 89, 90; CAA 1990, ss 137, 139(1)(2), 140(1)(2)(5); FA 1991, Sch 14 para 12; FA 1994, ss 211, 213(10); FA 2000, Sch 19 para 8, Sch 40 Pt II(7)*].

'*Research and development*' is as defined by *ICTA 1988, s 837A* and supporting regulations (see 71.70 SCHEDULE D, CASES I AND II), but also includes oil and gas exploration and appraisal (within *ICTA 1988, s 837B*). [*CAA 2001, s 437(2); CAA 1990, s 139(1)*].

'*Scientific research*' is defined as activities in the fields of natural or applied science for the extension of knowledge. [*CAA 1990, s 139(1)*]. Any question of whether, and to what extent, any activities constitute scientific research, or any asset is used for scientific research, is ultimately referred to the Secretary of State for a final decision. [*CAA 1990, s 139(3)*]. For a case in which allowances were refused on the grounds that the research was not related to the trade of publishing *inter alia* the findings of the research, see *Salt v Golding (Sp C 81), [1996] SSCD 269*.

For special provisions relating to oil licences, see *CAA 2001, ss 552–556, Sch 3 para 91*.

Disposal events and balancing charges. Where *CAA 2001* has effect (see 9.1 above), if a disposal value (see below) falls to be brought into account for the same chargeable period as that for which the related allowance falls to be given, the allowance is given on the excess (if any) of the expenditure over the disposal value; this previously operated slightly differently, but with a similar result, in that the allowance was given on the full expenditure and a balancing charge brought in as below.

If a disposal value falls to be brought into account for the chargeable period after that for which the related allowance is given, liability to a balancing charge arises for that later chargeable period. Effect is given to the charge by treating it as a trading receipt. The charge is equal to disposal value (or, where a reduced allowance was claimed, the excess, if any, of disposal value over unrelieved expenditure), except that it cannot exceed the allowance given (less any earlier balancing charges arising from 'additional VAT rebates' — see below).

A disposal value falls to be brought into account for a chargeable period in which a disposal event occurs, or, if such an event occurs later, for the chargeable period in which the trade is permanently discontinued. If, exceptionally, a disposal event occurs *before* the chargeable period for which the related allowance falls to be given, it is brought into account for the later chargeable period; before *CAA 2001* had effect (see 9.1 above), the resulting net allowance was given for the chargeable period *in which the disposal event occurred.*

Either of the following is a disposal event (unless it gives rise to a balancing charge under the rules for industrial buildings or plant and machinery allowances).

(*a*)   The trader ceases to own the asset representing the qualifying expenditure;

(*b*)   An asset representing the qualifying expenditure is demolished or destroyed before the trader ceases to own it.

On the sale of an asset, the seller is treated for these purposes as ceasing to own it at the earlier of the time of completion and the time when possession is given.

The amount of the disposal value depends on the nature of the disposal event, as follows.

*   If the event is a sale of the asset at not less than market value, it is the *net* sale proceeds; (before *CAA 2001* had effect, see 9.1 above, it was the sale proceeds).

*   If the event is the demolition or destruction of the asset, it is the net amount received for the remains, plus any insurance or *capital* compensation received (but see below as regards demolition costs); (before *CAA 2001* had effect, *any* compensation received had to be taken into account).

*   In any other event, it is the market value of the asset at the time of the event.

An 'additional VAT rebate' (see 9.2(viii) above) made in respect of qualifying expenditure, before the asset in question ceases to belong to the trader or has been demolished or destroyed, must be brought into account as a disposal value (or as an addition to a disposal value otherwise arising) for the chargeable period in which the rebate accrues or, if later, the chargeable period in which the trade commences.

[*CAA 2001, ss 441(1), 442–444, 448, 449–451; CAA 1990, s 138(1)–(4)(6)(7)(8), s 139(4); FA 1991, Sch 14 para 13; FA 1994, Sch 26 Pt V(24); FA 2000, Sch 19 para 8*].

Demolition costs. On demolition of an asset (within (*b*) above), the disposal value is reduced (or extinguished) by any demolition costs incurred by the trader. If the demolition costs exceed the disposal value, then, provided the asset had not begun to be used for non-qualifying purposes, the excess is itself treated as qualifying R & D expenditure, incurred at time of demolition (or, if earlier and where relevant, immediately before cessation of the trade). The demolition costs cannot be treated for any capital allowances purposes as expenditure on any replacement asset.

[*CAA 2001, s 445; CAA 1990, ss 138(5), 139(5)*].

Connected persons and other anti-avoidance provisions apply to substitute market value for sale consideration on certain 'sole or main benefit' transactions, sales without change of control and sales between connected persons. For most sales, the election referred to at 9.22(i) above is available, with the result that an asset representing expenditure for which an R & D allowance has been made as above will be treated as transferred for nil consideration. [*CAA 2001, ss 567–570; CAA 1990, ss 157, 158; FA 1993, s 117(3)–(5); FA 1994, s 119(1)*].

9.53 Capital Allowances

For R & D expenditure of a revenue nature, see 71.70 SCHEDULE D, CASES I AND II. For enhanced tax reliefs where such expenditure is incurred *by companies*, see Tolley's Corporation Tax under Research and Development.

Simon's Direct Tax Service. See B2.7.

9.53   *Example*

C is in business manufacturing and selling cosmetics, and he prepares accounts annually to 30 June. For the purposes of this trade, he built a new laboratory adjacent to his existing premises, incurring the following expenditure.

		£
April 2002	Laboratory building	50,000
June 2002	Technical equipment	3,000
March 2003	Technical equipment	4,000
July 2003	Plant	2,500
August 2004	Extension to existing premises comprising 50% further laboratory area and 50% sales offices.	30,000

In September 2003 a small fire destroyed an item of equipment originally costing £2,000 in June 2002; insurance recoveries totalled £3,000. In March 2004, the plant costing £2,500 in July 2003 was sold for £1,800.

The allowances due are as follows.

Y/e 30.6.02	£
Laboratory building	50,000
Technical equipment	3,000
	£53,000

Y/e 30.6.03	
Technical equipment	4,000
	£4,000

Y/e 30.6.04		
Net allowance on plant sold	(note (*a*))	**£700**
Balancing charge on equipment destroyed	(note (*b*))	**(£2,000)**

Y/e 30.6.05	
Extension (qualifying R & D expenditure only)	**£15,000**

Notes

(*a*)   As the plant is sold in the period of account in which the expenditure is incurred, the disposal value of £1,800 is set against the expenditure of £2,500, resulting in a net allowance of £700.

(*b*)   The destruction of the equipment in the year to 30 June 2004 results in a balancing charge limited to the allowance given. The charge accrues in the period of account in which the event occurs.

10   Capital Gains Tax

For full details of CGT provisions, see Tolley's Capital Gains Tax. For date due see 56.1 PAYMENT OF TAX.

10.1   CAPITAL GAINS TAX (CGT)

The legislation applying to individuals and companies was consolidated by the *Taxation of Chargeable Gains Act 1992* (*TCGA 1992*) and references to that Act are given throughout this book where appropriate. For full details see Tolley's Capital Gains Tax.

10.2   EXCLUSION OF AMOUNTS OTHERWISE TAXED

Gains for CGT purposes are calculated exclusive of receipts chargeable to income tax or corporation tax (except items giving rise to balancing charges or disposal values for CAPITAL ALLOWANCES (9) purposes). However, the capitalised value of a rentcharge, ground annual, feu duty or other series of income receipts can be taken into account for CGT purposes. [*TCGA 1992, s 37; CAA 2001, Sch 2 para 77*].

10.3   RATE OF CGT

For 1999/2000 and subsequent years, the rate of CGT applicable to an individual is equivalent to the lower rate of income tax or, where the individual is liable at the higher rate or Schedule F upper rate on any part of his income, the higher rate. Where there is no higher rate or Schedule F upper rate income tax liability, but the amount chargeable to CGT exceeds the unused part of the basic rate band, the CGT rate on the excess is equivalent to the higher rate of income tax. For this purpose, the basic rate band is the whole of the amount up to the basic rate limit. For 1999/2000, the starting rate of income tax does not apply to CGT; for 2000/01 onwards, it so applies to the extent that taxable gains, if treated as though they were the top slice of income, would fall within the starting rate band. See 1.3 ALLOWANCES AND TAX RATES for the lower rate, the higher rate, the basic rate limit and the starting rate, and 1.9 ALLOWANCES AND TAX RATES as regards the Schedule F upper rate.

For 1998/99 and earlier years, the rate of CGT was equivalent to the basic rate of income tax or, where the individual was liable at the higher rate on any part of his income, the higher rate. Similar provisions applied as above where the amount chargeable to CGT exceeded the unused part of the basic rate band. In addition, where part or all of the lower rate band was unused, a corresponding part of the chargeable gains was chargeable at a rate equivalent to the lower rate (instead of the basic rate) of income tax.

In determining for the above purposes whether income is liable at the higher or Schedule F upper rate of income tax, and the unused part of the basic rate band, account is taken of various provisions of the *Income Tax Acts* requiring additions to or deductions from total income.

For 1998/99 onwards, the rate of CGT applicable to gains accruing to the trustees of a settlement or the personal representatives of a deceased person is equivalent to the 'rate applicable to trusts' (see 81.5 SETTLEMENTS). Before 1998/99, this applied only to gains accruing to trustees of accumulation and discretionary settlements.

[*TCGA 1992, ss 4–6; F(No 2)A 1992, s 23; FA 1994, Sch 26 Pt V; FA 1995, Sch 29 Pt VIII(8); F(No 2)A 1997, Sch 4 paras 24, 25; FA 1998, s 120, Sch 27 Pt III(29); FA 1999, s 26; FA 2000, s 37*].

Before 1999/2000, special computational provisions applied for a year of assessment for which all or part of an individual's lower rate band was utilised by dividend or savings

10.4 Capital Gains Tax

income (see 1.9 ALLOWANCES AND TAX RATES) and he had chargeable gains. The effect was to allocate to the gains that part of the lower rate band which was so utilised, with the individual's basic rate limit being reduced by the amount so allocated (and the gains chargeable at the higher rate being correspondingly reduced or eliminated where relevant). [*TCGA 1992, s 4(3A)(3B); FA 1993, Sch 6 para 22; FA 1996, Sch 6 paras 27, 28; FA 1999, s 26(4), Sch 20 Pt III(1)*].

Simon's Direct Tax Service. See C1.107.

10.4 **SET-OFF OF INCOME TAX RELIEFS AGAINST CAPITAL GAINS**

See 46.5 LOSSES for set-off of trading losses against capital gains. See 62.4 POST-CESSATION ETC. RECEIPTS AND EXPENDITURE for relief for certain post-cessation expenditure, and 75.26 SCHEDULE E—EMPLOYMENT INCOME for relief for certain post-employment expenditure.

11   Cash Basis

General note. See 11.2 below as regards **withdrawal** of cash basis.

Simon's Direct Tax Service B4.202 *et seq.*

11.1   **Periods of account beginning before 7 April 1999.** Business profits should be computed on an earnings basis (see 71.30 SCHEDULE D, CASES I AND II) but in practice the cash basis (where profits measured by excess of cash receipts over cash outlay, ignoring debtors and creditors, accruals, unbilled or uncompleted work) or some other recognisable basis short of a full earnings basis, is accepted for individuals or partnerships carrying on professions or vocations (*not trades*) if desired and provided the profits computed on the new basis will not, taking one year with another, differ materially from the profits computed on the earnings basis. The Revenue do, however, insist on the earnings basis for the first three accounting years of a new profession including one treated as new on a partnership change (see 53.5 PARTNERSHIPS) and, on the change to a cash etc. basis, require a written undertaking that bills for services rendered for work done will be issued at regular and frequent intervals. See *Walker v O'Connor (Sp C 74), 1996 STI 709* for a case in which the cash basis was held not to be permissible in opening years.

The change must be a complete one. For example, receipts after the change for work done before the change must be brought into account on the cash basis notwithstanding that they have already been brought into the earnings basis (*Morrison CS 1932, 17 TC 325*) and similarly expenses accrued due but unpaid which were debited in the accounts on the earnings basis may again be charged in the subsequent accounts on the cash basis when they are paid. Receipts after a cessation or change of basis which would otherwise escape assessment are assessable as post-cessation receipts etc. (see 62 POST-CESSATION ETC. RECEIPTS AND EXPENDITURE). *Note.* There is no relief for this 'double charge' on any later charge to post-cessation receipts.

A change from the cash basis to the earnings basis will be accepted but not a subsequent claim to revert to a cash basis. (Revenue Pamphlet IR 131, A27). The above does not apply to barristers, see below.

See *Rankine v CIR CS 1952, 32 TC 520*, for limitation of Revenue's rights of revision on change-over of basis and *Wetton, Page & Co v Attwooll Ch D 1962, 40 TC 619*, for Revenue's rights to insist on earnings basis notwithstanding use of cash basis in other years. See also *McCash & Hunter v CIR CS 1955, 36 TC 170* (outgoing partner's share of receipts when cash basis applies).

Barristers are normally assessed on a cash basis but may elect to change to the earnings basis (or adopt that basis from commencement of practice). The earnings basis need not include work in progress. A change to the earnings basis or cessation of practice will attract a charge on POST-CESSATION ETC. RECEIPTS AND EXPENDITURE (63). (Revenue Pamphlet IR 131, A3).

11.2   **Position from 7 April 1999.** For periods of account beginning **on or after 7 April 1999** (subject only to the exemption referred to below for certain barristers and advocates), there is a statutory requirement for Schedule D, Case I and II profits to be computed on an accounting basis giving a 'true and fair view' (subject to any adjustment under specific legislation), for which see generally 71.30 SCHEDULE D, CASES I AND II. Broadly, this requires profits to be computed on the earnings basis, so that the cash basis (as above) may no longer be employed for tax purposes. Periods of account beginning before 7 April 1999 and still current on 7 April 2000 are treated for this purpose as having ended on 6 April 1999, with a new period having begun on 7 April 1999 (which is thus subject to these provisions). A period of account is any period for which accounts are drawn up. [*FA 1998, ss 42, 45; FA 2002, s 103(5)*].

Barristers and advocates are exempt from these requirements for periods of account ending not more than seven years after they first hold themselves out as available for fee-earning work. They may instead compute their profits either on the cash basis (as above) or by reference to fees earned whose amount has been agreed or in respect of which a fee note has been delivered, provided that a basis so adopted is applied consistently. If an accounting basis complying with *FA 1998, s 42* (as above) is adopted for a period of account, then that *section* applies for all subsequent periods of account. [*FA 1998, s 43*].

Change of accounting basis on which profits computed for tax purposes. The following provisions are **repealed**, and replaced by the wider provisions of *FA 2002, s 64, Sch 22* (which make similar provision but with a number of small changes, which are referred to below as appropriate), for (generally) periods of account ending **after 31 July 2001**. See 71.30 SCHEDULE D, CASES I AND II for the full details of the replacement provisions and for the circumstances in which they apply to earlier periods of account.

For any change after 5 April 1999, from one period of account to the next, from an accounting basis according with law and practice applicable immediately before the change to one according with law and practice applicable immediately after the change, an adjustment is required as follows for tax purposes (replacing the provisions of *ICTA 1988, s 104(4)*, see 62.2 POST-CESSATION ETC. RECEIPTS AND EXPENDITURE, and any rule of law as to the adjustments required in those circumstances).

A *positive* adjustment is treated as income arising on the first day (under the replacement provisions (see above), the last day) of the first period of account after the change (subject to the spreading provisions described below), chargeable under SCHEDULE D, CASE VI (74). For loss relief purposes it is treated as profits of the trade etc. for the chargeable period for which it is charged to tax, and in the case of an individual for whom the income from the trade etc. is 'relevant earnings' (see 60.8 PERSONAL PENSION SCHEMES, 66.7 RETIREMENT ANNUITIES) or earned income within *ICTA 1988, s 833(4)(c)* (see 1.7(iii) ALLOWANCES AND TAX RATES) it is similarly relevant earnings or earned income. (Under the replacement provisions (see above), if the charge is to corporation tax, the adjustment is treated as a trade etc. receipt arising on the last day of the first period of account after the change.) A *negative* adjustment is treated as an expense of the trade etc. for the first period after the change (under the replacement provisions (see above), arising on the last day of that period).

The amount of the adjustment is calculated as follows.

(*a*) The taxable receipts and allowable expenses of periods before the change are determined on the old and new bases, and the net understatement of profits (or overstatement of losses) on the old basis compared with the new basis determined (a negative figure resulting if there is a net overstatement of profits or understatement of losses).

(*b*) This figure is then adjusted for any difference between the closing stock or work in progress for the last period of account before the change and the opening stock or work in progress for the first period of account after the change. Under the replacement provisions (see above), account is taken for this purpose of any change in the basis of calculating those amounts.

(*c*) If the change of accounting basis is to comply with *FA 1998, s 42* (as above), a further adjustment may be made in respect of any change of accounting basis before 6 April 1999. This will reflect any receipts or expenses brought into account in more than one period of account or not brought into account in any period of account, and any difference between the closing stock or work in progress for the last period of account before the change and the opening stock or work in progress for the first period of account after the change.

(*c*) above does not apply under the replacement provisions (see above), but a further adjustment is introduced for depreciation to the extent that it was not the subject of an adjustment for tax purposes in the last period of account before the change but would be the subject of such an adjustment on the new basis. The replacement provisions also introduce modifications to the calculation of the adjustment charge in a number of cases, certain of which may apply to periods of account ending before 1 August 2001 (see 71.30(1)–(3) SCHEDULE D, CASES I AND II).

No further deduction is allowed in any period of account for amounts deducted in arriving in the figures at (*a*) or (*b*) above as representing an overstatement of profit. Similarly amounts may not be deducted in arriving in the figure at (*c*) above as representing an overstatement of profit if previously brought into account, and amounts which are deducted in arriving at the figure in (*c*) above may not be deducted again on a subsequent change of accounting basis.

For these purposes only items brought into account in the same trade etc., and in accordance with the law and practice then applicable, are considered. Deemed discontinuances under *ICTA 1988, s 113(1)* (see 71.15 SCHEDULE D, CASES I AND II) or *ICTA 1988, s 337(1)* (company beginning or ceasing to carry on a trade) prevent a trade etc. being the same trade etc. for this purpose.

Where an individual has been entitled to compute the profits of his profession or vocation (but *not* a trade) on a basis which does not meet the requirements of *FA 1998, s 42*, and the change of accounting basis is to comply with that *section*, either on its coming into effect or on the exemption for barristers and advocates coming to an end or ceasing to apply, any adjustment charge (as above) is (subject to the election described below) spread over ten years. In the year of assessment in which it would otherwise be chargeable in full and in each of the next eight years of assessment, the amount brought into charge is the lesser of one-tenth of the full amount of the adjustment charge and one-tenth of the Schedule D, Case II profits of the profession or vocation for the year of assessment (disregarding capital allowances and balancing charges). The balance of the adjustment charge is brought in in the following year of assessment. If the profession or vocation is (or is treated as) permanently discontinued before the whole of the adjustment charge has been charged to tax, the restriction of payments by reference to Schedule D, Case II profits ceases to apply. The individual may elect (by notice in writing to the Revenue before 31 January following a year of assessment) for the part of the adjustment charge treated as income of the year of assessment to be increased to a specified amount (up to the balance not previously brought into charge). Following such an election, the payments in later years are reduced as if the original amount of the adjustment charge had been reduced by the additional amount treated as arising in the year for which the election was made (subject to any further election). See Revenue Tax Bulletin February 1999 pp 625, 626 for a short article on the working of the 'catching-up' charge.

In the case of trades, professions or vocations carried on in *partnership*, the adjustment is calculated as if the partnership were an individual (or, for corporation tax purposes, a company) resident in the UK. Each partner's share is determined according to the profit-sharing arrangements for the twelve months immediately before the date of the change of accounting basis or, if the ten-year spreading provisions (as above) apply, the twelve months immediately preceding that date or the anniversary of that date falling in the year of assessment of charge. An election for accelerated payment in any year of assessment (as above) must be made by all persons who were partners in the twelve months immediately preceding the anniversary of the date of change in that year. If there is a discontinuance (or deemed discontinuance) before the whole of the adjustment charge has been charged to tax, each partner's share of any amount chargeable on or after the discontinuance is determined according to the profit-sharing arrangements

(i)   if the discontinuance occurs on the date of change of accounting basis, for the twelve months ending immediately before that date,

(ii) if it occurs after that date but before the first anniversary thereof, for the period between that date and the date of discontinuance,

(iii) if it occurs after the first anniversary of the date of change, for the period between the immediately preceding anniversary and the date of discontinuance,

and any election after the discontinuance for accelerated payment (as above) must be made by each former partner separately.

In the case of the death of an individual otherwise liable to payments of an adjustment charge spread over ten years (as above), the *personal representative* assumes the outstanding liabilities and may make any election for accelerated payment (as above).

[*FA 1998, s 44, Sch 6; FA 2002, s 64, Sch 22, Sch 40 Pt 3(8)*].

As regards valuation of professional work in progress, see 71.73 SCHEDULE D, CASES I AND II.

12   Certificates of Deposit

Simon's Direct Tax Service B3.736.

12.1   A certificate of deposit is any document relating to money, in any currency, which has been deposited with the issuer or some other person, being a document which recognises an obligation to pay a stated amount to bearer or to order, with or without interest, and being a document by the delivery of which, with or without endorsement, the right to receive that stated amount, with or without interest, is transferable. [*ICTA 1988, s 56(5)*]. It does not include bearer bonds. (CCAB Memorandum June 1973).

12.2   Profits or gains (other than in respect of interest) on certificates of deposit acquired after 6 March 1973 will be taxable under Schedule D, Case VI (if not taxable as a trading receipt). A loss on a certificate of deposit can be offset against interest assessable in respect of it. These provisions do not apply to exempt pension funds and charities. [*ICTA 1988, s 56(1)(a)(2)(3), s 398*].

12.3   Where, in a transaction in which no certificate of deposit or security (as defined by *TCGA 1992, s 132*) is issued, but an amount becomes payable with interest (by a bank, similar institution or person regularly engaging in similar transactions), then if the right to receive the amount or interest is disposed of or exercised, any profit (or loss) will be treated as in 12.2 above. [*ICTA 1988, s 56(1)(b)*]. Where a right to receive an amount (with or without interest) in pursuance of a deposit of money comes into existence without a certificate of deposit, but the person entitled to the right could call for the issue of such a certificate, a profit (or loss) on disposal of the right before the issue of such a certificate is similarly treated as in 12.2 above. [*ICTA 1988, s 56A; F(No 2)A 1992, Sch 8 para 1*].

12.4   12.1–12.3 above do not apply for corporation tax purposes for accounting periods ending after 31 March 1996 (subject to transitional provisions). [*ICTA 1988, s 56(4A)(4B); FA 1996, Sch 14 para 6*]. See now Tolley's Corporation Tax under Loan Relationships.

12.5   Neither 12.2 nor 12.3 above applies to a transfer of a right that is a *Pt 5* transfer under *Proceeds of Crime Act 2002* (as in 9.2(xi) CAPITAL ALLOWANCES) where no compensating payment is made to the transferor. [*Proceeds of Crime Act 2002, Sch 10 paras 6, 10*].

13 Certificates of Tax Deposit

Simon's Direct Tax Service A3.1335, A3.1336.

13.1 Taxpayers may make deposits, evidenced by Certificates of Tax Deposit, with Collectors of Taxes for the subsequent payment of their own tax and Class 4 NIC liabilities generally (other than PAYE and tax deducted from payments to construction sub-contractors and corporation tax — see further below). If a deposit is tendered in respect of any liability, that liability will be treated as paid on the later of the certificate date and the normal due date for that liability (see 56 PAYMENT OF TAX). The minimum initial deposit is £500 with minimum additions of £250. Deposits of £100,000 or over must be made by direct remittance to the Bank of England.

Series 7 Certificates are *not* available for purchase for use against corporation tax liabilities.

Deposits made after 5 April 2003 in a partnership name are not accepted in settlement of an individual partner's tax liability.

Interest, which is payable gross but taxable, will accrue for a maximum of six years from the date of deposit to the date of payment of tax or, if earlier, the 'deemed due date' for payment of the liability against which the deposit (plus accrued interest) is set. The *'deemed due date'* is generally the normal due date for payment of the tax under the relevant legislation, and does not change if for any reason an assessment is made late or the liability is not payable until later (e.g. following settlement of an appeal). A deposit may be withdrawn for cash at any time but will then receive a reduced rate of interest. Where a certificate is used in settlement of a tax liability, interest at the higher rate up to the normal due date may be less than interest at the encashment rate up to the reckonable date. In such circumstances the taxpayer may instruct the Revenue to calculate interest on the latter basis. (ICAEW Technical Release TAX 13/93, 30 June 1993). The rates of interest, published by the Treasury, and calculated by reference to the rate on comparable investment with the Government, vary with the size and period of the deposit, and the rate payable on a deposit is adjusted to the current rate on each anniversary of the deposit.

Deposits are not transferable except to personal representatives of a deceased person.

Rates of interest are given at 13.2, 13.3 and 13.4 below. Information on current rates may be obtained from www.inlandrevenue.gov.uk/howtopay/ctd_interest_rates.pdf, from any Revenue Tax Collecting Office or from Revenue Finance at 01903 509064 or 509066 or 01903 700222 ext. 2064/2066.

13.2 The rates of interest on date of deposit or anniversary on Series 6 and Series 7 Certificates for deposits of under £100,000 are (from 7 November 1997onwards)

	Used to pay tax	Withdrawals for cash
7 November 1997–8 October 1998	4%	2%
9 October 1998–5 November 1998	$3\frac{3}{4}$%	2%
6 November 1998–7 January 1999	$3\frac{1}{4}$%	$1\frac{3}{4}$%
8 January 1999–4 February 1999	$2\frac{1}{2}$%	$1\frac{1}{4}$%
5 February 1999–10 June 1999	$1\frac{3}{4}$%	1%
11 June 1999–8 September 1999	$1\frac{1}{2}$%	$\frac{3}{4}$%
9 September 1999–3 November 1999	$1\frac{3}{4}$%	1%
4 November 1999–13 January 2000	2%	1%
14 January 2000–10 February 2000	$2\frac{1}{4}$%	$1\frac{1}{4}$%
11 February 2000–8 February 2001	$2\frac{1}{2}$%	$1\frac{1}{4}$%

	Used to pay tax	Withdrawals for cash
9 February 2001–5 April 2001	$2\frac{1}{4}$%	$1\frac{1}{4}$%
6 April 2001–2 August 2001	2%	1%
3 August 2001–18 September 2001	$1\frac{1}{2}$%	$\frac{3}{4}$%
19 September 2001–4 October 2001	$1\frac{1}{4}$%	$\frac{3}{4}$%
5 October 2001–8 November 2001	1%	$\frac{1}{2}$%
9 November 2001–6 February 2003	$\frac{1}{2}$%	$\frac{1}{4}$%
7 February 2003–10 July 2003	$\frac{1}{4}$%	nil
11 July 2003–6 November 2003	nil	nil
7 November 2003–5 February 2004	$\frac{1}{4}$%	nil
6 February 2004–6 May 2004	$\frac{1}{2}$%	$\frac{1}{4}$%
6 May 2004–10 June 2004	$\frac{3}{4}$%	$\frac{1}{4}$%
11 June 2004 onwards	1%	$\frac{1}{2}$%

13.3 The rates of interest on date of deposit or anniversary on Series 6 or Series 7 Certificates for deposits of £100,000 or more used to meet a scheduled liability are (from 7 November 1997 onwards)

	Period of deposit in months				
	Under 1	1 but under 3	3 but under 6	6 but under 9	9 but under 12
7 November 1997–4 June 1998	4%	$6\frac{1}{2}$%	$6\frac{1}{4}$%	$6\frac{1}{4}$%	$6\frac{1}{4}$%
5 June 1998–8 October 1998	4%	$6\frac{1}{4}$%	$6\frac{1}{4}$%	$6\frac{1}{4}$%	6%
9 October 1998–5 November 1998	$3\frac{3}{4}$%	$6\frac{1}{4}$%	$5\frac{3}{4}$%	$5\frac{1}{2}$%	$5\frac{1}{4}$%
6 November 1998–10 December 1998	$3\frac{1}{4}$%	$5\frac{3}{4}$%	$5\frac{1}{4}$%	5%	$4\frac{3}{4}$%
11 December 1998–7 January 1999	3%	$5\frac{1}{4}$%	$4\frac{3}{4}$%	$4\frac{1}{2}$%	$4\frac{1}{4}$%
8 January 1999–4 February 1999	$2\frac{1}{2}$%	5%	$4\frac{1}{2}$%	4%	4%
5 February 1999–8 April 1999	$1\frac{3}{4}$%	$4\frac{1}{4}$%	4%	$3\frac{3}{4}$%	$3\frac{3}{4}$%
9 April 1999–10 June 1999	$1\frac{3}{4}$%	$4\frac{1}{4}$%	4%	$3\frac{3}{4}$%	$3\frac{3}{4}$%
11 June 1999–8 September 1999	$1\frac{1}{2}$%	4%	4%	4%	4%
9 September 1999–3 November 1999	$1\frac{3}{4}$%	$4\frac{1}{2}$%	$4\frac{1}{2}$%	$4\frac{1}{2}$%	$4\frac{1}{2}$%
4 November 1999–13 January 2000	2%	5%	$4\frac{3}{4}$%	$4\frac{3}{4}$%	$4\frac{3}{4}$%
14 January 2000–10 February 2000	$2\frac{1}{4}$%	5%	5%	5%	$5\frac{1}{4}$%
11 February 2000–8 February 2001	$2\frac{1}{2}$%	$5\frac{1}{4}$%	5%	$5\frac{1}{4}$%	$5\frac{1}{4}$%
9 February 2001–5 April 2001	$2\frac{1}{4}$%	$4\frac{3}{4}$%	$4\frac{1}{4}$%	$4\frac{1}{4}$%	4%
6 April 2001–10 May 2001	2%	$4\frac{1}{4}$%	4%	$3\frac{3}{4}$%	$3\frac{1}{2}$%
11 May 2001–2 August 2001	2%	4%	4%	$3\frac{3}{4}$%	$3\frac{3}{4}$%
3 August 2001–18 September 2001	$1\frac{1}{2}$%	4%	$3\frac{3}{4}$%	$3\frac{3}{4}$%	$3\frac{3}{4}$%
19 September 2001–4 October 2001	$1\frac{1}{4}$%	$3\frac{1}{2}$%	$3\frac{1}{4}$%	$3\frac{1}{4}$%	3%
5 October 2001–8 November 2001	1%	$3\frac{1}{4}$%	3%	3%	3%
9 November 2001–6 February 2003	$\frac{1}{2}$%	$2\frac{3}{4}$%	$2\frac{1}{2}$%	$2\frac{1}{4}$%	$2\frac{1}{4}$%
7 February 2003–10 July 2003	$\frac{1}{4}$%	$2\frac{3}{4}$%	$2\frac{1}{4}$%	$2\frac{1}{4}$%	2%
11 July 2003–6 November 2003	nil	$2\frac{1}{2}$%	$2\frac{1}{4}$%	2%	2%
7 November 2003–5 February 2004	$\frac{1}{4}$%	3%	3%	3%	3%
6 February 2004–6 May 2004	$\frac{1}{2}$%	3%	3%	3%	3%
6 May 2004–10 June 2004	$\frac{3}{4}$%	$3\frac{1}{4}$%	$3\frac{1}{4}$%	$3\frac{1}{4}$%	$3\frac{1}{4}$%
11 June 2004 onwards	1%	$3\frac{3}{4}$%	$3\frac{1}{2}$%	$3\frac{3}{4}$%	$3\frac{3}{4}$%

13.4 Certificates of Tax Deposit

13.4 The rates of interest on date of deposit or anniversary on Series 6 or Series 7 Certificates for deposits of £100,000 or more withdrawn for cash are (from 7 November 1997 onwards)

	Under 1	1 but under 3	3 but under 6	6 but under 9	9 but under 12
7 November 1997–4 June 1998	2%	$3\frac{1}{4}$%	$3\frac{1}{4}$%	$3\frac{1}{4}$%	$3\frac{1}{4}$%
5 June 1998–8 October 1998	2%	$3\frac{1}{4}$%	$3\frac{1}{4}$%	$3\frac{1}{4}$%	3%
9 October 1998–5 November 1998	2%	$3\frac{1}{4}$%	3%	$2\frac{3}{4}$%	$2\frac{3}{4}$%
6 November 1998–10 December 1998	$1\frac{3}{4}$%	3%	$2\frac{3}{4}$%	$2\frac{1}{2}$%	$2\frac{1}{2}$%
11 December 1998–7 January 1999	$1\frac{1}{2}$%	$2\frac{3}{4}$%	$2\frac{1}{2}$%	$2\frac{1}{4}$%	$2\frac{1}{4}$%
8 January 1999–4 February 1999	$1\frac{1}{4}$%	$2\frac{1}{2}$%	$2\frac{1}{4}$%	2%	2%
5 February 1999–10 June 1999	1%	$2\frac{1}{4}$%	2%	2%	2%
11 June 1999–8 September 1999	$\frac{3}{4}$%	2%	2%	2%	2%
9 September 1999–3 November 1999	1%	$2\frac{1}{4}$%	$2\frac{1}{4}$%	$2\frac{1}{4}$%	$2\frac{1}{4}$%
4 November 1999–13 January 2000	1%	$2\frac{1}{2}$%	$2\frac{1}{2}$%	$2\frac{1}{2}$%	$2\frac{1}{2}$%
14 January 2000–10 February 2000	$1\frac{1}{4}$%	$2\frac{1}{2}$%	$2\frac{1}{2}$%	$2\frac{1}{2}$%	$2\frac{3}{4}$%
11 February 2000–8 February 2001	$1\frac{1}{4}$%	$2\frac{3}{4}$%	$2\frac{1}{2}$%	$2\frac{3}{4}$%	$2\frac{3}{4}$%
9 February 2001–5 April 2001	$1\frac{1}{4}$%	$2\frac{1}{4}$%	$2\frac{1}{4}$%	$2\frac{1}{4}$%	2%
6 April 2001–10 May 2001	1%	$2\frac{1}{4}$%	2%	2%	$1\frac{3}{4}$%
11 May 2001–2 August 2001	1%	2%	2%	2%	2%
3 August 2001–18 September 2001	$\frac{3}{4}$%	2%	$1\frac{3}{4}$%	$1\frac{3}{4}$%	$1\frac{3}{4}$%
19 September 2001–4 October 2001	$\frac{3}{4}$%	$1\frac{3}{4}$%	$1\frac{3}{4}$%	$1\frac{3}{4}$%	$1\frac{1}{2}$%
5 October 2001–8 November 2001	$\frac{1}{2}$%	$1\frac{3}{4}$%	$1\frac{1}{2}$%	$1\frac{1}{2}$%	$1\frac{1}{2}$%
9 November 2001–6 February 2003	$\frac{1}{4}$%	$1\frac{1}{2}$%	$1\frac{1}{4}$%	$1\frac{1}{4}$%	$1\frac{1}{4}$%
7 February 2003–10 July 2003	nil	$1\frac{1}{4}$%	1%	1%	1%
11 July 2003–6 November 2003	nil	$1\frac{1}{4}$%	1%	1%	1%
7 November 2003–5 February 2004	nil	$1\frac{1}{2}$%	$1\frac{1}{2}$%	$1\frac{1}{2}$%	$1\frac{1}{2}$%
6 February 2004–10 June 2004	$\frac{1}{4}$%	$1\frac{1}{2}$%	$1\frac{1}{2}$%	$1\frac{1}{2}$%	$1\frac{1}{2}$%
11 June 2004 onwards	$\frac{1}{2}$%	$1\frac{3}{4}$%	$1\frac{3}{4}$%	$1\frac{3}{4}$%	$1\frac{3}{4}$%

14 Charities

(See also Detailed Guidance at www.inlandrevenue.gov.uk/charities/chapter_1.htm and Revenue Pamphlets IR 64 and IR 65, 'Giving to Charity: How businesses/individuals can get tax relief', IR 178, 'Giving shares and securities to Charities', IR 2001, 'Trading by Charities', and CWL 4, 'Fund Raising Events: Exemptions for Charities and other Qualifying Bodies'.)

Cross-references. See 12.2 CERTIFICATES OF DEPOSIT for exemption of gains; 29 EXEMPT ORGANISATIONS for other exempt organisations; 71.44 SCHEDULE D, CASES I AND II for employees seconded to charities.

Simon's Direct Tax Service C4.5.

Other sources. See Tolley's Charities Manual.

The headings in this chapter are as follows.

14.1 CHARITY, CHARITABLE PURPOSES — GENERAL PRINCIPLES

'**Charity**' means any body of persons or trust established for charitable purposes only. [*ICTA 1988, s 506(1)*]. The meaning of charity is also governed by general law. Under the *Recreational Charities Act 1958, s 1* the provision, in the interest of social welfare, of facilities for recreation or other leisure time occupation, is deemed to be charitable (subject to the principle that, unless the trust is for the relief of poverty (*Dingle v Turner HL 1972, 1 AER 878*), a trust or institution to be charitable must be for the public benefit). Charities may be registered under the *Charities Act 1993*. The CIR as an interested party may appeal to the High Court against a decision of the Charity Commissioners and *Charities Act 1993, s 10* provides for the exchange of information between the Charity Commissioners and the CIR.

Subject to the above, what is a charity rests largely on judicial interpretation. A leading case is *Special Commrs v Pemsel HL 1891, 3 TC 53* in which Lord Macnaghten laid down that 'charity' should be given its technical meaning under English law and comprises 'four principal divisions; trusts for the relief of poverty, trusts for the advancement of education, trusts for the advancement of religion and trusts beneficial to the community and not falling under any of the preceding heads. The trusts last referred to are not the less charitable ... because incidentally they affect the rich as well as the poor'. In the same case it was held that in relation to tax the English definition should be applied to Scottish cases (and cf. *Jackson's Trustees v Lord Advocate CS 1926, 10 TC 460* and *CIR v Glasgow Police Athletic Assn HL 1953, 34 TC 76*). The concept of 'charity' may change with changes in social values (cf. *CIR v Trustees of Football Association Youth Trust HL 1980, 54 TC 413*).

14.1 Charities

The charity reliefs are not available to overseas charities (*Gull KB 1937, 21 TC 374*; *Dreyfus Foundation Inc v CIR HL 1955, 36 TC 126*).

Where land given for educational and certain other charitable purposes ceases to be used for such purposes and, under the *Reverter of Sites Act 1987*, is held by the trustees on a trust for sale for the benefit of the revertee, then unless the revertee is known to be a charity, there is a deemed disposal and reacquisition for capital gains purposes, which may give rise to a chargeable gain. Any income arising from the property will be liable to income tax, and a chargeable gain may also arise on a subsequent sale of the land. By concession, where the revertee is subsequently identified as a charity or disclaims all entitlement to the property (or where certain orders are made by the Charity Commissioners or the Secretary of State), provided that charitable status is re-established within six years of the date on which the land ceased to be held on the original charitable trust, any capital gains tax paid as above in the interim period will be discharged or repaid (with repayment supplement where appropriate) as will any income tax (provided that the income charged was used for charitable purposes). Partial relief will be given where the above conditions are only satisfied in respect of part of the property concerned. A request by the trustees for postponement of the tax payable will be accepted by the Revenue where the revertee has not been identified and this concession may apply. (Revenue Pamphlet IR 1, D47).

The *Charitable Trusts (Validation) Act 1954* provides for validating as charitable a pre-1953 trust if its property was in fact applied for charitable purposes only, notwithstanding that the trust also authorised its application for non-charitable purposes (cf. *Vernon & Sons Ltd Employees Fund v CIR Ch D 1956, 36 TC 484*; *Buxton v Public Trustees Ch D 1962, 41 TC 235*).

A donation by one charity to another has been applied for charitable purposes even though merely added to the funds of the other charity (*Helen Slater Charitable Trust Ltd CA 1981, 55 TC 230*).

The application of income to the making of loans at interest to the subsidiaries from whom the income was derived was held to be for charitable purposes in *Nightingale Ltd v Price (Sp C 66), [1996] SSCD 116*.

As regards the time at which charitable purposes arise, see *Guild and Others (as Trustees of the William Muir (Bond 9) Ltd Employees' Share Scheme) v CIR CS 1993, 66 TC 1* (trustees of share scheme required to repay loans out of proceeds of distribution and to apply balance to charitable purposes; held not to apply proceeds of distribution for charitable purposes).

For general restrictions on reliefs, see 14.10 below.

The Revenue have issued a booklet 'Guidelines on the Tax Treatment of Disaster Funds' (obtainable free of charge from Customer Services Manager, IR Charities, St John's House, Merton Road, Bootle, Merseyside L69 9BB (tel. 0151–472 6036/7) or, in Scotland, Meldrum House, 15 Drumsheugh Gardens, Edinburgh EH3 7UG (tel. 0131–774 4040)) to help people organising disaster appeal funds to decide what form their fund should take and to deal with any tax implications. See generally Revenue publication 'Fund-Raising for Charity' (14.7 below), which also in particular replaces paras 27 and 28 of this booklet.

A leaflet 'Setting up a Charity in Scotland' is also available free of charge from IR Charities (Scotland), who may be contacted for enquiries on whether a body is charitable.

A 'Charity Fund-raising Pack' is available free of charge from Customer Services Manager, IR Charities (as above). It contains three booklets: 'Trading by Charities' (an Inland Revenue booklet); 'VAT — Charities' (Customs and Excise); and 'Charities and Fund-raising: A Summary' (Charity Commissioners). The Charity Commissioners for England and Wales have also published more comprehensive advice for charity trustees in 'Charities and Fund-raising' (CC20), available from any of their offices, including Harmsworth

House, 13–15 Bouverie Street, London EC4Y 8DP. Detailed guidance on the use of professional fund-raisers and commercial participation is available in the Home Office publication 'Charitable Fund-raising: Professional and Commercial Involvement' (ISBN 0 11 341133 2, £5.50 from HMSO, tel. 020–7873 9090).

The Revenue have published a Code of Practice (No 5) setting out their standards for the carrying out of inspections of charities' records.

IR Charities may be contacted at local call rates on 08453 020203 or by e-mail at Charities@inlandrevenue.gov.uk.

Simon's Direct Tax Service. See **C4.505**.

14.2   **CHARITY, CHARITABLE PURPOSES — EXAMPLES**

Relevant cases are summarised below under appropriate headings.

(*a*)   **Almshouse.** Inmates need not be destitute (*Mary Clark Home Trustees v Anderson KB 1904, 5 TC 48*).

(*b*)   **Arts.** A musical festival association and the Royal Choral Society have been held to be charitable (*Glasgow Musical Festival Assn CS 1926, 11 TC 154*; *Royal Choral Socy v CIR CA 1943, 25 TC 263*) but not companies formed to produce plays in association with the Arts Council (*Tennent Plays Ltd v CIR CA 1948, 30 TC 107*) or with the aim of furthering the theatre and dramatic taste (*Associated Artists Ltd v CIR Ch D 1956, 36 TC 499*).

(*c*)   **Benevolent funds etc.** for the relief of widows and orphans of members held charitable (*Society for the Relief of Widows and Orphans of Medical Men KB 1926, 11 TC 1*; *Baptist Union etc. Ltd v CIR KB (NI) 1945, 26 TC 335*) but not a death benefit fund (*Royal Naval etc. Officers' Assn Ch D 1955, 36 TC 187*) nor a fund set up to promote the formation of mutual provident associations (*Nuffield Foundation v CIR; Nuffield Provident Guarantee Fund v CIR KB 1946, 28 TC 479*).

(*d*)   **Education.** A trust for the advancement of education does not require an element of poverty to be charitable (*R v Special Commrs (ex p University College of N. Wales) CA 1909, 5 TC 408*). The technical college of a trade association was held to be charitable (*Scottish Woollen Technical College v CIR CS 1926, 11 TC 139*) as was the Students' Union of a medical college (*London Hospital Medical College Ch D 1976, 51 TC 365*) and a trust to promote sports in schools etc. (*CIR v Trustees of Football Association Youth Trust HL 1980, 54 TC 413*). See also *Educational Grants Assn Ltd CA 1967, 44 TC 93*; *Abdul Caffoor Trustees v Ceylon Income Tax Commr PC 1961, 40 ATC 93*. For 'public school' see (*h*) below.

(*e*)   **Hospital.** A Friendly Society's convalescent home was exempted (*Royal Antediluvian Order of Buffaloes v Owens KB 1927, 13 TC 176*).

(*f*)   **Political and similar objects** (including the reform of the law) are not charitable purposes. Objects held not to be charitable include the reform of the law on vivisection (*National Anti-Vivisection Socy HL 1947, 28 TC 311*) and temperance (*Temperance Council etc. of England KB 1926, 10 TC 748*), simplified spelling (*Hunter 'C' Trustees v CIR KB 1929, 14 TC 427*), fostering Anglo-Swedish relations (*Anglo-Swedish Socy v CIR KB 1931, 16 TC 34*), Jewish resettlement (*Keren Kayemeth Le Jisroel Ltd v CIR HL 1932, 17 TC 27*) and a memorial fund for Bonar Law (*Bonar Law Memorial Trust v CIR KB 1933, 17 TC 508*).

(*g*)   **Professional associations etc.** Professional associations are generally not admitted to be established for charitable purposes; they benefit their members, any wider public advantage being incidental (*R v Special Commrs (ex p Headmasters' Conference) KB 1925, 10 TC 73*; *General Medical Council v CIR CA 1928, 13 TC 819*;

Geologists' Assn v CIR CA 1928, 14 TC 271; Midland Counties Institution of Engineers v CIR KB 1928, 14 TC 285; General Nursing Council for Scotland v CIR CS 1929, 14 TC 645; Master Mariners (Honourable Company of) v CIR KB 1932, 17 TC 298). But contrast *Institution of Civil Engineers v CIR CA 1931, 16 TC 158,* where the Institution was held to be charitable, any benefit to members being incidental. Members' clubs and social clubs are not charitable (*Scottish Flying Club v CIR CS 1935, 20 TC 1; Sir H J Williams's Trustees v CIR HL 1947, 27 TC 409*). An agricultural society for the general promotion of agriculture was held charitable (*CIR v Yorkshire Agricultural Socy CA 1927, 13 TC 58*) but not a statutory Pig Marketing Board (*Pig Marketing Board (Northern Ireland) v CIR KB (NI) 1945, 26 TC 319*) nor a society to promote foxhound breeding (*Peterborough Royal Foxhound Show Socy v CIR KB 1936, 20 TC 249*) (but it was given relief under a predecessor to *ICTA 1988, s 510* on its annual show — see 29.1 EXEMPT ORGANISATIONS).

(*h*) **Public school.** A school may be for the public benefit and qualify for the relief notwithstanding that it derives substantial receipts from fees (*Blake v Mayor etc. of London CA 1887, 2 TC 209; Ereaut v Girls' Public Day School Trust Ltd HL 1930, 15 TC 529,* and contrast *Birkenhead School Ltd v Dring KB 1926, 11 TC 273*). A Quaker school exclusively for children of members of the Society of Friends was refused relief (*Ackworth School v Betts KB 1915, 6 TC 642*) but a Roman Catholic school which admitted non-Catholic pupils qualified for relief (*Cardinal Vaughan Memorial School Trustees v Ryall KB 1920, 7 TC 611*).

(*i*) **Religion.** Charitable relief was refused for trusts to advance the 'religious, moral, social and recreative life' of Presbyterians in Londonderry (*Londonderry Presbyterian Church House Trustees v CIR CA(NI) 1946, 27 TC 431*), for the promotion and aiding of 'Roman Catholicism' in a particular district (*Ellis v CIR CA 1949, 31 TC 178*) and for the 'religious, educational and other parochial requirements' of the Roman Catholic inhabitants of a parish (*Cookstown Roman Catholic Church Trustees v CIR QB (NI) 1953, 34 TC 350*). In each case, the objects included non-charitable elements which prevented the whole being charitable. Relief was also refused to the Oxford Group (*Oxford Group v CIR CA 1949, 31 TC 221*).

(*j*) **Miscellaneous.** A nursing home (*Peebleshire Nursing Assn CS 1926, 11 TC 335*) and a holiday home (*Roberts Marine Mansions Trustees CA 1927, 11 TC 425*) providing services for members etc. at reduced fees held to be charitable, as was a non-profit-making company for publishing law reports (*Incorpd. Council of Law Reporting v A-G CA 1971, 47 TC 321*). Relief refused to a trust to maintain an historic building because it also had a non-charitable object (*Trades House of Glasgow v CIR CS 1969, 46 TC 178*) and to a Society established mainly with philanthropic objects which, in the event, were not achieved (*Hugh's Settlement Ltd v CIR KB 1938, 22 TC 281*). The inclusion of an object 'to promote the development of industry, commerce and enterprise' and ancillary objects prevented the objects as a whole of a Training and Enterprise Council from being charitable (*Oldham TEC v CIR Ch D 1996, 69 TC 231*).

14.3   **SPECIFIC EXEMPTIONS AND RELIEFS FROM TAX**

Apart from the exemptions at 14.4–14.9 below, charities are subject to tax on investment and rental income and gains and on profits from trades carried on in order to raise funds. The Schedule D exemptions at 14.4, 14.5 and 14.7 below are not general exemptions and hence do not extend to trades not falling within 14.7 below or to Case VI income generally (cf. *Grove v Young Men's Christian Association KB 1903, 4 TC 613* and *Rotunda Hospital, Dublin v Coman HL 1920, 7 TC 517*).

The exemptions are subject to the restrictions at 14.10 below.

Claims can be made, generally within the time limit at 16.4 CLAIMS, to IR Charities, St John's House, Merton Road, Bootle, Merseyside L69 9BB or, in Scotland, Meldrum House, 15 Drumsheugh Gardens, Edinburgh EH3 7UG. [*ICTA 1988, s 505(1)*]. The Board have powers to require the production of books, documents etc. relevant to any claim for exemption under *ICTA 1988, s 505(1), s 507* (see 29.3, 29.9, 29.14, 29.20 EXEMPT ORGANISATIONS) or *s 508* (see 77.1 SCIENTIFIC RESEARCH ASSOCIATIONS) leading to the repayment of income tax or the payment of tax credits. [*F(No 2)A 1992, s 28*].

Simon's Direct Tax Service. See **C4.518** *et seq.*

14.4 **Rents — Schedules A and D.** Profits or gains in respect of rents or other receipts from an estate, interest or right in or over any land (whether in the UK or elsewhere) vested in any person for charitable purposes are exempt to the extent they are applied to charitable purposes only. [*ICTA 1988, s 505(1)(a); FA 1996, s 146(2)(5)*].

14.5 **Interest, distributions etc.** Income of a charity, or applicable for charitable purposes under an Act of Parliament, charter, decree, deed of trust or will, is exempt so far as applied to charitable purposes and consisting of **Schedule D, Case III** income (or equivalent overseas income within **Schedule D, Case IV or V**), **Schedule D, Case V** income consisting of distributions which would be within Schedule F if the paying company were UK resident or distributions within **Schedule F.** From 1 April 2002 this also applies to tax under **Schedule D, Case VI** in respect of non-trading gains of companies on intangible fixed assets under *FA 2002, Sch 29* (see Tolley's Corporation Tax under Intangible Assets).

Where under a will, a business was bequeathed to trustees to carry it on and pay the net profits to a charity, the amounts so paid were held to be annual payments (*R v Special Commrs (ex p Shaftesbury Homes) CA 1922, 8 TC 367*). In *Lawrence v CIR KB 1940, 23 TC 333* copyright royalties were held to be annual payments. For annual payments generally, see 22.10 DEDUCTION OF TAX AT SOURCE.

Schedule D income of trustees arising from public revenue dividends and which is applicable towards repairs of any cathedral, college, church, chapel etc., is also exempt so far as applied to those purposes only.

[*ICTA 1988, s 505(1)(c)(d); FA 1996, s 146(3)(5), Sch 7 para 19; FA 2002, Sch 30 para 3*].

For restrictions to the exemption in the case of certain distributions made before 6 April 1999, see 3.16, 3.17 ANTI-AVOIDANCE.

14.6 **Dividend tax credits.** Before 6 April 1993, the tax credit attached to a qualifying distribution was at the basic rate of income tax (i.e. 25% of the gross amount of the distribution, which is equivalent to one-third of the actual amount of the distribution). [*ICTA 1988, s 231(1)*]. From 6 April 1993 to 5 April 1999, the tax credit is at the lower rate of income tax (i.e. 20% of the gross amount of the distribution, equivalent to 25% of the actual amount of the distribution). [*FA 1993, s 78(1)(3)*]. From 6 April 1999, it is further reduced to 10% of the gross amount of the distribution, i.e. one-ninth of the actual amount of the distribution. Also from 6 April 1999, however, the tax credit attached to a qualifying distribution ceases to be repayable to exempt bodies, including charities. [*F(No 2)A 1997, s 30*]. For the compensatory transitional reliefs following each of these changes, see below. For restrictions on the recovery of tax credits in the case of certain distributions made before 6 April 1999, see 3.16, 3.17 ANTI-AVOIDANCE.

Transitional relief following reduction in rate of tax credit from 6 April 1993. As a transitional relief for charities (and for other bodies similarly treated under *ICTA 1988, s 507* (see 29.3,

14.6 Charities

29.9, 29.14, 29.20 EXEMPT ORGANISATIONS) or *s 508* (see 77.1 SCIENTIFIC RESEARCH ASSOCIATIONS)), a compensatory payment may be claimed by the charity etc. in respect of qualifying distributions received from UK companies between 6 April 1993 and 5 April 1997 inclusive, and in respect of which the charity etc. is entitled to payment of the attached tax credit. The payment is in addition to payment of the tax credit itself, and is treated for the purposes of *ICTA 1988, s 252* (see Tolley's Corporation Tax under Advance Corporation Tax) as if it were a payment of tax credit.

The claim must be made within two years after the end of the chargeable period in which the distribution is made. Where (and to the extent that) the claim is accepted, the charity etc. will be entitled to be paid by the Board, out of money provided by Parliament, a proportion of the amount or value of the distribution as follows:

(*a*) one-fifteenth for a distribution made in 1993/94;

(*b*) one-twentieth for a distribution made in 1994/95;

(*c*) one-thirtieth for a distribution made in 1995/96;

(*d*) one-sixtieth for a distribution made in 1996/97.

Any entitlement to a payment under these provisions is subject to a power of the Board to determine, whether before or after the payment is made, and having regard to *ICTA 1988, s 236, s 237* and *s 703* (see 3.16, 3.17 and 3.2 *et seq.* ANTI-AVOIDANCE respectively), that the charity etc. is to be treated as not entitled to the payment or to a part of it. An appeal may be made against any such decision by written notice to the Board within 30 days of receipt of written notification of the decision, the appeal being to the Special Commissioners.

[*FA 1993, s 80*].

Claims for payments under these transitional arrangements should be made on a special claim form R68 (TR), to be completed in addition to the usual form (R68) claiming payment of tax credits on dividends.

Transitional relief following abolition of repayment of tax credits from 6 April 1999. As a transitional relief for charities (and for other bodies similarly treated under *ICTA 1988, s 507* (see 29.3, 29.9, 29.14, 29.20 EXEMPT ORGANISATIONS) or *s 508* (see 77.1 SCIENTIFIC RESEARCH ASSOCIATIONS)), a compensatory payment may be claimed by the charity etc. in respect of qualifying distributions received from UK companies between 6 April 1999 and 5 April 2004 inclusive, provided that the charity is entitled to exemption from tax in respect of the distribution. The payment is treated for the purposes of *ICTA 1988, s 252* (see Tolley's Corporation Tax under Advance Corporation Tax) as if it were a payment of tax credit.

The claim must be made within two years after the end of the chargeable period in which the distribution is made. Where (and to the extent that) the claim is accepted, the charity etc. will be entitled to be paid by the Board, out of money provided by Parliament, a proportion of the amount or value of the distribution as follows:

(*a*) 21% for a distribution made in 1999/2000;

(*b*) 17% for a distribution made in 2000/01;

(*c*) 13% for a distribution made in 2001/02;

(*d*) 8% for a distribution made in 2002/03;

(*e*) 4% for a distribution made in 2003/04.

Any entitlement to a payment under these provisions is subject to a power of the Board to determine, whether before or after the payment is made, and having regard to *ICTA 1988, s 703* (see 3.2 *et seq.* ANTI-AVOIDANCE), that the charity etc. is to be treated as not entitled to the payment or to a part of it. An appeal may be made against any such decision by written notice to the Board within 30 days of receipt of written notification of the decision, the appeal being to the Special Commissioners. For the purposes of *section 703 et seq.*, the payment is treated as repayment of tax. *F(No 2)A 1997, Sch 5* similarly removes or restricts the right to payments under these provisions where anti-avoidance provisions in *ICTA 1988, ss 235–237* (see 3.16, 3.17 ANTI-AVOIDANCE) would have applied before 6 April 1999 to deny repayment of tax credits.

[*F(No 2)A 1997, s 35, Sch 5*].

14.7 **Trading profits — Schedule D.** Profits of trades carried on (in the UK or elsewhere) by, and applied solely for the purposes of, charities are exempted if either

(*a*)   the trade is exercised in the course of carrying out a primary purpose of the charity; or

(*b*)   the work is mainly carried on by its beneficiaries.

[*ICTA 1988, s 505(1)(e); FA 1996, s 146(4)(5)*].

See also the specific exemptions at (i)–(iv) below.

For trades held to fall within the exemption, see *Glasgow Musical Festival Assn CS 1926, 11 TC 154*; *Royal Choral Society v CIR CA 1943, 25 TC 263* and *Dean Leigh Temperance Canteen Trustees v CIR Ch D 1958, 38 TC 315*. For regular trading within Case I see *British Legion, Peterhead Branch v CIR CS 1953, 35 TC 509*. (In practice, the Revenue may in such cases allow a reasonable deduction for services etc. provided free.) For annual shows of agricultural societies, see 29.1 EXEMPT ORGANISATIONS.

A 'Charity Fund-raising Pack' is available from IR Charities (see 14.1 above for details), which includes a Revenue publication 'Trading by Charities' (available separately) giving advice on the tax treatment of particular types of trade commonly carried on by charities. This incorporates the guidance given in the earlier Revenue booklet 'Fund-Raising for Charity'. It includes guidance as to the type of fund-raising activities originally covered by ESC C4 (see (ii) below) and the conditions the activities must satisfy, the kind of profits covered by the concession and the consequences if an event is not covered by it, and offers a telephone helpline which charities may call for further advice.

(i)   **Exemption for small trades.** For 2000/01 onwards and for accounting periods of charity companies beginning on or after 1 April 2000, a tax exemption applies, on a claim made to the Board, to profits and other income which is chargeable to tax under Schedule D, Case I or Case VI and is not otherwise exempted from tax, provided the income is applied solely for the purposes of the charity and either

(*a*)   the gross income (potentially within this exemption and before deducting expenses) for the chargeable period, i.e. the tax year or company accounting period, does not exceed the 'requisite limit'; or

(*b*)   the charity had, at the beginning of the chargeable period, a reasonable expectation that its gross income (as above) would not exceed that limit.

The '*requisite limit*' is the greater of

(1)   £5,000, and

(2)   the lesser of £50,000 and 25% of the charity's total incoming resources for the chargeable period.

Both the above monetary limits are proportionately reduced for chargeable periods of less than twelve months.

14.8 Charities

The extension of the exemption to SCHEDULE D, CASE VI (74) income is intended to cover miscellaneous fund-raising activities not within Case I. Certain specified tax charges under Case VI are excluded.

[*FA 2000, s 46*].

The Revenue's interim guidance is that they will consider any evidence to satisfy the reasonable expectation test in (*b*) above. Such evidence may include minutes of meetings at which the expectations were discussed, copies of cash-flow forecasts and business plans prepared for these meetings and copies of the previous year's accounts.

(ii) **Small-scale fund-raising events.** Before 1 April 2000, profits from events such as bazaars, jumble sales, gymkhanas, carnivals etc., arranged by voluntary organisations or charities, held for, and promoted as being held for, the purpose of raising funds for charity, are not taxed if

(*a*) the organisation or charity is not regularly carrying on these trading activities,

(*b*) it is not competing with other traders, and

(*c*) the profits are transferred to charities or otherwise applied for charitable purposes.

After 31 March 2000, the exemption is extended to cover up to 15 of each type of event in any one location in any financial year of the charity etc. and includes events accessed electronically. Small events, e.g. jumble sales or coffee mornings, do not count toward the limit to the extent that the gross takings therefrom do not exceed £1,000 in any week. The limit of 15 is increased or reduced proportionately for financial years of more or less than 12 months.

The extended exemption brings the definition of a qualifying event in line with the corresponding VAT exemption for fund-raising events, for which see the corresponding chapter of Tolley's Value Added Tax. Any event meeting the criteria for the VAT exemption will automatically qualify for the income tax exemption if the condition at (*c*) above is satisfied.

(Revenue Pamphlet IR 1, C4 as revised).

(iii) **Lotteries.** Lottery profits applied solely to the charity's purposes are exempt, provided that the lottery is promoted and conducted in accordance with *Lotteries and Amusements Act 1976, s 3* or *s 5* (or NI equivalent). [*ICTA 1988, s 505(1)(f); FA 1995, s 138*].

(iv) **Underwriting commissions** are taxable, whether chargeable under Schedule D, Case I (as trading income) or Case VI.

See generally Revenue Pamphlet IR 2001.

14.8 **Capital gains.** Charities are exempt from capital gains tax on gains applicable, and applied, for charitable purposes. [*TCGA 1992, s 256(1)*]. But this exemption does not apply to gains arising where property which ceases to be subject to charitable trusts is then deemed to have been sold, and immediately re-acquired, at market value. Any CGT on such gains may be assessed within three years after the year of assessment in which the cessation occurs. [*TCGA 1992, s 256(2)*]. For payments made after 9 August 1998 (and for earlier payments in cases where the tax liability remains open), the exemption applies to liability under *TCGA 1992, s 87* in respect of capital payments received from offshore trusts. (Revenue Tax Bulletin August 1998 pp 573, 574). See also 52.8 OFFSHORE FUNDS as regards certain offshore gains.

14.9   **Miscellaneous.** Charities are exempt from tax on offshore income gains — see 52.8 OFFSHORE FUNDS.

Charitable unit trust schemes are excluded from the normal income tax treatment of unauthorised unit trusts, and are thus able to pass on their income to participating charities without deducting tax. [*SI 1988 No 267; SI 1994 No 1479*].

14.10   **Restrictions on exemptions.** A restriction of the exemptions in 14.3 above applies in any chargeable period in which a charity

(*a*)   has 'relevant income and gains' of £10,000 or more (but see below) which exceed the amount of its 'qualifying expenditure', and

(*b*)   incurs, or is treated as incurring, 'non-qualifying expenditure'.

Where (*a*) and (*b*) above apply, exemption under *ICTA 1988, s 505(1)* and *TCGA 1992, s 256* is not available for so much of the excess at (*a*) as does not exceed the 'non-qualifying expenditure' incurred in that period. Where the exemption is not so available, the charity may, by notice in writing, specify which items of its 'relevant income and gains' are wholly or partly to be attributed to the amount concerned (covenanted payments to the charity, see 14.17 below, being treated as a single item where due from individuals before 6 April 2000 or from companies before 1 April 2000). If, within 30 days of a request to do so, the charity does not give such notice, the Board determines the attribution. [*ICTA 1988, s 505(3)(6); FA 1995, Sch 17 para 7; FA 2000, s 41(5)(9)*].

The £10,000 *de minimis* limit in (*a*) above is proportionately reduced where a chargeable period is less than twelve months, and does not apply where two or more charities acting in concert are engaged in transactions aimed at tax avoidance and where the Board, by notice in writing, so direct. An appeal, as against a decision on a claim, may be made against such a notice. [*ICTA 1988, s 505(4)(7)(8)*].

'*Relevant income and gains*' means the aggregate of

(i)   income which, apart from *ICTA 1988, s 505(1)*, would not be exempt from tax, together with any income which is taxable notwithstanding *section 505(1)*, and

(ii)   gains which, apart from *TCGA 1992, s 256*, would be chargeable gains, together with any gains which are chargeable gains notwithstanding *section 256*. [*ICTA 1988, s 505(5)*].

'*Non-qualifying expenditure*' is expenditure other than 'qualifying expenditure'. If the charity invests any funds in an investment which is not a 'qualifying investment', or makes a loan (not as an investment) which is not a 'qualifying loan', the amount invested or lent is treated as non-qualifying expenditure. Where the investment or loan is realised or repaid in whole or in part in the chargeable period in which it was made, any further investment or lending of the sum realised or repaid in that period is, to the extent that it does not exceed the sum originally invested or lent, ignored in arriving at non-qualifying expenditure of the period.

Where the aggregate of the qualifying and non-qualifying expenditure incurred in a chargeable period (the '*primary period*') exceeds the relevant income and gains of that period, so much of the excess as does not exceed the non-qualifying expenditure constitutes '*unapplied non-qualifying expenditure*'. Except to the extent (if any) that it represents the expenditure of 'non-taxable sums' received in the primary period, the unapplied non-qualifying expenditure may be treated as non-qualifying expenditure of a chargeable period ending not more than six years before the end of the primary period. '*Non-taxable sums*' are donations, legacies and other sums of a similar nature which, apart from *ICTA 1988, s 505(1)* and *TCGA 1992, s 256*, are not within the charge to tax.

Where an amount of unapplied non-qualifying expenditure (the '*excess expenditure*') falls to be treated as non-qualifying expenditure of earlier periods, it is attributed only to those periods in which, apart from the attribution in question but taking account of any previous attribution, the relevant income and gains exceed the aggregate of the qualifying and non-qualifying expenditure in that period; and such attribution is not to be greater than the excess. Attributions are made to later periods in priority to earlier periods. Any excess expenditure which cannot be attributed to an earlier period is ignored altogether for attribution purposes. Adjustments by way of further assessments etc. are made in consequence of an attribution to an earlier period. [*ICTA 1988, s 506(1)(4)–(6), Sch 20 Pt III*].

'*Qualifying expenditure*' is expenditure incurred for charitable purposes only. A payment made (or to be made) to a body situated outside the UK is not qualifying expenditure unless the charity concerned has taken all reasonable steps to ensure that the payment will be applied for charitable purposes. Expenditure incurred in a particular period may be treated as incurred in another period if it is properly chargeable against income of that other period and is referable to commitments (contractual or otherwise) entered into before or during that other period. [*ICTA 1988, s 506(1)–(3)*].

'*Qualifying investments*' are the following.

(A) Investments within *Trustee Investments Act 1961, Sch 1 Pts I, II (para 13* (mortgages etc.) excepted) and *III*.

(B) Investments in a common investment fund established under *Charities Act 1960, s 22* (or NI equivalent) or *Charities Act 1993, s 24* or similar funds under other enactments.

(C) Investments in a common deposit fund established under *Charities Act 1960, s 22A* or *Charities Act 1993, s 25* or similar funds under other enactments (from 1 September 1992).

(D) Any interest in land other than a mortgage etc.

(E) Shares or securities of a company listed on a recognised stock exchange (within *ICTA 1988, s 841*) or dealt in on the Unlisted Securities Market.

(F) Units in unit trusts within *Financial Services and Markets Act 2000, s 237(1)*.

(G) Deposits with a recognised bank or licensed institution (but see below) in respect of which interest is payable at a commercial rate, but excluding a deposit made as part of an arrangement whereby the bank etc. makes a loan to a third party.

(H) CERTIFICATES OF DEPOSIT (12) within *ICTA 1988, s 56(5)*.

(I) Loans or other investments as to which the Board are satisfied, on a claim, that the loans or other investments are made for the benefit of the charity and not for the avoidance of tax (whether by the charity or by a third party). Loans secured by mortgage etc. over land are eligible.

Deposits within (G) above (and money placed within (3) below) on or after 29 April 1996 must be with a bank within *ICTA 1988, s 840A* (see 7.1 BANKS) rather than with a recognised bank or licensed institution.

There is guidance at www.inlandrevenue.gov.uk/charities/annex_iii.htm as to the approach the Revenue adopt in deciding whether or not a particular investment is a qualifying investment. As regards swap contracts, e.g. interest rate or currency swaps, see Revenue Tax Bulletin August 2003 p 1056.

'*Qualifying loans*'. A loan which is not made by way of investment is a qualifying loan if it is one of the following.

(1) A loan made to another charity for charitable purposes only.

(2) A loan to a beneficiary of the charity which is made in the course of carrying out the purposes of the charity.

(3)   Money placed on a current account with a recognised bank or licensed institution (as in (G) above) otherwise than under arrangements as in (G) above.

(4)   A loan, not within (1) to (3) above, as to which the Board are satisfied, on a claim, that the loan is made for the benefit of the charity and not for the avoidance of tax (whether by the charity or by a third party).

[*ICTA 1988, Sch 20 Pts I, II; Charities Act 1992, Sch 6 para 17; SI 1992 No 1900; FA 1996, Sch 37 paras 2, 5, 10, Sch 38 para 6; SI 2001 No 3629, Article 50*].

Payments between charities. Any payment received by one charity from another, other than in return for full consideration, which would otherwise not be chargeable to tax (and which is not of a description within any of the relieving provisions of *ICTA 1988, s 505(1)*, see 14.4–14.7 above), is chargeable to tax under Schedule D, Case III, but is eligible for relief under *ICTA 1988, s 505(1)(c)* (see 14.5 above) as if it were an annual payment. [*ICTA 1988, s 505(2)*].

Simon's Direct Tax Service. See **C4.527**.

14.11   **GIFT AID DONATIONS BY INDIVIDUALS**

Gifts of money made by individuals to charities which are 'qualifying donations' (see 14.13 below) attract tax relief under the Gift Aid scheme described below. Significant changes were made to the scheme with effect from 6 April 2000, including the removal of the £250 minimum limit on qualifying donations and the inclusion in Gift Aid of payments under deed of covenant. For the Gift Aid scheme as it applies to company donors, see the corresponding chapter of Tolley's Corporation Tax.

For the purposes of these provisions, '*charity*' has the meaning in 14.1 above but also includes the bodies listed in *ICTA 1988, s 507* (see 29.3, 29.9, 29.14, 29.20 EXEMPT ORGANISATIONS). [*FA 1990, s 25(12)(a)*]. For extension of the relief to gifts to community amateur sports clubs under *FA 2002, Sch 18*, see Tolley's Corporation Tax under Clubs and Societies.

A detailed guide to Gift Aid is available on the Revenue website at www.inlandrevenue.gov.uk/charities/chapter_3.htm.

Simon's Direct Tax Service. See **E1.504A**.

14.12   **Donations after 5 April 2000.** The provisions described below apply to gifts made after 5 April 2000 other than by deed of covenant, and also to covenanted payments (see 14.17 below) *due* after that date. [*FA 2000, s 39(10)*]. An amount due after 5 April 2000 under a pre-existing deed of covenant providing for payment of a fixed gross amount is determined as if basic rate tax continued to be deductible at source, even though this is not, in fact, the case (see 14.17 below). [*FA 2000, s 41(8)*].

The donor. Where a 'qualifying donation' to charity is made by an individual ('*the donor*') in a tax year, then, for that year, he is treated for the purposes of income tax (and capital gains tax) as if

(*a*)   the gift had been made after deduction of income tax at the basic rate; and

(*b*)   the basic rate limit (see 1.3 ALLOWANCES AND TAX RATES) were increased by an amount equal to the 'grossed up amount of the gift', i.e. the amount which, after deducting income tax at the basic rate for the tax year in which the gift is made, leaves the amount of the gift.

The donor obtains higher rate relief, where applicable, by virtue of (*b*) above. For this purpose, higher rate relief generally means relief for the excess of tax at the higher rate over tax at the basic rate for which relief is effectively given at source by virtue of (*a*) above (but see the second example at 14.15 below for the situation where there is savings income or dividend income). The increase in the basic rate limit does not apply for the purposes of computing top-slicing relief as in 45.13 LIFE ASSURANCE POLICIES.

To the extent, if any, necessary to ensure that he is charged to an amount of income tax and capital gains tax equal to the tax treated under (*a*) above as deducted from the gift, the donor is *not* entitled to personal reliefs. These include both reliefs given by deduction from total income (e.g. the personal allowance) and reliefs given as a tax reduction, but the restriction does not adversely affect the donor's ability to transfer unused children's tax credit to a partner as in 1.18 ALLOWANCES AND TAX RATES, or unused married couple's allowance to a spouse as in 47.1 MARRIED PERSONS. Where the tax treated as deducted nevertheless exceeds what would otherwise be his income tax and capital gains tax liability for the year, the donor is liable to income tax at the basic rate on so much of the gift as is necessary to recover an amount of tax equal to the excess. However, in determining *for this purpose* what would otherwise be his liability, the following charges and credits are disregarded:

(*a*) any basic rate tax charged by virtue of *ICTA 1988, ss 3, 348* or *ss 349, 350* (tax due by the maker of annual payments — see 22 DEDUCTION OF TAX AT SOURCE);

(*b*) any notional tax treated as having been paid under *ICTA 1988, s 233(1)(a)* (taxation of certain recipients of distributions — see 1.9 ALLOWANCES AND TAX RATES), *ICTA 1988, s 249(4)(a)* (see 85.1 STOCK DIVIDENDS), or *ICTA 1988, s 547(5)(a)* (gains on LIFE ASSURANCE POLICIES (45.13));

(*c*) any personal reliefs, or relief for maintenance payments, falling to be given by way of an income tax reduction (see 1.15, 1.16, 1.18 ALLOWANCES AND TAX RATES, 47.8 MARRIED PERSONS);

(*d*) any DOUBLE TAX RELIEF (24) (whether given under a double tax agreement or unilaterally);

(*e*) any set-off of tax deducted, or treated as deducted, from income *other than*

   (i) tax treated as deducted from income by virtue of *ICTA 1988, s 421(1)(a)* (taxation of borrower when loan released etc. — see 27.3 EXCESS LIABILITY), or

   (ii) tax treated as deducted from a relevant amount within the meaning of *ICTA 1988, s 699A* (untaxed sums comprised in the income of an estate — see 21.3 DECEASED ESTATES) except to the extent that the relevant amount is or would be paid in respect of a distribution chargeable to income tax under Schedule F; and

(*f*) any set-off of tax credits on dividends (see 1.9 ALLOWANCES AND TAX RATES).

For the purposes of applying the income limit for age-related personal allowance and married couple's allowance (see 1.14, 1.15 ALLOWANCES AND TAX RATES), the donor's total income is reduced by the aggregate grossed up amount of his qualifying donations for the tax year.

[*FA 1990, s 25(1)(6)(a)(c), (8)–(9A)(12)(d); FA 2000, s 39(6)*].

See the examples at 14.15 below.

Carry-back of relief. For gifts made after 5 April 2003, the donor may elect for a qualifying donation to be treated for the purposes of the relief as having been made in the previous tax year, provided that the grossed up amount of the gift would, if made in that previous year, be payable out of profits or gains brought into charge to income tax or capital gains tax for that year. The election must be made in writing to the Revenue by the date of delivery of the self-assessment return for the previous year, and not later than 31 January following the end of that year. The election affects only the tax position of the donor. As regards the recipient charity, the donation continues to be treated as made in the tax year in which it is in fact made. [*FA 2002, s 98*].

Giving through the self-assessment return. Where, as a result of his filing a personal self-assessment tax return for 2003/04 or any subsequent year, an individual is entitled to an income tax and/or capital gains tax repayment (after any set-off against liabilities) for one or more years, he may (within the tax return itself) authorise the Revenue to make the repayment (or a specified part of it) by means of a gift to a single charity specified by him (and for this purpose the amount of the repayment is taken as being inclusive of any repayment supplement due — see 41 INTEREST ON OVERPAID TAX). The specified charity must be included on the list maintained for these purposes by the Revenue. (Charities need to apply to the Revenue to be included on the list.) The gift must meet the conditions at 14.13(*b*), (*d*), (*e*) and (*f*) below. It is then treated as a qualifying donation made by the individual at the time the payment is received by the charity. The carry-back facility above is *not* available. [*FA 2004, s 83*]. In practice, taxpayers are required to enter on the return the unique reference code allocated to the charity of their choice; there is a search facility at www.inlandrevenue.gov.uk/charities/charities-search.htm to assist in finding the code required.

The charity. The receipt by a charity of a qualifying donation is treated as the receipt, under deduction of basic rate tax for the tax year in which the gift is made, of an annual payment equal to the grossed up amount of the gift. [*FA 1990, s 25(10)*]. The charity can reclaim the basic rate tax from the Revenue. In the case of a gift made via the self-assessment tax return (see above), the charity is treated as having made any necessary claim for exemption from tax under Schedule D, Case III (see 14.5 above), which means that it will receive back the basic rate tax without having to reclaim it. [*FA 2004, s 83(4)*].

14.13   *Qualifying donations.* A '*qualifying donation*' is a gift to a charity by the donor which meets the following conditions:

(*a*)   it takes the form of a payment of a sum of money;

(*b*)   it is not subject to a condition as to repayment;

(*c*)   it is not deductible under the payroll deduction scheme — see 14.18 below);

(*d*)   neither the donor nor any person connected with him (see 19 CONNECTED PERSONS) receives any benefit, in consequence of making it, in excess of specified limits (see 14.14 below);

(*e*)   it is not conditional on or associated with, or part of an arrangement involving, the acquisition of property by the charity, otherwise than by way of gift, from the donor or a person connected with him;

(*f*)   either

   (i)   at the time it is made the donor is UK-resident or is in Crown employment as defined by *ITEPA 2003, s 28(2)* (i.e. employment under the Crown which is of a public nature and the earnings from which are payable out of UK public revenue), or

   (ii)   the grossed up amount of the gift (see 14.12(*b*) above) would, if in fact made, be payable out of profits or gains brought into charge to income tax or capital gains tax; and

(*g*)   the donor gives the charity an 'appropriate declaration' in relation to it.

An '*appropriate declaration*' for the purposes of (*g*) above is a declaration which is given in the form and manner prescribed by regulations. It may be made in writing, by fax, over the internet or orally (e.g. by telephone). It must contain the donor's name and address, the name of the charity, a description of the gift(s) to which it relates, a statement that the gift(s) is (are) to be treated as qualifying donations for these purposes, and, where the declaration is in writing, a note explaining the requirement that the donor pays an amount of income tax or capital gains tax equal to the tax deducted from the donation. No signature is required. Oral declarations must be recorded in writing by the charity. A written record of the oral declaration must be sent to the donor by the charity, accompanied by a note explaining the requirement that the donor pays an amount of income tax or capital gains tax equal to the tax deducted from the donation. The written record must state the date on which it is sent to the donor, who may cancel the declaration by written notice to the charity within 30 days of that date. [*SI 2000 No 2074*]. Payments under a pre-6 April 2000 deed of covenant need not be covered by a declaration (see Inland Revenue Guidance Note for Charities, para 5.28).

[*FA 1990, s 25(1)–(3A)(11); FA 2000, s 39(1)–(4); ITEPA 2003, Sch 6 para 166; FA 2004, Sch 17 para 5*].

As regards (*d*) above, the benefit does not have to be received from the charity to be taken into account (see *St Dunstan's v Major (Sp C 127), [1997] SSCD 212*, in which the saving of inheritance tax by personal representatives as a result of the variation of a will to provide for a donation which would otherwise qualify under these provisions constituted a benefit).

The release of a loan not for consideration and not under seal cannot amount to a gift of money (see *Battle Baptist Church v CIR and Woodham (Sp C 23), [1995] SSCD 176*).

14.14   *Limits on donor benefits.* Where the donor or a person connected with him (see 19 CONNECTED PERSONS) receives a benefit or benefits in consequence of making the gift, the gift will not be a qualifying donation if either:

(*a*)   the aggregate value of the benefits received exceeds

     (i)   where the gift is £100 or less, 25% of the amount of the gift;

     (ii)   where the gift is greater than £100 but not more than £1,000, £25;

     (iii)   where the gift is greater than £1,000, 2.5% of the amount of the gift; or

(*b*)   the aggregate of the value of the benefits received in relation to the gift and the value of any benefits received in relation to any qualifying donations previously made to the charity by the donor in the same tax year exceeds £250.

Where a benefit:

(1)   consists of the right to receive benefits at intervals over a period of less than twelve months;

(2)   relates to a period of less than twelve months; or

(3)   is one of a series of benefits received at intervals in consequence of making a series of gifts at intervals of less than twelve months,

the value of the benefit and the amount of the gift are 'annualised' for the purposes of (*a*) above. Where a one-off benefit is received in consequence of making a gift which is one of a series of gifts made at intervals of less than twelve months, the amount of the gift (but not the value of the benefit) is likewise annualised. For these purposes a gift or benefit is '*annualised*' by multiplying the amount or value by 365 and dividing the result by the number of days in the period of less than twelve months or the average number of days in the intervals of less than twelve months as appropriate.

In applying the above limits, the benefit of a right of free or reduced-price admission for the donor or a member of his family

(A)   to view property, the preservation of which for the public benefit is the sole or main purpose of the charity; or

(B)   to observe wildlife, the conservation of which for the public benefit is the sole or main purpose of the charity;

is disregarded provided that the opportunity to make gifts which attract such a right is available to members of the public. For the wider application in practice of this relief, see para 3.48 of the Revenue guide referred to at 14.11 above.

[*FA 1990, s 25(2)(e), (4)–(5G)(11); FA 2000, s 39(1)(3)(5)*].

Acknowledgement of a donor in the charity's literature does not amount to a benefit *provided that* it does not take the form of an advertisement for the donor's business (see para 3.27 of the Revenue guide referred to at 14.11 above).

14.15   *Examples*

Higher rate taxpayer (1). Ronan, a single man under 65, has total income of £37,600 for 2004/05 which consists entirely of earned income. During that year, he makes various single donations and covenanted payments to charity, all of them qualifying donations, amounting in total to £585.

			£
Total income			37,600
Less Personal Allowance			4,745
Taxable Income			£32,855
Tax Liability			
	2,020	@ 10%	202.00
	30,130	@ 22%	6,628.60
	32,150		
	705	@ 40%	282.00
	£32,855		
			£7,112.60

Note

The basic rate limit of £31,400 is increased by the grossed up amount of the qualifying donations (£585 × 100/78 = £750) and becomes £32,150. Ronan thereby saves tax of £135 (£750 × 18% (40% – 22%)). The charities will reclaim basic rate tax of £165 (£750 × 22%) and will thus receive £750 in all. The net cost to Ronan is £450 (£585 – £135), a saving of 40%.

Higher rate taxpayer (2).The tax relief can, in fact, exceed 40% where the effect of extending the basic rate limit is that an additional amount of savings/dividend income falls within the basic rate band and is taxed at 20%/10% instead of at 40%/32.5%. Imagine the facts are as above but that £7,600 of Ronan's income is savings income (chargeable at 20% if within the basic rate band) with the remaining £30,000 being earned income as before.

14.16 Charities

		£
Total income		37,600
Less Personal Allowance		4,745
Taxable Income		£32,855

Tax Liability

2,020	@ 10%	202.00
23,235	@ 22%	5,111.70
6,895	@ 20%	1,379.00
32,150		
705	@ 40%	282.00
£32,855		
		£6,974.70

Note

Ronan now saves tax of £150 (£750 × 20% (40% – 20%)). The charities will still reclaim basic rate tax of £165 (£750 × 22%) and will receive £750 in all. The net cost to Ronan is £435 (£585 – £150), a saving of 42%.

Low income taxpayer. Rod, a single person of 66, has a State pension of £4,200 and dividends of £2,700 (with tax credits of £300) for 2004/05. He makes a qualifying donation of £390 to charity.

		£
Pension		4,200
Dividends plus tax credits		3,000
Total income		7,200
Less Personal Allowance	6,830	
Restricted by (note (*a*))	730	6,100
Taxable Income		£1,100

Tax Liability

£1,100 @ 10% (starting rate)	110.00
Deduct tax credits on dividends (note (*b*))	110.00
	Nil

Notes

(*a*)   The personal allowance is restricted by such amount as is necessary to leave tax of £110.00 in charge, this being the amount of basic rate tax deemed to have been deducted at source from the qualifying donation (£390 × 22/78 = £110). Although the donor's liability is, in fact, reduced to nil by dividend tax credits, no further charge arises in respect of the donation (as such credits are among the items to be disregarded for this purpose — see 14.12 above).

(*b*)   Although dividend tax credits of £300 are available, the deduction is limited to the amount necessary to reduce the liability to nil (as, for 1999/2000 onwards, dividend tax credits are not repayable — see 1.9 ALLOWANCES AND TAX RATES).

14.16   **Donations before 6 April 2000.** Where a 'qualifying donation' to charity is made by an individual before 6 April 2000, it is treated as if it were a covenanted payment (see 14.17

below) made at the same time as the gift, i.e. as if it were a payment of the corresponding grossed up amount paid under deduction of basic rate tax. Higher rate relief is available where appropriate in respect of the grossed up amount. Where the covenanted payment, had it been made, would not, or not wholly, have been payable out of income taxed at the basic (or higher) rate, the basic rate tax deemed to have been deducted (or the difference between that tax and tax at the lower or starting rate) or a corresponding proportion thereof, is chargeable on the donor.

ICTA 1988, ss 348 et seq. (annual payments — see 22.1 *et seq.* DEDUCTION OF TAX AT SOURCE) do not apply to such deemed payments. The charity may, however, claim repayment of tax deemed to have been deducted (as in 14.17(*a*) below).

A gift is a '*qualifying donation*' if it satisfies the conditions at 14.13(*a*)(*b*)(*c*) and (*e*) above, plus each of the following conditions:

(*a*) its amount is at least £250;

(*b*) it is not, in fact, a covenanted payment to charity;

(*c*) either of the following applies:

  (i) neither the donor nor a person connected with him (see 19 CONNECTED PERSONS) receives a benefit in consequence of the gift, or

  (ii) the aggregate value of all such benefits so received in consequence of the gift does not exceed one-fortieth of the amount of the gift, and the total value of such benefits so received in respect of the gift and any other gifts made by the donor to the charity earlier in the tax year does not exceed £250;

(*d*) the donor is UK resident at the time of the gift; and

(*e*) the donor gives the charity a certificate in prescribed form (i.e. Form R190(SD)) in relation to the gift, to the effect that the gift satisfies all the necessary conditions, and that the tax deemed to have been deducted has been or will be accounted for, either directly or by payment out of taxed income. (After 5 April 1999, charities no longer have to submit forms R190(SD) in support of a repayment claim, but need to retain the forms for inspection by IR Charities at any time.)

[*FA 1990, s 25; FA 1991, s 71(5)(6); FA 1993, s 67(2)(4); FA 1995, s 74, Sch 17 para 26*].

See 14.21 below for Millennium Gift Aid.

14.17 **COVENANTED PAYMENTS DUE BEFORE 6 APRIL 2000**

The separate tax relief below for payments to a charity made under a deed of covenant by an individual is withdrawn for payments *falling due* after 5 April 2000, as is the entitlement under *ICTA 1988, s 348(3)* and the requirement under *ICTA 1988, s 349(1)* to deduct tax at source. [*ICTA 1988, s 348(3), s 349(1); FA 2000, s 41(3)(4)(9)*]. Such payments are no longer charges on income (see 1.10 ALLOWANCES AND TAX RATES), but instead are dealt with under the Gift Aid regime (see 14.11–14.14 above). Where a covenanted payment falling due before 6 April 2000 is made on or after that date, the rules below continue to apply (with tax deductible at the basic rate in force when the covenanted payment fell due, rather than when it is made).

A '*covenanted payment to charity*' is a payment under a covenant in favour of a body of persons or trust established for charitable purposes only (including any of the bodies mentioned in *ICTA 1988, s 507* — see 29.3, 29.9, 29.14, 29.20 EXEMPT ORGANISATIONS) and under which the annual payments become payable for a period which can exceed three years. The covenant must not be for a consideration in money or money's worth and can

14.17 Charities

only be terminable within the three-year period with the consent of the charity. [*ICTA 1988, s 347A(7)(8); FA 1995, Sch 17 para 4(2); FA 2000, s 41(2)(9)*].

(a) **'Tax-free' subscriptions to charities.** If made by deed of covenant legally binding the taxpayer to pay for a period capable of exceeding three years such a sum as, after deduction of tax at the basic rate, will leave a stated amount, the charity benefits by treating that *gross* sum as its income and claiming refund of the difference as tax deducted from it. In practice, some covenants provide for payment of a fixed gross amount, in which case similar consequences ensue but the net payment to be made by the donor varies with changes in the basic rate of tax. An expiring deed must be renewed immediately if the arrangement is desired to continue; relief to charity has been refused on payments made between the expiry of the old deed and the coming into operation of the new. See 14.16 above as regards certain donations treated as made under covenant. See *Racal Group Services Ltd v Ashmore CA 1995 68 TC 86* for an unsuccessful attempt retrospectively to amend a deed to achieve the intended effect for tax purposes.

(b) Covenanted payments must be **pure income** in the hands of the charity and not a payment by the covenantor for goods, services or benefits to him (see 22.10 DEDUCTION OF TAX AT SOURCE and *Campbell & Anor v CIR HL 1968, 45 TC 427; National Book League CA 1957, 37 TC 455; Taw & Torridge Festival Socy Ltd v CIR Ch D 1959, 38 TC 603*). In relation to charities (and certain bodies treated as charities) for the preservation of property or the conservation of wildlife, certain admission rights in return for payments to the charity are ignored for this purpose. [*FA 1989, s 59; FA 2000, s 41(7)(9)*]. Generally, in the case of ordinary small subscriptions, benefits available to subscribers up to 25% of the subscription are ignored. (Revenue Press Release 20 March 1990).

(c) The long-standing practice of the Revenue, to accept **retrospective validation** of payments made earlier in the tax year in which the deed was made, ceased for covenants made after 30 July 1990. This followed the decision in *Morley-Clarke v Jones CA 1985, 59 TC 567*, see 47.8 MARRIED PERSONS. (Revenue Pamphlet IR 131, SP 4/90, 20 March 1990).

(d) The insertion of **escape clauses** in a deed which enable the covenantor of his own volition to terminate the covenant without the consent of the charity concerned (e.g. where payments cease on the covenantor voluntarily ceasing to work for his current employer) may invalidate the covenant for tax purposes. Covenants which had been accepted by the Revenue as valid, and on which repayments of tax had been made, but which were invalid as a result of escape clauses, were treated as effective until they expired. (Revenue Pamphlet IR 131, SP 4/90, 20 March 1990).

(e) For **claims** relating to deeds of covenant, from 6 April 1999, individuals are no longer required to complete form R185(Covenant) and companies are not required to complete form R185(AP). (The deeds themselves are now used by IR Charities for audit purposes.) All claims by a charity are made on a new single sheet form R68 accompanied by a schedule or schedules of income included in the claim (although previously approved computerised schedules could continue to be used until 5 April 2000). Previously, for deeds of covenant by individuals, forms R185(Covenant) were required for the first-year claims and, for covenants by companies, forms R185(AP) were required for all payments. The new single sheet form R68 replaced a four-page form requiring similar details. Proper records must be kept in support of claims, and should be retained for up to six years after the expiry of the covenants. (Revenue Press Release 7 May 1992). See generally the Charity Tax Pack obtainable from IR Charities, St John's House, Merton Road, Bootle, Merseyside L69 9BB.

(f)   To minimise any delay in making **repayments** of tax to charities, the Revenue will, in general, provisionally repay tax apparently suffered by deduction before the full verification procedure has been completed, but they reserve the right to make enquiries into the claim at a later date, which may result in a payment back to the Revenue. (Revenue Pamphlet IR 131, SP 3/87, 26 March 1987).

(g)   **Claims for repayment** must be made within five years after 31 January following the tax year in which the payment is due. A claim for repayment of tax deducted from covenanted donations was refused where the claim was made more than six years after the end of the years of assessment within which the payments were due, although the payments had in fact been made within the six years preceding the date of claim (*CIR v Crawley Ch D 1986, 59 TC 728*).

See Revenue Tax Bulletin October 1998 pp 597, 598 for additional commentary on the validity of covenants.

14.18   **PAYROLL GIVING SCHEMES**

Under an 'approved payroll giving scheme', an individual may make charitable donations, without limit for 2000/01 onwards (previously a limit of £1,200 per tax year applied), by deduction from earnings (or pension income or taxable social security income) subject to PAYE (55). At the individual's request, the employer (or other payer) withholds sums from gross pay as 'donations'. The amount of the donations is allowed as a deduction from gross pay for PAYE purposes and in calculating the individual's taxable income. For 2003/04 onwards, the deduction is made from the particular type of income (e.g. employment income) in respect of which the donations are made; previously, it was a global deduction in charging tax under Schedule E. The deduction is made for the tax year in which the donation is withheld or, for 2003/04 onwards (and, in practice, for earlier years also) as regards pension and social security income only, for the tax year in which the income out of which the deduction is made is chargeable to tax. A donation made under a payroll giving scheme is not a qualifying donation for Gift Aid purposes (see 14.13 above).

'*Donations*' are sums withheld by the payer under a scheme which at that time is an 'approved payroll giving scheme' and which constitute gifts by the individual to one or more charities specified by him and satisfy any conditions set out in the scheme. For 1999/2000 and earlier years, it was a further requirement that the gifts were not due under a deed of covenant. An '*approved payroll giving scheme*' is a scheme approved by (or of a kind approved by) the Revenue under which the payer is required to pay to an 'approved agent' the sums withheld and the agent is required to pass them on to the specified charities. An '*approved agent*' is a body approved by the Revenue for the purpose of paying donations to one or more charities; if the agent is itself a charity specified by the individual, it may retain any sum due to itself. A list of approved agents is available on the Revenue's website at www.inlandrevenue.gov.uk/payrollgiving/employers/index.htm.

For these purposes, '*charity*' is as defined in 14.1 above, but, as regards payroll deductions made for 2000/01 onwards, also includes the bodies listed in *ICTA 1988, s 507* (see 29.3, 29.9, 29.14, 29.20 EXEMPT ORGANISATIONS).

Administrative regulations may be made by statutory instrument regarding such matters as

(i)   the grant or withdrawal of approval by the Revenue of schemes and agents, and appeals to the Special Commissioners against the Revenue's decision,

(ii)   the requirements of kinds of schemes and qualifications of agents,

(iii)   the production of documents and records by a participating payer or agent within a specified time, and

(iv)   production of other information to the Revenue.

Such regulations are contained in *The Charitable Deductions (Approved Schemes) Regulations 1986 (SI 1986 No 2211)* as amended.

Penalties apply for failure to comply with (iii) and (iv) above under *TMA 1970, s 98*.

As regards payroll deductions made after 5 April 2000 and before 6 April 2004, the agent will pay to the nominated charity a supplement equal to 10% of the payroll deduction. The supplement is funded or reimbursed by the Revenue and must be paid by the agent etc. within a prescribed period. No claim for funding or reimbursement will be accepted after 5 April 2005. *SI 2000 No 2083* and *SI 2003 No 1745* (which amend the administrative regulations referred to above) make similar provision as regards accounting, record-keeping etc. in relation to the supplement as applies in relation to the donations themselves.

[*ITEPA 2003, ss 713–715, Sch 6 paras 137, 243, Sch 8; ICTA 1988, s 202; FA 1996, s 109; FA 2000, s 38; FA 2003, s 146*].

Administrative costs. Voluntary contributions made by an employer to assist an approved agent with its costs in managing a payroll giving scheme on the employer's behalf are deductible in computing the profits of a trade, profession or vocation, or as management expenses of an investment company. [*ICTA 1988, s 86A; FA 1993, s 69; ITEPA 2003, Sch 6 para 13*].

Simon's Direct Tax Service. See E4.948.

14.19   **GIFTS IN KIND TO CHARITIES**

With effect **from 27 July 1999**, relief is available to persons (including companies) carrying on a trade, profession or vocation who give certain articles to charities within *ICTA 1988, s 506* (see 14.1 above) or to bodies treated as such under *ICTA 1988, s 507(1)* (see 29.3, 29.9, 29.14, 29.20 EXEMPT ORGANISATIONS). The gift must consist of either:

(*a*)   articles manufactured, or of a type sold, in the course of the donor's trade; or

(*b*)   plant or machinery (see 9.25 CAPITAL ALLOWANCES) used in the donor's trade, profession, vocation or property business.

Where the donor is eligible for the relief, then

•   (where (*a*) above applies) no amount is required to be brought into account for tax purposes in respect of the donated article as a trading receipt; and

•   (where (*b*) above applies) the disposal value (see 9.29 CAPITAL ALLOWANCES) of the donated item is nil. (Before *CAA 2001* had effect, see 9.1 CAPITAL ALLOWANCES, this operated slightly differently in that no disposal value was required to be brought into account.)

However, if the donor or any connected person (see 19 CONNECTED PERSONS) receives any benefit in any way attributable to the gift, the donor is chargeable on an amount equal to the value of that benefit, for the chargeable period in which it is received, under either Schedule D, Case I or II or, if he is not chargeable to tax under either of those Cases for that period, under Schedule D, Case VI.

[*ICTA 1988, s 83A; FA 1999, s 55; CAA 2001, s 63(2)–(4), Sch 2 para 16*].

See 14.21 below for the earlier, more limited relief for gifts for third world health or education.

For extension of these reliefs to gifts to community amateur sports clubs under *FA 2002, Sch 18*, see Tolley's Corporation Tax under Clubs and Societies.

Simon's Direct Tax Service. See B3.1445A.

14.20   **GIFTS OF SHARES, SECURITIES AND REAL PROPERTY TO CHARITIES**

Income tax relief is available on a non-arm's length disposal after 5 April 2000, by an individual to a 'charity', of the whole of the beneficial interest in a 'qualifying investment'. This is in addition to the pre-existing capital gains tax relief for assets generally, for which see the corresponding chapter of Tolley's Capital Gains Tax. '*Charity*' has the meaning in 14.1 above, but also includes the bodies listed in *ICTA 1988, s 507* (see 29.3, 29.9, 29.14, 29.20 EXEMPT ORGANISATIONS). A '*qualifying investment*' is any of the following:

(*a*)   shares or securities listed or dealt in on a recognised stock exchange (within *ICTA 1988, s 841*);

(*b*)   units in an authorised unit trust (within *ICTA 1988, s 468*);

(*c*)   shares in an open-ended investment company (within *ICTA 1988, s 468* as modified for the purpose);

(*d*)   an interest in an OFFSHORE FUND (52.3); and

(*e*)   from 6 April 2002 (1 April 2002 in the case of a disposal by a company), a 'qualifying interest in land'.

On a claim to that effect (within the time allowed at 16.4 CLAIMS), the 'relevant amount' (see below) is deductible in computing the donor's total income for the tax year of disposal. See below as regards adjustments for incidental costs and consequential benefits. The deduction is disregarded for the purposes of computing top-slicing relief in respect of gains on LIFE ASSURANCE POLICIES (45.13). Where the claim is made, no relief is available under 14.19 above or any other provision in respect of the same disposal.

For disposals to a charity after 1 July 2004 (otherwise than in performance of a contract entered into on or before that date and not varied after that date), the '*relevant amount*' is the value of the 'net benefit to the charity' either at the time the disposal is made or immediately after that time (whichever gives the lower value), or the excess (if any) of that value over any consideration given for the disposal. The '*net benefit to the charity*' is normally the market value of the investment. Where, however, the charity is, or becomes, subject to a 'related obligation' to *any* person (whether or not the donor or a connected person), it is the market value of the investment reduced by the aggregate 'related liabilities' of the charity. An obligation is a '*related obligation*' if it is reasonable to suppose that the disposal would not have been made in its absence or if it relates to, or is framed by reference to, or is conditional upon the charity receiving, the investment in question or a related investment (as widely defined); 'obligation' is itself widely defined so as to include any scheme, arrangement or understanding (whether or not legally enforceable) and any series of obligations. A charity's '*related liabilities*' are its liabilities under the related obligation (or under each of them). Contingent obligations are taken into account if the contingency actually occurs.

Previously, the '*relevant amount*' was the market value of the investment at the time of the disposal, or the excess of that value over any consideration given for the disposal.

The market value of the investment is determined as for capital gains tax purposes, with an interest in an offshore fund being valued in a similar way for this purpose as units in a unit trust.

In computing the amount deductible, any consideration receivable at a future time, contingently or otherwise, is brought fully into account as it is for capital gains tax purposes (see Tolley's Capital Gains Tax under Disposal).

The amount deductible is increased by any incidental costs of disposal (construed as for capital gains tax purposes) incurred by the person making it. Where consideration is received for the disposal, this increase is limited to the excess, if any, of the deemed consideration for capital gains tax purposes (disposal deemed to be at no gain/no loss) over the actual consideration.

The amount deductible is reduced by the value of any benefits received, in consequence of the disposal, by the person making it or a person connected with him (within 19 CONNECTED PERSONS).

The cost of the asset to the charity for capital gains tax purposes is reduced by the amount deductible as above, or, if it is less than that amount, is reduced to nil.

A '*qualifying interest in land*' is a freehold interest (or a leasehold interest which is a term of years absolute) in UK land (but not an agreement to acquire freehold land or for a lease). The following two circumstances are additionally brought within the relief.

(i)   Where there is a disposal of the beneficial interest in a qualifying interest in land, and there is also a disposal to the charity of any easement, servitude, right or privilege so far as benefiting that land, relief is also available for the latter disposal.

(ii)   Where a person with a freehold or leasehold interest in UK land grants to a charity a lease, for (except in Scotland) a term of years absolute, of the whole or part of that land, this is regarded as a disposal for which the relief is available.

In the application of the above in Scotland:

(1)   references to a freehold interest in land are to the interest of the owner;

(2)   references to a leasehold interest in land which is a term of years absolute are to a tenant's right over or interest in a property subject to a lease; and

(3)   references to an agreement for a lease do not include missives of let that constitute an actual lease.

The following supplementary provisions apply to disposals of qualifying interests in land.

(A)   Where two or more persons are entitled jointly or in common to a qualifying interest in land, the relief applies only if each person disposes of the whole of his beneficial interest in the land to the charity. Relief is then allowed to each of those persons, being apportioned between or amongst them as they may agree.

(B)   The relief is dependent on the receipt by the person disposing of the interest of a certificate given by or on behalf of the charity specifying the description of the interest concerned and the date of the disposal, and stating that the charity has acquired the interest.

(C)   If a 'disqualifying event' occurs at any time in the period from the date of the disposal to the fifth anniversary of 31 January following the year of assessment of the disposal (in the case of a disposal by a company, to the sixth anniversary of the end of the accounting period of the disposal), the person (or each of the persons) making the disposal is treated as never having been entitled to the relief in respect of the disposal (and the Revenue has the necessary assessment etc. powers). A '*disqualifying event*' occurs if the person (or any one of the persons) who made the disposal, or any connected person within *ICTA 1988, s 839* (see 19 CONNECTED PERSONS), either becomes entitled to an interest or right in relation to all or part of the land to which the disposal relates, or becomes party to an arrangement under which he enjoys some right in relation to all or part of that land, otherwise than for full consideration in money or money's worth. This does *not* apply if the person became so entitled as a result of a disposition of property on death, whether by will, by intestacy or otherwise.

[*ICTA 1988, ss 587B, 587C; FA 2000, s 43; FA 2002, s 97; FA 2004, s 139*].

A similar relief is available to companies (see the corresponding chapter of Tolley's Corporation Tax).

See generally Revenue Pamphlet IR 178.

Simon's Direct Tax Service. See **E1.504C.**

14.21 **GIFTS FOR RELIEF OVERSEAS**

Two reliefs were introduced for a limited period for gifts to charities aimed at either the relief of poverty or the advancement of education.

Gifts of money ('Millennium Gift Aid'). Relief is available for gifts made by individuals in the period beginning on 31 July 1998 and ending on 31 December 2000 (though see below) to charities which have given the required notification to the Revenue, where it may reasonably be expected that the sum given will be applied for, or in connection with, one or more of the following.

(*a*)   The relief of poverty in one or more countries or territories designated for the purpose.

(*b*)   The advancement of education in one or more countries or territories designated for the purpose.

(*c*)   (In relation to gifts made after 5 April 1999) the relief of poverty in the case of persons from any country or territory designated for the purpose who are refugees or who have suffered displacement as a result of organised intimidation or oppression or of war or other armed conflict.

The countries or territories are in each case designated by Treasury order (or are of a description specified in such an order). As regards (*a*) and (*b*) above, see *SI 1998 No 1868* and Revenue Press Release 31 July 1998 — some 80 of the world's poorest countries are designated for this purpose. As regards (*c*) above, see *SI 1999 No 2118*, which designates refugees and displaced persons from Kosovo for this purpose.

The 'qualifying donations' provisions of *FA 1990, s 25* (see 14.16 above) apply to such gifts, but with a minimum gift of £100 (rather than £250). Gifts of less than £100 may be aggregated for this purpose and treated as a single gift made at the time of the last of the gifts so aggregated, provided that:

(i)   no gift of £250 or more, and not more than one gift of £100 or more, is so aggregated;

(ii)   the condition as regards consequential benefits (see 14.16(iii) above) would be satisfied by reference to that single gift; and

(iii)   the donor gives a certificate that each gift qualifies (or would but for the £100 minimum qualify), that (ii) above is satisfied, and that he or she has paid or suffered sufficient income tax to cover basic rate tax on the grossed-up amount of the aggregated gift.

Where gifts so aggregated include gifts made in different years of assessment, the single gift is treated as having suffered tax at the basic rate for the year in which the first of the gifts so aggregated was made.

These provisions are made largely redundant for donations after 5 April 2000 by the removal of the minimum limit for donations generally (see 14.11 above). However, these provisions can still be used to aggregate a gift made after 5 April 2000 (and on or before 31 December 2000) with one made in an earlier tax year, thus enabling the earlier gift to qualify for relief where it was less than £100 and the charity to reclaim tax at the higher basic rate prevailing at the time of the earlier gift. Amendments are made to link these provisions with the revised conditions at 14.13 above for qualifying donations generally. Where two or more gifts are treated as a single gift made after 5 April 2000, relief is given as in 14.12 above.

[*FA 1998, s 48; FA 1999, ss 56, 57; FA 2000, s 42*].

Gifts in kind. Relief is available for gifts made in the period beginning on 31 July 1998 and **ending on 26 July 1999** (the relief being replaced after that date by the wider relief described at 14.19 above) to persons (including companies) carrying on a trade, profession or vocation who give certain articles to charities for use, either for medical purposes (including medical research and health promotion) or by an educational establishment, in a country or territory designated for the purpose by Treasury order (or of a description specified in such an order). See *SI 1998 No 1868* and Revenue Press Release 31 July 1998 — some 80 of the world's poorest countries are designated for this purpose.

The gift must consist of either:

(*a*)   articles manufactured, or of a type sold, in the course of the donor's trade; or

(*b*)   plant or machinery (see 9.25 CAPITAL ALLOWANCES) used in the donor's trade, profession or vocation.

Where the donor claims the relief, no amount is required to be brought into account for tax purposes in respect of the donated article either as a trading receipt or (for capital allowance purposes) as a disposal value. However, if the donor or any connected person (see 19 CONNECTED PERSONS) receives any benefit in any way attributable to the gift, the donor is chargeable on an amount equal to the value of that benefit, for the chargeable period in which it is received, under either Schedule D, Case I or II or, if he is not chargeable to tax under either of those Cases for that period, under Schedule D, Case VI.

A claim must be made (for income tax purposes) by 31 January in the next year of assessment but one following the year in the basis period for which the gift was made (e.g. by 31 January 2001 for a gift made in a period of account ending 31 December 1998) or (for corporation tax purposes) within two years of the end of the accounting period in which the gift was made. It must specify the article given and the charity to which it was given.

[*FA 1998, s 47; FA 1999, s 55(2)(3)*].

See now 14.19 above for the wider relief which replaces this provision from 27 July 1999.

15   Children

Cross-references. See 28.3 EXEMPT INCOME for Child Trust Funds; 75.22 SCHEDULE E—EMPLOY-MENT INCOME for employer-provided childcare; 83.7 SOCIAL SECURITY for child tax credit.

15.1   Child allowances were phased out from 1977/78 onwards by the introduction of the non-taxable child benefit. The additional personal allowance in respect of children (see 1.17 ALLOWANCES AND TAX RATES), was abolished from 6 April 2000. A new children's tax credit (see 1.18 ALLOWANCES AND TAX RATES) was introduced from 6 April 2001. This in turn was replaced for 2003/04 onwards by the 'child tax credit', a social security type benefit payable directly to the main child carer.

15.2   All the income of a child is chargeable on him (subject to below) and he has full entitlement to personal allowances and reliefs. In most cases only the personal allowance (see 1.14 ALLOWANCES AND TAX RATES) will be claimable.

15.3   Returns and claims may be made by a child in respect of income within his control but otherwise these are the responsibility of his parent, guardian, tutor or any trustee [*TMA 1970, ss 72, 118*] who is also liable for payment of any tax in default of payment by the child, with right of recovery. [*TMA 1970, s 73*]. Where assessment should primarily be made on the guardian, tutor or trustee, an assessment in the name of the child is not precluded (*R v Newmarket Commrs (ex p Huxley) CA 1916, 7 TC 49*).

15.4   If a parent makes a settlement in favour of his child, then the income arising thereon is treated (subject to certain exceptions) as that of the parent and not of the child for tax purposes. The definition of 'settlement' for this purpose is wide enough to cover gifts e.g. of money, or shares. See 81.18 SETTLEMENTS. See also the other provisions in 81.13–81.20 SETTLEMENTS whereby income of a settlement can be treated as that of the settlor for tax purposes.

15.5   Any reference to a child in the *Tax Acts*, is to be construed as including reference to an adopted child. [*ICTA 1988, s 832(5)*].

16   Claims

Cross-references. See ALLOWANCES AND TAX RATES at 1.11 onwards for claims to personal allowances and reliefs; 9.2(ii) CAPITAL ALLOWANCES for capital allowances claims; 24 DOUBLE TAX RELIEF for claims under DTR agreements etc.; 43 INTEREST PAYABLE for relief for interest paid; 51.10 NON-RESIDENTS AND OTHER OVERSEAS MATTERS for reliefs claimable by non-residents; 65.7 RESIDENCE, ORDINARY RESIDENCE AND DOMICILE for residence etc. claims; 81 SETTLEMENTS for claims by beneficiaries and contingent trust claims.

16.1   **CLAIMS AND ELECTIONS UNDER SELF-ASSESSMENT**

Claims and elections may be made to an Inspector of Taxes or an officer of the Board of Inland Revenue (or to the Board itself in certain specified cases) whenever the *Taxes Acts* provide for relief to be given or other thing to be done.

A formal procedure applies under self-assessment as regards the making of claims and elections. A claim for a relief, allowance or tax repayment (other than one to be given effect by a PAYE coding adjustment — see also 16.3 below) must be for an amount quantified at the time of the claim. Where notice has been given by the Revenue requiring the delivery of a return (see 68.2, 68.13 RETURNS), a claim etc. (other than one to be given effect by a PAYE coding adjustment) can only be made at any time by inclusion in such a return (or by virtue of an amendment to a return) *unless it could not be so included* either at that time or subsequently. In the case of a partnership business, a claim or election under any of numerous provisions specified in *TMA 1970, s 42(7)* must be made by a partner nominated by the partnership if it cannot be included in a partnership return (or amendment thereto). See 16.3 below for provisions applying where a claim etc. is made otherwise than by inclusion in a return.

Where a claimant discovers an error or mistake has been made in a claim (whether or not made in a return), he may make a supplementary claim within the time allowed for making the original claim.

[*TMA 1970, s 42; FA 1994, ss 196, 199(2)(a), Sch 19 para 13; FA 1995, s 107(1)–(3)(7)(9); FA 1996, ss 128(1), 130; FA 1998, Sch 27 Pt III(4); CAA 2001, Sch 2 para 1; FA 2001, s 88, Sch 29 para 26; ITEPA 2003, Sch 6 para 128*].

Claims are personal matters and (except in the case of trustees for persons under disability etc.) can be made only by the person entitled to the relief (cf. *Fulford v Hyslop Ch D 1929, 8 ATC 588*). For claims to personal allowances etc. by persons receiving tax-free annuities, see 22.17 DEDUCTION OF TAX AT SOURCE. See 68.2 RETURNS for signing of claims by attorney.

Where an official form is provided for use in making a claim or election not included in a return, it is permissible to fill out a photocopy of the blank form, provided that, where double sided copying is not available, all the pages (including any notes) are present and attached in the correct order. Although such copying is in strictness a breach of HMSO copyright, this will only be pursued if forms are copied on a large scale for commercial gain. (Revenue Pamphlet IR 131, SP 5/87, 15 June 1987). See also 68.2 RETURNS.

See 16.5 below as regards the making of income tax claims by telephone or other method not in writing.

Simon's Direct Tax Service. See E1.830 *et seq.*

16.2   **Claims for relief involving two or more years.** The provisions described below are designed to facilitate the administration under self-assessment of claims, elections etc. which affect more than one tax year. They generally deem the claim to be that of the later year, with consequent effect on the dates from which interest on unpaid and overpaid tax will run.

Relief for losses and other payments. A claim, under whatever provision, for a loss incurred or payment made (for example, a personal pension contribution) in one year of assessment to be carried back to an earlier year need not be made in a return, is treated as a claim for the year of loss or payment (the later year), must be for an amount equal to what would otherwise have been the tax saving for the earlier year (after taking into account any associated claims, see below, to which effect has already been given) and is given effect *in relation to the later year* by repayment, set-off etc. or by treating the said amount for the purposes of 78.6 SELF-ASSESSMENT as a tax payment made on account. See Revenue Tax Bulletin April 1996 p 299 for the practical effect.

The Revenue have confirmed that under these provisions a carry-back claim (whether in the return for the year of loss or payment or not) will be given immediate effect provided that the tax return for the earlier year has been made and the tax calculated. Relief is given in terms of tax by set-off or repayment, and, provided that the claim (and, where appropriate, the payment) is made before 31 January in the year of loss or payment, may be by set-off against outstanding liabilities for the earlier year. Relief will be given by repayment where there are no outstanding liabilities. (Revenue Tax Bulletin December 1996 pp 361–365, June 1997 p 443; Revenue 'Working Together' Bulletin No 12, March 2003). See *Norton v Thompson (Sp C 399), [2004] SSCD 163* for an illustration, and confirmation, of the principles involved.

See also 41.1 INTEREST ON OVERPAID TAX.

Averaging of farming or market gardening profits. Where a farmer or market gardener makes a claim under *ICTA 1988, s 96* to average the profits of two consecutive years of assessment (see 71.47(a) SCHEDULE D, CASES I AND II), the claim is treated as a claim for the later of those years. To the extent that the claim would otherwise have affected the profits of the earlier of those years, it must be for an amount equal to the tax that would consequently have become payable or repayable for that earlier year (after taking into account any associated claims, see below, to which effect has already been given) and is given effect *in relation to the later year* by increasing the tax payable or treating the said amount for the purposes of 78.6 SELF-ASSESSMENT as a tax payment made on account, whichever is appropriate. Where the later year is included in a subsequent averaging claim, i.e. it is then averaged with the following year, the application of these provisions to the first claim is ignored in computing the effect of the subsequent claim.

See also 41.1 INTEREST ON OVERPAID TAX.

Where, having made an averaging claim, a person then makes, amends or revokes any other claim for relief for either of the two years affected, which would be out of time but for the provisions of *section 96*, the claim, amendment or revocation is treated as relating to the later of the two years. To the extent that it relates to income for the earlier year, the amount claimed (or, as appropriate, the increase or reduction therein) must be equal to the tax that would consequently have become payable or repayable for that earlier year (after taking into account any associated claims, see below, to which effect has already been given) and is given effect *in relation to the later year* by increasing the tax payable or treating the said amount for the purposes of 78.6 SELF-ASSESSMENT as a tax payment made on account, whichever is appropriate.

For articles on these rules and on the completion of the relevant tax returns, see Revenue Tax Bulletin February 1997 pp 392–394 and August 1998 p 575.

Election for post-cessation receipts to be treated as if received on date of discontinuance. Where a person elects under *ICTA 1988, s 108* (see 62.1 POST-CESSATION ETC. RECEIPTS AND EXPENDITURE) for a post-cessation receipt to be treated as if received on the date of cessation of trade rather than in the year of receipt (the later year), the election is treated as a claim for the later year, must be for an amount equal to what would otherwise have been the additional tax payable for the year of assessment (the earlier year) in which the sum is treated as received (after taking into account any associated claims, see below, to which effect has already been given) and is given effect *in relation to the later year* by increasing the tax payable for that year.

Averaging of profits of creative artists. For 2000/01 onwards, i.e. where the earlier of the years in question is 2000/01 or a subsequent year, on a claim in specified circumstances, the profits of creative artists, i.e. authors, designers, composers etc. for two consecutive tax years may be averaged — see 71.41 SCHEDULE D, CASES I AND II. Such an averaging claim is given effect in the same way as a claim to average the profits of a farmer or market gardener (see above). See also 41.1 INTEREST ON OVERPAID TAX. The consequent making, amending or revoking of any other claim, where this would otherwise be out of time, is also given effect in the same way as for farmers etc. (see above).

Backward spreading of lump sums for copyright etc. Where a claim is made under *ICTA 1988, s 534, s 537A* or *s 538* to spread back lump sum receipts for copyrights etc. over more than one year of assessment (see 71.41 SCHEDULE D, CASES I AND II), the claim is treated as a claim for the year of assessment into whose basis period the lump sum would have fallen had the claim not been made (the payment year). To the extent that the claim would otherwise have affected the profits of an earlier year of assessment, it must be for an amount equal to the additional tax that would consequently have become payable for that earlier year (after taking into account any associated claims, see below, to which effect has already been given) and is given effect *in relation to the payment year* by increasing the tax payable for that year. These spreading provisions are repealed for amounts receivable after 5 April 2001; see now averaging of profits of creative artists (above).

General. For the purposes of all the above provisions, two claims, elections etc. (including, where appropriate, amendments and revocations) by the same person are '*associated*' in so far as the same year of assessment is the earlier year in relation to both.

[*TMA 1970, s 42(11A), Sch 1B; FA 1996, s 128(2), Sch 17; ICTA 1988, s 95A, Sch 4A paras 7, 9, 12, 13; FA 2001, s 71(1)(2)(4), Sch 24 paras 1, 3, Sch 33 Pt II(6)*].

See Revenue Tax Bulletin August 2000 pp 774, 775 for an article concerning the admission of earlier year claims, including those affecting the liability of another taxpayer, consequential on carry-back claims as above.

Simon's Direct Tax Service. See E1.833.

16.3 **Claims etc. not included in returns.** Subject to any specific provision requiring a claim or election to be made to the Board, a claim or election made otherwise than in a return (see 16.1 above) must be made to an officer of the Board. The claim etc. must include a declaration by the claimant that all particulars are correctly stated to the best of his information or belief. No claim requiring a tax repayment can be made unless the claimant has documentary proof that the tax has been paid or deducted. The claim must be made in a form determined by the Board and may require, *inter alia*, a statement of the amount of tax to be discharged or repaid and (except as below) supporting information and documentation. In the case of a claim by or on behalf of a person who is not resident (or who claims to be not resident or not ordinarily resident or not domiciled) in the UK, the Revenue may require a statement or declaration in support of the claim to be made by affidavit.

A person who may wish to make a claim must keep all such records as may be requisite for the purpose and must preserve them until such time as the Revenue may no longer enquire into the claim (see below) or any such enquiry is completed. There is a maximum penalty of £3,000 for non-compliance in relation to any claim *actually made*. Similar provisions and exceptions apply as in 68.5 RETURNS as to the preservation of copies of documents instead of originals and the exception from penalty for non-compliance in relation to dividend vouchers, interest certificates etc.

Provisions similar to those in 68.4 RETURNS (amendments of self-assessments) apply to enable a claimant (within twelve months of the claim) or officer of the Board (within nine months of the claim) to amend a claim etc. The Revenue have power of enquiry into a claim etc. (or amendment thereof) similar to that in 68.6, 68.7 RETURNS (enquiries into returns). Notice of intention to enquire must be given by the first anniversary of 31 January following the year of assessment (or where the claim relates to a period other than a year of assessment the first anniversary of the end of that period) or, if later, the quarter day (meaning 31 January, 30 April etc.) next following the first anniversary of the date of claim etc. In the event of such an enquiry, they have power to call for documents similar to that in 68.8 RETURNS. Where an enquiry is in progress, an officer of the Board may give provisional effect to the claim etc. (or amendment thereof) to such extent as he thinks fit. Provisions similar to those in 68.9, 68.10 RETURNS apply as regards completion of enquiries and amendments of claims upon completion. The Revenue must give effect (by assessment, discharge or repayment) to an amendment arising out of an enquiry within 30 days after the date of issue of the closure notice (for enquiries completed before 11 May 2001 within 30 days after the amendment is made). An appeal may be made against any conclusion stated, or amendment made, by a closure notice by giving written notice to the relevant officer within 30 days after the date of issue of the closure notice (for enquiries completed before 11 May 2001 within 30 days after the amendment is made), extended to three months where certain specified issues concerning residence are involved. If an amendment is varied on appeal, the Revenue must give effect to the variation within 30 days. Where a claim etc. does not give rise to a discharge or repayment of tax (for example, a claim to carry forward trading losses), there are provisions for disallowance of the claim on completion of enquiry, with appeal procedures similar to those above.

Appeals as above are normally made to the General Commissioners. Where the claim was made to the Board or under certain specified provisions, appeal is to the Special Commissioners, and in other cases, there are rules, similar to those in 4.3 APPEALS, enabling the taxpayer to elect to bring the appeal before the Special Commissioners. If the taxpayer also has an appeal pending concerning an assessment and the appeals relate to the same income, both appeals must be to the same body of Commissioners.

[*TMA 1970, s 42(11), Sch 1A; FA 1994, ss 196, 199(2)(a), Sch 19 paras 13, 35; FA 1995, s 107(10)(11), Sch 20; FA 1996, s 124(4), s 130(6)–(8), Sch 19 paras 8–10, Sch 22 para 9; FA 1998, Sch 19 para 42; FA 2001, s 88, Sch 29 paras 10, 12, 34; ITEPA 2003, Sch 6 para 141*].

See 16.5 below as regards the making of income tax claims by telephone or other method not in writing and also the use of photocopied blank claim forms.

The Revenue now accept that, following a claim, any interest, surcharge or penalty charged for the year to which the claim relates may be amended in line with the revised tax liability. Repayment supplement may be due on any overpayment of penalty or surcharge (see 41.1 INTEREST ON OVERPAID TAX). Previously, the Revenue took the view that no such amendment was possible if the claim was made after the deadline for amending the return (see 68.4 RETURNS). Following this change of view, taxpayers are invited to submit written requests to revisit claims already processed that relate to 1996/97 and subsequent years. (Revenue 'Working Together' Bulletin June 2003 p 12).

Claims given effect by PAYE coding adjustment. Claims for a tax year may be made during that year, and thus before a tax return is issued, and given effect by adjustment to a PAYE code (see 55.4 PAY AS YOU EARN), for example a claim to married couple's allowance. Such in-year claims may subsequently be reflected in a tax return. Where no such return is issued, the claim will become final under the above provisions by the first anniversary of 31 January following the tax year, i.e. the final date for the Revenue to give notice of intention to enquire. Except in cases of 'discovery' (see 5.3 ASSESSMENTS), the Revenue will in practice apply the same deadline to claims rolled forward from one year to the next and automatically included in code numbers and to those included on the basis of preliminary information given by the taxpayer before the start of the tax year. (Revenue Tax Bulletin October 1996 pp 350, 351).

Simon's Direct Tax Service. See E1.832.

16.4   **TIME LIMITS FOR CLAIMS**

Unless otherwise prescribed, a claim with respect to income tax (or capital gains tax) must be made no later than the fifth anniversary of 31 January following the tax year to which it relates. [*TMA 1970, s 43(1); FA 1994, ss 196, 199(2)(a), Sch 19 para 14*].

See 16.8 below for claims following late assessments, and see generally 86 TIME LIM-ITS—FIXED DATES and 87 TIME LIMITS—MISCELLANEOUS.

Simon's Direct Tax Service. See E1.835.

16.5   **TELEPHONE CLAIMS AND OTHER SERVICES**

The Board have powers to accept income tax claims by telephone (or by any other method not in writing), where a written claim would otherwise be required, for which purpose they must publish general directions as regards the circumstances in which, and conditions subject to which, such claims will be accepted. The time for making the claim and the contents may not be altered by the directions. No directions may be given in relation to claims by an individual as trustee, partner or personal representative, to CAPITAL ALLOWANCES (9) claims or to claims under *TMA 1970, Sch 1B* (see 16.2 above). Directions may similarly be given as regards the making of elections, the giving of notice, the amendment or withdrawal of claims, elections and notices and the amendment of returns. [*FA 1998, s 118*].

All tax offices now offer certain telephone services, as set out in Revenue Pamphlet IR 131, SP 2/03 (replacing SP 2/98) and, for tax offices served by a Call Centre, Revenue Pamphlet IR 131, SP 3/03 (replacing SP 8/98) with which are published the appropriate directions. These include acceptance of telephone claims for personal allowances, interest relief and most employment expenses. They also enable taxpayers to notify changes in their details, including changes to employment benefits-in-kind. Call Centres will additionally accept telephone amendments to self-assessment tax returns. These services are available to individuals and, subject to identity and authorisation checks, to agents acting for individuals.

16.6   **TAX REPAYMENT CLAIMS**

A self-assessment tax return (see 68.2 RETURNS) may give rise to a tax repayment. Otherwise, a tax repayment claim can be made on form R40. The form and related Guidance Notes are available on the Revenue website or from tax offices. There is no requirement to send vouchers, certificates or other supporting documents with the claim (though these *can* be sent if the taxpayer so wishes) but they must be retained under the record-keeping requirements at 68.5 RETURNS as applied by 16.3 above. A tax repayment claim is also subject to the enquiry provisions at 16.3 above.

By virtue of *TMA 1970, s 43(1)* at 16.4 above, the time limit for making a claim is the fifth anniversary of 31 January following the tax year to which the claim relates. However, where an overpayment of tax has arisen because of official error, and there is no doubt or dispute as to the facts, claims to repayment of tax are accepted outside the statutory time limit (Revenue Pamphlet IR 1, B41).

A tax repayment claim can be made *before* the end of the tax year to which it relates, though the Revenue do not normally make in-year repayments of less than £50. If further income is expected between the making of the claim and the end of the tax year, i.e. the claim is an interim claim, a full-year estimate should be given for each such item of income as well as details of the actual income to date.

16.7   **ERROR OR MISTAKE RELIEF**

If an income tax (or capital gains tax) assessment (or self-assessment) proves to be excessive due to an error or mistake in a return, the taxpayer may give written notice to that effect to the Board (a claim for error or mistake relief) no later than the fifth anniversary of 31 January following the tax year to which the return relates. The Revenue may give such relief as is reasonable and just. The relief is given because the return was wrong and hence these provisions do not apply where the assessment simply does not agree with the return. No relief is given if the return was made on the basis or in accordance with the practice generally prevailing at the time it was made.

The relief, which is given by repayment, is determined by the Board, having regard to all relevant circumstances including, in particular, whether the granting of relief would result in income (or gains) being excluded from the charge to tax. They may take into account the taxpayer's liabilities, and assessments made on him, for years other than the year in question. The taxpayer may appeal to the Special Commissioners against the decision of the Board, and either party may then appeal to the High Court but only on a point of law arising in connection with the computation of the income (or gains). See *Rose Smith & Co Ltd v CIR KB 1933, 17 TC 586*; *Carrimore Six Wheelers Ltd CA 1944, 26 TC 301* and *CA 1947, 28 TC 422*; *Arranmore Investment Co Ltd v CIR CA(NI) 1973, 48 TC 623*; *Eagerpath Ltd v Edwards CA 2000, 73 TC 427.*

No relief is available in respect of an error or mistake in a claim which is included in a return (but see 16.1 above as regards supplementary claims).

[*TMA 1970, s 33; FA 1994, ss 196, 199, Sch 19 para 8; FA 1998, Sch 19 para 15*].

Error or mistake relief cannot be used to rectify a failure to claim a particular tax relief within a stipulated time limit where that claim could have been made outside a return (*Howard v CIR (Sp C 329), [2002] SSCD 408*).

Error or mistake relief is extended to cover an error or mistake in a partnership return (see 68.13 RETURNS) by reason of which the partners allege that their self-assessments were excessive. The claim to relief must be made by one of the partners within five years after the filing date for the partnership return. Where the claim results in an amendment to the partnership return, the Board will, by notice, make any necessary amendments to the tax returns of all persons who were partners at any time in the period covered by the partnership return. [*TMA 1970, s 33A; FA 1994, ss 196, 199(2)(a), Sch 19 para 9; FA 1996, Sch 22 para 5; FA 2001, s 88, Sch 29 para 25*].

A claim to error or mistake relief may still be made in relation to an amendment to a self-assessment notwithstanding an agreement with the inspector preceding that amendment (*Wall v CIR (Sp C 303), [2002] SSCD 122*).

The Revenue now accept that, following a successful error or mistake relief claim, any interest, surcharge or penalty charged for the year to which the claim relates may be amended in line with the revised tax liability. Repayment supplement may be due on any overpayment of penalty or surcharge (see 41.1 INTEREST ON OVERPAID TAX). The Revenue previously took the view that no such amendment was possible if the claim was made after the deadline for amending the return (see 68.4 RETURNS). Following this change of view, taxpayers are invited to submit written requests to revisit claims already processed that relate to 1996/97 and subsequent years. (Revenue 'Working Together' Bulletin June 2003 p 12).

For recovery of tax paid under *mistake of law*, see 56.11 PAYMENT OF TAX. For relief for double assessment, see 5.4 ASSESSMENTS. For re-opening of accounts in respect of 'late' receipts and payments, see 71.18 SCHEDULE D, CASES I AND II. For alteration of past claims on farming and market gardening profits, see 71.47 SCHEDULE D, CASES I AND II.

See generally Revenue Inspector's Manual IM 3750–3756.

Simon's Direct Tax Service. See E1.834.

16.8 **CLAIMS FOLLOWING FURTHER ASSESSMENTS**

A claim (including a supplementary claim) which could not have been allowed but for the making of an assessment to income tax or capital gains tax after the tax year to which it relates may be made before the end of the tax year following that in which the assessment was made. [*TMA 1970, s 43(2)*].

In the case of a discovery leading to an assessment under *TMA 1970, s 29* (see 5.3 ASSESSMENTS) which is made other than for the purpose of making good a loss of tax attributable to fraudulent or negligent conduct (see 30.3 FRAUDULENT OR NEGLIGENT CONDUCT),

(*a*)   any 'relevant' claim, election, application or notice which could have been made or given within the normal time limits may be made or given within one year after the end of the tax year in which the assessment is made, and

(*b*)   any 'relevant' claim etc. previously made or given, except an irrevocable one, can, with the consent of the person(s) by whom it was made or given (or their personal representatives), be revoked or varied in the manner in which it was made or given.

Certain elections for the transfer inter-spouse of the married couple's allowance and the transfer of children's tax credit are excluded from this treatment, as are, from 10 July 2003, capital gains re-basing elections (see Tolley's Capital Gains Tax under Assets held on 31 March 1982).

A claim etc. is '*relevant*' to an assessment for a tax year if

(i)   it relates to, or to an event occurring in, the tax year, and

(ii)   it, or its revocation or variation, reduces, or could reduce,

- the increased tax liability resulting from the assessment, or

- any other liability of the person for that tax year or a later one ending not more than one year after the end of the tax year in which the assessment is made.

The normal APPEALS (4) provisions apply, with any necessary modifications.

If the making etc. of a claim etc. (as above) would alter another person's tax liability, the consent of that person (or his personal representatives) is needed. If such alteration is an increase, the other person cannot make etc. a claim etc. under the foregoing provisions.

If the reduction, whether resulting from one or more than one claim etc., would exceed the additional tax assessed, relief is not available for the excess. If the reduction, so limited, involves more than one period, or more than one person, the inspector will specify by notice in writing how it is to be apportioned; but within 30 days of the notice (or last notice if more than one person is involved) being given, the person, or persons jointly, can specify the apportionment by notice in writing to the inspector.

[*TMA 1970, ss 43A, 43B; FA 1989, s 150; F(No 2)A 1992, Sch 5 para 9(4); FA 1993, Sch 14 para 2; FA 1994, ss 196, 199, Sch 19 para 15; FA 1998, Sch 19 para 22; FA 2003, s 207(2)*].

With effect after 10 July 2003, the provisions of *TMA 1970, ss 43(2), 43A, 43B* above are given similar effect in relation to a Revenue amendment to a self-assessment personal or partnership tax return as they would have in relation to a further assessment (see 68.9 RETURNS). Also, any late assessment required to give effect to a claim etc. as above, or as a result of allowing such a claim etc., can be made within a year after the claim etc. becomes final (i.e. becomes no longer capable of being varied, on appeal or otherwise); this applies to claims etc. made as a consequence of either an assessment as above or an amendment to a return. [*TMA 1970, s 43C; FA 2003, s 207(1)(3)*].

See also 30.3 FRAUDULENT OR NEGLIGENT CONDUCT.

17 Community Investment Tax Relief

Simon's Direct Tax Service E3.8.

17.1 INTRODUCTION

The Community Investment Tax Credit scheme provides tax relief to individuals and companies investing in Community Development Finance Institutions ('CDFIs') which have been accredited by the Government under the rules of the scheme. The intention is that CDFIs will use investors' funds to finance small businesses and social enterprises in disadvantaged communities. The relief takes the form of a reduction in the investor's income tax or corporation tax liability. The quantum of the relief is a maximum of 25% of the 'invested amount' (as defined — see 17.5 below), spread over five years, but relief cannot exceed in any year the amount needed to reduce the investor's tax liability to nil. The relief is available for investments made on or after 17 April 2002. Claims for relief may be made on or after 23 January 2003. A CDFI which is accredited at any time before 6 April 2003 is to have its accreditation backdated to 17 April 2002. (Treasury Explanatory Notes to Finance Bill 2002). [*FA 2002, s 57, Sch 16; SI 2003 No 88*].

No exemption is provided for chargeable gains on disposals of investments in CDFIs.

References in this chapter to the '*investment date*' are to the day on which the investment in the CDFI is made, and references to the '*five-year investment period*' are to the five years beginning with that day. [*FA 2002, Sch 16 para 3*]. The investment term need not, however, be limited to five years.

Guidance on the relief is available in Revenue Community Investment Tax Relief Manual.

The remainder of this chapter is set out under the following headings.

17.2 ELIGIBILITY FOR RELIEF

An individual or company who makes an investment in a body is eligible for community investment tax relief in respect of that investment if:

(*a*) the body is accredited as a CDFI (see 17.25 below) at the time the investment is made;

(*b*) the investment is a 'qualifying investment' (see 17.8 below); and

(*c*) the general conditions at 17.12 below are satisfied.

[FA 2002, Sch 16 para 1].

For these purposes, a person makes an investment in a body when:

(i)   he makes a loan (whether secured or unsecured) to the body (otherwise than by providing overdraft facilities or acquiring securities); or

(ii) an 'issue of securities or shares' (as defined) of or in the body, for which he has subscribed, is made to him.

Where a loan agreement authorises the body to draw down amounts of the loan over a period of time, the loan is treated for the purposes of (i) above as made when the first amount is drawn down.

[FA 2002, Sch 16 paras 2, 46].

17.3   **FORM OF RELIEF**

Income tax. Where an individual who is eligible for relief (see 17.2 above) makes a claim for relief for any one of the 'relevant tax years', his income tax liability for that year falls to be reduced by the lesser of:

(*a*)   5% of the 'invested amount' (see 17.5 below) in respect of the investment in question; and

(*b*)   an amount sufficient to reduce that liability to nil.

The '*relevant tax years*' are the tax year in which the investment date falls, and each of the four subsequent tax years.

The income tax reduction under this chapter is made in priority to any of the following:

(i)   an income tax reduction due in respect of personal reliefs (see 1.15, 1.18 ALLOWANCES AND TAX RATES) or qualifying maintenance payments (see 47.8 MARRIED PERSONS);

(ii) an income tax reduction due in respect of interest relief on a loan to purchase a life annuity (see 43.3, 43.24 INTEREST PAYABLE);

(iii) a reduction of liability to tax by way of DOUBLE TAX RELIEF (24);

The income tax reduction under this chapter is, however, made *after* any income tax reduction due under the ENTERPRISE INVESTMENT SCHEME (25) or in respect of investments in VENTURE CAPITAL TRUSTS (91).

In determining the individual's income tax liability from which the reduction under this chapter is to be made, no account is taken of any basic rate tax on income the tax on which the individual is entitled to charge against any other person or to deduct, retain or satisfy out of any payment. This includes any basic rate tax deemed to have been deducted at source from a charitable donation under the Gift Aid scheme (see 14.12 CHARITIES). Any such basic rate tax cannot, therefore, be extinguished by community investment tax relief.

Claims. The investor is entitled to make a claim for a 'relevant tax year' (see above) if it appears to him that the conditions for the relief are for the time being satisfied. He *must* also have received a tax relief certificate (see also 17.25 below) from the CDFI. No claim can be made before the end of the tax year to which it relates. Otherwise, by default, the general time limit for making claims applies (see 16.4 CLAIMS). See 17.7 below for specific circumstances in which no claim for relief can be made.

No application can be made to postpone tax (see 56.3 PAYMENT OF TAX), pending appeal, on the grounds that the appellant is entitled to community investment tax relief, unless a claim for the relief has been made.

17.4 Community Investment Tax Relief

[FA 2002, s 57, Sch 16 paras 19, 45, Sch 17 paras 2–4; ICTA 1988, s 289A(5)(ca), Sch 15B para 1(6)(da); FA 1990, s 25(6)(b), (7)(d)].

17.4   **Corporation tax.** Provisions similar to those at 17.3 above apply, where relevant, to company investors, but by reference to their corporation tax liability and by reference to 'relevant accounting periods' rather than tax years. The *'relevant accounting periods'* are the accounting period (as defined for corporation tax purposes) in which the investment date falls and each of the accounting periods in which fall the first four anniversaries of the investment date. The reduction in corporation tax liability is made after any reduction in respect of investment relief under the corporate venturing scheme (see Tolley's Corporation Tax) but before any double tax relief. The time limit for claims is six years after the end of the accounting period in question. *[FA 1998, Sch 18 para 8(1); FA 2002, s 57, Sch 16 para 20, Sch 17 para 5].*

17.5   **Meaning of the 'invested amount'.** For the purposes of 17.3 and 17.4 above, in respect of a **loan**, the *'invested amount'* is as follows.

(a)   In the tax year in which the investment date falls, it is the 'average capital balance' (see below) for the first year of the five-year investment period (see 17.1 above).

(b)   In each subsequent tax year (subject to (c) below), it is the average capital balance for the one year beginning with the anniversary of the investment date falling in that tax year.

(c)   For the third, fourth and fifth tax years for which relief may be claimed, it is initially determined as in (b) above but is restricted to, if less, the average capital balance for the six-month period beginning eighteen months after the investment date. (This is a consequence of the eighteen-month rule for drawdown facilities referred to at 17.9 below. (Treasury Explanatory Notes to Finance Bill 2002).)

For the purposes of (a)–(c) above, the *'average capital balance'* of a loan for any period of time is the mean of the daily balances of capital outstanding during that period. Where the investor is a company, all references to tax years in (a)–(c) above should be read as references to accounting periods.

In respect of **securities or shares**, the *'invested amount'* for any tax year or company accounting period is the amount subscribed for them (not necessarily in that tax year or accounting period).

[FA 2002, Sch 16 para 21].

See 17.19, 17.20 below for restriction of the invested amount in certain circumstances where value is received.

17.6   *Examples*

(A) Loans

Faith makes a £50,000 loan to a CDFI on 1 September 2003 on terms that it be repaid in annual £10,000 instalments beginning on 1 September 2005. She agrees to increase the loan outstanding by £40,000 on 1 September 2007 (repayable on 1 September 2009). The 'invested amount', and the 5% maximum income tax reduction available, for the five tax years for which relief may be claimed, are as follows.

	Invested amount £	Tax reduction £
2003/04	50,000	2,500
2004/05	50,000	2,500
2005/06	40,000	2,000
2006/07	30,000	1,500
2007/08	50,000*	2,500

* Initially determined at £60,000 (£20,000 + the £40,000 increase) but restricted to £50,000, being the average capital balance for the six-month period 1 March 2005 to 31 August 2005 inclusive (see 17.5(c) above).

(B) Securities or shares

Bill subscribes £50,000 for shares in a CDFI on 1 September 2003 and holds them for at least five years. The 'invested amount', and the 5% maximum income tax reduction available for each of the tax years 2003/04 to 2007/08 inclusive, the five years for which relief may be claimed, are £50,000 and £2,500 respectively.

17.7 **Circumstances in which no claim for relief can be made.** In the circumstances listed below, no claim for community investment tax relief can be made. For company investors, references to tax years should be read as references to accounting periods.

Loans: disposals and excessive repayments/receipts of value. No claim can be made for a tax year in respect of a loan if:

(a) the investor disposes of all or any part of the loan (disregarding any repayment of the loan) before the 'qualifying date' relating to that tax year; or

(b) at any time after the investment is made but before that 'qualifying date', the amount of the capital outstanding on the loan is reduced to nil; or

(c) before that 'qualifying date', cumulative loan repayments (or receipts of value treated as repayments — see 17.19 below) bring into play the withdrawal of relief provisions at 17.18 below.

The '*qualifying date*' relating to a tax year is the anniversary of the investment date next occurring after the end of that tax year.

[*FA 2002, Sch 16 para 22*].

Thus, if, for example, a loan made on 1 October 2003 is repaid in full by the CDFI on 1 July 2007 (i.e. before 1 October 2007, the qualifying date for 2006/07), no claim for relief can be made for 2006/07, even though the loan remained outstanding throughout that tax year. No claim can be made for 2007/08 either.

Securities or shares: disposals and excessive receipts of value. No claim can be made for a tax year in respect of any securities or shares other than those held by the investor (as sole beneficial owner) continuously (see 17.26 below) throughout the period beginning when the investment is made and ending immediately before the 'qualifying date' (as in (a) above) relating to that tax year. In addition, no claim can be made for a tax year if, before the 'qualifying date' (as in (a) above) relating to that tax year, cumulative receipts of value bring into play the withdrawal of relief provisions at 17.20 below. [*FA 2002, Sch 16 para 23*].

Loss of accreditation by the CDFI. Where the CDFI ceases to be accredited as such during the first year of the five-year investment period, no claim for relief can be made. Where accreditation is lost at any later time within the five-year investment period, no claim can be made for the tax year in which falls the most recent anniversary of the investment date preceding (or coinciding with) the date the accreditation is lost, or for any subsequent tax year. (There is no withdrawal of relief for any earlier tax year.) [*FA 2002, Sch 16 para 24*].

17.8 Community Investment Tax Relief

Accreditation of the investor (companies only). Provisions similar to those at (*c*) above apply if the investor, being a company, becomes accredited as a CDFI within the five-year investment period. [*FA 2002, Sch 16 para 25*].

17.8 **QUALIFYING INVESTMENTS**

An investment is a '*qualifying investment*' in a CDFI (and thus meets condition (*b*) at 17.2 above) if:

(*a*) the investment consists of a loan, securities or shares satisfying the conditions at 17.9 or, as the case may be, 17.10 below;

(*b*) the investor receives from the CDFI a valid tax relief certificate (see also 17.25 below); and

(*c*) the conditions at 17.11 below (pre-arranged protection against risks) are met.

[*FA 2002, Sch 16 para 8*].

17.9 **Conditions to be satisfied in relation to loans.** There are three such conditions. The first is that either the CDFI receives from the investor, on the investment date, the full amount of the loan or, in the case of a loan made under a drawdown facility, the loan agreement provides for the CDFI to receive the full amount of the loan within 18 months after the investment date. The second condition is that the loan must not carry any present or future right to be converted into, or exchanged for, a loan, securities, shares or other rights, any of which are redeemable within the five-year investment period. The third is that the loan must not be made on terms that allow any person to require:

(*a*) repayment within years 1 and 2 (of the five-year investment period) of any of the loan capital advanced during those two years; or

(*b*) repayment within year 3 of more than 25% of the balance of loan capital outstanding at the end of year 2; or

(*c*) repayment before the end of year 4 of more than 50% of the balance of loan capital outstanding at the end of year 2; or

(*d*) repayment before the end of year 5 of more than 75% of that balance.

Any of the above percentages may be altered by Treasury order, but only in relation to loans made on or after a date specified in the order. For the above purposes, there is disregarded any requirement to repay that may arise as a consequence of certain standard commercial default provisions in the loan agreement.

[*FA 2002, Sch 16 para 9*].

17.10 **Conditions to be satisfied in relation to securities or shares.** There are two such conditions. The first is that the securities or shares must be subscribed for wholly in cash and fully paid for (in the case of shares, fully paid up and with no undertaking for any further payment in connection with the acquisition) on the investment date. The second is that they must not carry:

(*a*) any present or future right to be redeemed within the five-year investment period; or

(*b*) any present or future right to be converted into, or exchanged for, a loan, securities, shares or other rights, any of which are redeemable within the five-year investment period.

[*FA 2002, Sch 16 paras 10, 11*].

17.11   **Pre-arranged protection against risks.** Any arrangements (as very broadly defined) under which the investment in the CDFI is made (or arrangements preceding the investment but relating to it) must not include arrangements a main purpose of which is to provide (by means of any insurance, indemnity, guarantee or otherwise) complete or partial protection for the investor against the normal risks attaching to the investment. Arrangements are, however, allowed if they do no more than provide the kind of commercial protection, e.g. the use of property as security for a loan, that might be expected if the investment were made by a bank. [*FA 2002, Sch 16 para 13*].

17.12   **GENERAL CONDITIONS FOR ELIGIBILITY**

No control of CDFI by investor. The investor must not control the CDFI at any time in the five-year investment period. 'Control' is construed in accordance with *ICTA 1988, s 840* where the CDFI is a body corporate, with similar rules applying in other cases, with any potential future rights and powers of the investor, and any rights and powers held or exercisable by another on his behalf, taken into account. References to 'the investor' include any person connected with him (within *ICTA 1988, s 839* — see 19 CONNECTED PERSONS).

Beneficial ownership. The investor must be the sole beneficial owner of the investment when it is made (which in the case of a loan means sole beneficial entitlement to repayment).

Investor not to be accredited. The investor must not itself be accredited as a CDFI as at the investment date. See 17.7(*d*) above as regards the situation where a company investor subsequently becomes a CDFI.

No acquisition of share in partnership. Where the CDFI is a partnership, the investment must not consist of or include any capital contributed by the investor on becoming a member of the partnership. This includes the provision of loan capital treated as partners' capital in the partnership accounts.

No tax avoidance purpose. The investment must not be made as part of a scheme or arrangement a main purpose of which is the avoidance of tax.

[*FA 2002, Sch 16 paras 14–18, 51(3)*].

17.13   **WITHDRAWAL OR REDUCTION OF RELIEF**

Community investment tax relief may fall to be withdrawn or reduced on a disposal of the investment (see 17.16 below), on repayment of an investment consisting of a loan (see 17.18 below), or if value is received in respect of the investment (see 17.19–17.22 below).

Where relief given falls to be withdrawn or reduced, and also where it is found not to have been due in the first place, the withdrawal etc. is achieved by means of an income tax or corporation tax assessment under Schedule D, Case VI for the tax year or company accounting period *for which the relief was obtained*. For income tax, no such assessment can be made by reason of any event occurring after the investor's death. [*FA 2002, Sch 16 para 27*].

17.14   **Information.** Certain events giving rise to withdrawal or reduction of investment relief must be notified to the Revenue by the investor. An individual investor must give such notice no later than 31 January following the tax year in which the event occurs. A company investor must do so within twelve months after the end of its accounting period in which the event occurs. If the requirement arises from the receipt of value by a connected person, each of the above deadlines is extended to, if later, the end of the period of 60 days beginning when the investor gains knowledge of the event. The penalty provisions of *TMA*

1970, s 98 apply in the event of non-compliance. [*FA 2002, s 57, Sch 16 para 42, Sch 17 para 1*].

17.15   **Attribution of relief.** Community investment tax relief is said to be 'attributable' to any investment in respect of a tax year or company accounting period if relief as in 17.3 or 17.4 above has been obtained in respect of that investment and has not been withdrawn (as opposed to reduced). Where for any tax year or accounting period relief has been obtained by reason of a single investment (i.e. one loan, or securities or shares comprised in one issue), the relief attributable to it is the reduction made in the investor's tax liability. Where the relief has been obtained by reason of two or more investments, it is attributed to those investments in proportion to the invested amounts (see 17.5 above) for the year or period. Relief attributable to any one issue of securities or shares is attributed *pro rata* to each security or share in that issue, and any reduction of relief is similarly apportioned between the securities or shares in question. For these purposes, any bonus shares, issued in respect of the original shares and being shares in the same company, of the same class and carrying the same rights, are treated as if comprised in the original issue, and relief is apportioned to them accordingly. This applies only if the original shares have been continuously held (see 17.26 below) by the investor (as sole beneficial owner) since their issue, and, where it does apply, the bonus shares are themselves treated as having been continuously held since the time of the original issue. [*FA 2002, Sch 16 paras 26, 51(2)*].

17.16   **Disposals.** For the purposes below, an investment is regarded as being disposed of if it is so regarded for the purposes of tax on chargeable gains, and see also 17.24 below (certain company reconstructions treated as disposals). [*FA 2002, Sch 16 para 48*]. For company investors, references below to tax years should be read as references to accounting periods.

Loans. Where the investment consists of a loan, and the investor disposes of the whole of it within the five-year investment period (see 17.1 above), otherwise than by way of a 'permitted disposal', or disposes of part of it during that period, any relief attributable to the investment (see 17.15 above), for any tax year, is withdrawn. See 17.13 above for consequences of withdrawal. Repayment of the loan does not count as a disposal. A disposal is a '*permitted disposal*' if it is:

(*a*)   by way of a distribution in the course of dissolving or winding up the CDFI; or

(*b*)   a disposal within *TCGA 1992, s 24(1)* (entire loss, destruction etc. of asset — see Tolley's Capital Gains Tax under Disposal); or

(*c*)   a deemed disposal under *TCGA 1992, s 24(2)* (assets of negligible value — see Tolley's Capital Gains Tax under Losses); or

(*d*)   made after the CDFI has ceased to be accredited as such.

[*FA 2002, Sch 16 para 28*].

Securities or shares. Where the investment consists of securities or shares, and the investor disposes of the whole or any part of the investment within the five-year investment period, any relief attributable to the investment (see 17.15 above), for any tax year, is withdrawn or reduced as set out below. This does not apply if the CDFI has ceased to be accredited before the disposal or if the disposal arises from the repayment, redemption or repurchase by the CDFI of any of the securities or shares. See 17.13 above for consequences of withdrawal etc.

In the case of a 'permitted disposal' (defined as for *Loans* above) or a disposal by way of a bargain made at arm's length for full consideration, the relief attributable to the investment for any tax year is withdrawn, or is reduced by 5% of the disposal consideration (if such reduction would not amount to full withdrawal). If the relief initially obtained for any tax year was less than 5% of the invested amount (see 17.5 above), i.e. because the investor's tax liability was insufficient to fully absorb the available relief, the reduction is correspondingly restricted. In the case of any other disposal, the relief for all tax years is withdrawn.

[*FA 2002, Sch 16 para 29*].

17.17 **Identification rules on disposal of securities or shares.** The rules below apply, for the purpose of identifying shares disposed of, where the investor makes a part disposal of a holding of shares of the same class in the same company, and the holding includes shares to which community investment tax relief is attributable (see 17.15 above) and which have been held continuously (see 17.26 below) since the time of issue. The rules apply for the purposes of 17.16 above and this chapter generally and for the purposes of taxing chargeable gains; as regards the latter, the normal identification rules are disapplied. They apply to securities as they apply to shares.

Where shares comprised in the holding have been acquired on different days, a disposal is identified with acquisitions on a first in/first out basis. In matching the shares disposed of with shares acquired on a particular day, shares to which relief is attributable, and which have been held continuously since issue, are treated as being disposed of *after* any other shares included in the holding and acquired on that day. If, on a reorganisation of share capital (e.g. a scrip issue), a new holding falls, by virtue of *TCGA 1992, s 127* (or any other chargeable gains enactment which applies that *section* — see Tolley's Capital Gains Tax under Shares and Securities, and see also 17.23 below), to be equated with the original shares, shares comprised in the new holding are deemed for these purposes to have been acquired when the original shares were acquired.

[*FA 2002, Sch 16 paras 47, 51(2)*].

17.18 **Excessive repayments of loan capital.** Where the investment consists of a loan, and the 'average capital balance' for the third, fourth or final year of the five-year investment period (see 17.1 above) is less than the 'permitted balance' for the year in question (other than by an amount of 'insignificant value'), any relief attributable to the investment (see 17.15 above), for any tax year or company accounting period, is withdrawn. See 17.13 above for consequences of withdrawal.

For these purposes, the '*average capital balance*' of the loan for any period of time is the mean of the daily balances of capital outstanding during that period, disregarding any 'non-standard repayments' made in that period or at any earlier time. The '*permitted balance*' of the loan is as follows:

(*a*)   for the third year of the five-year investment period, 75% of the average capital balance for the six months beginning eighteen months after the investment date;

(*b*)   for the fourth year, 50% of that balance; and

(*c*)   for the final year, 25% of that balance.

For these purposes, an amount is of '*insignificant value*' if it does not exceed £1,000, or in any other case is insignificant in relation to the average capital balance for whichever year of the five-year investment period is under consideration.

'Non-standard repayments' are repayments made:

(i)   at the choice or discretion of the CDFI and not under any obligation under the loan agreement; or

(ii)   as a consequence of certain standard commercial default provisions in the loan agreement.

[*FA 2002, Sch 16 para 30*].

17.19   **Value received by investor: loans.** Where the investment consists of a loan, and the investor 'receives value' (see 17.21 below), other than an amount of 'insignificant value', from the CDFI during the 'period of restriction', the investor is treated as having received a repayment equal to the amount of value received. This may have consequences for 17.5 above (determination of invested amount) and 17.18 above (withdrawal of relief where excessive repayments made). Where the value is received in the first or second year of the 'period of restriction', the repayment is treated as made at the beginning of that second year. Where the value is received in a later year, the repayment is treated as made at the beginning of the year in question. The repayment is not treated as a 'non-standard repayment' for the purposes of 17.18 above.

For these purposes, an amount is of '*insignificant value*' if it does not exceed £1,000, or in any other case is insignificant in relation to the 'average capital balance' for the year of the 'period of restriction' in which the value is received (treating any value received in the first year as received at the beginning of the second). There are provisions to aggregate a receipt of value, whether insignificant or not, with amounts of insignificant value received previously, and treating that aggregate, if it is not itself an amount of insignificant value, as an amount of value received at the time of the latest actual receipt. The '*average capital balance*' of the loan for any year is the mean of the daily balances of capital outstanding during that year, disregarding the receipt of value in question. [*FA 2002, Sch 16 paras 31, 34*].

The '*period of restriction*' is the period of six years beginning one year before the investment date. [*FA 2002, Sch 16 para 33*].

These provisions apply equally to receipts of value by and from persons connected (within *ICTA 1988, s 839* — see 19 CONNECTED PERSONS), at any time in the period of restriction, with the investor or, as the case may be, the CDFI. [*FA 2002, Sch 16 para 39*]. See 17.21 below for the meaning of 'value received' and the determination of the *amount* of value received.

17.20   **Value received by investor: securities or shares.** Where the investment consists of securities or shares, and the following circumstances are present, any relief attributable (see 17.15 above) to the 'continuing investment' (see (*b*) below), for any tax year or company accounting period, is withdrawn. See 17.13 above for consequences of withdrawal. The circumstances are that:

(*a*)   the investor 'receives value' (see 17.21 below), other than an amount of 'insignificant value', from the CDFI during the 'period of restriction' (defined as in 17.19 above);

(*b*)   the investment or a part of it has been continuously held (and see 17.26 below) by the investor (as sole beneficial owner) since the investment was made (the '*continuing investment*'); and

(*c*)   the receipt wholly or partly exceeds the permitted level of receipts (see below) in respect of the continuing investment (other than by an amount of 'insignificant value').

The permitted level of receipts is exceeded where:

(i)   any value is received by the investor (disregarding any amounts of 'insignificant value') in the first three years of the period of restriction; or

(ii)   the aggregate value received by the investor (disregarding any amounts of 'insignificant value') exceeds,

      (A)   before the beginning of the fifth year of the period of restriction, 25% of the amount subscribed for the securities or shares comprising the continuing investment;

      (B)   before the beginning of the final year of that period, 50% of that amount;

      (C)   before the end of that period, 75% of that amount.

Where a receipt of value in (a) above is not an amount of 'insignificant value' but is nevertheless insufficient to trigger any withdrawal of relief under the above rules, any tax relief subsequently due is computed as if the amount subscribed for the securities or shares comprising the continuing investment (and thus the invested amount at 17.5 above) were reduced by the amount of value received. This restriction applies for tax years and company accounting periods ending on or after the most recent anniversary of the investment date falling before (or coinciding with) the receipt of value.

For the above purposes, an amount is of '*insignificant value*' if it does not exceed £1,000, or in any other case is insignificant in relation to the amount subscribed by the investor for the securities or shares comprising the continuing investment. There are provisions to aggregate a receipt of value, whether insignificant or not, with amounts of insignificant value received previously, and treating that aggregate, if it is not itself an amount of insignificant value, as an amount of value received at the time of the latest actual receipt.

[*FA 2002, Sch 16 paras 32, 34, 38*].

These provisions apply equally to receipts of value by and from persons connected (within *ICTA 1988, s 839* — see 19 CONNECTED PERSONS), at any time in the period of restriction, with the investor or, as the case may be, the CDFI. [*FA 2002, Sch 16 para 39*]. See 17.21 below for the meaning of 'value received' and the determination of the *amount* of value received.

17.21   *Meaning of, and amount of, value received.* For the purposes of 17.19 and 17.20 above, the investor '*receives value*' from the CDFI at any time when the CDFI (and see 17.19, 17.20 above *re* connected persons):

(a)   repays, redeems or repurchases any securities or shares included in the investment;

(b)   releases or waives any liability of the investor to the CDFI (which it is deemed to have done if discharge of the liability is twelve months or more overdue) or discharges (or agrees to discharge) any liability of the investor to a third party;

(c)   makes a loan or advance to the investor which has not been repaid in full before the investment is made; for this purpose a loan includes any debt incurred, other than an ordinary trade debt (as defined), and any debt due to a third party which is assigned to the CDFI;

(d)   provides a benefit or facility for the investor, or for any associates (as defined) of the investor, or for any directors or employees of the investor (if a company) or any of their associates — except in circumstances such that, if a *payment* had been made of equal value, it would have been a 'qualifying payment';

(e)   disposes of an asset to the investor for no consideration or for consideration less than market value (as defined), or acquires an asset from the investor for consideration exceeding market value; or

(f)   makes a payment to the investor other than a 'qualifying payment'.

17.22 Community Investment Tax Relief

References above to a debt or liability do not include one which would be discharged by making a 'qualifying payment'. References to a payment or disposal include one made indirectly to, or to the order of, or for the benefit of, the person in question.

Each of the following is a '*qualifying payment*':

   (i)   a reasonable (in relation to their market value) payment for any goods, services or facilities provided by the investor in the course of trade or otherwise;

   (ii)   the payment of interest at no more than a reasonable commercial rate on money lent;

   (iii)   the payment of a dividend or other distribution which represents no more than a normal return on investment;

   (iv)   a payment to acquire an asset at no more than its market value;

   (v)   a payment not exceeding a reasonable and commercial rent for property occupied;

   (vi)   a payment discharging an 'ordinary trade debt' (as defined).

The amount of value received is:

   (1)   in a case within (*a*) above, the amount received;

   (2)   in a case within (*b*) above, the amount of the liability;

   (3)   in a case within (*c*) above, the amount of the loan etc. less any amount repaid before the making of the investment;

   (4)   in a case within (*d*) above, the cost to the CDFI (net of any consideration given for it by the investor or his associate) of providing the benefit etc.;

   (5)   in a case within (*e*) above, the difference between market value and the consideration received (if any); and

   (6)   in a case within (*f*) above, the amount of the payment.

[*FA 2002, Sch 16 paras 35, 36, 50, 51(4)*].

17.22   *Value received where more than one investment.* Where the investor makes more than one investment in the CDFI for which he is eligible for, and claims, relief, any value received (other than value within 17.21(*a*) above) is apportioned between the investments by reference to the average capital balances of loans and the amounts subscribed for securities or shares. [*FA 2002, Sch 16 para 37*].

17.23   **COMPANY RESTRUCTURING**

Reorganisations of share capital. The following apply where the CDFI is a company and the investment consists of shares or, in the case of 17.24 below, shares or securities.

Rights issues etc. Where

   (a)   a reorganisation (within *TCGA 1992, s 126*) involves an allotment of shares or debentures in respect of, and in proportion to, an existing holding of shares of the same class in the CDFI held by the investor in a single capacity,

   (*b*)   community investment tax relief is attributable (see 17.15 above) to the shares in the existing holding or to the allotted shares, and

   (*c*)   if the relief is attributable to the shares in the existing holding, those shares have been held continuously (and see 17.26 below) by the investor since they were issued,

the share reorganisation rules of *TCGA 1992, ss 127–130* are disapplied. The effect is that the allotted shares are treated as a separate holding acquired at the time of the reorganisation. This does not, however, apply in the case of bonus shares where these are issued in respect of shares comprised in the existing holding and are of the same class and carry the same rights as those shares. (For *TCGA 1992, ss 126–130*, see Tolley's Capital Gains Tax under Shares and Securities.)

Reorganisation involving issue of QCB. If, in a case otherwise within *TCGA 1992, s 116(10)* (see Tolley's Capital Gains Tax under Qualifying Corporate Bonds),

(i)   the old asset consists of shares to which community investment tax relief is attributable (see 17.15 above) and which have been held continuously (see 17.26 below) by the investor since they were issued, and

(ii)   the new asset consists of a qualifying corporate bond,

the usual treatment is disapplied. The effect is that the investor is deemed to have disposed of the shares at the time of the reorganisation, and the resulting chargeable gain or allowable loss crystallises *at that time*.

[*FA 2002, Sch 16 paras 40, 51(2)*].

17.24   **Company reconstructions.** *TCGA 1992, s 135* (exchange of securities for those in another company) and *s 136* (schemes of reconstruction involving issue of securities), which normally equate the new holding with the original shares, are disapplied in the following circumstances:

(*a*)   an investor holds shares in or debentures of a company (company A);

(*b*)   community investment tax relief is attributable (see 17.15 above) to those shares;

(*c*)   those shares have been held continuously (see 17.26 below) by the investor since they were issued; and

(*d*)   there is a reconstruction whereby another company issues shares or debentures in exchange for, or in respect of, company A shares or debentures.

The result is that the transaction is treated, both for the purposes of this chapter and for the purposes of taxing chargeable gains, as a disposal of the original securities or shares (and an acquisition of a new holding). (For *TCGA 1992, ss 135, 136*, see Tolley's Capital Gains Tax under Shares and Securities.)

[*FA 2002, Sch 16 paras 41, 48(2)*].

17.25   **ACCREDITATION AND TAX RELIEF CERTIFICATES**

Accreditation. A body may apply to the Secretary of State for Trade and Industry for accreditation as a CDFI. In practice, the accreditation process is administered by the Small Business Investment Taskforce, assisted by the Small Business Service (an Agency of the DTI). (Treasury Explanatory Notes to Finance Bill 2002). The body's principal objective must be to provide (directly or indirectly) finance, or finance and access to business advice, for enterprises for disadvantaged communities. The latter term includes enterprises located in disadvantaged areas and enterprises owned or operated by, or designed to serve, members of disadvantaged groups. The body must also satisfy such other criteria as may be specified in Treasury regulations. Such regulations may distinguish between 'wholesale' CDFIs, i.e. those whose objective is to finance other, generally smaller, CDFIs, and 'retail' CDFIs, i.e. those whose objective is to invest directly in enterprises. The terms and conditions of accreditation are also to be set by regulations; these may include a right of appeal against a refusal to accredit, and provision for the withdrawal of an accreditation, and the possible imposition of penalties, in consequence of any breach of terms and conditions. See now the *Community Investment Tax Relief (Accreditation of Community Development Finance Institutions) Regulations 2003 (SI 2003 No 96)*. [*FA 2002, Sch 16 paras 4–6*].

An accreditation normally has effect for three years. Where an application for accreditation is made before 6 April 2003, the accreditation may be backdated to 17 April 2002 (at the earliest) and have effect until immediately before the third anniversary of the date of grant. See also 17.1 above. A new accreditation may, if the CDFI so claims, displace an existing accreditation. [*FA 2002, Sch 16 para 7*].

Tax relief certificates. Before an investment in a CDFI can qualify for tax relief, the CDFI must issue to the investor a tax relief certificate (see 17.3, 17.8(*b*) above) in a specified form. In relation to an accreditation period, a CDFI may issue tax relief certificates in respect of investments made in it within that period of an aggregate value of up to £20 million in the case of a wholesale CDFI (see above) or £10 million in the case of a retail CDFI. The Treasury may substitute other figures by order but not so as to reduce them for periods beginning before the order takes effect. Any tax relief certificate issued wholly or partly in contravention of these limits is invalid (and thus the investment in question does not satisfy 17.8(*b*) above and does not attract tax relief). A CDFI is liable to a penalty of up to £3,000 for the issue of a tax relief certificate made fraudulently or negligently. [*FA 2002, Sch 16 para 12*].

17.26   MISCELLANEOUS

Circumstances in which investment not held 'continuously'. An investor is not treated for the purposes of this chapter as having held an investment (or a part of an investment) continuously throughout a period if:

(*a*)   under any provision of *TCGA 1992*, the investment (or part) has been deemed to be disposed of and immediately reacquired by the investor at any time in that period; or

(*b*)   there has been at any time in that period a transaction treated, by virtue of 17.24 above (company reconstructions etc.), as a disposal by the investor.

[*FA 2002, Sch 16 para 49*].

17.27   Nominees and bare trustees.
For the purposes of this chapter, actions of a person's nominee or bare trustee in relation to loans, shares or securities are treated as actions of that person. [*FA 2002, Sch 16 para 44*].

17.28   Disclosure of information.
There are provisions for the exchange of information between the Secretary of State and the Revenue insofar as this is necessary to enable them both to discharge their functions appertaining to community investment tax relief. Information thus obtained cannot be further disclosed except for the purposes of legal proceedings arising out of those functions. [*FA 2002, Sch 16 para 43*].

18   Compensation for Loss of Employment (and Damages)

Cross-references. See 71.38 SCHEDULE D, CASES I AND II ('Compensation, Damages etc. — Receipts') and 71.37 ('Compensation, Damages etc. — Payments') for treatment in relation to trading profits and 71.44 for allowability of payments to employees; 75.35 SCHEDULE E—EMPLOYMENT INCOME for Redundancy Payments, 75.37 for Restrictive Covenants, 75.44 for certain payments to MPs etc. and 75.48 for wages in lieu of notice.

Simon's Direct Tax Service E4.8.

18.1   The following paragraphs apply to lump sums paid on termination of an office or employment and, at 18.7 below, to the reduction of an award for damages by reference to the tax liability.

18.2   **PAYMENTS AND BENEFITS ON TERMINATION OF OFFICE OR EMPLOYMENT — SUMMARY**

In determining the correct treatment for tax purposes of a sum receivable by a director or employee on termination of his office or employment, it is first necessary to see whether it is taxable as employment income under the rules for taxing general earnings (see 75.1 SCHEDULE E—EMPLOYMENT INCOME). See 18.3 below for an outline of the principles to be applied. If it is within the general rules, it is taxable in full under PAYE (55) at the time of the payment.

If it is not within the general earnings rules, such a sum will generally be taxable as employment income by virtue of, and in accordance with, the special legislation in *ITEPA 2003, ss 401–416* (principally in *ICTA 1988, s 148* before 2003/04). See 18.4, 18.5 below for the application of this legislation, and 18.6 below for exemptions.

18.3   **COMPENSATION FOR TERMINATION OF OFFICE OR EMPLOYMENT — GENERAL TAX LAW**

The following principles apply in determining whether a sum received in compensation for termination of office or employment is taxable under the general earnings rules in 75 SCHEDULE E—EMPLOYMENT INCOME. See 18.4 *et seq.* below as regards such payments not within these rules.

A payment made to a director or employee by way of reward for services, past, present or future, is within the general earnings rules. It was considered by the Revenue that this could include any termination payment received under the terms of a contract of service, or where there was an expectation of receiving such a payment firm enough to allow the payment to be viewed as part of the reward for services. In *Mairs v Haughey HL 1993, 66 TC 273*, however, it was held that a non-statutory redundancy payment would not be within the general earnings charge, being compensation for the employee's not being able to receive emoluments from the employment rather than emoluments from the employment itself. (The case concerned a payment for the waiver of a contingent right to such a payment, which was to be accorded the same tax treatment.) Following the decision in *Mairs v Haughey*, the Revenue published Statement of Practice SP 1/94. This acknowledges that lump sum payments under a non-statutory redundancy scheme are liable to income tax only under what was then *ICTA 1988, s 148* (now *ITEPA 2003, ss 401–416*), provided that they are genuinely made solely on account of redundancy as defined in *Employment Rights Act 1996, s 139*, whether the scheme is a standing scheme forming part of the conditions of service or an *ad hoc* scheme devised to meet a particular situation. SP 1/94 indicates, however, that the Revenue is concerned to distinguish payments which are in reality terminal bonuses or other reward for services, which are fully taxable under the general earnings rules, and that in view of the often complex arrangements for redundancy, and the need to consider each scheme on its own facts, employers may submit proposed schemes (together with any explanatory letter to be sent to employees) to the inspector for advance clearance. (Revenue Pamphlet IR 131, SP 1/94).

The following decided cases reflect the different approaches the courts have adopted in relation to such compensation. Proper compensation for loss of office is usually exempt (see *Clayton v Lavender Ch D 1965, 42 TC 607*) except where payable under service agreement (see *Dale v De Soissons CA 1950, 32 TC 118*) or under rights conferred by company's articles (*Henry v Foster CA 1932, 16 TC 605*). But an agreed sum payable for waiving such rights was held not assessable (*Hunter v Dewhurst HL 1932, 16 TC 605*), as also a payment in lieu of agreed pension (*Wales v Tilley HL 1943, 25 TC 136*). Payment in settlement of claim re breach of service contract also exempt (*Du Cros v Ryall KB 1935, 19 TC 444*), but cf. *Carter v Wadman CA 1946, 28 TC 41* and *Richardson v Delaney Ch D 2001, 74 TC 167*. Voluntary payments on retirement held to be personal testimonials and not assessable (*Cowan v Seymour CA 1919, 7 TC 372; Mulvey v Coffey HC(I) 2 ITC 239*). A transfer fee paid by his old club to a professional footballer held to be assessable under general earnings rules and not as a termination payment (*Shilton v Wilmshurst HL 1991, 64 TC 78*).

Sums paid on cessation of office in lieu of future income were held not to be assessable in *Duff v Barlow KB 1941, 23 TC 633; Carter v Wadman CA 1946, 28 TC 41; Henley v Murray CA 1950, 31 TC 351*; and *Clayton v Lavender Ch D 1965, 42 TC 607*. *Hofman v Wadman KB 1946, 27 TC 192*, in which the decision was against the taxpayer, was not followed in *Clayton v Lavender*. But the following items paid during continuance of office were held liable: agreed sum paid to director to remain in office (*Prendergast v Cameron HL 1940, 23 TC 122*); for surrender of rights to fees or commission (*Leeland v Boarland KB 1945, 27 TC 71; Wilson v Daniels KB 1943, 25 TC 473; Bolam v Muller KB 1947, 28 TC 471* and *McGregor v Randall Ch D 1984, 58 TC 110*); and for accepting lower fees (*Wales v Tilley HL 1943, 25 TC 136*). See also *Williams v Simmonds Ch D 1981, 55 TC 17*. Statutory redundancy payments under *Employment Rights Act 1996* (or NI equivalent) are otherwise exempt from tax (see *ITEPA 2003, s 309*) but must be taken into account for the purposes of the special legislation in *ITEPA 2003, ss 401–416*. A proposed supplementary redundancy payment which, following a change in circumstances, was made to all employees whether or not made redundant, was held to be assessable under the general earnings rules where made to employees not made redundant (*Allan v CIR; Cullen v CIR CS 1994, 66 TC 681*). However, in *Mimtec Ltd v CIR (Sp C 277), [2001] SSCD 101* a Special Commissioner held that certain payments made following redundancy negotiations 'in recognition of any entitlements under the consultation process including pay in lieu of notice etc.' were not taxable as earnings.

See 75.48 SCHEDULE E—EMPLOYMENT INCOME for the Revenue view of payments in lieu of notice.

Sum paid as compensation for loss of benefit under an abandoned refuse salvage scheme held assessable (*Holland v Geoghegan Ch D 1972, 48 TC 482*).

See 3.9 ANTI-AVOIDANCE regarding capital sums received in lieu of earnings.

See generally Revenue Employment Income Manual EIM 12800 *et seq.*

18.4   **TERMINATION PAYMENTS AND BENEFITS — SPECIAL LEGISLATION**

The general legal position in 18.3 above is modified by special legislation as explained in 18.5, 18.6 below. A payment taxable under any other provisions is not within this special legislation, but *a compensation payment which does not fall within the special legislation nevertheless remains subject to the general law.*

For the interaction of these provisions and *Gourley* principles (see 18.7 below) see *Stewart v Glentaggart Ltd CS 1963, 42 ATC 318; Bold v Brough QB, [1963] 3 AER 849* and *Parsons v BNM Laboratories Ltd CA, [1963] 2 AER 658.*

18.5   **Termination payments and benefits — the charge to tax.** Under the special legislation in *ITEPA 2003, ss 401–416* (previously in *ICTA 1988, s 148*), payments and other benefits 'received' **after 5 April 1998** in connection with the termination of a person's office or employment (or with any change in the duties thereof or earnings therefrom), and not otherwise chargeable to income tax (see also 18.4 above), are chargeable to tax as employment income if *and to the extent that* they amount in aggregate to more than £30,000. The charge is as employment income for the tax year in which the payment or benefit is received. For these purposes, a cash benefit is treated as '*received*' when payment is made (including any payment on account) or when the recipient becomes entitled to require such payment. A non-cash benefit is treated as '*received*' when it is used or enjoyed. Where a payment or benefit, or the right to receive it, was brought into charge before 1998/99, it is not charged a second time on its receipt after 5 April 1998. See 18.6 below for exceptions from this charge.

A benefit includes anything which would be taxable earnings from the office or employment (or would be charged to tax as such) if received for performance of the duties thereof. However, a right to receive payments or benefits is not itself regarded as a benefit. A benefit also includes anything which would be taxable earnings, if received for the performance of duties, but for the availability of an 'earnings-only exemption'. After 5 April 2002, however, the following earnings-only exemptions can be disregarded.

- Any benefit received in connection with a change in duties or earnings to the extent that, were it received for the performance of duties, it would fall within the exemption at 75.36 SCHEDULE E—EMPLOYMENT INCOME (exempt removal benefits and expenses on relocation).

- Certain benefits received in connection with the termination of an office or employment which, were they received for the performance of duties, would fall within certain specified exemptions (see *ITEPA 2003, s 402(2)*).

An '*earnings-only exemption*' is defined in *ITEPA 2003, s 227*, but, unhelpfully, such exemptions are not listed; broadly, it is an exemption that removes a charge to tax as general earnings as opposed to a wider exemption that removes any charge to tax as employment income; this is explained in greater detail in the Explanatory Notes (on clause 227) to the Income Tax (Earnings and Pensions) Bill. See 75.45 SCHEDULE E—EMPLOYMENT INCOME for the termination-related exemptions of *ITEPA 2003, ss 310, 311* (counselling and retraining); these, for example, are not earnings-only exemptions and thus can be disregarded entirely for the purposes of these provisions.

The charge applies to payments and other benefits received directly or indirectly, in consideration or in consequence of, or otherwise in connection with, the termination (or change), by the employee himself, by a spouse, other relative or other dependant of his or by his personal representatives, or provided on his behalf or to his order. The charge is on the employee or, in the event of his death, on his personal representatives. Where an individual suffered constructive dismissal on grounds of discrimination, the amount awarded by a tribunal was within the charge to the extent that it related to loss of income but not to the extent that it covered injury to feelings (*Walker v Adams (Sp C 344), [2003] SSCD 269*). For the reporting requirements in relation to taxable termination payments, see 55.9 PAY AS YOU EARN.

Where a payment or benefit could fall to be taxed under both these provisions and the benefits code (see 75.12 SCHEDULE E — EMPLOYMENT INCOME), the benefits code takes priority after 5 April 2003. Previously, the Revenue took the opposite view. (There will not usually be any overlap between the two charging provisions where payments or benefits are received in connection with *termination* of employment, as opposed to a change of duties etc.) (Revenue Tax Bulletin June 2003 pp 1036, 1037).

Non-cash benefits. The amount of a non-cash benefit is normally its cash equivalent as determined under the benefits code (see 75.14 *et seq.* SCHEDULE E—EMPLOYMENT INCOME) as applied, with the necessary modifications (including a modified version of the rules for valuing the benefit of living accommodation) by *ITEPA 2003, s 415.* (Before 2003/04, non-cash benefits were valued in accordance with *ICTA 1988, s 596B,* see 67.9 RETIREMENT SCHEMES, as appropriately modified, producing broadly similar results.) If, however, a greater figure would thus result, the benefit is the amount of earnings it would give rise to if received by an employee for duties of the employment (money's worth), thus bringing into charge any appreciation in the value of an asset since its acquisition by the person providing it. Where the cash equivalent of a beneficial loan (see 75.20 SCHEDULE E—EMPLOYMENT INCOME) is charged under these provisions for any tax year, the taxpayer is treated as having paid interest for that year of an amount equal to that brought into charge (but not to the extent that the amount otherwise chargeable is covered by the £30,000 threshold); general principles then apply to determine whether such notional interest is allowable for tax purposes (see 43 INTEREST PAYABLE).

Application of £30,000 threshold. The £30,000 threshold is utilised against payments and benefits received in earlier tax years before those of later years. In any one tax year, the threshold (or so much of it as remains unutilised in earlier years) is set firstly against any cash benefits as they are received and any balance is set against the aggregate of non-cash benefits for the year. The threshold applies to the aggregate of payments and benefits provided in respect of the same person in respect of the same employment or of different employments with the same employer or 'associated' employers (as defined in *ITEPA 2003, s 404*) or successors.

[*ITEPA 2003, ss 401–404, 415, 416; ICTA 1988, s 148, Sch 11 paras 1, 2, 7, 8, 12–16; FA 1998, s 58(1)(2)(4), Sch 9 Pt 1; FA 2002, Sch 6 para 5*].

See Revenue Tax Bulletin October 1998 pp 582–587 for an article (with numerous examples) describing the changes brought about by the above provisions.

Similar rules applied to payments and other benefits 'received' (as above) before 6 April 1998, with the fundamental difference that all chargeable amounts were treated as received on the date of termination (or change) (or, in the case of a payment in commutation of annual or other periodical payments, the date the commutation was effected) and were thus taxable for the tax year in which that date fell. There was no statutory rule for valuing non-cash benefits. Any person making a payment within *ICTA 1988, s 148* in any tax year had to notify the inspector in writing within 30 days after the end of that year. [*ICTA 1988, ss 148, 188(4)(5)(7)*]. Continuing benefits (e.g. the use of a car or a beneficial loan) included in a termination settlement were taxable under *section 148* on the value of the right to receive the future benefits. See *George v Ward (Sp C 30), [1995] SSCD 230* (value of provision of car for limited period following termination held within *section 148,* but by reference to period actually made available rather than for longer period for which original termination agreement provided). For 1996/97 and 1997/98 only, pending new legislation, the Revenue were prepared to accept, as an alternative to the strict application of *section 148,* the adoption by the taxpayer of an alternative basis whereby the benefits are taxed as they are received or enjoyed (but not so as to alter the year for which they are taxable). The annual benefit is to be calculated as required by *ICTA 1988, s 596B* (see 67.9 RETIREMENT SCHEMES). The self-assessment return for the year of termination should include the benefit so calculated for that year; the Revenue will thereafter make separate assessments for that year in respect of the benefits enjoyed or received in subsequent years. Where, however, the taxpayer can demonstrate that the total benefits assessed on this basis exceed those assessable on the strict basis, the excess will not be collected. For details of how these arrangements are applied in practice, see Revenue Tax Bulletin June 1997 pp 427–429.

A payment or benefit within *ITEPA 2003, ss 401–416* is 'taxable specific income', which means that the charge is not dependent on the employee's residence or domicile status. See 75.1 SCHEDULE E—EMPLOYMENT INCOME and also *Nichols v Gibson CA 1996, 68 TC 611*.

A statutory redundancy payment under *Employment Rights Act 1996* (or NI equivalent) is specifically brought within these provisions. [*ITEPA 2003, s 309(3); ICTA 1988, s 580(3)*]. For the position as regards a payment under a non-statutory redundancy scheme, see 18.3 above.

For MPs see *ITEPA 2003, s 291*, and for European MPs, 75.44 SCHEDULE E—EMPLOYMENT INCOME.

Compensation for unfair dismissal, in a case in which the employment tribunal also made a reinstatement order, was held to be within these provisions (and thus subject to the £30,000 threshold) notwithstanding that the effect of the reinstatement order was to treat the taxpayer as if he had never been dismissed (*Wilson v Clayton Ch D, 2004 STI 1121*).

Expenses incurred by taxpayer in obtaining an award for unfair dismissal or securing fresh employment held not deductible (*Warnett v Jones Ch D 1979, 53 TC 283*).

See 75.26 SCHEDULE E—EMPLOYMENT INCOME for exemption from these provisions for payment made or benefit provided to reimburse the employee for cost of indemnity insurance or certain liabilities relating to the employment.

As to whether *compensation to auditor* and others falls within these provisions, see 75.27 SCHEDULE E—EMPLOYMENT INCOME.

Simon's Direct Tax Service. See E4.805 *et seq.*

18.6   The following are **excepted from the charge** under 18.5 above on termination payments and benefits (or, in the case of (vi) below, may be subject to reduction).

  (i)   Payments and other benefits where termination arises from death, injury or disability of the employee or office holder. [*ITEPA 2003, s 406; ICTA 1988, s 188(1)(a), Sch 11 para 3; FA 1998, Sch 9 para 3, Sch 27 Pt III(9)*]. 'Disability' covers not only a condition resulting from a sudden affliction but also continuing incapacity to perform the duties of an office or employment arising out of the culmination of a process of deterioration of physical or mental health caused by chronic illness. (Revenue Pamphlet IR 131, SP 10/81). See e.g. *Horner v Hasted Ch D, [1995] STC 766* (relief refused). (See, however, 67.12 RETIREMENT SCHEMES as regards certain *ex gratia* payments under unapproved arrangements which may be chargeable under *ITEPA 2003, ss 393–400.*)

  (ii) Benefits provided before 1 December 1993, or on or after that date under retirement benefit schemes entered into before that date and not varied on or after that date, for the provision of which the employee has been charged under *ICTA 1970, s 220* or *ICTA 1988, s 595* (now *ITEPA 2003, s 386*). [*ICTA 1988, s 188(1)(c); FA 1994, s 108(7)(8)*]. (See also now 67.9 RETIREMENT SCHEMES.)

  (iii) Any payment or other benefit provided under a tax-exempt pension scheme (as defined) by way of compensation for loss of office or employment or for loss or diminution of earnings, in either case because of ill-health, or properly regarded as earned by past service. [*ITEPA 2003, s 407; ICTA 1988, s 188(1)(d)(2), Sch 11 para 4; FA 1998, Sch 9 Pt I, Sch 27 Pt III(9)*].

  (iv) Certain payments and other benefits (including commutation of annual sums) provided to members of the armed forces. [*ITEPA 2003, s 411; ICTA 1988, s 188(1)(e), Sch 11 para 5; FA 1998, Sch 9 Pt I, Sch 27 Pt III(9)*].

(v)   A benefit provided under a pension scheme administered by a Commonwealth government or a payment of compensation, for loss of career, interruption of service etc. in connection with constitutional change in a Commonwealth country, to a person employed in the public service of that country. [*ITEPA 2003, s 412; ICTA 1988, s 188(1)(f), Sch 11 para 6; FA 1998, Sch 9 Pt I, Sch 27 Pt III(9); International Development Act 2002, Sch 3 para 10*].

(vi)   Payments and other benefits where the office or employment in question included foreign service (as defined). Depending on length of foreign service in relation to total service, payments etc. may be wholly excepted or the amount otherwise chargeable may be proportionately reduced. [*ITEPA 2003, ss 413, 414; ICTA 1988, s 188(3), Sch 11 paras 9–11; FA 1998, Sch 9 Pt I, Sch 27 Pt III(9)*].

(vii)   A contribution to a tax-exempt pension scheme (as defined) or approved personal pension scheme to provide benefits in accordance with the scheme as part of an arrangement relating to the termination of an office or employment. [*ITEPA 2003, s 408*]. Before 2003/04, this exception applied by virtue of SP 2/81, which also specifically excepted the purchase from a Life Office of an approved annuity for the employee. (Revenue Pamphlet IR 131, SP 2/81).

(viii)   Legal costs. Where an employee takes action to recover compensation for termination of office or employment, any legal costs recovered from the employer are strictly chargeable without any deduction for the costs incurred. By concession, tax will not be charged under 18.5 above on such recovered costs where either:

    (*a*)   the dispute is settled without recourse to the courts, and the costs are paid direct to the employee's solicitor under the settlement agreement, in full or partial discharge of the solicitor's bill of costs incurred by the employee only in connection with the termination of the office or employment; or

    (*b*)   the dispute goes to court, and the costs are paid in accordance with a court order (including where they are paid direct to the employee).

    Other professional costs, such as accountancy fees, are not covered by this concession, but it does cover legal costs incurred by the employee's solicitor in consulting other professionals for the specific claim or in paying the expenses of expert professional witnesses.

    (Revenue Pamphlet IR 1, A81; Revenue Tax Bulletin October 1994 p 170).

(ix)   From 6 April 2002,

-     any payment received in connection with a change in duties or earnings to the extent that, were it received for the performance of duties, it would fall within the exemption at 75.36 SCHEDULE E—EMPLOYMENT INCOME (exempt removal benefits and expenses on relocation); and

-     any contribution made, in connection with the termination of an office or employment, to the employee's approved personal pension scheme.

    [*ITEPA 2003, s 405; ICTA 1988, s 148(2A); FA 2002, Sch 6 para 5*].

Simon's Direct Tax Service. See E4.806, E4.807.

18.7   DAMAGES — REDUCTION FOR TAX

Tax liability is taken into account in fixing *damages* for injury, see *British Transport Commission v Gourley HL 1955, 34 ATC 305*. For application of *Gourley* principle see *West Suffolk CC v W Rought Ltd HL 1956, 35 ATC 315* and contrast *Stoke-on-Trent City Council v Wood Mitchell & Co Ltd CA 1978, [1979] STC 197* (compulsory purchase of land);

Lyndale Fashion Mfrs v Rich CA 1972, [1973] STC 32 (tax on damages calculated as if top slice of income after expenses deducted); *In re Houghton Main Colliery Ch D 1956, 23 ATC 320* (lump sum payable re pensions); *Stewart v Glentaggart CS 1963, 42 ATC 318*; *Parsons v BNM Labs CA 1963, 42 ATC 200* (damages for wrongful dismissal); *McGhie & Sons v BTC QB 1962, 41 ATC 144* (prohibition from mining under railway — cf. 71.38(*c*) SCHEDULE D, CASES I AND II); and *John v James Ch D, [1986] STC 352* (no deduction for tax paid by defendant on sums wrongfully retained or for tax plaintiff would have been liable for on these sums or on compound interest award). But cf. *Spencer v Macmillan's Trustees CS 1958, 37 ATC 388* (breach of contract). A PAYE refund was deducted in *Hartley v Sandholme QB, [1974] STC 434*. In a case involving taxable damages paid to a large group of Lloyd's Names, it was held that the fact that certain of the Names would receive a tax benefit, due to the differential tax rates applicable to the damages and the corresponding loss reliefs, did not require a departure from the general principle that no account is to be taken of taxation where both damages and lost profits are taxable (*Deeny and others v Gooda Walker Ltd HL 1996, 68 TC 458*).

As regards whether interest on awarded damages should take account of the extent to which the damages are taxable, see *Deeny and others v Gooda Walker Ltd (in liquidation) and others (No 4) QB, [1995] STC 696*.

Simon's Direct Tax Service. See E4.821 *et seq.*

19   Connected Persons

[*ICTA 1988, s 839* as amended]

Simon's Direct Tax Service C2.110.

19.1   For many tax purposes, certain persons are treated as being so closely involved with each other that they must either be viewed as the same person or that transactions between them must be treated differently from transactions 'at arm's length'. These 'connected persons' are generally defined for tax purposes as below. It should, however, be noted that a modified definition may be applied in relation to any specific legislation, to which reference is made as appropriate in the text describing that legislation.

19.2   **An individual** is connected with his spouse or with relatives (including their spouses) of his or his spouse. It appears that a widow or widower is no longer a spouse (*Vestey's Exors and Vestey v CIR HL 1949, 31 TC 1*). Spouses divorced by decree nisi remain connected persons until the decree is made absolute (*Aspden v Hildesley Ch D 1981, 55 TC 609*). See definition of relative in 19.8 below.

19.3   **A trustee of a settlement,** in his capacity as such, is connected with

(*a*)   the settlor (if an individual) (see 19.8 below), and

(*b*)   any person connected with the settlor (if within (*a*)), and

(*c*)   a body corporate connected with the settlement (see 19.8 below).

19.4   **A partner** is connected with the person with whom he is in partnership and with the spouse or relative of that person except in connection with acquisitions and disposals of partnership assets made pursuant to bona fide commercial arrangements.

19.5   **A company is connected with another company if**

(*a*)   the same person controls both, or

(*b*)   one is controlled by a person who has control of the other in conjunction with persons connected with him, or

(*c*)   a person controls one company and persons connected with him control the other, or

(*d*)   the same group of persons controls both, or

(*e*)   the companies are controlled by separate groups which can be regarded as the same by interchanging connected persons.

19.6   **A company is connected with another person who** (either alone or with persons connected with him) **has control of it.** It is understood that the Revenue will accept that a partnership and a company under common control are connected in relation to the treatment for capital allowances of assets transferred on a succession (Tolley's Practical Tax 1981 p 142).

19.7   **Persons acting together to secure or exercise control of a company** are treated in relation to that company as connected with each other and with any other person acting on the direction of any of them to secure or exercise such control. For the meaning of 'acting together to secure or exercise control', see *Steele v EVC International NV (formerly European Vinyls Corp (Holdings) BV) CA 1996, 69 TC 88*. Control may be 'exercised' passively. See *Floor v Davis HL 1979, 52 TC 609*.

19.8   '*Company*' includes any body corporate, unincorporated association or unit trust scheme (within *ICTA 1988, s 469*). It does not include a partnership.

'*Control*' is as defined by *ICTA 1988, s 416* (see Tolley's Corporation Tax under Close Companies) but see below as regards *ICTA 1988, s 840* definition.

'*Relative*' means brother, sister, ancestor or lineal descendant.

'*Settlement*' includes any disposition, trust, covenant, agreement, arrangement or, for 1995/96 onwards, transfer of assets. [*ICTA 1988, s 681(4) (repealed); ICTA 1988, s 660G(1); FA 1995, Sch 17 para 1*]. See also 81.16 SETTLEMENTS.

'*Settlor*' is any person by whom the settlement was made or who has directly or indirectly (or by a reciprocal arrangement) provided, or undertaken to provide, funds for the settlement. [*ICTA 1988, s 681(4) (repealed); ICTA 1988, s 660G(1)(2); FA 1995, Sch 17 para 1*].

'*A body corporate connected with the settlement*' is a close company (or one which would be close if resident in the UK) the participators in which include the trustees of the settlement, or a company of which such a close company etc. has control. 'Control' is as defined in *ICTA 1988, s 840*, i.e. the power of a person by shareholding or voting power (whether directly or through another company), or under Articles of Association or other regulating document, to secure that the company's affairs are conducted according to his wishes. [*ICTA 1988, s 681(5) (repealed); ICTA 1988, s 682A(2), s 839(3A); FA 1995, Sch 17 paras 11, 20*].

20 Construction Industry Scheme (CIS)

See also Revenue Pamphlets IR 14/15(CIS), IR 40(CIS), IR 109, IR 116(CIS), IR 117(CIS), IR 148, IR 157, IR 164(CIS) and IR 180(CIS).

Simon's Direct Tax Service E5.5.

Future changes. A new Construction Industry Scheme (CIS) is to be introduced from April 2006, based on legislation in *FA 2004*; in the meantime, the Revenue are increasing compliance activities in the sector. See 20.8 *et seq.* below for the new scheme.

20.1 **CIS APPLICABLE FROM 1 AUGUST 1999 TO APRIL 2006**

With effect for payments made on or after 1 August 1999, the scheme for deduction of tax from payments to construction sub-contractors who do not have a tax certificate entitling them to gross payment, and the arrangements and conditions for the issue of such certificates, are substantially revised. The revised scheme is described at 20.2 *et seq.* below. It is intended that, under the revised scheme, most sub-contractors will *not* hold tax certificates, but will hold registration cards (see 20.3 below) and receive payments after deduction on account of tax. The main changes from the scheme as it applied before 1 August 1999 are as follows.

(*a*) The 23% deduction is replaced by a deduction of a percentage determined by the Treasury by order, which may not exceed the basic rate (and is set at 18% from 6 April 2000).

(*b*) A minimum anticipated annual turnover (prescribed by regulation and, in the case of firms or companies, broadly geared to the number of individuals who are partners or directors) is a precondition for the issue of a tax certificate.

(*c*) The limited certificates for school leavers and where a bank guarantee is in force are withdrawn.

(*d*) A general exemption from deduction is provided where conditions to be prescribed are met in relation to a payment under any contract and to the person making the payment.

(*e*) All public offices and departments of the Crown, and such statutory bodies as are designated in regulations, are normally to be treated as contractors for the purposes of the deduction scheme. However, for these and the other public bodies treated as contractors, an exemption based on the average annual construction expenditure test already used for businesses is introduced. Government departments treated as contractors will be subject to the same obligations, sanctions and Revenue powers of enforcement as other contractors.

(*f*) The average annual expenditure on construction operations which renders the person incurring the expenditure a contractor for the purposes of the deduction scheme is increased from £250,000 to £1,000,000.

(*g*) The conditions for a tax certificate for an individual partner in a firm are generally aligned with those for sole traders, insofar as they relate to the circumstances of the individual. The individual conditions relating to the length of time the business has been carried on are removed.

(*h*) The fine (maximum £5,000) on summary conviction for certain fraudulent attempts to obtain or misuse a tax certificate is replaced by a penalty up to £3,000.

Exemption certificates covering periods beginning before and ending after 31 July 1999 cease to have effect after that date.

Registration cards. As referred to above, in conjunction with the revised deduction scheme, a mandatory registration card system is introduced for sub-contractors not holding a tax certificate. See 20.2, 20.3 below. In outline, the registration card system is as follows.

(i)   The card carries the sub-contractor's name and photograph, the tax reference and the national insurance number.

(ii) Contractors are required to check cards before making payments under deduction.

(iii) The cards are available on request to anyone working, or intending to work, in the construction industry.

(iv) A penalty of up to £3,000 applies for failure by a contractor to take the necessary steps to require the production of registration cards and to check their validity, or to make accurate returns in relation to registration card payments (unless there were reasonable grounds for accepting the validity of a card and all reasonable steps were taken to ensure the correctness of the return).

For detailed coverage of the scheme applicable before 1 August 1999, see the 1998/99 and earlier editions.

20.2   **Payments from which tax must be deducted.** Where a 'contractor' carrying on a business which includes 'construction operations' makes any payment (except as below) to, or to the nominee of, a 'sub-contractor' under a contract relating to 'construction operations' in the UK or on offshore installations within UK territorial waters, then, unless the recipient meets the conditions for gross payment (see 20.4 below), the payer must deduct, and pay over to the Revenue, a specified percentage of so much of the payment (excluding any VAT and CITB levy) as does not represent the cost of materials. Before making any such payment, the contractor must ensure that the sub-contractor produces a valid registration card (see 20.3 below), and must satisfy himself that the person producing it is the person to whom it was issued (or an authorised user of a company card, being a director or secretary of the company), unless he has done so on a previous occasion and has no reason to doubt that it remains valid for the person who produced it. Possession of a registration card by a sub-contractor does not, however, relieve the contractor of the responsibility to establish whether the sub-contractor is employed or self-employed (see 20.7 below). A penalty not exceeding £3,000 may apply for failure by a contractor to carry out these checks. These provisions do not apply to payments under a contract of employment, payments treated as earnings from an employment by virtue of *ITEPA 2003, ss 44–47* (workers supplied by agencies — see 75.49 SCHEDULE E—EMPLOYMENT INCOME), or payments excluded by regulations (including certain payments under contracts of value £1,000 or less). The percentage deduction rate is determined by the Treasury by order, and may not exceed the basic rate of income tax. [*ICTA 1988, s 559(1)–(4A), s 560(1), s 561(1), s 566(2B), s 567(1)(b); FA 1995, s 139, Sch 27 para 1; FA 1996, s 178(1); FA 1998, s 55(2)(3); ITEPA 2003, Sch 6 para 58; SI 1993 No 743, reg 7F; SI 1998 Nos 2620, 2622, reg 8; SI 2000 No 922*].

The specified rate of deduction is reduced from 23% to 18% with effect from 6 April 2000. [*SI 2000 No 921*].

The following items should be deducted in determining the amount subject to deduction: amounts paid by the sub-contractor for materials (including VAT if the subcontractor is not registered for VAT); the cost of manufacture or prefabrication of materials used in the construction operations; consumable stores; fuel (except fuel for travelling); plant hire used in the construction operations. Where a sub-contractor does not supply evidence of the cost to him of materials, the contractor should make a fair estimate of the actual cost. See Revenue Pamphlet IR 14/15(CIS), paras 3.3, 3.4.

20.2　Construction Industry Scheme (CIS)

A '*sub-contractor*' is a party to a contract relating to 'construction operations' who is under a duty to carry out, or to furnish his own, or others', labour in the carrying out of, such operations, or otherwise answerable to the contractor for the carrying out of such operations by others. See generally Revenue Pamphlet IR 14/15(CIS), paras 2.8–2.11.

A '*contractor*' is:

(*a*)　any person carrying on a business which includes 'construction operations';

(*b*)　any person carrying on a business at any time if his average annual expenditure on construction operations in the three years up to the end of his last period of account exceeded £1,000,000 or, where the business was not being carried on at the beginning of that three-year period, if his total expenditure on such operations up to the end of that last period of account exceeded £3,000,000. A person who is a contractor under this provision will continue within that definition until he satisfies the Board that his expenditure on construction operations has been below £1,000,000 in each of three successive years beginning in or after that period of account. For the purposes of these expenditure limits, where a trade is transferred from one company to another and *ICTA 1988, s 343* (no change of ownership) applies, the transferor's expenditure will be treated as the transferee's, with apportionment by the Board (subject to appeal) when only part of the trade is transferred; and

(*c*)　any public office or department of the Crown; any local authority; any development corporation or new town commission; the Commission for the New Towns; the Housing Corporation; the Secretary of State for Wales (in relation to a contract made under *Housing Associations Act 1985, s 89*); any housing association or trust; Scottish Homes; the Northern Ireland Housing Executive; any NHS trust (or NI equivalent); the Corporate Officers of the Houses of Parliament; and the Scottish Parliamentary Corporate Body. Apart from the Secretary of State for Wales, such offices, departments and bodies are, however, defined as contractors only at a time when their average annual expenditure on 'construction operations' in the three-year period to 31 March immediately preceding that time exceeded £1,000,000, but once so included they continue to be so until expenditure on 'construction operations' has been below £1,000,000 in each of three successive years after the end of the three-year period.

The definition includes a person who is himself a sub-contractor in relation to construction operations, e.g. a gang-leader.

[*ICTA 1988, s 559(1), s 560(2)–(5); FA 1995, Sch 27 para 2; FA 1998, Sch 8 para 2(2)–(4); Government of Wales Act 1998, Sch 16 para 58; SI 1993 No 743, reg 3A, Sch A1; SI 1998 No 2622, regs 4, 37; SI 1999 No 2159, reg 9; SI 2000 No 1880*].

Where payments by any of the bodies etc. which are contractors by virtue of (*b*) or (*c*) above are made under a contract in respect of which the total contract payments (excluding materials) do not exceed (and are not likely to exceed) £1,000, and the body etc. is approved by the inspector for the purpose, the payments are excluded from the application of these provisions. [*SI 1993 No 743, reg 20B; SI 1998 No 2622, reg 13*].

Private householders having work done on their own premises are *not* contractors for these purposes. See generally Revenue Pamphlet IR 14/15(CIS), paras 2.3–2.7.

'*Construction operations*' are widely defined to cover installing heating, lighting, drainage etc. systems, internal cleaning of buildings in the course of their construction, alteration or repair, and internal or external painting, as well as constructing, altering, repairing or demolishing buildings, walls, roadworks etc., but to *exclude* drilling for oil or gas, mining operations, the professional work of architects, surveyors etc., the installation etc. of sculptures, murals, and other artistic works, signwriting, advertisements, seating, blinds, shutters, security and public address systems, computer or telecommunications wiring through pre-existing ducts and the manufacture of components for heating, lighting, drainage etc. systems. The Treasury may add to these categories by order made by statutory instrument. [*ICTA 1988, s 567*]. Carpet fitting is outside the scope of the scheme. (Revenue Pamphlet IR 131, SP 12/81, 20 November 1981). For detailed guidance on the scope of 'construction operations', see chapter 7 and Appendix B to Revenue Pamphlet IR 14/15(CIS) and Revenue Construction Industry Scheme Manual CIS 1315 *et seq*.

A signed *tax payment voucher* (form CIS25) must be given by the contractor to the sub-contractor within 14 days of the end of a tax month in respect of all payments made under deduction of tax as above during the month. The contractor must also within 14 days of the end of each tax month either send the top copies of all forms CIS25 to the Inland Revenue (where three-part forms CIS25(I) or (M) have been used) or transmit specified particulars to them electronically (where single-part forms CIS25(E) have been used). [*SI 1993 No 743, reg 7; SI 1998 No 2622, reg 7*].

See generally Revenue Pamphlets IR 14/15(CIS), chapter 3 and IR 164(CIS) 'Advice to sub-contractors going onto deduction'. As regards disputes about, or corrections to, deductions, see IR 14/15(CIS), paras 8.3–8.5. For application of the scheme to non-residents, see IR 180(CIS).

20.3 **Registration cards** (see 20.2 above) are issued, renewed or replaced by an inspector or other person nominated by the Board. An inspector may require their surrender or cancel them. They must be produced for inspection, or surrendered, when required by any authorised officer of the Board. A refusal to issue or replace a registration card, or its cancellation, is subject to the normal right of appeal, although it is expected that cards will be available on request to anyone intending to commence work, or working, within the construction industry. They need only complete a form, supply a photograph and satisfy an identity check (see Revenue Pamphlet IR 14/15(CIS), para 1.6).

Cards (form CIS4(P)) other than temporary cards carry the sub-contractor's name, photograph and signature, the national insurance number (or, exceptionally, a 'system identifier'), and a distinctive reference number assigned to the card. They may also include a name under which the business is carried on. They have no expiry date. In the case of a partner in a firm, they must include the name of the firm for which the partner is acting. Company cards issued to a director or secretary of the company authorised to use the card must similarly include the name of the company for whom the director or secretary is acting. If a business name is included on a partner's or company card, it must be the same for all partners or directors and secretaries. Temporary registration cards (form CIS4(T)), which carry a date of expiry instead of the national insurance number, may be issued with a maximum validity of 12 months, or, if in exceptional cases the issuer deems it appropriate, 36 months; before 20 September 2002, the maximum was 3 months.

[*ICTA 1988, s 566(2A); FA 1996, s 178; SI 1993 No 743, regs 7A–7E, Sch 1; SI 1998 No 2622, regs 8, 38; SI 2002 No 2225, regs 3–5*].

See 20.7 below as regards penalties relating to registration card failures.

20.4 **Sub-contractors' tax certificates.** Where a tax certificate (form CIS5 or CIS6) has been issued to a sub-contractor and is in force when a payment is made, and the various regulatory requirements as regards production and validation etc. of the certificate (see below) are complied with, the deduction requirements under 20.2 above do not apply. Possession of a tax certificate by a sub-contractor does not, however, relieve the contractor of the responsibility to establish whether the sub-contractor is employed or self-employed (see 20.7 below). Certificates form CIS5 and (from 1 May 2001) CIS5 (Partner), which do not have to be produced to contractors (see alternative verification procedure described below) and which obviate the requirement to supply gross payment vouchers to contractors (see below), may only be issued when the inspector considers that a form CIS6 certificate would be inappropriate in all the circumstances. The Inland Revenue have indicated that a CIS5 certificate will only be issued to a company which either

(*a*)   is a plc or a subsidiary of a plc, or

(*b*)   has a turnover of at least £1 million (£3 million before December 2000), or has taken over and will continue an established concern with such a turnover which was previously owned by a director or directors of the company and which met certain other conditions as to previous compliance, or

(*c*)   is a subsidiary or associate of an established company holding a CIS5 (or predecessor 714C) certificate (and which would still qualify for a CIS 5 certificate), or

(*d*)   shows that operating with a CIS6 certificate would cause substantial difficulties.

As regards (*b*) above, following the reduction in the required turnover, a company already qualifying for a CIS6 certificate with a turnover of £1 million or more in its last set of accounts or tax return can apply for a CIS5 certificate. If it presently holds a CIS6 certificate with at least six months remaining, it may make a written request, and a CIS5 certificate issued in these circumstances will bear the same expiry date as the CIS6 certificate (which must be surrendered). If a CIS6 certificate with less than six months remaining is held, or the company does not currently hold a certificate, formal application for a CIS5 certificate must be made in the normal way. (Revenue Tax Bulletin December 2000 p 815).

As regards (*d*) above, evidence would have to be produced either of an administrative need, i.e. that using CIS6 certificates would involve either a high volume of vouchers — normally 300 or more per year but 150 or more per year may suffice in certain cases — or an excessive amount of time spent travelling specifically to present a certificate — at least 200 hours over a three-year period or 100 hours in any one of those years, or of a commercial need, i.e. where the applicant's trade is largely based on, or potentially involves, work for contractors who give work only to CIS5 certificate holders. (Revenue Tax Bulletin April 1999 pp 635, 636).

For more detailed guidance on the issue of CIS5 certificates, see Revenue Construction Industry Scheme Manual.

From 1 May 2001, a CIS5 (Partner) certificate may be issued, but only to a single partner in a particular firm, in his capacity as such, at any one time. The conditions for issue, and the alternative verification procedure, are similar to those applicable to CIS5 certificates.

Verification. Before a gross payment can be made, and subject to the alternative verification procedure described below for CIS5 certificate holders, the sub-contractor must produce the certificate to the contractor, who must satisfy himself by inspecting the certificate that the sub-contractor is the user of the certificate (or authorised to produce it on behalf of a company which is the user). Where the user receives the payment as a nominee, the person nominating the user must also produce his certificate for validation. Further inspections of the certificate are not required for so long as the contractor has no reason to doubt that it is still valid.

There is an alternative verification procedure where the user of a CIS5 certificate (not being a nominee) has notified the inspector of particulars of the company bank account into which payments, which must be under a written contract between the company and the contractor, are to be made. The user may produce to the contractor a 'certification document' signed by the secretary or a director of the company, and provided that the contractor has no reason to doubt that the information shown on the document is correct (and the payment date falls within the period of validity of the certificate referred to in the document), he may make payments gross. The certification document must certify that the company is the user of a valid company tax certificate form CIS5. It must specify the name, address (of the registered office) and registration number of the user, the distinctive number, expiry date (and, if any, commencement date) of the certificate, and details of the nominated bank account. It may also include the user's business name. To allay any doubt concerning the certification document, the contractor may, within 14 days of receipt of the document, apply to the inspector for confirmation that a valid certificate has been issued to the company and that the information on the certification document agrees with the inspector's records.

See above as regards CIS5 (Partner) certificates.

[*SI 1993 No 743, regs 33, 34; SI 1998 No 2622, reg 25; SI 2001 No 1531*].

Payments. Payment to a holder of a certification document should only be made by cheque or credit transfer, and *never* by cash, but payment to a sub-contractor presenting form CIS5 may be made in cash if certain procedures are followed (see Revenue Pamphlet IR 14/15(CIS), paras 5.12, 5.13).

Completion of vouchers. A sub-contractor with a certificate form CIS6 must, within 14 days after the end of each income tax month, give two signed copies of a gross payment voucher (form CIS24) containing specified particulars to the contractor in respect of all contract payments received gross in the month (or, if the contractor so requests, for each such payment). The contractor must complete the form with his distinctive reference number and deliver the appropriate copy to the sub-contractor. Where vouchers are not supplied, or are incorrectly completed, by the sub-contractor, and further payments are due, the contractor should reconsider the validity of the certificate. Duplicates should be requested of vouchers claimed to have been lost in the post. If a proper voucher is not supplied despite the contractor taking reasonable steps to obtain one, he should report the matter to the Revenue.

Where a sub-contractor has a certificate form CIS5, the contractor must complete a construction gross payment voucher (form CIS23(M) or CIS23(I)) containing specified particulars in respect of all gross payments in any income tax month (or transmit the specified particulars to the Inland Revenue electronically). Within 14 days after the end of each income tax month the contractor must forward to the Inland Revenue all forms CIS24, CIS23(M) or CIS23(I) given to or obtained or completed by him in the month. [*SI 1993 No 743, regs 35, 37A, 38, 39; SI 1998 No 2622, regs 26, 29–31*].

Issue of a certificate. Application for a tax certificate is made on form CIS2 or CIS3 as appropriate, and at least one month should be allowed for the application to be approved. Ten working days should be allowed after notification of approval for issue of the certificate.

For a tax certificate to be issued, the Revenue must be satisfied that the sub-contractor is carrying on a business in the UK consisting of or including the carrying out of construction operations (see 20.2 above), or the furnishing (or arranging for the furnishing) of labour for such operations, with proper premises, equipment, stock and other facilities. There must be a bank account through which the business is substantially conducted and proper records must be kept, and the applicant must also satisfy the 'turnover test' described at 20.5 below. Certificates are normally valid for either three years or one year, depending on the basis on which the turnover test is satisfied (see 20.5 below), although the initial issue of certificates under the new scheme will adjust the three-year period by up to six months to achieve an even rate of expiry of certificates. Certificates issued to partners in a firm or to a company at different times will have a common expiry date. The Board has wide powers to cancel certificates and require their surrender (and see 20.7 below).

An *individual applicant* (whether or not a partner in a firm) must have complied timeously with all tax and national insurance obligations (including supplying accounts and other information relating to any business of the applicant to the inspector on request) in respect of periods ending within the three years preceding the date of application (the '*qualifying period*'). There must be reason to expect that future such obligations will be complied with, and provided that this expectation is not rendered open to doubt, 'minor and technical failings' in relation to past obligations may be disregarded at the Board's discretion (but see *T & C Hill (Haulage) v Gleig (Sp C 227), [2000] SSCD 64* for a case in which refusal of a certificate was upheld on the grounds of late submission of returns and payment of tax liabilities after the due date). See Revenue Pamphlet IR 40(CIS), Appendix 2 for the Revenue interpretation of 'minor and technical failings'. Where the applicant claims not to have been subject to an obligation for these purposes, he must satisfy the Board of that fact by evidence prescribed by regulation, and where he claims to have been non-resident, he must also satisfy the Board by such evidence that any comparable foreign obligations have been met (see *SI 1993 No 743, regs 22–23B; SI 1998 No 2622, regs 15–17*). Any company of which the individual had control (within *ICTA 1988, s 416(2)–(6)*) during the qualifying period must also satisfy those conditions in respect of any accounting period ending within the qualifying period at a time when the applicant had such control.

A *company applicant* (whether or not a partner in a firm) must have a similarly satisfactory record of past and prospective compliance with all its taxation and national insurance and certain Companies Act obligations. In *Gorge Fabrications Ltd v Wilson (Sp C 214), [1999] SSCD 293*, the Special Commissioner upheld an inspector's refusal of a certificate to a company which had, within the three year period in question, entered into a voluntary arrangement with its creditors resulting in 75% of its outstanding corporation tax liabilities (amounting to £2,927) remaining unpaid (its PAYE/NIC liabilities of over £30,000 having been treated as preferential and met in full). The Board may also, in certain cases where there is a limited history of construction operations, or where there has been a change of control, issue a direction under *ICTA 1988, s 561(6)* that the directors (and, if the company is close, the beneficial shareholders) must satisfy any or all of the conditions imposed on individual applicants (see above). Where the introduction of a new shareholder into a close private company results in a change of control, the company must notify the inspector of the new shareholder within 30 days (see *SI 1993 No 743, reg 42*).

Each of the *partners in a firm* (applying as such), in addition to meeting the requirements for individual or company applicants (as above), as appropriate, must also satisfy the requirements as to the meeting of tax obligations (and requests by the inspector) in relation to the firm's business.

[*ICTA 1988, ss 561, 562, 564, 565; FA 1995, Sch 27 paras 3–7; ITEPA 2003, Sch 6 paras 59, 60; SI 1993 No 743, regs 25, 26; SI 1998 No 2622, regs 19, 20; SI 1999 No 2156*].

Refusal of a certificate on grounds of inadequate past compliance and uncertain future reliability did not contravene *Article 1* (peaceful enjoyment of possessions) or *Article 14* (right to enjoyment of convention rights without discrimination) of the *European Convention on Human Rights* (*Shaw v Vicky Construction Ltd Ch D 2002, 75 TC 26*).

Changes in a business. Where an individual or firm incorporates, or a partnership becomes a sole trader, the new business will require a new certificate. However, if the business is essentially the same, the new business may apply immediately on the basis of turnover of the old business, using either the three-year test (at 20.5 below), applied in the light of the particular circumstances of the case, or the six-month test (also at 20.5 below), depending on how long the old business existed. Changes in the number of partners in a firm or directors/shareholders in a company, without any change in the business, do not require the turnover test to be re-applied before the certificate falls to be renewed, unless the inspector suspects manipulation of the threshold provisions. New partners/directors can apply for additional certificates. (Revenue Pamphlet IR 40(CIS) pp 6, 7).

Old scheme certificates. Certificates issued under the scheme applicable before 1 August 1999 cease to have effect after 31 July 1999 regardless of the expiry date shown on the certificate. [*SI 1998 No 2620, reg 4*].

Simon's Direct Tax Service. See E5.510 *et seq.*

20.5   **Turnover test.** *Individuals (other than in relation to applications as partners in firms).* The turnover test requires the applicant to satisfy the Board that, during the period of validity of the certificate, the aggregate annual amount of 'relevant payments' received is likely to be not less than the 'individual turnover threshold' of £30,000. (It should, however, be noted that Revenue Pamphlet IR 40(CIS) states (at Appendix 1): 'If you are using the six-month test, you should show the actual amount you *received* in the period. Where you are using a three-year test on the basis of accounts, we would not expect you to adjust figures for gross construction turnover and materials for debtors or creditors to arrive at the net "payments received" in the three years. Just use the figures earned for construction operations, as shown in your accounts.'.) *'Relevant payments'* are all payments, net of the cost of materials, under contracts relating to, or to the work of individuals participating in the carrying out of, construction operations (see 20.2 above), whether or not within the scheme (i.e. including work for private householders etc.).

To satisfy the Board, either a six-month test or a three-year test must be satisfied (and depending on which test is satisfied, the certificate will generally be valid for one year or three years (subject to variation on the initial issue, see 20.4 above) respectively). The six-month test is not available where the applicant has been a sub-contractor for a continuous period of four years up to the date of application and three successive one-year certificates have been issued to him.

The six-month test requires the production of evidence (i.e. tax payment vouchers and gross payment vouchers and documentary evidence of relevant payments and of the direct cost of materials) that relevant payments (i.e. turnover) during a consecutive period of up to six tax months in the year preceding the date of application amounted to at least 70% of the individual turnover threshold (i.e. currently £21,000).

The three-year test requires the production of such evidence that relevant payments (i.e. turnover) in a consecutive period of three years in the four years preceding the date of application averaged at least 90% of the average of the individual turnover thresholds for those three years (i.e. currently £27,000) and were at least equal to that threshold in two of the three years. Accounts will also generally be required.

Companies. The turnover test requires a company applicant to satisfy the Board that either

(i)   the annual receipts test is satisfied, or

(ii)   all the company's shareholders are themselves companies limited by shares with current valid certificates.

The annual receipts test requires that, during the period of validity of the certificate, the aggregate annual amount of 'relevant payments' (as above) received is likely to be not less than the smaller of

(*a*)   the individual turnover threshold (currently £30,000), as above, multiplied by the number of 'relevant persons' in relation to the company, and

(*b*)   a specified amount (currently £200,000).

A person is a *'relevant person'* in relation to a company if he is a director of the company or (where the company is a close company) a beneficial owner of shares in the company. To satisfy the Board as regards (*a*) above, the six-month or three-year tests described above in relation to individual applicants are applied, but by reference to the '*multiple company turnover threshold*', i.e. (subject to special rules where a business is transferred by an individual or firm to a company as a going concern) the individual turnover threshold multiplied by the number of relevant persons. For the six-month test, the number of relevant persons is the maximum number at any time in the six-month (or shorter) period concerned. For the three-year test it is the maximum number at any time in the relevant year, except that for applications before 1 August 2001, by concession, the maximum number at any point during the last six months of the three-year period could be substituted for each of the three years if this assisted the sub-contractor to meet the test. (Revenue Pamphlet IR 1, B52). As regards (*b*) above (the '*alternative company turnover threshold*'), the three-year test is applied, but by reference to the £200,000 annual limit.

Individuals applying as partners in firms. The turnover test requires the partners in the firm to satisfy the Board that, during the period of validity of the certificate, the aggregate annual amount of 'relevant payments' (as above) received is likely to be not less than the smaller of

(A)   the sum of the individual turnover threshold (as above) multiplied by the number of individual partners and, for each corporate partner (other than a company within (ii) above), the turnover threshold which would have applied if the company had itself applied for a certificate (as above), and

(B)   a specified amount (currently £200,000).

To satisfy the Board as regards (A) above, the six-month or three-year tests described above in relation to individual applicants are applied, but by reference to the '*multiple partnership turnover threshold*', i.e. the individual turnover threshold multiplied by the sum of the number of individual partners and the number of relevant persons which would have been taken into account under (*a*) above in relation to company partners. For the six-month test, the number of partners is the maximum number at any time in the six-month (or shorter) period concerned. For the three-year test it is the maximum number at any time in the relevant year, except that for applications before 1 August 2001, by concession, the maximum number at any point during the last six months of the three-year period could be substituted for each of the three years if this assisted the subcontractor to meet the test. (Revenue Pamphlet IR 1, B52). As regards (B) above (the '*alternative partnership turnover threshold*'), the three-year test is applied, but by reference to the £200,000 annual limit.

[*ICTA 1988, s 562(2A)(2B), s 564(2A)–(2C), s 565(2A)–(2D); FA 1995, Sch 27 paras 4, 6, 7; FA 1998, Sch 8 paras 3–5; FA 1999, s 53; ITEPA 2003, Sch 6 para 60; SI 1993 No 743, regs 21A–21E; SI 1998 No 2622, reg 14; SI 1999 No 2159, regs 4–6*].

See generally Revenue Tax Bulletin December 1998 pp 615–617 and, as regards how the test is applied where the applicant's business changes (e.g. where a partnership becomes a sole trader or *vice versa* or a sole trader or partnership becomes a company, or where sole traders or partnerships merge to form a new partnership), June 1999 pp 667, 668.

Simon's Direct Tax Service. See E5.513 *et seq.*

20.6   **Renewal of certificates.** Applications for renewal of a certificate may be made at any time within six months before the date of expiry. The conditions are exactly the same as for the initial issue. [*SI 1993 No 743, reg 27*].

20.7   **Administration.** Detailed administrative arrangements for the operation of the scheme are contained in *The Income Tax (Sub-contractors in the Construction Industry) Regulations 1993 (SI 1993 No 743)* as amended by the *(Amendment) Regulations 1998 (SI 1998 No 2622), 1999 (SI 1999 No 825), 2000 (SI 2000 No 2742), 2002 (SI 2002 No 2225), 2003 (SI 2003 No 536)* and *2004 (SI 2004 No 1075)*. The arrangements for accounting for deductions (including electronic payment) and for interest on unpaid or overpaid tax (see *SI 1993 No 743, regs 8–19, 47–54; SI 1998 No 2622, regs 9, 10; SI 1999 No 825, reg 2; SI 2000 No 1151; SI 2003 No 536, regs 4–6; SI 2004 No 1075*) broadly follow those for PAYE (see 55.8 PAY AS YOU EARN, Revenue Pamphlet IR 14/15(CIS), chapter 6 and, as regards electronic payment, Revenue Directions 18 May 2004). There are detailed provisions governing the form and use of sub-contractor's tax certificates (see *SI 1993 No 743, reg 24, Sch 1; SI 1998 No 2622, regs 18, 38; SI 1999 No 2159, reg 10* and *SI 2002 No 2225, reg 6*) and the requirements for contractors' end of year returns of all payments to sub-contractors (see *SI 1993 No 743, reg 40A; SI 1998 No 2622, reg 33*). See also below under *Failure to deduct and under-deduction*. The Inland Revenue have powers to inspect records of contractors and sub-contractors (see *SI 1993 No 743, regs 41, 41A; SI 1998 No 2622, reg 34; SI 1999 No 2159, reg 8; SI 2003 No 536, reg 7*). Further regulations may be made by statutory instrument. [*ICTA 1988, s 566; FA 1995, Sch 27 para 9; FA 1998, Sch 8 para 6*]. See Revenue Pamphlet IR 109 as regards negotiation of settlements. The Revenue have published a Code of Practice (No 3, available from local tax offices) setting out their standards for the way in which inspections of contractors' records are conducted and the rights and responsibilities of taxpayers.

Interest on late payment of tax under these provisions is payable gross and is not deductible in computing any income, profits or losses for tax purposes. This was always the Revenue's view, but it is given legislative effect for only 2003/04 onwards. [*ICTA 1988, s 566(1A); FA 2003, s 147(1)(5)*].

Contractors are able to submit some of the vouchers information using electronic data interchange ('EDI'). [*SI 1993 No 743, reg 7(4)(b), reg 37A(2)(b), reg 40A(9)(b), reg 44A, reg 44B; SI 1998 No 2622, regs 7(4)(5), 29, 33, 35; SI 2003 No 536, reg 8*]. Full details should have been sent to all known contractors and sub-contractors by the end of 1998. For an outline of how EDI may be used, see Revenue Press Release 1 September 1998.

Multiple contractors. There are provisions allowing a contractor to elect to be treated as a different contractor for each of any specified groups of sub-contractors. [*SI 1993 No 743, reg 4*].

Appeals. There is a right of appeal (to the Commissioners, within 30 days) against the refusal or cancellation of a sub-contractor's tax certificate, and the Commissioners have the jurisdiction to review the exercise of any discretionary powers by the Board. [*ICTA 1988, s 561(9)*]. See also below under *Failure to deduct and under-deduction* and *Assessment*.

Cancellation. A certificate may at any time be cancelled by the Board, and its surrender demanded, if it was issued on false information, or has been misused by the holder, or if the holder no longer meets the requirements for the issue of a certificate or if, in the case of a company, there has been a change of control (within *ICTA 1988, s 840*) and the information required concerning that change has not been furnished. [*ICTA 1988, s 561(8)*].

Employment status. Where a worker in the construction industry is recategorised as an employee, the Revenue adopt a practical approach to the year of change. The liability for the year is calculated as if there was a Schedule D cessation, but with no prior year adjustments, and a commencement of employment on the date of the change. Schedule D profits of the year of cessation are generally taken either as those actually arising in the year or as the appropriate proportion of the profits from the end of the previous year's basis period to cessation, but any basis giving a reasonable result may be accepted. A due proportion of a full year's capital allowances is given for the final year, with no disposal value being brought in. See Taxation Vol 138, No 3596 p 643, 6 March 1997 for this and other aspects.

Possession of a registration card (see 20.3 above) or tax certificate (see 20.4 above) by a sub-contractor does not relieve the contractor of the responsibility to establish whether the sub-

20.7 Construction Industry Scheme (CIS)

contractor is employed or self-employed. A telephone helpline (0345–335588) is available for contractors and workers needing general assistance in determining whether workers are employed or self-employed.

See generally Revenue Pamphlets IR 56 and IR 148 and Revenue Tax Bulletin April 1997 pp 405–413.

Penalties. For fraudulent attempts to obtain or misuse a certificate, penalties of up to £3,000 may be exacted. [*ICTA 1988, s 561(10)(11); FA 1995, Sch 27 para 3*]. A maximum penalty of £3,000 similarly applies for failure to comply with obligations in relation to registration cards (see 20.2 above). [*ICTA 1988, s 566(2B)–(2F); FA 1996, s 178*]. Penalties under *TMA 1970, s 98A* apply in cases of failure to make required end-of-year returns. [*SI 1993 No 743, reg 40A(16); SI 1998 No 2622, reg 33*]. See also 57.10 PENALTIES as regards negotiated settlements.

Deduction of tax. If exemption is not obtained, but a registration card is produced, the sub-contractor will receive payments under deduction of tax as under 20.2 above, and will receive from the contractor(s) form(s) CIS25 vouching the tax deducted (see 20.2 above). He will be treated for tax purposes as having received the full amount, the tax deducted and vouched on forms CIS25 being treated as a payment in respect of his income or corporation tax liability on the profits of the trade in the year of assessment or accounting period in which the deduction was made. In the case of an individual, any excess is treated as a payment on account of his Class 4 contributions under the *Social Security Acts*, any further excess being repaid. In the case of a company, regulations will require the offset of amounts deducted from payments on or after 6 April 2002 against liabilities as an employer or contractor for the current year of assessment and then against profits of the trade before repayment is made. Previously the only offset for deductions suffered by companies was against profits of the trade. [*ICTA 1988, s 559(4)–(5A), s 559A; FA 1995, s 139(1); FA 1998, Sch 8 para 2(1); FA 2002, s 40, Sch 40 Pt 3(1)*].

To the extent that any liability for a year of assessment is met by tax deducted in that year, no interest charge will arise in e.g. a case of failure to notify liability. For the set-off of any corporation tax repayment due under these provisions against liabilities of certain intermediaries, see 61.12 PERSONAL SERVICE COMPANIES ETC.

Provisional repayments to individuals (or partners in firms) of tax vouched on forms CIS25 may, on application to the inspector, be made before the end of the tax year to which they relate. They may not be made after the end of the tax year. All earlier year income tax and Class 4 national insurance liabilities of the business must have been paid, and repayment is restricted to the excess of the deductions over the sum of the liability to income tax and Class 4 national insurance for the year on profits or gains of the business and on any income arising during the year up to the date of application from which tax has not been deducted (in either case whether or not yet due and payable) and any other sums due and payable from the applicant, including sums he has himself deducted as a contractor. A claim, accompanied by all the forms CIS25 relevant to the claim, is required on form CIS40 (obtainable from local tax offices), or form CIS41 in the case of a partner. In the case of a claim by a partner, the form must be signed by all individual partners and by the secretary or a director of all corporate partners. [*SI 1993 No 743, reg 20A; SI 1998 No 2622, reg 12*].

Failure to deduct and under-deduction. If the contractor fails to deduct the tax, he is nevertheless liable for the tax which should have been deducted (see *Ladkarn Ltd v McIntosh Ch D 1982, 56 TC 616*). However, where the Collector is satisfied that the contractor took reasonable care, and that the failure was due to an error made in good faith or to a genuine belief that the payment was not subject to deduction, the Collector may waive the liability. An appeal may be made (within 30 days) against a decision not so to waive liability. Liability in respect of such failure may also be waived at the contractor's request where the inspector is satisfied that the sub-contractor to whom the payment was made either was not chargeable to tax thereon or has made the appropriate return and paid the tax and any Class 4 contributions. [*SI 1993 No 743, reg 10*].

See Revenue Pamphlet IR 109 as regards negotiation of settlements.

Assessment. If the inspector considers it necessary to do so in all the circumstances, he may raise an assessment on the contractor in any amount which, to the best of his judgment, the contractor is liable to pay under the scheme regulations. The assessment is treated in the same way as an income tax assessment for assessment, appeal and recovery purposes. Tax is due and payable 14 days after the date of the assessment. [*SI 1993 No 743, reg 14*]. As regards interest on tax unpaid or overpaid on such assessments, similar provisions apply as in 55.8 PAY AS YOU EARN. [*SI 1993 No 743, regs 16–18*].

20.8   CIS APPLICABLE FROM APRIL 2006

A revised construction industry scheme is to be introduced in relation to payments made on or after a date to be appointed by Treasury order, expected to be in April 2006. [*FA 2004, s 77(1)(7)*]. The framework of the new scheme is provided for in *FA 2004*, but much of the detail is to be contained in regulations (see *FA 2004, ss 73, 75, 77(8)* for the principal regulation-making powers given to the Board and the Treasury); for draft regulations, still subject to consultation as at 1 July 2004, see www.inlandrevenue.gov.uk/cis/cis-secondary-regs.pdf

Change was felt to be necessary to reduce the administrative burden that the system of registration cards and tax certificates imposed on the industry; to improve the level of compliance within the industry; and to encourage the correct identification of employment status. Accordingly, features of the new scheme include:

(*a*)   the introduction of a verification service to enable contractors to check whether sub-contractors are registered for gross or net payment (see 20.18 below);

(*b*)   the introduction of periodic returns by contractors to replace the voucher system (see 20.18 below);

(*c*)   the introduction of an employment status declaration (see 20.18 below).

The Revenue anticipate being able to support much more electronic communication, and see the benefit of this not only in helping the industry to contact them but also in increasing the management information available to them.

In other respects the new scheme is very similar to the previous scheme. However, it should be emphasized that the new scheme will operate under a new legislative framework and regulations, and there are subtle differences from the previous scheme throughout.

For transitional measures on the introduction of the new scheme, see 20.19 below.

Outline of the new CIS. Where a contractor makes a contract payment to a sub-contractor under a construction contract, and that sub-contractor is either registered for payment under deduction (as opposed to being registered for gross payment), or is not registered at all, the contractor must make a deduction from the payment (see 20.13 below). The deduction is greater if the sub-contractor is unregistered. The terms 'contractor', 'contract payment', 'sub-contractor' and 'construction contract' are all defined by the legislation (see 20.9–20.13 below). The topic of registration is dealt with at 20.14–20.17 below.

It is up to the contractor to verify with the Revenue the registration status of a sub-contractor (see 20.18 below). The contractor must then make periodic returns to the Revenue concerning contract payments, as well as providing information about such payments to the sub-contractor (see 20.18 below).

20.9   Construction Industry Scheme (CIS)

20.9   **Payments from which tax must be deducted.** The scheme is concerned with payments (see 20.13 below) under a 'construction contract'. A contract of employment is specifically excluded from the definition of a construction contract, and it follows that the first question to be addressed before making any payment is whether the recipient is an employee. If so, the CIS is not in point (and the contractor will have to declare, in periodic returns to the Revenue, that none of the contracts to which the return relates is a contract of employment — see 20.18 below). For the indicators of employment status, see 61.18 PERSONAL SERVICE COMPANIES ETC. and 75.27 SCHEDULE E—EMPLOYMENT INCOME.

A '*construction contract*' must relate to 'construction operations' (see 20.10 below) and involve a 'sub-contractor' (see 20.11 below) and a 'contractor' (see 20.12 below).

[*FA 2004, s 57*].

20.10   '*Construction operations*' include

- construction, alteration, repair, extension, demolition or dismantling of buildings or structures, including offshore installations and temporary structures;

- construction, alteration, repair, extension or demolition of works forming part of the land, and this specifically includes walls, roadworks, power-lines, electronic communications apparatus, aircraft runways, docks and harbours, railways, inland waterways, pipe-lines, reservoirs, water-mains, wells, sewers, industrial plant and installations for purposes of land drainage, coast protection or defence;

- installation of heating, lighting, air-conditioning, ventilation, power supply, drainage, sanitation, water supply or fire protection;

- internal cleaning if carried out during construction, alteration, repair, extension or restoration; and

- painting or decorating (internal and external).

Operations which are an integral part of, or are preparatory to, the operations in the above list are also included, for instance: site clearance, earth-moving, excavation, tunnelling and boring, laying of foundations, erection of scaffolding, site restoration, landscaping and the provision of roadways and other access works.

Specifically excluded from the definition of construction operations are

- operations outside the UK;

- drilling for, or extraction of, oil or natural gas, and extraction of minerals;

- manufacture of building or engineering components or equipment, and delivery of these to site;

- manufacture of components for heating, ventilation etc. systems and delivery to site;

- the work of architects, surveyors and consultants;

- making, installing or repairing artistic works;

- signwriting, and erecting, installing or repairing signboards and advertisements;

- installation of seating, blinds and shutters; and

- installation of security systems and public address systems.

The Treasury may, by order, amend either of the above lists.

[*FA 2004, s 74*].

20.11   **Sub-contractors.** A person is a '*sub-contactor*' if the contract imposes on him a duty to

- carry out construction operations; or

- furnish his own labour or the labour of others in carrying out construction operations; or

- arrange for the labour of others to be furnished in carrying out construction operations.

Alternatively, a person may be a sub-contractor if, under the construction contract, he is answerable to the contractor for construction operations carried out by others (whether under a contract or other arrangements).

[*FA 2004, s 58*].

20.12   **Contractors.** The term '*contractor*' in relation to a construction contract includes someone who is at the same time a party to that contract and a sub-contractor in another construction contract relating to any or all of the same construction operations. [*FA 2004, s 57(2)(b)*]. This would include, for instance, a gang-leader.

Other than that, the definition of a '*contractor*' may be divided into three categories.

(i)   Persons who are automatically classed as contractors. These are:

- any person carrying on a business which includes construction operations; and

- the Secretary of State if the contract is made by him under *Housing Associations Act 1985, s 89*.

(ii)   Persons carrying on a business which exceeds a set level of expenditure on construction operations. That level is:

- £1 million per year on average over the period of three years ending at the same time as the last period of account; or

- where the business was not being carried on at the beginning of that three-year period, £3 million over the whole of the truncated period.

Once defined as a contractor under this category, the person is deemed to continue to be a contractor until the Board are satisfied that expenditure on construction operations has been less than £1 million for each of three successive years beginning in or after the period of account in which contractor status was acquired. For the purposes of all these limits, where a trade is transferred from one company to another and *ICTA 1988, s 343* (no change of ownership) applies, the transferor's expenditure will be treated as the transferee's, with apportionment by the Board (subject to appeal) when only part of the trade is transferred.

(iii)   Specified bodies or persons specified, provided their average annual expenditure on construction operations in any three-year period exceeds £1 million. Contractor status ceases to apply if, subsequently, there are three successive years in which expenditure on construction operations is less than £1 million. The bodies or persons specified are:

- any public office or department of the Crown (including any NI department and any part of the Scottish Administration);

- the Corporate Officer of the House of Lords, the Corporate Officer of the House of Commons, and the Scottish Parliamentary Corporate Body;

- any local authority;

- any development corporation or new town commission;

- the Commission for the New Towns;

- the Housing Corporation, a housing association, a housing trust, Scottish Homes, and the Northern Ireland Housing Executive;

- any NHS trust;

- any Health and Social Services trust.

The Revenue may add to this list by means of regulations.

[*FA 2004, s 59*].

20.13 **Deductions from contract payments.** *Contract payments.* Deductions on account of tax must be made from '*contract payments*'. These are defined as payments under a construction contract by the contractor to

- a sub-contractor; or

- a nominee of the sub-contractor or the contractor; or

- a nominee of a person who is a sub-contractor under another construction contract relating to the construction operations.

Where the contractor makes a payment to a third party which discharges his obligation to pay a person within the above list, that payment is deemed to have been made directly to that person.

There are three exceptions to this definition of a contract payment:

- payments to agency workers treated, by virtue of *ITEPA 2003, Pt 2 Ch 7* as earnings from employment (see 75.49 SCHEDULE E—EMPLOYMENT INCOME);

- payments where the recipient is registered for gross payment (see 20.14 below) when the payment is made (although this is subject to certain qualifications in the case of nominees and partnerships — see below); and

- payments excepted by regulations; these are expected to include small payments made by deemed contractors, reverse premiums, payments by local authority schools under devolved budgets and payments made by certain businesses in respect of property used in their own business and by their own staff (Explanatory Notes to 2004 Finance Bill).

The qualifications to the exception where the recipient is registered for gross payment are as follows.

- Where the recipient is a nominee, then the nominee, the person who nominated him and the person for whose labour (or the company for whose employees' labour) the payment is made must all be registered for gross payment when the payment is made.

- Where the recipient is registered for gross payment as a partner in a firm, the exception only applies to payments in respect of the firm's business (i.e. under contracts where the firm is a sub-contractor or, where the firm has been nominated to receive payments, the person who nominated the firm is a sub-contractor and is himself registered for gross payment).

- Where a person registered for gross payment other than as a partner in a firm becomes a partner in a firm, the exception does not apply to payments in respect of the firm's business (i.e. under contracts where the firm is a sub-contractor, or, where the firm has been nominated to receive payments, the person who nominated the firm is a sub-contractor).

[*FA 2004, s 60*].

Upon making a contract payment, the contractor must make a deduction on account of tax. The deductible amount is calculated by first excluding the cost of materials and then applying the 'relevant percentage', which is to be set by Treasury order. The *maximum* relevant percentage varies in accordance with the registration status of the person for whose labour (or, in the case of companies, for whose employees' labour) the payment is made, as follows.

- If registered for payment under deduction (see 20.14 below), the relevant percentage may not exceed the basic rate of tax for the tax year in which the payment is made;

- If unregistered, the relevant percentage may not exceed the higher rate of tax for that year.

The contractor must pay the amount deducted to the Revenue. For the purposes of computing the contractor's taxable profits, the full amount of the contract payment (i.e. the amount paid to the sub-contractor plus the amount paid to the Revenue) is allowed as a deduction (assuming the payment itself is allowable under general principles).

Where the sub-contractor is not a company, the amounts deducted from contract payments are treated as income tax paid in respect of the profits of the trade. Any excess of those amounts over the income tax liability on those profits is treated as discharging any Class 4 national insurance contributions payable in respect of those profits.

Where the sub-contractor is a company, the treatment of the amounts deducted is to be governed by regulations. The order of set-off is firstly against payments due to the Revenue, for the tax year in which the deduction is made, under the contractor's obligations as an employer or contractor (e.g. PAYE, Class 1 national insurance contributions, deductions under the CIS) and secondly against corporation tax. Any excess is repayable to the sub-contractor.

[FA 2004, ss 61, 62].

20.14   **Registration.** In order to be registered, an applicant must provide sufficient documents, records and information to establish, to the satisfaction of the Revenue, his identity and address. If the required documents etc. have been provided, the Revenue must register the applicant. If, in addition, the requirements for gross payment are met (see below) then the applicant must be registered for gross payment. There is provision for an appeal against the Revenue's refusal to register for gross payment (see below). Otherwise, the applicant must be registered for payment under deduction. Once again, there is provision for an appeal against a refusal by the Revenue to register.

There is a penalty of up to £3,000 for knowingly or recklessly making a statement, or supplying a document, which is false in a material particular (i.e. which contains a falsehood that is relevant to the decision regarding registration).

[FA 2004, ss 63, 72].

Registration for gross payment. The requirements for registration for gross payment vary, depending upon whether the applicant is:

- an individual (see 20.15 below);

- a company (see 20.17 below); or

- an individual or company applying as a partner in a firm (see 20.16 below).

Much of the detail is contained in regulations, and indeed the Treasury is specifically empowered to alter, by means of an order, the conditions relating to registration for gross payment. *[FA 2004, Sch 11 para 13].*

Cancellation of registration. Failure to comply with the requirements of the CIS may result in the cancellation of a person's registration.

In the case of registration for payment under deduction, the conditions relating to cancellation (and appeal against such a decision) are to be governed by regulations. [*FA 2004, s 68*].

In the case of registration for gross payment, the conditions relating to cancellation may be divided into two by reference to the gravity of the offence. Lesser offences are if:

- at the time in question, the Board would refuse a hypothetical application for gross payment registration;

- the person has made an incorrect return or provided incorrect information (whether as a contractor or a sub-contractor); or

- there is any failure to comply with the provisions of the CIS (whether as a contractor or a sub-contractor).

If it appears to the Board that any of these apply, a determination may be made cancelling a person's registration with effect from the end of a period to be prescribed by regulations. However, the effective date may be delayed by an appeal (see below) to the latest of:

- the abandonment of the appeal;

- determination by the Commissioners; or

- determination by the appropriate court (e.g. the High Court in England and Wales).

If gross payment registration is cancelled because of the above type of offence, the person must then be registered for payment under deduction.

More serious offences are:

- becoming registered for gross payment on the basis of false information;

- making a fraudulently incorrect return, or fraudulently providing incorrect information; or

- knowingly failing to comply with the provisions of the CIS.

The Board must have reasonable grounds to suspect such an offence, and if so they may make a determination cancelling registration with immediate effect. The Board then has discretion whether to register the person for payment under deduction. Note that it is possible to appeal against a refusal to register for payment under deduction. It is not clear whether, in this instance, the non-exercise of the Board's discretion would count as a refusal. If not, presumably it would be possible to make a formal application for registration for payment under deduction and appeal the resulting refusal.

On any cancellation, the Board must, without delay, give a notice stating the reasons for the cancellation. The person whose registration is cancelled may not re-apply for gross payment registration for at least a year.

[*FA 2004, ss 66, 67(5)*].

Appeals. An appeal may be made against the cancellation or refusal of a registration for gross payment by giving notice to the Revenue within 30 days of the decision. The notice must state the reasons why the decision is believed to be unjustified. Appeal is to the General Commissioners or, by election, to the Special Commissioners. The Commissioners may review any relevant decision made in relation to registration. [*FA 2004, s 67*].

20.15   **Registration for gross payment — individuals.** The conditions to be satisfied by individuals comprise three tests: a business test, a turnover test, and a compliance test.

The business test. The business carried on by the individual must be carried on in the UK. It must include either carrying out 'construction operations' (see 20.10 above), or furnishing labour for construction operations, or arranging for the furnishing of labour. Finally, it must, to a substantial extent, be carried on using an account with a bank; the phrase 'to a substantial extent' is not further defined in the legislation. The evidence required to prove the satisfaction of these conditions is to be prescribed in regulations.

The turnover test. The applicant must satisfy the Revenue that the likely receipt of 'relevant payments' in the year following the application is not less than a minimum to be set by regulations (expected to £30,000). There is provision for the Board to make regulations enabling a business that does not meet this test to be treated as if it did — this flexibility is designed to cover the situation where overall turnover exceeds the threshold but 'relevant payments' derive from an ancillary part of the business and are less than the threshold.

The evidence required for likely future turnover is to be prescribed in regulations (and likely to consist of data from the twelve months preceding the application). There is provision empowering regulations to presume what is likely to happen from what happened in the past.

'Relevant payments' means payments under contracts relating to 'construction operations' (see 20.10 above), or contracts relating to the work of individuals in the carrying out of construction operations. Payments representing the cost of materials are excluded.

The compliance test. In the twelve months prior to the application (the *'qualifying period'*) the individual must have complied with all his tax compliance obligations. Over the same period, the applicant must have supplied any requested information and accounts concerning any business of his (i.e. not just the business relating to the application). These requirements also apply to a company controlled by the applicant. Compliance must be within any required time limits or at the required time. That is to say, late compliance is no compliance at all for the purposes of this test.

The above compliance requirements are relaxed in two respects, as follows.

- There is a 'reasonable excuse' defence. This is accompanied by the usual requirement to have remedied any failure without unreasonable delay once the excuse ceased.

- There are to be disregards of specified compliance failures to be set out in regulations; this replaces the previous 'minor and technical failings' rule (see 20.4 above) and is intended to reduce uncertainty.

The applicant may state that he was not subject to compliance obligations, e.g. because of absence abroad, or unemployment, or being in full-time education, but must provide evidence to be prescribed by regulations. In the case of absence abroad, the applicant must also provide prescribed evidence of compliance with comparable obligations under the tax laws of the country in which he was living.

The applicant must have paid any national insurance contributions as they fell due. This is not subject to the 'reasonable excuse' defence.

Finally, there must be reason to expect that the applicant will continue to comply with compliance obligations and requests for documents etc., and continue to pay his national insurance contributions, after the qualifying period. There is no further statutory help as to the furnishing of such a reason, although it may perhaps be inferred that a satisfactory history of compliance is not a sufficient reason, since this is provided for elsewhere. Note that the existence of such a reason is a necessary condition of registration, and this would appear to give the Revenue very wide discretion to refuse registration for gross payment (albeit subject to appeal).

[*FA 2004, s 64(2), Sch 11 paras 1–4, 13–16*].

20.16 Construction Industry Scheme (CIS)

20.16 **Registration for gross payment — partners.** An individual applying for gross payment as a partner in a firm must first meet the compliance test for individuals (see 20.15 above). A company applying for gross payment as a partner in a firm must first meet all the tests applicable to companies (see 20.17 below). In addition, the firm itself must meet the following business, turnover and compliance tests.

The business test. The test for a firm's business is the same as that for a business carried on by an individual (see 20.15 above).

The turnover test. The partners must satisfy the Revenue that the likely receipt of 'relevant payments' (see 20.15 above) in the year following the application is not less than a threshold figure. The threshold is the smaller of:

- an amount to be specified in regulations (expected to be £200,000); and

- the 'multiple turnover threshold'.

The *'multiple turnover threshold'* is obtained by adding together:

(i) an amount found by multiplying the number of individuals in the partnership by the minimum turnover threshold for individuals (see 20.15 above); and

(ii) in respect of each company (if any) in the partnership, the threshold that would obtain were the company to be applying in its own behalf (see 20.17 below).

Where the number of partners has fluctuated, regulations will prescribe the number of partners to be used for the calculation in (i) above. In calculating the figure in (ii) above, there is disregarded any company whose only shareholders are other companies that are limited by shares and registered for gross payment.

There is provision for the Board to make regulations enabling a firm that does not meet this test to be treated as if it did (this is similar to the provision for individuals — see 20.15 above).

The compliance test. Each of the partners at the time of the application must, during the qualifying period (i.e. the twelve months prior to the application), have complied with all tax compliance obligations in relation to any income tax or corporation tax charge which was computed by reference to the firm's business. Over the same period, each partner must have supplied all requested information and accounts concerning the firm's business or his share of the profits of that business. Compliance must be within any required time limits or at the required time.

There are similar 'reasonable excuse' and regulatory relaxations as for individuals (see 20.15 above).

There must be reason to expect that, following the qualifying period, each of the persons who are from time to time partners in the firm will continue the record of compliance (see comments at 20.15 above on a similar provision relating to individuals).

[*FA 2004, s 64(3), Sch 11 paras 5–8, 13–16*].

20.17 **Registration for gross payment — companies.** In order to register for gross payment, a company must pass the business, turnover and compliance tests described below.

In addition to those tests, the Revenue may make a direction applying the conditions relating to individuals (see 20.15 above) to the directors of the company. If the company is a close company, this is extended to include the beneficial owners of shares. Rather than apply all the conditions to all of the directors or shareholders, the direction may specify which conditions are to apply, and to which directors or shareholders. In particular, the Revenue may make such a direction where there has been a change in control of a company that either is, or is applying to be, registered for gross payment. The Revenue are empowered to make regulations requiring the submission of information concerning changes in control of such companies. [*FA 2004, ss 64(5), 65*].

The business test. The test for a company's business is the same as that for a business carried on by an individual (see 20.15 above).

The turnover test. A company may pass this test in either of two ways:

- satisfying the Revenue that its only shareholders are companies limited by shares and registered for gross payment; or

- providing the Revenue with evidence (prescribed in regulations) that 'relevant payments' (see 20.15 above) received in the year following the application are likely to equal or exceed a set threshold.

The set threshold is the smaller of:

(i) an amount found by multiplying the number of 'relevant persons' in relation to the company by the minimum turnover threshold for individuals (see 20.15 above); and

(ii) a minimum turnover to be set by regulations (expected to be £200,000).

For a close company, a '*relevant person*' for the purposes of (i) above is a director or a beneficial owner of shares; for other companies, the definition is limited to a director. 'Director' is defined by reference to *ITEPA 2003, s 67*. Where the number of relevant persons has fluctuated, regulations will prescribe the number of relevant persons to be used for the calculation in (i) above.

There is provision for the Board to make regulations enabling a company that does not meet this test to be treated as if it did (this is similar to the provision for individuals — see 20.15 above).

The compliance test. The provisions relating to companies mirror those relating to individuals (see 20.15 above). However, in addition to this a company must have complied with specified *Companies Act 1985* (or NI equivalent) obligations during the qualifying period.

[*FA 2004, s 64(4), Sch 11 paras 9–16*].

20.18 **CIS procedures and administration.** *Verification of status of sub-contractors.* Anyone making contract payments must verify the registration status of the recipient. The Revenue will confirm whether the payment should be made gross or under deduction.

The verification system is a hallmark of the new CIS. It removes the need for the sub-contractor to present documents which the contractor must inspect, and thus reduces some of the bureaucratic burden of the old scheme.

The detail of the verification process is to be contained in regulations. However, it is intended that, once verified, the contractor may assume that the same status continues unless notified to the contrary by the Revenue.

[*FA 2004, s 69*].

Periodic returns by contractors. The Revenue are empowered to make regulations governing returns by contractors containing information about the payments they have made. These powers are drawn very widely, with the Revenue able to prescribe the time at which the return must be made, the period it is to cover, and the information required (including a requirement to make nil returns).

It is provided that the return may include two important declarations by the contractor:

- that none of the contracts to which the return relates is a contract of employment; and

- that in relation to any payment reported on the return, the contractor has complied with verification requirements.

The Revenue may make regulations governing the records to be kept in relation to contractors' returns, and the conditions relating to the examination of such records. The returns will be subject to the penalty provisions in *TMA 1970, s 98* and *s 98A* (see 57.9 PENALTIES).

Regulations may also specify that certain of the information on the return be provided to the sub-contractor concerned.

The contractor may appoint a 'scheme representative' to act on his behalf in relation to the requirement to make a return. The Revenue may make regulations governing the rights, obligations and liabilities of such a scheme representative.

[*FA 2004, ss 70, 76, Sch 12 paras 7, 8*].

Collection and recovery of sums deducted. The Revenue are empowered to make regulations governing the collection and recovery of sums required to be deducted from payments by contractors as in 20.13 above. [*FA 2004, s 71*].

20.19 **Transitional provisions.** There are transitional measures covering certificates and registration cards in force immediately before the appointed day for the commencement of the new CIS (expected to be in April 2006) and existing commercial relationships.

Existing certificates and registration cards. Where a sub-contractor's certificate is in force immediately before the appointed day, the sub-contractor is to be treated as if he had been registered for gross payment on the appointed day. Similarly, where a registration card is in force immediately before the appointed day, the sub-contractor is to be treated as having been registered for payment under deduction on the appointed day.

[*FA 2004, s 77(2)(3)*].

Existing relationships. When making the first payment under the new CIS to a particular sub-contractor, a contractor will not have to verify the status of that sub-contractor if

- he has already paid that sub-contractor under a construction contract;

- the last such payment was within either the same tax year as the first payment under the new CIS or the preceding two tax years;

- at the time of the last payment a certificate or registration card was in force; and

- the contractor has no reason to believe that the sub-contractor did not become automatically registered on the appointed day (under the rules above) and is not still so registered.

Where these conditions apply, the contractor may continue to assume the sub-contractor's registration status unless the Revenue notify him of a change in status.

[*FA 2004, s 77(4)–(6)*].

21   Deceased Estates

Cross-references. See 27.6 EXCESS LIABILITY, 42.5 INTEREST AND SURCHARGES ON UNPAID TAX and 43.6 and 43.23 INTEREST PAYABLE.

Simon's Direct Tax Service C4.1.

21.1   **Liability of personal representatives.** Personal representatives of a deceased person (being either executors appointed under the will or administrators if there was no will) are assessable for all tax due from the deceased to the date of his death. [*ICTA 1988, s 60(8), s 62(9), s 63(3) as originally enacted; ICTA 1988, s 60(4); TMA 1970, s 74; FA 1994, s 200*]. Personal allowances may be claimed in full for the year of death.

Income may be assessed and charged on and in the name of any one or more of the personal representatives to whom it arises (in the case of income consisting of life assurance policy gains arising after 5 April 1998, on any one or more of the personal representatives in the year of assessment in which the gains arise) or on any subsequent personal representatives of the deceased. [*FA 1989, s 151; FA 1998, Sch 14 paras 6, 7*].

See 71.9 SCHEDULE D, CASES I AND II for discontinuance of a business on death and 71.26 for trading (or not) by the executors. See 5.2 ASSESSMENTS and 30.4 FRAUDULENT OR NEGLIGENT CONDUCT for time limits for assessments. See Tolley's Capital Gains Tax for capital gains tax position on death.

21.2   Personal representatives are also liable to income tax at the basic or lower rate (as appropriate) on estate income which they receive subsequent to the death. Dividends falling due after death are treated as the income of the estate, and not of the deceased, for all tax purposes, including exemption claims, although they accrued before the death (*Reid's Trustees v CIR CS 1929, 14 TC 512; CIR v Henderson's Exors CS 1931, 16 TC 282*), and the same principle applies in respect of interest payments, including bank and building society interest, falling due after the date of death. An exception (for deaths before 6 April 1996) is interest falling within the accrued income scheme (see 74.14 SCHEDULE D, CASE VI). The accrued annuity to the date of death of an annuitant is income of his estate and not his income (*Bryan v Cassin KB 1942, 24 TC 468*) and similarly as to the accrued income of which he was life-tenant (*Wood v Owen KB 1940, 23 TC 541; Stewart's Exors v CIR Ch D 1952, 33 TC 184*).

Strictly, the personal representatives should notify the Revenue that they are liable to tax on estate income no later than six months after the tax year in which they become liable (in accordance with 57.1 PENALTIES) and should file self-assessment tax returns and pay any tax due on normal self-assessment payment dates (see 78.4–78.7 SELF-ASSESSMENT). However, the Revenue operate informal procedures as follows. For estates where date of death is after 5 April 2003, they will instead accept a single computation and one-off payment of an estate's self-assessment liability (presumably including capital gains tax where relevant) if the estate is not 'complex' and the liability (over the whole of the administration period) is less than £10,000. For these purposes, an estate is '*complex*' if probate value exceeds £2.5 million *or* if administration continues into the third tax year from date of death *or* the personal representatives have disposed of a chargeable asset of the estate for more than £250,000. For estates where date of death was on or before 5 April 2003, the Revenue allowed one-off payment only where probate value was less than £400,000. (Revenue Tax Bulletin August 2003 pp 1043, 1044). The Tax Bulletin article also provides information as to which tax office is likely to deal with an estate.

Simon's Direct Tax Service. See **C4.102** *et seq.*

21.3 Deceased Estates

21.3 **Income from deceased estates during administration.** [*ICTA 1988, ss 695–702*]. Residuary income of an estate comprises aggregate income therefrom *less* interest and annual payments charged thereon, sums payable out of residue under law of intestacy, admissible expenses of administration and any income from assets vesting during or on completion of administration. [*ICTA 1988, ss 697(1), 701(6)*]. An annual payment made by personal representatives in satisfaction of a liability of the deceased is treated as if made by an individual for the purpose of applying the provisions of *FA 1988, s 36* excluding such payments from being a charge on income (see 1.10(i) ALLOWANCES AND TAX RATES). [*ICTA 1988, s 347A(3); FA 1988, s 36(1)*].

Limited interests (e.g. life tenants). Sums paid (including assets transferred, debts released etc.) to a beneficiary *during administration* are treated as his income for the tax year of payment. Any amount which remains payable in respect of the limited interest *on completion of administration* is deemed to have been paid to the beneficiary as income for the tax year in which the administration period ends or, if that interest has ceased earlier (because of the beneficiary's death), as income for the tax year in which the interest ceased. [*ICTA 1988, s 695(2)(3), s 700, s 701(12); FA 1995, Sch 18 para 2*]. **Absolute interests.** Sums paid (including assets transferred, debts released etc.) to a beneficiary *during administration* are treated as his income for the tax year of payment except to the extent that aggregate payments of income for that and earlier years exceed the beneficiary's aggregate entitlement to the residuary income of the estate for that and earlier years. If *on completion of administration* the aggregate income entitlement exceeds the aggregate payments of income, the excess is deemed to have been paid to the beneficiary immediately before the end of the administration period. [*ICTA 1988, s 696(3)–(3B)(5), s 700, s 701(12); FA 1995, Sch 18 para 3*].

In each case payments out of a UK estate are 'grossed-up' at the basic, lower or (from 6 April 1999) Schedule F ordinary rate, as appropriate (see 1.9 ALLOWANCES AND RATES), for the year of assessment of receipt, and treated as received under deduction of such tax. For this purpose, payments are assumed to be made out of the beneficiary's share of income bearing tax at the basic rate before they are made out of his share of income bearing tax at the lower rate or (from 6 April 1999) at the Schedule F ordinary rate, and (from 6 April 1999) at the lower rate before the Schedule F ordinary rate. Payments out of a foreign estate are directly assessed, without grossing, under Schedule D, Case IV (although, for 1995/96 onwards, certain sums ('*relevant amounts*') treated as having suffered tax at source, e.g. life assurance gains and UK stock dividends, *are* grossed up at the basic, lower or (from 6 April 1999) Schedule F ordinary rate of tax as appropriate, no repayment of which may be made, and this applies also from 2 July 1997 to distributions within *ICTA 1988, s 233(1)* in respect of which the recipient is not entitled to a tax credit, and from 6 April 1999 to any distribution chargeable under SCHEDULE F (76) (see 1.9 ALLOWANCES AND TAX RATES)). [*ICTA 1988, s 246D(1)–(3A), s 695(4), s 696(3)–(6), s 699A, s 701(3A); FA 1993, Sch 6 para 11; FA 1994, Sch 16 para 1; FA 1995, s 76(1)(4); FA 1996, Sch 6 para 5; F(No 2)A 1997, ss 21, 23, Sch 6 paras 3, 12; FA 2003, s 173, Sch 35 para 4*]. Income bearing tax at the lower rate or the Schedule F ordinary rate is treated in the hands of the recipient as chargeable under *ICTA 1988, s 1A* at whichever of those rates applies (see 1.9 ALLOWANCES AND RATES), except that income paid indirectly through a trustee and taxable under *ICTA 1988, s 698(3)* on the ultimate recipient is instead so treated in the hands of the trustee (unless it is within *ICTA 1988, s 686*, see 81.5 SETTLEMENTS). [*ICTA 1988, s 698A; FA 1993, Sch 6 para 11(2); FA 1996, Sch 6 para 17; F(No 2)A 1997, s 33(1)(11)*].

In computing estate residuary income in the case of an absolute interest, any excess of allowable deductions over income for any year is carried forward and treated as an allowable deduction of the following year. [*ICTA 1988, s 697(1A); FA 1995, Sch 18 para 4(1)(3)*]. If the total benefits received by a beneficiary with an absolute interest on completion of administration are less than the amount taken to be his residuary income, the deficiency is

314

applied in reducing the said amount, firstly for the tax year in which the administration ends, then for the previous year and so on. [*ICTA 1988, s 697(2); FA 1995, Sch 18 para 4(2)(3)*].

Assessments may be made or adjusted and relief may be claimed by virtue of these provisions within three years after 31 January following the year of assessment in which administration was completed. [*ICTA 1988, s 700(3); FA 1996, s 135, Sch 21 para 20*].

By concession, a residuary legatee, or legatee with a limited interest, who is not resident or not ordinarily resident in the UK, may claim to have his tax liability on income from the estate adjusted to what it would be if such income had arisen to him directly from the respective sources of residuary income. For 1999/2000 and later years, the relief or exemption must be claimed within five years and ten months of the end of the year of assessment in which the beneficiary is deemed to have received the income, and is dependent upon the personal representatives having made all required estate returns, paid all tax and any interest, surcharge and penalties, and keeping available for inspection any relevant tax certificates and copies of the estate accounts for all years of the administration period showing details of all sources of estate income and payments to beneficiaries. No tax will be repayable in respect of income which, if received by a UK-resident beneficiary, would be a 'relevant amount' (as above) within *ICTA 1988, s 699A*. For 1998/99 and earlier years, relief or exemption must be claimed not later than three years after the end of the year of assessment in which the administration of the estate is completed, or within six years of the end of the year of assessment in which the estate income arose, whichever is the later. (Revenue Pamphlet IR 1, A14; Revenue Press Release 1 April 1999). However, where the legatee is resident in a country with which the UK has a double taxation agreement, and the 'Other Income' Article in that agreement gives sole taxing rights in respect of such income to that country, the above concession does not apply, and the tax paid by the personal representatives will be repaid to the legatee, subject to the conditions in the Article being met. (Revenue Pamphlet IR 131, SP 3/86, 2 April 1986).

The treatment of rights held by personal representatives in relation to other deceased estates, and of successive interests in the residue of an estate, are dealt with in *ICTA 1988, s 698(1)–(2); FA 1995, Sch 18 para 5*. Discretionary payments out of the income of the residue of an estate, whether made directly by the personal representatives or through a trustee etc., are income of the recipient when paid. [*ICTA 1988, s 698(3)*]. This applies whether the payments are out of income as it arises, or out of income arising to the personal representatives in earlier years and retained pending exercise of the discretion. See Revenue Pamphlet IR 131, SP 4/93, 16 March 1993, under which claims and supplementary claims on this basis are invited for 1986/87 onwards.

For Revenue information powers, see *ICTA 1988, s 700(4)*. A personal representative has a duty to supply a beneficiary on request with a statement of income and tax borne for a year of assessment. [*ICTA 1988, s 700(5)(6); FA 1995, Sch 18 para 6*].

For relief from overlapping of inheritance tax and excess liability on accrued income, see 27.6 EXCESS LIABILITY.

Simon's Direct Tax Service. See **C4.115** *et seq.*

21.4   *Examples*

Limited interest

Mrs D died on 5 January 2003 leaving her whole estate with a life interest to her husband and then the capital to her children on his death. The administration of the estate is completed on 7 February 2005. Mr D receives payments on account of income of £1,200 on 30 September 2003, £2,500 on 31 December 2004, £1,050 on 7 February 2005 and £336 on 31 May 2005.

21.4 Deceased Estates

The actual income and deductible expenses of the estate were as follows.

	2002/03 (from 6.1.03)	2003/04	2004/05 (to 7.2.05)
	£	£	£
Interest received (net)	750	2,400	2,000
Other income (gross)	400	600	200
Basic rate tax thereon	(88)	(132)	(44)
Expenses	(150)	(450)	(400)
Net income available for distribution	£912	£2,418	£1,756

D's income from the estate for tax purposes is calculated as follows.

	2002/03	2003/04		2004/05	
		Basic rate income	Lower rate income	Basic rate income	Lower rate income
	£	£	£	£	£
Net income	Nil	780*	420*	156**	3,730**
Basic rate tax		220		44	
Lower rate tax			105		932
Gross income	Nil	£1,000	£525	£200	£4,662

* The payments to the beneficiary in each year must be allocated between (i) income bearing tax at the basic rate and (ii) income bearing tax at the lower rate, (i) taking priority over (ii). Total basic rate income for 2002/03 and 2003/04 is £780 (£400 + £600 − £88 − £132), so £780 of the £1,200 payment in 2003/04 is deemed to have been made out of basic rate income.

** Total basic rate income for the three tax years is £936 (£400 + £600 + £200 − £88 − £132 − £44) of which £780 was paid out in 2003/04 leaving £156 of the 2004/05 payments to be allocated to basic rate income. The balance of the 2004/05 payments (£2,500 + £1,050 + £336 − £156 = £3,730) is deemed to have been made out of lower rate income.

Note

(a)   The £336 paid in May 2005 is deemed to have been paid in 2004/05, being the tax year in which the administration period ends.

Absolute interest

C died on 5 July 2002 leaving his estate of £400,000 divisible equally between his three children. The income arising and administration expenses paid in the administration period which ends on 25 January 2005 are as follows.

	Period to 5.4.03		Year to 5.4.04		Period to 25.1.05	
	£	£	£	£	£	£
Interest income (net)		15,000		8,850		3,000
Administration expenses charge-able to income		(1,500)		(750)		(300)
		13,500		8,100		2,700
Other income (gross)	10,000		3,200		1,000	
Basic rate tax thereon payable by executors	(2,200)		(704)		(220)	
		7,800		2,496		780
Net income distributed		£21,300		£10,596		£3,480
Each child's share		£7,100		£3,532		£1,160

Dates and amounts of payments to *each* child are as follows.

	Payment	Allocated to tax years (see 21.3 above)
	£	
30.4.03	5,000	2003/04
16.10.03	3,000	2003/04
21.6.04	2,000	2004/05
22.1.05	1,000	2004/05
30.7.05	792	2004/05

The children's income for tax purposes is as follows.

	2002/03	2003/04	2004/05
Each child's share of basic rate income	Nil	3,432*	260
Basic rate tax	Nil	968	73
Gross basic rate income	Nil	£4,400	£333

* £(7,800 + 2,496) × $\frac{1}{3}$ = £3,432

	2002/03	2003/04	2004/05
Each child's share of lower rate income	Nil	4,568	3,532
Lower rate tax	Nil	1,142	883
Gross lower rate income	Nil	£5,710	£4,415

Notes

(a)   Each beneficiary would receive tax certificates (Forms R185 (Estate Income)) showing the gross amount of his entitlement and the tax paid by the executors. Where the estate has income bearing tax at the lower rate (i.e. savings income), or dividend income bearing tax at the Schedule F ordinary rate, the tax certificate shows such income separately from income which has borne tax at the basic rate.

(b)   In the hands of a beneficiary, estate income which has borne tax at the lower rate or the Schedule F ordinary rate is treated as income within *ICTA 1988, s 1A*. Therefore, the beneficiary will have a further liability only to the extent that the income exceeds the basic rate limit. Where the income is subject to lower rate tax, the beneficiary will be able to reclaim tax at 20% to the extent that the income is covered by personal reliefs.

21.5 Deceased Estates

(*c*) Payments to a beneficiary of an estate are deemed to be made out of his share of income bearing tax at the basic rate in priority to his share of income bearing tax at the lower rate. Therefore, administration expenses chargeable to income are effectively relieved primarily against lower rate income.

21.5 **Residence of personal representatives.** See 65.5 RESIDENCE, ORDINARY RESIDENCE AND DOMICILE for special provisions where personal representatives are partly UK resident and partly non-UK resident.

21.6 Otherwise the tax position in respect of deceased estates is similar to that of settlements (or trusts as they are often called) and reference should be made to the following items under 81 SETTLEMENTS which contain details of tax cases relating to both deceased estates and settlements.

81.3 Assessments on trust income.   81.9   Annuities etc. out of capital.
81.7 Personal position of trustee.   81.10 Foreign trust income.
81.8 Income of beneficiaries.   81.11 Claims by trustees and beneficiaries.

22   Deduction of Tax at Source

Cross-references. See 3.18 ANTI-AVOIDANCE re annual payments for non-taxable consideration; 7 BANKS and 8 BUILDING SOCIETIES for interest; 14.17 CHARITIES regarding deeds of covenant; 20 CONSTRUCTION INDUSTRY SCHEME; 24.6 DOUBLE TAX RELIEF for reduced rate of deduction on payments abroad; 24.5(a) DOUBLE TAX RELIEF for alimony payable by non-resident; 32 FUNDING BONDS; 33.3 GOVERNMENT STOCKS for certain payments gross; 43 INTEREST PAYABLE; 44 INTEREST RECEIVABLE; 48 MEDICAL INSURANCE; 49 MINERAL ROYALTIES; 51.7 NON-RESIDENTS AND OTHER OVERSEAS MATTERS for non-resident entertainers and sportsmen; 55 PAY AS YOU EARN; 60.1 PERSONAL PENSION SCHEMES for personal pension scheme contributions; 66.1 RETIREMENT ANNUITIES for retirement annuity premiums; 67.5 RETIREMENT SCHEMES for additional voluntary contributions and for refunds of pension and superannuation contributions; 75.37 SCHEDULE E—EMPLOYMENT INCOME for payments for restrictive covenants; 81.5 SETTLEMENTS for distributions from discretionary and accumulation trusts; 89 UNDERWRITERS AT LLOYD'S for transfers to special reserves; 92 VOCATIONAL TRAINING RELIEF for vocational training costs.

Simon's Direct Tax Service A3.4.

22.1   Income tax (at the basic or lower rate, whichever is applicable) *may* legally be deducted by the payer from certain annuities and other annual payments and certain royalties, which are paid out of taxed income, within the terms of *ICTA 1988, s 348* (see 22.2 below) and *must* be deducted from the payments listed in 22.3 below. Tax may also be deducted from certain mortgage loan interest, see 22.13 below. See Revenue Tax Bulletin February 1996 pp 277–280 for a list showing the rate at which tax should be deducted from various types of payment and for commentary on the various deduction arrangements.

The **payer** thus obtains tax relief other than at the higher rate in respect of such payments. He may also be able to deduct the payments as charges on income in arriving at his EXCESS LIABILITY (27). For **companies** the payments may rank as charges on income for corporation tax, see Tolley's Corporation Tax under Profit Computations.

The **recipient** has, because of the deduction of tax, suffered income tax at the basic or lower rate (whichever is applicable) on the income. If he is not liable, or not wholly liable, on such income at that rate, he can recover from the Revenue any excess tax suffered so far as not adjusted in direct assessments on him. On the other hand, if his total income is high enough, further liability will arise on him at the higher rate of income tax. See 1.9 ALLOWANCES AND TAX RATES for the circumstances in which the recipient is liable at the lower rate (as opposed to the basic rate) on savings income.

A payment made under deduction of tax is income (equal to the grossed-up equivalent) of the year of assessment by reference to the basic or lower rate of tax for which tax is deducted from the payment, without regard to the period of accrual (and see *CIR v Crawley Ch D 1986, 59 TC 728*). [*ICTA 1988, s 835(6); FA 1996, Sch 6 paras 24, 28*].

For the deduction of tax from VAT-inclusive amounts, see Revenue Inspector's Manual IM 3900.

Headings in this chapter are as follows.

22.2	Circumstances where payer *may* deduct tax	22.6	Alterations in basic rate
		22.7	Certificate of tax deducted
22.3	Circumstances where payer *must* deduct tax	22.8	Omission to deduct tax
		22.9	Alimony, maintenance, separation allowances etc.
22.4	Deduction of tax under foreign agreements or by non-residents	22.10	Annual payments etc.
22.5	Rate of tax deductible	22.11	Annuities

22.2 Deduction of Tax at Source

22.2 CIRCUMSTANCES WHERE PAYER MAY DEDUCT TAX [*ICTA 1988, s 348; ITEPA 2003, Sch 6 para 50*]

The permissible tax deduction, as 22.1 above, applies to

(a) any annuity or other annual payment charged with tax under SCHEDULE D, CASE III (72) or, from 6 April 2003, under *ITEPA 2003, s 607* (annuities from retirement annuity contracts — see 58.2(*j*) PENSION INCOME) or, if sourced in the UK, *ss 609–611* (see 58.2(*k*) PENSION INCOME), not being interest (but see 1.8(i) ALLOWANCES AND TAX RATES for certain annual payments excluded from the charge to tax, 22.13 below for certain relevant loan interest, and also see 3.18 ANTI-AVOIDANCE re annual payments made for non-taxable consideration and 81.5 SETTLEMENTS re payments out of discretionary trusts),

(b) (i) any royalty or other sum paid in respect of the user of a patent, and

   (ii) (before 6 April 1997) electric line wayleaves [*ICTA 1988, s 120; FA 1997, Sch 18 Pt VI(2)*] (see 22.14 below),

provided that the payment is wholly out of profits or gains brought into charge to income tax. (N.B. As the profits of UK companies are not charged to income tax, *ICTA 1988, s 348* does not apply to them and payments by them will be within *ICTA 1988, s 349* — see 22.3 below.)

The payer is entitled to deduct tax and it will be detrimental to himself if he fails to do so. See 22.8 below regarding omission to deduct tax.

The tax deductible is at the basic rate for the year in which the payment became due, irrespective of the date of actual payment. Where the payment would constitute 'savings income' (see 1.9 ALLOWANCES AND TAX RATES) of the recipient (whatever his status), deduction is at the lower rate instead (although the only type of payment within *section 348* to which this should apply is a purchased life annuity). [*ICTA 1988, s 4; FA 1996, s 73(2)–(4), Sch 6 paras 2, 28*]. (Cf. *Re Sebright Ch D 1944, 23 TC 190.*) It is accordingly income of the recipient of the year when due — an important point if the recipient wishes to claim repayment of the tax deducted (*CIR v Crawley Ch D 1986, 59 TC 728*).

See 14.17 CHARITIES as regards covenanted donations.

Simon's Direct Tax Service. See A3.403.

22.3 CIRCUMSTANCES WHERE PAYER MUST DEDUCT TAX [*ICTA 1988, ss 349, 350; ITEPA 2003, Sch 6 para 51*]

Income tax *must* be deducted from the following.

(i) Payments specified in 22.2(*a*) and (*b*) above which are not payable, or not wholly payable, out of profits or gains brought into charge to income tax. [*ICTA 1988, s 349(1); FA 1995, Sch 29 Pt VIII(22); FA 1997, Sch 18 Pt VI(2)*]. See 74.2 SCHEDULE D, CASE VI as regards certain payments to theatrical 'angels'.

The payer must deduct tax from such payments, and must inform the Revenue, who will make an assessment to collect that tax. Appeals against that assessment are to the Special Commissioners. [*TMA 1970, s 31C(2)*]. Payments by UK companies are within *section 349(1)* but the tax is accounted for under *ICTA 1988, Sch 16*, see

Tolley's Corporation Tax. See, however, below under heading *Certain payments by companies and local authorities* as regards disapplication of the requirement to deduct tax from such payments.

The obligation to deduct is upon 'the person by or through whom' the payment is made and see *Rye & Eyre v CIR HL 1935, 19 TC 164*; *Aeolian Co Ltd v CIR KB 1936, 20 TC 547* and *Howells v CIR KB 1939, 22 TC 501*. But liability under *section 350* does not arise until the annual payment is actually 'paid'.

Tax is deductible at the basic rate in force at the time of payment. Where the payment would constitute 'savings income' (see 1.9 ALLOWANCES AND TAX RATES) of the recipient (whatever his status), deduction is at the lower rate instead (but the same comment applies as in 22.2 above as regards application). [*ICTA 1988, s 4; FA 1996, s 73(2)–(4), Sch 6 paras 2, 28*].

Where a payment from which tax should have been deducted is made in full, there is no right to recover the under-deduction by deduction from later payments (*Tenbry Investments Ltd v Peugeot Talbot Motor Co Ltd Ch D, [1992] STC 791*).

If a payment is made by an individual in a later year than the year when due and it could have been made out of taxed income in that due year, an allowance will be made in any assessment to collect the tax for the tax which could have been deducted if the payment had been made when due. A similar allowance may be made in the case of a trust or other non-trading institution (not within the charge to corporation tax) in cases of hardship. (Revenue Pamphlet IR 1, A16 as revised).

The profits or gains to be taken into account are those assessed (or received less tax) for the year of assessment in which the payment was made. Hence, except where the concession A16 applies, accumulated income of previous years cannot be taken into account (*Luipaard's Vlei Estate v CIR CA 1930, 15 TC 573*) and, for a trader, the Case I assessment for the year after deducting any losses forward and capital allowances is taken into account irrespective of the actual profits of the year (*A-G v Metropolitan Water Board CA 1927, 13 TC 294*; *Trinidad Petroleum Development Co Ltd v CIR CA 1936, 21 TC 1*). For the individual, *section 349(1)* will normally be applicable only if his annual payments etc. exceed his aggregate income of the year (cf. *CIR v Plummer HL 1979, 54 TC 1*). However, trustees may be liable under *section 350* where annual payments etc. are made out of capital of the trust fund irrespective of the trust income, see 81.9 SETTLEMENTS.

Loss Relief. Where payments are made under deduction of tax but the payer has no income assessable to income tax the tax deducted will be collected by assessment under *section 350*. But if this position arises by reason of a loss sustained in a trade etc. in the year, or brought forward, a sole trader or partnership may treat amounts so assessed as if they were trading losses under *ICTA 1988, s 385* and carry them forward for computing profits of the same business for the following years, except where they fall into the list given under 46.14(*a*) LOSSES. [*ICTA 1988, s 387*].

(ii) Subject to the exclusion, from 1 April 2001, of certain payments by companies and local authorities (see below), yearly interest of money chargeable to tax under Case III of Schedule D (disregarding the modifications made for corporation tax purposes, see 72.1 SCHEDULE D, CASE III), but only if paid

 (*a*) by a company or local authority (otherwise than in a fiduciary or representative capacity), or

 (*b*) by or for a partnership of which a company is a member, or

 (*c*) to a person whose usual place of abode is outside the UK. [*ICTA 1988, s 349(2); FA 1996, Sch 14 para 18*].

22.3 Deduction of Tax at Source

As regards (c) above, tax need not be deducted from payments of interest to the UK branch of a non-resident company trading in the UK through that branch, where the branch profits are liable to corporation tax under *ICTA 1988, s 11* and not exempted under a double tax treaty. (Revenue Tax Bulletin August 1993 p 87). See now below for the general exclusion of certain payments by companies and local authorities.

Where interest received by a company is charged to tax as a trading receipt (see Tolley's Corporation Tax under Loan Relationships), this does not affect the requirement for deduction of tax by the payer (see Revenue Tax Bulletin August 1999 pp 685, 686). See now below for the general exclusion of certain payments by companies and local authorities.

Interest under the *Late Payment of Commercial Debts (Interest) Act 1998* (or under a contractual right but for which that *Act* would have applied) is *not* 'yearly interest'. (Revenue Tax Bulletin August 1999 pp 686, 687).

For advances made on or after 29 April 1996, interest payable on an advance from a bank (within *ICTA 1988, s 840A*, see 7.1 BANKS) within the charge to corporation tax in respect of it, and interest paid by such a bank in the ordinary course of its business, is excluded. Previously, the exclusion applied to interest payable in the UK on an advance from a bank carrying on a *bona fide* banking business in the UK (see *Hafton Properties Ltd v McHugh Ch D 1986, 59 TC 420*) or paid by such a bank in the ordinary course of such a business (for which see Revenue Pamphlet IR 131, SP 4/96, 13 May 1996, revising SP 12/91, 9 October 1991). For whether interest is 'payable in the UK', see *Mistletoe Ltd v Flood (Sp C 351), [2003] SSCD 66*. There are transitional provisions preserving relief as regards interest payable or paid on or after 29 April 1996 on an advance made before that day. National Savings Bank interest is always paid without deduction of tax. [*ICTA 1988, s 349(3)(a)(b) (3AA)(3AB); FA 1996, Sch 37 Pt II; FA 1997, s 78*]. See, however, 22.13 below as regards 'relevant loan interest' and 7.2 BANKS as regards special deduction schemes. See 7.2 BANKS also for exclusion from *section 349(2)* of certain interest payments by bodies other than banks where those payments are not within the special deduction scheme. [*ICTA 1988, s 349(3)(h); FA 1993, s 59*]. See now below for the general exclusion of certain payments by companies and local authorities.

As regards payments by building societies, only interest and dividends on certain 'marketable securities' is within *section 349*. [*ICTA 1988, s 349(2)(3A); FA 1991, Sch 11 para 1*]. See BUILDING SOCIETIES (8) generally and at 8.3 in particular. Interest paid to a society is payable gross unless it is 'relevant loan interest', see 22.13 below. [*ICTA 1988, s 369(1); FA 1994, s 81(3)*]. See now below for the general exclusion of certain payments by companies and local authorities.

For interest payments after 30 September 2002, the requirement to deduct tax does not apply to a person authorised under the *Financial Services and Markets Act 2000* whose business consists wholly or mainly of dealing as principal in 'financial instruments' (as specially defined) and who pays the interest in the ordinary course of that business. [*ICTA 1988, s 349(3)(i)(5)(6); FA 2002, s 95*].

For interest payments after 13 April 2003, the requirement to deduct tax does not apply to

- interest paid by a recognised clearing house or recognised investment exchange, in the course of providing a central counterparty clearing service (as defined), on margin or other collateral deposited with it by users of the service; or

- price differentials on repos where treated (under *ICTA 1988, s 730A* — see 3.4 ANTI-AVOIDANCE) as interest paid by a recognised clearing house or recognised investment exchange in respect of contracts made by it as provider of a central counterparty clearing service.

[*ICTA 1988, s 349(3)(j)(k)(6); FA 2003, s 202*].

'*UK public revenue dividends*' (i.e. any income from securities which is paid out of the UK or NI public revenue, but excluding interest on local authority stock (see (*a*) above)) are, from 1 April 2001, payable under deduction of tax, subject to any provision to the contrary in the *Taxes Acts* (and see in particular 33.3 GOVERNMENT STOCKS for the general exemption of gilt-edged securities). The Board has wide powers to make regulations governing the accounting arrangements and modifying *ICTA 1988, ss 349, 350* in their application to UK public revenue dividends. [*ICTA 1988, ss 349(3C)(4), 350A; FA 2000, s 112(2)–(5)*]. For the deduction of tax from UK public revenue dividends by paying agents before 1 April 2001, see *ICTA 1988, ss 118A–118K* and regulations thereunder.

Interest paid on '*quoted Eurobonds*' (i.e. listed securities issued by a company and carrying a right to interest) is in all cases excluded from the above provisions for deduction of tax from interest from 1 April 2001. For payments made before that date, the exclusion applies only where the security is in bearer form and

(I)   the payment is made by or through a person who is not in the UK; or

(II)   where (I) above does not apply, either

    (i)   the bond is held in a 'recognised clearing system' (as designated by the Board), or

    (ii)   the beneficial owner of the bond is non–UK resident and is beneficially entitled to the interest.

The Board has regulatory powers to disapply (II) above unless certain declarations confirming eligibility are received by the payer or the Board has issued the appropriate notice (for regulations made under which see *SI 1996 No 1779*). Before 29 April 1996, different requirements applied in relation to (II) above. [*ICTA 1988, ss 124, 841A; FA 1996, Sch 7 para 26, Sch 29 para 4, Sch 38 para 6, Sch 41 Pt V(19); FA 2000, s 111(2)(6), Sch 40 Pt II(17)*]. See also Revenue Press Release 1 August 1984 as regards designation as a 'recognised clearing system', and *FA 1989, s 116* (repealed by *FA 1996, Sch 41 Pt V(3)*) as regards certain payments of interest to Netherlands Antilles subsidiaries which were treated as being within *section 124*.

Tax is deductible at the lower rate in force for the tax year in which payment is made. [*ICTA 1988, s 4; FA 1996, s 73(2)–(4), Sch 6 paras 2, 28*].

For the procedure under which companies pay income tax so deducted to the Revenue, see *ICTA 1988, Sch 16* and Tolley's Corporation Tax.

(iii)   The following, as under (i) above, except that they cannot qualify for the loss relief described.

    (*a*)   Sale of British patent rights by a non–resident. [*ICTA 1988, s 524*]. See 54 PATENTS.

    (*b*)   Copyright royalties, public lending right payments and design royalties payable to a non–resident. [*ICTA 1988, ss 536, 537, 537B; FA 1995, s 115(10)*]. See 22.15 below and 51.9 NON-RESIDENTS AND OTHER OVERSEAS MATTERS.

(iv)   (Before 1 April 2001) UK public revenue and foreign dividends etc. paid in UK through an agent (and see now (ii) above and 22.12 below).

See 14.17 CHARITIES as regards covenanted donations.

22.4 Deduction of Tax at Source

Certain payments by companies and local authorities. For payments made by one company to another after 31 March 2001, there is no requirement to deduct tax from interest, royalties, annuities or other annual payments where the recipient company is within the charge to corporation tax in respect of that income. There are detailed rules requiring the paying company to satisfy itself that the recipient company is eligible to receive the payment gross. For payments made after 30 September 2002, gross payment may also be made by companies to a wide range of tax-exempt bodies (and, after 30 November 2002, to their nominees), and the provisions are extended to apply to payments by local authorities subject to similar conditions. [*ICTA 1988, ss 349A–349D; FA 2001, s 85(1)–(3); FA 2002, s 94; SI 2002 No 2931*]. For details, see Tolley's Corporation Tax under Income Tax in Relation to a Company. See also Revenue Tax Bulletin August 2001 pp 867, 868 for an article outlining the original provisions.

Cross-border royalties. For payments made by companies after 30 September 2002 of royalties within (i) above in respect of which the company reasonably believes that, at the time the payment is made, the payee is entitled to relief under any double tax arrangements, the company may, if it thinks fit, calculate the sum to be deducted from the payment under (i) above by reference to the rate of income tax appropriate to the payee under the arrangements. If the payee was not so entitled, the company must account for the tax as if the above rule had never applied, and the Revenue have powers to direct the company that it is not to apply to a particular payment or payments. [*ICTA 1988, s 349E; FA 2002, s 96*]. For details, see Tolley's Corporation Tax under Income Tax in Relation to a Company.

EU Interest and Royalties Directive. This Directive (*Directive 2003/49/EC* of 3 June 2003) has effect from 1 January 2004 and provides for the elimination of source taxation on interest and royalty payments between associated companies in different Member States of the European Union. For details, see Tolley's Corporation Tax under Income Tax in Relation to a Company.

Simon's Direct Tax Service. See A3.404 *et seq.*

22.4	**DEDUCTION OF TAX UNDER FOREIGN AGREEMENTS, OR BY NON-RESIDENTS**

UK tax legislation cannot alter rights not within the jurisdiction of UK courts. See *Keiner v Keiner QB 1952, 34 TC 346* (tax not deductible from alimony under American agreement paid by UK resident ex-husband to non-resident ex-wife); *Bingham v CIR Ch D 1955, 36 TC 254* (maintenance payments under foreign Court Order not deductible in arriving at total income as tax not deductible); *Westminster Bank v National Bank of Greece HL 1970, 46 TC 472* (interest on foreign bonds paid in London by guarantor held within Case IV and tax not deductible). But where under a UK contract a non-resident paid interest to another non-resident and the payer died, held his executors (resident in UK) must deduct tax from interest they paid (*CIR v Broome's Exors KB 1935, 19 TC 667*). And where 'free of tax' alimony was payable under UK agreements etc., payments by the ex-husband no longer resident in the UK were held to have been paid subject to deduction of tax, the onus being on the Crown to collect the tax if the payments were within *section 349* (*Stokes v Bennett Ch D 1953, 34 TC 337*). See also *CIR v Ferguson HL 1969, 46 TC 1*.

22.5	**RATE OF TAX DEDUCTIBLE**

For *ICTA 1988, s 348* purposes, the basic (or lower) rate when payment becomes **due** applies, see 22.2 above.

For *ICTA 1988, s 349* purposes, the basic (or lower) rate when payment is **made** applies, see 22.3(i) and (ii) above.

In other words, the tax deductible is at the basic (or lower) rate in force for the year in which the payment is due if paid out of taxed profits or gains or, in any other case, the rate for the year in which the payment is made.

For 1995/96 and earlier years, tax is deductible at the basic rate. This continues for 1996/97 and later years except where the payment would constitute 'savings income' (including interest) (see 1.9 ALLOWANCES AND TAX RATES) of the recipient (whatever his status), in which case tax is deductible at the lower rate. [*ICTA 1988, s 4; FA 1996, s 73(2)–(4), Sch 6 paras 2, 28*].

22.6   ALTERATIONS IN TAX RATE

Where deductions are made by reference to a tax rate greater or less than the rate subsequently fixed for the tax year:

(*a*)   **under-deductions** in respect of any half-yearly or quarterly payments of interest, dividends or other annual payments, other than company dividends and other distributions, are charged under Schedule D, Case III. [*ICTA 1988, s 821(1); FA 1996, Sch 6 paras 22, 28*];

(*b*)   **under-deductions** in respect of any rent, interest, annuity or other annual payment, any copyright royalties or public lending right payments paid to non-residents and patent royalties (and, where previously applicable, mining rents etc. under *ICTA 1988, s 119* and *s 120*) may be deducted from future payments or, if none, recovered from the payee. [*ICTA 1988, s 821(2)(3); FA 1997, Sch 18 Pt VI(2)*]. See *Nesta v Wyatt KB 1940, 19 ATC 541*;

(*c*)   **over-deductions** of tax under *section 349* or from interest on government securities can generally be recovered from the Revenue provided that the tax has been accounted for and no adjustment made between the parties. See *Provisional Collection of Taxes Act 1968, s 2*; and

(*d*)   **over-deductions** of tax by a 'body corporate' on interest (not being a distribution) on its securities may be adjusted in the next payment but any repayments must be made no later than a year from the passing of the Act imposing the tax, and enure to the benefit of the person entitled at date of adjustment or repayment. [*ICTA 1988, s 822; FA 1996, Sch 6 paras 23, 28*].

22.7   CERTIFICATE OF TAX DEDUCTED

A certificate of tax deducted under *ICTA 1988, ss 339, 348, 349, 480A* or *687* (re payments under discretionary trusts), or under regulations made under *ICTA 1988, s 477A* (*SI 1990 No 2231*, see 8.3 BUILDING SOCIETIES) must be given by payer upon written request by recipient. [*ICTA 1988, s 352; FA 1990, Sch 5 para 11*].

22.8   OMISSION TO DEDUCT TAX

(*a*)   The provisions for the deduction of tax do not preclude assessment of the recipient if tax is not deducted (*Glamorgan County Quarter Sessions v Wilson KB 1910, 5 TC 537; Renfrew Town Council v CIR CS 1934, 19 TC 13; Grosvenor Place Estates Ltd v Roberts CA 1960, 39 TC 433*). These cases were decided when the legislation (cf. *subsection (1)(a)* (as originally enacted) of *ICTA 1970, s 52* (the predecessor to *ICTA 1988, s 348*)) precluded assessment on the recipient if the payment was out of taxed income. This provision was abolished for 1973/74 onwards by *FA 1971, Sch 14 Pt II*. However where in a case within *ICTA 1988, s 348* (22.2 above) tax is not deducted, the Crown nevertheless effectively collects from the payer the tax he failed to deduct [*ICTA 1988, s 3, s 256(3)(c)(ii), s 276(1)(1A); FA 1994, s 77(1), Sch 8 para 11*] and does not need to have recourse to the recipient.

22.9 Deduction of Tax at Source

(b)   Tax not deducted at the time of payment cannot generally be recovered afterwards. For this see *Shrewsbury v Shrewsbury CA 1907, 23 TLR 224*; *Re Hatch Ch D 1919, 1 Ch 351*; *Ord v Ord KB 1923, 39 TLR 437*; *Taylor v Taylor CA 1937, 16 ATC 218*; *Brine v Brine KB 1943, 22 ATC 177*; *Hemsworth v Hemsworth KB 1946, 25 ATC 466*; *Tenbry Investments Ltd v Peugeot Talbot Motor Co Ltd Ch D, [1992] STC 791*. But where trustees omitted to deduct tax from annuities through an honest error of fact, not an error of law, they were authorised to recoup the tax from future payments (*Re Musgrave, Machell v Parry Ch D, [1916] 2 Ch 417*). See also *Turvey v Dentons (1923) Ltd QB 1952, 31 ATC 470*. Only net amount of alimony available to satisfy contra account (*Butler v Butler CA 1961, 40 ATC 19*). See also *Fletcher v Young CS 1936, 15 ATC 531*; *Hollis v Wingfield CA 1940, 19 ATC 98*.

(c)   The Courts may rectify documents shown not to embody the intentions of the parties. For cases where rectification sought in relation to deduction of tax see *Burroughes v Abbott Ch D 1921, 38 TLR 167*; *Jervis v Howle & Talke Colliery Co Ltd Ch D 1936, 15 ATC 529*; *Fredensen v Rothschild Ch D 1941, 20 ATC 1*; *Van der Linde v Van der Linde Ch D 1947, 26 ATC 348*; *Whiteside v Whiteside CA 1949, 28 ATC 479*.

(d)   A penalty of £50 is incurred by refusal to allow the deduction of tax, and any 'agreement' not to deduct is void to that extent. [*TMA 1970, s 106*]. See 22.17 below for 'free of tax' payments.

22.9   ALIMONY, MAINTENANCE, SEPARATION ALLOWANCES ETC.

See 47.8 MARRIED PERSONS.

22.10   ANNUAL PAYMENTS ETC.

The broad rule is that annual payments are recurrent payments which, in the hands of the recipient, are 'pure income profit' and not e.g. elements in the computation of the profits of the recipient. Leading cases are *Earl Howe v CIR CA 1919, 7 TC 289* (insurance premiums under covenant not annual payments) and *CIR v Epping Forest Conservators HL 1953, 34 TC 293* (yearly contributions to meet the deficiencies of a charity held to be annual payments). Payments for the use of chattels not annual payments (*In re Hanbury, decd CA 1939, 38 TC 588*). See also *CIR v Whitworth Park Coal Co Ltd HL 1959, 38 TC 531*. Payments to a County Council under deed of covenant in consideration of the Council's paying special school fees of the covenantor's handicapped child held not annual payments (*Essex County Council v Ellam CA 1989, 61 TC 615*). The profits of a business bequeathed to a charity were held to be annual payments (*R v Special Commrs (ex p Shaftesbury Homes) CA 1922, 8 TC 367*). For covenanted subscriptions see *CIR v National Book League CA 1957, 37 TC 455* and *Taw & Torridge Festival Society Ltd v CIR Ch D 1959, 38 TC 603* (but see also 14.17(b) CHARITIES). Covenanted payments to a charity as part of arrangements under which it acquired the business of the payer not annual payments (*Campbell v CIR HL 1968, 45 TC 427*). Payments by a film company of a share of certain receipts as part of arrangements for cancellation of a contract were annual payments (*Asher v London Film Productions Ltd CA 1943, 22 ATC 432*) as were payments under a guarantee of the dividends of a company (*Aeolian Co Ltd v CIR KB 1936, 20 TC 547*; *Moss Empires Ltd v CIR HL 1937, 21 TC 264*). But not payments by the principal subscribers to a newsfilm service to make good its operating deficit (*British Commonwealth International Newsfilm Agency Ltd v Mahany HL 1962, 40 TC 550*).

Instalments of the purchase price of a mine held not annual payments (*Foley v Fletcher 1858, 7 WR 141*) nor instalment repayments of a debt (*Dott v Brown CA 1936, 15 ATC 147*). Where the Secretary of State for India acquired a railway in consideration of annuities for 48 years, tax held to be deductible only from the interest element actuarially ascertained (*Scoble v*

Secretary of State for India HL 1903, 4 TC 478, 618 and cf. the two *East India Railway* cases at *21 TLR 606* and *40 TLR 241*). Similarly where shares were sold for payments over 125 years, the actuarially ascertained interest element in the payments was held to be income in the hands of the recipient for surtax (*Vestey v CIR Ch D 1961, 40 TC 112*). See also *Goole Corporation v Aire etc. Trustees KB 1942, 21 ATC 156* (tax held deductible from interest element in yearly payments to local authority to meet street repairs). In *CIR v Church Commissioners HL 1976, 50 TC 516* rent charges paid as the consideration for property were held wholly income and not (as contended for Crown) partly income and partly capital. The HL judgments are an important review of the possibility of dissecting periodical payments in return for valuable consideration between income and capital and *Vestey v CIR* above, although not overruled, was called 'the high water of dissection cases' (Lord Wilberforce) and some of the reasoning in it was not approved. See also *Chadwick v Pearl Life Insce KB 1905, 21 TLR 456*. For reimbursement of expenditure calculated by reference to an interest factor, see *Re Euro Hotel (Belgravia) Ltd Ch D 1975, 51 TC 293* and *Chevron Petroleum (UK) Ltd v BP Petroleum Development Ltd Ch D 1981, 57 TC 137*.

Payments in satisfaction of the transfer of a business etc., and based on profits held not to be annual payments in *CIR v Ramsay CA 1935, 20 TC 79* and *CIR v Ledgard KB 1937, 21 TC 129* but contrast *CIR v Hogarth CS 1940, 23 TC 491*. Payments of a percentage of receipts over 40 years for the use of a secret process held to be annual payments (*Delage v Nugget Polish Co Ltd KB 1905, 21 TLR 454*) as were quarterly payments for the use of a firm's name etc. (*Mackintosh v CIR KB 1928, 14 TC 15*). See also *CIR v 36/49 Holdings Ltd CA 1943, 25 TC 173*. Where a business was bequeathed for life and the trustees were directed to carry a percentage of the profits to reserve, the amounts set aside were held to be annual payments (*Stocker v CIR KB 1919, 7 TC 304*).

In *Watkins v CIR KB 1939, 22 TC 696*, payments by a husband for the maintenance of his wife (of unsound mind) were held not to be annual payments. Payments to trustees as 'remuneration' are annual payments (*Baxendale v Murphy KB 1924, 9 TC 76*; *Hearn v Morgan KB 1945, 26 TC 478*) but not Schedule E remuneration (*Jaworski v Institution of Polish Engineers CA 1950, 29 ATC 385*).

For amounts taxable under *ICTA 1988, s 775* or *s 776* (see 3.9 and 3.10 ANTI-AVOIDANCE), if the person entitled is resident abroad the Revenue may direct that they be treated as annual payments subject to deduction of tax under *ICTA 1988, s 349(1)*. [*ICTA 1988, s 777(9)*]. Such a direction may, however, only be made once there is entitlement to the consideration, i.e. on execution of a contract (*Pardoe v Entergy Power Development Corp Ch D 2000, 72 TC 617*).

For annual payments under certain life assurance policies (e.g. Guaranteed Income Bonds) not treated as such for tax purposes, see 45.15(*i*) LIFE INSURANCE POLICIES.

See also 3.18 ANTI-AVOIDANCE where certain annual payments are made for non-taxable consideration.

Simon's Direct Tax Service. See B5.302.

22.11   **ANNUITIES**

(*a*)   **General.** In the absence of provisions to the contrary annuities are (i) within SCHEDULE D, CASE III (72) unless payable under foreign contracts etc. (when they are foreign possessions within SCHEDULE D, CASE IV (73), (ii) subject to deduction of tax under *ICTA 1988, ss 348, 349(1)* and (iii) this is so notwithstanding that the annuity may have been granted for valuable and sufficient consideration. Hence, (iv) an annuity cannot be dissected between the capital, if any, in consideration of the annuity and an 'interest element'. For a full discussion of this, see the HL opinions in *CIR v Church Commissioners HL 1976, 50 TC 516*. See also 22.10 above. For tax-free annuities see 22.17 below.

22.11 Deduction of Tax at Source

Statutory exceptions to this general rule are below.

(b) **Annuities for non-taxable consideration.** See 3.18 ANTI-AVOIDANCE.

(c) **Purchased life annuities.** The capital element in such annuities, whenever purchased, is **not treated as income** (except where, for other tax purposes, a lump sum payment has to be taken into account in computing profits or losses). This applies to any *life annuity* (i.e., one payable for a period ending with, or ascertainable only by reference to, the end of a life—notwithstanding that it may also end at a fixed term, or on the happening of a contingency, during the life or may extend beyond the end of the life) *purchased for money or money's worth* from a person whose business is to grant life annuities — but **not including any annuity**

    (i)   treated, for other tax purposes, as being partly payment or repayment of a capital sum, or

    (ii)   bought with sums ranking for relief under provisions for retirement annuities (see 66 RETIREMENT ANNUITIES) or as life assurance premiums etc. under *ICTA 1988, ss 266, 273* (see 45.1 *et seq.* LIFE ASSURANCE POLICIES), or

    (iii)   purchased under direction in a will, or in substitution for an annuity charged on income of settled property, or

    (iv)   purchased under any sponsored superannuation scheme (see *ICTA 1988, s 624* and 67 RETIREMENT SCHEMES), or retirement annuity scheme (see 66 RETIREMENT ANNUITIES), or in recognition of services, past or present, in any employment, or

    (v)   purchased under or for the purposes of a retirement benefits scheme approved under *ICTA 1988, s 591* (discretionary approval, see 67.4 RETIREMENT SCHEMES) or in pursuance of any obligation imposed, or offer or invitation made, under or in connection with any such scheme, or

    (vi)   payable under approved personal pension arrangements (see 60 PERSONAL PENSION SCHEMES), or

    (vii)   purchased, for purposes connected with giving effect to any pension-sharing order or provision under *Welfare Reform and Pensions Act 1999, s 24(1)*, for consideration which derives: from an approved retirement benefits scheme (see 67.1(*a*)–(*c*) RETIREMENT SCHEMES); from sums satisfying the conditions for relief under *ICTA 1988, s 619* (retirement annuity premiums, see 66.1 RETIREMENT ANNUITIES); from schemes or arrangements within (iv) or (vi) above; or from the surrender or partial surrender of an annuity within (v) above or this subparagraph, or of a contract for such an annuity.

[*ICTA 1988, ss 656(1), 657, 659D; FA 1999, s 80, Sch 10 paras 16, 17*].

Subject as below, the *capital element* is constant throughout and is, normally, that part of an annuity payment which bears to the full amount the same proportion as the purchase price of the annuity bears to the actuarial value of the total annuity payments, based on mortality tables but excluding any element of discounting, and calculated as at the date the first payment begins to accrue. For prescribed mortality tables see *SI 1956 No 1230* as amended by *SI 1991 No 2808*, and *Rose v Trigg Ch D 1963, 41 TC 365*.

Where the term but not the amount of the annuity does not depend solely on the duration of a life or lives, the calculation of the capital element is varied as may be just, and where the purchase price covers more than a pure annuity, that price is similarly apportioned.

But where the *amount* of any annuity payment depends on a contingency other than the duration of a life or lives the exempt capital element will not be calculated as above but will be arrived at by spreading the purchase price of the annuity rateably over its expected term (as at the date the first annuity payment begins to accrue) and allocating to each annuity payment a part corresponding to the length of the period for which the annuity payment is made. [*ICTA 1988, s 656; FA 1991, s 76*]. If the capital element exceeds the annuity payment, the excess may be carried forward for allowance in determining the capital element in the next payment or payments. (See Revenue Pamphlet IR 1, A46).

Sellers of annuities are notified of annuities affected by *ICTA 1988, s 656(1)–(4)* and of the capital element in them: until then they continue to deduct tax and account for it, where appropriate, as before. Any tax over- or under-deducted from payments made before the notification is repaid to or charged on the payee, subject to time limits. [*ICTA 1988, s 656(5)(6)*, and *IT (Purchased Life Annuities) Regulations 1956 (SI 1956 No 1230)*, and *Amendment Regulations 1960 (SI 1960 No 2308)* and *1990 (SI 1990 No 626)*].

The income element of a purchased life annuity is chargeable to income tax at the lower rate (to the extent that it does not fall within an individual's higher rate band) and tax is deductible at source at the lower rate (see 1.9 ALLOWANCES AND TAX RATES).

As to tax on sale, surrender etc., of rights under a life annuity contract see 45.15 LIFE ASSURANCE POLICIES and *ICTA 1988, ss 542, 543*.

Other life, or terminable, annuities are taxed under *ICTA 1988, s 348*.

See Simon's Direct Tax Service B5.314.

(*d*)   **Annuities** charged under *ITEPA 2003* as **pension income** (see 58.2 PENSION INCOME), other than those arising from retirement annuity contracts and certain employment-related annuities from UK sources (see 58.2(*j*)(*k*) PENSION INCOME and 22.2 above).

(*e*)   **'Capital and income'** policies are those where in the event of death within a selected period, a lump sum and an annuity for the rest of the period is paid. The annuity may (conditionally) be treated as instalments of capital, not subject to tax deduction. Some companies arrange for return of part of *capital* over a number of years, followed by an ordinary annuity subject to tax deduction. But if assigned or settled for benefit of a third party see 81.9 SETTLEMENTS.

(*f*)   For **children's education policies** see *Perrin v Dickson CA 1929, 14 TC 608* in which the yearly payments were held to be a return of the premiums with interest, only the interest being taxable. The decision was questioned in *Sothern-Smith v Clancy CA 1940, 24 TC 1*. Purchased life annuities are now regulated, see (*c*) above.

(*g*)   For **guaranteed income bonds** and similar life policies, see 45.15(*i*) LIFE INSURANCE POLICIES.

22.12   DIVIDENDS AND INTEREST

Banks etc. See 7 BANKS.

British companies etc. See 1.9 ALLOWANCES AND TAX RATES.

Building societies. See 8 BUILDING SOCIETIES.

Government stock. See 33 GOVERNMENT STOCKS.

Local authority and statutory corporation stock. Tax is deductible under *ICTA 1988, s 349(2)* (see 22.3(ii) above) but not if borrowing is in foreign currency (or, for securities issued before 6 April 1982, in the currency of a territory outside the scheduled territories) and Treasury so direct. Interest is then exempt from income tax (but not corporation tax) if the beneficial owner is not resident in UK. [*ICTA 1988, ss 349(2), 581*].

Foreign dividends (including foreign Government or public revenue dividends) are, before 1 April 2001, generally subject to deduction of tax at, from 6 April 1999 (see *FA 2000, s 33*) the Schedule F ordinary rate of tax (see 1.9 ALLOWANCES AND RATES) (previously, the lower rate of tax) under the paying and collecting agents arrangements under *ICTA 1988, ss 118A–118K* and associated regulations. For an article on the scope of these arrangements, see Revenue Tax Bulletin August 1996 p 329. There are reliefs *inter alia* for payments to non-UK residents, or to non-UK resident trustees of certain discretionary or accumulation trusts for non-UK resident beneficiaries, for certain payments held in 'recognised clearing systems' (see 22.3(ii) above), for dividends payable by non-UK resident companies to UK companies holding 10% or more of the voting power in the paying company, and for various payments constituting exempt income in the hands of the recipient. From 1 April 2001 these provisions are abolished by *FA 2000, s 111(1)(6)*, but see 22.3(ii) above as regards the deduction regime introduced in their place in relation to UK public revenue dividends. As regards the other sources, to which deduction no longer applies, enhanced information powers are available to the Revenue (see 68.15 RETURNS).

22.13   MORTGAGE INTEREST ('MIRAS')

Mortgage interest on home loans may be paid after deduction of tax if the interest is 'relevant loan interest' paid by a 'qualifying borrower' to a 'qualifying lender'. This scheme is commonly known as MIRAS: Mortgage Interest Relief At Source.

Where the loan is within (*a*)(ii) below (loans to purchase life annuities), tax was deducted at the basic rate for the year in which the payment becomes due up to 1999/2000, the rate being fixed at **23%** thereafter. Where it is within (*a*)(i) or (iii) below, the deduction was at 15% for interest due in 1996/97 and 1997/98, and at 10% for interest due after 5 April 1998, relief **ceasing altogether** for interest paid on such loans after (as a general rule) 5 April 2000 (see below and 43.3 INTEREST PAYABLE). No further tax relief is available, but nor is tax relief clawed back if the borrower has insufficient liability to cover it.

Payments of 'relevant loan interest' are not deductible in computing total income. Interest payments do not attract relief from income tax at the higher rate(s) (but see below as regards certain bridging loans).

It is understood that relief under MIRAS may be claimed retrospectively where interest under a mortgage meeting all the qualifying conditions for inclusion in the scheme was paid outside MIRAS, and relief for the interest thereby lost (e.g. where there was no taxable income). (Tolley's Practical Tax 1993 p 120).

Qualifying lenders are able to recover from the Government the tax deducted from interest payments received. Where the lender was not entitled to such a payment, the Board may assess and recover such overpayments and obtain interest and penalties where appropriate.

Relevant loan interest is not deductible from profits etc. under Schedule D, Case I or II or VI. [*ICTA 1988, ss 74(1)(o), 369; FA 1991, s 27(2); F(No 2)A 1992, s 19(3)(5); FA 1993, s 58, Sch 6 para 1; FA 1994, s 81(3)–(7), Sch 9 para 1; FA 1996, Sch 18 paras 6, 17(1)–(4)(8); F(No 2)A 1997 s 15(2)(3); FA 1999, s 38, Sch 4 para 4; FA 2000, s 83(3)(4)*]. Form Miras 5, a certificate of interest paid, is available on demand from the lender, although building societies normally notify the tax office direct.

For a general explanation of the scheme, see Revenue Pamphlet IR 63 'Mortgage interest relief at source'.

'**Relevant loan interest**' is interest which is paid and payable in the UK to a 'qualifying lender', where

(*a*)   it is interest

    (i)   paid before, generally, 6 April 2000 (see below) on loans for purchase of land, caravan or houseboat *in the UK* which, when the interest is paid, is used 'wholly or to a substantial extent' (see below) as the only or main residence of the borrower under *ICTA 1988, ss 354(1), 355* (as altered for this purpose), see 43.6 INTEREST PAYABLE, or where the borrower resides in job-related accommodation within *ICTA 1988, s 356*, see 43.16 INTEREST PAYABLE; or

    (ii)   on pre-9 March 1999 loans to a borrower aged 65 or over to purchase life annuities secured on land *in the UK* under *ICTA 1988, s 365*, see 43.24 INTEREST PAYABLE; or

    (iii)   paid before, generally, 6 April 2000 (see below) on an option mortgage in respect of which an option notice was in force on 31 March 1983 and to which the conditions in (*a*)(i) above apply (with minor modifications), and

(*b*)   apart from the current provisions, the whole of the interest in (*a*)(i) or (*a*)(ii) above (ignoring the tax relief limit — see 43.10 INTEREST PAYABLE) would be eligible for relief under *ICTA 1988, s 353* (see 43.3 INTEREST PAYABLE) or would be deductible from profits etc. under Schedule D, Case I or II or VI.

As regards (*a*)(i) and (iii) above, interest on such loans ceases to be relevant loan interest following the withdrawal of relief for such interest with effect, generally, for payments made after 5 April 2000 (and see 43.3 INTEREST PAYABLE).

The election referred to in 43.3 INTEREST PAYABLE (where interest is dually eligible for relief) also has effect for determining whether interest falls within (*a*)(i) above.

[*ICTA 1988, s 370; FA 1988, s 42(3)(c); FA 1994, Sch 9 para 10; FA 1995, Sch 29 Pt VIII(2); FA 1999, s 39, Sch 4 para 5*].

The Revenue normally regard the condition in (*a*)(i) above as satisfied if at least two-thirds of the property is used as the borrower's main residence. (Revenue Tax Bulletin August 1995 p 230). In practice, where no part of the home is used exclusively for business purposes, there will be only incidental business use. (MIRAS 30 (1996 Amendments) para 4.13). See *R v Inspector of Taxes (ex p Kelly) CA 1991, 64 TC 343* for disallowance of interest on mixed purpose loans.

Interest on home improvement loans and on loans for the purchase of property to be used, wholly or substantially, as the only or main residence of the borrower's dependent relative or separated or former spouse is within (*a*)(i) above if it would be eligible for tax relief (see 43.6 *et seq.* INTEREST PAYABLE), that is, broadly speaking, if the loan was made, or deemed to be made, before 6 April 1988, and if within (*b*) above.

If non-qualifying expenditure is added to otherwise qualifying loans, the loans must be taken out of MIRAS. In practice, however, lenders may treat as qualifying expenditure sums advanced:

(1)   by miscellaneous debits to the borrower's account by virtue of the mortgage deed or rules, e.g. buildings insurance premiums, legal costs in the event of arrears, or realisation expenses;

(2)   to pay premiums due on indemnity insurance, mortgage protection and guarantee policies, or loan protection policies (including limited costs of incidental sickness and redundancy cover); or

(3)   to pay costs of mortgage deed preparation, stamp duty, valuation and survey fees, and legal costs.

22.13 Deduction of Tax at Source

(MIRAS 30 (1995) para 10.22).

Certain administration fees charged to loan account are similarly disregarded, up to £300 in the first year and £150 p.a. thereafter. (MIRAS 30 (1995) para 10.23).

Where unauthorised arrears of interest are capitalised, the loan should strictly be excluded from the MIRAS scheme as being of a mixed quality. In practice, such action will only be taken where, when the loan is recalculated, the capitalised interest exceeds the greater of 12 months' arrears and £1,000, and no satisfactory arrangements have been made to reduce the arrears. Even then, in certain cases of hardship, no action will be taken. (MIRAS 30 (1995) paras 10.4, 10.5). See also 43.10 INTEREST PAYABLE as regards extension of the tax relief limit by up to £1,000 where interest is capitalised.

Interest on a *home improvement loan* (i.e. a loan applied wholly in improving or developing land or buildings or in paying off another similar loan), if otherwise eligible (see 43.6 *et seq.* INTEREST PAYABLE), is *not* relevant loan interest unless

   (i)   it is paid to a building society or a local authority or the NI Housing Executive, or

   (ii)   the qualifying lender has given notice to the Board that he is prepared to have such loans, made after such date as specified in the notice, brought within the tax deduction scheme, or

   (iii)   it is interest to which (*a*)(iii) above applies. [*ICTA 1988, s 372; FA 1999, Sch 4 para 6*].

Loans over the tax relief limit. (See 43.10 INTEREST PAYABLE.) Interest on such loans is not relevant loan interest unless all the loans to be taken into account are by the same qualifying lender, and only interest on loans up to the limit is then relevant loan interest. For loans made before 6 April 1987, there is an additional requirement that the lender has given notice to the Board that he is prepared to have such loans brought within the tax deduction scheme. [*ICTA 1988, s 373(1)–(5); FA 1988, s 42(3)(d); FA 1999, Sch 4 para 7*]. See also 43.10 INTEREST PAYABLE as regards extension of the limit by up to £1,000 where interest is capitalised.

Joint borrowers. Interest on a loan which is to joint borrowers who are not husband and wife (i.e. living together and not separated) is not relevant loan interest unless each of the borrowers is a qualifying borrower and in relation to each of them, considered separately, the whole of that interest is relevant loan interest. [*ICTA 1988, s 373(6)(7); FA 1999, Sch 4 para 7*].

'Penalty' interest charged on the early redemption of a loan within MIRAS is not relevant loan interest (although this does not apply to interest charged for the whole of the month in which redemption occurs). Similarly a penalty charged for changing the terms of a loan, including a penalty for changing from a fixed to a variable rate, is not relevant loan interest. However, a replacement loan need not be regarded as mixed purpose merely because, in part, it replaces such a charge. (MIRAS 30 (1995) para 10.46).

Option to deduct interest under Schedule A. Where a qualifying borrower carries on or proposes to carry on a Schedule A business (see 69.3 SCHEDULE A) and gives notice to the Board that relevant interest on a loan is to be deducted in computing profits, interest paid on that loan after the date specified in the notice is to be paid outside MIRAS. The notice is irrevocable and must be given within 22 months after the end of the tax year in which the specified date falls. The Board must notify the lender, and there are provisions whereby any tax deducted by the borrower after the specified date can be reclaimed by the Revenue and reimbursed to the lender. The loan remains outside MIRAS until the Board gives notice to both borrower and lender that it is to be brought back within the scheme, which they will do only when the Schedule A business is permanently discontinued or the proposal to carry it on is finally abandoned. [*ICTA 1988, s 375A; FA 1995, Sch 6 para 18; FA 1999, Sch 4 para 10*].

Property used for both residential and business purposes. See 43.2 INTEREST PAYABLE for Revenue Concession applicable where part of a borrower's main residence is used for business (including a Schedule A business) purposes. The concession applies equally to a loan within MIRAS. (Revenue Pamphlet IR 1, A89). This is, however, subject to the property being used 'wholly or to a substantial extent' as the borrower's residence (see (*a*)(i) above). Where this condition is satisfied, *all* the interest qualifies for relief through MIRAS (subject to the £30,000 maximum). Where the part of the loan attributed to residential use under Concession A89 is less than £30,000, all or part of the interest attributed to the business use will have been relieved through MIRAS. The business deduction is reduced accordingly (see Revenue Tax Bulletin August 1995 pp 230–232 for worked examples).

A **'qualifying borrower'** is an individual who pays 'relevant loan interest'. In relation to interest paid at a time when an individual (or spouse, if not permanently separated) holds an office or employment the earnings from which would otherwise be chargeable to tax as employment income, the individual is **not** a qualifying borrower if he or she has some special exemption or immunity (e.g. diplomatic) from such charge. [*ICTA 1988, s 376(1)–(3); ITEPA 2003, Sch 6 para 52*]. The exclusion of European Union employees from the scheme by virtue of their employment income exemption does not conflict with Community law (*Tither v CIR CJEC, [1990] STC 416*). Interest paid for and on behalf of a borrower may be treated as though paid by the borrower. (MIRAS 30 (1995) paras 10.43–10.45). Where a borrower dies, the loan should be removed from MIRAS immediately the lender is advised of the death by the personal representatives, except in the case of the death of a joint married borrower where the surviving borrower continues to use the property as the only or main residence. (MIRAS Central Unit Guidance Letter 31 May 1989).

A **'qualifying lender'** is any of the following: a building society; a local authority; the Bank of England; the Post Office; an insurance company authorised to carry on long-term business (e.g. life assurance) in the UK; a company successor to a trustee savings bank; a registered or incorporated friendly society or branch; a development corporation; the Commission for the New Towns; the Housing Corporation; Housing for Wales (or the Secretary of State if the loan is made by him under *Housing Associations Act 1985, s 79*); the Northern Ireland Housing Executive; the Scottish Special Housing Association; the Development Board for Rural Wales; the Church of England Pensions Board; and an existing lender under the mortgage option scheme.

The Board could also register as a qualifying lender any of the following bodies: a recognised bank or licensed deposit-taking institution; an insurance company authorised to carry on general insurance business in the UK; a 90% subsidiary of any such bank, institution or company; and any other body whose activities and objects it considers qualify the body for inclusion.

[*ICTA 1988, s 376(4)–(6), s 376A; Housing Act 1988, Sch 17 para 115; F(No 2)A 1992, Sch 9 para 3; FA 1994, s 142; Government of Wales Act 1998, Sch 16 para 55; FA 1999, Sch 4 para 11; SI 2001 No 3629, Articles 23, 24*].

Administration of the tax deduction scheme. The scheme does not apply to any relevant loan interest unless

(*a*)   the borrower, or each joint borrower, has given notice to the lender in the prescribed form certifying (i) that he is a qualifying borrower and (ii) that the interest is relevant loan interest and (iii) such other matters as may be prescribed; or

(*b*)   the Board have notified the lender and the borrower that the interest may be paid under deduction of tax; or (*c*)   the interest is on a loan which was, on 31 March 1983, an option mortgage loan; or

(*d*)   the loan was made before the commencement date (see above), and is of a description specified by regulations made by the Board.

Where any of the above requirements are met, tax may be deducted from the interest: on and after the date of the notice in (*a*); on and after the date specified in the Board's notification in (*b*), and where that date is retrospective the Board may repay the amount which was under-deducted from interim interest paid (together with INTEREST ON OVERPAID TAX (41)), subject to recovery powers for amounts wrongly repaid; on and after the commencement date (see above) for (*c*) and (*d*). [*ICTA 1988, ss 374, 375(8)(8A); FA 1995, s 112(4); FA 1999, s 41, Sch 4 paras 8, 9*].

Where the relevant loan interest is payable to a building society or other specified qualifying lender under a loan agreement requiring combined payments (i.e. a number of regular payments which are part repayment of capital and part payment of interest) on a loan made before 1 April 1983, the qualifying lender may give notice to the qualifying borrower that each net payment (i.e. each payment from the interest element of which tax has to be deducted) will be of the same amount (unless there is a change in the deductible rate of income tax or in the rate of interest charged by the borrower) and that payments will be determined so as to secure that the period of the loan remains unchanged. The borrower may, however, give counter-notice that each net payment must be of the same amount (again subject to deductible tax rate or interest rate changes) and that the amount of each combined payment must not exceed what would have been the amount of the first combined payment, less tax, after the giving of notice by the lender, apart from these provisions. If such notice is given the borrower may, whenever he chooses, make additional capital repayments so as to secure repayment of the loan within a period not shorter than that originally agreed. Subsequent variations may be made by agreement. [*ICTA 1988, s 377; FA 1994, s 81(8); FA 1999, Sch 4 para 12*].

Where tax is deducted from interest which has never been relevant loan interest or which is paid otherwise than by a qualifying borrower, the interest is treated as such providing either condition (*a*) or condition (*b*) above is fulfilled. The tax deducted is, however, recoverable from the borrower by assessment. Interest is chargeable under *TMA 1970, s 86* (see 42.1 INTEREST AND SURCHARGES ON UNPAID TAX) by reference to a due date of 1 December following the tax year in which the deduction was made). Where the borrower fraudulently or negligently makes a false statement or representation, he will be liable to a penalty not exceeding the amount of tax consequently deducted. [*ICTA 1988, s 374A; FA 1995, s 112(1)(5); FA 1996, Sch 18 paras 7, 17(5)(6)*].

Except as below, if at any time interest ceases to be relevant loan interest or a person paying relevant loan interest ceases to be a qualifying borrower, the borrower must notify the lender, and where tax has been deducted from a payment made between that time and the notification the payment is treated as relevant loan interest, but any excess relief or deduction above proper entitlement is recoverable from the borrower by assessment, with potential interest and penalties. If a qualifying lender has reason to believe that interest is no longer relevant loan interest or a borrower is no longer a qualifying borrower, he must inform the Board. Failure to do so incurs penalties.

Form Miras 3, available from the lender, enables the borrower to claim tax relief where a qualifying loan is excluded from MIRAS.

Where it appears to the Board that any qualifying condition under the scheme is not, or may not be, fulfilled, they must give notice to the lender and the borrower and the tax deduction scheme will not apply to the relevant loan interest due between dates specified in the notice and any subsequent notice.

These provisions do *not*, however, apply where interest ceases to be relevant loan interest by virtue of the general cessation of mortgage interest relief (see above and 43.3 INTEREST PAYABLE).

[*ICTA 1988, s 375(1)–(7)(8B); FA 1994, Sch 9 para 11; FA 1995, s 112(2)(3)(5); FA 1996, Sch 18 paras 8, 17(1); FA 1999, Sch 4 para 9*].

Where interest is treated as relevant loan interest only by virtue of *ICTA 1988, s 375(2)*, it may nevertheless be deductible against total income or for Schedule D, Case I or II purposes if it would be so deductible under general principles. [*ICTA 1988, s 74(1)(o), s 369(3); FA 1994, s 81(4), Sch 9 para 1*].

The Treasury may make regulations to apply the above provisions to housing associations and self-build societies which borrow from qualifying lenders and the Board may make regulations regarding the administration of the scheme, its application to personal representatives and trustees, the inspection of records, appeals and generally. [*ICTA 1988, s 378; FA 1999, Sch 4 para 13*]. The first such regulations made by the Board deal mainly with the bringing of loans into the scheme; with 'limited loans' (broadly those over the interest relief limit — see 43.10 INTEREST PAYABLE); with variations of amounts due under existing loans brought within the scheme; with the reimbursement of lenders for tax deducted by borrowers; and with information and penalty powers and appeal procedures. [*The Income Tax (Interest Relief) Regulations 1982 (SI 1982 No 1236) as amended*]. The *(No 2) Regulations 1983 (SI 1983 No 311)* supplement the principal regulations, and the *(No 3) Regulations 1985 (SI 1985 No 1252)* amend the procedures for bringing limited loans into the scheme. The *(Housing Associations) Regulations 1988 (SI 1988 No 1347)* and *(Amendment) Regulations 1995 (SI 1995 No 1212)* and *1996 (SI 1996 No 2616)* deal with housing associations and self-build societies.

Interest paid by a housing association or self-build society is not relevant loan interest if

(A)   it is interest on a home improvement loan made on or after 6 April 1988 (and not deemed to have been made before that date), or

(B)   by virtue of *FA 1988, s 44* (loans for residence of dependent relative etc.) it would not be relevant loan interest if paid by a member of the association or society.

(See 43.6 *et seq.* INTEREST PAYABLE.)

[*FA 1988, ss 43(3), 44(6); FA 1999, Sch 20 Pt III(7)*].

An explanatory lenders booklet (MIRAS 30) is available to existing MIRAS lenders and those thinking about coming into the scheme.

The Revenue have published a Code of Practice (No 4) setting out their standards for the carrying out of inspections of tax relief at source schemes operated by financial intermediaries.

Simon's Direct Tax Service. See A3.430–A3.435.

22.14   **RENTS ETC. UNDER ICTA 1988, S 119 AND S 120**

Under *ICTA 1988, s 119*, where rent (as defined) was payable before 1 May 1995 for any 'easement' (as defined) 'used, occupied or enjoyed' in connection with any of the 'concerns' specified in *ICTA 1988, s 55(2)*, tax was deductible as for patent royalties, see 22.15(*b*) below. See *New Sharlston Collieries CA 1936, 21 TC 69; Hope CS 1937, 21 TC 116* and *Fitzwilliam's Collieries Co v Phillips HL 1943, 25 TC 430*. Payments made on or after that date are made gross. [*FA 1995, s 145*]. If the rent is paid in produce of the concern the recipient is charged, on its value, under Schedule D, Case III. [*ICTA 1988, s 119(2)*].

Deduction at source as above continued to apply until 5 April 1997 to rents for easements in connection with electric telegraph or telephone wires or cables (including poles, pylons, related apparatus and transformers) except, by payer's election, to sums of £2.50 p.a. or under (which are then assessable on recipient under Schedule D, Case III) but if any such rent was paid under deduction of tax by a person carrying on a radio relay service the payment was nevertheless deductible in calculating profits for Schedule D, Case I but for purposes of *ICTA 1988, ss 348, 349* deemed not to be payable out of taxed profits. [*ICTA 1988, s 120; FA 1997, s 60*].

Other property rentals, including ground rents, are payable in full and assessable on recipient, see 69 SCHEDULE A.

22.15 ROYALTIES

(*a*) **Copyright royalties, public lending right payments** and **design royalties** paid to non-residents are taxed by deduction under *ICTA 1988, s 349(1)*. [*ICTA 1988, ss 536, 537, 537B; FA 1995, s 115(10)*]. This does not apply to professional authors (Hansard 10 November 1969, Vol 791, Col 31). Payer is assessable, even if he has not deducted the tax (*Rye & Eyre v CIR HL 1935, 19 TC 164*). See 51.9 NON-RESIDENTS AND OTHER OVERSEAS MATTERS.

(*b*) **Patent royalties** are payable under deduction of tax. [*ICTA 1988, s 348(2), s 349(1)(b)*]. Instalments of fixed amount for five-year use of patent held capital (*Desoutter Bros Ltd KB 1936, 15 ATC 49*). A lump sum payment on signing a ten-year agreement held capital but ten fixed yearly payments royalties (*CIR v British Salmson Aero Engines Ltd CA 1938, 22 TC 29*). Awards by a Royal Commission for use of inventions and patents in 1914–1918 war held patent royalties (*Constantinesco v Rex HL 1927, 11 TC 730; Mills v Jones HL 1929, 14 TC 769*). See also *Jones v CIR KB 1919, 7 TC 310; Wild v Ionides KB 1925, 9 TC 392; International Combustion Ltd v CIR KB 1932, 16 TC 532* and cf. *Rank Xerox Ltd v Lane HL 1979, 53 TC 185*.

For the treatment of capital sums for the acquisition or from the sale of patents, see 54 PATENTS.

(*c*) **Mining royalties,** see 22.14 above.

22.16 TAX-FREE ARRANGEMENTS

An agreement which provides for an annual payment without deduction of tax is void [*TMA 1970, s 106(2)*] but a provision to pay interest at a stated rate after deduction of tax is treated as requiring payment at the gross rate. [*ICTA 1988, s 818(2)*]. An agreement to make payments 'free of tax' is not avoided by *TMA 1970, s 106(2)* (*CIR v Ferguson HL 1969, 46 TC 1*). See 22.17 below for tax-free annuities.

22.17 TAX-FREE ANNUITIES ETC.

(*a*) **General.** A direction under a will or settlement for an annuity to be paid 'free of tax' (or similar wording) is a direction to pay an annuity of such an amount which after deduction of the tax will produce the specified figure (cf. *CIR v Ferguson HL 1969, 46 TC 1*). This is a matter, however, in which it is important the wording used should express clearly and unambiguously what is intended. The large number of court cases referred to below have arisen mostly because of the imprecision of the relevant wording.

The wording was held *not* to confer freedom from tax in *Abadam v Abadam 1864, 10 LT 53* ('payable without any deduction whatsoever'); *Shrewsbury v Shrewsbury Ch D 1906, 22 TLR 598* ('clear of all deductions'); *In re Loveless Ch D 1918, 34 TLR 356* ('clear'); *In re Well's Will Trusts Ch D 1940, 19 ATC 158* ('clear of all deductions');

In re Best's Marriage Settlement Ch D 1941, 20 ATC 235 ('such a sum as shall after deductions'); *CIR v Watson CS 1942, 25 TC 25* (annuity payable out of 'whole free residue' of income); *In re Hooper Ch D 1944, 1 AER 227* ('free of all duty ... and ... free of all deductions whatsoever'); *In re Wright Ch D 1952, 31 ATC 433* ('net'). The wording was held to confer freedom from tax in *In re Buckle 1894, 1 Ch 286* ('free of legacy duty and every other deduction' under a codicil to a will in which originally 'clear of all deductions whatsoever, except income tax'); *In re Shrewsbury Estate Acts CA 1923, 40 TLR 16* ('clear of all deductions whatsoever for taxes or otherwise'). *In re Hooper* above was not followed in *In re Cowlishaw Ch D 1939, 18 ATC 377* where the wording was similar, but in a later case (*In re Best's Marriage Settlement* above) *Cowlishaw* was described as special to its context.

(*b*)   **Surtax/excess liability.** All the decisions below relate to super-tax or surtax but it would seem that, suitably adapted, they are equally applicable to excess liability (see 27.1 EXCESS LIABILITY). Here it is relevant that an annuity is investment income.

An annuity of a sum such 'as after deduction of the income tax' would give the prescribed amount was held not to be free of super-tax (*In re Bates Ch D 1924, 4 ATC 518*). However an annuity 'free of income tax' was held to be free of surtax on the ground that surtax was an additional income tax and there was no indication in the will to restrict the wording to 'income tax as known for many years'. The previous decision was distinguished as there the wording referred to 'deduction' and surtax was not deductible at source (*In re Reckitt CA 1932, 11 ATC 429*; followed in *Prentice's Trustees CS 1934, 13 ATC 612*). A direction to pay an annuity free of super-tax was held to cover surtax (*In re Hulton Ch D 1930, 9 ATC 570*).

The surtax is normally taken as the part of the annuitant's total surtax proportionate to the ratio of the annuity grossed at the standard rate to the annuitant's total income (*In re Bowring 1918, 34 TLR 575*; followed in *In re Doxat 1920, 125 LT 60* and other cases). In *Baird's Trustees CS 1933, 12 ATC 407* the surtax was calculated on the basis that the annuity was the annuitant's only income, but this decision was distinguished in *Richmond's Trustees 1935 CS, 14 ATC 489* and *In re Bowring* was followed. See also *In re Horlick's Settlement CA 1938, 17 ATC 549*.

The surtax/excess liability borne on behalf of the annuitant by the trust fund is itself, grossed-up, income in his hands (*Meeking v CIR KB 1920, 7 TC 603*; *Lord Michelham's Trustees v CIR CA 1930, 15 TC 737*. See also *Shrewsbury & Talbot v CIR KB 1936, 20 TC 538* and compare *CIR v Duncanson KB 1949, 31 TC 257*). The practice is to treat the liability so borne for year 1 as an addition for grossing-up purposes to the annuity for year 2.

(*c*)   **Tax repayments of annuitants.** In a tax-free annuity the question arises whether the benefit conferred on the annuitant should be limited to the tax actually suffered by him after taking into account his allowances etc.

Where the annuity under a will was 'free of income tax' it was held that the annuitant must hand to the trustees a part of the tax repaid to her on account of her reliefs, in proportion to the ratio of the net annuity to her net income after tax (*In re Pettit, Le Fevre v Pettit Ch D 1922, 38 TLR 787*). But where the annuity was expressed to be of such an amount as after deduction of the tax at the current rate would give the prescribed sum it was held, distinguishing *In re Pettit*, that the annuitant was entitled to retain any tax repaid to him (*In re Jones Ch D 1933, 12 ATC 595*). For cases in which these two decisions were considered and applied as appropriate to the precise wording of the provision of the annuity, see *Richmond's Trustees CS 1935, 14 ATC 489*; *In re Maclennan CA 1939, 18 ATC 121*; *In re Eves Ch D 1939, 18 ATC 401*; *Rowan's Trustees CS 1939, 18 ATC 378*; *In re Jubb Ch D 1941, 20 ATC 297*; *In re Tatham Ch D 1944, 23 ATC 283*; *In re Williams Ch D 1945, 24 ATC 199*; *In re Bates's*

Will Trusts Ch D 1945, 24 ATC 300; In re Arno CA 1946, 25 ATC 412. Tatham and *Arno* give useful reviews of the subject as does *CIR v Cook HL 1945, 26 TC 489* (in which it was held that the Revenue must repay the tax on the grossed-up amount of a tax-free annuity notwithstanding that the annuitant would not be liable to tax if the annuity was not grossed-up and that the whole of the repayment would be handed over to the trustees). The annuitant must, if required by the trustees, exercise his right to repayment (*In re Kingcombe Ch D 1936, 15 ATC 37*). If the annuitant is a married woman *In re Pettit* applies to tax repayable to the husband but, if necessary, she must apply for separate assessment (*In re Batley CA 1952, 31 ATC 410*). It applies to loss relief (*In re Lyons CA 1951, 30 ATC 377*). For the effect of an *In re Pettit* refund on the annuitant's total income for surtax see *CIR v Duncanson KB 1949, 31 TC 257.*

(d)   **Tax-free alimony etc. payments.** The *In re Pettit* rule (see (c) above) does not apply to tax-free Court Orders and in *CIR v Ferguson HL 1969, 46 TC 1*, Lord Diplock explicitly refrained from deciding whether it applied to a separation agreement. Whether a free of tax Court Order would confer freedom from surtax/ excess liability does not seem to have arisen. Subject to the foregoing (*a*), (*b*) and (*c*) above apply, where appropriate, to tax-free alimony payments etc.

For tax-free alimony payments by non-residents, see *Ferguson* above and *Stokes v Bennett Ch D 1953, 34 TC 337.*

(e)   For **overseas taxes** under tax-free annuities, see *Re Frazer Ch D 1941, 20 ATC 73* and compare *Havelock v Grant KB 1946, 27 TC 363.*

22.18   VOLUNTARY ALLOWANCES

Not assessable on recipient (unless a misnomer for payments for services). But voluntary *pensions* and other annual payments by employers are taxable as PENSION INCOME (58.2) and subject to deduction under PAY AS YOU EARN (55).

23   Diplomatic etc. Immunity—Individuals and Organisations

Simon's Direct Tax Service D4.334, E5.401.

23.1   *Diplomatic Agents* (i.e. heads of mission or members of diplomatic staff) of foreign states (recognised by HM Government, see *Caglar v Billingham (Sp C 70), [1996] SSCD 150*) are exempt from tax except on income or capital gains arising from *private* investments or immovable property in the UK under *Diplomatic Privileges Act 1964*. Similar exemption is given to *Agents-General* and their staffs [*ICTA 1988, s 320; TCGA 1992, s 11*] (and see *SI 1997 No 1334* as regards certain Hong Kong officials). *Consuls* and *official agents* of foreign States in UK (not British subjects or citizens of Eire and not trading) are exempt on income from their official employment [*ITEPA 2003, ss 300, 301; ICTA 1988, s 321*]. Subject to any Order in Council, consular officers and employees, provided they are foreign nationals and not British (or overseas British) citizens, are exempt from tax on employment income. Provided they are either permanent employees or were not ordinarily resident in the UK immediately prior to the employment, and are not otherwise engaged in any UK trade, profession, vocation or employment, they are also exempt from tax on income within SCHEDULE D, CASES IV AND V (72) and certain foreign pensions, annuities and social security benefits. [*ITEPA 2003, s 302, Sch 6 para 44; ICTA 1988, s 322; FA 1990, Sch 14 para 4; FA 1996, Sch 7 para 15*]. See also *Consular Relations Act 1968*.

International organisations (e.g. the United Nations (*SI 1974 No 1261*)), their representatives, officers, members of committees, persons or missions etc. may be specified by Order in Council as exempt from certain taxes under *International Organisations Act 1968*. Also other bodies under the *European Communities Act 1972* (e.g. the North Atlantic Salmon Conservation Organisation (*SI 1985 No 1773*)) and certain financial bodies under the *Bretton Woods Agreements Act 1945* (e.g. the International Monetary Fund (*SI 1946 No 36*)). Also exemption from income tax is given to the remuneration of the Commissioners of the European Communities and their staffs under *Art. 13 of Chap. V of the Protocol on the Privileges and Immunities of the European Communities*. See *Hurd v Jones CJEC, [1986] STC 127* as regards exemption of certain payments out of Community funds, although see now *SI 1990 No 237*. See also *Tither v CIR CJEC, [1990] STC 416*, where exclusion of EU official from MIRAS scheme upheld. Experts seconded to the European Commission under the detached national experts scheme are exempt from income tax on their daily subsistence allowances, from 6 April 2003 by statute [*ITEPA 2003, s 304*], previously by concession (see Revenue Pamphlet IR 1, A84), and certain education allowances under the Overseas Services Aid Scheme are similarly exempt (see Revenue Pamphlet IR 1, A44). The Treasury may also designate any of the international organisations of which the UK is a member for the purpose of exemption from various requirements for the deduction of tax from payments made in the UK (see e.g. *SI 1997 No 168*). [*ICTA 1988, s 582A; FA 1991, s 118; FA 1996, Sch 7 para 22, Sch 29 para 6*].

See 65 RESIDENCE, ORDINARY RESIDENCE AND DOMICILE for definition of resident etc.

24 Double Tax Relief

[*ICTA 1988, ss 788–816*]

(See also Revenue Pamphlet IR 6.)

Cross-reference. See generally 51 NON-RESIDENTS AND OTHER OVERSEAS MATTERS.

Simon's Direct Tax Service Parts F1–F7.

Other sources. See Tolley's Double Taxation Relief.

24.1   Where the same income is liable to be taxed in both the UK and another country, relief may be available

    (*a*)   under the specific terms of a double tax agreement between the UK and that other country — see 24.2 below [*ICTA 1988, s 788*];

    (*b*)   under special arrangements with Ireland — see 24.3 below; or

    (*c*)   under the unilateral double tax relief provisions contained in UK tax legislation — see 24.4 below. [*ICTA 1988, s 790*].

24.2   **DOUBLE TAX AGREEMENTS** [*ICTA 1988, ss 788, 789 as amended*]

A list is given below of the bilateral agreements made by the UK which are currently operative. For texts of agreements, see Simon's Direct Tax Service Part F4. Representations on points interested parties would like to see addressed in negotiating particular treaties, or on other matters relating to the treaty negotiation programme or the treaty network, should be addressed to Mrs Jas Sahni, Revenue Policy International, Inland Revenue, Victory House, 30–34 Kingsway, London WC2B 6ES (email Jas.Sahni@ir.gsi.gov.uk).

Under these agreements certain classes of income derived from those countries by UK residents are given complete exemption from income taxes in the country from which they arise and reciprocal exemption from UK income tax or corporation tax is given to similar income derived from the UK by residents of those countries. Exemption may also be granted in respect of capital gains taxes, as provided for by *TCGA 1992, s 277*, and in respect of corporation tax on capital gains.

Other classes of income or gain derived from those countries are not exempted, or only partially exempted, by the agreements and in these cases relief from UK income tax etc., is generally given in the agreement (but to UK residents only [*ICTA 1988, s 794*]) in the form of a credit, calculated by reference to the foreign tax suffered, which is set against and reduces the UK tax chargeable on the doubly-taxed income or gain. [*ICTA 1988, s 793*]. See example in 24.8 below.

As regards the concept of 'permanent establishment' on which taxation rights are based under most treaties, the Revenue take the view that a website, or a server on which e-commerce is conducted through a website, is not of itself a permanent establishment. (Revenue Press Release 11 April 2000).

Double tax agreements normally contain a 'mutual agreement procedure' enabling a taxpayer who considers that the action of a tax authority has resulted, or will result, in taxation not in accordance with the agreement to present his case to the competent authority in his state of residence. The UK competent authority is the Inland Revenue, and the address to which all relevant facts and contentions should be sent is International Division, Melbourne House, Aldwych, London WC2B 4LL. For the presentation of such cases, and for giving effect to solutions and agreements reached under such procedures, see *ICTA 1988, s 815AA* introduced by *FA 2000, Sch 30 para 28*. Details of the administrative arrangements for operating the procedure with the USA are set out in Revenue Press Release 13 November 2000.

In *R v CIR (ex p Commerzbank AG) QB 1991, 68 TC 252,* INTEREST ON OVERPAID TAX (41) was held not to fall within the scope of double tax agreements, although on a reference to the European Court of Justice (see *68 TC 264*), the Court upheld the view that, in the case of companies resident in EC Member States, such discrimination against non-UK resident companies was prevented by the relevant Articles of the Treaty of Rome. See also 41.2 INTEREST ON OVERPAID TAX as regards treatment of EC resident individuals following this decision, and Revenue Double Taxation Relief Manual DT 1950 *et seq.* for Revenue approach to non-discrimination claims generally.

For the scope of 'dividends' attracting treaty relief, see *Memec plc v CIR CA 1998, 71 TC 77* (in which receipts under a silent partnership agreement were held not to attract relief), and see Revenue Tax Bulletin February 1999 p 627 for an article on the classification of foreign entities for UK tax purposes. See also Revenue Tax Bulletin December 2000 pp 809–812 for a list of overseas business entities on whose classification for UK tax purposes the Revenue has been asked to express a view. The general abolition of the repayment of tax credits after 5 April 1999 does not affect the entitlement of a non-UK resident to payment in respect of a tax credit under double tax agreements (although it should be noted that in practice, with the reduction after that date to one-ninth in the rate of tax credit, such repayments will be very limited). [*F(No 2)A 1997, s 30(9)(10)*]. Similarly, the tax credit payment restrictions applicable to pension funds in relation to distributions made after 1 July 1997 do not apply to non-residents' entitlements under such arrangements. [*ICTA 1988, s 231A(6)(b); F(No 2)A 1997, s 19(2), Sch 8 Pt II(9)*].

Special relationships: interest. Agreements under *ICTA 1988, s 788* making provision in relation to interest may also have a provision dealing with cases where, owing to a special relationship, the amount of interest paid exceeds the amount which would have been paid in the absence of that relationship, and requiring the interest provision to be applied only to that lower amount. Any such special relationship provision has to be construed:

(*a*)   as requiring account to be taken of all factors, including whether, in the absence of the relationship, the loan would have been made at all, or would have been in a different amount, or a different rate of interest and other terms would have been agreed. This does not apply, however, where the special relationship provision expressly requires regard to be had to the debt on which the interest is paid in determining the excess interest, and accordingly expressly limits the factors to be taken into account, and in the case of a loan by one company to another, the fact that it is not part of the lending company's business to make loans generally is disregarded; and

(*b*)   as requiring the taxpayer either to show that no special relationship exists or to show the amount of interest which would have been paid in the absence of that relationship.

[*ICTA 1988, s 808A; F(No 2)A 1992, s 52*].

See Simon's Direct Tax Service F1.221.

Special relationships: royalties. Agreements may make similar provision in relation to royalties. Where they are payable on or after 28 July 2000, any royalties special relationship provision, unless it expressly requires regard to be had to the use, right or information for which royalties are paid in determining the excess royalties, has to be construed as requiring account to be taken of all factors. These include:

(A)   in the absence of the relationship, whether the royalty agreement would have been made at all, or the rate or amount of royalties and other terms which would have been agreed; and

24.2 Double Tax Relief

(B) if the asset in respect of which the royalties are paid (or any asset which it represents or from which it is derived) had previously been in the beneficial ownership of

    (i) the person liable to pay the royalties,

    (ii) a person who has at any time carried on a business which, when the royalties fall due, is carried on in whole or part by the person liable to pay the royalties, or

    (iii) a person who is or has been an 'associate', as specially defined, of a person within (i) or (ii),

amounts paid under the transaction(s) which resulted in the asset falling into its present beneficial ownership, the amounts which would have been so paid in the absence of the special relationship, and the question as to whether the transaction(s) would have taken place at all in the absence of that relationship.

The taxpayer must also show either that no special relationship exists, or the amount of royalties which would have been paid in the absence of the relationship, and if he cannot show that (B) above does not apply, he must show that the transaction(s) mentioned therein would have taken place in the absence of a special relationship, and the amounts which would then have been paid under those transaction(s).

[ICTA 1988, s 808B; FA 2000, Sch 30 para 25].

See Simon's Direct Tax Service F1.222.

Under many double tax agreements, **employees working in the UK**, who are resident in the overseas country but not resident in the UK, and who are not physically present in the UK for more than 183 days in the year of assessment, are exempt from UK tax on earnings paid by or on behalf of a non-UK resident employer. For this purpose, fractions of days are counted. (CCAB Memorandum TR 508, 9 June 1983). This exemption does not usually apply to public entertainers (and see now 51.7 NON-RESIDENTS AND OTHER OVERSEAS MATTERS), nor, under certain agreements, does it extend to employees working on the UK continental shelf (see Revenue Press Release 3 March 1989). For employees commencing a work assignment in the UK, claims will be refused where the cost of an employee's remuneration is borne by a UK resident company acting as the 'economic employer'. This would apply where, for example, the employee is seconded to the UK company, which obtains the benefit and bears the risks in relation to work undertaken by the employee, and to which the non-resident employer recharges the remuneration costs. It would also apply where the non-resident employer carries on a business of hiring out staff to other companies. (Revenue Tax Bulletin June 1995 p 220). In the absence of a formal contract of employment, the Revenue would not consider a UK company to be the employer of a short-term business visitor who is in the UK for less than 60 days in a tax year (the '**60-day rule**'), provided that that period does not form part of a more substantial period (for example, a period spanning two tax years) when the taxpayer is in the UK (Revenue Tax Bulletins October 1996 p 358, December 2003 pp 1069–1071).

The specific provisions of the particular agreement concerned must be examined carefully. For relevant Court decisions, see Tolley's Tax Cases.

Where double tax relief applies no deduction for foreign tax is generally allowed in assessing the foreign income or gain [ICTA 1988, ss 795(2), 811(2)] but if a taxpayer elects not to take credit allowable by an agreement, any foreign tax paid on that income in the place where it arises is *deductible* from the income for purposes of UK assessment, *except* that it is not so deductible where the UK assessment is on the basis of *remittances* to the UK. [ICTA 1988, ss 805, 811]. See 24.5(b)(iii) below. Where tax on overseas income is not relieved, or is only partly relieved, under an agreement, unilateral relief (see 24.4 below) will normally apply.

The following provisions supersede those of *ICTA 1988, s 790* (Unilateral Relief) to the extent, and as from the operative dates, specified in the various reciprocal agreements currently operative with the countries and territories that follow (*SI* numbers in round brackets).

Antigua and Barbuda (1947/2865; 1968/1096), **Argentina** (1997/1777), **Australia** (1968/305; 1980/707; 2003/3199 (new treaty applying from *broadly* 6 April 2004 (UK) and 1 July 2004 (Australia) — see Revenue Press Release 19 January 2004)), **Austria** (1970/1947; 1979/117; 1994/768), **Azerbaijan** (1995/762),

Bangladesh (1980/708), **Barbados** (1970/952; 1973/2096), **Belarus** (1995/2706) (and see note below), **Belgium** (1987/2053), **Belize** (1947/2866; 1968/573; 1973/2097), **Bolivia** (1995/2707), **Bosnia-Hercegovina** (see note below), **Botswana** (1978/183), **British Honduras** (see Belize), **Brunei** (1950/1977; 1968/306; 1973/2098), **Bulgaria** (1987/2054), **Burma** (see Myanmar),

Canada (1980/709; 1980/780; 1980/1528; 1985/1996; 1987/2071; 1996/1782; 2000/3330; 2003/2619) (2003 protocol applies from 6 April 2005 (UK) and 1 January 2005 (Canada)), **Chile** (2003/3200 (not yet in force)), **China** (1981/1119; 1984/1826; 1996/3164) (and see note below), **Croatia** (see note below), **Cyprus** (1975/425; 1980/1529), **Czech Republic** (see note below),

Denmark (1980/1960; 1991/2877; 1996/3165),

Egypt (1980/1091), **Estonia** (1994/3207),

Falkland Islands (1997/2985), **Faroe Islands** (1961/579; 1971/717; 1975/2190) until 6 April 1997, **Fiji** (1976/1342), **Finland** (1970/153; 1980/710; 1985/1997; 1991/2878; 1996/3166), **France** (1968/1869; 1973/1328; 1987/466; 1987/2055),

Gambia (1980/1963), **Germany** (1967/25; 1971/874), **Ghana** (1993/1800), **Greece** (1954/142), **Grenada** (1949/361; 1968/1867), **Guernsey** (1952/1215; 1994/3209), **Guyana** (1992/3207),

Hungary (1978/1056),

Iceland (1991/2879), **India** (1981/1120; 1993/1801), **Indonesia** (1994/769), **Ireland** (see 24.3 below), **Isle of Man** (1955/1205; 1991/2880; 1994/3208), **Israel** (1963/616; 1971/391), **Italy** (1990/2590), **Ivory Coast** (1987/169),

Jamaica (1973/1329), **Japan** (1970/1948; 1980/1530), **Jersey** (1952/1216; 1994/3210), **Jordan** (2001/3924) from 6 April 2003 (UK) and 1 January 2003 (Jordan),

Kazakhstan (1994/3211; 1998/2567), **Kenya** (1977/1299), **Kiribati and Tuvalu** (1950/750; 1968/309; 1974/1271), **Korea (South)** (1996/3168), **Kuwait** (1999/2036),

Latvia (1996/3167), **Lesotho** (1997/2986), **Lithuania** (2001/3925, 2002/2847) from 6 April 2002 (UK) and 1 January 2002 (Lithuania)(subject to protocol), **Luxembourg** (1968/1100; 1980/567; 1984/364),

Macedonia (see note below), **Malawi** (1956/619; 1964/1401; 1968/1101; 1979/302), **Malaysia** (1973/1330; 1987/2056; 1997/2987), **Malta** (1995/763), **Mauritius** (1981/1121; 1987/467; 2003/2620) (2003 protocol applies from 6 April 2003 (UK) and 1 July 2003 (Mauritius)), **Mexico** (1994/3212), **Mongolia** (1996/2598), **Montserrat** (1947/2869; 1968/576), **Morocco** (1991/2881), **Myanmar** (1952/751),

Namibia (1962/2352; 1967/1490), **Netherlands** (1967/1063; 1980/1961; 1983/1902; 1990/2152; 2000/3330), **New Zealand** (1984/365; 2004/1274 (not yet in force)), **Nigeria** (1987/2057), **Norway** (1985/1998; 2000/3247),

Oman (1998/2568),

24.2　Double Tax Relief

Pakistan (1987/2058), **Papua New Guinea** (1991/2882), **Philippines** (1978/184), Poland (1978/282), Portugal (1969/599),

Romania (1977/57), **Russian Federation** (1994/3213),

St. Christopher (St. Kitts) and Nevis (1947/2872), **Sierra Leone** (1947/2873; 1968/1104), **Singapore** (1997/2988), **Slovak Republic** (see note below), **Slovenia** (see note below), **Solomon Islands** (1950/748; 1968/574; 1974/1270), South Africa (1969/864; 2002/3138) (new treaty applies from 6 April 2003 (UK) and 1 January 2003 (South Africa)), **South West Africa** (see Namibia), **Spain** (1976/1919; 1995/765), **Sri Lanka** (1980/713), **Sudan** (1977/1719), **Swaziland** (1969/380), **Sweden** (1961/619; 1984/366; 2000/3330), **Switzerland** (1978/1408; 1982/714; 1994/3215),

Taiwan (2002/3137) from 6 April 2003 (UK) and 1 January 2003 (Taiwan), **Thailand** (1981/1546), **Trinidad and Tobago** (1983/1903), **Tunisia** (1984/133), **Turkey** (1988/932),

Uganda (1993/1802), **Ukraine** (1993/1803), **USA** (1980/568; 2002/2848) (new treaty applies from 6 April 2003 (UK) and 1 January 2004 (USA) but from 1 May 2003 (UK *and* USA) in respect of tax withheld at source) (1946/1331, 1955/499, 1961/985, 1980/779, 1994/418, 1996/1781 all revoked from January 2001 — see 2000/3330)) (and see note below), **USSR** (see note below), **Uzbekistan** (1994/770),

Venezuela (1996/2599), **Vietnam** (1994/3216),

Yugoslavia (see note below),

Zambia (1972/1721; 1981/1816), **Zimbabwe** (1982/1842).

Shipping & Air Transport only—Algeria (Air Transport only) (1984/362), Argentina (but see now above), Belarus (but see now above), Brazil (1968/572), Cameroon (Air Transport only) (1982/1841), China (Air Transport only) (1981/1119), Ethiopia (Air Transport only) (1977/1297), Hong Kong (Air Transport only) (1998/2566) from 6 April 1998 (UK) and 1 April 1998 (Hong Kong), Hong Kong (Shipping only) (2000/3248) from 6 April 2002 (UK) and 1 April 2002 (Hong Kong), Iran (Air Transport only) (1960/2419), Jordan (1979/300), Kuwait (Air Transport only) (1984/1825), Lebanon (1964/278), Russia (but see now above), Saudi Arabia (Air Transport only) (1994/767), Venezuela (but see now above), USSR (see note below), Ukraine (but see now above), Uzbekistan (but see now above), Zaire (1977/1298).

Notes.

Agreements not yet in force. The above-mentioned Agreement with Belarus had not yet entered into force at 1 April 2003. (Revenue Tax Bulletin August 2003 p 1048).

China. The Agreement published as *SI 1984 No 1826* does not apply to the Hong Kong or Macao Special Administrative Regions which came into existence on 1 July 1997. (Revenue Tax Bulletin October 1996 p 357).

Czechoslovakia. The Agreement published as *SI 1991 No 2876* between the UK and Czechoslovakia is treated as remaining in force between the UK and, respectively, the Czech Republic and the Slovak Republic. (Revenue Pamphlet IR 131, SP 5/93).

USA. For the Revenue's understanding of how certain provisions of the Agreement published as *SI 2002 No 2848* will be interpreted and applied, see Revenue Tax Bulletin Special Edition 6, April 2003.

USSR. The Agreement published as *SI 1986 No 224* (which also continued in force the Air Transport agreement published as *SI 1974 No 1269*) between the UK and the former Soviet Union was to be applied by the UK as if it were still in force between the UK and the former Soviet Republics until such time as new agreements took effect with particular countries. It later came to light that Armenia, Georgia, Kyrgyzstan, Lithuania and Moldova did not consider themselves bound by the UK/USSR convention and were not operating it in relation to UK residents. Accordingly, the UK ceased to apply it to residents of those countries from 1 April 2002 for corporation tax and from 6 April 2002 for income tax and capital gains tax. (The Agreement published as *SI 2001 No 3925* between the UK and Lithuania has effect from those dates.) The position for other former Republics (Belarus, Tajikistan and Turkmenistan) with which new conventions are not yet in force remains as before. (Revenue Pamphlet IR 131, SP 4/01 (replacing SP 3/92) and Revenue Tax Bulletin June 2001 p 864).

Yugoslavia. The Agreement published as *SI 1981 No 1815* between the UK and Yugoslavia is regarded as remaining in force between the UK and, respectively, Croatia, Slovenia, Macedonia and the Federal Republic of Yugoslavia. The position as at 1 April 2003 with regard to the rest of former Yugoslavia remains undetermined. (Revenue Tax Bulletin August 2003 p 1048).

Copies of double tax agreements and other statutory instruments published from 1987 onwards are available on the Stationery Office website at www.hmso.gov.uk/stat.htm

24.3   **IRELAND** [*ICTA 1988, s 68; FA 1994, s 207(5); SI 1976 Nos 2151, 2152; SI 1995 No 764; SI 1998 No 3151*]

A Convention and Protocol 1976 (as subsequently amended) replace previous provisions between UK and Ireland. Shipping and air transport profits, certain trading profits not arising through a permanent establishment, interest, royalties, pensions (other than Government pensions and salaries which are normally taxed by the paying Government only) are taxed in the country of residence. Salaries, wages and other similar remuneration (including directors) is taxed in the country where earned unless the employer is non-resident and the employee is present for not more than 183 days in the fiscal year and is not paid by a permanent establishment.

The Revenue take the view that a website, or a server on which e-commerce is conducted through a website, is not of itself a permanent establishment. (Revenue Press Release 11 April 2000).

Where income is taxable in both countries, relief is given in the country of residence for the tax payable in the country of origin.

The recipient of a dividend from a company resident in the other country is entitled to the related tax credit (except where the recipient is a company which controls, alone or with associates, 10% or more of the voting power of the paying company). Income tax up to 15% of aggregate of dividend and tax credit may be charged in country of source (but not on charity or superannuation scheme exempt in other country).

Capital gains on immovable property (and assets of a permanent establishment or fixed base) are taxed in country where situate, and gains on other property in the taxpayer's country of residence with credit given in the other country if also taxed there.

A further Convention relates to inheritance tax (previously capital transfer tax) (UK) and capital acquisitions tax (Ireland). Relief attaches to the property subject to the charge and is given by each country allowing a credit against its own tax if the property is situated in the other country.

24.4   **UNILATERAL RELIEF BY UK** [*ICTA 1988, ss 790, 794*]

Taxes, other than those for which credit is available under the bilateral double tax agreements in 24.2 above, payable under the law of any territory outside the UK (and see

24.4 Double Tax Relief

24.3 above for Ireland) and computed by reference to income or gain *arising in that territory* are allowed (to the extent defined below) as a credit against UK income tax or corporation tax paid on that income or gain by UK residents. Relief is only available against UK tax chargeable under the same Schedule and Case as that under which the foreign income on which the foreign tax was borne is chargeable (*George Wimpey International Ltd v Rolfe Ch D 1989, 62 TC 597*). Where appropriate an apportionment must be made to determine what part of income may be regarded as 'arising in' the overseas territory, and in making that apportionment it is the principles of UK tax law which are to be applied (see *Yates v GCA International Ltd and cross-appeal Ch D 1991, 64 TC 37* and Revenue Pamphlet IR 131, SP 7/91, 26 July 1991). The machinery and limits (with modifications as below) are substantially the same as those under which the bilateral agreements operate and the credit given is, basically, such as would be allowable were a double taxation agreement in force with the territory concerned. [*ICTA 1988, s 790(1)–(4), s 794*]. See example in 24.8 below.

With effect from 21 March 2000, it is made clear that unilateral relief will not be allowed where credit could be claimed under a double tax agreement under 24.2 above, or in cases or circumstances in which such an agreement made on or after that date specifically prohibits relief. [*ICTA 1988, s 793A(2)(3); FA 2000, Sch 30 para 5*].

The modifications are:

(a)   The foreign taxes must be charged on income or profits and correspond to income tax or corporation tax in the UK, but may include similar taxes payable under the law of a province, state or part of a country, or a municipality or other local body. [*ICTA 1988, s 790(12)*]. See *Yates v GCA International Ltd and cross-appeal Ch D 1991, 64 TC 37* where a tax imposed on gross receipts less a fixed 10% deduction was held to correspond to UK income tax or corporation tax. Following that decision, the Revenue amended their practice. (Revenue Pamphlet IR 131, SP 7/91, 26 July 1991). For claims made on or after 13 February 1991, and earlier claims unsettled at that date, foreign taxes will be examined to determine whether, in their own legislative context, they serve the same function as UK income and corporation taxes in relation to business profits, and are thus eligible for unilateral relief. As regards those overseas taxes which the Inland Revenue considers admissible (or inadmissible) for relief, these are listed by country in the Revenue Double Taxation Relief Manual at DT 2100 *et seq.* See also Revenue Business Income Manual BIM 45905, and Revenue Tax Bulletin August 1995 p 244, October 1996 p 358 and December 2001 p 903 as regards re-classification of certain South African, Algerian, Argentinian, Brazilian, Peruvian, Chilean and Turkish taxes. Current information may be obtained on 020–7438 6643.

(b)   The restriction to tax on '*income or gain arising in the territory*' does not apply in the case of the Channel Islands or the Isle of Man, and credit is given for CI or IOM tax if the claimant is resident for the particular year of assessment or accounting period either in the UK or the Channel Islands, or IOM as the case may be. [*ICTA 1988, s 790(5)(a), s 794(2)(a)*].

(c)   Income from personal or professional services performed in a territory is deemed to arise in that territory, and credit for overseas tax on income from employments etc. (where duties wholly or mainly performed in the overseas territory) is given against income tax on employment income computed by reference to that income if the claimant is resident for the year of assessment either in UK or in the overseas territory. [*ICTA 1988, s 790(4), s 794(2)(b); ITEPA 2003, Sch 6 para 103*].

(d)   Where an overseas company carries on a banking business through a UK branch or agency and suffers foreign tax on interest on a foreign loan made through that branch etc., double tax relief is available as if the UK branch were a UK bank. Tax payable in a country where the overseas company is taxable by reason of its domicile, residence or place of management is excluded. [*ICTA 1988, s 794(2)(c)*]. For chargeable periods ending after 20 March 2000, this is replaced by a wider relief available on similar terms to all non-UK resident persons (whether companies or individuals) with UK branches or agencies/permanent establishments. [*ICTA 1988, s 794(2)(bb); FA 2000, Sch 30 para 4(4)–(6)(14); FA 2001, Sch 27 para 7; FA 2003, s 153(2)(4)*].

Foreign tax levied by reference to the value of assets employed to produce income chargeable to UK tax may, in practice, be allowed as a business expense under normal Schedule D, Case I rules. (Revenue International Tax Handbook, ITH 602).

24.5 **SPECIFIC MATTERS**

(*a*) **Alimony.** Where alimony payments etc. under UK Court Order or agreement (technically a UK source) are made by an overseas resident, concessional relief by way of credit is allowed where (i) the payments are made out of the overseas income of the payer and subject to tax there, (ii) UK income tax if deducted from the payments is duly accounted for, and (iii) the payee is resident in the UK and effectively bears the overseas tax. (Revenue Pamphlet IR 1, A12).

(*b*) (i) **Amounts assessable in UK on the remittance basis.** Where double tax credit for foreign tax is allowable in respect of it, any income which is assessable on the basis of *remittance* is treated, for UK assessment purposes, as increased by the *foreign tax* on that income (but ignoring any notional tax under (*i*) below). [*ICTA 1988, s 795(1)(3)*].

(ii) **Amounts assessable in UK on the arising basis.** Where income or gain is assessable to income tax or corporation tax on the basis of the full amount arising (not on remittance as in (i) above), and double tax credit is allowable in respect of foreign tax suffered on it, *no deduction* may be made for foreign tax on that, or any other, income or gain.

If the income is a dividend, credit is given for foreign taxes deducted from the dividend plus (either if provided for under the specific terms of a double tax agreement *or* if covered by unilateral relief under *ICTA 1988, s 790(6)*, which only applies to UK recipient companies with 10% holdings etc., in the overseas company) 'underlying tax', being overseas taxes paid on the profits of the paying company (but ignoring any notional tax under (*i*) below). If credit for underlying tax is available, then the dividend is grossed-up by such tax for UK assessment purposes. For dividends paid after 30 March 2001 by a non-resident company to a UK-resident company, certain further adjustments are made to the underlying tax taken into account for these purposes. [*ICTA 1988, s 795(2)(3A); FA 2001, Sch 27 para 1*]. See further details in Tolley's Corporation Tax.

(iii) **If the taxpayer does not take any credit** by way of either bilateral or unilateral relief, or if no UK double tax credit is otherwise allowable in respect of foreign income, any foreign tax paid on that income in the place where it arises is generally deductible from the income for purposes of UK assessment, *except* where the UK assessment is on the basis of *remittances* to the UK. Where foreign tax for which such a deduction has been given is subsequently adjusted after 20 March 2000, similar provisions to those which apply by virtue of *ICTA 1988, s 806(3)–(6)* in the case of foreign tax credits (see (*e*) below) apply as regards the requirement to notify the Revenue of the adjustment and extended time limit for assessments etc. [*ICTA 1988, ss 805, 811; FA 2000, Sch 30 para 27*].

24.5 Double Tax Relief

(c) **Business Profits.** Where a UK resident pays tax in an overseas country on *business profits* arising there, that tax is allowed as a business expense if no double tax credit is allowable against UK tax on those profits, or the right to credit is forgone.

(d) **Capital Gains.** Relief for foreign taxes on *capital gains* is given against, and is limited to, the amount of UK capital gains tax on those gains. [*TCGA 1992, s 277*]. Capital gains accruing to companies are subject to corporation tax, and relief is available accordingly.

(da) **Utilisation of unused relief.** The provisions which, from 31 March 2001, permit companies to pool certain dividends for the purposes of relief of eligible unrelieved tax, and also allow a limited carry back or carry forward or sideways of unused relief (see Tolley's Corporation Tax under Double Tax Relief) apply *mutatis mutandis* to unrelieved foreign tax in respect of any dividend income arising after 30 March 2001 to a UK branch or agency/permanent establishment of a non-UK resident person. Such relief must be claimed (specifying the amount to which each of the available options is to apply) within six years of the end of the chargeable period in which the unrelieved foreign tax arose (or, if later, within one year of the end of the chargeable period in which the foreign tax in question is paid). [*ICTA 1988, s 806K; FA 2000, Sch 30 para 22; FA 2003, s 153(2)(4)*].

(e) **Claims** for credit under double tax arrangements must be made within five years after 31 January following the tax year in which the income or gain falls to be charged to tax or, for corporation tax purposes, six years after the end of the accounting period concerned. After 20 March 2000, claims may be made (if later) up to (for income tax) 31 January following the tax year in which the foreign tax is paid or (for corporation tax) one year after the end of the accounting period in which the foreign tax is paid. [*ICTA 1988, s 806(1); FA 1996, s 135, Sch 21 para 23; FA 2000, Sch 30 para 20*]. Claims in respect of overlap profits (see (j) below) must be made within five years after 31 January following the latest tax year for which relief is due. [*ICTA 1988, s 804(7); FA 1996, s 135, Sch 21 para 22*].

Written notice must be given to the Revenue where any credit allowed for foreign tax has become excessive by reason of an adjustment of the amount of any foreign tax payable (except in the case of Lloyd's UNDERWRITERS (89) where the consequences of such an adjustment are dealt with under regulations). This applies to adjustments made on or after 17 March 1998, and the notice must be given within one year after the making of the adjustment. The maximum penalty for failure to comply is the amount by which the credit was rendered excessive by the adjustment. The time limit for assessments etc. to be revised following such an adjustment is extended to six years after the adjustment is finalised. [*ICTA 1988, s 806(2)–(6); FA 1998, s 107*]. For this and for the Revenue view of what constitutes an 'adjustment', and when an adjustment is made, see Revenue Double Taxation Manual DT 837.

Claims for relief other than by way of credit must made to the Board. [*ICTA 1988, s 788(6)*]. For appeals, see 65.8 RESIDENCE, ORDINARY RESIDENCE AND DOMICILE. Pending final agreement a provisional allowance can usually be obtained on application to the inspector.

(f) **Exchange rate.** Foreign tax is normally converted into sterling at the rate of exchange obtaining on the date it became payable. (Revenue Double Taxation Relief Manual DT 845). Where part of foreign tax repaid and sterling was devalued in the period between payment and repayment, held relief due on net tax in foreign currency at the old rate (*Greig v Ashton Ch D 1956, 36 TC 581*).

(g) **Limit on Relief.** Where income is chargeable to *UK income tax*, credit for foreign tax suffered on that income is set against the income tax chargeable in respect of the doubly-taxed income. [*ICTA 1988, ss 790(4), 793*]. But the relief is limited to the *difference* between the income tax (before double tax relief, but after any other income tax reduction) which would be borne by the claimant

(i)   if he were charged on his *total income* (computed as in (*b*) above), and

(ii)   if he were charged on that income *excluding* the income in respect of which the credit is to be allowed. [*ICTA 1988, s 796; FA 1994, Sch 8 para 12*].

In no case may total double tax credits exceed the total income tax payable by the claimant for the year of assessment (less any income tax he is entitled to charge against any other person and any tax deemed to have been deducted at source from a charitable donation made after 5 April 2000 under the Gift Aid scheme). [*ICTA 1988, s 796(3); FA 1990, s 25(6)(b); FA 2000, s 39(6)(10)*].

For claims made after 20 March 2000, it is in addition provided that relief is limited to that which would be allowed if all reasonable steps had been taken, including all relevant claims, elections etc., under the law of the territory concerned or under double tax arrangements with that territory, to minimise the foreign tax payable. [*ICTA 1988, s 795A; FA 2000, Sch 30 para 6*]. As regards what the Revenue considers taxpayers can and cannot reasonably be expected to do, the former is likely to include appeals against excessive assessments, claims for reliefs generally known to be available, and selection of any option which produces a lower tax liability, and the latter is likely to include claims to reliefs whose availability is uncertain, and where disproportionate expenditure would be required to pursue a claim, substituting carry-forward claims for carry-back claims and *vice versa*, and attempting to exercise influence the taxpayer does not have on the underlying tax paid by a subsidiary. See the brief note on the Revenue's website at www.inlandrevenue.gov.uk/international/dtr26.htm.

(*h*)   **Lloyd's** UNDERWRITERS (89). For special arrangements for double tax relief for underwriters, in particular under SELF-ASSESSMENT (78), see *SI 1997 No 405*.

(*i*)   **Notional Tax.** Under *ICTA 1988, s 788(5)* it may be provided that any tax which would have been payable in a foreign country but for a relief under the law of that territory given with a view to promoting industrial, commercial, scientific, educational or other development therein is nevertheless treated for purposes of credit against UK tax as if it had been paid. See, for example, Revenue Double Taxation Relief Manual at DT 12758 in the case of Malaysia and at DT 16911 in the case of Singapore. For restrictions on relief available to companies in respect of such notional tax, see Tolley's Corporation Tax under Double Tax Relief.

(*j*)   **Overlap profits** [*ICTA 1988, s 804; FA 1994, s 217; FA 1996, s 135, Sch 21 para 22*]. Credit for foreign tax paid in respect of 'overlap profits' (see 71.11 SCHEDULE D, CASES I AND II) arising in taxing a trade etc. is allowed against UK income tax chargeable for any year in respect of that income, notwithstanding that credit for that foreign tax has already been allowed in an earlier year. There are overriding provisions limiting the credit allowable for any year by reference to the total of credit due for all the relevant years as above, and for cases where the number of UK periods of assessment exceeds the number of foreign periods.

Recovery of excess credit applies where, and to the extent that, relief is given for overlap profits either on cessation of the trade or on a change of accounting date resulting in a basis period of longer than twelve months. Recovery is achieved by reducing the credit otherwise available for the year of relief and, if there is still an excess, by assessment under Case VI.

(*k*) **Partnerships.** It was held in the case of *Padmore v CIR CA 1989, 62 TC 352* that, where profits of a non-UK resident partnership were exempt under the relevant double tax treaty, the profit share of a UK resident partner was thereby also exempt. This decision was, however, reversed by subsequent legislation with retrospective effect, see 53.14 PARTNERSHIPS.

(*ka*) **Prevention of double relief.** For claims made after 20 March 2000, credit may not be given for foreign tax for which relief is available in the territory in which it would otherwise be payable, either under the law of that territory in consequence of any double tax agreement or in cases or circumstances in which such an agreement made on or after that date specifically prohibits relief. [*ICTA 1988, s 793A(1); FA 2000, Sch 30 para 5*].

(*l*) **Royalties and 'know-how' payments.** Notwithstanding that credit for overseas tax is ordinarily given only against income which arises (or is deemed to arise) in the overseas territory concerned, the Revenue treatment as regards this class of income is as follows.

Income payments made by an overseas resident to a UK trader for the use, in that overseas territory, of any *copyright, patent, design, secret process or formula, trade mark etc.*, may be treated, for credit purposes (whether under double tax agreements or by way of unilateral relief) as income arising outside the UK — *except* so far as they represent consideration for services (other than merely incidental) rendered in the UK by the recipient to the payer (Revenue Pamphlet IR 1, B8).

For the treatment of sales of 'know-how' etc., see 71.57 SCHEDULE D, CASES I AND II.

(*m*) **Transfer pricing.** Under Convention *90/463/EEC*, Member States are required to adopt certain procedures, and to follow the opinion of an advisory commission, in transfer pricing disputes. *ICTA 1988, s 815B* makes provision for domestic legislation and double tax agreements to be overridden where necessary under the Convention. [*F(No 2)A 1992, s 51*]. See 3.8 ANTI-AVOIDANCE.

24.6   **PAYMENTS ABROAD BY UK RESIDENTS**

Interest etc. Under *SI 1970 No 488* (as amended) a UK resident paying to a resident of a country with which the UK has a double tax agreement income which under that agreement is wholly or partially relieved (other than a dividend or other distribution by a company) may be required, by notice from the Board of Inland Revenue, to make such payments without deducting UK income tax, or under deduction of tax at, or not exceeding, a specified rate. Applications for such relief from deduction should be sent to IR International — Centre for Non-Residents, Fitz Roy House, PO Box 46, Nottingham NG2 1BD. Where a notice is given, the payer, if otherwise chargeable with, or liable to account for, tax on such payments (under *ICTA 1988, s 349* etc., see 22.3 DEDUCTION OF TAX AT SOURCE) is exempted from that liability if the notice requires him to pay the income gross, and in other cases need account for tax only at the rate specified. The payer may, nevertheless, treat the gross amount of the payment as a loss for relief purposes, while if the payment is made by a company it is treated for the purposes of treatment as a charge on income as if tax has been deducted from it and accounted for under *ICTA 1988, s 349, Sch 16*. Where the payer would have been entitled (under *ICTA 1988, s 348*) to retain the tax deducted (as having made the payment out of income subjected to income tax) he is given, against the income tax otherwise payable by him for that year, an allowance equal to the additional tax which, but for the notice, he would have been entitled to deduct from the payment.

For Revenue practice in relation to claims for payment of interest to non-residents without deduction of tax, and in particular where payments are made in full in advance of the issue (or refusal) of a gross payment notice, see Revenue Tax Bulletin August 1994 p 153.

For review of applications for relief from deduction where loans are re-denominated from one currency to another (e.g. to or from the euro), see Revenue Tax Bulletin February 1999 pp 631, 632.

Provisional relief. From 1 September 1999, a Provisional Treaty Relief scheme is introduced for two types of loan, the one-to-one company loan (provided that there is no common shareholding or ownership) and the syndicated loan, where there is a syndicate manager. This allows the UK borrower to apply for immediate authority to make payments incorporating the treaty relief, pending a Revenue decision on the issue of a formal notice. It is a condition of the scheme that the recipient's application for relief (certified by the overseas tax authority) is received by the Revenue within three months of the provisional authority, and if that condition is not met, or the relief is found not to be due, the Revenue will look to the payer for the tax that should have been deducted (and any interest thereon). In the case of a syndicated loan, the requirement is for a composite application for relief (which does not need overseas tax authority certification) which must be made by the syndicate manager within three months of the provisional authority. Application for provisional relief is made on form PTRPAY1 (in the case of one-to-one loans) or form PTRSM1 (in the case of syndicated loans), which may be obtained from Complex Claims Group (Provisional Treaty Relief Scheme), IR International — Centre for Non-Residents, Fitz Roy House, PO Box 46, Nottingham NG2 1BD (tel. 0115-974 1904, fax. 0115-974 1918). Explanatory 'Guidelines' may be obtained from the same address. For a summary of the scheme, see Revenue Tax Bulletin June 1999 pp 668–670.

Dividends. Under *SI 1973 No 317*, the Revenue may make arrangements with a UK resident company whereby it may pay to a non-resident shareholder that part of the tax credit relating to a dividend to which he is entitled under the terms of a double tax agreement. See Tolley's Corporation Tax (under Double Tax Relief). All such arrangements cease on 6 April 1999. [*SI 1999 No 1927*]. See generally Revenue Tax Bulletin February 1999 pp 626, 627.

Simon's Direct Tax Service. See F1.3.

24.7   COMPANIES

Companies enjoy the benefit of the foregoing double tax reliefs and they can in certain circumstances claim relief for underlying taxes in respect of overseas dividends receivable by them (being the overseas taxes borne by the paying company on its profits). See 24.5(*b*)(ii) above and Tolley's Corporation Tax (under Double Tax Relief).

24.8   EXAMPLE OF RELIEF BY CREDIT

A single man has, for 2004/05, UK earnings of £16,200 and foreign income from property of £2,000 on which foreign tax of £400 has been paid. He is entitled to the personal allowance of £4,745.

24.9   Double Tax Relief

(a)   *Tax on total income*   £

    Earnings   16,200

    Income from property   2,000   (foreign tax £400)

                                                          18,200

    Personal allowance   4,745

    Taxable income   £13,455

    Tax on £13,455 @ 10/22%   £2,717.70

(b)   *Tax on total income less foreign income*   £

    Earnings   16,200

    Personal allowance   4,745

    Taxable income   £11,455

    Tax on £11,455 @ 10/22%   £2,277.70

The difference in tax between (a) and (b) is £440. The foreign tax is less than this and full credit of £400 is available against the UK tax payable. If the foreign tax was £600, the credit would be limited to £440 and the balance of £160 would be unrelieved.

24.9   EU SAVINGS DIRECTIVE — SPECIAL WITHHOLDING TAX

Under the EU Savings Directive (*Directive 2003/48/EC* of 3 June 2003 — see 68.15 RETURNS), due to come into force sometime on or after 1 January 2005, three EU Member States (Austria, Belgium and Luxembourg) will, for a transitional period, impose a 'special withholding tax' on the interest and other 'savings income' of individuals resident in the EU but outside the State in question. This is expected to be levied at 15% for the first three years, 20% for the next three and 35% thereafter, and is an alternative to the automatic exchange of information on cross-border payments which is envisaged by the Directive. Some of the other countries applying similar measures as the Directive, and with which the UK makes equivalent arrangements, are also expected to impose a special withholding tax. Legislation introduced by *FA 2004* and described below provides for relief to be given for the special withholding tax against UK income tax and capital gains tax liabilities or, to the extent that set-off is not possible, by repayment. It also provides, as an alternative, for application to be made to the Inland Revenue for a certificate which can be presented to a paying agent to enable savings income to be paid to the individual without deduction of the special withholding tax.

In these provisions, '*special withholding tax*' means a withholding tax (however described) levied under the law of a territory outside the UK implementing the relevant provision (*Article 11*) of the EU Savings Directive or, in the case of a non-EU Member State, any corresponding provision of equivalent international arrangements (whatever the period for which the provision is to have effect). '*Savings income*' means income within the scope of the EU Savings Directive or the equivalent international arrangements in question. Pre-existing legislation giving double tax relief by way of credit, as described elsewhere in this chapter, does not apply for the purposes of special withholding tax, and such tax is not regarded as a foreign tax for the purposes of such provisions.

Relief by way of credit. Where a UK resident is chargeable to income tax for a tax year on a payment of savings income (or would be so chargeable but for any exemption or relief available) and special withholding tax is levied, the special withholding tax is treated, on the making of a claim, as if it were tax deducted at source from the payment of income. To the extent that the special withholding tax so treated exceeds his income tax liability for the year, the excess is set against any capital gains tax liability of his for the year and any balance repaid to him. If, however, he is also resident in another territory for that tax year, or is treated as such under a double tax treaty, and obtains relief for the special withholding tax under the law of that territory, he is not entitled to the above relief.

A similar relief applies where a UK resident makes a disposal of assets which is within the scope of capital gains tax and the consideration for the disposal consists of or includes an amount of savings income subjected to special withholding tax. On the making of a claim, a credit is given against his capital gains tax liability (if any) for the tax year, with any excess given against his income tax liability and any balance repaid. For the purposes of certain specified self-assessment provisions (for example in determining the amount of a balancing payment as in 78.6 SELF-ASSESSMENT) the credit is treated as if it were income tax deducted at source. For more details of the capital gains tax credit, see the equivalent coverage in Tolley's Capital Gains Tax.

Where, for any tax year, double tax relief by way of credit is available for any foreign tax suffered, the credit for foreign tax is given in priority to any credit due as above for special withholding tax. This is to ensure that the taxpayer gets maximum relief, since excess foreign tax is not repayable.

Special withholding tax is not deductible in computing amounts of chargeable income or chargeable gains.

Where an amount of savings income is chargeable to income tax on the REMITTANCE BASIS (64), the amount received is treated as increased by any special withholding tax levied in respect of it and claimed under these provisions.

Certificate to avoid levy of special withholding tax. A person may make written application to the Inland Revenue for a certificate which he may then present to his paying agent, who will not then levy special withholding tax on savings income from the investment covered by the certificate. The application must include the person's name, address and national insurance number, the account number of the investment in question (or, if there is no such number, a statement identifying the investment), the name and address of the paying agent, the period for which the applicant would like the certificate to be valid (the maximum period of validity is three years) and any documents required by the Revenue to verify the said information. The Revenue must issue the certificate within two months after the applicant provides the said information and documents. These requirements may be modified as necessary where international arrangements differ from the EU Savings Directive as regards the issue of such certificates.

If the Revenue are not satisfied that the applicant has provided them with the requisite information and documents, they must give the applicant written notice, stating their reasons, of their refusal to issue a certificate. The applicant may give written notice of appeal against the refusal within 30 days after the date of the refusal notice. The appeal is to the Special Commissioners, who may either confirm or quash the refusal notice.

[*FA 2004, ss 107–115*].

25   Enterprise Investment Scheme

(See also Revenue Pamphlet IR137.)

25.1   The Enterprise Investment Scheme ('EIS') was introduced by *FA 1994, s 137, Sch 15* in respect of shares issued on or after 1 January 1994. It replaced the earlier Business Expansion Scheme ('BES'), which was withdrawn for shares issued after 31 December 1993, for which see the 2000/01 or earlier editions.

The EIS is dealt with in this chapter under the following headings.

See generally Revenue Venture Capital Schemes Manual VCM 10000 *et seq.*

Simon's Direct Tax Service. See E3.1.

25.2   **CONDITIONS FOR RELIEF**

A 'qualifying individual' is eligible for relief under the EIS if

(*a*)   'eligible shares' in a 'qualifying company' for which he has subscribed are issued to him fully paid up;

(*b*)   those shares are issued to raise money (i.e. cash, see *Thompson v Hart Ch D 2000, 72 TC 543*) for the purpose of a 'qualifying business activity';

(*c*)   the 'money raised' is employed wholly (disregarding insignificant amounts) for that purpose by the end of the 24 months following the issue or, if the only 'qualifying business activity' falls within 25.6(*a*) or (*c*) below, and if later, by the end of the 24 months starting when the company (or, where applicable, a subsidiary) began to carry on the 'qualifying trade', and 80% of that money is so employed within 12 months after the issue/commencement of trade. This applies after 6 March 2001; previously, *all* the money had to be so employed within 12 months after the issue/ commencement of trade. Money whose retention can reasonably be regarded as necessary or advisable for financing current business requirements is regarded as employed for trade purposes (see Revenue Venture Capital Schemes Manual VCM 12080); and

(*d*)   the additional condition described below (which differs depending on whether the shares are issued after 16 March 2004 or on or before that date) is satisfied in relation to the 'qualifying company'.

See 25.3–25.7 below for the meaning of 'qualifying individual', 'eligible shares', 'qualifying company', 'qualifying business activity' and 'qualifying trade'.

For the purposes of (a) above, the shares must have been subscribed for wholly in cash, except for any shares issued after 16 March 2004 which are '*bonus shares*', i.e. shares issued otherwise than for payment (whether in cash or otherwise); and any such bonus shares are disregarded in determining whether shares are issued fully paid up. (Bonus shares issued after 16 March 2004 are similarly disregarded in establishing whether or not (b) above is satisfied.) Shares are not issued fully paid up if there is any undertaking to pay cash to any person at a later date in respect of the acquisition; for shares issued on or before 16 March 2004, this rule applied only by reference to an undertaking to pay cash to the company rather than to 'any person'.

In (c) above, the '*money raised*' means the money raised by the issue of the shares in question and all other eligible shares (if any) in the company of the same class which are issued on the same day; for shares issued on or before 16 March 2004, only shares comprised in the same issue were taken into account. In determining for the purposes of (c) above, in relation to shares issued after 16 March 2004, the time at which a qualifying trade begins to be carried on by a 'qualifying 90% subsidiary' of a company, any carrying on of the trade etc. by it before it became such a subsidiary is disregarded.

For shares issued after 16 March 2004, the additional condition referred to at (d) above is that at no time in the 'relevant period' (as defined in 25.6 below) must any of the following be carried on by a person other than the 'qualifying company' or a 'qualifying 90% subsidiary' (see 25.21 below) of that company:

- the '*relevant qualifying trade*', i.e. the 'qualifying trade' which is the subject of the 'qualifying business activity' referred to in (a) above;

- '*relevant preparation work*', i.e. preparations to carry on a 'qualifying trade' where such preparations are the subject of that 'qualifying business activity' (see 25.6(c) below);

- research and development which is the subject of that 'qualifying business activity' (see 25.6(d) below); and

- any other preparations for the carrying on of the 'qualifying trade'.

Where 'relevant preparation work' (as above) is carried on by the 'qualifying company' or a 'qualifying 90% subsidiary', the carrying on of the 'relevant qualifying trade' by a company other than the 'qualifying company' or one of its subsidiaries is disregarded for these purposes if it occurs before the 'qualifying company' or a 'qualifying 90% subsidiary' carries on that trade.

This additional condition is not regarded as failing to be met if, by reason only of a company being wound up or dissolved or being in administration or receivership (both as defined by *ICTA 1988, s 312(2A)*), the 'relevant qualifying trade' ceases to be carried on in the 'relevant period' by the 'qualifying company' or any 'qualifying 90% subsidiary' and is subsequently carried on by a person who is not connected (within *ICTA 1988, s 839* — see 19 CONNECTED PERSONS) with the company at any time in the 'period of restriction' (as in 25.16 below). This let-out applies only if the winding-up, dissolution or entry into administration or receivership (and everything done as a consequence of the company being in administration or receivership) is for *bona fide* commercial reasons and not part of a tax avoidance scheme or arrangements.

For shares issued on or before 16 March 2004, the additional condition referred to at (d) above is that the 'active company' must, throughout the 'relevant period' (as defined in 25.6 below), either:

(i)   be within 25.5(a) below; or

   (ii) be such a company as would be within (i) if its purposes were disregarded to the extent that they consist

   (A) in holding shares in or securities of, or making loans to, any of the company's subsidiaries, or

   (B) in holding and managing property used by the company or any of its subsidiaries either for research and development (as defined) from which a 'qualifying trade' (see 25.7 below) to be carried on by any of them is intended to be derived, or for the purposes of a 'qualifying trade' or trades carried on by any of them, or

   (C) in making loans to the parent company; or

   (iii) be a '90% subsidiary' of the 'qualifying company' which either

   (A) apart from purposes capable of having no significant effect (other than on incidental matters) on the extent of its activities, exists wholly for the purpose of carrying on activities consisting in holding and managing property used by the company or any of its subsidiaries either for research and development (as defined) from which a qualifying trade to be carried on by any of them is intended to be derived, or for the purposes of a qualifying trade or trades carried on by any of them, or

   (B) has no corporation tax profits and no part of its business consists in the making of investments.

The '*active company*' is the 'qualifying company' unless the 'qualifying business activity' consists in a subsidiary of the 'qualifying company' carrying on or preparing to carry on a 'qualifying trade', research and development or, before 7 March 2001, oil exploration (see below), in which case it is that subsidiary. Due to a defect in *Finance Act 1998*, it was sufficient as regards shares issued after 5 April 1998 and before 6 April 1999 for the active subsidiary to be a 75% subsidiary of the qualifying company. As regards shares issued after 5 April 1999, reverting to the rules for those issued before 6 April 1998, it must be a '90% subsidiary'.

For these purposes, a '*90% subsidiary*' is a subsidiary that would satisfy the conditions given at 25.21(*a*) below if references to 90% were substituted for references to 75% and, as regards shares issued after 5 April 1998, the let-out for *bona fide* commercial disposals of interests in the subsidiary were disregarded.

Although a winding-up or dissolution in the relevant period generally prevents a company meeting this additional condition, it is deemed met if the winding-up or dissolution is for *bona fide* commercial reasons and not part of a scheme a main purpose of which is tax avoidance, with the additional proviso before 21 March 2000 that any net assets are distributed to members (or dealt with as *bona vacantia*) before the end of the relevant period or (if later) the end of three years from the commencement of winding-up. After 20 March 2000 (both in relation to shares issued after that date and to pre-existing shares to which EIS income tax relief or capital gains tax deferral relief remains attributable), a company does not cease to meet the additional condition by reason of anything done as a consequence of its being in administration or receivership (both as defined by *ICTA 1988, s 312(2A)*), provided everything so done and the making of the relevant order are for *bona fide* commercial (and not tax avoidance) reasons.

[*ICTA 1988, s 289(1)–(1E)(3)(3A)(8A)(9), s 312(1); FA 1994, Sch 15 para 2; FA 1997, Sch 8 paras 1, 2; FA 1998, s 74, Sch 13 para 1(1)(2)(5); FA 1999, s 71; FA 2000, Sch 17 paras 9(2), 12, 15; FA 2001, Sch 15 paras 2(a), 6, 40; FA 2004, Sch 18 para 1(1)–(3)(5)–(7), paras 11(2), 21*].

Paragraph (*b*) above may be satisfied where money is raised to acquire shares in a company carrying on a qualifying trade, provided the target company has no non-trading assets and the hive up of the trade is not unnecessarily delayed. Money used to meet the expenses of issuing the shares should be regarded as employed in the same way as the remainder of the money raised. Where the company obtains a listing, for example on the Alternative Investment Market, at the same time as it issues the shares, the use of money to meet the expenses of flotation is normally acceptable. (Revenue Venture Capital Schemes Manual VCM 12070). Paragraphs (*b*) and (*c*) above are *not* satisfied if the money raised by the issue is used partly to pay dividends to investors (*Forthright (Wales) Ltd v Davies Ch D, [2004] STC 875*).

Relief is denied unless the shares are subscribed for and issued for *bona fide* commercial purposes and not as part of a scheme or arrangement a main purpose of which is the avoidance of tax. [*ICTA 1988, s 289(6); FA 1994, Sch 15 para 2; FA 1998, s 74, Sch 13 para 1(3)*].

Relief is available where eligible shares are held on a bare trust for two or more beneficiaries as if each beneficiary had subscribed as an individual for all of those shares, and as if the amount subscribed by each was the total subscribed divided by the number of beneficiaries. [*ICTA 1988, s 311(2); FA 1994, Sch 15 para 26(a)*].

Relief is also available where shares are subscribed for by a nominee for the individual claiming relief, including the managers of an investment fund approved by the Board for this purpose (an '*approved fund*'). With regard to an approved fund closed for the acceptance of further investments, the provisions of *ICTA 1988, ss 289A, 289B* (dealing with the form and attribution of relief, see 25.8 below) apply as if the eligible shares were issued at the time at which the fund was closed, provided that the amount subscribed on behalf of the individual for eligible shares issued within six months after the closure of the fund is not less than 90% of the individual's investment in the fund. [*ICTA 1988, s 311(1)(2A)(2B); FA 1988, s 53; FA 1994, Sch 15 para 26(b)*]. The Revenue have published guidelines setting out the principal criteria used in deciding whether to approve an investment fund for this purpose, and covering the procedures to be followed in applying for approval. They are available free of charge from Brian Lodde, Inland Revenue, Company Tax Division, Room M22, West Wing, Somerset House, London WC2R 1LB.

For the manner in which the scheme operates where a company wishes to raise money by a single issue of shares either partly for preparing to carry on a trade and partly for the subsequent carrying on of that trade, or for more than one qualifying business activity (e.g. for a trade carried on by one subsidiary and for research and development carried on by another), see Revenue Tax Bulletin April 1996 pp 305, 306.

For the date on which shares are issued, see *National Westminster Bank plc v CIR; Barclays Bank plc v CIR HL 1994, 67 TC 1*.

25.3   A '*qualifying individual*' is an individual who subscribes for the 'eligible shares' on his own behalf and who (except as below) is not at any time in the 'designated period' — see below (as regards shares issued before 6 April 1998, at any time in the 'relevant period' — see below) 'connected with' the issuing company (i.e. provided that there is no such connection at any time in that period, see *Wild v Cannavan CA 1997, 70 TC 554*). He is '*connected with*' the issuing company) if he is either:

(*a*)   an employee, partner, or director of, or an employee or director of a partner of, the issuing company or any 'subsidiary'; or

(*b*)   an individual who directly or indirectly possesses or is entitled to acquire (whether he is so entitled at a future date or will at a future date be so entitled)

(i)   more than 30% of the voting power, the issued ordinary share capital, or the loan capital and issued share capital of the issuing company or any 'subsidiary' (loan capital including any debt incurred by the company for money borrowed, for capital assets acquired, for any right to income created in its favour, or for insufficient consideration, but excluding a debt incurred for overdrawing a bank account in the ordinary course of the bank's business), or

(ii) such rights as would entitle him to more than 30% of the assets of the issuing company or any 'subsidiary' available for distribution to the company's equity holders (as under *ICTA 1988, Sch 18 paras 1, 3* — see Tolley's Corporation Tax under Groups of Companies); or

(*c*) an individual who has control (as defined by *ICTA 1988, s 840*, see 19.8 CONNECTED PERSONS) of the issuing company or any 'subsidiary'; or

(*d*) an individual who subscribes for shares in the issuing company as part of an arrangement providing for another person to subscribe for shares in another company with which, were that other company an issuing company, the individual (or any other individual party to the arrangement) would be connected as above,

and rights or powers of 'associates' (within *ICTA 1988, s 417(3)(4)* but excluding a brother or sister) are taken into account as regards (*b*) and (*c*) above (see *Cook v Billings CA, [2001] STC 16* on the similar wording under the earlier BES provisions.

As regards (*b*)(i) above, an individual is not connected with the company by virtue only of the fact that he or an associate is a shareholder if at that time the company has issued no shares other than subscriber shares and has neither commenced business nor made preparations for doing so. This applies by statute in relation to shares issued after 5 April 1998, but a similar exclusion, aimed at the investor who acquires one of two subscriber shares in a company from company formation agents, previously applied by concession (Revenue Pamphlet IR 1, A76).

A '*subsidiary*' for these purposes is a company more than 50% of whose ordinary share capital is at any time in the 'relevant period' owned by the issuing company, regardless of whether or not that condition is fulfilled while the individual falls within (*a*)–(*d*) above in respect of it.

As regards (*a*) above, directorships are taken into account only where the individual or an associate (or a partnership of which either of them is a member) receives or is entitled to receive, during the 'designated period' — see below (as regards shares issued before 6 April 1998, during the 'relevant period'), a payment (whether directly or indirectly or to his order or for his benefit) from the issuing company or a 'related person' other than by way of

(i) payment or reimbursement of allowable expenditure against employment income,

(ii) interest at no more than a commercial rate on money lent,

(iii) dividends etc. representing no more than a normal return on investment,

(iv) payment for supply of goods at no more than market value,

(v) rent at no more than a reasonable and commercial rent for property occupied, or

(vi) any reasonable and necessary remuneration for services rendered (other than secretarial or managerial services, or those rendered by the payer) which is chargeable under Schedule D, Case I or II,

and a '*related person*' is any company of which the individual or an associate is a director and which is a subsidiary of the issuing company, or a partner of the issuing company or a subsidiary, 'subsidiary' for this purpose requiring ownership of more than 50% of ordinary share capital at some time in the 'relevant period'.

For these purposes, in the case of a person who is both a director and an employee of a company, references to him in his capacity as a director include him in his capacity as an employee, but otherwise he is not treated as an employee.

The '*designated period*' for these purposes is

(1)   (for shares issued after 5 April 2000) the period beginning two years before the issue of the shares and ending immediately before the third anniversary of the issue date or, if later and where relevant, the third anniversary of the date of commencement of the intended trade referred to in 25.6(*a*) or (*c*) below; or

(2)   (for shares issued before 6 April 2000) the seven-year period beginning two years before the issue of the shares.

The '*relevant period*' for these purposes is the period beginning with the incorporation of the company or, if later, two years before the date of issue of the shares and ending

(I)   (for shares issued after 5 April 2000) immediately before the third anniversary of the issue date or, if later and where relevant, the third anniversary of the date of commencement of the intended trade referred to in 25.6(*a*) or (*c*) below; or

(II)   (for shares issued before 6 April 2000) five years after the issue date.

(In determining for the purposes of both the above definitions, in relation to shares issued after 16 March 2004, the time at which a qualifying trade begins to be carried on by any 'qualifying 90% subsidiary' (see 25.21 below) of a company, any carrying on of the trade by it before it became such a subsidiary is disregarded.)

An individual who is connected with the issuing company may nevertheless qualify for relief if he is so connected only by reason of his (or his associate's) being a director of (or of a partner of) the issuing company or any subsidiary receiving, or entitled to receive, remuneration (including any benefit or facility) as such, provided that:

(A)   the remuneration (leaving out any within (vi) above) is reasonable remuneration for services rendered to the company as a director;

(B)   he subscribed for eligible shares in the company at a time when he had never been either

(i)   connected with the issuing company, or

(ii)   involved (as sole trader, employee, partner or director) in carrying on its (or its subsidiary's) trade, business, profession or vocation (or any part thereof) (in relation to shares issued before 6 April 1998, an employee of a person who had previously carried on the issuing company's trade etc. or part thereof),

and where those conditions are satisfied in relation to an issue of eligible shares, subsequent issues are treated as fulfilling (B) where they would not otherwise do so, provided that they are made within three years (for shares issued before 6 April 2000, five years) of the date of the last issue which did fulfil (B). Where relevant, and in relation only to shares issued after 5 April 2000, the said three-year period is replaced by a longer period beginning with the date of the last such issue and ending with the date of commencement of the intended trade referred to in 25.6(*a*) or (*c*) below. (In determining for these purposes, in relation to shares issued after 16 March 2004, the time at which a qualifying trade begins to be carried on by any 'qualifying 90% subsidiary' (see 25.21 below) of a company, any carrying on of the trade by it before it became such a subsidiary is disregarded.) For examples of this 'business angels' exception, see Revenue Venture Capital Schemes Manual VCM 25080.

Parallel trades. For shares issued **before 29 November 1994**, relief may be denied if, on the date of issue of the shares (or, if later, the date on which the company commences trading) the individual is both one of a group of persons who either control the company (within *ICTA 1988, s 416*) or together own more than a half share (determined as under *ICTA 1988, s 344(1)(a)(b)(2)(3)*) in the trade carried on by the company, and also, individually or as one of a group, so controls another company or has such an interest in another trade, business, profession or vocation. Where the trade (or a substantial part of it) carried on by

25.4 Enterprise Investment Scheme

the issuing company is concerned with the same or similar types of property or provides the same or similar services or facilities, and serves substantially the same outlets or markets, as the other trade etc. or the trade etc. carried on by the other company, the individual will not qualify for relief in respect of any shares in the issuing company. Rights and powers of associates are taken into account, as are trades etc. carried on by companies more than 50% of whose ordinary share capital is, at the relevant date (as above), owned by the company concerned.

[*ICTA 1988, ss 291, 291A, 291B, 292, 312(1)(1A)(a)(1ZA); FA 1994, Sch 15 paras 5, 6; FA 1995, s 66(2); FA 1998, s 74, Sch 13 paras 6–8, 23, Sch 27 Pt III(14); FA 2000, Sch 17 paras 2, 3, 6(2)–(4); FA 2001, Sch 15 paras 10, 11, 40, Sch 33 Pt II(3); FA 2004, Sch 18 paras 11, 21*].

Simon's Direct Tax Service. See E3.106 *et seq.*

25.4   '*Eligible shares*' are new ordinary shares which, throughout the three years beginning with the date of issue (five years for shares issued before 6 April 2000), carry no present or future preferential right to dividends or to assets on a winding-up and no present or future right (for shares issued before 6 April 1998, present or future preferential right) to redemption. If, for shares issued after 5 April 2000, the company satisfied the qualifying business activity requirement by virtue of 25.6(*a*) or (*c*) below and the trade had not yet commenced on the issue date, these conditions must be satisfied throughout the period from date of issue to immediately before the third anniversary of commencement. (In determining for this purpose, in relation to shares issued after 16 March 2004, the time at which a qualifying trade begins to be carried on by any 'qualifying 90% subsidiary' (see 25.21 below) of a company, any carrying on of the trade etc. by it before it became such a subsidiary is disregarded.) [*ICTA 1988, ss 289(7), 312(1)(1ZA); FA 1994, Sch 15 para 2; FA 1998, s 74, Sch 13 para 1(4), Sch 27 Pt III(14); FA 2000, Sch 17 paras 1, 6(3), 8; FA 2004, Sch 18 paras 11, 21*].

25.5   A '*qualifying company*' may be resident in the UK or elsewhere. It must, throughout the 'relevant period' (see 25.6 below), either

(*a*)   exist wholly for the purpose of carrying on one or more 'qualifying trades' (see 25.7 below) (disregarding purposes incapable of having any significant effect on the extent of the company's activities), or

(*b*)   be the 'parent company of a trading group'.

For the ascertainment of the purposes for which a company exists, see Revenue Venture Capital Schemes Manual VCM 15070.

Before 7 March 2001, it was also a condition that the company be 'unquoted' throughout the 'relevant period' (as in 25.6 below). This is replaced from that date by a condition that it be 'unquoted' when the shares are issued and that no arrangements then exist for it to cease to be unquoted. If, at the time of issue, arrangements exist for the company to become a wholly-owned subsidiary of a new holding company by means of a share exchange within 25.23 below, no arrangements must exist for the new company to cease to be unquoted. A company is '*unquoted*' if none of its shares etc. are listed on a recognised stock exchange or on a foreign exchange designated for the purpose, or dealt in on the Unlisted Securities Market (now closed) or outside the UK by such means as may be designated for the purpose. Securities on the Alternative Investment Market ('AIM') are treated as unquoted for these purposes. (Revenue Press Release 20 February 1995). If it is unquoted at the time of the share issue, it does not cease to be unquoted in relation to those shares solely because they are listed on an exchange which becomes a recognised stock exchange or is designated by an order made after the date of the issue (see Revenue Venture Capital Schemes Manual VCM 15020).

The '*parent company of a trading group*' is a company all of whose subsidiaries are 'qualifying subsidiaries' (i.e. within 25.21 below) provided that, in relation to the business consisting of the activities, taken together, of the company and its subsidiaries, neither the business nor a substantial part of it (i.e. broadly 20% — see Revenue Venture Capital Schemes Manual VCM 17040) consists in either or both of

(I)   excluded activities within 25.7(*a*)–(*m*) below (with the same exceptions from (*e*) as are set out in the following text in 25.7), and

(II)   non-trading activities (not including, as regards shares issued after 5 April 1998, research and development (as defined) and, before 7 March 2001, oil exploration).

Activities are for this purpose disregarded to the extent that they consist (*a*) in holding shares in or securities of, or making loans to, any of the company's subsidiaries, or (*b*) in holding and managing property used by the company or any of its subsidiaries either for research and development (as defined) from which a 'qualifying trade' (see 25.7 below) to be carried on by any of them is intended to be derived, or for the purposes of a 'qualifying trade' or trades carried on by any of them. They are similarly disregarded to the extent that they consist in making loans to the company or, in the case of a subsidiary whose main purpose is the carrying on of 'qualifying trade(s)' and whose other purposes are incapable of significantly affecting the extent of its activities (other than in relation to incidental matters), in activities not in pursuance of its main purpose.

Although a winding-up or dissolution in the relevant period generally prevents a company meeting the above conditions, they are deemed met if the winding-up or dissolution is for *bona fide* commercial reasons and not part of a scheme a main purpose of which is tax avoidance, with the additional proviso before 21 March 2000 that any net assets are distributed to members (or dealt with as *bona vacantia*) before the end of the relevant period or (if later) the end of three years from the commencement of winding-up. After 20 March 2000 (both in relation to shares issued after that date and to pre-existing shares to which EIS income tax relief or capital gains tax deferral relief remains attributable), a company does not cease to meet the above conditions by reason of anything done as a consequence of its being in administration or receivership (both as defined by *ICTA 1988, s 312(2A)*), provided everything so done and the making of the relevant order are for *bona fide* commercial (and not tax avoidance) reasons. For shares issued after 16 March 2004, these provisions are extended to refer also to the winding-up, dissolution, administration or receivership of any of the company's subsidiaries.

The company must not at any time in the relevant period either

(i)   (in relation to shares issued before 6 April 1998) have share capital which includes any issued shares not fully paid up (or which would not be fully paid up if any undertaking to pay cash to the company at a future date were disregarded), or

(ii)   (subject to 25.23 below) control another company other than a qualifying subsidiary (see 25.21 below), 'control' being construed in accordance with *ICTA 1988, s 416(2)–(6)* and being considered with or without connected persons within *ICTA 1988, s 839*, or

(iii) (subject to 25.23 below) be a 51% subsidiary of another company or otherwise under the control of another company, 'control' being construed in accordance with *ICTA 1988, s 840* (after 20 March 2000, previously in accordance with *ICTA 1988, s 416(2)–(6)*) and again being considered with or without connected persons, or

(iv)   be capable of falling within (ii) or (iii) by virtue of any arrangements (as very broadly defined).

In relation to shares issued after 16 March 2004, the company must not at any time in the relevant period have a 'property managing subsidiary' which is not a 'qualifying 90%

25.6 Enterprise Investment Scheme

subsidiary' (see 25.21 below) of the company. A '*property managing subsidiary*' is a subsidiary whose business consists wholly or mainly in the holding or managing of 'land' or any 'property deriving its value from land' (both as defined in *ICTA 1988, s 776* (see 3.10 ANTI-AVOIDANCE).

Gross assets test. In relation to shares issued after 5 April 1998, the value of the company's gross assets must not exceed £15 million immediately before the issue of EIS shares and must not exceed £16 million immediately afterwards. If the company has 'qualifying subsidiaries' (see 25.21 below), the test applies by reference to the aggregate gross assets of the company and all such subsidiaries (disregarding certain assets held by any such company which correspond to liabilities of another). The general approach of the Revenue to the gross assets test is that the value of a company's gross assets is the sum of the value of all of the balance sheet assets. Where accounts are actually drawn up to a date immediately before or after the issue, the balance sheet values are taken provided that they reflect usual accounting standards and the company's normal accounting practice, consistently applied. Where accounts are not drawn up to such a date, such values will be taken from the most recent balance sheet, updated as precisely as practicable on the basis of all the relevant information available to the company. Values so arrived at may need to be reviewed in the light of information contained in the accounts for the period in which the issue was made, and, if they were not available at the time of the issue, those for the preceding period, when they become available. The company's assets immediately before the issue do not include any advance payment received in respect of the issue. Where shares are issued partly paid, the right to the balance is an asset, and, notwithstanding the above, will be taken into account in valuing the assets immediately after the issue regardless of whether it is shown in the balance sheet. (Revenue Pamphlet IR 131, SP 2/00, 3 August 2000).

The Treasury may, by statutory instrument, amend any of the above provisions in relation to shares issued after 16 March 1998.

[*ICTA 1988, ss 293, 298(4), 312(1)–(1E)(2A); FA 1994, Sch 15 para 7; FA 1997, Sch 8 paras 1, 4; FA 1998, ss 70(2)(4), 74, Sch 13 paras 9, 23, Sch 27 Pt III(14); FA 2000, Sch 17 paras 9(1)(4), 10–12, 14, 15; FA 2001, Sch 15 paras 4, 12–14, 40; FA 2004, Sch 18 paras 5, 21*].

Informal clearance. Enquiries from companies as to whether they meet the conditions of the EIS should be directed to Small Company Enterprise Centre, TIDO, Ty Glas, Llanishen, Cardiff CF14 5ZG (tel. 029–2032 7400; fax 029–2032 7398; e-mail enterprise.centre@ir.gsi.gov.uk). However, where subscribers to the same issue of shares are expected to include company applicants claiming relief under the Corporate Venturing Scheme (see Tolley's Corporation Tax under Corporate Venturing Scheme), and the issuing company seeks formal advance clearance under that scheme, any request for informal EIS clearance should accompany the Corporate Venturing Scheme clearance application.

Simon's Direct Tax Service. See E3.115 *et seq.*

25.6   Any of the following is a '*qualifying business activity*' in relation to the issuing company.

(*a*)   (In relation to EIS shares issued on or before 16 March 2004) the issuing company or any subsidiary (within *ICTA 1988, s 308* — see 25.21 below) carrying on a 'qualifying trade' which it is carrying on on the date of issue of the shares, or preparing to carry on such a trade which, on the date of issue of the shares, it intends to carry on 'wholly or mainly in the UK' and which it begins to carry on within two years after that date; provided that, at any time in the 'relevant period' when the qualifying trade is carried on, it is carried on wholly or mainly in the UK.

(*b*)   (In relation to EIS shares issued on or before 16 March 2004) the issuing company or any subsidiary carrying on either 'research and development' or, before 7 March

2001, oil exploration, which it is carrying on on the date of issue of the shares, or which it begins to carry on immediately afterwards, and from which it is intended will be derived a 'qualifying trade' which the company or a subsidiary will carry on 'wholly or mainly in the UK'; provided that, at any time in the 'relevant period' when the research and development or the 'qualifying trade' derived from it is carried on, it is carried on wholly or mainly in the UK.

(c)   (In relation to EIS shares issued after 16 March 2004) the issuing company or any 'qualifying 90% subsidiary' (see 25.21 below) (i) carrying on a 'qualifying trade' which, on the date of issue of the shares, the company or any such subsidiary is carrying on or (ii) preparing to carry on such a trade which, on the date of issue of the shares, is intended to be carried on 'wholly or mainly in the UK' by the company or any such subsidiary and which is begun to be so carried on within two years after that date or (iii) actually carrying on the trade mentioned in (ii) above; provided that, at any time in the 'relevant period' when the 'qualifying trade' is so carried on, it is carried on wholly or mainly in the UK.

(d)   (In relation to EIS shares issued after 16 March 2004) the issuing company or any 'qualifying 90% subsidiary' (see 25.21 below) carrying on 'research and development' which, on the date of issue of the shares, the company or any such subsidiary is carrying on or which company or any such subsidiary begins to carry on immediately afterwards, and from which it is intended will be derived a 'qualifying trade' which the company or any such subsidiary will carry on 'wholly or mainly in the UK'; provided that, at any time in the 'relevant period' when the research and development or the qualifying trade derived from it is carried on, it is carried on wholly or mainly in the UK.

As regards (a) and (c) above, 'preparing' to carry on a trade covers both the setting up of a new trade and the acquisition of an existing trade from its present owner. It does not cover preliminary activities such as market research aimed at discovering whether a trade would be likely to succeed or raising capital or research and development. (Revenue Venture Capital Schemes Manual VCM 20030).

As regards (b) above, in relation to oil exploration, there were further conditions relating to exploration and appraisal or development licences.

In relation to shares issued after 5 April 2000, '*research and development*' in (b) and (d) above has the meaning given by *ICTA 1988, s 837A* (see 71.70 SCHEDULE D, CASES I AND II and note that the latest DTI guidelines issued on 5 March 2004 have no effect in relation to shares issued before 6 April 2004). Previously, it meant any activity intended to result in a patentable invention (within *Patents Act 1977*) or in a computer program.

In determining for the purposes of (c) and (d) above the time at which a qualifying trade or research and development begins to be carried on by a qualifying 90% subsidiary of the issuing company, any carrying on of the trade etc. by it before it became such a subsidiary is disregarded.

The '*relevant period*' for these purposes is the period beginning with the date of issue of the shares and ending either three years after that date or, where (a) or (c) above applies and the company (or subsidiary) was not carrying on the 'qualifying trade' on that date, three years after the date on which it begins to carry on the trade. In determining for these purposes, in relation to shares issued after 16 March 2004, the time at which a qualifying trade begins to be carried on by any 'qualifying 90% subsidiary' (see 25.21 below) of a company, any carrying on of the trade by it before it became such a subsidiary is disregarded.

[*ICTA 1988, s 289(2)(3A)(4)(5)(8), s 312(1)(1A)(b)(1ZA); FA 1994, Sch 15 para 2; FA 2000, Sch 17 paras 6(4), 15; FA 2001, Sch 15 paras 2(b)(c), 40; FA 2004, Sch 18 para 1(4)(6), paras 11, 21*].

25.7 Enterprise Investment Scheme

In considering whether a trade is carried on '*wholly or mainly in the UK*', the totality of the trade activities is taken into account. Regard will be had, for example, to where capital assets are held, where any purchasing, processing, manufacturing and selling is done, and where the company employees and other agents are engaged in its trading operations. For trades involving the provision of services, both the location of the activities giving rise to the services and the location where they are delivered will be relevant. No one factor is itself likely to be decisive in any particular case. A company may carry on some such activities outside the UK and yet satisfy the requirement, provided that the major part of them, that is over one-half of the aggregate of these activities, takes place within the UK. Thus relief is not excluded solely because a company's products or services are exported, or because its raw materials are imported, or because its raw materials or products are stored abroad. Similar principles apply in considering the trade(s) carried on by a company and its qualifying subsidiaries.

In the particular case of a ship chartering trade, the test is satisfied if all charters are entered into in the UK and the provision of crews and management of the ships while under charter take place mainly in the UK. If these conditions are not met, the test may still be satisfied depending on all the relevant facts and circumstances.

(Revenue Pamphlet IR 131, SP 3/00, 3 August 2000).

For the manner in which the scheme operates where a company wishes to raise money by a single issue of shares for more than one qualifying business activity (e.g. for a trade carried on by one subsidiary and for research and development carried on by another), see Revenue Tax Bulletin April 1996 pp 305, 306.

Simon's Direct Tax Service. See E3.125 *et seq.*

25.7   To be a '*qualifying trade*' a trade may not, at any time in the 'relevant period' (as defined in 25.6 above), consist to a substantial extent of, or of a combination of:

(*a*)   dealing in land, commodities or futures, or in shares, securities or other financial instruments; or

(*b*)   dealing in goods otherwise than in an ordinary trade of wholesale or retail distribution (see below); or

(*c*)   banking, insurance or any other financial activities; or

(*d*)   (before 7 March 2001) oil extraction activities (but without prejudice to relief in respect of oil exploration (see 25.6(*b*) above) for which the activities would otherwise qualify); or

(*e*)   leasing or letting or receiving royalties or licence fees; or

(*f*)   providing legal or accountancy services; or

(*g*)   'property development';

(*h*)   farming or market gardening;

(*j*)   holding, managing or occupying woodlands, any other forestry activities or timber production;

(*k*)   operating or managing hotels or comparable establishments (including guest houses, hostels and other establishments whose main purpose is to offer overnight accommodation with or without catering) or property used as such;

(*l*)   operating or managing nursing homes or residential care homes (both as defined) or property used as such;

(*m*)   providing services or facilities for any trade, profession or vocation concerned in (*a*) to (*l*) and carried on by another person (other than a parent company), where one person has a 'controlling interest' in both trades.

As regards (*f*) above, the provision of the services of accountancy personnel is the provision of accountancy services (*Castleton Management Services Ltd v Kirkwood (Sp C 276), [2001] SSCD 95*).

Exclusions (*g*)–(*l*) (and the reference to those in exclusion (*m*)) apply in relation to shares issued **after 16 March 1998**. Exclusions (*k*) and (*l*) apply only if the person carrying on the activity in question has an estate or interest (e.g. a lease) in the property concerned or occupies that property.

Adventures and concerns in the nature of trade, and trades not carried on commercially and with a view to the realisation of profits, are also generally excluded.

The Revenue regard as 'substantial' for the above purposes a part of a trade which consists of 20% or more of total activities, judged by any reasonable measure (normally turnover or capital employed). (Revenue Venture Capital Schemes Manual VCM 17040). As regards (*a*) above, dealing in land includes cases where steps are taken, before selling the land, to make it more attractive to a purchaser; such steps might include the refurbishment of existing buildings. (Revenue Venture Capital Schemes Manual VCM 17050).

As regards (*b*) above, a trade of wholesale or retail distribution is a trade consisting of the offer of goods for sale either to persons for resale (or processing and resale) (which resale must be to members of the general public) by them ('*wholesale*') or to the general public ('*retail*'), and a trade is not an ordinary wholesale or retail trade if it consists to a substantial extent of dealing in goods collected or held as an investment (or of that and any other activity within (*a*)–(*m*) above), and a substantial proportion of such goods is held for a significantly longer period than might reasonably be expected for a vendor trying to dispose of them at market value. Whether such trades are 'ordinary' is to be judged having regard to the following features, those under (A) supporting the categorisation as 'ordinary', those under (B) being indicative to the contrary.

(A) (i) The breaking of bulk.

(ii) The purchase and sale of goods in different markets.

(iii) The employment of staff and incurring of trade expenses other than the cost of goods or of remuneration of persons connected (within *ICTA 1988, s 839*) with company carrying on such a trade.

(B) (i) The purchase or sale of goods from or to persons connected (within *ICTA 1988, s 839*) with the trader.

(ii) The matching of purchases with sales.

(iii) The holding of goods for longer than might normally be expected.

(iv) The carrying on of the trade at a place not commonly used for wholesale or retail trading.

(v) The absence of physical possession of the goods by the trader.

As regards the application of (*e*) above in relation to shares issued after 5 April 2000, a trade is not excluded from being a qualifying trade solely because at some time in the relevant period it consists to a substantial extent in the receiving of royalties or licence fees substantially attributable (in terms of value) to the exploitation of 'relevant intangible assets'. An intangible asset is an asset falling to be treated as such under generally accepted accounting practice (see 71.30 SCHEDULE D, CASES I AND II), including all intellectual property and also industrial information and techniques (see Revenue Venture Capital Schemes Manual VCM 17310). A '*relevant intangible asset*' is an asset the whole or greater part of which (in terms of value) has been created by the company carrying on the trade or by a company which throughout the creation of the asset was the 'parent company' of that company or a qualifying subsidiary (within 25.21 below) of that parent company. A '*parent*

25.7 Enterprise Investment Scheme

company' is for these purposes a company with one or more 51% subsidiaries which is not itself a 51% subsidiary. Where the asset is 'intellectual property', it is treated as created by a company only if the right to exploit it vests in that company (alone or with others). The term *'intellectual property'* incorporates patents, trade marks, copyrights, design rights etc. and foreign equivalents.

As regards the application of (*e*) above in relation to shares issued before 6 April 2000, a company engaged throughout the relevant period in the production of original master films, tapes or discs is not excluded from the scheme by reason only of its receipt by way of trade of royalties or licence fees, provided that all royalties and licence fees received by it in the relevant period are in respect of films etc. produced by it in that relevant period or in respect of by-products arising therefrom. The company may also be engaged in the distribution of films produced by it in the relevant period. Similarly royalties and licence fees attributable to research and development which a company carrying on a trade has engaged in throughout the relevant period do not prevent the trade being a qualifying trade.

Also as regards (*e*) above, a trade will not be excluded by reason only of its consisting of letting ships, other than offshore installations (previously oil rigs) or pleasure craft (as defined), on charter, provided that

(i) the company beneficially owns all the ships it so lets,

(ii) every ship beneficially owned by the company is UK-registered,

(iii) throughout the relevant period, the company is solely responsible for arranging the marketing of the services of its ships, and

(iv) in relation to every letting on charter, certain conditions as to length and terms of charter, and the arm's length character of the transaction, are fulfilled,

and if any of (i)–(iv) above is not fulfilled in relation to certain lettings, only those lettings are taken into account in determining whether a substantial part of the trade consists of activities within (*a*)–(*m*) above.

In relation to (*e*) above, in the Revenue Tax Bulletin August 2001 pp 877, 878, the Revenue set out their views on the scope of the exclusions. The *leasing and letting* exclusion covers all cases where (subject to reasonable conditions imposed by the trader) the customer is free to use the property for the purpose for which it is intended, e.g. television rental, video hire and the provision of self-storage warehousing facilities. In the case of car hire, a distinction has to be drawn between the provision of a *transportation service* and that of a *transportation facility*, only the latter falling within the exclusion. A taxi service would usually fall within the former category, a chauffeured car hire within the latter. *Royalties and licence fees* are received where property rights are exploited by the granting of permission to others to make use of the property. There will, however, be cases (e.g. the retailing of CDs) where, although the sales are made under licence, the receipts are nevertheless consideration for the supply of goods. In the case of *licence fees*, the grant of the right to use the property is often incidental to the supply of services (e.g. a cinema ticket), and the exclusion does not apply in such cases. The principle can be illustrated in relation to sports and leisure facilities provision. Simply making sports facilities available to the general public, with no service provision, would involve the receipt of licence fees. In the more commonly encountered activity of a health club providing a high level of services, including active supervision and advice from qualified staff, the licence to enter the premises and use the equipment would be merely incidental. Similarly where, although there is no direct provision of services, continuous work is required to keep the property in a fit state for use, the question to be considered is the extent to which the fees relate to the cost of such work.

'*Property development*' in (g) above means the development of land by a company, which has (or has had at any time) an 'interest in the land' (as defined), with the sole or main object of realising a gain from the disposal of an interest in the developed land.

As regards (*m*) above, a person has a '*controlling interest*' in a trade carried on by a company if he controls (within *ICTA 1988, s 416*) the company; or if the company is close and he or an 'associate' is a director of the company and the owner of, or able to control, more than 30% of its ordinary share capital; or if at least half of its ordinary share capital is directly or indirectly owned by him. In any other case it is obtained by his being entitled to at least half of the assets used for, or income arising from, the trade. In either case, the rights and powers of a person's 'associates' are attributed to him. '*Associate*' is as under *ICTA 1988, s 417(3)(4)*, but excluding brothers and sisters.

The Treasury may, by statutory instrument, amend any of the above conditions.

[*ICTA 1988, ss 297, 298; FA 1994, Sch 15 paras 10, 11; FA 1997, Sch 8 para 5; FA 1998, Sch 12 paras 1, 2, 5(1), Sch 13 paras 10, 11; FA 2000, Sch 17 para 13; FA 2001, Sch 15 paras 5, 40; FA 2004, Sch 27 para 4*].

Simon's Direct Tax Service. See E3.126 *et seq.*

25.8 **FORM OF RELIEF**

Relief is (except as below) given for the year of assessment in which the shares were issued, by a reduction in what would otherwise be the individual's income tax liability by the lesser of

(*a*)   tax at the lower rate (currently 20%) for the year on the amount (or aggregate amounts) subscribed for eligible shares in respect of which he is eligible for relief (subject to the minimum and maximum subscription figures at 25.10 below), and

(*b*)   an amount sufficient to reduce that liability to nil.

The income tax reduction under this chapter is made in priority to any of the following:

(i)   an income tax reduction due in respect of personal reliefs (see 1.15, 1.16, 1.17, 1.18 ALLOWANCES AND TAX RATES) or qualifying maintenance payments (see 47.8 MARRIED PERSONS);

(ii)   an income tax reduction due in respect of interest relief (see 43.5 INTEREST PAYABLE);

(iii)   an income tax reduction due in respect of medical insurance (see 48.1 MEDICAL INSURANCE);

(iv)   an income tax reduction due in respect of COMMUNITY INVESTMENT TAX RELIEF (17);

(v)   a reduction of liability to tax by way of DOUBLE TAX RELIEF (24).

The income tax reduction under this chapter is, however, made *after* any income tax reduction due in respect of investments in VENTURE CAPITAL TRUSTS (91).

In determining the individual's income tax liability from which the reduction under this chapter is to be made, no account is taken of any basic rate tax on income the tax on which the individual is entitled to charge against any other person or to deduct, retain or satisfy out of any payment. This includes any basic rate tax deemed to have been deducted at source from a charitable donation made after 5 April 2000 under the Gift Aid scheme (see 14.12 CHARITIES). Any such basic rate tax cannot, therefore, be extinguished by EIS income tax relief.

Where shares in respect of which the individual is eligible for relief are issued before 6 October in a year of assessment, he may claim relief as if up to one half of the shares had been issued in the preceding year of assessment, subject to an overall limit of £25,000 on the amount of subscriptions which may be so treated. See 16.2 CLAIMS for general provisions regarding claims for payments made in one year of assessment to be carried back to an earlier year.

[*ICTA 1988, s 289A(1)–(5); FA 1990, s 25(6)(b)(7); FA 1994, Sch 15 para 2; FA 1998, s 74, Sch 13 para 2; FA 2000, s 39(6)(10); FA 2002, s 57, Sch 17 para 2*].

Relief for loss on disposal. ICTA 1988, s 574 (see 46.15 LOSSES), which grants income tax relief for certain losses on shares in unquoted trading companies, applies on the disposal by an individual of shares to which relief is attributable (see below) as it applies to shares in 'qualifying trading companies' under that *section. ICTA 1988, ss 575(1)(3), 576(1)–(3)* are similarly applied for this purpose (though *section 576(1)* was not so applied for disposals before 6 April 1998). [*ICTA 1988, s 305A; FA 1994, Sch 15 para 20; FA 1998, Sch 13 para 18*].

Attribution of relief to shares. Subject to any reduction or withdrawal of relief (see 25.12 *et seq.* below), where an individual's income tax liability is reduced for a year of assessment as above by reason of an issue or issues of shares made (or treated as made) in that year, the income tax reduction is attributed to that issue or those issues (being apportioned in the latter case according to the amount subscribed for each issue). Issues of shares of the same class by a company to an individual on the same day are treated as a single issue for this purpose. A proportionate amount of the reduction attributed to an issue is attributed to each share in the issue (and adjusted correspondingly for any subsequent bonus issue of shares of the same class and carrying the same rights).

An issue to an individual part of which is treated as having been made in the preceding year (as above) is treated as two separate issues, one made on a day in the previous year, for the purposes of the above and other specified provisions.

Where relief attributable to an issue of shares falls to be withdrawn or reduced, the relief attributable to each of the shares in question is reduced to nil (if relief is withdrawn) or proportionately reduced (where relief is reduced).

[*ICTA 1988, s 289B; FA 1994, Sch 15 para 2; FA 1998, s 74, Sch 13 para 3; FA 2004, Sch 18 paras 3, 21*].

On a *reorganisation of share capital* falling within *TCGA 1992, s 126(2)(a)* (i.e. where shares or debentures are allotted in proportion to an existing holding), the relief attributable to shares is reduced where both the amount subscribed for the shares and their market value immediately before the reorganisation exceed their market value immediately after the reorganisation. The reduction is in the same proportion as the lower of those two excesses bears to the amount subscribed for the shares. A similar reduction applies where, at any time in the 'relevant period' (see 25.3 above), rights on such a reorganisation are disposed of, and the reduction would have applied had the rights not been disposed of but the allotment made by virtue of the rights. No reduction applies, however, where the reorganisation occurred, or the rights were disposed of, after 28 November 1994. [*ICTA 1988, s 305; FA 1994, Sch 15 para 19; FA 1995, s 66(4)*].

Simon's Direct Tax Service. See E3.140 *et seq.*

25.9 *Example*

Mr Jones is a married man with a salary of £55,000 per annum and no other income. Both he and his wife were born after 5 April 1935. In 2003/04 he subscribes for ordinary shares in two unquoted companies issuing shares under the enterprise investment scheme (EIS).

A Ltd was formed by some people in Mr Jones' neighbourhood to publish a local newspaper. 200,000 ordinary £1 shares were issued at par in August 2003 and the company started trading in September 2003. Mr Jones subscribed for 16,000 of the shares. Mr Jones becomes a director of A Ltd in September 2003, receiving director's fees of £5,000 per annum (£2,500 in 2003/04), a level of remuneration which is considered reasonable for services rendered by him to the company in his capacity as a director.

B Ltd, which is controlled by an old friend of Mr Jones, has acquired the rights to manufacture in the UK a new type of industrial cleaning solvent and requires additional finance. Mr Jones subscribed for 8,000 ordinary £1 shares at a premium of £1.50 per share in October 2003. The issue increases the company's issued share capital to 25,000 ordinary £1 shares.

Mr Jones will obtain tax relief in 2003/04 as follows.

Amount eligible for relief

	£
A Ltd notes (*a*) and (*b*)	16,000
B Ltd note (*c*)	Nil
Total (being less than the 2003/04 maximum of £150,000)	£16,000

	£
Salary	55,000
Director's remuneration (A Ltd)	2,500
Total income	57,500
Deduct Personal allowance	4,615
Taxable income	£52,885

	£
Tax payable:	
1,960 @ 10%	196.00
28,540 @ 22%	6,278.80
22,385 @ 40%	8,954.00
	15,428.80
Deduct EIS relief £16,000 @ 20%	3,200.00
Net tax liability 2003/04	£12,228.80

Notes

(*a*)   Mr Jones is entitled to relief on the full amount of his investment in A Ltd regardless of the amount of relief claimed by other investors.

(*b*)   The fact that Mr Jones becomes a paid director of A Ltd *after* an issue to him of eligible shares does not prevent his qualifying for relief in respect of those shares providing his remuneration as a director is reasonable and he is not otherwise connected with the company (see 25.3 above).

(*c*)   Mr Jones is not entitled to relief against his income for his investment of £20,000 in B Ltd. As a result of the share issue he owns more than 30% of the issued ordinary share capital (8,000 out of 25,000 shares) and is therefore regarded as connected with the company and denied relief. See 25.3 above.

In 2004/05 Mr Jones subscribes for shares in three more unquoted companies trading in the UK and issuing shares under the EIS.

25.9   Enterprise Investment Scheme

C Ltd is a local company engaged in the manufacture of car components. It issues a further 300,000 ordinary £1 shares at £1.80 per share in June 2004 and Mr Jones subscribes for 7,500 shares costing £13,500, increasing his stake in the company to 2%. He had originally held 13,500 shares, acquired by purchase at arm's length in May 2002 for £16,200.

D Ltd has been trading as a hotel and restaurant company for several years and requires an injection of capital to finance a new restaurant. Mr Jones and three other unconnected individuals each subscribe for 18,750 ordinary £1 shares at par in November 2004. The balance of 120,000 shares are held by Mr Jones' sister and niece.

E Ltd is an electronics company controlled by two cousins of Mr Jones. The company is seeking £2.5 million extra capital to enable it to expand and take advantage of new computer technology and raises it via the EIS. Mr Jones subscribes for 183,500 ordinary £1 shares at par in December 2004.

Mr Jones's salary is increased to £60,000 for 2004/05.

If he makes the optimum claims Mr Jones will obtain tax relief as follows

2003/04
C Ltd (note (*a*)) £6,750 @ 20% =   £1,350

2004/05

Amount eligible for relief

	£
C Ltd (£13,500 – £6,750 carried back)	6,750
D Ltd	18,750
E Ltd	183,500
Total	£209,000

But amount eligible for relief restricted to subscriptions of   £200,000

Relief given

	£
Salary	60,000
Director's remuneration	5,000
Total income	65,000
Deduct Personal allowance	4,745
Taxable income	£60,255

Tax payable:	
2,020 @ 10%	202.00
29,380 @ 22%	6,463.60
28,855 @ 40%	11,542.00
	18,207.60
Deduct EIS relief:	
£200,000 @ 20% = £40,000, but restricted to	18,207.60
Net tax liability 2004/05	Nil

Attribution of relief to shares (note (*b*))

$£$

C Ltd shares $\dfrac{6,750}{209,000} \times £18,208$ 588

D Ltd shares $\dfrac{18,750}{209,000} \times £18,208$ 1,633

E Ltd shares $\dfrac{183,500}{209,000} \times £18,208$ 15,987

$£18,208$

Notes

(*a*) Since the C Ltd shares were issued before 6 October 2004, Mr Jones may elect to carry back up to half the amount subscribed, subject to an overriding maximum of £25,000, to the preceding tax year. The relief will be given in addition to that previously claimed for 2003/04 (see above). If Mr Jones had previously claimed relief on say £148,000 in 2003/04 the amount carried back would be restricted to £2,000 as relief in any one year may not be given on subscriptions of more than the annual maximum for that year. See 25.8 above and 25.10 below.

(*b*) Relief is restricted by (i) the £200,000 maximum (see 25.10 below) and (ii) an insufficiency in Mr Jones' tax liability. The relief attributable to each issue of shares (which will be relevant in the event of a disposal of the shares or withdrawal of relief—see 25.12 *et seq.* below) is found by apportioning the income tax reduction by reference to the amounts subscribed for each issue. (For this purpose, half of the C Ltd shares are regarded as having been separately issued in the previous year.) The relief so attributed to each issue is then apportioned equally between all the shares comprised in that issue. See 25.8 above.

25.10 **MINIMUM AND MAXIMUM SUBSCRIPTIONS**

Except in the case of investments through 'approved funds' (see 25.2 above), relief is restricted to investments of £500 or more in any one company in any tax year.

There is in all cases an upper limit of £200,000 for 2004/05 onwards (previously £150,000) on the amount in respect of which an individual may obtain relief in a tax year (regardless of whether the shares were issued in that year or in the following year — see 25.8 above).

[*ICTA 1988, s 290, 311(3); FA 1988, s 53; FA 1994, Sch 15 para 3; FA 1998, s 74, Sch 13 para 4; FA 2004, Sch 18 para 4*].

As regards shares issued before 6 April 1998, there was also a restriction on the total amount of eligible shares which could be issued by a company within a specified period and attract relief. For details, see the 2003/04 and earlier editions.

Simon's Direct Tax Service. See E3.136, E3.141.

25.11 **CLAIMS FOR RELIEF**

A claim for relief in respect of eligible shares issued by a qualifying company in a year of assessment cannot be allowed until the trade (or research and development or, before

25.11 Enterprise Investment Scheme

7 March 2001, oil exploration) has been carried on for four months, but may otherwise be given at any time when it appears that the relief conditions may be satisfied. For shares issued after 16 March 2004, it is made explicit that the trade etc. must have carried on for those months by no person other than the qualifying company or a 'qualifying 90% subsidiary' (see 25.21 below) of that company.

A period shorter than four months is permitted (and a claim can thus be allowed after the trade ceases) if this is by reason only of the winding-up or dissolution of any company or (for shares issued after 20 March 2000) anything done as a consequence of a company being in administration or receivership, provided the winding-up etc. is for *bona fide* commercial reasons and not part of a tax avoidance scheme or arrangements. For shares issued after 16 March 2004, this relaxation applies to research and development (where applicable), having previously applied only to a trade.

[*ICTA 1988, s 289A(6)–(8A); FA 1994, Sch 15 para 2; FA 2000, Sch 17 paras 9(3), 12; FA 2001, Sch 15 paras 3, 40; FA 2004, Sch 18 paras 2, 21*].

A claim for relief must be made not earlier than the end of the four-month period referred to above, and not later than the fifth anniversary of 31 January following the year of assessment for which relief is claimed. The claimant must have received the said certificate before making the claim. The certificate must state that the conditions for relief, except insofar as they fall to be satisfied by the individual, are satisfied in relation to the eligible shares in question. A certificate may not be issued without the inspector's authority; where a notice under *ICTA 1988, s 310(2)* (see 25.25 below), or a notice of certain chargeable events under the EIS capital gains deferral provisions mentioned at 25.24 below, has been given to the inspector, an authority given before receipt of the notice, and not renewed thereafter, has no effect. For appeal purposes, the inspector's refusal to authorise a certificate is treated as the refusal of a claim by the company.

Before issuing such a certificate, the company must supply to the inspector a statement (Form EIS 1) that those conditions were fulfilled from the beginning of the 'relevant period' (see 25.6 above), and that statement must contain such information as the Board may reasonably require, and a declaration that it is correct to the best of the company's knowledge and belief. The statement must be furnished to the inspector within two years after the end of the year of assessment in which the shares in question were issued (or, if the four-month period referred to above ends in the following year, within two years after the end of that four-month period).

If a certificate or statement is made fraudulently or negligently, or a certificate was issued despite being prohibited (as above), the company is liable to a fine of up to £3,000.

Special provisions (see *ICTA 1988, s 311(4)–(6)*) apply in relation to the issue of certificates (Forms EIS 5) where shares are held through an approved fund (see 25.2 above).

No application for postponement of tax pending appeal can be made on the ground that relief is due under these provisions unless a claim has been duly submitted.

For the purposes of INTEREST ON UNPAID TAX (41), tax charged by an assessment is regarded as due and payable notwithstanding that relief is subsequently given on a claim under these provisions, but is regarded as paid on the date on which a claim is made resulting in relief being granted, unless it was either in fact paid earlier or not due and payable until later. Interest is not refunded in respect of any subsequent discharge or repayment of tax giving effect to relief under these provisions.

[*ICTA 1988, ss 306, 311(4)–(6); FA 1994, Sch 15 para 21; FA 1996, ss 134, 135, Sch 20 paras 22, 23, Sch 21 para 7; FA 1998, s 74, Sch 13 para 19, Sch 27 Pt III(14); FA 2001, Sch 15 para 22*].

Relief for a year can only be claimed after the end of the year, and any in-year claims for relief by repayment through self-assessment will be rejected. This does not affect the right to claim a reduction in payments on account (see 78.4 SELF-ASSESSMENT), and relief may still be given through a PAYE (55) coding. (Revenue Tax Bulletin April 2002 p 924).

Simon's Direct Tax Service. See E3.142, F3.143.

25.12   **RESTRICTION OR WITHDRAWAL OF RELIEF**

The following provisions apply to restrict or withdraw relief in certain circumstances. References to a reduction of relief include its reduction to nil, and references to the withdrawal of relief in respect of any shares are to the withdrawal of the relief attributable to those shares (see 25.8 above). Where no relief has yet been given, a reduction applies to reduce the amount which apart from the provision in question would be the relief, and a withdrawal means ceasing to be eligible for relief in respect of the shares in question. [*ICTA 1988, s 312(4); FA 1994, Sch 15 para 27*].

Where an event giving rise to complete withdrawal of relief occurs at the same time as a disposal at a loss, the disposal is regarded as occurring first, so that relief may be only partially withdrawn (as below). (Revenue Venture Capital Schemes Manual VCM 26010).

25.13   **Disposal of shares.** Where eligible shares to which relief is attributable (see 25.8 above) are disposed of (or an option granted the exercise of which would bind the grantor to sell them) before the end of the 'relevant period' (see 25.3 above):

(*a*)   if the disposal is at arm's length, relief attributable to those shares (see 25.8 above) is withdrawn or, if that relief exceeds an amount equal to lower rate tax (for the year in which the relief was given) on the disposal consideration, reduced by that amount;

(*b*)   otherwise, the relief is withdrawn.

Where the relief attributable to the shares was less than the lower rate of tax for the year of issue on the amount subscribed for the issue, the amount referred to in (*a*) above is correspondingly reduced. For this purpose, shares are treated as having been issued in an earlier year where relief was carried back as in 25.8 above.

A share exchange is treated as a disposal for these purposes (Revenue Assessment Procedures Manual AP 4977), unless it occurs after 5 April 1998 and is within *ICTA 1988, s 304A* — see 25.23 below).

For the above purposes, disposals are identified with shares of the same class issued earlier before shares issued later (i.e. first in/first out (FIFO)). For disposals after 5 April 1998, where shares within two or more of the categories listed below were acquired on the same day, any of those shares disposed of (applying the FIFO basis) are treated as disposed of in the order in which they are listed, as follows:

(i)   shares to which neither EIS income tax relief nor EIS capital gains deferral relief (see 25.24 below) is attributable;

(ii)   shares to which deferral relief, but not income tax relief, is attributable;

(iii)   shares to which income tax relief, but not deferral relief, is attributable;

(iv)   shares to which both of those reliefs are attributable.

Any shares within (iii) or (iv) above which are treated as issued on an earlier day by virtue of the carry-back provisions at 25.8 above are to be treated as disposed of before any other shares within the same category. Shares transferred between spouses living together are treated as if they were acquired by the transferee spouse on the day they were issued (see also 25.22 below). Shares comprised in a 'new holding' following a reorganisation to which *TCGA 1992, s 127* applies (see Tolley's Capital Gains Tax under Shares and Securities) are treated as having been acquired when the original shares were acquired.

Relief is also withdrawn where, during the relevant period, an option is granted to the individual, the exercise of which would bind the grantor to purchase shares. There are provisions for identifying the shares to which an option granted after 5 April 1998 relates, where these form part of a larger holding.

[*ICTA 1988, ss 299, 312(4B); FA 1994, Sch 15 para 12; FA 1998, s 74, Sch 13 paras 12, 23(5), Sch 27 Pt III(14)*].

Simon's Direct Tax Service. See E3.146.

25.14 **Loan linked investments.** Relief is denied where

(*a*) a loan is made to the individual subscribing for shares or to an 'associate' (see 25.3 above) by any person at any time in the 'relevant period' (see 25.3 above), and

(*b*) the loan would not have been made, or would not have been made on the same terms, if he had not subscribed, or had not been proposing to subscribe, for the shares.

The granting of credit to, or the assignment of a debt due from, the individual or associate is counted as a loan for these purposes.

[*ICTA 1988, s 299A; FA 1993, s 111(1); FA 1994, Sch 15 para 13*].

For this restriction to apply, the test is whether the lender makes the loan on terms which are connected with the fact that the borrower (or an associate) is subscribing for eligible shares. The prime concern is why the lender made the loan rather than why the borrower applied for it. Relief would not be disallowed, for example, in the case of a bank loan if the bank would have made a loan on the same terms to a similar borrower for a different purpose. But if, for example, a loan is made specifically on a security consisting of or including the eligible shares (other than as part of a broad range of assets to which the lender has recourse), relief would be denied. Relevant features of the loan terms would be the qualifying conditions to be satisfied by the borrower, any incentives or benefits offered to the borrower, the time allowed for repayment, the amount of repayments and interest charged, the timing of interest payments, and the nature of the security. (Revenue Pamphlet IR 131, SP 6/98, 30 November 1998, replacing SP 3/94, 9 May 1994, as revised).

Simon's Direct Tax Service. See E3.149.

25.15 **Pre-arranged exits.** In relation to shares issued after 1 July 1997, relief is denied if arrangements (as very broadly defined) under which the shares are issued to an individual (or arrangements preceding the issue but relating to it)

(*a*) provide for the eventual disposal by the investor of the shares in question or other shares or securities of the company; or

(*b*) provide for the eventual cessation of a trade of the company or of a person connected with it; or

(*c*) provide for the eventual disposal of all, or a substantial part of, the assets of the company or of a person connected with it; or

(*d*) provide (by means of any insurance, indemnity, guarantee or otherwise) complete or partial protection for investors against the normal risks attaching to EIS investment (but excluding arrangements which merely protect the company and/or its subsidiaries against normal trading risks).

Arrangements with a view to the company becoming a wholly-owned subsidiary of a new holding company within the terms of *ICTA 1988, s 304A* (see 25.23 below) are excluded from (*a*) above. Arrangements applicable only on an unanticipated winding-up of the company for commercial reasons are excluded from (*b*) and (*c*) above.

[*ICTA 1988, ss 299B, 312(1); FA 1998, s 71(1)(5); FA 2000, Sch 17 para 14, Sch 40 Pt II(5)*].

Simon's Direct Tax Service. See **E3.141**.

25.16   **Value received from company.** Where an individual subscribes for eligible shares in a company, and during the 'period of restriction' that individual 'receives value' (other than 'insignificant value') from the company, any relief attributable to those shares (see 25.8 above) and not previously reduced in respect of the 'value received' is withdrawn or, if that relief exceeds an amount equal to lower rate tax (for the year in which the relief was given) on the 'value received', reduced by that amount. That amount is correspondingly reduced where the relief attributable to the shares was less than the lower rate of tax for the year of issue on the amount subscribed for the issue.

The '*period of restriction*' is the period beginning one year before the issue of eligible shares and ending immediately before the third anniversary of the issue date or, if later and where relevant, the third anniversary of the date of commencement of the intended trade referred to in 25.6(*a*) or (*c*) above. (In determining for these purposes, in relation to shares issued after 16 March 2004, the time at which a qualifying trade begins to be carried on by any 'qualifying 90% subsidiary' (see 25.21 below) of a company, any carrying on of the trade by it before it became such a subsidiary is disregarded.)

As regards value received before 7 March 2001 in respect of shares issued before that date, these provisions operated by reference to receipts of value during the 'designated period' as in 25.3 above (as regards shares issued before 6 April 1998, during the 'relevant period' as in 25.3 above). There was no let-out for receipts of insignificant value.

As regards shares issued on or after 6 April 1998, the provisions apply equally to 'value received' from a person who is connected (within *ICTA 1988, s 839* — see 19 CONNECTED PERSONS) with the issuing company at any time in the relevant period (whether or not at the time value is received). As regards shares issued before that date, it applied to 'value received' from a company which is a 51% subsidiary of the issuing company (i.e. a company more than 50% of whose ordinary share capital it owns) at any time in the relevant period (whether before or after the value is received).

An individual '*receives value*' from a company if it:

(*a*)   repays, redeems or repurchases any part of his holding of its share capital or securities, or makes any payment to him for giving up rights on its cancellation or extinguishment; or

(*b*)   (in relation to shares issued after 16 March 2004) repays, in pursuance of any arrangements for or in connection with the acquisition of the shares in respect of which the relief is claimed, any debt owed to him other than one incurred by the company on or after the date of issue of those shares and otherwise than in consideration of the extinguishment of a debt incurred before that date; (but if the debt was incurred on or before 16 March 2004 but on or after the date the shares were subscribed for, (*ba*) below applies instead of the foregoing); or

(*ba*)   (in relation to shares issued on or before 16 March 2004) repays, whether or not in pursuance of any such arrangements as are referred to in (*b*) above, any debt owed to him other than one incurred by the company on or after the date on which he subscribed for the shares in respect of which the relief is claimed and otherwise than in consideration of the extinguishment of a debt incurred before that date; or

(c)   pays him for the cancellation of any debt owed to him other than an '*ordinary trade debt*' (i.e. one incurred for normal trade supply of goods or services on normal trade credit terms (not in any event exceeding six months)) or one in respect of a payment falling within 25.3(i) or (vi) above; or

(d)   releases or waives any liability of his to the company (which it is deemed to have done if discharge of the liability is twelve months or more overdue) or discharges or undertakes to discharge any liability of his to a third person; or

(e)   makes a loan or advance to him (defined as including the deferring by him of any debt either to the company (other than an 'ordinary trade debt' (as above)) or to a third person but assigned to the company) which has not been repaid in full before the issue of the shares; or

(f)   provides a benefit or facility for him; or

(g)   transfers an asset to him for no consideration or for consideration less than market value, or acquires an asset from him for consideration exceeding market value; or

(h)   makes any other payment to him except one either falling within 25.3(i)–(vi) above or in discharge of an 'ordinary trade debt' (as above); or

(j)   is wound up or dissolved in circumstances such that the company does not thereby cease to be a 'qualifying company' (see 25.5 above), and he thereby receives any payment or asset in respect of ordinary shares held by him.

However, an individual does *not* receive value from a company by reason only of the payment to him (or to an associate) of reasonable remuneration (including any benefit or facility) for services as a company director, and for this purpose, if the individual is also an employee of the company, references to him in his capacity as a director include him in his capacity as an employee.

The amount of value received by the individual is that paid to or received (as regards value received before 7 March 2001 in respect of shares issued before that date, receivable) by him from the company; or the amount of his liability extinguished or discharged; or the difference between the market value of the asset and the consideration (if any) given for it; or the net cost to the company of providing the benefit. In the case of value received within (a), (b) or (c) above, the market value of the shares, securities or debt in question is substituted if greater than the amount receivable.

Additionally, the individual '*receives value*' from the company if any person connected with the company (within 25.3 above) purchases any shares or securities of the company from him, or pays him for giving up any right in relation to such shares or securities. The value received is the amount received (as regards value received before 7 March 2001 in respect of shares issued before that date, receivable) or, if greater, the market value of the shares etc.

All payments or transfers, direct or indirect, to, or to the order of, or for the benefit of, an individual or 'associate' (see 25.3 above) are brought within these provisions, as are payments etc. made by any person connected with the company (within *ICTA 1988, s 839*).

Where relief is withdrawn or reduced by reason of a disposal (see above) after 5 April 1998, the individual is not treated as receiving value in respect of the disposal.

As regards value received after 5 April 1998, an individual who acquired eligible shares by means of an inter-spouse transfer within 25.22 below is treated for these purposes as having subscribed for the shares.

In relation to shares issued after 6 March 2001 and, for shares issued previously, in relation to value received after that date, where two or more issues of shares have been made by the same company to the same individual, in relation to each of which income tax relief is claimed, and value is received during a period of restriction relating to more than one such issue, the value received is apportioned between them by reference to the amounts subscribed for each of those issues.

Insignificant value. In relation to shares issued after 6 March 2001 and, for shares issued previously, in relation to value received after that date, an amount of '*insignificant value*' is an amount of value which

- does not exceed £1,000, or

- in any other case is insignificant in relation to the amount subscribed by the individual for the eligible shares.

If, at any time in the period beginning one year before the date of issue of the eligible shares and ending with the date of issue, there are in existence arrangements (as very broadly defined) providing for the individual (or an 'associate', within 25.3 above) to receive, or become entitled to receive, any value from the issuing company (or a 'connected person', within *ICTA 1988, s 839*) at any time in the 'period of restriction' (as above), no amount of value received by the individual is treated as an amount of insignificant value. References to an associate or person connected with the company include anyone who has such status at *any* time in the period of restriction.

There are provisions to aggregate a receipt of value, whether insignificant or not, with amounts of insignificant value received previously, and treating that aggregate, if it is not itself an amount of insignificant value, as an amount of value received at the time of the latest actual receipt.

[*ICTA 1988, ss 300, 301, 301A, 312(1)(1ZA); FA 1994, Sch 15 paras 14, 15; FA 1998, s 74, Sch 13 paras 13, 14; FA 2000, Sch 17 paras 4, 8; FA 2001, Sch 15 paras 15, 17, 18, 24, 40; FA 2004, Sch 18 paras 6, 11, 21*].

Replacement value. In relation to shares issued after 6 March 2001 and, for shares issued previously, in relation to value received after that date, the 'value received' provisions above (other than (*j*) above) are disapplied if the person from whom the value was received (the '*original supplier*') receives, by way of a 'qualifying receipt', and whether before or after the original receipt of value, at least equivalent replacement value from the original recipient. A receipt is a '*qualifying receipt*' if it arises by reason of:

(A)   any one, or any combination of, the following:

   (i)   a payment by the original recipient to the original supplier other than an 'excepted payment' (or a payment covered by (C) below);

   (ii)   the acquisition of an asset by the original recipient from the original supplier for consideration exceeding market value;

   (iii)   the disposal of an asset by the original recipient to the original supplier for no consideration or for consideration less than market value; or

(B)   (where the original receipt of value falls within (*d*) above) an event having the effect of reversing the original event; or

(C)   (where the original receipt of value arose from the purchase from the individual by a person connected with the company of shares or securities of the company, including for this purpose a payment for giving up any right in relation to them — see above) the repurchase by the original recipient of the shares or securities in question, or reacquisition of the right in question, for consideration not less than the original value.

The amount of replacement value is

- in a case within (A) above, the amount of any such payment plus the difference between the market value of any such asset and the consideration received;

- in a case within (B) above, the same as the amount of the original value; and

- in a case within (C) above, the consideration received by the original supplier.

The receipt of replacement value is disregarded if

- it occurs before the start of the 'period of restriction' (as above) in relation to the shares in question; or

- there was an unreasonable delay in its occurrence; or

- it occurs more than 60 days after the relief falling to be withdrawn (or reduced) has been determined on appeal.

Each of the following is an *'excepted payment'* for the purposes of (A)(i) above:

(1) a reasonable (in relation to their market value) payment for any goods, services or facilities provided (in the course of trade or otherwise) by the original supplier;

(2) a payment of interest at no more than a reasonable commercial rate on money lent to the original recipient;

(3) a payment not exceeding a reasonable and commercial rent for property occupied by the original recipient;

(4) a payment not exceeding market value for the acquisition of an asset;

(5) a payment in discharge of an 'ordinary trade debt' (as above);

(6) a payment for any shares or securities in any company in circumstances not within (A)(ii) above.

Each reference in (1)–(3) above to the original supplier or recipient includes a reference to any person who at any time in the period of restriction is an 'associate' (as in 25.3 above) of his or, in the case of the supplier, is 'connected' with him (within *ICTA 1988, s 839*).

Where

- the receipt of replacement value is a qualifying receipt (as above), and

- the event giving rise to the receipt is (or includes) a subscription for shares by the individual or by a person who is an 'associate' (as in 25.3 above) of his at any time in the period of restriction,

the subscriber is not eligible for EIS income tax relief or EIS capital gains deferral relief (see 25.24 below) in relation to those shares or any other shares in the same issue.

For the above purposes, any apportionment made of value received where there are two or more share issues (see above) is disregarded in determining the amount of the original receipt of value; and payments to a person include any made indirectly or to his order or for his benefit.

[*ICTA 1988, ss 300A, 301; FA 2001, Sch 15 paras 16, 17, 40*].

Simon's Direct Tax Service. See E3.147, 3.147A.

25.17 **Value received other than by claimant.** Relief is also restricted or withdrawn where an individual has obtained relief attributable (see 25.8 above) to eligible shares in a company, and at any time during the 'period of restriction', the company or any '51% subsidiary' of the company repays, redeems or repurchases any of its share capital belonging to a member other than

(i)   the individual or

(ii) another individual whose relief is thereby withdrawn or reduced (as above) or who thereby suffers a qualifying chargeable event under the capital gains deferral provisions mentioned at 25.24 below, or

(iii) a company whose investment relief under the Corporate Venturing Scheme (see Tolley's Corporation Tax) is thereby withdrawn or reduced,

or makes any payment to any such member for giving up rights on the cancellation or extinguishment of any of the share capital of the company or subsidiary. The relief is withdrawn or, if it exceeds an amount equal to lower rate tax (for the year in which the relief was given) on the sum received (as regards repayments etc. made before 7 March 2001 where the eligible shares were issued before that date, receivable) by the member, reduced by that amount. That amount is correspondingly reduced where the relief attributable to the shares was less than the lower rate of tax for the year of issue on the amount subscribed for the issue. That amount is also apportioned between individuals (by reference to amounts subscribed) where the receipt of value causes a withdrawal or reduction of more than one individual's relief. Where the receipt of value falls into the 'period of restriction' for more than one issue of eligible shares, the value received is similarly apportioned between issues.

A '51% subsidiary' of a company is one of which the company owns more than 50% of the ordinary share capital at any time in the relevant period (defined as in 25.3 above), whether or not at the time of the repayment etc.

In relation to shares issued after 6 March 2001 and, where the eligible shares were issued earlier, in relation to repayments etc. made after that date, the absence of any withdrawal or reduction of the kind referred to in (ii) and (iii) above is disregarded if it is due only to the amount received being of insignificant value.

The 'period of restriction' is the period beginning one year before the issue of eligible shares and ending immediately before the third anniversary of the issue date or, if later and where relevant, the third anniversary of the date of commencement of the intended trade referred to in 25.6(a) or (c) above. (In determining for these purposes, in relation to shares issued after 16 March 2004, the time at which a qualifying trade begins to be carried on by any 'qualifying 90% subsidiary' (see 25.21 below) of a company, any carrying on of the trade by it before it became such a subsidiary is disregarded.)

As regards repayments etc. made before 7 March 2001 where the eligible shares were issued before that date, these provisions operated by reference to repayments etc. during the 'designated period' as in 25.3 above. Slightly different provisions applied in relation to shares issued before 6 April 1998. In particular, the old provisions applied by reference to value received in the relevant period (defined as in 25.3 above) rather than the above-mentioned designated period and any apportionment between individuals was by reference to relief otherwise available rather than amounts subscribed. Also, the old provisions applied by reference to the nominal value of the share capital concerned if this was greater than the sum receivable by the member.

This restriction of relief does not apply to the redemption, within twelve months of issue, of any share capital of nominal value equal to the authorised minimum issued to comply with Companies Act 1985, s 117 (or NI equivalent) where the company subsequently issues eligible shares.

In relation to shares issued after 6 March 2001 and, where the eligible shares were issued earlier, in relation to repayments etc. made after that date, a repayment etc. is disregarded if the amount received by the member in question is insignificant in relation to the market value immediately after the event of the remaining issued share capital of the company or, as the case may be, 51% subsidiary. The assumption is made that the shares in question are cancelled at the time of the event. In applying the test, the market value, immediately before the event, of the shares to which the event relates is substituted for the amount received if this would give a greater amount. This let-out does not apply if, at any time in the period beginning one year before the date of issue of the eligible shares and ending with the date of issue, there are in existence arrangements (as very broadly defined) providing for a payment within these provisions to be made, or entitlement to such a payment to come into being, at any time in the period of restriction.

The following additional provisions apply as regards value received before 7 March 2001 where the eligible shares in question were issued before that date. Where, in the 'designated period' — as above (as regards shares issued before 6 April 1998, the 'relevant period' — as above), a member of the issuing company receives, or is or may become entitled to receive, any 'value' from the company or a '51% subsidiary' (as above), then in applying the 30% test under 25.3(*b*)(i) above at any subsequent time, the following amounts are treated as reduced:

(*a*) the amount of the company's ordinary share capital;

(*b*) the amount of that capital which, under 25.3(*b*) above, the individual directly or indirectly possesses or is entitled to acquire; and

(*c*) the amount at (*a*) not included in (*b*).

The reduction in (*b*) and (*c*) above is in each case the same proportion of the total amount as the value received by the member(s) entitled to the shares comprising the amount bears to the sum subscribed for those shares. The reduced amount at (*a*) is the sum of those at (*b*) and (*c*).

A member receives or is entitled to receive '*value*' where any payments etc. are made to him which, if made to an individual, would fall within (*d*)–(*h*) above, excluding those within (*h*) made for full consideration. The amount of value received is as described above in relation to such payments etc.

[*ICTA 1988, ss 303, 303AA, 312(1)(1ZA); FA 1994, Sch 15 para 17; FA 1998, s 74, Sch 13 para 15; FA 2000, Sch 16 para 2(2), Sch 17 paras 5, 8; FA 2001, Sch 15 paras 19, 20, 24, 40, Sch 33 Pt II(3); FA 2004, Sch 18 paras 7, 11, 21*].

Where, by virtue of provisions comparable to those above, a repayment, redemption etc. of share capital causes a withdrawal or reduction of investment relief given to one or more companies, in respect of the full amount repaid etc., under the Corporate Venturing Scheme ('CVS') (see Tolley's Corporation Tax), there is provision to ensure that no withdrawal or reduction is made under *section 303*. A withdrawal etc. of CVS investment relief is also disregarded for the purposes of *section 303* if the amount repaid etc. exceeds the amount in respect of which the relief was given by no more than £1,000. These exemptions are subject to the absence of any 'repayment arrangements' (as defined) throughout the one year ending with the date of issue of the shares to which the CVS investment relief is attributable. Where the above-mentioned excess (if any) is greater than the *de minimis* limit or the exemptions are prevented from applying, the amount of that excess is taken as the sum receivable by the member for the purposes of *section 303*.

Under the comparable CVS provisions mentioned above, a repayment etc. of an insignificant amount (judged by reference to the greater of the market value of the shares to which it relates and the amount received by the member in question, and to the market value of the remaining share capital) is disregarded. A repayment etc. disregarded under that provision is also disregarded for the purposes of *section 303*. Following the introduction of the insignificant repayments etc. provisions in 25.16 above, this rule becomes superfluous and is abolished.

[*ICTA 1988, s 303A; FA 2000, Sch 16 para 2(3); FA 2001, Sch 15 paras 21, 40; FA 2004, Sch 18 para 8*].

Simon's Direct Tax Service. See E3.148.

25.18   **Replacement capital.** Relief attributable (see 25.8 above) to any shares in a company held by an individual is withdrawn if, at any time in the 'relevant period' (see 25.3 above), the company (or any subsidiary, as specially defined for this purpose) begins to carry on as its trade, business, profession or vocation (or part) a trade etc. (or part) previously carried on at any time in that period otherwise than by the company or a subsidiary, or acquires the whole or the greater part of the assets used for a trade etc. previously so carried on, and the individual is a person who, or one of the group of persons who together, either

(a)   owned more than a half share (ownership and, if appropriate, respective shares being determined as under *ICTA 1988, s 344(1)(a)(b)(2)(3)* (see Tolley's Corporation Tax under Losses) at any such time in the trade etc. previously carried on, and also own or owned at any such time such a share in the trade etc. carried on by the company, or

(b)   control (within *ICTA 1988, s 416*), or at any such time have controlled, the company, and also, at any such time, controlled another company which previously carried on the trade etc.

For these purposes, interests etc. of 'associates' (see 25.3 above) are taken into account. There are special rules relating to shares held by certain directors of, or of a partner of, the issuing company or any subsidiary.

Relief is also withdrawn if the company, at any time in the relevant period, comes to acquire all the issued share capital of another company, and where the individual is a person who, or one of a group of persons who together, control or have, at any such time, controlled the company and who also, at any such time, controlled the other company.

[*ICTA 1988, s 302; FA 1994, Sch 15 para 16*].

Simon's Direct Tax Service. See E3.151.

25.19   **Assessments for withdrawing or reducing relief** are made under Schedule D, Case VI for the year of assessment for which the relief was given. Relief may not be withdrawn on the grounds that the company is not a qualifying company (see 25.5 above), that the requirements as to the purpose of the issue or the application of the proceeds are not fulfilled (see 25.2(*b*)(*c*) above) or that the requirements of 25.2(i)–(iii) above are not met, unless either the company has given notice under *ICTA 1988, s 310* (see 25.25 below) (or the equivalent capital gains deferral provisions) or the inspector has given notice to the company of his opinion that relief was not due (against which notice the company may appeal as though it were refusal of a claim by the company). Such notice by the inspector may not be given, nor any assessment withdrawing relief be made, more than six years after the end of the year of assessment in which the period mentioned in 25.2(*c*) above ends or, if later, the event giving rise to withdrawal occurs, but this restriction is without prejudice to the extension of time limits in cases of fraudulent or negligent conduct (see 30.3 FRAUDULENT OR NEGLIGENT CONDUCT). The determination of a comparable appeal under the capital gains deferral provisions mentioned at 25.24 below is conclusive for the purposes of an appeal under these provisions. No assessment may be made by reason of any event occurring after the death of the person to whom the shares were issued.

Where a person has made an arm's length disposal of all the eligible shares issued to him by a company in respect of which relief has been given, no assessment may be made in respect of those shares by reason of any subsequent event unless he is at the time of that event 'connected with' the company (as under 25.3 above). As regards shares issued before 6 April 1998, this rule operated by reference to disposals of all the *ordinary* shares.

25.20 Enterprise Investment Scheme

The relevant date for the purposes of 42.1 INTEREST AND SURCHARGES ON UNPAID TAX is the date on which the event took place which gave rise to the withdrawal of relief, *except that*:

(*a*) where relief is withdrawn under the general anti-avoidance provision of *ICTA 1988, s 289(6)* (see 25.2 above) or by virtue of the pre-arranged exit provisions of *ICTA 1988, s 299B* (see above), it is the date on which relief was granted or, if relief was given under PAYE, 5 April in the year of assessment in which relief was given;

(*b*) where relief is withdrawn due to failure to meet the condition at 25.2(*c*) above, it is the date on which relief was granted; and

(*c*) where relief is withdrawn as a result of the grant of an option the exercise of which would bind the grantor to purchase the shares (see above), it is the date of grant of the option.

[*ICTA 1988, s 307; FA 1989, s 149(4); FA 1993, s 111(3); FA 1994, Sch 15 para 22; FA 1996, Sch 18 paras 5, 17(3); FA 1998, s 71(2)(5), s 74, Sch 13 para 20; FA 2001, Sch 15 paras 7, 40*].

Simon's Direct Tax Service. See E3.152.

25.20   *Example*

In June 2005, Mr Jones, the investor in 25.9 above, sells 18,000 ordinary £1 shares in C Ltd (see 25.9 above), in an arm's length transaction, for £45,000.
The position is as follows.

Income tax

	£
2003/04	
Relief attributable to 3,750 shares treated as issued in 2003/04:	
3,750 shares at £1.80 per share = £6,750 @ 20%	1,350
Consideration received $\left(\dfrac{3,750}{18,000} \times £45,000\right) = £9,375$ @ 20%	1,875
Excess of lower rate tax on consideration over relief	£525
Relief withdrawn—Schedule D, Case VI assessment	£1,350
2004/05	£
Relief attributable to 750 shares	
750/3,750 × £588	118
Consideration received	
$\left(\dfrac{750}{18,000} \times £45,000\right) = £1,875 \times 118/(1,350$ @ 20%) = £819 @ 20%	164
Excess of lower rate tax on adjusted consideration over relief	£46
Relief withdrawn—Schedule D, Case VI assessment	£118

Capital gains tax

2005/06	£	£
Disposal proceeds (18,000 shares)		45,000
Cost: 13,500 shares acquired May 2002	16,200	
4,500 shares acquired June 2004	8,100	24,300
Chargeable gain (subject to taper relief)		£20,700

Notes

(a)   For both income tax and capital gains tax purposes, a disposal is matched with acquisitions on a first in/first out basis (see 25.13 above and Tolley's Capital Gains Tax). Thus, the 18,000 shares sold in June 2005 are matched with 13,500 shares purchased in May 2002 and with 4,500 of the 7,500 EIS shares subscribed for in June 2004. For these purposes, 3,750 of the 7,500 EIS shares are treated as having been issued in 2003/04 (by virtue of Mr Jones' carry-back claim — see 25.9 above). Therefore, those shares are treated as disposed of in priority to those on which relief was given in 2004/05.

(b)   EIS relief is withdrawn if shares are disposed of before the end of the requisite three-year period (five years for shares issued before 6 April 2000). In this example, relief attributable to the shares sold is fully withdrawn as consideration received, reduced as illustrated, exceeds the relief attributable. See below for where the reverse applies. The consideration is reduced where the relief attributable (A) is less than tax at the lower rate on the amount subscribed (B), and is so reduced by applying the fraction A/B. See 25.13 above.

(c)   Relief is withdrawn by means of a Schedule D, Case VI assessment for the year(s) in which relief was given (see 25.19 above).

(d)   The capital gain on the disposal is fully chargeable as the shares are not held for the requisite three-year period (see Tolley's Capital Gains Tax).

In December 2005 Mr Jones disposes of his 18,750 ordinary £1 shares in D Ltd (see 25.9 above), in an arm's length transaction, for £15,000.

The position is as follows.

Income tax

2004/05	£
Relief attributable to shares sold	1,633

Consideration received $£15,000 \times \dfrac{1,633}{£18,750 \times 20\%} = £6,532$ @ 20%   1,306

Excess of relief over lower rate relief on adjusted consideration	£327
Relief withdrawn—Schedule D, Case VI assessment	£1,306

Capital gains tax

2005/06	£	£
Disposal proceeds (December 2005)		15,000
Cost (November 2004)	18,750	
Less Relief attributable to shares £1,633 – £1,306	327	18,423
Allowable loss		£3,423

Notes

(a)   The EIS relief withdrawn is limited to the consideration received, reduced as illustrated, at the lower rate of tax for the year for which relief was given. If the disposal had been made otherwise than by way of a bargain made at arm's length, the full relief would have been withdrawn. See 25.13 above.

(b)   An allowable loss may arise for capital gains tax purposes on a disposal of EIS shares, whether or not the disposal occurs within the requisite three-year period. In computing such a loss, the allowable cost is reduced by EIS relief attributable to the shares (and not withdrawn). See Tolley's Capital Gains Tax.

(c)   A loss, as computed for capital gains tax purposes, may be relieved against income on a claim under *ICTA 1988, s 574* (losses on unquoted shares — see 46.15 LOSSES).

25.21   **SUBSIDIARY COMPANIES**

A qualifying company (see 25.5 above) is allowed to have one or more subsidiaries in the 'relevant period' (see 25.6 above) if each subsidiary meets the conditions described below (which differ according to whether the EIS shares in question are issued after 16 March 2004 or on or before that date). (See further below for the separate definition of 'qualifying 90% subsidiary' for the purposes of this chapter in relation to shares issued after 16 March 2004.)

In relation to EIS shares issued after 16 March 2004. More than 50% of the subsidiary's ordinary share capital must be owned directly or indirectly by the qualifying company (and *ICTA 1988, s 838(2)–(10)* apply in determining whether or not this is the case) and no person other than the qualifying company or another of its subsidiaries may have control (within *ICTA 1988, s 840* — see 19.8 CONNECTED PERSONS) of the subsidiary. Furthermore, no arrangements (as very broadly defined) may exist by virtue of which either of these conditions would cease to be satisfied.

However, the above conditions are not regarded as ceasing to be satisfied by reason only of the subsidiary or any other company being wound up or dissolved or by reason only of anything done as a consequence of any such company being in administration or receivership, provided the winding-up, dissolution, entry into administration or receivership or anything done as a consequence of its being in administration or receivership is for *bona fide* commercial reasons and is not part of a tax avoidance scheme or arrangements. Also, the above conditions are not regarded as ceasing to be satisfied by reason only of arrangements being in existence for the disposal of the interest in the subsidiary held by the qualifying company (or, as the case may be, by another of its subsidiaries) if the disposal is to be for *bona fide* commercial reasons and is not to be part of a tax avoidance scheme or arrangements.

In relation to EIS shares issued on or before 16 March 2004. The qualifying company, or another of its subsidiaries, must possess at least 75% of both the issued share capital and the voting power, and be beneficially entitled to at least 75% of the assets available for distribution to equity holders on a winding-up etc. (see *ICTA 1988, Sch 18 paras 1, 3*) and of the profits available for distribution to equity holders. No other person may have control (within *ICTA 1988, s 840* — see 19.8 CONNECTED PERSONS) of the subsidiary. Furthermore, no arrangements (as very broadly defined) may exist by virtue of which any of these conditions could cease to be satisfied.

The above conditions must continue to be satisfied until the end of the relevant period, except that the winding-up or dissolution, during that period, of the subsidiary or of the qualifying company does not prevent those conditions being satisfied, provided that the winding-up etc. meets the conditions applied in relation to qualifying companies (see 25.5

above). The conditions are also not regarded as ceasing to be satisfied by reason only of the disposal of the interest in the subsidiary within the relevant period if it can be shown to be for *bona fide* commercial reasons and not part of a tax avoidance scheme.

[*ICTA 1988, ss 308, 312(1); FA 1994, Sch 15 paras 23, 24; FA 1997, Sch 8 paras 1, 6; FA 1998, s 74, Sch 13 para 21; FA 2000, Sch 17 para 14; FA 2004, Sch 18 paras 9, 21*].

Qualifying 90% subsidiaries. In relation to EIS shares issued after 16 March 2004, the concept of a 'qualifying 90% subsidiary' is introduced (see 25.2, 25.5, 25.6 and 25.11 above). A company (the subsidiary) is a *'qualifying 90% subsidiary'* of another company (the holding company) if

- the holding company possesses at least **90%** of both the issued share capital of, and the voting power in, the subsidiary;

- the holding company would be beneficially entitled to at least **90%** of the assets of the subsidiary available for distribution to equity holders on a winding-up or in any other circumstances;

- the holding company is beneficially entitled to at least **90%** of any profits of the subsidiary available for distribution to equity holders;

- no person other than the holding company has control (within *ICTA 1988, s 840* — see 19.8 CONNECTED PERSONS) of the subsidiary; and

- no arrangements (as very broadly defined) exist by virtue of which any of the above conditions would cease to be met.

For the above purposes, *ICTA 1988, Sch 18 paras 1, 3* apply, with appropriate modifications, to determine the persons who are equity holders and the percentage of assets available to them.

The above conditions are not regarded as ceasing to be satisfied by reason only of the subsidiary or any other company being wound up or dissolved or by reason only of anything done as a consequence of any such company being in administration or receivership, provided the winding-up, dissolution, entry into administration or receivership or anything done as a consequence of its being in administration or receivership is for *bona fide* commercial reasons and is not part of a tax avoidance scheme or arrangements. Also, the above conditions are not regarded as ceasing to be satisfied by reason only of arrangements being in existence for the disposal of the holding company's interest in the subsidiary if the disposal is to be for *bona fide* commercial reasons and is not to be part of a tax avoidance scheme or arrangements.

[*ICTA 1988, s 289(9)–(13), s 312(1); FA 2004, Sch 18 paras 1(8), 21*].

Simon's Direct Tax Service. See E3.117.

25.22   **MARRIED PERSONS**

The provisions for withdrawal of relief on the disposal of shares in respect of which relief has been given (see 25.13 above) do not apply to transfers between spouses living together. On any subsequent disposal or other event, the spouse to whom the shares were so transferred is treated as if he or she were the person who subscribed for the shares, and as if his or her liability to income tax had been reduced in respect of those shares by the same amount, and for the same year of assessment, as applied on the subscription by the transferor spouse. Any assessment for reducing or withdrawing relief is made on the transferee spouse. As regards inter-spouse transfers after 5 April 1998, the identification rules for disposals at 25.13 above apply to determine the extent (if any) to which shares to which relief is attributable are comprised in the transfer. [*ICTA 1988, s 304; FA 1994, Sch 15 para 18; FA 1998, Sch 13 para 16*].

25.23 **EIS COMPANY BECOMING WHOLLY-OWNED SUBSIDIARY OF NEW HOLD-ING COMPANY**

Where a company (Company A) has issued eligible shares (the old shares) under the enterprise investment scheme (a certificate having been issued on Form EIS 3 — see 25.11 above) and, by means of an exchange of shares, all of its shares are acquired by a company (Company B) in which the only previously issued shares are subscriber shares, then, subject to the further conditions below being satisfied, the exchange is not regarded as involving a disposal of the old shares (and a consequent withdrawal of relief) and an acquisition of the Company B shares (the new shares). EIS relief attributable to the old shares is regarded as attributable instead to the new shares for which they are exchanged. For EIS purposes generally, the new shares stand in the shoes of the old shares, e.g. as if they had been subscribed for and issued at the time the old shares were subscribed for and issued and as if anything done by or in relation to Company A had been done by or in relation to Company B.

The further conditions are as follows.

(*a*)   The new shares must be issued after 5 April 1998.

(*b*)   The consideration for the old shares must consist entirely of the issue of the new shares.

(*c*)   The consideration for old shares of each description must consist entirely of new shares of the 'corresponding description'.

(*d*)   New shares of each description must be issued to holders of old shares of the 'corresponding description' in respect of and in proportion to their holdings.

(*e*)   Before the issue of the new shares, on the written application of either Company A or Company B, the Board must have notified to that company their satisfaction that the exchange

    (i)   is for *bona fide* commercial reasons; and

    (ii)   does not form part of a scheme or arrangements designed to avoid liability to corporation tax or capital gains tax.

    The Board may, within 30 days of an application, request further particulars, which must then be supplied within 30 days of the request (or such longer period as they may allow in any particular case).

For the purposes of (*c*) and (*d*) above, old and new shares are of a '*corresponding description*' if, assuming they were shares in the same company, they would be of the same class and carry the same rights.

References above to 'shares' (other than those to 'eligible shares' or 'subscriber shares') include references to 'securities'

An exchange within these provisions does not breach the conditions at 25.5(ii)–(iv) above (definition of 'qualifying company').

[*ICTA 1988, s 304A; TCGA 1992, s 138(2); FA 1998, Sch 13 para 17*].

Simon's Direct Tax Service. See E3.121.

25.24 **CAPITAL GAINS TAX**

In determining the gain or loss on a disposal of shares to which any income tax relief is attributable (see 25.8 above):

(*a*)   if a loss would otherwise arise, the consideration the individual is treated as having given for the shares is treated as reduced by the amount of the relief;

(*b*)   if the disposal is after the end of the 'relevant period' (see 25.3 above) and a gain would otherwise arise, the gain is not a chargeable gain (although this does not prevent a loss arising in these circumstances from being an allowable loss). Where the reduction in liability in respect of the issue of the shares was less than the amount corresponding to lower rate income tax on the amount subscribed for the shares (other than because there is insufficient income tax liability to make full use of the relief), there is a corresponding reduction in the amount of the gain which is not chargeable.

Where a gain (or part of a gain) on a disposal is not a chargeable gain under (*b*) above, but the income tax relief on the shares disposed of is reduced on account of value received from the company by the claimant or by other persons (see 25.16, 25.17 above) before the disposal, then a corresponding proportion of the gain is brought back into charge.

The identification rules of *ICTA 1988, s 299* (see 25.13 above) apply for the above purposes.

See further *TCGA 1992, ss 150A, 150B* as amended and introduced by *FA 1994, Sch 15 paras 28–34* and *FA 1995, Sch 13 paras 1–3*, and as further amended by *FA 1998, Sch 13 paras 24, 25, Sch 27 Pt III(14)*. For full coverage, see the corresponding chapter of Tolley's Capital Gains Tax.

Capital gains deferral relief. General reinvestment relief was available for reinvestment into qualifying shares acquired before 6 April 1998 but such relief for reinvestment into shares on which EIS income tax relief was claimed was prohibited by *TCGA 1992, s 164MA*. However, a specific relief was introduced by *FA 1995, s 67, Sch 13 para 4(3)* whereby any chargeable gain accruing after 28 November 1994 could be deferred to the extent that it could be matched with an investment in EIS shares to which income tax relief was attributable (see 25.8 above).

In relation to EIS shares issued after 5 April 1998, significant changes were made to the deferral relief provisions. In particular, it is no longer a requirement that the shares qualify for income tax relief nor that the individual be unconnected with the company. However, the company itself must be a qualifying company (as in 25.5 above) and certain other EIS income tax relief conditions are adopted. The provisions are also extended to trustees. These changes are intended to compensate for the abolition of general reinvestment relief. There is no limit on the amount of the gain that can be deferred under the new provisions (previously the income tax relief annual maximum at 25.10 above would have applied), but the gross assets test at 25.5 above does limit the amount that may be invested in any one EIS company (or group).

Deferral relief applies where

(*a*)   a chargeable gain would otherwise accrue to an individual

    (i)   on the disposal by him of any asset; or

    (ii)   on the occurrence of a chargeable event under these provisions or the provisions governing reinvestment into VCT shares (see 91.14 VENTURE CAPITAL TRUSTS); or

    (iii)   (as regards shares issued after 5 April 1998) to give effect to a withdrawal of general reinvestment relief;

(*b*)   the individual makes a 'qualifying investment'; and

(*c*)   the individual is UK resident or ordinarily resident both when the chargeable gain accrues to him and when he makes the qualifying investment, and is not, at the time he makes the investment, regarded as resident outside the UK for the purposes of any double taxation arrangements the effect of which would be that he would not be liable to tax on a gain arising on a disposal, immediately after their acquisition, of the shares comprising the qualifying investment, disregarding any exemption available under *TCGA 1992, s 150A* (see above).

Subject to the further conditions referred to above, a '*qualifying investment*' is a subscription for eligible shares (broadly, *new* ordinary, non-preferential, shares) in a qualifying EIS company which are issued within the one year immediately preceding or the three years immediately following the time the chargeable gain in question accrues. These time limits may be extended by the Board in individual cases. If the shares are issued *before* the gain accrues, they must still be held at the time it accrues. The deferred gain is brought back into charge on the occurrence of (and at the time of) any one of a number of specified chargeable events, in particular the disposal (at any time) of the shares in question.

[*TCGA 1992, s 150C, Sch 5B; FA 1995, Sch 13 para 4; FA 1998, s 74, Sch 13 paras 26–36, Sch 27 Pt III(14); FA 1999, s 73, Sch 8; FA 2000, Sch 17 para 7; FA 2001, Sch 15 paras 25–37, 40; FA 2004, Sch 18 paras 12–21*].

The above is intended as a brief summary only. For full coverage, see the corresponding chapter of Tolley's Capital Gains Tax.

Simon's Direct Tax Service. See C3.10.

25.25   NOTIFICATION REQUIREMENTS AND INFORMATION POWERS

Certain events leading to withdrawal or reduction of income tax relief must be notified to the inspector, generally within 60 days, by either the individual who received the relief, the issuing company, or any person connected with the issuing company having knowledge of the matter. The inspector may require such a notice and other relevant information where he has reason to believe it should have been made.

For events occurring after 6 March 2001,

(i)   the notification requirement extends to cases where income tax relief would have fallen to be withdrawn or reduced were it not for the 'replacement value' rules at 25.18 above; and in all cases a notice under these provisions should include details of any such replacement value received (or expected to be received) where this is within the knowledge of the person giving the notice; and

(ii)   the inspector's powers extend to cases where notice would have been required were it not for 'value received', or a repayment, redemption etc. of share capital, being of an insignificant amount (see 25.16–25.18 above), and he may require notice and other information from persons giving or receiving such value or making or receiving such a repayment etc.

The penalty provisions of *TMA 1970, s 98* apply for failure to comply with the notification requirements.

The inspector also has broad powers to require information in other cases where relief may be withdrawn, restricted or not due. The requirements of secrecy do not prevent his disclosing to a company that relief has been given or claimed on certain of its shares.

[*ICTA 1988, s 310; FA 1993, s 111(2); FA 1994, Sch 15 para 25; FA 1998, s 71(3)–(5), s 74, Sch 13 para 22, Sch 27 Pt III(14); FA 2001, Sch 15 paras 8, 23, 39, 40; FA 2004, Sch 18 para 10*].

Simon's Direct Tax Service. See E3.155.

26   European Community Legislation

26.1   Statements of the European Council and European Commission are Graded Under the *EC Treaty* as Follows.

(*a*)   **Regulations** are binding in their entirety and have general effect in all Member States. They are directly applicable in the legal systems of Member States and do not have to be implemented by national legislation.

(*b*)   **Directives** are binding as to result and their general effect is specific to named Member States. The form and methods of compliance are left to individual Member States, which are normally given a specific period in which to implement the necessary legislation.

(*c*)   **Decisions** are binding in their entirety and are specific to a Member State, commercial enterprise or private individual. They take effect on notification to the addressee.

(*d*)   **Recommendations and opinions** are not binding and are directed to specific subjects on which the Council's or Commission's advice has been sought.

26.2   European Community law is effective in the UK by virtue of *European Communities Act 1972, s 2*, and the European Court of Justice has held that 'wherever the provisions of a Directive appear . . . to be unconditional and sufficiently precise, those provisions may . . . be relied upon as against any national provision which is incompatible with the Directive insofar as the provisions define rights which individuals are able to assert against the State' (*Becker v Finanzamt Munster-Innenstadt [1982] 1 CMLR 499*). Judgments in the European Court of Justice also have supremacy over domestic decisions, even if the proceedings commenced in another Member State.

26.3   In contrast to the extensive application of EU legislation in the VAT sphere, direct taxes are currently subject to only the following specific measures.

(*a*)   *Council Regulation 2137/85* (25 July 1985) concerning European Economic Interest Groupings.

(*b*)   *Directive 90/434/EEC* (23 July 1990) concerning mergers, divisions, transfers of assets and exchanges of shares concerning companies of different Member States.

(*c*)   *Directive 90/435/EEC* (23 July 1990) concerning distributions of profits to parent companies.

(*d*)   *Directive 2003/48/EC* (3 June 2003) concerning the taxation of savings income.

(*e*)   *Directive 2003/49/EC* (3 June 2003) concerning interest and royalty payments.

As regards (*a*), see the related UK legislation at 53.19 PARTNERSHIPS. As regards (*b*), the UK legislation is dealt with in Tolley's Corporation Tax under Capital Gains. As regards (*c*), a minor amendment is dealt with at 22.12 DEDUCTION OF TAX AT SOURCE, and see also Tolley's Corporation Tax under Double Tax Relief. As regards (*d*), see 68.15 RETURNS and as regards (*e*), see Tolley's Corporation Tax under Income Tax in relation to a Company. The Revenue Consultative Document on EC Direct Tax Measures published in December 1991 sets out the manner in which (*b*) and (*c*) are considered to be implemented by the UK legislative changes.

For a case on the application of *Directive 90/434/EEC*, see *Leur-Bloem v Inspecteur der Belastingdienst/Ondernemingen Amsterdam 2 (Case C-28/95) ECJ, [1997] STC 1205*.

In addition to the above, *Convention 90/436/EEC* (23 July 1990), concerning arbitration in double taxation disputes arising from transfer pricing adjustments, came into force on

26.4 European Community Legislation

1 January 1995. See 3.8 ANTI-AVOIDANCE, 24.5(*m*) DOUBLE TAX RELIEF and 36.2(*o*), 36.4 INLAND REVENUE: CONFIDENTIALITY OF INFORMATION.

26.4   The European Commission has proposed to amend the Parent-Subsidiary Directive (*90/435/EEC*) and the Mergers Directive (*90/434/EEC*). See the corresponding chapter of Tolley's Corporation Tax.

The European Company Statute Regulation (Council Regulation (EC) No 2157/2001), which was adopted on 8 October 2001, will apply to all Member States with effect from 8 October 2004. It will create the legal framework for a new corporate entity, the European Company or 'Societas Europaea' (SE), to facilitate cross-border activities within the European Union including cross-border mergers. See the corresponding chapter of Tolley's Corporation Tax.

27   Excess Liability

Cross-references. See 1.3 ALLOWANCES AND TAX RATES for current unified tax rates (lower, basic and higher) and 1.4 for a description of the changeover to unified income tax in 1973/74.

27.1   'Excess Liability' means the excess of income tax liability over what it would be if all taxable income were charged at the basic rate (or, as appropriate, starting rate, lower rate or Schedule F ordinary rate) to the exclusion of the higher rate or Schedule F upper rate. (See 1.9 ALLOWANCES AND TAX RATES as regards Schedule F ordinary and upper rates, applicable for 1999/2000 onwards.) Although it is only so defined for certain specific purposes of the *Taxes Acts*, it is used for convenience in this chapter to refer to all such liabilities.

Returns, assessments and appeals. There is no provision for a return of total income for the purposes of excess liability. The ordinary annual return (see 68.2 RETURNS) will enable the total income and the relevant deductions – see 27.2(*a*) below – to be ascertained. The normal provisions for ASSESSMENTS (5) and APPEALS (4) apply to excess liability as they do to basic rate liability. Where the income is received untaxed, any appropriate excess liability is included with liabilities at other rates in the assessment on the income or, as regards employment income, dealt with under PAY AS YOU EARN (55). The excess rate liability on other income is separately assessed. [*ICTA 1988, s 5(4); FA 1994, Sch 26 Pt V(23); FA 1996, Sch 6 paras 3, 28*]. For due dates of payment and related matters, see 56.1 PAYMENT OF TAX, 78.4–78.7 SELF-ASSESSMENT.

Relationship to surtax. Excess liability replaced surtax which, similarly, was charged by reference to the total income of individuals. Court decisions on appeals against assessments to surtax (or its predecessor, super-tax) apply to excess liability where the relevant legislation is now applicable to it, and the majority of cases referred to below (and in other parts of this work to which reference is made) do in fact involve surtax etc. appeals.

27.2   **INCOME CHARGEABLE TO EXCESS LIABILITY—GENERAL**

(*a*)   Excess liability is charged by reference to the total income of an individual and any investment income included in it. [*ICTA 1988, s 1(2)*]. Total income is the aggregate income from all sources. [*ICTA 1988, s 835(1)*]. 'Charges on income' (27.4 below), personal allowances given by deduction [*ICTA 1988, s 256; FA 1994, s 77(1)*], any interest payments eligible for relief by deduction and any other such reliefs, e.g. allowable LOSSES (46), are deducted to give the amount on which the excess liability is calculated.

The personal allowances are deducted after any other deductions and will not reduce the investment income surcharge payable for years of assessment before 1984/85 unless they exceed in aggregate the earned income plus the investment income covered by the nil rate. Subject to this and to any express provisions to the contrary (e.g. those providing for the order in which losses are to be allowed), the deductions are treated as reducing income of different descriptions in the order which results in the greatest tax reduction. [*ICTA 1988, s 835(3)–(5); FA 1971, s 34(4)*]. Hence for years before 1984/85 if there is any investment income surcharge liability, charges on income or interest will normally be deducted against investment income first.

For what is investment income see 1.8 ALLOWANCES AND TAX RATES.

For 2000/01 onwards, qualifying donations to charity under Gift Aid are not a charge on income, but are relieved, in computing excess liability, by extending the basic rate band (see 14.12 CHARITIES).

(*b*)   There are various provisions under which amounts not within the normal charging rules of the Schedules and Cases are nevertheless to be treated as income of a person, or income of one person is to be deemed income of another. This legislation includes the following.

(i)   Much of the ANTI-AVOIDANCE (3) legislation.

(ii)   The settlements legislation in *ICTA 1988, ss 660–689*. See 81.13 *et seq.* SETTLEMENTS.

For other provisions relating specifically to excess liability, see 27.3 below.

(c)   **Assessments** which have become *final and conclusive* for income tax are also final and conclusive in estimating total income. [*ICTA 1988, s 835(7)*].

(d)   **Dividends, interest, annual payments etc. receivable.** Income received under deduction of tax is income of the year by reference to which the rate of tax is determined, irrespective of the period over which it accrued, and similarly for dividends within Schedule F. [*ICTA 1988, s 835(6)(a); FA 1996, Sch 6 paras 24, 28*]. Where securities are sold through the Stock Exchange, the interest or dividend for the period spanning the date of sale is income of the vendor or purchaser according to whether they were sold ex- or cum-dividend etc. irrespective of the period of accrual (cf. *Wigmore v Summerson KB 1925, 9 TC 577* and *CIR v Oakley KB 1925, 9 TC 582*). But see 74.5 *et seq.* SCHEDULE D, CASE VI as regards the accrued income scheme. Where the transfer of shares bequeathed under a will was delayed, dividends paid before the transfers were held to be income of the legatee (*CIR v Hawley KB 1927, 13 TC 327*). But where the controlling shareholder of a company set up a scheme under which the employees were contingently entitled to shares he owned, the dividends were held to be his pending the contingency (*CIR v Parsons CA 1928, 13 TC 700*). See also *Spence v CIR CS 1941, 24 TC 311* where dividends on shares sold and later recovered because of fraudulent misrepresentation by the purchaser were held to be income of the vendor.

Income due is not assessable before it is received (*Lambe v CIR KB 1933, 18 TC 212*, mortgage interest due but not received from company in hands of receiver not assessable) and this is so even though the non-receipt is because right to the income has not been exercised (*Dewar v CIR CA 1935, 19 TC 561; Woodhouse v CIR KB 1936, 20 TC 673*). But where a shareholder refused to accept dividends tendered to her, surtax assessments including the dividends were upheld (*Dreyfus v CIR Ch D 1963, 41 TC 441*). See also *St Lucia Usines v Colonial Treasurer PC 1924, 4 ATC 112*.

Interest receivable on National Savings Certificates and on Tax Reserve Certificates is exempt. Special treatment applies to certain interest from Building Societies (see 27.3(a) below), and to interest from National Savings Banks (see 28.15(iv) EXEMPT INCOME).

(e)   **Partnership income.** A partner's share of the partnership profits (arrived at as in 53.3 PARTNERSHIPS), is part of his total income. Where the ownership of partnership profits was subject to a future contingency and they were meanwhile carried to suspense, it was held that the profits could not meanwhile be assessed to super-tax (*Franklin v CIR KB 1930, 15 TC 464*). Similarly, amounts payable under a partnership agreement to the widow of a deceased partner, but not paid, were held not to be income of the widow (*Lebus's Exors CA 1946, 27 TC 136*). In *Dreyfus v CIR CA 1929, 14 TC 560*, it was held that the taxpayer's share of the profit of a French 'société en nom collectif' was not part of his total income.

(f)   **Settlements.** Where the legislation at (b)(iii) above does not apply, the income of a beneficiary under a settlement or trust (including a will trust) falls to be determined under general principles. For this see SETTLEMENTS at 81.8 and also at 81.10 for foreign trust income, 81.5 for discretionary and accumulation trusts, 81.9 for annuities and other annual payments and 22.17 DEDUCTION OF TAX AT SOURCE for 'free of tax' annuities. For income from deceased estates during administration see 21.3 DECEASED ESTATES.

(g) **Other matters.** A balancing charge is part of total income (*CIR v Lloyds Bank (Scott's Exors) Ch D 1963, 41 TC 294*). For income assigned for certain purpose see *CIR v Paterson CA 1924, 9 TC 163* and *Perkins' Exors v CIR KB 1928, 13 TC 851* (in which the income was held to be income of the assignor) and compare *Wolverton v CIR HL 1931, 16 TC 467*. For case where the ownership of income was in dispute, see *Shenley v CIR KB 1945, 27 TC 85*.

In *Vestey v CIR Ch D 1961, 40 TC 112* the taxpayer sold shares of an estimated value of £2m for £5.5m payable in equal instalments over 125 years. He was held to be assessable to surtax on the interest element in the instalments, calculated on actuarial lines. (Some of the reasoning in this decision was not approved by the HL in *CIR v Church Commissioners HL 1976, 50 TC 516*.)

27.3 **INCOME CHARGEABLE TO EXCESS LIABILITY—PARTICULAR PROVISIONS**

(a) The following are treated as income not liable to basic rate (or lower or Schedule F ordinary rate, see below) income tax but (after grossing-up at that rate) are subject to excess liability.

   (i) Close company loans to a participator or associate of a participator which are written off or released are grossed up at the Schedule F ordinary rate of income tax (before 6 April 1999, the lower rate) and taxed as if they were dividends (see 1.9 ALLOWANCES AND TAX RATES), with no entitlement to repayment of the notional tax credit. [*ICTA 1988, s 421; FA 1993, s 77(4); FA 1996, s 122(6), Sch 6 paras 9, 28; F(No 2)A 1997, Sch 4 para 11*].

   (ii) Restrictive covenant payments in respect of pre-9 June 1988 undertakings, in connection with an office or employment. [*ITEPA 2003, s 225; ICTA 1988, s 313*]. See 75.38 SCHEDULE E—EMPLOYMENT INCOME.

(b) **Gains on 'non-qualifying' insurance policies etc.** are subject to excess liability, with top-slicing relief. See 45.13 LIFE ASSURANCE POLICIES.

27.4 **CHARGES ON INCOME**

(a) **General.** The term 'charges on income' is derived from *TMA 1970, s 8(8)* (as originally enacted). The deduction, subject to (b) below, is for annuities or other annual payments (other than interest), patent royalties (and, previously, certain mining etc. rents and royalties) payable under DEDUCTION OF TAX AT SOURCE (22) out of the income. [*ICTA 1988, s 3; FA 1995, Sch 29 Pt VIII(22); FA 1997, Sch 18 Pt VI(2)*]. In *Bingham v CIR Ch D 1955, 36 TC 254* a deduction was refused for alimony payable under a foreign Court Order as the payer was not empowered to deduct tax at source (cf. *Keiner v Keiner QB 1952, 34 TC 346*). Tax is deductible only if the payment is 'pure income profit' in the hands of the recipient and not e.g. an element entering into the computation of his business receipts. Hence a deduction was refused for insurance premiums payable under covenant on policies lodged as part of a mortgage security (*Earl Howe v CIR CA 1919, 7 TC 289*).

Where an interest in a business is transferred in consideration for periodical payments based on subsequent profits, whether the payments are 'annual payments' rests on the facts. See *Ramsay CA 1935, 20 TC 79* and *Ledgard KB 1937, 21 TC 129* in which a deduction was refused and contrast *Hogarth CS 1940, 23 TC 491*.

Whether a payment is an 'annual payment' may arise in a number of contexts other than in arriving at total income. See 22.10 DEDUCTION OF TAX AT SOURCE for other cases.

(b)   **Statutory modifications** of the general rule include the following.

(i)   See the provisions at 81.13–81.18 SETTLEMENTS under which certain income of a settlement may fall to be treated for all tax purposes as that of the settlor.

(ii)   Annual payments made for a non-taxable consideration and not involving a settlement within the legislation (*CIR v Plummer HL 1979, 54 TC 1*) are payable in full and are not deductible for excess liability purposes. [*ICTA 1988, s 125*]. See 3.18 ANTI-AVOIDANCE.

(iii) Payments due after 14 March 1988 under non-charitable covenants are not, in any case, charges on income. [*ICTA 1988, s 347A; FA 1988, s 36; FA 1995, Sch 17 para 4(1); FA 1999, Sch 20 Pt III(6)*]. See 14.17 CHARITIES and (iv) below as regards charitable covenants.

(iv)   Payments falling due after 5 April 2000 under charitable deeds of covenant are not charges on income (see 14.17 CHARITIES) but are instead dealt with under the Gift Aid regime (see 14.12 CHARITIES).

(c)   **Timing and method of deduction.** Charges are deducted for the year which determines the rate of tax deductible, see 22.5 DEDUCTION OF TAX AT SOURCE. [*ICTA 1988, s 835(6)(b)*]. For the order of allowance against different types of income see 27.2(a) above.

27.5   INTEREST PAYABLE

Interest payable does not rank as a 'charge on income' within 27.4 above for income tax purposes, but may be allowable either as a deduction in computing business profits or as a deduction in arriving at total income or as a reduction in income tax liability. For this see 43 INTEREST PAYABLE. For the corporation tax position, see Tolley's Corporation Tax under Profit Computations.

27.6   OVERLAP BETWEEN EXCESS LIABILITY AND INHERITANCE TAX ON A DEATH

Where, on a death, income accrued at the death is treated both as capital of the estate for inheritance tax purposes and as residuary income of the estate in the hands of a beneficiary having an absolute interest in the residue, in arriving at the excess liability of the beneficiary the residuary income is reduced by the grossed-up amount of the inheritance tax attributable to the excess of the accrued income over any liabilities taken into account in both valuing the estate and arriving at the residuary income. [*ICTA 1988, s 699; FA 1993, Sch 6 para 6; FA 1996, Sch 6 paras 13, 28; F(No 2)A 1997, Sch 4 para 17; FA 1999, s 22(9)*].

27.7   OVERSEAS MATTERS

There are no special provisions regarding the excess liability treatment of non-residents or overseas income and accordingly the normal rules apply unless modified by double tax agreements. Subject to any such relevant agreement a non-resident will be within the charge to excess liability as regards his UK income (see *Brooke v CIR CA 1917, 7 TC 261*) and is assessable in his own name if he can be served with a notice of assessment (cf. *CIR v Huni KB 1923, 8 TC 466; Whitney v CIR HL 1925, 10 TC 88*).

For the treatment of personal allowances, see 51.10 NON-RESIDENTS AND OTHER OVERSEAS MATTERS.

28   Exempt Income

Cross-references. See 1 ALLOWANCES AND TAX RATES for the various personal allowances against income and 1.8(i) for certain annual payments not treated as taxable income; 16.6 CLAIMS for repayment of tax suffered; 22.11(*c*) DEDUCTION OF TAX AT SOURCE for exemption of capital portion of purchased life annuities; 29 EXEMPT ORGANISATIONS; 58.3, 58.4 PENSION INCOME; 69.10 SCHEDULE A for 'rent a room' relief; 81.21 SETTLEMENTS — re maintenance funds for historic buildings; 89 UNDERWRITERS AT LLOYD'S for transfers to special reserve funds.

The following income is exempt from income tax (to the extent and in the circumstances stated, where appropriate) and any tax suffered may be reclaimed.

28.1   **Adopters, financial support to.** Financial support paid by local authorities and adoption agencies to adopters or potential adopters, to assist towards the extra costs faced when adopting, or seeking to adopt, a child, is exempted from income tax by statute for 2003/04 onwards. The legislation lists the specific types of payment and reward within the exemption, by reference to *Adoption Act 1976* (and Scottish and NI equivalents) and *Adoption and Children Act 2002* (and to regulations under those Acts), and these extend to payment of legal and medical expenses in certain cases. The Treasury is given power to amend the list by order to take account of any future changes in the description of financial support payments. [*ICTA 1988, s 327A; FA 2003, s 175*]. Adoption allowances paid under the *Adoption Allowance Regulations 1991* (and Scottish equivalent) are included in this exemption and were previously exempted by concession (Revenue Pamphlet IR 1, A40).

28.2   **Bravery awards.** Pensions and annuities are exempt if paid to holders of certain awards for bravery in respect of the award (see 58.3(*b*) PENSION INCOME).

28.3   **Child Trust Funds.** Broadly, there is no tax on the income or gains of a child trust fund (see below for more details). Similarly, there will be no tax charges when the fund matures on the child's 18th birthday.

The child trust fund was established in order to provide all children with a financial asset at the start of adult life, to encourage savings and investment, and to help people to engage with financial institutions. Given these aims, it is not surprising that the legislation detailing the characteristics of an account that may qualify as a child trust fund, and those who may provide such accounts, is carefully drawn to protect the assets until the child reaches 18.

An account with an approved provider may be opened in respect of a child born after 31 August 2002 where (broadly) there is an entitlement to child benefit (an 'eligible child'). The majority of the regulatory framework becomes effective from an appointed day (yet to be determined at the time of writing), but it is possible to go through the formalities of opening an account at any time on or after 1 January 2005.

The process of opening an account begins with the Revenue issuing a voucher to the person who is entitled to child benefit in respect of an eligible child. The voucher must be given to an account provider within twelve months of issue. There is provision to appeal against a Revenue decision not to issue such a voucher.

An account may be opened by a responsible person (broadly, a person with parental responsibility) or (looking forward to September 2018 and beyond) by an eligible child who is over 16. If there is no responsible person, or if a voucher has been issued but not given to an account provider within twelve months, the Revenue will open an account. At any time only a single responsible person, or only the child if over 16, is able to give instructions to the account provider as to the management of the account. This person is designated the 'registered contact'.

In truth, the decisions to be made about the management of the account are limited. However, it is possible to swap to another account provider (at the cost only of incidental expenses) or to swap to an account of another description or type offered by the same account provider (once again, at the cost only of incidental expenses).

Accounts may be of two types: stakeholder accounts and non-stakeholder accounts. Stakeholder accounts are subject to stringent rules about the charges that may be deducted from them, and have a more restricted range of permissible investments and investment strategies (see below). Certain accounts, chiefly those opened by the Revenue, have to be stakeholder accounts.

Contributions to the account. The Revenue will make an initial payment into the account. The amount of this initial contribution is £250 (£500 for children in care), but there are small increases to this figure for eligible children born before the appointed day. The initial contribution is supplemented by a further £250 if (broadly) child tax credit is payable at the time child benefit is first paid and either (i) income is below the threshold for child tax credit (see 83.7 SOCIAL SECURITY) or (ii) income support or income-based job-seekers' allowance is being claimed. The amount of the supplementary payment is subject to small increases where child benefit was first paid prior to the appointed day.

The legislation provides for further contributions by the Revenue to the account, say, as the child reaches a certain age, dependent on any regulations that may be made. The detailed proposals document released by the Treasury indicate that a further contribution will be made when the child is 7, and that there will again be supplementary payments to children in families on lower incomes. As the first such payments are not due until 2009, the amounts have yet to be determined.

There is provision for the Revenue to recoup their contributions where the account is invalid and cannot be 'repaired' (see under Administration below) or where the basis for the supplementary contribution is removed because of a change in the tax credit/benefit position. Any decision not to pay a contribution, or to recoup contributions, is subject to a right of appeal.

In addition to these government payments, anyone, including the child, may pay into the account. However, there is a limit of £1,200 for such contributions in any one year. A "year" for this purpose is the period from the opening of the account to the child's next birthday, and each succeeding period of twelve months. If the limit is not reached in any year, it is not possible to carry forward the unused part. Neither is there any provision for a carry-back of contributions.

Only monetary payments may be accepted, so there is no possibility of gifting shares or other assets into a child trust fund.

Withdrawals from the account. Withdrawals from the account are not permitted before the child reaches the age of 18. There are only two exceptions to this. The first is that the account provider is allowed to make deductions in respect of management charges and incidental expenses. The second is where the child dies before reaching 18.

The investments under a child trust fund are inalienable — any charge over them, or assignment of them is void. If the child is made bankrupt, creditors may not gain access to the account.

Qualifying investments. There are extensive strictures regarding permitted investments for a child trust fund account. In order to help account providers, the structure of the regulations governing child trust fund accounts has been modelled on the provisions relating to Individual Savings Accounts. Qualifying investments for child trust funds are as follows.

(*a*)   Shares issued by a company (other than an investment trust, but see (*e*) below) wherever incorporated, and officially listed on a recognised stock exchange. There are rules to allow the official listing condition to be treated as satisfied in the case of shares issued under a public offer and due to be listed. However, shares do not qualify if they have been acquired on favourable terms because of a connection with the allocation or allotment of other shares, securities or rights thereto.

(b)   Securities issued by a company wherever incorporated, provided either the securities themselves, or the shares in the issuing company, or the shares in a parent company (of which the issuing company is a 75% subsidiary) are officially listed on a recognised stock exchange. In the case of securities in an investment trust, the investment trust must have no 'eligible rental income' (see Tolley's Corporation Tax under Unit and Investment Trusts).

(c)   Gilt-edged securities.

(d)   Securities issued by or on behalf of a government of any EEA State, and strips of such securities.

(e)   Shares in an investment trust listed in the Official List of the Stock Exchange. Broadly, in order to qualify, an investment trust must have no 'eligible rental income' (see Tolley's Corporation Tax under Unit and Investment Trusts).

(f)   Units in, or shares of, a securities scheme, warrant scheme or fund of funds scheme.

(g)   Units in, or shares of, a money-market scheme.

(h)   Units in, or shares of, a UCITS (Undertaking for Collective Investment in Transferable Securities).

(j)   A depositary interest.

(k)   Cash deposited in a share or deposit account with a building society or deposit account with a bank (as defined in *ICTA 1988, s 840A(1)(b)*) or a relevant European institution. However, a deposit or share account is not a qualifying investment if it is 'connected' with any other investment. For this purpose, an account is '*connected*' with another investment if either was opened or acquired with reference to the other, or with a view to enabling the other to be opened or acquired on particular terms, or with a view to facilitating the opening or acquisition of the other on particular terms *and* the terms on which the account was opened would have been significantly less favourable to the holder if the investment had not been acquired.

(l)   Designated national savings products.

(m)   Life insurance policies satisfying specified conditions (see below).

In order to qualify, a life insurance policy must insure the life of the child only. Its terms and conditions must provide:

• that the policy may only be owned or held as a qualifying investment for a child trust fund account;

• that the policy will terminate if it comes to the notice of the account provider that there has been a breach of the child trust fund regulations relating to insurance policies, and the breach cannot be remedied as a repair to an invalid account (see below under Administration);

• for the express prohibition of payments resulting from termination or partial surrender to the child before age 18;

• that the policy etc. cannot be assigned other than by transfer of title between approved account providers or by its vesting in the child's personal representatives.

28.3 Exempt Income

The contract of insurance must either fall within the *Financial Services and Markets Act 2000 (Regulated Activities) Order 2001, Sch 1 Pt 2* (contract of long-term insurance), *para 1* (life insurance) or *para 3* (life insurance where benefits linked to value of property), or be capable of falling within either of those paragraphs were the insurer to be a company with permission under *Financial Services and Markets Act 2000* to effect insurance contracts.

The policy must constitute life insurance and must not be a contract to pay a life annuity, a personal portfolio bond (see 45.13 LIFE ASSURANCE POLICIES) or a contract constituting pension business (as defined). There must be no contractual obligation to pay any premium other than the first (so regular premium policies are excluded). The making of loans by, or by arrangement with, the insurer to, or at the direction of, the child or registered contact is prohibited.

Stakeholder accounts. There are further restrictions on investment, and investment strategy, for stakeholder accounts. Broadly, they must not invest directly in investment trusts and certain types of insurance contract. Investment in authorised unit trusts and open-ended investment companies is subject to specific conditions. As regards investment strategy, there is a requirement for the account to be exposed to equities. The account provider must have regard to the need for diversification, and must consider investment options in the light of the purpose of the account. For the last five years or so of the account, the account provider must consider the need to minimise fluctuations in the capital value of the account resulting from market conditions.

Tax treatment. The basic proposition is that no tax is chargeable in respect of interest, dividends, distributions or gains on account investments. (For capital gains tax purposes, assets in the fund are treated as sold and immediately re-acquired at market value just prior to the child's 18th birthday). To maintain symmetry, capital gains tax losses on account investments are disregarded. Any income from account investments is not to be regarded as income for any income tax purposes — this exemption specifically embraces the children's settlements provisions at 81.18 SETTLEMENTS.

There are, in addition, disapplications of provisions taxing profits or gains under the accrued income scheme (see 74.5 SCHEDULE D, CASE VI), offshore income gains (see 52 OFFSHORE FUNDS), and discounts on relevant discounted securities (see 72.5 SCHEDULE D, CASE III). Life assurance gains (see 45.13 LIFE ASSURANCE POLICIES) are not taxable (and a deficiency on termination is not deductible from the child's total income) provided regulatory conditions are not breached (see below). Companies and local authorities may pay interest etc. gross.

It is up to the account provider to make tax claims, conduct appeals, and agree liabilities and reliefs on behalf of the child or registered contact. It is unlikely then that the child or registered contact will have to deal with any tax matters arising from the account. However, there is power for the Board to make an assessment under Schedule D, Case VI on the registered contact as an alternative to the account provider in order to withdraw relief or recover tax. This is subject to the right of appeal.

Where a life assurance policy becomes invalid because of a breach of the regulations (see above under Qualifying investments*)* a chargeable event then occurs. That event, and any prior chargeable event becomes taxable under the normal provisions relating to life assurance gains (see 45.13 *et seq.* LIFE ASSURANCE POLICIES). Lower rate tax is payable by the account provider (with the Revenue having the power to tax the registered contact). Any higher rate tax due is payable by the registered contact by assessment within five years after 31 January following the year in which the chargeable event or termination occurred.

Administration. Administration of the account largely rests with the account provider. Regulations cover: qualification as an account manager; Revenue approval and withdrawal thereof (and appeals against these decisions); appointment of UK tax representatives of non-UK account managers; account managers ceasing to act or qualify; transfer of accounts to other account providers; annual and fortnightly electronic returns of information; annual and interim tax repayment claims; record-keeping; and information to be provided to the named child (including annual statements).

The account provider and the registered contact are required to take any necessary steps to remedy any breach of the regulations surrounding the child trust fund account. Provided this is done the account remains valid during the period of the breach, although penalties may still be in point. There are, however, two breaches where no repair is possible:

- where the child has never been an eligible child; and

- where more than one account is held for the same child.

In the above circumstances, Revenue contributions, plus any consequent income and gains, will be recouped, the account provider, registered contact and named child being jointly and severally liable.

The Revenue have wide powers to require information and to inspect records in relation to child trust fund accounts. This is subject to a penalty regime analogous to that for special returns in *TMA 1970, s 98* (see 57.9 PENALTIES).

There is a penalty of up to £300 for fraudulently opening, or making a withdrawal from, a child trust fund account.

[*Child Trust Funds Act 2004; SI 2004 No 1450*].

28.4   **Compensation for loss of employment etc. up to £30,000.** See 18.4 COMPENSATION FOR LOSS OF EMPLOYMENT for details of exemptions and reliefs for these and other terminal payments at the end of an employment.

28.5   **Compensation for mis-sold pensions products (and interest thereon). Personal pensions etc.** Exemption from both income tax and capital gains tax is conferred on the receipt at any time of a capital sum (which may include a sum otherwise chargeable to income tax) by way of compensation for loss, or likely loss, caused by certain 'bad investment advice' concerning personal pensions etc. *'Bad investment advice'* is investment advice (as defined) in respect of which an action has been or may be brought against the adviser for negligence, breach of contract or fiduciary obligation or by reason of a contravention actionable under *Financial Services Act 1986, s 62* or *Financial Services and Markets Act 2000, s 150*. The exemption applies where a person (whether or not the person suffering loss), acting on such advice at least some of which was given after 28 April 1988 and before 1 July 1994 (at which date new regulatory safeguards came into force), either

(*a*)   joined a personal pension scheme or took out a retirement annuity contract (see 60 PERSONAL PENSION SCHEMES, 66 RETIREMENT ANNUITIES) whilst eligible, or reasonably likely to become eligible, to join an occupational pension scheme (i.e. an approved retirement benefits scheme, relevant statutory scheme or pre-6 April 1980 approved superannuation scheme — see 67.1, 67.13 RETIREMENT SCHEMES FOR EMPLOYEES); or

(*b*)   left, or ceased to pay into, an occupational pension scheme and instead joined a personal pension scheme or took out a retirement annuity contract; or

(*c*)   transferred to a personal pension scheme his accrued rights under an occupational pension scheme; or

(*d*)   left an occupational pension scheme and instead entered into arrangements for securing relevant benefits (see 67.1 RETIREMENT SCHEMES FOR EMPLOYEES) by means of an annuity contract with an insurance company.

Interest on the whole or part of a capital sum within the above exemption is itself exempt from income tax to the extent that it covers a period ending on or before the earliest date on which the amount of the capital sum is first determined, whether by agreement or by a court, tribunal, commissioner, arbitrator or appointee.

[*FA 1996, s 148; SI 2001 No 3629, Article 93*].

Freestanding additional voluntary contribution schemes ('FSAVCSs'). By concession, where liability would otherwise arise, the following payments will not be chargeable to income tax (although this will not apply to annuities or other annual payments arising from the compensation), and their receipt will not be treated as the disposal of an asset for capital gains tax purposes.

(i)   The payment of a capital sum by way of compensation determined in accordance with the Financial Services Authority guidance for the performance of the review required by the Authority of specified categories of FSAVCSs sold between 28 April 1988 and 15 August 1999 inclusive, and made as a result of the review.

(ii)   The payment of interest on the whole or part of the sum within (i) for a period ending on or before the earliest date on which the capital sum was determined.

(Revenue Pamphlet IR 1, A99).

28.6   **Damages and compensation for personal injury — periodical payments.** Income tax relief is available where an agreement is made settling a claim or action for damages for personal injury (as widely defined) under which the damages are to consist wholly or partly of periodical payments, or where a court order incorporates such terms. This applies equally in relation to interim court order payments and voluntary payments on account. Periodical payments are not regarded as income for income tax purposes, and are paid without deduction of tax under *ICTA 1988, s 348(1)(b)* or *s 349(1)* (see 22.2, 22.3 DEDUCTION OF TAX AT SOURCE). This applies as regards the person ('A') entitled to the damages under the agreement or order, and also

(*a*)   any person receiving the payments on behalf of A; and

(*b*)   any trustee receiving the payments on trust for A's benefit under a trust under which A is (during his lifetime) the sole beneficiary,

and sums paid on to (or for the benefit of) A by a person within (*b*) above are not regarded as A's income for income tax purposes.

Any or all of the periodical payments may (if the agreement etc., or a subsequent agreement, so provides) be under one or more annuities purchased or provided for (or for the benefit of) A by the person otherwise liable for the payments.

The above provisions apply equally to annuity payments under a compensation award under the Criminal Injuries Compensation Scheme. The Treasury may also apply them (with any necessary modifications) to any other scheme or arrangement making similar provision.

[*ICTA 1988, ss 329AA, 329AB; FA 1996, s 150, Sch 26*].

Simon's Direct Tax Service. See **E4.326**.

28.7   **Foreign service allowance** to a person in the service of the Crown representing compensation for the extra cost of living abroad. [*ITEPA 2003, s 299; ICTA 1988, s 319*].

28.8   **Foster care receipts** are exempt for 2003/04 onwards if they do not exceed a limit computed by reference to the individual recipient, and, if the recipient so elects, are subject to special computational rules if they do. See further below. Previously, under what was known as the 'reward system', local authorities were allowed to allocate their payments to foster carers between those that merely reimbursed expenditure and those that provided profit (i.e. reward) to the carer. To the extent that payments fell into the first category, they were not taxable. Otherwise, the carer's profits, after deducting allowable expenditure and any capital allowances, were liable to tax under Schedule D. (Hansard 26 October 1994, Vol 248, Col 628, Treasury Explanatory Notes to Finance Bill 2003, and see Revenue Business Income Manual BIM 52760).

An individual's 'foster care receipts' are potentially within the above exemption for 2003/04 onwards if, for the tax year under consideration, he derives no taxable income, other than 'foster care receipts', from any trade, profession, vocation or non-trading foster care arrangement from which he derives 'foster care receipts'. Receipts are *'foster care receipts'* of an individual for a tax year if

- they are receipts from the 'provision of foster care',

- they would (apart from these provisions) be chargeable under Schedule D, Case I, II or VI, and

- they accrue in the basis period for the trade, profession or vocation (see 71.3 SCHEDULE D, CASES I AND II) or, in the case of non-trading foster care arrangements within Case VI, in the tax year itself.

For these purposes, the *'provision of foster care'* means the provision of accommodation and maintenance for a child by an individual, other than an 'excluded individual', with whom the child has been placed under specified statutory provisions governing foster care in the UK. Receipts from *private* foster care arrangements do not qualify for the exemption. Anyone who is a parent of the child, or has parental responsibility in relation to the child, is an *'excluded individual'* for this purpose, as is (where relevant) anyone in whose favour a residence order (or, in Scotland, a contact order) has been made and was in force immediately prior to the child's being placed in care.

The exemption applies where the individual's total foster care receipts for the tax year or (as the case may be) the period of account, taking no account of any deduction for expenses etc., do not exceed the individual's limit. This limit is based on a fixed amount of £10,000 per 'residence' plus an amount per child per individual based on the number of weeks (or part weeks) during the income period (i.e. the basis period or, for non-trading arrangements, the tax year) in which the individual provides foster care for the child. The amount per child is £200 per week (or part week) for a child under 11 and £250 per week (or part week) for a child of 11 or over; a week in which the child reaches the age of 11 qualifies for the higher figure. A week, for these purposes, comprises the seven days beginning with a Monday. A week in which an income period ends is counted as belonging to that income period. Both the fixed and weekly amounts are subject to any amendment made by future Treasury order. If, *in the tax year*, the residence used to provide the foster care is also used for provision of foster care by one or more other individuals who also have foster care receipts for the year, the £10,000 fixed amount is divisible equally between them. If an individual's income period is not an exact year, the fixed amount or, where relevant, his share of it is apportioned *pro rata*. For these purposes, a *'residence'* is a building, or part of a building, occupied, or intended to be occupied, as a separate residence, with any temporary division of a single residence into two or more residences being disregarded; the term also extends to a caravan or houseboat.

Where the exemption applies, the individual is treated, for the tax year in question, as making nil profit and nil loss from the trade, profession or vocation or (as the case may be) from each non-trading foster care arrangement from which the foster care receipts arise. If, in the case of a trade etc., the individual would otherwise be entitled to relief for an overlap profit (see 71.11 SCHEDULE D, CASES I AND II), he is given the relief anyway. If, for the tax year or (as the case may be) the period of account, the individual's total foster care receipts would be within the exemption were it not for the fact that they exceed his limit, he may give written notice of election to an officer of the Board to be charged to income tax as if his profit were equal to the excess. The election for this alternative method of calculating profit must be made no later than the first anniversary of 31 January following the tax year (or such later date as the Board may allow in a particular case) and has effect for that tax year only. In the absence of an election, the normal rules for computing profits and losses apply. If no election is made before the deadline but his taxable foster care profits are adjusted after the deadline has passed, the individual is given additional time in which to make an election, the revised deadline being the first anniversary of 31 January following the tax year in which the adjustment is made (or, again, such later date as the Board may allow in a particular case).

In computing the individual's limit in a case where the foster care receipts are those of a period of account (other than one ending on 5 April), the fixed amount is that prescribed for the tax year in which the period of account ends, e.g. £10,000 for a period ending in 2003/04. For 2003/04, the amounts per child are computed by reference to the whole of the period of account (notwithstanding that part of it preceded 6 April 2003). If, in future, the prescribed amounts per child alter, so that different rates apply for two tax years in which the period of account falls, the rates for the first of those tax years apply in respect of children cared for during that part of the period of account preceding 6 April and the new rates will apply in respect of children cared for during that part of the period of account falling after 5 April.

Example

Dave and Holly, a couple living together, provide foster care by way of trade. Each prepares accounts to 31 December. During their respective periods of account covering the year ending 31 December 2004, they provide care to a twelve-year old (child 1) for the full 52 weeks and to a nine-year old (child 2) for 15 weeks. *Each* of their individual limits is computed as follows.

	£
Fixed amount for 2004/05: £10,000 ÷ 2	5,000
Amounts per child: child 1 (52 × £250)	13,000
child 2 (15 × £200)	3,000
	£21,000

For a chargeable period (see 9.2(i) CAPITAL ALLOWANCES) corresponding to an income period for a tax year for which either the exemption applies or an election is made to apply the alternative method of calculating profit, the individual is not entitled to capital allowances on plant and machinery used to provide foster care. Where such allowances *were* available for the preceding chargeable period, a disposal event is deemed to have occurred immediately after the start of the current chargeable period and a disposal value must be brought into account equal to the unrelieved qualifying expenditure brought forward from the preceding chargeable period; consequently, no balancing allowance or charge arises (see generally 9.28 CAPITAL ALLOWANCES). For the first chargeable period for which neither the exemption nor the alternative method applies, but for which foster care receipts still arise, *CAA 2001, s 13* is brought into effect as if, on the first day of that chargeable period, the individual had brought into use for the purposes of his provision of foster care any such plant or machinery that he still owns and any plant or machinery acquired for those purposes during the time that allowances were not available. Such plant or machinery will normally fall to be brought in at its then market value — see 9.38(E) CAPITAL ALLOWANCES.

[*FA 2003, s 176, Sch 36*].

28.9   **German and Austrian annuities and pensions for victims of Nazi persecution** under German or Austrian law are not treated as income for any income tax purpose. [*ITEPA 2003, s 642; ICTA 1988, s 330*].

28.10   **Guaranteed income bonds etc.** See 45.15(*i*) LIFE INSURANCE POLICIES as regards annuities and annual payments under certain life insurance policies which are excluded from treatment as such.

28.11   **Housing grants.** Except where the expense recouped is deductible from profits, amounts received, under any relevant Act, towards expenses incurred, by the recipient or another, in providing, maintaining or improving residential accommodation are not assessable. [*ICTA 1988, s 578*].

28.12   An annual payment made after 30 September 2004 under an '**immediate needs annuity**', otherwise chargeable under Schedule D, Case III or V, is exempt from income tax to the extent that it is made to a care provider (as defined) or local authority in respect of the provision of care (as defined) for the person for whose benefit the annuity was made. For this purpose, an '*immediate needs annuity*' is a life annuity contract

●   the purpose of which, or one of the purposes of which, is to protect a person against the consequences of his being unable, at the time the contract is made, to live independently without assistance, due to permanent mental or physical impairment, injury, sickness or other infirmity, and

●   under which benefits are payable in respect of the provision of care for that person.

The above definition, and the definition of care provider, may be amended by Treasury Order.

[*ICTA 1988, s 580C; FA 2004, s 147(3)(6)*].

28.13   **Individual savings accounts. From 6 April 1999,** individuals aged 18 or over (reduced to 16 from 6 April 2001 in the case of cash only accounts (as below)) who are resident and ordinarily resident in the UK are able to subscribe up to £7,000 in each tax year (reducing to £5,000 after 5 April 2006) to an individual savings account set up in accordance with regulations. The account may contain three components: cash (including National Savings); life insurance (but see below); and stocks and shares. Of the annual subscription, no more than £3,000 (reducing to £1,000 after 5 April 2006) may go into cash and £1,000 into life insurance. The restrictions on the scope of investments in stocks and shares are generally more relaxed than those which previously applied to personal equity plans (see 28.24 below). Shares acquired under approved profit-sharing or SAYE option schemes or share incentive plans (see 82.18, 82.47, 82.20 SHARE-RELATED EMPLOYMENT INCOME AND EXEMPTIONS) may be transferred in at market value (with no capital gains tax liability) within the annual subscription limits, but public offer and demutualisation issues may not be transferred in. Life insurance products have to be of the single premium type (i.e. there must be no obligation to keep up premium payments in order to obtain policy benefits), although policies with recurrent single premiums or regular monthly premiums are acceptable. There is no minimum subscription, no lifetime limit and no loss of relief on withdrawals. It is guaranteed that the arrangements will continue for at least ten years.

It was announced in the December 2003 Pre-Budget Report that the insurance component is to be abolished from April 2005. Life insurance products and newly-introduced medium-term stakeholder products will instead go into the stocks and shares component, except that products which provide a 'cash-like' return (i.e. which are relatively risk-free) will have to go into the cash component. The maximum subscription per tax year to a stocks and shares mini-account will be increased from £3,000 to £4,000.

Personal equity plans (see 28.24 below) held at 5 April 1999 may continue to be held without affecting the ability to invest in an individual savings account. Similarly investments in TESSAs started before 6 April 1999 do not affect individual savings account investments, and the capital (but *not* the accrued interest) in a maturing TESSA may be transferred to an individual savings account in addition to the normal investment limits.

There is an exemption from income tax and capital gains tax on the investments, and for the first five years for which the accounts are available (i.e. until 5 April 2004), *FA 1998, s 76* disapplies the rule introduced by *F(No 2)A 1997, s 30* preventing payment of the tax credit attached to UK dividends (see 1.9 ALLOWANCES AND TAX RATES), so that the 10% tax credit is payable (and regulations make similar provision in respect of non-resident holders of accounts — see below). (*FA 1998, s 76* also makes similar provision in relation to holders of personal equity plans, see 28.24 below.) Similar provision made in relation to insurance company and friendly society investments referable to individual savings account business.

The necessary regulation-making powers are provided in general by amendment to the personal equity plan regulations [*FA 1998, s 75*], and in relation to life insurance investments and FRIENDLY SOCIETIES (31) by *FA 1998, s 77*. Accounts, which must be administered by managers, may be offered by financial institutions or by independent providers. Managers will be able to offer accounts either accepting overall subscriptions (which must be able to accept the annual maximum, and so *must* offer a stocks and shares component and *may* offer either or both of the other two components) or accepting one of the three components (within the applicable annual maximum, including a £3,000 maximum in relation to a stocks and shares account).

The Individual Savings Account Regulations 1998 (*SI 1998 No 1870* as amended) provide for the setting up by Revenue-approved accounts managers of plans in the form of an account (an ISA) under which individuals may make certain investments, for the conditions under which they may invest and under which the accounts are to operate, for relief from tax in respect of account investments, and for general administration. The regulations, which are summarised below, generally took effect on 6 April 1999.

General. An application to subscribe to an ISA may be made by an individual who is 18 or over (16 or over from 6 April 2001 in the case of cash only accounts) and who is resident and ordinarily resident in the UK (or is a non-UK resident Crown employee whose duties are in effect treated as performed in the UK, see 75.4 SCHEDULE E—EMPLOYMENT INCOME, or, from 6 April 2001, the spouse of such an employee). Joint accounts are not permitted. An investor who subsequently fails to meet the residence requirement may retain the account and the right to tax exemptions thereunder but can make no further subscriptions to the account until he again comes to meet that requirement. After 7 January 2003, an application made on behalf of an individual suffering from mental disorder, by a parent, guardian, spouse, son or daughter of his, is treated as if made by that individual. This replaced a rule specific to Scotland whereby a *curator bonis* appointed in respect of a qualifying individual incapable of managing his affairs could subscribe to an ISA in his capacity as such without affecting his right to subscribe in any other capacity.

An ISA is made up of *one or more* of the following: a stocks and shares component, a cash component and an insurance component (see below re qualifying investments for each of these components and see above re the proposed abolition of the insurance component). It must be designated from the outset as a maxi-account, mini-account or TESSA only account, such designation continuing to have effect for any year in which the investor makes a subscription to the account.

A *maxi-account* must comprise a stocks and shares component (*with or without* other components). The maximum subscription per tax year is £7,000 (reducing to £5,000 after 5 April 2006) of which a maximum of £3,000 (reducing to £1,000 after 5 April 2006) may be allocated to a cash component and £1,000 to an insurance component. For 2001/02 and subsequent years, where the subscriber is 16 but under 18 at the end of the tax year, the limit is lowered to £3,000 (reducing to £1,000 after 5 April 2006), which may only be invested in a cash component, and in the year in which the subscriber attains the age of 18 that limit and restriction apply to subscriptions before his or her birthday. In any tax year in which an investor subscribes to a maxi-account he cannot subscribe to any other ISA apart from a TESSA only account.

A *mini-account* must consist of a single specified component. The maximum subscription (per tax year) is £3,000 if that component is stocks and shares, £1,000 if it is insurance and £3,000 (reducing to £1,000 after 5 April 2006) if it is cash. In any tax year in which an investor subscribes to a mini-account, he cannot subscribe to another mini-account consisting of the same component or to a maxi-account. From April 2005, as a consequence of the abolition of the insurance component (see above), the maximum subscription to a stocks and shares mini-account is expected to be increased to £4,000.

A *TESSA only account* is an account consisting of a cash component only and limited to capital (*not* accumulated interest) transferred from a TESSA (see 28.16(iii) below) within six months following its maturity after 5 April 1999 (or after 5 January 1999 where no follow-up TESSA is opened). Such transfers are not subject to any annual subscription limit, and may also be made to a maxi-account or to a cash component mini-account without counting towards the annual subscription limits for such accounts. Continuing subscriptions after 5 April 1999 to a TESSA or follow-up TESSA do not affect an individual's ISA annual subscription limits.

Subscriptions to an ISA must be made in cash (and must be allocated irrevocably to the agreed component or single component) *except that* shares acquired by the investor under a SAYE option scheme (see 82.47 SHARE-RELATED EMPLOYMENT INCOME AND EXEMPTIONS) or a share incentive plan (see 82.20 SHARE-RELATED EMPLOYMENT INCOME AND EXEMPTIONS) or appropriated to him under an approved profit sharing scheme (see 82.18 SHARE-RELATED EMPLOYMENT INCOME AND EXEMPTIONS) may be transferred to a stocks and shares component. Such transfers count towards the annual subscription limits, by reference to the market value of the shares at the date of transfer. No chargeable gain or allowable loss arises on the transfer. A transfer of SAYE scheme shares must be made within 90 days after the exercise of the option, and a transfer of share incentive plan shares must be made within 90 days of the shares ceasing to be subject to the plan. A transfer of shares appropriated under a profit sharing scheme must be made within 90 days after the earlier of the release date (see 82.19 SHARE-RELATED EMPLOYMENT INCOME AND EXEMPTIONS) and the date on which the investor instructed the scheme trustees to transfer ownership of the shares to him. From 13 December 2000, 'shares' in these cases includes a reference to those held in the form of depositary interests (see (*j*) below).

Compensation paid into ISAs for loss of income or capital growth due to failures or delays on the part of ISA managers will not count towards the subscription limit. This does not apply to compensation paid in respect of a delay in opening an ISA, or in accepting a subscription to an ISA. See Revenue Guidance Notes for ISA Managers paras 10.38, 10.39 and PEP and ISA Bulletin 4, 13 December 2001.

ISA investments cannot be purchased otherwise than out of cash held by the account manager and allocated to the particular component concerned, and cannot be purchased from the investor or the investor's spouse.

The title to ISA investments (other than cash deposits, national savings products and certain insurance policies) is vested in the account manager (or his nominee) either alone or jointly with the investor, though all ISA investments are in the beneficial ownership of the investor. The investor may elect to receive annual reports and accounts etc. in respect of ISA investments and/or to attend and vote at shareholders' etc. meetings.

The statements and declarations to be made when applying to subscribe to an ISA are specified. The maximum penalty for an incorrect statement or declaration is the amount (if any) of income tax and/or capital gains tax underpaid as a result. Assessments to withdraw tax relief or otherwise recover tax underpaid may be made (under SCHEDULE D, CASE VI (74)) in the case of income tax) on the account manager or investor. The Revenue have power to require information from, and to inspect records of, account managers and investors.

From 1 October 2002 (and with reference to pre-existing ISAs as well as new ones), the terms and conditions of an ISA cannot prevent the investor from withdrawing funds or from transferring his account (or a part of it) to another Revenue-approved account manager (subject to the conditions governing such transfers). The account manager is allowed a reasonable business period (not exceeding 30 days) to comply with the investor's instructions in this regard. By concession, an ISA opened before 24 August 2002 offering a fixed or guaranteed return under terms requiring the funds to be locked in for a period of up to five years may, if the manager wishes and with Revenue agreement, continue to maturity under its original terms, though no further subscriptions can be made after 5 April 2003. (Revenue Press Release 26 July 2002).

Tax exemptions. Except as stated below, no income tax or capital gains tax is chargeable on the account manager or the investor in respect of interest, dividends, distributions or gains on ISA investments. Capital losses are not allowable. As stated in the introduction above, tax credits on UK dividends paid before 6 April 2004 are repayable (via the account manager). An investor who ceases to be UK-resident is treated as continuing to be so resident as regards his entitlement to repayment of tax credits.

Interest on a cash deposit held within a stocks and shares component or insurance component is, however, taxable at the lower rate of income tax, such tax to be accounted for by the account manager (by set-off against tax repayments or otherwise). There is no further liability; the interest does not form part of the investor's total income and the tax paid cannot be repaid to the investor.

Life assurance gains on policies held within an insurance component are not subject to income tax (and a deficiency on termination is not deductible from the investor's total income). If it comes to the account manager's notice that such a policy is invalid, i.e. its terms and conditions do not provide (or no longer provide) that it be held only as a qualifying insurance component investment, a chargeable event then occurs, with any gain taxable under SCHEDULE D, CASE VI (74). If the policy has already terminated, the chargeable event is deemed to have occurred at the end of the final policy year (see 45.15(*a*) LIFE ASSURANCE POLICIES). Any previous chargeable event which actually occurred in relation to the policy is similarly taxed, by reference to the time it occurred. Basic rate income tax is payable by the account manager (with the Revenue also having power to assess the investor). Any higher rate tax due is payable by the investor by assessment within five years after 31 January following the year of assessment in which the chargeable event occurred or was deemed to occur. Top-slicing relief (see 45.13 LIFE ASSURANCE POLICIES) is available in the same way as for non-ISA-related chargeable events.

Exempt income and gains do not have to be reported in the investor's personal tax return.

Further capital gains matters. A transfer of ISA investments by an account manager to an investor is deemed to be made at market value, with no capital gain or allowable loss arising. An investor is treated as holding shares or securities in an ISA in a capacity other than that in which he holds any other shares etc. of the same class in the same company, so that share identification rules (see Tolley's Capital Gains Tax under Shares and Securities —

Identification Rules) are applied separately to ISA investments (and separately as between different ISAs held by the same investor). The normal share reorganisation rules are disapplied in respect of ISA investments in the event of a reorganisation of share capital involving an allotment for payment, e.g. a rights issue. Shares transferred to an ISA in the limited circumstances described above are deemed for these purposes to have been ISA investments from, in the case of SAYE option scheme shares, their acquisition by the investor, in the case of all-employee plan shares, their ceasing to be subject to the plan, and, in the case of profit sharing scheme shares, the earlier of the release date (see 82.19 SHARE-RELATED EMPLOYMENT INCOME AND EXEMPTIONS) and the date on which the investor instructed the scheme trustees to transfer ownership of the shares to him. Where the investor held shares eligible for transfer to an ISA and other shares of the same class but not so eligible, disposals are generally identified primarily with the latter, thus preserving to the greatest possible extent the eligibility of the remaining shares.

Qualifying investments

Stocks and shares component. Qualifying investments for a stocks and shares component are as follows.

(*a*) Shares issued by a company (other than an investment trust, but see (*e*) below) wherever incorporated, and officially listed on a recognised stock exchange (see below). There are rules to allow the official listing condition to be treated as satisfied in the case of shares issued under a public offer and due to be listed.

(*b*) Securities (i.e. secured or unsecured loan stock and similar) issued by a company wherever incorporated, and with a minimum residual term of five years from the date when first held under the ISA. Either the securities must be officially listed on a recognised stock exchange (see below) or the shares in the issuing company or its 75% holding company must be so listed. In the case of securities of an investment trust, the trust must satisfy the two qualifying conditions at (*e*) below.

(*c*) Gilt-edged securities and gilt strips with at least five years to run to maturity from the date when first held under the ISA.

(*d*) Securities issued by or on behalf of a government of a European Economic Area State (comprising the EU plus Norway, Iceland and Liechtenstein and excluding for this purpose the UK), and strips of such securities, with at least five years to run to maturity from the date when first held under the ISA.

(*e*) Shares in a qualifying investment trust listed in the Official List of the Stock Exchange. Broadly, in order to qualify, an investment trust must have no 'eligible rental income' (within *ICTA 1988, s 508A* — see Tolley's Corporation Tax under Unit and Investment Trusts) *and* not more than 50% in value of its investments can be securities otherwise within any of (*b*)–(*d*) above but having less than five years to run to maturity from the date when first acquired by the trust.

(*f*) (Before 6 April 2004) units in, or shares of,

  • a securities scheme (broadly an authorised unit trust or open-ended investment company ('OEIC') or part of an umbrella scheme — see 90.1 UNIT TRUSTS), or

  • a warrant scheme (broadly a type of authorised unit trust or OEIC investing in warrants or part of an umbrella scheme of that category), or

  • a relevant UCITS (an Undertaking for Collective Investment in Transferable Securities situated in and authorised by an EU Member State other than the UK, or part of such an undertaking equivalent to part of an umbrella scheme), where the scheme or UCITS satisfies the equivalent of the 50% condition in (*e*) above.

(*fa*)   (After 5 April 2004) units in, or shares of,

- a securities scheme (as in (*f*) above), or

- a warrant scheme (as in (*f*) above), or

- a relevant UCITS (an Undertaking for Collective Investment in Transferable Securities situated in and authorised by an EU Member State other than the UK, or part of such an undertaking equivalent to part of an umbrella scheme), or

- a fund of funds scheme (as defined),

where the units or shares satisfy the '5% test' outlined below.

(*g*)   (Before 6 April 2004) units in, or shares of, a fund of funds scheme (as defined), subject to the condition that not more than 50% in value of its investments can be investments which would otherwise be within (*f*) above but do not themselves satisfy the 50% condition therein mentioned.

(*ga*)   (After 16 November 2003) units in, or shares of, a Chapter 5 UCITS (an Undertaking for Collective Investment in Transferable Securities complying with Chapter 5 of the Collective Investment Schemes Sourcebook made by the Financial Services Authority) where the units or shares satisfy the '5% test' outlined below.

(*h*)   Shares acquired by the investor under a SAYE share option scheme or all-employee share ownership plan or appropriated to him under an approved profit sharing scheme which are transferred into the ISA as mentioned under '*General*' above.

(*j*)   (From 13 December 2000) a 'depositary interest' in or in relation to an investment which is itself a qualifying investment other than cash. A '*depositary interest*' means the rights of any person to investments held by another, effectively as his nominee. After 16 November 2003 or 5 April 2004 (as appropriate), the underlying investment, if within (*fa*) or (*ga*) above, must satisfy the '5% test' outlined below.

(*k*)   Cash held on deposit pending investment in any of the above.

By concession, a fund of funds scheme that invests in a Chapter 5 UCITS may be eligible for inclusion in an ISA if the Chapter 5 UCITS restricts its investment and borrowing powers to those of a securities scheme (Revenue PEP and ISA Bulletin No 13, 10 December 2003).

The term '*company*' does not for the above purposes include an OEIC, a UCITS or an industrial and provident society (or 51% subsidiary thereof).

As regards the 50% test in (*e*) (and consequently (*f*) and (*g*)) above, securities transferred under stock lending arrangements are still considered to be held by the trust or scheme, and any collateral obtained under those arrangements is ignored (Revenue PEP and ISA Bulletin No 5, 29 April 2002).

For the purposes of (*fa*), (*ga*) and (*j*) above, an investment satisfies the '5% test' if there is no time during the five years after the investment is first held in the ISA when, by virtue of any contract or any other transaction entered into or by virtue of the nature of the underlying investments, the investor is not exposed (or not exposed to any significant extent) to the risk of a loss (from fluctuations in value) exceeding 5% of the sum of the capital consideration paid (or payable) for the acquisition of the investment and the incidental costs of acquisition. Thus, if the investor is certain or near certain of receiving back at least 95% of the investment within five years, for example if he is given a guarantee to that effect or if the scheme or UCITS itself invests substantially in cash, the test is failed.

Investments held in an ISA on 6 April 2004 and within (*f*) or (*g*) above may continue to be held in the ISA notwithstanding the '5% test' introduced in (*fa*) above. The same applies to depositary interests (see (*j*) above) where the underlying investment is within (*f*) or (*g*) above.

Following a revision in the Revenue's interpretation of the phrase 'listed on a recognised stock exchange', securities admitted to trading on a European Economic Area exchange where securities traded are not listed by the relevant competent authority may have ceased to be a qualifying investment from 28 November 2001. Amending regulations were passed to preserve the qualifying status of securities held on that date within an ISA (where such status would otherwise have been lost for the aforementioned reason and no other) for as long as the above circumstances continue (and see Revenue Press Release 28 November 2001).

Cash component. Qualifying investments for a cash component are as follows.

(i) Cash deposited in a deposit account with a building society, a person within *ICTA 1988, s 840A(1)(b)* (see 7.1 BANKS) or certain European institutions entitled to accept deposits in the UK.

(ii) Cash deposited in a building society share account.

(iii) Units in, or shares of, a money market scheme (as defined).

(iv) Units in, or shares of, a fund of funds scheme (as defined) which permits investment only in units in, or shares of, money market schemes.

(v) Designated national savings products.

(vi) (After 16 November 2003) investments that would fall within (*ga*) above (stocks and shares component) but for their failing the '5% test'.

(vii) (After 16 November 2003) depositary interests (see (*j*) above) in or in relation to an investment which is itself a qualifying investment for a cash component.

(viii) (After 5 April 2004) investments that would fall within (*fa*) above (stocks and shares component) but for their failing the '5% test'.

A deposit or share account within (i) or (ii) above is not a qualifying investment if is 'connected' with any other account held within those categories (whether or not by the investor). For this purpose, accounts are '*connected*' if either was opened with reference to the other or with a view to enabling the other to be opened, or facilitating the opening of the other, on particular terms *and* the terms on which the cash component account was opened would have been significantly less favourable to the investor if the other had not been opened. The Revenue will accept that an account is not a connected account if it is a 'feeder' account opened to enable investors to fund future deposits into an ISA, provided that the interest on the feeder account is in line with the interest paid on the account manager's other savings accounts (see Revenue Guidance Notes for ISA Managers).

Insurance component. Qualifying investments for an insurance component are policies of life insurance satisfying specified conditions and cash held on deposit pending investment in such policies. The insurance must be on the life of the ISA investor only and its terms and conditions must provide:

(A) that the policy may only be owned or held as a qualifying investment for an ISA insurance component;

(B) that, if found to be in breach of (A) above, it shall automatically terminate (and see also above under 'Tax exemptions');

(C) for an express prohibition of any transfer to the investor of the policy or the rights conferred thereby or any share or interest therein (other than cash proceeds on termination or partial surrender); and

(D)   that the policy etc. cannot be assigned other than by transfer of title between approved ISA managers or by its vesting in the investor's personal representatives.

The policy must constitute life insurance and must not be a contract to pay a life annuity, a personal portfolio bond (see 45.13 LIFE ASSURANCE POLICIES) or a contract constituting pension business (as defined). There must be no contractual obligation to pay any premium other than the first (so regular premium policies are excluded). 'Connected' policies are excluded in much the same way as connected accounts are excluded from a cash component (see above). The making of loans by, or by arrangement with, the insurer to, or at the direction of, the ISA investor is prohibited.

Repairing of invalid accounts. Where, within a single tax year, an investor opens a valid ISA, closes it and opens a new ISA of the same designation and component, the new ISA used to be technically invalid (because transfers between ISAs can only be carried out by account managers). For 2003/04 onwards, where the account is a mini-account or TESSA only account, the new ISA (i.e. the first such ISA to be opened after the said closure and in the same tax year) is treated as valid (and thus qualifying for tax relief) from the date it is opened.

Where the above circumstances occurred in 2001/02 or 2002/03 and the Revenue give notice after 7 January 2003 that the new account is invalid, the account becomes 'eligible for repair', i.e. it qualifies for tax relief *but only from the date of the notice*. Similar consequences ensue for 2001/02 and all subsequent years (where the resulting Revenue notice is given after 7 January 2003) where an investor subscribes to an incompatible combination of maxi-accounts and mini-accounts in a single tax year. Accounts thus eligible for repair are the earliest invalid account opened in the year and any account to which the capital proceeds of a matured TESSA are transferred. Repairing of accounts is subject to normal subscription limits, and where necessary the Revenue will apportion (i.e. between valid accounts and any one or more accounts eligible for repair) the total amount subscribed in the tax year.

Account managers. The regulations cover qualification as an account manager, Revenue approval and withdrawal thereof, appointment of UK tax representatives of non-UK account managers, account managers ceasing to act or to qualify, claims for tax relief and agreement of liabilities, annual returns of income and of information, annual and interim tax repayment claims, record-keeping, and information to be provided to investors.

[*SI 1998 No 1870; SI 1998 No 3174; SI 2000 Nos 809, 3112; SI 2001 No 908; SI 2001 No 3629, Articles 168–178; SI 2001 No 3778; SI 2002 Nos 453, 1974, 3158; SI 2003 No 2747*].

Separate regulations modify existing tax legislation so far as it concerns individual savings account business of insurance companies. [*SI 1998 No 1871 as amended; SI 1998 No 3174; SI 2001 No 3629, Article 179*].

Closure and death. Subject to the ISA terms and conditions, an investor may close an ISA at any time without affecting tax exemptions up to the date of closure. Where an investor dies, income and gains in respect of ISA investments which arise after the date of death but before the date of closure are not exempt.

See generally Revenue Booklet IR 2008 'ISAs, PEPs and TESSAs' and the Revenue 'Guidance Notes for ISA Managers'. There is also a Revenue ISA helpline on 0845–604 1701, and PEP and ISA Bulletins are published on the Revenue website.

Simon's Direct Tax Service. See E3.7.

28.14   Income from **international organisations** may be exempt under specific provisions, see 23 DIPLOMATIC IMMUNITY.

28.15 Annual payments falling to be made under certain **insurance policies** are exempt from income tax. The exemption, described below, will most commonly apply to mortgage payment protection insurance, permanent health insurance, creditor insurance (to meet existing commitments, possibly including domestic utility bills, in event of accident, sickness, disability or unemployment) and certain kinds of long-term care insurance (but only where the policy is taken out before the need for care becomes apparent). (Revenue Press Release REV 6, 28 November 1995).

The exemption is generally restricted to payments that would otherwise be taxed under Schedule D, Case III or, in the case of equivalent non-UK policies, Schedule D, Case V. Payments to be taken into account in computing business profits are thus excluded. However, where an employer takes out a group policy to meet the cost of employees' sick pay and the policy would otherwise qualify under these provisions, the proportion of any payment attributable (on just and reasonable apportionment) to employees' contributions to premiums is not treated as employment or pension income. The exemption does not apply if any premiums under the policy (disregarding in the case of the employment or pension income exemption an employer's share of premiums) have to any extent qualified for tax relief, either as a deduction from total income or in computing income from any source (e.g. business profits).

For an annual payment to qualify for the exemption:

(*a*) it must be made under a policy (or part of a policy) providing insurance against a 'qualifying risk';

(*b*) the provisions of the policy which insure against that risk must be 'self-contained';

(*c*) the policy must make no provision for payments relating to that risk other than for a period throughout which the 'relevant conditions of payment' are satisfied; and

(*d*) the provisions of the policy relating to that risk must always have been such that the insurer runs a genuine risk of loss (i.e. proceeds payable must be capable of exceeding premiums received plus an investment return on those premiums).

A '*qualifying risk*' is either a risk of physical or mental illness, disability, infirmity or defect (including a risk of an existing condition deteriorating) or a risk of loss of employment (including loss of self-employment). The persons at risk may include the insured, his spouse and, for policies connected with the meeting of liabilities under an identified transaction, a person jointly liable with the insured or his spouse.

The '*relevant conditions of payment*' are satisfied for as long as the illness etc. or unemployment continues (including in the case of illness etc. any related period of convalescence or rehabilitation) or for as long as the income of the insured etc. (apart from benefits under the policy) is less, in circumstances so insured against, than it otherwise would be. If any such period ends as a result of the death of the insured etc., it is extended to any period immediately following (so that benefits paid to the deceased's spouse or estate are brought within the exemption).

The requirement for the relevant provisions of the policy to be '*self-contained*' is an anti-avoidance measure. The provisions of a policy covering different kinds of benefits are self-contained unless the terms of the policy (possibly including the fixing of the amount of premiums), or the way in which they are given effect, in relation to the qualifying risk would have been significantly different if the policy insured only against the qualifying risk (except where the only difference is that certain benefits are applied for reducing other benefits under the policy). A broadly similar rule applies where there are multiple policies. In each case, regard must be had to all the persons for whose benefit insurance is provided against the qualifying risk.

28.16   Exempt Income

There are provisions enabling benefits relating to illness etc. to qualify for the exemption if paid under an individual policy derived from and superseding an employer's group policy where an employee has left the employment as a consequence of the occurrence insured against.

For a simplified explanation of the exemption, see Revenue Pamphlet IR 153.

[*ICTA 1988, ss 580A, 580B; FA 1996, s 143; ITEPA 2003, Sch 6 para 65*].

Benefits which are wholly exempt are paid without deduction of tax. Where they are partially exempt (e.g. in the case of a company policy to which the employee contributes) or the policy holder's income, including the maximum benefits payable, is below taxable income limits, the insurer may pay benefits gross on receipt of an appropriate declaration from the recipient (on form R91). (Revenue Tax Bulletin December 1996 p 377).

28.16   **Interest —**

(i) on damages for personal injuries or death [*ICTA 1988, s 329*] including similar interest awarded by a foreign court if also exempt from tax in that country (Revenue Pamphlet IR 1, A30);

(ii) on certain UK government stocks held by non-residents (see 33.2 GOVERNMENT STOCKS) and certain borrowings in foreign currency by local authorities and certain STATUTORY BODIES (84) (see 22.12 DEDUCTION OF TAX AT SOURCE);

(iii) on **tax-exempt special savings accounts ('TESSAs')**. Bonuses are also exempt. An account is a 'TESSA' if the following conditions (and any others specified by regulation by the Board) are satisfied when the account is opened.

(*a*)   It must have been opened by an individual aged 18 or more **before 6 April 1999.**

(*b*)   It must be with a building society or an appropriately authorised deposit-taker; it must not be a joint account and must not be held on behalf of another person; it must be identified as a TESSA, and the account-holder must not simultaneously hold another TESSA; and it must not be 'connected with' any other account. An account is '*connected with*' another if either was opened with reference to the other, or with a view to enabling or facilitating the opening of the other on particular terms, and the terms on which either was opened would have been significantly less favourable to the holder if the other had not been opened. Accounts may be held with certain European authorised firms entitled to accept deposits in the UK (which must, however, appoint UK tax representatives or make similar arrangements for discharging their duties under the scheme).

(*c*)   There must not be a notice in force given by the Board to the society or other authorised person prohibiting it from operating new TESSAs.

(*d*)   It must be transferable from one society or other authorised person to another which is entitled to, and does, operate TESSAs, on terms agreed between the account-holder and any society or other authorised person concerned.

A society or other authorised person intending to cease to operate TESSAs must comply with notification requirements. The Board have powers (subject to appeal) to prohibit a society or other authorised person from operating TESSAs. An application by an individual for a TESSA had to contain information specified by regulation, and a statement that false statements in connection with the application could result in penalties or prosecution. On a transfer within (*d*) above, the transferor must supply the transferee with details of the account as specified by regulation.

An account continues to be a TESSA for five years from its being opened (or until the earlier death of the account-holder), or until any of the conditions set out above ceases to be satisfied or any of the following events occurs.

(I) The deposit of more than £3,000 in the first twelve months the account is open, of more than £1,800 in any succeeding twelve-month period, or of more than £9,000 in total.

(II) A withdrawal reducing the balance on the account below the aggregate of earlier deposits and lower or basic rate income tax (whichever is applicable) on any interest or bonus previously paid on the account. The rate applicable is the lower rate, except as regards interest etc. paid or credited before 6 April 1996 where it is the basic rate (being in each case the rate in force for the tax year in which the interest etc. was paid or credited).

(III) The assignment of any rights of the account-holder in respect of the account or the use of such rights as security for a loan.

When an account ceases to be a TESSA (other than on the expiry of the five-year period from its opening or the death of the account-holder), the *Income Tax Acts* have effect as if, immediately after it so ceased, the account were credited with an amount of interest equal to the interest and bonuses payable during the period it was a TESSA.

The Board have the necessary regulatory powers to require information, both aggregate and individual, and the maintenance and inspection of records, and to impose certain requirements as to UK tax representation on European authorised firms. Penalties apply in relation to notices under those powers.

[*ICTA 1988, ss 326A–326D; FA 1990, s 28; TCGA 1992, s 271(4); FA 1995, ss 62, 63; FA 1996, Sch 6 para 7; FA 1998, s 78; SI 1990 No 2361; SI 1995 Nos 1929, 3236, 3239; SI 1996 No 844; SI 2001 No 3629, Articles 20, 129–133*].

See 28.13 above as regards the introduction in 1999 of the individual savings account. The regulations governing such accounts permit the transfer in of the capital from maturing TESSAs (but *not* the accumulated interest) without affecting the amount which can be subscribed to an individual savings account, and TESSA subscriptions similarly do not affect the individual savings account limits;

(iv) to the extent of the first £70 for each individual of **National Savings Bank** interest on deposits other than investment deposits. [*ICTA 1988, s 325*]. In practice, this only applies to National Savings Bank ordinary accounts and not to any other National Savings Bank products; no new ordinary accounts can be opened after 28 January 2004;

(v) on **Government Savings Certificates**. See 33.5 GOVERNMENT STOCKS;

(vi) on **Save As You Earn** (SAYE) certified contractual savings schemes (bonuses under such schemes also being exempt), provided that they are linked to approved SAYE option schemes (see 82.51 SHARE-RELATED EMPLOYMENT INCOME AND EXEMPTIONS). Share option linked savings schemes may be offered by a wide range of providers, including certain European authorised institutions. Treasury authorisation is required for the operation of such schemes. [*ICTA 1988, s 326, Sch 15A; FA 1990, s 29, Sch 14 para 5; FA 1995, s 65, Sch 12; ITEPA 2003, Sch 6 para 120; SI 1995 No 1778; SI 2001 No 3629, Article 19*];

(vii) on overpaid inheritance tax. [*IHTA 1984, ss 233(3), 235(2)*];

(viii) on certain repayments, see 41 INTEREST ON OVERPAID TAX;

(ix) being loan interest paid by its members to a credit union. [*ICTA 1988, s 487; FA 1996, Sch 14 para 31*];

(x)   on refunds of amounts over-repaid by borrowers in respect of **student loans** made under specified statutory provisions. [*ICTA 1988, s 331A; FA 1999, s 60*];

(xi)   (by concession) consisting of compensation payments paid on bank accounts owned by Holocaust victims. (Revenue Pamphlet IR 1, A100).

Certain income (see 27.3(*a*) EXCESS LIABILITY) is exempt from basic or lower rate income tax only.

28.17   **Long service awards** to employees, within limitations set out in 75.29 SCHEDULE E—EMPLOYMENT INCOME.

28.18   **Meal vouchers** if the conditions shown in 75.33 SCHEDULE E—EMPLOYMENT INCOME are complied with.

28.19   **Members of Parliaments or Assemblies.** The following payments made pursuant to a House of Commons resolution are disregarded as income for tax purposes:

(i)   accommodation allowances paid for additional overnight expenses incurred in performing parliamentary duties (and see 75.32 SCHEDULE E—EMPLOYMENT INCOME); and

(ii)   European travel expenses, i.e. reimbursed costs relating to travel between the UK and a '*relevant European location*' meaning

●   (for costs incurred after 5 April 2004) an EU institution or agency or the national parliament of another Member State, of a candidate or applicant country or of a Member State of the European Free Trade Association; this definition may be varied by the Treasury by statutory instrument;

●   (previously) an EU institution in Brussels, Luxembourg or Strasbourg or (from 1 April 1999) the national parliament of another Member State or (from 1 April 2002) of a country which is a candidate for EU membership (as defined).

(See generally 75.46 SCHEDULE E—EMPLOYMENT INCOME.)

[*ITEPA 2003, ss 292, 294; ICTA 1988, s 200; FA 1993, s 124; FA 1999, s 51; FA 2002, s 41; FA 2004, s 82*].

Additionally, ministers and certain other office-holders in the UK Government, the Scottish Parliament or the Wales or Northern Ireland Assemblies are exempt from income tax in respect of the provision of transport or subsistence to them or their families or households by or on behalf of the Crown, or the reimbursement of expenditure on such provision. 'Transport' for this purpose includes any car (with or without a driver) and any other benefit in connection with such a car (including fuel). 'Subsistence' includes food, drink and temporary accommodation. The exemption does *not* extend to the provision of mobile telephones for 1998/99 and earlier years (see 75.19 SCHEDULE E—EMPLOYMENT INCOME), but see now 75.16(xxiii) SCHEDULE E—EMPLOYMENT INCOME as regards the general exemption of such provision thereafter. [*ITEPA 2003, s 295; ICTA 1988, s 200AA; FA 1996, s 108; FA 1999, s 44(5)(6), Sch 5 para 3*].

Payments to members of the Scottish Parliament or the Wales or Northern Ireland Assemblies in respect of necessary overnight expenses or European travel expenses (as in (ii) above) are similarly disregarded for income tax purposes from 6 April 1999. The former are additional expenses necessarily incurred for the purpose of performing duties as a member in staying away from home overnight, either where the body of which he is a member sits or in the area he represents. [*ITEPA 2003, ss 293, 294; ICTA 1988, s 200ZA; FA 1999, Sch 5 para 2(1); FA 2002, s 41; FA 2004, s 82*].

28.20   **Miners'** free coal or cash in lieu thereof is exempt by concession before 2003/04. (Revenue Pamphlet IR 1, A6). Now superseded by legislation (see 75.16(xi) SCHEDULE E—EMPLOYMENT INCOME and 58.3(j) PENSION INCOME).

28.21   **Non-residents** are exempt from tax on income and capital gains from: certain GOVERNMENT STOCKS (33); securities of the Inter-American Development Bank [*ICTA 1988, s 583*]; securities of the OECD Support Fund [*OECD Support Fund Act 1975, s 4*] and certain other international organisations designated by statutory instrument [*ICTA 1988, s 324*], including the Asian Development Bank (*SI 1984 No 1215*), the African Development Bank (*SI 1984 No 1634*), the European Bank for Reconstruction and Development (*SI 1991 No 1202*) and any of the European Communities or the European Investment Bank (*SI 1985 No 1172*); and from certain pensions, see 58.4 PENSION INCOME. See also 24.2 DOUBLE TAX RELIEF.

28.22   Certain **overseas income** is exempt from UK tax under specific DOUBLE TAX RELIEF (24) agreements. If not so exempt, double tax relief may nevertheless be claimable. In some circumstances, overseas income is only assessable on the REMITTANCE BASIS (64). See also 51 NON-RESIDENTS AND OTHER OVERSEAS MATTERS.

28.23   Certain **pensions** are exempt, see 58.3, 58.4 PENSION INCOME.

28.24   **Personal equity plans.** From 1 January 1987 and before 6 April 1999, a 'qualifying individual' could subscribe a specified maximum to a Personal Equity Plan (PEP) (to which no-one else could subscribe). New regulations came into force on 6 April 1989 (*SI 1989 No 469* — subsequently amended). Plans under the earlier 1986 Regulations operated by reference to calendar years rather than tax years.

No further subscriptions to PEPs can be made after 5 April 1999, but existing PEPs may continue, and independently of individual savings accounts (ISAs) (see 28.13 above). A 10% tax credit is payable on dividends received from UK equities before 6 April 2004.

A 'qualifying individual' had to be 18 years of age or over, and resident and ordinarily resident in the UK or a non-resident Crown employee serving overseas whose duties were treated as performed in the UK. Subscriptions up to specified limits could be made to one general plan and one 'single company plan' in any tax year. A 'single company plan' allowed investment only in shares of one designated company and was often known as a corporate PEP. After 5 April 2001, the distinctions between general plans and single company plans are abolished, allowing such plans to be merged if the investor wishes. Plans, or (after 5 April 2001) parts of plans, may be transferred between plan managers.

After 5 April 2001, the range of qualifying investments that may be held under a plan is brought into line with that applicable to the stocks and shares component of an ISA (see 28.13 above), except that qualifying investments held immediately before 6 April 2001 may be retained in the plan even if they no longer otherwise qualify. For the range of qualifying investments applicable before 6 April 2001, see the 2003/04 and earlier editions.

Investments may not be purchased from the plan investor or spouse. Subscription to a plan had to be by payment of cash to the plan manager for investment by him, except that

● qualifying shares allotted to the investor under public offers, and

● (in relation to single company plans) shares acquired by him under certain approved employee share schemes,

could be transferred into plans before 6 April 1999. This also applied to shares issued by a building society on conversion to plc status and, from 20 March 1997, to shares in a mutual insurer transferring its business to a company limited by shares (see Revenue Tax Bulletins April 1997 p 418 and April 1998 pp 522, 523). Where such would not otherwise have been the case, any shares sold during the period allowed for transfer were identified first with shares which were ineligible for transfer so as to ensure that investors were able to transfer the maximum number of shares into a PEP. There was no deemed disposal for capital gains purposes when the plan investor transferred shares into a plan, the investor retaining his beneficial ownership of plan investments even though legal ownership is held by the plan manager.

Cash held for reinvestment within a plan must be held in sterling and invested in a designated account with a deposit taker or building society. Interest is paid gross and is exempt from tax. However, if interest exceeding £180 in a tax year is paid by the plan manager to or for the plan investor in respect of cash held within a plan, the plan manager must account for a sum representing lower rate tax on all such interest payments in the year; the interest payments are for all purposes treated as interest taxable under Schedule D, Case III in the year in which they arise.

Otherwise, for so long as the various conditions continue to be met, dividends and interest on securities are tax-free, and, as regards pre-6 April 2004 dividends on UK equities, the plan manager may reclaim the related tax credits, including (from 21 August 1998) those pertaining to investors who have ceased to be UK-resident since subscribing to the plan.

No chargeable gain or allowable loss arises on the disposal of an investment within the plan. Where plan investments are withdrawn in specie, the plan investor is deemed to have made a disposal and reacquisition at market value, thus exempting any gain or loss arising and establishing a capital gains tax acquisition cost for future disposals. The plan investor is treated as holding securities within the plan in a capacity other than that in which he holds any other securities of the same class so that identification rules and, for acquisitions before 6 April 1998, share pooling rules are applied separately to plan investments. The normal share reorganisation rules are disapplied in respect of plan investments in the event of a reorganisation of share capital involving an allotment for payment, e.g. a rights issue.

[*TCGA 1992, ss 151, 287; ICTA 1988, ss 333, 333A, 828; FA 1988, s 116; SI 1989 No 469; FA 1991, s 70; SI 1990 No 678; SI 1991 Nos 733, 2774; SI 1992 No 623; SI 1993 No 756; FA 1993, s 85; FA 1995, s 64; SI 1995 Nos 1539, 3287; SI 1996 Nos 846, 1355; SI 1997 Nos 511, 1716; SI 1998 No 1869; SI 2000 No 3109; SI 2001 No 923; SI 2001 No 3629, Arts 120–125; SI 2001 No 3777; SI 2003 No 2748*].

A list of registered plan managers may be obtained by sending a self-addressed A4 size envelope to (or calling at) Inland Revenue Information Centre, South West Wing, Bush House, Strand, London WC2B 4RD.

Simon's Direct Tax Service. See E3.3.

28.25   **Profit-related pay** under a registered scheme is wholly or partly exempt within certain limits. See 75.34 SCHEDULE E—EMPLOYMENT INCOME.

28.26   **Redundancy payments** under *Employment Rights Act 1996* (or NI equivalent). [*ITEPA 2003, s 309, Sch 6 para 63; ICTA 1988, s 579*]. See also 75.35 SCHEDULE E—EMPLOYMENT INCOME.

28.27   **Repayment supplement** in respect of income tax or capital gains tax repayments (see 41 INTEREST ON OVERPAID TAX) or VAT repayments (under *VATA 1994, s 79*, see Tolley's Value Added Tax under Payment of Tax) is disregarded for income tax purposes. (*Note.* Interest payable on certain VAT repayments under *VATA 1994, s 80* is *not* exempt.) [*ICTA 1988, ss 824(8), 827(2)*].

28.28   Certain lump sums under PERSONAL PENSION SCHEMES (60), RETIREMENT ANNUITIES (66) and RETIREMENT SCHEMES (67).

28.29   **Sandwich courses.** Where an employee is released by employer to take a full-time educational course at a university, technical college or similar institution open to the public at large, payments for periods of attendance may be treated as exempt from income tax. Conditions are (i) that the course lasts at least one academic year, with an average of at least 20 weeks per year of full-time attendance, and (ii) that the rate of payment does not exceed the greater of (*a*) £7,000 p.a. and (*b*) the rate of payment an individual in similar personal circumstances would have received as a grant from one of the public awarding bodies on a scale fixed by the Secretary of State for Education and Science (e.g. a Research Council Studentship). For this purpose, university fees etc. paid or reimbursed by employer are ignored. Where the rate of payment exceeds the limit, the full payments are taxable, but where a rate of payment is increased during a course, only subsequent payments are taxable, and periods where payments are thus taxable nonetheless count towards the requisite periods of attendance. (Revenue Pamphlet IR 131, SP 4/86, 8 August 1986; Revenue Press Releases 12 April 1989, 18 November 1992). See 92 VOCATIONAL TRAINING RELIEF as regards certain training courses.

28.30   **Scholarship** income and bursaries. [*ICTA 1988, s 331*]. In *Clayton v Gothorp Ch D 1971, 47 TC 168*, discharge of loan made by employer for training course held not scholarship income but was emoluments. See 28.29 above and 75.23 SCHEDULE E—EMPLOYMENT INCOME for where scholarship awarded by employer of parent etc. Covenanted 'parental contributions' under *Education Act 1962* not an educational endowment (*Gibbs v Randall Ch D 1980, 53 TC 513*).

28.31   Certain **Social Security** benefits (see 83 SOCIAL SECURITY) and corresponding foreign benefits (Revenue Pamphlet IR 1, A24) and payments under Jobmatch programme (Revenue Pamphlet IR 1, A97). Disabled Person's Vehicle Maintenance Grants under *National Health Service Act 1977, Sch 2 para 2* or corresponding Scottish or NI Act. [*ICTA 1988, s 327*].

28.32   **Training allowances and bounties** for reserve and auxiliary forces and armed forces' **food, drink and mess allowances.** [*ITEPA 2003, ss 297, 298; ICTA 1988, s 316*]. Civil Defence Corps bounties are not exempt because these are paid by local authorities and therefore not 'out of the public revenue' (*Lush v Coles Ch D 1967, 44 TC 169*).

28.33   **Wages in lieu of notice** in some instances. See 75.48 SCHEDULE E—EMPLOYMENT INCOME.

28.34   **War widows etc.** Pensions payable in respect of death due to military or war service (see 58.3(*c*) PENSION INCOME).

28.35   **Wounds and disability pensions** to HM Forces (see 58.3(*d*) PENSION INCOME).

29   Exempt Organisations

Exemption is given to the organisations etc. below to the extent indicated.

29.1   **Agricultural societies** established to promote 'the interests of agriculture, horticulture, livestock breeding or forestry' are exempt from tax on profits or gains 'from any exhibition or show held for the purposes of the society . . . if applied solely to the purposes of the society'. [*ICTA 1988, s 510*]. See *Peterborough Royal Foxhound Show Society v CIR KB 1936, 20 TC 249*; *Glasgow Ornithological Assn CS 1938, 21 TC 445*. An agricultural society may also qualify for charitable relief, see 14.2(*g*) CHARITIES.

29.2   Non-resident central **banks** as specified by Order in Council are exempt from tax on certain classes of income [*ICTA 1988, s 516*] and the issue departments of the Reserve Bank of India and the State Bank of Pakistan are exempt from all taxes. [*ICTA 1988, s 517; TCGA 1992, s 271(8)*].

29.3   **The British Museum and Natural History Museum** may claim exemption as if they were charities. [*ICTA 1988, s 507; TCGA 1992, s 271(6)(a); FA 1989, s 60; Museums and Galleries Act 1992, Sch 8 para 1(8)(9)*].

29.4   **Charities** are generally exempt but see full details under 14 CHARITIES.

29.5   **Clubs and societies.** See 29.22 below.

29.6   **The Crown** is not generally within the taxing Acts; see *ICTA 1988, s 49(2)* and *s 829(2)*. See *ICTA 1988, s 829* as amended by *FA 1993, s 122* as to assessment, deduction and payment of tax by Crown public offices and departments.

29.7   Under DIPLOMATIC IMMUNITY ETC. (23), there are certain exemptions.

29.8   FRIENDLY SOCIETIES (31) have certain exemptions.

29.9   **Historic Buildings and Monuments Commission for England** may claim exemption as if it were a charity. [*ICTA 1988, s 507; TCGA 1992, s 271(7)*].

29.10   **Housing Associations** and approved self-build societies have certain exemptions. [*ICTA 1988, ss 488, 489*]. See Tolley's Corporation Tax.

29.11   **International Maritime Satellite Organisation.** An overseas signatory is exempt in respect of any receipt from the Organisation. [*ICTA 1988, s 515; TCGA 1992, s 271(5)*].

29.12   **Local authorities,** local authority associations and health service boards, as defined by *ICTA 1988, ss 842A, 519(3), 519A* respectively as amended, are exempt. [*ICTA 1988, ss 519, 519A as amended; TCGA 1992, s 271(3)*].

29.13   MUTUAL TRADING (50). There are some special tax provisions.

29.14   **National Heritage Memorial Fund** may claim exemption as if it were a charity. [*ICTA 1988, s 507; TCGA 1992, s 271(7)*].

29.15   SCIENTIFIC RESEARCH ASSOCIATIONS (77) are generally exempt.

29.16   Some STATUTORY BODIES (84) receive a measure of exemption.

29.17   Approved **Superannuation Funds, personal pension schemes** etc. are exempt from tax on investment income and on chargeable gains arising on investments the income of which is exempt from tax. See 60 PERSONAL PENSION SCHEMES, 66 RETIREMENT ANNUITIES and 67 RETIREMENT SCHEMES. Income from, or from transactions relating to, futures and options contracts is within the exemption. See further 71.22 SCHEDULE D, CASES I AND II.

29.18   TRADE UNIONS (88), including employers' associations and Police Federations, which are registered are exempt on provident benefit income under certain conditions.

29.19   Authorised UNIT TRUSTS (90), investment trusts and VENTURE CAPITAL TRUSTS (91) are exempt from corporation tax on their chargeable gains. [*TCGA 1992, s 100(1); FA 1995, s 72(2)*].

29.20   The **United Kingdom Ecolabelling Board** may claim exemption as if it were a charity (see 14 CHARITIES). [*ICTA 1988, s 507(1)(e); SI 1992 No 2383, reg 2*].

29.21   **Visiting forces** and associated civilians from designated countries. [*ITEPA 2003, s 303, Sch 6 para 45; ICTA 1988, s 323; FA 1990, Sch 14 para 4*]. See *SI 1961 No 580, SI 1964 No 924* and *SI 1998 Nos 1513, 1514*.

29.22   VOLUNTARY ASSOCIATIONS (93). There is restriction of liability in a few special circumstances.

30   Fraudulent or Negligent Conduct

Cross-references. See 5.3 ASSESSMENTS for discovery assessments; 42 INTEREST AND SURCHARGES ON UNPAID TAX; 57 PENALTIES; 68.6 *et seq.* RETURNS for enquiries into self-assessment tax returns.

Simon's Direct Tax Service A3.15, A3.16.

30.1   INTRODUCTION

Where the Revenue consider tax to have been lost by a taxpayer's fraudulent or negligent conduct (or, under earlier legislation, by his fraud, wilful default or neglect), they will seek to recover that tax, whether by formal assessment or by way of a contract settlement (see 30.11 below). In such cases, the normal time limits for assessment are extended (see 30.3 below), interest is chargeable on the understated tax (see 42 INTEREST AND SURCHARGES ON UNPAID TAX) and PENALTIES (57) are incurred, which the Board may mitigate in appropriate circumstances. In cases of serious fraud, the Revenue may pursue a criminal prosecution. In most cases, the amount of tax lost will be established by the use of the Revenue's enquiry powers, for which see 68.6 *et seq.* RETURNS, or the investigatory powers at 30.7–30.10 below. See also 5.3 ASSESSMENTS as regards the Revenue's power to make 'discovery' assessments. For cases relating to fraudulent or negligent conduct, see Tolley's Tax Cases.

Revenue Codes of Practice 8 and 9, dealing, respectively, with Special Compliance Office Investigations in cases other than suspected serious fraud and in cases of such fraud were first published in January 1995. Code 11, dealing with enquiries into self-assessment income tax returns by local tax offices is issued at the start of every enquiry (except that in certain simple cases a short, single-page version is issued instead). The latest versions of these Codes are available on the Revenue's website.

Inspectors will respect the right of confidentiality between husband and wife in all cases. However, in investigating one spouse, an inspector may need information from or concerning the other. Although inspectors will make every effort to avoid unwarranted disclosure and the gratuitous passing of information, it remains open to them to take such action as is necessary to enable them to perform their duties. In effect, married persons are in the same position with regard to confidentiality as are single persons. (ICAEW Memorandum TR 778, 8 January 1990).

For the validity of tax amnesties see *CIR v National Federation of Self-employed and Small Businesses Ltd HL 1981, 55 TC 133.*

30.2   CASE LAW ON FRAUDULENT OR NEGLIGENT CONDUCT

See 30.3 below as regards the replacement of 'fraud, wilful default or neglect' assessments by 'fraudulent or negligent conduct' assessments. The latter expression is not defined, and the following cases may be of continued assistance in this respect.

The onus of proving fraud or wilful default is on the Crown (see e.g. *Hurley v Taylor CA 1998, 71 TC 268*), but the onus is on the taxpayer to prove the assessments are excessive (*Johnson v Scott CA 1978, 52 TC 383; Jonas v Bamford Ch D 1973, 51 TC 1; Nicholson v Morris CA 1977, 51 TC 95* and cf. *Barney v Pybus Ch D 1957, 37 TC 106* and *R v Spec Commrs (ex p Martin) CA 1971, 48 TC 1*). Acceptance of an inadequate estimated assessment may amount to wilful default (*Nuttall v Barrett Ch D 1992, 64 TC 548*). Once the unreliability of one year's accounts has been demonstrated, the Commissioners are entitled to make their own estimate for other years (*Brittain v Gibbs Ch D 1986, 59 TC 374*). For the standard of proof required, see *Les Croupiers Casino Club v Pattinson CA 1987, 60 TC 196*. For finding required of Commissioners, see *Rea v Highnam Ch D 1990, 63 TC 287*.

Unexplained capital increases or admitted omissions may be held evidence of fraud or wilful default (*Amis v Colls Ch D 1960, 39 TC 148*; *Woodrow v Whalley Ch D 1964, 42 TC 249*; *Hudson v Humbles Ch D 1965, 42 TC 380*; *Hillenbrand CS 1966, 42 TC 617*; *Young v Duthie Ch D 1969, 45 TC 624*; *James v Pope Ch D 1972, 48 TC 142*; and cf. *Brimelow v Price Ch D 1965, 49 TC 41*). Taxpayer's deliberate exclusion of wife's income when making return held wilful default (*Brown v CIR Ch D 1965, 42 TC 583*) but not where husband unaware of wife's omissions (*Wellington v Reynolds Ch D 1962, 40 TC 209*). Wilful default may be by agent (*Clixby v Pountney Ch D 1967, 44 TC 515*; *Pleasants v Atkinson Ch D 1987, 60 TC 228*). Where Commissioners found fraud on the basis of the inspector's evidence at a hearing which the taxpayer or his agent did not attend, the case was remitted to be heard by different Commissioners (*Ottley v Morris Ch D 1978, 52 TC 375*).

Neglect means negligence or a failure to give any notice, to make any return or to produce or furnish any document or other information required by or under the *Taxes Acts*. [*TMA 1970, s 118 as previously enacted*]. Neglect may be by an agent (*Mankowitz v Special Commrs Ch D 1971, 46 TC 707*). See the note at 68.23 RETURNS as regards reasonable excuse for failure to make returns.

30.3   **EXTENDED TIME LIMITS**

Except where specifically provided, the normal time limit for assessments is five years after 31 January following the tax year. In relation to corporation tax it is six years after the end of the accounting period. [*TMA 1970, s 34; FA 1994, Sch 19 para 10; FA 1998, Sch 18 para 46(1), Sch 19 para 17*]. In certain cases, however, as described below, extended limits apply to assessments for the purpose of making good a loss of tax. There is an overriding deadline for deceased persons (see 30.4 below).

An objection to the making of any assessment on the grounds that it is out of time can only be made on an appeal against the assessment. [*TMA 1970, s 34(2); FA 1998, Sch 18 para 46(3)*].

Assessments made after 26 July 1989 relating to 1983/84 and subsequent years (or to company accounting periods ending after 31 March 1983). Where the loss of tax arises due to the *fraudulent or negligent conduct* of a person (or of a person acting on his behalf), an assessment may be made at any time not later than 20 years after 31 January following the tax year to which it relates. The equivalent corporation tax time limit is 21 years after the end of the accounting period. Persons in partnership with a person responsible for fraudulent or negligent conduct may similarly be assessed in respect of additional partnership profits. If the person assessed so requires, the assessment may give effect to reliefs or allowances to which he would have been entitled had he made the necessary claims within the relevant time limits (excluding certain elections for the transfer of the married couple's allowance or children's tax credit). [*TMA 1970, s 36; FA 1989, s 149; F(No 2)A 1992, Sch 5 para 9(2); FA 1994, ss 196, 199(2)(a), Sch 19 para 11(1); FA 1998, Sch 18 paras 46(2), 65, Sch 19 para 18; FA 1999, s 30(4)*]. With effect after 10 July 2003, the facility to claim late reliefs and allowances is similarly available in relation to a Revenue amendment to a self-assessment personal or partnership tax return (see 68.9 RETURNS). Also, any late assessment required to give effect to such a claim, or as a result of allowing such a claim, can be made within a year after the claim becomes final (i.e. becomes no longer capable of being varied, on appeal or otherwise); this applies to claims made as a consequence of either an assessment or an amendment to a return. [*TMA 1970, s 43C; FA 2003, s 207(1)(3)*].

For 1995/96 and earlier years and for corporation tax accounting periods ended before 1 July 1999, the equivalent time limit to those above was 20 years after the end of the tax year or corporation tax accounting period.

30.3 Fraudulent or Negligent Conduct

For a case in which appeals against assessments raised out of the normal time limit were allowed on the grounds that, on the balance of probabilities, the Revenue had not proved fraudulent or negligent conduct, see *York v Pickin (Sp C 160), [1998] SSCD 138*. For cases where 'fraudulent or negligent conduct' was found, see *Last Viceroy Restaurant v Jackson Ch D, [2000] STC 1093; Hurley v Taylor CA 1998, 71 TC 268; Hancock v CIR (Sp C 213), [1999] SSCD 287; Billows v Hammond (Sp C 252), [2000] SSCD 430*; and *Chartered Accountant v Inspector of Taxes (Sp C 358), [2003] SSCD 166* (and see 30.2 above).

Married couples. Where total income is increased as a result of fraudulent or negligent conduct assessments, this does not affect the validity of any blind person's allowance or certain other allowances transferred between spouses which are determined by reference to total income or given as a reduction in total income tax liability. The transferor's allowances are correspondingly not restored. [*TMA 1970, s 37A; FA 1988, Sch 3 para 30; FA 1989, s 149(4); F(No 2)A 1992, Sch 5 para 9(3); FA 1994, Sch 8 para 13*].

Assessments made before 27 July 1989 or relating to 1982/83 and earlier years (or to company accounting periods ending before 1 April 1983) (references below to *TMA 1970* being to those provisions as they stood prior to amendment under self-assessment). Note that whilst the overall 20-year time limit referred to above does not strictly apply to these earlier chargeable periods, the Revenue indicated, at IH 4151 in their now superseded Investigations Handbook, they do apply it in practice.

Fraud or wilful default. An assessment to make good tax lost through fraud or wilful default may be made at any time [*TMA 1970, s 36*] with the leave of a single General or Special Commissioner, who must be satisfied that there are reasonable grounds for believing that tax has or may have been so lost. [*TMA 1970, s 41*]. In applying for leave, the Revenue are only required to provide such information as will allow the Commissioner to so satisfy himself, and are not obliged to make full and frank disclosure of all facts known to them or to embark on a wide-ranging review of all the circumstances of the case (*Re McGuckian CA(NI) 1999, 72 TC 343*). Granting of leave by a Commissioner does not involve a hearing, and the taxpayer is not entitled to appear or be heard (*Day v Williams CA 1969, 46 TC 59; Pearlberg v Varty HL 1972, 48 TC 14* and *Nicholson v Morris CA 1977, 51 TC 95*). For jurisdiction of Commissioners see *CIR v Adams CA 1971, 48 TC 67; Murphy v Elders Ch D 1973, 49 TC 135* and cf. *F Lack Ltd v Doggett CA 1970, 46 TC 524*. See also *R v Special Commrs (ex p Morey) CA 1972, 49 TC 71* (use of prerogative orders disapproved) but contrast *R v Special Commrs (ex p Stipplechoice Ltd) (No 1) CA 1985, 59 TC 396* where judicial review was granted in the absence of any other adequate remedy (and see *R v Special Commrs (ex p Stipplechoice Ltd) (No 2) QB 1986, 59 TC 396* for the decision against the taxpayer on that review). The taxpayer may, of course, appeal against the assessment in the normal way. The Commissioner who gave leave to issue the assessment is not allowed to be present at the hearing of such an appeal. [*TMA 1970, s 41(2)*].

Neglect. Where, for the purpose of recovering tax lost due to fraud, wilful default, or neglect, an assessment has been made not later than six years after the end of the year for which the tax was lost (the '*normal year*'), the Revenue may make assessments for any of the six years prior to that normal year to make good a loss of tax attributable to neglect. Leave of a General or Special Commissioner is required (see below). Such an assessment must be made not later than the end of the year of assessment following that in which the normal year assessment is finally determined. [*TMA 1970, s 37(1)–(3)*]. Thus an assessment made in 1988/89 to recover tax lost for the year 1982/83 may support assessments for 1976/77 onwards. The decision in *O'Mullan v Walmsley QB (NI) 1965, 42 TC 573* that such assessments are invalid unless the assessment for the 'normal year' was expressly stated to be for making good tax lost by fraud, default or neglect was not followed in *Thurgood v Slarke Ch D 1971, 47 TC 130*. 'What matters is not the purpose of the assessor but of the assessment.' See also *R v Spec Commrs (ex p Rogers) CA 1972, 48 TC 46; Knight v CIR CA 1974, 49 TC 179* and *R v Holborn Commrs (ex p Rind) QB 1974, 49 TC 656*.

The Revenue may go back further if an assessment for any year has been made more than six years after the end of that year. The year for which the assessment has been made is called the '*earlier year*'. One of the following conditions must be satisfied.

(*a*)   The assessment has been made under *TMA 1970, s 37(3)* (see above).

(*b*)   The assessment is one of a number made under *TMA 1970, s 36* (see above) for years which are not more than six years apart and of which the latest is within six years prior to the normal year.

If (*a*) or (*b*) above applies, the Revenue may make an assessment for any of the six years immediately preceding the earlier year (and so on for other earlier years) with the leave of the General or Special Commissioners. The Commissioners must be satisfied that reasonable grounds exist for believing that tax for that year may have been lost through the taxpayer's neglect. The taxpayer is entitled to appear (or to be represented) and be heard. [*TMA 1970, s 37(4)–(7)*]. The Revenue must apply to the Commissioners not later than the end of the year following that in which liability under the assessment for the earlier year is finally determined.

In determining the tax to be charged for any year, the taxpayer is to be given the reliefs and allowances to which he would have been entitled for that year. [*TMA 1970, s 37(8)*].

The making of an assessment to income tax will not affect the time allowed for the making of a capital gains tax assessment under these provisions, and vice versa. [*TMA 1970, s 37(9)*].

Adaptation of these provisions to partnerships is provided by *TMA 1970, s 38* and to companies by *TMA 1970, s 39*.

Simon's Direct Tax Service. See A3.221–A3.226.

30.4   **Deceased persons.** Assessments on a deceased person's income or capital gains arising or accruing before death must normally be made on the personal representatives no later than the third anniversary of 31 January following the tax year in which death occurred. Assessments to make good tax lost due to the deceased's fraudulent or negligent conduct can be made (but *no later* than that third anniversary) for any of the six tax years preceding that of death. [*TMA 1970, s 40(1)(2); FA 1989, s 149(4), Sch 17 Pt VIII; FA 1994, ss 196, 199(2)(a), Sch 19 para 12*].

Simon's Direct Tax Service. See A3.227.

30.5   **UNDERSTATED PROFITS ETC.**

The measure of understated profits etc., is calculated from the available data, but if this is unsatisfactory, on the increase of capital from year to year, with adjustments for cost of living etc. See for this, cases mentioned at 30.2 and 30.3 above and *Deacon v Roper Ch D 1952, 33 TC 66; Horowitz v Farrand Ch D 1952, 33 TC 221; Moschi v Kelly CA 1952, 33 TC 442; Kilburn v Bedford Ch D 1955, 36 TC 262; Roberts v McGregor Ch D 1959, 38 TC 610; Chuwen v Sabine Ch D 1959, 39 TC 1; Erddig Motors Ltd v McGregor Ch D 1961, 40 TC 95; Hellier v O'Hare Ch D 1964, 42 TC 155; Hurley v Young Ch D 1966, 45 ATC 316; Hope v Damerel Ch D 1969, 48 ATC 461; Driver v CIR CS 1977, 52 TC 153; Kovak v Morris CA 1985, 58 TC 493* and cf. *Rose v Humbles CA 1971, 48 TC 103*. For a case in which similar principles were applied in determining directors' true remuneration, see *Billows v Robinson Ch D 1989, 64 TC 17*.

Inspectors will not automatically insist on annual capital statements (see above) where understated profits can be measured satisfactorily in other ways, such as by use of expected rates of gross trading profits (Revenue Press Release 1 August 1977).

30.6 Fraudulent or Negligent Conduct

30.6 CERTIFICATES OF FULL DISCLOSURE

Where it is established that tax has been lost due to fraudulent or negligent conduct, the Revenue may request that the taxpayer complete a 'certificate of full disclosure' stating that complete disclosure has been made of, inter alia, all banking, savings and loan accounts, deposit receipts, building society accounts, and accounts with other financial institutions; all investments including savings certificates and premium bonds and loans (whether interest-bearing or not); all other assets, including cash and life assurance policies, which the taxpayer now possesses, or has possessed, or in which he has or has had any interest or power to operate or control during the stated period; all gifts (in any form) by the taxpayer to his spouse, domestic partner, children or other persons during the stated period; all sources of income and all income derived therefrom; and all facts bearing on liability to income tax, capital gains tax and other duties for the stated period. Great care must be exercised before signing such a certificate, since subsequent discovery of an omission could lead to heavy penalties including, in serious cases, criminal prosecution. See also 57.10 PENALTIES.

30.7 INVESTIGATORY POWERS

TMA 1970, ss 20–20D contain the Revenue's powers to obtain the production of accounts, books and other information. These are described below and at 30.8–30.10 below. The enquiry procedures under self-assessment (see 68.6–68.9 RETURNS), including a separate power to call for documents, operate in tandem with these powers.

Revenue power to require documents and other particulars. For these purposes, '*document*' means anything in which information of any description is recorded, but (except in relation to orders under *TMA 1970, s 20BA*, see below) does not include personal records or journalistic material (within *Police and Criminal Evidence Act 1984, ss 12, 13*) (and those exclusions apply also to particulars contained in such records or material). The documents concerned are those in the possession or power of the person receiving the notice. Photographic etc. facsimiles may be supplied provided the originals are produced if called for, and documents relating to any pending tax appeal need not be delivered. In practice, the latter also applies to documents relating to a pending referral (see 68.11 RETURNS) during an enquiry (Hansard Standing Committee A 8 May 2001, Cols 172–174). There are special provisions relating to electronic records (see *FA 1988, s 127*). Documents in a person's 'possession or power' are those actually in existence at the time the notice is given, and not any which would have to be brought into existence in order to satisfy the notice.

(*a*) Where an **inspector** is of the reasonable opinion that documents contain, or may contain, information relevant to any tax liability of a person he may (with the Board's authority and the consent of a General or Special Commissioner (who is excluded from subsequent appeal proceedings)) by notice in writing require that person to deliver such documents to him (but only after that person has been given reasonable opportunity to produce them). Applications to a Commissioner for consent to issue a notice are held *ex parte* (see *Applicant v Inspector of Taxes (Sp C 189), [1999] SSCD 128*). A notice may not require disclosure of material subject to legal professional privilege (*R v A Special Commr ex p Morgan Grenfell & Co Ltd HL 2002, 74 TC 511*). For other challenges to the validity of notices, see *R v CIR (ex p T C Coombs & Co) HL 1991, 64 TC 124*; *R v CIR (ex p Taylor) CA 1988, 62 TC 562; (No 2) CA 1990, 62 TC 578*; also *Kempton v Special Commrs and CIR Ch D 1992, 66 TC 249*, where the validity of the notice was confirmed although the only evidence on which the inspector relied related to omissions from the returns of a fellow director of the taxpayer concerned, and *R v Macdonald and CIR (ex p Hutchinson & Co Ltd and others) QB 1998, 71 TC 1*, in which the notice was quashed in view of the failure of the Revenue either to put before the Commissioner a letter setting out the taxpayer's substantive response to precursor notices (which had failed for technical reasons), or to address the issues raised by the taxpayer in their summary of reasons (see below) for applying for consent to the notice. In *R v CIR (ex p Banque Internationale à Luxembourg SA) QB 2000, 72 TC 597*, an application for judicial review based *inter alia* on the protections afforded by the *European Convention on Human Rights* was refused, although an opposite view (albeit *obiter*) was expressed in *R v A Special Commr ex p Morgan Grenfell & Co Ltd HL 2002, 74 TC 511*.

(*b*)   An **inspector** may similarly by notice in writing require a person to furnish him with such particulars as he may reasonably require as being relevant to any tax liability of that person (again after reasonable opportunity has been given for their production).

(*c*)   An **inspector** may similarly by notice in writing require any other person (including the Director of Savings) to deliver to him (or, if the person so elects, make available for inspection by a named officer of the Board) documents relevant to any tax liability of a taxpayer. A copy of the notice must be sent to the taxpayer concerned unless, in a case involving suspected fraud, a General or Special Commissioner directs otherwise. Production of documents originating more than six years before the notice cannot be required (unless the Commissioner who gave consent to the notice specifically allows it on being satisfied there is reasonable ground for believing loss of tax through fraud).

For general limitations on these powers, see *R v O'Kane and Clarke (ex p Northern Bank Ltd) and related application QB 1996, 69 TC 187*, and for a review of the procedural and other requirements, see *R v CIR (ex p Ulster Bank Ltd) CA 1997, 69 TC 211*, in which *ex p Northern Bank Ltd* was in part disapproved.

A notice cannot require the production by a statutory auditor of his audit papers, nor by a tax adviser of communications with a client (or with any other tax adviser of his client) relating to advice about the client's tax affairs. This exemption does not, however, apply to explanatory documents concerning any other documents prepared with the client for, or for delivery to, the Revenue, unless the Revenue already has access to the information contained therein in some other document. Similarly, where a notice does not identify the taxpayer to which it relates (see below), the exemption does not apply to any document giving the name or address of any taxpayer to whom the notice relates (or of a person acting on their behalf) unless the Revenue already has access to the information contained therein. Where the exemption is so disapplied, either the document must be delivered or made available to the Revenue or a copy of the relevant parts must be supplied (which parts must be available if required for inspection). The Revenue's application of these provisions in practice is set out in a Statement of Practice (Revenue Pamphlet IR 131, SP 5/90, 11 April 1990). In particular, it is made clear that accountants' working papers will be called for only where voluntary access has not been obtained and it is considered absolutely necessary in order to determine whether a client's accounts or returns are complete and correct. Requests for access may on occasion extend to the whole or a particular part of the working papers, rather than just to information explaining specific entries, and the Revenue will usually be prepared to visit the accountants' or clients' premises to examine the papers and to take copies or extracts. These restrictions on the use of its powers by the Revenue do not apply in the circumstances described under (*d*) below. The restrictions also do not apply to 'link papers', i.e. those papers which show how the figures in a tax return are derived from the figures in the prime records (Revenue Tax Bulletin June 2003 pp 1031, 1032).

'*Taxpayer*' includes an individual who has died (but any notice must be given within six years of the death) and a company which has ceased to exist.

A notice may, subject to conditions, be given which does not specify the taxpayer to whom it relates, with the specific consent of a Special Commissioner, and subject to appeal (within 30 days) by the person on whom it is served on the ground that it would be onerous for him to comply with it. For an unsuccessful application for judicial review of the issue of such a notice, see *R v CIR (ex p Ulster Bank Ltd) QB 2000, 73 TC 209.*

(*d*) An **inspector** may similarly by notice in writing (with the Board's authority and the consent of a Circuit judge in England and Wales, a sheriff in Scotland or a County Court judge in NI) require a tax accountant (i.e. a person who assists another in the preparation of returns etc. for tax purposes) who has been convicted of a tax offence or incurred a penalty under *TMA 1970, s 99* (see 57.7 PENALTIES) (in relation to which no appeal is pending) to deliver documents relevant to any tax liability of any of his clients. The notice must be issued within twelve months of the final determination of the conviction or penalty award.

(*e*) The **Board** may require, by notice in writing, a person to deliver or furnish, to a named officer of theirs, documents or information as specified in (*a*) and (*b*) above. Notices will not, however, be given under this power unless there are reasonable grounds for believing that that person may have failed, or may fail, to comply with any provision of the *Taxes Acts*, and that any such failure is likely to have led, or to lead, to serious prejudice to the proper assessment or collection of tax.

Where notice is given under (*a*), (*b*) or (*c*) above, the taxpayer concerned must be provided with a written summary of the inspector's reasons for applying for consent to the giving of the notice (unless, in the case of (*c*), a Commissioner has directed that the taxpayer need not be sent a copy of the notice itself). Such a summary may exclude information which might identify an informant, or which the Commissioner is satisfied might prejudice the assessment or collection of tax, although a summary written so as not to compromise these requirements should nevertheless be provided. However, in a case within (*c*) above, the courts refused to quash such a notice where no written summary had been provided to the taxpayers whose liabilities were under investigation (*R v CIR (ex p Continental Shipping Ltd and Atsiganos SA) QB 1996, 68 TC 665*).

For guidance on the question of whether documents and records are the property of the client or of the accountant, see ICAEW Memorandum TR 781, 23 February 1990.

The notice must specify or describe the documents or particulars required, the time limit for production (generally not less than 30 days) and, except as above, the name of the taxpayer or client, as appropriate; and the person to whom they are delivered may take copies. There are severe penalties for the falsification, concealment, disposal or destruction of a document which is the subject of a notice or formal request (see (*a*) above), unless strict conditions and time limits are observed.

[*TMA 1970, ss 20–20BB, s 20D; FA 1989, ss 142–145, s 148, s 168(2); FA 1990, s 93; FA 1994, s 255; Civil Evidence Act 1995, Sch 1 para 6*].

For failure to comply with a notice, see 57.9 PENALTIES.

Notices (other than those under (*d*) above and those which relate to an unnamed taxpayer) may relate to tax liabilities in EU member States other than the UK [*FA 1990, s 125(1)(2)(6)*] or in any other territory with which the UK has entered into arrangements providing for the obtaining of information. [*FA 2000, s 146(3)(4)*].

For an article setting out the Revenue's view on the question of claims to legal or professional privilege in relation to requests for information under these provisions (other than where tax evasion or tax fraud is suspected), see Revenue Tax Bulletin April 2000 pp 743–746 (updated by Revenue Tax Bulletin December 2002 p 993 following the *Morgan Grenfell* case at (*a*) above).

30.8 **Order for delivery of documents in serious tax fraud cases.** Under *TMA 1970, s 20BA, Sch 1AA*, introduced by *FA 2000, s 149, Sch 39*, the Board may apply to the appropriate judicial authority (a Circuit judge in England and Wales, a sheriff in Scotland or a County Court judge in NI) for an order requiring any person who appears to have in his possession or power documents specified or described in the order to deliver them to an officer of the Board within ten working days after the day of service of the notice, or such longer or shorter period as may be specified in the order. The judicial authority must be satisfied, on information on oath given by an authorised officer of the Board, that there is reasonable ground for suspecting that an offence involving serious tax fraud has been or is about to be committed, and that the documents may be required as evidence in proceedings in respect of the offence. In Scotland, a single sheriff may make orders in respect of persons anywhere in Scotland as long as one of the orders relates to a person residing or having a place of business at an address in the sheriff's own sheriffdom. Orders may not be made in relation to items subject to legal privilege (as defined) unless they are held with the intention of furthering a criminal purpose. Failure to comply with an order is treated as contempt of court, and there are severe penalties for falsification of documents.

Schedule 1AA lays down detailed requirements in relation to such applications, and these may be supplemented by regulations. In particular, a person is entitled to notice of intention to apply for such an order, and to appear and be heard at the application, unless the judicial authority is satisfied that this would seriously prejudice investigation of the offence. Until the application has been dismissed or abandoned, or an order made and complied with, any person given such notice must not conceal, destroy, alter or dispose of any document to which the order sought relates, or disclose information etc. likely to prejudice the investigation, except with the leave of the judicial authority or the written permission of the Board. Professional legal advisers may, however, disclose such information etc. in giving legal advice to a client or in connection with legal proceedings, provided that it is not disclosed with a view to furthering a criminal purpose. Failure to comply with these requirements is treated as failure to comply with an order under these provisions. The procedural rules where documents are delivered in accordance with an order are as under *TMA 1970, s 20CC(3)–(9)* (see 30.9 below). For detailed procedural requirements, see *SI 2000 No 2875*.

See also Revenue Code of Practice COP 22.

Simon's Direct Tax Service. See A3.150 *et seq.*

30.9 **Search and seizure.** Where there is reasonable suspicion of serious tax fraud, and there are reasonable grounds for believing that use of the procedure under *TMA 1970, s 20BA* (see 30.8 above) might seriously prejudice the investigation, the Board may apply to a Circuit judge etc. (as in 30.7(*d*) above) for a warrant to enter premises within 14 days to search and to seize any things which may be relevant as evidence. There are detailed procedural rules governing searches and the removal of documents etc. [*TMA 1970, ss 20C, 20CC, 20D; FA 1989, ss 146, 147; FA 2000, s 150; Criminal Justice and Police Act 2001, Sch 2 para 13*]. The warrant need not specify the suspected fraud or the documents etc., searched for (*Rossminster Ltd HL 1979, 52 TC 160*). For the proper procedure in seeking and obtaining judicial review of a decision to grant such a warrant, and interim injunctions, see *R v CIR (ex p Kingston Smith (a firm)) QB 1996, 70 TC 264*. For the validity of warrants, see *R v CIR (ex p Tamosius & Partners) QB, [1999] STC 107*. If a Revenue officer executing a warrant has reasonable cause to believe that the data on a computer's hard drive might be required as evidence, he can seize and remove that computer even though it may also contain irrelevant material (*R (oao H) v CIR QB, [2002] STC 1354*).

Simon's Direct Tax Service. See A3.160 *et seq.*

30.10   Fraudulent or Negligent Conduct

30.10   **Barristers, advocates or solicitors.** A notice under 30.7(*a*), (*b*), (*c*) or (*d*) above to a barrister, advocate or solicitor can be issued only by the Board (although that power may be delegated, see *R v CIR (ex p Davis Frankel & Mead) QB 2000, 73 TC 185*) and he cannot (without his client's consent) be required to deliver under 30.7(*c*) and (*d*) above documents protected by professional privilege. [*TMA 1970, s 20B(3)(8)*]. As regards the search and seizure powers in 30.9 above, there is similarly an exclusion for documents protected by professional privilege or, from 28 July 2000, 'legal privilege' as more widely defined (but excluding items held with the intention of furthering a criminal purpose) [*TMA 1970, s 20C(4); FA 1989, s 146(4); FA 2000, s 150(4)*], and see also 30.8 above as regards similar protection in relation to an order under *TMA 1970, s 20BA* in cases involving serious tax fraud. See *R v CIR (ex p Goldberg) QB 1988, 61 TC 403* as regards nature of documents subject to privilege, but note that the decision in that case was doubted in *Dubai Bank Ltd v Galadari CA, [1989] 3 WLR 1044*, a non-tax case. In relation to search and seizure under 30.9 above, it was held in *R v CIR (ex p Tamosius & Partners) QB, [1999] STC 1077* that the presence of independent counsel to determine the issue of privilege was 'to be encouraged', although it would not prevent action by the courts if counsel was wrong. The issue and execution of warrants to search a lawyer's offices was held not to be in breach of *Article 8* of the *European Convention on Human Rights* (*Tamosius v UK ECHR, [2002] STC 1307*).

For an article setting out the Revenue's view on the question of claims to legal or professional privilege in relation to requests for information under these provisions (other than where tax evasion or tax fraud is suspected), see Revenue Tax Bulletin April 2000 pp 743–746 (updated by Revenue Tax Bulletin December 2002 p 993 following the *Morgan Grenfell* case at 30.7(*a*) above).

Simon's Direct Tax Service. See A3.153.

30.11   **CONTRACT SETTLEMENTS**

In cases of fraudulent or negligent conduct, the taxpayer may be invited to offer a sum in full settlement of liability for tax, interest and penalties (a 'contract settlement') and such offers are often accepted by the Board without assessment of all the tax. A binding agreement so made cannot be repudiated afterwards by the taxpayer or his executors.

See *CIR v Nuttall CA 1989, 63 TC 148* for confirmation of power to enter into such agreements. Amounts due under such an agreement which are unpaid may be pursued by an action for a debt, but the Crown does not rank as a preferential creditor in respect of the sums due (*Nuttall* above; *CIR v Woollen CA 1992, 65 TC 229*).

See 57.10 PENALTIES for mitigation of penalties.

Relief for retirement annuity premiums and personal pension contributions. Where an offer as above is made and accepted by the Board in settlement of liabilities which include tax on relevant earnings assessable for a year which ended more than six years earlier, unused retirement annuity and personal pension relief (see 66.5 RETIREMENT ANNUITIES and 60.6 PERSONAL PENSION SCHEMES) which would have arisen if an assessment had been made on such earnings may be set against premiums or contributions paid within six months of acceptance of the offer on election by the taxpayer, within the same six months, for such relief to be given. Relief is, however, only available to the extent that the premiums or contributions exceed the maximum applying for the year of assessment in which they are paid, although the normal time limits apply in relation to the payment of premiums up to that maximum. See now, however, 60.6 PERSONAL PENSION SCHEMES for the prohibition on carry forward of relief for personal pension contributions after 5 April 2001. This practice also applies where assessments have been made and appealed against but the appeals have not been formally determined, if the tax for the years concerned is included in the settlement. (Revenue Pamphlet IR 131, SP 9/91).

30.12   **BOARD'S PRACTICE IN CASES OF SERIOUS TAX FRAUD**

The practice of the Board of Inland Revenue in cases of suspected serious tax fraud, as set out in the so-called 'Hansard Statement' (last revised on 7 November 2002), is as follows.

(i)   The Board reserve complete discretion to pursue prosecutions in the circumstances they consider appropriate.

(ii)   Where serious tax fraud has been committed, they may accept a money settlement instead of pursuing a criminal prosecution.

(iii) They will accept a money settlement, and will not pursue a criminal prosecution, if the taxpayer, in response to being given a copy of the Hansard Statement by an authorised officer (meaning a current serving member of Inland Revenue Special Compliance Office), makes a full and complete confession of all tax irregularities.

(Revenue Internet Statement 8 November 2002; Revenue Tax Bulletin December 2002 pp 979–981). This replaces the previous Hansard Statement of 18 October 1990, which did not include the undertaking in (iii) above. Instead, the Board retained full discretion as to the course they would pursue. In considering this, it was the Board's practice to be *influenced* by the taxpayer's having made a full confession and given full co-operation during the investigation, but they gave no explicit assurance that they would not prosecute in such cases. In *R v Gill and another CA, [2003] STC 1229*, the facts in which pre-dated the November 2002 revision, it was held that Code C of *Police and Criminal Evidence Act 1984* applied to the 'Hansard' interview (in which, in the instant case, the taxpayers made statements later used by the Revenue in a successful criminal prosecution) and the taxpayers should, accordingly, have been cautioned and the interview taped. The Revenue have since adopted this approach; the taxpayer or his adviser should be provided with a copy of the tape.

See also Revenue Code of Practice COP 9 referred to at 30.1 above.

See *R v CIR (ex p Mead and Cook) QB 1992, 65 TC 1* as regards Revenue discretion to seek monetary settlements or institute criminal proceedings. See *R v CIR (ex p Allen) QB 1997, 69 TC 442* for an unsuccessful application for judicial review of a Revenue decision to take criminal proceedings. The Revenue have an unrestricted power to conduct a prosecution in the Crown Court, there being no requirement for the consent of the Attorney-General (*R (oao Hunt) v Criminal Cases Review Commission DC, [2000] STC 1110*). A case is more likely to be prosecuted by the Revenue if it contains features such as falsification of documents, lying during an investigation, conspiracy, discovery of false statements made during a previous investigation or dishonesty on the part of a professional tax adviser (Revenue Press Release 14 July 1999). See also 35.4 INLAND REVENUE: ADMINISTRATION.

The Crown Prosecution Service ('CPS') is not precluded from instituting criminal proceedings in circumstances where the Revenue has accepted a monetary settlement. (*R v W and another CA, [1998] STC 550*). The Attorney-General made it clear, however, in a Parliamentary Written Answer, that proceedings brought by the CPS will ordinarily encompass charges relating to tax evasion only in circumstances where that is incidental to allegations of non-fiscal criminal conduct. A 'Convention between Prosecuting Authorities to provide arrangements for ensuring effective co-ordination of decision making and handling in related cases which are the responsibility of different authorities' was established on 11 February 1998 (for which see the Attorney General's Press Release of that date). See Hansard Vol 310, No 155 at Cols 230, 231 and Revenue Tax Bulletin June 1998 pp 544, 545.

Statements made or documents produced by or on behalf of a taxpayer are admissible as evidence in proceedings against him notwithstanding that reliance on the Board's practice above or on their policy for mitigating penalties (see 57.10 PENALTIES) may have induced

30.13 Fraudulent or Negligent Conduct

him to make or produce them. [*TMA 1970, s 105; FA 1989, s 168(5); FA 2003, s 206(1)(2)(5)*].

Simon's Direct Tax Service. See A3.1638–A3.1648.

30.13 **OFFENCE OF FRAUDULENT EVASION OF INCOME TAX**

A person who is knowingly concerned in the fraudulent evasion of income tax (by him or any other person) is liable, on summary conviction, to imprisonment for up to six months and/or a fine not exceeding the statutory maximum (£5,000), or on conviction on indictment, to imprisonment for up to seven years and/or an unlimited fine. This applies to things done or omitted after 31 December 2000. [*FA 2000, s 144*].

For an article giving the Revenue's views on conduct amounting to this offence, see Revenue Tax Bulletin October 2000 pp 782, 783.

Simon's Direct Tax Service. See A3.1502A.

31 Friendly Societies

Simon's Direct Tax Service D4.601 et seq.

31.1 **Friendly societies** are within the charge to corporation tax on income and capital gains. There are, however, exemptions from tax for:

(i) unregistered societies with incomes not exceeding £160 p.a.; and

(ii) registered or incorporated societies, in respect of 'tax exempt life or endowment business'.

[*ICTA 1988, ss 459, 460(1)(2); F(No 2)A 1992, Sch 9 paras 4, 5*].

Incorporated societies, following enactment of the *Friendly Societies Act 1992*, attract the same exemptions etc. as registered societies, and there are provisions to ensure that no tax charges arise on the incorporation of a registered society under that *Act*. [*F(No 2)A 1992, Sch 9; ICTA 1988, ss 461A–461C, s 465A; TCGA 1992, ss 217A–217C; SI 2001 No 3629, Articles 34–36*].

Following the general abolition, from 6 April 1999, of dividend tax credit payments, and their temporary reinstatement in relation to individual savings account investments (see 28.13 EXEMPT INCOME), they are similarly reinstated in relation to distributions to friendly societies in respect of tax exempt business until 5 April 2004. [*FA 1998, s 90*].

'*Tax exempt life or endowment business*' is broadly life or endowment business consisting of the granting of annuities of annual amounts not exceeding £156, or of the assurance of gross sums under contracts under which the total premiums payable in any twelve-month period do not exceed a maximum figure as follows:

for contracts made after 30 April 1995	£270
for contracts made after 24 July 1991 and before 1 May 1995	£200
for contracts made after 31 August 1990 and before 25 July 1991	£150
for contracts made after 31 August 1987 and before 1 September 1990	£100

For contracts made after 13 March 1984 and before 1 September 1987, the limit on the assurance of gross sums was by reference to the amount of the gross sum assured, and was set at £750. For contracts made before 14 March 1984, the limit was £500, and that on the granting of annuities £104. Where the premium under a contract made after 31 August 1987 and before 1 May 1995 is increased by a variation after 24 July 1991 and before 1 August 1992 or after 30 April 1995 and before 1 April 1996, the contract is to be treated for these purposes as having been made at the time of the variation. In determining these limits, no account is taken of any bonus or addition declared upon an assurance or accruing thereon by reference to an increase in the value of any investments, or of any bonus or addition declared upon an annuity. In relation to premium limits, so much of any premium as relates to exceptional risk of death or disability is disregarded, as is 10% of premiums payable more frequently than annually. The reference here to 'disability' was added by *FA 2003* and deemed always to have had effect, except to the extent that this retrospection would have detrimental effect. [*ICTA 1988, s 460(2)(c)(d)(3)–(6); FA 1990, s 49(1)(2); FA 1991, Sch 9 para 1; F(No 2)A 1992, Sch 9 para 5; FA 1995, Sch 10 para 1; FA 2003, s 172(5)(6)*]. For detailed requirements for exemption, see Tolley's Corporation Tax under Friendly Societies.

31.2 **Individual limit.** The total amount of business which a person may have outstanding with registered or incorporated friendly societies is limited:

(i) to an annuity or annuities totalling not more than £156 p.a. (£416 p.a. where all the contracts were made before 14 March 1984); and

(ii) to a gross sum assured under a contract or contracts under which the total premiums payable in any twelve-month period do not exceed any of the following limits:

for all contracts	£270
for contracts made after 24 July 1991 and before 1 May 1995	£200
for contracts made after 31 August 1990 and before 25 July 1991	£150
for contracts made before 1 September 1990	£100

unless all the contracts were made before 1 September 1987. For these purposes, a premium under an annuity contract made before 1 June 1984 by a 'new society' (see 31.3 below) is brought into account as if the contract were for the assurance of a gross sum. For contracts made before 1 September 1987, a limit was imposed by reference to the gross sum(s) assured, the limit being £750 (£2,000 if all the contracts were made before 14 March 1984). Where the premium under a contract made after 31 August 1987 and before 1 May 1995 is increased by a variation after 24 July 1991 and before 1 August 1992 or after 30 April 1995 and before 1 April 1996, the contract is to be treated for these purposes as having been made at the time of the variation. No account is, however, taken of (*a*) so much of any premium as relates to exceptional death risk, (*b*) 10% of premiums payable more frequently than annually, and (*c*) £10 of the premiums payable in a twelve month period under any contract made before 1 September 1987 by a society which is not a 'new society' (see 31.3 below).

The restrictions on both gross sum and annuity contracts are applied without taking into account any bonus or addition declared upon an assurance or accruing thereon by reference to an increase in the value of any investments. An annuity contract made before 1 June 1984 by a 'new society' is for these purposes treated as providing both the annual sum assured and a gross sum equal to 75% of the premiums which would be payable if the annuity ran its full term or the person died at age 75. [*ICTA 1988, s 464; FA 1990, s 49(3)(4); FA 1991, Sch 9 para 3; F(No 2)A 1992, Sch 9 para 11; FA 1995, Sch 10 para 2*]. If, after 18 March 1985, a person obtains a policy which causes his contracts to exceed the above limits, the policy will not be a 'qualifying policy' (see 31.3 below), but without affecting earlier policies. [*ICTA 1988 Sch 15 para 6*].

31.3 **Qualifying policies** attract income tax relief on the premiums paid (for insurances made before 14 March 1984), and the proceeds are generally free of any income tax charge (see 45.1, 45.13 LIFE ASSURANCE POLICIES). Except as below, all policies issued by friendly societies before 19 March 1985 in the course of tax exempt life or endowment business (see 31.1 above) are qualifying policies. [*ICTA 1970, Sch 1 para 3 as originally enacted*]. A policy issued *or varied* after 18 March 1985 is a qualifying policy only if it satisfies the conditions in *ICTA 1988, Sch 15 paras 3, 4 as amended*. Broadly, these are the same as the conditions imposed under *ICTA 1988, s 462* on policies which a friendly society may issue in the course of its tax exempt life or endowment business (see Tolley's Corporation Tax under Friendly Societies), but in addition the minimum sum assured must be at least 75% of the total premiums payable, and contracts made before 25 July 1991 with a 'new society' must be with a person over the age of 18. [*ICTA 1988, Sch 15 para 3(1); FA 1991, Sch 9 para 4*]. For the detailed application of the 75% test, see *ICTA 1988, Sch 15 para 3(5)–(11) as amended*.

Certain policies issued under contracts made before 20 March 1991, and expressed at the outset not to be made in the course of tax-exempt life or endowment business, were subsequently determined to have been within the statutory definition of that business. A similar situation arose in relation to certain contracts for qualifying policies assumed, at the outset of the contract, not to be made in the course of tax-exempt life or endowment business (without being expressed either to be or not to be so). Where the society so elected, profits attributable to such contracts are treated as not being within the exemption. [*ICTA*

1988, s 462A; FA 1991, Sch 9 para 2]. However, such an election does not affect the tax position of the member holding the policy. By concession, the member will be taxed on the basis of the original assumption he will have been given that no charge to tax would arise on the surrender or maturity of the policy. (Revenue Press Release 12 June 1991). See Tolley's Corporation Tax under Friendly Societies for details of the society's election.

A '*new society*' is a society which either was registered after 3 May 1966 or was registered in the three months before that date but did not carry on any life or endowment business during that period (or a successor incorporated society). [*ICTA 1988, s 466(2); F(No 2)A 1992, Sch 9 para 14(5)*].

If any rights under a health insurance policy (within *Friendly Societies Act 1974, Sch 1 para 1*) issued by a new society (see above) are wholly or partly surrendered after 18 March 1985, the policy ceases to be a qualifying policy. [*ICTA 1988, Sch 15 para 4(3)(b)*].

31.4   **Non-qualifying policies.** A gain on a chargeable event in respect of a policy which is not a qualifying policy (see 31.3 above), or in respect of certain life annuity contracts, may give rise to a charge to income tax (see 45.13 LIFE ASSURANCE POLICIES). If such a gain arises on a policy issued in the course of a society's tax exempt life or endowment business (see 31.1 above), it is fully chargeable to income tax, with no notional tax credit but with 'top-slicing relief' (see 45.13 LIFE ASSURANCE POLICIES) applying to any higher rate tax. [*ICTA 1988, s 547(7)*].

31.5   **Qualifying distributions.** If a society registered after 31 May 1973, with certain exceptions, or one registered before that date if the Board so directs, makes a payment to a member (in excess of his contributions and not in the course of life or endowment business), this is a qualifying distribution for income and corporation tax purposes (see Tolley's Corporation Tax under Distributions). [*ICTA 1988, s 461(2)(3); SI 2001 No 3629, Article 33*].

31.6   See 3.16 ANTI-AVOIDANCE for restriction of tax recovery regarding pre-acquisition dividends etc. on 10% holdings, and 3.17 regarding certain bonus issues.

32.1 Funding Bonds

32 Funding Bonds

Simon's Direct Tax Service A3.425.

32.1 **Funding Bonds etc.** issued in respect of interest by any Government, public authority or institution, or company are treated as income equal to bonds' value when issued; but their eventual redemption is not treated as a payment of the interest. 'Bonds' includes 'stocks, shares, securities or certificates of indebtedness'. Persons by or through whom the bonds are issued and who, if the amount treated as income had been an actual payment of interest, would have been required to deduct tax therefrom, must retain a proportionate amount of these bonds equal to tax at the lower rate on their value, and are accountable to the Revenue accordingly, with the right to tender the bonds in payment. Where retention is impracticable they may be relieved of liability on their furnishing a list of recipients, who are then assessed direct under Schedule D, Case VI. [*ICTA 1988, s 582; FA 1996, s 134, Sch 6 para 14, Sch 20 para 32; FA 2002, Sch 25 para 50*].

33 Government Stocks

Cross-references. See 3 ANTI-AVOIDANCE for dividend-stripping and bond-washing transactions; 13 CERTIFICATES OF TAX DEPOSIT; 22 DEDUCTION OF TAX AT SOURCE.

Simon's Direct Tax Service A7.11.

33.1 GENERAL TAX PROVISIONS

For corporation tax purposes, all interest and profits or losses in respect of securities is brought in on revenue account, either on an accruals or on a mark to market basis. For income tax purposes, however, Government and foreign securities are chargeable under Schedule D, Case III, IV or V as appropriate, and, until 31 March 2001, are subject to the paying and collecting agents arrangements under *ICTA 1988, ss 118A–118K* and associated regulations. For an article on the scope of these arrangements, see Revenue Tax Bulletin August 1996 p 329. From 1 April 2001, these arrangements are abolished. [*FA 2000, s 111(1)(6)*]. See 33.3 below and, as regards continuing deduction arrangements for UK public revenue dividends (other than gilt-edged securities), 22.3(ii) DEDUCTION OF TAX AT SOURCE.

33.2 INTEREST—TAX EXEMPTION FOR NON-RESIDENTS

The Treasury has powers to issue securities ('FOTRA securities') on terms that the profits or gains arising from the securities are exempt from tax provided that they are beneficially owned by persons not ordinarily resident in the UK (see RESIDENCE, ORDINARY RESIDENCE AND DOMICILE (65)). From 6 April 1998, however, *FA 1998, s 161* provides for all gilt-edged securities issued before that date without that status to be treated as if they were FOTRA securities (except 3.5% War Loan, which is in effect treated in the same way as FOTRA securities under its terms of issue).

Further and current information relating to exempt stocks may be obtained from Gilt-Edged and Money Markets Division, Bank of England, Threadneedle Street, London EC2R 8AH (tel. 020–7601 4540). A restricted market operates in those stocks marked with an asterisk because of the small amounts still in issue.

Provided that any conditions imposed are complied with, nothing in the *Tax Acts* overrides such exemption, although this does not confer any exemption from charge where income is treated under anti-avoidance provisions as income of a UK resident etc. (see 81.17, 81.18 SETTLEMENTS, 3.7 ANTI-AVOIDANCE). See *FA 1996, s 154, Sch 28*. For 1995/96 and earlier years (and for company accounting periods ending before 1 April 1996), *ICTA 1988, s 47* (which is repealed by *FA 1996, Sch 28 para 1*) applied to broadly similar effect.

If interest forms part of the profits of a UK trade, exemption does not generally apply (depending on the Treasury conditions of issue) (see *Owen v Sassoon Ch D 1950, 32 TC 101*).

See 51.8 NON-RESIDENTS AND OTHER OVERSEAS MATTERS for the special position of *non-resident banks, insurance companies and dealers in securities* carrying on business in the UK.

For the exemption of non-residents from income tax on interest on local authority securities expressed in a foreign currency, see 22.12 DEDUCTION OF TAX AT SOURCE.

33.3 INTEREST — DEDUCTION OF TAX

From 6 April 1998, interest on gilt-edged securities (excluding, for payments made before 1 April 2001, those held in bearer form) is paid without deduction of tax [*ICTA 1988, s*

50(A1); F(No 2)A 1997, s 37(2)(8); FA 2000, s 112(1)], although the option of deduction continues to be available (see *F(No 2)A 1997, s 37* generally and below and, from 1 April 2001, 22.3(ii) DEDUCTION OF TAX AT SOURCE). See Revenue Tax Bulletin February 1998 pp 511, 512 for an article explaining the effect of the changes on gilt holders.

Before 6 April 1998, interest on gilt-edged securities was generally payable under deduction of tax, but the Treasury could direct that interest on certain securities should be paid gross [*ICTA 1988, ss 50(1), 51AA; FA 1996, s 155*], although the recipient could nevertheless apply to the Bank of England for income tax to be deducted. Gross payment applied to all existing strippable Government stocks from 7 June 1997, and to all subsequent strippable issues. Interest on 3.5% War Loan, on registered stocks and bonds on the National Savings Stock Register and stocks held through any Savings Bank was also paid gross.

The procedure whereby paying agents deduct and account for tax is laid down in *ICTA 1988, ss 118A–118K* (introduced by *FA 1996, s 156, Sch 29* and as subsequently amended) and regulations thereunder (see *SI 1996 No 1780, SI 1997 No 2705, SI 1999 No 823*), although these provisions are repealed from 1 April 2001 (and see now 22.3(ii) DEDUCTION OF TAX AT SOURCE). CHARITIES (14) generally receive payments gross on presentation to the paying agent of evidence of charitable status. For an article on the scope of these procedural rules, see Revenue Tax Bulletin August 1996 p 329.

Also until 5 April 1998, the Treasury had powers to make regulations for gross payment of interest on gilt-edged securities held by corporate bodies and in certain other circumstances under specified arrangements, and, until 5 April 1999, for periodic accounting for tax on such interest (which is, however, abolished for interest falling due on or after 1 April 1999). (These powers relate to the 'gilt repos' market introduced on 2 January 1996.) See *SI 1995 No 2934, SI 1996 No 21* (as amended). See also *SI 1995 Nos 3223, 3224, 3225* (as amended) and *SI 1999 Nos 623, 624*. [*ICTA 1988, ss 51A, 51B; FA 1995, ss 77, 78; FA 1996, Sch 6 para 4; F(No 2)A 1997, s 37(5)(8); FA 1998, s 37(1); SI 1995 No 2932; SI 1999 No 619*]. See Tolley's Corporation Tax under Income Tax in Relation to a Company.

33.4   **PREMIUM SAVINGS BONDS**

Prizes are free of both income tax and capital gains tax.

33.5   **SAVINGS CERTIFICATES**

All income arising from savings certificates (as defined) (and including index-linked) and tax reserve certificates is exempt from tax except that arising from

(i)   savings certificates purchased by or on behalf of a person in excess of the amount authorised under the regulations of the particular issue, or

(ii)   Ulster savings certificates, unless the holder is resident and ordinarily resident in NI when the certificates are repaid or he was so resident and ordinarily resident when he purchased them. [*ICTA 1988, s 46*]. By concession, where repayment is made after the death of the holder, who was resident and ordinarily resident in NI when he purchased them, the exemption is allowed. (Revenue Pamphlet IR 1, A34).

34 Herd Basis

See generally Revenue Business Income Manual BIM 55501–55640.

Simon's Direct Tax Service B3.515 et seq.

34.1 Animals and other living creatures kept for the purposes of farming or similar trades (e.g. animal or fish breeding) are generally treated as trading stock (see 71.73 SCHEDULE D, CASES I AND II) unless an election is made under *ICTA 1988, s 97, Sch 5* for the 'herd basis' to apply. [*ICTA 1988, s 97, Sch 5 paras 1, 9(1)(2)*]. Animals etc. are exempt from capital gains tax as wasting assets within *TCGA 1992, s 45.*

34.2 **Availability of election for herd basis.** An election for the herd basis may apply to animals etc., whether kept singly or as part of a production herd or flock etc., which are kept wholly or mainly for the sale of products of living animals or of their young, and to shares in such animals etc. [*ICTA 1988, Sch 5 para 1(2), para 8(1)(5), para 9(2)(4); FA 2000, s 76(2)(3)*]. An election must apply to all herds consisting of animals of the same species (irrespective of breed), kept for production of products of the same kind, which are kept by the farmer making the election, including herds which he ceased to keep before, or first keeps after, the making of the election. [*ICTA 1988, Sch 5 paras 2(1), 8(6)*].

Foot and mouth outbreak. For the full range of measures, including acceptance of herd basis elections, in relation to the 2001 foot and mouth disease outbreak, see Revenue Tax Bulletin Special Edition May 2001and Revenue Tax Bulletin October 2001 pp 890, 891. In particular, by concession, certain replacement animals slaughtered before giving birth may be regarded as having been mature for the purposes of *ICTA 1988, Sch 5 para 8(4)* (see 34.3 below), and hence treated as having been part of the herd rather than trading stock. (Revenue Pamphlet IR 1, B56).

34.3 An election for the herd basis **may not apply** to animals kept wholly or mainly for farm work or for public exhibition or racing or other competitive purposes. [*ICTA 1988, Sch 5 paras 7, 9(5)*]. Immature animals are not treated as part of a herd for these purposes unless the land on which the herd is kept is such that the replacement of animals which die or cease to form part of the herd can only be by animals bred and reared on that land (e.g. acclimatised hill sheep), and then only to the extent that they are necessarily bred and maintained in the herd for the purposes of replacement. Female animals become mature when they produce their first young (and laying birds when they first lay), but see 34.2 above as regards temporary concession during the 2001 foot and mouth outbreak. [*ICTA 1988, Sch 5 para 8(2)–(4), para 9(3)*].

34.4 The **election must be made** in writing, specifying the class of herd to which it applies, not later than:

(*a*) for individual farmers, twelve months after 31 January following the qualifying year of assessment, i.e. the first tax year (excluding that in which the trade commences) in the basis period for which a production herd of the class specified was first kept by the individual; and

(*b*) for partnerships, twelve months after 31 January following the year of assessment in which ends the qualifying period of account, i.e. the first period of account during the whole or part of which a production herd of the class specified was first kept by the partnership.

For corporation tax purposes, as respects accounting periods ending on or after the appointed day for the introduction of self-assessment for companies (see Tolley's

34.5 Herd Basis

Corporation Tax under Assessments and Appeals), the time limit is two years after the end of the qualifying accounting period, i.e. the first accounting period during the whole or part of which a production herd of the class specified was first kept by the company.

[*ICTA 1988, Sch 5 para 2(2)(3)(6); FA 1994, ss 196, 199(2), Sch 19 para 43(1)(3)*].

See, however, 34.8 below as regards compulsory slaughter.

The election is irrevocable and has effect for, respectively, the qualifying year of assessment, period of account or accounting period (see above) and subsequently. For individuals, the election also has effect for the tax year in which the trade commenced if that year immediately precedes the qualifying year of assessment. [*ICTA 1988, Sch 5 para 2(4)–(6); FA 1994, Sch 19 para 43(2)(3)*].

Previously, the election had to be made within two years after the end of either

(i) the first period of account for which an account was made up for farming, or

(ii) the first year of assessment or company accounting period for which farming profits were chargeable under Schedule D, Case I (or loss relief given under *ICTA 1988, s 380, s 393(2)* or *s 393A(1)*) and in which (or, where applicable, in the basis period for which) a production herd of the class specified in the election was kept,

and had effect from the first year of assessment or company accounting period affected by it. [*ICTA 1988, Sch 5 para 2(2)–(4), para 8(7)*].

Where there is a change in the persons carrying on a trade in partnership (see 53.5 PARTNERSHIPS), whether or not the trade is treated as continuing, a further election is required if the herd basis is to continue to apply (Revenue Business Income Manual BIM 55610).

See 34.5 below as regards renewal of right of election where there is a five-year gap in keeping a herd of a particular class.

34.5 **Consequences of election.** Where a herd basis election is in force, the animals in the herd are in effect treated as capital assets. The initial cost of the herd and of additions to the herd is not deductible as a trading expense, and its value is not brought into account. A profit or loss on the sale within a twelve-month period (without replacement, see 34.6 below) of the whole or a substantial (i.e. normally 20% or more) part of the herd is similarly not brought into account. Where, however, within five years of such a sale, another herd of the same class is (or begins to be) acquired (or replacement animals are or begin to be acquired), the normal replacement provisions (see 34.6 below) apply, the proceeds of the sale being treated as received at the time of the corresponding acquisition(s). However, the sale, for reasons beyond the farmer's control, of animals subsequently replaced by animals of inferior quality may not give rise to a greater trading receipt than the amount allowed as a deduction in respect of the replacement animals. [*ICTA 1988, Sch 5 para 3(1)(2)(8)(9)*].

Where a farmer ceases to keep any herd of a particular class for a period of at least five years, he is thereafter treated as if he had never previously kept a herd of that class. [*ICTA 1988, Sch 5 para 4*].

The addition to a herd of an animal previously treated as trading stock, otherwise than by way of replacement (see 34.6 below), gives rise to a trading receipt equal to the cost of acquiring or breeding it and rearing it to maturity. [*ICTA 1988, Sch 5 para 3(3)*]. In practice, if the animal is included in stock at market value (being lower than cost), that figure will similarly be substituted as the trading receipt on appropriation to the herd.

The sale without replacement (see 34.6 below) of an animal from a herd gives rise to a trading profit or loss, calculated by reference to the cost of acquiring or breeding it (or its market value if acquired other than for valuable consideration) and of rearing it to maturity. [*ICTA 1988, Sch 5 para 3(10)*]. This charge also covers disposals, without replacement, of more than one animal, where the number disposed of is less than 20% of the herd. For the Revenue's interpretation of this provision, including a change of view on how the profit on such sales is to be computed, see Revenue Tax Bulletin April 2003 pp 1024, 1025.

34.6   **Replacement animals.** The replacement of an animal dying or ceasing to be a member of a herd gives rise to a trading receipt of any proceeds of sale of the animal replaced, and a trading deduction of the cost of the replacement animal (so far as not otherwise allowable under Schedule D, Case I) but limited to the cost of an animal of similar quality to that replaced (for which see Revenue Tax Bulletin October 2001 pp 890, 891). Where the animal replaced was compulsorily slaughtered, and the replacement animal is of inferior quality, the trading receipt is restricted to the amount of the corresponding deduction. [*ICTA 1988, Sch 5 para 3(4)–(6)*]. See 34.5 above as regards animals not replaced. Whether a particular animal brought into the herd replaces an animal disposed of for these purposes is a question of fact, requiring a direct connection between the disposal and the later addition rather than a simple restoration of numbers. As a practical matter, inspectors will accept that replacement treatment is appropriate where animals are brought into the herd within twelve months of the corresponding disposal. Where disposal and replacement are in different accounting periods, the overall profit or loss may either be brought in in the first period and any necessary adjustment made in the second, or the profit or loss arising in the first period may be held over to the second period. Where the interval is more than twelve months, there is unlikely to be sufficient evidence to support the necessary connection where the new animal is bought in. Where animals are home bred, however, a longer interval may be reasonable where e.g. there is insufficient young stock to replace unexpected disposals. (Revenue Tax Bulletin October 1994 p 169, February 1997 p 396).

Where the whole herd is replaced, this is treated as the replacement of a number of animals, being the smaller of the number in the old herd and in the new. [*ICTA 1988, Sch 5 para 3(7)*]. Where the new herd is the larger, the net increase will be treated as additions to the herd. Where the new herd is the smaller, but not substantially so (i.e. the provisions described in 34.5 above in relation to a substantial reduction do not apply), the net reduction in the number of animals is treated as giving rise to a corresponding sale without replacement (see 34.5 above). [*ICTA 1988, Sch 5 para 3(11)*].

34.7   **Insurance, compensation etc.** Any reference to sale proceeds in the foregoing provisions includes a reference, in the case of the death or destruction of an animal, to insurance or compensation moneys received and to proceeds of carcass sales. [*ICTA 1988, Sch 5 para 3(12)*].

34.8   **Compulsory slaughter.** Where compensation is received for the whole, or a substantial part (i.e. normally 20% or more), of a herd compulsorily slaughtered by order under animal diseases laws, the farmer may, notwithstanding the time limits in 34.4 above, elect for the herd basis to apply. As respects 1996/97 and subsequent years, the election must be made not later than:

(*a*)   for individual farmers, twelve months after 31 January following the qualifying year of assessment, i.e. the first year of assessment in the basis period for which the compensation falls (or would otherwise fall) to be taken into account as a trading receipt; and

(*b*)   for partnerships, twelve months after 31 January following the year of assessment in which ends the qualifying period of account, i.e. the first period of account in which the compensation falls (or would otherwise fall) to be taken into account as a trading receipt.

For corporation tax purposes, as respects accounting periods ending on or after the appointed day for the introduction of self-assessment for companies (see Tolley's Corporation Tax under Assessments and Appeals), the time limit is two years after the end of the qualifying accounting period, i.e. the first accounting period in which the compensation falls (or would otherwise fall) to be taken into account as a trading receipt. The election has effect for, respectively, the qualifying year of assessment, period of account or accounting period and subsequently.

[*ICTA 1988, Sch 5 para 6; FA 1994, ss 196, 199(2), Sch 19 para 43(4)*].

Compensation paid under the BSE Suspects Scheme and the BSE Selective Cull (where the animal was born after 14 October 1990) is for compulsory slaughter, and for these purposes includes Selective Cull 'top-up' payments. Payments under the Calf Processing Scheme, the Over Thirty Month Scheme and the BSE Selective Cull where the animal was born before 15 October 1990 are *not* for compulsory slaughter. See Revenue Tax Bulletin February 1997 pp 396, 397 for this and for the application of these provisions to BSE compensation generally. Where the herd basis does not apply, see 71.47(*b*) SCHEDULE D, CASES I AND II.

34.9 **Anti-avoidance.** There are provisions for the prevention of avoidance of tax in the case of a transfer between connected persons or where the sole or main benefit relates to its effect on a herd basis election. [*ICTA 1988, Sch 5 para 5*].

34.10 **Information etc.** Where an election has effect, returns may be required as to the animals, and products thereof, kept by any person affected by the election. Repayments etc. may be made as required to give effect to the election. [*ICTA 1988, Sch 5 paras 10, 11*].

34.11 *Example*

A farmer acquires a dairy herd and elects for the herd basis to apply. The movements in the herd and the tax treatment are as follows.

Year 1	No	Value
		£
Mature		
Bought @ £150	70	10,500
Bought in calf @ £180		
(Market value of calf £35)	5	900
Immature		
Bought @ £75	15	1,125
Herd Account		£
70 Friesians		10,500
5 Friesians in calf (5 × £(180 − 35))		725
75 Closing balance		£11,225

	No	Value
Year 1		*£*
Trading Account		
5 Calves (5 × £35)		175
15 Immature Friesians		1,125
Debit to profit and loss account		£1,300

Year 2

	No	Value
		£
Mature		
Bought @ £185	15	2,775
Sold @ £200	10	2,000
Died	3	—
Immature		
Born	52	—
Matured @ 60% of market value of £200 note (*a*)	12	1,440

Herd Account		£	£
75	Opening balance		11,225
	Increase in herd		
15	Purchases	2,775	
12	Transferred from trading stock	1,440	
—			
27		4,215	
(13)	Replacement cost £4,215 × $\frac{13}{27}$	2,029	
—			
14	Non-replacement animals cost		2,186
—			
89	Closing balance		£13,411
—			

Trading Account	£
Sale of 10 mature cows replaced	(2,000)
Transfer to herd—14 animals	(2,186)
Cost of 13 mature cows purchased to replace those sold/deceased ($\frac{13}{15}$ × £2,775)	2,405
Net credit to profit and loss account note (*b*)	£(1,781)

Year 3

	No	Value
		£
Mature		
Jerseys bought @ £250	70	17,500
Friesians slaughtered @ £175 (market value £185)	52	9,100

34.11　Herd Basis

	No	Value £
Immature		
Friesians born	20	—
Matured		
Friesians @ 60% of market value of £190 note (*a*)	15	1,710

Herd Account	£	£
89　Opening balance		13,411
Increase in herd		
18　Jerseys		4,500
52 Improvement Jerseys @	250	
less Market value of Friesians	185	
52 @	65	3,380
Transfer from trading stock		
15　Friesians		1,710
122　Closing balance		£23,001

Trading Account	£
Compensation	(9,100)
Transfer to herd	(1,710)
Purchase of replacements note (*c*) (52 × £185)	9,620
Net credit to profit and loss account	£(1,190)

Year 4

The farmer ceases dairy farming and sells his whole herd.

	No	Value £
Mature		
Jerseys sold @ £320	70	22,400
Friesians sold @ £200	52	10,400
Immature		
Friesians sold @ £100	65	6,500

Herd Account	£
Opening balance	23,001
52　Friesians	
70　Jerseys	
(122)　Sales	(32,800)
—　Profit on sale note (*d*)	£(9,799)

Trading Account	£
Sale of 65 immature Friesians	(6,500)
Credit to profit and loss account	£(6,500)

Notes

(*a*)   The use of 60% of market value was originally by agreement between the National Farmers' Union and the Revenue (see now Revenue Business Economic Note 19: Farming — Stock Valuation for Income Tax purposes, at paragraph 7.2). Alternatively, the actual cost of breeding or purchase and rearing could be used.

(*b*)   As the cost of rearing the 12 cows to maturity will already have been debited to the profit and loss account, no additional entry is required to reflect that cost. Due to the fact that the animals were in opening stock at valuation and will not be in closing stock, the trading account will in effect be debited with that valuation.

(*c*)   The cost of the replacements is restricted to the cost of replacing like with like.

(*d*)   Provided these animals are not replaced by a herd of the same class within five years the proceeds will be tax-free (see 34.5 above).

35 Inland Revenue: Administration

35.1 The levying and collection of income tax, surtax and capital gains tax is administered by the **Commissioners of Inland Revenue** (normally referred to as the Board), Somerset House, London WC2R 1LB. [*TMA 1970, s 1(1)*].

Under them are local **inspectors of taxes**, permanent civil servants with an expert knowledge of tax law, who are responsible for making most assessments, and dealing with claims and allowances, and to whom all enquiries should be addressed.

The Inland Revenue maintains an internet website (www.inlandrevenue.gov.uk/home.htm) which provides access to detailed information on many aspects of the Revenue's activities, including publications, press releases and contact points.

The Chancellor of the Exchequer announced in his Budget speech on 17 March 2004 that the Inland Revenue and HM Customs & Excise are to merge.

35.2 **Collectors of Taxes** are also permanent civil servants and their duties for the most part relate only to the collection of tax. [*TMA 1970, ss 60–70*].

35.3 **Commissioners.** Appeals against assessments or amendments of self-assessments are heard by

(*a*) the General Commissioners (local persons appointed on a voluntary basis by the Lord Chancellor or, in Scotland, by the Secretary of State) [*TMA 1970, s 2; FA 1975, s 57; FA 1988, s 134(1)*], or

(*b*) the Special Commissioners (full-time civil servants, being barristers, advocates or solicitors etc. of at least ten years' standing, appointed for this purpose) [*TMA 1970, s 4; FA 1984, s 127, Sch 22 para 1; Courts and Legal Services Act 1990, Sch 10 para 30*].

The Lord Chancellor has powers, by regulation, to change the names by which the General and Special Commissioners are to be referred to. [*F(No 2)A 1992, s 75*].

With effect from 1 April 2001, provisions are introduced which

(*a*) prohibit courts from ordering a General Commissioner to pay costs relating to any acts or omissions in the execution of his duties as such (except in relation to proceedings in which he is being tried for an offence or is appealing against a conviction), the court being able instead to order the 'relevant Minister' to make such payment, and

(*b*) require the 'relevant Minister' to indemnify a General Commissioner or Clerk (or assistant) to the General Commissioners against certain costs or damages,

except in cases involving bad faith. The '*relevant Minister*' is the Lord Chancellor or, in Scotland, the Secretary of State.

[*TMA 1970, ss 2A, 3A; Access to Justice Act 1999, ss 102, 103; SI 2001 No 916*].

See 4.4, 4.7 APPEALS as regards jurisdiction of Commissioners and the conduct of appeals before them.

35.4 **'Care and management' powers.** For the validity of amnesties by the Board, see *CIR v National Federation of Self-Employed and Small Businesses Ltd HL 1981, 55 TC 133*. INLAND REVENUE EXTRA-STATUTORY CONCESSIONS (38) have been the subject of frequent judicial criticism (see Lord Edward Davies' opinion in *Vestey v CIR (No 1) HL 1979, 54 TC 503* for a review of this) but their validity has never been directly challenged in the Courts. In *R v HMIT (ex p Fulford-Dobson) QB 1987, 60 TC 168*, a claim that the Revenue had acted unfairly in refusing a concession where tax avoidance was involved was rejected, but the taxpayer's right to seek judicial review of a Revenue decision to refuse the benefit of a concession was confirmed in *R v HMIT (ex p Brumfield and Others) QB 1988, 61 TC 589*. A decision by the Revenue to revoke its authorisation to pay a dividend gross was upheld in *R v CIR (ex p Camacq Corporation) CA 1989, 62 TC 651*. For a general discussion of the Board's care and management powers and an example of a ruling by the Court that the Board had exercised a discretionary power reasonably, see *R v CIR (ex p Preston) HL 1985, 59 TC 1*. Where a discretionary power is given to the Revenue, it is an error in law to proceed on the footing that the power is mandatory (*R v HMIT and Others (ex p Lansing Bagnall Ltd) CA 1986, 61 TC 112*). See also *R v CIR (ex p J Rothschild Holdings) CA 1987, 61 TC 178*, where the Revenue were required to produce internal documents of a general character relating to their practice in applying a statutory provision.

The Revenue policy of selective prosecution for criminal offences in connection with tax evasion does not render a decision in a particular case unlawful or *ultra vires*, provided that the case is considered on its merits fairly and dispassionately to see whether the criteria for prosecution were satisfied, and that the decision to prosecute is then taken in good faith for the purpose of collecting taxes and not for some ulterior, extraneous or improper purpose (*R v CIR (ex p Mead and Cook) QB 1992, 65 TC 1*). See *R v CIR (ex p Allen) QB 1997, 69 TC 442* for an unsuccessful application for judicial review of a Revenue decision to take criminal proceedings.

The making of a 'forward tax agreement', by which the Revenue renounced their right and duty to investigate the true financial and other circumstances of the other party during the period of the agreement in return for payments of money, was not a proper exercise of the Revenue's care and management powers, and was accordingly *ultra vires* and illegal (*Al Fayed & Others v Advocate-General for Scotland and CIR CS, [2002] STC 910*).

The social security authorities are authorised to disclose information held by them to the Commissioners of Inland Revenue, or persons providing certain services to the Commissioners, for investigative purposes or in relation to national insurance contributions. [*FA 1997, s 110; Social Security Administration Act 1992, s 121F; Social Security Contributions (Transfer of Functions etc.) Act 1999, Sch 6 para 1; Tax Credits Act 1999, Sch 5 para 7; Tax Credits Act 2002, Sch 5 para 13; SI 1997 No 1603; SI 2002 No 1727*].

35.5   **Equitable liability.** For the circumstances in which the Revenue may accept a reduced sum in respect of certain assessed liabilities, see 56.12 PAYMENT OF TAX.

35.6   **Inland Revenue rulings.** For the extent to which taxpayers may rely on guidance given by the Revenue, see the letter from the Deputy Chairman to the various professional bodies following the decision in *R v CIR (ex p Matrix-Securities Ltd) HL 1994, 66 TC 587*.

The Revenue may provide a post-transaction ruling for a transaction after it has occurred but before the tax return is submitted. Rulings will only be given where the tax treatment of a transaction is in doubt, for example in relation to unusual transactions or transactions entered into in usual circumstances. See Code of Practice 10 (as revised April 1999) for the types of transactions on which a ruling can be given, the extent to which the Revenue will be bound by the ruling, the effect of the ruling on interest and penalties and the procedures in obtaining such a ruling.

35.7   **Taxpayer's Charter.** The Board of Inland Revenue and HM Customs and Excise have jointly produced a Taxpayer's Charter setting out the principles they try to meet in their dealings with taxpayers, the standards they believe the taxpayer has a right to expect, and what people can do if they wish to appeal or complain. Copies are available from local tax or collection offices and from local VAT offices.

A series of codes of practice, setting out the standards of service people can expect in relation to specific aspects of the Revenue's work, is published to support the Taxpayer's Charter. Each code states the standards which the Revenue sets itself and the rights of taxpayers in particular situations. The first three, covering mistakes by the Revenue and their complaints procedure (see 35.8 below), the conduct of tax investigations and the conduct of inspections of employers' and contractors' records (see 55.1 PAY AS YOU EARN) were first published in February 1993, and are available from local tax offices. Codes 4 and 5, relating to financial intermediaries and charities (see 14.1 CHARITIES) respectively, were first published in July 1993, copies being sent to the institutions concerned, and are available from IR Charities, Repayments, St John's House, Merton Road, Bootle, Merseyside L69 9BB. Codes 6 and 7, on collection of tax generally and collection from employers and construction industry contractors, were first published in November 1994 and are available from local tax offices. Codes 8 and 9, on Special Compliance Office Investigations in cases other than suspected serious fraud and cases of such fraud respectively (the latter significantly revised in November 2002), were first published in January 1995 and are available from the Special Compliance Office, Angel Court, 199 Borough High Street, London SE1 1HZ. Code 10, on the provision by the Revenue of information and advice, was first published in June 1995 and is available from local tax offices. Code 11, dealing with enquiries into self-assessment income tax returns by local tax offices, was first published in July 1996, superseding Code 2 as regards such returns. It will be issued at the start of every such enquiry (except that in certain simple cases a short, single-page version will be issued). Code 14, dealing with enquiries into self-assessment company tax returns, was first published in July 1999, superseding Code 2 as regards such returns. It will be given to the company concerned at the start of every enquiry (except that where a simple enquiry is expected to be settled by a brief exchange of correspondence and not to involve penalties, a single-page version of the Code will be issued instead). Code 17 concerns Working Families' and Disabled Person's Tax Credits, Codes 19 and 20 the National Minimum Wage and Code 22 orders for the delivery of documents. There is also a joint Revenue and Customs & Excise Code of Practice on the disclosure of information under the *Anti-terrorism, Crime and Security Act 2001, ss 19, 20*. Most of the above codes are also available on the Revenue's website.

35.8   **Revenue error.** Code of Practice 1 (COP 1), 'Putting things right: how to complain' (revised June 2003), outlines the complaints procedure and gives general advice on the circumstances in which payment may be claimed from the Revenue as a consequence of Revenue mistake or unreasonable delay. These fall into three categories.

(*a*)   *Claiming back costs.* Any reasonable costs paid as a direct result of Revenue error, such as postage, 'phone calls, travelling expenses, professional fees and financial charges, may be reclaimed. If the extra costs arose because of Revenue delay in dealing with the taxpayer's affairs, interest normally charged on overdue tax or national insurance owed by the taxpayer may be waived, and interest may be paid on money owed by the Revenue, during the unreasonable delay.

(*b*)   *Compensation for worry and distress.* If the Revenue's actions have affected the taxpayer particularly badly, the Revenue may pay compensation (usually in the range £25 to £500) to acknowledge and apologise for the way the taxpayer was treated.

(*c*)   *Further mistakes or delays in dealing with complaint.* If the Revenue handle a complaint badly, or take an unreasonable time to deal with it, compensation (usually in the range £25 to £500) may be paid, on top of any reasonable costs, to reflect this.

All payments made by the Revenue under this Code of Practice are non-taxable. The Revenue will not compensate for time spent sorting things out unless the taxpayer can show lost earnings as a direct result. Where there has been a difference of opinion between taxpayer and Revenue on a matter of law and the taxpayer's view prevails, the Revenue will consider paying compensation only if the view they had taken had been unreasonable. Compensation may be paid to agents but only in exceptional circumstances, for example if a mistake has affected all or most of the agent's clients.

35.9 **Adjudicator's Office.** A taxpayer who is not satisfied with the Revenue response to a complaint has the option of putting the case to an independent Adjudicator for the Inland Revenue. The Adjudicator's Office considers complaints about the Revenue's handling of a taxpayer's affairs, e.g. mistakes, delays, misleading advice, staff behaviour or the exercise of Revenue discretion. Matters subject to existing rights of appeal are excluded.

The Adjudicator also investigates complaints about Customs and Excise and the Valuation Office Agency.

The address is The Adjudicator's Office, Haymarket House, 28 Haymarket, London SW1Y 4SP (tel. 020–7930 2292, e-mail address: adjudicators@gtnet.gov.uk).

Complaints normally go to the Adjudicator only after they have been considered by, firstly, the Customer Relations or Complaints Manager and, secondly, the Director of the relevant Revenue office, and where the taxpayer is still not satisfied with the response received. The alternatives of pursuing the complaint to the Revenue's Head Office, to an MP, or (through an MP) to the Parliamentary Ombudsman continue to be available. The Adjudicator reviews all the facts, considers whether the complaint is justified, and, if so, settles the complaint by mediation or makes recommendations as to what should be done. The Revenue normally accept the recommendations.

The Adjudicator publishes an annual report to the Board.

See also Revenue leaflet AO1 'The Adjudicator's Office'.

Leave to apply for judicial review of the rejection by the Adjudicator of a complaint concerning the use of information from unidentified informants was refused in *R v Revenue Adjudicator's Office (ex p Drummond) QB 1996, 70 TC 235.*

35.10 **Open Government.** Under the Government's 'Code of Practice on Access to Government Information', the Revenue (in common with other Government departments) is to make information about its policies and decisions more widely available. Revenue Pamphlet IR 141 ('Open Government') sets out the information to be made available, and how it may be obtained, and the basis on which a fee may be charged in certain circumstances to offset the cost of providing the information. Copies of the Code of Practice may be obtained by writing to Open Government, Room 417b, Office of Public Service and Science, 70 Whitehall, London SW1A 2AS (tel. 0345–223242). The Revenue has also published its own Code of Practice on the provision of information and advice (see 35.7 above).

As part of the Revenue's response to this process, most internal Revenue guidance manuals are now available (subject to the withholding of certain material under the exemptions in the Code of Practice).

35.11 **Employers' helpline.** A joint employers' telephone helpline has been set up on 0345–143 143 by the Inland Revenue, Contributions Agency and Customs & Excise for general enquiries about PAYE, national insurance and value added tax registration. The service is available from 0830 to 1700 on working days. Calls will be charged at local rates. See also 20.7 CONSTRUCTION INDUSTRY SCHEME.

There is also a helpline for **new employers** on 0845–607 0143 (0800 to 2000 weekdays, 1000 to 1600 weekends), where the employer may register for PAYE, order an information pack on the operation of payroll tax and national insurance, and obtain help and information on payroll queries. Arrangements may also be made for access to business support teams and workshops providing further assistance.

35.12   **Use of electronic communications.** The Commissioners of Inland Revenue (and Customs and Excise) are given broad powers to make regulations, by statutory instrument, to facilitate two-way electronic communication in the delivery of information, e.g. tax returns (and see 68.14 RETURNS for existing legislation), and the making of tax payments. The regulations may allow or require the use of intermediaries such as Internet service providers. They will have effect notwithstanding any existing legislation requiring delivery or payment in a manner which would otherwise preclude the use of electronic communications or intermediaries. [*FA 1999, ss 132, 133*]. The intention is to develop a range of electronic services which taxpayers can use as an alternative to paper if they so wish. One of the first services to be offered was to allow taxpayers (and subsequently their agents) to file self-assessment tax returns via the internet (see 68.2 RETURNS). (Joint Revenue and Customs & Excise News Release CW 1, 9 March 1999).

See *The Income and Corporation Taxes (Electronic Communications) Regulations 2003* (*SI 2003 No 282*) (which replace the *Regulations 2000* (*SI 2000 No 945*) as amended) and directions thereunder by the Commissioners, which make provision for electronic communications in relation to delivery of returns and other information under *TMA 1970, ss 8–9, 9A–9D, 12AA, 12AB, 12AC–12AE, 59DA, 59E* or *Sch 1A* or *FA 1998, ss 30–36* or *Sch 18* and payments or repayments in connection with the operation of those provisions.

From 1 January 2004, regulations (*SI 2003 No 3143*) provide for electronic delivery of dividend vouchers, interest vouchers and other tax deduction certificates by prior agreement between sender and recipient.

Incentives for electronic communications. Regulations may be made by statutory instrument by the Commissioners of Inland Revenue in relation to matters under their care and management (and by the Commissioners of Customs and Excise in relation to theirs) for the provision of incentives to use electronic communications. These may include discounts (or payments or repayments), or additional time for compliance or payment, or more convenient intervals for the delivery of information or the making of payments. Anything received by way of incentive is not regarded as income for tax purposes. The regulations may make provision as to the conditions of entitlement to incentives and for their withdrawal (which may be authorised to be made by direction), and may provide for penalties up to £1,000 for failure to comply with any specified provision. They may make different provision for different cases, and may make such incidental, supplemental, consequential or transitional provision as the Commissioners think fit. [*FA 2000, s 143, Sch 38*]. See *SI 2001 No 56; SI 2001 No 1081, reg 22; SI 2003 No 2495*.

See 68.2 RETURNS for initial incentives for making certain returns over the internet and see 55.9 PAY AS YOU EARN as regards incentives for e-filing of PAYE returns where not mandatory.

Mandatory e-filing. The Commissioners of Inland Revenue have been given extremely wide powers to make regulations requiring the use of electronic communications for the delivery of information required or authorised to be delivered under tax legislation. [*FA 2002, ss 135, 136*]. See 55.9 PAY AS YOU EARN as regards e-filing of PAYE returns.

35.13   **INTERNATIONAL CO-OPERATION**

ICTA 1988, s 815C (introduced by *FA 2000, s 146* and amended by *FA 2003, s 198*) enables the UK to enter into agreements (Tax Information Exchange Agreements) with other governments for the exchange of information foreseeably relevant to the administration or enforcement of the law on income tax, corporation tax and capital gains tax (and corresponding law in the foreign territory). The Revenue may not, however, disclose information under any such agreements unless they are satisfied that the counterparty is bound by, or has undertaken to observe, rules of confidentiality at least as strict as those applying in the UK. The power under *TMA 1970, s 20(1)–(8)(8C)–(9)* (see 30.7 FRAUDULENT OR NEGLIGENT CONDUCT) to call for information relevant to income tax, corporation tax or capital gains tax liabilities is accordingly extended to liabilities to the corresponding taxes in a counterparty territory.

Similar provisions in relation to inheritance tax apply under *IHTA 1984, s 220A* introduced by *FA 2000, s 147*.

Recovery of taxes etc. due in other EU Member States. Provision is made for the recovery in the UK of amounts in respect of which a request for enforcement has been made in accordance with the Mutual Assistance Recovery Directive (*Directive 76/308/EEC* as amended by *Directive 2001/44/EC*) by an authority in another EU Member State. Disclosure of information by a UK tax authority (i.e. the Commissioners of Inland Revenue, the Commissioners of Customs and Excise or, in relation to certain agricultural levies, the relevant Minister) for these purposes (or for the purposes of a request for enforcement by the UK) is not generally precluded by any obligation of secrecy.

Broadly, the UK tax authority has the same powers it would have for a corresponding claim in the UK, in particular in relation to penalties and interest. Treasury regulations may make provision as to what UK claim corresponds to a foreign claim, and for other procedural and supplementary matters (see now *SI 2004 No 674*). Regulations may also be made by the relevant UK tax authority for the application, non-application or adaptation of the law applicable to corresponding UK claims, without prejudice to its application when not dealt with by such regulations.

No proceedings may be taken against a person under these provisions if he shows that proceedings relevant to the liability in question are pending (i.e. still open to appeal), or about to be instituted, before a competent body in the Member State in question. This does not apply if the foreign proceedings are not prosecuted or instituted with reasonable expedition, or if regulations made by the UK tax authority apply a UK enactment that permits proceedings in the case of a corresponding UK claim. If a final decision on the foreign claim (i.e. one against which no further appeal lies or would be in time), or a part of it, has been given in favour of the taxpayer by a competent body in the Member State in question, no proceeding may be taken under these provisions in relation to the claim (or part).

The Treasury may amend, replace or repeal any of the above provisions by regulations for the purpose of giving effect to future amendments to the Directive.

[*FA 2002, s 134, Sch 39*].

35.14   **REVENUE FUNCTIONS CARRIED OUT BY THE ASSETS RECOVERY AGENCY**

Under *Proceeds of Crime Act 2002, Pt 6*, the Director of the Assets Recovery Agency is empowered, after 23 February 2003, to carry out the functions vested in the Board and its officers. The Director must have reasonable grounds to suspect that

(*a*)   income arising or a gain accruing to a person in respect of a chargeable period is chargeable to income tax or is a chargeable gain and arises or accrues as a result (whether wholly or partly, directly or indirectly) of the 'criminal conduct' of that person or another, or (*b*)   a company is chargeable to corporation tax on its profits arising in a chargeable period and the profits arise as a result (whether wholly or partly, directly or indirectly) of the criminal conduct of the company or another person,

and must serve a notice on the Board specifying the person or company, the period or periods concerned, and the functions which he intends to carry out. The periods involved may include periods beginning before the *Act* was passed.

For the purpose of the exercise by the Director of any function so vested in him, it is immaterial that he cannot identify a source for any income. An assessment made by the Director under *TMA 1970, s 29* (discovery assessment — see 5.3 ASSESSMENTS) in respect of income charged to tax under Schedule D, Case VI cannot be reduced or quashed only because it does not specify (to any extent) the source of the income.

The Director may cease carrying out the functions specified in the notice at any time (by notifying the Board), but *must* so cease where the conditions allowing the notice to be made are no longer satisfied. Any assessment made by him under *TMA 1970, s 29* (see above) is subsequently invalid to the extent that it does not specify a source for income.

For the above purposes, '*criminal conduct*' is conduct which constitutes an offence anywhere in the UK or which would do so if it occurred there, but does not include conduct constituting an offence relating to a matter under the care and management of the Board.

It should be noted that the vesting of a function in the Director under these provisions does not divest the Board or its officers of the function (so that, for example, the Revenue can continue to carry out routine work). Certain functions, as listed in *Proceeds of Crime Act 2002, s 323(3)*, cannot be carried out by the Director. If the Director serves notice in relation to a company and in respect of a chargeable period or periods, the general Revenue functions vested in the Director do not include functions relating to any requirement which is imposed on the company in its capacity as an employer and relates to a tax year which does not fall wholly within the chargeable period(s).

Appeals in respect of actions carried out by the Director in the exercise of Revenue functions are to the Special Commissioners. In hearing such appeals, the Special Commissioners may be assisted by one or more assessors selected for their special knowledge and experience of the matter to which the appeal relates from a panel appointed for the purpose by the Lord Chancellor.

[*Proceeds of Crime Act 2002, ss 317, 318(1)(2), 319, 320(1)–(3), 323(1)(3), 326(1)(2); SI 2003 No 120*].

36 Inland Revenue: Confidentiality of Information

36.1 The Revenue consider that the confidentiality of information maintained by their Department 'is essential to their traditional approach to their task and is deeply embedded in their practice'. (*Royal Commission on Standards of Conduct in Public Life 1976, para 111*). All officers of the Inland Revenue, together with General and Special Commissioners, are required to make declarations that information received in the course of duty will not be disclosed except for the purposes of such duty or for the purposes of the prosecution of revenue offences or as may be required by law. [*TMA 1970, s 6, Sch 1*]. As to production in Court proceedings of documents in the possession of the Revenue, see *Brown's Trustees v Hay CS 1897, 3 TC 598*; *In re Joseph Hargreaves Ltd CA 1900, 4 TC 173*; *Shaw v Kay CS 1904, 5 TC 74*; *Soul v Irving CA 1963, 41 TC 517*; *H v H HC 1980, 52 TC 454*. For the overriding of confidentiality by the public interest in the administration of justice, see *Lonrho plc v Fayed and Others (No 4) CA 1993, 66 TC 220*.

Following the transfer of the functions of the Contributions Agency to the Inland Revenue, appropriate provision is made for the internal distribution of information. [*Social Security Contributions (Transfer of Functions etc.) Act 1999, s 7*].

36.2 The Inland Revenue are authorised to disclose information to the following.

(*a*) **Charity Commissioners for England and Wales.** There are wide powers under which information may be exchanged between the Charity Commissioners and the Commissioners of Inland Revenue, in particular enabling the Revenue to disclose details of institutions which they consider to have been carrying on non-charitable activities or applying funds for non-charitable purposes. [*Charities Act 1993, s 10*].

(*b*) **Business Statistics Office of the Department of Industry** or to the **Department of Employment.** The Revenue are authorised to disclose, for the purposes of statistical surveys, the names and addresses of employers and employees and the number of persons employed by individual concerns. [*FA 1969, s 58; F(No 2)A 1987, s 69; ITEPA 2003, Sch 6 para 122; SI 1990 No 1840*].

(*c*) **Tax authorities of other countries.** The Revenue are authorised to disclose information where it is necessary to do so for the operation of double taxation agreements. [*ICTA 1988, s 816; TCGA 1992, s 277(4); IHTA 1984, s 158(5)*]. Double taxation agreements may also authorise the exchange of information foreseeably relevant to the administration or enforcement of UK and foreign tax law, particularly with regard to the prevention of fiscal evasion. [*ICTA 1988, s 788(2); FA 2003, s 198*]. Disclosure may also be made to the tax authorities of other Member States of the EU which observe similar confidentiality and use only for tax purposes [*FA 1978, s 77; FA 1990, s 125(5)(6); FA 2003, s 197(1)–(6), Sch 43 Pt 5(1)*], and similar rules apply in relation to any information exchange arrangements under *ICTA 1988, s 815C* or *IHTA 1984, s 220A* (see 35.13 INLAND REVENUE: ADMINISTRATION). [*ICTA 1988, s 816(2ZA); IHTA 1984, s 220A(4)(5); FA 2000, ss 146(2), 147(1)*]. See also the 'working arrangement' between USA and UK in Revenue Press Release 2 March 1978.

(*d*) **Customs and Excise.** The Revenue and Customs and Excise are authorised to disclose information to each other for the purpose of their respective duties. [*FA 1972, s 127*].

(*e*) **Occupational Pensions Board.** The Revenue are authorised to disclose information about pension schemes. [*Social Security Act 1973, s 89(2)*].

(*f*) **Social Security Departments.** Information held by the Revenue relating to national insurance contributions, statutory sick pay or statutory maternity pay may, and must if an authorised social security officer so requires, be supplied to the social security authorities for use in relation to social security, child support or war pensions. Other information may similarly be supplied to those authorities in relation to the prevention, detection, investigation or prosecution of social security offences or in checking social security information. [*Social Security Administration Act 1992, ss 121E, 122; Social Security Administration (Fraud) Act 1997, s 1; Social Security Contributions (Transfer of Functions etc.) Act 1999, Sch 6 paras 1, 2*]. The Revenue will also supply the names and addresses of absent parents and, where appropriate, their employers, in cases where they are liable under the *Social Security Acts* to maintain lone parent families receiving income support. (Revenue Press Release 9 May 1990). (See 35.4 INLAND REVENUE: ADMINISTRATION for supply of information *by* social security authorities.) From 5 October 1999, the Board may, and must if an authorised social security officer so requires, supply to the social security authorities information held for the purposes of tax credit functions (see 83.6, 83.7 SOCIAL SECURITY) (extended from 1 August 2002 to functions relating to child benefit or guardian's allowance) for use by those authorities for the purposes of functions relating to social security benefits, child support, tax credits, war pensions or prescribed evaluation or statistical studies. [*Tax Credits Act 1999, Sch 5 para 2; Tax Credits Act 2002, Sch 5 para 4; SI 2002 Nos 1727, 3036*].

(*g*)   **Assistance to police investigation into suspected murder or treason.** [*Royal Commission on Standards of Conduct in Public Life 1976, para 93*].

(*h*)   **Non-UK resident entertainers and sportsmen.** In connection with the deduction of tax from certain payments to such persons, the Board may disclose relevant matters to any person who appears to the Board to have an interest. [*ICTA 1988, s 558(4)*].

(*i*)   **Land Registry.** Particulars of land and charges. [*Land Registration Act 1925, s 129*].

(*j*)   **Department of Environment.** Information regarding option mortgages and qualification of housing associations for certain grants. [*FA 1982, s 26, Sch 7 para 12; Housing Associations Act 1985, s 62*].

(*k*)   **Parliamentary Commissioner for Administration.** Information required for the purposes of his investigations. [*Parliamentary Commissioner Act 1967, s 8*].

(*l*)   **National Audit Office.** Information required for the purposes of the Office's examinations. [*National Audit Act 1983, s 8*].

(*m*)   **Data Protection.** Any information necessary for the discharge of the Registrar's or Tribunal's functions. [*Data Protection Act 1984, s 17*].

(*n*)   **Secretary of State for Scotland and Scottish Housing Association.** Information regarding status of housing associations and refusals of charitable exemption. [*Tenants' Rights etc. (Scotland) Act 1980, s 1*].

(*o*)   An **advisory commission** set up under the Convention (*90/463/EEC*) on the elimination of double taxation in connection with the adjustment of profits of associated enterprises (see 3.8 ANTI-AVOIDANCE). [*ICTA 1988, s 816(2A); F(No 2)A 1992, s 51(2)*].

(*p*)   As regards information held for the purposes of tax credit functions (see 83.6, 83.7 SOCIAL SECURITY) (extended from 1 August 2002 to functions relating to child benefit or guardian's allowance), a **local authority** (or authorised delegate) for use in the administration of housing benefit or council tax benefit. Information must also be provided in the opposite direction if the Board so require but only for use for purposes relating to tax credits etc. [*Tax Credits Act 1999, Sch 5 paras 4, 5; Tax Credits Act 2002, Sch 5 paras 7, 8; SI 2002 No 1727*].

(From 1 August 2002) as regards information held for the above-mentioned purposes, **Health Departments** for use for purposes of prescribed functions relating to health, relevant Government Departments for purposes of prescribed functions relating to **employment** or **training** (with provision also for certain information to pass in the opposite direction) and (as regards information held for child benefit and guardian's allowance functions only) any civil servant or other person for purposes of prescribed functions relating to provision of specified services concerning participation by young persons in **education and training**. [*Tax Credits Act 2002, Sch 5 paras 5, 6, 9, 10; SI 2002 No 1727*].

(*q*)   The **Health and Safety Executive**, the **Government Actuary's Department**, the **Office for National Statistics** or the **Occupational Pensions Regulatory Authority** in relation to national insurance contributions, statutory sick pay or statutory maternity pay. [*Social Security Administration Act 1992, s 122AA; Social Security Contributions (Transfer of Functions etc.) Act 1999, Sch 6 para 3*].

(*r*)   **Minimum wage legislation.** Any information obtained by an officer of the Board acting under *National Minimum Wage Act 1998, s 13(1)(b)* may be used for the purpose of any of the functions of the Board. The Secretary of State may similarly supply to the Board any information supplied to him under *section 16(2)* of that *Act.* [*FA 2000, s 148*].

(*s*)   **Financial Services Authority.** The Commissioners of Inland Revenue may authorise the disclosure of information to the Financial Services Authority or the Secretary of State for the purposes of investigations under *Financial Services and Markets Act 2000, s 168*. [*Financial Services and Markets Act 2000, s 350*].

(*t*)   Under the **Anti-terrorism, Crime and Security Act 2001, ss 19, 20**, the Revenue and Customs & Excise are authorised to disclose certain information required for the purposes of that *Act*. See 35.7 INLAND REVENUE: ADMINISTRATION for a Code of Practice published by those departments.

(*u*)   **Assets Recovery Agency.** After 23 February 2003, the Revenue may disclose information (including information obtained before that date) to the Director of the Assets Recovery Agency for the purpose of the exercise of his functions. [*Proceeds of Crime Act 2002, s 436; SI 2003 No 120*]. The Revenue may also disclose information to the Lord Advocate and the Scottish Ministers in connection with the exercise of their functions in Scotland under *Proceeds of Crime Act 2002, Pt 3* and *Pt 5* respectively. [*Proceeds of Crime Act 2002, s 439*].

36.3   From 5 October 1999, consequent upon the introduction of working families' tax credit and disabled person's tax credit (for which see 83.6 SOCIAL SECURITY), the Board may pool the information they hold for the purposes of their functions relating to those tax credits and to tax, national insurance contributions, statutory sick pay, statutory maternity pay and certain functions under *Pension Schemes Act 1993* (and corresponding NI legislation). There is also provision for the exchange of information held for the purposes of functions relating to the aforementioned tax credits between the Board and persons providing services to the Board, for use in the exercise of those functions. [*Tax Credits Act 1999, Sch 5 para 1*]. From 1 August 2002, these provisions are extended to include functions relating to the working tax credit and child tax credit (see 83.7 SOCIAL SECURITY), child benefit and guardian's allowance. [*Tax Credits Act 2002, Sch 5 paras 1, 2; SI 2002 No 1727*].

36.4   It is a criminal offence for a person to disclose information held by him in the exercise of tax functions about any matter relevant to tax in the case of an identifiable person. This applies equally as regards the Revenue's tax credit functions and social security functions. It does not apply if (or if he believes) he has lawful authority or the information has lawfully been made available to the public, or if the person to whom the matter relates has consented. [*FA 1989, s 182; FA 1995, Sch 29 Pt VIII(16); Government of Wales Act 1998, Sch 12 para 31; Social Security Contributions (Transfer of Functions etc.) Act 1999, Sch 6 para 9; Tax Credits Act 1999, s 12; SI 1999 No 527; Tax Credits Act 2002, Sch 5 para 11; SI 2002 No 1727*]. Similar provisions apply to members of an advisory commission set up under the Convention on transfer pricing arbitration (see 3.8 ANTI-AVOIDANCE). [*FA 1989, s 182A; F(No 2)A 1992, s 51(3)*].

37   Inland Revenue Explanatory Publications

Simon's Direct Tax Service Part H5.

The Board publish explanatory publications (with supplements from time to time) on Inland Revenue taxes, a catalogue of which is available. The majority of these are listed below, with the date of the latest edition in brackets, and are obtainable free of charge (with just a few exceptions) from any office of HM Inspector of Taxes, unless otherwise stated. Most of them (including some for which a charge is made for hard copy) are freely available on the Revenue website; a few are available *only* on the website. See Tolley's Inheritance Tax and Tolley's National Insurance Contributions for lists of explanatory publications available from the Revenue on those taxes. As regards Revenue internal guidance manuals, see 35.10 INLAND REVENUE: ADMINISTRATION.

IR 1	Extra-Statutory Concessions as at 31 August 2003 (December 2003).
IR 2	Occupational Pension Schemes — A Guide for Members of Tax Approved Schemes (February 2003).
IR 3	Personal Pension Schemes (including Stakeholder Pension Schemes) — A Guide for Members of Tax Approved Schemes (February 2003).
IR 4	Bankruptcy Proceedings in England and Wales (January 2003).
IR 5	Winding-Up Proceedings in England and Wales (October 2002).
IR 6	Double Taxation Relief for Companies (March 1994).
IR 8	Winding-Up Petitions (November 2002).
IR 12	Practice notes on the approval of occupational pension schemes. (Now available only on the Internet via the Revenue website. Those who subscribed to the looseleaf version, which was previously available, for the year to 31 March 2003 will continue to receive paper updates until 29 November 2003.)
IR 14/15(CIS)	Construction Industry Scheme (April 2003).
IR 20	Residents and Non-residents — Liability to Tax in the United Kingdom (December 1999).
IR 33	Income Tax and School Leavers (May 2000).
IR 40(CIS)	Construction Industry Scheme: Conditions for Getting a Sub-Contractor's Tax Certificate (July 2003).
IR 41	Income Tax and Job Seekers (April 2000).
IR 45	Income Tax, Capital Gains Tax and Inheritance Tax: What to do about Tax when Someone Dies (March 2001).
IR 46	Income Tax and Corporation Tax: Clubs, Societies and Voluntary Associations (January 2000).
IR 56	Employed or Self-employed?: A Guide to Employment Status for Tax and National Insurance Contributions (July 2004).
IR 59	Collection of Student Loans (April 2003).
IR 60	Income Tax and Students (June 2002).
IR 64	Giving to Charity by Businesses (February 2004).
IR 65	Giving to Charity by Individuals (February 2004).
IR 68	Accrued Income Scheme (December 2002).
IR 69	Expenses: Payments and Benefits in Kind — How to Save Yourself Work (April 2002).
IR 72	Inland Revenue Investigations: The Examination of Business Accounts (May 1995).
IR 73	Inland Revenue Investigations: How Settlements are Negotiated (January 1994).
IR 76	Personal Pension Schemes: Guidance Notes (2001). (Obtainable from Inland Revenue (Savings, Pensions, Share Schemes), Yorke House, PO Box 62, Castle Meadow Road, Nottingham NG2 1BG (tel. 0115–974 1670)).
IR 78	Looking to the Future: Tax Reliefs to help you save for Retirement (February 2001).

37 Inland Revenue Explanatory Publications

IR 87	Letting and Your Home (December 1999).
IR 95	Approved Profit Sharing Schemes — An Outline for Employees (June 1996).
IR 96	Approved Profit Sharing Schemes — Explanatory Notes (June 1996). (Obtainable from Inland Revenue Visitors' Information Centre, Ground Floor, SW Wing, Bush House, Strand, London WC2B 4RD).
IR 97	Approved SAYE Share Option Schemes — An Outline for Employees (June 1996).
IR 98	Approved SAYE Share Option Schemes — Explanatory Notes (August 2002). (Obtainable as IR 96 above).
IR 101	Approved Company Share Option Plans — An Outline for Employees (June 1996).
IR 102	Company Share Options — Explanatory Notes (June 1996). (Obtainable as IR 96 above).
IR 109	Employer Compliance Reviews and Negotiations (December 2002).
IR 110	Bank and Building Society Interest — A Guide for Savers (December 2003).
IR 115	Income Tax, National Insurance Contributions and Childcare (April 2003).
IR 116(CIS)	A Guide for Subcontractors with Tax Certificates (February 2003).
IR 117(CIS)	A Guide for Subcontractors with Registration Cards (November 2003).
IR 121	Income Tax and Pensioners (September 2003).
IR 122	Volunteer Drivers (April 2002).
IR 124	Using Your Own Vehicle for Work (April 2002).
IR 125	Using Your Own Car for Work (February 2002).
IR 126	Corporation Tax Pay and File — A General Guide (July 1995).
IR 131	Statements of Practice as at 31 August 2003 (February 2004). (Available online only.)
IR 134	Income Tax and Relocation Packages (November 2000).
IR 136	Income Tax and Company Vans — A Guide for Employees and Employers (April 2001).
IR 137	The Enterprise Investment Scheme (January 2003).
IR 138	Living or Retiring Abroad? (October 1995).
IR 139	Income from Abroad? (October 1995).
IR 140	Non-resident Landlords, their Agents and Tenants (September 2002).
IR 141	Open Government (March 2001).
IR 143	Income Tax and Redundancy (June 2000).
IR 144	Income Tax and Incapacity Benefit (May 2002).
IR 145	Low Interest Loans Provided by Employers: A Guide for Employees (August 2001).
IR 148	Construction Industry: Are your Workers Employed or Self-employed? (March 2001).
IR 150	Taxation of Rents — A Guide to Property Income (April 1999).
IR 152	Trusts — An Introduction (April 2002).
IR 153	Tax Exemption for Sickness or Unemployment Insurance Payments (February 1997).
IR 155	PAYE Settlement Agreements (February 2001).
IR 156	Our Heritage — Your Right to See Exempt Works of Art (December 1996).
IR 160	Inland Revenue Enquiries under Self-Assessment (December 2002).
IR 166	The Euro — Tax Implications for UK Individuals and Businesses from 1 January 2002 (February 2002).
IR 167	Charter for Inland Revenue Taxpayers (July 2003).
IR 168	How Tax Credit Settlements are Negotiated (July 2002).
IR 169	Venture Capital Trusts — A Brief Guide (November 2002).
IR 170	Blind Person's Allowance (November 2003).
IR 172	Income Tax and Company Cars (July 2003).
IR 175	Supplying Services through a Limited Company or Partnership (October 2001).

IR 176	Green Travel — A Guide for Employers and Employees on Tax and National Insurance Contributions (February 2003).
IR 177	Share Incentive Plans and Your Entitlement to Benefits (October 2001).
IR 178	Giving Shares and Securities to Charity (February 2004).
IR 179	R&D Tax Credits (August 2002).
IR 180(CIS)	Construction Industry Scheme — A Guide for Non-residents (March 2003).
IR 2000	The Corporate Venturing Scheme (January 2001).
IR 2001	Trading by Charities (January 2001).
IR 2002	Share Incentive Plans: A Guide for Employees (October 2001).
IR 2003	Supplying Services: How to Calculate the Deemed Payment (October 2001).
IR 2004	Setting up a Charity in Scotland (October 2003).
IR 2005	Share Incentive Plans — Guidance for Employers and Advisers (October 2001).
IR 2006	Enterprise Management Incentives — A Guide (October 2001).
IR 2007	Capital Allowances for Flats over Shops (October 2001).
IR 2008	ISAs, PEPs and TESSAs (January 2002).
IR 2009	Why Pay Cash? (November 2001).
IR 2010	Paying Tax and National Insurance Contributions Electronically (February 2004).
IR 2013	Record-keeping for Self-assessment (January 2002).
CGT 1	Capital Gains Tax — An Introduction (December 2003).
CGT/FS1	Capital Gains Tax — A Quick Guide (May 2002).
IHT 3	Inheritance Tax — An Introduction (April 2004).
480	Expenses and Benefits — A Tax Guide (November 2003).
490	Employee Travel — A Tax and NICs Guide for Employers (October 2003).
Misc 5	Help for your Business in the Construction Industry (October 2001).
CWG 2	Employer's Further Guide to PAYE and NICs (April 2004).
NE 1	First Steps as a New Employer (April 1999).
NE 3	New and Small Employers — Support with your Payroll (August 2001).
SA/BK4	Self-Assessment — A General Guide to Keeping Records (June 2003).
SA/BK6	Self-Assessment — Penalties for Late Tax Returns (March 2003).
SA/BK7	Self-Assessment — Surcharges for Late Payment of Tax (March 2003).
SA/BK8	Self-Assessment — Your Guide (June 2004).
AO1	The Adjudicator's Office (September 2003).
COP 1	Putting Things Right — How to Complain (June 2003).
COP 3	Review of Employers' and Contractors' Records (March 2003).
COP 4	Inspection of Schemes Operated by Financial Intermediaries (October 2002).
COP 8	Special Compliance Office Investigations — Cases Other Than Suspected Serious Fraud (January 2003).
COP 9	Special Compliance Office Investigations — Cases of Suspected Serious Fraud (December 2003).
COP 10	Information and Advice (April 1999).
COP 11	Enquiries into Tax Returns by Local Tax Offices (December 2002).
COP 21	Data Protection (August 2003)
COP 22	Orders for the Delivery of Documents (February 2001).
COP-AT	Anti-Terrorism, Crime and Security Act 2001: Code of Practice on the Disclosure of Information (February 2002).
CWL 2	National Insurance Contributions for Self-Employed People. Class 2 and Class 4 (June 2003).
CWL 4	Fund Raising Events: Exemption for Charities and other Qualifying Bodies (February 2001).
CWL 5	The Voluntary Arrangements Service (October 2002).
FEU 50	A Guide to Paying Foreign Entertainers (March 2000).
P/SE/1	Thinking of Working for Yourself? (April 2004).
P/TXB/1	Taxback — Are You Paying Too Much Tax on Your Savings? (September 2000).

37   Inland Revenue Explanatory Publications

SV 1	Shares Valuation — An Introduction (March 2004).
WTC1	Child Tax Credit and Working Tax Credit — An Introduction (October 2002).
WTC2	Child Tax Credit and Working Tax Credit — A Guide (May 2003).
WTC5	Child Tax Credit and Working Tax Credit — Help with the Costs of Childcare (April 2003).
WTC6	Child Tax Credit and Working Tax Credit — Other Types of Help You May Be Able To Get (August 2003).
WTC/AP	Child Tax Credit and Working Tax Credit — How to Appeal Against a Tax Credit Decision or Award (February 2003).
—	Tax Appeals: A Guide to Appealing against Decisions of the Inland Revenue on Tax and Other Matters (July 2004).
—	Digest of Double Taxation Treaties (June 2004).
—	The euro — Tax and national insurance options for UK businesses from 1 January 1999 (January 1999).
—	List of bodies approved by the Inland Revenue under *ITEPA 2003, ss 343, 344* (subscriptions to professional bodies). (Obtainable from Inland Revenue Library, 28 New Wing, Somerset House, Strand, London WC2R 1LB).
—	Explanatory notes on the provisions of *ICTA 1988, Pt XVII, Ch IV* (Controlled Foreign Companies). (Obtainable from Inland Revenue Library, 28 New Wing, Somerset House, Strand, London WC2R 1LB).
—	Charities — Payroll Giving Schemes, explaining how the proposals for tax relief are expected to work. (Obtainable from Customer Services Manager, IR Charities, St John's House, Merton Road, Bootle, Merseyside L69 9BB (tel. 0151–472 6036/7)).
—	Guidelines on the tax treatment of disaster funds, giving guidelines on the organisation of disaster appeal funds. (Obtainable from Customer Services Manager, IR Charities, St John's House, Merton Road, Bootle, Merseyside L69 9BB (tel. 0151–472 6036/7)).
—	Fund-raising for charity, giving guidance on the operation of Extra-statutory Concession C4 (see 14.7 CHARITIES). (Obtainable from Customer Services Manager, IR Charities, St John's House, Merton Road, Bootle, Merseyside L69 9BB (tel. 0151–472 6036/7)).
—	The tax treatment of top-up pension schemes. (Obtainable from Inland Revenue Library, 28 New Wing, Somerset House, Strand, London WC2R 1LB).
—	Business economic notes. See 71.18 SCHEDULE D, CASES I AND II.

'Appeals and Other Proceedings before the Special Commissioners', dealing with procedural and other points, is available free of charge from the Clerk to the Special Commissioners, 15/29 Bedford Avenue, London WC1B 3AS (tel. 020–7631 4242) and at www.financeandtaxtribunals.gov.uk There is also a supplement available on 'IR35 Appeals'.

The Board also issue Concessions, Press Releases and Statements of Practice, summaries of, and references to which, are included in the following three chapters and elsewhere under the appropriate chapter heading. A Revenue Tax Bulletin is also published bi-monthly (annual subscription £22), relevant items from which are referred to in the appropriate chapter. Tax Bulletin subscription applications should be made to Inland Revenue, Finance Division, Barrington Road, Worthing, West Sussex, BN12 4XH (cheques to be made payable to 'Inland Revenue'). Telephone enquiries can be made on 020–7438 6373 (subscription or distribution) and 020–7438 7842 (more general information). Tax Bulletin is also published online at http://www.inlandrevenue.gov.uk/bulletins/index.htm

38   Inland Revenue Extra-Statutory Concessions

Simon's Direct Tax Service Part H4.

The following is a summary of the concessions published in the Revenue Pamphlet IR 1 (December 2003) (or in earlier editions where still relevant) or subsequently announced, insofar as they relate to subjects dealt with in this book. It should be borne in mind that in a particular case there may be special circumstances which will require to be taken into account in considering the application of a concession. A concession will not be given in any case where an attempt is made to use it for tax avoidance (and see *R v HMIT (ex p Fulford-Dobson) QB 1987, 60 TC 168*). See also 35.4 INLAND REVENUE: ADMINISTRATION.

A.   APPLICABLE TO INDIVIDUALS

A1   **Flat rate allowances for cost of tools and special clothing** may be claimed. Superseded by *ITEPA 2003, s 367*. See 75.28 SCHEDULE E—EMPLOYMENT INCOME.

A2   **Meal vouchers.** Certain vouchers are exempt from income tax. Superseded by *ITEPA 2003, s 89*. See 75.33 SCHEDULE E—EMPLOYMENT INCOME.

A4   **Directors' travelling expenses.** Certain expenses paid by employers are not assessable. See 75.16(ix), 75.46 SCHEDULE E—EMPLOYMENT INCOME.

A6   **Miners: free coal and allowances in lieu** are exempt from income tax. Superseded by *ITEPA 2003, s 306* (see 75.16(xi) SCHEDULE E—EMPLOYMENT INCOME) and *ITEPA 2003, s 646* (see 58.3(*j*) PENSION INCOME).

A9   **Doctors' and dentists' superannuation contributions** under the NHS are allowable as deductions under Schedule D but alternatives apply where premiums for retirement annuities are also paid. See 67.11 RETIREMENT SCHEMES.

A10   **Overseas pension schemes.** Income tax is not charged on certain lump sums on termination of employment overseas. See 58.3(*k*) PENSION INCOME.

A11   **Residence in the UK: year of commencement or cessation of residence.** Liability to tax is computed by reference to the period of residence in that year. See 65.5 RESIDENCE, ORDINARY RESIDENCE AND DOMICILE.

A12   **Double taxation relief: alimony etc. under UK court order or agreement: payer resident abroad.** Relief by way of credit is allowed in certain circumstances. See 24.5(*a*) DOUBLE TAX RELIEF.

A14   **Deceased person's estate: residuary income received during the administration period.** A legatee resident abroad may have his tax liability on estate income adjusted as if the income had arisen to him directly. See 21.3 DECEASED ESTATES.

A16   **Annual payments (other than interest) paid out of income not brought into charge to income tax.** If payment is made in a year later than when due, and it could have been made out of taxed income in that due year, an allowance will be made (when collecting under *ICTA 1988, s 350*) for the tax which the payer would have been entitled to deduct (under *ICTA 1988, s 348*) and retain if the payment had been made at the due date. See 22.3(i) DEDUCTION OF TAX AT SOURCE.

A17   **Death of taxpayer before due date for payment of tax.** Interest on tax overdue may not begin to run until after probate or letters of administration are obtained. See 42.5 INTEREST AND SURCHARGES ON UNPAID TAX.

A19   **Arrears of tax arising through official error.** Relief is given. See 56.8 PAYMENT OF TAX for current details.

A22   **Long service awards** are exempt from tax within limitations. Superseded by *ITEPA 2003, s 323*. See 75.29 SCHEDULE E—EMPLOYMENT INCOME.

A24   **Foreign social security benefits.** Payments by foreign governments to UK residents which correspond to exempt UK benefits are also exempt from tax. Superseded by *ITEPA 2003, s 681*. See 28.31 EXEMPT INCOME, 83.4 SOCIAL SECURITY.

A25   **Crown Servants engaged overseas** may be exempted from UK tax. Superseded by *ITEPA 2003, s 28*. See 75.4 SCHEDULE E—EMPLOYMENT INCOME.

A27   **Mortgage interest relief: temporary absences from mortgaged property.** Absences of up to one year, or longer if occasioned by employment, are ignored in determining if a property is an only or main residence. See 43.6, 43.15 INTEREST PAYABLE.

A29   **Farming and market gardening: relief for fluctuating profits.** For this purpose, 'farming' includes the intensive rearing of livestock or fish on a commercial basis for the production of food for human consumption. See 71.47 SCHEDULE D, CASES I AND II.

A30   **Interest on damages for personal injuries (foreign court awards)** will be exempt from income tax if also exempt in the country in which award made. See 28.16(i) EXEMPT INCOME.

A31   **Life assurance premium relief by deduction: pre-marriage policies: premium relief after divorce** continues where one party pays on life of the other. See 45.4(*f*) LIFE ASSURANCE POLICIES.

A32   **Tax relief for life assurance premiums: position of certain pension schemes which are unapproved after 5 April 1980.** Relief is continued. See 45.10(ii) LIFE ASSURANCE POLICIES.

A33   **Lump sum retirement benefits: changes after 5 April 1980.** Previous tax exemption is continued under certain conditions. See 67.12 RETIREMENT SCHEMES.

A34   **Ulster savings certificates: certificates encashed after death of registered holder.** Accumulated interest is exempt from income tax if the deceased was resident and domiciled in NI at time of purchase. See 33.5 GOVERNMENT STOCKS.

A37   **Tax treatment of directors' fees received by partnerships and other companies.** Under certain conditions, such fees may be included in computing the partnership profits — see 75.27 SCHEDULE E—EMPLOYMENT INCOME, or in the corporation tax assessment of the other company — see 75.2(v) SCHEDULE E—EMPLOYMENT INCOME.

A38   **Retirement annuity relief: death and disability benefits.** An individual in a scheme providing a pension only on death or disability will not be treated as being in pensionable employment. See 66.7 RETIREMENT ANNUITIES.

A40   **Adoption allowances,** under approved schemes, are not taxable. Superseded by *FA 2003, s 175*. See 28.1 EXEMPT INCOME.

A41 **Qualifying life assurance policies: statutory conditions** may be relaxed in certain circumstances. See 45.12(*h*) LIFE ASSURANCE POLICIES.

A42 **Chargeable events: loans to policyholders** may not be treated as partial surrenders in certain circumstances. (Obsolete.) See 45.15(*f*) LIFE ASSURANCE POLICIES.

A43 **Interest relief: investment in partnerships and close companies** may continue to attract relief where the partnership is incorporated or the close company's shares reorganised. See 43.19–43.22 INTEREST PAYABLE.

A44 **Education allowances under Overseas Service Aid Scheme,** payable to officers in the public service of certain overseas territories, which the UK government has undertaken to exempt from income tax, are so exempted. See 23.1 DIPLOMATIC IMMUNITY.

A45 **Life assurance policies: variation of term assured policies.** A term assurance policy for a term of ten years or less will not be disqualified under *ICTA 1988, Sch 15 paras 17(2)(b), 18* because of a reduction in the rate of premium to less than half as a result of a similar reduction in the sum assured or an extension of the term (resulting in a total term still not exceeding ten years). See 45.12(*d*) LIFE ASSURANCE POLICIES.

A46 **Variable purchased life annuities: carry forward of excess of capital element.** Any excess of the capital element over the annuity payment may be carried forward for allowance in determining the capital element in future payments. See 22.11(*c*) DEDUCTION OF TAX AT SOURCE.

A47 **House purchase loans made before 6 April 2000 by life offices to staffs of insurance associations** may be treated in the same way as loans by a life office to a full-time employee. See 45.15(*f*) LIFE ASSURANCE POLICIES.

A49 **Widow's pension paid to widow of Singapore nationality, resident in the UK, whose husband was a UK national employed as a Public Officer by the Government of Singapore** is included in the exemption provided by *ITEPA 2003, s 643.* See 58.3(*f*) PENSION INCOME.

A51 **Repayment supplement: life assurance premium relief.** The repayment supplement provisions (see 41.2 INTEREST ON OVERPAID TAX) apply also to repayments of excessive clawback under *ICTA 1988, ss 268, 269* (see 45.5 LIFE ASSURANCE POLICIES) and to relief by repayment under *ICTA 1988, Sch 14 para 6(1)* where relief is not obtained by deduction (see 45.1 LIFE ASSURANCE POLICIES).

A56 **Benefits in kind: tax treatment of accommodation provided by employers.** The rules are modified in relation to Scotland. See 75.32 SCHEDULE E—EMPLOYMENT INCOME.

A57 **Suggestion schemes.** Awards to employees under such schemes are not charged to tax provided that certain conditions are satisfied. Superseded by *ITEPA 2003, ss 321, 322.* See 75.29 SCHEDULE E—EMPLOYMENT INCOME.

A58 **Travelling and subsistence allowance when public transport disrupted.** Such allowances, or the provision of facilities by the employer, are not charged to tax. Superseded by *ITEPA 2003, s 245.* See 75.16(v), 75.46 SCHEDULE E—EMPLOYMENT INCOME.

A59 **Disabled persons 'home to work travel'.** Provision of transport facilities or financial assistance is not charged to tax. Superseded by *ITEPA 2003, s 246.* See 75.16(vi), 75.18, 75.46 SCHEDULE E—EMPLOYMENT INCOME.

A60 **Agricultural workers' board and lodging** will, subject to conditions, not be charged to tax even where a higher wage in lieu could be taken. See 75.10 SCHEDULE E—EMPLOYMENT INCOME.

A61 **Clergymen's heating and lighting etc. expenses.** Certain sums paid or reimbursed are not charged to tax. See 75.13 SCHEDULE E—EMPLOYMENT INCOME.

A62 **Pensions to employees disabled at work.** The excess over the normal ill health retirement pension is not charged to tax. Superseded by *ITEPA 2003, s 644*. See 58.3(*g*) PENSION INCOME.

A65 **Workers on offshore oil and gas rigs or platforms — free transfers from or to mainland.** No charge to tax arises in respect of such transfers or certain mainland accommodation and subsistence. Superseded by *ITEPA 2003, s 305*. See 75.16(viii), 75.46 SCHEDULE E—EMPLOYMENT INCOME.

A66 **Employees' late night journeys from work to home.** Where the cost of occasional journeys is borne by the employer, the employee will not, subject to various conditions, be charged to tax on the benefit he receives. Superseded by *ITEPA 2003, s 248*. See 75.16(vii), 75.46 SCHEDULE E—EMPLOYMENT INCOME.

A68 **Payments out of a discretionary trust which are emoluments taxable under Schedule E.** Trustees may reclaim tax on certain payments to beneficiaries. See 81.5 SETTLEMENTS.

A69 **Composite rate tax: non-resident depositors.** Certain declarations made to a society are treated as having been made to a successor company. See 7.2 BANKS, 8.6 BUILDING SOCIETIES.

A70 **Small gifts to employees by third parties and staff Christmas parties** may be exempted from income tax. Superseded by *ITEPA 2003, ss 264, 270, 324*. See 75.16(xvi), 75.29 SCHEDULE E—EMPLOYMENT INCOME.

A71 **Company cars for family members.** In relation to the car scale charge: (*a*) a double charge is prevented where cars are supplied to members of the same family by the same employer; and (*b*) the charge is apportioned where use is shared. Superseded by *ITEPA 2003, ss 148, 169*. See 75.18 SCHEDULE E—EMPLOYMENT INCOME.

A72 **Pension schemes and accident insurance policies.** The exemption from the benefits charge for provision of death or retirement benefits is extended to all family and household beneficiaries. Superseded by *ITEPA 2003, s 307*. See 75.16(iii) SCHEDULE E—EMPLOYMENT INCOME.

A74 **Meals and light refreshments provided for employees** may escape charge to tax as a benefit. Superseded by *ITEPA 2003, s 317*. See 75.16(iv) SCHEDULE E—EMPLOYMENT INCOME.

A76 **Business expansion scheme and enterprise investment scheme subscriber shares.** Relief will not be denied to subscribers for such shares because they may, for a short period, hold in excess of 30% of the issued share capital. (This concession is superseded by *FA 1998, Sch 13 para 8(1)* as regards EIS shares issued after 5 April 1998.) See 25.3 ENTERPRISE INVESTMENT SCHEME.

A78 **Residence in the UK: accompanying spouse.** A concessional treatment is introduced for the determination of the residence and ordinary residence status of spouses accompanying individuals in full–time employment abroad. See 65.5, 65.6 RESIDENCE, ORDINARY RESIDENCE AND DOMICILE.

A81 **Termination payments and legal costs.** Certain legal costs recovered from the employer will not be charged under *ITEPA 2003, ss 401–416*. See 18.6(viii) COMPENSATION FOR LOSS OF EMPLOYMENT (AND DAMAGES).

A82 **Repayment supplement to individuals resident in EC Member States** will be paid in certain cases following the decision in the *Commerzbank AG* case. See 41.2 INTEREST ON OVERPAID TAX.

A84 **Allowances paid to Detached National Experts** on secondment to the European Commission are exempt from income tax. Superseded by *ITEPA 2003, s 304*. See 23.1 DIPLOMATIC IMMUNITY.

A85 **Transfers of assets by employees and directors to employers and others.** Certain employer's transaction costs will not be charged as a benefit. Superseded by *ITEPA 2003, s 326*. See 75.16(xxi) SCHEDULE E—EMPLOYMENT INCOME.

A86 **Blind person's tax allowance.** The allowance will be granted for the year before registration where the evidence on which registration was based was available at the end of that year. See 1.19 ALLOWANCES AND TAX RATES.

A89 **Mortgage interest relief — property used for residential and business purposes.** Interest relief may be obtained both under *ICTA 1988, s 353* and as a deduction in computing profits and losses. See 22.13 DEDUCTION OF TAX AT SOURCE, 43.2 INTEREST PAYABLE.

A91 **Living accommodation provided by reason of employment.** A charge will not be raised under the special provisions for accommodation costing £75,000 or more where the basic charge was based on the full market rent, and the combined charge under those *sections* will be restricted where the accommodation is provided to more than one director or employee. Second leg of this concession superseded by *ITEPA 2003, s 108*. See 75.32 SCHEDULE E—EMPLOYMENT INCOME.

A93 **Payments from offshore trusts to minor unmarried child of settlor: claim by settlor for credit of tax paid by trustees** against his liability to tax on income distributed to or for the benefit of the child will be allowed. See 81.5 SETTLEMENTS.

A94 **Profits and losses of theatre backers (angels)** may in certain cases be treated as within Schedule D, Case VI, and the requirement for deduction of tax from certain payments is waived. See 74.2 SCHEDULE D, CASE VI.

A95 **Small lump sum retirement benefits schemes.** Relief for employee contributions to personal pension schemes or retirement annuity contracts may not be withdrawn where certain lump sum retirement benefits accrue in respect of the same employment. See 60.11 PERSONAL PENSION SCHEMES, 66.7 RETIREMENT ANNUITIES.

A96 **Old life insurance policies — insurer stopping collection of premiums.** Such a change will, in certain circumstances, not be treated as an alteration of the policy for tax purposes. See 45.13 LIFE ASSURANCE POLICIES.

A97 **Jobmatch programme.** Income tax is not charged on payments under the Jobmatch programme or in respect of training vouchers received under its terms. See 28.31 EXEMPT INCOME.

A98   **Cessation adjustments under self-assessment transitional rules.** Interest otherwise arising due to cessation adjustments at the direction of the inspector during the transitional period will not generally be charged. See 42.1 INTEREST AND SURCHARGES ON UNPAID TAX.

A99   **Tax treatment of compensation for mis-sold freestanding additional voluntary contribution schemes.** Certain compensation payments are exempted from tax. See 28.5 EXEMPT INCOME.

A100   **Tax exemption for compensation paid on bank accounts owned by Holocaust victims.** Compensation paid on unclaimed accounts opened by Holocaust victims and frozen during the Second World War will be exempt from income tax and death duties. See 28.16(xi) EXEMPT INCOME.

A101   **Personal pension schemes: tax relief for contributions.** Higher rate relief is available regardless of whether such liability would otherwise arise in respect of income or chargeable gains. See 60.1 PERSONAL PENSION SCHEMES (AND STAKEHOLDER PENSIONS).

A102   **Contributions to approved personal pension plans from 6 April 2001 under ICTA 1988, s 639 and age-related allowances.** Contributions are deducted from the individual's total income *but only for the purposes* of determining the level of age-related personal and married couple's allowances. See 1.14, 1.15 ALLOWANCES AND TAX RATES, 60.1 PERSONAL PENSION SCHEMES (AND STAKEHOLDER PENSIONS).

A103   **Approved employee share schemes: armed forces reservists.** From 7 January 2003, Armed Forces Reservists called up to active service are enabled to maintain their participation in their civilian employers' approved share schemes during the period they are away on service. See 82.2 SHARE-RELATED EMPLOYMENT INCOME AND EXEMPTIONS.

B.   CONCESSIONS APPLICABLE TO INDIVIDUALS AND COMPANIES

B1   **Machinery or plant: changes from 'renewals' to 'capital allowances' basis.** Capital allowances may be claimed provided all items of the same class are changed to new basis. See 9.38(H) CAPITAL ALLOWANCES.

B4   **Maintenance and repairs of property obviated by alterations etc.: Schedule A assessments.** The estimated cost of the repairs etc. may be allowed. Withdrawn after 5 April 2001. See 69.5 SCHEDULE A.

B5   **Maintenance expenses of owner-occupied farms not carried on on a commercial basis** may be claimed under *ICTA 1988, s 33*. Withdrawn after 5 April 2001. See 71.47 SCHEDULE D, CASES I AND II.

B7   **Benevolent gifts by traders** are allowable in certain circumstances. See 71.74 SCHEDULE D, CASES I AND II.

B8   **Double tax relief: income consisting of royalties and 'know-how' payments** arising to a UK resident from abroad. See 24.5(*l*) DOUBLE TAX RELIEF.

B10   **Income of contemplative religious communities or of their members,** having a common fund and not being charities, is partly regarded as income of each monk or nun up to the amount of the basic personal allowance for the year (see 1.14 ALLOWANCES AND TAX RATES). Where the aggregate of 'allowable figures' exceeds income of the community, the excess may be set against chargeable gains of that year.

B11 **Compensation for compulsory slaughter of farm animals** may be treated as profits spread over the following three years. See 71.47 SCHEDULE D, CASES I AND II.

B16 **Fire safety: capital expenditure incurred on certain trade premises (a) in Northern Ireland, and (b) by lessors.** (*a*) Provisions relating to fire safety expenditure in the UK are extended to NI, and (*b*) relief is allowed where lessor incurs the expenditure himself, if similar expenditure by the tenant would have qualified for relief. See 9.25(i) CAPITAL ALLOWANCES.

B17 **Capital allowances: sale of invented patent to an associate.** Where an inventor sells a patent to his own controlled company at less than open market value, the actual sale price is taken for assessment and capital allowances, and (subject to the purchaser's agreement) for capital gains tax. Obsolete. See 9.50 CAPITAL ALLOWANCES.

B18 **Payments out of discretionary trusts.** Beneficiaries may claim certain reliefs as if they had received the income out of which the payment was made directly. See 81.5 SETTLEMENTS.

B20 **Capital allowances for buildings: sales by property developers of buildings which have been let.** Writing-down allowances are made to the purchaser even though the developer's expenditure on construction has been on revenue account. Superseded by legislation. See 9.14 CAPITAL ALLOWANCES.

B25 **Schedule D, Case V losses.** Deficiencies of income from overseas lettings could be carried forward for set-off against future income from the same property. Obsolete, subject to transitional arrangements. See 73.4 SCHEDULE D, CASES IV AND V.

B27 **Approved employee share schemes: jointly owned companies.** A scheme operated by a jointly owned company may nevertheless be granted approval. Superseded by legislation. See 82.2, 82.52, 82.65 SHARE-RELATED EMPLOYMENT INCOME AND EXEMPTIONS.

B29 **Treatment of income from caravan sites where there is both trading and associated letting income.** In such circumstances the receipts from caravan pitch site income and from letting caravans may be treated as receipts of the trading activities. See 69.3 SCHEDULE A.

B30 **Income from property in Scotland: property managed as one estate.** The tax treatment will continue to be by reference to 1978 gross rateable values where appropriate. See 69.5(*b*) SCHEDULE A—PROPERTY INCOME.

B37 **The herd basis: shares in animals.** The herd basis may be applied to a share in an animal in the same way as if the share were a whole animal. Now superseded by *FA 2000, s 76*. See 34.2 HERD BASIS.

B38 **Tax concessions on overseas debts.** Relief may be available where they form part of profits assessable under Schedule D, Case I or Case II. See 71.82 SCHEDULE D, CASES I AND II.

B40 **UK investment managers acting for non-resident clients.** The exemptions of *TMA 1970, ss 78(2), 82* are extended in certain cases. See 51.1, 51.5 NON-RESIDENTS AND OTHER OVERSEAS MATTERS.

B41 **Claims to repayment of tax.** Where an over-payment of tax has arisen because of official error, and there is no doubt or dispute as to the facts, claims to repayment of tax are accepted outside the statutory time limit (generally six years from the end of the tax year concerned). See 16.6 CLAIMS.

B42 **'Free gifts' and insurance contracts.** Certain incentive gifts offered in connection with the issue of insurance policies are disregarded. See 45.6 LIFE ASSURANCE POLICIES.

B43 **Alterations to old pension funds.** Certain minor rule amendments may be made without loss of exemption. See 67.13 RETIREMENT SCHEMES.

B44 **Profit-related pay: extraordinary items.** Existing treatment of certain items in the statutory profit and loss account is preserved following the replacement of SSAP6 by FRS3. See generally 75.34(K) SCHEDULE E—EMPLOYMENT INCOME.

B46 **Automatic penalties for late employers' and contractors' end-of-year returns.** A short period of grace is allowed for submission of annual returns. See 57.9 PENALTIES.

B47 **Furnished lettings of dwelling houses — wear and tear of furniture.** As an alternative to the renewals basis, an allowance of 10% of rent may be claimed. See 69.7 SCHEDULE A.

B49 **Capital allowances — repaid grants.** Capital allowances will be given for repayments of grants which were deducted from expenditure qualifying for capital allowances. See 9.2(vi) CAPITAL ALLOWANCES.

B50 **Capital allowances for caravans on holiday caravan sites.** An extended definition of 'caravan' applies for this purpose. Superseded by legislation in *CAA 2001*. See 9.26(19) CAPITAL ALLOWANCES.

B52 **Subcontractors in the construction industry: the multiple turnover tests.** Until 1 August 2001, the number of partners or directors taken into account in determining the three-year turnover threshold may be taken as the maximum number at any time in the last six months of the three-year period, rather than at any time in the whole period, where this is more favourable. See 20.5 CONSTRUCTION INDUSTRY SCHEME.

B53 **Non residents and insurance gains on life policies.** (i) The treatment, in the case of non-residents, of life assurance gains is brought more into line with that of other forms of income. (ii) The reporting requirements in relation to non-resident policy holders are relaxed. (iii) The transitional reliefs for holders of personal portfolio bonds issued before 17 March 1998 are extended. See 45.13 LIFE ASSURANCE POLICIES.

B54 **Tax relief for expenditure on films, tapes and discs confirmed.** Notwithstanding the changes made by *FA 2000, s 113(2)*, expenditure on the production of master audio tapes and discs will continue to be treated as of a revenue nature. See 71.48 SCHEDULE D, CASES I AND II.

B55 **Farming losses.** *ICTA 1988, s 397* is disapplied for 2000/01 and/or 2001/02 (and for accounting periods ending in the years to 31 March 2001 and/or 2002) provided certain conditions as to profits in earlier years are satisfied. See 46.8(*b*) LOSSES.

B56 **Slaughter of immature animals intended to be replacements.** For the duration of the 2001 foot and mouth outbreak, certain animals slaughtered before giving birth may be treated as having been mature. See 34.2 HERD BASIS.

C.   CONCESSIONS APPLICABLE TO COMPANIES ETC.

C1   Credit for underlying tax: dividends from trade investments in overseas companies. (*a*) A few UK double tax agreements provide relief for underlying tax on income from ordinary portfolio investments and where these are in force, credit is also given for underlying taxes along a chain of shareholdings (see 24.5(*b*) DOUBLE TAX RELIEF). (*b*) Insurance companies in receipt of dividends from overseas companies, in which there is at least 10% control of voting power or the dividend is referable to insurance business of the UK company, are given credit for underlying taxes along a chain of shareholdings. See Tolley's Corporation Tax.

C2   Loan and money societies. There is restricted liability to tax on dividends and interest to members. Withdrawn from April 2001. See 93.3 VOLUNTARY ASSOCIATIONS.

C3   Holiday clubs and thrift funds. There is restricted liability to tax on profits or interest to members. Withdrawn from April 2001. See 93.2 VOLUNTARY ASSOCIATIONS.

C4   Trading activities for charitable purposes. Profits are not taxed under certain conditions. See 14.7(ii) CHARITIES.

C30   Authorised unit trusts and open-ended investment companies — waivers of distributions. Distribution treatment is disapplied in the case of certain *de minimis* waivers of distributions (or accumulations). See 90.1 UNIT TRUSTS.

C31   Scientific research associations. Tax exemptions will temporarily continue under the previous practice following a change in the DTI guidance on the qualification requirements. See 77.1 SCIENTIFIC RESEARCH ASSOCIATIONS.

C32   Interest relief—companies with tax and NICs liabilities under the personal service rules where the payments for relevant contracts have been received after deduction of tax by virtue of the construction industry scheme provisions. Corporation tax repayments due may be set against certain liabilities in respect of deemed Schedule E payments for the purposes of interest on overdue tax and NICs on such payments. See 61.12 PERSONAL SERVICE COMPANIES ETC.

D.   CONCESSIONS RELATING TO CAPITAL GAINS

D46   Relief against income for capital losses on the disposal of unquoted shares in a trading company. Relief will be allowed in certain cases where a company without assets is dissolved and either no distribution is made during winding-up, or no final distribution is made. Superseded by statutory provision for events treated as disposals after 5 April 2000. See 46.15 LOSSES.

D47   Temporary loss of charitable status due to reverter of school and other sites. Liabilities which may arise in the period before charitable status is re-established will be discharged or repaid. See 14.1 CHARITIES.

39   Inland Revenue Press Releases

The following is a summary in date order of Press Releases referred to in this work (other than those containing Statements of Practice, as to which see 40 INLAND REVENUE STATEMENTS OF PRACTICE). Certain pre-18 July 1978 Press Releases were reissued as Statements of Practice on 18 June 1979 (see 40 INLAND REVENUE STATEMENTS OF PRACTICE).

Copies of any individual Press Release may be obtained from Inland Revenue Information Centre, SW Wing, Bush House, Strand, London WC2B 4RD (tel. 020–7438 6420/6425/7772). Copies of recent press releases are also available on the internet at www.inlandrevenue.gov.uk/home.htm

2.3.78	**Double taxation: exchange of information with the USA.** Notes on the 'working arrangement' with the US Internal Revenue Service. See 36.2(*c*) INLAND REVENUE: CONFIDENTIALITY OF INFORMATION.
26.7.79	**Administrative simplification to help pensioners.** The Revenue are notified by the Department of Health and Social Security (now the Department for Work and Pensions) of the amounts of retirement and widows pensions. See 83.3 SOCIAL SECURITY.
16.6.80	**Life assurance premium relief: ICTA 1988, Sch 15 para 14: disqualification of certain life policies.** Guidance is given as to the application of this legislation. See 45.11 LIFE ASSURANCE POLICIES.
26.1.81	**Transfer pricing of multinational enterprises: notes for guidance.** See 3.8 ANTI-AVOIDANCE.
4.2.81	**Life assurance premiums paid to the UK branch of an overseas life office.** Relief is available. See 45.4(*c*) LIFE ASSURANCE POLICIES.
13.2.81	**Travelling and subsistence allowances paid to site-based staff employees in the construction and allied industries.** Revenue practice is explained and extended. See 75.46 SCHEDULE E—EMPLOYMENT INCOME.
25.1.83	**Deferred listing of delay appeals.** See 4.6 APPEALS.
30.3.83	**'Freelance' workers in the film and allied industries.** Revised treatment of such workers operates from 6 April 1983. See 75.27 SCHEDULE E—EMPLOYMENT INCOME.
13.3.84	**Net of tax pay.** Special forms and tax tables are available to employers. See 75.43 SCHEDULE E—EMPLOYMENT INCOME.
15.3.84	**Cable television: capital allowances** are available on ducting. See 9.25 CAPITAL ALLOWANCES.
17.5.84	**Furnished holiday lettings and caravans.** The application of *ICTA 1988, s 503* to caravan lettings is clarified. See 69.3, 69.8 SCHEDULE A.
31.7.84	**Offshore funds: applications for certification as a distributing fund.** The procedure is explained. See 52.7 OFFSHORE FUNDS.
1.8.84	**ICTA 1988, s 124: interest on quoted Eurobonds.** The requirements for designation as a 'recognised clearing system' are outlined. See 22.3 DEDUCTION OF TAX AT SOURCE.
2.11.84	**Incentive awards and prizes for employees: taxed award schemes.** See 75.43 SCHEDULE E—EMPLOYMENT INCOME.

23.7.85   **Extra-statutory concession: benefits in kind: the tax treatment of accommodation provided for employees.** Annual value is in practice taken as gross rateable value. See 69.5(*b*) SCHEDULE A.

15.4.86   **Voluntary lifeboatmen: tax treatment of call-out fees.** See 55.44 PAY AS YOU EARN.

27.10.86   **Capital allowances: changes in accounting practice for plant and machinery under lease or subject to hire purchase.** The tax treatment is unaffected. See 9.24 CAPITAL ALLOWANCES.

22.12.87   **Inland Revenue further guidance on profit-related pay.** See 75.34 SCHEDULE E—EMPLOYMENT INCOME.

22.1.88   **Life assurance: variation of qualifying policies.** After 24 February 1988, the Revenue will not certify, as qualifying policies, any new life assurance policies which allow for variations such that, under contract law, a new policy would be created. See 45.12 LIFE ASSURANCE POLICIES.

1.2.88   **Annual return form for profit-related pay.** The form of return to be used is published. See 75.34 SCHEDULE E—EMPLOYMENT INCOME.

4.2.88   **Occupational pensions: publication of Inland Revenue model rules and guidance notes for simplified occupational pension schemes.** See 67.4 RETIREMENT SCHEMES.

15.3.88   **Alimony, maintenance etc.: retrospective Court Orders.** Revenue Statement of Practice SP 6/81 will not apply to Court Orders made or varied after 30 June 1988. See 47.8 MARRIED PERSONS.

15.3.88   **Reduction of basic rate of income tax.** The consequences are outlined, including the adjustments to be made where tax is deducted from certain payments. See 22.6 DEDUCTION OF TAX AT SOURCE.

14.4.88   **Unapproved employee share schemes.** A charge will not normally arise under *FA 1988, s 78* in respect of 'equity ratchets'. See 82.14(*a*) SHARE-RELATED EMPLOYMENT INCOME AND EXEMPTIONS.

2.9.88   **New tax unit for agricultural gangmasters.** See 71.47(*c*) SCHEDULE D, CASES I AND II.

19.12.88   **Tax appeals and other proceedings: place of hearing by General Commissioners.** See 4.4 APPEALS.

3.2.89   **Profit-related pay simplified.** A number of modifications are introduced either prior to enactment or by concession. See 75.34 SCHEDULE E—EMPLOYMENT INCOME.

3.3.89   **Double taxation: taxation of certain non-residents working on the UK continental shelf.** See 24.2 DOUBLE TAX RELIEF.

29.3.89   **Cutting the cost of handling claims for repayment of income tax.** From 6 April 1989, repayments under £50 will not be made during the tax year to which the claim relates. See 16.6 CLAIMS, 56.9 PAYMENT OF TAX.

12.4.89   **Scholarship and apprenticeship schemes for employees.** The exempt limit under Revenue Statement of Practice SP 4/86 is increased to £5,500 p.a.. See 28.29 EXEMPT INCOME.

39 Inland Revenue Press Releases

3.5.89   **Personal equity plans: relaxations to 75% test.** See 28.24 EXEMPT INCOME.

19.7.89   **Tax relief for medical insurance.** The permissible benefits are outlined. See 48.6 MEDICAL INSURANCE.

1.8.89   **Setting Revenue rates of interest** for repayment supplement, overdue tax, and official rate purposes. The rates are in future to be set automatically by reference to a formula based on certain bank base lending rates. See 41 INTEREST ON OVERPAID TAX, 42 INTEREST AND SURCHARGES ON UNPAID TAX.

6.10.89   **Personal equity plans: new issue shares** on slightly different terms from those offered to the general public will not thereby be excluded from transfer into a plan. See 28.24 EXEMPT INCOME.

7.11.89   **Simpler accounts for small businesses.** From April 1990, businesses with a turnover under £10,000, and landlords with gross rental income under £10,000, may submit simplified three-line accounts. See 69.6 SCHEDULE A.

18.1.90   **Incentives for employees: improvements to the taxed award scheme.** Schemes may cover higher rate as well as basic rate liabilities. See 75.43 SCHEDULE E—EMPLOY-MENT INCOME.

20.3.90   **New tax reliefs to encourage charitable giving.** Certain benefits available to subscribers to charitable organisations are ignored for the purposes of relief for covenanted payments. See 14.17(*b*) CHARITIES.

19.4.90   **Benefits in kind: valuation of living accommodation provided for employees in England and Wales.** The consequences of the ending of the domestic rates system are outlined. See 75.32 SCHEDULE E—EMPLOYMENT INCOME.

9.5.90   **Tracing of absent parents: Inland Revenue assistance to DSS.** The Revenue will supply to the DSS (now the Department for Work and Pensions) information relating to such parents where they are liable to maintain lone-parent families on income support. See 36.2(*f*) INLAND REVENUE: CONFIDENTIALITY OF INFORMATION.

17.10.90 **Changes to personal equity plans.** Pending the issue of revised regulations, certain changes to the rules for qualifying investments are applied by concession. The treatment of interest following abolition of composite rate tax is outlined. See 28.24 EXEMPT INCOME.

22.11.90 **Benefits in kind — employer-provided living accommodation.** Revenue practice is revised where employees are provided with more than one property. See 75.32 SCHEDULE E—EMPLOYMENT INCOME.

5.4.91   **Benefits in kind: loans provided by employers.** A new basis of determining the official rate of interest is introduced from 6 April 1991. See 75.20 SCHEDULE E—EMPLOY-MENT INCOME.

11.4.91   **Finance lease rental payments.** A new statement of practice (SP 3/91) is issued, and some aspects of finance leases clarified. See 71.58 SCHEDULE D, CASES I AND II.

12.6.91   **Finance Bill: friendly societies — tax-exempt policies.** An extra-statutory concession applies in relation to certain wrongly classified policies. See 31.3 FRIENDLY SOCIETIES.

1.11.91   **Simpler accounts for small businesses: increase in the numbers who can benefit.** The limit for the submission of three-line accounts is increased to £15,000 from 6 April 1992. See 69.6 SCHEDULE A.

16.12.91   **Enterprise zone capital allowances.** By concession, certain amounts payable before 16 December 1991 for the purchase of unused buildings are treated as incurred on the date the construction expenditure was incurred. See 9.19 CAPITAL ALLOWANCES.

7.5.92   **Charitable giving.** The requirements for repayment claims relating to deeds of covenant are revised. See 14.17(e) CHARITIES.

13.8.92   **Tax on savings — getting it right.** The Revenue's attitude to cases of incorrect registration for gross payment of interest is explained. See 7.2 BANKS.

12.11.92   **Enhanced capital allowances for plant, machinery and buildings.** First-year and initial allowances are reintroduced generally for a limited period. See 9.3, 9.13, 9.18, 9.27 CAPITAL ALLOWANCES.

18.11.92   **Scholarship and apprenticeship schemes at universities and technical colleges.** Revenue Statement of Practice SP 4/86 is amended and reprinted with an increased exemption limit. See 28.29 EXEMPT INCOME.

21.12.92   **Enhanced capital allowances for buildings.** The temporary reinstatement of initial allowances for agricultural and industrial buildings (see Revenue Press Release 12 November 1992 above) is also to apply to buildings purchased unused from traders in buildings. See 9.3, 9.13 CAPITAL ALLOWANCES.

21.1.93   **Deposit interest: amendment to tax deduction at source rules.** Deduction will not be required from interest paid by deposit-takers other than banks to certain non-ordinarily resident individuals. See 7.2 BANKS.

21.1.93   **Taxation of in-house benefits in kind.** The Revenue explain how they intend to deal with such benefits following the decision in *Pepper v Hart*. See 75.16 SCHEDULE E—EMPLOYMENT INCOME.

17.2.93   **Remission of tax in cases where information has not been used within a reasonable time.** The income limits for remission are increased. See 56.8 PAYMENT OF TAX.

16.3.93   **Council tax: income tax and corporation tax implications.** See 71.44, 71.68 SCHEDULE D, CASES I AND II, 75.10, 75.11(a) SCHEDULE E—EMPLOYMENT INCOME.

24.3.93   **Charitable giving: covenants.** Guidance is given concerning revocable covenants. See 14.17(a) CHARITIES.

14.4.93   **New statutory exemption for relocation packages.** Aspects of the operation of the provisions introduced by *FA 1993*, and of the phasing out of the previous extra-statutory concessions, are explained. See 75.36 SCHEDULE E—EMPLOYMENT INCOME.

23.7.93   **Tax repayments to EC resident companies.** Claims to repayment supplement may be made following the *Commerzbank AG* decision. See 41.2 INTEREST ON OVERPAID TAX.

17.12.93   **Capital allowances for plant and machinery.** The *FA 1994* provisions restricting the availability of allowances, and requiring notification of expenditure, are explained. See 9.25, 9.26 CAPITAL ALLOWANCES.

39   Inland Revenue Press Releases

2.2.94 **Tax treatment of interest paid by Government departments.** Following the decision in *Esso Petroleum Co Ltd v MOD*, no steps will be taken to seek out, nor make further payments to, the recipients of payments of interest other than on securities before the date of the decision. See 70.1 SCHEDULE C.

8.9.94 **Individuals coming to the UK to take up employment — administrative measures.** Procedures following arrival in the UK are explained. See 65.5 RESIDENCE, ORDINARY RESIDENCE AND DOMICILE.

29.11.94 **Self-assessment.** Deduction of tax from payments to non-resident landlords will not be required where the tax is included in payments on account made under self-assessment arrangements. See 69.13 SCHEDULE A.

29.11.94 **Taxation of income from property and self-assessment.** The renewals basis or wear and tear allowances will continue to be available for furnished lettings under the new Schedule A regime introduced by *FA 1995*. See 69.7 SCHEDULE A.

29.11.94 **Self-assessment: transition to current year basis — anti-avoidance provisions.** Guidance on the Revenue interpretation of certain expressions used in the legislation is contained in the commentary published with the draft legislation. See 71.12 SCHEDULE D, CASES I AND II.

29.11.94 **Investment managers.** Extra-statutory concession B40 may continue to apply until 5 April 2005 in certain cases which fall outside the *FA 1995* provisions limiting the chargeable income of non-residents. See 51.1 NON-RESIDENTS AND OTHER OVERSEAS MATTERS.

4.1.95 **Trusts and settlements — simplification of income tax 'benefit to settlor' rules.** See 81.13 *et seq.* SETTLEMENTS.

20.2.95 **The Stock Exchange alternative investment market (AIM) — tax reliefs for investment in companies joining AIM.** Shares in such companies are treated as unquoted for tax purposes. See 25.5 ENTERPRISE INVESTMENT SCHEME, 28.24(i) EXEMPT INCOME, 46.15 LOSSES, 91.3 VENTURE CAPITAL TRUSTS.

14.7.95 **Profit-related pay — interest and penalties** may apply for late and incorrect returns for 1994/95 and subsequent years. See 75.34 SCHEDULE E—EMPLOYMENT INCOME.

14.9.95 **Venture capital trusts.** Inadvertent breaches of the 70% 'qualifying holdings' limit will not generally result in withdrawal of approval. See 91.2 VENTURE CAPITAL TRUSTS.

19.10.95 **Insurance commissions rebated to ordinary policyholders will not be taxed.** Statement of Practice SP 5/95 is to be revised. See 71.54 SCHEDULE D, CASES I AND II.

28.11.95 **Taxation of car and mileage allowances (REV 32).** FPCS rates may be used in calculating taxable profits and allowable deductions in respect of business use of an employee's private car. See 75.46 SCHEDULE E—EMPLOYMENT INCOME.

21.3.96 **Carry-back of personal pension contributions made in 1996/97.** Contributions carried back to 1995/96 will be taken into account in determining the interim payment required for 1996/97. See 78.4 SELF-ASSESSMENT.

4.4.96 **Self-assessment — early settlement of a deceased taxpayer's tax affairs or those of a trust or estate following cessation.** Returns will, on request, be issued before the end of the tax year, and early written confirmation given if there is to be no enquiry into the return. See 68.2, 68.6 RETURNS.

29.4.96 **Bovine spongiform encephalopathy (BSE) and farm stock taking valuations.** The Revenue approach is clarified, and special arrangements instituted in the short term. See 71.47 SCHEDULE D, CASES I AND II.

30.4.96 **Tax treatment of premiums and benefits under locum and fixed practice expenses insurance policies.** The Revenue now consider premiums under such policies allowable, and benefits taxable. See 71.54 SCHEDULE D, CASES I AND II.

31.5.96 **Disclosure and discovery under self-assessment.** A Revenue paper discusses disclosure requirements, with particular reference to the possibility of a discovery assessment. See 5.3 ASSESSMENTS, 68.2 RETURNS.

4.2.97 **Self-assessment — valuations for capital gains tax.** The Revenue will, on request, check asset valuations. See 68.2 RETURNS.

4.2.97 **Old life insurance policies: insurer stopping collection of premiums — new extra-statutory concession.** Such a change will, in certain circumstances, not be treated as an alteration of the policy for tax purposes. See 45.13 LIFE ASSURANCE POLICIES.

12.12.97 **Self-assessment — provision of information from taxpayer statements of account to authorised agents.** See 78.4 SELF-ASSESSMENT.

18.12.97 **Taxation of offshore personal portfolio bonds and residence of transferors of assets.** The Revenue explain how they propose to deal with the taxation of transfers of assets following the House of Lords' decision in *CIR v Willoughby*. See 3.7 ANTI-AVOIDANCE.

23.2.98 **Ministers clarify scope of Scottish Parliament's tax varying power.** See 1.3 ALLOWANCES AND TAX RATES.

17.3.98 **Taxation of life insurance policy holders.** The annual charge on personal portfolio bonds will not commence before 6 April 1999. See 45.13 LIFE ASSURANCE POLICIES.

17.3.98 **Taxation of income from property.** Extra-statutory concessions B4 and B5 are to be withdrawn from 6 April 2001 (1 April 2001 for corporation tax). See 69.5 SCHEDULE A, 71.47 SCHEDULE D, CASES I AND II.

25.3.98 **Tax treatment of expenditure on films.** A revised Statement of Practice replaces those previously applicable with effect from 25 March 1998 (subject to transitional arrangements). See 71.48 SCHEDULE D, CASES I AND II.

31.3.98 **Inland Revenue launch 'faster working' scheme for their self-assessment enquiries.** See 68.7 RETURNS.

31.7.98 **Eighty countries eligible for millennium Gift Aid announced.** See 14.21 CHARITIES.

1.9.98 **The construction industry scheme trading electronically.** An outline is given of how electronic data interchange will be used. See 20.7 CONSTRUCTION INDUSTRY SCHEME.

23.10.98 **Construction industry tax scheme: type of certificate issued to limited companies.** Guidance is given on the conditions for issue of the CIS5 (previously 714C) rather than the CIS6 (previously 714P) certificate under the new scheme. See generally 20.4 CONSTRUCTION INDUSTRY SCHEME.

39   Inland Revenue Press Releases

5.3.99   **Employees to get help with uniform cleaning costs.** Fire service and healthcare workers are entitled to flat rate allowances. See 75.28 SCHEDULE E—EMPLOYMENT INCOME.

9.3.99   **New choice for taxpayers — returns via the Internet.** The planned extension of the use of electronic communication is outlined. (Joint Press Release with Customs and Excise.) See 35.12 INLAND REVENUE: ADMINISTRATION.

1.4.99   **Trusts and estates in administration: revised extra-statutory concessions.** Revenue Concessions A14, A93, B18 and D40 are revised. See 21.3 DECEASED ESTATES, 81.5 SETTLEMENTS.

28.5.99   **New deal for the unemployed.** Certain payments made in 1997/98 and 1998/99 are to be treated as tax-free. See 83.4 SOCIAL SECURITY.

20.7.99   **Tax provisions move closer to accounting practice.** The Revenue accept certain decisions moving the tax treatment of provisions closer to accounting practice. See 71.30, 71.39, 71.68, 71.69(*b*), 71.73 SCHEDULE D, CASES I AND II.

23.9.99   **Personal services provided through intermediaries.** The Revenue publish details of new rules to be included in *FA 2000* to 'tackle tax avoidance' using service companies and similar intermediaries such as partnerships. See 61.1, 61.12 PERSONAL SERVICE COMPANIES ETC.

9.11.99   **Rate of tax on savings income and chargeable gains.** The starting rate is to be applied to savings income with retrospective effect from 6 April 1999. See 1.9 ALLOWANCES AND TAX RATES.

14.12.99   **Authorised mileage rate for cars, pedal cycles and motorcycles.** The FPCS rates and pedal cycle rate are unchanged for 2000/01, and a fixed motor cycle rate introduced from 6 April 2000. See 75.46 SCHEDULE E—EMPLOYMENT INCOME.

25.1.00   **Deregulatory change setting official rate of interest on beneficial loans in advance.** See 75.20 SCHEDULE E—EMPLOYMENT INCOME.

7.2.00   **Personal services provided through intermediaries — guidance.** The Revenue publish detailed guidance to assist in deciding whether a worker would have been an employee if engaged by a client directly rather than through an intermediary such as a service company or partnership. They give specific advice on 'standard contracts' said to be common to service company workers in the information technology industry engaged through agencies. See 61.4 PERSONAL SERVICE COMPANIES ETC.

16.2.00   **Discounts to boost use of the internet.** Tax discounts for submitting returns via the internet and paying the tax due electronically are introduced for one year. See 55.9 PAY AS YOU EARN, 68.2, 68.14 RETURNS.

3.3.00   **New Revenue Pamphlet IR 1 published.** Concessions C2 and C3 are withdrawn from April 2001. See 93.2, 93.3 VOLUNTARY ASSOCIATIONS.

21.3.00 (BN1D)   **Extra discount for employers paying tax credits.** Following Press Release 16 February 2000 above, a further £50 discount will be available where employers pay working families' or disabled person's tax credits. See 55.9 PAY AS YOU EARN, 68.14 RETURNS.

11.4.00   **Electronic commerce — tax status of websites and servers.** The Revenue take the view that a website, or a server on which e-commerce is conducted through a website, is not of itself a permanent establishment. See 24.2, 24.3 DOUBLE TAX RELIEF.

13.11.00   **UK/US double taxation convention — mutual agreement procedure.** Details of the administrative arrangements are published. See 24.2 DOUBLE TAX RELIEF.

10.1.01   **Self-assessment — paying tax over the Internet.** A facility for payment by debit card through GiroBank is introduced. See 68.2 RETURNS.

7.3.01   **New statutory mileage rates.** The statutory rates introduced from 6 April 2002 may
(BN 2/01)   be used by the self-employed with small turnover and volunteer drivers. See 71.80 SCHEDULE D, CASES I AND II, 74.2 SCHEDULE D, CASE VI.

7.3.01   **100% capital allowances for flats over shops.** The purposes for which the ground
(BN 15/01)   floor premises must be used for the flat conversion allowances to apply are outlined. See 9.9 CAPITAL ALLOWANCES.

7.3.01   **Enterprise management incentives.** From 5 April 2001, the Revenue will give an
(BN 6/01)   advance assurance on whether a company will be a qualifying company for these purposes. See 82.35 SHARE-RELATED EMPLOYMENT INCOME AND EXEMPTIONS.

28.11.01   **Recognised stock exchanges.** Following a change in the Revenue interpretation of the expression 'listed on a recognised stock exchange', the status of certain individual savings account investments is preserved. See 28.13 EXEMPT INCOME.

17.4.02   **Supporting small businesses and entrepreneurs.** The planned implementation of
(REV/   payroll electronic filing is set out. See 35.12 INLAND REVENUE: ADMINISTRATION, 55.9 PAY
C&E 2/02)   AS YOU EARN.

26.7.02   **Individual savings accounts.** Certain ISAs opened before 24 August 2002 on terms denying the investor access to his funds for a fixed period may, with Revenue agreement, be allowed to continue to maturity, despite such terms being generally prohibited from 1 October 2002. See 28.13 EXEMPT INCOME.

23.9.02   **Electronic filing of self-assessment tax returns.** The period in which a return must be filed if an underpayment is to be coded out through PAYE (55) is extended for 2001/02 and subsequent years' returns if the return is filed electronically. See 68.3 RETURNS.

12.12.02   **Official rate of interest on beneficial loans.** This is set in advance at 5% for the tax year 2003/04. See 75.20 SCHEDULE E—EMPLOYMENT INCOME.

9.4.03   **Employer contribution to homeworker expenses.** The Revenue explain the circumstances in which the exemption in *ITEPA 2003, s 316A* introduced by *FA 2003* will apply without the need for supporting evidence. (Revenue Budget Press Release REV BN 03). See 75.10 SCHEDULE E — EMPLOYMENT INCOME.

9.4.03   **Enhanced capital allowances for water technologies.** From 1 April 2003, all businesses can claim 100% first-year allowances on designated plant and machinery to reduce water use and improve water quality. (Revenue Budget Press Release REV BN 26). See 9.27 CAPITAL ALLOWANCES under Environmentally beneficial plant or machinery.

12.1.04   **Official rate of interest on beneficial loans.** This is set in advance at 5% for the tax year 2004/05. See 75.20 SCHEDULE E—EMPLOYMENT INCOME.

30.1.04   **First-year allowances on plant and machinery.** New definitions of 'small or medium-sized enterprise' and 'small enterprise' come into effect. See 9.27 CAPITAL ALLOWANCES.

39   Inland Revenue Press Releases

22.6.04   **Disclosure of tax avoidance schemes.** Changes to the draft regulations are announced and transitional commencement rules are introduced. See 3.24 ANTI-AVOIDANCE.

40   Inland Revenue Statements of Practice

Simon's Direct Tax Service Part H3.

The following is a summary of those Statements of Practice published in Revenue Pamphlet IR 131 (February 2004), or subsequently announced, which are referred to in this book.

Statements are divided into those originally published before 18 July 1978 (which are given a reference letter (according to the subject matter) and consecutive number, e.g. A34) and later Statements (which are numbered consecutively in each year, e.g. SP 6/94).

Certain Statements marked in IR 131 as obsolete continue to be referred to in the text (having been relevant at some time within the tax years referred to in that particular text).

Copies of individual SP-denominated Statements are available free of charge from Inland Revenue Information Centre, SW Wing, Bush House, Strand, London WC2B 4RD (large SAE to accompany postal applications) (tel. 020–7438 6420/6425/7772).

As regards Inland Revenue internal guidance manuals, see 35.10 INLAND REVENUE: ADMINISTRATION.

A3   **Barristers: the cash basis.** Although normally assessed on a cash basis, barristers may elect to change to the earnings basis. Obsolete from 2000/01 onwards. See 11.1 CASH BASIS.

A6   **Employment income — VAT.** Expenses and other benefits chargeable on an employee must include VAT, if any. See 55.9 PAY AS YOU EARN, 75.16 SCHEDULE E—EMPLOYMENT INCOME. For PAYE purposes, VAT is excluded from payments for services supplied by a person holding an office in the course of carrying on a trade, profession or vocation. See 55.43 PAY AS YOU EARN.

A8   **Stock dividends.** The interpretation of *ICTA 1988, s 251(2)* is clarified. See 85.1 STOCK DIVIDENDS.

A9   **Schedule E assessments (1995/96 and earlier): repayment supplement.** Attribution of repayments etc. between years. Obsolete. See 41.2 INTEREST ON OVERPAID TAX.

A10   **Airline pilots.** Revenue practice re duties deemed to be performed in the UK. See 75.2(iii) SCHEDULE E—EMPLOYMENT INCOME.

A13   **Completion of return forms by attorneys.** In cases of illness, infirmity or old age of the taxpayer, the Revenue will accept the signature of an attorney who has full knowledge of the taxpayer's affairs. See 68.2 RETURNS.

A16   **Living expenses abroad: Schedule D, Cases I and II.** A UK resident living abroad for the purposes of his trade etc. will have his personal living expenses allowed. See 71.80 SCHEDULE D, CASES I AND II.

A27   **Accounts on a cash basis.** (Obsolete from 2000/01 onwards.) See 11.1 CASH BASIS.

A32   **Goods taken by traders for personal consumption.** The Revenue's practice in applying *Sharkey v Wernher* is stated. See 71.73 SCHEDULE D, CASES I AND II.

A33   **Relief for interest payments: loans applied in acquiring an interest in a partnership.** Salaried partners in a professional firm may claim relief in certain circumstances. See 43.22 INTEREST PAYABLE.

A34   **Relief for interest payments: loans for purchase or improvement of land.**

    (*a*)   Husband and wife living together are given relief for interest paid by either even if the property is owned wholly or partly by the other.

    (*b*)   A person who inherits property subject to a mortgage is entitled to tax relief for mortgage interest if, and only if, the person from whom he inherited the property was so entitled.

    See 43.12 INTEREST PAYABLE.

B1   **Treatment of VAT.** Guidance on the general principles applied in dealing with VAT in tax computations. See 71.83 SCHEDULE D, CASES I AND II.

B6   **Goods sold subject to reservation of title.** Such goods should normally be treated as purchases in the buyer's accounts and sales in the supplier's accounts provided that both parties agree. See 71.73 SCHEDULE D, CASES I AND II.

C1   **Lotteries and football pools.** Where part of the cost of a ticket is to be donated to a club etc., that part is, in certain circumstances, not treated as a trading receipt. See 71.20 SCHEDULE D, CASES I AND II.

SP 3/78   **Close companies: income tax relief for interest on loans applied in acquiring an interest in a close company.** Relief continues after company ceases to be close. See 43.19 INTEREST PAYABLE.

SP 4/79   **Life assurance premium relief — children's policies.** This is relaxed by SP 11/79 below. See 45.4(*g*) LIFE ASSURANCE POLICIES.

SP 7/79   **Benefits in kind: cheap loans — advances for expenses** to an employee will not be a taxable benefit provided certain conditions are met. Superseded by *ITEPA 2003, s 179.* See 75.20 SCHEDULE E—EMPLOYMENT INCOME.

SP 8/79   **Compensation for acquisition of property under compulsory powers.** Reimbursement of revenue costs are trading receipts. See 71.38(*d*) SCHEDULE D, CASES I AND II.

SP 11/79   **Life assurance premium relief — children's policies.** Relief will be given in certain circumstances on premiums on policies taken out by children under twelve. See 45.4(*g*) LIFE ASSURANCE POLICIES.

SP 3/80   **ICTA 1988, s 707: Cancellation of tax advantages from certain transactions in securities: procedure for clearance in advance.** The procedure is explained. See 3.2 ANTI-AVOIDANCE.

SP 4/80   **Industrial buildings allowance: industrial workshops constructed for separate letting to small businesses.** A global basis will be used for giving allowances. See 9.21 CAPITAL ALLOWANCES.

SP 6/80   **Small workshops allowance.** Clarifies eligibility for the allowance. (Revenue Press Release 9 July 1980). Obsolete. See 9.21 CAPITAL ALLOWANCES.

SP 10/80   **Mortgage interest relief: year of marriage.** Relief may be granted on more than one property. Obsolete. See 43.12 INTEREST PAYABLE.

SP 11/80   **Liability on gains arising on life and capital redemption policies and life annuities.** Non-residents will not be charged in certain circumstances. (Superseded by Revenue Concession B53.) See 45.13 LIFE ASSURANCE POLICIES.

SP 15/80 **Maintenance payments: payment of school fees.** Relief may be given to a parent paying fees direct to a school as part of a Court Order. See 47.8 MARRIED PERSONS.

SP 16/80 **Lorry drivers: relief for expenditure on meals** where there is a full-time travelling appointment. Also refers to subsistence etc. allowances when working temporarily away from home. See 75.46 SCHEDULE E—EMPLOYMENT INCOME.

SP 2/81 **Contributions to retirement benefit schemes on termination of employment.** Such payments by the employer on behalf of an employee will not be chargeable under *ICTA 1988, s 148.* Superseded by legislation for 2003/04 onwards. See 18.6(vii) COMPENSATION FOR LOSS OF EMPLOYMENT.

SP 5/81 **Expenditure on farm drainage.** The net cost of restoring drainage is allowable as revenue expenditure. See 71.47(*b*) SCHEDULE D, CASES I AND II.

SP 10/81 **Payments on account of disability resulting in cessation of employment.** The interpretation of 'disability' in *ITEPA 2003, s 406* (formerly in *ICTA 1988, Sch 11 para 3*) is extended. See 18.6(i) COMPENSATION FOR LOSS OF EMPLOYMENT.

SP 11/81 **Additional redundancy payments.** Allowance under *ICTA 1988, s 90* will also apply to a partial discontinuance of a trade. See 71.44 SCHEDULE D, CASES I AND II.

SP 12/81 **Construction industry tax deduction scheme: carpet fitting** is considered to be outside the scope of the scheme. See 20.2 CONSTRUCTION INDUSTRY SCHEME.

SP 1/82 **Interaction of income tax and inheritance tax on assets put into settlement.** Income of a settlement will not be treated as income of the settlor solely because the trustees have power to pay, or do pay, inheritance tax on assets put into the settlement by the settlor. See 81.16(*e*) SETTLEMENTS.

SP 1/84 **Trade unions: provident benefits: legal and administrative expenses.** See 88.1 TRADE UNIONS.

SP 5/84 **Employees resident but not ordinarily resident in the UK: general earnings chargeable under ITEPA 2003, ss 25, 26.** Revenue practice on apportionment of earnings between UK and non-UK duties of an employment is explained. See 75.4 SCHEDULE E—EMPLOYMENT INCOME.

SP 6/84 **Non-resident lessors: FA 1973, s 38.** The conditions under which profits of such lessors of mobile drilling rigs etc. are exempt from tax are outlined. See 51.12 NON-RESIDENTS AND OTHER OVERSEAS MATTERS.

SP 6/85 **Incentive awards.** The basis on which expenses are included is outlined. See 75.47(*a*) SCHEDULE E—EMPLOYMENT INCOME.

SP 1/86 **Capital allowances: plant and machinery: short-life assets.** Guidance is given on some practical aspects of the short-life asset provisions. See 9.30(F) CAPITAL ALLOWANCES.

SP 2/86 **Offshore funds.** Various aspects of the legislation are clarified. See 52.3, 52.4, 52.5 OFFSHORE FUNDS.

SP 3/86 **Payments to a non-resident from UK discretionary trusts or UK estates during the administration period: double taxation relief.** A change of practice replaces extra-statutory concessions A14 and B18 in certain cases. See 21.3 DECEASED ESTATES, 81.5 SETTLEMENTS.

40   Inland Revenue Statements of Practice

SP 4/86   **Scholarship and apprenticeship schemes for employees.** Certain payments to employees attending full-time educational courses are exempt from income tax. See 28.29 EXEMPT INCOME.

SP 9/86   **Income tax: partnership mergers and demergers.** The application of the succession rules is explained. See 53.7 PARTNERSHIPS.

SP 3/87   **Repayment of tax to charities on covenanted and other income.** Obsolete. See 14.17(*f*) CHARITIES.

SP 5/87   **Tax returns: the use of substitute forms.** The conditions for acceptance of facsimile and photocopied returns and other forms are set out. See 16.1 CLAIMS, 68.2 RETURNS.

SP 9/87   **Capital allowances: hotels.** The Revenue interpretation of the provision of breakfast and evening meals by a qualifying hotel is set out. See 9.18 CAPITAL ALLOWANCES.

SP 2/88   **Civil tax penalties and criminal prosecution cases.** The Revenue practice as regards pursuit of such penalties is set out. See 57.19 PENALTIES.

SP 3/90   **Stocks and long-term contracts.** The Revenue practice as regards bases of valuation and changes therein is explained. Obsolete. See 71.73 SCHEDULE D, CASES I AND II.

SP 4/90   **Charitable covenants.** Revised practices in relation to retrospective validation and escape clauses are explained. Now obsolete. See 14.17(*c*)(*d*) CHARITIES.

SP 5/90   **Accountants' working papers.** The Revenue's approach to the use of its information powers in relation to accountants' working papers is explained. See 30.7 FRAUDULENT OR NEGLIGENT CONDUCT.

SP 2/91   **Residence in the UK: visits extended because of exceptional circumstances.** Extra days spent in the UK may be ignored for certain purposes. See 65.5 RESIDENCE, ORDINARY RESIDENCE AND DOMICILE.

SP 3/91   **Finance lease rental payments.** The practice in relation to deduction of rental payments is explained. See 71.58 SCHEDULE D, CASES I AND II.

SP 7/91   **Double taxation: business profits: unilateral relief.** The practice as regards admission of foreign taxes for unilateral relief is revised. See 24.4 DOUBLE TAX RELIEF.

SP 8/91   **Discovery assessments.** The Revenue practice as regards the making of further assessments following 'discovery' is explained. See 5.3 ASSESSMENTS.

SP 9/91   **Investigation settlements: retirement annuities and personal pension relief.** Special premium relief is given where an investigation is settled by voluntary offer. See 30.11 FRAUDULENT OR NEGLIGENT CONDUCT.

SP 12/91   **Income tax: 'in the ordinary course' of banking business.** The Revenue interpretation of this expression is explained. (Replaced by SP 4/96 below.) See 22.3 DEDUCTION OF TAX AT SOURCE.

SP 13/91   **Ex gratia awards made on termination of an office or employment by retirement or death.** A revised practice, and extended system of approval, applies after 31 October 1991. See 67.12 RETIREMENT SCHEMES.

SP 16/91   **Accountancy expenses arising out of accounts investigations.** Revenue practice on the allowance of such expenses is explained. See 71.59 SCHEDULE D, CASES I AND II.

SP 17/91 **Residence in the UK: when ordinary residence is regarded as commencing where the period to be spent here is less than three years.** See 65.6 RESIDENCE, ORDINARY RESIDENCE AND DOMICILE.

SP 6/92 **Accident insurance policies: chargeable events and gains on policies of life insurance.** Certain accident insurance policies will no longer be considered policies of life insurance for these purposes. See 45.13 LIFE ASSURANCE POLICIES.

SP 7/92 **Profit-related pay — use of pool determination formulae** will not normally meet the scheme registration requirements after 2 August 1992. Obsolete. See 75.34 SCHEDULE E—EMPLOYMENT INCOME.

SP 1/93 **Tax treatment of expenditure on films and certain similar assets.** Guidance on procedural points relating to relief for film production and preliminary expenditure. (Incorporates updated guidance from SP 2/83 and SP 2/85. See also SP 1/98 below.) Obsolete. See 71.48 SCHEDULE D, CASES I AND II.

SP 4/93 **Deceased persons' estates: discretionary interests in residue.** Payments out of income of the residue are treated as income of the recipient for the year of payment, whether out of income as it arises or out of income arising in earlier years. See 21.3 DECEASED ESTATES.

SP 5/93 **UK/Czechoslovakia double taxation Convention.** The Convention is regarded as applying to the Czech and Slovak Republics. See 24.2 DOUBLE TAX RELIEF.

SP 15/93 **Business tax computations rounded to nearest £1,000** will be accepted from certain large businesses. See 71.18 SCHEDULE D, CASES I AND II.

SP 1/94 **Non-statutory redundancy payments.** Revenue practice following the decision in *Mairs v Haughey* is explained. See 18.3 COMPENSATION FOR LOSS OF EMPLOYMENT.

SP 2/94 **Enterprise investment scheme and venture capital trust scheme — location of activity.** The requirement that trade(s) be carried on 'wholly or mainly in the UK' is clarified. Replaced by SP 7/98 below. See 25.6 ENTERPRISE INVESTMENT SCHEME, 91.3(*b*) VENTURE CAPITAL TRUSTS.

SP 3/94 **Business expansion scheme, enterprise investment scheme, capital gains tax reinvestment relief and venture capital trust scheme — loans to investors.** The requirements for denial of relief on loan-linked investments are explained. Replaced by SP 6/98 below. See 25.14 ENTERPRISE INVESTMENT SCHEME, 91.5 VENTURE CAPITAL TRUSTS.

SP 4/94 **Enhanced stock dividends received by trustees of interest in possession trusts.** The Revenue view on the tax treatment of such dividends is explained. See 85.6 STOCK DIVIDENDS.

SP 5/95 **Taxation of receipts of insurance and personal pension scheme commissions.** The Revenue view of the taxation consequences of a number of different arrangements is set out. (Superseded by SP 4/97 below.) See 71.54 SCHEDULE D, CASES I AND II.

SP 6/95 **Legal entitlement and administrative practice** in relation to repayments of tax is revised (superseding SP 1/80 above). See 56.9 PAYMENT OF TAX.

SP 7/95 **Venture capital trusts — value of gross assets.** The Revenue's general approach to the valuation of gross assets in determining whether a holding is a 'qualifying holding' is explained. (Replaced by SP 5/98 below.) See 91.3(*e*) VENTURE CAPITAL TRUSTS.

SP 8/95   **Venture capital trusts — default terms in loan agreements.** Certain event of default clauses will not disqualify a loan from being a security for the purposes of approval. See 91.2 VENTURE CAPITAL TRUSTS.

SP 1/96   **Notification of chargeability to income tax and capital gains tax for tax years 1995/96 onwards.** Employees are relieved in certain circumstances of the obligation to notify chargeability in respect of benefits etc. See 57.1 PENALTIES.

SP 2/96   **Pooled cars: incidental private use.** The Revenue interpretation of the requirement that private use of pooled vehicles be 'merely incidental' to business use is explained. See 75.18(vi) SCHEDULE E—EMPLOYMENT INCOME.

SP 3/96   **ITEPA 2003, ss 225, 226 — termination payments made in settlement of employment claims.** The circumstances in which a charge will not arise are clarified. See 75.37 SCHEDULE E—EMPLOYMENT INCOME.

SP 4/96   **Income tax — interest paid in the ordinary course of a bank's business.** The Revenue interpretation of this requirement is explained (revising SP 12/91 above). See 22.3 DEDUCTION OF TAX AT SOURCE.

SP 5/96   **PAYE settlement agreements.** The detailed operation of the scheme is explained. See generally 55.12 PAY AS YOU EARN.

SP 1/97   **The electronic lodgement service.** The Revenue operation and detailed requirements of the scheme are explained. See 68.14 RETURNS.

SP 4/97   **Taxation of commission, cashbacks and discounts.** The Revenue's views are outlined. See 71.36 SCHEDULE D, CASES I AND II.

SP 1/98   **Tax treatment of expenditure on films.** SP 1/93 (and the earlier SP 2/83 and SP 2/85) are revised and replaced. Withdrawn with effect from 15 April 2003 and replaced by Revenue guidance material. See 71.48 SCHEDULE D, CASES I AND II.

SP 2/98   **Business by telephone.** Details are given of the services available by telephone from tax offices. Superseded by SP 2/03 below. See 16.5 CLAIMS.

SP 5/98   **Venture capital trusts and the enterprise investment scheme — value of 'gross assets'.** The Revenue's general approach to the valuation of gross assets is explained. Replaces SP 7/95 above and superseded by SP 2/00 below. See 25.5 ENTERPRISE INVESTMENT SCHEME, 91.3(*e*) VENTURE CAPITAL TRUSTS.

SP 6/98   **Enterprise investment scheme, venture capital trusts, capital gains tax reinvestment relief and business expansion scheme — loans to investors.** The requirements for denial of relief on loan-linked investments are explained. Replaces SP 3/94 above. See 25.14 ENTERPRISE INVESTMENT SCHEME, 91.5 VENTURE CAPITAL TRUSTS.

SP 7/98   **Enterprise investment scheme, venture capital trusts and capital gains tax reinvestment relief — location of activity.** The requirement that trade(s) be carried on 'wholly or mainly in the UK' is clarified. Replaces SP 2/94 above and superseded by SP 3/00 below. See 25.6 ENTERPRISE INVESTMENT SCHEME, 91.3(*b*) VENTURE CAPITAL TRUSTS.

SP 8/98   **Business by telephone — East Kilbride call centre.** Details are given of the expanded services available by telephone from the call centre on an experimental basis. Superseded by SP 3/03 below. See 16.5 CLAIMS.

SP 1/99   **Self-assessment enquiries — TMA 1970, ss 9A, 12AC.** Where an enquiry remains open for agreement of a capital gains tax valuation, the Revenue will not take advantage of this fact to raise further enquiries which could otherwise not be made. See 68.7 RETURNS.

SP 3/99   **Advance pricing agreements (APAs).** The detailed administration of the scheme of APAs relating to transfer pricing issues is explained. See 3.8 ANTI-AVOIDANCE.

SP 2/00   **Venture capital trusts, the enterprise investment scheme, the corporate venturing scheme and enterprise management incentives — value of 'gross assets'.** The Revenue's general approach to the valuation of gross assets is explained. Replaces SP 5/98 above. See 25.5 ENTERPRISE INVESTMENT SCHEME, 82.38 SHARE-RELATED EMPLOYMENT INCOME AND EXEMPTIONS, 91.3(e) VENTURE CAPITAL TRUSTS.

SP 3/00   **Enterprise investment scheme, venture capital trusts, corporate venturing scheme, enterprise management incentives and capital gains tax reinvestment relief — location of activity.** The requirement that trade(s) be carried on 'wholly or mainly in the UK' is clarified. Replaces SP 7/98 above. See 25.6 ENTERPRISE INVESTMENT SCHEME, 82.39 SHARE-RELATED EMPLOYMENT INCOME AND EXEMPTIONS, 91.3(b) VENTURE CAPITAL TRUSTS.

SP 1/01   **Treatment of investment managers and their overseas clients.** Guidance is given on the application of the *FA 1995* rules. See 51.5 NON-RESIDENCE AND OTHER OVERSEAS MATTERS.

SP 4/01   **Double taxation relief — status of the UK's double taxation conventions with the former USSR and with newly independent states.** The current position is clarified. See 24.2 DOUBLE TAX RELIEF.

SP 2/02   **Exchange rate fluctuations.** The Revenue set out their practice in relation to the tax treatment of exchange rate fluctuations in the tax computations of non-corporate traders. Replaces SP 1/87. See 71.46 SCHEDULE D, CASES I AND II.

SP 3/02   **Financial futures and options.** The Revenue set out their views on the circumstances in which transactions in financial futures and options would be regarded as trading rather than taxed under the chargeable gains rules. Replaces SP 14/91. See 71.22 SCHEDULE D, CASES I AND II.

SP 2/03   **Business by telephone — non-Contact Centre taxpayers.** Details are given of the services available by telephone from tax offices not served by a Contact Centre. Replaces SP 2/98. See 16.5 CLAIMS.

SP 3/03   **Business by telephone — Contact Centre taxpayers.** Details are given of the services available by telephone from Revenue Contact Centres. Replaces SP 8/98. See 16.5 CLAIMS, 68.4 RETURNS .

41 Interest on Overpaid Tax

[*ICTA 1988, s 824; FA 1988, Sch 13 para 7; FA 1989, ss 110(5), 114(4), 158(2), 178, 179; FA 1994, ss 196, 199(2)(a), Sch 19 para 41; FA 1997, s 92; FA 1999, s 41; FA 2001, s 90; ITEPA 2003, Sch 6 para 104; SI 1978 No 1117; SI 1979 No 1687; SI 1982 No 1587; SI 1985 No 563; SI 1986 Nos 1181, 1832; SI 1987 Nos 513, 898, 1492, 1988; SI 1988 Nos 756, 1278, 1621, 2185; SI 1989 Nos 1000, 1297; SI 1993 No 753; SI 1996 No 3187; SI 1997 Nos 2707, 2708*]

Cross-reference. See also 55.8 PAY AS YOU EARN.

Simon's Direct Tax Service A3.1330.

41.1 1996/97 ONWARDS (SELF-ASSESSMENT)

Under self-assessment for 1996/97 and subsequent years (1997/98 and subsequent years as regards partnership businesses commenced before 6 April 1994), a repayment by the Revenue of income tax (including payments on account (see 78.4 SELF-ASSESSMENT) and tax credits (where previously payable)) paid by or on behalf of an individual, a partnership, a trust or the personal representatives of a deceased person carries interest at the rate(s) listed below. The amount by which the repayment is so increased is known as a **repayment supplement**. The interest runs from the 'relevant time' until the date on which the order for the repayment is issued by the Revenue. Repayment supplement is added in similar fashion to any repayment of a penalty imposed under any provision of *TMA 1970* (see 57 PENALTIES) or of a surcharge imposed under *TMA 1970, s 59C* (see 42.2 INTEREST AND SURCHARGES ON UNPAID TAX) and to any payment under *ICTA 1988, s 375(8)* equal to the amount a borrower was entitled to deduct from mortgage interest payments (see 22.13 DEDUCTION OF TAX AT SOURCE). Repayment supplement does not count as a person's income for any tax purpose. The '*relevant time*' is:

(*a*)   as regards interim payments (see 78.4 SELF-ASSESSMENT) and other payments of income tax not deducted at source, the date of the payment;

(*b*)   as regards tax repaid as a result of a claim affecting two or more years (see 16.2 CLAIMS), 31 January following the *later* year in relation to the claim, i.e. on a claim to carry back a loss or a payment, e.g. a pension contribution, the tax year in which the loss arises or the payment is made; on an averaging claim (for farmers or, for 2000/01 onwards, creative artists), the later of the two tax years to be averaged;

(*c*)   as regards income tax deducted at source, 31 January following the year of assessment for which tax is deducted;

(*d*)   as regards a penalty or surcharge, the date on which the penalty or surcharge was paid; and

(*e*)   as regards a payment under *ICTA 1988, s 375(8)*, 31 January next following the year of assessment in which the mortgage interest was paid *unless* the interest was paid before 6 April 1996, in which case it is 5 April next following that year.

(*b*) above applies by law to repayments made on or after 11 May 2001 but was also applied by the Revenue in practice to earlier repayments. Income tax is deducted at source for a year of assessment for the above purposes if it is so deducted (or treated as deducted) from any income, or treated as paid on any income, in respect of that year, or if it is a tax credit in respect of that year (but excluding tax deducted under PAYE (55) in respect of previous years). Repayments in respect of income tax for a year of assessment are attributed first to the final payment (see 78.6 SELF-ASSESSMENT) of income tax for that year, secondly in two equal parts to the interim payments for that year, and finally to income tax deducted at source for that year. Where a payment was made in instalments, any repayment is attributed to later instalments before earlier ones.

Rates of interest are:

> **2.5% p.a. from 6 December 2003**
> 1.75% p.a.from 6 August 2003 to 5 December 2003
> 2.5% p.a.from 6 November 2001 to 5 August 2003
> 3.5% p.a.from 6 May 2001 to 5 November 2001
> 4% p.a.from 6 February 2000 to 5 May 2001
> 3% p.a.from 6 March 1999 to 5 February 2000
> 4% p.a.from 6 January 1999 to 5 March 1999
> 4.75% p.a.from 6 August 1997 to 5 January 1999
> 4% p.a.from 31 January 1997 to 5 August 1997

It will be noted that rates are considerably lower than those by reference to which interest is charged on late paid tax (see 42.1 INTEREST AND SURCHARGES ON UNPAID TAX). The rates are adjusted automatically by reference to changes in the average of base lending rates of certain clearing banks, and are announced by Revenue Press Release. For details of the relationship to base rates, see *SI 1989 No 1297, reg 3AB* as inserted from 31 January 1997 by *SI 1996 No 3187.*

In contrast to the position prior to 1996/97 (see 41.2 below), there is no requirement that the taxpayer be resident in the UK or EC.

Repayments relating to claims under *ITA 1952, s 228* (income accumulated under trusts, see 81.12 SETTLEMENTS) are treated as repayments of tax paid for the year of assessment in which the contingency happened. The above provisions do not apply to repayments of post-war credits or amounts paid by order of a court having power to allow interest (for which see 56.4 PAYMENT OF TAX).

Although interest on tax paid otherwise than at source runs from the date the tax was paid, even if this falls before the due date, the Revenue state that they will not pay repayment supplement on any amount deliberately overpaid. (Revenue Press Release 12 November 1996). This is intended to deter taxpayers from using the Revenue as a source of tax-free interest. Where a payment of tax is not set against any liability and repayment is not claimed, the payment remains on record until the next liability arises, but no repayment supplement will be given. (Revenue Tax Bulletin June 1999 p 674). As regards the date on which payment is treated as made, see 56.2 PAYMENT OF TAX. Repayment supplement is not paid in respect of out of date claims, since the amount repaid is regarded as an *ex gratia* payment made without acceptance of any legal liability. (Revenue Claims Manual RM 5104).

Repayment supplement applies also to Class 4 national insurance contributions (see 83.8 SOCIAL SECURITY) and to tax paid by employers under PAYE (see 55.8 PAY AS YOU EARN).

41.2   1995/96 AND EARLIER YEARS

The provisions described below apply where the tax repayable relates to 1995/96 and earlier years (and to 1996/97 in the case of tax repayable to a partnership commenced before 6 April 1994).

A repayment (or set-off) to an individual by the Revenue of income tax (including tax credits and tax deducted under PAYE), surtax, capital gains tax or the special charge under *FA 1968, Pt IV*, repaid more than twelve months after the year of assessment to which it relates, carries tax-free interest ('a repayment supplement'), which will not be a person's income for any tax purpose, provided that the individual was resident in the UK for that year of assessment. A payment under *ICTA 1988, s 375(8)* equal to the amount a borrower was entitled to deduct from mortgage interest payments (see 22.13 DEDUCTION OF TAX AT SOURCE) is treated for this purpose as a repayment of tax for the year of assessment in which the interest was paid. Repayment supplement applies also to Class 4 national insurance contributions (see 83.8 SOCIAL SECURITY).

41.2 Interest on Overpaid Tax

The **rates of interest** are adjusted automatically by reference to changes in the average of base lending rates of certain clearing banks, and are announced in Revenue Press Releases. (Revenue Press Release 1 August 1989). The relationship to base rates was revised from 31 January 1997 (see *SI 1996 No 3187*). The rates are as follows.

2.5% p.a. from 6 December 2003 to
1.75% p.a.from 6 August 2003 to 5 December 2003
2.5% p.a.from 6 November 2001 to 5 August 2003
3.5% p.a.from 6 May 2001 to 5 November 2001
4% p.a.from 6 February 2000 to 5 May 2001
3% p.a.from 6 March 1999 to 5 February 2000
4% p.a.from 6 January 1999 to 5 March 1999
4.75% p.a.from 6 August 1997 to 5 January 1999
4% p.a.from 31 January 1997 to 5 August 1997
6.25% p.a.from 6 February 1996 to 30 January 1997
7% p.a.from 6 March 1995 to 5 February 1996
6.25% p.a.from 6 October 1994 to 5 March 1995
5.50% p.a.from 6 January 1994 to 5 October 1994
6.25% p.a.from 6 March 1993 to 5 January 1994
7% p.a.from 6 December 1992 to 5 March 1993
7.75% p.a.from 6 November 1992 to 5 December 1992
9.25% p.a.from 6 October 1991 to 5 November 1992
10% p.a.from 6 July 1991 to 5 October 1991
10.75% p.a.from 6 May 1991 to 5 July 1991
11.5% p.a.from 6 March 1991 to 5 May 1991
12.25% p.a.from 6 November 1990 to 5 March 1991
13% p.a.from 6 November 1989 to 5 November 1990
12.25% p.a.from 6 July 1989 to 5 November 1989
11.5% p.a.from 6 January 1989 to 5 July 1989
10.75% p.a.from 6 October 1988 to 5 January 1989
9.75% p.a.from 6 August 1988 to 5 October 1988
7.75% p.a.from 6 May 1988 to 5 August 1988
8.25% p.a.from 6 December 1987 to 5 May 1988
9% p.a.from 6 September 1987 to 5 December 1987
8.25% p.a.from 6 June 1987 to 5 September 1987
9% p.a.from 6 April 1987 to 5 June 1987
9.5% p.a.from 6 November 1986 to 5 April 1987
8.5% p.a.from 6 August 1986 to 5 November 1986
11% p.a.from 6 May 1985 to 5 August 1986
8% p.a.from 6 December 1982 to 5 May 1985

See earlier editions for rates of interest before 6 December 1982.

It is understood that a denominator of 365 is used in calculations of repayment interest regardless of whether or not a leap year is involved.

The interest will run to the end of the tax month (i.e. sixth day of one calendar month to fifth day of following month) in which the repayment order is issued and will commence as follows.

Tax originally paid	*Interest commences*
More than 12 months after year of assessment	From end of year of assessment in which tax was paid
In any other case	From end of 12 months following year of assessment

Where a repayment relates to tax paid in two or more years of assessment, it shall be treated, as far as possible, as representing later rather than earlier years.

Repayments relating to claims under *ITA 1952, s 228* (income accumulated under trusts, see 81.12 SETTLEMENTS) are treated as repayment of tax paid for the year of assessment in which the contingency happened.

Repayment supplement is not paid in respect of out of date claims, since the amount repaid is regarded as an *ex gratia* payment made without acceptance of any legal liability. (Revenue Claims Manual RM 5104).

Tax on employment etc. income deducted under PAYE will be attributed to the year of assessment in which deducted, and repayments will be attributed to particular years according to regulations made by the Board. See Revenue Pamphlet IR 131, A9 and *SI 1975 No 1283*.

The above provisions also apply to partnerships, trusts and deceased estates, but not to repayments of post-war credits or amounts paid by order of a court having power to allow interest (for which see 56.4 PAYMENT OF TAX). They are extended to repayments of excessive clawback of life assurance premium relief, and to relief by repayment for such premiums where relief is not obtained by deduction (see 45.5, 45.1 LIFE ASSURANCE POLICIES). (Revenue Pamphlet IR 1, A51).

In *R v CIR (ex p Commerzbank AG) QB 1991, 68 TC 252*, repayment supplement was held not to fall within the scope of double tax agreements, although on a reference to the European Court of Justice (see *68 TC 264*), the Court upheld the view that, in the case of companies resident in EC Member States, such discrimination against non-UK resident companies was prevented by the relevant Articles of the Treaty of Rome. For repayment supplement payable to non-UK EC resident companies following this decision, see Revenue Press Release 23 July 1993. By concession, repayment supplement is also added to tax repayments to non-UK EC resident individuals on the same basis as applies to UK resident individuals. The concession also applies to repayments of income tax to individuals since 12 July 1987, and equally to partnerships, trustees and personal representatives. Claims should be sent to IR International — Centre for Non-Residents, Fitz Roy House, PO Box 46, Nottingham NG2 1BD or Claims (International), St John's House, Merton Road, Bootle, Merseyside L69 9BB (to the latter address in the case of claims relating to repayments made by other offices). (Revenue Pamphlet IR 1, A82 as revised).

See also 55.8 PAY AS YOU EARN.

41.3   UNAUTHORISED DEMANDS FOR TAX

There is a general right to interest under *Supreme Court Act 1981, s 35A* in a case where a taxpayer submits to such an unauthorised demand, provided that the payment is not made voluntarily to close a transaction (*Woolwich Equitable Building Society v CIR HL 1992, 65 TC 265*). (*Note.* The substantive decision against the Revenue which gave rise to the repayment was subsequently upheld in the HL. See *R v CIR (ex p Woolwich Equitable Building Society) HL 1990, 63 TC 589*.)

41.4   REVENUE ERROR

The Revenue have published a Code of Practice (No 1, available from local tax offices) setting out the circumstances in which they will consider paying a repayment supplement on money owed to the taxpayer for any period during which there has been undue delay on the part of the Revenue. See 35.8 INLAND REVENUE: ADMINISTRATION.

41.5   OVER-REPAYMENTS

Where a repayment supplement has been overpaid it may be recovered by an assessment under Schedule D, Case VI. See 56.10 PAYMENT OF TAX.

42   Interest and Surcharges on Unpaid Tax

Cross-references. See also 55.8 PAY AS YOU EARN.

Simon's Direct Tax Service A3.1321, E1.823.

42.1   **INTEREST ON UNPAID TAX**

The provisions of *TMA 1970, s 86*, as amended for self-assessment and described below, apply in respect of income tax (and capital gains tax) for 1996/97 and subsequent years (1997/98 and subsequent years as regards partnership businesses commenced before 6 April 1994) **and also** for 1995/96 and earlier years where the tax is charged by an assessment first raised after 5 April 1998. [*FA 1995, s 110(2)*]. Tax paid more than 28 days after the due date is subject also to a surcharge, with an additional surcharge where payment is more than six months late (see 42.2 below).

Interest is charged by the Revenue on late payments of income tax, whether they be interim payments or a balancing payment (see 78.4, 78.6 SELF-ASSESSMENT), or tax payable under an assessment made by the Revenue or as a result of a Revenue amendment to a self-assessment following an enquiry (see 68.10 RETURNS), or tax becoming payable under *TMA 1970, s 55* (payment and postponement of tax pending appeal, see 56.3 PAYMENT OF TAX). Interest accrues from the 'relevant date' (even if a non-business day) to the date of payment. For the two interim payments under 78.4 SELF-ASSESSMENT, the '*relevant dates*' are the due dates, i.e. 31 January in the year of assessment and the following 31 July. In any other case, the '*relevant date*' is 31 January following the year of assessment (with the one statutory exception that where the due date of a final payment is deferred until three months after notice is given to deliver a return — see 78.6 SELF-ASSESSMENT — the relevant date is identically deferred). Where the due date for payment is *later* than the relevant date, either under the circumstances in 78.7 SELF-ASSESSMENT or because a successful application is made to postpone tax (see 56.3 PAYMENT OF TAX), this does *not* alter the relevant date for interest purposes.

There are provisions to remit interest charged on interim payments to the extent that an income tax repayment is found to be due for the year. There are also provisions covering the situation where a taxpayer makes a claim to dispense with or reduce his interim payments (see 78.4 SELF-ASSESSMENT) and the total income tax liability for the year is found to be such that interim payments should have been made or should have been greater. Interest is chargeable as if each interim payment due had been equal to half the current year's liability or half the previous year's liability, whichever is less.

[*TMA 1970, s 86; FA 1995, s 110; FA 1996, s 131, Sch 18 paras 3, 17(1)(2)*].

In practice, where a self-assessment return is submitted by 30 September for calculation by the Revenue of the tax due (see 78.3 SELF-ASSESSMENT), the relevant date is deferred until 30 days after notification of the liability to the taxpayer if this occurs later than 31 December following the tax year (Revenue Self-Assessment Manual — Interest, penalties and surcharge section). This is of no significance where returns are filed over the internet (see 68.2 RETURNS) as the tax due is automatically computed during the filing process. See also 42.5 below re executors.

As regards the date on which payment of tax is treated as made, see 56.2 PAYMENT OF TAX.

Rates of interest are:

6.5% p.a.from 6 December 2003
5.5% p.a.from 6 August 2003 to 5 December 2003
6.5% p.a.from 6 November 2001 to 5 August 2003
7.5% p.a.from 6 May 2001 to 5 November 2001
8.5% p.a.from 6 February 2000 to 5 May 2001
7.5% p.a.from 6 March 1999 to 5 February 2000
8.5% p.a.from 6 January 1999 to 5 March 1999
9.5% p.a.from 6 August 1997 to 5 January 1999
8.5% p.a.from 31 January 1997 to 5 August 1997
6.25% p.a.from 6 February 1996 to 30 January 1997
7% p.a.from 6 March 1995 to 5 February 1996
6.25% p.a.from 6 October 1994 to 5 March 1995
5.5% p.a.from 6 January 1994 to 5 October 1994
6.25% p.a.from 6 March 1993 to 5 January 1994
7% p.a.from 6 December 1992 to 5 March 1993
7.75% p.a.from 6 November 1992 to 5 December 1992
9.25% p.a.from 6 October 1991 to 5 November 1992
10% p.a.from 6 July 1991 to 5 October 1991
10.75% p.a.from 6 May 1991 to 5 July 1991
11.5% p.a.from 6 March 1991 to 5 May 1991
12.25% p.a.from 6 November 1990 to 5 March 1991
13% p.a.from 6 November 1989 to 5 November 1990
12.25% p.a.from 6 July 1989 to 5 November 1989
11.5% p.a.from 6 January 1989 to 5 July 1989
10.75% p.a.from 6 October 1988 to 5 January 1989
9.75% p.a.from 6 August 1988 to 5 October 1988
7.75% p.a.from 6 May 1988 to 5 August 1988
8.25% p.a.from 6 December 1987 to 5 May 1988
9% p.a.from 6 September 1987 to 5 December 1987
8.25% p.a.from 6 June 1987 to 5 September 1987
9% p.a.from 6 April 1987 to 5 June 1987
9.5% p.a.from 6 November 1986 to 5 April 1987
8.5% p.a.from 6 August 1986 to 5 November 1986
11% p.a.from 1 May 1985 to 5 August 1986

See earlier editions for rates of interest before 1 May 1985.

Interest charges are calculated automatically and, however small, will appear on taxpayer statements of account under self-assessment. There is no *de minimis* limit for charging interest. It will be noted that the above rates are greater than those by reference to which interest is paid by the Revenue (see 41.1 INTEREST ON OVERPAID TAX). The rates are adjusted automatically by reference to changes in the average of base lending rates of certain clearing banks, and are announced by Revenue Press Release. For the relationship to base rates, see *SI 1989 No 1297, reg 3* as substituted from 31 January 1997 by *SI 1996 No 3187*.

Interest is also chargeable on late payment of surcharges (see 42.2 below) and PENALTIES (57). [*TMA 1970, ss 59C(6), 103A; FA 1994, Sch 19 para 33; FA 1995, s 115(8); SI 1989 No 1297, reg 3; SI 1998 Nos 310, 311*].

Interest is payable gross and recoverable (as if it were tax) as a Crown debt; it is not deductible from profits or income [*TMA 1970, ss 69, 90; FA 1998, s 33; FA 2001, s 89(2)*] and is refundable to the extent that tax concerned is subsequently discharged (and any repayment may be treated as a discharge for this purpose). [*TMA 1970, s 91; FA 1996, Sch 18 para 4(2), para 17(3)(4)*].

42.2 Interest and Surcharges on Unpaid Tax

Tax becoming due where notice of appeal given. See 56.3, 56.4 PAYMENT OF TAX as regards determination of the due and payable date where an assessment etc. is under appeal.

For 1996/97 and subsequent years, and as regards assessments for 1995/96 and earlier years first raised after 5 April 1998, the giving of notice of appeal, whether or not accompanied by a postponement application, does *not* affect the date from which interest accrues.

Tax becoming due after determination of an appeal by the Courts. See 56.4 PAYMENT OF TAX as regards the due and payable date where further tax is found to be chargeable on determination by the Courts of an appeal against an assessment etc..

For 1996/97 and subsequent years, and as regards assessments for 1995/96 and earlier years first raised after 5 April 1998, those rules do *not* affect the date from which interest accrues.

Foot and mouth outbreak — relief from interest on unpaid tax. Where the Revenue have agreed that payment of any tax be deferred because of the foot and mouth outbreak in 2001, no interest is chargeable on the amount so deferred for the period from 31 January 2001 (or, if the Revenue so direct, any later date from which the deferral agreement has effect) to the date on which the deferral agreement ceases to have effect (subject to any agreed extension of the deferral period because of the continued outbreak). If the agreement is for payment by instalments, the deferral period in relation to each instalment ends on the date by which the instalment is to be paid. However, if an instalment is not paid by the agreed date (without Revenue agreement to a further deferral), the whole agreement ceases to have effect on that date. Provision is also made for a deferral agreement to be assumed to have been made, with the like consequences to an actual agreement, where it was not made but the Revenue are satisfied that it could have been made. The terms of such a notional agreement are assumed to be such as the Revenue are satisfied would have been agreed in the circumstances. This relief applies until ended by the Treasury order, such cessation not to affect its continued operation in relation to deferral agreements already in effect. A deferral agreement is effective whether made before or after the enactment of this provision or before or after the due date for the tax concerned. [*FA 2001, s 107*]. For the full range of measures relating to the foot and mouth outbreak, see Revenue Tax Bulletin Special Edition May 2001. In particular this indicates that surcharges will not be payable for an agreed period of deferral of payment of tax or NICs.

Transitional matters. Where a business which commenced before 6 April 1994 ceased trading in 1998/99, the inspector may direct that the 1996/97 assessment be revised to the actual profits arising in the tax year (see 71.14 SCHEDULE D, CASES I AND II). By concession, where an interest charge under *TMA 1970, s 86* would otherwise arise as a result of the adjustments required following such a direction, such interest will not normally be sought. The concession does not apply to interest arising for any other reason. (Revenue Pamphlet IR 1, A98).

General. Interest is also charged on Class 4 national insurance contributions (see 83.8 SOCIAL SECURITY) and on tax paid by employers under PAYE (see 55.8 PAY AS YOU EARN).

42.2 SURCHARGES ON UNPAID TAX

The provisions described below apply **for 1996/97 and subsequent years** and **also apply** in respect of assessments for 1995/96 and/or earlier years which are raised after 5 April 1998. [*FA 1995, s 109(2)*].

Where income tax (or capital gains tax) has become payable, whether under a self-assessment in accordance with *TMA 1970, s 59B* (see 78.6, 78.7 SELF-ASSESSMENT) or an assessment raised by the Revenue or as a result of a Revenue amendment to a self-assessment following an enquiry (see 68.10 RETURNS), and any of the tax remains unpaid more than 28 days after the due date (i.e. at any time after the end of the 28th day, see *Thompson v Minzly Ch D 2001, 74 TC 340*), the taxpayer is liable to a surcharge of 5% of the unpaid tax. An additional 5% surcharge is levied on any tax still unpaid more than six months after the due date. The due date is normally 31 January following the year of assessment, but see 78.6, 78.7 SELF-ASSESSMENT for exceptions (and note also the postponement rules at 56.3 PAYMENT OF TAX). As regards a pre-1996/97 assessment first raised after 5 April 1998, the due date is 30 days after the issue of the notice of assessment, though this is deferred to the extent that any tax is postponed on appeal (see 56.3 PAYMENT OF TAX).

For payments due on 31 January 2001, no surcharge applies where payment was made on 1 March 2001, and no further surcharge applies where payment was made on 1 August 2001. This is a temporary relaxation from the strict position (as above) that payments must not be outstanding *at any time* during those days. (Revenue Tax Bulletin February 2001 pp 826, 827, December 2001 p 904).

Interest (at the rate in 42.1 above) will accrue on an unpaid surcharge with effect from the expiry of 30 days beginning with the date of the notice imposing the surcharge. An appeal may be made, within that same 30-day period, against the imposition of a surcharge as if it were an assessment to tax. The Commissioners may, on appeal, set aside the surcharge if it appears to them that, *throughout* the period from the due date until payment, the taxpayer had a reasonable excuse for not paying the tax. Inability to pay the tax, i.e. due to insufficient funds, is not to be regarded as a reasonable excuse. For the Revenue's general approach to what constitutes a 'reasonable excuse' for late payment, see Revenue Tax Bulletin April 1998 pp 527–529. Common examples which the Revenue might regard as reasonable are where a cheque is lost in the post or by the Revenue (although evidence may be required to show that every effort was made to pay by the due date); where a cheque is dishonoured solely through bank error (and payment made immediately after the taxpayer learned of the bank's action); serious illness of the taxpayer or a close relative or domestic partner which began shortly before the due date; or the death of a close relative or domestic partner at or around the due date. Examples of excuses *not* considered reasonable by the Revenue are the fact that the return had not been submitted; pressure of work; failure by a tax agent; not knowing how much to pay; or the absence of a reminder that the tax is due. It is, however, stressed that these are the Revenue's views, and that it is for the Commissioners to adjudicate where the taxpayer takes a different view. A taxpayer's political beliefs do not amount to a 'reasonable excuse' (*Gladders v Prior (Sp C 361), [2003] SSCD 245*). Although, as stated above, the 'reasonable excuse' must strictly continue throughout the period of default in payment, in practice the Revenue normally allow a further 14 days for payment to be made after the excuse has ceased (for which see also Revenue booklet SA/BK7).

See also *Steeden v Carver (Sp C 212), [1999] SSCD 283*, in which reliance on the Revenue's advice as to the practical extension of a deadline, unequivocally given, was held to be 'as reasonable an excuse as could be found'.

There are provisions to prevent a double charge where tax has been taken into account in determining the tax-geared penalties of *TMA 1970, s 7* (see 57.1 PENALTIES), *s 93(5)* (tax-geared penalty for failure to make return for income tax and capital gains tax; see 57.2 PENALTIES), *s 95* (incorrect return etc. for income tax or capital gains tax; see 57.3 PENALTIES) and *s 95A* (incorrect return etc. for partnerships; see 57.3 PENALTIES). Any such tax will not be subject to a surcharge. The Board have discretion to mitigate, or to stay or compound proceedings for recovery of, a surcharge and may also, after judgment, entirely remit the surcharge.

[*TMA 1970, s 59C; FA 1994, ss 194, 199(2)(a); FA 1995, s 109*].

42.3   Interest and Surcharges on Unpaid Tax

No surcharge will be imposed where a taxpayer has entered into a 'Time to Pay' arrangement (see 56.5 PAYMENT OF TAX), provided that the payment proposals are received by the Revenue before the relevant surcharge date, they lead to an acceptable agreement to settle the full liability for the self-assessment year, and the terms of the arrangement are adhered to, such that it is not cancelled. (Revenue Self-Assessment Manual — Payments section).

See 42.1 above as regards special arrangements in relation to the 2001 foot-and-mouth outbreak.

See generally Revenue booklet SA/BK7.

42.3   EXCHANGE RESTRICTIONS

Where foreign income cannot be remitted to the UK due to government action in the country of origin, and tax thereon is held over by agreement with the Board, interest ceases to run from the date when the Board were first in possession of relevant facts — *no interest* if that date within three months after tax due. Interest recommences from the date of any subsequent demand, but this *latter* interest remitted if payment made within three months of demand. [*TMA 1970, s 92*]. See 51.13 NON-RESIDENTS AND OTHER OVERSEAS MATTERS.

42.4   REVENUE ERROR

The Revenue have published a Code of Practice (No 1, available from local tax offices) setting out the circumstances in which they will consider waiving a charge to interest on unpaid tax where there has been undue delay on the part of the Revenue. See 35.8 INLAND REVENUE: ADMINISTRATION.

42.5   EXECUTORS

Executors unable to pay tax before obtaining probate may have concessional treatment so that interest on tax falling due after the date of death runs from 30 days after the date on which probate or letters of administration are obtained. (Revenue Pamphlet IR 1, A17). It is understood that the concession is similarly applied to surcharges (see 42.2 above).

42.6   VALUE ADDED TAX, INSURANCE PREMIUM TAX, LANDFILL TAX, CLIMATE CHANGE LEVY AND AGGREGATES LEVY

Interest on overdue or under-declared VAT, insurance premium tax, landfill tax, climate change levy or aggregates levy is not allowed as a deduction for income or corporation tax purposes. [*ICTA 1988, s 827(1)(1B)(1C)(1D)(1E); FA 1994, Sch 7 para 31; FA 1996, Sch 5 para 40; FA 2000, Sch 7 para 4; FA 2001, s 49(3)*].

43   Interest Payable

Cross-references. See 3.15 ANTI-AVOIDANCE; 7 BANKS; 8 BUILDING SOCIETIES; 22 DEDUCTION OF TAX AT SOURCE; 27.5 EXCESS LIABILITY for interest on loans to pay insurance premiums; 32 FUNDING BONDS for interest paid by issue of bonds; 42 INTEREST AND SURCHARGES ON UNPAID TAX.

Simon's Direct Tax Service E1.530 *et seq.*

Note. See Tolley's Corporation Tax under Loan Relationships for the special provisions applicable for accounting periods ending after 31 March 1996 to all profits and losses in respect of company 'loan relationships'.

The headings in this chapter are as follows.

43.1   DEDUCTION OF TAX FROM INTEREST PAYMENTS

In general, tax is deductible from annual interest paid by companies but not by individuals (except on certain home mortgage loans etc.), but see details under 22.3(ii) and 22.13 DEDUCTION OF TAX AT SOURCE. See also 7.2 BANKS and 8.3 BUILDING SOCIETIES.

43.2   BUSINESS INTEREST PAYABLE

Interest incurred wholly and exclusively for business purposes is an allowable deduction from profits assessable under Schedule D, Case I or II (including interest on money borrowed for use as capital in the business, see *ICTA 1988, s 74(1)(f)*). [*ICTA 1988, s 74(1)(m), s 817(1)(b)*]. Interest incurred wholly and exclusively for the purposes of a Schedule A business is similarly an allowable deduction from the profits of that business (see 69.4 SCHEDULE A). [*ICTA 1988, s 21(3); FA 1995, s 39*]. For disallowance of interest where capital account overdrawn, see *Silk v Fletcher (Sp C 201), [1999] SSCD 220* and

43.2 Interest Payable

(No 2)(Sp C 262), [2000] SSCD 565 and see Revenue Business Income Manual BIM 45705–45730.

Exceptions are as follows.

(i) **Interest payable to non-residents** is deductible only if the interest

    (*a*) is paid under deduction of tax in accordance with *ICTA 1988, s 349*, see 22.3(ii) DEDUCTION OF TAX AT SOURCE (in which case the gross amount of the interest is deductible from profits, see *ICTA 1988, s 82(5)*), or

    (*b*) is contractually payable abroad (and is in fact so paid) by a UK resident sole trader or partnership either on a liability incurred for purposes of the foreign activities of the trade etc., or in a currency other than sterling (for securities issued before 6 April 1982, in the currency of a territory outside the scheduled territories). But deduction of interest in these circumstances is not permitted if the recipient is a partner in the trade, or both payer and recipient are under common control.

[*ICTA 1988, s 82; FA 1995, Sch 6 para 13; FA 1998, Sch 27 Pt III(4)*].

Before 2004/05, there was specific provision to the effect that interest paid to a non-resident in excess of a reasonable commercial rate was disallowable. This is repealed, but note the likely similar effect of the transfer pricing rules at 3.8 ANTI-AVOIDANCE and the thin capitalisation rules for companies (for which see Tolley's Corporation Tax). [*ICTA 1988, s 74(1)(n); FA 2004, Sch 42 Pt 2(2)*].

(ii) **Anti-avoidance.** Where interest is paid, no relief will be allowed if, at any time, a scheme has been effected or arrangements made such that the sole or main benefit expected to accrue was a reduction in tax liability by means of the relief. [*ICTA 1988, s 787; FA 2002, Sch 25 para 53*]. See also *Cairns v MacDiarmid CA 1982, 56 TC 556* and *Lancaster v CIR (Sp C 232), [2000] SSCD 138*.

(iii) **'Relevant loan interest'**, see 22.13 DEDUCTION OF TAX AT SOURCE.

The restrictions in 43.3 *et seq.* below do not apply to interest deductible in computing business profits, but if interest so deductible is also allowable within those restrictions, relief may instead be claimable under *ICTA 1988, s 353*. See 43.3 below as to this. Where interest wholly and exclusively for business purposes is dealt with under *section 353* but not wholly relieved because of insufficiency of income, the unrelieved interest can be treated as a trading loss. [*ICTA 1988, s 390*]. See 46.14(*b*) LOSSES.

Where part of a borrower's main residence is used exclusively for business purposes, then, by concession, a loan to buy the property may be treated as proportionately divided into two separate loans, mortgage interest relief (see 43.3 below) and relief for interest as a business (including a Schedule A business) deduction being available respectively. Where the exclusive business use occurs only sometimes (but for a significant amount of time), the concession still applies but with duration of use also taken into account in apportioning the loan. (Revenue Pamphlet IR 1, A89). See 22.13 DEDUCTION OF TAX AT SOURCE for the MIRAS (mortgage interest relief by deduction at source) position, and see Revenue Tax Bulletin August 1995 pp 229–232 for worked examples. Mortgage interest relief ceases, however, to be available after 5 April 2000.

See generally Revenue Business Income Manual BIM 45650–45776.

Schedule D, Case VI. Where profits are assessable under Schedule D, Case VI, it is understood that in practice interest incurred wholly and exclusively for the purposes of earning those profits (e.g. on money borrowed to purchase properties let furnished) is an allowable deduction.

43.3   **RELIEF FOR INTEREST PAID—GENERAL**

Subject to the provisions in this and the following paragraphs, relief for interest may be given *for income tax purposes* for the year of assessment in which paid. For interest paid by companies within the charge to corporation tax, see Tolley's Corporation Tax. For the exclusion of double relief where the interest ranks as business interest, see 43.25 below.

Subject to the restrictions in this paragraph and in 43.5 *et seq. below*, relief is given on interest paid. [*ICTA 1988, s 353(1); FA 1994, s 81(1)*]. The following should, however, be noted.

(i)   **Interest on loan for property bought by partner for partnership use.** The following applies where interest is paid by a partnership, and charged as an expense in its accounts, on a loan taken out by a partner to purchase land occupied rent-free by the partnership and used for business purposes. Relief as a trading expense for interest payable by the partnership on the individual's behalf should be available in the normal way. The individual's Schedule A computation would include the interest payments made by the partnership on his behalf, but these would be offset by a deduction for interest payable by the individual (which would be allowable regardless of the interest payments actually having been met by the partnership). The Schedule A profit would therefore generally be nil. (Revenue Tax Bulletin June 1997 pp 437, 438).

(ii)   **Interest on loan for property bought by controlling director for company use.** The following applies where interest is paid by a company, and charged as an expense in its accounts, on a loan taken out by a controlling director to purchase land occupied rent-free by the company and used for business purposes. Relief as a trading expense for interest payable by the company on the director's behalf should be available in the normal way, and the payments would not normally constitute either emoluments or a benefit of the director. The director's Schedule A computation would include the interest payments made by the company on his behalf, but these would be offset by a deduction for interest payable by the director (which would be allowable regardless of the interest payments actually having been met by the company). The Schedule A profit would therefore generally be nil. (Revenue Tax Bulletin June 1997 pp 437, 438).

(iii)   **Hire purchase charges** (the excess of the hire purchase payments over the cash price) are not interest and therefore not within this relief. (Some hire purchase agreements may specify that the whole balance of the rental after the initial payment is payable within seven days but will leave the hirer the option of paying that balance over a defined period on interest terms. At the date the option is exercised a loan is created and the interest on that loan is true interest under *section 353* and will qualify for relief if other relevant conditions are satisfied, e.g. on a residential caravan.)

No relief is given to the extent that the interest exceeds a reasonable commercial rate. [*ICTA 1988, s 353(3)(b)*].

Where interest is business interest (see 43.2 above), see 43.25 below for the exclusion of double relief, 43.2 above where property used for both residential and business purposes and 46.14 LOSSES for the treatment of unrelieved interest as a trading loss.

No relief is given if the interest is within the anti-avoidance provisions of *ICTA 1988, s 787*, see 43.2(ii) above.

See 53.9, 53.17, 53.18 PARTNERSHIPS for restrictions on interest relief available to certain partners.

Note. Where interest is 'relevant loan interest' (see 22.13 DEDUCTION OF TAX AT SOURCE) the provisions under *section 353* (above) do not apply. [*ICTA 1988, s 353(2)*].

43.3 Interest Payable

Rate of relief and method of giving relief. Interest on certain types of loan is relieved by way of a deduction in computing total income, and thus attracts relief at marginal rates. The categories of loan in question are those for the purpose of

(A)   purchasing property let at a commercial rent (not generally applicable after 1994/95 — see 43.15 below), the deduction being available only against letting income,

(B)   purchasing plant or machinery (see 43.18 below),

(C)   purchasing an interest in, or, where appropriate, making a loan or advance to, a close company, co-operative, an employee-controlled company or a partnership (see 43.19 to 43.22 below), or

(D)   paying inheritance tax (see 43.23 below).

However, interest on the categories of loan within (I)–(III) below is relieved by way of a reduction in income tax liability and does not reduce total income. Interest within (I) or (II) below attracts relief at 10% for 1998/99 and 1999/2000, relief being **abolished thereafter** (the applicable rate being determined by reference to the year of actual payment, regardless of when payment was due). The abolition of relief also applies to payments made before 6 April 2000 (but after 8 March 1999) either under a scheme or arrangement etc. made after 8 March 1999 for a tax-avoidance purpose or of interest not due until after 5 April 2000. For when a scheme etc. is made for a tax-avoidance purpose, see *FA 1999, s 38(5)(6)*. Interest within (III) below continues to attract relief at the basic rate of tax in force for the year of payment up to 1999/2000, relief being fixed at **23%** thereafter. The loans in question are those for the purchase of

(I)   the borrower's only or main residence (see 43.6 to 43.12, and also 43.17, below),

(II)   a residence intended to become the borrower's only or main residence, where the borrower lives in job-related accommodation (see 43.16 below), or

(III)   a life annuity, where the loan is secured on land (see 43.24 below).

The reduction in liability is the smaller of the applicable percentage (as above) of the amount of interest eligible for relief and what would otherwise be the borrower's total income tax liability. For this purpose, 'total income tax liability' is as defined in 1.15 ALLOWANCES AND TAX RATES, except that it is before any reductions on account of personal reliefs and maintenance payments (where such items are also relieved by way of reduction in income tax liability — see 1.15–1.17 ALLOWANCES AND TAX RATES and 47.8 MARRIED PERSONS).

Where, for any tax year, an amount of interest is eligible for relief partly as a deduction and partly as a reduction in liability (for example, because the loan is a mixed loan or there is a change in the use of a property), it is apportioned by reference to the proportions of the amount borrowed (not the amount still outstanding) applied for different purposes and, where relevant, the different uses to which property is put from time to time.

Where particular interest payments would be eligible for relief both under (A) above and under (I) or (II) above, they will be treated as eligible under (A) above (so that relief is given by deduction) unless the borrower elects to the contrary. Such an election must take effect from the commencement of dual eligibility or from the beginning of a later tax year, remains in force until withdrawn with effect from the beginning of a tax year, and applies to all such interest payments made while it has effect. An election or withdrawal must be made by written notice, specifying the effective date, before the end of the tax year following that in which the effective date falls. See Revenue Tax Bulletin December 1994 p 173 for general commentary on the election. The provisions dealing with such dual eligibility are not relevant, and are repealed, following the repeal of the provisions at 43.15 below (interest on loans to purchase let property). Up to 1999/2000, a borrower who is eligible for mortgage interest relief in respect of a let property may choose each year whether to claim such relief (restricted to the applicable percentage on a maximum of £30,000) or to deduct the interest in computing the profits of the Schedule A business. As regards inclusion of the loan within MIRAS (mortgage interest relief by deduction at source), see 22.13 DEDUCTION OF TAX AT SOURCE.

[*ICTA 1988, s 353(1A)–(1H); FA 1994, s 81(2); FA 1995, s 42(2), Sch 29 Pt VIII(2); F(No 2)A 1997, s 15(1)(3); FA 1999, s 38, Sch 4 para 1; FA 2000, s 83(2)(4)*].

43.4   *Example*

Scott is a married man with the following details for 1999/2000: Schedule D, Case II £16,585, bank deposit interest (net) £640, dividend income (net) £900, investment made under enterprise investment scheme (EIS) £500, interest paid gross on a £40,000 endowment mortgage taken out some years ago for purchase of main residence £3,000, payment under charitable deed of covenant (net) £77. Scott's wife has no income. Scott's tax liability for 1999/2000 is computed as follows.

	£
Schedule D, Case II	16,585
Bank deposit interest (gross)	800
Dividends plus tax credits	1,000
	18,385
Deduct Charges (covenanted donation) (gross)	100
Total income	18,285
Deduct Personal allowance	4,335
Taxable income	£13,950

Tax payable;		
1,500	@ 10% (starting rate)	150.00
10,650	@ 23%	2,449.50
800	@ 20%	160.00
1,000	@ 10% (Schedule F ordinary rate)	100.00
13,950		2,859.50

Deduct EIS relief £500 @ 20%	100.00
	2,759.50

Deduct Mortgage interest relief:

$$£3,000 \times \frac{30,000}{40,000} = 2,250 \text{ @ } 10\% \qquad 225.00$$

	2,534.50
Deduct Married couple's allowance:	
£1,970 @ 10%	197.00
	2,337.50
Add Basic rate tax retained on covenanted donation	23.00
Total tax liability	2,360.50
Deduct Tax suffered at source on bank deposit interest	(160.00)
Tax credits on dividends	(100.00)
Net tax liability	£2,100.50

RELIEF FOR INTEREST PAID — RESTRICTED CATEGORIES OF LOAN — GENERAL PROVISIONS

Tax relief for interest paid on private borrowings will only be granted if the loan falls within any of the categories below (and even then will not be given on overdrafts, credit card or similar arrangements). [*ICTA 1988, s 353(1)(3)(a)*].

Relief is not granted unless the loan proceeds are so applied within a reasonable time, nor if the loan proceeds are used for some other purpose first. The giving of credit can be treated as a loan. Proportionate relief is granted where part only of a debt fulfils the required conditions. [*ICTA 1988, s 367(2)–(4)*].

Relief is available on similar terms on loans replacing either prior eligible loans under 43.6, 43.15 or 43.16 below, or loans which would have been eligible but for their inclusion in the MIRAS deduction scheme (see 22.13 DEDUCTION OF TAX AT SOURCE), subject to the abolition of such reliefs after 5 April 2000. [*ICTA 1988, s 354(1)(c); FA 1999, Sch 4 para 2*]. See *Lawson v Brooks Ch D 1991, 64 TC 462* for denial of relief for loan replacing overdraft relating to expenditure otherwise eligible for relief.

For loans to persons other than building societies or local authorities, claims to relief must be supported by a statement by the lender of the date and amount of the debt, the name and address of the debtor and the interest paid in the year of assessment. [*ICTA 1988, s 366*]. See generally Revenue Tax Bulletin April 1995 p 210.

Higher rate relief. Interest payments on a loan for the purchase of

(*a*)   the borrower's only or main residence (see 43.6 *et seq.* below), or

(*b*)   a residence intended to become the borrower's only or main residence, where the borrower lives in job-related accommodation (see 43.16 below), or

(*c*)   a life annuity, where the loan is secured on land (see 43.24 below),

for which relief is available do not attract relief from income tax at the higher rate(s). See 22.13 DEDUCTION OF TAX AT SOURCE for the application of this restriction in relation to loans within the MIRAS scheme. See 43.7 below for relief for certain bridging loans. [*ICTA 1988, s 353(4)(5); FA 1991, s 27(1); F(No 2)A 1992, s 19(3); FA 1993, Sch 6 para 1; FA 1994, Sch 9 para 3*].

See 43.3 above for further reductions, applying up to 1999/2000, in the rate of tax relief for interest within (*a*) and (*b*) above, and for the abolition of such relief from 6 April 2000.

43.6   **LOANS FOR PURCHASING PROPERTY AS ONLY OR MAIN RESIDENCE**

Relief is given for interest paid **before** (generally) **6 April 2000** (see 43.3 above) on a loan for the purchase of land by a person owning an estate or interest in the property, where the property is at the time the interest is paid used as the **only or main residence of the borrower.** Where that condition is not satisfied, relief is granted if the interest is paid less than twelve months after the loan and the property is so used within that twelve months. The Inland Revenue have power to extend such periods if it appears reasonable for them to do so. [*ICTA 1988, s 354(1)(a), s 355(1)(a)(2)(3); FA 1999, Sch 4 para 2*]. For what is the main residence, see *Frost v Feltham Ch D 1980, 55 TC 10*. See generally Simon's Direct Tax Service E1.535 *et seq.*

See 43.5 above for denial of higher rate relief (but see 43.7 below as regards certain bridging loans). See 43.3 above for the restriction of tax relief to 10% for 1998/99 and 1999/2000, and for the method of giving such relief.

Concessionally, temporary absences of up to one year are left out of account in determining whether a property is used as the owner's only or main residence for purposes of allowing mortgage interest relief. Up to four years are allowed if a person's employment requires him to move from a property occupied before his departure as his only or main residence for a period not expected to exceed four years and there is reasonable expectation of his return to the property. Where an individual has moved his home abroad by reason of his employment as a Crown servant (within *ICTA 1988, s 132(4)(a)*, see 75.4 SCHEDULE E—EMPLOYMENT INCOME), the concession applies without the four year time limit. The concession will also apply if a person acquires an interest in property, (e.g. by exchange of contracts) but is prevented from occupying it as his home by his move, or if a property is purchased and occupied for at least three months during a period of leave from an overseas tour of duty. The four year period will re-apply if the property is reoccupied for at least three months. If the property is let during the owner's absence, the benefit of the concession may be claimed, where appropriate, if this is more favourable than claiming a deduction in computing the Schedule A business profits (or, before 6 April 1995, relief against the lettings income) (see 43.15 below). (Revenue Pamphlet IR 1, A27).

Interest on an overdraft on the security of the deed of a residence is not allowable (*Walcot-Bather v Golding Ch D 1979, 52 TC 649*).

Additional interest charges. 'Penalty' interest charged on the early redemption of a loan within MIRAS does not qualify for relief (although this does not apply to interest charged for the whole of the month in which redemption occurs). Similarly a penalty charged for changing the terms of a loan, including a penalty for changing from a fixed to a variable rate, does not qualify for relief. However, a replacement loan need not be regarded as mixed purpose merely because, in part, it replaces such a charge. (MIRAS 30 (1995), para 10.46).

Administration fees. An allowance in respect of such fees reasonably incurred in arranging or servicing a qualifying loan will be regarded as qualifying expenditure up to £300 in respect of the first year of a loan, and up to £150 p.a. thereafter. (MIRAS 30 (1995) para 10.23).

Deceased persons. Interest paid by personal representatives of a deceased person, or by trustees of a settlement made by his will, is eligible for relief if the deceased used the property as his only or main residence at his death (or he resided in job-related living accommodation and the property was used by him as a residence or where he intended to use it in due course as his only or main residence) and, at the time the interest is paid, the property is used as the only or main residence of the widow or widower or, for interest paid before 6 April 1988, a dependent relative (or the widow or widower resides in job-related living accommodation and the property is used by such a relative or is intended to be used as the only or main residence). Interest paid after 5 April 1988 at a time when the property is used as the only or main residence of a dependent relative qualifies for relief only if the deceased died before 6 April 1988 *and* the property was so used by the dependent relative before that date. [*ICTA 1988, s 358; FA 1988, s 44(4); FA 1999, Sch 4 para 2*]. Interest paid by a person who has inherited property subject to a mortgage is allowable only if it was allowable when paid by the person from whom he inherited. See Revenue Pamphlet IR 131, A34.

House exchanges. Where houses are exchanged, so long as any loan on the old property is redeemed and a new loan on the new property taken out, the new loan (including any further loan to meet the difference in value) qualifies for relief in the normal way. (MIRAS 30 (1995) para 10.25).

Simon's Direct Tax Service. See E1.535A.

43.7   **Temporary relief following cessation of residence.** Relief under 43.6 above generally requires that, at the time the interest is paid, the land etc. is used as the only or main residence of the payer. Where the land etc. ceases at any time to be used as the only or main residence, and the borrower's intention at that time is to take steps within the following twelve months with a view to its disposal, that condition will be treated as satisfied until the end of those twelve months or, if earlier, until the borrower abandons his intention to dispose of the land etc. The Board may direct that the period of twelve months be extended in any particular case if it appears reasonable to do so.

Relief for interest on another loan used by the borrower for the purchase of a new property is eligible for relief to the extent it would be if no interest were payable on the loan on the former residence (in particular in relation to the qualifying limit, see 43.10 below).

[ICTA 1988, s 355(1A)(1B); FA 1993, s 57; FA 1994, Sch 9 para 12; FA 1999, Sch 4 para 2].

See also 75.20 SCHEDULE E—EMPLOYMENT INCOME for bridging loans from employers and reimbursement of interest paid.

43.8   **Home improvement loans.** Interest paid on 'home improvement loans' is also eligible for relief until 5 April 2000, subject to the general requirements described above and below, if paid on a loan made before 6 April 1988. A loan made after 5 April 1988 is deemed to have been made before 6 April 1988 if it is proved by written evidence that it is made in pursuance of an offer made by the lender before that date, such offer being either in writing or evidenced by a note or memorandum made by the lender before that date. A '*home improvement loan*' means a loan to defray money applied in improving or developing land or buildings on land, otherwise than by the erection of a new building (which is not part of an existing residence) on land which immediately before the improvement or development began had no building on it. The definition is extended to include a loan replacing, directly or indirectly, such a loan (so that a replacement loan taken after 5 April 1988 does not attract relief). *[ICTA 1988, s 354(1)(b), s 355(1)(a)(2A)–(2C); FA 1988, s 43(1); FA 1999, Sch 4 para 2].* Where interest on such a loan continues to qualify for relief up to 1999/2000, it does so at the reduced rate applicable for loans used to purchase the borrower's only or main residence, relief being given by way of reduction in tax liability (see 43.3 above).

43.9   **Dependent relatives, former or separated spouses.** Interest paid on loans made before 6 April 1988 (subject to the further condition below) is also eligible for relief until 5 April 2000 where the property is, at the time the interest is paid (or within a twelve month, or longer, period as described above), used as the only or main residence of

(i)   a dependent relative (incapacitated by old age or infirmity from maintaining himself, or the widowed, separated or divorced mother) of the borrower or his spouse, the residence being provided rent-free and without other consideration, or

(ii)   a separated (under Court Order, deed of separation or in circumstances likely to be permanent) or former spouse.

The further condition is that interest paid on the loan at a 'relevant time' was eligible for relief *only* because the property concerned was used as the only or main residence of *the same* dependent relative or former or separated spouse. '*Relevant time*' means either the last time when interest was paid on the loan before 6 April 1988 or, if no such interest was paid before that date, any time within twelve months (or such longer period as the Board may allow in the circumstances of a particular case) after the date on which the loan was made, except that the latter time does not apply if, at any time after the loan was made and before the property comes to be used as the only or main residence of the dependent relative etc., the property is used for any other purpose. A loan made after 5 April 1988 is deemed to have been made before 6 April 1988 in certain circumstances, these being identical to those described above for home improvement loans. *[ICTA 1988, s 355(1)(a); FA 1988, s 44(1)–(3)(5); FA 1999, Sch 4 para 2*]. Where interest on such a loan continues to qualify for relief up to 1999/2000, it does so at the reduced rate applicable for loans used to purchase the borrower's only or main residence, relief being given by way of reduction in tax liability (see 43.3 above).

43.10 **Limit on amount of loan eligible for relief.** For payments made after 31 July 1988 of '*qualifying interest*' (i.e. interest eligible for relief under 43.6–43.9 above or 43.16 below), the 'qualifying maximum' amount of loan on which interest may attract relief (currently £30,000) generally applies per residence (the '*residence basis*') rather than (as previously) per person. [*ICTA 1988, ss 356C(1), 356D(1), 367(5); FA 1988, s 41; FA 1989, s 46; FA 1990, s 71; FA 1991, s 26; FA 1992, s 10(4); FA 1993, s 55; FA 1994, s 80, Sch 9 para 7; FA 1996, s 76; FA 1997, s 57; F(No 2)A 1997, s 16; FA 1999, s 37, Sch 4 para 2*]. The residence basis does not, however, apply to a payment of qualifying interest if

(*a*)   the payment is under a loan made before 1 August 1988,

(*b*)   qualifying interest was payable in relation to the residence for 1 August 1988 by someone other than the person making the payment or his spouse,

(*c*)   qualifying interest is payable in respect of the residence throughout the period from 1 August 1988 to the date of payment by the person making the payment or by his spouse, and

(*d*)   someone other than the person making the payment or his spouse owns an estate, interest or property in the residence throughout the period in (*c*) above, and, at any time during that period, at least one such person is a person by whom qualifying interest is payable in respect of the residence at some time within the period.

A loan made after 31 July 1988 is treated as if made before 1 August 1988 if it is proved by written evidence both that it was made in pursuance of an offer made before that date and either made in writing or evidenced by a note or memorandum made by the lender before that date, and that it was used to defray money applied in pursuance of a binding contract entered into before that date. In relation to such loans, for the purpose of (*b*)–(*d*) above, the date on which interest first becomes payable (or the latest of such days where more than one loan is involved) is substituted for 1 August 1988. Where these exceptions to the residence basis apply to payments of qualifying interest under one loan, they also apply to such payments made under other loans if made by the same person or by his spouse in respect of the same residence in the same 'period'. The qualifying maximum in respect of a loan excepted as above is restricted to the lesser of £30,000 and the amount on which interest was payable immediately before 1 August 1988 or, if later, the first day for which interest is payable. Payments of interest which is qualifying interest due only to the residence in question being the only or main residence of a dependent relative or former or separated spouse of the person making the payment (but see 43.9 above for the restricted circumstances in which such interest is eligible for relief) are also excepted from the residence basis. Where payments of qualifying interest would otherwise be excepted from the residence basis, the persons liable to pay such interest may jointly elect that the residence basis should apply to all qualifying interest paid by any person in relation to the residence, such election being irrevocable. The election had to be made within twelve months after 31 January following the year of assessment in which fell the first 'period' for which it was made.

References above to a spouse do not include, except where stated, a separated spouse.

[*ICTA 1988, ss 356C, 357(1A)–(1C); FA 1988, s 42(1)(2); FA 1996, s 135, Sch 21 para 9; FA 1999, Sch 4 para 2*].

Where the residence basis does apply to a payment of qualifying interest, and all the interest payable for any 'period' in relation to a 'residence' is payable by one person, relief is

43.11   Interest Payable

available in full to the extent that the amount on which it is payable does not exceed the qualifying maximum. Where the interest payable for any 'period' in relation to a 'residence' is payable by more than one person, relief is available to each payer only to the extent that the amount on which the interest is payable by him does not exceed the 'sharer's limit' for the 'period' in his case. Prior loans on which interest is similarly eligible for relief operate to reduce the relief available in any event, and joint loans are for these purposes divided equally between the parties to the loan in determining the amount on which each pays interest. *[ICTA 1988, s 356A(1)(2), s 356D(6)–(8); FA 1999, Sch 4 para 2].*

'*Residence*' for these purposes means a building or part thereof occupied or intended to be occupied as a separate residence, or a caravan or house-boat. A building or part of a building designed for permanent use as a single residence is treated as a single residence even if it is temporarily divided into two or more parts which are, or are to be, occupied as separate residences.

A '*period*', in relation to any person, begins with any of the following:

(i)   a day which is the first day for which qualifying interest is payable by any person in respect of the residence in question (notwithstanding that such interest may previously have been payable in respect of the residence);

(ii)   a day immediately following a day on which any other person ceased to be liable for qualifying interest (notwithstanding that such interest continues to be payable in respect of the residence);

(iii)   the beginning of a year of assessment,

and ends with the day immediately preceding the next day within (i)–(iii) above or, if sooner, with the last day for which the person concerned is liable to pay qualifying interest.

[ICTA 1988, s 356D(2)(3); FA 1988, s 42(1); FA 1999, Sch 4 para 2].

The '*sharer's limit*' for any period is the amount arrived at by dividing the qualifying maximum for the year of assessment in which the period falls by the number of persons liable to pay qualifying interest for the period in respect of the residence. (Interest treated as falling within 43.15 below by virtue of the dual eligibility provisions in 43.3 above was treated as qualifying interest for the purpose of determining the number of persons so liable.) If, however, any person's limit then exceeds the amount on which he actually pays interest and another person's limit falls short of the amount on which he pays interest, the limits are adjusted accordingly, any excess being eliminated and any shortfall thereby reduced. Where two or more persons have shortfalls, the total excess is apportioned between them on a pro rata basis. *[ICTA 1988, s 356A(2)–(8), s 356D(4); FA 1988, s 42(1); FA 1994, Sch 9 para 6; FA 1995, Sch 29 Pt VIII(2); FA 1999, Sch 4 para 2].* See 43.12 below for special provisions relating to married couples.

In determining whether the amount on which interest is payable exceeds the qualifying maximum or any sharer's limit, no account is taken of any interest which has been added to the capital and which does not exceed £1,000. *[ICTA 1988, s 356D(10), s 357(6); FA 1988, s 42(1); FA 1999, Sch 4 para 2].*

43.11   *Examples*

On 1 April 1999, Mr Romeo and Miss Juliet took out a joint mortgage for £65,000 for the purchase of a London flat to be used as their main residence. Gross interest paid in 1999/2000 amounts to £4,850.

Interest relief for 1999/2000

Mr Romeo

Amount on which interest is payable	£32,500
Sharer's limit — £30,000 (qualifying maximum) ÷ 2 =	£15,000
Interest paid	£2,425

Relief restricted to $£2,425 \times \dfrac{15,000}{32,500} =$ £1,119

Miss Juliet
Identical calculation—relief restricted to   £1,119

Adjustment of sharer's limits

Three friends, A, B and C, decide to pool their resources and buy a house to be shared as their main residence. Each contributes his own savings and obtains a mortgage to fund the balance of his one-third share of the purchase price. The mortgages are all taken out in May 1999 and the amounts thereof, and interest paid thereon for 1999/2000, are as follows.

	Mortgage £	Interest payable (gross) £
A	7,000	560
B	14,000	1,120
C	16,000	1,280

Each has a sharer's limit of £10,000 (£30,000 ÷ 3). As A's limit exceeds the amount on which he pays interest, the excess is divided between B and C, each of whose limits falls short of the amount on which he pays interest. B and C have shortfalls of £4,000 and £6,000 respectively, a total shortfall of £10,000, so A's excess of £3,000 is divided between them as follows.

B— $\frac{4}{10} \times £3,000 = £1,200$ (revised sharer's limit £11,200)

C— $\frac{6}{10} \times £3,000 = £1,800$ (revised sharer's limit £11,800)

A's sharer's limit is reduced to £7,000.

Interest relief for 1999/2000 is then calculated as follows.

A— $\dfrac{7,000}{7,000} \times £560 = £560$

B— $\dfrac{11,200}{14,000} \times £1,120 = £896$

C— $\dfrac{11,800}{16,000} \times £1,280 = £944$

43.12   **Married couples.** Special provisions apply in relation to married couples who are not separated under Court Order or deed of separation or in circumstances such that the separation is likely to be permanent.

Application of qualifying maximum. A husband and wife who were not separated could jointly elect that, for the year in question (or for a period within that year), qualifying interest payable by either or both of them be allocated between them in whatever proportions they chose, and that either of their sharer's limits (see 43.10 above) be increased by any amount specified (with a corresponding reduction in the other's limit). The election had to be made in prescribed form (i.e. form 15 (1990)) within twelve months after 31 January following the first year of assessment for which it was to apply, and, once made, continued to have effect for subsequent years until withdrawn. A notice of withdrawal could be given by either husband or wife in prescribed form (i.e. form 15–1 (1990)) within twelve months after 31 January following the first year of assessment for which it was to apply, and had effect for subsequent years (without prejudice to the right to make a fresh election).

Where a married couple who are not separated have two residences, so that the husband pays interest on one, being his main or intended main residence, and the wife similarly pays interest on the other, the residence that was purchased first is to be regarded as the couple's only or main residence, the other residence being treated as the only or main residence of neither of them.

[*ICTA 1988, ss 356B, 367(1); FA 1988, s 42(1), Sch 3 para 14; FA 1995, s 42(2); FA 1996, s 135, Sch 21 para 8; FA 1999, Sch 4 para 2*].

See generally Revenue Pamphlet IR 86.

Where two people, each buying a main residence before marriage with the aid of a loan, buy a joint residence and sell their existing properties, the bridging loan provisions (see 43.7 above) will be regarded as applying to all three properties, whether or not the relevant property continues to be used as the owner's only or main residence (Revenue Pamphlet IR 131, SP 10/80, 24 September 1980).

See also 43.7 above as regards more general relief from 16 March 1993.

43.13   **Substitution of security.** Interest relief as under 43.6 above is extended in certain cases where a person purchases an estate or interest in land etc. (the '*new estate*') after 15 March 1993, and a 'security substitution arrangement' takes effect after that date in connection with the purchase.

A '*security substitution arrangement*' is an arrangement under which:

(*a*)   the new estate becomes security for an existing loan or loans, and another estate etc. ceases to be security for the loan(s);

(*b*)   the other estate etc. was not absorbed into, or given up to obtain, the new estate;

(*c*)   immediately before the arrangement took effect, interest on the loan(s) was eligible for relief under 43.6 above or 43.16 below (job–related accommodation); and

(*d*)   had the loan(s) been applied in purchasing the new estate, interest would have been so eligible for relief.

Where there is more than one loan and one or more of them would not satisfy (*c*) above, these provisions are applied only in relation to such of the loans as do fall within (*c*) above.

Where the above conditions are met, then as regards interest paid on the loan after the time the new estate became security for the loan, the loan is treated for the purposes of 43.6 above as if:

(i)   it had been made at that time; and

(ii)   the amount then outstanding (insofar as it did not exceed the 'relevant amount') had been used at that time to purchase the new estate,

and similarly where two or more loans are the subject of such arrangements.

The '*relevant amount*' is generally an amount equal to the purchase price of the new estate. The definition varies, however, where there is a loan (referred to below for convenience as an 'additional loan') eligible for relief under 43.6 above or 43.16 below, and actually used to any extent to purchase the new estate at or before the time the security substitution took place, or treated under an earlier security substitution arrangement as if before that time it had been so used. In those circumstances, the '*relevant amount*' is the difference between the purchase price of the new estate and the amount of the additional loan(s).

These provisions do not apply where the amount of any additional loan(s) (as above) equals the purchase price of the new estate. Where an additional loan is or was only partly used (or treated as used) in purchasing the new estate, it is only taken into account for the above purposes to the extent that it is or was or was treated as so used.

The exclusion from relief under 43.6 above of interest within the MIRAS scheme (see 22.13 DEDUCTION OF TAX AT SOURCE) does not affect the determination of eligibility for the purposes of these provisions.

[*ICTA 1988, ss 357A, 357C(1)–(3); FA 1993, s 56; FA 1994, Sch 9 para 7; FA 1995, s 42(2); FA 1999, Sch 4 para 2*].

Treatment of loans following security substitution. Where, after the above provision has applied to treat a loan as having been used to defray the purchase cost of a new estate, a new loan is actually used to any extent for that purpose and would otherwise be eligible for relief under 43.6 above or 43.16 below, such relief is restricted. As regards interest paid on the new loan after the time it is so used (the '*material time*'), any part so used is eligible for relief only to the extent that it does not exceed the 'applicable amount', and relief for a number of such loans is similarly restricted in the aggregate. The '*applicable amount*' is the difference between the purchase price of the new estate and any earlier eligible loans or part loans in respect of the purchase (including those eligible by virtue of an earlier application of these provisions). [*ICTA 1988, s 357B; FA 1993, s 56; FA 1994, Sch 9 para 7; FA 1995, s 42(2); FA 1999, Sch 4 para 2*].

Joint purchases. Where the purchase is a joint purchase, and any of the money applied in the purchase is not attributable to all the joint purchasers, these provisions apply to the share of the new estate, and the attributable part of the purchase cost, of each of the purchasers to whom it is attributable. [*ICTA 1988, s 357C(4)–(6); FA 1993, s 56; FA 1999, Sch 4 para 2*].

43.14   *Example*

James has outstanding the following loans (all with the same lender).

	£
House purchase (main residence)	80,000
Home improvement loan 1 (made before 6 April 1988)	20,000
Home improvement loan 2 (made in 1991)	3,000

In October 1999, James arranges to sell his home for £90,000 and to buy a new home for £95,000. The lender agrees to substitute the new property as security for the three existing loans and to make a further advance of £5,000 to cover the difference between the proceeds of the old property and the cost of the new. The new arrangements all take effect from 6 October 1999.

Interest rates charged by the lender throughout 1999/2000 are 7.5% on both the original house purchase loan and the new advance and 10% on both home improvement loans.

43.15 Interest Payable

The interest qualifying for tax relief for 1999/2000 is calculated as follows.

6.4.99–5.10.99 (six months)

	£
$£80,000 \times 7.5\% \times \frac{6}{12}$	3,000
$£20,000 \times 10\% \times \frac{6}{12}$	1,000
Total interest on qualifying loans	£4,000

$$\text{Allowable interest} = £4,000 \times \frac{30,000}{100,000} = \qquad £1,200$$

6.10.99–5.4.2000 (six months)

The existing loans, restricted as below but disregarding home improvement loan 2 which is a non-qualifying loan, are regarded as having been made on 6.10.99 for the purchase of the new property.

The existing loans qualifying for relief are restricted to the lesser of

(i)   the amount of the qualifying loans outstanding (i.e. £100,000), and

(ii) the purchase price of the new property (£95,000) *less* the loan actually used in purchasing the new property (£5,000) (i.e. £90,000).

The total loans outstanding (disregarding home improvement loan 2) are £105,000. Of this amount, £90,000 qualifies as above and the new advance of £5,000 qualifies under normal principles. Therefore, £95,000 of the total loans is a qualifying loan and the balance of £10,000 is not.

Allowable interest is calculated as follows.

					£
$85,000 \times 7.5\% \times \frac{6}{12}$	=	$3,188 \times \frac{95}{105}$	=		2,884
$20,000 \times 10\% \times \frac{6}{12}$	=	$1,000 \times \frac{95}{105}$	=		905
£105,000	total interest	£4,188	qualifying interest		£3,789

$$\text{Allowable interest} = £3,789 \times \frac{30,000}{95,000} = \qquad £1,197$$

Total allowable interest 1999/2000 £(1,200 + 1,197) £2,397

43.15   LOANS FOR PURCHASING PROPERTY LET AT A COMMERCIAL RENT

Relief is given for interest paid **before 6 April 1995** (see below) on a loan for the purchase of land by a person owning an estate or interest in the property where the property is, in any period of 52 weeks comprising the time at which the interest is payable and falling wholly or partly within the year of assessment, **let at a commercial rent** for more than 26 weeks and, when not so let, either available for letting at such a rent *or* used as in 43.6

above *or* prevented from being so available or used by construction or repair work. [*ICTA 1988, s 355(1)(b); FA 1995, s 42(1)*]. Interest is also eligible under this paragraph on loans applied in improving or developing land. Interest falling within *section 355(1)(b)* is allowable only against income from letting that or any other land, but unallowed interest may be carried forward against such income (while the land in respect of which the interest is paid continues to be eligible) of the following and subsequent years of assessment (but see below). [*ICTA 1988, s 355(4); FA 1994, Sch 9 para 4; FA 1995, Sch 29 Pt VIII(2)*].

If an individual lets his property at a commercial rent whilst he is away, the benefit of the concession re temporary absences in 43.6 above may be claimed, where appropriate, if this is more favourable than a claim for relief against letting income. (Revenue Pamphlet IR 1, A27). If the loan is within the MIRAS scheme, this should not prevent relief being obtained against the letting income, where appropriate, provided that an adjustment is made for the MIRAS relief. (Taxation Vol 125, No 3269 p 707, 20 September 1990). See 43.3 above for the election available for 1994/95 onwards where interest is eligible both under these provisions and under those in 43.6 above.

Interest may generally be relieved under these provisions against rent paid by a partnership to a partner, or by a company to a controlling director, in respect of land owned by the partner or director occupied for business purposes by the partnership or company. See 43.3(i)(ii) above where the interest is in these circumstances paid by the partnership or company direct.

Repeal of above provisions. The provisions of *ICTA 1988, s 355(1)(b)* and *s 355(4)* are repealed with effect in relation to interest paid on or after 6 April 1995. With effect for **1995/96 and subsequent years,** interest incurred wholly and exclusively for the purposes of a Schedule A business (see 69.3 SCHEDULE A) is an allowable deduction as an expense in arriving at the profits of that business. Extra-statutory Concession A27 (referred to above) continues to apply if the benefit of the concession is more favourable than a deduction in arriving at the Schedule A business profits. A borrower who is eligible for mortgage interest relief, before its abolition from 6 April 2000, in respect of a let property may choose each year whether to claim such relief (restricted to the applicable percentage on a maximum of £30,000) or to deduct the interest in computing the Schedule A business profits. As regards inclusion of the loan within MIRAS (mortgage interest relief by deduction at source), see 22.13 DEDUCTION OF TAX AT SOURCE.

Simon's Direct Tax Service. See E1.535B, E1.535C.

43.16   **LOANS FOR PURCHASING PROPERTY WHERE BORROWER IN JOB-RELATED LIVING ACCOMMODATION**

Relief is given for interest paid before (generally) 6 April 2000 (see 43.3 above) on a loan for the purchase of land by a person owning an estate or interest in the property who is in **job-related living accommodation** at the time the interest is paid, provided that:

(i)   the property is used by him as a residence, or is so used within twelve months of the loan if the interest is paid within that time; or

(ii)   the property is intended to be used in due course as his only or main residence.

Relief can relate to only one property in the case of any one borrower.

See 43.5 above as regards denial of higher rate relief. See 43.3 above for the restriction of tax relief to 10% for 1998/99 and 1999/2000, and for the method of giving such relief.

43.17 Interest Payable

As regards 'home improvement loans', rules identical to those described in 43.6 above apply, as they do to restrict the amount of loans eligible for relief by reference to a qualifying maximum.

'*Job-related living accommodation*' is living accommodation which is provided to a person or spouse either:

(A) by reason of employment where (*a*) it is necessary for the proper performance of his duties for the employee to reside in the accommodation, or (*b*) the employment is such that it is customary for employees to be provided with accommodation for the better performance of their duties, or (*c*) there is a special threat to the employee's security, and he resides in the accommodation as part of special security arrangements in force; or

(B) under an arm's length contract requiring him or his spouse to carry on a trade, profession or vocation on premises or other land provided (under a tenancy or otherwise) by another person and to live on the premises or on other premises provided by that other person.

Neither (A)(*a*) nor (A)(*b*) above applies to accommodation provided to a director by a company, or associated company, unless he has no material interest (5% with or without associates) in the company of which he is a director *and either* he is a full-time working director *or* the company is non-profit making (i.e. it does not carry on a trade, nor is its main function the holding of investments or other property) *or* the company is a charity. (B) above does not apply if the accommodation is provided, wholly or in part, by a company in which the borrower or spouse has a material interest (as above), or by any person(s) with whom the borrower or spouse is in partnership. [*ICTA 1988, s 356; FA 1988, s 43(2); FA 1994, Sch 9 para 5; FA 1995, s 42(2); FA 1999, Sch 4 para 2*].

It is understood that certain accommodation occupied by Ministry of Defence employees who extend their overseas tour beyond four years may be regarded as job-related for these purposes (Tolley's Practical Tax 1986 p 167).

Simon's Direct Tax Service. See E1.546.

43.17 **LOANS FOR PURCHASING PROPERTY — GENERAL MATTERS**

In relation to the reliefs described at 43.6–43.16 above, land includes buildings, caravans and house-boats in UK or Eire (but not elsewhere, see *Ockendon v Mackley Ch D 1982, 56 TC 1*). [*ICTA 1988, s 354(1); FA 1999, Sch 4 para 2*]. Loans replacing a prior eligible loan are themselves eligible. [*ICTA 1988, s 354(1)(c); FA 1999, Sch 4 para 2*]. See, however, 43.8 above as regards replacement home improvement loans. '*Improving or developing*' includes capital expenditure on making-up, sewering, lighting etc., adjoining or service roads. Also making good dilapidations in existence at the time of the purchase, but not other maintenance or repairs (but see below). [*ICTA 1988, s 354(2); FA 1995, Sch 29 Pt VIII(1); FA 1999, Sch 4 para 2*]. A tenant occupier who is in the process of purchasing property with money advanced by the landlord on loan is treated as the owner of that property in relation to any interest paid on the loan before the property actually passes to him. [*ICTA 1988, s 354(7); FA 1999, Sch 4 para 2*]. There are provisions preventing avoidance by sales between husband and wife, or connected persons etc. [*ICTA 1988, s 355(5); FA 1999, Sch 4 para 2*].

The further provisions in *ICTA 1988, s 367(2)–(4)* (see 43.5 above) apply to all loans within 43.6–43.23.

The Revenue have indicated that the following are considered to be '*improvements*' for these purposes.

Home extensions/Loft conversions
Insulation of roofs/walls
Connection to main drainage
Landscaping gardens
Major reconstruction, e.g.
  conversion to flats
Rebuilding a facade
Inserting or renewing damp-proof
  course
Extensive repointing,
  pebble-dashing, texture-coating or
  stone-cladding
Erecting garages, garden sheds,
  greenhouses or fences
Double glazing/Replacement of
  windows and doors
Central or solar heating installations
  (excluding portable and night
  storage radiators not fixed to a
  permanent spar outlet)

Installing kitchen or bedroom units fixed
  to and part of the building
Installation of bathrooms,
  showers etc.
Recovering/Reconstructing a roof
Construction of swimming pools,
  saunas etc.
Underpinning
Renewing electrical installations
Dry rot, wet rot or timber treatment
Extensive replacement of guttering
Installation of fire or burglar alarms
Fire precaution works
Laying driveways, patios or paths
Permanent installation of water
  softening equipment
Replacement of one form of central
  heating with another (e.g. moving
  from oil to gas)

(Taxation Vol 114, No 2988 p 483, 30 March 1985).

Caravans acquired under a hire purchase agreement may concessionally attract relief subject to certain conditions. The local inspector should be consulted as to the current position.

Loan replacing *bank overdraft*. Where an eligible property is acquired by means of an overdraft which is within twelve months replaced by a loan, the Board will concessionally allow relief for the loan interest (up to 5 April 2000) if it can be demonstrated that the overdraft was used solely for the property acquisition (Revenue Pamphlet IR 11, para 33). (*Note.* Although IR 11 is no longer available, it is understood that this concession still applies, see Tolley's Practical Tax 1990 p 15.) See *Lawson v Brooks Ch D 1991, 64 TC 462* for denial of relief for loan replacing overdraft where the overdraft was not a 'temporary accommodation'.

43.18   **LOANS FOR PURCHASING PLANT OR MACHINERY**

Relief is given for interest paid on a loan for the purchase of plant or machinery

(*a*)   for use in the trade etc. of a partnership of which the individual is a member and which is entitled to capital allowances on that item under *CAA 2001, s 264* (see 9.38(F) CAPITAL ALLOWANCES), or

(*b*)   for the purposes of an *office or employment* he holds, and in respect of which he is entitled to capital allowances under *CAA 2001, Pt 2* (or would be so entitled but for some contribution made by his employer) (and see 75.46 SCHEDULE E—EMPLOYMENT INCOME for special provisions relating to use of private car or cycle for such purposes).

Relief is not so granted on interest payable more than three years after the end of the year of assessment in which the debt was incurred, and is applied to a proportionate part of the interest where use is in part other than in (*a*) or (*b*) above. Where *CAA 2001* has effect (see 9.1 CAPITAL ALLOWANCES), and in relation to relief by virtue of (*a*) above, this restriction operates by reference to the period of account (rather than the tax year) in which the debt was incurred. [*ICTA 1988, s 359; CAA 2001, Sch 2 para 27*].

Simon's Direct Tax Service. See E1.533.

43.19 **LOANS FOR PURCHASING INTEREST IN CLOSE COMPANY**

Relief is given for interest paid on a loan (or replacement loan) for the purchase of ordinary shares in, or making a loan to, a close company, provided that the borrower is an individual either (i) with, together with certain associates, a 'material interest' (broadly more than 5% of ordinary share capital at the date of payment of the interest) in the close company or (ii) when the interest is paid, the individual holds any ordinary shares of the close company and (between purchase or loan and relevant interest payment) he has worked for the greater part of his time in the actual management or conduct of the business of that close company or an associated company. As regards this last condition, the facts of each particular case have to be considered, but individuals will normally be regarded as meeting the requirement if they are directors or have significant managerial or technical responsibilities. They must, however, be involved in the overall running and policy-making of the company as a whole—responsibility for just a particular area is not sufficient. (Revenue Tax Bulletin November 1993 p 102). See also Revenue Inspector's Manual IM 3804. If the company exists wholly or mainly to hold investments or property, the individual must not reside in property of the company unless he has worked for the greater part of his time in the actual management or conduct of that company or an associated company. [*ICTA 1988, ss 360, 360A(1), 363(4); FA 1989, s 48*]. The associates whose interests are taken into account in applying the 'material interest' test for loans made after 5 April 1987 do not include the trustees of approved profit sharing schemes (see 82.18, 82.19 SHARE-RELATED EMPLOYMENT INCOME AND EXEMPTIONS), and for loans made after 26 July 1989 do not generally include the trustees of an employee benefit trust (as defined), as a beneficiary of which the borrower has an interest in shares or obligations of the company, unless the 5% ordinary share capital test would be satisfied without their inclusion (for which purpose certain payments received from the trust are treated as giving rise to beneficial ownership of ordinary share capital). Certain other variations in the general definition of 'associate' in *section 360A(2)* apply to loans made before 14 November 1986. [*ICTA 1988, s 360(4), s 360A(2)–(7), Sch 9 para 39; FA 1989, s 48*].

Relief is denied in relation to shares in respect of which a claim is made to relief under the enterprise investment scheme (see 25 ENTERPRISE INVESTMENT SCHEME) or, in relation to shares acquired after 5 April 1998, for deferral of a chargeable gain on reinvestment in an enterprise investment scheme investment, by the person acquiring them or their spouse. [*ICTA 1988, s 360(3A); FA 1989, s 47; FA 1998, s 79*].

The close company (see Tolley's Corporation Tax) must, both at the time the shares are acquired (or the loan made) and throughout the accounting period in which the interest is paid, comply with *ICTA 1988, s 13A(2)* (as introduced by *FA 1989, s 105*) and thus satisfy the conditions for not being a close investment-holding company (see Tolley's Corporation Tax under Close Companies). [*FA 1989, Sch 12 para 12*]. The Revenue's practice in the case of investment in a start-up trading company is to allow relief so long as trading commences within a reasonable time after the investment is made, provided that the company remains close when trading starts. (ICAEW Technical Release TAX 15/92, 23 October 1992).

Where shares were subscribed for in a 'shell' company to enable it to acquire a business, but the business had not been acquired at the time of the subscription, it could fairly be said that the company existed for the purpose of carrying on that business, so that interest on a loan for the purchase of the shares qualified for relief under these provisions (*Lord v Tustain Ch D 1993, 65 TC 761*).

If relief is claimed on a loan to a close company, the money must be used within a reasonable time for the purposes of its business (or that of an associated close company as defined above). [*ICTA 1988, s 360(1)(b), s 367(2)*]. Capital recoveries by the individual (by sale or repayment of ordinary shares, repayment by the company of its loan, or the assignment of the debt due from it etc.) are treated as a reduction of the loan with corresponding reduction of the interest allowable. [*ICTA 1988, s 363(1)–(3)*]. The interest will continue to be allowed if the company ceases to be close after the application of the loan monies (Revenue Pamphlet IR 131, SP 3/78, 19 October 1978). Conversely, it is understood that relief will be given where a loan is used to purchase shares in an 'open' company which by that acquisition becomes a close company (Tolley's Practical Tax 1981 p 99).

Interest paid by the guarantor of a bank loan to a close company is not within the relief (*Hendy v Hadley Ch D 1980, 53 TC 353*).

Interest on a loan applied to the purchase of a close company's convertible loan stock can qualify for relief under these provisions. Relief will, however, cease from the date on which the loan stock is converted to ordinary share capital, since this constitutes a capital recovery (see above). (Revenue Tax Bulletin February 1992 p 13).

Relief on a loan qualifying as above will not be discontinued where shares in the close company are exchanged for, or replaced by, shares in another close company, or by shares in a co-operative (see 43.20 below), or by shares in an employee-controlled company (see 43.21 below), provided that relief would have been available if the loan had been a new loan taken out to invest in the new entity. The usual restriction applies where any capital recovered from the close company is not used to repay the loan. (Revenue Pamphlet IR 1, A43).

Simon's Direct Tax Service. See E1.547.

43.20   **LOANS FOR PURCHASING INTEREST IN CO-OPERATIVE**

Relief is given for interest paid on a loan (or replacement loan) for the purchase of a share or shares in, or making a loan to, a co-operative. Such relief only applies to interest on a loan made after 10 March 1981 and the individual must (between purchase or loan and the relevant interest payment) have worked for the greater part of his time as an employee of the co-operative, or of a subsidiary of that body, which continues to be a co-operative when the interest is paid. A loan to a co-operative must be used wholly and exclusively for the purposes of the business of that body or of a subsidiary. Capital recoveries by the individual (by sale or replacement of the shares, repayment by the co-operative of its loan, or the assignment of the debt due from it etc.) are treated as a reduction of the loan with corresponding reduction of the interest allowable.

'*Co-operative*' (and '*subsidiary*') means a common ownership enterprise or a co-operative enterprise as defined in the *Industrial Common Ownership Act 1976, s 2*. [*ICTA 1988, s 361(1)(2), s 363*].

Relief on a loan qualifying as above will not be discontinued where shares in the co-operative are exchanged for, or replaced by, shares in another co-operative, or by shares in a close company (see 43.19 above), or by shares in an employee-controlled company (see 43.21 below), provided that relief would have been available if the loan had been a new loan taken out to invest in the new entity. The usual restriction applies where any capital recovered from the co-operative is not used to repay the loan. (Revenue Pamphlet IR 1, A43).

Simon's Direct Tax Service. See E1.548.

43.21 Interest Payable

LOANS FOR PURCHASING INTEREST IN EMPLOYEE-CONTROLLED COMPANY

Relief is given for interest paid on a loan (or replacement loan) for the purchase of any part of the ordinary share capital of an employee-controlled company by an individual, provided that:

(*a*) the company is, from the date of purchase of the shares to that of payment of the interest, resident only in the UK, unlisted on the Stock Exchange, and either a trading company (i.e. its business consists wholly or mainly of the carrying on of trade(s)) or the holding company of a trading group (i.e. the business of its 75% subsidiaries, taken together, consists wholly or mainly of carrying on trade(s));

(*b*) the shares are acquired before, or not later than twelve months after, the company becomes an 'employee-controlled company';

(*c*) the company is an 'employee-controlled company' throughout a period of at least nine months in the year of assessment in which the interest is paid, unless it is the year in which it first becomes an employee-controlled company;

(*d*) the individual (or spouse, but see further below) is a full-time employee of the company (i.e. works for the greater part of his time as an employee or director of the company or of a 51% subsidiary) from the date of application of the loan proceeds to the date of payment of the interest (or, if the interest is paid after cessation of the employment, the later of the date of cessation and twelve months before the interest payment date i.e. interest is eligible for relief for twelve months after full-time employment ceases);

(*e*) the individual has, from the date of application of the loan proceeds to the interest payment date, not recovered any capital from the company other than amounts treated as reducing the loan (see below).

Capital recoveries by the individual (by sale or replacement of the shares, repayment of the loan etc.) are treated as reducing the loan and, correspondingly, the interest allowable.

A company is an '*employee-controlled company*' if more than 50% of both the issued share capital and the voting power is beneficially owned by full-time employees (see (*d*) above) (or spouses, but see below) of the company, but ignoring the excess over 10% of any holding of a person (and spouse, but see below) which exceeds 10% of either issued share capital or voting power. Where an individual and spouse are *both* full-time employees, this 10% test is applied to each separately ignoring the other's holding.

As regards (*d*) above and the definition of employee-controlled company, for interest paid after 5 April 1990 (unless the loan was used before that date as required for relief under these provisions) neither the employment of a spouse nor the shares held by a spouse are taken into account in determining whether the conditions for relief for interest paid on such loans are met. Replacement loans made after that date attract interest relief only if the loan replaced was applied after that date or would have attracted relief if it had been applied after that date. [*ICTA 1988, s 361(3)–(8), s 363; FA 1988, Sch 3 para 15*].

Relief on a loan qualifying as above will not be discontinued where shares in the employee-controlled company are exchanged for, or replaced by, shares in another such company, or by shares in a close company (see 43.19 above), or by shares in a co-operative (see 43.20 above), provided that relief would have been available if the loan had been a new loan taken out to invest in the new entity. The usual restriction applies where any capital recovered from the company is not used to repay the loan. (Revenue Pamphlet IR 1, A43).

Simon's Direct Tax Service. See E1.549.

43.22   LOANS FOR PURCHASING INTEREST IN PARTNERSHIP

Relief is given for interest on a loan (or replacement loan) for the purchase of a share of, or making an advance to, a partnership to an individual who (throughout the period between application of the proceeds of the loan and payment of relevant interest) has been a member of the partnership otherwise than as a limited partner in a limited partnership registered under the *Limited Partnerships Act 1907* or as a member of an 'investment limited liability partnership' (see 53.17, 53.18 PARTNERSHIPS). If relief is claimed on a loan to the partnership, the money must be used for the purposes of its trade, profession or vocation. [*ICTA 1988, s 362; Limited Liability Partnerships Act 2000, s 10(2); FA 2001, Sch 25 para 9*]. Salaried partners in a professional firm who are allowed independence of action in handling the affairs of clients and so to act that they will be indistinguishable from general partners in their relations with clients, can claim relief. (See Revenue Pamphlet IR 131, A33.)

For a case in which relief was denied where 'the true net result of the circular transaction [involving a series of payments between spouses] was that no money was contributed or advanced to the partnership which it did not already have', see *Lancaster v CIR (Sp C 232), [2000] SSCD 138.*

Capital recoveries by the individual (from sale of his partnership interest, repayment of capital or loan etc.) are treated as a reduction of the loan with corresponding reduction of the interest allowable. [*ICTA 1988, s 363*].

Relief on a loan qualifying as above will not be discontinued where the partnership is incorporated into a close company (see 43.19 above), a co-operative (see 43.20 above) or an employee-controlled company (see 43.21 above), or there is a partnership reconstruction involving a merger or demerger, provided that relief would have been available if the loan had been a new loan taken out to invest in the new entity. The usual restriction applies where any capital recovered from the partnership is not used to repay the loan. (Revenue Pamphlet IR 1, A43).

Anti-avoidance measures on changeover to current year basis of assessment. Anti-avoidance provisions apply where a claim for interest relief under the above provisions is made by a partner for 1997/98 in respect of a loan made after 31 March 1994 and there is a transitional overlap profit (see 71.13 SCHEDULE D, CASES I AND II) on the changeover to the current year basis. Subject to a *de minimis* limit of £7,500 for application of these provisions, that partner's transitional overlap profit (as reduced where applicable by the anti-avoidance provisions at 71.13) is reduced by the amount of interest paid in respect of the transitional overlap period on any part of the loan proceeds which was contributed or advanced by him to the partnership otherwise than wholly or mainly for *bona fide* commercial reasons or wholly or mainly for a purpose other than the reduction of partnership borrowings for a period falling wholly or partly within the transitional overlap period. Similar notice provisions and time limits apply as in 71.13 as to the amendment of a self-assessment to give effect to the foregoing. [*FA 1995, Sch 22 paras 5, 12; FA 2001, s 88, Sch 29 para 37(4)(5); SI 1997 No 1158*].

Simon's Direct Tax Service. See **E1.550.**

43.23   LOANS TO PAY INHERITANCE TAX

Relief is given for interest on a loan (or replacement loan) to personal representatives to pay inheritance tax or estate duty before a grant of representation or confirmation (payable on delivery of the affidavit etc.), or interest thereon, on personalty of which the deceased was competent to dispose at his death (and which passes to the personal representatives as such, or would if it were situate in UK). The interest must be paid in respect of the period of one year from the making of the loan. Unrelieved interest in a year of assessment can be carried to previous year(s) of assessment and then, if still unrelieved, to succeeding years of assessment. [*ICTA 1988, s 364*].

Simon's Direct Tax Service. See E1.552.

43.24   **LOANS FOR PURCHASING LIFE ANNUITY**

Relief is given for interest on a loan for the purchase of a life annuity by a borrower aged 65 or over under a scheme in which 90% or more of the proceeds of the loan are applied to the purchase by the borrower of an annuity ending with his death (or the last death of two or more annuitants aged 65 or over which include the borrower). The loan must be secured on land in the UK or Eire in which the borrower or one of the annuitants owns an estate or interest. Interest is not eligible unless payable by the borrower or one of the annuitants.

The loan must have been made before 9 March 1999, or in pursuance of an offer made by the lender before that date (and either written or evidenced by a note or memorandum made by the lender before that date). However, replacement loans made on or after 27 July 1999 qualify for relief if the old loan did so, and this applies where only part of the new loan is applied in paying off the old loan, provided that at least 90% of the balance of the new loan not applied in paying off the old loan is applied to the purchase of an annuity ending with the life of the person to whom the loan is made (or of the survivor of two or more persons including that person).

See 43.5 above as regards denial of higher rate relief. See 43.3 above for the method of giving relief.

As regards loans made from 27 March 1974 onwards (*a*) the borrower or each of the annuitants must use the land as his only or main residence when the interest is paid or (in relation to interest payments on or after 27 July 1999) have so used it immediately before 9 March 1999, and (*b*) relief is granted on loans up to £30,000 only, with apportionment where payable by two or more annuitants. In relation to interest paid after 15 March 1993 and before 27 July 1999, where the condition at (*a*) ceased at any time to be satisfied, and it was intended to take steps, within the twelve months following cessation of use as the only or main residence, with a view to disposal of the land, the condition is treated as satisfied until the end of those twelve months or, if earlier, until the intention to dispose of the land is abandoned. The twelve month period could be extended at the Board's discretion in any particular case (irrespective of whether the period began before 16 March 1993). In relation to interest paid on or after 27 July 1999, a similar provision allows the condition at (*a*) to be treated as satisfied where it ceased to be satisfied at a time within the twelve months ending with 8 March 1999 and it was then intended to take steps to dispose of the land within the following twelve months.

[*ICTA 1988, ss 357(1), 365; F(No 2)A 1983, s 3; FA 1984, s 22; FA 1985, s 37; FA 1986, s 20; FA 1987, s 25; FA 1988, s 41; FA 1989, s 46; FA 1990, s 71; FA 1991, s 26; FA 1992, s 10(4); FA 1993, ss 55, 57(3)(5); FA 1994, s 80; FA 1996, s 76; FA 1997, s 57; F(No 2)A 1997, s 16; FA 1999, ss 37, 39, 40; FA 2000, s 83(1)(4)*].

Simon's Direct Tax Service. See E1.553.

43.25   **EXCLUSION OF DOUBLE RELIEF**

Provisions for exclusion of double relief or relief by different methods are in *ICTA 1988, s 368*. The general rule is that any interest relieved under *ICTA 1988, s 353* is not deductible for any other purpose. If a payment of interest on a debt has been allowed under 43.2 above in computing the profits of a period, no relief can be given under *ICTA 1988, s 353* on that payment and on any interest on the same debt in any years of assessment for which the period is the basis period (see 71.3 SCHEDULE D, CASES I AND II onwards). Conversely, if a payment of interest has been relieved under *section 353*, that payment cannot be deducted in computing profits for any year of assessment and any payment of interest on the same debt cannot be deducted in computing the profits for assessment for the year in which *section 353* relief was given. For these purposes, all business overdrafts are treated as one debt. [*ICTA 1988, s 368; FA 1994, Sch 9 para 9; FA 1995, Sch 6 para 17*]. Also, if any interest is eligible for deduction of tax at source as 'relevant loan interest' (see 22.13 DEDUCTION OF TAX AT SOURCE), then relief under *section 353* will not apply. [*ICTA 1988, s 353(2)*]. See 43.2 above for concession where property used for both residential and business purposes.

Simon's Direct Tax Service. See E1.531A.

44   Interest Receivable

Note. See Tolley's Corporation Tax under Loan Relationships for the special provisions applicable to all profits and losses in respect of company 'loan relationships'.

44.1   Interest is receivable gross unless tax is deductible under *ICTA 1988, s 349* (see 22.3(ii) DEDUCTION OF TAX AT SOURCE) or under paying and collecting agent arrangements or unless received from a building society (see 8.3 BUILDING SOCIETIES) or from a bank (see 7.2 BANKS) without a gross payment certificate being in force.

44.2   The recipient of interest is assessable thereon under SCHEDULE D, CASE III (72), or under SCHEDULE D, CASES IV AND V (73) if the interest is from abroad. See 71.56 SCHEDULE D, CASES I AND II for the assessment of interest received in the course of a business.

See 1.8(iii) ALLOWANCES AND TAX RATES as regards taxation of 'savings income'.

Interest received under deduction of tax (see 44.1 above) is income of the year of assessment in which the payment falls due, without regard to the period of accrual.

Solicitors' client accounts. Designated client account interest passed on to the client by a solicitor is within SCHEDULE D, CASE III (72) and hence potentially 'savings income' (see 1.8(iii) ALLOWANCES AND TAX RATES). Payments made to clients in respect of money held in undesignated client accounts are similarly treated from 6 April 1998. Before that date, they are treated as within SCHEDULE D, CASE VI (74), and hence cannot be 'savings income'. (Revenue Tax Bulletin February 1998 pp 512, 513).

44.3   A list of certain types of interest which are exempt from tax is shown in 28.16 EXEMPT INCOME.

44.4   See 3 ANTI-AVOIDANCE for transactions regarding the transfer of interest etc., and see 74.5 *et seq.* SCHEDULE D, CASE VI as regards the accrued income scheme.

45   Life Assurance Policies

The headings in this chapter are as follows.

45.1   **LIFE ASSURANCE PREMIUM RELIEF**

Relief for premiums paid on qualifying life assurance policies (see 45.3 below) ceases to be available for insurances made after 13 March 1984, other than certain deferred annuity contracts (see 45.3(i) below), certain part payments to friendly societies (see 45.3(ii) below) and certain industrial assurance policies (see 45.12(*b*) below). See 60.2 PERSONAL PENSION SCHEMES, 66.2 RETIREMENT ANNUITIES as regards certain types of life assurance contract for persons not in pensionable employment which continue to attract full relief against income. Relief ceases for a contract made before 14 March 1984 if the policy is terminated or varied (including the exercise of an option to change the terms of the policy) so as to increase the benefits secured or extend the term of the insurance (disregarding increased benefits in consideration of the cessation of house to house collection of premiums). [*ICTA 1988, s 266(3)(c), Sch 14 para 8(3)–(8); FA 1996, s 167(5)(6)*].

As regards whether contracts of insurance purporting to be made prior to midnight on 13 March 1984 in relation to a wide range of differing circumstances had in fact been completed at that time, see *Legal & General Assurance Society Ltd v CIR; Legal & General (Unit Assurance) Ltd v CIR (Sp C 96), [1996] SSCD 419*. The Revenue have an immediate enforceable right to recover amounts deducted from premiums under *The Income Tax (Life Assurance Premium Relief) Regulations 1978 (SI 1978 No 1159), reg 10(6)*, without issuing assessments under *TMA 1970 (United Friendly Insurance plc v CIR Ch D 1998, 70 TC 627)*.

Tax relief where applicable is generally given to UK residents (except children under 12), whether they have taxable income or not, by deduction from admissible premiums (see 45.3 below) up to certain limits (see 45.2 below). The deduction is $12\frac{1}{2}\%$ (but see 45.3(ii) below where relief is by reduction of total income). The deductions will normally be calculated by the life offices etc. (who will recover from the Board) without a specific claim being required. The Board may make regulations by statutory instrument to implement this scheme of 'premium relief by deduction'. [*ICTA 1988, s 266(4)(5), Sch 14 para 7; FA 1988, s 29; FA 1996, Sch 18 para 11(3)(4), para 17(1)–(4)(8)*]. Under the scheme relief will normally be allowed without the intervention of a tax office and PAYE taxpayers do not require a coding allowance for premiums.

Simon's Direct Tax Service. See E2.10.

45.2   **Limits on amounts of admissible premiums.** Relief is not given on premiums to the extent that they exceed

45.3 Life Assurance Policies

(a) **£1,500 or one-sixth of total income,** whichever is the greater. [*ICTA 1988, s 274(1)*]. See also 45.4(*j*) below for married persons and 1.6 ALLOWANCES AND TAX RATES for definition of total income.

(b) **£100** for policies not securing a capital sum at death. [*ICTA 1988, s 274(2)*].

The restrictions in (*a*) and (*b*) are not to take into account any additional 'war insurance premiums'. [*ICTA 1988, s 274(4); FA 1996, s 134, Sch 20 para 20*]. Where the limits seem likely to be exceeded by the deductions, the Board may require some premiums to be paid in full. Any over- or under-deductions in a year will be adjusted by assessment or claim to repayment. [*ICTA 1988, Sch 14 paras 4–6; FA 1996, Sch 18 para 11(2), para 17(5)(7)*].

45.3   **Admissible premiums.** Subject to the cessation of relief for policies made after 13 March 1984 (see 45.1 above), admissible premiums are as follows.

(i) **Life assurance premiums** (and payments under **contracts for deferred annuities** (but see 45.4(*b*) below and note limit at 45.2(*b*) above)) paid by an individual in respect of policies (or deferred annuities) on either the individual's own life or that of his spouse. The insurance or contract must be made by the individual. Policies effected after 19 March 1968 must be 'qualifying policies', see 45.6 below. [*ICTA 1988, s 266(1)–(3)*]. See 60 PERSONAL PENSION SCHEMES, 66 RETIREMENT ANNUITIES for the special provisions relating to annuities under such arrangements.

(ii) Proportion of members' contributions to trade unions allocated to superannuation benefits in addition to any portion allocated to funeral benefits or life assurance.

Relief is given by deducting one-half of the portion from total income. A similar deduction applies to a part payment to a registered or incorporated friendly society in respect of an eligible insurance or contract (excluding certain sickness etc. insurances or contracts made after 31 August 1996). The deduction applies also to payments to an organisation of persons in police service provided the allocated portion is £20 or more per annum. [*ICTA 1988, s 266(6)(7)(13); F(No 2)A 1992, Sch 9 para 2; FA 1996, s 171(3)(4)*].

(iii) Statutory deductions from salary for deferred pension to widow or widower or provision for children after claimant's death, including similar compulsory deductions under any contract of employment — the relief for such deductions being given at the full basic rate. [*ICTA 1988, s 273; FA 1988, Sch 3 para 10*].

Employers' contributions under retirement schemes not approved by the Revenue may be relieved in some circumstances as if they were life assurance premiums paid by the employee, see 67.2 RETIREMENT SCHEMES.

45.4   *Notes.*

(a) Policies as under 45.3(i) above are only eligible for relief if they secure capital sum at *death* whether or not in conjunction with any other benefit e.g. disability benefit or option to receive an annuity.

(b) No allowance during period of deferment on '*deferred policies*'. [*ICTA 1988, s 266(3)(a)(d)*].

But neither (*a*) nor (*b*) applies to policies (i) in connection with *bona fide* employees' pension schemes as defined or for the benefit of persons engaged in any particular trade, profession, vocation or business, or (ii) taken out by teachers in secondary schools (as so called in 1918) pending setting up of a pension scheme. [*ICTA 1988, s 266(11)*].

(c) The payments must be made to either (i) insurance company legally established in UK, *or lawfully carrying on business in UK,* (ii) underwriters, (iii) registered or incorporated friendly society, (iv) (deferred annuities) National Debt Commissioners. From 1 December 2001, this is revised to require payments to be made to a person permitted under *Financial Services and Markets Act 2000, Pt 4* or *Sch 3 para 15* to effect or carry out long-term insurance contracts (as defined), or to a member of Lloyd's who effects or carries out such contracts in accordance with *Pt 19* of that *Act.* [*ICTA 1988, s 266(2)(a)(13); F(No 2)A 1992, Sch 9 para 2; SI 2001 No 3629, Article 18*]. *Note.* Included under (i) is a policy issued and managed overseas but where the premium is paid to the UK branch of the insurance company (Revenue Press Release 4 February 1981).

(d) Premiums allowed only so far as *paid* i.e. not covered by advances (*Hunter v A-G HL 1904, 5 TC 13*), nor repayment of advances (*R v Special Commissioners (ex parte Horner) KB 1932, 17 TC 362*). A premium paid otherwise than in the year in which it becomes due and payable is treated as paid in that year. [*ICTA 1988, s 266(4)*].

Non-residents must pay their premiums in full but will be given relief as appropriate under *ICTA 1988, s 278* (see 51.10 NON-RESIDENTS AND OTHER OVERSEAS MATTERS). Premiums to foreign life assurance companies etc. will be payable in full without relief but see Note in (*c*) above. A member of the armed forces or the wife or husband of such a member is treated as resident in the UK. [*ICTA 1988, s 266(8)(9), Sch 14 para 6; FA 1988, Sch 3 para 9; FA 1996, Sch 18 para 11(2), para 17(5)(7)*].

(e) No allowance for joint insurance on two directors' lives (*Wilson v Simpson KB 1926, 10 TC 753*).

(f) *Accident and Sickness Policies.* Relief allowed only on proportion of premium relative to death benefit.

(g) *Children's Policies.* Premiums allowable if paid by parent for (i) life endowment on his own life, maturing when school fees begin, or when child may go into business etc., or (ii) for securing series of payments on specified dates if parent dies earlier. But no relief to parent where policy is on life of *child* unless it is an industrial assurance policy or policy issued by a registered or incorporated friendly society on the life of a child or grandchild and the annual premiums do not exceed £64. [*ICTA 1988, Sch 14 paras 2, 3; F(No 2)A 1992, Sch 9 para 18*].

Policy by child on own life. The Board are of the opinion that no relief is in strictness due on premiums on a policy taken out by a child under age twelve, but are prepared to allow relief as follows. An industrial branch policy or friendly society policy as above will receive relief. Where an ordinary branch policy is taken out on the life of a child and is assigned to him or he possesses or acquires the whole interest in the policy, relief on premiums paid by him may be allowed (provided the other conditions are satisfied) where the policy was taken out (*a*) after the child had attained age twelve; (*b*) before 1 March 1979 and before the child attained age twelve; or (*c*) on or after 1 March 1979 before the child attained age twelve and he has attained that age. (Revenue Pamphlet IR 131, SP 11/79, 1 November 1979 relaxing SP 4/79, 28 February 1979.)

(h) *Borrowings* (at intervals) against life policies may be treated as taxable income. Payments by way of loan under a contract or arrangement, made after 6 April 1949, providing (i) for such payments to be made at intervals during a period dependent on human life, (ii) that the loans, being secured on a life policy, are *not repayable* until the capital benefit accrues payable, and that (iii) the capital benefit *increases* with the length of the period (otherwise than by reason of the insured's right to share in profits of the insurer) are taxable as annual payments under Schedule D, Case III, or Case V, if made to a resident under a foreign contract, as income from a foreign possession under *ICTA 1988, s 65(1)*. The section does not apply if the Board are satisfied that it is not one of the objects of the contract etc., to secure for recipient

45.5 Life Assurance Policies

the equivalent of an annuity equal to the periodic loan payments. [*ICTA 1988, s 554*]. But see 45.15(*f*) below.

(*j*)   *Married persons.* Premiums paid by one spouse on the life of the other (in addition to relief on premiums paid on his or her own life) will be eligible for relief to the paying spouse even after divorce, unless the divorce was before 6 April 1979. [*ICTA 1988, Sch 14 para 1(1)*]. This treatment is extended to premiums paid by a divorced person on policies taken out prior to the marriage (Revenue Pamphlet IR 1, A31).

The premium relief limits in 45.2 above apply separately and in full to each spouse.

(*k*)   See 45.6 and 45.13 below regarding Qualifying and Non-Qualifying Policies respectively, effected after 19 March 1968.

45.5   CLAWBACK OF LIFE ASSURANCE PREMIUM RELIEF

(i)   **Clawback of relief on early surrender etc. within four years**

There was a 'clawback' of the tax relief given on premiums payable on a qualifying policy (see 45.6 below) issued in respect of an insurance made after 26 March 1974 and before 14 March 1984 (when relief ceased to be available) where within four years

(*a*)   the policy was wholly or partly surrendered (including certain loans, see 45.15(*f*) below), or

(*b*)   there was a sum payable on the policy (other than on death) by way of participation in profits, or

(*b*)   the policy was wholly or partly made paid-up.

The body which issued the policy had to pay the clawback to the Revenue out of the sum falling due at the following rate for 1988/89 and earlier years.

Time of surrender etc.	*Clawback of total premiums payable to date*	*Clawback limit*
In year 1 or 2	$\frac{3}{6}$ths of 30% i.e. 15%	Surrender value less 85% of total premiums payable to date
In year 3	$\frac{2}{6}$ths of 30% i.e. 10%	Surrender value less 90% of total premiums payable to date
In year 4	$\frac{1}{6}$th of 30% i.e. 5%	Surrender value less 95% of total premiums payable to date

For partial surrenders etc. the clawback limit could not exceed the value withdrawn or the surrender value if the policy was made paid-up and account was taken of any earlier clawbacks on the same policy. If the annual premium on a policy was increased by more than 25% over the first annual premium (or the annual premium at 26 March 1974 where a policy was issued before that date), the additional premiums and rights obtained were treated as relating to a new policy.

The above provisions did not apply to policies issued in connection with sponsored superannuation schemes or certain approved retirement benefit schemes or if the event under (*a*) or (*c*) arose because of the winding-up of the issuing body. [*ICTA 1988, s 268*]. For replacement of one policy by another, see 45.12(*d*) below.

(ii)   **Clawback of relief on surrender etc. after four years**

If in the fifth or any later year from the making of an insurance either (*a*) or (*b*) (other than on death or maturity) in (I) above occurs and either event has occurred before, a clawback will be made of 12.5% (15% for 1988/89 and earlier years of assessment) on the lower of the premiums payable in that year and the sum payable by reason of the event.

If two or more events occur in the same year the total clawback is limited to the appropriate percentage (as above) of the premiums payable in that year. Account is taken of any clawback also due under *section 268* (above) on a policy treated as new because of an increase in premiums, see (I) above.

The above provisions apply to qualifying policies made after 26 March 1974 but not to industrial assurance policies. [*ICTA 1988, s 269*].

(iii)   **Reduction in relief where clawback occurs**

Where there has been a clawback under (I) or (ii) above, the tax relief on the relevant premiums is reduced by the same amount and the increased liability arising from the loss of the tax relief is set against the clawback suffered (earlier years first), with any excess clawback reclaimable by the taxpayer within six years after the end of the year of assessment in which the event happens.

The relevant premiums are, for (I) above, the total premiums payable under the policy up to the event giving rise to the clawback and, for (ii) above, the premiums payable in the year in which the event happens. [*ICTA 1988, s 270*].

(iv)   Provisions apply for the collection etc. of the clawback by the Revenue from the life office and for the taxpayer to be given, within 30 days by the life office, a statement of the clawback amount and how calculated. [*ICTA 1988, s 272*].

Simon's Direct Tax Service. See E2.1051 *et seq.*

45.6   **QUALIFYING POLICIES**

A policy effected after 19 March 1968 qualifies for life assurance relief only if it provides no 'benefits' other than a capital sum (see 45.12(*a*) below for definition) payable only on death (or on death or earlier disability) or survival for specified term and it also fulfils the conditions set out in 45.7–45.9 below, subject to the exemptions in 45.10 below. [*ICTA 1988, s 266(3)(b), Sch 15 Pt I*].

By concession, free gifts offered as incentives in connection with life insurance policies are disregarded in determining whether a policy is a qualifying policy (and in computing any gain arising in respect of a non-qualifying policy, see 45.13 below), provided that the aggregate cost to the insurer of all gifts in connection with a policy (or a 'cluster' of policies) does not exceed £30. The concession applies in relation to all liabilities unsettled at 7 December 1993. (Revenue Pamphlet IR 1, B42).

See 45.17 below for conditions relating to 'new non-resident policies' issued in respect of an insurance made after 17 November 1983 by a company not resident in the UK.

Note. From 1 April 1976, the certification of new qualifying policies (other than friendly society policies) was transferred from the issuing body to the Revenue (with right of appeal if certificate refused). Certification of policies issued before 1 April 1976 but varied on or after that date remained the responsibility of the life office. [*ICTA 1988, Sch 15 Pt II*]. See *R (oao Monarch Assurance plc) v CIR CA 2001, 74 TC 346* for the circumstances in which the Revenue may exercise its discretionary power to refuse certification. Certification of policies is to be **abolished** altogether from a day to be appointed for the purpose by the Board, except for certification in relation to a time before that day, and subject to the rights of appeal in relation to refusals. A certificate issued under the old rules continues to be conclusive evidence that a policy is a qualifying policy. [*FA 1995, s 55(1)–(3); FA 1996, s 162(1)*].

Simon's Direct Tax Service. See E2.1032 *et seq.*

45.7   **Policies payable only on death** (or earlier disability) **within a specified period** ('Term Assurance').

(*a*)   If the period *does not exceed ten years*, any surrender value must not exceed the return of premiums paid. [*ICTA 1988, Sch 15 para 1(4)*].

(*b*)   If the specified term *exceeds ten years*, premiums must be payable at yearly, or shorter intervals, during at least ten years or three-quarters of the term, whichever is less, or until the assured's earlier death (or disability), and those payable in any one year, excluding any loading for exceptional mortality risk, must not exceed

  (i)   twice the amount of the premiums payable in any other year, nor

  (ii)   one-eighth of the total premiums which would be payable if the policy ran for the full term (or, if appropriate, the sooner of ten years or three-quarters of the term). [*ICTA 1988, Sch 15 para 1(3)(8)*].

(*c*)   For policies issued on or after 1 April 1976, if the specified term ends after the age of 75 years and the policy provides for any payment on the whole or partial surrender of the policy, the capital sum payable on death must not be less than 75% of the total premiums payable if death occurred at 75 years of age. In the case of a policy payable on one of two lives, the age of the older is taken if the sum is payable on the death of the first, and the age of the younger is taken if payment arises on the death of the survivor. If limited to death after 16 (or some lower age) the benefit on earlier death must not exceed the return of premiums paid. [*ICTA 1988, Sch 15 para 1(5)*].

In calculating total premiums, there will be ignored any weighting due to premiums being payable at lesser than annual intervals (generally taken to be 10% if the reduction is not specified) and in calculating the capital sum, the smallest amount is used if more than one is payable. [*ICTA 1988, Sch 15 para 1(6)(9); FA 1996, s 167(7)*].

Short-term assurances. A policy will not be a qualifying policy under 45.6 above if the capital sum is payable only if death or disability occurs less than one year after making the insurance. [*ICTA 1988, Sch 15 para 10*].

45.8   **Endowment policies.** Term must be for at least ten years, or until the assured's earlier death (or disability). The policy must not provide for any capital benefit to be paid (other than on whole or part surrender of the policy or bonus additions to it or on disability) during its continuance, but it must guarantee on death (or death after 16 or some lower specified age) a sum at least equal to 75% of the total premiums (less any weighting due to premiums being paid at lesser than annual intervals, generally taken to be 10% if the reduction is not specified) which would be payable if the policy ran full term. For a policy effected on or after 1 April 1976 by a person over 55 years of age, the 75% requirement is reduced by 2% for each year the age exceeds 55. If limited to death after 16 (or some lower age) the benefit on earlier death must not exceed the return of premiums paid.

Premiums must be payable annually, or at shorter intervals, for a period of not less than ten years or until death etc. Limitations (I) and (ii) under 45.7(*b*) above apply, but with exclusion of wording in brackets at end of (ii). For a policy payable on one of two lives, the rules under 45.7(*c*) above apply. [*ICTA 1988, Sch 15 para 2; FA 1996, s 167(7)*].

45.9   **Whole-life policies.** Premiums must be payable annually, or at shorter intervals, until the assured's death (or his earlier disability, if so provided) or for a specified period of at least ten years should he live longer than that period. Premium limitations (I) and (ii) under 45.7(*b*) above apply except that the total premiums under (ii) are those for the first ten years or for the specified period, as above, if longer. The provisions under 45.7(*c*) above also apply. [*ICTA 1988, Sch 15 para 1(2)*].

45.10   **Exemptions.** The above restrictions do not apply to the following.

(i)   Policies solely for the payment on an individual's death (or disability) of a sum substantially equal to the then balance of a mortgage (repayable by annual, or shorter, instalments) on his residence or business premises. [*ICTA 1988, s 266(10)(a)*].

(ii)   Policies under a sponsored superannuation scheme (as defined by *ICTA 1988, s 624*), if at least half the cost of the scheme is borne by the employer. [*ICTA 1970, s 19(4)(b)*]. This provision was repealed on 6 April 1980 [*FA 1971, Sch 14 Pt 1*] but is continued, for policies issued before that date, by extra-statutory concession (Revenue Pamphlet IR 1, A32).

(iii) Policies issued in connection with approved occupational pension scheme under *ICTA 1988, s 590 et seq. [ICTA 1988, s 266(10)(b)*].

Although the above policies are not qualifying policies, relief under 45.1 to 45.4 above is available on premiums paid (subject to the general restrictions) and they are not subject to the charge on life assurance gains (see 45.13 and 45.15 below).

(iv)   Certain policies issued by a friendly society in the course of its tax-exempt life business are qualifying policies. See 31.3 FRIENDLY SOCIETIES.

45.11   **Disqualification of certain life policies.** A policy (issued in the UK or elsewhere) evidencing a contract of long-term insurance (within *SI 2001 No 544, Sch 1 Pt II*) is not a 'qualifying policy' if it is 'connected with' another policy the terms of which provide benefits greater than would reasonably be expected if any policy 'connected with' it were disregarded.

A policy is 'connected with' another policy if

(*a*)   they are at any time simultaneously in force, and

(*b*)   either of them is issued with reference to the other, or with a view to enabling or facilitating the other to be issued on particular terms. (See Revenue Press Release 16 June 1980 for guidelines.)

This applies to policies issued in respect of insurances made after 25 March 1980 and to an insurance made on or before that date which is connected with one made after it, but not in relation to premiums paid before that date on the earlier policy.

In relation to policies issued in respect of insurances made after 22 August 1983, the above restriction applies where either of the policies concerned provides such excessive benefits as are mentioned above. With respect to payments made after 22 August 1983, this extension of the restriction also applies to insurances made before that date if further premiums exceeding £5 p.a. are made after that date.

Before 1 December 2001 the policies concerned were those effected in the course of long-term business within *Insurance Companies Act 1982, s 1*. A revised definition applied before 23 August 1983.

A person issuing a policy which by virtue of the above is not a qualifying policy (or a policy which causes another policy to cease to be a qualifying policy) is required to give written notice of the fact to the Board within three months of issue. The Board may require any person who appears to them to be concerned in the issue of such a policy (but not a solicitor who only gave advice) to provide them with such information as they think necessary, and as that person has or can reasonably obtain, for the purposes of this provision within a specified time of not less than 30 days. The penalty provisions of *TMA 1970, s 98* apply. [*ICTA 1988, Sch 15 para 14; SI 2001 No 3629, Article 47*].

45.12   Notes.

(a)   '*Capital sum*' includes a series of capital sums, or a sum varying with the circumstances. Bonus additions, an option to take an annuity, a payment on whole or part surrender, or a waiver of premiums in the event of disability *do not constitute* '*benefits*'. [*ICTA 1988, Sch 15 para 1(7)(9)*].

(b)   For *industrial assurance* policies and *family income* and *mortgage protection* policies, see *ICTA 1988, Sch 15 paras 7–9*. After 1 April 1976, industrial insurance policies are generally regarded as qualifying policies although not within the appropriate conditions. In addition, industrial assurance policies issued in respect of insurances made after 13 March 1984 continue to attract premium relief (see 45.1 above) as if issued on or before that date provided that

   (i)   the proposal form was completed on or before that date,

   (ii)   the policy was prepared for issue before 1 April 1984, and

   (iii)   before 1 April 1984 the policy was permanently recorded in the issuer's books in accordance with its normal business practice. [*ICTA 1988, Sch 14 para 8(3)*].

Industrial assurance ceases to be a distinct form of business for tax purposes for accounting periods beginning after 31 December 1995. However, the special treatment afforded to industrial assurance policies will continue to be given to policies issued by any company on or after 1 December 2001, provided that the company had previously issued qualifying policies in the course of industrial assurance business and was, on 28 November 1995, offering such policies of the same type as those offered on or after 1 December 2001. [*ICTA 1988, Sch 15 para 8A; FA 1996, s 167(1)(8); SI 2001 No 3643*].

(c)   A variation after 19 March 1968 to a policy taken out before that date so as to increase benefits or extend term ranks as a new policy. [*ICTA 1988, Sch 14 para 8(1)(2)*]. See, however, 45.13 below as regards cessation of premium collection on certain old policies which is not regarded as a variation.

(d)   Where, after 24 March 1982, a qualifying policy is replaced by another qualifying policy as a result of a variation in the life or lives assured (e.g. on marriage or divorce), both policies are treated for the following purposes as a single qualifying policy made at the time of the earlier policy provided that (*a*) any sum becoming payable in connection with the earlier policy is retained by the insurer and applied towards any premium on the later policy and (*b*) no consideration (apart from the benefits under the new policy) is received by any person in connection with the ending of the earlier policy. Any sum applied as in (*a*) is treated neither as a premium for premium clawback purposes (see 45.5 above) nor for the purposes of life assurance gain computations (see 45.13 below) nor as a capital sum received for the latter purposes. The replacement policy is also treated as made at the same time as the original policy for relief purposes (see 45.1 above) provided that the benefits conferred by the replacement policy are substantially equivalent to those under the original policy. [*ICTA 1988, Sch 14 para 8(6), Sch 15 para 20*].

Where a premium increases or decreases in connection with an exceptional risk of disability or death, this is not considered for tax purposes as a variation in the terms of the policy and, consequently, there is no need to consider whether or not a qualifying policy retains its status as such. A similar disregard applies to any amendment made to the policy by the insertion, variation or removal of a provision under which, on the grounds of such exceptional risk, a sum may become chargeable as a debt against the capital sum guaranteed. These disregards were added by *FA 2003* and deemed always to have had effect, except to the extent that this retrospection would deny a policy qualifying status at any time before 9 April 2003. [*ICTA 1988, Sch 15 para 18(4); FA 2003, s 172(4)(6)*].

The transfer under a Court Order (between spouses as part of a divorce settlement) of the rights conferred by a policy is regarded as being for no consideration, and thus the policy may continue to attract life assurance premium relief. This represents a change of interpretation of the law by the Revenue, announced initially on their website on 4 November 2003. For full detail, and advice on claiming relief withheld in accordance with the previous interpretation, see Revenue Tax Bulletin December 2003 p 1073.

For the effect of other substitutions for and variations to policies generally, see *ICTA 1988, Sch 15 paras 17–20 as amended* and note concession in Revenue Pamphlet IR 1, A45.

(e) A body issuing a policy which is certified by the Board as being a qualifying policy (or which is in the appropriate standard form) must, within three months of receipt of a written request by the policyholder, supply a certificate to that effect. Such a certificate must similarly be supplied where a policy is varied in a significant respect, but continues to be a qualifying policy (although certain variations to pre-20 March 1968 policies are ignored for this purpose). [*ICTA 1988, Sch 15 para 22*]. This requirement will **cease to apply** following the abolition of certification (see 45.6 above). [*FA 1995, s 55(4); FA 1996, s 162(1)*].

(f) Any option to vary a policy issued before 1 April 1976 is disregarded until it is exercised and the policy is then subject to the new qualifying conditions. A policy issued after 1 April 1976 with an option to vary the terms or to have another policy issued in substitution for it is only a qualifying policy if all the specified conditions would continue to be satisfied after the exercise of the option. [*ICTA 1988, Sch 15 para 19*].

(g) As a result of legal advice received, the Revenue have not, since 24 February 1988, certified as a qualifying policy any new life assurance policy which may be converted or fundamentally restructured in such a way as to constitute, under contract law, a rescission of the original contract and the creation of a new one, e.g. the conversion of a whole life policy to an endowment policy or vice versa. Such conversions etc. may arise by means of an agreement between the policyholder and the insurer or by the exercising of an option contained in the terms of the policy. Previously, such alterations were regarded as variations of the existing contract which did not, therefore, prejudice the qualifying status of the policy. Policies certified and sold before 25 February 1988 will not lose their qualifying status even if subsequently converted or restructured. (Revenue Press Release 22 January 1988). Certification is to be abolished (see 45.6 above).

(h) The Revenue may concessionally disregard certain minor infringements of the conditions for recognition as a qualifying policy relating to:

(i) policies back-dated by not more than three months, which may for certain purposes be treated as if the assurance was made on the earlier date;

       (ii)   reductions in first year premiums which do not result in any value being credited to the policyholder;

       (iii)   trivial non-recurring infringements of arithmetical tests; and

       (iv)   policies which could have been certified as qualifying but which were not so certified when the assurance was made.

       (Revenue Pamphlet IR 1, A41).

    (j)   In determining whether any policy is a qualifying policy, there is to be disregarded so much of any premium as is charged on the grounds of exceptional risk of death or disability and any provision under which, on those grounds, a sum may become chargeable as a debt against the capital sum guaranteed on death or disability. References here to 'disability' were added by *FA 2003* and deemed always to have had effect, except to the extent that this retrospection would deny a policy qualifying status at any time before 9 April 2003. [*ICTA 1988, Sch 15 para 12; FA 2003, s 172(1)(2)(6)*].

45.13   LIFE ASSURANCE GAINS

If a life policy effected after 19 March 1968 is not a qualifying policy (see 45.6 above), then

    (a)   no life assurance relief is granted on the premiums [*ICTA 1988, s 266(3)(b)*] (cf. 45.1 above re pre-14 March 1984 qualifying policies), and

    (b)   on the happening of a 'chargeable event' within *ICTA 1988, s 540*, a gain (a 'chargeable event gain') is treated as arising. There is a charge to income tax at the excess of the higher rate over the basic rate on the amount of the chargeable gain. For chargeable event gains arising in 2004/05 onwards, the charge is increased to the excess of the higher rate over the *lower* rate of income tax (for which see 1.3 ALLOWANCES AND TAX RATES). The notional basic rate/lower rate tax credit is not in any circumstances repayable. The gain is treated as an addition to total income. Top-slicing relief (see below) may be available to reduce the tax chargeable. [*ICTA 1988, s 547(1)(a)(5); FA 2003, s 173, Sch 35 para 2(2)*]. See also (A) below as regards certain qualifying policies.

Certain types of policy are excluded from these provisions, namely certain mortgage protection policies, certain policies connected with pension schemes and, with effect on and after 9 April 2003, certain group life policies (as defined) providing protection for loans made to individuals by credit unions and other group life policies meeting specified conditions. Insurers and policy holders are given until 5 April 2004 to vary a pre-9 April 2003 group life policy so that it meets the conditions; provided no benefits became payable, other than on death or disability, between 9 April 2003 and the effective date of variation, the policy is deemed to have met the conditions since 9 April 2003. Pure protection group life policies (as defined) are excluded retrospectively in relation to events occurring before 9 April 2003 but thereafter have to meet the said conditions. [*ICTA 1988, ss 539(2)(3), 539A; FA 2003, s 171, Sch 34 paras 1–4*].

For the duty of insurers to inform the inspector of chargeable events, see *ICTA 1988, s 552* (which is revised, and supplemented by *ICTA 1988, s 552ZA*, with effect from 6 April 2002 by *FA 2001, s 83, Sch 28 Pt II*) and regulations (as amended) thereunder. For the duty of insurers to provide the policy holder with a certificate detailing the chargeable event, see *ICTA 1988, s 552* (see also the transitional modification made by *FA 2003, Sch 34 para 5* in relation to deaths covered by a group life policy). In relation to non-resident policy holders, see Revenue Pamphlet IR 1, B53 (as revised). For the requirement for most overseas insurers (as widely defined) to nominate a UK tax representative responsible for providing such information, see *ICTA 1988, ss 552A, 552B* (introduced by *FA 1998, s 87* with effect from 6 April 1999 and amended by *FA 2001, s 83, Sch 28 para 19* with effect from 6 April 2002) and regulations (as amended) thereunder.

See 45.19 below for 'new non-resident policies' which are not qualifying policies.

Before 9 April 2003, a charge under (*b*) above does not arise if a new policy is issued on exercise of an option under a maturing policy and the proceeds of the maturing policy are fully applied to pay premium(s) under the new policy, *unless* the new policy is issued to a person who was an infant when the maturing policy was issued, and the maturing policy secured a capital sum within a month of his attaining age 25, or on the policy anniversary following his attaining that age. This exemption is repealed with effect for policies maturing on or after 9 April 2003 (though the policy holder can continue to achieve similar deferral of tax by agreeing with the insurer to defer the policy's maturity). The repeal does not have effect where either the option under the maturing policy was exercised in writing before 9 April 2003 or that policy matures before 1 May 2003 and is not varied on or after 9 April 2003 so as to change its maturity date, change any option that it confers or confer any option. [*ICTA 1988, s 540(2); FA 2003, s 171, Sch 34 paras 14, 15*].

The 'gain' (taxable as in (*b*) above) is the excess, over premiums paid plus gains arising on certain prior chargeable events, of

(i)   the surrender value of the policy *immediately prior to the death* plus any 'relevant capital payments' received previously (e.g. by surrender of bonus rights etc.), or

(ii)   any sum received on the *maturity* of the policy, or for the *surrender*, or *assignment* for value, of rights under it (plus any prior 'relevant capital payments' and the amount or value of previous assignments, except that, in the case of assignments after 5 April 2002, a previous assignment made in a policy year beginning after 5 April 2001 is taken into account only where it was made for money or money's worth). [*ICTA 1988, s 541; FA 2001, Sch 28 para 4; FA 2002, s 87(2)–(4)(11)*]. But see 45.12(*d*) above for replacement of a policy and 45.15(*b*) below as regards certain assignments.

A '*relevant capital payment*' is any capital sum (not attributable to disability) paid or conferred before the chargeable event. See also 45.15(*I*) below.

See 45.6 above as regards certain 'free gifts' given as incentives in relation to the issue of a policy, which are disregarded for these purposes.

See Revenue Pamphlet IR 131, SP 6/92, 3 July 1992 as regards certain accident insurance policies providing cover against dying as a result of an accident, which, from the date of issue of the Statement, are not regarded as life insurance policies for these purposes. The Statement of Practice applies mainly to group policies, under which a gain might otherwise arise on payment of a death benefit as a result of earlier payments under the policy.

See 45.15 below for computation of the gain realised on partial surrenders etc.

If the gain arises to a trust, the settlor is liable as under (*b*) above. [*ICTA 1988, s 547(1)(a)*]. There is special provision from 6 April 1998 (but excluding certain cases where a settlor had died before 17 March 1998) where, immediately before the chargeable event, the settlor was dead or non-resident or (being a company or 'foreign institution' (as defined)) had come to an end, or the policy was held as security for a debt owed by the trustees. There is similarly special provision from that date where a policy is beneficially owned by, or held as security for a debt owed by, a foreign institution. [*ICTA 1988, s 547(1)(d)(e)(5AA)(9)–(13); FA 1998, Sch 14 paras 1, 7*]. For the right to recover tax paid from trustees, see *ICTA 1988, s 551* (individuals) or (for companies from 6 April 1998) *s 551A* (introduced by *FA 1998, Sch 14 para 3*) (both as amended).

After 8 April 2003, the above rule for trusts is restricted to non-charitable trusts. For charitable trusts, chargeable event gains are instead treated as income of the trustees and

45.13 Life Assurance Policies

charged at the basic rate of tax (reduced to the lower rate for 2004/05 onwards); because of the availability of the notional tax credit at (*b*) above, no further tax is payable. (This does not apply, however, where the trusts were created before 17 March 1998, the policy was issued before that date (and not varied on or after that date so as to increase benefits or extend the term) and at least one settlor died before that date.) There is also provision (effective after 8 April 2003) to ensure that, in the case of non-charitable trusts, the trustees will be liable (at the 'rate applicable to trusts', see 81.5 SETTLEMENTS, but with the benefit of the notional tax credit) if a gain is not chargeable on anyone else. (This does not apply, however, where the policy was effected before 9 April 2003, it was not varied on or after that date so as to increase benefits or extend the term and none of the rights were assigned to non-charitable trusts on or after that date.) [*ICTA 1988, s 539(3), s 547(1)(a), (b), (cc), (d)(I)(ia)(ii), (4A), (5AA), (9), (9A), (10); FA 2003, ss 171, 173, Sch 34 paras 6, 7, 12, Sch 35 para 2(3)*].

For the method of charging gains where two or more persons have an interest in a policy, see *ICTA 1988, s 547(3)* or (for chargeable events on or after 6 April 1998) *s 547A* (as introduced by *FA 1998, Sch 14 para 2* and subsequently amended). See also 45.15(*g*) below.

For the charge under *FA 1989, s 90, Sch 9* on gains arising on policies held by companies, see Tolley's Corporation Tax under Profit Computations.

There is an exemption for gains arising on retirement annuities approved under *ICTA 1988, s 621* and occupational pension schemes approved under *ICTA 1988, s 590 et seq.* See 66 RETIREMENT ANNUITIES, 67 RETIREMENT SCHEMES.

A charge on the gain, as under (*b*) above, also arises (if the policy was taken out after 19 March 1968 or varied, so as to increase benefits or extend term, after that date) on

(A)   a qualifying policy if, within the lesser of ten years from inception or three-quarters of its term, it is surrendered or assigned for value, in whole or in part. Also, if it is converted to a paid-up policy within that period and any of the events as in (I) or (ii) above occur. [*ICTA 1988, s 540(1)(b)*]. See 45.15 below.

(B)   life annuity contracts (including those issued in connection with 'Guaranteed Income Bonds'). The charge is on the excess of the total amount received by way of capital payment up to and including surrender or assignment (and the amount or value of previous assignments, except that, in the case of assignments made after 5 April 2002, a previous assignment made in a policy year beginning after 5 April 2001 is taken into account only if made for money or money's worth) over the sum of premiums etc. paid and gains arising on certain prior chargeable events. [*ICTA 1988, ss 539(3), 542, 543; FA 2002, s 87(5)–(7)(11); FA 2003, s 171, Sch 34 para 13*]. For contracts made after 26 March 1974, any gains will be fully chargeable to income tax, under Schedule D, Case VI, without the benefit of a notional tax credit. This does not apply to gains on certain policies issued by non-UK resident companies within the charge to tax in a territory within the European Economic Area. [*ICTA 1988, s 547(6)(6A); FA 1995, s 56(1)*]. Capital sums payable on death under contracts made after 9 December 1974 are treated as a surrender of the contract. [*ICTA 1988, s 542(2)*]. See also 45.15 below.

(C)   a capital redemption policy (under which a premium is paid for a return or returns on a specified date or dates in the future). The charge is on the total amounts received up to and including maturity, surrender or assignment (excluding the proportion of any annual receipts already taxed as income) less premium etc. paid. [*ICTA 1988, s 545*]. Also applicable to companies. See also 45.15(*h*) below.

Gains on certain policies issued by friendly societies are fully chargeable to income tax, without the benefit of a notional tax credit (see 31.4 FRIENDLY SOCIETIES).

Cessation of premium collection on old policies. Where an insurer decides to cease collecting premiums on certain types of policy held for a specified period, and any change to the benefits is limited to a deduction of no more than the premiums forgone, this will, by concession, not be treated as an alteration to the policy for these purposes (and for the purposes of 45.12(*c*) above). This is dependent upon the change not itself being a chargeable event, the policy being at least 20 years old at the time of the change, and there being no option under the policy (whether or not previously exercised) for reduction of the premiums to a nominal amount in connection with a right to make partial surrenders after the date of the reduction. (Revenue Pamphlet IR 1, A96).

'**Assignment**' for the above purposes does not include an assignment between *spouses living together* or by way of *security for debt*. [*ICTA 1988, s 540(4)*]. There are exemptions from the general charge under (*b*) above, and from the charge under (A) and (B) above, for *assignees* (for money or money's worth) in respect of policies or life annuity contracts issued or made before 26 June 1982 and assigned before that date, who will normally be liable to capital gains tax on their gains. But the original beneficial owner of a policy or contract which *has been re-assigned to him* is not exempt from the income tax charge on subsequent gains. Also, the exemption is denied where a policy or contract was assigned for money or money's worth before 26 June 1982 and, after 23 August 1982, either

(i)   the policy is reassigned for money or money's worth (other than between spouses or as security for a debt or on the discharge of a debt so secured), or

(ii)   further capital is injected, or

(iii) loans are taken against security of the policy etc., except that (iii) does not apply

    (*a*)   unless the policy etc. was issued in respect of an insurance or contract made after 26 March 1974, and the sum is lent to, or at the direction of, the individual who, at the time of the loan, owns the rights conferred by the policy etc., or

    (*b*)   if the policy is a qualifying policy (see 45.6 above), and either a commercial rate of interest is payable on the sum lent, or it is lent to a full-time employee of the issuing body to assist in the purchase or improvement of his only or main residence.

[*ICTA 1988, ss 540(3), 542(3), 544*].

Gains arising in policy years beginning before 6 April 2001 from partial surrenders prior to an assignment by gift are chargeable on the donor. See now 45.15(*b*) below. [*ICTA 1988, s 541(4); FA 2001, Sch 28 para 4(4)*].

'**Top-slicing relief**'. An individual may claim that the additional tax payable by him as a result of (*b*) above shall be calculated as follows. Divide the gain by the number of *complete* years the policy has run (i) since the previous chargeable event (see 45.15(*b*) below) or (ii) since the start of the policy if there is no previous chargeable event, or on final termination of the policy. Compute the excess of higher rate tax over basic rate tax (lower rate tax for 2004/05 onwards) on the resulting amount. Multiply the tax so calculated by the number of complete years the policy has run (as in (i) or (ii)). This gives the total liability on the full gain. This procedure is most likely to be of benefit where the gain straddles the basic rate limit, such that it is partly chargeable at the higher rate. [*ICTA 1988, s 550; F(No 2)A 1992, s 19(2); FA 1999, s 22(8); ITEPA 2003, Sch 6 para 57; FA 2003, s 173, Sch 35 para 3*]. For this purpose, disregard the fact that no notional tax credit is available in respect of gains on life annuity contracts (see (B) above) and friendly society policies (see 31.4 FRIENDLY SOCIETIES). [*ICTA 1988, s 547(6)(c)(7)*].

Transfers of shares in life policies etc. New rules are introduced by *FA 2001, s 83, Sch 28* which are intended:

45.13 Life Assurance Policies

(1)   (from 6 April 2001) to make the treatment clearer where part of the rights in a life policy etc. is transferred and there is some continuity of ownership. They ensure that

    (*a*)   the tax charge on transfers of part of the rights under a life policy etc. will be determined by reference to the part of the rights transferred (so that the tax charge will be the same in all parts of the UK),

    (*b*)   the person who gives up the interest will be liable for any tax that is due on the transfer, and

    (*c*)   transfers for no consideration of part of the rights under a life policy etc. will no longer be liable to income tax; and

(2)   (from 6 April 2002) to make it easier for policyholders with a taxable gain to complete their self-assessment by requiring insurers to inform them of the amount of any gain for income tax purposes.

See Revenue Press Release BN 19/01 7 March 2001 and, in particular, 45.15(*b*)(*g*) below.

Divorce settlements. The transfer under a Court Order (between spouses as part of a divorce settlement) of the rights conferred by a life policy etc. is not regarded as being for money or money's worth, and thus no taxable gain can arise. This represents a change of interpretation of the law by the Revenue, announced initially on their website on 4 November 2003. For full detail, and advice on amending tax returns prepared in accordance with the previous interpretation, see Revenue Tax Bulletin December 2003 pp 1071–1073.

Non-residents. By concession, individuals and companies which are non-UK resident throughout (respectively) a year of assessment or an accounting period beginning after 5 April 1999 are not liable to UK tax on gains on chargeable events occurring at any time during such a year, unless, in the case of a company, the policy or contract is held as property used or held by a UK branch or agency of the company. Certain benefits and gains treated as income are not affected by this concession. (Revenue Pamphlet IR 1, B53). For earlier years of assessment and accounting periods, non-residents are not charged to tax if the proceeds of the policy or contract were not payable in the UK and the policy or contract was made outside the UK by either an overseas branch of a resident insurance company or by a non-resident insurance company. (Revenue Pamphlet IR 131, SP 11/80).

Personal portfolio bonds. The Treasury has wide powers by regulation to impose a yearly charge in relation to 'personal portfolio bonds', in addition to any other charge under the life assurance gains provisions. Subject to any additional conditions imposed by regulation, a *'personal portfolio bond'* is a life assurance policy, life annuity contract or capital redemption policy under whose terms:

    (i)   some or all of the benefits are determined by reference to the value of, or income from, any description of property (whether or not specified in the policy or contract), or fluctuations in, or in an index of, the value of such property; and

    (ii)   some or all of the property, or such an index, may be selected by or on behalf of the holder (or any of two or more holders) of the policy or contract and/or CONNECTED PERSONS (19).

There may be an exclusion where the only property or index which may be selected is of a description prescribed by regulation.

The annual charge will be on a deemed gain of 15% of the sum of the total premiums paid up to the end of each policy year and the total of deemed gains of earlier years. A deemed gain will also arise when the policy terminates or any other chargeable event occurs. The additional charge will not be imposed in respect of any policy year ending before 6 April 1999. (Revenue Press Release 17 March 1998).

[*ICTA 1988, s 553C; FA 1998, s 89*].

For the regulations, see *SI 1999 No 1029* (as amended). See also Revenue Pamphlet IR 1, B53 (as revised) for concessional extension of the transitional relief under those regulations for policies taken out before 17 March 1998.

Guidance Notes for Insurers and Practitioners, setting out the Revenue's interpretation of the personal portfolio bond legislation and the way they apply the law in practice, are published by the Revenue on their website. Enquiries about the legislation or the Guidance Notes should be addressed to Personal Portfolio Bond Group, Financial Institutions Division, Room S21 West Wing, Somerset House, Strand, London WC2R 1LB (tel. 020–7438 7343/7595).

Simon's Direct Tax Service. See B7.5.

45.14 *Example*

A single policyholder realises, in 2004/05, a gain of £2,600 on a non-qualifying policy which she surrenders after $2\frac{1}{2}$ years. Her other income for 2004/05 comprises earned income of £31,000 and dividends plus tax credits amounting to £3,895.

The tax chargeable on the gain is calculated as follows.

	Normal basis £	Top-slicing relief claim £
Policy gain	2,600	1,300
Earnings	31,000	31,000
Dividends	3,895	3,895
	37,495	36,195
Personal allowance	4,745	4,745
	£32,750	£31,450

Tax applicable to policy gain Higher rate	£	£
£1,350 at 40%	540.00	—
£50 at 40%	—	20.00
	540.00	20.00
Deduct Lower rate		
£1,350 at 20%	270.00	—
£50 at 20%	—	10.00
		£10.00
Appropriate multiple 2 × £10.00		£20.00
Tax chargeable lower of	£270.00 &	£20.00

45.15 Life Assurance Policies

	Normal basis	Top-slicing relief claim £
Tax payable is therefore as follows.		
2,020 @ 10% (starting rate)		202.00
24,235 @ 22%		5,331.70
3,895 @ 10% (Schedule F ordinary rate)		389.50
1,250 @ 20% (policy gain)		250.00
31,400		
1,350 @ 40% (policy gain)		540.00
£32,750		
		6,713.20
Deduct: Tax credits on dividends (£3,895 @ 10%)	389.50	
Lower rate of tax on policy gain (£2,600 @ 20%)	520.00	
Top-slicing relief (£270.00 – £20.00)	250.00	1,159.50
Tax liability (subject to PAYE deductions)		£5,553.70

45.15 **Partial surrenders etc.** The following provisions apply in relation to the charging of income tax at the excess of the higher rate over the basic rate (lower rate for 2004/05 onwards) on gains realised on the *partial surrender* (or *partial assignment* for money's worth) of life policies, capital redemption policies and annuity contracts.

(*a*) **'Policy year'** is any twelve months reckoning from the commencement of the policy etc. and subsequent anniversaries. If the final policy year ends in the same year of assessment as the termination of the policy etc. by death, maturity or total surrender, the two periods shall be treated as the final year. [*ICTA 1988, s 546(4)*].

(*b*) **'Chargeable event'.** Partial surrenders and assignments in any policy year may give rise to a taxable chargeable event at the end of that year. Except as below, a chargeable event occurs where the 'reckonable aggregate value' (see below) exceeds the 'allowable aggregate amount' (see below). See also (*g*) below.

On termination of a policy (by death, maturity, total surrender or assignment) all gains arising from previous chargeable events are deducted from the overall gain on that policy. A deficiency arising on termination is deductible from total income, but only for the purposes of ascertaining EXCESS LIABILITY (27), insofar as it does not exceed the total gains on previous chargeable events. For policies effected after 2 March 2004, the amount of such deficiency relief due to an individual cannot exceed the aggregate amount of earlier gains on the policy that formed part of the same individual's total income for tax purposes for previous tax years; this applies equally where a policy was effected on or before 2 March 2004 but after that date is varied so as to increase the benefits (an exercise of rights conferred by the policy being treated for this purpose as a variation), assigned (in whole or in part) or becomes held as security for a debt.

[*ICTA 1988, ss 540–543, s 545, s 549; FA 2001, s 83, Sch 28; ITEPA 2003, Sch 6 para 56; FA 2004, s 140*].

For events in policy years beginning after 5 April 2001, *ICTA 1988, ss 546B–546D* (introduced by *FA 2001, s 83, Sch 28 para 10 and amended by FA 2002, s 87(8)–(10)(12)*) make special provision for the charge to tax on chargeable events in cases where there has been either a part assignment for money (or money's worth) or a part surrender followed by a gift by way of assignment or partial assignment. In particular these prevent the charge arising on the assignor in certain cases (see 45.13 above). (*Note.* These provisions were introduced to ensure that the legislation operates as originally intended as regards the person on whom a liability is imposed. See Revenue Press Release BN 19/01 7 March 2001 as regards the revised view of the application of the earlier legislation and for the adjustment of earlier liabilities in accordance with strict application of the earlier legislation where this is favourable to the taxpayer.)

(*c*)   **'Reckonable aggregate value'** is the total value of all surrenders and assignments of the policy since its commencement (but excluding any policy year prior to the first such year falling wholly after 13 March 1975), less the total of such values which have been brought into account in earlier chargeable events. [*ICTA 1988, s 546(1)(2)*].

(*d*)   **'Allowable aggregate amount'** is the total of annual fractions of one-twentieth (with a maximum of 20 twentieths) of the premiums, and lump sums, paid since the policy commenced (but excluding the fractions relating to policy years prior to the first such year falling wholly after 13 March 1975), less the total of such fractions which have been brought into account in earlier chargeable events. [*ICTA 1988, s 546(1)(3)*].

(*e*)   **Bonuses.** Surrender (or automatic payment) of a bonus is treated as a surrender of rights with consequent calculation under (*b*) above. [*ICTA 1988, s 539(4)*].

(*f*)   **Loans** by the body issuing the policy will be treated as surrenders (with consequent calculation under 45.5 above (clawback) or (*b*) above (chargeable event)) on policies made after 26 March 1974, except where lent on qualifying policies at a commercial rate of interest or (for loans made before 6 April 2000) to assist in the purchase or improvement of an only or main residence of a full-time employee of the issuing body or of an insurance association serving the insurance market (see Revenue Pamphlet IR 1, A47). Any repayment of the loan will be treated as a premium when the calculation of any gain is made for the final year. [*ICTA 1988, s 548; FA 1999, Sch 4 paras 16, 18(3); FA 2003, s 171, Sch 34 para 9*]. By concession, a loan-back option exercised in connection with a concurrent retirement annuity contract with the same insurer may not be treated as a surrender. (Revenue Pamphlet IR 1, A42). There is no tax charge on a loan to an elderly person in connection with a life annuity contract to the extent that the interest is eligible for relief under *ICTA 1988, s 365* (see 43.24 INTEREST PAYABLE). [*ICTA 1988, s 548(3)(b)*].

(*g*)   **Assignments etc. involving co-ownership.** For events in policy years beginning after 5 April 2001, where, as a result of any transaction, the whole or part of (or a share in) the rights conferred by a policy or contract (the '*material interest*') becomes beneficially owned by one person or by two or more persons jointly or in common (the '*new ownership*'), and immediately before that transaction the material interest was in the beneficial ownership of one person or two or more persons jointly (the '*old ownership*'), then if at least one person is common to both the old and the new ownership, the transaction is treated as having been the assignment by each of the old owners of so much (if any) of his old share as exceeds his new share (if any). The old and new shares in cases of joint ownership are treated as having been equal shares. [*ICTA 1988, s 546A; FA 2001, s 83, Sch 28 para 9*]. (*Note.* This provision was introduced to ensure that the legislation in England, Wales and NI operates as originally intended. It does not affect the position in Scotland. See Revenue Press Release BN 19/01 7 March 2001 as regards the adjustment of liabilities in relation to earlier part assignments in accordance with strict application of the earlier provisions where this is favourable to the taxpayer.)

(*h*) **Capital redemption policies.** Where the sums payable are chargeable as annual payments under Schedule D (or, from 6 April 2003, as income within 58.2(*k*) PENSION INCOME), no further charge to tax will arise under the above provisions. [*ICTA 1988, s 545(1)(a); ITEPA 2003, Sch 6 para 56*].

(*i*) **Payments under certain life policies (commonly 'Guaranteed Income Bonds').** Special provisions apply to any contract of insurance within *SI 2001 No 544, Sch 1 Pt II para I* or *para III* (before 1 December 2001, any contract of long-term business insurance within *Insurance Companies Act 1982, Sch 1 Class I* or *III*) which is neither an annuity contract nor a contract effected in the course of the insurer's pension business (within *ICTA 1988, s 431B* or appropriate earlier enactment). Such policies are often in the form of so-called Guaranteed Income Bonds. A '*relevant excepted benefit*' is so much of any payment by the insurer under such a policy as:

(*a*) falls (apart from the current provisions) to be treated as interest or an annual payment;

(*b*) is not payable under provisions of the policy which, taken alone, would constitute a different sort of policy (for which see below); and

(*c*) does not represent interest for late payment on any other part of the payment or on the whole or part of any other payment by the insurer under the policy.

As regards (*b*) above, a contract is a 'different sort of policy' if it falls within *SI 2001 No 544, Sch 1 Pt I* or *Pt II* (and not within *Pt II para I* or *II*) (before 1 December 2001, if it falls within *Insurance Companies Act 1982, Sch 1* or *Sch 2* other than *Sch 1 Classes I* and *III*), and would in most cases relate to sickness benefits. (*c*) above refers to any interest on the whole or part of a payment for a period beginning on or after the date of the event or contingency giving rise to the payment.

For all tax purposes (and with full retrospective effect):

(i) a relevant excepted benefit is treated as being neither interest nor an annual payment, and as being a 'relevant capital payment' within *ICTA 1988, s 541* (or earlier enactment) (see 45.13 above); and

(ii) on payment of a relevant excepted benefit, there is treated as having been a surrender of a part of the rights conferred by the policy in question or, in the case of the final payment, of all the remaining rights, the value of the rights (or part) surrendered being equal to the amount of the payment.

[FA 1997, s 79; SI 2001 No 3629, Article 98].

(*j*) **'Top-slicing relief'** applies as under 45.13 above.

45.16   *Example*

Jade took out a policy on 4 February 1997 for a single premium of £15,000. The contract permits periodical withdrawals.

(i) Jade draws £750 p.a. on 4 February in each subsequent year.

There is no taxable gain because at the end of each policy year the 'reckonable aggregate value' (RAV) does not exceed the 'allowable aggregate amount' (AAA).

	£	
At 3.2.01 withdrawals have been	2,250	(RAV)
Deduct 4 × $\frac{1}{20}$ of the sums paid in	3,000	(AAA)
	No gain	

(ii) On 20.7.01 Jade withdrew an additional £3,500.

	£	
At 3.2.02 withdrawals have been	6,500	(RAV)
Deduct 5 × $\frac{1}{20}$ of the sums paid in	3,750	(AAA)
Chargeable 2001/02	£2,750	

(iii) Jade made no annual withdrawal on 4.2.02 but on 4.2.03 made a withdrawal of £1,000.

In the year 2003/04 the position is

	£	£	
At 3.2.04 withdrawals have been		7,500	
Deduct Withdrawals at last charge		6,500	
		1,000	(RAV)
Deduct 7 × $\frac{1}{20}$ of the sums paid in	5,250		
less amount deducted at last charge	3,750		
		1,500	(AAA)
		No gain	

(iv) Jade surrendered the policy on 1.7.04 for £13,250, having made a further £1,000 withdrawal on 4.2.04.

In the year 2004/05, the position is

		£	£
Proceeds on surrender			13,250
Previous withdrawals			8,500
			21,750
Deduct:	Premium paid	15,000	
	Gains previously charged	2,750	
			17,750
Chargeable 2004/05			£4,000

Notes

(a) The gain on final surrender of the policy is calculated under *ICTA 1988, s 541* (see 45.13 above).

(b) The gains in (ii) and (iv) above are subject to any available top-slicing relief (see 45.13 above).

45.17 Life Assurance Policies

45.17 **OFFSHORE POLICIES**

Conditions. A policy issued in respect of an insurance made after 17 November 1983 by a company resident outside the UK (a '*new non-resident policy*') will not be a qualifying policy under *ICTA 1988, Sch 15 Pt II* (see 45.6 above) until either

(*a*)   the premiums are payable to, and are business receipts of, a UK branch/permanent establishment of the issuing company and the company is lawfully carrying on life assurance business in the UK; or

(*b*)   the policy holder is a UK resident and a portion of the issuing company's income from the investments of its life assurance fund is charged to corporation tax by virtue of *ICTA 1988, s 445*.

[*ICTA 1988, Sch 15 para 24; FA 1995, s 55(5); FA 2003. s 155, Sch 27 para 1(4)*].

Policies issued under insurances made before 18 November 1983 are not affected by the above unless they are varied after 17 November 1983 so as to increase the benefits secured or to extend the term of the insurance, in which event they are treated as issued after 17 November 1983. A variation includes the exercise of an option. [*ICTA 1988, Sch 15 para 27; FA 1995, s 55(7)*].

As regards chargeable events on or after 17 March 1998 in relation to policies issued in respect of insurances made (or varied to increase the benefits or extend the term) on or after that date, special provisions apply to life assurance policies with non-UK residents. If, immediately before the happening of the event, they are not 'new non-resident policies' (as above), they are treated as such, and they are in any event not treated as qualifying policies. The gains are fully chargeable to income tax, under Schedule D, Case VI as in 45.19 below, without the benefit of a notional tax credit. Similarly, for contracts made after the coming into force of the first regulations under *ICTA 1988, s 458A* (applying life assurance provisions generally to capital redemption business — see Tolley's Corporation Tax), a capital redemption policy with a non-UK resident which, immediately before a chargeable event, is not a 'new offshore capital redemption policy' (see 45.19 below) is treated as such in relation to that event. [*ICTA 1988, ss 553A, 553B; FA 1998, s 88*].

Simon's Direct Tax Service. See B7.525, E2.1048.

45.18   **Substitution of policies.** Where one policy is substituted for another and the old policy was a 'new non-resident policy' but the new policy is not, the rules in *ICTA 1988, Sch 15 paras 17–20* (see 45.12(*d*) above) are modified as follows.

(*a*)   If the old policy and any related policy (any preceding policy in a chain of substituted policies) would have been, or, where certification was required, would have been capable of being, a qualifying policy were it not for the 'new non-resident policy' rules, then it is assumed to have been a qualifying policy for the purposes of *ICTA 1988, Sch 15 para 17(2)*.

(*b*)   If the new policy would otherwise be, or, where certification is still required, be capable of being, a qualifying policy, it will nevertheless not qualify unless the circumstances are those specified in *ICTA 1988, Sch 15 para 17(3)* (regarding residence, benefits, the issuing company etc.).

(*c*)   The company issuing the new policy must certify that the old policy for which it is substituted was issued by a company outside the UK with whom they have arrangements for issuing substitute policies to persons coming to the UK.

The modification in (*c*) above also applied where the old policy was a qualifying policy issued on or before 17 November 1983 which would have been a non-qualifying 'new non-resident policy' if issued after that date while the new policy is issued after that date and is not a 'new non–resident policy'.

If the new policy confers an option to have another policy substituted for it or to have any of its terms changed and thereby falls within *ICTA 1988, Sch 15 para 19(3)* it is to be treated for the purposes of that sub-paragraph as having been issued in respect of an insurance made on the same day as the old policy. [*ICTA 1988, Sch 15 paras 25, 26; FA 1995, s 55(6)*].

45.19 **Tax on chargeable events.** Gains from non-qualifying new non-resident policies are fully chargeable to income tax, under Schedule D, Case VI, without the benefit of a notional tax credit. This also applies to *'new offshore capital redemption policies'*, i.e. capital redemption policies issued in respect of contracts made after 22 February 1984 by non-UK resident companies. It does not apply to gains on new non-resident policies if the conditions in (*a*) or (*b*) in 45.17 above are fulfilled at all times between the date of issue and the date of the gain, or to gains on certain policies issued by non-UK resident companies within the charge to tax in a territory within the European Economic Area. [*ICTA 1988, s 553(6)(6A)(7)(10); FA 1995, s 56(2); FA 1996, s 168(5)*].

Except as below, the gain which would be chargeable is reduced by multiplying it by the fraction of which the denominator is the number of days for which the policy (and any preceding related policy) has run before the chargeable event and the numerator is the number of those days when the policy holder was a UK resident. No reduction is, however, made where, at any time during the life of the policy, it was held either

(*a*) by a trustee resident outside the UK, or by two or more trustees any of whom was so resident, *unless* the policy was issued in respect of an insurance made on or before 19 March 1985 *and* it was on that date held by a trustee resident outside the UK or by two or more trustees any of whom was so resident, or

(*b*) (from 6 April 1998) by a *'foreign institution'* (i.e. a company or other institution of non-UK residence or domicile) *unless* the policy was issued in respect of an insurance made on or before 16 March 1998 *and* it was on that date held by a foreign institution.

The gain thus reduced is chargeable to tax in full under Schedule D, Case VI (see above) but any top-slicing relief due under *ICTA 1988, s 550* (see 45.13 above) is computed as if the notional tax credit were available. [*ICTA 1988, s 553(3)–(6); FA 1998, Sch 14 paras 4, 7*].

The denominator in the 'appropriate fraction' in the top-slicing relief calculation is altered for these purposes to the number of complete years the policy has run before the chargeable event less any complete years in which the policy holder was not resident in the UK. [*ICTA 1988, s 553(8)*].

Where there is a substitution of policies within 45.18 above and the new policy is a qualifying policy there is no chargeable event on the surrender of rights under the old policy and the new policy is treated as having been issued in respect of an insurance made on the same day as the old policy. [*ICTA 1988, s 553(1)*].

If at any time a previously qualifying 'new non-resident policy' ceases to fulfil the conditions of either (*a*) or (*b*) in 45.17 above it is brought within the chargeable events legislation of *ICTA 1988, s 539 et seq.* from that time onwards. [*ICTA 1988, s 553(2); FA 1995, s 55(8)*].

The provisions of *ICTA 1988, s 550(5)* regarding the operation of top-slicing relief when there is more than one chargeable event do not apply to 'new non-resident policies' or to 'new offshore capital redemption policies'. [*ICTA 1988, s 553(9)*].

46   Losses

Cross-references. See 16.2 claims for claims involving more than one tax year; 51.11 NON-RESIDENTS AND OTHER OVERSEAS MATTERS for trades carried on and controlled abroad; 53.9–53.11, 53.17, 53.18 PARTNERSHIPS; 69.12 SCHEDULE A; 71.34 SCHEDULE D, CASES I AND II for loss of money lent; 73.3 SCHEDULE D, CASES IV AND V for deficiencies on overseas lettings; 74.4 SCHEDULE D, CASE VI.

Simon's Direct Tax Service E1.6.

Other sources. See Tolley's Tax Losses. See also Revenue Business Income Manual BIM 75000–75760.

46.1   Headings in this chapter are as follows.

<table>
<tr><td>46.2</td><td>Trading losses</td><td>46.10</td><td>Losses in early years of a trade</td></tr>
<tr><td>46.3</td><td>Set-off of trading losses against other income</td><td>46.11</td><td>— example</td></tr>
<tr><td></td><td></td><td>46.12</td><td>Terminal losses</td></tr>
<tr><td>46.4</td><td>— examples</td><td>46.13</td><td>— example</td></tr>
<tr><td>46.5</td><td>Set-off of trading losses against capital gains</td><td>46.14</td><td>Treatment of annual payments and interest as losses</td></tr>
<tr><td>46.6</td><td>— example</td><td>46.15</td><td>Losses on shares in unlisted trading companies</td></tr>
<tr><td>46.7</td><td>Treatment of capital allowances</td><td></td><td></td></tr>
<tr><td>46.8</td><td>Restrictions on relief</td><td>46.16</td><td>— example</td></tr>
<tr><td>46.9</td><td>Trading losses carried forward</td><td></td><td></td></tr>
</table>

46.2   **TRADING LOSSES**

Unless otherwise stated or the context suggests otherwise, references in this chapter to **trading losses** are to losses sustained in the carrying on of a trade, profession or vocation.

Trading losses are generally computed according to the same rules as apply in computing profits. [*FA 1998, s 46(2)*]. Relief may be obtained for trading losses

(*a*)   by **Set-off** against other income of the same tax year or preceding year. See 46.3–46.8 below.

(*b*)   by **Carry-forward** against subsequent profits of the same trade. See 46.9 below.

(*c*)   by carry-back of **Losses in early years of a trade.** See 46.10 below.

(*d*)   by carry-back of a **Terminal Loss.** See 46.12 below.

(*e*)   by **Set-off** against **capital gains** of the same tax year or preceding tax year if and to the extent that the loss remains unrelieved after applying (*a*) above. See 46.5 below.

It is not possible to anticipate a loss by claiming it before the end of the period of account in which the loss arises (and similarly where the results of more than one period are required to determine the loss for a tax year, claims may not precede the end of the last such period). See *Jones v O'Brien Ch D 1988, 60 TC 706* and Revenue Tax Bulletin August 2001 pp 878, 879.

Where a loss can be relieved under more than one head and it is sufficiently large, the taxpayer can select the order in which the different heads are to be applied, but the whole of the income or profits available for relief under one head must be relieved before passing to the next (*Butt v Haxby Ch D 1982, 56 TC 547*).

Relief against income may be obtained for losses on shares in unlisted trading companies. See 46.15 below.

See 16.2 CLAIMS for further provisions regarding claims for a loss incurred in one tax year to be carried back to an earlier tax year.

The rules for relieving trading losses were substantially amended as a consequence of the introduction of a current year basis of assessment by *FA 1994*, replacing the preceding year basis of assessment that applied previously. The rules set out in this chapter are as amended. For the old rules, which applied to, broadly, losses sustained in 1995/96 and earlier years where the trade etc. commenced before 6 April 1994, and for transitional rules on the changeover, see the 2003/04 and earlier editions.

46.3   **SET-OFF OF TRADING LOSSES AGAINST OTHER INCOME** [*ICTA 1988, s 380*]

Where in any tax year a person sustains a loss in a trade, profession, vocation or employment, carried on solely or in partnership, he may make a claim on or before the first anniversary of 31 January following that tax year for relief against income (i) of the tax year in which the loss is incurred (under *ICTA 1988, s 380(1)(a)*), or (ii) of the tax year preceding that in which the loss is incurred (under *ICTA 1988, s 380(1)(b)*). Where, against income of the same year, claims are made both under (i) in respect of that year's loss and under (ii) in respect of the following year's loss, (i) takes precedence. [*ICTA 1988, s 380; FA 1994, s 209(1)(7), Sch 20 para 8; FA 1995, s 118*].

Where claims are made for a particular loss to be set against income of both the same tax year and the preceding tax year, no statutory order of priority is laid down; the claimant may choose which of the two claims should take precedence (Revenue booklet SAT 1(1995), para 4.15).

For the above purposes, a loss is computed in the same way *and in respect of the same basis period* as profits are computed under Schedule D, Case I or II (see 71.3–71.11 SCHEDULE D, CASES I AND II for basis period rules). Where, as a result of basis periods overlapping, an amount of loss would otherwise fall to be included in the computations for two successive tax years, it is not to be so included for the second of those years. [*ICTA 1988, s 382; FA 1994, s 209(3)(8); FA 1995, s 118*].

For restrictions on relief, see 46.8 below.

The income against which a loss is set is income *before* deduction of the personal allowance or, where applicable, blind person's allowance, which will thus be wasted if the income of a particular tax year is fully covered by a loss claim. The effect on personal allowances, rates of tax etc. needs to be carefully considered. See Tolley's Tax Losses for more detail. Also, if taxable income is extinguished, this may result in an *ICTA 1988, s 350* assessment on any annuities or other payments made net of tax (see 1.10 ALLOWANCES AND TAX RATES).Partial claims under *ICTA 1988, s 380* are not permitted; if a loss is set against income of a particular tax year, it must be fully set against that income until either the loss or the available income is exhausted. Claims under *ICTA 1988, s 380(1)(a)* and *s 380(1)(b)* are, however, entirely separate; in relation to a particular loss the taxpayer may make either or neither claim or both claims. By virtue of *ICTA 1988, s 835(4)*, the loss is treated as reducing income of different classes (e.g. dividend income, other savings income and non-savings income) in the order which results in the greatest reduction in tax liability.

See 16.2 CLAIMS for further provisions regarding claims for a loss incurred in one tax year to be carried back to an earlier tax year.

46.4   Losses

Late claims. Although there is no provision for the acceptance of late claims under *ICTA 1988, s 380* (or *ICTA 1988, s 381* at 46.10 below), such relief may be granted as would have been due if a timeous claim had been made where the taxpayer or agent either:

(*a*)   was misled by some relevant and uncorrected Revenue error; or

(*b*)   made an informal claim within the time limit which he or she reasonably believed to be an acceptable claim, and the need to formalise the claim was not pointed out by the Revenue within the time limit; or

(*c*)   was effectively prevented from making a timeous claim for reasons beyond his or her control,

and provided that the late claim is made within a reasonable period (not normally more than three months) after the expiry of the excuse. As regards (*c*) above, acceptable reasons do *not* normally include: delays in preparing the accounts (unless for reasons beyond the taxpayer's or agent's control); delays in the Revenue's agreeing the accounts (although valid claims may be made before the accounts are either submitted or agreed, provided that the loss is clearly identified); misunderstandings and failures to communicate between taxpayer and agent; oversight or neglect by current or previous agents; ignorance of the statutory time limits; or deliberate delays because it was unclear at the expiry of the time limit whether the claim was advantageous. (Revenue Tax Bulletin December 1994 p 183). See further Revenue Business Income Manual BIM 75225, 75230. See also BIM 75220 as regards withdrawal of claims.

Foot and mouth outbreak. For the full range of measures, including early claims to loss relief, in relation to the 2001 foot and mouth disease outbreak, see Revenue Tax Bulletin Special Edition May 2001.

Simon's Direct Tax Service. See E1.602, E1.604.

46.4   *Examples*

General

L, a single woman, commences to trade on 1 July 2000, preparing accounts to 30 June, and has the following results (as adjusted for tax purposes and after capital allowances) for the first four years.

	Profit/(loss)
	£
Year ended 30 June 2001	9,000
Year ended 30 June 2002	3,000
Year ended 30 June 2003	(1,000)
Year ended 30 June 2004	(7,000)

L has other income of £6,000 for 2003/04 and £7,000 for 2004/05, having had no other income in the earlier years.

The taxable profits for the first four tax years of the business are as follows.

	£
2000/01 (1.7.2000–5.4.01) (£9,000 × $\frac{9}{12}$)	6,750*
2001/02 (y/e 30.6.01)	9,000
2002/03 (y/e 30.6.02)	3,000
2003/04 (y/e 30.6.03)	Nil
2004/05 (y/e 30.6.04)	Nil

* Overlap relief accruing – £6,750.

L claims relief under *ICTA 1988, s 380(1)(a)* (set-off against income of the same year) for the 2003/04 loss (£1,000). She also claims relief under *ICTA 1988, s 380(1)(b)* (set-off against income of the preceding year) for the 2004/05 loss (£7,000), with a further claim being made under *ICTA 1988, s 380(1)(a)* for the balance of that loss.

The tax position for 2003/04 and 2004/05 is as follows.

	£
2003/04	
Total income before loss relief	6,000
Deduct Claim under *section 380(1)(a)* note (*a*)	1,000
	5,000
Deduct Claim under *section 380(1)(b)*	5,000
Revised total income	Nil
2004/05	
Total income before loss relief	7,000
Deduct Claim under *section 380(1)(a)* (balance)	2,000
Revised total income	5,000
Deduct Personal allowance	4,745
Taxable income	£255

Loss utilisation

	£
2003/04	
Loss available under *section 380(1)(a)*	1,000
Deduct Utilised in 2003/04	1,000
Loss available under *section 380(1)(b)*	7,000
Deduct Utilised in 2003/04	5,000
Loss available for relief in 2004/05 under *section 380(1)(a)*	£2,000
2004/05	
Balance of loss available under *section 380(1)(a)*	2,000
Deduct Utilised in 2004/05	2,000

Note

(*a*) Where losses of two different years are set against the income of one tax year, then, regardless of the order of claims, relief for the current year's loss is given in priority to that for the following year's loss (see 46.3 above). This is beneficial to the taxpayer in this example as it leaves £2,000 of the 2004/05 loss to be relieved in that year.

Losses in early years

Q commenced trading on 1 February 2004 and prepared accounts to 31 December. He made a trading loss of £20,900 in the 11 months to 31 December 2004 and profits of £18,000 and £16,000 in the years to 31 December 2005 and 2006 respectively. He has substantial other income for 2003/04 and 2004/05 and makes claims under *ICTA 1988, s 380* for both years.

46.5 Losses

Taxable profits/(allowable losses) are as follows.

		£	£
2003/04	(1.2.04–5.4.04) (£20,900) × $\frac{2}{11}$		(3,800)
2004/05	(1.2.04–31.1.05)		
	1.2.04–31.12.04	(20,900)	
	Less already allocated to 2003/04	3,800	
		(17,100)	
	1.1.05–31.1.05 £18,000 × $\frac{1}{12}$	1,500	
			(15,600)
2005/06	(y/e 31.12.05)		18,000
	(Overlap relief accruing—£1,500)		
2006/07	(y/e 31.12.06)		16,000

Notes

(a)   Losses available for relief for 2003/04 and 2004/05 are £3,800 and £15,600 respectively. If both years' losses are carried forward under *ICTA 1988, s 385* instead of being set against other income (under either *ICTA 1988, s 380* or *s 381*), the aggregate loss of £19,400 will extinguish the 2005/06 profit and reduce the 2006/07 profit by £1,400. Note that although the actual loss was £20,900, there is no further amount available for carry-forward: the difference of £1,500 has been used in aggregation in 2004/05.

(b)   The net profit for the first three accounting periods is £13,100 (£18,000 + £16,000 – £20,900). The net taxable profit for the first four tax years is £14,600 (£18,000 + £16,000 – £3,800 – £15,600). The difference of £1,500 represents the overlap relief accrued (see 71.11 SCHEDULE D, CASES I AND II). Note that the overlap profit of £1,500 is by reference to an overlap period of *three* months, i.e. 1.2.04 to 5.4.04 (two months — overlap profit nil) and 1.1.05 to 31.1.05 (one month — overlap profit £1,500).

46.5   **SET-OFF OF TRADING LOSSES AGAINST CAPITAL GAINS**

Where losses arise and a person makes a claim under *ICTA 1988, s 380* as in 46.3 above, a further claim may be made in the same notice of claim for the determination of the 'relevant amount', which is so much of the trading loss as

(a)   cannot be set off against the claimant's income for the year of claim, and

(b)   has not already been relieved for any other year.

A separate claim for relief under *FA 1991, s 72* will be accepted where (i) relief under *ICTA 1988, s 380* had previously been claimed and a claim under *FA 1991, s 72* could have been made, (ii) a separate claim under *FA 1991, s 72* is made within the time limits for the original *section 380* claim, (iii) after the *section 380* relief there is a balance of unrelieved trading losses, and (iv) all other conditions for *FA 1991, s 72* relief are satisfied. (Revenue Tax Bulletin August 1993 p 87). A claim under *FA 1991, s 72* may be made even though there is no income for the year of claim to justify making a claim under *section 380* alone. (Revenue Business Income Manual BIM 75425).

The claim is not deemed to be determined until the relevant amount for the year can no longer be varied, whether by the Commissioners on appeal or on the order of any court.

The relevant amount, as finally determined, is to be treated for the purposes of capital gains tax as an allowable loss accruing to the claimant (in the year whose income is covered by the *ICTA 1988, s 380* claim), except that it cannot exceed the '*maximum amount*', which is the amount on which the claimant would be chargeable to capital gains tax for that year, disregarding the effect of this provision and of the capital gains tax annual exemption. In relation to claims in respect of trading losses sustained in 2004/05 and subsequent years, taper relief (see Tolley's Capital Gains Tax under Taper Relief) is also disregarded (so that the maximum amount is equal to pre-tapered gains). An election may be made to apply this amendment in relation to trading losses sustained in 2002/03 and to so apply it in relation to chargeable gains of 2001/02 or 2002/03 or both. Similarly, an election may be made to apply it in relation to losses sustained in 2003/04 and to so apply it in relation to gains of 2002/03 or 2003/04 or both. Such an election must be made in writing to an officer of the Board within the time allowed for making the claim under *ICTA 1988, s 380* (and thus under *FA 1991, s 72*) for the year in question (see 46.3 above).

In computing the maximum amount, no account is taken of any event occurring after the determination of the relevant amount and in consequence of which the maximum amount might otherwise be reduced by virtue of any capital gains tax legislation. Thus if, as a result of a subsequent reduction in the chargeable gains against which the maximum amount is set, the maximum amount exceeds those chargeable gains, the excess is carried forward as an allowable capital loss.

No amount treated as an allowable loss under this provision may be deducted from chargeable gains accruing in a tax year which begins after the claimant has ceased to carry on the trade in which the loss was sustained.

[*FA 1991, s 72; FA 1994, Sch 26 Pt V(24); FA 2002, s 48*].

Simon's Direct Tax Service. See E1.603.

46.6   *Example*

M has carried on a trade for some years, preparing accounts to 30 June each year. For the year ended 30 June 2004 he makes a trading loss of £17,000. His assessable profit for 2003/04 is £5,000, and his other income for both 2003/04 and 2004/05 amounts to £2,000. He makes a capital gain of £12,500 and a capital loss of £1,000 for 2004/05 and has capital losses brought forward of £8,000. M makes claims for loss relief, against income of 2003/04 and income and gains of 2004/05, under *ICTA 1988, s 380(1)(b), s 380(1)(a)* and *FA 1991, s 72* respectively.

Calculation of 'relevant amount'

	£
Trading loss—year ended 30.6.04	17,000
Relieved against other income for 2004/05 (*section 380(1)(a)*)	(2,000)
Relieved against income for 2003/04 (*section 380(1)(b)*)	(7,000)
Relevant amount	£8,000

Calculation of 'maximum amount'

		£
Gains for 2004/05		12,500
Deduct Losses for 2004/05		(1,000)
Unrelieved losses brought forward		(8,000)
Maximum amount		£3,500

46.7 Losses

Relief under *FA 1991, s 72*

	£	£
Gains for the year		12,500
Losses for the year	1,000	
Relief under *FA 1991, s 72*	3,500	
		4,500
Gain (covered by annual exemption)		£8,000
Capital losses brought forward and carried forward		£8,000

Loss memorandum

	£
Trading loss	17,000
Claimed under *section 380(1)(a)*	(2,000)
Claimed under *section 380(1)(b)*	(7,000)
Claimed under *FA 1991, s 72*	(3,500)
Unutilised loss	£4,500

Notes

(a) In this example, £200 of the capital gains tax annual exemption of £8,200 is wasted, but the brought forward capital losses are preserved for carry-forward against gains of future years. If M had *not* made the claim under *FA 1991, s 72*, his net gains for the year of £11,500 would have been reduced to the annual exempt amount by deducting £3,300 of the losses brought forward. Only £4,700 of capital losses would remain available for carry-forward against future gains and a further £3,500 of trading losses would have been available for carry-forward against future trading profits. So the effect of the claim is to preserve capital losses at the expense of trading losses.

(b) For 2004/05 onwards, the gains to be taken into account in computing the 'maximum amount' are the gains *before* applying taper relief (see main commentary above).

46.7 TREATMENT OF CAPITAL ALLOWANCES

Under the old preceding year basis of assessment which applied up to and including, broadly, 1995/96, a loss for *ICTA 1988, s 380* purposes could be increased, or created, by capital allowances if the claimant so wished. [*ICTA 1988, s 383; FA 1994, s 214(1)(b)*]. See the 2002/03 and earlier editions for details.

Under the current year basis of assessment applicable for, broadly, 1996/97 onwards, capital allowances are treated as trading expenses of periods of account (see 9.1, 9.2(i) CAPITAL ALLOWANCES). They are thus automatically included in the amount of any trading loss (as adjusted for tax purposes).

46.8 RESTRICTIONS ON RELIEF

(a) **Non-commercial basis** [*ICTA 1988, s 384; FA 1994, s 214(1)(c), s 216(3)(d); FA 1996, s 134, Sch 20 para 25*]. Relief under *ICTA 1988, s 380* (see 46.3 above) will not be given for a tax loss unless, for the tax year in which the loss is sustained (or, if the trading method was changed during that year, by the end of it), the trade, profession or vocation was carried on

(i)   on a commercial basis, and

(ii)   with a view to realisation of profit in that trade etc., or any larger undertaking of which it forms part.

The test is a subjective one — see *Walls v Livesey (Sp C 4)*, *[1995] SSCD 12* on similar wording in *ICTA 1988, s 504(2)(a)*. In *Wannell v Rothwell Ch D 1996, 68 TC 719* an individual's speculative dealing in stocks and shares and commodity futures was held to be trading but not on a commercial basis. See also *Brown v Richardson (Sp C 129), [1997] SSCD 233*, and the Revenue Tax Bulletin article (October 1997 pp 472, 473) commenting on that decision, and *Delian Enterprises v Ellis (Sp C 186), [1999] SSCD 103*.

A trade is treated as complying with the requirement at (ii) above if at the relevant time it was being carried on so as to afford a reasonable expectation of profit.

For the Revenue approach generally, see Revenue Business Income Manual BIM 75705–75725.

(The above restrictions do not apply to losses incurred in the exercise of functions conferred by or under any enactment, including a local or private Act.)

(*b*)   **Farming and market gardening** [*ICTA 1988, s 397; FA 1994, s 214(3); FA 1996, s 134, Sch 20 para 27; CAA 2001, Sch 2 para 34*]. Except as below, relief will not be given under *ICTA 1988, s 380* for any loss incurred in a trade of farming or market gardening if losses from that trade, computed under the normal Schedule D, Case I rules but ignoring capital allowances, were also incurred in each of the five years preceding the tax year in which the loss is sustained. Similarly, if such a trade is carried on by a company a loss incurred in any accounting period may not be set off against total profits (under *ICTA 1988, s 393(2)* or *s 393A(1)* — see Tolley's Corporation Tax) if there would still be a loss if capital allowances were ignored and there was a loss (similarly computed) in each of the chargeable periods wholly or partly comprised in the five years preceding that accounting period.

Disallowance under *section 397* **does not apply** if:

(i)   the farming etc., is part of, and ancillary to, a larger trading undertaking, or

(ii)   the farming etc., activities in the year are carried on in a way which might reasonably be expected to produce profits in the future and the activities in the preceding five years could not reasonably have been expected to become profitable until after the year under review. [*ICTA 1988, s 397(3)(4)*].

By concession, there is also relief from the application of *section 397* for 2000/01 and 2001/02 in cases where 2000/01 is the sixth, or 2001/02 the sixth or seventh, consecutive year of losses, provided that the six or seven year period of losses was immediately preceded by a year of profit, and that in the three years immediately preceding that year of profit there was at least one other year of profit. For incorporated farmers the concession applies by reference to the accounting periods ending in the years to 31 March 2001 and 31 March 2002. (Revenue Pamphlet IR 1, B55).

See 71.47(*d*) SCHEDULE D, CASES I AND II for relief for repairs etc. on owner-occupied farms (no longer applicable after 5 April 2001).

Also by concession, the Revenue extend the five-year time limits above to eleven years from commencement in the case of stud farming, i.e. the breeding of thoroughbred horses, provided that the business is potentially profitable (Revenue Business Income Manual BIM 55725).

46.8 Losses

(c) **Leasing by individuals** [*ICTA 1988, s 384(6)–(8)(11); FA 1994, s 214(2); CAA 2001, Sch 2 para 29*]. Where an individual (alone or in partnership) incurs expenditure on plant or machinery for leasing in the course of a trade, any capital allowances are not to be included in calculating loss relief under *ICTA 1988, s 380* unless the individual carries on the trade for a continuous period of at least six months in, or beginning or ending in, the year of loss (i.e. the tax year in which the loss is sustained) and he devotes substantially the whole of his time (see Business Income Manual BIM 75730) to the trade throughout the year of loss or, if the trade begins or ceases (or both) in that year, for a continuous period of at least six months beginning or ending in that year. This prohibition also applies if the asset is not leased but payments in the nature of royalties or licence fees are to accrue from rights granted in connection with it. Any relief given will be withdrawn by assessment under Schedule D, Case VI. The foregoing provisions are without prejudice to (d) and (e) below.

First-year allowances [*ICTA 1988, s 384A; CAA 2001, Sch 2 para 30; CAA 1990, s 142*].

(d) **Leasing partnerships.** Where expenditure is incurred on plant or machinery for leasing in the course of a trade (or other qualifying activity — see 9.24 CAPITAL ALLOWANCES) carried on, or to be carried on, by a partnership including a company and an individual (with or without other partners), any loss arising from a first-year allowance (where available — see 9.27 CAPITAL ALLOWANCES) on that expenditure will not be allowed as set-off against the general income of the individual under *ICTA 1988, s 380*. For this purpose, letting a ship on charter is regarded as leasing.

(e) **Arrangements.** Where an individual incurs expenditure giving rise to a first-year allowance (see (d) above), no relief will be given to him for that allowance under *section 380* if, under an arrangement or scheme, such relief was expected as the sole or main benefit of the expenditure and (i) he was in partnership then or later, or (ii) he transferred the trade etc., or the relevant asset, to a CONNECTED PERSON (19), or (iii) he transferred the asset to any person at lower than its market value.

Any relief given will be withdrawn under (d) or (e) above by assessment under Schedule D, Case VI.

(f) **Losses derived from film tax reliefs.** There is a potential exit charge as described below where

  (i)   an individual has claimed relief under *ICTA 1988, s 380* in respect of a 'film-related loss' sustained by him in a trade (whether carried on solely or in partnership);

  (ii) there is a 'disposal' after **9 December 2003** of a right of the individual to profits arising from the trade (a '*relevant disposal*'); and

  (iii) an 'exit event' occurs.

A loss is a '*film-related loss*' if the computation of profits or losses that it results from is made in accordance with *F(No 2)A 1992, ss 40A–40C* or *ss 41–43* or *F(No 2)A 1997, s 48*, all of which give relief, as revenue expenditure, for production and acquisition expenditure on films (see 71.48 SCHEDULE D, CASES I AND II).

A '*disposal*' is very widely (but not exhaustively) defined (by *FA 2004, s 120*) for the purposes of (ii) above to include, for example, the disposal, surrender or loss of a right to income, a default in the payment of income, certain changes in profit- or loss-sharing ratios and the individual's leaving a partnership (including a case where the partnership is dissolved). The disposal may be part of a larger disposal.

An '*exit event*' occurs when, after 9 December 2003,

- the individual receives any consideration for the relevant disposal (whether or not as part of a larger sum) which is not otherwise chargeable to income tax; or

- the 'losses claimed' become greater than the individual's 'capital contribution' to the trade (whether because of a claim for losses or a decrease in that capital contribution); or

- there is an increase in the amount by which the losses claimed exceed the capital contribution.

A **chargeable event** occurs at the time the last of the conditions at (i)-(iii) above is satisfied (regardless of whether or not the individual is still carrying on the trade). The individual is treated as receiving at that time annual profits chargeable to income tax under Schedule D, Case VI of an amount equal to the total consideration received for relevant disposals and not otherwise chargeable to income tax plus the excess (if any) of 'losses claimed' over 'capital contribution' (such amounts being judged as at the time immediately after the chargeable event). There is provision to avoid double counting where there are successive chargeable events. The consideration to be taken into account is deemed to be increased by any deduction actually made from it in consideration of any person's agreeing to or facilitating a relevant disposal or exit event (e.g. an exit fee).

References above to '*losses claimed*' are to any film-related losses sustained in the trade in any tax year for which the individual has claimed relief under *ICTA 1988, s 380* or *s 381* (see 46.10 below) or *FA 1991, s 72* (see 46.5 above). An individual's '*capital contribution*' is the amount he has contributed to the trade as capital, less so much of that amount as

- he has, directly or indirectly, drawn out or received back, or

- he is entitled so to draw out or receive back, or

- he has had, directly or indirectly, reimbursed to him by any person, or

- he is entitled to require any person so to reimburse to him,

but not including any such amount drawn out or received back as is chargeable to income tax as profits of the trade. Anything brought into account on a chargeable event as consideration for a relevant disposal is not deducted in arriving at his capital contribution.

[*FA 2004, ss 119–123*].

See 53.11 PARTNERSHIPS for other anti-avoidance provisions concerning losses derived from exploiting films.

(*g*)   **Miscellaneous.** See 53.9–53.11 PARTNERSHIPS for restrictions on loss reliefs available to non-active members of partnerships. Special restrictions on the use of losses apply in relation to certain company partnership arrangements [*ICTA 1988, s 116*] — see 53.13 PARTNERSHIPS. See 53.17, 53.18 PARTNERSHIPS for restrictions on loss reliefs available to, respectively, limited partners and members of limited liability partnerships. Loss relief cannot be claimed in respect of the special type of bonus issue described in *ICTA 1988, s 237* (prior to its repeal from 6 April 1999 — see 3.17 ANTI-AVOIDANCE) nor for certain partnerships dealing in commodity futures (see 3.19 ANTI-AVOIDANCE). See also under 3 ANTI-AVOIDANCE generally for restrictions regarding certain transactions in securities etc.

Simon's Direct Tax Service. See E1.606.

46.9 Losses

TRADING LOSSES CARRIED FORWARD [*ICTA 1988, s 385*]

Any balance of trading loss not used as above (or otherwise under the Taxes Acts) may be carried forward without time limit as a set-off against the first following profits (or, if insufficient, the next, and so on) of the same business by the same owner. See *Bispham v Eardiston Farming Co Ch D 1962, 40 TC 322* as to effect of *ICTA 1988, s 53* (all farming by a person treated as one trade) on the carry-forward of farming losses. A loss carried forward must be set against the first available profits, although the latter might otherwise have been completely offset by personal allowances etc. for that year; partial claims are not permitted. A loss available for carry-forward is computed as in 46.3 above with the same rules governing overlapping basis periods; see also the second example at 46.4 above, particularly as regards losses used in aggregation (for which see *CIR v Scott Adamson CS 1932, 17 TC 379*).[*ICTA 1988, s 385; FA 1994, s 209(4)(5)(8), s 216(3)(e); FA 1995, s 118*].

Time limit for claims. A claim to carry forward a loss must be made on or before the fifth anniversary of 31 January following the tax year in which the loss arose. The loss is then relieved automatically against subsequent profits with no further claim being necessary. [*ICTA 1988, s 385(8); TMA 1970, s 43; FA 1994, s 196, s 199(2)(a), s 209(5), Sch 19 para 14*].

For a case turning on the failure to establish the year(s) in which losses from an abortive business venture arose, see *Richardson v Jenkins Ch D 1995, 67 TC 246*.

Relief against certain investment income. Where full relief under *ICTA 1988, s 385* cannot be given for any particular year because of an insufficiency of business profits, these are to be increased for the purpose by adding to them interest and dividends on investments arising in that year which, had they not been taxed under other provisions, would have formed part of the trading receipts. In that event repayment of tax may be due. [*ICTA 1988, s 385(4)*]. See also 71.56 SCHEDULE D, CASES I AND II.

Private businesses converted into companies [*ICTA 1988, s 386; FA 1994, s 216(3)(f)*]. Any unrelieved balance of loss from pre-conversion years may be made use of by individuals transferring their business mainly for shares allotted to themselves or their nominees, as follows.

For any year *throughout which* they retain the beneficial ownership of the shares and the company carries on the business, the loss may be used as a set-off (under *ICTA 1988, s 385*) against any income derived from the company. The set-off must be used first against direct assessments (e.g. on director's fees etc.) with any balance set against dividends etc. from the company. In practice, relief should not be refused so long as shares representing at least 80% of the consideration received for the business are retained (Revenue Business Income Manual BIM 75500).

Change of residence. Where, on a sole trader becoming or ceasing to be UK resident, the trade is deemed to be permanently discontinued and a new one commenced, losses of the 'old' trade may be carried forward under *ICTA 1988, s 385* and set against profits of the 'new' trade. See 71.17 SCHEDULE D, CASES I AND II (and see 53.14 PARTNERSHIPS for a similar rule as regards an individual trading in partnership).

For the treatment in certain circumstances of annual payments and interest as losses carried forward, see 46.14 below.

Simon's Direct Tax Service. See E1.610 *et seq.*

46.10 **LOSSES IN EARLY YEARS OF A TRADE** [*ICTA 1988, s 381*]

If an individual sustains a loss in a trade, profession or vocation in any of the first four tax years in which the trade etc. is first carried on by him, he may claim relief for that loss against his other income of the *three* tax years preceding the year of loss. Income of earlier years is relieved in priority to that of later years. The trade (or if part of a larger undertaking, the whole undertaking) must have been carried on during the period of loss on a commercial basis with a reasonable expectation of profits during that period or within a reasonable time thereafter (an objective test — see *Walls v Livesey (Sp C 4), [1995] SSCD 12* — and see generally *Walsh and Another v Taylor (Sp C 386) 2003, [2004] SSCD 48*). The relief is available to an individual trading etc. in partnership by reference to the first four tax years in which he is a partner. However, relief is not available to a married individual where the trade was being carried on by his or her spouse at a time earlier than the three tax years preceding the year of loss (which, for example, precludes relief to that extent where an individual takes his spouse into partnership). See 53.9–53.11 PARTNERSHIPS for other restrictions on relief available to certain partners. The anti-avoidance legislation at 46.8(*f*) above (losses derived from film tax reliefs) applies equally where the loss relief is claimed under these provisions.

Computation of losses is as for *ICTA 1988, s 380* purposes (see 46.3 above).

Time limit for claims. Claims must be made on or before the first anniversary of 31 January following the tax year in which the loss is sustained. For late claims, see 46.3 above.

See 16.2 CLAIMS for further provisions regarding claims for a loss incurred in one tax year to be carried back to an earlier tax year.

Capital allowances are subject to the same restrictions as in 46.8(*c*)(*d*)(*e*) above.

General. The income against which a loss is set is income *before* deduction of the personal allowance or, where applicable, blind person's allowance, which will thus be wasted if the income of a particular tax year is fully covered by a loss claim. The effect on personal allowances, rates of tax etc. needs to be carefully considered. See Tolley's Tax Losses for more detail. Also, if taxable income for a year is extinguished, this may result in an *ICTA 1988, s 350* assessment on any annuities or other payments made net of tax (see 1.10 ALLOWANCES AND TAX RATES).Partial claims under *ICTA 1988, s 381* are not permitted; if a loss is set against income of a particular tax year, it must be fully set against that income until either the loss or the available income is exhausted. Furthermore, it is not possible to claim to carry back a loss under these provisions against the income of particular years as opposed to all of the three years in question. By virtue of *ICTA 1988, s 835(4)*, a loss is treated as reducing income of different classes (e.g. dividend income, other savings income and non-savings income) in the order which results in the greatest reduction in tax liability.

[*ICTA 1988, ss 381, 382(3)(4); FA 1994, ss 209(2)(3)(7)–(9), 216(3)(c); FA 1995, s 118; FA 1996, ss 134, 135, Sch 20 para 24, Sch 21 para 10*].

See also 71.66 SCHEDULE D, CASES I AND II as regards **pre-trading expenditure**.

Simon's Direct Tax Service. See E1.621.

46.11   *Example*

F, a single person, commenced to trade on 1 December 2002, preparing accounts to 30 November. The first four years of trading produce losses of £12,000, £9,000, £2,000 and £1,000 respectively, these figures being as adjusted for tax purposes and after taking account of capital allowances. For each of the four tax years 1999/2000 to 2002/03, F had other income of £8,000.

The losses for tax purposes are as follows.

	£	£
2002/03 (1.12.02–5.4.03) (£12,000 × $\frac{4}{12}$)		4,000
2003/04 (y/e 30.11.03)	12,000	
Less already allocated to 2002/03	4,000	
		8,000
2004/05 (y/e 30.11.04)		9,000
2005/06 (y/e 30.11.05)		2,000
2006/07 (y/e 30.11.06) note (b)		1,000

Loss relief under *ICTA 1988, s 381* is available as follows.

	2002/03	2003/04	2004/05	2005/06
	£	£	£	£
Losses available	4,000	8,000	9,000	2,000
Set against total income				
1999/2000	4,000	—	—	—
2000/01	—	8,000	—	—
2001/02	—	—	8,000	—
2002/03	—	—	1,000	2,000
	£4,000	£8,000	£9,000	£2,000

Revised total income is thus £4,000 for 1999/2000, nil for 2000/01 and 2001/02 and £5,000 for 2002/03.

Notes

(a) Losses are computed by reference to the same basis periods as profits. Where any part of a loss would otherwise fall to be included in the computations for two successive tax years (as is the case for 2002/03 and 2003/04 in this example), that part is excluded from the computation for the second of those years.

(b) The loss for the year ended 30 November 2006 in this example is not available for relief under *ICTA 1988, s 381* as it does not fall into the first four *tax years* of the business (even though it is incurred in the first four years of trading). It is of course available for relief under *ICTA 1988, s 380* (depending on other income for 2005/06 and 2006/07) or for carry-forward under *ICTA 1988, s 385*.

46.12   **TERMINAL LOSSES** [*ICTA 1988, s 388*]

On the permanent discontinuance for income tax purposes of any trade, profession or vocation, a loss sustained in the *twelve months* before the date of cessation, so far as not otherwise relieved (for example, in a claim under *ICTA 1988, s 380* at 46.3 above), may be carried back and set off against the taxable profits (if any) of the business for the tax year in which the cessation occurs and the *three* preceding tax years. Relief is given against profits of later years in priority to those of earlier years. The terminal loss is computed by aggregating the loss (if any) sustained in the final tax year and the loss (if any) sustained in that part of the penultimate tax year that falls within the twelve months immediately preceding cessation, insofar as such losses have not otherwise been taken into account to reduce or relieve any charge to tax — see also the example and note at 46.13 below.

A terminal loss must be set against the latest available profits in full, although the latter might otherwise have been completely offset by personal allowances etc. for that year; partial claims are not permitted. Furthermore, it is not possible to claim to carry back a terminal loss against the income of particular years as opposed to all of the four years in question.

Time limit for claims. A claim for relief must be made on or before the fifth anniversary of 31 January following the tax year in which cessation occurs.

See 16.2 CLAIMS for further provisions regarding claims for a loss incurred in one tax year to be carried back to an earlier tax year.

Partnerships. Terminal loss relief is available to an outgoing member of a partnership in respect of losses sustained in his notional trade. All partners may claim terminal loss relief on a discontinuance of the actual partnership trade. See 53 PARTNERSHIPS.

Effect of charges on income. The profits against which a terminal loss may be set are treated as reduced by the gross amount of any payment made from which income tax was deducted at source but did not have to be accounted for to the Revenue, i.e. because the payment was made out of taxed profits. In other words, the profits are treated as reduced by charges on income within *ICTA 1988, s 348* (see 22.2 DEDUCTION OF TAX AT SOURCE), with no distinction between trade and non-trade charges. In such cases, the terminal loss itself is reduced by a like amount *unless* the payment in question (i) was made wholly and exclusively for the purposes of the trade etc., (ii) could have been assessed under *ICTA 1988, s 350* (see 22.2 DEDUCTION OF TAX AT SOURCE) if not made out of taxed profits, *and* (iii) if so assessed, could have been treated as a loss under the provisions at 46.14(*a*) below.

Relief against certain investment income. Where full relief under *ICTA 1988, s 388* cannot be given for any particular year because of an insufficiency of business profits, these are to be increased for the purpose by adding to them interest and dividends on investments arising in that year which, had they not been taxed under other provisions, would have formed part of the trading receipts. See also 71.56 SCHEDULE D, CASES I AND II.

Mines, oil wells etc. Where the trade discontinued is, or includes, the working of a mine, oil well etc., special provisions apply to dual claims under these provisions and under *CAA 2001, s 355.*

[*ICTA 1988, ss 388, 389; FA 1988, Sch 14 Pt V; FA 1994, s 209(6)(7), s 211(2), s 214(1)(d)(e), s 215(4)(5), s 216(3)(4), s 218; FA 1995, s 118*].

Overlap relief (see 71.11 SCHEDULE D, CASES I AND II) is a deduction in computing the profits of the final tax year (not the final period of account) and thus falls to be included in full in a terminal loss claim (and may itself create a terminal loss).

Simon's Direct Tax Service. See E1.622.

46.13   *Example*

B, a trader with a 30 September year end, ceases to trade on 30 June 2004. Tax-adjusted results for his last two accounting periods (disregarding overlap relief) are as follows.

	Trading profit/(loss)
Year ended 30 September 2003	£28,000
Nine months to 30 June 2004	(£9,000)

In addition, there is unused overlap relief (see 71.11 SCHEDULE D, CASES I AND II) of £2,000.

46.14 Losses

The terminal loss available is as follows.

		£	£
2004/05	(6.4.04 to 30.6.04)		
	£9,000 × $\frac{3}{9}$		3,000
	plus unused overlap relief		2,000
2003/04	(1.7.03 to 5.4.04)		
	1.10.03 to 5.4.04 £9,000 × $\frac{6}{9}$	6,000	
	1.7.03 to 30.9.03 (£28,000) × $\frac{3}{12}$	(7,000)	
		(1,000)	Nil
	Terminal loss		£5,000

Note

In determining the part of a terminal loss arising in a part of the final twelve months (the terminal loss period) that falls into any one tax year, a profit made in that period must be netted off against a loss sustained in that period. In this example, no net loss is incurred in that part of the terminal loss period falling within 2003/04. However, the two different tax years are considered entirely separately, so that the 'net profit' of £1,000 falling within 2003/04 does not have to be netted off against the 2004/05 loss and is instead treated as nil. The £6,000 losses which cannot form part of the terminal loss claim may be relieved under *ICTA 1988, s 380* (see 46.3 above), and in practice, where other income is sufficient, the whole of the £11,000 would in many cases be claimed under *ICTA 1988, s 380*.

46.14 **TREATMENT OF ANNUAL PAYMENTS AND INTEREST AS LOSSES**

(*a*) **Assessments under ICTA 1988, s 350** in respect of annual payments, royalties etc. not paid out of taxed income (see 22.3 DEDUCTION OF TAX AT SOURCE) may be treated as losses for the purposes of carry-forward under *ICTA 1988, ss 385, 386* (see 46.9 above) or allowed as terminal losses under *ICTA 1988, s 388* (see 46.12 above). Further, where such payments are made to residents of a country with which a DOUBLE TAX RELIEF (24) agreement is in force and are thereby exempt from UK tax, so that no assessment under *ICTA 1988, s 350* is made in respect of them, the amounts thereof can nevertheless be similarly carried forward (*SI 1970 No 488*). But these provisions do not apply to *section 350* assessments arising from

- payments not made wholly and exclusively for the purposes of the trade etc.,

- payments charged to capital, or not ultimately borne by the person assessed,

- yearly interest paid under deduction of tax under *ICTA 1988, s 349(2)* (see 22.3(ii) DEDUCTION OF TAX AT SOURCE),

- copyright royalties and design royalty and public lending right payments paid to non-residents (see *ICTA 1988, ss 536, 537, 537B*),

- sales of patent rights by non-residents (see *ICTA 1988, s 524* and 54 PATENTS),

[*ICTA 1988, ss 387, 389(1); FA 1997, Sch 18 Pt VI(2)(10)*].

(*b*) *Interest payments.* Where relief is claimed under *ICTA 1988, s 353* (see 43.3 INTEREST PAYABLE) in respect of interest paid wholly and exclusively for the purposes of a trade etc. and full effect cannot be given to such relief due to an insufficiency of income, the amount unallowed may be carried forward as a loss under *ICTA 1988, s 385* (see 46.9 above) or treated as a terminal loss under *ICTA 1988, s 388* (see 46.12 above). [*ICTA 1988, s 390*].

46.15   **LOSSES ON SHARES IN UNLISTED TRADING COMPANIES** [*ICTA 1988, ss 574–576*]

An individual may claim relief from income tax, instead of from capital gains tax, for an allowable loss (as computed for capital gains tax purposes) on a disposal of ordinary shares or stock in a qualifying trading company for which he subscribed and which were issued to him by the company in consideration of money or money's worth, or were transferred to him *inter vivos* by his spouse who had similarly subscribed for them. Where, for shares subscribed for before 10 March 1981, the consideration was deemed equal to the market value under *CGTA 1979, s 19(3)*, the loss allowable on disposal cannot exceed what the loss would have been without applying that subsection. For shares subscribed for after 9 March 1981, market value is not substituted where the consideration is less than market value. [*TCGA 1992, s 17(2)(b)*].

See generally Revenue Venture Capital Schemes Manual VCM 10000 *et seq.*, 45000 *et seq.*

Relief is available only if

(i)   the disposal is at arm's length for full consideration, or

(ii)   it is by way of a distribution on a winding-up, or

(iii)   the value of the shares has become negligible and a claim to that effect made under *TCGA 1992, s 24(2)* (see Tolley's Capital Gains Tax under Losses), or

(iv)   a deemed disposal occurs after 5 April 2000 under *TCGA 1992, s 24(1)* (which deems the entire loss, destruction, dissipation or extinction of an asset to be a disposal — see Tolley's Capital Gains Tax under Disposal).

By concession, relating to events before 6 April 2000, relief is not denied, provided that all the other conditions are fulfilled, where the company has no assets and is dissolved, the shareholder has not received a distribution in the course of dissolving or winding up the company (or an anticipated final distribution has not been made), and the shareholder has not made a deemed disposal of the shares under *TCGA 1992, s 24(2)*. (Revenue Pamphlet IR 1, D46). This concession is effectively replaced by (iv) above.

As regards shares issued **after 5 April 1998**, a '*qualifying trading company*' is a company which

(*a*)   either (i) is an 'eligible trading company' (see below) on the date of disposal, or (ii) has ceased to be an eligible trading company within three years before that date and has not since that cessation been an 'excluded company', an investment company or a non-eligible trading company, *and*

(*b*)   either (i) has been an eligible trading company for a continuous period of at least six years prior to the disposal (or prior to the cessation in (*a*)(ii) above, as the case may be), or (ii) has been an eligible trading company for a shorter continuous period ending with the disposal or cessation and has not previously been an excluded company, an investment company or a non-eligible trading company, *and*

(*c*)   has carried on its business wholly or mainly in the UK throughout the '*relevant period*' (i.e. the period ending with the date of disposal of the shares and beginning with the incorporation of the company, or, if later, one year before the date on which the shares were issued).

For shares issued before 7 March 2001, it was also a condition that the company be an 'unquoted' company (as defined for the purposes of the EIS — see 25.5 ENTERPRISE

INVESTMENT SCHEME) throughout that part of the relevant period (as defined in (c) above) that falls before 7 March 2001 (and see now below in the definition of 'eligible trading company').

As regards shares issued **before 6 April 1998**, a '*qualifying trading company*' is a company none of whose shares have at any time in the relevant period (i.e. ending with the date of disposal of the shares and beginning with the incorporation of the company, or, if later, one year before the date on which the shares were subscribed for) been listed on a recognised stock exchange and which

(*aa*) either (i) is a trading company (i.e. a company, other than an excluded company, whose business consists wholly or mainly of the carrying on of a trade or trades, or which is the holding company of a 'trading group') on the date of the disposal or (ii) has ceased to be a trading company within the previous three years and has not since that time been an investment company or an 'excluded company'; and

(*bb*) either (i) has been a trading company for a continuous period of six years ending on the date of disposal of the shares or the time it ceased to be a trading company; or (ii) if shorter, a continuous period ending on that date or that time and had not before the beginning of that period been an excluded company or an investment company; and

(*cc*) it has been resident in the UK since incorporation until the date of disposal.

Securities on the Alternative Investment Market ('AIM') are treated as unlisted for these purposes. (Revenue Press Release 20 February 1995).

An '*eligible trading company*' is a company which is, or would be, a qualifying company for the purposes of the EIS (see 25.5 ENTERPRISE INVESTMENT SCHEME). For this purpose, the EIS legislation is applied (by *ICTA 1988, s 576(4A)(4B)*) with appropriate minor modifications; for example, certain references to the relevant period for EIS purposes are replaced with references to the date of disposal or ceasing to be an eligible trading company (whichever is relevant) or whichever is the relevant continuous period (see (*b*) above). In relation to shares issued on or after 7 March 2001, in line with a change to the EIS rules, the company must be unquoted at the time of issue and no arrangements must then exist for it to cease to be unquoted (see 25.5 ENTERPRISE INVESTMENT SCHEME for further details). However, there is no requirement that the company *remain* unquoted, and this applies equally on and after 7 March 2001 in relation to shares issued before that date and after 5 April 1998. A winding-up does not prevent a company being an eligible trading company, but only for so long as it continues to be a trading company (within (*aa*) above); the condition now applies in relation to shares issued after 5 April 2001 (but did originally apply up to and including 20 March 2000, after which a drafting error inadvertently altered the law).

The above represents a narrowing of the loss relief against income rules as regards shares issued after 5 April 1998 in that the company which issued the shares must satisfy the EIS requirements as to, *inter alia*, qualifying activities, qualifying trades, gross assets and, where applicable, group structure. However, it is *not* a condition that the company issued the shares under the EIS, that the shares be held for a minimum period or that any EIS income tax relief has been, or could have been, claimed in respect of them.

An '*excluded company*' is a company whose trade consists mainly of dealing in land, in commodities or futures or in shares, securities or other financial instruments (as regards shares issued before 6 April 1998 — dealing in shares, securities, land, trades or commodity futures) or is not carried on on a commercial basis with a reasonable expectation of profit, or which is the holding company of a non-trading group, or which is a building society (see 8 BUILDING SOCIETIES) or a registered industrial and provident society within *ICTA 1988, s 486(12)*.

A *'trading group'* is a group (i.e. a company and its 51% subsidiaries) the business of the members of which, taken together, consists wholly or mainly in the carrying on of a trade or trades (disregarding any trade carried on by a subsidiary which is an excluded company or, as regards shares issued before 6 April 1998, which is non-UK resident).

Claims must be made in writing on or before the first anniversary of 31 January following the tax year *in which the loss is incurred.* A loss may be claimed against income.

(I)   of the year in which the loss is incurred, or

(II)   of the year preceding that in which the loss is incurred.

Where, against income of the same year, claims are made both under (I) in respect of that year's loss and under (II) in respect of the following year's loss, (I) takes precedence. Where both claims are made for the same loss, no order of priority is specified but it is considered that the Revenue would follow the same practice as for loss relief under *ICTA 1988, s 380* (see 46.3 above).

Relief under the above provisions is given in priority to relief under *ICTA 1988, s 380* (see 46.3 above) and *ICTA 1988, s 381* (see 46.10 above) for the same tax year. The relief cannot be allowed for capital gains tax as well as income tax purposes.

Identification. Where an individual holds shares of the same class only some of which qualify for the above relief because they were subscribed for, and both the subscription shares and the other shares form part of the same holding (i.e. a number of shares of the same class held by one person in one capacity, whether or not pooled for capital gains tax purposes), then in determining the extent (if any) to which a disposal relates to shares subscribed for (qualifying shares), disposals are to be identified with acquisitions on a last in/first out (LIFO) basis.

For disposals after 5 April 1998, there is an exception to the above rule where the holding includes *any* of the following:

(A)   Shares in respect of which Business Expansion Scheme (BES) was been given and was not withdrawn (see 25.1 ENTERPRISE INVESTMENT SCHEME);

(B)   Shares to which Enterprise Investment Scheme (EIS) income tax relief is attributable (see 25 ENTERPRISE INVESTMENT SCHEME);

(C)   Shares to which EIS capital gains deferral relief is attributable (see 25.24 ENTERPRISE INVESTMENT SCHEME).

In such a case, disposals are identified in accordance with the identification rules generally applicable to BES and EIS shares (broadly, first in/first out (FIFO) — see, for example, 25.13 ENTERPRISE INVESTMENT SCHEME).

Loss relief under these provisions on the disposal of qualifying shares forming part of a larger holding is restricted to the sums that would have been allowable as deductions in computing the loss if the qualifying shares had been acquired and disposed of as a separate holding (see Step 4 in the example at 46.16 below).

Revenue Venture Capital Schemes Manual VCM 47150 identifies four steps in the computation of loss relief under these provisions where a holding does not entirely consist of qualifying shares. Step 1 is to compute the allowable loss for capital gains tax purposes under normal capital gains tax principles and identification rules (see Tolley's Capital Gains Tax under Shares and Securities — Identification Rules). Step 2 is to identify the qualifying and non-qualifying shares included in the disposal (using the special identification rules described above). If it is found that the disposal comprises both, Step 3 is to apportion the loss, on a just and reasonable basis, between qualifying and non-qualifying shares. Step 4 is to compare the loss so attributed to the qualifying shares with the actual allowable expenditure incurred on those shares and to apply, if necessary, the restriction mentioned above.

Note that, for capital gains tax (though not corporation tax) purposes, share pooling is abolished for *acquisitions* after 5 April 1998, although existing pools at 5 April 1998 are retained. The *principal* identification rule for disposals (other than of EIS and BES shares) after that date is a LIFO basis. See Tolley's Capital Gains Tax.

Anti-avoidance. Any claim to relief will bring in the provisions of *TCGA 1992, s 30* (value-shifting to give a tax-free benefit) so that the relief may be adjusted for any benefit conferred whether tax-free or not.

Company reconstructions etc. Where the shares disposed of represent a new holding identifiable under *TCGA 1992, s 127* with 'old shares' after a reorganisation or reduction of share capital, relief is not available unless it could have been given (on the disposal of the old shares for full consideration) at the reorganisation etc. had this legislation been in force and had the reorganisation been a chargeable occasion producing a loss. Where the reorganisation did not so qualify, but new consideration was given for the new holding, relief is limited to such of that new consideration as is an allowable deduction. Where *TCGA 1992, s 137* operates to make a disposal of shares on a reconstruction etc., no relief is available under the above provisions. *'New consideration'* is money or money's worth but excluding any surrender or alteration to the original shares or rights attached thereto, and the application of assets of the company or distribution declared but not made out of the assets. See Revenue Venture Capital Schemes Manual VCM 48000 *et seq.*

[*ICTA 1988, ss 574–576; FA 1988, Sch 14 Pt VIII; FA 1989, Sch 12 para 14; FA 1994, s 210, Sch 20 para 8; FA 1995, s 119; FA 1996, Sch 38 para 6; FA 1998, s 80, Sch 27 Pt III(16); FA 2000, s 63(2)–(4), Sch 16 para 3(3); FA 2001, Sch 15 para 38, Sch 33 Pt II(3)*].

Application to EIS shares. It is formally provided that the provisions described above apply to a loss on the disposal by an individual of shares to which EIS income tax relief is attributable (see 25 ENTERPRISE INVESTMENT SCHEME). However, the above-mentioned LIFO identification rules do not apply to such disposals (whether made before or on or after 6 April 1998. [*ICTA 1988, s 305A; FA 1994, s 137, Sch 15 para 20; FA 1998, Sch 13 para 18*].

Simon's Direct Tax Service. See E1.627.

46.16   *Example*

X is a semi-retired business executive. Over the years he has acquired several shareholdings in unlisted companies and he has suffered the following losses.

(i)   500 shares in A Ltd (a qualifying trading company) which X subscribed for in 1993. Allowable loss for CGT purposes on liquidation in June 2003 — £12,000.

(ii)   500 shares in B Ltd which X subscribed for in 1995 at £10 per share. B Ltd traded as a builder until 1998 when it changed its trade to that of buying and selling land. X received an arm's length offer for the shares of £3 per share in May 2003 which he accepted.

(iii)   In 1990, X subscribed for 2,000 shares in C Ltd at £50 per share. In 1995 his aunt gave him a further 1,000 shares. The market value of the shares at that time was £60 per share.

      The company has been a qualifying trading company since 1986 but has fallen on hard times recently. A company offered X £20 per share in June 2004. X accepted the offer to the extent of 1,500 shares.

The treatment of these losses in relation to income tax would be as follows.

(i)   Loss claim — *ICTA 1988, s 574*, 2003/04 or 2002/03 — £12,000

(ii) No loss claim under *ICTA 1988, s 574* is possible as B Ltd is an 'excluded company' (see 46.15 above).

(iii) *Step 1.* Compute the allowable loss for capital gains tax purposes.

Share pool

	Shares	Qualifying expenditure £
1990 subscription	2,000	100,000
1995 acquisition	1,000	60,000
	3,000	160,000
2004 disposal	(1,500)	(80,000)
Pool carried forward	1,500	£80,000

(An indexed pool should also have been maintained but is ignored here for convenience and because indexation allowance cannot increase a loss in any case.)

	£
Disposal consideration 1,500 × £20	30,000
Allowable cost $\dfrac{1,500}{3,000} \times £160,000$	80,000
Allowable capital loss	£50,000

Step 2. Applying a LIFO basis, identify the qualifying shares (500) and the non-qualifying shares (1,000) comprised in the disposal.

Step 3. Calculate the proportion of the loss attributable to the qualifying shares.

Loss referable to 500 qualifying shares $\dfrac{500}{1,500} \times £50,000$ £16,667

Step 4. Compare the loss in *Step 3* with the actual cost of the qualifying shares, *viz.*

Cost of 500 qualifying shares $\dfrac{500}{2,000} \times £100,000$ £25,000

No restriction is necessary as the cost of the qualifying shares exceeds the loss in *Step 3*.

Loss claim — *ICTA 1988, s 574* for 2004/05 or 2003/04 — £16,667

(The loss not relieved against income (£50,000 – £16,667 = £33,333) remains an allowable loss for capital gains tax purposes.)

Utilisation of losses

X makes all possible claims under *ICTA 1988, s 574* so as to obtain relief against the earliest possible income. He has total income, before *section 574* relief, of £7,000 for 2002/03, £11,500 for 2003/04 and £9,000 for 2004/05.

46.16 Losses

The *section 574* losses available as above are as follows.

	2003/04 disposals £	2004/05 disposals £
A Ltd shares	12,000	
C Ltd shares		16,667

Section 574 claims are made as follows.

	£
2002/03	
Total income	7,000
Claim under *section 574(1)(b)*	(7,000)
Revised total income	Nil
2003/04	
Total income	11,500
Claim under *section 574(1)(a)* note (*b*)	(5,000)
	6,500
Claim under *section 574(1)(b)*	(6,500)
Revised total income	Nil
2004/05	
Total income	9,000
Claim under *section 574(1)(a)*	(9,000)
Revised total income	Nil

Loss utilisation

	£
2003/04 loss	
Loss available	12,000
Relief claimed for 2002/03 (*section 574(1)(b)*)	(7,000)
Relief claimed for 2003/04 (*section 574(1)(a)*)	(5,000)

	£
2004/05 loss	
Loss available	16,667
Relief claimed for 2003/04 (*section 574(1)(b)*)	(6,500)
Relief claimed for 2004/05 (*section 574(1)(a)*)	(9,000)
Unused balance note (*c*)	£1,167

Notes

(*a*)   In this example, losses have been set against preceding year's income first, as X wished to obtain relief against earliest possible income, but this need not be the case.

(*b*)   Where two years' losses are set against one year's income, the current year's loss is relieved in priority to that of the following year.

(*c*)   The unused balance of the 2004/05 loss cannot be relieved under *section 574* due to insufficiency of income and therefore reverts to being a capital loss available to reduce chargeable gains.

47   Married Persons

(See also Revenue Pamphlets IR 80, 83, 90, 91.)

Cross-references. See 1.14, 1.15 ALLOWANCES AND TAX RATES; 2 ALLOWANCES AND TAX RATES—EXAMPLES; 25.22 ENTERPRISE INVESTMENT SCHEME; 43.12 INTEREST PAYABLE; 53.12 PARTNERSHIPS; 65.5 RESIDENCE, ORDINARY RESIDENCE AND DOMICILE (residence); 81.16(*a*), 81.17 SETTLEMENTS as regards settlements not involving use of trusts.

Simon's Direct Tax Service E5.1.

The headings in this chapter are as follows.

47.1   PERSONAL RELIEFS

Husband and wife are each entitled to the personal allowance (see 1.14 ALLOWANCES AND TAX RATES) in their own right. The husband used to be entitled to the married couple's allowance (see 1.15 ALLOWANCES AND TAX RATES) for any year of assessment at any time during which his wife was living with him. For 2000/01 and subsequent years of assessment, the married couple's allowance is only available where one of the spouses was born before 6 April 1935, so that the allowance will in due course cease to be available at all. [*ICTA 1988, ss 257, 257A; FA 1988, s 33; FA 1994, s 77; FA 1996, s 134, Sch 20 para 14; FA 1999, s 31*].

Transfer of married couple's allowance. A wife may elect to be entitled to claim one-half of the married couple's allowance for any year of assessment (ignoring any age-related increase), the husband's entitlement being correspondingly reduced. Alternatively, they may jointly elect for the wife to be able to claim the full amount of the basic allowance, the husband's entitlement being restricted to any age-related increase, although the husband may then elect to be able to claim back one-half of the basic allowance (the wife's entitlement being correspondingly reduced). A woman may not, however, be entitled to more than one reduction under these provisions in any year of assessment.

For 1999/2000 and subsequent years, as a consequence of the abolition of the married couple's allowance after that year except where one of the spouses was born before 6 April 1935, the transfer is restricted to the minimum amount below which the allowance may not be reduced by reference to the income of the claimant. This is initially set at the amount of the basic allowance for 1999/2000 (i.e. £1,970), and is subject to the normal indexation provisions for subsequent years (see 1.15 ALLOWANCES AND TAX RATES for subsequent years' figures).

An election under these provisions has to be made in prescribed form (i.e. form 18) before the first year of assessment for which it is to have effect (or within the first 30 days of that year if prior notification of intention to elect has been given to the inspector before the beginning of that year), and has effect until withdrawn or until a different election is made. If an election is to have effect for the year of assessment of marriage, it may be made during that year, but will only apply for that year to the reduced basic or minimum allowance available. An election may be withdrawn with effect from the year following that in which notice of withdrawal is given.

47.2 Married Persons

[*ICTA 1988, s 257BA; F(No 2)A 1992, Sch 5 para 2; FA 1994, Sch 8 para 2; FA 1999, s 32*].

Where a spouse's entitlement to an income tax reduction in respect of the married couple's allowance (including, in the case of the husband, any age-related increase in the basic allowance) exceeds his or her total income tax liability (see 1.15 ALLOWANCES AND TAX RATES), the excess may, if he or she so notifies the inspector, be claimed as a reduction in the other spouse's income tax liability (in addition to any reduction to which he or she is entitled as above). The notification to the inspector must be given in prescribed form and is irrevocable. It must be given within five years after 31 January following the year of assessment to which it is to apply.

[*ICTA 1988, s 257BB; F(No 2)A 1992, Sch 5 para 2; FA 1994, Sch 8 para 3; FA 1996, s 135, Sch 21 para 4; FA 2000, s 39(8)(10)*].

Transfer of blind person's allowance. Blind person's allowance (see 1.19 ALLOWANCES AND TAX RATES) may be transferred from husband to wife and *vice versa* to the extent that the allowance exceeds the total income of the claimant. For this purpose total income is as reduced by all other deductions other than those in respect of payments for which relief is obtained by deduction of basic rate tax in respect of retirement benefit or personal pension scheme contributions (see 67.5(*a*) RETIREMENT SCHEMES, 60.1 PERSONAL PENSION SCHEMES) or vocational training costs (until abolition of the relief for such costs, see 92.1 VOCATIONAL TRAINING RELIEF). Transfer of the relief must be notified to the inspector in prescribed form within five years after 31 January following the year of assessment to which it is to apply. The notice is irrevocable. [*ICTA 1988, s 265; FA 1988, Sch 3 para 8; FA 1989, s 33(10), s 57(4); FA 1991, s 33(4); F(No 2)A 1992, Sch 5 para 8; FA 1994, Sch 8 para 10, Sch 10 para 3, Sch 26 Pt V; FA 1996, s 135, Sch 21 para 6; FA 1999, Sch 20 Pt III(15)*].

Simon's Direct Tax Service. See E2.302, E2.303, E2.802, E5.103.

47.2   *Example*

Transfer of surplus married couple's allowance

Mr Grey, who was born in 1933, is a sole trader and made a profit of £500 in the year to 30 April 2004. Mr Grey has been married for some years. He has a pension of £4,200 and building society interest of £1,040 (net) for 2004/05 and his wife, who was born in 1944, has a salary of £15,000 and building society interest of £1,880 (net). Mr and Mrs Grey receive interest of £2,240 (net) in 2004/05 from a bank deposit account in their joint names. Mr Grey elects under *ICTA 1988, s 257BB(2)* to transfer the unused balance of his married couple's allowance for 2004/05 to his wife.

The couple's tax position for 2004/05 is as follows.

	Mr Grey £	Mrs Grey £
Schedule D, Case I	500	—
Employment income	—	15,000
Pension income	4,200	—
Building society interest (gross)	1,300	2,350
Bank deposit interest (gross)	1,400	1,400
Total income	7,400	18,750
Deduct Personal allowance	6,830	4,745
Taxable income	£570	£14,005

	Mr Grey £	Mrs Grey £
Tax payable:		
570/2,020 @ 10%	57.00	202.00
8,235 @ 22%		1,811.70
3,750 @ 20%		750.00
	57.00	2,763.70
Deduct Married couple's allowance		
£5,725 @ 10% = £572.50, but restricted to	57.00	
Deduct Surplus married couple's		
allowance £(572.50 – 57.00)		515.50
Total tax liabilities	Nil	2,248.20
Deduct Tax at source:		
Building society interest	(260.00)	(470.00)
Bank deposit interest	(280.00)	(280.00)
Net tax (repayment)/liability (subject to wife's PAYE deductions)	£(540.00)	£1,498.20

47.3   **JOINTLY HELD PROPERTY**

Special rules apply for the apportionment between spouses living together of income arising from property held in their joint names. Provided that at least one of them is beneficially entitled to that income, they are treated as beneficially entitled to it in equal shares, except in the following circumstances.

(i)   Where the income is earned income or, not being earned income, is assessable in the name of a partnership.

(ii)   To the extent that the income is by any other provision of the *Income Tax Acts* treated as the income either of the spouse who is not beneficially entitled to the income, or of a third party.

(iii)   For 2004/05 onwards, where the income consists of a distribution in respect of shares in, or securities of, a close company (broadly a company controlled by five or fewer participators — see Tolley's Corporation Tax) to which the husband and wife are beneficially entitled (whether in equal or unequal shares) or to which one of them is beneficially entitled. (The intention behind this is to prevent the normal 50:50 rule being used to circumvent the application of the settlements legislation (see 81.16(*a*) SETTLEMENTS) where income is diverted to a spouse via the payment of dividends.)

(iv)   Where the husband and wife are not beneficially entitled to the income in equal shares, and they make a declaration of their beneficial interests in the income to which the declaration relates and the property from which that income arises, provided that the beneficial interests of the husband and wife in the property correspond to their beneficial interests in the income.

A declaration under (iv) above has effect in relation to income arising on and after the date of the declaration, and continues to have effect unless and until the beneficial interests of the spouses in either the income or the property cease to accord with the declaration. Notice of a declaration must be given to the inspector, in a prescribed form (i.e. form 17) and manner, within 60 days of the date of the declaration.

47.4   Married Persons

[*ICTA 1988, ss 282A, 282B; FA 1988, s 34; FA 2004, s 91*].

Simon's Direct Tax Service. See E5.103A.

47.4   **TRANSITIONAL RELIEFS**

Three reliefs were available following the transition to independent taxation of husband and wife for 1990/91 onwards. They **cease to have effect after 1999/2000.**

(*a*)   *Husband with excess allowances.* Where a husband and wife were living together at any time during 1990/91, and for the whole or any part of 1989/90 the wife's income is aggregated with that of the husband for income tax purposes (and no election for separate taxation was in force for 1989/90), the wife is entitled to a deduction from her total income for 1990/91 of an amount equal to the excess of the husband's 1989/90 allowances over the sum of the husband's total income for 1990/91 and the wife's allowances (apart from these transitional provisions) for 1990/91.

Where they were living together for part only of 1989/90, and the aggregation rules do not apply to them for any part of 1989/90, the wife is entitled to a deduction from her total income for 1990/91 of an amount equal to the excess of the husband's allowances (other than wife's earned income relief) for 1989/90 over his total income for 1990/91. The deduction is, however, reduced by the excess, if any, of the allowances to which the wife would be entitled for 1990/91 apart from these provisions over the lesser of

(i)   her total income for 1989/90, and

(ii)   her allowances for that year other than the additional relief for children, widow's bereavement allowance (see 1.17, 1.16 ALLOWANCES AND TAX RATES) and allowances transferred from her husband.

Transitional relief may also be available for 1991/92 or any subsequent year (the '*year in question*') at any time during which the husband and wife are living together, where they were also living together throughout the immediately preceding year of assessment, and the wife made a deduction from her total income under these transitional provisions for that immediately preceding year (see below). Where that deduction is greater than the excess of the wife's allowances given by deduction for the year in question over those for the immediately preceding year (in both cases apart from transitional relief under these provisions), and the husband's allowances given by deduction for the year in question (other than blind person's allowances (see 1.19 ALLOWANCES AND TAX RATES) and (before 1994/95) married couple's allowance (see 1.15 ALLOWANCES AND TAX RATES)) exceed his total income for that year, the wife is entitled to a deduction for the year in question of the lesser of

(A)   the deduction under these transitional relief provisions for the immediately preceding year of assessment *less* any increase in her allowances (*other than* under these transitional relief provisions) for the year in question over those for the immediately preceding year, and

(B)   the excess of her husband's allowances for the year in question (other than blind person's and married couple's allowances) over his total income for that year.

In determining for the above purpose the excess of the wife's allowances given by deduction for 1994/95 over those for 1993/94, deductions for 1993/94 in respect of allowances falling to be given by way of reduction in tax liability for 1994/95 are disregarded (so that like is compared with like). (In practice, this is likely to be relevant only as regards married couple's allowance — see 1.15 ALLOWANCES AND TAX RATES.)

In determining whether the wife made a deduction from her total income under these transitional provisions for the immediately preceding year, and the amount thereof, it is assumed that such deduction is made after all other deductions except any in respect of business expansion scheme investments.

Total income for all the purposes of these transitional reliefs is as reduced by all deductions other than those in respect of investments under the business expansion scheme (see 25 ENTERPRISE INVESTMENT SCHEME) and in respect of payments for which relief is obtained by deduction of basic rate tax in respect of retirement benefit or personal pension scheme contributions (67.5(*a*) RETIREMENT SCHEMES, 60.1 PERSONAL PENSION SCHEMES), relevant loan interest (22.13 DEDUCTION OF TAX AT SOURCE), MEDICAL INSURANCE (48) premiums, and vocational training costs (92 VOCATIONAL TRAINING RELIEF). Any separate assessment election for 1989/90 is similarly disregarded in determining the husband's excess allowances for that year. For 1994/95 and subsequent years, payments of relevant loan interest and medical insurance premiums are not relieved by deduction from total income, and are therefore no longer relevant.

Transitional relief under these provisions is available only if notice is given by the husband. The notice must be in writing and in prescribed form (i.e. form 575) to the inspector, and is irrevocable. The notice must be given within five years after 31 January following the year of assessment to which it relates.

These provisions cease to apply after 1999/2000.

[*ICTA 1988, s 257D; FA 1988, s 33; FA 1989, s 33(10), s 57(4); F(No 2)A 1992, Sch 5 para 3; FA 1994, Sch 8 para 4, Sch 10 para 3, Sch 26 Pt V; FA 1996, s 135, Sch 21 para 5; FA 1999, s 32(2)(4)*].

(*b*)   *The elderly.* Where, for 1989/90, a claimant was entitled (disregarding any separate assessment election) to the age allowance determined by reference to his wife's age and not his own (i.e. he was under 65 or under 75, as the case may be, throughout 1989/90), and the amount of that allowance exceeded the aggregate of the personal and married couple's allowances available for 1990/91 apart from these transitional provisions, then for any subsequent year at any time in which he had the same wife living with him, his personal allowance was £3,400 or £3,540, as appropriate (subject to restriction by reference to an income limit in the same way as the normal age increase, see above). The indexation provisions (see above) did *not* apply to these figures. The personal allowance was thus frozen at this figure until such time as the claimant became entitled himself to the increased personal allowance for those aged over 65 (or 75). [*ICTA 1988, s 257E; FA 1988, s 33; FA 1996, s 134, Sch 20 para 15; FA 1999, s 32(2)(4)*]. These provisions are of no practical application for 1996/97 onwards as the normal personal allowance is higher than £3,540 (and has been higher than £3,400 since 1992/93). They are formally repealed after 1999/2000.

(*c*)   *Separated couples.* Where, before 6 April 1990, a husband and wife ceased to live together, but they continued to be married to one another and the wife is wholly maintained by the husband, then, subject to conditions as below, they may be treated as continuing to live together for the purposes of entitlement to married couple's allowance and the transitional relief for the elderly (see (*b*) above), although not for the purposes of transfer of excess allowances to the wife (see (*a*) above) or of married couple's allowance (see 47.1 above). This applies to any year of assessment for which the husband is not entitled to make a deduction in respect of maintenance payments in computing his income for tax purposes, provided that, for 1989/90, he was entitled to the married person's allowance, and that, in relation to years of assessment after 1990/91, he has been entitled to the married couple's allowance under this provision in each intervening year.

47.5 Married Persons

These provisions cease to apply after 1999/2000.

[*ICTA 1988, s 257F; FA 1988, s 33; F(No 2)A 1992, Sch 5 para 4; FA 1994, Sch 8 para 5; FA 1996, s 134, Sch 20 para 16; FA 1999, s 32(2)(4)*].

Simon's Direct Tax Service. See **E2.203, E2.304.**

47.5 **'LIVING TOGETHER'**

A married woman is treated as '*living with her husband*' unless they are

(*a*)   separated under a Court Order or separation deed, or

(*b*)   in fact separated in circumstances which render permanent separation likely.

[*ICTA 1988, s 282*].

A husband and wife may be separated even though living under the same roof if they have become two households (*Holmes v Mitchell Ch D 1990, 63 TC 718*).

47.6 **DECREE OF NULLITY**

A decree of nullity does not operate retrospectively to disentitle the husband to the married allowance during the years the parties lived together (*Dodworth v Dale KB 1936, 20 TC 285*).

47.7 **WHEN THE MARRIAGE ENDS**

A marriage may end by death, by divorce or by separation (which for tax purposes is when the parties cease 'living together', as defined in 47.5 above). Effects are as below.

- The **husband** is entitled to the full married couple's allowance (see 1.15 ALLOW-ANCES AND TAX RATES) for the year of assessment in which the marriage ends. If he remarries in the same year, the proportionate reduction in such allowances by reference to the length of the part of the year of assessment before the marriage took place does not apply.

- The **wife**, in addition to her personal allowance for the year of assessment and, if appropriate, the additional personal allowance for children (see 1.17 ALLOWANCES AND TAX RATES), is entitled to any of the married couple's allowance not used against her husband's income and, if the husband dies, to the widow's bereavement allowance (see 1.16 ALLOWANCES AND TAX RATES). All these allowances may be set against any income of the year or, where relevant, used to reduce the total tax liability for the year.

- Prior to the abolition of mortgage interest relief (see 43.3 INTEREST PAYABLE), interest payable by each former spouse on a property held on a joint tenancy or as tenants in common will be allowable, subject to the usual conditions, but the allowance may be restricted where the amount of the mortgage on which a former spouse pays interest exceeds the value of his/her interest in the property. (CCAB Memorandum TR 500, 10 March 1983).

47.8 **Alimony, maintenance, separation allowances etc.** See generally Revenue Pamphlet IR 93 and Simon's Direct Tax Service E5.104 *et seq.*

Payments of alimony and maintenance falling due **after 14 March 1988** and made other than under an 'existing obligation' (see 1.8(i) ALLOWANCES AND TAX RATES) are not charges on the income of the person making the payment and tax is not deductible at source. Such payments do not form part of the taxable income of the person to whom they are made or of any other person. Where such payments are 'qualifying maintenance payments', the payer obtains relief as below. **For 2000/01 onwards,** relief is restricted to cases where at least one of the former spouses was aged 65 or over on 5 April 2000. Relief is available by reference to the lesser of

(a) the aggregate amount of 'qualifying maintenance payments' made by the payer which fall due in that year, and

(b) the amount of the married couple's allowance for that year (see 1.15 ALLOWANCES AND TAX RATES) or, from 2000/01 onwards and where still available, the minimum amount of that allowance available for couples at least one of whom was born before 6 April 1935,

reduced, for 1999/2000 and earlier years, by the aggregate amount of any other maintenance payments attracting relief for that year. Relief is given at a reduced rate of 15% for 1995/96 to 1998/99 inclusive, and 10% thereafter, by means of a reduction in the payer's income tax liability. The reduction is the smaller of the specified percentage (i.e. 10% for 1999/2000) of the amount established above and what would otherwise be the payer's total income tax liability. For this purpose, 'total income tax liability' is as defined in 1.15 ALLOWANCES AND TAX RATES, except that it is before any reductions on account of personal reliefs (where these are also given by way of reduction in income tax liability — see 1.15 to 1.17 ALLOWANCES AND TAX RATES).

So much of the aggregate of payments under existing obligations which attract tax relief as does not exceed the married couple's allowance is treated as if it were a qualifying maintenance payment made otherwise than under an existing obligation, and thus attracts the above relief subject to the overall limit.

A *'qualifying maintenance payment'* is a periodical payment (other than an instalment of a lump sum) which

(A) is made under a UK, European Community or European Economic Area Court Order, or under a written agreement the proper law of which is the law of a part of the UK, the European Community or the European Economic Area, or under a maintenance assessment or maintenance calculation made under the *Child Support Act 1991* (or NI equivalent),

(B) is made by one party to a marriage (or former marriage) either

    (i) to or for the benefit of, and for the maintenance of, the other party, or

    (ii) to the other party for the maintenance by that other party of a 'child of the family',

(C) is due at a time when

    (i) the two parties are not a married couple living together within *ICTA 1988, s 282(1)* and disregarding *section 282(2)* (see 47.5 above), and

    (ii) the party to whom or for whose benefit the payment is made has not remarried, and

(D) does not attract tax relief for the person making the payment, apart from the deduction specified above.

As regards (B) above, for payments falling due after 5 April 2000 there is an additional requirement that at least one of the parties to the marriage (or former marriage) was born before 6 April 1935.

As regards (C)(ii) above, the fact that the subsequent marriage may itself have been dissolved is irrelevant (*Norris v Edgson Ch D 2000, 72 TC 553*).

The above conditions were not satisfied by a payment made by the taxpayer to a former spouse for the maintenance of their child where the agreement required the payment to be made to the child (*Billingham v John Ch D 1998, 70 TC 380*), nor by payments made by one party to a marriage to pay off the joint mortgage on a house continuing to be occupied by the other (*Otter v Andrews (Sp C 181), [1999] SSCD 67*).

(B) above is treated as satisfied in relation to periodical payments made to or retained by the Secretary of State under a maintenance assessment or maintenance calculation under the *Child Support Act 1991* (or NI equivalent) by one party to a marriage (whether or not dissolved or annulled) where the other party is, for the purposes of that *Act*, a parent of the child(ren) to whom the assessment or calculation relates. Assessments or calculations under *section 7* of that *Act* (right of child in Scotland to apply for maintenance assessment or calculation) are excluded from this treatment. Payments to the Secretary of State under *Social Security Administration Act 1992, s 106* or *Jobseekers Act 1995, s 23* (or NI equivalent of either) by one party to a marriage (whether or not dissolved or annulled) in respect of income support or an income-based jobseeker's allowance claimed by the other party are similarly treated as satisfying (B) above in relation to payments falling due after 5 April 1993.

A '*child of the family*' is a person under 21 who is either a child of both parties to a marriage or has been treated by them both as a child of their family, but excluding a child who has been boarded out with them by a public authority or voluntary organisation.

[*ICTA 1988, s 347B; FA 1988, ss 36, 38(3A), 40, Sch 3 para 13; F(No 2)A 1992, ss 61, 62(1); FA 1994, s 79(1)(3)–(6)(8); Jobseekers Act 1995, Sch 2 para 15; FA 1998, s 27(1), Sch 27 Pt III(1); FA 1999, s 36(1)–(6)(8), Sch 20 Pt III(6); Child Support, Pensions and Social Security Act 2000, ss 26, 86, Sch 3 paras 8, 9; SI 1992 No 2612*].

Payments under 'existing obligations' (see 1.8(i) ALLOWANCES AND TAX RATES). Payments satisfying the conditions set out below are to be made without deduction of tax and are not charges on income. For payments due in *1989/90 to 1993/94 inclusive*, the payer could, in computing his total income, claim a deduction of the lesser of

(*aa*)   the aggregate amount of such payments falling due and made by him in the year of assessment, and

(*bb*)   the aggregate amount of payments due in 1988/89 which also satisfied the conditions set out below and for which he was entitled to tax relief for 1988/89.

For payments due in *1994/95 to 1999/2000 inclusive*, the deduction is limited to the excess, if any, of the amount established as above over the amount of the married couple's allowance (see 1.15 ALLOWANCES AND TAX RATES). So much of the amount established as above as does *not* exceed the married couple's allowance is treated as if it were a qualifying maintenance payment made otherwise than under an existing obligation, and relief is thus given (subject to an overall limit) at a reduced rate and by way of a reduction in income tax liability rather than by deduction in computing total income (see above).

Payments due in *1989/90 to 1999/2000 inclusive* will form part of the recipient's taxable income and be chargeable under Schedule D, Case III (generally on a current year basis), or Case V if arising outside the UK, but only to the extent of the aggregate amount of payments received from the same payer which satisfied the conditions below and which formed part of his taxable income for 1988/89 (disregarding the deduction of up to £1,490 for that year). In addition, where the payments meet the conditions in (B) and (C) above, the recipient may claim, in respect of such payments, a deduction not exceeding an amount equal to the married couple's allowance for the year (see 1.15 ALLOWANCES AND TAX RATES). Where part of the aggregate payments falls to be treated, as regards the payer, as a qualifying maintenance payment (see above), this does *not* affect the tax position of the recipient, who continues to be taxed as if such part were a payment under an existing obligation.

These provisions apply to annual payments falling due in 1989/90 or any subsequent year which

(AA)   are made in pursuance of an existing obligation under a Court Order, in the UK or elsewhere, or a written or oral agreement, or a maintenance assessment or maintenance calculation under the *Child Support Act 1991* (or NI equivalent),

(BB)   are made by an individual either

    (i)   to or for the benefit of, and for the maintenance of, his or her spouse or ex-spouse, or

    (ii)   to any person under 21 for his own benefit, maintenance or education, or

    (iii)   to any person for the benefit, maintenance or education of a person under 21, and

(CC)   are, apart from these provisions, within the charge to tax under Schedule D, Case III or Case V and are not, under any provision of *ICTA 1988, Pt XV* (see 81 SETTLEMENTS), regarded as the income of the payer.

Payments due **after 5 April 2000** under existing obligations cease to attract relief under these provisions and do not form part of the recipient's taxable income. If at least one of the parties to the former marriage was aged 65 or over on 5 April 2000 and the payments satisfy the other conditions for qualifying maintenance payments (see above), the payer is entitled to the limited relief still available under *ICTA 1988, s 347B* (see above).

[*FA 1988, s 38; F(No 2)A 1992, s 62(3); FA 1994, s 79(7)(8); FA 1999, s 36(7)(8), Sch 20 Pt III(6); Child Support, Pensions and Social Security Act 2000, ss 26, 86, Sch 3 para 9; FA 2004, Sch 17 para 10(3); SI 1992 No 2642*].

Where maintenance payments are made for 1999/2000 and earlier years under existing obligations such that the above rules would apply, the payer may elect that they be treated as maintenance payments other than under existing obligations, so that *ICTA 1988, s 347B* (above) will apply if they are qualifying maintenance payments. The election must cover all such payments falling due in a year of assessment for which it has effect. It must be made in prescribed form (i.e. Form 142) and within twelve months after 31 January following the first year of assessment to which it is to apply, will continue to have effect for subsequent years and is irrevocable. A person making such an election must, within 30 days of the date on which it is made, give notice thereof to every recipient of a payment affected by the election. [*FA 1988, s 39; FA 1996, s 135, Sch 21 para 25; FA 1999, Sch 20 Pt III(6)*].

General matters. Court Orders for alimony generally take into account the income and tax liabilities of both parties.

Maintenance receipts, where taxable, are investment income.

If, under a **Divorce Court Order**, payments are made *to the wife* for the maintenance of children, such income is for tax purposes the wife's and not the children's (see *Stevens v Tirard CA 1939, 23 TC 321; Spencer v Robson KB 1946, 27 TC 198*). Where a Court orders payment direct to the child, the income is that of the child. Under Scots law, where a child is entitled to aliment in his own right but payment is made to the parent with custody *qua tutrix* (or *tutor, curator, curatrix*), the income is that of the child for tax purposes. (*Huggins v Huggins 1981 SLT 179*). In strict law, the retrospective variation of an Order is not effective for tax purposes (*Morley-Clarke v Jones CA 1985, 59 TC 567*). For Orders made or varied after 30 June 1988 which provide for retrospective payments, only payments made on or after the date of the Order count towards the limit on which tax relief is available in any year. Payments made under a legally binding written agreement before the Court Order may of course qualify in their own right. (Revenue Press Release 15 March 1988). Payments made under an agreement voluntarily entered into by a father in favour of his children, for their maintenance following separation, and later confirmed by a Court Order, were not made under that Order and were thus ineffective for tax purposes (*CIR v Craw CS 1985, 59 TC 56*).

Where the Court orders maintenance payments by a former spouse direct to his/her child who is living with the other spouse and an element is included to cover school fees, those fees may be paid direct to the school in *full* out of the *net* amount due under the maintenance order after tax at the basic rate has been deducted (assuming deduction at source to be still applicable) from the total amount payable, including the school fees. The payments will form part of the taxable income of the child, subject to the general rules outlined above. The Order normally includes: 'that part of the Order which reflects the school fees shall be paid to the (headmaster/bursar/school secretary) as agent for the said child and the receipt of that payee shall be sufficient discharge'. The onus will be on the parties themselves to produce evidence, where requested, that the person receiving the school fees has agreed to act as agent for the child and that the contract for the payment of the fees (which is most easily proved if in writing) is between the child (not the spouse making the payments) and the school. (Revenue Pamphlet IR 131, SP 15/80, 14 November 1980 and see Tolley's Practical Tax 1983 p 124). From 6 April 2000, relief is no longer available for payments direct to children (see above).

See also *Sherdley v Sherdley HL, [1987] STC 217*, where the validity of such arrangements was considered and affirmed in a case where an Order was sought against himself by the parent having custody.

47.9 *Examples*

Maintenance payments (1999/2000 and earlier years): Court Orders before 15 March 1988
Mr Smith separated from his wife on 31 October 1987. For 1999/2000 he has assessable Schedule D, Case I profits of £23,000 and building society interest of £4,000 (net). He pays mortgage interest of £2,400 on a home loan of under £30,000 which is outside the MIRAS scheme. Under a Court Order dated 5 March 1988, Mr Smith paid £50 per week maintenance directly to his son, Paul, aged 17 in 1999/2000, who lives with Mrs Smith, and £70 per week maintenance to Mrs Smith. On 1 June 1990, the payments to Mrs Smith were increased by the Court to £100 per week. In 1999/2000, Mrs Smith has earnings of £6,000. Paul Smith has no other income.

1999/2000			£	£
Mr Smith				
Earned income				23,000
Building society interest			4,000	
Add Tax deducted at source			1,000	5,000
				28,000
Deduct:	Maintenance payments:			
	Wife £70 × 52	note (*a*)	3,640	
	Son £50 × 52		2,600	
			6,240	
	Less the first £1,970	note (*b*)	1,970	
				(4,270)
Total income				23,730
Deduct Personal allowance				4,335
Taxable income				£19,395

Mr Smith	£	£
Tax payable:		
1,500 @ 10%		150.00
12,895 @ 23%		2,965.85
5,000 @ 20%		1,000.00
		4,115.85
Deduct Mortgage interest relief £2,400 @ 10%		240.00
		3,875.85
Deduct Maintenance £1,970 @ 10% note (*b*)		197.00
Total tax liability		3,678.85
Deduct Tax paid on building society interest		1,000.00
Net tax liability		£2,678.85

Mrs Smith		
Earned income		6,000
Maintenance note (*a*)	3,640	
Deduction note (*a*)	1,970	
		1,670
Total income		7,670
Deduct Personal allowance note (*c*)		4,335
Taxable income		£3,335
Tax payable:		
1,500 @ 10%		150.00
1,835 @ 23%		422.05
		£572.05

Paul Smith		
Maintenance		2,600
Deduct Personal allowance (restricted)		2,600
Taxable income		Nil
Tax payable/repayable		Nil

Notes

(*a*)   The tax relief and the amount chargeable on the recipient is limited to the relief obtainable and the amount forming part of the recipient's income for 1988/89. The recipient may then deduct from the amount otherwise chargeable an amount equal to the married couple's allowance for the year, providing the payments are from a divorced or separated spouse. See 47.8 above.

(*b*)   For 1999/2000, the first £1,970 of allowable maintenance payments attracts relief at 10%, such relief being given as an income tax reduction (see 47.8 above).

(*c*)   Mrs Smith may also be entitled to the additional personal allowance in respect of Paul if all the conditions of *ICTA 1988, s 259* are satisfied (see 1.17 ALLOWANCES AND TAX RATES).

Maintenance payments: Court Orders after 14 March 1988

Mr Green, who was born on 7 October 1933, separated from his wife in June 1998 and, under a Court Order dated 15 July 1999, pays maintenance of £300 per month to his

47.9 Married Persons

ex-wife and £100 per month to his daughter, payments being due on the first of each calendar month commencing 1 August 1999. Mr Green has earned income of £13,000 and dividends of £4,500 for 2004/05. He re-marries on 6 October 2004.

	£	£
2004/05		
Mr Green		
Earned income		13,000
Dividends	4,500	
Add Tax credits (£4,500 × $\frac{1}{9}$)	500	5,000
Total income		18,000
Deduct Personal allowance		6,830
Taxable income		£11,170
Tax payable:		
2,020 @ 10% (starting rate)		202.00
4,150 @ 22%		913.00
5,000 @ 10% (Schedule F ordinary rate)		500.00
		1,615.00
Deduct Maintenance relief — wife:		
£3,600 paid, but restricted to £2,210 @ 10%		221.00
		1,394.00
Deduct Married couple's allowance		
£5,725 × $\frac{6}{12}$ = £2,863 @ 10%		286.30
Total tax liability		1,107.70
Deduct Tax credits		500.00
Net tax liability (subject to PAYE deductions)		£607.70

48   Medical Insurance

(See Revenue Pamphlet IR 103.)

Simon's Direct Tax Service E2.9.

Note. The provisions described in this chapter are repealed by the Finance (No 2) Act 1997. See 48.1 below.

48.1   Subject to the **abolition** of this relief (see below), where a UK resident individual makes a payment in respect of a private medical insurance premium under an 'eligible contract' insuring a UK resident individual or individuals who, or each of whom, is aged 60 or over at the date of the payment (or, where a married couple is insured, at least one of whom is aged 60 or over at that time), he may claim relief (see below) for the payment, provided that he is not entitled to any other relief or deduction in respect of the payment and does not make it out of resources provided by another person for the purpose of enabling it to be made. Crown employees treated as performing their duties in the UK under *ICTA 1988, s 132(4)(a)* (see 75.4 SCHEDULE E—EMPLOYMENT INCOME) are treated as UK resident for these purposes. Where a payment is made under a contract insuring a married couple one of whom is 60 or over, and the said spouse dies, a subsequent payment under the same contract is not disqualified from relief by virtue of the surviving spouse being under 60.

[*FA 1989, s 54(1)–(3C)(9); FA 1994, Sch 10 paras 2, 4*].

Regulations provide for the payment to be made under deduction of basic rate tax, the payee reclaiming the tax deducted from the Revenue, and for relief to be withdrawn, and the related tax accounted for, in prescribed circumstances. The Revenue consider that where a payment *may* be made under deduction of basic rate tax, basic rate relief can *only* be obtained by deduction. The tax deducted from payments is not clawed back where the individual is liable only at the lower rate of income tax or has no, or insufficient, income tax liability. For relief to be given by deduction at source, the individual must provide a notice of entitlement to relief, containing specified information and undertakings etc., to the person to whom payments are made under the contract. That person must be either a 'qualifying insurer' (see 48.4 below) or a managing agent, either with Lloyd's or for a 'qualifying insurer'. The insurer (or agent) must have no reason to doubt any of the information given by the individual, must have undertaken to observe the requirements of the regulations (and, in the event of failure, must satisfy the Board that he is able and willing to observe them in future), and must have undertaken that, before entering into a further contract, he will give notice to the individual of his obligation to notify the insurer of any relevant changes in his (or the insured's) circumstances. Any refunded payments must not exceed the payment actually made, and any amount recovered from the Board in respect of tax deducted from payments which are refunded must be accounted for to the Board. There are detailed regulations for the recovery from the Board of tax deducted from payments, and for approval of standard forms of contract. [*FA 1989, s 54(4)–(8); FA 1996, s 129; SI 1989 No 2387; SI 1994 Nos 1518, 1527*].

These provisions are **abolished** by *F(No 2)A 1997, s 17*. Relief ceases altogether for payments received by the insurer after 5 April 1999. It is not available for payments in respect of premiums under contracts entered into after 1 July 1997, unless either:

(*a*)   the contract was entered into (other than by way of renewal of an earlier contract) before 1 August 1997 in pursuance of a written proposal received by or on behalf of the insurer before 2 July 1997, and at least one payment in respect of a premium under the contract was received by the insurer before 1 August 1997; or

(*b*)   the contract was entered into before 1 August 1997, by way of renewal of an earlier contract the period of insurance under which ended before 2 July 1997, and at least one payment in respect of a premium under the renewal contract was received by the insurer before 1 August 1997.

As regards (*b*) above, a contract is treated as having been entered into by way of renewal of an earlier contract only if the earlier contract was with the same insurer and was an 'eligible contract' when it was entered into, and there was no gap between the periods of insurance under the two contracts.

48.2 A contract is an '*eligible contract*' if, at the date it was entered into, the insurer was a 'qualifying insurer' approved by the Board for these purposes, and the period of insurance does not exceed one year from that date. As regards approval of qualifying insurers, see *SI 1989 No 2387, regs 12–14* as amended by *SI 1994 No 1527, reg 11*. No benefit other than an 'approved benefit' must have been provided by virtue of the contract, and the contract must not be, or have been, 'connected with' another contract.

The contract must, at the time payment is made thereunder, meet the conditions at 48.6(*a*)–(*d*) below. Where a contract confers one or more 'material rights', but the total cost to the insurer of providing benefits in pursuance thereof would not exceed £30 (which amount is variable by Treasury order), this does not preclude eligibility. There is an anti-avoidance provision to prevent the above limit being by-passed by means of certain linked contracts. A '*material right*' is a right which does not otherwise meet the conditions for eligibility and is not a right to a cash benefit.

[*FA 1989, s 55(1)–(6)(11)–(13), s 56; FA 1994, Sch 10 paras 5, 6*].

There is no reason in principle why members of group schemes cannot come within the scope of the relief, provided that the scheme meets the qualifying conditions. (ICAEW Technical Release TAX 17/93, 28 September 1993).

48.3 A contract is '*connected with*' another contract at any time if they are both in force at that time; one was entered into with reference to the other or to enable the other to be entered into on particular terms or to facilitate the other being so entered into; and the terms on which one of the contracts was entered into would have been significantly less favourable to the insured but for the other being entered into. [*FA 1989, s 55(7)*].

48.4 A '*qualifying insurer*' is any insurer lawfully carrying on business in the UK of any of the classes specified in *Insurance Companies Act 1982, Sch 2 Pt I*, or an insurer not carrying on business in the UK but doing so in another EC country (or, from 1 January 1994, a country within the European Economic Area) and meeting certain other conditions as to status and location. [*FA 1989, s 55(8)*].

48.5 A benefit is an '*approved benefit*' if it is provided in pursuance of rights as under 48.6(*a*) below or as specified by regulations under 48.6(*b*) below. One or more benefits otherwise provided (and which are not cash benefits) are also approved benefits if their total cost to the insurer does not exceed £30 (which amount is variable by Treasury order). [*FA 1989, s 55(9)(10)(12)(13); FA 1994, Sch 10 para 5(6)(7)*].

48.6 The conditions a contract must meet are that:

(*a*) it either provides indemnity in respect of all or any of the costs of all or any of the treatments, medical services and other matters prescribed by regulations for these purposes or, in addition to such indemnity, provides cash benefits falling within rules prescribed by such regulations;

(*b*) it confers no other right except as may be specified by regulations;

(c)   the premium is reasonable; and

(d)   it satisfies such other requirements as may be specified by regulations.

As regards (a) above, the treatments etc. specified in the regulations are the treatment of the insured consisting of medical or surgical procedures (including diagnosis, drugs and dressings) for the relief of illness or injury, and services for the purposes of or consequent upon such treatment consisting of:

(i)   accommodation and other (including nursing) services in a hospital where the insured is a private patient charged for the accommodation or for treatments etc. (as above);

(ii)   home nursing;

(iii)   accommodation for up to 14 days' convalescence following discharge from hospital;

(iv)   transport by private ambulance (including by air ambulance) accompanied (where medically necessary) by one other person to or from hospital or to or from accommodation provided for convalescence; and

(v)   physiotherapy, occupational therapy, speech therapy, chiropody and podiatry, prosthesis and orthopty (including necessary equipment).

The treatment must either

(A)   be given to the insured as a private patient in a hospital by or under the supervision of a registered medical or dental practitioner, or

(B)   in the case of surgical procedures performed by a registered medical practitioner providing personal medical services for persons in a particular locality, be given to the insured as a private patient of that practitioner,

and physiotherapy services and equipment must be provided to the insured and must be associated with treatment given to the insured by or under the supervision of a registered medical practitioner.

Treatments are excluded if they were not provided free under the *National Health Service Act 1977* (or Scottish or NI equivalent), in the five years preceding the date the contract was entered into, more often than they were provided in the UK other than under that *Act*.

The allowable cash benefit may not exceed £5 for each night in a hospital as a private patient charged for the accommodation.

Other rights within (b) above are the right to terminate the contract and receive a refund in respect of the unexpired period of cover, waiver or refund by the insurer of payments for a period during which the insured is receiving treatment covered by the contract, and the right to enter into a further contract at the expiry of the current contract.

[*SI 1994 No 1518*].

Contracts are not permitted to cover charges for 'alternative medicine', dental procedures in a general dental practice, general ophthalmic procedures not carried out in hospital, and medical or surgical procedures (other than GP operations as above) not on an in-, out- or day-patient basis. (Revenue Press Release 19 July 1989).

48.7   Supplementary regulatory powers are provided, and the provisions of the *Taxes Management Act 1970* applied as necessary. [*FA 1989, s 57; FA 1996, s 129, Sch 18 paras 12, 17(1)–(4)(8)*].

49 Mineral Royalties

[*ICTA 1988, s 122; TCGA 1992, ss 201–203*]

Simon's Direct Tax Service. See C2.1111.

49.1   Where a person resident or ordinarily resident in the UK is entitled to receive mineral royalties (i.e. so much of any rents, tolls, royalties or periodical payments as relates to the winning and working of minerals other than water, peat, topsoil etc.) under a lease, licence or agreement conferring a right to win and work minerals in the UK or under a sale or conveyance of such minerals, only one-half of any such royalties receivable in any year of assessment or accounting period is treated as income for purposes of income tax or corporation tax on profits other than chargeable gains.

Management expenses available for set-off against those royalties, under *ICTA 1988, s 121* or under Schedule A, are similarly reduced by one-half.

Where Betterment Levy (which was abolished after July 1970) was not chargeable on the grant of the lease, or any subsequent renewal, extension or variation of it, the other half of the royalties receivable is treated as a chargeable gain for purposes of capital gains tax (or corporation tax on chargeable gains).

Where, on the last disposition (before 23 July 1970) affecting the lease, Betterment Levy was chargeable under Case B (as defined by *Land Commission Act 1967, Pt III*) the chargeable gain, as above, is limited to a fraction (base value of that disposition/consideration received) of one-half of the royalties received. After 5 April 1988, this limitation applies only if it applied to a chargeable period ending on or before that date. But if such a lease is renewed, extended or varied after 22 July 1970, one-half of any subsequent royalty receipt is treated as a chargeable gain.

Where payments under a mineral lease etc. relate both to the winning and working of minerals and to other matters, the part to be treated as mineral royalties for these purposes will be calculated under regulations made by the Board. See *SI 1971 No 1035*.

These chargeable gains are assessable in full, without any deduction on account of expenditure incurred.

Income tax was deductible from royalty payments made before 1 May 1995, but if the recipient was not a person chargeable to corporation tax the excess tax so suffered was set against CGT payable as above, any balance thereafter remaining being repaid.

Terminal Losses. If the mineral lease comes to an end while the person entitled to receive the royalties still has an interest in the land, and an allowable loss would then arise to him if he sold his interest for a price equal to its market value, he may claim to be treated for CGT (or corporation tax) purposes as if he had sold, and immediately reacquired, his interest at that price, the resultant loss being allowed, at his election, either (*a*) against CGT etc. for the year in which the lease expires, or (*b*) against chargeable gains, in respect of mineral royalties under the lease, within the previous 15 years.

50   Mutual Trading

Simon's Direct Tax Service B3.236 *et seq.*

50.1   A person cannot derive a taxable profit from trading with himself except in certain cases of self-supply by a trader of trading stock, see *Sharkey v Wernher HL 1955, 36 TC 275* and 71.73 SCHEDULE D, CASES I AND II. This is extended to a group of persons engaged in mutual activities of a trading nature, if there is an identifiable 'fund' for the common purpose with complete identity between contributors to, and participators in, the fund (the *mutuality principle*). A body not liable as regards transactions with members may nevertheless be liable under Schedule D, Case I on transactions with non-members and is liable in the ordinary way on any investment etc. income. Whether the mutuality principle applies depends on the facts. For mutual insurance see *Styles v New York Life Insce Co HL 1889, 2 TC 460* (an early leading case on the mutuality principle but there are now special provisions for life insurance companies — see Tolley's Corporation Tax); *Jones v South-West Lancs Coal Owners' Assn HL 1927, 11 TC 790*; *Cornish Mutual Assce Co Ltd HL 1926, 12 TC 841*; *Municipal Mutual Insce Ltd v Hills HL 1932, 16 TC 430*; *Faulconbridge v National Employers' Mutual General Insce Assn Ltd Ch D 1952, 33 TC 103*. For other cases see *Liverpool Corn Trade Assn Ltd v Monks KB 1926, 10 TC 442* (trade association providing corn exchange etc. held to be trading and not 'mutual' — but see 71.74 SCHEDULE D, CASES I AND II for special arrangement available for trade associations); *English & Scottish CWS Ltd v Assam Agricultural IT Commr PC 1948, 27 ATC 332* (wholesale co-operative with two members held to be trading and not mutual — there was no 'common fund'). Similarly a members' club is not trading and not liable on its surplus from the provision of its facilities for members (*Eccentric Club Ltd CA 1923, 12 TC 657*) but liable on the surplus attributable to non-members (*Carlisle and Silloth Golf Club v Smith CA 1913, 6 TC 48*; *NALGO v Watkins KB 1934, 18 TC 499*; *Doctor's Cave Bathing Beach (Fletcher) v Jamaica IT Commr PC 1971, 50 ATC 368*).

In the past, on the assumption that their constitutions/rules were such that their trades were mutual trades, the trading profits of Health Insurers were not usually charged to tax under Schedule D, Case I. However, the assumption proved to be incorrect. The Revenue have agreed that those Health Insurers who make the necessary changes to their constitutions/rules will be treated as having carried on a continuous mutual trade. For those who choose not to retain mutual trading status, the Revenue will not impose the change for current, or earlier, accounting periods and will seek to agree a date from which mutual trading status will no longer apply. (Revenue Internet Statement 16 April 2003).

For a detailed discussion of mutual trading, see Revenue Business Income Manual BIM 24000–24995.

For distribution of assets by a company carrying on mutual business, see Tolley's Corporation Tax.

51   Non-Residents and other Overseas Matters

Cross-references. See 65 RESIDENCE, ORDINARY RESIDENCE AND DOMICILE for the meaning of those terms. See also ANTI-AVOIDANCE at 3.7 regarding income payable to person abroad assessable on UK resident in certain circumstances; 3.8 for trading transactions with a non-resident under common control; 22 DEDUCTION OF TAX AT SOURCE for certain payments to non-residents; 23 DIPLOMATIC IMMUNITY, including international organisations etc.; 24 DOUBLE TAX RELIEF; 33.2 GOVERNMENT STOCKS for exemption on certain stocks held by non-residents; 53 PARTNERSHIPS; 58 PENSION INCOME; 64 REMITTANCE BASIS; 73 SCHEDULE D, CASES IV AND V under which assessments are raised on income from overseas securities and possessions; 75.1 to 75.9 SCHEDULE E—EMPLOYMENT INCOME for earnings from work done abroad and expenses.

The Revenue Centre for Non-Residents publishes an occasional Non-Residents Newsletter aimed at keeping agents who deal with non-residents up to date and informed about current issues that may affect them. The newsletter may be accessed on the Revenue's website. The November 1999 issue includes a useful list of telephone numbers on which advice may be sought on general matters or in relation to particular clients.

Headings in this chapter are as follows.

51.1   LIMIT ON INCOME CHARGEABLE ON NON-RESIDENTS

The income tax chargeable on the total income of a non-UK resident (other than a company) is not to exceed the aggregate of

(i)   the tax which would otherwise be chargeable if 'excluded income' and any personal allowances due (see 51.10 below) were both disregarded, and

(ii)   the tax deducted from so much of the 'excluded income' as is subject to deduction of income tax at source (including tax credits and tax treated as deducted at source).

Income is '*excluded income*' if it falls into one of the categories below and is not income in relation to which the non-resident has a UK representative for the purposes of the provisions at 51.3 to 51.6 below (i.e. income from or connected with a trade etc. carried on in the UK through a branch or agency, subject to the exclusions at 51.5 below). The categories are:

(*a*)   income chargeable under SCHEDULE D, CASE III (72) or SCHEDULE F (76);

(*b*)   income chargeable under Schedule D, Case VI by virtue of *ICTA 1988, s 56* (see 12 CERTIFICATES OF DEPOSIT);

(*c*)   certain social security benefits (including state pensions);

(*d*)   retirement annuities within 58.2(*j*) PENSION INCOME and UK-sourced employment-related annuities within 58.2(*k*) PENSION INCOME;

(*e*)   income not falling within (*a*)–(*c*) above and not being Lloyd's underwriting profits, which arises as mentioned in 51.5(2)(3) below (certain income from trading in the UK through a broker or investment manager); and

(*f*)   any income designated for these purposes by Treasury regulations.

These provisions do not apply to limit the income tax chargeable on a settlement if any actual or potential beneficiary, whether his interest is absolute or discretionary, is an individual ordinarily resident in the UK or a UK resident company.

These provisions replaced Revenue extra-statutory concessions B13 (which covered income within (*a*), (*b*), (*d*) and, in practice, (*c*) above) and B40 (which covered broadly the same ground as (*e*) above). There may 'exceptionally' be arrangements set up before 29 November 1994 which fall outside the statutory provisions and to which ESC B40 will continue to apply until, at the latest, 5 April 2005 (see Revenue Press Release IR 31, 29 November 1994).

[*FA 1995, s 128; ITEPA 2003, Sch 6 para 226; FA 2003, s 155, Sch 27 para 6*].

Simon's Direct Tax Service. See B3.126.

51.2   *Example*

Hugh and Elizabeth are non-UK resident throughout 2004/05. They are each entitled to a UK personal allowance under the provisions in 51.10 below. Their tax liabilities on total UK income for 2004/05, disregarding the limit under *FA 1995, s 128*, are as follows.

	Hugh £	Elizabeth £
Net rental income (Schedule A) (received gross)	2,000	5,000
Bank interest (received gross)	5,595	695
Dividends	3,600	—
Tax credits	400	—
Total UK income	11,595	5,695
Deduct Personal allowance	4,745	4,745
Taxable UK income	£6,850	£950

Tax on total UK income:

	£	£
£2,020/950 @ 10%	202.00	95.00
£830 @ 20% (lower rate on interest)	166.00	
£4,000 @ 10% (Schedule F ordinary rate)	400.00	
	768.00	95.00
Deduct Tax credits	400.00	
	£368.00	£95.00

But tax is limited under *FA 1995, s 128* as follows.

	£	£
Schedule A	2,000	5,000

(Bank interest and dividends are 'excluded income' — see 51.1 above.)

	£	£
£2,000/£2,020 @ 10%	200.00	202.00
£2,980 @ 22%		655.60
	£200.00	£857.60

Hugh's UK income tax liability is therefore restricted to £200.00 (plus £400.00 in tax credits, which cannot be reclaimed). Elizabeth's liability is not reduced under *FA 1995, s 128* and is thus £95.00.

51.3 NON-RESIDENTS TRADING IN UK

The provisions described below apply where a non-UK resident carries on a trade in the UK through a branch or agency (which for this purpose means any factorship, agency, receivership, branch or management). They establish the obligations and liabilities of UK representatives of such non-residents under self-assessment. See also 78.11 SELF-ASSESSMENT.

For whether activities of a non-resident person constitute trading in the UK, see Revenue Inspector's Manual IM 170 *et seq*.

Where a non-resident carries on a trade partly in and partly outside the UK, the charge to UK tax is limited, under general principles, to the profits from the part of the trade carried on in the UK (whether or not through a branch or agency). The Revenue have reaffirmed that the profits from a part of a trade carried on in the UK are to be measured on the arm's length principle set out in the OECD model tax convention and explained in OECD publications, irrespective of whether a double tax agreement applies. (Revenue Tax Bulletin August 1995 pp 237–239).

51.4 Meaning of 'UK representative'.

For the purposes of 51.6 below and subject to 51.5 below (persons not treated as UK representatives), a branch or agency in the UK through which a non-resident carries on (solely or in partnership) a trade, profession or vocation is his UK representative in relation to the following:

(*a*)　such income from the trade etc. as arises, directly or indirectly, through or from the branch or agency;

(*b*)　any income from property or rights used by, or held by or for, the branch or agency; and

(*c*)　capital gains arising in connection with the branch or agency and chargeable under *TCGA 1992, s 10* (see Tolley's Capital Gains Tax).

Where the non-resident ceases to carry on the trade etc. through the branch or agency, it continues to be his UK representative for tax purposes in relation to amounts arising during the period of the agency. A UK representative is a legal entity distinct from the non-resident. Where the branch or agency is a partnership, the partnership is the non-resident's UK representative. If a trade etc. is carried on in the UK by a non-resident in partnership with at least one UK resident partner, the partnership itself is the UK representative in relation to the non-resident's share of UK profits.

[*FA 1995, s 126; TMA 1970, s 118(1); FA 2003, s 155, Sch 27 para 4, Sch 43 Pt 3(6)*].

Simon's Direct Tax Service. See B3.125.

51.5 Persons not treated as UK representatives for tax purposes.

The following are not treated as UK representatives for the purposes of 51.6 below.

(1)   *Casual Agents.* An agent is not treated as a non-UK resident's UK representative in relation to income etc. arising from so much of any business as relates to transactions carried out through the agent otherwise than in the course of carrying on a regular agency for the non-resident.

(2)   *Brokers.* A broker is not treated as a non-resident's UK representative in relation to income etc. arising from so much of any business as relates to transactions carried out through the broker and satisfying all the following conditions:

   (i)   the broker was carrying on the business of broker at the time of the transaction;

   (ii)   the transaction was carried out in the ordinary course of that business;

   (iii) the remuneration for that transaction was at a rate not less than would have been customary for that class of business; and

   (iv)   the broker is not the non-resident's UK representative in relation to income chargeable to tax for the same chargeable period which is not excluded under these provisions.

(3)   *Investment managers.* An investment manager is not treated as a non-resident's UK representative in relation to income etc. arising from so much of any business as relates to investment transactions (as defined) carried out through the investment manager and satisfying all the following conditions:

   (i)   the manager was carrying on the business of providing investment management services at the time of the transaction;

   (ii)   the transaction was carried out in the ordinary course of that business;

   (iii) the manager, when acting on the non-resident's behalf in that transaction, did so in an independent capacity;

   (iv)   the '20% condition' is satisfied in relation to the transaction (see below);

   (v)   the remuneration for the investment management services in question was at a rate not less than would have been customary for that class of business; and

   (vi)   the manager is not the non-resident's UK representative in relation to income chargeable to tax for the same chargeable period which is not excluded under these provisions.

As regards (iii) above, Revenue Pamphlet IR 131, SP 1/01 clarifies the 'independent capacity' requirement. A person is not regarded as acting in an independent capacity on behalf of the non-resident unless, having regard to its legal, financial and commercial characteristics, their relationship is on an arm's length basis as between independent businesses. The test will be regarded as satisfied where any of the following applies (although this list is not exhaustive). (A subsidiary may be considered independently of its parent for these purposes.)

   (i)   The provision of services to the non-resident (and persons connected with the non-resident) is not a substantial part (i.e. it must be less than 70%) of the investment management business (or that condition is satisfied within 18 months from the start of a new investment management business).

   (ii)   An intention to satisfy (i) above was not met for reasons outside the manager's control, despite reasonable steps being taken to fulfil that intention.

   (iii) Investment management services are provided to a collective fund, the interests in which are quoted or otherwise freely marketed, e.g. as unit trust units.

(iv) Investment management services are provided to a widely held collective fund. (This will apply mostly to non-transparent overseas funds, and will be regarded as satisfied if either no majority interest in the fund was held by five or fewer persons (and persons connected with them), or no interest of more than 20% was held by a single person (and persons connected with that person).)

The '*20% condition*' (see (iv) above) is that, broadly, the investment manager and persons connected with him may not have a beneficial entitlement to more than 20% of the non-resident's excluded income (see 51.1 above) from transactions carried out by the investment manager on his behalf. The condition must be satisfied throughout a qualifying period which must at least consist of the chargeable period for which the income from the transaction in question is chargeable to tax and which may be no more than five years comprising two or more chargeable periods. Failure to satisfy the condition is disregarded if it was for reasons beyond the control of the manager and persons connected with him and they did not fail to take reasonable mitigating action. If a transaction satisfies the conditions at (i) to (vi) above except for the 20% condition, it is regarded as satisfying *all* conditions to the extent of any income etc. which does *not* represent excluded income to which the manager etc. has or has had a beneficial entitlement. Special rules apply to determine whether or not the 20% condition is satisfied in relation to a transaction carried out for a collective investment scheme (within *Financial Services and Markets Act 2000, s 235*) in which the non-resident is a participant; broadly, the condition is treated as satisfied by each participant if the scheme (were it taxable as a separate entity) would not be regarded as carrying on a trade in the UK or if it would be so regarded but the 20% rule is satisfied by reference to the scheme's taxable income.

Statement of Practice 1/01 (referred to above) also clarifies certain other aspects of the conditions for exclusion, and in particular the interaction between the 'independent capacity test' and the '20% condition'.

Persons are connected if they are connected within *ICTA 1988, s 839* (see 19 CONNECTED PERSONS).

Exceptionally, a non-resident who does not qualify for the limitation on charge under these investment manager rules may have enjoyed the protection of extra-statutory concession B40 up to 5 April 1995. Concession B40 will continue to apply in these circumstances, if the arrangements are in respect of a jointly-held fund marketed before 29 November 1994, for the intended life of the fund when marketed (or until 5 April 2005 if earlier). (Revenue Inspector's Manual IM 226).

(4) *Lloyd's members' agents and managing agents.* A Lloyd's members' agent or syndicate managing agent is not treated as a non-resident Lloyd's underwriter's UK representative in relation to income etc. arising from his Lloyd's business (or, in the case of a managing agent, from the syndicate in question). See 89 UNDERWRITERS AT LLOYD'S generally.

General. Where a person acts as broker or investment manager as part only of a business, that part is deemed to be a separate business for the purposes of (2) and (3) above. A person carries out a transaction on behalf of another where he either undertakes it himself or instructs a third party to do so. Income arising from so much of a business as results from transactions carried out through a branch or agency includes income from property or rights which as a result of the transactions are used by, or held by or for, that branch or agency.

[*FA 1995, s 127; FA 2003, s 155, Sch 27 para 5; SI 2001 No 3629, Article 89; SI 2003 No 2172*].

Simon's Direct Tax Service. See B3.125A.

51.6 **Obligations etc. imposed on UK representatives.** As regards the taxation of any amounts in relation to which a non-UK resident has a UK representative (see 51.4, 51.5 above), legislation making provision for, or in connection with, the assessment, collection and recovery of income tax, capital gains tax and interest on tax has effect as if the obligations and liabilities of the non-resident were *also* obligations and liabilities of the UK representative. The discharge of an obligation or liability by either the non-resident or the UK representative is treated as discharging the corresponding obligation or liability of the other. The non-resident is bound by any acts or omissions of his UK representative. Where an obligation or liability depends on the serving of a notice or other document or the making of a request or demand, it is not treated as having been imposed on the UK representative unless the notice etc. was served on or copied to him or he was notified of the request or demand. A person is not guilty of a criminal offence by virtue of these provisions except where he committed the offence himself or consented to or connived in its commission.

Independent agents. An '*independent agent*' of a non-resident is any person who is the non-resident's UK representative in respect of any agency from the non-resident in which he was acting on the non-resident's behalf in an independent capacity (see 51.5(3) above). The provisions above apply equally to independent agents as to other UK representatives, with the following applying in addition.

As regards his obligations to furnish information (including anything contained in a return, self-assessment, account, statement or report provided to the Revenue), the independent agent is not required to do anything beyond what is practicable by acting to the best of his knowledge and belief after having taken all reasonable steps to obtain the information. In such a case, the non-resident is not discharged from his own obligation to furnish the information, but is also not bound by any error or mistake in the information so furnished by the agent unless it results from the non-resident's own act or omission or one to which he consented or in which he connived. An independent agent is entitled to be indemnified in respect of any liability discharged by him on the non-resident's behalf under these provisions and to retain, out of monies due by him to the non-resident, amounts sufficient to cover any such liability, whether or not already discharged. An independent agent is not liable to any civil penalty or surcharge in respect of any act or omission which is neither his own nor one to which he consented or in which he connived, providing he can show that he could not recover the penalty etc. out of monies due to the non-resident after being indemnified for his other liabilities.

[*FA 1995, Sch 23*].

Simon's Direct Tax Service. See B3.125.

51.7 **NON-RESIDENT ENTERTAINERS AND SPORTSMEN**

Any person making a payment or transfer (including by way of loan) for, in respect of, or which in any way derives either directly or indirectly from, the performance of a 'relevant activity' performed in the UK by an entertainer or sportsman (as broadly defined) who is not resident in the UK in the year of assessment in which that activity is performed, is required to deduct and account to the Revenue for an amount representing income tax, at a rate which may not exceed the basic rate of income tax for the year of assessment. In the case of a transfer, the actual worth of what is transferred is treated as being a net amount corresponding to a gross amount from which income tax at the basic rate has been deducted. That gross amount is treated as the value of the transfer and the net value is the cost to the transferor less any contribution made by the entertainer or sportsman.

A '*relevant activity*' is an activity performed in the UK by an entertainer or sportsman in his character as such on or in connection with (including promotion of) a commercial occasion or event (including participation in live or recorded transmissions of any kind) for which he is entitled to receive a payment or transfer or which is designed to promote commercial sales or activity by any means. See *Set, Deuce and Ball v Robinson (Sp C 373), [2003] SSCD 382* which analysed this definition in relation to non-resident tennis players performing at Wimbledon; on appeal, it was further held that payments are within the scope of these provisions even if made by a foreign company with no UK tax presence (*Agassi v Robinson Ch D, [2004] STC 610*).

Payments or transfers from which tax need not be withheld under these provisions are as follows.

(i)   A payment subject to deduction of tax under some other provision of the *Taxes Acts* than *ICTA 1988, s 555(2)* and *The Income Tax (Entertainers and Sportsmen) Regulations 1987 (SI 1987 No 530)*.

(ii) An arm's length payment made to a person resident and ordinarily resident in the UK, who is not connected or associated with the payee, for services ancillary to the performance of a relevant activity.

(iii) Payments representing royalties from the sale of sound recordings.

(iv) Any total amount paid in a tax year by a payer, together with persons connected or associated with him, to a non-UK resident entertainer or sportsman, together with persons connected or associated with him, which does not exceed £1,000.

The *Regulations* provide for arrangements to be made in writing between the payer, the entertainer or sportsman, or other recipient of the payment, and the Board of Inland Revenue for a reduced tax payment representing, as nearly as may be, the actual liability of the entertainer or sportsman, to apply. Such application must be made not later than 30 days before the payment (or transfer) falls to be made and the full basic rate deduction must be made from any payment or transfer made before approval is given by the Board. There are provisions to prevent any payment suffering withholding tax more than once where it passes through an intermediary, and for reductions to apply where there is a double taxation agreement in force. Similarly, there are anti-avoidance provisions to prevent payments or transfers being routed through third parties such as controlled companies and similar entities.

The sum accounted for to the Revenue is treated as paid on account of the income or corporation tax liability of a person other than the person so accounting for it, whether a liability under the *Regulations*, under *ICTA 1988, ss 555 et seq.* or under any other provision of the *Taxes Acts*. The charge under *ICTA 1988, s 555(2)* applies in place of any charge on employment income (any amount charged on which is to be treated as an expense of the 'Schedule 11 trade' (see below)), under *ICTA 1988, ss 660–685* (settlements) or under Schedule D (where the connected payment is a receipt falling to be included in the computation of profits of a company which provides the services of the entertainer or sportsman). A recipient is entitled to claim in writing that a tax payment deducted is excessive and *TMA 1970, s 42* (see 4 APPEALS) applies to such claims.

Computation of liability of entertainer or sportsman. Where a payment or other transfer is made within these provisions, the relevant activity is treated as performed in the course of a trade, profession or vocation (the '*Schedule 11 trade*', so called because these provisions were originally enacted in *FA 1986, Sch 11*) exercised in the UK and thus chargeable to tax under Schedule D, Case I or II (to the extent that it would not otherwise be so treated) unless it is performed in the course of an office or employment.

Payment of tax is due, whether or not it has been withheld from the connected payment or transfer, before, or at the time when, a quarterly return (see below) is made, whether or not an assessment has been made.

Assessment to tax. An assessment may be made, in relation to a tax year or other period, on a current year (not a preceding year) basis and any apportionment, division or aggregation by reference to tax years or other periods may be made as is just and reasonable. The 'Schedule 11 trade' is thus treated separately from the 'world-wide trade' of an entertainer or sportsman, but for the purposes of loss relief under *ICTA 1988, ss 381, 385* they are treated as the same trade, although losses in early years will be relieved only by reference to the date of commencement of the world-wide trade. Terminal loss relief under *ICTA 1988, s 388* will only be given in respect of the Schedule 11 trade if the world-wide trade ceases in the same period.

All other provisions of the *Taxes Acts* as to the time within which an assessment may be made apply to such an assessment as do the provisions for out of time assessments. Tax charged by an assessment is payable within 14 days of the issue of the notice, or by the due date of payment of the tax (see above) if this is earlier. The collection and recovery procedures and the provisions relating to interest on overdue tax in *TMA 1970* apply to such assessments.

Returns (including returns of payments for which a nil deduction rate applied) must be made quarterly in respect of the periods to 30 June, 30 September, 31 December and 5 April within 14 days of the end of each period. The Board may require, in writing, within a specified time, certain information regarding payments, payees and relevant activities. The penalty provisions of *TMA 1970, s 98* apply to failure to submit returns (see 57.9 PENALTIES).

[*ICTA 1988, ss 555–558; SI 1987 No 530*].

Simon's Direct Tax Service. See E5.8.

51.8   **NON-RESIDENT BANKS, INSURANCE COMPANIES AND DEALERS IN SECURITIES** carrying on business in the UK.

(i)   Where exempt on $3\frac{1}{2}$% War Loan 1952 or later, an amount equal to interest at the average rate for the period under review on all money borrowed for purposes of the business up to the total cost of any such tax-free securities held is disallowed in the computation of profits or losses and excluded from relief as a loan relationship debit (see Tolley's Corporation Tax). Expenses of acquiring, holding or dealing with the tax-free securities and any profits or losses arising therefrom are also excluded from computation. [*ICTA 1988, s 475; FA 1995, Sch 8 para 25(1); FA 1996, Sch 14 para 27, Sch 28 para 3*].

(ii)   Where receipts of interest or dividends have been treated as tax-exempt under double taxation arrangements, they are not to be excluded from trading income etc. so as to give rise to losses for set-off against income etc. [*ICTA 1988, s 808*].

(iii)   See also Tolley's Corporation Tax.

51.9   **PAYMENTS OF ANNUAL SUMS TO NON-RESIDENTS**

Copyright royalties, public lending right payments and **design royalties** (or 'sums paid periodically') paid '*by or through* any person' in the UK to a person whose usual place of abode is outside the UK are subject to deduction of tax on the net sum (i.e. less commission). [*ICTA 1988, ss 536, 537, 537B; FA 1995, s 115(10)*]. This does not apply to professional authors (Hansard 10 November 1969, Vol 791, Col 31). See Revenue Inspector's Manual IM 4005 as regards meaning of 'usual place of abode'.

Payment to foreign author for right to sell translation, held to be within *ICTA 1988, s 536* (*Longmans, Green KB 1932, 17 TC 272*). Also that solicitors of the payers remitting royalties to non-residents must deduct tax and account to Revenue (*Rye & Eyre v CIR HL 1935, 19 TC 164*).

The Inland Revenue may call for a return of payments. [*TMA 1970, s 16*]. See 68.17 RETURNS.

51.10 Non-Residents and other Overseas Matters

51.10 **PERSONAL ALLOWANCES FOR CERTAIN NON-RESIDENTS** [*ICTA 1988, s 278; FA 1988, s 31; FA 1996, ss 134, 145, Sch 20 para 21; FA 1999, Sch 20 Pt III(3)*]

As mentioned under 65.3 RESIDENCE, ORDINARY RESIDENCE AND DOMICILE, a non-resident is liable to UK tax without any deduction for personal allowances etc. except under specific double tax treaties or in cases where the individual concerned is eligible for relief as below. (Foreigners resident here have the same rights to relief as British subjects, and where assessments are made on the ground of '*residence*' here, the taxpayer is entitled to the full allowances. But this does not apply to persons assessed because temporarily employed here, but not technically 'resident'.)

The non-resident individuals eligible for reliefs are as follows.

   (i) All Commonwealth citizens and citizens of Republic of Ireland.

   (ii) All nationals of States within the European Economic Area (EEA), which comprises all EU States plus Norway, Iceland and Liechtenstein.

  (iii) Persons who are or who have been in service of the Crown.

  (iv) Missionaries.

   (v) Servants of British Protectorates.

  (vi) Residents in the Isle of Man or Channel Islands.

 (vii) Persons abroad for health reasons (including health of wife or family) after residence in UK.

(viii) Widows or widowers of Crown Servants.

For the status of Hong Kong residents who were previously British Dependent Territories citizens following the transfer of sovereignty on 30 June 1997, see Revenue Tax Bulletin October 1996 pp 357, 358. It is expected that most will continue to be able to claim allowances under *ICTA 1988, s 278* either as British Nationals (Overseas) or as British Overseas citizens.

All personal reliefs under *ICTA 1988, Pt VII, Ch 1* are available in full to non-resident individuals within (i)–(viii) above, except that no relief is given to a wife under *ICTA 1988, s 257D* (see 47.4 MARRIED PERSONS), prior to its abolition after 5 April 2000, in respect of excess allowances of her husband where the husband is not UK resident.

Claims are made to the Board. Claimants should contact IR International—Centre for Non-Residents, Fitz Roy House, PO Box 46, Nottingham NG2 1BD, except that Crown employees or Crown pensioners should contact Inland Revenue, Public Departments (Technical Unit) Foreign Section, Ty-Glas, Llanishen, Cardiff, Wales, CF14 5FN. A right of appeal to the Special Commissioners, within three months of the notice of the Board's decision, is given by *TMA 1970, Sch 1A paras 9(2), 10*.

Simon's Direct Tax Service. See E6.2.

51.11 **TRADES ETC. CARRIED ON AND CONTROLLED ABROAD**

A trade, profession or vocation carried on by a UK resident is within Schedule D, Case I or II if carried on wholly or partly in the UK but within Case V if carried on wholly abroad [*ICTA 1988, s 18(1)(a)(ii)(3); FA 1995, Sch 6 para 2*] subject to special rules as regards trades etc. in Eire. [*ICTA 1988, s 68; FA 1994, s 207(5)*]. This is so notwithstanding the wide wording of the Case I charging rule in *ICTA 1988, s 18(3)* (*Colquhoun v Brooks HL 1889, 2 TC 490*). A non-resident is chargeable on trading etc. in the UK (see 51.3 above).

Where a business is 'carried on' for this purpose depends on from where it is managed and controlled, irrespective of where the day-to-day business activities are conducted. See for this *Trustees of Ferguson, decd v Donovan Supreme Court (IFS) 1927, 1 ITC 214* (trustees delegated control of Australian business to Australian company and did not interfere in any way; held not within Case I) and contrast *Ogilvie v Kitton CES 1908, 5 TC 338* (Canadian business managed by Canadians but 'head and brains' in UK where owners resided; Case I applied) and *Spiers v Mackinnon KB 1929, 14 TC 386*. For trades carried on by companies, see 51.8 above, and for trades carried on by partnerships, see 53.14 PARTNERSHIPS.

Where assessments are under Schedule D, Case V (see 73 SCHEDULE D, CASES IV AND V), income is nevertheless computed under the rules applicable to SCHEDULE D, CASES I AND II (71). For 1994/95 and subsequent years as regards businesses commenced after 5 April 1994 and for 1997/98 and subsequent years as regards businesses commenced on or before that date, the basis period rules in 71.3 to 71.11 SCHEDULE D, CASES I AND II apply, as does *ICTA 1988, s 113* (see 53.5 PARTNERSHIPS) (see also 73.9 SCHEDULE D, CASES IV AND V). [*ICTA 1988, s 65(3); FA 1994, s 207(2)(6), s 218*]. Loss relief under *ICTA 1988, ss 380–386* and *s 388* (see 46 LOSSES) is available only against other overseas trading etc. income, certain overseas earnings (see 75.4 SCHEDULE E—EMPLOYMENT INCOME), overseas government pensions (as in 58.2(*l*) PENSION INCOME) or foreign pensions falling to be taxed as if under Schedule D, Case V (see 58.2(*b*)(*k*)(*p*)(*q*) PENSION INCOME. [*ICTA 1988, s 391; ITEPA 2003, Sch 6 para 53*]. These provisions apply equally to income from Eire. [*ICTA 1970, Sch 12 Pt III; ICTA 1988, s 68*].

The REMITTANCE BASIS (64) applies to persons not domiciled in the UK and to persons who, being Commonwealth or Eire citizens, are not ordinarily resident in the UK. [*ICTA 1988, s 65(4); FA 1996, s 134, Sch 20 para 3*].

Travelling expenses. A deduction may be claimed for expenses incurred in a business carried on abroad (and not assessable on the REMITTANCE BASIS (64)) in travelling between any place in the UK and any place where the business is carried on, either

(*a*)   for the individual, provided that his absence is wholly and exclusively for the performance of the functions of the business, or

(*b*)   where there is absence from the UK for a continuous period of 60 days or more, for the spouse and any children under 18 (at beginning of outward journey) accompanying the individual at the beginning of the period of absence or visiting him during that period, including the return journey, but with a limit of two outward and return journeys per person in any year of assessment.

Where (*a*) above applies, a deduction may also be claimed for expenditure incurred on board and lodging at the overseas location.

Where more than one business is carried on at the overseas location, travelling etc., expenses are apportioned between them. [*ICTA 1988, s 80*].

Travelling between overseas businesses. Where more than one business is carried on abroad (and at least one is within *section 80*, as above), and absence from the UK is solely for business purposes, a deduction may be claimed for travelling between them. The deduction will normally be given in taxing the trade at the place of destination, but, exceptionally, where this trade is not within *section 80*, as above, it will be given in taxing the trade at the place of departure. Where more than one business is carried on at the place of destination or, exceptionally, at the place of departure, the expenses are apportioned between them. [*ICTA 1988, s 81*].

See 71.17 SCHEDULE D, CASES I AND II for provisions applying where an individual carrying on a business wholly or partly abroad **becomes or ceases to be UK resident.**

Partnerships abroad. See 53.14 PARTNERSHIPS.

Simon's Direct Tax Service. See **B3.103, E1.330.**

51.12 Non-Residents and other Overseas Matters

51.12 UNITED KINGDOM

The United Kingdom for tax purposes comprises England, Scotland, Wales and Northern Ireland. The Channel Islands and the Isle of Man are not included. Great Britain comprises England, Scotland and Wales only.

Territorial extension of tax area. The territorial sea of the UK is regarded as part of the UK for tax purposes. Earnings, profits and gains from exploration or exploitation activities in a designated area (under *Continental Shelf Act 1964, s 1(7)*), are treated as arising in the UK. A resident licence holder under *Petroleum (Production) Act 1934* or *Petroleum Act 1998, Pt I* may be held accountable for the liability of a non-resident and may be required by inspector to provide information concerning transactions with other persons and payments of earnings and other payments made. [*ITEPA 2003, s 41, Sch 6 paras 106, 144–146; ICTA 1988, s 830; FA 1973, s 38, Sch 15; TCGA 1992, 276; Petroleum Act 1998, Sch 4 para 5*]. As regards liability of non-resident lessors of mobile drilling rigs, vessels or equipment used in conjunction with exploration or exploitation activities, see Revenue Pamphlet IR 131, SP 6/84, 31 July 1984 (as revised). See 24.2 DOUBLE TAX RELIEF as regards certain UK exemptions *not* extended to continental shelf workers.

51.13 UNREMITTABLE OVERSEAS INCOME

Where the '*income arising*' basis applies, such income which

(i)   cannot, despite reasonable endeavour, be remitted to the UK, by reason of laws or executive action of, or the impossibility of obtaining foreign currency in, the territory concerned, and

(ii) the person chargeable has not realised outside that territory for sterling or an unblocked currency

may be omitted from assessments. The relief must be claimed within twelve months after 31 January following the year of assessment in which the income arises.

When the Inland Revenue consider that the above conditions are no longer satisfied at any time, the income is treated as arising *at that time* and is taxable accordingly (valued as at that time, taking into account foreign taxes, and, if source of income ceased before that time, charged under SCHEDULE D, CASE VI (74)). Disputes are settled by appeal to the Special Commissioners. [*ICTA 1988, s 584; FA 1996, s 134, Sch 20 para 33*].

Delayed remittances of overseas income. Where income under Schedule D, Cases IV or V is assessable on the REMITTANCE BASIS (64) the taxpayer may claim that so much of any remittance in the basis year for a year of assessment as consists of income which **arose before that basis year** shall be excluded from that year and treated as income of the basis year(s) for the year(s) of assessment in which it arose, provided that, despite reasonable endeavour, the income could not previously be remitted, by reason of the laws or executive action of, or the impossibility of obtaining foreign currency in, the territory of origin. The claim must be made within five years after 31 January following the tax year of remittance. Before 6 April 2003, these provisions applied equally to income within Schedule E, Case III, but from that date similar provision is made specifically in relation to employment income under *ITEPA 2003, ss 35–37* (see 75.6 SCHEDULE E—EMPLOYMENT INCOME). [*ICTA 1988, s 585; FA 1996, ss 134, 135, Sch 20 para 34, Sch 21 para 16; ITEPA 2003, Sch 6 para 66*].

Interest does not run on the unpaid tax if Inland Revenue are informed promptly, see details under 42.3 INTEREST AND SURCHARGES ON UNPAID TAX.

See 71.82 SCHEDULE D, CASES I AND II for relief for certain unremittable income forming part of the profits of trades within Case I of Schedule D.

Simon's Direct Tax Service. See E1.326.

52   Offshore Funds

Simon's Direct Tax Service B7.4.

52.1   INTRODUCTION

After 31 December 1983 'offshore income gains' arising on disposals of certain interests in offshore funds which are considered not to distribute sufficient income are charged to income tax or corporation tax under Schedule D, Case VI rather than to capital gains tax. Broadly, the capital gains tax regime applies to any part of such a gain accruing before 1 January 1984 but the whole of the gain arising thereafter (without indexation) is taxed as income. Special provisions apply to funds operating equalisation arrangements.

See generally Revenue Inspector's Manual IM 4075–4121.

Disposal of material interests in non-qualifying offshore funds. The offshore fund rules apply to a disposal by any person of an asset:

(*a*)   if, at the time of the disposal, the asset constitutes a '**material interest**' in an '**offshore fund**' (see 52.3 below) which is or has at any 'material time' been a '**non-qualifying offshore fund**' (see 52.4 below); or

(*b*)   if

  (i)   at the time of the disposal, the asset constitutes an interest in a UK resident company or in a unit trust scheme within *ICTA 1988, s 469(7)* which has UK resident trustees, and

  (ii)   at a 'material time' after 31 December 1984 the interest was a material interest in a 'non-qualifying offshore fund'. (For account periods (see 52.4 below) ending before 22 July 2004, this condition was that the company or unit trust was a 'non-qualifying offshore fund' and the asset constituted a 'material interest' in that fund.) For this purpose the provisions of *TCGA 1992, s 127*, equating original shares with a new holding on reorganisation, apply.

[*ICTA 1988, s 757(1); FA 1984, s 92(1); FA 2004, s 145, Sch 26 para 4(2)*].

A '*material time*' is any time after 31 December 1983 or, if later, the earliest date on which any 'relevant consideration' was given for the acquisition of the asset. '*Relevant consideration*' is that given by or on behalf of the person making the disposal or a predecessor in title which would be taken into account in determining any gain or loss on disposal under *TCGA 1992*. [*ICTA 1988, s 757(7); FA 1990, Sch 14 para 10*].

With some modifications, a disposal occurs for offshore fund purposes if there would be a disposal under *TCGA 1992*. Death is an occasion of charge as the deceased is deemed to have made a disposal at market value, immediately before his death, of any asset which was or had at any time been a 'material interest' in a 'non-qualifying offshore fund'. In addition, neither *TCGA 1992, s 135* nor *s 136* will apply, and there will therefore be a disposal at market value, if an exchange or arrangement is effected in such a way that an interest in a 'non-qualifying offshore fund', is exchanged for an interest in a distributing fund. The same principle applies to exchanges of different classes of interest where they form separate funds in their own right (see 52.3 below). [*ICTA 1988, s 757(2)–(6), s 762A; FA 2002, Sch 9 para 4(5); FA 2004, s 145, Sch 26 para 4(3)(4), para 15(1)*].

A *Pt 5* transfer under *Proceeds of Crime Act 2002* (as in 9.2(xi) CAPITAL ALLOWANCES) of an asset within (*a*) or (*b*) above is not treated as a disposal for offshore fund purposes where no compensating payment is made to the transferor. [*Proceeds of Crime Act 2002, Sch 10 paras 7, 10*].

52.2 Offshore Funds

52.2 **Offshore funds operating equalisation arrangements.** There are specific provisions to enable funds operating 'equalisation arrangements' to satisfy the 'distribution test' (see 52.5 below) which the nature of such funds might otherwise preclude. As a corollary, provision is also made to ensure that the 'accrued income' paid to outgoing investors as part of their capital payments is treated as income for tax purposes when the fund qualifies as a distributor.

Definition. For these purposes, an offshore fund operates '*equalisation arrangements*' where the first distribution paid to a person acquiring a 'material interest' by way of 'initial purchase' includes a payment which is a return of capital (debited to the fund's 'equalisation account') determined by reference to the income which had accrued to the fund in the period before that person's acquisition. An acquisition is by way of '*initial purchase*' if it is by way of direct purchase from the fund's managers in their capacity as such.

'Accrued income' chargeable to income tax — application of offshore fund rules. A disposal is one to which the offshore fund provisions apply, subject to exception below, if it is a disposal by any person of a 'material interest' in an 'offshore fund' operating equalisation arrangements where

(i) the disposal proceeds are not a trading receipt; and

(ii) the fund *is not*, and *has not been*, at any material time (see above) a 'non-qualifying offshore fund' (see 52.4 below)

(i.e. the provisions apply also to *distributing* funds (see 52.5 below) with equalisation arrangements).

Capital gains tax rules for disposals apply as they do for other offshore fund disposals (see 52.1 above) with some variations. Death is not treated as a disposal in this context. In addition, *TCGA 1992, s 127* (reorganisations etc.) (including that section as applied by certain other *TCGA 1992* provisions) does not apply and there is a disposal at market value in such circumstances.

Exception. The offshore fund legislation does *not* apply as indicated above to a disposal where the fund's income for the period preceding the disposal is of such a nature that the part relating to the interest in question is in any event chargeable under Schedule D, Case IV or Case V on the person disposing of the interest (or would be so chargeable if residence/domicile/situation of assets requirements were met).

[*ICTA 1988, s 757(2)(3), s 758; FA 1989, s 81; FA 2002, Sch 9 para 4(6)*].

52.3 **MATERIAL INTERESTS IN OFFSHORE FUNDS**

An 'offshore fund' is a collective investment scheme (as defined by *Financial Services and Markets Act 2000, s 235*) constituted by

(*a*) a company resident outside the UK; or

(*b*) a unit trust scheme within *ICTA 1988, s 469(7)* which has non-UK resident trustees; or

(*c*) any other arrangements taking effect under overseas law which create rights in the nature of co-ownership under that law.

For account periods (see 52.4 below) ending on or after 22 July 2004, sub-funds and different classes of interest in a fund constitute separate offshore funds. This allows the test for distributing status (see 52.5 below) to be applied to them independently.

[*ICTA 1988, ss 756A–756C, s 759(1)(1A); FA 1995, s 134(1)–(3)(8); SI 2001 No 3629, Article 45;FA 2004, s 145, Sch 26 paras 3, 6(2)*].

A **'material interest'** is one which, when acquired, could reasonably be expected to be realisable (by any means, either in money or in asset form) within seven years for an amount reasonably approximate to its proportionate share of the market value of the fund's assets. For these purposes, an interest in an offshore fund which at any time is worth substantially more than its proportionate share of the fund's underlying assets is not to be regarded as so realisable. [*ICTA 1988, s 759(2)–(4)*]. If shares in a quoted overseas company have habitually been traded at or near net asset value, and an investor in these shares had a reasonable expectation, on acquisition, of a future sale at or near such value, those shares are likely to represent a 'material interest'. (Revenue Pamphlet IR 131, SP 2/86, 7 March 1986).

Exceptions. The following are not material interests.

(i)   Interests in respect of loans etc. made in the ordinary course of banking business.

(ii)   Rights under insurance policies.

(iii)   Shares in a company resident outside the UK where

    (*a*)   the shares are held by a company and the holding is necessary or desirable for the maintenance and development of a trade carried on by the company, or by an associated company within *ICTA 1988, s 416*; and

    (*b*)   the shares confer at least 10% of the voting rights and, on winding-up, a right to at least 10% of the assets after discharging all prior liabilities; and

    (*c*)   the shares are held by not more than ten persons and all confer both voting rights and a right to assets on winding-up; and

    (*d*)   at the time of acquisition of the shares the company could reasonably expect to realise its interest for market value within seven years only by virtue of (I) an arrangement requiring the company's fellow participators to purchase its shares and/or (II) provisions of either the overseas company's constitution or an agreement between the participators regarding that company's winding-up.

(iv)   Interests in companies resident outside the UK at any time when the holder is entitled to have the company wound up and to receive in that event in the same capacity more than 50% of the assets after discharging all prior liabilities.

[*ICTA 1988, s 759(5)–(8)*].

The Revenue have also indicated that normal commercial loans or other debt instruments entitling the lender to no more than a fixed return of principal on redemption, and which are not geared to the underlying asset value of the borrower's business, are not regarded as 'material interests'. (Revenue Pamphlet IR 131, SP 2/86, 7 March 1986).

'Market value' for the purposes of the offshore funds legislation is determined according to capital gains tax rules with necessary modifications of *TCGA 1992, s 272(5)* (market value in relation to rights in unit trust schemes) where appropriate. [*ICTA 1988, s 759(9)*].

52.4   **NON-QUALIFYING OFFSHORE FUNDS**

An offshore fund is **'non-qualifying'** except during an 'account period' in respect of which it is certified by the Board as a distributing fund pursuing a 'full distribution policy' (see 52.5 below). For these purposes, the first *'account period'* begins when the fund begins to carry on its activities or, if later, on 1 January 1984. An *'account period'* ends on the fund's accounting date or, if earlier, twelve months from the beginning of the period or on the fund's ceasing to carry on its activities. In addition, if the fund is a non-UK resident

52.4 Offshore Funds

company, an *'account period'* ends when it becomes UK resident, and if the fund is a unit trust with non-UK resident trustees, it ends when those trustees become UK resident. Where a sub-fund or class of interest is treated as a fund in its own right (see 52.3 above) references to *'account period'* are to the account period of the main fund. [*ICTA 1988, s 760(1)(2)(8)–(10A); FA 1984, s 95(8); FA 2004, s 145, Sch 26 para 7(3)*].

Conditions for certification. The investment conditions for certification are significantly relaxed in relation to account periods ending on or after 22 July 2004. For earlier account periods, and subject to the modifications of conditions for certification in certain cases noted below, an offshore fund is not to be certified as a 'distributing fund' for any account period if, at any time in that period:

(*a*)   more than 5% by value of the fund's assets consists of interests in other offshore funds (but see below); or

(*b*)   more than 10% by value of the fund's assets consists of interests in a single company. For this purpose

    (i)   the value of an interest in a single company is determined as at the most recent occasion (in that account period or earlier) on which the fund acquired an interest in that company for money or money's worth. However an occasion is disregarded if it is one on which *TCGA 1992, s 127* (equation of original shares and new holding) applied, including that *section* as applied by later provisions of *TCGA 1992* (reorganisations, conversion of securities etc.), and on which no consideration is given for the interest other than the interest in the original holding,

    (ii)   an interest is disregarded, except for determining the total value of the fund's assets, if it consists of a current or deposit account provided in the normal course of its banking business by a company whose business it is to provide such account facilities in any currency for members of the public and bodies corporate, and

    (iii)   Government-owned national or supra-national bodies whose activities are directed not with a view to commercial profits, but to the exercise of a wider social or economic function, are not regarded as companies for this purpose (Revenue Pamphlet IR 131, SP 2/86, 7 March 1986); or

(*c*)   the fund's assets include more than 10% of the issued share capital, or any class of it, in any company; or

(*d*)   there is more than one class of material interests (see 52.3 above) in the fund and, were each class and the assets represented by it in a separate offshore fund, each such separate fund does not pursue a 'full distribution policy'. For this purpose, interests held solely by persons involved in the management of the fund's assets are disregarded if they carry no right or expectation to participate in profits and no right to anything other than the return of the price paid on winding-up or redemption.

For account periods ending on or after 22 July 2004, all of the above conditions are removed apart from (*a*). It follows that the commentary below on inadvertent failures and modifications of conditions apply, in relation to such account periods, only to condition (*a*). As a transitional measure, sub-funds that constitute an offshore fund in their own right as a result of *FA 2004* (see 52.3 above) may have regard to the investments of the main fund (the umbrella fund) in applying the test at (*a*) above for account periods ending between 22 July 2004 and 31 December 2005 inclusive.

Where the Board are satisfied that an apparent failure to comply with any of (*a*)–(*c*) above occurred inadvertently and was remedied without unreasonable delay, that failure may be disregarded.

[ICTA 1988, s 760(3)–(7), Sch 27 para 14; FA 2004, Sch 26 paras 13, 14(7), 17].

Modifications of conditions for certification. The conditions for certification in (*a*)–(*d*) above are modified in certain cases.

(A) **Investments in second tier funds.** If offshore funds ('primary funds') would fail to meet the conditions in (*a*) to (*c*) above because of investments in other offshore funds (referred to below as 'second tier funds') which could themselves be certified as qualifying distributing funds (without any modification of the (*a*) to (*c*) conditions), then the primary funds' interests in the second tier funds are left out of account, except for determining the total value of the primary funds' assets, in establishing whether the primary funds are prevented by (*a*) to (*c*) above from being certified as distributing funds. In addition, where the above applies, if at any time in a primary fund's account period that fund's assets include an interest in another offshore fund or in any company and the qualifying second tier fund's assets also include an interest in that other fund or company, then the primary fund's interest is aggregated with its proportionate share of the second tier fund's interest in determining whether the primary fund is within the limits in (*a*) to (*c*) above. Its share of the second tier fund's interest is the proportion which the average value during its account period of its own holding of interests in the second tier fund bears to the average value during the period of all interests in the second tier fund. [*ICTA 1988, s 760(3), Sch 27 paras 6, 7, 9; FA 2004, Sch 26 para 14(2)(3)*].

(B) **Investments in trading companies.** Where the assets of an offshore fund include an interest in a company whose business is wholly the carrying on of trade(s) the limit of 10% of a fund's assets invested in a single company in (*b*) above is increased to 20% and the 10% limit on the proportion of a class of share in any company in (*c*) above is increased to allow holdings of less than 50%. For these purposes companies are excluded if their business consists to any extent of banking or moneylending or of dealing, including dealing by way of futures contracts and traded options, in commodities, currency, securities, debts or other assets of a financial nature. [*ICTA 1988, s 760(3), Sch 27 paras 4(2), 10; FA 2004, Sch 26 para 14(4)*]. Dealing in commodities, currency and financial assets incidental to the business of a company will be disregarded in determining whether the company is trading. (Revenue Pamphlet IR 131, SP 2/86, 7 March 1986).

(C) **Wholly-owned subsidiaries.** Where an offshore fund has a wholly-owned subsidiary company, the receipts, expenditure, assets and liabilities of the fund and the subsidiary are aggregated so that the fund and the subsidiary are treated as one for the purposes of determining whether the fund is within the limits in (*a*) to (*d*) above. In the same way, the interest of the fund in the subsidiary and any distributions or other payments between the fund and the subsidiary are left out of account. A wholly-owned subsidiary is one owned either directly and beneficially by the fund, or directly by the trustees of the fund for the benefit of the fund, or, in the case of a fund within 52.3(*c*) above, in some other equivalent manner. Where the subsidiary has only one class of issued share capital, ownership of at least 95% of that capital by the offshore fund constitutes the subsidiary a wholly-owned subsidiary for this purpose, and only a corresponding proportion of the subsidiary's receipts, expenditure, assets and liabilities are then aggregated with those of the offshore fund. [*ICTA 1988, s 760(3), Sch 27 para 11; FA 2004, Sch 26 para 14(5)*].

(D) **Subsidiary dealing and management companies.** The investment restriction in (*c*) above does not apply to so much of an offshore fund's assets as consists of share capital of a company which is either

(1) a wholly-owned subsidiary of the fund (as defined in (C) above) whose sole function is dealing in material interests in the offshore fund for management

591

and administrative purposes and which is not entitled to any distribution from the fund; or

(2)   a subsidiary management company of the fund whose sole function is to provide the fund, or other funds with an interest in the company, with advisory services or administrative, management and related property holding services on arm's length commercial terms. For the purposes of determining whether a company is a subsidiary management company of a fund, that company and any wholly-owned subsidiary companies it may itself have are regarded as a single entity. [*ICTA 1988, s 760(3), Sch 27 para 12; FA 2004, Sch 26 para 14(6)*].

(E)   **Disregard of certain investments.** Certain holdings which would otherwise fall within the restriction at (*c*) above are not taken into account for the purposes of that restriction. This applies where no more than 5% of the value of the offshore fund's assets consists of such holdings and of interests in other non-qualifying offshore funds. [*ICTA 1988, s 760(3), Sch 27 para 13; FA 2004, Sch 26 para 14(6)*].

52.5   THE DISTRIBUTION TEST

An offshore fund pursues a '**full distribution policy**' with respect to an account period if

(*a*)   a distribution is made for that account period or for some other period falling wholly or partly within that period; and

(*b*)   subject to modifications below, the distribution represents at least 85% of the fund's income and not less than 85% of its 'UK equivalent profits' for that period; and

(*c*)   the distribution is made during or within six months after the end of the account period (the six month limit may be extended at the Board's discretion); and

(*d*)   the distribution is in a form such that any part of it received in the UK by a UK resident which is not part of the profits of a trade etc. is chargeable under Schedule D, Case IV or Case V.

These conditions may equally be satisfied by any two or more distributions taken together. [*ICTA 1988, Sch 27 para 1(1)*].

The basic conditions in (*a*) to (*d*) above are modified in certain cases (see 52.6 below).

A fund is treated as pursuing a full distribution policy for any account period in which there is no income and no 'UK equivalent profits', or for account periods ending after 28 November 1994 for which gross fund income does not exceed 1% of the average value of fund assets during the period, but it will not be so treated for any account period for which no accounts are prepared. [*ICTA 1988, Sch 27 para 1(2)(3); FA 1995, s 134(4)(9)*].

Non-UK legal restrictions. Where in an account period an offshore fund is subject to non-UK legal restrictions on making distributions by reason of an excess of losses over profits as computed according to the law in question, a deduction is allowed from the fund's income of any amount which cannot be distributed but which would otherwise form part of the fund's income for that account period. [*ICTA 1988, Sch 27 para 1(6)*].

Apportionment of income and distributions between account periods. Where a period for which accounts are made up or for which a distribution is made covers the whole or part of two or more account periods of the fund, the income or distribution is apportioned on a time basis according to the number of days in each period. A distribution made out of specified income but not for a specified period is attributed to the account period in which the income arose. Where no period or income is specified, a distribution is treated as made for the last account period ending before the distribution. If the distribution made, or treated as made, for an account period exceeds the income of that period the excess is reallocated to previous periods, to later periods before earlier ones, until exhausted, unless the distribution was apportioned on a time basis as mentioned above in which case the excess is first reapportioned on a just and reasonable basis to the other account period(s). [*ICTA 1988, Sch 27 para 1(4)(5)*].

'UK equivalent profits' of an offshore fund are the total profits, excluding chargeable gains, on which, after allowing for any deductions available, corporation tax would be chargeable, assuming that

(i)   the offshore fund is a UK resident company in the account period in question, but in no other; and

(ii)   the account period is an accounting period of that company; and

(iii) any dividends or distributions from a UK resident company are included.

The special corporation tax rules for loan relationships and derivative contracts (see Tolley's Corporation Tax under Loan Relationships and under Financial Instruments and Derivative Contracts) used to be disregarded for this purpose, and it was assumed that income tax, rather than corporation tax, rules applied, as they did for unauthorised unit trusts. However, for account periods ending on or after 22 July 2004, the corporation tax rules relating to creditor loan relationships and profits/losses from derivative contracts apply as if the fund were an authorised unit trust. This change in treatment does not apply to funds in existence on or before 22 July 2004 unless they elect for it to apply. Such an election, once made, is irrevocable.

Any UK government securities or securities of foreign states which are exempt from tax (see 33.2 GOVERNMENT STOCKS) must be brought into account in determining the fund's total profits.

Whether a fund is trading will turn on the particular facts, but in general a fund would not normally be regarded as trading in respect of relatively infrequent transactions, or where the intention was merely to hedge specific investments which were not associated with trading activities. (Revenue Pamphlet IR 131, SP 2/86, 7 March 1986).

The deductions referred to above include a deduction equal to that allowed against a fund's income where non-UK legal restrictions prevent distribution (see above) and a deduction equal to any foreign capital tax allowed as a deduction in determining the fund's income for the account period in question.

Interest paid to a non-UK resident is deductible in the same way as if it were paid to a UK resident. UK income tax (whether suffered by deduction or by assessment) is available as a deduction. (Revenue Pamphlet IR 131, SP 2/86, 7 March 1986).

[*ICTA 1988, Sch 27 para 5; FA 1994, s 176(2); FA 1996, Sch 10 para 3; FA 2002, Sch 26 para 35; FA 2004, s 145, Sch 26 paras 1, 2*].

52.6   **MODIFICATIONS OF DISTRIBUTION TEST**

The basic rules of the distribution test in 52.5(*a*) to (*d*) above are modified in various circumstances.

(*a*)   **Funds operating equalisation arrangements.** Where an offshore fund operates such arrangements (see 52.2 above) throughout an account period (see 52.4 above), an amount equal to any 'accrued income' which is part of the consideration for certain disposals in that period is treated as a distribution for the purposes of the distribution test. This applies to a disposal

(i)   which is a disposal of a material interest in the fund to either the fund or the fund managers in their capacity as such; and

(ii)   which is one to which the offshore fund rules apply (whether or not by virtue of their application to disposals from distributing funds with equalisation arrangements — see 52.2 above), or which is one to which the rules would apply if the provisions regarding the non-application of *TCGA 1992, ss 127, 135* applied generally and not only for the purpose of determining whether a disposal from a distributing fund with equalisation arrangements is brought within the rules (see 52.2 above); and

(iii)   which is not a disposal within the *exception* at 52.2 above (where the income of the fund is, or would be, chargeable to tax under Schedule D, Case IV or V in any event).

The '*accrued income*' referred to above is that part of the consideration which would be credited to the fund's equalisation account if the interest were resold to another person by way of 'initial purchase' (see 52.2 above) on the same day. However there are provisions to ensure that this accrued income figure is reduced where the interest disposed of was acquired by way of initial purchase (by any person) after the beginning of the account period by reference to which the accrued income is calculated. In addition, where an offshore commodity dealing fund (see also (*c*) below) operates equalisation and there is a disposal within (i) to (iii) above, one half of the accrued income representing commodity profits is left out of account in determining what part of the disposal consideration represents accrued income.

For the purposes of the distribution test, the distribution which the fund is treated as making on a disposal is treated as being paid to the person disposing of his interest, in the income form required by 52.5(*d*) above, out of the income of the fund for the account period of disposal. Where a distribution is made to the managers (in their capacity as such) of a fund operating equalisation arrangements it is disregarded for the purposes of the distribution test except to the extent that it relates to that part of the period for which the distribution is made during which the managers (in that capacity) held that interest. [*ICTA 1988, Sch 27 paras 2, 4(4)*].

(*b*)   **Funds with income taxable under Schedule D, Case IV or V on investors.** Where sums forming part of the income of an offshore fund within 52.3(*b*) or (*c*) above are chargeable to tax under Schedule D, Case IV or V on the holders of interests in the fund (or would be so chargeable were the necessary residence etc. rules met), any such sums which are not actually part of a distribution complying with the part of the distribution test in 52.5(*c*) and (*d*) above are treated as distributions which do so comply made out of the income of which they are part and paid to the holders of the interests in question. [*ICTA 1988, Sch 27 para 3*].

(*c*)   **Funds with commodity dealing income.** Where an offshore fund's income includes commodity dealing profits, half of those profits are left out of account in determining the fund's income and UK equivalent profits for the purposes of the distribution test in 52.5(*b*) above. '*Commodities*' are defined as tangible assets dealt with on a commodity exchange, excluding currency, securities, debts or other financial assets. '*Dealing*' includes dealing by way of futures contracts and traded options. Where the fund's income includes both commodity dealing profits and other income, its expenditure is apportioned on a just and reasonable basis and the non-commodity dealing business is treated as carried on by a separate company when determining what expenditure, if any, is deductible under *ICTA 1988, s 75* (management expenses of investment companies). See also (*a*) above for position where a commodity dealing fund operates equalisation arrangements. [*ICTA 1988, Sch 27 para 4; FA 1988, Sch 13 para 12*].

(*d*) **Wholly-owned commodity dealing subsidiaries.** In a situation within 52.4(C) above, the fund and the subsidiary dealing company are similarly treated as a single entity for the purposes of the distribution test. [*ICTA 1988, Sch 27 para 11*].

(*e*) **Investments in second tier funds.** In a situation within 52.4(A) above, the UK equivalent profits of the primary fund for the period are increased by its 'share' of the 'excess income' (if any) of the second tier fund in determining whether not less than 85% of the primary fund's UK equivalent profits are distributed. The '*excess income*' of the second tier fund is the amount by which its UK equivalent profits exceeds its distributions. There are provisions for apportioning excess income between periods on a time basis when the account periods of the primary and second tier funds do not coincide. The primary fund's '*share*' of the excess income is the proportion which the average value during its account period of its own holding of interests in the second tier fund bears to the average value of all interests in that fund. [*ICTA 1988, Sch 27 paras 6, 8, 9*].

52.7 **CERTIFICATION PROCEDURE**

Fund requesting certification. Application for certification as a distributing fund for an account period must be made within six months of the end of that period and should be sent to Inland Revenue Technical Division (Offshore Funds), Room 208, St John's House, Merton Road, Bootle, Merseyside, L69 9BB (tel 0151–922 6363 ext 2100). The application must be accompanied by a copy of the fund's accounts covering or including the account period for which certification is sought (including balance sheet, income and expenditure account, and, where prepared, the report for investors and the statement of source and application of funds), and provision of the following information in relation to the account period in question will assist the Board in its consideration of the application.

(1) The fund's full name.

(2) The account period for which certification is sought.

(3) A copy of any fund prospectus or explanatory memorandum.

(4) Details of any equalisation arrangements in force.

(5) An analysis of the fund's investment portfolio at the last accounting date, unless supplied in the accounts. This should include the percentage value of the fund's assets represented by each investment, and the percentage interest of the fund in each class of share capital of any unquoted company, and should identify any holding in other offshore funds (including whether they are considered to be distributing funds).

(6) A copy of the accounts of any wholly-owned subsidiary of the fund dealing either in commodities or in material interests in the fund.

(7) A copy of the accounts of any subsidiary management company in which the fund has an interest.

(8) A computation of the fund's UK equivalent profits or, failing this, a summary analysis of surpluses on realisation taken directly to the fund reserves.

(9) In respect of each class of share in the fund, the amount and date of each distribution (actual or projected) in respect of the account period, and the aggregate amount of deemed distributions made in respect of the period by way of equalisation.

(Revenue Press Release 31 July 1984).

Where the Board is satisfied that the necessary conditions are met it must certify the fund as a distribution fund for the period in respect of which application was made. The Board must give written notice if, after application, it determines that no certificate should be issued. It must also give notice where it appears that the accounts or other information provided do not make full and accurate disclosure of all relevant matters, in which case any notice of certification previously given is void. The fund may appeal to the Special Commissioners against Board decisions within ninety days. The Special Commissioners have jurisdiction to review any decision of the Board relevant to a ground of the appeal. [*ICTA 1988, Sch 27 paras 15, 16*].

A list of offshore funds which have been granted UK distributor status is available on the Revenue's website.

Investor requesting certification. No appeal may be brought against a tax assessment (see 52.8 below) on the grounds that a fund should have been certified as a distributing fund in respect of an account period. However, where a fund does not apply for certification, an investor, who is assessed to tax for which he would not be liable if the fund were certified, may by notice in writing require the Board to take action with a view to determining whether the fund should be so certified.

If more than one request from an investor is received, the Board is taken to have complied with each if it complies with one.

Broadly, the procedure is as follows.

(i)   The Board invites the fund to apply for certification. The time limit for application (see above) is then extended, if necessary, to 90 days from the date of the Board's invitation.

(ii)   If the fund does not then apply for certification the Board must determine the question as if such application had been made having regard to any accounts or information provided by the investor.

(iii) If, after the Board has determined that the fund should not be certified, other accounts or information are provided which were not previously available, the Board must reconsider their determination.

(iv)   The Board must notify the investor who requested the Board to take action of their decision.

(v)   The Revenue has wide powers enabling it to disclose to interested parties information regarding Board or Special Commissioner decisions or details of any notice given to a fund regarding a lack of full and accurate disclosure of information (see above).

[*ICTA 1988, Sch 27 paras 17, 18, 20*].

Postponement of tax. There are provisions to enable an investor to apply for tax assessed to be postponed pending the Board's determination of the question of certification. [*ICTA 1988, Sch 27 para 19*].

52.8   **CHARGE TO INCOME OR CORPORATION TAX OF OFFSHORE GAIN**

Where a disposal to which the offshore fund rules apply (including a disposal of a holding in a distributing fund operating equalisation arrangements — see 52.2 above) gives rise to an 'offshore income gain', then subject to below, that gain is treated for all purposes as income assessable under Schedule D, Case VI arising to the investor at the time of disposal.

For the Revenue practice as regards identification of part disposals out of mixed holdings where a non-qualifying offshore fund has subsequently obtained distributor status, see Revenue Inspector's Manual IM 4120, 4121.

The following provisions have effect in relation to income tax or corporation tax on offshore income gains as they have in relation to capital gains tax (or corporation tax) on chargeable gains.

(*a*)   *TCGA 1992, s 2* (persons chargeable).

(*b*)   *TCGA 1992, s 10* (gains accruing to non-residents carrying on a trade in the UK through a branch or agency) except that assets need not be situated in the UK.

(*c*)   *TCGA 1992, s 12* (foreign assets of UK resident or ordinarily resident persons with foreign domicile chargeable on remittance basis).

Charitable exemption applies similarly to that for capital gains (see 14.8 CHARITIES).

Where a disposal to which the offshore fund rules apply is one of settled property, any offshore income gain will escape the Schedule D, Case VI charge provided that the general administration of the trust is ordinarily carried on outside the UK and a majority of the trustees are not resident or not ordinarily resident in the UK.

[*ICTA 1988, s 761; FA 1990, Sch 14 para 11*].

52.9   **COMPUTATION OF OFFSHORE INCOME GAIN**

The computation of the gain depends upon whether the disposal is of an interest in a non-qualifying fund (see 52.10 below) or of an interest involving an equalisation element (see 52.11 below).

52.10   **Disposals of interests in non-qualifying funds.** A '*material disposal*' (one to which the offshore fund rules apply otherwise than by virtue of the provisions regarding distributing funds operating equalisation arrangements — see 52.2 above and 52.11 below) gives rise to an '*offshore income gain*' equal to the 'unindexed gain' or, if less, the 'post-1983 gain'.

Subject to the modifications to the CGT rules mentioned in 52.1 above and to exceptions below, the '*unindexed gain*' is the gain calculated under CGT rules without indexation allowance and without regard to any income tax or corporation tax charge arising under the offshore fund rules. The exceptions are as follows.

(*a*)   Where there has been indexation on an earlier disposal on a no gain/no loss basis within *TCGA 1992, s 56(2)*, the unindexed gain on the material disposal is computed as if indexation had not been available on the earlier disposal and, subject to that, as if the earlier disposal had produced neither gain nor loss.

(*b*)   If the material disposal forms part of a transfer to which *TCGA 1992, s 162* applies (rollover relief on transfer of business), the unindexed gain is computed without any deduction falling to be made under that section in computing a chargeable gain.

(*c*)   Any claim for relief under *FA 1980, s 79* (relief for gifts) does not affect the computation of the unindexed gain on the disposal. (See now *TCGA 1992, s 67*.)

(*d*)   In the case of an insurance company carrying on life assurance business, where a profit from overseas life assurance business, attributable to a material disposal, is taken into account in the computation under *ICTA 1988, s 441*, the unindexed gain, if any, accruing on disposal is computed as if *TCGA 1992, s 37(1)* did not apply. For accounting periods beginning before 1 January 1992, this applies equally where a profit arising from general annuity business attributable to a material disposal is taken into account (or would be but for the provisions relating to offshore income gains of insurance companies (see 52.12 below)) in the computation under *ICTA 1988, s 436*.

(*e*)   Where the computation of the unindexed gain would otherwise produce a loss, the unindexed gain is treated as nil so that no loss can arise on a material disposal.

52.11   Offshore Funds

[*ICTA 1988, Sch 28 paras 1–3, 5; FA 1990, Sch 7 para 7; FA 1991, Sch 7 para 10*].

'**Post-1983 gains**'. A person making a material disposal who acquired, or is treated as having acquired, his interest in the offshore fund before 1 January 1984, is treated as having disposed of and immediately reacquired his interest at market value on that date. The offshore income gain from 1 January 1984 to the date of disposal is then calculated in the ordinary way. If the person making the material disposal acquired his interest by way of a deemed no gain/no loss disposal (other than those arising by virtue of the indexation provisions of *FA 1982, s 86(5), Sch 13*) any previous owner's acquisition of the interest is treated as his acquisition of it. [*ICTA 1988, Sch 28 para 4*].

52.11   **Disposals involving an equalisation element**. A disposal is a '*disposal involving an equalisation element*' if it is a disposal to which the offshore fund rules apply by virtue of the provisions relating to distributing funds operating equalisation arrangements (see 52.2 above). Such a disposal gives rise to an '*offshore income gain*' of an amount equal, subject to below, to the 'equalisation element' relevant to the asset disposed of. [*ICTA 1988, Sch 28 para 6(1)(3)*].

The '**equalisation element**' is the amount which would be credited to the fund's equalisation account in respect of accrued income if, on the date of the disposal, the asset disposed of were acquired by another person by way of 'initial purchase' (see 52.2 above). However, where the person making the disposal acquired the asset in question after the beginning of the account period by reference to which the accrued income is calculated, or at or before the beginning of that period where that period began before and ended after 1 January 1984, there are provisions to ensure that the equalisation element is reduced to exclude any part which accrued prior to either 1 January 1984 or to the investor's period of ownership. Where any of the accrued income represents commodity dealing profits (within 52.6(*c*) above) half of that income is left out of account in determining the equalisation element. [*ICTA 1988, Sch 28 para 6(2)(4)–(6)*].

'**Part I gains**'. Where the offshore income gain as computed above would exceed the 'Part I gain', the offshore income gain is reduced to the lower figure. If there is no 'Part I gain' there can be no offshore income gain. The '*Part I gain*' is, broadly, the amount which would be the offshore income gain on the disposal if the disposal were a 'material disposal' within 52.10 above (i.e. within *ICTA 1988, Sch 28 Part I*) as modified by certain consequential amendments. [*ICTA 1988, Sch 28 paras 7, 8*].

52.12   **MISCELLANEOUS**

Offshore income gains accruing to persons resident or domiciled abroad. There are consequential provisions made in connection with gains accruing to certain non-resident investors in offshore funds which modify, for the purposes of the offshore fund legislation, provisions relating to

(*a*)   chargeable gains accruing to certain non-resident companies under *TCGA 1992, s 13*;

(*b*)   gains of non-resident settlements under *TCGA 1992, ss 80–98*;

(*c*)   avoidance of tax by the transfer of assets abroad under *ICTA 1988, ss 739, 740*.

To the extent that an offshore income gain is treated by virtue of (*a*) or (*b*) above as having accrued to any person resident or ordinarily resident in the UK, that gain is not deemed to be the income of any individual under *ICTA 1988, s 739* or *s 740* or any provision of *ICTA 1988, Pt XV* (settlements). [*ICTA 1988, s 762*].

Capital gains tax. There are provisions to prevent a double charge to tax when a disposal gives rise to both an offshore income gain and a chargeable gain for capital gains tax purposes.

Where an offshore income gain arises on a 'material disposal' within 52.10 above, that gain is deducted from the sum which would otherwise constitute the amount or value of the consideration in the calculation of the capital gain arising under *TCGA 1992* (on 'the 1992 Act disposal'), although the offshore gain is not to be taken into account in calculating the fraction under *TCGA 1992, s 42(2)* (part disposal).

Where the 1992 Act disposal forms part of a transfer within *TCGA 1992, s 162* (rollover relief on transfer of business wholly or partly for shares) then, in determining the amount of the deduction from the gain on the old assets, the offshore income gain is deducted from the value of the consideration received in exchange for the business.

Where an exchange of shares or securities constitutes a disposal of an interest in an offshore fund (see 52.1 and 52.2 above), the amount of any offshore income gain to which the disposal gives rise is treated as consideration for the new holding.

Where the offshore fund provisions apply to a disposal of an interest in a fund operating equalisation arrangements (see 52.2 above) and the disposal

(*a*)   is not to the fund or to its managers in their capacity as such, and

(*b*)   gives rise to an offshore income gain in accordance with 52.11 above, and

(*c*)   is followed subsequently by a distribution to either the person who made the disposal or to a person connected with him (within *ICTA 1988, s 839*, see 19 CONNECTED PERSONS) and that distribution is referable to the asset disposed of,

then the subsequent distribution (or distributions) is (are) reduced by the amount of the offshore income gain.

[*ICTA 1988, s 763*].

For disposals on or after 6 March 1998, exemption from capital gains tax under *TCGA 1992, s 76(1)* is disapplied where the disposal is of an interest in a trust which has at any time been an offshore trust, or where the interest disposed of originated in a trust which has at any time been an offshore trust. [*TCGA 1992, s 76(1A)(1B)(3); FA 1998, s 128*]. See Tolley's Capital Gains Tax under Offshore Settlements.

Offshore income gains of insurance companies. Income attributable to offshore income gains, so far as referable to general annuity business, is deducted from the receipts to be taken into account in computing the insurance company's profits from that business. [*ICTA 1988, s 437(2)(a); FA 1990, Sch 6 para 6*].

Offshore income gains of trustees. Any offshore income gains arising to trustees and assessable under Schedule D, Case VI will be charged at the rate applicable to trusts (see 81.5 SETTLEMENTS) for the year in question. [*ICTA 1988, s 764; FA 1993, Sch 6 para 13*]. However such tax paid is available for set-off against the amount assessable on discretionary trustees under *ICTA 1988, s 687(2)(b)* (see 81.5 SETTLEMENTS). [*ICTA 1988, s 687(3)(e)*].

Where trustees hold assets for a person who would be absolutely entitled as against the trustees but for being a minor, any offshore income gains liable to income tax which accrue on the disposal of those assets are deemed to be paid to that person for the purposes of the provisions regarding settlements on children in *ICTA 1988, s 660B* — see 81.18 SETTLEMENTS. [*ICTA 1988, s 660B(4); FA 1995, Sch 17 para 1*].

52.13   *Example*

R, who is resident, ordinarily resident and domiciled in the UK, invests in non-qualifying offshore funds as follows.

52.13 Offshore Funds

(i) **ABC fund**   £
   30.11.82   1,000 shares purchased at £10 per share   10,000
   1.1.84   Market value per share = £20   20,000
   1.4.05   On amalgamation with XYZ fund (an offshore fund which is not and has not been non-qualifying) the 1,000 original shares are exchanged for 2,000 new shares in XYZ which have a value of £15 per share   30,000

(ii) **DEF fund**   £
   1.8.83   500 units purchased at £25 per unit   12,500
   1.1.84   Market value per unit = £20   10,000
   1.2.05   500 units sold for £40 per unit   20,000

R has offshore income gains and capital gains/losses in 2004/05 as follows.

Offshore income gains

Disposal on 1.2.05 of 5000 DEF units

	Post-1983 gain £	Unindexed gain £
Disposal proceeds	20,000	20,000
Market value at 1.1.84	10,000	
Cost		12,500
	£10,000	£7,500

As the unindexed gain is less than the post-1983 gain, the offshore income gain chargeable under Schedule D, Case VI is £7,500.

Disposal on 1.4.05 of 1,000 ABC shares

Disposal consideration	30,000	30,000
Market value at 1.1.84	20,000	
Cost		10,000
	£10,000	£20,000

The offshore income gain chargeable under Schedule D, Case VI is the £10,000 post-1983 gain as this is less than the unindexed gain.

Capital gains computation

Disposal on 1.2.05 of 500 DEF units

	£
Disposal proceeds	20,000
Offshore income gain	7,500
	12,500
Cost	12,500
Chargeable gain/allowable loss	Nil

Disposal on 1.4.05 of 1,000 ABC shares

There is no capital gains tax liability as the share exchange is not treated as a disposal for capital gains tax purposes. [*TCGA 1992, s 135*]. See Tolley's Capital Gains Tax.

Note

(*a*)   The £10,000 offshore income gain arising on the exchange of ABC shares for XYZ shares will be treated as part of the acquisition cost for capital gains tax purposes on a subsequent disposal of XYZ shares (see 52.12 above).

53 Partnerships

[ICTA 1988, ss 111–115]

Cross-reference. See also 61 PERSONAL SERVICE COMPANIES ETC.

Simon's Direct Tax Service E5.3.

Other sources. See Tolley's Partnership Taxation.

53.1 INTRODUCTION

An English partnership is not a legal entity in the same way as a company, but a collection of separate persons. In Scotland, a firm is a legal person, see *Partnership Act 1890, s 4(2)*. However, the *Taxes Acts* are in general applied to Scottish partnerships in the same way as they are applicable to the rest of the UK.

The profits of a trade, profession or other business carried on in partnership used to be assessed jointly on the partnership itself, and to this extent it was treated for tax purposes as an entity distinct from its members. This does not apply for 1997/98 and subsequent tax years and did not apply from the outset to partnership trades etc. commenced after 5 April 1994. Instead, the taxable profits of the trade etc. are apportioned between the partners, each of whom is then taxed on his own share. See 68.9, 68.13 RETURNS for self-assessment provisions regarding partnership returns and general compliance.

See the 2003/04 and earlier editions for full coverage of the old (i.e. pre-1997/98) rules and the transitional provisions on changeover to the new rules. For a general discussion of the tax treatment of partnerships where the old rules applied, see *R v City of London Commrs (ex p Gibbs) HL 1942, 24 TC 221*.

Headings in this chapter are as follows.

53.2 NATURE OF PARTNERSHIP

Whether a partnership exists and, if so, from what date is a question of fact (*Williamson CS 1928, 14 TC 335; Calder v Allanson KB 1935, 19 TC 293*). The existence of a formal partnership agreement is not conclusive of the existence of a partnership (*Hawker v Compton KB 1922, 8 TC 306; Dickenson v Gross KB 1927, 11 TC 614*). Equally, whether a partnership can ante-date the date of the agreement is a question of fact (*Ayrshire Pullman*

Services v CIR CS 1929, 14 TC 754; Waddington v O'Callaghan KB 1931, 16 TC 187; Taylor v Chalklin KB 1945, 26 TC 463; Alexander Bulloch & Co v CIR CS 1976, 51 TC 563; Saywell v Pope Ch D 1979, 53 TC 40).

Joint transactions may amount to a partnership or joint trading for tax purposes—see *Morden Rigg & Eskrigge v Monks CA 1923, 8 TC 450* (joint cotton transactions); *Gardner & Bowring Hardy v CIR CS 1930, 15 TC 602* (temporary joint coal merchanting); *Lindsay Woodward & Hiscox v CIR CS 1932, 18 TC 43* (joint transactions in whisky in violation of USA law); *George Hall & Son v Platt Ch D 1954, 35 TC 440* (joint crop growing). See also *Fenston v Johnstone KB 1940, 23 TC 29*.

Where a partnership terminated with open forward contracts, subsequently completed, it was held to continue trading notwithstanding that some of the partners had formed a new partnership to carry on a similar business (*Hillerns & Fowler v Murray CA 1932, 17 TC 77*). A doctor who sold his practice, helping the purchaser for a short time on a profit-sharing basis, was held not to be a partner (*Pratt v Strick KB 1932, 17 TC 459*).

A partnership set up for tax avoidance purposes may nevertheless be a true partnership (*Newstead v Frost HL 1980, 53 TC 525*).

A Rotary Club is not a partnership (*Blackpool Marton Rotary Club v Martin Ch D 1988, 62 TC 686*).

See 69.4 SCHEDULE A as regards joint ownership and exploitation of property.

See the corresponding chapter of Tolley's Capital Gains Tax as regards the chargeable gains of partnerships and individual partners.

See generally Revenue Business Income Manual BIM 72001–72035.

See 53.17 below as regards limited partnerships and 53.18 below as regards limited liability partnerships (LLPs).

See Simon's Direct Tax Service E5.302.

53.3 TAXATION OF PARTNERSHIP INCOME

Trading profits and losses. A partnership is not generally treated for tax purposes as an entity which is separate and distinct from its members. The profits or losses of the partnership trade or profession are computed in like manner as if the partnership were a UK resident individual. Each individual's share (see below) of the partnership profit or loss (as adjusted for income tax purposes) is taxed or relieved as if it derived from a trade or profession (the notional trade) carried on by him alone. The notional trade is treated as commencing at the time the individual becomes a partner, or, if the actual trade or profession was previously carried on by him alone, at the time the actual trade commenced. Similar rules apply as regards cessations.

The notional trade is taxed in accordance with the normal basis period rules including the overlap relief rules (see 71.3–71.11 SCHEDULE D, CASES I AND II). A change of accounting date of the actual partnership trade that would result in a change of basis period if it were a sole trade (i.e. the necessary conditions are satisfied) changes the basis periods for each partner's notional trade. Notice of the change of accounting date must be given in a partnership tax return by a nominated partner. The rule whereby the necessary conditions do not have to be satisfied if the change occurs in the second or third tax year of the business applies only by reference to the second or third tax year of the actual partnership trade and not to the second or third tax year of a partner's notional trade. Where a change of accounting date in the second or third tax year of a partner's notional trade fails to result in a change of basis period (because the necessary conditions are not satisfied), the 'opening years' rules (see 71.4 SCHEDULE D, CASES I AND II) apply to determine the basis period of the notional trade for that tax year by reference to the old accounting date. See 71.7 SCHEDULE D, CASES I AND II for the detailed rules on changes of accounting date and 68.13 RETURNS for partnership tax returns.

Where the partnership trade or profession commenced before 6 April 1994, transitional overlap relief (see 71.13 SCHEDULE D, CASES I AND II) applies to individual partners' notional trades as it does to sole trades, providing they were partners in 1997/98. See the 2003/04 and earlier editions for full coverage of the old (i.e. pre-1997/98) rules and the transitional provisions on changeover to the current rules described above.

The taxable profits or allowable losses of the partnership for a period of account are apportioned between the individual members in accordance with their profit/loss sharing ratios under the partnership agreement for that period of account.

The above rules apply equally to a partnership business other than a trade or profession.

[*ICTA 1988, s 111(1)–(6)(10)–(13); FA 1994, s 215(1)(4)(5); FA 1995, s 117(1)(a)(2)(4)*].

Adjustments to partnership profits for tax purposes will include any of the items below.

(i) **Legal costs** and stamps re partnership deeds are not normally permissible deductions.

(ii) **Partners'** salaries, domestic and personal expenses, interest credited on capital and any benefit of financial value given to a partner are not permissible deductions for tax purposes, being regarded as part of the taxable profits. See e.g. *PDC Copyprint (South) v George (Sp C 141), [1997] SSCD 326* as regards partners' salaries (and see the example at 53.6 below). But this does not necessarily apply to payments to a partner for goods or services 'altogether disconnected with the partnership business as such' and where the firm's premises are owned by a partner, *bona fide* rent paid to him under legal agreement is a proper deduction for tax purposes (*Heastie v Veitch CA 1933, 18 TC 305*). Contributions towards partners' removal expenses, where partner moved in the interests of the firm, are not deductible (*MacKinlay v Arthur Young McClelland Moores & Co HL 1989, 62 TC 704*).

(iii) **Taxed charges,** payable out of firm's income, are added back in computing the firm's taxable profits, and tax on them has to be accounted for. The Revenue accept the view that a partner's personal taxed investment income is available to cover his share of partnership charges. Should there be an excess of partnership taxed charges over partnership income, an assessment under *ICTA 1988, s 350* would therefore be made only to the extent that each individual partner's share of the excess is not covered by his own private investment income.

See *MacKinlay v Arthur Young McClelland Moores & Co HL 1989, 62 TC 704* as to prohibition on deduction of certain payments made to partners in connection with partnership business.

See also 71 SCHEDULE D, CASES I AND II for adjustments to profits generally and 75.27 SCHEDULE E—EMPLOYMENT INCOME for director's fees received by professional partnership.

Non-trading income. In the case of a trading or professional partnership to which non-trading income (or a relievable non-trading loss) accrues, each individual partner is taxed on his share, computed by reference to profit sharing ratios for the period of account of the trade etc. In the case of untaxed income (as defined) from one or more sources, the normal basis period rules for trading income (see 71.3–71.11 SCHEDULE D, CASES I AND II) apply as if each individual's share of the income (or loss) were profits (or losses) of a notional trade carried on by him alone. The notional trade is treated as commencing at the time the individual becomes a partner and ceasing when he ceases to be a partner, with each source of the income treated as continuing until he ceases to be a partner. The same comments apply as above as regards changes of partnership accounting date. Where overlap relief (see 71.11) in respect of untaxed income falls to be deducted in a tax year (because of a change of accounting date or a permanent discontinuance of the notional trade) and the deduction exceeds the partner's share of untaxed income for that year, the excess is deductible in computing his taxable income for that year. [*ICTA 1988, s 111(7)–(9)(12)(13); FA 1994, s 215(1); FA 1995, s 117(1)(a)(2)*].

These special rules for non-trading untaxed income apply only where the associated trade or profession is carried on *in partnership*, so that, for example, if one partner is left to carry on the partnership business as a sole trader, his notional trade ceases at that time and his untaxed income is subsequently taxed on a fiscal year basis.

General. The assignment by a partner of part of his share in the partnership was ineffective for the purpose of displacing his liability to income tax on that part of his share of partnership profits (*Hadlee and Another v Commissioner of Inland Revenue (NZ) PC, [1993] STC 294*).

If a **company** is a partner, see 53.13 below.

Capital gains which arise from the disposal of partnership assets are charged on the partners separately. [*TCGA 1992, s 59; FA 1995, Sch 29 Pt VIII(16)*]. See Tolley's Capital Gains Tax.

Simon's Direct Tax Service. See E5.311 *et seq.*, E5.321 *et seq.*

53.4   *Example*

X and Y began to trade in partnership on 1 July 2000, preparing first accounts to 30 September 2001 and sharing profits equally. Z joins the firm as an equal partner on 1 October 2002. Y leaves the firm on 31 March 2004. Accounts are prepared to that date to ascertain Y's entitlement, but the accounting date then reverts to 30 September and the partnership does not give notice to the Revenue of a change of accounting date, so that there is no change of basis period. In addition to trading profits, the partnership had a source of lettings income which ceased in September 2003, and is in receipt of both taxed and untaxed interest, the latter from a source commencing in October 2001. Taxed interest is received on 31 March each year. Revised figures as adjusted for tax purposes are as follows.

	Schedule D, Case I	Schedule A	Schedule D, Case III	Taxed interest (gross)
	£	£	£	£
15 months to 30.9.01	30,000	4,500	—	750
Year to 30.9.02	24,000	5,000	1,000	1,500
Year to 30.9.03	39,000	3,000	600	300
6 months to 31.3.04	19,500	—	225	165
6 months to 30.9.04	14,000	—	140	—

The partners' shares of taxable income from the partnership for the years 2000/01 to 2004/05 inclusive are as follows. (See 53.5 below as regards changes in the membership of a partnership.)

53.4 Partnerships

Schedule D, Case 1	X £	Y £	Z £
2000/01			
1.7.2000–5.4.01 (£30,000 × $\frac{9}{15}$)	9,000	9,000	
2001/02			
1.10.2000–30.9.01 (£30,000 × $\frac{12}{15}$)	12,000*	12,000*	
* Overlap relief accrued:			
1.10.2000–5.4.01 (£30,000 × $\frac{6}{15}$)	6,000	6,000	
2002/03			
Y/e 30.9.02	12,000	12,000	
1.10.02–5.4.03 (£39,000 × $\frac{6}{12}$ × $\frac{1}{3}$)			6,500
2003/04			
Y/e 30.9.03	13,000	13,000	13,000*
1.10.03–31.3.04		6,500	
		19,500	
Less overlap relief		(6,000)	
		13,500	
* Overlap relief accrued			
1.10.02–5.4.03 (as above)			6,500
2004/05			
Y/e 30.9.04			
1.10.03–31.3.04	6,500		6,500
1.4.04–30.9.04	7,000		7,000
	13,500		13,500
Schedule A			
2000/01			
1.7.2000–5.4.01 (£4,500 × $\frac{9}{15}$)	1,350	1,350	
2001/02			
1.10.2000–30.9.01 (£4,500 × $\frac{12}{15}$)	1,800*	1,800*	
* Overlap relief accrued			
1.10.2000–5.4.01 (£4,500 × $\frac{6}{15}$)	900	900	
2002/03			
Y/e 30.9.02	2,500	2,500	
1.10.02–5.4.03 (£3,000 × $\frac{6}{12}$ × $\frac{1}{3}$)			500
2003/04			
Y/e 30.9.03	1,000	1,000	1,000*
1.10.03–31.3.04		—	
		1,000	
Less overlap relief		(900)	
		100	
* Overlap relief accrued			
1.10.02–5.4.03 (as above)			500

Schedule D, Case III	X £	Y £	Z £
2002/03			
Y/e 30.9.02	500	500	
1.10.02–5.4.03 ($£600 \times \frac{6}{12} \times \frac{1}{3}$)			100
2003/04			
Y/e 30.9.03	200	200	200*
1.10.03–31.3.04		75	
		275	
* Overlap relief accrued			
1.10.02–5.4.03 (as above)			100
2004/05			
Y/e 30.9.04			
1.10.03–31.3.04	75		75
1.4.04–30.9.04	70		70
	145		145
Taxed interest			
2000/01 (received 31.3.01)	375	375	
2001/02 (received 31.3.02)	750	750	
2002/03 (received 31.3.03)	100	100	100
2003/04 (received 31.3.04)	55	55	55
2004/05	**	—	**

** Each to be based on one-half of interest received 31.3.05.

Note

Taxed investment income is taxed on a fiscal year basis as for an individual, but is apportioned between the partners according to their shares for the accounting period in which the income arises.

53.5   CHANGES IN MEMBERS OF A PARTNERSHIP

A partnership trade or profession is *not* treated as discontinued and recommenced when a partner joins or leaves the firm providing there is at least one continuing partner (which also includes the situation where a sole trader begins to carry on the trade in partnership or a former partner begins to carry it on as a sole trader). Where, exceptionally, there is no such continuing partner, the trade etc. is treated as permanently discontinued, with a new trade treated as being commenced. [*ICTA 1988, s 113; FA 1994, s 215(4)(5), s 216(1)(2)*]. New partners are taxed on their profit share under the opening years provisions at 71.4 SCHEDULE D, CASES I AND II and outgoing partners are taxed on their share under the closing year provisions at 71.9 SCHEDULE D, CASES I AND II (see also 53.3 above).

53.6   *Example*

P, Q and R have carried on a profession in partnership for a number of years (since before 6 April 1994) sharing profits in the ratio 2:2:1. Accounts are made up to 30 June. P leaves the partnership on 30 June 2001 and Q and R share profits 3:2 for the year to 30 June 2002 and equally thereafter. On 30 June 2004, Q leaves the partnership and on 1 July 2004, S becomes a partner. Profits are then shared between R and S in the ratio 2:1 until 30 September 2006 when the practice comes to an end, neither partner continuing to carry it on as a sole practitioner thereafter. P, Q and R have transitional overlap relief of £18,400, £18,400 and £9,200 respectively by reference to an overlap period of nine months. Results for the seven periods of account up to 30 September 2006 are as follows.

Period ended	Partners' salaries				Adjusted Profit
	P	Q	R	S	
	£	£	£	£	£
30.6.2000	4,000	4,000	2,000	—	75,000
30.6.01	18,000	13,000	13,500	—	60,000
30.6.02	—	12,500	12,500	—	80,000
30.6.03	—	12,000	17,000	—	85,000
30.6.04	—	4,000	11,000	—	95,000
30.6.05	—	—	5,000	—	101,000
30.9.06	—	—	3,000	—	58,000

The adjusted profit figures above are after adding back partners' salaries (see 53.3(ii) above).

The taxable profits for the years 2000/01 to 2006/07 are as follows.

Taxable profits of P, Q & R individually for 2000/01 and 2001/02

	P	Q	R
	£	£	£
2000/01			
Y/e 30.6.2000			
Profits £75,000 – £(4,000 + 4,000 + 2,000)	26,000	26,000	13,000
Salaries	4,000	4,000	2,000
Taxable profits	£30,000	£30,000	£15,000
2001/02			
Y/e 30.6.01			
Profits £60,000 – £(18,000 + 13,000 + 13,500)	6,200	6,200	3,100
Salaries	18,000	13,000	13,500
	24,200	19,200	16,600
Less transitional overlap relief	18,400	—	
Taxable profits	£5,800	£19,200	£16,600

Taxable profits of Q, R & S individually from 2002/03 to 2006/07

	Q	R	S
	£	£	£
2002/03			
Y/e 30.6.02			
Profits £80,000 – £(12,500 + 12,500)	33,000	22,000	
Salaries	12,500	12,500	
Taxable profits	£45,500	£34,500	

	Q £	R £	S £
2003/04			
Y/e 30.6.03			
Profits £85,000 − £(12,000 + 17,000)	28,000	28,000	
Salaries	12,000	17,000	
Taxable profits	£40,000	£45,000	
2004/05			
Y/e 30.6.04			
Profits £95,000 − £(4,000 + 11,000)	40,000	40,000	
Salaries	4,000	11,000	
Taxable profits	44,000	51,000	
Less transitional overlap relief	18,400	—	
Taxable profits	£25,600	£51,000	
Y/e 30.6.05			
Profits £101,000 − £5,000 × $\frac{1}{3}$ = £32,000			
Taxable profit 1.7.04–5.4.05			
£32,000 × $\frac{9}{12}$			£24,000
2005/06			
Y/e 30.6.05			
Profits £101,000 − £5,000		64,000	32,000
Salary		5,000	—
Taxable profits		£69,000	£32,000*
*Overlap relief accrued			
1.7.04–5.4.05 as above			£24,000
2006/07			
15 months to 30.9.06			
Profits £58,000 − £3,000		33,000	22,000
Salary		3,000	—
		36,000	22,000
Less overlap relief		9,200	24,000
Taxable profit/(allowable loss)		£26,800	(£2,000)

Note

See 53.4 above for a further example of partners joining and leaving a firm, which also illustrates the position where there is non-trading as well as trading income.

53.7 **Partnership mergers and demergers.** Where two businesses carried on in partnership merge, it is a question of fact whether the new partnership has succeeded to the businesses of the old partnerships, or whether the old businesses have ceased and a new business resulted from the merger which is different in nature from either of the two old businesses. Disparity of size between the old partnerships will not of itself be a significant matter. Clearly the former is more likely to be the case where the two old businesses carried on the same sort of activities, and the latter where they were themselves different in nature. Where the former applies, both businesses are treated as continuing. Where the new partnership does not succeed to the old businesses, the trades are treated as discontinued and the closing year rules (see 71.9 SCHEDULE D, CASES I AND II) will apply to the notional trades of the partners in both old partnerships; the opening year rules (see 71.4 SCHEDULE D, CASES I AND II) will then apply to the notional trades of the partners in the new partnership.

Similar considerations apply where a partnership is divided up and two or more partnerships are formed, in determining whether any of the separate partnerships has succeeded to the business of the original partnership.

Similar principles apply where sole traders merge into partnership or a partnership business is demerged and carried on by sole traders.

(Revenue Pamphlet IR 131, SP 9/86). For an updated discussion of the principles involved, see Revenue booklet SAT 1(1995), chapter 8.

See *C Connelly & Co v Wilbey Ch D 1992, 65 TC 208* for a case in which it was held that neither part of a demerged partnership succeeded to the former partnership trade (and in which legal costs relating to the dissolution were disallowed).

The amalgamation of two sole traders into partnership in *Humphries v Cook KB 1934, 19 TC 121* was held to result in the commencement of a new business and the cessation of both the old businesses, but this is applied sparingly by the Revenue, mainly where the new partnership business is of a different nature from those previously carried on.

Simon's Direct Tax Service. See E5.333.

53.8 **LOSSES**

Partnership losses, as computed for tax purposes, are apportioned between the individual partners in the same way as are profits. The loss of each partner may (*a*) be set off against his other income (under *ICTA 1988, s 380* or, where applicable, *ICTA 1988, s 381*) or (*b*) be carried forward against his share of subsequent profits of the partnership (under *ICTA 1988, s 385*), including in certain circumstances where a partnership business is converted into a company (*ICTA 1988, s 386*) or (*c*) be used in a terminal loss claim (under *ICTA 1988, s 388*) where either the partnership trade or profession ceases or the individual leaves the partnership. For full details of these loss claims, see 46 LOSSES. It is for each partner to choose how to utilise his own losses and to make his own claim.

Similarly, losses made by a partner in other businesses may be set-off against his share of partnership profits under *ICTA 1988, s 380*.

Where the firm as a whole makes a profit (as adjusted for tax purposes) but, after the allocation of prior shares (e.g. salaries) the result is that *an individual partner makes a loss*, it is established practice that the loss-making partner cannot claim tax relief for his loss; similarly, where there is an overall partnership loss, the aggregate amount available to loss-making partners cannot exceed that loss and no partner can be taxed on a share of *profit*.

For restrictions on, and claw-back of, loss reliefs in the case of non-active partners, see 53.9–53.11 below. For restrictions in the case of limited partners and members of limited liability partnerships, see, respectively, 53.17 and 53.18 below.

53.9 **NON-ACTIVE PARTNERS: RESTRICTION OF LOSS RELIEFS AND INTEREST RELIEF**

With effect from, broadly, **10 February 2004** (see below), relief under *ICTA 1988, s 380* or *s 381* (see, respectively, 46.3 and 46.10 LOSSES) for trading losses against total income (and, consequently, relief under *FA 1991, s 72* against chargeable gains) is restricted in the case of an individual partner who is '*non-active*', i.e. who does not devote 'a significant amount of time' to the trade. The relief available, otherwise than against profits of the trade, is restricted to the amount of the partner's 'contribution to the trade' as at the end of the tax year in which the loss is sustained. The restriction applies to losses sustained in the tax year in which the partner first carries on the trade and in any of the next three tax years. A similar restriction applies to relief under *ICTA 1988, s 353* (see 43.3 INTEREST PAYABLE) for interest paid by a partner in connection with the carrying on of the trade.

The restrictions potentially apply to a loss sustained or interest paid in any tax year

- the basis period for which ends on or after 10 February 2004 (see 53.3 above as regards partners' basis periods and see below for transitional provisions),

- at any time during which the individual carried on the trade as a partner (other than a limited partner within 53.17 below) or as a member of a limited liability partnership (LLP) within 53.18 below and at no time during which he carried it on as a limited partner,

- which is the first, second, third or fourth tax year in which the individual carried on the trade, and

- in which he did not devote 'a significant amount of time' to the trade.

Where relief under the aforementioned *sections* has previously been given for losses sustained in, or interest paid in, tax years which meet the above conditions, all such reliefs must be aggregated. The relief that can then be given, otherwise than against profits of the trade, for the current loss or interest is limited to the excess (if any) of the amount of the partner's 'contribution to the trade' at the end of the current tax year over the aggregate amount. This aggregate must also include any relief given for losses sustained in, or interest paid in, any tax year at any time during which the partner carried on the trade as a limited partner or member of an LLP and the basis period for which ends on or after 10 February 2004. It does not include any 'pre-announcement allowance' (see the transitional provisions below).

These rules do not prevent or restrict a loss from being carried forward under *ICTA 1988, s 385* (see 46.9 LOSSES) against subsequent profits of the trade. They do not apply at all to UNDERWRITERS AT LLOYD'S (89) in connection with their underwriting business.

A partner devotes a '*significant amount of time*' to the trade in a tax year if, for the whole of the basis period for that tax year, he spends an average of at least 10 hours a week personally engaged in activities of the trade. Any relief erroneously given on the assumption that this requirement will be met will be withdrawn by means of a Schedule D, Case VI assessment. If the basis period is less than six months because the tax year is the one in which the individual joined or left the partnership, the requirement must instead be met by reference to the six months beginning with his commencement date or ending with his cessation date. The legislation is silent as to what is meant by personal engagement in the activities of the trade. The Explanatory Notes to the 2004 Finance Bill suggest that this may include, for example, a management or service role such as personnel, accountancy or purchasing, but does not include time spent deciding whether or not to invest, and/or how much to invest, in the partnership or its trade.

A partner's '*contribution to the trade*' at any time ('*the relevant time*') is the sum of the 'amount subscribed' by him, any profits of the trade to which he is entitled but has not received in money or money's worth and (where relevant) any amount he has contributed to the partnership assets on a winding-up. For this purpose, the '*amount subscribed*' by a partner is the amount of his capital contributions net of capital withdrawals. This includes capital contributed before 10 February 2004 but this must be reduced by any 'pre-announcement allowance' (see the transitional provisions below) and by any relief claimed under the aforementioned *sections* for losses sustained in, or interest paid in, any tax year whose basis period ended before 10 February 2004 and which either (i) would otherwise be a tax year to which the restrictions potentially apply or (ii) is a tax year at any time during which the partner carried on the trade as a limited partner or member of an LLP. Capital withdrawals are treated as made out of capital contributed on or after 10 February 2004 in priority to capital contributed earlier. They are widely defined so as to include amounts of capital

- that the partner has previously, directly or indirectly, drawn out or received back, or
- that he so draws out or receives back during the five years beginning with the relevant time, or
- that he is or may be entitled so to draw out or receive back at any time when he carries on the trade as a member of the partnership, or
- that he is or may be entitled to require another person to reimburse to him,

but not so as to include any such amount drawn out or received back which is chargeable to income tax as profits of the trade.

Where a partner's loss relief or interest relief has been restricted as above, the total amount thereby unrelieved is carried forward to subsequent tax years in which he continues to carry on the trade in partnership. For any such subsequent tax year, that total amount (including both losses and interest), or so much of it as still remains unrelieved, is treated for the purposes of *ICTA 1988, s 380* and *s 381* as a loss sustained in that year (or as an increase to any loss actually sustained in that year). In ascertaining how much remains unrelieved, any relief given under general rules (e.g. carry-forward of losses under *ICTA 1988, s 385*) is taken into account as is any relief given (or which could have been given had a claim been made) by virtue of this carry-forward rule. For the purpose only of determining whether an amount can be relieved in a subsequent year by virtue of this rule, that year is treated as a year to which these restrictions potentially apply even it is not actually so. Thus, this carry-forward rule does enable restricted relief to be obtained in a subsequent year but only to the extent that capital contributions have increased sufficiently. Any amount remaining unrelieved after applying this rule is again carried forward and the rule once more applied in the following year. An unrelieved amount can also be carried forward to a year in which the partner no longer carries on the trade but makes a contribution to the assets of the partnership on a winding-up, and in this case certain conditions that otherwise apply to loss reliefs under *ICTA 1988, s 380* and *s 381* (in particular the condition that the trade be carried on commercially with a view to profit) are relaxed in relation to the carried-forward amount.

Transitional provisions. Special rules apply to the tax year the basis period for which includes 10 February 2004 (the '*first restricted year*'). If there is more than one tax year whose basis period includes that date (for example, under the opening years rules at 71.4 SCHEDULE D, CASES I AND II), the first restricted year is the first such tax year and the rules apply to that year only. Losses and interest for the first restricted year are split into two parts; the first part (the '*pre-announcement allowance*') is the loss sustained, and interest paid in, the part of the basis period ending with 9 February 2004 and the second part is the loss sustained, and interest paid in, the remaining part of the basis period. The first part is allowable in full and the second part is allowable only to the extent that it does not exceed the partner's contribution to the trade at the end of the tax year. Each part of the basis period has to be treated as a separate period of account for the purpose of determining how much (if any) of a loss is sustained in that part; the loss cannot simply be time-apportioned. However, any capital allowances derived from expenditure incurred before 10 February 2004 are regarded as belonging to the first part of the basis period; a similar rule applies to any film production or acquisition expenditure incurred before that date but deductible over a three-year period (see 71.48 SCHEDULE D, CASES I AND II). A loss for either part of the basis period is allocated between partners in accordance with their sharing arrangements for that part. This would normally prevent an individual who joined the partnership after 9 February 2004 from having any share of the loss for the part of the basis period ending on that date but if he joined before 26 March 2004 he can nevertheless be allocated such a share provided he was a partner at some time in the basis period for the first restricted year. Interest is allocated to the different parts of the basis period in accordance with when it was actually paid.

For tax years after the first restricted year, capital allowances on pre-10 February 2004 expenditure and any film production or acquisition expenditure incurred before that date are again excluded from the losses subjected to the restrictions; the extent to which a loss derives from such allowances or expenditure is determined on a just and reasonable basis.

[*ICTA 1988, ss 118ZE–118ZK; FA 2004, s 124(1)*].

53.10   **NON-ACTIVE PARTNERS: CLAW-BACK OF LOSSES DERIVED FROM EXPLOITING A LICENCE**

There is a potential exit charge as described below where

(*a*)   an individual carries on a trade in partnership or has done so previously;

(*b*)   he has claimed relief under *ICTA 1988, s 380* or *s 381* (see, respectively, 46.3, 46.10 LOSSES) for trading losses against his total income (or, effectively, relief under *FA 1991, s 72* against his chargeable gains) for a 'licence-related loss' sustained in the first, second, third or fourth tax year in which he carried on the trade;

(*c*)   the tax year in which the loss was sustained was one in which he did not devote a '*significant amount of time*' (as defined in 53.9 above) to the trade;

(*d*)   there is a 'disposal' on or after **10 February 2004** of any licence acquired in carrying on the trade or any rights to income under any agreement 'related' to, or which contains, such a licence; and

(*e*)   the individual receives any consideration for that disposal (whether or not as part of a larger sum) which is not otherwise chargeable to income tax.

In (*b*) above, a '*licence-related loss*' means a loss derived to any extent from expenditure incurred in the partnership trade in exploiting the licence referred to in (*d*) above. For an individual who carried on the trade at any time before 26 March 2004 (i.e. normally one who joined the partnership before that date), a loss is not a licence-related loss to the extent that it derives from any such expenditure incurred before 10 February 2004.

For the purposes of (*d*) above, an agreement is '*related*' to a licence if they are entered into (in whatever order) in pursuance of the same arrangement. An agreement which imposes an obligation to do something (as opposed to conferring a right to do it) may itself be a licence for the purposes of these provisions; and fulfilling such obligations may therefore count as exploiting the licence.

A '*disposal*' is very widely (but not exhaustively) defined (by *FA 2004, s 129*) for the purposes of (*d*) above to include, for example, a revocation of the licence, the disposal, surrender or loss of rights or income, certain changes in profit- or loss-sharing ratios and the individual's leaving the partnership (including a case where the partnership is dissolved). The disposal may be part of a larger disposal.

Consideration is not within (*e*) above if its receipt is an exit event under 46.8(*f*) LOSSES in relation to film-related losses.

A **chargeable event** occurs at the time the claim in (*b*) above is made or at the time the consideration in (*e*) above is received, whichever is the later (provided at least one of those times is on or after 10 February 2004). So much of the 'total consideration' as does not exceed the 'chargeable amount' is treated as annual profits of the individual for any tax year in which one or more chargeable events occur and as chargeable to income tax under Schedule D, Case VI. The *'total consideration'* is the aggregate of all the otherwise non-chargeable consideration received in that tax year *and* in previous tax years (but not before 10 February 2004) in relation to the licence in question. The *'chargeable amount'* is found by taking so much of the total consideration as does not exceed the 'net licence-related loss' and reducing that amount by so much (if any) of the consideration as has been taxed in previous years under these provisions. The *'net licence-related loss'* is the amount, computed as at the end of the tax year concerned and in relation to the licence in question, by which the individual's 'claimed licence-related losses' exceed the total of his 'licence-related profits' for all tax years. An individual's *'claimed licence-related losses'* are so much of the losses claimed by the individual under the aforementioned *sections* and potentially subject to claw-back under these provisions as derive from expenditure incurred in the partnership trade in exploiting the licence. Again, for an individual who carried on the trade at any time before 26 March 2004, pre-10 February 2004 expenditure is not taken into account. An individual's *'licence-related profits'* are so much of his profits as derive from income arising from any agreement that is related to or contains the licence. The extent to which a loss or profit is derived from any particular expenditure or income is determined on a just and reasonable basis.

[*FA 2004, ss 126–130*].

53.11 **NON-ACTIVE PARTNERS: RESTRICTION OF LOSS RELIEFS DERIVED FROM EXPLOITING FILMS**

With effect from, broadly, **26 March 2004** (see below), relief under *ICTA 1988, s 380* or *s 381* (see, respectively, 46.3 and 46.10 LOSSES) for trading losses derived from exploiting films is restricted in certain circumstances in the case of an individual partner who is *'non-active'*, i.e. who does not devote 'a significant amount of time' to the trade. Such relief can be given only against income consisting of profits (if any) arising from the trade in question and not against other income or against chargeable gains. This measure is aimed at avoidance schemes which apparently use generally accepted accounting practice to generate large initial losses followed by a guaranteed income stream over several years, thus producing a tax deferral. The rules do not prevent a loss from being carried forward under *ICTA 1988, s 385* (see 46.9 LOSSES) against subsequent profits of the trade.

The restriction potentially applies to a loss sustained by an individual, in a trade consisting of or including the exploitation of films, in any tax year

- in which he carried on the trade in partnership,

- which is the first, second, third or fourth tax year in which he carried on the trade,

- in which he did not devote '*a significant amount of time*' (as defined in 53.9 above) to the trade, and

- at any time during which there existed a 'relevant agreement' guaranteeing him an amount of income.

For these purposes, a *'relevant agreement'* is an agreement made with a view to the individual's carrying on the trade or in the course of his carrying it on (including any agreement under which he is, or may be, required to contribute an amount to the trade). The definition is extended to include an agreement relating to such an agreement. An agreement guarantees an amount of income if it, or any part of it, is designed to secure the receipt by the individual of that amount (or at least that amount); it is irrelevant as to *when* the income would be received.

To the extent (if any) that the loss derives from 'exempt expenditure', the restriction does not apply. Expenditure is *'exempt expenditure'* if it is

- expenditure incurred before 26 March 2004 (but only in a case where the individual carried on the trade before that date); or

- expenditure which is deducted, in computing the partnership loss, under the statutory relief provisions for qualifying films, i.e. under either *F(No 2)A 1992, s 41* (preliminary expenditure) or *s 42* (production or acquisition expenditure) — see 71.48 SCHEDULE D, CASES I AND II; or

- incidental expenditure (i.e. expenditure on management, administration or obtaining finance) that, whilst deductible other than under the statutory relief provisions for qualifying films, was incurred in connection with the production or the acquisition (as defined) of a film in relation to which expenditure was deducted under the said provisions.

Exempt expenditure does not, therefore, include expenditure on distribution of a film or 'print and advertising' or production of a film as trading stock (Explanatory Notes to 2004 Finance Bill).

The extent to which a loss derives from exempt expenditure and the extent to which expenditure qualifies as incidental expenditure are to be determined on a just and reasonable basis.

Where a loss sustained in one tax year is treated, by virtue of 53.9 above or 53.18(2) below, as if sustained in a later tax year, these provisions apply to that loss as if it were indeed sustained in that later year.

[*ICTA 1988, ss 118ZL, 118ZM; FA 2004, s 125*].

See 46.8(*f*) LOSSES for other anti-avoidance provisions concerning losses derived by individuals (whether trading in partnership or not) from the exploitation of film tax reliefs.

53.12 SPOUSE AS PARTNER

Where a spouse is taken into partnership, perhaps to maximise the benefit of personal reliefs and rate bands, the Revenue cannot challenge the apportionment of profits as they could the payment of a salary to a spouse. There is no requirement for the spouse to contribute capital or to participate in management or even to take an active part in the business. Note, however, the possible application of the settlements legislation at *ICTA 1988, s 660A* where one spouse takes the other into partnership with a share of profits but with no requirement, or insufficient requirement, to contribute capital and/or personal time and effort (see 81.16(*a*) SETTLEMENTS and Revenue Tax Bulletin April 2003 pp 1011–1016). See also Revenue Business Income Manual BIM 72065, which, as well as discussing the above, also covers the less frequent event of minor children being taken into partnership.

53.13 CORPORATE PARTNERS

Where one of the partners carrying on a trade, profession or business in partnership is a company, the partnership profits are notionally computed as for corporation tax (see Tolley's Corporation Tax) but ignoring distributions, charges on income, capital allowances, pre-trading expenditure (see 71.66 SCHEDULE D, CASES I AND II) and any losses brought forward, and without regard to any change in the partners carrying on the trade etc. The company is chargeable to corporation tax as if its apportioned share of those profits, and of the other items above, arose from a trade it carried on alone.

53.14 Partnerships

The individual partners are charged tax in respect of their profit shares and given relief for losses in the same way as if all the partners were individuals, the partnership profit or loss being computed as for income tax purposes.

[*ICTA 1988, ss 111(2), 114; FA 1994, s 215; FA 1995, ss 117, 125(4)*].

Yearly interest of money chargeable to tax under SCHEDULE D, CASE III (72) (as it applies for income tax purposes) paid by a partnership of which a company is a member must be paid under deduction of income tax at the lower rate in force for the year in which the payment is made. [*ICTA 1988, s 349(2)(b)*].

Anti-avoidance. There are restrictions that apply in certain circumstances (where there are arrangements for transferring relief for losses etc.) on the use (*a*) by a partner company's losses in a partnership against its other income and (*b*) of a partner company's losses outside the partnership against its partnership profits. [*ICTA 1988, s 116*]. From 17 March 2004, there are provisions aimed at schemes which allocate profit shares disproportionate to the shares of capital contributed so as to enable a company to realise profits as capital rather than as taxable income. [*FA 2004, ss 131–133*]. See Tolley's Corporation Tax (under Losses). See 3.19 ANTI-AVOIDANCE for withdrawal of losses from a company partnership dealing in commodity futures.

Simon's Direct Tax Service. See **D4.8**.

53.14 **NON-RESIDENT PARTNERS AND PARTNERSHIPS CONTROLLED ABROAD**

Partner non-UK resident. The general assessment and computation rules of *ICTA 1988, s 111* (see 53.3 above) are applied to a non-UK resident member of a trading etc. partnership in such a way as to ensure that he is taxed only on his share of profits earned in the UK (whereas UK resident partners are taxed on their share of worldwide profits). A similar rule applies to a non-resident company partner.

Individual partner's change of residence. Where a partnership trade or profession is carried on wholly or partly outside the UK and an individual partner becomes or ceases to be UK resident, he is treated for income tax purposes as ceasing to be a partner at that time and becoming a partner again immediately afterwards. His share of a loss sustained before the change may nevertheless be carried forward under *ICTA 1988, s 385* and set against his share of profits after the change.

Individual partner resident but not domiciled etc. in the UK. Where a partnership trade etc. is carried on wholly or partly outside the UK and controlled and managed outside the UK, an individual partner who is UK resident, but to whose overseas trading income the REMITTANCE BASIS (64.1) would normally apply, is taxed under Case V on that basis in respect of his share of the partnership profits earned outside the UK.

[*ICTA 1988, s 112(1)–(1B), s 115(4); FA 1995, s 125(1)(2)(5)*].

Subject to the exception above, UK-resident partners are chargeable under Case I on both UK and foreign profits, regardless of where the partnership is controlled.

Double tax arrangements. In the case of *Padmore v CIR CA 1989, 62 TC 352*, it was held that, where profits of a non-UK resident partnership were exempt under the relevant double tax treaty, the profit share of a UK resident partner was thereby also exempt. This decision is, however, reversed by *ICTA 1988, s 112(4)(5)*, to the effect that arrangements under a double tax treaty relieving partnership income or capital gains from UK tax are not to affect any UK tax liability in respect of a UK resident partner's share of such income or gains. Such a partner is similarly entitled to the corresponding share of the tax credit in respect of a UK company qualifying distribution to a share of which he is entitled. Where a partnership includes a company, these provisions apply equally for corporation tax purposes. The provisions apply where the partnership either resides outside the UK or carries on any trade etc. the control and management of which is outside the UK. [*ICTA 1988, s 112(4)–(6), s 115(5); FA 1995, s 125(3)(5)*]. These changes are deemed always to have had effect. [*F(No 2)A 1987, s 62(2)*]. An appeal based on a claim that *ICTA 1988, s 112(4)(5)* was ineffective in bringing about the changes as detailed above was dismissed in *Padmore v CIR (No 2) Ch D 2001, 73 TC 470.*

Simon's Direct Tax Service. See E5.324.

53.15   **PARTNERSHIP RETIREMENT ANNUITIES**

Although *ICTA 1988, s 628* below remains on the statute book, it should be noted that the distinction between earned and investment income has had little or no significance for income tax purposes since 1990/91.

Annual payments for the benefit of a former partner (who has ceased to be a partner on retirement, because of age or ill-health, or on death), or the widow, widower or dependant of a former partner, are treated as earned income up to the limit below and, up to that limit, do not reduce the investment income of the payer.

The payments must be made under (*a*) the partnership agreement, or (*b*) an agreement replacing or supplementing the partnership agreement, or (*c*) an agreement with an individual who acquires the whole or part of the partnership business.

The limit referred to above is 50% of the average of the former partner's share of profits or gains (included in his tax return) in the best three of the last seven years of assessment in which he was required to devote substantially the whole of his time to the partnership (or to any other partnership of which he was a member — in which case the profits or gains of that partnership can be included in the calculations). Profits or gains not assessable to income tax are included in the calculation as if they were so assessable. [*ICTA 1988, s 628; FA 1988, Sch 3 para 19*].

To the extent that they exceed or are outside the above provisions, partnership retirement annuities are investment income in the hands of the recipients.

Indexation. The above limit of profits on which the earned income element of the annuity is calculated can be increased by the same percentage increase as the increase in the retail prices index between the December in the year of assessment in which the former partner left the partnership and the December preceding the year in which the annuity income is assessed. [*ICTA 1988, s 628(4)*]. The first six years of the last seven years of assessment which are the basis for computing the limit (as above) are also to be increased by indexation. The increase for each of these six years is to be by the same percentage increase as the percentage increase in the retail prices index for the month of December in the seventh year over that for the month of December in each of the previous six years. [*ICTA 1988, s 628(3)*].

Incorporation. Where a partnership business is incorporated, or a company takes over a partnership, and the agreement in either case refers to the company assuming responsibility for payment of an annuity to a former partner, then provided that the annuity is commercial in amount, the payment is not prevented by the fact that the liability was not incurred for a valuable and sufficient consideration from being treated by the company as a charge on income. *ICTA 1988, s 125* (annual payments for non-taxable consideration, see 3.18 ANTI-AVOIDANCE) is not in practice considered to apply to such payments in respect of a *bona fide* commercial transaction. (Revenue Tax Bulletin August 1994 p 151).

53.16   **LOANS FOR PURCHASING INTEREST ETC. IN A PARTNERSHIP**

See 43.22 INTEREST PAYABLE as regards relief for interest on a loan to an individual for purchasing a share of or making an advance to a partnership.

LIMITED PARTNERSHIPS

The *Limited Partnership Act 1907* allows the formation of limited partnerships, in which the liability of one or more (but not all) of the partners for the firm's debts is limited to a specified amount.

Restriction on loss and interest reliefs. In *Reed v Young HL 1986, 59 TC 196*, it was held that the share of the loss of a limited partner for the purposes of *ICTA 1988, s 380* (see 46.3 LOSSES) was not restricted to the amount of her contribution to the partnership capital. The decision was, however, reversed by legislation. Where an individual 'limited partner' in a partnership sustains a loss in the partnership trade, or pays interest in connection with it, relief may be restricted.

A *'limited partner'* is a partner carrying on a trade:

(*a*)   as a limited partner in a limited partnership registered under the *Limited Partnerships Act 1907*; or

(*b*)   as a general partner in a partnership, but who is not entitled to take part in the management of the trade, and who is entitled to have his liabilities for debts or obligations incurred for trade purposes discharged or reimbursed by some other person, in whole or beyond a certain limit; or

(*c*)   who, under the law of any territory outside the UK, is not entitled to take part in the management of the trade, and is not liable beyond a certain limit for debts or obligations incurred for trade purposes.

The restriction applies to any excess of the loss etc. sustained by a limited partner in respect of a trade as above for a year of assessment over his 'contribution' to the trade at the end of that year of assessment (or at the time he ceased to carry on the trade if he did so during that year of assessment). That excess may not be relieved under:

(i)   *ICTA 1988, s 380* (see 46.3 LOSSES);

(ii)   *ICTA 1988, s 381* (see 46.10 LOSSES); or

(iii)   *ICTA 1988, s 353* (see 43.3 INTEREST PAYABLE),

other than against profits arising from the same trade.

If relief has previously been given under any of the provisions at (i)–(iii) above to the individual for a loss etc. in the partnership trade in any year of assessment at any time during which the individual carried on the trade as a limited partner (or to which the restrictions at 53.9 above potentially apply), relief for the loss etc. for the year of assessment in question is restricted by the excess of the sum of the loss etc. for that year of assessment and earlier amounts so relieved, over the 'contribution'.

The partner's *'contribution'* to the trade at any time is the aggregate of:

(A)   capital contributed and not directly or indirectly withdrawn (excluding any the partner is or may be entitled to withdraw at any time he carries on the trade as a limited partner, or which he is or may be entitled to require another person to reimburse to him); and

(B)   any profits of the trade to which he is entitled but which he has not received in money or money's worth.

These provisions also operated to restrict relief for capital allowances where they were used to create or augment a trading loss by virtue of *ICTA 1988, s 383(1)* (under the now defunct preceding year basis rules — see 46.7 LOSSES) or were given by way of discharge or repayment of tax (no longer applicable to traders). (For the purposes of the former, an allowance was treated as made for the year of loss, and not for the year of assessment for which the year of loss was the basis year.) The amount of any such allowances given for any tax year at any time during which the individual carried on the trade as a limited partner continues to be taken into account in restricting losses/interest for subsequent tax years as above.

Similar provisions apply to company partners (see Tolley's Corporation Tax under Partnerships).

[*ICTA 1988, s 117; CAA 2001, Sch 2 para 22; FA 2004, s 124(2)*].

See generally Revenue Business Income Manual BIM 72101, 72105.

Simon's Direct Tax Service. See E5.305, E5.347.

53.18   **LIMITED LIABILITY PARTNERSHIPS (LLPS)**

From 6 April 2001, where a trade, profession or other business is carried on by an LLP (within *Limited Liability Partnerships Act 2000, s 1*) with a view to profit, all the activities of the LLP (i.e. anything it does) are treated as carried on in partnership by its members and not by the LLP as such. Anything done by, to or in relation to the LLP for the purposes of, or in connection with, any such activities is treated as done by, to or in relation to the members as partners, and property of the LLP is treated as held by the members as partnership property. In the *Tax Acts*, references to a partnership or to members of a partnership include an LLP to which the above applies and members of such an LLP, and references to a company or to members of a company do not include an LLP or members of an LLP.

Where an LLP no longer carries on any trade, profession or other business with a view to profit, the above provisions continue to apply if the cessation is only temporary or during a winding up following a permanent cessation (provided, in the latter case, that the winding up is not for reasons connected in whole or part with tax avoidance and is not unreasonably prolonged). They cease to apply on the appointment of a liquidator or (if earlier) on the making of a winding-up order by the court, or on the occurrence of any corresponding event under the law of a country or territory outside the UK.

[*ICTA 1988, s 118ZA; Limited Liability Partnerships Act 2000, s 10(1); FA 2001, s 75(1)*].

Similar provisions apply for capital gains tax purposes (see *TCGA 1992, s 59A* inserted by *Limited Liability Partnerships Act 2000, s 10(3)* and amended by *FA 2001, s 75(2)*, *TCGA 1992, s 156A* inserted by *Limited Liability Partnerships Act 2000, s 10(4)* and *TCGA 1992, s 169A* inserted (with effect from 3 May 2001) by *FA 2001, s 75(3)*). See Tolley's Capital Gains Tax under Partnerships and Hold-Over Reliefs.

For the Revenue's views on how the members of a limited liability partnership carrying on a trade or profession are to be taxed, see Revenue Tax Bulletin December 2000 pp 801–805.

Restrictions on loss and interest reliefs. *ICTA 1988, s 117* (see 53.17 above) applies to members of LLPs as it does to limited partners, except as follows.

(1)   A member's contribution to a trade at any time (a 'relevant time') is the greater of the 'amount subscribed' by him and the amount of his liability on a winding up (see below). The '*amount subscribed*' by a member is the amount contributed to the LLP as capital, less so much of that amount (if any) as:

(*a*)   he has previously, directly or indirectly, drawn out or received back; or

(*b*)   he so draws out or receives back during the five years beginning with the relevant time; or

(c) he is or may be entitled so to draw out or receive back at any time when he is a member of the LLP; or

(d) he is or may be entitled to require another person to reimburse to him.

The amount of the liability of a member on a winding up is the amount which he is liable to contribute to the assets of the LLP in the event of its being wound up, and which he remains liable so to contribute for at least the period of five years beginning with the relevant time (or until it is wound up if that happens before the end of that period).

(2) Amounts relating to a trade carried on by a member of an LLP which, apart from this provision, are prevented from being given or allowed by *section 117* are referred to as the member's '*total unrelieved loss*'. In each subsequent year of assessment in which the member continues to carry on the trade and any of the total unrelieved loss remains outstanding (see below), the balance of the total unrelieved loss is treated for the purposes of *ICTA 1988, ss 380, 381* (see 46.3, 46.10 LOSSES), and *section 117* as it applies in relation to those *sections*, as increasing any loss incurred in the trade in that year of assessment or, if no such loss is incurred, as consisting of such a loss. The amount of the total unrelieved loss remaining outstanding in a year of assessment is the total amount less any part of it for which relief has been given in that or any earlier year of assessment *other than* by virtue of this provision and any part for which relief has been given for an earlier year of assessment *under* this provision (or would have been so given had a claim been made).

The restrictions at 53.9 above also apply to members of LLPs, and do so in priority to *ICTA 1988, s 117* where both sets of restrictions would otherwise apply to the same loss or interest.

[*ICTA 1988, ss 118ZB–118ZD; Limited Liability Partnerships Act 2000, s 10; FA 2004, s 124(3)(4)*].

Investment LLPs and property investment LLPs. A number of tax exemptions for income and gains are disapplied where they are received by a member of a 'property investment LLP' as such, and interest relief under *ICTA 1988, s 362* (loan to individual to purchase interest in partnership — see 43.22 INTEREST PAYABLE) is denied where the partnership is an 'investment LLP'. An '*investment LLP*' is an LLP whose business consists wholly or mainly in the making of investments and the principal part of whose income is derived therefrom, and a '*property investment LLP*' is similarly defined by reference to investments in land. The status of an LLP in this respect is determined for each period for which partnership accounts are drawn up.

Exemptions are *disapplied* in the case of property investment LLPs as follows.

(a) *Pension funds, etc.*. (i) Exemptions under *ICTA 1988, ss 592(2), 608(2)(a), 613(4), 614(3)–(5), 620(6), 643(2)* (see 60.1 PERSONAL PENSION SCHEMES (AND STAKE-HOLDER PENSIONS), 67.5(*b*), 67.13, 67.11, 67.15 RETIREMENT SCHEMES, 66.8 RETIRE-MENT ANNUITIES), including exemptions for related stock lending fees and income from related futures and options. (ii) Corresponding exemption from the trusts rate of income tax under *ICTA 1988, s 686* (accumulation and discretionary trusts — see 81.5 SETTLEMENTS). (iii) Corresponding exemptions under *TCGA 1992, s 271(1)* (see Tolley's Capital Gains Tax under Exemptions and Reliefs).

(b) *Insurance companies.* The policyholders' share (as specially determined) of certain income and gains is treated as referable to basic life assurance and general annuity business, rather than pension business, and double tax credit relief and capital allowances are attributed to different categories of business accordingly.

(c)   *Friendly societies.* Exemption under *ICTA 1988, s 460* of profits from life and endowment business, or under *ICTA 1988, s 461* or *s 461B* of profits from other business of registered or incorporated societies.

[*ICTA 1988, ss 362(2)(ii), 438B, 438C, 460(2)(cb), 461(3A), 461B(2A), 659E, 686(6A), 804B(2)(4), 842B; TCGA 1992, s 271(12); FA 2001, s 76, Sch 25*].

See generally Revenue Business Income Manual BIM 72110–72155.

Simon's Direct Tax Service. See **E5.306, E5.348.**

53.19   **EUROPEAN ECONOMIC INTEREST GROUPINGS (EEIGS)** [*FA 1990, s 69, Sch 11*]

A European Economic Interest Grouping (EEIG) within *EEC Directive No. 2137/85* (which applies to all EEIGs established within the European Economic Area), wherever it is registered, is regarded as acting as the agent of its members. Its activities are regarded as those of its members acting jointly, each member being regarded as having a share of EEIG property, rights and liabilities, and a person is regarded as acquiring or disposing of a share of the EEIG assets not only where there is an acquisition or disposal by the EEIG while he is a member but also where he becomes or ceases to be a member or there is a change in his share of EEIG property.

A member's share in EEIG property, rights or liabilities is that determined under the contract establishing the EEIG or, if there is no provision determining such shares, it will correspond to the profit share to which he is entitled under the provisions of the contract. If the contract makes no such provision, members are regarded as having equal shares.

Where the EEIG carries on a trade or profession, the members are regarded for the purposes of tax on income and gains as carrying on that trade or profession in partnership.

[*ICTA 1988, s 510A; FA 1990, Sch 11 paras 1, 5; FA 1995, Sch 29 Pt VIII(16); FA 2002, Sch 25 para 49*].

Contributions to an EEIG from its members are not assessable on the EEIG, and the members are not assessable on distributions from the EEIG (which is equally not obliged to account for ACT thereon). (Revenue EEIGs Manual EEIG 34).

For the purposes of securing that members of EEIGs are assessed to income tax, corporation tax or capital gains tax, an inspector may, in the case of an EEIG which is registered, or has an establishment registered, in Great Britain or Northern Ireland, by notice require the EEIG to make a return containing such information as the notice may require, accompanied by such accounts and statements as the notice may require, within a specified time. In any other case, he may issue a similar notice to any UK resident member(s) of the EEIG (or if none is so resident, to any member(s)). Notices may differ from one period to another and by reference to the person on whom they are served or the description of EEIG to which they refer. Where a notice is given to an EEIG registered in Great Britain or Northern Ireland (or having an establishment registered there), the EEIG must act through a manager, except that if there is no manager who is an individual, the EEIG must act through an individual designated as a representative of the manager under the *Directive.* The return must in all cases include a declaration that, to the best of the maker's knowledge, it is correct and complete, and where the contract establishing the EEIG requires two or more managers to act jointly for the EEIG to be validly bound, the declaration must be given by the appropriate number of managers. [*TMA 1970, s 12A; FA 1990, Sch 11 para 2; FA 1994, ss 196, 199, Sch 19 para 2*]. See 68.1 RETURNS as regards the form and content of returns.

A penalty not exceeding £300 (and £60 per day for continued failure) may be imposed in the case of failure to comply with a notice under the above provisions. No penalty may be imposed after the failure has been remedied, and if it is proved that there was no income or chargeable gain to be included in the return, the maximum penalty is £100. Fraudulent or negligent delivery of an incorrect return etc. or of an incorrect declaration may result in a penalty not exceeding £3,000 for each member of the EEIG at the time of delivery. The £300 and £60 penalties are multiplied by the number of members of the EEIG (but subject to the overall £100 maximum in the circumstances described above); the daily penalty may only be imposed by the Commissioners (on an application to them by the Revenue) and has effect from the day following notification of imposition. [*TMA 1970, s 98B; FA 1990, Sch 11 para 3; FA 1994, ss 196, 199, Sch 19 para 30*].

The provisions of *TMA 1970, ss 36, 40* for extended time limits for assessments in cases of fraudulent or negligent conduct (see 30.3, 30.4 FRAUDULENT OR NEGLIGENT CONDUCT) are amended so that any act or omission on the part of the EEIG or a member thereof is deemed to be the act or omission of each member of the EEIG. [*TMA 1970, s 36(4), s 40(3); FA 1990, Sch 11 para 4*].

Simon's Direct Tax Service. See D4.901 *et seq.*

54   Patents

[*ICTA 1988, ss 524–529*]

Cross-references. See 9.50 CAPITAL ALLOWANCES for allowances on capital expenditure in acquiring patent rights; 22.15(b) DEDUCTION OF TAX AT SOURCE for patent royalties; 24.5(l) DOUBLE TAX RELIEF for DTR treatment of patent royalties from abroad and 71.63 SCHEDULE D, CASES I AND II for trading receipts and expenses re patents.

Simon's Direct Tax Service B3.841 *et seq.*

54.1   **Patent rights** means the right to do or authorise the doing of anything which would, but for the right, be an infringement of a patent. [*ICTA 1988, s 533(1)*].

54.2   **Expenses** (otherwise than for the purpose of a trade) of devising inventions, agents' charges, patent office fees etc. (including fees, expenses etc. for rejected or abandoned applications) are allowable from income from patents (after any CAPITAL ALLOWANCES (9.50)) with a right to carry forward indefinitely unallowed balances against future assessable patent income. [*ICTA 1988, ss 526, 528; CAA 2001, Sch 2 para 46*].

54.3   **Patent income** of inventors is treated as earned income. [*ICTA 1988, s 529*].

54.4   **Patent royalties** are always assessable (*Kirke CA 1944, 26 TC 208*). Where royalties are received, less tax, for user of a patent which comprises two or more complete years, the income tax or corporation tax liabilities are reducible, on application, to the total that would have been payable if the royalties had been paid by equal instalments (corresponding to the number of complete years concerned, but not exceeding six years) made at yearly intervals ending with the date of actual receipt. [*ICTA 1988, s 527*].

54.5   **Sales of patent rights** (including receipts for rights for which a patent has not yet been granted [*ICTA 1988, s 533(5)(6)*]) are treated according to the residence of the vendor.

(*a*)   **Resident** (*all patents*). Any capital sum received is assessable under Schedule D, Case VI (after deducting capital cost where purchased [*ICTA 1988, s 524(7)–(9)*]), but spread equally over year of receipt and five succeeding years thereafter, or wholly charged in year of receipt if written election made. [*ICTA 1988, s 524(1)(2)*]. See also *Green v Brace Ch D 1960, 39 TC 281*.

(*b*)   **Non-Resident** (*UK patents only*). Purchaser must deduct tax at basic rate from purchase money and account to Revenue under *ICTA 1988, s 349(1)* [*ICTA 1988, s 524(3)*]. But this procedure may be modified by DOUBLE TAX RELIEF (24) agreements. The non-resident may, however, (i) claim relief for the cost to him of acquiring the patent, and (ii) elect to have the net sum treated as arising over that and subsequent periods, to a total of six years. [*ICTA 1988, s 524(4)*].

The election in (*a*) above must be made within twelve months after 31 January following the year of assessment in which the sum was received or, for corporation tax purposes, two years after the end of the accounting period in which it was received. The election in (*b*) above applies only for income tax, with the same time limits as above. [*ICTA 1988, s 524(2)(2A)(4); FA 1996, s 135, Sch 21 para 15*].

54.6   **On death, winding-up or partnership change,** any charges under *ICTA 1988, s 524* above for subsequent years become assessable, but personal representatives of deceased person, or each partner, may claim (within 30 days of the assessment) that such amount be spread back equally to the years beginning with the year of receipt and ending with the year in which the death or change occurred. [*ICTA 1988, s 525*].

55 Pay As You Earn

Cross-references. See also 61.12 PERSONAL SERVICE COMPANIES ETC., 78.12 SELF-ASSESSMENT.

Simon's Direct Tax Service E4.9.

Other sources. See Tolley's Employment Tax Planning and Tolley's Tax Compliance Manual.

55.1 **Introduction.** Pay As You Earn (PAYE) is a system of collection of tax from salaries, wages, pensions etc. See under 75 SCHEDULE E—EMPLOYMENT INCOME for provisions regarding amount chargeable, allowable deductions etc. and see 83.3 SOCIAL SECURITY for taxable State benefits.

PAYE is subject to regulations (the 'PAYE regulations'), which were last consolidated, with effect from 6 April 2004, in the *Income Tax (Pay As You Earn) Regulations 2003 (SI 2003 No 2682)*, a product of the Tax Law Rewrite Project. The previous regulations were the *Income Tax (Employments) Regulations 1993 (SI 1993 No 744)* as amended by subsequent statutory instruments. The main regulation-making powers are in *ITEPA 2003, s 684* (as modernised by *FA 2003, s 145*) and enable provision to be made for, *inter alia*, requiring persons making a payment of, or on account of, PAYE income (see 55.2 below) to deduct, at the time of payment, an amount of income tax computed in accordance with Revenue tax tables (see 55.5 below). Specific regulation-making powers enable provision to be made for acceptance by the Revenue of the use of electronic means of transmission by employers (and see now *SI 2003 No 2682, Pt 10*, Revenue Directions 7 April 2004 and Revenue Directions made under the equivalent pre-consolidated regulations). [*ITEPA 2003, s 684(2), Sch 7 para 89; ICTA 1988, s 203(10); FA 1998, s 119*].

It does not matter for the purposes of PAYE if income is wholly or partly income for a tax year other than that in which payment is made. [*ITEPA 2003, s 684(6); ICTA 1988, s 203(1)*].

See Revenue Pamphlet P7 (Employer's Guide to PAYE) and IR 34 (Income Tax — PAYE), IR 109 (Employer Compliance Reviews and Negotiations) and IR 173 (Tax Credits — A Summary for Employers (Working Families' Tax Credit and Disabled Person's Tax Credit)).

The Revenue have published a Code of Practice (No 3) setting out their standards for the way in which inspections of employers' records are conducted and the rights and responsibilities of taxpayers.

The outline of PAYE is stated below but reference should be made to the Revenue publications noted above.

For PAYE audits and investigations, see Tolley's Employment Tax Planning.

Getting payroll records in order. The Revenue offer a free service to employers to ensure their payroll records are in order, and that errors in employees' personal details and national insurance numbers are identified and corrected before end-of-year returns are required. Employers may also ask for their records to be cross-checked with Revenue records, so that the Revenue may pursue any discrepancies directly with employees and make appropriate amendments. To register for this service, employers should contact Customer Account Services in Kings Lynn (tel. 0155 36 66 866) or Newcastle (tel. 0191 22 56 110).

See also 35.11 INLAND REVENUE: ADMINISTRATION as regards telephone helplines available to employers.

55.2 **Scope of PAYE.** PAYE income (i.e. income potentially within the scope of PAYE) embraces taxable earnings from an employment (see 75 SCHEDULE E—EMPLOYMENT INCOME), 'taxable specific income' from an employment, most taxable pension income and taxable social security income. [*ITEPA 2003, s 683*]. '*Taxable specific income*' includes, in accordance with *ITEPA 2003, s 10(3)*, payments to and from non-approved pension schemes (see 67.1, 67.9 RETIREMENT SCHEMES), payments and benefits on termination of office or employment within the special legislation at 18.4–18.6 COMPENSATION FOR LOSS OF EMPLOYMENT (AND DAMAGES), and, subject to the specific inclusions and exclusions in (*a*) and (*e*)–(*h*) below, amounts falling to be taxed as employment income under 82 SHARE-RELATED EMPLOYMENT INCOME AND EXEMPTIONS. Not all PAYE income is subject to deduction of tax under PAYE but all *payments* of such income are subject to such deduction. See (*a*)–(*h*) below for items not normally regarded as payments but brought specifically within the scope of PAYE deductions.

Payments only part of which are PAYE income have been held to be outside the scope entirely (*CIR v Herd HL 1993, 66 TC 29*). It was held in *Paul Dunstall Organisation Ltd v Hedges (Sp C 179), [1999] SSCD 26* that 'payment', for PAYE purposes, need not be payment in money (but see Taxation Vol 142, No 3692 p 429, 4 February 1999 for an article doubting the correctness of this decision). In *Black and others v Inspector of Taxes (Sp C 260), [2000] SSCD 540* it was held that, where units in unit trusts were provided in satisfaction of a pre-existing legal entitlement to a payment in money or money's worth, tax should have been deducted and the units provided out of the net sum.

Extension of scope. The following items, not otherwise regarded as *payments* of income, are specifically brought within the scope of PAYE deductions.

(*a*)   'Readily convertible assets'. The amount subject to PAYE is computed on the basis of the best estimate that can reasonable be made of the amount likely to be chargeable to tax.

For this purpose, 'asset' is widely defined to include any property but specifically *excludes*

●   non-cash vouchers, credit tokens and cash vouchers (but see the separate provisions at (*b*)–(*d*) below); and

●   shares acquired under an approved SAYE option scheme, CSOP scheme or profit sharing scheme, and any shares acquired as the result of exercising a right obtained before 27 November 1996 (though this last exclusion does not apply after 17 June 2004 if the avoidance of tax or national insurance contributions is one of the main purposes of any arrangements under which the right was obtained or is exercised). In each case, the reference to shares is to ordinary shares in (i) the employer company, or (ii) a company that controls it, or (iii) a member of a consortium (as defined) that owns a company within (i) or (ii), or (iv) a company that controls a consortium member within (iii), and 'share' includes stock. In relation to shares acquired on or after 9 April 2003 under an approved CSOP scheme, the exclusion does not apply (and PAYE therefore does apply) if the shares are acquired by exercise of an option within three years after it was granted (other than in permissible circumstances — see 82.63 SHARE-RELATED EMPLOYMENT INCOME AND EXEMPTIONS) or more than ten years after it was granted.

After 17 June 2004 (regardless of the date of acquisition), the exclusions for shares apply only at the instant of their acquisition and therefore do not exclude post-acquisition events from the scope of PAYE.

A '*readily convertible asset*' is an asset (defined as above) capable of being sold on a recognised investment exchange or other specified market, an asset for which 'trading arrangements' exist or are likely to come into existence, an asset consisting of rights in respect of a money debt, property subject to a warehousing regime (as defined) (or rights in respect of such property), or anything likely (without any action by the employee) to give rise to, or become, a right enabling a person to obtain (by any means at all, including the use of the asset as security for a loan) an amount of money similar to or greater than the amount expended in providing the asset (see *ITEPA 2003, s 702*).

For this purpose, '*trading arrangements*' are arrangements, not excluded by regulation, which enable the recipient of the asset (or a member of his family or household) to obtain (by any means at all, including the use of the asset as security for a loan) an amount of money similar to or greater than the amount expended in providing the asset (see *ITEPA 2003, s 702(2)–(5)*).

These provisions extend to anything *enhancing* the value of an asset in which the employee (or a member of his family or household) has an interest, where the asset, with its value enhanced, would be a readily convertible asset if provided at the time of enhancement (see *ITEPA 2003, s 697*).

From 10 July 2003, an asset consisting in securities within 82.3 SHARE-RELATED EMPLOYMENT INCOME AND EXEMPTIONS is treated as a readily convertible asset in all cases unless the securities are shares (or interests therein) that are 'corporation tax deductible'. Shares (and interests) are '*corporation tax deductible*' if they are acquired by reason of employment, or pursuant to an option granted by reason of employment, and the employer company is entitled to corporation tax relief under *FA 2003, Sch 23* (see 71.44 SCHEDULE D, CASES I AND II and, for detailed coverage, Tolley's Corporation Tax) or would have been so entitled if its accounting period had not begun before 1 January 2003. See *ITEPA 2003, s 702(5A)–(5D)* inserted by *FA 2003, Sch 22 para 15*.

See Revenue Employment Income Manual EIM 11900 for further notes on the meaning of 'readily convertible assets'. See Revenue Tax Bulletin August 1998 pp 563–573 for a detailed Revenue view of the application of PAYE to such assets. For notes on the status of shares as readily convertible assets where there is either a long stop provision or a prohibition on employees selling shares, see Revenue Tax Bulletin April 2000 pp 735, 736.

Before 6 April 1998, these provisions applied by reference to 'tradeable assets' rather than readily convertible assets, the former term being more narrowly defined. Transitory provisions applied from 2 July 1997 to 5 April 1998 which widened the definition of 'tradeable assets' to apply to the assignment or transfer of trade debts to employees.

(b) 'Non-cash vouchers' (see 75.47(a) SCHEDULE E—EMPLOYMENT INCOME), not excluded by regulation, where the voucher is capable of being exchanged for anything which, if provided at the time the voucher is provided, would be a readily convertible asset or pre-6 April 1998 equivalent (see (a) above) or the voucher would itself be such an asset but for the exclusion of non-cash vouchers from (a) above. For PAYE purposes, the payment is deemed to be made at the later of the time its cost of provision is incurred and the time of receipt by the employee. If, however, the voucher is a 'cheque voucher' (see 75.47(a) SCHEDULE E—EMPLOYMENT INCOME), the payment is deemed to be made when the voucher is exchanged for money, goods or services.

(c) 'Credit tokens' (see 75.47(d) SCHEDULE E—EMPLOYMENT INCOME), not excluded by regulation or used to meet expenses, on each occasion they are used to obtain money or anything which, if provided at that time, would be a readily convertible asset or pre-6 April 1998 equivalent (see (a) above).

(d) 'Cash vouchers' (see 75.47(b) SCHEDULE E—EMPLOYMENT INCOME), not excluded by regulation or used to meet expenses, when received by the employee.

(*e*) (From 6 April 1998) a gain on the exercise of a share option where the gain is chargeable as in 82.16 SHARE-RELATED EMPLOYMENT INCOME AND EXEMPTIONS and the shares acquired are readily convertible assets (as in (*a*) above). For PAYE purposes, the payment is deemed to be made at the time the option is exercised and in respect of the employment by reason of which the chargeable person was granted the option. The amount subject to PAYE is the best estimate of the amount chargeable to tax. In arriving at that amount in relation to an exercise after 28 July 2000, account is taken of any deduction likely to be available for employer national insurance contributions borne by the employee.

(*f*) (From 6 April 1998) a gain on the assignment or release of a share option where the gain is chargeable as in 82.16 SHARE-RELATED EMPLOYMENT INCOME AND EXEMPTIONS and regardless of whether or not the shares subject to the option are readily convertible assets. PAYE applies, at the time of the chargeable event, where the consideration for the assignment or release takes the form of a payment or the provision of a readily convertible asset (as in (*a*) above), and the amount subject to PAYE is as in (*e*) above. On and after 1 September 2003, the application of PAYE extends to a chargeable event within 82.16(*d*) (receipt of benefit in connection with the option) where the benefit takes the form of a payment or the provision of a readily convertible asset.

(*g*) (From 6 April 1998) an amount chargeable under 82.5 or 82.7 SHARE-RELATED EMPLOYMENT INCOME AND EXEMPTIONS on (i) the cessation of a conditional interest in shares (because the conditionality itself ceases or the employee makes a disposal) or (ii) the conversion of shares into shares of a different class. Where (i) applies, a further (non-conditional) interest in the shares is deemed to have been provided at that time. Where (ii) applies, the 'new' shares are deemed to have been provided at that time. Whether PAYE applies will depend on whether the asset thereby provided is a readily convertible asset (as in (*a*) above). The amount subject to PAYE is the best estimate of the amount chargeable to tax. Superseded by (*h*) below, except, as regards conditional interests, in relation to shares (or interests in shares) acquired before 16 April 2003.

(*h*) (On and after 1 September 2003, but *not* so as to displace (*g*) above in relation to shares acquired before 16 April 2003 insofar as it affects conditional interests), any amount taxable as employment income, in relation to 'employment-related shares', by virtue of a chargeable event under 82.4 or 82.6 SHARE-RELATED EMPLOYMENT INCOME AND EXEMPTIONS, the charge on acquisition under 82.8 SHARE-RELATED EMPLOYMENT INCOME AND EXEMPTIONS, the charge under 82.9 SHARE-RELATED EMPLOYMENT INCOME AND EXEMPTIONS, the charge on discharge of a notional loan under 82.10 SHARE-RELATED EMPLOYMENT INCOME AND EXEMPTIONS, or the charge under 82.11 or 82.12 SHARE-RELATED EMPLOYMENT INCOME AND EXEMPTIONS. PAYE applies as if the employee were provided with PAYE income in the form of the employment-related shares by the employer on the date of the event in question (or, in the case of 82.9, on the valuation date in question). (See 82.4 for the meaning of '*employment-related shares*' and 82.3 SHARE-RELATED EMPLOYMENT INCOME AND EXEMPTIONS for the extended meaning of '*shares*' in this connection.) The amount subject to PAYE is the best estimate of the amount chargeable to tax. Where the employment-related shares are not themselves readily convertible assets (as in (*a*) above) but the event is one involving the receipt of consideration or a benefit (whether in the form of a payment or the provision of an asset), PAYE applies to the payment or, if it is a readily convertible asset, to the provision of the asset.

[*ITEPA 2003, ss 693–702, 712; ICTA 1988, ss 203F, 203FA, 203FB, 203G–203I, 203K, 203L; FA 1994, ss 127–131; FA 1998, ss 64–69; FA 2000, s 56(2); FA 2003, Sch 21 para 18, Sch 22 paras 12–15; FA 2004, s 85, s 88(9)–(11), Sch 16 para 4; SI 2003 No 1997*].

See 55.4 below under Notional payments as regards accounting for tax in respect of items within (*a*)–(*h*) above. See Revenue Tax Bulletins May 1994 p 212, February 1997 p 385 and April 2000 pp 734, 735 for practical considerations in operating PAYE in these circumstances.

For the application of the *Ramsay* principle (see 3.1 ANTI-AVOIDANCE) to a PAYE avoidance scheme, see *DTE Financial Services Ltd v Wilson CA 2001, 74 TC 14.*

See Simon's Direct Tax Service E4.909A *et seq.*

For arrangements for relief where both foreign tax and tax under PAYE have to be deducted from the earnings of employees sent to work abroad, see Revenue Tax Bulletin February 2003 p 999.

Employee not resident, or not ordinarily resident, in the UK. Where such an employee works (or is likely to work) both inside and out of the UK in a tax year, and it appears to them that some of the income paid to the employee is PAYE income and some may not be, the Revenue may, on application by the employer or a person designated by the employer, by notice direct that a proportion of any payment made in the year is to be dealt with under PAYE. If no direction is made, the whole of any payment must be so dealt with. The direction may similarly be withdrawn (with at least 30 days notice) by a further notice. For 2003/04 onwards, it is made explicit that these provisions apply only to payments made by the employer and to payments by a person acting on the employer's behalf and at the expense of the employer or a person connected with him (within *ICTA 1988, s 839* — see 19 CONNECTED PERSONS). They are without prejudice to any income assessment on the employee and to any rights to repayment, or obligations to repay, income tax over- or underpaid. For 2003/04 onwards, the provisions enable direction to be given, where both these provisions and those of *ITEPA 2003, s 689* (see 55.3 below under Non-UK employer) apply, on application made by whoever is the 'relevant person' for the purposes of *section 689.* [*ITEPA 2003, ss 690, 718; ICTA 1988, s 203D; FA 1994, s 126*]. See Simon's Direct Tax Service E4.988. For a brief article on the correct application of *section 203D*, and the relaxation of strict PAYE rules in respect of certain short-term business visitors, see Revenue Tax Bulletin February 2003 pp 998, 999.

Right to make a return. A person within PAYE for a tax year will not necessarily be required to file a self-assessment tax return but may, by written notice, require the Revenue to send him such a return for completion and filing. Notice must be given no later than the fifth anniversary of 31 October following the tax year. [*ITEPA 2003, s 711; ICTA 1988, s 205(4); FA 1995, s 111(1)*].

55.3 **All persons making payments of such emoluments** are required to deduct the appropriate amount of tax from each payment (or repay over-deductions) by reference to PAYE Tax Tables, which are so constructed that, as near as may be, tax deducted from payments to date from previous 5 April corresponds with the correct time proportion to date of the net total tax liability (after allowances and reliefs) of the recipient on those emoluments for the year. See *Andrews v King Ch D 1991, 64 TC 332* as regards extended definition of 'employer' and *Booth v Mirror Group Newspapers plc QB, [1992] STC 615* as regards application of the PAYE regulations where emoluments are paid by a third party. The 'total tax' may include adjustments for any previous year and it 'may be assumed' that payments to date bear the same proportion to the total emoluments as that part of the year bears to the whole. [*ITEPA 2003, s 685; ICTA 1988, s 203(6)–(8); FA 2003, s 145(3)(4)*]. Employers are also required to deduct national insurance contributions at the same time as PAYE tax is deducted.

There are provisions to determine the time at which a payment of income is treated as being made for PAYE purposes. These equate to the rules in 75.5 SCHEDULE E—EMPLOYMENT

INCOME for determining when money earnings are to be treated as being received. [*ITEPA 2003, s 686; ICTA 1988, s 203A; FA 1989, s 45*].

Employers may elect to operate separate PAYE schemes for different groups of employees. [*SI 2003 No 2682, regs 98, 99*].

Payments by intermediaries. Where a payment of, or on account of, PAYE income is made by an 'intermediary' of the employer (i.e. a person acting on behalf, and at the expense, of the employer or a person 'connected' (within *ICTA 1988, s 839* — see 19 CONNECTED PERSONS) with the employer, or trustees holding property for persons including the employee), then unless the intermediary deducts and accounts for tax under PAYE (whether or not the PAYE regulations apply to him), the employer is to be treated for PAYE purposes as having made the payment (grossed up where the recipient is entitled to the amount after deduction of any income tax). [*ITEPA 2003, ss 687, 712, 718; ICTA 1988, ss 203B, 203L; FA 1994, ss 125, 131*]. See 55.4 below as regards the method of accounting for tax in respect of such notional payments.

Non-UK employer. Where, during any period, an employee works for a person (the 'relevant person') other than his employer, and any payment of, or on account of, his PAYE income for work done in that period is made by the employer (or by an intermediary (see above) of the employer or, from 6 April 1998, of the relevant person) outside the scope of PAYE, the relevant person is treated for PAYE purposes as having made the payment (grossed up where the employee is entitled to the payment after deduction of any income tax). From 6 April 1998 this applies also to any items brought within the scope of PAYE under 55.2(*a*)–(*h*) above. [*ITEPA 2003, s 689; ICTA 1988, s 203C; FA 1994, s 126; FA 1998, s 69*].

Agency workers. (From 6 April 1998) where an individual's remuneration under a contract falls to be treated under the agency worker rules at 75.49 SCHEDULE E—EMPLOYMENT INCOME as earnings from an employment, *ITEPA 2003, ss 687, 689* (see above) and *ss 693–702* (see 55.2 above) have effect as if the agency, and not the client, were the employer. However, where payment is made on behalf of, and at the expense of, the client or a person connected with him (within *ICTA 1988, s 839* — see 19 CONNECTED PERSONS), the rules above on payments by intermediaries have effect as if the client, and not the agency, were the employer. [*ITEPA 2003, ss 688, 718; ICTA 1988, s 203L(1A)–(1C); FA 1998, s 69*].

Mobile UK workforce. Where a person (the 'relevant person') has entered, or is likely to enter, into an agreement that employees of another person (the 'contractor') will work for him, but not as his employees, for a period, and it is likely that PAYE will not be deducted or accounted for in accordance with the regulations on payments made by (or on behalf of) the contractor of, or on account of, PAYE income of those employees for that period, the Board may by notice to the relevant person direct that he apply PAYE to any payments made by him in respect of work done in that period by such employees of the contractor. So much of the payment as is attributable to the work done by each such employee is treated for this purpose as a payment of PAYE income of that employee. The notice must specify the relevant person and the contractor to whom it relates, and may similarly be withdrawn by further notice, and notices must, where reasonably practicable, be copied to the contractor. [*ITEPA 2003, s 691; ICTA 1988, s 203E; FA 1994, s 126*].

55.4   **The tax deductions to be made** are those appropriate to the employee's 'PAYE code' (calculated by the Revenue, and notified to both employer and employee, to take account of personal allowances and reliefs due, certain higher rate liabilities and reliefs, underpayments from earlier years, and items within the benefits code (see 75.14 SCHEDULE E—EMPLOYMENT INCOME) from which deductions cannot be made). The PAYE code generally represents the total allowances due omitting the final digit. Notice of objection to a code or revised code may be made to the inspector and in default of agreement an appeal can be taken to General

Commissioners. See 89.5 UNDERWRITERS AT LLOYD'S for a case concerning a request to include an anticipated underwriting loss in a PAYE code.

See, respectively, 68.3 RETURNS and 16.3 CLAIMS as regards the coding out of self-assessment liabilities and as regards claims for reliefs etc. given effect by adjustments to codes.

Tax offices only notify an employer if there is a change in an employee's code. Until such notification an employer will continue to use the same code from year to year.

[*SI 2003 No 2682, Pt 2*].

Notional payments: accounting for tax. A '*notional payment*' of PAYE income is a payment treated as made by virtue of any of 55.2(*a*)–(*h*) above or, with the exception of grossed up payments, under the 'payment by intermediary' rules or 'non-UK employer' rules in 55.3 above. Where a notional payment of PAYE income is made, the income tax thereon is to be deducted, at a prescribed time, from any *actual* payment(s) of PAYE income to the employee. Where, due to an insufficiency of actual payments, all or part of the tax cannot be so deducted, the employer (or person treated as such) must account to the Board, within a prescribed time, for any tax he is required, but unable, to deduct. The amount so deducted or accounted for is treated as an amount paid by the employee in respect of his own liability to income tax. For 2003/04 onwards, it is made clear that it is so treated *at the time the notional payment is made*.

As regards any amount the employer has accounted for (being unable to deduct it from any payments made to the employee), if the employee does not make good the amount to the employer within 90 days of the date on which the employer is treated as making the notional payment (30 days for notional payments treated as made before 9 April 2003), the employee is treated as receiving earnings (or, before 2002/03, income) of that amount on that date.

[*ITEPA 2003, ss 222, 710; ICTA 1988, ss 144A, 203J; FA 1994, ss 131, 132; FA 1998, s 69; FA 2002, Sch 6 para 4; FA 2003, ss 144, 145(6)*].

For notes on the application of these provisions to share-related benefits, see Revenue Tax Bulletin April 2000 pp 734, 735. For a case in which directors were held to have made good an amount of tax despite the amount in question having erroneously been held in their loan account beyond the 30-day time limit, see *Ferguson and others v CIR (Sp C 266), [2001] SSCD 1*.

55.5   **Tax Tables** show, in relation to each 'code', the cumulative 'free pay' for each weekly (or monthly) period, which is subtracted from the total gross pay down to that period leaving 'taxable pay' on which is calculated the tax due from (or refundable to) the employee.

The Revenue may authorise the use of simplified tax tables for personal employees, i.e. those employed in the home to provide personal or domestic services or those employed to personally assist a disabled employer. [*SI 2003 No 2682, regs 34, 35*].

55.6   **Deductions working sheets** (Form P11) must be kept in each fiscal year by every employer in respect of each employee for recording the employee's pay, tax and related national insurance contributions. [*SI 2003 No 2682, reg 66*].

55.7   As to **recovery from employee** of tax under-deducted see *SI 2003 No 2682, reg 72* as amended by *SI 2004 No 851, reg 3*. Recovery from employee is subject to the condition that either the employer (i) made an error in good faith having taken reasonable care or (ii) with the employee's acquiescence, the employer wilfully failed to deduct the correct tax. See also *Bernard & Shaw Ltd v Shaw KB 1951, 30 ATC 187*, and for wilful failure by employer to deduct correct tax, *R v CIR (ex p Chisholm) QB 1981, 54 TC 722, R v CIR (ex p Sims) QB 1987, 60 TC 398* and *R v CIR (ex p Cook) QB 1987, 60 TC 405*. In *R v CIR (ex p McVeigh) QB 1996, 68 TC 121*, accounting entries purporting to deduct tax, where tax not paid over to Revenue, were held not to constitute deduction of tax for these purposes.

After 11 April 2004, an appeals procedure is introduced. Where (i) applies, the employer may request the Revenue to make a direction to the effect that the employer is not liable. If the Revenue agree, they will issue a direction notice, subject to right of appeal by the employee within 30 days. If not, they will issue a refusal notice, subject to similar right of appeal by the employer. Where (ii) applies, the Revenue will issue a direction notice, to the effect that the employer is not liable, to the employee, who again has 30 days in which to appeal. [*SI 2003 No 2682, regs 72A–72D; SI 2004 No 851, reg 4*]. See also Revenue Tax Bulletin April 2004 pp 1108–1110.

Likewise, the Revenue may direct that the employer be relieved of tax determined under *SI 2003 No 2682, reg 80* (see 55.8 below), with similar right of appeal available to the employee after 11 April 2004. [*SI 2003 No 2682, regs 81, 81A; SI 2004 No 851, regs 5, 6*]. See also Revenue Tax Bulletin April 2004 pp 1108–1110.

For tax accounted for by employer in respect of certain notional payments, see 55.4 above.

55.8   **The net tax deducted by the employer must be paid to the Revenue** within 14 days after the end of each tax month (17 days for electronic payments for 2004/05 onwards), except in certain cases where payment may be made quarterly. Quarterly payment applies either where simplified tax tables are in use for personal employees (see 55.5 above) or where the employer has reasonable grounds for believing that the 'average monthly amount' otherwise payable to the Revenue will be less than £1,500 and chooses to pay quarterly instead of monthly. The '*average monthly amount*' is the average, for tax months falling within the current tax year, of

(*a*)   amounts deducted under PAYE and the CONSTRUCTION INDUSTRY SCHEME (20) (disregarding any adjustment thereto in respect of working tax credit),

(*b*)   national insurance contributions (again disregarding working tax credit adjustments and also disregarding any contributions for which liability has been transferred to the employee), and

(*c*)   student loan repayments,

less any payments of

(i)   working tax credit,

(ii)   statutory maternity pay, statutory paternity pay, statutory sick pay or statutory adoption pay, and

(iii)   (in the case of company employers only) amounts suffered by deduction under the construction industry scheme.

Where quarterly payment applies, payment to the Revenue must be made within 14 days (or 17 days) after the end of the tax quarter. A tax month ends on the 5th of each month; a tax quarter ends on 5 July, 5 October, 5 January and 5 April.

[*SI 2003 No 2682, regs 2, 68–71*].

If no tax has been paid within that 14 days (or 17 days), or the Revenue are not satisfied that any payment made satisfies the employer's liability, the Revenue, if they are not aware of the amount the employer is liable to pay, can give notice requiring a return within 14 days showing the amount of that liability. [*SI 2003 No 2682, reg 77*]. The Revenue have powers to determine to the best of their judgement the amount of tax payable where it appears to them that tax may have been payable under these regulations but has not been paid. The determination applies as if it were an assessment to tax. [*SI 2003 No 2682, reg 80*]. See 55.7 above as regards recovery of tax from employee in certain cases.

Interest is charged at the prescribed rate (as in 42.1 INTEREST AND SURCHARGES ON UNPAID TAX) on tax unpaid in respect of determinations for 1991/92 and earlier years made after 19 April 1988, from 14 days after the end of the tax year to which the determination relates (or from 19 April 1988 if later). [*ITEPA 2003, s 684(2); ICTA 1988, s 203(2)(d); FA 1988, s 128(1); SI 1993 No 744, reg 50; SI 2003 No 2682, Sch 1 para 20*]. In respect of tax payable for 1992/93 and subsequent years, interest is so charged on tax unpaid by 19 April in the tax year following that for which it was payable (22 April for electronic payments for 2004/05 onwards) whether or not it is the subject of a determination. Also in respect of tax payable for 1992/93 and subsequent years, interest on overpaid tax runs at the prescribed rate (see 41.1, 41.2 INTEREST ON OVERPAID TAX) from (for tax paid for 1996/97 and subsequent years) the 14th day after the end of the year in respect of which the tax was paid (or, if later, from the date of payment of the tax), or (for tax paid for 1995/96 and earlier years) the end of the year after that in respect of which the payment was made (or in the case of a repayment of tax paid more than twelve months after the end of the year for which it was paid, from the end of the year in which the tax was paid). [*ITEPA 2003, s 684(2); ICTA 1988, s 203(2)(dd); FA 1988, s 128(1); FA 1994, ss 196, 199, Sch 19 para 38; SI 1993 No 744, reg 53; SI 2003 No 2682, regs 82, 83, Sch 1 para 23*]. In either case, such interest is paid without deduction of tax and is not taken into account in computing income for tax purposes. [*ITEPA 2003, s 684(2); ICTA 1988, s 203(9); FA 1988, s 128(2)*]. Cheque payments are normally treated as made on the day of receipt by the Revenue (and see 56.2 PAYMENT OF TAX). [*SI 2003 No 2682, reg 219*].

Interest may also arise in the case of late paid or overpaid Class 1 or 1A national insurance contributions (see Tolley's National Insurance Contributions).

Employer is not entitled to charge Revenue with costs of PAYE collection (*Meredith v Hazell QB 1964, 42 TC 435*). Revenue have power to inspect wages sheets and other records to ensure regulations being observed. [*ITEPA 2003, s 684(2); ICTA 1988, s 203(2)(b); SI 2003 No 2682, reg 97*]. Where money is stolen, the employer is liable (*A-G v Antoine KB 1949, 31 TC 213*).

Mandatory electronic payment for 'large employers'. For 2004/05 and subsequent years, employers who at the 'specified date' were 'large employers' (i.e. they were paying PAYE income to at least 250 recipients) are required, upon receipt of an e-payment notice issued by the Revenue by 31 December in the tax year preceding the year of payment, to use an approved method of electronic payment of PAYE liabilities. An appeal may be made (within 30 days) against an e-payment notice on the grounds that the employer is not a 'large employer'. In relation to 2004/05, the '*specified date*' is 26 October 2003. A system of default surcharges, ranging from 0.17% to 0.83% of the annual net PAYE liability, applies for persistent failure to make payments in full by the due dates; a person is not in default if he has a reasonable excuse (excluding inability to pay). Appeals may be made against default notices and surcharge notices. [*FA 2003, ss 204, 205; SI 2003 No 2682, regs 190, 191, 199–204; Revenue Direction 21 October 2003*]. See also Revenue Tax Bulletin February 2004 p 1085 and Revenue Handbook 'Do it online: online filing and electronic payment handbook' available at www.inlandrevenue.gov.uk/employers/doitonline.pdf

55.9   **After the end of each tax year the employer must**, in respect of each employee for whom he was required to maintain a deductions working sheet, send the following to the Revenue.

(*a*)   Not later than 19 May

  (i)   an End of Year Return P14,

  (ii)   a declaration on form P35 (including a nil return where appropriate).

[*SI 2003 No 2682, reg 73*].

(*b*)   Not later than 6 July, annual returns of other earnings on form P9D and, for 'P11D employees' only, form P11D. '*P11D employees*' are employees who are not in 'lower-paid employment' (see 75.14 SCHEDULE E—EMPLOYMENT INCOME) and all directors (other than those excluded under 75.14). Particulars (including, where applicable, amounts) of the following are required for *any* employee or director:

- earnings received otherwise than in money, whether from the employer or a 'related third party';

- payments made on the employee's behalf (and not repaid), whether by the employer or a 'related third party';

- non-cash vouchers and credit tokens falling to be treated as earnings (see 75.47(*a*)(*d*) SCHEDULE E—EMPLOYMENT INCOME), whether provided by the employer or a 'related third party';

- any tax on 'notional payments' of PAYE income which has not been made good by the employee (see 55.4 above);

- living accommodation provided for the employee or his family (see 75.32 SCHEDULE E—EMPLOYMENT INCOME), whether by the employer or a 'related third party';

- any removal benefits or removal expenses in excess of the qualifying limit (see 75.36 SCHEDULE E—EMPLOYMENT INCOME);

- whether any earnings relating to business entertainment will be disallowed in computing the employer's profits (see 71.45 SCHEDULE D, CASES I AND II, 75.11(*b*) SCHEDULE E—EMPLOYMENT INCOME).

Particulars of the following are additionally required for a P11D employee:

- expenses payments, whether made by the employer or a 'related third party';

- sums put at the employee's disposal, whether by the employer or a 'related third party', and paid away by the employee;

- details (including amounts) of taxable benefits provided (see 75.14 *et seq.* SCHEDULE E—EMPLOYMENT INCOME), whether by the employer or a 'related third party'.

For the above purposes, a '*related third party*' is any person who makes payments or provides benefits to an employee by arrangement with the employer, which includes the employer's guaranteeing or in any way facilitating the payments etc.

For the use of substitute forms P11D, see Revenue Tax Bulletin August 1996 p 334.

[*SI 2003 No 2682, regs 85–89*].

Supplementary returns (form P38A) must be submitted with form P35 for all employees for whom a deductions working sheet is not required. [*SI 2003 No 2682, reg 74*].

See 57.9 PENALTIES as regards a period of grace for submission of returns under (*a*) above.

A return by the employer is also required not later than 6 July following the end of the tax year in respect of any employee (or former employee) awarded termination payments and other benefits within *ITEPA 2003, ss 401–416* (see 18.5 COMPENSATION FOR LOSS OF EMPLOYMENT (AND DAMAGES)) totalling more than £30,000 in the tax year. [*SI 2003 No 2682, regs 91–93, 96*].

As regards information to be supplied by employers to employees, see 78.12 SELF-ASSESSMENT.

Value added tax paid, if any (and whether or not recoverable), must be included in amounts of expenses and benefits. (Revenue Pamphlet IR 131, A6). See also 55.43 below.

Returns are also required under 55.16 below (cars provided for private use).

See 68.16 RETURNS for employers' returns generally.

Internet filing discount. From April 2001 for one year only, small businesses filing their PAYE end-of-year returns via the internet and paying any tax due electronically received a discount of £50. A further £50 was available where there were one or more working families' or disabled person's tax credit cases. (Revenue Press Releases 16 February 2000, 21 March 2000 (BN1D)). See 68.14 RETURNS as regards other electronic filing discounts.

Mandatory e-filing. The Commissioners of Inland Revenue have been given extremely wide powers to make regulations requiring the use of electronic communications for the delivery of information required or authorised to be delivered under tax legislation. [*FA 2002, ss 135, 136*]. The Government has adopted a three-stage move towards e-filing of PAYE returns (i.e. the information required at (*a*) above), as follows.

(A) Employers with 250 or more employees are required to file electronically from 2004/05.

(B) Employers with 50 or more employees are required to file electronically from 2005/06.

(C) Employers with less than 50 employees are required to file electronically from 2009/10, with an incentive for earlier adoption.

(Revenue/C&E Budget Press Release 2/02, 17 April 2002).

Under the regulations giving effect to (A) and (B) above, the mandatory e-filing requirement applies for 2004/05 to employers who at 26 October 2003 were 'large employers' (i.e. they were paying PAYE income to at least 250 recipients) and who received an e-filing notice issued by the Revenue no later than 31 December 2003. Similar provisions apply for subsequent years but by reference to employers who at the specified date (to be announced by Revenue Direction) were 'large or medium-sized employers' (i.e. they were paying PAYE income to at least 50 recipients) and who received an e-filing notice issued by the Revenue no later than 31 December preceding the tax year in question. An appeal may be made (within 30 days) against an e-filing notice on the grounds that the employer does not fall into the specified category. There are let-outs for members of any religious orders whose beliefs are incompatible with electronic communication. Penalties for failure to comply range from £600 to £3,000 depending upon the number of employees, the maximum penalty applying where there are 1,000 or more. Appeals may be made against penalty determinations on specified grounds including reasonable excuse throughout the default period. [*SI 2003 No 2682, regs 190, 191, 205–210; Revenue Direction 21 October 2003*].

Regulations have also been made to give effect to (C) above. The incentives are available to employers who at a specified date (to be announced by Revenue Direction) preceding the tax year in question were 'small employers' (i.e. they were paying PAYE income to less than 50 recipients) or who first started paying PAYE income after that date. The payments receivable are £250 for each of 2004/05 and 2005/06, £150 for 2006/07, £100 for 2007/08 and £75 for 2008/09. These are not chargeable to tax. Appeals are possible (within 30 days of the notice) against an officer's decision not to make an incentive payment or to recover a payment already made. [*SI 2003 No 2495; Revenue Direction 21 October 2003*]. Employers can either use incentive payments to reduce a subsequent PAYE liability or claim a repayment, but repayments will not be sent to the employer's agent (Revenue Tax Bulletin February 2004 p 1085).

See also Revenue Tax Bulletins February 2003 pp 995, 996, February 2004 pp 1084, 1085 and Revenue Handbook 'Do it online: online filing and electronic payment handbook' available at www.inlandrevenue.gov.uk/employers/doitonline.pdf

Mandatory e-payment for 'large employers'. See 55.8 above.

Foot and mouth outbreak. For the full range of measures, including extra time for submission of end-of-year returns, in relation to the 2001 foot and mouth disease outbreak, see Revenue Tax Bulletin Special Edition May 2001.

Simon's Direct Tax Service. See E4.965 *et seq.*

55.10   Employers must give each employee annually **a certificate** (form P60) showing his total taxable earnings for the year and total tax deducted therefrom, his appropriate code, national insurance number, and the employer's name and address etc. [*SI 2003 No 2682, reg 67*]. This certificate is produced automatically as the third sheet of the End of Year Return, or a substitute form P60 may be used or other document approved by the Revenue. See 78.12 SELF-ASSESSMENT for the time limit for supplying form P60 and for other information to be supplied by employers to employees.

55.11   For **Penalties** see 57.9 PENALTIES and *TMA 1970, ss 98, 98A*. See also Revenue Pamphlet IR 109.

55.12   **PAYE settlement agreements.** The Revenue and an employer may make a non-statutory agreement, known as an 'annual voluntary settlement', whereby the employer settles by way of lump sum an amount approximating to the tax otherwise payable by his employees on items covered by the settlement, which will be minor, incidental benefits and expenses payments, e.g. reimbursement of telephone expenses, late night taxis home and benefits shared between a number of employees. The employer is then relieved of including such benefits and expenses in the returns at 55.9(*b*) above and the employees do not have to declare them or include them in their total income.

A statutory framework for such arrangements, known as 'PAYE settlement agreements', is established by regulations provided for originally by *ICTA 1988, s 206A* (introduced by *FA 1996, s 110*) and now by *ITEPA 2003, ss 703–707*. See *SI 2003 No 2682, regs 105–117* and Revenue Statement of Practice SP 5/96, 15 October 1996 (as revised) for the detailed rules governing such agreements and the scope of payments and benefits covered. These are described in some detail in an article in the Revenue Tax Bulletin December 1996 pp 365–369. Separate legislation enables national insurance contributions to be comprised in such settlements (and see 71.44 SCHEDULE D, CASES I AND II).

See also Revenue Pamphlet IR 155.

Simon's Direct Tax Service. See E4.968.

55.13   **Annual payments.** Tax on certain periodic redundancy and other similar payments by a former employer which are strictly assessable under Schedule D, Case III as annual payments, and payable under deduction of basic rate tax, may, where it is convenient and with the agreement of the parties and the inspector, be dealt with instead under PAYE (Revenue Tax Bulletin February 1995 p 196).

55.14 **Annuities** paid out of superannuation funds approved under *ICTA 1970, s 208* which have not sought approval under subsequent legislation and to which no contributions have been made since 5 April 1980 (see 67.13 RETIREMENT SCHEMES) continue to be taxable pension income and subject to PAYE. [*ITEPA 2003, ss 590–592, 594, 683(3); ICTA 1988, s 608*].

55.15 **Benefits in kind** constitute PAYE income (see 55.2 above) but are not payments and are not, therefore, directly subject to PAYE deductions. They are usually dealt with by set-off against allowances in arriving at an employee's PAYE code (see 55.4 above and *R v Walton Commrs (ex p Wilson) CA, [1983] STC 464*). However, see 55.2(*a*)–(*h*) above for items not normally regarded as payments but brought within the scope of PAYE deductions.

55.16 **Cars provided for private use.** See 75.18(i)(ii) SCHEDULE E—EMPLOYMENT INCOME for computation of the charge. A return is required no later than 28 days after a tax quarter (see 55.8 above) if, during that quarter, a company car on which a benefits charge will arise is newly provided to an employee or ceases to be provided to an employee, or an employee to whom a car is provided becomes a P11D employee (see 55.9(*b*) above). The return form asks for specified particulars required to compute the benefits charge. [*SI 2003 No 2682, reg 90*].

55.17 **Charitable donations** are an allowable deduction for PAYE purposes where made under an approved payroll giving scheme. See 14.18 CHARITIES.

55.18 **Crown priority (now abolished).** The provisions of *Insolvency Act 1986, s 386, Sch 6* applied to PAYE which the bankrupt was liable to deduct from PAYE income paid in the twelve months before the date of the bankruptcy order or, if earlier, the date of appointment of an interim receiver. This priority was *abolished* by *Enterprise Act 2002, s 251* from 15 September 2003. See 56.7 PAYMENT OF TAX.

55.19 **Director's remuneration.** Credit of remuneration voted to a director to an account with the company constitutes 'payment' for PAYE purposes. See generally ICAEW Technical Release TAX 11/93, 9 July 1993, as regards tax implications of payments to directors. [*ITEPA 2003, s 686(1); ICTA 1988, s 203A(1)(c); FA 1989, s 45*]. See 55.3 above and 75.5 SCHEDULE E—EMPLOYMENT INCOME.

55.20 **Disabled person's tax credit** due to an individual in receipt of earnings within PAYE is payable by the employer from 6 April 2000, such payment to be funded by the Revenue. [*Tax Credits Act 1999, s 6; ITEPA 2003, Sch 6 para 240; SI 1999 No 3219*]. See Revenue Tax Bulletin October 1999 pp 691–693, and see 83.6 SOCIAL SECURITY. The same applies to its replacement, **working tax credit** (see 83.7 SOCIAL SECURITY), from 6 April 2003. [*Tax Credits Act 2002, ss 25, 65, 67; ITEPA 2003, Sch 6 para 265; SI 2002 No 2172*].

55.21 **Domestic workers and nannies.** See Revenue Pamphlet IR 53 for simplified guidelines on the operation of PAYE by taxpayers likely to be employing domestic workers or nannies for the first time. See also 55.5 above and the Revenue's website at www.inlandrevenue.gov.uk/simple_deduction/index.htm

55.22 **Employee arriving.** A new employee should produce a form P45 and the employer should start a Deductions Working Sheet from the particulars on that form and send Part 3 to the tax office. If a form P45 (or other code authorisation) is not produced, the employer should complete form P46, ask the employee to sign the appropriate certificate, and send to the tax office on making the first payment exceeding the PAYE threshold (see 55.25 below). A Deductions Working Sheet must be prepared and tax deducted in accordance with the emergency code or basic rate code as appropriate. [*SI 2003 No 2682, regs 40–53*].

55.23   **Employee dying.** On death of employee, the employer must forthwith send all parts of completed form P45 to the Revenue. [*SI 2003 No 2682, regs 38, 39*].

55.24   **Employee leaving** must be given certificate (form P45) by former employer showing code, pay and tax deducted to date of leaving (split if more than one employment). [*SI 2003 No 2682, reg 36*]. This produced to new employer [*SI 2003 No 2682, reg 40*] ensures continuity and provides data for commencement of new deduction working sheet.

Payments to employees who have left and which are not included in P45 must have tax deducted at the basic rate. [*SI 2003 No 2682, reg 37*].

Employee retiring. At retirement on pension of an employee, no P45 need be completed and tax must be deducted from the pension on a non-cumulative basis. The employer/pension payer must then complete a 'retirement statement' containing specified details and send it to the Revenue with a copy to the pensioner. [*SI 2003 No 2682, regs 36(3), 55*].

55.25   **Exemption.** Where a new employee has no other employment and rate of payment is less than a weekly or monthly rate equal to $\frac{1}{52}$nd or $\frac{1}{12}$th respectively of the personal allowance (the 'PAYE threshold'), no tax is deductible. [*SI 2003 No 2682, regs 9, 47(2), 48(2), 49(2)*].

55.26   **Expense payments etc.** must (except as regards pure reimbursement to subordinate employees of specific outlay incurred) be included with pay and taxed with it, unless given a dispensation by the Revenue under *ITEPA 2003, s 65* (or corresponding earlier legislation — see *ITEPA 2003, Sch 7 para 15*).

55.27   **Free of tax payments, awards etc.** For remuneration payable free of tax, taxed incentive awards etc., see 75.40 SCHEDULE E—EMPLOYMENT INCOME.

55.28   **H.M. Forces.** Members of the reserve and auxiliary forces will generally have basic rate tax deducted from pay. [*SI 2003 No 2682, regs 122–133*].

55.29   **Holiday pay funds.** Holiday pay paid by a holiday pay fund is taxed at the basic rate at the time of payment. [*SI 2003 No 2682, regs 134, 136*].

55.30   **Incapacity benefit,** where taxable (see 83.3 SOCIAL SECURITY), is brought within PAYE by *SI 2003 No 2682, regs 173–180.*

55.31   **Jobseekers allowance** (so far as taxable, see 83.3 SOCIAL SECURITY) is brought within PAYE by *SI 2003 No 2682, regs 148–172*. The Department for Work and Pensions (or in NI, the Department for Social Development) maintain a record of the claimant's previous cumulative pay and tax in the tax year and of any taxable benefit paid to him. At the end of the claimant's period of benefit claim (or at the end of the tax year, if earlier) the Department calculate his tax position, make any repayments of tax due to him and notify the details to him and to his tax office. See also 55.40 below and Revenue Pamphlet IR 41.

55.32 **Local councillors' attendance allowances.** The councillor may opt for deduction of basic rate tax from such allowances (net of an appropriate amount in respect of allowable expenditure) rather than deduction by reference to the appropriate code. [*SI 2003 No 2682, regs 118–121*].

55.33 **Maternity, paternity and adoption pay** is taxable social security income. [*ITEPA 2003, ss 658, 660; ICTA 1988, s 150; FA 2002, s 35*].

55.34 **Overseas matters.** Where an employee works abroad, see Employer's Guide to PAYE. See *SI 2003 No 2682, reg 57* as regards pensions. A non-resident employer must operate PAYE in respect of any taxable earnings of his employees if he has a 'trading presence' in the UK (*Clark v Oceanic Contractors Incorporated HL 1982, 56 TC 183*). See also *Bootle v Bye; Wilson v Bye (Sp C 61), [1996] SSCD 58* and Revenue Employment Procedures Manual EP 8116. See also 55.3 above as regards payments by intermediaries.

55.35 **PAYE threshold.** See 55.25 above.

55.36 **Pension contributions** (the 'net pay arrangement'). Employees' allowable pension contributions deducted from salary (see *SI 2003 No 2682, reg 3*) are also allowable for the purposes of computing PAYE deductions (though not for the purposes of computing national insurance contributions).

55.37 **Records.** Wages sheets, deductions working sheets, certificates and other records required to be maintained under the PAYE regulations and not required to be sent to the Revenue must be retained by the employer for not less than three years after the end of the year to which they relate. [*SI 2003 No 2682, reg 97(8)*]. There are special provisions relating to inspection of computer records (see *FA 1988, s 127* and *SI 2003 No 2682, reg 97(7)*). See Revenue Pamphlets IR 71 and IR 109 as regards inspection of records and negotiation of settlements. See also Revenue Tax Bulletin October 1998 pp 588, 589.

55.38 **Religious Centres.** If a Local Religious Centre does not expect to pay anyone £100 or more in a tax year, no action is required under PAYE. For anyone to whom the Centre does expect to pay £100 or more in a tax year, but who has no other job, records need to be kept for three years of name, address, national insurance number and the amount paid in the tax year. For any such person who has (or may have) another job, the Centre does not need to deduct tax, but should write to TIDO(LRC), Ty Glas, Llanishen, Cardiff CV4 5ZG giving details of name, address and national insurance number and of both the amount paid to the following 5 April and the amount expected to be paid in a full tax year. (Taxation, 16 February 1995, p 462).

55.39 **Seamen** are subject to standard PAYE procedures on wages from employment. Travelling expenses and subsistence allowances paid to seafarers making regular journeys to the same UK port are subject to PAYE. (Hansard 26 February 1981 Vol 999 Col 442).

55.40 **Tax refunds** arising during unemployment are made directly by the Revenue, but refunds are withheld from the unemployed who claim jobseeker's allowance and from strikers until the end of the strike. [*ITEPA 2003, s 708; ICTA 1988, s 204; SI 2003 No 2682, regs 64, 65*].

55.41 **Termination payments.** For the reporting requirements in relation to taxable termination payments, see 55.9 above.

55.42   **Tips, organised arrangements for sharing.** Gratuities and service charge shares under such arrangements (sometimes known as a 'tronc') are within PAYE and the 'tronc-master' (i.e. the person running the arrangements, being a person other than the employer) is regarded as responsible for the tax deductions. For arrangements coming into existence after 5 April 2004, the employer, on becoming aware of their existence, must notify the Revenue and give the name of the person running them, if known. [*ITEPA 2003, s 692; SI 2003 No 2682, reg 100*]. For a case in which informal arrangements, under which directors of the employing company collected gratuities and divided them between themselves and the employees, were held not to constitute organised arrangements, see *Figael Ltd v Fox CA 1991, 64 TC 441*.

The above rules apply where the troncmaster acts independently of the employer. If the employer himself acts as troncmaster, or appoints an employee to make distributions in accordance with the employer's own formula or is otherwise involved in the distribution of monies from the tronc, payments made under the arrangements must be dealt with through the employer's own PAYE system. (Revenue Tax Bulletin February 2004 p 1081).

See generally Revenue Employment Procedures Manual EP 1155 *et seq.*, Revenue booklet E24 'Tips, Gratuities, Service Charges and Troncs: A Guide to Income Tax, National Insurance contributions, National Minimum Wage issues and VAT' (distributed to employers) and Revenue Tax Bulletin February 2004 pp 1081–1084.

55.43   **Value added tax.** Earnings paid to a person holding an office in the course of carrying on a trade, profession or vocation and subject to VAT on services supplied by him should exclude the VAT element for PAYE purposes (Revenue Pamphlet IR 131, A6). See also 55.9 above.

55.44   **Voluntary lifeboatmen** call-out fees, although taxable, are not subject to deduction of tax under PAYE (Revenue Press Release 15 April 1986).

55.45   **Working tax credit** (see 83.7 SOCIAL SECURITY) due to an individual in receipt of earnings within PAYE is payable by the employer from 6 April 2003, such payment to be funded by the Revenue. [*Tax Credits Act 2002, ss 25, 65, 67; ITEPA 2003, Sch 6 para 265; SI 2002 No 2172*]. The same applied to its predecessor, **working families' tax credit** (see 83.6 SOCIAL SECURITY) from 6 April 2000. [*Tax Credits Act 1999, s 6; ITEPA 2003, Sch 6 para 240; SI 1999 No 3219*].

56 Payment of Tax

Cross-references. See 42 INTEREST ON UNPAID TAX and 55 PAY AS YOU EARN.

Simon's Direct Tax Service A3.13, E1.820 *et seq.*

Payment in euros. Tax payments may be made in euros through automated banking systems, from euro accounts or (at certain locations) in euro bank notes (but not coins). Costs incurred in respect of a euro payment drawn on an overseas bank account will be borne by the taxpayer, but other administrative costs will not be passed on. The exchange rate used is the one in force when the payment is presented by the clearing bank. If the conversion rate used leaves a shortfall, the difference will have to be paid. If it results in an overpayment, any repayment arising will be made in sterling.

56.1 DUE DATES FOR PAYMENT

A final payment is due for a year of assessment if a person's combined income tax and capital gains tax liabilities contained in his self-assessment (see 68.3 RETURNS) exceed the aggregate of any payments on account (whether under *TMA 1970, s 59A*, see 78.4 SELF-ASSESSMENT, or otherwise) and any income tax deducted at source. If the second total exceeds the first, a repayment will be made. Tax deducted at source has the same meaning as in 78.4(*b*) SELF-ASSESSMENT.

Subject to the further provisions referred to below, the normal due date for payment (or repayment) is 31 January following the year of assessment. Where, however, the person gave notice of chargeability under *TMA 1970, s 7* (see 57.1 PENALTIES) within six months after the end of the year of assessment, but was not given notice under *TMA 1970, s 8 or s 8A* (see 68.2 RETURNS) until after 31 October following the year of assessment, the due date is the last day of the three months beginning with the date of the said notice.

[*TMA 1970, s 59B(1)–(4)(7)(8); FA 1994, ss 193, 199(2)(a); FA 1996, s 122(2), s 126(2); ITEPA 2003, Sch 6 para 131*].

See 78.7 SELF-ASSESSMENT for deferral of the due date for payment (or repayment) of an amount of tax as a result of an amendment or correction to a self-assessment or a consequential amendment arising from an amendment or correction to a partnership return or partnership statement (see 68.13 RETURNS). It should, however, be noted that those rules do *not* defer the date from which interest accrues (for which see 42.1 INTEREST AND SURCHARGES ON UNPAID TAX (or 41.1 INTEREST ON OVERPAID TAX), although they *do* determine the due date for surcharge purposes (see 42.2 INTEREST AND SURCHARGES ON UNPAID TAX).

Where an officer of the Board enquires into a return (see 68.6 RETURNS) and a repayment is otherwise due, the repayment is not required to be made until the enquiry is completed (see 68.9 RETURNS), although the officer may make a provisional repayment at his discretion.

Subject to the appeal and postponement provisions in 4.1 APPEALS and 56.3 below, the due date for payment of tax charged by assessment *otherwise* than by self-assessment (e.g. a discovery assessment under *TMA 1970, s 29*, see 5.3 ASSESSMENTS) is 30 days after the date on which the notice of assessment is given (but see also 42.1 INTEREST AND SURCHARGES ON UNPAID TAX).

[*TMA 1970, s 59B(4A)(6); FA 1994, s 193, s 199(2)(a); FA 1995, s 103(7), s 115(6); FA 1996, s 127; FA 2001, s 88, Sch 29 paras 14(2), 16*].

As regards due dates for payment of tax for **1995/96 and earlier years**, i.e. before the introduction of self-assessment, see the 2003/04 and earlier editions.

For the full range of special measures in relation to the 2001 foot and mouth disease outbreak, including deferment of payment of tax liabilities, see Revenue Tax Bulletin Special Edition May 2001.

See 78.4 SELF-ASSESSMENT as regards notifications to agents.

56.2   EFFECTIVE DATES OF PAYMENT

The Revenue take the date of payment in respect of each payment method to be as follows.

(1)   *Cheques, cash, and postal orders* handed in at the Revenue office or received by post — the day of receipt by the Revenue *unless* received by post following a day on which the office was closed for whatever reason, in which case it is the day on which the office was first closed.

(2)   *Electronic funds transfer* — payment by BACS (transfer over two days) or CHAPS (same day transfer) — one day prior to receipt by the Revenue (not applicable after 18 May 2004 to payments by employers under PAY AS YOU EARN (55) and by contractors under the CONSTRUCTION INDUSTRY SCHEME (20)).

(3)   *Bank giro or Girobank* — the date on which payment was made at the bank or post office.

(Revenue 'Working Together' Bulletin July 2000 p 3).

For the purposes of *TMA 1970* and *ICTA 1988, s 824* (see 41 INTEREST ON OVERPAID TAX), *s 825* and *s 826*, where any payment to an officer of the Board or the Board itself is received by cheque after 5 April 1996 and the cheque is paid on its first presentation to the bank on which it is drawn, the payment is treated as made on the date of receipt of the cheque by the officer or the Board. [*TMA 1970, s 70A; FA 1994, s 196, Sch 19 para 22*].

56.3   PAYMENT AND POSTPONEMENT OF TAX PENDING APPEAL

The provisions described below apply for 1996/97 and subsequent years in the case of appeals against:

(i)   (for enquiries completed on or after 11 May 2001) a conclusion stated or amendment made by a closure notice on completion of enquiry (see 68.9 RETURNS);

(ii)   (for enquiries completed before 11 May 2001) a Revenue amendment of a self-assessment following enquiry (see 68.10 RETURNS);

(iii)   a Revenue amendment to a self-assessment during enquiry to prevent potential loss of tax (see 68.10 RETURNS); and

(iv)   an assessment other than a self-assessment.

In the absence of any application for postponement of tax as below, tax is due and payable as if there had been no appeal.

If the appellant has grounds for believing that he is overcharged to tax by the amendment or assessment or as a result of the conclusion stated, as the case may be, he (or his agent) may, by notice in writing stating those grounds and given to the inspector or Revenue officer in question within 30 days after the 'relevant date', apply to the Appeal Commissioners for postponement of a specified amount of tax pending determination of the appeal. The '*relevant date*' is the date of issue of the notice of amendment or assessment or, in the case of an appeal within (i) above, the date of issue of the closure notice.

The taxpayer and the Revenue officer may then come to an agreement in writing as to the amount of tax (if any) to be postponed. An agreement not in writing is nevertheless treated as such provided that its existence and terms are confirmed in writing by notice given by either party to the other. (In *Sparrow Ltd v Inspector (Sp C 289), [2001] SSCD 206*, an obvious error by the Revenue, notifying a full rather than the nil postponement previously notified, was held not to constitute such an agreement.) Where the parties do not come to an agreement, the matter is referred to the Appeal Commissioners who, if they consider that there are reasonable grounds for believing that an amount of tax has been overcharged, must postpone that amount pending determination of the substantive appeal. For a case in which no such 'reasonable grounds' were found, see *Sparrow Ltd* (above).

On the determination of (or agreement as to) the amount of tax to be postponed, the balance of tax *not postponed* (if any) becomes due and payable as if it had been charged by an amendment or assessment issued on the date of that determination or agreement (or on the date of notice of confirmation of the latter) and in respect of which there had been no appeal.

Application for postponement may be made outside the normal 30-day time limit if there is a change in the circumstances of the case giving grounds for belief that the appellant is overcharged. In the Revenue view, this requires a change in the circumstances in which the original decision not to apply for postponement was made, not just a change of mind, e.g. further accounts work indicating a substantially excessive assessment, or further reliefs becoming due (see CCAB Statement TR 477, 22 June 1982). A late application does not defer the due date of any balance of tax not postponed.

If, after the determination of an amount of tax to be postponed and as a result of a change in the circumstances of the case, either party has grounds for believing that the amount postponed has become either excessive or insufficient, he may, by written notice to the other party (at any time before the determination of the substantive appeal), apply to the Appeal Commissioners for a further determination of the amount to be postponed. The notice must state the amount of the excess or shortfall believed to have arisen and the grounds for that belief. If, on a consequent further determination, an amount of tax ceases to be postponed, that amount is treated as charged by an assessment issued on the date of the further determination and in respect of which there had been no appeal. If, on the other hand, an amount of tax has been overpaid, it is repaid.

A postponement application is heard in the same way as the appeal, and consideration of the application does not preclude the same Commissioners from hearing and determining the appeal or from considering a further application as above. Any transfer of proceedings from one body of Commissioners to another does not affect the validity of a postponement determination.

[*TMA 1970, s 55; F(No 2)A 1975, s 45; FA 1982, s 68; FA 1989, s 156(2); FA 1990, s 104(2)(4); FA 1994, ss 196, 199, Sch 19 para 18; FA 1996, Sch 18 paras 1, 17(1)(2); FA 2001, s 88, Sch 29 para 31*].

The giving of notice of appeal, whether or not accompanied by a postponement application, does *not* affect the date from which interest accrues, for which see 42.1 INTEREST AND SURCHARGES ON UNPAID TAX, and this applies also to assessments for 1995/96 and earlier first raised after 5 April 1998.

56.4 **PAYMENT OF TAX ON DETERMINATION OF APPEAL**

Tax payable in accordance with the determination of an appeal within 56.3(i)–(iv) above, being either postponed or additional tax, becomes due and payable as if it were charged by an amendment or assessment issued on the date on which the Revenue issued to the taxpayer a notice of the total amount payable in accordance with the determination, and in respect of which no appeal was made. Any tax found to be overpaid becomes repayable. [*TMA 1970, s 55(9); F(No 2)A 1975, s 45; FA 1989, s 156(2); FA 1994, ss 196, 199, Sch 19 para 18*].

In cases of appeals to the Courts, any tax so notified must be paid first in accordance with the determination of the Commissioners. Tax overpaid consequent on the Court's decision is repaid (with, at the Court's discretion, interest) even though further appeal is possible (see e.g. *T & E Homes Ltd v Robinson CA 1979, 52 TC 567*), and any tax not previously charged is due and payable 30 days after the date of notification by the inspector of the total amount payable in accordance with the order or judgment of the Court. [*TMA 1970, ss 56(9), 56A(8)(9); F(No 2)A 1975, s 45; FA 1989, s 156(3); SI 1994 No 1813*].

56.5   COLLECTION AND GENERALLY

The Collector may distrain. [*TMA 1970, ss 61–64; FA 1989, ss 152–155*]. See also *Herbert Berry Associates Ltd v CIR HL 1977, 52 TC 113*. Where amount due (or any instalment) is less than £2,000, Collector may within six months of due date take summary magistrates' court proceedings. The Collector may recover the tax by proceedings in the County Court. [*TMA 1970, ss 65, 66; FA 1984, s 57; SI 1989 No 1300; SI 1991 Nos 724, 1625*]. But for limitations in Scotland and N. Ireland see *TMA 1970, s 65(4), s 66(3)(4), s 67; FA 1976, s 58; FA 1995, s 156*, and for time limits for proceedings see *Mann v Cleaver KB 1930, 15 TC 367* and *Lord Advocate v Butt CS 1992, 64 TC 471*. Unpaid tax (and arrears) may also be recovered (with full costs) as a Crown debt in the High Court. [*TMA 1970, s 68*]. The amount of an assessment which has become final cannot be re-opened in proceedings to collect the tax (*Pearlberg CA 1953, 34 TC 57; CIR v Soul CA 1976, 51 TC 86*), and it is not open to the taxpayer to raise the defence that the Revenue acted *ultra vires* in raising the assessment (*CIR v Aken CA 1990, 63 TC 395*).

For whether unpaid tax is a business liability for commercial etc. purposes, see *Conway v Wingate CA 1952, 31 ATC 148; Stevens v Britten CA 1954, 33 ATC 399; R v Vaccari CCA 1958, 37 ATC 104; In re Hollebone's Agreement CA 1959, 38 ATC 142*.

'Time to Pay' arrangements. By concession, under a 'time to pay' arrangement, a taxpayer enters into a negotiated agreement with the Revenue, which takes full account of his circumstances (e.g. illness, unemployment, unforeseen short-term business difficulties), and thereby commits to settle his tax liabilities by regular instalments. Clear reasons for allowing settlement over an extended period that runs beyond the due date must be established during negotiations and any such arrangement is normally subject to adequate provision being made to settle future liabilities on time. INTEREST AND SURCHARGES ON UNPAID TAX (42) is chargeable in the normal way on the full amount unpaid at the due date and not just on overdue instalments. However, a surcharge may be avoided where a 'Time to Pay' arrangement is in force (see 42.2 INTEREST AND SURCHARGES ON UNPAID TAX). (Revenue HINT/Self-Assessment Manual para 7.2.1, Personal Contact Manual para 4.8).

56.6   COMPANIES

Companies resident in the UK pay corporation tax and are not assessable to income tax on their profits.

They must deduct income tax from payments of yearly interest (see 22.3(ii) DEDUCTION OF TAX AT SOURCE) as well as from other annual payments, and account for such income tax to the Revenue. See Tolley's Corporation Tax.

56.7   CROWN PRIORITY

Crown priority in bankruptcy was abolished with effect from 29 December 1986, except for sums due at the 'relevant date'

(*a*)   on account of net tax deductions the bankrupt was liable to make under PAYE (55) from taxable earnings paid during the twelve months before that date, and (*b*)   in respect of deductions required to be made in the twelve months before that date under the CONSTRUCTION INDUSTRY SCHEME (20).

The '*relevant date*' is the date of the making of the bankruptcy order, or, if an interim receiver was appointed before that date, the date on which he was first appointed after presentation of the bankruptcy petition. [*Insolvency Act 1986, s 386, Sch 6* and corresponding Scottish legislation].

This remaining Crown priority is *abolished* by *Enterprise Act 2002, s 251* from 15 September 2003. [*SI 2003 No 2093*].

56.8   REMISSION OR REPAYMENT OF TAX IN CASES OF OFFICIAL ERROR

Arrears of tax. Arrears of income or capital gains tax may be waived if they result from the Revenue's failure to make proper and timely use of information supplied by:

(*a*)   a taxpayer about his or her own income, gains or personal circumstances;

(*b*)   an employer, where the information affects a taxpayer's coding; or

(*c*)   the Department for Work and Pensions (previously the DSS) about a taxpayer's retirement, disability or widow's State pension.

The waiver will normally apply only where the taxpayer could reasonably have believed that his or her tax affairs were in order, and either:

(i)   was notified of the arrears more than twelve months after the end of the tax year in which the Revenue received the information indicating that more tax was due; or

(ii)   was notified of an over-repayment after the end of the tax year following the year in which the repayment was made.

Exceptionally, arrears notified less than twelve months after the end of the relevant tax year may be waived if the Revenue either failed more than once to make proper use of the facts they had been given about one source of income, or allowed the arrears to build up over two whole tax years in succession by failing to make proper and timely use of information they had been given.

(Revenue Pamphlet IR 1, A19).

Where an **overpayment** of tax has arisen because of official error, and there is no doubt or dispute as to the facts, claims to repayment of tax are accepted outside the statutory time limits. (Revenue Pamphlet IR 1, B41).

56.9   OVERPAYMENT OF TAX

The Revenue's administrative practice relating to repayments of tax is as below.

(i)   Where an assessment has been made and this shows a repayment due to the taxpayer, repayment is invariably made of the full amount.

(ii)   Under SELF-ASSESSMENT (78), any amount repayable will be repaid on request.

(iii)   Where the end-of-year check applied to PAYE taxpayers who have not had a tax return for the year in question shows an overpayment of £10 or less, the repayment is not made automatically.

(iv)   Where tax assessed has been paid to the Collector in excess of the amount due, and the discrepancy is not noted before the payment has been processed, the excess is not repaid routinely by the computer system unless it is £1 or more, or where clerical intervention is required unless it is £10 or more.

The above tolerances are to minimise work which is highly cost ineffective, they cannot operate to deny a repayment to a taxpayer who has claimed it. (Revenue Pamphlet IR 131,

SP 6/95, 31 March 1995 as revised). Provisional repayments will not be made during the tax year to which a claim or claims relate if the tax involved does not exceed £50 in total. (Revenue Press Release 29 March 1989).

See 56.8 above as regards claims in cases of official error. See also 16.6 CLAIMS as regards repayment procedures.

Allocation of overpayments against underpayments. Where there are underpayments of tax, overpayments will automatically be reallocated against any other tax or Class 4 NICs (or interest thereon) outstanding in respect of the amended assessment unless the amendment is processed before 1 June following the end of the year of assessment and either the amount to be reallocated to the second instalment is £1,000 or more or the tax is not yet due and the taxpayer requests that no reallocation should be made. (Revenue Assessed Taxes Manual AT 8.701 *et seq.*). For an article on Revenue practice re allocations of overpayments under SELF-ASSESSMENT (78), see Revenue Tax Bulletin June 1999 pp 673, 674.

56.10   **OVER-REPAYMENTS OF TAX**

For **1995/96 and earlier years,** tax over-repaid (by actual payment or set-off) and not assessable in the normal way under *TMA 1970, s 29* (see 5.1, 5.3 ASSESSMENTS) may be recovered by assessment under Schedule D, Case VI as if it were unpaid tax. Any excess repayment supplement may be included in such an assessment or assessed separately. The time limit for such assessment is, if necessary, extended to the end of the chargeable period following that in which the repayment was made (without prejudice to the extended time limits which apply in cases of fraudulent or negligent conduct, see 30.3 FRAUDULENT OR NEGLIGENT CONDUCT). [*TMA 1970, s 30 as originally enacted; FA 1982, s 149; FA 1989, s 149(3); FA 1990, s 105*].

TMA 1970, s 30 continues to apply for **1996/97 and subsequent years,** but subject to the same exceptions (modified as appropriate) as apply to discovery assessments (see 5.3 ASSESSMENTS). The normal time limit for such an assessment is extended, if necessary, to the later of the end of the chargeable period following that in which the repayment was made and, where relevant, the day on which an officer of the Board's enquiries into a return delivered by the person concerned are statutorily completed (see 68.9 RETURNS), again subject to extension in cases of fraudulent or negligent conduct. [*TMA 1970, s 30(1B)(5); FA 1994, ss 196, 199(2)(a), Sch 19 para 4; FA 2001, s 88, Sch 29 para 23*].

The exercise by the Revenue of their discretion to raise an assessment under *TMA 1970, s 30* can be challenged only by way of judicial review (see 4.24 APPEALS) and not by appeal to the Appeal Commissioners (*Guthrie v Twickenham Film Studios Ltd Ch D 2002, 74 TC 733*).

56.11   **RECOVERY OF TAX PAID UNDER MISTAKE OF LAW**

It was held in *R v CIR (ex p. Woolwich Equitable Building Society) HL 1990, 63 TC 589* that at common law taxes extracted *ultra vires* are recoverable as of right and without need to invoke mistake of law by the taxpayer (and see 41.3 INTEREST ON OVERPAID TAX).

It was further held, *inter alia*, in *Deutsche Morgan Grenfell Group plc v CIR and A-G Ch D, [2003] STC 1017* that the common law remedy of restitution of payment made under a mistake of law applies to payments of tax as it does to other payments. By virtue of *Limitation Act 1980, s 32(1)(c)*, the six-year period of limitation in such a case does not begin to run until the plaintiff discovers the mistake (or could with reasonable diligence have discovered it). However, under legislation in *FA 2004* (reversing the effect of *Deutsche Morgan Grenfell*), *Limitation Act 1980, s 32(1)(c)* (and Scottish equivalent) does *not* apply in relation to a mistake of law relating to taxes administered by the Inland Revenue where the action for restitution is brought **after 7 September 2003**. The effect is that court actions for restitution based on mistake of law must generally be brought within six years (or five years under Scottish law) of the tax having been paid. If, after 19 November 2003, a pre-existing action is amended to include additional years, the amendment is no longer treated as backdated to the date of the original action. [*FA 2004, ss 320, 321*].

56.12   EQUITABLE LIABILITY

Where all other possible remedies have been exhausted by the taxpayer, the Revenue may be prepared to consider applying 'equitable liability' where it is clearly demonstrated that a liability assessed is greater than it would have been had the returns and supporting documentation been submitted at the proper time, provided that acceptable evidence is produced of what the correct liability should have been. It will not be sufficient to seek to replace the assessment with the taxpayer's (or accountant's) estimate of the liability. In such cases, the Revenue may be prepared to accept a reduced sum based on the evidence provided, having regard to all the relevant circumstances of the case, and not to pursue its right of recovery of the full amount. Full payment of the reduced sum would be expected.

The application of equitable liability is conditional on the taxpayer's affairs being brought fully up to date, and would be very unlikely to be applied more than once in favour of the same taxpayer.

Under self-assessment, even where, in the absence of a return, the Revenue has determined a taxpayer's liability, the taxpayer has until five years after the statutory filing date (or, if later, one year after the determination) to displace the determination with their own self-assessment (see 68.12 RETURNS). The point should therefore not often be reached where a determination can no longer be replaced, but where that does occur and the above conditions are fulfilled, equitable liability may be extended to meet this situation.

(Revenue Tax Bulletin August 1995 pp 245, 246).

57   Penalties

Cross-references. See 30 FRAUDULENT OR NEGLIGENT CONDUCT. See also 16.3 CLAIMS, 68.5 RETURNS as regards failure to keep records and 68.23 RETURNS as regards reasonable excuse for failure to make returns.

Simon's Direct Tax Service A3.802 *et seq.*

57.1   NOTIFICATION OF CHARGEABILITY

A person chargeable to income tax or capital gains tax for a particular tax year who has not been required by a notice under *TMA 1970, s 8* (see 68.2 RETURNS) to deliver a return for that year must, within six months after the end of that year, notify an officer of the Board that he is so chargeable. The maximum penalty for non-compliance is the amount of tax in which the person is assessed for that year which is not paid on or before 31 January following that year. A person is not required to give notice under these provisions if his total income for the year consists of income from the sources below and he has no chargeable gains. The said sources are those in respect of which

(*a*)   all payments etc. are dealt with under PAYE, or

(*b*)   all income has been or will be taken into account either in determining the chargeable person's liability to tax or under PAYE, or

(*c*)   the income is chargeable under Schedule F or is other income from which income tax has been, or is treated as having been, deducted, provided that the chargeable person is not liable for that year at the higher rate or (from 6 April 1999) the Schedule F upper rate, or

(*d*)   all income for that year is income on which the chargeable person could not become liable to tax under a self-assessment under *TMA 1970, s 9* (see 68.3 RETURNS) in respect of that year.

These provisions also apply with the appropriate modifications to 'relevant trustees' (as defined in 78.11 SELF-ASSESSMENT) of settlements.

[*TMA 1970, s 7; FA 1994, s 196, Sch 19 para 1; FA 1995, s 103(1)(2), s 115(1), Sch 21 para 1; F(No 2)A 1997, Sch 4 para 1; FA 1999, s 22(11); ITEPA 2003, Sch 6 para 124*].

As regards items within (*b*) above, the Revenue will normally accept that employees in receipt of copy form P11D (or equivalent particulars) from their employer (see 78.12 SELF-ASSESSMENT) can assume that any items on it not already taken into account for PAYE will be so taken into account, so there is no need to notify chargeability in respect of such items. Notice of chargeability is, however, necessary to the extent that the P11D is incorrect or incomplete or if the employee knows that the actual form has not been submitted to the Revenue. Employees are not relieved of any obligation to notify chargeability if they have not received a copy P11D or in respect of non-P11D items which ought to have been reported by the employer to the Revenue on other returns. (Revenue Pamphlet IR 131, SP 1/96, 1 February 1996).

Pension schemes. The trustees of approved occupational pension schemes with income or capital gains are within these provisions. See Pension Schemes Office Update No 49, 24 August 1998 and, for the detailed administrative arrangements, Revenue Tax Bulletin February 1999 pp 628, 629.

Simon's Direct Tax Service. See A3.816.

57.2   FAILURE TO DELIVER TAX RETURN ON OR BEFORE FILING DATE

A person (the taxpayer) who fails to deliver a return on or before the 'filing date' when required to do so by notice under *TMA 1970, s 8 or s 8A* (see 68.2 RETURNS) is liable to a

57.2 Penalties

penalty of £100. The *'filing date'* is 31 January following the tax year in question or, if later, the last day of the period of three months beginning with the day on which the said notice is given.

For continuing failure, a further penalty of up to £60 per day may be imposed by the Commissioners (but not at any time after the failure has been remedied) on application by an officer of the Board, such daily penalty to start from the day after the taxpayer is notified of the Commissioners' direction (but not for any day for which such a daily penalty has already been imposed). Although the Revenue is responsible for setting the amount of any daily penalty, it is understood that the Commissioners should not in practice impose a daily penalty of an unspecified amount.

If the failure continues for more than six months beginning with the filing date (i.e. the due date for delivery of the return — see 68.2 RETURNS), and no application for a daily penalty was made within those six months, the taxpayer is liable to a further £100 penalty. If failure continues after the anniversary of the filing date, and there would have been a liability under *TMA 1970, s 59B* (see 78.6 SELF-ASSESSMENT), based on a proper return promptly delivered, the taxpayer is liable to a further penalty of an amount not exceeding that liability. See 78.11 SELF-ASSESSMENT below as regards trustees.

If the taxpayer proves that his liability under *TMA 1970, s 59B*, based on a proper return promptly delivered, would not have exceeded a particular amount, his liability to penalties other than the daily and tax-geared penalties is reduced to that amount. Thus a payment on account, made under *TMA 1970, s 59A* or otherwise, which reduces the liability outstanding at 31 January to less than £100 will similarly reduce any automatic penalty otherwise chargeable (see Revenue Enquiry Manual EM 4562, Revenue Income Tax Self-Assessment Manual: The Legal Framework SALF 208, paras 2.68, 2.69). Where a number of tax years are being finalised together following late returns, the Revenue will not regard earlier years' overpayments as set against later years' underpayments so as to reduce or extinguish fixed penalties for the later years. (Tolley's Practical Tax 2002 p 152).

On an appeal against either of the £100 penalties (reduced where appropriate), the Commissioners may either confirm the penalty or, if it appears to them that throughout the period of failure the taxpayer had a reasonable excuse for not delivering the return, set it aside.

[TMA 1970, s 93; FA 1994, ss 196, 199(2)(a), Sch 19 para 25].

For the Revenue's approach to 'reasonable excuse' for failure to deliver a return, see Revenue Tax Bulletin April 1998 pp 527–529. Common examples which the Revenue might regard as reasonable are where they are satisfied that the taxpayer did not receive the return; where the return was posted in good time but held up by an unforeseen disruption to the postal service; where the taxpayer's records were lost through fire, flood or theft and could not be replaced in time to meet the deadline; where serious illness immediately before the filing date made timeous submission impossible; or the death of a close relative or domestic partner shortly before the deadline (provided that all necessary steps to meet the deadline had been taken). Examples of excuses *not* considered reasonable by the Revenue are claims that the return is too difficult to complete; pressure of work on the taxpayer or agent; failure by an agent; unavailability of information needed to complete the return; or the absence of a reminder that the return was overdue. It is, however, stressed that these are the Revenue's views, and that it is for the Commissioners to adjudicate where the taxpayer takes a different view. In this connection, see the National Association of Tax Commissioners website at www.natax.org.uk A taxpayer's political beliefs do not amount to a 'reasonable excuse' (*Gladders v Prior (Sp C 361), [2003] SSCD 245*). Although, as stated above, the 'reasonable excuse' must strictly continue throughout the period of default, in practice the Revenue normally allow a further 14 days for submission of the return after the excuse has ceased.

See also *Steeden v Carver (Sp C 212), [1999] SSCD 283*, in which reliance on the Revenue's advice as to the practical extension of a deadline, unequivocally given, was held to be 'as reasonable an excuse as could be found'. Following the decision in this case, the Revenue's practice for 1999/2000 returns onwards is as follows. They regard a return due on 31 January as delivered on time if found in a tax office post box when first opened on 1 February (or if delivered before midnight on 31 January by hand, courier or electronically). They do not charge a late filing penalty for returns subsequently delivered to the post box no later than first opening on 2 February (or delivered any time on 1 February by other means); however, such returns are nevertheless late, and the enquiry window is automatically extended as in 68.6(*b*) RETURNS (though in practice the Revenue did not take that point for 1998/99 returns — see Revenue 'Working Together' Bulletin April 2000 p 8). The same approach applies to later filing dates where the return is issued after 31 October (see 68.2 RETURNS). (Revenue Enquiry Manual EM 4563). This practice also applied, but in a slightly different form, for 1998/99 returns.

The Revenue's original intention was to use the daily penalty sanction above where the tax at risk was substantial and they believed the fixed penalties to be an insufficient deterrent (Revenue booklet SAT 2 (1995), para 2.74 (now out of print)), but they have since stated that they will be increasing their use of such sanctions. (Revenue Tax Bulletins February 2002 p 915, December 2003 p 1067).

See generally Revenue booklet SA/BK6.

Unsatisfactory returns. By concession, the Revenue do not charge a fixed late-filing penalty where

(*a*)   they reject a return as being 'unsatisfactory',

(*b*)   they consequently send it back (to whoever submitted it — taxpayer or agent) with an explanatory letter no earlier than the 13th day before the filing date (e.g. 18 January where the filing date is 31 January), and

(*c*)   they then receive a satisfactory return within 14 days from the date of the said letter.

An 'unsatisfactory' return is not the same as an incomplete return (for example, a return omitting income) for which the correct redress would be an enquiry (see 68.6 RETURNS) rather than rejection. A return is '*unsatisfactory*' if, for example, it is unsigned or incorrectly signed (see 68.2 RETURNS), it is not on the standard Revenue form (or agreed alternative — see 68.2 RETURNS) or supplementary pages are missing (see 78.1 SELF-ASSESSMENT). The 14-day period of grace will not be given where the original return is itself late or where the taxpayer appears to be using deliberate delaying tactics. This concession applies for 2000/01 returns onwards and will be kept under review. A similar concession applied to earlier years' self-assessment returns. (Revenue Tax Bulletin June 2001 pp 848, 849, February 2002 p 916). See 68.2 RETURNS for the circumstances in which a return is likely to be accepted even though it contains a provisional figure.

Partnership returns. The same fixed penalties (including the daily penalty) as under *TMA 1970, s 93* (above) apply in the case of failure to submit a partnership return as required by a notice under *TMA 1970, s 12AA* (see 68.13 RETURNS). However, there is no tax-geared penalty and no provision for reducing the £100 penalties. Each person who was a partner at any time during the period in respect of which the return was required is separately liable to each penalty. The penalties apply by reference to failure by the representative partner, i.e. the partner required by the notice under *TMA 1970, s 12AA* to deliver the return, or his successor (see 68.13 RETURNS). Where penalties are imposed on two or more partners, an appeal cannot be made otherwise than by way of composite appeal by the representative partner (or successor). The same reasonable excuse provisions apply as under *TMA 1970, s 93* but by reference to the representative partner (or successor).

57.3 Penalties

[*TMA 1970, s 93A; FA 1994, ss 196, 199(2)(a), Sch 19 para 26; FA 1996, s 123(8)–(11)*].

General. Political objections do not justify failure to make returns (*Turton v Birdforth Commrs Ch D 1970, 49 ATC 346*), nor do objections to the system of taxation (*Walsh v Croydon Commrs Ch D 1987, 60 TC 442*). The submission of a return marked 'to be advised' or some similar phrase does not satisfy the requirements and penalties may be incurred (*Cox v Poole General Commrs Ch D 1987, 60 TC 445*).

Pre-self-assessment. The following applies to returns for 1995/96 and earlier years where the notice to deliver was served after 5 April 1989. If a person other than a company fails to make a return when required to do so under *TMA 1970, s 8, s 8A*, or *s 9* (as applied for capital gains tax purposes by *TMA 1970, s 12*), he incurs a maximum penalty of £300. If his failure continues beyond the end of the tax year following that in which notice was served under one of those provisions, he is liable to a further penalty not exceeding the amount of tax (no amount being taken into account more than once) charged under assessments made on him or his personal representatives after that year on gains which should have been included in the return. A further penalty of up to £60 per day, not continuing after the failure has been remedied, is incurred if the failure continues after the non-tax-based penalty has been imposed (but not for any day for which such a daily penalty has already been imposed). Except in cases where a tax-based penalty is incurred, the rendering of the return prevents the imposition of a penalty. In addition, if the person proves that there was no income or chargeable gain to be included in the return, the overall penalty under the foregoing cannot exceed £100. [*TMA 1970, s 93(1)(2)(5)–(8) as previously enacted; FA 1988, Sch 3 para 28; FA 1989, s 162; FA 1990, s 90(3)*].

Simon's Direct Tax Service. See A3.805, A3.806.

57.3   **NEGLIGENCE OR FRAUD IN CONNECTION WITH RETURN OR ACCOUNTS**

Where a person fraudulently or negligently

- delivers an incorrect tax return under *TMA 1970, s 8* or *s 8A* (personal or trustees' return — see 68.2 RETURNS);

- makes any incorrect return, statement or declaration in connection with any claim for an allowance, deduction or relief; or

- submits to the Revenue or the Appeal Commissioners any incorrect accounts;

he is liable to a maximum penalty of an amount equal to the resulting tax underpayment. In arriving at the latter, one takes into account the tax year *in which* the return is delivered etc., the following tax year and any previous tax year. [*TMA 1970, s 95; FA 1988, Sch 14 Pt VIII; FA 1989, s 163; FA 1994, ss 196, 199(2), Sch 19 para 27*]. Liability to a penalty is supplementary to the liability to make good the tax underpayment itself.

For the above purposes, an innocent error is attributed to negligence unless it is rectified without unreasonable delay after its discovery by the taxpayer (or, following his death, by his personal representatives). Accounts submitted on a person's behalf are deemed to have been submitted by him unless he proves that they were submitted without his consent or connivance. [*TMA 1970, s 97*].

Use of a provisional or estimated figure in a return may result in its being incorrect, and subject to a penalty, if the figure was calculated without reasonable care or if the final figure could have been obtained before the return was filed (Revenue Tax Bulletin February 2002 p 916).

Partnerships. For 1996/97 and subsequent years, where a partner (the representative partner) delivers an incorrect partnership return (see 68.13 RETURNS), or, in connection with such a return, makes an incorrect statement or declaration or submits incorrect accounts, and either he does so fraudulently or negligently or his doing so is attributable to fraudulent or negligent conduct on the part of a 'relevant partner' (i.e. any person who was a partner at any time in the period covered by the return). Each relevant partner is liable to a penalty not exceeding the income tax (or corporation tax) underpaid by him as a result of the incorrectness. Where penalties are imposed on two or more partners, an appeal cannot be made otherwise than by way of composite appeal by the representative partner, or his successor (see 68.13 RETURNS). [*TMA 1970, s 95A; FA 1994, ss 196, 199(2)(a), Sch 19 para 28; FA 1996, s 123(12)(13); FA 2001, s 88, Sch 29 para 32*]. For earlier years, the general provisions described above apply equally to partnership returns.

Simon's Direct Tax Service. See A3.810.

57.4   FAILURE TO PRODUCE DOCUMENTS

A penalty applies where a person fails to comply with a notice or requirement under *TMA 1970, s 19A* or *TMA 1970, Sch 1A para 6(2)(3A)(b)* (notice requiring production of documents etc. for purpose of Revenue enquiry into a return — see 68.8 RETURNS). He is liable to a fixed penalty of £50 and, for continuing failure after the fixed penalty is imposed, a daily penalty not exceeding the 'relevant amount'. No penalty may be imposed after the failure has been remedied. An officer of the Board may determine the daily penalty under *TMA 1970, s 100* (see 57.12 below), in which case the '*relevant amount*' is £30, or may commence proceedings under *TMA 1970, s 100C* (see 57.14 below) for determination of the penalty by the Commissioners, in which case the '*relevant amount*' is £150. [*TMA 1970, s 97AA; FA 1994, ss 196, 199(2)(a), Sch 19 para 29; FA 1996, Sch 19 para 3(4); FA 1998, Sch 19 para 36*]. See Revenue 'Working Together' Bulletin April 2000 p 8 as regards discharge of penalties raised after 14 December 1998 for non-compliance with notices subsequently determined to be invalid because they did not allow 30 days *from receipt* for compliance.

Simon's Direct Tax Service. See A3.809.

57.5   FAILURE TO KEEP AND PRESERVE RECORDS

The maximum penalty for non-compliance with *TMA 1970, s 12B* (records to be kept and preserved for the purposes of self-assessment tax returns — see 68.5 RETURNS) in relation to any tax year is £3,000. [*TMA 1970, s 12B(5)–(5B); FA 1994, ss 196, 199(2)(3), Sch 19 para 3; FA 1995, s 103(7), s 105(6)(7); FA 1996, s 124(4)(5); FA 1998, Sch 19 para 6*]. The same applies for companies under corporation tax self-assessment. [*FA 1998, s 117, Sch 18 para 23*].

A separate maximum £3,000 penalty applies in relation to records relating to a claim made otherwise than in a self-assessment tax return (see 16.3 CLAIMS). [*TMA 1970, Sch 1A para 2A(4)(5); FA 1994, ss 196, 199, Sch 19 para 35; FA 1995, s 107(11), Sch 20 para 2; FA 1996, s 124(6)–(8); FA 1998, s 117, Sch 19 para 42*]. This also applies in relation to certain claims by companies under corporation tax self-assessment. [*FA 1998, s 117, Sch 18 para 57(4), para 58(3), para 59*].

Simon's Direct Tax Service. See A3.808.

57.6   TWO OR MORE TAX-RELATED PENALTIES IN RESPECT OF THE SAME TAX

Where two or more tax-related penalties are determined by reference to the same income tax, capital gains tax or corporation tax liability, the aggregate penalty is reduced to the greater or greatest of those separate penalties. [*TMA 1970, s 97A; FA 1988, s 129; FA 1998, s 117, Sch 18 para 90, Sch 19 para 37*]. See 57.10 below for mitigation of penalties.

57.7 Penalties

57.7 ASSISTING IN PREPARATION OF INCORRECT RETURN ETC.

Assisting in or inducing the preparation or delivery of any information, return, accounts or other document known to be incorrect and to be, or to be likely to be, used for any tax purpose carries a maximum penalty of £3,000. [*TMA 1970, s 99; FA 1989, s 166*]. For the taxpayer's position where an agent has been negligent or fraudulent, see *Mankowitz v Special Commrs & CIR Ch D 1971, 46 TC 707* and cf. *Clixby v Pountney Ch D 1967, 44 TC 515* and *Pleasants v Atkinson Ch D 1987, 60 TC 228*.

57.8 INTEREST ON PENALTIES

All of the above penalties carry interest, calculated from the due date (broadly, 30 days after issue of a notice of determination by an officer of the Board — see 57.12 below, or immediately upon determination by Appeal Commissioners or judgment of the High Court — see 57.14, 57.15 below) to the date of payment. [*TMA 1970, s 103A; FA 1994, ss 196, 199(2)(3), Sch 19 para 33; FA 1995, s 103(7), s 115(8); FA 1998, s 117, Sch 19 para 40; SI 1998 No 311*]. For income tax and capital gains tax, rates of interest on penalties are synonymous with those on unpaid tax — see 42.1 INTEREST AND SURCHARGES ON UNPAID TAX.

57.9 SPECIAL RETURNS

Failure to render any information or particulars or any return, certificate, statement or other document which is required, whether by notice or otherwise, under the provisions listed in *TMA 1970, s 98* is the subject of a maximum penalty of £300, plus £60 for each day the failure continues after that penalty is imposed (but not for any day for which such a daily penalty has already been imposed). These penalties are increased by a factor of ten in the case of a failure under *ICTA 1988, s 765A* (movements of capital between residents of EC Member States). The maximum penalty for an incorrect return etc. given fraudulently or negligently is £3,000. Penalties for failure to render information etc. required by notice cannot be imposed after the failure is rectified, and daily penalties can similarly not be imposed where the information etc. was required other than by notice. [*TMA 1970, s 98; FA 1980, s 121; FA 1989, s 164(1)–(4)(7); FA 1990, s 68(3)(4)*].

Failure to allow access to computers renders a person liable to a maximum £500 penalty. [*FA 1988, s 127*].

See 53.19 PARTNERSHIPS as regards penalties under *TMA 1970, s 98B* in relation to European Economic Interest Groupings.

PAYE returns etc. Special penalties are imposed for failure to make annual returns required under PAYE (see 55.9(*a*) PAY AS YOU EARN) or the construction industry scheme (see 20.7 CONSTRUCTION INDUSTRY SCHEME) by the statutory filing date, i.e. by 19 May following the end of the tax year for which the return is required. These are a penalty of £100 for each month or part month (up to twelve) during which the failure continues and for each 50 persons (or part where the total is not a multiple of 50) in respect of whom particulars should have been included in the return, and, if the failure continues beyond twelve months, an additional penalty of the amount payable for the tax year to which the return relates which remained unpaid at 19 April following that year. If an incorrect return is fraudulently or negligently made, the penalty is the difference between the amount payable under the return and the amount which would have been payable had the return been correct. [*TMA 1970, s 98A; FA 1989, s 165; ITEPA 2003, Sch 6 para 138; SI 1993 No 743, reg 40A; SI 1998 No 2622, reg 33; SI 2003 No 2682, regs 73, 146*].

By concession, no penalty is charged if the return is received on or before the last business day within seven days following the filing date (Revenue Pamphlet IR 1, B46).

See the 2003/04 and earlier editions as regards PAYE etc. returns for 1996/97 and earlier years.

See 20.7 CONSTRUCTION INDUSTRY SCHEME for other penalties specifically relating to that scheme.

Simon's Direct Tax Service. See A3.817, A3.818.

57.10 **MITIGATION OF PENALTIES**

The Board may mitigate penalties before or after judgment. [*TMA 1970, s 102; FA 1989, s 168(4)*]. In considering mitigation, credit will be given for co-operation of taxpayer (Revenue Press Release 1 August 1977). A binding agreement by a taxpayer to pay an amount in composition cannot be repudiated afterwards by him or his executors (*A-G v Johnstone KB 1926, 10 TC 758; A-G v Midland Bank Trustee Co KB 1934, 19 TC 136; Richards KB 1950, 33 TC 1*).

Negotiated settlements. In the case of tax-based penalties where a maximum penalty of 100% is in strict law exigible, the inspector will start with the figure of 100% and then take the following factors into account in arriving at the penalty element which he will expect to be included in any offer in settlement of liabilities.

(*a*)   Disclosure. A reduction of up to 20% (or 30% where there has been full voluntary disclosure), depending on how much information was provided, how soon, and how that contributed to settling the investigation.

(*b*)   Co-operation. A reduction of up to 40%, depending upon a comparison of the extent of co-operation given in the investigation with the co-operation which the inspector believes would have been possible.

(*c*)   Gravity. A reduction of up to 40%, depending upon the nature of the offence, how long it continued and the amounts involved.

(Revenue Pamphlet IR 73). See, for example, *Caesar v Inspector of Taxes (Sp C 142), [1998] SSCD 1*.

For power of Revenue to enter into agreements in full settlement of liabilities in investigation cases, see 30.11 FRAUDULENT OR NEGLIGENT CONDUCT.

See also 68.23 RETURNS as regards *TMA 1970, s 118(2)* (reasonable excuse for failure etc.).

For the validity of tax amnesties, see *R v CIR (ex p. National Federation of Self-Employed and Small Businesses Ltd) HL 1981, 55 TC 133*.

Simon's Direct Tax Service. See A3.826.

57.11 **COMMISSIONERS' PRECEPTS**

Summary penalties (to be treated as tax assessed and due and payable) may be determined by Commissioners against any party to proceedings before them who fails to comply with a precept, order for inspection etc. (see 4.10 APPEALS). The maximum penalty is £300 in the case of the General Commissioners, £10,000 in the case of the Special Commissioners (and in the case of the General Commissioners, a daily penalty up to £60 may also be imposed for continuing failure). A penalty up to £10,000 may similarly be imposed for failure to comply with any other direction of the Special Commissioners (including in relation to a preliminary hearing). [*SI 1994 No 1811, reg 24(1)(3); SI 1994 No 1812, reg 10(1)(3)(4)*]. If a person on whom a witness summons is served (see 4.9 APPEALS) fails to attend in obedience thereto, or attends but refuses to be sworn or to affirm, or refuses to answer any lawful question, or refuses to produce any document required by the summons, the Commissioners may summarily determine a penalty against that person, to be treated as tax assessed and due and payable. The maximum penalty is £1,000 in the case of the General

57.12 Penalties

Commissioners, £10,000 in the case of the Special Commissioners. [*SI 1994 No 1811, reg 24(2)(3); SI 1994 No 1812, reg 4(12)(13)*].

Appeal against such summary penalties lies to the High Court (or Court of Session). [*TMA 1970, s 53 (as inserted by SI 1994 No 1813)*]. For the procedure on such appeals, see *QT Discount Foodstores Ltd v Warley Commrs Ch D 1981, 57 TC 268* and, for a case in which penalties were quashed because the taxpayer's evidence that he was unable to supply the information in question was not properly tested, *Boulton v Poole Commrs Ch D 1988, 60 TC 718*.

For appeals against penalties for non-compliance with precepts etc. see *Shah v Hampstead Commrs Ch D 1974, 49 TC 651; Chapman v Sheaf Commrs Ch D 1975, 49 TC 689; Toogood v Bristol Commrs Ch D 1976, 51 TC 634* and *[1977] STC 116; Campbell v Rochdale Commrs Ch D 1975, 50 TC 411; B & S Displays Ltd v Special Commrs Ch D 1978, 52 TC 318; Galleri v Wirral Commrs Ch D 1978, [1979] STC 216; Beach v Willesden Commrs Ch D 1981, 55 TC 663; Stoll v High Wycombe Commrs and CIR Ch D 1992, 64 TC 587; Wilson v Leek Commrs and CIR Ch D 1993, 66 TC 537.*

57.12 PROCEDURE

The following applies in relation to events occurring after 26 July 1989. For the procedure as respects events occurring on or before that date, see the 2003/04 and earlier editions.

Except in the case of

(a) penalty proceedings instituted before the courts in cases of suspected fraud (see 57.15 below); or

(b) penalties under

- *TMA 1970, s 93(1)(a)* as it applied before self-assessment (£300 late filing penalty — see 57.2 above);

- *TMA 1979, s 94* as it had effect for notices served before 1 January 1994 (late company tax return filing penalty for pre-Pay and File accounting periods, i.e. those ended before 1 October 1993);

- *TMA 1970, s 98(1)(i)* (£300 penalty for non-filing of returns etc. under the provisions listed in *TMA 1970, s 98* — see 57.9 above);

- *TMA 1970, s 98B(2)(a)* as it applied before self-assessment (£300 late filing penalty for European Economic Interest Groupings); or

- *TMA 1970, s 98C(1)(a)* (penalty of up to £5,000 under 3.24 ANTI-AVOIDANCE); or

(c) penalties in respect of which application to the Commissioners is specifically required, as mentioned where relevant in the preceding paragraphs of this chapter (for example, the daily penalty for late income tax and capital gains tax returns as in 57.2 above),

an authorised officer of the Board may make a determination imposing a penalty under any tax provision and setting it at such amount as, in his opinion, is correct or appropriate.

The notice of determination must state the date of issue and the time within which an appeal can be made. It cannot be altered unless

- there is an appeal (see 57.13 below), or

- an authorised officer of the Board discovers that the penalty is or has become insufficient (in which case he may make a further determination), or

- the penalty is an automatic or tax-related penalty under *TMA 1970, s 93* (late delivery of personal or trustees' tax returns — see 57.2 above) or arises under *TMA*

1970, s 94(6) or *FA 1998, Sch 18 para 18(2)* (tax-related penalty for late filing of company tax returns), and an authorised officer of the Board subsequently discovers that the amount of tax is or has become excessive (in which case it is to be revised accordingly).

A penalty under these provisions is due for payment 30 days after the issue of the notice of determination, and is treated as tax charged in an assessment which is due and payable. A determination which could have been made on a person who has died can be made on his personal representatives, and is then payable out of his estate.

[*TMA 1970, ss 100, 100A; FA 1989, s 167; FA 1990, Sch 11 para 3(2), para 5; FA 1998, s 117, Sch 19 para 38; FA 2001, s 91; FA 2004, s 315(2); SI 1994 No 1813*].

Simon's Direct Tax Service. See A3.820.

57.13 **Appeals.** Subject to the following points, the general APPEALS (4) provisions apply to an appeal against a determination of a penalty as in 57.12 above.

TMA 1970, s 50(6)–(8) (see 4.11 APPEALS) do not apply. Instead (subject to below), on appeal the Commissioners can

- in the case of a penalty which is required to be of a particular amount, set the determination aside, confirm it, or alter it to the correct amount, and

- in any other case, set the determination aside, confirm it if it seems appropriate, or reduce it (including to nil) or increase it as seems appropriate (but not beyond the permitted maximum).

Neither *TMA 1970, s 50(6)–(8)* nor the above apply on an appeal against a determination of an automatic late filing penalty for personal or partnership tax returns (see 57.2 above), where the 'reasonable excuse' let-out may have effect (see 57.2 above for the options open to the Commissioners in those cases).

Without prejudice to any right to have a case stated by the General Commissioners for the opinion of the High Court, or to appeal against a Special Commissioners' decision (see 4.19, 4.23 APPEALS), an appeal lies to the High Court (in Scotland, the Court of Session).

[*TMA 1970, s 100B; FA 1989, s 167; FA 1994, ss 196, 199, Sch 19 para 31; FA 1995, s 115(7); SI 1994 No 1813*].

Simon's Direct Tax Service. See A3.824.

57.14 **Proceedings before Commissioners.** For a penalty within 57.12(*b*) above or the higher daily penalty within 57.4 above (failure to produce documents), an authorised officer of the Board can commence proceedings before the General or Special Commissioners (except for a penalty under *TMA 1970, s 98C(1)(a)*, where proceedings can be brought only before the Special Commissioners). The proceedings are by way of information in writing to the Commissioners, upon summons to the defendant (or defender); and they are heard and decided in a summary way. An appeal lies to the High Court (or Court of Session) on a question of law, or by the defendant (defender) against the amount. The court can set the determination aside, confirm it if it seems appropriate, or reduce it (including to nil) or increase it as seems appropriate (but not beyond the permitted maximum). The penalty is treated as tax charged in an assessment and due and payable. [*TMA 1970, s 100C; FA 1989, s 167; FA 2004, s 315(3)*].

Simon's Direct Tax Service. See A3.821.

57.15 **Proceedings before court.** If the Board considers that liability for a penalty arises from fraud by any person, proceedings can be brought in the High Court (or Court of Session).

57.16 Penalties

If the court does not find fraud proved, it can nevertheless impose a penalty to which it considers the person liable. [*TMA 1970, s 100D; FA 1989, s 167*].

Simon's Direct Tax Service. See **A3.822**.

57.16 **General matters.** Non-receipt of notice of the hearing at which the Commissioners awarded penalties is not a ground of appeal to the courts *(Kenny v Wirral Commrs Ch D 1974, 50 TC 405; Campbell v Rochdale Commrs Ch D 1975, 50 TC 411).*

A mere denial of liability to penalties implies an intention by the taxpayer to set up a case in refutation, and details must be supplied (*CIR v Jackson CA 1960, 39 TC 357*).

For the validity of penalty proceedings while assessments remain open, see *A-G for Irish Free State v White SC (RI) 1931, 38 TC 666* and *R v Havering Commrs (ex p. Knight) CA 1973, 49 TC 161.* For other procedural matters, see *Collins v Croydon Commrs Ch D 1969, 45 TC 566; Bales v Rochford Commrs Ch D 1964, 42 TC 17; Sparks v West Brixton Commrs Ch D, [1977] STC 212; Moschi v Kensington Commrs Ch D 1979, 54 TC 403;* and for other appeals against penalties for failure to make returns, see *Dunk v Havant Commrs Ch D 1976, 51 TC 519; Napier v Farnham Commrs CA, [1978] TR 403; Garnham v Haywards Heath Commrs Ch D 1977, [1978] TR 303; Cox v Poole Commrs and CIR (No 1) Ch D 1987, 60 TC 445; Montague v Hampstead Commrs & Others Ch D 1989, 63 TC 145; Cox v Poole Commrs (No 2) Ch D 1989, 63 TC 277.*

For variation etc. of penalties by the court, see *Dawes v Wallington Commrs Ch D 1964, 42 TC 200; Salmon v Havering Commrs CA 1968, 45 TC 77; Williams v Special Commrs Ch D 1974, 49 TC 670; Wells v Croydon Commrs Ch D 1968, 47 ATC 356; Taylor v Bethnal Green Commrs Ch D 1976, [1977] STC 44; Stableford v Liverpool Commrs Ch D 1982, [1983] STC 162; Sen v St. Anne, Westminster Commrs Ch D, [1983] STC 415; Jolley v Bolton Commrs Ch D 1986, 65 TC 242; Lear v Leek Commrs Ch D 1986, 59 TC 247; Walsh v Croydon Commrs Ch D 1987, 60 TC 442; Fox v Uxbridge Commrs & CIR Ch D 2001, [2002] STC 455.*

For the test used by the court in considering whether penalties are excessive, see *Brodt v Wells Commrs Ch D 1987, 60 TC 436.* Per Scott LJ, penalties awarded by different bodies of Commissioners 'should, in relation to similar cases, bear some resemblance to one another'.

Statements made or documents produced by or on behalf of a taxpayer are admissible as evidence in proceedings against him notwithstanding that reliance on the Board's practice in cases of full disclosure (the 'Hansard Statement' — see 30.12 FRAUDULENT OR NEGLIGENT CONDUCT) or their policy on mitigating penalties (see 57.10 above) may have induced him to make or produce them. [*TMA 1970, s 105; FA 1989, s 168(5); FA 2003, s 206(1)(2)(5)*].

57.17 **TIME LIMITS**

The following applies in relation to events occurring after 26 July 1989. For the position as respects events occurring on or before that date, see the 2003/04 and earlier editions.

The time within which a penalty can be determined, or proceedings can be commenced, depends on the penalty, as follows.

(*a*)   If the penalty is ascertainable by reference to tax payable, the time is

    (i)   six years after the date the penalty was incurred, or

    (ii)   (subject to below) a later time within three years after the final determination of the amount of tax.

(*b*) If the penalty arises under *TMA 1970, s 99* (assisting in preparation of incorrect return etc. — see 57.7 above) the time is twenty years after the date it was incurred.

(*c*) In any other case, the time is six years from the time when the penalty was, or began to be, incurred.

Where the person liable has died, and the determination falls to be made in relation to his personal representatives, the extension in (*a*)(ii) above does not apply if the tax is charged in an assessment made more than six years after 31 January following the chargeable period for which it is charged. For 1995/96 and earlier years, this applied by reference to tax charged in an assessment made more than six years after the chargeable period for which it is charged.

[*TMA 1970, s 103; FA 1989, s 169; FA 1994, ss 196, 199, Sch 19 para 32*].

Final determination of amount of tax. Provisional agreement of the amount due subject to the inspector being satisfied later with statements of assets, etc. is not final determination (*Carco Accessories Ltd v CIR CS 1985, 59 TC 45*).

Simon's Direct Tax Service. See A3.823.

57.18   BANKRUPTS

Penalties awarded after a bankruptcy are provable debts, but in practice the Revenue does not proceed for penalties during a bankruptcy where there are other creditors. The trustee may agree to compromise any penalties awarded but the compromise must also be agreed by the bankrupt. (*Re Hurren Ch D 1982, 56 TC 494*).

57.19   LIABILITY UNDER CRIMINAL LAW

'False statements to the prejudice of the Crown and public revenue' are criminal offences (*R v Hudson CCA 1956, 36 TC 561*). False statements in income tax returns, or for obtaining any allowance, reduction or repayment may involve liability to imprisonment for up to two years, under *Perjury Act 1911, s 5*, for 'knowingly and wilfully' making materially false statements or returns for tax purposes. Also, in Scotland, summary proceedings may be taken under *TMA 1970, s 107*.

In relation to any criminal prosecution case, the Revenue will

(*a*) refrain from taking steps to recover civil money penalties on the basis of fraud in respect of an offence which has been before the criminal courts;

(*b*) seek appropriate civil money penalties in respect of any offence which has not been brought before the courts; and

(*c*) reserve the right to seek, where there are grounds to do so, a civil penalty in respect of negligence by a taxpayer who has been acquitted of criminal intent in respect of a prosecution for fraud.

(Revenue Pamphlet IR 131, SP 2/88).

The Revenue have an unrestricted power to conduct a prosecution in the Crown Court, there being no requirement for the consent of the Attorney-General (*R (oao Hunt) v Criminal Cases Review Commission DC, [2000] STC 1110*).

See 30.11 FRAUDULENT OR NEGLIGENT CONDUCT as regards acceptance of money settlements instead of institution of criminal proceedings. See 35.4 INLAND REVENUE: ADMINISTRATION as regards Revenue powers generally.

Penalties imposed for non-declaration of income and calculated as a percentage of the tax lost have been held to be criminal (rather than civil) penalties for the purposes of the

57.20 Penalties

European Convention on Human Rights (King v United Kingdom (No 2) ECHR, [2004] STC 911).

Falsification etc. of documents which are required to be produced as in 30.7 FRAUDULENT OR NEGLIGENT CONDUCT is a criminal offence punishable, on summary conviction, by a fine of the statutory maximum or, on indictment, by a fine or imprisonment for up to two years or both. [*TMA 1970, s 20BB; FA 1989, s 145*].

Offence of fraudulent evasion of income tax. A person who is knowingly concerned in the fraudulent evasion of income tax (by him or any other person) is liable, on summary conviction, to imprisonment for up to six months and/or a fine not exceeding the statutory maximum (£5,000), or on conviction on indictment, to imprisonment for up to seven years and/or an unlimited fine. This applies to things done or omitted after 31 December 2000. [*FA 2000, s 144*]. For an article giving the Revenue's views on conduct amounting to this offence, see Revenue Tax Bulletin October 2000 pp 782, 783.

Simon's Direct Tax Service. See A3.830.

57.20 VALUE ADDED TAX, EXCISE DUTIES ETC.

VAT penalties and surcharge are not allowed as a deduction for tax purposes. [*ICTA 1988, s 827(1)*]. See Tolley's Value Added Tax under Penalties. Excise penalties under *FA 1994, ss 8–11* are similarly disallowed. [*ICTA 1988, s 827(1A); FA 1994, s 18(7)*]. So are penalties under *FA 2003, ss 25, 26* (evasion of, or breach of rules relating to, import and export taxes and duties). [*ICTA 1988, s 827(1E); FA 2003, s 40*].

57.21 INSURANCE PREMIUM TAX, LANDFILL TAX, CLIMATE CHANGE LEVY AND AGGREGATES LEVY

Penalties and interest under the insurance premium tax, landfill tax, climate change levy and aggregates levy provisions are not allowed as a deduction for tax purposes. [*ICTA 1988, s 827(1B)(1C)(1D)(1E); FA 1994, Sch 7 para 31; FA 1996, Sch 5 para 40; FA 2000, Sch 7 para 4; FA 2001, s 49(3)*].

58   Pension Income

Simon's Direct Tax Service E4.126.

58.1   CHARGE TO TAX ON PENSION INCOME

The pensions, annuities etc. listed in 58.2 below are chargeable to tax as pension income. *Except where otherwise stated* in 58.2,

- the chargeable amount is the full amount accruing in the tax year (regardless of when paid); and

- the chargeable person is the person receiving or entitled to the income.

The chargeable amount is subject to any deductions due under the payroll giving scheme (see 14.18 CHARITIES) and the 10% deduction mentioned in 58.2(*l*) below.

[*ITEPA 2003, ss 565–568*].

Except where otherwise stated in 58.2 below, and subject also to the exemptions in 58.4 below, the charge applies regardless of the residence status of the recipient. See 58.3, 58.4 below for exempt pension income generally.

Most taxable pension income is within the scope of PAYE (55) (see the list at *ITEPA 2003, s 683(3)*).

Before 2003/04, except in the case of certain overseas pensions within Schedule D, Case V, the charge to tax on pensions was under Schedule E. However, a pension is not an employment, so retired employees are not chargeable on the provision of benefits in kind (see 75.16 SCHEDULE E—EMPLOYMENT INCOME). For example, they are not chargeable in respect of the provision after retirement of medical insurance under the former employer's group medical scheme, except where the expense of providing such insurance represents a specific part of the retired person's pension, a supplementary pension, part of an unapproved pension scheme or part of a termination package (Revenue Employment Income Manual EIM 21764).

A disability benefit paid to a redundant employee from the former employer company pension fund was held to be chargeable as a pension (*Johnson v Holleran Ch D 1988, 61 TC 428; Johnson v Farquhar Ch D 1991, 64 TC 385*).

58.2   TAXABLE INCOME

The chargeable pensions, annuities etc. referred to in 58.1 above are as listed below. These are subject to the exemptions in 58.3, 58.4 below.

(*a*)   **UK pensions,** i.e. any pension paid by or on behalf of a person within the UK and not within any of (*c*)–(*p*) below. These include voluntary pensions and pensions capable of being discontinued. [*ITEPA 2003, ss 569–572; ICTA 1988, s 19(1), paras 2, 3, s 133(2); FA 1989, s 41*].

(*b*)   **Foreign pensions,** i.e. any pension paid by or on behalf of a person outside the UK to a person resident in the UK and not within any of (*c*)–(*p*) below. These include voluntary pensions, and pensions capable of being discontinued, paid by former employers or their successors. The chargeable amount is computed as for the purposes of Schedule D, Case V (before 2003/04 the charge was *under* Case V) and is **90%** of the amount of income arising in the tax year, other than where the remittance basis applies (for which see 73.5 SCHEDULE D, CASES IV AND V and 64 REMITTANCE BASIS). [*ITEPA 2003, ss 573–576; ICTA 1988, s 18(1)–(3), ss 58, 59(1), s 65(1)(2)(4)–(9), s 68; FA 1994, ss 207(1)(3), 218*]. See 51.13 NON-RESIDENTS AND

OTHER OVERSEAS MATTERS for reliefs potentially available for unremittable overseas income; these apply equally to foreign pensions.

(c)   **UK social security pensions**, i.e. the State pension and similar benefits included in the list at 83.3 SOCIAL SECURITY, subject to the partial exemption at 58.3(*h*) below for child dependency additions. [*ITEPA 2003, ss 577–579; ICTA 1988, s 19(1), para 2, s 617(1); FA 1989, s 41; FA 2004, Sch 17 para 9(4)*].

(d)   **Pensions and annuities** paid under a **retirement benefits scheme** (see 67 RETIREMENT SCHEMES) that is approved or being considered for approval, and annuities acquired using funds held for such a scheme. [*ITEPA 2003, ss 580–582, 586, Sch 6 para 76; ICTA 1988, s 597; FA 1989, s 41; FA 1994, s 110*]. The charge also covers annuities paid under, or acquired using funds held for, a former approved superannuation fund (as in 67.13 RETIREMENT SCHEMES). The chargeable amount is the full amount of the annuity paid in the tax year. [*ITEPA 2003, ss 591–592, 594, Sch 6 para 81; ICTA 1988, s 608(1)(4)*].

(e)   **Unauthorised payments** (including any transfer of assets or other money's worth but excluding anything within (*n*) below) from an **approved retirement benefits scheme** (see 67 RETIREMENT SCHEMES) to (or for the benefit of) an employee (or, after 30 November 2000, an ex-spouse of an employee) other than in the course of payment of a pension or annuity. The chargeable amount is the total amount or value of payments made in the tax year. The chargeable person is the person to whom (or for whose benefit) the payment is made. The charge also covers unauthorised payments from a former approved superannuation fund (as in 67.13 RETIREMENT SCHEMES). Before 2003/04, an unauthorised payment by a marine pilots' benefit fund (see 67.11 RETIREMENT SCHEMES) was instead taxable under Schedule D, Case VI. [*ITEPA 2003, ss 583–588, 593, 594, Sch 6 para 80(6); ICTA 1988, s 599A(9), s 600, s 607(3)(b)(iv), s 608(1); FA 1989, Sch 6 paras 12, 13; FA 1999, Sch 10 para 8; SI 2000 No 1093*].

(f)   **Annuities** acquired from funds held for the purposes of an **approved personal pension scheme** (see 60 PERSONAL PENSION SCHEMES (AND STAKEHOLDER PENSIONS)). For 2003/04 onwards, it is made explicit that the chargeable amount is the full amount of the annuity received in the tax year. [*ITEPA 2003, ss 595–597, Sch 6 para 96; ICTA 1988, s 648A; FA 1994, s 109*].

(g)   **Income withdrawals** (within 60.2(ii) or (iv) PERSONAL PENSION SCHEMES (AND STAKEHOLDER PENSIONS)) under **approved personal pension arrangements**. The chargeable amount is the total amount of income withdrawals made in the tax year. [*ITEPA 2003, ss 598–600, 604, Sch 6 para 91; ICTA 1988, s 643(5); FA 1995, Sch 11 para 11*].

(h)   **Unauthorised payments** (as defined, and including any transfer of assets or other money's worth) from a **personal pension scheme** (see 60 PERSONAL PENSION SCHEMES (AND STAKEHOLDER PENSIONS)). The chargeable amount is the total amount or value of payments made in the tax year. The chargeable person is the individual who made the personal pension arrangements and to whom (or for whose benefit) the payment is made. [*ITEPA 2003, ss 601–604; ICTA 1988, s 647*].

(j)   **Annuities** paid under an **approved retirement annuity contract** (see 66 RETIREMENT ANNUITIES). The chargeable amount is the full amount of the annuity arising in the tax year. [*ITEPA 2003, ss 605–608*]. Such annuities are *not* within PAYE (see 66.1). Before 2003/04, such annuities were chargeable under Schedule D, Case III (see 66.1).

(k)   **Other employment-related annuities** (where not covered by any of (*d*)–(*j*) above but including annuities from a non-UK source if paid to a UK resident). These comprise annuities purchased by someone in recognition of another's services in an office or employment, annuities under a 'sponsored superannuation scheme' (as defined by *ICTA 1988, s 624(1)*) and certain annuities for the benefit of dependants. The chargeable amount is

- (if the annuity arises from a UK source) the full amount of the annuity arising in the tax year; or

- (if the annuity arises from a non-UK source), the amount on which tax would be chargeable if the charge were under Schedule D, Case V (i.e. as for foreign pensions in (*b*) above).

[*ITEPA 2003, ss 609–614*].

Such annuities are *not* within PAYE but are instead subject to DEDUCTION OF TAX AT SOURCE (22.2). Before 2003/04, such annuities were chargeable under, depending on the source, Schedule D, Case III or Schedule D, Case V itself.

(*l*)   **Overseas government pensions** payable in the UK *to* a UK resident (or to his widow, widower, child, relative or dependant) in respect of overseas government service, and *by* (or on behalf of) the government of a British dominion or protectorate or a country mentioned in *British Nationality Act 1981, Sch 3* and otherwise than out of UK or NI public revenue. These include voluntary pensions and pensions capable of being discontinued. A **10%** deduction is allowed from the amount otherwise chargeable. [*ITEPA 2003, ss 615–618; ICTA 1988, s 19(1), para 4, s 133(2), s 196; FA 1989, s 41*]. In *Magraw v Lewis KB 1933, 18 TC 222*, the taxpayer was given no reduction for foreign exchange differences and no deduction for costs of unsuccessful litigation against the overseas government.

(*m*)   Periodical payments out of the **House of Commons Members' Fund**. The chargeable amount is the total amount of payments made in the tax year. [*ITEPA 2003, ss 619–622; ICTA 1988, s 613(3)*].

(*n*)   **Surplus additional voluntary contributions** paid to or for an employee (or office holder) in pursuance of a duty to return surplus funds (see 67.8 RETIREMENT SCHEMES under Payments to employees). Payment includes any transfer of assets or other money's worth. The chargeable amount is the grossed up (at basic rate) equivalent of the total amount or value of the payments made in the tax year. The chargeable person is the employee to whom (or for whose benefit) the payment is made. He is deemed to have paid basic rate tax on the amount chargeable, but that tax is not repayable. [*ITEPA 2003, ss 623–628, Sch 6 para 77; ICTA 1988, s 599A(5)–(8); FA 1989, Sch 6 para 12; FA 1996, s 122(7)*]. Before 2003/04, the charge was under Schedule D, Case VI but was similarly computed.

(*p*)   **Pre-1973 pensions previously paid by Commonwealth governments** and for which, under *Overseas Pensions Act 1973*, the British Government took over responsibility for payment. (Any part of the pension representing statutory increases is excluded from this heading and instead falls within (*a*) above.) The chargeable amount is the amount on which tax would be chargeable if the charge were under Schedule D, Case V (i.e. as for foreign pensions in (*b*) above). [*ITEPA 2003, ss 629–632; ICTA 1988, s 616(3)(4)*]. See also 58.3(*f*) below.

(*q*)   **Annual payments** made **voluntarily**, or **capable of being discontinued**, by former employers or their successors (including payments from a non-UK source to a UK resident). If the payment is from a UK source, the chargeable amount is computed as in 58.1 above. If from a non-UK source, the chargeable amount is the amount on which tax would be chargeable if the charge were under Schedule D, Case V (i.e. as for foreign pensions in (*b*) above); before 2003/04, the charge was under

58.3 Pension Income

Case V itself. [*ITEPA 2003, ss 633–636; ICTA 1988, ss 58(2), 133(1); FA 1989, s 41*].

58.3 **GENERAL EXEMPTIONS**

General exemptions from the charge to tax on pension income are as listed below. See 59.4 below for exemptions specific to non-UK residents.

(*a*)   **Lump sums** provided by a tax-exempt pension scheme (see 67.12 RETIREMENT SCHEMES for exceptions), approved personal pension arrangements (see 60 PERSONAL PENSION SCHEMES (AND STAKEHOLDER PENSIONS) or a retirement annuity contract (see 66.1 RETIREMENT ANNUITIES). See also (*k*) below.

(*b*)   Pensions and annuities paid to holders of an '**award for bravery**' in respect of the award. For this purpose, an '*award for bravery*' means the Victoria Cross, George Cross, Albert Medal, Edward Medal, Military Cross, Distinguished Flying Cross, Distinguished Conduct Medal, Conspicuous Gallantry Medal, Distinguished Service Medal, Military Medal or Distinguished Flying Medal. [*ITEPA 2003, s 638; ICTA 1988, s 317*].

(*c*)   Pensions in respect of **death due to military or war service**, comprising pensions or allowances payable by the UK Government in respect of death due to service in the armed forces (including peacetime service before the 1939–1945 war), wartime service in the merchant navy or war injuries, and comparable pensions etc. paid under foreign law. Where such a pension is abated because of entitlement to another pension, the exemption extends to so much of the other pension as is equal to the abatement. [*ITEPA 2003, ss 639, 640; ICTA 1988, s 318*].

(*d*)   Certain **wounds, disablement, disability** and **injury** pensions granted to members of the armed forces (including nurses) or payable under War Risks Compensation Schemes for the Mercantile marine or under certain War Compensation Acts and Armed Forces Pensions Acts, and **retired pay** granted to a disabled officer on account of service-related medical unfitness. Where a pension or retired pay is certified by the Secretary of State as only partly attributable to disablement etc., only the part attributable attracts the exemption. [*ITEPA 2003, s 641; ICTA 1988, s 315*]. Otherwise, the whole of the disability pension or retired pay is exempt provided that the immediate occasion of retirement was service-related disability, notwithstanding that a 'long service' element enters into the computation of the award. Further, where a member of the armed forces is invalided out in circumstances which qualify him for both a service-related disability pension and a service pension, the combined pension is regarded as within the above exemption. (Revenue Assessment Procedures Manual AP 844).

Tax was in the past incorrectly deducted from certain Army pensions paid in addition to pensions from the War Pensions Agency where the pensioner was medically discharged/invalided from the Army before 31 March 1973. Although most cases have been identified and a refund made, pensioners (or spouses or prime beneficiaries) may contact the Army Personnel Centre, Kentigern House, 65 Brown Street, Glasgow G2 8EX to ascertain whether a tax refund arises. Further information can be obtained from the Army Pensions Helpline on 0141–224 2719.

(*e*)   Pensions and annuities payable under provision of German or Austrian law for **victims of Nazi persecution**. [*ITEPA 2003, s 642; ICTA 1988, s 330*].

(*f*)   Certain **pre-1973** pensions paid in respect of **government service** in **Malawi, Trinidad and Tobago** and **Zambia**. [*ITEPA 2003, s 643; ICTA 1988, s 616(1)(2)(4)*]. See also Revenue Pamphlet IR 1, A49.

(g)   Where a person has ceased to hold an employment or office because of **disablement**, such amount (if any) of any pension as exceeds what would have been payable if the disablement had not been attributable to the performance of the duties of the employment or office or to war injuries. [*ITEPA 2003, s 644*]. Before 2003/04, this exemption operated by concession (Revenue Pamphlet IR 1, A62).

(h)   So much of any **social security pension** (as in 58.2(*c*) above or a foreign equivalent) as is attributable to an increase in respect of a child. [*ITEPA 2003, s 645; ICTA 1988, s 617(1)(b)*].

(j)   **Coal or smokeless fuel** provided to former colliery workers and their widow(er)s for personal use (and allowances paid in lieu of such provision). [*ITEPA 2003, s 646*]. Before 2003/04, this exemption operated by concession (Revenue Pamphlet IR 1, A6 as extended by Revenue Schedule E Manual SE 66695 as then drafted).

(k)   (By concession) **lump sums** paid by **overseas pension schemes**, i.e. lump sum 'relevant benefits' (see 67.1 RETIREMENT SCHEMES) received by an employee (or by his dependants or personal representatives) from

    (i)   a superannuation fund for overseas employees accepted as being within *ICTA 1988, s 615(6)* (see 67.15 RETIREMENT SCHEMES), or

    (ii)   an overseas retirement benefits scheme or provident fund where certain conditions as to the employee's foreign service are met.

As regards (ii) above, exemption may be total or partial depending on the length of foreign service, and this is determined in the same way as the statutory exemption from charge under *ITEPA 2003, ss 413, 414* for foreign service payments (see 18.6(vi) COMPENSATION FOR LOSS OF EMPLOYMENT (AND DAMAGES)).

(Revenue Pamphlet IR 1, A10).

Where pensions are paid to or from overseas, relief from double taxation may be available under the specific terms of a double tax treaty with the country concerned or by means of unilateral relief granted in the UK. See 24 DOUBLE TAX RELIEF.

58.4   **EXEMPTIONS SPECIFIC TO NON-UK RESIDENTS**

The exemptions listed below apply only if the Board are satisfied, on his making a claim to that effect, that the person to whom the pension is payable is not resident in the UK. For the purposes of these exemptions, 'pension' includes a gratuity or any sum payable on death and a return of contributions (including any interest or other addition included therein). [*ITEPA 2003, s 647; ICTA 1988, s 615(1)(7)*].

(a)   Pensions paid from the **Central African Pension Fund**. [*ITEPA 2003, s 648; ICTA 1988, s 615(2)(f)*].

(b)   Pensions paid out of a fund established in the UK by a **Commonwealth government** (as defined) for the sole purpose of providing pensions payable in respect of service under that government. [*ITEPA 2003, s 649; ICTA 1988, s 615(2)(b), (5)(7), (8)(a)*].

(c)   Pensions paid under the **Oversea Superannuation Scheme**. [*ITEPA 2003, s 650; ICTA 1988, s 615(2)(c), (8)(c); Overseas Superannuation Act 1991, s 2*].

(d)   Pensions paid under *Overseas Pensions Act 1973, s 1*, whether or not out of a fund established under a scheme made under that *section* but excluding certain statutory increases. [*ITEPA 2003, s 651; ICTA 1988, s 615(2)(d), (4)(7)*].

(e)   Pensions paid under the authority of the *Overseas Service Act 1958* to the extent that the pension is certified by the Secretary of State as attributable to the employment

58.4 Pension Income

of a person in the public services of an overseas territory. [*ITEPA 2003, s 652; ICTA 1988, s 615(2)(e), (8)(b)(c)*].

(f) Pensions paid out of the **Overseas Service Pensions Fund**. For this purpose only, 'pension' also includes any sum payable in respect of ill-health. [*ITEPA 2003, s 653; ICTA 1988, s 615(2)(g), (7)*].

(g) Pensions paid under the authority of the *Pensions (India, Pakistan and Burma) Act 1955*, excluding certain statutory increases. [*ITEPA 2003, s 654; ICTA 1988, s 615(2)(a), (4)(7), (8)(c)*].

See also 51.1 NON-RESIDENTS AND OTHER OVERSEAS MATTERS for limitation on income tax liability of non-UK residents and 51.10 NON-RESIDENTS AND OTHER OVERSEAS MATTERS for availability of UK personal allowances to British and certain other residents abroad.

59   Pension Provision after 5 April 2006

59.1   INTRODUCTION AND KEY POINTS

With effect for **2006/07** and subsequent years, the various pre-existing pension scheme regimes described in 60 PERSONAL PENSION SCHEMES (AND STAKEHOLDER PENSIONS), 66 RETIREMENT ANNUITIES and 67 RETIREMENT SCHEMES FOR EMPLOYEES are replaced by *FA 2004, ss 149–284, Schs 28–36* with a single universal regime for tax-privileged pension provision. Key points are as follows.

- The pre-existing requirement for pension schemes to obtain Revenue approval is replaced by a requirement to register the scheme with the Revenue. Pre-6 April 2006 approved schemes are automatically treated as registered schemes unless, before 6 April 2006, they give notice to opt out of deemed registration. See 59.2 below.

- A registered scheme is exempt from income tax on its investment income and from capital gains tax on disposals of investments. See 59.3 below.

- Contributions to registered schemes are not limited by reference to a fraction of earnings and there is no earnings cap. An individual may make unlimited contributions and tax relief is available on contributions of up to the full amount of his relevant earnings or, if lower and provided the scheme operates tax relief at source, on contributions of up to £3,600. There is no provision for the carry-back or carry-forward of contributions to tax years other than the year of payment. See 59.4 below.

- Employer contributions to registered schemes are deductible for tax purposes, with statutory provision for the spreading of abnormally large contributions over a period of up to four years, and do not count as taxable income of the employee. See 59.5 below.

- The maximum permissible 'tax-free' lump sum payment by a registered scheme to a member is broadly the lower of 25% of the value of the pension rights and 25% of the member's lifetime allowance (see below). *[FA 2004, Sch 29 paras 2, 3]*. All registered schemes are able to offer lump sums. There is transitional protection of lump sum rights accrued before 6 April 2006 (see *FA 2004, Sch 36 paras 24–35*). The general tax exemption for lump sums received is set out by *ITEPA 2003, s 636A* (inserted by *FA 2004, Sch 31 para 11*), but is subject to the lifetime allowance below.

- Each individual has a **lifetime allowance** (set at £1.5 million for 2006/07 but rising annually). When benefits crystallise, most commonly when a pension begins to be paid, the amount crystallised is measured against the individual's lifetime allowance and any excess taxed at 55% if taken as a lump sum and 25% in other cases. Any tax due may be deducted by the administrator from the individual's benefits. See 59.6 below.

- Each individual also has an **annual allowance** (set at £215,000 for 2006/07 but rising annually). To the extent (if any) that the annual increase in an individual's rights under all registered schemes of which he is a member exceeds the annual allowance, the excess is chargeable to tax at 40% with the individual being liable for the tax. See 59.7 below.

- The minimum pension age will rise from 50 to 55 on 6 April 2010. *[FA 2004, s 279(1)]*. Except on ill-health grounds, a pension cannot be paid before the minimum age is reached. *[FA 2004, s 165(1)]*. Those with certain existing contractual rights to draw a pension earlier will have those rights protected (see *FA 2004, Sch 36 para 22*) and there is special protection for members of pre-6 April 2006 approved schemes with early retirement ages, e.g. sports persons (see *FA 2004, Sch 36 para 23*). However, except in the case of certain professions to be prescribed by regulations, e.g. police and armed forces, a reduced lifetime allowance will apply in the case of early retirement before age 50 (see *FA 2004, Sch 36 para 19*).

- Benefits must be taken by the age of 75 at the latest. A member of a money purchase scheme may take a pension from the age of 75 by way of income withdrawal, known as an '*alternatively secured pension*', instead of taking a scheme pension or purchasing a lifetime annuity; the maximum alternatively secured pension is 70% of a comparable annuity.

- It is no longer necessary for an employee to leave his employment before accessing his occupational pension. Members of occupational schemes may, where permitted by the scheme rules, continue to work for the same employer whilst drawing retirement benefits from the employer's scheme.

- Pre-existing limits and restrictions on the investment powers of various types of pension scheme will be lifted and replaced with a single set of investment rules for all schemes; subject to Department for Work and Pensions requirements, pension schemes may invest in all kinds of investments, including residential property (Revenue Budget Note BN 39, 17 March 2004).

- Non-registered pension schemes are permitted to exist but without the tax advantages of registered schemes; they are treated like any other arrangement to provide employees with benefits. On the other hand, they are not subject to restrictions such as the lifetime allowance. Transitional protection will be available for pension rights accrued before 6 April 2006 within non-registered schemes. (Revenue Budget Note BN 39, 17 March 2004). See *FA 2004, ss 245–249, Sch 36 paras 53–55*.

The Revenue are expected to publish detailed guidance some time in 2005.

59.2 REGISTERED PENSION SCHEMES

A '*pension scheme*' for these purposes is a scheme or other arrangements comprised in one or more instruments or agreements, having effect (or capable of having effect) so as to provide benefits to (or in respect of) persons on retirement, on death, on having reached a particular age, on the onset of serious ill-health or incapacity or in similar circumstances to these. [*FA 2004, s 150(1)*]. *FA 2004, s 151* defines a 'member' in relation to a pension scheme, and *FA 2004, s 152* defines, *inter alia*, money purchase schemes and defined benefits (usually final salary) schemes, both already well-known concepts.

A scheme administrator may make application, containing specified information and declarations, to the Inland Revenue to register a pension scheme. The Revenue must register the scheme unless it appears that it contains incorrect information or a false declaration. The scheme must be an occupational pension scheme (as defined by *FA 2004, s 150(5)* — i.e. an employer scheme) or a public service pension scheme (as defined by *FA 2004, s 150(3)* — broadly a scheme established by Government) or else must be a scheme established by an insurance company, unit trust scheme, a recognised EEA (i.e. European Economic Area) collective investment scheme, an authorised open-ended investment company, a bank, a building society or an EEA investment portfolio manager. The Treasury has power to amend this list by statutory instrument. A deferred annuity contract which will eventually provide the benefits due from a registered scheme is treated as having become a registered scheme on the day it was made.

The Revenue must notify the scheme administrator of their decision whether or not to register the scheme; no time limit is stipulated. An appeal may be made, within 30 days of the notice, against a decision not to register.

The Revenue may by notice withdraw a pension scheme's registration on any one or more of a number of grounds specified by *FA 2004, s 158*. An appeal may be made, within 30 days of the notice, against the decision to de-register the scheme. See 59.8(*g*) below as regards the tax charge on de-registration.

[*FA 2004, ss 153–159*].

There are rules as to the payments a registered scheme is and is not permitted to make (see *FA 2004, ss 160–181, Schs 28–30*) and dealing with unauthorised borrowing by registered schemes (see *FA 2004, ss 163, 182–185*); registered schemes may borrow up to 50% of the value of total scheme assets. The rules relating to payment of pensions are in *FA 2004, s 165, Sch 28 Pt 1*, those relating to pension death benefits are in *FA 2004, s 167, Sch 28 Pt 2*, those relating to payment of lump sums are in *FA 2004, s 166, Sch 29 Pt 1* and those relating to lump sum death benefits are in *FA 2004, s 168, Sch 29 Pt 2*.

Transitional. Subject to the opt-out below, a pension scheme which, immediately before 6 April 2006, falls into one of the following categories becomes automatically a registered scheme:

- a retirement benefits scheme approved for purposes of *ICTA 1988, Pt 14 Ch 1* (see 67 RETIREMENT SCHEMES FOR EMPLOYEES);

- a superannuation fund approved as at 5 April 1980 for purposes of *ICTA 1970, s 208* which has not since been approved for purposes of *ICTA 1988, Pt 14 Ch 1* and to which no contribution has since been made (see 67.13 RETIREMENT SCHEMES FOR EMPLOYEES);

- a relevant statutory scheme or a scheme treated as such by the Revenue as at 6 April 2006 (see 67.1 RETIREMENT SCHEMES FOR EMPLOYEES);

- a deferred annuity contract providing for the eventual payment of benefits under any of the above-listed schemes;

- a scheme or fund within *ICTA 1988, s 613(4)(b)–(d)* (Parliamentary pension schemes or funds) (see 67.11 RETIREMENT SCHEMES FOR EMPLOYEES);

- a retirement annuity contract approved under *ICTA 1988, s 620* or *s 621* (see 66 RETIREMENT ANNUITIES) (or a substituted contract within *ICTA 1988, s 622(3)*);

- a personal pension scheme approved under *ICTA 1988, Pt 14 Ch 4* (which includes a stakeholder scheme) (see 60 PERSONAL PENSION SCHEMES (AND STAKEHOLDER PENSIONS)).

Where only part of a retirement benefits scheme was approved, only that part becomes automatically a registered scheme. A retirement benefits scheme or personal pension scheme approved after 5 April 2006 with retrospective effect for a period ending with that date becomes automatically a registered scheme with effect from 6 April 2006.

A scheme may opt out of becoming automatically a registered pension scheme by giving the Revenue notice to that effect before 6 April 2006. Except in the case of a Parliamentary scheme or fund, this action gives rise to an income tax charge at 40% on the aggregate of the sums held for the purposes of the scheme immediately before 6 April 2006 and the market value of the scheme assets at that time.

[*FA 2004, Sch 36 paras 1–6*].

Compliance. A compliance regime for registered pension schemes is set out at *FA 2004, ss 250–274*. This covers such matters as completion and filing of returns, the providing of information to the Revenue outside of returns, accounting for income tax on a quarterly basis and the making of assessments. It also provides a penalty regime for non-compliance.

59.3 Pension Provision after 5 April 2006

59.3   **TAX EXEMPTIONS**

A registered pension scheme is exempt from income tax on income derived from investments (including futures contracts and option contracts) or deposits held for the purposes of the scheme. (The exemption does not apply in relation to investments or deposits held as a member of a property investment LLP — see 53.18 PARTNERSHIPS.) [*FA 2004, s 186*]. A gain accruing on a disposal of scheme investments is not a chargeable gain for capital gains tax purposes. [*TCGA 1992, s 271(1A); FA 2004, s 187(4)*].

59.4   **RELIEF FOR CONTRIBUTIONS BY INDIVIDUAL MEMBERS**

An individual is entitled to full tax relief on the contributions he makes to a pension scheme during a tax year if he is a 'relevant UK individual' for that year. An individual is a *'relevant UK individual'* for a tax year if

- he has 'relevant UK earnings' 'chargeable to income tax' for the year; or

- he is resident in the UK at some time during the year; or

- he was resident in the UK both at some time within the period of five years immediately preceding the tax year and at the time he became a member of the scheme; or

- he, or his spouse, has general earnings for the tax year from overseas Crown employment subject to UK tax (within *ITEPA 2003, s 28* — see 75.4 SCHEDULE E—EMPLOYMENT INCOME).

'Relevant UK earnings' means

- employment income;

- Schedule D income from a trade, profession or vocation (whether carried on individually or in partnership); or

- income from patent rights within *ICTA 1988, s 529* (see 54 PATENTS).

The individual is entitled to relief on contributions up to the total amount of his relevant UK earnings 'chargeable to income tax' for the year. Provided, however, the scheme operates tax relief at source (see below), contributions of up to £3,600 (gross) attract relief even if total relevant UK earnings are less than that amount or there are no such earnings. (The £3,600 minimum may be increased from time to time by Treasury order.)

Relevant UK earnings are treated as *not* being *'chargeable to income tax'* if, by virtue of a double tax treaty, they are not taxable in the UK.

In the case of an employer scheme, the relief may be given under the so-called net pay arrangements, whereby the contributions are deducted by the employer from salary before applying PAY AS YOU EARN (55) and the individual's employment income to be included in his total income for tax purposes is net of such contributions.

Otherwise, a registered pension scheme must normally operate relief at source arrangements, whereby tax relief at the basic rate is deducted from the amount of the contribution payable and the scheme administrator recovers the tax deducted from the Revenue. If the individual is a higher rate taxpayer, he then claims relief for the excess of the higher rate over the basic rate in his self-assessment tax return. Such relief is achieved by increasing his basic rate limit for the year by the gross amount of the contribution. The increased basic rate limit applies for the purposes of both income tax and capital gains tax. For the purposes only of age-related personal and married couple's allowances, the gross contribution is treated as reducing total income. (Revenue ESCs A101 and A102 — see 60.1 PERSONAL PENSION SCHEMES (AND STAKEHOLDER PENSIONS) — are thereby given statutory effect after 5 April 2006.) The individual retains the basic rate relief given at source even if his tax liability is insufficient to cover it. Any excess of contributions over an individual's relevant UK earnings (but within the £3,600 minimum referred to above) can *only* be relieved if the scheme operates relief at source (and cannot be relieved under net pay arrangements).

Contributions to pre-6 April 2006 retirement annuity contracts that have become registered pension schemes (see 59.2 above) are not required to be included in relief at source arrangements but can instead be relieved by deduction from total income on the making of a claim.

There are other limited circumstances in which relief can be given by deduction from total income on the making of a claim. These apply to contributions to public service pension schemes or marine pilots' benefits funds by individuals who are not employees in relation to the scheme or fund and third party contributions made on behalf of individuals who are within net pay arrangements.

In contrast to the pre-6 April 2006 position for personal and stakeholder pensions and retirement annuity contracts, there is no provision for the carry-back of contributions/premiums to tax years preceding the year of payment. A retirement annuity premium paid in 2005/06 may still be carried back in accordance with 66.4 RETIREMENT ANNUITIES by election made on or before 31 January 2007. Likewise, there is no provision for the carry-forward of contributions/premiums or of unused relief.

There is provision for shares acquired under an approved share incentive plan or SAYE option scheme (see, respectively, 82.20, 82.47 SHARE-RELATED EMPLOYMENT INCOME AND EXEMPTIONS) to be transferred to a registered scheme and treated as contributions made. The amount of the contribution is the market value of the shares at the date of transfer, and the transfer must be made within, broadly, 90 days after the shares are acquired by the individual.

[*FA 2004, ss 188–195, Sch 36 paras 39, 40*].

59.5   EMPLOYER CONTRIBUTIONS

Contributions made by an employer to a registered pension scheme in respect of an individual are deductible in computing profits for the period of account in which they are made (subject to the spreading provisions below). The contributions must meet the normal conditions for deduction under Schedule D, Case I or II, in particular the 'wholly and exclusively' rule (see 71.30 SCHEDULE D, CASES I AND II), but it is specifically provided that they are not treated as capital expenditure even if they would fall to be so treated under general principles. In like manner, such contributions are deductible under *ICTA 1988, s 75* as management expenses of a company with investment business or under *ICTA 1988, s 76* as expenses of an insurance company.

Certain payments an employer may make to discharge his statutory obligations in relation to an under-funded defined benefits scheme are treated as contributions to the scheme for the above purposes and, if made after cessation of the employer's business, are treated as if made immediately before cessation. Otherwise, no sums other than contributions are deductible in connection with the cost of providing benefits under the employer pension scheme; this overrides any contrary rule that might apply under generally accepted accounting practice.

[*FA 2004, ss 196, 199, 200*].

Spreading of abnormally large contributions. Where the contributions paid by an employer in a period of account exceed 210% of the contributions paid in the previous period of account, relief for the excess contributions may fall to be spread over more than one period of account as follows. Firstly, identify the amount of current period contributions that exceeds 110% of previous period contributions (the '*relevant excess contributions*').

If this amount is less than £500,000, spreading does not apply. Otherwise, relief for the relevant excess contributions is spread over the current and following periods of account as follows.

Amount of relevant excess contributions	Spread equally over
£500,000 to £999,999 inclusive	2 periods of account
£1,000,000 to £1,999,999 inclusive	3 periods of account
£2,000,000 or more	4 periods of account

This gives statutory effect to existing Revenue practice. If the current and previous periods of account are unequal in length, the amount of the previous period contributions is adjusted proportionately in order to determine the excess (if any). Any contributions paid in the current period to fund cost of living increases in current pensions are disregarded in determining any excess, as are any contributions to fund a future service liability for employees joining the scheme in the current period. If the employer ceases business, such that some of the excess contributions would otherwise remain unrelieved, the otherwise unrelieved amount is relieved in the period of account which ends with the date of cessation or, at the employer's option, is apportioned on a daily basis over the whole of the spreading period up to the date of cessation.

[*FA 2004, ss 197, 198*].

No tax charge on employee. An employee is not liable to income tax in respect of a contribution by his employer to a registered pension scheme, i.e. it is not treated as a benefit-in-kind. [*ITEPA 2003, s 308; FA 2004, s 201(2)*].

59.6   **LIFETIME ALLOWANCE**

Each individual has a '*lifetime allowance*' for the purposes of these provisions. This is set at £1.5 million for 2006/07 and will rise each year for the first five years as follows.

2006/07	£1.5 million
2007/08	£1.6 million
2008/09	£1.65 million
2009/10	£1.75 million
2010/11	£1.8 million

Future increases will be pre-announced at five-yearly intervals. (Revenue Budget Note BN 39, 17 March 2004).

Whenever a 'benefit crystallisation event' occurs in relation to an individual, the amount crystallised is measured against the individual's lifetime allowance (or so much of it, if any, as remains after previous benefit crystallisation events). Any excess is chargeable to tax (the '*lifetime allowance charge*').

On a second or subsequent benefit crystallisation event, the *proportion* of the lifetime allowance utilised in relation to previous events is taken into account in computing how much lifetime allowance remains. Thus, if an amount of £500,000 is crystallised in 2006/07, one-third of the lifetime allowance of £1.5 million is utilised against it (and no charge applies). If a further amount is crystallised in 2010/11, the lifetime allowance remaining to be utilised against it is £1.2 million, i.e. two-thirds of the 2010/11 figure.

The legislation lists eight different '*benefit crystallisation events*' and gives the amount crystallised in each case. These events are intended to cover (i) the commencement of the individual's entitlement to receive a pension (and the various different ways in which this can occur), (ii) increases in an individual's pension (already being paid) by more than a permitted margin (applied on a cumulative basis), (iii) the attainment of age 75 by an individual in a defined benefits scheme without his having received a pension or lump sum, (iv) an individual's becoming entitled to receive a lump sum, (v) the payment of certain lump sum death benefits and (vi) the transfer of funds from registered schemes to certain overseas schemes. The amount crystallised when an individual starts to receive a pension is generally the amount of pension that will be payable in the first 12 months, disregarding any actual increases during that period, multiplied by a factor of 20. If, however, the scheme is a money purchase scheme and the pension is an unsecured pension or lifetime annuity, the amount crystallised is the total sum (including market value of any assets) designated for the payment of the unsecured pension or used to purchase the annuity. In the case of a lump sum payment, the amount crystallised is the amount of the lump sum. See *FA 2004, s 216, Sch 32*.

To the extent that the amount chargeable to tax is paid as a lump sum to the individual (or as a lump sum death benefit in respect of the individual), the tax charge is at **55%**. Otherwise it is at **25%**. The tax is the joint and several liability of the individual and the scheme administrator (except in the case of a lump sum death benefit, where the tax is the liability of the person to whom the benefit is paid). The tax will normally be paid by the scheme administrator (see *FA 2004, s 254*). The charge is not dependent upon any person's being resident, ordinarily resident or domiciled in the UK. Although chargeable to income tax, the chargeable amount is not treated for any tax purposes as income, which means that, for example, losses, reliefs and allowances cannot be set against it and it does not count as income for the purposes of any double tax treaty. The scheme administrator may meet the liability out of scheme funds or by deducting it from the individual's scheme benefits. To the extent that it is not fully deducted from the individual's scheme benefits, the tax is itself added to the chargeable amount.

An individual's lifetime allowance is enhanced (in accordance with *FA 2004, ss 221–223*) if, at any time during his membership of a registered pension scheme (treated for this purpose as commencing no earlier than 6 April 2006), either (i) he is not a 'relevant UK individual' (see 59.4 above) or (ii) he is such an individual only because he was UK resident at some time in the previous five tax years *and* he is not employed by a person resident in the UK. This is to reflect the fact that his pension provision will not have entirely benefited from UK tax reliefs. An individual's lifetime allowance is also enhanced (in accordance with *FA 2004, ss 224–226*) if pension rights of his are transferred from a recognised overseas pension scheme into a UK registered scheme, again reflecting the fact that rights will have built up without the benefit of UK tax relief. An individual who intends to benefit from either of these enhancements must give notice of that intention to the Revenue in accordance with regulations to be made by the Board.

[*FA 2004, ss 214–226, Sch 32*].

Transitional. There are two kinds of protection available in relation to pension rights built up before 6 April 2006 — 'primary protection' and 'enhanced protection'.

'*Primary protection*' applies where an individual's 'relevant pre-commencement pension rights' exceed £1.5 million (the amount of the lifetime allowance for 2006/07). The individual's lifetime allowance for each tax year is enhanced by the proportion which the excess bears to £1.5 million; for example, an individual with relevant pre-commencement pension rights of £2 million will have his lifetime allowance increased by one-third. An individual's '*relevant pre-commencement pension rights*' is the aggregate of (i) the value of his uncrystallised pension rights under all schemes of the kind listed at 59.2 above (under Transitional), rights being 'uncrystallised' if at 5 April 2006 the individual has not become entitled to the present payment of benefits, and (ii) the value of his crystallised rights (if any) at 5 April 2006, calculated at 25 times the annual rate of pensions payable at that date. In the case of occupational schemes, the value of uncrystallised pension rights is limited by a ceiling of 20 times the maximum permitted pension (as defined). [*FA 2004, Sch 36 para*

9.] An individual who intends to benefit from this enhancement must give notice of that intention to the Revenue in accordance with regulations to be made by the Board.

'*Enhanced protection*' exempts an individual from the lifetime allowance charge if he has ceased active membership of a pre-existing pension scheme that becomes a registered scheme on 6 April 2006 and continues for so long as he does not resume active membership or join any registered scheme. An individual is taken to have resumed active membership if, in the case of a money purchase scheme, a contribution to the scheme is made by him or his employer or, in the case of a defined benefits scheme, crystallised benefits exceed the 'appropriate limit' set out in *FA 2004, Sch 36 para 15* or if pensionable earnings exceed a permitted maximum set out at *FA 2004, Sch 36 paras 16, 17*. An individual who intends to benefit from this exemption must give notice of that intention to the Revenue in accordance with regulations to be made by the Board.

[*FA 2004, Sch 36 paras 7–20*].

59.7 **ANNUAL ALLOWANCE**

In addition to the lifetime allowance at 59.6 above, each individual has an '*annual allowance*' for the purposes of these provisions. This is set at £215,000 for 2006/07 and will rise each year for the first five years as follows.

2006/07	£215,000
2007/08	£225,000
2008/09	£235,000
2009/10	£245,000
2010/11	£255,000

Future increases will be pre-announced at five-yearly intervals. (Revenue Budget Note BN 39, 17 March 2004; Explanatory Notes to 2004 Finance Bill).

The annual increase in an individual's rights under all registered pension schemes of which he is a member is measured against his annual allowance, and any excess over the annual allowance is chargeable to tax (the '*annual allowance charge*') at the rate of **40%**. The individual himself is liable to the tax. The charge is not dependent upon the residence, ordinary residence or domicile status of the individual or the scheme administrator. Although chargeable to income tax, the chargeable amount is not treated for any tax purposes as income, which means that, for example, losses, reliefs and allowances cannot be set against it and it does not count as income for the purposes of any double tax treaty.

The annual increase in an individual's pension rights is computed in terms of his total '*pension input amount*' for the tax year. This is found by aggregating the pension input amounts for all registered schemes of which he is a member. There is no pension input amount in respect of a pension arrangement if, before the end of the tax year, all the benefits under that arrangement have crystallised or the individual dies. The calculation of the pension input amount depends on the type of scheme and on the 'pension input period' that ends in the tax year. For money purchase schemes (other than cash balance arrangements — as defined by *FA 2004, s 152(3)*), the pension input amount is broadly the amount of contributions paid by or on behalf of the individual (including contributions by his employer) in that pension input period. For defined benefits schemes and cash balance arrangements, it is the excess (if any) of the value of his pension rights at the end of that pension input period over the value of his pension rights at the beginning of that pension input period. For this purpose, the value of an individual's pension rights at a particular time is

- (in the case of a defined benefits scheme) the aggregate of any lump sum to which the individual would have been entitled (otherwise than by commutation of pension)

if he had become entitled to payment of it at that time and 10 times the annual pension that would have been payable if the individual had become entitled to payment of it at that time;

- (in the case of a cash balance arrangements) the amount that would have been available for provision of benefits if the individual had become entitled to the benefits at that time.

In determining any amount to which an individual would have been entitled if he became entitled to it at a particular time, certain assumptions are made as set out in *FA 2004, s 277*.

In ascertaining the pension input amount, the value of the pension rights at the beginning of the pension input period is increased by the greatest of 5%, the increase in the retail prices index during that period and such percentage as may be determined by regulations made by the Board, *but* in the case of a defined benefits scheme this uprating applies only if no pension rights accrue to the individual during the pension input period (whether by means of contributions or by accruing years of pensionable service). There is also provision for the adjustment in certain circumstances of the value of the pension rights at the end of the pension input period.

The first '*pension input period*' begins on the day the pension rights begin to accrue or, in the case of a money purchase scheme (other than cash balance arrangements) the day on which the first contribution to the scheme is made. The period ends a year after commencement or, if earlier, on a day nominated for the purpose. This enables the period to end on a convenient date, e.g. the end of the tax year or the date to which the scheme prepares its accounts; the nomination is made by the scheme administrator but, in the case of a money purchase scheme (other than cash balance arrangements), may also be made by the individual. Each subsequent pension input period begins immediately after the end of the previous one and ends a year later or, if earlier, on a nominated date falling in the tax year following that in which the previous pension input period ended. The final pension input period in relation to a scheme comes to an end on the first day on which the individual has no benefits remaining to be provided.

[*FA 2004, ss 227–238*].

Transitional. Where an individual has notified the Revenue of his intention to benefit from *enhanced protection* from the *lifetime allowance charge* (see 59.6 above under Transitional), the individual is exempt from the annual allowance charge for any tax year throughout the whole of which the enhanced protection continues to apply. If at some point during a tax year the enhanced protection terminates (because the individual resumes active membership of a scheme or joins a new scheme), the annual allowance charge applies in full for that tax year. [*FA 2004, Sch 36 para 49*]. There is also provision for the pension input amount for the pension input period ending in 2006/07 to be reduced by any employer contribution made between 6 April 2006 and 7 July 2006 inclusive to consolidate unfunded unapproved pension promises made before 6 April 2006 into a registered scheme. [*FA 2004, Sch 36 para 48*].

59.8   **OTHER TAX CHARGES**

In addition to the lifetime allowance charge at 59.6 above and the annual allowance charge at 59.7 above, other income tax charges may arise in relation to registered schemes as listed below. These are in addition to the normal taxation under *ITEPA 2003* of individuals' pension income, which is covered at 58 PENSION INCOME; that chapter will be updated for the 2006/07 edition to cover pension income from registered schemes, for which see *FA 2004, s 204, Sch 31* (and the relevant transitional provisions within *FA 2004, Sch 36 Pt 4*).

59.8 Pension Provision after 5 April 2006

(a) **Short service refund lump sum charge.** This is a charge on the scheme administrator at **20%** or, to the extent that the lump sum exceeds £10,800, **40%**. A '*short service lump sum*' is defined by *FA 2004, Sch 29 para 5* and is broadly a refund in specified circumstances of a member's contributions to an occupational pension scheme. The charge is not dependent upon the residence, ordinary residence or domicile status of the scheme administrator or the person to whom the lump sum is paid. Although chargeable to income tax, a short service refund lump sum is not treated for any tax purposes as income. The tax may be deducted at source by the scheme administrator from the lump sum payment if the scheme rules so permit. [*FA 2004, s 205*].

(b) **Special lump sum death benefits charge.** This is a charge on the scheme administrator at **35%** where a pension protection lump sum death benefit, an annuity protection lump sum death benefit or an unsecured pension fund lump sum death benefit is paid. These terms are defined by *FA 2004, Sch 29 paras 14, 16, 17*. The same comments apply as in (a) above as regards residence status etc., non-treatment as income and deduction at source. [*FA 2004, s 206*].

(c) **Authorised surplus payments charge.** This is a charge on the scheme administrator at **35%** where an authorised surplus payment (i.e. a return of surplus funds) is made to the employer by an occupational scheme. The charge is not dependent upon the residence, ordinary residence or domicile status of the scheme administrator or the employer. Although chargeable to income tax, an authorised surplus payment is not treated for any tax purposes as income. If the employer is a charity or is otherwise exempt from tax, the charge does not apply. [*FA 2004, s 207*].

(d) **Unauthorised payments charge.** Where an unauthorised payment is made, a charge at **40%** arises on the amount thereof. The person liable is the scheme member to whom (or in respect of whom) the payment is made (or, if made after the member's death, the recipient) or, where applicable, the employer to whom (or in respect of whom) it is made. If more than one person is liable, liability is joint and several. The charge is not dependent upon the residence, ordinary residence or domicile status of the scheme administrator or any person who is liable. Although chargeable to income tax, an unauthorised payment is not treated for any tax purposes as income. [*FA 2004, s 208*].

See *FA 2004, ss 164–181* as regards authorised and unauthorised payments by registered schemes.

(e) **Unauthorised payments surcharge.** This is payable at **15%**, in addition to the unauthorised payments charge at (d) above, in respect of

- unauthorised payments to or for a member where, broadly, such payments made over a 12-month period use up at least 25% of the value of the member's pension fund; and

- unauthorised payments to or for a scheme employer where, broadly, such payments made over a 12-month period use up at least 25% of the aggregate value of sums and assets held for the purposes of the pension scheme.

[*FA 2004, ss 209–213*].

(f) **Scheme sanction charge.** This is a charge on the scheme administrator at **40%** in respect of unauthorised payments made by the scheme (with certain specified exemptions) and payments which the scheme is treated as having made by virtue of *FA 2004, s 183* or *s 185* (unauthorised borrowing). The charge is not dependent upon the residence, ordinary residence or domicile status of any person liable. If payments subjected to this charge are also charged under (d) above, credit is given for the tax *paid* (as opposed to the tax charged) under (*d*); however, the available credit is limited to 25% of the chargeable payment. [*FA 2004, ss 239–241*].

(*g*) **De-registration charge.** This is a charge on the scheme administrator at **40%** of the aggregate value of sums and assets held for the purposes of the pension scheme immediately before the withdrawal by the Revenue of the scheme's registration (see 59.2 above). It is not dependent upon the residence, ordinary residence or domicile status of any person liable. [*FA 2004, s 242*].

59.9   **OVERSEAS PENSION SCHEMES — CONTRIBUTIONS AND CHARGES**

Migrant member relief. Where an individual comes to work in the UK and is already a member of an overseas pension scheme, UK tax relief may be available for his contributions to the scheme and on his employer contributions. This is known as '*migrant member relief*'. It replaces the pre-existing 'corresponding relief' in *ITEPA 2003, s 355* (see 75.9 SCHEDULE E—EMPLOYMENT INCOME), although where an individual obtains relief under that *section* for contributions made in 2005/06, the Board may in certain circumstances continue to allow such relief for contributions made in subsequent years to the same scheme (see *FA 2004, Sch 36 para 51*).

Migrant member relief is available for contributions made by an individual

- who is a 'relevant migrant member' of a 'qualifying overseas pension scheme',

- who has relevant UK earnings chargeable to income tax for the tax year in which the contributions are made (see 59.4 above), and

- who has notified the scheme manager of his intention to claim the relief.

Relief is given as in 59.4 above, but is so given by deduction from total income on the making of a claim rather than by deduction at source and extension of the basic rate band. Relief for employer contributions applies as in 59.5 above.

An individual is a '*relevant migrant member*' of an overseas pension scheme if he

- was non-UK resident when he joined the scheme;

- was a member of the scheme at the beginning of the period of UK residence in which the contributions in question are made;

- was, immediately before that period of UK residence, entitled to tax relief on his contributions in the country in which he was then resident; and

- has been notified by the scheme manager that information on benefit crystallisation events (see 59.6 above) will be given to the Inland Revenue.

A '*qualifying overseas pension scheme*' is an overseas pension scheme which has provided certain notifications, evidence and undertakings to the Revenue, including an undertaking to comply with information requirements regarding benefit crystallisation events, and which has not been excluded by the Revenue from being a qualifying overseas pension scheme by reason of previous significant failures to comply with such information requirements. A scheme manager has the right of appeal to the General Commissioners (or, by election, to the Special Commissioners) against a decision of the Revenue to exclude the scheme from qualifying.

[*ITEPA 2003, s 308A; FA 2004, s 243, Sch 33*].

Lifetime allowance charge. The lifetime allowance charge at 59.6 above applies, with appropriate modifications, in relation to a member of a non-UK pension scheme if

- UK tax relief has been given, on contributions to the scheme made by the member or on his behalf, either under the 'migrant member relief' provisions above or under a double tax treaty; or

- the member has been given exemption under *ITEPA 2003, s 307* (see 75.16(iii) SCHEDULE E—EMPLOYMENT INCOME) in respect of provision for retirement or death benefits made under the scheme at a time after 5 April 2006 when it was an overseas scheme.

[*FA 2004, s 244, Sch 34 paras 13–20*].

Annual allowance charge. The annual allowance charge at 59.7 above applies, with appropriate modifications, in relation to a member of a non-UK pension scheme for any tax year in respect of which

- UK tax relief is obtained, on contributions to the scheme made by the member or on his behalf, either under the 'migrant member relief' provisions above or under a double tax treaty; or

- the member is given exemption under *ITEPA 2003, s 307* (see 75.16(iii) SCHEDULE E—EMPLOYMENT INCOME) in respect of provision for retirement or death benefits made under the scheme while it is an overseas scheme

[*FA 2004, s 244, Sch 34 paras 8–12, 20*].

Other tax charges. The charges at 59.8(*a*)(*b*)(*d*) and (*e*) above apply, in certain circumstances and with appropriate modifications, in relation to payments made to or in respect of a member of a non-UK pension scheme at a time when he is UK resident, if

- UK tax relief has been given, on contributions to the scheme made by the member or on his behalf, either under the 'migrant member relief' provisions above or under a double tax treaty; or

- the member has been given exemption under *ITEPA 2003, s 307* (see 75.16(iii) SCHEDULE E—EMPLOYMENT INCOME) in respect of provision for retirement or death benefits made under the scheme at a time after 5 April 2006 when it was an overseas scheme; or

- the member's pension rights have been transferred from a registered pension scheme to the non-UK scheme at a time when it was a 'qualifying recognised overseas pension scheme' (see *FA 2004, s 150(7)(8), s 169*).

The charges at 59.8(*a*)(*b*)(*d*) and (*e*) above similarly apply in relation to payments made to or in respect of a member of a non-UK scheme at a time when he is non-UK resident, provided he has been UK resident at some time earlier in the tax year in which the payment is made or at some time in the five preceding tax years.

[*FA 2004, s 244, Sch 34 paras 1–7, 20*].

60   Personal Pension Schemes (and Stakeholder Pensions)

(See Revenue Pamphlet IR 3 and the Revenue Guidance Notes on Personal Pension Schemes IR 76.)

Cross-references. See 59 PENSION PROVISION AFTER 5 APRIL 2006; 66 RETIREMENT ANNUITIES; 67 RETIREMENT SCHEMES.

Simon's Direct Tax Service E7.4.

General note. The provisions under *ICTA 1988, ss 618–629* for retirement annuity contracts for the self-employed and those in non-pensionable employment were, for new schemes, replaced, after 30 June 1988, by the regime for personal pension schemes under *ICTA 1988, ss 630–655*, designed to encourage employees who wish to do so to opt out of company pension schemes in favour of independent arrangements not linked to any one employment. Retirement annuity schemes contracted before 1 July 1988 continue, however, to be dealt with under the earlier provisions now in ICTA 1988, ss 618–629 (see 66 RETIREMENT ANNUITIES) and the new personal pension scheme provisions adopt many of the features of those earlier provisions.

Stakeholder pensions. Provision is made from 1 October 2000 for the establishment of stakeholder pension schemes under The Stakeholder Pension Schemes Regulations 2000 (*SI 2000 No 1403*) (as amended), and the personal pension scheme provisions are accordingly adapted, generally from 6 April 2001, to accommodate their introduction. Thus, except to the extent that it relates to tax years before 2001/02, the content of this chapter applies to stakeholder schemes as it does to other personal pension schemes. Stakeholder pensions have to be facilitated by most employers (subject to alternative provision of the opportunity to join a conventional personal pension scheme in certain cases), and offer a simplified form of scheme with low annual charges, on a contract basis as an alternative to the pre-existing trust regime. The major new element is the ability to pay up to £3,600 into a scheme without reference to earnings, but a number of other significant changes are also made, as described below.

Stakeholder pension schemes must be contracted out of the additional State pension, i.e. SERPS or the State Second Pension (see Pensions Updates Nos 119, 25 February 2002 and 138, 17 March 2003).

Application for approval under the new regime (or amendment of an existing scheme to incorporate the revised provisions) cannot be made before 1 October 2000. [*FA 2000, Sch 13 para 30*]. Schemes approved before 6 April 2001 are deemed to include certain of the new provisions on or after that date (for which see further below). [FA 2000, Sch 13 para 28].

A booklet 'Stakeholder pensions — a guide for employers', explaining what action firms have to take to prepare for the introduction of stakeholder pensions, from choosing a pension scheme to managing payroll deductions, was sent to all employers with five or more employees in September 2000. It can be found on the internet at www.dwp.gov.uk, or copies obtained on 0845-7646 646.

The headings in this chapter are as follows.

60.1	Outline of provisions	60.9	— presumption of same level
60.2	Contract requirements		of net relevant earnings for five
60.3	Limits of relief		years
60.4	— example	60.10	— examples
60.5	Contributions related back	60.11	Small lump sum retirement
60.6	Unused relief carried forward		benefits schemes
60.7	— example	60.12	Mis-sold personal pensions etc.
60.8	Relevant earnings		

New pension schemes regime after 5 April 2006. A new pension schemes tax regime was introduced by *FA 2004* and comes into force on **6 April 2006**. It fully replaces the pre-existing rules for occupational pension schemes, personal (and stakeholder) pension schemes and retirement

60.1 Personal Pension Schemes (and Stakeholder Pensions)

annuity schemes. **The rules described in this chapter remain valid for 2004/05 and 2005/06.** For the new regime, see 59 PENSION PROVISION AFTER 5 APRIL 2006.

60.1 **OUTLINE OF PROVISIONS**

Relief is available in respect of contributions payable by an individual under arrangements made in accordance with a 'personal pension scheme' (see 60.2 below). Before 6 April 2001, eligibility to make contributions to a scheme is determined by the possession of 'relevant earnings' (see 60.8 below). From that date, in consequence of the introduction of stakeholder pensions (contributions to which may, to a limited extent, be made without reference to earnings), a scheme may not be approved if it accepts contributions from a member (or his employer) during a year of assessment unless one of the following applies.

(*a*)   The member has actual (i.e. not presumed) net relevant earnings (see 60.8 below) for that year.

(*b*)   The member does not have actual net relevant earnings but is, for some part of that year, *not* in 'pensionable employment' (see 60.8 below), and either

    (i)   at some time in that year the member is UK-resident and ordinarily resident, or

    (ii)   at some time in that year the member was, or was the spouse of, a person in an employment the duties of which are in effect treated as performed in the UK (Crown servants, see 75.4 SCHEDULE E—EMPLOYMENT INCOME), or

    (iii)   the member was UK-resident and ordinarily resident both at some time in the preceding five years of assessment and when the personal pension arrangements were made.

(*c*)   Where neither (*a*) nor (*b*) above applies, and throughout that year the member *is* in 'pensionable employment' (see 60.8 below), and

    (i)   the member satisfies either (*b*)(i), (*b*)(ii) or (*b*)(iii) above,

    (ii)   the member is not, and has not been, a 'controlling director' (see 60.8 below) of any company at any time in that year or in the preceding five years of assessment (disregarding years before 2000/01),

    (iii)   for at least one of the preceding five years of assessment (but excluding years before 2000/01), the aggregate of the member's 'grossed-up remuneration' from each office and each employment held on 5 April in that year does not exceed the 'remuneration limit' (initially set at £30,000 but variable by Treasury order) for the year in which the contributions are made, and

    (iv)   the total of the contributions made in that year by the member or his employer, together with any other such contributions made in that year under approved personal pension arrangements made by the member, does not exceed the 'earnings threshold' (see 60.3 below) for that year.

'*Grossed-up remuneration*' in (iii) above is the total emoluments for PAYE purposes multiplied, where the office or employment was not held throughout the year, by the figure obtained by dividing twelve by the number of months for which it was held (rounded up to a whole number of months) and rounding the result to the nearest single decimal place.

Persons claiming to be so eligible to make contributions are required to provide to the scheme administrator, before or when making the first contribution, a certificate in support of the claim containing prescribed information (see *SI 2000 No 2318, reg 4*).

There must be provision for repayment of ineligible contributions (which, in the case of a contribution causing the limit in (c)(iv) above to be exceeded, requires repayment only of the excess over the earnings threshold and of any subsequent contributions in the year, to enable that condition to be met).

Schemes approved before 6 April 2001 are deemed to include provision prohibiting acceptance of contributions from (or in respect of) members not satisfying any of the above conditions.

[*ICTA 1988, ss 632A, 632B; FA 2000, Sch 13 paras 8, 28(2)(3)(8); SI 2000 No 2318*].

For 2000/01 and earlier years, the contributions paid in a year of assessment may, subject to certain limits (see 60.3 below), be deducted from the individual's 'relevant earnings' (see 60.8 below) as assessed for that year. In the case of Schedule E employees, and subject to conditions prescribed by regulations (see *SI 1988 No 1013; SI 2000 No 2315*), relief is given by deduction of basic rate tax, which may be recovered by the scheme administrator. Relief other than by deduction at source, and higher rate relief in all cases, is given on a claim being made (on form PP120 or in the income tax return) by deduction or set off in an assessment.

For 2001/02 and subsequent years, relief for contributions in any year is given up to a maximum of the greater of the 'earnings threshold' for the year and, where (c) above does not apply, the 'maximum amount' for the year (see 60.3 below). Relief for all contributions is given by deduction of basic rate tax, recoverable by the administrator, subject to conditions prescribed by regulations (see *SI 1988 No 1013 as amended by SI 2000 No 2315*). Higher rate relief is, on a claim, given by an addition to the basic rate limit of the amount of contributions in respect of which relief is available for the year. (Due to a drafting omission this strictly applies only where higher rate liability would otherwise arise in respect of income, but by Revenue concession relief is extended to cases where higher rate liability would otherwise arise in respect of chargeable gains (see Revenue Pamphlet IR 1, A101).) Also by concession, contributions are deducted from the individual's total income *but only for the purposes* of determining the level of age-related personal and married couple's allowances (see 1.14, 1.15 ALLOWANCES AND TAX RATES). (Revenue Pamphlet IR 1, A102).

In addition, any contribution to such a scheme by the employer is not chargeable to income tax on the individual. There are provisions for adjustment of relief following alterations in the individual's liability to tax, and for the prevention of double relief.

The Revenue consider that where a payment *may* be made under deduction of basic rate tax, basic rate relief can *only* be obtained by deduction. The tax deducted from valid contributions is not clawed back where the individual is liable only at less than the basic rate of income tax or has no income tax liability. IR Savings, Pensions, Share Schemes may be contacted in relation to personal pensions on 0115–974 1777.

[*ITEPA 2003, s 308; ICTA 1988, ss 639, 643(1); FA 2000, Sch 13 paras 15, 28(6)–(8)*].

Income and gains on scheme investments are exempt from income tax and capital gains tax, and there are similar reliefs in relation to authorised unit trusts which are also approved personal pension schemes. [*ICTA 1988, s 643(2); TCGA 1992, s 271(1)(h)(j)*]. See 71.22 SCHEDULE D, CASES I AND II as regards futures and options contracts.

There are special provisions relating to salaries of members of the House of Commons or the Scottish Parliament. [*ICTA 1988, s 654; FA 1999, Sch 5 para 6*].

An annuity payable under such a scheme is treated as earned income of the annuitant to whom it is made payable by the terms of the arrangements. [*ICTA 1988, s 643(3)(4)*]. Annuity payments are taxable under *ITEPA 2003* as pension income for 2003/04 onwards (see 58.2(*f*) PENSION INCOME) (and were previously taxable under Schedule E) and are thus

60.2 Personal Pension Schemes (and Stakeholder Pensions)

within the scope of PAYE (see 55.2 PAY AS YOU EARN). Income withdrawals (within 60.2(ii) or (iv) below) are treated as earned income of the recipient. [*ICTA 1988, s 643(5); FA 1995, Sch 11 para 11; ITEPA 2003, Sch 6 para 91*]. They are taxed in the same way as annuity payments (see 58.2(*g*) PENSION INCOME). Unauthorised payments from a scheme are taxed in similar manner (see 58.2(*h*) PENSION INCOME). Contributions by an employer under non-approved personal pension arrangements are taxable as earnings of the employee for the tax year in which made. [*ITEPA 2003, s 224; ICTA 1988, s 648*]. Lump sums provided under approved personal pension arrangements are not chargeable to income tax. [*ITEPA 2003, s 637(1)(a), (5); ICTA 1988, s 189(1)(c)*].

Where a lump sum refund of contributions is paid under 60.2(viii) below in a case where the member's death occurred after he had elected for income withdrawals under 60.2(ii) below, the scheme administrator is charged under Schedule D, Case VI on the gross payment at the rate of 35% (variable by Treasury order). [*ICTA 1988, s 648B; FA 1995, Sch 11 para 12*].

Contributions to personal pension schemes are not deductible in arriving at profits for Class 4 national insurance purposes (see 83.8 SOCIAL SECURITY). [*Social Security Contributions and Benefits Act 1992, Sch 2 para 3(2)(g)*].

Administrators. A charge on the administrator of a scheme is treated as charged on all present and future administrators and is assessable in the name of the administrator, but is not assessable on persons who are no longer administrators. [*ICTA 1988, s 658A; FA 1998, s 98(1); ITEPA 2003, Sch 6 para 98*]. SELF-ASSESSMENT (78) does not apply to charges on administrators. [*TMA 1970, s 9(1A); FA 1998, s 98(2)(3)*]. Where there is no scheme administrator or he cannot be traced, there is provision for notices etc. to be delivered to certain other persons. [*ICTA 1988, s 653A; FA 1998, s 97*].

Information and penalties. From 1 October 2000, new information and inspection powers are made available to the Revenue (see *SI 2000 No 2316 as amended*), displacing those previously available under *ICTA 1988, s 652*. There are penalties for giving false information in support of an application for approval (see 60.2 below) or for the purpose of obtaining relief from or repayment of tax under these provisions, or for failure to supply information as above or in relation to the regulations regarding deduction of tax from contributions (see above). [*ICTA 1988, ss 651A, 652, 653; TMA 1970, s 98; FA 1989, s 170(4); FA 1998, s 96, Sch 27 Pt III(21); SI 2000 Nos 2316, 2319; SI 2001 No 3629, Article 188*].

See generally Revenue Pamphlet IR 78.

Simon's Direct Tax Service. See E7.401 *et seq.*

60.2 **CONTRACT REQUIREMENTS**

For approval under ICTA 1988, s 631 (which, from 6 April 2001, may be conditional), a personal pension scheme must be established by:

(*a*)   a person who has permission under *Financial Services and Markets Act 2000, Pt 4* to effect or carry out 'contracts of long-term insurance' (within *SI 2001 No 544, Sch 1 Pt II*) or to manage unit trust schemes authorised under that *Act* (see 90.1 UNIT TRUSTS);

(*b*)   an EEA firm within *Financial Services and Markets Act 2000, Sch 3 para 5(d)* which has permission under *para 15* of that *Schedule* (as a result of qualifying for authorisation under *para 12*) to effect or carry out contracts of long-term insurance (as in (*a*) above) and which fulfils the requirements of *ICTA 1988, s 659B(5), (6)* or *(7)* (definition of insurance company, see below);

(c)   an institution which is an EEA firm within *Financial Services and Markets Act 2000, Sch 3 para 5(a)*, (*b*) or (*c*) qualifying for authorisation under *para 12(1)* or *(2)* of that *Schedule* and permitted under that *Act* to manage portfolios of investments;

(d)   a firm which has permission under *Financial Services and Markets Act 2000, Sch 4 para 4* (as a result of qualifying for authorisation under *para 2* of that *Schedule*) to manage unit trust schemes authorised under that *Act* (see 90.1 UNIT TRUSTS);

(e)   a person qualifying for authorisation under *Financial Services and Markets Act 2000, Sch 5*;

(f)   a building society (see 8 BUILDING SOCIETIES);

(g)   a person falling within *ICTA 1988, s 840A(1)(b)* (i.e. (subject to certain exclusions) a person who has permission under *Financial Services and Markets Act 2000, Pt 4* to accept deposits) or a body corporate which is a subsidiary or holding company (or a subsidiary of the holding company) of such a person; or

(h)   such other person as the Treasury may specify by order.

(Before 1 December 2001, schemes had to be established by:

(a)   a person authorised under *Financial Services Act 1986, Pt I, Ch III* to carry on investment business, and who carries on business either of issuing insurance policies or annuity contracts or of managing authorised unit trust schemes (see 90.1 UNIT TRUSTS). This may include an authorised corporate director of an open-ended investment company (see Pensions Update No 74, 6 November 2000);

(b)   a building society (see 8 BUILDING SOCIETIES);

(c)   a pension company which is an associate of a building society;

(d)   an institution authorised under *Banking Act 1987* or a subsidiary or holding company (or a subsidiary of the holding company) of such an institution;

(e)   a recognised bank or licensed institution within *Banking Act 1979*;

(f)   (from 24 October 1997) an EC insurance company lawfully carrying on long term business, or providing long-term insurance, in the UK, and certain European banking institutions; or

(g)   such other person as the Treasury may specify by order.)

There must be a person responsible for administration of the scheme who is resident in the UK.

The Board may approve a scheme established other than by a person within (*a*)–(*h*) (or (*a*)–(*g*)) above if the scheme is established under a trust or trusts, subject to certain restrictions where the scheme is *not* registered as a stakeholder pension scheme under *Welfare Reform and Pensions Act 1999, s 2* (or NI equivalent). See Pensions Updates Nos 118, 25 February 2002 and 140, 17 March 2003.

[*ICTA 1988, ss 631, 632, 638(1); FA 1988, s 54; FA 2000, Sch 13 para 6; SI 1988 No 993; SI 1997 No 2388; SI 2000 Nos 2314, 2317; SI 2001 No 3629, Article 41*].

The scheme may not provide for benefits to an individual participant other than the following.

(i)   A life annuity payable to the participant, commencing not earlier than age 50 and not later than age 75 (except as follows) and which, except as detailed at (v) below, must not be capable of assignment or surrender other than for the purpose of giving effect to a pension-sharing order or provision under *Welfare Reform and Pensions Act 1999, s 24(1)*. An annuity may commence earlier than age 50 in the event of the participant becoming physically or mentally incapacitated from carrying on his occupation, or any similar one, or if earlier retirement is customary in his occupation. As regards the latter, the following early retirement ages have been agreed by the Superannuation Funds Office.

30	Downhill skiers.
35	Athletes; badminton players; boxers; cyclists; dancers; footballers; ice hockey players; models; national hunt jockeys; real tennis players; rugby league players; rugby union players; squash players; table tennis players; tennis players; wrestlers.
40	Cricketers; divers (saturation, deep sea and free swimming); golfers; motorcycle riders (motocross or road racing); motor racing drivers; WPBSA snooker players; speedway riders; trapeze artistes.
45	Flat racing jockeys; members of the reserve forces.

These pension ages apply only to arrangements funded by contributions in respect of relevant earnings from the occupation or profession in question. For professional sportsmen, the earnings must arise from activities as such, e.g. tournament earnings and appearance and prize money, and not from sponsorship or coaching (for which separate arrangements may be made). (Revenue Pamphlet IR 76, Appendix 10).

(ii)   Where schemes (or amendments) are approved on or after 1 May 1995, income withdrawals, i.e. payments of income other than by way of annuity, during a period of deferral of the purchase of an annuity under (i) above, where the participant so elects. Income withdrawals may not commence before the participant attains the age of 50 (subject to provision for earlier commencement as under (i) above) and must not continue after the participant attains the age of 75. The right to such income withdrawals must not be capable of assignment or surrender other than for the purpose of giving effect to a pension-sharing order or provision under *Welfare Reform and Pensions Act 1999, s 24(1)*. The aggregate income withdrawals in each successive twelve month period starting with the 'pension date' must be between 35% and 100% (inclusive) of the annual amount of the annuity purchasable on the 'relevant reference date'. The *'pension date'* for this purpose is the date on which the member elects to make income withdrawals, and the *'relevant reference date'* is the pension date for the first three years of withdrawals, and thereafter the first day of each successive three year period. The annuity purchasable on any such date is determined by reference to the value on that date, as determined by the scheme administrator, of the accrued rights under the scheme (net of any lump sum payable on that date) and the Government Actuary's annuity rate tables (copies of which may be obtained free of charge from Supplies Section, Audit and Pension Schemes Services, Yorke House, PO Box 62, Castle Meadow Road, Nottingham NG2 1BG (tel. 0115–974 1670)). The basis on which those Tables are prepared is prescribed in *The Personal Pension Schemes (Tables of Rates of Annuities) Regulations 1996 (SI 1996 No 1311)*.

For schemes approved on or after 1 October 2000, provision is made for the alignment of different relevant reference dates where income withdrawals are taken from schemes with multi-segmented arrangements. Broadly, reviews of all such arrangements are aligned on the relevant reference date for the arrangement with the earliest pension date (disregarding certain arrangements no longer in operation). Provision is also made from that date allowing reviews after the initial period to be by reference to a particular day in the 60 days before the relevant reference date.

From 6 April 2001, where income withdrawals have been taken, schemes may make provision for different parts of the fund to be used to purchase different annuities (which may commence on different days), with corresponding provision for the review dates for continuing income withdrawal arrangements.

(iii)   A life annuity payable after the death of the participant to the surviving spouse or to a dependant, which, except as detailed at (v) below, must not be capable of assignment or surrender other than for the purpose of giving effect to a pension-sharing order or provision under *Welfare Reform and Pensions Act 1999, s 24(1)*. Such an annuity may, however, cease on the marriage of the annuitant or, in the case of an annuity to a surviving spouse, if there ceases to be any dependant under the age of 18 before the surviving spouse attains age 45. An annuity to a dependant under 18 at the time the annuity first becomes payable *must* cease on his attaining age 18 or on the later of his attaining age 18 and ceasing full-time education, unless the dependency was not only because of his being under age 18.

The aggregate of such annuities (or if they vary the initial aggregate) must not exceed the annuity (or highest annuity) payable to the participant under the scheme or, if he died before receiving an annuity under the scheme, the highest annuity that would have been payable under the scheme (ignoring any lump sum commutation, see (vi) below) had it been purchased on the day before his death. Where payments of such an annuity were or would have been affected by the making of any pension-sharing order or provision under *Welfare Reform and Pensions Act 1999, s 24(1)*, those amounts are determined as if the only payments of the annuity to be taken into account were those that have been or would have been so affected.

An annuity to a surviving spouse who is under 60 at the time of the participant's death may be deferred to a time not later than the attainment of that age or, if an annuity is payable for a term certain under (v) below which terminates after attainment of that age, the termination of that annuity.

(iv)   Where schemes (or amendments) are approved on or after 1 May 1995, income withdrawals (as under (ii) above) during a period of deferral of the purchase of an annuity under (iii) above, where the person entitled to the annuity so elects. The limitations and conditions on the amount of withdrawals are as under (ii) above, but by reference to the date of death of the participant rather than the date of election for income withdrawals, and without the provisions for alignment of review dates under multi-segmented arrangements. Withdrawals may not be made where an annuity under (iii) above has been deferred until the surviving spouse attains age 60, or after the payments under an annuity purchased under (iii) above by the person concerned would have ceased, or after that person attains the age of 75 or (if earlier) after the participant would have attained that age. The right to such income withdrawals must not be capable of assignment or surrender other than for the purpose of giving effect to a pension-sharing order or provision under *Welfare Reform and Pensions Act 1999, s 24(1)*.

(v)   An annuity as at (i) or (iii) above may continue for a term certain not exceeding ten years if the original annuitant dies within that term, and such an annuity may be assigned by will or by the annuitant's personal representatives in distributing his estate. The annuity is regarded as being for a term certain even if it may terminate on the happening, after the original annuitant's death but within that term, of the marriage of the annuitant to whom it becomes payable, or of his attaining age 18, or of the later of his attaining age 18 and ceasing full-time education.

(vi)   If the participant so elects, the benefits under the scheme may be partially commuted for a lump sum at the time when the annuity at (i) above is first payable or the time at which he elects to make income withdrawals under (ii) above. The lump sum must not exceed one-quarter of the difference between the total value at that time of the benefits under the scheme and the value at that time of the protected rights under *Social Security Act 1986* (or NI equivalent) (except that where the scheme came into existence before 27 July 1989, the protected rights reduction does not apply as regards arrangements made before that day), and must not be capable of assignment or surrender other than for the purpose of giving effect to a pension-sharing order or provision under *Welfare Reform and Pensions Act 1999, s 24(1)*. In relation to schemes approved before 27 July 1989, the reduction for protected rights was not required, but is nevertheless treated as being included in the rules where the lump sum arrangements are made on or after that date. There was also an overriding limit on the lump sum of £150,000 (variable by Treasury order), but any scheme rule applying a fixed limit (other than in relation to lump sums payable out of transfer payments) is treated as not applying to lump sums payable on or after that date.

(vii) A lump sum may be payable on the death of the participant before age 75.

(viii) If no annuity under (i) or (iii) above has become payable at the time of the participant's death, a lump sum representing a return of contributions with reasonable interest or bonuses (or if contributions are invested in a unit trust scheme, the sale or redemption price of the units) may be payable. Where schemes (or amendments) are approved on or after 1 May 1995, the lump sum may be payable on or after the participant's death, but, where the death occurred after the participant had elected for income withdrawals (within (ii) above), within two years after the death (and see 60.1 above as regards charge to tax on lump sums so payable). Also in relation to such approvals, a refund of contributions is after allowing for any withdrawals within (ii) or (iv) above, no lump sum may be paid to a surviving spouse who has elected for deferral to age 60 under (iii) above, and the prohibition where an annuity has become payable under (iii) above applies only to a lump sum payable to the person who purchased the annuity. Where schemes (or amendments) are approved on or after 29 April 1996, a lump sum may also be payable (without time limit) on the death of a person who has deferred an annuity and taken income withdrawals under (iv) above (the lump sum being required to take account of any annuity purchased under (iii) above in favour of another person).

A scheme may also make provision for insurance against a risk relating to the non-payment of contributions, so that the premiums attract relief (although any contributions paid on a claim do not do so), but this ceases to apply to insurance contracts made after 5 April 2001. Premiums on existing contracts (including those under personal pension arrangements taken out before 6 April 2001 with an option for such insurance, whether or not exercised before that date, and notwithstanding any premium variations on or after that date) will continue to attract relief. Where premiums on a contract taken out after 5 April 2001 accordingly do not attract relief, any contributions paid from claim proceeds will be capable of doing so.

Where a scheme is approved on or after 1 May 1995, it must (except in such cases as may be prescribed by regulations) prohibit the acceptance of further contributions and the making of transfer payments after the date on which an annuity within (i) above is first payable or the participant elects for income withdrawals within (ii) above. In the latter case, minimum contributions within (C) below may continue to be accepted with effect from 6 April 1996. [*SI 1996 No 805*].

An annuity within (i) or (iii) above or a lump sum within (vii) above must be payable by an authorised insurance company, which in the case of (i) and (iii) above may be chosen by the participant or the annuitant. For the definition of 'authorised insurance company', see *ICTA 1988, s 630* and, from 1 May 1995, *ICTA 1988, s 659B, 659C* introduced by *FA 1995, s 59(4)(5), s 60* and amended (from 1 December 2001) by *SI 2001 No 3629, Article 42*.

As regards the requirements relating to pension-sharing arrangements (which apply from 1 December 2000) referred to in (i)–(iv) and (vi) above, these apply in relation to approvals from 10 May 2000. For pension-sharing generally, see Pensions Update No 62, 28 April 2000.

[ICTA 1988, s 630, ss 633–637A; FA 1989, Sch 7 paras 2, 11, 12; F(No 2)A 1992, Sch 9 para 17; FA 1995, Sch 11 paras 1–8; FA 1996, s 172; FA 1999, Sch 10 paras 12–14; FA 2000, Sch 13 paras 5, 6, 9–12, 28(4); SI 2000 No 1093].

A scheme must also satisfy any requirements laid down by the Board as to the making, acceptance and application of transfer payments. *[ICTA 1988, s 638(2)]*. See *The Personal Pension Schemes (Transfer Payments) Regulations 2001 (SI 2001 No 119)*, replacing (generally with effect from 6 April 2001) the *(Transfer Payments) Regulations 1988 (SI 1988 No 1014)* (as amended), and Pensions Update No 121, 25 February 2002.

Contributions may only be accepted from

(A)   the individual participants in the scheme,

(B)   their employers, and

(C)   in respect of certain minimum contributions (the 'contracted-out' rebate), the Board of Inland Revenue (or, before 1 April 1999, the Secretary of State).

Contributions within (A) and (B) above by or in respect of a participant, together with those under any other schemes arranged by the participant, must not exceed the 'maximum amount' (within 60.3 below) for the year of assessment or (for 2001/02 onwards), if greater, the earnings threshold for that year (see 60.3 below). Any excess must be repaid to the participant to the extent of his contributions, otherwise to the employer. A scheme must not accept contributions within (C) above in respect of service as a director whose earnings are excluded from being relevant earnings (see 60.8 below), and such minimum contributions may only be accepted where either the participant is not in pensionable employment at the time the contributions are paid, or the scheme rules prohibit acceptance of contributions from the participant or employer. Schemes must (unless regulations prescribe to the contrary) prohibit the acceptance of contributions, or the making of transfer payments, after the date on which benefits are first taken under (i) or (ii) above (subject, from 6 April 2001, to *ICTA 1988, s 638ZA*, see below, which provides for benefits to be taken separately in respect of different parts of the scheme funds). For 2001/02 onwards, schemes may accept contributions in cash or equivalent (as previously) or in the form of the transfer (at market value) of shares acquired under a SAYE option scheme, an approved profit-sharing scheme or a share incentive plan (see 82.47, 82.18, 82.20 SHARE-RELATED EMPLOYMENT INCOME AND EXEMPTIONS), provided that the transfer takes place within 90 days of the right to acquire the shares being exercised.

[ICTA 1988, s 638(3)–(13); FA 1988, s 55(2)(4); FA 1995, Sch 11 para 9; Social Security Contributions (Transfer of Functions etc.) Act 1999, Sch 1 para 3; FA 2000, Sch 13 para 13; ITEPA 2003, Sch 6 para 90; FA 2003, s 174(2)].

From 6 April 2001, schemes may provide for multiple annuities, and for different annuities to commence on different days, and for deferral elections to be made at different times in relation to different portions of the fund (and for corresponding availability of multiple lump sums, each subject to corresponding limitations). There are detailed provisions for applying the general restrictions on benefits where such multiple arrangements are made, effectively treating each annuity or withdrawal arrangement as deriving from a separate scheme. *[ICTA 1988, s 638ZA; FA 2000, Sch 13 para 14].*

Approval by the Board cannot be effective before 1 July 1988. Regulations provide for provisional approval to be granted. *[ICTA 1988, s 655(4)(5); FA 1988, s 54(2)(c); SI 1987 No 1765; SI 1988 No 1437; FA 1989, Sch 7 para 9].*

The Revenue have available from 31 July 1998 extensive further regulatory powers to prescribe restrictions on approval of personal pension schemes. *[ICTA 1988, s 638A; FA 1998, s 94].* See *The Personal Pension Schemes (Restriction on Discretion to Approve) (Permitted Investments) Regulations 2001 (SI 2001 No 117)*(as amended), which broadly permit schemes to invest in any assets except assets owned by scheme members and most residential property (with special rules applying to self-invested schemes).

Withdrawal of approval. If, in the Board's opinion, the facts concerning a personal pension scheme do not warrant the continuance of approval, it may be withdrawn. Approval may similarly be withdrawn in relation to any individual arrangements made under such a scheme. Withdrawal must be by written notice to the scheme administrator (and to the individual if appropriate), and must state the grounds for withdrawal and the date from which it is effective (which must not be before the date when the facts first warranted withdrawal). Approval may be withdrawn from the date on which arrangements were made where, in the Board's opinion, the securing of the provision of benefits under the arrangements was not the sole purpose of the individual in making them. [*ICTA 1988, s 650*]. There is provision for notice of withdrawal to be given to certain other persons where there is no scheme administrator or he cannot be traced. [*ICTA 1988, s 653A; FA 1998, s 97*]. See Pensions Update No 33, 26 September 1997, as regards rebated and shared commissions on transfer of funds between investment vehicles.

Where approval of any personal pension arrangements is withdrawn (as above) after 16 March 1998, tax at 40% is charged under Schedule D, Case VI on the value, immediately before approval was withdrawn, of the properly attributable part of the assets held for the purposes of the scheme under which the arrangements were made. The value of assets is their market value, except that rights or interests in respect of money lent directly or indirectly to any person who made or contributed to the arrangements (or CONNECTED PERSONS (19)) are valued at the amount owing (including unpaid interest). The person liable for the tax is the scheme administrator, but there is provision for recourse to the person who made the arrangements in certain cases. Approval of arrangements may be withdrawn for these purposes notwithstanding that approval may simultaneously be withdrawn from the whole scheme. [*ICTA 1988, ss 650(6), 650A; FA 1998, s 95*]. Assets which are the subject of a charge under *ICTA 1988, s 650A* (as above) are treated for capital gains tax purposes as acquired at the time of withdrawal of approval for a consideration equal to the amount on which tax was charged (without there being any deemed disposal at that time). [*TCGA 1992, s 239B; FA 1998, s 95(3)*].

Appeals against refusal or withdrawal of approval (including approval of conversion of a retirement benefits scheme under *ICTA 1988, Sch 23ZA*, see below) must be made to the Board within 30 days of the notice of refusal or withdrawal, and lie to the Special Commissioners. Their decision on an appeal against withdrawal may be to alter the effective date of the withdrawal. [*ICTA 1988, s 651; FA 2000, Sch 13 para 24*].

Refunds of contributions. For the circumstances in which contributions are repaid, and the procedural requirements, see Revenue Guidance Notes IR 76, Pt 18.

Trivial funds. Where a member's fund under a scheme is insufficient to provide an annuity of at least £260 p.a. or the fund does not exceed £2,500, the fund may be repaid to the member (net of expenses) if certain conditions are met (including the member's not being a member of another scheme or in receipt of an annuity from any scheme). The repayment (net of any permissible lump sum payment under the scheme) is chargeable on the member as if it were an unauthorised payment within 58.2(*h*) PENSION INCOME. (Revenue Guidance Notes IR 76, para 9.32).

Conversion of certain approved retirement benefits schemes to approved personal pension schemes. From 1 October 2000, the trustees of any retirement benefits scheme (see 67.1 RETIREMENT SCHEMES) which is eligible (broadly, money purchase schemes which could be approved as personal pension schemes under *ICTA 1988, s 631* as above, for which purpose retirement benefits schemes may be treated as consisting of different elements so as to identify those eligible for conversion) may apply to the Board of Inland Revenue for approval of the scheme (or part) as a personal pension scheme instead of as a retirement benefits scheme (or part). If the application is granted, it will apply from a specified date (not earlier than 6 April 2001). For the detailed conditions, see *ICTA 1988, Sch 23ZA*. In particular, in considering approval, the Board may require valuations of benefits and assets to be undertaken in respect of specified individual members and may require any excess assets to be dealt with in a particular way. The Board may also impose conditions as to the contributions which may be made between the date of any such valuation and the date of conversion to a personal pension scheme. [*ICTA 1988, ss 611(3), 631A, Sch 23ZA; FA 2000, Sch 13 paras 4, 7, 27*]. See *The Personal Pension Schemes (Conversion of Retirement Benefits Schemes) Regulations 2001 (SI 2001 No 118)*, which came into force on 6 April 2001, and Pensions Updates No 89, 23/30 March 2001 and No 96, 14 May 2001.

Simon's Direct Tax Service. See E7.403.

60.3   **LIMITS OF RELIEF**

For **2000/01 and earlier years,** a contribution paid by an individual under approved personal pension arrangements may be deducted from or set off against 'relevant earnings' for the year of assessment in which the payment is made. The maximum amount for which relief is available is $17\frac{1}{2}$% of 'net relevant earnings' (see 60.8 below), with increased limits for older individuals as indicated in the following table where the individual is in the age range indicated at the beginning of the tax year.

36 to 45	20%
46 to 50	25%
51 to 55	30%
56 to 60	35%
61 or more	40%

Any excess of 'net relevant earnings' over an allowable maximum (known as the earnings cap) is disregarded. The allowable maximum is the same as the 'permitted maximum' (aka the earnings cap) referred to at 67.4 RETIREMENT SCHEMES (i.e. £87,600 for 1998/99, £90,600 for 1999/2000, £91,800 for 2000/01, £95,400 for 2001/02, £97,200 for 2002/03, £99,000 for 2003/04 and **£102,000 for 2004/05**). It is increased in line with the retail prices index (unless Parliament sets a different figure) but is not reduced if the retail prices index falls. Any employer contribution is deducted from the overall contribution limit, but contributions within 60.2(C) above are ignored for this purpose. Within the overall limit, contributions to secure a lump sum payable on the death of the participant are limited to 5% of 'net relevant earnings'. [*ICTA 1988, ss 639(1), 640, 640A; FA 1989, Sch 7 paras 3, 4; FA 1995, Sch 11 para 10*].

For the deduction of basic rate tax from certain contributions, see 60.1 above.

For **2001/02 and subsequent years,** relief for contributions in any year is given up to a maximum of the greater of the 'earnings threshold' for the year and (except in the case of 'concurrent' schemes within 60.1(c) above) the 'maximum amount' for the year (which remains as for 2000/01 and earlier years, see above, including the cap on net relevant earnings). The *'earnings threshold'* is £3,600, subject to variation by the Treasury by order. As previously, any employer contribution (but not any contribution within 60.2(C) above paid by the Board) must be taken into account in arriving at the maximum contribution for which the employee can obtain relief. In relation to contributions paid after 8 April 2003, it is made clear that the earnings cap applies so as to limit the aggregate contributions paid by the individual *and* his employer (though the Revenue view is that this was always the case).

Within the overall limit, contributions to secure a lump sum payable on the death of the participant are restricted:

(*a*)   where the life assurance contract was made (or could have been made) before 6 April 2001, to **5%** of net relevant earnings; or

60.4   Personal Pension Schemes (and Stakeholder Pensions)

(*b*)   where the contract was made on or after that date (and not by exercise of an option available before that date), to **10%** of the aggregate allowable contributions made by employer and employee for that year other than for death benefits (i.e. $\frac{1}{11}$ of the *total* contributions).

[*ICTA 1988, ss 630(1)(1A), 639(1), 640, 640A; FA 2000 Sch 13 paras 16, 28(6)–(8); FA 2003, s 174(1)(2)(4)*].

For the deduction of basic rate tax from contributions, see 60.1 above.

Where relief is also available for qualifying retirement annuity premiums in a year of assessment, the relief available for personal pension contributions is correspondingly reduced. [*ICTA 1988, s 655(1)(a); FA 2000, Sch 13 para 25*]. See following Example.

Simon's Direct Tax Service. See E7.407.

60.4   *Example*

C is an employee whose date of birth is 30 April 1952 and who does not participate in his employer's occupational pension scheme. His earnings for tax purposes for 2003/04 and 2004/05 are £102,000 and £106,000 respectively. C pays annual retirement annuity premiums of £6,000 under long-standing contracts.

In August 2003, C makes a contribution of £18,000 (less basic rate tax) to a personal pension scheme. In December 2003, his employer contributes £750 to this scheme.

In the year ended 5 April 2005, C and his employer make contributions of £23,900 (less basic rate tax) and £1,000 respectively to the scheme.

The maximum relief is calculated as follows.

2003/04

	£	£
Maximum relief for personal pension contributions:		
25% of capped net relevant earnings of £99,000		24,750
Deduct retirement annuity relief claimed	6,000	
employer's contribution	750	6,750
Relief due		18,000
Amount paid		18,000
Maximum relief for retirement annuity premiums:		£
$17\frac{1}{2}$% of net relevant earnings of £102,000		17,850
Amount paid		6,000
		11,850
Less relief claimed for personal pension contributions		18,000
Unused relief		Nil
Total relief due (£18,000 + £6,000)		£24,000

688

2004/05

	£	£
Maximum relief for personal pension contributions:		
30% of capped net relevant earnings of £102,000		30,600
Deduct retirement annuity relief claimed	6,000	
employer's contribution	1,000	7,000
Relief due		23,600
Amount paid		23,900*
Maximum relief for retirement annuity premiums:		£
20% of net relevant earnings of £106,000		21,200
Amount paid		6,000
		15,200
Less relief claimed for personal pension contributions		23,600
Unused relief		Nil
Total relief due (£23,600 + £6,000)		£29,600

* For 2004/05, there are excess contributions of £300 which do not qualify for relief, and which must be repaid. Such an excess is deemed to relate primarily to contributions made by the individual rather than by his employer (see 60.2 above).

60.5   **CONTRIBUTIONS RELATED BACK**

For contributions paid **before 6 April 2001**, an individual who makes a qualifying contribution in a year of assessment (whether or not he has relevant earnings for that year) may elect that the contribution (or part) be treated as paid

(*a*)   in the last preceding year of assessment, or

(*b*)   if he had no net relevant earnings in the last preceding year, in the last preceding year but one.

Form PP43 is available from the inspector for the purpose of such an election, which must be made on or before 31 January following the year of assessment in which the contribution is paid.

Where such an election is made, the contribution is treated as having been paid in the year elected and not in the year actually paid. See 16.2 CLAIMS as regards how relief for contributions carried back to 1996/97 and subsequent years is given. An election is in practice treated by the Revenue as operative only up to the maximum available for relief for the year specified in the election. If the amount specified in the election becomes excessive as a result of an adjustment to the assessment for the year specified, the unrelievable proportion will fall back into the actual year of payment.

[*ICTA 1988, s 641; FA 1993, s 183(3); FA 1994, s 228(2)(4); FA 1996, s 135, Sch 21 para 18; FA 2000, Sch 13 para 17*].

For contributions paid **after 5 April 2001**, a person who pays a contribution on or before 31 January in any year of assessment may, at or before the time the contribution is paid, irrevocably elect for the contribution (or part) to be treated as having been paid in the preceding year of assessment and not in the year in which it was actually paid. In relation to contributions paid after 8 April 2003, it is made clear, as originally intended, that the facility to carry back contributions is available only for contributions paid by the individual who made the personal pension arrangements (and not, for example, for employer contributions). [*ICTA 1988, s 641A; FA 2000, Sch 13 para 18; FA 2003, s 174(3)(4)*].

Simon's Direct Tax Service. See E7.410.

60.6   **UNUSED RELIEF CARRIED FORWARD**

For **2000/01 and earlier years,** relief available for a year of assessment which is not used in that year may be carried forward and used to cover that part of a qualifying contribution paid in any of the next six years which exceeds the relief limit (see 60.3 above) for that year. Relief is given in the year in which the contribution is paid although the maximum relief for that year must be used first. Unused relief for earlier years must be used before that for later years. Form PP42 is available from the inspector for claiming such relief.

Where an assessment on an individual's earnings becomes final and conclusive more than six years after the end of the year to which it relates, and as a result there is an amount of unused relief for that year, that amount shall not be available for any of the following six years. However, that relief may be covered by a qualifying contribution paid within six months of the date on which the assessment becomes final and conclusive. Relief is given in the year of assessment in which the contribution is paid but is not allowed unless the maximum contribution allowable for that year (see 60.3 above) is paid. Although the extra contribution representing the unused relief must be paid within the specified six months, the maximum contribution for the year of assessment in which the extra contribution is paid may be paid at any time within the normal time limits for that year. If relief is given for a contribution in this way, it may not be given under the normal carry-forward rule. Relief is given in a similar way where relevant earnings for a year which ended more than six years previously are not formally assessed but are taken into account in a contract settlement in a case involving fraudulent or negligent conduct. See 30.11 FRAUDULENT OR NEGLIGENT CONDUCT.

Where contributions are made under both approved personal pension arrangements and retirement annuity contracts (see 66 RETIREMENT ANNUITIES) in a year of assessment, the unused relief that may be utilised in that year is correspondingly reduced. For the method of calculating the reduction, see *Brock v O'Connor (Sp C 118), [1997] SSCD 157.*

No unused relief for personal pension contributions may be carried forward to 2001/02 or any later year.

[*ICTA 1988, s 642; FA 2000, Sch 13 para 19*].

60.7   *Example*

P, who was born in 1975, entered non-pensionable employment in September 1997 and his recent personal pension scheme contribution record, assuming no unused relief before 6 April 1997, is as follows.

Year	Net relevant earnings £	Maximum relief due £	Amount paid £	Unused relief £
1997/98	15,000	2,625	2,425	200
1998/99	19,000	3,325	2,200	1,125
1999/2000	22,000	3,850	3,375	475

In 2000/01, P pays a personal pension scheme contribution of £5,000 (less basic rate tax). His net relevant earnings for that year are £24,000.

P has excess contributions for 2000/01 as follows.

Net relevant earnings	£24,000

	£
Maximum relief (£24,000 × 17½%)	4,200
Contributions made	5,000
Excess contributions	£800

Tax relief on the excess contributions can be obtained in the following way.

In 1999/2000

£475 may be related back to 1999/2000 and relief obtained for that year (see 60.5 above).

In 2000/01

The remainder (£325) is matched on a first in, first out basis with the unused relief brought forward (see 60.6 above).

	£	£
Excess contributions as above		800
Deduct amount related back to 1999/2000		475
		325
Unused relief 1997/98	200	
Unused relief 1998/99	125	325

Thus, full relief is obtained for the £5,000 paid in 2000/01 and P's revised relief record is as follows.

Year	Net relevant earnings	Maximum relief due	Amount relieved	Unused relief	Unused relief c/f
	£	£	£	£	£
1997/98	15,000	2,625	2,425	200	200
1998/99	19,000	3,325	2,200	1,125	1,325
1999/2000	22,000	3,850	3,850	—	1,325
2000/01	24,000	4,200	4,525	(325)	1,000

Notes

(a)   The balance of the 1998/99 unused relief, i.e. £1,000, can no longer be carried forward.

(b)   As an alternative to carrying back £475 to 1999/2000, P could have utilised an additional £475 of his 1998/99 unused relief and obtained relief in 2000/01 for the whole of the £5,000 paid in that year. The £475 unused relief for 1999/2000 would then be carried forward together with £525 of the 1998/99 relief. A further possibility is to carry back £1,800 to 1999/2000, thus utilising all unused relief in that year and leaving £1,000 unused relief for 2000/01. This would be advantageous if the taxpayer's marginal tax rate were higher in the earlier year.

(c)   Unused relief in 2001/02 and subsequent years cannot be carried forward.

60.8   **RELEVANT EARNINGS**

'*Relevant earnings*' of an individual for the purposes of such schemes is chargeable income which is included in one of the following categories.

60.8 Personal Pension Schemes (and Stakeholder Pensions)

(*a*)   Income from an office or employment which is not 'earnings from pensionable employment', and income from property which is either attached thereto or forms part of the earnings therefrom.

(*b*)   Income chargeable under Schedule D immediately derived from the carrying on, individually or in partnership, of his trade, profession or vocation. This includes enterprise allowances (see 71.75 SCHEDULE D, CASES I AND II) and POST-CESSATION RECEIPTS (62).

(*c*)   Income from patent rights treated as earned income under *ICTA 1988, s 529*.

It does not include any amount in respect of which tax is chargeable under *ITEPA 2003* (previously Schedule E) which arises from acquisitions or disposals of shares or interests in shares, or from rights to acquire shares, or any amount in respect of which tax is chargeable under *ITEPA 2003, s 403* or, before 2003/04, under *ICTA 1988, s 148* (see 18.5 COMPENSATION FOR LOSS OF EMPLOYMENT (AND DAMAGES)), or income of the individual as director of a company whose income is wholly or mainly investment income and which is controlled (within *ICTA 1988, s 840*) by the individual, with or without past or present directors of the company. Nor does it include earnings of a person who is a 'controlling director' at any time in the year of assessment in question, or who has been one at any time during the period of ten years prior to that year, if at any time in the year of assessment any of the following circumstances apply to him.

(i)   He is in receipt of benefits under a 'relevant superannuation scheme' payable in respect of past service with the company.

(ii)   He is in receipt of benefits under a personal pension scheme, the scheme has received a transfer payment from a 'relevant superannuation scheme', and the transfer payment was in respect of past service with the company.

(iii)   He is in receipt of benefits under a 'relevant superannuation scheme', the benefits are payable in respect of past service with another company, and the emoluments are for a period during which the company of which he is a 'controlling director' has carried on a trade or business previously carried on by the second company, which itself carried on the trade or business at any time during the period of service in respect of which the benefits are payable.

(iv)   He is in receipt of benefits under a personal pension scheme, the scheme received a transfer payment from a 'relevant superannuation scheme', the transfer payment was in respect of past service with another company, and the emoluments are for a period during which the company of which he is a 'controlling director' has carried on a trade or business previously carried on by the second company, which itself carried on the trade or business at any time during the period of service in respect of which the transfer payment was made.

For these purposes benefits which would have been received in respect of past service but for the transfer of rights under a pension-sharing order or provision under *Welfare Reform and Pensions Act 1999, s 24(1)* are treated as being received in respect of such service. Benefits received *as* an ex-spouse are, however, excluded. Transfer payments similarly do not include any made for the purpose of giving effect to a pension-sharing order or provision.

A person is a '*controlling director*' if he is a director within *ICTA 1988, s 612(1)* and comes within the meaning of *ICTA 1988, s 417(5)(b)* (which broadly refers to ownership, or direct or indirect control, with or without associates, of 20% or more of ordinary share capital). '*Relevant superannuation scheme*' has the same meaning as in *ICTA 1988, s 645(1)* (see below). References to benefits and transfer payments payable in respect of past service include benefits and transfer payments partly so payable.

In determining 'net relevant earnings' (see below), relevant earnings are determined before deducting capital allowances (other than those deductible in computing profits) but inclusive of any balancing charges.

A married woman's relevant earnings are *not* relevant earnings of her husband for these purposes.

[*ICTA 1988, s 644; FA 1989, Sch 7 para 5, Sch 12 para 16; FA 1999, Sch 10 para 15; ITEPA 2003, Sch 6 para 92*].

'*Earnings from pensionable employment*' are earnings from an office or employment in respect of service in which the individual is a participant in a 'relevant superannuation scheme'. Such schemes under which benefits are restricted to an annuity to a surviving spouse or dependant and/or a lump sum on death in service are disregarded for this purpose. See also below as regards concessional relief in the case of certain small lump sum retirement benefits schemes. Where the only benefit paid under a scheme in respect of a period of employment was a refund of contributions (or where no benefit accrued in a non-contributory scheme), earnings from that employment are relevant earnings for the purposes of carry-forward of unused relief (see 60.6 above). (Revenue Guidance Notes IR 76, para 7.12).

A '*relevant superannuation scheme*' is a scheme established by a person other than the individual concerned, an object of which is the provision of retirement benefits, and which is (or, in the case of certain foreign earnings, corresponds to) a scheme within 67.1(*a*)–(*c*) RETIREMENT SCHEMES. It does not include a scheme converted to a personal pension scheme under *ICTA 1988, Sch 23ZA* (see 60.2 above).

It is irrelevant for this purpose where the duties of the office or employment are performed, and whether or not the individual is chargeable to tax in respect of it.

[*ICTA 1988, s 645; FA 1989, Sch 7 para 6; FA 2000, Sch 13 para 20; ITEPA 2003, Sch 6 para 93*].

'*Net relevant earnings*' are relevant earnings, as above, less deductions which would be made therefrom in computing the individual's total income for income tax, being:

(i)   deductions which but for *ICTA 1988, s 74(1)(m), (p) or (q)* could be made in computing his profits or gains (i.e. various payments, subject to deduction of tax at source, made for business purposes, but excluding e.g. annuities to former partners, which would be prohibited under *ICTA 1988, s 74(1)(a)*);

(ii)   deductions made by virtue of *ITEPA 2003, ss 232, 336, 343, 344 or 351* or for travelling or subsistence expenses by virtue of *ITEPA 2003, Pt 5* (previously those made by virtue of *ICTA 1988, ss 197AG, 198 or 201*), which refer to allowable expenses, mileage allowances, professional fees and subscriptions and certain travelling and subsistence expenses, or clergymen's expenses under *ICTA 1988, s 332(3)*; or

(iii) deductions in respect of losses, or of capital allowances, relating to activities any profits from which would be relevant earnings of the individual.

'Relevant earnings' for this purpose are those earnings before giving effect to any capital allowance not an allowable deduction in arriving at profits, but after taking account of balancing charges.

Other amounts deducted in charging the individual's income to tax (e.g. for earnings from work done abroad, see 75.7 SCHEDULE E—EMPLOYMENT INCOME, or under the current provisions) do not reduce net relevant earnings.

Where

(A)   in any year of assessment 2000/01 or earlier, contributions are relieved against relevant earnings, or

(B)   in any year of assessment 2001/02 or later, higher rate relief for contributions is given by an extension of the basic rate limit (see 60.1 above),

and a deduction for a loss or allowance under (iii) above is treated as made to any extent out of income other than relevant earnings, net relevant earnings for the next year are treated as reduced to that extent, any balance being carried forward to the third year, and so on.

In the case of partnership profits, net relevant earnings are the share of partnership income (as computed for tax purposes) after allowable deductions for partnership payments and capital allowances.

[*ICTA 1988, s 646; FA 2000, Sch 13 para 21; FA 2001, Sch 12 Pt II para 14; ITEPA 2003, Sch 6 para 94*].

However, where an individual holds two or more 'associated' employments in a year, at least one of which is pensionable (as above) and one not, the earnings from the non-pensionable employment(s) are taken into account only to the extent that those from the pensionable employment(s) do not exceed the allowable maximum (see 60.3 above). Employments are '*associated*' if one employer controls the other, or both are controlled by a third person, directly or indirectly, at any time in the year. [*ICTA 1988, s 646A; FA 1989, Sch 7 para 8; ITEPA 2003, Sch 6 para 95*].

Simon's Direct Tax Service. See **E7.408** *et seq.*

60.9   **Presumption of same level of net relevant earnings for five years.** Where a member of a personal pension scheme provides evidence (as prescribed by regulations made by the Board) of the amounts needed to calculate his net relevant earnings for any year of assessment (the '*basis year*') to the scheme administrator (whether or not he was a member of the scheme in the basis year), it is presumed that those amounts, and hence the net relevant earnings, are the same in each of the five years of assessment following the basis year. The earliest year to which such a presumption may apply is 2001/02. This is subject to such conditions or exceptions as may be prescribed by regulations made by the Board.

From 23 April 2002, the earnings cap (see 60.3 above) for the current year is applied to the net relevant earnings for the nominated basis year, so that there is no need to re-nominate the basis year simply to take account of the increased earnings cap each year. Previously, the Revenue considered that the net relevant earnings of the basis year were subject to the earnings cap for that year. (Pensions Update No 130, 23 April 2002).

Certain particulars furnished under the *Personal Pension Schemes (Relief at Source) Regulations 1988* (*SI 1988 No 1013*), *reg 5* for years before 2001/02 are treated as satisfying the evidence requirement in relation to a basis year for the purposes of the above presumption.

Where such evidence is provided for a later basis year, it supersedes that provided for the earlier basis year. If the actual net relevant earnings are higher in the later year, the supersession has effect for the later basis year and subsequent years of assessment In any other case, it has effect only for years of assessment later than the last of the five years following the earlier basis year. The order in which evidence is presented in relation to different basis years is immaterial for these purposes.

Where the member has no actual (as opposed to presumed) relevant earnings for a year of assessment not earlier than 2001/02 (the '*break year*'), but had actual relevant earnings for the preceding year (the '*cessation year*') and was entitled to make contributions in excess of the earnings threshold (see 60.3 above) in any one or more of the six years of assessment preceding the break year (the '*reference years*'), special rules apply to any of the five years of assessment following the cessation year other than a year or years

(a)   for which there were actual relevant earnings, or

(b)   throughout which the member held a pensionable office or employment (as above), or

(c)   immediately following a year excluded under (a) or (b).

Under these special rules, the member may, by providing the requisite evidence, choose *any one* of the six reference years as his basis year. It does not matter if the basis year chosen is more than five years earlier than the post-cessation year under review. If the member has provided the requisite evidence for two or more reference years, he may, by written notice to the scheme administrator, nominate which of those is to be the basis year. The supersession rules above do not apply. Years excluded by (a)–(c) above are not thereby excluded in relation to a different break year.

[*ICTA 1988, ss 646B–646D; FA 2000, Sch 13 paras 22, 23, 28(8), 29*].

See Simon's Direct Tax Service E7.407.

60.10   *Examples*

(A) Presumption of NRE for five years (ICTA 1988, s 646B)
Alistair (born on 10 August 1966) is self-employed and has net relevant earnings (NRE) as follows.

Year	NRE
	£
1996/97 to 1998/99	16,000 p.a.
1999/2000	24,000
2000/01	20,000
2001/02	18,000
2002/03	21,000
2003/04	23,000
2004/05	40,000
2005/06	28,000

Alistair joins a personal pension scheme in 2000/01 and wishes to make the maximum allowable contributions for each year (ignoring unused relief for 1999/2000 and earlier years — see 60.6 above). If no basis year is chosen, Alistair's maximum allowable contributions are as follows.

Year	Age at start of year	% of NRE allowable	NRE	Maximum allowable contributions
			£	£
2000/01	33	$17\frac{1}{2}$%	20,000	3,500
2001/02	34	$17\frac{1}{2}$%	18,000	3,600*
2002/03	35	$17\frac{1}{2}$%	21,000	3,675
2003/04	36	20%	23,000	4,600
2004/05	37	20%	40,000	8,000
2005/06	38	20%	28,000	5,600

* Maximum allowable contributions are equal to 'earnings threshold' of £3,600 as this is greater than the appropriate percentage of NRE (£18,000 @ $17\frac{1}{2}$% = £3,150) (see 60.3 above)

However, if Alistair chooses, say, 1999/2000 as his basis year (by providing evidence of earnings — see 60.9 above), his NRE for each of the following five years are presumed to be the same as for 1999/2000 (though the presumption cannot have effect for any year earlier than 2001/02). Maximum allowable contributions are now as follows.

Year	Age at start of year	% of NRE allowable	NRE £	Maximum allowable contributions £
2000/01	33	$17\frac{1}{2}$%	20,000	3,500
2001/02	34	$17\frac{1}{2}$%	24,000	4,200
2002/03	35	$17\frac{1}{2}$%	24,000	4,200
2003/04	36	20%	24,000	4,800
2004/05	37	20%	24,000	4,800
2005/06	38	20%	28,000	5,600

Clearly, for 2004/05, actual NRE are greater than presumed NRE. If Alistair now chooses 2004/05 as his basis year (again by providing evidence of earnings), this supersedes the earlier presumption for that year, and his NRE for 2004/05 and each of the following five years are based on the new presumption. Maximum allowable contributions are finally as follows.

Year	Age at start of year	% of NRE allowable	NRE £	Maximum allowable contributions £
2000/01	33	$17\frac{1}{2}$%	20,000	3,500
2001/02	34	$17\frac{1}{2}$%	24,000	4,200
2002/03	35	$17\frac{1}{2}$%	24,000	4,200
2003/04	36	20%	24,000	4,800
2004/05	37	20%	40,000	8,000
2005/06	38	20%	40,000	8,000

Notes

(*a*) For 2001/02 onwards, contributions are payable net of basic rate tax regardless of the payer's tax position (see 60.1 above), so for 2001/02, for example, Alistair would pay £3,276 (£4,200 less tax at 22%). If his taxable income exceeds the basic rate limit, that limit is increased, on a claim, by the gross amount of the contribution, so as to give higher rate relief.

(*b*) If Alistair wished to attribute part of his contributions to a term assurance contract so as to secure death benefits, the maximum so attributable for 2001/02 onwards is $\frac{1}{11}$ of the *total* allowable contributions paid, e.g. for 2001/02, £382 (£4,200 × $\frac{1}{11}$) (see 60.3 above).

(B) Presumption of NRE following cessation of earnings (ICTA 1988, s 646D)

Rowena (born on 20 April 1955) is in non-pensionable employment, joins a personal pension scheme in 2001/02 and wishes to make the maximum allowable contributions for each year (ignoring unused relief for 2000/01 and earlier years — see 60.6 above). In May 2003, she gives up work to care for a sick child (but can continue to fund the maximum pension contributions). In January 2009, she takes up a new non-pensionable employment. Set out below are Rowena's net relevant earnings (NRE) and maximum allowable contributions, the latter computed on the assumption that the most beneficial basis years are chosen (by providing evidence of earnings — see 60.9 and *Example (A)* above).

Year	Actual NRE	Age at start of year	% of NRE allowable	Basis year chosen	Presumed NRE	Maximum allowable contributions
	£				£	£
1996/97	30,000	—	—	—	—	—
1997/98	31,000	—	—	—	—	—
1998/99	36,000	—	—	—	—	—
1999/00	33,000	—	—	—	—	—
2000/01	34,000	—	—	—	—	—
2001/02	35,000	45	20%	1998/99	36,000	7,200
2002/03	35,000	46	25%	1998/99	36,000	9,000
2003/04*	6,000	47	25%	1998/99	36,000	9,000
2004/05**	Nil	48	25%	1998/99	36,000	9,000
2005/06	Nil	49	25%	1998/99	36,000	9,000
2006/07	Nil	50	25%	1998/99	36,000	9,000
2007/08	Nil	51	30%	1998/99	36,000	10,800
2008/09	10,000	52	30%	2008/09	10,000	3,600 (note (a))
2009/10	40,000	53	30%	2009/10	40,000	12,000
2010/11	38,000	54	30%	2009/10	40,000	12,000

*   the 'cessation year' (see 60.9 above)
**   the 'break year' (see 60.9 above)

Notes

(a)   The year 2008/09 is the fifth post-cessation year, but is also a year in which there are actual relevant earnings, so the special rules for post-cessation years do not apply (see 60.9 above). Instead, under the general rules in *Example (A)* above, Rowena could choose any of the five years immediately preceding 2008/09 as her basis year. She would not, in fact, do so, as her actual NRE for 2008/09 are greater than for any of those years. Her maximum allowable contributions based on the appropriate percentage of NRE are £3,000 (£10,000 @ 30%) but the 'earnings threshold' of £3,600 (see 60.3 above) is greater and thus applies instead.

(b)   By a combination of the post-cessation rules and the general rules, the same year's actual NRE can potentially be used to support contributions for up to eleven years. In this example, the 2007/08 contributions are based on NRE for 1998/99, nine years previously.

(c)   A new regime for pension provision takes effect on 6 April 2006 (see 59 PENSION PROVISION AFTER 5 APRIL 2006) and supersedes this chapter. This example includes years after 2005/06 but has been retained here in its original form purely for illustrative purposes.

60.11   SMALL LUMP SUM RETIREMENT BENEFITS SCHEMES

Concessional relief applies where an employee has

(A)   paid contributions to a personal pension scheme (or premiums on a retirement annuity contract), or the employer has made such contributions for the employee's benefit, for a year of assessment (see 60.3 above), and

(B)   accrued benefits, for the same year and in respect of the same office or employment, under an approved retirement benefits scheme

    (i)   under the rules of which the only benefit on retirement (other than from additional voluntary contributions) is a lump sum not exceeding £400 per year of pensionable service, and

(ii) whose rules provide for no such lump sum to accrue (or for the lump sum to be waived) in respect of any period for which contributions are made to a personal pension scheme or retirement annuity contract.

The tax relief for the personal pension contributions (or retirement annuity premiums) will not be withdrawn provided that

(1) the lump sum benefit entitlement for the period is waived or does not accrue, and

(2) the personal pension scheme (or retirement annuity contract) is not cancelled.

(Revenue Pamphlet IR 1, A95).

60.12   MIS-SOLD PERSONAL PENSIONS ETC.

See 28.5 EXEMPT INCOME for the exemption from income and capital gains tax of compensation awards for mis-sold personal pensions etc.

The Revenue has issued guidance on how such compensation payments should be applied and the consequences for tax purposes. The general recommendation is that compensation should be paid into an appropriate pensions vehicle to secure the benefits lost as a result of the bad advice. Where possible this should result in reinstatement or instatement into an occupational pension scheme. Payments of cash in hand would be appropriate only where the individual concerned has already retired (or died) and catching-up payments are required or, exceptionally, where it is impractical for redress to be achieved by the provision of retirement benefits. Regulations provide for the conditions under which such reinstatements may be achieved and for the disapplication of provisions under which they might otherwise be prevented, e.g. earnings cap provisions. (Pensions Updates Nos 21, 22 August 1996 and 26, 24 March 1997). See *The Occupational Pension Schemes (Transitional Provisions) (Amendment) Regulations 1996 (SI 1996 Nos 3115, 3234)*, *The Retirement Benefits Schemes (Continuation of Rights of Members of Approved Schemes) (Amendment) Regulations 1996 (SI 1996 Nos 3114, 3233)* and *The Retirement Benefits Schemes (Tax Relief on Contributions) (Disapplication of Earnings Cap) (Amendment) Regulations 1996 (SI 1996 No 3113)*, all effective from 1 January 1997.

See generally Revenue Booklet IR 12, paras 10.55 *et seq.*

61   Personal Service Companies etc.

Simon's Direct Tax Service E4.10.

61.1   INTRODUCTION

With effect for 2000/01 and subsequent tax years (and see 61.2 below), provisions are introduced 'to remove opportunities for the avoidance of tax and Class 1 national insurance contributions (NICs) by the use of intermediaries, such as [personal] service companies or partnerships, in circumstances where an individual worker would otherwise be an employee of the client or the income would be income from an office held by the worker'. (Annex to Revenue Press Release 23 September 1999). These are based on rules first published as Revenue Budget Press Release IR35 on 9 March 1999 (though significant changes were made subsequently) and thereafter commonly referred to as the 'IR35' proposals.

The rules do not prevent an individual providing his services through an intermediary. Instead, where the individual would otherwise have been categorised under pre-existing case law and practice as an employee in relation to a particular engagement, his income from that engagement is deemed to have been paid to him (if not *actually* paid to him) by the intermediary as earnings from an employment and is subject to PAY AS YOU EARN (55) and NICs. This applies even if the income is, in fact, paid to the individual in some other way, for example in the form of dividends from a personal service company (but see 61.14 below) or as a share of partnership profits within Schedule D, Case I or II, or is retained within the intermediary. Some allowance is made for deductible expenses (see 61.8, 61.9 below). Although proposed as an attack on avoidance, the provisions apply to any situation within their ambit (see 61.3, 61.5 below) and are not dependent on the taxpayer's motive.

The tax provisions are contained in *ITEPA 2003, ss 48–61* (originally *FA 2000, s 60, Sch 12*) and are described in this chapter. For the NIC position, see *The Social Security Contributions (Intermediaries) Regulations 2000 (SI 2000 No 727)* (or, as regards Northern Ireland, *SI 2000 No 728*), and see Tolley's National Insurance Contributions.

The Revenue have published on a dedicated website — at www.inlandrevenue.gov.uk/ir35 — their answers to a number of so-called 'Frequently Asked Questions' (FAQs) on both the tax and NICs aspects of these provisions. A selection of these is reproduced, together with a worked example, in Revenue Tax Bulletin June 2000 pp 751–757. See also Revenue Pamphlets IR 175 and IR 2003.

There is also a general article in the Revenue Tax Bulletin February 2001 pp 819–826 explaining who is affected by these provisions and what actions need to be considered where they do apply. It also explains step-by-step how the deemed payment (see 61.7 *et seq.* below) is calculated.

The detailed Revenue internal instructions on the operation of these provisions are contained in the Employment Status Manual ESM 3000 *et seq.*

The operation of *ITEPA 2003, ss 44–47* (workers supplied by agencies — see 75.49 SCHEDULE E—EMPLOYMENT INCOME) is not affected by these provisions. Those *sections* apply only where the worker engaged through the agency is an individual. If a service company, for example, is engaged by a client via an independent agency, the provisions in this chapter may well apply but will not directly affect the agency. Nothing in this chapter applies to a payment subject to deduction of tax under *ICTA 1988, s 555* (payments to non-resident entertainers and sportsmen — see 51.7 NON-RESIDENTS AND OTHER OVERSEAS MATTERS). [*ITEPA 2003, s 48(2); FA 2000, Sch 12 paras 6, 24*].

Simon's Direct Tax Service. See E4.1001.

The remainder of this chapter is set out under the following headings.

61.2 Personal Service Companies etc.

61.2 COMMENCEMENT

The provisions have effect for **2000/01 and subsequent tax years in relation to services performed after 5 April 2000**. Payments and other benefits received on or before that date in respect of services performed after that date are treated for these purposes as received in the tax year 2000/01 and are thus brought within the scope of these provisions. [*FA 2000, Sch 12 para 22*]. As regards non-corporate intermediaries, see also the transitional measure at 61.17 below.

61.3 SERVICES PROVIDED THROUGH AN INTERMEDIARY

The provisions apply in relation to an engagement where the following conditions are all present:

(*a*)   an individual (the worker) personally performs, or is under an obligation personally to perform, services for another person (the client);

(*b*)   the services are provided not under a contract directly between worker and client but under arrangements involving a third party (the 'intermediary') to which these provisions apply (see 61.5 below); and

(*c*)   if the services had been provided under a direct contract as mentioned in (*b*) above, the worker would have fallen to be categorised for income tax purposes as an employee of the client (see 61.4, 61.18 below).

The term '*intermediary*' in (*b*) above can refer to a company or to an individual. It is expressly provided that the term also refers to a partnership or unincorporated body of which the worker is a member.

In relation to services performed, and due to be performed, before 10 April 2003, it was a further condition that the services be performed for the purposes of a 'business' carried on by another person. For these purposes, a '*business*' includes any activity carried on by a government or public or local authority (in the UK or elsewhere) or by a body corporate, unincorporated body or partnership. It also implicitly includes a business, but not any other activity, carried on by an individual. For the purposes of these provisions generally, a business means a trade, profession or vocation and also includes a Schedule A business (as in 69.3 SCHEDULE A). Domestic or other services provided to an individual not in business (a householder for example) were therefore outside the scope of the provisions, regardless of the test in (*c*) above. From 10 April 2003, however, domestic workers such as nannies and butlers are brought within the scope of the provisions.

[*ITEPA 2003, ss 49, 61(1); FA 2000, Sch 12 paras 1, 21(1); FA 2003, s 136*].

61.4   **Whether or not employment?** In applying the test at 61.3(*c*) above, i.e. whether or not the worker would have been an employee if engaged directly, the circumstances to be taken into account include the terms on which the services are provided, having regard to the terms of contracts forming part of the arrangements (as in 61.3(*b*) above) under which the services are provided. [*ITEPA 2003, s 49(4); FA 2000, Sch 12 para 1(4)*]. Otherwise, no statutory rules are provided, the test instead being based on pre-existing case law and practice as to the distinction between employment and self-employment — see 75.27 SCHEDULE E—EMPLOYMENT INCOME, Tolley's National Insurance Contributions under Categorisation and Revenue Pamphlet IR 56. See also Revenue Tax Bulletin February 2000 pp 715–723 for a comprehensive article and practical illustrations devoted to the provisions in this chapter. The main text of this article is summarised at the end of this chapter — at 61.18 below. It is the reality of the working relationship that counts, irrespective of whether the parties have chosen to attach a different label to it (*Massey v Crown Life Insurance Co CA 1977, [1978] 2 All ER 576*).

Taxpayers may seek an opinion from the Revenue as to whether or not a contract falls within the provisions in this chapter. The request, together with copies of contracts and any other relevant information, should be sent to North East Metropolitan, IR35 Unit, 1st Floor, Tyne Bridge Tower, Gateshead, Tyne & Wear, NE8 2DQ (fax 0845–302 3535). No opinion will be given on a *draft* agreement. (Revenue Tax Bulletin February 2001 p 820). See also Revenue Employment Status Manual ESM 3280 *et seq.*

Since the introduction of the legislation in 2000, a number of cases have come before the Special Commissioners and the Courts on the question of whether an individual would have been an employee if engaged directly by the client rather than via a service company. These have tended to be brought under the equivalent national insurance legislation referred to in 61.1 above, and each turns entirely on its own facts. For summaries of these cases, see Tolley's Tax Cases under National Insurance Contributions.

The Revenue have also identified a standard contract said to be common to service company workers engaged, through agencies, in the information technology industry. Such a contract requires the worker

(*a*)   to work where the client requests, for an agreed number of hours per week, and at an agreed hourly rate;

(*b*)   to keep a timesheet for checking by the client;

(*c*)   to be subject to the client's control; and

(*d*)   not to sub-contract the work to anyone else.

Where a worker is engaged for a month or more on a contract of this type, and cannot demonstrate a recent history of work including engagements which have the characteristics of self-employment, the Revenue will treat the engagement as being within the provisions in this chapter. (Note that whilst this may be a convenient rule of thumb, the taxpayer is not precluded from arguing for a different treatment.) Where the contract is for less than a month, the Revenue will consider each case on its merits. (Revenue Press Release 7 February 2000 and Revenue Tax Bulletin February 2000 p 717).

The income tax legislation on personal service companies does not bite if the worker's only relationship with the client is as non-executive director of the client, as the wording in 61.3(*c*) above refers to an 'employee' rather than an office-holder. (There is no such exemption for national insurance purposes.) If, however, a non-executive director performs other services for the client through an intermediary, such that under a direct contract he would have been an employee as well as an office-holder, those services do fall within the legislation. (Revenue Internet Statement 29 April 2003).

See Simon's Direct Tax Service E4.205–E4.222.

61.5 Personal Service Companies etc.

61.5 INTERMEDIARIES TO WHICH THESE PROVISIONS APPLY

The provisions apply only if the intermediary meets the relevant conditions below.

Where the intermediary is a company, the provisions apply in relation to an engagement if either

(*a*)   the worker has a 'material interest' (see below) in the intermediary, or

(*b*)   the payment or benefit in 61.7(ii) below is received or receivable by the worker directly from the intermediary and can reasonably be taken to represent remuneration for services provided by the worker to the client.

The provisions do not, however, apply if either of the above is satisfied but the intermediary is an associated company (within *ICTA 1988, s 416*) of the client by reason of both the client and itself being under the control of the worker (or of the worker and, for 2003/04 onwards, other persons (previously one other person)).

For these purposes, the worker has a *'material interest'* in a company if he, and/or certain 'associates' of his (within *ITEPA 2003, s 60* (originally *FA 2000, Sch 12 para 19*) and with the extended meaning of 'husband and wife' at 61.6(*c*) below),

(i)   beneficially owns or is able to control (directly or indirectly) more than 5% of the ordinary share capital, or

(ii)   possesses, or is entitled to acquire, rights to more than 5% of any distributions that the company may make, or

(iii)   (where the company is a close company) possesses, or is entitled to acquire, rights to more than 5% of the assets available for distribution among the participators (within *ICTA 1988, s 417(1)*) in a winding-up or in any other circumstances.

[*ITEPA 2003, ss 51, 61(1); FA 2000, Sch 12 paras 3, 21(1)*].

Providing (*a*) or (*b*) above is satisfied, the provisions apply equally to a 'composite service company' employing several workers as to a service company employing only one or two workers. (Revenue Tax Bulletin August 2002 pp 956, 957).

In both places in which it is mentioned above, *'control'* is as defined by *ICTA 1988, s 840* for 2003/04 onwards; previously it was given no statutory definition. [*ITEPA 2003, s 719*].

Where the intermediary is a partnership, the provisions apply in relation to payments or benefits received or receivable by the worker as a member of the partnership if

(A)   the worker, *alone or with one or more 'relatives'*, is entitled to at least 60% of partnership profits; or

(B)   most of the partnership profits derive from provision of services under engagements within 61.3 above to a single client (or to a single client and his 'associates' — within *ITEPA 2003, s 60* (originally *FA 2000, Sch 12 para 19*)); or

(C)   the partnership profit sharing arrangements are such that the income of any of the partners is based on the income which that partner generates from engagements within 61.3 above.

'Relative' is broadly defined to include a spouse (or cohabitant treated as such — as in 61.6(*c*) below), parent or child or remoter relation in the direct line, or brother or sister). Most family partnerships are thus potentially within these rules.

In addition, the provisions apply in relation to payments or benefits received or receivable by the worker directly from the partnership, but in a capacity other than as a member of the partnership, if they can reasonably be taken to represent remuneration for services provided by the worker to the client.

[ITEPA 2003, ss 52, 61(4); FA 2000, Sch 12 paras 4, 21(4)].

Where (exceptionally) the intermediary is an individual, the provisions apply in relation to a payment or benefit if it is received or receivable by the worker directly from the intermediary and can reasonably be taken to represent remuneration for services provided by the worker to the client. *[ITEPA 2003, s 53; FA 2000, Sch 12 para 5]*.

Overseas intermediaries. There is no requirement that the intermediary be resident or incorporated in the UK. An offshore service company, for example, can fall within these provisions (and see 61.11 below as regards place of business). See also Revenue FAQs — as in 61.1 above.

61.6 **Supplementary.** For the purposes of the above (and of these provisions generally),

(*a*) whether a person is an '*associate*' of an individual is construed in accordance with *ICTA 1988, s 417(3)(4)* (with the extended meaning of 'husband and wife' at (*c*) below), except that special rules apply to determine whether an individual is an associate of an employee benefit trust of which he is a beneficiary;

(*b*) a payment or benefit receivable from a partnership or unincorporated association includes any such payment or benefit to which a person may be entitled in his capacity as a member of the partnership or association;

(*c*) a payment or benefit provided to a member of an individual's family or household (within *ITEPA 2003, s 721(4)(5)* but treating a man and woman cohabiting as a couple as if they were husband and wife) is treated as provided to the individual; and

(*d*) anything done by an 'associate' (as defined) of an intermediary is treated as done by the intermediary.

[ITEPA 2003, s 60(1)(a), (2)–(6), s 61(2)–(4); FA 2000, Sch 12 para 19(1)(a), (2)–(6), para 21(2)–(4)].

61.7 **THE 'DEEMED EMPLOYMENT PAYMENT'**

If, as regards any engagement within 61.3 above, in any tax year

(i) the intermediary is within these provisions by virtue of 61.5 above, and

(ii) the worker (or an 'associate' of his) receives, is entitled to receive, or has rights entitling him to receive, from the intermediary (directly or indirectly) a payment or benefit that is not employment income,

the intermediary is deemed to have made to the worker, normally on 5 April in that tax year (though see 61.15 below for exceptions), a payment (a '*deemed employment payment*') the amount of which is computed as in 61.8 below and which is treated as earnings from an employment. Where such payments would be treated as having been made in respect of multiple engagements, a single such payment is deemed to have been made. See 61.12 below as regards the application of PAYE. *[ITEPA 2003, s 50; FA 2000, Sch 12 para 2]*.

See 61.6 above for the meaning of 'associate' in relation to an individual and other supplementary provisions.

61.8 **Computation of deemed employment payment.** The deemed payment in 61.7 above is computed as follows (and see the supplementary points at 61.9 below).

(1) Take the total of all 'payments' and 'benefits' (see 61.9 below) received by the intermediary in the tax year in respect of engagements falling within 61.7 above by

61.8 Personal Service Companies etc.

reference to the worker (the *'relevant engagements'*) and reduce it by 5% (see 61.9 below).

Where a payment received by the intermediary has been subjected to deduction of tax at source under the CONSTRUCTION INDUSTRY SCHEME (20), it is the gross amount before tax that must be brought into account in arriving at this total.

(2)　Add in any 'payments' and 'benefits' (see 61.9 below) received direct by the worker (and see 61.6(*c*) above) in that tax year in respect of the relevant engagements, *from anyone other than the intermediary*, that are not chargeable as employment income but would have been if the worker had been employed by the client.

(3)　Deduct

    (*a*)　any expenses met by the intermediary (see below) in that tax year which, if incurred by the worker as an employee of the client, would have been deductible under normal rules — see 75.11 SCHEDULE E—EMPLOYMENT INCOME,

    (*b*)　any capital allowances which on that basis could have been deducted by the worker from employment income under *CAA 2001, s 262* (plant and machinery allowances — see 9.32 CAPITAL ALLOWANCES), and

    (*c*)　any contributions made to an approved occupational or personal pension scheme by the intermediary in that tax year for the benefit of the worker which, if made by an employer for the benefit of an employee, would not be regarded as the employee's income for tax purposes — see 60 PERSONAL PENSION SCHEMES (AND STAKEHOLDER PENSIONS) and 67 RETIREMENT SCHEMES. Exclude any excess contributions made and later repaid.

(4)　Deduct

    (*a*)　any 'payments' and 'benefits' (see 61.9 below) received in that tax year by the worker from the intermediary and chargeable as employment income in his hands (but excluding anything already deducted under (3)(*a*) above), and

    (*b*)　any employer's Class 1 and Class 1A NICs (on salary and benefits) payable by the intermediary for that tax year in respect of the worker.

If the result is a negative amount, or is nil, there is no deemed employment payment. In any other case, the deemed employment payment is the amount which, together with employer's NICs thereon, is equal to the result of applying steps (1)–(4) above. In other words, allowance is made at this point for the fact that employer's NICs are chargeable on the deemed payment itself (see Tolley's National Insurance Contributions).

[ITEPA 2003, s 54(1)(2), s 61(1); FA 2000, Sch 12 paras 7, 8, 21(1); CAA 2001, Sch 2 para 107].

For the purposes of (3)(*a*) above, an intermediary 'meets' an expense on the date it pays the bill. (Revenue FAQs — as in 61.1 above). For 2002/03 onwards, expenses met by an intermediary include expenses met by the worker and reimbursed by the intermediary and also, in the case of a partnership intermediary of which the worker is a member, expenses met by the worker for and on behalf of the intermediary. Also for 2002/03 onwards, in a situation where the intermediary provides a vehicle for the worker, expenses deductible under (3)(*a*) above include any 'mileage allowance relief' (see 75.46 SCHEDULE E—EMPLOY-MENT INCOME) that would have been due to the worker if he had been an employee of the client and had provided the vehicle himself. This also applies, in the case of a partnership intermediary of which the worker is a member, in a situation where the worker provides the vehicle for the purposes of the partnership business. Any 'approved mileage allowance payments' or 'approved passenger payments' made by the intermediary to the worker and exempt from the charge to tax on EMPLOYMENT INCOME (75.46) are deductible under (4)(*a*) above (if not deductible under (3)(*a*) above), notwithstanding the said exemption. For 2003/04 onwards (but apparently applied in practice before then — see Change 13 listed in Annex 1 to the Explanatory Notes to the Income Tax (Earnings and Pensions) Bill), the duties performed under the relevant engagements are treated, for the purpose of determining the deductibility under (3)(*a*) above of any travelling expenses (see 75.8, 75.11(*a*) SCHEDULE E—EMPLOYMENT INCOME), as duties of a continuous employment with the intermediary. [*ITEPA 2003, s 54(3)–(7); FA 2000, Sch 12 paras 7A, 7B; FA 2002, s 38(2)(5)*].

See the Example at 61.10 below and Revenue Pamphlet IR 2003.

Simon's Direct Tax Service. See **E4.1011** *et seq.*

61.9　　**Supplementary.** For the purposes of computing the deemed employment payment as in 61.8 above, any amounts received by the intermediary that refer to more than one worker, or partly to a worker and partly to other matters, are to be apportioned on a just and reasonable basis. [*ITEPA 2003, s 54(8); FA 2000, Sch 12 para 9*].

For the purposes of 61.8(1), (2) and (4) above, a "*payment*" or "*benefit*" means anything that, if received by an employee for performing the duties of an employment, would be earnings from the employment. The amount of a payment or cash benefit is taken to be the amount received. The amount of a non-cash benefit is computed in the same way as if it were earnings of an employment, which means that it will normally, in practice, be computed under the employee benefit rules at 75.16–75.24 SCHEDULE E—EMPLOYMENT INCOME. A payment or cash benefit is treated as received when payment is actually made (or a payment is made on account). A non-cash benefit calculated by reference to a period within the tax year is treated as received, for 2003/04 onwards, at the end of that period; otherwise the time of receipt is determined under normal rules (see 75.12 SCHEDULE E—EMPLOYMENT INCOME). (Before 2003/04, a non-cash benefit was treated as received when it was used or enjoyed.) [*ITEPA 2003, s 55; FA 2000, Sch 12 para 10*].

Where the intermediary is VAT-registered, the amount to be brought into account at 61.8(1) above is the VAT-exclusive amount, and this applies even where the optional flat-rate scheme introduced by *FA 2002* is used (though in that case the VAT-exclusive amount is the amount inclusive of output VAT at the normal rate less the flat-rate VAT payable). (Revenue Tax Bulletin April 2003 p 1024).

The 5% deduction at 61.8(1) above is a standard allowance intended to cover the intermediary's running costs. It is given regardless of the actual occurrence or amount of such running costs, and does not have to be justified or supported by records. The limited deductions at 61.8(3) above, based on actual expenditure, are given in addition to the 5% deduction. The 5% deduction applies purely for the purpose of computing the deemed employment payment under these provisions, and is not deductible in computing the business profits of the intermediary (actual running costs being deductible or not, as the case may be, under normal rules — see 71 SCHEDULE D, CASES I AND II and see also 61.13 below as regards partnerships). See 61.13 below as regards deductibility of the deemed employment payment itself.

61.10　　*Example*

Harry is a systems analyst trading through his own personal service company, ABC Ltd, in which he owns 99% of the ordinary shares. During 2004/05, he is engaged at different times by two independent companies, DEF Ltd and GHJ Ltd (the client companies), in each case under a contract between the client company and ABC Ltd. It is accepted that each engagement is in the nature of employment and is within the provisions covered in this

61.11 Personal Service Companies etc.

chapter. ABC Ltd is paid £40,000 by DEF Ltd and £20,000 by GHJ Ltd for the services provided by Harry.

For 2004/05, Harry draws a salary of £28,000 from ABC Ltd which is taxed under PAYE and on which employer's NICs of, say, £3,000 are due. He is also provided with a company car on which the taxable benefit is £4,000 and on which Class 1A NICs of, say, £510 are due. ABC Ltd makes pension contributions of £3,100 into an approved scheme on Harry's behalf and reimburses motor expenses of £1,500 which, if Harry had been employed directly by the client companies, would have been qualifying travelling expenses within 75.11(a) SCHEDULE E—EMPLOYMENT INCOME. It pays a salary of £4,700 to Harry's wife who acts as company secretary and administrator.

The deemed employment payment for 2004/05 is computed, using steps numbered in accordance with 61.8 above, as follows.

		£	£	£
Step (1)	Total amount from relevant engagements			60,000
	Deduct 5%			3,000
				57,000
Step (2)	Not applicable			
Step (3)	*Deduct* (a) Expenses	1,500		
	(b) Not applicable	—		
	(c) Pension contributions	3,100	4,600	
Step (4)	*Deduct* Salary	28,000		
	Benefits	4,000		
	Employer's Class 1 NICs	3,000		
	Employer's Class 1A NICs	510	35,510	40,110
Total				£16,890

Deemed employment payment £16,890 × $\dfrac{100}{112.8}$ 14,973

Employer's NICs due on deemed payment £14,973 @ 12.8%   1,917

Total as above   £16,890

Note

The salary paid by ABC Ltd to Harry's wife is not deductible in arriving at the deemed employment payment, except to the extent that it, and other expenses of the company, are covered by the 5% deduction at 61.8(1) above. (The salary may of course be deductible under the rules of SCHEDULE D, CASE I (71) in computing ABC Ltd's taxable business profits.)

61.11   TAX TREATMENT OF DEEMED EMPLOYMENT PAYMENT

The deemed employment payment is generally treated in the same way as an actual payment of employment income, as if the worker were employed by the intermediary and as if the relevant engagements (see 61.8(1) above) were undertaken by him in the course of performing the duties of that employment. The PAYE provisions are applied as in 61.12 below. Where

(a)   the worker is UK-resident,

(*b*)   the services in question are provided in the UK, and

(*c*)   (for services performed, and due to be performed, before 10 April 2003) the client carries on business in the UK,

the intermediary is treated as having a place of business in the UK (and is thus obliged to operate PAYE for example — see 55.34 PAY AS YOU EARN) even if this is not, in fact, the case.

To the extent that, by reason of any combination of

(i)   the worker being resident, ordinarily resident or domiciled outside the UK,

(ii)   the client being resident or ordinarily resident outside the UK, and

(iii)   the services in question being provided outside the UK,

the worker would not be chargeable if employed directly by the client, he is not chargeable to tax in respect of the deemed employment payment. (See 75.4 SCHEDULE E—EMPLOYMENT INCOME for the relevant charging provisions.)

In particular, the deemed employment payment counts

(A)   to determine whether the worker is a higher- or lower-paid employee for the purpose of applying the benefits code (see 75.14 SCHEDULE E—EMPLOYMENT INCOME);

(B)   as taxable earnings for the purpose of deducting qualifying travelling expenses and other necessary expenses incurred by the worker (see 75.11(*a*) SCHEDULE E—EMPLOY-MENT INCOME) or (from 6 April 2002) mileage allowance relief (see 75.46 SCHEDULE E—EMPLOYMENT INCOME); and

(C)   as relevant earnings for personal pension contributions purposes (see 60.8 PERSONAL PENSION SCHEMES (AND STAKEHOLDER PENSIONS)).

[*ITEPA 2003, ss 56, 218(1)(d); FA 2000, Sch 12 para 11; FA 2001, Sch 12 Pt II para 16; FA 2003, s 136(3)(4)*].

Where the work is carried out outside the UK, and the worker is UK-resident and ordinarily resident, a service company may suffer foreign tax. Where the company's tax liability is insufficient to give full effect to DOUBLE TAX RELIEF (24), the Revenue suggest that the balance of foreign tax may be allowed against UK tax (but not NICs) on the deemed employment payment, but only where it is possible to directly link the work in the overseas country and the deemed payment. (Revenue FAQs — as in 61.1 above).

For an article, including case studies, on the international issues surrounding the personal service company legislation, concentrating mainly on the national insurance aspects, see Revenue Tax Bulletin April 2003 pp 1016–1020.

61.12   **PAYE.** By virtue of 61.11 above, the intermediary must account for tax under PAY AS YOU EARN (55) as if the deemed employment payment to the worker were an actual payment of employment income. Where, as is normally the case, the employment payment is deemed to be made on 5 April in the tax year (see 61.7 above), then, strictly, the total tax, employee's NICs and employer's NICs due in respect of the deemed payment must be paid over to the Revenue on or before 19 April following the tax year (as in 55.8 PAY AS YOU EARN), which may leave insufficient time for the amount of the deemed payment to be computed. In practice, the Revenue will accept a lower, provisional amount on account. They must be notified on Employer's Annual Return Form P35 (due by the following 19 May — see 55.9 PAY AS YOU EARN) that the amount paid is provisional (if this remains the case). The balance due must be paid (and a supplementary P35 submitted) by the following 31 January. Provided that deadline is met, the Revenue will not seek to recover the underpaid tax in the meantime and will not seek PENALTIES (57.9). Subject to the concession described below, **interest on**

overdue tax will, however, accrue from 19 April following the tax year as normal (see 55.8 PAY AS YOU EARN). (Revenue FAQs — as in 61.1 above, Revenue Pamphlet IR 175).

See Simon's Direct Tax Service E4.1020.

Where the intermediary fails to account for PAYE on a deemed employment payment, then, in addition to their powers to recover such tax and impose interest and penalties, the Revenue also have the option of using pre-existing rules (see 55.7 PAY AS YOU EARN) to collect the tax and NICs direct from the worker. (Annex to Revenue Press Release 23 September 1999).

See 61.16 below as regards joint and several liability of multiple intermediaries.

Interaction with construction industry scheme — concession. Where a deemed employment payment is based on amounts received by a company under deduction under the CONSTRUCTION INDUSTRY SCHEME (20), the amounts deducted are treated as corporation tax paid in respect of company profits, and are therefore not available for offset against any liability in respect of the deemed employment payment. By concession, where, as a result of such deductions, a company is entitled to a corporation tax repayment for an accounting period which overlaps a tax year for which a deemed employment payment is treated as made, the company may claim to set off the corporation tax repayment against any outstanding tax and NICs due in respect of the deemed employment payment, using 19 April in the following tax year as the effective date of payment for the set-off. Provided that the claim is made by the following 31 January (and is accepted), no interest will be charged on the amount of any late-paid tax and NICs in respect of the deemed employment payment which is matched by the corporation tax repayment. This concession first applies in relation to deemed employment payments arising on 5 April 2001 on which the tax and NICs are due by 19 April 2001. (Revenue Pamphlet IR 1, C32). See also Revenue Tax Bulletin June 2001 p 861 and Revenue Employment Status Manual ESM 3262, 3269 *et seq.*

61.13   **Computation of intermediary's business profits.** Subject to the special rules below for partnerships, a deemed employment payment (and related employer's NICs) is an allowable expense in computing the business profits (or losses) of the intermediary, for the purposes of SCHEDULE D, CASES I AND II (71), for the period of account in which the payment is treated as made (but for no other period of account). [*FA 2000, Sch 12 para 17; ITEPA 2003, Sch 6 para 244(2)*].

Partnerships — special rules. The above applies equally where the intermediary is a partnership except that:

(*a*)   the deduction for the deemed employment payment can reduce the partnership profits to nil for tax purposes but it cannot create a trading loss; and

(*b*)   the expenses of the partnership in connection with the relevant engagements (see 61.8(1) above) are deductible only to the extent that in any tax year they do not exceed the sum of

  (i)   the 5% deduction at 61.8(1) above, and

  (ii)   the deduction at 61.8(3)(*a*) above.

[*FA 2000, Sch 12 para 18; FA 2002, s 38(4)(5); ITEPA 2003, Sch 6 para 244(3)*].

Simon's Direct Tax Service. See E4.1021.

61.14   **RELIEF WHERE DIVIDENDS ETC. PAID BY INTERMEDIARY**

A relief from double taxation is available where a **company** intermediary is treated as making a deemed employment payment in any tax year and also pays a dividend (or otherwise makes a distribution) in that or a subsequent tax year. A claim for relief must be made in writing by the intermediary within five years after 31 January following the tax year in which the dividend is paid. Relief is given by reducing the dividend (not the deemed employment payment) but only if the Revenue are satisfied that this is necessary to avoid a double charge to tax. The reduction is made, as far as practicable, by setting the amount of the deemed payment against

(a)   dividends etc. of the same tax year in priority to those of other years;

(b)   dividends etc. received by the worker before those received by another person; and

(c)   dividends etc. of earlier years before those of later years.

Where a dividend is reduced, the associated tax credit is correspondingly reduced. See 1.9 ALLOWANCES AND TAX RATES for taxation of dividends and other distributions generally.

[*ITEPA 2003, s 58; FA 2000, Sch 12 para 13*].

Simon's Direct Tax Service. See **E4.1025**.

61.15   **EARLIER DATE OF DEEMED EMPLOYMENT PAYMENT IN CERTAIN CASES**

As stated in 61.7 above, the deemed employment payment is normally treated as made on 5 April in the relevant tax year. If, however, a 'relevant event' occurs in relation to the intermediary in that tax year and before that date, the deemed employment payment is treated as made immediately before that event, or, if there is more than one, immediately before the first of them. The fact that the deemed payment is treated as made before the end of the tax year does not affect the way in which it is computed and the receipts and other matters that are taken into account.

In relation to a **company** intermediary, any of the following is a '*relevant event*':

(a)   where the worker is a member of the company (which normally means a share-holder), his ceasing to be a member;

(b)   where the worker holds an office with the company (for example, as a director), his ceasing to hold that office;

(c)   where the worker is an employee of the company, his ceasing to be an employee;

(d)   (for 2002/03 onwards) the company ceasing to trade.

In relation to a **partnership** intermediary, any of the following is a '*relevant event*':

(i)   the dissolution of the partnership or cessation of the partnership trade;

(ii)   a partner ceasing to act as such;

(iii) where the worker is an employee of the partnership, his ceasing to be an employee.

Where the intermediary is an **individual** and the worker is employed by him, a '*relevant event*' occurs if the worker ceases to be so employed.

[*ITEPA 2003, s 57; FA 2000, Sch 12 para 12; FA 2002, s 38(3)(5)*].

61.16   **MULTIPLE INTERMEDIARIES**

Where, in the case of an engagement within 61.3 above, the arrangements (as in 61.3(*b*) above) involve one or more intermediaries within 61.5 above, then, except as below, these provisions apply separately in relation to each such intermediary.

61.17 Personal Service Companies etc.

Where a payment or other benefit has been made or provided, directly or indirectly, by one such intermediary to another in respect of the engagement, the amount taken into account at 61.8(1) or (2) above (computation of deemed employment payment) in relation to any intermediary is to be reduced as necessary so as to avoid double-counting.

All such intermediaries are jointly and severally liable to account for PAYE (55) on a deemed employment payment treated as made by any of them in respect of the engagement in question, or in respect of multiple engagements which include the engagement in question, except that an intermediary is excepted from such liability if has not received any payment or benefit in respect of the engagement(s).

[*ITEPA 2003, s 59; FA 2000, Sch 12 paras 14–16*].

Simon's Direct Tax Service. See **E4.1026**.

61.17 **TRANSITION**

An **individual or partnership intermediary** carrying on a pre-existing business at 6 April 2000 and treated under these provisions as making one or more deemed employment payments for 2000/01 could elect that the business be deemed to have been permanently discontinued on 5 April 2000 and that a new business be deemed to have commenced on 6 April 2000. The opening years and closing year rules at 71.4, 71.9 SCHEDULE D, CASE I have effect, but for the purpose of enabling trading losses to be carried forward under *ICTA 1988, s 385* (see 46.9 LOSSES) the 'old' and 'new' businesses are treated as the same business. The election had to be included in a personal or partnership tax return (as the case may be) delivered on or before its due date (see 68.2, 68.13 RETURNS). [*FA 2000, Sch 12 para 23*].

The purpose of providing for such an election was to give an unincorporated business the option of obtaining tax relief for the same tax year as that in which the first deemed employment payment fell to be taxed in the worker's hands. Otherwise, for example, a continuing intermediary business making a deemed payment on 5 April 2001 in relation to income received for its period of account ending on, say, 30 April 2001 would not have obtained relief for that payment (as a business expense) until the tax year 2001/02, whereas the payment fell to be taxed under PAYE (and attracts NICs) for 2000/01.

61.18 **DECIDING EMPLOYMENT STATUS — SUMMARY OF REVENUE TAX BULLETIN ARTICLE**

The following is a summary of the main text of the article in Revenue Tax Bulletin February 2000 pp 716–723 referred to at 61.4 above. The views expressed are those of the Revenue, who emphasise that their role is 'to provide advice and guidance about the employment status resulting from a given set of circumstances, not to impose any particular status. The terms and conditions of any engagement are entirely a matter for the parties involved.' See also 61.4 above as regards the Revenue's identification of a 'standard contract' and their advice thereon (which is included in the said article but not covered again below). See also 75.27 SCHEDULE E—EMPLOYMENT INCOME, particularly as regards relevant case law.

Whether a worker would have fallen to be treated as an employee of the client if engaged directly by the client rather than though an intermediary depends on a range of factors. However, it is not a mechanical exercise of running through a checklist with a view to adding up, and comparing, the number of factors pointing towards employment and self-employment respectively. The overall effect must be evaluated, which is not necessarily the same as the sum of the individual factors; the factors may not be of equal weight or importance in a given situation and may also vary in importance from one situation to another. See also *Hall v Lorimer CA 1993, 66 TC 349*. The intention of the parties may be conclusive if, but only if, the evidence is otherwise evenly balanced.

It is first necessary to establish the terms and conditions of the engagement, which is usually achieved mainly by considering the contract (whether written, oral or implied — or a mixture of those) between the client and the intermediary. Next, it is necessary to consider any relevant surrounding facts, for example whether the worker has other clients and a business organisation. In this context, other contracts under which the worker's services are supplied by the intermediary may be taken into account, as may any business organisation of the intermediary which is relevant to that supply.

Relevant factors in determining whether a contract is a 'contract for service' (i.e. employment) or a 'contract for services' (self-employment) are listed below.

(*a*)   Does the client have the right to exercise **control** over the worker? This may be a right to control what work is done, where or when it is done and/or how it is done. A working relationship involving no control at all is unlikely to be employment. Where the client has the right to determine *how* the work is done or *what* work is carried out, this is, in either case, a strong pointer towards employment.

(*b*)   Personal service is an essential element of a contract of employment. If the worker has the freedom to choose whether to do the job himself or hire a **substitute** to do it for him or a helper to provide substantial help, this points towards self-employment.

(*c*)   The provision by the worker of significant **equipment** and/or materials which are fundamental to the engagement is a strong pointer towards self-employment. If the client provides the office space (where relevant) and equipment, this points towards employment. Note that in some trades it is not uncommon for *employees* to provide their own small tools.

(*d*)   The taking on by the worker of **financial risk**, for example his buying significant assets and materials and/or quoting a fixed price for the job with the consequent risk of bearing the extra costs if it overruns, is a strong pointer towards self-employment.

(*e*)   **Basis of payment.** Employees tend to be paid a fixed wage or salary, weekly or monthly, and possibly bonuses or overtime. A self-employed contractor tends to be paid a fixed sum for a particular job. (Piece work or payment by commission can be a feature of both employment and self-employment.)

(*f*)   A person who may **profit from sound management**, i.e. his reward for the job varies according to his ability to organise the work effectively and reduce overheads, may well be self-employed. Though not mentioned in the Tax Bulletin text, an obligation to correct unsatisfactory work in the worker's own time and at his own expense suggests self-employment.

(*g*)   A person who becomes **'part and parcel' of the client's organisation** may well be an employee.

(*h*)   A **right of dismissal** is a common feature of employment. A contract for services, on the other hand, usually ends only when it is completed or is breached.

(*j*)   The right to sick pay, holiday pay, pensions, expenses and/or other **employee benefits** points towards employment, though their absence does not necessarily indicate self-employment — especially where the engagement is short-term.

(*k*)   **Length of engagement.** A long period working for one engager is typical of employment, but is not conclusive. Where a single engagement is covered by a series of short contracts, it is the length of the engagement that is relevant, and not the length of each contract.

(*l*)   It may be appropriate to take into account factors which are personal to the worker and have little to do with the terms of the particular engagement. For example, if a

61.18 Personal Service Companies etc.

skilled worker works for a number of clients and has a business-like approach to securing his engagements (perhaps involving expenditure on office accommodation, office equipment etc.), this points towards self-employment. Such **personal factors** carry less weight in the case of an unskilled worker, where factors like a high degree of control exercised by the client are more likely to be conclusive of employment.

62 Post-Cessation etc. Receipts and Expenditure (Trades, professions and vocations)

[*ICTA 1988, ss 103–110; FA 1995, s 90*]

Cross-reference. See 11 CASH BASIS.

Simon's Direct Tax Service B4.221 *et seq.*

62.1 POST-CESSATION ETC. RECEIPTS

Earnings basis. Where a trade etc., the profits of which are computed 'by reference to earnings' (as defined by *ICTA 1988, s 110(3)*) is permanently discontinued (or treated as such) all **sums received on or after the discontinuance** (other than those exempted below) arising from the carrying on of the trade etc., during any period before its discontinuance (including the amount, or arm's length value, of any consideration for a transfer of the right to receive them, and any recoveries or releases of items previously allowed as bad or doubtful debts) which are not otherwise chargeable to tax nor already brought into account for any period before the discontinuance are chargeable under Schedule D, Case VI.

Where the profits are not computed 'by reference to earnings' there is a similar charge on amounts received after the discontinuance which, if the earnings basis had applied, would have been left out of account because the date on which they became due or the date on which the amount was ascertained fell after the discontinuance. [*ICTA 1988, s 103(1)(2)(4); FA 1994, s 144(3)*]. Receipts within the legislation will include, *inter alia*, royalties and similar amounts which under decisions such as *Carson v Cheyney's Exor HL 1958, 38 TC 240*, prior to the legislation, had been held not to be taxable.

The charge is for the year of receipt (or as if received on the date of discontinuance if received by the person who carried on the trade before the discontinuance (or his personal representatives) in a tax year beginning within six years after the discontinuance *and election made* within one year after 31 January following the year of receipt). [*ICTA 1988, s 108; FA 1996, s 128(4)*]. Where an election is made, the charge is still under Case VI of Schedule D, so that the Case I cessation provisions do not apply in relation to it (*Gilmore v Inspector of Taxes (Sp C 206), [1999] SSCD 269*). See 16.2 CLAIMS for the way in which effect is given to this election.

Deductions. Deductions may be made of any expenses or losses (other than arising from the discontinuance) which are not otherwise allowable (and have not been allowed under any other provision) but which would have been allowable to the previous owner if the trade etc., had not ceased (or, before 6 April 1999, changed its 'conventional' basis, see below) and any unused balance of his CAPITAL ALLOWANCES (9) down to the date of discontinuance (or change). [*ICTA 1988, s 105; FA 1995, s 78(6); FA 1998, Sch 27 Pt III(6)*].

Exemptions.

(i) Sums received by a non-resident (or his agent) for income arising outside the UK,

(ii) a lump sum received by an author's executor etc., for total or partial assignment of copyright or public lending right in his literary, dramatic, musical or artistic work or of design right in his design,

(iii) sums realised for transfer of closing trading stock or professional work in progress (these are already dealt with by *ICTA 1988, ss 100, 101* see 71.73 SCHEDULE D, CASES I AND II). [*ICTA 1988, s 103(3)*].

Deemed discontinuance. The above provisions also apply on a change of ownership which, under *ICTA 1988, s 113* (see 71.15 SCHEDULE D, CASES I AND II) or *ICTA 1988, s 337(1)* (company beginning or ceasing to carry on a trade), is treated as a permanent discontinuance, but if, on such a change, the right to receive sums as above is transferred from the previous owner to his successor the only liability under these sections is on the latter, who has to include as normal trade receipts, for the periods in which they are received, all such sums arising from the transfer. [*ICTA 1988, s 106(2)*]. Deduction may be made for any debts taken over on the discontinuance which prove bad, so far as not already allowed to the previous owner in computations for periods before the change. [*ICTA 1988, s 89*]. The provisions also apply to an individual leaving a partnership such that his notional trade is permanently discontinued (see 53.3 PARTNERSHIPS). [*ICTA 1988, s 110(2); FA 1994, s 215(1A); FA 1995, s 117(1)(b)(3)*].

Simon's Direct Tax Service. See **B4.221** *et seq.*

62.2 **'Conventional' basis.** Where a trade, profession or vocation previously taxed on a 'conventional' basis, i.e. on the CASH BASIS (11) or otherwise than 'by reference to earnings' (see 62.1 above), is permanently discontinued (or treated as such), treatment as above applies to all receipts on or after the discontinuance arising from carrying on the trade etc. so far as their amount or value was not taken into account in computing the profits before the discontinuance. Similarly chargeable is any amount received for work in progress transferred or realised after discontinuance. The charge does not extend to amounts otherwise chargeable (including amounts chargeable under 62.1 above) nor to the sums referred to in exemptions (i) and (ii) in 62.1 above. [*ICTA 1988, s 104(1)–(3)(6)*].

Where, before 6 April 1999, a trade etc. changes from a 'conventional' basis to an earnings basis or to a different 'conventional' basis so that receipts drop out of computation, there is a similar charge on receipts after the change (and before any discontinuance). [*ICTA 1988, s 104(4)(5); FA 1998, Sch 27 Pt III(6)*]. For changes on or after that date, see 11.2 CASH BASIS.

Professional work in progress. Where, in the case of a profession or vocation, there has been a change, before 6 April 1999, from a conventional basis to an earnings basis or a different conventional basis *and* the work in progress at the change has been allowed as a deduction after the change, the amount of that work in progress (if not counterbalanced by a previous credit) will be charged as above under Schedule D, Case VI. [*ICTA 1988, s 104(7); FA 1998, Sch 27 Pt III(6)*]. For changes on or after that date, see 11.2 CASH BASIS.

Relief. In the case of an individual who was carrying on the trade etc., on 18 March 1968 (profits of the trade etc., not having been computed on an earnings basis at any time between that date and the discontinuance, or change, as above) any net amount chargeable on him under *section 104* above (but not any amount chargeable under *section 103*), is (subject as below) reduced by 5% for each year, or part year, by which his age at 5 April 1968 exceeded 51, up to a maximum of 75%, if he was then 65 or over. [*ICTA 1988, s 109*]. But the above reduction does not apply to any excess of a partner's share in post-cessation receipts over the amount which would have been apportioned to him had his share been calculated at the same rate as his average participation in partnership profits for the three tax years ending with that in which the discontinuance, or change, took place. [*ICTA 1988, s 109(5)*].

62.3   **Earned income.** Receipts assessable as above are treated as earned income if profits before the discontinuance or change of basis were previously so treated. [*ICTA 1988, s 107*].

62.4   **POST-CESSATION EXPENDITURE**

Relief against total income (and capital gains, see below) is available for certain payments made in connection with a trade etc. which has been permanently discontinued (or treated as such — see 62.1 above) and within seven years after the discontinuance. Relief is given for the year in which the payment is made and unused relief cannot be carried forward (but may qualify as a deduction under *ICTA 1988, s 105* from post-cessation receipts of later years — see 62.1 above). The relief is not available to companies.

Payments qualifying for this relief are those made wholly and exclusively:

(*a*)   in remedying defective work done, goods supplied or services rendered or by way of damages (awarded or agreed) in respect of defective work etc.;

(*b*)   in meeting legal and professional fees in connection with a claim that work done etc. was defective;

(*c*)   in insuring against such a claim or against the incurring of such legal etc. fees; or

(*d*)   for the purpose of collecting a debt taken into account in computing profits of the former trade etc.

In addition, where an unpaid debt taken into account in computing profits of the former trade etc. proves to be bad in any part of the year of claim (and the claimant gives notice of that fact in making the claim) or is wholly or partly released as part of a voluntary arrangement or compromise (see 71.34 SCHEDULE D, CASES I AND II), then, to the extent that the former trader is entitled to the benefit of that debt, he is treated as making a payment qualifying for relief under these provisions and equal to the amount lost or released. To the extent that relief is then given under these provisions, any subsequent recovery of the debt is taxed as a post-cessation receipt (see 62.1 above) with no deduction available against it under *section 105*.

Where relief becomes available in respect of a payment within any of (*a*) to (*d*) above, the following are taxed as post-cessation receipts with no deduction available against them under *section 105*: (i) in the case of (*a*) or (*b*), any insurance proceeds, or similar, to allow the payment to be made or to reimburse it, (ii) in the case of (*c*), any refund of the insurance premium, or similar receipt, and (iii) in the case of (*d*), any sum received to meet the costs of collecting the debt. Where the receipt occurs in an earlier tax year than the related payment, it is treated as instead having been received in the year of payment.

Set-off of unpaid expenses against relief. Where a deduction was made in computing profits or losses of the former trade etc. in respect of an expense not actually paid, relief otherwise due and claimed under these provisions is reduced by the amount of any such expenses remaining unpaid at the end of the year to which the claim relates (to the extent that those expenses have not so reduced relief for an earlier year). If an unpaid expense has reduced relief but is subsequently paid, wholly or partly, the amount paid (or, if less, the amount of the reduction) is treated as a payment qualifying for relief under these provisions for the year of payment.

Exclusion of double relief. Relief is not available in respect of an amount for which income tax relief is otherwise available. In determining whether an amount could otherwise be relieved under *section 105* (deduction from post-cessation receipts — see 62.1 above), amounts not available for relief under these provisions are assumed to be relieved under *section 105* in priority to amounts that are so available.

Time limit. The relief must be claimed within twelve months after 31 January following the tax year of payment.

Relief against capital gains. Where a claim is made as above and the claimant's income for the year is insufficient to fully utilise the relief, he may include in his claim an additional claim to have the excess relief treated as an allowable loss for that year for capital gains tax purposes. The allowable loss may not exceed the amount of the claimant's gains for the year *before* deducting any losses brought forward, the capital gains tax annual exemption or any relief available under *FA 1991, s 72* for trading losses (see 46.5 LOSSES); any excess over that amount is *not* available to carry forward against gains of a later year.

[*ICTA 1988, ss 109A, 110; FA 1995, s 90; FA 1996, s 134, Sch 20 para 5*].

See generally Revenue Tax Bulletin October 1995 pp 256, 257.

Simon's Direct Tax Service. See **B4.231** *et seq.*

62.5   *Example*

Simcock ceased trading in October 2003. In 2004/05 the following events occur in connection with his former trade.

(i)   He pays a former customer £9,250 by way of damages for defective work carried out by him in the course of the trade.

(ii)   He incurs legal fees of £800 in connection with (i) above.

(iii)   He incurs debt collection fees of £200 in connection with trade debts outstanding at cessation and which were taken into account as receipts in computing profits.

(iv)   He writes off a trade debt of £500, giving the Revenue notice of his having done so.

(v)   He incurs legal fees of £175 in relation to a debt of £1,000 owing by him to a supplier which, although disputed, was taken into account as an expense in computing his trading profits.

(vi)   He eventually agrees to pay £500 in full settlement of his liability in respect of the debt in (v) above, paying £250 in March 2005 and the remaining £250 in May 2005.

In 2005/06 he receives £3,000 from his insurers in full settlement of their liability with regard to the expense incurred in (i) above.

For 2004/05, his total income before taking account of the above events is £9,000, and he also has capital gains of £9,400 (with £1,000 capital losses brought forward from 2003/04).

He makes a claim under *ICTA 1988, s 109A* for 2004/05 and a simultaneous claim under *FA 1995, s 90(4)* to have any excess relief set against capital gains.

Simcock's tax position is as follows.

2004/05

	£	£
Income		
Total income before *section 109A* claim		9,000
Deduct post-cessation expenditure —		
(i)	9,250	
(ii)	800	
(iii)	200	
(iv)	500	
(v)	—	
(vi) *less* expenses unpaid at 5.4.05		
(£1,000 – £250)	(750)	
	10,000	
Restricted to total income	(9,000)	(9,000)
Excess relief	£1,000	
Capital gains		
Gains before losses brought forward and annual exemption		9,400
Deduct excess post-cessation expenditure (as above)		1,000
Net gains for the year		8,400
Losses brought forward	1,000	
Used 2003/04	200	200
Losses carried forward	£800	
Net gains (covered by annual exemption)		£8,200

2005/06

He will have taxable post-cessation receipts of £3,000 arising from the insurance recovery. He will be able to offset expenses of £175 under (v) above which, whilst not within *section 109A*, should qualify as a deduction under *section 105* (see 62.1 above). He will also have post-cessation expenditure of £250 in respect of the further payment under (vi) above, the 2004/05 post-cessation expenditure having been restricted by more than that amount.

| 63 | Qualifying Employee Share Ownership Trusts (QUESTs) |

Simon's Direct Tax Service. See E4.591 *et seq.*

63.1   Under provisions introduced by *FA 1989, ss 67–74, Sch 5*, companies could claim an allowable deduction, for corporation tax, for payments to qualifying employee share ownership trusts (QUESTS), being, broadly, trusts set up to acquire shares in the employer company and distribute them to employees. This deduction was abolished for payments made in accounting periods beginning on or after 1 January 2003. A deduction continues to be available for the costs of setting up such a trust. See 71.44 SCHEDULE D, CASES I AND II for details of these deductions. Investment companies may also obtain the deductions, where available, by treating payments as management expenses. Neither the QUEST nor its beneficiaries qualify for any special income tax or capital gains tax reliefs, although such a trust may be used in conjunction with an approved profit sharing scheme (see 82.18 SHARE-RELATED EMPLOYMENT INCOME AND EXEMPTIONS) or, for trusts established on or after 29 April 1996, an approved SAYE option scheme (see 82.47 SHARE-RELATED EMPLOYMENT INCOME AND EXEMPTIONS), thus enabling beneficiaries to receive shares free of income tax. In certain circumstances (see 63.8 below), where the above-mentioned deduction has been made, the tax relief given to the company may, effectively, be clawed back by means of a charge under Schedule D, Case VI on the trustees, with powers to recover the tax so charged from the company.

63.2   **Definition.** A trust is a QUEST at any time (the relevant time) if it was a 'QUEST' at the time it was established, regardless of whether or not it is a QUEST at the relevant time. A '*QUEST*' is a trust established, by means of a trust deed, by a UK resident company (the 'founding company') which is not controlled by another company, and which, at the time of establishment, satisfies the conditions in *FA 1989, Sch 5 paras 3–11* as summarised at 63.3–63.6 below. A trust is established when the deed under which it is established is executed. [*FA 1989, Sch 5 paras 1, 2, 13, 17; FA 1994, Sch 13 para 8*].

See *FA 1989, Sch 5 paras 14–16* as regards interpretation of the provisions of *Schedule 5*.

63.3   The trust deed must deal with the appointment, retirement, removal and replacement of **trustees**. The trustees must number at least three, must all be UK resident and must include a trust corporation or a solicitor (or member of such other professional body as the Board may allow). Most of the trustees must be employees, either of the founding company or of a UK resident company controlled by it, who have never had a material interest (broadly more than 5% of ordinary share capital) in any such company, and those trustees must be selected by a majority of employees or by the employees' elected representatives. Most of the trustees must never have been directors of either the founding company or a UK resident company controlled by it.

For QUESTs set up after 3 May 1994, two other possible trust structures are permitted: a 'paritarian' trust structure; or a UK resident corporate trustee controlled by the founding company and with directors composed in the same way as the trustees in a 'paritarian' trust structure. The 'paritarian' trust structure requires three or more UK resident trustees, of whom at least one must be, and at least two must not be, 'professional' trustees. A '*professional*' trustee is a trust corporation or a solicitor (or member of such other professional body as the Board may allow), other than an employee or director of the founding company (or of a UK resident company controlled by it), selected by the non-professional trustees. Also, at least half of the non-professional trustees must be employees of the founding company (or of a UK resident company controlled by it) who have never had a material interest (as above) in any such company and who are selected either by election (with all such employees being able to stand for election or to vote) or by selection by elected representatives of those employees.

A trust is not a QUEST at any time when the requirements as to trustees are not satisfied.

[*FA 1989, Sch 5 paras 3–3C, 12, 12A; FA 1994, s 102, Sch 13 paras 2–5*].

63.4 The terms of the trust deed must be such that a person is a **beneficiary** at a particular time if

(*a*) he is then an employee or director of the founding company or a UK resident company then under its control, and

(*b*) he has been an employee or director of such a company throughout a period specified in the trust deed, which must not be more than five years (and which, for trusts established before 29 April 1996, had to be at least one year), ending at that time, working for at least twenty hours a week (ignoring holidays and sickness). (For trusts established under deeds executed on or after 1 May 1995, the minimum hours restriction applies only to directors.)

The trust deed *may* provide that where a person has been an employee or director as required under (*a*) above throughout a period of the length specified in the trust deed as under (*b*) above and ending when the employment/directorship ceased or the company ceased to be controlled by the founding company, that person may continue to be a beneficiary for 18 months thereafter. For trusts established on or after 29 April 1996, the deed *may* also provide for a person to be a beneficiary at a given time if at that time he is eligible to participate in an approved SAYE option scheme (see 82.47 SHARE-RELATED EMPLOYMENT INCOME AND EXEMPTIONS) established by a member of the founding company's group; the deed must then provide that the only powers and duties the trustees may exercise in relation to such beneficiaries (if they would not otherwise be beneficiaries) are those exercisable under such a scheme. A trust deed *may* also provide for a charity to be a beneficiary if the trust is being wound up in consequence of there being no qualifying beneficiaries under the deed. All persons not satisfying these conditions at a particular time must be excluded from being beneficiaries at that time. Notwithstanding the fact that a person satisfies these conditions, he cannot be a beneficiary at a particular time if he then has, or has had at any time in the previous twelve months, a material interest (broadly more than 5% of ordinary share capital) in the founding company (but this restriction does not apply to persons who qualify as beneficiaries only by virtue of their being eligible to participate in a SAYE scheme).

[*FA 1989, Sch 5 para 4; FA 1995, s 137(5)(9); FA 1996, ss 119, 120(1)(5)–(7)(12)*].

63.5 The **general functions of trustees** must be to receive sums and to acquire, retain and manage and eventually to transfer sums or securities (i.e. shares and debentures) to beneficiaries or transfer securities at not less than market value to trustees of approved profit sharing schemes (see 82.18 SHARE-RELATED EMPLOYMENT INCOME AND EXEMPTIONS) or, for trusts established on or after 29 April 1996, grant rights to acquire shares (i.e. under approved SAYE option schemes — see 82.47 SHARE-RELATED EMPLOYMENT INCOME AND EXEMPTIONS) to beneficiaries. Any sum received, whether from the founding company or by way of loan or otherwise, must be expended, within the 'relevant period', for a qualifying purpose (see 71.44 SCHEDULE D, CASES I AND II), being retained in cash or in a bank or building society account in the meantime. The '*relevant period*' is the period of nine months after the end of the period of account, of the company making the payment to the trust, for which the payment is charged as an expense, or, in the case of sums received other than from the founding company or a company under its control, nine months from the date of receipt of the sum in question.

Sums received are to be treated as being expended on a first in/first out basis, and all sums paid to different beneficiaries at the same time must be paid on similar terms (although variations according to remuneration, length of service or similar factors are permitted). The trust deed must not contain features which are not essential or reasonably incidental to the purposes herein described as being the general functions of the trustees.

[*FA 1989, Sch 5 paras 5, 6, 10; FA 1996, s 120(8)(11)(12)*].

63.6   The **securities** to be acquired by the trust must be fully paid up, non-redeemable ordinary shares in the founding company which are free of restrictions other than those attaching to all shares of the same class or certain restrictions imposed by the company's articles of association. The deed must preclude the trustees from acquiring shares either at greater than open market value or at a time when the founding company is under the control of another company. It *may* allow for the trustees to acquire securities other than shares in the founding company if they are acquired as a result of a company reorganisation or reconstruction within *TCGA 1992, s 126* or *s 135* and the shares originally held were shares in the founding company. The trustees must transfer securities to beneficiaries within seven years (twenty years in the case of trusts established under deeds executed after 3 May 1994) of their acquisition (securities acquired being deemed to be transferred on a first in/first out basis) and on 'qualifying terms'. A transfer is made on '*qualifying terms*' if

(i)   all securities transferred at the same time (other than to savings-related share option scheme participants — see below) are transferred on similar terms (allowing, if desired, for differences in levels of remuneration, length of service or similar factors),

(ii)   securities have been offered to all existing beneficiaries (disregarding those who would be not be beneficiaries but for their being participants in a savings-related scheme) at the time of transfer, and

(iii)   securities are transferred to all such persons who have accepted.

As regards trusts established on or after 29 April 1996, a transfer of securities is also made on '*qualifying terms*' if made to a person exercising a right to acquire shares under an approved SAYE option scheme (see 82.47 SHARE-RELATED EMPLOYMENT INCOME AND EXEMPTIONS) established by the founding company or a company under its control, where the consideration for the transfer is payable to the trustees.

The trust deed must contain specified provisions determining the time at which the trustees are deemed to acquire and transfer securities and when they are considered to retain securities.

[*FA 1989, Sch 5 paras 7, 8, 9, 11; FA 1994, Sch 13 para 7; FA 1996, s 120(9)(10)(12)*].

63.7   **Clearance.** Requests for clearance that a trust is a QUEST, supported by copies of the trust deed or draft deed and any other relevant information, should be sent to Inland Revenue, Business Profits Division (Employee Share Schemes), Room 111A, New Wing, Somerset House, Strand, London WC2R 1LB.

63.8   **Tax charge on trustees.** Where a 'chargeable event' occurs in relation to the trustees of a QUEST, they will be charged tax under Schedule D, Case VI, for the year of assessment in which the event occurs, on the 'chargeable amount' at the rate applicable to trusts (see 81.5 SETTLEMENTS) for that year. If they fail to pay the tax in full within six months of the assessment's becoming final and conclusive, a notice of liability for the unpaid tax may be served either on the founding company or on any company which has previously made a payment to the trust and obtained tax relief thereon. The company is also liable for any interest, accruing before or after the date of the notice, on the unpaid tax. If any tax and/or interest still remains unpaid three months after the date of notice, it may be recovered from the trustees without prejudice to the right to recover it instead from the company.

A *'chargeable event'* occurs whenever the trustees of a QUEST do any of the following:

(A) make a transfer, other than a 'qualifying transfer', of securities;

(B) make a transfer of securities, other than on 'qualifying terms' (see 63.6 above), to beneficiaries;

(C) retain securities for more than twenty years (for QUESTs established under deeds executed after 3 May 1994 — previously more than seven years);

(D) make a payment other than for a 'qualifying purpose' (see 71.44 SCHEDULE D, CASES I AND II);

(E) make a 'qualifying transfer' to the trustees of an approved share incentive plan (see below) for a consideration, and fail to apply the whole of that consideration (or an equivalent amount) for 'qualifying purposes' (see 71.44 SCHEDULE D, CASES I AND II) within the period beginning with the transfer and ending nine months after the end of the period of account (of the company which established the QUEST) in which the transfer took place; the chargeable event is the expiry of that permitted period.

A *'qualifying transfer'* is a transfer made either to a beneficiary, or at not less than open market value to the trustees of an approved profit sharing scheme (see 82.18 SHARE-RELATED EMPLOYMENT INCOME AND EXEMPTIONS), or (after 31 December 1991) by way of exchange of shares within *TCGA 1992, s 135(1)*. A transfer is also a *'qualifying transfer'* if it is a transfer of 'relevant shares' to the trustees of a share incentive plan (see 82.20 SHARE-RELATED EMPLOYMENT INCOME AND EXEMPTIONS), approved at the time of transfer, for a consideration (if any) not exceeding market value. *'Relevant shares'* are shares held by the trustees of the QUEST at midnight on 20 March 2000 or purchased with funds held (in a bank or building society account) at that time. For these purposes, all payments of any kind made by the trustees after 20 March 2000 are deemed to be made as far as possible out of such funds, and any disposal or transfer of shares of a particular class by the trustees after that date is treated as far as possible as a transfer or disposal of relevant shares. To assist companies in winding up QUESTs, if they wish, as a consequence of the abolition of corporation tax relief (see 63.1 above), these rules are extended so as to apply equally in relation to shares and funds held at midnight on 26 November 2002.

The *'chargeable amount'* is determined as follows:

(I) if the event falls within (A), (B) or (C) above, the chargeable amount, if the event constitutes a disposal for capital gains tax purposes, is the amount of allowable expenditure under *TCGA 1992, s 38(1)(a)(b)*, or, if the event does not constitute such a disposal, is the amount that would have been so allowable if it did so;

(II) if the event falls within (D) above, the chargeable amount is the amount of the payment made;

(III) if the event falls within (E) above, the chargeable amount is the amount of consideration not so applied within the permitted period;

but see below for limitation on the chargeable amount.

Once a chargeable event as defined above has occurred, then if at that time there was outstanding any principal of any borrowings by the trustees and if the chargeable amount was limited as described below, a further chargeable event will occur at the end of any year

63.9 Qualifying Employee Share Ownership Trusts (QUESTs)

of assessment in which any part of such principal is repaid by the trustees. Amounts borrowed earlier are for these purposes taken to be repaid before amounts borrowed later. The chargeable amount in this case is the amount repaid (but subject to limitation, see below) and is chargeable and recoverable in the same way as on other chargeable events. There are provisions to prevent a double charge in respect of the same borrowings where two or more chargeable events, of the kind first described above, occur at different times.

The chargeable amount, however arising, is limited to the total amount of payments received by the trustees before the chargeable event in question which have either qualified for corporation tax relief or would so qualify if a claim to that effect were made immediately before the occurrence of the event. For the purpose of determining whether or not the limit has been exceeded, any previous chargeable amounts must be aggregated with the chargeable amount in question. There is also a limitation on the chargeable amount in respect of repaid borrowings by reference to earlier chargeable amounts.

[FA 1989, ss 68–72; F(No 2)A 1992, s 36; FA 1993, Sch 6 para 20; FA 1994, Sch 13 para 6; FA 1996, s 120(3)(4)(12); FA 2000, s 55; FA 2003, s 142(2)].

63.9   **Capital gains relief on introduction of shares.** A form of capital gains rollover relief may be available on the transfer of shares into a QUEST before 6 April 2001. See Tolley's Capital Gains Tax under Employee Share Schemes for details.

63.10   **Information.** Where any payments to a QUEST have been allowed for tax purposes, the inspector must notify the trustees, stating the amount involved. He may, by written notice to the trustees, require the submission by them, with penalties for failure to comply, of a return containing such further information as is specified in the notice. This may include information about sums received, sums borrowed, expenditure incurred, assets acquired, transfers of assets made etc. [FA 1989, s 73]. Similar provisions apply in relation to claims for capital gains tax relief on the introduction of shares. [TCGA 1992, s 235].

64 Remittance Basis

Cross-references. See RESIDENCE, ORDINARY RESIDENCE AND DOMICILE at 65.4 for domicile, 65.5 for residence, 65.6 for ordinarily resident; NON-RESIDENTS AND OTHER OVERSEAS MATTERS at 51.11 for trades etc. carried on abroad and 51.13 for unremittable overseas income; see 24.3 DOUBLE TAX RELIEF regarding Ireland.

Simon's Direct Tax Service E1.323 *et seq.*

64.1 APPLICATION

The remittance basis (i.e. UK tax assessments are restricted to sums actually remitted to the UK out of such income or gains (grossed up in certain cases where credit for foreign tax is allowable, see 24.5(*b*)(i) DOUBLE TAX RELIEF)) applies to UK residents in respect of overseas income and gains as follows.

(A) **Persons not domiciled in the UK.**

  (i) **Capital gains** from disposal of assets abroad (with no allowance for losses arising abroad).

  (ii) **Taxable earnings** from an employer not resident in UK or Ireland where the duties are performed wholly abroad (see 75.4 SCHEDULE E—EMPLOYMENT INCOME) but this only applies if the employee is also ordinarily resident in the UK (otherwise see (B) below).

  (iii) **Investment income etc.** from abroad assessable under SCHEDULE D, CASES IV AND V (73). [*ICTA 1988, s 65(4)(5); FA 1994, s 207(3); FA 1996, s 134, Sch 20 para 3*]. But such income from Ireland is assessable on the full amount arising, whether remitted or not. [*ICTA 1988, s 68; FA 1994, s 207(5)*].

  (iv) **Pensions** from overseas (see 58.2(*b*)(*k*)(*p*)(*q*) PENSION INCOME).

  (v) **Trades etc.** controlled abroad, see under 51.11 NON-RESIDENTS AND OTHER OVERSEAS MATTERS. Except trades etc. in Ireland. [*ICTA 1988, s 68; FA 1994, s 207(5)*].

(B) **Persons not ordinarily resident in the UK.**

  Taxable earnings in respect of duties performed wholly abroad, see 75.4 SCHEDULE E—EMPLOYMENT INCOME.

(C) **Persons not ordinarily resident in the UK who are also either British subjects or Irish citizens.**

  Investment income etc. — per (A)(iii) above.

  Pensions — per (A)(iv) above.

  Trades etc. — per (A)(v) above.

Note. Employments are not treated as being abroad for the above purposes if they comprise certain Crown duties or sea or air duties. See 75.4 SCHEDULE E—EMPLOYMENT INCOME.

64.2 BASIS OF ASSESSMENT

The charge is normally on the actual remittances in the tax year (subject to the addition of any foreign tax for which credit is allowable — see 24.5(*b*)(i) DOUBLE TAX RELIEF). See also 73.9 SCHEDULE D, CASES IV AND V.

64.3 REMITTANCES—GENERAL

A remittance of capital is not taxable as such (unless within the provisions of capital gains tax, see Tolley's Capital Gains Tax) but a taxable remittance may include the proceeds of investments made abroad out of overseas income (*Scottish Provident Institution v Farmer CS 1912, 6 TC 34*). Where the proceeds were of investments made before the taxpayer came to reside in the UK, there was no liability (*Kneen v Martin CA 1934, 19 TC 33*). Similarly a remittance from a foreign bank into which overseas income had been paid may be assessable, dependent on the circumstances. For this see *Walsh v Randall KB 1940, 23 TC 55* (sterling draft on foreign bank in favour of London hospital received by taxpayer before handing to hospital, held to be remittance) and *Thomson v Moyse HL 1960, 39 TC 291* (dollar cheques on US bank sold to Bank of England held to be remitted) and compare *Carter v Sharon KB 1936, 20 TC 229* (drafts on foreign bank posted abroad to taxpayer's daughter for maintenance, held not to be remittance as, under relevant foreign law, gift to daughter completed on posting of draft). See also *Fellowes-Gordon v CIR CS 1935, 19 TC 683*. In *Harmel v Wright Ch D 1973, 49 TC 149* an amount received via two South African companies, ending as a loan from one of them, was held to be a remittance of South African emoluments within Schedule E, Case III. Where, contrary to the customer's instructions, a bank erroneously remitted untaxed overseas income to him, it was held there was no liability (*Duke of Roxburghe's Exors v CIR CS 1936, 20 TC 711*). In *Grimm v Newman & Another CA, [2002] STC 1388* (a negligence case in which the Revenue were not a party), an absolute inter-spousal gift, perfected abroad, of overseas assets subsequently used to purchase a matrimonial home in the UK was held not to be a remittance.

64.4   **CONSTRUCTIVE REMITTANCES** [*ICTA 1988, s 65(6)–(9)*]

Income arising abroad to a person *ordinarily resident* in the UK and which he applies abroad towards the satisfaction of

(*a*)   a debt (or interest thereon) for money lent him in the UK, or

(*b*)   a debt for money lent to him abroad and brought here, or

(*c*)   a debt incurred to satisfy such debts,

is treated as received by him in the UK.

Where an ordinarily resident person imports money lent to him abroad the debt for which has at that time already been wholly or partly satisfied, the loan is treated as a remittance at the date of importation to the extent that the debt is satisfied.

Income **hypothecated in any form to the lender** so that the amount of a loan debt, or the time of its repayment, depends directly or indirectly on the amount of property so available to the lender, is treated as having been applied towards satisfaction of the loan. '*Lender*' includes any person for the time being entitled to repayment.

These provisions regarding constructive remittances are contained in Schedule D, Cases IV and V legislation and are applied to employment income by *ITEPA 2003, ss 33, 34*, to certain foreign pensions by *ITEPA 2003, ss 575, 613, 631, 635* (see 58.2(*b*)(*k*)(*p*)(*q*) PENSION INCOME) and to capital gains tax by *TCGA 1992, s 12(2)*.

Simon's Direct Tax Service. See E1.324.

65   Residence, Ordinary Residence and Domicile

Cross-reference. See 51 NON-RESIDENTS AND OTHER OVERSEAS MATTERS for situations in which the residence, ordinary residence or domicile of an individual may be of relevance for income tax purposes. See generally Revenue Pamphlets IR 20, to which reference is made throughout this chapter, IR 138 and IR 139.

Simon's Direct Tax Service Part E6.

65.1   UK tax liability may depend on a person's **domicile** (the country or state which is his 'natural home', see 65.4 below), on whether or not he is **resident** in the UK for tax purposes in a particular tax year (which is primarily a matter of physical presence, see 65.5 below) or, occasionally, on whether or not he is ordinarily resident in the UK (see 65.6 below). EU law does not prevent a Member State from imposing more onerous fiscal charges on nationals resident in another Member State than those imposed on its own resident nationals (*Werner v Finanzamt Aachen-Innenstadt (Case C–112/91) CJEC, [1996] STC 961*).

Possible future changes? In the 2002 Budget, the Government announced a review of the residence and domicile rules as they affect the taxation of individuals. A year later, in April 2003, a background paper was published on the subject, but this does little more than describe the current rules and outline the underlying principles to which any changes should adhere; it contains no specific proposals.

65.2   A person who is **resident** in the UK is liable to UK tax on all his income and gains, whether from UK or overseas sources, subject to limited categories of EXEMPT INCOME (28).

Assessments are limited to remittances to the UK out of the income or gains in the circumstances listed under REMITTANCE BASIS (64).

Deductions are made from the amounts assessable as follows.

Employment income. Employments wholly abroad where the employee is abroad for a qualifying period (as defined) of 365 days or more — a deduction of 100% is made (i.e. complete exemption) in limited circumstances. See 75.7 SCHEDULE E—EMPLOYMENT INCOME.

Overseas pensions. A deduction of 10% may be made, as set out in 58.1(iv) and 58.2 PENSION INCOME.

65.3   **Non-residents** are liable to UK tax on UK income, including income from property etc. in the UK, income from trades, professions etc. exercised in the UK [*ICTA 1988, s 18(1)(a)(iii)*] and on employment income for duties performed in the UK. [*ITEPA 2003, s 27; ICTA 1988, s 19(1)*].

See also 28.21 EXEMPT INCOME and 33.2 GOVERNMENT STOCKS for the special exemption to non-residents in respect of certain government stocks and 22.12 DEDUCTION OF TAX AT SOURCE for a similar relief in respect of the interest or dividends on certain foreign stocks and securities payable in the UK.

The appropriate double tax agreement should be examined for exemptions and for restrictions on the rates of tax to be borne. Otherwise non-residents are chargeable at the full rate and not entitled to personal or other reliefs. Thus a person carrying on a business in the UK but claiming to be non-resident may thereby have his tax allowances reduced or even refused. But see 51.10 NON-RESIDENTS AND OTHER OVERSEAS MATTERS for reliefs available to certain Commonwealth subjects and others.

Non-residents have no liability on overseas income.

65.4 Residence, Ordinary Residence and Domicile

65.4 DOMICILE

It may be necessary to determine domicile in relation, *inter alia*, to the assessment of income from foreign possessions and securities (see 73.5 SCHEDULE D, CASES IV AND V), of 'chargeable overseas earnings' (see 75.4 SCHEDULE E—EMPLOYMENT INCOME) and of certain chargeable gains (see Tolley's Capital Gains Tax).

A person may have only one place of domicile at any given time denoting the country or state considered his permanent home. He acquires a **domicile of origin** at birth (normally that of his father). It may be changed to a **domicile of choice** (to be proved by subsequent conduct). If a domicile of choice is established but later abandoned (by actual action, not by intention or declaration only — see *Faye v CIR* below) reversion to domicile of origin is automatic.

Domicile is a highly technical matter and does not necessarily correspond with either residence or nationality (see *Earl of Iveagh v Revenue Commissioners Supreme Court (IFS) [1930] IR 431, Fielden v CIR Ch D 1965, 42 TC 501*, and *CIR v Cohen KB 1937, 21 TC 301*). This last case shows how difficult it is to displace a domicile of origin by a domicile of choice, but contrast *In re Lawton Ch D 1958 37 ATC 216*. A new domicile of choice may be acquired whilst continuing to be resident in the domicile of origin, but only if the residence in the domicile of choice is the 'chief residence' (*Plummer v CIR Ch D 1987, 60 TC 452*). See also *In re Wallach HC 1949, 28 ATC 486, Faye v CIR Ch D 1961, 40 TC 103, Buswell v CIR CA 1974, 49 TC 334, Steiner v CIR CA 1973, 49 TC 13, CIR v Bullock CA 1976, 51 TC 522, In re Furse decd., Furse v CIR Ch D, [1980] STC 597, Re Clore decd. (No 2) Ch D, [1984] STC 609, Anderson v CIR (Sp C 147), [1998] SSCD 43, Mrs F and S2 (personal representatives of F (dec'd)) v CIR (Sp C 219), [2000] SSCD 1, Civil Engineer v CIR (Sp C 299), [2002] SSCD 72, Moore's Executors v CIR (Sp C 335), [2002] SSCD 463* and *Surveyor v CIR (Sp C 339), [2002] SSCD 501*.

In determining domicile for tax purposes at any time **after 5 April 1996**, no action taken at any time in relation to registration as an 'overseas elector', or in voting as such, is taken into account in determining domicile, unless the person whose liability is being determined (whether or not the person whose domicile is in question) wishes it to be taken into account (in which case the domicile determination applies only for the purpose of ascertaining the liability in question). An *'overseas elector'* is broadly a non-resident British citizen to whom the parliamentary franchise is extended under *Representation of the People Act 1985, s 1* or *s 3*. [*FA 1996, s 200*].

See 65.5 below for administrative procedures for determination of domicile in certain cases.

Married women. Up to 31 December 1973, a woman automatically acquired the domicile of her husband on marriage. From 1 January 1974 onwards, the domicile of a married woman is to be ascertained 'by reference to the same factors as in the case of any other individual capable of having an independent domicile' except that a woman already married on that date will retain her husband's domicile until it is changed by acquisition or revival of another domicile. [*Domicile and Matrimonial Proceedings Act 1973, ss 1, 17(5)*]. But an American woman who married a husband with UK domicile before 1974 will be treated, for determining her domicile, as if the marriage had taken place in 1974. See Article 4(4) of the US/UK Double Tax Agreement. A **widow** retains her late husband's domicile unless she later acquires a domicile of choice (and see *CIR v Duchess of Portland Ch D 1981, 54 TC 648*).

Minors. The domicile of a minor normally follows that of the person on whom he is legally dependent. Under *Domicile and Matrimonial Proceedings Act 1973, s 3* (which does not extend to Scotland), a person first becomes capable of having an independent domicile when he attains 16 or marries under that age. Under *section 4* of that *Act*, where a child's father and mother are alive but living apart, his domicile is that of his mother if he has his home with her and has no home with his father.

Simon's Direct Tax Service. See E6.3.

65.5   RESIDENCE

General. There is relatively little statutory guidance on the determination of the 'residence' of an individual, despite its importance in determining the individual's tax liabilities (see 65.1–65.3 above). It has been held by the courts that residence is a question of fact for the Appeal Commissioners to decide on the particular circumstances of each case, and there are a number of important decisions indicative of the courts' views (see below). See also 65.8 below regarding appeals. A person can be resident for a particular tax year in more than one country for tax purposes (or may even be resident in none).

For practical purposes, the Revenue's interpretation as set out in Pamphlet IR 20 and other sources referred to below is, subject to appeal, likely to determine the issue in any particular case.

There are three circumstances in which the residence status of an individual is subject to statutory provisions.

(*a*)   An individual in the UK for some temporary purpose only, and not with the intention of establishing his residence here, is UK resident for any year of assessment in which he is physically present in the UK for six months or more in aggregate, and is not resident for any year of assessment in which he is not physically present in the UK for six months or more. In determining whether the individual is in the UK for some temporary purpose only and not with the intention of establishing his residence here one of the considerations is that an individual is regarded as resident if visits to the UK average 91 days or more per tax year, calculated over a maximum of four years (see Revenue Pamphlet IR 20, para 2.10 for method of averaging). (Revenue Pamphlet IR 131, SP 2/91, 19 March 1991). The question is determined without regard to any 'available accommodation' in the UK (see below). [*ICTA 1988, s 336; FA 1993, s 208(1)(4); ITEPA 2003, Sch 6 para 48; FA 2004, Sch 17 para 10(2)*]. Strictly, periods of time in terms of hours are relevant in determining a period of presence in the UK (see *Wilkie v CIR Ch D 1951, 32 TC 495*) but in practice six months are regarded as 183 days, ignoring (normally) days of arrival and departure. (Revenue Pamphlet IR 20, para 1.2).

(*b*)   A Commonwealth or Eire citizen whose ordinary residence (see 65.6 below) has been in the UK, and who has left the UK for the purpose only of occasional residence abroad, continues to be UK resident. [*ICTA 1988, s 334*]. 'Occasional residence' is not defined, but generally refers to short stays on holiday or business trips (and see *Reed v Clark Ch D 1985, 58 TC 528*).

(*c*)   The residence of an individual working full time in a trade, profession or vocation no part of which is carried on in the UK, or in an office or employment all of the duties of which are performed outside the UK (other than any whose performance is merely incidental to the duties abroad), is determined without regard to any place of abode maintained for his use in the UK. [*ICTA 1988, s 335*]. As to whether duties are incidental, see *Robson v Dixon Ch D 1972, 48 TC 527* (airline pilot employed abroad but occasionally landing in UK where family home maintained, held UK duties more than incidental). See also Revenue Pamphlet IR 20, paras 5.7, 5.8. 'Full-time' employment (here and in relation to Revenue concession A11 referred to below), in an ordinary case involving a standard pattern of hours, requires an individual working hours clearly comparable with those in a typical UK working week. See Revenue Pamphlet IR 20, para 2.5 for this and for the Revenue interpretation of the requirement in less straightforward cases.

65.5 Residence, Ordinary Residence and Domicile

'Available accommodation' does not depend on ownership but whether any accommodation is in fact maintained for occupation at any time by the individual concerned. A house owned and let out on a lease which denies availability is ignored, as is a renting of less than two years of furnished accommodation (or one year of unfurnished accommodation) during temporary stay. A house owned but left empty of furniture, or only available during a part of the year when the person is not in the UK, or situated too far away from a UK destination visited briefly on business for its use to be practical, may similarly be ignored. (Revenue Pamphlet IR 20 (1996), paras 4.2, 4.3, 4.4).

Case law. Resident in Eire making monthly visits to UK as director of British company (having no UK residence, but a permanent one in Eire) held to be resident and ordinarily resident in UK (*Lysaght v CIR HL 1928, 13 TC 511*) (but cf. *CIR v Combe CS 1932, 17 TC 405*). Officer succeeding to Eire estate, intending to return there permanently but prevented by military duties in UK, held on facts to be resident in both countries (*Lord Inchiquin v CIR CA 1948, 31 TC 125*). In *CIR v Brown KB 1926, 11 TC 292* and *CIR v Zorab KB 1926, 11 TC 289*, however, held that retired Indian civil servants making periodical visits to the UK, but having no business interests here, were not UK resident.

An American holding a lease of a shooting box in Scotland and spending two months there every year (*Cooper v Cadwalader CES 1904, 5 TC 101*), and a merchant usually resident and doing business in Italy but owning house in UK where he resided less than six months (*Lloyd v Sulley CES 1884, 2 TC 37*) were both held to be UK resident.

A Belgian who had at his disposal, for the visits he paid here, a house owned not by him but by a company which he controlled, so that it was in fact available whenever he chose to come, was held to be UK resident (*Loewenstein v De Salis KB 1926, 10 TC 424*). In *Withers v Wynyard KB 1938, 21 TC 724*, however, an actress (after 18 months abroad) performing in UK, and for $3\frac{1}{2}$ months in 1933/34 occupying a leasehold flat (unable to be disposed of and sublet when possible), was held to be non-resident for that year.

Where neither the individual nor spouse physically present in UK during tax year, although children here, the individual was non-resident (*Turnbull v Foster CES 1904, 6 TC 206*). See also *Reed v Clark Ch D 1985, 58 TC 528*, where individual held non-resident for tax year of absence from UK during which continuing trade carried on. If, however, either an individual or spouse, while they are still living together, has established a UK family home, any visit during a tax year, however short, to that home, may render the individual UK resident for that tax year (although cf. *Withers v Wynyard* above).

Revenue practice. Revenue Pamphlet IR 20 (to which paragraph numbers in the following text refer) considers the application of the above tests first generally, then in relation to those leaving the UK, then in relation to those coming to the UK.

General. Some physical presence in the UK during a tax year is normally required for an individual to be regarded as UK resident for that year, and the individual will invariably be so regarded where that physical presence is for six months or more in the year (as in (*a*) above). (para 1.2).

Strictly, residence status applies only by reference to whole tax years. By concession, however, an individual coming to the UK to take up permanent residence or to stay for at least two years, or leaving the UK to live abroad permanently (or for at least three years), is treated as UK resident only from the date of arrival or up to and including the date of departure, tax liabilities which are affected by residence status being calculated on the basis of the period of residence. In either case, the Revenue must be satisfied that the person was not ordinarily resident in the UK (see 65.6 below) prior to arrival or on departure. Similarly, subject to the further conditions as described below in relation to leaving the UK, an individual (and accompanying spouse) going abroad under a contract of employment will be so treated only up to and including the date of departure and from the date of return to the

UK. The provisions limiting the income chargeable on non-residents (see 51.1 NON-RESIDENTS AND OTHER OVERSEAS MATTERS) do not apply to the non-resident part of a split year. This concession previously applied to temporary visitors coming to stay for at least three years, with a shorter period applying only in the case of those coming to the UK to take up employment expected to last at least two years, but the concession has been revised to apply the two year period for all temporary visitors. (paras 1.5–1.7; Revenue Pamphlet IR 1, A11 and A78 (as revised)). See also 73.10, 73.11 SCHEDULE D, CASE VI.

Full personal allowances are available for the year permanent residence begins or ends. (para 7.4).

For detailed Revenue procedures in relation to matters concerned with residence, see Revenue Residence Guide Manual.

For commentary on aspects of Revenue practice in relation to available accommodation, see ICAEW Technical Release TAX 20/94, 30 November 1994.

Leaving the UK. Short trips abroad, e.g. on holiday or business trips, do not alter the residence status of a person who usually lives in the UK (see (*b*) above). (para 2.1).

An individual (and accompanying spouse) leaving to work abroad 'full-time' (see (*c*) above) under a contract of employment is treated as non-UK resident provided that both the absence from the UK and the employment cover a complete tax year, and that any interim visits to the UK do not amount to either 183 days or more in any tax year or an average of 91 days or more per tax year (averaged over a maximum of four years (see para 2.10 for method of averaging), and ignoring days spent in the UK for exceptional circumstances beyond the person's control, for example own or family illness). Similar conditions apply to an individual leaving to work abroad full-time in a trade, profession or vocation. These conditions are applied separately in relation to the employee and the accompanying spouse, but must be satisfied by the employee for the concession to be available to the accompanying spouse. See also 65.6 below as regards ordinary residence of the accompanying spouse. (paras 2.2–2.6).

An individual leaving the UK permanently is nevertheless treated as continuing to be UK resident if visits to the UK average 91 days or more per tax year (subject to exceptional circumstances, as above). (para 2.7). Some evidence will normally be required in support of a claim to have become non-resident (and non-ordinarily resident, see 65.6 below), e.g. steps taken to acquire a permanent home abroad, and, if UK property is retained, a reason consistent with the stated aim of permanent residence abroad. If such evidence is satisfactory, or, where such evidence is not available, if the absence abroad is for a settled purpose, UK residence (and ordinary residence) will be treated as ceasing on the day after departure from the UK, provided that absence from the UK has covered at least a whole tax year and that interim visits to the UK have not exceeded 182 days in any tax year and have averaged less than 91 days per tax year (as above). If such evidence is lacking, and the absence abroad is not for a settled purpose, UK residence and ordinary residence will be treated as continuing, subject to review if the absence actually extends to three years after departure or if evidence becomes available to show that the absence is permanent (and provided that the 182- and 91-day tests (as above) are satisfied). (paras 2.8, 2.9).

Coming to the UK. UK residence (and ordinary residence, see 65.6 below) will commence on the date of arrival in the UK where an individual whose home has been abroad comes to the UK to live here permanently or intending to stay for three years or more (disregarding holidays or short business trips abroad). (para 3.1). Otherwise, short-term visitors will be treated as resident for a tax year in which they are in the UK for 183 days or more in the year (see (*a*) above), or from the fifth tax year where in the preceding four tax years regular visits have been made to the UK averaging 91 days or more per tax year (subject to exceptional circumstances, as above). If such visits are clearly intended on arrival in the UK, residence will commence with the first of those four years, and if the decision to make such visits is taken before the start of the fifth year, residence will commence with the year in which the decision was taken. (para 3.3). Longer-term visitors are treated as resident throughout any period for which they come to the UK for a purpose (such as employment) that will mean remaining (apart from holidays or short business trips) for at least two years. This will also apply if accommodation is owned or is acquired or taken on a lease of three years or more in the year of arrival. Otherwise (and subject to the usual 183-day rule) such visitors will be treated as resident from the beginning of the tax year in which such accommodation is acquired or leased. (paras 3.7, 3.11).

It is understood that, in practice, an individual arriving in the UK with no fixed intentions regarding residence but who during the visit sets up a permanent residence in the UK is deemed resident and ordinarily resident from the date of arrival, provided that that date and the date of change of plan fall within the same tax year. Back assessments are understood to be made only where the visitor's intentions on arrival were admitted or quite clear.

An individual who comes to the UK not as a short-term visitor but with the intention of remaining in the UK may be regarded as UK resident even if UK visits are within the above limits. Whether an individual is a short-term visitor will depend on e.g. the reason for coming to the UK and the general background to the normal living pattern. An habitual visitor who stays in accommodation owned or available for less than 91 days in each tax year is unlikely to have the intention of remaining in the UK for at least three years and would, if this is so, be treated as a short-term visitor. (Taxation Practitioner October 1994, p 26).

As regards visits for education, see 64.6 below.

Mobile workers. For how the Revenue consider the residence and ordinary residence rules apply to individuals who usually live in the UK but make frequent and regular trips abroad in the course of their employment or business (e.g. lorry or coach drivers driving to and from the Continent and those working on cross-Channel transport), see the article in the Revenue Tax Bulletin April 2001 pp 836–838. For this purpose individuals 'usually live' in the UK if their home and settled domestic life continue to be there, and trips abroad are 'frequent and regular' where they are made every two or three weeks or more often. Only in exceptional cases are the Revenue likely to accept that such workers are other than resident and ordinarily resident in the UK.

Administrative procedures. Individuals who come to the UK to take up employment are asked to complete Form P86 to enable their residence status to be considered. This form also includes a section on domicile so that, in straightforward cases (where, e.g., a person never domiciled in the UK comes here only to work and with the intention of leaving the UK when the employment ceases), the two matters may be dealt with together. In less straightforward cases, Form DOM1 has been introduced to obtain the information necessary to the determination of domicile. On leaving the UK, a shortened Form P85 (Form P85(S)) enables any repayment to be claimed in straightforward cases. Otherwise, Form P85 continues to be used.

As regards individuals who are not regarded as ordinarily resident in the UK on arrival, enquiries as to any change in circumstances now begin only after a complete tax year has elapsed since arrival, although individuals are expected to report any actual changes in their circumstances without delay, whether or not that period has elapsed. (Revenue Press Release 8 September 1994).

Under *self-assessment* from 1996/97 onwards, Forms P85, P85(S), P86 and DOM1 continue in operation, but individuals who regard themselves as not resident, not ordinarily resident or not domiciled in the UK are required to self-certify their status in the self-assessment tax return and to complete the 'NON-RESIDENCE ETC.' supplementary pages to the return. The Revenue no longer provide residence 'rulings' but will give specific advice in limited circumstances. Revenue queries on residence status and domicile aspects may be made as part of an enquiry into the self-assessment return or into an initial claim made outside the return (see 68.6 RETURNS, 16.3 CLAIMS). See Revenue Tax Bulletin June 1997 pp 425–427.

Residence of trustees and personal representatives. Where at least one of the trustees of a settlement is non-UK resident and at least one is UK resident, then provided that the settlor (including any person providing or undertaking to provide funds directly or indirectly for the settlement) satisfies a further condition (or, if there is more than one settlor, that at least one of them satisfies that condition), the non-UK resident trustee(s) is (are) treated as UK resident for income tax purposes. Otherwise, the UK resident trustee(s) is (are) treated as not resident in the UK and as resident elsewhere for those purposes.

Similar rules apply to determine the residence of personal representatives.

The condition to be met in relation to trustees is that the settlor is resident, ordinarily resident or domiciled in the UK at a 'relevant time'. A *'relevant time'* is the time of the settlor's death in relation to a testamentary disposition or intestacy, otherwise it is the time, or each of the times, when he has provided funds for the settlement. In relation to personal representatives, the condition is that the deceased was resident, ordinarily resident or domiciled in the UK at the time of his death.

See 3.7 ANTI-AVOIDANCE as regards certain circumstances in which the above rules do not apply. [*FA 1989, ss 110, 111*].

Special provision is made for the assessment of trustees and personal representatives to income tax. See 81.3 SETTLEMENTS.

Simon's Direct Tax Service. See **E6.1.**

65.6   ORDINARY RESIDENCE

The term 'ordinary residence' is not defined in the *Taxes Acts*. See below for the case law on its interpretation. Broadly, it denotes greater permanence than the term 'residence' (see 65.5 above), and is equivalent to habitual residence; if an individual is resident year after year, he is ordinarily resident. An individual may be resident in the UK under the six months rule of *ICTA 1988, s 336* (see 65.5(*a*) above) without becoming ordinarily resident. Equally, he may be ordinarily resident without being resident in a particular year, e.g. because he usually lives in the UK but is absent on an extended holiday throughout a tax year. (Revenue Pamphlet IR 20, para 1.3).

An individual will be treated as ordinarily resident in the UK if he visits the UK regularly and either has available accommodation (see 65.5(*c*) above) or his visits average (for which see Revenue Pamphlet IR 20, para 3.6) 91 days or more per tax year (ignoring days spent in the UK for exceptional circumstances beyond his control, for example his own or family illness). Ordinary residence will commence from 6 April in the tax year of first arrival if the intention to make such visits to the UK for at least four tax years is clear on that first visit, or from 6 April in the fifth tax year after four years of such visits (unless the decision to make regular visits was made in an earlier tax year, in which case it applies from 6 April in that earlier year). (Revenue Pamphlet IR 20, paras 3.4, 3.5).

If an individual regarded as ordinarily resident solely because of the availability of accommodation disposes of it and leaves the UK within three years of arrival, he is normally treated as not ordinarily resident for the duration of his stay (assuming this is to his advantage). (Revenue Pamphlet IR 20, para 3.12).

See 65.5 above for administrative procedures in certain cases.

Longer-term visitors — commencement of ordinary residence. If it is clear on arrival in the UK that the intention is to stay for at least three years (disregarding holidays and short business trips abroad), ordinary residence commences on arrival. An individual coming to the UK, but not intending to stay more than three years (and not buying or leasing for three years or more accommodation for use in the UK), is treated as ordinarily resident from the beginning of the tax year following the third anniversary of arrival. If, before the beginning of that tax year, either there is a change in the individuals' intention (i.e. to an intention to stay in the UK for three years or more in all) or accommodation for use in the UK is bought (or leased for three years or more), ordinary residence is treated as commencing at the beginning of the tax year in which either of those events happens (or from the date of arrival in the UK if later). (Revenue Pamphlet IR 131, SP 17/91, 4 December 1991 and Revenue Pamphlet IR 20, paras 3.8–3.11).

Education. A student who comes to the UK for a period of study or education and will be in the UK for less than four years will be treated as not ordinarily resident providing (i) he does not own or buy (or lease for three years or more) accommodation in the UK, and (ii) he will not, following his departure from the UK, be returning regularly for visits averaging 91 days or more (see Revenue Pamphlet IR 20, para 3.6) per tax year. (Revenue Pamphlet IR 20, para 3.13).

Spouse accompanying employee working overseas. Where a person going abroad for full-time employment (see 65.5 above) was accompanied by a spouse who was within the concession (Revenue Pamphlet IR 1, A11) described at 65.5 above, and who retained available accommodation in the UK, the accompanying spouse was treated as not ordinarily resident throughout the period of absence, provided that the absence was three years or more and UK visits averaged less than 91 days per tax year. Where an intended period of absence of three years or more was cut to less than three years because of the unexpected termination of the spouse's employment, the shorter period might qualify provided that it included a complete tax year and UK visits averaged less than 91 days per tax year. (Revenue Pamphlet IR 1, A78 (as revised)).

Mobile workers. See 65.5 above.

Cases

In *Reid v CIR SC 1926, 10 TC 673*, British subject held '*ordinarily resident*' here although no fixed residence either here or abroad and regularly absent abroad $8\frac{1}{2}$ months every year. But she had here an address, family ties, banking account and furniture stored.

Levene v CIR HL 1928, 13 TC 486 was decided similarly. (British subject abroad for health reasons since 1918, no fixed residence here since (or abroad till 1925), but having ties with this country and in the 'usual ordering of his life', making habitual visits to UK 20 weeks yearly for definite purposes.) The judgments in this case interpreted the meaning of 'ordinarily resident' by the following phrases: 'habitually resident', 'residence in a place with some degree of continuity', and 'according to the way a man's life is usually ordered'. In *Peel v CIR CS 1927, 13 TC 443*, although appellant had his business and house in Egypt, he was held ordinarily resident here because he also had a house here, and spent an average of 139 days of each year in the UK.

In *Kinloch v CIR KB 1929, 14 TC 736*, a widow living mostly abroad with a son at school here, who had won an appeal in previous years but continued regular annual visits, was held to be resident and ordinarily resident.

In *Elmhirst v CIR KB 1937, 21 TC 381* appellant held on facts to have been ordinarily resident although denying any intention at the time to become so. And see *Miesegaes v CIR CA 1957, 37 TC 493* (minor at school here for five years, spending the occasional vacation with his father in Switzerland, held ordinarily resident). See also cases under 65.5 above.

In *R v Barnet London Borough Council (ex p Nilish Shah) HL 1982, [1983] 1 AER 226* (a non-tax case), the words 'ordinarily resident' were held to mean 'that the person must be habitually and normally resident here, apart from temporary or occasional absence of long or short duration'.

Simon's Direct Tax Service. See E6.1.

65.7   **VISITS ABROAD AND CLAIMS TO NON-RESIDENCE (AND TO NON-ORDINARY RESIDENCE)**

Visits abroad are differentiated as follows.

(*a*)   **Absence from UK for full-time work abroad.** An individual working abroad in the circumstances specified in 65.5(*c*) above will normally be regarded as not resident and not ordinarily resident for his period of absence if the period includes at least one complete tax year and if his visits to the UK do not exceed the limits specified in 65.5(*a*) and (*b*) above. (Revenue Pamphlet IR 20, para 2.2).

(*b*)   **Absence from UK for other reasons.** Where an individual goes abroad and intends to remain abroad for at least three years, he may claim to be treated as neither resident nor ordinarily resident from the day after departure, provided that he has been absent for at least a whole tax year and visits to the UK have not exceeded 182 days in any tax year or averaged more than 90 days in any tax year (as regards both of which tests see further 65.5 above). Such a claim must be supported by suitable evidence (e.g. acquiring permanent living accommodation abroad and making appropriate arrangements in relation to any property owned in the UK). (Revenue Pamphlet IR 20, paras 2.7, 2.8).

In the absence of such evidence, the same treatment may be claimed where the absence abroad is for a settled purpose, e.g. where there is a fixed object or intention in which the individual is going to be engaged for an extended period of time. Otherwise, UK residence and ordinary residence will be treated as continuing, subject to review if the absence actually extends beyond three years or if evidence becomes available to show that the absence is permanent (and provided that the 182- and 91-day tests (as above) are satisfied). (Revenue Pamphlet IR 20, para 2.9).

In any event, an individual will be regarded as resident in the UK in the circumstances described in 65.5(*a*) above, and as both resident and ordinarily resident in the circumstances described in 65.5(*b*) above. (Revenue Pamphlet IR 20, paras 3.3, 3.4).

See 65.5 above as regards the relevance of available accommodation in the UK for 1992/93 and earlier years.

65.8   **APPEALS**

Ordinary residence and domicile in relation to employment income and CGT are determined by the Board. [*ITEPA 2003, s 42; ICTA 1988, s 207*]. Claims to the remittance basis in respect of overseas income on the grounds of ordinary residence or domicile outside the UK (see 73.5 SCHEDULE D, CASES IV AND V), claims to the special reliefs referred to at 65.3 above and certain double tax claims (see 24.5(*e*) DOUBLE TAX RELIEF) are made to the Board. Any appeal from a Board decision is to the Special Commissioners [*TMA 1970, Sch 1A para 10, Sch 2 para 3*] and the normal time limit of 30 days is extended to three months if on a question of residence, ordinary residence or domicile. [*TMA 1970, Sch 1A para 9(2)(b)*]. Other disputes regarding residence are settled by way of appeal against the relevant assessment in the ordinary way.

66 Retirement Annuities

Cross-references. See 59 PENSION PROVISION AFTER 5 APRIL 2006; 60 PERSONAL PENSION SCHEMES (AND STAKEHOLDER PENSIONS). See also 53.15 PARTNERSHIPS for partnership retirement annuities and 67 RETIREMENT SCHEMES generally.

Simon's Direct Tax Service E7.3.

General note. The provisions under *ICTA 1988, ss 618–629* for retirement annuity contracts for the self-employed and those in non-pensionable employment were, for new schemes, replaced, after 30 June 1988, by the regime for personal pension schemes under *ICTA 1988, ss 630–655*, designed to encourage employees who wish to do so to opt out of company pension schemes in favour of independent arrangements not linked to any one employment. See 60 PERSONAL PENSION SCHEMES (AND STAKEHOLDER PENSIONS). Retirement annuity schemes contracted before 1 July 1988 continue, however, to be dealt with under the earlier provisions as described in this chapter.

The headings in this chapter are as follows.

66.1	Outline of provisions	66.7	Relevant earnings
66.2	Contract requirements	66.8	Trust schemes
66.3	Limits of relief	66.9	Interaction between retirement
66.4	Premiums related back		annuity premiums and personal
66.5	Unused relief carried forward		pension contributions
66.6	Cancellation of retirement annuity contract		

New pension schemes regime after 5 April 2006. A new pension schemes tax regime was introduced by *FA 2004* and comes into force on **6 April 2006**. It fully replaces the pre-existing rules for occupational pension schemes, personal (and stakeholder) pension schemes and retirement annuity schemes. **The rules described in this chapter remain valid for 2004/05 and 2005/06.** For the new regime, see 59 PENSION PROVISION AFTER 5 APRIL 2006.

66.1 OUTLINE OF PROVISIONS

Where an individual pays a 'qualifying premium' in a year of assessment under a contract made before 1 July 1988 and approved by the Board of Inland Revenue under *ICTA 1988, s 620* or *s 621*, the amount of that premium may, subject to certain limits (see 66.3 below), be deducted from his 'relevant earnings' (see 66.7 below) as assessed for that year from a trade, profession, vocation, office or employment. [*ICTA 1988, ss 618(1), 619(1), 620(1); FA 1988, s 54*]. These arrangements do not apply to income from a pensionable office or employment (see 66.7 below). Retirement annuity premiums are not deductible in arriving at profits for Class 4 national insurance purposes (see 83.8 SOCIAL SECURITY). [*Social Security Contributions and Benefits Act 1992, Sch 2 para 3(2)(f)*].

Relief may be granted on a provisional basis in respect of renewal premiums, whether fixed or variable, without proof of payment being required before the due date for payment of tax (although proof of payment is of course required in due course). (Revenue Tax Bulletin May 1992 p 19).

An annuity payable under such a contract (so far as it derives from premiums in respect of which relief was given) is treated as earned income when received by an annuitant to whom it is made payable under the terms of the contract. [*ICTA 1988, s 619(1)*]. For 2003/04 onwards, such an annuity is taxable under *ITEPA 2003* as pension income (see 58.2(j) PENSION INCOME), though PAYE (55) does not apply (see *ITEPA 2003, s 683(3)*). For earlier years, it was taxable under Schedule D, Case III. For all years, it is normally paid under deduction of tax at source (see 22.11 DEDUCTION OF TAX AT SOURCE), although non-taxpayers can request (on form R89) that payments be made gross (Revenue Pamphlet IR 121). A lump sum provided (as in 66.2 below) under a retirement annuity contract is not chargeable to income tax. [*ITEPA 2003, s 637(1)(c)(4)(5)*].

Simon's Direct Tax Service. See E7.301.

66.2   **CONTRACT REQUIREMENTS**

For approval under ICTA 1988, s 620, the annuity contract must have as its main object the provision for an individual of a life annuity in old age. It must be made by an individual with a person carrying on life annuity business in the UK, and, subject as follows, **must preclude**

(*a*)   any payment during the life of the individual other than a life annuity to him commencing not earlier than age 60 and not later than age 75, and

(*b*)   any payment after his death other than

    (i)   a life annuity (not greater than his original annuity) to his surviving spouse, or

    (ii)   if no annuity becomes payable either to the individual or his spouse, the return of premiums paid, with reasonable interest or bonuses out of profits.

An annuity under *section 620* may, if so provided and if the individual so elects before the annuity first becomes payable, be *partially commuted* for a lump sum not exceeding three times the annual amount of the remaining part of the annuity, but subject to this all annuities must be incapable of total or partial surrender, commutation or assignment.

For approved contracts made after 16 March 1987 (but before 1 July 1988), however, the maximum lump sum which may be paid to the individual is £150,000 (or such other sum as may be specified by Treasury order), regardless of the terms of the contract. Alternatively, the individual and the person(s) to whom premiums are payable were able jointly to elect (before the end of January 1988) for the approval of the contract to be cancelled *ab initio*.

But the Inland Revenue may, conditionally, approve a contract, otherwise satisfying the above, even though it contains one or more of the following provisions:

(i)   the individual's life annuity to commence at age earlier than 60 in the event of his becoming incapacitated from carrying on his occupation, or any similar one,

(ii)   the individual's life annuity to commence earlier than age 60 if his occupation is one in which retirement before that age is customary (see below),

(iii)   a life annuity, after the individual's death, for a dependant other than the surviving spouse,

(iv)   an annuity to continue for a term certain (not exceeding 10 years) despite death within that term, and for such an annuity to be capable of assignment by will, or by the annuitant's personal representatives in distributing his estate,

(v)   suspension, or termination, of the annuity, in the event of marriage, remarriage, or otherwise,

(vi)   the value of the accrued rights to be paid as a premium for another approved annuity contract or personal pension scheme, if required by the individual, widow, widower or dependant having the accrued rights.

[*ICTA 1988, s 618(2)(4), s 620(1)–(4); FA 1988, s 54*].

66.3 Retirement Annuities

As regards (ii) above, the following early retirement ages have been agreed by Superannuation Funds Office.

30   Downhill skiers

35   Athletes; badminton players; boxers; cyclists; dancers; footballers; ice hockey players; models; national hunt jockeys; real tennis players; rugby league players; rugby union players; squash players; table tennis players; tennis players; wrestlers.

40   Cricketers; divers (saturation, deep sea and free swimming); golfers; motorcycle riders (motocross or road racing); motor racing drivers; WPBSA snooker players; speedway riders; trapeze artistes.

45   Flat racing jockeys; members of the reserve forces.

50   Circus animal trainers; croupiers; interdealer brokers and moneybroker dealers; martial arts instructors; TV newsreaders; offshore riggers; Royal Navy reservists; rugby league referees; territorial army members.

55   Air pilots; brass instrumentalists; distant water trawlermen; firemen (part-time); inshore fishermen; moneybroker dealer directors and managers responsible for dealers; nurses, physiotherapists, midwives or health visitors who are females; psychiatrists (who are also maximum part-time specialists employed within the NHS solely in the treatment of the mentally disordered); singers.

These pension ages apply only to arrangements funded by premiums in respect of relevant earnings from the occupation or profession in question. For professional sportsmen, the earnings must arise from activities as such, e.g. tournament earnings and appearance and prize money, and not from sponsorship or coaching (for which separate arrangements may be made).

For approval under ICTA 1988, s 621, (term assurance or family income cover) the contract must be made by an individual with a person carrying on life annuity business in the UK. It must either

(*a*)   have as its main object the provision of a life annuity for the surviving spouse or other dependants of the individual, or

(*b*)   have as its sole object the provision of a lump sum on the death of the individual before age 75.

Unless the Revenue otherwise allow, a contract within (*a*) must also satisfy the following conditions:

(i)   any annuity payable must be incapable of total or partial surrender, commutation or assignment;

(ii)   if payable to the individual's surviving spouse or dependant, it must be a life annuity commencing on the individual's death;

(iii)   if payable to the individual, it must be a life annuity commencing after the age of 60 and, unless payable as a result of the death of a person to whom an annuity would otherwise have been payable, commencing before the age of 75;

(iv)   if, as a result of death, no annuity is payable, the only sums which may be paid under the contract are by way of return of premiums, reasonable interest on premiums or bonuses out of profits.

[*ICTA 1988, s 621(1)–(4)*].

Simon's Direct Tax Service. See E7.302.

66.3   **LIMITS OF RELIEF**

Relief is given only by deduction from relevant earnings, and the amount of qualifying premiums which may be deducted from relevant earnings in any year of assessment is subject to an overall limit which is a percentage of 'net relevant earnings' in that year (see 66.7 below). See 66.5 below for relief carry-forward. [*ICTA 1988, s 619(2)(3)*].

The overall limit is $17\frac{1}{2}\%$ of net relevant earnings although older individuals are allowed a higher percentage (see below). Premiums paid under *ICTA 1988, s 621* approved contracts may not exceed 5% of net relevant earnings, and are included in the overall limit of $17\frac{1}{2}\%$.

Increased limits for older individuals. The overall limits are increased as indicated in the following table where the individual is in the age range indicated at the beginning of a year of assessment.

51 to 55	20%
56 to 60	$22\frac{1}{2}\%$
61 or more	$27\frac{1}{2}\%$

[*ICTA 1988, s 626*].

Where relief is also available for personal pension scheme contributions in a year of assessment, the relief available for those contributions is correspondingly reduced. [*ICTA 1988, s 655(1)(a)*]. See examples at 60.4 PERSONAL PENSION SCHEMES (AND STAKEHOLDER PENSIONS) and 66.9 below.

Simon's Direct Tax Service. See E7.321.

66.4   **PREMIUMS RELATED BACK**

An individual who pays a qualifying premium in a year of assessment (whether or not he has relevant earnings for that year) may elect that the premium (or part of it, see Tolley's Practical Tax 1982 p 132) be treated as paid

(*a*)   in the last preceding year of assessment, or

(*b*)   if he had no net relevant earnings in the last preceding year, in the last preceding year but one.

The election must be made on or before 31 January following the year of assessment in which the premium is paid.

Where such an election is made, the premium is treated as having been paid in the year elected and not in the year actually paid. [*ICTA 1988, s 619(4); FA 1996, s 135, Sch 21 para 17*]. See 16.2 CLAIMS as regards how relief for premiums carried back to 1996/97 and subsequent years is given. An election is in practice treated by the Revenue as operative only up to the maximum available for relief for the year specified in the election. If the amount specified in the election becomes excessive as a result of an adjustment to the assessment for the year specified, the unrelievable proportion will fall back into the actual year of payment. (Tolley's Practical Tax 1984 p 158).

Simon's Direct Tax Service. See E7.324.

66.5   **UNUSED RELIEF CARRIED FORWARD**

Relief available for a year of assessment which is not used in that year may be carried forward and used to cover that part of a qualifying premium paid in any of the next six years which exceeds the relief limit (see 66.3 above) for that year. Relief is given in the year in which the premium is paid although the maximum relief for that year must be used first. Unused relief for earlier years must be used before that for later years.

Where an assessment on an individual's earnings becomes final and conclusive more than six years after the end of the year to which it relates, and as a result there is an amount of unused relief for that year, that amount shall not be available for any of the following six years. However that relief may be covered by a qualifying premium paid within six months of the date on which the assessment becomes final and conclusive. Relief is given in the year of assessment in which the premium is paid but is not allowed unless the maximum premium allowable for that year (see 66.3 above) is paid. Although the extra premium representing the unused relief must be paid within the specified six months, the maximum premium for the year of assessment in which the extra premium is paid may be paid at any time within the normal time limits for that year. If relief is given for a premium in this way, it may not be given under the normal carry-forward rule. [*ICTA 1988, s 625*]. Relief is given in a similar way where relevant earnings for a year which ended more than six years previously are not formally assessed but are taken into account in a contract settlement in a case involving fraudulent or negligent conduct. See 30.11 FRAUDULENT OR NEGLIGENT CONDUCT.

Where contributions are made under approved personal pension arrangements (see 60.1 PERSONAL PENSION SCHEMES (AND STAKEHOLDER PENSIONS)) in a year of assessment, the unused relief that may be utilised in that year is correspondingly reduced. [*ICTA 1988, s 655(1)(b)*]. For the method of calculating the reduction, see *Brock v O'Connor (Sp C 118), [1997] SSCD 157*. See example at 66.9 below.

Simon's Direct Tax Service. See E7.323.

66.6   **CANCELLATION OF CONTRACT**

The Revenue has indicated that cancellation of a policy under a retirement annuity contract may be agreed to where there has been some fundamental misconception as to the nature of the policy. Where the Life Office accepts that a valid case of misapprehension by the taxpayer has arisen, and is anxious to cancel the policy *ab initio* and refund the premiums paid, the matter would be viewed sympathetically. Such a case may be settled on the basis that there was no valid contract at the outset, so that *ICTA 1988, s 620(2)* would not be breached. It is for the taxpayer to contact the Life Office, who should then approach the Revenue. This would not extend to the case where a contract has been in existence for a number of years, and a premium is subsequently paid which for some reason is not fully tax-relieved. (Tolley's Practical Tax 1983 p 157, 1985 p 22).

66.7   **RELEVANT EARNINGS**

'*Relevant earnings*' of an individual is chargeable income which is included in one of the following categories.

(*a*)   Income from an office or employment which is not a 'pensionable office or employment', and income from property which is either attached thereto or which forms part of the earnings therefrom. This includes amounts assessed as benefits in kind. In contrast to the position for personal pension schemes (see 60.8 PERSONAL PENSION SCHEMES (AND STAKEHOLDER PENSIONS)), SHARE-RELATED EMPLOYMENT INCOME (82) is not excluded from being relevant earnings, and neither is the excess over the exempt limit of any lump sum termination payment within 18.4, 18.5 COMPENSATION FOR LOSS OF EMPLOYMENT (AND DAMAGES).

(*b*)   Income chargeable under Schedule D immediately derived from the carrying on, individually or in partnership, of his trade, profession or vocation. This includes enterprise allowances (see 71.75 SCHEDULE D, CASES I AND II) and POST-CESSATION RECEIPTS (62).

(*c*)   Income from patent rights treated as earned income under *ICTA 1988, s 529*.

It does not include remuneration of a controlling director of an investment company. A married woman's relevant earnings are her own and not her husband's for the purpose of determining entitlement to retirement annuity relief. The amount from each such source is the statutory income of the year of assessment (i.e. ignoring any 'conventional' basis of assessment) before deducting capital allowances (other than those actually deductible in computing profits) but inclusive of any balancing charges. [*ICTA 1988, s 623(1)(2)(5), s 624(3); FA 1989, Sch 12 para 15*].

A '*pensionable office or employment*' is one to which any sponsored superannuation scheme applies which provides for retirement etc., and under which any part of the cost is borne otherwise than by the holder of the office etc. (and is not chargeable to tax as his earnings). See, however, below for concessional relief in the case of certain small lump sum retirement benefits schemes. An office or employment may be 'pensionable' even if the holder performs the duties partly outside the UK or is not chargeable to tax in respect of it. If the holder of such an office etc., having an option, does not join the scheme, his office is treated, for this purpose, as non-pensionable. [*ICTA 1988, s 623(3)(4), s 624(1)(2); ITEPA 2003, Sch 6 para 89*]. By concession, where an individual is treated as in pensionable employment solely because provision is made under a scheme or arrangement existing on 14 October 1980, fully or partly at the cost of the employer, for a benefit in pension form payable only on death or disability, the employment will be treated as non-pensionable for any tax year in which the individual has not become entitled to benefit as a result of that provision. Relief will be available on a year to year basis for the period of employment or until benefit becomes payable. Employment in the tax year in which such a contingency occurs will be regarded as pensionable and no retirement annuity relief will be available for that year, but relief given for previous years will not be affected. (Revenue Pamphlet IR 1, A38). The Revenue has ruled that an office or employment is non-pensionable up to the date on which the employee etc. first becomes entitled to benefits under a retirement scheme, even if these benefits are calculated by reference to earlier periods of service. (Tolley's Practical Tax 1982 p 131). It is, however, understood that where an employee receives a refund of premiums paid while in pensionable employment, that employment is *not* thereby rendered non-pensionable. (Tolley's Practical Tax 1986 p 135, 1990 p 95). See below, however, as regards personal pension schemes.

'*Net relevant earnings*' are relevant earnings, as above, less deductions which would be made therefrom in computing the individual's total income for income tax, being

(i)   deductions which but for *ICTA 1988, s 74(1)(m), (p) or (q)* could be made in computing his profits or gains (i.e. various payments, subject to deduction of tax at source, made for business purposes – excluding e.g. annuities to former partners, which would be prohibited under *ICTA 1988, s 74(1)(a)* – see Tolley's Practical Tax 1983 p 73), or

(ii)   deductions in respect of losses, or of capital allowances, relating to activities any profits from which would be relevant earnings of the individual. [*ICTA 1988, s 623(6)*].

Other amounts deducted in charging the individual's income to tax (e.g. for earnings from work done abroad, see 75.7 SCHEDULE E—EMPLOYMENT INCOME, or under the current provisions) do not reduce net relevant earnings.

If, in any year for which an individual claims relief, a deduction for a loss or allowance under (ii) above is treated as made to any extent out of income other than relevant earnings, his net relevant earnings for the next year are treated as reduced to that extent, any balance being carried forward to the third year, and so on. [*ICTA 1988, s 623(7)*].

In the case of partnership profits, net relevant earnings are the share of partnership income (as computed for tax purposes) after allowable deductions for partnership payments and capital allowances. [*ICTA 1988, s 623(9)*].

Simon's Direct Tax Service. See E7.322.

66.8 Retirement Annuities

Small lump sum retirement benefits schemes. Concessional relief applies where an employee has

(*a*)   paid premiums to a retirement annuity contract (or the employee or employer had made personal pension scheme contributions) for a year of assessment (see 66.3 above), and

(*b*)   accrued benefits, for the same year and in respect of the same office or employment, under an approved retirement benefits scheme

    (i)   under the rules of which the only benefit on retirement (other than from additional voluntary contributions) is a lump sum not exceeding £400 per year of pensionable service, and

    (ii)   whose rules provide for no such lump sum to accrue (or for the lump sum to be waived) in respect of any period for which premiums are paid to a retirement annuity contract (or personal pension scheme).

The tax relief for the retirement annuity premiums (or personal pension contributions) will not be withdrawn provided that

(1)   the lump sum benefit entitlement for the period is waived or does not accrue, and

(2)   the retirement annuity contract (or personal pension scheme) is not cancelled.

(Revenue Pamphlet IR 1, A95).

66.8   TRUST SCHEMES

The retirement annuity provisions also apply to contributions under a trust scheme, approved by the Inland Revenue, administered in the UK and established under irrevocable trusts by *a body representing a substantial proportion of the individuals engaged* (in UK, or in England, Scotland, Wales or NI) *in a particular occupation* (or group of occupations), for providing retirement annuities for them, with or without subsidiary benefits for their families or dependants. If the scheme is approved, income from investments or deposits of any fund maintained for the purpose of that fund is exempt from income tax. Gains are similarly exempt from capital gains tax. [*ICTA 1988, s 620(5)(6), s 621(5); TCGA 1992, s 271(1)(d)*]. See 71.22 SCHEDULE D, CASES I AND II as regards futures and options contracts.

Relief ceases to be available under such schemes to a person by whom contributions are first paid after 30 June 1988, even though the scheme may have been established on or before that date. [*ICTA 1988, s 618; FA 1988, s 54*].

66.9   INTERACTION BETWEEN RETIREMENT ANNUITY PREMIUMS AND PERSONAL PENSION CONTRIBUTIONS

Example

Y is self-employed and pays both retirement annuity premiums (RAPs), under a pre-1 July 1988 contract, and contributions to a personal pension scheme (PPCs). He had no unused relief brought forward at 6 April 1992, on which date he was 48 years of age. His net relevant earnings (NRE), RAPs paid and PPCs paid in each of the years 1992/93 to 2004/05 are as set out below. At no time does Y elect to carry back an RAP or a PPC to a previous year.

	NRE	Earnings cap	PPCs paid	RAPs paid
	£	£	£	£
1992/93	74,000	75,000	3,000	10,000
1993/94	78,000	75,000	5,000	10,000
1994/95	90,000	76,800	10,000	10,000
1995/96	120,000	78,600	14,000	10,000
1996/97	125,000	82,200	16,000	10,000
1997/98	127,500	84,000	16,500	10,000
1998/99	140,000	87,600	17,000	10,000
1999/00	155,000	90,600	20,930	10,000
2000/01	90,000	91,800	21,500	10,000
2001/02	110,000	95,400	23,390	10,000
2002/03	115,000	97,200	24,020	10,000
2003/04	100,000	99,000	20,000	10,000
2004/05	101,000	102,000	20,000	10,000

Y's records of amounts paid and tax relief given will look as follows

Personal pension contributions (PPCs)

	NRE	Maximum PPC relief	RAPs relieved	PPCs paid	Unused relief For year	Unused relief Cumulative
	£	£	£	£	£	£
1992/93	74,000	18,500 (1)	(10,000)	(3,000)	5,500	5,500
1993/94	75,000	18,750 (1)	(10,000)	(5,000)	3,750	9,250
1994/95	76,800	19,200 (1)	(10,000)	(10,000)	(800)	8,450
1995/96	78,600	23,580 (2)	(10,000)	(14,000)	(420)	8,030
1996/97	82,200	24,660 (2)	(10,000)	(16,000)	(1,340)	6,690
1997/98	84,000	25,200 (2)	(10,000)	(16,500)	(1,300)	5,390
1998/99	87,600	26,280 (2)	(10,000)	(17,000)	(720)	3,750 (4)
1999/00	90,600	27,180 (2)	(10,000)	(20,930)	(3,750)	Nil
2000/01	90,000	31,500 (3)	(10,000)	(21,500)	Nil	Nil
2001/02	95,400	33,390 (3)	(10,000)	(23,390)	Nil	Nil
2002/03	97,200	34,020 (3)	(10,000)	(24,020)	Nil	Nil
2003/04	99,000	34,650 (3)	(10,000)	(20,000)	Nil*	Nil*
2004/05	101,000	35,350 (3)	(10,000)	(20,000)	Nil*	Nil*

(1)   =   Relief at 25%

(2)   =   Relief at 30%

(3)   =   Relief at 35%

(4)   =   £5,390 b/f *less* £720 relieved in 1998/99 *less* £920 remaining for 1992/93 which cannot be carried forward beyond 1998/99 (although relief for the £920 could have been obtained by an election to treat part of the 1999/2000 premium as having been paid in 1998/99). The £3,750 is the unused relief for 1993/94.

* Unused personal pension relief for 2001/02 and subsequent years cannot be carried forward, so is shown here as nil even though £4,650 and £5,350 was unrelieved for 2003/04 and 2004/05 respectively.

The aggregate for each year of the 'RAPS relieved' and 'PPCs paid' columns above represents the total relief given in each year.

66.9 Retirement Annuities

Retirement annuity premiums (RAPs)

	NRE	Maximum RAP relief	RAPs relieved	Unused relief	PPCs paid	Unused relief c/f
	£	£	£	£	£	£
1992/93	74,000	12,950 (5)	(10,000)	2,950	(3,000)	Nil*
1993/94	78,000	13,650 (5)	(10,000)	3,650	(5,000)	Nil*
1994/95	90,000	15,750 (5)	(10,000)	5,750	(10,000)	Nil*
1995/96	120,000	24,000 (6)	(10,000)	14,000	(14,000)	Nil
1996/97	125,000	25,000 (6)	(10,000)	15,000	(16,000)	Nil*
1997/98	127,500	25,500 (6)	(10,000)	15,500	(16,500)	Nil*
1998/99	140,000	28,000 (6)	(10,000)	18,000	(17,000)	1,000
1999/00	155,000	31,000 (6)	(10,000)	21,000	(20,930)	1,070
2000/01	90,000	20,250 (7)	(10,000)	10,250	(21,500)	Nil*
2001/02	110,000	24,750 (7)	(10,000)	14,750	(23,390)	Nil*
2002/03	115,000	25,875 (7)	(10,000)	15,875	(24,020)	Nil*
2003/04	100,000	22,500 (7)	(10,000)	12,500	(20,000)	Nil*
2004/05	101,000	22,725 (7)	(10,000)	12,725	(20,000)	Nil*

(5) = Relief at 17.5%

(6) = Relief at 20%

(7) = Relief at 22.5%

* Unused relief carried forward cannot be reduced to a negative figure, so is merely reduced to nil.

Notes

(a) The maximum relief for PPCs for any year is reduced by any RAPs relieved in that year. One effect of this is that if a combination of RAPs and PPCs is to be relieved in any year, the maximum relief available for that year (excluding unused relief brought forward) is restricted by reference to the earnings cap.

(b) In computing unused retirement annuity relief for any year, any PPCs relieved in that year must be deducted.

(c) The maximum potential relief for the 13 years illustrated (taking the higher of the two maxima for each year) is £358,860. The total relief given is £341,340. Of the difference of £17,520, £920 is unused relief for 1992/93 which is lost under the six-year rule, £6,600 arises from the operation of the earnings cap and the balance of £10,000 represents unused relief for 2003/04 and 2004/05 which cannot be carried forward.

(d) As regards the method of calculation of unused relief, see *Brock v O'Connor (Sp C 118), [1997] SSCD 157.*

Simon's Direct Tax Service. See E7.420.

67 Retirement Schemes for Employees

(See also Revenue Pamphlets IR 2 and IR 12. The latter is now available only on the Internet via the Revenue website. Those who subscribed to the looseleaf version, which was previously available, for the year to 31 March 2003 should have continued to receive paper updates until 29 November 2003. For tax district practice generally, see Revenue Inspector's Manual IM 8000 *et seq.*)

Cross-references. See 58 PENSION INCOME; 59 PENSION PROVISION AFTER 5 APRIL 2006; 60 PERSONAL PENSION SCHEMES (AND STAKEHOLDER PENSIONS); and 66 RETIREMENT ANNUITIES.

Simon's Direct Tax Service E7.2.

The headings in this chapter are as follows.

New pension schemes regime after 5 April 2006. A new pension schemes tax regime was introduced by *FA 2004* and comes into force on **6 April 2006**. It fully replaces the pre-existing rules for occupational pension schemes, personal (and stakeholder) pension schemes and retirement annuity schemes. **The rules described in this chapter remain valid for 2004/05 and 2005/06.** For the new regime, see 59 PENSION PROVISION AFTER 5 APRIL 2006.

67.1 WHETHER PAYMENTS BY EMPLOYER ARE ASSESSABLE ON EMPLOYEE

Payments by an employer pursuant to a 'retirement benefits scheme' for the provision of 'relevant benefits' for, or in respect of, an employee are treated as employment income of that employee for the tax year of payment, with apportionment of composite payments, unless

(*a*) the scheme is approved by the Inland Revenue, or

(*b*) the scheme is a 'relevant statutory scheme', or

(*c*) the scheme is set up by a non-UK government for the benefit (or primarily for the benefit) of its employees, or

(*d*) the earnings from the employment for that year are not (or would not have been if there were any) general earnings within *ITEPA 2003, s 15* (employee resident, ordinarily resident and domiciled in the UK), *ITEPA 2003, s 21* (employee resident and ordinarily resident but not domiciled in the UK), *ITEPA 2003, s 25* (employee resident but not ordinarily resident in the UK) or *ITEPA 2003, s 27* (UK-based earnings for year when employee not resident in the UK) (see 75.3, 75.4 SCHEDULE E—EMPLOYMENT INCOME), or

(*e*) the employee is not of UK domicile and the employment is with a 'foreign employer' (see 75.4 SCHEDULE E—EMPLOYMENT INCOME), or

(f) the payment is made for a period for which the employee is a seafarer entitled to the foreign earnings deduction, see 75.7 SCHEDULE E—EMPLOYMENT INCOME (this exemption being statutory from 6 April 2003, having previously applied by Revenue practice), or

(g) the payment is otherwise chargeable to income tax as income of the employee (other, from 6 April 2002, than under *ITEPA 2003, s 403* or *ICTA 1988, s 148* (see 18.5 COMPENSATION FOR LOSS OF EMPLOYMENT (AND DAMAGES)), over a charge under which a charge under the current provisions takes precedence).

[*ITEPA 2003, ss 386–391; ICTA 1988, s 595(1), s 596(1)(2); FA 1989, Sch 6 para 8; FA 2002, Sch 6 para 6; FA 2004, Sch 17 para 2*].

See Revenue Explanatory Booklet 'The Tax Treatment of Top-Up Pension Schemes' for the Revenue view of when a charge arises under *section 595(1)*. Where a payment has been the subject of such a charge, the employer should provide the employee with a notice of the charge, which the employee should retain in order to show that benefits arising under the scheme are not chargeable to tax under *ITEPA 2003, s 394* or *ICTA 1988, s 596A* (see 67.9 below).

Where payments have been treated as income of an employee as above, but the employee (or his personal representatives) subsequently proves to the satisfaction of the Board that no payment in respect of the benefits has so far been made and that some event has occurred by reason of which no such payment will be made (in both cases other than as a consequence of a pension-sharing order or provision under *Welfare Reform and Pensions Act 1999, s 24(1)*), the tax paid will be repaid or otherwise relieved on application within six years of the event in question. Partial repayment may also be given on a just and reasonable basis. [*ITEPA 2003, s 392; ICTA 1988, s 596(3)(4); FA 1999, Sch 10 para 5*].

'*Retirement benefits scheme*' is defined as including any scheme, deed or arrangement (even if for single employee and even if the pension is to commence immediately) providing 'relevant benefits'. Approved personal pension schemes providing such benefits (see 60.2 PERSONAL PENSION SCHEMES) and national schemes are not included. [*ICTA 1988, s 611; FA 1999, Sch 10 para 9; FA 2000, Sch 13 para 4*]. Benefits provided for the employee's wife or husband (or widow or widower), children, dependants or personal representatives are included. [*ITEPA 2003, s 386(6); ICTA 1988, s 595(5); FA 1999, Sch 10 para 4*].

'*Relevant benefits*' are any pension, lump sum, gratuity etc. either (i) on retirement or death, or (ii) by virtue of a pension-sharing order or provision under *Welfare Reform and Pensions Act 1999, s 24(1)*, or (iii) in anticipation of retirement, or (iv) in connection with past service, after retirement or death, or (v) in anticipation of or in connection with any change in the nature of the employee's service, *other than* benefits afforded solely by reason of accidental disablement or death by accident during employment. [*ICTA 1988, s 612(1); FA 1999, Sch 10 para 10*].

A '*relevant statutory scheme*' is a statutory scheme established before 14 March 1989, or established on or after that date and entered in the register maintained by the Board for that purpose, or a parliamentary pension scheme (as defined). [*ICTA 1988, s 611A; FA 1989, Sch 6 para 15; FA 1999, Sch 5 para 5*].

As regards certain lump sum payments on retirement etc., see 67.12 below.

'*Employee*' is widely defined in *ICTA 1988, s 612(1)* and includes a director.

67.2 LIFE ASSURANCE RELIEF

Where approval was not obtained, and the payment by the employer is made under such an insurance or contract that life assurance relief (see 45.1 LIFE ASSURANCE POLICIES) would be obtained if made by the individual, then that individual is eligible for life assurance relief thereon. [*ICTA 1988, ss 266A, 595(1)(b); ITEPA 2003, s 386(7)(b), Sch 6 para 36*].

67.3   **CONDITIONS FOR APPROVAL — HISTORY**

Up to 5 April 1973, schemes for employees generally could be approved under *ICTA 1970, s 208* and a scheme for specific individuals (often referred to as a 'top-hat' scheme) could be approved under *ICTA 1970, s 222*.

After 5 April 1973, new schemes, or existing schemes materially altered, had to comply with new provisions which apply to *all* schemes after 5 April 1980 when *ICTA 1970, s 208, ss 220–225* were repealed. [*FA 1971, Sch 3*]. See 67.13 below.

Schemes existing at 5 April 1973 accordingly had to be amended to comply with the new provisions on or before 5 April 1980, in order for approval to be continued after that date.

67.4   **CONDITIONS FOR APPROVAL AFTER 5 APRIL 1973** [*ICTA 1988, Pt XIV, Ch 1; FA 1988, Sch 3 para 18; FA 1989, Sch 6 paras 3, 4; FA 1991, ss 34–36*]

Subject to provision for discretionary approval (see below), the following conditions apply.

(*a*)   The scheme must be established in connection with a trade or undertaking carried on in the UK by a UK resident, and there must be a UK resident who will be responsible for carrying out all statutory duties imposed on the administration of the scheme.

(*b*)   The employer must contribute to the scheme and both he and the employees to whom the scheme relates must recognise it, every employee who is, or has a right to be, a member of the scheme being given particulars of all essential features of it which concern him.

(*c*)   The sole purpose of the scheme must be to provide employees (or their widows or widowers, children, dependants or personal representatives) with 'relevant benefits' (see 67.1 above)

     (i)   on, after, or in anticipation of, *retirement at a specified age*, which must be not later than 75 or earlier than 60,

     (ii)   on, or after, *death*,

     (iii)   on, or in anticipation of, or in connection with, *a change in the nature* of the employee's service with the employer.

'Retirement' in (i) above means retirement from the service of the company whether as an employee or as a director but not necessarily from both positions; an individual who retired from paid employment but continued as an unpaid non-executive director was held by the HL to have duly retired and to have been entitled to receive payments from the company's pension scheme (*Venables and Others v Hornby HL 2003, [2004] STC 84*).

(*d*)   Employee's contributions must not be returnable in any circumstances (but see 67.5(*c*) below regarding existing schemes).

(*e*)   The employee's pension must not exceed *one-sixtieth* of his final remuneration for each year of service up to a maximum of 40. '*Final remuneration*' is the average annual remuneration of the last three years' service.

(*f*)   No pension may be commuted except where the scheme allows an employee to do so. A lump sum so obtained must not exceed *three-eightieths* of the employee's final remuneration for each year of service up to a maximum of 40; i.e. the maximum lump sum is $1\frac{1}{2}$ years' pay. (For schemes approved after 16 March 1987 and before 27 July 1989, and for any person who before 1 June 1989 became a member of a scheme which came into existence before 14 March 1989 but was not approved before 27 July 1989, there is excluded from final remuneration for this purpose any excess over £100,000.)

(g) The normal pension payable to the widow or widower of an employee dying after retirement must not exceed *two-thirds of the pension.*

(h) Approval may be withdrawn if in the Board's opinion its continuance is not warranted, from a specified date (not earlier than that on which the facts first ceased to warrant approval). An alteration to a scheme invalidates any earlier approval unless the alteration has been approved by the Board, either specifically or in general regulations.

(i) Where more than one retirement benefits scheme applies to a particular class or description of employees, approval of any such scheme, so far as it relates to such employees, is considered by reference to all such schemes. The schemes to be considered are specified as schemes approved or seeking approval under these provisions, funds within *ICTA 1988, s 608* (see 67.13 below) and any relevant statutory schemes (see 67.1 above).

With effect from 10 May 2000, the conditions for approval are amended to make provision for pension-sharing arrangements under e.g. *Welfare Reform and Pensions Act 1999, s 24(1)* (or NI equivalent), and generally for the provision of benefits for ex-spouses (or their widows or widowers, children, dependants or personal representatives). Where a scheme member's rights are transferred under such arrangements, they may not be replaced with rights the scheme member would not have been able to acquire had there been no such transfer. Schemes approved before 10 May 2000 which continue to be approved on and after 1 December 2000 (when the pension-sharing rules come into operation) are treated as containing certain of the provisions for automatic approval. This does not apply to simplified defined contribution schemes or in certain cases where the member is a 'moderate earner' (broadly an employee who is not a controlling director and whose earnings at the date the marriage ends do not exceed one-quarter of the 'permitted maximum' (see below) for the year in which it ends), and the provisions are modified in certain other cases. See *The Retirement Benefits Schemes (Sharing of Pensions on Divorce or Annulment) Regulations 2000 (SI 2000 No 1085)*. As regards pension-sharing generally, see Pensions Update No 62, 28 April 2000 and Revenue Pamphlet IR 12 at, in particular, Pt 6A and Appendix XIII.

[*ICTA 1988, ss 590, 591B, 612(1); FA 1989, Sch 6 para 3(4); FA 1991, ss 34, 36; FA 1999, Sch 10 paras 2, 18(5); SI 2000 No 1093*].

As regards (*a*) above there are detailed provisions for determining who is the administrator of a scheme, responsible for all the tax affairs of the scheme. Broadly, the administrator of a scheme set up under a trust is the trustee or trustees of the scheme, and the administrator of a scheme not set up under a trust is the sponsor or sponsors of the scheme. In either case a different person or persons (who must be UK resident) may be appointed as administrator by written notice, and such person(s) must be so appointed if none of the trustees or sponsors, as the case may be, is UK resident. Such an appointment made after the establishment of the scheme is an alteration of the scheme requiring Revenue approval. [*ICTA 1988, s 611AA; FA 1994, s 103(1)*]. There are provisions dealing with the position where a scheme has no administrator (e.g. where the trustees or sponsors are non-UK resident and have made no appointment), or no administrator can be traced, or the administrator is in default (considered serious by the Board). In such cases responsibilities and liabilities pass to any UK resident trustee or sponsor who can be traced (where a different administrator has been appointed), or ultimately to the employer (provided that the employer is a contributor to the scheme — failing which, if the scheme is a trust scheme, they pass to the sponsor(s) of the scheme) or the UK representative of a non-UK resident employer. [*ICTA 1988, s 606; FA 1994, s 104; FA 1998, Sch 15 para 5; ITEPA 2003, Sch 6 para 79; FA 2003, s 155, Sch 27 para 1(2)*]. A charge on the administrator of a scheme is treated as charged on all present and future administrators (without prejudice to the exclusion from charge under *ICTA 1988, s 591C* of certain independent trustees, see below) and is assessable in the name of the administrator. It is not assessable on persons who are no longer administrators. SELF-ASSESSMENT (78) does not apply to charges on administrators (or on persons to whom the Revenue has recourse for tax on administrators under *section 606* (see above) or *section 606A* (see below)). [*ICTA 1988, s 658A; TMA 1970, s 9(1A); FA 1998, s 98; ITEPA 2003, Sch 6 para 98*].

Further restrictions were introduced by *FA 1989, Sch 6* which apply to schemes approved after 26 July 1989, but, where a scheme came into existence before 14 March 1989, only as regards new members after 31 May 1989.

(i)   Where an employee is a member of a scheme by virtue of two or more 'relevant associated employments', or of a scheme which, in relation to the employee, is 'connected with' one or more other approved schemes, new limits on pension and commuted pension are applied by reference to a 'relevant amount' and to the aggregate payable in respect of all such employments or schemes.

(ii)   In arriving at an employee's final remuneration for the purposes of (*e*) or (*f*) above, any excess over the 'permitted maximum' for the year in which his participation in the scheme ceases is disregarded. Where this restriction applies, the earlier permitted maximum referred to in (*f*) above is abolished.

Employments are '*relevant associated employments*' for this purpose if an employee has held both or all of them, and become entitled to benefits in respect of both or all of them, during a period during which both or all of the employers were 'associated', and a scheme is '*connected with*' another in relation to an employee if a period of service under both of two 'associated' employers gives rise to entitlement to benefits under one scheme by reference to service with one employer and under the other scheme by reference to service with the other employer. Employers are '*associated*' if one is 'controlled' by the other or both are 'controlled' by a third person. '*Control*' may be direct or indirect and in relation to companies is determined in accordance with *ICTA 1988, s 840* (or, if the company is a close company, *ICTA 1988, s 416*).

The '*relevant amount*' is, in the case of pensions, $\frac{1}{60}$th, and in the case of commuted pension, $\frac{3}{80}$ths of the 'permitted maximum' for the year of assessment in which the benefits become payable, for each year of qualifying service (up to a maximum of 40), with a corresponding allowance for part years. Where there are relevant associated employments, all periods counting for benefit at the time the benefits become payable are taken into account, but periods counting by virtue of more than one such employment are included only once. Where schemes are connected with one another in relation to the employee, all periods counting for benefit for the purposes of all the connected schemes at the time the benefits become payable are taken into account, but periods counting for the purposes of more than one scheme are included only once.

The '*permitted maximum*' (aka the earnings cap) is £87,600 for 1998/99, £90,600 for 1999/2000, £91,800 for 2000/01, £95,400 for 2001/02, £97,200 for 2002/03, £99,000 for 2003/04 and **£102,000 for 2004/05**. It is increased in line with the retail prices index (unless Parliament sets a different figure) but is not reduced if the retail prices index falls.

[*ICTA 1988, s 590(3), ss 590A–590C; FA 1989, Sch 6 para 3(2)(3), para 4; SI 1991 No 734; SI 1992 No 624; FA 1993, ss 106, 107; SI 1996 No 2951; SI 1998 No 758; SI 1999 No 592; SI 2000 No 807; SI 2001 No 637; SI 2002 No 700; SI 2003 No 843; SI 2004 No 773*].

67.4 Retirement Schemes for Employees

Remuneration does not include anything chargeable as employment income arising from the acquisition or disposal of shares (or interests in shares) or from rights to acquire shares, nor anything in respect of which tax is chargeable under *ITEPA 2003, s 403* or, before 2003/04, under *ICTA 1988, s 148* (see 18.5 COMPENSATION FOR LOSS OF EMPLOYMENT (AND DAMAGES)). [*ICTA 1988, s 612(1); ITEPA 2003, Sch 6 para 82*].

Discretionary approval. The Board are given discretion, subject to regulations, to approve a scheme not fully complying with the above conditions (e.g. by allowing retirement up to 10 years before the ages prescribed in (*c*)(i) above, or earlier if incapacitated; by providing benefits in excess of the limits in (*e*) above on retirement after less than 40 years' service; by modifying the definition of 'final remuneration'; by providing a pension, and a lump sum up to four times final remuneration, for the widow(er) or dependants of an employee dying in service; by permitting certain increases in pensions in payment; by providing for the commutation in full of trivial pensions (i.e. up to £260 p.a.); by including a trade carried on partly overseas or by a non-resident; or by allowing the return of employees' contributions in certain contingencies) and, in respect of schemes in existence on 6 April 1980, will exercise that discretion to preserve benefits earned, or rights arising out of prior service, before the date of the approval of the scheme under the new code or 5 April 1980, whichever is the earlier, and to preserve any rights to death-in-service benefits existing under the scheme at 26 February 1970. Discretion is also given to approve schemes which allow members to have their benefits secured by means of an annuity contract with an insurance company of their choice, and schemes to which the employer is not a contributor which provide benefits additional to those under the employer's scheme. A condition for discretionary approval is that the employee's contribution must not exceed 15% of remuneration (and see now 67.5(*a*) below). [*ICTA 1988, s 591; FA 1994, s 107; FA 1995, ss 59(2), 60(1); FA 1999, Sch 10 para 3*]. Restrictions relating to the discretionary approval of small self-administered schemes (generally those with less than twelve members) are contained in *The Retirement Benefits Schemes (Restriction on Discretion to Approve) (Small Self-administered Schemes) Regulations 1991* (*SI 1991 No 1614*) (as amended) — see also Pensions Updates Nos 69 and 70, 29 August 2000, No 137, 11 March 2003 and No 143, 25 March 2003. As regards the requirement under those *regulations* for a 'pensioneer trustee', see *Lambert and others v Glover (Sp C 292), [2001] SSCD 250*. Restrictions relating to discretionary approval of additional voluntary contribution schemes are contained in *The Retirement Benefits Schemes (Restriction on Discretion to Approve) (Additional Voluntary Contributions) Regulations 1993* (*SI 1993 No 3016*) (as amended), from which existing approved schemes were excepted by *The Retirement Benefits Schemes (Restriction on Discretion to Approve) (Excepted Schemes) Regulations 1996* (*SI 1996 No 1582*) and *2000* (*SI 2000 No 1087*) — see also Pensions Update No 18, 11 July 1996. See generally Revenue Pamphlet IR 12 and Pensions Updates No 47, 24 July 1998, No 48, 24 August 1998, No 83, 22 January 2001, Nos 110–112, 18 December 2001, Nos 120, 122, 25 February 2002 and No 135, 20 December 2002.

For easements on benefit restrictions where pension ages have been equalised, see Pensions Update No 68, 29 August 2000.

The Revenue have published model rules and guidance notes for simplified occupational pension schemes, satisfying certain specified criteria and aimed primarily at the smaller employer. There are two types of simplified scheme: 'final salary' and 'defined contribution' (although the Revenue will no longer consider new applications for approval of simplified defined contribution schemes, see Pensions Update No 91, 23 March 2001). The model scheme documents, if used unaltered, will enable schemes to obtain immediate tax approval. (Revenue Press Release 4 February 1988; SFO Memorandum No 94 February 1988).

Discretionary approval may be *withdrawn* in the same way as mandatory approval (see (*h*) above). Where regulations place certain restrictions on approval by reference to circumstances other than the provision of benefits, 36 months grace is given before withdrawal of approval after the regulations concerned come into effect. [*ICTA 1988, ss 591A, 591B; FA 1991, ss 35, 36*].

For the conditions for *abandonment* of schemes which have not received exempt approval, see Pensions Update No 100, 18 June 2001.

The Board has wide information powers, including prescriptive regulation-making powers, in relation to approved and statutory schemes, and penalties of up to £3,000 may be imposed in cases of fraudulent or negligent false statements or representations. [*ICTA 1988, ss 605, 605A; FA 1994, ss 105, 106; FA 1998, Sch 15 para 4; SI 1995 Nos 3103, 3125; SI 2002 No 3006*]. See also Pensions Updates No 39, 25 February 1998, No 47, 24 July 1998, No 48, 24 August 1998, No 79, 20 November 2000, No 83, 22 January 2001, No 113, 21 January 2002 and No 134, 20 December 2002. For inspection visit procedure, see Pensions Update No 32, 26 September 1997.

Changes to increase flexibility of schemes. The Revenue have announced changes to the requirements for scheme approval in two areas. These are introduced with effect from 30 June 1999. Trustees of existing schemes may choose whether or not to amend scheme rules to offer these options to members.

(I)   *Additional voluntary contributions ('AVCs').* Benefits from AVCs may be allowed to be taken at any time between ages 50 and 75 (and earlier if the member leaves employment due to incapacity), whether or not a person has retired or is drawing the main scheme benefits. (Currently, AVC benefits must be taken at the same time as the main scheme benefits.) Thus they may be able to be taken early (e.g. on a move from full- to part-time employment) or late (to boost income later in retirement).

(II) *Money purchase occupational schemes (including free-standing AVCs).* On retirement, members may have the option to defer purchase of the annuity up to (at latest) age 75 and to make income withdrawals (which are taxable under PAYE) during the deferral period, on terms similar to those already available in relation to personal pension schemes (see 60.2 PERSONAL PENSION SCHEMES).

For details, see Pensions Updates No 54, 30 June 1999, No 90, 23 March 2001, No 97, 11 June 2001 and No 105, 31 August 2001, and Revenue Pamphlet IR 12, Appendix XII.

Insured loanback arrangements. See Pensions Update No 43, 22 April 1998 as regards the actions expected of trustees to avoid loss of approval of wholly insured schemes in cases where loans by the life office to the employer, which are secured on a policy or polices held by the scheme to provide benefits for a controlling director, are subject to foreclosure.

Tax on cessation of approval of certain schemes. A special charge to tax applies where approval of certain schemes is withdrawn (under *ICTA 1988, s 591A* or *s 591B*, see above), unless the scheme is instead approved as a personal pension scheme under *ICTA 1988, Sch 23ZA para 3* (see 60.2 PERSONAL PENSION SCHEMES). This applies to any scheme which either:

(A)   immediately before the date of cessation of approval, had less than twelve individual members; or

(B)   at any time within the year preceding that date, had a member who has at any time been a 'controlling director' (within *ICTA 1988, s 417(5)(b)*) of a company which has contributed to the scheme; or

(C)   (where that date is after 16 March 1998) has, at any time in the three years ending with that date, received, in respect of any person, a transfer value represented in which were contributions made to *any* 'approved pension arrangements', by or in respect of that person, by reference to:

  (i)   service by him with a company of which he is or has been a controlling director; or

(ii) remuneration in respect of any such service; or

(iii) income chargeable under Schedule D immediately derived from his carrying on or exercising (including in partnership) a trade, profession or vocation.

As regards (C) above, a scheme receives a 'transfer value' when it comes to hold for its own purposes any sum or asset held for the purposes of any other 'approved pension arrangements'. 'Contributions' to such arrangements include any made in accordance with, or for the purposes of, the arrangements, and any premium or other consideration under an annuity contract for which the arrangements provide. '*Approved pension arrangements*' are those approved, or being considered for approval, under the current provisions, personal pension schemes, annuity contracts entered into for the purposes of any such scheme or arrangements, and retirement annuity contracts.

Any person to whom, at any particular time, a benefit under a scheme is being or may be provided in respect of his past or present employment is a member of the scheme at that time for these purposes.

Tax is charged under SCHEDULE D, CASE VI (74) at a rate of 40% on the value, as it stands immediately before the date approval ceases, of the assets held for the purposes of the scheme. The value of such assets is the market value, except that rights or interests in respect of money lent directly or indirectly to certain persons are valued at the amount owing (including unpaid interest). The charge is on the scheme administrator, except that where the scheme administrator is constituted by persons including a person who is an 'approved independent trustee', that person is not liable for the tax. An '*approved independent trustee*' is a person approved by the Board as a trustee of the scheme who is not connected (within *ICTA 1988, s 839*) with either a member or fellow trustee of the scheme or an employer who has contributed to the scheme. There are provisions (for schemes approved on or before 17 March 1998) which, subject to limited exceptions, prevent the removal of such a trustee on or after that date without his being immediately replaced.

Where an employer has become liable under *ICTA 1988, s 606* (see above) to any tax arising under these provisions on a cessation of approval after 16 March 1998, but has failed to pay the tax in full, there are provisions for recourse to scheme members who are or have been controlling directors (or by reference to whom the condition in (C) above was satisfied for the purpose of the tax charged) *pro rata* to their share of the scheme.

For the purposes of taxation of capital gains, assets in respect of which a charge arises as above are treated as having been acquired immediately before the date of cessation of approval for a consideration equal to the amount on which tax is charged under these provisions, without any corresponding deemed disposal.

For the procedures leading to withdrawal of approval, see Revenue Tax Bulletin August 1995 p 233.

[*ICTA 1988, ss 591C, 591D, 606A; FA 1995, s 61; FA 1998, Sch 15 paras 1, 2, 6, 7; FA 2000 Sch 13 para 3*].

See Pensions Update No 10, 1 November 1995 (with subsequent changes in Update No 25, 24 March 1997 and No 31, 5 September 1997) or Revenue Tax Bulletin December 1995 p 266 as regards measures to prevent avoidance of a charge under *ICTA 1988, s 591C* by payment of a transfer value to a pension scheme subsequently transferred offshore (and see further 67.9 below), and Update No 109, 29 October 2001, as regards permitted transfers of benefits at or after normal retirement date. See also Update No 33, 26 September 1997, as regards rebated and shared commissions on transfer of funds between investment vehicles.

An **exempt approved scheme** is any approved scheme as above which is established under irrevocable trusts, or any other approved scheme which the Board may direct as exempt. [*ICTA 1988, s 592(1)*].

Simon's Direct Tax Service. See E7.214, E7.215.

67.5   **EFFECTS OF APPROVAL**

(*a*)   **Payments by employer** of ordinary annual contributions to an exempt approved scheme are deductible as an expense for tax purposes in the tax year (or chargeable period) in which paid. A payment by the employer to the scheme discharging the employer's liability under *Social Security Pensions Act 1975, s 58B* or *Pension Schemes Act 1993, s 144* (or NI equivalent) is treated as a contribution to the scheme, and if the trade etc. has ceased before the payment is made, is deductible as if paid on the last day on which the trade etc. was carried on. Contributions other than ordinary annual contributions are also deductible, but the Revenue may require these to be spread. Tax relief is given only for contributions actually paid, and not e.g. for any provision for such contributions. [*ICTA 1988, s 592(4)–(6A)*]. See Revenue Pamphlet IR 12 para 5.7 *et seq.* and Pensions Update No 16, 30 May 1996 for practice on spreading of contributions (broadly over up to four years where special contributions amount to £500,000 or more in a chargeable period). A Revenue decision on spreading is not subject to review on appeal (*Kelsall v Investment Chartwork Ltd Ch D 1993, 65 TC 750*). Where employer's business changes hands see *Clarke v Musker Ch D 1956, 37 TC 1*. Legal and other expenses of establishing a scheme and running expenses of a revenue nature will be allowed. (Revenue Pamphlet IR 12 paras 5.9, 5.10). For repayments out of overfunded schemes, see 67.8 below. See Simon's Direct Tax Service E7.231.

Payments by employees of contributions to exempt approved schemes are allowed as an expense in the tax year in which paid, provided that they do not in total exceed 15% (or such higher percentage as the Board may prescribe) of remuneration of that year. Remuneration in excess of the permitted maximum (see 67.4 above) is disregarded for this purpose (although this limitation does not apply in the circumstances prescribed by regulation by the Board for this purpose, see *SI 1990 No 586 (as amended); SI 1993 No 3221; SI 1996 No 3113*), and where there is more than one employment, the 15% limit must not be exceeded in respect of any one of them. Where contributions are to a scheme to which the employer does not contribute, regulations provide for them to be made under deduction of basic rate tax. The tax deducted from payments is not clawed back where the individual is liable only at less than the basic rate of income tax or has no income tax liability. [*ICTA 1988, s 592(7)(8), s 593; FA 1989, Sch 6 paras 5, 21; ITEPA 2003, Sch 6 para 72; SI 1987 No 1749; SI 1990 No 585*]. See Simon's Direct Tax Service E7.232.

Retrospective membership. For relief for employer and employee contributions where part-time employees are given back-dated rights to membership of schemes (following a House of Lords ruling on the issue), see Pensions Update No 131, 23 April 2002. Broadly, employer contributions are allowable when paid but tax relief for employee contributions is subject to the normal 15% annual limit.

(*b*)   The exempt approved fund itself is exempt from income tax on income from investments or deposits held for the purposes of the scheme and from liability under capital gains tax on gains from disposals of investments so held. [*ICTA 1988, s 592(2)(3), s 659; TCGA 1992, s 271(1)(g); FA 1996, s 134, Sch 20 para 63*]. See 71.22 SCHEDULE D, CASES I AND II as regards futures and options contracts, and *Clarke v British Telecom Pension Fund Trustees CA 2000, 72 TC 472* as regards sub-underwriting commissions. See also 67.13 below.

67.6 Retirement Schemes for Employees

See 90.2 UNIT TRUSTS as regards certain pooled pension funds.

(c) **Repayments to employee.** Where contributions are repaid to an employee during his lifetime from an exempt approved scheme or a relevant statutory scheme, the administrator is chargeable at 20% under Schedule D, Case VI on lump sums and contributions repaid, and has no statutory right to deduct tax, but deduction may be made where the rules of the scheme so authorise. The charge does not apply where the employment was carried on outside the UK (i.e. if the employee worked abroad for at least 75% of the period of scheme membership, see Revenue Inspector's Manual IM 8133). [*ICTA 1988, s 598; SI 1988 No 504; FA 1989, Sch 6 para 10*].

The rate of 20% will also generally apply to any excess of a lump sum paid, in special circumstances, in commutation of an employee's entire pension over the sums specified in *ICTA 1988, s 599*.

Certain other unauthorised payments to employees may be taxable as pension income (see 58.2(*e*) PENSION INCOME).

As regards repayments from overfunded schemes, see 67.8 below.

(d) **Pensions payable** are chargeable to tax as pension income (see 58.2(*d*) PENSION INCOME). Pensions under the unapproved voluntary pension scheme of a foreign company were held to be assessable under Case V (*Bridges v Watterson Ch D 1952, 34 TC 47*).

67.6 **SCHEMES APPROVED BEFORE 27 JULY 1989**

Approved schemes: general. *FA 1989, Sch 6 Pt II* came into effect on 14 March 1989, and applies in relation to any retirement benefits scheme approved by the Board before 27 July 1989, notwithstanding anything to the contrary in the scheme rules or (in relation to schemes approved before 23 July 1987, see 67.7 below) in *ICTA 1988, Sch 23*. The Board may, however, make regulations disapplying or modifying any of its provisions where appropriate (and certain such disapplications and modifications are contained in *The Retirement Benefits Schemes (Continuation of Rights of Members of Approved Schemes) Regulations 1990 (SI 1990 No 2101)* (as amended), which also give the Board power to disapply any of the provisions by direction in any particular case). Also, the administrator of a scheme could, before the end of 1989, elect for it not to apply and for approval of the scheme to cease from the date of approval or, if the scheme came into existence before 14 March 1989, from 1 June 1989 if earlier. [*FA 1989, Sch 6 para 19*]. The revised rules are applied to all members of schemes which came into existence after 13 March 1989, but only as regards employees who became members after 31 May 1989 of schemes which were in existence on 13 March 1989. An employee who became a member of a scheme after 16 March 1987 and before 1 June 1989 may, for these purposes, elect (by written notice in prescribed form to the scheme administrator) to be treated as having become a member of the scheme on 1 June 1989. [*FA 1989, Sch 6 para 29*].

Remuneration. Any excess of '*relevant annual remuneration*' (i.e. the annual remuneration on which scheme benefits are based) over the 'permitted maximum' (see 67.4 above) is disregarded in calculating benefits and any excess of remuneration over that maximum is disregarded for the purposes of any restriction on the aggregate of employee and employer contributions. The maximum allowable employee contribution is restricted as described in 67.5(*a*) above. [*FA 1989, Sch 6 paras 20, 22, 30*].

Accelerated accrual. If the scheme permits commutation of pension for a lump sum, that lump sum may not exceed the greater of $\frac{3}{80}$ths of relevant annual remuneration for each year of service up to a maximum of 40 and the initial pension payable in the first year (assuming the employee survives the year and ignoring the effects of commutation or allocation to provide benefits for survivors) multiplied by 2.25. Where any lump sum is payable otherwise than by way of commutation, it must not exceed $\frac{3}{80}$ths of relevant annual remuneration for each year of service up to a maximum of 40, or, if greater, the number of eightieths of relevant annual remuneration by reference to which the pension payable under the scheme is calculated (up to a maximum of 120). [*FA 1989, Sch 6 paras 23, 24*].

Associated employments and connected schemes. The provisions described in 67.4 above are applied in relation to pensions payable in respect of service in any of 'relevant associated employments' or in 'connected schemes', except that the permitted rate of accrual is $\frac{1}{30}$th of the permitted maximum for each year of qualifying service, with a maximum of 20 years. [*FA 1989, Sch 6 paras 25, 26*].

Augmentation. Where an employee has contributed to an approved voluntary scheme to which the employer did not contribute, to supplement benefits under the main scheme, then in relation to any augmentation of benefits after the employee has ceased to be a member of the scheme, the limits on benefits under the main scheme rules are reduced by any benefits provided by the voluntary scheme. [*FA 1989, Sch 6 para 27*].

Centralised schemes. In relation to such schemes, the references above to the date the scheme came into existence are replaced by a reference to the date the employee commenced participation in the scheme. A *'centralised scheme'* is a retirement benefits scheme established to enable any employer, other than an employer 'associated' with the person by whom the scheme is established, to participate in it as regards his employees. An employer is *'associated'* with a person if one controls the other or both are under the control of a third person (whether directly or indirectly). [*FA 1989, Sch 6 para 28*].

Additional voluntary contributions. *FA 1989, Sch 6 Pt III* applies to schemes approved before 27 July 1989 which make provision for the payment by employees of voluntary contributions (again subject to variation by regulation by the Board) notwithstanding anything to the contrary in the scheme rules.

(*a*)   Where the employer does not contribute to the scheme and the provision for voluntary contributions is freestanding, a limit is imposed on benefits, equal to the main scheme limit on such benefits reduced by benefits under that scheme plus any similar benefits under other schemes providing additional benefits. This applies only to benefits provided after 26 July 1989. [*FA 1989, Sch 6 para 32*].

(*b*)   The scheme administrator must repay surplus funds to the employee or his personal representatives (deducting therefrom the amount he is required to account for under *ICTA 1988, s 599A*, see 67.8 below), where total benefits exceed the relevant limits. The method of calculating the surplus is to be prescribed by regulations. [*FA 1989, Sch 6 paras 33, 34*].

Simon's Direct Tax Service. See E7.226.

67.7   **SCHEMES APPROVED BEFORE 23 JULY 1987**

ICTA 1988, Sch 23 (or its predecessor) came into effect on 17 March 1987, and applies in relation to any retirement benefits scheme approved by the Board before 23 July 1987, notwithstanding anything to the contrary in the scheme rules. The Board may, however, make regulations disapplying or modifying any of its provisions where appropriate (and certain such disapplications and modifications are contained in *The Occupational Pension Schemes (Transitional Provisions) Regulations 1988* (*SI 1988 No 1436*) and *(Amendment) Regulations 1993* (*SI 1993 No 3219*) and *1996* (*SI 1996 Nos 3115, 3234*), which also give the Board power to disapply any of these provisions by direction in any particular case). Also, the administrator of a scheme could, before the end of 1987, elect for it not to apply and for approval of the scheme to cease on and after 17 March 1987 (or the date of approval if later). [*ICTA 1988, Sch 23 para 1; FA 1988, s 56*]. See also 67.6 above for further supplementary rule changes which apply notwithstanding the provisions of *Schedule 23*.

Accelerated accrual. Where an employee joins a scheme after 16 March 1987, the maximum rate of accrual of pension is one-thirtieth of *'relevant annual remuneration'* (i.e. the annual remuneration on which scheme benefits are based) for each year up to a maximum of 20. If commutation for a lump sum is allowed, a formula is laid down for determining the maximum lump sum which may be paid. This is in no case less than three-eightieths of relevant annual remuneration for each year of service up to a maximum of 40 (the *'basic rate lump sum'*) and is increased by a percentage of the difference between the basic rate lump sum and a maximum rate lump sum as prescribed by the Board by regulation. That percentage derives from the ratio between the full pension under the scheme and the maximum allowable pension (as above), in both cases after deducting a pension of one-sixtieth of average annual remuneration for each year of service up to a maximum of 40. If the scheme provides for a lump sum other than by commutation of pension, similar limits apply, but with a somewhat faster accrual rate. [*ICTA 1988, Sch 23 paras 2–4, 9; SI 1987 No 1513*].

Final remuneration. Where a scheme member retires after 16 March 1987, his relevant annual remuneration is determined with the meaning of 'remuneration' restricted as in 67.4 above. In the case of an employee who at any time in his last ten years of service has been a 'controlling director' of the employer company (broadly a director controlling 20% of its ordinary share capital), relevant annual remuneration is restricted to his highest average annual remuneration for any period of three or more years ending in his last ten years of service. A similar restriction applies to an employee whose relevant annual remuneration, so far as ascertained by reference to years beginning after 5 April 1987, would otherwise exceed £100,000 (or such other figure as is prescribed by Treasury order), but if he retires before 6 April 1991, a higher limit of his 1986/87 remuneration may apply where appropriate. [*ICTA 1988, Sch 23 para 5*].

Lump sums. Where an employee joins a scheme after 16 March 1987, any lump sum calculated by reference to relevant annual remuneration must disregard any excess of that remuneration over £100,000 (or such other figure as may be prescribed by Treasury order). [*ICTA 1988, Sch 23 para 6*].

Additional voluntary contributions. No commutation of a pension for a lump sum is permitted where an employee enters into arrangements to pay such contributions after 7 April 1987, to the extent that the pension is secured by those contributions. Benefits provided before 27 July 1989 from such voluntary contribution schemes acted to reduce any maxima otherwise applicable to benefits under the employer's scheme (and see now 67.6 above). [*ICTA 1988, Sch 23 paras 7, 8; FA 1989, Sch 6 para 17*].

Simon's Direct Tax Service. See E7.227.

67.8   **PENSION SCHEME SURPLUSES**

Payments to employers. A charge may arise on any payment (or transfer of money's worth) out of a scheme which is or has been an exempt approved scheme (see 67.4 above). For payments on or after 11 May 2001 the rate of charge is 35% (variable by Treasury order). Previously it was 40%. No charge arises where:

(*a*)   the employer is a charity (see 14 CHARITIES) or would otherwise be entitled to exemption in respect of the payment apart from the current provisions; or

(*b*)   the payment was made before the scheme was approved; or

(*c*)   the payment was made

　(i)   in winding up the scheme, provided the winding-up was commenced before 19 March 1986, or

　(ii)   following application to the Board before that date for assurance that the payment would not lead to withdrawal of approval; or (*d*)   the payment was of a description prescribed for this purpose by regulation. Under *The Pension Scheme Surpluses (Administration) Regulations 1987 (SI 1987 No 352)*, this exclusion applies to reimbursement of certain expenditure by the employer on behalf of the scheme; commercial loans to, or repayment of loans or interest to, the employer; certain payments in respect of members' obligations to the employer; and reimbursement of a state scheme premium to which *Social Security Pensions Act 1975, s 42* or *s 45* applies.

Where a charge arises, the payment to which it relates is treated neither as income for tax purposes nor as brought into charge to tax.

The amount charged is recoverable by the Board from the employer, and the Treasury is empowered to make regulations (see below) regarding the assessment and collection of the amount recoverable, which is treated for this purpose as an amount of income tax chargeable under Schedule D, Case VI (or, where the employer is a company, an amount of corporation tax). It is not, however, available for any exemption, relief or set-off. *The Pension Scheme Surpluses (Administration) Regulations 1987 (SI 1987 No 352)* require the scheme administrator to deduct the amount charged in making the payment to the employer, and, within 14 days of making the payment, to make a return to the Board and account for the amount deducted without the making of any assessment. An assessment may be made on the employer under which the tax due is reduced by any amount deducted and accounted for by the administrator, and if the full amount of tax and interest thereon is not paid within 60 days of the date of the notice of assessment, the tax and interest unpaid may be assessed on the administrator in the name of the employer, becoming due and payable within 14 days of the date of the notice of assessment. The administrator may recover any amount so assessed and paid from the employer.

The *Regulations* referred to above also provide for appeals and postponement applications to be made in the normal way against assessments under these provisions, and for interest on unpaid tax so assessed to run from the 15th day after the date of the payment to the employer. The Board may require information from the administrator or employer where there is reason to believe that a surplus payment has been made in respect of which no return, or an incorrect return, has been made. The penalty provisions of *TMA 1970, s 98* (see 57.9 PENALTIES) apply where information is not provided.

[*ICTA 1988, ss 601, 602; FA 2001, s 74*].

Where scheme assets transferred to an employer in breach of trust were returned to the trustees, the tax paid under *ICTA 1988, s 601* was recoverable from the Revenue (*Hillsdown Holdings plc v CIR Ch D, [1999] STC 561*).

Certain payments out of an exempt approved scheme, to which the above provisions do not apply, are charged to tax on the employer as a trading receipt or, if the scheme did not relate to a trade, under Schedule D, Case VI. [*ICTA 1988, s 601(5)*].

Insured loanback arrangements. See Pensions Update No 43, 22 April 1998 as regards the possibility of a charge under the above provisions in the case of wholly insured schemes where loans by the life office to the employer, which are secured on a policy or polices held by the scheme to provide benefits for a controlling director, are subject to foreclosure.

Payments to employees. Where a payment or transfer of money's worth is made to or for an employee or to his personal representatives in pursuance of a duty to return surplus funds held for an exempt approved or relevant statutory scheme (see 67.6 above), the payment is grossed up at 32% (33% before 6 April 2000, variable by Treasury order) and the scheme administrator is charged to tax under Schedule D, Case VI at that rate on the grossed-up amount. See 58.2(*n*) PENSION INCOME as regards taxation of the employee on the sum received. A payment so chargeable is not chargeable under *ICTA 1988, ss 598, 599, 600* (see 67.5(*c*) above) or under certain regulations relating to old schemes. [*ICTA 1988, s 599A(1)–(4)(9)(10); FA 1989, Sch 6 para 12; SI 2000 No 600*].

67.8 Retirement Schemes for Employees

Restriction of surpluses. *The Pension Scheme Surpluses (Valuation) Regulations 1987 (SI 1987 No 412)* (subsequently amended by *SI 1989 No 2290*) apply to all exempt approved schemes. The administrator of the scheme is required to provide, within three months of its being signed, either a written valuation of the scheme assets and liabilities (on the basis prescribed in those *Regulations*) or a certificate in prescribed form stating that such assets do not exceed such liabilities by more than 5%, with the signatory in either case being an actuary within the regulatory prescription. Such a valuation or certificate is required whenever scheme assets and liabilities are valued, and in any event within three and a half years (five years in certain cases) of the previous valuation (or the establishment of the scheme). Where such assets exceed such liabilities by more than 5%, the administrator must, within six months of the date of signature of the valuation or certificate, submit proposals for reducing or eliminating the surplus by any or all of the following means.

(A) Making payments to the employer.

(B) Suspending or reducing (for five years or less) employer's and/or employees' contributions.

(C) Providing new or improved scheme benefits.

(D) Any other way which may be prescribed by regulation.

The proposals must secure that, within a prescribed time, the excess will be reduced to not more than 5% (and where the proposals include any repayments to the employer, the excess must not be reduced *below* 5%). The prescribed time for this purpose is

(i) where (A) applied, six months,

(ii) where (B) applies, a maximum of five years,

(iii) where (C) applies, six months,

(iv) in any other case, such period as is agreed with the Board,

beginning 30 days after the Board has notified its approval of the proposals (or 30 days after the final determination of an appeal). Under (D), a longer period is allowed in certain cases where a scheme has been in existence less than 15 years, or has ceased to admit new members, or has less than 30 members.

If proposals are not submitted within the prescribed time, or are not agreed, or are not carried out, only a fraction of the scheme income and gains attract exemption from the date of the valuation or certificate referred to above until the Board is satisfied that the excess no longer exceeds 5%. The fraction continuing to attract exemption is that obtained by dividing the Board's estimate of scheme liabilities, increased by 5%, by their estimate of scheme assets, both as at the date of the valuation or certificate.

The above provisions are modified in their application to schemes with twelve members or less and insured schemes (i.e. schemes the contributions to which (other than members' voluntary contributions) are invested wholly by way of insurance premiums) which require that contribution levels take account of surpluses. They are similarly modified in their application to schemes approved by reference to limitations on aggregate contributions and lump sum and death benefits, and to insured schemes providing only lump sum death benefits before retirement age.

There are appeal provisions, and penalties apply under *TMA 1970, s 98* for failure to supply a valuation or certificate, or to furnish the Board with certain additional information. [*ICTA 1988, Sch 22*].

Simon's Direct Tax Service. See E7.248, E7.249.

67.9   **UNAPPROVED RETIREMENT BENEFIT SCHEMES**

A charge applies in respect of any benefit provided pursuant to a funded unapproved retirement benefit scheme ('FURBS'), i.e. a scheme not within 67.1(*a*)–(*c*) above. The amount of the benefit is treated as employment income or, where the recipient is not an individual, is chargeable under Schedule D, Case VI (in the latter case being a charge on the administrator of the scheme at a special rate of 40% (variable by Treasury order)). There are various exemptions (see below), and no income tax liability arises under any other provision of *ITEPA 2003* (previously under *ICTA 1988, s 19(1)* or *s 148*) in respect of a benefit within these provisions. The charge is made for the year of assessment in which the benefit is received. Except as mentioned below, the amount of the charge is:

(*a*)   in the case of a cash benefit, the amount received; or

(*b*)   in the case of a non-cash benefit, the cash equivalent of the benefit or, for 1998/99 and subsequent years and if greater, the amount chargeable under the normal employment income rules if the benefit were taxable as an emolument. The cash equivalent of the benefit is determined under the benefits code rules, see 75.16–75.24, 75.32 SCHEDULE E—EMPLOYMENT INCOME, modified as appropriate in the case of living accommodation, and, for 1998/99 and subsequent years, where the benefit is a beneficial loan, with relief being available in respect of the notional interest as under those rules (see 75.20 SCHEDULE E—EMPLOYMENT INCOME).

With effect from 6 April 2003, the above provisions do not apply to any benefit charged to tax under *ITEPA 2003, Pt 9* as PENSION INCOME (58). Previously, where the scheme was entered into after 30 November 1993, or varied after that day with a view to the provision of the benefit, there was an exemption for any pension or annuity to the extent that it was chargeable under *ICTA 1988, s 19(1)* (see 75.1 SCHEDULE E—EMPLOYMENT INCOME), and for any pension or other benefit chargeable under *ICTA 1988, s 58* (see 58.2(*b*) PENSION INCOME). There is also an exemption for any lump sum provided under the scheme to the employee or certain other persons where the employee has been taxed on an amount treated as employment income by virtue of *ITEPA 2003, s 386* or under *ICTA 1988, s 595(1)* (see 67.1 above) in respect of contributions by the employer, except that if any of the income or gains of the scheme out of which the lump sum is provided cannot be shown to have been brought into charge to UK tax (where the income or gains were chargeable to tax in the first place — see ICAEW Technical Release TAX 9/94, 7 June 1994), the exemption does not apply, although certain deductions may be made from the lump sum brought into charge in respect of employee contributions and employer contributions charged on the employee. Income and gains are not for this purpose treated as brought into charge to tax merely because a tax charge arose on cessation of approval of the scheme under *ICTA 1988, s 591C* (see 67.4 above). A proportionate deduction is allowed where the lump sum is provided on the part disposal of an asset, and there is an expectation that a further lump sum will be received.

Where the scheme was entered into on or before 30 November 1993 and has not been varied after that day, there is an exemption to the extent that the payment or benefit is chargeable as employment income (see 75.1 SCHEDULE E—EMPLOYMENT INCOME), or can be shown to be attributable to the payment of a sum treated as income and charged to tax under *ITEPA 2003, s 386(1)* or, before 2003/04, *ICTA 1988, s 595(1)* (see 67.1 above).

[*ITEPA 2003, ss 393–400, Sch 6 para 71, Sch 7 para 41; ICTA 1988, s 591D(6), ss 596A–596C; FA 1989, Sch 6 para 9; FA 1994, s 108(1)–(6); FA 1995, s 61(1); FA 1998, s 93; FA 1999, Sch 10 para 6*].

For a case in which approval was withdrawn from a scheme on transfer of the scheme assets to an unapproved scheme, see *R v CIR (ex p Roux Waterside Inn Ltd)* QB 1997, 70 TC 545 (and see *R (oao Mander) v CIR* QB, *[2002] STC 631* for refusal of judicial review of a Revenue withdrawal of approval in similar circumstances). See also 67.4 above.

67.10 Retirement Schemes for Employees

See 58.3(*k*) PENSION INCOME as regards lump sum benefits from overseas schemes, and generally Revenue Explanatory Booklet 'The Tax Treatment of Top-Up Pension Schemes'.

See generally Revenue Employment Income Manual EIM 15000 *et seq.*

Simon's Direct Tax Service. See E7.257.

67.10 DEDUCTIBILITY BY EMPLOYER

See 67.5(*a*) above regarding exempt approved schemes. Expenses incurred in, or with a view to, providing benefits pursuant to a non-approved scheme, i.e. a scheme not within 67.1(*a*)–(*c*) above, are not allowed as a SCHEDULE D, CASES I AND II (71) deduction (nor as a management expense under *ICTA 1988, s 75*) unless the benefits are within the charge to income tax on receipt or payments made are treated as income when paid (see 67.1, 67.2, 67.9 above), and those exceptions do not apply unless the sums concerned have actually been expended. These restrictions do not, however, apply to contributions to overseas superannuation funds within *ICTA 1988, s 615(6)* (see 67.15 below), or to retirement benefits schemes established outside the UK which correspond to schemes within 67.1(*a*)–(*c*) above and under which payments or provisions are made for the benefit either of non-UK domiciled employees of a foreign employer or of employees not resident in the UK whose duties are performed wholly outside the UK or are incidental to duties so performed. [*FA 1989, s 76; FA 1996, Sch 39 para 2; ITEPA 2003, Sch 6 para 161; FA 2004, Sch 17 para 10(4)*].

In cases not involving approved funds, a company's initial lump sum to cover past service on the setting up of a contributory pension scheme was disallowed as capital (*Atherton v British Insulated & Helsby Cables Ltd HL 1925, 10 TC 155*) as was a lump sum contribution to an employees' benevolent fund (*Rowntree & Co Ltd v Curtis CA 1924, 8 TC 678*). However, a series of payments to trustees to build up an indeterminate fund for the benefit of employees for whom pension arrangements might prove inadequate was allowable (*Jeffs v Ringtons Ltd Ch D 1985, 58 TC 680*). The cost of an annuity to replace a pension was allowed (*Hancock v General Reversionary & Investment Co Ltd KB 1918, 7 TC 358*) but not the cost of a policy for payment to a company of annuities equal to (allowable) pensions it paid (*Morgan Crucible Co Ltd v CIR KB 1932, 17 TC 311*). A gratuity on retirement was allowed (*Smith v Incorporated Council of Law Reporting KB 1914, 6 TC 477*) as was a lump sum in commutation of (allowable) premiums under a staff assurance scheme (*Green v Cravens Railway Wagon Co Ch D 1951, 32 TC 359*) but not premiums paid by a 'family company' to secure pensions for its directors (*Samuel Dracup & Sons Ltd v Dakin Ch D 1957, 37 TC 377*) nor payments to commute voluntary pensions on the cessation of trading (*Anglo Brewing Co Ltd KB 1925, 12 TC 803*).

A sum transferred from an unapproved fund on reconstruction as approved was allowed, under facts of that case (*Lowe v Peter Walker & R Cain CA 1935, 20 TC 25*).

Simon's Direct Tax Service. See E7.257.

67.11 OTHER SCHEMES

Doctors and Dentists. For NHS practitioners assessable under Schedule D who pay both superannuation contributions and retirement annuity premiums, the statutory basis of relief is for full relief to be given for retirement annuity premiums based on net relevant earnings (including NHS earnings) within the normal relief limits, with no relief for the superannuation contributions. By concession, relief may instead be allowed in full for the superannuation contributions, with retirement annuity premiums attracting relief on one of the following bases.

(*a*)   In respect of non-NHS earnings only (taken as net relevant earnings less superannuation contributions multiplied by $16\frac{2}{3}$), with unused relief brought forward being calculated using the concessionary basis applied for years in which relief has been given.

(*b*)   Up to the amount of the largest premium on which relief was allowed for 1969/70, 1970/71 or 1971/72, restricted, if necessary, to keep the total relief (on NHS contributions and retirement annuity premiums) within the appropriate pre-1971/72 limits (with no carry-forward of surplus premiums).

(Revenue Pamphlet IR 1, A9). It is understood that this concession is treated as applying equally to personal pension scheme contributions. See Simon's Direct Tax Service E7.322A.

Members of Parliaments and Assemblies. Periodical payments out of the House of Commons Members' Fund are taxable as pension income (see 58.2(*m*) PENSION INCOME). Trustees of the Fund and of other pension funds maintained for the UK or Scottish Parliaments or the Wales or Northern Ireland Assemblies are exempt from income tax on fund income. [*ICTA 1988, s 613(4); FA 1999, Sch 5 para 4*].

Marine pilot's benefit fund. The Board may approve a fund established under the *Pilotage Act 1983* as if it were a retirement benefits scheme notwithstanding that some of the usual conditions are not satisfied. Contributions will be allowable as an expense under Schedule D and pensions paid out will be earned income. Certain unauthorised payments previously chargeable under SCHEDULE D, CASE VI (74) are, from 6 April 2003, within *ITEPA 2003, s 583.* [*ICTA 1988, s 607; ITEPA 2003, s 587, Sch 6 para 80*]. See also 58.2(*e*) PENSION INCOME.

Relevant statutory scheme established under a public general Act (but not any national scheme). Employees' contributions are allowable deductions from employment income, subject to the same limits as under 67.5(*a*) above. [*ICTA 1988, s 594; FA 1989, Sch 6 para 6; ITEPA 2003, Sch 6 para 73*]. For contributions repaid to employees see 67.5(*c*) above.

67.12   **LUMP SUM ON RETIREMENT ETC.**

With the exceptions below, no liability to income tax arises on a lump sum provided (whether on retirement or otherwise) under a tax-exempt pension scheme, i.e. an approved retirement benefits scheme (as in 67.1 above), a 'relevant statutory scheme' (as in 67.1 above), a scheme set up by a government outside the UK for the benefit of its employees or a scheme within *ICTA 1970, s 221(1)(2)*. The exemption does not apply to a lump sum taxable as in 58.2(*e*) PENSION INCOME (unauthorised payments) or 58.2(*n*) PENSION INCOME (return of surplus AVCs). Where a lump sum is paid as compensation for loss of office or employment, or for loss or diminution of earnings, the exemption applies only if the loss or diminution is due to ill-health or the payment is properly regarded as earned by past services. [*ITEPA 2003, s 637(1)(b)(2)(3)(5)–(7); ICTA 1988, s 189(1)(a)(2)(3); FA 1988, s 57; FA 1998, s 58, Sch 9 para 1*]. See also 18.3, 18.6 COMPENSATION FOR LOSS OF EMPLOYMENT (AND DAMAGES). As regards unapproved schemes, see 67.9 above.

Lump sums paid from *ICTA 1970, s 208* schemes which have not sought approval under the new code (see 67.3 and 67.4 above and 67.13 below) will by concession continue to enjoy exemption from tax. (Revenue Pamphlet IR 1, A33).

Ex gratia payments. Where *ex gratia* lump sum payments of 'relevant benefits' (see 67.1 above) are made on retirement or death by virtue of any 'arrangement', the Revenue consider that the arrangement constitutes a retirement benefits scheme, and unless that scheme has obtained Revenue approval, the benefits paid will be taxable under *ITEPA 2003, s 394* or, before 2003/04, under *ICTA 1988, s 596A* (see 67.1 above). Where Revenue approval *has* been obtained, the payments will not be chargeable to tax.

The question of what constitutes 'retirement' for these purposes depends on the facts of each particular case. See ICAEW Technical Release TAX 15/92, 23 October 1992 for the Revenue view of a number of borderline hypothetical cases.

'*Arrangement*' for these purposes includes any system, plan, pattern or policy connected with the payment, and this would include e.g. a decision at a meeting to make a payment on an employee's retirement, a decision to make a payment under a delegated authority, or the existence of a common practice for the making of such payments to a particular class of employee. Revenue approval may be given in relation to such non-contractual arrangements provided that:

(i) the payment is the only lump sum relevant benefit potentially payable in respect of the employment (unless the payment is made on retirement and there is a scheme providing death in service benefits); and

(ii) the normal requirements for approval of contractual retirement benefits schemes (e.g. as regards limits on benefits) are met.

Approval in these circumstances should be sought from the Revenue, and PAYE applied to any payments made before such approval is received. Approval need *not* be sought for a single payment to a particular employee, provided that it meets the condition at (i) above and that the total of payments in connection with the retirement etc. (including any from 'associated employers' (see 67.4 above)) does not exceed one-twelfth of the 'permitted maximum' for the year of payment (see 67.4 above).

(Revenue Pamphlet IR 131, SP 13/91).

Payments on redundancy or loss of office, or because of death or disability due to accident, are not covered by the above practice. This applies equally to cases of unfair dismissal (see Law Society Press Release 7 October 1992) and to ill-health early retirement (see Revenue Employment Income Manual EIM 15024).

Where exceptionally an *ex gratia* payment is not covered by the above practice, the payment will, unless taxable under the general rules for employment income, be taxable under *ITEPA 2003, s 403* (subject to the usual exemptions) (see 18.2 *et seq.* COMPENSATION FOR LOSS OF EMPLOYMENT (AND DAMAGES)).

Simon's Direct Tax Service. See E4.802.

67.13 **SCHEMES CEASING TO BE APPROVED AT APRIL 1980**

Where a scheme was an approved superannuation scheme under *ICTA 1970, s 208* immediately before 6 April 1980 and has not been approved under the new rules above and no contributions have been paid to it since 5 April 1980, exemption from income tax may be claimed on income from investments or deposits, underwriting commissions and transactions in certificates of deposit (otherwise taxable under Schedule D, Case VI), and from capital gains tax on gains from investments held for the purposes of the scheme. [*ICTA 1988, s 608(1)–(3); TCGA 1992, s 271(2); FA 1996, s 134, Sch 20 para 63*]. An annuity paid under, or acquired using funds held for, such a scheme is chargeable to tax as pension income, as are certain unauthorised payments from such a scheme (see 58.2(*d*)(*e*) PENSION INCOME). By concession, certain minor rule amendments may be made to benefits provided under such schemes without the loss of tax exemptions (see Revenue Pamphlet IR 1, B43 as revised). For the implementation of pension-sharing orders under the *Welfare Reform and Pensions Act 1999*, see Pensions Update No 95, 23 April 2001.

See 71.22 SCHEDULE D, CASES I AND II as regards futures and options contracts.

67.14   **MIS-SOLD FREESTANDING ADDITIONAL VOLUNTARY CONTRIBUTION SCHEMES**

See 28.5 EXEMPT INCOME as regards concessionary tax exemption of certain compensation payments (and interest thereon) for mis-sold schemes.

67.15   **OVERSEAS PENSIONS FUNDS**

Income from investments or deposits of any fund within 58.4(*a*)–(*d*) PENSION INCOME is exempt from tax. Any tax deducted from such income is repayable by the Board to the recipient. [*ICTA 1988, s 614(3); ITEPA 2003, Sch 6 para 84*].

Exemption (as for a person not domiciled, resident or ordinarily resident in the UK) applies to income from investments or other property of a fund (i) established under irrevocable trusts in connection with a trade carried on wholly or partly overseas (ii) solely to provide superannuation benefits to overseas employees (incidental duties in UK being ignored), and (iii) recognised by both employer and employees. Annuities to non-UK residents are payable gross, and trustees are not liable under *ICTA 1988, s 349(1)*. [*ICTA 1988, s 614(5), s 615(3)(6); FA 1999, Sch 10 para 11*].

See also 90.2 UNIT TRUSTS as regards certain pooled funds in which overseas funds participate.

68.1 Returns

68 Returns

Cross-reference. See 57.1–57.3 PENALTIES as regards duty to notify chargeability to tax and penalties for late or incorrect returns. See also generally 78 SELF-ASSESSMENT.

Simon's Direct Tax Service A3.1, E1.806 *et seq.*

The headings in this chapter are as follows.

68.1 INTRODUCTION

The Revenue have considerable powers to obtain information and these are generally exercised initially by the requirement to complete and submit various returns, with PENALTIES (57) for non-compliance, omissions or incorrect statements. Explanatory notes are usually issued with the returns. See 68.23 below as regards reasonable excuse for failure to comply with any such requirement.

68.2 ANNUAL RETURNS OF INCOME AND CHARGEABLE GAINS

For the purposes of establishing a person's income, chargeable gains and net income tax liability for 1996/97 or a subsequent year of assessment, an officer of the Board may by notice require that person to deliver a return on or before 31 January following the year or, if later, within three months beginning with the date of the notice. See 57.2 PENALTIES as regards failure to deliver the return on time. The return must contain such information and be accompanied by such accounts, statements, documents and other records as may reasonably be required. The return must include a declaration that, to the best of the knowledge of the person making it, it is complete and correct. The information, accounts and statements required by the notice may differ in relation to different periods, or different sources of income, or different descriptions of person. [*TMA 1970, ss 8, 12; FA 1988, s 127; FA 1990, s 90(1); FA 1994, s 178(1), s 199(2)(a); FA 1995, s 104(1)–(3); FA 1996, s 121(1)–(3)*]. Similar provisions apply in relation to returns by trustees, by reference to any 'relevant trustee' (see 78.11 SELF-ASSESSMENT). [*TMA 1970, ss 8A, 12; FA 1990, s 90(1); FA 1994, s 178(2), s 199(2)(a); FA 1995, s 103(3), s 104(1); FA 1996, s 121(1)–(3)*]. See 68.13 below as regards partnership returns. See 68.3 below for circumstances in which compliance by a date earlier than 31 January is required.

The Revenue will, on request, issue a return before the end of the tax year (*a*)   in which the taxpayer dies (or administration of the estate is completed), to the personal representatives of the deceased, or

(*b*)   in which a trust is wound up, to the trustees.

(Revenue Press Release 4 April 1996).

See 3.2(vii) ANTI-AVOIDANCE as regards the exclusion from self-assessment of possible charges under *ICTA 1988, s 703 et seq.*

Before making their return, taxpayers may ask their Tax Office (on Form CG34) to check their valuation for capital gains tax purposes of an asset they have disposed of. (Revenue Press Release 4 February 1997).

As regards returns for 1995/96 and earlier years, see the 2003/04 and earlier editions.

Persons in receipt of taxable income belonging to others. Returns may also be required from any person who, in whatever capacity, receives money or value etc. belonging to another person who is chargeable to income tax in respect thereof, or could be so chargeable if resident in UK and not an incapacitated person (although information may not be sought in relation to years of assessment ending more than three years before the date of the notice). [*TMA 1970, s 13; FA 1988, s 123(1)*]. This applies whether a person is in receipt of chargeable profits or gains of another or of gross receipts representing an element in the determination of such profits or gains (*Fawcett v Special Commrs and Lancaster Farmers' Auction Mart Co Ltd CA 1997, 69 TC 279*). In practice, returns may be restricted to receipts of the following nature:

(*a*)   those from Schedule A or D sources which have not suffered deduction of tax;

(*b*)   those exceeding £250 in aggregate in respect of any one person or estate;

(*c*)   those which have not been included on any other return or repayment claim;

(*d*)   those received by an agent acting on behalf of an individual not domiciled in, or (being a British subject) not ordinarily resident in, the UK.

(Law Society Press Release 29 May 1991).

Provisional figures. A return containing a provisional figure will be accepted provided that the figure is reasonable, taking account of all available information, and is clearly identified as such. An explanation should be given as to why the final figure is not available, all reasonable steps having been taken to obtain it, and when it is expected to be available (at which time it should be notified without unreasonable delay). The absence of such explanation and expected date will influence the Revenue in selecting returns for enquiry (see 68.6 below). Before 23 October 2001, Revenue practice in such cases was to reject the return as unsatisfactory (see also 57.2 PENALTIES) and to send it back to whoever submitted it (taxpayer or agent). Pressures of work and complexity of tax affairs are not regarded as acceptable explanations. If the final figure is not provided by the expected date the Revenue will take appropriate action to obtain it, which may mean opening an enquiry. See Revenue Tax Return Guide, Revenue Tax Bulletins October 1998 pp 593–596, December 1999 p 705, June 2001 p 848 and February 2002 p 916, and Revenue 'Working Together' Bulletin July 2000 p 5. Note that a provisional figure is different in concept to an estimate that is not intended to be superseded by a more accurate figure. See also 57.2 PENALTIES.

Where the replacement of a provisional figure by a final figure leads to a *decrease* in the self-assessment, and the time limit for making amendments (see 68.10 below) has passed, the amendment may be made by way of error or mistake relief claim (see 16.7 CLAIMS) where the conditions for such relief are otherwise met. Where such replacement leads to an *increase* in the self-assessment, a discovery assessment (see 5.3 ASSESSMENTS) may be made to collect the additional tax due. (Revenue Tax Bulletin December 2000 p 817).

68.2 Returns

Rounding. As regards the use of pence in returns, see Revenue Tax Bulletin October 1997 pp 470, 471. Broadly, income (or aggregate income) figures may be rounded down and tax credits and deductions (or aggregate figures) rounded up.

Accounts. Business accounts are not required with the return except in the case of partnerships with an annual turnover exceeding £15 million. Instead, the return includes a section in which standard accounts information (SAI) *must* be completed as well as space for additional information. See 5.3 ASSESSMENTS re the option of submitting accounts (in addition to completing SAI) to possibly reduce the risk of a discovery assessment. Accounts should otherwise be retained in case of enquiry (see 68.6 below). (Revenue Press Release 31 May 1996, Tax Bulletins June 1996 pp 313–315, June 1997 p 436 and Revenue Income Tax Self-Assessment: The Legal Framework Manual SALF 203, paras 2.18, 2.19).

Tax equalisation. For details of special instructions on practical measures to make the completion of the Employment Pages of returns more straightforward for foreign nationals working in the UK who have made tax equalisation arrangements with their employer, see Revenue Tax Bulletin October 1997 pp 467–469 and June 1998 p 551. (See also Help Sheet IR212 issued with the Employment Pages of the return, which reflects these instructions.) Interim tax payments (see 78.4 SELF-ASSESSMENT) made by an employer on any employee's behalf, as part of tax equalisation arrangements where full in-year gross up is used, should not figure in the employment pages of the employee's self-assessment tax return (see Revenue Tax Bulletin June 1998 p 551).

Signature of returns etc. The Revenue will accept returns signed by an attorney acting under a general or enduring power where the taxpayer is physically unable to sign (and not merely unavailable to do so). The attorney must have full knowledge of the taxpayer's affairs, and provide the original power or a certified copy when such a return is first made. In cases of mental incapacity, the signature of an attorney appointed under an enduring power registered with the Court of Protection (or of a receiver or committee appointed by that Court) will be accepted. Similar requirements apply to the signature of claims on behalf of physically or mentally incapacitated taxpayers, and to other documents. (Revenue Pamphlet IR 131, A13 as revised and Revenue Tax Bulletin February 1993 p 51). Although this practice pre-dates self-assessment, the Revenue have published further information in their Tax Bulletin, which confirms that the only exceptions to the personal signature requirement are where, due to his age, physical infirmity or mental incapacity, the taxpayer is unable to cope adequately with the management of his affairs or where his general health might suffer if he were troubled for a personal signature. In all other cases, the Revenue expect the return to be signed personally and will reject the return as unsatisfactory, and send it back to whoever submitted it (taxpayer or agent), if it is not (see also 57.2 PENALTIES). In the case of a return submitted via the internet (see below), the taxpayer's personal authentication (password and User ID) takes the place of his signature. Where a return is lodged electronically by an agent (see 68.14 below), the taxpayer must sign a copy before the electronic version is sent. (Revenue Tax Bulletin June 2001 pp 847, 848).

Substitute return forms. The Revenue have issued a Statement of Practice (Revenue Pamphlet IR 131, SP 5/87, 15 June 1987) concerning the acceptability of facsimile and photocopied tax returns. Whenever such a substitute form is used, it is important to ensure that it bears the correct taxpayer's reference.

Facsimiles must satisfactorily present to the taxpayer the information which the Board have determined shall be before him when he signs the declaration that the return is correct and complete to the best of his knowledge. They should be readily recognisable as a return when received in the Revenue office, and the entries of taxpayers' details should be distinguishable from the background text. Approval must be obtained from Inland Revenue, Corporate Communications Office, Room 9/3A, 9th Floor, NW Wing, Bush House, London WC2B 4PP before a facsimile return is used, and the facsimile must bear an agreed unique imprint for identification purposes.

Photocopies must bear the actual, not photocopied, signature of the relevant person. They are acceptable provided that they are identical (except as regards use of colour) to the official form. Where double-sided copies are not available, it is sufficient that all pages are present and attached in the correct order. Although the copying of official forms is in strictness a breach of HMSO copyright, action will be taken only where forms are copied on a large scale for commercial gain.

Internet filing. For one year only from April 2000, small businesses and individual taxpayers who personally filed their self-assessment tax return via the internet and paid any tax due electronically were entitled to a discount of £10. (Revenue Press Releases 16 February 2000, 10 January 2001). See 68.14 below as regards other electronic filing discounts. After 20 August 2001, agents are authorised to file individual clients' personal tax returns via the internet, subject to conditions as to authorisation of the agent by the client, authentication of the information by the client and use of Revenue approved software. (Revenue Directions under *SI 2000 No 945, reg 3*, 21 August 2001). For internet filing and payment generally, see Revenue Tax Bulletin June 2000 pp 757, 758, and see the Revenue website at www.ir-portal.gov.uk/index.jsp which includes a link to 'Frequently Asked Questions'.

Simon's Direct Tax Service. See E1.806 *et seq.*

68.3   **Self-assessments.** For 1996/97 and subsequent years, every return under *TMA 1970, s 8* or *s 8A* (see 68.2 above) must include, subject to the exception below, an assessment (a self-assessment) of the amounts in which, based on the information in the return and taking into account any reliefs and allowances claimed therein, the person making the return is chargeable to income tax and capital gains tax for the year of assessment and of his net income tax liability for the year, taking into account tax deducted at source and tax credits on dividends. In the event of non-compliance, an officer of the Board *may* make the assessment on his behalf, based on the information in the return, and send the person a copy.

The tax to be self-assessed does not include any chargeable on the administrator of a retirement benefits scheme or personal pension scheme (see 60.1 PERSONAL PENSION SCHEMES, 67.4, 67.9 RETIREMENT SCHEMES).

A person need not comply with this requirement if he makes and delivers his return on or before 30 September following the year of assessment or, if later, within two months beginning with the date of the notice to deliver the return. For returns submitted outside these time limits, the Revenue will still, if the taxpayer so requests, carry out the computations based on the return, but will not guarantee that the relevant filing date will be met. In the event of a person making no self-assessment under this option, an officer of the Board *must* make the assessment on his behalf, based on the information in the return, and send the person a copy. If, by reason only of Revenue delay, the assessment is made less than 30 days before the due date for payment of the tax, the date from which any interest or surcharge is triggered (see 42.1, 42.2 INTEREST AND SURCHARGES ON UNPAID TAX) is 30 days after the issue of the assessment. (ICAEW Technical Release TAX 9/94, 7 June 1994). The 30 September deadline is of no significance where returns are filed over the internet (see 68.2 above) as the tax due is automatically computed during the filing process.

Assessments made as above by an officer of the Board are treated as self-assessments by the person making the return and as included in the return.

A self-assessment must not show as repayable any notional tax treated as deducted from certain income deemed to have been received after deduction of tax, for example STOCK DIVIDENDS (85).

[*TMA 1970, s 9(1)–(3A); FA 1994, ss 179, 199(2)(a); FA 1995, s 104(4), s 115(2); FA 1996, s 121(4), s 122(1); FA 1998, s 98(2)(3); FA 2001, s 88, Sch 29 para 1; ITEPA 2003, Sch 6 para 125*].

68.4 Returns

The Revenue need not give notice to deliver a return under 68.1 above, and thus a self-assessment will not be required, in cases where tax deducted under PAY AS YOU EARN (55) equates to the total tax liability for the year. The taxpayer may, however, give notice requiring a return to be issued so that he can make a self-assessment, such notice to be given within the five years after 31 October following the year of assessment. [*ITEPA 2003, s 711; ICTA 1988, s 205; FA 1995, s 111(1)*].

Taxpayers who wish to have a liability of less than £2,000 coded out through PAYE (55) are advised to file their return by an earlier date than the 31 January deadline at 68.2 above (whether or not they wish the Revenue to compute the liability). As regards returns for 2001/02 onwards, that date is 30 September (following the year of assessment) if the return is filed manually, 29 December if it is filed via the electronic lodgement service (see 68.14 below) and 30 December if it is filed via the internet (see 68.2 above). As regards returns for 2000/01 and earlier years, the date was 30 September in all cases (and before 2000/01 the limit was £1,000). A 2001/02 underpayment, for example, will be coded out for 2003/04. (Revenue Income Tax Self-Assessment: The Legal Framework Manual SALF 204, para 2.33; Revenue Tax Bulletin June 1996 p 315; Revenue 'Working Together' Bulletin February 2001 p 2; Revenue Press Release 23 September 2002). Coding out of an underpayment for a tax year has the consequential effect of reducing any payments on account (see 78.4 SELF-ASSESSMENT) due for the following tax year.

Simon's Direct Tax Service. See E1.807.

68.4   **Amendments of returns other than where enquiries made.** At any time within twelve months after the filing date (i.e. the date by which the return must be delivered, as in 68.1 above), a person may by notice to an officer of the Board amend his return. It should, however, be noted that amendment of a return does not preclude penalty action by the Revenue where there is evidence that the taxpayer has acted fraudulently or negligently (see Revenue Tax Bulletin October 1998 p 597).

At any time within nine months after the delivery of a person's return, an officer of the Board may by notice to that person amend his return to correct obvious errors and omissions (whether of principle, arithmetical or otherwise). Where the correction is required in consequence of an amendment by the taxpayer as above, then as from 11 May 2001 the nine-month period begins immediately after the date of the taxpayer's amendment. Also as from 11 May 2001 the taxpayer has a legal right to reject an officer's correction, by notice within 30 days beginning with the date of the notice of correction. In practice the Revenue will reverse a correction regardless of this 30-day limit, unless they are no longer empowered to do so, i.e. if all deadlines for corrections and amendments (by Revenue or taxpayer) have passed and the Revenue enquiry window (see 68.6 below) has closed. (Revenue Tax Bulletin June 2001 pp 850, 851).

[*TMA 1970, s 9(4)(6), s 9ZA, s 9ZB; FA 1994, s 179; FA 2001, s 88, Sch 29 para 2*].

Individuals whose tax office is served by a Call Centre may notify certain amendments by telephone (Revenue Pamphlet IR 131, SP 3/03). See also 16.5 CLAIMS. From April 2004, the Revenue will itself make increased use of the telephone to resolve minor queries arising in connection with completed returns (Revenue Tax Bulletin February 2004 p 1080).

See 68.10 below for amendments to returns where the Revenue make enquiries into the return.

Simon's Direct Tax Service. See E1.807A, E1.807B.

68.5   **Record-keeping.** Any person who may be required to make and deliver a return under 68.1 above (personal and trustee's returns) or 68.13 below (partnership returns) for a year of assessment or other period is statutorily required to keep all necessary records and to preserve them until the end of the 'relevant day'. The '*relevant day*' is normally (*a*)   in the case of a person carrying on a trade (including, for these purposes, any letting of property), profession or business alone or in partnership or a company, the fifth anniversary of 31 January following the year of assessment or, for partnership or company returns, the sixth anniversary of the end of the period covered by the return; and

(*b*)   in any other case, the first anniversary of 31 January following the year of assessment.

Where, as is normal, notice to deliver the return is given before the day in whichever is the applicable of (*a*) or (*b*) above, the '*relevant day*' is the *later* of that day and whichever of the following applies:

(i)   where Revenue enquiries are made into the return, the day on which the enquiries are statutorily completed (see 68.9 below);

(ii)   where no such enquiries are made, the day on which the Revenue no longer have power to enquire (see 68.6 below).

Where notice to deliver the return is given *after* the day in whichever is the applicable of (*a*) and (*b*) above, (i) and (ii) above still apply to determine the relevant day but only in relation to such records as the taxpayer has in his possession at the time the notice is given.

In the case of a person within (*a*) above, the records in question include records concerning business receipts and expenditure and, in the case of a trade involving dealing in goods, all sales and purchases of goods. All supporting documents (including accounts, books, deeds, contracts, vouchers and receipts) relating to such items must also be preserved. Generally, copies of documents may be preserved instead of the originals and are admissible in evidence in proceedings before the Commissioners. (See Revenue Tax Bulletin February 1996 p 283 as regards the use of optical imaging to preserve records.) Exceptions to this are vouchers, certificates etc. which show tax credits or deductions at source of UK or foreign tax, e.g. dividend vouchers, interest vouchers (including those issued by banks and building societies) and evidence of tax deducted from payments to sub-contractors under the CONSTRUCTION INDUSTRY SCHEME (20), which, with effect on or after 29 April 1996, must be preserved in their original form.

The maximum penalty for non-compliance in relation to any year of assessment or accounting period is £3,000. This penalty does not apply where the failure relates to records which might have been requisite only for the purposes of claims, elections or notices which are *not* included in the return (but see 16.3 CLAIMS for the requirement as regards records relating to such claims etc. and the penalty for non-compliance), or to vouchers, certificates etc. showing UK tax credits or deductions at source (e.g. dividend vouchers and interest certificates) where the inspector is satisfied that other documentary evidence supplied to him proves any facts he reasonably requires to be proved and which the voucher etc. would have proved.

[*TMA 1970, s 12B; FA 1994, s 196, Sch 19 para 3; FA 1995, s 105; FA 1996, s 124(2)–(5)(9); FA 2001, s 88, Sch 29 para 20*].

The Revenue have published guidance notes as to the type of records to be kept (Revenue Pamphlet SA/BK4).

Simon's Direct Tax Service. See E1.809.

68.6   **ENQUIRIES INTO RETURNS**

Notice of enquiry. An officer of the Board may enquire into a personal or trustees' return, and anything (including any claim or election) contained (or required to be contained) in it. He must give notice that he intends to do so (notice of enquiry) within whichever of the following periods is appropriate:

(a)   in the case of a return delivered on or before the filing date (i.e. the date on or before which the return must be delivered — see 68.1 above), the twelve months after the filing date (the twelve months beginning with that date as regards returns for 2000/01 and earlier years);

(b)   in the case of a return delivered after the filing date, the period ending with the 'quarter day' next following the first anniversary of the delivery date;

(c)   in the case of a return amended by the taxpayer under 68.4 above, the period ending with the 'quarter day' next following the first anniversary of the date of amendment.

For these purposes, the '*quarter days*' are 31 January, 30 April etc. A return cannot be enquired into more than once, except in consequence of an amendment (or further amendment). If notice under (c) above is given at a time when the deadline in (a) or (b) above, as the case may be, has expired or after a previous enquiry into the return has been completed, the enquiry is limited to matters affected by the amendment.

[*TMA 1970, s 9A; FA 1994, s 180; FA 1996, Sch 19 para 2; FA 2001, s 88, Sch 29 para 4; FA 2004, Sch 5 para 1*].

As regards (a) above, it was held by a Special Commissioner that service of a notice is treated as effected at the time at which the letter would be delivered in the ordinary course of post, i.e. on the second working day after posting for first class mail or on the fourth working day after posting for second class mail (*Wing Hung Lai v Bale (Sp C 203), [1999] SSCD 238*). See also *Holly v Inspector of Taxes (Sp C 225), [2000] SSCD 50*. The Revenue now accept that it is the time of receipt of the notice, rather than that of its issue, by reference to which the time limit applies. See Revenue 'Working Together' Bulletin April 2000 p 8 for this and for the appropriate action which may be taken by taxpayers or their agents in respect of 1996/97 notices issued shortly before 30 January 1999 but received after that date. As regards (b), where a 1998/99 return is treated as filed on 1 February 2000, but with no late filing penalty (see 57.2 PENALTIES), no enquiry will be opened in the three months to 30 April 2001. (Revenue 'Working Together' Bulletin April 2000 p 8).

In the case of a return by the personal representatives of a deceased taxpayer (for the year of death or of completion of administration of the estate), the Revenue will give early written confirmation if they do not intend to enquire into the return (although, in exceptional circumstances, an enquiry at a later date would not thereby be precluded if the return was discovered to be incomplete or incorrect). Such early confirmation will also be given to trustees in relation to the return for the year in which the trust is wound up. (Revenue Press Release 4 April 1996). See also 68.1 above as regards early issue of returns in such cases.

See 68.13 below as regards similar provisions as regards enquiries into partnership returns.

There are provisions concerning enquiries into a personal or partnership return which includes amounts which may be taxed using more than one method, with the Revenue having the right to choose which method is to be used (the 'Crown Option'). These are restricted to cases where amounts may be taxed either under Case I or II or under any of Cases III to V of Schedule D (applicable normally to dividends and interest forming part of a financial trader's profits). [*TMA 1970, s 9D, s 12AE, s 28A(7A)–(7C), s 28B(6A)(6B); FA 1994, ss 188, 189; FA 1996, Sch 19 para 4(3), para 5(2); FA 2001, s 88, Sch 29 paras 4(1), 5(1), 8, 9*].

Simon's Direct Tax Service. See E1.810 *et seq.*

68.7   **Conduct of enquiry.** A Code of Practice (COP 11, see 35.7 INLAND REVENUE: ADMINISTRA-
TION, or, in certain simple cases, a short, single-page version) is issued at the start of every
such enquiry. This sets out the rules under which enquiries are made into income tax
returns and explains how taxpayers can expect the Revenue to conduct enquiries. It
describes what the Revenue do when they receive a return and how they select cases for
enquiry, how they open and carry out enquiries, and what happens if they find something
wrong.

Where an enquiry remains open after the time by which notice to enquire into the return
had to be given solely because of an unagreed capital gains tax valuation, the Revenue will
not raise further enquiries into matters unrelated to that capital gains tax computation
unless, had the enquiry already been completed, a discovery under *TMA 1970, s 29* (see 5.3
ASSESSMENTS) could have been made. (Revenue Pamphlet IR 131, SP 1/99, 28 January
1999).

The Revenue have also published an Enquiry Manual as part of their series of internal
guidance manuals (see 35.10 INLAND REVENUE: ADMINISTRATION) and, as an extended
introduction to the material on operational aspects of the enquiry regime covered in the
manual, a special edition of their Tax Bulletin (Special Edition 2, August 1997). The
following points are selected from the Bulletin.

(i)   Early submission of a tax return will not increase the likelihood of selection for
        enquiry.

(ii)   The Revenue do not have to give reasons for opening an enquiry — and they *will not
        do so.*

(iii)   Enquiries may be full enquiries or 'aspect enquiries'. An aspect enquiry will fall
        short of an in-depth examination of the return (though it may develop into one), but
        will instead concentrate on one or more aspects of it.

(iv)   Greater emphasis than before will be placed on examination of underlying records.
        The Revenue will make an informal request for information before, if necessary,
        using their powers under *TMA 1970, s 19A* (see 68.8 below).

(v)   Where penalties are being sought, the Revenue will aim to conclude the enquiry by
        means of a contract settlement (see 30.11 FRAUDULENT OR NEGLIGENT CONDUCT)
        rather than by the issue of a closure notice under *TMA 1970, s 28A* (see 68.9
        below).

In March 2002, the Revenue published a framework within which enquiries will be worked
and to which professional advisers are encouraged to adhere. Particular topics covered are
the opening enquiry letter, requests for and conduct of interviews and meetings, and
requests for non-business bank and building society accounts (plus credit/charge/store
card details). (Revenue 'Working Together' Bulletin March 2002 pp 1–6).

Where income is received from co-owned property where the letting activity does not
amount to a partnership (see 69.4 SCHEDULE A), and the name and address of the managing
co-owner is provided in co-owners' returns, the Revenue will confine initial enquiries
relating to that income to the managing co-owner's return. (Revenue Tax Bulletin October
1996 p 350).

For the allowability of additional accountancy expenses incurred in connection with self-
assessment enquiries, see 71.59 SCHEDULE D, CASES I AND II and Revenue Tax Bulletin
October 1998 p 596.

See ICAEW Technical Release TAX 23/98, 30 September 1998, paras 3–40 and Appendix
for Revenue comment on various procedural matters in relation to self-assessment
enquiries.

68.8   Returns

Power to call for documents. At the same time as giving notice of enquiry under 68.6 above to any person, or subsequently, an officer of the Board may by notice in writing require that person, within a specified period of at least 30 days (from the date of receipt of the notice — see *Self-assessed v Inspector of Taxes (Sp C 207), [1999] SSCD 253* and Revenue 'Working Together' Bulletin April 2000 p 8), to produce to the officer such documents (including computer records) as are in the person's possession or power, and such accounts or particulars as the officer may reasonably require to check the validity of the return (or, where applicable, the amendment to the return). Copies of documents may be produced but the officer has power to call for originals, and may himself take copies of, or make extracts from, any document produced. A person is not obliged under these provisions to produce documents etc. relating to the conduct of any pending appeal by him or any pending referral (see 68.11 below) to which he is a party. There is provision for a person to appeal, within 30 days beginning with the date of the notice, against any requirement imposed by a notice as above. In restricted cases, an officer may, alternatively or in addition, require documents, accounts etc. to enable him to exercise the 'Crown Option' (see 68.6 above). [*TMA 1970, s 19A; FA 1988, s 127; FA 1994, s 187; FA 1996, Sch 19 para 3, Sch 22 para 2; FA 2001, s 88, Sch 29 para 21*]. For cases on the scope of such notices, see *Mother v Inspector of Taxes (Sp C 211), [1999] SSCD 279, Accountant v Inspector of Taxes (Sp C 258), [2000] SSCD 522, Parto v Bratherton (Sp C 414), 2004 STI 1516*. See 57.4 PENALTIES as regards penalties for non-compliance. See ICAEW Technical Release TAX 23/98, 30 September 1998, paras 3–15 for the Revenue approach to the obtaining and retention of records in relation to self-assessment enquiries.

The provisions of *TMA 1970, s 19A* 'override the contractual duty of confidence owed by a solicitor to his clients', and 'the rule of legal professional privilege is excluded because it is not expressly preserved by *section 19A*' (*Guyer v Walton (Sp C 274), [2001] SSCD 75*). See also Revenue Tax Bulletin April 2000 pp 743–746. However, in *R v A Special Commr ex p Morgan Grenfell & Co Ltd HL 2002, 74 TC 511*, the HL quashed a notice under *TMA 1970, s 20(1)* (see 30.7(*a*) FRAUDULENT OR NEGLIGENT CONDUCT) on the grounds that the inspector was not entitled to require delivery of documents subject to legal professional privilege (of the person under enquiry), a fundamental human right not expressly overridden by that *subsection*; the Revenue accept that the same reasoning applies as regards their power under *section 19A* (see Revenue Tax Bulletin December 2002 p 993).

68.9   **Completion of enquiry.** An enquiry is completed when an officer of the Board gives the taxpayer notice (closure notice) that he has completed his enquiries and states his conclusions. The closure notice takes effect when it is issued and must either make the necessary amendments to the return to give effect to the stated conclusions or state that no amendment of the return is required. Before the enquiry is complete, the taxpayer may apply to the Commissioners for a direction requiring the Revenue to give closure notice within a specified period, such application to be heard and determined in the same way as an appeal. The Commissioners must give the direction unless satisfied that there are reasonable grounds for not giving closure notice within a specified period. These provisions apply to enquiries commenced (i.e. where notice of enquiry has been given) on or after 11 May 2001 or in progress at that date. Largely similar provisions applied previously (and see also 68.10 below). [*TMA 1970, s 28A; FA 1994, s 188; FA 1996, Sch 19 paras 2, 4(1)(2); FA 2001, s 88, Sch 29 para 8*].

Similar provisions apply in the case of an enquiry into a partnership return. Where a partnership return is amended under these provisions, the Revenue will, by notice, make any necessary consequential amendments to the partners' returns (including those of company partners). [*TMA 1970, s 28B; FA 1994, s 189; FA 1996, Sch 19 paras 2, 5(1); FA 1998, Sch 19 para 10; FA 2001, s 88, Sch 29 para 8*].

For enquiries completed before 11 May 2001, the Revenue consider that the day of completion of an enquiry is the day the taxpayer receives the closure notice. If the notice is handed to the taxpayer, it is thus the day it is handed over, and if there is evidence of the day on which the notice was received by post, it is that day. Otherwise the notice is assumed to be received two working days after being posted first class or four working days after being posted second class. (Revenue Tax Bulletin August 2000 p 769).

See 4.1 APPEALS for right of appeal against any conclusion stated or amendment made by a closure notice.

Where a personal or partnership return is amended by notice issued after 10 July 2003, the taxpayer is given the same rights to make, revise and withdraw claims, elections, applications and notices as he would have had if a 'discovery' assessment had been raised under *TMA 1970, s 29* (see 5.3 ASSESSMENTS). This is achieved by giving effect to *TMA 1970, ss 43A, 43B* (see 16.8 CLAIMS) in cases not involving fraudulent or negligent conduct, to *TMA 1970, s 36(3)* (which in a case involving fraudulent or negligent conduct enables the same reliefs and allowances to be given as if the necessary claims etc. had been made within the relevant time limits — see 30.3 FRAUDULENT OR NEGLIGENT CONDUCT), and to *TMA 1970, s 43(2)* (extended time limit for claims — see 16.8 CLAIMS). These *sections* are given similar effect in relation to an amendment as they would have in relation to an assessment. Any late assessment required to give effect to such a claim etc., or as a result of allowing such a claim etc., can be made within a year after the claim etc. becomes final (i.e. becomes no longer capable of being varied, on appeal or otherwise). [*TMA 1970, s 43C; FA 2003, s 207(1)(3)*].

68.10   **Amendment of returns where enquiries made.** As from 11 May 2001, if a return is amended by the taxpayer under 68.4 above while an enquiry into it is in progress (i.e. during the inclusive period between notice of enquiry and closure notice), the amendment does not restrict the scope of the enquiry but may itself be taken into account in the enquiry. The amendment does not take effect to alter the tax payable until the enquiry is completed and closure notice is issued (see 68.9 above). It may then be taken into account separately or, if the officer so states in the closure notice, in arriving at the amendments contained in the notice. It does not take effect if the officer concludes in the closure notice that the amendment is incorrect. [*TMA 1970, s 9B; FA 2001, s 88, Sch 29 para 4(1)*]. See 68.13 below as regards similar provisions for partnership returns. Before 11 May 2001, no amendment could be made by a taxpayer to a personal, trustees' or partnership tax return while an enquiry was in progress. [*TMA 1970, s 9(5), s 12AB(3); FA 1994, ss 179, 185, 199; FA 2001, s 88, Sch 29 para 2(1), para 3(1)*].

If in his opinion there is otherwise likely to be a loss of tax to the Crown, an officer may amend a self-assessment contained in the return while an enquiry is still in progress. If the enquiry is itself limited to an amendment to the return (see 68.6 above), the officer's power in this respect is limited accordingly. [*TMA 1970, s 9C, s 28A(2); FA 1994, ss 188, 199; FA 2001, s 88, Sch 29 para 4(1)*]. No similar power exists in the case of partnership returns.

For enquiries completed before 11 May 2001, a set procedure applied for amending a self-assessment following completion of an enquiry into the return. This is in part replaced by the procedure at 68.9 above and in part rendered unnecessary by the rules above on taxpayer amendments to returns during an enquiry. The earlier procedure is as follows. The taxpayer is given 30 days beginning with the day of completion of the officer's enquiries to amend his self-assessment in accordance with the officer's conclusions. The Revenue consider that the amendment must be *received* by the Revenue within those 30 days, which start on the day of completion and end 29 days later (see Revenue Tax Bulletin August 2000 p 769). Where the enquiry was into a return rather than an amendment, and the return was made before the expiry of twelve months beginning with the due date for delivery (see 68.2

above), the taxpayer also has this 30-day period to amend his self-assessment in accordance with any amendments to the return which he has notified to the officer. The officer then has a further 30 days in which to amend the self-assessment himself (i.e. the amendment must be received (see above) by the taxpayer by the 59th day after the day of completion of the enquiry, see Revenue Tax Bulletin August 2000 pp 769, 770). [*TMA 1970, s 28A(3)(4); FA 1994, ss 188, 199; FA 1996, Sch 19 para 4(1)*].

68.11   **Referral of questions during enquiry.** For enquiries commenced (i.e. where notice of enquiry has been given) on or after 11 May 2001 or in progress at that date, provisions are introduced to enable specific contentious points to be litigated while the enquiry is still open, instead of waiting until it is completed. Enquiries into personal, trustees' and partnership returns are all included. The system cannot be used until the necessary enabling regulations have been made.

At any time whilst the enquiry is in progress (i.e. during the inclusive period between notice of enquiry as in 68.6 above and closure notice as in 68.9 above), any one or more questions arising out of it may be referred, jointly by the taxpayer and an officer of the Board and by written notice, to the Special Commissioners for their determination. More than one notice of referral may be given in relation to the enquiry. Either party may withdraw a notice of referral before the first hearing, by giving written notice to the other party and to the Special Commissioners. Until the questions referred have been finally determined (or the referral withdrawn), no closure notice may be given or applied for in relation to the enquiry. The Lord Chancellor is given power to make regulations by statutory instrument to govern the operation of the referral process and in particular to deal with procedure before the Special Commissioners, appeals to the High Court and proceedings in NI, and specified pre-existing regulations and regulatory powers relating to appeals are adapted so as also to relate to such referrals.

The determination of the question(s) by the Special Commissioners is binding on both parties in the same way, and to the same extent, as a decision on a preliminary issue in an appeal. The Revenue must take account of it in concluding their enquiry. Following completion of the enquiry, the question concerned may not be reopened on appeal except to the extent (if any) that it could have been reopened had it been determined on appeal following the enquiry rather than on referral during the enquiry.

[*TMA 1970, ss 28ZA–28ZE; FA 2001, s 88, Sch 29 para 6; SI 2001 No 4024*].

68.12   **DETERMINATION OF TAX WHERE NO RETURN DELIVERED**

Where a notice has been given under *TMA 1970, ss 8, 8A* (notice requiring an individual or trustee to deliver a return — see 68.2 above) and the return is not delivered by the due date (the filing date), an officer of the Board may make a determination of the amounts of taxable income, capital gains and income tax payable which, to the best of his information and belief, he estimates for the year of assessment. The officer must serve notice of the determination on the person concerned. Tax is payable as if the determination were a self-assessment, with no right of appeal. No determination may be made after the expiry of five years beginning with the filing date.

A determination is automatically superseded by any self-assessment made (whether by the taxpayer or the Revenue), based on information contained in a return. Such self-assessment must be made within the five years beginning with the filing date or, if later, within twelve months beginning with the date of the determination. Any tax payable or repayable as a result of the supersession is deemed to have fallen due for payment or repayment on the normal due date, usually 31 January following the year of assessment (see 78.6 SELF-ASSESSMENT).

Any recovery proceedings commenced (restricted for proceedings commenced before 11 May 2001 to those commenced by an officer of the Board) before the making of such a self-assessment may be continued in respect of so much of the tax charged by the self-assessment as is due and payable and has not been paid.

[*TMA 1970, ss 28C, 59B(5A); FA 1994, s 190; FA 1996, s 125; FA 2001, s 88, Sch 29 para 17(1)(3)*].

Simon's Direct Tax Service. See E1.814.

68.13   **PARTNERSHIPS**

The following provisions apply for 1996/97 and subsequent years (or, as regards corporate partners, for accounting periods ending on or after 1 July 1999).

Any partner may be required by notice to complete and deliver a return of the partnership profits (a 'partnership return') together with accounts, statements, documents and other records (and see further below). The return must include information as to taxable partnership income, reliefs and allowances claimed, tax at source and tax credits plus the names, residences and tax references of all persons (including companies) who were partners during the period specified in the notice and such other information as may reasonably be required by the notice, which may include information relating to disposals and acquisitions of partnership property. The general requirements are similar to those for personal returns under *TMA 1970, s 8* (see 68.2 above). The notice will specify the period (the relevant period) to be covered by the return and the date by which the return should be delivered (the filing date). For a partnership including at least one individual, the filing date will be no earlier than 31 January following the year of assessment concerned (normally that in which the relevant period ends). For a partnership including at least one company, the filing date will be no earlier than the first anniversary of the end of the relevant period. In both cases, the filing date will be deferred until, at the earliest, the last day of the three-month period beginning with the date of the notice, if this is a later date than that given above.

Where the partner responsible for dealing with the return ceases to be available, a successor may be nominated for this purpose by a majority of the persons (or their personal representatives) who were partners at any time in the period covered by the return. A nomination (or revocation of a nomination) does not have effect until notified to the Revenue. Failing a nomination, a successor will be determined according to rules on the return form or will be nominated by the Revenue.

[*TMA 1970, s 12AA; FA 1988, s 127; FA 1994, ss 184, 199; FA 1995, s 104(6), s 115(4); FA 1996, s 121(6)(7), s 123(1)–(4); FA 1998, Sch 19 para 3; FA 2001, s 88, Sch 29 para 18*].

See 57.2 PENALTIES as regards penalties for non-compliance.

It is not possible for individual partners to make, in their personal tax returns, supplementary claims for expenses incurred on the partnership's behalf or capital allowances on personal assets used in the partnership. If not included in the accounts, adjustments for such expenditure etc. must be included in the tax computation forming part of the partnership return. (Revenue booklet SAT 1(1995), para 5.17 and see Revenue Tax Bulletin August 1997 p 453).

Provisions similar to those in 68.4 above apply as regards amendments and corrections to partnership returns. Where a return is so amended or corrected (and the correction is not rejected by the taxpayer), the partners' returns will be amended by the Revenue accordingly, by notice to each partner concerned. [*TMA 1970, ss 12AB, 12ABA, 12ABB; FA 1994, s 185; FA 1995, s 104(7)(8); FA 1996, s 123(5)(6); FA 1998, Sch 19 para 4; FA 2001, s 88, Sch 29 paras 3, 19*].

Enquiries into returns. Provisions similar to those in 68.6 above apply as regards enquiries into partnership returns. The notice of enquiry may be given to a successor (see above) of the person who made the return. The giving of such notice is deemed to include the giving of notice under *TMA 1970, s 9A* (or, where applicable, the equivalent corporation tax provision) to each partner affected. Similarly the rules in 68.9–68.11 above apply in relation to partnership returns, except that there is no provision equivalent to *TMA 1970, s 9C* for amendment of returns by the Revenue while an enquiry remains in progress. There is also appropriate provision to consequentially amend partners' own returns, including those of company partners. [*TMA 1970, ss 12AC, 12AD, 28ZA–28ZE, 28B; FA 1994, s 186; FA 1996, s 123(7), Sch 19 para 2; FA 1998, Sch 19 para 5; FA 2001, s 88, Sch 29 para 5*].

Partnership statements. Every partnership return as above must include a statement (a partnership statement) showing, in respect of the period covered by the return and each period of account ending within that period,

(*a*)   the partnership income or loss from each source, after taking into account any relief or allowance due to the partnership and for which a claim is made under any of the provisions in *TMA 1970, s 42(7)* (see 16.1 CLAIMS),

(*b*)   the amount of consideration for each disposal of partnership property,

(*c*)   the amounts of any tax deducted at source from or tax credits on partnership income, and

(*d*)   the amount of each charge on partnership income,

and each partner's share of that income, loss, consideration, tax, credit or charge.

In the case of an individual carrying on a trade etc. in partnership, the return under *TMA 1970, s 8* (see 68.2 above) must include each amount which, according to any '*relevant partnership statement*' (i.e. one falling to be made, as respects the partnership, for a period which includes all or any part of the year of assessment or its basis period), is the individual's share of any income, loss, tax, credit or charge for the period covered by the statement. [*TMA 1970, s 8(1B)(1C); FA 1994, s 178(1), s 199(2); FA 1995, s 103(7), s 104(2)*].

Simon's Direct Tax Service. See E1.808 *et seq.*, E1.813.

68.14   **ELECTRONIC LODGEMENT OF TAX RETURNS ETC.**

Certain returns required to be made to the Board or to an officer of the Board may, subject to the conditions detailed below, be lodged electronically. The provision under which the return is required must be specified for this purpose by Treasury order, which will also appoint a commencement day. For returns under *TMA 1970, ss 8, 8A* and *12AA* (see 68.2, 68.13 above), the appointed day was 1 March 1997, so that returns due from 6 April 1997 under self-assessment are eligible. Any supporting documentation (including accounts, statements or reports) required to be delivered with a return may similarly be lodged electronically if the return is so lodged (or may instead be delivered by the last day for submission of the return).

The normal powers and rights applicable in relation to returns etc. delivered by post are applied to information transmitted electronically. A properly made and authenticated hard copy (see (*c*) below) is treated in any proceedings as if it were the return or other document in question, but if no such copy is shown to have been made, a hard copy certified by an officer of the Board to be a true copy of the information transmitted is so treated instead.

There are four conditions for electronic lodgement.

(*a*)   A person seeking approval must be given notice of the grant or refusal of approval, which may be granted for the transmission of information on the person's own behalf or on behalf of another person or persons. Approval may be withdrawn by notice from a given date, and any notice refusing or withdrawing approval must state the grounds. An appeal against refusal or withdrawal must be made within 30 days of such notice having been given, and lies to the Special Commissioners, who may grant approval from a specified date if they consider the refusal or withdrawal to have been unreasonable in all the circumstances.

(*b*)   The transmission must comply with any requirements notified by the Board to the person making it, including in particular any relating to the hardware or software to be used.

(*c*)   The transmission must signify, in an approved manner, that a hard copy was made under arrangements designed to ensure that the information contained in it is the information in fact transmitted.

(*d*)   The information transmitted must be accepted under a procedure selected by the Board for this purpose, which may in particular consist of or include the use of specifically designed software.

As regards (*c*) above, the hard copy must have been authenticated by the person required to make the return:

(i)   in the case of a return required by notice, by endorsement with a declaration that it is to the best of his knowledge correct and complete; or

(ii)   otherwise by signature.

[*TMA 1970, s 115A, Sch 3A; FA 1995, s 153, Sch 28; SI 1997 No 57*].

Agents may pre-register for the electronic lodgement service. Copies of an information pack and registration form are available from the Agent Educator in all local tax offices. Revenue Statement of Practice SP 1/97, 16 January 1997, describes how the Revenue operate electronic lodgement and the detailed requirements.

The above provisions are to be repealed from a date (or dates) to be appointed. [*FA 1999, s 133(3)(4)*].

After 20 August 2001, agents are authorised to file individual clients' personal tax returns over the internet subject to certain conditions (see 68.2 above). For the time being, this facility is available in addition to the electronic lodgement service described above and does not displace it. The electronic lodgement service is to continue until at least April 2005 (for 2003/04 returns) (Revenue 'Working Together' Bulletin June 2003 p 11).

Incentives for electronic communications. Regulations may be made by statutory instrument by the Commissioners of Inland Revenue in relation to matters under their care and management (and by the Commissioners of Customs and Excise in relation to theirs) for the provision of incentives to use electronic communications. These may include discounts (or payments or repayments), or additional time for compliance or payment, or more convenient intervals for the delivery of information or the making of payments. Anything received by way of incentive is not regarded as income for tax purposes. The regulations may make provision as to the conditions of entitlement to incentives and for their withdrawal (which may be authorised to be made by direction), and may provide for penalties up to £1,000 for failure to comply with any specified provision. They may make different provision for different cases, and may make such incidental, supplemental, consequential or transitional provision as the Commissioners think fit. [*FA 2000, s 143, Sch 38*].

Internet filing discount. Regulations as above provided for a number of one-off incentives to encourage internet filing of returns. For the 1999/2000 return, small businesses and individual taxpayers filing their self-assessment returns over the internet by the due date and paying any tax due electronically received a tax discount of £10. Similarly for the 2000/01 returns, small businesses filing their VAT returns and/or their PAYE end-of-year returns by the due date via the internet and paying any tax due electronically received a discount of £50, or £100 for both VAT and PAYE filing, and a further £50 where there was one or more working families' or disabled person's tax credit cases. The discounts were available only for the one year for each service. (Revenue Press Releases 16 February 2000, 21 March 2000 (BN1D)). See *SI 2001 No 56; SI 2001 No 1081, reg 22*.

Mandatory e-filing. See 55.9 PAY AS YOU EARN as regards the phasing in of mandatory electronic returns by employers.

Simon's Direct Tax Service. See E1.806D.

68.15   **BANKERS ETC. AND PAYING AGENTS — RETURNS OF INTEREST**

On receipt of notice, any person (including the National Savings Bank and a building society) paying or crediting interest on money received or retained, in the UK, in the ordinary course of his business, and any bank (within *ICTA 1988, s 840A*, see 7.1 BANKS), must make a return, for any specified year of assessment (ending not more than three years previously), showing the names and addresses of the recipients and the gross amount of interest paid or credited to each and the amount (if any) of tax deducted therefrom. The payer may exclude from that return interest paid to a person who has so requested and has given written notice that the person beneficially entitled to the interest is a non-UK resident company. Similarly, where a declaration of non-ordinary residence has been given to the payer to enable interest to be paid gross (see 7.2 BANKS, 8.3 BUILDING SOCIETIES), and the person who made that declaration has so requested, the payer is not required to include interest paid, credited or received before 6 April 2001 in the return under this provision. Notices may be issued re parts or branches of a business. The Board have powers by statutory instrument to make regulations requiring further prescribed information with the return, or providing that prescribed information is *not* required, or requiring information or returns to be in prescribed form, or providing for inspection of books, documents, records etc. [*TMA 1970, s 17; FA 1988, s 123(2); FA 1990, s 92; F(No 2)A 1992, s 29; FA 1996, Sch 37 para 11; FA 2000, s 145; SI 1990 No 2231; SI 1992 No 2915; SI 2001 Nos 404, 405*].

Returns may similarly be required from any other person paying interest (including building society dividends) or receiving it on behalf of others [*TMA 1970, s 18; FA 1988, s 123(3); FA 1990, s 92; FA 1991, Sch 11 para 5; FA 1996, Sch 37 para 11; FA 2000, s 145; SI 2001 No 405*] and from persons collecting interest on securities on behalf of others who are resident in UK. [*TMA 1970, s 24; FA 1996, Sch 37 para 11*].

With effect for interest payments on or after 6 April 2001, *SI 2001 No 405* excludes a wide range of payments from the application of *TMA 1970, s 17* and *s 18*. In particular, the automatic reporting of payments to non-residents now applies only to interest paid to individuals. For guidance on the making of information returns under *TMA 1970, s 17* and *s 18*, see the notes (under 'Publications, specialist') on the Revenue's website.

EU Savings Directive. Under *FA 2003, s 199*, the Treasury may make regulations by statutory instrument (see now *SI 2003 No 3297*) to implement into UK law the EU Directive on the Taxation of Savings (*Directive 2003/48/EC*, 3 June 2003), designed to counter cross-border tax evasion by individuals on their savings income and due to come into effect on 1 January 2005. Under the Directive, prescribed UK paying agents, e.g. businesses and public bodies that pay savings income to, or collect savings income for, individuals resident elsewhere in the EU will have to report details of the income and the payee to the Revenue, who will then pass on the information to the corresponding tax authority in the payee's country of residence. Similar information regarding UK-resident payees will flow in the opposite direction. (Austria, Belgium and Luxembourg are expected to impose, for a transitional period, a withholding tax as an alternative to exchanging information.) The regulations prescribe the types of paying agent and payee within the scheme, the information required, the time limits for compliance and the penalties for non-compliance, and they provide for inspection of paying agents' records. For these purposes, '*savings income*' means interest (including premium bond winnings but not interest unrelated to a money debt or penalty charges for late payments), interest accrued or capitalised at the sale, refund or redemption of a money debt, and certain income distributed by or realised upon the sale, refund or redemption of shares or units in a collective investment fund. Treasury regulations may also implement any similar arrangements made with non-EU countries. See the Revenue's detailed Savings Income Reporting Guidance Notes at www.inlandrevenue.gov.uk/esd-guidance/esd-guidance-notes.pdf and www.inlandrevenue.gov.uk/esd-guidance/contractualrelations.pdf See also Treasury Explanatory Notes to Finance Bill 2003, European Commission Press Release 4 June 2003, Revenue Press Releases 30 June 2003, 22 September 2003 and Revenue Internet Statement 19 December 2003.

Where, under the Savings Directive or equivalent arrangements made with non-EU Member States, a withholding tax is levied as an alternative to exchanging information, relief is available for such withholding tax against UK income tax and capital gains tax liabilities or, to the extent that set-off is not possible, by repayment. As an alternative, application may be made to the Revenue for a certificate which can be presented to a paying agent to enable savings income to be paid to the applicant without deduction of such withholding tax. See, in both cases, 24.9 DOUBLE TAX RELIEF.

Simon's Direct Tax Service. See **A3.120–A3.122, F1.119.**

68.16   **EMPLOYERS**

Employers (including deemed employers of agency workers) must, on application by the Revenue (made no later than the fifth anniversary of 31 January following the tax year(s) specified), furnish particulars, for employees (i.e. any person whose earnings are within the charge to tax on employment income) and periods specified, of

- payments made by the employer to employees, including expenses, payments made on employees' behalf and not repaid and payments made for services rendered in connection with a trade or business (whether or not rendered in the course of the employment), and taxable benefits provided by the employer to employees;

- payments (as above) made, and benefits provided, by third parties by arrangement with the employer (including name and business address of third party);

- payments (as above) made, and benefits provided, to the employer's knowledge, by third parties other than by arrangement with the employer (including name and business address of third party).

Third parties may similarly be required by notice to furnish particulars of payments made and benefits provided to employees of other persons. A similar time limit applies.

As regards benefits, particulars required may include the amounts chargeable to tax.

[*TMA 1970, ss 15, 16A; FA 1995, s 106; ITEPA 2003, Sch 6 paras 126, 127*].

See also 55.9 PAY AS YOU EARN as regards employers' returns.

Person in UK treated as employer. Where a person performs duties for a continuous period of not less than 30 days in the UK for a non-resident employer but for the benefit of a person resident or carrying on a trade etc. in the UK, then the latter person must include him in any returns of employees and the employee may be required to include any such earnings in his tax return. [*FA 1974, s 24; FA 1976, Sch 9 para 5; ITEPA 2003, Sch 6 para 147*].

68.17 Returns

FEES, COMMISSIONS, COPYRIGHTS ETC.

Any person carrying on any trade etc., and any body of persons carrying on any non-trading activity (including Crown departments, public or local authorities and any other public bodies), may, by notice, be required to give particulars of all payments made (including commissions or expenses), or valuable consideration given, for services rendered by persons not employed by him, including, in the case of a trade etc., services in connection with the formation, acquisition, development or disposal thereof. Applies also to periodical or lump-sum payments in respect of any copyright or public lending right or design right. But returns are limited to payments from which tax is not deductible, and those (*a*) exceeding £15 in total to any one person, or (*b*) made during the three tax years ending prior to the notice. [*TMA 1970, s 16; FA 1983, s 27; FA 1988, s 124*]. See Revenue Pamphlet 46Q re payments to entertainers etc. for total payments exceeding £250 in a year.

68.18 GRANTS, SUBSIDIES, LICENCES ETC.

Any person paying grants or subsidies directly or indirectly out of public funds (whether UK or European Union), or issuing licences or approvals or maintaining entries in a register which subsist after that date, may be required to furnish particulars to the inspector where they may be relevant to the determination of any tax liability. [*TMA 1970, s 18A; FA 1988, s 125*].

68.19 HOTELS AND BOARDING HOUSES

Returns of all lodgers and inmates resident in any dwelling house must be made by the proprietor, if required by notice from the inspector. [*TMA 1970, s 14*].

68.20 ISSUING HOUSES, STOCKBROKERS, AUCTIONEERS ETC.

For the purposes of obtaining particulars of chargeable gains, an inspector may require a return of parties to transactions and description and consideration of assets dealt with from (i) an issuing house or any other person concerned in effecting public issues or placing of shares etc. or (ii) a member of a stock exchange (other than a market maker) or any other person acting as an agent or broker in share transactions or (iii) any person or body managing a clearing house for any terminal market in commodities or (iv) an auctioneer and any person carrying on a trade of dealing in any description of tangible movable property or acting as agent in such where the value in the hands of the recipient exceeds £6,000. Returns are limited to transactions effected within three years prior to the issue of the notice requiring the return. [*TMA 1970, s 25; FA 1978, s 45(5); FA 1982, s 81*].

The Board may make regulations by statutory instrument, effective from a day to be appointed therein, making appropriate provision in regard to recognised investment exchanges other than the Stock Exchange. [*FA 1986, s 63, Sch 18 para 8*].

See also *TMA 1970, s 21* as amended by *FA 1997, Sch 10 para 14* as regards other transactions by market makers. See Simon's Direct Tax Service A3.126.

68.21 PAY AS YOU EARN

See 55.9 PAY AS YOU EARN and 78.12 SELF-ASSESSMENT.

68.22 TRUSTEES

A return may be required from a trustee under *TMA 1970, ss 8A, 13* — see 68.2 above.

68.23 REASONABLE EXCUSE

It is generally provided that a person is deemed not to have failed to do anything required to be done where there was a reasonable excuse for the failure and, if the excuse ceased, provided that the failure was remedied without unreasonable delay after the excuse had ceased. Similarly, a person is deemed not to have failed to do anything required to be done within a limited time if he did it within such further time as the Board, or the Commissioners or officer concerned, may have allowed. [*TMA 1970, s 118(2); F(No 2)A 1987, s 94*]. In *Creedplan Ltd v Winter (Sp C 54), [1995] SSCD 352*, the Special Commissioner, in confirming a penalty under *TMA 1970, s 94(1)(a)*, considered that 'there is no reasonable excuse ... for sending in a return which was less than was required' (but cf. *Akarimsons Ltd v Chapman (Sp C 116), [1997] SSCD 140* in which a penalty under *TMA 1970, s 94(1)(b)* was quashed). See, however, *Steeden v Carver (Sp C 212), [1999] SSCD 283*, in which reliance on the Revenue's advice as to the practical extension of a deadline, unequivocally given, was held to be 'as reasonable an excuse as could be found'.

Under **self-assessment**, there are separate 'reasonable excuse' let-outs as regards penalties for late returns (see 57.2 PENALTIES) and surcharges for late payment of tax (see 42.2 INTEREST AND SURCHARGES ON UNPAID TAX).

69   Schedule A—Property Income

[ICTA 1988, s 15, ss 21–43; FA 1995, s 39, Sch 6]

Simon's Direct Tax Service Part A4.

Other sources. See Revenue Booklet IR 150, Revenue Property Income Manual and Tolley's Property Taxes.

69.1   Schedule A applies to **property income.** Tax is charged on rents etc. (see 69.3 below) after deducting allowable expenses (see 69.4, 69.5 below). Certain lease premiums etc. are also taxable (see 69.16 below). See 9.9 CAPITAL ALLOWANCES for flat conversion allowances and 9.10 *et seq.* CAPITAL ALLOWANCES for allowances available in respect of leased industrial buildings.

Headings in this chapter are as follows.

69.2   **HISTORY**

The legislation was introduced in *FA 1963* and assessments up to 1969/70 were made under Schedule D, Case VIII. From 1970/71 onwards, assessments have been made under Schedule A. A new regime, incorporating the concept of a 'Schedule A business' and *including furnished lettings* (previously chargeable under Schedule D, Case VI), was introduced by *FA 1995* for income tax purposes only (see 69.3–69.12 below). This regime was extended to corporation tax with effect from 1 April 1998 with the necessary amendments and modifications (see Tolley's Corporation Tax under Profit Computations). See the 2003/04 and earlier editions for the old regime and for Revenue guidelines on the transition from the old to the new. The treatment of premiums and other matters are dealt with at 69.13 *et seq.* below.

Commencement of current regime. The provisions of *FA 1995* mentioned above have effect for income tax purposes for 1995/96 and subsequent tax years, subject to transitional provisions affecting 1995/96 only.

[FA 1995, s 39(4)(5)].

69.3   **AMOUNTS CHARGEABLE**

Schedule A applies to the annual profits arising from a business carried on for the exploitation, as a source of rents or other 'receipts', of any estate, interest or rights in or over land in the UK. To the extent that any transaction is entered into for such exploitation, it is taken to have been entered into in the course of such a business; this brings into charge, for example, one-off or casual lettings. Income tax under Schedule A is charged on the persons receiving or entitled to the chargeable income. See below for exclusions from Schedule A and 69.4 below for computation of amounts chargeable.

'*Receipts*', in relation to any land, includes

(a)   any payment in respect of any licence to occupy or otherwise to use any land or in respect of the exercise of any other right over land; and

(b)   rentcharges, ground annuals and feu duties and any other annual payments reserved in respect of, or charged on or issuing out of, that land.

Income from the letting of immobile caravans or permanently moored houseboats is specifically brought within the charge to Schedule A. Income from letting caravan pitches, i.e. site rents, is chargeable under Schedule A to the extent that it arises from exploitation of land, but, by concession, where the site proprietor carries on associated activities (e.g. shops) which constitute trading and account for a substantial part of the income, the letting income may be included as receipts of the trade under Schedule D, Case I. (Revenue Press Release 17 May 1984 and see Revenue Pamphlet IR 1, B29).

A '*Schedule A business*' means any business the profits or gains of which are chargeable to income tax under Schedule A, including the business in the course of which any such transaction as is mentioned above is treated as entered into. All such businesses and transactions entered into by a particular person or partnership are treated as, or as transactions entered into in the course of carrying on, *a single business*. (This is subject to a special rule for non-UK resident companies partly within the charge to income tax.)

In the case of a **furnished letting** (including that of a caravan or houseboat), any consideration receivable for the use of furniture is chargeable under Schedule A in the same way as rent (and expenditure incurred in providing furniture is treated accordingly). This does not apply to any amount taken into account in computing profits of a trade involving the making available of furniture for use in premises.

Schedule A does not include the following.

(i)   Profits arising from the *occupation of land*.

(ii)   *Farming and market gardening*. Profits or gains charged under *ICTA 1988, s 53(1)* (Schedule D, Case I).

(iii)   *Mineral rents, royalties etc.* charged to tax under Schedule D by virtue of *ICTA 1988, s 55, s 119 or s 120(1)*, see under 22.2 and 22.14 DEDUCTION OF TAX AT SOURCE. However, wayleave payments within *ICTA 1988, s 120* are charged under Schedule A (instead of Schedule D) where for the same period some or all of the land to which the easement relates is included in land by reference to which a Schedule A charge arises on the same person.

(iv)   Receipts/expenses taken into account as trading receipts/expenses under *ICTA 1988, s 98* (tied premises — see 71.35 SCHEDULE D, CASES I AND II).

[*ICTA 1988, s 15, s 21(1), s 120(1A), s 832(1); FA 1995, s 39(1)(2), Sch 6 paras 1, 28; FA 1997, s 60; FA 1998, s 38, Sch 5 paras 1, 2*].

Receipts from sales of turf have been held to be within Schedule A although they may alternatively be taxed as trading receipts within Schedule D, Case I (*Lowe v J W Ashmore Ltd Ch D 1970, 46 TC 597*); but receipts from sale of colliery dross bings held to be capital (*Roberts v Lord Belhaven's Exors CS 1925, 9 TC 501*). Sums received for licence to tip soil on land held to be capital (*McClure v Petre Ch D 1988, 61 TC 226*). These cases were decided under the old regime referred to at 69.2 above.

69.4 Schedule A—Property Income

See also the comprehensive Revenue booklet IR 150 and Revenue Property Income Manual.

Simon's Direct Tax Service. See A4.102.

69.4 **COMPUTATION OF AMOUNTS CHARGEABLE**

Tax under Schedule A is computed on the full amount of profits arising in the tax year. The Revenue will not allow any deviation from a strict fiscal year basis (except as regards trading partnerships with ancillary Schedule A income — see below). The profit (or loss) should be arrived at by use of ordinary accounting principles and by applying the computational provisions of SCHEDULE D, CASE I (71) contained in *ICTA 1988, Pt IV, Chapter V* (*ICTA 1988, s 74 et seq.* but see also below), and the further provisions listed below, as if the Schedule A business were a trade (although Schedule A income continues to be investment income rather than trading income), i.e. on an earnings basis (see 71.30 SCHEDULE D, CASES I AND II). By concession, a cash basis may be used where gross annual receipts do not exceed £15,000, provided that it is used consistently and gives a reasonable overall result not substantially different from that produced on the earnings basis (see Revenue Pamphlet IR 150, paras 90–92). Loan interest, to the extent that it is incurred wholly and exclusively for the purposes of the letting business, is deductible under general principles. See 43.6 INTEREST PAYABLE as regards alternative concessionary relief for interest in certain cases of temporary absence from owner-occupied property, and see also below.

The following provisions relating to the computation of profits of trades and professions also apply for Schedule A purposes.

(*a*) *ICTA 1988, s 72* (method of apportioning profits) — see 71.3 SCHEDULE D, CASES I AND II.

(*b*) *ICTA 1988, s 577* (entertainment expenses) — see 71.45 SCHEDULE D, CASES I AND II.

(*c*) *ICTA 1988, s 577A* (illegal payments etc.) — see 71.53 SCHEDULE D, CASES I AND II.

(*d*) *ICTA 1988, ss 579, 580* (redundancy payments), *ICTA 1988, s 588* (training courses for employees), and *ICTA 1988, s 589A* (counselling services for employees) — see 71.44 SCHEDULE D, CASES I AND II.

(*e*) *FA 1988, s 73(2)* (deductibility of sums paid as consideration for restrictive undertakings) — see 75.37 SCHEDULE E—EMPLOYMENT INCOME.

(*f*) *FA 1989, s 43* (timing of deduction for remuneration) — see 71.44 SCHEDULE D, CASES I AND II.

(*g*) *FA 1989, s 76* (expenses in connection with non-approved retirement benefits schemes) — see 67.10 RETIREMENT SCHEMES FOR EMPLOYEES.

(*h*) *FA 1989, ss 112, 113* (expenditure on security) — see 71.71 SCHEDULE D, CASES I AND II.

(*j*) *FA 1998, ss 42, 46(1)(2)* (requirement that accounts give a true and fair view etc.) — see 46.2 LOSSES, 71.30 SCHEDULE D, CASES I AND II.

The following further provisions apply for Schedule A purposes.

(i) *ICTA 1988, ss 103–106, s 108, s 109A, s 110* — see 62 POST-CESSATION ETC. RECEIPTS AND EXPENDITURE.

(ii) *ICTA 1988, s 113* (change in the members of a partnership) — see 53.5 PARTNERSHIPS.

(iii)   *ICTA 1988, s 401(1)* (relief for pre-trading expenditure) — see 71.66 SCHEDULE D, CASES I AND II.

(iv)   *FA 1998, s 44, Sch 6* (change of accounting basis) — see 11.2 CASH BASIS.

The following provisions of *ICTA 1988, Pt IV, Chapter V* are excluded from applying for Schedule A purposes.

(1)   *ICTA 1988, s 82* (restriction on deductibility of interest paid to non-UK residents) — see 43.2(i) INTEREST PAYABLE.

(2)   *ICTA 1988, s 87* (deductibility of premiums paid) — see 71.88 SCHEDULE D, CASES I AND II.

(3)   *ICTA 1988, s 96* (averaging of farming profits) — see 71.47(*a*) SCHEDULE D, CASES I AND II.

(4)   *ICTA 1988, s 98* (tied premises) — see 71.35 SCHEDULE D, CASES I AND II.

ICTA 1988, s 74(1)(d) (disallowance of provisions for future repairs) applies for Schedule A purposes in a suitably modified form. For a general article on what constitutes an allowable repair for Schedule A, see Revenue Tax Bulletin June 2002, pp 935, 936.

[*ICTA 1988, ss 21, 21A, 21B; FA 1995, s 39(2), Sch 6 paras 13–16, para 20, paras 22–25; FA 1998, s 38, Sch 5 para 4, Sch 27 Pt III(4); ITEPA 2003, Sch 6 para 7*].

See also the comprehensive Revenue booklet IR 150 and Revenue Property Income Manual.

Profits or losses on contracts taken out to hedge interest payments deductible in computing profits or losses of the Schedule A business (as above) will normally be taxed or relieved as receipts or deductions of that business. Such profits or losses would generally be computed on an accruals basis in accordance with normal accountancy practice. Similarly deposits paid to landlords by tenants or licensees will ordinarily be receipts of the business, to be recognised in accordance with generally accepted accountancy practice, normally by being deferred and matched with the related costs. Excess deposits which are refunded should be excluded from the business receipts. (Revenue Tax Bulletin October 1996 p 349). As regards allowable legal and professional costs, see paras 213–218 of Revenue Pamphlet IR 150 and Revenue Tax Bulletin December 1996 p 375.

A borrower who was eligible for mortgage interest relief prior to its abolition for 2000/01 onwards in respect of a let property could choose each year whether to claim such relief (restricted to 10%, for 1998/99 and 1999/2000, on a maximum of £30,000) or to deduct the interest in computing the Schedule A business profits. As regards inclusion of the loan within MIRAS (mortgage interest relief by deduction at source), see 22.13 DEDUCTION OF TAX AT SOURCE. See also 43.2 INTEREST PAYABLE for concession available where part of a borrower's main residence is used for business (including a Schedule A business) purposes.

Partnerships. Ancillary Schedule A income of a trading or professional partnership is taxable on an accounts year basis (see 53.3 PARTNERSHIPS). Joint ownership of property does not, of itself, create a partnership. Where the letting is not ancillary to a trade or profession, there will only be a partnership if, exceptionally, the exploitation of property constitutes the carrying on of a business (using that term without regard to the concept of a Schedule A business) jointly with a view to profit. See Revenue Tax Bulletin December 1995 pp 271, 272.

Mutual businesses. The normal exemption for MUTUAL TRADING (50) does not extend to Schedule A activities, the transactions and relationships involved in mutual business being instead treated as if they were between persons between whom no relationship of mutuality existed. The taxable person is the person who would be taxable if the business were not mutual business. (This does not affect the treatment of Co-operative Housing Associations — see Tolley's Corporation Tax). [*ICTA 1988, s 21C; FA 1998, s 38, Sch 5 para 5*].

Foot and mouth outbreak. For the full range of measures, in particular in relation to rent waivers, in relation to the 2001 foot and mouth disease outbreak, see Revenue Tax Bulletin Special Edition May 2001.

69.5   DEDUCTIONS — MISCELLANEOUS

(*a*)   *Capital allowances on plant and machinery.* A Schedule A business is a qualifying activity for the purposes of such allowances under *CAA 2001, Pt 2* (see 9.24 CAPITAL ALLOWANCES). Capital allowances were similarly available under *CAA 1990, Pt II* on plant or machinery as if the Schedule A business were a separate trade for which the item was provided (subject to further separation where there are furnished holiday lettings, see 69.8 below). Allowances are thus given as expenses, and charges treated as receipts, of the business. Plant or machinery provided for use in a dwelling-house is excluded (with a just and reasonable apportionment of expenditure where such use is partial). [*CAA 2001, ss 15, 16, 35; ICTA 1988, s 32; CAA 1990, s 28A; FA 1995, Sch 6 para 8; FA 1997, Sch 15 paras 1, 3, 9; FA 1998, Sch 27 Pt III(4)*].

(*b*)   *Land managed as one estate.* Where, at 5 April 1963, land was in one ownership and managed as one estate, the owner was able to elect, for tax years before 2001/02, to be treated as receiving, for any part of the estate not let (other than premises he occupies for estate management or trade) and for any part let at less than its annual value, rent at a rate equal to its annual value. The estate is thus split into two parts, the part for which rent is determined as above (Part A) and the remainder (Part B). Expenditure relating to Part A must first be set against the rents as so determined (the deemed receipts); any balance is set against Part B receipts, with any excess treated as Part A expenditure for the following chargeable period. The excess cannot be set against income from outside the estate or form part of a Schedule A loss (see 69.12 below). Expenditure relating to Part B is deductible against any balance of Part A deemed receipts (after deducting Part A expenditure, including any excess brought forward as above). Any excess Part B expenditure is treated as a Schedule A loss.

Election, applying to all subsequent years before 2001/02 in which the estate was in the same ownership, had to be made within one year after the first tax year for which the owner could have made it, and then (except in the case of the first possible election) was valid only if the previous owner had made a similar election. Except in the case of certain trusts [*ICTA 1988, s 26(5)*] property acquired after 5 April 1963 did not form part of the estate. [*ICTA 1988, s 26(4)*]. The election did not generally cease to be effective if part of the estate became comprised in a maintenance fund (see 81.21 SETTLEMENTS), but also see *ICTA 1988, s 27; FA 1995, Sch 6 para 6; FA 1998, s 38, Sch 5 para 8.* [*ICTA 1988, s 26; FA 1995, Sch 6 para 5; FA 1998, s 38, Sch 5 para 7, Sch 27 Pt III(4)*].

These provisions are **repealed** with effect for 2001/02 and subsequent tax years. [*FA 1998, s 39*].

Annual value, see *ICTA 1988, s 837,* is the rent reasonably to be expected from a letting on terms of the tenant paying tenant's rates etc. and the landlord bearing repairs, insurance and expenses necessary to maintain the property so as to command that rent. In practice, a property's gross rateable value is taken as its annual value. (Revenue Press Release 23 July 1985). In the case of Scottish estates, 1978 gross rateable values will continue to be used for this purpose, despite the 1985 rating revaluation, 'for the time being'. (Revenue Pamphlet IR 1, B30).

(c)   *Sea walls.* For allowances for expenditure on making sea walls, see *ICTA 1988, s 30; FA 1995, Sch 6 para 7; FA 1998, s 38, Sch 5 para 11* and *Hesketh v Bray CA 1888, 2 TC 380.*

(d)   By concession, the estimated cost of any maintenance and repairs obviated by alterations etc., was allowed provided the alterations were not so extensive as to amount to reconstruction, and there had been no such change in the use of the property as would have rendered the repairs etc., unnecessary. (Revenue Pamphlet IR 1, B4). This concession is **withdrawn** after 5 April 2001. (Revenue Press Release 17 March 1998).

(e)   *Landlord's expenditure on energy-saving items.* Where the land in question consists of or includes a dwelling-house, a deduction can be claimed, in computing Schedule A profits for income tax (*not* corporation tax) purposes, for expenditure incurred within any of the tax years **2004/05 to 2008/09** inclusive which

- is capital expenditure incurred in the acquisition, and installation in the dwelling-house, of a '*qualifying energy-saving item*', defined as cavity wall insulation or loft insulation (but see the Treasury's regulatory powers below); and

- is incurred wholly and exclusively for the purposes of the Schedule A business, is not otherwise deductible in computing the profits of that business and does not qualify for any capital allowance.

The deduction is limited to a maximum of £1,500 per building, irrespective of the number of dwelling-houses contained in it (*Draft Regulations 21 May 2004*).

The deduction cannot be claimed if, at the time the item is installed, the dwelling-house is under construction or is comprised in land in which the claimant does not have an interest or is in the course of acquiring an interest or a further interest. The Schedule A business must not consist in the commercial letting of furnished holiday accommodation (within 69.8 below) or, if it does so consist to any extent, the dwelling-house must not itself constitute any of that accommodation. The claimant must not also be claiming 'rent a room' relief (within 69.10 below) in respect of any qualifying residence which consists of or includes the dwelling-house.

Where the qualifying conditions are satisfied in relation to part only of any expenditure, a deduction is allowed on the basis of a just and reasonable apportionment of the expenditure. Relief under *ICTA 1988, s 401* for *pre-trading expenditure* (see 71.66 SCHEDULE D, CASES I AND II as applied by 68.4(iii) above) is allowed only for expenditure incurred within the *six months* before the claimant commences the Schedule A business.

The Treasury are given wide powers to vary these provisions by regulation; this includes the power to vary the definition of a 'qualifying energy-saving item' and to impose conditions by reference to which a specified item will qualify. They may also make regulations determining (i) entitlement to the deduction where different people have different interests in the land in question and (ii) the method of apportioning relief between members of a partnership, joint tenants or tenants in common; in both cases, a just and reasonable apportionment applies (*Draft Regulations 21 May 2004*). (Where a part of the relief falls to be apportioned to a company, that part will lapse as the relief does not apply for corporation tax purposes.) Any contribution received from another person towards the expenditure must be deducted in arriving at the claimable amount (*Draft Regulations 21 May 2004*).

[*ICTA 1988, ss 31A, 31B; FA 2004, s 143*].

Simon's Direct Tax Service. See **A4.330** *et seq.*

69.6 Schedule A—Property Income

69.6 **SIMPLIFIED RETURNS**

Landlords with a total annual gross income from property under £15,000 are required to state on their income tax returns only the gross property income, the total amount of allowable expenses and the net income or profit. There is, of course, still a need to keep accurate records to ensure the correctness of the three-line accounts. (Revenue Press Releases 7 November 1989, 1 November 1991). See generally 68.2, 68.5 RETURNS.

69.7 **FURNISHED LETTINGS**

Furnished lettings are taxable as, or as part of, a Schedule A business (and the computational rules at 69.4 above thus apply). See 69.8, 69.10 below for furnished holiday lettings and 'rent a room' relief respectively.

Dependent on the nature of the lettings, including their frequency and the extent to which the landlord provides services, e.g. cleaning, laundry and meals, the letting may amount to a trade of providing serviced accommodation and be within Schedule D, Case I rather than Schedule A. Alternatively, the provision of services may amount to a trade separate to the letting (cf. *Salisbury House Estate Ltd v Fry HL1930, 15 TC 266*). In *Gittos v Barclay Ch D 1982, 55 TC 633*, the letting of two villas in a holiday village was held not to amount to trading. A similar decision was reached in *Griffiths v Jackson; Griffiths v Pearman Ch D 1982, 56 TC 583* in relation to the extensive letting of furnished rooms to students. Note that all the decisions cited were made before 1995/96 when non-trading furnished lettings were within Schedule D, Case VI rather than Schedule A.

Capital allowances are not due on plant or machinery let for use in a dwelling house (see 9.24 CAPITAL ALLOWANCES) (but see 69.8 below as regards furnished holiday lettings). Furniture and furnishing may be dealt with on the renewals basis but an alternative Revenue concession is to allow as depreciation 10% of the rents received as reduced by any council tax and water rates or material payments for services borne by landlord but normally a tenant's burden. Where the 10% deduction is allowed, no further deduction is given for the cost of renewing furniture or furnishings, nor for fixtures such as cookers, dishwashers or washing machines which, in unfurnished accommodation, the tenant would normally provide for himself. However, the cost of renewing fixtures which are an integral part of the building (e.g. baths, toilets, washbasins) may be claimed in addition, provided that they are revenue repairs to the fabric. Both bases, which applied under Case VI, are maintained under Schedule A. Any different basis in use for a particular case prior to 1975/76 will not normally be disturbed (Revenue Pamphlet IR 1, B47; Revenue Press Release IR28, 29 November 1994). See *Abidoye v Hennessey Ch D 1978, [1979] STC 212*.

69.8 **Furnished holiday lettings.** In so far as a Schedule A business consists in the 'commercial letting' of 'furnished holiday accommodation' in the UK (a 'furnished holiday lettings business'), it is treated for the following purposes as a trade.

(i) Relief for losses under *ICTA 1988, ss 380–390* (see 46 LOSSES);

(ii) Classification as earned income;

(iii) Personal pension contribution relief and retirement annuity premium relief (see 60 PERSONAL PENSION SCHEMES, 66 RETIREMENT ANNUITIES).

In addition, a furnished holiday lettings business is a qualifying activity for the purposes of capital allowances on plant and machinery (see 9.24 CAPITAL ALLOWANCES). In contrast to furnished lettings generally, plant or machinery provided for use in a dwelling-house is not precluded, but the 10% wear and tear allowance in 69.7 above cannot be claimed as an alternative. All commercial lettings of furnished holiday accommodation by a particular person are treated as a single qualifying activity, separate from any other qualifying activity carried on by that person, e.g. a trade or the remainder of his Schedule A business.

Any necessary apportionments, where letting of accommodation qualifies only in part under these provisions, is on a just and reasonable basis.

Relief as at (i) above under *ICTA 1988, s 381* (see 46.10 LOSSES) is not available for a tax year if any of the accommodation concerned was first let by the same person as furnished accommodation more than three years before the beginning of that tax year. Loss may not be relieved both under (i) above and under any other relief provision. *ICTA 1988, s 384(6)–(8)* (restriction on relief for capital allowances etc. in a part-time letting trade, see 46.8(*c*) LOSSES) do not apply for these purposes.

The Revenue consider that the requirement under *section 381* that there be a reasonable expectation of profits in the period concerned or in a 'reasonable time thereafter' normally requires a reasonable and realistic expectation of profits emerging within five years from the date of commencement of furnished holiday letting activities. (Revenue Tax Bulletin October 1997 p 473).

'*Commercial letting*' is letting (whether or not under a lease) on a commercial basis and with a view to the realisation of profits, and accommodation is let '*furnished*' if the tenant is entitled to use of the furniture. For a case in which the 'commercial letting' test was satisfied despite a significant excess of interest over letting income, see *Walls v Livesey (Sp C 4), [1995] SSCD 12*, but see also *Brown v Richardson (Sp C 129), [1997] SSCD 233* in which the opposite conclusion was reached. See Revenue Tax Bulletin October 1997 pp 472, 473 for the Revenue view of the requirements in this respect.

'*Holiday accommodation*' is accommodation which

(*a*)   must be available for commercial letting to the public generally as holiday accommodation for at least 140 days in a twelve month period (see below), and

(*b*)   is so let at least 70 such days.

It must, however, not normally be in the same occupation for more than 31 consecutive days at any time during a period (although not necessarily a continuous period) of seven months in that twelve month period which includes any months in which it is let as in (*b*) above. The words 'in the same occupation' refer to tenants and do not prevent relief being due where the owner himself occupies the property outside the holiday season (Revenue Property Income Manual PIM 4110).

In the case of an individual or partnership, these conditions must be satisfied in the tax year in which the profits or gains arise, unless

(1)   the accommodation was not let furnished in the preceding tax year but is so let in the following tax year, in which case they must be satisfied in the twelve months from the date such letting commenced in the current tax year, or

(2)   the accommodation was let furnished in the preceding tax year but is not so let in the following tax year, in which case they must be satisfied in the twelve months ending with the date such letting ceased in the current tax year.

In the case of a company, the conditions must be satisfied in the twelve months ending on the last day of the accounting period in which the profits or gains arise, with similar variations as in (1) and (2) above where the accommodation was not let furnished in the twelve months preceding or following the period in question.

In satisfying the 70 day test (as above) averaging may be applied to letting periods of any or all of the accommodation let by the same person which would be holiday accommodation if it satisfied the 70 day test. A claim for averaging must be made within twelve months after 31 January following the tax year to which it is to apply. Only one such claim may be made in respect of accommodation in a tax year or accounting period.

69.9   Schedule A—Property Income

[*ICTA 1988, ss 503, 504; CAA 2001, ss 15, 17; CAA 1990, s 29; FA 1995, Sch 6 paras 21, 31; FA 1996, ss 134, 135, Sch 20 paras 30, 44, Sch 21 para 14; FA 1997, Sch 15 paras 2(2), 4, 9; FA 1998, s 38, Sch 5 paras 42, 51*].

Furnished holiday accommodation may include caravans (Revenue Press Release 17 May 1984).

See Tolley's Capital Gains Tax as regards relief from capital gains tax in respect of furnished holiday lettings.

Foot and mouth outbreak. For the full range of measures, including easing of restrictions on relief for furnished holiday lettings losses, in relation to the 2001 foot and mouth disease outbreak, see Revenue Tax Bulletin Special Edition May 2001.

Simon's Direct Tax Service. See **A4.108A.**

69.9   *Example*

Mr B owns and lets out furnished holiday cottages. None is ever let to the same person for more than 31 days. Three cottages have been owned for many years but Rose Cottage was acquired on 1 June 2004 (and first let on that day) while Ivy Cottage was sold on 30 June 2004 (and last let on that day).
In 2004/05, days available for letting and days let are as follows.

	Days available	Days let
Honeysuckle Cottage	180	160
Primrose Cottage	130	100
Bluebell Cottage	150	60
Rose Cottage	150	60
Ivy Cottage	30	5

Additional information

Rose Cottage was let for 30 days between 6 April and 31 May 2005.

Ivy Cottage was let for 50 days in the period 1 July 2003 to 5 April 2004 but was available for letting for 110 days in that period.

Qualification as 'furnished holiday accommodation'

Honeysuckle Cottage qualifies as it meets both the 140-day availability test and the 70-day letting test.

Primrose Cottage does *not* qualify although it is let for more than 70 days as it fails to satisfy the 140-day test. Averaging (see below) is only possible where it is the 70-day test which is not satisfied.

Bluebell Cottage does not qualify by itself as it fails the 70-day test. However it may be included in an averaging claim.

Rose Cottage qualifies as furnished holiday accommodation. It was acquired on 1 June 2004 so qualification in 2004/05 is determined by reference to the period of twelve months beginning on the day it was first let, in which it was let for a total of 90 days.

Ivy Cottage was sold on 30 June 2004 so qualification is determined by reference to the period from 1 July 2003 to 30 June 2004 (the last day of letting). It does not qualify by itself as it was let for only 55 days in this period but it may be included in an averaging claim.

Averaging claim for 2004/05

	Days let
Honeysuckle Cottage	160
Bluebell Cottage	60
Rose Cottage	90
Ivy Cottage	55

$$\frac{160 + 60 + 90 + 55}{4} = 91.25 \text{ days} \quad \text{note } (a)$$

Note

(*a*)   All four cottages included in the averaging claim qualify as furnished holiday accommodation as each is deemed to have been let for 91.25 days in the year 2004/05. If the average had been less than 70, any three of these cottages could have been included in an averaging claim leaving the other as non-qualifying. If this still did not produce the desired result, an average of any two could be tried. More than one averaging claim is possible for a tax year, but no cottage may be included in more than one claim.

69.10   **'Rent a room' relief for letting of rooms in private residence.** The taking in of domestic lodgers may be treated as the carrying on of a trade, where services other than accommodation are provided, or as furnished lettings.

A special relief applies to an individual receiving sums for the use of furnished accommodation in a 'qualifying residence' or residences, or for ancillary services consisting of the provision of meals, cleaning, laundry etc., in respect of all of which the individual would otherwise be chargeable to income tax under Schedule D, Case I and/or Schedule A. Unless the taxpayer elects otherwise (see below), and provided that the gross sums received (i.e. without any deduction for expenses) do not exceed the individual's limit for the year (see below), the profits or gains (or losses) of the basis period for the tax year are treated as nil. No plant and machinery capital allowances or balancing charges are made to or on the individual in relation to the letting of the accommodation. If, however, the addition of such balancing charges which would otherwise be made for the tax year to the gross sums received would result in the individual's limit for the year being exceeded, the exemption does not apply. An election for the exemption not to apply for a tax year must be made, and may be withdrawn, within twelve months after 31 January following that year (or such longer time as the Board may allow — see Revenue Property Income Manual PIM 4050) by written notice, and any necessary assessment is not out of time if made within twelve months after 31 January following the tax year in which the election was made (or withdrawal notice given). The exemption (and the further provisions described below) do not apply for a tax year for which the source(s) for income tax purposes of the gross sums concerned also include sums which are not within the reliefs.

Where the gross sums received exceed the individual's limit for the tax year, the individual may elect for the profits or gains of the basis period to be treated as equal to that excess. If the gross sums are treated for income tax purposes as arising from more than one source, the individual's limit is apportioned amongst those sources on the basis of the proportion of the gross sums taxable under each source. No plant and machinery capital allowances are made to the individual in relation to the letting of the accommodation. An election for this treatment to apply for a tax year must be made (and may be withdrawn) within twelve months after 31 January following that year (or such longer time as the Board may allow — see above) by written notice, and the election (or withdrawal) applies for all subsequent tax years (but, in the case of a withdrawal, without prejudicing the right to make a fresh election). Any necessary assessment is not out of time if made within twelve months after 31 January following the tax year in which the election was made (or withdrawal notice given). Where an election applies to a tax year for which the gross sums do *not* exceed the individual's limit, the individual is deemed to have withdrawn the election for that year and subsequent tax years (again without prejudicing the right to make a fresh election for a subsequent year).

A *'qualifying residence'* is a 'residence' which is the individual's only or main residence at any time in the basis period for the tax year in relation to the source in question. The furnished accommodation let within the qualifying residence may be in a self-contained flat provided that the division into a self-contained unit is only temporary (Revenue Property Income Manual PIM 4004).

'Residence' means a building (or part) occupied or intended to be occupied as a separate residence (ignoring any temporary division into separate residences of a building (or part) designed for permanent use as a single residence), or a caravan or house-boat.

'Rent a room' relief will not normally be available to taxpayers who are living abroad (or in job-related accommodation) and letting their home while they are away; this applies even in the years of departure and return since the property will not normally have been their residence at any time during the basis periods for those years. If, however, the letting commences *before* departure and/or ceases *after* return, relief may then be due for the year of departure and/or return. (Revenue Property Income Manual PIM 4010, 4015).

The individual's limit for a tax year is **£4,250** (or such sum as may be specified by Treasury order), but is reduced to one-half of that amount in certain cases where sums accrue to another person in respect of use of furnished accommodation in the individual's only or main residence or in respect of services ancillary (as above) to that use.

[*F(No 2)A 1992, s 59, Sch 10; FA 1995, Sch 6 para 38; FA 1996, s 135, Sch 21 para 47; CAA 2001, Sch 2 para 86; SI 1996 No 2953*].

The Revenue consider that 'rent a room' relief is inapplicable to the letting of a residence (or part) as an office or for other trade or business purposes (other than the business of providing furnished living accommodation) (Revenue Tax Bulletin August 1994 p 154).

Simon's Direct Tax Service. See A4.108B.

69.11   *Example*

Emily and Charlotte are single persons sharing a house as their main residence. They have for some years taken in lodgers to supplement their income. As Emily pays the greater share of the mortgage interest on the house, she and Charlotte have an agreement to share the rental income in the ratio 2:1, although expenses are shared equally.

For the year ended 5 April 1999, gross rents amounted to £5,700 and allowable expenses were £1,100. In the year ended 5 April 2000, the pair face a heavy repair bill after uninsured damage to one of the rooms. Gross rents for that year amount to £3,600 and expenses to £4,400. For the years ended 5 April 2001 and 2002, gross rents are £6,600 and expenses £2,200, and for the year ended 5 April 2003 they are £6,000 and £2,500 respectively. For the year ended 5 April 2004, they are £8,100 and £4,500 respectively. For the year ended 5 April 2005, they are £9,000 and £3,000 respectively.

For 1998/99, the position is as follows

Normal Schedule A computation

	Emily	Charlotte
	£	£
Gross rents (y/e 5.4.99)	3,800	1,900
Allowable expenses	550	550
Net rents	£3,250	£1,350

Charlotte's share of *gross* rents is less than her one half share (£2,125) of the basic amount (£4,250). It is assumed that she would not make the election under *F(No 2)A 1992, Sch 10 para 10* for the exemption under *Sch 10 para 9* ('rent a room' relief) not to apply. Her share of net rents is thus treated as nil.

Emily's share of gross rents exceeds £2,125, so the exemption in *Sch 10 para 9* cannot apply. She can, however, elect under *Sch 10 para 12* for *Sch 10 para 11* to apply. Under *Sch 10 para 11*, she is taxed on the excess of *gross* rents over £2,125. It is assumed that she will make the election as she will then be taxed on £1,675 rather than £3,250.

For 1999/2000, the position is as follows

Normal Schedule A computation

	Emily	Charlotte
	£	£
Gross rents (y/e 5.4.2000)	2,400	1,200
Allowable expenses	2,200	2,200
Net rents/(loss)	£200	£(1,000)

Charlotte's share of gross rents continues to be less than her one half share of the basic amount. Under *Sch 10 para 9*, her share of net rents will be treated as nil. However, she will obtain no relief, by carry-forward or otherwise, for her loss. In order to preserve her loss, she could elect under *Sch 10 para 10* for *Sch 10 para 9* not to apply, the election having effect for 1999/2000 only.

Emily's share of gross rents exceeds her one half share of the basic amount. Therefore, her previous election under *Sch 10 para 12* will not automatically be deemed to be withdrawn. She will be taxed under *Sch 10 para 11* on £275 (£2,400 – £2,125). However, this is greater than the amount taxable on a normal Schedule A computation (£200), so it is assumed she would withdraw the election with effect for 1999/2000 and subsequent years. The notice of withdrawal does not prejudice the making of a fresh election for 2000/01 or any subsequent year.

For 2000/01, the position is as follows

Normal Schedule A computation

	Emily	Charlotte
	£	£
Gross rents (y/e 5.4.01)	4,400	2,200
Allowable expenses	1,100	1,100
Net rents	£3,300	£1,100

Charlotte's share of gross rents now exceeds her share of the basic amount, so the exemption will not apply. She could elect for *Sch 10 para 11* to apply, and her chargeable income will then be reduced to £75 (£2,200 – £2,125). This is further reduced to nil by the bringing forward of her £1,000 loss for 1999/2000. (Although a loss cannot enter into the ascertaining of the amount chargeable under *Sch 10 para 11*, there appears to be no reason why a loss cannot be set off against the amount so ascertained.) If Charlotte did not make the election, her chargeable income would be £100 with the whole of her 1999/2000 loss having been utilised.

Emily can make a fresh election for *Sch 10 para 11* to apply, with effect from 2000/01, and she will then be taxed on £2,275 (£4,400 – £2,125).

For 2001/02, the position is as follows.

The normal Schedule A computation is as for 2000/01. Assuming Emily and Charlotte both elected under *Sch 10 para 11* for 2000/01, the elections will continue to apply for 2001/02, so that their respective chargeable incomes under Schedule A are £2,275 and £75. Charlotte's chargeable income is reduced to nil by the brought forward balance of £925 of the 1999/2000 loss (of which the balance of £850 is carried forward to 2002/03).

For 2002/03, the position is as follows.

Normal Schedule A computation

	Emily	Charlotte
	£	£
Gross rents (y/e 5.4.03)	4,000	2,000
Allowable expenses	1,250	1,250
Net rents	£2,750	£750

Charlotte's share of gross rents is now below her one-half share of the basic amount, so that the election under *Sch 10 para 11* is deemed to have been withdrawn, and under *Sch 10 para 9* her share is treated as nil (assuming no election under *Sch 10 para 10*). The balance of £850 of her 1999/2000 loss is carried forward to 2003/04. Emily's election under *Sch 10 para 11* will continue to apply (unless withdrawn), so that her chargeable income under Schedule A will be £1,875 (£4,000 – £2,125).

For 2003/04, the position is as follows.

Normal Schedule A computation

	Emily	Charlotte
	£	£
Gross rents (y/e 5.4.04)	5,400	2,700
Allowable expenses	2,250	2,250
Net rents	£3,150	£450

For both Emily and Charlotte their share of gross rents now exceeds their share of the basic amount, so that the exemption will not apply, and since their share of the expenses also exceeds their share of the basic amount, the election under *Sch 10 para 11* will be unfavourable. It is therefore assumed that Emily withdraws her election (by 31 January 2006). They are accordingly both charged to tax on the basis of the normal Schedule A computation, with Charlotte's £850 loss brought forward being set against her share, the balance of £400 being carried forward to 2004/05.

For 2004/05, the position is as follows.

Normal Schedule A computation

	Emily £	Charlotte £
Gross rents (y/e 5.4.05)	6,000	3,000
Allowable expenses	1,500	1,500
Net rents	£4,500	£1,500

Both could now elect for *Sch 10 para 11* to apply (by 31 January 2007). Emily's chargeable income will be reduced to £3,875 (£6,000 – £2,125) and Charlotte's to £875 (£3,000 – £2,125). Charlotte's is further reduced to £475 by the balance of her 1999/2000 loss brought forward.

69.12   **LOSSES**

Carry-forward. Where a loss (a '*Schedule A loss*'), computed in like manner as Schedule A profits, is incurred by any person in a Schedule A business, carried on alone or in partnership, it is carried forward without time limit as a set-off against the first following profits of the business, or, if insufficient, the next, and so on. [*ICTA 1988, s 379A(1)(7); FA 1995, Sch 6 para 19(1)*].

Set-off against other income. Where a Schedule A loss is incurred in a tax year (the year of loss) and as regards that year,

(*a*)   there is a net amount of capital allowances, (i.e. capital allowances exceed any balancing charges), *and/or*

(*b*)   the Schedule A business has been carried on in relation to land which consists of or includes an 'agricultural estate' to which 'allowable agricultural expenses' (see below) are attributable,

a claim may be made under *ICTA 1988, s 379A(3)* to set an amount of loss relief against total income for the year of loss or the following year. The amount of loss relief is restricted to the lowest of the following:

(i)   the loss,

(ii)   the 'relievable income' for the year to which the claim relates, and

(iii)   the net capital allowances (where (*a*) above applies) or the allowable agricultural expenses (where (*b*) applies) or the sum of those two items (where *both* (*a*) and (*b*) apply).

Relief cannot normally be claimed for both years in respect of the same loss, but where relief is restricted for one year by virtue of (ii) above, the balance (i.e. the excess of the lower of (i) and (iii) above over the relief given) may be claimed for the other year. A person's '*relievable income*' is his total income after taking into account any Schedule A loss brought forward under *ICTA 1988, s 379A(1)* (see above) from a year prior to the year of loss and, where the claim relates to the year of loss, after giving effect to any *section 379A(3)* claim in respect of a loss for the preceding year. A loss carried forward under *section 379A(1)* from the year of loss is restricted or extinguished by relief given for that loss under *section 379A(3)*.

A claim under *section 379A(3)* must be made within 12 months after 31 January following *the year to which the claim relates*, and must be accompanied by any necessary amendments to the claimant's tax return (including self-assessment) for that year.

An *'agricultural estate'* (see (*b*) above) means any land (including any houses or other buildings) which is managed as one estate and which consists of or includes any agricultural land, i.e. land in the UK occupied wholly or mainly for husbandry. *'Allowable agricultural expenses'* (see (*b*) above) are any deductible disbursements or expenses attributable to the agricultural estate in respect of maintenance, repairs, insurance or estate management (but excluding loan interest). For these purposes, disbursements and expenses are taken into account only to the extent that they are attributable to the parts of it used for husbandry, with those attributable to parts used partly for other purposes being proportionately reduced.

[*ICTA 1988, s 379A(2)–(10); FA 1995, Sch 6 para 19(1)(4); FA 1997, Sch 15 paras 2(1), 9; FA 2001, s 88, Sch 29 para 35(2)*].

Simon's Direct Tax Service. See A4.410.

Application to overseas property business. The provisions of *ICTA 1988, s 379A* apply equally to an overseas property business (see 73.4 SCHEDULE D, CASES IV AND V which also covers the position for unrelieved losses carried forward at 5 April 1998). [*ICTA 1988, s 379B; FA 1998, s 38, Sch 5 para 27*].

69.13   **NON-RESIDENT LANDLORDS—COLLECTION FROM AGENTS OR TENANTS**

Where a landlord is non-resident (i.e. his usual place of abode is outside the UK), tax is to be deducted at source by the agent for the property or, where there is no agent, the tenant, with a final settling up with the non-resident landlord. [*ICTA 1988, s 42A; FA 1995, s 40(1)–(3)(8); FA 1998, s 38, Sch 5 para 22, Sch 27 Pt III(4)*]. The regulations giving effect to these requirements provide broadly as follows.

(i)   Letting agents who receive or have control over UK property income of a non-resident must operate the scheme.

(ii)   Where there is no letting agent acting, tenants of a non-resident must operate the scheme.

(iii) Tenants who pay less than £100 per week do not have to operate the scheme unless asked to do so by the Revenue.

(iv)   Letting agents and tenants who have to operate the scheme must pay tax at the basic rate each quarter on the non-resident's UK property income less certain allowable expenses and deductions, and must give the non-resident an annual certificate showing details of tax deducted.

(v)   Non-residents whose property income is subject to deduction of tax may set the tax deducted against their UK tax liability through their self-assessment.

(vi)   Non-residents may apply to the Revenue for approval to receive their UK property income without deduction of tax provided that:

(*a*)   their UK tax affairs are up to date;

(*b*)   they have never had any obligations in relation to UK tax; or

(*c*)   they do not expect to be liable to UK income tax,

and that they undertake to comply with all their UK tax obligations in the future. An appeal may be made against refusal or withdrawal of approval.

The regulations also make provision for interest on unpaid tax and for payments on account under self-assessment, and set out details of the annual information requirements on those operating the scheme, and of other information to be supplied on request. Penalties apply under *TMA 1970, s 98* for non-compliance with these return and information provisions.

[*ICTA 1988, s 42A(4)–(7); FA 1995, s 40(2); SI 1995 No 2902*].

The Revenue have issued detailed guidance notes for those required to operate the scheme. See also Revenue Pamphlet IR 140 'Non-resident landlords, their agents and tenants' and Revenue Tax Bulletin December 1995 pp 261–263.

Simon's Direct Tax Service. See A4.503.

69.14   APPORTIONMENT OF RECEIPTS AND OUTGOINGS ON SALE OF LAND

Where a property is purchased or sold during the year, income or expenditure before contract, or between contract and completion, which is apportioned to the purchaser is treated as having been received or paid by him immediately after completion. Similarly, where part of a receipt or payment after completion is apportioned to the vendor that part is treated as if he had received or paid it in the period immediately before completion, and the purchaser is relieved accordingly. [*ICTA 1988, s 40; FA 1995, Sch 6 para 4(f); FA 1998, s 38, Sch 5 para 20, Sch 27 Pt III(4)*].

69.15   INFORMATION RE LEASES

Information, including consideration for their grant or assignment etc., may be required, under penalty, from present or former lessees or occupiers, or from agents managing property or receiving rents etc. [*TMA 1970, ss 19, 98; FA 1988, s 123(4)*].

69.16   PREMIUMS ETC. ON LEASES OF UP TO 50 YEARS —RECIPIENT'S TAX POSITION [*ICTA 1988, ss 34–39; FA 1995, Sch 6 paras 9–12; FA 1998, ss 38, 40, Sch 5 paras 15–18*]

Premiums. A premium receivable by the landlord (or by another person, see Note (ii) below) under a lease of land in the UK not exceeding 50 years, or otherwise under the terms subject to which a lease is granted, is treated as additional rent, received at the date the lease is granted, equivalent to the amount of the premium less $\frac{1}{50}$th for each full year (minus one) in the lease's duration (e.g. if the lease is for 10 years, $\frac{41}{50}$ths of any premium will be chargeable). An amount so treated is taken into account in full in computing Schedule A profits for the tax year in which it is treated as received (but see Note (iii) below). [*ICTA 1988, s 34(1)(7A); FA 1998, Sch 5 para 15(5)*, and see Note (ii) below]. For this purpose, where under the terms of the lease the tenant is required to carry out work on the premises (other than normal repairs or maintenance) the value of the benefit accruing to the landlord is treated as a premium receivable at the commencement of the lease. Similarly, any sum payable by the tenant (*a*) for varying or waiving any of the terms of a lease, or (*b*), under the terms of the lease, for surrendering it, or in lieu of the whole or part of the rent, is treated as if it were a premium (received, under (*a*), at the date of the contract for variation or, under (*b*), when the sum is payable) on a lease for the period affected by the variation etc. [*ICTA 1988, ss 34(2)–(5); FA 1995, Sch 6 paras 9, 40(1); FA 1998, s 40(3)–(5), Sch 5 para 15(3)*]. Note that these provisions refer to leases granted and not to leases assigned. See *Banning v Wright* under 69.17 below. Also see 3.12 ANTI-AVOIDANCE concerning *ICTA 1988, s 780*, and under 71.56 SCHEDULE D, CASES I AND II.

Example (i):

A person grants a 14-year lease of premises for a premium of £50,000. The amount chargeable on him in that year is

69.16 Schedule A—Property Income

	£
Premium	50,000
Less $\dfrac{14-1}{50} \times 50,000$	13,000
Chargeable	£37,000

Note. Only complete years are taken into account. For allowance to payer, see 69.17 below.

But where a lease etc., which gave rise to a liability as above (or would have done so but for relief as under Note (iii) below, or any exemption) is **subleased or sold,** any potential further liability on that latter event is compared with a fraction of the liability on the first transaction (proportionate to the period covered by the sublease etc., as compared with that covered by the first lease etc., with adjustment where the sub-lease relates to part only of the property) and only any *excess* is chargeable. [*ICTA 1988, s 37(1)–(3)(7); FA 1990, Sch 14 para 2; FA 1995, Sch 6 para 12; FA 1998, Sch 5 para 18, Sch 27 Pt III(4)*].

Example (ii):

If, after 4 years, the payer of the premium in (*i*) above grants a sub-lease of 10 years for which he receives a premium of £60,000, the amount chargeable on him is

	£
Premium	60,000
Less $\dfrac{10-1}{50} \times 60,000$	10,800
	49,200
Less 'appropriate fraction' of amount chargeable on superior landlord (see (*i*) above): $\frac{10}{14} \times £37,000$	26,428
Chargeable	£22,772

For these purposes, the amount chargeable on the superior landlord is calculated ignoring any obligation on the tenant to carry out work on the premises in respect of which capital allowances have been or will be granted.

See also 69.17 below as regards relief where the 'appropriate fraction' of the amount chargeable on the superior landlord exceeds the amount of the premium chargeable on the intermediate landlord.

Anti-avoidance provisions. Where a lease granted at less than market value is assigned for a consideration exceeding any premium for which it was granted (or the consideration on any previous assignment) the excess, up to the limit of the amount of any premium, or additional premium, which the grantor forwent when granting the lease, is charged on the assignor to the same extent that an additional premium would have been charged on the grantor. The amount chargeable is treated as received when the consideration becomes payable and is taken into account in computing Schedule A profits for the tax year in which that time falls. [*ICTA 1988, s 35; FA 1995, Sch 6 para 10; FA 1998, Sch 5 para 16*].

Similarly, where an interest in land is sold on terms requiring it to be subsequently reconveyed (or leased, later than one month after the sale) to the vendor, or a person connected with him, and the price at which the interest is sold exceeds that at which it is to be reconveyed (or, in the case of a lease-back, the value of the reversionary interest plus any premium for the lease), the excess less $\frac{1}{50}$th for each full year (minus one) between the sale and the date (if at least two years after the sale) of the earliest possible reconveyance (or lease-back) is treated, at the time of sale (as defined), as a receipt of a Schedule A business carried on by the vendor. [*ICTA 1988, s 36; FA 1995, Sch 6 para 11; FA 1998, Sch 5 para 17*]. For the so-called 'Treasury Arrangement' to avoid a charge under *ICTA 1988, s 36* where there is a genuine commercial reason for the restricted sale, see Revenue Assessment Procedures Manual AP 1560. See also 3.12 ANTI-AVOIDANCE.

Notes on above.

(i)   For the above purposes the duration of a lease is governed by *ICTA 1988, s 38, Sch 30 paras 2–4*, and the tenant's rights of extension, or entitlement to a further lease, may be taken into account.

(ii)   Where a premium, payment in lieu of rent or for surrender, is payable to a person other than the landlord, or where a payment for variation is due not to the landlord but to some person connected with him, the receipt is treated as a receipt of a Schedule A business (see 69.3 above) carried on by the recipient. [*ICTA 1988, s 34(6)(7); FA 1995, Sch 6 para 9; FA 1998, Sch 5 para 15(4)*].

(iii)   Where any premium etc., is receivable by instalments the recipient may, at his option, pay the tax by instalments over a period not exceeding eight years (or the period during which the premium instalments are receivable if less). [*ICTA 1988, s 34(8); FA 1998, Sch 5 para 15(6)*].

(iv)   See Tolley's Capital Gains Tax for the treatment of chargeable gains arising from disposal by way of a lease. Note particularly that the part of the premium chargeable to income tax is omitted from the computation of the chargeable gain.

Simon's Direct Tax Service. See A4.2.

69.17   **PREMIUMS ETC. ON LEASES OF UP TO 50 YEARS — ALLOWANCE TO PAYER** [*ICTA 1988, ss 37, 87; FA 1995, Sch 6 paras 12, 14; FA 1998, s 38, Sch 5 paras 18, 34*]

See generally Revenue Property Income Manual PIM 2300–2340.

Where a premium paid on the grant of a lease etc. falls to be included in computing Schedule A profits of the recipient (see 69.16 above), or would have done so but for exemption etc., the person for the time being entitled to that lease etc., is treated as paying additional rent at a rate equivalent to the amount of that charge spread over the period to which it relates. See example below. In *Banning v Wright HL 1972, 48 TC 421* an agreed payment for waiving termination for sub-letting in breach of covenant was held to be a premium deductible from rents received. Adjustments arise in respect of sub-leases of the whole or part of the property.

The 'additional rent' so ascertained is allowable against property income, e.g. on a sub-letting [*ICTA 1988, s 37; FA 1995, Sch 6 para 12; FA 1998, s 38, Sch 5 para 18*] or against profits if the property is used in connection with a trade, profession or vocation. [*ICTA 1988, s 87; FA 1995, Sch 6 para 14; FA 1998, s 38, Sch 5 para 34*].

Example: For a premium paid as in example (i) in 69.16 above, the 'additional rent' is $\frac{1}{14}$th of £37,000 which is £2,643 per annum (allocated on a daily basis). If, however, a sub-lease is granted for a premium (as in example (ii) in 69.16 above) the 'additional rent' is restricted to the 'appropriate fraction' not used to reduce the charge on that later premium. In the example, the 'appropriate fraction' is entirely used and no 'additional rent' is available.

Anti-avoidance provision. Relief under *ICTA 1988, s 37* or *s 87* will not be allowed in respect of any amount which has become chargeable under *ICTA 1988, s 36* (see 69.16

above). [*ICTA 1988, s 37(1)(a), s 87(1)(a); FA 1995, Sch 6 paras 12, 14; FA 1998, s 38, Sch 5 paras 18, 34*].

Simon's Direct Tax Service. See **A4.221** *et seq*.

69.18 REVERSE PREMIUMS

Legislation (*FA 1999, s 54, Sch 6*) has been introduced to ensure that reverse premiums are taxable as revenue receipts. It applies in relation to any 'reverse premium' (as defined but broadly a payment made or benefit provided by a landlord to a prospective tenant as an inducement to enter into a lease) due and received on or after 9 March 1999. Other than in cases where the transaction is entered into for purposes of the recipient's trade etc. (or prospective trade etc.), a reverse premium is to be treated as a receipt of a Schedule A business, or (as the case may be) an overseas property business (see 73.4 SCHEDULE D, CASES IV AND V), carried on by the recipient. Subject to a specific anti-avoidance rule, it is understood that accountancy principles require the receipt to be brought into account by spreading over the period of the lease or, if shorter, to the first rent review. See 71.68 SCHEDULE D, CASES I AND II for the full provisions, and also the Revenue's views on the treatment of reverse premiums due before 9 March 1999.

69.19 RENT FACTORING

ICTA 1988, ss 43A–43G, introduced by *FA 2000, s 110*, apply from 21 March 2000 to companies participating in rent factoring schemes. They provide for amounts received for giving up the right to future rental income from UK land, whether by transferring the rights to receive rents or by granting a lease at a premium, to be charged to tax as income of a Schedule A business. They do not apply to genuine property investment or to capital allowance based finance leasing. For details of the legislation, see Tolley's Corporation Tax under Profit Computations.

Rent factoring of leases of plant or machinery. Where, after 1 July 2004, a person arranges to transfer his right to receive taxable rentals under a lease of plant or machinery for consideration all or some of which is neither chargeable (to income tax or corporation tax) as income nor liable to be treated as a disposal receipt for plant and machinery capital allowances purposes, the otherwise non-taxable consideration is taxable as rental income by reference to the period(s) of account in which it is receivable. A transfer of a right to receive rentals includes any arrangement that results in the rental receipts otherwise ceasing to be taxed as income, and 'lease' is widely defined to include, for example, an underlease, sublease, tenancy or licence. [*ICTA 1988, s 785A; FA 2004, s 135*].

69.20 SCHEDULE A ALLOWANCE ON SALE OF TRADING PREMISES — TRANSITIONAL

Where a trader occupied property before 6 April 1963 for the purpose of his trade, profession or vocation and subsequently sells that property, or otherwise ceases to occupy it, he will normally be entitled (unless he permanently ceases to carry on the trade) to a special deduction from his profits amounting to the excess of the net annual value deductions for the years 1963/64 and 1964/65 to which he would have been entitled but for the Schedule A charge in *FA 1963* over certain deductions actually made for those years. [*ICTA 1988, Sch 30 para 5*].

70 Schedule C—Paying and Collecting Agents

[ICTA 1988, ss 17, 44–52, Sch 3; FA 1996, s 79, Sch 7]

70.1 For **1995/96 and earlier years** (and for company accounting periods ending before 1 April 1996), **Schedule C** applied to paying agents (bankers and others) entrusted with the payment in the UK of 'interest, public annuities, dividends or shares of annuities' out of the public revenue of any government and the revenue of any public authority or institution outside UK. [*ICTA 1988, s 17(1) para 1, s 45*]. The agents had to deduct tax and pay the net amount to the persons entitled to the interest etc.

Schedule C is abolished for 1996/97 and subsequent years of assessment and for company accounting periods ending after 31 March 1996, the charge being transferred to Schedule D, Case III, IV or V as appropriate. [*ICTA 1988, s 18(3B)–(3E); FA 1996, s 79, Sch 7, Sch 14 para 5*]. For the provisions for paying and collecting agents effective from that date until 31 March 2001, see *ICTA 1988, ss 118A–118K* and regulations thereunder (see *SI 1996 No 1780, SI 1997 No 2705, SI 1999 No 823*). For an article explaining the scope of these rules, see Revenue Tax Bulletin August 1996 p 329. The paying and collecting arrangements are abolished from 1 April 2001. [*FA 2000, s 111(1)(6)*]. See now 22.3(ii), 22.12 DEDUCTION OF TAX AT SOURCE.

71 Schedule D, Cases I and II—Profits of Trades, Professions etc.

Cross-references. See subjects dealt with separately under 3 ANTI-AVOIDANCE; 9 CAPITAL ALLOW-ANCES; 11 CASH BASIS; 24 DOUBLE TAX RELIEF; 34 HERD BASIS; 43 INTEREST PAYABLE; 44 INTEREST RECEIVABLE; 46 LOSSES; 51 NON-RESIDENTS AND OTHER OVERSEAS MATTERS; 53 PARTNERSHIPS; 56 PAYMENT OF TAX; 61 PERSONAL SERVICE COMPANIES ETC.; 62 POST-CESSATION ETC. RECEIPTS AND EXPENDITURE; 78 SELF-ASSESSMENT and 94 WOODLANDS.

For 'Whether a Trade Carried On', see 71.19–71.29 below and for 'Chargeable Income and Allowable Deductions', see 71.30–71.84 below. There is a sub-index preceding each of these divisions.

The headings in this chapter are as follows.

71.1 CHARGE TO TAX

Tax is charged under **Schedule D, Case I and II** on the profits or gains of trades (Case I) and professions or vocations (Case II) carried on wholly or partly in the UK by UK residents or exercised within the UK by non-residents. [*ICTA 1988, s 18*]. Businesses carried on wholly abroad are 'possessions' within SCHEDULE D, CASES IV AND V (73) but a business controlled from the UK is within Cases I and II even though the day-to-day trading activities are carried on wholly abroad. For this see 51.11 NON-RESIDENTS AND OTHER OVERSEAS MATTERS and for trades exercised within the UK by non-residents see 51.3 NON-RESIDENTS AND OTHER OVERSEAS MATTERS.

Trade 'includes every trade, manufacture, adventure or concern in the nature of trade' [*ICTA 1988, s 832(1)*]. For what is a trade, see generally 71.19–71.29 below and in particular, in relation to isolated or speculative transactions, 71.25 below. For a discussion on the *scope* of a trade, see Revenue Business Income Manual BIM 21000–21040. There is no statutory definition of 'profession or vocation'. There are certain provisions applicable only to trades and others applicable only to professions or vocations but the distinction between the two is of limited practical importance. There is no reported case in which it was necessary to decide between the two for income tax purposes, but in a Hong Kong case it was held that stockbrokers were carrying on a trade, not a profession or business (*Kowloon Stock Exchange Ltd v Commr of Inland Revenue PC, [1984] STC 602*). There are a number of cases turning on whether a business was an exempt profession as specially defined for the purposes of excess profits duty and similar taxes. For these see Tolley's Tax Cases. For professions or vocations (e.g. actor) which necessarily involve carrying out numerous engagements see 71.33 below and 75.27 SCHEDULE E—EMPLOYMENT INCOME.

In the rest of this chapter 'trade' includes 'profession or vocation' unless the context indicates otherwise and similarly Case I includes Case II.

For whether the liability is under Schedule D or as employment income see 75.27 SCHEDULE E—EMPLOYMENT INCOME. See also 71.21 below for special treatment of certain divers and diving supervisors.

The Schedules are mutually exclusive, see 5.1 ASSESSMENTS. The general principle is that rents and other income derived from the exploitation of proprietary interests in land are within Schedule A and not income derived from a trade. The leading case is *Salisbury House Estate Ltd v Fry HL 1930, 15 TC 266*. For illustrations see *Sywell Aerodrome Ltd v Croft CA 1941, 24 TC 126*; *Webb v Conelee Properties Ltd Ch D 1982, 56 TC 149*. However, profits arising out of land are charged under Case I in the case of mines, quarries, gravel pits, sand pits, brickfields, ironworks, gas works, canals, railways, rights of markets, fairs and tolls and like concerns. *[ICTA 1988, s 55]*. Farming and market gardening within the UK is treated as trading. *[ICTA 1988, s 53(1)]*. All the farming carried on by a particular person, partnership or body of persons is treated as one trade *[ICTA 1988, s 53(2)]* (*Bispham v Eardiston Farming Co Ch D 1962, 40 TC 322*) but this does not apply to farming outside the UK (*Sargent v Eayrs Ch D 1972, 48 TC 573*). See 94 WOODLANDS for the exemption of woodlands managed on a commercial basis.

71.2   COMPANIES

Companies (and other bodies corporate, unincorporated associations and authorised unit trusts — but not partnerships, local authorities or local authority associations *[ICTA 1988, s 832(1)(2)]*) are assessable to corporation tax on their trading income as computed under the law and practice applying to Schedule D, Case I or II. *[ICTA 1988, s 9]*. The provisions below, from 71.19 onwards (relating to chargeable income, allowable deductions and other Schedule D, Case I and II matters) apply generally to companies etc. Items 71.3–71.14 below referring to the current year basis of assessment and the opening/closing year and change of accounting date provisions do not apply to companies etc. See 71.15 below for 'notional' commencements or cessations by companies. See generally Tolley's Corporation Tax.

71.3   INDIVIDUALS — CURRENT YEAR BASIS OF ASSESSMENT

The basis period rules set out in detail in 71.4–71.11 below (the current year basis of assessment) apply for 1996/97 and subsequent years as regards businesses commenced before 6 April 1994 (see 71.12–71.14 below for transitional provisions on the changeover from the preceding year basis of assessment). They apply from the outset to businesses commenced after 5 April 1994. *[FA 1994, s 218(1)(2)(5)]*. The current year basis of assessment has no application to a partnership as an entity in itself but does apply to individual partners in the same way as to sole traders (see 53.3 PARTNERSHIPS).

Businesses commenced before 6 April 1994 were on a preceding year basis of assessment for all years up to and including 1995/96. See the 2003/04 and earlier editions for the detailed rules.

A detailed Revenue booklet SAT 1(1995) 'The new current year basis of assessment — A guide for Inland Revenue officers and tax practitioners' should have been sent by tax offices to all tax practices with which they deal in August/September 1995. Further copies were available (price £7.50) from Inland Revenue Library, New Wing, Somerset House, Strand,

London WC2R 1LB. Also, a series of explanatory articles on self-assessment appeared in the Revenue Tax Bulletin from August 1993 onwards, many of which illustrated different aspects of the current year basis.

In summary the basis periods are generally as follows (subject to any change of accounting date — see 71.7 below).

Opening years (see 71.4 below)

Year 1   Actual

Year 2   12 months ending with the accounting date in the year or, if the period from commencement to the accounting date in the year is less than 12 months, the first 12 months or, if there is no accounting date in the first or second year, actual

Year 3   Normally current year basis (see 71.4 below for exception)

See 71.11 below for relief (overlap relief) where the above rules have the effect of the same profits being taxed in each of two successive years of assessment.

Intermediate years (see 71.6 below)

Current year basis.

Closing year (see 71.9 below)

Period from the end of the basis period in the penultimate year to the date of cessation in the year (which may exceed 12 months).

General. Current year basis normally means that the assessment is based on the profits shown by the annual accounts ended within the current tax year.

Power is given to apportion profits or losses, on a time basis in proportion to the number of days in the respective periods, if required for purpose of assessments under Cases I and II. [*ICTA 1988, s 72; FA 1995, s 121*]. This applies only where such time apportionment is necessary (see *Marshall Hus & Partners Ltd v Bolton Ch D 1980, 55 TC 539*) and only to the *extent* that it is necessary (see *Lyons v Kelly (Sp C 334), [2002] SSCD 455*). In practice, the Revenue will accept any reasonable time-based apportionment that is applied consistently. If the taxpayer wishes, they will treat an accounting date of 31 March as being equivalent to one of 5 April (Revenue booklet SAT 1(1995), paras 1.17, 1.98, 1.99).

Simon's Direct Tax Service. See **E1.203, E1.205–E1.212**.

71.4   **Opening years.** On the **commencement of a business** by an individual (which includes his commencing to carry on an existing business in partnership), the following rules apply. As to what constitutes a commencement etc. see 71.15 below.

First tax year. The assessment will be on the profits (as adjusted for tax purposes) from the commencement date to the following 5 April. [*ICTA 1988, s 61(1); FA 1994, s 201*].

Second tax year. If there is an accounting date (i.e. a date to which accounts are made up) in the year, the assessment is based on the twelve months to that date. If the period from commencement to the accounting date in the second year is less than twelve months, the assessment is based on the profits for the first twelve months of the business. If there is no accounting date in the first or second year, the second year's assessment will be on the actual profits for the year, i.e. 6 April to 5 April. Where there is more than one accounting date in the year, reference to the accounting date in the year is to the latest of such dates (see also the rules for changes of accounting date in 71.7 below). [*ICTA 1988, s 60(1)(2)(3)(a)(5), s 61(2)(a); FA 1994, ss 200, 201*].

Third tax year. If the year is the first year in which there is an accounting date falling not less than twelve months after the date of commencement, the assessment is based on the twelve months ending with the accounting date. Otherwise, the rule for intermediate years (see 71.6 below) applies as regards the third year. [*ICTA 1988, s 60(1)–(3); FA 1994, s 200*].

See 71.11 below for relief (overlap relief) where the above rules have the effect of the same profits being taxed in each of two successive years of assessment.

Simon's Direct Tax Service. See **E1.205–E1.209.**

71.5   *Example*

Owen commences trade on 1 September 2003 and prepares accounts to 30 April, starting with an eight-month period of account to 30 April 2004. His profits (as adjusted for tax purposes) for the first three accounting periods are as follows.

	£
Eight months to 30 April 2004	24,000
Year to 30 April 2005	39,000
Year to 30 April 2006	40,000

His taxable profits for the first four tax years are as follows.

	Basis period		£	£
2003/04	1.9.03 – 5.4.04	£24,000 × $\frac{7}{8}$		21,000
2004/05	1.9.03 – 31.8.04:			
	1.9.03 – 30.4.04		24,000	
	1.5.04 – 31.8.04	£39,000 × $\frac{4}{12}$	13,000	
				37,000
2005/06	Y/e 30.4.05			39,000
2006/07	Y/e 30.4.06			40,000

Overlap relief accrued:	
1.9.03 – 5.4.04 — 7 months	21,000
1.5.04 – 31.8.04 — 4 months	13,000
Total overlap relief accrued (see 71.11 below)	£34,000

71.6   **Intermediate years** (i.e. tax years for which the special rules for Opening Years, as in 71.4 above, or for the Closing Year, see 71.9 below, do not apply).

Assessment on individuals (including those trading in partnership) is on the current year basis, i.e. the profits (as adjusted for tax purposes) of the trading account ending in the current tax year (subject to any change of accounting date — see 71.7 below). [*ICTA 1988, s 60(1)(2)(3)(b); FA 1994, s 200*].

71.7   **Change of accounting date.** Where a change (an accounting change) from one accounting date (the old date) to another (the new date) is made in a year of assessment, the conditions below must be satisfied if the change of accounting date is to result in a change of basis period. (This does not apply if the year is the second or third year of assessment of the business.) An accounting change is made in a year of assessment if accounts are not made up to the old date in that year or are made up to the new date in that year. The conditions, *all of which must be satisfied*, are as follows.

71.7 Schedule D, Cases I and II—Profits of Trades etc.

(1) The first accounting period (i.e. period for which accounts are made up) ending with the new date does not exceed 18 months.

(2) Notice of the change is given to an officer of the Board in a personal (or, where appropriate, a partnership) tax return on or before the day on which that return is required to be delivered (see 68.2, 68.13 RETURNS).

(3) Either

    (i) no accounting change resulting in a change of basis period has been made in any of the previous five years of assessment;

    or

    (ii) the notice in (2) above sets out the reasons for the change and the Revenue do not, within 60 days of receiving the notice, give notice to the trader that they are not satisfied that the change is made for *bona fide* commercial reasons (which does not include the obtaining of a tax advantage). (An appeal may be made against such a Revenue notice, within 30 days beginning with the date of issue, and the Commissioners may either confirm the notice or set it aside.)

Where all the conditions are satisfied, or the accounting change is made in the second or third tax year of the business, the basis period for the year of assessment is as follows.

(*a*) If the year is the second year of assessment of the business, the basis period is the twelve months ending with the new date in the year (unless the period from commencement of the business to the new date in the second year is less than twelve months, in which case the basis period is the first twelve months of the business).

(*b*) If the 'relevant period' is a period of less than twelve months, the basis period is the twelve months ending with the new date in the year.

(*c*) If the 'relevant period' is a period of more than twelve months, the basis period consists of the relevant period.

The '*relevant period*' is the period beginning immediately after the end of the basis period for the preceding year and ending with the new date in the year.

It will be seen that a basis period can be of more than twelve months' duration but cannot be less than twelve months. If not all of the above conditions are satisfied (and the year is not the second or third tax year of the business), the basis period for the year is the twelve months beginning immediately after the end of the basis period for the preceding year. However, the accounting change is then treated as made in the following year of assessment and can thus result in a change of basis period for that following year if all the above conditions are satisfied as regards that year. An accounting change can continue to be 'carried forward' in this way until such time, if any, as a change of basis period results or the old accounting date is reverted to.

[*ICTA 1988, s 60(3)(b), s 61(2)(b), s 62, s 62A; FA 1994, ss 200–203; FA 1996, s 135, Sch 21 para 1*].

See 71.11 below for relief (overlap relief) where the above rules in (*a*) or (*b*) above have the effect of the same profits being taxed in each of two successive years of assessment, and for the use of overlap relief brought forward in computing profits in a situation within (*c*) above.

For partnership trades, notice in (2) above and an appeal within (3)(ii) above may be given or brought by such one of the partners as may be nominated by them for the purpose (any resulting change of basis period affecting the notional trades of individual partners — see 53.3 PARTNERSHIPS). [*ICTA 1988, s 111(6); FA 1994, s 215(1); FA 1995, s 117*].

Simon's Direct Tax Service. See E1.218.

71.8   *Examples*

(i) Change to a date earlier in the tax year

Miranda commenced trade on 1 September 2001, preparing accounts to 31 August. In 2004, she changed her accounting date to 31 May, preparing accounts for the nine months to 31 May 2004. The conditions of *ICTA 1988, s 62A* are satisfied in relation to the change. Her profits (as adjusted for tax purposes) are as follows.

	£
Year ended 31 August 2002	18,000
Year ended 31 August 2003	21,500
Nine months to 31 May 2004	17,000
Year ended 31 May 2005	23,000

Taxable profits for the first five tax years are as follows.

	Basis period		£	£
2001/02	1.9.01 – 5.4.02	£18,000 × $\frac{7}{12}$		10,500
2002/03	Y/e 31.8.02			18,000
2003/04	Y/e 31.8.03			21,500
2004/05	1.6.03 – 31.5.04:			
	1.6.03 – 31.8.03	£21,500 × $\frac{3}{12}$	5,375	
	1.9.03 – 31.5.04		17,000	
				22,375
2005/06	Y/e 31.5.05			23,000

Overlap relief accrued (see 71.11 below)

	£
1.9.01 – 5.4.02 — 7 months	10,500
1.6.03 – 31.8.03 — 3 months	5,375
Total overlap relief accrued	£15,875

Note

(a)   In this example, the 'relevant period' is that from 1 September 2003 (the day following the end of the basis period for 2003/04) to 31 May 2004 (the new accounting date in the year 2004/05 — the year of change). As the relevant period is less than 12 months, the basis period for 2004/05 is the 12 months ending on the new accounting date.

(ii) Change to a date later in the tax year

Dennis starts a business on 1 July 2001, preparing accounts to 30 June. In 2004, he changes his accounting date to 31 December, preparing accounts for the six months to 31 December 2004. The conditions of *ICTA 1988, s 62A* are satisfied in relation to the change. His profits (as adjusted for tax purposes) are as follows.

	£
Year ended 30 June 2002	18,000
Year ended 30 June 2003	21,500
Year ended 30 June 2004	23,000
Six months to 31 December 2004	12,000
Year ended 31 December 2005	27,000

Taxable profits for the first five years are as follows.

	Basis period		£	£
2001/02	1.7.01 – 5.4.02	£18,000 × $\frac{9}{12}$		13,500
2002/03	Y/e 30.6.02			18,000
2003/04	Y/e 30.6.03			21,500
2004/05	1.7.03 – 31.12.04:			
	1.7.03 – 30.6.04		23,000	
	1.7.04 – 31.12.04		12,000	
			35,000	
	Deduct Overlap relief		9,000	
				26,000
2005/06	Y/e 31.12.05			27,000

Overlap relief accrued:

1.7.01 – 5.4.02 — 9 months	13,500
Less utilised in 2004/05	9,000
Carried forward	£4,500

Utilisation of overlap relief in 2004/05

Apply the formula: $A \times \dfrac{B - C}{D}$ (see 71.11 below)

where

A = aggregate overlap relief accrued (£13,500);

B = length of basis period for 2004/05 (18 months);

C = 12 months; and

D = the length of the overlap period(s) by reference to which the aggregate overlap profits accrued (9 months).

Thus, the deduction to be given in computing profits for 2004/05 is

$$£13,500 \times \frac{18 - 12}{9} = £9,000$$

Notes

(a) In this example, the 'relevant period' is that from 1 July 2003 (the day following the end of the basis period for 2003/04) to 31 December 2004 (the new accounting date in the year 2004/05 — the year of change). As the relevant period is more than 12 months, the basis period for 2004/05 is equal to the relevant period. Note that a basis period of 18 months results in this case, even though accounts were prepared for a period of only 6 months to the new date.

(b) The overlap relief accrued (by reference to an overlap period of 9 months) is given on cessation or, as in this example, on a change of accounting date resulting in a basis period exceeding 12 months (the relief given depending on the extent of the excess). The balance of overlap relief (£4,500) is carried forward for future relief on the happening of such an event. See 71.11 below. If Dennis had changed his accounting date to 31 March or 5 April (instead of 31 December), the use of the formula in *ICTA 1988, s 63A(2)* would have resulted in overlap relief of £13,500 being given in full in 2004/05.

71.9   **Closing year.** If there is a **discontinuance of a business** carried on by an individual (which includes his ceasing to carry on an existing business in partnership and his transferring the ownership of a business, e.g. on sale, incorporation or death), the following rule applies. As to what constitutes a discontinuance etc. see 71.15 below.

The basis period for the **final year of assessment**, i.e. that in which cessation occurs, is the period beginning immediately after the end of the basis period for the penultimate year and ending with the date of cessation. [*ICTA 1988, s 63; FA 1994, s 204*]. The basis period may thus exceed twelve months, but see 71.11 below as regards the use of overlap relief brought forward in computing profits for the final year. There are no special rules for the penultimate and ante-penultimate years of assessment (but see 71.14 below for transitional provisions where a business commenced before 6 April 1994 ceased in any of the years 1996/97 to 1998/99).

See 46.12 LOSSES for terminal losses and 46.9 LOSSES for the carry-forward of certain losses where a private business is converted into a company.

Simon's Direct Tax Service. See E1.211.

71.10   *Example*

Robin commenced to trade on 1 May 2000, preparing accounts to 30 April. He permanently ceases to trade on 30 June 2004, preparing accounts for the two months to that date. His profits (as adjusted for tax purposes) are as follows.

	£
Year ended 30 April 2001	24,000
Year ended 30 April 2002	48,000
Year ended 30 April 2003	96,000
Year ended 30 April 2004	36,000
Two months ended 30 June 2004	5,000
	£209,000

Taxable profits for the five tax years of trading are as follows.

	Basis period		£	£
2000/01	1.5.2000 – 5.4.01	£24,000 × $\frac{11}{12}$		22,000
2001/02	Y/e 30.4.01			24,000
2002/03	Y/e 30.4.02			48,000
2003/04	Y/e 30.4.03			96,000
2004/05	1.5.03 – 30.6.04:			
	1.5.03 – 30.4.04		36,000	
	1.5.04 – 30.6.04		5,000	
			41,000	
	Deduct Overlap relief		22,000	
				19,000
				£209,000

Overlap relief accrued (see 71.11 below):

1.5.2000 – 5.4.01 — 11 months	22,000
Utilised in 2004/05	(22,000)

71.11 Schedule D, Cases I and II—Profits of Trades etc.

71.11   **Overlap relief.** An 'overlap profit' is an amount of profits which, by virtue of the basis period rules above, is included in the computations for two successive years of assessment. It may arise as a result of the opening year rules in 71.4 above or on a change of basis period within 71.7(*a*) or (*b*) above (i.e. resulting from a change of accounting date). An 'overlap period' in relation to an overlap profit is the number of days in the period for which the overlap profit arose. For example (working in terms of months for simplicity), if a business commences on 1 May 2003 and prepares its first accounts for the year to 30 April 2004 showing tax-adjusted profits of £24,000, the 2003/04 assessment is based on the period 1 May 2003 to 5 April 2004 (£24,000 × $\frac{11}{12}$ = £22,000) and the 2004/05 assessment is based on the year ended 30 April 2004 (£24,000). The overlap profit is £22,000 by reference to an overlap period of 11 months.

Relief for an overlap profit is given, by way of a deduction in computing profits, on a change of accounting date resulting in a basis period of more than twelve months (see 71.7(*c*) above) and/or in the final year of assessment of the business (see 71.9 above). On the first such change of accounting date, if any, the deduction is

$$A \times \frac{B - C}{D}$$

where

A =   the aggregate of any overlap profits;

B =   the number of days in the basis period (i.e. more than 365 or 366);

C =   the number of days in the year of assessment (365 or 366); and

D =   the aggregate of the overlap periods by reference to which the overlap profits in A are calculated.

For example (working in terms of months for simplicity), if the overlap profit brought forward is £22,000 by reference to an overlap period of 11 months, and the basis period for a year of assessment is 15 months, the overlap relief deductible in computing profits for that year is £22,000 × $\frac{3}{11}$ = £6,000, leaving an overlap profit of £16,000, by reference to an overlap period of eight months, to be carried forward. On subsequent applications of this formula, A and D are reduced by, respectively, the overlap profit previously relieved and the number of days referable to the previous relief.

On cessation, the deduction in computing profits for the final year of assessment is equal to the total overlap profits previously unrelieved.

Relief for an overlap profit is not restricted to the amount of profits available, and may convert a taxable trading profit into an allowable trading loss, or increase an allowable trading loss, which may be relieved in the same way as any other trading loss (see 46 LOSSES). Where it creates or augments a terminal loss claim (see 46.12 LOSSES), the full amount of the overlap profit is included, without any apportionment.

[*ICTA 1988, s 63A(1)–(3)(5); FA 1994, s 205*].

The Revenue will accept a calculation of overlap relief by reference otherwise than to days, e.g. using months or fractions of months, providing the same method is used consistently so that, over the lifetime of the business, the total profits assessed exactly equal the profits made (Revenue booklet SAT 1(1995), para 1.86).

See 71.13 below for overlap profits arising under transitional rules for businesses commenced before 6 April 1994.

Overlap losses. Where an amount of loss would otherwise fall to be included in the computations for two successive years of assessment, that amount (the 'overlap loss') is not to be so included for the second of those years. [*ICTA 1988, s 63A(4); FA 1994, s 205*].

Simon's Direct Tax Service. See E1.211, E1.218.

71.12 **Transitional rules for businesses commenced before 6 April 1994 — Basis period for 1996/97.** A business commenced before 6 April 1994 was within the preceding year basis period rules for all years up to and including 1995/96. In order to bridge what would otherwise have been a gap between the basis periods for 1995/96 and 1996/97, the basis period for 1996/97 was determined according to special rules (subject to 71.14 below for businesses ceasing before 6 April 1999). For these transitional rules, and for the preceding year basis period rules, see the 2003/04 and earlier editions.

71.13 **Transitional rules for businesses commenced before 6 April 1994 — Overlap profit for 1997/98.** A business commenced before 6 April 1994 is treated as having a transitional overlap profit for 1997/98 (subject to 71.14 below for businesses ceasing before 6 April 1999). This is equal to the amount of profits taxable for 1997/98, but before deduction/ addition of capital allowances/balancing charges (except in the case of a partnership with a corporate partner), which arises after the end of the basis period for 1996/97 and before 6 April 1997. For example, if accounts are regularly made up to 30 June and those for the year to 30 June 1997 show tax-adjusted profits of £20,000 before capital allowances, the 1997/98 assessment will be £20,000 *less* capital allowances and there will be a transitional overlap profit of £15,000 by reference to a transitional overlap period of nine months, 1 July 1996 to 5 April 1997 (working in terms of months rather than days, for simplicity). The transitional overlap profit is carried forward and relieved in the same way as other overlap profits (see 71.11 above). [*FA 1994, Sch 20 para 2(4)–(4B); FA 1995, s 122(2)(3)*]. The computation of transitional overlap profits is not affected by averaging claim(s) by farmers (see 71.47(*a*) below). (Revenue Tax Bulletin August 1998 pp 574, 575).

Anti-avoidance measures were introduced to deter and penalise attempts to exploit the above rules by moving profits into the basis period for 1997/98, of which the transitional overlap period forms part, so as to otherwise increase the transitional overlap profit. Their effect was to reduce the transitional overlap profit by 1.25 times the profits so moved. See the 2003/04 and earlier editions for full commentary.

An officer of the Board could not amend a self-assessment tax return to give effect to these anti-avoidance provisions unless he gave notice stating the aggregate of the amounts on which the adjustment was based. He was able to give such notice at any time until a return for 1998/99 had been made and was no longer capable of being amended (see 68.4 RETURNS generally). Such a notice was conclusive of the matters stated in it, subject to the right of the taxpayer to appeal within 30 days beginning with the date of the notice, the same procedures applying as for an appeal against an assessment, with the Commissioners able to confirm, set aside or modify the notice. [*FA 1995, Sch 22 para 12; FA 2001, s 88, Sch 29 para 37(4)(5)*].

71.14 **Transitional rules for businesses commenced before 6 April 1994 — cessation in 1996/97 to 1998/99.** A business commenced before 6 April 1994 and ceasing in the tax year 1996/97 was subject not to the basis period rules in 71.3–71.11 above but to the cessation rules that applied under the preceding year basis of assessment (for which see the 2003/04 and earlier editions).

In the case of a business commenced before 6 April 1994 and ceasing in the tax year 1997/98, an officer of the Board could direct that the basis period rules in 71.3—71.11 above should not apply. Theoretically the cessation could be dealt with as under the preceding year basis of assessment, but Revenue practice was to make a direction only if it was to replace the preceding year basis for 1995/96 and the transitional basis for 1996/97 (see 71.12 above) with an actual basis (6 April to 5 April) for both years (and they would not normally amend 1997/98). (Revenue booklet SAT 1(1995), para 6.39).

71.15   Schedule D, Cases I and II—Profits of Trades etc.

In the case of a business commenced before 6 April 1994 and ceasing in the tax year 1998/99, a comparison was made between the profits assessable for 1996/97 under the transitional rules referred to in 71.12 above (ignoring any brought-forward losses) and those arising on an actual basis (6 April 1996 to 5 April 1997). If the latter figure was the greater, an officer of the Board could direct that 1996/97 should be taxed on an actual basis. The assessments for 1997/98 and 1998/99 were unaffected.

The Revenue may make all such adjustments, whether by assessment or otherwise, to give effect to either of the above-mentioned directions.

[*FA 1994, Sch 20 para 3*].

Simon's Direct Tax Service. See E1.215.

71.15   **WHETHER OR NOT THERE HAS BEEN A COMMENCEMENT OR DISCONTINUANCE**

The rules at 71.4 and 71.9 above for the opening and closing years apply (i) on the commencement of a new business or the permanent discontinuance of a business by an individual (including a transfer of the ownership of a business, e.g. when it is sold or incorporated or it passes on death) and (ii) on an individual becoming or ceasing to be a member of a partnership (*but not so as to affect the continuing partners*) — see 53.3 PARTNERSHIPS.

See 53.7 PARTNERSHIPS as regards partnership mergers and demergers.

Although these rules do not apply to companies (see 71.2 above) the income of a company is to be computed on the basis of a commencement/cessation of a trade when it commences/ceases to carry on a trade whether or not there has been a permanent commencement/discontinuance. [*ICTA 1988, s 337(1)*]. This provision is necessary so that a provision operating on a notional cessation/commencement as well as a permanent one may, if required, be applied to companies as well as individuals. (For examples, see *ICTA 1988, ss 102(2), 110(2)*.)

For a short article on the distinction between succession to a trade, extension of an existing trade and commencement of a new trade, see Revenue Tax Bulletin February 1996 pp 285, 286. For an in-depth discussion, see Revenue Business Income Manual BIM 70500–70690.

Simon's Direct Tax Service. See B3.248–B3.251, B3.3.

71.16   **Case law.** Whether or not a person has commenced/ceased trading and, if so, the date, are questions of fact. Preliminary activities in setting up a business do not amount to trading (*Birmingham & District Cattle By-Products Co Ltd v CIR KB 1919, 12 TC 92*). For pre-trading expenditure, see 71.66 below. For whether the sale of a business can be effective for tax purposes before the vending agreement, see *Todd v Jones Bros Ltd KB 1930, 15 TC 396* and contrast *Angel v Hollingworth & Co Ch D 1958, 37 TC 714*. 'Permanent discontinuance' does not mean a discontinuance which is everlasting (see *Ingram v Callaghan CA 1968, 45 TC 151*) but a trade may continue notwithstanding a lengthy break in active trading (*Kirk & Randall Ltd v Dunn KB 1924, 8 TC 663* but contrast *Goff v Osborne & Co (Sheffield) Ltd Ch D 1953, 34 TC 441*). An intensification by a freelance television producer of his freelance activities could not effect a discontinuance and commencement of a new business (*Edmunds v Coleman Ch D 1997, 70 TC 322*).

The trade was held to have been continuous when the owner of a drifter continued to manage it after its war-time requisition (*Sutherland v CIR CS 1918, 12 TC 63*); when a merchant sold stock on hand after announcing retirement (*J & R O'Kane v CIR HL 1922, 12 TC 303*); when a flour miller and baker gave up a mill (*Bolands Ltd v Davis KB(IFS)*

1925, 4 ATC 532); when a barrister took silk (*Seldon v Croom-Johnson KB 1932, 16 TC 740*); when a partnership was dissolved but completed open forward contracts (*Hillerns & Fowler v Murray CA 1932, 17 TC 77*); when a building partnership transferred construction activities to a company but retained building land and continued to sell land with houses built thereon by the company (*Watts v Hart Ch D 1984, 58 TC 209*). A new trade was held to have commenced when the vendor of a business retained the benefit of outstanding hire-purchase agreements (*Parker v Batty KB 1941, 23 TC 739*) and when the vendor of a business got commission on open contracts completed by the purchaser (*Southern v Cohen's Exors KB 1940, 23 TC 566*).

It is similarly a question of fact whether a trader expanding by taking over an existing business and operating it as a branch has succeeded to the trade. See e.g. *Bell v National Provincial Bank of England Ltd CA 1903, 5 TC 1* (bank succeeded to trade of single-branch bank taken over); *Laycock v Freeman Hardy & Willis Ltd CA 1938, 22 TC 288* (shoe retailer did not succeed to trade of manufacturing subsidiaries taken over); *Briton Ferry Steel Co Ltd v Barry CA 1939, 23 TC 414* (steel manufacturer succeeded to trade of tinplate manufacturing subsidiaries taken over); and *Maidment v Kibby Ch D 1993, 66 TC 137* (fish and chip shop proprietor did not succeed to trade of existing business taken over). See also *H & G Kinemas Ltd KB 1933, 18 TC 116* (cinema company disposed of existing cinemas and opened new one, held to commence new trade).

Whether or not there has been a commencement etc. has arisen in a number of cases where the activities of a company have altered on e.g. a change of shareholdings or a group reconstruction or on its absorption of another trade or part-trade. Such decisions are now of limited importance to companies (see 71.15 above) and where the facts are such that they are unlikely to arise in relation to individuals, they are not referred to here. For such cases, see Tolley's Tax Cases.

71.17   **Change of residence.** A special rule applies where a sole trader carrying on his trade wholly or partly outside the UK either becomes or ceases to be resident in the UK. The trade is deemed to have been permanently discontinued at the time of the change of residence and, in so far as the individual continues to carry on the actual trade, a new trade is deemed to have been set up immediately afterwards. This applies equally for the purposes of loss reliefs except that a loss incurred in the 'old' trade may be carried forward under *ICTA 1988, s 385* (see 46.9 LOSSES) and set against profits of the 'new' trade. [*ICTA 1988, s 110A; FA 1995, s 124*].

Similar rules apply to individuals trading in partnership (see 53.14 PARTNERSHIPS).

71.18   **ACCOUNTS**

Under self-assessment, it is not a requirement that accounts should accompany returns, although (except in cases where the annual turnover is less than £15,000) standardised accounts information has to be provided. (Where turnover is less than £15,000, only turnover, purchases and expenses totals need to be shown in the return.) There are, however, strict requirements as to maintenance and preservation of records. See 68.2, 68.5 RETURNS.

See 71.59 below for allowability of accountancy expenses.

Rounding of tax computations. To reduce the compliance burden on large businesses whose statutory accounts are produced in round thousands, the Revenue are generally prepared to accept profit returns for tax purposes in figures rounded to the nearest £1,000 from single businesses or companies with an annual turnover of at least £5 million (including investment and estate income) in the accounts in question or in the preceding year, where rounding at least to that extent has been used in preparing the accounts. (Turnover of groups of companies is not aggregated for this purpose.) Such returns must be accompanied by a certificate by the person preparing the computations stating the basis of rounding, and confirming that it is unbiased, has been applied consistently and produces a fair result for tax purposes (and stating the program or software used where relevant), or, if there have been no changes from the previous year in these respects, confirming the unchanged basis. The rounding may not extend to the tax payable or other relevant figures of tax. Rounding is not acceptable where it would impede the application of the legislation, or where recourse to the underlying records would normally be necessary to do the computation. Thus it is not acceptable e.g. in computations of chargeable gains (except in relation to the incidental costs of acquisition and disposal), in accrued income scheme computations (see 74.5 SCHEDULE D, CASE VI), in computations of tax credit relief or in certain capital allowance computations. The inspector may exceptionally insist that roundings are not used in other circumstances. (Revenue Pamphlet IR 131, SP 15/93, 18 May 1993).

Enquiries into returns. For the investigative powers of inspectors under self-assessment, see 68.6 *et seq.* RETURNS. The system of in-depth examination of accounts which applied for earlier years may continue to apply where returns for such years are subject to investigation without any self-assessment return being brought into question (e.g. following cessation).

The Revenue have published a Code of Practice (No 2, available from local tax offices) setting out their standards for the way in which investigations are conducted and the rights and responsibilities of taxpayers. Codes of Practice 8 and 9, dealing with Special Compliance Office Investigations in cases other than suspected serious fraud and cases of such fraud respectively, were published in January 1995 and are available from the Special Compliance Office, Angel Court, 199 Borough High Street, London SE1 1HZ.

See also 57.3, 57.10 PENALTIES. See generally Revenue Pamphlets IR 72 and IR 73.

Business Economic Notes relating to various trades, which are used by inspectors as background information in investigating returns, are available on the Revenue's website at www.inlandrevenue.gov.uk/bens/index.htm. They may alternatively be purchased from the Inland Revenue, Room 28 New Wing, Somerset House, London WC2R 1LB (price £1.60 (£2.00 for no. 23 onwards) post free). Those currently available are:

1. Travel agents.
2. Road haulage (revised 1995).
3. The lodging industry.
4. Hairdressers.
5. Waste materials reclamation and disposals.
6. Funeral directors.
7. Dentists.
8. Florists.
9. Licensed victuallers.
10. The jewellery trade.
11. Electrical retailers.
12. Antiques and fine art dealers.
13. Fish and chip shops.
14. The pet industry.
15. Veterinary surgeons.
16. Catering — general.
17. — restaurants.
18. — fast-foods, cafes and snack-bars.
19. Farming — stock valuation for income tax purposes.
20. Insurance brokers and agents.
21. Residential rest and nursing homes.
22. Dispensing chemists.
23. Driving instructors.
24. Independent fishmongers.
25. Taxicabs and private hire vehicles.
26. Confectioners, tobacconists and newsagents.

WHETHER A TRADE CARRIED ON

See also 50 MUTUAL TRADING and 84 STATUTORY BODIES. See 71.1 above for statutory definition of 'trade'; meaning of 'profession or vocation'; application of Cases I and II to overseas business activities; and the principle that income within Schedules A and B is not derived from trading. Special types of activity are dealt with below in alphabetical order.

Simon's Direct Tax Service. See B3.2.

71.19 **AVOIDANCE SCHEMES**

A line is drawn between transactions of a trading nature which remain trading even though entered into to secure tax advantages and transactions so remote from ordinary trading as to be explicable only as fiscal devices and hence not trading.

In *Ransom v Higgs and Kilmorie (Aldridge) Ltd v Dickinson etc. HL 1974, 50 TC 1* the taxpayers entered into complex arrangements to siphon development profits into the hands of trustees. They succeeded, the Crown failing to establish that, looked at as a whole, the arrangements constituted trading. In *Johnson v Jewitt CA 1961, 40 TC 231* an elaborate and artificial device to manufacture trading losses was held not to amount to trading, but see *Ensign Tankers (Leasing) Ltd v Stokes HL 1992, 64 TC 617*, where the company's investment in two film production partnerships was entered into with a view to obtaining first-year capital allowances. See also *Black Nominees Ltd v Nicol Ch D 1975, 50 TC 229* and *Newstead v Frost HL 1980, 53 TC 525*. See generally ANTI-AVOIDANCE (3).

71.20 **BETTING**

Betting by professional bookmakers is assessable (*Partridge v Mallandaine QB 1886, 2 TC 179*) even if carried on in an unlawful way (*Southern v A B KB 1933, 18 TC 59*) but not private betting however habitual (*Graham v Green KB 1925, 9 TC 309*). Also exempt from CGT. [*TCGA 1992, s 51(1)*]. Receipts from newspaper articles based on betting system held assessable in *Graham v Arnott KB 1941, 24 TC 157*.

Lotteries and football pools promotion constitutes trading, but where a pool or small lottery is run by a supporters club or other society on terms that a specified part of the cost of the ticket is to be donated to a club or body within the purposes in *Lotteries and Amusements Act 1976, s 5(1)*, the donation element is not treated as a trading receipt (Revenue Pamphlet IR 131, C1). For further detail, see Revenue Business Income Manual BIM 61600–61615. See 14.7(iii) CHARITIES as regards charitable lotteries.

71.21 **DIVERS AND DIVING SUPERVISORS**

The emoluments of a person employed in the UK (including a designated area under *Continental Shelf Act 1964, s 1(7)*, see 51.12 NON-RESIDENTS AND OTHER OVERSEAS MATTERS) as a diver in operations to exploit the sea-bed, or as a supervisor in relation to such operations, are to be dealt with under Schedule D, Case I as if he were carrying on a trade and not as employment income. [*ICTA 1988, s 314; ITEPA 2003, Sch 6 para 40*]. See Simon's Direct Tax Service E5.7.

71.22 **FUTURES, OPTIONS AND SWAP CONTRACTS**

As far as companies are concerned, almost all futures, options and swaps fall within the derivative contracts rules applicable for accounting periods beginning on or after 1 October 2002 (see Tolley's Corporation Tax under Financial Instruments and derivative contracts), so the following now applies mainly for income tax purposes.

Futures and options. Any gain arising in the course of dealing, other than in the course of trade, in commodity or financial futures or in traded or financial options on a recognised exchange, and not chargeable under *ICTA 1988, Sch 5AA* (see 3.21 ANTI-AVOIDANCE), is dealt with under the chargeable gains rules and is not chargeable to tax under Schedule D. [*ICTA 1988, s 128; TCGA 1992, s 143; FA 1994, s 95; FA 1997, s 80(3); FA 2002, Sch 27 para 3*]. See Tolley's Capital Gains Tax under Disposal.

Where dealing is in the course of a trade, any profit or loss is chargeable under Schedule D, Case I. In general, relatively infrequent transactions, and transactions to hedge specific investments, would not be regarded as trading, nor would purely speculative transactions. For the Revenue view on what constitutes trading in this context, see Revenue Pamphlet IR 131, SP 3/02 (replacing SP 14/91).

Special rules are applied (by regulation) to the market formed by the merger of the London International Financial Futures Exchange (LIFFE) and the London Traded Options Market (LTOM), which operates outside the Stock Exchange. These relate to bond-washing and to stamp duty and stamp duty reserve tax. See *SI 1992 Nos 568, 570*.

Pension schemes etc. For the purposes of approved retirement benefit schemes (see 67.5(*b*), 67.13 RETIREMENT SCHEMES), personal pension schemes and retirement annuity trust schemes (see 60.1 PERSONAL PENSION SCHEMES, 66.8 RETIREMENT ANNUITIES), futures and options contracts are treated as investments (and thus as attracting tax exemption for income and capital gains). Any income derived from transactions relating to such a contract is regarded as arising from the contract, and a contract is not excluded from these provisions by the fact that any party is, or may be, entitled to receive and/or liable to make only a payment of a sum in full settlement of all obligations, as opposed to a transfer of assets other than money. [*ICTA 1988, s 659A; TCGA 1992, s 271(10)(11); FA 1990, s 81(2)(3)(5)(6)*].

Swaps. The word 'swap' is not defined for tax purposes but is taken to mean any financial arrangement that would be regarded by the financial markets as a swap. Profits or losses on a swap are within Schedule D, Case I if on trading account and are otherwise within Schedule D, Case VI (if not of a capital nature). When considering whether a swap transaction is within Case I or Case VI, the Revenue apply the general principles set out in Statement of Practice SP 3/02 referred to above, and for an overview see also Revenue Tax Bulletin August 2003 pp 1054, 1055.

Pension schemes etc. ICTA 1988, s 659A referred to above has no bearing on the tax status of swaps. Where a swap transaction by an approved scheme falls close to the trading/investment borderline, the Revenue judge the case on its merits. Where an approved scheme uses interest rate swaps, currency swaps, equity swaps, credit derivatives or similar instruments to hedge risks inherent in, or as part of a strategy to enhance the return from, its existing investment portfolio or (in line with its normal policies of investing directly in such investments) to create a synthetic exposure to investments of a particular type or in a particular market, the Revenue normally regard such swaps as investments (and thus as attracting tax exemptions for income and capital gains). (Revenue Tax Bulletin August 2003 pp 1055, 1056).

71.23   HORSE RACING ETC.

'Private' horse racing and training is not normally trading (cf. *Sharkey v Wernher HL 1955, 36 TC 275*). But racing and selling the progeny of a brood mare held within Schedule D in *Dawson v Counsell CA 1938, 22 TC 149* and in *Norman v Evans Ch D 1964, 42 TC 188* share of prize monies for letting racehorses held within Case VI. Profits from stallion fees are assessable and assessments under both Case I and Case VI have been upheld (*Malcolm v Lockhart HL 1919, 7 TC 99; McLaughlin v Bailey CA (I) 1920, 7 TC 508; Jersey's Exors v Bassom KB 1926, 10 TC 357; Wernher v CIR KB 1942, 29 TC 20; Benson v Counsell KB 1942, 24 TC 178*) but wear and tear allowances (the forerunner of modern capital allowances on plant etc.) for stallions refused in *Derby v Aylmer KB 1915, 6 TC 665*. Profits from greyhound breeding held trading in *Hawes v Gardiner Ch D 1957, 37 TC 671*.

71.24   ILLEGAL TRADING

Crime, e.g. burglary, is not trading but the profits of a commercial business are assessable notwithstanding the business may be carried on in an unlawful way, e.g. 'bootlegging' (*Canadian Minister of Finance v Smith PC 1926, 5 ATC 621* and cf. *Lindsay Woodward & Hiscox v CIR CS 1932, 18 TC 43*), operating 'fruit machines' illegal at the time (*Mann v Nash KB 1932, 16 TC 523*), street bookmaking illegal at the time (*Southern v A B KB 1933, 18 TC 59*) and prostitution (*CIR v Aken CA 1990, 63 TC 395*). But penalties for trading contrary to war-time regulations held not deductible (*CIR v E C Warnes & Co KB 1919, 12 TC 227; CIR v Alexander von Glehn & Co CA 1920, 12 TC 232*). See also 71.20 above. See Simon's Direct Tax Service B3.247.

See 71.53 below as regards prohibition on deduction of expenditure involving crime.

71.25   ISOLATED OR SPECULATIVE TRANSACTIONS

For futures, property transactions and share dealing see 71.22, 71.28 and 71.29 respectively.

Whether the surplus on the purchase and resale of assets, otherwise than in the course of an established commercial enterprise, is derived from an 'adventure or concern in the nature of trade' (see 71.1 above) depends on the facts. Para 116 of the Final Report of the Royal Commission on the Taxation of Profits and Income (1955 HMSO Cmd. 9474) lists six 'badges of trade': (i) the subject matter of the realisation; (ii) length of period of ownership; (iii) frequency or number of similar transactions; (iv) supplementary work on assets sold; (v) reason for sale; (vi) motive. Other relevant factors may be the degree of organisation, whether the taxpayer is or has been associated with a recognised business dealing in similar assets and how the purchases were financed. For a recent review of the factors to be considered, see *Marson v Morton Ch D 1986, 59 TC 381*.

Although in disputed cases the Revenue may make alternative Case I and Case VI assessments, it would seem from *Pearn v Miller KB 1927, 11 TC 610* and *Leeming v Jones HL 1930, 15 TC 333* (see 71.28 below) that as regards isolated transactions the income tax liability, if any, will be under Case I. As regards commodity futures, see 71.22 above.

Case I assessments were upheld on a purchase and resale of war surplus linen (*Martin v Lowry HL 1926, 11 TC 297* — a leading case); a purchase, conversion and resale of a ship (*CIR v Livingston CS 1926, 11 TC 538*); transactions in brandy (*Cape Brandy Syndicate v CIR CA 1921, 12 TC 358*), whisky (*Lindsay Woodward* at 71.24 above), whisky in bond (*P J McCall decd v CIR KB(IFS) 1923, 4 ATC 522; CIR v Fraser CS 1942, 24 TC 498*); 'turning over' cotton mills (*Pickford v Quirke CA 1927, 13 TC 251*); purchase and resale of cotton spinning plant (*Edwards v Bairstow & Harrison HL 1955, 36 TC 207*); and purchase and resale of toilet rolls (*Rutledge v CIR CS 1929, 14 TC 490*). But in *Jenkinson v Freedland CA 1961, 39 TC 636* the Commissioners' finding that a profit on the purchase, repair and sale (to associated companies) of stills was not assessable, was upheld, and in *Kirkham v Williams CA 1991, 64 TC 253*, the Commissioners' decision that the sale of a dwelling house built on land partly acquired for storage etc. was an adventure in the nature of trade was reversed in the CA.

Simon's Direct Tax Service. See **B3.211** *et seq.*

71.26 **LIQUIDATORS ETC. AND PERSONAL REPRESENTATIVES**

Whether a liquidator or receiver is continuing the company's trade or merely realising its assets as best he can, is a question of fact and similarly for the personal representatives of a deceased trader. For liquidators or receivers see *Armitage v Moore QB 1900, 4 TC 199*; *CIR v 'Old Bushmills' Distillery KB(NI) 1927, 12 TC 1148*; *CIR v Thompson KB 1936, 20 TC 422*; *Wilson Box v Brice CA 1936, 20 TC 736*; *Baker v Cook KB 1937, 21 TC 337*.

Personal representatives were held to be trading while winding up the deceased's business in *Weisberg's Executrices v CIR KB 1933, 17 TC 696*; *Wood v Black's Exor HC 1952, 33 TC 172*; *Pattullo's Trustees v CIR CS 1955, 36 TC 87* but not in *Cohan's Exors v CIR CA 1924, 12 TC 602* (completion of ship under construction at death) and *CIR v Donaldson's Trustees CS 1963, 41 TC 161* (sale of pedigree herd). For property sales after death of partner in property dealing firm, see *Marshall's Exors v Joly KB 1936, 20 TC 256* and contrast *Newbarns Syndicate v Hay CA 1939, 22 TC 461*.

71.27 **MISCELLANEOUS**

Assessments under Case I were upheld on a committee operating golf links owned by a Town Council (*Carnoustie Golf Course Committee v CIR CS 1929, 14 TC 498*); trustees under a private Act managing a recreation ground (*CIR v Stonehaven Recreation Ground Trustees CS 1929, 15 TC 419*); temporary joint coal merchanting (*Gardner and Bowring Hardy & Co v CIR CS 1930, 15 TC 602*); promotion of mining companies to exploit mines (*Murphy v Australian Machinery etc. Co Ltd CA 1948, 30 TC 244* and cf. *Rhodesia Metals v Commr of Taxes PC 1940, 19 ATC 472*); purchase and resale of amusement equipment (*Crole v Lloyd HC 1950, 31 TC 338*).

A company which made loans to another company to finance a trading venture was held not to be trading itself (*Stone & Temple Ltd v Waters*; *Astrawall (UK) Ltd v Waters Ch D 1995, 67 TC 145*).

The activities of the British Olympic Association (which included the raising of funds through commercial sponsorship and the exploitation of its logo, but many of which were non-commercial) were held as a whole to be uncommercial and not to constitute a trade (*British Olympic Association v Winter (Sp C 28), [1995] SSCD 85*).

For whether or not an *athlete* is taxable under Case I, see Revenue Business Income Manual BIM 50605; for the treatment of Lottery Sports Fund Athlete Personal Awards, see BIM 50651–50690.

For whether *ostrich farming* (i.e. the ownership of ostriches which are looked after on the owner's behalf by others) amounts to trading, and for the consequences of such trading, see Revenue Tax Bulletin June 1996 pp 318, 319.

See also *Smith Barry v Cordy CA 1946, 28 TC 250* in which a taxpayer was held liable on his surplus from the sale or maturing of endowment policies he had purchased, *J Bolson & Son Ltd v Farrelly CA 1953, 34 TC 161* (deals in vessels by company operating boat services held a separate adventure) and *Torbell Investments Ltd v Williams Ch D 1986, 59 TC 357* (dormant company revived for purpose of acquiring certain loans held to have acquired them as trading stock). But a company formed to administer a holidays with pay scheme for the building etc. industry was held not trading (*Building & Civil Engineering etc. Ltd v Clark*

Ch D 1960, 39 TC 12). Assessments on profits from promoting a series of driving schools were upheld in *Leach v Pogson Ch D 1962, 40 TC 585*; in concluding that the profit from *first* sale was assessable, Commissioners were entitled to take into account the subsequent transactions.

For circumstances in which the profits of a trade may not accrue to the proprietor, see *Alongi v CIR CS 1991, 64 TC 304.*

71.28   **PROPERTY TRANSACTIONS**

This paragraph relates to transactions in land and buildings otherwise than in the course of an established business of property development, building etc. For the Revenue view, see Revenue Business Income Manual BIM 60000–60165. For other sales of property see 71.67 below.

A line is drawn between realisations of property held as an investment or as a residence and transactions amounting to an adventure or concern in the nature of trade. The principles at 71.25 above apply suitably adapted.

In *Leeming v Jones HL 1930, 15 TC 333* an assessment on the acquisitions and disposal of options over rubber estates was confirmed by Commissioners. The Crown had defended the assessment under both Case I and Case VI. In a Supplementary Case the Commissioners found there had been no concern in the nature of the trade. The Court held there was no liability. Per Lawrence LJ 'in the case of an isolated transaction ... there is really no middle course open. It is either an adventure in the nature of trade, or else it is simply a case of sale and resale of property.' See also *Pearn v Miller KB 1927, 11 TC 610* and *Williams v Davies* below.

Property transactions by companies held to be trading in *Californian Copper Syndicate v Harris CES 1904, 5 TC 159* (purchase of copper bearing land shortly afterwards resold); *Thew v South West Africa Co CA 1924, 9 TC 141* (numerous sales of land acquired by concession for exploitation); *Cayzer, Irvine & Co v CIR CS 1942, 24 TC 491* (exploitation of landed estate acquired by shipping company); *Emro Investments v Aller* and *Lance Webb Estates v Aller Ch D 1954, 35 TC 305* (profits carried to capital reserve on numerous purchases and sales); *Orchard Parks v Pogson Ch D 1964, 42 TC 442* (land compulsorily purchased after development plan dropped); *Parkstone Estates v Blair Ch D 1966, 43 TC 246* (industrial estate developed—land disposed of by sub-leases for premiums); *Eames v Stepnell Properties Ltd CA 1966, 43 TC 678* (sale of land acquired from associated company while resale being negotiated). See also *Bath & West Counties Property Trust Ltd v Thomas Ch D 1977, 52 TC 20.* Realisations were held to be capital in *Hudson's Bay v Stevens CA 1909, 5 TC 424* (numerous sales of land acquired under Royal Charter — contrast *South West Africa Co* above); *Tebrau (Johore) Rubber Syndicate v Farmer CES 1910, 5 TC 658* (purchase and resale of rubber estates — contrast *Californian Copper* above).

In *Rand v Alberni Land Co Ltd KB 1920, 7 TC 629* sales of land held in trust were held not trading but contrast *Alabama Coal Iron Land v Mylam KB 1926, 11 TC 232; Balgownie Land Trust v CIR CS 1929, 14 TC 684; St Aubyn Estates v Strick KB 1932, 17 TC 412; Tempest Estates v Walmsley Ch D 1975, 51 TC 305.* Sales of property after a period of letting held realisations of investments or not trading in *CIR v Hyndland Investment Co Ltd CS 1929, 14 TC 694; Glasgow Heritable Trust v CIR CS 1954, 35 TC 196; Lucy & Sunderland Ltd v Hunt Ch D 1961, 40 TC 132* but held trading in *Rellim Ltd v Vise CA 1951, 32 TC 254* (notwithstanding that company previously admitted as investment company); *CIR v Toll Property Co CS 1952, 34 TC 13; Forest Side Properties (Chingford) v Pearce CA 1961, 39 TC 665.* But sales by liquidator of property owned by companies following abandonment of plan for their public flotation held not trading in *Simmons v CIR HL 1980, 53 TC 461* (reversing Commissioners' decision). In *Rosemoor Investments v Inspector of Taxes (Sp C 320), [2002] SSCD 325,* it was not open to the Commissioners to recharacterise as trading a complex transaction routed via an investment company subsidiary and structured to produce capital.

Property transactions by individuals and partnerships. Profits held assessable in *Reynold's Exors v Bennett KB 1943, 25 TC 401*; *Broadbridge v Beattie KB 1944, 26 TC 63*; *Gray & Gillitt v Tiley KB 1944, 26 TC 80*; *Laver v Wilkinson KB 1944, 26 TC 105*; *Foulds v Clayton Ch D 1953, 34 TC 382* and *Kirkby v Hughes Ch D 1992, 65 TC 352*; in all of which the taxpayers were or had been associated with building or estate development, and contrast *Williams v Davies KB 1945, 26 TC 371* in which the taxpayers were closely associated with land development but a profit on transactions in undeveloped land in the names of their wives held not assessable. The acquisition and resale of land for which planning permission had been or was obtained held trading in *Cooke v Haddock Ch D 1960, 39 TC 64; Turner v Last Ch D 1965, 42 TC 517* and *Pilkington v Randall CA 1966, 42 TC 662* (and cf. *Iswera v Ceylon Commr PC 1965, 44 ATC 157*), but contrast *Taylor v Good CA 1974, 49 TC 277* in which a house bought as a residence was found unsuitable and resold to a developer after obtaining planning permission and held not an adventure. In *Burrell v Davis Ch D 1948, 38 TC 307; Johnston v Heath Ch D 1970, 46 TC 463; Reeves v Evans, Boyce & Northcott Ch D 1971, 48 TC 495* and *Clark v Follett Ch D 1973, 48 TC 677* the short period of ownership or other evidence showed an intention to purchase for resale at a profit and not for investment, but contrast *CIR v Reinhold CS 1953, 34 TC 389, Marson v Morton Ch D 1986, 59 TC 381* and *Taylor v Good* above. For other cases in which profits held assessable see *Hudson v Wrightson KB 1934, 26 TC 55* and *MacMahon v CIR CS 1951, 32 TC 311*.

For sales after a period of letting see *Mitchell Bros v Tomlinson CA 1957, 37 TC 224* and *Cooksey & Bibby v Rednall KB 1949, 30 TC 514*.

For sale of houses built by taxpayer and used as residences see *Page v Pogson Ch D 1954, 35 TC 545* and *Kirkham v Williams CA 1991, 64 TC 253*.

For sales after death of partner in property dealing transactions, see cases at 71.26 above. See also re partnership sales *CIR v Dean Property Co CS 1939, 22 TC 706* and *Dodd and Tanfield v Haddock Ch D 1964, 42 TC 229*.

Simon's Direct Tax Service. See B3.6.

71.29   SHARE DEALING

Share dealing with the public is strictly controlled by the *Financial Services and Markets Act 2000*. This paragraph is concerned with share transactions entered into (generally through the Stock Exchange) by persons not authorised to deal under that Act and the question arises whether they amount to an adventure or concern in the nature of trade. The principles of 71.25 above apply suitably adapted. The prudent management of an investment portfolio may necessitate changes in the holdings but this is not normally trading. Stock Exchange speculation, particularly by individuals, may be quasi-gambling and not trading — see Pennycuick J in *Lewis Emanuel & Son Ltd v White Ch D 1965, 42 TC 369* in which, reversing the Commissioners' finding, he held that the Stock Exchange losses of a fruit etc. merchanting company were from a separate trade of share dealing but observed that gambling by the company would have been *ultra vires*. Subsequent *Companies Act* changes have, however, removed any such restriction on the activities of most companies (see Revenue Inspector' Manual IM 129a). In *Cooper v C & J Clark Ltd Ch D 1982, 54 TC 670*, the losses of a manufacturing company on its sale of gilts, in which it had invested temporarily surplus cash, were allowed as a set-off against its general trading profits. An individual speculating in stocks and shares and commodity futures was held to be trading in *Wannell v Rothwell Ch D 1996, 68 TC 719* (although loss relief was refused on the grounds that the trading was 'uncommercial', see 46.8(a) LOSSES), but the opposite conclusion was reached in *Salt v Chamberlain Ch D 1979, 53 TC 143*.

For share dealing by investment companies see *Scottish Investment Trust Co v Forbes CES 1893, 3 TC 231* and *Halefield Securities Ltd v Thorpe Ch D 1967, 44 TC 154*. For trading in secured loans, see *Torbell Investments Ltd v Williams Ch D 1986, 59 TC 357*.

For share sales connected with an existing business see 71.72 below.

CHARGEABLE INCOME AND ALLOWABLE DEDUCTIONS

See also 9 CAPITAL ALLOWANCES. Headings below after 71.30 are in alphabetical order.

See Revenue Business Income Manual BIM 50000 *et seq.* for Revenue guidance on measuring the profits of a wide range of particular trades.

The provisions for computing business profits are in *ICTA 1988, ss 74–99*. The general rules for expenses are in *ICTA 1988, s 74*. These are few and simple and, in content and wording, little changed since Napoleonic times. There are no corresponding rules for receipts. Hence practice is largely based on principles evolved over the years and endorsed by the Courts. It has, however, been clarified that the words 'receipts' and 'expenses' refer generally to items brought into account as credits or debits in computing profits, and contain no implication that an amount has actually been received or expended. [*FA 1998, s 46(1)*].

True and fair view requirement. For periods of account (i.e. any period for which accounts of a trade, profession or vocation are drawn up) beginning **after 6 April 1999**, *FA 1998, s 42* provides that the profits of a trade, profession or vocation must generally be computed for tax purposes on an accounting basis giving a true and fair view, subject to any adjustment required or authorised by law. This imposes a general requirement to apply an earnings basis (see below) for tax purposes, whilst at the same time importing the accountancy concept of 'materiality', allowing a practical view to be taken of the time when immaterial amounts are recognised. The 'true and fair view' rule requires neither the auditing of accounts, nor additional disclosure, nor the preparation of a true and fair view balance sheet. Neither does it require accounts to be drawn up on any particular basis (provided the necessary adjustments are made in the tax computation). See Revenue Press Release 17 March 1998. For the Revenue view of what is meant by 'true and fair view', see Revenue Tax Bulletin December 1998 pp 606–615. See Revenue Business Income Manual BIM 31045–31047 as regards the concept of materiality.

With effect from 24 July 2002, the reference to accounts drawn up 'on an accounting basis which gives a true and fair view' is replaced by a reference to accounts drawn up in accordance with '*generally accepted accounting practice*' (GAAP), which is however defined by reference to such practice with respect to UK company accounts drawn up to give a true and fair view (whether in its application to such companies or to individuals, entities other than companies or non-UK companies). The expression is now employed (and has that meaning) in many places in the *Taxes Acts*. '*For accounting purposes*' similarly means for the purposes of accounts drawn up in accordance with such practice. With effect for periods of account beginning after 31 December 2004, 'generally accepted accounting practice' also incorporates international accounting standards in cases where accounts are prepared in accordance with such standards; in all other cases, the expression is restricted to UK GAAP.

The special computational rules for UNDERWRITERS AT LLOYD'S (89) are not affected by these changes.

Transition to 'true and fair view'. There is a transitional exemption, allowing the continued use of the cash basis for a transitional period, for barristers and advocates, and an ongoing exemption for barristers and advocates in the early years of practice. See 11.2 CASH BASIS. Generally, a period of account beginning before 7 April 1999 which is still current on 7 April 2000 is treated as having ended on 6 April 1999, and a new period of account as having begun on 7 April 1999 (to which the 'true and fair view' rule thus applies).

[*ICTA 1988, s 836A; FA 1998, ss 42, 43, 45; FA 2002, s 103; FA 2004, s 50*].

See 71.39 below as regards future and contingent liabilities generally.

For the earlier application of the cash basis in practice in certain cases, see 11.1 CASH BASIS. Case law had previously established that the legal basis is the **earnings basis** with provision for debtors, creditors, accruals and stock and work in progress (cf. *CIR v Gardner Mountain & D'Ambrumenil Ltd HL 1947, 29 TC 69*). Hence profits and losses which have not accrued cannot be anticipated (cf. *Willingale v International Commercial Bank Ltd HL*

1977, 52 TC 242) nor can future expenses. Conversely an expense actually incurred is allowable in full even though the benefit from it will not accrue until later years (*Vallambrosa Rubber Co Ltd v Farmer CES 1910, 5 TC 529*; *Duple Motor Bodies Ltd v Ostime HL 1961, 39 TC 537*).

Accountancy principles. See above as regards the adoption of GAAP in the computation of taxable profits. Even prior to this, it had always been the case that, since the starting figure in computing profits was that brought out by the accounts of the business, accountancy principles were of the greatest importance. They could not, however, override established income tax principles (*Heather v P-E Consulting Group Ltd CA 1972, 48 TC 293*; *Willingale v International Commercial Bank Ltd HL 1977, 52 TC 242*; but see *Threlfall v Jones CA 1993, 66 TC 77*; *Johnston v Britannia Airways Ltd Ch D 1994, 67 TC 99*). See also *RTZ Oil & Gas Ltd v Elliss Ch D 1987, 61 TC 132*. A 'provision for a future operating loss', whose inclusion could not be said to have 'violated existing accounting principles', was disallowed in *Meat Traders Ltd v Cushing (Sp C 131), [1997] SSCD 245*). See *Robertson v CIR (Sp C 137), [1997] SSCD 282* as regards timing of inclusion of insurance agents' advance commission. See also *Herbert Smith v Honour Ch D 1999, 72 TC 130* for the timing of deductions in respect of future rents under leases of premises ceasing to be used for business purposes, and Revenue Press Release 20 July 1999 for Revenue practice following that decision.

Per Sir Thomas Bingham MR in *Threlfall v Jones*: ' . . . I find it hard to understand how any judge-made rule could override the application of a generally accepted rule of commercial accountancy which (a) applied to the situation in question, (b) was not one of two or more rules applicable to the situation in question and (c) was not shown to be inconsistent with the true facts or otherwise inapt to determine the true profits or losses of the business'. FRS 18 now requires companies to choose accounting policies that are most appropriate to their particular circumstances (see Revenue Tax Bulletin April 2002 p 924).

If an entity has correctly followed an International Accounting Standard or USA standard, which does not conflict with UK GAAP, including the requirements of FRS 18 (accounting policies), and this accurately reflects the facts, the accountancy treatment will comply with the requirement of *FA 1998, s 42* above (Revenue Business Income Manual BIM 31027).

For the Revenue view on the relationship between accountancy and taxable profits, see Revenue Business Income Manual BIM 31000–31120 and Revenue Tax Bulletin December 1997 pp 485, 486, February 1999 pp 623–625, April 1999 pp 636–641, December 1999 pp 707–709, June 2001 pp 859, 860. For generally accepted accounting practice and accounting standards, see BIM 31020–31070. For the timing of deductions where an expense is taken to the balance sheet rather than charged immediately against profits, i.e. *deferred revenue expenditure*, see Revenue Business Income Manual BIM 42215, 42220. For *provisions*, see Revenue Business Income Manual BIM 46500 *et seq.* and Revenue Press Release 20 July 1999, Revenue Tax Bulletin December 1999 pp 707–709.

Capital receipts and expenses must, unless the Acts explicitly provide otherwise, be excluded. This principle is derived, as regards expenses, from *ICTA 1988, s 74(1)(f)(g)* and generally because the charge to tax is on *income*. See also *ICTA 1988, s 817(2)*. 'No part of our law of taxation presents such almost insoluble conundrums as the decision whether a receipt or outgoing is capital or income for tax purposes' (Lord Upjohn in *Strick v Regent Oil Co Ltd HL 1965, 43 TC 1* q.v. for a comprehensive review of the law). A widely used test is the 'enduring benefit' one given by Viscount Cave in *Atherton v British Insulated & Helsby Cables Ltd HL 1925, 10 TC 155*. For recent reviews of the cases, see *Lawson v Johnson Matthey plc HL 1992, 65 TC 39* and *Halifax plc v Davidson (Sp C 239), [2000] SSCD 251*. In the latter case, costs incurred by a building society on conversion to a public limited company were disallowed as capital expenditure to the extent that they related to payment of statutory cash bonuses to non-voting members of the society, but otherwise allowed.

It is by virtue of *ICTA 1988, s 74(1)(f)* that depreciation of fixed assets is not allowable in computing profits (see 9.1 CAPITAL ALLOWANCES) (*In re Robert Addie & Sons CES 1875, 1 TC 1*). Where the depreciation charge in the accounts was reduced by capitalising part of it and including that part in the balance sheet value of stock (i.e. as an overhead cost), only the net depreciation (i.e. the amount after reduction) fell to be added back to trading profits in order to arrive at taxable profits (*Mars UK Ltd v Small; William Grant & Sons Distillers Ltd v CIR (Sp C 408), 2004 STI 1282*).

A gain or loss on the sale of a capital asset not included in trading profits is dealt with according to the provisions relating to capital gains tax. A sale of a fixed asset on which capital allowances have been claimed may result in a balancing charge or allowance, see 9 CAPITAL ALLOWANCES.

The revenue or capital nature of a payment is fixed at the time of its receipt (*Tapemaze Ltd v Melluish Ch D 2000, 73 TC 167*, following *Morley v Tattersall CA 1938, 40 TC 671*).

For a brief note on the Revenue approach to challenging schemes or arrangements designed to turn income into capital (or capital expenditure into a revenue deduction), see Revenue Tax Bulletin June 1997 p 438.

For the Revenue's own guidance on capital *v* income, see Revenue Business Income Manual BIM 35000–35910.

Wholly and exclusively. Any expense to be deductible must, *inter alia*, have been incurred 'wholly and exclusively ... for the purposes' of the trade etc. [*ICTA 1988, s 74(1)(a)*]. This provision underlies, explicitly or implicitly, the very large number of 'expenses' cases noted in the paragraphs below. For a review of the leading cases see *Harrods (Buenos Aires) Ltd v Taylor-Gooby CA 1964, 41 TC 450* and for a frequently quoted analysis of the words see *Bentleys, Stokes & Lowless v Beeson CA 1952, 33 TC 491*. Since that case the '*dual purpose rule*' has figured prominently in Court decisions. If an expense is for a material private or non-business purpose, the whole is strictly disallowable as it is thereby not wholly and exclusively for business purposes. For examples of its application see 71.64 and 71.80 below. 'Dual expenditure is expenditure that is incurred for more than one reason. If one of the reasons is not for business purposes, the expenditure fails the statutory test and there is no provision that allows a "business" proportion' (Revenue Business Income Manual BIM 37007). *However*, in practice, where an identifiable part or proportion of an expense has been laid out wholly and exclusively for the purposes of the trade, the Revenue do not disallow that part or proportion on the grounds that the expense is not *as a whole* laid out wholly and exclusively for the purposes of the trade (BIM 37007). For rent etc. of premises used both for business and as residence, see 71.68 below.

See *Mallalieu v Drummond* (71.64) for an important HL discussion of *ICTA 1988, s 74(1)(a)*, in which it was held that the purposes of the relevant expenditure involved looking into the taxpayer's mind at the time of the expenditure, later events being irrelevant except as a reflection of that state of mind. However, the taxpayer's conscious motive at the time was not conclusive; an object, not a conscious motive (in this case the human requirement for clothing), could be taken into account.

A purely incidental consequence of a business expense does not, however, preclude its being wholly and exclusively for business purposes (Revenue Business Income Manual BIM 37007, 37400). See, for example, *Robinson v Scott Bader Ltd*, 71.44 below and *McKnight v Sheppard HL 1999, 71 TC 419*, 71.69, 71.64 below. *Mallalieu v Drummond* was applied in *Watkis v Ashford, Sparkes and Harward Ch D 1985, 58 TC 468*, where expenditure on meals supplied at regular partners' lunchtime meetings was disallowed, overruling the Commissioner's finding that the expenditure was exclusively for business purposes. Expenditure on accommodation, food and drink at the firm's annual weekend conference was, however, allowed. For deduction of payments by partnerships to individual partners generally, see *MacKinlay v Arthur Young McClelland Moores & Co HL 1989, 62 TC 704*. Salaries paid to partners are not deductible as trading expenses (*PDC Copyprint (South) v George (Sp C 141), [1997] SSCD 326*).

See also 71.64 below as regards personal expenses.

It should be borne in mind that the trade for whose purposes the expenditure is incurred must be that in which the expense arose. For a successful appeal against a decision in favour of the Revenue on this point, see *Vodafone Cellular Ltd v Shaw CA 1997, 69 TC 376*.

For the Revenue's own guidance on the 'wholly and exclusively' rule, see Revenue Business Income Manual BIM 37000–38600.

Adjustments on change of basis. The tax adjustment described below is required where there is, from one period of account of a trade etc. to the next, a 'change of basis' in computing Schedule D, Case I or II profits, and the bases adopted before and after the change accorded with the law or accepted practice applicable in relation to the respective periods of account. A *'change of basis'* for this purpose is either (i) a change of accounting principle or practice which, in accordance with 'generally accepted accounting practice' (see above), gives rise to a prior period adjustment, or (ii) a change in the statutory tax adjustments applied (including a change resulting from a change of view as to application of the statute but excluding a change made to comply with an amendment to the statute which was not applicable to the earlier period of account). Except as detailed below, these provisions apply to changes taking effect in periods of account ending **on or after 1 August 2001**, and replace the similar earlier provisions of *FA 1998, s 44, Sch 6* (see 11.2 CASH BASIS), which, however, dealt only with changes of accounting basis.

Subject to the special cases referred to below, the adjustment required is calculated as follows.

(A)   Taxable receipts and allowable expenses of the trade etc. for periods of account before the change are determined on the old and new bases, and the net understatement of profits (or overstatement of losses) on the old basis compared with the new basis determined (a negative figure indicating a net overstatement of profits (or understatement of losses)).

(B)   That figure is then adjusted for any difference between the closing stock or work in progress for the last period of account before the change and the opening stock or work in progress for the first period of account after the change, also taking account of any change in the basis of calculating those amounts.

(C)   Finally an adjustment is made for depreciation to the extent that it was not the subject of an adjustment for tax purposes in the last period of account before the change but would be the subject of such an adjustment on the new basis.

Subject to the spreading provisions described below, a *positive* adjustment is treated for income tax purposes as income arising on the last day of the first period of account for which the new basis is adopted, chargeable under SCHEDULE D, CASE VI (74). For loss relief purposes it is treated as profits of the trade etc. for the chargeable period for which it is charged to tax, and in the case of an individual for whom the income from the trade etc. is 'relevant earnings' (see 60.8 PERSONAL PENSION SCHEMES, 66.7 RETIREMENT ANNUITIES) or earned income within *ICTA 1988, s 833(4)(c)* (see 1.7(iii) ALLOWANCES AND TAX RATES) it is similarly relevant earnings or earned income. (For corporation tax purposes, it is treated as a trade etc. receipt arising on the last day of the first period of account after the change.) A *negative* adjustment is treated as an expense of the trade etc. arising on that day. No further deduction is allowed for amounts taken into account in calculating the adjustment.

71.30 Schedule D, Cases I and II—Profits of Trades etc.

Special rules modify (A)–(C) above in a number of cases.

(1) *Expenses spread over more than one period of account after the change* on the new basis which were brought into account before the change on the old basis are excluded from the calculation at (A) above, but may not be deducted for any period of account after the change.

(2) *Adjustment not required until asset realised or written off.* Where the change of basis results from a tax adjustment affecting the calculation of amounts within (B) or (C) above, the adjustment required by (B) or (C) is brought into account only when the asset concerned is realised or written off.

(3) *Change from realisation basis to mark to market*, i.e. from recognition of a profit or loss on an asset only when it is realised to bringing assets into account in each period of account at fair value. Any adjustment required by (A) above for an understatement of profit (or overstatement of loss) in relation to an asset that is trading stock within *ICTA 1988, s 100* is not given effect until the period of account in which the value of the asset is realised. An election may, however, be made for the adjustment charge to be spread over six periods of account beginning with the first period after the change. The election must be made in writing to an officer of the Board within twelve months after the end of the first accounting period to which the new basis applies. If the trade etc. is permanently discontinued before the whole of the adjustment charge has been brought into charge, the uncharged balance is charged as if it arose immediately before the discontinuance. Special provision is made for the application of this rule in the case of insurance business transfers.

(4) *Barristers and advocates.* See 11.2 CASH BASIS.

As regards changes of basis within (1) or (3) above, the current provisions apply to a change taking effect in a period of account ending before 1 August 2001 if the relevant tax return for the period of the change (or for a later period ending before that date) is delivered or voluntarily amended by the taxpayer on or after that date. Any resulting adjustment is given effect for the first period of account ending on or after that date if it would otherwise be given effect in an earlier period.

Partnerships. In the case of trades, professions or vocations carried on in partnership, the adjustment (as above) is calculated as if the partnership were an individual (for corporation tax purposes, a company) resident in the UK. Each partner's share is determined according to the profit-sharing arrangements for the twelve months immediately before the first day of the first period of account for which the new basis was adopted, and an election for spreading of an adjustment under (3) above must be made jointly by all persons who were partners in that twelve-month period.

Personal representatives. In the case of the death of an individual otherwise chargeable to tax on an amount representing part of an adjustment charge (as above), the personal representatives assume the outstanding liabilities and may make any election under these provisions which the deceased might have made.

[*FA 2002, s 64, Sch 22*].

See Revenue Business Income Manual BIM 34000–34135.

Employment income received by a trader should in law be excluded from his Case I and II income (see 5.1 ASSESSMENTS) but in practice the legal position is modified in certain circumstances. See Revenue Employment Income Manual EIM 03002. See *Walker v Carnaby Harrower Ch D 1969, 46 TC 561* and *CIR v Brander & Cruickshank HL 1970, 46 TC 574* for the inclusion in the Case II assessment of professions of remuneration as auditor etc. For the tax treatment of directors' fees received by partnerships and other companies and the distinction between employment income and Schedule D, see 75.2(v) and 75.27

SCHEDULE E—EMPLOYMENT INCOME. See 75.35 SCHEDULE E—EMPLOYMENT INCOME as regards certain payments to redundant steel workers.

For **ancillary trading income** see 71.56 below.

Private Finance Initiative ('PFI') projects. For a series of articles on the tax aspects of PFI projects (dealing with the introduction by the public sector body of surplus land, or cash derived therefrom, with stamp duty considerations, with income arising from leases of fully serviced accommodation and with the scope of a PFI operator's trade), see Revenue Tax Bulletin April 1999 pp 642–645, October 1999 pp 694–697, August 2002 p 950. See also Revenue Business Income Manual BIM 64000–64405.

Simon's Direct Tax Service. See B3.9, B3.12.

71.31   **ADVERTISING**

Expenditure generally is allowable (but not capital outlay such as fixed signs (but see *Leeds Permanent Building Society v Proctor Ch D 1982, 56 TC 293*), nor initial costs etc. of new business). Contribution to campaign for Sunday opening held allowable (*Rhymney Breweries Ch D 1965, 42 TC 509*). As to political campaign see *Tate & Lyle HL 1954, 35 TC 367*, contrasted with *Boarland v Kramat Pulai Ch D 1953, 35 TC 1*. See Revenue Business Income Manual BIM 42550–42555.

71.32   **APPLICATION OF PROFITS**

A requirement that a trading surplus is to be applied in a particular way does not remove the trade from Case I (*Mersey Docks and Harbour Board v Lucas HL 1883, 2 TC 25*) and applications of the profits under the requirement are not allowable deductions (*City of Dublin Steam Packet Co v O'Brien KB(I) 1912, 6 TC 101*; *Hutchinson & Co v Turner HC 1950, 31 TC 495*; *Young v Racecourse Betting Control Board HL 1959, 38 TC 426* and cf. *Pondicherry Rly Co PC 1931, 10 ATC 365*; *Tata Hydro-Electric Agencies PC 1937, 16 ATC 54*; *India Radio & Cable Communication Co PC 1937, 16 ATC 333*).

For circumstances in which the profits of a trade may not accrue to the proprietor, see *Alongi v CIR CS 1991, 64 TC 304*.

71.33   **ARTISTES**

For creative artists, see 71.41 below.

An actress based in the UK but with engagements abroad was held to be carrying on a single profession. Hence receipts from her overseas engagements fell to be included in her Case II assessment (*Davies v Braithwaite KB 1933, 18 TC 198* and compare *Withers v Wynyard KB 1938, 21 TC 724*).

An artiste engaged by a theatre under a standard contract was held to be within Schedule E (*Fall v Hitchen Ch D 1972, 49 TC 433*), but see now 75.27 SCHEDULE E—EMPLOYMENT INCOME as regards application of Schedule D to artistes generally.

A sum received by a company, formed to exploit the services of an actor, on cancellation of an agreement giving another his exclusive services was held a trading receipt (*John Mills Productions Ltd v Mathias Ch D 1967, 44 TC 441*). Payment to actor for entering into restrictive covenant held not assessable (*Higgs v Olivier CA 1952, 33 TC 136*).

For deductibility of expenses of actors and other entertainers, including clothing, costume, grooming and cosmetic surgery, see Revenue Business Income Manual BIM 50160.

See 3.9 ANTI-AVOIDANCE for the treatment as income of certain capital sums received in lieu of earnings and 51.7 NON-RESIDENTS AND OTHER OVERSEAS MATTERS as regards certain non-resident entertainers and sportsmen.

71.34 Schedule D, Cases I and II—Profits of Trades etc.

BAD AND DOUBTFUL DEBTS

See generally Revenue Business Income Manual BIM 42700–42750.

Bad debts, and doubtful debts to the extent they are estimated to be bad, are deductible. Where the debtor is bankrupt or insolvent, the debt is deductible except to the extent that any amount may reasonably be expected to be received on it.

Debts (or parts) released wholly and exclusively for trade purposes as part of a voluntary arrangement under or by virtue of *Insolvency Act 1986* or a compromise or arrangement under *Companies Act 1985, s 425* (or NI equivalent) do not require any write-back for tax purposes. [*ICTA 1988, s 74(1)(j); FA 1994, s 144(1)(2)(6); FA 1996, s 134, Sch 20 para 4*]. Profit and loss credits for trade debts written back do not generally require adjustment for tax purposes [*ICTA 1988, s 94; FA 1994, s 144(3)(a)*] except that, for accounting periods starting before 1 January 2002 (following *British Mexican Petroleum Co Ltd v Jackson HL, 16 TC 570*), where a trade debt is written back *without* being released, a computational adjustment is required for tax purposes to deduct the amount written back. (Revenue Tax Bulletin December 2001 pp 901, 902). See also Revenue Business Income Manual BIM 40201, 42740.

Where a trade is treated as notionally discontinued (see 71.15 above), the allowance extends to debts taken over by the successor, and similar treatment applies to recoveries. [*ICTA 1988, ss 89, 106(2)*].

For debt recoveries and releases after the cessation of a trade, see 62 POST-CESSATION ETC. RECEIPTS AND EXPENDITURE. Bad debt allowances are not applicable where the business is assessed on a CASH BASIS (11). For VAT on bad debts, see 71.83 below.

The provision for a bad or doubtful debt for a period of account may reflect events after the balance sheet date insofar as they furnish additional evidence of conditions that existed at the balance sheet date. See Revenue Tax Bulletin August 1994 p 154, which also outlines the evidence which inspectors may require in support of the allowance of a provision.

Where as part of a transfer of assets and liabilities between group companies creditors consent to the release of the transferor company from its obligations in return for the transferee assuming those obligations, no charge arises under *section 94*. (Revenue Tax Bulletin August 1993 p 88).

Where an asset accepted in satisfaction of a trading debt is of market value (as at the date of acceptance) less than the outstanding debt, the deficit may be allowed as a deduction, provided the trader agrees that, on a disposal of the asset, any excess of disposal proceeds over that value (up to the amount by which the debt exceeds that value) will be brought in as a trading receipt (such receipt being excluded from any chargeable gain computation on the disposal) (Revenue Business Income Manual BIM 42735).

An allowance agreed under conditions of full disclosure cannot be withdrawn because of a subsequent change in the circumstances (*Anderton & Halstead Ltd v Birrell KB 1931, 16 TC 200*) but an allowance for year 1 may be revised, upwards or downwards, in the year 2 computation by reference to the circumstances for year 2 and similarly for later years. The amount of the allowance depends on the likelihood of recovery. This is a question of fact but the fact that the debtor is still in business is not itself a reason for refusing an allowance (*Dinshaw v Bombay IT Commr PC 1934, 13 ATC 284*). See also *Lock v Jones KB 1941, 23 TC 749*.

The allowance is made in respect of a particular debt and general bad debt provisions are not allowed. However where there are a large number of comparatively small debts, making the 'valuation' of individual debts impracticable, the Revenue will normally agree to an allowance in accordance with a formula based on the bad debt experience of the business. Typical businesses are mail-order firms and firms with a large proportion of hire-purchase sales. Where hire-purchase is involved the formula may also cover the spread of the profit on hire-purchase sales. But no provision for the estimated cost of collecting future debt instalments is permissible (*Monthly Salaries Loan Co Ltd v Furlong Ch D 1962, 40 TC 313*).

For small credit traders who collect their debts by weekly instalments (sometimes called travelling drapers or Scotch drapers) a special arrangement is available. For details see Form 189 obtainable from inspectors.

Where a builder sold houses leaving part of the sale proceeds with Building Societies as collateral security for mortgages by the purchasers, held the amounts should be brought in at valuation when houses sold and if practicable and otherwise when released by Building Society (*John Cronk & Sons Ltd v Harrison HL 1936, 20 TC 612* and cf. *Chibbett v Harold Brookfield & Son Ltd CA 1952, 33 TC 467*). A similar decision was reached in *Absalom v Talbot HL 1944, 26 TC 166* where amounts were left on loan to the purchasers. See also *Lock v Jones* above. The HL judgments in *Absalom v Talbot* are an important review of the treatment of trading debts.

The normal debt considered for allowance under *ICTA 1988, s 74(1)(j)* is one for goods or services supplied or one in a business, such as banking or money-lending, which consists of advancing money (see e.g. *AB Bank v Inspector of Taxes (Sp C 237), [2000] SSCD 229*). Losses on advances by a brewery company to its customers were allowed as on the evidence it habitually acted as banker for them in the course of its brewing business (*Reid's Brewery v Male QB 1891, 3 TC 279*). But losses on advances to clients by solicitors were refused as there was no evidence that they were money-lenders (*CIR v Hagart & Burn-Murdoch HL 1929, 14 TC 433; Rutherford v CIR CS 1939, 23 TC 8*. See also *Bury & Walkers v Phillips HC 1951, 32 TC 198* and contrast *Jennings v Barfield Ch D 1962, 40 TC 365*). An allowance was refused for an irrecoverable balance due from the managing director of a company as outside the company's trade (*Curtis v J & G Oldfield Ltd KB 1925, 9 TC 319*). See also *Roebank Printing Co Ltd v CIR CS 1928, 13 TC 864*.

Advances to finance or recoup the losses of subsidiary or associated companies are capital. Allowances were refused in *English Crown Spelter v Baker KB 1908, 5 TC 327* and *Charles Marsden & Sons v CIR KB 1919, 12 TC 217* for losses on advances to facilitate the supply of materials for the trade of the lender as were losses on an advance to a company under the same control (*Baker v Mabie Todd & Co Ltd KB 1927, 13 TC 235*), amounts written off in respect of the losses of a subsidiary (*Odhams Press Ltd v Cook HL 1940, 23 TC 233*) and payments to meet the operating losses of a subsidiary (*Marshall Richards Machine Co Ltd v Jewitt Ch D 1956, 36 TC 511*). See also *CIR v Huntley & Palmers Ltd KB 1928, 12 TC 1209; Henderson v Meade-King Robinson & Co Ltd KB 1938, 22 TC 97;* and *Stone & Temple Ltd v Waters; Astrawall (UK) Ltd v Waters Ch D 1995, 67 TC 145*. (N.B. The loss of subsidiary may now be eligible for group relief — see Tolley's Corporation Tax.)

Losses relating to trade debts with a subsidiary were, however, held allowable in *Sycamore plc and Maple Ltd v Fir (Sp C 104), [1997] SSCD 1*.

Payments by the purchaser to discharge the unpaid liabilities of the vendor to preserve goodwill etc. allowed in *Cooke v Quick Shoe Repair Service KB 1949, 30 TC 460*.

See 71.82 below for relief for certain unremittable overseas debts of trades within Schedule D, Case I.

Note. Loans made to a trader for the setting up or purposes of his trade and irrecoverable are in certain circumstances allowable as a loss for capital gains tax — see Tolley's Capital Gains Tax.

For losses under guarantees see 71.51 below.

Simon's Direct Tax Service. See B3.1461 *et seq.*

71.35 Schedule D, Cases I and II—Profits of Trades etc.

71.35 BREWERIES, DISTILLERIES, LICENSED PREMISES

Tied houses. Receipts and expenses in respect of 'tied premises' which would otherwise be brought into account under SCHEDULE A (69) are instead brought in as trading receipts or expenses. Premises outside the UK are for this purpose treated as if they were in the UK. Any necessary apportionment (e.g. where rents etc. relate only in part to the tied premises or where only part of the premises qualifies) is on a just and reasonable basis. '*Tied premises*' are premises through which goods supplied by a trader are sold or used by another person, where the trader has an estate or interest in the premises which he treats as property employed for trade purposes. Slightly different rules applied before 17 March 1998 (see *ICTA 1988, s 98* as originally enacted). Receipts or expenses taken into account under the previous rules are not taken into account again, but any which would have been allowed under the new rules before 17 March 1998 but which were not previously taken into account are brought into account on that date. [*ICTA 1988, s 98; FA 1998, s 41*]. (*Note.* These rules are of general application, although of most common application in the licensed trade.)

Case law. Repairs, rates, insurance premiums paid on behalf of tied tenants allowable (*Usher's Wiltshire Brewery v Bruce HL 1914, 6 TC 399*) but not extra expenditure incurred to keep licensed houses open while undergoing rehabilitation (*Mann Crossman & Paulin Ltd v Compton KB 1947, 28 TC 410*) or compensation to a tenant displaced on a licence transfer (*Morse v Stedeford KB 1934, 18 TC 457*). For compensation paid on the termination of tenancies of tied houses, see *Watneys (London) Ltd v Pike Ch D 1982, 57 TC 372*. Losses on advances to 'customers and connections' held allowable (*Reid's Brewery v Male QB 1891, 3 TC 279*).

The expenses of an unsuccessful application for licences were held not allowable (*Southwell v Savill Bros KB 1901, 4 TC 430* — it was conceded that expenses of successful applications are capital) nor expenses of applying for licence transfers (*Morse v Stedeford* above; *Pendleton v Mitchells & Butlers Ch D 1968, 45 TC 341*). Contributions by a brewer to a trade association to promote Sunday opening in Wales allowed in *Cooper v Rhymney Breweries Ch D 1965, 42 TC 509*. Compensation Fund levies deductible (*Smith v Lion Brewery HL 1910, 5 TC 568*) but not monopoly value payments (*Kneeshaw v Albertolli KB 1940, 23 TC 462; Henriksen v Grafton Hotels Ltd CA 1942, 24 TC 453*).

Damages paid to hotel guest injured by falling chimney held not allowable — see *Strong & Co v Woodifield* at 71.37 below. For accrued whisky storage rents see *Dailuaine-Talisker Distilleries v CIR CS 1930, 15 TC 613; CIR v Oban Distillery Co CS 1932, 18 TC 33* and *CIR v Arthur Bell & Sons CS 1932, 22 TC 315*.

Where a brewery company ceased brewing but continued to sell beer brewed for it by another company it was held to have discontinued its old trade and commenced a new one (*Gordon & Blair Ltd v CIR CS 1962, 40 TC 358*).

Simon's Direct Tax Service. See B3.1121 *et seq.*

71.36 COMMISSION, CASHBACKS AND DISCOUNTS

Revenue Statement of Practice SP 4/97 sets out the Revenue's views on the tax treatment of commissions, cashbacks and discounts. The types of payment with which the Statement is concerned are as follows.

Commissions. Sums paid by the providers of goods, investments or services to agents or intermediaries as reward for the introduction of business, or in some cases paid directly by the provider to the customer. Sums paid to an agent or intermediary may be passed on to the customer or to some other person.

Cashbacks. Lump sums received by a customer as an inducement for entering into a transaction for the purchase of goods, investments or services and received as a direct

828

consequence of having entered into that transaction. The payer may be either the provider or another party with an interest in ensuring that the transaction takes place.

Discounts, i.e. where the purchaser's obligation to pay for goods, investments or services is less than the full purchase price, other than as a result of commissions or cashbacks.

The Statement also deals with commissions or cashbacks which are netted off, or invested or otherwise applied for the benefit of the purchaser, or where extra value is added to the goods, investments or services supplied (e.g. the allocation of bonus units in an investment) (although in the case of the addition of value to investments this may represent a return on the investment, which is outside the scope of the Statement).

The Statement provides detailed guidance on the circumstances in which Schedule D liability may arise under either Case I or II or Case VI, and on deductibility of the payments under those Cases. It also considers possible liabilities under Schedule E or to capital gains tax, and the effect of commissions etc. on life insurance policies and personal pension contributions.

Generally, ordinary retail arm's length customers will not be liable to income or capital gains tax. The Statement outlines the circumstances in which receipts are treated as tax-free, or payments qualify for tax relief, and contains an element of concession for those who, in the ordinary course of their business, earn commission relating to their own transactions. It contains a warning that the principles outlined may not be followed where tax avoidance schemes are involved, or where the arrangements for the commission etc. include an increase in the purchase price of the goods etc. involved. The tax treatment of the payer and the recipient are in all cases considered independently of one another.

(Revenue Statement of Practice SP 4/97, 27 November 1997).

For an article explaining the legal basis of this approach, see Revenue Tax Bulletin February 1998 pp 505–509.

71.37   **COMPENSATION, DAMAGES ETC. — PAYMENTS**

For compensation and redundancy payments to directors or employees see 71.44 below. An important case is *Anglo-Persian Oil Co Ltd v Dale CA 1931, 16 TC 253* in which a substantial payment by a company for the cancellation of its principal agency, with ten years to run, was held to be allowable. It was not for a capital asset nor to get rid of an onerous contract (cf. *Mallett v Staveley Coal CA 1928, 13 TC 772*) but to enable it to rationalise its working arrangements. The decision was applied in *Croydon Hotel & Leisure Co Ltd v Bowen (Sp C 101), [1996] SSCD 466*, in which a payment for the termination of a hotel management agreement was held to be allowable. See also *Vodafone Cellular Ltd v Shaw CA 1997, 69 TC 376* (payment for release from onerous agreement), in which the principle underlying the decision in *Van den Berghs Ltd v Clark* (see 71.38(*b*) below) was applied, but cf. *Tucker v Granada Motorway Services Ltd HL 1979, 53 TC 92*, where a payment to modify the method of calculating the rent was held to be capital, and *Whitehead v Tubbs (Elastics) Ltd CA 1983, 57 TC 472*, where a payment to alter the terms of a capital loan by removing borrowing restrictions on the borrower was held to be capital.

A payment by a shipping company for cancelling an order it had placed for a ship was held capital (*'Countess Warwick' SS Co Ltd v Ogg KB 1924, 8 TC 652* and contrast *Devon Mutual Steamship Insce v Ogg KB 1927, 13 TC 184*). A payment to an associated company in return for its temporarily ceasing production held allowable (*Commr of Taxes v Nchanga Consolidated Copper Mines PC 1964, 43 ATC 20*) as were statutory levies on a brewery for a Compensation Fund where a licence is not renewed (*Smith v Lion Brewery Co Ltd HL 1910, 5 TC 568*) and a payment to secure the closure of a rival concern (*Walker v The Joint Credit Card Co Ltd Ch D 1982, 55 TC 617*). Payments by a steel company to secure the closure of railway steel works were held capital (*United Steels v Cullington (No 1) CA 1939,*

23 TC 71) as were payments to safeguard against subsidence on a factory site (*Bradbury v United Glass Bottle Mfrs CA 1959, 38 TC 369*; compare *Glenboig Union Fireclay* at 71.38(*c*) below) and a payment for cancelling electricity agreement on closure of a quarry (*CIR v Wm Sharp & Son CS 1959, 38 TC 341*). For compensation paid on the termination of tied houses of breweries, see *Watneys (London) Ltd v Pike Ch D 1982, 57 TC 372*.

Where damages awarded by a Court against a solicitor were later compounded, the compounded amount (accepted as allowable) was held to be an expense of the year in which the Court award was made (*Simpson v Jones Ch D 1968, 44 TC 599*). See also *CIR v Hugh T Barrie Ltd CA(NI) 1928, 12 TC 1223*.

Damages paid by a brewery to a hotel guest injured by a falling chimney were held to have been incurred by it *qua* property owner and not *qua* trader and not deductible (*Strong & Co of Romsey Ltd v Woodifield HL 1906, 5 TC 215*). Penalties for breach of war-time regulations and defence costs not allowed (*CIR v Warnes & Co KB 1919, 12 TC 227*; *CIR v Alexander von Glehn & Co Ltd CA 1920, 12 TC 232*), nor fines imposed by professional regulatory body (*McKnight v Sheppard Ch D 1996, 71 TC 419*), nor damages for breach of American 'anti-trust' law (*Cattermole v Borax & Chemicals Ltd KB 1949, 31 TC 202*). See also *G Scammell & Nephew v Rowles CA 1939, 22 TC 479*; *Fairrie v Hall KB 1947, 28 TC 200*; *Golder v Great Boulder Proprietary HC 1952, 33 TC 75*; *Knight v Parry Ch D 1972, 48 TC 580*; *Hammond Engineering v CIR Ch D 1975, 50 TC 313*.

Simon's Direct Tax Service. See A1.212, B3.1466, B3.1509.

71.38   **COMPENSATION, DAMAGES ETC. — RECEIPTS**

(*a*)   **Capital sums** (i.e. sums not taken into account in computing income) received as compensation for damage, injury, destruction or depreciation of assets are subject to capital gains tax [*TCGA 1992, s 22(1)*] (or corporation tax in the case of a company), but this does not apply to compensation or damages to an individual for wrong or injury to his person or in his profession or vocation. [*TCGA 1992, s 51(2)*].

(*b*)   **Cancellation or variation of trading contracts and arrangements.** An important case is *Van den Berghs Ltd v Clark HL 1935, 19 TC 390* in which a receipt on the termination of a profit-sharing arrangement was held to be capital. The arrangement related to the whole structure of the recipient's trade, forming the fixed framework within which its circulating capital operated. Compensation etc. receipts were also held to be capital in *Sabine v Lookers Ltd CA 1958, 38 TC 120* (varying car distributor's agreement); *British–Borneo Petroleum v Cropper Ch D 1968, 45 TC 201* (cancelling a royalty agreement); *Barr Crombie & Co Ltd v CIR CS 1945, 26 TC 406* (terminating agreement as ship-managers); but the opposite conclusion was reached in *Consultant v Inspector of Taxes (Sp C 180), [1999] SSCD 63* (termination of profit participation agreement). A payment by the liquidator of a shipping company to its managers as authorised by the shareholders held not assessable (*Chibbett v Robinson & Sons KB 1924, 9 TC 48*).

Compensation etc. receipts on the cancellation of contracts receipts from which, if completed, would have been trading receipts are normally themselves trading receipts, to be credited in the computations for the period in which cancelled. See *Short Bros Ltd v CIR* and *Sunderland Shipbuilding Co Ltd v CIR CA 1927, 12 TC 955* (cancellation of order for ships); *CIR v Northfleet Coal Co KB 1927, 12 TC 1102*; *Jesse Robinson & Sons v CIR KB 1929, 12 TC 1241* (cancellation of contracts for sale of goods etc.); *Greyhound Racing Assn v Cooper KB 1936, 20 TC 373* (cancellation of agreement to hire greyhound track); *Shove v Dura Mfg Co Ltd KB 1941, 23 TC 779* (cancellation of commission agreement). Similarly compensation to a merchanting company on cancellation of a contract to supply goods to it was held a trading receipt (*Bush, Beach & Gent Ltd v Road KB 1939, 22 TC 519*). See also *United Steel v*

Cullington (No 1) CA 1939, 23 TC 71; Shadbolt v Salmon Estates KB 1943, 25 TC 52; Sommerfelds Ltd v Freeman Ch D 1966, 44 TC 43; Creed v H & M Levinson Ltd Ch D 1981, 54 TC 477.

Compensation received on the termination of agencies is a trading receipt unless the agency, by reason of its relative size etc., is part of the 'fixed framework' (see *Van den Berghs* above) of the agent's business. See *Kelsall Parsons CS 1938, 21 TC 608; CIR v Fleming & Co CS 1951, 33 TC 57; CIR v David MacDonald & Co CS 1955, 36 TC 388; Wiseburgh v Domville CA 1956, 36 TC 527; Fleming v Bellow Machine Co Ch D 1965, 42 TC 308; Elson v James G Johnston Ltd Ch D 1965, 42 TC 545* (in all of which the compensation etc. was held to be a trading receipt). See also *Anglo-French Exploration Co Ltd v Clayson CA 1956, 36 TC 545.*

For payments received on termination of building society agencies, see Revenue Capital Gains Tax Manual CG 13050 *et seq.*

The treatment of compensation on the termination of posts held in the course of a business (particularly a profession), the yearly remuneration having been included in the business receipts (see 75.27 SCHEDULE E—EMPLOYMENT INCOME), has arisen in a number of cases. In *Blackburn v Close Bros Ltd Ch D 1960, 39 TC 164,* compensation on the cancellation of an agreement by a merchant banker to provide secretarial services was held to be a trading receipt but in *Ellis v Lucas Ch D 1966, 43 TC 276* compensation on the termination of an auditorship was held to be within the ambit of the special legislation on termination payments (see 18.4 COMPENSATION FOR LOSS OF EMPLOYMENT (AND DAMAGES)) and hence could not be included in the profits for Case II purposes (except a small part of the payment held to be compensation for the loss of general accountancy work). Similar decisions were reached in *Walker v Carnaby Harrower, Barham & Pykett Ch D 1969, 46 TC 561* (loss of auditorship by firm of accountants) and *CIR v Brander & Cruikshank HL 1970, 46 TC 574* (loss of company secretaryships by firm of Scottish advocates) and in *Carnaby Harrower* the payment was also held not to be a professional receipt because of its *ex gratia* nature. For *ex gratia* payments, see also (*e*) below. For compensation on cancellation of contracts of actors, authors etc. see 71.33 above, 71.41 below.

(*c*) **Compensation etc. relating to capital assets.** Compensation to a company making fireclay goods for refraining from working a fireclay bed under a railway line was held to be capital (*Glenboig Union Fireclay Co Ltd v CIR HL 1922, 12 TC 427* and cf. *Thomas McGhie & Sons v BTC QB 1962, 41 ATC 144* and *Bradbury v United Glass Bottle CA 1959, 38 TC 369*), but compensation to a colliery from the Government for requisition of part of its mining area was held to be a trading receipt (*Waterloo Main Colliery v CIR (No 1) KB 1947, 29 TC 235*). Compensation to a shipping company for delay in the overhaul of a ship was held to be a trading receipt (*Burmah Steam Ship Co v CIR CS 1930, 16 TC 67*) as was compensation to a jetty owner for loss of its use after damage by a ship (*London & Thames Haven v Attwooll CA 1966, 43 TC 491*) and compensation for the detention of a ship (*Ensign Shipping Co v CIR CA 1928, 12 TC 1169* but contrast *CIR v Francis West CS 1950, 31 TC 402*).

For insurance recoveries see 71.54 below.

(*d*) **Compensation on compulsory acquisition etc.** Where compensation is paid for the acquisition of business property by an authority possessing powers of compulsory acquisition, any amounts included as compensation for temporary loss of profits or losses on trading stock or to reimburse revenue expenditure, such as removal expenses and interest, are treated as trading receipts. (See Revenue Pamphlet IR 131, SP 8/79, 18 June 1979. This Statement of Practice was originally issued as consequence of *Stoke-on-Trent City Council v Wood Mitchell & Co Ltd CA 1978, [1979] STC 197*.)

(e) **Other compensation etc. receipts.** Voluntary payments to an insurance broker on the loss of an important client company (made by its parent company) were held, approving *Chibbett v Robinson* and *Carnaby Harrower* (see (*b*) above), not to be assessable (*Simpson v John Reynolds & Co CA 1975, 49 TC 693*) and similarly for voluntary payments from a brewer to a firm of caterers for the surrender of the leases of tied premises (*Murray v Goodhews CA 1977, 52 TC 86*) but *ex gratia* payments to an estate agent who had not been given an agency he expected were held, on the facts, to be additional remuneration for work already done and assessable. (*McGowan v Brown & Cousins (Stuart Edwards) Ch D 1977, 52 TC 8*). A payment to a diamond broker under informal and non-binding arbitration as damages for the loss of a prospective client was held assessable (*Rolfe v Nagel CA 1981, 55 TC 585*). Compensation for 'loss of profits' following the destruction of the premises of a business not recommenced was held to be of a revenue nature in *Lang v Rice CA (NI) 1983, 57 TC 80*. For compensation receipts relating to the terms on which business premises are tenanted, see 71.68 below.

For the treatment of compensation received by businesses as customers of e.g. utility companies for interruptions and other service deficiencies, see Revenue Tax Bulletin December 1997 pp 490, 491.

Financial loss allowances paid to e.g. jurors, members of certain local authorities and magistrates to compensate them for loss of profit in their trade or profession are assessable under Schedule D, Case I or II as trading receipts. (Revenue Tax Bulletin May 1992 p 20). Such payments are not taxable as employment income (see 75.10 SCHEDULE E—EMPLOYMENT INCOME).

Damages awarded to a theatrical company for breach of a licence it had, were held to be assessable (*Vaughan v Parnell & Zeitlin KB 1940, 23 TC 505*) as was compensation received by a development company under legislation for restricting development (*Johnson v W S Try Ltd CA 1946, 27 TC 167*). A retrospective award for a war-time requisition of trading stock was held to be a trading receipt of the year of requisition (*CIR v Newcastle Breweries Ltd HL 1927, 12 TC 927*).

71.39 CONTINGENT AND FUTURE LIABILITIES

For forward contracts see 71.40 below.

Where a company is required under overseas legislation to make leaving payments to its employees, a provision in its accounts for its prospective liability is permissible if capable of sufficiently accurate calculation (*Owen v Southern Railway of Peru HL 1956, 36 TC 602*). The allowance each year is the actual payments as adjusted for any variation between the opening and closing provisions but the deductible provision for the year in which the legislation was enacted may include an amount in respect of previous services of the employees (*CIR v Titaghur Jute Factory Ltd CS 1978, 53 TC 675*).

No deduction is normally permissible for future repairs or renewals (*Clayton v Newcastle-under-Lyme Corpn QB 1888, 2 TC 416; Naval Colliery Co Ltd v CIR HL 1928, 12 TC 1017; Peter Merchant Ltd v Stedeford CA 1948, 30 TC 496*). However, this rule is now subject to Financial Reporting Standard FRS 12 (see 71.69(*b*) below). No deduction is permissible for the future cost of collecting debts (*Monthly Salaries Loan Co v Furlong Ch D 1962, 40 TC 313*) or for future payments of damages in respect of accidents to employees unless liability has been admitted or established (*James Spencer & Co v CIR CS 1950, 32 TC 111*). See also *Albion Rovers Football Club v CIR HL 1952, 33 TC 331* (wages deductible when paid). A provision for regular major overhaul work accrued due on aircraft engines was allowed in

Johnston v Britannia Airways Ltd Ch D 1994, 67 TC 99 (but see now Revenue Tax Bulletin February 1999 p 624 and further below as regards changes in accounting practice superseding this decision).

For provisions by insurance companies for unexpired risks etc., see *Sun Insurance Office v Clark HL 1912, 6 TC 59*. For the liability of cemetery companies in receipt of lump sums for the future maintenance of graves, see *Paisley Cemetery Co v Reith CES 1898, 4 TC 1* and *London Cemetery Co v Barnes KB 1917, 7 TC 92*.

A provision by a company engaged in the exploitation of a North Sea oil field, for anticipated future expenditure on the completion of the exploitation, in dismantling installations used and (as required under its licence) in 'cleaning up' the sea bed, was disallowed as capital when incurred in *RTZ Oil & Gas Ltd v Elliss Ch D 1987, 61 TC 132*.

See generally Revenue Business Income Manual BIM 42201, 46500–46565. See also Revenue Press Release 20 July 1999, and FRS 12 and articles in the Revenue Tax Bulletin April 1999 pp 636–639 and December 1999 pp 707–709 commenting on its implications for the treatment of provisions in tax computations.

Simon's Direct Tax Service. See B3.916, B3.1211 *et seq.*

71.40   **CONTRACTS**

For compensation etc. on the cancellation or variation of contracts see 71.37 and 71.38 above. For work in progress under contracts see 71.73 below.

Where a taxpayer took over a coal merchanting business on the death of his father, an amount paid for the benefit of contracts between his father and suppliers was held capital (*John Smith & Son v Moore HL 1921, 12 TC 266* and see *City of London Contract Corpn v Styles CA 1887, 2 TC 239*). The completion of outstanding contracts following a partnership dissolution (*Hillerns & Fowler v Murray CA 1932, 17 TC 77*) and on a company going into liquidation (*Baker v Cook KB 1937, 21 TC 337*) held to be trading.

Where under a long-term contract goods were invoiced as delivered, the sale proceeds are receipts of the year of delivery (*J P Hall & Co Ltd v CIR CA 1921, 12 TC 382*). If contract prices are varied retrospectively the resultant further sums are assessable or deductible for the years applicable to the sums at the original prices (*Frodingham Ironstone Mines Ltd v Stewart KB 1932, 16 TC 728*; *New Conveyor Co Ltd v Dodd KB 1945, 27 TC 11*). Compare *English Dairies Ltd v Phillips KB 1927, 11 TC 597*; *Isaac Holden & Sons Ltd v CIR KB 1924, 12 TC 768* and contrast *Rownson Drew & Clydesdale Ltd v CIR KB 1931, 16 TC 595*.

Losses because of a fall in prices fixed under forward contracts etc. cannot be anticipated (*Edward Collins & Sons Ltd v CIR CS 1924, 12 TC 773*; *Whimster & Co v CIR CS 1925, 12 TC 813*) and cf. *Wright Sutcliffe Ltd v CIR KB 1929, 8 ATC 168*; *J H Young & Co v CIR CS 1924, 12 TC 817*; *CIR v Hugh T Barrie Ltd CA(NI) 1928, 12 TC 1223*.

71.41   **CREATIVE ARTISTS**

General. A taxpayer who, after writing plays in his spare time which were not sold, wrote a successful play was held to be carrying on the vocation of dramatist (*Billam v Griffith KB 1941, 23 TC 757*). Receipts from the occasional writing of articles are normally assessable under SCHEDULE D, CASE VI (74) but Case II assessments on a regular newspaper contributor were upheld in *Graham v Arnott KB 1941, 24 TC 157*. Receipts from the sale of an author's notebooks and memorabilia were held to be taxable as part of the fruits of his profession (*Wain v Cameron Ch D 1995, 67 TC 324*).

A sum received by an author on cancellation of his contract as script writer was held a revenue receipt (*Household v Grimshaw Ch D 1953, 34 TC 366*). Film writer's loss under guarantee of indebtedness of film company held allowable (*Lunt v Wellesley KB 1945, 27 TC 78*).

Whether a literary prize or award is a receipt of the author's profession depends on the precise facts, see Revenue Business Income Manual BIM 50710, 50715.

See below as regards copyright, royalties etc. and see 71.33 above for the taxation of *artistes*. See 3.9 ANTI-AVOIDANCE for the treatment as income of certain capital sums received in lieu of earnings.

Averaging of profits from 2000/01 onwards. The averaging provisions below apply for 2000/01 onwards, i.e. the first pair of tax years for which averaging may be possible are 2000/01 and 2001/02. They apply in respect of profits of a 'qualifying trade, profession or vocation', i.e. one whose profits derive wholly or mainly from 'qualifying creative works' and are within Schedule D, Case I or II. '*Qualifying creative works*' means literary, dramatic, musical or artistic works, or designs, created by the individual personally or, in the case of a partnership, by one or more of the partners personally. Averaging does not apply to profits chargeable to corporation tax.

Where, in relation to two consecutive tax years, the profits for one year are less than 75% of the profits for the other (or the profits for one year, but not both, are nil, e.g. where a loss is incurred), an averaging claim can be made, with the following results. If the profits for either year do not exceed 70% of the profits for the other (or are nil), the profits for each year are adjusted to half the total of both. If either year's profits exceed 70% of the other's, but are less than 75%, the profits are adjusted by adding to the lower and subtracting from the higher the amount obtained by multiplying the difference by three and deducting 75% of the higher figure. (Thus, if the profits are £29,200 and £40,000, the averaged profits would be £31,600 and £37,600.)

'*Profits*' for this purpose are those before any adjustment for losses sustained in any tax year. An averaging claim does not prevent a claim for loss relief. (Thus, if there were a loss of £10,000 for one tax year and a profit of £30,000 for the other, the averaged profits for each year are £15,000, but the loss of £10,000 remains eligible for loss relief in the normal way.)

If an averaging claim is made for a pair of tax years, Years X and Y, a claim is also permitted for Years Y and Z, the profits for Year Y being taken as those adjusted on the first claim, and so on for subsequent years. However, no averaging claim is subsequently permissible involving any year prior to Year X. No averaging claim can be made involving the tax year in which the business commences or that in which it is permanently discontinued; neither can a claim be made involving any tax year in which the business begins, or ceases, to be a 'qualifying trade, profession or vocation' (see above).

An averaging claim must be made on or before the first anniversary of 31 January following the later of the two tax years to which it relates. An averaging claim can be made only by an individual. In the case of a partnership, an individual partner may make his own claim, based on his own profit shares, irrespective of whether or not other partners make claims.

If, after a claim, the profits of either or both years are adjusted for some other reason, the claim lapses but a new one may then be made, in respect of the adjusted profits, on or before the first anniversary of 31 January following the tax year in which the adjustment is made.

See 16.2 CLAIMS for the method of giving effect to an averaging claim.

A claim for relief under any other provision of the *Income Tax Acts* for a tax year included in an averaging claim can be made, amended or revoked at any time on or before the last date on which the averaging claim itself could have been made. See 16.2 CLAIMS for the method of giving effect to such a claim, amendment or revocation that would otherwise be out of time.

[*ICTA 1988, s 95A, Sch 4A paras 1–6, 8, 10, 11, 14; FA 2001, s 71(1)(2), Sch 24 para 1*].

Example

Richard is an established author by profession and has the following profits/losses as adjusted for Schedule D, Case II purposes (including a deduction for capital allowances) for the five years mentioned.

Year ended	Schedule D, Case II profit/loss
	£
31.12.2000	35,000
31.12.01	30,000
31.12.02	6,000
31.12.03	25,000
31.12.04	(2,000)

Averaged profits for all years would be

		No averaging claims	Averaging claims for all possible years
		£	£
2000/01	note (i)	35,000	35,000
2001/02	note (ii)	30,000	18,000
2002/03	note (iii)	6,000	20,250
2003/04	note (iv)	25,000	11,375
2004/05	note (iv)	Nil	11,375
		£96,000	£96,000

Notes

(i)	2000/01	35,000
	2001/02	30,000
		£65,000

As £30,000 is not less than 75% of £35,000, no averaging claim is possible.

(ii)	2001/02	30,000
	2002/03	6,000
		£36,000 ÷ 2 = £18,000

As £6,000 does not exceed 70% of £30,000, straight averaging applies. Still no claims can be made to average 2001/02 (as adjusted) with 2000/01, even though this would now be possible purely on the figures.

(iii) 2002/03   18,000
      2003/04   25,000

                                £43,000

As £18,000 exceeds 70% of £25,000 (but is less than 75%), the adjustment proceeds as follows.

Difference £7,000 × 3		21,000	
Deduct 75% × £12,000		18,750	
Adjustment		2,250	(2,250)
Existing 2002/03		18,000	
Existing 2003/04			25,000
Averaged profits 2002/03/2003/04		£20,250	£22,750

(iv) 2003/04   22,750
      2004/05   Nil

             22,750 ÷ 2 = £11,375

The loss of £2,000 for 2004/05 does not enter into the averaging claim, but is available to reduce either the 2003/04 or the 2004/05 averaged profits of £11,375 on a claim under *ICTA 1988, s 380* (see 46.3 LOSSES).

The 2004/05 averaged profits of £11,375 may themselves be averaged with 2005/06 profits if the 75% rule is satisfied. Any loss claim against income of 2004/05 is disregarded for this purpose.

Copyright, royalties etc. *General.* Amounts held to be assessable include advance payments of gramophone royalties to a singer (*Taylor v Dawson KB 1938, 22 TC 189*); commutations of future royalties paid to an authoress (*Glasson v Rougier KB 1944, 26 TC 86*); receipts from sale of film rights in books (*Howson v Monsell HC 1950, 31 TC 529*); sales of copyright in novels written when the author was non-resident (with no deduction for his expenses then incurred — *Mackenzie v Arnold CA 1952, 33 TC 363*). But contrast *Mitchell v Rosay CA 1954, 35 TC 496. Sharkey v Wernher* (see 71.73 below) does not apply to a gift of copyright (*Mason v Innes CA 1967, 44 TC 326*). Royalties etc. arising after an author etc. dies or otherwise ceases to carry on his profession or vocation may be chargeable as POST-CESSATION ETC. RECEIPTS AND EXPENDITURE (62).

Copyright and design royalties or public lending right payments paid by publisher etc. are deductible in computing their profits but royalties to non-residents must be paid less tax, the tax being accounted for to the Revenue under *ICTA 1988, s 536, s 537* or *s 537B*.

Spreading of income before 6 April 2001. ICTA 1988, s 534, s 535, s 537A and *s 538*, as described below, and *ICTA 1988, s 537* insofar as it applies the provisions of *ss 534, 535* to public lending rights, cease to have effect in relation to payments *actually* receivable after 5 April 2001. [*FA 2001, s 71(3)(4), Sch 24 para 4*]. They are superseded by the rules above for averaging profits of creative artists for 2000/01 onwards.

Where copyrights or public lending rights in literary, dramatic, musical or artistic works, taking more than twelve months to produce, were assigned for a lump sum in circumstances which would have rendered the proceeds assessable as profits of a single year of assessment, an option was given to spread the sum retrospectively (as set out in *ICTA 1988, s 534(2)(3)*) over that and the preceding tax year and (if the work took more than 24 months to produce) the tax year before that. [*ICTA 1988, ss 534, 537*]. This treatment applied also to sale prices etc. of paintings, sculptures or other works of art taking more than twelve months to produce [*ICTA 1988, s 538; FA 1996, s 128(10)*] and to periodical payments, including royalties, due within two years of date of first publication etc. A claim had to be made within one year after 31 January following the year of assessment (or in the case of periodical payments the latest year of assessment) into whose basis period the payments would otherwise have fallen. Where the claim relates to periodical payments, it must cover all such payments from the same work, and where payments fall into more than one year of assessment the claim is treated as if it were two or more separate claims, being one for each of the years concerned. [*ICTA 1988, s 534(4)(b)(5)–(5B); FA 1996, s 128(5)*]. See 16.2 CLAIMS for the method of giving effect to claims.

Broadly similar provisions applied in the case of design rights in a design. [*ICTA 1988, s 537A; Copyright, Designs and Patents Act 1988, Sch 7 para 36(6); FA 1996, s 128(9)*].

Alternatively, where an author assigned, wholly or partially, for *two years or more* (or similarly grants by licence an interest in) the copyright or public lending right in a literary, dramatic, musical or artistic work of his (first published ten or more years previously) for a lump sum which would normally have been treated as profits of a single year, he could claim to treat that sum as receivable by equal yearly instalments (up to a maximum of six) during the period covered by the assignment or licence, the first of such sums being treated as due on the date the lump sum became receivable. But if the author permanently discontinues his profession, or dies, any subsequent instalments as above are treated as having been receivable together with the last instalment due before the cessation or death unless the author (or his personal representatives) elected for recomputation as if the assignment etc. had been for a lesser period ending with the day before the cessation or death. A claim under these provisions had to be made within one year after 31 January following the year of assessment into whose basis period the lump sum would otherwise have fallen. [*ICTA 1988, s 535; FA 1996, s 128(7)(8)*].

ICTA 1988, s 534 and *s 535* were mutually exclusive. [*ICTA 1988, ss 534(6), 535(9)*].

None of the above provisions applied for corporation tax, nor could any claim be made by a partnership. [*ICTA 1988, s 534(6A); FA 1996, s 128(6)*].

Simon's Direct Tax Service. See **B3.814** *et seq.*, **B3.835** *et seq.*

71.42   **DEDUCTION OF TAX AT SOURCE—AMOUNTS PAID UNDER**

The combined effect of *ICTA 1988, s 74(1)(m)(p)* is to prohibit the deduction in computing profits of annuities, annual payments (other than interest), patent royalties etc. payable under DEDUCTION OF TAX AT SOURCE (22) but see 22.13 re certain mortgage interest. For interest see 71.55 below and for copyright royalties see 71.41 above. For the treatment of such payments as 'charges on income' for companies see Tolley's Corporation Tax. See 46.14 LOSSES where payments exceed the profits.

ICTA 1988, s 74(1)(m) applies only to amounts 'payable out of the profits' (cf. similar wording in *ICTA 1988, s 348*). Payments made before the profits can be ascertained are not payable out of the profits and therefore not within the *section 74(1)(m)* prohibition. For this see *Gresham Life Assce v Styles HL 1890, 3 TC 185* and *Paterson Engineering Co Ltd v Duff KB 1943, 25 TC 43*. See also *Ogden v Medway Cinemas Ltd KB 1934, 18 TC 691* and *Moss Empires Ltd v CIR HL 1937, 21 TC 264*.

71.43   **EMBEZZLEMENT ETC.**

Losses allowed but not misappropriation by partner or director. See *Bamford v ATA Advertising Ch D 1972, 48 TC 359* and cf. *Curtis v J & G Oldfield Ltd KB 1925, 9 TC 319*. Where defalcations were made good by the auditor who admitted negligence, refund held to be a trading receipt for the year in which made (*Gray v Penrhyn KB 1937, 21 TC 252*).

See 71.53 below as regards prohibition on deduction of expenditure involving crime.

EMPLOYEES (AND DIRECTORS)

Bona fide remuneration is deductible including bonuses, commissions, tax deducted under PAYE and the cost of board, lodging, uniforms and benefits provided. The deduction is for the remuneration etc. payable; future payments cannot be anticipated (*Albion Rovers Football Club v CIR HL 1952, 33 TC 331*). The remuneration etc. must be shown to be wholly and exclusively for the purposes of the trade. In *Stott & Ingham v Trehearne KB 1924, 9 TC 69* an increase in the rate of commission payable to the trader's sons was disallowed as not on a commercial footing. See also *Johnson Bros & Co v CIR KB 1919, 12 TC 147, Copeman v Wm Flood & Sons Ltd KB 1940, 24 TC 53* and *Earlspring Properties Ltd v Guest CA 1995, 67 TC 259*. Payments by a farming couple to their young children for help on the farm were disallowed in *Dollar v Lyon Ch D 1981, 54 TC 459*. For excessive payments to 'service company' see *Payne, Stone Fraser* at 71.62 below. For wife's wages see *Thompson v Bruce KB 1927, 11 TC 607*; *Moschi v Kelly CA 1952, 33 TC 442*. The salary etc. of an employee for service in an overseas subsidiary was allowed in computing the profits of the parent in *Robinson v Scott Bader & Co Ltd CA 1981, 54 TC 757*. The secondment was wholly and exclusively for the purposes of the parent's business, notwithstanding the benefit to the subsidiary's business.

Any excess of the market value over the par value of shares issued to employees at par is not deductible (*Lowry v Consolidated African Selection Trust Ltd HL 1940, 23 TC 259*). For payments to trustees to acquire shares for the benefit of employees, see *Heather v P-E Consulting Group CA 1972, 48 TC 293*, *Jeffs v Ringtons Ltd Ch D 1985, 58 TC 680* and *E Bott Ltd v Price Ch D 1985, 59 TC 437*, and contrast *Rutter v Charles Sharpe & Co Ltd Ch D 1979, 53 TC 163* and *Mawsley Machinery Ltd v Robinson (Sp C 170), [1998] SSCD 236*. See also below under Employee share schemes.

Timing of deductions. In calculating profits for a period of account, no deduction is allowed for an amount charged in the accounts in respect of employees' remuneration unless it is paid no later than nine months after the end of the period of account. Remuneration paid at a later time (and otherwise deductible) is deductible for the period of account *in which* it is paid. For these purposes, 'remuneration' includes any amount which is, or falls to be treated as, earnings for income tax purposes, and includes remuneration of office holders as well as other employees. Remuneration is treated as paid when it falls to be treated for tax purposes as received by the employee (see 75.5 SCHEDULE E—EMPLOYMENT INCOME). These provisions apply whether the amount charged is in respect of particular employments or employments generally and apply equally to remuneration for which provision is made in the accounts (or, for periods ended before 27 November 2002 and see now below under Employee benefit contributions, which is held by an intermediary) with a view to its becoming employees' remuneration. Computations prepared before the end of the said nine-month period must be prepared on the basis that any still unpaid remuneration will not be paid before the expiry of that nine-month period and thus will not be deductible for the period of account in question. If, in fact, such remuneration *is* paid by the end of the nine-month period, the computation may be adjusted accordingly on a claim being made to an officer of the Board no later than two years after the end of the period of account in question.

For 2003/04 only (and for corporation tax accounting periods ending after 5 April 2003 but before 6 April 2004), due to a drafting error in *ITEPA 2003*, these provisions applied only to trades and not to professions or vocations.

[*FA 1989, s 43; ITEPA 2003, Sch 6 para 157; FA 2003, Sch 24 paras 10(1), 11; FA 2004, Sch 17 para 4*].

Payments to an employee benefit trust were held to fall within these restrictions in *Macdonald v Dextra Accessories Ltd and Others CA, [2004] STC 339* (and see now below under Employee benefit contributions).

Similar provisions apply in relation to investment and insurance companies. [*FA 1989, s 44; ITEPA 2003, Sch 6 para 158; FA 2003, Sch 24 paras 10(1), 11*].

Council tax. An employer who pays the council tax for an employee will normally be able to claim a deduction for it. If such payments are also made on behalf of members of the employee's family, they too are deductible if part of the employee's remuneration package (which would normally mean they were paid under the contract of employment). (Revenue Press Release 16 March 1993).

Employee share schemes. A statutory corporation tax deduction has been introduced by *FA 2003, s 141, Sch 23* (and significantly amended by *FA 2003, Sch 22 paras 59–73*) for the cost of providing shares for employee share schemes where the employees are taxable in respect of shares acquired or would be taxable if the scheme were not an approved share option scheme, or in the case of an enterprise management incentive scheme option (see 82.35 SHARE-RELATED EMPLOYMENT INCOME AND EXEMPTIONS) if the option were non-qualifying, or if the employee were UK-resident and ordinarily resident and the duties of the employment were performed in the UK. The relief applies in respect of shares acquired by employees in accounting periods beginning on or after 1 January 2003. The deduction is normally based on the market value of the shares, at the time they are awarded or the share option is exercised (whichever is applicable), less any contribution given (by the recipient or anyone else) in respect of the shares. It is restricted by any relief given in earlier accounting periods, in respect of the same shares, under pre-existing rules. The relief relates only to the cost of providing shares; it does not affect, and is not restricted by, pre-existing reliefs for costs of setting up or administering schemes, costs of borrowing and incidental expenses of acquiring shares, e.g. fees, commissions, stamp duty. The shares themselves must be fully-paid, non-redeemable, ordinary shares in a listed company, a subsidiary of a listed company or an unlisted company not under the control of another company. The relief is generally given for the accounting period in which the employee acquires the shares. There are, however, special rules for restricted shares (within 82.4 SHARE-RELATED EMPLOYMENT INCOME AND EXEMPTIONS) and convertible shares (within 82.6 SHARE-RELATED EMPLOYMENT INCOME AND EXEMPTIONS) that also give relief, in subsequent accounting periods in which chargeable events occur, in amounts broadly equal to the amounts chargeable on employees as a result of such events. Where the restricted shares rules do not have effect, special rules apply instead to shares subject to forfeiture (as defined) and give relief on the lifting of the condition for forfeiture rather than on acquisition. For full details of the above provisions, see Tolley's Corporation Tax under Profit Computations. For an article on the interaction of the provisions with the transfer pricing rules (see 3.8 ANTI-AVOIDANCE), see Revenue Tax Bulletin February 2003 pp 1002–1007.

Other reliefs available in connection with employee share schemes are described below.

Share incentive plans. Subject to the exceptions below, the following are allowable deductions (in computing company trading profits or as management expenses) in connection with an approved share incentive plan within *ITEPA 2003, Sch 2* (see 82.11–82.25 SHARE-RELATED EMPLOYMENT INCOME AND EXEMPTIONS):

(*a*)   the market value (at time of acquisition by the plan trustees, and see below) of free and matching shares awarded to employees under the plan (the deduction being given *to the employer company* for the period of account in which the shares are awarded);

(*b*)   any excess of the market value (at time of acquisition by the plan trustees, and determined as for capital gains tax purposes) of partnership shares over the amounts paid by participating employees to acquire them (the deduction being given *to the employer company* for the period of account in which the shares are acquired on participants' behalf);

(c)   expenditure incurred by a company in establishing a plan (the deduction being given for the period of account in which the expenditure is incurred, unless the Revenue approve the plan more than nine months after the end of that period, in which case the deduction is given for the period of account in which approval is given);

(d)   contributions by a company to the expenses of plan trustees in operating a plan, *excluding* expenses in acquiring shares (other than incidental costs such as fees, commission, stamp duty etc.) but *including* interest on money borrowed to acquire shares.

Once a deduction is made under (a) or (b) above, no other deduction (other than any within (c) or (d) above) may be made by the employer company or any associated company (as defined) in respect of the provision of the shares, and no deduction within (a) or (b) above may then be made by any other company in that respect. Once a deduction is made under (c) above, no other deduction may be made in respect of the costs of setting up the plan.

For the purposes of (a) above, market value is determined as for capital gains tax purposes, and, for the purposes of that determination (and also for those of (iii) below), shares acquired by the trustees on different days are deemed to be awarded under the plan on a first in/first out basis. In the case of a group plan (i.e. a plan established by a parent company and extending to one or more companies under its control), the total market value of the shares awarded is apportioned between the relevant employer companies by reference to the number of shares awarded to the employees of each company.

No deduction is allowed under (a) or (b) above:

(i)   in respect of shares awarded to an individual whose earnings from the eligible employment are not, at the time of the award, taxable earnings (whether or not subject to the remittance basis as regards overseas earnings);

(ii)   in respect of shares that are liable to depreciate substantially in value for reasons that do not apply generally to shares in the company;

(iii)   if a deduction has been made (on whatever basis), by the company, or an associated company (as defined) in respect of providing the same shares for the plan trust or for another trust (whatever its nature or purpose); or

(iv)   in respect of the subsequent award of shares previously forfeited by participants (such shares being treated as acquired by the trustees at time of forfeit for no consideration).

No deduction is allowed under (c) above if any employee acquires rights under the plan, or the trustees acquire any shares, before the plan receives Revenue approval. Subject to (d) above, no deduction is allowed for expenses in providing dividend shares.

On withdrawal of Revenue approval to a plan, the Revenue may, by notice, direct that any deductions made under (a) or (b) above be withdrawn also, in which case the aggregate deductions made are treated as a trading receipt of the company concerned for the period of account in which the Revenue notify withdrawal of approval (or, in the case of an investment company, as income chargeable under Schedule D, Case VI arising at the time of notice of withdrawal). See 82.24 SHARE-RELATED EMPLOYMENT INCOME AND EXEMPTIONS for right of appeal.

A payment made after 5 April 2003 by the employer company to the trustees sufficient to enable them to acquire (other than from a company) a significant block of shares (at least 10% of the employer company's ordinary share capital) attracts a deduction (in computing trading profits etc.) which, in contrast to the above, is not deferred until the shares are awarded to employees. The deduction falls to be given for the period of account in which falls the first anniversary of the date of acquisition, provided the 10% requirement is then met. The deduction will, however, be clawed back unless at least 30% of those shares are awarded within five years of acquisition by the trustees and all of the shares are awarded within ten years; if all the shares are subsequently awarded, the deduction is reinstated at that later time. An appropriate proportion of the original deduction is also subject to clawback if the plan terminates before all the shares have been awarded or if shares are awarded to an individual within (i) above. In the event of the Revenue withdrawing their approval to the plan, the same provisions apply as above as regards potential withdrawal of deductions.

[*ICTA 1988, s 85B, Sch 4AA; FA 2000, Sch 8 para 2(1), para 3(1), paras 105–114, para 121(10)(11), paras 125, 126; ITEPA 2003, Sch 2 paras 92, 94, Sch 6 paras 12, 109*].

Employee share ownership trusts. For accounting periods beginning before 1 January 2003, payments made by a UK resident company by way of contribution to a trust which at the time of payment is a qualifying employee share ownership trust (QUEST) from which at least some of its employees (or those of a company which it controls (within *ICTA 1988, s 840*)) are eligible to benefit are allowable on a claim to that effect being made within two years after the end of the period of account in which the payment is charged as an expense. In order for the payment to qualify for relief, the sum received must be expended by the trustees within nine months (or such longer period as the Board may, by notice, allow) after the end of the said period of account (all sums received by the trustees being deemed to be expended by them on a first in/first out basis) for one or more of the following qualifying purposes:

(*a*)   the acquisition of shares in the company which established the trust;

(*b*)   the repayment of borrowings;

(*c*)   the payment of interest on borrowings;

(*d*)   the payment of sums to beneficiaries;

(*e*)   the meeting of expenses (including payment of income tax or capital gains tax — see Revenue Business Income Manual BIM 44025).

Contributions received are deemed to be used first to meet expenditure for qualifying purposes, expenditure for non-qualifying purposes being treated as far as possible as met out of other income (e.g. dividends or interest) (Revenue Business Income Manual BIM 44030).

In view of the new statutory deduction for the cost of providing shares for employee share schemes (see above), this relief is repealed in respect of contributions made in company accounting periods beginning on or after 1 January 2003.

[*FA 1989, s 67; FA 2003, s 142(1)*].

See 63 QUALIFYING EMPLOYEE SHARE OWNERSHIP TRUSTS for the definition of a QUEST and for provisions enabling a charge to tax to be made, in certain circumstances, on the trustees, but recoverable also from the company, where the above relief has previously been given.

Expenditure on establishing a QUEST is deductible in computing the company's trading profits (or as a management expense). If the deed establishing the trust is executed more than nine months after the end of the period of account in which the expenditure is incurred, it is treated as incurred in the period in which the deed is executed. [*ICTA 1988, s 85A; FA 1991, s 43*].

Non-qualifying employee share ownership trusts. For the treatment of contributions to employee share ownership trusts not within the above provisions which are not capital expenditure on general principles but which are required under UITF 13 to be treated as giving rise to an asset in the employer's accounts, see Revenue Tax Bulletin February 1997 pp 399, 400. Broadly, relief for the contributions is deferred until the rights in the shares are transferred to employees, although this would not prevent a deduction for a properly calculated provision reflecting employees' accruing entitlement to such benefits.

Profit sharing and share option schemes. Expenditure on establishing an approved profit sharing scheme, SAYE option scheme or CSOP scheme (see 82.18, 82.47, 82.61 SHARE-RELATED EMPLOYMENT INCOME AND EXEMPTIONS) is deductible in computing the company's trading profits (or as a management expense) provided that:

(*a*)   in the case of a profit sharing scheme, the trustees acquire no shares under the scheme before it is approved; or

(*b*)   in the case of a SAYE or CSOP scheme, no employee or director obtains rights under the scheme before it is approved.

If the scheme is approved more than nine months after the end of the period of account in which the expenditure is incurred, it is for these purposes treated as incurred in the period in which the approval is given. (Note that, under the provisions for phasing out approved profit sharing schemes, the Revenue will not approve a scheme unless the application was received by them before 6 April 2001 — see 82.18 SHARE-RELATED EMPLOYMENT INCOME AND EXEMPTIONS).

[*ICTA 1988, s 84A; FA 1991, s 42; ITEPA 2003, Sch 6 para 11*].

In the case of an approved profit sharing scheme, a similar deduction is available for payments made to the scheme trustees which are either (i) necessary to meet their reasonable administration expenses or (ii) applied by them, within nine months after the end of the period of account in which the expense is charged (or such longer time as the Revenue may allow), in acquiring shares for appropriation to participants. As a consequence of the phasing out of approved profit sharing schemes (see 82.18 SHARE-RELATED EMPLOYMENT INCOME AND EXEMPTIONS), no deduction is available under (i) above for any payment made more than three years after the last appropriation made in accordance with the scheme before 1 January 2003. Similarly, no deduction is available under (ii) above for (1) any payment made after 5 April 2002 or (2) any payment made after 20 March 2000 and before 6 April 2002 unless the shares thus acquired are appropriated no later than nine months after the end of the period of account in which the payment was made and before 1 January 2003. [*ICTA 1988, s 85; FA 2000, s 50*].

Retirement and benevolent provisions for employees. See 67.5(*a*), 67.10 RETIREMENT SCHEMES for the deductibility of payments by the employer under such schemes. *Bona fide* voluntary pensions and retirement gratuities, including pensions to widows, are allowed (*Smith v Incorporated Council of Law Reporting KB 1914, 6 TC 477*). The cost of an annuity to replace a pension is allowed but not the cost of a policy to secure payment *to the employer* of an annuity equal to pensions payable by him (*Hancock v General Reversionary & Investment Co Ltd KB 1918, 7 TC 358; Morgan Crucible Co Ltd v CIR KB 1932, 17 TC 311*). For provisions for directors of 'family companies' see *Samuel Dracup & Sons Ltd v Dakin Ch D 1957, 37 TC 377*.

Payments directly or indirectly for the benefit of employees are allowable including donations to hospitals and charities (see 71.74 below) unless capital or abnormal (*Rowntree & Co v Curtis CA 1924, 8 TC 678; Bourne & Hollingsworth v Ogden KB 1929, 14 TC 349*). See also *Hutchinson & Co v Turner HC 1950, 31 TC 495*. Subscriptions to BUPA and similar group schemes for employees are allowed (see 75.40 SCHEDULE E—EMPLOYMENT INCOME for position regarding the employees).

See also below under Employee benefit contributions.

Redundancy payments, or other employer's payments, under *Employment Rights Act 1996* (or NI equivalent) allowable. Rebates recoverable are trading receipts. [*ICTA 1988, ss 579, 580; FA 1998, s 38, Sch 5 para 43, Sch 27 Pt III(4); ITEPA 2003, s 309, Sch 6 paras 63, 64*].

Non-statutory redundancy and similar payments are normally allowable unless made on the cessation of trading (but now see following paragraphs) (*CIR v Anglo-Brewing Co Ltd KB 1925, 12 TC 803; Godden v Wilson's Stores CA 1962, 40 TC 161; Geo Peters & Co v Smith Ch D 1963, 41 TC 264*) or as part of the bargain for the sale of shares of the company carrying on the business (*Bassett Enterprise Ltd v Petty KB 1938, 21 TC 730; James Snook & Co Ltd v Blasdale CA 1952, 33 TC 244*). See also *Overy v Ashford Dunn & Co KB 1933, 17 TC 497* and contrast *CIR v Patrick Thomson Ltd CS 1956, 37 TC 145*. A payment to secure the resignation of a life-director who had fallen out with his co-directors was allowed in *Mitchell v B W Noble Ltd CA 1927, 11 TC 372*. See also *O'Keeffe v Southport Printers Ltd Ch D 1984, 58 TC 88*. For provisions for future leaving payments see 71.39 above.

Payments made to employees taken on for trade purposes, under a pre-existing contractual or statutory obligation which was a consequence of their being so taken on, are not disallowed by *ICTA 1988, s 74(1)(a)* (see 71.30 above) just because it is the cessation of the trade that crystallises the liability to pay. (Revenue Tax Bulletin February 1999 pp 630, 631).

Payments in addition to the statutory payment made on cessation of trading (including deemed cessation on a partnership change) will be allowed if they would have been allowed had there been no cessation. Allowance is up to three times the statutory payment and payment made after cessation is treated as made on last day business carried on. [*ICTA 1988, s 90*]. In practice, allowance will also be given for such payments on a partial cessation (i.e. where an identifiable part of a trade is discontinued). (Revenue Pamphlet IR 131, SP 11/81, 6 November 1981).

Relief under *ICTA 1988, s 579* or *s 90* (as above) is due for the period of account in which the payment is made (or, if paid after discontinuance, for the last day on which the business is carried on). Where instead relief is due under general principles, a provision for future payments may be allowed for a period of account provided that:

(*a*)   it appears in the commercial accounts in accordance with generally accepted accounting principles;

(*b*)   it was accurately calculated (normally requiring the identification of the individual employees affected) using the degree of hindsight permitted by SSAP 17;

(*c*)   a definite decision to proceed with the redundancies was taken during the period; and

(*d*)   payment was made within nine months of the end of the period.

(Revenue Tax Bulletin February 1995 p 195).

See generally Revenue Business Income Manual BIM 46600–46615.

Counselling services etc. Expenditure on counselling and other outplacement services which falls within the earnings exemption of *ITEPA 2003, s 310* (see 75.45 SCHEDULE E—EMPLOYMENT INCOME) is deductible either in computing the profits of the employer's trade or as a management expense under *ICTA 1988, s 75*. [*ICTA 1988, ss 589A, 589B; FA 1993, s 108; ITEPA 2003, Sch 6 paras 69,70*].

Key employee insurance. Premiums on policies in favour of the employer insuring against death or critical illness of key employees are generally allowable, and the proceeds of any such policies trading receipts. However, in *Beauty Consultants Ltd v Inspector of Taxes (Sp C 321), [2002] SSCD 352*, premiums on a policy insuring a company against the death of either of its controlling shareholder-directors were disallowed; the 'dual purpose rule' at 71.30 above applied, in that the premiums benefited the shareholders personally by improving the value of their shares. In *Greycon Ltd v Klaentschi (Sp C 372), [2003] SSCD 370*, it was held that the company's sole purpose in taking out key man policies was to meet a requirement of an agreement under which funding and other benefits were obtained from another company, that the policies had a capital purpose and that, consequently, the proceeds were not trading receipts. See generally Revenue Business Income Manual BIM 45525, 45530.

National insurance contributions ('NICs'). Under *ICTA 1988, s 617(4)*, secondary Class 1 NICs (payable by an employer in respect of employees' earnings) are deductible if they would be so but for the general prohibition in *section 617(3)*. Relief is similarly available for Class 1A NICs (payable by an employer where cars are provided to employees wholly or partly for private use) and for Class 1B NICs (payable from 6 April 1999 in respect of PAYE settlement agreements — see 55.12 PAY AS YOU EARN). [*ICTA 1988, s 617(3)(4); FA 1997, s 65; FA 1999, s 61; ITEPA 2003, Sch 6 para 87(3)*].

Training costs. Costs incurred by an employer in respect of employee training are generally allowable as a trading expense. For a Revenue view of the circumstances in which such relief may be prohibited by *ICTA 1988, s 74(1)(a)* (see 71.30 above), see Revenue Tax Bulletin February 1997 pp 400, 401 (which also indicates that it is extremely unlikely that such expenditure would be disallowed on the grounds that it was of a capital nature).

Retraining course expenses paid or reimbursed by an employer and within the earnings exemption of *ITEPA 2003, s 311* at 75.44 SCHEDULE E—EMPLOYMENT INCOME are deductible either in computing the profits of the employer's trade or as a management expense under *ICTA 1988, s 75*. The provisions relating to recovery of tax, information and penalties in relation to the earnings exemption apply equally in relation to this deduction. [*ICTA 1988, s 588; FA 1996, Sch 18 paras 10, 17(1)(2); ITEPA 2003, Sch 6 para 67*]. See 71.74 below as regards contributions to training and enterprise councils, and 92 VOCATIONAL TRAINING RELIEF as regards relief for self-employed.

Employees seconded to charities or educational bodies. If an employer seconds an employee temporarily to a charity (as defined in *ICTA 1988, s 506*, see 14.1 CHARITIES), any expenditure attributable to the employment incurred by the employer is deductible in computing its profits to the extent to which it would have been deductible if the employee's services had continued to be available for its business. This relief is extended to secondments to certain educational bodies. The bodies concerned include education authorities and educational institutions maintained by such authorities, and certain other educational bodies, the descriptions of which were updated from 1999/2000 onwards. [*ICTA 1988, s 86; FA 1999, s 58*].

Employee benefit contributions (timing of deductions). Legislation was introduced in *FA 2003* to 'counter the avoidance of tax and national insurance contributions (NICs) through the abuse of employee benefit trusts' (Pre-Budget Report Press Release REV/C&E 1, 27 November 2002). It provides rules for the timing of deductions for 'employee benefit contributions'. To this extent, these rules replace those of *FA 1989, s 43* (see above under Timing of deductions). They apply in relation to deductions otherwise allowable in computing profits for periods ending after 26 November 2002 in respect of contributions made after that date. For these purposes, an *'employee benefit contribution'* is a payment of money, or the transfer of an asset, by the employer to a third party (e.g. the trustees of an employee benefit trust) who is entitled or required, under the terms of an employee benefit scheme, to hold or use the money or asset to provide benefits to employees. A deduction is allowed only to the extent that, during the period in question or within nine months after the end of it, 'qualifying benefits' are provided, or 'qualifying expenses' are paid, out of the contributions. (If the employer's contribution is itself a qualifying benefit, it is sufficient that the contribution be made during the period or within those ensuing nine months.) Any amount thus disallowed remains available for deduction in any subsequent period during which it is used to provide qualifying benefits. For these purposes, qualifying benefits are treated as provided, and expenses are treated as paid, as far as possible out of employee benefit contributions, with no account being taken of any other receipts or expenses of the third party.

A '*qualifying benefit*' is a payment of money or transfer of assets (other than by way of loan) that gives rise to *both* a charge to tax on employment income and a charge to NICs (or would do so but for available exemptions for duties performed outside the UK or in connection with termination of employment). Money benefits are treated for these purposes as provided at the time the money is treated as received (applying the rules at 75.5 SCHEDULE E — EMPLOYMENT INCOME). '*Qualifying expenses*' are those expenses (if any) of the third party in operating the scheme that would have been deductible in computing profits if incurred by the employer. Where a qualifying benefit takes the form of the transfer of an asset, the amount provided is the aggregate of the amount that would otherwise be deductible by the employer (in a case where the third party acquired the asset from the employer) and the amount expended on the asset by the third party. If, however, the amount charged to tax under *ITEPA 2003* (or which would be so charged if the duties of employment were performed in the UK) is lower than that aggregate, any amount deductible under these provisions at any time is limited to that lower amount; this rule is aimed at a situation where the asset falls in value after its acquisition by the third party but before its transfer to the employee (Treasury Explanatory Notes to Finance Bill 2003).

These restrictions do not apply to disallow deductions for consideration given for goods or services provided in the course of a trade or profession, contributions to a retirement benefits scheme, approved personal pension scheme or accident benefit scheme (as defined) and specified statutory deductions available in connection with employee share schemes (for which see above under Employee share schemes).

Computations prepared before the end of the said nine-month period must be prepared by reference to the facts at the time of computation. If any contributions are used for qualifying purposes after that time, but within the nine months, the computation may be adjusted accordingly (subject to the normal time limits for amending self-assessment tax returns).

[*FA 2003, s 143, Sch 24*].

Payments for restrictive undertakings are deductible in computing profits (or as management expenses under *ICTA 1988, s 75*) if falling to be treated as earnings of the employee under *ITEPA 2003, s 225* (or, before 2003/04, *ICTA 1988, s 313*). [*FA 1988, s 73(2)–(4); ITEPA 2003, Sch 6 para 155*].

Payroll giving schemes. See 14.18 CHARITIES.

Simon's Direct Tax Service. See B3.1424 *et seq.*, B3.1513.

71.45   ENTERTAINMENT EXPENSES

Entertainment expenses are not allowed, except for staff entertainment. The disallowance applies to gifts to any person unless they (*a*) carry a prominent advertisement, (*b*) do not consist of food, drink, tobacco etc., and (*c*) do not cost in total more than a specified limit. For 2001/02 and subsequent years (and for company accounting periods beginning after 31 March 2001), the limit per person is £50 in the year of assessment (or, where applicable, in the basis period as determined under *ICTA 1988, ss 60–63*, see 71.4 *et seq.* above) or accounting period. Previously, it was £10 per year. [*ICTA 1988, s 577; CAA 2001, Sch 2 para 51; FA 2001, s 73; ITEPA 2003, Sch 6 para 62*]. Deductions were allowed for items provided in the ordinary course of a trade of providing entertainment (see *Fleming v Associated Newspapers Ltd HL 1972, 48 TC 382*) or provided gratuitously for advertising to the public generally. [*ICTA 1988, s 577(10)*]. See also the VAT cases of *C & E Commissioners v Shaklee International and Another CA, [1981] STC 776* and *Celtic Football and Athletic Co Ltd v C & E Commissioners CS, [1983] STC 470*. There is also a restriction on capital allowances where plant or machinery is used to provide entertainment, with similar exceptions as above where relevant (see 9.24 CAPITAL ALLOWANCES).

71.46 Schedule D, Cases I and II—Profits of Trades etc.

For an article on the scope and application of *ICTA 1988, s 577*, see Revenue Tax Bulletin August 1999 pp 679–682 as supplemented by Revenue Tax Bulletin February 2000 p 729. For further comprehensive guidance on business entertainment, see Revenue Business Income Manual BIM 45000–45090.

See 71.74 below as regards gifts to charitable bodies.

Simon's Direct Tax Service. See B3.1438.

71.46 **(FOREIGN) EXCHANGE GAINS AND LOSSES**

See Tolley's Corporation Tax for special provisions applying in the case of transactions by certain 'qualifying companies' for accounting periods beginning before 1 October 2002, and for the inclusion of foreign exchange gains and losses in the loan relationship provisions thereafter.

In general, where the special provisions referred to above do not apply, foreign exchange differences are taken into account in computing trading profits if they relate to the circulating capital of the business but not otherwise. In *Overseas Containers (Finance) Ltd v Stoker CA 1989, 61 TC 473*, exchange losses arising on loans transferred to a finance subsidiary set up to convert the losses to trading account were held not to arise from trading transactions.

In *Davies v The Shell Co of China Ltd CA 1951, 32 TC 133*, a petrol marketing company operating in China required agents to deposit Chinese dollars with it, repayable on the ending of the agency. Exchange profits it made on repaying the deposits were held to be capital. In *Firestone Tyre & Rubber Co Ltd v Evans Ch D 1976, 51 TC 615*, a company repaid in 1965 a dollar balance due to its US parent, the greater part of which represented advances in 1922–1931 to finance the company when it started. The Commissioners' finding that 90% of the resultant large exchange loss was capital and not allowable, was upheld. A profit by an agent on advances to the principal to finance purchases by the agent on behalf of the principal, was held to be a trading receipt (*Landes Bros v Simpson KB 1934, 19 TC 62*) as was a profit by a tobacco company on dollars accumulated to finance its future purchases (*Imperial Tobacco Co v Kelly CA 1943, 25 TC 292*). See also *McKinlay v H T Jenkins & Son KB 1926, 10 TC 372; Ward v Anglo-American Oil KB 1934, 19 TC 94; Beauchamp v F W Woolworth plc HL 1989, 61 TC 542*; and contrast *Radio Pictures Ltd v CIR CA 1938, 22 TC 106*. Where a bank operated in foreign currencies and aimed at, and generally succeeded in, matching its monetary assets and liabilities in each currency, it was held that there could be no profit or loss from matched transactions where there were no relevant currency conversions (*Pattison v Marine Midland Ltd HL 1983, 57 TC 219*). In *Whittles v Uniholdings Ltd (No 3) CA 1996, 68 TC 528* it was held that a dollar loan and a simultaneous forward contract with the same bank for dollars sufficient to repay the loan had to be treated, for tax purposes, as separate transactions, each giving rise to its own tax consequences.

Following the *Marine Midland Ltd* case (above) the Revenue issued a Statement of Practice setting out their views on the general treatment of exchange differences for tax purposes. The principles outlined in this Statement, as subsequently revised, are broadly summarised below. These extend to trades, professions, Schedule A businesses and overseas property businesses but, for accounting periods beginning on or after 1 October 2002, are of no application at all to companies.

Following *FA 1998, s 42*, which requires taxable profits to be computed on a basis that reflects a true and fair view (see 71.30 above), tax computations should follow the accounting treatment where the latter is based on generally accepted accounting practice (and, in particular, on SSAP 20). Where, for example, under SSAP 20, gains and losses on monetary assets and liabilities are taken to reserve rather than profit and loss account, then, even if they are not capital items, they should not be recognised for tax purposes. Previously, the nature of the assets and liabilities had to be considered to determine whether or not a tax adjustment was required.

Where currency assets are matched by currency liabilities in a particular currency, so that a translation adjustment on one would be cancelled out by a translation adjustment on the other, no adjustment is required for tax purposes.

Where currency assets are not matched, or are incompletely matched, with currency liabilities in a particular currency, the adjustment required to the net exchange difference debited or credited in the profit and loss account is determined along the following lines:

(i)   the aggregate exchange differences, positive and negative, on capital assets and liabilities in the profit and loss account figure are ascertained;

(ii)   if there are no differences as at (i), no adjustment is required;

(iii)   if the net exchange difference as at (i) is a loss, and the net exchange difference in the profit and loss account is also a loss, the smaller of the two losses is the amount disallowed for tax purposes as relating to capital transactions;

(iv)   if the net exchange difference as at (i) is a profit, and the net exchange difference in the profit and loss account is also a profit, the smaller of the two profits is allowed as a deduction for tax purposes;

(v)   if the net exchange difference as at (i) is a loss, and the net exchange difference in the profit and loss account is a profit, or *vice versa*, no adjustment is required for tax purposes.

In considering whether a trader is matched in a particular foreign currency, *forward exchange contracts* and *currency futures* entered into for hedging purposes may be taken into account, provided the hedging is reflected in the accounts on a consistent basis from year to year and in accordance with accepted accounting practice. *Currency swap agreements* are treated as converting the liability in the original currency into a liability in the swap currency for the duration of the swap. Hedging through *currency options* does not result in any matching.

Where the profits on disposal of assets held by a financial concern other than as trading stock fall to be treated as trading receipts and the concern does not account for those assets on a mark to market basis, such profits are taxable only on disposal (the 'realisation basis'). It may, however, be the practice to revalue the assets in the accounts to reflect exchange rate fluctuations. Where the resulting exchange differences are taken to profit and loss account or set against exchange differences on liabilities, the accounts treatment *must* now be followed for tax purposes. (Previously, the Revenue would normally accept such treatment if applied consistently and if appropriate to the facts of the particular case.)

Where an *overseas trade*, or an *overseas branch* of a trade, is carried on primarily in a non-sterling economic environment, accounts are usually drawn up in the local currency and translated into sterling using the 'closing rate/net investment' method (SSAP 20 paras 25, 46). Under the revised Statement of Practice, tax computations *must* now be based on those translated accounts. (Under the original Statement of Practice, other specified methods of preparing computations were allowed if applied consistently.) The principles outlined in the

Statement of Practice should be applied in considering any adjustment necessary in respect of exchange differences in the foreign currency accounts.

(Revenue Pamphlet IR 131, SP 2/02 (replacing SP 1/87)).

For further discussion, see Revenue Business Income Manual BIM 39500–39528.

If not taken into account in computing trading profits, a profit/loss on the sale of currency is within the ambit of CGT unless exempted by *TCGA 1992, s 269* as currency required for an individual's (or his dependant's) personal expenditure abroad (including provision or maintenance of a residence abroad).

Simon's Direct Tax Service. See B3.17.

71.47   FARMING AND MARKET GARDENING

(*a*)   **Averaging of profits.** Where for two consecutive years of assessment the profits of an individual or partnership from a trade of farming or market gardening in the UK for one year are less than 75% of the profits for the other, a claim for relief may be made as described below. The relief does not extend to corporation tax.

'*Farming*' for this purpose includes the intensive rearing of livestock or fish on a commercial basis for the production of food for human consumption. (Revenue Pamphlet IR 1, A29).

If the profits for either year do not exceed seven-tenths of the profits of the other (or are nil), the profits for each year are adjusted to half the total of both. If either year's profits exceed seven-tenths of the other's, but are less than three-quarters, the profits are adjusted by adding to the lower and subtracting from the higher the amount obtained by multiplying the difference by three and deducting three-quarters of the higher figure. (Thus, if the profits are £21,900 and £30,000, the adjusted profits after relief would be £23,700 and £28,200.)

'*Profits*' for this purpose are those before any adjustment for losses.

The adjustments made under the relief are effective for all income tax purposes but do not prevent a claim for loss relief. Thus, if there was a loss of £5,000 in the basis period for one year and a profit of £15,000 in that for the other, the profits chargeable for each year become £7,500 but the loss of £5,000 remains eligible for loss relief in the normal way.

A claim must be made in writing on or before the first anniversary of 31 January following the *second* year. If a claim has been made for years 1 and 2, a claim may also be made for years 2 and 3, the profits for year 2 being taken as those adjusted on the first claim, and similarly for subsequent years. In the case of a partnership, an individual partner may make his own claim, based on his share of profits, regardless of whether or not other partners make claims. See 16.2 CLAIMS for further provisions regarding claims.

No claim is available for a year of assessment in which the trade is commenced or discontinued or treated as having been discontinued.

If, after a claim, the profits of either or both years are adjusted for some other reason, the claim lapses but a new one may then be made, in respect of the adjusted profits, within the year of assessment following the year in which the adjustment is made. The deadline for the new claim is 31 January following the year immediately after that in which the adjustment is made.

A claim for other relief for either of the two years affected by an averaging claim can be made, amended or revoked within the period during which the averaging claim can be revoked by amendment of a return or otherwise (which, other than in enquiry cases, will normally end twelve months after the filing date for the return in which the averaging claim is made — see 68.4 RETURNS). See also 16.2 CLAIMS for the way in which claims for other relief are given effect.

[ICTA 1988, s 96; FA 1994, s 196, s 214(1)(a)(7), s 216(3)(a)(5), Sch 19 para 37, Sch 26 Pt V(24); FA 1995, Sch 6 para 15; FA 1996, s 128(3); FA 1998, Sch 27 Pt III(4)].

For articles on the making, calculating and implementing of averaging claims under self-assessment and on the completion of the relevant tax returns, see Revenue Tax Bulletin February 1997 pp 392–394 and August 1998 p 575.

Example

A, who has been farming for many years, earns the following profits as adjusted for Schedule D, Case I.

Year ended	Schedule D, Case I Profit/(loss)
	£
30.9.98	8,500
30.9.99	12,000
30.9.2000	15,000
30.9.01	10,000
30.9.02	4,000
30.9.03	(1,000)
30.9.04	(10,000)
30.9.05	1,600

Averaged profits for all years would be

		No averaging claims	Averaging claims for all years
		£	£
1998/99	note (i)	8,500	10,000
1999/2000	notes (i)(ii)	12,000	12,750
2000/01	note (ii)(iii)	15,000	12,750
2001/02	notes (iii)(iv)	10,000	7,000
2002/03	notes (iv)(v)	4,000	3,500
2003/04	notes (v)(vi)	Nil	1,750
2004/05	notes (vii)(viii)	Nil	1,750
2005/06	note (ix)	1,600	1,600
		£51,100	£51,100

Notes

(i)   1998/99   8,500
       1999/2000   12,000
                                          ————
                                         £20,500

As £8,500 exceeds $\frac{7}{10}$ of £12,000 but is less than $\frac{3}{4}$, the adjustment is computed as follows.

Difference £3,500 × 3	10,500	
Deduct $\frac{3}{4}$ × £12,000	9,000	
Adjustment	1,500	(1,500)
Existing 1998/99	8,500	
Existing 1999/2000		12,000
Revised averaged profits 1998/99 & 1999/2000	£10,000	£10,500

(ii)   1999/2000   10,500
       2000/01   15,000
                                         ————
                                 £25,500 ÷ 2 = £12,750

As £10,500 does not exceed $\frac{7}{10}$ of £15,000, the straight average applies.

(iii) 2000/01   12,750
       2001/02   10,000
                                         ————
                                         £22,750

As £10,000 is not less than $\frac{3}{4}$ of £12,750, no averaging is permitted.

(iv)   2001/02   10,000
       2002/03   4,000
                                         ————
                                 £14,000 ÷ 2 = £7,000

As £4,000 does not exceed $\frac{7}{10}$ of £10,000, the straight average applies.

(v)   2002/03   7,000
       2003/04   Nil
                                         ————
                                  £7,000 ÷ 2 = £3,500

(vi)   The loss for the year to 30 September 2003 is not taken into account for averaging, but would be available to reduce the averaged profits for 2003/04 on a claim under *ICTA 1988, s 380* (see 46.3 LOSSES).

(vii) 2003/04   3,500
       2004/05   Nil
                                         ————
                                  £3,500 ÷ 2 = £1,750

(viii) The loss for the year to 30 September 2004 is not taken into account for averaging, but would be available to set off against the balance of the averaged profits for 2003/04 and against the averaged profits for 2004/05 on a claim under *ICTA 1988, s 380* (see 46.3 LOSSES), with the balance being carried forward.

(ix) 2004/05   1,750
      2005/06   1,600
                                       ———————
                                         £3,350

As £1,600 is not less than $\frac{3}{4}$ of £1,750, no averaging is permitted.

See generally Revenue Business Income Manual BIM 73000–73190.

The computation of transitional overlap profits for 1997/98 (see 71.13 above) is not affected by averaging claim(s) by farmers. (Revenue Tax Bulletin August 1998 pp 574, 575).

(b) **Compensation for compulsory slaughter.** Where compensation is received for compulsory slaughter of animals to which the HERD BASIS (34) does not and could not apply, any excess of the amount received over the book value or cost of those animals may, by concession, be excluded from the year of receipt and treated, by equal instalments, as profits of the next three years. (Revenue Pamphlet IR 1, B11). (In practice, the profit on an animal born in the year of slaughter is deemed to be 25% of the compensation received.) For a worked example of this spreading relief, see Revenue Business Income Manual BIM 55185; see also Revenue Tax Bulletin October 2001 p 890 as regards certain aspects of the concession, in particular with regard to its application during the 2001 foot and mouth outbreak.

Compensation paid under the BSE Suspects Scheme and the BSE Selective Cull (where the animal was born after 14 October 1990) is for compulsory slaughter, and for these purposes includes Selective Cull 'top-up' payments. Payments under the Calf Processing Scheme, the Over Thirty Month Scheme and the BSE Selective Cull where the animal was born before 15 October 1990 are *not* for compulsory slaughter. (Revenue Tax Bulletin February 1997 pp 396, 397).

(c) **Drainage.** Where land is made re-available for cultivation by the restoration of drainage or by re-draining, the net expenditure incurred (after crediting any grants receivable) will be allowed as a revenue expenditure in farm accounts provided it excludes (i) any substantial element of improvement (e.g. the substitution of tile drainage for mole drainage) and (ii) the capital element in cases in which the present owner is known to have acquired the land at a depressed price because of its swampy condition. (Revenue Pamphlet IR 131, SP 5/81).

(d) **Farmhouses.** The apportionment of the running costs of a farmhouse between business and private use should be based on the facts of the case for the year of account in question, and may require revision to reflect the fact that many farmhouses are now used only to a limited extent for business purposes. The long-standing practice of accepting a one-third business/two-thirds private split will in many cases no longer be appropriate. (Revenue Tax Bulletin February 1993 p 54).

Maintenance expenses of owner-occupied farms not carried on on a commercial basis. Where a loss claim against general income is precluded by *ICTA 1988, ss 384, 397* (see 46.8 LOSSES) or *s 393A(3)* (see Tolley's Corporation Tax under Losses), relief for maintenance etc. of land, houses etc. may be claimed under *ICTA 1988, s 33.* (Revenue Pamphlet IR 1, B5). Despite the repeal of *section 33* for income tax purposes, the Revenue still allow relief to be claimed, by virtue of this concession, for expenditure incurred after 5 April 1995 which would have qualified under *section 33* if it was still in force. The concession is withdrawn after 5 April 2001 (31 March 2001 for corporation tax). (Revenue Press Release 17 March 1998; Revenue Business Income Manual BIM 75610).

71.47 Schedule D, Cases I and II—Profits of Trades etc.

(*da*) **Foot and mouth outbreak.** For the full range of special measures in relation to the 2001 foot and mouth disease outbreak, see Revenue Tax Bulletin Special Edition May 2001 and Revenue Tax Bulletin October 2001 pp 890, 891.

(*e*) **Gangmasters.** A special unit within the Revenue monitors compliance by agricultural gangmasters, in relation to PAYE and national insurance in respect of their workers and their own returns. It is the Agricultural Compliance Unit, Sovereign House, 40 Silver Street, Sheffield S1 2EN (tel. 01142 739099). (Revenue Press Release 2 September 1988). For whether a worker also responsible for selection of other workers acts as gangmaster, see *Andrews v King Ch D 1991, 64 TC 332*.

(*f*) **Grants and subsidies.** See generally 71.75 below. As regards the time at which a receipt should be brought in for tax purposes, a distinction should be drawn between grants to meet particular costs and those subsidising the sale proceeds of a specific crop. The former should reduce the costs in question (and if those costs are included in the closing stock valuation, the net cost should be used), whereas the latter should be recognised as income of the year in which the crop is sold. (Revenue Tax Bulletin February 1993 p 53). A grant subsidising trading income generally is a trading receipt of the period when the entitlement to the grant was established, provided that it can be quantified with reasonable accuracy. As regards instalments of grant, the tax treatment should follow accounting practice, which provides that information available before accounts are completed and signed should be taken into account as regards those to which entitlement arose in the period of account. (Revenue Tax Bulletin February 1994 p 108).

As regards animal grants and subsidies, these are generally recognised either at the end of the retention period or on receipt. Either of these bases will be accepted for tax purposes provided that it is consistently applied, as will any other basis which reflects generally accepted accounting practice provided that it does not conflict with tax law. A change of basis should be made only where the need for change outweighs the requirement for accounts to be prepared on a consistent basis, and will be dealt with in accordance with Revenue Statement of Practice SP 3/90 (see 71.73 below) (and regard should be had to the anti-avoidance provisions under the current year basis transitional rules, see 71.12, 71.13 above). (Revenue Tax Bulletin December 1994 p 182).

The following relate to specific types of farm support payment.

(i) *Advances under British Sugar Industry (Assistance) Act 1931*, linked with sugar production and prices, were held to be assessable as trading receipts (*Smart v Lincolnshire Sugar Co Ltd HL 1937, 20 TC 643*).

(ii) *Arable area payments.* Payments under the 1992 scheme for land set aside may be treated as sales subsidies, and hence recognised when the crops are sold. Valuations based on 75% of market value (see (*j*) below) should include the same proportion of the related arable area payments. (Revenue Tax Bulletin February 1994 p 109). See (*f*)(v) below for specific comment on oilseed support payments.

(iii) *Dairy herd conversion scheme.* Grants for changing from dairying to meat production were held to be assessable as trading receipts (*White v G & M Davis Ch D 1979, 52 TC 597; CIR v Biggar CS 1982, 56 TC 254*).

(iv) *Flood rehabilitation grants* in excess of rehabilitation costs (admitted to be capital) were held to be capital receipts (*Watson v Samson Bros Ch D 1959, 38 TC 346*).

(v) *Oilseed support scheme.* Payments of aid under the 1992 scheme are a subsidy towards the selling price, and as such should be recognised as income at the time of sale. If the final amount is not known when the accounts are prepared, but it is reasonably certain that a further payment will be received, the tax computations should be kept open to admit the final figure. If a reasonable estimate is included in the accounts and the difference when the final amount is known has only a small effect on the overall tax liability, the inspector may agree to recognise the difference in arriving at profits of the following year. (Revenue Tax Bulletin February 1993 p 53).

(vi) *Ploughing subsidies* were held to be assessable as trading receipts (*Higgs v Wrightson KB 1944, 26 TC 73*).

(g)   **Milk.** *SLOM compensation.* The Revenue view is that such compensation is on revenue account, and should be recognised for income tax purposes in one sum in the accounting period in which legal entitlement to it arises and the amount can be quantified with reasonable certainty using information available at the time of preparation of the accounts. Additions for interest to the date of payment should be dealt with under the normal Schedule D, Case III rules. (Revenue Tax Bulletin May 1994 p 127).

Superlevy. The Revenue view is that superlevy is an allowable Schedule D, Case I deduction, but that the purchase of additional quota to avoid superlevy does not give rise to a deduction for either the superlevy thus avoided or the sum which would have been paid to lease rather than purchase the additional quota. (Revenue Tax Bulletin August 1994 p 151).

Residuary Milk Marketing Board receipts. B Reserve Fund distributions and sums repaid to producers under the Rolling Fund arrangements on the flotation of Dairy Crest (in the latter case whether taken in cash or in shares) are income receipts of the trade. Any element of a B Reserve Fund payment described as interest may also be treated as a trade receipt. Post-cessation treatment (see 62.1 POST-CESSATION ETC. RECEIPTS AND EXPENDITURE) will apply where appropriate. (Revenue Tax Bulletin August 1997 p 461).

Milk Marque Ltd shares. Bonus preference shares (or loan stock) issued in October 1998 to dairy farmers supplying the company form part of the trading receipts of the farmer, the appropriate measure of the income (and of the capital gains tax base cost) being the nominal value of the shares (Revenue Tax Bulletin August 1999 p 685).

For capital gains tax considerations generally, see Tolley's Capital Gains Tax under Assets and Rollover Relief.

(h)   **Share farming.** The Inland Revenue consider that both parties to a share farming agreement based on the Country Landowners Association model may be considered to be carrying on a farming trade for tax purposes. In the case of the landowner, he must take an active part in the share farming venture, at least to the extent of concerning himself with details of farming policy and exercising his right to enter onto his land for some material purpose, even if only for the purposes of inspection and policy-making. (Country Landowners Association Press Release 19 December 1991). This reverses an earlier Revenue decision to deny such treatment in respect of the landowner's share of income under a share farming agreement, which was itself a change of view from that previously held by the Revenue.

(i)   **Short rotation coppice.** The cultivation of 'short rotation coppice' (i.e. a perennial crop of tree species planted at high density, the stems of which are harvested above ground level at intervals of less than ten years) is treated for tax purposes as farming and not as forestry, so that UK land under such cultivation is farm or agricultural land and not woodlands. [*FA 1995, s 154*]. For the Revenue view of the taxation implications of short rotation coppice, see Revenue Tax Bulletin October 1995 p 252.

(*j*) **Single trade.** All farming carried on by any particular person or partnership or body of persons is treated for all tax purposes as one trade. [*ICTA 1988, s 53(2)*]. This applies, however, only to farming of land in the UK (see *ICTA 1988, s 832(1)* and *Sargent v Eayrs Ch D 1972, 48 TC 573*).

(*k*) **Stock valuations.** See generally Business Economic Notes No 19 'Farming — stock valuations for income tax purposes' (for which see 71.18 above) and, for a commentary thereon relating particularly to changes in the basis of valuation, Revenue Tax Bulletin May 1993 p 63. See also 34 HERD BASIS and, for trading stock generally, 71.73 below. In general, livestock is treated as trading stock unless the herd basis applies, and home-bred animals may be valued, if there is no adequate record of cost, at 75% for sheep and pigs (60% for cattle) of open market value. Deadstock may be taken at 75% of market value.

Where an animal grant or subsidy for which application has been made has not been taken into account for a particular period but has been applied for, and that application materially affects the value of the animal, the grant or subsidy should be taken into account as a supplement to the market value when deemed cost is computed. Grants or subsidies applied for but not recognised as income in the period concerned should also be taken into account in arriving at net realisable value for stock valuation purposes. (Revenue Tax Bulletin December 1994 p 182).

(*l*) **Subscriptions** to the **National Farmers Union** are allowable in full.

(*la*) **Sugar beet outgoers scheme.** Receipts and payments derived from the disposal of contract tonneage entitlement under contracts between farmers and British Sugar are to be dealt with on revenue and not capital account, i.e. as taxable receipts and allowable deductions in computing profits. Payments for entitlement which are amortised in the accounts over the period for which the entitlement may reasonably be expected to be of value to the business are similarly allowed for tax purposes. (Revenue Tax Bulletin October 2001 pp 891, 892).

(*m*) **Trading profits.** Proceeds from the sale of trees (mostly willows planted by the taxpayer) were held to be farming receipts (*Elmes v Trembath KB 1934, 19 TC 72*), but no part of the cost of an orchard with nearly ripe fruit purchased by a fruit grower was an allowable deduction in computing his profits, which included receipts from the sale of the fruit (*CIR v Pilcher CA 1949, 31 TC 314*). Proceeds from sales of turf were held to be trading receipts from farming (*Lowe v J W Ashmore Ltd Ch D 1970, 46 TC 597*).

For these and other aspects of farming taxation, see Revenue Business Income Manual BIM 55000–55730, 73000–73190 and 75600–75650.

Simon's Direct Tax Service. See B3.5.

71.48 **FILM AND AUDIO PRODUCTS**

For a detailed explanation, with examples, of how these provisions are applied in practice, see Revenue Business Income Manual BIM 56000–56530. This replaced, with effect from 15 April 2003, Statement of Practice SP 1/98, which itself replaced the earlier Statement of Practice SP 1/93 (which in turn replaced SP 2/83 and SP 2/85).

In the absence of special legislation, the master negative and soundtrack of a film (or the electronic equivalent) would generally be plant for tax purposes, so that the production costs would attract capital allowances (see 9.24 *et seq.* CAPITAL ALLOWANCES), although this would not apply to e.g. expenditure on the acquisition of exhibition rights in a film. Under special provisions, however, expenditure on the production or acquisition of a 'master version' of a film is to be regarded as revenue rather than capital expenditure, and any receipts from the disposal of any interest or right or insurance or compensation or similar moneys derived from the master version are revenue receipts. See below, however, as regards election for these provisions *not* to apply to expenditure on certain 'qualifying films' etc. The *'master version'* of a film means the original master negative of the film and its soundtrack (if any), the original master film tape or original master audio tape of the film, or the original master audio disc of the film, and includes references to any rights in the film (or its soundtrack) held or acquired with them.

For expenditure on the acquisition of a film, tape or disc incurred before 6 April 2000, the above provisions apply with two minor differences.

(*a*)   The provisions apply only to expenditure which would otherwise have constituted expenditure on plant or machinery for capital allowance purposes (see 9.25 CAPITAL ALLOWANCES).

(*b*)   References to a master version of a film are to an original master negative of the film and its soundtrack if any, an original master film or audio tape, or an original master film or audio disc (but see below as regards concessional treatment), and any reference to the acquisition of a film, tape or disc includes a reference to the acquisition of any description of rights in a film, tape or disc.

These differences similarly apply in relation to expenditure on the production of a film where principal photography commences on or after 21 March 2000, or if it commenced before that date and the film is completed on or after that date and the person incurring the expenditure so (irrevocably) elects. A film is completed for this purpose when it is in a form in which it can reasonably be regarded as ready for copies to be made and distributed for public exhibition.

[*F(No 2)A 1992, s 40A; CAA 1990, s 68(1)(2)(8)(10); FA 2000, s 113(1)(2)(5)(6); CAA 2001, Sch 2 para 82, Sch 3 para 116*].

By concession, notwithstanding the changes made by *FA 2000, s 113(2)*, non-film master audio tapes and discs continue to be treated as being within the special provisions. (Revenue Pamphlet IR 1, B54).

All revenue expenditure on the production or acquisition of a master version of a film is allocated to periods of account on a just and reasonable basis having regard to the expenditure unallocated at the beginning of a period, the proportion which the estimated value of the master version realised in the period (whether by way of income or otherwise) bears to the aggregate of the value so realised and the estimated remaining value at the end of the period, and the need to bring the whole expenditure into account over the time during which the value of the master version is expected to be realised. Additional expenditure (so far as not previously allocated to the period or to any earlier period) may be claimed for a period bringing the total expenditure allocated to the period up to the value of the master version which is realised in the period (whether by way of income or otherwise). The claim must be made (i) for income tax, within twelve months after 31 January following the tax year in which the period in question ends, and (ii) for corporation tax, within two years after the end of the period in question. [*F(No 2)A 1992, s 40B; CAA 1990, s 68(3)–(6); FA 1996, Sch 21 para 32(2)(3); CAA 2001, Sch 2 para 82, Sch 3 para 116*].

Expenditure in respect of which a deduction has been made for a period of account under *F(No 2)A 1992, s 42* (see below) is not allocated under these provisions, and where this applies, no other expenditure on the master version concerned is allocated to that period. Neither the above provisions, nor the relief under *F(No 2)A 1992, s 42* (see below), apply to revenue expenditure in relation to trades in which the master version concerned constitutes trading stock under *ICTA 1988, s 100(2)* (see 71.73 below). [*F(No 2)A 1992, s 40C, s 42(8), s 69(1)(2); CAA 1990, s 68(6A)(6B)(7); CAA 2001, Sch 2 para 82, Sch 3 para 116*].

Qualifying films, tapes or discs. Unless an application for certification (as below) was received before 17 April 2002, the following special reliefs are restricted, for films completed after 16 April 2002, or completed before 1 January 2002 but not certified before 17 April 2002, to films genuinely intended for theatrical release, i.e. for exhibition to the paying public at the commercial cinema (subject to the transitional relief referred to below). The relevant intention for this purpose is the intention, at the time the film is completed (i.e. when it can first reasonably be regarded as ready for copies to be made and distributed for presentation to the general public), of the person then entitled to determine how the film is to be exploited. A film is not regarded as genuinely intended for theatrical release unless it is intended that a significant proportion of the film's earnings should be obtained by such exhibition. A film commissioned before 18 April 2002 and on which the principal photography commenced before 1 July 2002 is **not** so excluded from the reliefs *provided that* it is a drama with an average production expenditure greater than £500,000 per hour of running time of the completed film. 'Production expenditure' for this purpose includes all expenditure on production of the film, whenever and by whomsoever incurred, other than any which, at the time of completion, has not been paid and is not the subject of an unconditional obligation to pay within four months after that time. It is increased to an arm's length amount in the case of certain connected person transactions. 'Drama' does not include anything in the nature of an advertisement or promotional film, a training film, a discussion programme, news or current affairs programme, quiz show, panel show, variety show or similar entertainment, or a film of a live event, or of a theatrical or artistic performance given otherwise than for the purpose of being filmed, but does include a documentary involving the dramatic reconstruction of events if the dramatic content forms 50% or more of the running time. [*FA 2002, s 99*].

A person carrying on a trade or business consisting of, or including, the exploitation of master versions of films may elect for the special provisions of *F(No 2)A 1992, ss 40A, 40B* above not to apply to expenditure which is incurred on the production or acquisition of a master version of a film which is certified by the Secretary of State as being a 'qualifying film, tape or disc', and the value of which is expected to be realisable over a period of not less than two years. The election, which is irrevocable, must relate to the whole of the expenditure incurred on the master version in question. The election must be made (i) for income tax, within twelve months after 31 January following the tax year in which ends the period of account in which the master version of the film is completed, and (ii) for corporation tax, within two years after the end of such period. The master version of a film is completed when it is first in a form in which it can reasonably be regarded as ready for copies to be made and distributed for public exhibition or, in relation to expenditure incurred on acquisition of the master version, the time of that acquisition, if later. No election is available in respect of expenditure in relation to any of which a claim has been made under *F(No 2)A 1992, s 41* or *s 42* (see below). [*F(No 2)A 1992, ss 40D, 69; CAA 1990, s 68(9)–(9B); FA 1996, Sch 21 para 32(4)–(6); CAA 2001, Sch 2 para 82, Sch 3 paras 116, 117*].

A film etc. is a '*qualifying film*' if it is within the definition applied for this purpose by *Films Act 1985, s 6, Sch 1*, broadly a film meeting certain criteria as to EU and Commonwealth content, and '*qualifying tape*' and '*qualifying disc*' are similarly defined. See Leaflet FB1 'Evidence of British Nature of a Film', available from Department of National Heritage, 2nd Floor, Grey Core, 151 Buckingham Palace Road, London SW1W 9SS. Regulations relating to certification are contained in *The Films (Certification) Regulations 1985 (SI 1985 No 994)*.

In relation to qualifying films etc. completed (as above) after 9 March 1992, an alternative deduction may be claimed for a period, in respect of any expenditure of a revenue nature incurred in producing a film completed in or before the period, of up to one-third (proportionately reduced for periods of less than twelve months) of the total production expenditure (reduced by any preliminary expenditure already deducted under *F(No 2)A 1992, s 41*, see below), subject to a maximum of the total such expenditure not already deducted. Similar relief is available in respect of expenditure of a revenue nature on the acquisition of the original master negative of a film and its soundtrack (if any) or the original master film or audio tape of a film or the original master film or audio disc of a film, where the film was completed (as above) in the period to which the claim relates (or in an earlier period), and the master negative, tape or disc is a qualifying film, tape or disc. This also applies to such expenditure on the acquisition of any rights in the film (or its soundtrack) that are held or acquired with the original master negative, tape or audio disc of the film. (For acquisition expenditure incurred before 6 April 2000, the restriction to expenditure on films completed after 9 March 1992 is not specifically applied to acquisition expenditure, the extension to expenditure on ancillary rights is to 'any description of rights in' the original master negative, tape or disc of the film, and the reference to the date of completion of the film is to the date of the acquisition if later.) These provisions do not apply where an election has been made in respect of the expenditure under *F(No 2)A 1992, s 40D* (see above), or where a deduction has been made in respect of it under *F(No 2)A 1992, s 40B* (see above), and where a deduction has been allowed for a period under *section 40B*, no deduction is allowed under these provisions for that period in respect of any expenditure on the film concerned. A claim is irrevocable and must be made within twelve months after 31 January following the tax year in which ends the period to which the claim relates (for corporation tax purposes, two years after the end of the period to which it relates). [*F(No 2)A 1992, ss 42, 43; FA 1996, s 135, Sch 21 para 46; FA 2000, s 113(3)(4)(6); CAA 2001, Sch 2 paras 84, 85*].

F(No 2)A 1992, s 42 is further amended to grant enhanced allowances for expenditure incurred in the period **from 2 July 1997 to 1 July 2005 inclusive** on a film completed after 1 July 1997 with a 'total production expenditure' of £15 million or less. As regards the time expenditure is incurred, see 9.2(iv) CAPITAL ALLOWANCES. A film is for this purpose completed when it can first reasonably be regarded as ready for copies to be made and distributed for presentation to the general public. '*Total production expenditure*' includes all production expenditure, whenever incurred and whether or not incurred by the claimant, but increased to an arm's length amount in the case of certain connected person transactions. Where these conditions are met, the allowable deduction for a period is increased from one-third (as above) to the whole of the production or acquisition expenditure (net of earlier deductions). In the case of acquisition expenditure, the deduction is limited to the total production expenditure. Where only a part of expenditure on a film falls within the 100% deduction rules, the amount deductible for a period is limited to the sum of the maximum amount deductible under the 100% deduction rules and the maximum amount deductible under the one-third deduction rules disregarding expenditure within the 100% deduction rules (and restricted on the assumption that the maximum 100% deduction has already been given). For the purposes of this relief, production expenditure on a film completed after 16 April 2002 does not include any which at the time of completion has not been paid and which is not the subject of an unconditional obligation to pay within four months after that time. [*F(No 2)A 1992, s 42(4); F(No 2)A 1997, s 48; FA 1999, s 62; CAA 2001, Sch 2 para 99; FA 2001, s 72; FA 2002, s 100*]. For expenditure incurred **on or after 30 June 2002**, such enhanced allowances do **not** apply to acquisition expenditure unless the acquisition is by, or directly from, the producer (i.e. the person who commissions the making of the film and is entitled to control its exploitation) and is the first such acquisition. [*FA 2002, s 101*].

Preliminary expenditure. A deduction may be claimed for a period for any expenditure payable in the period (or in an earlier period) which can reasonably be said to have been incurred in deciding whether or not to make a film (as defined in *Films Act 1985, Sch 1 para 1*), and which is not payable under a contract etc. whereby it may be repaid if the film is not made. If the decision taken is to make the film, this applies to expenditure incurred before commencement of principal photography, up to a maximum of 20% of the budgeted expenditure as at the first day of principal photography, provided that the film etc. is a qualifying film etc. or, if it has not been completed at the time the claim is made, it is reasonably likely that, if completed, it would be a qualifying film etc. If the decision taken is not to make the film, it applies only where it is reasonably likely that it would have been a qualifying film etc. had it been completed. No relief may be claimed where a deduction has previously been made for the expenditure, or an election made in respect of it under *F(No 2)A 1992, s 40D* (see above). A claim must be made within twelve months after 31 January following the tax year in which ends the period in which the expenditure becomes payable (for corporation tax purposes, two years after the end of such period). [*F(No 2)A 1992, ss 41, 43; FA 1996, s 135, Sch 21 para 45; CAA 2001, Sch 2 paras 83, 85*].

Anti-avoidance. For claw-back in certain circumstances of reliefs for trading losses derived from film reliefs under *F(No 2)A 1992, ss 40A–40C* or *ss 41–43* or *F(No 2)A 1997, s 48* above, see 46.8(*f*) LOSSES. For restrictions on relief for partnership losses derived from expenditure *other* than under *F(No 2)A 1992, s 41* or *s 42* in a trade involving the exploitation of films, see 53.11 PARTNERSHIPS.

Leasing. See 71.58 below as regards restrictions on relief under the above provisions where finance leasing arrangements are involved.

Simon's Direct Tax Service. See B3.1307–B3.1307B.

71.49   **FRANCHISING**

Under a business system franchising agreement (i.e. an agreement under which the franchisor grants to the franchisee the right to distribute products or perform services using that system), there is generally an initial fee (payable in one sum or in instalments) and continuing, usually annual, fees.

The capital or revenue treatment of the initial fee depends on what it is for. To the extent that it is paid wholly or mainly for substantial rights of an enduring nature, to initiate or substantially extend a business, it is a capital payment (as are any related professional fees). (See 71.30 above for general principles.) It is immaterial that the expenditure may prove abortive, and the treatment of the payment in the hands of the franchisor is irrelevant. However, where goods or services of a revenue nature are supplied at the outset (e.g. trading stock or staff training), the Revenue will accept that an appropriate part of the initial fee is a revenue payment, provided that the sum claimed fairly represents such items, and that it is clear that the items are not separately charged for in the continuing fees. The costs of the franchisee's own initial training are not normally allowable.

The continuing fee payable by the franchisee is generally a revenue expense.

(Revenue Tax Bulletin June 1995 p 224).

See generally Revenue Business Income Manual BIM 57600–57620.

For *companies* acquiring and selling franchises after 31 March 2002, the intangible assets regime (see Tolley's Corporation Tax under Intangible Assets) is likely to apply and takes precedence over the above.

71.50   **GIFTS AND OTHER NON-CONTRACTUAL RECEIPTS AND PAYMENTS**

See also generally 71.44 above, 71.74 and 71.75 below and CHARITIES (14).

The fact that a receipt is gratuitous is not in itself a reason for its not being a trading receipt. See *Severne v Dadswell Ch D 1954, 35 TC 649* (payments under war-time arrangements held trading receipts although *ex gratia*); *CIR v Falkirk Ice Rink CS 1975, 51*

TC 42 (donation to ice rink from associated curling club held taxable); *Wing v O'Connell Supreme Court (IFS) 1926, [1927] IR 84* (gift to professional jockey on winning race taxable).

In recent years the problem has arisen in relation to *ex gratia* payments on the termination of long-standing business arrangements. A distinction is drawn between parting gifts as personal testimonials (not taxable as business receipts) and payments which, on the facts, can be seen as additional rewards for services already rendered or compensation for a loss of future profits (taxable). For cases see 71.38(*e*) above and compare the position for employees, see 75.29 SCHEDULE E—EMPLOYMENT INCOME. For gifts and donations made, see 71.74 below.

Cremation fees (often known as 'ash cash') assigned in advance, and paid directly, to a medical charity may escape liability under Schedule D, Case VI where the doctor entitled to them is not chargeable under Case II, but liability under Case II is not affected by such assignment. See Revenue Business Income Manual BIM 54015.

Gifts to educational establishments. A relief is available for certain gifts by traders for the purposes of 'designated educational establishments'.

Where the gift is of an article manufactured by the trader, or of a type sold by him, in his trade, and would have been classified as plant or machinery for capital allowance purposes if the educational establishment had incurred expenditure on it for the purposes of a trade carried on by it, the trader is not required to bring in any amount as a trading receipt in respect of the gift.

The relief must be claimed within twelve months after 31 January following the year of assessment in whose basis period the gift was made (or, for corporation tax where self-assessment applies, within two years after the end of the accounting period in which it was made). The claim must specify the article and educational establishment concerned.

Similarly, where the gift is of an item of plant or machinery used in the course of the donor's trade, its disposal value (see 9.29 CAPITAL ALLOWANCES) is nil. (Before *CAA 2001* had effect, see 9.1 CAPITAL ALLOWANCES, the relief applied only if a plant and machinery allowance had been claimed on the item, and operated slightly differently in that no disposal value was required to be brought into account. Also, the relief was given only on the making of a claim, within the same time limits as above.)

The value of any benefit received by the donor or by a person connected with him (see 19 CONNECTED PERSONS), which is in any way attributable to the making of a gift for which relief has been given, will be assessed on the donor under Case I, Case II or Case VI of Schedule D, as appropriate.

'*Designated educational establishment*' means any educational establishment designated (or of a category designated) in regulations, broadly all UK universities, public or private schools and further and higher educational institutions (see *SI 1992 No 42* as amended by *SI 1993 No 561*).

[*ICTA 1988, s 84; FA 1991, s 68; FA 1996, s 135, Sch 21 para 2; CAA 2001, s 63(2)–(4), Sch 2 para 17*].

Gifts in kind to charities. See 14.19 CHARITIES for relief for gifts in kind (i.e. of trading stock or plant or machinery used in the trade etc.) to charities and certain other bodies on or after 27 July 1999, and 14.21 CHARITIES for the earlier, more limited relief for gifts for third world health or education. Where such reliefs do not apply, donations of trading stock to charities are dealt with on normal Case I principles. See Revenue Tax Bulletin June 1996 p 319 for the Revenue's view of the application of those principles.

Simon's Direct Tax Service. See **B3.1441** *et seq.*, **B3.1508.**

71.51 Schedule D, Cases I and II—Profits of Trades etc.

71.51 GUARANTEES

Losses under guarantees of the indebtedness of another are analogous to bad debt losses (see 71.34 above) and similar principles apply. Losses allowed to a solicitor under the guarantee of a client's overdraft (*Jennings v Barfield Ch D 1962, 40 TC 365*) and to a film-writer under guarantee of loans to a film company with which he was associated (*Lunt v Wellesley KB 1945, 27 TC 78*) but refused to a company under a guarantee of loans to an associated company with which it had close trading connections (*Milnes v J Beam Group Ltd Ch D 1975, 50 TC 675*) and a guarantee of loans to a subsidiary (*Redkite Ltd v Inspector of Taxes [1996] SSCD 501*). See also *Bolton v Halpern & Woolf CA 1980, 53 TC 445* and *Garforth v Tankard Carpets Ltd Ch D 1980, 53 TC 342*.

A loss by an asphalt contractor under a guarantee to an exhibition (for which he hoped but, in the event, failed to work) allowed (*Morley v Lawford & Co CA 1928, 14 TC 229*). For commission paid to guarantors see *Ascot Gas Water Heaters Ltd* at 71.55 below.

Payments under guarantees made to a trader for the setting up or the purposes of his trade and irrecoverable are in certain circumstances allowable as a loss for capital gains tax. [*TCGA 1992, s 253; FA 1996, Sch 21 para 40*]. See Tolley's Capital Gains Tax.

71.52 HIRE-PURCHASE

Where assets are purchased under hire-purchase agreements, the charges (the excess of the hire-purchase price over the cash price, sometimes called interest but not true interest) are, appropriately spread, allowable deductions (*Darngavil Coal Co Ltd v Francis CS 1913, 7 TC 1*). See 71.34 above for the bad debt etc. provisions of hire-purchase traders. For relief on capital element, see 9.38(A) CAPITAL ALLOWANCES.

For whether goods sold under hire-purchase are trading stock, see *Lions Ltd v Gosford Furnishing Co Ltd & CIR CS 1961, 40 TC 256* and cf. *Drages Ltd v CIR KB 1927, 46 TC 389*.

See generally Revenue Business Income Manual BIM 40550–40555 (hire-purchase receipts) and BIM 45350–45365 (hire-purchase payments).

Simon's Direct Tax Service. See B3.1161 et seq., B3.1310.

71.53 ILLEGAL PAYMENTS ETC.

In computing profits chargeable under Schedule D, no deduction may be made in respect of expenditure (including incidental costs) incurred (*a*) in making a payment the making of which constitutes the commission of a criminal offence, or (*b*) after 31 March 2002 in making a payment outside the UK where the making of a corresponding payment in any part of the UK would constitute a criminal offence there. A deduction is similarly denied for any payment induced by a demand constituting blackmail or extortion. Relief as a management expense is similarly denied. [*ICTA 1988, s 577A; FA 1993, s 123; FA 1994, s 141; FA 1998, Sch 27 Pt III(4); FA 2002, s 68*]. For a discussion of the circumstances in which these provisions may apply, see Revenue Business Income Manual BIM 43100–43185.

Simon's Direct Tax Service. See B3.1447.

71.54 INSURANCE

Premiums for business purposes are normally allowable including insurance of assets, insurance against accidents to employees, insurance against loss of profits and premiums under mutual insurance schemes (cf. *Thomas v Richard Evans & Co HL 1927, 11 TC 790*; for trade associations see 71.74 below). For war risk premiums see *ICTA 1988, s 586*.

Any corresponding recoveries are trading receipts (or set off against trading expenses (see *ICTA 1988, s 74(1)(l)*) or capital, according to the nature of the policy. If capital, the recovery may be taken into account, where appropriate, for the purposes of CAPITAL ALLOWANCES (9) or capital gains tax. The whole of a recovery in respect of the destruction of trading stock is a trading receipt of the year of destruction, notwithstanding that it exceeds the market value of the stock lost or not all the stock was replaced (*Green v J Gliksten & Son Ltd HL 1929, 14 TC 364; Rownson Drew & Clydesdale Ltd v CIR KB 1931, 16 TC 595*). The total recovery under a loss of profits was held a trading receipt although in excess of the loss suffered (*R v British Columbia Fir & Cedar PC 1932, 15 ATC 624*). See also *Mallandain Investments Ltd v Shadbolt KB 1940, 23 TC 367*. For recoveries under accidents to employees see *Gray & Co v Murphy KB 1940, 23 TC 225; Keir & Cawder Ltd v CIR CS 1958, 38 TC 23*. Where a shipping company insured against late delivery of ships being built for it, both premiums and recoveries held capital (*Crabb v Blue Star Line Ltd Ch D 1961, 39 TC 482*).

Premiums on policies in favour of the employer insuring against death or critical illness of key employees are generally allowable, and the proceeds of any such policies trading receipts. However, in *Beauty Consultants Ltd v Inspector of Taxes (Sp C 321), [2002] SSCD 352*, premiums on a policy insuring a company against the death of either of its controlling shareholder-directors were disallowed; the 'dual purpose rule' at 71.30 above applied, in that the premiums benefited the shareholders personally by improving the value of their shares. In *Greycon Ltd v Klaentschi (Sp C 372), [2003] SSCD 370*, it was held that the company's sole purpose in taking out key man policies was to meet a requirement of an agreement under which funding and other benefits were obtained from another company, that the policies had a capital purpose and that, consequently, the proceeds were not trading receipts.

For mutual insurance trading, see 50 MUTUAL TRADING.

Health insurance. See 28.15 EXEMPT INCOME.

Locum and fixed practice expenses insurance. With effect for periods of account beginning after 30 September 1996, the Revenue take the view that premiums for such policies are deductible, and benefits taxable, under Schedule D, Case II, whether the professional person is obliged to insure (e.g. under NHS regulations) or does so as a matter of commercial prudence. This view relates to premiums paid by professional people such as doctors and dentists to meet locum and/or fixed overhead costs. It does not apply to any part of a premium relating to other, non-business, risks such as the cost of medical treatment for accident or sickness. (Revenue Press Release 30 April 1996).

Professional indemnity insurance premiums are normally allowable on general principles, and the Revenue will not seek to disallow a premium paid prior to cessation of trading on the grounds that the cover extends to claims lodged after cessation. (Premiums paid after cessation will generally be relievable as post-cessation expenditure, see 62.4 POST-CESSATION ETC. RECEIPTS AND EXPENDITURE.) (Revenue Tax Bulletin October 1995 p 257).

As regards **accountancy fee protection insurance**, see 71.59 below.

Commissions. Revenue Statement of Practice SP 4/97 (see 71.36 above) deals widely with commissions, cashbacks and discounts.

See also *Robertson v CIR (Sp C 137), [1997] SSCD 282* as regards timing of inclusion of insurance agents' advance commission.

71.55   **INTEREST AND OTHER PAYMENTS FOR LOANS**

Interest paid for business purposes if not claimed as a relief under *ICTA 1988, s 353* is deductible, subject to certain restrictions, as described at 43.2 INTEREST PAYABLE. For 'hire-purchase interest' see 71.52 above.

Premium on repayment of mortgage (*Arizona Copper Co v Smiles CES 1891, 3 TC 149*) and on repayment of loan to finance estate development (*Bridgwater v King KB 1943, 25 TC 385*) held not allowable, as were exchange losses attendant on foreign borrowings by a company to finance its purchase of a controlling interest in another company (*Ward v Anglo-American Oil Co Ltd KB 1934, 19 TC 94*). A share of profits paid as partial consideration for a loan was held to be distribution of profits and not allowed in *Walker & Co v CIR KB 1920, 12 TC 297*.

Prior to *FA 1969*, interest paid in full on capital advances was disallowed (cf. *European Investment Trust Ltd v Jackson CA 1932, 18 TC 1*). The legislation was amended by *FA 1969*. In a case under the old law, commission paid for a guarantee of a trading liability was allowed but not for guarantee of a debenture loan (*Ascot Gas Water Heaters Ltd v Duff KB 1942, 24 TC 171*).

INTEREST ON UNPAID TAX (42) is not an allowable deduction in computing profits or losses. This applies equally to interest on unpaid or under-declared value added tax, insurance premium tax, landfill tax, climate change levy or aggregates levy. [*TMA 1970, s 90; ICTA 1988, s 827(1)(1B)(1C)(1D)(1E); FA 1994, Sch 7 para 31; FA 1996, Sch 5 para 40; FA 2000, Sch 7 para 4; FA 2001, s 49(3)*].

For the treatment of the incidental costs of obtaining loan finance, see 71.60 below. See also 43.16 INTEREST PAYABLE regarding interest relief for persons living in job-related accommodation.

Companies. For the special provisions applicable to all profits and losses in respect of company 'loan relationships', see Tolley's Corporation Tax under Loan Relationships.

71.56 **INVESTMENT INCOME (DIVIDENDS, INTEREST, RENTS, ROYALTIES)**

Income received under deduction of tax may not be included in a Case I or II assessment (cf. *F S Securities Ltd v CIR HL 1964, 41 TC 666; Bucks v Bowers Ch D 1969, 46 TC 267; Bank Line Ltd v CIR CS 1974, 49 TC 307*) nor, subject to the Crown option between Cases (see 5.1 ASSESSMENTS), may income received in full from sources within Cases III, IV or V (cf. *Northend v White & Leonard & Corbin Greener Ch D 1975, 50 TC 121*) and also from sources *explicitly* within Case VI. See 46 LOSSES for treatment of certain investment income as trading profits for loss relief purposes and Tolley's Corporation Tax for similar provisions for companies. Rents receivable within Schedule A may not be assessed under Schedule D (see 5.1 ASSESSMENTS) but in practice the Revenue do not generally object to the inclusion in trading profits of rents from the letting of business accommodation temporarily surplus to requirements, provided that the premises in question continue to be partly used for the business and the rental income is comparatively small (see Revenue Tax Bulletin February 1994 p 115). See also 71.68 below.

Investment income may be treated as a trading receipt where it is the fruit derived from a fund employed and risked in the business (see *Liverpool and London and Globe Insurance Co v Bennett HL 1913, 6 TC 327*). This treatment is not confined to financial trades, but the making and holding of investments at interest must be an integral part of the trade. See *Nuclear Electric plc v Bradley HL 1996, 68 TC 670*, in which (in refusing the company's claim) the crucial test was considered to be whether the investments were employed in the business (of producing electricity) in the year of assessment in question. The Court of Appeal, whose judgment was approved, considered decisive the facts that the liabilities against which the investments were provided were liabilities to third parties, not to customers, and that, in view of the long-term nature of the liabilities, the business could be carried on for a long period without maintaining any fund of investments at all. See also *Bank Line Ltd v CIR* (above).

Payments received in lieu of dividends in contango operations held trading receipts (*Multipar Syndicate Ltd v Devitt KB 1945, 26 TC 359*); also co-operative society 'dividends' on trading purchases (*Pope v Beaumont KB 1941, 24 TC 78*). For interest received by underwriters on securities deposited with Lloyd's see *Owen v Sassoon HC 1950, 32 TC 101* and for discount receivable on bills see *Willingale v International Commercial Bank Ltd HL 1978, 52 TC 242*.

For the purposes of the excess profits tax and similar taxes it was necessary to determine whether rents and royalties were 'investment income'. For cases dealing with this, not involving the Case I or II treatment of the income, see Tolley's Tax Cases.

71.57　KNOW-HOW

'Know-how' is any industrial information and techniques of assistance in (*a*) manufacturing or processing goods or materials, (*b*) working, or searching for etc., mineral deposits, or (*c*) agricultural, forestry or fishing operations. [*ICTA 1988, s 533(7)*]. Where know-how which has been used in the vendor's trade (the trade thereafter continuing) is disposed of, the consideration received (including any consideration for a restrictive covenant connected with the disposal) is a trading receipt (if not already taxable). [*ICTA 1988, s 531(1)*]. It should, however, be noted that, in relation to know-how on which expenditure is incurred after 31 March 1986, a disposal value will normally fall to be brought into account instead in these circumstances (see 9.23 CAPITAL ALLOWANCES). A non-trading vendor is assessable under Schedule D, Case VI, on his net gain (treated as earned income if he devised the know-how) after deducting expenditure on acquisition or disposal. [*ICTA 1988, s 531(4)–(6)*].

But the above provisions do not apply to a sale between bodies of persons (which includes partnerships) under the same control. [*ICTA 1988, s 531(7)*].

If know-how is sold together with a trade, or part trade, both the vendor and the purchaser are treated as if the consideration for the know-how were a payment for goodwill. They may, however, jointly elect to disapply this treatment (within two years of the disposal, and provided they are not bodies under common control), and it is disapplied in any event where the trade acquired was previously carried on wholly outside the UK. In either case, the purchaser may then claim capital allowances on his expenditure (see 9.23(iii) CAPITAL ALLOWANCES). [*ICTA 1988, s 531(2)(3)(7); CAA 2001, Sch 2 para 48*]. If goodwill, capital gains tax may apply.

For capital allowances on purchases of know-how, see 9.23 CAPITAL ALLOWANCES.

In *Delage v Nugget Polish Co Ltd KB 1905, 21 TLR 454*, payments for the use of a secret process, payable for 40 years and based on receipts, were held to be annual payments subject to deduction of tax at source. See also *Paterson Engineering v Duff KB 1943, 25 TC 43*.

For patents, see 71.63 below.

Simon's Direct Tax Service. See **B3.861** *et seq.*

71.58　LEASE RENTAL PAYMENTS

Car hire. Where a 'car' of which the retail price when new (i.e. unused and not second-hand) exceeded £12,000 is hired for business purposes, the hire charge is reduced for tax purposes by multiplying it by the fraction

$(12,000 + P) \div 2P$

where P is the retail price in pounds when new. If the price paid for the car by the lessor when new is known, it can be used as the retail price when new, but otherwise the manufacturer's list price, net of any discount generally available but inclusive of extras and VAT, should be used (Revenue Tax Bulletin April 2000 p 746). For this purpose, a '*car*' is a mechanically propelled road vehicle which is neither (1) of a construction primarily suited for the conveyance of goods or burden of any description nor (2) of a type not commonly used as a private vehicle and unsuitable for such use; a 'car' thus includes a motor cycle. As regards (2), see the case law referred to at 9.27(ii) CAPITAL ALLOWANCES. The restriction does not apply to cars used wholly or mainly for a trade of hire to, or carriage of, members of the public and satisfying the same conditions as apply for the similar exception at 9.27(A) CAPITAL ALLOWANCES. As regards hire-purchase agreements under which there is an option to purchase for a sum not more than one per cent of the retail price when new, the finance charge element, which strictly falls within the definition of a hire charge, is also excluded from the restriction.

Also excluded from the restriction is expenditure incurred *after 16 April 2002* on hiring cars (other than motorcycles) first registered after that date which are 'electrically-propelled' or have 'low carbon dioxide emissions' (for which see 9.27 CAPITAL ALLOWANCES) for hire periods beginning before 1 April 2008 under a contract entered into before that date.

'Hire charges' for these purposes were held to include payments under a finance lease providing a revolving facility for the purchase of vehicles for use in a contract hire operation (*Lloyds UDT Finance Ltd and Another v Britax International GmBH and Another CA 2002, 74 TC 662*).

Where the above restriction has applied, any subsequent rental rebate (or other release within *ICTA 1988, s 94* — see 71.34 above) is reduced for tax purposes in the same proportion as the hire charge restriction.

[*ICTA 1988, ss 578A, 578B; CAA 1990, s 35(2)–(4); FA 1991, s 61; F(No 2)A 1992, s 71; FA 1996, Sch 39 para 1(3)(4); CAA 2001, Sch 2 para 52, Sch 3 para 113; FA 2001, Sch 12 Pt II para 11; FA 2002, s 60*].

See Revenue Business Income Manual BIM 47715–47720.

See 9.30(A) CAPITAL ALLOWANCES for the restriction of writing-down allowances in respect of *capital* expenditure on the acquisition of a car costing over £12,000.

Finance lease rentals — Statement of Practice. In relation to finance leases entered into after 11 April 1991, the Revenue practice described below applies to rentals payable by a lessee under a finance lease, i.e. a lease which transfers substantially all the risks and rewards of ownership of an asset to the lessee while maintaining the lessor's legal ownership of the asset. The treatment of such rentals depends upon whether or not SSAP 21 has been applied. This practice has no implications for the tax treatment of rentals receivable by the lessor, nor for the availability of capital allowances to the lessor. (Revenue Pamphlet IR 131, SP 3/91 and Revenue Press Release 11 April 1991).

Finance lease rentals are revenue payments for the use of the asset, and, both under normal accounting principles and for tax purposes, should be allocated to the periods of account for which the asset is leased in accordance with the accruals concept. Where there is an option for the lessee to continue to lease the asset after expiry of the primary period under the lease, regard should be had, in allocating rentals to periods of account, to the economic life of the asset and its likely period of use by the lessee, as well as to the primary period.

Under SSAP 21, the lessee is required to treat a finance lease as the acquisition of an asset subject to a loan, to be depreciated over its useful life, with rentals apportioned between a finance charge and a capital repayment element. This treatment does not, however, affect the tax treatment, which remains as described above.

Where SSAP 21 has not been applied, the lessee's accounting treatment of rental payments is normally accepted for tax purposes, provided that it is consistent with the principles described above. If not, computational adjustments are made to secure the proper spreading of the rental payments.

Where SSAP 21 has been applied, the finance charge element of the rental payments for a period of account is normally accepted as a revenue deduction for that period. In determining the appropriate proportion of the capital repayment element to be deducted for tax purposes, a properly computed commercial depreciation charge to profit and loss account will normally be accepted. Where, however, the depreciation charge is not so computed, the appropriate proportion for tax purposes will be determined in accordance with the principles described above.

For comment on the principles set out in SP 3/91, and on their application to particular arrangements, see Revenue Tax Bulletin February 1995 pp 189–193. This considers in particular: sums paid before the asset comes into use; depreciation of leased assets (and the interaction with SSAP 21); long-life assets; termination adjustments; fixtures leases; and the interaction of SP 3/91 with statutory restrictions on relief for rental payments.

See generally Revenue Business Income Manual BIM 61000–61075 (leasing: general) and BIM 61100–61195 (finance leasing).

Lease rental anti-avoidance — return in capital form. *FA 1997, Sch 12 Pt I* applies from 26 November 1996 in relation to asset leasing arrangements which are dealt with by generally accepted accounting practice (see 71.30 above) as finance leases or loans, and whose effect is that some or all of the investment return is or may be in non-rental form and would not, apart from these provisions, be wholly taxed as lease rental. The principal purposes of the provisions are to charge any person entitled to the lessor's interest to tax by reference to the income return for accounting purposes (taking into account the substance of the matter as a whole, e.g. as regards connected persons or groups of companies); and to recover reliefs etc. for capital and other expenditure as appropriate by reference to sums received which fall within the provisions. The provisions are described below.

FA 1997, Sch 12 Pt I applies where an asset lease (as widely defined) is or has at any time been granted in the case of which the following conditions are or have been satisfied at some time (the '*relevant time*') in a period of account of the current lessor. Where the conditions have been satisfied at a relevant time, they are treated as continuing to be satisfied unless and until the asset ceases to be leased under the lease or the lessor's interest is assigned to a person not 'connected' with the assignor or certain other prior or subsequent lessors. Persons who are CONNECTED PERSONS (19) (within *ICTA 1988, s 839*) at any time in the period from the earliest time at which any of the leasing arrangements were made to the time when the current lessor finally ceases to have an interest in the asset or any arrangements relating to it are for these purposes treated as so connected throughout that period.

[*FA 1997, Sch 12 paras 1, 2, 23, 25, 30*].

The conditions referred to above are as follows.

(*a*)   At the relevant time, and under generally accepted accounting practice, the leasing arrangements fall to be treated as a finance lease or loan in relation to which either:

   (i)   the lessor (or a connected person) is the finance lessor; or

   (ii) the lessor is a member of a group of companies for the purposes of whose consolidated accounts (within *Companies Act 1985, s 227* or NI equivalent) the finance lease or loan is treated as subsisting.

(*b*)   A sum (a '*major lump sum*') is or may be payable to the lessor (or a connected person) under the leasing arrangements which is not rent but which falls to be treated, under generally accepted accounting practice, partly as repayment of some or all of the investment in respect of the finance lease or loan and partly as a return on that investment.

(*c*)   Not all of the part of the major lump sum which is treated as a return on the investment (as in (*b*) above) would, apart from these provisions, be brought into account for tax purposes, as 'normal rent' from the lease for periods of account of the lessor, in chargeable periods of the lessor ending with the 'relevant chargeable period'. The *'relevant chargeable period'* is the chargeable or basis period (or latest such period) consisting of or including all or part of the period of account in which that sum is or may be payable under the arrangements. A *'normal rent'* for a period of account is the amount which (apart from the current provisions) the lessor would bring in for tax purposes in the period as rent arising from the lease.

(*d*)   The period of account of the lessor in which the relevant time falls (or an earlier period during which he was the lessor) is one for which the 'accountancy rental earnings' in respect of the lease exceed the normal rent. The *'accountancy rental earnings'* for a period are the greatest of the *'rental earnings'* for the period in respect of the lease (i.e. the amount treated under generally accepted accounting practice as the gross return on investment for the period):

  (i)   of the lessor;

  (ii)   of any person connected with the lessor; and

  (iii)   for the purposes of consolidated group accounts of a group of which the lessor is a member.

Where (ii) or (iii) applies and the lessor's period of account does not coincide with that of the connected person or the consolidated group accounts, amounts in the periods of account of the latter are apportioned as necessary by reference to the number of days in the common periods.

The normal rent for a period of account for these purposes is determined by treating rent as accruing and falling due evenly over the period to which it relates (unless a payment falls due more than twelve months after any of the rent to which it relates is so treated as accruing).

(*e*)   At the relevant time, either:

  (i)   arrangements exist under which the lessee (or a connected person) may directly or indirectly acquire the leased asset (or an asset representing it — see *FA 1997, Sch 12 para 26*) from the lessor (or a connected person), and in connection with that acquisition the lessor (or a connected person) may directly or indirectly receive a *'qualifying lump sum'* from the lessee (or a connected person) (i.e. a non-rental sum part at least of which would be treated under generally accepted accounting practice as a return on investment in respect of a finance lease or loan); or

  (ii)   in the absence of such arrangements, it is in any event more likely that the acquisition and receipt described in (i) above will take place than that, before any such acquisition, the leased asset (or the asset representing it) will have been acquired in an open market sale other than by the lessor or lessee (or persons connected with either of them).

[*FA 1997 Sch 12 paras 3, 4, 20–24; FA 1998, Sch 27 Pt III(4); FA 2002, Sch 40 Pt 3(16)*].

Where *Part I* applies to a lease for a period of account of the current lessor, the consequences are as follows.

Current lessor to be taxed by reference to accountancy rental earnings.

Where the accountancy rental earnings in respect of the lease for a period of account exceed the normal rent for that period, the accountancy rental earnings are substituted for the normal rent for tax purposes. The substituted amount is treated as having accrued evenly over the period of account (disregarding periods for which the asset was not leased).

Where the reverse applies (i.e. the normal rent exceeds the accountancy rental earnings), and there is a 'cumulative accountancy rental excess', the rent otherwise taxable for the period (the *'taxable rent'*) is reduced (although not below the accountancy rental earnings) by setting it against that excess. An *'accountancy rental excess'* for a period to which these provisions apply is the excess (if any) of the accountancy rental earnings over the normal rent for the period, and the *'cumulative accountancy rental excess'* is so much of the aggregate of accountancy rental excesses of previous periods (after allowing for certain bad debts, see below) as has not been set against taxable rents for previous periods or against certain chargeable gains disposal consideration (see below). *'Normal rental excess'* and *'cumulative normal rental excess'* (see below) are correspondingly defined, except that the normal rental excess for a period for which the taxable rent is reduced as above is the excess (if any) of the normal rent (reduced by a similar amount) over the accountancy rental earnings.

If there is a cumulative normal rent excess (as above) for a period of account for which the taxable rent is increased in amount to the accountancy rental earnings, the taxable rent for the period (as so increased) is reduced (but not below the normal rent) by set-off against that excess, and the accountancy rental excess for the period (as above) is the excess (if any) of the taxable rent as so determined over the normal rent.

On an assignment of the current lessor's interest under the lease treated under *TCGA 1992, s 35(3)(d)* as at neither gain nor loss (see Tolley's Capital Gains Tax under Assets Held on 31 March 1982), a period of account of the assignor is treated as ending, and of the assignee as beginning, with the assignment. Any unused cumulative accountancy rental excess or cumulative normal rental excess at the time of the assignment is transferred to the assignee.

Where accountancy rental earnings for a period of account are substituted for normal rent for tax purposes (as above), and a bad debt deduction in excess of the accountancy rental earnings falls to be made for the period, any cumulative accountancy rental excess for the period is reduced (but not below nil) by that excess. If the accountancy rental earnings do not exceed the normal rent, any bad debt deduction acts to reduce the amount of the normal rent against which a cumulative accountancy rental excess may be set, and the cumulative accountancy rental excess is reduced (but not below nil) by any excess of the bad debt deduction over the normal rent. There is provision for such reductions in the cumulative accountancy rental excess to be reversed in the event of subsequent bad debt recoveries or reinstatements.

There are corresponding provisions relating to the effect of bad debt deductions on cumulative normal rental excesses.

In determining the *chargeable gain on a disposal* by the current lessor (or a connected person) of his interest under the lease (or of the leased asset or an asset representing it), the disposal consideration is reduced (but not below nil) by setting against it any cumulative accountancy rental excess (as above) for the period of account of the disposal. This does not preclude the exclusion from the disposal consideration under *TCGA 1992, s 37* of any amount chargeable to tax on income, except to the extent (if any) that it is represented by any cumulative accountancy rental excess set off under this provision (on the current disposal or previously). On a part disposal, the cumulative accountancy rental excess is apportioned in the same manner as the associated acquisition costs, and any further apportionment is on a just and reasonable basis where there is more than one simultaneous disposal. For all purposes of *FA 1997, Sch 12*, the period of account of the current lessor is treated as ending, and a new period as beginning, immediately before such a disposal (or simultaneous such disposals).

If these provisions come to apply to a lease to which the provisions of *FA 1997, Sch 12 Pt II* (see below) already apply, the cumulative accountancy rental excess or cumulative normal rent excess are determined as if these provisions had applied throughout the period for which *Part II* in fact applied.

[FA 1997, Sch 12 paras 5–10, 12, 14, 30; FA 1998, Sch 27 Pt III(4)].

Capital allowances

Where an occasion occurs on which a major lump sum (as in (*b*) above) falls to be paid, there are provisions for the withdrawal of earlier reliefs etc. for expenditure incurred by the current lessor in respect of the leased asset. This applies to reliefs etc. for capital expenditure under *CAA 2001* or *ICTA 1988, ss 91–91B* (cemeteries etc., see 9.5 CAPITAL ALLOWANCES, or waste disposal sites, see 71.84 below). Deductions allowed under *F(No 2)A 1992, s 40B(1)* or *s 42* (films etc., see 71.48 above) are similarly withdrawn. The earlier reliefs etc. are withdrawn either by the bringing in of a disposal value or by the imposition of a balancing charge or, in the case of film, cemetery or waste disposal site expenditure allowed as a deduction, by the bringing in of a countervailing receipt. These provisions apply equally to capital allowances for contributors to capital expenditure under *CAA 2001, ss 537–542*. *[FA 1997, Sch 12 para 11; CAA 2001, Sch 2 para 98]*.

Existing schemes for which (a)–(e) above become satisfied after 26 November 1996

Where a lease of an asset forms part of an 'existing scheme' (as below) for which conditions (*a*)–(*e*) above only become satisfied after 26 November 1996, *FA 1997, Sch 12* applies as if a period of account of the current lessor ended and another began both immediately before and immediately after those conditions came to be satisfied, i.e. as if there was a brief separate period of account during which they became satisfied. Any cumulative accountancy rental excess which would have arisen for that period, had the conditions been satisfied at all times on or after 26 November 1996, is treated as so arising, and the current lessor is treated as if, at the end of the immediately preceding period, there had accrued an additional amount of rent equal to that excess (which rent is, however, left out of account in determining normal rent for comparison with accountancy rental earnings, as above). Similarly a cumulative normal rent excess which would have arisen on those assumptions is treated as having arisen in the period in which the conditions came to be satisfied.

A lease of an asset forms part of an '*existing scheme*' if a contract in writing for the lease was made before 26 November 1996 and either:

(i)   no terms of the contract remained to be agreed on or after that date, and any conditions were satisfied before that date; or

(ii)   the requirements in (i) are satisfied before the end of the period ending with the later of 31 January 1997 and the expiry of six months after the making of the contract, or within such further time as the Commissioners of Inland Revenue may allow in any particular case, and in its final form the contract does not differ materially from how it stood when originally made. *[FA 1997, Sch 12 paras 13, 27; FA 1998, Sch 27 Pt III(4)]*.

Insurance companies. If the current lessor under the lease of an asset is a company carrying on life assurance business, the provisions of *FA 1997, Sch 12 Pt I* (and *Pt II* below) are modified. See *FA 1997, Sch 12 Pt III*.

For the Revenue's views on various points of interpretation regarding these provisions, see Revenue Tax Bulletin April 1997 pp 414–417.

Finance leases not within anti-avoidance provisions. *FA 1997, Sch 12 Pt II* applies from 26 November 1996 to arrangements, not within *Part I* (above), which involve the lease of an asset and are of a kind which would be treated under generally accepted accounting practice as finance leases or loans. The main purpose of the provisions is to charge tax on amounts equal to the income return on investment under generally accepted accounting practice (taking into account the substance of the matter as a whole, e.g. as regards connected persons or groups of companies). *Part II* accordingly applies where a lease of an asset forming part of a new scheme is granted on or after 26 November 1996, and condition (*a*) above is satisfied at some time on or after that date in a period of account of the current lessor, but the anti-avoidance provisions of *Part I* described above do not apply because not all of conditions (*b*)–(*e*) above are or have been satisfied at such a time. Where condition (*a*) was satisfied at some time on or after 26 November 1996, it is treated as continuing to be satisfied until either the asset ceases to be leased under the lease or the lessor's interest is assigned to (i) a person not connected with the assignor, (ii) any other person who was the lessor before the assignment, or (iii) any person who becomes the lessor after the assignment under arrangements made by a person who was the lessor (or a person connected with the lessor) at some time before the assignment. A lease which ceases to be within *Part II* following assignment will come within the provisions again if the conditions are again satisfied. [*FA 1997, Sch 12 paras 15, 16; FA 2002, Sch 40 Pt 3(16)*].

Where *Part II* applies, the provisions of *FA 1997, Sch 12 paras 5–10, 12* for the taxation of the current lessor by reference to accountancy rental earnings (see above) apply to the lease. [*FA 1997, Sch 12 para 17*].

See above as regards special provisions relating to insurance companies.

For the Revenue's views on various points of interpretation regarding these provisions, see Revenue Tax Bulletin April 1997 pp 414–417.

Finance leasing generally. See 9.28, 9.38(A)(C) CAPITAL ALLOWANCES for other finance lease capital allowance restrictions. It was held in *Caledonian Paper plc v CIR (Sp C 159), [1998] SSCD 129* that annual or semi-annual payments of commitment fees, guarantee fees and agency fees relating to guarantees required in relation to finance leasing arrangements were deductible in computing profits, but that a one-off management fee was not.

Simon's Direct Tax Service. See B3.1310.

71.59   **LEGAL AND PROFESSIONAL EXPENSES**

The costs of forming a company are capital but in so far as they relate to loan capital may qualify for relief by virtue of *ICTA 1988, ss 77, 401* (see 71.60 and 71.66 below).

The expenses of a company incorporated by charter in obtaining a variation of its charter etc. were allowed (*CIR v Carron Co HL 1968, 45 TC 18*). See also *McGarry v Limerick Gas HC(IFS) [1932] IR 125* and contrast *A & G Moore & Co v Hare CS 1914, 6 TC 572*. In general, the costs of maintaining existing trading rights and assets are revenue expenses (*Southern v Borax Consolidated KB 1940, 23 TC 597; Bihar etc. IT Commr v Maharaja of Dharbanga PC 1941, 20 ATC 337* and compare *Morgan v Tate & Lyle Ltd HL 1954, 35 TC 367*). But the incidental costs of acquiring new assets etc. are part of their capital cost. The expenses of obtaining or renewing a lease of business premises are strictly capital but, in practice, the expenses of renewing leases under 50 years are generally allowed (although a proportionate disallowance may apply where a lease premium is involved — see Revenue Business Income Manual BIM 46420). The cost of an unsuccessful application to vary a carrier's licence was disallowed (*Pyrah v Annis & Co CA 1956, 37 TC 163*) as was the cost of an unsuccessful application for planning permission (*ECC Quarries Ltd v Watkis Ch D 1975, 51 TC 153* but see 9.11(*b*) CAPITAL ALLOWANCES). For excise licences, see 71.35 above.

Legal expenses in defending charges brought by a professional regulatory body were allowed on the grounds that they were incurred to prevent suspension or expulsion and thus to protect the taxpayer's business (applying *Tate & Lyle Ltd* (above)), although the fines imposed were disallowed (see 71.37 above) (*McKnight v Sheppard HL 1999, 71 TC 419*).

Costs incurred by a partner in connection with the dissolution of the partnership were disallowed in *C Connelly & Co v Wilbey Ch D 1992, 65 TC 208*.

The cost of tax appeals even though successful is not allowable (*Allen v Farquharson Bros & Co KB 1932, 17 TC 59*; *Smith's Potato Estates v Bolland HL 1948, 30 TC 267*; *Rushden Heel Co v Keene HL 1948, 30 TC 298*). Where an accountant etc. agrees the tax liabilities based on the accounts he prepares, normal annual fees are allowed but not fees for a special review of settled years (*Worsley Brewery Co v CIR CA 1932, 17 TC 349*).

Additional accountancy expenses incurred as a result of an 'in-depth' examination by the Revenue of a particular year's accounts (see 71.18 above) will normally be allowed if the investigation does not result in an adjustment to the profits of any earlier year or in the imposition of interest or interest and penalties in relation to the current year. Where the investigation reveals discrepancies and additional liabilities for earlier years, or results in a settlement for the current year including interest (with or without penalties), the expenses will be disallowed. (Revenue Pamphlet IR 131, SP 16/91, 3 December 1991). In its application to self-assessment enquiries (see 68.6 RETURNS), the Statement of Practice is reworded to make it clear that the prohibition on allowance of accountancy expenses applies only where the enquiry reveals negligent or fraudulent conduct (and see Revenue Tax Bulletin October 1998 p 596).

It is the Revenue's view that premiums for a fee protection insurance policy, which entitles the policy holder to claim for the cost of accountancy fees incurred in negotiating additional tax liabilities resulting from negligent or fraudulent conduct, are not allowable. Even if the policy covers other risks as well, the premiums cannot be apportioned between allowable and non-allowable elements. (Revenue Tax Bulletin June 2003 p 1036).

Simon's Direct Tax Service. See B3.1515.

71.60   **LOAN FINANCE INCIDENTAL COSTS**

Expenditure may qualify for relief under *ICTA 1988, s 77*. The relief applies to the incidental costs of obtaining finance by means of a loan or issue of loan stock (*a*) the interest on which would be deductible in computing profits (see 71.55 above and 43.2 INTEREST PAYABLE), and (*b*) which does not carry a right, exercisable within three years, of conversion into, or to the acquisition of, shares or other (non-qualifying) securities.

(*b*) does not apply if the right is not wholly exercised within the three-year period, and where part only of the loan etc. is so converted, only the corresponding part of the incidental costs is disallowed. For this purpose, incidental costs incurred before the end of the three-year period are treated as incurred immediately after that period. [*ICTA 1988, s 77*].

The incidental costs deductible are those incurred wholly and exclusively for the purpose of (i) obtaining the loan finance, whether actually obtained or not, or (ii) providing security for it, or (iii) repaying it. They include fees, commissions, advertising, printing, and other incidental matters but not stamp duty nor does the relief extend to exchange losses (or sums paid for protection against them) or a premium on repayment. [*ICTA 1988, s 77(6)*]. Costs incidental to the taking out of a life insurance policy as a condition of obtaining the loan finance are deductible, but not premiums payable on such a policy. (Revenue Tax Bulletin February 1992 p 13). Costs of a flotation the proceeds of which were used to repay loan finance were held not allowable as the motive of the company in arranging for the flotation was not wholly and exclusively to repay the debt (*Focus Dynamics plc v Turner (Sp C 182), [1999] SSCD 71*).

It was held in *Cadbury Schweppes plc v Williams (Sp C 302), [2002] SSCD 115* that the period for which the relief is available is that in which the finance is obtained, rather than that in which the facility is used, notwithstanding the accountancy treatment. See, however,

Revenue Tax Bulletin April 1996 p 306 for the Revenue view that the timing of the deduction is in accordance with normal principles (i.e. it follows the accounting treatment, provided that the accounts are correctly drawn up in accordance with applicable UK accounting standards).

Where loan finance costs are incurred on the formation of a company before it commences trading, see 71.66 below.

These provisions do not apply for corporation tax purposes for accounting periods ending after 31 March 1996. [*ICTA 1988, s 77(8); FA 1996, Sch 14 para 9*]. See Tolley's Corporation Tax under Loan Relationships.

Simon's Direct Tax Service. See B3.1321.

71.61   MINES, QUARRIES ETC.

See 9.39 *et seq.* CAPITAL ALLOWANCES for mining etc. expenditure so allowable. The relevant legislation which applied before 1 April 1986 originated from 1945 and may therefore affect any pre-1945 decisions below.

The cost of sinking (*Coltness Iron Co v Black HL 1881, 1 TC 287*), deepening (*Bonner v Basset Mines KB 1912, 6 TC 146*) or 'de-watering' (*United Collieries v CIR CS 1929, 12 TC 1248*) a pit is capital.

A lump sum paid at the end of a mining lease for surface damage was held capital (*Robert Addie & Sons v CIR CS 1924, 8 TC 671*) but not periodic payments during the currency of the lease based on acreage worked (*O'Grady v Bullcroft Main Collieries KB 1932, 17 TC 93*). *Bullcroft* was decided before the enactment of what is now *ICTA 1988, s 119* and rents and tonnage payments for the right to withdraw surface support are easements within *section 119* (*CIR v New Sharlston Collieries CA 1936, 21 TC 116*). For the deduction of tax under *section 119* see 22.14 DEDUCTION OF TAX AT SOURCE and also for periodic payments for rights to minerals, sand and gravel etc. For shortworkings, see *Broughton & Plas Power v Kirkpatrick QB 1884, 2 TC 69*; *CIR v Cranford Ironstone KB 1942, 29 TC 113*. Provision for the future costs of abandoning an oil field and of restoring hired equipment used therein to its original state held capital (*RTZ Oil and Gas Ltd v Elliss Ch D 1987, 61 TC 132*).

For the Revenue's view of the treatment of payments by mining concerns to landowners for restoration for surface damage, see Revenue Business Income Manual BIM 62025. In particular, a payment of compensation for ascertained past damage is allowable, as is a provision for such expenditure where made in accordance with generally accepted accounting practice and accurately quantified.

Purchase of unworked deposits by sand and gravel merchant held capital (*Stow Bardolph Gravel Co Ltd v Poole CA 1954, 35 TC 459*) as was purchase of land with nitrate deposits by chemical manufacturer (*Alianza Co v Bell HL 1905, 5 TC 172*) and payment by oil company for unwon oil in wells it took over (*Hughes v British Burmah Petroleum KB 1932, 17 TC 286*). See also *Golden Horse Shoe v Thurgood CA 1933, 18 TC 280* (purchase of tailings for gold extraction, allowable) and *CIR v Broomhouse Brick CS 1952, 34 TC 1* (purchase of blaes for brick manufacture, allowable).

See generally Revenue Business Income Manual BIM 62000–62085.

Production wells etc. The costs of drilling the second and subsequent production wells in an area are not allowable. Such costs may attract mineral extraction capital allowances (see 9.39 *et seq.* CAPITAL ALLOWANCES). [*ICTA 1988, s 91C; FA 1997, s 66*].

71.62   MISCELLANEOUS EXPENSES AND RECEIPTS

Card winnings of club proprietor, trading receipts (*Burdge v Pyne Ch D 1968, 45 TC 320*). For lotteries and football pools, see 71.20 above.

Carers. Any profits arising from payments by local authorities for taking the elderly or infirm into the home as family are assessable under Schedule D, Case I or II (although the availability of 'rent-a-room' exemption (see 69.10 SCHEDULE A) will often obviate the need for further enquiry). See Revenue Business Income Manual BIM 52780–52800 for the Revenue approach to determination of the chargeable profit (if any) in such cases.

Computer software. The Revenue's views on the treatment of expenditure on computer software are summarised as follows.

Software acquired under licence. Regular payments akin to a rental are allowable revenue expenditure, the timing of deductions being governed by correct accountancy practice (see 71.30 above). A lump sum payment is capital if the licence is of a sufficiently enduring nature to be considered a capital asset in the context of the licencee's trade (see 71.30 above), e.g. where it may be expected to function as a tool of the trade for several years. Equally the benefit may be transitory (and the expenditure revenue) even though the licence is for an indefinite period. Inspectors will in any event accept that expenditure is on revenue account where the software has a useful economic life of less than two years. Timing of the deduction in these circumstances will again depend on correct accountancy practice.

Where the licence is a capital asset, capital allowances are available (see 9.25 CAPITAL ALLOWANCES).

Expenditure on a package containing both hardware and a licence to use software must be apportioned before the above principles are applied.

Software owned outright. The treatment of expenditure on such software (including any in-house costs) follows the same principles as are described above in relation to licensed software.

(Revenue Tax Bulletin November 1993 p 99).

For the treatment of expenditure on systems modification work relating to the Year 2000 problem and to EMU conversion, see Revenue Tax Bulletin April 1998 p 531. Broadly, such work will always be a revenue matter unless it is carried out as part of a major new project instituting changes on such a scale as to be of a capital nature in relation to the business.

See Revenue Business Income Manual BIM 35800–35865 for a detailed analysis of the Revenue's views generally. See also Simon's Direct Tax Service B3.1518.

Overpayments received, due to errors by customers or their banks which the taxpayer neither caused nor facilitated, held not to be trading receipts (*Anise Ltd and Others v Hammond (Sp C 364), [2003] SSCD 258*).

Purchases/sales of assets. See *T Beynon & Co v Ogg KB 1918, 7 TC 125* (profits of colliery agent from deals in wagons held trading receipts); *Gloucester Railway Carriage v CIR HL 1925, 12 TC 720* (sale by wagon manufacturer of wagons previously let, held trading receipts); *Bonner v Frood KB 1934, 18 TC 488* (sale of rounds by credit trader, held trading receipts).

Reimbursements of capital expenditure spread over 30 years held capital as regards both payer and recipient (*Boyce v Whitwick Colliery CA 1934, 18 TC 655*). For allowances from railway in respect of traffic on sidings paid for by trader see *Westcombe v Hadnock Quarries KB 1931, 16 TC 137*; *Legge v Flettons Ltd KB 1939, 22 TC 455*.

Excessive payments to **service company** of professional firm held not deductible (*Stephenson v Payne, Stone Fraser & Co Ch D 1967, 44 TC 507*).

Solicitor's fees as trustee held professional receipts (*Jones v Wright KB 1927, 13 TC 221*) even though also a beneficiary (*Watson & Everitt v Blunden CA 1933, 18 TC 402*).

Sub-postmasters. Introductory fees paid by sub-postmasters were held not to be allowable (*Dhendsa v Richardson (Sp C 134), [1997] SSCD 265*).

Timber purchases and sales. For purchases and sales of standing timber by timber merchants see *Murray v CIR CS 1951, 32 TC 238*; *McLellan, Rawson & Co v Newall Ch D 1955, 36 TC 117*; *Hood Barrs v CIR (No 2) HL 1957, 37 TC 188*; *Hopwood v C N Spencer Ltd Ch D 1964, 42 TC 169*; *Russell v Hird and Mercer Ch D 1983, 57 TC 127*. For sales of trees by farmer see *Elmes v Trembath KB 1934, 19 TC 72*.

Trade marks or designs. Fees and expenses of applications for registration and extensions are allowable. [*ICTA 1988, s 83*].

Transfer fees. The accounting treatment of transfer fees paid by football or other sports clubs may be affected by either FRS 10 issued by the Accounting Standards Board on 4 September 1997 or the FRS for Smaller Entities issued by the Board on 10 December 1998. Where a transfer fee is paid under a contract entered into before the beginning of the first accounting period for which either of those standards has effect, then unless the club elects to the contrary (within two years after the end of that accounting period), the tax treatment of the payment is not affected by anything in the standard. Any necessary adjustments to give effect to this provision may be made, notwithstanding any relevant time limits. [*FA 1999, s 63*].

Video tape rental. Relief for the cost of acquiring video tapes for hire may be obtained by way of either:

(i)   capital allowances (provided the useful economic life is at least two years);

(ii)   valuation basis (where the useful economic life is two years or less); or

(iii)   renewals basis.

See Revenue Tax Bulletin October 1995 pp 254, 255 for a discussion of each of these methods in this context. See also Revenue Business Income Manual BIM 67200–67220.

Websites. The cost of setting up a website is likely to be capital expenditure; the regular update costs are likely to be revenue expenses (see Revenue Business Income Manual BIM 35870).

General. See also *Thompson v Magnesium Elektron CA 1943, 26 TC 1* (payments based on purchases, held trading receipts); *British Commonwealth International Newsfilm v Mahany HL 1962, 40 TC 550* (payments to meet operating expenses, trading receipts); *CIR v Pattison CS 1959, 38 TC 617* (weekly instalments for business, capital).

71.63 PATENTS

Expenses (agent's charges, patent office fees etc.) in obtaining, or extending the term of, a patent for the purposes of a trade (including rejected or abandoned applications) are allowable. [*ICTA 1988, s 83*]. For capital expenditure on the purchase of patent rights see 9.50 CAPITAL ALLOWANCES.

Sums received on the sale of patent rights may, dependent on the facts, be trading receipts (*Rees Roturbo Development v Ducker HL 1928, 13 TC 366*; *Brandwood v Banker KB 1928, 14 TC 44*; *CIR v Rustproof Metal Window CA 1947, 29 TC 243* and cf. *Harry Ferguson (Motors) v CIR CA(NI) 1951, 33 TC 15*). Other sums are taxable under *ICTA 1988, s 524*, see 54 PATENTS.

Where a company held a patent for renovating car tyres, lump sums received by it under arrangements for giving the payer a *de facto* franchise in his area, were held to be capital receipts (*Margerison v Tyresoles Ltd KB 1942, 25 TC 59*).

Patent royalties are payable less tax and not deductible — see 71.42 above. For spreading of patent royalties received less tax, see 54 PATENTS and for DTR treatment of royalties from abroad, see 24.5(*l*) DOUBLE TAX RELIEF.

71.64 Schedule D, Cases I and II—Profits of Trades etc.

For copyright, know-how and trade marks, see 71.51, 71.57 and 71.62 respectively.

Simon's Direct Tax Service. See **B3.841** *et seq.*, **B3.1406** *et seq.*

71.64   PERSONAL EXPENSES

Expenditure for domestic and private purposes is explicitly disallowable under *ICTA 1988, s 74(1)(b)* and is, in any event, not wholly and exclusively for business purposes and disallowable under *ICTA 1988, s 74(1)(a)*. The 'dual purpose rule' (see 71.30 above) is relevant here. Hence the cost of treatment at a nursing home was disallowed even though motivated by need for room from which to conduct business (*Murgatroyd v Evans-Jackson Ch D 1966, 43 TC 581*) as was the cost of a minor finger operation to enable a professional guitarist to continue playing as, on the evidence, he also played the guitar as a hobby (*Prince v Mapp Ch D 1969, 46 TC 169*) and expenditure on child care by a graphic designer working from home (*Carney v Nathan (Sp C 347), [2003] SSCD 28*). Medical expenses where illness said to be due to working conditions were not allowed in *Norman v Golder CA 1944, 26 TC 293*. Expenditure on ordinary clothing is not normally allowable, the leading case here being *Mallalieu v Drummond HL 1983, 57 TC 330*, in which, reversing the decisions in the lower Courts, it was held that the cost of sober clothing worn by a lady barrister to comply with Bar Council guidelines was for the dual purpose of her profession and her requirements as a human being, and not allowable. See also 71.30 above and the 'clothing' cases at 75.11(*b*) SCHEDULE E—EMPLOYMENT INCOME. In *Watkis v Ashford, Sparkes and Harward Ch D 1985, 58 TC 468*, expenditure on meals at regular partners' lunchtime meetings was disallowed, whilst expenditure on accommodation, food and drink at the firm's annual weekend conference was allowed. In *McKnight v Sheppard HL 1999, 71 TC 419*, legal expenses in defending charges brought by a professional regulatory body were allowed despite the fact that the taxpayer's 'personal reputation was inevitably involved'. In *MacKinlay v Arthur Young McClelland Moores & Co HL 1989, 62 TC 704*, contributions towards the removal expenses of a partner moved in the interests of the firm were not allowed. For rent etc. of premises used both as residence and for business see 71.68 below and for travelling and subsistence expenses see 71.80 below. See also *Mason v Tyson Ch D 1980, 53 TC 333* (expenses of occasional use of flat) and *McLaren v Mumford Ch D 1996, 69 TC 173* (expenses of residential accommodation required to be occupied with licensed premises).

The personal costs (e.g. accommodation, food and drink) of a UK resident individual chargeable under Schedule D, Case I or Case II of living abroad on business are not disallowed under *ICTA 1988, s 74(1)(a)* or *(b)* (Revenue Business Income Manual BIM 47710 and Revenue Pamphlet IR 131, A16).

For the 'dual purpose rule' in relation to expenditure with an intrinsic duality of purpose, e.g. food, warmth, health and shelter, see Revenue Business Income Manual BIM 37900–37970.

Simon's Direct Tax Service. See **B3.1435** *et seq.*

71.65   POOLING OF PROFITS

Where traders pool profits or act together in consortia but so as not to form PARTNERSHIPS (53) or trade jointly (cf. *Gardner and Bowring Hardy v CIR CS 1930, 15 TC 602*; *Geo Hall & Son v Platt Ch D 1954, 35 TC 440*) each trader's share of the pooled profits will normally be treated as a receipt of his main trade and any payment under the arrangement by one trader to another will be deductible in computing his profits (*Moore v Stewarts & Lloyds Ltd CS 1905, 6 TC 501* and cf. *United Steel v Cullington (No 1) CA 1939, 23 TC 71*). In *Utol Ltd v CIR KB 1943, 25 TC 517* payments by one company to another under a profit sharing arrangement were held to be dividends payable less tax under the law in force before

SCHEDULE F (76). For compensation received on the termination of a profit sharing arrangement see *Van den Berghs* at 71.38(*b*) above.

71.66 **PRE-TRADING EXPENDITURE**

The general rule is that trading expenditure is deductible when incurred and hence is not allowable if incurred before trading commenced (cf. *Birmingham & District Cattle By-Products Ltd v CIR KB 1919, 12 TC 92*). The rule is modified for certain pre-trading capital expenditure, including scientific research expenditure and abortive exploration expenditure by mining concerns (see 9 CAPITAL ALLOWANCES).

There is also a special relief for expenditure incurred by a person in the seven years before he commenced to carry on a trade which, had it been incurred after he commenced, would have been deductible in computing the profits. The relief does not extend to expenditure already deductible in computing profits, e.g. pre-trading purchases of stock or advance payments of rent. The expenditure is treated as incurred on the day the person commences the trade. Where a company carries on the trade in partnership, see 53.13 PARTNERSHIPS. [*ICTA 1988, s 401; FA 1993, s 109(1)(4); FA 1995, s 120, Sch 6 para 20; FA 1998, Sch 27 Pt III(4)*].

The relief also applied to unrelieved trade charges paid by companies before commencement. However, for accounting periods ending after 31 March 1996 this is replaced by a special relief for non-trading debits arising under the loan relationship provisions introduced in *FA 1996* (see Tolley's Corporation Tax under Loan Relationships). [*ICTA 1988, s 401(1A)–(1AC); FA 1993, s 109(2)(4); FA 1996, Sch 14 para 20*].

Simon's Direct Tax Service. See B3.1204.

71.67 **PROPERTY SALES AND OTHER PROPERTY RECEIPTS**

For property dealing see 71.28 above and for rents received see 71.56 above. For builders and property developers generally, see Revenue Business Income Manual BIM 51500–51665.

Sales of property by builders in special circumstances have been considered in a number of cases. Profits held trading receipts in *Spiers & Son v Ogden KB 1932, 17 TC 117* (building activities extended); *Sharpless v Rees KB 1940, 23 TC 361* (sale of land acquired for hobby abandoned for health reasons); *Shadford v H Fairweather & Co Ch D 1966, 43 TC 291* (sale of site after development plan dropped); *Snell v Rosser, Thomas & Co Ch D 1967, 44 TC 343* (sale of land surplus to requirements); *Bowie v Reg Dunn (Builders) Ch D 1974, 49 TC 469* (sale of land acquired with business); *Smart v Lowndes Ch D 1978, 52 TC 436* (sale of land in wife's name). Sales of property built but let meanwhile held trading in *J & C Oliver v Farnsworth Ch D 1956, 37 TC 51*; *James Hobson & Sons v Newall Ch D 1957, 37 TC 609*; *W M Robb Ltd v Page Ch D 1971, 47 TC 465* and this notwithstanding active building given up (*Speck v Morton Ch D 1972, 48 TC 476*; *Granville Building Co v Oxby Ch D 1954, 35 TC 245*). But in *Harvey v Caulcott HC 1952, 33 TC 159* the sales were held realisations of investments and in *West v Phillips Ch D 1958, 38 TC 203* some houses were treated as investments and others as trading stock. See also *Andrew v Taylor CA 1965, 42 TC 557*. Sales of houses retained after business *transferred* held sales of investments in *Bradshaw v Blunden (No 1) Ch D 1956, 36 TC 397*; *Seaward v Varty CA 1962, 40 TC 523*. See also *Hesketh Estates v Craddock KB 1942, 25 TC 1* (profit on sale of brine baths held trading receipt of mixed business including land development).

For house sales subject to ground rents etc., see *CIR v John Emery & Sons HL 1936, 20 TC 213*; *B G Utting & Co Ltd v Hughes HL 1940, 23 TC 174*; *McMillan v CIR CS 1942, 24 TC 417*; *Heather v Redfern & Sons KB 1944, 26 TC 119*. For ground rents (England) and feu duties (Scotland) there should be credited the lower of their market value and cost, the cost being taken as the proportion of the cost of the land and building in the ratio of the market value to the sum of the market value and the sale price. For ground annuals (Scotland) which are perpetual the realisable value is brought in. The right to receive the rent then becomes part of the fixed capital of the trade, whose subsequent sale is not taken into account for income tax purposes. Any premiums on the grant of leases are part of the sale proceeds.

Turf sales by a farmer were held to be farming receipts in *Lowe v J W Ashmore Ltd Ch D 1970, 46 TC 597*. For timber sales see 71.62 above and for woodlands managed on a commercial basis see 94 WOODLANDS.

A lump sum received by a property investment company in return for the assignment for a five-year term of a stream of rental income was held to be a capital receipt for part disposal of the company's interest (*CIR v John Lewis Properties plc CA, [2003] STC 117*), but see now 69.19 SCHEDULE A as regards special rent factoring provisions.

Any excess of SCHEDULE A (69) deductions over rent received by a builder from property held as trading stock may be allowed as a trading expense (Revenue Business Income Manual BIM 51555).

Annuities under *Agriculture Act 1967* for giving up (after attaining age of 55) uncommercial agricultural land are treated as earned income [*ICTA 1988, s 833(5)(d)*] and receipts of grants under the same *Act* for the same reason are exempt from capital gains tax. [*TCGA 1992, s 249*].

Where sales of land etc., are capital, the profits on assets disposed of are liable to capital gains tax. See also 3.10 ANTI-AVOIDANCE for provisions affecting land or land development. [*ICTA 1988, s 776*].

For transactions not at market value see 71.73 below.

Simon's Direct Tax Service. See B3.1128, B3.1129.

71.68　**RENTS ETC. FOR BUSINESS PREMISES**

are allowable. For repairs see 71.69 below.

Where partly used privately (e.g. shop with residential accommodation above), *ICTA 1988, s 74(1)(c)* provides for the allowance of not more than two-thirds of the rent unless the circumstances justify a higher proportion. In practice, the allowance is normally two-thirds for retail businesses and, although not provided for in the legislation, rates and 'common' repairs are similarly apportioned. For this see *Wildbore v Luker HC 1951, 33 TC 46*. For allowance for use of home for business, see *Thomas v Ingram Ch D 1979, 52 TC 428*. See also *Mason v Tyson Ch D 1980, 53 TC 333* (expenses of flat used occasionally to enable professional man to work late not allowed).

For rents from letting surplus business accommodation see 71.56 above. Where premises became redundant or were closed down, continuing rents (less sub-letting receipts) were allowed (*CIR v Falkirk Iron CS 1933, 17 TC 625; Hyett v Lennard KB 1940, 23 TC 346*) but not payments to secure the cancellation of leases no longer required (*Mallett v Staveley Coal & Iron CA 1928, 13 TC 772* (the leading case here); *Cowcher v Richard Mills & Co KB 1927, 13 TC 216; Union Cold Storage v Ellerker KB 1939, 22 TC 547; Dain v Auto Speedways Ch D 1959, 38 TC 525; Bullrun Inc v Inspector of Taxes (Sp C 248), [2000] SSCD 384*). See also *West African Drug Co v Lilley KB 1947, 28 TC 140*. Where the rent of a motorway service station was calculated by reference to takings, a lump sum payment for the exclusion of tobacco duty from takings was held capital (*Tucker v Granada Motorway Services HL 1979, 53 TC 92*), but, distinguishing *Granada Motorways*, an amount received by a company in respect of its agent's negligent failure to serve its landlord with counter-notice of a notice of an increase in its rent, was held to be a trading receipt in *Donald Fisher*

(Ealing) Ltd v Spencer CA 1989, 63 TC 168. Rent for a building not required for occupation for business purposes but to control access to the lessee's works was held deductible (less sub-let rents) in *Allied Newspapers v Hindsley CA 1937, 21 TC 422*.

For allowance of a provision in respect of future rents under leases of premises ceasing to be used for business purposes, see *Herbert Smith v Honour Ch D 1999, 72 TC 130*. Following that decision, the Revenue now accept that there is no longer a tax rule which denies provisions for anticipated loses or expenses (see Revenue Press Release 20 July 1999). See the article in the Revenue Tax Bulletin December 1999 pp 707–709 summarising the Revenue's current view, in particular in relation to error or mistake relief claims (see 16.7 CLAIMS) arising from the change of view.

Additional rent liability incurred to obtain the freehold reversion to premises already rented held capital (*Littlewoods Mail Order v McGregor CA 1969, 45 TC 519* following *CIR v Land Securities HL 1969, 45 TC 495*), as were periodical payments to reimburse capital expenditure incurred by landlord (*Ainley v Edens KB 1935, 19 TC 303*) and payments based on production for grant of sisal estates (*Ralli Estates v East Africa IT Commr PC 1961, 40 ATC 9*). But payments for the use of a totalisator calculated by reference to its cost were allowed (*Racecourse Betting Control Board v Wild KB 1938, 22 TC 182*) as were rents subject to abatement dependent on profits (*Union Cold Storage v Adamson HL 1931, 16 TC 293*). For Scottish duplicands see *Dow v Merchiston Castle School CS 1921, 8 TC 149*. Rent paid by partnership to partner owning business premises allowed (*Heastie v Veitch & Co CA 1933, 18 TC 305*). For excessive payments to professional 'service company' see *Payne, Stone Fraser* at 71.62 above.

Rates and council tax. Business rates are deductible in the same way as rent, and before their replacement by the council tax, domestic rates were deductible to the extent that domestic premises were used for trade purposes. Council tax may similarly be deducted where it is attributable to premises (or part) used for trade purposes. (Revenue Press Release 16 March 1993).

Premiums. Certain lease premiums etc., in relation to leases not exceeding 50 years are chargeable on the landlord to an extent which varies with the length of the lease (see 69.16 SCHEDULE A). For any part of the 'relevant period' (the duration of the lease etc. as defined in *ICTA 1988, s 87(9)*) during which the lessee occupies the premises for purposes of a trade etc. or (with certain limitations) deals with his interest therein as property employed for trade, he is treated as paying *additional rent* for the property, allowable against profits under Schedule D, Case I or II, at a rate calculated by spreading over the relevant period the amount which falls to be included in computing the landlord's Schedule A profits (or would fall to be so included but for certain claims which he can make) proportionately reduced for any part of the premium etc. paid which gives rise to an allowance under *CAA 2001, s 403* (mineral asset expenditure — see 9.40(*b*) CAPITAL ALLOWANCES), or in respect of which any other CAPITAL ALLOWANCES (9) have been, or will be, made. Partial allowance is given where part only of the property is occupied for trade etc. purposes [*ICTA 1988, s 87; FA 1995, Sch 6 para 14; FA 1998, s 38, Sch 5 para 34, Sch 27 Pt III(4)*], otherwise lease premiums not allowable. Lease premiums not within the legislation are not allowable (cf. *MacTaggart v Strump CS 1925, 10 TC 17*).

Reverse premiums. In *New Zealand Commissioner of Inland Revenue v Wattie and another PC 1998, 72 TC 639*, the decision in which has persuasive authority in the UK, it was held that a lump sum paid by a landlord to a prospective tenant as an inducement to enter into a lease at an above-market rental (generally known as a reverse premium) was a receipt of a capital nature. Legislation has been introduced to counter this decision, and it applies in relation to any 'reverse premium' received on or after 9 March 1999 except where, disregarding any arrangements made on or after that date, the recipient was entitled to the premium immediately before that date. For these purposes, a '*reverse premium*' is a payment or other benefit received by way of inducement in connection with a transaction (the *'relevant transaction'*) entered into by the recipient or a person 'connected' with him (see below), where

(a) the relevant transaction is one under which the recipient or connected person becomes entitled to an estate or interest in, or a right in or over, land; and

(b) the payment (or other benefit) is made (or provided) by

  (i) the person (the *'grantor'*) by whom that estate, interest or right is granted, or was granted at an earlier time, or

  (ii) a person 'connected' with the grantor, or

  (iii) a nominee of (or a person acting on the directions of) the grantor or a person connected with the grantor.

As regards (b)(i) above, the use of the word 'grantor' means that the provisions do not apply when a freehold is conveyed. The most common occasion on which the provisions will apply will be a payment by a landlord as an inducement to a tenant to take a new lease, but they may apply where an existing tenant pays a new tenant an inducement to take over the remaining term of a lease if (and only if) (b)(ii) or (iii) applies to the existing tenant. (Revenue Tax Bulletin December 1999 pp 711–713).

For the purposes of these provisions, persons are *'connected'* with each other if they are connected within *ICTA 1988, s 839* (see 19 CONNECTED PERSONS) at any time during the period when the 'relevant arrangements' are entered into. The *'relevant arrangements'* comprise the relevant transaction and any arrangements entered into in connection with it (whether earlier, simultaneously or later).

A reverse premium is to be regarded as a revenue receipt. Where the relevant transaction is entered into by the recipient of the reverse premium and for the purposes of a trade profession or vocation carried on (or to be carried on) by him, the reverse premium is to be taken into account in computing the trading profits under Schedule D, Case I or II. In any other case, the reverse premium is to be treated as a receipt of a SCHEDULE A (69) business, or (as the case may be) an overseas property business (see 73.4 SCHEDULE D, CASES IV AND V), carried on by the recipient.

It is understood that accountancy principles require the receipt to be brought into account by spreading over the period of the lease or, if shorter, to the first rent review. This treatment must normally be followed for tax purposes (see 71.30 above) but, as an anti-avoidance measure, is overridden where

(A) two or more parties to the relevant arrangements (see above) are connected persons (see above), and

(B) the terms of the those arrangements differ significantly from those which, at that time and under prevailing market conditions, would be regarded as reasonable and normal between persons dealing at arm's length in the open market.

In such case, the full amount or value of the reverse premium must be brought into account in the period of account in which the relevant transaction (see above) is entered into or, where applicable, the first period of account of the trade which the recipient subsequently begins to carry on.

None of these provisions apply where the recipient is an individual and the property in question is, or will be, occupied by him as his only or main residence. Nor do they apply to the extent that the payment or benefit is consideration for the first leg of a sale and leaseback arrangement within *ICTA 1988, s 779* or *s 780(1)* (see 3.11, 3.12 ANTI-AVOIDANCE) or is taken into account under *CAA 2001, s 532* (contributions to expenditure) to reduce expenditure qualifying for capital allowances (see 9.2(vi) CAPITAL ALLOWANCES).

Special provisions apply where the reverse premium is received by a company carrying on life assurance.

[FA 1999, s 54, Sch 6; CAA 2001, Sch 2 para 104].

It will be seen that a reverse premium within the above provisions is not confined to a lump sum payment and that 'other benefit' may include, for example, a contribution to the tenant's costs or an assumption of the recipient's liabilities under an existing lease. 'Other benefit' must, however, represent money or something capable of being turned into money. It does not include a sum foregone or deferred by the provider, rather than actually expended, such as a rent free period. See the article in the Revenue Tax Bulletin December 1999 pp 711–713, in particular in relation to the meeting of the tenant's costs.

As regards any reverse premium to which the recipient became entitled before 9 March 1999 (and therefore outside the scope of the above legislation), the Revenue will be guided by the decision in *Wattie* (see above). Reversing their earlier view, they accept that the linkage of a reverse premium to an increased rental does not give it the character of a revenue receipt and that the rental itself retains its character as a revenue payment. However, a reverse premium may still be a revenue receipt if, on the evidence, it is in fact a contribution to revenue expenditure, e.g. relocation costs. If, again on the evidence, the reverse premium is in fact a contribution to expenditure qualifying for capital allowances, the expenditure so qualifying may fall to be reduced by virtue of *CAA 2001, s 532* (see 9.2(vi) CAPITAL ALLOWANCES). (Revenue Tax Bulletin April 1999 p 641). See also Tolley's Capital Gains Tax under Land.

Payment of reverse premium. The payment of a reverse premium by a company to achieve the assignment of a lease which had become disadvantageous (due to the company's failure to meet its obligations under a repairing covenant) was held to be on capital account (*Southern Counties Agricultural Trading Society Ltd v Blackler (Sp C 198), [1999] SSCD 200*). The Revenue take the view that where a reverse premium is paid by a developer trading in property, it is deductible in computing his trading profits. (Revenue Press Release 9 March 1999).

For the Revenue approach to these rules, see Revenue Business Income Manual BIM 41050–41145.

See Simon's Direct Tax Service A4.235.

General. See 3.11 ANTI-AVOIDANCE [*ICTA 1988, s 779*] regarding restrictions where there is a lease-back at a non-commercial rent and 3.12 ANTI-AVOIDANCE [*ICTA 1988, s 780*] for taxation of capital sums received on certain lease-backs.

For deductibility of rents for wayleaves paid by Radio Relay services see 22.14 DEDUCTION OF TAX AT SOURCE.

Simon's Direct Tax Service. See B3.1341 *et seq.*

71.69   **REPAIRS AND RENEWALS**

(*a*)   **General.** Expenditure held to be capital as described at (*b*) and (*c*) below may now qualify for CAPITAL ALLOWANCES (9). Any allowable expenditure is deductible in the period when incurred and not when the repairs etc. accrued (*Naval Colliery Co Ltd v CIR HL 1928, 12 TC 1017*). Provisions for future repairs and renewals were held not allowable in *Clayton v Newcastle-under-Lyme Corpn QB 1888, 2 TC 416* and *Peter Merchant Ltd v Stedeford CA 1948, 30 TC 496*, but see now 71.30, 71.38 above, and Revenue Business Income Manual BIM 46515, 46901, for the wider current acceptance of the application of normal accountancy principles in this context. Hence a provision for regular major overhaul work accrued due on aircraft engines was allowed in *Johnston v Britannia Airways Ltd Ch D 1994, 67 TC 99* (but see now Revenue Tax Bulletin February 1999 p 624 as regards changes in accounting practice superseding this decision).

(b)   **Business premises.** The general rule is that expenditure on additions, alterations, expansions or improvements is capital but the cost of repairs, i.e. restoring a building to its original condition, is allowable. However, the use of modern materials in repairing an old building does not make the expenditure capital (*Conn v Robins Bros Ltd Ch D 1966, 43 TC 266*), and the Revenue now consider that this applies to the replacement of single-glazed windows by double-glazed equivalents (see Revenue Tax Bulletin June 2002 p 936). If the expenditure is capital, the estimated cost of 'notional repairs' obviated by the work is not allowable (see *Wm P Lawrie* and *Thomas Wilson (Keighley)* below).

As regards provisions for such expenditure, *ICTA 1988, s 74(1)(d)* prohibits any deduction 'beyond the sum actually expended' for repairs of premises, and the Revenue previously considered that this debarred any allowance for such provisions (see Revenue Business Income Manual BIM 46901). A Revenue contention to this effect was rejected by the Special Commissioners in *Jenners Princes Street Edinburgh Ltd v CIR (Sp C 166), [1998] SSCD 196*. The Revenue now accept that provisions properly made under Financial Reporting Standard 12 are tax deductible except where there is an express rule to the contrary (e.g. provisions for capital expenditure). (Revenue Press Release 20 July 1999). FRS 12 imposes a requirement for accounting periods ending after 22 March 1999 that for a provision to be allowable it must be a present obligation (either legal or constructive) as a result of a past event; it must be probable that a transfer of economic benefits will be required to settle the obligation; and it must be possible to make a reliable estimate of the amount of that obligation. See Revenue Tax Bulletin April 1999 pp 636–639. See also the article in the Revenue Tax Bulletin December 1999 pp 707–709 summarising the Revenue's current view, in particular in relation to error or mistake relief claims (see 16.7 CLAIMS) arising from the change of view. It should be noted that the Revenue view is that *Jenners* would have been decided differently if FRS 12 had been in operation at the time (see Revenue Business Income Manual BIM 46550).

A renewal of a building, i.e. a complete re-construction, is capital (*Fitzgerald v CIR Supreme Court (IFS) 1925, 5 ATC 414; Wm P Lawrie v CIR CS 1952, 34 TC 20*). The cost of rebuilding a factory chimney was held capital in *O'Grady v Bullcroft Main Collieries KB 1932, 17 TC 93* but allowed in *Samuel Jones & Co v CIR CS 1951, 32 TC 513* where the chimney was an integral part of the building. For roof replacements see *Wm P Lawrie* (above) and *Thos Wilson (Keighley) v Emmerson Ch D 1960, 39 TC 360*. The replacement of the ring in a cattle auction mart and of a stand in a football ground were held not to be repairs in *Wynne-Jones v Bedale Auction Ltd Ch D 1976, 51 TC 426* and *Brown v Burnley Football Co Ltd Ch D 1980, 53 TC 357* respectively in which the problem is reviewed.

Cost of barrier against coastal erosion held capital (*Avon Beach & Cafe v Stewart HC 1950, 31 TC 487*); also replacing a canal embankment (*Phillips v Whieldon Sanitary Potteries HC 1952, 33 TC 213*) and building new access road (*Pitt v Castle Hill Warehousing Ch D 1974, 49 TC 638*).

For a modern case (involving the insertion of plastic pipes within dilapidated metal ones over substantial lengths of a gas pipe network, held to be capital), see *Auckland Gas Co Ltd v CIR PC, [2000] STC 527. Auckland Gas* was considered but distinguished in *Transco plc v Dyall (Sp C 310), [2002] SSCD 199*, in which the insertion of plastic pipes in cast iron ones was on a selective basis and had not changed the character of the pipeline system as a whole.

Where on taking a lease of dilapidated property the dilapidations were made good under a covenant in the lease, the cost was held disallowable as attributable to the previous use of the premises (*Jackson v Laskers Home Furnishers Ch D 1956, 37 TC 69*) but when cinemas were acquired in a state of disrepair (but still fit for public showings) because of war-time restrictions on building work, the cost of the repairs was allowed (*Odeon Associated Theatres Ltd v Jones CA 1971, 48 TC 257*). See also (*c*) below. In practice, expenditure on repairing and redecorating newly acquired premises is allowed unless abnormal (and likely to be reflected in the purchase price or rent payable). See generally Revenue Business Income Manual BIM 46906.

Dilapidations of a repair nature on the termination of a lease are generally allowed.

For repairs to tied premises see 71.35 above.

(*c*)　**Plant and other business assets etc.** The general rules at (*b*) above apply to plant with the important modification that expenditure on the renewal of plant is allowed as an alternative to capital allowances. For this see 9.38(H) CAPITAL ALLOWANCES. Renewals of utensils and loose tools are allowable, see *ICTA 1988, s 74(1)(d)*. The cost of additional utensils and loose tools is capital but if not ranking for capital allowances (cf. *Hinton v Maden & Ireland Ltd HL 1959, 38 TC 391*) the Revenue may in suitable cases agree to spread the cost forward.

For repairs soon after the acquisition of an asset see *Law Shipping v CIR CS 1923, 12 TC 621* and *CIR v Granite City SS Co CS 1927, 13 TC 1* in which the cost of repairs to ships attributable to their use before acquisition, was held capital. But see *Odeon Associated Theatres* at (*b*) above in which *Law Shipping* was distinguished. See also *Bidwell v Gardiner Ch D 1960, 39 TC 31* in which the replacement of the furnishings of a newly acquired hotel was held capital.

Expenditure on renewal of railway tracks was allowed in *Rhodesia Railways v Bechuanaland Collector PC 1933, 12 ATC 223*, distinguishing *Highland Railway v Balderston CES 1889, 2 TC 485* in which held capital. Abnormal expenditure on dredging a channel to a shipyard was held capital in *Ounsworth v Vickers Ltd KB 1915, 6 TC 671* but the cost to a Harbour Board of removing a wreck (*Whelan v Dover Harbour Board CA 1934, 18 TC 555*) and of renewing moorings (*In re King's Lynn Harbour CES 1875, 1 TC 23*) was allowed. For shop fittings see *Eastmans Ltd v Shaw HL 1928, 14 TC 218*; *Hyam v CIR CS 1929, 14 TC 479*. See also *Lothian Chemical v Rogers CS 1926, 11 TC 508.*

(*d*)　**Assets held under an operating lease.** A deduction may be allowed for a provision to cover future repairs of assets held under an operating lease which contains a repairing obligation (for example, tenants' repairing leases of property). The obligation, required under FRS 12 (see (*b*) above), subsists from the signing of the lease. (Revenue Business Income Manual BIM 46535). It is unlikely the Revenue would have accepted such a deduction prior to the decision in *Jenners* at (*b*) above.

See generally Revenue Business Income Manual BIM 46900–46970.

Simon's Direct Tax Service. See B3.1344, B3.1514.

71.70　**RESEARCH AND DEVELOPMENT AND SCIENTIFIC RESEARCH**

Revenue expenditure incurred by a trader on 'research and development' (previously, for 1999/2000 and earlier years, on scientific research) related to his trade, whether undertaken directly or on his behalf, is allowable as a deduction from profits. Expenditure incurred in the acquisition of rights in, or arising out of, the research and development is excluded, but the allowable expenditure otherwise includes all expenditure incurred in, or providing facilities for, carrying it out. Research and development 'related' to a trade includes any which may lead to or facilitate an extension of the trade, or which is of a medical nature and has a special relation to the welfare of workers employed in the trade. These provisions apply equally to expenditure on oil and gas exploration and appraisal (within *ICTA 1988, s 837B*). From a date to be appointed by the Treasury, revenue expenditure *by a company* on research and development is not precluded from deduction under these provisions by reason only of the fact that it is brought into account in determining the value of an intangible asset, but there are rules to prevent double relief in respect of the same expenditure. [*ICTA 1988, s 82A; CAA 1990, ss 136, 139(1)(3); FA 2000, s 68, Sch 19 para 5; FA 2004, s 53*].

Relief is similarly given for any sum paid to a scientific research association having as its object 'scientific research' related (with the extended meaning referred to above) to the class of trade concerned, or to any approved university etc. for such research. The association or university etc. must be approved for the purpose by the Secretary of State. *'Scientific research'* means any activities in the fields of natural or applied science for the extension of knowledge. Any question as to what constitutes scientific research is to be referred by the Board to the Secretary of State, whose decision is final. [*ICTA 1988, s 82B; CAA 1990, ss 136, 139(1)(3); FA 2000, Sch 19 para 5*].

It should be noted that these reliefs are given to trades and *not* to professions or vocations.

For *capital* outlay, see 9.52 CAPITAL ALLOWANCES.

'Research and development' means activities that fall to be treated as such in accordance with generally accepted accounting practice (see 71.30 above). However, this is subject to Treasury regulations which narrow the definition by reference to guidelines issued by the Department of Trade and Industry (DTI). [*ICTA 1988, s 837A; FA 2000, Sch 19 para 1*]. The latest regulations have effect for 2004/05 onwards and refer to DTI guidelines issued on 5 March 2004 (for which see www.dti.gov.uk/support/rd-guidelines-2004.htm). [*SI 2004 No 712*]. The previous regulations referred to guidelines issued on 28 July 2000 (see www.dti.gov.uk/support/rndguide.htm) which are revoked from 2004/05 onwards. [*SI 2000 No 2081*].

For enhanced tax reliefs for research and development expenditure *by companies*, see Tolley's Corporation Tax under Profit Computations.

71.71   **SECURITY**

A deduction may be allowed from profits of a trade etc. carried on by an individual (or partnership of individuals) for certain expenditure incurred in connection with the provision for or use by the individual (or any of them) of an asset or service which improves personal security. The asset or service must be provided or used to meet a special threat to the individual's personal physical security arising wholly or mainly by virtue of the trade, profession or vocation, and the sole object of the provider must be the meeting of that threat. In the case of an asset, relief is available only to the extent that the provider intends the asset to be used solely to improve personal physical security (ignoring any other incidental use), and in the case of a service, the benefit to the individual must consist wholly or mainly in such an improvement. Any improvement in the personal physical security of the individual's family resulting from the asset or service provided is disregarded for these purposes.

Excluded from relief is provision of a car, ship or aircraft, or of a dwelling (or grounds appurtenant thereto); but relief may be obtained in respect of equipment or a structure (such as a wall), and it is immaterial whether or not an asset becomes affixed to land and whether or not the individual acquires the property in the asset or (in the case of a fixture) an estate or interest in the land. [*FA 1989, ss 112, 113*]. See also 9.25 CAPITAL ALLOWANCES, 75.38 SCHEDULE E—EMPLOYMENT INCOME.

Simon's Direct Tax Service. See B3.1436.

71.72   **SHARE, SECURITY ETC. ISSUES, PURCHASES, SALES AND EXCHANGES**

For whether a trade of 'share dealing' carried on see 71.29 above. For transactions not at market value see 71.73 below.

Profits and losses on realisations of investments by a bank in the course of its business enter into its Case I profits (*Punjab Co-operative Bank v Lahore IT Commr PC 1940, 19 ATC 533* and see *Frasers (Glasgow) Bank v CIR HL 1963, 40 TC 698*) and similarly for insurance companies (*Northern Assce Co v Russell CES 1889, 2 TC 551*; *General Reinsurance Co v Tomlinson Ch D 1970, 48 TC 81* and contrast *CIR v Scottish Automobile CS 1931, 16 TC 381*). Profits/losses held capital in *Stott v Hoddinott KB 1916, 7 TC 85* (investments acquired by architect to secure contracts); *Jacobs Young & Co v Harris KB 1926, 11 TC 221* (shares held by merchanting company in subsidiary wound up); *Alliance & Dublin Consumers' Gas Co v Davis HC(IFS) 1926, 5 ATC 717* (investments of gas company earmarked for reserve fund). A profit by a property dealing company on the sale of shares acquired in connection with a property transaction was held a trading receipt (*Associated London Properties v Henriksen CA 1944, 26 TC 46*) but contrast *Fundfarms Developments v Parsons Ch D 1969, 45 TC 707* and see now 3 ANTI-AVOIDANCE.

Shares allotted for mining concessions granted by company dealing in concessions held trading receipts at market value (*Gold Coast Selection Trust v Humphrey HL 1948, 30 TC 209*). See also *Murphy v Australian Machinery & Investment Co CA 1948, 30 TC 244* and *Scottish & Canadian Investment Co v Easson CS 1922, 8 TC 265*.

For options, see *Varty v British South Africa Co HL 1965, 42 TC 406* (no profits or loss until shares sold). See also *Walker v Cater Securities Ch D 1974, 49 TC 625*.

Conversion etc. of securities held as circulating capital. Where a new holding of securities (as defined) is issued in exchange for an original holding beneficially owned by a person carrying on a business of banking, insurance or dealing in investments, the transaction, for purposes of Schedule D, Case I, shall be treated as not involving any disposal of the original holding; the new holding being treated as the same asset. This applies to securities where a profit on their sale would normally be a trading profit and to transactions which result in the new holding being equated with the original holding under *TCGA 1992, ss 132, 136* (capital gains rollover relief in cases of conversions etc.) or *TCGA 1992, s 134* (compensation stock) but does not apply to a transaction on or before 31 July 1998 under *ICTA 1988, s 471* (see below) whether or not a notice has been given under that *section*. For periods of account ending on or after 1 August 2001, it also does not apply to securities for which unrealised profits or losses (computed on a mark to market basis by reference to fair value) are brought into account in the period of account in which the transaction takes place. Where there is consideration in addition to the new holding, apportionment will apply. [*ICTA 1988, s 473; FA 1998, Sch 27 Pt III(23); FA 2002, s 67*].

Gilt-edged securities: stripping and reconsolidation. Where the computation of profits from a trade etc. requires amounts in respect of the acquisition or redemption of a gilt-edged security to be brought into account, there are special provisions dealing with the exchange of such a security for strips of the security and for reconsolidation on the exchange of strips for the security from which they derived.

On an exchange for strips, the security is treated as having been redeemed at its market value, and the strips as having been acquired at that market value apportioned *pro rata* to their market value at the time of the exchange. Similarly on a consolidation, each strip is treated as having been redeemed at its market value, and the security as having been acquired at the aggregate market value of the strips. The Treasury may make regulations for determining market value for these purposes.

ICTA 1988, s 473 (conversion etc. of securities held as circulating capital, see above) does not apply where these provisions apply.

These provisions do not apply for the purposes of corporation tax, for which see Tolley's Corporation Tax under Loan Relationships (special cases).

[*ICTA 1988, s 730C; FA 1996, Sch 40 para 7*].

Stock lending fees. Such fees relating to investments eligible for relief under *ICTA 1988, s 592(2), s 608(2)(a), s 613(4), s 614(3), s 620(6) or s 643(2)* (pension scheme funds etc., see 67.5, 67.13, 67.11, 67.15 RETIREMENT SCHEMES, 66.8 RETIREMENT ANNUITIES and 60.1 PERSONAL PENSION SCHEMES) are themselves eligible for relief under those *sections*. [*ICTA 1988, s 129B; FA 1996, s 157; FA 1997, Sch 10 para 2*].

Dealers in securities. Any distribution by a UK-resident company (or payment representative of such a distribution) *received by* a dealer in securities is taken into account (exclusive of any tax credit) in computing the dealer's Schedule D, Case I or II profits. Accordingly:

(*a*)   income tax under SCHEDULE F (76) is not chargeable; and

(*b*)   the normal exemption from corporation tax of UK company distributions under *ICTA 1988, s 208* does not apply.

Any payment *made by* a dealer which is representative of a UK company distribution is similarly brought into the Case I or II computation.

A person is for these purposes a dealer in relation to a distribution if, on a sale of the shares or stock in respect of which the distribution is made, the price would be taken into account in computing Schedule D, Case I or II profits (assuming that it would not fall to be treated as a distribution) other than insurance business profits.

See 3.22 ANTI-AVOIDANCE as regards arrangements to pass on the value of tax credits.

[*ICTA 1988, s 95; FA 1997, Sch 7 para 8(1)(3); F(No 2)A 1997, s 24; FA 2003, Sch 43 Pt 3(6); FA 2004, s 137(2)(6)*].

Extra return on new issues of securities. Where

(*a*)   securities of a particular kind are issued (being the original issue of securities of that kind),

(*b*)   new securities of the same kind are issued subsequently,

(*c*)   a sum (the 'extra return') is payable by the issuer in respect of the new securities, to reflect the fact that interest is accruing on the old securities and calculated accordingly, and

(*d*)   the issue price of the new securities includes an element (separately identified or not) representing payment for the extra return,

the extra return is treated for all tax purposes (except corporation tax) as a payment of interest, but the issuer is not entitled to tax relief, either as a deduction in computing profits or otherwise as a deduction or set-off, for the payment. [*ICTA 1988, s 587A; FA 1991, Sch 12 paras 1, 5; FA 1996, Sch 14 para 33*].

General. See also 3 ANTI-AVOIDANCE, including transactions in securities to obtain tax advantage [*ICTA 1988, s 703*] and dividend-stripping [*ICTA 1988, s 736*].

For share transactions entered into to secure tax advantages see 71.19 above and for transactions in dividend-stripping before the enactment of existing legislation see Tolley's Tax Cases.

71.73   **STOCK IN TRADE AND WORK IN PROGRESS**

See generally Revenue Business Income Manual BIM 33000–33630. Following the adoption for tax purposes of the 'true and fair view' accounting basis (subject to any statutory adjustment) for periods of account beginning after 6 April 1999 (see 71.30 above), Revenue Statement of Practice SP 3/90 (to which a number of references are made below) is generally superseded and is accordingly withdrawn. However, the principles drawn from that Statement continue to be relevant for subsequent accounting periods (except as referred to below).

Basis of valuation. The general rule has long been that stock is to be valued at the lower of cost and market value. Leading cases are *Minister of National Revenue v Anaconda American Brass Co PC 1955, 34 ATC 330* and *BSC Footwear v Ridgway HL 1971, 47 TC 495*. Market value held to be replacement price for a merchant (*Brigg Neumann & Co v CIR KB 1928, 12 TC 1191*) and retail price for a retailer in *BSC Footwear* above (Revenue prepared to take price net of any selling commission). Stock may be valued partly at cost and partly at market value where lower (*CIR v Cock Russell & Co KB 1949, 29 TC 387*). The base stock method is not permissible (*Patrick v Broadstone Mills CA 1953, 35 TC 44*) nor is 'LIFO' (*Anaconda American Brass* above). See also *Ryan v Asia Mill HL 1951, 32 TC 275*. The cost should include as a minimum the cost of materials and direct labour but the accounts treatment of overheads is normally accepted (*Duple Motor Bodies v Ostime HL 1961, 39 TC 537*).

However, the Revenue now take the view that any valuation of stock included in financial statements prepared in accordance with generally accepted accounting practice (see 71.30 above) should be accepted provided that

- it reflects the correct application of the principles of normal accountancy,

- the method pays sufficient regard to the facts, and

- the basis does not violate the taxing statutes as interpreted by the courts.

(Revenue Business Income Manual BIM 33115).

A mark to market basis of valuation, used mainly by financial institutions and commodity dealers and under which stock is valued at market value, may also be acceptable (Revenue Business Income Manual BIM 33160).

The principal accounting standard governing stock is SSAP 9.

For the use of formulae in computing stock provisions and write-downs, see Revenue Tax Bulletin December 1994 p 184. Broadly, inspectors will accept formulae which reflect a realistic appraisal of future income from the particular category of stock and which result in the stock being included at a reasonable estimate of net realisable value. Where computations are accepted without enquiry, it is on the assumption that profits are arrived at in accordance with such principles. (Revenue Tax Bulletin December 1994 p 184).

For the treatment of depreciation taken into account in arriving at stock valuations, see Revenue Tax Bulletin June 2002 pp 936, 937.

For motor dealer stock valuations, see Revenue Tax Bulletin August 1994 p 156.

As regards valuation of professional work in progress, it is understood that the following principles are, in broad terms, currently accepted by the Revenue:

(i) nothing should be included for partners' time;

(ii) direct employment costs of fee-earners and direct overheads applicable, such as secretarial salaries, stationery, telephone costs etc. should be included;

(iii) general production overheads for general office areas, conference rooms etc. should be excluded, whilst those for individual office areas directly applicable should be discounted by, say, 30% for non-productive time; and

(iv) contingent fees should be included.

(Taxation Vol 141, No 3654 p 126, 30 April 1998). For further guidance on valuation of professional work in progress, see the detailed note agreed between the Revenue and the ICAEW in Revenue Tax Bulletin December 1998 pp 607–615. It has been suggested that an amendment by the Accounting Standards Board to FRS 5 'Reporting the Substance of Transactions' requires professional work in progress to be valued at *selling price* beginning with accounts ended on after 23 December 2003 (Taxation Vol 152, No 3941 p 376, 22 January 2004); however, not all commentators interpret the amendment in this way (Taxation Vol 152, No 3944 p 447, 12 February 2004).

Changes in basis of valuation. Where the stock was found to be grossly undervalued it was held that an assessment to rectify the closing undervaluation must be reduced by the opening undervaluation to bring out the true profits (*Bombay IT Commr v Ahmedabad New Cotton Mills Co PC 1929, 9 ATC 574*). But where a company altered its method of dealing with accrued profits on long-term contracts and the closing work in progress in the year 1 accounts on the old basis was substantially below the opening figure in the year 2 accounts on the new basis, held, distinguishing *Ahmedabad*, the difference must be included in the year 2 profits (*Pearce v Woodall-Duckham Ltd CA 1978, 51 TC 271*). See also Revenue Pamphlet IR 131, SP 3/90, 10 January 1990.

Where there is a change in the basis of valuation, the following practice is applied for tax purposes. If the bases of valuation both before and after the change are valid bases, the opening figure for the period of change must be the same as the closing figure for the preceding period. If the change is from an invalid basis to a valid one, the opening figure for the period of change must be arrived at on the same basis as the closing figure for that period, and liabilities for earlier years will be reviewed where it is possible to do so. (Revenue Pamphlet IR 131, SP 3/90, 10 January 1990 and see now Revenue Business Income Manual BIM 33199). See, however, *Woodall-Duckham Ltd* (above) as regards long-term contracts.

Long-term contracts. The Revenue now accept that accurate provisions for foreseen losses on long-term contracts (e.g. in the construction industry) made in accordance with correct accounting practice are tax deductible. (Revenue Press Release 20 July 1999 and see now Revenue Business Income Manual BIM 33025). Previously, their practice was to permit provision for a proportion of an overall loss, calculated either on a time basis or by reference to expenditure, provided that all contracts, profitable or otherwise, were similarly dealt with. Provisions for foreseeable further expenditure, representing obligations up to final delivery, were normally allowed where work was substantially completed (likely to require at least 90% completion) and the financial outcome of the contract was reasonably certain. Reasonable provision for future expenditure under guarantees or warranties was also normally allowed. Beyond these limits, no provision was permitted for future loss apportionable to the remainder of the contract. (Revenue Pamphlet IR 131, SP 3/90, 10 January 1990). This practice did not apply to professional work in progress.

In *Symons v Weeks and Others Ch D 1982, 56 TC 630*, it was held that progress payments under the long-term contracts of a firm of architects did not fall to be brought into account for tax before the relevant contract was completed, notwithstanding that they exceeded the figure brought in for work in progress, calculated on the correct principles of commercial accounting.

See above for changes of basis.

Goods sold subject to reservation of title. Where the supplier of goods reserves the title in them until payment is made (as a protection should the buyer become insolvent) and meanwhile the goods are treated by both parties for accountancy purposes as having been sold/purchased, the Revenue will follow the accounts treatment. (Revenue Pamphlet IR 131, B6). See Note A of Financial Reporting Standard No 5 and Revenue Business Income Manual BIM 33375.

Goods on consignment stock are normally treated as stock in the hands of the supplier until disposed of by the consignee (e.g. sale or return). (Revenue Pamphlet IR 131, B6).

For **forward contracts**, see 71.40 above.

Insurance recoveries. See 71.54 above.

Transactions not at market value. Where trading stock is disposed of otherwise than by way of trade, the realisable value is to be credited for tax purposes. This was established by *Sharkey v Wernher HL 1955, 36 TC 275* approving *Watson Bros v Hornby KB 1942, 24 TC 506*. It applies, *inter alia*, to goods taken out of stock by a retailer for his own use (see below). It was applied in *Petrotim Securities Ltd v Ayres CA 1963, 41 TC 389* to a disposal of shares at gross under-value as part of a tax avoidance scheme, but in *Ridge Securities Ltd v CIR Ch D 1963, 44 TC 373*, dealing with the other end of the same scheme, it was held that the same principle applied to acquisitions of trading stock otherwise than by way of trade, market price being substituted for the actual purchase price. But the principle is not applicable to sales or purchases by way of trade notwithstanding not at arm's length. Hence when a share dealing company acquired shares at substantial overvalue from an associated company, the claim by the Revenue for market value failed (*Craddock v Zevo Finance Co HL 1946, 27 TC 267*), and when a property dealing company acquired property from its controlling shareholder at substantial undervalue, its claim to substitute market value failed (*Jacgilden (Weston Hall) v Castle Ch D 1969, 45 TC 685*). See also *Skinner v Berry Head Lands Ch D 1970, 46 TC 377* and *Kilmorie (Aldridge) v Dickinson HL 1974, 50 TC 1*.

Appropriations to trading stock of assets held in another capacity are generally treated as a disposal and reacquisition at market value. Where a chargeable gain or allowable loss would otherwise arise for capital gains tax purposes under *TCGA 1992, s 161(1)*, the trader may elect for the market value to be reduced for these purposes by the amount of the chargeable gain (or increased by the amount of the allowable loss), the trading profits being computed accordingly and the appropriation being disregarded for capital gains tax purposes. The election must be made within twelve months after 31 January following the tax year in which ends the period of account in which the asset is appropriated, or for corporation tax purposes where self-assessment applies, two years after the end of the accounting period in which the asset is appropriated. [*TCGA 1992, s 161(3)(3A); FA 1996, s 135, Sch 21 para 36*].

Stock taken for own use or disposed of otherwise than by sale in the normal course of trade. The case of *Sharkey v Wernher HL 1955, 36 TC 275* established the principle that such a transfer should be treated as if it were a sale at market value. Inspectors have been authorised to take a reasonably broad view in applying this principle. The case is not considered to apply to

(a)   services rendered to the trader personally or to his household the cost of which should be disallowed under *ICTA 1988, s 74(1)(b)*;

(b)   the value of meals provided for proprietors of hotels, boarding houses, restaurants etc. and members of their families, the cost of which should be disallowed under *ICTA 1988, s 74(1)(b)*;

(c)   expenditure incurred by a trader on the construction of an asset which is to be used as a fixed asset in the trade.

(Revenue Pamphlet IR 131, A32).

For the Revenue's view of the application of normal Schedule D, Case I principles to donations of trading stock to charities, see Revenue Tax Bulletin June 1996 p 319.

What constitutes stock. Greyhounds kept by greyhound racing company not trading stock (*Abbot v Albion Greyhounds (Salford) KB 1945, 26 TC 390*). Payments by cigarette manufacturer for cropping trees (not owned by it) for leaves used in manufacture, held to be for materials (*Mohanlal Hargovind of Jubbulpore v IT Commr PC 1949, 28 ATC 287*). For payments for unworked minerals, sand and gravel etc., (including tailings etc.) by mines, quarries etc. see 71.61 above. For payments for oil by oil companies, see *Hughes v British Burmah Petroleum KB 1932, 17 TC 286*; *New Zealand Commr v Europa Oil (NZ) PC 1970, 49 ATC 282*; *Europa Oil (NZ) v New Zealand Commr PC, [1976] STC 37*. For timber see 71.62 above and *Coates v Holker Estates Co Ch D 1961, 40 TC 75*.

Valuation on discontinuance of business. Under *ICTA 1988, s 100* where a trade is discontinued (or so treated for tax purposes by *ICTA 1988, s 113* or *s 337(1)*) otherwise than on the death of a sole trader, the following provisions apply.

(1) Where the stock is '*sold or transferred for valuable consideration*' to a person carrying on (or intending to carry on) a trade in the UK who can deduct the cost as an expense for tax purposes, the stock is normally to be valued at the amount realised on the sale (or the value of the consideration). However, where the two parties to the sale or transfer are connected persons (defined more broadly than by *ICTA 1988, s 839* — see *ICTA 1988, s 100(1F)*), arm's length value is to be taken instead. Neither rule applies to a transfer of farm animals where the anti-avoidance rules at 34.9 HERD BASIS apply. Where arm's length value exceeds both (i) actual sale price and (ii) acquisition value (broadly, the amount that would have been deductible in respect of the stock had it been sold in the course of trade immediately before cessation), connected persons may jointly elect to substitute the greater (taking all the stock sold or transferred together) of (i) and (ii), the election to be made within two years after the end of the chargeable period in which cessation occurs. The stock valuation determined under these provisions applies both to transferor and transferee. For a case involving a simultaneous discontinuance and stock transfer, see *Moore v Mackenzie Ch D 1971, 48 TC 196*.

Where, on or after 24 July 2002, stock is sold or transferred (other than to a connected person) together with other assets, the amount realised on the sale or the value of the consideration given, as the case may be, is apportioned on a just and reasonable basis to each of the assets concerned. (Previously no provision was made for such apportionment of a composite amount.)

Any dispute as to the application of these provisions is dealt with as if it were an appeal. If both trades are within the jurisdiction of the same body of General Commissioners, such appeals are dealt with by them, otherwise by the Special Commissioners. See *Bradshaw v Blunden (No 2) Ch D 1960, 39 TC 73*; *CIR v Barr (No 2) CS 1955, 36 TC 455*.

ICTA 1988, s 100 is not applicable to woodlands managed on a commercial basis (*Coates v Holker Estates* above). For its application to 'hire-purchase debts' see *Lions Ltd v Gosford Furnishing Co Ltd & CIR CS 1961, 40 TC 256*.

(2) In all other cases stock is to be valued at the price it would have realised if sold in open market at date of discontinuance.

This section applies to all kinds of property real or personal sold in usual course of the trade, materials used in manufacture etc. and services etc., which would be treated as work in progress if the trade were a profession (see below).

For 2004/05 onwards, these provisions are disapplied in relation to any stock if a transfer pricing adjustment (see 3.8 ANTI-AVOIDANCE) falls to be made in connection with any provision made or imposed in relation to that stock and having effect in connection with the discontinuance of the business.

[*ICTA 1988, ss 100, 102(1); FA 1995, s 140; FA 1996, Sch 22 para 11; FA 2002, ss 105(1), 106; FA 2004, s 30(9), s 37(1)(2), Sch 5 para 2*].

If, following the death of a sole trader, the executors continue trading, or if the business passes direct to a beneficiary, the opening stock can be brought in at market value even if valued at cost on death. (Revenue Business Income Manual BIM 33520).

Similar provisions are applied, *mutatis mutandis*, to work in progress at the date when a profession or vocation is, or is treated as, discontinued. But taxpayer may elect that for computing his profits to the date of cessation w.i.p. shall be taken at cost, and that any realised excess over cost shall be treated as POST-CESSATION ETC. RECEIPTS (62) under *ICTA 1988, s 103*. The election must be made within twelve months after 31 January following the year of assessment of cessation (or, for corporation tax where self-assessment applies, within two years after the end of the accounting period of cessation). [*ICTA 1988, s 101; FA 1996, s 135, Sch 21 para 3*].

See ICAEW Technical Release TAX 7/95, 15 February 1995, for a guidance note on the taxation implications of various treatments of transfers of work in progress and debtors on incorporation of a professional partnership.

Recovery of assets under *Proceeds of Crime Act 2002, Pt 5*. Where the transfer of trading stock is a *Pt 5* transfer under *Proceeds of Crime Act 2002* (as in 9.2(xi) CAPITAL ALLOWANCES) and the stock is to be treated, as a result of the transfer, as if sold in the course of the trade, it is treated, for the purpose of computing taxable profits and notwithstanding *ICTA 1988, s 100* above (if applicable), as sold at cost price. [*Proceeds of Crime Act 2002, Sch 10 para 11*].

Simon's Direct Tax Service. See **B3.10, B3.1517.**

71.74   **SUBSCRIPTIONS   ETC.   INCLUDING   TRADE   ASSOCIATION CONTRIBUTIONS**

Gifts to charitable bodies are deductible under general rules of business expenses (i.e. requiring the outlay to be wholly and exclusively for purposes of the trade etc.) notwithstanding *ICTA 1988, s 577(8)* (see 71.45 above). [*ICTA 1988, s 577(9)*]. Concessionally, other gifts are allowed provided that they are (i) wholly and exclusively for the purposes of the business, (ii) made for the benefit of a body or association established for educational, cultural, religious, recreational or benevolent purposes which is local to the donor's business activities and not restricted to persons connected with the donor and (iii) reasonably small in relation to the scale of the donor's business. (Revenue Pamphlet IR 1, B7). In *Bourne & Hollingsworth v Ogden KB 1929, 14 TC 349* an abnormally large donation was disallowed. For donations of part of cost of ticket in football pools and lotteries, see 71.20 above. See 14.17 CHARITIES for three year covenants to charities, and see 14.11, 14.18 CHARITIES as regards certain other donations by individuals. See Tolley's Corporation Tax as regards qualifying donations by companies to charities.

Trade and professional associations. Ordinary annual subscriptions to local associations, including Chambers of Commerce, are normally allowed. Subscriptions to larger associations are allowable, and receipts therefrom assessable, if the association has entered into an arrangement with the Revenue under which it is assessed on any surplus of receipts over allowable expenditure (the association should be asked). Most associations enter into the arrangement but if not the allowance is restricted to the proportion applied by the association for purposes such that it would have been allowed if so applied by the subscriber (*Lochgelly Iron & Coal Co Ltd v Crawford CS 1913, 6 TC 267*). For other cases see Tolley's Tax Cases. Subscriptions to the Economic League are not allowed (*Joseph L Thompson & Sons Ltd v Chamberlain Ch D 1962, 40 TC 657*).

Contributions to mutual insurance associations are allowable even though used to create a reserve fund (*Thomas v Richard Evans & Co Ltd HL 1927, 11 TC 790*). See also 50 MUTUAL TRADING.

Local enterprise agencies. Expenditure incurred in making any contribution (whether in cash or kind) to an 'approved local enterprise agency' is allowable if not otherwise deductible. There is no allowance if any related benefit is receivable by the contributor, or any person connected with him (see 19 CONNECTED PERSONS), from the agency or from any other person, and any relief already given will be recovered by a charge under Schedule D, Cases I or II or VI to the extent of the benefit.

'*Approved local enterprise agency*' is any body approved by the Secretary of State who is satisfied (i) its sole objective is the promotion or encouragement of industrial and commercial activity or enterprise in a particular area of the UK and with particular reference to small businesses, or (ii) one of its principal objectives is as in (i) *and* it maintains a separate fund for that objective. The agency must be precluded from making dividends, gifts etc. to its members or managers. Approval may be conditional and may be withdrawn retrospectively. [*ICTA 1988, s 79; FA 1990, s 75; FA 1994, s 145(1); FA 2000, s 88*].

Training and enterprise councils, local enterprise companies and business link organisations. Identical provisions to those described above in relation to local enterprise agencies apply to a contribution to a training and enterprise council which has an agreement with the Secretary of State to act as such, or to a local enterprise company which has an agreement with Scottish Enterprise or Highlands and Islands Enterprise to act as such, or to a business link organisation authorised by the Secretary of State to use a service mark designated for these purposes. [*ICTA 1988, s 79A; FA 1990, s 76; FA 1994, s 145; FA 2000, s 88, Sch 40 Pt II(9)*].

Urban regeneration companies. Identical provisions to those described above in relation to local enterprise agencies apply to a contribution made after 31 March 2003 to an urban regeneration company designated as such by Treasury order. A body of persons (corporate or otherwise) may be designated if its sole or main function is to co-ordinate the regeneration of a specific urban area in the UK in association with public and local authorities. Designation orders may be backdated by up to three months or, in the case of the first such order, to 1 April 2003. [*ICTA 1988, s 79B; FA 2003, s 180*]. The first designations are made by *SI 2004 No 439*.

71.75 **SUBSIDIES, GRANTS ETC.**

Payments under the **Business Start up scheme**, to assist unemployed people in setting up their own businesses, are made under *Employment and Training Act 1973, s 2(2)(d)* or *Enterprise and New Towns (Scotland) Act 1990, s 2(4)(c)* (or NI equivalent). They are chargeable to tax under Schedule D, Case VI rather than Case I. This treatment does not, however, prevent the payments being treated as earned income or as 'relevant earnings' for personal pension scheme and retirement annuity purposes (see 60.8 PERSONAL PENSION SCHEMES, 66.7 RETIREMENT ANNUITIES). They also give rise to liability to Class 4 national insurance contributions. [*ICTA 1988, s 127, Sch 29 para 14*]. The payments are made by Training and Enterprise Councils (in Scotland, Local Enterprise Councils). The legislation refers to payments of *Enterprise Allowance* (which preceded the Business Start up scheme), but applies equally to payments under the current scheme provided they retain the essential characteristics of Enterprise Allowance, in particular that the applicant is unemployed or working notice and that the allowance is a flat rate weekly amount. (Lump sum payments are outside the scope of the above and are likely to be taxable as Case I trading receipts.) Where the business is run through a company, the payments are made to the individual as agent of the company and are treated as Case VI income of the company. (Revenue Business Income Manual BIM 40400, 40405).

Farming support payments. See 71.47 above.

Fishing grants. For the tax treatment of decommissioning grants, laying-up grants, exploratory voyage grants and joint venture grants under *SI 1983 No 1883*, see Revenue Business Income Manual BIM 57001.

Football pools promoters. Certain contributions to the Football Trust 1990 by pools promoters for football ground improvements are allowable as deductions in the pools promoter's trade, as are certain payments by them to other trustees established mainly for the support of athletic sports or games (but with power to support the arts). [*FA 1990, s 126; FA 1991, s 121*]. See also 9.2(vi) CAPITAL ALLOWANCES.

Regional development grants. Grants under *Industry Act 1972, ss 7, 8* (and similar NI legislation) and certain other NI payments, not made towards specified capital expenditure or compensation for loss of capital assets, are trading receipts. [*ICTA 1988, s 93*]. An earlier interest relief grant under the *Act* was held to be assessable in *Burman v Thorn Domestic Appliances (Electrical) Ltd Ch D 1981, 55 TC 493*, as was a similar grant undifferentiated between revenue and capital in *Ryan v Crabtree Denims Ltd Ch D 1987, 60 TC 183*, applying *Gayjon Processes Ltd* (below) and distinguishing *Seaham Harbour* (below). Grants under *Industrial Development Act 1982, Part II* to traders etc. or investment companies are exempt from income tax. [*ICTA 1988, s 92*].

Research grant by trading company to medical practitioner held assessable (*Duff v Williamson Ch D 1973, 49 TC 1*). For research grants and fellowships generally, see Revenue Business Income Manual BIM 65151.

Temporary employment subsidy was paid under *Employment and Training Act 1973, s 5* (as amended by *Employment Protection Act 1975, Sch 14 para 2*) as a flat-rate weekly payment or (in the textile, clothing and footwear industries) by way of reimbursement of payments made to workers on short time.

Such payments were held to be taxable as trading receipts in *Poulter v Gayjon Processes Ltd Ch D 1985, 58 TC 350*, distinguishing the grants made by the Unemployment Grants Committee in *Seaham Harbour* (below).

Unemployment grants. Subsidy to dock company (from Unemployment Grants Committee) for extension work to keep men in employment held, although grant made in terms of interest, not a 'trade receipt' for tax purposes (*Seaham Harbour v Crook HL 1931, 16 TC 333*).

See 9.2(vi) CAPITAL ALLOWANCES for effect thereon of grants and subsidies.

See 68.18 RETURNS as regards returns of certain grant and subsidy payments.

Simon's Direct Tax Service. See B3.929.

71.76 **TAXATION**

Income tax and corporation tax are not deductible in computing profits (cf. *Allen v Farquharson Bros & Co KB 1932, 17 TC 59*). Overseas taxes may be subject to DOUBLE TAX RELIEF (24) but any such tax not relieved by credit on overseas income included in the profits may generally be deducted [*ICTA 1988, s 811*] but not on UK income, e.g. profits of UK branches (*CIR v Dowdall O'Mahoney & Co Ltd HL 1952, 33 TC 259*).

In *Harrods (Buenos Aires) v Taylor-Gooby CA 1964, 41 TC 450* an annual capital tax imposed by the Argentine on foreign companies trading there was not a tax on the profits and was allowable.

As regards relief for national insurance contributions by employers in respect of employees, see 71.44 above. For deduction of part of Class 4 National Insurance contributions from total income, see 1.10 ALLOWANCES AND RATES.

For taxation appeals see 71.59 above. For VAT see 71.83 below.

Simon's Direct Tax Service. See B3.1451 *et seq.*, B3.1516.

71.77 Schedule D, Cases I and II—Profits of Trades etc.

71.77 TELECOMMUNICATIONS LICENCES

Special rules apply in relation to licences granted under *Wireless Telegraphy Act 1949, s 1* as a result of bidding for such licences under *Wireless Telegraphy Act 1998, s 3* regulations, and to rights derived directly or indirectly therefrom. They also apply to indefeasible rights to use a telecommunications cable system ('IRUs') acquired after 20 March 2000 other than from an 'associate' (within *ICTA 1988, s 417(3)(4)*) or an 'associated company' (within *ICTA 1988, s 416(1)* or, in relation to an individual, being a company of which that individual has control under *ICTA 1988, s 416(2)–(6)*) which acquired them on or before that date, and to derived rights.

Acquisition costs and disposal proceeds in respect of such rights which, in accordance with generally accepted accounting practice (see 71.30 above), may be taken into account in determining accounting profit or loss, and which are so taken into account in any relevant statutory accounts required under *Companies Act 1985, s 226* (or NI or foreign equivalent), are treated as being of a revenue nature in computing profits chargeable to income tax or corporation tax. This applies equally to costs of extension of attached rights or of cancellation or restriction of rights attached to derivative rights, and to receipts from cancellation or restriction of attached rights or from granting derivative rights or extensions of rights attached to derivative rights.

Similar treatment applies to amounts in respect of the revaluation of such rights provided that, in accordance with generally accepted accounting practice, they fall to be taken into account for accounting purposes, whether or not they may be so taken into account in determining profit or loss or are so taken into account in any relevant statutory accounts. The period of account for which such an amount is taken into account for tax purposes is that in which it is recognised for accounting purposes in accordance with generally accepted accounting practice.

Where the taxpayer company is a member of a group of companies (within *Companies Act 1985, s 262(1)* or NI or foreign equivalent) which is required to produce consolidated group accounts (within *Companies Act 1985, s 227* or NI or foreign equivalent), the company's accounting policies, and method of applying those policies, in respect of rights within these provisions must not be more cautious than that adopted in the group accounts. This applies in relation to each group of which the company is a member, if there is more than one.

[*FA 2000, s 87, Sch 23*].

For articles giving the Revenue's view on the interpretation of *FA 2000, Sch 23*, see Revenue Tax Bulletins December 2000 pp 815–817, February 2004 p 1094. For corporation tax purposes, *FA 2000, Sch 23* is superseded for accounting periods ending on or after 1 April 2002 by *FA 2002, Sch 29* (see Tolley's Corporation Tax under Intangible Assets).

71.78 TIED PETROL STATIONS ETC.

For tied licensed premises see 71.35 above.

'Exclusivity payments' by petrol company to retailers undertaking to sell only its goods were allowed in computing its profits in *Bolam v Regent Oil Co Ltd Ch D 1956, 37 TC 56* (payments for repairs carried out by retailer), *BP Australia Ltd PC 1965, 44 ATC 312* (lump sums paid for sales promotion) and *Mobil Oil Australia Ltd PC 1965, 44 ATC 323*, but held capital in *Strick v Regent Oil HL 1965, 43 TC 1* where the payment took the form of a premium to the retailer for a lease of his premises (immediately sub-let to him).

In the hands of the retailer, exclusivity payments were held capital when for capital expenditure incurred by him (*CIR v Coia CS 1959, 38 TC 334*; *McLaren v Needham Ch D 1960, 39 TC 37*; *Walter W Saunders Ltd v Dixon Ch D 1962, 40 TC 329*; *McClymont and Another v Jarman (Sp C 387) 2003, [2004] SSCD 54*) but revenue when for repairs etc.

(*McLaren v Needham* above) or sales promotion (*Evans v Wheatley Ch D 1958, 38 TC 216*) or where petrol sales were a relatively small part (some 30%) of the company's turnover (*Tanfield Ltd v Carr (Sp C 200), [1999] SSCD 213*).

For a summary of the Revenue view of such arrangements, see Revenue Tax Bulletin August 1993 p 88.

71.79   **TRAINING**

Costs incurred by an employer in respect of employee training are generally allowable as a trade expense. See 71.44 above for this and as regards certain other allowable employee training costs, and 71.74 above as regards contributions to training and enterprise councils. See also 92 VOCATIONAL TRAINING RELIEF.

In general, the expenses of a training course undertaken by a self-employed person are allowed as a trade deduction under general principles only where the training is undertaken for the purposes of the trade and relates to the updating of existing expertise rather than the acquisition of new skills. See Revenue Business Income Manual BIM 47651.

71.80   **TRAVELLING AND SUBSISTENCE EXPENSES**

The cost of travelling in the course of the business activities is allowable but not that of travelling between home and the place at or from which the business is conducted. For this see *Newsom v Robertson CA 1952, 33 TC 452* in which the expenses of a barrister between his home and his chambers were refused and contrast *Horton v Young CA 1971, 47 TC 60* in which a 'self-employed' bricklayer was allowed his expenses between his home and the sites at which he worked as, on the evidence, his business was conducted from his home. In *Jackman v Powell Ch D, [2004] STC 645*, a milkman was not allowed the costs of travelling between his home and the dairy-owned depot from which he collected his supplies and to which his milk round was adjacent. Any expenses of an employment ancillary to a profession that are not allowable against employment income may not be deducted in computing the profits of the profession (*Mitchell & Edon v Ross HL 1961, 40 TC 11*).

The 'dual purpose rule' (see 71.30 above) entails the disallowance of *all* travelling expenses with a material private purpose, i.e. the part attributable to business purposes is not allowable. Thus the expenses of a solicitor in travelling abroad partly for a holiday and partly to attend professional conferences were disallowed in *Bowden v Russell & Russell Ch D 1965, 42 TC 301* (but the expenses of an accountant in travelling abroad to attend a professional conference abroad were allowed in *Edwards v Warmsley, Henshall & Co Ch D 1967, 44 TC 431*). Similarly the expenses of a dentist in travelling between his home and surgery were disallowed even though he collected dentures from a laboratory on the way (*Sargent v Barnes Ch D 1978, 52 TC 335*). The expenses of a farmer in visiting Australia with a view to farming there were held inadmissible (*Sargent v Eayrs Ch D 1972, 48 TC 573*). In practice, the Revenue normally allow a fair proportion of overseas trips partly for holidays if there was a genuine business purpose. (In *Bowden v Russell* above, the Revenue considered the business purpose too remote to justify apportionment.) Car expenses are also apportioned if used partly for private purposes. Parking and other motoring fines are normally disallowed in their entirety either under the 'dual purpose rule' (see 71.30 above) or under the general principles applicable to allowable trading deductions (see *CIR v Alexander von Glehn & Co Ltd CA 1920, 12 TC 232*, in which penalties for breach of wartime regulations were disallowed), although reimbursement of employee normally allowable (but see 75.10 SCHEDULE E—EMPLOYMENT INCOME as regards employee's liability).

Similar principles apply to hotel etc. expenses incurred when travelling for business purposes. The reasonable cost of overnight stays is allowed but not the cost of lunches

71.81   Schedule D, Cases I and II—Profits of Trades etc.

(*Caillebotte v Quinn Ch D 1975, 50 TC 222*). In practice, reasonable costs of evening meals and breakfast taken in conjunction with overnight accommodation are similarly allowed, and this treatment is extended to such costs incurred by long distance lorry drivers who sleep in their cabs. (Revenue Tax Bulletin August 1993 p 88). Normally there is no restriction for 'home saving' (cf. 75.46 SCHEDULE E—EMPLOYMENT INCOME). Nor will there be any disallowance of personal living expenses (i.e. accommodation, food and drink of self but not family or other dependants) incurred on longer business trips abroad. (Revenue Pamphlet IR 131, A16).

Motoring expenses. As an alternative to claiming their actual business motoring costs in their accounts, taxpayers with a turnover not exceeding the VAT registration threshold (currently £58,000), judged at the time they first used the vehicle, are permitted to use the authorised (from 6 April 2002, the statutory) tax-free mileage rates applicable to employees (see 75.46 SCHEDULE E—EMPLOYMENT INCOME) to arrive at the accounts figure. No other motoring expenses or related capital allowances may then be claimed (other than interest on a loan to purchase the vehicle). The basis of claim may only be changed when a vehicle is replaced. (Revenue Business Income Manual BIM 47701; Revenue Press Release BN 2/01 7 March 2001).

See 51.11 NON-RESIDENTS AND OTHER OVERSEAS MATTERS for extended relief for travelling expenses in overseas trade.

For car hire, see 71.58 above. For travelling and subsistence generally, see Revenue Business Income Manual BIM 47700–47710. For the 'dual purpose rule' in relation to travel and subsistence costs, see BIM 37600–37630, 37660.

Simon's Direct Tax Service. See B3.1437.

71.81   UNCLAIMED BALANCES

Unclaimed balances for which a firm was liable to account were held not assessable despite their being distributed to partners (*Morley v Tattersall CA 1938, 22 TC 51*). Such balances held by a pawnbroker are, however, assessable when claimants' rights expire (*Jay's, the Jewellers v CIR KB 1947, 29 TC 274*), and deposits on garments not collected were held trade receipts assessable when received (*Elson v Prices Tailors Ch D 1962, 40 TC 671*). The fact that trading receipts were subsequently, and correctly, treated for accountancy purposes as an element in a sale of fixed assets did not alter their nature for tax purposes (*Tapemaze Ltd v Melluish Ch D 2000, 73 TC 167*). See 71.34 above for releases of debts owing.

71.82   UNREMITTABLE RECEIPTS, DEBTS ETC.

Where a trade is carried on partly in the UK and partly overseas, so that liability to tax arises on all trade profits, the following amounts will be included in profits, with no relief being available under *ICTA 1988, s 584* (unremittable overseas income, see 51.13 NON-RESIDENTS AND OTHER OVERSEAS MATTERS) or *ICTA 1988, s 74(1)(j)* (bad and doubtful debts, see 71.34 above):

(a)   amounts received overseas but not remittable to the UK;

(b)   amounts owed to the trader overseas which temporarily cannot be paid; and

(c)   amounts owed to the trader overseas which, even when paid, will not be remittable to the UK.

By concession, where any of (a)–(c) above applies solely as a result of local foreign exchange control restrictions, and continues to apply twelve months after the end of the accounting period in which the amount concerned was received or the debt arose, relief may be claimed, provided that:

(i)   the assessment in question is not final and conclusive;

(ii)   all reasonable endeavours have been made to secure payment and remittance to the UK of funds;

(iii)   receipts or debts have not been used to finance expenditure or investment outside the UK;

(iv)   (in the case of debts) the debt cannot be discharged in the UK; and

(v)   the taxpayer agrees to the withdrawal of relief by an addition to profits for the period in which the concessional relief ceases to be available (see below).

As regards (iii) above, debts are regarded as having been used to finance expenditure outside the UK where they are used, or might have been used, to meet expenditure or guarantee a liability incurred in the same territory by the trader or by a person with whom the trader has a special relationship, or where they remain unpaid by reason of such a relationship.

Relief for debts is available only to the extent that they are not insured. Relief is given by a deduction from trading profits for the accounting period in which the receipt or debt is recognised as unremittable. Any excess may be carried forward against trading profits of subsequent periods.

Relief is withdrawn where (a)–(c) or (iii) above cease to apply, or the receipt or debt is otherwise applied outside the UK or exchanged for or discharged in a remittable currency.

This concession also applies to unremittable bank interest in appropriate circumstances.

(Revenue Pamphlet IR 1, B38).

71.83   VALUE ADDED TAX

For treatment in computing business profits see Revenue Pamphlet IR 131, B1.

In general, if the trader is not a 'taxable person' for VAT his expenditure *inclusive* of any VAT on it, is treated in the ordinary way.

If he is a taxable person, the receipts and expenses (including capital items) to be taken into account will generally be exclusive of VAT but if he suffers VAT on any expenditure which does not rank as 'input tax' (e.g. entertaining expenses and certain expenditure relating to motor cars) that expenditure inclusive of VAT will be taken into account for income tax etc. purposes (although any such inclusive sum in respect of entertaining expenses may also be disallowed for income tax purposes). Any allowance for bad debts (see 71.34 above) is inclusive of any VAT not recovered but accounted for to HM Customs and Excise. (*VATA 1994, s 36* and regulations made thereunder now provide for VAT on bad debts to be refunded in certain cases.)

VAT interest, penalties and surcharge are not allowed as a deduction for income tax purposes, and repayment supplement is disregarded for income tax purposes. [*ICTA 1988, s 827*].

Where the trader uses the optional *flat-rate scheme* for smaller businesses introduced by *FA 2002*, receipts and expenses to be taken into account will generally be *inclusive* of normal output and input VAT, but the flat-rate VAT itself can either be deducted from turnover or treated as a separate expense and in either case is an allowable deduction for income tax purposes. Any irrecoverable VAT on capital items will form part of their cost for the purposes of CAPITAL ALLOWANCES (9). (Revenue Tax Bulletin April 2003 pp 1023, 1024).

VAT refunds. See Revenue Tax Bulletin October 1995 pp 255, 256 for the timing of the recognition, for the purposes of computing trading profits, of certain VAT refunds (specifically, of refunds to opticians following acceptance by Customs and Excise that they had incorrectly required VAT to be charged on certain outputs).

See Revenue Business Income Manual BIM 31500–31625 and, generally, Tolley's Value Added Tax.

71.84   **WASTE DISPOSAL**

Expenditure on purchase and reclamation of tipping sites by a company carrying on a waste disposal business was held to be capital in *Rolfe v Wimpey Waste Management Ltd CA 1989, 62 TC 399*, as were instalment payments for the right to deposit waste material in *CIR v Adam CS 1928, 14 TC 34*. See also *McClure v Petre Ch D 1988, 61 TC 226*, where the receipt of sum for licence to tip soil was also held to be capital.

Site preparation and restoration expenditure. A person making a 'site restoration payment', in the course of carrying on a trade, may deduct the payment in computing profits for the period of account (i.e. a period for which an account is drawn up) in which the payment is made. A payment will not qualify for relief to the extent that it represents either expenditure allowed as a trading deduction for prior periods or capital expenditure qualifying for capital allowances.

A *'site restoration payment'* is a payment made

(*a*)   in connection with the restoration of a site (or part thereof), and

(*b*)   in order to comply with any condition of a 'relevant licence', or any condition imposed on the grant of planning permission to use the site for the carrying out of 'waste disposal activities', or any term of a 'relevant agreement'.

For restoration expenditure generally (including provisions for such expenditure), see Revenue Tax Bulletin April 1998 p 534.

'Waste disposal activities' are the collection, treatment, conversion and final depositing of waste materials, or any of those activities.

A *'relevant licence'* is a disposal licence under the *Control of Pollution Act 1974, Pt I* (or NI equivalent), a waste management licence under the *Environmental Protection Act 1990, Pt II* (or NI equivalent), a permit under regulations under *Pollution Prevention and Control Act 1999, s 2* or an authorisation for the disposal of radioactive waste or a nuclear site licence.

A *'relevant agreement'* is an agreement under *Town and Country Planning Act 1971, s 52, Town and Country Planning (Scotland) Act 1972, s 50* or *Town and Country Planning Act 1990, s 106* (or NI equivalent) regulating the development or use of land.

[*ICTA 1988, s 91A; FA 1990, s 78; FA 1993, s 110(1)(3); SI 2000 No 1973*].

A deduction is available of the 'allowable amount' where a person incurs, in the course of a trade, 'site preparation expenditure' in relation to a 'waste disposal site', and, at the time when he first deposits waste materials on the site in question, he holds a relevant licence (as above) which is in force. It is not available where the person incurring the expenditure recharges it to another person who holds the licence when first depositing waste (see Revenue Tax Bulletin April 1998 p 533). A claim for the relief to apply will have to be made in the prescribed manner and the Board may also require plans and other documents to verify it. Expenditure incurred for trade purposes by a person about to carry on the trade is for this purpose treated as incurred on the first day of trading.

A '*waste disposal site*' is a site used (or to be used) for the disposal of waste materials by their deposit on the site, and in relation to such a site, '*site preparation expenditure*' is expenditure on preparing the site for the deposit of waste materials (and may include expenditure on earthworks). This includes expenditure incurred before the relevant licence is granted, and in particular expenses associated with obtaining the licence itself. (Revenue Tax Bulletin November 1992 p 45). For preparation expenditure generally, see Revenue Tax Bulletin April 1998 p 533, February 2001 p 828.

In relation to the period of account in question, the '*allowable amount*' of the expenditure is

$$(A - B) \times \frac{C}{C + D}$$

where

'A' is the site preparation expenditure incurred by the person at any time before the beginning of, or during, the period in question in relation to the site in question and in the course of carrying on the trade. It does not include any expenditure which either has been allowed as a trading deduction for a prior period or is capital expenditure qualifying for capital allowances. In addition, where any expenditure which would otherwise be included in 'A' was incurred before 6 April 1989, 'A' is reduced by an amount determined by

$$E \times \frac{F}{F + G}$$

where

'E' is so much of the initial expenditure (that is, the expenditure which would otherwise be included in 'A') as was incurred before 6 April 1989,

'F' is the volume of waste materials deposited on the site in question before 6 April 1989,

'G' is the capacity (expressed in volume) of the site in question not used up for the deposit of waste materials immediately before 6 April 1989;

'B' is the amount (or aggregate of amounts) allowed as a trading deduction under this provision in prior periods and as regards expenditure incurred in relation to the site in question;

'C' is the volume of waste materials deposited on the site in question during the period in question, excluding any deposited before 6 April 1989;

'D' is the capacity of the site in question not used up for the deposit of waste materials as at the end of the period in question.

71.85 Schedule D, Cases I and II—Profits of Trades etc.

Where, after 20 March 2000, a person (the 'predecessor') who has incurred site preparation expenditure as above in the course of a trade ceases to carry on the trade, or to carry it on so far as it relates to that site, and another person (the 'successor') begins to carry it on, or to carry on in the course of a trade the activities formerly carried on by the predecessor in relation to that site, then provided that

(i) the whole of the site is transferred to the successor (although not necessarily the same estate or interest in the site), and

(ii) the successor holds a relevant licence in relation to the site which is in force when he first deposits waste material on the site,

the successor's trade is treated for these purposes as the same as that carried on by the predecessor, and the successor stands in the predecessor's shoes as regards allowances in relation to the site.

[*ICTA 1988, ss 91B, 91BA; FA 1990, s 78; FA 1993, s 110(2)(3); FA 2000, s 89*].

See generally Revenue Business Income Manual BIM 67405–67520.

Leasing. See 71.58 above as regards restrictions on relief under the above provisions where finance leasing arrangements are involved.

See Simon's Direct Tax Service B3.1345.

Landfill tax. The Revenue's views on the deductibility of landfill tax under Schedule D, Case I or II are as follows.

Site operators. Treatment of landfill tax charged on to customers will follow the generally accepted accounting practice. As regards self-generated waste, landfill tax (net of any credit following a contribution to an environmental trust) will be allowed as a deduction so long as the other costs incurred in disposing of the waste are deductible.

Customers of site operators. The landfill tax element of the global charge does not need to be separately invoiced, and deductibility of the landfill tax element will follow that of the non-landfill tax element of the charge.

Environmental trust contributions. Site operators may obtain relief from landfill tax by making such contributions, the deductibility of which is to be determined in the circumstances of each particular case under the normal test of whether the expenditure is incurred wholly and exclusively for trade purposes. In the case of an unconnected trust engaged in projects of possible use to the operator, the payment would *prima facie* be deductible. If the operator has some degree of control over the trust, or the income of the trust is ultimately received by a person connected with the operator, it might be less clear that the payment was for the purposes of the operator's own trade. Similarly if the trust's objects were insufficiently related to the operator's trade, it might be considered that contributions were for a general philanthropic, and hence non-trade, purpose.

(Revenue Tax Bulletin June 1996 pp 317, 318).

71.85 GENERAL EXAMPLE

A UK trader commences trading on 1 October 2003. His profit and loss account for the year to 30 September 2004 is

			£	£
Sales				110,000
Deduct	Purchases		75,000	
	Less	Stock and work in progress at 30.9.04	15,000	
				60,000
Gross profit				50,000
Deduct				
Salaries (all paid by 30.6.05)			15,600	
Rent and rates			2,400	
Telephone			500	
Heat and light			650	
Depreciation			1,000	
Motor expenses			2,700	
Entertainment			600	
Bank interest			900	
Hire-purchase interest			250	
Repairs and renewals			1,000	
Accountant's fee			500	
Bad debts			200	
Sundries			700	
				27,000
Net profit				23,000
Gain on sale of fixed asset				300
Rent received				500
Bank interest received (net)				150
Profit				£23,950

Further Information

(i) Rent and rates. £200 of the rates bill relates to the period from 1.6.03 to 30.9.03.

(ii) Telephone. Telephone bills for the trader's private telephone amount to £150. It is estimated that 40% of these calls are for business purposes.

(iii) Motor expenses. All the motor expenses are in respect of the proprietor's car. 40% of the annual mileage relates to private use and home to business use.

			£
(iv)	Entertainment	Staff	100
		UK customers	450
		Overseas customers	50
			£600

(v) Hire-purchase interest. This is in respect of the owner's car.

(vi) Repairs and renewals. There is an improvement element of 20% included.

(vii) Bad debts. This is a specific write-off.

(viii) Sundries. Included is £250 being the cost of obtaining a bank loan to finance business expenditure, £200 for agent's fees in obtaining a patent for trading purposes and a £50 inducement to a local official.

(ix)   Other. The proprietor obtained goods for his own use from the business costing £400 (retail value £500) without payment.

(x)   Capital allowances for the year to 30 September 2004 amount to £1,520.

Schedule D, Case I Computation — Year to 30.9.04

	£	£
Profit per the accounts		23,950
Add		
Repairs — improvement element		200
Hire-purchase interest (40% private)		100
Entertainment note (*e*)		500
Motor expenses (40% private)		1,080
Depreciation		1,000
Telephone (60% × £150)		90
Goods for own use		500
Illegal payment note (*f*)		50
		27,470
Deduct		
Bank interest received — Taxed income	150	
Rent received — Schedule A	500	
Gain on sale of fixed asset	300	
		950
		26,520
Less Capital allowances		1,520
Schedule D, Case I profit		£25,000

Notes

(*a*)   Costs of obtaining loan finance are specifically allowable (see 71.60 above).

(*b*)   Capital allowances are deductible as a trading expense (see 9.1 CAPITAL ALLOWANCES).

(*c*)   The adjusted profit of £25,000 would be subject to the commencement provisions for assessment purposes (see 71.4 above).

(*d*)   Pre-trading expenses are treated as incurred on the day on which trade is commenced if they are incurred within seven years of the commencement and would have been allowable if incurred after commencement. See 71.66 above.

(*e*)   All entertainment expenses, other than staff entertaining, are non-deductible (see 71.45 above).

(*f*)   Expenditure incurred in making a payment which itself constitutes the commission of a criminal offence is specifically disallowed. This includes payments which are contrary to the Prevention of Corruption Acts. See 71.53 above.

72 Schedule D, Case III—Interest Receivable etc.

[ICTA 1988, ss 18, 64, 66, 67]

Cross-references. See generally under 22 DEDUCTION OF TAX AT SOURCE; 33 GOVERNMENT STOCKS; 44 INTEREST RECEIVABLE; 71.41 SCHEDULE D, CASES I AND II re copyrights and royalties.

Simon's Direct Tax Service Part B5.

72.1 **INTRODUCTION AND CHARGEABILITY**

Case III of Schedule D is principally concerned with the taxation of interest and annual payments. There were, however, significant changes following the abolition of Schedule C, and the introduction of a new corporation tax regime for the taxation of most profits and gains from securities (by reference to 'loan relationships', for which see Tolley's Corporation Tax under Loan Relationships). Both of these changes took effect for 1996/97 and subsequent years and for accounting periods ending after 31 March 1996, and the charges under Cases III to V of Schedule D are accordingly now defined separately for income tax and for corporation tax purposes.

For corporation tax, Case III now includes all profits and gains from loan relationships, any annuity or other annual payment (not chargeable under Schedule A) payable in or out of the UK, and at whatever intervals, in respect of anything other than a loan relationship and any discount arising other than in respect of a loan relationship. Thus, for corporation tax purposes, Case IV is subsumed into Case III, and Case V is redefined to exclude profits or gains from loan relationships.

For income tax purposes, the abolition of Schedule C has led to the inclusion under Case III of income from the UK (and NI) public revenue previously dealt with under that Schedule. Case IV is similarly extended to include all income from securities out of the UK (including foreign public revenue income previously within Schedule C), and Cases IV and V now include income realised by disposal of coupons on overseas holdings (again previously within Schedule C). Thus income tax is now charged under Schedule D, Case III in respect of:

- any interest of money, and any annuity or other annual payment (not chargeable under SCHEDULE A (69)) either as a charge on or reservation out of property of the payer or as a personal contractual debt or obligation, whether payable in or out of the UK and at whatever intervals received and payable;

- all discounts; and

- income from securities payable out of UK (or NI) public revenue.

[ICTA 1988, s 18(3)–(3E); FA 1996, Sch 7 para 4(2)(3), Sch 14 para 5].

The following items are additionally brought within the charge under Case III.

- Profits and losses from discounts on securities. *[FA 1996, Sch 13].* See 72.5 below.

- Share or loan interest paid by a registered industrial and provident society. *[ICTA 1988, s 486(4)].*

- Borrowings against life policies in certain circumstances. *[ICTA 1988, s 554].* See 45.4(*h*) LIFE ASSURANCE POLICIES.

- Mining rents and royalties payable in produce. *[ICTA 1988, s 119(2)].* See 22.14 DEDUCTION OF TAX AT SOURCE.

For general exemptions from charge to tax, see EXEMPT INCOME (28). Annuities charged under *ITEPA 2003* as pension income are not within Schedule D. *[ICTA 1988, s 18(1)(b);*

ITEPA 2003, Sch 6 para 5(2)]. See the list at 58.2 PENSION INCOME. The following items are additionally excluded from Case III.

- Distributions within SCHEDULE F (76). *[ICTA 1988, s 20(2)]*.

- Certain annual payments by individuals. *[ICTA 1988, s 347A]*. See 1.8(i) ALLOWANCES AND TAX RATES.

- The capital portion of purchased life annuity payments. *[ICTA 1988, s 656]*. See 22.11(c) DEDUCTION OF TAX AT SOURCE.

- Certain payments to redundant steel workers, see 75.35 SCHEDULE E—EMPLOYMENT INCOME.

- Certain payments to theatrical angels, see 74.2 SCHEDULE D, CASE VI.

Various of the above items are payable after deduction of tax by the payer under *ICTA 1988, ss 348, 349*. See under 22 DEDUCTION OF TAX AT SOURCE for the provisions relating to such deductions and for annuities and annual payments etc. See also under 43 INTEREST PAYABLE.

Chargeability under Case III depends upon there being a UK source. The Revenue regard the most important factors supporting the existence of a UK source of interest to be (i) the debtor's residence (i.e. the place in which the debt will be enforced), (ii) the source from which interest is paid, (iii) where the interest is paid, and (iv) the nature and location of the security for the debt. If all of these are located in the UK, it is likely that the interest will have a UK source. (Revenue Tax Bulletin November 1993 p 100).

Income from overseas securities and possessions is assessable under SCHEDULE D, CASES IV AND V (73).

For whether solicitors' client account interest is within Case III, see 44.2 INTEREST RECEIVABLE.

72.2   SCOPE AND ASSESSMENT

(a)   **Assessment.** Certain interest and certain annuities and annual payments are payable under deduction of tax at source. If so paid, the deduction is treated as tax paid by the recipient who is then liable, if his total income is high enough, at the excess of the higher rate(s) of tax over the basic or lower rate (whichever is applicable) on the gross amount.

If the payer omits to deduct tax an assessment may be made on either the payer or payee. See 22.8 DEDUCTION OF TAX AT SOURCE for omission to deduct tax.

All other income not taxed at source is charged by direct assessment on the recipient. Loss relief and capital allowances are not applicable.

The person receiving or entitled to the income is assessable. *[ICTA 1988, s 59(1)]*. See also *Aplin v White Ch D 1973, 49 TC 93*. A non-resident may be assessed under Case III through an agent under *TMA 1970, s 82* (*Scales v Atalanta SS Co KB 1925, 9 TC 586*) (and see also 51.3 to 51.6 NON-RESIDENTS AND OTHER OVERSEAS MATTERS).

Bank interest is generally received when credited to the account (*Dunmore v McGowan Ch D 1978, 52 TC 307; Peracha v Miley CA 1990, 63 TC 444*), but there may be no receipt or entitlement if the bank has the right to refuse payment out of the account and the interest is not in fact paid out (*Macpherson v Bond Ch D 1985, 58 TC 579*). Interest paid by cheque is received when the sum is credited to the recipient's account, not when the cheque is received. (*Parkside Leasing Ltd v Smith Ch D 1984, 58 TC 282*). Interest credited by the deposit-taker to a suspense account in advance of the payment date was held to arise only when paid (*Girvan v Orange Personal Communications Services Ltd Ch D 1998, 70 TC 602*).

See Simon's Direct Tax Service B5.102.

(*b*) **Interest and discount.** Whether an amount described as interest in a Court or arbitration award is true interest or an element entering into the calculation of the award and capital depends on the facts. See *Schulze v Bensted (No 1) CS 1915, 7 TC 30*; *Westminster Bank Ltd v Riches HL 1947, 28 TC 159* and *Barnato CA 1936, 20 TC 455* and contrast *Ballantine CS 1924, 8 TC 595*. A premium on the repayment of a loan was held to be interest in *Davies v Premier Investment Co Ltd KB 1945, 27 TC 27*, but a premium on the repayment of securities quoted on the Stock Exchange or issued on terms similar to those of quoted securities is normally regarded as capital and similarly as regards the discount on securities issued at a discount. A discount within Case III is a profit of an income nature received on a discounting transaction. See *National Provident Institution v Brown HL 1921, 8 TC 57* and *Ditchfield v Sharp CA 1983, 57 TC 555* and contrast *Lomax v Peter Dixon & Son Ltd CA 1943, 25 TC 453*. Where credit balances on accounts held by members of a group of companies were set against the overdrawn balance on a current account held at the same bank by another member (C) of the group, it was held that the arrangements did not provide for C to receive interest on the credit balance, but for its obligation to pay interest to be reduced (*Cooker v Foss (Sp C 165), [1998] SSCD 189*).

Payments in pursuance of a guarantee of the capital of a company were held to be interest in *Blake v Imperial Brazilian Rly Co CA 1884, 2 TC 58*. See also *Wilson v Mannooch KB 1937, 21 TC 178* and *Ruskin Investments Ltd v Copeman CA 1943, 25 TC 187*. The interest element in loan repayments after the death of a money-lender was held to be assessable on his administrator under Case III (*Bennett v Ogston KB 1930, 15 TC 374*). Accrued interest on securities sold (if not sold 'ex-dividend') is income of the purchaser (*Wigmore v Thomas Summerson & Sons Ltd KB 1925, 9 TC 577* and *Schaffer v Cattermole CA 1980, 53 TC 499*). Arrears of interest are not assessable until received — see *St Lucia Usines v Colonial Treasurer PC 1924, 4 ATC 112* and the cases noted in 27.2(d) EXCESS LIABILITY.

See Simon's Direct Tax Service B5.201 *et seq.*

See now the special provisions at 72.5 below.

(*c*) **Annual payments and annuities.** For cases where deduction of tax is involved, see 22.10 and 22.11 DEDUCTION OF TAX AT SOURCE.

Case III assessments were upheld in respect of periodical payments to a newspaper company after a merger (*Morning Post Ltd v George KB 1940, 23 TC 514*), payments to an actress from the exploitation of a film (*Mitchell v Rosay CA 1954, 35 TC 496*) and annual payments to the executors of a deceased director pursuant to an agreement entered into by him relating to special services he had rendered (*Westminster Bank Ltd v Barford Ch D 1958, 38 TC 68*). Compensation payments by the USA Government to a wounded American soldier were held not to be assessable in *Laird v CIR CS 1929, 14 TC 395* but in *Forsyth v Thompson KB 1940, 23 TC 374* periodical disability payments from a mutual insurance society were held to be assessable. But see now 75.40 SCHEDULE E—EMPLOYMENT INCOME.

(*d*) **Deductions.** The full amount of the income is assessable without any deduction. Cf. *Lord Inverclyde's Trustees v Millar CS 1924, 9 TC 14* and *A B (Committee of) v Simpson KB 1928, 14 TC 29*.

72.3   Schedule D, Case III—Interest Receivable etc.

72.3   BASIS OF ASSESSMENT

For 1996/97 and subsequent years as regards income from a source first arising on or before that date and from the outset as regards income from a source first arising after 5 April 1994, the charge is on actual income of the current tax year (without any deduction). [*ICTA 1988, s 64; FA 1994, s 206*]. There are no special rules for opening and closing years as there are for Schedule D, Cases I and II.

For the preceding year basis of assessment that applied previously, and for transitional rules (and associated anti-avoidance provisions) on the changeover to the current year basis of assessment, see the 2003/04 and earlier editions.

72.4   APPLICABLE RATE OF INCOME TAX

Most types of Schedule D, Case III income, including interest and discounts, are chargeable to income tax at the *lower rate* (to the extent that the income does not exceed the basic rate limit in the case of an individual, in which case it is chargeable at the higher rate). See 1.9 ALLOWANCES AND TAX RATES for more detail.

72.5   RELEVANT DISCOUNTED SECURITIES

Charge to and relief from tax for profits and losses realised. For any year of assessment in which a person transfers a 'relevant discounted security', or becomes entitled, as holder, to any payment on its redemption, and where the amount payable on the transfer or redemption exceeds the amount he paid for its acquisition, he is chargeable to income tax under Schedule D, Case III (or Case IV as appropriate) on the amount of the excess. The chargeable amount used to be reduced by any costs incurred in connection with the acquisition of the security or with its transfer or redemption, but no relief is given for any such costs incurred on or after 27 March 2003, unless the person transferring or redeeming the security had held it continuously since before that date *and* the security was listed on a recognised stock exchange (within *ICTA 1988, s 841(1)*) at some time before that date.

A loss on the transfer or redemption (together with any such costs as above) could be relieved against income of the tax year in which the transfer or redemption took place. Relief had to be claimed by no later than the first anniversary of 31 January following that tax year. No relief is available where the transfer or redemption takes place on or after 27 March 2003, unless the person transferring or redeeming the security had held it continuously since before that date *and* the security was listed on a recognised stock exchange (within *ICTA 1988, s 841(1)*) at some time before that date.

'Transfer' for these purposes means transfer by way of sale, exchange, gift or otherwise. A transfer or acquisition under an agreement is treated as taking place when the agreement is made if entitlement to the security passes at that time. A conditional agreement is treated as made when the condition is satisfied. Where the holder dies, he is treated as having transferred the security at market value immediately before his death, and his personal representative as acquiring it at that value on his death. Except in relation to certain strips of government securities (see below), 'redemption' includes the extinguishment of a security (under rights conferred by the security) by conversion into shares in a company or into any other securities, the amount payable on that deemed redemption being the market value of the replacement shares or securities.

Where a conversion into euros of relevant discounted securities from the currency of a State which has adopted the euro (a '*euroconversion*', see *SI 1998 No 3177, reg 3*) is effected solely by means of an exchange or conversion of those securities, the conversion is not treated as constituting either a transfer within *FA 1996, Sch 13 para 4* or a conversion within *FA 1996, Sch 13 para 5*. Provision is made for an adjustment to the acquisition cost in respect of any cash payment received as a result of the conversion.

Where a security is issued to a person in accordance with the terms of a 'qualifying earn-out right', the issue price, and the amount paid for the acquisition, is taken to be the sum of the market value, immediately before the issue, of the right to be issued with the security in accordance with those terms and any amount payable for the issue in accordance with those terms. A *'qualifying earn-out right'* is so much of any right conferred on a person as:

(A)   constitutes the whole or any part of the consideration for the transfer by him of shares in or debentures of a company or for the transfer of the whole or part of a business or interest in a business carried on alone or in partnership;

(B)   consists in either a right to be issued with securities of another company or a right which is capable of being discharged in accordance with its terms by the issue of such securities; and

(C)   is such that the value of the consideration referred to in (A) above is unascertainable at the time when the right is conferred.

A *'relevant discounted security'* is, except as below, any security such that the amount payable on redemption (excluding interest) is or might be an amount involving a *'deep gain'*, i.e. the issue price is less than the amount payable on redemption by 15% of that amount or, if less, by $\frac{1}{2}$% per annum of that amount (counting months and part months as $\frac{1}{12}$th of a year) to the earliest possible redemption date. This comparison is made as at the time of issue of the security and assuming redemption in accordance with the terms of issue. 'Redemption' for these purposes referred originally to redemption on maturity or, if the holder of the security could opt for earlier redemption, the earliest occasion on which the holder might require redemption. In relation to any transfer of a security after 14 February 1999 or any occasion after that date on which a holder of a security becomes entitled to payment on redemption, the definition is widened so that one must consider, in addition to redemption on maturity, possible earlier occasions on which a security might be redeemed. The security will be a relevant discounted security if it would be such by reference to at least one such occasion. One need not take into account any occasion on which there may be a redemption other than at the option of the holder *unless* issuer and holder are connected or the obtaining of a tax advantage (as defined) is a main benefit that might be expected to accrue from the redemption provision. Additionally, where the holder has an option entitling him to redeem only on the occurrence of an 'event adversely affecting the holder' (as defined) or of a person's default *and* such entitlement is unlikely, judged at time of issue, to arise, the potential redemption is disregarded.

The following are not relevant discounted securities:

(*a*)   shares in a company;

(*b*)   gilt-edged securities (other than strips, see below);

(*c*)   'excluded indexed securities';

(*d*)   LIFE ASSURANCE POLICIES (45);

(*e*)   capital redemption policies (see 45.13(C) LIFE ASSURANCE POLICIES); and

(*f*)   securities issued under the same prospectus as other securities issued previously but not themselves relevant discounted securities.

Also after 14 February 1999, however, securities within (*c*) and (*f*) above may be treated as relevant discounted securities in certain circumstances involving their being held by a person connected with the issuer. *ICTA 1988, s 839* (see 19 CONNECTED PERSONS) applies to determine whether persons are connected for these purposes, but without taking any account of the security under review or any security issued under the same prospectus.

Strips of government securities (see below) are always relevant discounted securities, without regard to their issue terms. As regards (*f*) above, if none of the securities originally issued under a prospectus would otherwise be a relevant discounted security, and some of those subsequently issued under the prospectus would be but for (*f*) above, and the aggregate nominal value of the latter at any time exceeds that of all other securities issued under the prospectus, then all securities issued under that prospectus are, from that time, treated as relevant discounted securities acquired as such.

A security is an '*excluded indexed security*' within (*c*) above if, in pursuance of any provision having effect for the purposes of the security, the amount payable on redemption (as above) is determined by applying to the amount for which the security was issued a percentage change, over the 'relevant period', in the value of chargeable assets of any particular description (or in an index of the value of such assets — the retail prices index or similar foreign general prices index is not such an index). If, however, there is such a provision which is made subject to any other provision applying to the determination of the amount payable on redemption, whose only effect is to place a lower limit on the discharge payment of a specified percentage (which must not be more than 10%) of the amount for which the security is issued, then that other provision is disregarded for this purpose. An asset is for these purposes a chargeable asset if any disposal gain would be a chargeable gain (assuming the asset (not being trading stock etc.) to belong to the person in question (and that that person does not have the benefit of exemption under *TCGA 1992, s 100* (authorised unit trusts etc.)), and disregarding gains previously deferred under *TCGA 1992, s 116* on a capital reorganisation etc. involving a qualifying corporate bond, see Tolley's Capital Gains Tax under Qualifying Corporate Bonds). The '*relevant period*' is the period between the time of issue and redemption, or any other period in which almost all of that period is comprised and which differs from it exclusively for valuation purposes.

These provisions do not apply for corporation tax purposes, for which a separate regime applies, broadly dealing with all interest and profits or losses on securities on revenue account, either on an accruals basis or on a mark-to-market basis. See Tolley's Corporation Tax under Loan Relationships.

Treatment of losses where income exempt. Where a loss is sustained on transfer or redemption in a case where a profit on the transaction would have been an 'exempt profit' for the tax year, the loss (if otherwise allowable) can be relieved only against income chargeable under these provisions. An '*exempt profit*' for this purpose is income:

(1)   which is eligible for relief under *ICTA 1988, s 505(1)* (or which would be so eligible but for *ICTA 1988, s 505(3)*) (charitable exemptions and restrictions, see 14.4–14.7, 14.10 CHARITIES); or

(2)   which is eligible for relief under *ICTA 1988, s 592(2), s 608(2)(a), s 613(4), s 614(2)–(5), s 620(6)* or *s 643(2)* (pension scheme funds etc., see 67.5, 67.13, 67.11, 67.15 RETIREMENT SCHEMES, 60.1 PERSONAL PENSION SCHEMES, 66.8 RETIREMENT ANNUITIES).

As regards (2) above, where the exemption under *ICTA 1988, s 592(2)* applies, there is special provision for the interaction with the pension fund surplus provisions of *ICTA 1988, Sch 22* (see 67.8 RETIREMENT SCHEMES).

[*FA 1996, ss 102, 105(1)(b), Sch 13 paras 1–5, 7, 10, 13, 14(1), 16; FA 1999, s 65(1)–(8); FA 2003, s 182, Sch 39 paras 1, 2, 5(1)(2), 6; SI 1998 No 3177, reg 12*].

Trustees. Amounts chargeable under these provisions on the transfer or redemption of a security by trustees are treated for the purposes of *ICTA 1988, ss 660A–682A* (see 81.13–81.19 SETTLEMENTS) as income arising under the settlement from the security, and for the purposes of *ICTA 1988, ss 686 et seq.* (see 81.5 SETTLEMENTS) as income arising to the trustees. To the extent that tax on such an amount is chargeable on the trustees, it is chargeable at the rate applicable to trusts (see 81.5 SETTLEMENTS). This does not apply to trustees of unauthorised unit trusts (see 90.2 UNIT TRUSTS) to the extent that the amount is treated as income in the scheme accounts.

In the case of trustees, relief for losses under these provisions (where available) can be given only against income chargeable under these provisions. Where, in any tax year up to and including 2001/02, losses exceed amounts chargeable, the excess is carried forward and treated as a loss sustained under these provisions in the next tax year (although this does not apply to the extent that the loss arises in circumstances such that a profit would have been exempt — see above). No losses can be carried forward to any tax year later than 2002/03. The restriction on set-off does not apply to losses sustained on or after 27 March 2003 on transfers/redemptions of strips of government securities (see below).

Non-resident trustees. Charges and reliefs under these provisions do not apply to securities held under a settlement the trustees of which are non-UK resident.

[FA 1996, Sch 13 para 6(1)–(6), para 7(2); FA 2003, Sch 39 paras 5(1)(2), 6].

Personal representatives. On the transfer of a relevant discounted security to a legatee, personal representatives are deemed to obtain market value consideration. A 'legatee' is any person taking under a testamentary disposition or on an intestacy or partial intestacy (including an appropriation in or towards satisfaction of a legacy or other interest or share in the deceased's property). *[FA 1996, Sch 13 para 6(7)(8)].*

Strips of government securities. (See Tolley's Corporation Tax under Income Tax in Relation to a Company as regards strips generally.) For the purposes of these provisions, a 'strip' originally meant a strip of a UK Government (i.e. a gilt-edged) security. In relation to securities acquired on or after 27 March 2003, its meaning is extended to include strips of overseas government securities. Every strip is a relevant discounted security within these provisions. For these purposes:

- on the exchange of a security for strips of that security, the acquisition cost of each strip is determined by apportioning the market value of the security *pro rata* to the market value of each strip;

- when a person consolidates strips into a single security by exchanging them for that security, each strip is treated as being redeemed at market value;

- any person holding a strip on 5 April in any year of assessment, and not transferring or redeeming it on that day, is deemed to have transferred it at market value on that day and to have re-acquired it at the deemed disposal value on the following day (without incurring any costs in connection with the deemed transactions); and

- the Treasury has wide powers by regulation to modify these provisions in their application to strips.

In relation to exchanges and deemed transfers and re-acquisitions after 16 March 2004, the market value of a strip or of any security exchanged for strips of that security is determined in accordance with *FA 1996, Sch 13 para 14E* which requires use of prices quoted in the London Stock Exchange Daily Official List or, for overseas government strips or securities not quoted in that list, the equivalent foreign stock exchange list for the territory of the issuing government.

[FA 1996, Sch 13 paras 14, 14E, 15(1); FA 2003, Sch 39 paras 4, 5(3), 6; FA 2004, s 138(4)(8)(9)(11)].

The provisions for claiming loss relief, generally abolished from 27 March 2003 subject to transitional provisions (see above), are retained for any loss sustained on the transfer (including a deemed transfer on 5 April — see above) or the redemption of a strip, except that costs of acquisition, transfer or redemption cannot be included in the relief for transfers/redemptions on or after 27 March 2003 (except under the transitional provisions). This relief applies equally on transfers and redemptions by UK-resident trustees.

The following anti-avoidance provisions apply.

72.5 Schedule D, Case III—Interest Receivable etc.

    (i)   With effect in relation to any strip held on 15 January 2004 or subsequently acquired (disregarding any deemed re-acquisition as above): where, as a result of a scheme or arrangement aimed at securing a tax advantage, a person acquires (or acquired) a strip at more than market value or transfers or redeems a strip at less than market value (disregarding any costs incurred in connection with any acquisition, transfer or redemption), market value is substituted for the purpose of determining both profits and losses. Market value for these purposes is determined in accordance with *FA 1996, Sch 13 para 14E* (referred to above).

    (ii)   With effect in relation to losses accruing after 16 March 2004: where, as a result of a scheme or arrangement aimed at securing a tax advantage or producing an allowable loss for capital gains tax purposes, the circumstances are (or might have been) as in (i) above and a payment resulting in a capital loss falls to be made other than in respect of the acquisition or disposal of a strip, that loss is not allowable for capital gains tax purposes.

    (iii)   With effect in relation to any strip acquired on or after 15 January 2004 (disregarding any deemed re-acquisition as above): a loss on the transfer, deemed transfer or redemption of a strip is restricted for tax purposes is restricted *by* the amount (if any) by which proceeds are less than 'original acquisition cost'. A profit is restricted *to* the amount (if any) by which disposal proceeds exceed 'original acquisition cost'. These rules cannot reduce a loss or a profit to a negative amount, i.e. a profit cannot be converted into a loss or *vice versa*. '*Original acquisition cost*' is determined without taking account of any earlier deemed transfers and re-acquisitions by the person concerned but otherwise takes account of any rule requiring market value to be substituted for actual cost.

[*FA 1996, Sch 13 paras 14A–14D; FA 2003, Sch 39 paras 3, 6; FA 2004, s 138(5)–(7)(12)–(15)*].

Market value transfers. In addition to the deemed transfer on death and in relation to personal representatives and strips (see above), the following transfers of relevant discounted securities are deemed to take place at market value.

- Transfers between CONNECTED PERSONS (19) (within *ICTA 1988, s 839*).

- Where the consideration for the transfer is not all money or money's worth.

- Where the transfer is not by way of a bargain made at arm's length.

Where the security is a strip and the transfer takes place after 16 March 2004, market value is determined in accordance with *FA 1996, Sch 13 para 14E* (referred to above under Strips of government securities).

[*FA 1996, Sch 13 paras 8, 9; FA 2004, s 138(2)(3)(10)*].

Restriction of loss: connected persons transactions. For transfers on or after 26 March 2002, no loss relief is available to a person (the 'relevant person') where he transfers a relevant discounted security to a 'connected person' within *ICTA 1988, s 839* (see 19 CONNECTED PERSONS), and:

- the relevant person acquired the security on issue;

- the amount paid by the relevant person in respect of the acquisition exceeds the market value of the security at the time of issue; and

- either

    (*a*)   the relevant person was, at the time of issue, connected (as above) with the issuer, or

    (*b*)   the following conditions are satisfied:

(i)   the security was issued by a close company (as in *ICTA 1988, s 414*, but without the exclusion of non-UK resident companies);

(ii)   at the time of issue the relevant person was not connected (as above) with the issuing company;

(iii)   securities of the same kind as that issued to the relevant person were also issued to other persons; and

(iv)   the relevant person and some or all of those other persons, taken together, controlled (within *ICTA 1988, s 416*) the issuing company.

[*FA 1996, Sch 13 para 9A; FA 2002, s 104; FA 2003, Sch 39 paras 5(2), 6*].

Accrued income scheme. Relevant discounted securities within these provisions are outside the accrued income scheme (see 74.6 SCHEDULE D, CASE VI).

Transfer of assets abroad. For the purposes of *ICTA 1988, ss 739, 740* (transfer of assets abroad, see 3.7 ANTI-AVOIDANCE), a profit chargeable under these provisions realised by a person resident or domiciled outside the UK is taken to be income of that person.

Recovery of assets under *Proceeds of Crime Act 2002, Pt 5.* Where the transfer of a relevant discounted security is a *Pt 5* transfer under *Proceeds of Crime Act 2002* (as in 9.2(xi) CAPITAL ALLOWANCES) and no compensating payment is made to the transferor, it is not treated as a transfer for the purposes of these provisions. [*Proceeds of Crime Act 2002, Sch 10 paras 5, 10*].

Simon's Direct Tax Service. See A7.6.

73 Schedule D, Cases IV and V—Overseas Income

[ICTA 1988, ss 18, 65–67]

Cross-references. See RESIDENCE, ORDINARY RESIDENCE AND DOMICILE at 65.4 for domicile, 65.5 for residence; NON-RESIDENTS AND OTHER OVERSEAS MATTERS at 51.11 for trades etc. carried on and controlled abroad, 51.13 for unremittable overseas income; 53.14 PARTNERSHIPS for partnerships abroad; 56 PAYMENT OF TAX; 58.2(*b*)(*k*)(*p*)(*q*) PENSION INCOME for foreign pensions; 64 REMITTANCE BASIS for remittances; 75.4, 75.9 SCHEDULE E—EMPLOYMENT INCOME for foreign employment.

Simon's Direct Tax Service Part B6.

73.1 Persons resident in the UK are chargeable under Schedule D, Cases IV and V on overseas income, except from the carrying on in the UK of a trade, profession or vocation, either solely or in partnership (chargeable under Schedule D, Cases I or II) or employment, pension or social security income (previously chargeable under Schedule E, now chargeable as employment income under *ITEPA 2003*).

Case IV applies to interest on overseas **securities**.

Case V applies to income from overseas **possessions**. *[ICTA 1988, s 18(3); FA 1996, Sch 7 para 4(2)(b); ITEPA 2003, Sch 6 para 5]*.

See 72.1 SCHEDULE D, CASE III for interaction with that Case, and for variations for corporation tax purposes.

73.2 **'Securities'** are debts or claims secured on some fund or property, i.e. debenture or mortgage. (Cf. *dicta* in *Williams v Singer HL 1920, 7 TC 419*).

'Possessions' include all sources of income other than securities. The distinction between the two has ceased to be of any general practical importance.

73.3 **Overseas income** within Cases IV or V includes foreign bank interest; income as partner (*Colquhoun v Brooks HL 1889, 2 TC 490*; *Padmore v CIR CA 1989, 62 TC 352*); alimony paid under a foreign decree (*Anderstrom CS 1927, 13 TC 482*) (and see below); annuity paid under foreign deed of separation (*Chamney v Lewis KB 1932, 17 TC 318*); interest on unpaid instalments of a debt (*Hudson's Bay Co v Thew KB 1919, 7 TC 206*). Where the aggregate face value of foreign promissory notes exceeded the consideration for them, the excess was held to be interest within Case V (*Lord Howard de Walden v Beck KB 1940, 23 TC 384*).

Alimony, maintenance payments etc. arising outside the UK which fall due after 14 March 1988 and before 6 April 2000 and are made in pursuance of 'existing obligations' (see 1.8(i) ALLOWANCES AND TAX RATES) are within the charge to tax under Case V, but subject to the deductions and limitations described at 47.8 MARRIED PERSONS. Other maintenance payments which, if they had arisen in the UK, would not have been within the charge to tax under Case III (see 47.8 MARRIED PERSONS) are similarly exempted from charge under Case V if arising abroad. *[ICTA 1988, s 347A(4); FA 1988, ss 36(1), 38(8); FA 1999, Sch 20 Pt III(6)]*.

Promissory notes issued in satisfaction of arrears were held to be assessable (*Lilley v Harrison HL 1952, 33 TC 344*) and in *Westminster Bank v National Bank of Greece HL 1970, 46 TC 472* interest on foreign bonds paid, as guarantor, by the London branch of a foreign bank was held to be within Case IV. A dividend from a foreign company out of a capital profit was held to be within Case V (*Reid's Trustees HL 1949, 30 TC 431*) but see *Lazard Inv Co v Rae HL 1963, 41 TC 1*, where different treatment by application of Maryland law. In *Lawson v Rolfe Ch D 1969, 46 TC 199*, bonus shares received, by operation of Californian law, by the UK resident life tenant under a US will trust were held not assessable under Case V. And see *Courtaulds Investments v Fleming Ch D 1969, 46 TC 111*, distribution out of the share premium reserve of an Italian company (released, under Italian law, by accumulating out of profits a corresponding reserve fund) held a return of capital. See also *Pool v Guardian Investment Trust Co Ltd KB 1921, 8 TC 167* and *Associated Insulation Products Ltd v Golder CA 1944, 26 TC 231*. Compensation paid by a foreign government, following redundancy, in substitution for a proportion of salary was held to be assessable as income (*Beveridge v Ellam (Sp C 62), [1996] SSCD 77*).

Whether **premiums and discounts** are assessable to income tax depends upon whether recipient received altogether more than commercial interest reasonable on a sound investment (*Lomax v Peter Dixon CA 1943, 25 TC 353*, compared with *Thomas Nelson & Sons Ltd CS 1938, 22 TC 175*, and *Davis v Premier Investment KB 1945, 27 TC 27*). If exempt from income tax they may be assessable to capital gains tax.

Simon's Direct Tax Service. See **B6.101, B6.201** *et seq.*

Overseas lettings of property, caravans and houseboats are assessed under Case V. See 73.4 below. For foreign pensions, see 58.2(*b*)(*k*)(*p*)(*q*) PENSION INCOME and cf. *Bridges v Watterson Ch D 1952, 34 TC 47*. For foreign trust income, see 81.10 SETTLEMENTS. For Crown option between Cases of Schedule D, see 5.1 ASSESSMENTS. For treatment of blocked currency cases, see 51.13 NON-RESIDENTS AND OTHER OVERSEAS MATTERS and *ICTA 1988, ss 584, 585*.

73.4   **Overseas lettings.** Except where the REMITTANCE BASIS (64) applies (see 73.5 below), income arising from any business (other than a trade, profession or vocation) carried on for the exploitation, as a source of rents or other receipts, of any estate, interest or rights in or over land outside the UK is chargeable under Case V but is to be computed under the rules applicable to a Schedule A business. All such businesses carried on by one person are treated as a single business (an overseas property business). The question of whether income falls within the above description is determined as for Schedule A purposes. See 69.3, 69.4 SCHEDULE A. The following do *not*, however, apply as they would under Schedule A: (i) *ICTA 1988, ss 80, 81* — travelling expenses (see 51.11 NON-RESIDENTS AND OTHER OVERSEAS MATTERS), but see below, and (ii) *ICTA 1988, ss 503, 504* — special rules for furnished holiday lettings (see 69.8 SCHEDULE A). Where a person carries on both a Schedule A business and an overseas property business, each is treated as a separate business without regard to the other. Domestic concepts of law are to be interpreted to produce the result most closely corresponding to that under Schedule A for land in the UK. [*ICTA 1988, s 65(2A)(2B)(4), s 65A; FA 1995, s 41(1)–(3)(10); FA 1996, s 134, Sch 20 para 3; FA 1998, s 38, Sch 5 paras 23, 24, Sch 27 Pt III(4); CAA 2001, Sch 2 para 13*]. Under general principles, relief is available for travelling expenses incurred wholly and exclusively for the purposes of the overseas letting business. Interest on a loan to purchase an overseas property is deductible as an expense to the extent that it is incurred wholly and exclusively for the purposes of the letting business, with the interest being apportioned accordingly where the owner occupies the property, or it is otherwise unavailable for letting, for part of the year or if only part of the property is used exclusively for letting. (Revenue booklet SAT 1(1995), paras 9.151–9.153). For the application of capital allowances to an overseas property business, see 9.17, 9.24(iii) CAPITAL ALLOWANCES. Although all overseas let properties are regarded as a single letting business, the income from each must be calculated separately for the purposes of computing DOUBLE TAX RELIEF (24) (SAT 1(1995), para 9.160).

The above rules apply for 1995/96 and subsequent years. For the transitional rules on changeover to the current system, see the 2003/04 and earlier editions; these do not affect any year later than 1997/98 except as regards losses (see below).

73.5   Schedule D, Cases IV and V—Overseas Income

For years before 1998/99, deficiencies of income from overseas lettings may by concession be carried forward for set-off against future income from the same property. For 1998/99 onwards, the loss regime at 69.12 SCHEDULE A operates instead (by virtue of *ICTA 1988, s 379B*), but any unrelieved losses at 5 April 1998 (including any incurred after 5 April 1995 on properties where letting ceases before 1998/99) may by concession be carried forward against future profits of the single overseas letting business. (Revenue Pamphlet IR 1, B25; Revenue Booklet SAT 1(1995), paras 9.157–9.159).

Simon's Direct Tax Service. See B6.204.

73.5   **Assessment** on income chargeable under Cases IV and V is normally on **income arising** whether remitted to this country or not but the **remittance basis** (see 64 REMITTANCE BASIS) applies to

(*a*)   persons not domiciled in the UK.

(*b*)   Commonwealth subjects, or citizens of Republic of Ireland, not ordinarily resident in the UK.

[*ICTA 1988, s 65(1)(4)(5); FA 1994, s 207(1)(3); FA 1996, s 134, Sch 20 para 3*].

For certain foreign pensions, the amount taxable on the arising basis is 90% of the amount of income arising in the tax year (see 58.2(*b*)(*k*)(*p*)(*q*) PENSION INCOME).

Other than where the remittance basis applies, interest, discounts etc. within Case IV or V are chargeable to income tax at the lower rate (to the extent that such income does not exceed the basic rate limit in the case of an individual, in which case it is chargeable at the higher rate). See 1.9 ALLOWANCES AND TAX RATES for more detail.

Simon's Direct Tax Service. See E1.3.

73.6   **Ireland.** Income from whatever source in Ireland (i.e. the Republic of Ireland) is chargeable on the amount arising in the year of assessment whether remitted to this country or not, subject to certain deductions in the case of income not remitted. [*ICTA 1988, s 68; F(No 2)A 1992, s 60; FA 1994, s 207(5)*].

73.7   **Deductions.** In general the assessment is on the full amount of the income with no deductions (cf. *Aikin v Macdonald Trustees CES 1894, 3 TC 306*), but where the assessment is on the arising basis (see 73.5 above) there may be deducted from income not received in the UK (*a*) the same deductions and allowances as if it had been so received, and (*b*) any annuities or other annual payments (not being interest) payable out of the income to a resident abroad. No deduction is permitted either in respect of any annuity or annual payment which would not have been chargeable under Schedule D, Case III if made to a UK resident, nor in respect of any payment of maintenance within *FA 1988, s 38* (see 47.8 MARRIED PERSONS). [*ICTA 1988, ss 65(1), 347A(5); FA 1988, ss 36(1), 38(9); FA 1994, s 207(1)*].

Foreign tax for which no double tax credit is allowable (see 24.2 DOUBLE TAX RELIEF) may generally be deducted where the arising basis applies. [*ICTA 1988, ss 811, 795(2)*]. Where the remittance basis applies, see *ICTA 1988, s 795(1)*.

Simon's Direct Tax Service. See E1.331.

73.8   No assessment can be made for years during which the source of income was taxed by **deduction at source.** See 5.4 ASSESSMENTS (and cf. *Bradbury v Eng. Sewing Cotton HL 1923, 8 TC 481*).

73.9   **BASIS OF ASSESSMENT**

For 1994/95 and subsequent years (1996/97 and subsequent years as regards income from a source first arising (or, where the remittance basis applies, see 73.5 above, income first remitted to the UK) before 6 April 1994), the assessment under Case IV or V is on the income arising (or, where applicable, remitted) in the current year of assessment. [*ICTA 1988, s 65; FA 1994, s 207(1)(3)(4), s 218(1)(4)*]. Generally, there are no special rules for opening and closing years (i.e. new and discontinued sources). But, in the case of a trade, profession or vocation chargeable under Case IV or V, the basis period rules in 71.3–71.11 SCHEDULE D, CASES I AND II apply, as does *ICTA 1988, s 113* (see 53.5 PARTNERSHIPS). [*ICTA 1988, s 65(3); FA 1994, s 207(2)(6)*].

For the preceding year basis of assessment that applied previously, and for transitional rules, including associated anti-avoidance provisions, on the changeover to the current year basis as above, see the 2003/04 and earlier editions.

73.10   **NEW RESIDENTS**

As regards a *trade, profession or vocation* carried on by an individual wholly or partly outside the UK, the comments and concessions below are superseded by the statutory provisions at 71.17 SCHEDULE D, CASES I AND II.

Strictly, an individual who becomes resident (see 65.5 RESIDENCE, ORDINARY RESIDENCE AND DOMICILE) in the UK during a tax year is treated as resident throughout that year. He is chargeable on income arising or remitted as appropriate (see 73.5 above and *Back v Whitlock KB 1932, 16 TC 723*; *Carter v Sharon KB 1936, 20 TC 229*; *Joffe v Thain Ch D 1955, 36 TC 199*).

For the year in which an individual whose home has previously been abroad becomes permanently resident in the UK, however, certain concessions are generally available, provided that he was not previously ordinarily resident in the UK.

(i)   The individual may be treated as resident only from the date of his arrival in the UK to take up permanent residence.

(ii)   No assessment is made in respect of a source ceasing before the date of arrival in the UK to take up permanent residence.

(iii)   Where untaxed income is chargeable on the 'arising' basis (see 73.5 above),

(*a*)   if the source ceases in the period between arrival and the end of the tax year of arrival, assessment will be restricted to the amount arising in that period;

(*b*)   if the source ceases in the tax year following that of arrival, assessment for the year of arrival will be on a proportion of the income for the year of arrival. The proportion is that which corresponds to the period of UK residence in the year of arrival. For the following year, assessment will be on the income arising during that year to the date the source ceased;

(*c*)   if income from a continuing source first arose in the tax year of arrival but before arrival, assessment for the year of arrival is restricted to the same proportion as in (*b*) above of the income of that year.

(iv)   Where untaxed income is chargeable on the 'remittance' basis (see 73.5 above),

(*a*)   if the source ceases in the period between arrival and the end of the tax year of arrival, assessment is restricted to the lesser of remittances in the tax year and income arising between arrival and cessation;

(*b*)   if the source ceases in the tax year following that of arrival, the assessment for the year of arrival is restricted to the lesser of (A) remittances in that year (or,

73.11 Schedule D, Cases IV and V—Overseas Income

if the source was in existence at 5 April 1994, and if greater, in the previous year) and (B) a proportion (as in (iii)(*b*) above) of the income arising in that year (or, if the source was in existence at 5 April 1994, and if greater, in the previous year). The sum of the assessments for the year of arrival and the following year is then restricted to the sum of the amount arrived at under (B) above and income arising in the year following that of arrival up to the date the source ceased.

These concessions do not, however, apply to income received from a source in Ireland (see 73.6 above) and are of limited application to individuals previously resident there.

As regards overseas income received through a UK paying or collecting agent, tax is charged only on income received on or after the date of arrival.

(Revenue Pamphlet IR 20, paras 1.5, 5.4, 6.17, 6.19, 6.20).

See also Revenue Pamphlet IR 20, para 5.14 as regards whether a change of residence brings about a cessation of a trade etc.

73.11   **INDIVIDUALS PERMANENTLY LEAVING UK**

As regards a *trade, profession or vocation* carried on by an individual wholly or partly outside the UK, the comments and concessions below are superseded by the statutory provisions at 71.17 SCHEDULE D, CASES I AND II.

Strictly, an individual who is resident in the UK (see 65.5 RESIDENCE, ORDINARY RESIDENCE AND DOMICILE) continues to be so for the remainder of the tax year after his permanent departure from the UK. Certain concessions are, however, available, provided that he ceases to be ordinarily resident in the UK on his departure.

   (i)   Where untaxed income is chargeable on the 'arising' basis (see 73.5 above), the assessment for the year in which permanent residence ceases is restricted to the lesser of

       (*a*)   income arising between 6 April in that year and the date of his departure, and

       (*b*)   the proportion of the income otherwise chargeable for the year corresponding to the period of UK residence in the year.

   (ii)   Where untaxed income is chargeable on the 'remittance' basis (see 73.5 above), concessions apply as in (i) above, substituting 'remitted' for 'arising'.

These concessions do not, however, apply to income received from a source in Ireland (see 73.6 above), and are of limited application to persons leaving to take up residence there.

(Revenue Pamphlet IR 20, paras 1.5, 5.4, 6.15, 6.16).

As regards overseas income received through a paying or collecting agent, tax is charged only on income received on or before the date of departure (but see IR 20, para 6.14).

74   Schedule D, Case VI—Miscellaneous Income

[*ICTA 1988, ss 18, 69*]

Simon's Direct Tax Service Part B7.

74.1   Tax is charged under Schedule D, Case VI in respect of any annual profits or gains not falling under any other case of Schedule D and not charged by virtue of any other Schedule. [*ICTA 1988, s 18(3)*].

Case VI is also specifically applied to various kinds of income including, for example, amounts chargeable under the accrued income scheme, see 74.5 *et seq.* below; various charges under ANTI-AVOIDANCE (3); withdrawal of relief under 25.19 ENTERPRISE INVEST-MENT SCHEME; sale of patent rights, see 54 PATENTS; CERTIFICATES OF DEPOSIT (12); easements not falling under *ICTA 1988, ss 119, 120* and certain under-deductions where tax rate changed, see 22 DEDUCTION OF TAX AT SOURCE; interest paid by issue of bonds, see 32 FUNDING BONDS; gains on certain offshore life insurance policies, see 45.17–45.19 LIFE ASSURANCE POLICIES; formerly unremittable overseas income where source has ceased, see 51.13 NON-RESIDENTS AND OTHER OVERSEAS MATTERS; offshore income gains, see 52 OFFSHORE FUNDS; recovery of tax over-repaid, see 56.10 PAYMENT OF TAX; certain POST-CESSATION ETC. RECEIPTS (62); lease premiums and assignments at under-value etc. see 69.16 SCHEDULE A; certain settlement income, see 81.15 SETTLEMENTS; charges on trustees of QUESTS, see 63.8 QUALIFYING EMPLOYEE SHARE OWNERSHIP TRUSTS; recovery of various excess reliefs for double taxation [*ICTA 1988, ss 788, 790, 804*], losses [*ICTA 1988, s 383(11), s 384A(6)*], capital allowances [*CAA 1990, s 9(6), s 15(2) (both now superseded); CAA 2001, s 258(4)*] etc. See Simon's Direct Tax Service B7.102.

Case VI income is not earned income unless specifically provided, e.g. in *ICTA 1988, s 107* (POST-CESSATION ETC. RECEIPTS (62)), in *ICTA 1988, s 491(5)* (distribution of assets of mutual companies), in *ICTA 1988, s 531(6)* (sale of know-how — see 71.57 SCHEDULE D, CASES I AND II), in *ICTA 1988, s 775(2)* (capitalisation of earnings — see 3.9 ANTI-AVOIDANCE).

74.2   Following held to be income within Case VI: commission for guaranteeing overdrafts (*Ryall v Hoare KB 1925, 8 TC 521* and *Sherwin v Barnes KB 1931, 16 TC 278*); underwriting commission (*Lyons v Cowcher KB 1926, 10 TC 438*); commission for negotiating a sale of shares (*Grey v Tiley CA 1932, 16 TC 414*); commission from an insurance company (*Hugh v Rogers Ch D 1958, 38 TC 270* and see *Way v Underdown CA 1974, 49 TC 648*); shipping dues (the two *Forth Conservancy Board cases HL 1928, 14 TC 709, HL 1931, 16 TC 103*); share of prize monies for letting racehorses (*Norman v Evans Ch D 1964, 42 TC 188*).

Held to be capital were shares allotted to members of a mining finance development scheme (*Whyte v Clancy KB 1936, 20 TC 679*) and shares allotted for a guarantee of dividends (*National United Laundries v Bennet KB 1933, 17 TC 420*).

A payment to an architect for his services relating to a property deal was held income within Case VI in *Brocklesby v Merricks KB 1934, 18 TC 576*, but payments for services in deals are not income if made gratuitously in such circumstances that the recipient has no enforceable right to them. For cases in which such payments held *not* income see *Bradbury v Arnold Ch D 1957, 37 TC 665*; *Bloom v Kinder Ch D 1958, 38 TC 77*; *Dickinson v Abel Ch D 1968, 45 TC 353*. See also *Scott v Ricketts CA 1967, 44 TC 303* in which a payment to an estate agent linked with a development scheme was held not to be income even though embodied in a contract.

Receipts of the use of copyright material were held income within Case VI in *Hobbs v Hussey KB 1942, 24 TC 153* (sale of rights in life story to newspaper) and *Housden v*

74.3 Schedule D, Case VI—Miscellaneous Income

Marshall Ch D 1958, 38 TC 233 and *Alloway v Phillips CA 1980, 53 TC 372* (receipt for material for newspaper articles by 'ghost writer') but held capital in *Earl Haig Trustees v CIR CS 1939, 22 TC 725* (payment to trustees for permission to use diaries of deceased); *Beare v Carter KB 1940, 23 TC 353* (payment for permission to re-print book); *Nethersole v Withers HL 1948, 28 TC 501* (sale of film rights in work by deceased author).

For other copyright sales see 71.33 and 71.41 SCHEDULE D, CASES I AND II. For the line between Cases I and VI as regards surpluses on the sales of assets see 71.25 SCHEDULE D, CASES I AND II.

See Simon's Direct Tax Service B7.2.

Volunteer drivers (e.g. hospital car service drivers) are taxable in the normal way under Case VI on the profit element in any mileage allowances. They may use the authorised (from 6 April 2002, the statutory) tax-free mileage rates applicable to employees (see 75.46 SCHEDULE E—EMPLOYMENT INCOME) in determining any profit element, although they have the option of claiming their actual motoring expenses (see Revenue Press Release BN 2/01 7 March 2001). See also Revenue explanatory leaflet IR 122.

Theatrical angels. UK-resident backers of theatrical productions ('angels'), although strictly assessable under SCHEDULE D, CASE III (72) on any return over and above their original investment (with the capital gains tax rules applicable to any losses), may treat the profit or loss arising on any particular transaction as within Case VI, thereby being able to utilise such losses against similar (or any other) Case VI profits. Losses so utilised cannot also qualify as capital losses. The Revenue will not insist on deduction of tax being applied to payments to angels whose usual place of abode is in the UK where it is strictly required under *ICTA 1988, s 349.* (Non-resident angels may apply for authority for tax not to be deducted, see 24.6 DOUBLE TAX RELIEF.) (Revenue Pamphlet IR 1, A94).

74.3 BASIS OF ASSESSMENT

The income tax charge under Case VI is on the income arising in the current year of assessment. [*ICTA 1988, s 69; FA 1994, ss 208, 218(1)*]. For corporation tax, the charge is on the income of the current accounting period.

74.4 LOSSES

Losses on transactions which, if profitable, would have been assessable under Schedule D, Case VI (other than losses on transactions falling under *ICTA 1988, ss 34–36*, see 69.16 SCHEDULE A), can be set off against any profit or gains charged under Case VI for the same year of assessment or carried forward against the next subsequent profits chargeable under that Case. Claims relating to the amount of losses must be made within five years after 31 January following the tax year in which they arose. A further claim for relief for losses brought forward must be made within five years after 31 January following the tax year for which relief is claimed. From 6 April 2003, certain types of pension income previously charged under Case VI are charged as employment income under *ITEPA 2003* (see 58.2(*e*)(*n*) PENSION INCOME), but Case VI losses may still be set against such income. [*ICTA 1988, s 392; FA 1996, s 135, Sch 21 para 11; ITEPA 2003, Sch 6 para 54*].

Simon's Direct Tax Service. See E1.626.

74.5 ACCRUED INCOME SCHEME (BONDWASHING)

Introduction. Bondwashing is the practice of converting income into capital gains by disposing of securities at a time when the price obtained reflects a significant element of accrued interest. Under the accrued income provisions, interest on securities is treated as accruing on a day to day basis between 'interest payment days', and on transfer of the securities a person is charged to income tax on the interest that accrues during the 'final interest period' of his ownership with appropriate adjustments to the taxable incomes of transferor and transferee.

A Revenue Pamphlet (IR 68) is available describing in brief terms the basic rules of the scheme. See generally Revenue Inspector's Manual IM 4230–4285.

Simon's Direct Tax Service. See A7.5.

These provisions are disapplied for the purposes of corporation tax for accounting periods ending after 31 March 1996, except as respects transfers taking place on or before that date, and subject to transitional provisions. [*ICTA 1988, s 710(1A); FA 1996, Sch 14 para 36, Sch 15 para 18*]. For the corporation tax loan relationships regime introduced for accounting periods ending after 31 March 1996, including (where still relevant) the transitional provisions, see Tolley's Corporation Tax under Loan Relationships.

74.6   The **main definitions** of terms used in the accrued income legislation are in *ICTA 1988, ss 710–712*.

'*Securities*' include any loan stock or similar security of any government, or public or local authority, or any company, or other body, whether or not secured or carrying a right to interest of a fixed amount or at a fixed rate per cent and whether or not in bearer form. *Not included* are shares in a company (other than certain building society shares); (for 2003/04 and earlier years) securities on which the whole of the return is a distribution under *ICTA 1988, s 209(2)(da)* (issued by a subsidiary to its non-resident parent, see Tolley's Corporation Tax under Distributions); national and war savings certificates (including Ulster savings certificates); CERTIFICATES OF DEPOSIT (12) and certain other rights for which a certificate of deposit could be, but has not been, issued (see 12.3 CERTIFICATES OF DEPOSIT); relevant discounted securities within *FA 1996, Sch 13* (see 72.5 SCHEDULE D, CASE III); and any security redeemable at a price exceeding its issue price and carrying no other return. [*ICTA 1988, s 710(2)(3); FA 1991, Sch 10 para 2; F(No 2) A 1992, Sch 8 para 5; FA 1996, Sch 13 para 11; FA 2003, Sch 39 paras 5(2)(4), 6; FA 2004, Sch 42 Pt 2(2)*].

Securities are '*of the same kind*' if so treated by a recognised stock exchange or if they would be so treated if dealt with on such an exchange. [*ICTA 1988, s 710(4)*].

'*Transfer*' in relation to securities means transfer by way of sale, exchange, gift or otherwise, but does not include their vesting in personal representatives on a death after 5 April 1996, or exchanges of gilt-edged securities for strips (or reconsolidation of strips) except as provided by *ICTA 1988, s 722A* (see 74.23 below). It does not include an exchange or conversion of securities solely as a result of actions to effect a '*euroconversion*', i.e. a change from the currency of a State which has adopted the euro into euros (see *SI 1998 No 3177, regs 3, 32*). A transfer takes effect when an agreement for transfer is made and not at any later date. Except for this, a person '*acquires*' securities when he becomes entitled to them and '*holds*' them on any day if he is entitled to them at the end of that day. Partners in Scottish partnerships are treated as being entitled to securities held by the firm and as carrying out themselves any partnership dealings. [*ICTA 1988, s 710(5)–(9)(10); FA 1996, s 158(1)(5)*].

'*Interest*' includes dividends and any other return (however described) except a return consisting of the excess of a security's redemption amount over its issue price. [*ICTA 1988, s 711(9)*].

An '*interest payment day*' is a day on which interest is payable or, where payment may be made on more than one day, the first such day. [*ICTA 1988, s 711(2)*].

An '*interest period*' is normally the period beginning with the day after one interest payment day (or the day after issue) and ending with the next (or first) such day. If, however, an interest period would otherwise exceed twelve months, it is divided into successive twelve month interest periods with any remaining months also a separate interest period. [*ICTA 1988, s 711(3)(4)*].

The '*interest applicable to securities*' for an interest period is that due at the end of the period, unless the period does not end on an interest payment day. Where the interest period is part of a long period as above, the interest applicable is a pro rata proportion of that due at the end of the long period of which the interest period is part. [*ICTA 1988, s 711(7)(8)*].

The '*settlement day*', where securities are transferred through a recognised market such as the Stock Exchange, is the agreed settlement day or, if the transferee may settle on more than one day, the day he settles. If the transfer is not through such a market and the consideration is money alone and there is no interest payment day between the agreement for transfer and the agreed payment day or days, that day (or the latest such day) is the settlement day. If the transfer is not through such a market and either there is no consideration, or it is treated as a transfer by virtue of special provisions in *ICTA 1988, s 710(13), s 715(3), s 717(8), s 720(4), s 721, s 722, s 722A* or *s 724(1A)* (see 74.16, 74.20, 74.18, 74.11, 74.14, 74.15, 74.23 or 74.26 below), the settlement day is the day of transfer. If the settlement day is not established by one of the above, it is decided by an inspector, subject to review by the General or Special Commissioners on appeal. [*ICTA 1988, s 712; FA 1990, Sch 6 paras 9, 11; FA 1996, Sch 40 para 5*].

74.7 **Determination of accrued income.** When securities are transferred, the 'interest applicable to the securities' for 'the interest period' in which the 'settlement day' falls is apportioned between the old and new owners so that the former is charged to income tax on the interest accrued up to the date of transfer while the latter is similarly charged on the interest accruing from that date.

The interest actually received is chargeable to tax in the normal way. It may, however, be reduced, or a further charge may arise, as below.

Subject to exceptions in 74.9 below, if the transfer is *with accrued interest* (i.e. with the right to receive the next interest due, or 'cum div'), the transferor is treated as entitled to a sum equal to the 'accrued amount' while the transferee is treated as entitled to relief of the same amount. If, on the other hand, the transfer is *without accrued interest* (i.e. 'ex div') the transferor is treated as entitled to relief equal to the 'rebate amount' while the transferee is treated as entitled to a sum of the same amount.

The '*accrued amount*' is either the gross interest accruing to the settlement day (see 74.6 above) where this is accounted for separately by the transferee (as happens with short-dated gilts), or the 'accrued proportion' of the interest applicable for that interest period (see 74.6 above) in any other case. The '*accrued proportion*' is A/B where A is the number of days in the interest period up to and including the settlement day and B is the number of days in the whole period.

Conversely, the '*rebate amount*' is either the gross interest accruing from the settlement day to the next interest payment date where the transferor accounts to the transferee for this, or the 'rebate proportion' of the interest applicable for that interest period in any other case. The '*rebate proportion*' is (B − A)/B where A and B have the same meanings as for the accrued proportion above. Where the transfer of securities is a *Pt 5* transfer under *Proceeds of Crime Act 2002* (as in 9.2(xi) CAPITAL ALLOWANCES) and no compensating payment is made to the transferor, these provisions do not apply. [*ICTA 1988, ss 711(5), 713; Proceeds of Crime Act 2002, Sch 10 paras 4, 10*].

Euroconversions. Where, in any interest period, there is both a transfer of securities and a '*euroconversion*' of those securities, i.e. a change from the currency of a State which has adopted the euro into euros, the accrued or rebate amount arising on the transfer is such amount as is just and reasonable. A euroconversion does not generally of itself give rise to a transfer within these provisions (see 74.6 above), but certain capital sums received in connection with euroconversions of securities which, on a just and reasonable view, may be attributable to a reduction or deferral of interest on those securities may give rise to adjustments under these provisions. [*SI 1998 No 3177, regs 3, 34, 35*].

74.8   **Tax charge (or relief).** The various sums and reliefs to which a person is deemed to be entitled as in 74.7 above and which relate to securities of a particular kind in an interest period (see 74.6 above) are aggregated. If the overall result is a sum chargeable to tax, it is taxed under Schedule D, Case VI as if it were income received at the end of the interest period. If, on the other hand, the overall result shows entitlement to relief, the relief is given by way of a reduction in the actual interest received at the end of the interest period so that only the reduced amount is charged to tax. If this reduction is not possible because no interest is received at the end of the interest period, the relief is carried forward to be taken into account in calculating the accrued income or relief in the next interest period. Provision is also made (where relevant) to ensure that a company does not escape liability where the date on which an interest period ends does not fall within an accounting period. [*ICTA 1988, s 714; FA 1996, Sch 41 Pt V(3)*].

For 1998/99 and subsequent years, the lower rate (rather than the basic rate) of income tax is applied to charges under these provisions (subject to any higher rate liability). This does not affect the charge on trustees at the rate applicable to trusts (see 74.11 below). [*ICTA 1988, s 1A(1)(2)(aa); FA 1998, s 100*].

74.9   **Exceptions to deeming provisions.** The following are excluded from the accrued income scheme.

(*a*)   Transfers by persons who account for such transfers in the computation of their trading profits or losses (e.g. financial traders).

(*b*)   Transfers by individuals, personal representatives and trustees of mentally disabled persons or persons in receipt of attendance allowance, provided that the nominal value of securities held in the capacity in question does not exceed £5,000 on any day in the year of assessment in which the interest period ends or in the preceding year of assessment.

(*c*)   Transfers by persons neither resident nor ordinarily resident in the UK in the chargeable period in which the transfer is made, unless trading in the UK through a branch or agency. However, where such a person does so trade in the UK, the accrued income scheme only applies to securities used, or held, or acquired for use, for the purposes of the branch or agency, if the person is a company, and only to such of those securities as are situated in the UK (within the meaning of *TCGA 1992, s 275*) in other cases.

(*d*)   Transfers of FOTRA securities (see 33.2 GOVERNMENT STOCKS) where the appropriate conditions are met. (For securities treated as FOTRA securities from 6 April 1998 by virtue of *FA 1998, s 161(1)*, exemption applies in relation to amounts a person is treated as receiving on or after that date (see *FA 1998, s 161(2)(a)*).)

(*e*)   For foreign securities only, transfers by individuals who would be liable to tax on the remittance basis on actual interest on the securities under Schedule D, Case IV or V (i.e. persons not domiciled in the UK, or Commonwealth subjects or citizens of the Republic of Ireland not ordinarily resident in the UK).

The exceptions apply separately by reference to the circumstances of the transferor and the transferee. [*ICTA 1988, ss 710(9), 715; FA 1996, s 154, Sch 41 Pt V(18)*].

74.10   Schedule D, Case VI—Miscellaneous Income

74.10   *Example*

The following transactions take place between individuals during the year ended 5 April 2005.

Settlement day	Sale by	Purchase by	Securities
14.8.04	X (cum div)	Y	£4,000 6¼% Treasury Loan 2010
17.9.04	X (ex div)	P	£4,000 8% Treasury Loan 2013
4.4.05	S (cum div)	Y	£2,500 4% Treasury Loan 2009

Interest payment days are as follows.

6¼% Treasury Loan 2010	25 May, 25 November
8% Treasury Loan 2013	27 March, 27 September
4% Treasury Loan 2009	7 March, 7 September

Both X and Y owned chargeable securities with a nominal value in excess of £5,000 at some time in either 2003/04 or 2004/05, and both are resident and ordinarily resident in the UK. P is not resident and not ordinarily resident in the UK throughout 2004/05. The maximum value of securities held by S at any time in 2004/05 and 2005/06 is £4,000.

14.8.04 transaction

The transaction occurs in the interest period from 26.5.04 to 25.11.04 (inclusive).

Number of days in interest period	184
Number of days in interest period to 14.8.04	81
Interest payable on 25.11.04	£125

The accrued amount is

$$£125 \times \frac{81}{184} = £55$$

X is treated as receiving income (chargeable under Schedule D, Case VI) of £55 on 25.11.04.

Y is given credit for £55 against the interest of £125 he receives on 25.11.04. £70 remains taxable.

17.9.04 transaction

The transaction occurs in the interest period from 28.3.04 to 27.9.04 (inclusive).

Number of days in interest period	184
Number of days in interest period to 17.9.04	174
Interest payable on 27.9.04	£160

The rebate amount is

$$£160 \times \frac{184 - 174}{184} = £9$$

X is given credit for £9 against the interest of £160 he receives on 27.9.04. £151 remains taxable.

P is not chargeable on any notional income as he is neither resident nor ordinarily resident in the UK.

4.4.05 transaction

The transaction occurs in the interest period from 8.3.05 to 7.9.05 (inclusive).

Number of days in interest period   184
Number of days in interest period to 4.4.05   28
Interest payable on 7.9.05   £50

The accrued amount is

$$£50 \times \frac{28}{184} = £7$$

S is not chargeable on any notional income. He is not within the accrued income scheme provisions as his holdings do not exceed £5,000 at any time in 2004/05 or 2005/06 (the year in which the interest period ends).

Y is given credit for £7 against the interest of £50 he receives on 7.9.05. £43 remains taxable.

74.11 **ACCRUED INCOME SCHEME: SPECIAL CASES**

Nominees and trustees. Transfers made by or to a nominee, or by or to a trustee of a person or persons absolutely entitled as against the trustee (including persons who would be so entitled if not an infant or under a disability), are treated for accrued income scheme purposes as being made by or to the person on whose behalf the nominee or trustee acts. [*ICTA 1988, s 720(1)(2)*].

A person who becomes entitled to securities as trustee immediately after holding them in another capacity is treated as making a transfer within the new legislation. Such a transfer is 'with accrued interest' (see 74.7 above) if the person was entitled to receive any interest payable on the day of transfer or on the next interest payment day. [*ICTA 1988, ss 711(6), 720(4)*].

Trustees' accrued income (i.e. excluding that deemed to be that of a beneficiary, see above) is chargeable at the rate applicable to trusts (see 81.5 SETTLEMENTS). This tax is set against any subsequent tax charge under *ICTA 1988, s 687* (payments by trustees of discretionary trusts). The charge does not apply to certain funds in court within *ICTA 1988, s 328* (which is, however, repealed from 6 April 1999), and special rules apply to calculation of the income of such funds in receipt of interest on securities. [*ICTA 1988, s 720(5); FA 1993, Sch 6 para 13; FA 1999, Sch 20 Pt III(17)*].

Where a trustee is treated as receiving accrued income (see 74.8 above), or where he would have been treated as receiving, or receiving a greater amount of, accrued income if he had been UK resident or domiciled, the SETTLEMENTS (81) provisions apply with the effect that the accrued amount is, broadly, treated as income of the settlor where any actual income would be so treated. Similarly, any actual income received in those circumstances is reduced where the trustee is entitled to relief under the accrued income scheme (see 74.8 above). [*ICTA 1988, s 720(6)–(8); FA 1995, Sch 17 para 17*].

74.12 **Interest payable in foreign currency.** Provision is made for establishing the rate of exchange to be used in converting into sterling certain figures used in calculating the accrued income charge.

The accrued amount and the rebate amount (see 74.7 above). Where accrued interest is accounted for separately and the parties specify a sterling equivalent themselves, this figure is used. Otherwise accrued interest is converted at the rate of exchange (the London closing rate) on the settlement day.

Nominal values are converted at the London closing rate for the day in question.

[*ICTA 1988, s 710(12), s 713(7)–(9)*].

74.13   Schedule D, Case VI—Miscellaneous Income

74.13   **Foreign securities: delayed remittances.** A person (or his personal representatives) may claim to postpone all or part of sums which would be chargeable under the accrued income provisions if

(a)   he makes a claim within six years of the end of the interest period in which the transfer occurred, and

(b)   he was unable (through no want of reasonable endeavour) to remit the proceeds of transfer(s) to the UK, either because of the laws or government action of the territory in question or because of the impossibility of obtaining foreign currency there.

The postponed sums are taken into account in the chargeable period in which (b) above ceases to apply. [*ICTA 1988, s 723*].

74.14   **Death** is *not* treated as giving rise to a transfer to the personal representatives. Where a transfer by the personal representatives to a legatee takes place in the interest period in which the death occurs, the transfer is disregarded for the purposes of the current provisions. [*ICTA 1988, ss 711(6), 721; FA 1996, s 158*].

74.15   **Trading stock: appropriations etc.** A transfer is deemed to be made under the new provisions where a person appropriates to trading stock securities previously held as investments, and vice versa. The transfer is 'with accrued interest' (see 74.7 above) if the person was entitled to receive any interest payable on the day of transfer or on the next interest payment day thereafter. [*ICTA 1988, ss 711(6), 722*].

74.16   **Conversions.** On a conversion of securities within *TCGA 1992, s 132*, the person entitled to them immediately before the conversion is treated as transferring them on the day of the conversion (if there is no actual transfer). The transfer is 'with accrued interest' (see 74.7 above) if the person was entitled to receive any interest payable on the day of conversion or on the next interest payment day thereafter. The 'interest period' (see 74.6 above) in which the conversion is made is treated as ending on the day on which it would have ended but for the conversion. [*ICTA 1988, ss 710(13), 711(6)*].

74.17   **Transfer of unrealised interest (bearer securities).** Provision is made to ensure that accrued interest which has already become payable before the settlement day (e.g. on bearer securities) does not escape the accrued income scheme. The transferor is treated as entitled to that interest and taxed accordingly while the transferee is not taxed when he actually receives the interest. The exceptions at 74.9 above apply to a charge so arising on the transferor and to the relief arising to the transferee. The capital gains tax calculation of the gain on the disposal by the transferor is adjusted to exclude the accrued interest from the consideration received and the transferee's base cost is similarly reduced by the amount of the relief obtained as above. Where necessary, the unrealised interest is converted into sterling at the London closing rate of exchange on the settlement day. Where the transfer of securities is a *Pt 5* transfer under *Proceeds of Crime Act 2002* (as in 9.2(xi) CAPITAL ALLOWANCES) and no compensating payment is made to the transferor, these provisions do not apply. [*ICTA 1988, s 716; TCGA 1992, s 119(4); Proceeds of Crime Act 2002, Sch 10 paras 4, 10*]. See also 74.19 below where there is a default in interest payments.

74.18   **Variable rate bonds.** Special rules apply to the transfer of securities unless either

(a)   they carry interest from issue to redemption at one, and only one, of the following rates:

(i)   a constant fixed rate; or

(ii)   a rate fixed in relation to a standard published base rate or the retail prices index (or foreign equivalent), or

(b)   they were deep discount securities (prior to their abolition from 6 April 1996) for which the rate of interest for each interest period did not exceed the yield to maturity.

Where an interest rate change may arise solely from provision for actions required to effect a 'euroconversion' of a security, i.e. a change from the currency of a State which has adopted the euro into euros, this does not of itself bring the security concerned within these provisions (see *SI 1998 No 3177, regs 3, 33*).

Where securities not within (a) or (b) above are transferred at any time between issue and redemption, then:

(1)   if they are transferred without accrued interest, they are treated as transferred with accrued interest;

(2)   the transferor is treated as entitled to a sum equal to such amount (if any) as is just and reasonable;

(3)   no relief is available to the transferee; and

(4)   the person entitled to the securities immediately before their redemption is treated as transferring them with accrued interest on the day of redemption, giving rise to a charge as in (2) and (3) above.

Where there is a deemed transfer as a result of (4) above, in relation to which the settlement day falls after the end of the only or last interest period in relation to the securities the period from the day following that interest period to the settlement day (inclusive) is treated as an interest period (even if it is longer than twelve months). [*ICTA 1988, s 717; FA 1996, s 134, Sch 20 para 35; FA 1998, Sch 27 Pt III(22)*].

74.19   **Interest in default.** Where there has been a failure to pay interest on the securities, the charge under the accrued income scheme on transfer is calculated by reference to the value of the right to receive the interest on the interest payment day in question rather than the full amount of the interest payable. The provisions regarding transfers of unrealised interest (see 74.17 above) similarly apply by reference to the value of the right to receive the interest (if less than the amount of the unrealised interest). If the transferee subsequently receives the unrealised interest, the assessment on the interest is reduced by the amount of the value of the right to receive the interest at the time of purchase (i.e. the relief given to him at that time). If he transfers the securities with the unrealised interest, the charge on him under the current provisions is restricted to any increase in the value of the right to receive the interest between purchase and re-sale. Special rules apply where unrealised interest is partially repaid and where part of a holding of securities is transferred. [*ICTA 1988, ss 718, 719; TCGA 1992, s 119(5)*]. For the application of these provisions in practice, see Revenue Inspector's Manual IM 4257.

74.20   **Charities** are excluded from the accrued income scheme if any interest actually received would be exempt under *ICTA 1988, s 505(1)(c)(d)*, but where securities cease to be subject to charitable trusts the trustees are treated for the purposes of the legislation as making a transfer at that time. Such a transfer is 'with accrued interest' (see 74.7 above) if the trustees were entitled to receive any interest payable on the day of transfer or on the next interest payment day thereafter. [*ICTA 1988, s 711(6), s 715(1)(d)(2)(3)*].

74.21   **Retirement schemes.** Transfers to or by pension funds are excluded from the accrued income scheme as regards the pension fund if any interest received would be exempt under *ICTA 1988, s 592(2)*. [*ICTA 1988, s 715(1)(k)(2)*].

74.22 **Sale and repurchase of securities.** On a sale and repurchase of securities the accrued income scheme provisions are disapplied to both transfers. A sale and repurchase of securities involves an agreement (or agreements entered into under the same arrangement) for securities to be sold and the transferor, or a person connected with him (within *ICTA 1988, s 839*) to buy them, or similar securities, back. The repurchase may be triggered by an obligation to purchase, or the exercise of an option (put or call) under the agreement or a related agreement. However, for agreements made after 8 April 2003, if the sale and repurchase rules are themselves disapplied because the agreements are not arm's length or the interim holder assumes the risks and benefits of ownership, then the accrued income scheme provisions will apply.

Securities are 'similar' for this purpose if they entitle the holder to the same rights against the same persons as to capital and interest, and to the same enforcement remedies, and where securities are converted from the currency of a State which has adopted the euro into euros (a *'euroconversion'*), the new securities are treated as 'similar' (see *SI 1998 No 3177, regs 3, 14*).

[*ICTA 1988, s 727A; FA 1995, s 79; FA 2003, Sch 38 paras 4, 15, 21(2)*].

The Treasury has broad powers to make regulations providing for the above provisions to apply with modifications (including exceptions and omissions) in relation to cases involving any arrangement for the sale and repurchase of securities where the obligation to repurchase is not performed, or the repurchase option not exercised, or where provision is made by or under any agreement:

(*a*) for different or additional securities to be treated as, or included with, securities which, for the purposes of the repurchase, are to represent securities transferred in pursuance of the original sale; or

(*b*) for any securities to be treated as not included with securities which, for repurchase purposes, are to represent securities transferred in pursuance of the original sale; or

(*c*) for the sale or repurchase price to be determined or varied wholly or partly by reference to fluctuations, in the period from the making of the agreement for the original sale, in the value of securities transferred in pursuance of that sale, or in the value of securities treated as representing those securities, or for any person to be required, where there are such fluctuations, to make any payment in the course of that period and before the repurchase price becomes due.

Regulations may also make such modifications in relation to cases where corresponding arrangements are made by an agreement, or by related agreements, in relation to securities which are to be redeemed in the period after their sale, those arrangements being such that the vendor (or a person connected with him), instead of being required to repurchase the securities or acquiring an option to do so, is granted rights in respect of the benefits that will accrue from their redemption.

[*ICTA 1988, s 737E; FA 1995, s 83(1); FA 2003, Sch 38 paras 8, 21(2)*].

74.23 **Gilt strips.** Where a person exchanges a gilt-edged security for strips of that security, that person is deemed to have transferred the security with accrued interest (unless the exchange is after the balance has been struck for a dividend on the security but before the day the dividend becomes payable), without any person being treated as the transferee within *ICTA 1988, s 713(2)(b)* (see 74.7 above), and without affecting the end of the interest period in which the exchange takes place. Similarly where strips are reconstituted by any person into the security from which they derived, the security is deemed to have been transferred to that person with accrued interest (unless the reconstitution is after the balance has been struck for a dividend on the security but before the day the dividend becomes payable) without any person being treated as the transferor, and the interest period in which the reconstitution takes place is deemed to have begun on the day specified for that purpose in the security. [*ICTA 1988, s 710(13A)(13B), s 722A; FA 1996, Sch 40 paras 3, 4, 6*].

74.24 **Stock lending.** The accrued income scheme provisions are specifically disapplied in relation to stock lending transactions disregarded for chargeable gains purposes under *TCGA 1992, s 263B(2)*. [*ICTA 1988, s 727; FA 1997, Sch 10 para 5(3), Sch 18 Pt VI(10)*].

74.25 **Interest etc. on debts between associated companies or to associates of banks.** Certain debts owed by non-UK resident companies (or certain third parties) to UK resident 'associated' companies (within *ICTA 1988, s 416*), or by any company to a UK resident company associated with a company carrying on a UK banking business, are classed as 'qualifying debts'. Where the debt on a 'security' (within 74.6 above) is a qualifying debt, it is treated as transferred for the purposes of the accrued income scheme on becoming or ceasing to be a qualifying debt, at the end of each accounting period, and on the provisions in question coming into force. [*FA 1993, ss 61–63, s 66; FA 1995, ss 88, 89; FA 1996, Sch 41 Pt V(3)*]. See Tolley's Corporation Tax under Profit Computations for the detailed provisions, and under Loan Relationships for the provisions substituted for later accounting periods.

74.26 **Insurance companies.** See Tolley's Corporation Tax under Loan Relationships.

74.27 **New issues.** Where

(*a*) securities of a particular kind are issued (being the original issue of securities of that kind),

(*b*) new securities of the same kind are issued subsequently, and after 18 March 1991,

(*c*) a sum (the 'extra return') is payable by the issuer in respect of the new securities, to reflect the fact that interest is accruing on the old securities and calculated accordingly, and

(*d*) the issue price of the new securities includes an element (separately identified or not) representing payment for the extra return,

then, for the purposes of the accrued income scheme,

(i) the new securities are treated as having been issued on the '*relevant day*' (being the last 'interest payment day' (see 74.6 above) prior to the actual day of issue, or, if there is no such day, the day on which the original securities were issued);

(ii) they are treated as transferred *to* the person to whom they are issued, but are not treated as transferred *by* any person; and

(iii) the transfer is treated as being 'with accrued interest' (see 74.7 above) and as made on the actual day of issue of the new securities, that day being treated as the settlement day (notwithstanding *ICTA 1988, s 712* — see 74.6 above).

If *ICTA 1988, s 717* (see 74.18 above) applies to the new securities, after applying (i) above, (ii) and (iii) above do not apply.

The 'accrued amount' (see 74.7 above) in respect of the transfer in (ii) above is the 'accrued proportion' (see 74.7 above) of the interest applicable for the interest period in which the settlement day falls. If, however, the new securities are issued under an arrangement whereby the 'extra return' (see (c) above) is accounted for separately to the issuer by the person to whom the securities are issued, the accrued amount is equal to the extra return so accounted for (or to its sterling equivalent calculated by reference to the London closing rate of exchange on the settlement day, in cases where interest on the new securities is payable in a foreign currency).

[*ICTA 1988, s 726A; FA 1991, Sch 12 paras 2, 5*].

74.28   **INTERACTION WITH OTHER TAXES**

Corporation tax. The accrued income scheme provisions are disapplied for the purposes of corporation tax for accounting periods ending after 31 March 1996, except as respects transfers taking place on or before that date, and subject to transitional provisions. [*ICTA 1988, s 710(1A); FA 1996, Sch 14 para 36, Sch 15 para 18*]. For the corporation tax loan relationships regime introduced for accounting periods ending after 31 March 1996, including (where still relevant) the transitional provisions, see Tolley's Corporation Tax under Loan Relationships.

Capital gains tax. Adjustments are necessary to capital gains tax computations where the accrued income scheme applies. The consideration for the disposal is adjusted to exclude or add the accrued or rebate amounts as appropriate (see 74.7 above) and the sums allowed as a deduction to the transferee on a future disposal are correspondingly adjusted. [*TCGA 1992, s 119(1)–(3)*]. Where there is a CGT disposal which is not a transfer (see 74.6 above) for accrued income scheme purposes but which would be within the scheme if it were such a transfer, a transfer is deemed to be made on the day of the disposal and the capital gains tax consideration and sums deductible are adjusted accordingly as above. [*TCGA 1992, s 119(6)–(9)*]. Where there is a conversion of securities within *TCGA 1992, s 132* or an exchange not involving a disposal within *TCGA 1992, Pt IV, Ch II* (reorganisations etc.) a capital gains tax adjustment is made to allow for the effect of the accrued income scheme. Any accrued amount which the transferor is treated as receiving (see 74.7 above) is first treated as reducing any consideration receivable on the conversion etc., and then as consideration given for the conversion etc., while any rebate amount is treated as consideration received for the conversion etc. [*TCGA 1992, s 119(10)(11)*].

74.29   **Double taxation relief.** Where a person is treated as receiving accrued income taxable under Schedule D, Case VI (see 74.8 above) and any interest actually received would be liable both to UK tax under Schedule D, Case IV or V (foreign securities) and to foreign tax, he is allowed credit against UK tax on accrued income for foreign tax at the rate at which tax would be payable on interest on the securities. The credit is treated as if it were allowed under *ICTA 1988, s 790(4)*. See 24.4 DOUBLE TAX RELIEF.

Where a person is entitled to double tax relief under *ICTA 1988, ss 788, 790(4)* against UK tax on interest which is treated as reduced under the accrued income scheme (see 74.8 above), the credit is reduced to the same proportion that the interest actually taxable bears to the interest which would have been taxable without the reduction. There is a similar reduction where relief is allowed by way of deduction of foreign tax from interest received under *ICTA 1988, s 811(1)*. The proportionate reduction in the credit does not apply if the person entitled to it is an individual unless the interest arises from securities to which he became or ceased to be entitled during the interest period.

[*ICTA 1988, s 807*].

Section 807 does not apply for corporation tax purposes for accounting periods ending after 31 March 1996 [*ICTA 1988, s 807(6); FA 1996, Sch 14 para 45*], but an equivalent corporation tax relief is provided for such periods by *ICTA 1988, s 807A* introduced by *FA 1996, Sch 14 para 46*.

74.30   **Anti-avoidance.** Several anti-avoidance measures are affected by this legislation.

Transfer of assets abroad. Where a non-UK resident or non-UK domiciled person would have been treated as receiving income under the accrued income scheme (see 74.8 above) if he had been so resident or domiciled, the accrued income which he would have been treated as receiving is treated as income becoming payable to him for the purposes of *ICTA 1988, ss 739–741* (transfer of assets abroad). A corresponding reduction in interest payable for these purposes is made where it would have been made under the accrued income scheme. See 3.7 ANTI-AVOIDANCE. [*ICTA 1988, s 742(4)–(7)*].

Other matters. Securities within the accrued income scheme are excluded from *ICTA 1988, s 734* (see 3.5 ANTI-AVOIDANCE). [*ICTA 1988, s 731(9)*].

ICTA 1988, Sch 23A (manufactured dividends and interest — see 3.6 ANTI-AVOIDANCE) takes precedence over the accrued income scheme, which does not apply to the extent that the transfer is covered by those provisions [*ICTA 1988, s 715(6)(7); FA 1994, s 123(1)(6); FA 1997, Sch 18 Pt VI(10)*].

74.31   **POWER TO REQUIRE INFORMATION**

Inspectors have power by notice in writing to require Stock Exchange members and other persons acting as UK agents or brokers to provide information about transactions in securities effected by them. Information may not be required about transactions effected more than three years before service of the inspector's notice.

Market makers are excluded from these information requirements. The Board has powers, by regulation by statutory instrument, to broaden the scope of information requirements to include other recognised investment exchanges.

Similarly, any person in whose name securities are registered can be required to state who is the beneficial owner.

The penalty provisions of *TMA 1970, s 98* (failure to comply with notices etc.) apply. See 57.9 PENALTIES.

[*ICTA 1988, s 728*].

75 Schedule E—Employment Income

Cross-references. See 18 COMPENSATION FOR LOSS OF EMPLOYMENT (AND DAMAGES); 24 DOUBLE TAX RELIEF; 65 RESIDENCE, ORDINARY RESIDENCE AND DOMICILE for definitions of those terms; 55 PAY AS YOU EARN; 56 PAYMENT OF TAX; 58 PENSION INCOME; 60 PERSONAL PENSION SCHEMES; 61 PERSONAL SERVICE COMPANIES ETC.; 64 REMITTANCE BASIS; 66 RETIREMENT ANNUITIES; 67 RETIREMENT SCHEMES; 82 SHARE-RELATED EMPLOYMENT INCOME AND EXEMPTIONS; 83 SOCIAL SECURITY for taxation of benefits.

Simon's Direct Tax Service Part E4.

Other sources. See Tolley's Employment Tax Planning and Tolley's Tax Compliance.

The headings in this chapter are as follows.

75.1 INTRODUCTION

Under the Tax Law Rewrite programme, the law relating to income from employment, previously within Schedule E, was rewritten as *Pts 2 to 8* of the *Income Tax (Earnings and Pensions) Act 2003* ('*ITEPA 2003*'), which has effect for income tax purposes for 2003/04 and subsequent years. For corporation tax purposes it has effect for accounting periods ending after 5 April 2003, subject to special rules for accounting periods straddling that date (see Tolley's Corporation Tax under Profit Computations). [*ITEPA 2003, s 723, Sch 7 paras 90–92*].

Pensions and social security benefits, which were previously within Schedule E, are now dealt with in, respectively, *Part 9* and *Part 10* of the new *Act* (see 58 PENSION INCOME, 83 SOCIAL SECURITY).

Before the rewriting, Schedule E was divided into three Cases.

Case I applied to employees *resident and ordinarily resident* in the UK wherever the duties were performed (but with the exclusion of those receiving 'foreign emoluments' in respect of duties performed wholly abroad).

Case II applied to employees *not resident (or if resident, not ordinarily resident)* in the UK in respect of duties performed in the UK, subject to a deduction from 'foreign emoluments'.

Case III applied to employees *resident (whether ordinarily resident or not)* in the UK so far as the emoluments did not fall within Case I or II.

Cases I and II operated on the 'receipts basis', Case III on the remittance basis (see 75.5, 75.6 below).

[*ICTA 1988, ss 19(1), 192–195*].

See now 75.3, 75.4 below.

Although Schedule E and the division into three Cases, and the concept of 'foreign emoluments', are abolished after 5 April 2003, the effect of the Schedule E provisions is generally unchanged. The opportunity has, however, been taken to incorporate into the legislation applicable Revenue concessions and practices and certain well-established aspects of case law, and to restructure the legislation where the law as it is applied in practice can thereby be more clearly stated.

One particular area where a new approach has been adopted without changing the impact of the legislation is the limitation on deductions from earnings. Previously most deductions were required to be for expenditure met 'out of the emoluments' from the employment. This is replaced by a general provision that a deduction (or aggregate deductions) may not exceed the earnings from which it is (or they are) deductible (see *ITEPA 2003, s 329*). The general rules for deductions are now brought together in *ITEPA 2003, ss 327–332*.

Where significant changes *have* been made, these are noted, with appropriate references. In the remainder of this chapter at 75.2 *et seq.* below, the text follows the approach adopted in the rewritten provisions. Where the old provisions are closely mirrored, the earlier statutory references, practice statements etc. are cited. Otherwise, more general references are provided to the earlier provisions where relevant. The Explanatory Notes accompanying the precursor Bill set out in detail all the changes which have been made, and their likely impact (if any).

For the detailed pre-rewriting provisions, reference should be made to Tolley's Income Tax 2002/03 or earlier edition.

General operation of tax charge

'Employment' is not exhaustively defined, but includes any employment under a contract of service or apprenticeship or in the service of the Crown. [*ITEPA 2003, s 4*]. Except as otherwise provided, the provisions apply equally to any 'office', which in particular includes any position which has an existence independent of the person holding it and may be filled by successive holders (and see Revenue Employment Status Manual ESM 2502 *et seq.*). [*ITEPA 2003, s 5*].

The charge to tax on employment income is divided into a charge on 'general earnings' (see 75.10 below) and a charge on '*specific employment income*', i.e. amounts which count as employment income (in particular payments to and benefits from pension schemes, see 67 RETIREMENT SCHEMES; payments and benefits on termination of employments etc., see 18 COMPENSATION FOR LOSS OF EMPLOYMENT (AND DAMAGES); and share-related income, see 82 SHARE-RELATED EMPLOYMENT INCOME AND EXEMPTIONS). The latter charge is not dependent on the residence, ordinary residence or domicile of the employee, so that the provisions described in 75.2–75.6 below relate only to the charge on general earnings. [*ITEPA 2003, ss 6, 7*].

The amount of *general earnings* chargeable for a particular year from an employment is the net taxable earnings for the year from the employment. The taxable earnings are determined as described in 75.2–75.6 below.

The amount of *specific employment income* chargeable for a particular year from an employment is the net taxable specific income from the employment. The taxable specific income is the full amount which counts as employment income for that year under the relevant provision.

The deductions allowed in arriving at *net taxable earnings* or *net taxable specific income* from an employment are as described in 75.11 below, but such deductions may not reduce the taxable amount from any source below nil. If there is more than one kind of specific employment income from an employment in a year, a separate calculation is required for each.

[*ITEPA 2003, ss 9–12*].

75.2　Schedule E—Employment Income

Person liable for tax. On *general earnings*, the person liable to tax thereon is the person to whose employment the earnings relate. If the tax is on such earnings received, or remitted to the UK, after the death of that person, the liability falls on the personal representatives, and is payable out of the estate. On *specific employment income*, the person liable to tax thereon is the person in relation to whom the income is to count as employment income under the provision in question. [*ITEPA 2003, s 13*]. See, however, Revenue Concession A37, referred to at 75.2(v) below.

75.2　**GENERAL EARNINGS FROM EMPLOYMENT — BASIS OF ASSESSMENT**

The basis on which taxable general earnings for a tax year are determined depend on whether the employee is, in that year, (*a*) resident, ordinarily resident and domiciled in the UK, or (*b*) either resident, ordinarily resident or domiciled outside the UK (for which see 65 RESIDENCE, ORDINARY RESIDENCE AND DOMICILE). Subject to any specific provision requiring earnings to be treated as 'for' a particular tax year, general earnings are earned 'for' a period if they are earned in, or in respect of, the period. If the period is or is within a tax year, they are earned for that year: if the period extends over two or more tax years, they are apportioned between those years on a just and reasonable basis. Earnings (other than benefits in kind, see 75.16 below) which would accordingly be treated as for a tax year in which the employee does not hold the employment are instead treated as for the first year in which the employment is held (if later) or the last such year (if earlier)(but not if any of the years concerned is earlier than 1989/90). [*ITEPA 2003, ss 14, 16, 17, 20, 29, 30, Sch 7 para 8(4); ICTA 1988, s 19(1)*].

Disputes on ordinary residence or domicile in relation to employment income are referred to, and decided by, the Board of Inland Revenue, subject to appeal (by written notice within three months of the Board's decision) to the Special Commissioners. [*ITEPA 2003, ss 42, 43, Sch 7 para 12; ICTA 1988, s 207*].

General matters

(i)　*Leave periods etc.* If a person ordinarily performs the whole or part of the duties of an employment in the UK, general earnings for periods of absence from the employment are treated as for duties performed in the UK except insofar as, but for that absence, they would have been for duties performed outside the UK. [*ITEPA 2003, s 38; ICTA 1988, s 132(1)*]. An airline pilot, the great majority of whose work was performed outside the UK, could not rely on this provision to treat his days of absence from work as days of absence from the UK in the same proportion as his working days (*Leonard v Blanchard CA 1993, 65 TC 589*).

(ii)　*Incidental duties in the UK.* If an employment is substantially one where the duties for a year fall to be performed outside the UK, any duties incidental thereto performed in the UK are treated as if performed abroad. [*ITEPA 2003, s 39; ICTA 1988, s 132(2)(3)*]. As to whether duties 'incidental' to foreign duties see *Robson v Dixon Ch D 1972, 48 TC 527* (airline pilot employed abroad but occasionally landing in UK where family home maintained, held UK duties more than incidental). The Revenue will normally disregard a single take-off and landing on *de minimis* grounds. (Revenue Pamphlet IR 131, A10). See also Revenue Pamphlet IR 20, paras 5.7, 5.8. Different rules apply in relation to the 100% foreign earnings deduction available to seafarers (see 75.7 below).

(iii)　*Duties deemed to be performed in the UK.* As regards certain overseas *employments under the Crown*, see 75.4 below.

Duties of *seafarers and aircraft crew* are treated as performed in the UK if (i) the voyage does not extend to a port outside the UK or (ii) the person concerned is UK-resident and either (*a*) the voyage or flight begins or ends in the UK or (*b*) it is a part, beginning or ending in the UK, of a voyage or flight which does not begin or end in the UK. As regards seafarers' duties on board ship, this does *not* apply for the purposes of *ITEPA 2003, s 24(1)(b)* (see 75.4 below) in determining whether the duties of an 'associated employment' are performed wholly outside the UK; for this purpose, duties performed on a ship during a voyage beginning or ending outside the UK (other than any part of it beginning and ending there), or on a part beginning or ending outside the UK of any other voyage, are treated as performed outside the UK. The UK includes areas designated under *Continental Shelf Act 1964, s 1(7)* for this purpose. A 'ship' does not include an offshore installation (within *ICTA 1988, s 837C*). [*ITEPA 2003, s 40; ICTA 1988, s 132(4), Sch 12 para 5; FA 1998, s 63(4)(b); FA 2004, Sch 27 paras 12, 16*]. See 75.7 below for the meaning of 'seafarer'.

(iv) *United Kingdom* for these purposes includes the UK sector of the continental shelf (under *Continental Shelf Act 1964, s 1(7)* as regards duties performed there in connection with exploration or exploitation activities. [*ITEPA 2003, s 41; ICTA 1988, s 830*].

(v) *Directors' fees received by other companies.* Where a company has the right to appoint a director to the board of another company and the director is required to hand over to the first company any fees or other earnings received from the second company and does so, and the first company agrees to accept liability to corporation tax on the fees etc., the director is not charged to tax on thereon. Where the first company is not chargeable to corporation tax but to income tax (e.g. a non-resident company not trading through a branch or agency/permanent establishment in the UK) and agrees to accept liability, tax is deducted at the basic rate from the fees etc. This practice is extended to the case where the first company has no formal right to appoint the director to the board but the director is required to, and does, hand over his fees etc., provided the first company is (*a*) chargeable to corporation tax on its income and (*b*) not a company over which the director has control. '*Control*' for this purpose has the meaning given by *ICTA 1988, s 840* (see 19.8 CONNECTED PERSONS), but in determining whether the director has control of the company the rights and powers of his spouse, his children and their spouses and his parents, will also be taken into account. (Revenue Pamphlet IR 1, A37). For directors' fees received by professional partnerships, see 75.27 below.

(vi) *Changes in practice.* Where income dealt with under PAYE (55) was received more than twelve months before the beginning of the year *in* which the assessment on the income is made, that assessment, if made after the period of twelve months following the year *for* which it is made, is to accord with the practice generally prevailing at the end of that period. [*ITEPA 2003, s 709; ICTA 1988, s 206*]. This cannot, however, displace an unqualified statutory exemption relating to the income in question (*Walters v Tickner CA 1993, 66 TC 174*).

(vii) *Divers.* See 71.21 SCHEDULE D, CASES I AND II for treatment of earnings of certain divers etc. under Schedule D, Case I.

Simon's Direct Tax Service. See E4.101 *et seq.*

As regards remuneration planning generally, see Tolley's Employment Tax Planning.

75.3   **Employee resident, ordinarily resident and domiciled in the UK**

Where general earnings are for a tax year in which the employee is resident, ordinarily resident and domiciled in the UK, the full amount of such earnings 'received' in a tax year (see 75.5 below) is taxable earnings in that year, whether they are for that or another year and whether or not the employment is held when the earnings are received. Before 6 April

75.4 Schedule E—Employment Income

2003, such earnings were within Schedule E, Case I (see 75.1 above). [*ITEPA 2003, s 15; ICTA 1988, s 19(1)*].

75.4 **Employee resident, ordinarily resident or domiciled outside the UK**

Where the employee is resident, ordinarily resident or domiciled outside the UK for a tax year, determination of taxable general earnings depends upon which of the following applies. [*ITEPA 2003, s 20*].

Earnings for a year when the employee is resident and ordinarily resident, but not domiciled, in the UK

The determination depends on whether the earnings are 'chargeable overseas earnings' for the year or not.

If they are not, the full amount of such earnings 'received' (see 75.5 below) in a tax year is taxable earnings in that year, whether they are for that or another year and whether or not the employment is held when the earnings are received.

If they are 'chargeable overseas earnings', the full amount of such earnings 'remitted' to the UK (see 75.6 below) in a tax year is taxable earnings in that year, whether they are for that or another year and whether or not the employment is held when the earnings are remitted. See also below as regards relief for certain delayed remittances.

'*Chargeable overseas earnings*' are earnings from an employment with a 'foreign employer', the duties of which are performed wholly outside the UK. They are reduced by any deductions which would be allowed if they were taxable earnings. Where the duties of any 'associated' employment are not performed wholly outside the UK, then the chargeable overseas earnings are limited to a reasonable proportion of the aggregate earnings (after allowable deductions) from all the employments, having regard to the nature of and the time devoted to duties performed outside and in the UK and to all other relevant considerations. Any amount deducted by virtue of this limitation falls back into general earnings. Employments are '*associated*' if they are with the same employer, or the employers are under common control or one controls the other, control being as in *ICTA 1988, s 416* (for companies) and *s 840* (for individuals and partnerships, see 19.8 CONNECTED PERSONS).

A '*foreign employer*' is one resident outside, and not resident within, the UK (and, in relation to a UK-resident employee, not resident in the Republic of Ireland).

Before 6 April 2003, such earnings were within Schedule E, Case I or, in the case of chargeable overseas earnings, Case III (see 75.1 above). Chargeable overseas earnings were previously one type of 'foreign emoluments' (the other type being where the duties of the employment were not performed wholly outside the UK, for which see 75.9 below). Certain deductions did *not* reduce the amount of the foreign emoluments, which could result in a higher amount chargeable under Case III.

[*ITEPA 2003, ss 21–24, 721(1); ICTA 1988, ss 19(1), 192*].

Earnings for a year when the employee is resident, but not ordinarily resident, in the UK

The determination depends on whether the earnings are UK-based or foreign earnings. The former applies if they are either in respect of duties performed in the UK or from overseas Crown employment subject to UK tax (for which see further below). The latter applies otherwise.

If they are UK-based earnings, the full amount of such earnings 'received' (see 75.5 above) in a tax year is taxable earnings in that year, whether they are for that or another year and whether or not the employment is held when the earnings are received.

If they are foreign earnings, the full amount of such earnings 'remitted' to the UK (see 75.6 below) in a tax year is taxable earnings in that year, whether they are for that or another year

Schedule E—Employment Income 75.5

and whether or not the employment is held when the earnings are remitted. See also below as regards relief for certain delayed remittances.

General earnings are *'from overseas Crown employment subject to UK tax'* if they are from employment of a public nature under the Crown and payable out of UK or NI public revenue (which includes civil servants (*Graham v White Ch D 1971, 48 TC 163* and *Caldicott v Varty Ch D 1976, 51 TC 403*) and HM Forces), unless excluded by an order made by the Board of Inland Revenue. (The exclusion of certain categories of employee by order of the Board applies from 6 April 2003, and replaces the concession in Revenue Pamphlet IR 1, A25, under which no tax was charged in the case of locally engaged unestablished staff working abroad who are not UK resident and for whose grade the maximum pay is less that that of an executive officer in the UK Civil Service in Inner London. The statutory exclusion should continue to operate at least as widely as the previous concession.) See also 75.30 below and 28.7, 28.32 EXEMPT INCOME.

A Revenue Statement of Practice covers the *apportionment of earnings* where a person resident but not ordinarily resident in the UK performs duties of a single employment both inside and outside the UK. In such cases, the earnings will be taxable in full under *ITEPA 2003, s 25* in respect of the UK duties, but under *ITEPA 2003, s 26* on amounts remitted to the UK in respect of the non-UK duties. Apportionment of the earnings between UK and non-UK duties is a question of fact, but time apportionment based on working days inside and outside the UK will normally be applied, unless clearly inappropriate. Where part of the earnings are paid in the UK, the Revenue practice is to accept that, where a reasonable apportionment has been made between earnings chargeable under *section 25* and *section 26*, liability arises under *section 26* only on any excess of the aggregate of earnings paid and benefits received in the UK and earnings remitted to the UK over the amount chargeable under *section 25*. Where none of the earnings are paid in the UK, remittances are generally taken in the first instance as out of income liable under *section 25*. (Revenue Pamphlet IR 131, SP 5/84). See also Revenue Tax Bulletin February 2003 pp 996–998 for examples of how apportionment is applied in practice.

As regards *tax equalisation* payments to non-UK ordinarily resident employees, for 1997/98 and subsequent years these are treated as being chargeable wholly under Case II. (Revenue Tax Bulletin February 1997 pp 386, 387). They are treated as being wholly in respect of the UK duties to which they relate (i.e. they are not apportioned between UK and non-UK duties) (*Perro v Mansworth (Sp C 286), [2001] SSCD 179*). For an article on the treatment of tax equalisation payments following the decision in that case, see Revenue Tax Bulletin June 2002, pp 931–934. For self-assessment returns in cases involving tax equalisation, see Revenue Tax Bulletin October 1997 pp 467, 468 and June 1998 p 551. It is presumed that a similar approach will be adopted in relation to UK-based and foreign earnings after 5 April 2003.

[*ITEPA 2003, ss 25, 26, 28; ICTA 1988, ss 19(1), 132(4)*].

Before 6 April 2003, such earnings were within Schedule E, Case II or, if foreign earnings, Case III (see 75.1 above).

UK-based earnings (see above) for a year when the employee is not resident in the UK

The full amount of such earnings 'received' (see 75.5 below) in a tax year is taxable earnings in that year, whether they are for that or another year and whether or not the employment is held when the earnings are received. Before 6 April 2003, such earnings were within Schedule E, Case II (see 75.1 above). [*ITEPA 2003, s 27; ICTA 1988, s 19(1)*].

75.5 **Receipts basis.** General earnings consisting of money (including money payments chargeable under the benefits code, see 75.14 below) are *'received'* at the earliest of the following times:

75.6 Schedule E—Employment Income

    (*a*)   the time when payment is actually made of, or on account of, the earnings;

    (*b*)   the time when a person becomes entitled to such payment; and

    (*c*)   where the person concerned is a 'director' of a company at any point in the tax year in which the time falls and the earnings are from employment with that company (whether or not as director), the earliest of:

        (i)   the time when sums on account of earnings are credited in the company's accounts or records (regardless of any restriction on the right to draw those sums);

        (ii)   the time when a period of account ends and the amount of earnings for that period has already been determined; and

        (iii)   the time when the amount of earnings for a period of account is determined and that period has already ended.

A '*director*' is defined as being any of the following:

    (1)   a member of a board of directors, or similar body, which manages the company;

    (2)   a single director, or similar person, who manages the company;

    (3)   a member of the company, in cases where the company is managed by its members;

    (4)   any person in accordance with whose directions or instructions, given other than in a professional capacity, the directors, as defined in (1)–(3) above, are accustomed to act.

Non-money general earnings (e.g. benefits in kind) are generally treated as received in the tax year for which they are treated as earnings. Before 6 April 2003, this applied also to money payments within the benefits code (see 75.14 below).

[*ITEPA 2003, ss 18, 19, 31, 32; ICTA 1988, s 202B*].

75.6   **Remittances.** Earnings are '*remitted to the UK*' at the time when they are paid, used or enjoyed in the UK, or transmitted or brought to the UK in any manner or form. There are special provisions treating as a remittance the use of earnings of employees not ordinarily resident in the UK to satisfy UK-linked debt. These are similar to the general 'constructive remittances' provisions of *ICTA 1988, s 65(6)–(9)* (see 64.4 REMITTANCE BASIS). [*ITEPA 2003, ss 33, 34; ICTA 1988, s 132(5)*]. Certain pre-1989/90 earnings remitted in 2003/04 or later are excluded. [*ITEPA 2003, Sch 7 para 8(3)*].

Relief for delayed remittances. Relief is available in respect of general earnings taxable on the remittance basis in a tax year (under *ITEPA 2003, s 22(2)* or *s 26(2)*, see above) which were received outside the UK before that year but which were not transferred to the UK until that year and could not be transferred to the UK before that year because of the laws of the country or territory in which they were received, the executive action of its government or the impossibility of obtaining non-local currency which could be transferred to the UK. A claim may be made for remittances to be taxable instead in an earlier tax year or years. This is normally the year(s) in which the earnings were received outside the UK. An irrevocable election may, however, be made as part of the claim for the earnings to be allocated to certain years (before that of receipt in the UK) for which there were '*blocked earnings*' from the employment, i.e. earnings which would have been taxable had they been remitted to the UK in that year but which could not be transferred to the UK in that year for the reasons referred to above. The amount which may be allocated to a particular tax year by election is restricted to the excess of the blocked earnings for that year over the amount of delayed remittances previously treated as taxable in that year. (Before 6 April 2003 no such election was available, but the Revenue practice was to allow allocation on a reasonable basis to similar effect.) Claims for relief on delayed remittances must be made within five years after 31 January following the tax year of remittance to the UK. Where appropriate, these provisions apply to the personal representative of the taxpayer as they would have to the taxpayer. [*ITEPA 2003, ss 35–37; ICTA 1988, s 585*]. Special provision is made where any of the years concerned is before 2003/04, to ensure that the appropriate legislation applies. [*ITEPA 2003, Sch 7 paras 9–11*].

Allowable deductions. Expenses which would be allowable (see 75.11 below) against earnings taxed on the receipts basis are generally allowable against earnings taxed on the remittance basis. No deduction is, however, allowable for an amount paid in respect of the duties of an employment to which earnings taxed other than on the remittance basis relate. Capital allowances are not available for expenditure on plant and machinery (see 9.24(ii) CAPITAL ALLOWANCES). [*ITEPA 2003, ss 353, 354, Sch 7 para 39; ICTA 1988, s 198(2)(3); CAA 2001, s 20*].

75.7   **FOREIGN EARNINGS DEDUCTION**

Where the duties of a 'seafarer' resident and ordinarily resident in the UK are performed wholly or partly outside the UK, a deduction may be allowed from taxable earnings (other than chargeable overseas earnings) within 75.3 or 75.4 above. Employment as a '*seafarer*' for this purpose means an employment (other than certain employments under the Crown) consisting of the performance of duties on a ship (disregarding incidental duties elsewhere). For this purpose, a 'ship' does not include an offshore installation (within *ICTA 1988, s 837C*).

Duties performed on a ship during a voyage beginning or ending outside the UK (other than any part of it beginning and ending there), or on a part beginning or ending outside the UK of any other voyage, are treated as performed outside the UK for these purposes. Overseas duties merely incidental to a UK employment are treated as performed in the UK, as are duties on a voyage not extending to a port outside the UK.

Where such duties are performed in the course of an 'eligible period' of 365 days or more (which can include days outside the tax year concerned), a deduction is made of 100% of the earnings for those duties attributable to that period (i.e. they are completely relieved from tax). Earnings for a tax year for this purpose are as reduced by capital allowances and all allowable deductions (including mileage allowance relief (see 75.46 below) and certain superannuation contributions). An '*eligible period*' consists either (*a*) entirely of consecutive days of absence from the UK or (*b*) of days of absence from the UK *plus* any earlier eligible period *plus* an intervening period in the UK not exceeding 183 days, provided that the total number of days in the UK in the intervening period and in the earlier eligible period is not more than one-half of the total number of days in the new eligible period. Successive intervening periods and periods of absence may continue to be eligible as long as these conditions are met in relation to each new period of absence.

A day of absence from the UK requires absence from the UK at the end of the day.

A period spent in the UK during a contract of employment but not followed by a period abroad may not be included in the eligible period (*Robins v Durkin Ch D 1988, 60 TC 700*).

The seafarer must have been resident and ordinarily resident in the UK for tax purposes throughout the eligible period (for which see *Carstairs v Sykes Ch D 2000, 73 TC 225*). It may therefore be more favourable for a taxpayer departing from or returning to the UK to be treated, in strict accordance with the statute, as UK resident throughout the year of assessment of departure or return, rather than only being so treated for the part of that year falling before the departure or after the return under Revenue Extra-statutory Concession

A11 (see 65.5 RESIDENCE, ORDINARY RESIDENCE AND DOMICILE). Liabilities on earnings from employment are normally calculated on the basis that the concession applies unless the application of the statutory basis is requested. (Revenue Tax Bulletin November 1992 p 40).

Leave periods. Earnings for duties attributable to an eligible period include earnings from that employment for a period of leave immediately following that period (and so qualify for the 100% deduction) to the extent that they are earnings for the tax year in which the eligible period ends.

Associated employments. Where the duties of the employment or any 'associated employment' (see 75.4 above) are not performed wholly outside the UK, the earnings relievable as above may not exceed a reasonable proportion of the total earnings from all such employments, having regard to the nature of, and time devoted to, duties performed outside and in the UK and to all other relevant considerations.

For earnings attributable to qualifying periods beginning *before 17 March 1998* and received on or before that date, a similar relief was available to all employees, but with a more restrictive definition of 'qualifying period'.

[*ITEPA 2003, ss 378–385; ICTA 1988, s 192A, Sch 12; FA 1998, s 63; FA 2004, Sch 27 paras 14, 16*].

75.8 **OVERSEAS DUTIES — TRAVEL ETC. EXPENSES**

For travelling expenses generally, see 75.46 below. For certain EU travel expenses of MPs etc., see 28.19 EXEMPT INCOME.

Where duties of an employment by an employee resident and ordinarily resident in the UK are performed abroad, the following deductions may be made from taxable earnings (if not 'chargeable overseas earnings', see 75.4 above). In each case, apportionment applies where expenses are only partly attributable to the purpose in question.

Where duties performed wholly outside the UK

(*a*) Travelling expenses incurred by the employee from any place in the UK to take up the overseas employment and to return on its termination.

(*b*) Board and lodging expenses outside the UK provided or reimbursed by the employer to enable the employee to perform the duties of the overseas employment.

Incidental duties performed in the UK are for these purposes treated as performed outside the UK.

[*ITEPA 2003, ss 341, 376; ICTA 1988, s 193(2)–(4)*].

Where duties are performed partly outside the UK

Travel facilities, provided or reimbursed to the employee (so far as included in the taxable earnings), between any place in the UK and the place of performance outside the UK of any of the duties of an employment, either:

(i) for the employee, provided that the duties concerned can only be performed outside the UK, and that either the outward and return journeys are wholly exclusively for the purpose of performing those duties or returning after performing them, or the absence from the UK is wholly and exclusively for the purpose of performing those duties and the journeys are from the place of employment of the duties to the UK and return; or

(ii) where there is absence from the UK for a continuous period of 60 days or more, for the spouse and any children under 18 (at beginning of outward journey) accompanying the employee at the beginning of the period of absence or visiting him during that period, including the return journey, but with a limit of two outward and return journeys per person in any year of assessment.

For these purposes, duties performed on a ship on a voyage extending to a port outside the UK are not treated under *ITEPA 2003, s 40(2)* (see 75.2(iii) above) as performed in the UK, and the requirements as to place of performance of duties are correspondingly modified.

[*ITEPA 2003, s 370–372; ICTA 1988, s 194*].

More than one employment

Where two or more employments are held and at least one of them is performed wholly or partly outside the UK, and travelling expenses are incurred by the employee in travelling from one place where duties of one employment were performed to another place to perform duties of another, and either or both places are outside the UK, the expenses are deductible from the taxable earnings from the second employment.

[*ITEPA 2003, s 342; ICTA 1988, s 193(5)(6)*].

For travel on leave by HM Forces, see 75.30 below.

Simon's Direct Tax Service. See E4.709.

75.9   **EMPLOYEES OF NON-UK DOMICILE — TRAVEL COSTS ETC.**

A deduction may be allowed from taxable earnings for duties performed in the UK for the cost of certain travel facilities provided or reimbursed to a non-UK domiciled employee (so far as included in taxable earnings) for journeys ending on the date of arrival in the UK to perform the duties of the employment, or within five years after that date. This applies to facilities provided

(*a*)   for any journey between the employee's usual place of abode (i.e. the country outside the UK where he normally lives) and any place in the UK in order to perform, or after performing, any duties of the employment, and

(*b*)   where the employee is in the UK for the purpose of performing the duties of any such employment for a continuous period of 60 days or more, for any outward and return journey by his spouse or child (under 18 at the beginning of the journey to the UK) between his usual place of abode and the place where any of those duties are performed in the UK, either to accompany him at the beginning of the period or to visit him during it (but limited to two outward and return journeys by any person in a year of assessment).

No deduction is, however, available unless, on a date on which he arrives in the UK to perform the duties, either

(i)   he was not resident in the UK in either of the two tax years immediately preceding that in which that date falls, or

(ii)   he was not in the UK for any purpose at any time in the two years ending immediately before that date,

and if condition (i) is satisfied on more than one date in a year of assessment, relief is given by reference to the first such date only.

As regards the 60-day requirement under (*b*) above, since 14 December 2001 the Revenue have accepted that the 60-day requirement is satisfied where at least two-thirds of working days are spent in the UK over a period of 60 days or more, at both the start and end of which the employee is in the UK for the purpose of performing the duties of the employment. This will apply to any self-assessment made on or after 14 December 2001

75.10 Schedule E—Employment Income

and to any self-assessment that can be amended on or after that date within the usual time limits. (Revenue Tax Bulletin December 2001 pp 900, 901 and Revenue Employment Income Manual EIM 35050, 35055). It had previously been accepted by the Revenue that an occasional day's absence abroad on business could be ignored.

[*ITEPA 2003, ss 373–375, Sch 7 para 40; ICTA 1988, s 195*].

Foreign employer. Certain payments made by a non-UK domiciliary out of earnings from an employment with a 'foreign employer' (see 75.4 above) which do not reduce the employee's liability to UK income tax, but which are made 'in circumstances corresponding to those in which it would do so', may be allowed as a deduction from those earnings. [*ITEPA 2003, s 355; ICTA 1988, s 192(3)*]. See Revenue Employment Income Manual EIM 32661 *et seq.*

Simon's Direct Tax Service. See E4.709.

Assessable income, allowable deductions etc.

The section headings in the remainder of this chapter are as follows.

See also cross-references at the head of this chapter.

For treatment of particular occupations, see Revenue Employment Income Manual EIM 50000 *et seq.* See generally Tolley's Employment Tax Planning.

75.10 GENERAL EARNINGS

The income taxable as '*general earnings*' from employment (see 75.1, 75.2 above) consists of '*earnings*', i.e. any salary, wages or fee, any gratuity or other incidental benefit of any kind obtained by an employee consisting of money or 'money's worth', and anything else constituting an emolument of the employment, together with anything treated under any statutory provision as earnings (e.g. benefits, see 75.12 below). '*Money's worth*' means something of direct monetary value to the employee or capable of being converted into money or something of such value. [*ITEPA 2003, ss 7(3)(5), 62*].

Before 6 April 2003, tax was chargeable on employment income (as well as certain other related income) under Schedule E on the emoluments of offices and employments [*ICTA 1988, s 19*], including 'all salaries, fees, wages, perquisites and profits whatsoever'. [*ICTA 1988, s 131(1)*]. The new description of the charge does not entail any change in the scope of the charge on employment income, although the well-established case law concept of 'money's worth' being assessable is made statutory (as referred to above). For an early and important statement of the 'money's worth' concept, see *Tennant v Smith HL 1892, 3 TC 158*. The case law referred to below accordingly continues to be of application (although in some cases superseded by the new legislation), with references to 'emoluments' now being relevant to 'general earnings'.

The emoluments assessable are those arising from the office or employment, regardless of by whom they are provided (see e.g. *Shilton v Wilmshurst HL 1991, 64 TC 78*).

Where an employee was granted a share option, the emolument was the granting of the option (any subsequent increase in value not being an emolument) (*Abbott v Philbin HL 1960, 39 TC 82*). See, however, *Bootle v Bye; Wilson v Bye (Sp C 61), [1996] SSCD 58*, where payments under an agreement with a third party, and not the rights under the agreement, were held to be emoluments.

Whether 'money's worth' received by an employee comes to him as an emolument may be a difficult question of fact. For modern examples see *Hochstrasser v Mayes HL 1959, 38 TC 673* (compensation for loss on sale of house on transfer, held not assessable); *Wilcock v Eve Ch D 1995, 67 TC 223* (payment for loss of rights under share option scheme, held not assessable), and contrast *Hamblett v Godfrey CA 1986, 59 TC 694* (payment for loss of trade union etc. rights, held assessable); *Laidler v Perry HL 1965, 42 TC 351*; *Brumby v Milner HL 1976, 51 TC 583*; *Tyrer v Smart HL 1978, 52 TC 533*. The meeting by the employer of a **pecuniary liability** of the employee constitutes money's worth, see e.g. *Hartland v Diggines HL 1926, 10 TC 247* (tax liability), *Nicoll v Austin KB 1935, 19 TC 531* (rates etc. of employee's residence), and *Glynn v CIR PC 1990, 63 TC 162* (payment direct to school of child's school fees); this applies to payment of the employee's council tax (Revenue Press Release 16 March 1993), and may apply to payment of employees' parking fines. In the latter case, the tax treatment depends on whether the vehicle is owned by employer or by employee and whether the fixed penalty notice is affixed to the car or handed to the driver (see Revenue Employment Income Manual EIM 21686 for a full summary). Congestion charges paid by an employer in connection with an employee-owned vehicle are taxable (see Revenue Employment Income Manual EIM 21680). For specific items and legislation modifying the general rule, see 75.12 onwards below.

Hence, subject to any special legislation, board, lodging, uniforms etc. provided by the employer and not convertible into money are not assessable, but cash allowances *in lieu* are generally assessable, e.g. a clothing allowance to a 'plain-clothes' policeman (*Fergusson v Noble CS 1919, 7 TC 176*); a meals allowance when working abnormal hours (*Sanderson v Durbridge Ch D 1955, 36 TC 239*); lodging allowances to army personnel (*Nagley v Spilsbury Ch D 1957, 37 TC 178*); an allowance to meet extra cost of living abroad (*Robinson v Corry CA 1933, 18 TC 411*). Allowances in lieu of uniform to uniformed staff are, however, not treated as emoluments (see Revenue Employment Income Manual EIM 10400). See 75.33 below for meal vouchers. See also 28.19 EXEMPT INCOME as regards accommodation allowances for Members of Parliament and 75.32 below as regards living accommodation generally. Where deductions were made from salary for board etc., held gross amount assessable (*Cordy v Gordon KB 1925, 9 TC 304; Machon v McLoughlin CA 1926, 11 TC 83*). Where a higher salary may be taken in lieu of the provision of free board and lodging, the value of the provision is taxable, but see Revenue Pamphlet IR 1, A60 as regards concessional treatment of agricultural workers. It is understood that a similar concession is applied to stable lads employed by racehorse trainers.

Where an employee used his car in the course of his duties, a lump sum and mileage allowances were held to be emoluments (*Perrons v Spackman Ch D 1981, 55 TC 403*). See 75.46 below as regards mileage allowances and travelling and subsistence allowances generally. 'Garage allowances' to salesmen with company cars were held to be assessable in *Beecham Group Ltd v Fair Ch D 1983, 57 TC 733*, but expenditure on the provision of car (or, for 1999/2000 onwards, cycle or motor cycle or, for 2005/06 onwards, van) parking facilities for an employee at or near his place of work does not constitute an emolument (see *ITEPA 2003, s 237; ICTA 1988, s 197A; FA 1999, s 49; FA 2004, s 80, Sch 14 para 8*).

Payments made by an employer after 5 April 2003 to a 'homeworker employee' in respect of reasonable additional 'household expenses' incurred by him after that date in carrying out the duties of his employment at home are exempt from income tax. For these purposes, a '*homeworker employee*' is one who, by arrangement with the employer, regularly performs all or some of those duties at home, and '*household expenses*' are expenses connected with the day-to-day running of his home. [*ITEPA 2003, s 316A; FA 2003, s 137*]. Up to £2 per week can be paid without the need to justify the amount paid or to provide supporting evidence of the expenses incurred; for larger payments, the employer must be able to provide supporting evidence that the payment falls wholly within the above exemption (Revenue Press Release REV BN 3, 9 April 2003). See also Revenue Employment Income Manual EIM 01472–01478 and Revenue Tax Bulletin December 2003 pp 1068, 1069.

Financial loss allowances, or payments for loss of earnings, to members of public bodies, or to magistrates or those on jury service, are not taxable as employment income (although when received by the self-employed they are taxable as business receipts, see 71.38(*e*) SCHEDULE D, CASES I AND II) (Revenue Employment Income Manual EIM 01120). For the PAYE treatment of local councillors' attendance allowances, see 55.32 PAY AS YOU EARN.

For the exemption of cash allowances paid to miners in lieu of free coal, see 75.16(xi) below.

Employer's gift of clothing assessable on *second-hand* value (*Wilkins v Rogerson CA 1960, 39 TC 344*), but gift voucher available for use only in specified shop assessable on face value (*Laidler v Perry HL 1965, 42 TC 351*) but see 75.47 below for legislation now applicable although the case remains an important authority on what constitutes an emolument. Also see *Heaton v Bell HL 1969, 46 TC 211* (assessment on free use of car connected with reduction in wages, but see company car legislation at 75.18 below).

Interest on money loaned interest-free, subject to conditions and repayable on demand, by the employer to a trust for the benefit of an employee held to be assessable emoluments (*O'Leary v McKinlay Ch D 1990, 63 TC 729*).

Endowment premiums paid by employers are assessable (*Richardson v Lyon KB 1943, 25 TC 497*). But trustees' payments out of fund set up by employers for assisting education of employees' children held not assessable on parent (*Barclays Bank v Naylor Ch D 1960, 39 TC 256*) but see now educational scholarships under 75.23 below. In *Ball v Johnson Ch D 1971, 47 TC 155*, a discretionary payment to employee for passing an examination was held not assessable (but see Revenue Employment Income Manual EIM 01100, and see also 75.16 below for treatment of such awards as benefits-in-kind). Commission applied in taking up shares held assessable (*Parker v Chapman CA 1927, 13 TC 677*). In *Clayton v Gothorp Ch D 1971, 47 TC 168*, a loan to a former employee for improving qualifications, which became non-repayable when the employee returned to employer's service after qualification, was held assessable for year in which it became non-repayable. Where wages paid in gold sovereigns, held their market value to be taken as the measure of the emoluments (*Jenkins v Horn Ch D 1979, 52 TC 591*).

Whether lump sum payments etc. on taking up an employment are emoluments of the employment or non-taxable inducements is a question of fact. Signing-on fees to an amateur footballer on joining a Rugby League club were held to be assessable in *Riley v Coglan Ch D 1967, 44 TC 481*, distinguishing *Jarrold v Boustead CA 1964, 41 TC 701*. In *Shilton v Wilmshurst HL 1991, 64 TC 78*, a transfer fee paid by his old club to a professional footballer was taxable as an emolument of his new employment. In *Sports Club plc and others v Inspector of Taxes (Sp C 253), [2000] SSCD 443*, payments by a sports club via third party companies under separate promotional contracts relating to employees' services were held not to be chargeable under Schedule E.

The value of shares allotted to an accountant on becoming managing director of a company was held not to be assessable in *Pritchard v Arundale Ch D 1971, 47 TC 680*, but an opposite conclusion was reached on the facts in *Glantre Engineering Ltd v Goodhand Ch D 1982, 56 TC 165*. See now 75.37 below. A lump sum payment for giving up rights to trade union representation was assessable (*Hamblett v Godfrey CA 1986, 59 TC 694*).

For the effectiveness of 'salary sacrifice' arrangements, see Revenue Internet Statement 25 February 2003.

The reimbursement by an employer of an employee's bank charges, where these arise solely because of the employer's failure to make a salary payment on time, does not give rise to a tax charge. Any employer who believes that the Revenue have failed to apply this rule correctly in the past, and who, on his employees' behalf, has paid tax (or national insurance contributions) in respect of such bank charges, may be entitled to a refund and should contact the tax office concerned. (Revenue Tax Bulletin June 2003 p 1039).

For the Revenue view of the taxation implications of guaranteed selling price (or similar) schemes for houses as part of employee relocation packages, see Revenue Tax Bulletin May 1994 p 122 and April 1995 p 211.

Simon's Direct Tax Service. See E4.1.

75.11 **ALLOWABLE DEDUCTIONS**

Following the rewriting of the legislation for the taxation of employment income with effect from 6 April 2003 in *ITEPA 2003* (see 75.1 above), the provisions allowing deductions from taxable earnings from employment are substantially restructured, although without significant change to their application in practice. The Explanatory Notes published with the precursor Bill sets out in detail the reasoning behind the changes, which are generally aimed at achieving uniformity in the way in which deductions are allowed and setting them in an overall context. In particular, the previous requirement (in most cases) that payments be made 'out of the emoluments' from the employment is replaced by a prohibition on expenses exceeding earnings, and the allowance of reimbursed expenses provided the reimbursed amount is treated as earnings is made explicit. *ITEPA 2003, ss 327–335* provide the general rules within which the specific provisions operate as regards these and other matters, such as the income from which expenses may be deducted, order of deductions, prevention of double deduction etc. As noted more generally at 75.1 above, the following text describes the rules as they are applied after 5 April 2003, with a note of any significant changes with practical effect.

(a) **General.** For 1998/99 and subsequent years, a deduction is generally allowed from earnings from employment charged on the receipts basis (see 75.3, 75.4 above) for expenses the holder of an office or employment is obliged to incur and pay which are either 'qualifying travelling expenses' or other amounts incurred wholly, exclusively and necessarily in the performance of the duties of the employment. A deduction is similarly allowed for amounts paid on behalf of, or reimbursed to, the employee and included in the earnings from the employment. The deductions allowable against earnings may not exceed those earnings. There is a general prohibition on obtaining more than one deduction for any cost or expense. For travelling expenses generally, see 75.46 below. For deductions from earnings charged on the remittance basis, see 75.6 above.

'*Qualifying travelling expenses*' are amounts necessarily expended on travelling in the performance of the duties of the office or employment, or other travel expenses which

(i)   are attributable to necessary attendance at any place of the holder of the office or employment in the performance of those duties, and

(ii)   are not expenses of either 'ordinary commuting' or 'private travel'.

Expenses of travel between two places at which duties are performed of different offices or employments under or with companies in the same group are treated as necessarily expended in the performance of the duties to be performed at the destination. Companies are members of the same group for this purpose if one is a 51% subsidiary (by reference to ordinary share capital) of the other or both are 51% subsidiaries of a third company.

'*Ordinary commuting*' means travel between home (or a place other than a 'workplace' in relation to the office or employment) and a place which is a 'permanent workplace' in relation to the office or employment. (See *Kirkwood v Evans Ch D 2002, 74 TC 481* for a case in which weekly home to office travel by a homeworker was held to be ordinary commuting.) '*Private travel*' means travel between home and a place that is not a 'workplace', or between two places neither of which is a 'workplace'. Travel which for practical purposes is substantially ordinary commuting or private travel is treated as such. As regards emergency call-outs, see 75.46 below.

A '*workplace*' in relation to an employment is a place at which attendance is necessary in the performance of the duties of the office or employment. It is a '*permanent workplace*' if it is not a 'temporary workplace' and attendance there in the performance of those duties is regular. Except as below, it is a '*temporary workplace*' if the purpose of attendance there is to perform a task of limited duration or some other temporary purpose.

A workplace is *not* a 'temporary workplace' if attendance there is in the course of a 'period of continuous work' at that place lasting more than 24 months or comprising all (or almost all) of the period for which the office or employment is likely to be held, or if it is reasonable to assume that it will be in the course of such a period. See *Phillips v Hamilton; Macken v Hamilton (Sp C 366), [2003] SSCD 286.* A '*period of continuous work*' at a place is a period over which the duties of the employment fall to be performed to a significant extent at that place (i.e. 40% or more of working time is spent there, see Revenue Booklet 490 para 3.12). Actual or contemplated modifications of the place at which the duties are performed which do not have any substantial effect on the journey or on the travelling expenses are disregarded.

A place regularly attended in the performance of the duties of the office or employment which forms the base from which those duties are performed, or which is the place at which the tasks to be carried out in the performance of those duties are allocated, is treated as a permanent workplace. Similarly where the duties are defined by reference to an area (whether or not requiring attendance outside the area), and attendance is required at different places in the area (none of them a permanent workplace) in the performance of the duties, then that area is treated as a permanent workplace if it would be so treated (as above) were it a place.

From 6 April 2002, where a vehicle other than a company vehicle is used for business travel, and either mileage allowance payments are received or mileage allowance relief is available in respect of that use (see 75.46 below), no deduction is available for qualifying travelling expenses incurred in connection with that use.

[*ITEPA 2003, s 328(1), s 329(1)–(3), s 330, s 333(1)(2), s 334(1)(2), s 335(1)(2), ss 336–340, s 359*].

For leading articles explaining the above rules, with numerous examples, see Revenue Tax Bulletin December 1997 pp 477–485, February 1998 pp 497–505 and April 1998 pp 524–527. See also Revenue Tax Bulletin December 2000 pp 805–809 for an article explaining the Revenue's approach to benefits and expenses paid to employees sent on secondments not exceeding 24 months, in particular those sent by an overseas employer to work in the UK. Revenue Booklet 490 'Employee Travel: A Tax and NICs Guide for Employees' also provides comprehensive general guidance, and see generally Revenue Employment Income Manual EIM 32005 *et seq.*

For **1998/99 to 2002/03** inclusive, the above provisions are contained in *ICTA 1988, s 198(1)(1A)(1B)(5), Sch 12A* as amended and introduced by *FA 1998, s 61, Sch 10; FA 2001, Sch 12 Pt II para 6.*

For **1997/98** and earlier years, the deductions allowed are expenses necessarily incurred on travelling in the performance of the duties of the office or employment and any other expenses incurred wholly, exclusively and necessarily in the performance of those duties (and certain other equine expenses). [*ICTA 1988, s 198(1) as originally enacted*].

For **all years**, the requirements that expenditure be incurred 'necessarily' and (other than in the case of qualifying travelling expenses within (i) above) 'in the performance of the duties' impose additional restrictions on the allowability of deductions from earnings compared with those generally deductible under Schedule D. 'Necessarily' has been held to require that every holder of the office or employment would have to incur the expenditure, regardless of personal circumstances (see *Ricketts v Colquhoun HL 1925, 10 TC 118*). As regards 'in the performance of the duties', it follows that expenses incurred prior to entering upon duties or merely in preparation for them are not allowed (see e.g. *Ansell v Brown Ch D 2001, 73 TC 338* and, in relation to a training post, *Snowdon v Charnock (Sp C 282), [2001] SSCD 152*). See *Nolder v Walters KB 1930, 15 TC 380*, air pilot allowed hotel expenses because incurred *in course of duty*, but not car and telephone *merely in preparation for it*, and *Bhadra v Ellam Ch D 1987, 60 TC 466* where a doctor's travelling and secretarial expenses in relation to locum posts obtained through medical agencies were not allowed, as his duties commenced only on arrival at the hospital concerned. But contrast *Pook v Owen HL 1969, 45 TC 571* where a GP with a part-time Schedule E hospital appointment was allowed his expenses of travelling to the hospital from his home (where his surgery was), not covered by his mileage allowance, because, on the facts, his home as well as the hospital was a place where he carried out the duties of his appointment. See also *Gilbert v Hemsley Ch D 1981, 55 TC 419* and 75.46 below generally.

Employees' costs of provision, upkeep, replacement or repair of protective clothing or of uniforms (recognisable as such) are allowable where their duties require them to be worn (Revenue Employment Income Manual EIM 32465 *et seq.*).

Use of room at home for business purposes allowed (*Newlin v Woods CA 1966, 42 TC 649* but cf. *Kirkwood v Evans Ch D 2002, 74 TC 481*) but not alternative room for son's homework (*Roskams v Bennett Ch D 1950, 32 TC 129*) or mortgage interest on loan to purchase property used as office (*Baird v Williams Ch D 1999, 71 TC 390*). A deduction may be due for a proportion of the council tax payable where a room or rooms are used exclusively for work purposes. (Revenue Press Release 16 March 1993). See Revenue Employment Income Manual EIM 32815 for a list of other expenses deductible in these circumstances. For the exemption available after 5 April 2003 where the employer makes a contribution to the extra costs of the employee's working at home, see 75.10 above.

Rental of *second* telephone line at employee's home allowed where used exclusively for business calls and there is a genuine business need for the line (but rental of first line or single line not allowed) (Revenue Employment Income Manual EIM 32940).

Expenses of a part-time Schedule E appointment not allowable under Schedule E may not be deducted in computing the profits of an associated business within Schedule D (*Mitchell & Edon v Ross HL 1961, 40 TC 11*).

(*b*)　**Expenses not allowed** include: employment agency fees (*Shortt v McIlgorm KB 1945, 26 TC 262*); meal expenses paid out of meal allowances (*Sanderson v Durbridge Ch D 1955, 36 TC 239*); living expenses paid out of living allowances when working away from home (*Elderkin v Hindmarsh Ch D 1988, 60 TC 651*); headmaster's course to improve background knowledge (*Humbles v Brooks Ch D 1962, 40 TC 500*); articled clerk's examination fees (*Lupton v Potts Ch D 1969, 45 TC 643*); cost of ordinary clothing (*Hillyer v Leeke Ch D 1976, 51 TC 90; Woodcock v CIR Ch D 1977, 51 TC 698; Ward v Dunn Ch D 1978, 52 TC 517*); rental of telephone installed at employer's behest, but not used *wholly* and *exclusively* in performance of duties (*Lucas v Cattell Ch D 1972, 48 TC 353*); telephone and other expenses of consultant anaesthetist (*Hamerton v Overy Ch D 1954, 35 TC 73*); journalists' expenditure on newspapers and periodicals (*Fitzpatrick and Others v CIR, Smith v Shuttleworth and Others HL 1994, 66 TC 407*); and rugby player's expenditure on dietary supplements (*Ansell v Brown Ch D 2001, 73 TC 338*).

Any excess cost of living in place where required by work (*Bola v Barlow KB 1949, 31 TC 136; Collis v Hore (No 1) KB 1949, 31 TC 173; Robinson v Corry CA 1933, 18 TC 411*); cost of domestic assistance where wife employed (*Bowers v Harding QB 1891, 3 TC 22*); cost of looking after widower's children (*Halstead v Condon Ch D 1970, 46 TC 289*).

Entertaining expenses are not allowed, but see 71.45 SCHEDULE D, CASES I AND II for exceptions. However where an employer is not allowed a deduction for expenditure on business entertainment paid by him, directly or indirectly, to a member of staff, and that sum is also taxable earnings of the employee, the employee is allowed an equivalent deduction from taxable earnings for expenses defrayed out of that sum. [*ITEPA 2003, ss 356–358; ICTA 1988, s 577*].

No deduction permitted for broadband internet access where employee is able to use the internet for non-business purposes (Revenue Employment Income Manual EIM 32940).

(*c*)　For travelling, subsistence and incidental overnight expenses etc. generally, see 75.46 below, and for other specific deductions, see below at 75.28 (flat rate expenses), 75.42 (subscriptions) and 75.45 (training etc.).

(*d*)　For provision of security assets and services for employees, see 75.38 below.

(*e*)　For capital allowances where plant or machinery is provided for the purposes of an employment, see 9.24 CAPITAL ALLOWANCES. See also 75.46 below.

(*f*)　For expenditure by Members of Parliament on accommodation, see 75.32(2) below.

(*g*)　For charitable donation payroll deduction scheme, see 14.18 CHARITIES.

(*h*)　For deduction of agents' fees by artistes, see 75.27 below.

(j)   For expenditure on indemnity insurance and on certain liabilities such as legal costs in relation to the employment, see 75.26 below.

For the Revenue view on specific employments and expenses, see Revenue Employment Income Manual EIM 31622 *et seq.*

Simon's Direct Tax Service. See E4.7.

75.12   **BENEFITS**

Generally, if an employee receives money or money's worth from his employment he is chargeable to tax on that amount (see 75.10 above). However, he or his family may receive benefits by reason of his employment where special legislation is required if taxation is to apply. Such legislation is now contained in the 'Benefits Code' contained in *ITEPA 2003, Pt 3 Chs 2–11.* For benefits derived by directors and certain employees from their employment, see 75.14 *et seq.* below. For other taxable benefits of general application, see 75.32, 75.47 below. A benefit provided by a third party (e.g. a car provided by a car dealer to a football player for promotional purposes) is potentially within the benefits charging provisions where it is provided by reason of the employment.

Where the provision charging a particular benefit does not specify the year of charge, the earnings are treated as received at the time the benefit is provided. [*ITEPA 2003, ss 19(4), 32(4)*].

See 58.1 PENSION INCOME as regards the provision of benefits to retired employees.

Many of the exceptions listed at 75.16 below from the special charge on benefits apply also to amounts in respect of which a charge might also arise under the general charge on employment income. As a general rule there is a relief from all income tax liability in respect of such amounts. Where an amount is assessable both as general earnings and under the benefits code, only the amount (if any) by which the charge under the benefits code exceeds that as general earnings is brought in under the benefits code. This does not apply to the provision of living accommodation (see 75.32 below) or in relation to certain employee shareholdings taxed under the benefits code (see 82.10 SHARE-RELATED EMPLOYMENT INCOME AND EXEMPTIONS). [*ITEPA 2003, s 64; FA 2003, Sch 22 para 21*]. See also Revenue Employment Income Manual EIM 21640.

See 55.12 PAY AS YOU EARN as regards PAYE settlement agreements whereby employer accounts for tax on minor benefits, which do not then count as employees' income.

75.13   **CLERGYMEN ETC.**

A clergyman or other minister of a religious denomination in full-time employment as such is not taxable on any sums paid for or reimbursed to him in respect of any statutory amount payable, or statutory deduction made, under any *Act* in connection with the residence made available to him by a charity or ecclesiastical corporation for carrying out his duties (except in so far as they relate to any part of the premises which he lets) and, unless he is in 'director's or higher-paid' employment (see 75.14 below), no account is taken of the value of any expenses relating to his own living accommodation so provided. [*ITEPA 2003, s 290; ICTA 1988, s 332(1)(2)(4)*]. By concession, no liability arises in respect of payment or reimbursement of his heating, lighting, cleaning or gardening expenses. (Revenue Pamphlet IR 1, A61).

Expenses wholly, exclusively and necessarily incurred in performance of duties (e.g. postage, stationery, telephone, car etc.) may be deducted from earnings from any employment as a minister (although from 6 April 2002, where a vehicle other than a company vehicle is used for business travel, and either mileage allowance payments are received or mileage allowance relief is available in respect of that use (see 75.46 below), no deduction is available for qualifying travelling expenses (see 75.11 above) incurred in connection with that use). If he pays rent in respect of a dwelling-house any part of which is used mainly or substantially for his duties, up to one-quarter thereof may be deducted from earnings, and in addition he may claim in total one-quarter of the aggregate of any expenses of maintenance, repair, insurance or management of the premises borne by him. Such deductions are also allowed from profits or fees chargeable under Schedule D. [*ITEPA 2003, ss 351, 328(2), Sch 6 para 47; ICTA 1988, s 332(3)(3A)(3B); FA 2001, Sch 12 Pt II para 10*]. Relief may also be available for the cost of *locum tenens* for illness or holidays and lighting, heating, cleaning and rates of study (see Revenue Employment Income Manual EIM 60046, 60048).

See generally Revenue Employment Income Manual EIM 60001–60055.

The expenses of a minister in visiting his congregation were allowed (*Charlton v CIR CS 1890, 27 SLR 647*) but not expenses of a curate in moving from one curacy to another (*Friedson v Glyn-Thomas KB 1922, 8 TC 302*). In *Mitchell v Child KB 1942, 24 TC 511*, cost of opposing a Bill which would have dispossessed rector of parsonage was allowed.

Gifts to a clergyman including voluntary subscriptions and collections (*In re Strong C/E/S 1878, 1 TC 207; Slaney v Starkey KB 1931, 16 TC 45*), Easter offerings (*Cooper v Blakiston HL 1908, 5 TC 347*) and grants (*Herbert v McQuade CA 1902, 4 TC 489; Poynting v Faulkner CA 1905, 5 TC 145*) are taxable but not where in recognition of past service (*Turner v Cuxson QB 1888, 2 TC 422*). The cost of maintenance of a priest living in communal presbytery held not taxable as not convertible into money (*Daly v CIR CS 1934, 18 TC 641*).

An unbeneficed clergyman was held to be within the charge on employment income (*Slaney v Starkey* above) as was a professed nun employed as a teacher (*Dolan v K Supreme Court (IFS), 2 ITC 280*) but not the headmaster of a school established by a congregation of secular priests (*Reade v Brearley KB 1933, 17 TC 687*).

For the concessional treatment of contemplative religious communities, see Revenue Pamphlet IR 1, B10.

Simon's Direct Tax Service. See E4.712.

75.14   **DIRECTORS AND EMPLOYEES (OTHER THAN LOWER-PAID EMPLOYEES) — BENEFITS CODE**

The provisions of the benefits code described at 75.15–75.24 below apply to all directors (as widely defined, but subject to the exclusion below) and to employees who are not in 'lower-paid employment'. [*ITEPA 2003, ss 63, 66, 67, 216*]. See 75.32, 75.47 below as regards those parts of the benefits code which apply to *all* employees and directors.

A director is excluded if he has no material interest (i.e. broadly if his and/or his associates' interests in the company do not exceed 5%) in the company *and either* is a full-time working director (i.e. he devotes substantially the whole of his time to the service of the company in a managerial or technical capacity) *or* the company is either non-profit-making (i.e. it does not carry on a trade nor is its main function the holding of investments or other property) or charitable. [*ITEPA 2003, ss 67–69, 216(3)*]. A director so excluded will nevertheless be subject to these provisions if he is not in 'lower-paid employment'.

An employee is in *'lower-paid employment'* for a tax year if the earnings rate for the employment for that year is less than £8,500. The earnings rate for an employment for a year is calculated as follows.

(*a*)   Determine the aggregate (after deducting any exempt income) of:

(i)   the earnings (see 75.10 above) from the employment for that year;

(ii)   the total of amounts treated as earnings for that year. This includes all amounts which would be so treated under the benefits code, disregarding the exclusion of lower-paid employees where it might otherwise apply; and

(iii)   any deemed employment payment for the year under *ITEPA 2003, s 54* (see 61.7 PERSONAL SERVICE COMPANIES ETC.).

As regards (ii) above: in the case of provision of living accommodation under 75.32 below, the additional charge where cost exceeds £75,000 does not apply for this purpose, the basic charge being applied regardless of the cost; in the case of fuel provided for private use of a company car, see *Allcock v King (Sp C 396), [2004] SSCD 122,* but note that the decision in this case is superseded by an extra-statutory concession (Revenue ESC A104) published on 5 July 2004.

(*b*)   Where an alternative is offered to a company car such that, if it had been taxable as earnings rather than under the benefits code, the taxable amount would have exceeded the car and fuel benefits charge computed as in 75.18(i)(iv) below, the excess is added to the amount determined under (*a*) above.

(*c*)   From the amount resulting from (*a*) and (*b*) above, subtract specified 'authorised deductions', which do *not* include general allowable deductions within 75.11(*a*) above or most general travelling expenses. The '*authorised deductions*' are those within 75.8 (other than those under *ITEPA 2003, s 341* or *s 342* (travelling expenses on commencement or termination of employment or between employments)) and 75.9 above, 75.26 (employee liabilities), 75.27 (artiste's percentage deduction) and 75.38 (personal security provision) below, 9.32 CAPITAL ALLOWANCES (machinery and plant allowances), 14.18 CHARITIES (payroll deduction scheme) and 67.5, 67.11 RETIREMENT SCHEMES (contributions).

(*d*)   The earnings rate is the figure resulting from (*a*)–(*c*) above, proportionately increased if the employment is held for less than the full number of days in the tax year concerned.

Earnings rates from different but 'related' employments during a year are aggregated and compared with £8,500 p.a. in determining whether all or none of them is lower-paid employment. Employments are '*related*' for this purpose where either they are with the same employer or one is with a body or partnership ('A') and the other either with an individual, partnership or body ('B') that controls A or with another partnership or body controlled by B.

[*ITEPA 2003, ss 216–220*].

Detailed application of the provisions is covered in 75.14–75.24 below, in which references to an 'employee' should (unless the context requires otherwise) be taken as referring to any director or employee to whom the provisions relate.

Before 6 April 2003, the corresponding provisions were contained in *ICTA 1988, ss 154, 167,* and see *ITEPA 2003, Sch 7 para 17* as regards transitional matters.

Simon's Direct Tax Service. See E4.6.

75.15   **Expenses.** All payments to an employee by reason of the employment in respect of expenses, including sums put at employee's disposal and paid away by him, are taxable. All payments by the employer are 'by reason of the employment' unless the employer is an individual and the payment is made in the normal course of his domestic, family or personal relationships. Deductions may be made as under 75.6 (remittances), 75.8 (under *ITEPA 2003, s 341* or *s 342* or *ICTA 1988, s 193* (travelling expenses on commencement or termination of employment or between employments)), 75.11(*a*) (general allowable deductions), 75.13 (clergymen etc.), 75.26 (employee liabilities) and 75.42 (professional fees and subscriptions). [*ITEPA 2003, ss 70–72; ICTA 1988, s 153, 168(3)*]. This includes use of employer's credit card. See 55.12 PAY AS YOU EARN as regards PAYE settlement agreements whereby employer accounts for tax on minor payments of expenses within the agreement, which do not then count as employees' income.

75.16   **Benefits-in-kind generally.** All benefits or facilities of any kind (other than those within the special charging provisions at 75.18–75.23 below) provided for an employee (or for an employee's family or household) by reason of the employment are taxable on the cash equivalent of the benefit (see below). Benefits are 'provided' by those at whose cost they are provided, and benefits provided by someone other than the employer may be included. All benefits provided by the employer are 'by reason of the employment' unless the employer is an individual and the provision is made in the normal course of his domestic, family or personal relationships. [*ITEPA 2003, ss 201, 202, 209; ICTA 1988, ss 154, 168(3)*]. See also 75.32, 75.47 below as regards provisions for the taxation of certain benefits which apply to *all* employees and directors.

The Treasury does, however, have powers to exempt minor benefits by order, such exemption being conditional on the benefit(s) in question being made available to the employer's employees generally on similar terms. From 6 April 2002, provision of a voucher evidencing entitlement to such an exempt minor benefit is also exempt from charge under *ITEPA 2003, s 87* (non-cash vouchers, see 75.47(*a*) below). The following minor benefits have been the subject of such regulatory exemption.

- (From 21 August 2000) welfare counselling (excluding medical treatment and advice on finance (other than debt problems), tax, leisure or recreation and legal advice).

- (From 6 April 2002) cyclists' breakfasts (limited before 25 June 2003 to the first six breakfasts per tax year, thereafter unlimited).

- (From 6 April 2002) provision of buses for journeys of ten miles or less from the workplace to shops etc. on a working day.

- (From 9 July 2002) certain benefits provided to disabled employees (e.g. hearing aids or wheelchairs) to enable them to perform the duties of the employment.

[*ITEPA 2003, ss 210, 266(4); ICTA 1988, s 155ZB; FA 2000, s 57, Sch 10 para 3; FA 2002, s 36; SI 2000 No 2080; SI 2002 Nos 205, 1596; SI 2003 No 1434*].

In relation to the timing of a benefit, 'provided' refers to the receipt by the employee of the benefit, rather than to steps taken or costs incurred by the employer (*Templeton v Jacobs Ch D 1996, 68 TC 735*).

See 58.1 PENSION INCOME as regards benefits provided to retired employees.

Following the decision in *Wicks v Firth HL 1982, 56 TC 318*, payments of cash are potentially within the benefits legislation, so that for example examination awards which would otherwise not be taxable following *Ball v Johnson* (see 75.10 above) fall within the benefits charge. (ICAEW Technical Memorandum TR 786, 15 March 1990).

Legal expenses incurred by a company in defending a dangerous driving charge against a director were held to be a benefit (*Rendell v Went HL 1964, 41 TC 641*). Parking etc. fines met by employer would generally constitute a benefit (see 75.10 above).

Allocations of moneys by trustees of an *employee benefit trust* to sub-funds for individual employees were not taxable as benefits-in-kind (*Macdonald v Dextra Accessories Ltd and Others Ch D, [2003] STC 749*).

Exceptions

(i)   (From 6 April 2000) provision of accommodation, supplies or services used by the employee in performing the duties of the employment, provided that either:

(A)   if the benefit is provided on premises occupied by the employer or other person providing it, any private use (i.e. use other than in performing those duties) by the employee (or by the employee's family or household) is not significant; or

(B)   in any other case, the sole purpose of providing the benefit is to enable the employee to perform those duties, any private use (as in (A)) is not significant, and the benefit is not an 'excluded benefit'.

Whether private use under (B) above is 'significant' will depend on all the circumstances of any given case, but provided that

(a)   the employer's policy is clearly stated to employees, setting out the circumstances in which occasional private use may be made, and

(b)   any policy not to recover costs of such use is taken because the administrative costs would exceed the amounts involved, rather than to reward the employee,

and that there are reasonable checks to ensure the policy is followed in practice, then provided the amount of private use is small compared to work use, the Revenue accept that the exemption will apply. (Revenue Tax Bulletin October 2000 pp 779, 780).

Subject to Treasury regulations (which may provide that a benefit is an 'excluded benefit' only if prescribed conditions are met as to the terms on which, and persons to whom, it is provided), 'excluded benefit' consists of the provision of a motor vehicle, boat or aircraft, or of a benefit which involves the extension, conversion or alteration of any living accommodation or the construction, extension, conversion or alteration of a building or other structure on land adjacent to and enjoyed with living accommodation.

[ITEPA 2003, s 316; ICTA 1988, s 155ZA; FA 2000, s 57, Sch 10 para 2].

The exemption can extend to the provision of a telephone line and/or broadband internet access in the employee's home (Revenue Employment Income Manual EIM 21615, 21616). See generally EIM 21610–21614.

Before 6 April 2000, the exemption applied only to the provision, in premises occupied by the employer or other person providing it, of accommodation, supplies or services used by the employee solely in performing duties of the employment. [ICTA 1988, s 155(2); FA 2000, Sch 40 Pt II(2)].

(ii)   Provision of living accommodation and connected expenses in certain circumstances, see 75.32 below. [ITEPA 2003, ss 313–315; ICTA 1988, ss 154(2), 155(3), 163].

(iii)   Provision made by the employer for any pension, annuity, lump sum, gratuity or other like benefit to be given to the employee, his dependants or any other members of his family or household on his retirement or death (although see 67.1 RETIREMENT SCHEMES). [ITEPA 2003, s 307; ICTA 1998, s 155(4)]. Before 6 April 2003, the extension to benefits payable to any member of the employee's family or household (e.g. including a parent or a son- or daughter-in-law) was by concession (see Revenue Pamphlet IR 1, A72).

(iv)   Provision by the employer of free or subsidised meals in a canteen or on the employer's business premises where, in either case, the meals are provided on a reasonable scale and all of the employer's employees (or all of them at a particular location) may obtain such a meal or a voucher, ticket, pass etc. to enable them to obtain such a meal. Light refreshments are regarded as meals for these purposes. If the meals are provided in the restaurant or dining-room of a hotel or a catering etc.

business at a time when meals are served to the public, the exemption applies only if the staff meals are taken in a part designated for staff use only. [*ITEPA 2003, ss 266(3)(e), 317; ICTA 1988, s 155(5); FA 2004, Sch 17 para 1*]. For 2003/04 only, due to a drafting error in *ITEPA 2003*, the full conditions above did not apply to meals provided in a canteen. Before 2003/04, these provisions applied by a combination of legislation, concession (see Revenue Pamphlet IR 1, A74) and Revenue practice.

(v) Provision of travel, accommodation and subsistence during public transport disruption caused by industrial action. From 6 April 2003, this exemption is statutory [*ITEPA 2003, s 245*], having previously applied by concession (see Revenue Pamphlet IR 1, A58). See also 75.46 below.

(vi) Provision of means of transport between home and place of employment (or training) for disabled employees. From 6 April 2003, this exemption is statutory [*ITEPA 2003, ss 246, 247*], having previously applied by concession (see Revenue Pamphlet IR 1, A59). See also 75.18, 75.46 below.

(vii) Provision of transport for occasional late night journeys from work to home, or following a failure of car-sharing arrangements, subject to certain conditions. From 6 April 2003, this exemption is statutory [*ITEPA 2003, s 248*], having previously applied by concession (see Revenue Pamphlet IR 1, A66). See also 75.46 below.

(viii) Provision of transport between mainland and offshore rig etc., and necessary overnight accommodation on the mainland, for offshore oil and gas workers. From 6 April 2003, this exemption is statutory [*ITEPA 2003, s 305; FA 2004, Sch 27 paras 13, 16*], having previously applied by concession (see Revenue Pamphlet IR 1, A65).

(ix) Travelling expenses (including reasonable hotel expenses) of

(A) a director of two or more companies within a group of companies, between his main place where he acts as director and other places within the UK in the course of his duties as a director. Similarly where a person is a director of one company and an employee of another company in the same group;

(B) an unremunerated director of a company not managed with a view to dividends (e.g. a club);

(C) a director who holds the position as part of a professional practice, provided no claim is made to a deduction under Schedule D;

(D) a spouse accompanying a director on his or her duties abroad because of his or her precarious health.

(Revenue Pamphlet IR 1, A4). See also 75.46 below and, as regards (A), 75.11(*a*) above for comparable statutory relief for 1998/99 onwards.

(x) Removal expenses. For the statutory relief from charge as employment income of certain payments and benefits received in connection with job-related residential moves, see 75.36 below.

For the Revenue view of the taxation implications of guaranteed selling price (or similar) schemes for houses as part of employee relocation packages, see Revenue Tax Bulletin May 1994 p 122 and, in relation in particular to the application of the concession at (xxi) below, April 1995 p 211.

(xi) Miners' free coal and allowances in lieu thereof. From 6 April 2003, this exemption is statutory [*ITEPA 2003, s 306*], having previously applied by concession (see Revenue Pamphlet IR 1, A6).

(xii) Meal vouchers. See 75.33 below.

(xiii) Medical insurance for treatment and medical services where the need for treatment arises while abroad in performance of duties. [*ITEPA 2003, s 325; ICTA 1988, s 155(6)*].

(xiv) Car parking facilities. No benefit arises from the provision for the employee of a car (or, for 1999/2000 onwards, a cycle or motor cycle or, for 2005/06 onwards, a van) parking space at or near his place of work. [*ITEPA 2003, s 237(1)(3); ICTA 1988, s 155(1A); FA 1999, s 49; FA 2004, s 80, Sch 14 para 8*]. See also 75.10 above, 75.47 below.

(xv) Entertainment by third parties. No income tax liability arises from the provision of hospitality of any kind for the employee (or for his family or household), unless it is provided either

    (*a*)   in recognition or anticipation of particular services by the employee in the course of the employment, or

    (*b*)   directly or indirectly by or on behalf of the employer or by any person connected with the employer (within *ICTA 1988, s 839*, see 19 CONNECTED PERSONS).

[*ITEPA 2003, s 265; ICTA 1988, s 155(7)*].

'Hospitality' covers dinners, parties, hospitality tents at sporting events etc., and events such as theatrical performances or sporting events where a host invites someone to accompany him as a guest. It includes associated costs, such as transport or overnight accommodation. (Revenue Employment Income Manual EIM 21836).

See also 75.47 below and, as regards concessionary relief in respect of gifts from third parties, 75.29 below.

(xvi) Christmas parties etc. No benefit arises from expenditure on an annual Christmas party or similar annual function open to the staff generally, or to staff at a particular location, of up to £150 per head per annum (£75 for 2002/03 and earlier years), including VAT and any transport or accommodation costs, or of non-cash vouchers for obtaining such provision (see 75.47 below). Where expenditure exceeds this amount the full amount will be taxable. The total cost is for this purpose divided by the total number of people attending the function to determine whether the limit is exceeded. The expenditure may be split between more than one annual event, and where the total expenditure for the year exceeds the £150 (or £75) limit, a function or functions whose cost or the sum of whose costs is within the limit will not be taxed, the cost of the remaining functions being taxed in full. Casual hospitality is not regarded as constituting an annual function for these purposes. No P11D return (see 55.9 PAY AS YOU EARN) is required in respect of expenditure not exceeding the limit. From 6 April 2003, this exemption is statutory, having previously applied by concession (see Revenue Pamphlet IR 1, A70). [*ITEPA 2003, s 264; SI 2003 No 1361, regs 1, 2*].

(xvii) Childcare facilities. For 2004/05 and earlier years, no benefit arises from the provision of care for a child to the extent that

    (*a*)   either the employee has parental responsibility (as under *Children Act 1989, s 3(1)*) for the child or the child is resident with or (being a child or step child of the employee) maintained by the employee,

    (*b*)   the care is provided other than on premises wholly or mainly used as a private dwelling,

    (*c*)   the care is provided either on premises made available by the employer alone or under arrangements made by persons who include the employer, on premises made available by one or more of them, with the employer being 'wholly or partly responsible for financing and managing the provision of the care' (for the Revenue interpretation of which expression see Revenue Tax Bulletin April 1998 pp 531-533), and

(*d*)   the premises or the person providing the care are registered if so required under the applicable legislation.

'Care' means any form of care or supervised activity, whether or not provided on a regular basis, other than supervised activity provided primarily for educational purposes. 'Child' means a person under 18.

[*ITEPA 2003, s 318 as originally enacted; ICTA 1988, s 155A as amended; FA 1990, s 21*].

The exemption is extended from 6 April 2005 to childcare away from the workplace, in which case the benefit is tax-free up to a maximum of £50 per week. See 75.22 below for details.

(xviii) Certain training and counselling expenses, see 75.45 below.

(xix) It is understood that the provision of driver training courses for employees will not be taxed as a benefit.

(xx) Medical check-ups. The provision of routine health checks or medical screening for employees does not confer a chargeable benefit, whether carried out by the employer's own medical staff or by an outside firm. (Revenue Tax Bulletin May 1993 p 74). This applies also to such provision for members of the employee's family or household (Revenue Employment Income Manual EIM 21765).

(xxi) Asset acquisition costs. Normal purchaser's costs in relation to the sale or transfer of an asset by the employee to the employer (or to some other person by reason of the employment) are disregarded in calculating any benefit arising to the employee. From 6 April 2003, this exemption is statutory [*ITEPA 2003, s 326*], having previously applied by concession (see Revenue Pamphlet IR 1, A85). See Revenue Tax Bulletin April 1995 p 210 as regards the application of this exemption in relation to guaranteed selling price (or similar) schemes for houses as part of employee relocation packages (and see (x) above).

(xxii) Incidental overnight expenses. A benefit is exempt from tax where its provision is incidental to the employee's being away from home on business during a 'qualifying absence' in relation to which the authorised maximum (£5 per night spent in the UK and £10 per night spent abroad) is not exceeded, being a benefit the cost of which is not otherwise deductible from earnings. [*ITEPA 2003, ss 240, 241, Sch 7 paras 33, 34; ICTA 1988, s 155(1B)(1C); FA 1995, s 93(3)*]. See also 75.46 below.

(xxiii) Mobile telephones. For 1999/2000 and subsequent years, no benefit arises from the making available (without any transfer of property) of a 'mobile telephone' to an employee (or to his family or household). The exemption covers the telephone itself, any line rental and any calls, business or private, paid for by the employer on that telephone (Revenue Employment Income Manual EIM 21780). This exemption replaces the flat rate charge applicable for earlier years (see 75.19 below).

A '*mobile telephone*' is defined to include provision in connection with a car, van or heavier commercial vehicle, whether or not a company car etc., but to exclude cordless extensions to fixed telephones and certain short-range radio apparatus.

[*ITEPA 2003, s 319; ICTA 1988, s 155AA; FA 1999, s 44*].

(xxiv) Computer equipment. For 1999/2000 and subsequent years, the making available (without any transfer of property) of certain computer equipment to an employee (or to his family or household) gives rise to a benefits charge only to the extent that the aggregate cash equivalent of the benefit exceeds £500 for a year of assessment. For example, the provision of the use of £2,000 of equipment (at 20% cash equivalent) plus £100 of related expenses, or the provision of equipment rented at an annual rental of £500, would be within the exemption. The arrangements by the employer for providing employees with computer equipment must not be limited to directors, and must not make more favourable provision in relation to any director(s).

'Computer equipment' includes printers, scanners, modems, discs and other peripheral devices designed to be used with a computer, and the provision of a right to use software together with the provision of hardware is included (but not provision of access to, or use of, any public telecommunications system (within *Telecommunications Act 1984*)).

For 2004/05 onwards, computer equipment provided as above is also exempt from the general charge under *ITEPA 2003, s 62* on earnings (see 75.10 above), thus avoiding a charge where the employee is given the choice of the loan of computer equipment or additional salary.

[*ITEPA 2003, s 320; ICTA 1988, s 156A; FA 1999, s 45; FA 2004, s 79*].

For the interaction between this exemption and *ITEPA 2003, s 206* (cost of benefit on subsequent transfer of asset), see Revenue Employment Income Manual EIM 21652.

(xxv) Bus services. For 1999/2000 and subsequent years, two exemptions apply in relation to bus services for employees.

(a) No benefit arises from the provision for employees of a '*works transport service*', i.e. a service provided by means of a 'bus' or (from 6 April 2002) a 'minibus' for conveying employees of one or more employers on 'qualifying journeys'. For this purpose a '*bus*' is a road passenger vehicle with a seating capacity of 12 or more, and a '*minibus*' is a vehicle constructed or adapted for the carriage of 9, 10 or 11 passengers (no account being taken in the case of a minibus of seats which do not meet the relevant 'construction and use requirements' under *Road Traffic Act 1988 Pt II* or NI equivalent). Seating capacity is determined as under *Vehicle Excise and Registration Act 1994, Sch 1 Pt III*. A '*qualifying journey*' for an employee is a journey (or, from 6 April 2003, part of a journey) between home and workplace (i.e. a place at which the employee's attendance is necessary in performance of the duties of the employment) or thereabouts (see Hansard Standing Committee B, 25 May 1999), or between workplaces, in connection with the performance of those duties. The service must be available generally to employees of the employer(s) concerned, and the main use must be for qualifying journeys by those employees. The service must also substantially be used only by those employees or their children aged under 18 (including step- and illegitimate children). Provision of a voucher for use of such a service is similarly exempt from charge under *ICTA 1988, s 141* (non-cash vouchers, see 75.47(a) below), and from 6 April 2002 it is made clear that the company car provisions (see 75.18(ii) below) cannot apply to a works bus service.

(b) No income tax liability arises in respect of financial or other support for a public passenger transport service provided by means of a road vehicle and used by employees of one or more employers for 'qualifying journeys'. A '*qualifying journey*' is as under (a) above, except that it includes part of such a journey from 6 April 2002 rather than 2003. The service must be available generally to employees of the employer(s) concerned. The terms on which it is available must not be more favourable than those available to other passengers, although for 2002/03 onwards this condition does not apply in the case of a 'local bus service' within *Transport Act 1985, s 2* and provision of a voucher for use of the service is similarly exempt from charge under *ICTA 1988, s 141* (non-cash vouchers, see 75.47(a) below).

[*ITEPA 2003, ss 242, 243, 249, 266(2); ICTA 1988, ss 197AA, 197AB; FA 1999, s 48; FA 2001, s 60; FA 2002, s 33*].

See also above as regards exemption of minor benefits of provision of transport to shops etc.

(xxvi) Cycles and cyclists' safety equipment. For 1999/2000 and subsequent years, no benefit arises from the provision (without any transfer of property) for an employee of a cycle or cyclist's safety equipment, provided that

(a)   the facility is available generally to employees of the employer concerned, and

(b)   the employee uses the cycle or equipment mainly for 'qualifying journeys' (as under (xxv)(a) above). Employers are not, however, expected to monitor employees' other cycling journeys (see Hansard Standing Committee B, 25 May 1999).

Provision of a voucher for use of a cycle or safety equipment is similarly exempt from charge under *ICTA 1988, s 141* (non-cash vouchers, see 75.47(a) below).

See also (xiv) above, 75.10 above and 75.47(a)(d) below as regards cycle parking facilities at work places.

[*ITEPA 2003, ss 244, 249, 266(2); ICTA 1988, s 197AC; FA 1999, s 50(1)(3)*].

See also above as regards exemption of minor benefit of cyclists' breakfasts.

(xxvii) Emergency vehicles. For 2004/05 onwards, no benefit arises where an emergency vehicle (as defined) is made available to a person employed in an emergency service (i.e. police or a fire, fire and rescue, ambulance or paramedic service) if the terms on which it is made available prohibit its private use otherwise than when the person is 'on call' or 'engaged in on-call commuting' and the person does not, in fact, make private use of the vehicle outside these terms. For this purpose, a person is '*on call*' when liable, as part of normal duties, to be called upon to use the vehicle to respond to emergencies. A person is '*engaged in on-call commuting*' when he is using the vehicle for ordinary commuting (see 75.11 above) (or for travel between two places that is for practical purposes substantially ordinary commuting) and is required to do so in order that the vehicle is available for use in responding to emergencies. [*ITEPA 2003, s 248A; FA 2004, s 81(1)(3)*].

See 75.38 below as regards provision of security assets and services for employees.

See 55.12 PAY AS YOU EARN as regards PAYE settlement agreements whereby employer accounts for tax on minor benefits within the agreement, which do not then count as employees' income.

Cash equivalent of the benefit is the cost of the benefit (including a proper proportion of any expense relating partly to the benefit and partly otherwise) less any part made good by the employee to those providing the benefit. [*ITEPA 2003, ss 203, 204; ICTA 1988, s 156(1)(2)*]. VAT is included whether or not recoverable by the employer (Revenue Pamphlet IR 131, A6). The cost of 'in-house' benefits (i.e. those consisting of services or facilities enjoyed by the employee which it is part of the employer's business to provide to members of the public) is the additional or marginal cost of their provision to the employee, rather than a proportionate part of total costs incurred in their provision both to employees and to the public. See *Pepper v Hart HL 1992, 65 TC 421*, in which only the marginal cost of providing school places for the children of masters at the school was assessable, regardless of whether or not the children occupied places which would otherwise have been provided to members of the public. (*Note*. This decision was based on consideration of statements by the Financial Secretary to the Treasury in Standing Committee debates on the enacting legislation. See 4.22 APPEALS as regards the circumstances in which this is permissible.)

Following this decision, the Revenue have set out their view of how the marginal cost rule should apply in practice. In particular, nil or negligible cost arises in the case of:

(i)   rail or bus travel by employees (provided fare-payers are not displaced);

(ii)   goods sold to employees for not less than the wholesale price; and

(iii) provision of professional services not requiring additional staffing (excluding disbursements).

It is accepted that no additional benefit arises where teachers pay 15% or more of normal school fees.

The decision also affects the calculation of the benefit of the provision of assets for part business, part private use. Fixed costs need not now be taken into account where the private use is incidental to the business use. The cash equivalent is the proper proportion of the 'annual value' of the asset (see below) together with any *additional* running expenses. (Revenue Press Release 21 January 1993).

See 75.47(*a*) below as regards valuation of incentive awards.

Where the benefit is the *use of an asset* other than a car or van (as to which see 75.18 below), the cash equivalent is the annual value (or if higher, the rent or hire charge paid by those providing the benefit) plus any expenses related to the asset's provision (excluding the cost of acquiring or producing it and excluding also any rent or hire charge payable for the asset by those providing the benefit). [*ITEPA 2003, s 205; ICTA 1988, s 156(5)(7)*].

Where the benefit is the *transfer of an asset after it has been used or depreciated* since the transferor acquired it, the cost of the benefit is the market value at the time of the transfer. However, if the asset (not a car or van) was first applied for the provision of any benefit for a person or for members of his family or household by reason of his employment after 5 April 1980 and a person (whether or not the present transferee) has been chargeable to tax on its use, the cost of the benefit (unless a higher benefit is obtained by taking market value at the time of transfer) is its market value when it was first so applied less the total amounts charged to tax for its use in the years up to and including the year of transfer. [*ITEPA 2003, s 206, Sch 7 para 32(2); ICTA 1988, s 156(3)(4)*].

Annual value of the use of an asset is:

for land, from 6 April 2003, its 'annual rental value' under *ITEPA 2003, s 207* (which in practice follows the earlier definition by reference to *ICTA 1988, s 837*, for which see 69.5(*b*) SCHEDULE A);

for any other case, 20% of market value at time asset was first provided as a benefit.

[*ITEPA 2003, ss 205(3), 207, 208; ICTA 1988, s 156(6)*].

Apportionment of cost or annual or market value. Where appropriate, e.g. where an asset is not available for the whole of a year of assessment or where it is available to more than one person, only a corresponding proportion of the cost etc. of the benefit (determined as above) is brought in. See *ITEPA 2003, s 204, ICTA 1998, s 156(2)*, Revenue Employment Income Manual EIM 21200 *et seq.* and *Kerr v Brown; Boyd v Brown (Sp C 333, 333A), [2002] SSCD 434, [2003] SSCD 266*.

Deductions. From 6 April 2003, deductions may be claimed from the cash equivalent calculated as above for payments falling within 75.6, 75.8–75.9, 75.11 or 75.13 above or

75.26 (employee liabilities), 75.27 (artiste's percentage deduction), 75.38 (personal security provision) or 75.42 (professional fees and subscriptions) below. [*ITEPA 2003, s 365*]. Previously, relief was restricted to amount falling within *ICTA 1988, s 198* (expenses 'wholly and necessarily incurred', see 75.11 above), *ICTA 1988, s 201* (professional subscriptions, see 75.42 below), *ICTA 1988, s 201AA* (employee liabilities and indemnity insurance, see 75.26 below) and *ICTA 1988, s 332(3)* (clergymen, see 75.13 above). [*ICTA 1988, s 156(8)*].

Part business and part private use. A deduction may be available under *ITEPA 2003, s 365* (as above) from the full cash equivalent of a benefit within the general charge where there is mixed use of the benefit, or the cost of the benefit may be apportioned under *ITEPA 2003, s 204* (see above) if the expense relates partly to the benefit and partly to other matters. This does not apply to benefits for which there are special computational rules (see 75.18 *et seq.* below). See Revenue Tax Bulletin October 2000 pp 779–782 for an article on this subject and for the application of *Pepper v Hart* (see above) in cases of mixed use. The article also deals in particular with the provision of home telephones.

Simon's Direct Tax Service. See E4.611 *et seq.*

75.17   *Example*

During 2004/05 P Ltd transferred to R a television set which it had previously leased to him for a nominal rent of £2 per month. The company also leased a suit to R under the same arrangements. R's salary is £30,000 p.a.
Television

First leased to R in April 2003 (when its market value was £560); transferred to R on 6 March 2005 for £50, the market value at that time being £175.

R's benefits are	£	£
2003/04		
Cost of benefit 20% × £560		112
Deduct Rent paid by R		24
Cash equivalent of benefit		£88
2004/05		
Cost of benefit 20% × £560 × $\frac{11}{12}$		103
Deduct Rent paid by R (11 months)		22
Cash equivalent of benefit		81
Greater of		
(i) Market value at transfer	175	
Deduct Price paid by R	50	
	£125	
And		
(ii) Original market value	560	
Deduct Cost of benefits note (*b*)	215	
	345	
Deduct Price paid by R	50	
	£295	
		295
Total		£376

Suit

First leased to R on 6 November 2004 (when its market value was £340).

R's benefit for 2004/05 is	
Cost of benefit 20% × £340 × $\frac{5}{12}$	28
Deduct Rent paid by R (5 months)	10
Cash equivalent of benefit	£18

Notes

(*a*) On the transfer of the television set, the cost of the benefits to date (£112 + 103), not the cash equivalents, is deducted from the original market value.

(*b*) It is assumed that the television set and suit have been bought by P Ltd and are not goods provided from within its own business. If the latter was the case, R would be assessed on the marginal cost to P Ltd in providing the benefit (in accordance with *Pepper v Hart* — see 75.16 above).

75.18   **Motor vehicles provided for private use.** The provision by an employer, by reason of the employment, of a car or van partly or wholly for 'private use' by an employee (or by a member of his family or household), without the transfer of any property in it, is the subject of a special basis of charge. A car provided by the employer is provided 'by reason of the employment' unless the employer is an individual and the provision is made in the normal course of his domestic, family or personal relationships. *'Private use'* means any use other than for travel the expenses of which would, if incurred and paid by the employee, have been deductible from his earnings, and a car or van is deemed to be available for private use unless the terms on which it is made available prohibit such use *and* it is not so used. [*ITEPA 2003, ss 114, 116, 117, 118, 171(1); ICTA 1988, s 157(1), s 159AA(1), s 168(5)(5A)(6), Sch 6 para 10, Sch 6A para 12; FA 1993, Sch 4 paras 4, 6; FA 1996, s 134, Sch 20 para 10(2); FA 1997, s 62(4); FA 2001, Sch 12 Pt II para 4; FA 2004, s 80, Sch 14 paras 2, 3*]. See 75.46 below as regards business use where more than one place of work. See also *Gilbert v Hemsley Ch D 1981, 55 TC 419*. Where a car salesman or demonstrator has to take a car home as part of his normal duties in order to call on a prospective customer, this will not of itself make the car available for his private use. The use of test or experimental cars by engineers in the motor and components industries will be considered on the facts of each particular case. (Revenue Booklet 480). See also Revenue Employment Income Manual EIM 23640 *et seq*. See 75.16(xxvii) above for an exemption for 2004/05 onwards for emergency vehicles.

The special basis of charge continues to apply where the car is in the *co-ownership* of the employer and employee (*Christensen v Vasili Ch D, [2004] STC 935*).

A car provided by a third party (e.g. by a car dealer to a football player for promotional purposes) is within these provisions where it is provided by reason of the employment (Revenue Employment Income Manual EIM 23062).

Where such a special basis of charge applies, no other charge arises in respect of any expenses or reimbursements etc. in relation to the vehicle or in respect of vouchers for their provision (e.g. insurance, road tax, congestion charges). It appears that this does not apply to the payment of fines by the employer (although parking fines may escape liability in certain circumstances — see Revenue Employment Income Manual EIM 21686). The provision of a driver is a separate benefit under 75.16 above (subject to an expense claim for business use). [*ITEPA 2003, ss 239, 269; ICTA 1988, s 154(2), s 155(1), s 157(3), s 159AA(3), s 159AC(3); FA 1993, Sch 4 paras 2–4; FA 2002, Sch 6 para 3*]. See 75.19 below for flat rate charge on mobile telephones for 1998/99 and earlier years, and 75.16(xxiii) above for the general exemption of the provision of mobile telephones thereafter. The provision of a personalised registration number does not enter into the computation under the special basis of charge, whether under (i) or (ii) below, and is normally excluded from charge as above. (Revenue Tax Bulletin December 1994 p 177). The provision of a benefit which could equally be enjoyed by the employee when using a car of his own (e.g. a season ticket for a toll bridge) is not excluded from charge (Revenue Employment Income Manual EIM 23005).

The mere fact that an employee is offered an alternative (for example, a cash alternative) to a company car (or, for 2005/06 onwards, a van) does not make the benefit chargeable under the general earnings rules as opposed to the special company car (or van) provisions. [*ITEPA 2003, s 119; ICTA 1988, s 157A; FA 1995, s 43(1)(4); FA 2004, s 80, Sch 14 para 4*].

A car is any mechanically propelled road vehicle *except* (i) a vehicle constructed primarily for carrying goods, (ii) a vehicle of a type unsuitable and not commonly used as a private vehicle, (iii) a motor cycle and (iv) an invalid carriage. [*ITEPA 2003, s 115; ICTA 1988, s 168(5)(a)*]. A car owned by the fire brigade and equipped with a flashing light and other emergency equipment was held to be within (ii) (*Gurney v Richards Ch D 1989, 62 TC 287*).

A van is a mechanically propelled road vehicle, other than a motor cycle, of a construction primarily suited for the conveyance of goods or burden and designed (or adapted) not to exceed a laden weight of 3,500 kgs. in normal use. [*ITEPA 2003, s 115; ICTA 1988, s 168(5A)(a)(e); FA 1993, Sch 4 para 6*]. There is apparent confusion about the status of 'double cab pick-ups', and for 2002/03 onwards the Revenue work in line with definitions used by Customs & Excise for VAT purposes (Revenue Employer's Bulletin September 2002 p 8). For further details, see www.inlandrevenue.gov.uk/cars/company_vans_info.htm

There is a limited exemption for '*disabled employees*', i.e. those with a physical or mental impairment which has a substantial and long-term adverse effect on their ability to carry out normal day-to-day activities. Where a car is made available to such an employee, without any transfer of the property in it, no benefits charge arises on provision of the car, provided that

(*a*) the car has been adapted for the employee's special needs (or has an automatic transmission (see (ii) below) because the employee can only drive such a car), and

(*b*) the terms of its provision prohibit private use except for home-to-work travel or travel in connection with certain training course, and those terms are complied with.

Permitted use within (*b*) above is treated as business use for the purposes of the mileage limits applicable for 2001/02 and earlier years. The provision of, or payment or reimbursement of the cost of, fuel for the car similarly does not give rise to an income tax liability where those conditions are met. From 6 April 2003, this exemption is statutory [*ITEPA 2003, s 247*], having previously applied by Revenue practice and concession (see Revenue Booklet 480, Revenue Pamphlet IR 1, A59 and Revenue Employment Income Manual EIM 23601). See also 75.46 below.

The provision of car (and, for 2005/06 onwards, van) parking facilities for an employee at or near his place of work (including such provision in relation to a privately-owned vehicle) constitutes neither earnings nor a benefit. [*ITEPA 2003, s 237; ICTA 1988, s 155(1A); FA 1988, s 46; FA 2004, s 80, Sch 14 para 8*].

Where two members of the same family or household are each supplied with a car for their private use by the same employer, and neither is in lower-paid employment, each will be charged separately according to his/her own usage but will not be charged in respect of the car supplied to the other. Similarly, if one of them is not in such employment, but is supplied with the car in his/her own right either in equivalent circumstances to other employees in similar employment or in accordance with normal commercial practice for a job of that kind, the other will not be charged in respect of the car supplied to the lower-paid employee. This applies equally to any fuel scale charge. Where two or more persons are chargeable in respect of their shared use of the same car, the charge applicable to each of them will be reduced on a just and reasonable basis (and a similar reduction is made in any fuel scale charge). From 6 April 2003, these reliefs are statutory [*ITEPA 2003, ss 148, 153, 169*], having previously applied by Revenue practice and concession (see in particular Revenue Pamphlet IR 1, A71). The reliefs for members of the same family or household are extended to vans for 2005/06 onwards. [*ITEPA 2003, s 169A; FA 2004, s 80, Sch 14 para 6*]. (A reduction for shared vans was already available — see (iii) and (iiia) below.)

Compensation to an employee from whom a company car was withdrawn following a change of policy by the employer was held to be an assessable emolument in *Bird v Martland; Bird v Allen Ch D 1982, 56 TC 89*.

Where the special basis of charge applies to provision of a car, a separate charge also arises in respect of provision of any fuel for private use (see (iv) below). In the case of provision of a van, no separate charge arises before 2007/08 on provision of fuel; for 2007/08 onwards, see (iiia) below.

As regards mileage allowances for the provision by employees of fuel for business travel in company cars, see 75.46 below.

Simon's Direct Tax Service. See E4.625.

(i) *Cars for private use: 1994/95 to 2001/02.* For 1994/95 to 2001/02 inclusive, the cash equivalent of the benefit of provision of a company car for private use is **35%** of the 'price of the car as regards a year'. Where the employee is required by the nature of his employment to use, and does use, the car for at least 18,000 miles of business travel in a year, this is reduced to **15%** for 1999/2000 and subsequent years (for 1998/99 and earlier years, by two-thirds, i.e. to $11\frac{2}{3}$%). Where such use amounts to at least 2,500 but less than 18,000 business miles, the reduction is to **25%** for 1999/2000 and subsequent years (for 1998/99 and earlier years, by one-third, i.e. to $23\frac{1}{3}$%). Where an employee is taxable in respect of the benefit of the provision of two or more cars available concurrently, for all such cars other than the one used to the greatest extent for business travel in the period of concurrent availability the reduction for 18,000 or more business miles is to **25%** instead of 15% for 1999/2000 and subsequent years (by one-third to $23\frac{1}{3}$% instead of by two-thirds to $11\frac{2}{3}$% for 1998/99 and earlier years), and no reduction is made where business miles are less than 18,000. The figures of 2,500 and 18,000 are reduced *pro rata* where the car is 'unavailable' for part of the year. Where there is a change in the vehicle provided during a year of assessment, they are similarly reduced *pro rata* and applied to the period for which each vehicle was provided (*Henwood v Clarke Ch D 1997, 69 TC 611*).

The cash equivalent is reduced, or further reduced, by one-quarter (one-third for 1998/99 and earlier years) where the car is four or more years old at the end of the year of assessment in question. It is similarly reduced *pro rata* where the car is 'unavailable' for part of the year.

Where the employee is required, as a condition of the car being available for private use, to pay for that use, the cash equivalent determined as above for a year is reduced (or extinguished) by the amount so paid in respect of the year. No reduction was allowed for a payment made to the employer to obtain a better car (*Brown v Ware (Sp C 29) [1995] SSCD 155*) or for a payment made for the insurance of the car for both private and business use (*CIR v Quigley CS, [1995] STC 931*).

A car is '*unavailable*' on a day falling before the first day on which it is made available to the employee (or a member of his family or household) or after the last day on which it is made so available, or on a day falling within a period of 30 or more consecutive days throughout which it is not so available. See below as regards regulations modifying these provisions in cases where a replacement car is provided during a period in which the car normally available to an employee is not so available for a period of less than 30 days.

The '*price of a car as regards a year*' is its 'list price' (or its 'notional price' if it has no list price) on the '*relevant day*', i.e. the day immediately before the date on which the car was first registered under the *Vehicle Excise and Registration Act 1994* or corresponding legislation, plus the price of certain accessories and net of certain capital contributions, and the age of a car commences with the date of its first registration. For 1998/99 and subsequent years, in the case of a car manufactured so as to be capable of running on 'road fuel gas' (as defined), e.g. LPG, the price as so determined is reduced by so much of it as is reasonably attributable to the car's being manufactured to be so capable rather than only being capable of running on petrol.

The '*list price*' of a car is the price published by the manufacturer, importer or distributor (as the case may be) as the inclusive price (including delivery charges and taxes, but not vehicle excise duty) appropriate for a car of that kind (including any standard accessories) sold in the UK singly in an open market retail sale, plus the price so published (including any fitting charges) of any optional accessories with the car when it was first made available to the employee (or to a member of his family or household). The price advertised by a car dealer cannot be used instead of that published by the manufacturer etc. (see Revenue Tax Bulletin December 1994 p 177). If no such price is available for an optional accessory, no adjustment is made to the list price in respect of the accessory (which may, however, be the subject of a separate addition, see below). The accessories taken into account for these purposes are those attached to the car (whether or not permanently) for use with the car (without any transfer of the property) and not necessarily provided for use in the performance of the employee's duties. The following are excluded from being taken into account as accessories for this purpose:

(*a*)   mobile telephones (see 75.16(xxiii) above and 75.19 below);

(*b*)   equipment either designed solely for use by a chronically sick or disabled person or made available to enable an employee holding, at the time the car is first made available to him, a disabled person's badge (an 'orange badge') to use the car in spite of the disability which entitles him to hold that badge at that time; and

(*c*)   (for 1998/99 onwards) equipment by means of which the car is capable of running on 'road fuel gas' (as defined), e.g. LPG (and see above as regards cars manufactured with that capability).

The charge is based on the list price of an individual car at the time it is first registered, not on average prices. However, where there are very frequent changes of car, inspectors may agree to arrangements under which average prices are used (see Revenue Employment Income Manual EIM 23641 *et seq.*).

The '*notional price*' of a car or accessory is that which might reasonably be expected to have been its list price (as above) (including accessories in the case of a car) had such a price been published.

There is, however, an overall limit of £80,000 (or such greater sum as the Treasury may specify by order) on the price, whether list or notional, after taking account of accessories (as below), to be taken into account under these provisions.

Optional accessories not having a list price and hence not taken into account as above, are the subject of a separate addition to the price of the car equal to their price delivered and fitted (list or notional, as above, as appropriate). A separate addition is similarly made where such accessories are fitted after the car is first made available to the employee (or to a member of his family or household), but ignoring for this purpose any accessory whose price is less than £100 (or such greater sum as the Treasury may specify by order). Again, mobile telephones, accessories designed solely for use by the disabled and road fuel gas conversions (see (a)–(c) above) are excluded.

The Treasury may make regulations (which may make different provision for different cases) as regards the fitting of replacement accessories, to provide either that the price of the car will remain the same as if the accessory replaced had continued in use, or that the above provisions are to be modified in some other way to take account of the replacement.

Where the employee makes a capital contribution to the cost of the car or accessories taken into account as above, the price of the car for the purposes of the charge on the employee for the year in which the contribution is made and subsequent years is reduced by the lesser of the amount of the contribution (or the sum of such contributions) and £5,000 (or such greater sum as may be specified by Treasury order). An agreement for the employee to receive a proportionate return of his capital contribution on disposal of the car will not prejudice relief in respect of the contribution, and will not give rise to any Schedule E charge on the amount repaid. An agreement to refund the contribution in full will result in the contribution being disregarded. (Revenue Tax Bulletin December 1994 p 177).

[ICTA 1988, s 157(2), ss 168A–168E, s 168G, Sch 6; FA 1993, Sch 3 paras 1–5, 7; FA 1995, s 44; FA 1996, s 134, Sch 20 para 40; FA 1998, s 60; FA 1999, s 44(4), s 47].

Classic cars. There are special provisions substituting market value for the price determined as above where the market value is at least £15,000 (or such greater sum as the Treasury may specify by order) and exceeds that price, and the car is 15 years or more old at the end of the year concerned. Capital contributions are taken into account on a similar basis to that described above, and the £80,000 overall limit similarly applies. [*ICTA 1988, ss 168F, 168G; FA 1993, Sch 3 para 4*].

Replacement cars and accessories. Regulations provide for the situation where a double charge would otherwise arise where a temporary replacement car is provided while the normal car is unavailable for use for less than 30 days. The replacement car is ignored, and mileage in it treated as mileage in the normal car, provided that either it is of a similar quality to the normal car (in practice, that it is not materially better than the normal car) or it is not provided as part of an arrangement to supply a better car. Similarly, where an accessory is fitted which replaces another, regulations provide that the 'price' of the car will not be affected where the replacement is of the same kind and does not cost more than the price of the old accessory (or, if greater, the current price of an equivalent to the old accessory). The addition to the 'price' in respect of a more costly replacement accessory is restricted to the excess cost over the amount (if any) included in the 'price' in respect of the old accessory. [*SI 1994 Nos 777, 778*].

Administration. See generally Revenue Pamphlet IR 172. See also 55.16 PAY AS YOU EARN.

See Simon's Direct Tax Service E4.626.

75.18 Schedule E—Employment Income

Example

A, B and C are employees of D Ltd. Each earns at least £8,500 per annum and each is provided with a company car throughout 2001/02. The company also bears at least part of the cost of petrol for private motoring (see (iv) below).

A is provided with a 1,800 cc car first registered in October 1998 with a list price (including VAT, car tax (but not road tax), delivery charges and standard accessories) of £19,000. The car was made available to A in April 1999. An immobiliser was fitted in September 1999 at a cost of £200. A's business mileage is 20,000 for 2001/02. He is required to pay the company £250 per year as a condition of using the car for private motoring, and duly pays this amount.

B is provided with a 1,400 cc car first registered in March 1997 with a list price of £9,000. B drives 8,000 business miles in 2001/02. He was required to make a capital contribution of £1,000 on provision of the car in January 2000.

C is provided with a luxury car first registered in February 2000 with a list price of £85,000 (which includes optional accessories). He made a capital contribution of £3,000 in 1999/2000. C's business mileage was 2,000 in 2001/02.

Car and fuel benefits for 2001/02 are as follows.

	A £	B £	C £
List price	19,000	9,000	85,000
Later optional accessories	200	—	—
	19,200		
Capital contributions	—	(1,000)	(3,000)
			£82,000
Price cap for expensive cars			80,000
Price of car	£19,200	£8,000	£80,000
Cash equivalent — 35% of price of car			28,000
— 15%	2,880		
— 25%		2,000	
Reduction for older cars ($\frac{1}{4}$)	—	(500)	—
Contribution for private use	(250)	—	—
Car benefit	2,630	1,500	28,000
Fuel benefit (see (iv) below)	2,460	1,930	3,620
Total car and fuel benefits	£5,090	£3,430	£31,620

(ii) *Cars for private use: 2002/03 and subsequent years.* For 2002/03 and subsequent years, the basis of charge for 2001/02 and earlier years (see (i) above) continues, but instead of the fixed charge of 35% of list price subject to reduction in respect of business travel and age of the car, the cash equivalent of the benefit is a percentage of the list price dependent on carbon dioxide emissions and certain related factors. Thus the detailed provisions described at (i) above, apart from the first two paragraphs, continue to apply (except in relation to certain bi-fuel cars, see (c) below), and the pro-rata reduction for periods of unavailability continues to apply with a minor revision to take account of leap years.

The percentage of list price which determines the cash equivalent of the benefit (the '*appropriate percentage*') varies (except as further detailed below) from 15% to 35%

depending on the 'applicable carbon dioxide emissions figure' for the car, expressed in grams per kilometre (g/km). If it does not exceed the '*lower threshold*' for the year (165g/km for 2002/03, 155g/km for 2003/04, 145g/km for 2004/05, 140 g/km for 2005/06 and subsequent years, subject (after 5 April 2006) to a different figure being substituted by the Treasury by order), the 15% figure applies. For each 5g/km by which it exceeds the lower threshold (rounding the emissions figure down to the nearest multiple of 5), the 15% figure is increased by 1%, up to a maximum of 35%.

The 'applicable carbon dioxide emissions figure' is determined as follows.

(*a*)   If the car was first registered after 31 December 1997 but before 1 October 1999 and conformed to a vehicle type with an 'EC type-approval certificate' (as defined), or had a 'UK approval certificate' (as defined), specifying a carbon dioxide emissions figure in terms of g/km driven, it is that figure.

(*b*)   If the car is first registered after 30 September 1999 on the basis of an 'EC certificate of conformity' (as defined) or UK approval certificate specifying a carbon dioxide emissions figure in terms of g/km driven, it is that figure or, if more than one figure is quoted, the carbon dioxide emissions (combined) figure.

(*c*)   If a bi-fuel car is first registered after 31 December 1999 on the basis of an EC certificate of conformity or UK approval certificate specifying separate carbon dioxide emissions figures in terms of g/km driven for the different fuels, it is the lowest figure specified or, if more than one figure is specified in relation to each fuel, the lowest carbon dioxide emissions (combined) figure. (In the case of such bi-fuel cars, the specific list price provisions applicable for 2001/02 and earlier years to cars capable of running on 'road fuel gas' are disapplied.)

The official carbon dioxide emissions figures referred to in (*a*)–(*c*) above are recorded on the vehicle registration document from November 2000. For earlier registrations, an online carbon dioxide emissions enquiry service has been set up by the Society of Motor Manufacturers and Traders under an agreement with the Revenue.

Cars with no carbon dioxide emissions figure. If the car is first registered after 31 December 1997 but (*a*)–(*c*) above do not apply, then if the car has an internal combustion engine with reciprocating piston(s), the appropriate percentage is 15% if the cylinder capacity is 1,400cc or less, 25% if it is 1,401–2,000cc inclusive, 35% if it is more than 2,000cc. If a car which does not have such an engine is an '*electrically propelled vehicle*' (i.e. if it is propelled solely by electrical power derived from an external source or from a battery not connected to any source of power when the vehicle is in motion), it is 15%. Otherwise it is 35%.

Automatic cars made available to disabled drivers. Where an employee holding a disabled person's badge (an 'orange badge') can only drive a car with automatic transmission, and an automatic car to which (*a*) or (*b*) above applies is made available to him or her (and not merely deemed to be made available to him or her because it is made available to a member of his or her family or household), then if the applicable carbon dioxide emissions figure for the car is higher than that for the 'equivalent manual car', the manual figure is substituted. The '*equivalent manual car*' is the closest non-automatic variant available of the same make and model of car first registered at or about the same time. A car has automatic transmission for these purposes if the gear ratio cannot be varied by the driver independently of the accelerator and brakes, or if the driver can independently vary the gear ratio but not by means of a manually-operated clutch pedal or lever.

Diesel car supplement. Where a car propelled solely by diesel is first registered after 31 December 1997, the appropriate percentage, determined as above, is increased by 3%, subject to a maximum of 35%.

Discounts. The Treasury may make regulations providing for a reduction in any of the appropriate percentage figures as above in such circumstances, and subject to such conditions, as may be prescribed. Under *SI 2001 No 1123*, reductions are accordingly provided for as follows.

(1)   Cars first registered after 31 December 1997, propelled solely by diesel and meeting the European standard for cleaner cars (Council Directive 70/220/EEC, Annex 1, section 5.3.1.4, table row B): the amount of the diesel supplement (as above).

(2)   Electrically-propelled cars (as above) first registered after 31 December 1997: 6%.

(3)   Cars first registered after 31 December 1997 and capable of being propelled by electricity and petrol: 2% + 1% for each 20g/km by which the carbon dioxide emissions figure is less than the lower threshold (as above).

(4)   Cars first registered after 31 December 1997 and propelled solely by road fuel gas (e.g. LPG), and bi-fuel cars within (*c*) above: 1% + 1% for each 20g/km by which the carbon dioxide emissions figure is less than the lower threshold (as above).

(5)   Cars first registered after 31 December 1997 which are bi-fuel cars either when first registered or by virtue of the subsequent addition of equipment, but which are not within (*c*) above: 1%.

Cars registered before 1 January 1998. If the car has an internal combustion engine with reciprocating piston(s), the appropriate percentage is 15% if the cylinder capacity is 1,400cc or less, 22% if it is 1,401–2,000cc inclusive, 32% if it is more than 2,000cc. If the car is an electrically propelled vehicle, it is 15%. In any other case it is 32%.

[*ITEPA 2003, ss 116, 120–147, 170(1)–(4), 171, 172, Sch 7 paras 22, 23; ICTA 1988, ss 157, 157A, 168(5)(6), 168A–168G, Sch 6; FA 1995, s 44; FA 1998, s 60; FA 1999, s 44(4); FA 2000, s 59, Schs 11, 40 Pt II(3); FA 2003, s 138; SI 1994 Nos 777, 778*].

See Simon's Direct Tax Service E4.626A.

Example

A, B and C in the example at (i) above continued to enjoy the benefit of the provision of the same cars in 2002/03 onwards on the same terms. The details as regards list prices and contributions are accordingly unchanged.

A's car (which has a diesel engine) has an emissions figure of 185g/km.

B's 1,400cc car was, as previously noted, first registered before 1 January 1998.

C's car has an emissions figure of 280g/km.

Car and fuel benefits for 2004/05 are as follows.

	A	B	C
Price of car (as for 2001/02)	£19,200	£8,000	£80,000
Cash equivalent — 26% (including 3% diesel supplement)	4,992		
— 15%		1,200	
— 35%			28,000
Contribution for private use	(250)	—	—
Car benefit	4,742	1,200	28,000
Fuel benefit (see (v) below)	3,744	2,160	5,040
Total car and fuel benefits	£8,486	£3,360	£33,040

(iii)   *Vans for private use: 2004/05 and earlier years* (for subsequent years, see (iiia) below). Where a 'van' (for which see the opening paragraphs of this section) is available for an employee's private use, the employee is to be taxed on the benefit in accordance with a standard scale.

Unless the van is a 'shared van' (see below) for all or part of the year, the scale benefit is **£500**, reduced to **£350** for a van aged four years or more at the end of the year. The scale benefit is reduced pro-rata if for any part of the year it is either 'unavailable' or is a shared van. A van is *'unavailable'* on a day falling before the first day on which it is made available to the employee (or a member of his family or household) or after the last day on which it is made so available, or on a day falling within a period of 30 or more consecutive days throughout which it is not so available. The scale benefit is reduced (or extinguished) by any monetary contribution which the employee is required to make, and does make, as a condition for private use. The age of a van commences with the date of its first registration.

A van is a *'shared van'* for any period throughout which it is available concurrently or otherwise to two or more employees of the same employer, and in which there is no period exceeding 30 consecutive days during which it is exclusively available to one employee. A van shared for part of a day is treated as shared throughout that day. Each employee to whom one or more shared vans are available for private use while they are shared vans and who makes private use of the van (or at least one of them) while it is a shared van is a *'participating employee'*.

Scale benefits of £500 or £350 (depending on the van's age) are allocated to each shared van, these amounts being reduced pro-rata where for any part of the year the van is not a shared van or where the van is incapable of use for 30 or more consecutive days. The aggregate scale benefit for all shared vans is then divided equally among the participating employees, and the result is the amount on which each such employee is taxed for the year, except that if that amount is more than £500 it is reduced to £500.

A participating employee may claim an alternative method of calculation (such a claim being counted as a claim for relief for the purposes of penalties under *TMA 1970, s 95*, see 57.3 PENALTIES), as follows.

(*a*)   For each van involved, take the number of days in the year of assessment during which the employee (or a member of his family or household) makes private use of a van while it is a shared van.

(*b*)   Aggregate the numbers arrived at under (*a*) (where more than one van is involved).

(*c*)   Multiply the number in (*a*) or, where applicable, the number in (*b*) by £5.

The result is the amount on which the employee is taxed.

The amount on which the employee would otherwise be taxed, whether calculated under the standard or the alternative method, is reduced, or extinguished, by any monetary contribution which the employee is required to make, and does make, as a condition for private use of a shared van while it is a shared van. Where more than one van is involved, the aggregate of such contributions is taken.

Where, in respect of the same van, an employee has a taxable benefit for a year under both the non-shared van and the shared van provisions as above, the benefits are aggregated to arrive at his total taxable benefit for the year.

There is an overall limit of £500 on the charge under these provisions on an employee for a year at no one time during which more than one van was available for the private use of the employee or a member of his family or household.

[*ITEPA 2003, ss 154–166 as originally enacted, Sch 7 para 24; ICTA 1988, s 159AA(1)(2), s 168(5A), Sch 6A; FA 1993, Sch 4 paras 4, 6–8*].

For 2006/07 and earlier years, there is no separate charge for fuel provided for private motoring in a van.

Revenue Pamphlet IR 136 provides an employees' and employers' guide to the taxation of company vans.

See Simon's Direct Tax Service E4.630.

Example

L is an employee of N Ltd, earning £18,000 per annum. From 1 October 2004 to 5 April 2005, L is provided by his employer with exclusive use of a one-year old company van (Van A) on terms which do not prohibit private use and which provide for a deduction of £4 per month to be made from his net salary at the end of each month in consideration for private use. For the period 6 April 2004 to 30 September 2004 inclusive, L had shared the van with another employee, M. Either L or a member of his family or household had made private use of the shared van for 42 days during that period, and M also made private use of the van. No payment for private use was required.

In addition to the van mentioned above, four other company vans are shared between five employees of N Ltd (excluding L and M) throughout the year ended 5 April 2005, three of which vans are aged less than four years at the end of that year. All the employees make some private use of one or more of the vans. One of the vans is off the road and incapable of use for three weeks in March 2005.

All vans mentioned have a normal laden weight not exceeding 3,500 kilograms.

The taxable benefit to L for 2004/05 of company vans is calculated as follows.

Non-shared van

	£
Cash equivalent of benefit before adjustment	500
Exclude Period for which van is a shared van:	
£500 × $\dfrac{178}{366}$ (6.4.04 – 30.9.04)	243
	257
Deduct Payment for private use (6 × £4 per month)	24
Cash equivalent of benefit	£233

Shared van

	£	£
Basic values:		
Van A	500	
Exclude Period for which van is not a shared van:		
$£500 \times \dfrac{188}{366}$ (1.10.04 – 5.4.05)	257	243
Other vans ((3 × £500) + (1 × £350))		1,850
Sum of basic values		£2,093
Divide £2,093 equally between seven participating employees		£299
Cash equivalent of benefit to L (maximum £500)		£299

Total benefits to L

	£
Non-shared van	233
Shared van	299
Total cash equivalent of benefit	£532
But restricted by *ITEPA 2003, s 166* to	£500

L will thus be taxed on a van benefit of £500 for 2004/05.

In relation to the shared van, L then makes a claim for the alternative calculation under *ITEPA 2003, s 164*.

Number of relevant days for Van A	42
Number of relevant days for other shared vans	Nil
Aggregate number of relevant days	42
Cash equivalent of benefit to L (42 × £5 per day)	£210

Total benefits to L (revised)

	£
Non-shared van	233
Shared van	210
Total cash equivalent of benefit	£443

L will thus be taxed on a van benefit of £443 for 2004/05.

(iiia)   *Vans for private use: 2005/06 and subsequent years.* The cash equivalent of the benefit of a 'van' (for which see the opening paragraphs of this section) depends on the degree to which private use is permitted or does, in fact, occur.

If the van is made available to the employee mainly for business travel and the terms on which it is made available prohibit its private use otherwise than for the purposes of 'ordinary commuting' (for which see 75.11 above), the cash equivalent of the benefit is **nil**. For this purpose, the term 'ordinary commuting' is extended to include travel between two places that is for practical purposes substantially ordinary commuting. It is a further condition that neither the employee nor any member of his family or household does, in fact, make private use of the van outside these terms.

These requirements must be met throughout the tax year (or throughout that part of the tax year during which the van is available to the employee), but 'insignificant' private use is disregarded.

If the restricted private use requirements above are not met, the cash equivalent of the benefit is

- (for 2005/06 and 2006/07) £500 if the van is less than four years old at the end of the tax year or £350 if is not;

- (for 2007/08 and subsequent years) £3,000 regardless of the age of the van.

The above figures are subject to reductions as outlined below for periods when the van is unavailable or if the van is shared or if the employee makes payments for private use. There is a separate fuel benefit charge (see below).

If the van is 'unavailable' on any one or more days during the tax year, the cash equivalent as above is reduced proportionately. For these purposes, a van is *unavailable* on any day in the tax year if that day falls before the first day on which it is available to the employee or after the last day on which it is so available or within a period of 30 days or more throughout which it is not so available.

If a van is shared, i.e. if it is made available to two or more employees concurrently by the same employer and is available concurrently for each of those employees' private use (or private use by any member of their family or household), the cash equivalent as above to each such employee (reduced in each case for any periods of unavailability) is reduced on a just and reasonable basis. If any of the employees in question is a member of the family or household of another of them and the first-mentioned employee is outside the charge to tax on van benefits by virtue of his being in lower-paid employment (see 75.14 above), the availability of the van to him is disregarded in applying any reduction in the case of the second-mentioned employee.

If, as a condition for private use of a van, an employee is required to pay an amount of money (whether by deduction from earnings or otherwise) and does, in fact, make such payment, the cash equivalent (after applying any reductions as above) is reduced by the amount paid (or by so much of that amount as is required to reduce the cash equivalent to nil).

If the van normally available to the employee is not available to him for a period of less than 30 days and is replaced for all or part of that period by another van, the above provisions generally apply as if the replacement van were the normal van.

The cash equivalent figures of nil and £3,000 above may be altered by the Treasury by statutory instrument.

Fuel charge. If fuel is provided for a van by reason of the employment and the cash equivalent of the benefit of the van itself falls to be computed on the basis that the restricted private use requirements above are not met, then **for 2007/08 onwards**, and subject to the exceptions below, there is a tax charge on fuel as well as on the van itself. Fuel is treated as provided if *inter alia* a liability for such fuel is discharged, a non-cash voucher or credit-token is used to obtain fuel or to obtain money to buy fuel or if any sum is paid for expenses incurred in providing fuel. The supply of electrical energy for an electrically-propelled vehicle does not count as provision of fuel for these purposes.

The cash equivalent of the benefit of fuel is £500. However, no charge applies for a tax year if either

- the fuel is made available for business travel only; or

- the employee is required to make good the full cost of fuel provided for private use and does, in fact, do so.

Where for any part of the tax year either

- fuel is not provided for the van at all, or

- it is made available only for business travel, or

- the requirements for the 'making good' exemption referred to above are met,

and there is no subsequent time in the year when none of these three conditions is met, the cash equivalent of the fuel benefit is reduced in the proportion that the number of days on which at least one of these conditions is met bears to the number of days in the year. (For example, if for part of a year an employee makes good the cost of all fuel for private use but then ceases to do so later in the same tax year, without one of the other conditions being met, no reduction can be made to the cash equivalent of the benefit for that year.)

The cash equivalent of the fuel benefit is also proportionately reduced if the van is 'unavailable' (see above) at any time in the tax year. As above, a replacement van generally counts as the normal van.

If the cash equivalent of the benefit of the van itself falls to be reduced because the van is shared (see above), a corresponding reduction is made in the cash equivalent of the fuel benefit.

The cash equivalent figure of £500 above may be altered by the Treasury by statutory instrument.

[*ITEPA 2003, ss 154–164, 170(1A)(2)(5); FA 2004, s 80, Sch 14 paras 5, 7*].

(iv) *Car fuel for private use: 2002/03 and earlier years.* A scale charge applies to free fuel provided for private motoring in 'company' cars, i.e. a vehicle which attracts, or could attract, a charge within (i) or (ii) above. The charge varies with the cylinder capacity of the car. Separate scales apply for petrol and diesel cars. The scale charge does not apply to fuel provided for vans (see (iii) above).

The scale charges are as follows.

Table for 2002/03

		Petrol/LPG (£)	Diesel (£)
(a)	With cylinder capacity of		
	Up to 1,400 cc	2,240	2,850
	1,401 cc to 2,000 cc	2,850	2,850
	2,001 cc or more	4,200	4,200
(b)	without a cylinder capacity	£4,200	

[*SI 2002 No 706*]

Table for 2001/02

		Petrol/LPG (£)	Diesel (£)
(a)	with cylinder capacity of		
	Up to 1,400 cc	1,930	2,460
	1,401 cc to 2,000 cc	2,460	2,460
	2,001 cc or more	3,620	3,620
(b)	without a cylinder capacity	£3,620	

[*SI 2001 No 635*]

Table for 2000/01

		Petrol/LPG (£)	Diesel (£)
(a)	with cylinder capacity of		
	Up to 1,400 cc	1,700	2,170
	1,401 cc to 2,000 cc	2,170	2,170
	2,001 cc or more	3,200	3,200
(b)	without a cylinder capacity	£3,200	

[SI 2000 No 810]

Table for 1999/2000

		Petrol/LPG (£)	Diesel (£)
(a)	with cylinder capacity of		
	Up to 1,400 cc	1,210	1,540
	1,401 cc to 2,000 cc	1,540	1,540
	2,001 cc or more	2,270	2,270
(b)	without a cylinder capacity	£2,270	

[SI 1999 No 684]

Table for 1998/99

		Petrol/LPG (£)	Diesel (£)
(a)	with cylinder capacity of		
	Up to 1,400 cc	1,010	1,280
	1,401 cc to 2,000 cc	1,280	1,280
	2,001 cc or more	1,890	1,890
(b)	without a cylinder capacity	£1,890	

[FA 1998, s 59]

Table for 1997/98

		Petrol/LPG (£)	Diesel (£)
(a)	With cylinder capacity of		
	Up to 1,400 cc	800	740
	1,401 cc to 2,000 cc	1,010	740
	2,001 cc or more	1,490	940
(b)	without a cylinder capacity	£1,490	

[SI 1996 No 2954]

Where the charge for private use of a car is reduced by reason of its being unavailable for part of the year (see (i) and (ii) above), the scale rate for private fuel is similarly reduced. There are no special rules for second cars, cars with low business mileage or older cars. If the employee is required to make good to his employer the cost of *all* company fuel used for private purposes (including travel between home and work), and in fact does so during the year in question (or without unreasonable delay thereafter), the scale charge is cancelled, but there is no reduction where fuel is provided for part only of a year. Fuel provided only for home-to-work travel of severely and permanently disabled employees is ignored for this purpose (see Revenue Booklet 480). Where the scale charge applies, there is no charge under other provisions (e.g. on expense allowances or use of credit cards or vouchers which enable the employee to obtain private fuel) and, accordingly, the *method* by which private fuel is obtained does not affect the employee's tax liability. The rates do not apply to fuel provided for private use in individuals' own cars, hire cars etc., where the general charging rules continue to apply (i.e. the employer will notify the Revenue on form P11D of the actual cost of fuel provided by him). For fuel provided *by the employee* for business use in such cars, see 75.46 below. The Treasury may alter the Table by statutory instrument.

[ICTA 1988, s 158; F(No 2)A 1992, s 53; FA 1993, s 71(2)(3), Sch 3 paras 6, 7; FA 1995, s 43(2)].

Providing that all the miles of private travel have been properly identified, the Revenue will accept that there is no fuel charge where the employer uses the appropriate advisory rate from the table in (v) below, first published in January 2002, to work out the cost of fuel used for private travel that the employee must make good (Revenue Employment Income Manual EIM 23781). See (v) below for further detail.

See Simon's Direct Tax Service E4.629.

(v) *Car fuel for private use: 2003/04 and subsequent years.* A new method is introduced from 5 April 2003 for calculating the cash equivalent of the benefit of provision of free fuel for private motoring in a 'company car', i.e. a vehicle which attracts, or could attract, a charge within (ii) above. This particular charge does not apply to fuel provided for vans (see (iii) and (iiia) above), but a separate charge for van fuel applies for 2007/08 onwards, for which see (iiia) above. The cash equivalent is obtained by applying the 'appropriate percentage' (see (ii) above) used in determining the benefit of use of the car to an amount initially fixed at £14,400 (and variable by Treasury order). Within the normal range for the 'appropriate percentage' of 15% to 35%, the fuel charge is thus from £2,160 to £5,040. 'Fuel' for these purposes does *not* include electrical energy for an electrically propelled vehicle.

If the employee is required to make good to his employer the cost of *all* company fuel used for private purposes, and in fact does so during the year in question (or without unreasonable delay thereafter), the charge is reduced to nil. Travel between home and work is private for these purposes.

Where for any part of the tax year either

- fuel is not provided for the car at all, or

- it is made available only for business travel, or

- the requirements for the 'making good' exemption referred to above are met,

and there is no subsequent time in the year when none of these three conditions is met, the cash equivalent of the fuel benefit is reduced in the proportion that the number of days on which at least one of these conditions is met bears to the number of days in the year. (For example, if for part of a year an employee makes good the cost of all fuel for private use but then ceases to do so later in the same tax year, without one of the other conditions being met, no reduction can be made to the cash equivalent of the benefit for that year.)

The cash equivalent of the fuel benefit is also proportionately reduced if the car is 'unavailable' (see (i) above) at any time in the tax year.

Where there is a charge under these provisions, there is no charge under other provisions in respect of the supply of fuel (e.g. on expense allowances or use of credit cards or vouchers which enable the employee to obtain private fuel). The *method* by which private fuel is obtained does not affect the employee's liability.

These provisions do not apply to fuel provided for private use in individuals' own cars, hire cars etc., where the general charging rules continue to apply (i.e. the employer will notify the Revenue on form P11D of the actual cost of fuel provided by him). For fuel provided *by the employee* for business use in a car *other than* a company car, see 75.46 below.

[*ITEPA 2003, ss 149–152, 170(5)(6); ICTA 1988, s 158; FA 2002, s 34*].

Providing that all the miles of private travel have been properly identified, the Revenue will accept that there is no fuel charge where the employer uses the appropriate rate from the table below (or any higher rate) to work out the cost of fuel used for private travel that the employee must make good. These advisory rates are not binding where the employer can demonstrate that employees cover the full cost of private fuel by repaying at a lower rate per mile. Even if it seems that the actual cost of the fuel could be more than, for example, 14p a mile for a 2.5 litre petrol car, it is only in exceptional cases that they will argue that a higher repayment rate should apply; they will always accept the use of the advisory rates where the engine size is 3 litres or less.

Engine size	Petrol	Diesel	LPG*
1400 cc or less	10p	9p	7p (6p)
1401 cc to 2000cc	12p	9p	8p (7p)
Over 2000 cc	14p	12p	10p (9p)

* LPG = Liquid Petroleum Gas. Figures shown are for 2004/05 with previous years' figures in brackets.

(Revenue Employment Income Manual EIM 23781, Revenue Internet Statement 29 March 2004).

See also the opening paragraphs of this section for relief from the fuel scale charge in the cases of certain cars supplied to disabled employees or to members of the same family, and of shared cars, where there is relief from the charge on provision of the car.

(vi) *Pooled vehicles.* Cars or vans provided as *pooled cars* or *pooled vans* will not be treated as being available for private use by any employee.

Conditions are

(a) the vehicle must have been included for the year in a car or van pool for use of employees of one or more employers and actually used by more than one of those employees by reason of their employment and not ordinarily used by one of them to the exclusion of the others, and

(b) any private use of the vehicle in the year by an employee was merely incidental to his other use of it, and

(c) the vehicle was not normally kept overnight at or near any of the residences of the employees concerned (except on the employer's premises).

As regards (b) above, the Revenue interpret the requirement that private use is 'merely incidental to' other use as a qualitative test requiring consideration, in the case of each employee using the vehicle during the year, of whether the private use is independent of the employee's business use (so that it is not 'merely incidental' to it) or follows from the business use (so that it is). Thus if a business journey requiring an early start cannot reasonably be undertaken starting from the normal place of work, the journey from work to home the previous day (although private) is merely incidental to the business use. Similarly minor private use (e.g. to visit a restaurant) while away from home on a business trip is merely incidental to the business use. On the other hand use for an annual holiday would not be merely incidental to business use, no matter how small in comparison to business travel in the year. As regards cars with drivers, carrying and working on confidential papers, whilst a factor in determining whether a journey is business or private (and if private whether merely incidental to business use), is not determinative of the issue. The need to deliver papers to a client, or to have them available for a meeting at the employee's home, may be additional relevant factors. Where a chauffeur is obliged to take the car home for the night, in order to collect or deliver passengers, this does not disqualify the car from treatment as a pooled vehicle. (Revenue Pamphlet IR 131, SP 2/96).

[*ITEPA 2003, ss 167, 168; ICTA 1988, ss 159, 159AB; FA 1993, Sch 4 para 4; FA 1996, s 134, Sch 20 para 8*].

The Revenue accept that condition (*c*) above is satisfied if the occasions on which the vehicle is taken home by employees do not amount to more than 60% of the year. However, where a vehicle is garaged at employees' homes on a large number of occasions (although less than 60% of the year), they consider it 'unlikely' that all home-to-work journeys would satisfy the 'merely incidental' test in (*b*) above. Such use by a chauffeur employed to drive a car does not prevent its being a pooled car. (Revenue Booklet 480).

See Simon's Direct Tax Service E4.630A.

(vii)   *Heavier commercial vehicles.* Where a 'heavier commercial vehicle' is made available to an employee in such circumstances that had it been a van it would have been chargeable under the provisions described at (iii) or (iiia) above, no charge will arise in respect of its provision unless the vehicle is wholly or mainly used for private purposes. A benefit will, however, arise on the provision of any driver for the vehicle. A '*heavier commercial vehicle*' is defined in the same terms as a van under (iii) above, but with a design laden weight limit exceeding 3,500 kgs. in normal use. From 6 April 2003, this exemption is extended to apply to any income tax charge in these circumstances. [*ITEPA 2003, s 238; ICTA 1988, s 159AC; FA 1993, s 74*]. See Simon's Direct Tax Service E4.630.

75.19   **Mobile telephones. For 1998/99 and earlier years,** where a 'mobile telephone' is made available to a director or employee (or to a member of his family or household) by the employer, and is available for private use, an amount of £200 (which may be increased by Treasury order) is treated as an emolument of the employment (unless the benefit is otherwise chargeable to tax as income). If in any year there is no private use, or the employee is required to, and does, make good the full cost of private use, the charge is reduced to nil. The full cost of private use for this purpose is the cost of private calls, plus a proportionate share of the higher of the equipment rental and 20% of the market value of the equipment when first used to provide a benefit (plus, unless the purpose of the provision of the telephone was to make it available for business use, a proportionate share of any other expenses incurred, e.g. line rental, in connection with its provision) (see Revenue Tax Bulletin August 1994, p 158). Only outgoing private calls (and incoming reversed charge private calls) are taken into account for this purpose. A call is private unless made wholly, exclusively and necessarily in the performance of the duties of the employment. Although the requirement to reimburse must be imposed in advance, where the telephone is provided for business use only but a non-business call is made entirely due to an exceptional and genuine emergency, reimbursement for that call by the employee will be regarded as satisfying the condition. (Revenue Tax Bulletin May 1992 p 20).

The charge is reduced *pro rata* for days on which the telephone is unavailable, either before or after it is provided at all or during a period of 30 consecutive days on which it is incapable of being used at all. A further charge applies for each additional mobile telephone made available, but the fact that different apparatus may be supplied on different days is disregarded.

'*Mobile telephone*' is defined to include provision in connection with a car or a van or heavier commercial vehicle, whether or not a company car etc., but to exclude cordless extensions to fixed telephones and certain short-range radio apparatus.

These provisions are repealed for 1999/2000 and subsequent years. See now 75.16(xxiii) as regards exclusion of mobile telephones from benefits charge.

75.20 Schedule E—Employment Income

[*ICTA 1988, s 159A; FA 1991, s 30; FA 1993, s 74(2), Sch 4 para 5; FA 1999, s 44(2)(6)*].

Simon's Direct Tax Service. See E4.617.

75.20   **Cheap loan arrangements.** Where a director or employee within 75.14 above obtains an 'employment-related loan', and the loan is a 'taxable cheap loan' in relation to that year, the cash equivalent of the benefit of the loan is treated as earnings from the employment for that year, subject to the exceptions referred to below.

An '*employment-related loan*' is a loan (including any form of credit) made to an employee (or a 'relative' of an employee) by the employer, by a company or partnership under the employer's control, by a company or partnership controlling the employer (being a company or partnership), or by a company or partnership under common control with the employer (being a company or partnership). It also includes a loan by a person having a 'material interest' (broadly 5%, see *ITEPA 2003, s 68*) in a close company which was the employer or had control of or was controlled by the employer, or in a company or partnership controlling that close company. It does not include a loan made by an individual in the normal course of his domestic, family or personal relationships, or one made to a 'relative' of the employee from which the employee derives no benefit. Loans by a prospective employer are included, and 'making a loan' includes arranging, guaranteeing or in any way facilitating a loan or the continuation of an existing loan, and the assumption of the rights and liabilities of the person who originally made the loan. '*Relative*' means spouse of the employee, or parent, ancestor, lineal descendant, brother or sister (or those persons' spouses) of the employee or spouse.

A '*taxable cheap loan*' is an employment-related loan for a tax year if it is outstanding at any time during that year when the employment is held and the interest (if any) paid on the loan for that year is less than would have been payable at the 'official rate'. The cash equivalent of the benefit of a loan (which applies to each loan separately) is the excess of the interest which would have been payable at the 'official rate' over the interest (if any) actually paid. A loan ceases to be outstanding on the death of the employee.

For *2002/03 and earlier years*, the amount chargeable in respect of a loan for a tax year is calculated in the same way, and is treated as an emolument chargeable under Schedule E.

It is not necessary for the application of these provisions that there be any benefit from the loan in terms of something of an advantage to the employee (*Williams v Todd Ch D 1988, 60 TC 727*). A loan secured by a charge on a house purchased by a relocated employee, with an agreement that when the charge was called in the employing company would receive the same proportion of the sale price or valuation as the loan bore to the purchase price, was within these provisions (*Harvey v Williams (Sp C 49), [1995] SSCD 329; (Sp C 168), [1998] SSCD 215*). The payment of the expenses of an estate agency by a service company of which one of the partners in the agency was a director was within the provisions from the time the services were provided for so long as the payments were not reimbursed (with agreed mark-up) to the company (*Grant v Watton and cross-appeal Ch D 1999, 71 TC 333*).

Before 2000/01, the 'official rate' was adjusted with changes in typical mortgage rates. With effect for 2000/01 and subsequent years, it is set in advance for the whole year, although it may be decreased during the year should there be a sharp fall in typical mortgage rates (but will *not* be increased during the year). (Revenue Press Release 25 January 2000). Subject to this *caveat* as regards the rate set for 2000/01 onwards, the prescribed rate from 6 August 1997 is as follows.

7.25%p.a. from 6 August 1997 to 5 March 1999
6.25%p.a. from 6 March 1999 to 5 January 2002
5%p.a. from 6 January 2002 to 5 April 2005

See *SI 1997 No 1681; SI 1999 No 419; SI 2001 No 3860*; Revenue Press Releases 12 December 2002, 12 January 2004.

The *average* rate for 2001/02 was 5.94% (1998/99 7.16%, 1997/98 7.08%).

Regulations may provide for a different official rate of interest in relation to a loan in the currency of a country or territory outside the UK, the benefit of which is obtained by reason of the employment of a person who normally lives in that country or territory and who has lived there at some time in the year in question or the preceding five years. In this context, 'lives' and 'has lived' are considered to connote a degree of continuance if not permanence, i.e. more than a return for a short holiday. (Revenue Tax Bulletin October 1994 p 162). The following different rates are applicable.

Japan	3.9% p.a.
Switzerland	5.5% p.a.

[*SI 1994 Nos 1307, 1567*]. For the circumstances in which loans taken out prior to an employee coming to work in the UK are within the beneficial loan provisions, see Revenue Tax Bulletin October 1994 p 161.

The amount taxable in respect of the loan for a year of assessment is treated as interest paid by the employee on the loan in that year of that amount (other than for the purpose of this or any other benefit charge). It is not treated as 'relevant loan interest' (i.e. it is not within MIRAS, see 22.13 DEDUCTION OF TAX AT SOURCE), nor is it treated as income of the lender, but it is treated as accruing during, and paid at the end of, the year (or, if different, the period during the year when the employee was in the employment and the loan was outstanding).

Aggregation of loans (which applied before 1996/97) no longer applies, except that, where the lender is a close company (see Tolley's Corporation Tax under Close Companies) and the borrower a director, the lender may elect, by notice to the Revenue on or before 6 July following the tax year, to treat as a single loan all loans with that borrower which are in the same currency, are not 'qualifying loans (see below), were obtained by reason of employment, and the rate of interest on which has been below the official rate throughout the year.

A claim may be made for late payments of interest to be related to the year to which they apply, and for assessments to be adjusted accordingly.

The above provisions do not apply where a loan made for a fixed and unvariable period and at a fixed and unvariable rate of interest (originally not less than the official rate) becomes a taxable cheap loan only by reason of an increase in the official rate, or on similar unvariable loans made before 6 April 1978 where the rate of interest is not less than could have been expected to apply between persons not connected with each other.

[*ITEPA 2003, ss 173–175, 177, 181, 184, 187, 190(2), 191(2); ICTA 1988, ss 160, 161(2)–(4), 161A, Sch 7 paras 1–3; FA 1995, s 45(2); FA 1996, ss 107(1)(4), 134, Sch 20 paras 9, 41; FA 2000, Sch 10 para 4*].

'Qualifying loans': interest qualifying for relief. For 2000/01 and subsequent years, the above provisions do not apply to a loan in any year of assessment in which, if interest were paid on the loan (whether or not it is in fact so paid), the whole of the interest paid on it would either be eligible for relief under *ICTA 1988, s 353* (or would be so but for being relevant loan interest, see 22.13 DEDUCTION OF TAX AT SOURCE) or would be an allowable deduction to the payer under Schedule D, Case I or II or in a Schedule A business (see 71.55 SCHEDULE D, CASES I AND II, 69.4 SCHEDULE A). [*ITEPA 2003, s 178; ICTA 1988, s 161A; FA*

2000, s 57, Sch 10 para 4]. For loans interest on which would only partly so qualify for relief, and for years before 2000/01, such loans are within *section 160*, the amount chargeable being treated as interest paid and therefore attracting relief as appropriate in the normal way. [*ITEPA 2003, s 184; ICTA 1988, s 160(1); FA 1994, s 88(1)(6)*].

Ordinary commercial loans. For 2000/01 and subsequent years, the above provisions do not apply to a loan on '*ordinary commercial terms*', i.e. a loan made in the ordinary course of business by a lender whose business includes either the lending of money or the supply of goods or services on credit, and in relation to which one of the following conditions is satisfied.

(*a*)   When the loan was made, loans for the same or similar purposes and on the same terms and conditions were available to all those who might be expected to avail themselves of the services provided by the lender in the course of business, and a substantial proportion (broadly 50% or more, see Revenue Employment Income Manual EIM 26160) of such loans (including the loan in question) made at or about that time were made to members of the public (i.e. those with whom the lender deals at arm's length). All such loans so made to members of the public at or about that time must be held on the same terms as the loan in question, and any change in those terms since that time must have been imposed in the ordinary course of the lender's business. As regards loans made before 1 June 1994, terms and conditions are considered for this purpose disregarding any fees, commission or other incidental expenses incurred by the borrower to obtain the loan.

(*b*)   If the loan was varied before 6 April 2000, a substantial proportion (as in (*a*) above) of the loan in question, any existing loans varied at or about the same time so as to be held on the same post-variation terms and any new loans made by the same lender at or about the time of the variation must have been made to members of the public. All such loans so made to members of the public at or about the time of the variation must be held on the same terms as the loan in question, and any change in those terms since that time must have been imposed in the ordinary course of the lender's business. Terms and conditions are considered for these purposes disregarding any fees, commission or other incidental expenses incurred by the borrower to obtain the loan and any penalties, interest or similar amounts incurred by the borrower as a result of varying the loan.

(*c*)   If the loan is varied on or after 6 April 2000, a substantial proportion (as in (*a*) above) of the loan in question, of any existing loans varied at or about the same time so as to be held on the same post-variation terms and of any new loans made by the same lender at or about the time of the variation must have been made to members of the public. At the time of the variation, members of the public who had loans from the lender for similar purposes must have had a right to vary their loans on the same terms and conditions as applied in relation to the variation of the loan in question, and the post-variation terms on which any existing loans so varied and the loan in question are held must be the same. Any change in those terms since that time must have been imposed in the ordinary course of the lender's business. Terms and conditions are considered for these purposes disregarding any fees, commission or other incidental expenses incurred by the borrower to obtain the loan and any penalties, interest or similar amounts incurred by the borrower as a result of varying the loan.

[*ITEPA 2003, s 176; ICTA 1988, s 161B, Sch 7A; FA 2000, s 57, Sch 10 para 5*].

For 1999/2000 and earlier years, a similar exclusion applies in relation to loans made in the ordinary course of a business which includes the lending of money and which is carried on by the lender, if

(A)   at the time the loan was made, loans made for the same or similar purposes, and on the same terms and conditions, were available to all the lender's usual customers,

(B)   of all such loans (including the loan in question) made at or about the same time by the lender, a substantial proportion (broadly 50% or more, see Revenue Employment Income Manual EIM 26160) was made at arm's length to members of the public,

(C)   the loan in question and all arm's length loans referred to in (B) are held on the same terms, and

(D)   if the terms on which the loan in question is held are altered, such alteration was imposed in the ordinary course of business.

As regards (A) above, a loan not within the exception at the time it was made, but the terms of which were subsequently varied so as to fall within (A)–(D) above, did not come within the exception (*West v Crossland; West v O'Neill Ch D 1999, 71 TC 314*).

As regards (A), (C) and (D) above, for loans made before 1 June 1994, differences in fees, commission or other incidental expenses incurred by the borrower for the purpose of obtaining the loan are disregarded in determining whether the same terms and conditions apply to that and other loans.

For loans made on or after 1 June 1994, the terms and conditions must be exactly the same, so that the exemption would *not* apply where e.g. the lending criteria were relaxed in favour of employees or any normal application or loan fees or charges were waived or reduced in their favour. For this and generally, see Revenue Tax Bulletin August 1994 p 157.

[*ICTA 1988, s 161(1)–(1B); FA 1994, s 88; FA 2000, s 57, Sch 10 para 5(4)*].

De minimis exemption. No amount is treated as earnings (or as interest paid) in respect of a loan within the above provisions if the loan (or aggregate taxable loans) at no time in the year exceed £5,000. Similarly if a loan which is not a 'qualifying loan' (as above), or the aggregate of such loans, does not exceed £5,000, the above provisions do not apply to that loan or those loans. The Revenue have confirmed that, in consequence of the general abolition of mortgage interest tax relief for 2000/01 onwards (see 43.3 INTEREST PAYABLE), affected loans must be aggregated with other non-qualifying loans in applying the £5,000 exemption, possibly resulting in the latter becoming taxable. (Revenue Tax Bulletin December 1999 p 706).

[*ITEPA 2003, s 180; ICTA 1988, s 161(1); FA 1994, s 88(3)(6)*].

Bridging loans. By concession, reimbursement by an employer of the net interest on a bridging loan is not charged to tax, nor is the benefit of a bridging loan advanced by an employer in excess of the relief limit. See 75.36 below.

Expense advances. There is also no charge on advances for an employee's incidental overnight expenses (see 75.46 below) or other expenses necessarily incurred in performance of the duties of the employment, provided that (*a*) the maximum amount outstanding at any one time in the tax year does not exceed £1,000 (or such higher figure as may be set by Treasury order); (*b*) the advances are spent within six months; and (*c*) the employee accounts to his employer at regular intervals for the expenditure of the sum advanced. Where there are good reasons for exceeding the limits, the employer may apply for their increase. Where the conditions are met, no entry is required on form P11D for taxable loans but details of expense payments are still necessary. From 6 April 2003, this exemption is statutory [*ITEPA 2003, s 179*], having previously applied by Revenue practice (see Revenue Pamphlet IR 131, SP 7/79, 11 April 1979).

Calculation of interest at the official rate. The normal method for any year of assessment ('the relevant year') is (*a*) to take the average of the maximum amounts of the loan outstanding on 5 April immediately preceding and 5 April in the relevant year (or at the date the loan was made or discharged (or the employee died) if falling within that year), (*b*) multiply that figure by the number of whole months (a month begins on sixth day of each calendar month) during which the loan was outstanding in that year and divide by twelve, (*c*) multiply the result by the official rate of interest in force, or if the rate changed, the average rate (on a daily basis), for the period during which the loan was outstanding during the year. [*ITEPA 2003, ss 182, 190(1); ICTA 1988, Sch 7 para 4(1)*]. A replacement loan is treated for averaging purposes as being the same loan as the original if it is a 'further employment-related loan' which replaces (i) the original loan or (ii) a non-employment related loan which itself replaced the original, the second replacement occurring in the same tax year, or within 40 days thereafter, as the first. A '*further employment-related loan*' is a loan the benefit of which is obtained by reason of the same employment or other employment with the same employer or a person connected with him (within *ICTA 1988, s 839* — see 19 CONNECTED PERSONS). [*ITEPA 2003, s 186; ICTA 1988, Sch 7 para 4(2)–(4); FA 1995, s 45(4)(5)*].

An alternative method may be required by the inspector or elected by the employee. Notice of requirement or election must be given within twelve months after 31 January following the relevant year of assessment. The alternative method is to calculate the figures by reference to the daily amounts of the loan and official rates of interest (leap years being ignored for years before 2003/04 in determining the effective daily rate of interest). [*ITEPA 2003, s 183, Sch 7 para 26; ICTA 1988, Sch 7 para 5; FA 1996, s 107(2)–(4)*].

For 2000/01 and subsequent years, where two or more employees are chargeable under the above provisions in respect of the same loan, the cash equivalent is apportioned between them in a fair and reasonable manner, the portion allocated to each being treated as the cash equivalent as far as that employee is concerned. Any election for the alternative method of calculation in such a case must be made by all the employees concerned. [*ITEPA 2003, ss 183(4), 185; ICTA 1988, Sch 7 para 5A; FA 2000, s 57, Sch 10 para 6*].

General. See Revenue Pamphlet IR 145 'Low Interest Loans Provided by Employers: A Guide for Employees' for a general guide to these provisions. See also ICAEW Technical Release TAX 11/93, 9 July 1993 as regards loans to directors.

Interest on money loaned interest-free, subject to conditions and repayable on demand, by the employer to a trust for the benefit of an employee held to be taxable earnings (*O'Leary v McKinlay Ch D 1990, 63 TC 729*).

Loans written off. Any amount released from, or written off, an 'employment-related loan' (see above) will be charged as taxable earnings, unless otherwise taxable as income. Where, however, it would be taxable under *ITEPA 2003, s 403* (see 18.5 COMPENSATION FOR LOSS OF EMPLOYMENT (AND DAMAGES)) it will instead be taxable under this provision, and where the loan is one which is a capital sum within *ICTA 1988, s 677* (see 81.19 SETTLEMENTS) the charge will be on the excess of the amount released over sums previously treated as the employee's income under *section 677*. These provisions continue to apply after termination of employment, and to a loan replacing the original loan, but they cease on death of the employee. If the loan is wholly or partly repaid after a charge has arisen under this provision, a claim may be made for the appropriate relief. They do not apply to arrangements to protect a person from a fall in value of shares acquired before 6 April 1976. [*ITEPA 2003, ss 188–190, 191(3), Sch 7 paras 25, 27; ICTA 1988, s 160(2)–(7), s 161(4)–(7); FA 1995, s 45(3)*].

Where the lender is a company in which the employee is also a participator and a charge arises under this provision, the Revenue would not seek to treat the amount written off as a distribution. Similarly, where the lending company is close and a charge arises under *ICTA 1988, s 421* (see 27.3 EXCESS LIABILITY), the Revenue would not seek to treat the amount written off as a distribution or to raise an assessment under this provision. (Tolley's Practical Tax 1993 p 144).

Simon's Direct Tax Service. See E4.631 *et seq.*

75.21   *Examples (i)*

D, who is an employee of A Ltd earning £25,000 per annum, obtained a loan of £10,000 from the company on 10 October 2001 for the purpose of buying a car. Interest at a nominal rate is charged on the outstanding balance while the principal is repayable by instalments of £1,000 on 31 December and 30 June commencing 31 December 2001. The interest paid by D amounted to £50 in 2001/02 and to £250 in 2002/03. The official rate of interest is 6.25% until 5 January 2002, 5% thereafter, the average rate for the period 10 October 2001 to 5 April 2002 accordingly being 5.62%.
D is assessed for 2001/02 as follows.

Normal method (averaging)   £

Average balance for period $\dfrac{£10,000 + £9,000}{2}$ £9,500

£9,500 × $\frac{5}{12}$ £3,958

£3,958 × 5.62%   222

Deduct Interest paid in year   50

Cash equivalent of loan benefit   £172

Alternative method

Period	Balance of loan in period £	Interest at official rate on balance	£
10.10.01 – 31.12.01	10,000	£10,000 × 6.25% × $\frac{83}{365}$	142
1.1.02 – 5.1.02	9,000	£9,000 × 6.25% × $\frac{5}{365}$	8
6.1.02 – 5.4.02	9,000	£9,000 × 5% × $\frac{90}{365}$	111

261

Deduct Interest paid in year   50

Cash equivalent of loan benefit   £211

Amount chargeable to tax note (*b*)   £211

D is assessed for 2002/03 as follows.

Normal method (averaging)   £

Average balance for period $\dfrac{£9,000 + £7,000}{2}$ £8,000

£8,000 × 5%   400
Deduct   Interest paid in year   250

Cash equivalent of loan benefit   £150

75.21 Schedule E—Employment Income

Alternative method

Period	Balance of loan in period	Interest at official rate on balance	
	£		£
6.4.02 – 30.6.02	9,000	$£9,000 \times 5\% \times \frac{86}{365}$	106
1.7.02 – 31.12.02	8,000	$£8,000 \times 5\% \times \frac{184}{365}$	202
1.1.03 – 5.4.03	7,000	$£7,000 \times 5\% \times \frac{95}{365}$	91
			399
Deduct Interest paid in year			250
Cash equivalent of loan benefit			£149
Amount chargeable to tax note (*b*)			£150

Notes

(*a*)   The period 10 October 2001 to 5 April 2002 is, for the purpose of calculating the average balance, five complete months (months begin on the sixth day of each calendar month). However, in applying the interest rate change, the actual number of days during which the loan was outstanding is taken into account.

(*b*)   The inspector will probably require the alternative method to be applied for 2001/02. It is assumed that no election will be made for 2002/03 as the difference is negligible.

(*c*)   Assuming that the official rate remains unchanged at 5% as expected, the computations for 2003/04 and 2004/05 will follow the same principles as for 2002/03.

(ii)

B, another employee of A Ltd, earns £33,000 per annum and obtained a loan from the company of £50,000 in January 1999 for house purchase (B's principal private residence). At 5 April 1999, no capital had been repaid but on 1 August 1999 B repays £10,000 of the loan. The rate of interest on the loan is 2.5% per annum on the daily outstanding balance and interest paid in 1999/2000 is £1,080. The official rates of interest are as in 75.20 above. B has no other source of taxable income for 1999/2000. He is a single man.

A Ltd also gives B a season ticket loan of £2,400, interest-free and repayable in equal monthly instalments, on 10 January 2000.

The cash equivalent of the loan benefit for 1999/2000 is computed as follows.

(i) Normal method (averaging)

		£
Average balance for period $\dfrac{£9,000 + £7,000}{2}$		45,000
$£45,000 \times 6.25\%$		2,812
Deduct Interest paid in year		1,080
Cash equivalent of loan benefit		£1,732

980

(ii) Alternative method

Period	Balance of loan in period	Interest at official rate on balance	
	£		£
6.4.99 – 1.8.99	50,000	£50,000 × 6.25% × $\frac{118}{365}$	1,010
2.8.99 – 5.4.00	40,000	£40,000 × 6.25% × $\frac{247}{365}$	1,692
			2,702
Deduct Interest paid in year			1,080
Cash equivalent of loan benefit			£1,622
Amount chargeable to tax (on assumption that B elects for the alternative method)			£1,622

B is also treated as having paid notional interest on the loan of an amount equal to that chargeable to tax. Interest eligible for tax relief is as follows.

(i) Interest actually paid

Interest paid		Interest eligible for relief	
	£		£
6.4.99 – 1.8.99 (118 days)			
£50,000 × 2.5% × $\frac{118}{365}$	404	£404 × $\dfrac{30,000}{50,000}$	243
2.8.99 – 5.4.00 (247 days)			
£40,000 × 2.5% × $\frac{247}{365}$	676	£676 × $\dfrac{30,000}{40,000}$	507
	£1,080		£750

(ii) Notional interest paid

Interest paid		Interest eligible for relief	
	£		£
6.4.99 – 1.8.99	1,010	£1,010 × $\dfrac{30,000}{40,000}$	606
2.8.99 – 5.4.00	1,692	£1,692 × $\dfrac{30,000}{40,000}$	1,269
	2,702		1,875
Deduct actual interest	1,080		750
	£1,622		£1,125

B's tax liability for 1999/2000 is computed as follows.

	£	£
Salary		33,000
Benefit (home loan)		1,622
Schedule E income		34,622
Other income		—
Total income		34,622
Deduct Personal allowance		4,335
Taxable income		£30,287

	£	£
Tax payable:		
1,500 @ 10%		150.00
26,500 @ 23%		6,095.00
2,287 @ 40%		914.80
		7,159.80
Deduct Interest relief:		
Actual interest	750	
Notional interest	1,125	
	£1,875	
£1,875 @ 10%		187.50
Tax liability		£6,972.30

Notes

(a)   The season ticket loan does not give rise to a taxable benefit as it is not a qualifying loan and at no time in the tax year does the amount outstanding exceed £5,000.

(b)   Mortgage interest is abolished for 2000/01 and subsequent years.

75.22   **Childcare provision.** *Employer-provided childcare.* For **2005/06** onwards, no liability to income tax arises in respect of the provision for an employee of 'care' for a 'child' where *all* of the following conditions are met:

- the child is the employee's child or stepchild and is maintained (wholly or partly) at his expense *or* is resident with the employee *or* is a person for whom the employee has parental responsibility (as defined);

- the premises on which the care is provided are not used wholly or mainly as a private dwelling, and any applicable registration requirement (under *Children Act 1989, Pt 10A* or Scottish or NI equivalents) is met;

- those premises are made available by the employer operating the childcare scheme (the scheme employer) or, where the care is provided under arrangements made by the scheme employer and other persons, those premises are made available by one or more of those persons with the scheme employer being wholly or partly responsible for financing and managing the care provision; and

- the childcare scheme is open to all the scheme employer's employees or to all those at a particular location and the employee in question is either an employee of the scheme employer or works at the same location as employees of the scheme employer to whom the scheme is open.

If the conditions are met in respect of part only of the childcare provision (for example if the arrangements change partway through the tax year), the exemption applies to that part.

For the above purposes

- '*care*' means any form of care or supervised activity not provided in the course of the child's compulsory education; and

- a person is regarded as a '*child*' until 1 September following his 15th birthday (or 16th birthday if he is disabled, as defined) and on until the end of the week in which that date falls.

[*ITEPA 2003, ss 318, 318B; FA 2004, s 78, Sch 13 para 1*].

As regards 2004/05 and earlier years, see the similar (though not identical) exemption at 75.16(xvii) above.

Other employer-contracted childcare — limited exemption. Also for **2005/06** onwards, in cases where the above exemption does not apply, no liability to income tax arises in respect of the provision for an employee of 'care' for a 'child' *except* to the extent that the cash equivalent of the benefit (see 75.16 above) exceeds £50 per week and the employee is not in lower-paid employment (see 75.14 above). *All* of the following conditions must be met:

- the child must be the employee's child or stepchild and must be maintained (wholly or partly) at his expense *or* must be both resident with the employee and a person for whom the employee has parental responsibility (as defined);

- the care must be 'qualifying childcare' (see below); and

- the care scheme is open to all the employer's employees or to all those at a particular location.

If the conditions are met in respect of part only of the childcare provision, the exemption applies to that part. '*Care*' and '*child*' have the same meanings as for employer-provided childcare above.

The £50 per week exemption is applied to a tax year by multiplying it by the number of 'qualifying weeks' in the tax year to give an annual exempt amount. For employees not in lower-paid employment (see 75.14 above), income tax is chargeable on the excess, if any, of the cash equivalent of the benefit for the year over that exempt amount. For this purpose, a week begins on the first day of the tax year and on every 7th day after that, with the last day of the tax year (or 2 days if the tax year ends in a leap year) being treated as a week in itself. Any week in which care is provided in compliance with the above conditions counts as a '*qualifying week*'. An employee is entitled to only one exempt amount regardless of the number of children for whom care is provided, but two or more people can be entitled to an exempt amount in respect of the same child. If an employee would otherwise be entitled to an exemption both under these provisions and under the childcare vouchers provisions described below, he is entitled to only one such exemption for any one week. The Treasury has power to alter the amount of the weekly exemption by statutory instrument.

'*Qualifying childcare*' means 'registered or approved care'. This is defined by one of *subsections (2)–(6)* of *ITEPA 2003, s 318C* depending on whether the care is being provided for a child in England, Wales, Scotland, NI or outside the UK. In England, for example, it includes care provided by a person registered under *Children Act 1989, Pt 10A*, by schools or other establishments exempted from such registration requirements, (in the case of care provided out of school hours for a child aged 8 or over) by a school on school premises or by a local authority (as defined), and by certain other approved childcare providers and domiciliary care workers. Care provided by the employee's domestic partner is excluded in all cases from being qualifying childcare, as is care provided by a relative (as defined) of the child wholly or mainly in the child's home or, if different, the home of a person having parental responsibility for the child.

[*ITEPA 2003, ss 318A–318D; FA 2004, s 78, Sch 13 para 1*].

Childcare vouchers. Also for **2005/06** onwards, no liability to income tax arises in respect of the provision for an employee of 'qualifying childcare vouchers' *except* to the extent that the cash equivalent of the benefit (see 75.16 above) exceeds £50 per week. A '*qualifying childcare voucher*' is a non-cash 'childcare voucher' in relation to which *all* of the following conditions are met:

- the voucher is provided to enable the employee to obtain 'care' for a 'child' who is the employee's child or stepchild and is maintained (wholly or partly) at his expense *or* who is both resident with the employee and a person for whom the employee has parental responsibility (as defined);

- the voucher can be used only to obtain 'qualifying childcare'; and
- the voucher is provided under a scheme that is open to all the employer's employees or to all those at a particular location.

'*Care*', '*child*' and '*qualifying childcare*' have the same meanings as above.

The £50 per week exemption is applied to a tax year by multiplying it by the number of 'qualifying weeks' in the tax year to give an annual exempt amount. Income tax is chargeable on the excess, if any, of the cash equivalent of the benefit for the year over that exempt amount. For this purpose, a week begins on the first day of the tax year and on every 7th day after that, with the last day of the tax year (or 2 days if the tax year ends in a leap year) being treated as a week in itself. Any week in respect of which a qualifying childcare voucher is received counts as a '*qualifying week*'. An employee is entitled to only one exempt amount regardless of the number of children for whom care is provided, but two or more people can be entitled to an exempt amount in respect of the same child. If an employee would otherwise be entitled to an exemption both under these provisions and those for employer-contracted childcare above, he is entitled to only one such exemption for any one week. The Treasury has power to alter the amount of the weekly exemption by statutory instrument.

See 75.47 below as regards tax liability on vouchers, including non-cash vouchers, generally. A '*childcare voucher*' is a voucher, stamp or similar document intended to enable a person to obtain childcare (whether or not in exchange for the voucher).

[*ITEPA 2003, ss 84(2A), 270A; FA 2004, s 78, Sch 13 paras 2, 3*].

75.23   **Scholarships.** Where payments are made under scholarship awards, *ICTA 1988, s 331* (see 28.30 EXEMPT INCOME) is not to be construed as conferring exemption from tax on any person other than the holder of the scholarship. If a scholarship (including an exhibition, bursary or other similar educational endowment) is provided to a member of the family or household of a director or non-lower-paid employee by reason of the latter's employment the payments are chargeable on such director etc. under the benefits code. A scholarship is taken to have been provided by reason of a person's employment if provided, directly or indirectly, under arrangements entered into by, or by a person connected with, the employer, unless the employer is an individual and the arrangements are made in the normal course of his domestic, personal or family relationships.

However, the benefits code will not bring into charge a payment under a scholarship awarded out of a trust fund, or under a scheme, to a person receiving full-time instruction at an educational establishment, where 25% or less of the payments made out of the fund etc. in any year of assessment are scholarship payments provided, or treated as provided, by reason of a person's employment (regardless of whether or not the employment is director's or non-lower-paid or in the UK).

Payments which are *in fact* provided by reason of a person's employment are taxable even if the fund meets the 25% test.

[*ITEPA 2003, ss 211–215, Sch 7 para 32(3); ICTA 1988, s 165*].

For administrative procedures in relation to educational trust scholarships, see Revenue Employment Income Manual EIM 30006–30008.

See also 28.29 EXEMPT INCOME for payments to employees to attend sandwich courses.

Simon's Direct Tax Service. See E4.618.

75.24   **Sporting and recreational facilities.** The provision to an employee (or to a member of his family or household) of (*a*)   any benefit consisting in, or in a right or opportunity to make use of, any sporting or other recreational facilities made available generally to, or for use by, the employees of the employer in question, or

(*b*)   any non-cash voucher (see 75.47 below) capable of being exchanged only for such a benefit

is exempted from any charge to income tax.

Excluded from the relief (unless prescribed by regulation) is any benefit consisting in

(i)   an interest in, or the use of, any mechanically propelled vehicle (including ships, boats, aircraft and hovercraft),

(ii)   an interest in, or the use of, any holiday or other overnight accommodation or associated facilities,

(iii)   a facility provided on domestic premises (i.e. premises used wholly or mainly as a private dwelling, or belonging to or enjoyed with such premises),

(iv)   a facility available to, or for use by, the general public,

(v)   a facility not used wholly or mainly by persons whose right or opportunity to use it derives from employment, or

(vi)   a right or opportunity to make use of any facility within (i)–(v) above.

As regards (iv) above, where employers group together to provide facilities for members of all their staffs, this does not of itself mean that they are available to members of the general public. In practice, the opening of facilities to a restricted section of the public (e.g. those living in the immediate vicinity) as well as to employees will similarly not result in loss of the relief. (Revenue Employment Income Manual EIM 22860, 22862).

As regards (v) above, a right or opportunity derives from employment only if it derives from the person's being (or having been) an employee of a particular employer (or a member of such a person's family or household) and the facility is available generally to employees of that employer.

The Treasury may by regulation prescribe exceptions from, and conditional inclusions in, this relief.

[*ITEPA 2003, ss 261–263; ICTA 1988, s 197G; FA 1993, s 75*].

Simon's Direct Tax Service. See E4.612.

75.25   **Dispensations** (notices of nil liability). If an employer supplies the inspector with a statement of the cases and circumstances in which particular types of expense payments and benefits are made or provided by him for any employees (whether his own or those of anyone else) and the inspector is satisfied that such benefits etc. give rise to no tax liability, he shall issue a notice of nil liability, but this can be revoked later. [*ITEPA 2003, s 65, Sch 7 para 15; ICTA 1988, s 166*]. Dispensations are not generally available for 'round sum' expense allowances, but are frequently given for e.g. travelling and subsistence expenses on an approved scale for business journeys in the UK. They cease to have effect from 6 April 2002 insofar as they relate to expenses in connection with the use of a vehicle for business travel where mileage allowance payments are made or mileage allowance relief is available in respect of that use (see 75.46 below). [*ITEPA 2003, Sch 7 para 16; FA 2001, s 58*]. This does not, however, prevent the inclusion of congestion charges in a dispensation (see Revenue Internet Statement 6 February 2003). Scale rate payments merely reimbursing average expenditure are not regarded as round sum allowances (see Revenue Employment Income Manual EIM 05200). The effect is to exclude such items from the PAYE scheme, returns etc. Dispensations are not given, however, where the effect would be to remove the employee from liability under the benefits legislation (see 75.14 above). A dispensation may be considered for a controlling director who decides his own expenses provided that there is independent documentation to vouch for the expenditure.

See Revenue Pamphlets IR 69 for conditions and 480 generally. See also Revenue Employment Income Manual EIM 30050 *et seq.*

Provided that the circumstances under which a dispensation was issued have not changed, it will also be accepted as evidence that the expenses covered are not earnings for national insurance contributions purposes. (Revenue Tax Bulletin August 1995 p 245).

Simon's Direct Tax Service. See E4.651.

75.26 **EMPLOYEE LIABILITIES AND INDEMNITY INSURANCE**

There may be deducted from earnings from an employment which continues to be held:

(*a*) any amount paid in or towards the discharge of a 'qualifying liability' of the employee;

(*b*) costs or expenses incurred in connection with any claim that the employee is subject to a 'qualifying liability' or with any related proceedings; and

(*c*) so much of any premium (or similar payment) paid under a 'qualifying contract' of insurance as relates to the indemnification of the employee against a 'qualifying liability' or to the payment of such costs and expenses as in (*b*) above.

Where any amount in (*a*)–(*c*) above is met by the employer or a third party, there may be made a deduction to offset a resultant taxable benefit (see 75.14 above). However, no deduction may be made for any such liability, costs or expenses if it would have been unlawful for the employer to insure against them (for example, costs arising from criminal convictions, and see Revenue Tax Bulletin October 1995 p 258).

A liability is a '*qualifying liability*' of the employee if it is imposed either

(i) in respect of any acts or omissions of the employee in his capacity as such or in any other capacity in which he acts in the performance of his duties, or

(ii) in connection with any proceedings relating to or arising from claims in respect of such acts or omissions.

A '*qualifying contract*' of insurance is one

(A) which, as regards the risks insured against, relates exclusively to one or more of the following

(i) indemnification of any employee against any qualifying liability,

(ii) indemnification of any person against any vicarious liability in respect of acts or omissions giving rise to a qualifying liability of another,

(iii) payment of costs and expenses in connection with any claim that a person is subject to a liability to which the insurance relates or with related proceedings, and

(iv) indemnification of any employer against any loss from the payment by him to an employee of his of any amount in respect of either a qualifying liability or costs and expenses as in (iii) above;

(B) which is not 'connected' with any other contract (see below);

(C) a significant part of the premium for which does not relate to rights to payments or benefits other than cover for the risks insured against and any right of renewal; and

(D)   the period of insurance under which is not more than two years (disregarding renewals) and which the insured is not required to renew.

Two contracts are '*connected*' (see (B) above) if either was entered into by reference to the other or to enable the other to be, or to facilitate the other being, entered into on particular terms *and* the terms of either contract would have been significantly different if it had not been for the other. Connected contracts, each of which satisfy (A), (C) and (D), are qualifying contracts despite (B) above, where the only significant difference in terms consists in certain premium reductions.

Where applicable, for the purposes of these provisions, an insurance premium may be reasonably apportioned as between the different risks, persons or employments to which the contract relates.

[*ITEPA 2003, ss 346–350; ICTA 1988, s 201AA; FA 1995, s 91*].

For clarification of certain points on operation of the relief, see Revenue Tax Bulletin October 1995 pp 257, 258.

See below as regards payments made after the employment has ceased.

See Simon's Direct Tax Service E4.718A.

Post-employment deductions. Relief against total income (and capital gains, see below) may be claimed for payments made by a former employee or office-holder which are made after the day the employment ceases and no later than six years after the end of the year of assessment in which it ceased and which would have been deductible under *ITEPA 2003, s 346* (see above) if the employment had continued. Relief is given for the year in which the payment is made and unused relief cannot be carried forward. In determining whether the payment would have been deductible under *section 201AA*, only acts or omissions relating to the actual period of employment are taken into account.

Payments made by the former employer, by a successor to the former employer's business or to his liabilities, or by a person connected with any of them (see 19 CONNECTED PERSONS), is not deductible from total income of the former employee *except* insofar as the payment falls to be treated either as general earnings received after the cessation of the employment by the former employee or as a taxable benefit received by the former employee under an unapproved retirement benefit scheme (see 67.9 RETIREMENT SCHEMES). Similarly where a payment made by the former employee is borne wholly or partly by the former employer or other persons mentioned above, so much of the payment as is such taxable earnings or taxable benefit of the former employee is deductible from his or her total income. Before 6 April 2003, payments made or borne by the employer were similarly relieved, but by deduction from the taxable earnings or benefit concerned.

Relief against capital gains. Where a claim is made as above and the claimant's income for the year is insufficient to fully utilise the relief, he may claim to have the excess relief treated as an allowable loss for that year for capital gains tax purposes. The allowable loss may not exceed the amount of the claimant's gains for the year *before* deducting any losses brought forward, the capital gains tax annual exemption, any relief available under *FA 1991, s 72* for trading losses (see 46.5 LOSSES) or any relief available to a former trader etc. for post-cessation expenditure (see 62.4 POST-CESSATION ETC. RECEIPTS AND EXPENDITURE); any excess over that amount is *not* available to carry forward against gains of a later year.

[*ITEPA 2003, ss 555–564, Sch 6 para 217; TCGA 1992, s 263ZA; FA 1995, s 92(1)–(9); FA 1998, s 58, Sch 9 para 5*].

No tax is charged under *ITEPA 2003, s 403* (see 18.5 COMPENSATION FOR LOSS OF EMPLOYMENT (AND DAMAGES)) in respect of any amount paid, or benefit provided, to reimburse the former employee for a payment, which, had he not been reimbursed, would have attracted relief under the above provisions; the same applies as regards amounts paid etc. to the former employee's executors or administrators. [*ITEPA 2003, ss 409, 410; FA 1995, s 42(10)*].

See Simon's Direct Tax Service E4.718B.

75.27   EMPLOYMENT OR PROFESSION?

Whether a person holds an office or employment or carries on a profession or vocation depends on the facts including the relevant contract(s). A distinction is drawn between a contract *of service* (employment) and a contract *for services* (profession or vocation). A vision mixer engaged under a series of short-term contracts was within Schedule D (*Hall v Lorimer CA 1993, 66 TC 349*), as was an artiste who entered into a series of engagements (*Davies v Braithwaite KB 1933, 18 TC 198*), but contrast *Fall v Hitchen Ch D 1972, 49 TC 433* in which a ballet dancer engaged by a theatrical management under a standard form of contract, but able to work elsewhere when not required by the management, was held to be in employment. See now below as regards artistes. A barristers' clerk was not the holder of an office (*McMenamin v Diggles Ch D 1991, 64 TC 286*), but in *Horner v Hasted Ch D, [1995] STC 766* an unqualified accountant contributing capital to, and sharing profits of, a firm of accountants was held not to be a partner. The provision of catering services under contract at a golf club was held to be within Schedule D, Case I (*McManus v Griffiths Ch D 1997, 70 TC 218*). See *Andrews v King Ch D 1991, 64 TC 332* as regards agricultural gangmasters.

See also *Barnett v Brabyn Ch D 1996, 69 TC 133* for a case in which the taxpayer unsuccessfully appealed against Schedule D, Case I additional assessments on the grounds that he was employed, where the original assessments had been agreed on the basis of his contention that he was self-employed.

Problems may arise in relation to part-time activities. A part-time medical appointment of a doctor in private practice assessable under Schedule D was held to be an employment (*Mitchell & Edon v Ross HL 1961, 40 TC 11*) as were the lecture fees of a full-time employed consultant (*Lindsay v CIR CS 1964, 41 TC 661*) and a non-practising barrister (*Sidey v Phillips Ch D 1986, 59 TC 458*), the evening class fees of a teacher (*Fuge v McClelland Ch D 1956, 36 TC 571*) and the remuneration as lecturer of a professional singer (*Walls v Sinnett Ch D 1986, 60 TC 150*), but *ad hoc* Crown appointments were held to be within Schedule D (*Edwards v Clinch HL 1981, 56 TC 367*). Salaries of sub-postmasters carrying on a retail trade from the same premises as the sub-post office are in practice treated as part of their Schedule D income. Where a company operates sub-post offices in its shops with its directors as nominee sub-postmasters, and the directors are required to, and do, hand over their salaries as sub-postmasters to the company, the salaries will similarly be brought into the company's Schedule D, Case I computation and not assessed on the directors as employment income. (Revenue Employment Status Manual ESM 4400). As regards sub-postmasters generally, see *Dhendsa v Richardson (Sp C 134), [1997] SSCD 265.*

Certain appointments, such as auditorships and registrarships, are strictly offices, but if held by practising accountants or solicitors the annual remuneration therefrom is, in practice, usually included in computing the business profits of the profession. Fees from directorships of professional partnerships may be included in profits provided that the directorship is a normal incident of the profession and the practice concerned, and that the fees are only a small part of total profits and are pooled for division among the partners under the partnership agreement. A written undertaking must be given that the full fees received will be included in gross income of the basis period whether or not the directorship is still held in the year of assessment or the partner concerned is still a partner. (Revenue Pamphlet IR 1, A37). For directors' fees received by other companies see 75.1(1) above. However, any compensation etc. payments on the termination of such appointments are dealt with under *ITEPA 2003, ss 401–416* (previously under *ICTA 1988, s 148*) — see 18.4 COMPENSATION FOR LOSS OF EMPLOYMENT (AND DAMAGES) and *Brander & Cruickshank HL 1970, 46 TC 574* and the cases referred to therein.

See generally Revenue Employment Status Manual ESM 0500 *et seq.* and, for the Revenue approach to case law in this area, ESM 7000 *et seq.* For questions likely to be raised in any interview in relation to the question of employment or self-employment, see ESM 0525. See also Revenue Pamphlet IR 56.

See also 61.4, 61.18 PERSONAL SERVICE COMPANIES ETC. which are concerned with the question of whether an individual providing his services through an intermediary would be an employee if engaged directly by a client, but which are also of wider application.

An **apprenticeship** is an employment (see Revenue Employment Status Manual ESM 1111).

Artistes (i.e. actors, singers, musicians, dancers and theatrical artists). It is understood that the Revenue accept that the earnings of most artistes should be assessed under Schedule D, Case I. Circumstances in which such earnings are employment income subject to PAYE (55) would e.g. be where the artiste is engaged for a regular salary to perform in a series of different productions at the direction of the engager, and with a period of notice stipulated before termination of the contract. This might apply e.g. to permanent members of an opera, ballet or theatre company or an orchestra. (*Taxation* 8 September 1994, p 553). See Revenue Business Income Manual BIM 50151 for a general discussion of this distinction. In such cases, a deduction of up to 17.5% of earnings may be claimed in respect of percentage fees (and VAT thereon) paid out of those earnings to a licensed employment agency within *Employment Agencies Act 1973* or to a *bona fide* non-profit-making co–operative society acting as agent for the artiste. [*ITEPA 2003, s 352; ICTA 1988, s 201A; FA 1990, s 77; FA 1991, s 69*].

See generally Revenue Employment Status Manual ESM 4121 *et seq.*

A **dentist** employed by a Panamanian company, which contracted with a UK practice to supply his services in return for a proportion of the NHS fees and a management charge, was held to be employed, although the legality of the arrangements was in question (*Cooke v Blacklaws Ch D 1984, 58 TC 255*). See generally Revenue Employment Status Manual ESM 4030.

Divers etc. employed in UK area of the Continental Shelf are assessed under Schedule D, Case I, see 71.21 SCHEDULE D, CASES I AND II. See also Revenue Employment Status Manual ESM 4050.

Film etc. technicians. From 6 April 1983, the Revenue reclassified certain grades of such technicians as employed persons, subject to the usual rights of appeal, so that only grades included on the Schedule D grading lists issued by the Revenue's Film, Television and Radio Industry Units continue to be treated as self-employed. (Revenue Press Release 30 March 1983). A vision mixer was held to be self-employed in *Hall v Lorimer CA 1993, 66 TC 349*. See Revenue Employment Status Manual ESM 4101 *et seq.* See also Revenue Tax Bulletin August 2000 pp 775, 776 and the Guidance Notes published on the Revenue's website (www.inlandrevenue.gov.uk/specialist/fi_guidance_notes2003.pdf).

Simon's Direct Tax Service. See E4.2.

75.28   **FLAT RATE EXPENSES FOR EMPLOYEES**

Deductions are allowed for tools, special clothing etc. necessarily provided by an employee without reimbursement, and which the employer does not make available. If tools or protective clothing are supplied, but not both, or if some of the tools are provided, the rate of allowance may be reduced accordingly. These are mostly agreed with trade unions, but the agreed rates do not preclude further claims, if justified, under the general deduction

75.28 Schedule E—Employment Income

provisions (see 75.11 above). From 6 April 2003, this exemption is statutory [*ITEPA 2003, ss 330(2), 367*], having previously applied by concession (see Revenue Pamphlet IR 1, A1 Appendix). See also *Ward v Dunn Ch D 1978, 52 TC 517.*

Industry Code	Industry Group	Occupation	Allowances from 6 April 1995 (1991) £
10	Agriculture	All Workers	70 (60)
20	Forestry	All Workers	70 (60)
30	Seamen	a. Carpenters (Seamen) — Passenger Liners	165 (140)
		b. Carpenters (Seamen) — Cargo Vessels, Tankers, Coasters and Ferries	130 (110)
40	Fire Service	Uniformed Fire Fighters and Fire Officers	60(45)
50	Iron Mining	a. Fillers, Miners and Underground Workers	100 (85)
		b. All Other Workers	75 (65)
60	Quarrying	All Workers	70 (60)
70	Iron and Steel	a. Day Labourers, General Labourers, Stockmen, Time Keepers, Warehouse Staff and Weighmen	60 (50)
		b. Apprentices	45 (40)
		c. All Other Workers	120 (105)
80	Healthcare Staff in the NHS, Private Hospitals and Nursing Homes	a. Ambulance Staff on Active Service	110(95)*
		b. Nurses, Midwives, Chiropodists, Dental Nurses, Occupational, Speech, Physios and Other Therapists, Phlebotomists and Radiographers	70(60)*
		c. Plaster Room Orderlies, Hospital Porters, Ward Clerks, Sterile Supply Workers, Hospital Domestics, Hospital Catering Staff	60(50)*
		d. Laboratory Staff, Pharmacists and Pharmacy Assistants	45(40)*
		e. Uniformed Ancillary Staff — Maintenance Workers, Grounds Staff, Drivers, Parking Attendants and Security Guards, Receptionists and Other Uniformed Staff	45(40)*
90	Brass and Copper	All Workers	100 (85)
100	Aluminium	a. Continual Casting Operators, Process Operators, De-Dimplers, Driers, Drill Punchers, Dross Unloaders, Firemen, Furnace Operators and their helpers, Leaders, Mouldmen, Pourers, Remelt Department Labourers, Roll Flatteners	130 (110)

Industry Code	Industry Group	Occupation	Allowances from 6 April 1995 (1991) £
		b. Cable Hands, Case Makers, Labourers, Mates, Truck Drivers and Measurers, Storekeepers	60 (50)
		c. Apprentices	45 (40)
		d. All Other Workers	100 (85)
110	Engineering	a. Pattern Makers	120 (105)
		b. Labourers, Supervisory and Unskilled Workers	60 (50)
		c. Apprentices and Storekeepers	45 (40)
		d. Motor Mechanics in Garage Repair Shops	100 (85)
		e. All Other Workers	100 (85)
120	Shipyards	a. Blacksmiths and their Strikers, Boilermakers, Burners, Carpenters, Caulkers, Drillers, Furnacemen (Platers), Holders Up, Fitters, Platers, Plumbers, Riveters, Sheet Iron Workers, Shipwrights, Tubers and Welders	115 (95)
		b. Labourers	60 (50)
		c. Apprentices and Storekeepers	45 (40)
		d. All Other Workers	75 (65)
130	Vehicles	a. Builders, Railway Wagon etc. Repairers and Railway Wagon Lifters	105 (90)
		b. Railway Vehicle Painters and Letterers, Railway Wagon etc. Builders' and Repairers' Assistants	60 (50)
		c. All Other Workers	40 (30)
140	Particular Engineering	a. Pattern Makers	120 (105)
		b. All Chainmakers; Cleaners, Galvanisers, Tinners and Wire Drawers in the Wire Drawing industry; Toolmakers in the Lockmaking Industry	100 (85)
		c. Apprentices and Storekeepers	45 (40)
		d. All Other Workers	60 (50)
150	Constructional Engineering	a. Blacksmiths and their Strikers, Burners, Caulkers, Drillers, Erectors, Fitters, Chippers, Holders Up, Markers Off, Platers, Riggers, Riveters, Rivet Heaters, Scaffolders, Sheeters, Template Workers, Turners and Welders	115 (95)
		b. Banksmen, Labourers, Shop-helpers, Slewers and Straighteners	60 (50)
		c. Apprentices and Storekeepers	45 (40)

75.28 Schedule E—Employment Income

Industry Code	Industry Group	Occupation	Allowances from 6 April 1995 (1991) £
		d. All Other Workers	75 (65)
160	Precious Metals	All Workers	70 (60)
170	Electrical and Electricity Supply	a. Those workers incurring laundry costs only	25 (20)
		b. All Other Workers	90 (75)
180	Textiles	a. Carders, Carding Engineers, Overlookers (all), and Technicians in Spinning Mills	85 (70)
		b. All Other Workers	60 (50)
190	Clothing	a. Lacemakers, Hosiery Bleachers, Dyers, Scourers and Knitters, and Knitwear Bleachers and Dyers	45 (40)
		b. All Other Workers	30 (25)
200	Textile Prints	All Workers	60 (50)
210	Leather	a. Curriers (Wet Workers), Fell-mongering Workers and Tanning Operatives (Wet)	55 (45)
		b. All Other Workers	40 (30)
220	Food	All Workers	40 (30)
230	Printing	a. The following occupations in the Letterpress Section, Electrical Engineers (Rotary Presses), Electrotypers, Ink and Roller Makers, Machine Minders (Rotary), Maintenance Engineers (Rotary Presses) and Stereotypers	105 (90)
		b. Bench Hands (P&B), Compositors (Lp), Readers (Lp), T&E Section Wireroom Operators, Warehousemen (Ppr box)	30 (25)
		c. All Other Workers	70 (60)
240	Glass	All Workers	60 (50)
250	Building Materials	a. Stone Masons	85 (70)
		b. Tilemakers and Labourers	40 (30)
		c. All Other Workers	55 (45)
255	Police Force	Uniformed Police Officers (ranks up to and including Chief Inspector)	55(45)
260	Wood and Furniture	a. Carpenters, Cabinet Makers, Joiners, Wood Carvers and Woodcutting Machinists	115 (95)
		b. Artificial Limb Makers (other than in wood), Organ Builders and Packaging Case Makers	90 (75)
		c. Coopers not providing own tools, Labourers, Polishers and Upholsterers	45 (40)
		d. All Other Workers	75 (65)
270	Building	a. Joiners and Carpenters	105 (95)
		b. Cement Works, Roofing Felt and Asphalt Labourers	55 (45)

Industry Code	Industry Group	Occupation	Allowances from 6 April 1995 (1991) £
		c. Labourers and Navvies	40 (30)
		d. All Other Workers	85 (70)
280	Heating	a. Pipe Fitters and Plumbers	100 (90)
		b. Coverers, Laggers, Domestic Glaziers, Heating Engineers and all their Mates	90 (75)
		c. All Gas Workers and All Other Workers	70 (60)
290	Railways	All Workers except Craftsmen (For craftsmen see the appropriate industry code lists e.g. engineering)	70 (60)
300	Public Service	i. Dock and Inland Waterways	
		a. Dockers, Dredger Drivers and Hopper Steerers	55 (45)
		b. All Other Workers	40 (30)
		ii. Public Transport	
		a. Garage Hands (including Cleaners)	55 (45)
		b. Conductors and Drivers	40 (30)
320	Prisons	Uniformed Prison Officers	55 (45)
330	Banks	Uniformed Bank Employees	40 (30)

* Introduced for 1998/99 onwards. Employees may claim allowances for up to six years previously, i.e. from 1992/93 onwards. (Revenue Press Release 5 March 1999).

Notes.

1. Industry Code is an industry identification term used for Inland Revenue computer purposes.

2. The expressions 'all workers' and 'all other workers' refer only to manual workers, or certain other workers who have to bear the cost of upkeep of tools or special clothing. They do not extend to other employees such as office staff.

3. 'Cost of upkeep' means the cost of replacement, repair or cleaning, but not the initial cost of providing the tools or special clothing.

4. 'Special clothing' means overalls or other protective clothing or uniform, but does not include ordinary clothing of the sort which is also worn off duty.

75.29   GIFTS, AWARDS ETC. RECEIVED

Gifts etc. are taxable when they arise out of the employment but not if they are given to the recipient in a personal capacity. The line between the two may be fine. Although payments may be voluntary and irregular, they are assessable. Also all commissions, Xmas presents, 'cost of living', cash and other bonuses. For 'tax-free' payments and awards, see 75.43 below. For payments to clergymen, see 75.13 above.

Bonus to a director described as a gift held assessable (*Radcliffe v Holt KB 1927, 11 TC 621*), and *ex gratia* payments to the retiring chairman of an action group for the successful outcome of litigation similarly held assessable (*McBride v Blackburn (Sp C 356), [2003]*

75.29 Schedule E—Employment Income

SSCD 139). Proceeds of a *public benefit match* for a cricketer held to be a gift and not chargeable (*Reed v Seymour HL 1927, 11 TC 625*), but see *Moorhouse v Dooland CA 1954, 36 TC 1* re collections. In *Davis v Harrison KB 1927, 11 TC 707, Corbett v Duff and other cases KB 1941, 23 TC 763*, payments to professional football players *in lieu of benefit* or on *transference to another club*, held assessable. World Cup bonus to professional footballer not assessable (*Moore v Griffiths Ch D 1972, 48 TC 338*). Present to *successful jockey* by owner of racehorse assessable (*Wing v O'Connell Supreme Court (Ireland) 1926, 1 ITC 170*) also *taxi-driver's tips* (*Calvert v Wainwright KB 1947, 27 TC 475*) and gifts to Hunt servant (*Wright v Boyce CA 1958, 38 TC 160*). Betting winnings on own games by professional golfer not assessable (*Down v Compston KB 1937, 21 TC 60*).

Gift to employee by company to which his services were lent by employer held not assessable, *Morris CS 1967, 44 TC 685*. But amount to company secretary, agreed by directors for negotiating sale of works and paid by liquidator, held assessable (*Shipway v Skidmore KB 1932, 16 TC 748*) as were payments to a director for negotiating sale of a branch (*Mudd v Collins KB 1925, 9 TC 297*) and to a director for special services abroad (*Barson v Airey CA 1925, 10 TC 609*). Commission for work outside ordinary duties assessable (*Mudd v Collins KB 1925, 9 TC 297*). Sums paid as compensation for loss of benefit under an abandoned salvage scheme held assessable (*Holland v Geoghegan Ch D 1972, 48 TC 482*), also assets distributed to employees on termination of profit-sharing trust fund before termination of employment (*Brumby v Milner HL 1976, 51 TC 583*). See, however, *Bray v Best HL 1989, 61 TC 705* as regards such a distribution after termination of employment.

See 75.39 below regarding gifts of shares.

Pensions (voluntary or otherwise) to retired employees are taxable (see 58.2 PENSION INCOME) as are certain payments in consideration of, in consequence of, or in connection with the termination, or change, of employment (see 18 COMPENSATION FOR LOSS OF EMPLOYMENT (AND DAMAGES)).

Suggestion scheme awards are not liable to income tax provided that there is a formally constituted scheme open to all employees (or to a particular description of them) on equal terms, and that:

(*a*)   the suggestion relates to the employer's activities;

(*b*)   it could not reasonably have been expected to be made by the employee in the course of the duties of the employment in the light of the employee's experience; and

(*c*)   it is not made at a meeting held for that purpose.

Awards under the scheme must either be 'encouragement' awards of £25 or less, for suggestions with intrinsic merit or showing special effort, or 'financial benefit' awards for suggestions relating to improvements in efficiency or effectiveness which the employer has decided to adopt with a reasonable expectation of financial benefit. The amount of a financial benefit award must not exceed 50% of the first year's expected net benefit, or 10% of the expected benefit over a period of up to five years, with an overall limit of £5,000. Any excess over £5,000 is not covered by the exemption. Where a suggestion is put forward by more than one employee, the award is limited *pro rata*, and any subsequent award(s) for the same suggestion must not exceed the residue of the maximum award. From 6 April 2003, this exemption is statutory [*ITEPA 2003, ss 321, 322*], having previously applied by concession (see Revenue Pamphlet IR 1, A57), but with continuity of treatment as regards the limits on payments. [*ITEPA 2003, Sch 7 para 38*].

Long service awards to employees, including directors, for service of 20 years or more, are not liable to income tax to the extent that the cost to the employer does not exceed £50 for each year of service (£20 per year for awards made before 13 June 2003) and provided that no similar award has been made to the recipient within the previous ten years. Service may include that with predecessor employers. The award must consist of tangible articles, of shares in the employing company (or in another group company), or of other benefits provided that they are not payments (or cash vouchers or credit-tokens) or other shares or securities (or interests in or rights over them). From 6 April 2003, this exemption is statutory, having previously applied by concession (see Revenue Pamphlet IR 1, A22). [*ITEPA 2003, s 323; SI 2003 No 1361, reg 3*]. Cash awards are assessable (*Weston v Hearn KB 1943, 25 TC 425*).

Gifts from third parties. Gifts received by an employee (or a member of the employee's family or household) from a person other than the employer (or person connected with the employer, see 19 CONNECTED PERSONS), and not directly or indirectly procured by the employer or a connected person, are not liable to income tax, provided that:

(*a*)   they are not made in recognition or anticipation of particular services by the employee in the course of the employment;

(*b*)   they are of goods (i.e. not of cash, securities or the use of a service), or of non-cash vouchers or credit-tokens only capable of being used to obtain goods; and

(*c*)   the total cost to the donor of all such gifts relating to an employee in a tax year is not more than £250 (inclusive of any VAT) (£150 for 2002/03 and earlier years).

From 6 April 2003, this exemption is statutory, having previously applied by concession (see Revenue Pamphlet IR 1, A70). [*ITEPA 2003, ss 270, 324; SI 2003 No 1361, regs 1, 4*].

Simon's Direct Tax Service. See **E4.461** *et seq.*

75.30   **HM FORCES**

Mess and ration allowances and certain bounties and gratuities are exempt. [*ITEPA 2003, s 297; ICTA 1988, s 316*]. No tax allowance may be claimed for lodging expenses paid out of assessable lodging allowance (*Evans v Richardson, Nagley v Spilsbury Ch D 1957, 37 TC 178*), nor for mess expenses (*Lomax v Newton Ch D 1953, 34 TC 558*).

Territorial Army pay assessable but not annual bounty and training expenses. [*ITEPA 2003, s 298; ICTA 1988, s 316(4)*]. Certain payments and other benefits (including commutation of annual sums) are exempt from any charge under *ITEPA 2003, s 403* (see 18 COMPENSATION FOR LOSS OF EMPLOYMENT (AND DAMAGES)). [*ITEPA 2003, s 411; ICTA 1988, s 188(1)(e), Sch 11 para 5; FA 1998, Sch 9 Pt I, Sch 27 Pt III(9)*]. See also 28.7 and 28.32 EXEMPT INCOME and 58.3 PENSION INCOME. Travel facilities (including allowances, vouchers and warrants) for going on, or returning from, leave are exempt from tax. [*ITEPA 2003, ss 266(3), 296; ICTA 1988, s 197*].

Uniform allowances. Serving officers generally receive an annual tax-free allowance which, taking one year with another, covers the costs they are obliged to incur in maintaining their uniforms. The allowance is automatically included in their earnings, with a corresponding deduction being made. [*ITEPA 2003, ss 328(3), 368; ICTA 1988, s 199*]. No further action is thus generally required. Pending a general review of the system of allowances, they are as follows.

75.31 Schedule E—Employment Income

Army	£
Officers serving at full mounted duty	1,012.88
Male dismounted Officers, Colonels and above	749.78
Female Officers, Colonels and above (except QARANC (below))	499.84
Dismounted Officers (Household Division) below Colonel	673.19
Male dismounted Officers below Colonel (except Household Division)	589.29
Female Officers below Colonel (except QARANC (below))	488.30
QARANC: Female Nursing Officers, Colonels and above	671.48
Female Nursing Officers below Colonel	652.87
Male SSLC and SSVC Officers	186.55
Female SSLC and SSVC Officers	201.20

Royal Air Force	£
Male RAF Officers (including PMRAFNS)	
Air Officers	422.76
Group Captains	402.72
Wing Commander and below	361.10
Female officers of PMRAFNS	
Air Officers	589.16
Group Captains	586.00
Wing Commander and below	579.70
Female RAF Officers	
Air Officers	477.98
Group Captains	460.74
Wing Commander and below	421.69

Royal Navy and Royal Marines	£
Officers Flag and equivalent ranks	1,071.00
Officers below Flag rank	792.12
WRNS Officers: seagoing only	853.80
non-seagoing	680.52
Women Medical and Dental Officers: seagoing	792.60
non-seagoing	567.48
QARNNS Officers (female)	
Matron and above	544.68
Below Matron	828.00
QARNNS Officers (male)	
Chief Nursing Officer and above	489.36
Below Chief Nursing Officer	456.48

75.31 LEGAL

In *Eagles v Levy KB 1934, 19 TC 23* held (*a*) costs of action to recover remuneration not an allowable deduction, and (*b*) lump sum amount in settlement of action for balance remuneration assessable in full.

Where company had special need of director's services and paid more than necessary in legal costs of defence on motoring charge, no apportionment between benefits to company and employee and all assessable (*Rendell v Went HL 1964, 41 TC 641*).

Simon's Direct Tax Service. See E4.718.

75.32   LIVING ACCOMMODATION ETC.

Provision of living accommodation etc., for an employee may be taxable earnings under general principles (see 75.10 above), but see below. In *Nicoll v Austin KB 1935, 19 TC 531*, a company maintained a large house owned and occupied by its managing director and controlling shareholder, paying the rates, fuel bills and other outgoings. The expenditure was held to be assessable on him as emoluments of his office.

There may also be liability under special legislation as described below, the charge under which takes priority over any charge under general principles, the latter applying only if, and to the extent that, the charge would exceed that under the special legislation described below. [*ITEPA 2003, s 109; ICTA 1988, s 146A; FA 1996, s 106(2)(3)*]. This is an anti-avoidance measure aimed at salary sacrifices.

'Living accommodation' for these purposes includes all kinds of residential accommodation – e.g. mansions, houses, flats, houseboats, holiday homes or apartments – but not overnight or hotel accommodation or board and lodging (Revenue Employment Income Manual EIM 11321). Whether such accommodation is provided for an employee is a question of fact — see Revenue Employment Income Manual EIM 11405, 11406.

Basic charge

For any employee, the 'cash equivalent' of any living accommodation provided to him, or to members of his family or household, by his employer for any period during or comprising a tax year is treated as earnings for that year *unless* it is provided in the normal course of domestic, family and personal relationships, or by a local authority under its usual terms for non-employees. A deduction is allowed for any amounts which would have been allowed had the employee paid for the accommodation out of earnings.

A charge similarly arises where the accommodation is provided by someone other than the employer but 'by reason of' the employment, i.e. where the accommodation would not have been provided but for the employment. In practice the Revenue normally assume that a benefit which is provided by someone other than the employer but which is plainly connected with the employment has been provided by reason of the employment. (Revenue Employment Income Manual EIM 11408, 20503).

The '*cash equivalent*' of the provision of accommodation for a period is the 'rental value' of the accommodation for that period less any sum made good by the employee to the person at whose cost the accommodation is provided and attributable to that provision. The '*rental value*' is normally an amount equal to rent for the period at an annual rent equal to the annual value ascertained under *ITEPA 2003, s 110* (or, before 6 April 2003, *ICTA 1988, s 837*), which for UK property is equivalent to the gross rateable value (see 69.5(*b*) SCHEDULE A). In Scotland, where the 1985 rating revaluation produced annual values out of line with those in the rest of the UK, a figure lower than the gross rateable value is, by concession, used as annual value. The 1985 valuation figure is scaled back by the average increase in Scottish rateable values between 1978 and 1985 (170%), e.g. a 1985 value of £270 becomes £100 for this purpose. (Revenue Pamphlet IR 1, A56). For new properties which do not appear on the domestic rating lists, and for those where there has been a material change since the lists ceased to be maintained, estimates will be agreed of what the gross annual value would have been had domestic rates been continued. In the case of Scotland these will then be scaled back to 1978 values. (Revenue Press Release 19 April 1990).

For determination of the annual value of property situated outside the UK, see Revenue Employment Income Manual EIM 11440, 11441. Disputes as to annual value are determined by the General Commissioners in the same way as appeals.

Alternatively, if the person at whose cost the accommodation is provided pays actual rent for the whole or part of the period at an annual rate greater than the annual value (as above), then that actual rent is the rental value for the period (or part).

75.32 Schedule E—Employment Income

[*ITEPA 2003, ss 97, 98, 102, 103, 105, 110, 111, 364; ICTA 1988, s 145(1)–(3)(6)(7); FA 1996, s 106(1)(3)*].

Where a property is provided as living accommodation to more than one employee or director in the same period, the total of the basic and additional charges (see below) will not exceed the amount which would have been chargeable if the property had been provided to a single employee in that period. From 6 April 2003, this exemption is statutory [*ITEPA 2003, s 108*], having previously applied by concession (see Revenue Pamphlet IR 1, A91).

Exemptions to the above charge are:

(*a*)   where it is necessary for the proper performance of his duties for the employee to reside in the accommodation;

(*b*)   where the employment is such that it is customary for employees to be provided with accommodation for the better performance of their duties. (For employees to whom the Revenue normally accept this exemption applies, see Revenue Employment Income Manual EIM 11350, 11352.);

(*c*)   where there is a special threat to the employee's personal security, and he resides in the accommodation as part of special security arrangements in force; and

(*d*)   accommodation in Chevening House or certain related premises where the employee is a person nominated in accordance with the Chevening Estate trusts.

[*ITEPA 2003, ss 99(1)(2), 100, 101; ICTA 1988, s 145(4); FA 1996, s 134, Sch 20 para 7*].

See *Vertigan v Brady Ch D 1988, 60 TC 624* as regards the scope of (*a*) and (*b*) above.

Notes to above.

(A)   *Council tax etc.* Where (*a*), (*b*) or (*c*) above applies, there is also no liability if the water or sewerage charges or rates or council tax are paid or reimbursed by the employer (otherwise there could be liability under general principles, see above). [*ITEPA 2003, s 314; ICTA 1988, s 145(4)*].

(B)   *Directors.* Neither (*a*) nor (*b*) above applies to accommodation provided by a company, or associated company, to its director unless for each such directorship he has no material interest in the company (i.e. broadly if his and/or his associates' interests in the company do not exceed 5%) *and either* he is a full-time working director *or* the company is non-profit-making (i.e. it does not carry on a trade nor is its main function the holding of investments or other property) *or* the company is established for charitable purposes only. [*ITEPA 2003, ss 68, 99(3)–(5); ICTA 1988, s 145(5)(8)*].

(C)   As regards (*b*) above, it is accepted that the following employees are within the exemption: police officers; MOD police; prison governors, officers and chaplains; clergymen and ministers of religion (unless engaged on purely administrative duties); members of HM forces; members of the Diplomatic Service; managers of newsagent shops with paper rounds; managers of off-licence shops with opening hours broadly equivalent to those of public houses; head teachers and teachers with 24-hour pastoral duties provided with accommodation on or adjacent to the school premises. Veterinary surgeons assisting in veterinary practices and managers of camping and caravan sites living on or adjacent to the site will be accepted as meeting the test that provision of accommodation is 'customary', but must individually satisfy the test that the provision is for the 'better performance' of their duties. (Revenue Employment Income Manual EIM 11346 *et seq.*).

Simon's Direct Tax Service. See E4.412.

Additional charge in respect of properties costing over £75,000

For all employees, if there is a liability to tax on living accommodation under the basic charge (as above), or there would be a liability if the employee's contributions towards the cost were disregarded, and the cost of providing the accommodation exceeds £75,000, the employee will, in addition to any basic charge (as above), be taxable on the 'additional value' to him of the accommodation. Where, however, the basic charge is based on the full open market rent the property might fetch, the Revenue will, by concession, not seek to impose an additional charge. (Revenue Pamphlet IR 1, A91). Any rent paid by the employee which exceeds the value of the accommodation as determined for the purposes of the basic charge is deducted from the additional value. The '*additional value*' is the rent which would have been payable for the period if the annual rent was the 'appropriate percentage' of the amount by which the cost of providing the accommodation exceeds £75,000. The '*appropriate percentage*' is the 'official rate' in force, for the purposes of taxing cheap loan arrangements under *ITEPA 2003, s 181* (see 75.20 above), at the beginning of the year of assessment (i.e. 5% for 2003/04).

The cost of providing the accommodation is the aggregate of expenditure incurred by any 'relevant person' in acquiring the property together with any improvement expenditure incurred before the year of assessment in question *less* any payments by the employee to any relevant person as reimbursement of such expenditure or as consideration for the grant of a tenancy, or subtenancy, to him. Where the employee first occupies the property on a date after 30 March 1983 and an estate or interest in the property was held by a relevant person throughout the period of six years ending with that date (i.e. the date of first occupation), then the cost of providing the accommodation, for the purposes of calculating the additional value (but not for determining whether the additional charge applies), is the aggregate of the market value of the property at that date, together with any improvement expenditure incurred after that date and before the year of assessment, *less* any payments by the employee to any relevant person as reimbursement of any part of the cost of acquiring the estate or interest held when the employee first occupied the property (up to the market value on that date) or of the improvement expenditure, or as consideration for the grant of a tenancy, or subtenancy, to him. A '*relevant person*' is the person providing the accommodation, or, if different, the employee's employer, and any person, other than the employee, connected with such persons under *ICTA 1988, s 839* (see 19 CONNECTED PERSONS). '*Market value*' is open market value assuming vacant possession and disregarding any options on the property held by the employee, a person connected with him or any relevant person as defined above.

Where an employee is provided with more than one property, the £75,000 limit is applied separately to each property. (Revenue Press Release 22 November 1990). Where a property is provided as living accommodation to more than one employee or director in the same period, the total of the basic and additional charges will not exceed the amount which would have been chargeable if the property had been provided to a single employee in that period. From 6 April 2003, this exemption is statutory [*ITEPA 2003, s 108*], having previously applied by concession (see Revenue Pamphlet IR 1, A91).

It is understood that the Revenue would not normally seek to revise the cost of providing the accommodation for these purposes where the property in question happens to be transferred for administrative reasons within a group, although continuing to be provided for the same employee. (Tolley's Practical Tax 1985 p 120).

[*ITEPA 2003, ss 104, 106, 107, 112, Sch 7 para 21; ICTA 1988, s 146*].

Example

S, the founder and managing director of S Ltd, a successful transport company, has since April 1999 occupied a mansion house owned by S Ltd. The house was acquired by S Ltd in August 1993 for £150,000 and, since acquisition, but before 6 April 2003, £80,000 has been spent by S Ltd on alterations and improvements to the house. The gross annual value of the house for rating purposes before 1 April 1990 (when the community charge replaced general rates) was £1,663. S pays annual rental of £2,000 to the company in respect of 2004/05 only. He pays all expenses relating to the property.

S will have assessable benefits in respect of his occupation of the house for 2003/04 and 2005/06 as follows.

	£	£
2003/04		
Gross annual value		1,663
Additional charge		
Acquisition cost of house	150,000	
Cost of improvements	80,000	
	230,000	
Deduct	75,000	
Additional value	£155,000	
Additional value at 5%		7,750
		£9,413
2004/05		
Gross annual value		Nil*
Additional charge		
Acquisition cost of house	150,000	
Cost of improvements	80,000	
	230,000	
Deduct	75,000	
Additional value	£155,000	
Additional value at 5%		7,750
		7,750
Rental payable by S	2,000	
Deduct Gross annual value	1,663	
		337*
		£7,413

* No taxable gross annual value arises in 2004/05 because the rental of £2,000 payable by S exceeds the gross annual value of £1,663. The excess is deductible from the amount of the benefit arising under the additional charge.

Simon's Direct Tax Service. See E4.413.

Related expenses

Certain expenses connected with the provision of living accommodation which are met on behalf of, or reimbursed to, the employee may give rise to liability either as benefits-in-kind for directors and certain employees or directly as earnings for all employees. The following reliefs apply.

(i)   *Alterations and repairs* to accommodation provided for directors and non-lower-paid employees (see 75.16 above) will not be treated as benefits if

(A)   the alterations or additions are of a structural nature, or

(B)   the repairs would be the obligation of the lessor if the premises were leased and *Landlord and Tenant Act 1985, s 11* applied. [*ITEPA 2003, s 313; ICTA 1988, s 155(3)*].

(ii)   Where one of the exemptions in (*a*), (*b*) or (*c*) above applies, any amount to be treated as earnings in respect of expenditure on *heating, lighting, cleaning, repairs, maintenance, decoration, provision of furniture etc.* normal for domestic occupation is limited to 10% of the net earnings from the employment for the period concerned less any sum made good by the employee. Earnings include any from an associated company (i.e. where one company has control of the other or both are under control of the same person). Net earnings are (ignoring the benefit in question) after deducting capital allowances, allowable expenses, mileage allowance relief, superannuation, retirement annuities and approved retirement benefits scheme payments. Before 6 April 2003, this applied only to directors and those in non-lower-paid employment (see 75.14 above), but thereafter it applies without that restriction. [*ITEPA 2003, s 315; ICTA 1988, s 163*]. The earnings to be taken into account are those for the year under review, regardless of the year in which they are chargeable (Revenue Employment Income Manual EIM 21723).

See Simon's Direct Tax Service E4.620.

Example

N is employed by the G Property Co Ltd, earning £12,000 p.a.. He occupies, rent-free, the basement flat of a block of flats for which he is employed as caretaker/security officer. The annual value of the flat is determined at £250. In 2004/05, G Ltd incurred the following expenditure on the flat.

	£
Heat and light	700
Decoration	330
Repairs	210
Cleaning	160
Conversion of large bedroom into two smaller bedrooms	3,000

In addition, the company pays N's council tax which amounts to £500.

As the company does not have a pension scheme, N pays a stakeholder pension premium of £200 (net) on 31 October 2004, but apart from his personal allowance, he has no other reliefs.

N's taxable income for 2004/05 is

	£
Salary	12,000
Annual value of flat	—
Heat and light, decoration, repairs, cleaning £1,400 restricted to	1,200
	13,200
Deduct	
Personal allowance	4,745
Taxable	£8,455

Notes

(*a*)   N is not assessed on the annual value of the flat as long as he can show that it is necessary for the proper performance of his duties for him to reside in the accommodation.

(*b*)   The structural alterations costing £3,000 will not be regarded as a benefit.

(*c*)   The earnings treated as having arisen in respect of the heat and light, decoration, repairs and cleaning costs will be restricted to the lesser of

(i)   the expenses incurred £1,400

(ii)   10% × £12,000 (net earnings) £1,200

The stakeholder pension contribution is not deductible in arriving at net earnings for this purpose, although retirement annuity premiums and occupational pension scheme contributions are so deductible. (The contribution is not shown above as a deduction from taxable income as basic rate relief has been given at source and higher rate relief is not applicable.)

Case law

The following cases, decided under earlier legislation, may be relevant to a charge under the benefits code in respect of expenses related to living accommodation. *Butter v Bennett CA 1962, 40 TC 402* ('representative occupier' held to be assessable on provisions for fuel and gardening); *Doyle v Davison QB(NI) 1961, 40 TC 140* (repairs paid for by employer held to be benefits); *McKie v Warner Ch D 1961, 40 TC 65* (flat provided at reduced rent held to be benefit); *Luke HL 1963, 40 TC 630* (certain expenses held not to be benefits — house owned by employer); *Westcott v Bryan CA 1969, 45 TC 476* (apportionment approved where company house provided to accommodate company guests).

Other matters relating to living accommodation etc.

(1)   **Compulsory transfers.** *Guarantee payments* making good loss on sale of employee's house when compulsorily transferred were held not assessable in *Hochstrasser v Mayes, Jennings v Kinder HL 1959, 38 TC 673.*

(2)   **Members of Parliaments and Assemblies.** Members of the House of Commons, the Scottish Parliament or the Wales or Northern Ireland Assemblies are not allowed a deduction for expenditure incurred on residential or overnight accommodation to enable duties to be performed where the body of which they are a member sits or in the area which they represent. [*ITEPA 2003, s 360; ICTA 1988, s 198(4); FA 1999, Sch 5 para 2(2)*]. See 28.19 EXEMPT INCOME as regards exempt accommodation allowances. See Simon's Direct Tax Service E4.334.

As regards board and lodging allowances, see 75.10 above and for subsistence allowances, see 75.46 below. For deductibility of the cost of living accommodation etc., see 75.11(*b*) above.

75.33   **MEAL VOUCHERS**

No assessment on employee if vouchers are (i) non-transferable, (ii) used for meals on working days only, (iii) limited to 15 pence per day, (iv) if limited in issue, available to staff in lower-paid employment (see 75.14 above).

The value of any voucher or part voucher not satisfying these conditions is taxable (e.g. the excess over 15p where the voucher otherwise qualifies). From 6 April 2003, this exemption is statutory [*ITEPA 2003, s 89, Sch 7 para 18*], having previously applied by concession (see Revenue Pamphlet IR 1, A2). See 75.16(iv) above for canteen meals.

75.34   **PROFIT-RELATED PAY** [*ICTA 1988, ss 169–184, Sch 8; FA 1989, s 61, Sch 4; FA 1991, s 37; FA 1994, ss 98, 99; FA 1995, ss 136, 137(1)(6); FA 1997, s 61, Sch 18 pt vi(3); FA 1999, s 46*]

Profit-related pay is charged in accordance with the receipts basis (see 75.5 above) subject to the exemption (until phased out — see below) from tax of so much of the profit-related pay as does not exceed the lower of:

(*a*)   one-fifth of the aggregate, for the employment to which the scheme relates, of non-profit-related pay (within PAYE but excluding benefits) in the '*profit period*' (i.e. the accounting period by reference to which the profit-related pay is calculated), or in the part of that period by reference to which eligibility for profit-related pay arises, and the profit-related pay itself, and

(*b*)   £4,000 (proportionately reduced where the profit period is less than twelve months or the employee is entitled to profit-related pay by reference to part only of that period).

The £4,000 limit in (*b*) above is reduced to £2,000 for profit periods beginning on or after 1 January 1998 and before 1 January 1999, and to £1,000 for profit periods beginning on or after 1 January 1999 and before 1 January 2000. The relief is **abolished** altogether for profit periods beginning **on or after 1 January 2000**. Registration of schemes (see below) is accordingly restricted. *FA 1998, s 62, Sch 11* prevent exploitation of the phasing-out provisions, by preventing employees in a registered scheme from obtaining a higher relief limit for a longer period by joining another scheme on or after 17 March 1998. This applies where the scheme employers of the two schemes are the same person or are CONNECTED PERSONS (19). The cancellation by the Revenue of a new scheme designed to obtain such an advantage, before enactment of these provisions, was upheld on the general anti-avoidance principles laid down in *Furniss v Dawson* (see 3.1 ANTI-AVOIDANCE) (*Colours Ltd (formerly Spectrum Ltd) v CIR (Sp C 156), [1998] SSCD 93*).

The profit-related pay must be paid under a registered scheme (see below) under which a part of the emoluments in the 'employment unit' to which the scheme relates is determined by reference to the profits in a profit period of that 'employment unit'. '*Employment unit*' means the undertaking (or part) to which a scheme relates.

[*ICTA 1988, ss 169–171; FA 1989, s 42(4), Sch 4 para 2, Sch 17 Pt IV; FA 1991, s 37*].

Example

E is employed by C Ltd and receives, on 1 May 2000, profit-related pay of £4,200 for the year to 31 March 2000 (the profit period). His earnings received in the year to 31 March 2000, excluding profit-related pay, amounted to £16,600 and he was also provided with a company car on which both car and fuel benefits arise.

The amount of profit-related pay to be included in E's taxable emoluments for 2000/01 is as follows.

	£	£
Amount received		4,200
Deduct Tax-free amount, being the *lower* of		
(i) 20% of £20,800	4,160	
(ii) Overriding maximum	1,000	
		1,000
Taxable profit-related pay		£3,200

Relief is denied where either

(i) the profit-related pay relates to a period when the employee had another employment in respect of which he receives profit-related pay which is exempt under these provisions, or

(ii) no Class 1 National Insurance contributions are payable by the employer in respect of the profit-related pay (unless they are not payable only because the employee's earnings are below the earnings threshold (before 6 April 1999, the lower earnings limit) — see 83.8 SOCIAL SECURITY). [*ICTA 1988, s 172; Social Security Act 1998, Sch 7 para 16*].

Excluded employments. Crown and local authority employments (as widely defined) cannot be covered by a scheme seeking registration (see below). [*ICTA 1988, s 174*].

Conditions for registration. To qualify for registration, a scheme must satisfy the following conditions.

(A) Its terms must be set out in writing.

(B) It must identify

    (i) the 'scheme employer' and any other person by whom emoluments of scheme employees are paid, and

    (ii) the undertaking (or distinct part) to which the scheme relates (which must be carried on with a view to profit).

(C) It must enable employees to whom it relates to be identified.

(D) It must exclude employees (or their associates, as defined) with a 'material interest' (broadly, a 25% interest) in the company throughout a profit period.

(E) It must ensure that payments are not made under the scheme by reference to any profit period at the beginning of which less than 80% of the employees in the employment unit are covered by the scheme (ignoring employees excluded under (D) above and certain short service and (in relation to schemes registered before 1 May 1995) part-time employees who are excluded from the scheme).

(F) It must identify the accounting period(s) by reference to which profit-related pay is to be calculated. Any such period must be of twelve months' duration unless either the scheme is cancelled with effect from a date after the start of the period, or the scheme is a 'replacement scheme' in which case it may only provide for two periods, the first of which may be less than twelve months. Some leeway is allowed where an employer makes up his financial accounts to slightly varying dates; the twelve month period may be increased or reduced by up to seven days. (Revenue Press Release 22 December 1987).

(G) It must provide for a method for calculating the '*distributable pool*' (i.e. the amount which may be paid to scheme employees in respect of a profit period). Except in the case of a 'replacement scheme', one of two methods must be specified. These are set out as 'Method A' and 'Method B' in *ICTA 1988, Sch 8 paras 13–14A*, which broadly allow the distributable pool to be equal *either* to a fixed percentage of the profits of the employment unit in the profit period *or* to a percentage of the distributable pool for the previous profit period (with a notional pool being specified for the first profit period). In either case, there is a formula for ensuring that, where profits remain unchanged, the pool is at least 5% of the annual equivalent of scheme employees' pay (within PAYE but excluding benefits) at the beginning of the first profit period (as reasonably estimated at the time of application for registration). Equally, either method may provide for profit increases in excess of 60% (or a specified higher figure) to be disregarded in arriving at the pool, and for there to be no pool when profits are below a specified level (which must be below that giving rise to the 5% minimum referred to above). Where there is accordingly no pool for a profit period and the following year's pool is to be a set percentage of the earlier year's pool, the percentage is applied to the pool that would have arisen but for the special provision for there to be no pool.

The requirement for a 5% minimum was abolished in relation to schemes registered after 2 February 1989. (Revenue Press Release 3 February 1989). In consequence, the requirement to be met for there to be no distributable pool was replaced by a requirement that the profits limit below which there is to be no pool must not exceed profits representing a zero increase. Any of the rules included in a scheme which moderate the effect of profit changes on the distributable pool may take effect either from the first profit period or from any later profit period determined in accordance with the scheme.

For schemes registered after 2 August 1992, the requirement that the scheme specify a fixed percentage (Method A) or the amount of a notional pool (Method B) will *not* be met where a formula is specified rather than an actual figure, unless the factors used in the formula are ascertained at the time the scheme is written, so that the actual figure derived from the formula may be fully and finally identified at that time. (Revenue Pamphlet IR 131, SP 7/92, 3 August 1992).

Schemes registered after 30 November 1993 which include a 60% (or higher) limit on profit increases to be taken into account in arriving at the pool must also include a provision for that upper limit to be increased where there is a fall in the taxable pay (ignoring PRP) by comparison with the previous profit period (or the base year) (or, in the case of Method B, the previous twelve months). The percentage decrease must be applied as an increase in the amount of the 160% (or higher) limit. Also, where a scheme registered after 30 November 1993 includes provision for either a 60% (or higher) upper profits limit or a lower profits level below which there is no pool, profit-related pay and secondary Class 1 national insurance contributions must be accorded the same accountancy treatment in arriving at the profits for both the current and the previous profit period (or the base year) (or, in the case of Method B, the previous twelve months).

A 'replacement scheme' must provide for the distributable pool to be a specified percentage of the profits of the profit period.

(H) It must provide for the whole of the distributable pool to be paid to employees in the employment unit, and for the timing of such payments.

(J) Its provisions must ensure that employees participate on similar terms, although payments may vary according to objective factors such as length of service or level of remuneration.

(K) It must provide for the preparation of a profit and loss account giving a true and fair view of the profit or loss of the employment unit to which the scheme relates in respect of each profit period (and any other necessary period). *Companies Act 1985, Sch 4* (or NI equivalent) applies, with appropriate modification, to such accounts which must not, however, include a deduction for the remuneration (as widely defined) of any person excluded from the scheme as having a material interest (see above). Certain other restrictions apply as to what the scheme may require to be included in or excluded from the accounts notwithstanding *Companies Act* require-ments, and as to what changes in accounting policy between periods may be permitted (see *ICTA 1988, Sch 8 paras 19–20 as amended* and Revenue Pamphlet IR 1, B44). The permitted adjustments include PRP itself (and see Revenue Tax Bulletin August 1997 pp 457, 458 as regards dealing with differences between PRP charged in the accounts and the full amount of PRP for a period). See also Revenue

Tax Bulletin June 2000 pp 759, 760 for Revenue practice as regards the impact of the revised FRS11 in preparing PRP accounts.

(L)   In relation to schemes registered after 26 July 1989, where the employment unit is part of an undertaking, and the scheme requires the profits to be taken as equivalent to those of the whole (identified) undertaking, the provisions of *ICTA 1988, Sch 8* apply as if those profits were the profits of the employment unit. The scheme must, however, contain provisions ensuring that no payments are made under it by reference to a profit period unless, at the beginning of the period, the number of scheme employees does not exceed 33% of the total number of employees in other registered schemes relating to employees of the same undertaking (disregarding other schemes whose rules require the profits for scheme purposes to be taken as equivalent to those of the whole undertaking, or under which no payments could be made for the profit period concerned by virtue of the rules required by (E) above). Where two or more schemes relating to employment units which are parts of the same undertaking both have rules requiring their profits for scheme purposes to be taken as equivalent to those of the whole undertaking, an employee to whom another scheme relates cannot be included for the purposes of the above 33% test in connection with more than one of those schemes.

For schemes registered after 30 November 1993, there is a further condition that the scheme must ensure that its fixed percentage (in the case of schemes employing Method A) or notional or distributable pool (in the case of schemes employing Method B) (see (G) above) does not exceed a limit calculated by reference to the ratio of PRP to total pay in the other scheme or schemes registered for the business. The ratio is calculated by reference to the figures for pay and PRP paid for a specified earlier period.

The '*scheme employer*' is the person by whom the emoluments of all employees to whom the scheme relates are paid or, if there is no one such person, the parent company of the group of companies (i.e. consisting of the parent company and its 51% subsidiaries) where all the persons paying such emoluments are members of the group. Changes in the members of a partnership which is a scheme employer are ignored for these purposes.

A scheme is a '*replacement scheme*' if it relates to employees to not less than one-half of whom another registered scheme (or schemes) applied, and the registration of the previous scheme was cancelled because of changes in the employment unit or in the circumstances relating to the scheme which occurred within the three months before the start of the first profit period of the new scheme. The Board must also be satisfied as to certain other matters.

[*ICTA 1988, ss 169, 173, 183, Sch 8; FA 1989, Sch 4 paras 9–15; FA 1994, ss 98, 99; FA 1995, s 136*].

Registration. Application for registration of a profit-related pay scheme had to be in such form, and supported by such information, as the Board required, and had to specify the profit period(s) to which it relates. It had to be made to the Board by the scheme employer, and had to contain a declaration that the scheme complied with the conditions referred to above. It previously had to contain an undertaking that any requirements under minimum wage legislation would be met without taking profit-related pay into account, but this requirement was abolished with effect from 28 July 1998. The application had also to be accompanied by a report by an 'independent accountant', in a form prescribed by the Board, to the effect that, in his opinion, the scheme complied with the conditions referred to above, and the books and records were adequate for preparation of the annual return required (see below). If it was made more than three months before the beginning of the period (or first period) to which the scheme related, it was guaranteed that the scheme would, if approved, be registered from the beginning of that period. There was provision for further information in support of the application to be sought by the Board. If the Board were not satisfied that the application met the various requirements, the application was refused (subject to appeal, see below). Later applications could, if the Board were satisfied, lead to registration before the beginning of the first period to which they related, but would otherwise be regarded as having been refused (again, subject to appeal). Notice of registration or refusal had to be in writing.

An '*independent accountant*' is a qualified auditor who does not employ scheme employees and who is not (and is not an employee of) a partner, officer, employee or partner of an employee of a person who employs scheme employees or whose subsidiary or holding company or fellow subsidiary employs scheme employees. A report may be signed in the name of a firm of accountants, provided that all partners meet these qualifications. (Revenue Press Release 22 December 1987).

[*ICTA 1988, ss 173, 175, 176, 184; FA 1989, Sch 4 para 10(2); SI 1991 No 1997; FA 1999, s 46(1)*].

Change of employer. Where there is a change in the scheme employer, and the successor would have been eligible to apply for registration, and there is no other material change in the employment unit to which the scheme relates or in the circumstances affecting the scheme, the predecessor and successor may, within one month of the change, jointly elect for the scheme registration to be amended by substitution of the successor for the predecessor. Provided that there are not other grounds for cancellation of the scheme, it will continue to operate under the amended registration as if the successor had been the original applicant. [*ICTA 1988, s 177*]. A scheme registration may be amended following the death of the scheme employer to substitute his personal representatives, on written application within one month of the grant of probate etc., provided that there would be no grounds apart from the death for cancellation of the registration. The provisions then apply as if the personal representatives had been the scheme employer throughout. The scheme registration may be cancelled with effect from the date of death if the personal representatives so request within the same period. [*ICTA 1988, ss 177A, 178(5A); FA 1989, Sch 4 paras 3, 4(4)*].

Alteration of scheme terms. Where the terms of a registered scheme are altered, the Board may cancel the registration with effect from the beginning of the profit period during which the alteration took place or any later profit period, although such alteration does not of itself invalidate the registration. The scheme employer may, however, apply to the Board, in a prescribed form and within one month of the alteration, for registration of the alteration, which precludes cancellation of the registration by virtue of the alteration. Provided that the alteration meets one of the conditions listed below, and the scheme employer declares (and a report in a prescribed form by an independent accountant confirms) that it does so and that the scheme as altered complies with *ICTA 1988, Sch 8* (as at the date the scheme was registered subject to any specified subsequent amendments to that *Schedule*), the Board will register such an alteration. The Board's decision on the application must in any event be given within three months of receipt and notified to the scheme employer. If it subsequently appears to the Board that the application did not meet the above requirements or that the declaration by the scheme employer was false, the registration may be cancelled with effect as if the alteration had not been registered.

The conditions referred to above are that the alteration either:

(*a*)   relates to a term not relevant to the scheme's complying with the requirements of *ICTA 1988, Sch 8*; or

(*b*)   relates to a term identifying any person (other than the scheme employer) who pays scheme employees' emoluments; or

(*c*)   consists of the addition of a term providing for an abbreviated profit period following cancellation of registration; or (*d*) amends the provisions identifying scheme employees for subsequent profit periods; or

(*e*) relates to a scheme provision dealing with the computation under Method A or Method B (see (G) above) for subsequent profit periods; or

(*f*) amends the provisions as to when payments are made to employees for subsequent profit periods; or

(*g*) is made to bring the scheme into compliance with the requirements of *ICTA 1988, Sch 8* (as it had effect either at the time of registration or at the date of application for registration of the alteration) if it did not so comply at the time of registration, provided that

(i) it is made for the purposes of all profit periods to which the scheme relates,

(ii) it is made within two years of the beginning of the first profit period, and

(iii) it does not wholly or partly invalidate any payment of profit-related pay already made under the scheme.

[*ICTA 1988, ss 177B, 178(3A)(3B); FA 1989, Sch 4 paras 3, 4(3)*].

Cancellation of registration. The Board may (subject to appeal, see below) cancel registration of a scheme, by notice in writing, where certain conditions have not been complied with or where losses have arisen, or if the scheme employer so requests in writing. The cancellation generally applies from the beginning of the profit period in which the change giving rise to the cancellation takes place. Any shortfall in tax deducted from profit-related pay as a result of cancellation of registration is payable by the scheme employer (or by his personal representatives or by the UK payer if the scheme employer is non-UK resident) to the Board, and PAYE regulations provide for collection and recovery and interest on unpaid amounts. [*ICTA 1988, ss 178, 179; FA 1989, Sch 4 paras 4, 5, 10(2); FA 1999, s 46(2)(3); SI 1995 No 917*]. With effect from 14 July 1995, interest is charged on tax recovered from employers in respect of payments incorrectly made tax-free under PRP schemes for 1994/95 and subsequent years. Penalties will be sought where there has been fraud or negligence in making late or incorrect returns for such years. (Revenue Press Release 14 July 1995).

See also the preceding paragraphs as regards death of the scheme employer and scheme alterations.

Appeals. An appeal against refusal or cancellation of registration, or against refusal to register an alteration or amend a registration on the death of the scheme employer, must be made within 30 days of notification of the refusal etc., and lies to the Special Commissioners. [*ICTA 1988, s 182; FA 1989, Sch 4 para 8*].

Returns and other information. An annual return and a report by an independent accountant (including confirmation that the scheme terms have been complied with in the period) are required, as laid down by the Board (see Revenue Press Release 1 February 1988), within ten months of the end of each scheme accounting period (seven months in the case of public companies). The time limit may be extended by three months in certain cases where a company has overseas interests.

There is a general requirement to provide relevant information requested by the Board, and for the scheme employer to notify the Board of anything of which he becomes aware which may be a ground for cancellation of that registration. The personal representatives of a deceased scheme employer must inform the Board of his death within one month of the grant of probate etc. [*ICTA 1988, ss 180, 181; FA 1989, Sch 4 paras 6, 7*].

Penalties apply for failure to furnish information as above. [*TMA 1970, s 98*].

Guidance notes and model rules on profit-related pay schemes are available from Profit Related Pay Office, Inland Revenue, St Mungo's Road, Cumbernauld, Glasgow G67 1YZ.

Simon's Direct Tax Service. See **E4.301** *et seq.*

75.35   **REDUNDANCY PAYMENTS**

Amounts received under *Employment Rights Act 1996*, or NI equivalent, may be taken into account for purposes of *ITEPA 2003, s 403*, see 18.5 COMPENSATION FOR LOSS OF EMPLOYMENT (AND DAMAGES), but are otherwise exempt earnings. [*ITEPA 2003, s 309; ICTA 1988, ss 579, 580*]. Other redundancy payments may be taxable earnings, see 18.5 *et seq.* COMPENSATION FOR LOSS OF EMPLOYMENT (AND DAMAGES). See Simon's Direct Tax Service E4.327.

75.36   **RELOCATION PACKAGES**

Certain payments and benefits received in connection with job-related residential moves are exempted from charge as taxable earnings. The statutory exemption applies to

(*a*)   any sums paid to the employee, or to another person on behalf of the employee, in respect of 'qualifying removal expenses', and

(*b*)   any 'qualifying removal benefit' provided for the employee or for members of his family or household (including sons- and daughters-in-law, servants, dependants and guests),

to the extent that they do not exceed a 'qualifying limit'.

'*Qualifying removal expenses*' are 'eligible removal expenses' reasonably incurred by the employee, and '*qualifying removal benefits*' are 'eligible removal benefits' reasonably provided, on or before the 'limitation day' in connection with a change of the employee's sole or main residence. The change of residence does not require the disposal of the former residence, but the new residence must, on the facts of the particular case, become the main residence of the employee (see Revenue Press Release 14 April 1993).

The change of residence must result from the employee commencing employment with the employer, or from an alteration of his duties in the employment, or from an alteration of the place where those duties are normally to be performed. The change must be made wholly or mainly to bring the employee's residence within a reasonable daily travelling distance of the place he normally performs, or is to perform, those duties. What is a 'reasonable daily travelling distance' is not defined, but is a matter for common sense, taking account of local conditions. It may depend on either or both travelling time or distance (see Revenue Tax Bulletin November 1993 p 94).

The '*limitation day*' is the last day of the year of assessment following that in which the commencement or change of duties etc. took place, unless the Board grants an extension in a particular case to the end of a later year of assessment.

'*Eligible removal expenses*' fall into seven different categories.

(i)   Expenses of disposal, i.e. legal expenses, loan redemption penalties, estate agents' or auctioneers' fees, advertising costs, disconnection charges, and rent and maintenance etc. costs during an unoccupied period, relating to the disposal of his interest (or of the interest of a member of his family or household) in the employee's former residence. Expenses of a sale which falls through are eligible provided that the residence is in fact still changed.

(ii)   Expenses of acquisition, i.e. legal expenses, loan procurement fees, insurance costs, survey fees, Registry fees, stamp duty and connection charges, relating to the acquisition by the employee (and/or by a member of his family or household) of an interest in his new residence.

(iii) Expenses of abortive acquisition, i.e. expenses which would have been within (ii) above but for the interest not being acquired, for reasons beyond the control of the person seeking to acquire it or because that person reasonably declined to proceed with it.

(iv) Expenses of transporting belongings, i.e. expenses, including insurance, temporary storage and disconnection and reconnection of appliances, connected with transporting domestic belongings of the employee and of members of his family or household from the former to the new residence.

(v) Travelling and subsistence expenses (subsistence meaning food, drink and temporary accommodation). These are restricted to:

(a) such costs of the employee and members of his family or household on temporary visits to the new area in connection with the change;

(b) the employee's travel costs between his former residence and new place of work;

(c) (other than in the case of a new employment) the employee's travel costs, before the change in the employment, between his new residence and old place of work or temporary living accommodation;

(d) the employee's subsistence costs (not within (a));

(e) the employee's travel costs between his old residence and any temporary living accommodation;

(f) the travel costs of the employee and members of his family or household between the former and new residences;

(g) certain costs (the scope of which is widened slightly from 6 April 2003) incurred to secure continuity of education for a member of the employee's family or household who is under 19 at the beginning of the tax year in which the commencement or change of duties etc. takes place.

Expenses for which a deduction is allowable under *ITEPA 2003, ss 341, 342, 369–375* (certain foreign travel expenses, see 75.8, 75.9 above) are excluded, so that these are in effect allowed in addition to expenses up to the 'qualifying limit' referred to below (Revenue Employment Income Manual EIM 03116).

(vi) Bridging loan expenses, i.e. interest payable by the employee (or by a member of his family or household) on a loan raised at least partly because there is a gap between the incurring of expenditure in acquiring the new residence and the receipt of the proceeds of disposal of the former residence. Interest on so much of the loan as either

(a) exceeds the market value of his interest (or the interest of a member of his family or household) in the former residence (at the time the new residence is acquired), or

(b) is not used for the purpose of either redeeming a loan raised by the employee (or by a member of his family or household) on his former residence or acquiring his interest (or the interest of a member of his family or household) in the new residence

is excluded.

(vii) Duplicate expenses, i.e. expenses incurred as a result of the change on the replacement of domestic goods used at the former residence but unsuitable for use at the new residence. (Before 6 April 2003, the exemption applied only to the excess of the replacement cost over any sale proceeds from the assets replaced. No such deduction was required in relation to the benefit of replacement of such items (see below), and the requirement is abolished altogether from 6 April 2003.)

The Treasury may by regulation amend these categories so as to add any expenses from a day to be specified in the regulations, with effect for commencements or changes of duties etc. taking place on or after that day.

'*Eligible removal benefits*' fall into six different categories, consisting of the benefit of services corresponding, as applicable, to the expenses specified under (i)–(v) and (vii) above in relation to eligible removal expenses (but, under (v), excluding the provision of a company car or van also available for general private use (see 75.18 above) in the same tax year in which it is provided for the move). They may include administration fees of a relocation management company charged to the employer. From 6 April 2003, they also include the benefit of the provision of vouchers or credit-tokens for the obtaining of goods or services within these reliefs. The Treasury has similar powers to those applicable in the case of eligible removal expenses.

The '*qualifying limit*' as regards any change of residence applies to the aggregate of qualifying removal expenses paid and the value of qualifying removal benefits received in respect of the change. The value attributed to such benefits is their cash equivalent under the general benefits legislation (75.16 above) or, as appropriate, the amount of the living accommodation charge under 75.32 above (net of any attributable contribution by the employee and certain allowable deductions).

The amount of the '*qualifying limit*' is £8,000. This may be varied upwards by Treasury order from a day to be specified in the order, with effect for commencements or changes of duties etc. taking place on or after that day.

Bridging loan finance obtained before the 'limitation day' (as above) by reason of the employment within the cheap loan provisions of *ITEPA 2003, s 173* (see 75.20 above) on a move meeting the above conditions may attract a measure of relief where the expenses and benefits for which relief is obtained in respect of the move are in total less than the £8,000 (or increased) limit. Relief is obtained by delaying the implementation of the cheap loan provisions for a number of days after the making of the loan such that the interest (at the official rate at the time the loan was made, see 75.20 above) on the maximum sum borrowed for those days would equate to the amount by which the £8,000 (or increased) limit exceeds the amount of expenses and benefits otherwise relieved. If the loan is discharged before those days have expired, no liability arises. Otherwise, the cheap loan provisions apply as if the loan had been made on the day after the last of the days for which the exemption applies. The tax payable by virtue of those provisions for a tax year ending before the limitation day may be decided on the basis that the maximum relief would be utilised against qualifying removal expenses and benefits, and subsequently adjusted if that is not in fact the case.

[*ITEPA 2003, ss 191(4), 271–289, Sch 7 paras 35, 36; ICTA 1988, ss 191A, 191B, Sch 11A; FA 1993, s 76, Sch 5; FA 2004, Sch 17 para 9(2)*].

PAYE should not be applied to payments made under a relocation package, even if the qualifying limit is exceeded. Flat rate allowances may be paid gross, provided that the inspector is satisfied that they do no more than reimburse employees' eligible expenses. Any taxable payments are to be included in the annual return of benefits (see 55.9 PAY AS YOU EARN). See Revenue Press Release 14 April 1993.

For the application of these provisions to relocation company management fees, and in particular to guaranteed sale price schemes, see Revenue Employment Income Manual EIM 03127–03137. See generally EIM 03101 *et seq.*

Simon's Direct Tax Service. See E4.637.

75.37 Schedule E—Employment Income

75.37 RESTRICTIVE COVENANTS

Where the present, past or future holder of an office or employment, the earnings from which are taxable on the receipts basis (see 75.3, 75.4 above), gives, in connection therewith, an undertaking (whether qualified or legally valid or not) restricting his conduct or activities, any sum paid to any person in respect of the giving or fulfilment (in whole or part) of the undertaking is, if it would not otherwise be so, treated as earnings from the office or employment for the tax year of payment. If such a payment is made after the death of the individual concerned, it is treated as having been paid immediately before his death. Where valuable consideration rather than money is given, a sum equal to the value of that consideration is treated as having been paid. [*ITEPA 2003, ss 225, 226; ICTA 1988, s 313; FA 1988, s 73*].

Termination settlements. Financial settlements relating to the termination of an employment may require the employee to undertake that the agreement is in 'full and final settlement' of his claims relating to the employment, and/or not to commence, or to discontinue, legal proceedings in respect of those claims. They may also reaffirm undertakings about the employee's conduct or activity after termination which formed part of the employment terms. The Revenue accept that such undertakings do not give rise to a charge under the above provisions, without prejudice to the treatment of other restrictive undertakings, whether or not contained in the settlement. (Revenue Pamphlet IR 131, SP 3/96).

Where a compromise agreement made at termination of employment includes a repayment clause (typically a clause requiring full or partial repayment by the employee of the sum settled if he subsequently initiates litigation in respect of the employment or its termination), the attribution of any of the sum settled to the undertaking not to litigate would be outside SP 3/96 and thus within the above charging provisions. Other than in exceptional cases, e.g. where the sum settled is clearly excessive in the circumstances, the Revenue will not seek to make such an attribution and a charge under the above provisions will not arise. It should be noted that if, exceptionally, a charge *does* arise, there can be no subsequent adjustment to the charge if a repayment is, in fact, made under the clause. (Revenue Tax Bulletin October 2003 p 1063).

75.38 SECURITY OF EMPLOYEES

Where an asset or service which improves personal security is provided for an employee by reason of his employment, or is used by the employee, and the cost was (wholly or partly) borne by (or on behalf of) a person other than the employee, then a deduction is allowed to the extent that the provision gives rise to taxable earnings of the employee. The asset or service must be provided or used to meet a special threat to the employee's personal physical security arising wholly or mainly by virtue of the employment, and the sole object of the provider must be the meeting of that threat. In the case of an asset, relief is available only to the extent that the provider intends the asset to be used solely to improve personal physical security (ignoring any other incidental use), and in the case of a service, the benefit to the employee must consist wholly or mainly in such an improvement. Any improvement in the personal physical security of the employee's family resulting from the asset or service provided is disregarded for these purposes.

Excluded from relief is provision of a car, ship or aircraft, or of a dwelling (or grounds appurtenant thereto); but relief may be obtained in respect of equipment or a structure (such as a wall), and it is immaterial whether or not an asset becomes affixed to land and whether or not the employee acquires the property in the asset or (in the case of a fixture) an estate or interest in the land.

Similar relief applies where the employee incurs the expenditure out of his earnings and is reimbursed by some other person, and to office holders.

[*ITEPA 2003, ss 369(1), 377; FA 1989, ss 50–52*].

In *Lord Hanson v Mansworth (Sp C 410), 2004 STI 1365* (involving the meeting of a potential terrorist threat to the high profile executive chairman of a prominent public company), the above deduction was allowed on appeal.

See also 9.25 CAPITAL ALLOWANCES, 71.71 SCHEDULE D, CASES I AND II.

Simon's Direct Tax Service. See E4.622.

75.39   **SHARES ETC.**

The value of a gift or transfer of shares to a director or employee, if regarded as a reward for services or part of his earnings, is taxable on him. Held, liability did not arise in *Bridges v Bearsley CA 1957, 37 TC 289* (because gift of shares in default of legacy held to be testimonial not remuneration). Where shares were issued to employees at par value which was less than market value, the difference was held taxable (*Weight v Salmon HL 1935, 19 TC 174; Ede v Wilson KB 1945, 26 TC 381; Patrick v Burrows Ch D 1954, 35 TC 138; Bentley v Evans Ch D 1959, 39 TC 132; Tyrer v Smart HL 1978, 52 TC 533*).

A payment received from the parent company of a group after the employing company left the group, in consideration of loss of rights under the parent company's SAYE option scheme (see 82.47 SHARE-RELATED EMPLOYMENT INCOME AND EXEMPTIONS), was not taxable (*Wilcock v Eve Ch D 1995, 67 TC 223*).

For capital gains tax, such gifts are treated as an acquisition for nil consideration where there is no corresponding disposal of the shares, i.e. where the shares are issued by the company concerned. [*TCGA 1992, s 17*].

For the circumstances in which the Revenue will accept that shares or share options were acquired by a director or employee in a different capacity and not by reason of the office or employment, see Revenue Share Schemes Manual SSM 4.4.

For priority allocations of shares for employees etc., see 82.76 SHARE-RELATED EMPLOYMENT INCOME AND EXEMPTIONS.

Phantom share schemes. Some employers may set up incentive schemes involving 'phantom' or hypothetical shares; the employee is 'allocated' a number of shares in the employer company and potentially receives a future cash bonus linked to the value of those shares. No tax is chargeable at the time of the award (as no value passes), the bonus being chargeable as general earnings for, usually but not invariably, the tax year of receipt. After 15 April 2003, an employee's rights under a phantom share scheme are a 'security' for the purposes of the employee shares legislation (being rights under a contract for differences or similar contract — see 82.3 SHARE-RELATED EMPLOYMENT INCOME AND EXEMPTIONS); consequently the bonus may alternatively be taxed as a post-acquisition benefit from securities (see 82.12 SHARE-RELATED EMPLOYMENT INCOME AND EXEMPTIONS). (Revenue Employment Income Manual EIM 01600).

75.40   **SICK PAY AND HEALTH INSURANCE**

Continuing pay from an employer during sickness or other absence from work is taxable as earnings from employment. Any payments of statutory sick pay under *Social Security Contributions and Benefits Act 1992, s 15* are similarly taxable. [*ITEPA 2003, s 660; ICTA 1988, s 150(c)*].

Any sum paid to, or to the order or for the benefit of, an employee in respect of absence from work through sickness or disability (or to his spouse, a son or daughter or spouse, or a parent or dependant) is taxable earnings of the employee for the period of absence (unless otherwise taxable) where it is paid as a result of any arrangements entered into by the employer. There is no charge under the benefits code (see 75.16 above) on the right to receive such sums, and there is no liability to the extent that the contributions funding the arrangements are paid by the employee. [*ITEPA 2003, ss 202(1), 221; ICTA 1988, ss 149, 154(2)*]. See further below as regards treatment of self-funded arrangements.

A lump sum received under a life, accident or sickness or insurance policy is not normally taxable.

See 28.15 EXEMPT INCOME for provisions exempting annual payments falling to be made under certain insurance policies.

See generally Revenue Employment Income Manual EIM 01550, 06400 *et seq.*

See also 71.54 SCHEDULE D, CASES I AND II.

75.41   **SOCIAL SECURITY BENEFITS**

See 83 SOCIAL SECURITY.

75.42   **SUBSCRIPTIONS**

Professional subscriptions etc. [*ITEPA 2003, ss 343–345; ICTA 1988, s 201*]. There may be deducted from taxable earnings:

(*a*)   provided the registration, retention etc. is a condition of the performance of the duties, professional fees listed in the *Table* in *ITEPA 2003, s 343*. These include fees payable by health (or animal health) professionals, legal professionals, architects, teachers, patent and trade mark agents, driving instructors, aircraft maintenance engineers, air traffic controllers, aircraft flight crew, flight information service officers, HGV drivers and seafarers (including certain related technical and medical examination fees). The Board of Inland Revenue may add to the list by order — see *SI 2003 No 1652* adding, from 1 July 2003, fees paid by an airport employee (or prospective employee) for a criminal records check needed to qualify him for a security pass, and *SI 2004 No 1360* adding, from 17 May 2004, fees paid by employees in the private security industry on application for a licence from the Security Industry Authority;

(*b*)   annual subscriptions, or parts thereof, to bodies approved by the Board whose activities are directed, otherwise than for profit, to advancing or spreading knowledge, maintaining or improving professional conduct and competence, or indemnifying or protecting professional persons against claims incurred in exercising their profession, and are relevant to the office or employment. The body must not be of a mainly local character.

As regards (*b*) above, for approval of bodies by the Board, withdrawal of approval, apportionment of subscriptions and appeals generally, see *ITEPA 2003, ss 344(4)–(6), 345* (previously *ICTA 1988, s 201(3)(4)(6)(7)*). Applications for approval should be made in writing to Inland Revenue, Personal Tax Division 5, Sapphire House, 550 Streetsbrook Road, Solihull, West Midlands B91 1QU. A list of bodies approved by the Board for this purpose is available on the Revenue website at www.inlandrevenue.gov.uk/list3

Other subscriptions. Bank manager's club subscriptions reimbursed by bank not allowed, *Brown v Bullock CA 1961, 40 TC 1*, but subscriptions to clubs to obtain cheaper accommodation on visits to London were allowed, *Elwood v Utitz CA (NI) 1965, 42 TC 482*.

75.43   **'TAX-FREE PAYMENTS'**

If an employer pays an employee's tax, this constitutes the payment of a pecuniary liability of the employee as in 75.10 above. If, however, it is agreed between them that the employer will pay the employee such amount as leaves the employee with a stated sum after PAY AS YOU EARN (55) deductions, it follows that the employer must account for those deductions to the Revenue under the PAYE system and that the employee's taxable earnings are equal to the gross amount before PAYE and not the net amount he actually receives. See *North British Rly v Scott HL 1922, 8 TC 332; Hartland v Diggines HL 1926, 10 TC 247; Jaworski v Institution of Polish Engineers CA 1950, 29 ATC 385*). See also Revenue Pamphlet P7 (Employer's Guide to PAYE).

Special forms and tax tables are available to assist employers who pay employees on a 'net of tax' basis to calculate how much tax is due (Revenue Press Release 2 March 1984).

Where an employer paying earnings of a director fails, in whole or in part, to deduct and account for PAYE tax at the proper time, and that tax is subsequently accounted for by someone other than the director, such tax paid, less so much as is made good by the director, will be treated as taxable earnings unless the director has no material interest in the company and either he is a full-time working director or the company is non-profit-making. Any amounts accounted for after cessation of employment are treated as having arisen in the tax year in which the employment ended but no amounts accounted for after the death of the director will be chargeable. [*ITEPA 2003, s 223; ICTA 1988, s 164*].

An agreement to reimburse tax as 'expenses' was held not to be enforceable as the contract was illegal (*Miller v Karlinski CA 1945, 24 ATC 483*, and see also *Napier v National Business Agency CA 1951, 30 ATC 180*).

Interim payments of tax under self-assessment made by an employer on an employee's behalf, as part of *tax equalisation* arrangements where full in-year gross up is used, should not figure in the employment pages of the employee's self-assessment tax return (see Revenue Tax Bulletin June 1998 p 551).

See Simon's Direct Tax Service E4.451.

Taxed award schemes. Employers may, if they wish, enter into arrangements with the Revenue to meet the liability of employees on the grossed-up value of non-cash incentive prizes and awards. The arrangements involve a legally binding contract for payment of the related tax together with simplified reporting arrangements. The arrangements may involve payment of tax at the basic rate or at the higher rate or both, although separate contracts are required in relation to basic rate and higher rate schemes. Where only basic rate liabilities are met, higher rate liabilities continue to be collected from employees in the usual way. Valuation of an award will depend on details of the scheme and whether or not the recipient is in director's or non-lower-paid employment (see 75.14 above). Details of the arrangements may be obtained from Inland Revenue, Incentive Award Unit, Manchester Blackfriars TDO, Trinity Bridge House, 2 Dearmans Place, Salford M3 5BH (tel. 0161–261 3269), which also deals with national insurance aspects. (Revenue Press Releases 2 November 1984, 18 January 1990; Revenue Tax—Bulletin April 2000 p 747).

See generally Revenue Employment Income Manual EIM 11235 *et seq*.

For the valuation of incentive awards generally, see 75.47 below and Revenue Pamphlet IR 131, SP 6/85.

75.44   **TERMINATION PAYMENTS**

See 18.3 COMPENSATION FOR LOSS OF EMPLOYMENT (AND DAMAGES) for the assessment of such payments under general principles (see 75.10 above). See also 75.35 above for statutory redundancy payments and 75.48 below for wages in lieu of notice.

Certain payments to persons ceasing to be members of the House of Commons, the European Parliament, the Scottish Parliament, the Assembly for Wales or the Northern Ireland Assembly, or to persons ceasing to hold a ministerial (or equivalent) office, are exempted from the general charge on earnings. They are, however, liable in the normal way under *ITEPA 2003, s 403* (see 18 COMPENSATION FOR LOSS OF EMPLOYMENT (AND DAMAGES)). [*ITEPA 2003, s 291; ICTA 1988, s 190; FA 1998, s 58, Sch 9 para 2; FA 1999, Sch 5 para 1*].

75.45   **TRAINING, COUNSELLING ETC.**

Employer training costs. No income tax liability arises in respect of expenditure incurred by the employer in paying or reimbursing retraining course expenses of an employee (or past employee). The employee must begin the course during, or within one year of leaving, the employment, must have left that employment by two years after the end of the course, and must not be re-employed by the employer within two years of leaving. If, after the relief has been given, any of these conditions fail to be met, an assessment may be raised to withdraw the relief within six years of the end of the year of assessment in which the failure occurred. The employer must notify such failure to the inspector within 60 days of coming to know of it, and the inspector may require information from the employer in relation to any such failure where he has reason to believe that the employer has failed to give such notice. Penalties apply under *TMA 1970, s 98* for failure to give such notice or furnish such information.

The retraining course must

(*a*)   be designed to impart or improve skills or knowledge relevant to, and intended to be used in the course of, gainful employment (or self-employment) of any description, and

(*b*)   be devoted entirely to the teaching and/or practical application of such skills or knowledge (which, before 6 April 2003, had to take place within the UK, although in practice this requirement was not enforced by the Revenue), and

(*c*)   not last more than one year, and

(*d*)   be available on similar terms to all, or to a particular class or classes of, past or present employees,

and the employee must

(i)   attend the course on a full-time or substantially full-time basis, and

(ii)   be employed full-time in the employment throughout the two years prior to starting the course (or prior to his earlier leaving that employment — see above).

The qualifying expenses are

(A)   course attendance and examination fees, and

(B)   costs of essential course books, and

(C)   travelling expenses where, if attendance at the course was a duty of the employment and the employee was in that employment when the expenses were incurred and paid them himself, either they would have been deductible under *ITEPA 2003, Pt 5* (see 75.11 above) or, from 6 April 2002, mileage allowance relief would have been available if no mileage allowance had been paid (see 75.46 below).

[*ITEPA 2003, ss 311, 312, Sch 7 para 37; ICTA 1988, ss 588, 589; FA 1996, Sch 18 paras 10, 17(1)(2); FA 2001, Sch 12 Pt II para 12*].

For relief to the employer, see 71.44 SCHEDULE D, CASES I AND II.

Work-related training. Subject to the exceptions below, where an employer pays or reimburses the cost of providing 'work-related training' to employees, no income tax liability arises in respect of such expenditure or of any benefit. Similar relief applies to any incidental costs incurred as a result of the employee's undertaking the training, any expenses in connection with an assessment of what the employee has gained from the training, and the costs of obtaining for the employee any consequent qualification, registration or award.

'*Work-related training*' means any training course or other activity designed to impart, instil, improve or reinforce any knowledge, skills or personal qualities likely to prove useful to the employee in performing the duties of the employment or a 'related employment', or which will qualify (or better qualify) the employee to perform such duties or to participate in any charitable or voluntary activities available to be performed in association with any such employment. Participation in a genuine Employee Development Scheme which seeks to improve the employee's attitude towards training by commencing with an enjoyable course, as an introduction to more concentrated job-related training, will qualify, as will participation in activities such as Outward Bound, Raleigh International or Prince's Trust where leadership skills are appropriate to the employee. (Revenue Employment Income Manual EIM 01220). A '*related employment*' is an employment, with the same employer or a person connected with him (within *ICTA 1988, s 839*), which the employee is to hold, has a serious opportunity of holding or can realistically expect to have a serious opportunity of holding in due course.

Exceptions. The above exemption does not apply to the extent that facilities or other benefits are provided or made available for any of the following purposes:

(*a*)   to enable the employee to enjoy them for entertainment or recreational purposes, or in the course of any leisure activity, unconnected with the promotion of knowledge, skills or personal qualities (as above);

(*b*)   to reward the employee for the performance of the duties of his employment or for the manner of their performance; or

(*c*)   to provide the employee with an inducement, unconnected with the promotion of knowledge, skills or personal qualities (as above), to remain in or accept an employment with the employer or a connected person.

The cost of provision of any asset, or of the use of any asset, to the employee is excluded except where:

(i)   the asset is not for use other than in the course of the training or in the performance of the duties of the employment;

(ii)   it consists of training materials, e.g. stationery, books, tapes, disks etc.; or

(iii)   it consists in something made by the employee during the training, or incorporated into something so made.

Expenditure exempted under *FA 1991, s 32* (vocational training, see 92 VOCATIONAL TRAINING RELIEF) was excluded.

Travelling and subsistence expenses are not excluded provided that, if the training had been undertaken in the performance of the duties of the employment and the expenses incurred and paid by the employee, either they would have been allowable under the general deductions provisions or, from 6 April 2002, mileage allowance relief would have been available if no mileage allowance had been paid (see 75.46 below).

Third party expenditure. Before 6 April 2003, benefits consisting in, or provided in connection with, work-related training as above but at the expense of a person other than the employer were exempt to the same extent that they would have been had they been provided at the employer's expense. From 6 April 2003, the exemptions apply without regard to the source of the benefit, payment or reimbursement.

[*ITEPA 2003, ss 250–254; ICTA 1988, ss 200B–200D; FA 1997, s 63(1)(3); FA 2001, Sch 12 Pt II para 8*].

An MBA course costing £18,000 and reimbursed by way of a 'signing bonus' was held on the facts to be for the purpose of qualifying the taxpayer to undertake the employment as opposed to inducing her to accept the employment and was within the exemption; it did not matter that the training took place outside the currency of the employment (*Silva v Charnock (Sp C 332), [2002] SSCD 426*). However, the Revenue do not see this case as supporting a general exemption for reimbursements of training costs incurred by individuals before the employment commences, though they will not pursue arrears of tax where such reimbursements have been made tax-free in accordance with specific advice given by tax offices (some of which may have given conflicting advice). The Revenue do allow exemption for reimbursement of pre-commencement training costs where there is a strong and demonstrable link between the training and the employment, for example where an individual undergoes training for a job he has already accepted and which he is due to start in the near future. (Revenue Tax Bulletin April 2003 pp 1022, 1023).

See generally Revenue Employment Income Manual EIM 01200 *et seq.*

See Simon's Direct Tax Service E4.717A.

Individual learning account training. For 2000/01 and subsequent years, and subject to the exceptions below, where an employer makes a payment to the provider in respect of the costs of providing 'individual learning account training' to a qualifying employee of the employer, no income tax liability arises in respect of such expenditure or of any benefit. Similar relief applies in respect of the payment or reimbursement of any incidental costs incurred as a result of the employee's undertaking the education or training, any expenses in connection with an assessment of what the employee has gained from the education or training, and the costs of obtaining for the employee any consequent qualification, registration or award.

For the exemption to apply the expenditure must be incurred in giving effect to 'fair opportunity arrangements' in place when the employer agreed to incur the expenditure. This requires that, at that time, arrangements are in place which provide for such employer contributions to be generally available, on similar terms, to all current office-holders or employees of the employer. Special provisions apply in relation to Crown servants (for which see also *SI 2000 No 2076*).

'*Individual learning account training*' is education or training of a kind which qualifies for grants authorised by regulations under *Learning and Skills Act 2000, s 108* or *s 109* or by corresponding provision in Scotland. To qualify, an employee must hold an account qualifying under *Learning and Skills Act 2000, s 104*, or be a party to arrangements which qualify under *Learning and Skills Act 2000, s 105* or *s 106* or Scottish equivalent.

Exceptions. The above exemptions do not apply to expenditure to the extent that facilities or other benefits are thereby provided or made available to the employee:

(*a*)   for entertainment or recreation (including in the course of any leisure activity); or

(*b*)   to reward the employee for the performance of the duties of his office or employment or for the manner of their performance.

Travelling and subsistence expenses are excluded unless, if the education or training had been undertaken in the performance of the duties of the office or employment and the expenses incurred and paid by the employee, either they would have been allowable under the general deductions provisions or, from 6 April 2002, mileage allowance relief would have been available if no mileage allowance had been paid (see 75.46 below).

The cost of provision of any asset, or of the use of any asset, to the employee is excluded except where:

(i)   the asset is for use only in the course of the training;

(ii)   it is for use in the course of the education or training and in the performance of the duties of the office or employment and not to any significant extent for any other use;

(iii) it consists of training materials, e.g. stationery, books, tapes, disks etc., provided in the course of the education or training; or

(iv)   it consists in something made by the employee during the education or training, or incorporated into something so made.

Third party expenditure. Before 6 April 2003, benefits consisting in, or provided in connection with, education or training as above but at the expense of a person other than the employer are exempt to the same extent that they would have been had they been provided at the employer's expense. From 6 April 2003, the exemptions apply without regard to the source of the benefit or expenditure.

[*ITEPA 2003, ss 255–260; ICTA 1988, ss 200E–200J; FA 2000, s 58; FA 2001, Sch 12 Pt II para 9; SI 2000 No 2076*].

See Simon's Direct Tax Service E1.449.

Counselling services provided by employers. No income tax liability arises in respect of qualifying counselling services and certain necessary related travelling expenses provided for, or paid or reimbursed on behalf of, an employer in connection with the termination of his employment. This applies whether or not the services or expenses are provided or paid by the employer.

The counselling services which qualify are those consisting wholly of giving advice and guidance, imparting or improving skills, and/or providing or making available the use of office equipment or similar facilities to enable an employee to adjust to his job loss and/or find other employment. The employee must have been in the employment full-time throughout the period of two years to the date the services are provided or, if earlier, the time he ceases to be employed. The opportunity to receive the services must be generally available to employees or a particular class of employees. Before 6 April 2003, the services had to be provided in the UK, with just and reasonable apportionment where they were provided partly outside the UK, but this requirement was not in practice enforced by the Revenue.

[*ITEPA 2003, s 310; ICTA 1988, ss 589A, 589B; FA 1993, s 108; FA 2001, Sch 12 Pt II para 13*].

For relief to the employer, see 71.44 SCHEDULE D, CASES I AND II.

See Simon's Direct Tax Service B3.1432, E4.327.

Employee training costs. See 92 VOCATIONAL TRAINING RELIEF.

75.46   **TRAVELLING, SUBSISTENCE ETC.**

See generally Revenue Booklet 490 'Employee Travel — A Tax and NICs Guide for Employers' and Revenue Employment Income Manual EIM 31800 *et seq.*

For 1998/99 onwards, the normal statutory relief for expenses in employment is extended to include certain additional travelling and associated expenses, broadly those of travelling to temporary workplaces (excluding ordinary commuting and private travel). See 75.11(*a*) above. Previously, only certain equine travelling expenses were the subject of specific statutory provision, although relief was in practice given for certain travel to temporary workplaces (see below). The following commentary applies to all travelling and associated expenses which are not the subject of specific statutory relief (or exclusion).

The general relief for deductions from employment income is for expenses necessarily incurred in the performance of the duties of the office or employment (see 75.11(*a*) above).

75.46 Schedule E—Employment Income

Subject to the special reliefs mentioned above and below relating to temporary workplaces, this excludes expenses of travelling to the place of employment from home or from a place at which a business or another employment is carried on. A leading case here is *Ricketts v Colquhoun HL 1925, 10 TC 118* in which a barrister practising in London was refused his expenses of travelling to Portsmouth where he was employed as Recorder. See also *Cook v Knott QB 1887, 2 TC 246; Revell v Directors of Elworthy Bros & Co Ltd QB 1890, 3 TC 12; Nolder v Walters KB 1930, 15 TC 380; Burton v Rednall Ch D 1954, 35 TC 435; Bhadra v Ellam Ch D 1987, [1988] STC 239* (see 75.11(*a*) above); *Parikh v Sleeman CA 1990, 63 TC 75; Smith v Fox Ch D 1989, 63 TC 304; Miners v Atkinson Ch D 1995, 68 TC 629; Warner v Prior (Sp C 353), [2003] SSCD 109* and contrast *Pook v Owen* (see below and 75.11(*a*) above) and *Taylor v Provan HL 1974, 49 TC 579* in both of which *Ricketts v Colquhoun* was distinguished. The deduction is refused notwithstanding that the taxpayer is unable to live nearer his place of employment (*Andrews v Astley KB 1924, 8 TC 589; Phillips v Keane HC(IFS), 1 ITC 69*). No allowance to an assistant required to attend classes (*Blackwell v Mills KB 1945, 26 TC 468*). For extra-statutory concession for directors and employees of two or more group companies, see 75.16(ix) above (and note the comparable statutory relief for 1998/99 onwards at 75.11(*a*) above).

If an employee with a normal place of work travels directly from home to another place at which he is required to perform duties of the employment, or *vice versa*, the allowable travel and subsistence expenditure (including business mileage) is the lesser of that actually incurred and that which would have been incurred if the journey (by the same mode of transport) had started or finished at the normal place of work. In general, business travel by a route other than the shortest possible is acceptable, provided that the longer route was selected for good business reasons. (Revenue Booklet 480; Revenue Tax Bulletin December 1994 p 185). For 1998/99 onwards, this is replaced by the statutory relief at 75.11(*a*) above.

If an emergency call-out requires an employee to travel from home to the normal place of employment, reimbursed travel expenses will be taxable earnings unless the conditions underlying the decision in *Pook v Owen HL 1969, 45 TC 571* (for which see also 75.11(*a*) above) are met, i.e. (i) advice on handling the emergency is given on receipt of the telephone call; (ii) responsibility for those aspects appropriate to the employee's duties is accepted at that time; and (iii) the employee has a continuing responsibility for the emergency whilst travelling to the normal place of employment. A claim for a deduction for expenses not reimbursed will be allowed on the same basis. Where an emergency call-out requires travel from home to a place other than the normal place of employment, reimbursed expenses are not chargeable emoluments, and a claim for expenses not reimbursed should be allowed. (Revenue Employment Income Manual EIM 10040, 10050).

Reasonable reimbursement of expenses of home to work travel (or the provision of vouchers etc. for such travel, see 75.47 below) is not taxed where the expenses are incurred either (*a*) as a result of public transport disruption owing to industrial action, or (*b*) by disabled employees. From 6 April 2003, these exemptions are statutory [*ITEPA 2003, ss 245, 246*], having previously applied by concession (see Revenue Pamphlet IR 1, A58, A59). See also 75.16(v)(vi) above.

The provision by an employer of private transport, e.g. taxis, hired cars etc., for the journey home of employees required to work late (or of vouchers etc. for such travel, see 75.47 below) will not result in a charge to income tax on the employee, provided that (*a*) the employee is occasionally required to work late, i.e. until 9 p.m. or later, but those occasions are not regular, i.e. they do not follow a predictable pattern, and (*b*) either public transport between the employee's place of work and his home has ceased for the day or it would not be reasonable to expect him to use it, for example if the journey would take much longer than usual due to low availability or reliability of services at that hour. From 6 April 1999, this concession is extended to cover the payment for or provision of transport home by the employer where regular home to work car-sharing arrangements with other employees fail on a particular occasion due to unforeseen or exceptional circumstances. This includes circumstances where travel home is at the normal time but, for reasons beyond the employee's control, he cannot travel in the shared car at that time, and where he expects to travel in the shared car at the normal time (and the car travels at that time) but in the event he needs to travel home at a different time. They do not include circumstances where, on any occasion, inability to travel home in the shared car might reasonably have been anticipated. The exemption applies to a maximum of 60 journeys in a tax year, and from 6 April 1999 this applies to the aggregate of journeys under both legs of the concession (i.e. late night journeys and car-share breakdowns). From 6 April 2003, this exemption is statutory [*ITEPA 2003, s 248*], having previously applied by concession (see Revenue Pamphlet IR 1, A66).

Insofar as the statutory relief for 'qualifying travelling expenses' for 1998/99 onwards (see 75.11(*a*) does not apply, travel and subsistence expenditure is allowed, and reimbursement thereof not taxed, when working temporarily away from home and normal place of employment. This is intended to cover the extra cost of travelling and subsistence incurred because of being away on duty — but not the cost of travelling from home to normal place of work or usual expenses on food or meals taken when at normal place of work. (Revenue Pamphlet IR 131, SP 16/80, 20 November 1980). An absence is regarded as temporary where it is not expected to, and does not, exceed twelve months, and the employee returns to the normal place of work at the end of it. Where it becomes clear during such a period that the absence will extend beyond twelve months, the exemption will apply only to amounts paid up to the date the change of circumstances became known. (Revenue Tax Bulletin May 1994 p 130). As regards what is meant by the 'normal place of employment', the Revenue normally accept that it is the place where an employee spends more than 50% of his working time, and a lower proportion may be acceptable depending on the circumstances of each business and the employee's pattern of work. Employers should be able to agree with their local inspector to divide employees into groups for these purposes. (ICAEW Technical Memorandum TR 760, 6 September 1989).

A claim for a deduction corresponding to living allowances paid while working away from home was refused where an engineer without a permanent work base was required to undertake assignments necessitating his living away from home for long periods (*Elderkin v Hindmarsh Ch D 1988, 60 TC 651*).

In addition, reasonable reimbursement of expenditure on subsistence etc. is, by concession, not taxed where (*a*) an employee occupies overnight accommodation near his normal place of work as a result of public transport disruption owing to industrial action, or (*b*) it is necessary for an offshore oil or gas worker to take overnight accommodation near the point of his departure from the mainland for the offshore rig etc. From 6 April 2003, these exemptions are statutory [*ITEPA 2003, ss 245, 305; FA 2004, Sch 27 paras 13, 16*], having previously applied by concession (see Revenue Pamphlet IR 1, A58, A65). See also 75.16(v)(vi) above.

See 75.16(x) as regards certain removal expenses.

Incidental overnight expenses. Payments made to or on behalf of an employee in respect of his overnight personal incidental expenses (e.g. laundry, newspapers, telephone calls home) while away from home on business are exempt from income tax provided that they do not exceed certain limits. Payments exceeding the limits are taxable in full. The exemption covers expenses incidental to the employee's being away from home during a 'qualifying absence' other than one in relation to which the overall exemption limit is exceeded, being expenses which would not otherwise be deductible. A '*qualifying absence*' is a continuous period throughout which the employee is obliged to stay away from home and which includes at least one overnight stay but does not include any such stay at a place the expenses of travelling to which would not be either deductible under normal rules or, for 1997/98 onwards, exempt under *ITEPA 2003, s 250* (work-related training costs, see 75.45 above) or, for 2000/01 onwards, exempt under *ITEPA 2003, s 255* (individual learning account training, see 75.45 above). The overall exemption limit, in relation to a qualifying absence, is £5 for each night spent in the UK and £10 for each night any part of which is spent outside the UK (such amounts being subject to increase by Treasury Order from a date specified therein). In determining whether the authorised maximum is exceeded, payments by non-cash voucher or credit token and the providing of benefits are taken into account as well as cash payments. [*ITEPA 2003, ss 240, 241, Sch 7 paras 33, 34; ICTA 1988, s 200A; FA 1995, s 93(4)(5); FA 1997, s 63(2)(3); FA 2000, s 58(2)(3)*]. Inland Revenue guidance notes for employers on the practical application of these provisions (see Revenue Booklet 480 and the Employer's Guide to PAYE (P7)) are available.

Working Rule Agreements. Where Working Rule Agreements are drawn up between employers and trade unions and include payments of allowances for daily travel and subsistence, the Revenue have agreed that certain of these payments (or part) should not be taxed because of the high degree of mobility required in the industries concerned. Consistent treatment is accorded to site-based staff who work alongside operatives who are covered by a Working Rule Agreement and who have broadly the same working circumstances. Employers must obtain authority from their local tax district before making any such tax-free payments. (Revenue Press Release 13 February 1981).

Lodging allowances may generally be paid tax-free to an employee engaged under the terms of a Working Rule Agreement, provided that he is married, or has dependants living with him, and incurs extra expense while working away from home in addition to the cost of maintaining a permanent home. This treatment is extended to single men without dependants who maintain a permanent home. (ICAEW Memorandum TR 713, August 1988).

Travelling appointments. Excess expenditure on meals away from home may be claimed by employees holding full-time travelling appointments (e.g. lorry drivers) not restricted to a limited area. Bills, receipts etc. must be produced as evidence. Estimated figures will not be accepted. Relief is not restricted by amount saved by not having meals at home or a fixed place of work. (Revenue Pamphlet IR 131, SP 16/80, 20 November 1980). The Revenue has agreed a tax-free overnight subsistence allowance of £26.00 (from 1 January 2004 — £25.15 for calendar year 2003, £24.50 for 2002, £24.30 for 2001, £23.55 for 2000, £23.22 for 1999, £22.55 for 1998) (reduced by 25% where a sleeper cab is available) under certain industry agreements (Revenue Employment Income Manual EIM 66100–66190).

Employment abroad. Tax will not be charged on the reimbursement to an employee, whose duties are carried on wholly abroad and who retains an abode in the UK, of expenses, including reasonable hotel expenses necessarily incurred, in travelling (whether alone or with his wife and family) to the country where his duties are performed and returning to the UK. Similar relief applies for persons of non-UK domicile travelling between the UK and their abode in the home country. See 75.8, 75.9 above. For allowances for travelling etc. expenses to members of the European Parliament, see *Lord Bruce of Donington v Aspden CJEC, [1981] STC 761*.

For **overseas trips** generally, see *Newlin v Woods CA 1966, 42 TC 649* (cost of journey for health reasons disallowed); *Maclean v Trembath Ch D 1956, 36 TC 653* (business trip accompanied by wife; expenses attributable to wife disallowed); *Thomson v White Ch D 1966, 43 TC 256* (expenses of farmers and wives on organised trip partly for sightseeing and partly to see farms overseas disallowed); *Owen v Burden CA 1971, 47 TC 476* (expenses of county surveyor voluntarily to attend overseas road conference disallowed). Expenses of spouse of director or higher-paid employee who accompanies director on business journey abroad because his or her health is too precarious for travel alone are not assessable on employee. (Revenue Pamphlet IR 1, A4). See 28.19 EXEMPT INCOME as regards certain overseas travel costs of MPs.

Private transport used for office or employment — 2001/02 and earlier years. A proportion of the costs of running privately-owned transport used partly in the performance of the duties of an office or employment is allowable as a deduction from emoluments where the normal requirements of *ICTA 1988, s 198* are met (see 75.11 above). Similar proportionate relief is available by way of capital allowances (under *CAA 1990, s 27; CAA 2001, s 80*), for expenditure incurred on provision of a 'car' (or, for 1999/2000 and subsequent years, a cycle), and interest relief (under *ICTA 1988, s 359*, see 43.18 INTEREST PAYABLE), for interest on a loan for its purchase. 'Car' is defined for this purpose as any mechanically propelled road vehicle, and thus includes a motor cycle.

In considering capital allowances and interest relief, there is no requirement that the vehicle (or cycle) be 'necessarily' provided for use in the office or employment (i.e. that the duties of the office or employment could not be carried out without its provision, see 75.11(a) above). Where *CAA 2001* has effect (see 9.1 CAPITAL ALLOWANCES), the provisions are extended to vehicles (and cycles) provided partly for travelling of such kind as would give rise to 'qualifying travelling expenses' (see 75.11(a) above). Any balancing allowance (see 9.28 CAPITAL ALLOWANCES) on the vehicle (or cycle) being disposed of, or starting to be used wholly for purposes other than those of the office or employment, is reduced to the proportion that the number of years of assessment for which capital allowances have been claimed for use of the vehicle (or cycle) in the office or employment bears to the number of years of assessment for which allowances were available for such use. [*ICTA 1988, s 359(3); CAA 2001, s 80, Sch 3 para 54; CAA 1990, s 27; FA 1990, s 87; FA 1999, s 50(2)(3)*]. Following the introduction of statutory mileage allowances from 6 April 2002 (see below), any vehicle (or cycle) for which capital allowances are claimed up to 5 April 2002 is treated as ceasing to be owned by the employee immediately before 6 April 2002. [*FA 2001, s 59(4)*]. This would normally give rise to a disposal value being brought in equal to the market value of the vehicle (or cycle) at that date. In the unusual situation where the open market value exceeds the tax written-down value at the deemed date of disposal, the Revenue will accept claims to treat the open market value as being equal to the written-down value at that date. (Hansard Standing Committee A 1 May 2001, Cols 78, 79).

As an alternative to keeping detailed records of costs, until 5 April 2002 employees may apply the 'tax-free' rates under the Fixed Profit Car Scheme (see below) to their business mileage to support a tax deduction for allowable motoring expenses (after allowing for any mileage allowances received). (Revenue Press Release (REV 32) 28 November 1995). See also below as regards similar schemes for cyclists and motor cyclists.

Mileage allowances. As a general rule, the excess of such allowances paid to an employee (or office-holder) over the costs necessarily incurred in travelling in the performance of the duties of the employment is taxable on the employee, but the treatment of a particular payment will depend on the facts of the case. In *Pook v Owen HL 1969, 45 TC 571* (see 75.11(a) above) the mileage allowance paid to a doctor was held not to be part of his emoluments, and this decision was applied in *Donnelly v Williamson Ch D 1981, 54 TC 636* (mileage allowance paid to a schoolteacher for use of her car when attending parents' meetings) but distinguished in *Perrons v Spackman Ch D 1981, 55 TC 403* (lump sum and mileage allowances to a county council employee treated as part of his emoluments, but he was allowed to deduct his actual car expenses on official duties, including a proportion of his repairs and standing expenses). Deductions for car expenses in excess of the employer's allowance were refused to a Regional Hospital Board employee (*Hamerton v Overy Ch D 1954, 35 TC 73*) and a civil servant (*Marsden v CIR Ch D 1965, 42 TC 326*).

Strictly, the employer should return the full amount of such allowances paid, and the employee submit a detailed claim for relief based on actual expenses and business/private mileage. The Revenue, however, operate with some employers a simplified administrative arrangement known as the Fixed Profit Car Scheme (FPCS) under which an employee's taxable business mileage profit is determined by reference to engine size and the excess of the mileage allowance paid over the authorised mileage rates, which are as follows (*a*) for the first 4,000 miles in the year and (*b*) for mileage in excess of 4,000.

Capacity	Up to 1,000cc		1,001–1,500cc		1,501–2,000cc		Over 2,000cc	
	(*a*)	(*b*)	(*a*)	(*b*)	(*a*)	(*b*)	(*a*)	(*b*)
	28p	17p	35p	20p	45p	25p	63p	36p

The two lower bands are increased to (*a*) 40p and (*b*) 25p for 2001/02 (the two upper bands remaining unchanged).

The rates for years before 1997/98 were as follows.

1996/97	27p	16p	34p	19p	43p	23p	61p	33p
1995/96	27p	15p	34p	19p	43p	23p	60p	32p
1994/95	27p	15p	33p	19p	41p	23p	56p	31p
1993/94	26p	15p	32p	18p	40p	22p	54p	30p

Banded payments by employers are matched as closely as possible to the authorised mileage rate bands, and where uniform allowances are paid, the average of the two middle bands is used. Relief for interest on a loan for purchase of the car (see 43.18 INTEREST PAYABLE) is not included in the authorised mileage rates, and needs to be claimed separately. (Revenue Press Release 14 December 1999). As the authorised mileage rates include an allowance for depreciation, it follows that capital allowances cannot be claimed in addition.

Where the employer has not entered into the FPCS, employees may, for 1996/97 and subsequent years, nevertheless use the authorised mileage rates to calculate any taxable profit on mileage allowances received. (Revenue Press Release (REV 32) 28 November 1995).

For cars provided by the employer ('company cars'), see 75.18 above.

See generally Revenue Pamphlet IR 125.

Similar schemes for *cyclists* and *motor cyclists* permit the payment from 6 April 1999 (cyclists) or 6 April 2000 (motor cyclists) of a tax- and NIC-free allowance of up to 12p per mile (cyclists) or 24p per mile (motor cyclists). (Revenue Press Releases (IR 5) 9 March 1999, 14 December 1999).

Private transport used for office or employment — 2002/03 and later years The system described above for 2001/02 and earlier years is replaced by a system of statutory mileage allowances for employees (which includes office holders) which are exempt from income tax when paid by the employer and which form the basis of a claim by the employee where no (or smaller) mileage allowances are payable. The alternative of claiming actual expenses (including capital allowances and interest relief on purchase of a vehicle (or cycle)) is no longer available (see *ICTA 1988, s 198(5); FA 2001, s 59, Sch 12 Pt II para 6*). Dispensations relating to payments for 2001/02 and earlier years accordingly ceased to be valid from 6 April 2002, except that they could be extended to cover payments made in 2002/03 for business travel in 2001/02.

The statutory exemption applies to:

(*a*)   'approved mileage allowance payments' for a 'qualifying vehicle', *provided that* the employee is not a passenger in the vehicle and the vehicle is not a 'company vehicle' (as broadly defined, see *ITEPA 2003, s 236(2)*); and

(*b*)   'approved passenger payments' made to an employee for a car or van, *provided that* 'mileage allowance payments' are made to the employee for the vehicle and, if it is made available to the employee by reason of the employment, the employee is chargeable in respect of it as a benefit-in-kind under 75.18(ii)(iii)(iiia) above.

'*Mileage allowance payments*' are payments (other than 'passenger payments') paid to an employee in respect of expenses in connection with the use by the employee of a 'qualifying vehicle' for 'business travel'. They are '*approved*' if and to the extent that, for a tax year, the total payments made to the employee for the kind of vehicle in question do not exceed the 'approved amount' for mileage allowance payments applicable to that kind of vehicle. A '*qualifying vehicle*' is a car, van, motor cycle or cycle (each as defined in *ITEPA 2003, s 235*), and '*business travel*' is travel the expenses of which would be deductible under the general provisions (see 75.11(*a*) above) if incurred and paid by the employee. The '*approved amount*' for this purpose is obtained from the formula

$$M \times R$$

where M is the number of business miles travelled by the employee (other than as a passenger) using the kind of vehicle in question, in the tax year; and

R is the rate applicable for that kind of vehicle. For a car or van, it is 40p per mile for the first 10,000 miles, 25p per mile thereafter. For motor cycles it is 24p per mile and for cycles it is 20p per mile. The 10,000 mile limit is applied by reference to business travel by car or van in all 'associated employments' (as defined, broadly where the employments are under the same employer or the employers are under common control). All these rates may be altered by the Treasury by regulation.

'*Passenger payments*' are payments made to an employee because, while using a car or van for business travel, he carries one or more '*qualifying passengers*', i.e. fellow employee(s) for whom the travel is also business travel. They are '*approved*' if and to the extent that, for a tax year, the total passenger payments made to the employee do not exceed the 'approved amount' for passenger payments. The '*approved amount*' for this purpose is

$$M \times R$$

where M is the number of business miles travelled by the employee by car or van carrying any qualifying passenger in the tax year and in respect of which passenger payments are made. If more than one qualifying passenger is carried, a separate addition is made to the amount in respect of each passenger; and

R is 5p per mile (alterable by the Treasury by regulation).

[*ITEPA 2003, ss 229, 230, 233–236; ICTA 1988, ss 197AD, 197AE, 197AH, Sch 12AA Pt I; FA 2001, s 57, Sch 12; FA 2004, s 81(2)(3)*].

An employee (or office holder) who uses a qualifying vehicle for business travel is entitled to '*mileage allowance relief*' for a tax year if the approved amount for mileage allowance payments (as above) applicable to the kind of vehicle in question exceeds the total amount of mileage allowance payments (if any) made to the employee for the tax year for that kind of vehicle. As in (*a*) above, the relief is not available where the employee is a passenger in a vehicle or the vehicle is a company vehicle. The amount of the relief is the excess of the approved amount over any mileage allowance payments. It is allowed as a deduction from earnings taxable on the receipts basis (see 75.3, 75.4 above). Any amount of relief which cannot be so given may be deducted from earnings taxable on the remittance basis (see 75.4 above), the deduction for any tax year being of amounts of relief available and otherwise unrelieved for that tax year and for any earlier tax year in which the employee was UK resident, and which would have been deductible from earnings for each such year if the receipts basis had applied. [*ITEPA 2003, ss 231, 232; ICTA 1988, ss 197AF–197AH, Sch 12AA Pt I; FA 2001, s 57, Sch 12*].

Mileage allowances where fuel provided by employee for business travel in company car. Employers may negotiate dispensations for payments to employees for fuel provided by the employee for business travel. Advisory rates are as follows, although it is open to the employer to make a case for paying higher rates in particular circumstances.

Engine size	Petrol	Diesel	LPG*
1400cc or less	10p	9p	7p (6p)
1401cc to 2000cc	12p	9p	8p (7p)
Over 2000cc	14p	12p	10p (9p)

* LPG = Liquid Petroleum Gas. Figures shown are for 2004/05 with previous years' figures in brackets.

(www.inlandrevenue.gov.uk/cars/fuel_company_cars.htm).

Parking provision and expenses. No income tax liability arises in respect of expenditure on the provision of car parking facilities for an employee at or near his place of work, whether the car etc. is company-owned or private. This exemption extends to parking facilities for cycles and motor cycles for 1999/2000 onwards and for vans for 2005/06 onwards. [*ITEPA 2003, s 237; ICTA 1988, s 155(1A); FA 1999, s 49; FA 2004, s 80, Sch 14 para 8*].

Volunteer drivers (e.g. hospital car service drivers). See 74.2 SCHEDULE D, CASE VI.

Car hire. The restriction at 71.58 SCHEDULE D, CASES I AND II, on the deductibility of expenditure on the hire of a car whose retail price when new exceeded £12,000 (previously £8,000), applies equally where such expenditure falls to be allowed as a deduction from taxable earnings. [*ICTA 1988, s 578A(1)(c); CAA 1990, s 27(1)(a), s 35(2)–(4); CAA 2001, Sch 2 para 52*].

Simon's Direct Tax Service. See E4.708 *et seq.*

75.47   VOUCHERS AND CREDIT-TOKENS

The following, when provided for an employee (or a '*relation*', i.e. his spouse, parent, child or spouse of his child or any dependant of the employee) by reason of the employment, are taxable earnings of the employment. [*ITEPA 2003, ss 74, 81, 83, 87, 91, 94; ICTA 1988, ss 141(1), 142(1), 143(1), 144(4)(5)*]. Their supply by the employer is regarded as 'by reason of the employment' unless the employer is an individual and the supply is made in the normal course of his domestic, family or personal relationships (the latter relief being applied by Revenue practice before 6 April 2003). [*ITEPA 2003, ss 73(2), 82(2), 90(2); ICTA 1988, s 144(4)*]. The provisions do not apply to vouchers etc. of a kind made available to the public generally and provided to the employee (or family) on no more favourable terms than to the public generally (this relief being statutory from 6 April 2003 [*ITEPA 2003, ss 78, 85, 93*], and having previously applied by Revenue practice). Where they do apply (or would do so but for a dispensation, see below), no liability arises in respect of the money goods or services obtained for the voucher. [*ITEPA 2003, s 95; ICTA 1988, ss 141(1), 142(1), 143(1); FA 2004, s 78, Sch 13 para 2(4)*].

Dispensations. The provisions do not apply if a person supplies the inspector with a statement of the cases and circumstances in which vouchers are provided to any employee (whether his own or not) and the inspector is satisfied that no additional tax is payable under these provisions and notifies that person accordingly. Such notification may be revoked retrospectively, and ceased automatically to have effect from 6 April 2002 insofar as it related to expenses in connection with the use of a vehicle for business travel where mileage allowance payments were made or mileage allowance relief available in respect of that use (see 75.46 above). [*ITEPA 2003, s 96, Sch 7 paras 19, 20; ICTA 1988, s 144(1)(2); FA 1994, s 89(12)–(14); FA 2001, s 58*].

For the exemption from income tax liability of the provision of vouchers which can be used to obtain anything the direct provision of which would be exempt, see *ITEPA 2003, ss 266, 267*.

For a summary of the amounts chargeable and the tax year in which liability arises, see Revenue Employment Income Manual EIM 16140.

For the application of PAYE, see 55.2 PAY AS YOU EARN.

(*a*)   **Non-cash vouchers** (i.e. vouchers, stamps or similar documents or tokens capable of being exchanged, either singly or together, immediately or later, for money, goods or services or any combination of these but excluding cash vouchers — see also Revenue Employment Income Manual EIM 16040). The tax charge is on the expense incurred by the person at whose cost the voucher, and the money, goods or services for which it is capable of being exchanged, are provided, and in or in connection with that provision, with 'just and reasonable' apportionment in the case of schemes relating to groups of employees, and less any amounts made good by the employee. The charge is reduced to the extent that general deductions would have been allowable if the costs had been incurred by the employee. The tax year in which the earnings are treated as received is the year in which the expense is incurred by the employer or, if different and later, the year in which the voucher is received by, or appropriated to, the employee, but for cheque vouchers it is the year in which the voucher is handed over in exchange for money, goods or services (time of posting is treated as time of handing over). [*ITEPA 2003, ss 82, 83, 84(1)(2), 87, 88, 362; ICTA 1988, s 141(1)–(5)(7), s 144(3); FA 1994, s 89(1)(2); FA 1995, s 91(2); FA 2004, s 78, Sch 13 para 2(2)(3)*]. This provision does not affect the treatment of meal vouchers as in 75.33 above.

Expense incurred by the employer in providing vouchers or any other incentive awards includes expenses beyond the direct cost of buying the goods or services provided where the expenses contribute more or less directly to the advantage enjoyed by the employee, e.g. costs of selecting and testing goods or services, or of after-sales service, or of storage and distribution. More remote expenses, e.g. costs of planning or administering a scheme or of promotional literature etc., are excluded. See Revenue Pamphlet IR 131, SP 6/85.

Transport vouchers are specifically included in the above provisions but *not included* is a voucher provided for an employee of a passenger transport undertaking under arrangements in operation on 25 March 1982 to enable that employee (including spouse or family, as above) to obtain passenger transport services from his employer or his employer's subsidiary or parent company or another passenger transport undertaking. 'Transport voucher' means any ticket, pass or other document or token intended to enable a person to obtain passenger transport services (whether or not in exchange for it). [*ITEPA 2003, ss 84(3), 86, 87(4); ICTA 1988, s 141(6)(7)*]. See also 75.16(xxv)(xxvi) above.

For a limited exemption in respect of *childcare vouchers* for 2005/06 onwards, see 75.22 above.

Cheque vouchers are also included in the above provisions. '*Cheque voucher*' means a cheque provided for an employee and intended for his use wholly or mainly for payment for particular goods or services or for goods or services of one or more particular classes. [*ITEPA 2003, s 84(4); ICTA 1988, s 141(7)*].

A voucher used by an employee to obtain the use of a *car parking space* (or, for 1999/2000 and subsequent years, a cycle or motor cycle parking space) at or near his place of work is excluded from these provisions [*ITEPA 2003, s 266(1); ICTA 1988, s 141(6A); FA 1999, s 49*], and a voucher provided neither by the employer nor by a person connected with the employer (within *ICTA 1988, s 839*, see 19 CONNECTED PERSONS) and used to obtain *entertainment* for the employee (or a relation) is similarly excluded, subject to the same conditions as are specified in 75.16(xv) above. [*ITEPA 2003, s 266(1); ICTA 1988, s 141(6B); FA 1994, s 89(3)*]. See also 75.24 above for the exclusion of vouchers relating to certain sports and recreational facilities.

Incidental overnight expenses. There is excluded from these provisions a voucher used to obtain goods or services (or to obtain money to buy goods or services) incidental to the employee's being away from home on business during a 'qualifying absence' in relation to which the authorised maximum (£5 per night spent in the UK and £10 per night spent abroad) is not exceeded, where the cost of such goods or services is not otherwise deductible from earnings. [*ITEPA 2003, s 268, Sch 7 paras 33, 34; ICTA 1988, s 141(6C)(6D); FA 1995, s 93(1)*]. See also 75.46 above.

See Simon's Direct Tax Service E4.432.

(*b*) **Cash vouchers** (as defined below). Where, as in some holiday pay schemes, a cash voucher is provided for an employee for redemption for cash which will be an emolument, tax is to be charged on the redemption amount when the voucher is received by, or appropriated to, the employee, with 'just and reasonable' apportionment in the case of schemes relating to groups of employees, *unless* the voucher is issued under a scheme which is approved by the Board as being practicable for PAYE to be applied at the time the vouchers are exchanged for cash.

'*Cash voucher*' means any voucher, stamp or similar document capable of being exchanged, either singly or together, immediately or later, for a sum of money not substantially less than the cost to the person at whose cost it is provided, but excluding any document for a sum which would not have been employment income if paid to the employee directly and excluding any savings certificate on which accumulated interest is exempt from tax. Where the sum of money is substantially less than the cost, any part of the difference representing benefits in connection with sickness, personal injury or death will be disregarded in deciding if the voucher is a cash voucher.

[*ITEPA 2003, ss 73, 75–77, 79–81; ICTA 1988, ss 143, 144(3); FA 1994, s 89(8)–(14)*].

See Simon's Direct Tax Service E4.431.

(*c*) **Meal Vouchers.** See 75.33 above.

(*d*) **Credit-tokens.** Tax is charged when the employee (or, from 6 April 2002, a relation, see above) uses a credit token to obtain money, goods or services, on the expense incurred by the person at whose cost the money, goods or services are provided, in or in connection with that provision, with 'just and reasonable' apportionment in the case of schemes relating to groups of employees. See (*a*) above as regards valuation of expenses incurred. The charge is reduced by any amounts made good by the employee and by deductions which would have been allowable if the costs had been incurred by the employee. [*ITEPA 2003, ss 90, 94, 363; ICTA 1988, s 142(1)–(3), s 144(4A); FA 1994, s 89(5)(6); FA 1995, s 91(2); FA 2002, Sch 6 para 2*].

A token used by an employee to obtain the use of a *car parking space* (or, for 1999/2000 and subsequent years, a cycle or motor cycle parking space) at or near his place of work is excluded from these provisions [*ITEPA 2003, s 267(2); ICTA 1988, s 142(3A); FA 1999, s 49*], and a token provided neither by the employer nor by a person connected with the employer (within *ICTA 1988, s 839*, see 19 CONNECTED PERSONS) and used to obtain *entertainment* for the employee (or a relation) is similarly excluded, subject to the same conditions as are specified in 75.16(xv) above. [*ITEPA 2003, s 267(2); ICTA 1988, s 142(3B); FA 1994, s 89(7)*].

Incidental overnight expenses. There is excluded from these provisions a token used to obtain goods or services (or to obtain money to buy goods or services) incidental to the employee's being away from home on *business* during a 'qualifying absence' in relation to which the authorised maximum (£5 per night spent in the UK and £10 per night spent abroad) is not exceeded, where the cost of such goods or services is not otherwise deductible from earnings. [*ITEPA 2003, s 268, Sch 7 paras 33, 34; ICTA 1988, s 142(3C)(3D); FA 1995, s 93(2)*]. See also 75.46 above.

'*Credit-token*' means a card, token or other thing given to a person by another person who undertakes that (*a*) on the production of it (whether or not some other action is also required) he will supply money, goods or services on credit or (*b*) on *similar* production to a third party, he will pay that third party for the money etc. supplied (whether or not taking any discount or commission). '*Production*' includes the use of an object provided to operate a machine. Not included is a cash voucher and a non-cash voucher within (*b*) or (*c*) above. [*ITEPA 2003, s 92; ICTA 1988, s 142(4)(5)*].

See Simon's Direct *Tax* Service E4.433.

75.48   **WAGES IN LIEU OF NOTICE**

The taxation treatment of payments in lieu of notice ('PILONs') is governed by the general principles applying to payments on cessation of employment, for which see 18.3 *et seq.* COMPENSATION FOR LOSS OF EMPLOYMENT (AND DAMAGES). Where the payment is not within the general employment income charge, it will generally fall within *ITEPA 2003, s 403*, subject to the exemptions from charge under that *section*.

The Revenue have set out their approach to the application of general Schedule E principles to PILONs, as follows.

(*a*)   Where contractual arrangements provide for a PILON, the contract is terminated in accordance with its terms on a summary dismissal. The compensation is a contractual entitlement rather than liquidated damages and is chargeable as an emolument under general Schedule E principles.

(*b*)   Where the employer and employee agree at the time of termination that the employment is to be terminated without proper notice but on the making of a PILON, and there was no existing understanding in this respect which could be construed as a contractual provision or amendment, the source of the payment lies only in the agreement to terminate the employment. The payment is therefore not an emolument from the employment.

(*c*)   In establishing whether contractual arrangements provide for a PILON, all relevant factors, e.g. rules in staff handbooks or wage agreements, or oral agreements, have to be considered. Even in the absence of any direct contractual arrangements, there may be an implied contractual term of service where an employer has established a practice of making PILONs instead of giving due notice (but see below for a change in the Revenue view on this aspect).

(*d*)   Where neither (*a*) nor (*b*) above applies, failure to give due notice is a breach of contract, and a payment made for such a breach represents liquidated damages and is not an emolument from the employment.

(*e*)   The existence of a reserved right or discretion of the employer to make a PILON where due notice is not given is not a determining factor where the right or discretion is not exercised. Where it is exercised, (*a*) above applies.

The Revenue reject the view that a contractual PILON is properly analysed as a payment of damages for breach of contract (in particular by analysis of the true effect of (what is now) *Employment Rights Act 1996, s 86*). They also reject the view that a PILON is a redundancy payment.

Payments for a period where notice is given but not in fact worked ('gardening leave') are emoluments from the employment.

(Revenue Tax Bulletin August 1996 pp 325–327).

A further article in Revenue Tax Bulletin February 2003 pp 999–1001 updates the above in a number of respects.

(i)   In the employment law case *Cerberus Software Ltd v Rowley [2001] ICR 376*, the Court of Appeal held that a contractual clause providing that an employer 'may' make a PILON meant that the employer was free to give neither notice nor a PILON, but instead to breach the contract and pay damages for that breach. Such damages would fall within *ITEPA 2003, s 403* (see 18.5 COMPENSATION FOR LOSS OF EMPLOYMENT AND DAMAGES) rather than the normal Schedule E charging provisions. Whether such discretion has been thus exercised in any particular case is a question of fact, but the Revenue sets out its views of indicative factors.

(ii)   The Revenue do not consider that *Cerberus* overrules the *EMI* case referred to below, since the general Schedule E charge is not expressed in contractual terms, so that many taxable payments are not dependent on any contractual obligation. What is required is that the source of the payment is the employer/employee relationship.

(iii)   As regards (*c*) above, although the Revenue now accept that it is unlikely that an implied contractual term in relation to PILONs can exist, they nevertheless consider that where, for example, a PILON is paid as an automatic response to a termination, the payment may be an 'integral part of the employer/employee relationship for the workplace', and as such be assessable under the normal Schedule E rules.

In *EMI Group Electronics Ltd v Coldicott CA 1999, 71 TC 455*, it was held that payments following exercise by the employer of a reserved right as under (*e*) above were chargeable earninmgs. However, in *Mimtec Ltd v CIR (Sp C 277), [2001] SSCD 101* a Special Commissioner held that certain payments made following redundancy negotiations 'in recognition of any entitlements under the consultation process including pay in lieu of notice etc.' were not taxable earnings.

Simon's Direct Tax Service. See E4.805.

75.49   **WORKERS SUPPLIED BY AGENCIES**

Where an individual worker (including a partner in a firm and a member of an unincorporated body) has a contract or arrangement with another person (e.g. with an agency, which term includes an unincorporated body of which the worker is a member) under which he is obliged to render personal services to another person ('the client') which are subject to supervision, direction or control as to the manner in which the services are rendered, those services will be treated as duties performed under an employment with the agency. Any remuneration, whether from the agency or the client, is treated as earnings from that employment (if not already so chargeable), as is any remuneration paid by the agency during a period when the worker is not assigned to any particular client. 'Remuneration' includes every form of payment, gratuity, profit and benefit, but not anything which would not otherwise be receivable from an office or employment. [*ITEPA 2003, ss 44–46, 47(1)(3), Sch 7 para 13; ICTA 1988, s 134*]. For the existence of a contract, see *Brady v Hart Ch D 1985, 58 TC 518*.

See also *Bhadra v Ellam Ch D 1987, 60 TC 466*, where a doctor obtaining locum posts through medical agencies was held to be within *section 134*.

The above provisions do not apply (*a*) to entertainers or fashion etc. models, or (*b*) if the services are wholly rendered in the worker's own home or at other premises which are neither under the control or management of the client nor at which the services are required by their nature to be rendered, or (*c*) as regards payments made in respect of services rendered (or to be rendered) after 5 April 1998, if the worker is a sub-contractor within the

CONSTRUCTION INDUSTRY SCHEME (20) (and see below). [*ITEPA 2003, s 47(2); ICTA 1988, s 134(5); FA 1998, s 55(1)(3), Sch 27 III(7)*].

The deemed employer must include the worker in his return of employees under *TMA 1970, s 15*, see 68.16 RETURNS. Where a worker is engaged through a foreign agency which does not have a branch or permanent agency in the UK, the client is responsible for operating PAYE and National Insurance arrangements (see Revenue Employment Status Manual ESM 2012).

See 55.3 PAY AS YOU EARN as regards application of PAYE generally.

As regards the scope of the legislation on agency workers, see generally Revenue Employment Status Manual ESM 2003. These provisions are independent of, and are not affected by, the rules at 61 PERSONAL SERVICE COMPANIES ETC.

Transitional provisions for sub-contractors. Where a trade

(i)   consisted of or included the rendering of services under contracts relating to construction operations (as defined in 20.2 CONSTRUCTION INDUSTRY SCHEME),

(ii)   was being carried on at the end of 1997/98,

(iii)   included receipts which would have been chargeable under Schedule E for 1997/98 had it not been for the exemption at (*c*) above (now removed),

then *unless the trader elected to the contrary* (see below), the trade was treated as permanently discontinued at 5 April 1998 and, to the extent that the trade included activities in addition to agency engagements chargeable under Schedule E, a new trade was deemed to commence on 6 April 1998. Losses could nevertheless be carried forward under *ICTA 1988, s 385* (see 46.9 LOSSES) from the old trade to the new (and this also applied where there was no deemed recommencement of the old trade as above but an actual new construction trade was commenced during 1998/99). The deemed cessation at 5 April 1998 could not give rise to a Revenue direction revising the basis of assessment for 1995/96 and 1996/97 in the case of a business commenced before 6 April 1994 (see 71.14 SCHEDULE D, CASES I AND II). An election to disapply these provisions had to be made in a self-assessment tax return or, as the case may be, a partnership return. It was a further condition that the return be submitted on or before the statutory filing date. See 68.2, 68.13 RETURNS. [*FA 1998, s 56; ITEPA 2003, Sch 7 para 14*].

Simon's Direct Tax Service. See E4.204.

76   Schedule F—Dividends etc.

Schedule F—Dividends etc.

Simon's Direct Tax Service Part D1.

76.1   Schedule F commenced on 6 April 1966 and applies to dividends and other distributions of UK companies. [*ICTA 1988, s 20; FA 1993, s 183(1)*].

76.2   Up to 5 April 1973, the company was required to account (to the Revenue) for the standard rate of income tax on the dividends etc.

76.3   Until 5 April 1999, the company paid (to the Revenue) advance corporation tax (at a prescribed rate) on paying the dividend etc. and the recipient obtained an equivalent 'tax credit' (subject to special provisions for 1993/94) except in the case of certain 'foreign income dividends'—see 1.9 ALLOWANCES AND TAX RATES. From 6 April 1999, following the abolition of advance corporation tax, the tax credit is set at one-ninth of the amount of the dividend etc. [*ICTA 1988, ss 231, 246C; FA 1993, s 78(3); FA 1994, Sch 16 para 1; F(No 2)A 1997, s 30, Sch 6 para 3; FA 1998, s 31*].

From 6 April 1999, following the change referred to above in the rate of tax credit, special rates of tax apply to Schedule F income and 'equivalent foreign income' (see 1.9 ALLOWANCES AND TAX RATES). Where the income falls within the basic rate limit (treating it as the top slice of total income), the rate is the 'Schedule F ordinary rate', initially set at 10%, so that the liability is met by the tax credit. To the extent that the income exceeds the basic rate limit, the rate is the 'Schedule F upper rate', initially set at 32.5% (equivalent to a further liability of 25% of the amount of the dividend etc., which is the same as that applicable before 6 April 1999). [*ICTA 1988, ss 1A, 1B; F(No 2)A 1997, s 31*]. See 1.9 ALLOWANCES AND TAX RATES as regards dividend taxation generally and in particular the treatment of tax credits.

See also Tolley's Corporation Tax under Advance Corporation Tax and Distributions.

77   Scientific Research Associations

Simon's Direct Tax Service C4.535.

77.1   Scientific research associations are, on a claim, granted the same exemptions from tax as CHARITIES (14), including exemptions from tax on capital gains, if

(a)   object is scientific research which may lead to extension of any class(es) of trade, and association is approved for this purpose by the Secretary of State, and

(b)   the Association is prohibited by Memorandum or similar instrument from distribution of income or property, in any form, to its members (other than reasonable payments for supplies, labour, power, services, interest and rent). [*ICTA 1988, s 508; TCGA, s 271(6)(b)*].

The Department of Trade and Industry (which is primarily responsible for determining whether a body is a scientific research association) issued new guidance on 4 September 1998 on the criteria they will apply, with effect from that date, in making such determinations. By concession, tax exemptions will continue to be granted on the previous basis for accounting periods beginning before 1 September 1999, provided that exemption would have continued to apply under the previous practice and the association continues to satisfy (b) above. This applies also to bodies established before 4 September 1998 which would have obtained approval under the previous practice. (Revenue Pamphlet IR 1, C31).

See also 71.70 SCHEDULE D, CASES I AND II as regards relief for contributions to scientific research associations.

78.1 Self-Assessment

78 Self-Assessment

Cross-reference. See also 79 SELF-ASSESSMENT—KEY DATES.

Simon's Direct Tax Service E1.8.

(See also Revenue Pamphlet IR 142.)

The headings in this chapter are as follows.

78.1 INTRODUCTION

Self-assessment generally has effect for 1996/97 and subsequent years of assessment, although certain aspects of the system came into effect in earlier or later years. The term 'self-assessment' refers to the system whereby the annual tax returns filed by individuals and trustees should include a self-assessment of the taxpayer's liability for income tax and capital gains tax. Payment of tax will then be due automatically, based on the self-assessment. The main body of legislation is contained in *Finance Act 1994*, although there have been further provisions in subsequent Finance Acts.

Two detailed Revenue booklets, SAT 1 'The new current year basis of assessment' and SAT 2 'Self Assessment: the legal framework', both guides for Inland Revenue officers and tax practitioners, should have been sent by tax offices to all practices with which they deal in August/September 1995. SAT 2 was replaced in October 2003 by a Revenue Manual, 'Income Tax Self-Assessment: The Legal Framework'. A booklet SAT 3 'Self Assessment: what it will mean for employers' should also have been sent to employers as part of an information pack in July 1995; further copies are available free from tax offices, as are the following explanatory pamphlets:

SA/BK4 Self Assessment: a general guide to keeping records
SA/BK6 Self Assessment: penalties for late tax returns
SA/BK7 Self Assessment: surcharges for late payment of tax
SA/BK8 Self Assessment: your guide

A series of articles has been published in the Revenue Tax Bulletin from August 1993 onwards on various aspects of self-assessment. See 79 SELF-ASSESSMENT—KEY DATES for a calendar of key dates and events.

Returns. The return for individuals consists of a basic eight pages to which will be attached any supplementary pages relevant to the individual concerned, forming a single 'customised' tax return. The supplementary pages are colour-coded and cover employment, share schemes, self-employment, partnership income, land and property, foreign income, trust income, capital gains and non-residence etc. Each individual will also receive a tax return guide containing explanatory notes relevant to his circumstances. It is the individual's responsibility to obtain any supplementary pages he needs but has not received, which he may do by telephoning a Revenue Orderline, by which means he may also obtain the relevant explanatory notes and/or 'helpsheets' on specific topics. Each return sent out will be accompanied by a tax calculation guide designed to assist the individual in calculating his tax liability if he chooses to do so. See generally 68.2 RETURNS. Partnership returns follow a similar pattern (see 68.13 RETURNS).

Returns must normally be filed by 31 January following the year of assessment (see 68.2 RETURNS). Taxpayers who would prefer not to compute their own liabilities do not have to do so providing they file their return early, normally by 30 September following the year of assessment, though this does not apply to internet filers (see 68.3 RETURNS). Taxpayers with employment income must file their return by earlier specified dates than 31 January if they wish to have a liability of less than £2,000 coded out through PAYE (55) (see 68.3 RETURNS). Penalties will be imposed for late submission of returns, subject to appeal on the grounds of reasonable excuse (see 57.2 PENALTIES). There are provisions for making amendments to returns (see 68.4 RETURNS). The Revenue are given broadly one year from the filing date to give notice of their intention to enquire into the return (see 68.6 RETURNS). A formal procedure is laid down for such enquiries (see 68.6–68.11 RETURNS). If the Revenue do not give such notice, the return becomes final and conclusive, subject to any 'error or mistake' claim by the taxpayer (see 16.7 CLAIMS) or 'discovery' assessment by the Revenue (see 5.3 ASSESSMENTS). In the event of non-submission of a return, the Revenue will be able to make a determination of the tax liability; there will be no right of appeal but the determination may be superseded upon submission of the return (see 68.12 RETURNS). Capital losses must be quantified if they are to be allowable losses (see Tolley's Capital Gains Tax).

A special return has to be filed by partnerships. This must include a statement of the allocation of partnership income between the partners. See 68.13 RETURNS.

An electronic version of the tax return (SA/BK5) is available from tax offices.

A four-page Short Tax Return (STR) for those with relatively simple tax affairs is being piloted and is expected to be rolled out nationwide in April 2005. Under new criteria applicable from April 2004, fewer taxpayers (including higher rate taxpayers) whose affairs can be adequately dealt with using the PAYE system will be asked to complete a tax return of any kind, though they may choose to do so if they wish. See also Guidelines for Individuals completing Tax Returns at www.inlandrevenue.gov.uk/sa/guidelines.htm From April 2004, the Revenue will make increased use of the telephone to resolve minor queries arising in connection with completed returns. (Revenue Tax Bulletin February 2004 pp 1079, 1080).

Payment of tax. Income tax (on all sources of taxable income) for a year of assessment is payable by means of two interim payments of equal amounts, based normally on the liability for the previous year and due on 31 January in the year of assessment and the following 31 July, and a final balancing payment due on the following 31 January (on which date any capital gains tax liability is also due for payment). Taxpayers have the right to reduce their interim payments if they believe their liability will be less than that for the previous year or to dispense with interim payments if they believe they will have no liability. Interim payments are not in any case required where substantially all of a taxpayer's liability is covered by deduction of tax at source, including PAYE, or where the amounts otherwise due are below *de minimis* limits prescribed by regulations. See 78.4–78.7 below.

Interest on overdue payments runs from the due date to the date of payment (see 42.1 INTEREST AND SURCHARGES ON UNPAID TAX). There is also a 5% surcharge on any tax unpaid by 28 February following the year of assessment and a further 5% surcharge on any tax unpaid by the following 31 July, such surcharges being subject to appeal on the grounds of reasonable excuse (see 42.2 INTEREST AND SURCHARGES ON UNPAID TAX). Interest on tax overpaid runs from the due date (or date of payment if later) to the date of repayment (see 41.1 INTEREST ON OVERPAID TAX); the rate of interest is lower than that on overdue tax.

Miscellaneous. Numerous consequential amendments have been made to taxes management provisions and time limits. There is a statutory requirement for taxpayers to keep records for the purpose of making returns and to preserve such records for specified periods

78.2 Self-Assessment

(see 68.5 RETURNS). A formal procedure now applies to the making of claims and elections and the giving of notices (see 16.1 CLAIMS).

78.2 INTERPRETATION OF REFERENCES TO ASSESSMENTS ETC.

Following the introduction of self-assessment, references to an individual (or trustee) being assessed to tax, or being charged to tax by an assessment, are to be construed as including a reference to his being so assessed, or being so charged, by a self-assessment under *TMA 1970, s 9* (see 78.3 below) or by a determination under *TMA 1970, s 28C* (see 68.12 RETURNS) which has not been superseded by a self-assessment. [*FA 1994, s 197*].

78.3 SELF-ASSESSMENTS

Every return under *TMA 1970, s 8* or *s 8A* (see 68.2 RETURNS) must include, subject to the exception below, an assessment (a self-assessment) of the amounts in which, based on the information in the return and taking into account any reliefs and allowances claimed therein, the person making the return is chargeable to income tax and capital gains tax for the year of assessment and of his net income tax liability for the year, taking into account tax deducted at source and tax credits on dividends. In the event of non-compliance, an officer of the Board *may* make the assessment on his behalf, based on the information in the return, and send the person a copy.

The tax to be self-assessed does not include any chargeable on the administrator of a retirement benefits scheme or personal pension scheme (see 60.1 PERSONAL PENSION SCHEMES, 67.4, 67.9 RETIREMENT SCHEMES).

A person need not comply with this requirement if he makes and delivers his return on or before 30 September following the year of assessment or, if later, within two months beginning with the date of the notice to deliver the return. For returns submitted outside these time limits, the Revenue will still, if the taxpayer so requests, carry out the computations based on the return, but will not guarantee that the relevant filing date will be met. In the event of a person making no self-assessment under this option, an officer of the Board *must* make the assessment on his behalf, based on the information in the return, and send the person a copy. If, by reason only of Revenue delay, the assessment is made less than 30 days before the due date for payment of the tax, the date from which any interest or surcharge is triggered (see 42.1, 42.2 INTEREST AND SURCHARGES ON UNPAID TAX) is 30 days after the issue of the assessment. (ICAEW Technical Release TAX 9/94, 7 June 1994). The 30 September deadline is of no significance where returns are filed over the internet (see 68.2 above) as the tax due is automatically computed during the filing process.

Assessments made as above by an officer of the Board are treated as self-assessments by the person making the return and as included in the return.

A self-assessment must not show as repayable any notional tax treated as deducted from certain income deemed to have been received after deduction of tax, for example STOCK DIVIDENDS (85).

[*TMA 1970, s 9(1)–(3A); FA 1994, ss 179, 199(2)(a); FA 1995, s 104(4), s 115(2); FA 1996, s 121(4), s 122(1); FA 1998, s 98(2)(3); FA 2001, s 88, Sch 29 para 1; ITEPA 2003, Sch 6 para 125*].

Taxpayers with employment income who wish to have a liability of less than £2,000 coded out through PAYE (55) are advised to file their return by an earlier date than the 31 January deadline at 68.2 RETURNS (whether or not they wish the Revenue to compute the liability). As regards returns for 2001/02 onwards, that date is 30 September (following the year of assessment) if the return is filed manually, 29 December if it is filed via the electronic lodgement service (see 68.14 RETURNS) and 30 December if it is filed via the internet (see

68.2 RETURNS). As regards returns for 2000/01 and earlier years, the date was 30 September in all cases (and before 2000/01 the limit was £1,000). A 2001/02 underpayment, for example, will be coded out for 2003/04. (Revenue Income Tax Self-Assessment: The Legal Framework Manual SALF 204, para 2.33; Revenue Tax Bulletin June 1996 p 315; Revenue 'Working Together' Bulletin February 2001 p 2; Revenue Press Release 23 September 2002). Coding out of an underpayment for a tax year has the consequential effect of reducing any payments on account (see 78.4 below) due for the following tax year.

Simon's Direct Tax Service. See E1.807.

78.4   **INTERIM PAYMENTS OF TAX ON ACCOUNT**

For 1997/98 and subsequent years (special transitional rules having applied for 1996/97), where, as regards the year immediately preceding the year of assessment in question,

(*a*)   a person is assessed to income tax under *TMA 1970, s 9* (self-assessment — see 68.3 RETURNS),

(*b*)   the assessed amount exceeds any income tax deducted at source (including tax deducted under PAYE, taking in any deduction in respect of that year but to be made in a subsequent year but subtracting any amount paid in that year but in respect of a previous year, tax treated as deducted from, or as paid on, any income, and tax credits on dividends), and

(*c*)   the said excess (the 'relevant amount') and the proportion which the relevant amount bears to the assessed amount are not less than, respectively, £500 and 20%,

the person must make two interim payments on account of his income tax liability for the year of assessment in question, each payment being equal to 50% of the relevant amount (see (*c*) above) and the payments being due on or before, respectively, 31 January in the year of assessment and the following 31 July. If the preceding year's self-assessment is made late or is amended, the relevant amount is determined as if the liability as finally agreed had been shown in a timeous self-assessment, with further payments on account then being required where appropriate. If a discovery assessment (see 5.3 ASSESSMENTS) is made for the preceding year, each payment on account due is deemed always to have been 50% of the relevant amount plus 50% of the tax charged by the discovery assessment as finally determined.

At any time before 31 January following the year of assessment, the taxpayer may make a claim stating his belief that he will have no liability for the year or that his liability will be fully covered by tax deducted at source and his grounds for that belief, in which case each of the interim payments is not, and is deemed never to have been, required to be made. Within the same time limit, the taxpayer may make a claim stating his belief that his liability for the year after allowing for tax deducted at source will be a stated amount which is less than the relevant amount, and stating his grounds for that belief, in which case each of the interim payments required will be, and deemed always to have been, equal to 50% of the stated amount. Either claim should be made on form SA 303. The maximum penalty for an incorrect statement made fraudulently or negligently in connection with either claim is the amount or additional amount he would have paid on account if he had made a correct statement. Interim payments of tax are subject to the same recovery provisions as any other payments of tax.

An officer of the Board may direct, at any time before 31 January following a year of assessment, that a person is not required to make payments on account for that year, such adjustments being made as necessary to give effect to the direction. For the circumstances in which such a direction will be made, see Revenue Tax Bulletin August 2001 p 875.

An erroneous repeal in *ITEPA 2003* made unintended changes (not included in the above coverage) to *TMA 1970, s 59A*. The position is corrected by *FA 2004, Sch 17 para 6* but not so as to affect anything done after 5 April 2003 and before 22 July 2004 in reliance on the said repeal.

[*TMA 1970, s 59A; FA 1994, s 192; FA 1995, s 108; FA 1996, s 126(1), Sch 18 paras 2, 17(1); ITEPA 2003, Sch 6 para 130; FA 2003, s 145(7); FA 2004, Sch 17 para 6; SI 1996 No 1654; SI 1997 No 2491*].

For an article on payments on account (including the special arrangements for 1996/97), see Revenue Tax Bulletin October 1996 pp 353–356. For an article on Revenue practice on repayment, and allocations and reallocations of overpayments, see Revenue Tax Bulletin June 1999 pp 673, 674. For the interaction of loss relief claims and payments on account, see Revenue Tax Bulletin August 2001 pp 878, 879.

Interim payments made by an employer on an employee's behalf, as part of *tax equalisation* arrangements where full in-year gross up is used, should not figure in the employment pages of the employee's self-assessment tax return (see Revenue Tax Bulletin June 1998 p 551).

These provisions, and those described at 78.6 and 78.7 below (and, as regards surcharges, 42.2 INTEREST AND SURCHARGES ON UNPAID TAX), apply equally (with the necessary modifications) to Class 4 national insurance contributions. [*Social Security Contributions and Benefits Act 1992, s 16(1)(b); FA 1994, Sch 19 para 45*].

Agents for whom the Revenue holds the taxpayer's authority on form 64–8, for information to be copied, are automatically provided in June and December each year with Clients' Account Information, i.e. details (though not true copies) of their clients' taxpayer statements of account (advisory statements issued to taxpayers notifying them of payments due and outstanding). A customised payslip is attached to the agent statement. A taxpayer may also elect, again using form 64–8, for his statement of account to be sent to his agent instead of to him. Agents registered for electronic lodgement (see 68.14 RETURNS), and authorised to receive copy information, automatically receive electronic copies of statements of account. From June 2003, taxpayers and agents registered to use the Revenue's internet services can also view issued statements of account online. (Revenue Press Release 12 December 1997; Revenue Tax Bulletins December 1998 pp 618–620 and December 1999 pp 703–705; and Revenue 'Working Together' Bulletins July 2000 p 4, November 2000 p 3 and June 2003 p 1).

Simon's Direct Tax Service. See E1.821.

78.5   *Example*

Calculation of interim payments for 2005/06
For 2004/05, Kylie's self-assessment shows the following.

	£
Total income tax liability	8,664
Capital gains tax liability	2,122
Class 4 NIC liability	198
PAYE tax deducted (all relating to 2004/05)	3,740
Tax credits on dividends received	200
Tax deducted from interest received	300

The payments on account for 2005/06 (unless Kylie claims to pay different amounts) are based on relevant amounts as follows.

	£
Income tax (£8,664 − £3,740 − £200 − £300 =)	4,424
Class 4 NIC	198

Half of the relevant amounts is due on each of 31 January 2005 and 31 July 2005. No payment on account is required in respect of capital gains tax liability.

78.6   **FINAL PAYMENT (REPAYMENT) OF TAX**

For 1996/97 and subsequent years, a final payment (known as a '*balancing payment*') is due for a year of assessment if a person's combined income tax and capital gains tax liabilities contained in his self-assessment (see 68.3 RETURNS) exceed the aggregate of any payments on account (whether under *TMA 1970, s 59A*, see 78.4 above, or otherwise) and any income tax deducted at source. If the second total exceeds the first, a repayment will be made. Tax deducted at source has the same meaning as in 78.4(*b*) above.

Subject to 78.7 below, the due date for payment (or repayment) is 31 January following the year of assessment. The one exception is where the person gave notice of chargeability under *TMA 1970, s 7* (see 57.1 PENALTIES) within six months after the end of the year of assessment, but was not given notice under *TMA 1970, s 8 or s 8A* (see 68.2 RETURNS) until after 31 October following the year of assessment; in such case, the due date is the last day of the three months beginning with the date of the said notice.

[*TMA 1970, s 59B(1)–(4)(7)(8); FA 1994, ss 193, 199(2)(a); FA 1996, s 122(2), s 126(2); ITEPA 2003, Sch 6 para 131; FA 2003, s 145(7)*].

See 78.4 above as regards notifications to agents.

Foot and mouth outbreak. For the full range of special measures in relation to the 2001 foot and mouth disease outbreak, including deferment of payment of tax liabilities, see Revenue Tax Bulletin Special Edition May 2001.

Simon's Direct Tax Service. See E1.822.

78.7   **Due date: further provisions.** Where an amount of tax is payable (repayable) as a result of an amendment or correction to an individual's or trustees' self-assessment under any of (*a*)–(*e*) below, then, subject to the appeal and postponement provisions in 4.1 APPEALS and 56.3 PAYMENT OF TAX, the due date for payment (repayment) is as stated below (if this is later than the date given under the general rules in 78.6 above). Note that these rules do *not* defer the date from which interest accrues, which is as in 42.1 INTEREST AND SURCHARGES ON UNPAID TAX or 41.1 INTEREST ON OVERPAID TAX, although they do determine the due date for surcharge purposes — see 42.2 INTEREST AND SURCHARGES ON UNPAID TAX.

(*a*)   Taxpayer amendment to return as in 68.4 RETURNS: 30 days after the date of the taxpayer's notice of amendment.

(*b*)   Revenue correction to return as in 68.4 RETURNS: 30 days after the date of the officer's notice of correction.

(*c*)   Taxpayer amendment to return whilst enquiry in progress as in 68.10 RETURNS, where accepted by the Revenue: 30 days after the date of the closure notice (see 68.9 RETURNS).

(*d*)   Revenue amendment to return where amendment made by closure notice following enquiry (see 68.9 RETURNS): 30 days after the date of the closure notice.

(*e*)   Revenue amendment of self-assessment to prevent potential loss of tax to the Crown (see 68.10 RETURNS): 30 days after the date of the notice of amendment.

As regards amendments and corrections to partnership returns, (*e*) above is not relevant, and the equivalent date in each of (*a*)–(*d*) above as regards each partner is 30 days after the date of the officer's notice of consequential amendment to the partner's own tax return. The same applies in the case of a consequential amendment by virtue of any of the following: an amendment of a partnership return on discovery (see 5.3 ASSESSMENTS), a partnership error or mistake relief claim (see 16.7 CLAIMS), or a reduction or increase in the partnership tax liability made by the Appeal Commissioners (see 4.1, 4.11 APPEALS).

These rules apply where the notice referred to in (*a*)–(*e*) above (or, for partnerships, the notice of consequential amendment) is given on or after 11 May 2001. Previously, where a self-assessment was amended under the relevant provisions in 68.4, 68.10 RETURNS (disregarding amendments to those provisions applying from 11 May 2001) or 68.13 RETURNS, then subject to the same point as above as regards interest (and subject to the appeal and postponement rules), the due date was 30 days after the date of the notice of amendment (if such due date was later than that given under 78.6 above).

[*TMA 1970, s 59B(5), Sch 3ZA; FA 1994, ss 193, 199(2)(a); FA 2001, s 88, Sch 29 paras 14(3), 15, 16*].

Where an officer of the Board enquires into the return (see 68.6 RETURNS) and a repayment is otherwise due, the repayment is not required to be made until the enquiry is completed (see 68.9 RETURNS) although the officer may make a provisional repayment at his discretion.

Subject to the appeal and postponement provisions in 4.1 APPEALS and 56.3 PAYMENT OF TAX, the due date for payment of tax charged by any assessment other than a self-assessment, e.g. a discovery assessment under *TMA 1970, s 29* (see 5.3 ASSESSMENTS), is 30 days after the date of the assessment (but, for interest consequences, see 42.1 INTEREST AND SURCHARGES ON UNPAID TAX).

[*TMA 1970, s 59B(4A)(6); FA 1994, ss 193, 199(2)(a); FA 1995, s 115(6); FA 1996, s 127; FA 2001, s 88, Sch 29 paras 14(2), 16*].

78.8   APPEALS

For appeals generally, see 4.1 *et seq.* APPEALS, and in particular for jurisdiction of Commissioners see 4.3, 4.4 APPEALS. For postponement of tax pending appeal and payment of tax on determination of the appeal, see respectively 56.3 and 56.4 PAYMENT OF TAX.

78.9   CLAIMS ETC.

For full details as to the making of, and the ramifications of, claims and elections under self-assessment, see 16.1–16.4 CLAIMS.

78.10   COLLECTION AND RECOVERY

For 1996/97 and subsequent years, miscellaneous amendments are made to provisions covering the collection and recovery by the Revenue of tax, interest on tax, surcharges and penalties. The limit of £1,000 referred to in 56.5 PAYMENT OF TAX is raised to £2,000. Further minor amendments are made from, broadly, 11 May 2001. [*TMA 1970, ss 65–67, 69, 70; FA 1994, ss 196, 199(2)(a), Sch 19 paras 19–21; FA 2001, s 89; ITEPA 2003, Sch 6 para 135*].

78.11   LIABILITY OF RELEVANT TRUSTEES

In relation to income and chargeable gains, the '*relevant trustees*' of a settlement are the persons who are the trustees when the income arises or in the year of assessment in which the chargeable gain or life assurance policy gain accrues or arises and, in both cases, any persons who subsequently become trustees. Where the relevant trustees are liable to a penalty under the self-assessment regime, to interest on a penalty, to a surcharge and/or interest thereon, to make interim and final payments of income tax and payments on an assessment to recover tax over-repaid, or to interest on unpaid tax, the penalty etc. may be recovered (but only once) from any one or more of them. As regards penalties and surcharges (and interest on either), the liability of any relevant trustee is, however, restricted to those incurred after the day that he became a relevant trustee (a daily penalty being regarded as incurred on a daily basis). The 'reasonable excuse' provisions in 42.2 INTEREST

AND SURCHARGES ON UNPAID TAX and 57.2 PENALTIES have effect by reference to each of the relevant trustees. [*TMA 1970, ss 7(9), 107A; FA 1995, s 103; FA 1998, Sch 14 para 5*].

Trustees of 'bare' (or 'simple') trusts treated as such for tax purposes are not required to complete self-assessment returns or make payments on account, the beneficiaries under such trusts being liable to give details of the income and gains in their own tax returns. The trustees may, if they and the beneficiaries so wish, make returns of income (but *not* of capital gains or capital losses), accounting for tax at the basic or lower rate (or, from 6 April 1999, the Schedule F ordinary rate), as appropriate to the class of income, provided that they so notify the trust district and follow this course consistently from year to year. This does not, however, affect the liability of the beneficiaries to make the appropriate self-assessment returns of income and gains. (Revenue Tax Bulletin February 1997 p 395, December 1997 pp 486, 487).

78.12   **INFORMATION TO BE PROVIDED TO EMPLOYEES**

With effect for 1996/97 and later years, amendments were made to the *Income Tax (Employments) Regulations 1993 (SI 1993 No 744)*, i.e. the PAY AS YOU EARN (55) Regulations, to ensure that sufficient information is given to employees, and in good time, to enable them to complete their self-assessment returns. The Revenue undertook to provide an education and assistance programme for employers, which included a booklet SAT 3 'Self Assessment: what it will mean for employers' sent out to employers as part of an information pack in July 1995. The *1993 Regulations* have since been superseded by the *Income Tax (Pay As You Earn) Regulations 2003 (SI 2003 No 2682)*. The amendments were as follows.

(*a*)   A time limit was introduced for providing an employee with form P60 (certificate of pay and tax deducted — see 55.10 PAY AS YOU EARN). It must be provided no later than 31 May following the tax year to which it relates. [*SI 2003 No 2682, reg 67*].

(*b*)   The deadline for submitting to the Revenue forms P9D and P11D (returns of benefits and expenses payments — see 55.9 PAY AS YOU EARN) is extended to no later than 6 July (previously 6 June) following the tax year. Within the same time limit, there is also a requirement for the employer to provide each employee for whom such a form is relevant with particulars of the information stated therein. (For 2001/02 and earlier years, where an employer operates the Fixed Profit Car Scheme (FPCS) (see 75.46 SCHEDULE E—EMPLOYMENT INCOME), he must provide each scheme employee with either his taxable business mileage profit figure or the figures for allowances paid and mileage covered.) An employer is not obliged to provide any of the above particulars to an employee who left during the tax year in question unless requested to do so within three years after the end of that tax year, the information to be provided within 30 days of receipt of the request if later than the normal 6 July deadline. [*SI 2003 No 2682, regs 85(1), 94, Sch 1 para 16*].

(*c*)   Where a third party makes payments or provides benefits which if done by arrangement with the employer would have fallen to be included on forms P11D and P9D (see 55.9 PAY AS YOU EARN), he must provide particulars, including cash equivalents, to the *employee* by 6 July following the tax year. (The third party is not obliged to provide such particulars to the Revenue unless required to do so by notice under *TMA 1970, s 15* (see 68.16 RETURNS).) [*SI 2003 No 2682, reg 95*].

There were also changes to form P45 (for employees changing jobs — see 55.22–55.24 PAY AS YOU EARN). The form now contains an additional part for retention by the employee.

Penalties under *TMA 1970, s 98* for failure to provide information to the Revenue (see 57.9 PENALTIES) apply equally to failure to comply with the above requirements for providing particulars to employees.

78.13   Self-Assessment

78.13   TAXATION OF NON-RESIDENTS

Non-UK residents are taxed on the shoreline principle, i.e. on income arising in or connected with the UK. New rules were introduced by *Finance Act 1995* to simplify the procedures for taxing non-residents and align them with self-assessment. See 51.3 to 51.6 NON-RESIDENTS AND OTHER OVERSEAS MATTERS for rules under *FA 1995, ss 126, 127, Sch 23* which apply where a non-resident carries on a trade in the UK through a branch or agency and for the obligations and liabilities of his UK representative. See 69.13 SCHEDULE A for provisions of *FA 1995, s 40* on income from UK property. See 51.1 NON-RESIDENTS AND OTHER OVERSEAS MATTERS for provisions of *FA 1995, s 128* which limit the income tax chargeable on a non-resident's total UK income. See Revenue Tax Bulletin August 1995 p 237 for a summary of the rules for taxing various types of income of non-residents under self-assessment.

Individuals who regard themselves as not resident, not ordinarily resident or not domiciled in the UK are required to self-certify their status in the self-assessment tax return. See 65.5 RESIDENCE, ORDINARY RESIDENCE AND DOMICILE under Administrative procedures.

79   Self-Assessment—Key Dates

Cross-references. See also 78 SELF-ASSESSMENT.

79.1   The Table below sets out key dates and events in the operation of the self-assessment regime.

Date	Event
31 January 2004	2002/03 tax return to be filed on or before this date (see 68.2 RETURNS).
31 January 2004	Balancing payment of income tax and payment of capital gains tax due for 2002/03 (see 78.6 SELF-ASSESSMENT).
31 January 2004	First interim payment on account due for 2003/04 (see 78.4 SELF-ASSESSMENT).
February 2004	Revenue begin to issue fixed penalty notices, and in some cases take daily penalty action, for non-filing of 2002/03 tax returns (see 57.2 PENALTIES).
February 2004	Revenue may issue determinations of tax due for 2002/03 where no tax return filed (see 68.12 RETURNS).
28 February 2004	Initial surcharge due of 5% of any 2002/03 income tax and capital gains tax due on 31 January 2004 and remaining unpaid after this date (see 42.2 INTEREST AND SURCHARGES ON UNPAID TAX).
April 2004	Revenue issue majority of 2003/04 self-assessment tax returns (see 68.2 RETURNS).
31 May 2004	Deadline for employers to provide employees with Form P60 for 2003/04 (see 78.12 SELF-ASSESSMENT).
June 2004	Revenue provide taxpayer agents (where authority held on form 64-8) with Clients' Account Information, i.e. details of their clients' taxpayer statements of account (see 78.4 SELF-ASSESSMENT).
6 July 2004	Deadline for employers to provide both the Revenue and employees with P11D/P9D information etc. for 2003/04 (see 55.9 PAY AS YOU EARN and 78.12 SELF-ASSESSMENT).
31 July 2004	Second interim payment on account due for 2003/04 (see 78.4 SELF-ASSESSMENT).
31 July 2004	Further surcharge due of 5% of any 2002/03 income tax and capital gains tax due on 31 January 2004 and remaining unpaid on this date (see 42.2 INTEREST AND SURCHARGES ON UNPAID TAX).
1 August 2004	Further £100 penalty due where 2002/03 tax return due to be filed on 31 January 2004 not filed before this date (see 57.2 PENALTIES).
1 August 2004	If 2003/04 tax return issued after this date, normal 30 September deadline for filing return if Revenue to calculate tax is deferred until two months from date of issue (see 78.3 SELF-ASSESSMENT).

79.1 Self-Assessment—Key Dates

30 September 2004	2003/04 tax return to be filed on or before this date if *either* (*a*) taxpayer filing manually wishes Revenue to calculate tax *or* (*b*) taxpayer filing manually wishes 2003/04 tax underpayment of less than £2,000 to be collected by adjustment to 2005/06 PAYE code (see 78.3 SELF-ASSESSMENT).
5 October 2004	Chargeability to tax for 2003/04 to be notified to Revenue on or before this date if no tax return received (see 57.1 PENALTIES).
1 November 2004	If 2003/04 tax return issued on or after this date, normal 31 January deadline for filing return if taxpayer to calculate tax liability is deferred until three months from date of issue (see 68.2 RETURNS) as is due date of balancing payment and payment of capital gains tax provided notice of chargeability given timeously (see above, and 78.6 SELF-ASSESSMENT).
December 2004	Revenue provide taxpayer agents (where authority held on form 64-8) with Clients' Account Information, i.e. details of their clients' taxpayer statements of account (see 78.4 SELF-ASSESSMENT).
29 December 2004	2003/04 tax return to be filed on or before this date if taxpayer filing via the electronic lodgement service wishes 2003/04 tax underpayment of less than £2,000 to be collected by adjustment to 2005/06 PAYE code (see 78.3 SELF-ASSESSMENT).
30 December 2004	2003/04 tax return to be filed on or before this date if taxpayer filing via the internet wishes 2003/04 tax underpayment of less than £2,000 to be collected by adjustment to 2005/06 PAYE code (see 78.3 SELF-ASSESSMENT).
31 January 2005	2003/04 tax return to be filed on or before this date (see 68.2 RETURNS).
31 January 2005	Balancing payment of income tax and payment of capital gains tax due for 2003/04 (see 78.6 SELF-ASSESSMENT).
31 January 2005	First interim payment on account due for 2004/05 (see 78.4 SELF-ASSESSMENT).
February 2005	Revenue begin to issue fixed penalty notices, and in some cases take daily penalty action, for non-filing of 2003/04 tax returns (see 57.2 PENALTIES).
February 2005	Revenue may issue determinations of tax due for 2003/04 where no tax return filed (see 68.12 RETURNS).
28 February 2005	Initial surcharge due of 5% of any 2003/04 income tax and capital gains tax due on 31 January 2005 and remaining unpaid after this date (see 42.2 INTEREST AND SURCHARGES ON UNPAID TAX).
April 2005	Revenue issue majority of 2004/05 self-assessment tax returns (see 68.2 RETURNS).
31 May 2005	Deadline for employers to provide employees with Form P60 for 2004/05 (see 78.12 SELF-ASSESSMENT).
June 2005	Revenue provide taxpayer agents (where authority held on form 64-8) with Clients' Account Information, i.e. details of their clients' taxpayer statements of account (see 78.4 SELF-ASSESSMENT).

6 July 2005	Deadline for employers to provide both the Revenue and employees with P11D/P9D information etc. for 2004/05 (see 55.9 PAY AS YOU EARN and 78.12 SELF-ASSESSMENT).
31 July 2005	Second interim payment on account due for 2004/05 (see 78.4 SELF-ASSESSMENT).
31 July 2005	Further surcharge due of 5% of any 2003/04 income tax and capital gains tax due on 31 January 2005 and remaining unpaid on this date (see 42.2 INTEREST AND SURCHARGES ON UNPAID TAX).
1 August 2005	Further £100 penalty due where 2003/04 tax return due to be filed on 31 January 2005 not filed before this date (see 57.2 PENALTIES).
1 August 2005	If 2004/05 tax return issued after this date, normal 30 September deadline for filing return if Revenue to calculate tax is deferred until two months from date of issue (see 78.3 SELF-ASSESSMENT).
30 September 2005	2004/05 tax return to be filed on or before this date if *either* (*a*) taxpayer filing manually wishes Revenue to calculate tax *or* (*b*) taxpayer filing manually wishes 2004/05 tax underpayment of less than £2,000 to be collected by adjustment to 2006/07 PAYE code (see 78.3 SELF-ASSESSMENT).

80	Self-Employed Persons

80.1   The individual in business, whether full-time or part-time, on his own or in partnership with others, is subject to particular tax legislation and practices. Such legislation etc. is included in this book under various subject headings and the following paragraphs indicate where the detailed provisions are to be found.

See 75.27 SCHEDULE E—EMPLOYMENT INCOME as regards the distinction between employment and self-employment.

See 61 PERSONAL SERVICE COMPANIES ETC. as regards individuals providing their services through an intermediary in circumstances such that they would fall to be categorised as employees if engaged directly.

80.2   **CHARGE TO INCOME TAX ETC.**

Profits and income are chargeable to tax under SCHEDULE D, CASES I AND II (71). Special provisions relate to the opening and closing years of a business. Particular items of expenditure or receipt may, or may not, be included in the computation of taxable profits. Where a business is discontinued, see also 62 POST-CESSATION ETC. RECEIPTS AND EXPENDITURE. Partnership matters are dealt with under 53 PARTNERSHIPS. Farmers may elect for the HERD BASIS (34) to apply to their animals. Special provisions apply to UNDERWRITERS AT LLOYD'S (89).

Some transactions may result in an assessment because they contravene legislation on ANTI-AVOIDANCE (3).

For general procedure, see SELF-ASSESSMENT (78). See also 5 ASSESSMENTS and 4 APPEALS.

Property. Property income is assessed under SCHEDULE A (69).

Assets. The acquisition or ownership of business assets may give rise to CAPITAL ALLOWANCES (9) as the tax substitute for the disallowable depreciation charge (if any) in the accounts. The disposal of assets may result in balancing adjustments, and also to a charge to capital gains tax (see Tolley's Capital Gains Tax) unless certain exemptions and reliefs apply.

Overseas. Income from trades etc. carried on wholly abroad is assessed under SCHEDULE D, CASES IV AND V (73). See 51.3 NON-RESIDENTS AND OTHER OVERSEAS MATTERS for non-residents trading in the UK.

Losses. If trading losses are incurred, relief may be obtained by various alternatives, see under 46 LOSSES.

80.3   **EMPLOYEES**

If staff are employed, then the regulations under the PAY AS YOU EARN (55) system must be complied with.

80.4   **PAYMENT OF TAX**

For times of payment, see under SELF-ASSESSMENT (78). See also 56 PAYMENT OF TAX and 42 INTEREST AND SURCHARGES ON UNPAID TAX. Special provisions relate to the construction industry, see CONSTRUCTION INDUSTRY SCHEME (20).

See 13 CERTIFICATES OF TAX DEPOSIT for a method of payment.

80.5   **PROVISION FOR RETIREMENT**

Special legislation allows tax relief for payments made for PERSONAL PENSION SCHEMES (60) and RETIREMENT ANNUITIES (66).

80.6   **NATIONAL INSURANCE CONTRIBUTIONS**

Class 4 contributions will be levied and included with certain assessments of business profits, see 83 SOCIAL SECURITY. For partial deduction from total income, see 1.10 ALLOWANCES AND TAX RATES.

80.7   **VALUE ADDED TAX**

The detailed provisions of VAT are outside the scope of this book but registration is generally required when the 'taxable turnover' of the business will exceed £58,000 (£56,000 before 1 April 2004) in a year. For detailed information, see Tolley's Value Added Tax.

81   Settlements

Cross-references. See 3.7 ANTI-AVOIDANCE for transfer of assets abroad; 22 DEDUCTION OF TAX AT SOURCE generally and at 22.10 for annuities etc. and 22.17 for tax-free annuities under wills etc.; 65.5 RESIDENCE, ORDINARY RESIDENCE AND DOMICILE for residence of trustees; 57.1 PENALTIES, 68.2 RETURNS, 78.11 SELF-ASSESSMENT for management provisions relating to trustees under self-assessment. See also Revenue Pamphlet IR 152.

Simon's Direct Tax Service Part C4.

81.1   Legislation providing specially for the tax treatment of settlements is dealt with at 81.13–81.21 below. The general tax treatment of trust income and trustees is in 81.2–81.12 below and, where appropriate, is applicable to trusts created by a will. For the income of estates of deceased persons in course of administration, see 21 DECEASED ESTATES.

The headings in this chapter are as follows.

It was announced in the December 2003 Pre-Budget Report that the Government are to consult on a new and modernised income tax and capital gains tax regime for trusts, to be implemented from 6 April 2005. Details of the proposals are on the Revenue's website.

81.2   **GENERAL POINTS ON TRUST TAXATION**

(*a*)   **Trustees** of settlements are taxed in their representative capacities under the Schedule appropriate to the income received (see 81.3 below). They are charged to income tax at the basic rate or the lower rate or, from 6 April 1999 the Schedule F ordinary rate (see 1.9 ALLOWANCES AND TAX RATES) as appropriate to the class of income, except in the case of discretionary and accumulation trusts (see 81.5 below). The latter are generally charged at the 'rate applicable to trusts' or, in respect of dividends and other similar income from 6 April 1999, the 'Schedule F trust rate' (see 81.5 below for detailed provisions).

Trustees of 'bare' (or 'simple') trusts treated as such for tax purposes are not required to deduct tax from payments to beneficiaries or to complete self-assessment returns or make payments on account. The beneficiaries under such trusts are liable to give details of the income and gains in their own tax returns. The trustees may, if they and the beneficiaries so wish, make returns of income (but *not* of capital gains or capital losses), accounting for tax at the basic or lower rate or, from 6 April 1999, the Schedule F ordinary rate, as appropriate to the class of income, provided that they so notify the trust district and follow this course consistently from year to year. This does not, however, affect the liability of the beneficiaries to make the appropriate self-assessment returns of income and gains. (Revenue Tax Bulletin February 1997 p 395, December 1997 pp 486, 487).

(b)   **Beneficiaries** receive income from settlements which is treated as net of the tax accounted for by the trustees. The grossed-up amount of the income is treated as part of the total income of the beneficiary for tax purposes. If the total income of a beneficiary is high enough, he will suffer income tax at the excess of the higher rate or, from 6 April 1999, the Schedule F upper rate over the tax accounted for by the trustees on the grossed-up income from the trust. He may alternatively be entitled to a repayment of some or all of the tax suffered by the trustees where it exceeds his own liability (although this does not extend to non-repayable tax or non-payable tax credits of the trustees). See also 81.5 below for tax repayments to non-residents.

In determining the income of beneficiaries, trustees' expenses, so far as properly chargeable to income (or so chargeable but for any express provisions of the trust) are to be treated as set against, broadly, income chargeable at the lower rate in priority to other income and, from 6 April 1999, against dividends and similar income before other savings income (see 1.9 ALLOWANCES AND TAX RATES). [*ICTA 1988, s 689B; FA 1993, s 79(3); FA 1996, Sch 6 paras 16, 28, Sch 41 Pt V(1); F(No 2)A 1997, Sch 4 para 16, Sch 6 para 11*]. See also 81.3, 81.5 below for rules on trustees' expenses.

(c)   **Scottish trusts.** Provided that the trustees are UK resident, the rights of a beneficiary of a Scottish trust are deemed to include an equitable right in possession to any trust income to which such a right would have arisen if the trust had effect under the law of England and Wales. [*FA 1993, s 118*]. This enables such beneficiaries to obtain the benefit of the application of the lower rate of tax to dividend income.

(d)   **Demergers.** For the income and capital gains tax treatment of shares received by trustees as a result of exempt demergers under *ICTA 1988, s 213* (for which see Tolley's Corporation Tax under Groups of Companies), see Revenue Tax Bulletin October 1994 pp 162–165 and Revenue Capital Gains Tax Manual CG 33900 *et seq.*

(e)   Trustees are also liable to capital gains tax.

(f)   For the allocation of trust work amongst Revenue Trusts Offices, see Revenue Tax Bulletin April 2001 pp 842, 843.

81.3   **ASSESSMENTS ON TRUST INCOME**

General. Income may be assessed and charged on and in the name of any one or more of the trustees to whom settlement income arises, or (from 6 April 1998) in the year of assessment in which life assurance policy gains arise, and any subsequent trustees of the settlement. [*FA 1989, s 151; FA 1998, Sch 14 paras 6, 7*]. See also 78 SELF-ASSESSMENT.

The untaxed income of a trust within Schedules A or D may be assessed on the trustee as the person receiving it [*ICTA 1988, ss 21(1), 59(1)* and cf. *Reid's Trustees v CIR CS 1929, 14 TC 512*] but if, under his authority, it is paid direct to the beneficiary and he returns it under *TMA 1970, s 13*, he will not be assessable. [*TMA 1970, s 76*]. See also *Williams v Singer HL 1920, 7 TC 387* (trustees not assessable where overseas income paid direct to non-resident beneficiary) and compare *Kelly v Rogers CA 1935, 19 TC 692* (UK trustee of foreign trust held assessable in respect of overseas income as there was no ascertainable non-resident beneficiary entitled to the income) and *Dawson v CIR HL 1989, 62 TC 301* (sole UK resident trustee of foreign trust with three trustees held not assessable

81.4 Settlements

in respect of income not remitted). See, however, 65.5 RESIDENCE, ORDINARY RESIDENCE AND DOMICILE as regards special residence provisions. Held in *Pakenham HL 1928, 13 TC 573* that settlement trustees not assessable in respect of beneficiary's super-tax liability; presumably this will apply to excess liability.

Expenses of administering the trust are not deductible in the assessments on the trustee (*Aikin v Macdonald Trustees CES 1894, 3 TC 306*; *Inverclyde's Trustees v Millar CS 1924, 9 TC 14*) even though deductible in arriving at the beneficiaries' income as at 81.8 below.

In computing the amount of a beneficiary's taxable income from a trust, and subject to *ICTA 1988, s 689A* (see below), trust expenses, in so far as they are properly chargeable to income (or would be so chargeable but for any express provisions of the trust) are to be set firstly against certain specified types of income (for example, foreign income dividends, stock dividends) which carry a notional and non-repayable tax credit, secondly against other 'savings income' chargeable at the lower rate (see 1.9 ALLOWANCES AND TAX RATES) and finally against other income. From 6 April 1999, dividends and similar income (see 1.9 ALLOWANCES AND TAX RATES) are included in the income against which expenses are first set, and they are then set against foreign income equivalent to dividends etc. before other savings income. [*ICTA 1988, s 689B; FA 1996, Sch 6 paras 16, 28; F(No 2)A 1997, Sch 4 para 16, Sch 6 para 11*]. See the examples at 81.4 below.

Where a beneficiary is not liable to income tax on part of his share of the trust income, by virtue wholly or partly of his being non-UK resident or being deemed under a double tax agreement to be resident in a territory outside the UK, the management expenses otherwise deductible in computing his income are reduced in the same proportion as that which such non-taxable income bears to his full share of income (using in each case the income net of UK and foreign tax). Where the beneficiary's income tax liability is limited under the provisions at 51.1 NON-RESIDENTS AND OTHER OVERSEAS MATTERS, excluded income (see 51.1), other than that which is subject to deduction of tax at source, must be included in non-taxable income for the purposes of this apportionment. [*ICTA 1988, s 689A; FA 1996, Sch 6 paras 16, 28*].

A trustee may be required to make a return under *TMA 1970, s 8A* (as inserted by *FA 1990, s 90(1)*) of the income chargeable on him or on the settlor or beneficiaries. In practice, trustees normally make an annual statement of all the trust income, expenses etc. from which is ascertained any tax payable by the trustees and each beneficiary's share of the net trust income. Trustees are within the self-assessment regime (see 68.2 RETURNS, 78.3, 78.11 SELF-ASSESSMENT).

See 81.5 below for trustees' liability where trust income is accumulated.

81.4   *Examples*

A is sole life-tenant of a settlement which has income and expenses in the year 2004/05 of

	£	£
Property income		500
Taxed investment income (tax deducted at source £300)		1,500
Dividends	900	
Add Tax credits	100	
		1,000
		£3,000
Expenses chargeable to revenue		£400

The tax assessable on the trustees will be £110 (£500 at 22%). The expenses are not deductible in arriving at the tax payable by the trustees. The 10% starting rate band applies only to individual taxpayers and not to trustees, although the 10% Schedule F ordinary rate and the 20% rate on, respectively, dividend and interest income (see 1.9 ALLOWANCES AND TAX RATES) do apply to trustees.

A is sole life-tenant of the above settlement and as such is absolutely entitled to receive the whole settlement income.

A's income for 2004/05 will include the following.

	£	£	£
Trust dividend income (gross)	1,000		
Trust interest income		1,500	
Other trust income			500
Deduct: Schedule F ordinary rate tax (10%)	(100)		
Lower rate tax (20%)		(300)	
Basic rate tax (22%)			(110)
	900	1,200	390
Deduct Expenses (note (*b*))	400		
Net income entitlement	500	£1,200	£390
Grossed-up amounts: $£500 \times \frac{100}{90}$	£556		
$£1,200 \times \frac{100}{80}$		£1,500	
$£390 \times \frac{100}{78}$			£500

Notes

(*a*)   This income falls to be included in A's return even if it is not actually paid to him, as he is absolutely entitled to it. He will receive a tax certificate (form R185 (Trust Income)) from the trust agents, showing three figures for gross income (£556, £1,500 and £500), tax deducted (£56, £300 and £110) and net income (£500, £1,200 and £390).

(*b*)   The trust expenses are deducted from income falling within *ICTA 1988, s 1A* (savings income) in priority to other income, firstly against dividend and similar income and then against other savings income (see 81.3 above).

(*c*)   That part of A's trust income which is represented by dividend and other savings income (£500 and £1,200 net) is treated in A's hands as if it were such income received directly by A. It is thus chargeable at the Schedule F ordinary rate and lower rate only, the liability being satisfied by the 10% and 20% tax credit respectively, except to the extent, if any, that it exceeds his basic rate limit.

81.5   **DISCRETIONARY AND ACCUMULATION TRUSTS**

Income received by a trust which is to be accumulated, or payable at the discretion of the trustees or some other person, is taxed at the 'rate applicable to trusts' rather than at the basic or (where otherwise applicable, see 1.9 ALLOWANCES AND RATES) lower rate. The '*rate applicable to trusts*' is **40%** for 2004/05 onwards (previously 34%). For 1999/2000 onwards, a special 'Schedule F trust rate' applies, instead of the 'rate applicable to trusts', to 'Schedule F type income', i.e. income falling within any of the categories at (i)–(v) below. The '*Schedule F trust rate*' is **32.5%** for 2004/05 onwards (previously 25%).

(i)   UK company dividends and other distributions chargeable under Schedule F, and 'equivalent foreign income' (see 1.9 ALLOWANCES AND TAX RATES).

81.5 Settlements

(ii)   Qualifying distributions arising to non-UK resident trustees (who are thus not entitled to any tax credit).

(iii)   Distributions which are not qualifying distributions.

(iv)   Certain stock dividends and loans or advances written off or released which, by virtue of *ICTA 1988, s 249(6)(b)* or *s 421(1)(a)* respectively, are treated as giving rise to income of the trustees. (See also *Red Discretionary Trustees v Inspector of Taxes (Sp C 397) 2003, [2004] SSCD 132* as regards the application of the Schedule F trust rate to stock dividends.)

(v)   Distributions within *ICTA 1988, s 686A* (see below) consisting of the purchase etc. by a company of its own shares.

See Revenue Tax Bulletin February 1999 pp 629, 630 for an illustrative Revenue interpretation of the application of the Schedule F trust rate.

The special charge does not apply where (*a*) the trust is exempt as a charity (see 14 CHARITIES), (*b*) the income arises from property held for the purposes of certain retirement benefit or personal pension schemes, or (*c*) the income is income of any person other than the trustees or treated as income of a settlor (see 81.13 to 81.21 below). As regards (*c*), the position is considered *before* the income is distributed, so that income paid to the settlor's unmarried minor children does not fall within the exemption. The trustees may offset management expenses against trust income for the purpose of determining income chargeable at the rate applicable to trusts or the Schedule F trust rate, although income so relieved remains subject to basic rate, lower rate or Schedule F ordinary rate tax, as the case may be. They must, however, be expenses properly chargeable to income (or which would be so chargeable but for any express provisions of the trust) (see *Carver v Duncan; Bosanquet v Allen HL 1985, 59 TC 125*). The order of set-off, subject to the apportionment of expenses in the circumstances described below, is determined by *ICTA 1988, s 689B* (broadly first against dividend income, then against other savings income, and finally against other income) (see 81.3 above), disregarding for this purpose the fact that all income is in fact chargeable at the rate applicable to trusts or the Schedule F trust rate (the tax saving being the difference between whichever of those rates applies and the basic, lower or Schedule F ordinary rate, as appropriate to the class of income — see the examples at 81.6 below). Where the trust has income not chargeable to income tax, by virtue wholly or partly of the trustees being non-UK resident or being deemed under a double tax agreement to be resident in a territory outside the UK, the management expenses otherwise available for offset are reduced in the same proportion as that which such non-taxable income bears to the total trust income for the year. Where the trustees' income tax liability is limited under the provisions at 51.1 NON-RESIDENTS AND OTHER OVERSEAS MATTERS, excluded income (see 51.1), other than that which is subject to deduction of tax at source, must be included in non-taxable income for the purposes of this apportionment. 'Income' of the trustees for the purposes of these provisions includes income receipts by trustees (which will be treated as net of tax at the applicable rate) from personal representatives during administration of estate.

[*ICTA 1988, ss 686, 832(1); FA 1988, ss 24(4), 55(3); FA 1989, Sch 17 Pt V; FA 1990, Sch 5 para 13; FA 1993, Sch 6 para 8; FA 1995, Sch 17 para 13; FA 1996, Sch 6 paras 13, 15, 28; FA 1997, s 54(3)(4), Sch 7 para 12, Sch 18 Pt VI(1); F(No 2)A 1997, s 32; FA 2004, s 29*].

Certain payments made on the redemption, repayment or purchase by a company of its own shares, or on the purchase of rights to acquire its own shares, are treated as income to which *section 686* applies from, broadly, 5 December 1996 (see 3.20 ANTI-AVOIDANCE). With effect from 6 April 1999, following the repeal of those provisions, *ICTA 1988, s 686A* (introduced by *F(No 2)A 1997, s 32(9)(11)*) applies to similar effect (and see (v) above as regards applicable tax rate from that date).

For certain capital proceeds of mineral lease rents and timber cropping previously considered to be accumulations within *section 686*, see Revenue Tax Bulletin December 1996 p 374.

Where the income of the trustees includes a distribution other than a qualifying distribution, liability is restricted to the difference between the Schedule F trust rate (before 6 April 1999, the rate applicable to trusts) and the Schedule F ordinary rate (before 6 April 1999 the lower rate) on so much of the distribution as otherwise falls to be assessed at the Schedule F trust rate (or the rate applicable to trusts). [*ICTA 1988, s 233(1B); FA 1993, Sch 6 para 2; F(No 2)A 1997, Sch 4 para 6*]. Where the income of non-resident trustees includes a qualifying distribution which is grossed up at the Schedule F ordinary rate (see 1.9 ALLOWANCES AND RATES) or, before 6 April 1999, the lower rate, a credit is allowed for the Schedule F ordinary or lower rate tax (which may not, however, be repaid). [*ICTA 1988, s 233(1)(1A); FA 1993, Sch 6 para 2; FA 1996, s 122(3)(4); F(No 2)A 1997, Sch 4 para 6*]. See *ICTA 1988, s 246D(4)* (introduced by *FA 1994, Sch 16 para 1*) as regards receipt of foreign income dividends within *ICTA 1988, Pt VI, Ch VA* prior to their abolition from 6 April 1999.

Discretionary payments by trustees, if treated for tax purposes as income of the payee, are treated as net after tax at the rate applicable to trusts. This also applies to payments to the settlor's unmarried minor children which are treated under *ICTA 1988, s 660B* as the settlor's income (see 81.18 below). [*ICTA 1988, s 687(1)(2)(a); FA 1995, Sch 17 para 14*]. For whether a payment is received as income, see *Stevenson v Wishart and Others (Levy's Trustees) CA 1987, 59 TC 740*.

The tax treated as deducted from the payments is assessable on the trustees but the amount will be reduced by

(a) tax suffered by them at the rate applicable to trusts or, in the case of dividends and other distributions within Schedule F made after 5 April 1999, at the excess of the Schedule F trust rate over the Schedule F ordinary rate, and

(b) tax suffered up to 5 April 1973, which for this purpose is deemed to be two-thirds of net amount of income available for distribution at 5 April 1973.

Amounts of tax within (a) and (b) above are known collectively as the 'Section 687(3) tax pool'. After 5 April 1999, in contrast to the position previously, tax credits on UK dividends do not form part of this pool. See Revenue Tax Bulletins February 1999 p 630, June 2004 pp 1120, 1121. Certain notional tax credits, for example on scrip dividends, continue to be excluded from the pool as before.

[*ICTA 1988, s 687(2)(b)(3); FA 1989, s 96(2); FA 1990, Sch 5 para 14; FA 1993, s 79(2), Sch 6 para 9; FA 1994, Sch 16 para 15; FA 1996, Sch 14 para 35; F(No 2)A 1997, Sch 4 para 15, Sch 6 para 10*].

By concession, tax paid by trustees of a non-resident trust may, subject to conditions, similarly be set against any liability of the settlor under *section 660B*. (Revenue Pamphlet IR 1, A93; Revenue Press Release 1 April 1999).

Employee trusts which are discretionary trusts are, by concession, and subject to conditions as regards returns and evidence, able to reclaim from the Revenue tax at the rate applicable to trusts on payments to employee beneficiaries made in any year which are taxable earnings in the hands of the employees without credit being available for the tax deducted from the payments (but limited to the total tax which the trustees would have available to set against their liability in respect of payments to beneficiaries in the year). (Revenue Pamphlet IR 1, A68).

Taxed overseas income included in payments by trustees may be certified as such by them and recipient may claim appropriate double tax relief within six years of the end of the tax year in which the income arose to the trustees. [*ICTA 1988, s 809*].

81.5 Settlements

Where *section 687* applies (as above) to a payment made after 1 July 1997 to a company within the charge to corporation tax other than a charity (within *ICTA 1988, s 506(1)*, see 14.1 CHARITIES) or a body treated as a charity under *ICTA 1988, ss 507, 508* (see 29.3, 29.9, 29.14, 29.20 EXEMPT ORGANISATIONS, 77.1 SCIENTIFIC RESEARCH ASSOCIATIONS), the payment is disregarded for corporation tax purposes, and no credit is given, or repayment made, of the tax deducted. In the case of non-UK resident companies, this applies to so much (if any) of the payment as is comprised in the company's profits for corporation tax purposes. [*F(No 2)A 1997, s 27*].

Payments to beneficiaries — concessionary reliefs. A non-resident beneficiary of a UK resident discretionary trust who receives income treated as net of tax may claim relief in respect of the tax exemption on 'FOTRA' securities (see 33.2 GOVERNMENT STOCKS) or under the terms of a double taxation agreement, where such relief would have been available had the beneficiary received the income directly instead of through the trustees. Repayment may similarly be claimed where the beneficiary would not have been chargeable to UK tax in those circumstances. Relief is granted provided that the payment is out of income which arose to the trustees not earlier than six years before the end of the year of assessment in which the payment was made to the beneficiary. The trustees must have submitted trust returns supported by tax certificates and relevant information. For 1999/2000 and subsequent years, the trustees must also have paid all tax, interest, surcharge and penalties and keep available for inspection any relevant tax certificates, and the beneficiary must claim the relief or exemption within five years and ten months after the end of the year of assessment in which the payment was received from the trustees.

A similar concession applies where a beneficiary receives a payment from discretionary trustees which is not within *ICTA 1988, s 687(2)* (see above) (e.g. from a non-resident trust). A non-resident beneficiary who, had he received the income out of which the payment was made, would have been liable to UK tax thereon may claim relief under *ICTA 1988, s 278* (personal reliefs, see 51.10 NON-RESIDENTS AND OTHER OVERSEAS MATTERS) and may be treated as if he received the payment from a UK resident trust, but credit may be claimed only for UK tax actually paid by the trustees on the income out of which the payment was made. For 1999/2000 and later years, exemption may also be claimed in respect of income arising from 'FOTRA' securities (as above). A UK resident beneficiary of a non-UK resident trust may similarly claim credit for tax actually paid by the trustees on the income out of which the payment was made as if the payment were from a UK resident trust. In all cases, the trustees must have submitted trust returns supported by tax certificates and relevant information, and have paid tax under *section 686* (see above) at the applicable rate on the UK income of the trust. For 1999/2000 and subsequent years, the trustees must have paid *all* tax due and any interest, surcharge and penalties, and keep available for inspection any relevant tax certificates, and the beneficiary must claim the relief or exemption within five years and ten months after the end of the year of assessment in which the payment was received from the trustees. No credit is given for tax treated as paid on income received by the trustees which would not be available for set-off under *section 687(2)* (see above) if that section applied, and that tax is not repayable and is not taken into account in calculating the beneficiary's gross income.

(Revenue Pamphlet IR 1, B18; Revenue Press Release 1 April 1999).

However, where the beneficiary is resident in a country with which the UK has a double taxation agreement, and the 'Other Income' Article in that agreement gives sole taxing rights in respect of such income to that country, the above concession does not apply, and the tax paid by the trustees will be repaid in full to the beneficiary, subject to the conditions in the Article being met. (Revenue Pamphlet IR 131, SP 3/86, 2 April 1986).

Simon's Direct Tax Service. See C4.203.

81.6   *Examples*

An accumulation and maintenance settlement set up by W for his grandchildren in 1981 now comprises quoted investments and an industrial property. The property is let to an engineering company. Charges for rates, electricity etc. are paid by the trust and recharged yearly in arrears to the tenant. As a result of the delay in recovering the service costs, the settlement incurs overdraft interest.

The relevant figures for the year ended 5 April 2005 are as follows.

	£
Property rents (Schedule A)	40,000
UK dividends (including tax credits of £500)	5,000
Taxed interest (before tax deducted at source £700)	3,500
	£48,500

	£
Trust administration expenses — proportion chargeable to revenue	1,350
Overdraft interest	1,050
	£2,400

The tax liability of the trust for 2004/05 is as follows

	£	£
Schedule A £40,000 at 40%		16,000
Gross interest at 20% (40 – 20)		700
Net dividends	4,500	
Deduct Expenses	(2,400)	
	£2,100	
£2,100 grossed at $\frac{100}{90}$ = £2,333 @ 22.5% (32.5 – 10)		525
Tax payable by assessment		17,225
Add: Tax deducted at source		700
Tax credits		500
Total tax borne		£18,425

Notes

(*a*)   Expenses (including in this example the overdraft interest) are set firstly against the Schedule F income and then against the other savings income falling within *ICTA 1988, s 1A* before other income (*ICTA 1988, s 689B*). The effect is that the expenses, grossed-up at 10%, save tax at 22.5% (the difference between the 10% rate applicable to dividend income and the Schedule F trust rate of 32.5%).

(*b*)   The net revenue available for distribution to the beneficiaries, at the trustees' discretion, will be £27,675 (£48,500 – £18,425 – £2,400), but see note (*c*) below.

(*c*)   Of the tax borne, only £17,925 goes into the Section 687(3) tax pool. For 1999/2000 onwards, tax credits on dividends cannot enter the pool. Unless there is sufficient balance brought forward from earlier years, the effect is that if the whole of the distributable income is in fact distributed, there will be insufficient tax in the pool to frank the distribution (£27,675 × 40/60 = £18,450), and the trustees will have a further liability which they may not have the funds to settle.

81.7 Settlements

M, the 17-year old grandson of W, is one of the beneficiaries to whom the trustees can pay the settlement income. The trustees make a payment of £3,200 to M on 31 January 2005. He has no other income in the year 2004/05.

M's income from the trust is

	£
Net income	3,200.00
Tax at $\frac{40}{60}$	2,133.33
Gross income	£5,333.33

He can claim a tax repayment for 2004/05 of

	£
Total income	5,333
Deduct Personal allowance	4,745
	£588

Tax thereon at 10% (within starting rate band)	58.80
Tax accounted for by trustees	2,133.33
Repayment due	£2,074.53

Note

(a)   Unlike the position with interest in possession trusts (see 81.4 above), no distinction is made between dividend and interest income and other income in the beneficiary's hands, the full amount of the payment to him having suffered tax at a single rate of 40% in the hands of the trustees.

81.7   PERSONAL POSITION OF TRUSTEE

Annual remuneration paid to a trustee under a will or settlement is an annual payment within Case III of Schedule D from which tax is deductible at source, and is not chargeable on him under any other case or schedule (*Baxendale v Murphy KB 1924, 9 TC 76; Hearn v Morgan KB 1945, 26 TC 478* and cf. *Clapham's Trustees v Belton Ch D 1956, 37 TC 26*). Where a trustee is empowered to, and does, charge for his professional services, his fees are part of his receipts for Schedule D, Case II purposes (*Jones v Wright KB 1927, 13 TC 221*) even where he is also a beneficiary (*Watson & Everitt v Blunden CA 1933, 18 TC 402*).

81.8   INCOME OF BENEFICIARIES

In the case of life-tenants and those with similar interests in trust income, the beneficiary's income for tax purposes (see 81.2(b) above) is the grossed-up amount of the net income after deducting any trust outgoings payable out of the income (*Lord Hamilton of Dalzell CS 1926, 10 TC 406; Murray v CIR CS 1926, 11 TC 133; MacFarlane v CIR CS 1929, 14 TC 532*) — see 81.3 above re trust expenses generally. In other cases, the tax treatment of payments under a trust depends on the circumstances. Payments to a parent for the maintenance of children were held to be income of the children assessable on the parent in *Drummond v Collins HL 1915, 6 TC 525* (remittances to mother as guardian of minors, all resident in UK, of income of American trust) and *Johnstone v Chamberlain KB 1933, 17 TC 706*. Payments for the rates etc. and the super-tax of a beneficiary and payments for the maintenance of beneficiaries were held to be income in their hands in *Lord Tollemache v CIR KB 1926, 11 TC 277; Shanks v CIR CA 1928, 14 TC 249; Waley Cohen v CIR KB*

1945, 26 TC 471. In a number of cases, the outgoings of a residence provided for the beneficiary, grossed-up, have been held to be income of the beneficiary (*Donaldson's Exors v CIR CS 1927, 13 TC 461; Sutton v CIR CA 1929, 14 TC 662; Lady Miller v CIR HL 1930, 15 TC 25*). Income applied in reducing charges on the trust fund was held not to be income of the life-tenant (*Wemyss CS 1924, 8 TC 551*). Shares allotted to trustees in consideration of arrears of dividends were held to be income and not capital of the trust fund (*In re MacIver's Settlement Ch D 1935, 14 ATC 571*).

Interest on money loaned interest-free, subject to conditions and repayable on demand, by the employer to a trust for the benefit of an employee held to be emoluments within Schedule E (*O'Leary v McKinlay Ch D 1990, 63 TC 729*).

The tax treatment of income accumulated (e.g. during the minority of a beneficiary) has arisen in a number of cases. The test is whether the beneficiary's interest under the trust is vested or contingent. If vested, the accumulated income is his income as it arises. (N.B. If the accumulated income is the beneficiary's, 81.5 above does not apply. If the interest was contingent, see 81.12 below). Decision involves the general law of trusts, outside the scope of this book. For tax cases in which the accumulated income has been treated as income of the beneficiary, see *Gascoigne v CIR KB 1926, 13 TC 573; Stern v CIR HL 1930, 15 TC 148,* and *Brotherton v CIR CA 1978, 52 TC 137;* for cases where the income was held not to be the beneficiary's, see *Stanley v CIR CA 1944, 26 TC 12* (where the position under the *Trustee Act 1925, s 31* was considered); *Cornwell v Barry Ch D 1955, 36 TC 268,* and *Kidston CS 1936, 20 TC 603.* For the release of accumulated income on the termination of a trust, see *Hamilton-Russell's Exors v CIR CA 1943, 25 TC 200,* and on termination of legally permissible period of accumulation, see *Duncan v CIR CS 1931, 17 TC 1.*

See also 21 DECEASED ESTATES.

Simon's Direct Tax Service. See C4.220 *et seq.*

81.9 ANNUITIES AND OTHER ANNUAL PAYMENTS

Annuities and other annual payments under settlements or wills are subject to the normal rules for DEDUCTION OF TAX AT SOURCE (22). Annual remuneration to a trustee is an annual payment for this purpose (see 81.7 above). Where the annuity etc. is paid out of the capital of the trust fund, the tax deducted is assessed on the trustees under *ICTA 1988, s 350.* (Where tax is not deducted, the beneficiary may be assessed under Case III.) Payments out of capital may be directed or authorised by the settlor or testator, as where he directs a stipulated annual amount to be paid out of capital (*Jackson's Trustees v CIR KB 1942, 25 TC 13; Milne's Exors v CIR Ch D 1956, 37 TC 10*) or authorises the beneficiary's income to be augmented to a stipulated amount out of capital (*Brodie's Trustees v CIR KB 1933, 17 TC 432; Morant Settlement Trustees v CIR CA 1948, 30 TC 147*), or direct payments out of capital for the maintenance etc. of the recipient (*Lindus & Hortin v CIR KB 1933, 17 TC 442; Esdaile v CIR CS 1936, 20 TC 700*) even though discretionary (*Cunard's Trustees v CIR CA 1945, 27 TC 122*). For position if annuity exceeds income of fund on which charged, see *Lady Castlemaine KB 1943, 25 TC 408.* Annuities directed to be paid out of capital but paid out of accumulated income forming part of the capital were held to have been paid out of income (*Postlethwaite v CIR Ch D 1963, 41 TC 244*).

For 'free of tax' annuities, see 22.17 DEDUCTION OF TAX AT SOURCE.

81.10 FOREIGN TRUST INCOME

There are no special provisions for the income tax treatment of foreign trust income. For the liability of trustees within the jurisdiction as regards foreign trust income, see the case of *Williams v Singer, Dawson v CIR* and *Kelly v Rogers* at 81.3 above.

The income of a life-tenant of a foreign trust fund depends first on the nature of his interest under the relevant foreign law. See for this the cases of *Archer-Shee v Baker HL 1927, 11*

81.11   Settlements

TC 749 and *Garland v Archer-Shee HL 1930, 15 TC 693,* dealing with the same life-tenancy. In the first, with no evidence as to the foreign law, the life-tenant was held to be assessable on the basis that the investments forming part of the fund were separate foreign possessions or securities. In the second case, relating to later years, it was held that having regard to evidence given as to the foreign law, she was assessable on the basis that the income was from a single foreign possession. (N.B. The decisions have lost some of their practical importance because of subsequent changes in the basis rules of Schedule D, Cases IV and V, but the principles established remain important.) See also *Nelson v Adamson KB 1941, 24 TC 36* and *Inchyra v Jennings Ch D 1965, 42 TC 388.* Stock dividends received by trustees of an American trust fund were part of the trust income under the relevant American law but held not to be income of a UK life-tenant, as not of an income nature under UK principles (*Lawson v Rolfe Ch D 1969, 46 TC 199*).

Discretionary remittances from foreign trustees are assessable and become income when the discretion is exercised (*Drummond v Collins HL 1915, 6 TC 525*) but cf. *Lawson v Rolfe,* see 73.3 SCHEDULE D, CASES IV AND V.

See 51.13 NON-RESIDENTS AND OTHER OVERSEAS MATTERS for unremittable foreign income and 73 SCHEDULE D, CASES IV AND V for assessments on overseas income generally.

81.11   CLAIMS BY TRUSTEES AND BENEFICIARIES

Only such claims as relate to the Trust can be made by the trustee — except as regards incapacitated persons for whom he is assessable, e.g., under *TMA 1970, s 72.* [*TMA 1970, s 42(6)*]. Beneficiaries other than these must claim in their own (or husband's) name. See 81.2(*b*) and 81.5 above. Beneficiaries claiming refund on their share of trust income must each make a separate claim showing their total income from all sources and tax paid on it.

In claim by non-resident life-tenants of residue subject to annuity, held that (where no 'appropriation') latter not to be treated as paid out of UK taxed income but rateably out of all investments. (*Crawshay CA 1935, 19 TC 715*).

81.12   CLAIMS FOR PERSONAL ALLOWANCES ETC. ON INCOME UP TO 1968/69 — FROM SPECIFIED 'CONTINGENT INTERESTS' ON OBTAINING A SPECIFIED AGE OR MARRYING

Under *ITA 1952, s 228,* where an individual has an interest under a will or settlement that is contingent on his or her attaining a specified age or marrying, and income is directed to be accumulated meantime, claims by that individual for personal allowances etc. may be made within six years after the end of the tax year in which the contingency happens, in respect of all income so compulsorily accumulated prior to 6 April 1969. [*ICTA 1970, Sch 14 para 1*]. Such claims cannot be made in respect of income which is deemed to be the income of the settlor as below. See 41 INTEREST ON OVERPAID TAX.

Where income is legally vested in beneficiaries, relief as above is refused; it is important, therefore, to ascertain whether income legally vested or contingent (*Roberts v Hanks KB 1926, 10 TC 351; Jones v Down KB 1936, 20 TC 279*), and when the 'contingency' happens (*Stonely v Ambrose KB 1925, 9 TC 389,* and *Lynch v Davies Ch D 1962, 40 TC 511*).

The section applies only when the contingency is the claimant's attainment of a specified age or marriage (*Bone CS 1927, 13 TC 20* and *White v Whitcher KB 1927, 13 TC 202*). Claimant's right must depend solely on happening of one of these contingencies *and on nothing else,* and no claim can be made if right to receive income is wholly at trustee's discretion (*Dain v Miller KB 1934, 18 TC 478,* and see *Maude-Roxby CS 1950, 31 TC 388*). See also *Cusden v Eden KB 1939, 22 TC 435* as to accumulations.

Tax on income accumulated but directed to be capitalised on happening of contingency may nevertheless be claimed under this section (*Dale v Mitcalfe CA 1927, 13 TC 41*).

The amount recovered belongs to the beneficiary (*Fulford v Hyslop Ch D 1929, 8 ATC 588*). In *Chamberlain v Haig Thomas KB 1933, 17 TC 595* where accumulations directed (from 1913 onwards) for infant children subject to power of appointment (which not in fact exercised until 1922), section held to apply to income of intervening period.

81.13 LIABILITY OF SETTLOR

In 81.17, 81.18 below, there are set out the provisions of *ICTA 1988, ss 660A, 660B*, introduced by *FA 1995, s 74, Sch 17*, which treat the income of settlements as the income of the settlor in certain circumstances. They are intended as a simplification of those in *ICTA 1988, ss 660–676, ss 679–681* and *ss 683–685* which applied for 1994/95 and earlier years and which they replaced. [*FA 1995, s 74(2)*]. The rules in *ICTA 1988, ss 677, 678* dealing with loans etc. to the settlor continue to apply and are covered at 81.19 below. The Finance Act 1995 provisions are divided into two areas:

(*a*)   income under settlements where settlor retains an interest [*ICTA 1988, s 660A*] (see 81.17 below); and

(*b*)   payments out of, or, in certain cases, income accumulated in, a settlement to or for an unmarried minor child of the settlor [*ICTA 1988, s 660B*] (see 81.18 below).

Settlors have an obligation to notify their tax office of any liability under the new provisions even if they do not normally receive a tax return. (Revenue Press Release 4 January 1995).

Simon's Direct Tax Service. See **C4.301** *et seq.*

81.14 Exclusion for income given to charity.

81.14   **Exclusion for income given to charity.** *ICTA 1988, ss 660A, 660B* do not apply to 'qualifying income' which arises to a 'UK trust' after 5 April 2000 and which either

(*a*)   is given by the trustees to a 'charity' in the tax year in which it arises, or

(*b*)   is income to which a 'charity' is entitled under the terms of the trust.

For these purposes, a '*UK trust*' is a trust the trustees of which are UK-resident, for which see the appropriate rules at 65.5 RESIDENCE, ORDINARY RESIDENCE AND DOMICILE. '*Charity*' has the meaning in 14.1 CHARITIES but also includes the bodies listed in *ICTA 1988, s 507* (see 29.3, 29.9, 29.14, 29.20 EXEMPT ORGANISATIONS). '*Qualifying income*' is widely defined to cover the income of accumulation, discretionary and interest in possession trusts.

Where the qualifying income arises from different sources (e.g. interest, dividends etc.) and *part* of that income for any tax year is excluded as above, the remainder is rateably apportioned for tax purposes between the different sources. However, this rule is overridden by any requirement in the terms of the trust that the whole or part of a *particular* source of income be given to charity. Any trust management expenses are rateably apportioned between income excluded as above, with the effect that relief is to that extent available for such expenses, and any remainder.

Where there is more than one settlor, *ICTA 1988, s 660E* (see 81.16(*c*) below) is applied *before* taking account of the above provisions.

[*FA 2000, s 44*].

81.15   **The charge to tax** under *ICTA 1988, ss 660A, 660B* is under Schedule D, Case VI (except for dividends and other distributions (and certain similar types of income), which are chargeable as for dividend income generally (see 1.9 ALLOWANCES AND TAX RATES)). Income treated under these provisions as income of the settlor is deemed to be the top slice of his income, but before taking into account income chargeable under *ITEPA 2003, s 403*

81.16 Settlements

(payments on loss of office, see 18.5 COMPENSATION FOR LOSS OF EMPLOYMENT (AND DAMAGES)) or *ICTA 1988, s 547(1)(a)* (life assurance gains, see 45.13 LIFE ASSURANCE POLICIES). The same deductions and reliefs are allowed as if the income had actually been received by the settlor. *[ICTA 1988, s 660C; FA 1995, Sch 17 para 1; F(No 2)A 1997, Sch 4 para 14]*. The settlor is entitled to recover the tax paid from any trustee or any person to whom the income is payable under the settlement, and to that end can obtain from the Revenue a certificate specifying the amount of income charged on him and the tax paid. If the settlor receives a tax repayment by virtue of setting an allowance or relief against income chargeable on him under these provisions, he must pay it over to the trustee or any person(s) to whom the income is payable under the settlement, with the General Commissioners having the final decision on any question as to the amount payable or how it should be apportioned. Nothing in these provisions precludes tax being charged on the trustees as persons by whom any income is received. *[ICTA 1988, s 660D; FA 1995, Sch 17 para 1]*.

Revenue information powers. An officer of the Board can, by notice, require from any party to a settlement such particulars as he thinks necessary (subject to penalty under *TMA 1970, s 98* for non-compliance). *[ICTA 1988, s 660F; FA 1995, Sch 17 paras 1, 23]*. See *Cutner v CIR QB 1974, 49 TC 429* and *Wilover Nominees v CIR CA 1974, 49 TC 559* in connection with similar information powers under the pre-Finance Act 1995 provisions.

81.16   **Definitions etc.** The following apply for the purposes of *ICTA 1988, ss 660A, 660B*, covered in 81.17, 81.18 below.

(a)   '*Settlement*' includes any disposition, trust, covenant, agreement, arrangement or transfer of assets. *[ICTA 1988, s 660G(1); FA 1995, Sch 17 para 1]*. The latter includes a gift of shares (*Hood Barrs v CIR CA 1946, 27 TC 385*) or of National Savings Bank deposit (*Thomas v Marshall HL 1953, 34 TC 178*). For shares in new company issued at par, see *Butler v Wildin Ch D 1988, [1989] STC 22*. See also *Yates v Starkey CA 1951, 32 TC 38* re Court Orders and *Harvey v Sivyer Ch D 1985, 58 TC 569* re provision for children whether under compulsion or not.

The creation of a new class of preference shares in a company, and their allotment to the wives of the directors, who had previously also been the sole shareholders, was held to be a settlement by the directors (*Young v Pearce; Young v Scrutton Ch D 1996, 70 TC 331*).

Revenue views on settlements not involving trusts. The Revenue have published guidance, including some examples, as to how they apply the settlements legislation at *ICTA 1988, ss 660A, 660B* in situations not involving trusts and especially in relation to businesses carried on by companies and partnerships. Situations in which the settlements legislation might be applied include: the issue or gifting of shares (to spouses or other relatives, for example) carrying no right (or a restricted right) to a share of the assets on a winding-up, and the payment of dividends on those shares; the issue or gifting to another person, typically a spouse, of shares in a company with minimal capital value that derives its income from the work of one person; the gifting, or transfer at undervalue, of a share of profits in a partnership; the waiving of dividends by one or more shareholders so that other shareholders can receive larger dividends; the payment of larger dividends than would otherwise be possible on one or more classes of shares but not on others; and the gifting to children of share by a parent, or by someone other than a parent where the company's profits, and decisions on the level of dividends, are made by a parent. The guidance also includes examples of situations in which the settlements legislation would not be applied, mainly involving transactions in which there is no element of bounty and outright gifts between spouses which are not wholly or substantially a right to income (see 81.17(*a*) below). (Revenue Tax Bulletin April 2003 pp 1011–1016).

A detailed joint response by seven professional bodies, including CIOT and ICAEW, was published on 11 September 2003 (and reproduced at *2003 STI 1605* and at www.tax.org.uk/attach.pl/1932/753/s660A%20paper%20final100903.doc).   This reflects the bodies' concerns both as to the Revenue's interpretation of the settlements legislation as summarised above and as to its retrospective nature and makes clear that they do not accept a number of key technical issues that underpin the above guidance.

The Revenue responded with a further article. It contains no relaxation of their views. The examples included in the original article are revisited purely for the purpose of setting out the entries required on self-assessment tax returns where the settlements legislation applies. A number of new examples are also included. (Revenue Tax Bulletin February 2004 pp 1085–1094).

Miscellaneous. Parent's release of expectant life interest is a settlement (*Buchanan CA 1957, 37 TC 365*) and see *D'Abreu v CIR Ch D 1978, 52 TC 352.*

A distinction can be made between arrangements which amount to a settlement and bona fide commercial transactions without any element of bounty which do not (*Copeman v Coleman KB 1939, 22 TC 594*; *Bulmer v CIR Ch D 1966, 44 TC 1*) and this notwithstanding that tax avoidance was a motive for the transactions (*CIR v Plummer HL 1979, 54 TC 1*). See also *CIR v Levy Ch D 1982, 56 TC 67*. For whether 'arrangements' are a settlement, see also *Prince-Smith KB 1943, 25 TC 84*; *Pay Ch D 1955, 36 TC 109*; *Crossland v Hawkins CA 1961, 39 TC 493*; *Leiner Ch D 1964, 41 TC 589*; *Wachtel Ch D 1970, 46 TC 543*; *Mills v CIR HL 1974, 49 TC 367*; *Chinn v Collins HL 1980, 54 TC 311*; *Butler v Wildin Ch D 1988, 61 TC 666.*

For 'property comprised in a settlement', see *Vestey v CIR HL 1949, 31 TC 1*. Where the settlement is of shares in a company controlled by the settlor, the assets of the company are not comprised in the settlement (*Chamberlain v CIR HL 1943, 25 TC 317*; *Langrange Trust v CIR HL 1947, 28 TC 55*).

Where the trust is imperfect, income not disposed of reverts to the settlor (*Hannay's Exors v CIR CS 1956, 37 TC 217*).

A foreign settlement of UK income by a non-resident was held to be within the ambit of the pre-Finance Act 1995 settlements legislation (*Kenmare HL 1957, 37 TC 383*).

A settlement does not include any arrangement consisting of a loan of money by an individual to a charity (as defined in 81.14 above) either for no consideration or for a consideration consisting only of interest. This exclusion has effect in relation to income arising after 5 April 2000 on any such loans, whenever made. [*FA 2000, s 45*]. Previously, an interest-free or low interest loan to a charity constituted a settlement, with the result that any income received by the charity on investment of the loan monies could be treated as the lender's income; it is understood that the Revenue did not always apply this in practice. (Treasury Explanatory Notes to Finance Bill 2000).

(*b*)   '*Settlor*', in relation to a settlement, means any person by whom the settlement was made. A person is deemed to have made a settlement if he has made or entered into it directly or indirectly and/or has provided or undertaken to provide funds directly or indirectly for the purpose of the settlement or has made reciprocal arrangements for another person to make or enter into the settlement. [*ICTA 1988, s 660G(1)(2); FA 1995, Sch 17 para 1*]. See *Crossland v Hawkins CA 1961, 39 TC 493, Leiner Ch D 1964, 41 TC 589* and *Mills HL 1974, 49 TC 367.*

(c)   If there is *more than one settlor*. Each is to be treated as the sole settlor, but only in respect of income or property he has himself provided, directly or indirectly. [*ICTA 1988, s 660E; FA 1995, Sch 17 para 1; FA 1999, s 64(7)*].

(d)   '*Income arising under a settlement*' includes any income chargeable to income tax, by deduction or otherwise, or which would have been so chargeable if received in the UK by a person domiciled, resident and ordinarily resident in the UK, but not income on which the settlor, if he were himself entitled to it, would not have been chargeable by reason of non-domicile, non-residence etc. (but such income *is* treated as arising under the settlement in a year of assessment in which it is subsequently remitted to the UK if, were the settlor entitled to the income when remitted, he would be chargeable to income tax by reason of his UK residence). [*ICTA 1988, s 660G(3)(4); FA 1995, Sch 17 para 1*].

(e)   *Payment of inheritance tax by trustees on assets put into settlement by settlor.* Where the trustees have power to pay, or do in fact pay, inheritance tax on assets which the settlor puts into the settlement, the Revenue will not argue that such a power renders that income the settlor's income for income tax purposes. This is because both the settlor and the trustees are liable for such inheritance tax. (Revenue Pamphlet IR 131, SP 1/82, 6 April 1982).

81.17   **SETTLOR RETAINING AN INTEREST** [*ICTA 1988, s 660A; FA 1995, Sch 17 para 1; FA 2000, Sch 13 para 26*]

See also 81.13, 81.14, 81.16 above.

Income arising under a settlement during the life of the settlor is treated for all income tax purposes as the income of the settlor (and not of any other person), *unless* the income arises from property in which the settlor has no interest (see below).

For the purposes of these provisions, a settlement does not include:

(a)   an outright gift between spouses of property from which income arises (but a gift which does not carry a right to the whole of that income is not excluded, nor is a gift of a right to income); or

(b)   (for 2000/01 and earlier years) an irrevocable allocation of pension rights between spouses under a relevant statutory scheme (see 67.1 RETIREMENT SCHEMES) (and see (iv) below as regards wider exclusion in later years).

As regards (a) above, a gift is not an outright gift if it is conditional or if the property or any 'derived property' could in any circumstances become payable to the donor or be applied for his benefit.

The following income is excluded from these provisions:

(i)   income arising under a marriage settlement made between spouses after separation, divorce or annulment, being income payable to or for the benefit of the spouse being provided for;

(ii)   annual payments by an individual for *bona fide* commercial reasons in connection with his trade, profession or vocation;

(iii)   qualifying donations within 14.13 CHARITIES made after 5 April 2000, and both qualifying donations and covenanted payments to charity made before 6 April 2000 (see 14.16, 14.17 CHARITIES); and

(iv)   (for 2001/02 and subsequent years) benefits under 'approved pension arrangements' (as widely defined).

A settlor has an *interest in property* if that property or any 'derived property' could in any circumstances become payable to the settlor or his spouse or be applied for the benefit of either. For this purpose, a spouse does not include a possible future spouse, a separated spouse or a widow/widower of the settlor. A settlor does *not* have an interest in property if it could become so payable or be so applied only in the event of

(A)   the bankruptcy of a current or potential beneficiary,

(B)   an assignment of, or charge on, the property or 'derived property' being made or given by a current or potential beneficiary,

(C)   in the case of a marriage settlement, the death of both spouses and all or any of their children, or

(D)   the death of a child of the settlor who has become beneficially entitled to the property etc. at an age not exceeding 25,

or if (and so long as) there is a beneficiary alive under the age of 25 during whose life the property etc. cannot become so payable etc. except in the event of the beneficiary becoming bankrupt or assigning or charging his interest.

'*Derived property*', in relation to any property, means income from that property or any other property directly or indirectly representing proceeds of, or of income from, that property or income therefrom.

Simon's Direct Tax Service. See **C4.310–C4.312.**

81.18   **CHILDREN'S SETTLEMENTS** [*ICTA 1988, s 660B; FA 1995, Sch 17 para 1; FA 1999, s 64*]

See also 81.13, 81.14, 81.16 above.

Income arising under a settlement which during the life of the settlor is paid to or for the benefit of an unmarried minor child (i.e. a child under 18, including a stepchild or illegitimate child) of the settlor in any year of assessment is treated for all income tax purposes as income of the settlor (and not of any other person) for that year. However, this does *not* apply for any tax year if the aggregate amount that would otherwise be treated as the settlor's income for that year in relation to any particular child does not exceed £100. Nor does it apply if the income falls to be treated under 81.17 above as that of the settlor.

As regards income arising under a settlement made on or after 9 March 1999, and income arising directly or indirectly from funds added on or after that date to a pre-existing settlement (any necessary apportionment being made on a just and reasonable basis), the provisions are extended to apply the same treatment as above to undistributed income which would otherwise be treated as income of an unmarried minor child of the settlor in any year of assessment. This is intended to catch income accumulated in a bare trust. The above-mentioned £100 limit applies, per parent per child, by reference to the aggregate of income paid out or accumulated.

Retained or accumulated income. Any payment made on or after 9 March 1999 under the settlement to or for the child is taken into account as above to the extent that there is available retained or accumulated income, i.e. aggregate income arising since the settlement was entered into exceeds the aggregate amount of such income which has been:

(*a*)   treated as income of the settlor; or

(*b*)   paid (as income or capital) to or for the benefit of, or otherwise treated as the income of, a beneficiary other than an unmarried minor child of the settlor; or

(*c*)   treated as the income of an unmarried minor child of the settlor, and 'subject to tax', in any of the years 1995/96, 1996/97 or 1997/98; or

(*d*)   used to pay expenses of the trustees which were properly chargeable to income (or would have been so chargeable but for express provisions of the trust).

For the purposes of (*c*) above, the income so treated is '*subject to tax*' to the extent that it does not exceed the child's taxable income (i.e. total income, inclusive of the settlement income, after allowances and deductions). For payments made before 9 March 1999, similar rules applied as above, the main difference being that any income treated as the income of an unmarried minor child, whether charged to tax or not, was deductible in arriving at available retained or accumulated income.

Any provision by a parent for his child may create a settlement, whether made under compulsion or merely under parental obligation (*Harvey v Sivyer Ch D 1985, 58 TC 569*), although in practice the Revenue do not treat payments made under a Court Order as being under a settlement for this purpose. '*Stepchild*' includes a child of the wife by a previous marriage (*CIR v Russell CS 1955, 36 TC 83*).

Simon's Direct Tax Service. See **C4.315, C4.316.**

81.19 **CAPITAL SUMS, LOANS AND REPAYMENTS OF LOANS TO SETTLOR FROM SETTLEMENT OR CONNECTED BODY CORPORATE — TREATED AS INCOME OF SETTLOR TO EXTENT THAT SETTLEMENT HAS UNDISTRIBUTED INCOME** [*ICTA 1988, ss 677, 678*]

Where in any year of assessment the trustees of a settlement pay any 'capital sum' to the settlor or spouse (or to the settlor jointly with another person), such an amount (grossed up at the rate applicable to trusts) is treated as income of the settlor to the extent that it falls within the amount of 'income available in the settlement' up to the end of that year of assessment or, to the extent that it does not fall within that amount, to the end of the next and subsequent years of assessment up to a maximum of eleven years after the year of payment. [*ICTA 1988, s 677(1)(6)(9); FA 1993, Sch 6 para 7*]. There is a corresponding deduction for any amount included in the settlor's income under *ICTA 1988, s 421* (see 27.3(*a*) EXCESS LIABILITY) in respect of a loan. [*ICTA 1988, s 677(3)*]. See also 81.21 below.

Any 'capital sum' paid before 6 April 1981 and not treated as income under these provisions before that date is for these purposes treated as having been paid on that date. [*FA 1982, s 63(4)*].

'*Income available in the settlement*' up to the end of any tax year is the aggregate amount of income arising under the settlement (see 81.16 above), for that and any previous year, which has not been distributed, less

(*a*)   any amount of that income which has already been 'matched' against a capital payment for assessment on the settlor (see above), and

(*b*)   any income taken into account under these provisions in relation to capital sums previously paid to the settlor, and

(*c*)   sums treated as income of the settlor under *ICTA 1988, ss 671–674A, s 683* or *ss 660A, 660B* (see 81.13–81.18 above), and

(*d*)   sums not allowed as an income deduction to the settlor under *ICTA 1988, s 676*, and

(*e*)   sums from an accumulation settlement for children treated as income of the settlor under *ICTA 1988, s 664(2)(b)*, and

(*f*)   the tax at the rate applicable to trusts on the accumulated undistributed income less the amounts in (*c*) to (*e*) above.

[*ICTA 1988, s 677(2); FA 1993, Sch 6 para 7; FA 1995, Sch 17 para 9; FA 2004, Sch 4 paras 1, 3*].

'*Capital sum*' includes a loan or loan repayment and any other sum (other than income) paid otherwise than for full consideration (but excluding sums which could not have become payable to the settlor except in one of the events mentioned in 81.17(A)–(D) above (or on the death under the age of 25 of the person referred to in the paragraph following 81.17(A)–(D) above) or under earlier legislation. [*ICTA 1988, s 677(9); FA 1995, Sch 17 para 9*]. As regards loans and repayment of loans, see *Potts' Exors v CIR HL 1950, 32 TC 211; De Vigier HL 1964, 42 TC 24; Bates v CIR HL 1966, 44 TC 225; McCrone v CIR CS 1967, 44 TC 142; Wachtel Ch D 1970, 46 TC 543* and *Piratin v CIR Ch D 1981, 54 TC 730.*

There is also treated as a capital sum paid to the settlor any sum paid to a third party at the settlor's direction or by assignment of his right to receive it (where the direction or assignment is after 5 April 1981) and any other sum otherwise paid or applied for the settlor's benefit. [*ICTA 1988, s 677(10)*].

Loan to settlor. Where the capital sum represents a loan to the settlor, there will be no tax charge on him for any tax year after the year in which the loan is repaid. If previous loans have been made and wholly repaid, any new loan will only be charged on its excess, if any, over so much of the earlier loans as have been treated as his income. [*ICTA 1988, s 677(4)*].

Repayment to settlor of loan. Where the capital sum is repayment of a loan by a settlor, a charge arises on him but will not apply for any year after the year in which he makes a further loan at least equal in amount to the loan repaid. [*ICTA 1988, s 677(5)*].

The tax charge under Schedule D, Case VI on the settlor is at the rate or rates in excess of the rate applicable to trusts (i.e. he will receive credit for the grossing up at that rate). For 2004/05 onwards, the credit is restricted to the tax actually paid by the trustees on the equivalent amount of income. Such deductions and reliefs are allowed as would have been given if the sum treated as income had actually been received as income. [*ICTA 1988, s 677(7)(7A)–(7C)(8); FA 1993, Sch 6 para 7; FA 2004, Sch 4 paras 1, 3*].

ICTA 1988, ss 660E (more than one settlor — see 81.16 above), *660F* (Revenue information powers — see 81.15 above) and *660G* (definitions — see 81.16 above) apply for the purposes of these provisions as they apply for those of *ICTA 1988, ss 660A, 660B*. [*ICTA 1988, s 682A; FA 1995, Sch 17 para 11*].

Payment of IHT by trustees, see 81.16 above.

Connected companies. A capital sum (as above) paid to a settlor by a company connected with the settlement (see 19.8 CONNECTED PERSONS) is treated as paid to him by the trustees of the settlement irrespective of whether or not the funds originated from that settlement if there has been an 'associated payment' (made directly or indirectly) to the company (or to another company associated with that company under *ICTA 1988, s 416* at that time) from the settlement (which, before 6 April 1995, was assumed to be the case unless the settlor showed otherwise). Such company payments to the settlor in a tax year will be 'matched' with associated payments from the trustees to the company up to the end of that year (less any amounts already 'matched') in order to determine the amount deemed paid to the settlor by the trustees in the year, any 'unmatched' balance being 'matched' with associated payments in subsequent years. Such amounts are then 'matched' with the 'income available in the settlement' as above. [*ICTA 1988, s 678(1)(2)(4)(5)(7); FA 1995, Sch 17 para 10*].

'*Associated payment*' is any capital sum paid, or any other sum paid or asset transferred for less than full consideration, to the company by the trustees within five years before or after the capital sum paid to the settlor by the company. [*ICTA 1988, s 678(3)*].

Loans. The above provisions do not apply to any payment to the settlor by way of loan or repayment of a loan if (i) the whole of the loan is repaid within twelve months and (ii) the

81.20 Settlements

total period during which loans are outstanding in any period of five years does not exceed twelve months. [*ICTA 1988, s 678(6)*].

Simon's Direct Tax Service. See C4.321–C4.324.

81.20 *Example*

The trustees of a settlement with undistributed income of £1,375 at 5 April 2002 made a loan of £15,000 to B, the settlor, on 30 September 2002.
B repays the loan on 31 December 2004. Undistributed income of £3,500 arose in 2002/03, £6,500 in 2003/04 and £5,500 in 2004/05. B has taxable income of £40,000 in each year (excluding savings income). The trustees duly settle all their liabilities to tax on trust income.

B will be treated as receiving the following income.

		£
2002/03	£4,875 × $\frac{100}{66}$	7,386
2003/04	£6,500 × $\frac{100}{66}$	9,848
2004/05	£3,625 × note (*a*)	6,041

B will pay additional tax of

		£
2002/03	£7,386 at 6% (40% – 34%)	443
2003/04	£9,848 at 6% (40% – 34%)	591
2004/05	£6,041 at 0% (40% – 40%)	—
		£1,034

Note

(*a*) The amount treated as income in 2004/05 is limited to the amount of the loan less amounts previously treated as income (£15,000 – (£4,875 + £6,500)).

81.21 **MAINTENANCE FUNDS FOR HISTORIC BUILDINGS — TAX EXEMPTION FOR SETTLORS ETC.** [*ICTA 1988, s 691*]

Where the Treasury has directed under *IHTA 1984, Sch 4 para 1* that funds put into a settlement for the maintenance, repair or preservation of qualifying property are exempt for inheritance tax purposes, the trustees may elect in writing for any year of assessment that (*a*) any income arising shall not be treated as income of the settlor (see 81.13 to 81.20 above) and (*b*) any sum applied for the purposes (as above) of the settlement shall not be treated as income of any person by virtue of his interest in, or occupation of, the building or land or by virtue of *ICTA 1988, s 677* (see 81.19 above). The election must be made within, for 1996/97 and later years, twelve months after 31 January following the year of assessment to which it relates (for earlier years, two years after the end of that year of assessment). If no election made, then (*b*) still applies to any sums so applied in excess of the income for that tax year. Under certain circumstances, an election (as above) may be made separately for different parts of a year of assessment. [*ICTA 1988, ss 690, 691; FA 1996, s 135, Sch 21 para 19*].

An income tax charge will arise when any property (whether capital or income) of a fund is applied for purposes other than within a Treasury direction as above (i.e. (i) the maintenance of, or public access to, the property, or (ii) for the benefit of specified national bodies, or (iii) for charities whose sole or main object is the preservation for public benefit of buildings, land etc. of historic, national etc. interest) or when any settlement property devolves on any body or charity other than mentioned in (ii) or (iii). The charge will also apply if property devolves on a body or charity mentioned in (ii) and (iii) *and* at or before that time an interest under the settlement is or has been acquired for money or money's worth by that or another such body or charity (but any acquisition from another such body or charity will be disregarded). The charge is on all income which has arisen from the property since the last charge under this provision or, otherwise, since the creation of the settlement, and has not been applied as in (i), (ii) or (iii) above. The charge will not apply to income which is treated as income of the settlor under *ICTA 1988, ss 660–689* (see 81.13 *et seq.* above) and sums applied otherwise than in (i) to (iii) above will be treated as paid first out of such income treated as the settlor's and only the excess charged in this way. There is no charge where the whole of the settlement property is transferred to another exempt settlement within 30 days of any charge otherwise arising as above or where immediately before and after the transfer the property is subject to a Treasury direction as above. The charge is assessed on the trustees and is in addition to tax charged under any other provision. The rate of charge is the higher rate of income tax *less* the rate applicable to trusts, i.e. 6% from 1996/97 to 2003/04 inclusive. [*ICTA 1988, s 694; FA 1993, Sch 6 para 10; FA 1995, Sch 17 para 16; FA 1997, s 54(3); FA 2004, Sch 4 para 2*].

Reimbursement of settlor. Where a settlor incurs expenditure on the maintenance of an historic building which the Treasury has approved for the purposes of capital transfer or inheritance tax (under *IHTA 1984, Sch 4 para 1*, see above) and the settlor is carrying on a trade of showing the property to the public or a SCHEDULE A (69) business, and that expenditure is reimbursed to the settlor by the trustees of the settlement, then the reimbursement will not reduce the expenditure deductible in computing the profits of the trade or business and will only be taxed as income of the settlor under *ICTA 1988, ss 660–685* (see 81.13 to 81.20 above). [*ICTA 1988, s 692; FA 1995, Sch 6 para 26*].

Simon's Direct Tax Service. See C4.340–C4.342.

82 Share-Related Employment Income and Exemptions

(See Revenue Pamphlets IR 16, 17, 95 to 98, 101, 102, 2002, 2005 and 2006 and the Revenue's dedicated website at www.inlandrevenue.gov.uk/shareschemes)

Simon's Direct Tax Service E4.5.

82.1   For general tax liability in respect of shares given to directors or other employees as part of their employment income, see 75.39 SCHEDULE E—EMPLOYMENT INCOME. For tax deductions (against trading profits etc.) available to employer companies in connection with employee share schemes, see 71.44 SCHEDULE D, CASES I AND II.

The expression 'shares' is used in this chapter in its broadest sense. For the application of the chapter to stocks and securities, as well as shares, see 82.3 below.

82.2   Legislation applies where there are arrangements to allow a person to acquire shares by reason of their (or in some cases another person's) employment, as follows.

(*a*)   Restricted shares under *ITEPA 2003, ss 422–432* as substituted by *FA 2003* — see 82.4 below.

(*b*)   Conditional interests in shares under *ITEPA 2003, ss 422–434* as originally enacted (previously under *ICTA 1988, s 140A*) — see 82.5 below.

(*c*)   Convertible shares under *ITEPA 2003, ss 435–444* as substituted by *FA 2003* — see 82.6 below.

(*d*)   Convertible shares under *ITEPA 2003, ss 435–446* as originally enacted (previously under *ICTA 1988, s 140D*) — see 82.7 below.

(*e*)   Shares with artificially depressed market value, under *ITEPA 2003, ss 446A–446J* — see 82.8 below.

(*f*)   Shares with artificially enhanced market value, under *ITEPA 2003, ss 446K–446P* — see 82.9 below.

(*g*)   Shares disposed of for more than market value, under *ITEPA 2003, ss 446X–446Z* — see 82.11 below.

(*h*)   Post-acquisition benefits under *ITEPA 2003, ss 447–450* as substituted by *FA 2003* — see 82.12 below.

(*j*)   Post-acquisition benefits under *ICTA 1988, s 138* or *ITEPA 2003, ss 447–470* as originally enacted (previously under *ICTA 1988, s 138* or *FA 1988, Pt III, Ch II*) — see 82.13–82.15 below.

(*k*)   Unapproved share options under *ITEPA 2003, ss 471–484* as substituted by *FA 2003* or under *ITEPA 2003, ss 471–487* as originally enacted (previously under *ICTA 1988, s 135*) — see 82.16 below.

(*l*)   (Before 1 January 2003) profit sharing schemes under *ICTA 1988, s 186*, see 82.18 below.

(*m*)   Share incentive plans under *ITEPA 2003, ss 488–515, Sch 2* (previously under *FA 2000, Sch 8*) — see 82.20 below.

(*n*)   Enterprise management incentives under *ITEPA 2003, ss 527–541, Sch 5* (previously under *FA 2000, Sch 14*) — see 82.35 below.

(*o*)   SAYE option schemes under *ITEPA 2003, ss 516–520, Sch 3* (previously under *ICTA 1988, s 185(1)(a)*) — see 82.47 below.

(*p*) Executive share option schemes under *ICTA 1988, s 185(1)(b)* — see 82.75 below. Superseded by (*q*) below.

(*q*) Company share option plan (CSOP) schemes under *ITEPA 2003, ss 521–526, Sch 4* (previously under *ICTA 1988, s 185(1)(b)* and *FA 1996*) — see 82.61 below.

(*r*) Priority share allocations under *ITEPA 2003, ss 542–548* (previously under *FA 1988, s 68*) — see 82.76 below.

See also the notional loan provisions of *ITEPA 2003, ss 446Q–446W* at 82.10 below for shares acquired partly-paid.

Before 2003/04, a *jointly owned company* (or subsidiary of such a company) could not strictly participate in an approved scheme under (*l*), (*o*), (*p*) or (*q*) which was a group scheme established by either of its joint owners, because it was not controlled by the company which established the scheme as the legislation required. (As regards (*m*) above, see 82.21 below.) By concession for 2002/03 and earlier years, a group scheme expressed to extend to a jointly owned company will normally be approved upon application by the company establishing the scheme, provided that:

(i) the jointly owned company is not controlled (under *ICTA 1988, s 840*) by any single person;

(ii) it is controlled between them by two persons, one of whom established the scheme; and

(iii) in relation to each of (*l*), (*o*), (*p*) and (*q*) it only participates in a scheme established by one of the companies controlling it.

This concession applies similarly in relation to subsidiaries of a jointly owned company which satisfies (i) and (ii) above, provided that (iii) above would also be satisfied if it related both to the jointly owned company and to its subsidiaries.

Such concessionary approval is conditional upon the scheme ceasing to apply to the jointly owned company or its subsidiaries where (i) or (ii) above ceases to be satisfied (unless the companies thereby pass into the control of the company which established the scheme). It must similarly cease to apply to a company which ceases to be a subsidiary of the jointly owned company (again, unless it thereby passes into the control of the company which established the scheme). The company establishing the scheme for which the concession is sought must undertake to notify the Revenue of any change of control of any of the companies concerned.

(Revenue Pamphlet IR 1, B27).

In its application to SAYE option schemes and CSOP schemes ((*l*) and (*p*) above being no longer relevant), the above concession is superseded by legislation for 2003/04 onwards which enables a jointly owned company to take part in a group scheme (see 82.52, 82.65 below).

Revenue Share Focus Newsletter. Starting in July 2002, the Revenue publish sporadically a newsletter, Share Focus, designed to provide practitioners with information on new interpretations on technical employee share schemes issues, together with guidance on practical issues, and to publicise the work of the Revenue Employee Share Schemes Team — see www.inlandrevenue.gov.uk/shareschemes

Self-assessment implications. See Revenue Tax Bulletin October 1996 pp 351–353 for an article on the self-assessment implications (i.e. reporting requirements for employees, arrangements for payment of tax due and interim payments on account) of income tax liability arising for 1996/97 onwards from shares or share options received by reason of employment. See Revenue Share Focus Newsletter December 2003 pp 1, 2 for new Revenue procedures for dealing with late filing of returns by employers and by others with reporting obligations.

82.3 Share-Related Employment Income and Exemptions

Armed Forces Reservists. By concession, backdated to 7 January 2003 (the date of the first call-up order for service in Iraq), a reservist called up for service under *Reserve Forces Act 1996* will have his consequent employment with the Ministry of Defence (MOD) treated as fulfilling the employment conditions for the approved schemes at 82.20, 82.47 and 82.61 below and for enterprise management incentives at 82.35 below. In addition, employers and scheme providers may take such action as is necessary to maintain the reservist's participation in the scheme for the period they are away serving with the MOD; provided the action does no more than that, it will not compromise the approval of the scheme. (Revenue Pamphlet IR 1, A103). Guidance notes for employers, setting out possible courses of action within the concession, are attached to the published concession.

Earn-outs. Where the consideration passing on the sale of a business includes an earn-out, typically a right to receive securities in the purchasing company after a certain period of time has elapsed and dependent on the performance of the newly taken-over business, any element of remuneration for services as an employee or prospective employee included in the earn-out may give rise to a tax charge under the provisions at 82.4 below (restricted shares), 82.6 below (convertible shares) or 82.16 below (unapproved share options) as it has effect after *FA 2003*, whichever is relevant, always bearing in mind the extended meaning of 'shares' at 82.3 below. Guidance has been issued as to how the rules will be applied and how to identify if an earn-out is 'remuneration' or further sale consideration or an element of both. See www.inlandrevenue.gov.uk/shareschemes/faq_emprelatedsecurity-ch5.htm#1

Two *Memoranda of Understanding* between the Revenue and the British Venture Capital Association, covering certain matters arising from the substantial changes made by *FA 2003* to the provisions at 82.3–82.17 below, were published on 25 July 2003 and are available at the Revenue's website.

University spin-out companies. See the 'Memorandum of Understanding between University Companies Association (UNICO) and the Inland Revenue — 14 April 2004' published on 26 April 2004. This concerns the treatment of shares acquired by university employees (usually academics) in spin-out companies in the light of the provisions described in this chapter on unapproved share schemes. Spin-outs are arrangements varying from requiring university employees to risk their own money by buying shares to rewarding those employees under the university's Intellectual Property Sharing Policy. The shares acquired by the employees in the spin-out company may be acquired wholly as an investment, wholly as a reward for services, or as a combination of both. The Memorandum describes a shareholding structure agreed with the Revenue and designed to produce certainty of tax treatment and to ensure that the employees do not incur significant tax liabilities until they realise the value of their shares.

82.3   EXTENDED MEANING OF 'SHARES'

For the purposes of 82.5 and 82.13–82.15 below, and also of 82.16 below as it had effect before the *FA 2003* changes detailed therein, 'shares' includes stock and also includes most securities issued by companies (though with little clarification as to exactly which types of security are and are not included).

For the purposes of 82.4, 82.6, 82.8–82.12 below, and also of 82.16 below as it has effect after the *FA 2003* changes detailed therein, the meaning of 'shares' is extended to embrace a broader range of financial products, including, for example, government and local authority stocks. All of the following are now 'shares' for these purposes:

- shares (including stock) in any body corporate, wherever incorporated, or in any unincorporated body constituted under the law of a foreign country;

- debentures, debenture stock, loan stock, bonds, certificates of deposit and other instruments creating or acknowledging indebtedness;

- warrants and other instruments entitling the holders to subscribe for securities;

- certificates and other instruments conferring rights in respect of securities held by persons other than the persons on whom the rights are conferred and which may be transferred without the consent of those persons;

- units in a collective investment scheme (as defined by *ITEPA 2003, s 420(2)*);

- futures (as defined by *ITEPA 2003, s 420(3)*);

- rights under contracts for differences (or under similar contracts — as defined by *ITEPA 2003, s 420(4)*) (see 75.39 SCHEDULE E—EMPLOYMENT INCOME as regards 'phantom' share schemes).

However, none of the following are 'shares' for these purposes:

- cheques, bills of exchange, bankers' drafts and letters of credit (other than bills of exchange accepted by a banker);

- money and statements showing balances on a current, deposit or savings account;

- leases and other dispositions of property and heritable securities;

- rights under insurance contracts; and

- options.

The above lists can be amended by Treasury order.

It is important to note that the above extended meaning of 'shares' does *not* apply for the purposes of the Revenue-approved schemes at 82.18 *et seq.* below. For the purposes of 82.18 and 82.35 *et seq.* below, 'shares' includes stock but not securities, and see also the specific rules at 82.18, 82.30, 82.41, 82.55 and 82.69 below.

An '*interest in shares*', for the purposes of 82.4, 82.6, 82.8–82.12 below, and also of 82.16 below as it has effect after the *FA 2003* changes detailed therein, means an interest which is less than full beneficial ownership. It includes an interest in their sale proceeds but not a right to acquire them.

[*ITEPA 2003, s 420, ss 434(1), 470(1), 487(1) as originally enacted, ss 516(4), 521(4), 548(1), Sch 5 para 58; ICTA 1988, s 136(5), s 139(11), s 140A(9), s 140H(8), s 187(2); FA 1988, s 87(1); FA 2000, Sch 14 para 71(1); FA 2003, Sch 22 para 2*].

See FAQs at www.inlandrevenue.gov.uk/shareschemes/faq_emprelatedsecurity-ch1.htm for further detail.

82.4   RESTRICTED SHARES

The following provisions have effect on and after 1 September 2003 in relation to shares (or interests in shares) acquired after 15 April 2003. See 82.5 below as regards shares etc. acquired on or before that day and for the position before these provisions take effect in relation to shares etc. acquired subsequently.

These provisions apply to 'employment-related shares' if, at the time of acquisition, they are 'restricted shares' (or a 'restricted interest in shares'). For the extended meaning of 'shares', in relation to these provisions, see 82.3 above. See below for the possibility of electing to disapply or moderate these provisions and for exclusions from the charge. See 82.17 below as regards reporting obligations. See also the anti-avoidance provisions at 82.8, 82.9 below.

'*Employment-related shares*' are shares (or an interest in shares) acquired by a person by virtue of a right or opportunity made available by reason of the employment (present, past or prospective) of that or any other person. For this purpose, shares are deemed to be acquired when the beneficial entitlement to them is acquired and not, if different, at the time of conveyance or transfer. Any right or opportunity made available by a person's employer, or by a person connected (within *ICTA 1988, s 839* — see 19 CONNECTED PERSONS) with a person's employer, is treated as made available by reason of the employment of that person, other than in the case of an individual conferring a right or opportunity in the normal course of his domestic, family or personal relationships. There are rules dealing with company reorganisations (such as conversions, scrip issues and rights issues); these treat replacement shares or additional shares acquired on such a reorganisation as acquired by virtue of the same right or opportunity as the original interest and treat any consequent reduction in the market value of the original shares as consideration given for the replacement shares or additional shares.

A right etc. is made available to the taxpayer even though he may himself have stipulated its being granted (*CIR v Herd CS 1992, 66 TC 29*).

An increase in a person's interest in shares is treated for the purposes of these provisions as a separate interest acquired by virtue of the same right or opportunity as the original interest. A decrease in a person's interest is treated as a disposal, otherwise than to an 'associated person', of a separate interest proportionate to the reduction.

For the purposes of these provisions, consideration given for the acquisition of employment-related shares includes consideration given by the employee or by the person who acquired the shares (if not the employee) and any consideration given for a *right* to acquire the shares. Any consideration given partly for one thing and partly for another is apportioned as is just and reasonable. Rules similar to those at 82.16 below (under Option exchanged for another) apply to determine the amount of consideration where a right to acquire the shares is assigned or released for consideration consisting of or including another right to acquire the shares.

Employment-related shares are '*restricted shares*' (or a '*restricted interest in shares*') if there is a contract, agreement, arrangement or condition that imposes any of the three types of restriction listed below *and* the market value of the shares or interest (determined as for capital gains purposes) is less than it otherwise would have been. The types of restriction covered are as follows:

(*a*)   any provision for the transfer, reversion or forfeiture of the shares etc. if certain circumstances arise or do not arise, such that the holder will cease to be beneficially entitled to them and will not be entitled to receive an amount at least equal to their unfettered market value;

(*b*)   any restriction (not within (*a*) above) on the freedom of the holder to dispose of the shares etc. (or to retain the proceeds if they are sold) or on his right to retain the shares or proceeds or on any right conferred by the shares themselves;

(*c*)   any provision (not within (*a*) or (*b*) above) whereby the disposal or retention of the shares etc., or the exercise of a right conferred by them, may result in a disadvantage to the holder or (if different) the employee or a connected person (within *ICTA 1988, s 839* — see 19 CONNECTED PERSONS) of either.

However, none of the following is sufficient in itself to confer 'restricted shares' status on employment-related shares:

●   (in the case of unpaid or partly paid shares) a provision for forfeiture in the event of non-payment of calls (provided the meeting of calls is not itself restricted);

●   a requirement that the shares be offered for sale or transfer in the event of the employee's losing his employment by reason of misconduct;

●   the fact that the shares may be redeemed on payment of any amount.

Exclusions. These provisions do not apply

- (before 18 June 2004) to shares acquired under an approved share incentive plan (as in 82.20 below), SAYE option scheme (as in 82.47 below) or CSOP scheme (as in 82.61 below); or

- if, at the time of acquisition, the earnings from the employment in question were not (or would not have been if there were any) general earnings within *ITEPA 2003, s 15* or *s 21* (earnings for year when employee resident and ordinarily resident in UK); or

- (in the case of a former employment) if they would not have applied had the acquisition taken place in the last tax year in which the employment was held; or

- (in the case of a prospective employment) if they would not apply if the acquisition had taken place in the first tax year in which the employment is held; or

- in relation to shares acquired under the terms of a public offer (including an 'employee offer' as in 82.76 below); but this exclusion does not apply after 17 June 2004 (whatever the date of acquisition) if one of the main purposes of the arrangements under which the shares are acquired, or for which the shares are held, is the avoidance of tax or national insurance contributions.

These provisions cease to apply to shares (or an interest in shares):

- following a disposal to a person other than an 'associated person', or

- immediately before the death of the employee (so that no charge arises on death), or

- on the seventh anniversary of the first date on which the employee is employed neither by the employer who made available the right or opportunity to acquire the shares nor by the company that issued the shares (where applicable) nor by a connected person (within *ICTA 1988, s 839* — see 19 CONNECTED PERSONS) of either that employer or that issuing company.

Associated persons. For the purposes of these provisions, any of the following are '*associated persons*' in relation to employment-related shares:

- the person who acquired them;

- (if different) the employee; and

- any 'relevant linked person'.

A '*relevant linked person*' is any person who is either connected (within *ICTA 1988, s 839* — see 19 CONNECTED PERSONS) with, or is a member of the same household as, either the person who acquired the shares or the employee. (After 17 June 2004, the definition is tightened to embrace past connections etc. so as to ensure the link cannot be broken.) However, a *company* cannot be a relevant linked person if it is the employer or (if different) the person by whom the right or opportunity to acquire the shares was made available or the person from whom the shares were acquired or by whom they were issued.

Tax exemption in certain cases on acquisition. No liability to income tax arises on the *acquisition* of employment-related shares under the normal rules at 75.39 SCHEDULE E—EMPLOYMENT INCOME if the shares are restricted under (*a*) above and will cease to be so within five years after the acquisition (whether or not they may remain restricted under either (*b*) or (*c*) above). However, the employer and employee may jointly and irrevocably elect to disapply this exemption. The point of an election would be to reduce the charge to tax on a future chargeable event (see below). (See below for the separate possibility of electing to disapply or moderate *all* these provisions.) The election is implemented by way of an agreement (between employer and employee), in a form approved by the Revenue, that must be made no later than 14 days after the acquisition; there is no requirement for it to be submitted to the Revenue or for Revenue approval to be sought. Prescribed forms of election were published on the Revenue's website on 22 July 2003. Whether or not the election is made, and where relevant, income tax charges may arise on acquisition under 82.16 below (unapproved share options), 82.6 below (conversion) or 82.10 below (acquisition for less than market value).

Charge to tax on occurrence of a chargeable event. If a chargeable event occurs in relation to restricted shares, there is a charge to tax on the employee for the tax year in which it occurs; the amount chargeable, computed as below, counts as employment income for tax purposes. This is subject to the exception from charge detailed below. Any of the following is a chargeable event:

(i)   the employment-related shares ceasing to be restricted shares (or a restricted interest in shares) without their having been disposed of to a person who is not an 'associated person' (see above);

(ii)   the variation or removal of any restriction without the employment-related shares having been disposed of to a person who is not an associated person and without their ceasing to be restricted shares (or a restricted interest in shares);

(iii) the disposal for consideration of the employment-related shares (or any interest in them) by an 'associated person' otherwise than to another associated person at a time when they are still restricted shares (or a restricted interest in shares).

Computation of chargeable amount. The chargeable amount is found by applying a formula, $UMV \times (IUP - PCP - OP) - CE$ (see *ITEPA 2003, s 426* as substituted by *FA 2003, Sch 22 para 3*), where

UMV =   Unrestricted Market Value, i.e. what would be the market value of the employment-related shares immediately after the chargeable event but for any restrictions;

IUP =   Initial Uncharged Proportion. This is that part, expressed as a proportion (e.g. 0.25), of the Initial Unrestricted Market Value ($IUMV$) in respect of which an income tax charge is still required. It is found by taking the difference between $IUMV$ and any deductible amounts and dividing it by $IUMV$. $IUMV$ is what would have been the market value of the shares at the time of acquisition but for any restrictions. Deductible amounts include any consideration given for the shares and amounts previously charged to income tax;

PCP =   Previously Charged Proportion. This is the aggregate obtained by applying the formula, $IUP - PCP - OP$, on each previous chargeable event since acquisition. If there has not been a previous chargeable event, PCP is nil;

OP =   Outstanding Proportion. This is the proportion of the share value that is still reduced by restrictions and is found by taking the difference between UMV and the actual market value of the shares immediately after the chargeable event and dividing it by UMV; and

CE =   Consideration and Expenses. This consists of any consideration given by the shareholder for, and any expenses incurred by him in connection with, the lifting or variation of restrictions, plus (where relevant) any expenses incurred by him in connection with the disposal of the shares.

If the employment-related shares are convertible shares (see 82.6 below), or an interest in convertible shares, their market value is to be determined for the purposes of the above formula as if they were not.

If the chargeable event is a disposal for less than actual market value, the chargeable amount as determined above is reduced in the proportion that the consideration given on the disposal bears to the market value of the shares.

The employer and employee may jointly and irrevocably elect to omit OP from the above formula. The effect is to preclude any further application of these provisions. The election is implemented by way of an agreement (between employer and employee), in a form approved by the Revenue, that must be made no later than 14 days after the chargeable event; there is no requirement for it to be submitted to the Revenue or for Revenue approval to be sought. Prescribed forms of election were published on the Revenue's website on 22 July 2003.

The Revenue can provide a calculator (based on an Excel 97 spreadsheet) to apply the above formula — see www.inlandrevenue.gov.ukshareschemes/faq_emprelatedsecurity-ch2.htm#c

PAYE. For the requirement to operate PAYE on chargeable amounts, see 55.2(*h*) PAY AS YOU EARN.

Relief for employer national insurance contributions. From a date to be appointed by Treasury order, where, under a voluntary agreement or a joint election under *Social Security Contributions and Benefits Act 1992, Sch 1 para 3A* or *para 3B* (or NI equivalent), whenever made, a liability to secondary Class 1 national insurance contributions (i.e. employer contributions) on an amount chargeable to tax under these provisions is borne by the employee, the amount so borne is deductible from the chargeable amount computed as above. In the case of a voluntary agreement, or an election to which Revenue approval is withdrawn, no such amount is deductible to the extent that it is borne by the employee later than 4 June following the tax year in which the chargeable event occurs.

Exception from charge. No charge to tax arises on the occurrence of a chargeable event if the restriction in question applies to all the company's shares of the same class, all the company's shares of that class are affected by an event similar to the chargeable event (disregarding the references in (i)–(iii) above to associated persons) and *either* of the conditions below is satisfied. (The extended meaning of shares in 82.3 above does not apply for this purpose.) After 6 May 2004, there is a further requirement that the arrangements under which the right or opportunity to acquire the shares was made available did not have as one of its main purposes the avoidance of tax or national insurance contributions.

The first of the conditions mentioned above is that, immediately before the event, the company is 'employee-controlled' (within *ITEPA 2003, s 421H*) by virtue of holdings of shares of the class in question. After 6 May 2004, the second condition is that, immediately before the event, the majority of the company's shares of the class in question are not 'employment-related shares' (see above). Previously, this condition was that, immediately before the event, the majority of the company's shares of the class in question were not held by or for the benefit of

- employees of the company;

- persons who are 'related persons' of an employee of the company;

- associated companies (within *ICTA 1988, s 416*) of the company;

- employees of any associated company of the company; or

- persons who are 'related persons' of an employee of any such associated company.

For the above purposes, a person is a '*related person*' of an employee if he acquired the shares pursuant to a right or opportunity made available by reason of the employee's employment or if he is connected with a person who so acquired the shares or with an employee and acquired the shares from the employee or a related person of the employee in a non-arm's length transaction.

Election to disapply or moderate the above provisions. The employer and employee may jointly and irrevocably elect to disapply the above provisions in full and to disregard the restrictions attaching to the shares when computing their acquisition value for the purposes of any charge to tax on employment income (including the charge on conversion at 82.6(*a*) below and the provisions at 82.10 and 82.16 below). The election is implemented by way of an agreement (between employer and employee), in a form approved by the Revenue, that must be made no later than 14 days after the acquisition; there is no requirement for it to be submitted to the Revenue or for Revenue approval to be sought. Prescribed forms of election were published on the Revenue's website on 22 July 2003 and 6 October 2003 (the latter being specially for use where the restricted shares are acquired on exercise of a qualifying enterprise management incentives option — see 82.35 below).

Alternatively, an election may be made, in similar manner, to disregard one or more specified restrictions in applying the above provisions and in computing acquisition value for the above-mentioned purposes.

Either election could also be made, with appropriate modifications, in relation to shares acquired after 15 April 2003 but before 1 September 2003. In this case, the deadline for implementing the election was 15 September 2003. Such an election could not, however, be made if, in relation to the shares, a tax charge arose under 82.5 or 82.14(*a*) below.

After 17 June 2004, the employer and the employee are deemed to have made the election to disapply the above provisions in full if the shares in question are acquired under an approved share incentive plan (as in 82.20 below), SAYE option scheme (as in 82.47 below) or CSOP scheme (as in 82.61 below) or by the exercise of an enterprise management incentive qualifying option (as in 82.35 below) in circumstances such that (in each case) no income tax liability arises on acquisition. In relation to shares so acquired before 18 June 2004, the election is deemed to have been made on that date.

[*ITEPA 2003, ss 419, 421, 421A–421D, 421E(1)(3)–(5), 421F–421I, 422–432, 718, 721(1); FA 2003, Sch 22 paras 2, 3; FA 2004, s 85, s 86(1)–(5)(8), s 88(2)(3)(11)(12), s 89(1)–(4), s 90(2)(5), Sch 16 paras 1, 7(2); SI 2003 No 1997*].

See also www.inlandrevenue.gov.uk/shareschemes/faq_emprelatedsecurity-ch2.htm

For *capital gains tax* purposes, the consideration for the acquisition is taken as the aggregate of the actual amount or value given for the restricted shares (or restricted interest in shares), any amount charged to income tax as earnings in relation to the acquisition and any amount charged on the occurrence of a chargeable event. (No account is taken of any relief given for employer national insurance contributions — see above.) This does not affect the calculation of the consideration received by the person from whom the acquisition is made. [*TCGA 1992, ss 119A, 149AA; FA 2003, Sch 22 paras 50, 52; FA 2004, s 85, Sch 16 para 6*]. See Tolley's Capital Gains Tax for full details.

82.5   CONDITIONAL INTERESTS IN SHARES

The following provisions are replaced by those at 82.4 above but still have effect in relation to shares (or interests in shares) acquired before 16 April 2003. In relation to shares etc. acquired subsequently, these provisions continue to have effect prior to 1 September 2003 (at which point the provisions at 82.4 above come into effect).

Where a conditional beneficial interest in company shares is acquired on or after 17 March 1998 by any person (the 'employee') as a director (as widely defined) or employee of that or any other company, there is no charge to tax in respect of that acquisition (other than any charge under 82.10 or 82.16 below) provided the interest will cease to be conditional within five years after its acquisition. As regards shares acquired before 27 July 1999 on terms such that the interest could continue to be conditional for more than five years, there was a specific charge under *ICTA 1988, s 140A(2)* on the basis that the interest was emoluments of the employment. As regards shares acquired on or after that date on such terms, there is no such specific charge, but a charge to tax may nevertheless arise under the normal rules at 75.39 SCHEDULE E—EMPLOYMENT INCOME.

Shares for these purposes includes securities. See below as regards whether shares are acquired by a person as a director or employee of a company.

Whether or not the conditionality may or will continue for more than five years, if and when it ceases without the employee's beneficial interest ceasing, or the employee disposes of any beneficial interest in the shares before the conditionality ceases, a charge to tax on employment income arises for the tax year in which such event occurs. The charge is on the amount (if any) by which the open market value of the interest immediately after the event in question exceeds the sum of

(*a*)   any consideration given for the interest,

(*b*)   any amount brought into charge, as earnings of the employee, in respect of the acquisition of the interest, and

(*c*)   any amount brought into charge under 82.14(*a*) or (*b*) below in respect of the shares on an earlier or simultaneous event.

The consideration referred to in (*a*) above includes consideration given by the employee or by any other person whose acquisition of the shares is within these provisions (see below). The amount of consideration taken into account includes any given for a right to acquire the shares or by virtue of which the interest in the shares ceases to be conditional (with apportionment, on a just and reasonable basis, of any amount given partly in respect of other matters). The performance by the director or employee of any duties of, or in connection with, the office or employment by reference to which the interest was acquired is not counted as consideration for this purpose. No amount is to be counted more than once in arriving at any amount of consideration given. In determining the consideration given for a right to acquire shares in a case where one share option has been exchanged for another, provisions identical to the relevant provisions in 82.16 below apply. As regards events occurring on and after 16 April 2003, see also the anti-avoidance provisions at 82.8 below.

These provisions do not apply if the earnings from the office or employment in question were not (or would not have been if there were any) general earnings within *ITEPA 2003, s 15* or *s 21* (earnings for year when employee resident and ordinarily resident in UK). They do not apply in relation to a right or opportunity conferred or offered after the office or employment has ceased if they would not have applied had the right or opportunity been conferred or offered in the last tax year in which the office or employment was held.

A *Pt 5* transfer of shares, or an interest in shares, under *Proceeds of Crime Act 2002* (as in 9.2(xi) CAPITAL ALLOWANCES) does not give rise to an income tax charge under the above rules.

Treatment of interest in shares as conditional. A beneficial interest in shares is treated as conditional for these purposes for so long as the terms (however imposed) on which the employee is entitled to the interest:

(i)   provide that if certain circumstances arise, or do not arise, there will be a transfer, reversion or forfeiture as a result of which the employee will cease to be entitled to any beneficial interest in the shares; and

(ii)   are not such that the employee will thereon be entitled to receive an amount equal to or more than the open market value of the interest at that time (disregarding the provision for transfer, reversion or forfeiture).

The 'circumstances' under (i) above may include the expiration of a period specified in or determined under the terms, the death of any person, and the exercise by any person of any power conferred on the person by or under the terms.

The employee's interest in a company's shares is *not* treated as conditional by reason only that:

(A)   where there is no restriction on the meeting of calls by the employee, the shares are unpaid or partly paid and may be forfeited for non-payment of calls; or

(B)   the articles of association of the company require the employee to offer the shares for sale, or transfer them, on ceasing to be an officer or employee of the company or of any one or more companies in the same 51% group; or

(C)   the employee may be required to offer the shares for sale, or transfer them, on ceasing, by reason of misconduct, to be an officer or employee of the company or of any one or more companies in the same 51% group; or

(D)   in the case of securities, the securities may be redeemed on payment of any amount.

The Revenue were originally of the view that the term 'articles of association' in (B) above did not include foreign company equivalents. (For this and other points concerning (A)–(D) above, see Revenue Tax Bulletin April 2000 pp 731–733, 736.) They have since reversed this view; for this and their proposed action in cases where their previous interpretation had been applied, see Revenue Tax Bulletin August 2002 pp 953, 954. Their revised interpretation is given statutory effect for 2003/04 onwards.

Shares acquired as director or employee. For the above purposes a person ('E') acquires an interest in shares as a director or employee of a company if he acquires the interest in pursuance of

• a right conferred on, or opportunity offered to, E by reason of E's office or employment as a director or employee (past, present or future) of the company; or

• a right or opportunity assigned to E, having previously been conferred on or offered to another person by reason of E's office or employment as above; or

• an assignment to E, the interest having previously been acquired by another person by reason of E's office or employment as above.

Where

• a person has (or is treated as having) acquired a conditional interest in any shares as a director or employee of a company, and

• as a result of any two or more transactions he ceases to be entitled to that interest and he or a connected person (see 19 CONNECTED PERSONS) becomes entitled to another conditional interest in any shares,

that person is treated as if the interest to which he becomes entitled were also acquired by him as a director or employee of the company in question.

The above rules interact with those in 82.7 below, so as to include within these provisions a conditional interest in shares which itself derives from convertible shares, or an interest in convertible shares, acquired as a director or employee.

Death of the employee. Where the employee dies holding the original interest, the above provisions apply as if he had disposed of that interest immediately before his death, and as if the open market value at that time were to be determined on the basis that it is known that the disposal is being made immediately before the employee's death and that any restriction on disposal subject to which the shares were held is to be disregarded in so far as it is a restriction terminating on death.

Reporting requirements. Where any person provides an individual with a conditional interest in shares in circumstances such that a charge may arise under these provisions, each 'relevant person' must provide the Revenue with written particulars of the shares and their provision. Similarly where an employee has a conditional interest in shares and a charge arises as above on the conditionality ceasing, or on the shares being disposed of or the employee dying, each 'relevant person' must provide the Revenue with written particulars of the shares and the event giving rise to the charge. The *'relevant persons'* are the person who provided the shares in question and the employer company. In each case the particulars must be provided before 7 July following the end of the tax year in which the shares are provided or the event occurs. For 2002/03 and earlier years, the time limit was 30 days after the end of the tax year in question. A penalty may arise under *TMA 1970, s 98* in the event of non-compliance. Particulars should be sent to Inland Revenue, Employee Share Schemes, Second Floor, New Wing, Somerset House, Strand, London, WC2R 1LB.

[*ITEPA 2003, ss 420, 422–434 as originally enacted, Sch 6 para 137, Sch 7 paras 44–48; ICTA 1988, ss 140A–140C, s 140G, s 140H; FA 1998, ss 50, 52, 53; FA 1999, ss 42, 43; Proceeds of Crime Act 2002, Sch 10 para 31; FA 2003, Sch 22 para 46(6)–(9)*].

For the requirement to operate PAYE on amounts chargeable by virtue of the conditionality ceasing or any disposal of the employee's beneficial interest, see 55.2(g) PAY AS YOU EARN.

For notes on the interaction between the above provisions and both *ICTA 1988, s 162* (now *ITEPA 2003, ss 446Q–446W*) (see 82.10 below) and *FA 1988, ss 78, 79* (now *ITEPA 2003, ss 449–456*) (see 82.14 below), see Revenue Tax Bulletin April 2000 pp 733, 734.

For *capital gains tax* purposes, an acquisition within the above provisions is not treated under *TCGA 1992, s 17* as an acquisition at market value. Instead, the consideration for the acquisition is taken as the actual amount of the consideration (determined as above), increased by any amount brought into charge to income tax under the above provisions. This does not affect the calculation of the consideration received by the person from whom the acquisition is made. [*TCGA 1992, s 120(2)(5A)(8), s 149B; FA 1998, s 54; ITEPA 2003, Sch 6 paras 210, 211; FA 2003, Sch 22 paras 51, 53*].

As regards shares acquired **before 17 March 1998** and subject to risk of forfeiture, it was originally the Revenue's view that an income tax charge arose when that risk was lifted and by reference to the value of the shares at that time. Following legal advice received on 26 May 1995, they now take the view that a charge arises at the time of acquisition and by reference to the then value of the shares taking into account the risk of forfeiture, with no charge arising on the risk being lifted. Where the relevant tax return was made before 27 March 1995 on the basis of the original Revenue view, the position will not be reconsidered. In the case of later returns made on that basis, and subject to an error or mistake claim (see 16.7 CLAIMS) where a tax liability has otherwise become final, the Revenue will charge tax according to their revised view but will postpone collection of tax thereby due for the tax year of acquisition (and also the date from which interest on unpaid tax accrues) until after risk of forfeiture is lifted. Such tax will not be charged, or will be written off, if the shares are forfeited. The capital gains tax acquisition cost of the shares will follow the income tax treatment. See Revenue Tax Bulletin June 1998 pp 545–548.

82.6 **CONVERTIBLE SHARES AFTER FA 2003**

The following provisions replace those at 82.7 below and have effect on and after 1 September 2003 irrespective of when the shares were acquired, except that the tax relief on acquisition (see below) applies only to acquisitions on and after that date. If shares were acquired before that date and a chargeable event occurs on or after that date, relief will be given for any amount charged to tax on acquisition in respect of the right to convert (see FAQs at www.inlandrevenue.gov.uk/shareschemes/faq_emprelatedsecurity-ch3.htm).

These provisions apply to 'employment-related shares' if, at the time of acquisition, they are 'convertible shares' (or an interest in 'convertible shares'). For the extended meaning of 'shares', in relation to these provisions, see 82.3 above. See below for exclusions from the charge. See 82.17 below as regards reporting obligations. See also the anti-avoidance provisions at 82.8 below.

82.6 Share-Related Employment Income and Exemptions

'*Employment-related shares*' are defined as in 82.4 above. There are rules dealing with company reorganisations (such as conversions, scrip issues and rights issues); these treat replacement shares or additional shares acquired on such a reorganisation as acquired by virtue of the same right or opportunity as the original interest and treat any consequent reduction in the market value of the original shares as consideration given for the replacement shares or additional shares.

An increase in a person's interest in shares is treated for the purposes of these provisions as a separate interest acquired by virtue of the same right or opportunity as the original interest. A decrease in a person's interest is treated as a disposal, otherwise than to an 'associated person' (as defined in 82.4 above), of a separate interest proportionate to the reduction.

For the purposes of these provisions, consideration given for the acquisition of employment-related shares includes consideration given by the employee or by the person who acquired the shares (if not the employee) and any consideration given for a *right* to acquire the shares. Rules similar to those at 82.16 below (under Option exchanged for another) apply to determine the amount of consideration where a right to acquire the shares is assigned or released for consideration consisting of or including another right to acquire the shares.

Employment-related shares are '*convertible shares*' if

- they confer on the holder an immediate or conditional entitlement to convert them into shares of a different description, or

- a contract, agreement, arrangement or condition authorises or requires the grant of such an entitlement to the holder if certain circumstances arise, or do not arise (for example, where the shares can only be converted following a stipulated period after acquisition) or makes provision for the conversion of the shares (otherwise than by the holder) into shares of a different description.

Exclusions. The same exclusions from charge apply as in 82.4 above.

Tax relief on acquisition. In relation to acquisitions on and after 1 September 2003, for the purposes of any liability to tax in respect of the acquisition of shares (under the general charging rules at 75.39 SCHEDULE E—EMPLOYMENT INCOME, under 82.16 below (unapproved share options) or under 82.10 below (acquisition for less than market value)), the market value of the employment-related shares is to be determined as if they were not convertible shares or an interest in convertible shares. Thus, if the market value per share is £1,100 with a conversion right and would be £1,000 without the conversion right, only £1,000 is taxed; previously, any tax charge on acquisition would have been calculated by reference to the full market value (£1,100).

Charge to tax on occurrence of a chargeable event. If a chargeable event occurs in relation to convertible shares, there is a charge to tax on the employee for the tax year in which it occurs; the amount chargeable, computed as below, counts as employment income for tax purposes. This is subject to the exception from charge referred to below. Any of the following is a chargeable event:

   (*a*)   the conversion of the employment-related shares (or the shares in which they are an interest) into shares of a different description, where an 'associated person' (see 82.4 above) is beneficially entitled to the shares into which the employment-related shares are converted;

   (*b*)   the disposal for consideration of the employment-related shares (or any interest in them) by an associated person otherwise than to another associated person at a time when they are still convertible shares (or an interest in convertible shares);

   (*c*)   the release, for consideration, of the conversion right;

(*d*)   the receipt by an associated person of a benefit in money or money's worth in connection with the conversion right; this could be, for example, compensation for loss of the conversion right but excludes any benefit received on account of disability (as defined) or anything within (*a*)–(*c*) above.

Computation of chargeable amount. The chargeable amount is found by computing the gain (if any) realised on the occurrence of the chargeable event (see below) and deducting from it any consideration given for the conversion right and any expenses incurred by the shareholder in connection with the conversion, disposal, release or receipt (whichever is applicable). For this purpose, consideration given for the conversion right is the excess (if any) of the consideration given for the acquisition of the shares (or interest in shares) over their market value, at the time of acquisition, determined as if they were not convertible shares (or an interest in convertible shares).

The gain realised on the chargeable event depends on the nature of the event, as follows:

(i)   on an event within (*a*) above, it is the amount given by the formula, CMVCS − (CMVERS + CC), see below;

(ii)   on an event within (*b*) above, it is the amount given by the formula, DC − CMVERS, see below;

(iii)   on an event within (*c*) above, it is the amount of the consideration received by an associated person in respect of the release; and

(iv)   on an event within (*d*) above, it is the amount or market value of the benefit.

For the purposes of (i) and (ii) above:

CMVCS =   the market value, at the time of the event, of the shares acquired on conversion (determined, if those shares are themselves convertible shares, as if they were not); in the case of an interest in shares, a proportionate amount of the market value is taken instead;

CMVERS =   the market value, at the time of the event, of the convertible shares (or the interest in them), again disregarding the effect on value of the conversion right;

CC =   the amount of any consideration given for the conversion; and

DC =   the amount of any consideration given on the disposal in (*b*) above.

For the purposes of these provisions generally, market value is determined as for capital gains tax purposes and *ITEPA 2003, ss 421(2), 421A* apply in determining the amount of any consideration given.

PAYE. For the requirement to operate PAYE on chargeable amounts, see 55.2(*h*) PAY AS YOU EARN.

Relief for employer national insurance contributions. From a date to be appointed by Treasury order, where, under a voluntary agreement or a joint election under *Social Security Contributions and Benefits Act 1992, Sch 1 para 3A or para 3B* (or NI equivalent), whenever made, a liability to secondary Class 1 national insurance contributions (i.e. employer contributions) on an amount chargeable to tax under these provisions is borne by the employee, the amount so borne is deductible from the chargeable amount computed as above. In the case of a voluntary agreement, or an election to which Revenue approval is withdrawn, no such amount is deductible to the extent that it is borne by the employee later than 4 June following the tax year in which the chargeable event occurs.

Exception from charge. The exception from charge detailed at 82.4 above, in relation to chargeable events under the restricted shares provisions, applies equally, subject to the necessary modifications, in relation to chargeable events under these provisions.

[*ITEPA 2003, ss 419, 421, 421A–421D, 421E(1)(3)–(5), 421F–421I, 435–444, 721(1); FA 2003, Sch 22 paras 2, 4; FA 2004, s 85, s 86(1)–(5)(8), s 88(2)(11), s 89(1)–(4), s 90(2)(5), Sch 16 paras 2, 7(2); SI 2003 No 1997*].

For *capital gains tax* purposes, the consideration for the acquisition is taken as the aggregate of the actual amount or value given for the convertible shares (or interest in convertible shares), any amount charged to income tax as earnings in relation to the acquisition and any amount charged on the occurrence of a chargeable event within (*a*) above. (No account is taken of any relief given for employer national insurance contributions — see above.) This does not affect the calculation of the consideration received by the person from whom the acquisition is made. [*TCGA 1992, ss 119A, 149AA; FA 2003, Sch 22 paras 50, 52; FA 2004, s 85, Sch 16 para 6*]. See Tolley's Capital Gains Tax for full details.

82.7 **CONVERTIBLE SHARES BEFORE FA 2003**

The following provisions have effect before 1 September 2003 (see also 82.6 above).

A special charge to tax on employment income may arise where, on or after 17 March 1998, a person (the 'employee') acquires 'convertible' shares in a company (or an interest in such shares) as a director (as widely defined) or employee of that or any other company. Shares are '*convertible*' for this purpose if they confer on the holder an immediate or conditional entitlement to convert them into shares of a different class, or if they are held on terms (however imposed) that authorise or require the grant of such an entitlement to the holder if certain circumstances arise or do not arise. Such 'circumstances' may include the expiration of a period specified in or determined under the terms, the death of any person, and the exercise by any person of any power conferred on him by or under the terms.

See below as regards whether shares are acquired by a person as a director or employee of a company.

Subject to the exceptions referred to below, the charge arises if, at a time when the employee has a beneficial interest in the shares, they are converted into shares of a different class in pursuance of a conversion entitlement, and is made for the tax year in which the conversion occurs.

The charge is on the amount (if any) by which the open market value, at the time of the conversion, of the shares into which the convertible shares are converted exceeds the sum of

(*a*)   any consideration given for the convertible shares or for the interest in them or for the conversion,

(*b*)   any amount brought into charge, as earnings of the employee, in respect of the acquisition of the shares or interest,

(*c*)   any amount brought into charge under 82.14(*a*) or (*b*) below in respect of the shares on an earlier or simultaneous event, and

(*d*)   if the convertible shares or interest were acquired through a series of conversions within these provisions, the taxable amount for each such conversion (so far as not within (*b*) above).

The consideration referred to in (*a*) above includes consideration given for acquisition of the shares (or interest) by the employee or by any other person whose acquisition of the shares (or interest) is within these provisions (see below). The amount of consideration taken into account includes any given for a right to acquire the shares (or interest), and sums partly in respect of one thing and partly in respect of another are apportioned on a just and reasonable basis. The performance by the director or employee of any duties of, or in connection with, the office or employment by reference to which the shares (or interest) were acquired is not counted as consideration for this purpose. No amount is to be counted more than once in arriving at any amount of consideration given. In determining the consideration given for a right to acquire shares in a case where one share option has been exchanged for another, provisions identical to the relevant provisions in 82.16 below apply.

Exceptions. These provisions do not apply if the earnings from the office or employment in question were not (or would not have been if there were any) general earnings within *ITEPA 2003, s 15* or *s 21* (earnings for year when employee resident and ordinarily resident in UK). They do not apply in relation to a right or opportunity conferred or offered after the office or employment has ceased if they would not have applied had the right or opportunity been conferred or offered in the last tax year in which the office or employment was held.

No charge arises under these provisions if the conversion is of all the shares of one class only into shares of one other class only, and immediately before the conversion the majority of the company's shares of the original class are either:

(i)   held otherwise than by or for the benefit of

     (*a*)   directors (as widely defined) or employees of the company or of an associated company (within *ICTA 1988, s 416*), or

     (*b*)   an associated company; or

(ii)   (disregarding any held by or for the benefit of an associated company) held by or for the benefit of directors or employees of the company, or of a company controlled (within *ICTA 1988, s 840*) by the company, who are together able as holders of those shares to control the company.

There is similarly no charge under these provisions where the employee's interest in the shares into which the convertible shares are converted is a conditional interest within 82.5 above.

Shares acquired as director or employee. For the above purposes a person ('E') acquires shares (or an interest in shares) as a director or employee of a company if he acquires the shares or interest in pursuance of

•   a right conferred on, or opportunity offered to, E by reason of E's office or employment as a director or employee (past, present or future) of the company; or

•   a right or opportunity assigned to E, having previously been conferred on or offered to another person by reason of E's office or employment as above; or

•   an assignment to E, the shares or interest having previously been acquired by another person by reason of E's office or employment as above.

Rights and opportunities for this purpose include any arising from the fact that any shares acquired (or treated as acquired) as a director or employee are convertible. Without prejudice to this, where

•   a person has (or is treated as having) acquired any convertible shares (or an interest therein) as a director or employee of a company, and

•   as a result of any two or more transactions he ceases to be entitled to those shares (or that interest) and he or a connected person (see 19 CONNECTED PERSONS) becomes entitled to any convertible shares (or to an interest therein),

that person is treated as if the shares (or interest) to which he becomes entitled were also acquired by him as a director or employee of the company in question. This rule interacts with the equivalent rule in 82.5 above, in that references to an interest in convertible shares include also an interest in shares which is 'conditional'.

Death of the employee. Where convertible shares in which the employee has an interest at the time of his death are, wholly or partly as a consequence of his death, converted into shares of a different class on, or within twelve months after, the death, these provisions apply as if the conversion had taken place immediately before the death in pursuance of a conversion entitlement conferred on the deceased.

Reporting requirements. Where any person provides an individual with convertible shares, which are subsequently converted into shares of a different class in circumstances such that a charge may arise under these provisions, each 'relevant person' must provide the Revenue with written particulars of the shares and their conversion. The *'relevant persons'* are the person who provided the shares in question and the employer company. The particulars must be provided before 7 July following the end of the tax year in which the conversion takes place. For 2002/03 and earlier years, the time limit was 30 days after the end of the tax year in question. A penalty may arise under *TMA 1970, s 98* in the event of non-compliance. Particulars should be sent to Inland Revenue, Employee Share Schemes, Second Floor, New Wing, Somerset House, Strand, London, WC2R 1LB.

[*ITEPA 2003, ss 420, 435–446 as originally enacted, Sch 6 para 137, Sch 7 paras 49–53; ICTA 1988, ss 140D–140H; FA 1998, ss 51–53; FA 2003, Sch 22 para 46(10)–(12)(26)*].

For the requirement to operate PAYE on amounts chargeable under the above provisions, see 55.2(*g*) PAY AS YOU EARN.

For *capital gains tax* purposes, any amount charged to income tax under the above provisions in respect of the conversion of shares is added to their acquisition cost. [*TCGA 1992, s 120(2)(5B); FA 1998, s 54; ITEPA 2003, Sch 6 para 210; FA 2003, Sch 22 para 51*]. See Tolley's Capital Gains Tax for full details.

82.8   **ANTI-AVOIDANCE — SHARES WITH ARTIFICIALLY DEPRESSED MARKET VALUE**

The following provisions are 'designed to ensure that if the value of employment-related securities is depressed by means of non-commercial transaction(s), then that reduction in value is taxed on the employee' (Treasury Explanatory Notes to Finance Bill 2003). Subject to qualifications noted below where relevant, these provisions apply on and after 16 April 2003 irrespective of the date the shares in question were acquired. They apply in certain cases where the market value of 'employment-related shares' (or, where relevant, other shares or interests in shares) is reduced by things done otherwise than for genuine commercial purposes; this specifically includes anything done as part of a scheme or arrangement a main purpose of which is to avoid tax *or national insurance contributions* and any transaction (other than a payment for corporation tax group relief) between members of a 51% group of companies otherwise than on arm's length terms. See 82.3 above for the extended meaning of 'shares', in relation to these provisions.

For these purposes, *'employment-related shares'* and 'consideration given for the acquisition of employment-related shares' are defined as in 82.4 above.

Exclusions. The same exclusions from charge apply as in 82.4 above, except that the second of the full exclusions (nature of earnings from the employment) is given wider application and the exclusion for shares acquired under the terms of a public offer does not apply after 17 June 2004 (whatever the date of acquisition of the shares).

Subject to the rules below requiring the importing of certain fictions into the determination of **market values**, such values are to be determined as for capital gains tax purposes.

Charge on acquisition. If anything done otherwise than for genuine commercial purposes within the seven years ending with the acquisition reduces the market value of employment-related shares at acquisition by at least 10%, there is a charge to tax on the employee for the tax year in which the acquisition occurs; the amount chargeable (see below) counts as employment income for tax purposes. This applies in relation to acquisitions on and after 16 April 2003 but does not apply in the case of *restricted shares* if the tax exemption on acquisition at 82.4 above applies. The charge does not displace other income tax charges that may arise on acquisition.

The chargeable amount is the amount by which market value has been reduced. If the consideration given for the shares is greater than actual market value, the chargeable amount is reduced by the excess. Where the shares are convertible shares as in 82.6 above (or an interest in convertible shares), the chargeable amount is determined as if they were not. Where the shares are restricted shares as in 82.4 above (or a restricted interest in shares), the chargeable amount is the excess of what would have been their market value, disregarding both the avoidance device and the effect of restrictions, over their actual market value taking account of restrictions; in such circumstances though, there is no charge under 82.4 above on any chargeable event.

Other tax charges. *Restricted shares.* The consequences described below ensue where the market value of restricted shares (or a restricted interest in shares) as in 82.4 above is 'artificially low' at any of the following times:

(*a*)   immediately after a chargeable event within 82.4;

(*b*)   (after 6 May 2004) immediately before the shares are disposed of (in circumstances not giving rise to a chargeable event within (*a*) above) or are cancelled without being disposed of; or

(*c*)   on 5 April in any year.

For this purpose, market value is '*artificially low*' where it has been reduced by at least 10% as a result of anything done otherwise than for genuine commercial purposes within the 'relevant period'. The '*relevant period*' is normally the seven years ending with the event in question or , in the case of (*c*) above, with that 5 April. If, however, the tax exemption on acquisition at 82.4 applied in relation to the shares, the start of the relevant period is extended back to a point seven years before the acquisition. For the purposes of (*b*) above, in a case where the shares were acquired on or before 6 May 2004, the relevant period begins on 7 May 2004 at the earliest.

The consequences are as follows.

- In a case within (*b*) above, a chargeable event within 82.4(i) (lifting of restrictions) is deemed to occur on the date of disposal or cancellation. The reference to OP (Outstanding Proportion) in the formula in 82.4 (for charging tax on chargeable events) is deemed to be omitted (so that all remaining untaxed proportions are brought into charge).

- In a case within (*c*) above, a chargeable event within 82.4(i) is deemed to occur on that 5 April.

- In *all* cases, the value of UMV (Unrestricted Market Value) in the formula in 82.4 (for charging tax on chargeable events) is suitably modified so as to disregard the things done otherwise than for commercial purposes and also, where (*b*) above applies, the fact that the shares are about to be disposed of or cancelled.

- After 6 May 2004, in a case within (*a*) above, where the chargeable event concerned is a disposal for less than actual market value, the normal reduction in the chargeable amount determined by the formula in 82.4 is disapplied.

The above do not affect shares (or interests in shares) acquired before 16 April 2003 and, in relation to shares acquired subsequently, apply only on and after 1 September 2003.

Conditional interests in shares. Where the conditionality ceases without the employee's beneficial interest ceasing, or the employee disposes of any beneficial interest in the shares before the conditionality ceases, such that a charge arises as in 82.5 above, the chargeable amount is increased by bringing back into account any reduction by 10% or more in the market value of the shares immediately after the event in question that results from anything done otherwise than for genuine commercial purposes within the period beginning seven years before the event or on 16 April 2003, whichever is later. This applies in relation to conditional interests acquired before 16 April 2003 and, in relation to conditional interests acquired subsequently, applies during the period beginning on that day and ending immediately before 1 September 2003.

Convertible shares. As detailed in 82.6 above, any consideration given for the right to convert shares enters into the computation of the chargeable amount on a chargeable event. If anything done otherwise than for genuine commercial purposes within the seven years ending with the acquisition reduces the market value of the shares (or interest in shares) at acquisition by at least 10%, the market value of the shares at acquisition (determined as if they were not convertible shares or an interest in convertible shares) is taken as what would be their market value (as so determined) if it were not for the reduction. This has the effect of reducing the amount deductible in the said computation.

If, on a chargeable event within 82.6(*a*) above (conversion of the shares), the market value, at the time of conversion, of the shares *into which* the shares are converted is reduced by 10% or more as a result of anything done otherwise than for genuine commercial purposes within the seven years ending with the event, the value of CMVCS in the formula at 82.6(i) above is adjusted to what it would have been without the reduction.

Adjustments to consideration etc. Where the consideration or benefit referred to in specific provisions contained in 82.4, 82.6 above and 82.11, 82.12 below (as listed at *ITEPA 2003, s 446I(1)*) consists wholly or partly of shares (or an interest in shares) whose market value at that time is reduced by 10% or more as a result of anything done otherwise than for genuine commercial purposes within the seven years ending with the receipt of the consideration or benefit, that market value is taken for the purpose of that provision to be what it would have been if it were not for the reduction. This rule also applies for the purpose of determining 'consideration given for the shares' under 'Charge on acquisition' above.

Exceptions from charge disapplied. After 6 May 2004, the exception from charge in 82.4 above (restricted shares) and the similar exceptions in 82.6 above (convertible shares), 82.10 below (shares acquired for less than market value) and 82.12 below (post-acquisition benefits) do not apply if a charge or an adjustment to market value or consideration would otherwise arise under the above provisions.

[*ITEPA 2003, ss 419, 421, 421A–421D, 421E(2)–(5), 421F–421I, 446A–446J; FA 2003, Sch 22 paras 2, 5; FA 2004, s 86(6)(8), s 87, s 88(2)(11), s 89(1)–(4), s 90(2)(5); SI 2003 No 1997*].

PAYE. For the requirement to operate PAYE on chargeable amounts, see 55.2(*h*) PAY AS YOU EARN.

82.9 **ANTI-AVOIDANCE — SHARES WITH ARTIFICIALLY ENHANCED MARKET VALUE**

The following provisions are 'designed to ensure that if the value of employment-related securities is enhanced by means of non-commercial transaction(s) during any tax year, then that appreciation in value is taxed on the employee at the earlier of the disposal of the employment-related securities or 5 April.' (Treasury Explanatory Notes to Finance Bill 2003). Subject to qualifications noted below where relevant, these provisions apply on and after 16 April 2003 irrespective of the date the shares in question were acquired. They apply in certain cases where the market value of 'employment-related shares' is increased by things done otherwise than for genuine commercial purposes (a '*non-commercial increase*'); this specifically includes anything done as part of a scheme or arrangement a main purpose of which is to avoid tax *or national insurance contributions* and any transaction (other than a payment for corporation tax group relief) between members of a 51% group of companies otherwise than on arm's length terms. See 82.3 above for the extended meaning of 'shares', in relation to these provisions. See 82.17 below as regards reporting obligations.

For these purposes, '*employment-related shares*' are defined as in 82.4 above.

Exclusions. The same exclusions from charge apply as in 82.4 above, except that the second of the full exclusions (nature of earnings from the employment) is given wider application and the exclusion for shares acquired under the terms of a public offer does not apply after 17 June 2004 (whatever the date of acquisition of the shares).

Subject to the rules below requiring the importing of certain fictions into the determination of **market values,** such values are to be determined as for capital gains tax purposes.

Charge on non-commercial increases. Where, on the 'valuation date' for a 'relevant period', the market value of employment-related shares is at least 10% greater than it would be if any 'non-commercial increases' (see above) during the relevant period were disregarded, the whole of the excess is taxed as employment income of the employee for tax purposes for the tax year in which the valuation date falls. In determining both actual and notional market values for this purpose, one must ignore any restrictions (of the kind at 82.4(*a*)–(*c*) above) having effect in relation to the shares on the valuation date and any non-commercial reductions (i.e. the opposite to non-commercial increases) during the relevant period. For these purposes,

- the '*valuation date*' is the last day of the 'relevant period'; and

- the '*relevant period*' means any tax year, except that the first such period runs from date of acquisition (or from 16 April 2003 if later) to the following 5 April and the last runs from 6 April to the date in the tax year on which the provisions cease to apply (see 82.4 above under Exclusions). If these provisions cease to apply to an interest in the shares, the relevant period ends at that time in relation to that interest, but these provisions apply separately to that interest and to what remains. Where these provisions apply in relation to shares acquired before 18 June 2004 under approved schemes or under the terms of a public offer, the shares are deemed to have been acquired on that date for the purpose of determining the relevant period.

Special provision applies where on the valuation date the employment-related shares are restricted shares (as in 82.4 above) (or a restricted interest in shares) and no election has been made to wholly disapply the restricted shares provisions in full or to ignore outstanding restrictions (i.e. to omit OP from the formula) in relation to a chargeable event preceding the valuation date. See 82.4 above for these elections. The chargeable amount determined above (i.e. the excess) is reduced by the proportion of the non-commercial increase that remains to be taxed when the restriction is eventually lifted. This is achieved by multiplying the otherwise chargeable amount by $(1 - OP)$, where OP is determined in accordance with 82.4 above on the assumption that a chargeable event (resulting in no tax charge) occurs on the valuation date. This rule is suitably modified where an election has been made to disregard one or more specified restrictions in applying the restricted shares provisions.

Where the employment-related shares have been restricted shares (or a restricted interest in shares) at any time during the relevant period and there have been one or more chargeable events during that period, the otherwise chargeable amount under these provisions is reduced by the excess of chargeable amounts under 82.4 above over what they would have been if one were to disregard non-commercial increases during the relevant period (and before the chargeable event).

82.10 Share-Related Employment Income and Exemptions

The above interactions with the restricted shares provisions do not affect shares (or interests in shares) acquired before 16 April 2003 and, in relation to shares acquired subsequently, apply only on and after 1 September 2003.

Exceptions from charge disapplied. After 6 May 2004, the exception from charge in 82.4 above (restricted shares) and the similar exceptions in 82.6 above (convertible shares), 82.10 below (shares acquired for less than market value) and 82.12 below (post-acquisition benefits) do not apply if the market value of the shares in question at the time of acquisition has been increased by at least 10% by non-commercial increases in the seven years preceding acquisition. Also after 6 May 2004, if the above charge on non-commercial increases applies in relation to any shares, the exception from charge in 82.4 above does not subsequently apply in relation to those shares.

[*ITEPA 2003, ss 419, 421, 421B–421D, 421E(2)–(5), 421F–421H, 446K–446P; FA 2003, Sch 22 paras 2, 6; FA 2004, s 86(7)(8), s 88(2)(11)(13), s 89, s 90(2)(5); SI 2003 No 1997*].

PAYE. For the requirement to operate PAYE on chargeable amounts, see 55.2(*h*) PAY AS YOU EARN.

82.10 SHARES ACQUIRED FOR LESS THAN MARKET VALUE

The following provisions deal with the acquisition of 'employment-related shares' for less than their market value and do so by creating the fiction of a notional interest-free loan on the amount of the under-value. The current provisions have effect in relation to shares (and interests in shares) acquired on or after 16 April 2003, but broadly similar provisions applied, as part of the 'benefits code' (see 75.14 SCHEDULE E—EMPLOYMENT INCOME), under *ITEPA 2003, ss 192–197* (and previously under *ICTA 1988, s 162(1)–(5)*) in relation to shares etc. acquired before that date but after 6 April 1976. The current provisions apply to all employees whereas the earlier provisions were excluded from applying to those in 'lower-paid employment' (see 75.14 SCHEDULE E—EMPLOYMENT INCOME). The provisions are aimed principally at shares that are acquired partly-paid, such that the employee pays an amount for the shares (which may well be equal to their market value) but does so wholly or partly by instalments.

For these purposes, *'employment-related shares'* are defined as in 82.4 above. The pre-16 April 2003 provisions were of narrower application in that they applied only where the shares (or interest in shares) were acquired by the employee, or by a person connected with him (within 19 CONNECTED PERSONS), by reason of the employee's employment.

For the extended meaning of 'shares', in relation to the current provisions, see 82.3 above. For the purposes of the pre-16 April 2003 provisions, 'shares' included stock and also included securities within *ICTA 1988, s 254(1)*.

See 82.17 below as regards reporting obligations.

Exclusions. The same exclusions from charge under the current provisions apply as in 82.4 above, except that the second of the full exclusions (nature of earnings from the employment) is given wider application. *Broadly* similar exclusions applied previously.

The provisions apply, subject to the exception referred to below, where, at the time of acquisition of employment-related shares, either no payment is (or has been) made for them or a payment is (or has been) made of an amount which is less than market value (determined as for capital gains tax purposes and as if, where it is not the case, the shares were fully paid up). For this purpose, any obligation to make further payment(s) after the time of acquisition is disregarded.

If the tax exemption at 82.4 above applies on an acquisition of restricted shares, the current provisions apply as if the acquisition took place at the first occurrence of a chargeable event within 82.4 above.

The application of these provisions does not displace the application of other tax charges arising in respect of the acquisition of employment-related shares under specified provisions at *ITEPA 2003, s 446V.*

Exception from charge. An exception similar to that applying on chargeable events in 82.4 above is imported into the current provisions; the provisions are disapplied if *all* the company's shares of the same class are acquired at an under-value and *either* of the conditions detailed at 82.4 above is satisfied. (The extended meaning of shares in 82.3 above does not apply for this purpose.) After 6 May 2004, there is a further requirement that the arrangements under which the right or opportunity to acquire the shares was made available did not have as one of its main purposes the avoidance of tax or national insurance contributions.

Where these provisions do apply, an **interest-free notional loan** is deemed to have been made to the employee by the employer at the time the employment-related shares are acquired. For so long as the employment continues, the loan counts as an 'employment-related loan' for the purposes of applying *ITEPA 2003, s 175* (benefit of cheap loan arrangements) and related provisions (see 75.20 SCHEDULE E—EMPLOYMENT INCOME). The initial amount of the loan is the market-value of the shares (or the interest in them) at the time of acquisition (determined as above) less any payment made at or before that time by the employee or (if different) the person who acquired the shares, any amount on which tax is charged as earnings by reason of the acquisition and any amounts on which tax is charged under specified other provisions relating to unapproved share options, restricted shares and convertible shares (see *ITEPA 2003, s 446T(3)*). The loan may be reduced subsequently by payments or further payments for the shares.

The notional loan is treated as discharged upon

(*a*)   the disposal, otherwise than to an 'associated person' (as defined at 82.4 above), of the shares (or the interest in shares); or

(*b*)   (in the case of shares not fully paid up at time of acquisition) the release, transfer or adjustment, so as no longer to bind any associated person, of the outstanding or contingent liability to pay for the shares; or

(*c*)   the making by associated persons of sufficient payments to clear the loan; or

(*d*)   the death of the employee.

If the discharge of the loan is within (*a*) or (*b*) above, the amount outstanding immediately before the discharge is taxed as employment income of the employee for the tax year of discharge, and this applies regardless of whether or not the employment has terminated.

For shares acquired before 16 April 2003, the concept of 'associated persons' did not apply and these provisions were instead framed by reference to the narrower concept of employee and persons connected with him.

[*ITEPA 2003, ss 192–197, 419, 421, 421B–421D, 421E(2)–(5), 421F–421H, 446Q–446W, Sch 7 paras 28, 29; ICTA 1988, s 162(1)–(5)(9)–(11); FA 2003, Sch 22 paras 2, 7, 22; FA 2004, s 86(1)–(5)(8), s 88(2)(11), s 89(1)–(4), s 90(2)(5)*].

See also FAQs at www.inlandrevenue.gov.uk/shareschemes/faq_emprelatedsecurity-ch3c.htm

PAYE. For the requirement to operate PAYE on the chargeable amount on discharge of the loan, see 55.2(*h*) PAY AS YOU EARN.

For *capital gains tax* purposes, any amount taxed as employment income on discharge of the notional loan normally counts as part of the acquisition cost of the shares. [*TCGA 1992, ss 119A, 120; FA 2003, Sch 22 paras 50, 51*]. See Tolley's Capital Gains Tax under Employee Share Schemes for full details.

82.11 Share-Related Employment Income and Exemptions

82.11 SHARES DISPOSED OF FOR MORE THAN MARKET VALUE

The following provisions impose an income tax charge on the employee when an 'associated person' (as defined at 82.4 above) disposes of 'employment-related shares' for more than their market value. The current provisions have effect in relation to shares (and interests in shares) disposed of on or after 16 April 2003, but broadly similar provisions applied, as part of the 'benefits code' (see 75.14 SCHEDULE E—EMPLOYMENT INCOME), under *ITEPA 2003, ss 198–200* (and previously under *ICTA 1988, s 162(6)–(11)*) in relation to shares etc. disposed of before that date. The current provisions apply to all employees whereas the earlier provisions were excluded from applying to those in 'lower-paid employment' (see 75.14 SCHEDULE E—EMPLOYMENT INCOME).

For these purposes, *'employment-related shares'* are defined as in 82.4 above. The pre-16 April 2003 provisions were of narrower application in that they applied only where the shares (or interest in shares) were acquired by the employee, or by a person connected with him (within 19 CONNECTED PERSONS), by reason of the employee's employment.

For the extended meaning of 'shares', in relation to the current provisions, see 82.3 above. For the purposes of the pre-16 April 2003 provisions, 'shares' included stock and also included securities within *ICTA 1988, s 254(1)*.

See 82.17 below as regards reporting obligations.

Exclusions. The same exclusions from charge under the current provisions apply as in 82.4 above, except that the second of the full exclusions (nature of earnings from the employment) is given wider application and the exclusion for shares acquired under the terms of a public offer does not apply after 17 June 2004 (whatever the date of acquisition of the shares). *Broadly* similar exclusions applied previously. In addition, neither the current nor the earlier provisions apply to shares (or an interest in shares) acquired before 6 April 1976.

The charge to income tax arises where employment-related shares are disposed of by an associated person, such that no associated person is any longer beneficially entitled to them, for consideration which exceeds their market value (determined as for capital gains tax purposes) at the time of disposal. *ITEPA 2003, ss 421(2), 421A* apply in determining the amount of any consideration given. For disposals before 16 April 2003, the concept of 'associated persons' did not apply and these provisions were instead framed by reference to the narrower concept of employee and persons connected with him.

The chargeable amount is the excess of the consideration given for the shares (or the interest in shares) over the market value of the shares (or interest). For disposals on or after 16 April 2003, any expenses incurred in connection with the disposal are also deductible in arriving at the chargeable amount. The chargeable amount is taxed as employment income of the employee for the tax year of disposal.

A *Pt 5* transfer of shares under *Proceeds of Crime Act 2002* (as in 9.2(xi) CAPITAL ALLOWANCES) does not give rise to an income tax charge under these provisions.

[*ITEPA 2003, ss 198–200, 419, 421, 421A–421D, 421E(2)–(5), 421F–421H, 446X–446Z, Sch 7 paras 30, 31, 61A; ICTA 1988, s 162(6)–(11); Proceeds of Crime Act 2002, Sch 10 para 32; FA 2003, Sch 22 paras 2, 8, 23, 46(2)(19)(26); FA 2004, s 88(2)(11), s 89(1)–(4), s 90(2)(5)*].

PAYE. For the requirement to operate PAYE on chargeable amounts, see 55.2(*h*) PAY AS YOU EARN.

82.12 POST-ACQUISITION BENEFITS FROM SHARES AFTER FA 2003

The following provisions supersede those at 82.14, 82.15 below and generally have effect on and after 16 April 2003 irrespective of when the shares were acquired. However, some of the provisions in 82.14 below (as noted therein) continue to apply in relation to shares (and interests in shares) acquired before 16 April 2003 and, in relation to shares etc. acquired subsequently, continue to apply prior to 1 September 2003. Note that the current provisions are not dissimilar to those at 82.14(*c*) below (chargeable benefits), but are of wider application.

For these purposes, '*employment-related shares*' are defined as in 82.4 above. See 82.17 below as regards reporting obligations.

Exclusions. The same exclusions from charge apply as in 82.4 above, except that the exclusion for shares acquired under the terms of a public offer does not apply after 17 June 2004 (whatever the date of acquisition of the shares). In addition, these provisions do not apply in relation to shares (or interests in shares) acquired before 26 October 1987 (for which see 82.13 below).

The charge. These provisions apply if an 'associated person' (as defined at 82.4 above) receives a benefit by virtue of the ownership of 'employment-related shares', whether by him or another associated person. The amount or market value (determined as for capital gains tax purposes) of the benefit is taxed as employment income of the employee for the tax year in which the benefit is received.

Exceptions. These provisions do not apply if the benefit is otherwise chargeable to income tax. In addition, an exception similar to that applying on chargeable events in 82.4 above is imported into the current provisions; the provisions are disapplied if a similar benefit is received by the owners of *all* the company's shares of the same class and *either* of the conditions detailed at 82.4 above is satisfied. (The extended meaning of shares in 82.3 above does not apply for this purpose, though the term does include stock.) After 6 May 2004, there is a further requirement that the arrangements under which the right or opportunity to acquire the shares was made available did not have as one of its main purposes the avoidance of tax or national insurance contributions.

[*ITEPA 2003, ss 421, 421B–421D, 421E(1)(3)–(5), 421F–421H, 447–450, Sch 7 para 54; FA 2003, Sch 22 paras 2, 9, 46(13)(26); FA 2004, s 86(1)–(5)(8), s 88(2)(11), s 89(1)–(4), s 90(2)(5); SI 2003 No 1997*].

PAYE. For the requirement to operate PAYE on chargeable amounts, see 55.2(*h*) PAY AS YOU EARN.

82.13   POST-ACQUISITION BENEFITS FROM SHARES BEFORE FA 2003

Shares acquired before 26 October 1987. The provisions in *ICTA 1988, ss 138–140* described below **do not apply to shares acquired after 25 October 1987,** for which see the provisions of *ITEPA 2003, ss 447–470* (formerly in *FA 1988, Pt III, Ch II*) described at 82.14 below and the subsequent provisions at 82.12 above. In relation to shares acquired before 26 October 1987, the following continues to apply, but see also the transitional provisions at 82.15 below.

Where (unless exempted as below) the holder of an office or employment, the emoluments from which are chargeable to tax under *ITEPA 2003, s 15* or *s 21* (earnings of employee resident and ordinarily resident in UK) (or, before 2003/04, under Case I of Schedule E), acquires shares (or an interest in shares) in a company under a right or opportunity given him by reason of that office or employment, he is chargeable to income tax under the employment income Parts of *ITEPA 2003* (or, before 2003/04, under Schedule E)

(*a*)   on the value of any benefit, not applicable to the majority of the ordinary shareholders, which he receives in respect of such shares acquired after 5 April 1972 and before 26 October 1987, and

(*b*)   at the end of seven years from the acquisition (or, if earlier, when he parts with the shares or they cease to be subject to specified restrictions (see *ICTA 1988, s 138(6)(9)(c)*) on any excess of their market value then over their value when acquired.

A right etc. is 'offered' to the taxpayer although he may himself have stipulated its being granted (*CIR v Herd CS 1992, 66 TC 29*).

For the circumstances in which the Revenue will accept that shares or share options were acquired by a director or employee in a different capacity and not by reason of the office or employment, see Revenue Share Schemes Manual SSM 4.4.

Neither (*a*) nor (*b*) above applies if the shares are acquired:

(i) in pursuance of an offer to the public; or

(ii) under an arrangement whereby a company gives its employees, as part of their emoluments, shares as a predetermined participation in profits, and for new schemes (or existing schemes modified) after 22 March 1973 if (A) equal participation is allowed to all full-time employees taxable under Case I of Schedule E over 25 years of age and with five years continuous service, (B) shares are in a company which is either quoted on a recognised stock exchange or not controlled by another company, (C) shares have no restrictions which may result in subsequent increase in value and (D) shares cannot be exchanged or converted into shares subject to such restrictions,

and (*b*) above does not apply:

(1) where immediately after the shares were acquired (A) the shares were not subject to specified restrictions (see *section 138(6)*), nor exchangeable into such shares, and the majority of available shares (exclusive of associated company shareholdings) of the same class were acquired otherwise than by reason of employment, or (B) the shares were not subject to specified restrictions (see *section 138(6)(a)(b)*), nor exchangeable into such shares, and the majority of the available shares of the same class (as above) were acquired by present or past employees or directors (of the company or a subsidiary) who together had control of the company; or

(2) for acquisitions after 5 April 1984 of shares in authorised unit trusts (see 90.1 UNIT TRUSTS) approved by the Board for this purpose, provided that shares in the employer company (or in any associated company) do not make up more than 10% of the value of the trust investments for a continuous period of one month or more throughout which a director or employee of the employer company has such a right as is dealt with under these provisions to acquire unit trust shares, or retains an interest in shares so acquired.

Before 19 March 1986, the ending of the restrictions specified in *FA 1972, s 79(2A)* (the predecessor to *section 138(6)*) triggered the charge under (*b*) above, but where such restrictions cease after 18 March 1986, the charge is triggered only if, had the shares been acquired immediately after the restrictions were lifted, they would have been excluded from the operation of (*b*) above by virtue of (1) above.

Additional shares (or an interest therein), acquired after 18 March 1986 by virtue of a holding of (or of an interest in) shares which are not excluded from (*b*) above, are for the purposes of (*b*) above treated with the original holding as one holding acquired at the same time and in the same circumstances as the original holding, the market value of the original holding being attributed proportionately over all shares in the new holding. Any consideration given for the additional shares is treated as an increase in the consideration for the original holding and thus as reducing any charge arising under (*b*) above.

The Board has information and penalty powers as regards approval of authorised unit trusts under (2) above.

As regards (i) above, shares (or an interest in shares) acquired by a director or employee are treated as acquired in pursuance of an offer to the public where

(A)   they were acquired at a discount under an offer (the 'discount offer') to directors or employees in their capacity as such;

(B)   the discount offer was made in conjunction with an offer to the public on the same terms but without the discount;

(C)   the director or employee is chargeable under Schedule E on an amount equal to the discount on shares acquired by him; and

(D)   at least 75% of the shares acquired under the discount offer and the offer to the public together were acquired under the offer to the public.

The amount of the charge under (*b*) is reduced where, under acquisition terms, any increased consideration is subsequently payable or the shares are disposed of at less than market value.

A profit on the sale of shares was held to be assessable under the legislation, notwithstanding that the employee had purchased the shares through the Stock Exchange (*Cheatle v CIR Ch D 1982, 56 TC 111*).

Company reconstructions etc. Where shares are disposed of after 18 March 1986 in circumstances such that a 'new holding' of shares is acquired which is treated as the same asset as the original holding under *TCGA 1992, ss 127–130*, the new holding is similarly treated for the purposes of *section 138*. Any consideration given for the new holding is treated as an increase in the consideration for the original holding, and thus as reducing any charge under (*b*) above. Any consideration received for the original holding, other than the new holding, is treated as proportionately increasing the market value of the shares comprised in the new holding at any subsequent time.

[*ICTA 1988, ss 138, 139; TMA 1970, s 98; ITEPA 2003, s 418(4), Sch 6 para 16, Sch 7 para 57*].

Simon's Direct Tax Service. See **E4.541** *et seq.*

82.14   **Shares acquired after 25 October 1987.** The provisions at 82.13 above do not apply in respect of shares acquired after 25 October 1987, and are replaced by the following. (All references below to *ITEPA 2003, ss 447–470* are to those *sections* as originally enacted, and see 82.12 above.)

Where a person acquires shares, or an interest in shares, in a company in pursuance of a right conferred on him, or opportunity offered him, by reason of his being a director or employee, past, present or future, of that or any other company, a charge to tax may arise on him (by reason of a subsequent event as below) unless the acquisition is made under the terms of an offer to the public. Where such a right is assigned to a person, and the right was conferred on some other person by reason of the assignee's office or employment, the assignee is treated as having acquired the shares in pursuance of a right conferred on him by reason of that office or employment. These provisions do not apply to an acquisition if the earnings from the office or employment in question were not (or would not have been if there were any) general earnings within *ITEPA 2003, s 15* or *s 21* (earnings for year when employee resident and ordinarily resident in UK). [*ITEPA 2003, ss 447(1)–(4), 448(1)(2), 470, Sch 7 para 58(2); FA 1988, ss 77, 87(1)(4); FA 1998, s 50(2); FA 2003, Sch 22 para 46(16)(26)*]. An option to acquire shares does not constitute an interest in the shares for this purpose. (ICAEW Memorandum TR 739, para 32, 13 February 1989). A right etc. is 'offered' to the taxpayer although he may himself have stipulated its being granted (*CIR v Herd CS 1992, 66 TC 29*).

82.14 Share-Related Employment Income and Exemptions

For the circumstances in which the Revenue will accept that shares or share options were acquired by a director or employee in a different capacity and not by reason of the office or employment, see Revenue Share Schemes Manual SSM 4.4.

In a case within *ITEPA 2003, s 544(1)* (broadly where a combination of shares in two or more companies is offered to the public, and at the same time shares in one or more but not all of those companies are offered to directors or employees — see 82.76 below) any acquisition under either the public offer or the employee offer is treated as made under the terms of a public offer so as to be outside these provisions. [*ITEPA 2003, s 448(3)(4), Sch 7 para 58(3); FA 1988, s 77(4); FA 1991, s 44(9); FA 2003, Sch 22 para 46(16)(26)*].

A charge to tax on employment income will arise in the following situations.

(a) *Removal of restrictions etc.* Insofar as the provisions below deal with the removal or variation of a restriction applying to the shares in question, they continue to apply in relation to shares (and interests in shares) acquired before 16 April 2003 and, in relation to shares etc. acquired subsequently, continue to apply prior to 1 September 2003. In both cases, they apply without any reference to dependent subsidiaries. In other respects, these provisions cease to apply on and after 16 April 2003, irrespective of when the shares etc. in question were acquired. [*FA 2003, Sch 22 para 9(2)–(4); SI 2003 No 1997*]. See now the restricted shares provisions at 82.4 above.

If a 'chargeable event' occurs while he still has a beneficial interest in the shares, and the shares are in a company which was not a 'dependent subsidiary' at the time either of his acquisition or of the 'chargeable event', the charge will be made for the tax year in which the 'chargeable event' occurs on the amount by which that event increases the value of the interest (or would do so but for some other event).

A *'chargeable event'* is the removal or variation of a restriction, or the creation or variation of a right, relating to the shares, or the imposition or variation of a restriction, or removal or variation of a right, relating to other shares in the company, which increases (or would do so but for another event) the value of the shares. This does not normally apply on the triggering of certain kinds of performance-related rights or restrictions attached at the outset to the shares acquired (known as 'equity ratchets') which are commonly found in management buy-outs. Under these, the managers' share of the company's equity is increased on some predetermined basis by reference to the company's performance. (Revenue Press Release 14 April 1988). It is understood that this applies equally to such arrangements in situations other than management buy-outs. (Tolley's Practical Tax 1995 p 15).

An event is *not* a *'chargeable event'* if, in relation to all shares of the same class, it is a removal etc. as above and, at the time of the event, either

(i)   the majority of shares of that class are held 'by outside shareholders', or

(ii) the company is 'employee-controlled' by virtue of holdings of shares of that class, or

(iii) the company is a 51% subsidiary with shares of a single class.

No charge arises under these provisions if at no time in the seven years immediately preceding the event has the person acquiring the shares been a director or employee of the company whose shares they are, or of the company as director or employee of which he acquired the shares, or of an 'associated company' of either. Nor does a charge arise under these provisions if a charge arises under *ITEPA 2003, s 427* (charge on interest ceasing to be conditional — see 82.5 above) in relation to the chargeable event.

[*ITEPA 2003, ss 449–452; FA 1988, s 78*].

(b)   *Shares in dependent subsidiaries.* These provisions cease to have effect on and after 16 April 2003, irrespective of when the shares were acquired.

If the shares are in a company which

(i)   was a 'dependent subsidiary' at the time of the acquisition, or

(ii)   became one before the person acquiring the shares ceased to have a beneficial interest in them,

and there is a 'chargeable increase' in the value of the shares, the charge is made on the amount of the increase (or appropriate part where the interest in the shares is less than full beneficial ownership). If, under the terms of the acquisition, the consideration for the acquisition is subsequently increased, the amount taxable is correspondingly reduced. If, under those terms, the person acquiring the shares subsequently ceases to have any beneficial interest in them as a result of a disposal for consideration less than the value of the shares at the time of the disposal, the amount taxable is reduced by

- (where (i) above applies and also, before 2003/04, where (ii) above applies) the excess of the disposal consideration over the value of the shares at the time of acquisition; or

- (for 2003/04 onwards where (ii) above applies) the excess of the disposal consideration over the value of the shares at the time the company became a 'dependent subsidiary'.

Where (i) above applies, there is a *'chargeable increase'* if the value of the shares, at the earlier of seven years from acquisition and the time when the taxpayer ceases to have any beneficial interest in the shares, exceeds their value at the time of acquisition.

Where (ii) above applies, there is a *'chargeable increase'* if the value of the shares, at the earliest of

(A)   seven years from the time of the company becoming a 'dependent subsidiary',

(B)   the time when the taxpayer ceases to have any beneficial interest in the shares, and

(C)   the time when the company ceases to be a 'dependent subsidiary',

exceeds their value at the time when the company became a 'dependent subsidiary', but only if, at some time during the seven years before the company became a 'dependent subsidiary', the taxpayer was a director or employee of the company, or of the company as a director or employee of which he acquired the shares, or of an 'associated company' of either of them.

The charge is made for the tax year in which falls the time by reference to which the chargeable increase is determined.

If, before the time by reference to which the chargeable increase is determined, an event occurs in respect of the shares by virtue of which an amount counts as employment income (of the person who acquired the shares) under 82.5 above (conditional interests in shares), disregarding any charge on acquisition, or 82.7 above (convertible shares), that amount is deductible in arriving at the charge described here.

No charge arises under these provisions by virtue of a disposal if a charge arises under *ITEPA 2003, s 427* (charge on interest ceasing to be conditional — see 82.5 above) in respect of the disposal.

82.14 Share-Related Employment Income and Exemptions

A *Pt 5* transfer of shares, or an interest in shares, under *Proceeds of Crime Act 2002* (as in 9.2(xi) CAPITAL ALLOWANCES) does not give rise to an income tax charge under the above rules.

[*ITEPA 2003, ss 453–456, Sch 7 para 59; FA 1988, s 79; FA 1998, ss 50(3), 51(2); Proceeds of Crime Act 2002, Sch 10 para 33; FA 2003, Sch 22 para 46(17)(26)*].

(c) *Other chargeable benefits.* The provisions below cease to have effect on and after 16 April 2003, irrespective of when the shares were acquired, and are replaced by those at 82.12 above.

If the person acquiring the shares receives a 'chargeable benefit' through his ownership of them, and was at some time during the previous seven years a director or employee as mentioned under (*b*) above, then unless the benefit is otherwise chargeable to income tax, the charge is made for the tax year in which it is received. The amount to be brought into account as employment income is the amount which the recipient of the benefit might reasonably expect to obtain from a sale in the open market.

A benefit is a '*chargeable benefit*' if,

- when the benefit becomes available, it is available to less than 90% of holders of shares of the same class as the shares in question, or,

- at the time the benefit is received, the company whose shares they are is a 'dependent subsidiary' and its shares are of a single class.

If neither of the above applies, a benefit is nevertheless a '*chargeable benefit*' unless, at the time it is received,

- the majority of shares in respect of which the benefit is received are held 'by outside shareholders', or

- the company is 'employee-controlled' by virtue of holdings of the same class as the shares in question, or

- the company is a 51% subsidiary (other than a 'dependent subsidiary') and the majority of its shares in respect of which the benefit is received are held otherwise than by, or for the benefit of, (i) directors or employees of the company or of an 'associated company' or (ii) a company which is the first-mentioned company's 'associated company' but not its parent company.

[*ITEPA 2003, ss 457–460; FA 1988, s 80; F(No 2)A 1992, s 37*].

For the purposes of these provisions, an '*interest in shares*' does not include a share option. [*ITEPA 2003, s 470(1)*]. Any increase or reduction in a person's interest in shares is treated for the purposes of these provisions as a proportionate acquisition or disposal of a separate interest. [*ITEPA 2003, s 464; FA 1988, s 81*].

For these purposes, a company's shares are held '*by outside shareholders*' if they are held otherwise than by, or for the benefit of, directors or employees of the company or of an 'associated company' or an 'associated company' itself. [*ITEPA 2003, s 469; FA 1988, s 78(6)*].

A company is '*employee-controlled*' for these purposes by virtue of shares of a class if the majority of shares of that class (other than those held by or for an 'associated company') are held by or for employees or directors of the company or a company which it controls, and those employees and directors as holders of the shares are together able to control the company. Control is defined by *ICTA 1988, s 840*. [*ITEPA 2003, ss 468, 719; FA 1988, s 87(2)(3)*].

'*Associated company*' is as defined by *ICTA 1988, s 416*. [*ITEPA 2003, s 470(1); FA 1988, s 87(1)*].

A 51% subsidiary is a *'dependent subsidiary'* throughout a period of account unless

(i) the whole (or substantially the whole) of its business during that period is carried on with persons who are not members of the same group (consisting of a principal company, which is not itself a 51% subsidiary, and all its 51% subsidiaries), and

(ii) during that period, any increase in the value of the company as a result of intra-group transactions not on arm's length terms (other than group relief payments) does not exceed 5% of the company's value at the beginning of the period (or pro rata for periods other than twelve months), and

(iii) the directors of the principal company give the inspector, within two years after the end of the period, a certificate that in their opinion conditions (i) and (ii) above are satisfied for that period, and attached to that certificate is a report from the subsidiary's auditors that, after enquiry, they are not aware of anything to indicate that the directors' opinion is unreasonable.

As regards (i) above, business carried on by a company with its own 51% subsidiary is treated as carried on with a non-member of the group unless all (or substantially all) of the business of that or any other 51% subsidiary during the period of account is carried on with members of the group other than the company and its 51% subsidiaries.

[*ITEPA 2003, s 467; FA 1988, s 86*].

Also as regards (i) above, the Revenue consider that, to meet this condition, at least 90% of the company's business must be carried on outside the group, although a higher percentage may be required in any particular case (Revenue Share Schemes Manual SSM 5.9).

Connected persons. Shares acquired by a person connected with a director or employee (within *ICTA 1988, s 839* — see 19 CONNECTED PERSONS) are deemed to be acquired by the director or employee for these purposes, as is any chargeable benefit received by such a connected person. [*ITEPA 2003, ss 447(5), 457(2), 718; FA 1988, ss 83(1)(4), 87(3)*].

The director or employee is treated for the purposes of these provisions as continuing to have a beneficial interest in the shares until such time as they are disposed of either by way of a bargain at arm's length with a non-connected person or, under the terms on which the acquisition was made, to the company whose shares they are. In other words, disposals to connected persons are disregarded for these purposes until there is an onward disposal satisfying the aforementioned conditions. Chargeable benefits received in such circumstances by other persons are treated as if received by the director or employee. [*ITEPA 2003, ss 457(2), 463, 718; FA 1988, ss 83(2)–(4), 87(3)*]. (Deficiencies in the wording of the pre-2003/04 legislation mean that, in certain limited circumstances, it may not strictly have achieved its intention in these respects — see Change 114 listed in Annex 1 to the Explanatory Notes to the Income Tax (Earnings and Pensions) Bill.)

Related acquisitions of additional shares. Any additional shares acquired by virtue of a holding within these provisions is treated as having been acquired at the same time, and in like manner, as the originally-acquired shares (whether or not consideration was given for the additional shares). As regards (*b*) above, all the shares are treated as one holding, their value being determined accordingly and the acquisition value allocated proportionately, and any consideration given for the additional shares is treated as additional consideration for the originally-acquired shares under the terms of the original acquisition. [*ITEPA 2003, s 461; FA 1988, s 82(1)(2)*].

Company reorganisations etc. If the shares originally acquired are converted into a new holding (within *TCGA 1992, ss 127–130*), the original and new holdings are equated for the purposes of these provisions, any new consideration *given* is treated as additional consideration under the terms of the original acquisition, and any consideration *received* is apportioned among the shares in the new holding, whose value is increased accordingly. [*ITEPA 2003, s 462; FA 1988, s 82*].

Capital gains tax. Where an amount is chargeable under these provisions on a person who acquires (or is treated as acquiring) shares or an interest in shares, then on the first disposal of the shares following that acquisition (whether that disposal is made by that or any other person, for example a connected person — see above), the amount so chargeable forms part of the CGT acquisition cost of the shares to the person making the disposal. [*TCGA 1992, s 120(1)–(1B); ITEPA 2003, Sch 6 para 210(2); FA 2003, Sch 22 para 51*].

Reporting requirements. The company whose shares are acquired (and, if different, the company as a director or employee of which they were acquired) must provide written particulars of the acquisition to the Revenue before 7 July following the end of the tax year in which the acquisition is made. For 2003/04 onwards, this requirement is expressly extended to related acquisitions of additional shares and to new holdings following a company reorganisation. Any such company must also provide the Revenue with written particulars of any chargeable event within (*a*) above or chargeable benefit within (*c*) above within 92 days (for 2003/04 onwards — previously 60 days) after the event occurs or the benefit is received. Both information requirements are subject to penalty under *TMA 1970, s 98* for non-compliance. [*ITEPA 2003, ss 465, 466, Sch 6 para 137, Sch 7 paras 60, 61; FA 1988, s 85; FA 2003, Sch 22 para 46(18)*]. Particulars should be sent to Inland Revenue, Employee Share Schemes, Second Floor, New Wing, Somerset House, Strand, London, WC2R 1LB.

Simon's Direct Tax Service. See E4.531 *et seq.*

82.15   **Transitional provisions.** If tax was chargeable under the earlier provisions applying to shares acquired before 26 October 1987 (see 82.13 above) by reference to the market value after that date of shares in a company which was not a dependent subsidiary (see above) on that date, and that market value was greater than the market value on that date, the latter was substituted.

Except as regards 82.14(*b*) and (*c*), the provisions at 82.14 above apply to shares acquired before 26 October 1987 if the company was not a dependent subsidiary on that date. However, the removal of a restriction on such shares is not a chargeable event (see 82.14(*a*) above) if it would have been excluded from being a chargeable event before that date by *FA 1973, Sch 8 para 7*.

[*ITEPA 2003, Sch 7 paras 54–56; FA 1988, s 88; FA 2003, Sch 22 para 46(13)–(15)(26)*].

82.16   **UNAPPROVED SHARE OPTIONS**

This section is essentially concerned with *unapproved* share options. For EMI options, approved SAYE option schemes and approved CSOP schemes, see respectively 82.35, 82.47 and 82.61 below. For approved 'executive share option schemes' (superseded by CSOP schemes), see 82.75 below. However, as noted in those sections where relevant, the breach of certain conditions under EMI options and approved schemes can lead to a charge under the provisions described below.

Meaning of 'share option'. A *'share option'* is a right to acquire 'shares'. Before 1 September 2003, *'shares'*, for the purposes of these provisions, includes stock and also includes securities as defined in *ICTA 1988, s 254(1)*. On and after that date, *'shares'* is given the extended meaning in 82.3 above. This extended meaning applies from the earlier date of 16 April 2003 in relation to options to acquire securities that would not have fallen within the original definition of 'shares'.

Application of these provisions. These provisions apply to a share option (an *'employment-related share option'*) acquired by a person where the right or opportunity to acquire it is available by reason of the employment (past, present or prospective) of that person or any other person. On and after the dates indicated above under 'Meaning of "share option"', depending on the type of share that may be acquired under the option, any right or opportunity made available by a person's employer, or by a person connected (within *ICTA 1988, s 839* — see 19 CONNECTED PERSONS) with a person's employer, is treated as made available by reason of the employment of that person, other than in the case of an individual conferring a right or opportunity in the normal course of his domestic, family or personal relationships. Also on and after those dates, a right to acquire a share option becoming available by reason of an existing holding of 'employment-related shares' (as defined at 82.4 above) is treated for these purposes as available by reason of the employment by reason of which the right or opportunity to acquire those shares was available.

For the circumstances in which the Revenue will accept that shares or share options were acquired by an employee in a different capacity and not by reason of the employment, see Revenue Share Schemes Manual SSM 4.4.

A gain realised following cessation of the employment on the exercise, assignment, release etc. of an employment-related share option falls within *these* provisions and not those at 18 COMPENSATION FOR LOSS OF EMPLOYMENT (AND DAMAGES) (*Bluck v Salton (Sp C 378), [2003] SSCD 439*).

Grant of option. Following changes made by *FA 2003*, if an employment-related share option is potentially within the charge to tax below on exercise, assignment, release etc., no income tax liability arises in respect of the receipt of the option (regardless of when it can be exercised). The *FA 2003* changes have effect on and after 16 April 2003 or on and after 1 September 2003, depending on the type of 'share' that can be acquired under the option (see above under 'Meaning of "share option"').

Prior to the *FA 2003* changes, if a share option was potentially within the charge to tax below on exercise, assignment, release etc. and could not be exercised after the tenth anniversary of the date on which it was obtained (the seventh anniversary where the option was obtained before 6 April 1998), no income tax liability arose in respect of the receipt of the option. Where such an option could be exercised after that anniversary, a charge could arise on receipt of the option (as earnings or as a benefit — under general principles) as well as on its exercise etc. Where both charges arise, the amount charged on receipt is deductible in arriving at the amount chargeable on exercise etc. (Before 6 April 2002, this relief was by reference to tax payable rather than amounts chargeable.) For the purpose of any charge to tax as earnings on receipt of the option, its value is taken to be the excess of

- the market value (at the time the option is obtained) of the shares that are its subject (of, if higher, of any shares for which those shares may be exchanged) over

- the consideration (or, if variable, the least consideration) for which the subject shares may be acquired.

Before 2003/04, slightly different rules applied for computing the option value (see Changes 119, 120 listed in Annex 1 to the Explanatory Notes to the Income Tax (Earnings and Pensions) Bill).

Where the option is outside the charge to tax below on exercise, assignment, release etc. (because the earnings from the employment in question were not general earnings within *ITEPA 2003, s 15* or *s 21* (earnings for year when employee resident and ordinarily resident in UK)), a charge to tax can arise on receipt of the option (regardless of when it is capable of being exercised) but not on its exercise etc. See also *Abbott v Philbin HL 1960, 39 TC 82* and Revenue Share Scheme Manual SSM 3.3.

Exercise, assignment or release of option or other chargeable event. Subject to the exceptions detailed below, the occurrence of a chargeable event in relation to an employment-related share option results in the chargeable amount (computed as below) being taxed as employment income of the employee for the tax year in which the event occurs. For these purposes, any of the following is a chargeable event:

(a)   the acquisition of shares on the exercise of the option by an 'associated person' (see below);

(b)   the assignment (for consideration) of the option by an associated person otherwise than to another associated person;

(c)   the release (for consideration) of the option by an associated person;

(d)   (following the *FA 2003* changes) the receipt by an associated person of a benefit in connection with the option.

Following the *FA 2003* changes, the reference in (a) above to the '*exercise*' of an option embraces any acquisition of shares in pursuance of a right to acquire them, which includes, for example, a right under a so-called long-term incentive plan to receive shares after a specified period of time without the need to exercise the right. Previously, these provisions did not apply if the acquisition did not involve an act of exercise.

For the purposes of (a) above, shares are deemed to be acquired when the beneficial interest is acquired and not, if different, at the time of conveyance or transfer. Specifically included in (d) above is consideration received for omitting, or undertaking to omit, to exercise the option, or granting, or undertaking to grant, to another person a right to acquire the option shares (or an interest in them). Such consideration was, in fact, within the charge to tax before *FA 2003*, as if it derived from the assignment or release of the option, and an agreement to restrict the exercise of an option counted for tax purposes as the release of the option, but the wording of the *FA 2003* provisions widens the scope of the charge to include, for example, sums received for varying the option or as compensation for the cancellation of the option (Treasury Explanatory Notes to Finance Bill 2003). Specifically excluded from (d) above is any benefit received on account of disability (as defined) and anything already covered by (a)–(c) above.

For the purposes of these provisions, any of the following are '*associated persons*' in relation to an employment-related share option:

● the person who acquired it;

● (if different) the employee; and

● any 'relevant linked person'.

A '*relevant linked person*' is any person who is either connected (within *ICTA 1988, s 839* — see 19 CONNECTED PERSONS) with, or is a member of the same household as, either the person who acquired the option or the employee. (After 17 June 2004, the definition is tightened to embrace past connections etc. so as to ensure the link cannot be broken.) However, a *company* cannot be a relevant linked person if it is the employer or (if different) the person by whom the right or opportunity to acquire the option was made available or the person from whom the option was acquired.

The **chargeable amount** depends on the type of chargeable event. On an event within (a) above (exercise of option), it is the excess (if any) of

● the market value, at time of acquisition, of the shares acquired, over

● the consideration given (if any) for the shares acquired.

If the chargeable event is within (b) or (c) above, the chargeable amount is the amount of consideration given for the assignment or release of the option. On an event within (d) above, it is the amount or market value of the benefit. Following the *FA 2003* changes, however, if that consideration or that benefit consists wholly or partly of shares (or an interest in shares) the market value of which has been reduced by 10% or more as a result of things done otherwise than for genuine commercial purposes (see 82.8 above) within the preceding seven years, such reduction is added back.

For the purposes of these provisions generally, market value is determined as for capital gains tax purposes and *ITEPA 2003, ss 421(2), 421A* apply in determining the amount of any consideration given for anything.

Whatever the type of event, any consideration given for the option itself (on its original acquisition) is also deductible, as are (following the *FA 2003* changes) any expenses incurred in connection with the exercise, assignment or release or the receipt of benefit. Following the *FA 2003* changes, where, in consequence of the acquisition of the option itself or the acquisition of shares under the option or any transaction of which either forms part, there is a reduction in the market value of any employment-related shares held by an associated person, the amount of that reduction is deductible as if it were consideration given for the option. Any amount charged on *grant* of the option, usually under the pre-*FA 2003* rules (see above), is also deductible (whether the chargeable event occurs before or after the *FA 2003* changes take effect). Where there is more than one chargeable event in relation to the same option, the same deductions cannot be made more than once.

Before the *FA 2003* changes, the concept of 'associated persons' did not exist for the above purposes, and (*a*)–(*c*) above applied only by reference to the exercise, assignment or release of the option by the employee by reason of whose employment it was granted. However, there were additional rules dealing with the situation where a gain on exercise, assignment or release of a share option was realised by a person other than the employee. The gain was taxed as employment income of the employee for the tax year in which the option was exercised etc. if either:

(i)   the option was granted to the other person; or

(ii)   the other person acquired it otherwise than by assignment by way of bargain at arm's length; or

(iii)   the employee and the other person were CONNECTED PERSONS (19) at the time the gain was realised.

The chargeable amount was computed in the same way as if the gain were realised by the employee except that, in a case within (ii) or (iii) above, the amount of any taxable gain realised by a previous holder on an assignment of the option was deductible. Any such amount previously unrelieved remains deductible on the occurrence of a chargeable event after the *FA 2003* changes take effect.

The *FA 2003* changes have effect on and after 16 April 2003 or on and after 1 September 2003, depending on the type of 'share' that can be acquired under the option (see above under 'Meaning of "share option"').

The charge on exercise etc. is independent of any charge on grant of the option (see also above), and depends solely on the above conditions being satisfied (*Ball v Phillips Ch D 1990, 63 TC 529*).

A special rule applies if an employee is divested of a share option by operation of law; in such case, the tax charge on a chargeable event is under Schedule D, Case VI and is on the person who exercises the option or receives the consideration or benefit (whichever is applicable).

Exceptions from charge. No charge arises on any event within (*a*)–(*d*) above

●   if it occurs on or after the death of the employee; or

●   if, at the time the option is acquired, the earnings of the employment were not (or would not have been if there had been any) general earnings within *ITEPA 2003, s 15* or *s 21* (earnings for year when employee resident and ordinarily resident in the UK); or

- (in the case of an option acquired after the employment has ceased) if no charge would have arisen had the acquisition taken place in the last tax year in which the employment was held; or

- (in the case of an option acquired before the employment has begun) if no charge would have arisen had the acquisition taken place in the first tax year in which the employment is held; this exception applies only after the *FA 2003* changes take effect (see above).

Where one option has been exchanged for another (see below) the acquisition referred to is that of the 'old' option.

Before the *FA 2003* changes, the first of these exceptions was expressed so as to apply where the option was exercised etc. after the grantee's death by his personal representatives or any person on whom it devolved by will or otherwise; this applied by law from 6 April 2003 but previously applied in practice, albeit to a lesser extent (see Change 121 listed in Annex 1 to the Explanatory Notes to the Income Tax (Earnings and Pensions) Bill).

Option exchanged for another. The following rules apply where an employee-related share option is assigned or released for consideration consisting of or including another share option. For the purpose of computing the chargeable amount (if any) on the assignment or release, the new option is not treated as consideration given for the old. For the purposes of computing the charge on any future chargeable event, the consideration (if any) given for the new option consists of any actual consideration given (apart from the old option) plus the excess (if any) of any consideration given for the old option over any consideration received (apart from the new option) for its assignment or release. There are provisions (see *ITEPA 2003, s 483(5)(6)* as substituted by *FA 2003*, or *ITEPA 2003, s 485(5)(6)* as originally enacted) which in specified circumstances treat for these purposes two or more transactions as a single transaction by which an option is assigned for consideration consisting of or including another share option.

Relief for employer national insurance contributions. Where, under a voluntary agreement or a joint election under *Social Security Contributions and Benefits Act 1992, Sch 1 para 3A* or *para 3B* (or NI equivalent), whenever made, a liability to secondary Class 1 national insurance contributions (i.e. employer contributions) on a share option gain chargeable to tax under these provisions is borne by the employee who realised the gain, the amount so borne is deductible in arriving at the amount on which the employee is chargeable to tax. In the case of a voluntary agreement, or an election to which Revenue approval is withdrawn, no such amount is deductible to the extent that it is borne by the employee later than 4 June following the tax year in which the chargeable event occurs. (Any deduction for national insurance contributions is disregarded in determining the allowable cost of the shares for capital gains tax purposes — see also below.)

A similar deduction is available for any one-off special contribution under *Social Security Contributions (Share Options) Act 2001, s 2* paid by an employee before 11 August 2001 (or within such further period as the Board directed) where notice was given to the Revenue under *section 1* of that Act before that date (for further details, see Tolley's National Insurance Contributions).

[*ITEPA 2003, ss 419, 421–421B, 421D, 471–484, ss 485, 487 as originally enacted, ss 718, 721(1), Sch 7 paras 62–67; ICTA 1988, ss 135, 136, 140, 187A; FA 1998, s 49; FA 2000, s 56(1)(3)(4); FA 2002, Sch 6 para 1; Proceeds of Crime Act 2002, Sch 10 para 30; FA 2003, Sch 22 paras 2, 10, 46(20)–(26); FA 2004, s 85, s 90(3)–(5), Sch 16 paras 3, 7(1)(2); SI 2003 No 1997*].

For reporting obligations, see 82.17 below.

For FAQs on the *FA 2003* changes, see www.inlandrevenue.gov.uk/shareschemes/faq_emprelatedsecurity-ch5.htm

PAYE. For the requirement to operate PAYE on chargeable events, see 55.2(*e*)(*f*) PAY AS YOU EARN. For an article on the imposition of income tax charges under the above provisions in the case of internationally mobile employees, see Revenue Tax Bulletin October 2001 pp 883–887. For associated national insurance contributions liabilities, see Revenue Tax Bulletin December 2001 pp 895–899. For a follow-up to these articles, see Revenue Tax Bulletin August 2002 pp 951–954.

Example

An employee is granted an option exercisable within five years to buy 1,000 shares at £5 each. The option costs 50p per share. He exercises the option in 2004/05 when the shares are worth £7.50. The option is not granted under an approved scheme.

The amount taxable as employment income in 2004/05 is as follows

		£	£
Open market value of shares 1,000 × £7.50			7,500
Price paid	1,000 × £5 — shares	5,000	
	1,000 × 50p — option	500	
			5,500
Amount taxable as employment income			£2,000

Notes

(a)   The result would be the same if, instead of exercising the option, the employee transferred his option to a third party for £2,500.

(b)   The capital gains tax cost of the shares is £7,500 (£5,000 + £500 + £2,000) — see below.

Capital gains tax. For capital gains tax purposes, when shares acquired on exercise of an employment-related share option are disposed of, any sum charged to income tax as employment income is normally treated as part of the cost of acquiring the shares. The Revenue's defeat in *Mansworth v Jelley CA 2002, 75 TC 1* in December 2002 meant that persons exercising unapproved share options (or options granted under approved schemes but exercised in breach of the statutory provisions) could deduct the market value of the shares at time of exercise plus any amount charged to income tax on the exercise (see Revenue Internet Statements 8 January 2003, 17 March 2003). However, with effect for options exercised after 9 April 2003, *FA 2003* reverses the effect of the decision in *Mansworth v Jelley*, so that the cost of acquisition for capital gains tax purposes once again comprises the actual consideration given for the shares, any consideration given for the option itself, and, as stated above, any amount charged to income tax on the exercise. In computing the latter amount, for this purpose only, relief given for national insurance contributions (see above) is added back, as is any deduction made in respect of any tax charged on *grant* of the option (mainly relevant to long-term options under the pre-*FA 2003* rules — see above). [*TCGA 1992, ss 119A, 120; ITEPA 2003, Sch 6 para 210; FA 2003, Sch 22 paras 50, 51; FA 2004, s 85, Sch 16 para 6*]. For full coverage of this subject, see Tolley's Capital Gains Tax under Employee Share Schemes.

Valuations. As regards obtaining, from the Revenue Shares Valuation Division, valuations of unquoted company shares (where either an option which may be exercised after more than ten (or seven) years is granted, or income tax liability arises on exercise of an option), see Revenue Tax Bulletin December 1996 pp 374, 375.

Payment of tax. Tax on a charge under these provisions, on a gain realised by the exercise of a right to acquire shares obtained before 6 April 1984, could be paid by instalments if certain conditions were met. [*ICTA 1988, s 137; ITEPA 2003, Sch 8*]. For details, see the 2002/03 and earlier editions.

Simon's Direct Tax Service. See E4.521 *et seq.*

82.17 **REPORTING OBLIGATIONS**

For the purposes generally of 82.4, 82.6, 82.8–82.12 and 82.16 above, there are extensive requirements for employers and others to provide the Revenue with information concerning any of the events listed below. See 82.5, 82.7 and 82.14 above for separate reporting requirements under those provisions. The reportable events are as follows:

- an acquisition (or event treated as such) of shares, an interest in shares or a share option pursuant to a right or opportunity available by reason of employment;

- chargeable events within either 82.4 above (restricted shares) or 82.6 above (convertible shares);

- the doing of anything that gives rise to an income tax charge under 82.9 above (shares with artificially enhanced market value);

- an event discharging a notional loan as in 82.10 above (shares acquired for less than market value);

- a disposal within 82.11 above (shares disposed of for more than market value);

- the receipt of a benefit within 82.12 above (post-acquisition benefits from shares);

- the assignment or release of a share option acquired pursuant to a right or opportunity available by reason of employment;

- the receipt of a benefit in money or money's worth received in connection with a share option (see 82.16(*d*) above).

See 82.3 above for the extended meaning of 'shares' in these respects. The persons obliged to report such events are the employer, the 'host employer' if any, the person from whom the shares, interest or option was acquired and, unless the shares are excluded from these requirements, the person by whom they were issued. A '*host employer*' is a person for whom the employee works at the time of the event and who would be treated as making payments of PAYE income if such payments were actually made by a non-UK employer (see 55.3 PAY AS YOU EARN under 'Non-UK employer'). Shares excluded from these requirements are, broadly, government and local authority stocks/bonds and quoted shares issued by a person who, at the time of the event, is not connected (within 19 CONNECTED PERSONS) with the employer.

Every person obliged to report the event in question must give the Revenue written particulars of the event (in specified form) before 7 July following the end of the tax year in which the event took place, but once one such person complies there is no need for others to comply in relation to the same event. In addition, the Revenue may give notice to any person, requiring him to provide written particulars of reportable events which take place during a period specified in the notice (and in relation to which that person is a person obliged to report such events) or to state that there are no such events. Such notice must specify a deadline for compliance, which must be at least 30 days after the notice is given. Again, once such particulars are provided in relation to a particular event, others are released from their original obligation to report the event. In both cases, penalties are exigible under *TMA 1970, s 98* for non-compliance.

[*ITEPA 2003, ss 421J–421L, 718; FA 2003, Sch 22 paras 2, 47*].

Particulars should be sent to Inland Revenue, Employee Share Schemes, Second Floor, New Wing, Somerset House, Strand, London, WC2R 1LB. The standard form for reporting the events listed above is Form 42; the Revenue have no obligation to issue Form 42 to employers but, in cases where they did not do so, they allowed a two-month extension to the deadline for reporting events in 2003/04 only, i.e. such events had to be reported before 7 September 2004; see Revenue Internet Statement 23 June 2004, which also includes 'frequently asked questions' on the need to report events and the acceptable methods of doing so.

To the extent that these reporting obligations arise from 82.16 above (unapproved share options), they apply on and after 16 April 2003 or on and after 1 September 2003, depending on the type of 'share' that can be acquired under the option (see 82.16 above under 'Meaning of "share option"'). However, there were previously separate reporting requirements under *ITEPA 2003, s 486* as originally enacted, though these were of narrower application.

82.18   **PROFIT SHARING SCHEMES — APPROVAL**

The provisions of *ICTA 1988, ss 186, 187, Sch 9* allow directors and employees of companies to receive shares free of income tax under certain conditions.

Approved profit sharing schemes are being **phased out** following the introduction of share incentive plans (see 82.20 below). A scheme could not be approved by the Board unless the application for approval, accompanied by necessary particulars, was received by them before 6 April 2001. No appropriations of shares to employees may be made after 31 December 2002 under approved schemes. [*ICTA 1988, s 186(1); FA 2000, s 49*]. Approval will be withdrawn if shares are appropriated to a participant who has already had *free shares* appropriated to him in the same tax year under an approved share incentive plan (see 82.20 below) established by the same company (or by a 'connected company', as defined) (or to a participant who would have had such shares appropriated to him but for his failure to meet set performance targets). [*ICTA 1988, Sch 9 para 3(2)(4)–(6); FA 2000, s 51*].

Otherwise, under a scheme approved by the Board a company provides funds to UK resident trustees who purchase certain defined shares (see below) and appropriate such shares to eligible employees (see below). The limit on the market value of shares which may be appropriated to any one individual in any year of assessment is the greater of £3,000 and 10% of his salary (net of pension contributions — CCAB Memorandum TR 511, 26 August 1983) for PAYE purposes (less any benefits taxable, see 75.14 *et seq.*, 75.32 SCHEDULE E—EMPLOYMENT INCOME) for that year (or for the preceding year if greater), subject to a ceiling of £8,000. An employee to whom the trustees have appropriated shares ('a participant') contracts (i) not to assign or dispose of his beneficial interest in the shares within a 'period of retention' (see below); (ii) to permit the trustees to retain his shares for that period; (iii) to pay to the trustees a sum equal to income tax at the basic rate on the 'appropriate percentage' of the 'locked-in value' (see 82.19 below) should he direct them to transfer the shares to him before the 'release date', and (iv) not to direct them to dispose of his shares before the release date other than by sale for the best consideration obtainable or, if the shares are redeemable shares in a workers' co-operative (as defined), by redemption. The participant may, however, at any time direct the trustees to accept, in respect of his shares, certain share exchanges or other offers (including, in certain cases, qualifying corporate bonds) made to all holders of the same class of shares. Any contravention of (i) above renders him ineligible for the tax relief (and he is charged to tax as at the time the shares were appropriated to him). With effect after 20 March 2000, the Board must be satisfied both that the arrangements (as widely defined) of the scheme do not provide, directly or otherwise, for loans to be made to any of the employees of the company or of a participating company in a group scheme and that the operation of the scheme is in no way associated with such loans. Alterations to the scheme must be approved. Approval of a scheme may be withdrawn if Board ceases to be satisfied with conditions. Appeal is available to the Special Commissioners within thirty days of notification of the Board's decision to refuse approval of a scheme or of an alteration in a scheme or in the trust deed.

[*ITEPA 2003, s 418(3); ICTA 1988, s 186(1), s 187(2)(5)(10), Sch 9 para 2(2)–(2B), para 3(2), paras 4–6, Sch 10 para 1, para 6(1)(2); FA 1986, s 24; FA 1989, s 63; FA 1991, s 41; FA 1994, s 101; FA 2000, s 53*]. See *CIR v Burton Group plc Ch D 1990, 63 TC 191*, where an appeal against Revenue refusal of approval of a share option scheme under identical statutory provisions was upheld.

'*Period of retention*' begins on the date the shares are appropriated to the participant and ends two years later or, if earlier, at cessation of employment due to injury, disability, redundancy or death, or on reaching the 'relevant age' or, if the shares are redeemable shares in a workers' co-operative, on his ceasing to be employed by, or by a subsidiary of, the co-operative. [*ICTA 1988, Sch 10 para 2; FA 1991, s 38(3)*].

The '*relevant age*' must be specified in the scheme rules, must be the same for men and women, and must not be less than 60 or more than 75. In relation to schemes approved before 25 July 1991, it is the normal state pensionable age (although in practice the Revenue have permitted the alteration of scheme rules to make the relevant age 60 for both men and women for this purpose). [*ICTA 1988, Sch 9 para 8A; FA 1991, s 38(5)*].

The '*release date*' is the third anniversary of the date of appropriation of the shares to the participant if that anniversary occurs on or after 29 April 1996. Previously, it was the fifth anniversary of the date of appropriation, except that 29 April 1996 is itself the release date if it falls after the third anniversary but before the fifth anniversary. [*ICTA 1988, s 187(2); FA 1996, s 116*].

A non-technical explanatory booklet (IR 95) aimed at employees is available from local tax offices and tax enquiry centres and on the Revenue website.

The shares must be (*a*) quoted on a recognised stock exchange or (*b*) in a company not controlled by another company or (*c*) in a company controlled by a quoted company (other than a company which is, or would be if resident in the UK, a close company); and they must be ordinary shares of the company concerned, its controlling company or a company (or its controlling company) which is a member of a consortium owning the company concerned (or its controlling company). The shares must be fully paid up, not redeemable (unless they are shares in a workers' co-operative) and (except as below) not subject to any restrictions differing from those attaching to other shares of the same class. Certain restrictions connected with cessation of employment may apply to scheme shares without applying to all shares of the same class. The articles of association may impose a restriction requiring all shares held by directors or employees to be disposed of on cessation of the employment, and all shares acquired by persons who are not directors or employees, but which were acquired in pursuance of rights or interests obtained by directors or employees, to be disposed of immediately they are so acquired. The required disposal must be by sale for money on specified terms, and the articles must also provide that any person disposing of shares of the same class (however acquired) may be required to sell them on the same terms. The restriction must not, however, require a disposal before the release date of shares the ownership of which has not been transferred to the participant, unless the shares are redeemable shares in a workers' co-operative. After 20 March 2000, but not so as to affect shares acquired by the scheme trustees on or before that date, scheme shares must not carry any restrictions affecting the rights attaching to them as regards dividends or assets on a winding-up, unless those restrictions apply to all other ordinary shares in the company.

Where there is more than one class of shares, the majority of the class of shares appropriated under the scheme must either (i) be held by persons other than directors or employees who received special rights of acquisition, or trustees for such persons or where shares are within (*c*) above and not within (*a*) above, companies which control the company whose shares are in question or of which that company is an associated company (as defined), or (ii) be '*employee-control shares*', i.e. shares held by persons who are or have been directors or employees, and who are together able to control the company by virtue of their holdings.

After 20 March 2000, but not so as to affect shares acquired by the scheme trustees on or before that date, the shares must not be shares in companies ('*employer companies*') whose business is substantially the provision of the services of its employees either to businesses, including partnerships, who control the company or to associated companies. The prohibition extends to shares in certain companies which have control of employer companies.

[*ICTA 1988, Sch 9 paras 10–12, 14; FA 1989, s 64; FA 2000, s 52*].

Persons eligible must include all employees (for schemes approved before 1 May 1995, all full-time employees) and full-time directors subject to tax under Case I of Schedule E (and may include any person who was such during the eighteen months preceding appropriation of shares to him, part-timers, and those chargeable under Case II or Case III of Schedule E) and employed for a maximum qualifying period of five years by the company or group concerned and all those who do participate must do so on similar terms (although variations by reference to salary, length of service etc. do not prevent this condition being met). The terms must not in effect either discourage any description of eligible participant, or confer benefits wholly or mainly on directors or the highest-paid employees in a group scheme. A person is not eligible if, in the same year of assessment, shares have been appropriated to him under another approved scheme by the company or group concerned, or if within the preceding twelve months he and/or certain associates of his had a material (broadly more than 25% of ordinary share capital) interest in such a company which was a close company or would be if it were resident in the UK or if its shares were not publicly quoted. [*ICTA 1988, s 187(3), Sch 9 para 2(3)(4), para 8, paras 35–40; FA 1989, s 65; FA 1995, s 137(4)(7)*].

See 71.44 SCHEDULE D, CASES I AND II as regards deduction available to company for expenses in setting up the scheme and in meeting expenses of trustees in administering the scheme and acquiring shares under the scheme.

Simon's Direct Tax Service. See E4.561–E4.571.

82.19   **PROFIT SHARING SCHEMES — THE CHARGE TO TAX**

Note that profit sharing schemes are being **phased out** and that no appropriations of shares to employees may be made after 31 December 2002 under approved schemes (see 82.18 above).

There is no charge to income tax on an eligible employee when the shares are appropriated to him. [*ICTA 1988, s 186(2)*]. On disposal or other chargeable event before the 'release date', the following percentage of the 'locked-in value' (see below) is chargeable to tax as employment income for the tax year in which the disposal or event takes place.

Disposals etc. on or after 29 April 1996:
Before third anniversary of appropriation	100%

Disposals etc. before 29 April 1996:
Before fourth anniversary of appropriation	100%
On or after fourth anniversary and before fifth anniversary	75%
On or after fifth anniversary	No charge

The '*release date*' is the third anniversary of the date of appropriation of the shares to the participant if that anniversary occurs on or after 29 April 1996. Previously, it was the fifth anniversary of the date of appropriation, except that 29 April 1996 is itself the release date if it falls after the third anniversary but before the fifth anniversary.

If the participant ceases employment with the company because of injury, disability, redundancy or reaching the 'relevant age' before the disposal and before the third anniversary (for disposals before 29 April 1996, before the fifth anniversary), the appropriate percentage is 50%. The '*relevant age*' in relation to schemes approved on or after 25 July 1991 must be specified in the scheme rules, must be the same for men and women, and must not be less than 60 or more than 75. For schemes approved before that date, it is generally the normal state pensionable age. However, in practice, such older schemes have been permitted to alter their rules to make 60 the relevant age for men as well as women for the purposes of the period of retention rules (see 82.18 above), and where this has been the case, for events occurring after 29 November 1993 (and after the scheme rules were altered), the relevant age for men for the purposes of determining the appropriate percentage is also 60.

[*ICTA 1988, s 186(4), s 187(2), Sch 10 para 3; FA 1991, s 38; FA 1994, s 100; FA 1996, ss 116, 117; ITEPA 2003, Sch 6 paras 26(3), 113(2)*].

Locked-in value of shares is their initial market value when appropriated to the employee (or any earlier dates as agreed in writing between the Board and the trustees) as reduced by any capital receipt charged to income tax under these provisions (see below), or the disposal proceeds, if less.

Proceeds are reduced by any payment to the trustees previously made for a rights issue but payments received from a disposal of rights are disregarded. Disposals are allocated to appropriations on a first in, first out basis. [*ICTA 1988, s 186(5)–(10), s 187(8), Sch 9 para 30(4); FA 1996, s 117(2), s 134, Sch 20 para 11; ITEPA 2003, Sch 6 para 26(4)*].

Any **excess or unauthorised shares** (i.e. in excess of the limit (see 82.18 above) or appropriated to a person not eligible (see 82.18 above)) are chargeable to tax on the market value at whichever is the earlier: date of disposal; release date; or death. The charge on anniversary of appropriation is applied by reference to authorised shares before excess or unauthorised shares. [*ICTA 1988, Sch 10 para 6; ITEPA 2003, Sch 6 para 113(2)*].

Capital receipts are charged on the appropriate percentage (as above) and after any appropriate allowance (see below) for the year in which the trustees or the participant become entitled to them but do not include (*a*) taxable income in hands of recipient or (*b*) disposal proceeds on any of the chargeable events referred to above or (*c*) new shares issued in a company reconstruction under *TCGA 1992, ss 132, 136* (except redeemable shares not issued for new consideration or bonus issues following repayment of share capital and stock dividends) or (*d*) proceeds of rights used to exercise other rights. Capital receipts are charged only on the excess over the 'appropriate allowance', which, for any tax year, is £20 multiplied by one plus the number of years which fall within the three years (before 1997/98, five years) immediately preceding the year in question and in which the shares were appropriated to the participant, up to a maximum of £60 (before 1997/98, £100). If more than one capital receipt arises to the trustees or the participant in any year (before the release date), the receipts are set against the appropriate allowance in the order received. [*ICTA 1988, s 186(3)(12), Sch 10 paras 4, 5; FA 1978, s 56(6); FA 1980, s 46(6); FA 1982, s 42(1)(2); FA 1985, s 45(4); FA 1996, s 118; ITEPA 2003, Sch 6 para 26(2)*].

PAYE applies to disposals as above. The trustees shall pay to the company out of the disposal proceeds, the sum of money on which tax is chargeable and the company must deduct tax under PAYE and pay the balance to the participant. The company is the employing company or, if more than one, whichever company the Board directs. If there is no appropriate company, the Board may direct the trustees to apply PAYE as if the participant were a former employee of theirs. [*ICTA 1988, Sch 10 para 7; ITEPA 2003, Sch 6 para 113(3)*].

Capital gains tax is chargeable on disposal of the shares by the participants, without deduction for any amount determined for purposes of charging income tax under the above provisions. For this purpose, a participant is absolutely entitled to his shares as against the trustees. The allowable cost is the initial market value of the shares. No CGT arises to the trustees if they appropriate shares to participants within eighteen months of acquisition. [*TCGA 1992, s 238(1)(2); ITEPA 2003, Sch 6 para 215*].

Dividends received on shares by the trustees are not liable to the Schedule F trust rate (or, before 6 April 1999, the 'rate applicable to trusts') (see 81.5 SETTLEMENTS) if the shares are appropriated within eighteen months of acquisition. [*ICTA 1988, s 186(11)*].

Simon's Direct Tax Service. See E4.572 *et seq.*

82.20 SHARE INCENTIVE PLANS

Introduction. A share incentive plan ('SIP') is a plan established by a company, and approved **on or after 28 July 2000** by the Revenue (see 82.33 below), providing for shares to be appropriated without payment to employees ('*free shares*' — see 82.22 below) and/or for shares to be acquired on employees' behalf from sums deducted from their salary ('*partnership shares*' — see 82.23 below). A plan providing for partnership shares may also provide for shares to be appropriated without payment to employees ('*matching shares*' — see 82.24 below) in proportion to the partnership shares acquired by them. See 82.26, 82.27 below for tax consequences in each case. See 82.25 below as to reinvestment of dividends on plan shares. Where a plan provides for more than one of the above kinds of shares, it may leave it to the company to decide when each such provision is to have effect. A plan established by a company which controls (within *ICTA 1988, s 840*) other companies (a '*parent company*') may extend to one or more of those other companies, whereupon it is known as a '*group plan*'. Companies that for the time being are party to a group plan are known as '*constituent companies*'. [*ITEPA 2003, ss 488, 719, Sch 2 paras 1–4; FA 2000, s 47, Sch 8 paras 1, 2, 129(1)*].

The remainder of this coverage is set out under the following headings.

See 71.44 SCHEDULE D, CASES I AND II as regards deductions which the employer company may make for corporation tax purposes.

Guidance, including model plan rules, trust deed and share agreements, is provided by the Revenue via a dedicated website at www.inlandrevenue.gov.uk/shareschemes/sip_employers.htm

82.21

General requirements. The purpose of the plan must be to provide benefits to employees by way of shares which give them a continuing stake in a company. A plan must contain no features which are neither essential nor reasonably incidental to that purpose. It *must* provide that every employee who is eligible (as in 82.28 below) in relation to an award of shares under the plan, and who is a 'UK resident taxpayer', may participate in the award and be invited to do so, and it should not contain any features (other than those required or authorised under these provisions) to discourage participation. It *may* provide for an eligible employee to be invited to participate in an award even though he is not a 'UK resident taxpayer'. An individual who *must* be invited, or who under terms as above *may* be invited, to participate in an award is a '*qualifying employee*' in relation to that award.

For the above purposes, an employee is a '*UK resident taxpayer*' if his earnings, from the employment by reference to which he meets the employment requirement at 82.28 below, are (or would be if there were any) general earnings within *ITEPA 2003, s 15* or *s 21* (earnings for year when employee resident and ordinarily resident in UK).

All employees invited to participate in an award must be invited to participate on the same terms, and those who do participate must actually do so on the same terms. Free shares may be awarded by reference to remuneration, length of service or hours worked, or (within confines) more than one of these factors, but not by reference to other factors. Free shares may, however, be allocated, in accordance with 82.29 below, by reference to performance. Subject to the above, no feature of the plan must have the likely effect of conferring benefits wholly or mainly on directors or on employees receiving higher levels of remuneration. In the case of a group, the identity of the company, or of the constituent companies in a group plan, must not be such as to have similar likely effect. No conditions may be imposed on an employee's participation in an award, except as required or permitted under these provisions. The arrangements (as broadly defined) for the plan must not provide for loans to employees of the company (or of constituent companies in a group plan), and neither those arrangements nor the operation of the plan must in any way be associated with any such loans.

[*ITEPA 2003, Sch 2 paras 6–12; FA 2000, Sch 8 paras 6–12*].

Awards of shares. Shares are '*awarded*' under a plan on each occasion when, in accordance with the plan, free or matching shares are appropriated to employees or partnership shares are acquired on behalf of employees. Shares are awarded to a particular employee (a '*participant*') when free or matching shares are appropriated to him, or partnership shares are acquired on his behalf, as part of the global award. [*ITEPA 2003, Sch 2 para 5; FA 2000, Sch 8 para 3*].

Shares leaving the plan. Shares '*cease to be subject to the plan*' when

(*a*)   they are 'withdrawn from the plan'; or

(*b*)   the participant ceases to be in '*relevant employment*' (which term comprises employment by the company and employment by any 'associated' company), in which case his shares cease to be subject to the plan on the date of leaving (but see below for exception); or

(*c*)   the plan trustees dispose of the shares in order to meet PAYE obligations (see 82.26 below).

For the purpose of determining any charge to income tax, shares cease to be subject to the plan in the order in which they were awarded to the participant. Shares awarded on the same day cease to be subject to the plan in the order which results in the lowest income tax charge. (For 2003/04 onwards, and in practice for earlier years also, dividend shares are treated as awarded when the trustees acquire them on behalf of, or appropriate them to, the participant.)

Shares are '*withdrawn from the plan*' (see (*a*) above) when, on the direction of the participant (or, after his death, of his personal representatives), the plan trustees either transfer them (whether to the participant etc. or to another person) or dispose of them and similarly account for the proceeds, or when the participant etc. assigns, charges or otherwise disposes of his beneficial interest in them.

For the purposes of (*b*) above and of these provisions generally (except where otherwise stated), two companies are '*associated*' if one controls the other or they are under common control, 'control' being interpreted in accordance with *ICTA 1988, s 416(2)–(6)*.

Where an individual ceases to be in relevant employment during the 'acquisition period' relating to an award of partnership shares, he is treated for the purposes of (*b*) above as ceasing to be in such employment immediately after the shares are awarded. The '*acquisition period*' begins with the deduction from salary and ends with the 'acquisition date' or, where relevant, begins with the end of the 'accumulation period' and ends immediately before the 'acquisition date' (see 82.23 below for meaning of terms used here).

[*ITEPA 2003, s 508, Sch 2 paras 94–97; FA 2000, Sch 8 paras 122, 123, 126*].

Jointly owned companies. To enable a jointly owned company to take part in a group plan (though it cannot thereby take part in more than one), such a company, and any company under its control (within *ICTA 1988, s 840*), is treated as being under the control of each of its two joint owners (though not for the purposes of 82.30(ii) below). From 6 April 2002, a company controlled *by* a jointly owned company may not take part in more than one group plan or in a different plan to that (if any) in which the jointly owned company (or any other company controlled by it) takes part (although this does not prevent its continued participation in a plan in which it took part immediately before 24 July 2002). [*ITEPA 2003, s 719, Sch 2 para 91, Sch 7 para 70; FA 2000, Sch 8 paras 127, 129(1); FA 2002, s 39(5)(7)(8)*].

In the case of a company registered outside the UK, **shares** include fractions of shares for the purposes of these provisions, where such fractions are recognised under local law. [*ITEPA 2003, Sch 2 para 99(2); FA 2000, Sch 8 para 129(3)*].

82.22   **Free shares.** The 'initial market value' of free shares awarded (see 82.21 above) to a participant in any tax year under a plan providing for free shares (see 82.20 above) must not exceed £3,000. The '*initial market value*' of shares is their market value (determined as for capital gains tax purposes) on the date of the award. Where the market value of shares on any date falls to be determined, the Revenue and the plan trustees may agree that it be determined by reference to a different date or a number of specified dates. In arriving at the market value of restricted shares as in 82.4 above (previously shares subject to restrictions, or to risk of forfeiture such that the interest that may be acquired is only conditional — see 82.5 above), the restrictions (or risk of forfeiture) are disregarded. [*ITEPA 2003, Sch 2 paras 34, 35, 92; FA 2000, Sch 8 paras 23, 24, 125; FA 2003, Sch 22 para 43*].

As regards each award of free shares, the plan must require the company to specify a period (the holding period) during which a participant is bound by contract, for so long as he remains in relevant employment (see 82.21 above), to permit his shares to remain in the hands of the trustees and not to assign, charge or otherwise dispose of his beneficial interest. The holding period must not be less than three years, nor more than five, beginning with the date the shares are awarded to the participant, and must be the same for all shares in the same award. See 82.26 below for income tax consequences of free shares leaving the plan. The plan *may* enable different holding periods to be specified from time to time, though not so as to increase the holding period for free shares already awarded. Notwithstanding the foregoing, the participant may direct the trustees to accept or agree to

(*a*)   an offer resulting in a new holding being equated with his original free shares for capital gains tax purposes (see Tolley's Capital Gains Tax under Shares and Securities); or

(*b*)   an offer of cash and/or a qualifying corporate bond (see Tolley's Capital Gains Tax), with or without other assets, which is part of a general offer designed to give the person making it control of the company; or

(*c*)   a transaction pursuant to a compromise, arrangement or scheme affecting all the shares or all the shares of the particular class concerned or all those held by a class of shareholders (identified otherwise than by reference to employment or participation in the plan).

[*ITEPA 2003, Sch 2 paras 36, 37; FA 2000, Sch 8 paras 31, 32*].

The holding period requirement is subject to the provisions for termination of plans (see 82.34 below) and those requiring the trustees to be enabled to meet certain PAYE obligations (see 82.26 below).

82.23   **Partnership shares.** A plan providing for partnership shares (see 82.20 above) must provide for qualifying employees (see 82.21 below) to enter into agreements ('*partnership share agreements*') with the company whereby the employee authorises the employer company to make deductions from his salary for the purchase of partnership shares to be awarded to him under the plan. It must specify the amount or percentage to be deducted from salary and the intervals at which deductions are to be made, although the company and employee may agree to vary both of these. It must also contain a notice giving prescribed information in prescribed form (see *SI 2000 No 2090*) as to the possible effect of deductions on an employee's entitlement to social security benefits, statutory sick pay and statutory maternity pay.

The amount deducted from salary must not exceed £1,500 in any tax year. Furthermore, it must not exceed 10% of the employee's salary for the tax year. Before 2003/04, these limits were expressed in terms of months. Thus, the amount deducted from salary could not exceed £125 in any month (or proportionate amount in the case of non-monthly pay intervals) and could not exceed 10% of salary, i.e. if the plan provided for an accumulation period (see below), 10% of the salary payments over that period, or, if it did not, 10% of the salary payment from which the deduction was made. The plan may authorise the setting of maximum limits which are lower than the aforementioned; different limits may be set for different awards. A lower limit may be expressed in terms of a monetary amount, a percentage or, on or after 10 July 2003, a stipulation that earnings of a specified kind (e.g. overtime payments, bonuses etc.) be excluded from employees' salaries for these purposes. Any amount deducted from salary in excess of the applicable limits must be returned to the employee. The plan may also set a minimum amount that can be deducted on any occasion (previously in any month, regardless of actual pay intervals); the specified minimum must not exceed £10.

Subject to the above, for these purposes an employee's salary means his earnings (from the employment in question) otherwise subject to PAYE, excluding any taxable benefits and expenses within 75.16–75.24 SCHEDULE E—EMPLOYMENT INCOME. The Revenue take this to mean salary after deduction of allowable pension contributions and charitable donations made under payroll giving schemes (Revenue Share Focus Newsletter December 2003 p 8). Where eligibility in respect of an award falls to be judged (see 82.28 below) on or after 11 May 2001, the term is extended to include emoluments which are outside the scope of the charge to tax on employment income, excluding benefits etc., which would have been chargeable had the individual been within the scope of that charge. See 82.26 below as regards tax relief for amounts deducted.

[*ITEPA 2003, Sch 2 paras 43–48; FA 2000, Sch 8 paras 33–38, 48; FA 2001, Sch 13 para 3; FA 2003, Sch 21 paras 7, 8*].

Amounts deducted from salary are to be paid over to the trustees and held by them (in a bank, building society etc.) on the employee's behalf until applied in acquiring partnership shares on his behalf (which includes their appropriating to him shares already held by them). If such monies are held in an interest-bearing account, the plan must require the trustees to account to the employee for the interest.

If the plan does not provide for an accumulation period (see below), it must provide for deductions from salary to be applied as above on the '*acquisition date*', which for *this* purpose is a date which is set by the trustees and is within 30 days after the date of the last salary deduction in relation to the partnership share award in question. Subject to any restriction imposed in accordance with the plan (see below), the number of shares awarded (see 82.21 above) to each employee is to be determined by reference to market value at the acquisition date.

A plan may provide for accumulation periods not exceeding 12 months. If it does so, the partnership share agreement must specify when each such period begins (which in the case of the first period must be no later than the date of the first salary deduction) and ends. The accumulation period for each award of shares must be same for all individuals entering into the partnership share agreements. Subject to this, the agreement may specify that an accumulation period shall end on the occurrence of a specified event, and may additionally provide that salary deductions be in such cases returned to participants. The plan may provide for continuity in the event of certain share exchanges. The plan must provide for deductions from salary to be applied by the trustees in acquiring, on the employee's behalf, partnership shares on the '*acquisition date*', which for *this* purpose is a date which is set by the trustees and is within 30 days after the end of the accumulation period applicable to the partnership share award in question. Subject to any restriction imposed in accordance with the plan (see below), the number of shares awarded to each employee is to be determined by reference to the lower of market value at the beginning of the accumulation period and market value at the acquisition date. If an employee ceases to be in relevant employment (see 82.21 above) during an accumulation period, salary deductions made must be paid over to him.

Any surplus monies held after acquiring shares as above may, with the employee's agreement, be carried forward to the next deduction or, where applicable, carried forward to the next accumulation period; otherwise they must be paid over to the employee.

The plan *may* authorise the company to restrict the number of shares to be included in a particular partnership share award to a specified maximum, subject to its giving employees advance notification. Where necessary, in such case, the number of shares in each individual award is to be scaled down.

[*ITEPA 2003, Sch 2 paras 43(3), 49–53; FA 2000, Sch 8 paras 39–43*].

An employee may, by written notice to the company, stop salary deductions under a partnership share agreement. He may similarly re-start deductions (though the plan *may* impose a limit of one re-start per accumulation period, where applicable) but is not permitted to make up deductions missed. The company must give effect to a notice to stop or re-start within 30 days of receiving it, unless the employee specifies a later date in the notice. An employee may also, again by written notice to the company, withdraw from a partnership share agreement, such notice to take effect within 30 days unless a later date is specified therein. Any monies deducted and still held on his behalf must then be paid over to him. On withdrawal of Revenue approval to a plan (see 82.33 below) or on the issue of a plan termination notice (see 82.34 below), any monies deducted and still held on an employee's behalf must be paid over to him as soon as practicable. [*ITEPA 2003, Sch 2 paras 54–56; FA 2000, Sch 8 paras 44–46*].

Access to partnership shares. An employee may at any time withdraw from the plan any or all of the partnership shares awarded to him. See 82.26 below for income tax consequences of withdrawal. [*ITEPA 2003, Sch 2 para 57; FA 2000, Sch 8 para 47*].

82.24   **Matching shares.** In a plan providing for matching shares (see 82.20 above), the partnership share agreement (see 82.23 above) must specify the ratio of matching shares to partnership shares for the time being offered by the company and the circumstances and manner in which the ratio may be changed. The ratio must apply by reference to the *number* of shares and must not be greater than **two matching shares to each partnership share**.

If the ratio changes before partnership shares are awarded under the agreement, employees must be notified accordingly. Matching shares must be of the same class and carry the same rights as the partnership shares to which they relate. They must be awarded (see 82.21 above) on the day the related partnership shares are awarded and must be awarded to all participants on exactly the same basis. See 82.30 below as to permitted provision for forfeiture. The provisions of *ITEPA 2003, Sch 2 paras 36, 37* (holding period and related matters — see 82.22 above) apply to matching shares as they apply to free shares. [*ITEPA 2003, Sch 2 paras 58–61; FA 2000, Sch 8 paras 49–52*].

82.25   **Dividend shares.** The plan *may* provide that, where the company so directs and subject to the limit below, all cash dividends on plan shares are to be reinvested in further shares ('*dividend shares*') on participants' behalf. Participants may be allowed to choose whether or not to reinvest. The company may revoke a direction. Where cash dividends are not required to be reinvested, they must be paid over to the participants.

The maximum dividend reinvestment per participant per tax year is £1,500. This is a global limit embracing all approved SIPs established by the company and its associated companies (within *ITEPA 2003, Sch 2 para 94*). Any cash dividends in excess of the limit must be paid over to the participant.

Dividend shares must be of the same class and carry the same rights as the shares on which the dividend is paid and must not be subject to any provision for forfeiture. The trustees must acquire dividend shares on participants' behalf (which includes their appropriating to participants shares already held by them) on the '*acquisition date*', which for this purpose is a date which is set by the trustees and is within 30 days after they receive the dividend. The number of shares acquired on behalf of each participant is to be determined by reference to market value at the acquisition date. There are provisions for carrying forward for future reinvestment, as a separately identifiable amount, any remaining balance, and for such amounts to be paid over to the participant in certain circumstances.

The holding period, during which dividend shares must not leave the plan (other than on cessation of employment), must be three years. In other respects, the provisions of *ITEPA 2003, Sch 2 paras 36, 37* (holding period and related matters — see 82.22 above) apply to dividend shares as they apply to free shares.

[*ITEPA 2003, Sch 2 paras 62–69; FA 2000, Sch 8 paras 53–58*].

82.26   **Income tax consequences for participants.** *General.* An award of shares (see 82.21 above) to an employee, or an acquisition of dividend shares (see 82.25 above) on his behalf, under an approved SIP does not attract an income tax charge. In addition, the following charging provisions are disapplied:

(i)   (as regards the removal or variation of a permitted provision for forfeiture — see 82.30 below) *ITEPA 2003, s 427* (conditional interests in shares — see 82.5 above) and *ITEPA 2003, s 449* (removal of restrictions — see 82.14(*a*) above), both as originally enacted;

(ii)   (if the chargeable event, as in 82.14(*a*) above, is the end of the holding period for free, matching or dividend shares) *ITEPA 2003, s 449* as originally enacted (as above); and

(iii)   (as regards any shares of the participant that are subject to the plan at or immediately before the time by reference to which the chargeable increase is determined) *ITEPA 2003, s 453* as originally enacted (charge on increase in value of shares in dependent subsidiaries — see 82.14(*b*) above).

For 2001/02 onwards, neither the employer's nor the plan trustees' incidental expenses in running the plan can give rise to any income tax charge on employees. For 2003/04 onwards, this exemption is extended to cover any such incidental expenses of the company which established the plan (if different from the employer).

Neither the above exemptions nor the income tax consequences below apply to an individual if, at the time of the award in question, his earnings (from the employment by reference to which he meets the employment requirement at 82.28 below) are not (or would not be if there were any) within the charge to UK tax on employment income.

After 17 June 2004, the income tax exemptions do not apply if the shares are awarded or acquired under arrangements one of the main purposes of which is the avoidance of tax or national insurance contributions.

[*ITEPA 2003, ss 489–491, 494, 495, 499, 500; FA 2000, Sch 8 paras 77, 78, 80; FA 2001, Sch 13 para 4; FA 2003, Sch 22 paras 26–28; FA 2004, s 88(4)(11)*].

Capital receipts. Where a 'capital receipt' is received by a participant in respect of, or by reference to, free, matching or partnership shares awarded to him fewer than five years previously or dividend shares acquired on his behalf fewer than three years previously, the amount or value of that receipt is chargeable to tax as employment income of the participant for the tax year of receipt (see below as regards PAYE). For these purposes, a *'capital receipt'* means any money or money's worth except to the extent that

(A)   it constitutes taxable income of the recipient (or would do so but for the exemptions conferred by these provisions);

(B)   it consists of the disposal proceeds of the shares;

(C)   it consists of the proceeds of a part disposal by the trustees (at the direction of the participant) of rights under a rights issue where those proceeds are used to take up other such rights;

(D)   it consists of 'new shares' following a company reconstruction (see 82.31 below); or

(E)   it is received by the participant's personal representatives after his death.

[*ITEPA 2003, ss 501, 502, Sch 2 para 99; FA 2000, Sch 8 para 79*].

Free or matching shares leaving plan. If free shares (see 82.22 above) or matching shares (see 82.24 above) cease to be subject to the plan (see 82.21 above) within less than five years of their being awarded to him, an amount is chargeable to tax as employment income of the participant (subject to the exceptions at (*a*)–(*c*) below) for the tax year in which the shares cease to be subject to the plan. If the shares leave the plan in less than three years, the chargeable amount is their market value (determined as in 82.22 above) when they leave the plan. If they leave the plan after three years or more but less than five years, the chargeable amount is the lower of their market value when they leave the plan and their market value at the date they were awarded. If the latter, the tax is reduced by any tax paid on 'capital receipts' (see above) in respect of the shares.

After 17 June 2004, any tax due as above is reduced by any tax paid by virtue of 82.9 above (shares with artificially enhanced market value) in relation to the shares.

If, within the holding period (see 82.22, 82.24 above) specified for the award of free or matching shares, the participant, in breach of his obligations under the plan, assigns, charges or otherwise disposes of his beneficial interest, then, instead of the above, the market value of the shares at the time they cease to be subject to the plan is chargeable to tax as employment income of the participant for the tax year in which that time falls.

There is no charge on free or matching shares leaving the plan after five years or more, nor is there any charge on the forfeiture of such shares.

[*ITEPA 2003, ss 497(1), 505, 507; FA 2000, Sch 8 paras 81, 82; FA 2001, Sch 13 para 5; FA 2004, s 88(5)(11)*].

There is no income tax charge on shares ceasing to be subject to the plan within five years by reason of the participant's ceasing to be in relevant employment (see 82.21 above) due to

(*a*)   injury, disability, redundancy (as defined), his employer company losing its 'associated company' status (see 82.21 above), or a transfer within the *Transfer of Undertakings (Protection of Employment) Regulations 1981 (SI 1981 No 1794)*; or

(*b*)   his retirement on or after reaching a retirement age specified in the plan, which must be not less than 50 and the same for men and women; or

(*c*)   his death.

[*ITEPA 2003, s 498, Sch 2 paras 98, 99; FA 2000, Sch 8 para 87*].

Partnership shares generally. Deductions from an employee's salary in accordance with a partnership share agreement (see 82.23 above) are allowable deductions for income tax purposes. Such deductions are, however, disregarded for the purposes of ascertaining the employee's remuneration for the purposes of RETIREMENT SCHEMES (67) or his relevant earnings for the purposes of PERSONAL PENSION SCHEMES (60) and RETIREMENT ANNUITIES (66). [*ITEPA 2003, s 492; FA 2000, Sch 8 para 83*].

Any amount deducted from an individual's salary but subsequently returned to him under any of the relevant provisions in 82.23 above is chargeable to tax as employment income of the individual for the tax year in which the amount is paid over to him. Any money or money's worth received by an individual in respect of the cancellation of a partnership share agreement entered into by him is chargeable to tax as employment income of the individual for the tax year of receipt. [*ITEPA 2003, ss 503, 504; FA 2000, Sch 8 paras 84, 85*].

Partnership shares leaving plan. If partnership shares (see 82.23 above) cease to be subject to the plan (see 82.21 above) within less than five years of the 'acquisition date', an amount is chargeable to tax as employment income of the participant (subject to the same exceptions as for free and matching shares — see (*a*)–(*c*) above) for the tax year in which the shares cease to be subject to the plan. (The '*acquisition date*' depends on whether or not there is an accumulation period, and is separately defined in 82.23 above for each such possibility.) If the shares leave the plan in less than three years, the chargeable amount is their market value (determined as in 82.22 above) when they leave the plan. If they leave the plan after three years or more but less than five years, the chargeable amount is the lower of their market value when they leave the plan and the amount of salary deductions used to acquire them. If the latter, the tax is reduced by any tax paid on 'capital receipts' (see above) in respect of the shares. After 17 June 2004, any tax due is reduced by any tax paid by virtue of 82.9 above (shares with artificially enhanced market value) in relation to the shares. There is no charge on partnership shares leaving the plan after five years or more. [*ITEPA 2003, ss 497(2), 506; FA 2000, Sch 8 para 86; FA 2004, s 88(5)(11)*].

Dividend shares generally. The amount applied by the trustees in acquiring dividend shares (see 82.25 above) on behalf of a participant is not treated as his income for any tax purposes. He is not entitled to a dividend tax credit in respect of amounts so applied. Any balance carried forward as in 82.25 above is treated in the same way, but any amount eventually paid over to the participant is chargeable to income tax under Schedule F (or Schedule D, Case V in the case of a foreign dividend) as if it were a dividend received by him (with accompanying tax credit) in the tax year in which it is paid over (see 1.9 ALLOWANCES AND TAX RATES for taxation of dividends generally). [*ITEPA 2003, ss 493, 496, Sch 2 para 80(4), Sch 6 paras 10, 34; ICTA 1988, ss 68A–68C, ss 251A, 251B, 251D; FA 2000, Sch 8 paras 89–92*].

Dividend shares leaving the plan. If dividend shares (see 82.25 above) cease to be subject to the plan (see 82.21 above) within less than three years after their acquisition on the participant's behalf, the participant is chargeable to income tax on a notional dividend (subject to the same exceptions as for free and matching shares — see (a)–(c) above). The notional dividend is equal to the amount of cash dividend applied to acquire the shares, and is chargeable to income tax under Schedule F (or Schedule D, Case V in the case of a foreign dividend) as if it were a dividend received by the participant (with accompanying tax credit) in the tax year in which the shares cease to be subject to the plan (see 1.9 ALLOWANCES AND TAX RATES for taxation of dividends generally). The tax due (after deduction of tax credits) is reduced by any tax paid on 'capital receipts' (see above) in respect of the shares. There is no charge on dividend shares leaving the plan after three years or more. [*ITEPA 2003, s 497(3), Sch 2 para 80(4)(5), Sch 6 paras 10, 34; ICTA 1988, ss 68A–68C, ss 251A, 251C, 251D; FA 2000, Sch 8 para 93; FA 2001, Sch 13 para 7*].

PAYE. Where a tax charge arises as above on any shares leaving the plan and those shares are 'readily convertible assets', PAYE must be applied by the 'employer company'. A '*readily convertible asset*' is as defined in *ITEPA 2003, s 702* (see 55.2(*a*) PAY AS YOU EARN) except that, in determining for these purposes whether or not shares fall within that definition, there is disregarded:

- any market for the shares which is created by virtue of the trustees acquiring shares for the plan and which exists solely for the purposes of the plan; and

- *ITEPA 2003, s 702(5A)–(5D)*, which in certain circumstances treat shares and securities as readily convertible assets even if they would otherwise not be (see 55.2(*a*) PAY AS YOU EARN).

The '*employer company*' is the company which employs the participant in 'relevant employment' (see 82.21 above) at the time the shares cease to be subject to the plan, or (for 2002/03 onwards), if the participant is not employed in relevant employment at that time, the company which last so employed him. The plan may require the participant to pay to the employer company a sum sufficient to meet the PAYE liability. Otherwise, the trustees must make such payment to the employer company (see 82.32 below as regards the raising of the necessary funds). The company must account for PAYE and return any unused balance to the participant. If there is no employer company, or if the Revenue consider that it is impracticable for the employer company to make a PAYE deduction and they so direct, the obligation to make the deduction falls on the trustees instead. *ITEPA 2003, s 689* (non-UK employers — see 55.3 PAY AS YOU EARN) is then disapplied.

[*ITEPA 2003, ss 509–512; FA 2000, Sch 8 paras 94, 95, 128; FA 2002, s 39; FA 2003, Sch 22 para 11*].

Where the trustees receive a sum of money by way of a capital receipt chargeable to tax on receipt by the participant (see above), the trustees must pay to the 'employer company' (defined as above but by reference to the time of receipt by the trustees) the amount on which such tax is chargeable. The employer company must make a PAYE deduction and account to the participant for the net amount. The obligation to deduct PAYE and account for the net amount may be transferred to the trustees in similar circumstances to those described above. [*ITEPA 2003, ss 513, 514; FA 2000, Sch 8 para 96; FA 2002, s 39(4)(7)*].

Plan trustees. For the tax position of the trustees in respect of dividends on unappropriated shares, see 82.32 below.

82.27   **Capital gains tax.** A participant is treated for capital gains tax purposes as absolutely entitled as against the plan trustees to any shares awarded to him under an approved SIP. Shares ceasing to be subject to the plan (see 82.21 above) at any time are deemed to have been disposed of and immediately reacquired by the participant at their then market value, but no chargeable gain or allowable loss arises on the deemed disposal. If any of a participant's shares are forfeited (see 82.30 below as regards provision for forfeiture), they are deemed to have been disposed of by the participant and acquired by the plan trustees at their market value at the date of forfeiture, but again no chargeable gain or allowable loss arises. [*TCGA 1992, Sch 7D paras 1, 3, 5, 7; FA 2000, Sch 8 paras 99, 101, 102; ITEPA 2003, Sch 6 para 221*]. A form of rollover relief is available for shares transferred (other than by a company) to the trustees of an approved SIP. [*TCGA 1992, s 236A, Sch 7C; FA 2000, s 48, Sch 9; ITEPA 2003, Sch 6 paras 214, 220*].

For details, see Tolley's Capital Gains Tax under Employee Share Schemes.

82.28 **Eligibility of employees.** An approved SIP must provide that only an individual who is eligible may participate in an award of shares (see 82.21 above), such eligibility to be judged, in the case of free shares, at the time the award is made and, in the case of partnership shares (and related matching shares), at the time of the salary deduction relating to the award or, if there is an accumulation period (see 82.23 above), the first such salary deduction. An individual is eligible only if the requirements (as detailed below) as to employment, no material interest and participation in other schemes are met. An individual who is not a 'UK resident taxpayer' (as defined in 82.21 above)must satisfy any further eligibility requirements set out in the plan. [*ITEPA 2003, Sch 2 para 14; FA 2000, Sch 8 para 13; FA 2003, Sch 21 para 4*].

Employment. The individual must be an employee of the company which established the plan or, in the case of a group plan, of a constituent company (see 82.20 above). The plan *may* provide for a qualifying period, in which case the individual is required to have been at all times during that period an employee of the company or of a company that is a constituent company at the end of that period. For awards made on or after 11 May 2001, this condition can also be satisfied by reference to employment with an associated company (as in 82.21 above and judged as at the time of that employment) and, in the case of a group plan, with a company that was a constituent company at the time of that employment or with a then associated company of such a company. The qualifying period, if any, must be

(i) (in the case of free shares) a period of not more than 18 months ending with the date of the award; and

(ii) (in the case of partnership shares and related matching shares) a period of not more than 18 months ending with the salary deduction related to the award, or, where relevant, a period of not more than six months ending with the start of the accumulation period (see 82.23 above) related to the award.

In relation to an award, the same qualifying period must apply in relation to all employees of the company or, where applicable, of the constituent companies. The plan may authorise the company to specify different qualifying periods in respect of different awards.

[*ITEPA 2003, Sch 2 paras 15–17; FA 2000, Sch 8 para 14; FA 2001, Sch 13 para 2*].

No material interest. An individual is not eligible to participate in an award if he has, or has had within the preceding 12 months, a 'material interest' in

(*a*) a close company whose shares may be awarded under the plan; or

(*b*) a company which has control (within *ICTA 1988, s 840*) of such a company or is a member of a consortium which owns such a company. (For this purpose, a company is a member of a consortium owning another company if it is one of a number of companies which between them beneficially own at least 75% of, and each of which beneficially owns at least 5% of, the other company's ordinary share capital.)

For these purposes, an individual has a '*material interest*' in a company if he, and/or certain associates of his (within *ITEPA 2003, Sch 2 paras 22–24; FA 2000, Sch 8 paras 20–22*),

(1)   beneficially owns or controls (directly or indirectly) more than 25% of ordinary share capital; or

(2)   (where the company is a close company, or would be but for being a non-UK resident company or a quoted company) possesses or is entitled to acquire rights to more than 25% of the assets available for distribution among the participators (within *ICTA 1988, s 417(1)*) in a winding-up or in any other circumstances.

Rights to acquire shares must be taken into account (in accordance with *ITEPA 2003, Sch 2 para 21*). Shares or rights held by trustees of an approved profit sharing scheme (see 82.18 above) or an approved SIP and *not* appropriated to, or acquired on behalf of, any individual are disregarded.

[*ITEPA 2003, s 719, Sch 2 paras 19–24, 99(3), Sch 7 para 87; FA 2000, Sch 8 paras 15, 17–19, 129(1)(4)*].

Participation in other schemes. An individual is not eligible to participate in an award of free, matching or partnership shares under an approved SIP at the same time as participating in an award under another approved SIP established by the same company or by a 'connected company' (simultaneous participation). Before 10 July 2003, an individual was also not eligible to participate in an award if he had in the same tax year participated in an award under another approved SIP established by the same company or by a 'connected company' (successive participation). On or after that date, successive participation is permitted but the limits on the number of free shares an individual can obtain, the amount of salary he can invest in partnership shares and the amount that can be reinvested on his behalf in dividend shares apply as if all such plans were a single plan. For 2002/03 and earlier years, an individual was also not eligible to participate in an award of *free* shares under an approved SIP in a tax year if shares had been (or were at the same time to be) appropriated to him under an approved profit sharing scheme (see 82.18 above) established by the same company or by a 'connected company'. For these purposes, an individual is treated as having participated in an award of free shares under a SIP if he would have done so but for his failure to obtain a performance allowance (see 82.29 below).

For these purposes, a *'connected company'* is

(I)   a company which controls (within *ICTA 1988, s 840*) the first company, or which is controlled by the first company, or which is controlled by a company which also controls the first company; or

(II)   a company which is a member of a consortium (as in (*b*) above) owning the first company or which is owned in part by the first company as a member of a consortium.

[*ITEPA 2003, s 719, Sch 2 paras 18, 18A; FA 2000, Sch 8 paras 16, 129(1); FA 2003, Sch 21 paras 2, 5*].

82.29   **Performance allowances.** If the plan provides for performance allowances, i.e. for the award of free shares, or the number or value of free shares awarded, to be conditional on performance targets being met, the company must use one of the two methods described below.

Under *Method 1*, in relation to a particular award of shares (see 82.21 above),

(*a*)   at least 20% of the shares must be awarded other than by reference to performance; and

(*b*)   the highest performance-related award (in terms of the number of shares) made to any individual must not exceed four times the highest non-performance-related award so made.

If different classes of share are awarded, the above applies separately in relation to each class. The overall requirement (at 82.21 above) to award free shares on similar terms to all participating employees is disapplied as regards the performance-related shares.

Under *Method 2*, in relation to a particular award of shares, some or all of the shares must be awarded by reference to performance, and the overall requirement to award free shares on similar terms to all participating employees is applied separately as regards each performance unit. The performance targets set must be consistent, which means they must be capable of being reasonably viewed as being comparable in terms of the likelihood of their being met by the performance units to which they apply.

Whichever method is used, performance allowances in relation to an award must be available to each qualifying employee. Performance targets must be set for performance units comprising one or more employees, and performance measures must be based on business results or other objective criteria and be fair and objective measures of the performance of the applicable units. An employee cannot belong to more than one performance unit for the purposes of a particular award of free shares. The plan must require

(i)   performance targets and measures to be notified to prospective participants, and

(ii) (in general terms and subject to reasonable considerations as to commercial confidentiality) performance measures to be notified to all qualifying employees (see 82.21 above) of the company (or of all constituent companies under a group plan),

such notifications to be given as soon as reasonably practicable.

[*ITEPA 2003, Sch 2 paras 34(4), 38–42; FA 2000, Sch 8 paras 25–30*].

82.30 **Requirements as to type of share used.** The requirements below must all be met with respect to any shares (*'eligible shares'*) that may be awarded under an approved SIP.

Eligible shares must form part of the ordinary share capital of:

(*a*)   the company which established the plan;

(*b*)   a company which has control (within *ICTA 1988, s 840*) of the company in (*a*) above;

(*c*)   a company which is a member of a consortium (as in 82.28(*b*) above) owning either the company in (*a*) above or a company within (*b*) above; or

(*d*)   a company which has control of a company within (*c*) above.

Eligible shares must be

(i)   shares of a class listed on a recognised stock exchange ;

(ii) shares in a company not under the control (within *ICTA 1988, s 840*) of another company; or

(iii) shares in a company under the control of a company (other than a close company) whose shares are listed on a recognised stock exchange. Reference here to a close company includes a company which would be a close company if it were UK resident.

Eligible shares must be fully paid up and, except in relation to shares in certain co-operatives (as defined), not redeemable (or capable of becoming redeemable). Shares are not fully paid up for this purpose if there is any undertaking to pay cash to the company at a future date.

Eligible shares must not be subject to any restrictions (as to their disposal or the exercise of rights conferred etc. — see *ITEPA 2003, Sch 2 para 30(2)–(4)* for full definition and disregards) other than

(A)   those involved in there being a holding period (i.e. for free, matching and dividend shares — see respectively 82.22, 82.24, 82.25 above);

(B)   those affecting all ordinary shares in the company; or

(C)   permitted restrictions as to voting rights, provision for forfeiture or pre-emption conditions (see below in each case).

Eligible shares must not be shares in an *'service company'*, i.e. a company whose business is substantially the provision of the services of its employees either to persons, including partnerships, who control the company or to associated companies (as specially defined for this purpose). The prohibition extends to shares in certain companies which have control of service companies. *'Control'* for these purposes is determined in accordance with *ICTA 1988, s 416(2)–(6)*.

[ITEPA 2003, s 719, Sch 2 paras 2(2), 25–30; FA 2000, Sch 8 para 1(4), paras 59–63, 67, 129(1)].

Voting rights. Eligible shares may be shares carrying no voting rights or limited voting rights.

Provision for forfeiture (i.e. provision to the effect that a participant shall cease to be beneficially entitled to the plan shares on the occurrence of certain events). As regards free or matching shares (see 82.22, 82.24 above), provision may be made for forfeiture if the participant

(1)   ceases to be in relevant employment (see 82.21 above), or

(2)   withdraws the shares from the plan (see 82.21 above),

within the *'forfeiture period'*, i.e. a period not exceeding three years as specified in the plan and beginning with the date on which the shares were awarded (see 82.21 above) to the participant. However, shares cannot be made subject to provision for forfeiture in the event of shares ceasing to be subject to the plan for any of the reasons at 82.26(*a*)–(*c*) above. As regards matching shares only, provision may be made for forfeiture if the participant withdraws from the plan, within the said forfeiture period, the partnership shares in respect of which the matching shares were awarded to him. Forfeiture cannot be linked to performance, and the same provision for forfeiture, if any, must apply to all free or matching shares included in the same award.

Pre-emption conditions. Eligible shares may be made subject to provision requiring shares awarded to an employee and held by him (or by a permitted transferee under the company's articles) to be offered for sale on his ceasing to be in relevant employment (see 82.21 above). Such provision can be made only if, under the company's articles, the same provision applies to all employees, the shares must be offered for sale at a specified price, and anyone disposing of shares of the class in question (whether or not as an employee) is required to offer them for sale on no better terms.

[ITEPA 2003, Sch 2 paras 31–33, 99(1); FA 2000, Sch 8 paras 64–66].

82.31   **Company reconstructions.** For the purposes of the SIP provisions (and subject to the rules below for rights issues),

(a)   a company reconstruction (see below) is treated as not involving a disposal of shares comprised in the original holding;

(*b*)   new shares (see below) are deemed to have been awarded to (or acquired on behalf of) a participant on the date the corresponding original shares were awarded or so acquired;

(*c*)   the requirements at 82.30 above are treated as fulfilled with respect to new shares if they were fulfilled (or treated as fulfilled) with respect to the original shares;

(*d*)   references throughout the provisions to a participant's plan shares are to be construed as including any new shares; and

(*e*)   the tax provisions at 82.26, 82.27 above apply to new shares as they would have applied to the original shares.

If, as part of a company reconstruction, the trustees become entitled to a capital receipt, their entitlement is deemed to arise before the new holding comes into being.

For the above purposes, a '*company reconstruction*' is a transaction in relation to any of a participant's plan shares

(i)   which results in a new holding being equated with the original holding for capital gains tax purposes (see Tolley's Capital Gains Tax under Shares and Securities), or

(ii)   which would do so but for the new holding consisting of or including a qualifying corporate bond (see Tolley's Capital Gains Tax under Qualifying Corporate Bonds);

and '*new shares*' means shares, securities and rights comprised in the new holding. Certain share issues treated as distributions chargeable to income tax are treated for the purposes of these provisions as *not* forming part of the new holding.

[*ITEPA 2003, Sch 2 paras 86, 87; FA 2000, Sch 8 para 115*].

Rights issues. Subject to the exceptions below, where the trustees take up rights under a rights issue in respect of a participant's plan shares, the resulting new shares or securities or rights are treated as synonymous with the original shares. This does not apply where

(A)   the funds used to acquire the new shares etc. are provided other than by the part disposal of rights in order to take up other rights under the issue; or

(B)   the rights are not conferred in respect of all ordinary shares in the company.

Where the rule is disapplied, the new shares etc. are not plan shares and do not fall to be equated with the original shares for capital gains tax purposes.

[*ITEPA 2003, Sch 2 paras 88, 99(1); FA 2000, Sch 8 para 116*].

82.32   **The plan trustees.** A SIP must provide for the establishment of a trust, constituted under UK law and consisting of UK-resident trustees, the principal duties of the trustees being to acquire shares and appropriate them as free or matching shares to employees, and to acquire partnership and dividend shares on behalf of employees, in accordance with the plan. The trustees' other duties must include:

(*a*)   giving an employee notice of shares awarded to him and of dividend shares acquired on his behalf, such notice to include specified information;

(*b*)   maintaining such records as may be necessary for the purposes of their own, and the employer's, plan-related PAYE obligations (see 82.26 above);

(*c*)   (where relevant) giving a participant notice of any foreign tax deducted at source from plan share dividends from a non-UK resident company;

(*d*)   informing a participant of the facts relevant to determining any income tax liability which he incurs under these provisions; and

(*e*)   (from 10 July 2003) maintaining records of individuals who have participated in other approved SIPs established by the same company or a connected company (see 82.28 above).

The trust instrument must require the trustees to act only at the direction of a participant as regards disposing of his plan shares and dealing with rights issues, but, except in the case of partnership shares, must also prohibit them from disposing of shares (to the participant or otherwise), except in certain specified circumstances, within the holding period for those shares (see 82.22, 82.24, 82.25 above), unless the participant has ceased to be in relevant employment (see 82.21 above). The plan may provide for participants' directions to be given in general terms. Subject to the above, the trustees may partly dispose of rights under a rights issue in order to raise funds to take up other rights under the issue. With certain exceptions, the trust instrument must require the trustees to account to participants for any money or money's worth received by them in respect of or by reference to plan shares.

The plan must provide for the trustees to raise funds to meet PAYE obligations on shares leaving the plan (see 82.26 above), either by disposing of a participant's plan shares (including a disposal to themselves as trustees) or by obtaining the necessary amount from the participant.

If authorised by the trust instrument, the trustees may borrow to acquire shares and for other specified purposes.

The trust instrument

(i)   must provide that shares acquired by the trustees by way of qualifying transfer of relevant shares from a QUEST (see 63 QUALIFYING EMPLOYEE SHARE OWNERSHIP TRUSTS) are not awarded under the plan as partnership shares but are otherwise awarded in priority to other available shares; and

(ii) must not contain any terms which are neither essential nor reasonably incidental to complying with the statutory requirements.

From 6 April 2003, the trust instrument *may* contain provision for at least half of the non-professional trustees to be selected from the employees of participating companies.

[*ITEPA 2003, Sch 2 paras 70–80, 99(1); FA 2000, Sch 8 paras 68–73, 75, 76, 129(1); FA 2003, s 142(3), Sch 21 para 6*].

Tax exemption for dividends on unappropriated shares. Tax is not chargeable at the Schedule F trust rate (see 81.5 SETTLEMENTS) in respect of dividends or other distributions on shares held by the trustees on their own account, provided that the shares satisfy the requirements at 82.30 above as to the type of share that may be used in the plan and are awarded (see 82.21 above) (or acquired as dividend shares) within a statutory period. The period within which shares must be awarded depends on whether or not any of the shares in the company in question are 'readily convertible assets' (see 82.26 above under PAYE) at the time of the acquisition of shares by the trustees. If they are, the period is the two years from acquisition. Otherwise, it is five years from acquisition, but if within those five years any of the shares in the company (for shares acquired before 11 May 2001, the shares acquired) become readily convertible assets the period ends no later than two years after the date on which they did so. For these purposes,

(A) shares of a particular class are deemed to be awarded by the trustees on a first in/first out basis; and

(B) shares subject to provision for forfeiture (see 82.30 above) are deemed to be acquired by the trustees if and when forfeiture occurs.

From 6 April 2003, the period within which shares must be awarded is extended to ten years from acquisition if the shares are part of a significant block of shares acquired by the trustees in relation to which the employer company has been given an up-front corporation tax deduction (see 71.44 SCHEDULE D, CASES I AND II).

[*ITEPA 2003, ss 686B, 686C, Sch 6 para 100; FA 2000, Sch 8 para 88*].

For *capital gains tax* matters relevant to the trustees, see Tolley's Capital Gains Tax under Employee Share Schemes.

82.33 Share-Related Employment Income and Exemptions

82.33 **Revenue approval.** On written application by the company, the Revenue will approve a SIP if they are satisfied that it meets the statutory requirements. Applications must contain such particulars and be supported by such evidence as the Revenue may require. The company may appeal within 30 days against refusal of Revenue approval; the appeal lies to the Special Commissioners. On a successful appeal, the Special Commissioners may direct the Revenue to approve the plan from a specified date no earlier than the original date of application. [*ITEPA 2003, Sch 2 paras 81, 82; FA 2000, Sch 8 paras 4, 5*].

Withdrawal of approval. If any disqualifying event occurs, the Revenue may by notice withdraw their approval of the plan with effect from, at the earliest, the time of the disqualifying event. The withdrawal does not affect the treatment of shares awarded to participants (see 82.21 above) before the effective time of withdrawal. Any of the following is a disqualifying event:

(*a*) a contravention, in relation to the operation of the plan, of any of the statutory requirements, the plan itself or the plan trust;

(*b*) an alteration made in a 'key feature' of the plan or in the terms of the plan trust without Revenue approval (see further below);

(*c*) the setting under *Method 2* of performance targets that are not consistent (see 82.29 above);

(*d*) an alteration in the share capital of the company whose shares are the subject of the plan, or in the rights attaching to any of its shares, that materially affects the value of plan shares;

(*e*) plan shares of a particular class receiving different treatment from the other shares of that class, particularly in respect of dividends (other than in limited circumstances as specified), repayment, restrictions, or any offer of substituted or additional shares, securities or rights of any kind in respect of the shares (see further below);

(*f*) the trustees, the company, or, in the case of a group plan, any company which is or has been a constituent company failing to furnish any information called for under the Revenue's information powers below.

The Revenue are not to withhold approval to an alteration within (*b*) above unless it appears to them that the plan, as altered, would not receive approval on an initial application. As regards (*e*) above, there is no disqualifying event where the difference in treatment arises from a 'key feature' or from any participants' shares being subject to provision for forfeiture (see 82.30 above). For the above purposes, a '*key feature*' of a plan is a provision of the plan that is necessary in order to meet the statutory requirements.

The company may appeal, within 30 days, against a withdrawal of approval, an associated withdrawal of corporation tax relief (see 71.44 SCHEDULE D, CASES I AND II), or a refusal to approve an alteration as in (*b*) above; the appeal lies in each case to the Special Commissioners.

[*ITEPA 2003, Sch 2 paras 83–85, Sch 7 para 68(4); FA 2000, Sch 8 paras 118, 119*].

Applications for approval should be sent to Inland Revenue, Employee Share Schemes, Second Floor, New Wing, Somerset House, Strand, London, WC2R 1LB.

Revenue information powers. The Revenue have wide-ranging powers to require any person to furnish them with such information as they reasonably require and as that person possesses or can reasonably obtain. The information must be supplied within a period specified in the notice, which must not be less than three months. Penalties under *TMA 1970, s 98* are exigible for non-compliance. [*ITEPA 2003, Sch 2 para 93, Sch 6 para 137; FA 2000, Sch 8 para 117*].

82.34   **Termination of plan.** A SIP may provide for the company to terminate the plan in such circumstances as the plan may specify. This is accomplished by the issue of a plan termination notice, a copy of which must be given without delay to the Revenue, the plan trustees and each individual who has plan shares or has entered into a current partnership share agreement. Any money held on an individual's behalf by the plan trustees must be paid over to him as soon as practicable after the plan termination notice is issued. Plan shares must be removed from the plan as soon as practicable after the end of three months following the distribution of the plan termination notice or, if later, after the first date on which they may be removed without giving rise to an income tax charge (see 82.26 above). Shares may be removed earlier with the consent of the participant (or, after his death, his personal representatives). The trustees can remove shares from the plan either by transferring them to, or at the direction of, the participant (or his personal representatives) or by disposing of them and similarly accounting for the proceeds.

[*ITEPA 2003, Sch 2 paras 89, 90; FA 2000, Sch 8 paras 120, 121(1)–(9)*].

82.35   **ENTERPRISE MANAGEMENT INCENTIVES**

Introduction. With effect **on and after 28 July 2000**, 'small higher risk' trading companies are able to grant options over shares worth up to £100,000 (at time of grant) to eligible employees without income tax consequences (except to the extent that the option is to acquire shares at less than their market value at time of grant). In relation to options granted on or after 11 May 2001, the total value of shares in respect of which unexercised options exist must not exceed £3 million. This replaced a rule limiting the number of employees who could hold options at any one time to 15. Any gain on sale of the shares by the employee is chargeable to capital gains tax (see 82.37 below).

The company may be quoted or unquoted but must be an independent company trading or preparing to trade wholly or mainly in the UK and whose gross assets do not exceed £30 million (£15 million for options granted before 1 January 2002). A company carrying on certain specified activities deemed to be lower risk activities does not qualify, such exclusions being similar to those at 25.7(*a*)–(*c*)(*e*)–(*l*) ENTERPRISE INVESTMENT SCHEME. Broadly, an employee is eligible if he is employed by the company for at least 25 hours per week or, if less, at least 75% of his total working time, and he controls no more than 30% of the company's ordinary share capital. Companies are not required to obtain Revenue approval to schemes but must give notification to the Revenue within 92 days after an option is granted (30 days for options granted before 11 May 2001).

[*ITEPA 2003, ss 527–541, Sch 5; FA 2000, s 62, Sch 14; FA 2001, Sch 14*].

From 5 April 2001, the Revenue will on request give written advance assurance that a company will be a qualifying company for these purposes, though not about any other aspect of the scheme. Applications should be made in writing to Inland Revenue, Small Company Enterprise Centre, TIDO. Ty Glas, Llanishen, Cardiff, CF14 5ZG and must be accompanied by all relevant information, including latest accounts, memorandum and articles, and details of trading activities, covering in each case the company and each of its subsidiaries. (Revenue Press Release BN6, 7 March 2001).

The coverage below is set out under the following headings.

82.36 Share-Related Employment Income and Exemptions

Qualifying options. A qualifying option is an option (i.e. a right to acquire shares) in relation to which the general requirements below and the further requirements at 82.38–82.41 below are met at the time it is granted, and of which notice is given to the Revenue as in 82.43 below. [*ITEPA 2003, s 527, Sch 5 para 1; FA 2000, Sch 14 paras 1, 71(1)*].

The option must be granted for commercial reasons in order to recruit or retain an employee (for options granted before 11 May 2001, a key employee) in a company, and not as part of a tax avoidance scheme or arrangement. It must be granted to the employee by reason of his employment with the '*relevant company*' (i.e. the company whose shares are the subject of the option) or, if the relevant company is a parent company, his employment with that company or another member of the group. See 82.38 below as to qualifying companies and 82.40 below as to eligible employees. See 82.41 below for requirements as to the terms of the option, including the type of share that may be acquired.

In relation to options granted on or after 11 May 2001, the total value (see below) of shares in the relevant company in respect of which unexercised qualifying options exist must not exceed £3 million. If the limit is already exceeded at the time an option is granted, that option is not a qualifying option. If the grant of an option causes the limit to be exceeded, that option is not a qualifying option so far as it relates to the excess. For this purpose, where more than one option is granted simultaneously, the excess is divided *pro rata* between them according to the value of shares which each represents. These rules replaced a rule to the effect that not more than 15 employees could hold qualifying options in respect of shares in the relevant company at the same time.

Maximum entitlement. An employee cannot at any time hold unexercised qualifying options in respect of shares with a total value (see below) of more than £100,000. If the limit is already exceeded at the time an option is granted, that option is not a qualifying option. If the grant of an option causes the limit to be exceeded, that option is not a qualifying option so far as it relates to the excess. Where an employee has been granted qualifying options in respect of shares with a total value of £100,000, then, whether or not those options remain unexercised (and disregarding any release of options), no further *qualifying* option may be granted to him within three years after the date of grant of the last qualifying option. If, at the time an option is granted under these provisions, the employee holds unexercised options under an approved CSOP scheme (as in 82.49 below), those options count towards the limit as if they were qualifying options.

The £100,000 limit is a global limit covering options granted by reason of employment with one company or with any number of companies in the same group. The legislation is framed to prevent the above provisions being circumvented if options are granted to an individual by reference to his employment with different companies within a group.

For the above purposes, the value of shares is the market value (determined as for capital gains tax purposes), *at the time the option is granted*, of shares of the same class, and an option is treated as granted in respect of the maximum number of shares that may be acquired under it. Where the market value of shares on any date falls to be determined for any purpose of these provisions, the Revenue and the employer company may agree that it be determined by reference to a different date or a number of specified dates. If market value is not agreed between the Revenue and the employer company, the Revenue have power to determine it. The employer company may appeal within 30 days against a notice of determination (see also 82.46 below as regards compliance with time limits). Alternatively, the company may, by notice to the Revenue before a notice of determination is given, refer the question of market value to the Commissioners, who must then determine it in like manner as on appeal. The appeal or referral lies to the General Commissioners, unless the company elects under *TMA 1970, s 46(1)* (see 4.3 APPEALS) for the Special Commissioners. In arriving at the market value of restricted shares as in 82.4 above (previously shares subject to restrictions, or to risk of forfeiture such that the interest that may be acquired is only conditional — see 82.5 above), the restrictions (or risk of forfeiture) are disregarded.

The £100,000 limit may be amended in the future by Treasury Order.

[*ITEPA 2003, Sch 5 paras 1(3)(d), 2–7, 54–57; FA 2000, Sch 14 para 1(2)(d), paras 8–11, 66, 67, 69; FA 2001, Sch 14 paras 4–6, 13; FA 2003, Sch 22 para 45(2)(4)*].

See 82.43 below re possibility and consequences of Revenue enquiry into an option.

82.37   **Income tax consequences of qualifying option.** No income tax is chargeable on the *receipt* of a qualifying option. The *exercise* of a qualifying option attracts the following special treatment (but only if it occurs within ten years after the time of the grant). Subject to any disqualifying event (see below), no income tax charge arises under 82.16 above on the exercise of a qualifying option to acquire shares at not less than their market value at the time of the grant. On the exercise on or after 11 May 2001 of a qualifying option to acquire shares at nil cost or otherwise at less than their market value at the time of the grant, an amount is chargeable under 82.16 above, but is limited (if it would otherwise be greater) to the excess of the 'chargeable market value' over the aggregate of any consideration given for the option itself and (if any) the amount for which the shares are acquired. If there is no such excess, no charge arises. The *'chargeable market value'* is the lower of

(*a*)   the market value of the shares at the time of grant, and

(*b*)   the market value of the shares at the time the option is exercised.

For options exercised before 11 May 2001, these rules operated similarly except that no account was taken of any consideration given for the option itself. In the case of a replacement option (see 82.42 below), all references above to the time of the grant are to the time of grant of the original option.

[*ITEPA 2003, ss 419, 475, 528–531, 532(6); FA 2000, Sch 14 paras 42–46, 53(3); FA 2001, Sch 14 paras 7, 8, 13; FA 2003, Sch 22 paras 2, 10, 36, 37*].

For guidance on the interaction between the above rules and the restricted shares rules at 82.4 above (where the shares acquired on exercise are restricted shares), see www.inland revenue.gov.uk/shareschemes/faq_emprelatedsecurity-ch2.htm#w

In their application in relation to a 'UK resident employee', the notional loan provisions at 82.10 above in respect of shares acquired at less than market value do not apply in relation to shares acquired by the exercise of a qualifying option (whether or not at a discount). For this purpose, an employee is a *'UK resident employee'* if, judged at the time of grant or exercise of the option, the earnings from the employment are (or would be if there were any) general earnings within *ITEPA 2003, s 15* or *s 21* (earnings for year when employee resident and ordinarily resident in UK). (Before 2003/04, this strictly fell to be judged at the time of exercise only, though it is understood that, in practice, the Revenue judged it at the time of grant only — see Change 131 listed in Annex 1 to the Explanatory Notes to the Income Tax (Earnings and Pensions) Bill.) [*ITEPA 2003, s 540; FA 2000, Sch 14 para 54(1); FA 2003, Sch 22 para 40*].

Other than on *exercise* of the qualifying option, there is no exemption from the charge at 82.16 above (e.g. on release of the option). In addition, the provisions at 82.4–82.9, 82.11, 82.12 and 82.14 above all apply to shares acquired under a qualifying option as they would to other employment-related shares. However, amounts deductible in computing the chargeable amount under 82.4 above (restricted shares), i.e. in ascertaining the value of IUP in the given formula, include the amount (or additional amount) that would have been chargeable under 82.16 above on exercise if the shares had not been acquired under a qualifying option. [*ITEPA 2003, s 541; FA 2000, Sch 14 paras 54(2), 55; FA 2003, Sch 22 para 41*].

Disqualifying events. Where a 'disqualifying event' occurs in relation to a qualifying option before it is exercised, and the option is not exercised within 40 days after the date of that event, an amount is chargeable under 82.16 above on the eventual exercise of the option. The amount chargeable where the option is exercised on or after 11 May 2001 is

- (where there would otherwise be no charge) the 'post-event gain' (if any) less any consideration given for the option itself; or

- the amount otherwise chargeable under *ITEPA 2003, s 531* (above) plus the 'post-event gain',

but not so as to substitute a greater chargeable amount than would be the case if these provisions (including *ITEPA 2003, ss 530, 531*) were disregarded. The *'post-event gain'* is the amount (if any) by which the market value of the shares on exercise exceeds their market value immediately before the disqualifying event. For options exercised before 11 May 2001, these provisions operated similarly except that no account was taken of any consideration given for the option itself.

Any of the following is a *'disqualifying event'* in relation to a qualifying option.

(i) The 'relevant company' (see 82.36 above) becomes a 51% subsidiary of another company or otherwise comes under the control of another company (with or without the aid of CONNECTED PERSONS (19)). In a case where a replacement option has been granted (see 82.42 below), such an event is not a disqualifying event in relation to the original option if it occurred during the period beginning at the same time as the period within which the replacement had to be granted and ending with the release of rights under the old option.

(ii) The relevant company ceases to meet the trading activities requirement (see 82.38 below).

(iii) The relevant company was a qualifying company by virtue only of its *preparing to carry on* a qualifying trade (see 82.38, 82.39 below), and either the preparations cease or two years elapse from the date of grant without the relevant company or any company in its group commencing that trade.

(iv) The employee ceases to be an eligible employee in relation to the relevant company by reason of his ceasing to satisfy the requirements at 82.40(*a*) or (*b*) below (and see also below as to actual working time).

(v) A variation is made of the terms of the option, the effect of which is to increase the market value of the option shares or that the statutory requirements would no longer be met in relation to the option.

(vi) An alteration of a specified kind (see *ITEPA 2003, s 537(2)*) is made to the share capital of the relevant company where the effect is either

- to increase the market value of the option shares, where the alteration is not made by the relevant company for commercial reasons or the said increase is one of its main purposes; or

- that the statutory requirements would no longer be met in relation to the option.

For alterations of the specified kind made before 11 May 2001, these conditions were not specified, but a disqualifying event occurred if the alteration was made without prior Revenue approval. Approval was not to be withheld unless, in the Revenue's view, the effect of the alteration would be to increase the market value of the option shares or that the statutory requirements would no longer be met in relation to the option. Refusal of approval was subject to notice of appeal being given to the Revenue within 30 days by the employer company. The appeal lay to the General

Commissioners, unless the company elected under *TMA 1970, s 46(1)* (see 4.3 APPEALS) for the Special Commissioners.

(vii)   Any of the shares to which the option relates are converted to shares of a different class. There is an exception similar to that in 82.7 above, and subject to similar conditions, where all the shares of one class only are converted into shares of one other class only.

(viii) The employee is granted a CSOP option (i.e. an option under an approved CSOP scheme — see 82.61 below) by reason of his employment with the same company or by a company in the same group as that company, *and* immediately afterwards holds unexercised 'employee options' in respect of shares with a total value of over £100,000. For this purpose, *'employee options'* include the qualifying option in question and any other qualifying option or CSOP option granted by reason of employment with the same company or group.

In addition, a disqualifying event is treated as occurring in relation to a qualifying option *at the end of any tax year* if, during that year (disregarding any part of it before the option was granted), the average amount per week of the employee's 'reckonable time in relevant employment' was less than 25 hours or, if less, 75% of his 'working time' (as defined in 82.40(*b*) below). An employee's *'reckonable time in relevant employment'* is the time he spent, as an employee in 'relevant employment' (as defined in 82.40(*b*) below), on the business of the relevant company or, if it is a parent company, its group (inclusive of any permissible periods of absence as in 82.40(*b*) below). This rule applies for 2003/04 onwards; previously, a similar but more complex rule applied, requiring the cumulative working time to be examined at the end of each calendar month and with a disqualifying event treated as occurring at the end of the previous month (or, if the examination was being carried out at the end of April, at the end of the previous tax year) if the working time requirement was found not to be met; this rule continued to apply for the purpose of determining whether a disqualifying event was to be treated as having occurred at the end of 2002/03.)

[*ITEPA 2003, ss 419, 532–539, 718, Sch 5 paras 2, 54, Sch 7 para 78(2); FA 2000, Sch 14 para 1(3), paras 47–53, 71(2); FA 2001, Sch 14 paras 9–11, 13; FA 2003, Sch 22 paras 2, 38, 39*].

The comments in 82.36 above regarding the market value of shares apply equally for the above purposes.

Internationally mobile employees. For an article on the imposition of income tax charges under the above provisions in the case of internationally mobile employees, see Revenue Tax Bulletin October 2001 pp 883–887. For associated national insurance contributions liabilities, see Revenue Tax Bulletin December 2001 pp 895–899. For a follow-up to these articles, see Revenue Tax Bulletin August 2002 pp 951–954.

Capital gains tax consequences of qualifying option. The cost of acquisition of shares acquired under a qualifying option is computed according to the rules at 82.16 above. In contrast to the rule for other types of option though, the period of ownership of the shares for taper relief normally runs from the date a qualifying option is granted and not the date it is exercised, though special rules apply if a disqualifying event (as above) occurs. For the detailed provisions, see Tolley's Capital Gains Tax under Employee Share Schemes.

82.38   **Qualifying companies.** The company whose shares are the subject of the option must be a qualifying company. [*ITEPA 2003, Sch 5 para 1(3)(b); FA 2000, Sch 14 para 1(2)(b)*]. To be a qualifying company, it must, at the time the option is granted, meet the requirements detailed below as to independence, qualifying subsidiaries, property managing subsidiaries (for options granted after 16 March 2004), gross assets and trading activities. [*ITEPA 2003, Sch 5 paras 1(4), 8; FA 2000, Sch 14 para 12; FA 2004, s 96(6)*]. The company may be quoted or unquoted, and there is no requirement that it be UK resident (though see 82.39(i) below as regards qualifying trades).

Independence. The company must not be a 51% subsidiary of another company or otherwise under the control (within *ICTA 1988, s 840*) of another company, or of another company and persons connected with it (within *ICTA 1988, s 839* — see 19 CONNECTED PERSONS). No arrangements must exist whereby the company could become such a subsidiary or fall under such control. 'Arrangements' is very broadly defined, but for this purpose any arrangements with a view to a 'qualifying exchange of shares' (see 82.42 below) are disregarded. [*ITEPA 2003, ss 718, 719, Sch 5 paras 9, 58; FA 2000, Sch 14 paras 13, 71(1)(2)*].

Qualifying subsidiaries. If the company has subsidiaries, each 'subsidiary' must be a 'qualifying subsidiary'. A '*subsidiary*' is a company which the company controls (within *ICTA 1988, s 416(2)–(6)*), with or without the aid of CONNECTED PERSONS (19). A subsidiary is a '*qualifying subsidiary*' of a company (the holding company) if the conditions below are met.

(1)   In relation to options granted **after 16 March 2004**. The subsidiary must be a 51% subsidiary (see *ICTA 1988, s 838*) of the holding company and no person other than the holding company or another of its subsidiaries may have control (within *ICTA 1988, s 840* — see 19.8 CONNECTED PERSONS) of the subsidiary. Furthermore, no arrangements (as very broadly defined) may exist by virtue of which either of these conditions would cease to be satisfied.

The above conditions are not regarded as ceasing to be met by reason only of the subsidiary or any other company being in the process of being wound up or by reason only of anything done as a consequence of its being in administration or receivership (both as defined by *ICTA 1988, s 312(2A)*), provided the winding-up, entry into administration or receivership or anything done as a consequence of its being in administration or receivership is for commercial reasons and is not part of a tax avoidance scheme or arrangements.

(2)   In relation to options granted **on or before 16 March 2004**. The holding company must possess at least **75%** of the issued share capital of, and the voting power in, the subsidiary, and be beneficially entitled to at least **75%** of the assets available for distribution to shareholders on a winding-up etc. and of the profits available for distribution to shareholders. For these purposes, the 'holding company' means either the holding company by itself or the holding company and/or one or more of its other subsidiaries (if any). (A narrower definition applied before 2003/04 — see Change 174 listed in Annex 1 to the Explanatory Notes to the Income Tax (Earnings and Pensions Bill.) No other person may have control (within *ICTA 1988, s 840* — see 19.8 CONNECTED PERSONS) of the subsidiary. Furthermore, no arrangements (as very broadly defined) may exist by virtue of which any of these conditions would cease to be satisfied. A subsidiary does not fail these conditions by reason only of the fact that it or any other company is being wound up, provided that the winding-up is for commercial reasons and not part of a tax avoidance scheme or arrangements.

The conditions at (1) or (2) above are not regarded as ceasing to be satisfied by reason only of arrangements being in existence for the disposal of the interest in the subsidiary held by the holding company (or, as the case may be, by another of its subsidiaries) if the disposal is to be for commercial reasons and is not to be part of a tax avoidance scheme or arrangements.

[*ITEPA 2003, ss 718, 719, Sch 5 paras 10, 11, 58; FA 2000, Sch 14 paras 14, 15, 71(1)(2); FA 2004, s 96(3)(4)(6)*].

Property managing subsidiaries. In relation to options granted **after 16 March 2004**, the company must not have a 'property managing subsidiary' which is not a 'qualifying 90% subsidiary' (see below) of the company. A *'property managing subsidiary'* is a qualifying subsidiary (see above) whose business consists wholly or mainly in the holding or managing of 'land' or any 'property deriving its value from land' (both as defined in *ICTA 1988, s 776* (see 3.10 ANTI-AVOIDANCE).

A company (the subsidiary) is a *'qualifying 90% subsidiary'* of another company (the holding company) if

- the holding company possesses at least **90%** of both the issued share capital of, and the voting power in, the subsidiary;

- the holding company would be beneficially entitled to at least **90%** of the assets of the subsidiary available for distribution to shareholders on a winding-up or in any other circumstances;

- the holding company is beneficially entitled to at least **90%** of any profits of the subsidiary available for distribution to shareholders;

- no person other than the holding company has control (within *ICTA 1988, s 840* — see 19.8 CONNECTED PERSONS) of the subsidiary; and

- no arrangements (as very broadly defined) exist by virtue of which any of the above conditions would cease to be met.

The above conditions are not regarded as ceasing to be met by reason only of the subsidiary or any other company being in the process of being wound up or by reason only of anything done as a consequence of its being in administration or receivership (both as defined by *ICTA 1988, s 312(2A)*), provided the winding-up, entry into administration or receivership or anything done as a consequence of its being in administration or receivership is for commercial reasons and is not part of a tax avoidance scheme or arrangements. Nor are they regarded as ceasing to be met by reason only of arrangements being in existence for the disposal of the holding company's interest in the subsidiary if the disposal is to be for commercial reasons and is not to be part of a tax avoidance scheme or arrangements.

[*ITEPA 2003, s 719, Sch 5 paras 11A, 11B, 58; FA 2004, s 96(5)(6)*].

Gross assets. The value of the company's gross assets must not exceed £30 million (£15 million for options granted before 1 January 2002). If the company is the parent company of a group, that limit applies by reference to the aggregate value of the gross assets of the group (disregarding certain assets held by any member of the group which correspond to liabilities of another member). The limit may be amended in the future by Treasury Order. [*ITEPA 2003, Sch 5 paras 12, 54; FA 2000, Sch 14 paras 16, 69; SI 2001 No 3799*].

See Revenue Pamphlet IR 131, SP 2/00, 3 August 2000 (at 25.5 ENTERPRISE INVESTMENT SCHEME) for the Revenue's approach to the gross assets requirement.

Trading activities. If the company is a single company (i.e. not the parent company of a group), it must exist wholly for the purpose of carrying on one or more qualifying trades (see 82.39 below) and must actually be carrying on such a trade or preparing to do so. Purposes having no significant effect (other than in relation to incidental matters) on the extent of the company's activities are disregarded. For the ascertainment of the purposes for which a company exists, see Revenue Venture Capital Schemes Manual VCM 15070.

If the company is a parent company, the business of the group (treating the activities of the group companies, taken together, as a single business) must not consist wholly or as to a substantial part (i.e. broadly 20% — see Revenue Venture Capital Schemes Manual VCM 17040) in the carrying on of 'non-qualifying activities', and at least one group company must satisfy the above trading activities requirement for a single company. *'Non-qualifying activities'* means 'excluded activities' (as in 82.39 below) and non-trading activities.

Purposes for which a company exists are disregarded to the extent that they consist of

(i)   (as regards a single company) the holding and managing of property used by the company for one or more qualifying trades carried on by it; or

(ii)   (as regards a group company) any activities within (*a*)–(*c*) below.

For the purposes of determining the business of a group, activities of a group company are disregarded to the extent that they consist of

(*a*)   holding shares in or securities of, or making loans to, another group company;

(*b*)   holding and managing property used by a group company for the purposes of one or more qualifying trades carried on by a group company; or

(*c*)   incidental activities of a company which meets the above trading activities requirement for a single company.

Amendments to the trading activities requirement (including the provisions at 82.39 below) may be made in the future by Treasury Order.

[*ITEPA 2003, Sch 5 paras 13, 14, 58; FA 2000, Sch 14 paras 17, 69*].

Informal clearance. Enquiries from companies as to whether they meet the conditions of the enterprise management incentives scheme should be directed to Small Company Enterprise Centre, TIDO, Ty Glas, Llanishen, Cardiff CF14 5ZG (tel. 029–2032 7400; fax 029–2032 7398; e-mail enterprise.centre@ir.gsi.gov.uk).

82.39   **Qualifying trades.** A trade is a qualifying trade (see the trading activities requirement at 82.38 above) if

(i)   it is carried on wholly or mainly in the UK;

(ii)   it is conducted on a commercial basis and with a view to profit;

(iii) it does not consist wholly or as to a 'substantial' part in the carrying on of 'excluded activities' (see below).

See Revenue Pamphlet IR 131, SP 3/00, 3 August 2000 (at 25.6 ENTERPRISE INVESTMENT SCHEME) for the Revenue's approach to the requirement at (i) above. '*Substantial*' in (iii) above is not defined, but in its application to similar legislation is taken by the Revenue to mean 20% or more of total activities (see 25.7 ENTERPRISE INVESTMENT SCHEME).

Activities of 'research and development' from which it is intended that a 'connected qualifying trade' will be derived or will benefit are treated as a notional qualifying trade, but preparing to carry on such activities is not treated as preparing to carry on a qualifying trade. A '*connected qualifying trade*' is a qualifying trade carried on either by the company carrying out the research and development or, where applicable, by another member of the group. '*Research and development*' is as defined by *ICTA 1988, s 837A* (see 71.70 SCHEDULE D, CASES I AND II and note that the latest DTI guidelines issued on 5 March 2004 have no effect in relation to share options granted before 6 April 2004).

'*Excluded activities*' are as follows:

(*a*)   dealing in land, commodities or futures, or in shares, securities or other financial instruments;

(*b*)   dealing in goods otherwise than in an ordinary trade of wholesale or retail distribution (see further below);

(*c*)   banking, insurance, money-lending, debt-factoring, hire purchase financing or other financial activities;

(*d*)   leasing (including letting ships on charter or other assets on hire) or receiving royalties or licence fees (see further below);

(*e*)   providing legal or accountancy services;

(*f*)   property development (see further below);

(*g*)   farming or market gardening;

(*h*)   holding, managing or occupying woodlands, any other forestry activities or timber production;

(*j*)   operating or managing hotels or comparable establishments (including guest houses, hostels and other establishments whose main purpose is to offer overnight accommodation with or without catering) or property used as such (see further below);

(*k*)   operating or managing nursing homes or residential care homes (both as defined) or property used as such (see further below);

(*l*)   providing services or facilities for any business consisting to a substantial extent of activities within (*a*)–(*k*) above and carried on by another person, where a person (other than a parent of the service provider company) has a controlling interest (see below) in both that business and the business of the service provider company.

The exclusions at (*j*) and (*k*) above apply only if the person carrying on the activity has an estate or interest (e.g. a lease) in the property concerned or occupies that property.

As regards (*b*), (*d*), (*e*), (*f*) and (*l*) above, the additional comments in 25.7 ENTERPRISE INVESTMENT SCHEME, on the similar list of exclusions there, apply equally to the current provisions.

[*ITEPA 2003, Sch 5 paras 15–23, 58; FA 2000, Sch 14 paras 18–26, 71(1); FA 2004, Sch 27 para 17*].

82.40   **Eligible employees.** The individual to whom the option is granted must be an eligible employee in relation to the 'relevant company' (see 82.36 above). An individual is an eligible employee in relation to the relevant company if he satisfies the following three requirements at the time the option is granted.

(*a*)   *Employment.* He must be an employee of that company or, if it is a parent company, of that company or a qualifying subsidiary (see 82.38 above).

(*b*)   *Commitment of working time.* The average amount per week of his 'committed time' must be at least 25 hours or, if less, 75% of his 'working time'. (See 82.39 above for disqualifying event where *actual* working time falls below this average.) His '*committed time*' is the time he is required, as an employee in 'relevant employment', to spend on the business of the relevant company or, if it is a parent company, of its group (inclusive of certain permissible periods of absence, for example through ill-health, maternity leave, reasonable holiday entitlement, gardening leave etc.) His '*working time*' is time spent on 'remunerative work' as an employee or self-employed person (including the same permissible periods of absence). '*Remunerative work*' means work undertaken to produce income taxable as employment income or under Schedule D, Case I or II (or which would be so taxable if the employee were UK resident and ordinarily resident). An employee is in '*relevant employment*' if he is employed by the relevant company or, if it is a parent company, by any company in its group.

Before 2003/04, the individual's committed time (*not* the average weekly amount of it) had to amount to at least 25 hours per week or, if less, 75% of his working time.

(*c*)   *Material interest test.* He must not have a 'material interest' in the company or, where applicable, in any of its subsidiaries. For these purposes, an individual has a '*material interest'* in a company if he, and/or certain 'associates' of his (within *ITEPA 2003, Sch 5 paras 31–33*),

(i)   beneficially owns or controls (directly or indirectly) more than 30% of ordinary share capital (as defined by *ICTA 1988, s 832(1)*), or,

(ii)   (where the company is a close company, or would be but for its being non-UK resident or having a stock exchange quotation) possesses or is entitled to acquire rights to more than 30% of the assets available for distribution among the participators (within *ICTA 1988, s 417(1)*) in a winding-up or in any other circumstances.

Rights to acquire shares must be taken into account (in accordance with *ITEPA 2003, Sch 5 para 30*, though see below as regards qualifying options). Shares or rights held by trustees of an approved profit sharing scheme (see 82.18 above) or approved share incentive plan (see 82.20 above) and *not* appropriated to, or acquired on behalf of, any individual are disregarded.

In applying the material interest test, no account is taken of shares that the individual may acquire under a qualifying option, although account *is* taken of shares already so acquired.

[*ITEPA 2003, Sch 5 para 1(3)(c), (4), paras 24–33, 59, Sch 7 para 87; FA 2000, Sch 14 para 1(2)(c), paras 27–36, 71(1)*].

82.41   **Requirements as to terms of option etc.** An option is not a qualifying option unless all the requirements set out below are met at the time of grant. [*ITEPA 2003, Sch 5 para 34; FA 2000, Sch 14 para 37*].

The *shares that can be acquired* under the option must be fully paid up shares forming part of the 'ordinary share capital' (within *ICTA 1988, s 832(1)*) of the 'relevant company' (see 82.36 above), and must be neither redeemable nor capable of becoming redeemable. Shares are not fully paid up for this purpose if there is any undertaking to pay cash to the company at a future date. [*ITEPA 2003, Sch 5 paras 35, 59; FA 2000, Sch 14 paras 38, 71(1)*].

The option must be *capable of being exercised within ten years* beginning with the date of grant. If the exercise of the option is dependent on conditions being fulfilled, it is treated as so capable if the conditions may be fulfilled within those ten years. [*ITEPA 2003, Sch 5 para 36; FA 2000, Sch 14 para 39*].

The option must take the form of a *written agreement* between the person granting the option and the employee, which states

(a)   the date on which the option is granted;

(b)   that it is granted under *ITEPA 2003, Sch 5* (*FA 2000, Sch 14* before 2003/04);

(c)   the number, or maximum number, of shares that may be acquired;

(d)   the price (if any) for which the shares may be acquired, or the method by which that price is to be determined;

(e)   when and how the option may be exercised;

(f)   any conditions, e.g. performance conditions, affecting the employee's entitlement;

(g)   where the shares that may be acquired on exercise are restricted shares within 82.4 above, details of the restrictions;

(h)   (other than where 82.4 above has effect) details of any restrictions attaching to the shares; and

(j)   (other than where 82.4 above has effect) where the interest that may be acquired is only conditional (within 82.5 above) details of those conditions.

[*ITEPA 2003, Sch 5 para 37; FA 2000, Sch 14 para 40; FA 2003, Sch 22 para 45(3)(4)*].

Non-assignability of rights. The terms on which the option is granted must prohibit the grantee from transferring any of his rights under it. The terms *may* permit the option to be exercised within up to one year after the grantee's death. [*ITEPA 2003, Sch 5 para 38; FA 2000, Sch 14 para 41*].

82.42   **Replacement options.** A company (the acquiring company) which obtains control (within *ICTA 1988, s 840*) of a company whose shares are subject to an as yet unexercised qualifying option (as a result of a general offer to acquire the whole of its issued share capital or all the shares of the same class as those to which the option relates) may grant to the holder of a qualifying option (by agreement with him, and in consideration of his releasing his rights under the option) equivalent rights (a '*replacement option*') relating to shares in the acquiring company. The replacement option must be granted within six months after the acquiring company obtains control and any condition subject to which the offer is made is satisfied. The replacement is a qualifying option only if the requirements listed below are met.

The same applies where the acquiring company obtains such control in pursuance of a compromise or arrangement with creditors and members which is sanctioned by the court under *Companies Act 1985, s 425* (or NI equivalent) (in which case the replacement option must be granted within six months after the acquiring company obtains control) or becomes bound or entitled to acquire shares (of the same class as those to which the option relates) under *Companies Act 1985, ss 428–430* (or NI equivalent) (in which case the replacement option must be granted within the period during which the acquiring company remains so bound or entitled).

The above also applies where the acquiring company obtains all the shares of the company (the old company) whose shares are subject to such an option as a result of a 'qualifying exchange of shares' (in which case the replacement option must be granted within six months after the acquiring company obtains control). A '*qualifying exchange of shares*' means arrangements whereby the old company becomes a wholly-owned subsidiary of a new holding company (the new company) by means of an exchange of shares. All the following conditions must be met (and for these purposes, references to 'shares', other than to 'subscriber shares', include references to securities).

(1)   The consideration for the shares in the old company (the old shares) must consist wholly of the issue of shares (new shares) in the new company.

(2)   The new shares must be issued only at times when the new company has no issued shares other than subscriber shares (and any new shares already issued in consideration of old shares).

(3)   The consideration for new shares of each description must consist wholly of old shares of the corresponding description (i.e. shares of equivalent class and carrying equivalent rights).

(4)   New shares of each description must be issued to holders of old shares of the corresponding description in respect of, and in proportion to, their holdings.

(5)   The exchange of shares must not fall to be treated as a disposal and acquisition for capital gains tax purposes.

Requirements for replacement option to be a qualifying option. The replacement option is itself a qualifying option if it is granted to the holder of the old option by reason of his employment with the acquiring company or with a member of a group of which it is the parent company, and (*a*)   at the time of the release of rights under the old option,

    (i)   the replacement option is granted for the reasons given in 82.36 above,

    (ii)   the limit on the total value of unexercised qualifying options (previously the limit of 15 on the number of employees holding qualifying options) (see 82.36 above) is met in relation to the replacement option,

    (iii) the requirements in 82.38 above as to independence and trading activities are met in relation to the acquiring company,

    (iv)   the individual to whom the replacement option is granted is an eligible employee (see 82.40 above) in relation to the acquiring company, and

    (v)   the requirements at 82.41 above (terms of option etc.) are met in relation to the replacement option;

(*b*)   the total market value, immediately before the release, of shares which were subject to the old option is equal to the total market value, immediately after the grant of the replacement option, of the shares in respect of which it is granted; and

(*c*)   the total amount payable by the employee for shares under the option remains the same.

General. For the purposes of the enterprise management incentives provisions, a replacement option which is a qualifying option is treated as if granted on the date the original option was granted. (This does not apply for the purposes of the 'notice of grant' provisions at 82.43 below — Revenue Share Focus Newsletter December 2003 pp 8, 9.) Such a replacement option may be replaced by a further replacement option if one of the above circumstances and the above qualifying requirements are again satisfied. For the purpose of applying the monetary tests at 82.36 above, the value of the shares in the acquiring company that are subject to a replacement option is taken to be equal to the value of the shares that were subject to the old option immediately before the release of rights under the old option (or the appropriate proportion of that value in a case where the replacement option has been partially exercised). This applies by law for 2003/04 onwards but is understood to have previously applied in practice (see Change 177 listed in Annex 1 to the Explanatory Notes to the Income Tax (Earnings and Pensions) Bill).

[*ITEPA 2003, s 719, Sch 5 paras 39–43; FA 2000, Sch 14 paras 59–63; FA 2001, Sch 14 paras 12, 13*].

82.43   **Notice of grant of option.** Notice (in prescribed form) of an option must be given to the Revenue by the employer company within 92 days after the option is granted (30 days for options granted before 11 May 2001), failing which the option is not a qualifying option (see 82.36 above). The notice must incorporate such information as the Revenue may require (the standard form can be downloaded from the Revenue website), and must contain

    (i)   a declaration by a director or the company secretary (of the employer company) that, in his opinion, the statutory requirements are met in relation to the option and that the information provided is to the best of his knowledge correct and complete; and

    (ii)   a declaration by the employee that he meets the requirement at 82.40(*b*) above as to commitment of working time.

The notice should be sent to the Revenue's Small Company Enterprise Centre at the address given at 82.35 above

The Revenue may correct obvious errors or omissions in the notice. They must give notice of such correction to the employer company within nine months after the notice of grant is given, and the company may give notice to the Revenue rejecting the correction within three months from the date of issue of the notice of correction.

Revenue enquiry. Where notice of grant of an option is given as above, the Revenue may

(*a*) enquire into the option, by giving the employer company notice of enquiry; and/ or

(*b*) enquire into the employee's commitment of working time, in which case notice of enquiry must be given to the employee, with a copy to the employer company.

In either case, notice of enquiry must normally be given no later than 12 months after the end of the period within which notice of the grant of the option must be given (see above), but it may be given at any time if the Revenue *discover* that any of the information provided was false or misleading in a material respect. In the absence of such discovery, no more than one enquiry can be made under either of (*a*) or (*b*) above.

While an enquiry under (*a*) above remains open, the employer company may apply to the Commissioners for a direction that it be closed within a specified period, such application to be heard and determined in the same way as an appeal. The Commissioners must give such a direction unless satisfied that the Revenue have reasonable grounds for keeping the enquiry open. On completion of the enquiry, the Revenue must issue a 'closure notice' informing the company that the enquiry is complete and stating their decision as to whether the statutory requirements are met in relation to the option. If that decision is negative, the Revenue must also notify the employee. The employer company may appeal, within 30 days after a closure notice is given, against a Revenue decision that the statutory requirements have not been met or that notice of grant was not properly given. Both an application for closure and an appeal lie to the General Commissioners, unless, in either or both cases, the company elects under *TMA 1970, s 46(1)* (see 4.3 APPEALS) for the Special Commissioners. These provisions also apply, with appropriate modifications, to an enquiry under (*b*) above.

In the absence of an enquiry, the option can be taken to be a qualifying option. In the event of an enquiry, the Revenue's decision, as stated in the closure notice, is conclusive, subject to any appeal and, where the option has been found to be a qualifying option, to any further enquiry as a result of a Revenue discovery (see above).

[*ITEPA 2003, Sch 5 paras 1(4), 44–50; FA 2000, Sch 14 paras 2–7; FA 2001, Sch 14 paras 2, 3, 13*].

See also 82.46 below as regards compliance with time limits.

82.44   **Returns.** A company whose shares are the subject of a qualifying option at any time in a tax year is required to make a return, containing such information as the Revenue may require, before 7 July following the end of that tax year. Penalties are exigible under *TMA 1970, s 98* for non-compliance. [*ITEPA 2003, Sch 5 para 52, Sch 6 para 137; FA 2000, Sch 14 para 65*]. See also 82.46 below as regards compliance with time limits.

82.45   **Revenue information powers.** The Revenue have wide-ranging powers to require any person to furnish them with such information as they reasonably require and as that person possesses or can reasonably obtain. The information must be supplied within a period specified in the notice, which must not be less than three months. Penalties are exigible under *TMA 1970, s 98* for non-compliance. [*ITEPA 2003, Sch 5 para 51, Sch 6 para 137; FA 2000, Sch 14 para 64*]. See also 82.46 below as regards compliance with time limits.

The reporting obligations at 82.17 above also apply in relation to options under these provisions, but not in relation to particulars given in a notice under 82.43 above. [*ITEPA 2003, s 421J(11); FA 2003, Sch 22 para 2*].

82.46 Share-Related Employment Income and Exemptions

82.46 **Compliance with time limits.** For the purposes of 82.43–82.45 above and for determining market value as in 82.36 above, a person is not taken to have failed to do anything within a time limit if he had a reasonable excuse and, if the excuse ceased, did it without unreasonable delay thereafter. In such circumstances, any further time limit expressed by reference to the original time limit operates by reference to the actual time of performance of the original task. [*ITEPA 2003, Sch 5 para 53; FA 2000, Sch 14 para 70*].

82.47 **SAYE OPTION SCHEMES**

Approved SAYE option schemes (also known as savings-related share option schemes) were introduced in 1980 and are now covered by *ITEPA 2003, ss 516–520, Sch 3*. A company may establish a scheme, subject to Revenue approval, for its directors and employees to obtain options to acquire shares in itself or another company without any charge to income tax on the receipt of the options and on any increase in value of the shares between the date of the option being granted and the date on which it is exercised. The shares must be paid for from the proceeds of an approved savings scheme (see 82.51 below). Up to a limit (see 82.56(*a*) below), the share option price may be set at a discount to the value of the shares at the time the option is granted, and such discount is also exempt from income tax.

The remainder of this coverage is set out under the following headings.

82.48	General	82.54	— Eligibility of employees
82.49	Income tax treatment	82.55	— Scheme shares
82.50	Capital gains tax treatment	82.56	— Share options
82.51	Approved savings schemes	82.58	— Exchange of share options
82.52	Group schemes	82.59	Revenue approval
82.53	Requirements for approval	82.60	Revenue information powers

See 71.44 SCHEDULE D, CASES I AND II as regards deductions available to the employer company for corporation tax purposes.

Simon's Direct Tax Service. See E4.581 *et seq.*

82.48 **General.** To qualify for the favourable income tax treatment described at 82.49 below, the share option must be granted to an individual under an approved SAYE option scheme (see 82.53 below as regards the requirements for approval and 82.59 below for the approval procedure) and by reason of his office or employment as a director or employee of a company (not necessarily the company whose shares are the subject of the option). [*ITEPA 2003, ss 516, 517; ICTA 1988, s 185(1)*]. The taxation of *unapproved* share options is covered at 82.16 above.

82.49 **Income tax treatment.** No income tax liability arises in respect of the receipt of the option. [*ITEPA 2003, ss 475, 518; ICTA 1988, s 185(2); FA 2003, Sch 22 paras 10, 29*]. No income tax liability arises in respect of the exercise of the option if it is exercised in accordance with the scheme at a time when the scheme is approved (or treated as still approved — see 82.59 below). The exemption on exercise does not, however, apply if the option is exercised before the third anniversary of the date of grant by virtue of the inclusion in the scheme of a non-compulsory provision within 82.56(*h*) or 82.57(*b*) below. After 17 June 2004, the exemption on exercise does not apply if the option was granted, or is exercised, under arrangements one of the main purposes of which is the avoidance of tax or national insurance contributions. Where the exemption does not apply, 82.16 above (exercise of unapproved share options) applies instead. Subject to the same condition as above, and with similar exception, no liability arises by virtue of *ITEPA 2003, s 449* (see 82.14(*a*) above) or *s 453* (see 82.14(*b*) above), both as originally enacted, in respect of shares acquired by the exercise of the option. [*ITEPA 2003, ss 519, 520; ICTA 1988, s 185(3)(4); FA 1991, s 39(2)(4)(8); FA 2003, Sch 22 paras 30, 31; FA 2004, s 88(6)(11)*].

Other than on *exercise* of the qualifying option, there is no exemption from the charge at 82.16 above (e.g. on release of the option).

For an article on the imposition of income tax charges on exercise in the case of internationally mobile employees, see Revenue Tax Bulletin October 2001 pp 883–887, and for associated national insurance contributions liabilities see Revenue Tax Bulletin December 2001 pp 895–899. For a follow-up to these articles, see Revenue Tax Bulletin August 2002 pp 951–954.

82.50 **Capital gains tax treatment.** There is no special capital gains tax treatment on the disposal of shares acquired under an approved SAYE option scheme and exempt from income tax on exercise of the option, except that *TCGA 1992, s 17(1)* (under which acquisitions are treated as made at their market value rather than their actual cost) is disapplied in relation to such acquisitions. [*TCGA 1992, Sch 7D paras 9, 10; ICTA 1988, s 185(3)(b); ITEPA 2003, Sch 6 para 221*]. The date of acquisition of the shares is the date the option is exercised. For details, see Tolley's Capital Gains Tax under Employee Share Schemes.

82.51 **Approved savings schemes.** As a condition of approval, a SAYE option scheme must provide for shares acquired on the exercise of options granted under the scheme to be paid for from the proceeds (including any interest or bonus added) of a certified contractual savings scheme (within the meaning of *ICTA 1988, s 326(2)–(6)* — see also 28.16(vi) EXEMPT INCOME) which has been approved by the Revenue for these purposes. The SAYE scheme must link the amount of a person's contributions under the savings scheme to the total amount needed to acquire at the option price the number of shares in respect of which options are granted to him. The maximum total amount of contributions a person may make at any time to savings schemes linked to approved SAYE schemes cannot exceed £250 per month. A SAYE scheme may impose a minimum contribution, but this must not exceed £10 per month. These amounts can be altered by Treasury Order. Subject to any such minimum that may be imposed, monthly contributions of as low as £5 are permitted (Revenue Pamphlet IR 98). The savings scheme may provide for a bonus to be added in respect of a person's contributions; this is to be determined at the time the options are granted and is to be taken into account in linking the contributions made to the number of shares that may be acquired. [*ITEPA 2003, Sch 3 paras 23–26; ICTA 1988, Sch 9 paras 16(1), 17, 24; FA 1990, s 40; FA 2003, Sch 21 para 10; SI 1991 No 1741*].

Interest and bonuses from the savings scheme are exempt from income tax. [*ICTA 1988, s 326(1); FA 1990, s 29*]. Three- or five-year savings contracts are available, and five-year contracts may offer the option of repayment on the seventh anniversary. The Treasury may alter permitted levels of interest and bonuses, but not so as to affect pre-existing savings contracts. Following such an alteration from 1 October 2001, bonuses are subject to automatic annual adjustment by reference to market swap rates from 1 September 2002 onwards (with provision for interim adjustments if the swap rates change dramatically); see Treasury Press Release 16 August 2001.

82.52 **Group schemes.** A SAYE option scheme established by a company that controls (within *ICTA 1988, s 840*) one or more other companies may extend to all or any of those other companies. A scheme which so extends is a '*group scheme*' and each company to which it extends (including the parent) are '*constituent companies*'. [*ITEPA 2003, s 719, Sch 3 para 3; ICTA 1988, Sch 9 para 1(3)(4)*].

Jointly owned companies. To enable a jointly owned company to take part in a group scheme (though it cannot thereby take part in more than one), such a company, and any company under its control (within *ICTA 1988, s 840*), is treated as being under the control of each of its two joint owners. A company controlled by a jointly owned company may not take part in more than one group scheme or in a different scheme to that (if any) in which the jointly owned company (or any other company controlled by it) takes part. [*ITEPA 2003, s 719, Sch 3 para 46*]. This supersedes, with effect for 2003/04 onwards, ESC B27 at 82.2 above.

82.53   **Requirements for approval.** In order to qualify for Revenue approval, a SAYE option scheme must meet the requirements at 82.54–82.58 below as well as the savings scheme requirement at 82.51 above. It must not contain features that are neither essential nor reasonably incidental to the purpose of providing director and employee benefits in the form of share options. [*ITEPA 2003, Sch 3 paras 1, 4, 5; ICTA 1988, Sch 9 paras 1(1), 2(1)*].].

82.54   *Eligibility of employees.* Eligible employees must include every person who

(*a*)   is an employee (for schemes approved before 1 May 1995, a full-time employee) or a full-time director of the company which established the scheme or, in the case of a group scheme, a constituent company, and

(*b*)   has been such an employee or director at all times during a qualifying period, not exceeding five years, and

(*c*)   whose earnings from the office or employment in question are (or would be if there were any) general earnings within *ITEPA 2003, s 15* or *s 21* (earnings for year when employee resident and ordinarily resident in UK), and

(*d*)   is not excluded by the 'no material interest' test below.

The scheme *must* ensure that, other than as required or authorised under the statutory provisions, no-one is eligible to participate in the scheme at a particular time unless he is at that time a director or employee of the company or, as regards a group scheme, a constituent company. It *may*, however, include part-time directors and any employees and directors whose earnings are not within (*c*) above and/or who do not meet the condition in (*b*) above.

The scheme must not contain any feature, other than as required or authorised under the statutory provisions, which is likely to discourage any description of persons within (*a*)–(*d*) above from participating. Every person within (*a*)–(*d*) above must be eligible to participate on similar terms, and those who participate must actually do so on similar terms. However, the rights of participants to obtain and exercise share options may vary according to such factors as remuneration levels and length of service. If the company which established the scheme is a member of a group (comprising for this purpose a company and any companies it controls) the scheme must not have the likely effect of conferring benefits wholly or mainly on directors or on the more highly-paid employees.

[*ITEPA 2003, Sch 3 para 2(2), paras 4–10; ICTA 1988, Sch 9 para 1(1), para 2(1)(3)(4), paras 7, 26; FA 1995, s 137(2)(7); FA 1996, s 113(3)*].

No material interest. The scheme must ensure that an individual is not eligible to participate in the scheme if he has, or has had within the preceding 12 months, a 'material interest' in a 'close company'

•   whose shares may be acquired under the scheme, or

•   which has control (within *ICTA 1988, s 840*) of a company whose shares may be acquired under the scheme, or

•   is a member of a consortium which owns a company whose shares may be acquired under the scheme. (For this purpose, a company is a member of a consortium owning another company if it is one of a number of companies which between them beneficially own at least 75% of, and each of which beneficially owns at least 5% of, the other company's ordinary share capital.)

For these purposes, an individual has a '*material interest*' in a company if he, and/or certain associates of his (within *ITEPA 2003, Sch 3 paras 14–16*),

● beneficially owns or controls (directly or indirectly) more than 25% of ordinary share capital; or

● possesses or is entitled to acquire rights to more than 25% of the assets available for distribution among the participators (within *ICTA 1988, s 417(1)*) in a winding-up or in any other circumstances.

Rights (including SAYE options — see Revenue Pamphlet IR 98) to acquire shares must be taken into account (in accordance with *ITEPA 2003, Sch 3 para 13*). Shares or rights held by trustees of an approved profit sharing scheme (see 82.18 above) or, for 2003/04 onwards, an approved SIP (see 82.20 above) and not appropriated to, or acquired on behalf of, any individual are disregarded.

For these purposes, '*close company*' has the meaning given by *ICTA 1988, s 414* but also includes a company which would be a close company but for its being a non-UK resident company or a quoted company.

[*ITEPA 2003, s 719, Sch 3 paras 11–16, 48(2), Sch 7 para 87; ICTA 1988, s 187(3)(4)(7), Sch 9 paras 8, 37–40; FA 1989, s 65, Sch 12 para 9*].

82.55   *Scheme shares.* Scheme shares (i.e. the shares which may be acquired under the scheme) must be fully paid up and not redeemable and must

(*a*)   form part of the ordinary share capital of

(i)   the company which established the scheme, or

(ii)   a company which has control (within *ICTA 1988, s 840*) of that company, or

(iii)   a member of a consortium (as in 82.54 above) which owns the company within (i) above or a company within (ii) above, or

(iv)   a company which has control of a member of a consortium within (iii) above; and

(*b*)   be either shares of a class listed on a recognised stock exchange, or shares in a company not under the control of another company, or shares in a company under the control of a listed company (other than a company which is, or would be if UK resident, a close company).

Scheme shares must not be subject to any restrictions (as to their disposal or the exercise of rights conferred etc. — see *ITEPA 2003, Sch 3 para 21(4)–(6)* for full definition and disregards) other than those attaching to all shares of the same class. Scheme shares can, however, be subject to a restriction imposed by the company's articles of association (or foreign company equivalent) which requires (i) shares held by directors or employees to be disposed of, or offered for sale, on cessation of the office or employment and (ii) shares acquired by persons who are not directors or employees, but in pursuance of rights or interests obtained by directors or employees, to be disposed of, or offered for sale, when they are acquired. The required disposal must be a sale for money on specified terms, and the articles must also provide that anyone disposing of shares of the same class (however acquired) may be required to sell them on those same specified terms.

Except where the scheme shares are in a company whose ordinary share capital consists of shares of one class only, the majority of the issued shares of the same class as the scheme shares must be either 'open market shares' or 'employee-control shares'. '*Open market shares*' are shares held by persons other than (i) persons who acquired them by virtue of their being directors or employees, or (ii) trustees for such persons, or (iii) (in the case of unlisted shares in a company under the control of a listed company — see (*b*) above) companies which control the company concerned or of which that company is an 'associated company' (within the meaning of *ITEPA 2003, Sch 3 para 47*). '*Employee-control shares*' are shares held by persons who are or have been directors or employees, and who are together able to control the company by virtue of their holdings.

[*ITEPA 2003, s 719, Sch 3 paras 2(2), 17–22, 48(2); ICTA 1988, Sch 9 paras 9(1), 10, 11, para 12(1)(1A)(2)(3), para 13(1)(2), para 14(1)(3); FA 1989, s 64*].

82.56   *Share options.* A SAYE option scheme *must* meet all the following requirements.

(*a*)   The price at which shares may be acquired under the scheme must be fixed and stated at the time the option is granted and must not be less than 80% of the market value of shares of the same class at that time (or, if the company and the Revenue agree in writing, at a stated earlier time). The scheme *may* provide for (i) the stated price, or (ii) the number or description of shares that may be acquired, to be varied as necessary, subject to prior Revenue approval, to take account of any variation in the share capital of which the scheme shares form part. As regards (ii) and the requirement for prior approval in both (i) and (ii), these apply by law for 2003/04 onwards but applied in practice for earlier years as well (see Change 169 listed in Annex 1 to the Explanatory Notes to the Income Tax (Earnings and Pensions) Bill).

(*b*)   Options granted under the scheme must be non-transferable.

(*c*)   Except as otherwise permitted under any of (*d*)–(*h*) below and 82.57 below, options granted under the scheme must not be capable of being exercised before the 'bonus date' or more than six months after it. The '*bonus date*' is the date on which the proceeds of the approved savings scheme are due to be released to the participant; that date is taken to be, in a case where those proceeds will include the maximum bonus under the scheme, the earliest date on which that bonus is payable and, in any other case, the earliest date on which a bonus is payable.

(*d*)   The scheme must provide that, if a participant dies before exercising his options and before the bonus date (defined as in (*c*) above), the options may be exercised after death, provided they are so exercised within twelve months after the date of death. It must also provide that, if death occurs before exercise and on, or within six months *after*, the bonus date, the options may be exercised within twelve months after the bonus date.

(*e*)   The scheme must provide that, if a participant continues in the office or employment (by reference to which he is eligible for the scheme) after reaching the 'specified age' (see below), he may exercise his options within six months after reaching that age. (This is subject to the overriding six-month rule at (*c*) above.)

(*f*)   The scheme must provide that, if a participant 'ceases to hold scheme-related employment' (see below) because of injury, disability or redundancy or because of retirement upon reaching the 'specified age' (see below) (or, if different, an age at which his employment contract requires him to retire), he has six months (after so ceasing) in which to exercise his options. (This is subject to the overriding six-month rule at (*c*) above.)

(*g*)   The scheme must provide that, if a participant 'ceases to hold scheme-related employment' (see below) for any reason other than those in (*f*) above, options granted more than three years previously either may not be exercised at all or may only be exercised within six months after so ceasing, whichever of those alternatives is specified in the scheme. (This is subject to the overriding six-month rule at (*c*) above.)

(*h*) The scheme must provide that, if a participant 'ceases to hold scheme-related employment' (see below) for any reason other than those in (*f*) above, options granted within the immediately preceding three years may not be exercised at all. The scheme *may*, however, permit such exercise where the scheme-related employment ceases only because it is in a company of which the company that established the scheme ceases to have control (within *ICTA 1988, s 840*) or because it relates to a business (or part) which is transferred to a person other than an 'associated company' (within the meaning of *ITEPA 2003, Sch 3 para 47*). If the scheme does permit such exercise, it must provide either that the options may be exercised within six months after the participant 'ceases to hold scheme-related employment' or, with effect from 10 July 2003 only, that they may be exercised within six months after the participant subsequently leaves the employment for the reasons given in (*f*) above. (This is subject to the overriding six-month rule at (*c*) above.) Note that the income tax exemptions on exercise are forgone in these circumstances (see 82.49 above).

The scheme must specify the age that is to be the '*specified age*' for the purposes of (*e*) and (*f*) above. This must be between 60 and 75 (inclusive) and the same for men and women.

For the purposes of (*f*)–(*h*) above, a participant normally '*ceases to hold scheme-related employment*' on the date when he ceases (other than by reason of his death) to hold the office or employment by reference to which he is eligible for the scheme. If, however, he continues after that date to hold office or employment with the company that established the scheme or with any 'associated company' (within the meaning of *ITEPA 2003, Sch 3 para 35(4)*), he '*ceases to hold scheme-related employment*' not on that earlier date but on the date he ceases to hold office or employment with any company of such description.

[*ITEPA 2003, s 719, Sch 3 paras 2(2), 27–35, Sch 6 para 168; ICTA 1988, s 187(2), Sch 9 paras 8A, 17–20, para 21(1)(e), (3), paras 22, 23, 25; FA 1989, s 62(3); FA 1991, s 38(2)(4)–(6); FA 2003, Sch 21 para 11*].

82.57 A SAYE option scheme *may* make provision as follows.

(*a*) It may provide that options may be exercised within six months after the bonus date (defined as in 82.56(*c*) above) if at that date the participant holds an office or employment in a company which is not a constituent company in a group scheme but which is an 'associated company' (within the meaning of *ITEPA 2003, Sch 3 para 47*) of the company that established the scheme. (This applies to options granted on or after 29 April 1996 but could also be applied to options granted before that date if the necessary alteration was made to the scheme before 5 May 1998 and approved by the Revenue; such alteration was not itself regarded as giving rise to the acquisition of new rights by the participant.)

(*b*) It may provide that options may be exercised in any of the following circumstances (in relation to the company whose shares may be obtained under the scheme) within six months after the 'relevant date'.

(i) A person obtains control of the company as a result of making a general offer to acquire the whole of its issued share capital or of all the shares of the same class as the scheme shares. In this case, the '*relevant date*' is the date when the person obtains unconditional control. For this purpose, a person obtains control of a company if he and others acting in concert obtain control of it (within *ICTA 1988, s 840*).

(ii)   A court sanctions, under *Companies Act 1985, s 425* (or NI equivalent), a compromise or arrangement proposed in connection with a scheme for the reconstruction or amalgamation of the company. In this case, the *'relevant date'* is the date of the sanction.

(iii)   The company passes a resolution for voluntary winding up. In this case, the *'relevant date'* is the date the resolution is passed.

Options may also be exercised at any time when any person is bound or entitled to acquire shares in the company under *Companies Act 1985, ss 428–430* (or NI equivalent) (power to acquire shares of dissenting shareholders).

All of the above are subject to the overriding six-month rule at 82.56(*c*) above. Note that the income tax exemptions on exercise are forgone in any of the above circumstances if the option is thus exercised within three years after it was granted (see 82.49 above).

[*ITEPA 2003, s 719, Sch 3 paras 27, 36, 37; ICTA 1988, Sch 9 para 21(1)(2)(4); FA 1996, s 113*].

82.58   *Exchange of share options.* A SAYE option scheme *may* provide that, if any other company (the 'acquiring company') obtains control of the company whose shares are scheme shares, or is bound or entitled to acquire shares in the company, in any of the circumstances described in 82.57(*b*) above (disregarding (*b*)(iii) above), a participant may agree with the acquiring company to release his options to acquire scheme shares in consideration of being granted options to acquire shares in the acquiring company (or in some other company falling within 82.55(*a*)(ii)–(iv) above). The new share options must be equivalent to the options under the pre-existing scheme as regards their being subject to the provisions of the scheme, the manner in which they are exercisable, the total market value of shares to which they are subject and the total amount payable by the participant on exercise. The new options are then treated as having been granted at the time the original options were granted. The agreement must be made within six months of the acquiring company's obtaining unconditional control or of the court's sanctioning the compromise or arrangement or within the period during which the acquiring company remains bound or entitled to acquire shares, whichever of these is applicable.

[*ITEPA 2003, Sch 3 paras 38, 39; ICTA 1988, Sch 9 para 15*].

82.59   **Revenue approval.** On written application by the company, containing such particulars and supported by such evidence as the Revenue require, the Revenue will approve a SAYE option scheme if satisfied that it meets the statutory requirements outlined above. They must give notice of their decision to the company, who may appeal to the Special Commissioners within 30 days against a refusal to give approval. On a successful appeal, the Special Commissioners may direct the Revenue to approve the scheme from a specified date no earlier than the original date of application.

Withdrawal of approval etc. If any of the statutory requirements ceases to be met or the company fails to provide information requested by the Revenue under their powers at 82.60 below or a 'key feature' of the scheme is altered without Revenue approval, the Revenue may by notice withdraw their approval of the scheme with effect from, at the earliest, the time of the failure in question. The withdrawal does not affect the favourable tax treatment of options granted before withdrawal and exercised afterwards; in its application to such options, the scheme is treated for these purposes as if it were still approved at the time of exercise. The Revenue are not to withhold approval to an alteration unless it appears to them that the scheme, as altered, would not receive approval on an initial application. For these purposes, a *'key feature'* is a provision of the scheme that is necessary in order to meet the statutory requirements. The company may appeal, within 30 days, to the Special Commissioners against a withdrawal of approval or a decision to refuse approval of an alteration.

[*ITEPA 2003, Sch 3 paras 2(2), 40–44, Sch 7 para 71(4); ICTA 1988, Sch 9 para 1(1)(2), paras 3(1), 4, 5; FA 2003, Sch 21 para 12, Sch 22 para 44*].

See *CIR v Burton Group plc Ch D 1990, 63 TC 191* where an appeal against a Revenue refusal to approve an alteration imposing performance conditions was upheld. In *CIR v Reed International plc and cross-appeal CA 1995, 67 TC 552*, a similar decision was reached where the alteration removed a contingency on which options would be exercisable and would be required to be exercised within a specified period; this did not amount to the acquisition of a new and different right to acquire scheme shares. For the Revenue's interpretation of this decision, see Revenue Employee Share Scheme Unit Manual ESSU 2086–2096. See also *CIR v Eurocopy plc Ch D 1991, 64 TC 370*.

Applications for approval should be sent to Inland Revenue, Employee Share Schemes, Second Floor, New Wing, Somerset House, Strand, London, WC2R 1LB. A specimen set of scheme documents is contained in the explanatory notes for employers, Revenue Pamphlet IR 98. (A non-technical explanatory pamphlet (IR 97) aimed at employees is also available.)

82.60   **Revenue information powers.** The Revenue have wide-ranging powers to require any person to furnish them with such information as they reasonably require, in relation to a SAYE option scheme, and as that person possesses or can reasonably obtain. The information must be supplied within a period specified in the notice, which must not be less than three months (30 days for 2002/03 and earlier years). Penalties are exigible under *TMA 1970, s 98* for non-compliance. [*ITEPA 2003, Sch 3 para 45, Sch 6 para 137; ICTA 1988, Sch 9 para 6*].

82.61   **COMPANY SHARE OPTION PLAN (CSOP) SCHEMES**

Company share option plan (CSOP) schemes are Revenue-approved share option schemes introduced in 1996 to replace approved 'executive share option schemes' (for which see 82.75 below) and are now covered by *ITEPA 2003, ss 521–526, Sch 4*. Unlike SAYE schemes above, CSOP schemes are discretionary schemes, in that there is no requirement to include all employees. The CSOP provisions apply in relation to options granted on or after 29 April 1996, but see 82.75 below as regards their effective application to certain options granted before that date under pre-existing executive share option schemes. CSOP schemes are more restrictive than their predecessors in that they place a lower ceiling on the value of options an individual may hold at any one time and do not permit the option price to be discounted by reference to the current share price (see also 82.75 below).

As regards options granted on or after 29 April 1996, pre-existing approved executive share option schemes (also known as 'discretionary share option schemes') were deemed to have incorporated into their rules the more restrictive conditions introduced under the CSOP rules (limit of £30,000 on value of shares subject to outstanding options — see 82.67 below — and requirements as to price for acquisition of shares — see 82.70 below) so that the schemes effectively became CSOP schemes. Such deemed alterations were treated as having been approved by the Revenue before 29 April 1996. If, however, a company did not wish to adopt those conditions into its scheme, it could have given the Revenue notice to that effect before 1 January 1997. The scheme would then have ceased to be an approved scheme as from the date of the notice. [*FA 1996, s 114(9), Sch 16; ITEPA 2003, Sch 7 paras 73–75*].

82.62 Share-Related Employment Income and Exemptions

The remainder of this coverage is set out under the following headings.

See 71.44 SCHEDULE D, CASES I AND II as regards deductions available to the employer company for corporation tax purposes.

Simon's Direct Tax Service. See E4.591 *et seq.*

82.62 **General.** To qualify for the favourable income tax treatment on exercise described at 82.63 below, the share option must be granted to an individual under an approved CSOP scheme (see 82.66 below as regards the requirements for approval and 82.73 below for the approval procedure) and by reason of his office or employment as a director or employee of a company (not necessarily the company whose shares are the subject of the option). [*ITEPA 2003, ss 521, 522; ICTA 1988, s 185(1)*]. The taxation of *unapproved* share options is covered at 82.16 above.

82.63 **Income tax treatment.** If, exceptionally, the aggregate of

- the amount payable by the grantee, on exercise, in order to acquire the maximum number of shares that may be acquired under the option, and

- the amount or value of consideration given (if any) for the grant of the option,

is less than the market value, at the time the option is granted, of a similar quantity of issued shares of the class in question (in other words, if the option is granted at a discount), the difference is taxed as employment income of the grantee for the tax year in which the option is granted. Any amount thus taxed is deductible in computing any amount that subsequently falls to be taxed under 82.16 above (charge on exercise, assignment or release etc. of unapproved share option), e.g. because the scheme has ceased to be approved, or in determining the amount of any notional loan as in 82.10 above.

Except as above, no income tax liability arises in respect of the receipt of a CSOP option.

[*ITEPA 2003, ss 475, 523, 526; ICTA 1988, s 185(2)(6)(8); FA 1996, s 114; FA 2003, Sch 22 paras 10, 32, 35*].

No income tax liability arises in respect of the *exercise* of an option if it is exercised in accordance with a CSOP scheme at a time when the scheme is approved, provided that the option is exercised no earlier than the third anniversary of the date it was granted and no later than the tenth anniversary of that date. There is an exception for options exercised within three years of grant but no later than six months after the individual ceases to be a full-time director or qualifying employee of the scheme organiser (or of a constituent company in a group scheme — see 82.65 below) because of injury, disability or redundancy or because he retires on or after reaching an age specified in the scheme (where the scheme rules allow such early exercise — see 82.71 below). (Any retirement age so specified must be the same for both sexes and must be at least 55.) For options exercised before 9 April 2003, this exception did not apply and the income tax exemption also depended on the further condition that the grantee had not made an exempt exercise of another option under the scheme (or under any other approved CSOP scheme) within the three years ending with the date of exercise of the option in question (but disregarding any other option exercised on that date itself).

After 17 June 2004, the exemption on exercise does not apply if the option was granted, or is exercised, under arrangements one of the main purposes of which is the avoidance of tax or national insurance contributions.

Where the exemption does not apply, 82.16 above (exercise of unapproved share options) applies instead. Before 2003/04, an exemption on exercise by personal representatives applied only if the exercise occurred within ten years after the option was granted but the conditions above did not otherwise have to be met.

Subject to the same conditions as those above as respects the exercise of an option, no liability arises by virtue of *ITEPA 2003, s 449* (see 82.14(*a*) above) or *s 453* (see 82.14(*b*) above), both as originally enacted, in respect of shares acquired by such exercise.

[*ITEPA 2003, ss 524, 525, Sch 4 para 35A; ICTA 1988, s 185(3)(5); Sch 9 para 27(3); FA 2003, Sch 21 paras 14, 15, Sch 22 paras 33, 34; FA 2004, s 88(7)(11)*].

Other than on *exercise* of the qualifying option, there is no exemption from the charge at 82.16 above (e.g. on release of the option).

For an article on the imposition of income tax charges on exercise in the case of internationally mobile employees, see Revenue Tax Bulletin October 2001 pp 883–887, and for associated national insurance contributions liabilities see Revenue Tax Bulletin December 2001 pp 895–899. For a follow-up to these articles, see Revenue Tax Bulletin August 2002 pp 951–954.

82.64 **Capital gains tax treatment.** There is no special capital gains tax treatment on the disposal of shares acquired under an approved CSOP scheme and exempt from income tax on exercise of the option, except that

- *TCGA 1992, s 17(1)* (under which acquisitions are treated as made at their market value rather than their actual cost) is disapplied in relation to such acquisitions; and

- where, exceptionally, an income tax charge arose on receipt of the option (see 82.63 above), the amount thus taxed forms part of the cost of acquisition of the shares for capital gains tax purposes; this applies equally if the scheme has ceased to be approved at time of exercise or if the exercise is made otherwise than in accordance with the scheme and/or if the income tax charge arose under earlier legislation preceding 82.63 above.

[*TCGA 1992, Sch 7D paras 11–13; ICTA 1988, s 185(3)(b), (7); FA 1996, s 114; ITEPA 2003, Sch 6 para 221*].

The date of acquisition of the shares is the date the option is exercised. For further detail, see Tolley's Capital Gains Tax under Employee Share Schemes.

82.65 **Group schemes.** A CSOP scheme established by a company that controls (within *ICTA 1988, s 840*) one or more other companies may extend to all or any of those other companies. A scheme which so extends is a '*group scheme*' and each company to which it extends (including the parent) are '*constituent companies*'. [*ITEPA 2003, s 719, Sch 4 para 3; ICTA 1988, Sch 9 para 1(3)(4)*].

Jointly owned companies. To enable a jointly owned company to take part in a group scheme (though it cannot thereby take part in more than one), such a company, and any company under its control (within *ICTA 1988, s 840*), is treated as being under the control of each of its two joint owners. A company controlled by a jointly owned company may not take part in more than one group scheme or in a different scheme to that (if any) in which the jointly owned company (or any other company controlled by it) takes part. [*ITEPA 2003, s 719, Sch 4 para 34*]. This supersedes, with effect for 2003/04 onwards, ESC B27 at 82.2 above.

82.66 Share-Related Employment Income and Exemptions

82.66   **Requirements for approval.** In order to qualify for Revenue approval, a CSOP scheme must meet the requirements at 82.67–82.72 below. It must not contain features that are neither essential nor reasonably incidental to the purpose of providing director and employee benefits in the form of share options. [*ITEPA 2003, Sch 4 paras 1, 4, 5; ICTA 1988, Sch 9 paras 1(1), 2(1)*].

82.67   *Limit on value of shares subject to options.* The scheme must provide that an individual cannot be granted options under it which would cause the value referred to below to exceed (or to further exceed) £30,000. The value in question is the aggregate market value (determined at time of grant or, where applicable, at the earlier time mentioned in 82.70 below) of the shares which the individual may acquire by exercising outstanding share options under the scheme or under any other approved CSOP scheme established by the same company or by an 'associated company' (within the meaning of *ITEPA 2003, Sch 4 para 35*). [*ITEPA 2003, Sch 4 paras 2(2), 6, 36(1); ICTA 1988, Sch 9 para 28; FA 1996, s 114(2)*]. Where an option is granted that causes the £30,000 limit to be exceeded, the whole of that option (and not just the excess) becomes an unapproved share option (Revenue Share Focus Newsletter December 2003 p 3). (A more generous limit applied for executive share option schemes, the forerunners of CSOP schemes, for which see 82.75 below.)

82.68   *Eligibility of employees.* The scheme *must* ensure that no-one is eligible to be granted share options under it at a particular time unless he is at that time a 'full-time' director or an employee (full-time or part-time) of the company or, as regards a group scheme, a constituent company. For schemes approved before 1 May 1995, an employee had to be a full-time employee to be eligible, which was treated as being the case if his terms of employment required him to work at least 20 hours per week; such schemes can be altered on or after that date to bring them into line with the current rules above. [*ITEPA 2003, Sch 4 paras 2(2), 7, 8; ICTA 1988, Sch 9 para 27(1)(4); FA 1995, s 137(3)(8)*]. A director is treated as a 'full-time' director for these purposes if he works at least 25 hours per week for the company or, as regards a group plan, for constituent companies (Revenue Pamphlet IR 102). See also 82.71 below.

No material interest. The scheme must ensure that an individual is not eligible to participate in the scheme if he has, or has had within the preceding 12 months, a 'material interest' in a 'close company'

- whose shares may be acquired under the scheme, or

- which has control (within *ICTA 1988, s 840*) of a company whose shares may be acquired under the scheme, or

- is a member of a consortium which owns a company whose shares may be acquired under the scheme. (For this purpose, a company is a member of a consortium owning another company if it is one of a number of companies which between them beneficially own at least 75% of, and each of which beneficially owns at least 5% of, the other company's ordinary share capital.)

For these purposes, an individual has a '*material interest*' in a company if he, and/or certain associates of his (within *ITEPA 2003, Sch 4 paras 12–14*),

- beneficially owns or controls (directly or indirectly) more than 25% of ordinary share capital; or

- possesses or is entitled to acquire rights to more than 25% of the assets available for distribution among the participators (within *ICTA 1988, s 417(1)*) in a winding-up or in any other circumstances.

Before 10 July 2003, these tests applied by reference to a figure of 10% rather than 25%. In applying the test on or after that date, the larger percentage has effect for the whole of the preceding 12 months notwithstanding that part of that period may have fallen before 10 July 2003.

Rights (including CSOP options — see Revenue Pamphlet IR 102) to acquire shares must be taken into account (in accordance with *ITEPA 2003, Sch 4 para 11*). Shares or rights held by trustees of an approved profit sharing scheme (see 82.18 above) or, for 2003/04 onwards, an approved SIP (see 82.20 above) and not appropriated to, or acquired on behalf of, any individual are disregarded.

For these purposes, '*close company*' has the meaning given by *ICTA 1988, s 414* but also includes a company which would be a close company but for its being a non-UK resident company or a quoted company.

[*ITEPA 2003, s 719, Sch 4 paras 9–14, 36(2), Schedule 7 para 87; ICTA 1988, s 187(3)(4)(7), Sch 9 paras 8, 37–40; FA 1989, s 65, Sch 12 para 9; FA 2003, Sch 21 para 16*].

82.69   *Scheme shares.* Scheme shares (i.e. the shares which may be acquired under the scheme) must satisfy the same conditions as apply for SAYE option schemes, for which see 82.55 above, except that the restrictions to which CSOP scheme shares must not be subject do not include any terms for repayment of, or security for, a loan.

[*ITEPA 2003, Sch 4 paras 15–20; ICTA 1988, Sch 9 paras 9(1), 10, 11, para 12(1)(1A)(2)(3), para 13, para 14(1)(3); FA 1988, s 69(1); FA 1989, s 64*].

82.70   *Share options.* A CSOP scheme *must* meet the following requirement. The price at which shares may be acquired must be stated at the time the option is granted and must not be less than the market value of shares of the same class at that time (or, if the company and the Revenue agree in writing, at a stated earlier time). The scheme *may* provide for (i) the stated price, or (ii) the number or description of shares that may be acquired, to be varied as necessary, subject to prior Revenue approval, to take account of any variation in the share capital of which the scheme shares form part. As regards (ii) and the requirement for prior approval in both (i) and (ii), these apply by law for 2003/04 onwards but applied in practice for earlier years as well (see Change 169 listed in Annex 1 to the Explanatory Notes to the Income Tax (Earnings and Pensions) Bill). (More generous rules applied for executive share option schemes, the forerunners of CSOP schemes, for which see 82.75 below. See the 2002/03 and earlier editions for the different rules that applied to options granted on or before 31 December 1991.)

The scheme must also ensure that share options granted are non-transferable.

[*ITEPA 2003, Sch 4 paras 21–23; ICTA 1988, Sch 9 paras 27(2), 29; FA 1996, s 114(3)(10), Sch 41 Pt V(5)*].

82.71   A CSOP scheme *may* make provision for share options to be exercised after a grantee has ceased to meet the requirement in 82.68 above to be a full-time director or an employee.

A CSOP scheme *may* also provide that a participant's options can be exercised within the twelve months following his death.

[*ITEPA 2003, Sch 4 paras 24, 25; ICTA 1988, Sch 9 para 27(1)(2)*].

82.72   *Exchange of share options.* A CSOP scheme *may* make provision comparable to that for SAYE option schemes in 82.58 above to allow old options to be exchanged for new in the event of a company takeover etc. and for the new options to be treated as having been granted at the time the original options were granted. [*ITEPA 2003, Sch 4 paras 26, 27; ICTA 1988, Sch 9 para 15*].

82.73   **Revenue approval.** On written application by the company, containing such particulars and supported by such evidence as the Revenue require, the Revenue will approve a CSOP scheme if satisfied that it meets the statutory requirements outlined above. They must give notice of their decision to the company, who may appeal to the Special Commissioners within 30 days against a refusal to give approval. On a successful appeal, the Special Commissioners may direct the Revenue to approve the scheme from a specified date no earlier than the original date of application.

Withdrawal of approval etc. If any of the statutory requirements ceases to be met or the company fails to provide information requested by the Revenue under their powers at 82.74 below or a 'key feature' of the scheme is altered without Revenue approval, the Revenue may by notice withdraw their approval of the scheme with effect from, at the earliest, the time of the failure in question. The Revenue are not to withhold approval to an alteration unless it appears to them that the scheme, as altered, would not receive approval on an initial application. For these purposes, a *'key feature'* is a provision of the scheme that is necessary in order to meet the statutory requirements. The company may appeal, within 30 days, to the Special Commissioners against a withdrawal of approval or a decision to refuse approval of an alteration.

[*ITEPA 2003, Sch 4 paras 2(2), 28–32, Sch 7 para 73(4); ICTA 1988, Sch 9 para 1(1)(2), paras 3(1), 4, 5; FA 2003, Sch 21 para 17*].

The Revenue's refusal to accept an alteration to the rules of an approved scheme, allowing for the imposition or variation, after the date of grant of options, of 'key task' conditions on whose fulfilment the number of shares to which an employee was entitled under the scheme depended, was reversed on appeal in *CIR v Burton Group plc Ch D 1990, 63 TC 191*. A similar conclusion was reached in *CIR v Reed International plc and cross-appeal CA 1995, 67 TC 552*, where the alteration removed a contingency on which options would be exercisable and would be required to be exercised within a specified period; this did not amount to the acquisition of a new and different right to acquire scheme shares. For the Revenue's interpretation of this decision, see Revenue Employee Share Scheme Unit Manual ESSU 2086–2096. In *CIR v Eurocopy plc Ch D 1991, 64 TC 370*, however, the Revenue's refusal to accept (in relation to existing options) an alteration to a scheme, bringing forward the earliest date on which options could be exercised, was upheld; a different right would be acquired as a result of the alteration, so that the option price set at the time of the original grant would be less than the market value of the shares at the time the new right was acquired.

The existence of a 'phantom' scheme alongside an approved scheme, designed merely to provide the employee with the cash needed to exercise options under the approved scheme, does not affect either the approval of the option scheme or the tax relief on exercise of the option. If, however, the phantom scheme effectively gave a participant a choice between exercising an option and receiving a cash payment, the arrangements would not meet the conditions for approval. (Revenue Tax Bulletin May 1992 p 19). For further points on phantom schemes, see 75.39 SCHEDULE E—EMPLOYMENT INCOME.

Applications for approval should be sent to Inland Revenue, Employee Share Schemes, Second Floor, New Wing, Somerset House, Strand, London, WC2R 1LB. A specimen set of scheme documents is contained in the explanatory notes for employers, Revenue Pamphlet IR 102. (A non-technical explanatory pamphlet (IR 101) aimed at employees is also available.)

82.74   **Revenue information powers.** The Revenue have wide-ranging powers to require any person to furnish them with such information as they reasonably require, in relation to a CSOP scheme, and as that person possesses or can reasonably obtain. The information must be supplied within a period specified in the notice, which must not be less than three months (30 days for 2002/03 and earlier years). Penalties are exigible under *TMA 1970, s 98* for non-compliance. [*ITEPA 2003, Sch 4 para 33, Sch 6 para 137; ICTA 1988, Sch 9 para 6*].

82.75   EXECUTIVE SHARE OPTION SCHEMES

These were Revenue-approved discretionary schemes that were superseded by CSOP schemes in relation to options granted on or after 29 April 1996 (but see also the transitional provisions below). See 82.61 above for CSOP schemes.

The executive share option scheme rules differed from those for CSOP schemes in the following material respects.

(*a*)   It was a condition of approval (superseded by the more restrictive condition for CSOP schemes at 82.67 above) that the aggregate market value (at the time of grant) of shares over which an individual could hold unexercised rights under a scheme (and any other approved share option scheme, other than a SAYE scheme, established by the company or an associated company) could at no time exceed the greater of £100,000 and four times his emoluments (as defined).

(*b*)   Subject to certain conditions being fulfilled (see the 2002/03 and earlier editions), and with effect after 31 December 1991, the scheme could contain provision for the option price (i.e. the price at which shares could be acquired) to be set as low as 85% of the market value of the shares at the time of grant.

Where the conditions referred to in (*b*) above were met and the scheme contained the provision mentioned, an income tax charge on receipt of the option arose only if the aggregate of the option price and any consideration for the option itself was less than 85% of the then market value of the shares.

[*ICTA 1988, ss 185, 187, Sch 9 as previously enacted; FA 1991, s 39*].

Under *transitional provisions*, the CSOP rules were applied to pre-existing approved executive share option schemes in relation to options granted on or after 17 July 1995 (other than within 30 days of a written offer or invitation to apply for them made before that date) and before 29 April 1996 as if the scheme had adopted them. See 82.61 above as regards options granted on or after 29 April 1996 under pre-existing schemes. In the event of the CSOP rules not being met in relation to options granted in that transitional period, the options were treated as unapproved share options and taxed accordingly. In considering whether or not the £30,000 limit at 82.67 above had been breached, the value of unexercised options granted before 17 July 1995 had also to be taken into account. [*FA 1996, s 115; ITEPA 2003, Sch 7 para 76*].

82.76   PRIORITY SHARE ALLOCATIONS

Where a director or employee (or future or past director or employee and whether or not of the company in question) is entitled, as such, to priority allocation of shares in a genuine public offer at fixed price or by tender, no liability to income tax in respect of earnings arises by virtue of any benefit derived therefrom, provided that

(*a*)   the shares reserved for such priority allocation do not exceed

- 10% of the total shares subject to the offer, or

- (if the offer is part of arrangements under which shares of the same class are offered to the public under more than one offer), either 40% of the total shares subject to the offer or 10% of all the shares of that class subject to any such offers,

(*b*) all persons entitled to priority allocation are so entitled on similar terms (which may, however, vary according to level of remuneration, length of service or similar factors), and

(*c*) the persons entitled to priority allocation are not restricted to directors or to those whose remuneration exceeds a particular level.

Paragraph (*b*) above is still satisfied where allocations to directors and employees of the company are greater than those to other persons, provided that

- the aggregate value of priority allocations made under the offer and under other public offers made at the same time in respect of the shares of other companies to those persons, and

- the aggregate value of the shares allocated to comparable directors and employees of the company

are, as nearly as reasonably practicable, the same.

The above exemption does not apply to the benefit of any discount given to the director or employee on the fixed price or lowest price successfully tendered. Any 'registrant discount' is disregarded for this purpose. Broadly, the '*registrant discount*' is any discount which, subject to any conditions imposed, may be available in respect of all or some part of the shares allocated to any person, whether a member of the public or an employee or director applying for shares as such. For the disregard to apply, at least 40% of the shares allocated to members of the public (other than employees or directors entitled, as such, to priority allocation) must be allocated to individuals entitled either to the discount or to some alternative benefit of similar value for which they may elect.

The above exemption is extended to cases where

- there is a genuine offer to the public of a combination of shares in two or more companies at a fixed price or by tender (the '*public offer*'), and

- there is at the same time an offer (the '*employee offer*') of shares, or a combination of shares, in one or more but not all of those companies to directors or employees (with or without others) of any company, and

- any of those directors or employees is entitled, by reason of his office or employment, to an allocation of shares under the employee offer in priority to any allocation to members of the public under the public offer.

The conditions at (*a*)–(*c*) above apply in relation to this extended exemption, and, for each company included in the employee offer, the limits in (*a*) above must be satisfied by reference to both offers. Where the extended exemption applies, the denial of exemption on any director- or employee-discount on the offer price (see above) is imposed by reference to an '*appropriate notional price*' for shares in each company concerned, i.e. the fixed price at which the shares might reasonably have been expected to be offered in a separate offer to the public, proportionately varied where the sum of the notional prices for all the companies concerned would otherwise differ from the actual fixed price, or lowest successfully tendered price, for the combination of shares subject to the public offer.

For 2003/04 onwards, the term '*director*' is widely defined for the purposes of these provisions (see *ITEPA 2003, s 548(1)(2)*) and includes, for example, any person in accordance with whose instructions (disregarding advice given in a professional capacity) the directors are accustomed to act.

Share-Related Employment Income and Exemptions 82.76

[*ITEPA 2003, ss 542–548; FA 1988, s 68; FA 1989, s 66; FA 1990, s 79; FA 1991, s 44*].

For capital gains tax purposes, *TCGA 1992, s 17(1)* (under which acquisitions are treated as made at their market value rather than their actual cost) is disapplied in relation to acquisitions within the above exemption. [*TCGA 1992, s 149C; FA 1988, s 68(4); ITEPA 2003, Sch 6 para 212*].

Simon's Direct Tax Service. See **E4.515** *et seq.*

83 Social Security

83.1 The *Social Security Acts* of 1973 and 1975 were designed to assimilate earlier national insurance and industrial injuries legislation. Subsequent *Acts* have introduced many detailed changes and extended the scope of the social security system. The legislation was consolidated in 1992. For details of individual benefits, see Tolley's Social Security and State Benefits.

With effect from 6 April 2003, the provisions for the taxation of social security benefits are in *ITEPA 2003, Pt 10*. Previously benefits were taxable under Schedule E.

83.2 **Contributions** by an employee are not allowable for tax purposes. An employer is allowed his contributions for employees as an expense or deduction. [*ICTA 1988, s 617(3)(4); FA 1997, s 65; FA 1999, s 61*]. See 71.44 SCHEDULE D, CASES I AND II. See also 1.10 ALLOWANCES AND TAX RATES as regards Class 4 contributions.

83.3 **Benefits taxable** (as earned income) are

Bereavement allowance
Carer's allowance (previously invalid care allowance)
Incapacity benefit (see below)
Income support when paid to strikers (see below)
Industrial death benefit (if paid as pension)
Invalidity allowance when paid with retirement pension

Jobseeker's allowance (up to 'taxable maximum')
Old persons' pension
Retirement pension
Statutory adoption pay
Statutory maternity pay
Statutory paternity pay
Statutory sick pay
Widowed parent's allowance

[*ITEPA 2003, ss 577—579, 660–662, 670—675; ICTA 1988, ss 150–151A, 617(1)(2)(6); FA 1994, s 139; FA 2002, s 35; FA 2004, Sch 17 para 9(4)*].

See 28.34 EXEMPT INCOME for certain exemptions on war widow's pension and 28.31 for other exemptions. See inside back cover for **rates** of main taxable benefits.

To reduce the administration of receiving returns before assessing retirement pensions and widow's pensions, the Revenue are generally notified by the DSS (now the Department for Work and Pensions) of the amounts each year. (Revenue Press Release 26 July 1979).

Incapacity benefit is taxable (and may be within PAYE) *except for* short-term benefit payable otherwise than at the higher rate, i.e. benefit payable for the first 28 weeks of incapacity (and except for any child addition). There is also an exclusion for certain payments where invalidity benefit was previously payable in respect of the same period of incapacity. [*ITEPA 2003, ss 663, 664; FA 1994, s 139; FA 1995, s 141*]. For the application of PAYE to taxable payments of incapacity benefit, see *SI 2003 No 2682, regs 173–180*.

Income support is taxable only if the claimant is one of a couple (whether or not married) and *Social Security Contributions and Benefits Act 1992, s 126* (or NI equivalent) (trade disputes) applies to the claimant but not to the other person (i.e. broadly if the claimant is on strike). There is a maximum amount in any period which is taxable, and this maximum applies to the sum of income support and jobseeker's allowance where both are in payment. There is provision for notification of, and objection to, determination of the taxable amount by the benefit officer. [*ITEPA 2003, ss 665–669; ICTA 1988, ss 151, 152*]. See Revenue Pamphlet IR 41 (Income Tax and Job Seekers). Although the provisions relating to receipt of unemployment benefit are no longer of application, they remain on the statute book.

See also 55.40 PAY AS YOU EARN regarding the withholding of tax refunds from the unemployed and strikers.

Statutory sick pay, statutory maternity pay, statutory paternity pay and statutory adoption pay paid by employers is taxable. See 75.41 SCHEDULE E—EMPLOYMENT INCOME.

Simon's Direct Tax Service. See E4.129.

83.4   **Benefits not taxable are**

Income-related benefits

Child tax credit (see 83.7 below)
Council tax benefit
Educational maintenance allowance
Hospital patients' travelling expenses
Housing benefit
Income support (if not taxable as in 83.3 above)
Social fund payments
State pension credit
Student grants
Working tax credit (see 83.7 below)
(previously Working Families' Tax Credit and Disabled Person's Tax credit, see 83.6 below)

Industrial injury benefits

Industrial death benefit child allowance
Disablement benefit, including
Constant attendance allowance
Exceptionally severe disablement allowance
Reduced earnings allowance
Retirement allowance
Unemployability supplement

Short-term benefits

Incapacity benefit (not at the higher rate, see 83.3 above)
Maternity allowance

War disablement benefits

Disablement pension, including
Age allowance
Allowance for lowered standard of occupation
Clothing allowance
Comforts allowance
Constant attendance allowance
Dependant allowance
Education allowance
Exceptionally severe disablement allowance
Invalidity allowance
Medical treatment allowance
Mobility supplement
Severe disablement occupational allowance
Unemployability allowance

Other benefits

Attendance allowance
Back to work bonus (paid by way of jobseeker's allowance or income support)
Bereavement payment
Child benefit
Child dependency additions *paid with* widowed mother's allowance, retirement pension, invalid care allowance or unemployment benefit
Child's special allowance
Christmas bonus for pensioners
Cold weather payments
Disability living allowance
Employment rehabilitation allowance
Employment training allowance
Fares to school
Guardian's allowance
Home renovation grants
Invalidity allowance when paid with invalidity pension
Invalidity pension

83.5   Social Security

Jobfinder's grant
Jobmatch payments and training vouchers
Jobseeker's allowance (in excess of 'taxable maximum')
Job search allowances
Severe disablement allowance
Vaccine damage payment
War orphan's pension
War widow's pension
Winter fuel payments

[*ITEPA 2003, ss 641, 645, 656, 677, Sch 7 para 88, Sch 8; ICTA 1988, s 315, s 614(1), s 617(1)(2), s 617A; FA 1996, s 152; Tax Credits Act 2002, Sch 3 para 14; FA 2004, Sch 17 para 9(5)*]. See also 83.3 above.

New Deal Employment Option. Payments made during 1997/98 and 1998/99 to employees whose employer received a subsidy in respect of their employment under the Department of Education and Employment's New Deal programme are taxable only to the extent that they exceeded that weekly subsidy (which ranged from £40 to £75 per week). A refund may be claimed from the local tax office in appropriate cases. (Revenue Press Release 28 May 1999).

New Deal 50 plus programme. Employment credits and in-work training grants under the New Deal 50 plus programme are disregarded for income tax purposes (and consequently exempt from Class 4 NICs). [*FA 2000, s 84*]. Exemption from Class 1 NICs applies under *SI 1999 No 2736*.

Employment Zones programme. Payments to a person as a participant in an Employment Zones programme are disregarded for income tax purposes (and consequently exempt from Class 4 NICs). [*FA 2000, s 85*]. Exemption from Class 1 NICs applies under *SI 2000 No 723*.

Foreign benefits. Before 6 April 2003, there was no explicit charge on foreign social security benefits substantially similar to UK taxable benefits. They were therefore taxable under the general rules of SCHEDULE D, CASE V (73). With effect from that date, they are brought into charge by *ITEPA 2003, ss 678–680*, the taxable amount remaining as if they were taxed under Case V. There is an exemption if the corresponding UK benefit is exempt, the exemption being statutory from 6 April 2003 [*ITEPA 2003, s 681*], having previously applied by concession (see Revenue Pamphlet IR 1, A24).

83.5   **Benefits under Government pilot schemes.** The question as to whether or not, or to what extent, any benefit under a Government pilot scheme is to be within the charge to income tax is to be determined by Treasury Order. The Treasury may also by order provide for any such benefit to be wholly or partly left out of account in determining whether expenditure otherwise qualifying for capital allowances has been met by the Crown etc. (see 9.2(vi) CAPITAL ALLOWANCES). For these purposes, a Government pilot scheme means, broadly, any arrangements made for a trial period by the Government which provide for new social security benefits or benefits under work incentive schemes. [*FA 1996, s 151; CAA 2001, Sch 2 para 95*]. The first such Order exempts payments made under the scheme known as Earnings Top-up. [*SI 1996 No 2396*]. A further Order exempts from 1 October 2003 payments made under the two schemes known as the Employment Retention and Advancement Scheme and the Return to Work Credit Scheme. [*SI 2003 No 2339*]. A further Order exempts from 6 April 2004 payments made under the two schemes known as Working Neighbourhoods Pilot and In-Work Credit. [*SI 2004 No 575*].

83.6   **Working families' tax credit** ('WFTC') and **disabled person's tax credit** ('DPTC') are payable to eligible claimants **after 4 October 1999 and before 7 April 2003**, replacing family credit and disability working allowance respectively (although awards already in payment at 5 October 1999 were allowed to run their course before the change to WFTC or DPTC came into effect). Both tax credits are non-taxable and are not related to the amount of a claimant's tax liability. Both are administered by the Revenue through their Tax Credit Office. For 1999/2000 and continuing thereafter as regards the self-employed and those not in employment, the tax credits are payable by the Revenue direct to recipients. On and after 6 April 2000 as regards employees, they are payable by employers via the PAYE system, such payment being funded by the Revenue (see further below). The main provisions are in *Tax Credits Act 1999*, with much of the detail provided by regulations made by statutory instrument. See in particular *SI 1999 Nos 2487, 2570 (as amended), 2571, 2572, 3110, 3219* (and NI equivalents).

Awards are normally fixed for a period of 26 weeks but where a claim is made after 4 June 2002, the awards were extended to run until 7 April 2003 to facilitate the transition to the new tax credits at 83.7 below. [*SI 2002 No 1334*].

WFTC is payable to UK resident single parents and couples, married or otherwise, who are responsible for children and who work (or one of whom works) at least 16 hours per week (being entitled to work in the UK), and with savings not exceeding £8,000. It consists of a basic adult credit (one per family), a child credit in respect of each child (varying according to age), a 30-hour credit if the claimant or at least one partner works at least 30 hours per week, and, subject to further qualifying conditions, a childcare credit reimbursing up to 70% of eligible childcare costs up to maximum costs of £100 per week for one child or £150 per week for two or more children. From October 2000, a further component, a disabled child's credit, will be added where relevant. The total credit is reduced by 55 pence for each £1 of the single parent's or couple's income (net of tax and national insurance contributions) over £90 per week (£91.45 for 2000/01, £92.90 for 2001/02, £94.50 for 2002/03). Couples eligible for WFTC may choose which partner applies for and receives the credit.

Eligibility for DPTC is based on illness or disability affecting a claimant's capacity to work. DPTC is payable to UK resident claimants, with or without children, who work at least 16 hours per week (being entitled to work in the UK), qualify for certain disability benefits (or have done so within a stipulated time prior to the claim) and have savings not exceeding £16,000. It consists of the same components as the WFTC with the addition of a higher adult credit for couples and including from the outset a disabled child's credit where applicable. The total credit is reduced by 55 pence for each £1 of net income over £70 per week for single persons without children and £90 per week for single parents and couples (for 2000/01 £71.10 and £91.45 per week respectively, for 2001/02 £72.25 and £92.90 per week respectively, and for 2002/03 £73.50 and £94.50 respectively). For claims made on or after 1 October 2000, entitlement to DPTC will extend to certain people who become long-term sick or disabled while in work.

Payment by employers. For 2000/01 onwards, payments of WFTC and DPTC (other than initial payments) are made by employers to their employees through the payroll at their normal pay intervals. The Revenue will give an employer advance notice of credits due to any of his employees. The employer obtains reimbursement by deducting the total amount of credits paid from his monthly (or quarterly) PAYE, NIC and student loan remittances. If, for any month (or quarter) the employer expects to incur a shortfall (i.e. total credits exceed the total otherwise due to the Revenue), he may apply to the Revenue for advance funding. Entries relating to tax credits are required on End of Year Returns P14 and P35 and, where relevant, employees' P60s (see 55.9, 55.10 PAY AS YOU EARN, the former also as regards an initial £50 discount where returns are filed over the internet and payments made electronically). *TMA 1970, s 20* (Revenue's power to call for documents etc.) and *s 20B* (restrictions on such powers) (see 30.7 FRAUDULENT OR NEGLIGENT CONDUCT) are applied with appropriate modifications to employer's obligations with regard to tax credits. See *SI 1999 No 3219* for detailed provisions. See also below re penalties.

To ease the transition to the new tax credits at 83.7 below, the Revenue assumed responsibility for payment of all WFTC and DPTC awards made on or after 27 August 2002 and reassumed responsibility for payment of pre-existing awards after 26 weeks.

Penalties and recovery. Where a person fraudulently or negligently makes any incorrect statement or declaration in connection with a claim for WFTC or DPTC, he is liable to a penalty not exceeding the amount overclaimed. Employers are liable to penalties similar to those of *TMA 1970, s 98* (see 57.9 PENALTIES) in relation to their obligations regarding delivery and accuracy of returns and other documents, and also face a maximum penalty of £3,000 (per employee affected) for refusal or repeated failure to make payment of tax credits as required (such that the Revenue have to take over the payment obligation) or for making or receiving inaccurate payments. Company directors may be held personally liable for fraudulent or negligent misuse of funds provided by the Revenue to pay tax credits.

There are provisions to recover an overpayment of tax credit as if it were tax charged by an assessment. Where the claimant is liable to a penalty as above, interest will also be charged on the overpayment. Interest is also chargeable on penalties themselves. In relation to penalties, procedural rules mirror those of *TMA 1970, ss 100–100D*, the Board's power to mitigate mirrors that of *TMA 1970, s 102*, and there are time limits similar to those of *TMA 1970, s 103* (see 57.10, 57.12–57.15, 57.17 PENALTIES).

See also Revenue leaflet 'Working Families Tax Credit and Disabled Person's Tax Credit' (November 1999) and Revenue Tax Bulletin October 1999 pp 691–693 (as regards employers' obligations).

83.7   **Child tax credit** ('CTC') and **working tax credit** ('WTC') are payable to eligible claimants **from 6 April 2003**, replacing children's tax credit (see 1.18 ALLOWANCES AND TAX RATES), working families tax credit (see 83.6 above) and disabled person's tax credit (see 83.6 above). They also replace (subject to a transition period in some cases) the child-related elements of retirement pension, income support, income-based jobseeker's allowance and certain other social security benefits.

For further reading, see Tolley's Tax Digest (Issue 7) 'A Practical Guide to the New Tax Credits'.

Both CTC and WTC are administered by the Revenue through their Tax Credit Office, are awarded in respect of a tax year and, for 2004/05 onwards, are computed initially on the claimant's income of the preceding tax year (see further below). They are non-taxable and are neither related to nor deducted from the claimant's income tax liability. Thus, they are not 'tax credits' in the conventional sense, but social security benefits. CTC and any childcare costs within WTC are paid direct by the Revenue to the main child carer (see further below). WTC, apart from any element of childcare costs, is similarly paid to a self-employed claimant by the Revenue but employee claimants receive such credits from their employer via the PAYE system, the payment being funded by the Revenue (see further below). The main provisions are in *Tax Credits Act 2002*, but most of the detail is provided by regulations made by statutory instrument. See in particular *SI 2002 Nos 2005–2008, 2014, 2172, 2173, 2926*.

Child tax credit is payable to UK resident single parents and couples, married or otherwise, who are responsible for a child aged under 16 (tax credits will continue to be paid until 1 September following their 16th birthday) or a young person (generally a person aged over 16 and under 19 in full-time, non-advanced, education) and whose income is within a set limit (see further below). It includes: a family element for all who qualify for CTC (£545 for 2003/04 and 2004/05), increased where the family has a child under the age of one year (to £1,090 for 2003/04 and 2004/05), and a child element for each child or young person (£1,445 for 2003/04, £1,625 for 2004/05), increased if the child or young person is disabled (to £3,600 for 2003/04, £3,840 for 2004/05) and further increased where the child or young person is severely disabled (to £4,465 for 2003/04, £4,730 for 2004/05).

Working tax credit is payable to UK residents who are at least 16 years old and who work (or in the case of a couple, one of whom works) at least 16 hours a week and whose income is within a set limit (see further below). Additionally, the claimant (or one of the claimants in the case of a couple) must either

- have dependent children, or a mental or physical disability which puts them at a disadvantage in getting a job and have been previously in receipt of some form of disability benefit, or be over 50 and qualify for the 50+ element of WTC (see below); or

- be at least 25 years old and work for at least 30 hours a week.

It may consist of

- a basic element which is paid to all who qualify for WTC (£1,525 for 2003/04, £1,570 for 2004/05);

- a second adult element in the case of a couple cohabiting (whether married or unmarried) or a lone parent element where the claimant has a dependent child (£1,500 for 2003/04, £1,545 for 2004/05);

- a 30 hour element where the claimant works (or, in the case of a couple, one of whom works) at least 30 hours a week or where the couple have a dependent child or young person and one of the couple works at least 16 hours a week and in aggregate they work at least 30 hours a week (£620 for 2003/04, £640 for 2004/05);

- a disability element where the claimant satisfies (or, in the case of a couple, one of whom satisfy) one of a wide range of disability conditions (£2,040 for 2003/04, £2,100 for 2004/05);

- a severe disability element where the claimant receives (or, in the case of a couple, one of whom receives) either higher rate attendance allowance or the higher rate care component of the disability living allowance (or would do so if not in hospital) (£865 for 2003/04, £890 for 2004/05);

- a 50+ element (paid for up to 12 months) for a claimant who is (or, in the case of a couple, one of whom is) 50 or over and has been out of work for at least six months and claiming certain benefits and who starts work after 5 April 2003 and within the three months preceding the claim (for 2003/04 £1,045 where the claimant works at least 16 hours a week and £1,565 where the claimant works at least 30 hours a week; for 2004/05 £1,075 and £1,610 respectively); and

- a childcare element equal to 70% of eligible childcare costs up to a maximum of £135 a week for one child or £200 a week for two or more children.

Income thresholds. The tax credits are subject to tapering if relevant gross annual income, or in the case of a couple aggregate joint income, exceeds specified thresholds. For claimants entitled to only WTC or to both CTC and WTC, the maximum credits, apart from the family element of CTC, are withdrawn at the rate of 37p for each £1 of the excess of relevant income (see below) over £5,060 (for 2003/04 and 2004/05). For claimants entitled only to CTC the maximum credits, apart from the family element, are withdrawn at the rate of 37p for each £1 of the excess of relevant income over (£13,230 for 2003/04; £13,480 for 2004/05). For all claimants, the family element of CTC is withdrawn at the rate of £1 for every £15 (6.67%) of the excess of relevant income over £50,000. The taper is applied first to the non-childcare elements of WTC, then to the childcare element of WTC then to

CTC. Where the tax credits are awarded at different rates within the same tax year, the figures are calculated for each relevant period (in which the rates remain the same) on a daily basis and the amounts for each period then aggregated.

Relevant income. The income taken into account is the annual gross income of the claimant or, in the case of a couple (of opposite sex) cohabiting (whether married or unmarried), the aggregate gross annual income of the couple. A claim for tax credits for 2003/04 is based on income for the tax year 2001/02. Claims for 2004/05 onwards will be based on income for the preceding tax year. These awards are provisional only and will be altered retrospectively to the extent that income in the year in which tax credits are received (the current year) increases or decreases by more than £2,500 from that in the year on which the award is based. Any resulting underpayment will be paid to the claimant and any overpayment collected from him (see further below).

Gross annual income includes the aggregate amount (if it exceeds £300) of pension income, investment income, property income, foreign income and notional income (as defined in *SI 2002 No 2006, regs 5, 10–17*). It also includes taxable income from employment (including most taxable benefits-in-kind), trading income, social security benefits (with some specific exclusions), student grants (other than for dependent children, travel, books or equipment) and other income not covered above by the regulations and taxable under Schedule D, Case VI. Certain types of income are specifically excluded such as maintenance payments and student loans, and certain deductions are allowed such as trading losses, charitable donations and pension contributions

Claims. Claims for CTC and WTC can be made on form TC600 or via the internet (www.inlandrevenue.gov.uk). Couples must make a joint claim. For 2003/04, claims can be made before the commencement of the tax year. For 2004/05 onwards, claims must be made after the commencement of the tax year but must be made within three months after commencement if maximum entitlement is to be awarded, as claims can only be backdated for a maximum of three months (providing the claimant is entitled to the tax credit in that earlier period).

Payment by the Revenue. CTC and any childcare costs within WTC are paid by the Revenue, at weekly or four-weekly intervals, to the main carer, normally through a bank account. In the case of a joint claim, the couple may jointly nominate the main carer, otherwise the Revenue will decide who is the main carer (normally the mother or the person who receives child benefit). Payments of WTC to a self-employed claimant are made by the Revenue.

Payment by employers. WTC, apart from any element of childcare costs, is paid to employees by their employers (except for an initial period when it is paid direct by the Revenue) through the payroll at normal pay intervals. In the case of a joint claim, the couple can jointly nominate which employer is to make the payment, otherwise the Revenue will choose. The payment by the employer is funded by deducting the credits from the monthly (or quarterly) remittances of PAYE, student loan repayments, NICs and tax withheld under the construction industry scheme. An employer can apply to the Revenue for additional funding if a shortfall is expected to be incurred.

End-of-year return. The claimant must make a return, by notice from the Revenue and normally by 6 July following the tax year to which the claim relates, confirming his circumstances and his income for that year.

Notifiable changes in circumstances. Certain in-year changes of circumstances must be notified to the Revenue, normally within three months of the change, if tax credit entitlement will fall to be reduced as a result. Notifiable changes include marriage, start of cohabitation, separation, and decreases in average weekly childcare charges where the childcare element of WTC is claimed.

Underpayments and overpayments. After the year-end, once entitlement to tax credits for the tax year has been determined, any underpayment will be paid by the Revenue in a lump sum to the designated claimant. Overpayments are recovered by deduction from tax credit entitlement in the following year, or through the PAYE system, or by assessment as if they were unpaid tax. The Revenue must serve notice on the claimants of the overpayment to be recovered specifying how it is to be recovered. Liability for the overpayment in the case of a couple is joint and several.

Interest and penalties. If a person fraudulently or negligently makes an incorrect statement or declaration in connection with a claim for CTC or WTC or incorrectly notifies a change of circumstances or provides incorrect information or evidence, a penalty may be imposed up to a maximum of £3,000. A penalty up to £3,000 may also be imposed on the other claimant in a joint claim (but not exceeding £3,000 in aggregate for both claimants) unless the other claimant was not, and could not reasonably have been expected to have been, aware of the fraud or neglect. Interest may also be charged on overpayments arising through fraud or neglect of the claimant(s). If a person fails to provide any information or evidence which is required in connection with the claim or fails to notify in-year changes of circumstances (where these must be notified), a penalty may be imposed of up to £300. If the failure persists, an additional penalty of up to £60 a day can be imposed for each day the failure continues after the initial penalty has been imposed..

See also Revenue leaflets WTC1 *et seq.* (listed at 37 INLAND REVENUE EXPLANATORY PUBLICATIONS).

83.8   **National Insurance contributions for 2004/05** (and for 2003/04 in brackets where different) are as follows.

Class 1 (earnings-related)

Not contracted out

The employee contribution is **11%** of earnings between £91 p.w. (£89 p.w.) and £610 p.w. (£595 p.w.) and 1% of all earnings above £610 p.w. (£595 p.w.).

The employer contribution is **12.8%** of all earnings in excess of the first £91 p.w. (£89 p.w.).

Contracted out

The 'not contracted out' rates for employees are reduced on the band of earnings from £91 p.w. (£89 p.w.) to £610 p.w. (£595 p.w.) by **1.6%**. For employers, they are reduced on the band of earnings from £91 p.w. (£89 p.w.) to £610 p.w. (£595 p.w.) by **3.5%** for employees in salary-related schemes or **1.0%** for employees in money purchase schemes. In addition, there is an employee rebate of **1.6%** and an employer rebate of **3.5%** or **1.0%**, as appropriate, on earnings from £79 p.w. (£77 p.w.) up to £91 p.w. (£89 p.w.).

Married women

The reduced employee rate for certain married women and widows with a certificate of election is **4.85%** of earnings between £91 p.w. (£89 p.w.) and £610 p.w. (£595 p.w.) and 1% of all earnings above £610 p.w. (£595 p.w.).

Class 1A (cars and car fuel and other benefits)

Employer contributions at **12.8%** are required on a scale charge value of cars and fuel made available to employees for private use and on most other employment-related benefits.

Class 1B (PAYE settlement agreements)

Employer contributions at **12.8%** are required on the value of all items included in a PAYE settlement agreement and the tax paid under the agreement (see 55.12 PAY AS YOU EARN).

Class 2 (self-employed, flat rate)

The flat weekly rate of contribution is £2.05 (£2.00). The annual limit of net earnings for exception from Class 2 liability is £4,215 (£4,095).

83.9   Social Security

Class 3 (voluntary contributions)

The flat weekly rate of contribution is £7.15 (£6.95).

Class 4 (self-employed, profit-related) (see Revenue Pamphlet IR 24)

The 2004/05 contribution rate is 8% on the band of profits between £4,745 and £31,720 and 1% on all profits above £31,720. See below for earlier years' figures (and note that the 1% charge on profits above the upper limit does not apply prior to 2003/04). Class 4 contributions are levied, generally, on profits chargeable to income tax under Schedule D, Case I or II (plus any enterprise allowance — see 71.75 SCHEDULE D, CASES I AND II). They are shown separately on the self-assessment tax return (or notice of assessment where applicable) and are payable at the same time as the income tax on the profits (see 78.4–78.7 SELF-ASSESSMENT). Profits for this purpose are after capital allowances and certain interest and annual payments for trade purposes. [*Social Security Contributions and Benefits Act 1992, Sch 2 paras 2, 3(5); CAA 2001, Sch 2 para 75*]. Trading losses set against other income may, *for Class 4 purposes*, be carried forward and set against the first available profits. [*SSCBA 1992, Sch 2 para 3(4)*]. Contributions to personal pension schemes and retirement annuity premiums are not deductible in arriving at profits for Class 4 purposes by virtue of *Social Security Contributions and Benefits Act 1992, Sch 2 para 3(2)(f)(g)*. There are various exceptions from Class 4 liability, including persons over State pensionable age, divers etc. assessed under Schedule D (see 71.21 SCHEDULE D, CASES I AND II) and, on application, those under 16 at the beginning of the year of assessment. [*SI 1979 No 591, regs 58–60*]. Non-UK residents and sleeping partners are not within the scope of Class 4.

Interest is chargeable on overdue Class 4 contributions under *TMA 1970, s 86* as it is for income tax purposes (see 42 INTEREST AND SURCHARGES ON UNPAID TAX), and repayment supplement (see 41 INTEREST ON OVERPAID TAX) is similarly available. [*SSCBA 1992, Sch 2 para 6; SI 1993 No 1025*].

The Class 4 rates and bands for earlier years are as follows.

	Rate	Band
2003/04	8% + 1%	£4,615 – £30,940
2002/03	7%	£4,615 – £30,420
2001/02	7%	£4,535 – £29,900
2000/01	7%	£4,385 – £27,820
1999/2000	6%	£7,530 – £26,000
1998/99	6%	£7,310 – £25,220

83.9   See Tolley's Social Security and State Benefits and Tolley's National Insurance Contributions for full details of this subject.

84   Statutory Bodies

84.1   *Marketing Boards.* Payments by Marketing Boards into certain compulsory reserve funds for maintaining guaranteed prices etc., allowed (on conditions) as deductions, and withdrawals (generally) treated as trading receipts. [*ICTA 1988, s 509*].

84.2   *Atomic Energy Authority and National Radiological Protection Board* are entitled to certain exceptions. [*ICTA 1988, s 512; TCGA 1992, s 271(7)*].

84.3   *Harbour reorganisation schemes* are subject to special tax treatment. [*ICTA 1988, s 518; TCGA 1992, s 221*].

84.4   *Local authorities, local authority associations and health service bodies* are exempt from tax. [*ICTA 1988, ss 519, 519A, 842A as amended; TCGA 1992, s 271(3)*].

84.5   Subject to the special provisions above and, where appropriate, to the Crown exemption (see 29.6 EXEMPT ORGANISATIONS), statutory bodies are liable in the ordinary way to corporation tax on their income and capital gains. Whether their activities amount to trading depends on the facts. See *Mersey Docks and Harbour Board v Lucas HL 1883, 1 TC 385, 2 TC 25* (held to be chargeable under legislation now in *ICTA 1988, s 55*) and *Port of London Authority v CIR CA 1920, 12 TC 122* and contrast the *Forth Conservancy Board cases, 14 TC 709, 16 TC 103* (liable under Case VI on surplus from shipping dues) and *British Broadcasting Corporation v Johns CA 1964, 41 TC 471* (liable under Case I on profits from publications etc. but not on rest of surplus; not entitled to Crown exemption). See also *Sowrey v King's Lynn Harbour Mooring Commrs QB 1887, 2 TC 201; Humber Conservancy Board v Bater KB 1914, 6 TC 555*.

84.6   *Statutory corporation borrowing in foreign currency.* Interest on securities issued by, or on a loan to, a statutory corporation (as defined) in foreign currency (for securities issued before 6 April 1982, in a currency outside the scheduled territories) shall, if the Treasury directs, be paid without deduction of income tax and be exempt from income tax (but not corporation tax) in the hands of a non-resident beneficial owner of such securities or, in the case of a loan, in the hands of the person for the time being entitled to repayment or eventual repayment of the loan. [*ICTA 1988, s 581*].

85 Stock Dividends

Simon's Direct Tax Service D1.202.

85.1   Shares issued by a UK company in lieu of a cash dividend are chargeable on the individual beneficial shareholder on an amount equal to the cash they replace grossed up at, from 6 April 1999, the Schedule F ordinary rate (previously the lower rate) of tax, as if it was dividend income (see 1.9 ALLOWANCES AND TAX RATES). No charge to, or repayment of, the Schedule F ordinary (or lower) rate tax is made, and the gross amount is not available to cover charges. Where there is no cash equivalent or this equivalent is substantially above or below (i.e. more than one or two percentage points outside 15% either way: Revenue Pamphlet IR 131, A8) the market value of shares issued, the market value is used. Similarly chargeable are bonus shares issued in respect of shares held under terms which carry the right to the bonus. The shareholder is treated as receiving the shares on the due date of issue i.e. the earliest date the company was required to issue the shares. Where more than one person is entitled to the shares issued, apportionment is made according to their respective interests. [ICTA 1988, s 249(1)–(4), s 251; F(No 2)A 1992, s 19(4); FA 1993, s 77(3); FA 1996, s 122(5), Sch 6 paras 6, 28, Sch 41 Pt V(1); F(No 2)A 1997, Sch 4 para 10].

85.2   **Capital gains tax.** With effect from 6 April 1998, the issue of shares treated as income as in 85.1 above (or 85.4, 85.5 below) does not constitute a reorganisation of share capital within TCGA 1992, ss 126–128. The person acquiring the shares is treated for capital gains tax purposes as having acquired them for whichever of the cash equivalent or market value was used in determining the amount treated as income under 85.1 above. [TCGA 1992, s 142; FA 1998, s 126]. Previously, the shares were treated as acquired for that consideration as part of the new holding following the reorganisation of share capital, except that where the shares were issued to a bare or nominee trustee, the position is as applies generally after 5 April 1998 (as above). [TCGA 1992, ss 141, 142 as originally enacted].

85.3   **Companies.** For provisions affecting companies issuing and receiving stock dividends, see Tolley's Corporation Tax.

85.4   **Deceased estates.** Stock dividends issued to personal representatives during the administration period are grossed as in 85.1 above and deemed part of the aggregate income of the estate, see 21 DECEASED ESTATES. [ICTA 1988, s 249(5)].

85.5   **Discretionary and accumulation trusts.** The provisions in 85.1 above apply to trustees as they do to individuals, with any necessary modifications. See 81.5 SETTLEMENTS as regards the application of ICTA 1988, s 686. [ICTA 1988, s 249(6); F(No 2)A 1997, Sch 4 para 10].

85.6   **Enhanced stock dividends received by trustees of interest in possession trusts.** Where the trustees of an interest in possession trust have concluded that either

(a)   an enhanced stock dividend belongs to the income beneficiary, or

(b)   it forms part of the trust's capital, or

(c)   while adding the enhanced stock dividend to capital, the trustees should compensate the income beneficiary for the loss of the cash dividend he would otherwise have received, and the view they have taken of the trust law position is supportable on the facts, the Revenue will not seek to challenge what the trustees have done. The income tax consequences of each view are as follows.

(*a*)   Since the beneficiary is beneficially entitled to the shares comprised in the dividend, the provisions described at 85.1 above apply.

(*b*)   Since the stock dividend is regarded as capital, there is no income tax liability.

(*c*)   The payment to the beneficiary is an annual payment from which basic rate tax must be deducted.

For full details of this treatment and of the capital gains tax consequences, and for differences under Scottish law, see Revenue Pamphlet IR 131, SP 4/94.

86 Time Limits—Fixed Dates

Note. This chapter lists fixed date time limits falling in the year to 30 September 2005. See also 87 TIME LIMITS—MISCELLANEOUS, and see 55.9 PAY AS YOU EARN, 78.12 SELF-ASSESSMENT, 79 SELF-ASSESSMENT—KEY DATES.

Simon's Direct Tax Service A3.620 *et seq.*

86.1 TIME LIMITS OF ONE YEAR OR LESS

(*a*) **5 October 2004** for action in respect of 2003/04.

Notification of chargeability. Any person who is chargeable to tax for a year of assessment must give notice to the Revenue that he is so chargeable, unless his income comes solely from certain sources (e.g. income dealt with under PAYE or dividend income chargeable at Schedule F ordinary rate) and he has no chargeable gains. [*TMA 1970, s 7 as amended*]. See 57.1 PENALTIES.

(*b*) **31 January 2005** for action in respect of 2003/04 or 2004/05 (whichever is stated).

(i) *Returns under self-assessment* for 2003/04 when required by notice given before 2 November 2004. See 68.2 RETURNS.

(ii) *Retirement annuity premiums.* Election for premiums paid in 2003/04 to be relieved as if paid in 2002/03, or in 2001/02 if no net relevant earnings in 2002/03. See 66.4 RETIREMENT ANNUITIES.

(iii) *Personal pension and stakeholder pension contributions.* Election for contributions paid in 2004/05 (but on or before 31 January 2005) to be relieved as if paid in 2003/04; election must be made at or before the time of payment. See 60.5 PERSONAL PENSION SCHEMES.

(iv) *Gift Aid donations to charity by individuals.* Election for qualifying donation(s) made in 2004/05 to be relieved as if made in 2003/04; election must be made no later than the date the 2003/04 self-assessment tax return is filed. See 14.12 CHARITIES.

(v) *Change of accounting date.* Notice of change to be given (in a return) where it affects basis period for 2003/04. See 71.7 SCHEDULE D, CASES I AND II.

(vi) *Cash basis withdrawal.* Election for increased adjustment charge to be made for 2003/04 under the transitional provisions. See 11.2 CASH BASIS.

(*c*) **5 April 2005** — advance time limit for action in respect of 2005/06.

Transfer of married couple's (where available) and blind person's allowances. Election by wife to receive one-half of the married couple's allowance, or by spouses jointly for wife to receive the whole of the allowance, or by husband to receive one-half where a joint election has been made for wife to receive the whole of the allowance, must be made before the start of the first year of assessment to which the election is to apply (subject to a 30 day extension where notice of intention to elect was given to the inspector before the start of that year). Withdrawals of such elections similarly do not have effect until the year of assessment after that in which notice of withdrawal was given. Similar rules apply to transfers inter-spouse of blind person's allowance. See 47.1 MARRIED PERSONS.

(*d*) **5 April 2005** for action in respect of 2003/04.

Claims following late assessments. A claim (including a supplementary claim) which could not have been allowed but for the making of an assessment to income tax or capital gains tax after the tax year to which it relates may be made before the end of the tax year of assessment following that in which the assessment was made. After 10 July 2003, this applies in relation to a Revenue amendment to a self-assessment personal or partnership tax return as it does in relation to an assessment. See 16.8 CLAIMS, 68.9 RETURNS.

(e)   **6 July 2005** for action in respect of 2004/05.

   (i)   *Election for treatment as a single loan of beneficial loans to director* by close company lender. [*ITEPA 2003, s 187; ICTA 1988, s 160(1B); FA 1996, s 107(1)*]. See 75.20 SCHEDULE E—EMPLOYMENT INCOME.

   (ii)   *Employment-related shares (outside approved employee share schemes).* Information on 'reportable events' to be supplied to Revenue by employer or other specified parties. See 82.17 SHARE-RELATED EMPLOYMENT INCOME AND EXEMPTIONS.

86.2   TIME LIMITS ONE TO TWO YEARS

(a)   **31 January 2005** for action in respect of 2002/03.

   (i)   *Capital allowances.* The following time limits apply.

      (A)   *Agricultural buildings and works.* Election for balancing adjustments to apply on a disposal etc. See 9.3 CAPITAL ALLOWANCES.

      (B)   *Ships.* Notice requiring the postponement of first-year allowances, see 9.27 CAPITAL ALLOWANCES. Also notice requiring postponement of writing-down allowances, and disapplying the 'single ship pool' provisions, see 9.30(B) CAPITAL ALLOWANCES. Also claim for deferment of balancing charge, see 9.30(B) CAPITAL ALLOWANCES.

      (C)   *Short-life assets.* Election for certain expenditure to be treated as on short-life assets. See 9.30(F) CAPITAL ALLOWANCES.

      (D)   *Equipment leasing.* Election for fixtures to be treated as belonging to the lessor and not the lessee. See 9.34(*b*) CAPITAL ALLOWANCES.

   (ii)   *Herd basis.* Election where 2002/03 was either the first year of assessment (after that in which trading commenced) during the basis period for which a herd was kept, or the first year of assessment in the basis period for which compensation was received for compulsory slaughter. See 34.4, 34.8 HERD BASIS.

   (iii)   *Claim for loss in trade etc.* to be set off against general income (see 46.3 LOSSES) or capital gains (see 46.5 LOSSES) or be carried back (see 46.10 LOSSES).

   (iiia)   *Trading losses set against chargeable gains.* Election to disregard taper relief in computing the 'maximum amount' when relieving a trading loss of 2002/03 (whether against gains for 2001/02 or for 2002/03 or for both). See 46.5 LOSSES.

   (iv)   *Claim for losses on shares* in unlisted companies. See 46.15 LOSSES.

   (v)   *Unremittable overseas income.* Claim for relief from assessment. See 51.13 NON-RESIDENTS AND OTHER OVERSEAS MATTERS.

   (vi)   *Patent rights* election where capital sum received. See 54.5 PATENTS.

   (vii)   *Post-cessation receipts.* Election for such receipts to be treated as received on date of discontinuance. See 62.1 POST-CESSATION ETC. RECEIPTS AND EXPENDITURE.

(viii) *Post-cessation expenditure.* Claim for relief against total income. See 62.4 POST-CESSATION ETC. RECEIPTS AND EXPENDITURE.

(ix) *Furnished holiday lettings.* Election for averaging treatment. See 69.8 SCHEDULE A.

(x) *Rent-a-room relief.* Election (or withdrawal) for relief not to apply, or for profits or gains to be treated as equal to excess of gross rents over relief limit. See 69.10 SCHEDULE A.

(xi) *Schedule A losses.* Claim for relief, against general income, for certain capital allowances and agricultural expenses. See 69.12 SCHEDULE A.

(xii) *Farming.* Claim to average profits of 2001/02 and 2002/03, see 71.47(*a*) SCHEDULE D, CASES I AND II.

(xiii) *Creative artists.* Claim to average profits of 2001/02 and 2002/03, see 71.41 SCHEDULE D, CASES I AND II.

(xiv) *Films.* Certain expenditure on production or acquisition may be reallocated to other periods or, alternatively, treated as capital expenditure on plant. See 71.48 SCHEDULE D, CASES I AND II.

(xv) *Gifts to educational establishments.* Claim for gifts of certain articles to be excluded from trading accounts. See 71.50 SCHEDULE D, CASES I AND II.

(xvi) *Appropriations to and from trading stock.* Election for market value to be adjusted in certain cases where a chargeable gain or allowable loss would otherwise arise. See 71.73 SCHEDULE D, CASES I AND II.

(xvii) *Work in progress on cessation.* Election for work in progress to be taken at cost on cessation in 2002/03. See 71.73 SCHEDULE D, CASES I AND II.

(xviii) *Relevant discounted securities.* Claim for relief for losses on transfer or redemption. See 72.5 SCHEDULE D, CASE III and note abolition of loss relief, except in limited circumstances, for transfers etc. on or after 27 March 2003.

(xix) *Beneficial loan arrangements.* Election (or requirement by inspector) for alternative method of calculating benefit. See 75.20 SCHEDULE E—EMPLOYMENT INCOME.

(xx) *Amendment of self-assessment tax return.* Amendments by taxpayer to return must be made within 12 months after the filing date (itself normally 31 January after the year of assessment). See 68.4 RETURNS.

(xxi) *Settlements for maintenance of historic buildings.* Election for tax exemption on income. See 81.21 SETTLEMENTS.

(*b*) **5 April 2005** for action in respect of 2002/03.

Valuation of trading stock on discontinuance. Election for transfers between CONNECTED PERSONS (19) to be reduced below market value in certain cases. See 71.73 SCHEDULE D, CASES I AND II.

86.3 TIME LIMITS THREE TO FOUR YEARS

31 January 2005 for action in respect of 2000/01.

Deceased estates. Claim for adjustment of assessments where administration was completed in 2000/01. See 21.3 DECEASED ESTATES.

86.4 TIME LIMITS MORE THAN FIVE YEARS

Claims by 31 January 2005 in respect of 1998/99. Except where other time limits are prescribed, claims must be made by the fifth anniversary of 31 January following the year of assessment to which the claim relates. [*TMA 1970, s 43(1); FA 1994, Sch 19 para 14*].

(*a*)   *Error or mistake claims.* See 16.7 CLAIMS.

(*b*)   *Claim for additional personal allowances etc.* omitted from the taxpayer's tax return.

(*c*)   *Claim against double assessment* where the same person has been assessed 'for the same cause' in the same year. [*TMA 1970, s 32*].

(*d*)   DOUBLE TAX RELIEF (24).

(*e*)   INTEREST PAYABLE (43).

(*f*)   *Claim for loss in trade etc.* for 1998/99 to be carried forward against future profits of the same trade (see 46.9 LOSSES).

(*g*)   *Claim for terminal loss relief* in relation to a trade etc. that ceased in 1998/99 (see 46.12 LOSSES).

(*h*)   MINERAL ROYALTIES (49).

(*j*)   NON-RESIDENTS AND OTHER OVERSEAS MATTERS at 51.13. Delayed remittances of overseas income or gains.

(*k*)   *Post-employment deductions* (for employee liabilities and indemnity insurance) to be relieved against total income of former employee. See 75.26 SCHEDULE E—EMPLOYMENT INCOME.

(*l*)   RETIREMENT ANNUITIES (66). Unused relief may be claimed.

(*m*)   ENTERPRISE INVESTMENT SCHEME at 25.11. Claim for income tax relief in respect of shares issued in 1998/99.

(*n*)   VENTURE CAPITAL TRUSTS at 91.5. Claim for income tax relief in respect of investments.

(*p*)   Any other matter not specified in 86.1–86.3 above for which relief from income tax is claimed.

Claims by 31 October 2004 in respect of 1998/99. *PAYE taxpayer* to request that a return be issued to him. See 68.3 RETURNS.

86.5 COMPANIES

Claims and elections in respect of companies, where applicable, usually have similar time limits as shown above except that:

- the expiry date is by reference to the end of the company's accounting period instead of the end of the tax year; and

- 31 January time limits of one to two years for income tax are normally two-year time limits for corporation tax; and 31 January time limits of five to six years for income tax are normally six-year time limits for corporation tax.

87 Time Limits—Miscellaneous

See also 78.4–78.7 SELF-ASSESSMENT as regards payment of tax, 79 SELF-ASSESSMENT—KEY DATES, 86 TIME LIMITS—FIXED DATES above. Time limits other than to fixed dates are set out below. In some (but not all) cases, the periods can be extended at the discretion of the Inland Revenue.

Simon's Direct Tax Service A3.620 *et seq.*

87.1 TIME LIMITS OF ONE YEAR OR LESS

(*a*) **14 days**

Various elections to disapply or moderate the restricted shares provisions at 82.4 SHARE-RELATED EMPLOYMENT INCOME AND EXEMPTIONS. Such elections are implemented by way of agreement between employer and employee to be made no later than 14 days after acquisition or after a chargeable event (whichever is applicable); there is no requirement for elections to be submitted to the Revenue.

(*b*) **30 days**

(i) Rejection of Revenue corrections to self-assessment tax return or partnership return. See 68.4, 68.13 RETURNS.

(ii) Appeals against assessments, amendments to self-assessment return or partnership return or claim made outside return, and Revenue conclusions on completion of enquiry. Lodging of notice of appeal. See 4 APPEALS, 16.3 CLAIMS.

(iii) Appeals to High Court. Request for Stated Case within 30 days of determination of appeal. The Case Stated must be transmitted to the High Court within 30 days of its receipt. See 4.19 APPEALS.

(iv) Patent rights election after death, winding-up or partnership change. See 54.6 PATENTS.

(v) Generally, appeals against refusal or withdrawal of Revenue approval to an employee share scheme. See e.g. 82.33 SHARE-RELATED EMPLOYMENT INCOME AND EXEMPTIONS.

(vi) There are many instances in which Revenue information powers and clearance procedures require a response within 30 days, see e.g. 3.2 ANTI-AVOIDANCE.

(*c*) **40 days**

Qualifying option under Enterprise Management Incentives scheme to be exercised within 40 days after a disqualifying event, if adverse tax consequences would otherwise ensue. See 82.37 SHARE-RELATED EMPLOYMENT INCOME AND EXEMPTIONS.

(*d*) **60 days**

(i) There are a number of circumstances in which information is required to be provided within 60 days, see e.g. 25.25 ENTERPRISE INVESTMENT SCHEME.

(ii) Notice of declaration by husband and wife of their beneficial interests in jointly held property, and income arising from it, where these are not equal. See 47.3 MARRIED PERSONS.

(*e*) **Three months**

(i) Returns of income, partnership returns etc., following notice requiring delivery (if this gives a date later than 31 January following year for which return required). See 68.2, 68.13 RETURNS.

(ii) Appeals relating to questions of (i) personal reliefs for non-residents, (ii) residence, ordinary residence or domicile, (iii) pension funds for service abroad. [*TMA 1970, Sch 1A para 9; ICTA 1988, s 207; ITEPA 2003, s 43(2)*].

(iii) Application for judicial review must be made within three months of the date when the grounds for application arose. See 4.24 APPEALS.

(iv) There are instances in which Revenue information powers require a response within three months. See e.g. 82.33, 82.45, 82.60, 82.74 SHARE-RELATED EMPLOYMENT INCOME AND EXEMPTIONS.

(*f*)   **92 days**

Notice of grant of option under Enterprise Management Incentives scheme to be given to Revenue within 92 days after option granted. See 82.43 SHARE-RELATED EMPLOYMENT INCOME AND EXEMPTIONS.

(*g*)   **Six months**

Payment of retirement annuity premiums by an individual (if not made during the tax year) may be made within six months of the agreed assessment for that year, together with an election, in certain circumstances. See 66.5 RETIREMENT ANNUITIES.

(*h*)   **Twelve months**

Double tax relief. Notice must be given to the Revenue within one year of a foreign tax credit becoming excessive. See 24.5(*e*) DOUBLE TAX RELIEF.

87.2   **TWO-YEAR TIME LIMITS**

(*a*)   *Industrial buildings.* Election for allowances to apply to holder of long lease out of relevant interest within two years of lease taking effect. See 9.14 CAPITAL ALLOWANCES.

(*b*)   *Sales without change of control.* Election for transfer of assets at tax written-down value. See 9.22(i) CAPITAL ALLOWANCES.

(*c*)   *Short-life assets.* Election for certain transfers between connected persons to be treated as at tax written-down value. See 9.30(F) CAPITAL ALLOWANCES.

(*d*)   *Equipment leasing.* Election for certain fixtures on which expenditure incurred by incoming lessee to be treated as belonging to lessee within two years of date of lease taking effect. See 9.34(*d*) CAPITAL ALLOWANCES.

(*e*)   *Successions.* Election for transfers between 'connected persons' to be at tax written-down value. See 9.38(G) CAPITAL ALLOWANCES.

(*f*)   *Late-paid remuneration.* Claim to adjust profits computation for remuneration paid after computation made but within nine months after end of period of account. See 71.44 SCHEDULE D, CASES I AND II.

(*g*)   *Know-how payment.* Election within two years of disposal for it not to be treated as a payment for goodwill. See 71.57 SCHEDULE D, CASES I AND II.

88   Trade Unions

Simon's Direct Tax Service D4.636.

88.1   Trade Unions are entitled to the tax exemptions below providing they are registered (which means listed under the *Trade Union and Labour Relations Act 1974* or NI equivalent) and providing they are precluded from assuring more than £4,000 by way of gross sum or £825 by way of annuity (excluding retirement annuities approved under *ICTA 1988, s 620(9)*) in respect of any one person. The limits may be increased by the Treasury by order. [*ICTA 1988, s 467; ICTA 1970, s 338; FA 1987, s 31; FA 1991, s 74*].

Exemption is then granted on income which is not trading income and is applicable and applied to *provident benefits* (as defined in *ICTA 1988, s 467(2)* as amended by *FA 1988, Sch 3 para 17*) which include legal expenses incurred in representing members at Industrial Tribunal hearings of cases alleging unfair dismissal, or in connection with a member's claim in respect of accident or injury suffered, and general administrative expenses of providing such benefits. (Revenue Pamphlet IR 131, SP 1/84, 17 February 1984). See also *R v Special Commrs (ex p NUR) QB 1966, 43 TC 445*. Similar exemption is granted on capital gains so applied. [*ICTA 1988, s 467(1)(b)*].

Similar provisions apply to employers' associations registered as trade unions [*ICTA 1988, s 467(4)(b)*] and to the Police Federations for England and Wales, Scotland and Northern Ireland and other police organisations with similar functions. [*ICTA 1988, s 467(4)(c)*].

89   Underwriters at Lloyd's

Simon's Direct Tax Service E5.6.

Other sources. For a full and detailed treatment of this highly specialised subject, see Tolley's Taxation of Lloyd's Underwriters.

89.1   Special tax provisions for Lloyd's underwriters were contained in *ICTA 1988, ss 450–457* and *Sch 19A*, for which see the 2003/04 and earlier editions. With effect generally for 1992/93 and subsequent years, but with some changes taking effect later than 1992/93, these provisions were repealed and replaced with a new tax regime for underwriters contained in *FA 1993, ss 171–184, Schs 19, 20* (as amended). Further changes in *FA 1994, s 228, Sch 21* facilitated the introduction of self-assessment by revising the relationship between the underwriting year and the tax year. Various further provisions are contained in *SI 1974 Nos 896, 1330* (amending), *SI 1990 No 2524* (amending) and other regulations (see, for example, *SI 1995 No 351*).

Following the admission of corporate members to Lloyd's from 1 January 1994, special provisions are contained in *FA 1994* for the application of corporation tax to such members. Broadly, the effect of these is as follows.

(*a*)   Corporation tax continues to be chargeable in the normal way.

(*b*)   Schedule D, Case I rules apply in determining the income from the Lloyd's underwriting trade, and in addition profits and gains from syndicate participation, premium trust funds, ancillary funds etc. are included.

(*c*)   Profits and gains from syndicate participation are treated as accruing uniformly over the underwriting year in which they are declared and apportioned to the concurrent accounting periods.

(*d*)   Non-syndicate income and gains are taxable as income (as for corporate insurers generally).

(*e*)   There are special rules for items such as stop-loss insurance, reinsurance to close, premium trust fund assets and cessation.

(*f*)   There is no provision for a special reserve fund.

See *FA 1994, ss 219–227, 229, 230, 248* (as amended).

As regards Scottish limited partnerships, see *SI 1997 No 2681*.

89.2   **Basis of assessment.** To enable the self-assessment rules to be applied for 1997/98 and subsequent years, a revised basis of assessment applies to profits or losses from syndicate membership (including syndicate investment income) and arising from assets forming part of the premium trust fund. The profits or losses in a tax year are those declared in the underwriting year ending in the tax year, i.e. profits of underwriting year 1998 are generally declared in 2001 and assessed for 2001/02. [*FA 1993, s 172(1); FA 1994, Sch 21 para 2*]. For transitional arrangements for years up to and including 1997/98, see the 2003/04 and earlier editions.

On cessation (on death or otherwise), the final tax year is that which corresponds to the underwriting year in which the underwriter's Lloyd's deposit is paid over to him or his personal representatives or assigns. Any underwriting profits or losses which do not fall to be taken as profits or losses of an earlier tax year are taken to be profits or losses of the final tax year. [*FA 1993, s 179; FA 1994, Sch 21 para 6(1)(2)*]. Where a member dies,

(*a*)   he is treated for these purposes as having died on 5 April in the underwriting year in which he actually died, and (*b*)   the business is treated as continuing until the member's deposit is paid over to his personal representatives, whose carrying on of the business is not treated as a change in the persons so engaged. [*FA 1993, s 179A; FA 1994, Sch 21 para 6(2)(3)*].

If underwriting commenced before 2 January 1971 and a cessation occurs, a claim may be made for assessments (*a*) for the final tax year for which underwriting profits or losses fall to be included (being profits or losses declared in the underwriting year following the closing year) to be based on the actual profits from 6 April to 31 December in that underwriting year, and (*b*) for the preceding year to be reduced by the lesser of (i) the whole of the profits of that year and (ii) the underwriting profits for the underwriting year 1972. [*SI 1995 No 351, reg 13*].

For double tax relief arrangements, see *SI 1997 No 405.*

89.3   UNDERWRITING PROFITS

The aggregate of a member's **underwriting profits** is chargeable under Schedule D, Case I. Underwriting profits include income from premium trust fund assets and income from 'ancillary trust fund' assets. An '*ancillary trust fund*' does not include a premium trust fund or special reserve fund but otherwise means any trust fund required or authorised by Lloyd's rules or required by an underwriter's member's agent. [*FA 1993, s 171(1)(2)(4), s 184(2)(b); FA 1994, Sch 21 para 8(1)*].

Foreign income dividends within *ICTA 1988, Pt VI, Ch VA* are included in premium trust fund income until their abolition after 5 April 1999 at the actual amount received. [*FA 1993, s 171(2A); FA 1994, Sch 21 para 1(1)(3)(a); F(No 2)A 1997, Sch 6 para 20*]. Distributions made after 1 July 1997 in respect of any asset of a premium trust fund do not carry any entitlement to a tax credit (and see the provisions against arrangements to pass on the value of tax credits at 3.22 ANTI-AVOIDANCE). [*F(No 2)A 1997, s 22(1)(7)*].

Annual appreciation in value of and profits on disposal of premium trust fund assets are included in underwriting profits for income tax purposes and annual depreciation in value and losses on disposal are deducted in arriving at such profits. For the purposes of computing appreciation and depreciation in value of premium trust fund assets, there is an exemption similar to that in 74.9(*d*) SCHEDULE D, CASE VI (FOTRA securities). [*FA 1993, ss 174, 184(2); FA 1994, Sch 21 para 3; FA 1996, s 154, Sch 41 Pt V(18); FA 1997, Sch 18 Pt VI(10)*]. Gains and losses on ancillary trust fund assets are subject to the capital gains tax regime. [*FA 1993, s 176(2)*].

Underwriting profits are treated as derived from the carrying on of a business and thus as **earned income.** [*FA 1993, s 180*].

Stop-loss insurance premiums are allowable as an expense in computing underwriting profits, and insurance money received in respect of a loss is a trading receipt of the tax year corresponding to the underwriting year in which the loss was declared. This treatment is extended to payments into and receipts out of the High Level Stop Loss Fund, i.e. the fund of that name established under Lloyd's rules. A repayment of insurance money received etc. is likewise allowed as an expense, as is any amount payable under a quota share contract, i.e. a contract made in accordance with Lloyd's rules and practice between the underwriter and another person which provides for that other person to take over any rights and liabilities of the underwriter under any of his syndicates. As regards quota share contracts, the deduction may be limited by reference to certain prior 'transferred losses', and if such losses exceed the amount payable under the contract, a trading receipt will arise. Amounts paid in respect of conditional contracts which do not come into effect are, however, allowed in full, and certain cash calls in respect of undeclared transferred losses are treated as payments under the contract. The treatment of insurance receipts etc. is modified where the inspector is not notified of the receipt in time to raise the necessary assessment for the year corresponding to that in which the loss arose; in such a case, the trading receipt is treated as arising in the tax year corresponding to the underwriting year in which the payment of insurance money etc. was made to the underwriter. [*FA 1993, ss 178, 184(1); FA 1994, Sch 21 para 5; FA 2002, s 86, Sch 32 paras 1–5*].

Reinsurance premiums. A restriction is placed on relief for such premiums payable in respect of liabilities outstanding at the end of an underwriting year for the purpose of closing the accounts for the underwriting year, where the member by whom the premium is payable is also a member of the syndicate as a member of which the reinsurer is entitled to receive it. Relief is restricted to an amount which must not exceed an assessment, arrived at with a view to producing neither profit nor loss to the member to whom it is payable, of the value of the liabilities in respect of which it is payable, and a corresponding reduction is made in his profits or gains as a member of the reinsurer syndicate. [*FA 1993, s 177; FA 1994, Sch 21 para 4*].

See Revenue Tax Bulletin October 1998 p 599 as regards the proportion of such premiums generally allowable for tax purposes, in particular in relation to the 1994 underwriting account.

Bank guarantee fees paid initially to secure membership as a Lloyd's underwriter are not deductible, but annual payments for the maintenance of such facilities are deductible.

General insurance reserves. For periods of account beginning after 1 January 2000, there are provisions for bringing in as a trading receipt or expense an amount representing interest on any allowance in respect of technical provisions to the extent that it subsequently becomes apparent that it was excessive or insufficient. [*FA 2000, s 107; SI 2001 No 1757 as amended*]. For guidance notes, including rates of interest, see www.inlandrevenue.gov.uk/specialist/gir.htm

Association of Lloyd's members. It is understood that subscriptions to the Association are allowable, as is the cost of League Tables and Syndicate Results. Two-thirds of the cost of prospective names seminars, and one-half of the cost of most other conferences and meetings, is also allowable, with proportionate allowance of travelling expenses other than to or from London (the place of business).

Personal accountancy fees are allowed on the usual 'wholly and exclusively' basis applicable to traders generally, by reference to the amount paid in the year of account.

Compensation payments from managing or members' agents are likely to be treated as trading receipts of the underwriting year in which the entitlement to compensation arises, and thus as not being chargeable to capital gains tax. Any legal fees incurred, together with any payments out of the compensation to stop-loss insurers, are deductible for tax purposes. (Revenue Tax Bulletin May 1992 p 17). For confirmation that such compensation payments are taxable, see *Deeny and others v Gooda Walker Ltd HL 1996, 68 TC 458*.

Members' agent pooling arrangements ('MAPAs'). For the tax treatment from 6 April 1999 of individuals' shares of the various syndicate membership rights held through each MAPA, see Tolley's Capital Gains Tax under Underwriters at Lloyd's. [*FA 1999, ss 82–84*].

Simon's Direct Tax Service. See E5.611 *et seq.*

89.4   The general administrative arrangements for assessment and collection of tax (see below) are contained in *FA 1993, Sch 19*. Annual arrangements for 1997/98 onwards are contained in *SI 1995 No 351*.

These arrangements broadly enable the inspector to require a return of syndicate profits at any time after the beginning of a tax year, and a payment on account of basic rate tax. Penalties apply for failure to comply with a notice requiring such a return.

The return must be submitted by 1 September in the tax year or three months after service of the notice requiring the return if later. The inspector may determine the syndicate profit or loss either in accordance with the return or, subject to the usual appeal procedures, to the best of his judgment if he is not satisfied with the return, and the determination is conclusive as regards the tax liability of each member. A return may be required apportioning the profits so determined between syndicate members, again subject to penalty for failure to comply.

The return of syndicate profit or loss is to be made by the managing agent, who may also, within six years from 1 March next following the end of the closing year (i.e. the underwriting year next but one following the underwriting year concerned), claim repayment of tax suffered by deduction on syndicate investment income. Any such repayment must be apportioned and, where there is a syndicate profit available for distribution, paid to the members' agents within 90 days of receipt. No repayment supplement is available.

There are special provisions relating to stop-loss insurance, to reasonable excuse for certain failures to deliver returns, to determinations and to cessations.

Member's liability. The amount of basic rate tax apportioned to a member as above is regarded as a payment on account of the member's liability in respect of his share of the profits, any additional liability or repayment being dealt with directly between the member and the Revenue. Tax is due in respect of profits from all a member's syndicates under the normal SELF-ASSESSMENT (78) rules, with credit being given for the basic rate tax accounted for as above by the member's agents.

For the purposes of assessment in cases involving fraudulent or negligent conduct, anything done or omitted to be done by the managing agent is treated as having been done or omitted by each syndicate member.

[*FA 1993, ss 173, 184(1), Sch 19; FA 1994, Sch 21 paras 9–11; F(No 2)A 1997, Sch 8 Pt II(5); FA 2001, s 88, Sch 29 para 36*].

89.5   **LOSSES**

An underwriting loss can be **carried forward** for relief against underwriting profits in subsequent tax years (under the normal provisions for carry-forward of losses under *ICTA 1988, s 385(1)*).

An underwriting loss for a tax year can also be **offset against other income** of the underwriter under the normal provisions of *ICTA 1988, s 380(1)*.

An underwriting loss in the early years of the business may be carried back and offset against other income under *ICTA 1988, s 381*.

See 46 LOSSES.

An *anticipated* underwriting loss may not be taken into account in a PAYE coding until title to it has been established, i.e. until it has actually been sustained (*Blackburn v Keeling CA, [2003] STC 1162*). Whilst awaiting this decision of the CA, which reversed an earlier Ch D decision, the Revenue were prepared to take account of provisional 2001 underwriting losses (i.e. 2004/05 losses) in 2003/04 PAYE codes if requested to do so, i.e. on the assumption that the loss would be carried back (Lloyd's Market Bulletin 28 May 2003).

Carry-forward of losses against income from successor company or partnership. Where, after 5 April 2004, under a conversion arrangement made under the rules or practice of Lloyd's (conversion to limited liability underwriting), a member transfers the whole of his outstanding syndicate capacity to a company (the successor company) for a consideration consisting entirely of shares in the company, any income which he derives from the company (e.g. earnings or dividends) is treated for the purposes of carry-forward of losses under *ICTA 1988, s 385* as if it were profits of the member's former underwriting business, thus enabling any unrelieved losses brought forward to be set against it. The successor company must be one which the member controls (within the meaning of *ICTA 1988, s 416*) and of which he owns more than 50% of the ordinary share capital and, for the relief to apply in respect of income of a particular tax year, these conditions must continue to be satisfied from the time of transfer until the end of that tax year. Losses are set firstly against any income which falls to be directly assessed, e.g. against earnings in priority to dividends. The transfer of syndicate capacity must take effect from the beginning of the underwriting year immediately following the member's final underwriting year, and the successor company must commence underwriting in that following year. The member must also have given notice of resignation to Lloyd's and must not undertake any new insurance business at Lloyd's after the end of his final underwriting year. If the member withdraws his resignation after claiming relief under these provisions, the relief fails; the member must give the Revenue written notice of the withdrawal within six months after it occurs, subject to penalty under *TMA 1970, s 95* (see 57.3 PENALTIES) in the event of his fraudulently or negligently failing to do so.

A similar relief applies if, after 5 April 2004, a member transfers the whole of his outstanding syndicate capacity to a Scottish limited partnership, provided he is the only person who disposes of syndicate capacity under a conversion arrangement to that partnership. The income to which the relief applies is the profits of the successor partnership's underwriting business to which the member is beneficially entitled and, for the relief to apply in respect of income of a particular tax year, the member must be beneficially entitled to more than 50% of such profits throughout the period from the time of transfer to the end of that tax year.

[*FA 1993, s 179B, Sch 20A paras 1, 2, 5–11; FA 2004, s 144, Sch 25*].

For capital gains tax reliefs on conversion to corporate underwriting, see the corresponding chapter of Tolley's Capital Gains Tax.

Simon's Direct Tax Service. See **E5.621** *et seq.*

89.6   **SPECIAL RESERVE FUND**

An underwriter may set up a Special Reserve Fund into which he may make payments (eligible for tax relief — see below) for the purpose of meeting future losses.

A special reserve fund may be set up in relation to each underwriter under arrangements complying with the requirements of *FA 1993, Sch 20 Pt I* and approved by the Revenue (who may consent to any variation of the arrangements). The fund must be vested in trustees who have control over it, and there must be appointed a fund manager, authorised under Lloyd's rules and who may be the trustees or one or more of them, to invest the capital and vary the investments. Payments into and out of the fund (which, unless a contrary intention appears in the legislation, must be in money) must be allowed only where required or permitted (expressly or by necessary implication) by the provisions of Schedule 20. Otherwise, the income arising from the fund must be added to capital and retained in the fund. The underwriter is absolutely entitled as against the trustees to the fund assets, but subject to the rules of cessation (see below) and without affecting the operation of capital gains tax on a disposal of an asset by the underwriter to the trustees. The fund manager must value the fund in a manner to be prescribed by regulations (see *SI 1995 No 353*) as at the end of each underwriting year, and must report the value (and such other matters as may be prescribed by regulations) to the underwriter. [*FA 1993, s 175(1)(2), Sch 20 paras 1(1), 2, 6(1), 8; FA 1994, Sch 21 paras 12(1), 13; FA 1995, s 143; SI 1999 No 3308, reg 4*].

Payments into and out of the special reserve fund are, respectively, deductions and additions in arriving at the underwriter's profit. [*FA 1993, Sch 19 para 10(2)(a)(3)(a), Sch 20 para 10*].

Tax exemption. Profits arising from special reserve fund assets are exempt from both income tax and capital gains tax, and losses are not allowable. The fund manager may, at any time after the end of an underwriting year, claim repayment of income tax deducted from such profits for that year and (before 6 April 1999) of tax credits in respect of qualifying distributions forming part of the fund income for that year. [*FA 1993, Sch 20 para 9; F(No 2)A 1997, Sch 4 para 30*].

For the purposes of the provisions described below, an underwriter's '*syndicate profit*' for an underwriting year is the excess of his aggregate profits over his aggregate losses, profits or losses being those shown in syndicate accounts as arising to him and disregarding payments into or out of the special reserve fund. Profits of a run-off underwriting year are attributable to the last underwriting year but one preceding the run-off year. An underwriter's '*syndicate loss*' is to be construed accordingly. [*FA 1993, Sch 20 para 1; SI 1995 No 353; F(No 2)A 1997, Sch 4 para 30*].

Payments into the fund out of syndicate profits. If an underwriter has made a syndicate profit for an underwriting year, he may pay into his special reserve fund, before the end of a period to be prescribed by regulations (see *SI 1995 No 353*), the lesser of

(i)   50% of that profit, and

(ii)   the excess, if any, of an amount equal to 50% of the underwriter's 'overall premium limit' for the closing year (i.e. the year next but one following the underwriting year) over the value of the fund at the end of that year.

An underwriter's '*overall premium limit*' for an underwriting year means the maximum amount which, under Lloyd's rules, he may accept by way of premiums in that year. If the underwriter did not accept premiums in the closing year, the reference in (ii) above to the closing year is to be taken as a reference to the latest underwriting year in which he did so. The above provisions are not to apply, in the case of any underwriter, to any tax year after a tax year in which the Revenue cancel their approval of the arrangements referred to above, having first given notice to Lloyd's of their intention to do so.

The payment into the fund in respect of an underwriting year is deductible as an expense in arriving at underwriting profits. From 1997/98 onwards, it is made for the tax year next but two after the tax year to which the underwriting year corresponds (i.e. a payment made in underwriting year 1998 is deducted in 2001/02 — see also 89.2 above). [*FA 1993, s 175(3), Sch 20 paras 1(1), 3, 10(1); FA 1994, Sch 14*].

Payments out of the fund. Payments *must* be made out of the fund in the following circumstances.

(1)   To cover 'cash calls'. A '*cash call*' means a request for funds made to the underwriter by an agent of a syndicate of which he is a member, being made in pursuance of a contract made in accordance with Lloyd's rules and practices. If a cash call is made in respect of an underwriting year, there must be paid out of the underwriter's special reserve fund into a premium trust fund of his an amount equal to the amount of the call (or, if less, the amount of the special reserve fund). There are provisions for a payment to be made back into the special reserve fund if a stop-loss payment (i.e. a payment of insurance money under a stop-loss insurance or a payment out of the High Level Stop Loss Fund — see 89.3 above) is made to the underwriter, and for a further payment out of the fund if a stop-loss payment is wholly or partly repaid. [*FA 1993, Sch 20 para 4; SI 1995 No 353*].

(2)   To cover syndicate losses. If an underwriter sustains a syndicate loss for an underwriting year, there must be paid out of his special reserve fund into a premium

trust fund of his an amount equal to the 'net amount of the loss' (or, if less, the amount of the special reserve fund). The *'net amount of the loss'* is the amount of the syndicate loss as reduced by any payment made out of the special reserve fund for the year to cover a cash call (see (1) above). As in (1) above, there are provisions for payments into and out of the special reserve fund in the event of stop-loss payments and repayments of stop-loss payments. If a stop-loss payment is made in respect of the loss before any payment out of the special reserve fund in respect of the loss, no payment is required into the fund but the said payment out of the fund is determined as if the net amount of the loss were reduced by the amount of the stop-loss payment. [*FA 1993, Sch 20 para 5*].

(3)   To eliminate excess amounts. If on the valuation (see above) of the special reserve fund at the end of the underwriting year, it is found that the value of the fund exceeds 50% of the higher of the underwriter's overall premium limit (see above) for that year and the corresponding figure for the previous year (or 50% of his overall premium limit for the last year in which he accepted premiums), the excess must be paid to the underwriter (or to his personal representatives or assigns). Before 31 December 1999, the overall premium limit for the preceding year was not taken into account. [*FA 1993, Sch 20 para 6(2); SI 1999 No 3308, reg 3*].

(4)   On cessation. On a person ceasing to be an underwriter (on death or otherwise), the amount of his special reserve fund (net of any amount required to be paid out to cover cash calls or syndicate losses) must be paid over to the underwriter (or to his personal representatives or assigns), the payment to be in money or in assets forming part of the fund, as the recipient may direct. [*FA 1993, Sch 20 para 7; FA 1994, Sch 21 para 12(2)*].

Any payments required to be made out of or into the fund under (1)–(3) above must be made before the end of a period to be prescribed in each case by regulations (see *SI 1995 No 353*). [*FA 1993, Sch 20 paras 4(8), 5(10), 6(3)*].

In computing underwriting profits for a tax year, payments into the special reserve fund under (1) and (2) above in respect of the 'relevant' underwriting year are deductible as expenses, and the following are treated as trading receipts:

(A)   payments out of the fund in respect of the 'relevant' underwriting year to cover cash calls and losses;

(B)   payments out of the fund as a result of the repayment of stop-loss payments (see (1) and (2) above) in the 'relevant' underwriting year; and

(C)   any payment out of the fund under (3) above in respect of the 'relevant' underwriting year's closing year (i.e. the underwriting year next but one following the 'relevant' underwriting year).

The *'relevant'* underwriting year for this purpose is the underwriting year next but two before the corresponding underwriting year, i.e. for 2001/02, for which the corresponding underwriting year is 2001, the relevant underwriting year is 1998.

[*FA 1993, Sch 20 para 10(2)–(4); FA 1994, Sch 21 para 14*].

Cessation. The aggregate of any payments made out of the special reserve fund under (4) above is treated, in computing underwriting profits for the 'relevant tax year', as made immediately after the end of the 'relevant underwriting year' and as being a trading receipt. Where cessation occurs by reason of death, such payments are treated for the purposes of INTEREST AND SURCHARGES ON UNPAID TAX (42) as if made immediately after the beginning of the member's final tax year. The amount of the said trading receipt is the value of the fund at the end of the 'penultimate underwriting year' as reduced by subsequent payments out (other than under (3) or (4) above) and as increased by:

(I) subsequent payments in (excluding payments made before 1 January 2000 out of syndicate profits);

(II) subsequent repayments of tax (and, in respect of 1998/99 and earlier years, tax credits) in respect of fund income;

(III) (for 2000/01 and subsequent years) the amount of any subsequent profits, net of any losses, arising to the trustees from assets (any net deficit being deducted), leaving aside any gain or loss on an asset transferred to the member etc. and treated as an acquisition by him for capital gains tax purposes (see below); and

(IV) any payments made before the end of the penultimate underwriting year (and after 31 December 1999) by the trustees to the member etc., whether under (4) above or otherwise than out of the special reserve fund, including the market value of any asset transferred by way of such payment.

On the transfer of an asset by the trustees to the member, his personal representatives or assigns, whether under (4) above or otherwise, there are rules to determine for capital gains tax purposes both the date and cost of acquisition by the member etc., for which see the corresponding chapter of Tolley's Capital Gains Tax.

The *'relevant tax year'* is the final tax year except that, where a member dies before the occurrence of certain events, it is the tax year at the end of which he is treated as having died (see 89.2 above). The events in question are where the member's deposit is paid over to any person (or a substituted arrangement ceases) or the last open year of account of any syndicate of which he was a member is closed or is regarded as having closed. The *'relevant underwriting year'* is the underwriting year corresponding to the tax year immediately preceding the final tax year except that, where the member dies before the occurrence of certain events (as above), it is the underwriting year immediately preceding that corresponding to the relevant tax year (as above). The *'penultimate underwriting year'* is the underwriting year corresponding to the tax year immediately preceding the final tax year. [*FA 1993, Sch 20 para 11; FA 1994, Sch 21 para 15; SI 1995 No 353, reg 8; SI 1995 No 1185, reg 5; F(No 2)A 1997, Sch 4 para 30; SI 1999 No 3308, reg 6*].

Death. Where a member dies and his personal representatives carry on his underwriting business after his death, the above provisions are modified to apply to the personal representatives. [*SI 1995 No 353, regs 7, 7A; SI 1995 No 1185, reg 4*].

Simon's Direct Tax Service. See E5.645.

90   Unit Trusts

Cross-references. For corporation tax provisions applicable to authorised unit trusts, see Tolley's Corporation Tax under Unit and Investment Trusts. See 52 OFFSHORE FUNDS for unit trusts which are offshore funds.

Simon's Direct Tax Service D4.413 *et seq.*

90.1   AUTHORISED UNIT TRUSTS

An '*authorised unit trust*' is a 'unit trust scheme' which is the subject of an order under *Financial Services and Markets Act 2000, s 243* for the whole or part of an accounting period. A '*unit trust scheme*' is as defined under *Financial Services and Markets Act 2000*, but subject to certain exclusions by Treasury order (see *SI 1988 Nos 266, 267, 268 as amended; SI 1992 Nos 571, 3133; SI 1994 No 1479; SI 2000 Nos 2549, 2550, 2551*). [*ICTA 1988, ss 468(6), 469(7); TCGA 1992, s 99(2); Financial Services and Markets Act 2000, Sch 20 para 4(3)(4)*]. The *Tax Acts* have effect as if the trustees were a company resident in the UK, and the rights of unit holders were shares in the company (but without prejudice to the making of 'interest distributions' (see below)). Expenses of management (including managers' remuneration) are allowed as if the company were an investment company. [*ICTA 1988, s 468(1)(4); FA 1994, Sch 14 para 3*]. For capital gains purposes, any unit trust scheme is treated as if the scheme were a company and the rights of the unit holders shares in the company, and, in the case of an authorised unit trust, as if the company were UK resident and ordinarily resident. [*TCGA 1992, s 99(1)*].

A special rate of corporation tax applies to the trustees of an authorised unit trust, equivalent to the lower rate of income tax (currently 20%) for the year of assessment beginning in the financial year concerned. [*ICTA 1988, s 468(1A); FA 1996, Sch 6 para 10(1)(2); FA 1999, s 28(3)*]. For the special corporation tax loan relationship provisions, see Tolley's Corporation Tax under Loan Relationships (special cases).

'*Umbrella schemes*' (i.e. schemes which provide separate pools of contributions between which participants may switch) which are authorised unit trusts may treat each of the separate pools as an authorised unit trust. [*ICTA 1988, s 468(7)–(9); FA 1994, s 113*].

Futures and options. For accounting periods beginning before 1 October 2002, income derived from transactions relating to futures or options contracts is exempt from tax under Schedule D, Case I in the hands of the trustees. A contract is not excluded from this exemption by the fact that any party is, or may be, entitled to receive and/or liable to make only a payment of a sum (rather than a transfer of assets other than money) in full settlement of all obligations. For subsequent accounting periods, the exemption becomes unnecessary, as profits from derivative contracts normally fall to be taxed under the special regime for such contracts (for which see Tolley's Corporation Tax), and is repealed; see also Revenue Tax Bulletin August 2002 pp 948–950. [*ICTA 1988, s 468AA; FA 1990, s 81(1); FA 1999, Sch 20 Pt III(17); FA 2002, Sch 27 para 6*].

Distributions. The total amount available for distribution to unit holders is to be shown in the distribution accounts as available for distribution either as dividends which are not foreign income dividends within *ICTA 1988, Ch VI, Pt VA* (a 'dividend distribution'), or as foreign income dividends (a 'foreign income distribution'), or as yearly interest (which may not include any amount deriving from Schedule A income) (an 'interest distribution') or as divided between the first two categories (in which case no discrimination between unit holders is permitted). For distribution periods ending after 25 November 1996, amounts deriving from distributions to which *FA 1997, Sch 7* applies (see 3.20 ANTI-AVOIDANCE) must be shown as available for distribution as foreign income dividends, as must other amounts which would fall to be treated as distributions to which *FA 1997, Sch 7* applies if they were shown as available for distribution as dividends. Foreign income dividends are abolished from 6 April 1999 (and *FA 1997, Sch 7* is repealed from that date), and these requirements are correspondingly modified from that date. These provisions do not apply to an authorised unit trust which is an approved personal pension scheme (see 60.1 PERSONAL PENSION SCHEMES). [*ICTA 1988, ss 468H(6), 468I; FA 1994, Sch 14 paras 2, 7; F(No 2)A 1997, Sch 6 para 8*].

For these purposes, the making of a distribution includes the investment of an amount on behalf of the unit holder in respect of his accumulation units. [*ICTA 1988, s 468H(2); FA 1994, Sch 14 para 2; FA 1997, Sch 7 para 11*]. See, however, Revenue Pamphlet IR 1, C30 as regards concessional relief from such treatment in the case of certain *de minimis* distribution (or accumulation) waivers.

As regards *dividend distributions*, they are treated as dividends on shares paid on the '*distribution date*' (i.e. the date specified under the trust or, if there is no such date, the last day of the distribution period), in respect of which no foreign income dividend election may be made (pending the abolition of foreign income dividends after 5 April 1999). See 1.9 ALLOWANCES AND TAX RATES as regards taxation of dividends. [*ICTA 1988, s 468J; FA 1994, Sch 14 para 2; F(No 2)A 1997, Sch 6 para 8*]. Special provisions apply to dividend distributions to unit holders within the charge to corporation tax (see *ICTA 1988, s 468Q* introduced by *FA 1994, Sch 14 para 2*).

As regards *foreign income distributions* (prior to the abolition of foreign income dividends after 5 April 1999), they are treated as foreign income dividends on shares paid on the '*distribution date*' (as above) to which *ICTA 1988, ss 246A, 246B* (elections for foreign income dividend treatment), *ss 246K–246M* (subsidiaries) and *ss 246S–246W* (international headquarters companies) do not apply (and for which provisions see Tolley's Corporation Tax under Foreign Income Dividends). [*ICTA 1988, s 468K; FA 1994, Sch 14 para 2; F(No 2)A 1997, Sch 6 paras 3, 8*]. Special provisions apply where, on the distribution date, the unit holder is within the charge to corporation tax (see *ICTA 1988, s 468R* introduced by *FA 1994, Sch 14 para 2*).

As regards *interest* distributions, they are treated as payments of yearly interest made on the '*distribution date*' (as above). They are not charges on income within *ICTA 1988, s 338(1)*, but if paid under deduction of tax (see below) they are deductible from total profits (see *ICTA 1988, s 468L(5)–(7)* (as amended), introduced by *FA 1994, Sch 14 para 2*).

For interest distributions made **on or after 16 October 2002**, lower rate tax is deductible under *ICTA 1988, s 349(2)* unless either:

(*a*)   the unit holder to whom the payment is made is either a company or the trustees of a unit trust scheme, or

(*b*)   either the 'residence condition' or the 'reputable intermediary condition' is fulfilled with respect to the unit holder on the distribution date.

The '*residence condition*' (in *ICTA 1988, ss 468O, 468P* as amended by *FA 2003, s 203(4)–(8)*) requires broadly that a valid declaration is made to the trustees of the authorised unit trust, in prescribed form, that either the recipient is non-UK ordinarily resident or, if the units are held as personal representative of a deceased holder, the deceased was non-UK ordinarily resident at the time of his death.

The '*reputable intermediary condition*' (in *ICTA 1988, ss 468O(1A)–(1B), 468PA* as inserted by *FA 2003, s 203(6)(9)*) requires broadly that the interest distribution is paid on behalf of the unit holder to a company which is subject to certain money laundering controls, and that the trustees of the authorised unit trust have reasonable grounds for believing the unit holder to be non-UK ordinarily resident. If it subsequently transpires that the unit holder was in fact ordinarily resident, the tax which should have been deducted is payable by the trustees of the authorised unit trust under *ICTA 1988, s 350, Sch 16*. See *TMA 1970, s 98(4E)* for penalty provisions.

The Revenue have wide-ranging powers to make provision by regulations to give effect to the deduction provisions. See *SI 2003 No 1830* which modifies the deduction provisions in relation to interest distributions made to or received under a trust and also provides the Revenue with general powers to obtain information from trustees of unit trusts, and inspect their records, for the purpose of determining whether interest distributions made gross were properly so made. In the case of distributions made to or received under a trust, the residence condition requirement is for a valid declaration from the trustees both that they are non-UK resident and that each beneficiary known to them is non-UK ordinarily resident or, in the case of a corporate beneficiary, non-UK resident. If, however, the whole of the distribution is, or falls to be treated as, income of a person other than the trustees, the normal provisions apply as if that person were the unit holder.

For interest distributions made **before 16 October 2002**, lower rate tax was deductible unless the 'residence condition' was fulfilled with respect to the unit holder on the distribution date. That condition required a declaration as described above in relation to later distributions, except for company and trustee unit holders. In relation to company unit holders, the declaration had to be that the company was not UK resident. In the case of distributions made to or received under a trust, under *SI 1994 No 2318* the requirement was for a valid declaration from the trustees both that they were non-UK resident and that each beneficiary known to them satisfied the individual or company residence conditions as appropriate (except that where the whole of the distribution was, or was treated as, income of a person other than the trustees, the residence conditions applied only to that person). If the gross income in the distribution accounts derived entirely from 'eligible income', payments to unit holders satisfying the appropriate residence condition could be made without deduction of tax. There was a formula for determining the amount which could be so paid where the gross income did not derive entirely from 'eligible income' (see *ICTA 1988, s 468N(4)–(6)*). *SI 1994 No 2318* also provided the Revenue with the appropriate powers to determine whether interest distributions were properly paid gross. '*Eligible income*' was defined in *ICTA 1988, s 468M(4)(5)* (as amended) broadly as income which would not be subject to deduction if received directly by a non-UK resident.

An interest distribution may be made only if the authorised unit trust satisfies the qualifying investments test throughout the distribution period, which it does if, at all times in that period, the market value of 'qualifying investments' exceeds 60% of the market value of all the investments of the trust (disregarding cash awaiting investment). '*Qualifying investments*' are defined as

(*a*)   money placed at interest,

(*b*)   building society shares,

(*c*)   securities (other than company shares),

(*d*)   entitlements to shares in the investments of other authorised unit trusts provided that, throughout the distribution period in question, more than 60% of the market value of the other unit trust's investments is represented by investments falling within (*a*)–(*c*) above and (*f*) and (*g*) below,

(*e*)   (from 25 February 1997) shares in open-ended investment companies provided that, throughout the distribution period in question, more than 60% of the market value of the company's investments is represented by investments falling within (*a*)–(*c*) above,

(*f*)   (for accounting periods beginning after 30 September 2002) derivative contracts (within *FA 2002, Sch 26 Pt 2*, see Tolley's Corporation Tax under Financial

Instruments and Derivative Contracts), or certain contracts treated as such, whose underlying subject matter consists wholly of any of (*a*)–(*e*) above, and

(*g*)   contracts for differences (within *FA 2002, Sch 26 para 12*) whose underlying subject matter consists wholly of interest rates or creditworthiness or both,

but the Treasury may, by order, extend or restrict the meaning of 'qualifying investments', including any necessary or expedient transitional provisions.

[*ICTA 1988, ss 468L–468PB; FA 1994, Sch 14 para 2; FA 1996, Sch 6 para 11, Sch 7 para 17, Sch 14 para 26; FA 2002, Sch 27 para 7; FA 2003, s 203, Sch 43 Pt 5(3); SI 1997 No 212*].

Subject to appropriate modifications (see *SI 1997 No 1154* as amended), the tax legislation relating to authorised unit trusts has effect in like manner in relation to **open-ended investment companies**.

Simon's Direct Tax Service. See D4.413–D4.419.

90.2   UNIT TRUSTS NOT TREATED AS AUTHORISED UNIT TRUSTS

Special provisions apply to the income of a unit trust scheme not within 90.1 above unless the trustees are non-UK resident. Such a trust is outside the scope of *ICTA 1988, s 468* (see 90.1 above). Income arising to the trustees is treated as income of the trustees (rather than the unit holders), and is subject to basic rate tax. Capital allowances are available to the trustees (but, since the trustees are not treated as a company, there is no relief for management expenses). The unit holders are treated as receiving annual payments, under deduction of basic rate tax, equal to their respective entitlements to the grossed-up income available for distribution or investment. The date the payment is treated as having been made is the latest (or only) date for distribution under the terms of the trust or (if there is no such date or it is more than twelve months after the end of the distribution period) the last day of the distribution period. For the definition of 'distribution period', see *ICTA 1988, s 469(6)* as amended by *FA 1994, Sch 14 para 5*.

The income of the trustees, and thus of the unit holders, is chargeable at the basic rate, as opposed to the lower rate (or, from 6 April 1999, the Schedule F ordinary rate), even if the nature of the income is such that the lower (or Schedule F ordinary) rate would otherwise apply (see 1.9 ALLOWANCES AND TAX RATES).

UK company qualifying distributions (see 1.9 ALLOWANCES AND TAX RATES) made after 1 July 1997 but before 6 April 1999 which are income of the trustees are treated as foreign income dividends (see 1.9 ALLOWANCES AND TAX RATES) if they would not otherwise be so treated. This does not, however, apply to common investment funds under *Administration of Justice Act 1982, s 42* (but see 90.3 below from 6 April 1999) or if, were it not treated as income of the trustees, the whole of a distribution would be income either of a charity (within *ICTA 1988, s 506(1)*, see 14.1 CHARITIES) or of a body treated as a charity under *ICTA 1988, ss 507, 508* (see 29.3, 29.9, 29.14, 29.20 EXEMPT ORGANISATIONS, 77.1 SCIENTIFIC RESEARCH ASSOCIATIONS). With effect from 6 April 1999, no tax credit is attached to any qualifying distributions received by the trustees, who are not treated as having paid income tax thereon (and the latter applies also to distributions other than qualifying distributions received by the trustees). See also 3.22 ANTI-AVOIDANCE as regards arrangements to pass on the value of a tax credit.

The liability of the trustees to account for tax deducted from annual payments treated as made by them, so far as not covered by tax deducted from income received, is reduced where there is a cumulative uncredited surplus of income on which they are chargeable to tax over such annual payments.

[*ICTA 1988, s 469; FA 1988, s 71; FA 1994, Sch 14 para 5; FA 1996, Sch 6 paras 12, 28, Sch 41 Pt V(1); FA 1997, s 80(5); F(No 2)A 1997, s 29, Sch 4 paras 4, 12*].

Pension fund pooling. Regulations which came into force on 11 July 1996 make special provision to ensure that certain international pooled pension funds (registered as 'pension fund pooling vehicles') are transparent for UK tax purposes, by disapplying the tax rules for unauthorised unit trusts (as above). Participants in such schemes must be approved by the Revenue, and are treated for income tax, capital allowances and capital gains tax purposes as though they themselves owned directly a share of each of the trust assets. There is also relief from stamp duty (or stamp duty reserve tax) on transfers of assets (other than land or buildings) by participants into the scheme. Participation in pension fund pooling vehicles is restricted to exempt approved pension schemes, UK-based superannuation funds used primarily by companies employing British expatriates working overseas, and pension funds established outside the UK broadly equivalent to UK exempt approved pension schemes. [*SI 1996 Nos 1583, 1584, 1585 as amended*]. See generally Revenue Inspector's Manual IM 4227–4227h. The position in the country in which any overseas participator is based will of course be crucial to the operation of such schemes.

Simon's Direct Tax Service. See D4.420.

90.3   **COURT COMMON INVESTMENT FUNDS**

Court common investment funds (CCIFs) are a form of unit trust set up by the Lord Chancellor under *Administration of Justice Act 1982, s 42(1)*. They are available only for individuals whose money is under control of certain Courts, e.g. road accident victims and the mentally incapacitated. As regards any income arising to a CCIF after 5 April 1999 and any distribution made for a distribution period beginning after that date, CCIFs are treated for tax purposes as authorised unit trusts within 90.1 above. The investment manager is treated as the trustee, and the persons with qualifying interests are treated as the unit holders. (Previously, CCIFs fell to be treated as unauthorised unit trusts within 90.2 above. For these purposes, a distribution period of a CCIF in existence on 5 April 1999 was deemed to have ended on that date, and its first accounting period and distribution period under the authorised unit trust regime were deemed to begin on 6 April 1999.) For the above purposes, the persons with qualifying interests are, in relation to shares in the fund held by the Accountant General (or other person authorised by the Lord Chancellor), the persons whose interests entitle them, as against him, to share in the fund's investments. In relation to income arising to a CCIF after 5 April 2003, they also include any persons authorised by the Lord Chancellor to hold shares in the fund on their own behalf. [*ICTA 1988, s 469A; FA 1999, s 68; FA 2003, s 183, Sch 43 Pt 3(17)*].

91   Venture Capital Trusts

Simon's Direct Tax Service C3.11, E3.6.

91.1   The venture capital trust scheme described at 91.2 *et seq.* below was introduced in 1995 to encourage individuals to invest in unquoted trading companies through such trusts. The provisions dealing with the approval of companies as venture capital trusts, and with the reliefs for investors, are introduced in *FA 1995, ss 70–72, Schs 14–16*. The Treasury has wide powers to make regulations governing all aspects of the reliefs applicable to venture capital trust investments, and for the requirements as regards returns, records and provision of information by the trust. [*FA 1995, s 73; FA 1996, Sch 18 paras 16, 17(1)(3); FA 2002, s 109, Sch 33 paras 14–16*]. See now *SI 1995 No 1979; SI 1999 No 819*.

See generally Revenue Venture Capital Schemes Manual VCM 10000–17320, 60000 *et seq.*

91.2   **CONDITIONS FOR APPROVAL** [*ICTA 1988, s 842AA; FA 1995, s 70; FA 1997, s 75; FA 1998, s 73(1)(6), Sch 27 Pt III(13); FA 1999, s 69(4)(5); FA 2002, s 109, Sch 25 para 57, Sch 33*]

A '*venture capital trust*' ('VCT') is a company approved for this purpose by the Board, close companies being excluded. The time from which an approval takes effect is specified in the approval, and may not be earlier than the time the application for approval was made.

Except as detailed further below, approval may not be given unless the Board are satisfied that the following conditions are met.

(*a*)   The company's income in its most recent complete accounting period has been derived wholly or mainly from shares or securities, and an amount greater than 15% of its income from shares and securities has not been retained.

(*b*)   Throughout that period at least 70% by value of the company's investments has been represented by shares or securities in 'qualifying holdings' (see 91.3 below), at least 30% of which (by value) has been represented by holdings of '*eligible shares*', i.e. ordinary shares carrying no present or future preferential right to dividends or to assets on a winding up and no present or future right (before 6 April 1998, present or future preferential right) to redemption.

(*c*)   The company's ordinary shares (or each class thereof) have been listed in the Official List of the Stock Exchange throughout that period.

(*d*)   No holding in any company other than a VCT (or a company which could be a VCT but for (*c*) above) has at any time in that period represented more than 15% of the value of the company's investments.

'Securities' for these purposes are deemed to include liabilities in respect of certain loans not repayable within five years, and any stocks or securities relating to which are not re-purchasable or redeemable within five years of issue. Provided that the loan is made on normal commercial terms, the Revenue will not regard a standard event of default clause in the loan agreement as disqualifying a loan from being a security for this purpose. If, however, the clause entitled the lender (or a third party) to exercise any action which would cause the borrower to default, the clause would not be regarded as 'standard'. (Revenue Pamphlet IR 131, SP 8/95, 14 September 1995).

As regards (*a*) and (*d*) above, the provisions which apply to the similar restrictions on investment trusts (see Tolley's Corporation Tax under Unit and Investment Trusts) apply modified as appropriate.

Where (a)–(d) above are met, the Board must also be satisfied that they will be met in the accounting period current at the time of application for approval. Where any of (a)–(d) above are not met, approval may nevertheless be given where the Board are satisfied as to the meeting of those conditions (and in certain cases other conditions imposed by regulations) in future accounting periods.

On a second and subsequent issues by an approved VCT, the requirements of condition (b) above similarly do not have to be met, in relation to the money raised by the further issue, in the accounting period of the further issue or any later accounting period ending no more than three years after the making of the further issue. For shares issued on or after 17 April 2002, the Treasury may make regulations to disapply this provision in specified cases or to apply it in specified cases only to a specified extent or only if specified conditions are met. The intention is to enable some of the money raised from an issue made as part of merger arrangements to be used to buy out those who do not wish to continue as members. (Treasury Explanatory Notes to Finance Bill 2002).

Where the 70% limit in (b) is breached inadvertently, and the position corrected without delay after discovery, approval will in practice not be withdrawn on this account. Full details of any such inadvertent breach should be disclosed to the Revenue as soon as it is discovered. (Revenue Press Release 14 September 1995).

The value of any investment for the purposes of (b) and (d) above is the value when the investment was acquired, except that where it is added to by a further holding of an investment of the same description, or a payment is made in discharge of any obligation attached to it which increases its value, it is the value immediately after the most recent such addition or payment.

Company restructuring and share conversions. With effect from 16 June 1999, certain transactions in shares held by a VCT are in effect disregarded in considering the value of holdings for the purposes of the 70%, 30% and 15% tests in (b) and (d) above. The transactions concerned are as follows.

(i)   Where, as part of a restructuring, shares or securities in a company are exchanged for corresponding shares and securities in a new holding company. Certain deemed securities (see above) which are not thus acquired by the new company may be disregarded where these provisions would otherwise be prevented from applying.

(ii)   Where a VCT exercises conversion rights in respect of certain convertible shares and securities.

In these circumstances, and subject to detailed conditions (see *ICTA 1988, Sch 28B paras 10C, 10D* introduced by *FA 1999, s 69*), the value of the new shares is taken to be the same as the value of the old shares when they were last valued for these purposes.

Where, after 20 March 2000 under a company reorganisation, takeover or scheme of reconstruction,

- a VCT exchanges a qualifying holding for other shares or securities (with or without other consideration), and

- the exchange is for *bona fide* commercial reasons and not part of a tax avoidance scheme or arrangements,

regulations provide a formula which values the new shares or securities, for the purposes of the 70%, 30% and 15% tests in (b) and (d) above, by reference to the proportion of the value of the old shares or securities that the market value of the new shares or securities bears to the total consideration receivable. If no other consideration is receivable, the value of the new is identical to that of the old. The provisions extend to new shares or securities received in pursuance of an earn-out right (see Tolley's Capital Gains Tax under Shares and Securities) conferred in exchange for a qualifying holding, in which case an election is available (under *Reg 10*) to modify the formula by effectively disregarding the earn-out right itself. [*SI 2002 No 2661*].

Approval may be **withdrawn** where there are reasonable grounds for believing that either:

(A)   the conditions for approval were not satisfied at the time the approval was given; or

(B)   a condition that the Board were satisfied (as above) would be met has not been or will not be met; or

(C)   in either the most recent complete accounting period or the current one, one of conditions (*a*)–(*d*) above has failed or will fail to be met (unless the failure was allowed for as above); or

(D)   where, in relation to a second or further issue by an approved VCT, (*b*) above does not have to be met in the period of issue or certain following accounting periods (see above), one of conditions (*a*)–(*d*) above will fail to be met in the first period for which (*b*) above must be met; or

(E)   any other conditions prescribed by regulations have not been met in relation to, or to part of, an accounting period for which (*b*) above does not have to be met.

The withdrawal is effective from the time the company is notified of it, except that:

(1)   where approval is given on the Board's being satisfied as to the meeting of the relevant conditions in future accounting periods, and is withdrawn before all the conditions (*a*)–(*d*) above have been satisfied in relation to either a complete twelve-month accounting period or successive complete accounting periods constituting a continuous period of twelve months or more, the approval is deemed never to have been given; and

(2)   for the purposes of relief for capital gains accruing to a VCT under *TCGA 1992, s 100* (see 91.11 below), withdrawal may be effective from an earlier date, but not before the start of the accounting period in which the failure occurred (or is expected to occur).

An assessment consequent on the withdrawal of approval may, where otherwise out of time, be made within three years from the time notice of the withdrawal was given.

For the detailed requirements as regards granting, refusal and withdrawal of approval, and appeals procedures, see *SI 1995 No 1979, Pt II.*

Mergers. For mergers (as defined) of two or more VCTs which take place after 16 April 2002, the Treasury may make regulations to enable the merging VCTs to retain VCT status and to provide for investors in the merged VCTs who continue as investors in the successor company (as defined) not to lose their tax reliefs. The regulations can apply only to mergers carried out for *bona fide* commercial reasons and which are not part of tax avoidance arrangements. [*FA 2002, Sch 33 Pt 2*].

Winding-up. The Treasury may make regulations to enable a VCT commencing winding-up after 16 April 2002 to retain its status as a VCT during the winding-up period (or a prescribed part of it) and to prescribe the time at which approval is to be treated as withdrawn. The intention is to provide a period of grace (expected to be two years) during which investors' reliefs may continue. This grace period will not, however, prevent a withdrawal of income tax investment relief (see 91.7 below), and the consequent crystallising of any deferred chargeable gain (see 91.14 below and Tolley's Capital Gains Tax), where the minimum holding period is not otherwise met. (Treasury Explanatory Notes to Finance Bill 2002).

The regulations may also permit a VCT-in-liquidation ('VCT1') to dispose of investments to another VCT ('VCT2') in consideration for shares in VCT2. In certain circumstances, such investments may be treated as meeting the requirements of a qualifying holding (see 91.3 below), and the conditions at (*a*)–(*d*) above treated as met, in relation to VCT2. Shares in VCT2 issued to, or distributed to, members of VCT1 may fall to be treated for the purposes of capital gains deferral relief (see 91.14 below) as if they were shares in VCT1.

In all cases, the winding-up must be for *bona fide* commercial reasons and not part of tax avoidance arrangements.

[*FA 2002, Sch 33 Pt 1*].

Simon's Direct Tax Service. See **E3.610** *et seq.*

91.3   **Qualifying holdings.** Shares or securities in a company are comprised in a VCT's '*qualifying holdings*' at any time if they were first issued to the VCT, and have been held by it ever since, and the following conditions are satisfied at that time.

(*a*)   The company is an '*unquoted company*' (whether or not UK resident), i.e. none of its shares, stocks, debentures or other securities is

    (i)   listed on a recognised stock exchange, or a designated exchange outside the UK, or

    (ii)   dealt in on the Unlisted Securities Market, or outside the UK by such means as may be designated for the purpose by order.

Securities on the Alternative Investment Market ('AIM') are treated as unquoted for these purposes. (Revenue Press Release 20 February 1995).

If the company ceases to be an unquoted company at a time when its shares are comprised in the qualifying holdings of the VCT, this condition is treated as continuing to be met, in relation to shares or securities acquired before that time, for the following five years.

(*b*)   Either

    (i)   the company must exist wholly for the purpose of carrying on one or more 'qualifying trades' (disregarding any purpose having no significant effect on the extent of its activities as a whole), or

    (ii)   it must be the 'parent company of a trading group'.

See also the related condition at (*ba*) below.

A trade is a '*qualifying trade*' if it meets the same conditions as apply in relation to the Enterprise Investment Scheme (EIS) (see 25.7 ENTERPRISE INVESTMENT SCHEME), but without the exclusion (before 7 March 2001) of oil extraction activities, and taking references to the 'relevant period' in relation to that scheme as references to the period since issue of the shares to the VCT. The exclusions that apply in relation to EIS shares issued after 16 March 1998 have effect for the purpose of determining whether any shares or securities are, as at any time after that date, to be regarded as comprised in the qualifying holdings of a VCT. However, those exclusions do not apply in relation to shares and securities acquired by the VCT by means of the investment of:

●   money raised by the issue before 17 March 1998 of shares in or securities of the VCT; or

●   money derived from the investment by the VCT of money so raised.

The changes in the rules concerning receipt of royalties and licence fees which apply in relation to EIS shares issued after 5 April 2000 also have effect for the purpose of determining whether shares or securities issued after that date are to be regarded as comprised in a VCT's qualifying holdings.

The definition of 'controlling interest' in relation to the above-mentioned conditions is also revised to permit holdings of non-voting fixed-rate preference shares, and rights as a loan creditor, to be disregarded. 'Research and development' from which it is intended that there will be derived a qualifying trade carried on 'wholly or mainly in the UK' is treated as the carrying on of a qualifying trade. For the purpose of determining whether shares or securities issued after 5 April 2000 are to be regarded as comprised in a VCT's qualifying holdings, '*research and development*' has the meaning given by *ICTA 1988, s 837A* (see 71.70 SCHEDULE D, CASES I AND II and note that the latest DTI guidelines issued on 5 March 2004 have no effect in relation to shares or securities issued before 6 April 2004). Previously, it meant any activity intended to result in a patentable invention (within *Patents Act 1977*) or in a computer program.

In considering whether a trade is carried on '*wholly or mainly in the UK*', the totality of the trade activities is taken into account. Regard will be had, for example, to where capital assets are held, where any purchasing, processing, manufacturing and selling is done, and where the company employees and other agents are engaged in its trading operations. For trades involving the provision of services, both the location of the activities giving rise to the services and the location where they are delivered will be relevant. No one factor is itself likely to be decisive in any particular case. A company may carry on some such activities outside the UK and yet satisfy the requirement, provided that the major part of them, that is over one-half of the aggregate of these activities, takes place within the UK. Thus relief is not excluded solely because a company's products or services are exported, or because its raw materials are imported, or because its raw materials or products are stored abroad. Similar principles apply in considering the trade(s) carried on by a company and its qualifying subsidiaries.

In the particular case of a ship chartering trade, the test is satisfied if all charters are entered into in the UK and the provision of crews and management of the ships while under charter take place mainly in the UK. If these conditions are not met, the test may still be satisfied depending on all the relevant facts and circumstances.

(Revenue Pamphlet IR 131, SP 3/00, 3 August 2000).

A company is the '*parent company of a trading group*' if it has one or more subsidiaries, each of which is a 'qualifying subsidiary' (see below), and if, taking all the activities of the company and its subsidiaries as one business, neither that business nor a substantial part of it (i.e. broadly 20% — see Revenue Venture Capital Schemes Manual VCM 17040) consists in either or both of:

(*aa*)   activities within 25.7(*a*)–(*c*)(*e*)–(*m*) ENTERPRISE INVESTMENT SCHEME (other than those within 25.7(*e*) which do not result in a trade being excluded from being a qualifying trade); and

(*bb*)   non-trading activities.

To the extent that the activities in (*aa*) above apply for EIS purposes in relation to shares issued after 16 March 1998 (see 25.7), they have effect for VCT purposes as described above under the definition of 'qualifying trade'.

Activities are for these purposes disregarded to the extent that they consist in:

(AA)   holding shares in or securities of, or making loans to, one or more of the company's subsidiaries; or

(BB)   holding and managing property used by the company or any of its subsidiaries for the purposes of either

(i)   'research and development' (see above) from which it is intended that a qualifying trade to be carried on by the company or any of its subsidiaries will be derived, or

(ii)   one or more qualifying trades so carried on.

Activities of a subsidiary are similarly disregarded to the extent that they consist in the making of loans to the company or, where the subsidiary exists wholly for the purpose of carrying on one or more qualifying trades (apart from '*insignificant purposes*', i.e. purposes capable of having no significant effect, other than in relation to incidental matters, on the extent of the subsidiary's activities), of activities carried on in pursuance of those insignificant purposes.

A subsidiary is a '*qualifying subsidiary*' of the issuing company if the following conditions are satisfied in relation to that subsidiary and every other subsidiary of the issuing company.

(1)   In relation to shares or securities issued to the VCT **after 16 March 2004**. The subsidiary must be a **51%** subsidiary (see *ICTA 1988, s 838*) of the issuing company and no person other than the issuing company or another of its subsidiaries may have control (within *ICTA 1988, s 840* — see 19.8 CONNECTED PERSONS) of the subsidiary. Furthermore, no arrangements may exist by virtue of which either of these conditions would cease to be satisfied.

The above conditions are not regarded as ceasing to be satisfied by reason only of the subsidiary or any other company being in the process of being wound up or by reason only of anything done as a consequence of its being in administration or receivership, provided the winding-up, entry into administration or receivership or anything done as a consequence of its being in administration or receivership is for *bona fide* commercial reasons and is not part of a tax avoidance scheme or arrangements.

(2)   In relation to shares or securities issued to the VCT **on or before 16 March 2004**. The issuing company, or another of its subsidiaries, must possess at least **75%** of the issued share capital of, and the voting power in, the subsidiary, and be beneficially entitled to at least **75%** of the assets available for distribution to equity holders on a winding-up etc. (see *ICTA 1988, Sch 18 paras 1, 3*) and of the profits available for distribution to equity holders. No other person may have control (within *ICTA 1988, s 840* — see 19.8 CONNECTED PERSONS) of the subsidiary. Furthermore, no arrangements may exist by virtue of which any of these conditions could cease to be satisfied. A subsidiary does not fail these conditions by reason only of the fact that it is being wound up, provided that the winding-up is for *bona fide* commercial reasons and not part of a tax avoidance scheme or arrangements.

The conditions at (1) or (2) above are not regarded as ceasing to be satisfied by reason only of arrangements being in existence for the disposal of the interest in the subsidiary held by the issuing company (or, as the case may be, by another of its subsidiaries) if the disposal is to be for *bona fide* commercial reasons and is not to be part of a tax avoidance scheme or arrangements.

(*ba*)   In relation to shares or securities issued to the VCT **after 16 March 2004**, a 'qualifying company' (whether or not the same such company at all times) must, when the shares were issued to the VCT and at all times since, have been either

●   carrying on a 'qualifying trade' (see (*b*) above) 'wholly or mainly in the UK' (see (*b*) above); or

- preparing to carry on a qualifying trade which, at the time the shares were issued, was intended to be carried on wholly or mainly in the UK;

but the second of these conditions is relevant only for a period of two years after the issue of the shares, by which time the intended trade must have been commenced by a 'qualifying company', and ceases to be relevant at any time within those two years after the intention is abandoned.

For these purposes, '*qualifying company*' means the issuing company itself or any 'relevant qualifying subsidiary' of that company. (In determining the time at which a qualifying trade begins to be carried on by a 'relevant qualifying subsidiary', any carrying on of the trade by it before it became such a subsidiary is disregarded.)

In relation to shares or securities issued to a VCT after 16 March 2004, a company (the subsidiary) is a '*relevant qualifying subsidiary*' of the issuing company at any time when

- the issuing company possesses at least **90%** of both the issued share capital of, and the voting power in, the subsidiary;

- the issuing company would be beneficially entitled to at least **90%** of the assets of the subsidiary available for distribution to equity holders on a winding-up or in any other circumstances;

- the issuing company is beneficially entitled to at least **90%** of any profits of the subsidiary available for distribution to equity holders;

- no person other than the issuing company has control (within *ICTA 1988, s 840* — see 19.8 CONNECTED PERSONS) of the subsidiary; and

- no arrangements exist by virtue of which any of the above conditions would cease to be met.

For the above purposes, *ICTA 1988, Sch 18 paras 1, 3* apply, with appropriate modifications, to determine the persons who are equity holders and the percentage of assets available to them. The above conditions are not regarded as failing to be satisfied by reason only of the subsidiary or any other company having commenced winding up or by reason only of anything done as a consequence of any such company being in administration or receivership, provided the winding-up, entry into administration or receivership (both as defined) or anything done as a consequence of its being in administration or receivership is for *bona fide* commercial reasons and is not part of a tax avoidance scheme or arrangements. Also, the above conditions are not regarded as ceasing to be satisfied by reason only of arrangements being in existence for the disposal of the issuing company's interest in the subsidiary if the disposal is to be for *bona fide* commercial reasons and is not to be part of a tax avoidance scheme or arrangements.

In relation to shares or securities issued to the VCT **on or before 16 March 2004**, the issuing company or a 'relevant qualifying subsidiary' must, when the shares were issued to the VCT and at all times since, have been either

- carrying on a qualifying trade wholly or mainly in the UK; or

- preparing to carry on a qualifying trade which, at the time the shares were issued, it intended to carry on wholly or mainly in the UK;

but the second of these conditions is relevant only for a period of two years after the issue of the shares, by which time the trade must have commenced as intended, and ceases to be relevant at any time within those two years after the intention is abandoned. For this purpose, a '*relevant qualifying subsidiary*' is, broadly, a company which is 90% owned by the issuing company (or by a subsidiary of the issuing company) and which otherwise satisfies the conditions of *ICTA 1988, Sch 28B para 10* (as amended prior to *FA 2004*).

(*c*)   The money raised by the issue of shares to the VCT must be employed *wholly* (disregarding insignificant amounts) for the purposes of the qualifying trade. At any time within 12 months after the issue (or after the date of commencement of the qualifying trade where this is later than the date of issue) this condition is treated as satisfied if at least 80% of that money has been, or is intended to be, so employed. At any time within the following 12 months, the condition is treated as satisfied if at least 80% of that money *has been* so employed. Money used for the purposes of *preparing* to carry on a trade is treated as used for the purposes of the trade. The above rules apply for the purpose of determining whether any shares or securities are, as at any time after 6 March 2001, to be regarded as comprised in the qualifying holdings of the VCT. Previously, the condition was treated as satisfied at any time within the first 12-month period if *all* the money was intended to be so employed, and no special treatment applied in the following 12 months.

Money whose retention can reasonably be regarded as necessary or advisable for financing current business requirements is regarded as employed for trade purposes (Revenue Venture Capital Schemes Manual VCM 12080, 62150–62153).

In relation to shares or securities issued to the VCT **after 16 March 2004**, the above requirements as to money employed are *not* regarded as satisfied if either the required qualifying trade or (where relevant — see (*ba*) above) any preparations for that trade are carried on, at any time after the issue of the shares, by a person other than the issuing company or a 'relevant qualifying subsidiary' (within (*ba*) above) of that company. Where any such preparations are carried on the issuing company or a relevant qualifying subsidiary at any time following the issue of the shares, the fact that the trade may previously have been carried on by another person is disregarded for this purpose. The carrying on of the trade by a partnership of which the issuing company or a relevant qualifying subsidiary is a member, or by a joint venture to which any such company is a party, is permitted.

The condition immediately above is not regarded as failing to be met if, by reason only of a company being wound up or dissolved or being in administration or receivership (both as defined), the qualifying trade ceases to be carried on by the issuing company' or a relevant qualifying 90% subsidiary and is subsequently carried on by a person who has not been connected (within *ICTA 1988, s 839* — see 19 CONNECTED PERSONS — but with the modifications mentioned in (*f*) below) with the issuing company at any time in the period beginning one year before the shares were issued. This let-out applies only if the winding-up, dissolution or entry into administration or receivership (and everything done as a consequence of the company being in administration or receivership) is for *bona fide* commercial reasons and not part of a tax avoidance scheme or arrangements.

In relation to shares or securities issued to the VCT **on or before 16 March 2004**, where the company is a 'parent company of a trading group' within (*b*)(ii) above, the '*trader company*' (i.e. the company carrying on (or preparing to carry on) the required qualifying trade) must either:

(i)   satisfy the requirements in (*b*)(i) above; or

(ii)   be a company in relation to which those requirements would be satisfied if activities within (*b*)(AA) or (*b*)(BB) above, or consisting of a subsidiary making loans to its parent, were disregarded; or

(iii)   be a 'relevant qualifying subsidiary' which either

(1)   exists wholly for the purpose of carrying on activities within (*b*)(BB) above (disregarding purposes capable of having no significant effect (other than in relation to incidental matters) on the extent of its activities), or

(2)   has no corporation tax profits and no part of its business consists in the making of investments.

A '*relevant qualifying subsidiary*' is, broadly, a company which is 90% owned by the investee company (or by a subsidiary of that company) and which otherwise satisfies the conditions of *ICTA 1988, Sch 28B para 10* (as amended prior to *FA 2004*).

(*d*)   The aggregate of money raised from shares issued by the company to the VCT must not have exceeded the 'maximum qualifying investment' of £1 million in the period from six months before the issue in question (or, if earlier, the beginning of the year of assessment of the issue) to the time of the issue in question. Disposals are treated as far as possible as eliminating any such excess. The £1 million limit is proportionately reduced where, at the time of the issue, the qualifying trade is carried on, or to be carried on, in partnership or as a joint venture, and one or more of the other parties is a company.

(*e*)   The value of the company's 'relevant assets' did not exceed £15 million immediately before the issue or £16 million immediately thereafter. As regards shares and securities issued by investee companies before 6 April 1998, these limits were £10 million and £11 million respectively. '*Relevant assets*' are the gross assets of the company and, at any time when it has one or more qualifying subsidiaries, of all such subsidiaries. In the latter case, assets consisting in rights against, or shares in or securities of, another member of the group consisting of the company and its qualifying subsidiaries are disregarded.

The general approach of the Revenue is that the value of a company's gross assets is the sum of the value of all the balance sheet assets. Where accounts are actually drawn up to a date immediately before or after the issue, the balance sheet values are taken provided that they reflect usual accounting standards and the company's normal accounting practice, consistently applied. Where accounts are not drawn up to such a date, such values will be taken from the most recent balance sheet, updated as precisely as practicable on the basis of all the relevant information available to the company. Values so arrived at may need to be reviewed in the light of information contained in the accounts for the period in which the issue was made, and, if they were not available at the time of the issue, those for the preceding period, when they become available. The company's assets immediately before the issue do not include any advance payment received in respect of the issue. Where shares are issued partly paid, the right to the balance is an asset, and, notwithstanding the above, will be taken into account in valuing the assets immediately after the issue regardless of whether it is stated in the balance sheet. (Revenue Pamphlet IR 131, SP 2/00, 3 August 2000).

(*f*)   The company must not 'control' (with or without 'connected persons') any company other than a 'qualifying subsidiary' (see (*b*) above), nor must another company (or another company and a person connected with it) control it. Neither must arrangements be in existence by virtue of which such control could arise. For these purposes, '*control*' is as under *ICTA 1988, s 416*, except that possession of, or entitlement to acquire, fixed-rate preference shares (as defined) of the company which do not, for the time being, carry voting rights is disregarded, as is possession of, or entitlement to acquire, rights as a loan creditor of the company. '*Connected persons*' are as under *ICTA 1988, s 839* (see 19 CONNECTED PERSONS) except that the definition of 'control' therein is similarly modified. For the application of the 'control' test to co-investors in a company, and in particular the question of whether co-investors are connected by virtue of their 'acting together to secure or exercise control' of the company, see Revenue Tax Bulletin October 1997 pp 471, 472.

(*g*) Where the company is being wound up, none of the conditions listed here are regarded on that account as not being satisfied provided that those conditions would be met apart from the winding up, and that the winding up is for *bona fide* commercial reasons and is not part of a scheme or arrangement a main purpose of which is the avoidance of tax. After 20 March 2000, the company does not cease to meet condition (*b*) or (*ba*) above by reason only of anything done as a consequence of its being in administration or receivership (both as defined), provided everything so done and the making of the relevant order are for *bona fide* commercial (and not tax avoidance) reasons.

(*h*) The holding in question must not include any securities (as defined in 91.2 above) relating to a guaranteed loan. A security relates to a guaranteed loan if there are arrangements entitling the VCT to receive anything (directly or indirectly) from a 'third party' in the event of a failure by any person to comply with the terms of the security or the loan to which it relates. It is immaterial whether or not the arrangements apply in all such cases. '*Third party*' includes any person other than the investee company itself and, if it is a parent company of a trading group (see (*b*) above), its subsidiaries. This condition applies for accounting periods (of the VCT) ending after 1 July 1997, but does not apply in the case of shares or securities acquired by the VCT by means of investing money raised by the issue by it before 2 July 1997 of shares or securities (or money derived from the investment of any such money raised).

(*j*) At least 10% (by value) of the VCT's *total* holding of shares in and securities of the company must consist of 'eligible shares' (as defined in 91.2(*b*) above — broadly, ordinary, non-preferential, shares). For this purpose, the value of shares etc. at any time is taken to be their value immediately after the most recent of the events listed below, except that it cannot thereby be taken to be less than the amount of consideration given by the VCT for the shares etc. The said events are as follows.

   (i)   The acquisition of the shares etc. by the VCT.

   (ii) The acquisition by the VCT (other than by way of bonus issue for no consideration) of any other shares etc. in the same company which are of the same description as those already held.

   (iii) The making of any payment in discharge (or part discharge) of any obligation attached to the shares etc. in a case where such discharge increases the value of the shares etc.

   This condition applies for accounting periods (of the VCT) ending after 1 July 1997, but, if necessary in order to satisfy the condition, one may disregard shares and securities acquired by the VCT by means of investing money raised by the issue by it before 2 July 1997 of shares or securities (or money derived from the investment of any such money raised).

(*k*) In relation to shares or securities issued to the VCT **after 16 March 2004**, the company must not have a 'property managing subsidiary' which is not a 'relevant qualifying subsidiary' (see (*ba*) above) of the company. A '*property managing subsidiary*' is a qualifying subsidiary (see (*b*) above) whose business consists wholly or mainly in the holding or managing of 'land' or any 'property deriving its value from land' (both as defined in *ICTA 1988, s 776* (see 3.10 ANTI-AVOIDANCE).

91.3 Venture Capital Trusts

As regards (c) and (d) above, where either condition would be met as to only part of the money raised by the issue, and the holding is not otherwise capable of being treated as separate holdings, it is treated as two separate holdings, one from which that part of the money was raised, the other from which the rest was raised, with the value being apportioned accordingly to each holding. In the case of (c), this does not require an insignificant amount applied for non-trade purposes to be treated as a separate holding.

As regards (c) above, in relation to buy-outs (and in particular management buy-outs), the Revenue will usually accept that where a company is formed to acquire a trade, and the funds raised from the VCT are applied to that purchase, the requirement that the funds be employed for the purposes of the trade is satisfied. Where the company is formed to acquire another company and its trade, or a holding company and its trading subsidiaries, this represents an investment rather than employment for the purposes of the trade. However, the Revenue will usually accept that the requirement is satisfied if the trade of the company, or all the activities of the holding company and its subsidiaries, are hived up to the acquiring company as soon as possible after the acquisition. In the case of a holding company and its subsidiaries, to the extent that the trades are not hived up, the holding cannot be a qualifying holding. (Revenue Tax Bulletin August 1995 pp 243, 244).

As regards (b)–(f) and (j) above, with effect from 16 June 1999, certain transactions in shares held by a VCT are in effect disregarded in considering whether the relevant condition is satisfied. The transactions concerned are as follows.

(A)   Where, as part of a restructuring, shares or securities in a company are exchanged for corresponding shares and securities in a new holding company. Certain deemed securities (see 91.2 above) which are not thus acquired by the new company may be disregarded where these provisions would otherwise be prevented from applying.

(B)   Where a VCT exercises conversion rights in respect of certain convertible shares and securities.

In these circumstances, and subject to detailed conditions (see *ICTA 1988, Sch 28B paras 10C, 10D* introduced by *FA 1999, s 69*), to the extent that the condition was satisfied in relation to the old shares, it will generally be taken to be satisfied in relation to the new shares.

Where, after 20 March 2000 under a company reorganisation, takeover or scheme of reconstruction,

• a VCT exchanges a qualifying holding for other shares or securities (with or without other consideration), and

• the exchange is for *bona fide* commercial reasons and not part of a tax avoidance scheme or arrangements,

the new shares or securities may be treated as being qualifying holdings for a specified period even if some or all of the above requirements are not otherwise satisfied. Regulations specify the circumstances in which, and conditions subject to which, they apply and which requirements are to be treated as met. Where the new shares or securities are those of a different company than before and they do not meet any one or more of the above requirements (disregarding (c) and (d)), those requirements are treated as met for, broadly, three years in the case of shares or five years in the case of securities, reduced in either case to, broadly, two years where the company is not, or ceases to be, an unquoted company as in (a) above. A formula is provided for valuing the new shares or securities for the purposes of (j) above. The provisions extend to new shares or securities received in pursuance of an earn-out right (see Tolley's Capital Gains Tax under Shares and Securities) conferred in exchange for a qualifying holding, in which case an election is available (under *Reg 10*) to modify the said valuation formula by effectively disregarding the earn-out right itself. [*SI 2002 No 2661*].

The Treasury have power by order to modify the requirements of (*b*) and (*ba*) above as they consider expedient, and to alter the cash limits referred to in (*d*) and (*e*) above.

[*ICTA 1988, s 842AA(5AD)(5AE)(13), Sch 28B; FA 1995, Sch 14; FA 1996, s 161; F(No 2)A 1997, s 25; FA 1998, s 70(1)(3), s 72, s 73(2)–(6), Sch 12 paras 3, 4, 5(2)(3); FA 1999, s 69(2)(3)(5); FA 2000, Sch 18 paras 4–8; FA 2001, Sch 16 paras 1, 2; FA 2004, Sch 19 paras 8–16, Sch 27 para 5*].

Informal clearance. Enquiries from companies as to whether they meet the conditions for investment by a venture capital trust should be directed to Small Company Enterprise Centre, TIDO, Ty Glas, Llanishen, Cardiff CF14 5ZG (tel. 029–2032 7400; fax 029–2032 7398; e-mail enterprise.centre@ir.gsi.gov.uk).

Simon's Direct Tax Service. See E3.620 *et seq.*

91.4   INCOME TAX RELIEFS [*ICTA 1988, s 332A, Sch 15B; FA 1995, s 71, Sch 15*]

Relief from income tax is granted in respect of both investments in VCTs and distributions from such trusts.

91.5   Relief in respect of investments. Subject to the conditions described below, an individual may claim relief ('investment relief') for a tax year for the amount (or aggregate amounts) subscribed by him on his own behalf for 'eligible shares' issued to him in the tax year by a VCT (or VCTs) for raising money. There is a limit of £200,000 (£100,000 for 2003/04 and earlier years) on the amount in respect of which relief can be claimed for any one tax year.

'*Eligible shares*' means new ordinary shares in a VCT which, throughout the three years following issue (five years for shares issued before 6 April 2000), carry no present or future preferential right to dividends or to assets on a winding up and no present or future right (before 6 April 1998, present or future preferential right) to redemption.

Relief is given by a reduction in what would otherwise be the individual's income tax liability for the tax year by whichever is the smaller of the following:

(i)   (for shares issued in 2004/05 and 2005/06 only) tax at the higher rate (40%) on the amount eligible for relief;

(ii)   (for shares issued in any tax year other than 2004/05 or 2005/06) tax at the lower rate (currently 20%) on the amount eligible for relief;

(iii) (for all years) such amount as reduces that income tax liability to nil.

The income tax reduction under these provisions is made in priority to any of the following:

(A)   an income tax reduction due in respect of personal reliefs (see 1.15, 1.16, 1.17, 1.18 ALLOWANCES AND TAX RATES) or qualifying maintenance payments (see 47.8 MARRIED PERSONS);

(B)   an income tax reduction due in respect of interest relief (see 43.5 INTEREST PAYABLE);

(C)   an income tax reduction due in respect of medical insurance (see 48.1 MEDICAL INSURANCE);

(D)   an income tax reduction due in respect of EIS investments (see 25.8 ENTERPRISE INVESTMENT SCHEME);

(E)   an income tax reduction due in respect of COMMUNITY INVESTMENT TAX RELIEF (17);

(F)   a reduction of liability to tax by way of DOUBLE TAX RELIEF (24).

In determining the individual's income tax liability from which the reduction under this chapter is to be made, no account is taken of any basic rate tax on income the tax on which the individual is entitled to charge against any other person or to deduct, retain or satisfy out of any payment. This includes any basic rate tax deemed to have been deducted at source from a charitable donation made after 5 April 2000 under the Gift Aid scheme (see 14.12 CHARITIES). Any such basic rate tax cannot, therefore, be extinguished by income tax relief on VCT investments.

An individual is **not** entitled to relief where:

(*a*)   he was under 18 years of age at the time of issue of the shares;

(*b*)   circumstances have arisen which, had the relief already been given, would have resulted in the withdrawal or reduction of the relief (see 91.7 below);

(*c*)   the shares were issued or subscribed for other than for *bona fide* commercial purposes or as part of a scheme or arrangement a main purpose of which was the avoidance of tax; or

(*d*)   a loan is made to the individual (or to an 'associate' within *ICTA 1988, s 417*, but excluding a brother or sister) by any person at any time in the period beginning with the incorporation of the VCT (or, if later, two years before the date of issue of the shares) and ending three years after the date of issue of the shares (five years for shares issued before 6 April 2000), and the loan would not have been made, or would not have been made on the same terms, if he had not subscribed, or had not been proposing to subscribe, for the shares. The granting of credit to, or the assignment of a debt due from, the individual or associate is counted as a loan for these purposes.

An individual is *not* eligible for relief by reference to any shares *treated as* issued to him by virtue of *FA 2003, s 195(8)*, which provides for a disposal to a person by a company of its own shares (so-called 'treasury shares') to be treated as a new issue of shares and for the recipient to be treated as having subscribed for them. In such a case, the VCT must, at the time the shares are issued, give the individual a notice stating that he is not eligible for relief, and must copy that notice to the Revenue within three months after the issue.

[*ICTA 1988, Sch 15B paras 1, 2, 6; FA 1990, s 25(6)(b)(7); FA 1995, Sch 15 paras 1, 2, 6; FA 1998, s 73(1)(6), Sch 27 Pt III(13); FA 2000, s 39(6)(10), Sch 18 paras 1(2)(4), 3; FA 2001, Sch 16 para 3; FA 2002, s 57, Sch 17 para 3; FA 2003, s 195(10)(12), Sch 40 para 1; FA 2004, s 94(1), Sch 19 paras 1, 3; SI 2003 No 3077*].

As regards (*d*) above, for this restriction to apply, the test is whether the lender makes the loan on terms which are connected with the fact that the borrower (or an associate) is subscribing for eligible shares. The prime concern is why the lender made the loan rather than why the borrower applied for it. Relief would not be disallowed, for example, in the case of a bank loan if the bank would have made a loan on the same terms to a similar borrower for a different purpose. But if, for example, a loan is made specifically on a security consisting of or including the eligible shares (other than as part of a broad range of assets to which the lender has recourse), relief would be denied. Relevant features of the loan terms would be the qualifying conditions to be satisfied by the borrower, any incentives or benefits offered to the borrower, the time allowed for repayment, the amount of repayments and interest charged, the timing of interest payments, and the nature of the security. (Revenue Pamphlet IR 131, SP 6/98, 30 November 1998, replacing SP 3/94, 9 May 1994, as revised).

An individual subscribing for eligible shares may obtain from the VCT a certificate giving details of the subscription and certifying that certain conditions for relief are satisfied. [*SI 1995 No 1979, reg 9*].

Relief for a year can only be claimed after the end of the year, and any in-year claims for relief by repayment through self-assessment will be rejected. This does not affect the right to claim a reduction in payments on account (see 78.4 SELF-ASSESSMENT), and relief may still be given through a PAYE (55) coding. (Revenue Tax Bulletin April 2002 p 924).

Simon's Direct Tax Service. See E3.641.

91.6   *Example*

On 1 May 2004, Miss K, who has annual earnings of £75,000, subscribes for 80,000 eligible £1 shares issued at par to raise money by VCT plc, an approved venture capital trust. On 1 September 2004 she purchases a further 180,000 £1 shares in VCT plc for £140,000 on the open market. The trust makes no distribution in 2004/05. Miss K's other income for 2004/05 consists of dividends of £16,200. PAYE tax deducted is £22,207.60.

Miss K's tax computation for 2004/05 is as follows.

	£	£
Earnings		75,000
Dividends	16,200	
Add Tax credit	1,800	18,000
Total income		93,000
Deduct Personal allowance		4,745
Taxable income		£88,255
Tax payable:		
2,020@ 10% (starting rate)		202.00
29,380@ 22%		6,463.60
38,855@ 40%		15,542.00
18,000@ 32.5% (Schedule F upper rate)		5,850.00
		28,057.60
Deduct Relief for investment in VCT plc: 40% of £80,000 subscribed = £32,000		
but restricted to		28,057.60
Net tax payable		—

PAYE tax of £22,207.60 is repayable. Dividend tax credits are not repayable for 1999/2000 onwards.

91.7   **Withdrawal of investment relief.** *Disposal of investment.* Where an individual disposes of eligible shares, in respect of which relief has been claimed as under 91.5 above, within three years of their issue (five years for shares issued before 6 April 2000) and other than to a spouse when they are living together (see below), then:

(*a*)   if the disposal is otherwise than at arm's length, relief given by reference to those shares is withdrawn;

(b)   if the disposal is at arm's length, the relief given by reference to those shares is reduced by an amount equivalent to tax at the lower rate (for the year for which relief was given) on the consideration received for the disposal (or withdrawn if the relief exceeds that amount). Where the year for which relief was given was 2004/05 or 2005/06, the maximum reduction is by an amount equivalent to tax at the *higher* rate (for whichever of those years is the year in question) on that consideration (see rates of relief at 91.5 above).

Relief is **not** withdrawn where the disposal is by one spouse to the other at a time when they are living together. However, on any subsequent disposal the spouse to whom the shares were transferred is treated as if he or she were the person who subscribed for the shares, as if the shares had been issued to him or her at the time they were issued to the transferor spouse, and as if his or her liability to income tax had been reduced by reference to those shares by the same amount, and for the same year of assessment, as applied on the subscription by the transferor spouse. Any assessment for reducing or withdrawing relief is made on the transferee spouse.

Identification of shares. For the above purposes, disposals of eligible shares in a VCT are identified with those acquired earlier rather than later. As between eligible shares acquired on the same day, shares by reference to which relief has been given are treated as disposed of after any other eligible shares.

Withdrawal of approval. Where approval of a company as a VCT is withdrawn (but not treated as never having been given) (see 91.2 above), relief given by reference to eligible shares in the VCT is withdrawn as if on a non-arm's length disposal immediately before the withdrawal of approval.

Assessments withdrawing or reducing relief, whether because relief is subsequently found not to have been due or under the above provisions, are made under SCHEDULE D, CASE VI (74) for the year of assessment for which the relief was given. No such assessment is, however, to be made by reason of an event occurring after the death of the person to whom the shares were issued.

Information. Particulars of all events leading to the reduction or withdrawal of relief must be notified to the inspector by the person to whom the relief was given within 60 days of his coming to know of the event. Where the inspector has reason to believe that a notice so required has not been given, he may require that person to furnish him, within a specified time not being less than 60 days, with such information relating to the event as he may reasonably require. The requirements of secrecy do not prevent the inspector disclosing to a VCT that relief has been given or claimed by reference to a particular number or proportion of its shares. Penalties under *TMA 1970, s 98* apply for failure to comply with these requirements.

[*ICTA 1988, Sch 15B paras 3–5; FA 1995, s 71(3), Sch 15 paras 3–5; FA 2000, Sch 18 paras 1(3), 3; FA 2004, s 94(2)*].

Simon's Direct Tax Service. See E3.642.

91.8   *Example*

On 1 May 2006, Miss K in the *Example* at 91.6 above, who has since 2004/05 neither acquired nor disposed of any further shares in VCT plc, gives 50,000 shares to her son. On 1 January 2007, she disposes of the remaining 210,000 shares for £170,000. The relief given as in 91.6 above is withdrawn as follows.

Disposal on 1 May 2006

The shares disposed of are identified, on a first in/first out basis, with 50,000 of those subscribed for, and, since the disposal was not at arm's length, the relief given on those shares is withdrawn.

$£$

Relief withdrawn $\dfrac{50,000}{80,000} \times 28,057$ 17,536

Disposal on 1 January 2007

The balance of $£10,521$ of the relief originally given was in respect of 30,000 of the shares disposed of. The disposal consideration for those 30,000 shares is

$$170,000 \times \dfrac{30,000}{210,000} = £24,286$$

The relief withdrawn is the lesser of the relief originally given ($£10,521$) and 40% of the consideration received, i.e. 40% of $£24,286 = £9,714$

Relief withdrawn is therefore   9,714

The 2004/05 Schedule D, Case VI assessment is therefore $£27,250$

91.9   **Relief on distributions.** A 'relevant distribution' of a VCT to which a 'qualifying investor' is beneficially entitled is not treated as income for income tax purposes, provided that certain conditions are fulfilled as regards the obtaining of an 'enduring declaration' from the investor, and that the VCT claims the related tax credit, which it is required to pass on to the investor.

A *'qualifying investor'* is an individual aged 18 or over who is beneficially entitled to the distribution either as the holder of the shares or through a nominee (including the trustees of a bare trust).

A *'relevant distribution'* is a dividend (including a capital dividend) in respect of ordinary shares in a company which is a VCT which were acquired at a time when it was a VCT by the recipient of the dividend, and which were not shares acquired in excess of the 'permitted maximum' for the year. Shares acquired after 8 March 1999 must also have been acquired for *bona fide* commercial purposes and not as part of a tax avoidance scheme or arrangements. A relevant distribution does not include any dividend paid in respect of profits or gains of any accounting period ending when the company was not a VCT.

Shares are acquired in excess of the *'permitted maximum'* for a year where the aggregate value of ordinary shares acquired in VCTs by the individual or his nominee(s) in that year exceeds **£200,000** (£100,000 for 2003/04 and earlier years), disregarding shares acquired other than for *bona fide* commercial reasons or as part of a scheme or arrangement a main purpose of which is the avoidance of tax. Shares acquired later in the year are identified as representing the excess before those acquired earlier, and in relation to same-day acquisition of different shares, a proportionate part of each description of share is treated as representing any excess arising on that day. Shares acquired at a time when a company was not a VCT are for these purposes treated as disposed of before other shares in the VCT. Otherwise, disposals are identified with earlier acquisitions before later ones, except that as between shares acquired on the same day, shares acquired in excess of the permitted maximum are treated as disposed of before any other shares. There are provisions for effectively disregarding acquisitions arising out of share exchanges where, for capital gains purposes, the new shares are treated as the same assets as the old.

[*ICTA 1988, Sch 15B paras 7–9; FA 1995, Sch 15 paras 7–9; FA 1999, s 70; FA 2004, Sch 19 paras 2, 3; SI 1995 No 1979, reg 10*].

For the detailed requirements as regards obtaining relief for distributions before 6 April 1999, including the obtaining of the 'enduring declaration' and the claiming of tax credits, see *SI 1995 No 1979, regs 10–21*. For distributions on or after that date, entitlement to tax credits on qualifying distributions is limited to individuals chargeable to tax on the distributions (see 1.9 ALLOWANCES AND TAX RATES), and those *regulations* are revoked.

Simon's Direct Tax Service. See E3.643 *et seq.*

91.10   *Example*

In 2005/06, Miss K in the *Example* at 91.6 above, whose circumstances are otherwise unchanged, receives a distribution from VCT plc of 9p per share.

The shares in VCT plc were acquired in 2004/05 for £220,000, so that distributions in respect of shares representing the £20,000 excess over the permitted maximum of £200,000 are not exempt. The 80,000 shares first acquired for £80,000 are first identified, so that the shares representing the excess are one-seventh (20,000/140,000) of the 180,000 shares subsequently acquired for £140,000, i.e. 25,714 of those shares.

Miss K's tax computation for 2005/06 (assuming no changes in rates and allowances since 2004/05) is as follows.

	£	£
Earnings		75,000
Dividends (other than VCT plc)	16,200	
Add Tax credit	1,800	18,000
VCT plc distribution in respect		
of 25,714 shares	2,314	
Add Tax credit ($\frac{1}{9}$)	257	2,571
Total income		95,571
Deduct Personal allowance		4,745
Taxable income		£90,826
Tax payable:		
2,020 @ 10% (starting rate)		202.00
29,380 @ 22%		6,463.60
38,855 @ 40%		15,542.00
20,571 @ 32.5% (Schedule F upper rate)		6,685.57
Tax payable		28,893.17
Deduct Tax credits		2,057.10
Net tax liability (subject to PAYE)		£26,836.07

91.11   **CAPITAL GAINS TAX RELIEFS** [*TCGA 1992, ss 151A, 151B, Sch 5C; FA 1995, s 72, Sch 16*]

The capital gains of a VCT are not chargeable gains. [*TCGA 1992, s 100(1); FA 1995, s 72(2)*]. In addition, individual investors in VCTs are entitled to the following reliefs:

(*a*)   on disposal of VCT shares (see 91.12 below); and

(*b*)   by deferral of chargeable gains on re-investment in VCT share issues (see 91.14 below) — but this relief is abolished in relation to VCT shares issued after 5 April 2004.

Various provisions of *TCGA 1992* which are superseded for these purposes by specific provisions (as below) are disapplied or applied separately to parts of holdings which do not fall within the reliefs.

Withdrawal of approval. Where approval of a company as a VCT is withdrawn (but not treated as never having been given) (see 91.2 above), shares which (apart from the withdrawal) would be eligible for the relief on disposal (see 91.12 below) are treated as disposed of at their market value at the time of the withdrawal. For the purposes of the relief on disposal, the disposal is treated as taking place while the company is still a VCT, but the re-acquisition is treated as taking place immediately after it ceases to be so.

91.12   **Relief on disposal.** A gain or loss accruing to an individual on a 'qualifying disposal' of ordinary shares in a company which was a VCT throughout his period of ownership is not a chargeable gain or an allowable loss. A disposal is a *'qualifying disposal'* if:

(*a*)   the individual is 18 years of age or more at the time of the disposal;

(*b*)   the shares were not acquired in excess of the 'permitted maximum' for any year of assessment; and

(*c*)   the shares were acquired for *bona fide* commercial purposes and not as part of a scheme or arrangement a main purpose of which was the avoidance of tax.

The identification of those shares which were acquired in excess of the *'permitted maximum'* is as under 91.9 above (in relation to income tax relief on distributions — broadly those in excess of an annual limit of £200,000 — £100,000 for 2003/04 and earlier years), and the identification of disposals with acquisitions for this purpose is similarly as under 91.9 above.

[*TCGA 1992, ss 151A, 151B; FA 1995, s 72(3)*].

See 91.11 above as regards relief on withdrawal of approval of the VCT.

Simon's Direct Tax Service. See **C3.1103.**

91.13   *Example*

On the disposals in the *Example* at 91.8 above, a chargeable gain or allowable loss arises only on the disposal of the shares acquired in excess of the permitted maximum for 2004/05. As in the *Example* at 91.10 above, these are 25,714 of the shares acquired for £140,000 on 1 September 2004. The disposal identified with those shares is a corresponding proportion of the 210,000 shares disposed of for a consideration of £170,000 on 1 January 2007.

Miss K's capital gains tax computation for 2006/07 is therefore as follows.

91.14   Venture Capital Trusts

£

Disposal consideration for 25,714 shares —

$$170,000 \times \frac{25,714}{210,000} =$$ 20,816

Deduct Cost —

$$140,000 \times \frac{25,714}{180,000} =$$ 20,000

Chargeable gain (subject to taper relief)   £816

91.14   **Deferred charge on re-investment.** In relation to VCT shares issued **before 6 April 2004**, *TCGA 1992, Sch 5C* (introduced as *FA 1995, Sch 16* by *FA 1995, s 72(4)*) applies where:

(a)   a chargeable gain accrues to an individual on the disposal of any asset (or on the occurrence of certain events in relation to enterprise investment scheme investments, see *TCGA 1992, Sch 5B paras 4, 5* introduced as *FA 1995, Sch 13 para 4(3)*, or under the current provisions, see below);

(b)   the individual makes a 'qualifying investment'; and

(c)   the individual is UK resident or ordinarily resident both when the chargeable gain accrues to him and when he makes the 'qualifying investment', and is not, at the latter time, regarded as resident outside the UK for the purposes of any double taxation arrangements the effect of which would be that he would not be liable to tax on a gain arising on a disposal, immediately after their acquisition, of the shares comprising the 'qualifying investment', disregarding the exemption under *TCGA 1992, s 151A(1)* (see 91.12 above).

A *'qualifying investment'* is a subscription for shares in a company which is a VCT, by reference to which relief is obtained under 91.5 above, within twelve months (extendible by the Board) before or after the time of the accrual of the chargeable gain in question, and, if before, provided that the shares are still held at that time.

Broadly, the provisions allow a claim for the chargeable gain to be deferred, and for it to become chargeable on certain events in relation to the VCT shares (including, in particular, on their disposal). For the detailed provisions, see *TCGA 1992, Sch 5C paras 2–6*, introduced as *FA 1995, Sch 16 paras 2–6*, and see Tolley's Capital Gains Tax under Venture Capital Trusts.

This deferral relief is **abolished** in relation to VCT shares issued after 5 April 2004 (see *FA 2004, Sch 19 paras 4–7*).

Simon's Direct Tax Service. See **C3.1110** *et seq.*

92   Vocational Training Relief

92.1   Where, **before 1 September 2000**, a UK-resident individual (or a Crown employee whose duties are in effect treated as performed in the UK, see 75.4 SCHEDULE E—EMPLOYMENT INCOME) pays fees in connection with his own training under a 'qualifying course of vocational training', he is entitled to income tax relief on the amount so paid, provided that

(a)   at the time of the payment, he has not received, and is not entitled to receive, public financial assistance (as defined by Treasury order, see *SI 1992 No 734; SI 1993 No 1074; SI 1995 No 3274; SI 1996 No 3049; SI 1997 No 635*) in relation to the course, and

(b)   he is not otherwise entitled to tax relief in respect of the payment,

(c)   at the time of the payment, the individual is aged 16 or over, and, if under 19, he is not being provided with full-time education at a school (including any institution at which such education is provided to persons at least some of whom are under 16), and

(d)   he undertakes the course neither wholly nor mainly for recreational purposes or as a leisure activity.

Qualifying payments made before 6 April 1999 are treated as deductions from income of the tax year of payment and thus attract relief at the individual's marginal tax rate. Payments made after 5 April 1999 are not so treated and attract relief at the basic rate only. Subject to conditions specified by the Board in regulations (see *SI 1992 No 746; SI 1993 Nos 1082, 3118; SI 1996 No 1185; SI 1997 No 661*), basic rate relief may be obtained by deduction of basic rate tax from the payment, with the recipient recovering the amount deducted from the Board on a claim. The Board consider that where a payment *may* be made under deduction of basic rate tax, basic rate relief can *only* be obtained by deduction. The tax deducted from payments is not clawed back where the individual is liable only at the lower or starting rate of income tax or has no income tax liability.

Where relief may not be obtained by deduction (e.g. where fees are paid to a non-UK provider), and for higher rate purposes before 1999/2000, relief must be claimed by the individual. For 1999/2000 onwards, the basic rate relief is given by way of an income tax reduction, and this is restricted as necessary to such amount as reduces the individual's liability to nil. The reduction is, however, given in priority to any income tax reductions due in respect of personal reliefs (see 1.15–1.17 ALLOWANCES AND TAX RATES), qualifying maintenance payments (see 47.8 MARRIED PERSONS) or loan interest (see 43.5 INTEREST PAYABLE), any reduction of tax liability by way of DOUBLE TAX RELIEF (24), or any basic rate tax on income the tax on which the individual is entitled to charge against any other person or to deduct, retain or satisfy out of any payment.

The Treasury could make regulations requiring either the individual or the recipient of the fees (as the regulations may prescribe) to account for the tax from which relief was given. *SI 1992 No 734 (amended by SI 1996 No 3049)* deals with payments refunded to the trainee by the training provider, and with awards by the training provider to the trainee by virtue merely of the course being undertaken, completed or completed successfully.

A '*qualifying course of vocational training*' is any programme of activity capable of counting towards a qualification accredited as a National or Scottish Vocational Qualification by the appropriate Council.

In relation to payments made **after 5 May 1996** by individuals *aged 30 or over* at the time the payment is made, a '*qualifying course of vocational training*' also includes any course of training, whether or not leading towards a qualification as above, which

92.1 Vocational Training Relief

    (i)   is designed to impart or improve skills or knowledge relevant to, and intended to be used in the course of, gainful employment (including self-employment) of any description,

   (ii)   is devoted entirely to the teaching and/or practical application within the UK of such skills or knowledge (treating time devoted to study in connection with the course as such practical application),

  (iii)   requires participation on a full-time, or substantially full-time, basis, and

  (iv)   extends for a period consisting of or including four *consecutive* weeks but does not last more than one year.

The Revenue have appropriate regulatory powers. Penalties under *TMA 1970, s 98* apply for failure to furnish information etc. required under such regulations, and various assessment, interest and penalty provisions apply in relation to invalid claims by the recipients of fees for repayment of tax deducted therefrom.

[*FA 1991, ss 32, 33; FA 1994, s 84; FA 1996, ss 129, 144, Sch 18 paras 14, 17(1)–(4)(8); FA 1999, s 59, Sch 20 Pt III(15); SI 2000 No 2004*].

See also 71.79 SCHEDULE D, CASES I AND II and 75.45 SCHEDULE E—EMPLOYMENT INCOME.

See generally Simon's Direct Tax Service E2.13 and Revenue Leaflet IR 119.

These provisions are abolished after 31 August 2000.

93   Voluntary Associations

93.1   A club or society is liable to corporation tax on its taxable income and capital gains which includes interest received and profits from trading activities with non-members (see under 50 MUTUAL TRADING). See *CIR v Worthing Rugby Football Club Trustees CA 1987, 60 TC 482* and *Blackpool Marton Rotary Club v Martin Ch D 1988, 62 TC 686* and, for non-proprietary members' golf clubs, Revenue Tax Bulletin August 1994 p 156. See also 93.5 below. For a case in which the Special Commissioner declined to make a distinction between profits arising from ordinary members and those arising from associate members, see *Westbourne Supporters of Glentoran Club v Brennan (Sp C 22), [1995] SSCD 137*. Generally, see Revenue explanatory pamphlet IR 46 'Clubs, Societies and Voluntary Associations'.

See also Revenue Tax Bulletin October 1998 p 600 for the Revenue approach to such bodies with trivial liabilities.

93.2   **Holiday clubs and thrift funds** formed annually are not legally entitled to relief, but where income is received which has not been subjected to composite rate tax, tax assessed on income paid or applied to members is restricted to the tax charge which would have arisen had the members received the income directly. (Revenue Pamphlet IR 1, C3). The concession is withdrawn with effect from April 2001. See Revenue Press Release 3 March 2000.

93.3   **Loan and Money Societies.** Society may account for income tax at average rate (calculated by reference to the average rate which would be applicable if investors were charged directly) on dividends etc. grossed up at that average rate, after taking into account contributions from members to meet management expenses. The grossed-up amount is deductible in computing corporation tax liability of society. (Revenue Pamphlet IR 1, C2). The concessional treatment is withdrawn with effect from April 2001. See Revenue Press Release 3 March 2000.

93.4   **Lotteries etc.** See 71.20 SCHEDULE D, CASES I AND II.

93.5   **Members' sports clubs.** For the Revenue's views on the circumstances in which a members' sports club's commercial activities can give rise to taxable trading profits (or to allowable trading losses), see Revenue Tax Bulletin December 1997 pp 488–490.

For corporation tax reliefs for community amateur sports clubs under *FA 2002, Sch 18*, see Tolley's Corporation Tax under Clubs and Societies.

VAT repayments. See Revenue Tax Bulletin April 1995 p 209.

93.6   **Transfer fees.** See 71.62 SCHEDULE D, CASES I AND II as regards transfer fees paid by football and other sports clubs.

94   Woodlands

Simon's Direct Tax Service Part A5.

94.1   For 1987/88 and earlier years (after which it was abolished), a special tax charge under what was known as Schedule B applied to the 'occupation of woodlands in the UK managed on a commercial basis and with a view to the realisation of profit'. [*ICTA 1970, s 91; FA 1988, s 65, Sch 6 para 2*].

Profits or gains from the commercial occupation of woodlands are not chargeable under SCHEDULE A (69). [*ICTA 1988, s 15(1)*].

The commercial occupation of land which comprises woodlands or is being prepared for use for forestry purposes is thus not within the charge to income tax [*ICTA 1988, s 54(4); FA 1988, Sch 6 para 6(7)*], and their non-commercial occupation has always been. In *Jaggers (trading as Shide Trees) v Ellis Ch D 1997, 71 TC 164*, land on which trees were planted and cultivated in a manner normally associated with Christmas tree production was held not to be woodland. Short rotation coppice cultivation is treated for tax purposes as farming and not forestry, so that UK land under such cultivation is not woodlands. [*FA 1995, s 154*].

95 Finance Act 2004—Summary of Income Tax Provisions

(Royal Assent 22 July 2004)

s 23	**Income tax: charge and rates for 2004/05.** The annual charge to income tax is renewed, and the starting, basic and higher rates remain at 10%, 22% and 40% respectively. See 1.3 ALLOWANCES AND TAX RATES.
s 24	**Age-related personal allowances.** The amounts of these allowances are set for 2004/05. See 1.14 ALLOWANCES AND TAX RATES.
s 29, Sch 4	**Rates of tax applicable to discretionary and accumulation trusts.** The 'rate applicable to trusts' is increased from 34% to 40% and the 'Schedule F trust rate' from 25% to 32.5%, both with effect for 2004/05 onwards, and consequential amendments are made. See 81.5, 81.19 SETTLEMENTS.
ss 30–33, 37, Sch 5 paras 1, 2	**Transfer pricing.** With effect for 2004/05 onwards, the transfer pricing rules, previously applicable only to cross-border transactions, are extended so as to apply to transactions between persons both within the charge to UK tax. Exemption from the rules is introduced for small and medium-sized enterprises. For 2004/05 and 2005/06, there is a temporary relaxation of liability to penalties in certain circumstances. See 3.8 ANTI-AVOIDANCE.
s 50	**International accounting standards.** For periods of account beginning on or after 1 January 2005, accounts drawn up in accordance with international accounting standards will be treated for tax purposes as conforming with generally accepted accounting practice. See 71.30 SCHEDULE D, CASES I AND II.
s 53	**Research and development expenditure by companies.** From a date to be appointed, research and development expenditure by companies is not prevented from being deductible for tax purposes by reason only of its being accounted for as part of the cost of an intangible asset. See 71.70 SCHEDULE D, CASES I AND II.
ss 57–77, Schs 11, 12	**Construction industry scheme.** A revised scheme providing for deductions to be made on account of tax from certain payments made in the construction industry is to be introduced from a date to be appointed, expected to be in April 2006. See 20.8–20.19 CONSTRUCTION INDUSTRY SCHEME.
s 78, Sch 13	**Employer-provided childcare.** New tax exemptions from the benefit-in-kind charge are introduced for 2005/06 onwards in respect of employer-contracted childcare and childcare vouchers. See 75.22 SCHEDULE E—EMPLOYMENT INCOME.
s 79	**Employer-provided computer equipment.** For 2004/05 onwards, computer equipment made available to an employee is exempt from the general charge to tax on earnings, thus avoiding a charge where the employee is given the choice of the loan of computer equipment or additional salary. See 75.16(xxiv) SCHEDULE E—EMPLOYMENT INCOME.
s 80, Sch 14	**Employer-provided vans.** For 2005/06 onwards, a new regime is introduced for taxing the benefit of private use of a van; for 2007/08 onwards a van fuel charge is introduced. See 75.18(iiia) SCHEDULE E—EMPLOYMENT INCOME.
s 81	**Emergency vehicles.** For 2004/05 onwards, where an emergency vehicle is made available to an emergency services employee, no taxable benefit arises by virtue only of his taking the vehicle home whilst on call. See 75.16(xxvii) SCHEDULE E—EMPLOYMENT INCOME.

s 82   **European travel expenses of MPs etc.** For costs incurred after 5 April 2004, the pre-existing tax exemption for reimbursed 'European travel expenses' of MPs, MSPs and Assembly Members is amended. See 28.19 EXEMPT INCOME.

s 83   **Gift Aid donations via the self-assessment return.** Where, as a result of his filing a personal tax return for 2003/04 or any subsequent year, an individual is entitled to an income tax and/or capital gains tax repayment, he may (within the tax return itself) authorise the Revenue to make the repayment (or a part of it) as a Gift Aid donation to a single nominated charity. See 14.12 CHARITIES.

s 84, Sch 15   **Benefits from pre-owned assets.** Subject to certain exemptions, a *de minimis* limit and the right to elect to disapply the provisions (with inheritance tax consequences), an income tax charge applies for 2005/06 onwards on the annual benefit of using property previously owned by the user and not disposed of by him at arm's length. The legislation is intended to counter avoidance schemes which bypass the inheritance tax 'gifts with reservation' rules, but is not restricted to such cases. See 3.23 ANTI-AVOIDANCE.

s 85, Sch 16   **Employee share schemes: national insurance contributions met by employee.** From a date to be appointed, where a liability to employer Class 1 national insurance contributions on an amount chargeable to tax under the rules for restricted shares or convertible shares is borne by the employee, the amount so borne is deductible from the amount so chargeable. See 82.4, 82.6 SHARE-RELATED EMPLOYMENT INCOME AND EXEMPTIONS.

s 86   **Unapproved employee share schemes: restriction of exceptions from charge.** With effect from 7 May 2004, various amendments are made to ensure that certain relieving provisions do not apply if the shares form part of arrangements to avoid tax or national insurance contributions. The changes include, but are not limited to, cases where the value of employment-related shares has been increased or decreased by things done otherwise than for genuine commercial purposes. See 82.4, 82.6, 82.8, 82.9, 82.10, 82.12 SHARE-RELATED EMPLOYMENT INCOME AND EXEMPTIONS.

s 87   **Unapproved employee share schemes: shares with artificially depressed market value.** With effect from 7 May 2004, amendments are made to ensure that artificially-depreciated restricted shares, disposed of or cancelled in a manner that would not otherwise create a charge, are brought within the restricted shares rules. See 82.8 SHARE-RELATED EMPLOYMENT INCOME AND EXEMPTIONS.

s 88   **Shares acquired from approved employee share schemes: post-acquisition events.** With effect from 18 June 2004, various amendments are made to bring post-acquisition events within the charge to tax in certain circumstances. A general anti-avoidance rule is introduced for the various approved schemes. See 82.4, 82.6, 82.8–82.12, 82.26, 82.49, 82.63 SHARE-RELATED EMPLOYMENT INCOME AND EXEMPTIONS and 55.2 PAY AS YOU EARN.

s 89   **Unapproved employee share schemes: shares acquired under public offer.** With effect from 18 June 2004, various amendments are made to bring post-acquisition events within the charge to tax in certain circumstances. See 82.4, 82.6, 82.8–82.12 SHARE-RELATED EMPLOYMENT INCOME AND EXEMPTIONS.

s 90   **Unapproved employee share schemes: associated persons.** With effect from 18 June 2004, amendments are made to ensure that the link between the employee and the shares (or share option) acquired by reason of the employment, once in place, cannot be broken. See 82.4, 82.6, 82.8–82.12, 82.16 SHARE-RELATED EMPLOYMENT INCOME AND EXEMPTIONS.

s 91   **Spouses: income from jointly held property.** For 2004/05 onwards, income from shares in close companies held jointly by husband and wife is taxed in accordance with each spouse's true share of the income and not automatically split 50:50. See 47.3 MARRIED PERSONS.

s 92, Sch 17   **Minor amendments of or connected with** *ITEPA 2003.* A number of errors to the drafting of *ITEPA 2003* are corrected. See, for example, 5.2 ASSESSMENTS, 71.44 SCHEDULE D, CASES I AND II, 75.16(iv) SCHEDULE E—EMPLOYMENT INCOME, 78.4 SELF-ASSESSMENT.

s 93, Sch 18   **Enterprise investment scheme (EIS).** For 2004/05 onwards, the annual subscription limit is raised from £150,000 to £200,000. With effect generally from 17 March 2004, a number of other changes are made to the EIS rules, in particular to the rules covering subsidiaries. See 25 ENTERPRISE INVESTMENT SCHEME.

s 94, Sch 19   **Venture capital trusts.** For 2004/05 onwards, the annual subscription limit is doubled to £200,000. For 2004/05 and 2005/06 only, the rate of income tax relief is doubled to 40%. In relation to shares issued after 5 April 2004, capital gains tax deferral relief is abolished. With effect generally from 17 March 2004, a number of other changes are made to the VCT rules, in particular to the rules covering subsidiaries. See 91 VENTURE CAPITAL TRUSTS.

s 96   **Enterprise management incentives.** In relation to options granted on or after 17 March 2004, the rules covering subsidiaries of the company granting the option are amended. See 82.38 SHARE-RELATED EMPLOYMENT INCOME AND EXEMPTIONS.

ss 107–115   **EU Savings Directive: relief for withholding tax.** These *sections* provide for relief to be given for tax withheld under the EU Savings Directive or equivalent arrangements from individuals' savings income. They also provide, as an alternative, for application to be made to the Revenue for a certificate which can be presented to a paying agent to enable savings income to be paid without deduction of such withholding tax. See 24.9 DOUBLE TAX RELIEF.

ss 119–123   **Film-related losses: disposal of a right to profits.** With effect from, broadly, 9 December 2003, there is a potential exit charge where an individual has claimed loss relief under *ICTA 1988, s 380* or *s 381* for a 'film-related loss' sustained by him in a trade, there is a disposal of a right of the individual to profits arising from the trade and an 'exit event' occurs. See 46.8(*f*), 46.10 LOSSES.

s 124   **Partnership losses: non-active partners.** With effect from, broadly, 10 February 2004, loss relief under *ICTA 1988, s 380* or *s 381* and interest relief under *ICTA 1988, s 353* is restricted in the case of an individual partner who does not devote 'a significant amount of time' to the trade. The relief available, otherwise than against profits of the trade, is restricted to the amount of the partner's 'contribution to the trade' as at the end of the tax year in which the loss is sustained. The restriction applies to losses sustained in the tax year in which the partner first carries on the trade and in any of the next three tax years. See 53.9, 53.18 PARTNERSHIPS.

s 125   **Partnership losses derived from exploiting films: non-active partners.** With effect from, broadly, 26 March 2004, relief under *ICTA 1988, s 380* or *s 381* for trading losses derived from exploiting films is restricted in certain circumstances in the case of an individual partner who does not devote 'a significant amount of time' to the trade. Such relief can be given only against income consisting of profits from the trade in question and not against other income or against chargeable gains. The restriction applies to losses sustained in the tax year in which the partner first carries on the trade and in any of the next three tax years. See 53.11 PARTNERSHIPS.

ss 126–130   **Partnership losses from exploiting a licence: non-active partners.** This is an anti-avoidance measure to tackle schemes used by individuals in a partnership to reduce the tax charge on income from a licence or similar agreement. The schemes aim to generate trading losses followed by a disposal of income rights for a sum not otherwise chargeable to income tax. The legislation has effect from, broadly, 10 February 2004 but only in relation to a partner who does not devote 'a significant amount of time' to the trade at the time the losses are generated. See 53.10 PARTNERSHIPS.

s 134, Sch 23   **Capital allowances on plant and machinery: finance leasebacks.** Anti-avoidance measures are introduced for periods ending after 16 March 2004 (but subject to transitional provisions) in connection with the sale and finance leaseback or the lease and finance leaseback of plant and machinery. The aim is to prevent businesses gaining an unintended tax advantage from the double benefit of retaining capital allowances and obtaining deductions for lease rentals. See 9.38(C)(iv) CAPITAL ALLOWANCES.

s 135   **Rent factoring of leases of plant or machinery.** Where, after 1 July 2004, a person arranges to transfer his right to receive taxable rentals under a lease of plant or machinery for otherwise non-taxable consideration, that consideration is taxable as rental income by reference to the period(s) of account in which it is receivable. See 69.19 SCHEDULE A.

s 136, Sch 24   **Manufactured dividends.** Where a person receives a real or manufactured dividend in respect of UK shares acquired under a repo or stock lending arrangement on terms requiring him to manufacture an equivalent payment, then, with effect from, broadly, 5 November 2003 in the case of an individual and 17 March 2004 in the case of a trust, this legislation seeks to ensure that the manufactured payment is deductible only from the dividend receipt (or so much of it as is chargeable to tax) and not from total income as previously. In addition, no tax is treated as having been paid at source on the dividend received. See 3.6 ANTI-AVOIDANCE.

s 138   **Relevant discounted securities: gilt strips.** This *section* amends the income tax treatment of relevant discounted securities in the form of strips of government bonds, particularly in relation to losses. It applies partly from 15 January 2004 and partly from 17 March 2004. See 72.5 SCHEDULE D, CASE III.

s 139   **Gifts of shares, securities and real property to charities.** For donations of shares etc. to a charity after 1 July 2004 (otherwise than in performance of a contract entered into on or before that date and not varied after that date), this anti-avoidance measure is intended to prevent donors from obtaining tax relief in excess of the benefit received by the charity from the donation. See 14.20 CHARITIES.

s 140   **Life policies etc.: restriction of corresponding deficiency relief.** With effect from, broadly, 3 March 2004, the amount of such deficiency relief due to an individual cannot exceed the aggregate amount of earlier gains on the policy that formed part of the same individual's total income for tax purposes for previous tax years. See 45.15(*b*) LIFE ASSURANCE POLICIES.

s 142   **First-year allowances on plant and machinery: small enterprises.** In the case of a 'small enterprise' only (as distinct from a 'small or medium-sized enterprise') the rate of first-year allowance is increased from 40% to 50% for expenditure incurred within the tax year 2004/05 only. See 9.27(*a*) CAPITAL ALLOWANCES.

s 143 **Landlord's expenditure on energy-saving items.** A deduction of up to £1,500 per building can be claimed, in computing Schedule A profits for income tax (not corporation tax) purposes, for capital expenditure incurred within any of the tax years 2004/05 to 2008/09 inclusive on the acquisition and installation of cavity wall insulation or loft insulation in a let residential property. See 69.5(e) SCHEDULE A.

s 144, Sch 25 **Lloyd's underwriters.** Where after 5 April 2004, an individual Lloyd's member converts to limited liability underwriting by transferring his syndicate capacity to a successor company or Scottish limited partnership and certain qualifying conditions are met, he can carry forward unused trading losses against income from the company or partnership. See 89.5 UNDERWRITERS AT LLOYD'S.

s 145, Sch 26 **Offshore funds.** With effect generally for account periods of offshore funds ending on or after date of Royal Assent (see above), various changes are made to the rules that determine whether or not an offshore fund can be certified as a distributing fund. Pre-existing funds are given the option of continuing to apply some of the pre-existing rules. See 52.1 and 52.3–52.5 OFFSHORE FUNDS.

s 146, Sch 27 **Meaning of 'offshore installation'.** A new definition of 'offshore installation' is provided for various tax purposes, and a number of pre-existing references in tax legislation to 'oil rigs' are replaced with references to 'offshore installations'.

s 147 **Immediate needs annuities.** An annual payment made after 30 September 2004 under an 'immediate needs annuity' (as defined) is exempt from any income tax charge to the extent that it is made to a care provider or local authority in respect of the provision of care for the person for whose benefit the annuity was made. See 28.12 EXEMPT INCOME.

ss 149–284, Schs 28–36 **Registered pension schemes.** With effect for 2006/07 and subsequent years, the various pre-existing pension scheme regimes described in 60 PERSONAL PENSION SCHEMES (AND STAKEHOLDER PENSIONS), 66 RETIREMENT ANNUITIES and 67 RETIREMENT SCHEMES FOR EMPLOYEES are replaced with a single universal regime for tax-privileged pension provision. See 59 PENSION PROVISION AFTER 5 APRIL 2006.

ss 306–319 **Disclosure of tax avoidance schemes.** With effect on and after 1 August 2004, promoters of certain tax avoidance schemes, and in some cases persons entering into transactions under such schemes, are obliged to disclose those schemes to the Revenue. See 3.24 ANTI-AVOIDANCE.

ss 320, 321 **Recovery of tax paid under mistake of law.** Court actions brought after 7 September 2003 for restitution based on mistake of law must generally be brought within six years (or five years under Scottish law) of the tax having been paid. See 56.11 PAYMENT OF TAX.

96   Table of Leading Cases

This Table lists those of the approximately 2,000 cases referred to in this book which are considered to be of most general application and interest. For fuller details of these cases, and of all other tax cases relevant to current or recent legislation, see Tolley's Tax Cases.

A

B

P

T

97 Table of Statutes

This index is referenced to the chapter and paragraph number. The entries printed in bold capitals are main subject headings in the text.